D1259579

ANNOTATED TEACHER'S EDITION

ELEMENTS OF Literature

SIXTH COURSE

LITERATURE OF BRITAIN WITH WORLD CLASSICS

This royal throne of kings,
this scepter'd isle . . .

— from *Richard II* by
William Shakespeare

HOLT, RINEHART AND WINSTON
Harcourt Brace & Company
Austin • New York • Orlando • Atlanta • San Francisco • Boston • Dallas • Toronto • London

Credits

EDITORIAL

Project Director:	Kathleen Daniel
Managing Editors:	Richard Sime, Bill Wahlgren
Project Editor:	Hester Weeden
Book Editors:	Mairead Stack, Leslie Griffin
Editorial Staff:	Steven Fechter, Abigail Winograd, Susan Kent Cakars, Dorothy M. Coe, Edward S. Cohen, Lanie Lee, Christine de Lignières, and Ron Ottaviano; David Knaggs and Sharon Churchin; Vicky Aeschbacher, Jane Archer-Feinstein, Roger Boylan, James Decker, Eric Estlund, Peggy Ferrin, Emily Gavin, Mikki Gibson, Annie Hartnett, Sean Henry, Julie Hoover, Eileen Joyce, Marcia Kelley, Linda Miller, Chi Nguyen, Carla Robinson, Deanna Roy, Tressa Sanders, Errol Smith, Suzanne Thompson, and Stephen Wesson
Editorial Support Staff:	Dan Hunter, Laurie Muir, Su Gordon, Leila Jamal, David Smith, Elizabeth Butler, Ruth Hooker, Kelly Keeley, Marie Price, Margaret Sanchez
Permissions:	Ann B. Farrar, Sacha Frey, Mark Hughs
Research and Development:	Joan Burditt

PRODUCTION AND DESIGN

Text Design:	Preface, Inc.
Design Coordinator:	Betty Mintz
Electronic Files:	TSI Graphics, Banta Digital
Production and Manufacturing:	Athena Blackorby
Marketing Design:	Bob Bretz

COVER

Cover Artist:	Greg Geisler
Photo Credits:	Front cover: (Bodiam Castle, East Sussex, England), Roy Rainford/Robert Harding Picture Library; (Sutton Hoo helmet), The Granger Collection, New York; (sky), Jim Ong/SuperStock; (Scottish thistles), Grace Davies/Omni-Photo Communications and W. Paton/Planet Earth Pictures. Back cover: (Baron Carlo Marochetti's sculpture of Richard Coeur de Lion), photograph by Janet Balmforth, courtesy of Benedict Read.
Quotation on Cover:	From *Richard II*, Act II, Scene I, by William Shakespeare

Copyright © 2000 by Holt, Rinehart and Winston

All rights reserved. No part of this publication may be reproduced or transmitted in any form or by any means, electronic or mechanical, including photocopy, recording, or any information storage and retrieval system, without permission in writing from the publisher.

Requests for permission to make copies of any part of the work should be mailed to the following address: Permissions Department, Holt, Rinehart and Winston, 1120 South Capital of Texas Highway, Austin, Texas 78746-6487.

Acknowledgments appear on pages 5 and 1266–1268, which are extensions of the copyright page.

Printed in the United States of America

ISBN 0-03-052118-1 5 6 048 03 02 01 00

Program Authors

Robert E. Probst established the pedagogical framework for the 1997 and 2000 editions of *Elements of Literature.* Dr. Probst is Professor of English Education at Georgia State University. For several years he was an English teacher in Maryland and Supervisor of English for the Norfolk, Virginia, Public Schools. He is the author of *Response and Analysis: Teaching Literature in Junior and Senior High School.* He has also contributed chapters to such books as *Literature Instruction: A Focus on Student Response; Reader Response in the Classroom: Evoking and Interpreting Meaning in Literature; Handbook of Research on Teaching the English Language Arts; Transactions with Literature: A Fifty-Year Perspective;* and *For Louise M. Rosenblatt.* Dr. Probst is a member of the National Council of Teachers of English and has worked on the council's Committee on Research, the Commission on Reading, and the Commission on Curriculum. Dr. Probst has also served on the board of directors of the Adolescent Literature Assembly and is a member of the National Conference on Research in Language and Literacy.

Robert Anderson wrote the special essay "Contemporary British Drama." Mr. Anderson is a playwright, novelist, screenwriter, and teacher. His plays include *Tea and Sympathy; Silent Night, Lonely Night; You Know I Can't Hear You When the Water's Running;* and *I Never Sang for My Father.* His screenplays include *The Nun's Story* and *The Sand Pebbles.* Mr. Anderson has taught at the Writers' Workshop at the University of Iowa, the American Theater Wing Professional Training Program, and the Salzburg Seminar in American Studies. He is a past president of the Dramatists' Guild, a past vice president of the Authors' League of America, and a member of the Theater Hall of Fame.

John Malcolm Brinnin wrote the biographies of the poets in all collections as well as the Critical Comments on selected poems. He also wrote the special essays "Twentieth-Century British Poetry" and "T. S. Eliot: The Voice of an Age." Mr. Brinnin is the author of six volumes of poetry, which received many prizes and awards. He was a member of the American Academy and Institute of Arts and Letters. He was also a critic of poetry and a biographer of poets and was for a number of years director of New York's famous Poetry Center. His teaching career, begun at Vassar College, included long terms at the University of Connecticut and Boston University, where he succeeded Robert Lowell as Professor of Creative Writing and Contemporary Letters. Mr. Brinnin's books include *Dylan Thomas in America: An Intimate Journal* and *Sextet: T. S. Eliot & Truman Capote & Others.*

John Leggett wrote biographies for the fiction writers in "The Victorian Period" and "The Twentieth Century." He also wrote the historical introduction for "The Twentieth Century." Mr. Leggett is a novelist, a biographer, and a former teacher. He went to the Writers' Workshop at the University of Iowa in the spring of 1969, expecting to work there for a single semester. In 1970, he assumed temporary charge of the program, and for the next seventeen years he was its director. Mr. Leggett's novels include *Wilder Stone; The Gloucester Branch; Who Took the Gold Away?; Gulliver House;* and *Making Believe.* He also wrote the highly acclaimed biography *Ross and Tom: Two American Tragedies.*

Richard Vacca established the conceptual basis for the reading strand in Grades 9 through 12 of the 2000 edition of *Elements of Literature.* Dr. Vacca is Professor of Education at Kent State University. He has also taught at Northern Illinois University and the University of Connecticut and at the middle school and high school levels. Dr. Vacca is co-author of *Content Area Reading; Reading and Learning to Read; Whole Language in Middle and Secondary Classrooms;* and *Case Studies in Whole Language.* For several years he served as the project director of the Cleveland Writing Project, a collaborative effort of Kent State University and the Cleveland Public Schools. In 1989, he was the College Reading Association's recipient of the A. B. Herr Award for Outstanding Contributions to Reading Education. Dr. Vacca served as a member of the board of directors of the International Reading Association and recently completed a term as the association's forty-second president. As this book goes to press, he is co-chair of the IRA's Commission on Adolescent Literacy.

Special Contributors

John Algeo wrote the essay "The English Language." Dr. Algeo was Professor of English at the University of Georgia at Athens. He is co-author, with Thomas Pyles, of *The Origins and Development of the English Language*.

Harley Henry wrote the historical introduction for "The Romantic Period." Dr. Henry is Professor of English at Macalester College in St. Paul, Minnesota. He has also been a senior Fulbright lecturer in Zimbabwe and a Redfield Visiting Professor at the University of Chicago. In addition to the Romantic Period, his teaching specialties include the literature of Zimbabwe; William Faulkner; American fiction from 1945 to 1960; and fiction about baseball.

Donald Gray wrote the historical introduction for "The Victorian Period." Dr. Gray is Professor of English at Indiana University, Bloomington. Dr. Gray has written essays on Victorian poetry and culture and has been editor of *College English*.

David Adams Leeming wrote the historical introduction for "The Anglo-Saxons" and "The Middle Ages" as well as the material on *Beowulf*. Dr. Leeming was for many years a Professor of English and Comparative Literature at the University of Connecticut. He is the author of several books on mythology, including *Mythology: The Voyage of the Hero; The World of Myth;* and *Encyclopedia of Creation Myths*. For several years Dr. Leeming taught English at Robert College in Istanbul, Turkey. He also served as secretary and assistant to the writer James Baldwin in New York and Istanbul. He has published two biographies, *James Baldwin* and *Amazing Grace: A Biography of Beauford Delaney.*

C. F. Main wrote the historical introductions for "The Renaissance" and "The Restoration and the Eighteenth Century," the biographies of writers in those periods, the Critical Comments on *Macbeth,* and the special essay "Women Writers of the Restoration and the Eighteenth Century." Dr. Main was for many years Professor of English at Rutgers University in New Brunswick, New Jersey. He is the editor of *Poems: Wadsworth Handbook and Anthology* and has written reviews and articles on sixteenth-, seventeenth-, and eighteenth-century literature.

William V. Costanza wrote the special essay "Film as Literature: More than Meets the Eye." Dr. Costanza is Professor of English and Film at Westchester Community College, State University of New York. He is active in the National Council of Teachers of English and has chaired the NCTE Commission on Media, the Committee on Film Study, and the Assembly on Media Arts.

Katharina M. Wilson wrote the special essay "The Example of a Queen: Elizabeth I." Dr. Wilson is Professor of Comparative Literature at the University of Georgia and the author of several books on early women writers. She is also the editor of encyclopedias and diverse anthologies of works by early women writers.

Writers

The writers prepared instructional materials for the text under the supervision of Dr. Probst and the editorial staff.

Ellen Ashdown
Former Teacher
Educational Writer and Editor
Tallahassee, Florida

Barbara Dodson
Editor and Creator of Educational Software
Cambridge, Massachusetts

Lynn Hovland
Former Teacher
Educational Writer and Editor
Berkeley, California

Carole S. Lambert
Educational Writer and Editor
Waterville, Maine

Mary E. McCurnin
Educational Writer and Editor
Tallahassee, Florida

Carroll Moulton
Former Teacher
Educational Writer and Editor
Southampton, New York

Elisabeth H. Piedmont-Marton
Former Teacher
Coordinator of the Writing Program
Austin, Texas

Carolyn C. Walter
Educational Writer and Editor
Oak Park, Illinois

Acknowledgments

For permission to reprint copyrighted material in the Annotated Teacher's Edition, grateful acknowledgment is made to the following sources:

Aitken Stone Ltd.: Quotes by V. S. Naipaul from *Words and Their Masters* by Israel Shenker. Copyright © 1974 by V. S. Naipaul.

Basic Books, a member of Perseus Books, LLC: From *Ancients and Moderns* by J. Cropsey. Copyright © 1964 by Basic Books.

Blackwell Publishers: From "The Witches" from *Shakespeare's Tragic Frontier* by Willard Farnham. Copyright © 1950 by Blackwell Publishers.

Robert Bly: Excerpt from commentary by Robert Bly from *Lorca and Jiménez: Selected Poems,* chosen and translated by Robert Bly. Copyright © 1973 by Robert Bly.

Georges Borchardt, Inc.: From *The Life and Times of Geoffrey Chaucer* by John Gardner (New York: Barnes & Noble Books, 1999). Copyright © 1977 by Boskydell Artists.

Cambridge University Press: From "Art, Drama and the People" from *Tolstoy: A Critical Introduction* by R. F. Christian. Copyright © 1969 by Cambridge University Press.

Chatto and Windus, an imprint of Random House UK Ltd.: From *Shakespeare and Society* by Terence Eagleton. Copyright © 1967 by Terence Eagleton.

Rosica Colin Ltd.: From *The Decameron* by Giovanni Boccaccio, translated by Richard Aldington. Copyright © 1957, 1985 by the Estate of Richard Aldington.

Daedalus, Journal of the American Academy of Arts and Sciences: From "Society and Culture" by Hannah Arendt from *Daedalus,* vol. 89, no. 2, Spring 1960. Copyright © 1960 by Daedalus, Journal of the American Academy of Arts and Sciences.

Darhansoff & Verrill Literary Agency: "Requiem" from *Poems of Akhmatova,* translated by Stanley Kunitz and Max Hayward. Copyright © 1967, 1968, 1972, 1973 by Stanley Kunitz and Max Hayward.

Doubleday, a division of Random House, Inc.: From "Source and Motive in *Macbeth* and *Othello*" from *From Shakespeare to Joyce* by Elmer Edgar Stoll. Copyright 1944 by Elmer Edgar Stoll. From "Ode to Liberty" from *Pushkin* by Henri Troyat, translated by Nancy Amphoux. Copyright © 1970 by Doubleday, a division of Random House, Inc.

Farrar, Straus & Giroux, Inc.: From "Visit" from *Birthday Letters* by Ted Hughes. Copyright © 1998 by Ted Hughes.

Martin Gardner: From *The Annotated "Ancient Mariner,"* with Introduction and Notes by Martin Gardner. Copyright © 1965 by Martin Gardner.

Harcourt, Inc.: From "Why I Write" from *Such, Such Were the Joys* by George Orwell. Copyright 1953 by Sonia Brownell Orwell; copyright renewed © 1981 by Mrs. George K. Perutz, Mrs. Miriam Gross, and Dr. Michael Dickson, Executors of the Estate of Sonia Brownell Orwell.

Alfred A. Knopf, Inc.: Quotes by Pablo Neruda from *Seven Voices: Seven Latin American Writers Talk to Rita Guibert,* translated by Frances Partridge. Copyright © 1972 by Alfred A. Knopf, Inc.

Macmillan Press Ltd., London: From *Twentieth-Century English Literature* by Harry Blamires. Copyright © 1982 by Harry Blamires.

Thomas Nelson and Sons Ltd.: Quotes by Kenneth Muir from *Macbeth* by William Shakespeare, edited by Kenneth Muir. Editorial matter copyright © 1962 by Methuen & Co.

W. W. Norton & Company, Inc.: From *Victorian People and Ideas* by Richard Altick. Copyright © 1973 by W. W. Norton & Company, Inc.

Prentice-Hall, Inc.: From *Literature of the Western World,* vol. 1, edited by Brian Wilkie and James Hurt. Copyright © 1984 by Prentice-Hall, Inc.

Rogers, Coleridge & White Ltd.: From *Green Blades Rising: The Anglo-Saxons* by Kevin Crossley-Holland. Copyright © 1975 by Kevin Crossley-Holland.

St. Martin's Press, LLC: From "The Violent Tenor of Life" from *The Waning of the Middle Ages* by J. Huizinga. Copyright 1949 by J. Huizinga.

Simon & Schuster: From Introduction from *Pope: A Collection of Critical Essays,* edited by J. V. Guerinot. Copyright © 1972 by Prentice-Hall, Inc.

W. D. Snodgrass: From "A Rocking-Horse: The Symbol, the Pattern, the Way to Live" by W. D. Snodgrass from *The Hudson Review,* XI, Summer 1958. Copyright © 1958 by W. D. Snodgrass.

Amber Coverdale Sumrall: Quotes by Nadine Gordimer from *Write to the Heart: Wit & Wisdom of Women Writers,* edited by Amber Coverdale Sumrall. Copyright © 1992 by Amber Coverdale Sumrall.

The University of Chicago Press: From Translator's Introduction from *The Panchatantra,* translated from the Sanskrit by Arthur W. Ryder. Copyright © 1956 by Mary E. and Winifred Ryder.

Yale University Press: From *The Guest Hall of Eden* by Alvin A. Lee. Copyright © 1972 by Yale University.

SOURCES CITED:

Letter to Louis Gillet, June 7, 1924, from *Claybook for James Joyce* by Louis Gillet. Published by Abelard-Schuman, London, 1958.

Quotes by Alexander Pushkin and Henri Troyat from *Pushkin* by Henri Troyat, translated by Nancy Amphoux. Published by Doubleday, New York, 1970.

From "Filthy Weed or Divine Plant" from *Nightshades: The Paradoxical Plants* by Charles B. Heiser, Jr. Published by W. H. Freeman and Company, San Francisco, 1969.

From *On Becoming a Novelist* by John Gardner. Published by HarperCollins Publishers, New York, 1983.

From *Victoria's Heyday* by J. B. Priestley. Published by HarperCollins Publishers, New York, 1972.

Letter to James Joyce, April 12, 1927, from *James Joyce's Letters to Sylvia Beach, 1921-1940,* edited by Melissa Banta and Oscar A. Silverman. Published by Indiana University Press, Bloomington, 1987.

From *Blake* by Peter Ackroyd. Published by Alfred A. Knopf, Inc., New York, 1995.

From *The Sacred Wood* by T. S. Eliot. Published by Alfred A. Knopf, Inc., New York, 1921.

Quote by D. H. Lawrence from *D. H. Lawrence: A Biography* by Jeffrey Meyers. Published by Alfred A. Knopf, Inc., New York, 1990.

From *Literature of the Western World,* vols. 1 and 2, edited by Brian Wilkie and James Hurt. Published by Macmillan Publishing Co., Inc., New York, 1984.

From "Chaucer's Pardoner, the Scriptural Eunuch, and The Pardoner's Tale" by Robert P. Miller from *Speculum,* XXX, 1955. Published by the Medieval Academy of America, 1955.

From "Chaucer the Pilgrim" by E. Talbot Donaldson from *Publications of the Modern Language Association,* LXIX, 1954.

From "Revolution and the Rule of Law" by Christopher Harvie from *The Oxford Illustrated History of Britain,* edited by Kenneth O. Morgan. Published by Oxford University Press, Oxford, 1984.

From *For Queen and Country: Britain in the Victorian Age* by Margaret Drabble. Published by The Seabury Press, New York, 1978.

Quote from Najib Mahfouz's interview from *UNESCO Courier,* December 1989. Published by UNESCO, France, 1989.

From *Samuel Beckett* by Ronald Hayman. Published by Frederick Ungar Publishing Co., New York, 1973.

From *The Story of English* by Robert McCrum, William Cran, and Robert MacNeil. Published by Viking Penguin Inc., New York, 1986.

From Introduction from *The Portable Voltaire,* edited by Ben R. Redman. Published by Viking Penguin Inc., New York, 1977.

From "Directing Pinter" by Sir Peter Hall from *Harold Pinter: You Never Heard Such Silence,* edited by Alan Bold. Published by Vision Press Ltd., London, 1984.

CONTENTS

The Anglo-Saxons 449–1066

Collection 1

Songs of Ancient Heroes

COLLECTION PLANNING GUIDE T16A–16D

The Middle Ages 1066–1485

Collection 2

The Gift of Story

COLLECTION PLANNING GUIDE T88A–T88D

The Renaissance 1485–1660

Collection 3

Love, Death, and Time

Joseph Papp
presents
Macbeth
The Public Theater

Communications Workshops

Collection 4

Under a Hand Accursed

Collection 5

The Power of the Word

COLLECTION PLANNING GUIDE T402A–T402D

COMMUNICATIONS WORKSHOPS

The Restoration and the Eighteenth Century 1660–1800

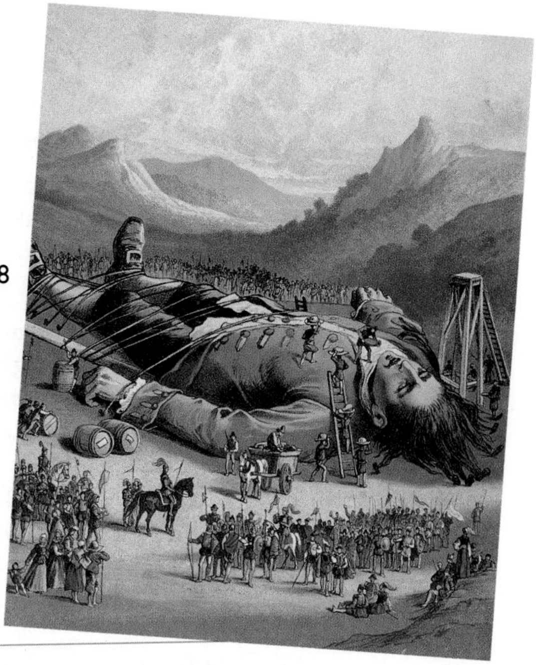

Collection 6

The Sting of Satire

Collection 7

An Appetite for Experience

COLLECTION PLANNING GUIDE T540A–T540D

The Romantic Period 1798–1832

Collection 8

The Power of Imagination

Collection 9

The Quest for Beauty

Collection Planning Guide T708A–708D

The Victorian Period 1832–1901

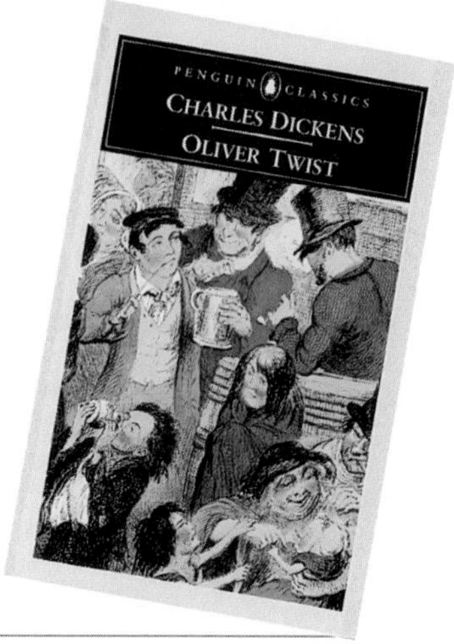

Collection 10

Love and Loss

COLLECTION PLANNING GUIDE T800A–T800D

Collection 11

The Paradox of Progress

COLLECTION PLANNING GUIDE T844A–T844D

The Twentieth Century

Collection 12

The Center Cannot Hold

Collection 13

The Transforming Imagination

Collection 14

Ourselves Among Others

Collection 15

Clashes of Culture

Collection Planning Guide T1120A–1120D

Resource Center

ELEMENTS OF Literature

OVER THE YEARS, *Elements of Literature* *has earned the trust of teachers across the country and generated tremendous enthusiasm in the literature and language arts classroom. The success of this unique program is due in large part to the authentic authorship team that shaped it. In no other literature textbook can you find the expertise of professional writers who have made the instruction focused and connected. These authors have given* ***Elements of Literature*** *its unique voice—a voice that speaks to students and gets them excited about reading and writing.*

CREATED BY LEADING EDUCATORS AND AUTHORS

Robert Anderson, John Malcolm Brinnin, and John Leggett, program authors since the inception of ***Elements of Literature,*** have been determined to involve students in the experience of literature, reflected in the program's respectful tone to students. The authors' motivational approach to instruction, through the use of anecdotes, story, and media, has helped establish the literary framework of this outstanding literature series. Dr. Robert Probst, respected nationally for his response approach, has been instrumental in shaping the student-centered pedagogy of the program. His commitment to making literature meaningful to students and relevant to their lives and experiences is the central focus of ***Elements of Literature.***

AN INCREASED EMPHASIS ON READING SKILLS

With this edition of ***Elements of Literature,*** Dr. Richard Vacca, national reading and literacy expert, joins the authorship team. As special advisor, Dr. Vacca assisted in developing the conceptual framework for the reading strand in the *Pupil's Editions* for grades nine through twelve. Dr. Kylene Beers, well known for her expertise in the area of reading, brings to the program the classroom experiences necessary to answer an increasingly urgent need in today's classrooms—reaching struggling and reluctant readers. Dr. Beers helped to integrate the strong reading development strand in the *Pupil's* and *Annotated Teacher's Editions* with a major new program component, *Reading Skills and Strategies: Reaching Struggling Readers.* This invaluable resource binder includes model lessons, instructional transparencies, and easy readings that help teach students the strategies needed to develop good reading skills.

The lessons in *Reading Skills and Strategies: Reaching Struggling Readers* correlate directly to the *Pupil's Edition* and provide a more thorough and detailed approach for students who are having difficulty. The binder includes the following resources:

- **MiniRead Skill Lessons** are based on short, easy selections enabling students to practice the reading strategies in a less-challenging situation. A complete lesson plan models instruction for the teacher.

- **Selection Skill Lessons** provide opportunities for students to apply the reading strategies they've learned to the literature selections in their textbook.

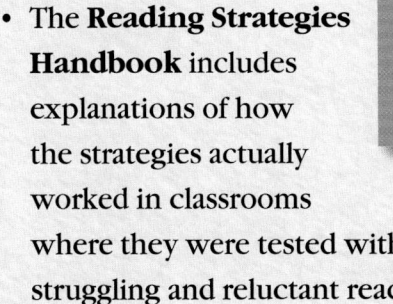

- The **Reading Strategies Handbook** includes explanations of how the strategies actually worked in classrooms where they were tested with struggling and reluctant readers.

- The **QuickGuide** provides a concise, convenient reference guide for using the instructional materials effectively.

Expanding the Role

THIS EDITION OF *Elements of Literature* expands the role of technology, bringing students face-to-face with the media that will shape their understanding of the role of language in their world.

INTERNET RESOURCES ENCOURAGE INVOLVEMENT

The *Elements of Literature* Web resources extend, enhance, and support the series by linking students to carefully researched resources.

When students use the **go.hrw.com** logo and keyword from their textbook, they will be instantly linked to specific resources ranging from biographical information about authors, to extensions of in-text activities and writing assignments, to cross-curricular support for selections. These Internet connections provide a fun and easy way to reach relevant sites without spending valuable time surfing the Web.

INTERACTIVE CD-ROMS MAKE GRAMMAR AND WRITING PRACTICE FUN

The **Language Workshop Interactive Multimedia CD-ROMs** offer a complete course of study in grammar, usage, and mechanics. Sound effects, animation, fine art, and other visuals complement interactive exercises so that students actually enjoy honing their grammar skills.

The **Writer's Workshop Interactive Multimedia CD-ROMs** guide students step-by-step through eight different writing assignments, such as writing a personal narrative, an informative report, or a persuasive essay.

MULTIMEDIA RESOURCES MAKE LITERATURE COME ALIVE

The **Audio CD Library** includes professional readings of nearly every selection in the textbook and reflects a wide range of genres, periods, and cultures.

The **Visual Connections Videocassette Program** features video segments directly related to course content. Author biographies, interviews, historical summaries, and cross-curricular connections enrich and extend instruction.

# of Technology

THE ALL-IN-ONE RESOURCE TOOL

The new **One-Stop Planner CD-ROM with Test Generator** is an all-in-one, comprehensive management tool that makes planning your lessons easier and more efficient. Two CD-ROMs for each grade level include all your teaching resources—organized in easy-to-understand, point-and-click menus.

Here are just a few of the teaching resources you can access on the **One-Stop Planner:**

- Editable lesson plans, importable into several word-processing formats
- Video previews of the *Visual Connections Videocassette Program*
- *Viewing and Representing* Transparencies and Worksheets
- Selection Tests and Answer Keys

LESSON PLANS FOR EVERY CLASSROOM NEED

Lesson Plans Including Strategies for English-Language Learners are designed to help make literature more accessible to students whose first language is not English.

Block Scheduling Lesson Plans help you manage instruction and activities for each day of the 90-day block.

ASSESSMENT TOOLS MATCHED TO THE WAY YOU TEACH

Elements of Literature provides a rich variety of assessment tools—including traditional, alternative, and standardized—that allows you to evaluate students' performance according to your teaching methods.

- *Formal Assessment*
- *Portfolio Management System with Rubrics for Assignments*
- *Standardized Test Preparation* and *Preparation for College Admission Exams*
- *Test Generator* (included on the *One-Stop Planner CD-ROM*)

ADDITIONAL TEACHING RESOURCES

Elements of Literature includes an array of flexible resources correlated to the *Pupil's Edition*.

- *Workshop Resources Transparencies and Worksheets*
- *Literary Elements Transparencies and Worksheets*
- *Daily Oral Grammar Transparencies and Worksheets*
- *Viewing and Representing* (Fine Art Transparencies and Worksheets, and the HRW Multimedia Presentation Maker)
- *Language Handbook Worksheets*
- *Grammar and Language Links Worksheets*
- *Cross-Curricular Activities*
- *Words to Own Worksheets*
- *Graphic Organizers for Active Readers*
- *Spelling and Decoding Worksheets (for grades 6–8)*

Literature

AN INVITATION TO A DIALOGUE

Dr. Robert Probst, *Georgia State University*

The classroom is the place for students to learn to read and reflect on visions of human possibilities offered them by the great literature and to begin to tell their own visions and stories.

Literature and Life

Surely, of all the arts, literature is most immediately implicated with life itself. The very medium through which the author shapes the text—language—is grounded in the shared lives of human beings. Language is the bloodstream of a common culture, a common history.

— Louise Rosenblatt

Mathematicians, scientists, and engineers build bridges and send people to the moon, statisticians calculate our insurance premiums and life expectancies, and accountants figure our taxes and amortize our house payments, but the poets, dramatists, novelists, and story-writers have nonetheless remained at the center of life. They bind us together as a society, and they define us as individuals within that society.

When we're very young we need stories almost as much as we need food and protection. Stories entertain us and help us sleep, but they also teach us how to get through the world. They tell us there are pots of gold waiting for us at the end of the rainbow, and they warn us about the trolls hiding under the bridges. They teach us about hope, fear, courage, and all the other elements of our lives. As we grow out of childhood, the great stories, poems, and plays of the world's literature encourage us to reflect on the issues that have intrigued men and women for centuries, inviting us into a continuing dialogue about human experience. When we're older, our own stories represent what we've done, capturing for us what we've made of our lives. Some we'll tell happily, some we'll tell with great pain, and some we may not tell at all, but they're all important because they are a way of making sense of our lives.

If literature is the ongoing dialogue about what it means to be human, then the language arts classroom is society's invitation to students to join that conversation. The texts we use represent the reflections of the world's cultures on the nature of human experience, and the writings we elicit from our students are their first efforts to join in that reflection. The classroom is the place for students to learn to read and reflect on visions of human possibilities offered them by the great literature and to begin to tell their own stories.

Literature offers an invitation to reflect, but it doesn't offer formulas to memorize or answers to write dutifully in notes so that later on, when life presents us with problems, we can pull out our tattered old notebooks and find our path sketched out for us. Literature is an invitation to a dialogue.

That, perhaps more than any other reason, is why it's so important that we teach literature and writing well. It's too easy to avoid the responsible thought demanded by the significant issues, too tempting to accept someone else's formulation of the truth. "Life imitates art," Richard Peck said in a speech in New Orleans in 1974, "especially

bad art." By that he meant, I think, that we may too often give in to tempting laziness and allow our lives to be governed by visions of human possibilities that we take from film, television, or graffiti. The problem for teachers, of course, is to lead students not simply to absorb unthinkingly what art offers, but to reflect on it.

This textbook series tries to support teachers' efforts to lead students to think, to feel, and to take responsibility for themselves. It will have much in common with other textbooks. After all, we'd miss "The Raven" if he didn't land croaking on our window sill one morning just before homeroom, and twelfth grade wouldn't be the same without an evening or two around the hearth with Beowulf. But if this series has much in common with other textbooks, it will also have much that differs—including new authors, perhaps authors we haven't met before, exploring lives and circumstances that previously may not have been well represented in the pages of school texts. And similarly, there will be familiar approaches to teaching—perhaps specific activities—that we've all come to rely upon, but there will be other suggestions that emphasize aspects of literary experience, writing, and discussion that may not have been prominent in other books.

Principles of the Program

❶ First among the principles of the program is that *the subject matter of the language arts classroom is human experience comprehended and expressed in language.* The classroom invites the student into the dialogue about the big issues of human experience. The content of literature is the content of our days, and we think and feel about these issues before we enter the classroom and open the text.

When we do finally come to the text, it offers students an opportunity to begin to make sense of experience and to see it captured in the literature.

❷ Implicit in this vision of the language arts is a second principle, *that learning in the English classroom is a creative act,* requiring students to make things with language. Reading literature is a process of engaging the text, weighing it against the experiences readers bring to it.

Similarly, writing isn't simply a matter of learning and applying the rules of grammar and usage or of memorizing the structure and strategies of narratives, descriptions, and arguments.

Literature offers us access to hidden experiences and perceptions.

❸ *The third principle focuses on the encounter between student and content.* It doesn't focus exclusively on the information and skills that have at times provided the framework for our instruction.

Nor, on the other hand, is teaching planned with thought only for the student's interests, needs and desires, and thus organized around whatever concerns happen to predominate at the moment. It is, to borrow Rosenblatt's term, transactional.

❹ For this series, *the integration of the several aspects of the English language arts program* is the fourth governing principle. Literature can't be taught effectively without work in composition. Writing, without the inspiration offered by good literature, remains shallow and undeveloped. Oral language has to be acquired in the context of groups working collaboratively. And so, these texts will suggest ways of interrelating instruction in literature, writing, and language.

Working With the Series

You will find, as you work with selections in this textbook, that students have immediate responses to what they've read. That may be the place to start. The students' responses are very likely to lead you back to the issues you would have wanted to discuss anyway, and so the questions we've suggested might be addressed naturally during the flow of the discussion. Look for the potential in students' reactions and their questions even before turning to the questions in the "First Thoughts" section. Then, the questions in the text can extend or expand the discussion.

The same might be said about the writing. The series has been designed so that experiences with literature, with writing, and with group processes will often be interconnected. We hope that the literature will inspire and shape the students' writing, that their writing will lead back to further reading, and that the discussions and group activities suggested will build a supportive community in which all this work can take place.

The objective in all of this is for students to be able to draw upon their literary heritage and their developing skill with written and spoken language so that, as humane and reasoning people, they may be responsibly engaged with the world around them. If the language arts class helps to achieve that goal, we should be well satisfied with our labors.

Reading Matters

Dr. Richard T. Vacca, *Kent State University*

As is the case with many teachers, I have had my fair share of unforgettable students, the "usual suspects," who have made a difference in the way I think about teaching and learning literature. Two such students quickly come to mind.

Tommy was an English teacher's dream; Johnny, a saboteur-in-training. They were contemporaries, but I'm sure their paths never crossed in school. One was a high achiever; the other, a low achiever. The classroom lessons I learned from each of them changed the way I think about reading and literature in English classrooms.

A Tale of Two Students

Johnny was just three years younger than I when I began teaching in a high school just outside Albany, New York. He was one of the forgotten students at school who went unnoticed until he got into trouble. Johnny couldn't read well, but he knew how to take apart a carburetor and replace a timing belt with his eyes closed. (As it turned out, he dropped out of school on his nineteenth birthday and went to work at his uncle's garage.) He and his cohorts tried to sabotage my teaching plans whenever I initiated the study of literature, no matter how relevant the text was to their lives. If the literature study required reading, Johnny could dismantle the lesson as skillfully as he could dismantle a car engine. I held my ground the best I could, but often to little avail. The more I urged him and others in the class to learn about what it means to be human through literature, the more they resisted.

I was tough on Johnny, always challenging him to do better, and I believe there was a measure of respect between the two of us. Even though it's been more than three decades since I saw him, I won't soon forget our last encounter. I remember running into Johnny at his uncle's garage and telling him that I had resigned my teaching position to go back to school to be a reading specialist. "Man," he said, "you read good already." Then he added somewhat wistfully, somewhat defiantly, "Reading robbed me of my manhood."

I had never heard the inability to read put in such human terms. Johnny helped me to understand how much reading matters, not only in students' literate lives but also in their human lives outside of school. What I learned from Johnny, and from other students who struggle with reading literature, is this: Reading gets in the way of too many students' understanding, enjoyment, and appreciation of literary texts. I made assumptions about Johnny's ability to use reading to learn that, in hindsight, were ill-informed. I assumed, for example, that by the time he reached high school he should be using reading to make meaning with literary texts. Because reading was second nature to me, I often assigned literary texts as if reading were second nature to my students. But I couldn't reach Johnny with literature because he didn't have the skills and strategies of an accomplished reader. I, on the other hand, didn't have the instructional know-how to bridge the gap between potentially difficult texts and the literacy capital that Johnny brought to the classroom and the study of literature.

Tommy, on the other hand, made teaching literature smooth sailing. He was tracked in an above-average class with others who knew how to do school well. I recall that his class was in the midst of reading Thornton Wilder's *Our Town* during the birth of my first (and only) child. I shared with the class every heartfelt moment of my ascent into fatherhood and connected the experience to Wilder's play. Unbeknownst to me, Tommy took it upon himself to write a letter to Thornton Wilder, which he mailed to Wilder's publisher. In the letter he shared how much the play (and my journey into fatherhood) had changed the way he thought about life and about relationships that he would have taken for granted. Several weeks later, Tommy received a letter from Wilder's sister explaining that her brother, who was nearly blind at the time and quite ill, enjoyed having the letter read to him. She went on to say that he insisted that she write to Tommy and apologized for not being able to do so directly. Wilder wanted Tommy to know that the letter brightened his spirits and reaffirmed his reasons for writing *Our Town*. Wilder's sister concluded by telling Tommy that her brother was especially grateful for readers such as Tommy who made writing well worth the effort. I remember Tommy saying, "I'll treasure this letter forever."

Reading matters to accomplished students such as Tommy who know how to use literary texts to explore the significance of what they are reading. Often, they are high achievers who are skillful and thoughtful in their approach to reading. But not all average and above-average students are accomplished readers. What I learned early on as a literature teacher is that many academically oriented students—adolescents who were most like me in high school, promising students who sometimes worked hard and sometimes didn't—struggle with reading literature as much as low-achieving students. In between the Johnnys and the Tommys are students who often go through the motions of reading literary texts but are likely to conceal some of their difficulties. These students have developed the ability to read print smoothly and accurately, but they don't know what to do with texts beyond just reading the words. They appear *skillful* in the mechanics of reading, but they aren't *strategic* in their ability to explore and interpret meaning.

Bringing Literature and Reading Together

Technologically advanced societies like ours value literate behavior and demand that citizens acquire literacy for personal, social, academic, and economic success. The pressure to hold teachers accountable for students' reading development is greater today than at any time in our nation's history. To the extent that texts are an integral part of learning in all content areas, *every* teacher has a role to play in helping students become readers, writers, and oral communicators. Yet the responsibility for teaching literacy usually lies with English teachers and with reading specialists in middle and high schools. English teachers, however, are not reading specialists and shouldn't view their roles as such. Showing students how to use reading strategies in the literature classroom doesn't require the specialized training of a reading specialist. Nor does the development of reading skills and strategies in the context of the literature classroom diminish the teacher's role as a subject matter specialist. It is far more realistic and effective to integrate the skills and strategies that readers actually need. The real value of reading lies in the way it is used. To be literate in literature classrooms, students must learn how to use reading to construct meaning from literary texts. Because literacy use is situational, the most meaningful way for students to develop reading skills and strategies is in the context in which they must be used. A student using reading to find meaning in literature gains confidence in his or her ability to read and to interpret texts.

Scaffolding reading experiences is the key to bringing literature and reading together in the literature classroom. The term *scaffolding* is a metaphor used in teaching and learning to suggest a means by which you help students do what they cannot do at first. In other words, scaffolding reading experiences allows teachers to provide the instructional support and guidance that students need to be successful. Instructional scaffolding allows teachers to support students' efforts to think clearly, critically, and creatively about literary texts *while* showing them how to use skills and strategies that will allow them to read more effectively than if left to their own devices.

Developing Skills and Strategies

Because skills and strategies are best learned through meaningful use, the lesson organization for the literary selections in ***Elements of Literature*** provides numerous opportunities to scaffold students' exploration and interpretation of literary texts. Each lesson creates an instructional framework that respects the nature of the literary experience while making provisions to scaffold students' use of reading skills and strategies. Instructional scaffolding before reading, for example, demonstrates to students the importance of anticipation, making predictions, raising questions, and other strategies that connect their world to the world of the text.

Students are in a strategic position to learn with literature whenever they use their prior knowledge to construct meaning. Prior knowledge includes the experiences, conceptual understandings, attitudes, values, skills, and strategies the reader brings to a text situation. How readers *activate* prior knowledge is the mechanism by which they connect their world to the world of the text. Prior knowledge, when activated, allows readers to seek, organize, retain, and elaborate meaning. In ***Elements of Literature***, features such as *Make the Connection* and *Quickwrites* activate prior knowledge in relation to the issues, problems, conflicts, or themes to be studied through the literary experience. These scaffolds provide students with an imaginative entry into the text by raising expectations, arousing curiosity, and anticipating what is ahead in the literature selection.

Making students aware of *why, how,* and *when* they should use strategies to activate prior knowledge and anticipate content is as important as understanding *what* the strategies are. For example: Why is activating what students already know about a topic through a quickwrite (or any prereading strategy) important? How can students connect what they know to what they are about to read? When should a technique such as quickwrite be used and when shouldn't it? From a strategy-learning perspective, these discussions provide students with a rationale for skill and strategy use and build *procedural knowledge*, which is knowledge about why, how, and what skill and strategy to use.

Providing instructional support during and after reading also encourages struggling readers to develop and use skills and strategies as they explore, clarify, and extend their understandings of the text. A skilled reader recognizes the important parts of a text. A struggling reader doesn't. Instead, the student who struggles with text tends to read each word, each sentence, each paragraph with equal emphasis and reverence.

While readers explore meaning before and during reading, they often need to engage in clarification and elaboration after reading. Postreading questions and activities at the end of each literary selection in ***Elements of Literature*** create another type of instructional support for students. They help students extend their thinking and evaluate the significance of the literary experience.

In addition to scaffolding reading experiences at the point of use, there are other features of ***Elements of Literature*** that will help you support and guide students' reading development. For example, the MiniRead lessons in the reading binder, *Reading Skills and Strategies: Reaching Struggling Readers,* are instructional resources that provide *explicit instruction* for students who need additional guidance and support. The MiniRead lessons allow students to share insights and knowledge that they might otherwise never discover. These explicit lessons create a framework that unifies skill and strategy development. They provide methods for struggling readers to become aware of, to use, and to develop control over skills and strategies that can make a difference in their literate lives.

DR. RICHARD T. VACCA

Reaching Struggling Readers

AN INTERVIEW WITH

DR. KYLENE BEERS

Dr. Kylene Beers

from the Editor's Desk

As we have listened to teachers over the past few years, one dominant issue has emerged: How do we teach literature to struggling readers? In our search for an answer, we read the research, attended workshops, and interviewed teachers and students. It was obvious that fill-in-the-blank drill worksheets weren't the answer. It was time for a change, but nothing we encountered seemed to offer a real solution to the problem of teaching literature to struggling readers.

Finally, one day Dr. Robert Probst suggested we contact Dr. Kylene Beers. He told us she knew a great deal about reading and might be the person with the answers. During our first meeting with Dr. Beers, she explained the link between reading skills and strategies and discussed the difference she had seen strategies make in the lives of struggling readers. She made a lot of sense to those of us who can recite whole sections of the *Iliad* but had never heard the words *reading* and *strategy* in the same sentence. A year and a half later we see the results of that first meeting: the *Reading Skills and Strategies: Reaching Struggling Readers* binder. This wasn't the easiest project in the history of publishing. Drill worksheets would have been easier to produce, but it was time for a change—time to turn struggling readers into successful ones.

Here are some of the questions we asked Dr. Beers during the course of this project.

The curriculum demands on English teachers are enormous. Teachers often ask us why they should add reading skills and strategies to an already loaded course.

"I used to ask myself the same thing. Twenty years ago, when I began teaching, I expected that I'd carefully guide excited students through the prose and poetry of literary giants like Whitman, Emerson, Dickinson, Thoreau, Kipling, Joyce, Márquez, Angelou, and well, you know the names. I expected that students would arrive early for literature class and leave late for their next class. I expected I'd never have to worry about teaching someone to read—that was for the elementary teachers. I was going to teach *Literature*. Those expectations changed quickly. First, I didn't have students who loved literature. Most of my students didn't even like literature. Second, I didn't have students who could already read. When I didn't get the students I expected, I didn't know what to do.

Twenty years later, I'm still not getting what I expected when it comes to teaching. But I've learned that if I understand students' strengths and have some ideas about how to address their weaknesses, then they'll often give me more than I ever expected.

I've spent the past twenty years learning how to help these secondary students who can't read and don't like to read become better readers. I've worked with students at all grade levels and all ability levels. I've gone back to school to study how to teach reading, and now I see myself as a reading/literature teacher. The teaching of literature and the teaching of reading are integral to one another, so interconnected that separating them seems an abomination."

How can a teacher use a literature anthology with the increasing numbers of students who have serious difficulty reading any text?

"After many years of working with all types of readers, but especially struggling and reluctant readers, I've learned some things that have helped me reach those students. I've found that struggling readers have difficulty reading for a myriad of reasons. Often they don't know a lot of words, so limited vocabulary keeps them from understanding what they've read. Sometimes they lack decoding ability, so they don't know how to get through big words. Other times, they can call words well, but they don't know how to make sense of what they've read. And sometimes, their distaste for reading makes them think reading is meaningless, so they see no reason for putting any effort into it. As I work with students and address those issues, I keep what I call the ABCDE rules in mind. A look at the diagram below will quickly show you what these rules are."

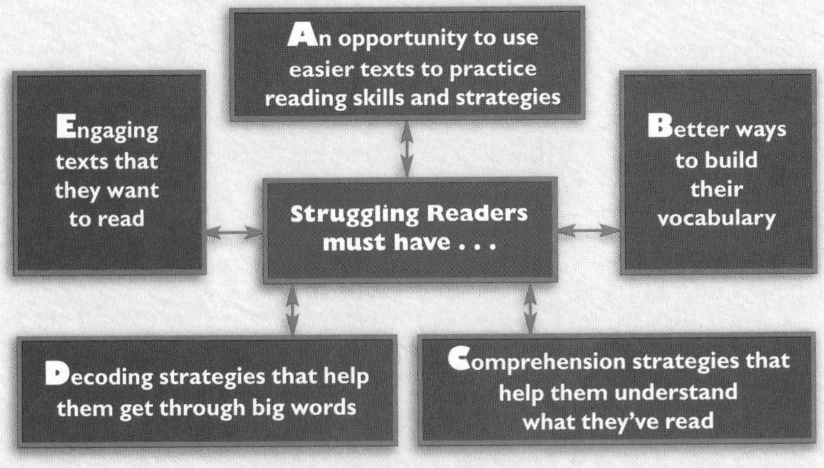

An opportunity to use easier texts to practice reading skills and strategies
Engaging texts that they want to read
Struggling Readers must have . . .
Better ways to build their vocabulary
Decoding strategies that help them get through big words
Comprehension strategies that help them understand what they've read

To help provide this ABCDE rule for struggling readers, what should a literature program include?

"A literature program should help teachers with each of those areas, particularly A, B, C, and E. If publishers want to help, they will have to develop specialized materials that complement the basal text. Here's what we did with the *Reading Skills and Strategies* binder for *Elements of Literature*:

❶ Easier Selections Provide Practice for Skills and Strategies.
We hired a group of professional writers to write easy fiction and nonfiction pieces. These selections, or MiniReads, are short texts written at an easier level than the selections in the literature book. The purpose of the MiniReads is to give students the opportunity to practice decoding skills, comprehension strategies, and vocabulary strategies with a text that is not only easier but engaging as well.

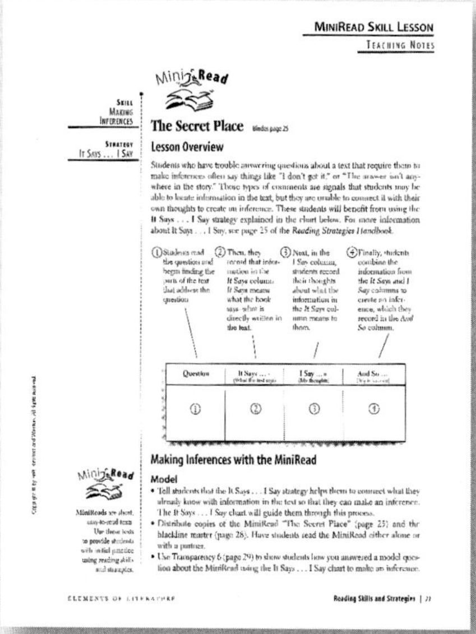

❷ Our MiniRead Lessons Include Modeling.
Each MiniRead includes a complete lesson plan that provides modeling of the skill and strategy. Transparencies help teachers focus students on the strategies. Blackline masters give students a chance to practice the strategies before applying them to selections in the Pupil's Edition.

❸ Reading Skills and Strategies Are Connected to the Selections in *Elements of Literature*.

All skills and strategies are *applied* to selections in the anthology. The detailed lesson plans can be used not only with struggling readers, but with all readers.

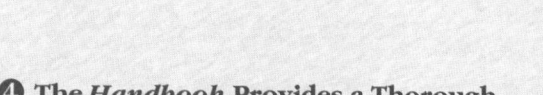

❹ The *Handbook* Provides a Thorough Explanation of the Research.
Without research to back them up, the lessons would have no foundation. The *Reading Strategies Handbook* includes transcripts from actual classrooms in which the strategies have been tested with struggling readers. The handbook *shows* rather than just *tells* how to initiate specific strategies, what pitfalls to avoid, and how to document progress. Articles about each of the strategies help teachers become more comfortable with using the strategies with any selection."

The Leader in Literature Presents

HRW LIBRARY

WITH CONNECTIONS THAT MATTER

Attractive hardcover editions with contemporary art that captures students' imaginations

Readings from a variety of authors and genres—poems, short stories, essays, memoirs, biographical sketches, interviews, and many more—that complement the theme

Study guides with support for both the novel and the Connections:

- **Pacing suggestions, vocabulary activities, inclusion strategies, and cross-curricular and multimedia projects**
- **Reproducible masters for reading skills, vocabulary, literary elements, and assessments**
- **One-page news sheets, Novel Notes, that provide high-interest background information relating to historical, cultural, or literary elements of the novel**

Elements of Literature on the Internet

To the Student

Discover more about the stories, poems, and essays in *Elements of Literature* by logging on to the Internet. At **go.hrw.com** we help you complete your homework assignments, learn more about your favorite writers, and find facts that support your ideas and inspire you with new ones. Here's how to log on:

1. Start your Web browser and enter **go.hrw.com** in the location field.

2. Note the keyword in your textbook.

go.hrw.com
LEO 12-1

3. In your Web browser, enter the keyword and click on GO.

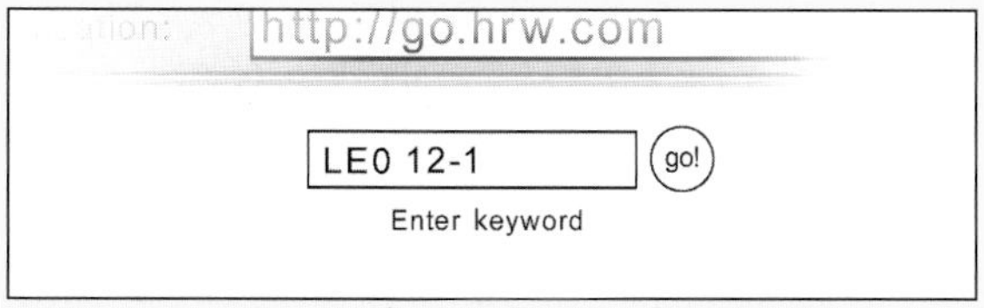

Now that you've arrived, you can peek into the palaces and museums of the world, listen to stories of exploration and discovery, or view fires burning on the ocean floor. As you move through *Elements of Literature,* use the best on-line resources at **go.hrw.com.**

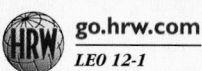

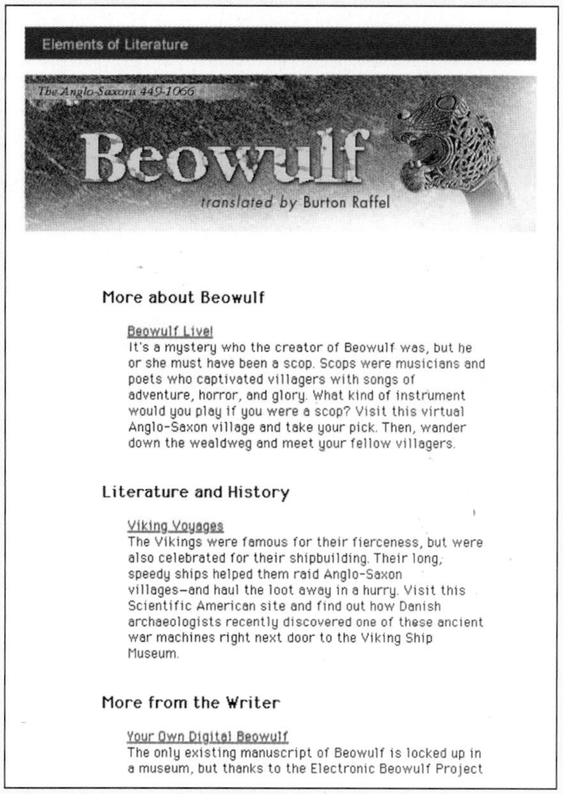

Elements of Literature
The Anglo-Saxons 449-1066
Beowulf
translated by Burton Raffel
More about Beowulf
Beowulf Live!
It's a mystery who the creator of Beowulf was, but he or she must have been a scop. Scops were musicians and poets who captivated villagers with songs of adventure, horror, and glory. What kind of instrument would you play if you were a scop? Visit this virtual Anglo-Saxon village and take your pick. Then, wander down the wealdweg and meet your fellow villagers.
Literature and History
Viking Voyages
The Vikings were famous for their fierceness, but were also celebrated for their shipbuilding. Their long, speedy ships helped them raid Anglo-Saxon villages—and haul the loot away in a hurry. Visit this Scientific American site and find out how Danish archaeologists recently discovered one of these ancient war machines right next door to the Viking Ship Museum.
More from the Writer
Your Own Digital Beowulf
The only existing manuscript of Beowulf is locked up in a museum, but thanks to the Electronic Beowulf Project

Enjoy the Internet, but be critical of the information you find there. Always evaluate your sources for credibility, accuracy, timeliness, and possible bias.

Web sites accessed through **go.hrw.com** are reviewed regularly. However, on-line materials change continually and without notice. Holt, Rinehart and Winston cannot ensure the accuracy or appropriateness of materials other than our own. Students, teachers, and guardians should assume responsibility for checking all on-line materials. A full description of Terms of Use can be found at **go.hrw.com.**

The British Isles

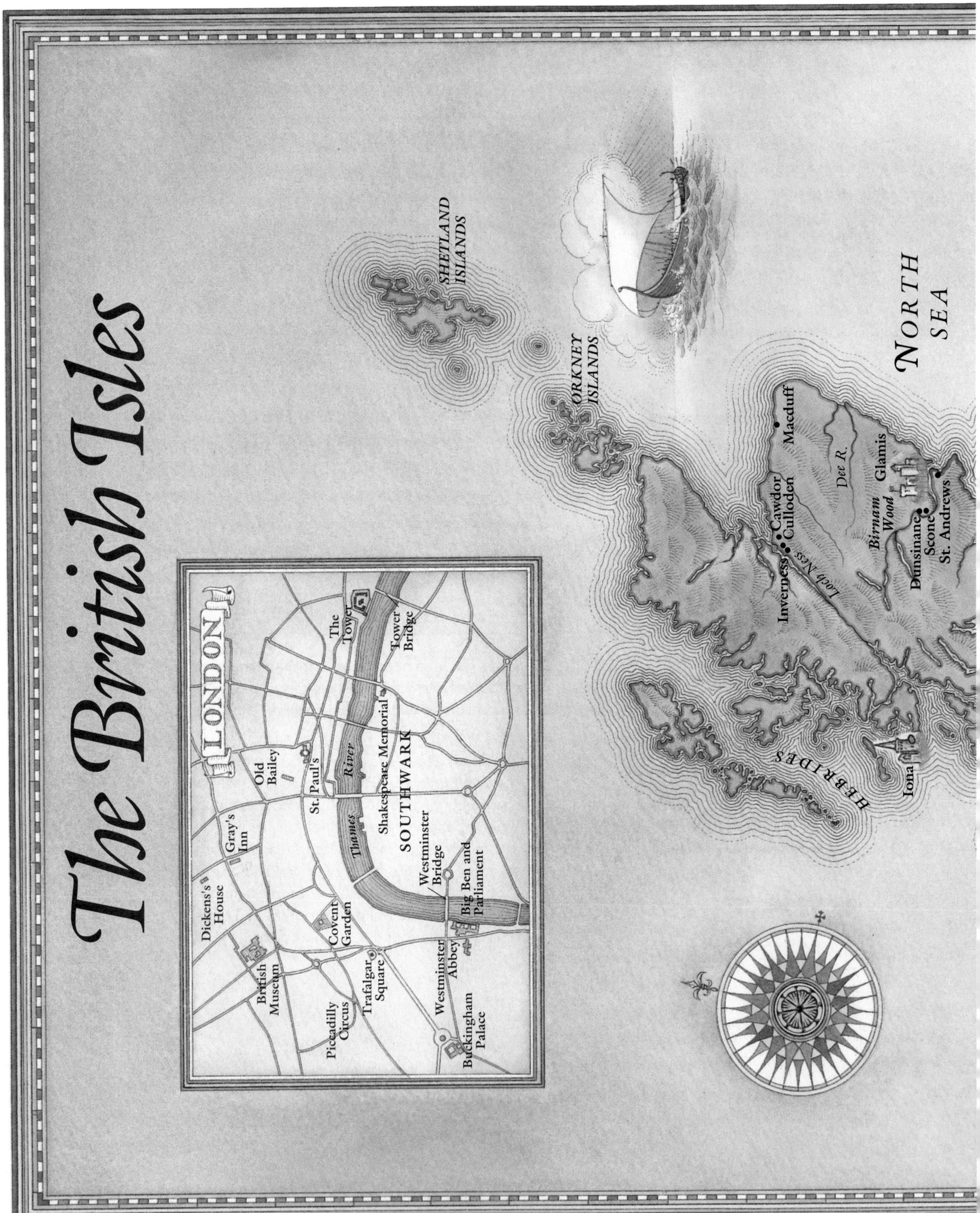

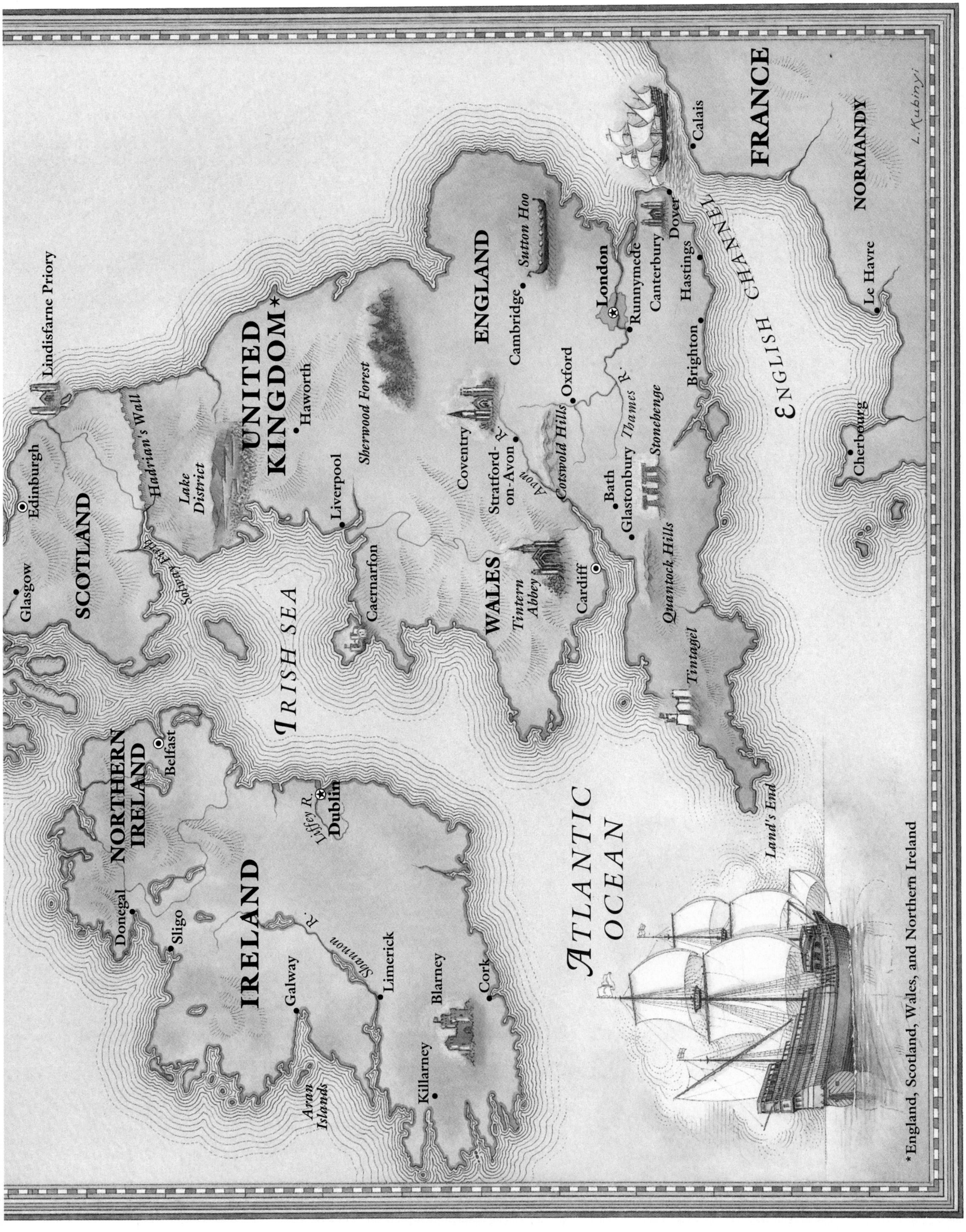
Lindisfarne Priory
Edinburgh
Glasgow
SCOTLAND
Hadrian's Wall
Lake District
Solway Firth
UNITED KINGDOM*
Haworth
Liverpool
Sherwood Forest
Coventry
Stratford-on-Avon
Avon R.
ENGLAND
Cambridge
Sutton Hoo
London
Runnymede
Canterbury
Dover
Hastings
Brighton
Oxford
Thames R.
Cotswold Hills
Bath
Glastonbury
Stonehenge
Quantock Hills
Cardiff
Tintern Abbey
WALES
Caernarfon
IRISH SEA
Tintagel
Land's End
NORTHERN IRELAND
Belfast
Liffey R.
Dublin
IRELAND
Donegal
Sligo
Galway
Shannon R.
Limerick
Blarney
Cork
Killarney
Aran Islands
ATLANTIC OCEAN
ENGLISH CHANNEL
FRANCE
Calais
NORMANDY
Le Havre
Cherbourg
L. Kubinyi
*England, Scotland, Wales, and Northern Ireland

Map of

Map labels indicate the homelands of writers included in this anthology.

the World

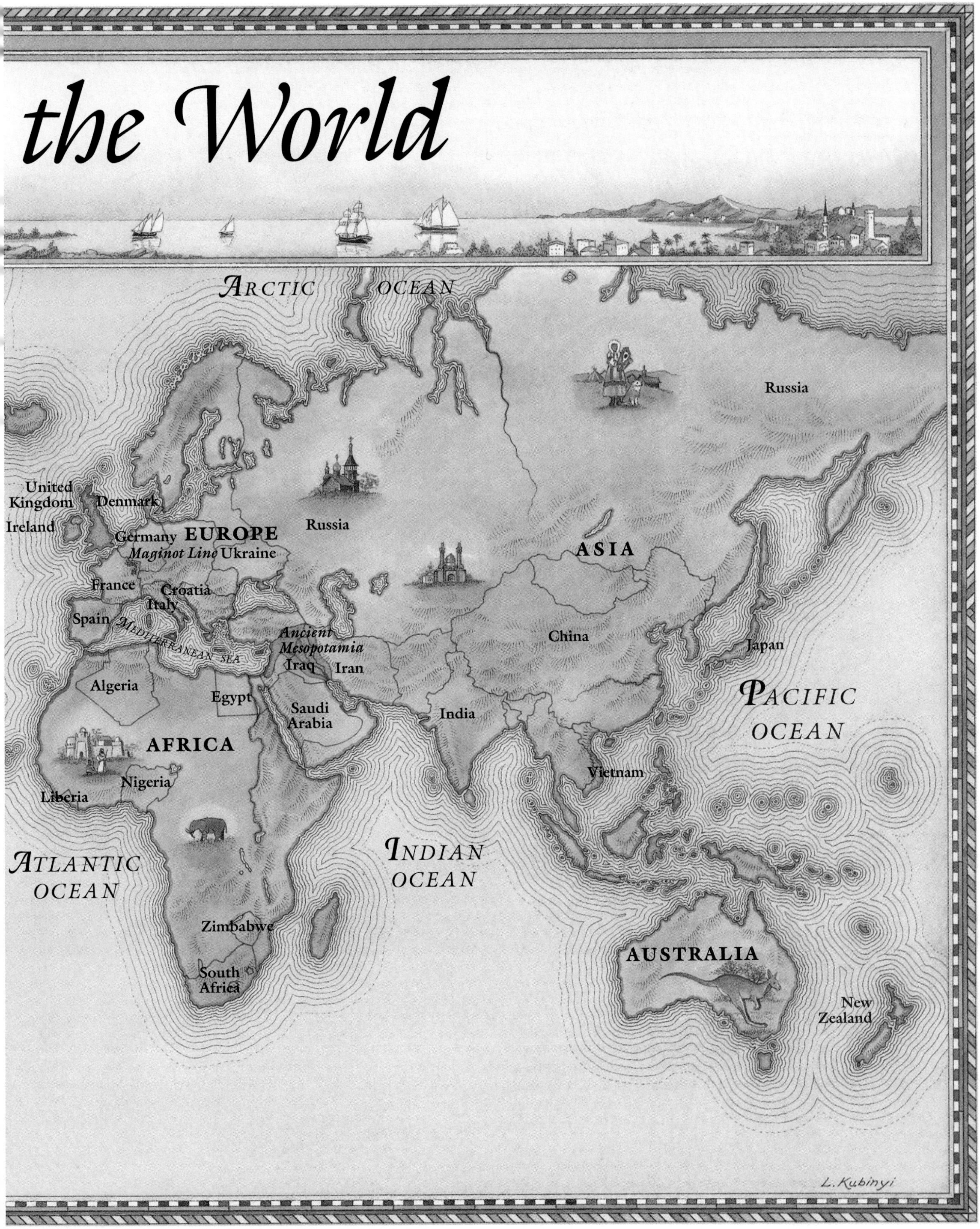
ARCTIC OCEAN
Russia
United Kingdom
Denmark
Ireland
Germany
EUROPE
Russia
Maginot Line
Ukraine
ASIA
France
Croatia
Italy
Spain
MEDITERRANEAN SEA
Ancient Mesopotamia
Iraq
Iran
China
Japan
Algeria
Egypt
Saudi Arabia
India
PACIFIC OCEAN
AFRICA
Nigeria
Liberia
Vietnam
ATLANTIC OCEAN
INDIAN OCEAN
Zimbabwe
AUSTRALIA
South Africa
New Zealand
L. Kubinyi

OBJECTIVES

1. Read the literature of the Anglo-Saxon period on the subject of "Songs of Ancient Heroes"
2. Interpret literary elements with special emphasis on alliteration and kennings
3. Apply a variety of reading strategies, including using context clues
4. Respond to the literature in a variety of modes
5. Learn and use new words
6. Learn about the birth and development of Old English
7. Plan, draft, revise, edit, proofread, and publish a literary analysis
8. Develop skill in sentence combining
9. Demonstrate an ability to evaluate a news feature
10. Explore the meaning of group membership through various projects

Selection Readability

This Annotated Teacher's Edition provides a summary of each selection in the student book. Following each Summary heading, you will find one, two, or three small icons. These icons indicate, in an approximate sense, the reading level of the selection.

- ■ One icon indicates that the selection is easy.
- ■■ Two icons indicate that the selection is on an intermediate reading level.
- ■■■ Three icons indicate that the selection is challenging.

The Anglo-Saxons 449–1066

The Saxon Infantry (in chain mail, visor helmets, and shields) holds off the Norman attack. Detail from the Bayeux Tapestry (11th century).

Responding to the Art

The French Bishop of Bayeux commissioned this tapestry to commemorate the story of the Normans' conquest of England under his half brother, William the Conqueror. The conquest itself makes up little more than half the length of the tapestry. Composed of half a dozen pieces of coarse linen, the tapestry depicts funerals, a coronation, a feast, and even the appearance of Halley's Comet. Three-inch borders at the bottom and top illustrate aspects of country life and humor, images of animals, and scenes from Aesop's fables. In the scene shown here, the English fight on foot, holding spears and two-handed axes above their heads in an attempt to resist the Normans.

Activity. Shields and spears were weapons all Anglo-Saxons possessed. Swords, helmets, and mail shirts, made of linked iron rings, were reserved for leaders. Ask students what they can tell about these soldiers from this tapestry. [These soldiers are large, strong men who wear armor reserved for leaders.]

Resources

Viewing and Representing

Videocassette A, Segment 3, "The Anglo-Saxons"
Available in English and Spanish.
Use the video to introduce students to life among the Anglo-Saxons.
For full lesson plans and worksheets, see the *Visual Connections Teacher's Manual.*

Videocassette A, Segment 1, "A Living Language, Part 1"
Available in English and Spanish.
Use the video to introduce students to the earliest phases of the development of the English language and literature.

OBJECTIVES

1. Understand the historical and social forces that shaped the Anglo-Saxon era
2. Interpret the way historical context influenced literary works in the Anglo-Saxon era
3. Read and understand a time line
4. Understand the relevance of the Anglo-Saxon era to our day
5. Take notes on and discuss the possibility that our language and literature might disappear

Responding to the Quotation

? In a society dominated by aggression, what would you expect to be the Anglo-Saxon attitude toward family life, the role of women, art, literature, ethics, and work? [Answers will vary.] After they have read the historical introduction, ask students to return to their initial notions to confirm or reject them.

RESPONDING TO THE ART

Built in three stages, Stonehenge (c. 3000–1848 B.C.) is the best known of many stone sites in the British Isles. Using radiocarbon dating methods on charcoal taken from pits within the circle of stones, historians have postulated that Stonehenge was in use around 1848 B.C. Some archaeologists believe the ring of stones served as a gathering place and ceremonial center. The huge bluestones are found only in southwestern Wales, 240 miles away, and some weigh up to four tons. How the stones were moved to their present location and why they were arranged in their positions is a great mystery. Scholars do know, however, that the arrangement of the slabs indicates the timing of important astronomical events such as the summer solstice.

Activity. Ask students to speculate about how such heavy stones were put in place. [Possible answers: log rollers, a pulley system, other devices.]

The Anglo-Saxons

by David Adams Leeming

Anglo-Saxon England was born of warfare, remained forever a military society, and came to its end in battle.

—J. R. Lander

Aerial view of Stonehenge (c. 3000–1848 B.C.), located near Salisbury, England.

go.hrw.com
LEO 12-Anglo-Saxons

Using Students' Strengths

Visual Learners

Have visual learners study the headings and captions, as well as the various illustrations, to make some predictions about what they will learn about life in Anglo-Saxon times. Students might also complete a K-W-L chart.

Verbal Learners

Engage students in dialogue about what they would and would not have liked about living in Anglo-Saxon times. Small groups of students might work together to brainstorm ideas about where and how they would have lived, what they might have worn, and what they would have loved and feared most.

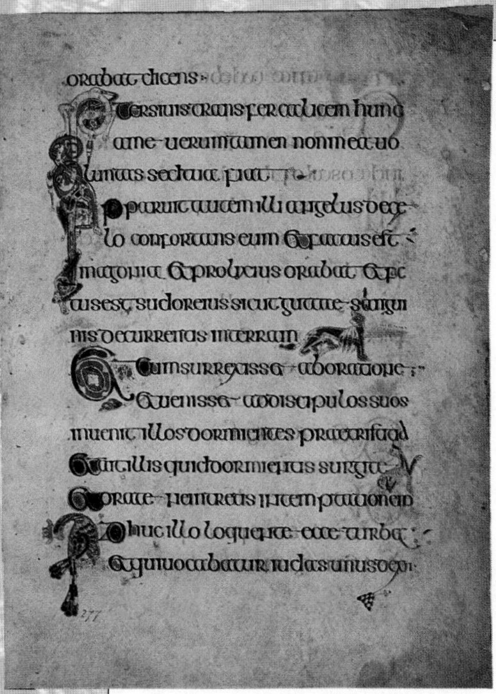

The Board of Trinity College, Dublin. Photograph by The Green Studio Ltd, Dublin.

Page from the Book of Kells (8th century).

Isolated from the European continent, rain-drenched and often fogged in, but also green and dotted with thatched cottages, quaint stone churches, and mysterious stone ruins, the island of Great Britain seems made for elves, legends, and poets. Yet if this land of mystery, beauty, and melancholy weather has produced Stonehenge, Robin Hood, and Shakespeare, it has also produced the theory of gravity, the Industrial Revolution, radar, penicillin, and the Beatles. We tend to associate the British with their monarchy and their former empire. But we should also remember that while most of the world suffered under various forms of tyranny, the English from the time of the Magna Carta (1215) were gradually creating a political system "by and for the people" that remains today a source of envy and inspiration for many nations. Although Americans rebelled against British rule in 1776, America would not be what it is today without the legacy of English common law—with its emphasis on personal rights and freedom. Nor would America be what it is today without the English parliamentary government, English literature, and the English language.

Stonehenge, consisting of large sandstone blocks and smaller bluestone pillars.

A Exploring the Historical Period

Isolation

Students may need to be reminded that ancient civilizations, some of which were quite advanced, had arisen in other parts of the world well before this time. For example, the great pyramids had already been built along the Nile. City-states had risen and fallen in Mesopotamia. Persia had already united many lands, and China was a unified, powerful empire. The beginnings of democracy had already come and gone in Greece. By contrast, England was a green, dark, isolated, sleepy island where civilization and empire had yet to bloom.

B Exploring the Historical Period

Stonehenge

The name *Stonehenge* is from the Saxon, combining *stone* and *henge,* "hang," thus a place of hanging stone. Stonehenge stands at the top of a gentle slope among the dry grasslands of the Salisbury Plain. The earthen mounds of the Bronze Age chieftains of the period surround the site. These ancient Britons were farmers, warriors, and traders. Ornaments found in the mounds include amber from the Baltic Sea and beads from Central Europe. Weathered carvings of bronze daggers, like those found in the burial mounds, appear on the upright slabs of Stonehenge itself.

Reaching All Students

Struggling Readers

Take time to go over with students the way this essay is organized, with a title, subheads, boldface summaries at the end of each section, boxed lists of key ideas (as on p. 9), boxed quotations from other sources that enrich or expand on the text (as on pp. 6, 7, 12, and 14), and boxed mini-essays on related topics (as on p. 10). Also discuss the role of illustrations and point out that most have captions.

English Language Learners

As you work through the essay, help students understand the idioms. Explain the general concept of nonliteral language, using these examples:

- p. 6: "... who *left their permanent stamp* in one of the names ..."
- p. 7: "... Christianity ... gradually *took hold* ...."
- p. 11: "Warfare was *the order of the day.*"

Advanced Learners

As students read each selection in this collection, have them write brief analyses on how each piece of literature reflects a topic covered in this historical essay. Such critical thinking will help students gain a deeper understanding of the connection between literature and social history. You may want students to maintain a notebook for this purpose throughout the year.

Time Line

This time line shows major events that occurred both in England and around the world between the time of the Celts and the Norman Conquest.

• **307–1 B.C.**

Roman Government

Well before the coming of the Anglo-Saxons to England, Rome already had what Roman writers proudly called a "balanced government." A republic had been created as early as c. 509 B.C., with a senate of distinguished citizens and assemblies made up of citizen-soldiers.

• **A.D. 1–399**

London

London grew from two ancient cities; the City of London and the City of Westminster. The Romans established the City of London as a trading center; a thousand years later, around the eleventh century, the City of Westminster, a few miles away, served as the residential area for London's elite. Present-day London encompasses approximately six hundred ten square miles along the River Thames.

• **500–599**

Japanese Religion

Shinto, which involves worship of ancestors and gods found in nature, is the native religion of Japan; however, many who practice Shinto are open to other philosophies as well. In the fifth century the Japanese began importing ideas and technology, including Buddhism, which came from China and Korea. Today, approximately seventy-five percent of the Japanese practice Buddhism, a religion that seeks the attainment of spiritual freedom and inner tranquillity.

Paper, Books, and Printing in China

The Chinese had been writing books on bamboo by 1,000 B.C. They had already invented paper in A.D. 105 and were printing books by 591. By approximately 1045, they had gone beyond the carved wooden blocks and ink of the sixth century to create movable type, about four hundred years in advance of Gutenberg.

The Anglo-Saxons, 449–1066

• **Detail from the Book of Kells (8th century).** The Board of Trinity College, Dublin. Photograph by The Green Studio Ltd, Dublin.

• **King Arthur in battle. From a French manuscript.**

	307–1 B.C.	A.D. 1–399	400–499	500–599
LITERARY EVENTS	Roman poet Virgil born, 70 B.C. Alexandria is center of Greek learning; library begun under Ptolemy, 307 B.C.	Throughout Europe, scrolls begin to be replaced by vellum books, c. 360 Roman poet Ovid writes *Metamorphoses*, c. 5		In China, books printed by the late 500s
CULTURAL/HISTORICAL EVENTS	Celts called "Brythons" live in Britain, 300s B.C. Julius Caesar invades Britain, 55 B.C. Cleopatra VII becomes last queen of Egypt, 51 B.C.	Londinium (present-day London) founded by Romans as a supply port, c. 50 Queen Boadicea leads her eastern British tribe in an uprising against the Romans, 61 Christianity proclaimed lawful religion in the Roman Empire, c. 313	Roman legions withdraw from Britain, 409 Patrick brings Christianity to Ireland, 432 Angles, Saxons, and Jutes invade Britain, c. 449 Roman Empire falls to Germanic tribes, 476	Semilegendary King Arthur rules Celtic tribe, c. 516 Death of King Arthur at Battle of Camlann, 537 Widespread plague reaches Britain from Europe, 547 Buddhism introduced to Japan, 552 Saint Augustine converts Anglo-Saxon King Ethelbert and establishes monastery at Canterbury, 597

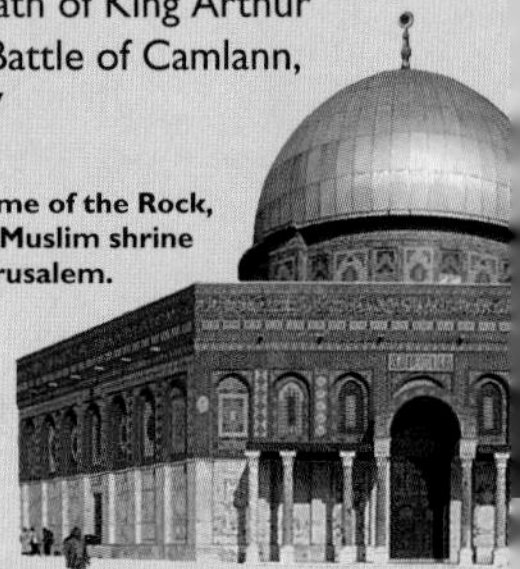

• **Dome of the Rock, holy Muslim shrine in Jerusalem.**

• **Roman helmet.** © British Museum, London.

• **Chinese sculpture of a seated Buddha (c. 650) from the T'ang dynasty.** The Metropolitan Museum of Art, Rogers Fund, 1919. (19.186). Photograph by Lynton Gardiner. © 1989 The Metropolitan Museum of Art.

Using the Time Line

Have students use a print or nonprint encyclopedia or a database to place the following events in science, mathematics, and the arts on the time line.

- Euclid publishes *The Elements of Geometry.* [c. 300 B.C.]
- Li Po writes poetry during China's "golden age of literature." [A.D. 701–762]
- The Maya, during their classical period, devise an extremely accurate calendar system consisting of 260 ritual days in a 365-day year forming a longer cycle of 52 years. [A.D. 320–900]
- In India, Aryabhata calculates the value of *pi* to four decimal places and the length of the solar year to 365.3586805 days. [c. A.D. 500]
- Muslim mathematician al-Khwarizimi introduces algebra. [A.D. 825]

600–699

Hymns produced by Caedmon, the earliest English Christian poet, c. 670

At Alexandria, Arabs discover the famous library with 300,000 papyrus scrolls, 640

Lyric poetry of the T'ang period promotes everyday use of Chinese language, 600s

Paulinus is first Roman missionary to arrive in northern England, 601

Golden Age of T'ang dynasty begins in China, 618

Mohammed (b. 570), founder of Islam, begins to dictate the *Koran,* c. 625

Egyptian caliphs introduce the first organized news and postal service, 650

Synod of Whitby unites British Christian Church with Roman Church, 664

• Mayan figure holding tortillas.

700–799

Monks begin the Book of Kells, an illuminated manuscript of Latin Gospels, 760

Compilation of *Manyoshu* ("Collection of Ten Thousand Leaves"), Japanese anthology of about 4,500 poems, c. 759

The Venerable Bede, an English cleric, writes the *Ecclesiastical History of the English People,* 730

Beowulf first recorded, c. 700

Moors invade Spain, 711

Pueblo period begins in southwestern North America, c. 750

Vikings invade Britain, beginning a century of invasions, 793

• Danes attacking an East Anglian town.

800–899

• Crown of the Holy Roman Empire (10th century, with later additions).

Anglo-Saxon Chronicle begun, 891

Composition of the Poetic Edda, a famous cycle of Norse mythological poems, c. 850

In France, Charlemagne crowned emperor of the West by Pope Leo III, 800

Decline of great Mayan civilization in Central America, 800s

Incas build fortress-city of Machu Picchu in Peru, c. 800

Algebra devised in Persia, c. 810

School of Astronomy founded at Baghdad, 813

Alfred the Great (849–899) becomes king of England, 871; he forces the Danes from Wessex, 878

900–1066

Japanese court attendant Sei Shōnogan writes diary, *The Pillow Book,* c. 1000

In Japan, Lady Murasaki Shikibu writes the world's first novel, *The Tale of Genji,* c. 1000

The Exeter Book, a collection of English poetry, first copied, c. 975

Beginnings of the Arabian tales, *The Thousand and One Nights,* 900

Kingdom of Ghana in Africa flourishes, 900s

High King Brian Boru drives the Danes from Ireland at the Battle of Clontarf, 1014

Normans defeat Saxons; William the Conqueror becomes English king, 1066

• Machu Picchu, Peru, lost city of the Incas.

• **700–799**

The Moors

The Moors of northwestern Africa (called the Mauri by the Romans) were a Berber people, many of whom spoke Arabic in addition to their own language. Converted to Islam, they conquered Spain with the Arabs in the 700s and ruled there during the Middle Ages, establishing a Moorish civilization. After losing most of their Spanish holdings by the 1200s, the Moors settled primarily in North Africa.

Bede the Venerable

A monk and a scholar, Bede (672/673–735) is the man most responsible for our knowledge of England before the eighth century. The purpose of his *Ecclesiastical History* is to show how the Church brought unity to England, ending an era of violence and barbarism.

• **800–899**

Alfred the Great

In addition to being the only ruler able to successfully resist Danish invasions, Alfred was a patron of learning who furthered the education of his people. He invited scholars to his court, and he himself translated scholarly works.

• **900–1066**

Anglo-Saxon Chronicle

The *Anglo-Saxon Chronicle,* a history of England from the beginning of the Christian era until the middle of the twelfth century, is the first important prose work in English.

Using the Time Line

Ask students to examine the time line and answer the following critical thinking questions:

1. What four peoples invaded England in the period covered by this time line? [the Romans in 55 B.C., the Anglo-Saxons c. 449, the Vikings in 793, and the Normans in 1066] What effects might a series of invasions—one every 300–500 years—have on a culture? [Students might speculate that such a history would make a culture adaptable; that people would learn to live with those who spoke differently or worshipped different gods.]
2. What thread unites all the literary events that take place in Britain up to the time of Bede? [Catholic monks initiated every literary event.] What inference can students make about the monks' cultural role during the Anglo-Saxon era? [The monks' role was critical because they preserved the Latin Gospels and also produced the first written works.]
3. What native military leaders are identified? [Queen Boadicea, King Arthur, Alfred the Great] Why were these people revered? [Possible response: They united warring tribes and tried to fight off invaders.]

A Exploring the Historical Period

Iberians

The earliest settlers in England were called Iberians because it is thought they originally came from the Iberian Peninsula (the peninsula of present-day Portugal and Spain).

B Exploring the Culture

Celts

From about 700 B.C., the Celts dominated most of what is now western and central Europe. Skilled artisans, they introduced the use of iron to the rest of Europe. They also had a highly developed religion, mythology, and legal system that specified individual rights. The Celts were also adept at curing hams, keeping bees, and making wooden barrels. The language of the Celts was dominant in Britain until around the fifth century A.D. Welsh, Scots Gaelic, and Irish are forms of the Celtic language that may still be heard in Wales, Scotland, and Ireland today.

C Cultural Connections

Celtic Descendants

Descendants of the Celts still live in Cornwall, the highlands of Scotland, Ireland, Wales, and Brittany. The Welsh refer to themselves as *cymry,* meaning "fellow countrymen," emphasizing their role as the true native Britons. Cymraeg, the language of Wales, shares origins with languages still spoken in geographic areas that range from the Hebrides Islands in the northwest Atlantic to Brittany in northwest France. For centuries the Cambrian Mountains of central Wales provided safety for the Britons from the victorious Anglo-Saxons, enabling the Welsh to preserve many Celtic customs along with their language.

D Exploring the Culture

Druids

The Druids of Britain thought that the soul was immortal, passing in death from one person to another. They considered mistletoe and oak trees sacred and generally held their rites in old oak forests.

This relatively small island of Great Britain has been invaded and settled many times: first by ancient people we call the Iberians, then by the Celts (kelts), by the Romans, by the Angles and Saxons, by the Vikings, and by the Normans. Whatever we think of as "English" today owes something to each of these invaders.

A small, isolated country, England is nevertheless the origin of a legal and political system that many other countries, including the United States, have since imitated. Over the centuries, English traditions and language have been reshaped by the island's invaders.

The Celtic Heroes and Heroines: A Magical World

When Greek travelers visited what is now Great Britain in the fourth century B.C., they found an island settled by tall blond warriors who called themselves Celts. Among these island Celts was a group called Brythons (or Britons), who left their permanent stamp in one of the names (Britain) eventually adopted by the land they settled.

A monk's cell (7th or 8th century) on Skellig Michael, off the coast of Kerry, Ireland.

The religion of the Celts seems to have been a form of **animism,** from the Latin word for "spirit." The Celts saw spirits everywhere—in rivers, trees, stones, ponds, fire, and thunder. These spirits or gods controlled all aspects of existence, and they had to be constantly satisfied. Priests called Druids acted as intermediaries between the gods and the people. Sometimes ritual dances were called for, sometimes even human sacrifice. Some think that Stonehenge—that array of huge stones on Salisbury Plain in Wiltshire—was used by the Druids for religious rites having to do with the lunar and solar cycles.

The mythology of the Celts has influenced English and Irish writers to this day. Sir Thomas Malory (page 169) in the fifteenth century, having time on his hands in jail, gathered together the Celtic legends about a warrior named Arthur. He mixed these stories generously with chivalric legends from the Continent and produced *Le Morte Darthur,* about the king who ultimately became the very embodiment of English values.

Early in the twentieth century, William Butler Yeats (page 978) used the Celtic myths in his poetry and plays in an attempt to make the Irish aware of their lost heroic past.

The Celtic stories are very different from the Anglo-Saxon tales that came later (see page 18), although it is the Anglo-Saxon myths that we tend to

> All the Britons dye their bodies with woad, which produces a blue color, and this gives them a more terrifying appearance in battle. They wear their hair long, and shave the whole of their bodies except the head and the upper lip.
>
> —Julius Caesar

Making the Connections

Cross-Cultural Connections: Storytellers

Like the Greek bards or rhapsodes before them, the Irish *ollamhs* were both historians and entertainers who preserved their culture's myths and legends. They studied philosophy, astronomy, and magic and had to know two hundred fifty basic tales and hundreds more variations. The Irish *shanachies,* the tellers of tales of history, were entrusted with one hundred seventy-eight important accounts. Other cultures have their traditional storytellers, too. These include Navajo singers who recite stories in Blessingway ceremonies that last for days and the Inuit of the Far North who trace scenes from their traditional stories in the snow and mud with whalebone knives. All these storytellers preserve oral traditions and in the end influence the written literature of their people.

study in school. Unlike the male-dominated Anglo-Saxon stories, the Celtic legends are full of strong women, like the tall and fierce and very beautiful Queen Maeve of Connacht (kân′ôt) in Ireland. Maeve once led her troops in an epic battle over the ownership of a fabulous white herd bull whose back was so broad fifty children could play upon it. Celtic stories, unlike the later, brooding Anglo-Saxon stories, leap into the sunlight (no matter how much blood is spilled). Full of fantastic animals, passionate love affairs, and fabulous adventures, the Celtic myths take you to enchanted lands where magic and the imagination rule.

The first British settlers were the Celts, a people whose daily lives were influenced by their magical religion. Their beliefs survive in Celtic mythology, which has influenced generations of later writers.

The Romans: The Great Administrators

Beginning with an invasion led by Julius Caesar in 55 B.C. and culminating in one organized by the emperor Claudius about a hundred years later, the Britons were finally conquered by the legions of Rome. Using the administrative genius that enabled them to hold dominion over much of the known world, the Romans provided the armies and organization that prevented further serious invasions of Britain for several hundred years. They built a network of roads (some still used today) and a great defensive wall seventy-three miles long. During Roman rule, Christianity, which would later become a unifying force, gradually took hold under the leadership of European missionaries. The old Celtic religion began to vanish.

Boadicea, queen of a Briton tribe, was flogged by the Romans after they had plundered her dead husband's property. She led the Britons to a fierce retaliation.

Boadicea's tribe, at once the most powerful and hitherto the most submissive, was moved to frenzy against the Roman invaders. They flew to arms. Boadicea found herself at the head of a numerous army, and nearly all the Britons within reach rallied to her standard. There followed an up-rush of hatred from the abyss, which is a measure of the cruelty of the conquest. It was a scream of rage against invincible oppression. . . . Her monument on the Thames Embankment opposite Big Ben reminds us of the harsh cry of liberty or death which has echoed down the ages.

—Winston S. Churchill

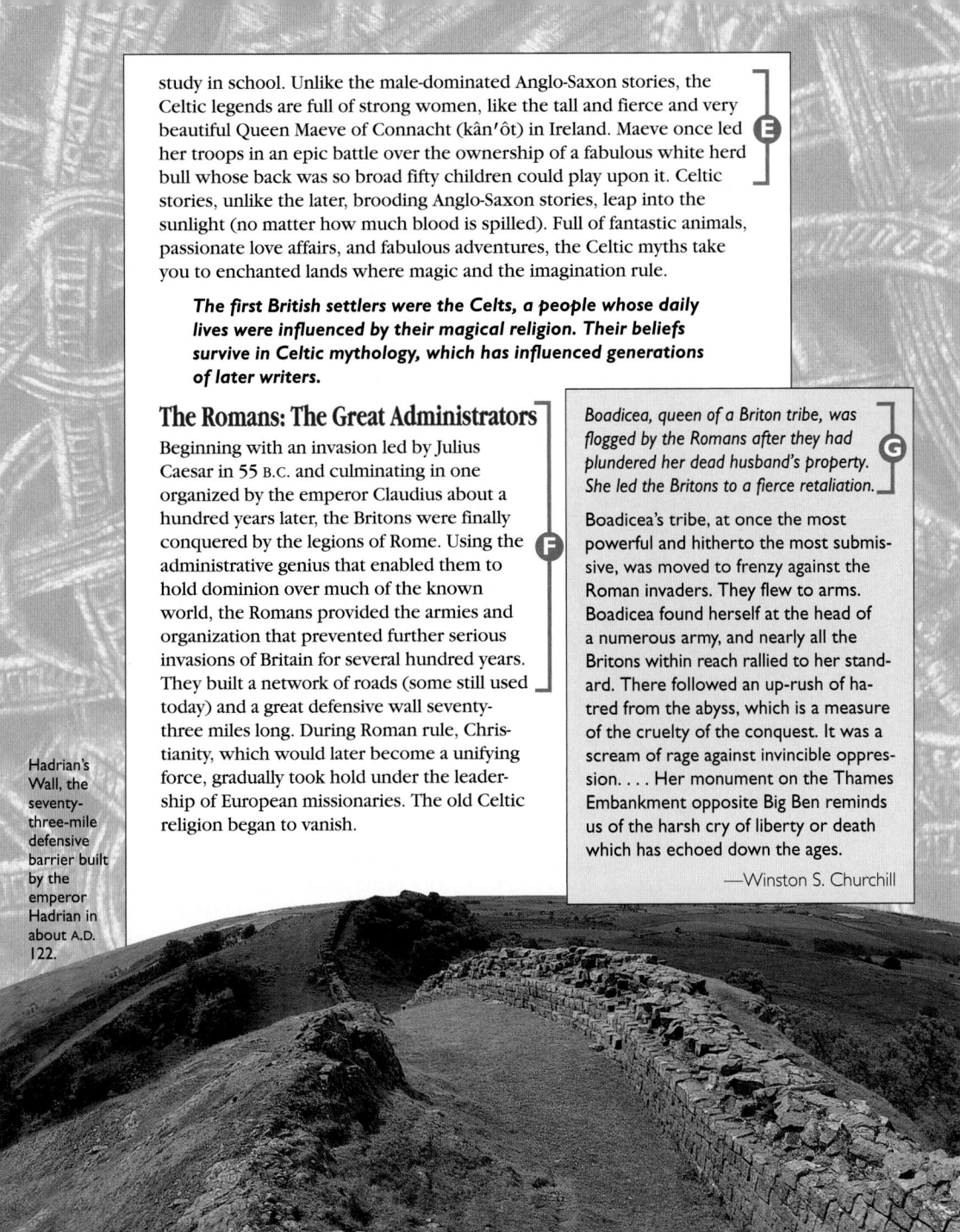

Hadrian's Wall, the seventy-three-mile defensive barrier built by the emperor Hadrian in about A.D. 122.

E Literary Connections

Irish Myths and Tales

Irish tales are also full of fairies, the good folk, and the wee people. These tales reflect (some say) the ancient Druidic tradition, plus a love of magic and the joy of storytelling.

F Exploring the Historical Period

Roman Roads and Walls

The five thousand miles of stone roads the Romans built linked tribal capitals and towns, especially London, York, and Winchester. These roads facilitated trade, the collection of taxes, and the movement of troops. The great defensive wall referred to in this text is Hadrian's Wall, which linked the North Sea and the Atlantic near the present-day border between England and Scotland, and held back the marauding Picts and Scots for two hundred fifty years. Along this wall were seventeen large stone forts to house the Roman legions guarding the frontier.

G Exploring the Historical Period

Boadicea

In *Roman History,* Dio Cassius described Boadicea like this: "She was very tall, the glance of her eye most fierce; her voice harsh. A great mass of the reddest hair fell down to her hips. Around her neck was a large golden necklace, and she always wore a tunic of many colours over which she fastened a thick cloak with a broach. Her appearance was terrifying."

Getting Students Involved

Cooperative Learning

Have students work in groups of four and assign each group two or more of the nine sections of the introduction. Direct each group to teach or present the information in that section by means of a ten-minute presentation that includes either handouts, posters, overhead projections, or other visuals that help make the material more interesting and accessible. Each group should divide responsibilities in this way: a leader to assign tasks and lead discussions, an artist to prepare visual materials, a writer to create written materials and take notes, and a speaker to present the information to the class.

Reading Celtic Tales

Have students find a Celtic myth or tale, read it, and report on the kinds of characters they encounter as well as on the aspects of the plot that make the story memorable.

Ⓐ Exploring the Historical Period

Tacitus on the Angles

At the height of the Roman Empire, the Roman historian Tacitus (c. 56–c. 120) described the Germanic tribes of the north, including the Angles, as having these positive attributes: love of freedom, chaste women, and lack of public extravagance.

Ⓑ Literary Connections

King Arthur

Students may read more about the heroic Celtic leader King Arthur in Sir Thomas Malory's treatment of the King Arthur legend in *Le Morte Darthur* (c. 1469), in Tennyson's *Idylls of the King* (1859–1885), or in T. H. White's *The Once and Future King* (1958), upon which the musical *Camelot* is based. (pp. 171, 826)

Ⓒ Exploring the Historical Period

King Alfred the Great

King Alfred may be one king who truly deserves the appellation "the great." Not only did he help save Wessex and other kingdoms in England from the Danes, but he also helped create a cohesive English society from a collection of small, fractious kingdoms. In addition, he restored cities destroyed during invasions and revived interest in learning and in the English language.

RESPONDING TO THE ART

The Alfred Jewel shows an enameled figure of a man holding two scepters. The inscription around the edge reads: "Alfred ordered me to be made."

Activity. Ask students what symbolic significance the two scepters might have. [Possible answer: Alfred was trying to unite the various kingdoms within the Anglo-Saxon dominion.]

If the Romans had stayed, Londoners today might speak Italian. But the Romans had troubles at home. By A.D. 409, they had evacuated their troops from Britain, leaving roads, walls, villas, and great public baths, but no central government. Without Roman control, Britain was a country of separate clans. The result was weakness, which made the island ripe for a series of successful invasions by non-Christian peoples from the Germanic regions of Continental Europe.

Roman conquerors remained in Britain for more than four hundred years. They built roads and the walls that fended off attacks on Britain for several centuries. When the Romans finished withdrawing in A.D. 409, Britain was left without a centralized government—again susceptible to other invaders.

A picture stone (8th century) from Gotland showing a Viking ship under sail.

Statens Historiska Museer, Stockholm.

The Anglo-Saxons Sweep Ashore

Ⓐ This time the attack came from the north. In the middle of the fifth century, the invaders, Angles and Saxons from Germany and Jutes from Denmark, crossed the North Sea. They drove out the old Britons before them and eventually settled the greater part of Britain. The language of the Anglo-Saxons became the dominant language in the land which was to take a new name—Engla land, or England—from the Angles.

But the latest newcomers did not have an easy time of it. The Celts put up a strong resistance before they retreated into Wales in the far west of the country. There, traces of their culture, especially their language, can still be found. One of the heroic Celtic leaders Ⓑ was a Welsh chieftain called Arthur, who developed in legend as Britain's "once and future king."

At first, Anglo-Saxon England was no more politically unified than Celtic Britain had been. The country was divided into several Ⓒ independent principalities, each with its own "king." It was not until King Alfred of Wessex (r. 871–899), also known as Alfred the Great, led the Anglo-Saxons against the invading Danes that England became in any true sense a nation. The Danes were one of the fierce Viking peoples who crossed the cold North Sea in their dragon-prowed boats in the eighth and ninth centuries. Plundering and destroying everything in their path, the Danes eventually took over and settled in parts of northeast and central England.

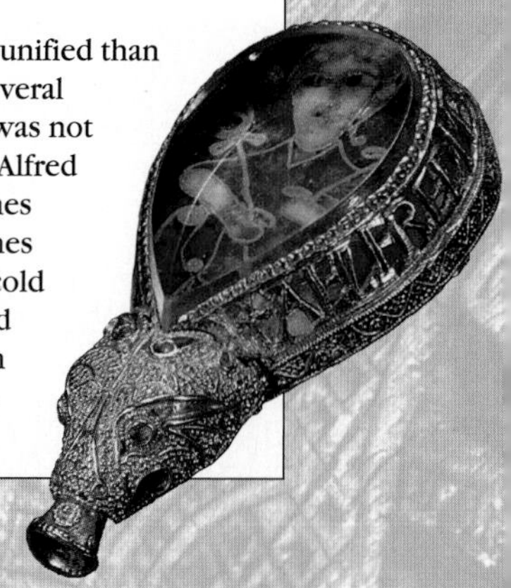

Gold and enamel jewel (9th century) thought to have belonged to King Alfred.

Ashmolean Museum, Oxford.

It is possible that even King Alfred would have failed to unify the Anglo-Saxons had it not been for the gradual reemergence of Christianity in Britain. Irish and Continental missionaries converted the Anglo-Saxon kings, whose subjects converted also. Christianity provided a common faith and common system of morality and right conduct; it also linked England to Europe. Under Christianity and Alfred, Anglo-Saxons fought to protect their people, their culture, and their church from the ravages of the Danes. Alfred's reign began the shaky dominance of Wessex kings in southern England. Alfred's descendants—Ethelfleda, a brilliant military leader and strategist, and her brother Edward—carried on his battle against the Danes.

The battle continued until both the Anglo-Saxons and the Danes were defeated in 1066 by William, Duke of Normandy, and his invading force of Normans from northwestern France.

The reemergence of Christianity and the role of Alfred the Great combined to unify Anglo-Saxon England. Alfred and his descendants fought the Danish invaders until the Norman Conquest in 1066.

What does "Anglo-Saxon England" mean?

Here are some key features of this age of warriors:

- Anglo-Saxon society developed from kinship groups led by a strong chief.
- The people farmed, maintained local governments, and created fine crafts, especially metalwork.
- Christianity eventually replaced the old warrior religion, linking England to Continental Europe.
- Monasteries were centers of learning and preserved works from the older oral tradition.
- English—not just the Church's Latin—gained respect as a written language.

The coronation of King Harold, from the Bayeux Tapestry (11th century).

Musée de la Tapisserie, Bayeux.

D Exploring the Historical Period

King Alfred's Legacy

In the preface to Boethius's *Consolation of Philosophy* (which Alfred translated), Alfred writes about his own legacy: "To be brief, I may say that it has always been my wish to live honorably, and after my death to leave to those who come after me my memory of good works." Ask students if Alfred's philosophy of leadership is still applicable. [Answers will vary. Students may say that leaders still need to be honorable; they may say that all leaders must build for the future.]

E Exploring the Culture

Christianity

The gradual emergence of Christianity among the Anglo-Saxons was to a great extent due to the work of Irish and Continental missionaries, the most important of whom was probably Saint Augustine (the second of that name), who converted King Ethelbert of Kent in A.D. 597, founded the cathedral at Canterbury, and became the first archbishop of Canterbury, or leader of the Church in England. His mission, however, was not immediately or permanently successful, since the old pagan Anglo-Saxon religion persisted.

Responding to the Art

This scene from the Bayeux Tapestry shows the coronation of Harold, the Anglo-Saxon king who was later defeated by the Normans in 1066. Although tapestry usually involves the weaving of thread, this "tapestry" is actually an embroidered band of linen, 231 feet long, and 19 1/2 inches wide. Of particular value to historians are the details of battle tactics and equipment depicted in the work. **Activity.** Ask students to identify the participants in the ceremony and the details that prompt this conclusion. [The participants on the left are lords as indicated by the upraised sword and the participant on the right is a bishop as indicated by his clerical robes and tonsure.]

Crossing the Curriculum

Geography

To give students a clear picture of the geographic locations of key events in this period, provide a large outline map of Europe. As students read, have them add names and events to the map as well as labeled arrows showing the invasions. Or, if it is available, students may use an atlas program or CD-ROM to locate key areas in Great Britain. Ask students to import these maps to a paintbrush program. Using the draw feature, they can illustrate the raids on England.

Art

Invite students to research art from this period, such as the Bayeux tapestry or objects from Sutton Hoo (see p. 10) and other archaeological sites. Ask them to choose one object to present to the class. Their presentation should include a drawing or photocopy of the object and a discussion of the insight the object provides into life in Anglo-Saxon times.

Ⓐ Exploring the Culture

The Role of Women

The wife of an earl (or *thane*) would supervise the weaving and dyeing of clothes, the slaughter of livestock, the baking of bread, and, most importantly, the brewing of mead—fermented honey that was kept in soft, gray-brown pottery bowls. Because honey was so essential, beekeeping was also an important chore.

Ⓑ Background

Whitby Abbey

Hild, sometimes called St. Hilda, originally founded Whitby Abbey for both monks and nuns. Until it was destroyed by the Danes in 867, it was the chief school of learning in the north. Later reestablished by the Benedictines, the abbey sits in a commanding spot on an exposed cliff two hundred feet above the sea, where people still come today to peer in wonder.

Ⓒ Exploring the Historical Period

Sutton Hoo

As extraordinary a find as Sutton Hoo was for the history of art and archaeology, it may be even more significant in terms of history, for it suggests that England was influenced by Scandinavia even before the Viking attacks began.

A CLOSER LOOK

Ⓐ Women in Anglo-Saxon Culture

Anglo-Saxon culture, with its emphasis on warfare, sounds as if it would be an inhospitable place for women. But women had rights in this society that were sharply curtailed after the Norman Conquest in 1066.

Evidence from wills first used during the later Anglo-Saxon period shows that women inherited and held property. Even when married, women still retained control over their own property. In fact, a prospective husband had to offer a woman a substantial gift (called the *morgengifu*, the "morning-gift") of money and land. The woman (not her family or her husband) had personal control over this gift; she could give it away, sell it, or bequeath it as she chose.

Christianity also offered opportunities for women. Women joined religious communities, and some women became powerful abbesses. These abbesses, usually women from noble families, were in charge of large double houses that included both a monastery and a nunnery. Ⓑ Hild (614–680), the abbess of Whitby (in present-day Yorkshire), was one of the most famous of these women. Hild accumulated an immense library and turned Whitby into a center of learning. Vikings sacked Whitby Abbey in the ninth century. The ruins of a monastery later founded at the same site still stand today, high atop cliffs overlooking the wild, gray North Sea.

Silver figurine (c. 9th–11th century) of Viking woman, from Grödinge, Söndermanland, Sweden.
Statens Historiska Museer, Stockholm.

Silver dish from the Sutton Hoo burial treasure (7th century).

Anglo-Saxon Life: The Warm Hall, the Cold World

Ⓒ In 1939, in Sutton Hoo in Suffolk, England, archaeologists discovered a treasure that had been under the earth for thirteen hundred years. This enormous ship-grave contained the imprint of a huge wooden ship and a vast treasure trove—all of which had been buried with a great king or noble warrior. There was no trace left of the king or warrior himself, but his sword lay there, along with other meticulously decorated treasures of gold, silver, and bronze—his purse, coins, helmet, buckle, serving vessels, and harp. This grave can't help but remind us of the huge burial mound erected in memory of the king Beowulf.

Skill Link

Discussing and Comparing Cultures

This essay contains a great deal of cultural information. Help students compare and contrast it to their own life and times.

- Have students identify the types of cultural information found in this essay. [Possible answers: information on social organization, the importance of law and order, the need for protection and military preparedness, as well as information on men and women's roles and their relationship to one another and to the community]
- Ask students to work in pairs or small groups to discuss how the specific cultural characteristics of the Anglo-Saxons are similar to or different from the cultural characteristics of their own times.

As these Sutton Hoo ship treasures show, the Anglo-Saxons were not barbarians, though they are frequently depicted that way. However, they did not lead luxurious lives either, or lives dominated by learning or the arts. Warfare was the order of the day. As *Beowulf* shows, law and order, at least in the early days, were the responsibility of the leader in any given group, whether family, clan, tribe, or kingdom. Fame and success, even survival, were gained only through loyalty to the leader, especially during war, and success was measured in gifts from the leader. Beowulf, for instance, makes his name and gains riches by defeating the monsters who try to destroy King Hrothgar.

This pattern of loyal dependency was basic to Anglo-Saxon life. Such loyalty grew out of a need to protect the group from the terrors of an enemy-infested wilderness—a wilderness that became particularly frightening during the long, bone-chilling nights of winter. In most of England, the Anglo-Saxons tended to live close to their animals in single-family homesteads, wooden buildings that surrounded a communal court or a warm, fire-lit chieftain's hall. This cluster of buildings was protected by a wooden stockade fence. The arrangement contributed to a sense of security and to the close relationship between leader and followers. It also encouraged the Anglo-Saxon tendency toward community discussion and rule by consensus.

Anglo-Saxon life was dominated by the need to protect the clan and home against enemies. All groups, from family to kingdom, were organized around a leader who commanded absolute loyalty.

Reconstructed Anglo-Saxon village in West Stow, Suffolk, England. The communal hall is at the right.

Ⓓ Exploring the Culture

Social Classes

An agricultural, semi-nomadic people, Anglo-Saxons had a two-class society: the earls, or thanes, who ruled and who were related to the founder of the tribe; and the churls, bondservants whose ancestors had been captured by the tribe. Although they admired their warriors, the Anglo-Saxons insisted on a social organization based on more than courage, a society with strict laws and a sense of obligation to others. An absolute ruler and mighty warrior, the Anglo-Saxon king nevertheless consulted with the *witan* ("wise men"), an assembly of respected earls. The churls provided the hard labor for this agricultural society and were bound to the earls' service unless they could earn possessions and special royal favor to become freemen (independent landholders). A woman received honor and power only as a queen, as a wife of a powerful earl, or as a churchwoman.

Ⓔ Exploring the Culture

Anglo-Saxon Art

Many gifts from a chieftain to his loyal followers were objects that had been decorated. In fact, the art of the Anglo-Saxons was functional art—drinking horns, buckles, clasps, purses, and above all beautifully engraved weapons. Weapons such as swords were sometimes engraved with runes, letters from an alphabet known as the *futhark*, thought to provide magical protection from harm. This runic alphabet, however, was used strictly for ornamentation, not writing.

Ⓕ Exploring the Culture

Chieftains and Followers

The chieftain and his followers were bound till death. If the lord was killed, his warriors had to avenge his death or die beside him. After a battle, the warriors gathered in the mead hall of the lord and feasted at trestle tables and mead benches studded with gold.

Crossing the Curriculum

Science

Ask students to research the diversity of plant and animal life in Great Britain and to find explanations for the fact that there is almost no genuine wilderness in the British Isles other than remote moorland and rocky mountain tops. Though forested when the Romans arrived, today only seven percent of England is woodland. From Anglo-Saxon times onward, the village—surrounded by its fields, hedgerows, and copses—dominated the landscape, "the sweet especial rural scene," in the words of Gerard Manley Hopkins.

The oldest villages are those whose names end in *-ham*, *-ingham*, and *-wich* (the latter from the Latin *vicus*, "village"); some of these still feature thatched roofs made of straw, leaves, branches, or reeds.

Ⓐ Exploring the Culture
Fate and Glory

The word *wyrd* was used by the Anglo-Saxons to represent one's fate in life. The early Anglo-Saxons did not believe strongly in an afterlife; instead, they believed immortality or *lof*—fame that survives death—could be earned through heroic action.

Ⓑ Exploring the Culture
Dragons

The dragon to the Anglo-Saxons was the living embodiment of evil and death, in part because it was associated with the fierce Vikings (called Danes), who sailed boats with prows carved in the shapes of dragons' heads and fangs. In 793, the *Anglo-Saxon Chronicle* (pp. T5, T16) records, "In this fierce year, forbidding omens came over the land of Northumbria, and wretchedly terrified the people. There were excessive whirlwinds, lightning storms, and fiery dragons were seen flying in the sky. . . . Shortly after in the same year, on January 8th, the ravaging of heathen men [Vikings] destroyed God's church at Lindisfarne. . . ."

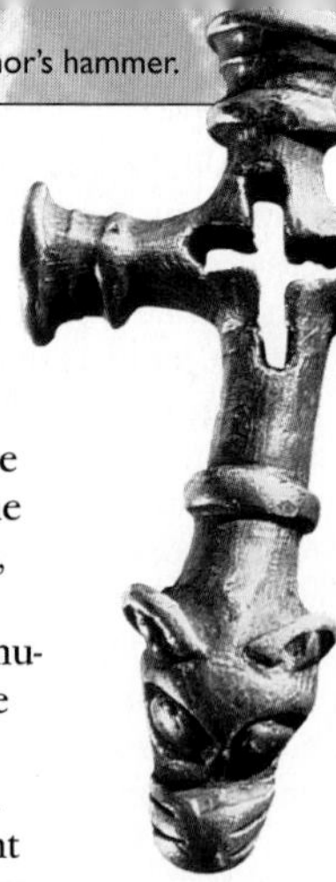

A pendant depicting Thor's hammer.

National Museum, Reykjavik.

The Anglo-Saxon Religion: Gods for Warriors

Ⓐ Despite the influence of Christianity, the old Anglo-Saxon religion with its warrior gods persisted. A dark, fatalistic religion, it had come with the Anglo-Saxons from Germany and had much in common with what we think of as Norse or Scandinavian mythology.

One of the most important Norse gods was Odin, the god of death, poetry, and magic. The Anglo-Saxon name for Odin was Woden (from which we have *Wednesday*, "Woden's day"). Woden could help humans communicate with spirits, and he was especially associated with burial rites and with ecstatic trances, important for both poetry and religious mysteries. Not surprisingly, this god of both poetry and death played an important role in the lives of people who produced great poetry and who also maintained a somber, brooding outlook on life.

The Anglo-Saxon deity named Thunor was essentially the same as Thor, the Norse god of thunder and lightning. His sign was the hammer and possibly also the twisted cross we call the swastika, which is found on so many Anglo-Saxon gravestones. (Thunor's name survives in *Thursday,* "Thor's day.")

Ⓑ Still another significant figure in Anglo-Saxon mythology is the dragon, which seems always, as in *Beowulf,* to be the protector of a treasure. Some scholars suggest that the fiery dragon should be seen as both a personification of "death the devourer" and as the guardian of the grave mound, in which a warrior's ashes and his treasure lay.

On the whole, the religion of the Anglo-Saxons seems to have been more concerned with ethics than with mysticism—with the earthly virtues of bravery, loyalty, generosity, and friendship.

Coifi, the Anglo-Saxon chief priest, advises King Edwin to give up the old gods and accept the new religion of Christianity. Here is his argument.

Your Majesty, when we compare the present life of man on earth with that time of which we have no knowledge, it seems to me like the swift flight of a single sparrow through the banqueting hall where you are sitting at dinner on a winter's day with your thanes and counselors. In the midst there is a comforting fire to warm the hall; outside, the storms of winter rain or snow are raging. This sparrow flies swiftly in through one door of the hall, and out through another. While he is inside, he is safe from the winter storms; but after a few moments of comfort, he vanishes from sight into the wintry world from which he came. Even so, man appears on earth for a little while; but of what went before this life or of what follows, we know nothing. Therefore, if this new teaching has brought any more certain knowledge, it seems only right that we should follow it.

—The Venerable Bede, quoting Coifi in *Ecclesiastical History of the English People*

Despite the growth of Christianity, the Anglo-Saxon religion remained strong. Although it drew many of its deities and rites from Scandinavian mythology, the Anglo-Saxon religion was more concerned with ethics than with mysticism.

Three standing figures (Odin, Thor, and Freyr) in tunics, from a Viking tapestry (12th century).

Statens Historiska Museer, Stockholm.

The Bards: Singing of Gods and Heroes

The Anglo-Saxon communal hall, besides offering shelter and a place for holding council meetings, also provided space for storytellers and their audience. As in other parts of the ancient world (notably in Homeric Greece more than one thousand years earlier), skilled storytellers, or bards, sang of gods and heroes. The Anglo-Saxons did not regard these bards (called scops) as inferior to warriors. To the Anglo-Saxons, creating poetry was as important as fighting, hunting, farming, or loving. C

RESPONDING TO THE ART

Activity. **Ask students to speculate about why Norse gods are featured in this tapestry and what purpose such tapestries served.** [Possible answers: Perhaps the Vikings wanted to pay homage to their gods through art or to depict a story about the gods. Tapestries might have served to educate people, to praise their gods, or to leave behind a record of their history. In an age of widespread illiteracy, pictures were more meaningful to most people than writing was.]

C Reading Skills and Strategies

Extending the Text

The text points out the high esteem in which the bard (or scop) was held in Anglo-Saxon society. Ask students to discuss the role of the writer in our society today. [Possible answer: Some of today's best-selling writers have access to the media and draw large audiences when they appear on television or in person. Their celebrity, however, is minor in comparison to movie stars and professional athletes.]

Taking a Second Look

Review: Identifying Main Idea and Supporting Details

Remind students that identifying main ideas and details is a useful strategy for understanding and recalling nonfiction.

Activities

1. Ask students to identify the main idea of the second paragraph on p. 12. [Woden, the god of poetry, death, and magic, was one of the important figures in the Anglo-Saxon religion.]
2. Ask students to point out some details in this paragraph that specifically "support" the main idea. [Woden helped people communicate with spirits, perform burial rites, and reach ecstatic trances, all important roles for a people who were obsessed with death and poetry.] Sometimes, however, details are used to elaborate on a subject. What is an example of an elaborating detail? [Woden is the word from which we get Wednesday.]
3. Have students identify the details in each paragraph and decide which are supporting details, which are elaborating details, and which are transitional details.

Ⓐ Literary Connections

Scops

The literature of the Anglo-Saxons was handed down orally by scops who sang in the mead halls of the lords where warriors gathered to celebrate the happenings of the day. In the words of the Beowulf poet, the scops "unlocked the wordhoard" and shared their songs with the tribe. These scops, like the Greek poets before them, remembered their stories by using accents and many stock phrases. The rhythms of the story may also have carried them along. In general, a line of Old English poetry has four main stresses and is divided in half by a pause, or caesura (see p. 49).

Ⓑ Cultural Connections

A Modern Point of View

Borges incorporates several elements of Anglo-Saxon culture into this passage. First, Anglo-Saxons often lived among their animals, a practice which protected the animals and warmed the people. Churches and abbeys were built of stone. The *Angelus* he hears is the ringing of bells that calls Roman Catholics to devotion in the morning, at noon, and in the evening; these might have tolled from a local monastery. Woden, sometimes called Odin, was the supreme god, the all-father, of Norse mythology who dominated the culture before the spread of Christianity among the Anglo-Saxons. The Roman coins probably remained behind from the occupation of the British Isles by the Romans from 55 B.C. to 449 A.D.

A knight, from a chess set carved from walrus ivory (12th century).
British Museum, London.

Ⓐ The poets sang to the strumming of a harp. As sources for their improvisational poetry, the storytellers had a rich supply of heroic tales that reflected the concerns of a people constantly under threat of war, disease, or old age. We are told of the king in *Beowulf:*

> . . . sometimes Hrothgar himself, with the harp
> In his lap, stroked its silvery strings
> And told wonderful stories, a brave king
> Reciting unhappy truths about good
> And evil—and sometimes he wove his stories
> On the mournful thread of old age, remembering
> Buried strength and the battles it had won.
> He would weep, the old king.
>
> —Lines 2107–2114

Anglo-Saxon literature contains many works in this same elegiac strain. Poems such as "The Seafarer" (page 56), for example, stress the transience of a life frequently identified with the cold and darkness of winter. For the non-Christian Anglo-Saxons, whose religion offered them no hope of an afterlife, only fame and its reverberation in poetry could provide a defense against death. Perhaps this is why the Anglo-Saxon bards, uniquely gifted with the skill to preserve fame in the collective memory, were such honored members of their society.

The Anglo-Saxon bard's ability to recite poetic stories was considered as important a skill as fighting. Fame in the bard's mournful poetry—and a place in the community's memory—was a hero's only consolation against death.

A modern Argentine writer imagines the last Anglo-Saxon:

Ⓑ In a stable which is almost in the shadow of the new stone church, a man with gray eyes and gray beard, lying amidst the odor of the animals, humbly seeks death as one would seek sleep. The day, faithful to vast and secret laws, is shifting and confusing the shadows inside the poor shelter; outside are the plowed fields and a ditch clogged with dead leaves and the tracks of a wolf in the black mud where the forests begin. The man sleeps and dreams, forgotten. He is awakened by the bells tolling the Angelus. In the kingdoms of England the ringing of bells is now one of the customs of the evening, but this man, as a child, has seen the face of Woden, the divine horror and exultation, the crude wooden idol hung with Roman coins and heavy clothing, the sacrificing of horses, dogs, and prisoners. Before dawn he will die and with him will die, and never return, the immediate images of these pagan rites; the world will be a little poorer when this Saxon has died. . . .

—Jorge Luis Borges,
translated by James E. Irby

RESPONDING TO THE ART

Activity. Ask students to discuss how this page from an illuminated manuscript reflects Winston Churchill's words that Irish Christianity "burned and gleamed through the darkness" of early medieval Europe?

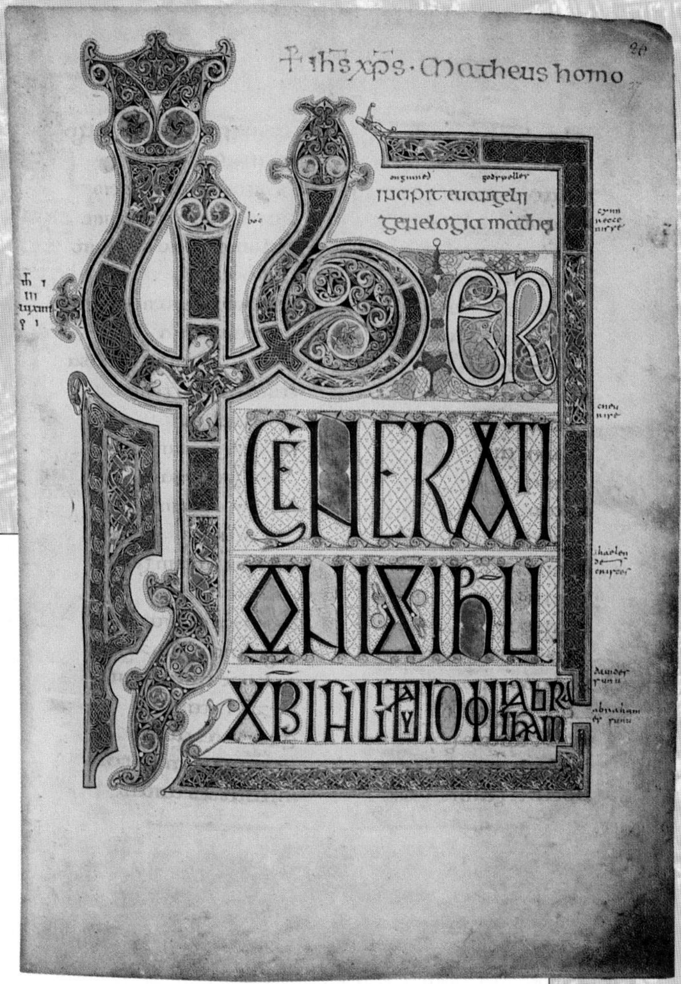

Opening of *St. Matthew's Gospel*, from the Lindisfarne Gospels (7th century). Note the scribe's comments in the margins.

A Light from Ireland

Ireland had historical good luck in the fifth century. Unlike England and the rest of Europe, Ireland, isolated and surrounded by wild seas, was not overrun by the Germanic invaders. Then, in 432, the whole of Celtic Ireland was converted to Christianity by a Romanized Briton named Patricius (Patrick). Patrick had (C) been seized by Irish slave traders when he was a teenager and had been held in bondage by a sheepherder in Ireland for six years. He escaped captivity, became a bishop, and returned to convert his former captors. His success was speedy and undying. From 432 to 750, while Europe and England sank into constant warfare, confusion, and ignorance, Ireland (D) experienced a Golden Age. The Irish monks founded monasteries that became sanctuaries of learning for refugee scholars from Europe and England. Thus, it was in Ireland that Christianity, in the words of Winston Churchill, "burned and gleamed through the darkness."

(C) Exploring the Historical Period

Saint Patrick

Historians have suggested that Patrick's reported use of the shamrock as an illustration of the Trinity, the three-person god of Christianity, led to the shamrock's becoming an Irish symbol.

(D) Exploring the Historical Period

Irish Civilization

The flowering of Irish civilization was eventually—and perhaps inevitably—stemmed by the arrival of Scandinavian invaders near the end of the eighth century. These raids continued to disrupt progress for more than two centuries.

Ⓐ Exploring the Historical Period

Monasteries

Before Henry VIII destroyed the English monasteries in the early sixteenth century, there were, in Yorkshire alone, twenty-eight abbeys, twenty-six priories, twenty-three convents, thirty friaries, and thirteen cells. All are in ruin today.

Ⓑ Literary Connections

The Anglo-Saxon Chronicle

This chronicle, kept by unknown clerics, tells of weak kings, greedy abbots, and proud barons. It also chronicles natural events. Here is one such record:

671 *There was the great death of birds.*

Call students' attention to the lack of any attempt to explain the event scientifically.

Ⓒ Exploring the Culture

The English Language

After defeating the Danes, King Alfred maintained political control over southwest England, which was not part of his Wessex domain, by encouraging a common loyalty to England and promoting the use of the English language. To that end, Alfred used English, not the customary Latin, to educate his people. In his preface to the English translation of Bede's *Historia Ecclesiastica,* King Alfred explains this emphasis on English: "Therefore it seems better to me . . . that we should all translate certain books which are most necessary for all men to know, into the language that we can all understand, and also arrange it . . . so that all the youth of freemen now among the English people . . . are able to read English writing as well."

Resources

Assessment

Formal Assessment

- Literary Period Introduction Test, p. 1

The Christian Monasteries: The Ink Froze

In the death-shadowed world of the Anglo-Saxons, the poets or bards provided one element of hope: the possibility that heroic deeds might be enshrined in the society's memory. Another element of hope was supplied by Christianity. The monasteries served as centers of learning in this period, just as they would in the Middle Ages. In England the cultural and spiritual influence of monasteries existed right Ⓐ alongside the older Anglo-Saxon religion. In fact, the monasteries preserved not only the Latin and Greek classics but also some of the great works of popular literature, such as *Beowulf.*

Monks assigned to the monastery's scriptorium, or writing room, probably spent almost all their daylight hours copying manuscripts by hand. (Printing was still eight hundred years away in England.) The scriptorium was actually in a covered walkway (the cloister) open to a court. Makeshift walls of oiled paper or glass helped somewhat, but the British Isles in winter are cold; the ink could freeze. Picture a shivering scribe, hunched over sheepskin "paper," pressing with a quill pen, obeying a rule of silence: That's how seriously the Church took learning.

Latin alone remained the language of "serious" study in England until the time of King Alfred. During his reign, Alfred Ⓑ instituted the *Anglo-Saxon Chronicle,* a lengthy running history of England that covered the earliest days and continued until 1154. Partly because of King Alfred's efforts, English began to gain respect as a language of culture. Only then did the Old Ⓒ English stories and poetry preserved by the monks come to be recognized as great works of literature.

> Here and there in the surviving manuscripts . . . we find the bored scribblings of the Irish scribes, who kept themselves awake by writing out a verse or two of a beloved Irish lyric—and so, by accumulation, left for our enjoyment a whole literature that would otherwise be unknown. . . . For the most part they enjoy their work and find themselves engrossed in the stories they are copying. Beneath a description of the death of Hector on the Plain of Troy, one scribe, completely absorbed in the words he is copying, has written most sincerely: "I am greatly grieved at the above mentioned death." Another, measuring the endurance of his beloved art against his own brief life span, concludes: "Sad it is, little parti-colored white book, for a day will surely come when someone will say over your page: 'The hand that wrote this is no more.' "
>
> —Thomas Cahill

Christian monks preserved the literature of the ancient world as well as works of popular culture.

Quickwrite

Think about the importance of preserving a society's literature and language. Suppose that the monasteries had not preserved the classics of Greek and Latin literature. What might we have lost? Is there any possibility that our own literature and language could disappear from the earth? Write your thoughts on these questions.

(Opposite) Norse chessmen, carved from walrus ivory, found on Isle of Lewis, Scotland.

Assessing Learning

Check Test: True-False

1. Celtic and Anglo-Saxon stories are so similar that they are often confused. [False]
2. The Roman occupation provided several hundred years of stability for Britain. [True]
3. When the Anglo-Saxons conquered Britain, renaming it England, the Celts retreated to Ireland. [False]
4. *Scop* is another word for "warrior." [False]
5. Before King Alfred, tales and poems in English were not considered great literature. [True]

Informal Assessment

Performance Assessment. Ask students to imagine the life of an Anglo-Saxon cleric and to write a diary entry that could have been written by that person, using specific information from this essay. You might assess the work not only for specificity in terms of historical detail but also for organization, clarity, creativity, tone, and use of language.

Collection 1

Songs of Ancient Heroes

Theme

Heroic Deeds: A Way to Immortality *The recounting of heroic deeds is a major feature of Anglo-Saxon literature. The ancient heroes quested to overcome evil, even loneliness, and by so doing, they hoped to win a place in the memory of their people.*

Reading the Anthology

Reaching Struggling Readers

The *Reading Skills and Strategies: Reaching Struggling Readers* binder provides materials coordinated with the Pupil's Edition (see the Collection Planner, p. T16B) to help students who have difficulty reading and comprehending text or students who are reluctant readers. The binder for twelfth grade is organized around ten individual skill areas and offers the following options:

- MiniRead MiniReads are short, easy texts that give students a chance to practice a particular skill and strategy before reading selections in the Pupil's Edition. Each MiniRead Skill Lesson can be taught independently or used in conjunction with a Selection Skill Lesson.
- **Selection Skill Lessons** Selection Skill Lessons allow students to apply skills introduced in the MiniReads. Each Selection Skill Lesson provides reading instruction and practice specific to a particular piece of literature in the Pupil's Edition.

Reading Beyond the Anthology

Read On

Collection 1 includes an annotated bibliography of books suitable for extended reading. The suggested books are related to works in this collection by theme, by author, or by subject. To preview the Read On for Collection 1, please turn to p. T62.

HRW Library

The *HRW Library* offers novels, plays, and short-story collections for extended reading. Each major work in the Library includes thematically or topically related Connections. The Connections are magazine articles, poems, or other pieces of literature. Each book in the *HRW Library* is also accompanied by a Study Guide that provides teaching suggestions and worksheets. For Collection 1, the following title is recommended.

READINGS IN WORLD LITERATURE

This collection of readings in world literature includes episodes from two classic epics: "The Death of Hector" from Homer's *Iliad*, and "The Fall of Troy" from Virgil's *Aeneid*. Both episodes provide interesting, cross-cultural counterparts of Beowulf's epic struggle.

Collection 1 Songs of Ancient Heroes

Resources for this Collection

Note: All resources for this collection are available for preview on the *One-Stop Planner CD-ROM 1 with Test Generator.* All worksheets and blackline masters may be printed from the CD-ROM.

Internet Resources
go.hrw.com LE0 12-1

Selection or Feature	Reading and Literary Skills	Vocabulary, Language, and Grammar
from **Beowulf** (p. 18) *translated by* Burton Raffel **Connections:** *from* **Grendel** (p. 36) John Gardner **Connections: A Collaboration Across 1,200 Years** (p. 39) D. J. R. Bruckner **Connections: Life in 999: A Grim Struggle** (p. 47) Howard G. Chua-Eoan **Elements of Literature: Alliteration and Kennings** (p. 49)	• *Reading Skills and Strategies: Reaching Struggling Readers* • MiniRead Skill Lesson, p. 1 • Selection Skill Lesson, p. 9 • *Graphic Organizers for Active Reading,* Worksheet p. 1 • *Literary Elements:* Transparencies 1, 2 Worksheet pp. 4, 7	• *Words to Own,* Worksheet p. 1 • *Grammar and Language Links:* Nouns, Pronouns, and Adjectives, Worksheet p. 1; Verbs, Prepositions, Conjunctions, and Interjections, Worksheet p. 3 • *Language Workshop CD-ROM:* Nouns, Pronouns, and Adjectives; Verbs and Adverbs • *Daily Oral Grammar,* Transparency 1
World Literature: Mesopotamia The Head of Humbaba, *from* **Gilgamesh** (p. 52) *retold by* Herbert Mason	The World Literature feature offers students the opportunity to explore thematically linked literature from different world cultures. Structured activities called Finding Common Ground are provided in the Pupil's Edition to guide students' explorations of these thematic connections between British and other world literature.	
The Seafarer (p. 55) *translated by* Burton Raffel **Primary Sources: The Original Language and the Translator's Task** (p. 59) **Spotlight On: Anglo-Saxon Riddles** (p. 61)	• *Graphic Organizers for Active Reading,* Worksheet p. 2	• *Grammar and Language Links:* Sentence Fragments, Worksheet p. 5 • *Language Workshop CD-ROM,* Sentence Fragments • *Daily Oral Grammar,* Transparency 2
The English Language: Where English Came From (p. 63) John Algeo		
Writer's Workshop: Analyzing a Literary Work (p. 67)		
Language Workshop: Sentence Combining (p. 69)		• *Workshop Resources,* p. 45 • *Language Workshop CD-ROM,* Sentence Combining
Learning for Life: Analyzing Groups (p. 71)		

Other Resources for this Collection

- *Cross-Curricular Activities*, p. 1
- *Portfolio Management System*, Introduction to Portfolio Assessment, p. 1
- *Formal Assessment:*
  Literary Period Introduction Test, p. 1
  Literary Period Test, p. 11
- *Test Generator*, Collection Test

Writing	Listening and Speaking Viewing and Representing	Assessment
• *Portfolio Management System*, Rubrics for Choices, p. 89	• *Audio CD Library*, Disc 1, Track 2 • *Viewing and Representing:* Fine Art Transparency 1 Worksheet p. 4 • *Portfolio Management System*, Rubrics for Choices, p. 89	• *Formal Assessment*, Selection Test, p. 3 • *Test Generator (One-Stop Planner CD-ROM)* • *Preparation for College Admission Exams*, pp. 1, 3 • *Formal Assessment*, Literary Elements Test, p. 9
	• *Audio CD Library*, Disc 1, Track 3	
• *Portfolio Management System*, Rubrics for Choices, p. 91	• *Audio CD Library*, Disc 1, Tracks 4, 5, 6, 7 • *Portfolio Management System*, Rubrics for Choices, p. 91	• *Formal Assessment*, Selection Test, p. 5 • *Test Generator (One-Stop Planner CD-ROM)*
		• *Formal Assessment*, The English Language Test, p. 7

• *Workshop Resources*, p. 1
• *Writer's Workshop 2 CD-ROM*, Interpretation
	• *Viewing and Representing*, HRW Multimedia Presentation Maker	• *Portfolio Management System*
		  • Prewriting, p. 93
		  • Peer Editing, p. 94
		  • Assessment Rubric, p. 95

		• *Portfolio Management System*, Rubrics, p. 96

Transparency   CD-ROM   Video   Audio CD

Collection 1 Songs of Ancient Heroes

Skills Focus

Selection or Feature	Reading Skills and Strategies	Elements of Literature and Language	Writing	Listening and Speaking	Viewing and Representing
from **Beowulf** (p. 18) *translated by* Burton Raffel	Contrast, p. 38 Symbolic Meaning, pp. 38, 48 Analyze Text, p. 48	Epic Hero, pp. 20, 38 Epic, p. 20 Images, pp. 38, 48 Character, p. 38 Tone, p. 48 Theme, p. 48 Setting, p. 48 Alliteration, p. 48 Kenning, p. 48	Analyze Character, p. 50 Write an Autobiographical Incident, p. 50 Retell an Episode from Another Point of View, p. 50 Compare Heroes of Film and Epic, p. 50	Retell an Episode from *Beowulf,* p. 50	
Reading Skills and Strategies: Using Context Clues (p. 51)	Using Context Clues, p. 51 • Restatement • Comparison • Contrast • Synonym		Construct Sentences Incorporating Context Clues, p. 51		
World Literature: Mesopotamia **The Head of Humbaba,** *from* **Gilgamesh** (p. 52) *retold by* Herbert Mason	Responding to the Text, pp. 52, 54	The World Literature feature offers students the opportunity to explore thematically linked literature from different world cultures. Structured activities called Finding Common Ground are provided in the Pupil's Edition to guide students' explorations of these thematic connections between British and other world literature.			
The Seafarer (p. 55) *translated by* Burton Raffel		Elegy, p. 55 Elegiac Tone, p. 59 Metaphor, p. 59	Identify Elements of Tone, p. 60 Write an Essay Comparing Texts Across Cultures, p. 60 Create a Personal "Seafarer" Poem, p. 60	Debate a Proposition, p. 60	Create a Collage, p. 60
The English Language: Where English Came From (p. 63) John Algeo		Proto-Indo-European Languages, p. 63 Borrowed Words, p. 64 Old English, p. 64 Root Words, p. 66 Affixes, p. 66 Etymologies, p. 66 Runic Alphabet, p. 66			Use a Map for Research, p. 66
Writer's Workshop: Analyzing a Literary Work (p. 67)			Analyze a Literary Work, pp. 67–68		
Language Workshop: Sentence Combining (p. 69)			Sentence Combining, p. 69 • Combine with Phrases • Combine Ideas • Subordinate Ideas Revise Short, Choppy Sentences, p. 69		
Reading for Life: Evaluating a News Feature (p. 70)	Evaluate a News Feature, p. 70 • Source • Writer's Stance and Motivation • Credibility and Context • Tone				
Learning for Life: Analyzing Groups (p. 71)				Present a Panel Discussion on How People Build a Sense of Community, p. 71	Create a Photo-Essay, p. 71 Create a Graphic, p. 71

Collection 1

SONGS OF ANCIENT HEROES

from **Beowulf**
from **Gilgamesh**
"The Seafarer"

And sometimes a proud old soldier
Who had heard songs of the ancient heroes
And could sing them all through, story after story,
Would weave a net of words for Beowulf's
Victory, tying the knot of his verses
Smoothly, swiftly, into place with a poet's
Quick skill, singing his new song aloud
While he shaped it, and the old songs as well.

—*from Beowulf, translated by* Burton Raffel

OBJECTIVES

1. Read literature of the Anglo-Saxon period on the subject of "Songs of Ancient Heroes"
2. Interpret literary elements with special emphasis on alliteration and kennings
3. Apply a variety of reading strategies including using context clues
4. Respond to the literature in a variety of modes
5. Learn and use new words
6. Learn about the birth and development of Old English
7. Plan, draft, revise, proof, and publish a literary analysis
8. Develop skill in sentence combining
9. Evaluate a news feature
10. Explore the meaning of group membership through various projects

Responding to the Quotation

Explore with students what this verse reveals about the role of storytelling in Anglo-Saxon society. What heroes are celebrated in poems and songs today? [Anglo-Saxon men could be poets as well as warriors, creating their own retellings of heroic deeds. Both roles were important to the Anglo-Saxons. Possible answers: Today one might hear songs or poems about King Arthur, Joan of Arc, Daniel Boone, Ulysses, Paul Revere, Charlemagne, El Cid, or Kamehameha.]

Writing Focus: Analyzing a Literary Work

The following **Work in Progress** assignments build to a culminating **Writer's Workshop** at the end of this collection.

- Beowulf — Gather details to analyze character (p. 50)
- The Seafarer — List details that create tone (p. 60)

Writer's Workshop: Expository Writing / Analyzing a Literary Work (p. 67)

Ⓐ Literary Connections

Epics

An **epic** is sometimes called a heroic poem; *Beowulf,* the *Iliad,* and the *Odyssey* are all heroic poems or epics. They are long narratives about the adventures of larger-than-life characters. Some later long narrative poems are called literary epics, because they were consciously created to be like the earlier heroic poems. These include Virgil's *Aeneid* and Milton's *Paradise Lost.* Epics tend to have these characteristics:

- The hero is a great leader strongly identified with a particular people or society.
- The setting is broad and often includes the upper and lower worlds.
- The hero does great deeds in battle or undertakes an extraordinary journey.
- Sometimes the gods or other supernatural or fantastic beings take part in the action.
- The story is told in heightened language.

Ⓑ Background

A Poem About War Heroes

The first three lines of *Beowulf* (the excerpt in this anthology begins with l. 86) in Burton Raffel's translation begin: "Hear me! We've heard of Danish heroes, /Ancient kings and the glory they cut/For themselves, swinging mighty swords!"

Background

The *Beowulf* manuscript here is part of a volume, or codex, that also contains four other works in Old English: *The Passion of St. Christopher, The Wonders of the East, Alexander's Letter to Aristotle,* and a fragment of *Judith.* Interestingly, Beowulf is the only character who does not appear anywhere other than in the epic; every other character is found in earlier legends or in actual history. The Grendel character, for example, almost surely has his roots in the Old Norse stories of the *draugar,* or animated corpses, dead men of supernatural strength who walked at night spreading evil and terror. Often a *draugar* had a mother even more terrible than he, known as a *ketta,* or "she-cat."

Page from the *Beowulf* manuscript (c. 1000). Cotton MS Vitellius A XV, f.133.

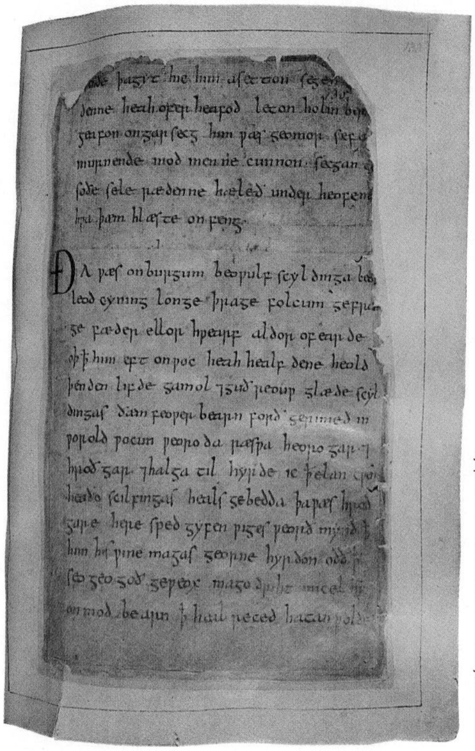

By permission of the British Library, London.

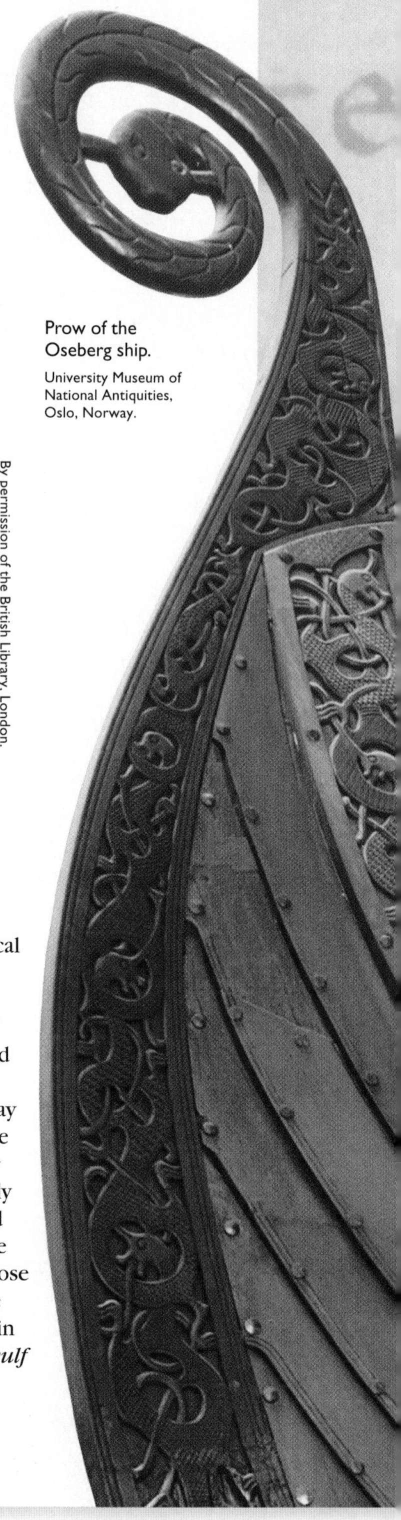

Prow of the Oseberg ship.
University Museum of National Antiquities, Oslo, Norway.

Beowulf

Ⓐ *Beowulf* is to England what Homer's *Iliad* and *Odyssey* are to ancient Greece: It is the first great work of the English national literature—the mythical and literary record of a formative stage of English civilization. It is also an epic of the heroic sources of English culture. As such, *Beowulf* uses a host of traditional motifs, or recurring elements, associated with heroic literature all over the world.

Ⓑ The epic tells the story of Beowulf (his name may mean "bear"), a Geat from Sweden who crosses the sea to Denmark in a quest to rescue King Hrothgar from the demonic monster Grendel. Like most early heroic literature, *Beowulf* is oral art. It was handed down, with changes and embellishments, from one minstrel to another. The stories of *Beowulf,* like those of all oral epics, are traditional ones, familiar to the audiences who crowded around the harpist-bards in the communal halls at night. The tales in the *Beowulf*

Professional Notes

Critical Comment: Where Kings Are Warriors

In his introduction to his translation of *Beowulf,* Burton Raffel explains the importance of battle in Anglo-Saxon culture: "Battle is a way of life, a necessary function of the worthiest members of society. Kings, and warriors generally . . . are the successful men of the time, the corporation presidents, the space explorers, and the movie stars. They are the people to be known about, to be emulated, but not blindly, not only because they are successful (death being the supreme product of their occupation). Theirs is the good and the true path; in their thoughts, their words, and their deeds they are the embodiment of the Anglo-Saxon way of life."

epic are the stories of dream and legend, of monsters and of god-fashioned weapons, of descents to the underworld and of fights with dragons, of the hero's quest and of a community threatened by the powers of evil.

By the standards of Homer, whose epics run to nearly 15,000 lines, *Beowulf* is relatively short—approximately 3,200 lines. It was composed in Old English, probably in Northumbria in northeast England, sometime between the years 700 and 750. The world it depicts, however, is much older, that of the early sixth century. Much of the poem's material is based on early folk legends—some Celtic, some Scandinavian. Since the scenery described is the coast of Northumbria, not Scandinavia, it has been assumed that the poet who wrote the version that has come down to us was Northumbrian. Given the Christian elements in the epic, this poet may also have been a monk.

The only manuscript we have of *Beowulf* dates from the year 1000 and is now in the British Museum in London. Burned and stained, it was discovered in the eighteenth century: Somehow it had survived Henry VIII's destruction of the monasteries two hundred years earlier.

Beowulf: People, Monsters, and Places

Beowulf: a Geat, son of Edgetho and nephew of Higlac, king of the Geats. Higlac is both Beowulf's feudal lord and his uncle.

Brecca: chief of the Brondings, a tribe, and Beowulf's friend.

Grendel: man-eating monster who lives at the bottom of a foul mere, or mountain lake. His name might be related to the Old Norse *grindill,* meaning "storm," or *grenja,* "to bellow."

Herot: golden guest-hall built by King Hrothgar, the Danish ruler. It was decorated with the antlers of stags; the name means "hart [stag] hall." Scholars think Herot might have been built near Lejre on the coast of Zealand, in Denmark.

Hrothgar: king of the Danes, builder of Herot. He had once befriended Beowulf's father. His father was called Healfdane (which probably means "half Dane"). Hrothgar's name might mean "glory spear" or "spear of triumph."

Unferth: one of Hrothgar's courtiers, reputed to be a skilled warrior. His sword, called Hrunting, is used by Beowulf in a later battle.

Welthow: Hrothgar's wife, queen of the Danes.

Wiglaf: a Geat warrior, one of Beowulf's select band, and the only one to help him in his final fight with the dragon. Wiglaf might be related to Beowulf.

Viking coin minted in England (10th–11th century). Most such coins consist of precious metals extorted from the English as tribute.

British Museum, London.

C Background

Length of the Text

The original, complete *Beowulf* consists of 3,182 lines. Of Raffel's modern retelling, 842 lines divided into seventeen parts, are reprinted here.

D Cultural Connections

Religion in *Beowulf*

This poem is actually full of religious elements, even though its basis may be a pagan heroic code. The poet sings to the "Almighty," and many references are made to God, God's creation, and the need to thank God. Perhaps most important of all, it is God who leads Beowulf to victory over Grendel's mother.

RESPONDING TO THE ART

The Oseberg ship, unearthed in 1904, may have been the burial ship of Asa, a Viking queen whose active life belied the passive role women were believed to have played at this time in history. Married against her will to a Norwegian king, Asa had her husband killed and ruled alone until her death in 850. Accompanying Asa on her voyage to the afterlife was the body of a maidservant, priceless gold and gems (which subsequently were stolen by looters), and objects such as sleds and a wagon. These would permit Asa to travel in the afterlife as much as the Vikings enjoyed traveling while living.

Activity. Ask students how funerals for great leaders are conducted today.

OBJECTIVES

1. Read and interpret the poem
2. Identify and analyze the epic hero
3. Identify alliteration and kennings
4. Understand word meanings through context clues
5. Express understanding through writing and speech
6. Demonstrate understanding of new words

SKILLS

Literary
- Identify and analyze the epic hero
- Identify alliteration and kennings

Writing
- Collect ideas for a literary analysis
- Relate an autobiographical incident
- Retell the story from a different point of view
- Compare the story to a film

Speaking/Listening
- Retell an episode

Vocabulary
- Use new words

Viewing and Representing
- Sketch a brooch (ATE)

Planning

- **Block Schedule**
  Block Scheduling Lesson Plans with Pacing Guide
- **Traditional Schedule**
  Lesson Plans Including Strategies for English-Language Learners
- **One-Stop Planner**
  CD-ROM with Test Generator

Before You Read

FROM **BEOWULF**

Make the Connection

The Dragon Slayer

This is a story about a hero from the misty reaches of the English past, a hero who faces violence, horror, and even death to save a people in mortal danger. The epic's events take place many centuries ago, but this story still speaks to people today—perhaps because there are so many people in need of a rescuer, a hero. Beowulf is ancient England's hero. In other times, in other cultures, the hero takes the shape of King Arthur, or Gilgamesh, or Sundiata, or Joan of Arc. In twentieth-century America, the hero may be a real person, like Martin Luther King, Jr., or a fictional character like Shane in the Western novel. This hero-type is the dragon slayer, representing a besieged community facing evil forces that lurk in the cold darkness. And Grendel, the monster lurking in the depths of the lagoon, may represent all those threatening forces.

Quickwrite

Take notes on several contemporary fictional heroes from novels, films, or even comics or television. Pick one of them, and briefly analyze him or her using these questions:

- What sort of evil or oppression does he confront?
- Why does she do it? What's her motivation?
- For whom does he do it?
- What virtues does she represent?

Now discuss some of the heroes you and your classmates chose. Do they all seem to qualify as hero-types, or do some of them fall short in one way or another?

Elements of Literature

The Epic Hero

Beowulf, like all epic heroes, has superior physical strength and is supremely ethical. In his quest, he must defeat monsters that embody dark, destructive powers. At the end of the quest, he is glorified by the people he has saved. If you watch current events, particularly about people emerging from years of oppression, you will see this impulse toward glorification still at work. You might also see such glorification in the impressive monuments that are great tourist attractions in Washington, D.C.

The **epic hero** is the central figure in a long narrative that reflects the values and heroic ideals of a particular society. An **epic** is a quest story on a grand scale.

For more on the Epic, see the Handbook of Literary Terms.

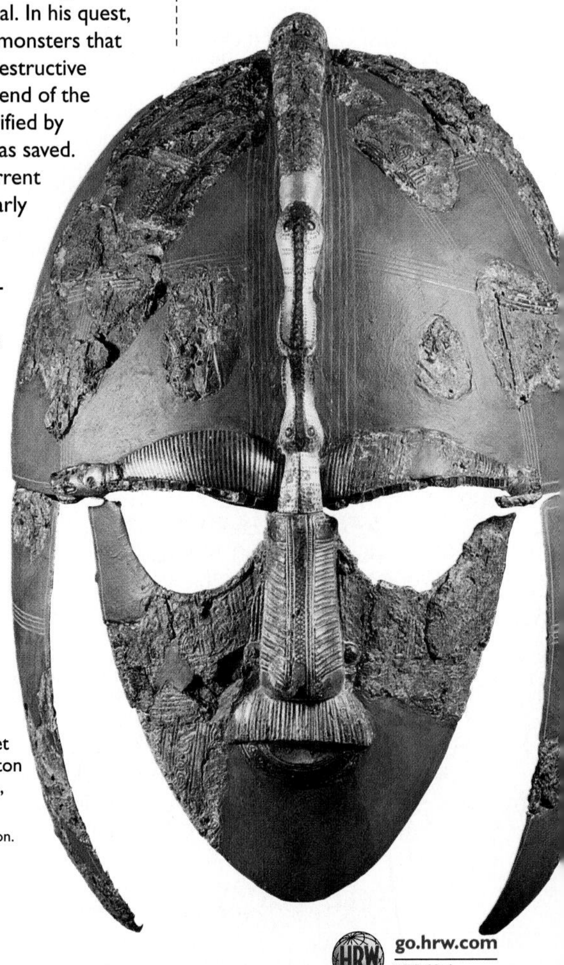

Sutton Hoo helmet (7th century). Sutton Hoo ship treasure, Suffolk, England.
British Museum, London.

go.hrw.com
LEO 12-1

Resources: Print and Media

Reading
- *Reading Skills and Strategies*
  MiniRead Skill Lesson, p. 1
  Selection Skill Lesson, p. 9
- *Graphic Organizers for Active Reading,* p. 1
- *Words to Own,* p. 1
- *Audio CD Library*
  Disc 1, Tracks 2, 3

Elements of Literature
- *Literary Elements*
  Transparencies 1, 2
  Worksheets, pp. 4, 7

Writing and Language
- *Daily Oral Grammar*
  Transparency 1
- *Grammar and Language Links*
  Worksheets, pp. 1, 3
- *Language Workshop CD-ROM*

Viewing and Representing
- *Viewing and Representing*
  Fine Art Transparency 1
  Fine Art Worksheet, p. 4
- *Visual Connections*
  Videocassette A, Segment 3

Assessment
- *Formal Assessment,* p. 3
- *Portfolio Management System,* p. 89
- *Preparation for College Admission Exams,* pp. 1, 3
- *Test Generator (One-Stop Planner CD-ROM)*

Internet
- go.hrw.com (keyword: LE0 12-1)

from Beowulf

translated by **Burton Raffel**

The Monster Grendel

1

. . . A powerful monster, living down
In the darkness, growled in pain, impatient
As day after day the music rang
Loud in that hall,° the harp's rejoicing
Call and the poet's clear songs, sung
Of the ancient beginnings of us all, recalling
The Almighty making the earth, shaping
These beautiful plains marked off by oceans,
Then proudly setting the sun and moon
To glow across the land and light it;
The corners of the earth were made lovely with trees
And leaves, made quick with life, with each
Of the nations who now move on its face. And then
As now warriors sang of their pleasure:
So Hrothgar's men lived happy in his hall
Till the monster stirred, that demon, that fiend,
Grendel, who haunted the moors, the wild
Marshes, and made his home in a hell
Not hell but earth. He was spawned in that slime,
Conceived by a pair of those monsters born
Of Cain, murderous creatures banished
By God, punished forever for the crime
Of Abel's death. The Almighty drove
Those demons out, and their exile was bitter,
Shut away from men; they split
Into a thousand forms of evil—spirits
And fiends, goblins, monsters, giants,
A brood forever opposing the Lord's
Will, and again and again defeated.

2

Then, when darkness had dropped, Grendel
Went up to Herot, wondering what the warriors
Would do in that hall when their drinking was done.
He found them sprawled in sleep, suspecting
Nothing, their dreams undisturbed. The monster's
Thoughts were as quick as his greed or his claws:
He slipped through the door and there in the silence

4. hall: guest-hall or mead-hall. (Mead is a fermented drink made from honey, water, yeast, and malt.) The hall was a central gathering place where Anglo-Saxon warriors could feast, listen to a bard's stories, and sleep in safety.

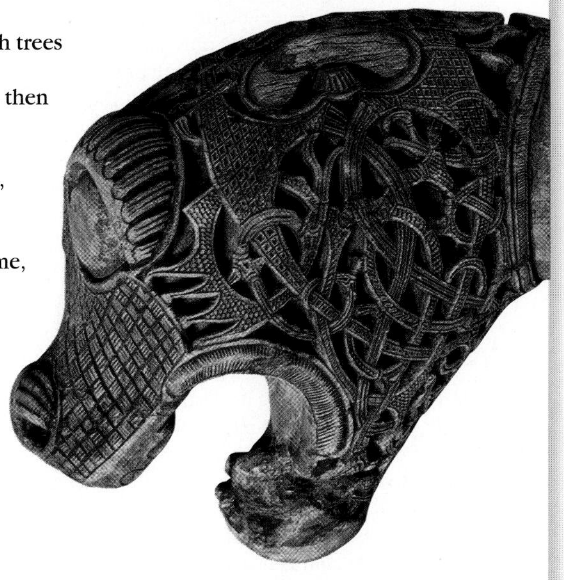

Animal head from Viking ship (c. 800).
University Museum of National Antiquities, Oslo, Norway. Photo by Eirik Irgens Johnsen.

Lines have been renumbered and do not correspond with the New American Library edition.

Summary ■■■

The poem begins by contrasting two settings: the dark, desolate lair of the monster Grendel and the noisy, joyous hall at Herot, home of the Danish King Hrothgar and his warriors. The characters are also contrasted. Hrothgar and his men are convivial and loyal while Grendel is exiled and murderous. The conflict between these symbols of good and evil begins when Grendel attacks Herot at night, killing about thirty of Hrothgar's men. *(This summary is continued on p. T24.)*

Background

The Anglo-Saxon scholar Kevin Crossley-Holland states that few works of literature represent the mood of a time as completely as *Beowulf.* The epic also showcases all the stylistic devices of Anglo-Saxon poetry: the use of four-beat rhythm, caesuras, alliteration, kennings, and the intermingling of pagan and Christian values.

A Critical Thinking

Interpreting

? What phrase points to Grendel's evil nature? ["Down in the darkness" suggests an evil lower world.]

B Humanities Connections

Cain and Abel

Explain that Cain, one of the Biblical sons of Adam and Eve, murdered his brother Abel and was cursed by God (Genesis 4:8–14). According to legend, Cain fathered a brood of monsters.

C Cultural Connections

Herot Hall

Herot means "hart" or "stag." The hart was an Anglo-Saxon symbol of kingship.

Preteaching Vocabulary

Words to Own

Ask students to form small groups to read the definitions of the Words to Own listed at the bottom of the selection pages and to work together to suggest a time, place, and reason when each of the following might occur: *laments, solace, reprisal, reparation,* and *pilgrimage.* Then ask students to complete the following sentences with one of these Words to Own. Have them use context clues to help them fill in the blanks.

1. We made a [pilgrimage] to the shrine.
2. Was there any cash [reparation] for the crime?
3. Most people find [solace] in meditation.
4. The [laments] of the mourners rose up.
5. She acted in [reprisal]for her son's murder.

Resources

Viewing and Representing

Videocassette A, Segment 3
Available in English and Spanish. This segment provides an overview of Anglo-Saxon life and times. For full lesson plans and worksheets, see the *Visual Connections Teacher's Manual.*

Fine Art Transparency
A fine art transparency of Robert Ingpen's *Beowulf Battling Grendel* can be used with this lesson to evoke a sense of victory following the first two battles. See the *Viewing and Representing Transparencies and Worksheets:*

- Transparency 1
- Worksheet, p. 4

A Struggling Readers

Getting the Main Idea

? What does Grendel do at night? [He slaughters men sleeping at Herot.]

B Reading Skills and Strategies

Drawing Conclusions

? Why do none of Hrothgar's men challenge Grendel? [Sample answer: They are afraid for their lives.] Students will learn later, from Hrothgar (ll. 214–222), that the men did make some ineffectual attempts.

C Cultural Connections

Wergild

When the poet says that Grendel pays no reparation for the deaths he causes, he is referring to the Anglo-Saxon custom of *wergild.* According to this code, an Anglo-Saxon who killed someone had to pay a price for his deed or accept the fact that the victim's relatives would seek revenge.

Snatched up thirty men, smashed them
Unknowing in their beds, and ran out with their bodies,
The blood dripping behind him, back
To his lair, delighted with his night's slaughter.
At daybreak, with the sun's first light, they saw
How well he had worked, and in that gray morning
Broke their long feast with tears and laments
A For the dead. Hrothgar, their lord, sat joyless
In Herot, a mighty prince mourning
The fate of his lost friends and companions,
Knowing by its tracks that some demon had torn
His followers apart. He wept, fearing
The beginning might not be the end. And that night
Grendel came again, so set
On murder that no crime could ever be enough,
No savage assault quench his lust
For evil. Then each warrior tried
To escape him, searched for rest in different
Beds, as far from Herot as they could find,
B Seeing how Grendel hunted when they slept.
Distance was safety; the only survivors
Were those who fled him. Hate had triumphed.
So Grendel ruled, fought with the righteous,
One against many, and won; so Herot
Stood empty, and stayed deserted for years,
Twelve winters of grief for Hrothgar, king
Of the Danes, sorrow heaped at his door
By hell-forged hands. His misery leaped
The seas, was told and sung in all
Men's ears: how Grendel's hatred began,
How the monster relished his savage war
On the Danes, keeping the bloody feud
Alive, seeking no peace, offering
No truce, accepting no settlement, no price
C In gold or land, and paying the living
For one crime only with another. No one
Waited for reparation from his plundering claws:
That shadow of death hunted in the darkness,
Stalked Hrothgar's warriors, old
And young, lying in waiting, hidden
In mist, invisibly following them from the edge
Of the marsh, always there, unseen.
So mankind's enemy continued his crimes,
Killing as often as he could, coming
Alone, bloodthirsty and horrible. Though he lived

Dragonhead from a Viking horse collar (detail) (10th century). Denmark.
National Museum, Copenhagen.

WORDS TO OWN
laments (lə·ments′) *n. pl.:* cries of grief.
reparation (rep′ə·rā′shən) *n.:* payment to compensate for wrongdoing.

Reaching All Students

Struggling Readers

For a lesson directly tied to this selection that teaches students to use context clues, see the *Reading Skills and Strategies* binder:

- MiniRead Skill Lesson, p. 1
- Selection Skill Lesson, p. 9

English Language Learners

This poem is especially challenging because of the long complicated sentences and the unusual breaks in the middles of lines. To help students, first play the *Audio CD* recording of Part 1, then read the text along with students, and finally have students listen again to the *CD* while following along in their textbooks.

Advanced Learners

Have students focus on the pagan-Christian struggle depicted in this poem. To do so, have them research or explain all Biblical allusions, such as the ones to creation (ll. 5–13) and Cain and Abel (ll. 19–29). Also ask them to look for all other Christian symbols and allusions, such as references to God, the devil, and hell, as well as for such Christian interludes as the lecture to the unfaithful (ll. 93–104).

In Herot, when the night hid him, he never
Dared to touch king Hrothgar's glorious
Throne, protected by God—God,
Whose love Grendel could not know. But Hrothgar's
Heart was bent. The best and most noble
Of his council debated remedies, sat
In secret sessions, talking of terror
And wondering what the bravest of warriors could do.
And sometimes they sacrificed to the old stone gods,
Made heathen vows, hoping for Hell's
Support, the Devil's guidance in driving
Their affliction off. That was their way,
And the heathen's only hope, Hell
Always in their hearts, knowing neither God
Nor His passing as He walks through our world, the Lord
Of Heaven and earth; their ears could not hear
His praise nor know His glory. Let them
Beware, those who are thrust into danger,
Clutched at by trouble, yet can carry no solace
In their hearts, cannot hope to be better! Hail
To those who will rise to God, drop off
Their dead bodies, and seek our Father's peace!

3

So the living sorrow of Healfdane's son°
Simmered, bitter and fresh, and no wisdom
Or strength could break it: That agony hung
On king and people alike, harsh
And unending, violent and cruel, and evil.
In his far-off home Beowulf, Higlac's
Follower° and the strongest of the Geats—greater
And stronger than anyone anywhere in this world—
Heard how Grendel filled nights with horror
And quickly commanded a boat fitted out,
Proclaiming that he'd go to that famous king,
Would sail across the sea to Hrothgar,
Now when help was needed. None
Of the wise ones regretted his going, much
As he was loved by the Geats: The omens were good,
And they urged the adventure on. So Beowulf
Chose the mightiest men he could find,
The bravest and best of the Geats, fourteen
In all, and led them down to their boat;
He knew the sea, would point the prow°
Straight to that distant Danish shore. . . .

104. Healfdane's son: Hrothgar.

110. Higlac's follower: Higlac is Beowulf's uncle and feudal lord.

123. prow (prou): front part of a boat.

WORDS TO OWN
solace (säl′is) *n.:* peace.

D Reading Skills and Strategies
Noting Important Details

? Why does Grendel not touch Hrothgar's throne? [The throne is protected by God.]

E Struggling Readers
Determining the Author's Purpose

? Why is this background information about Grendel and Hrothgar in the poem? [Possible answer: It shows how desperately Hrothgar needs a hero like Beowulf.]

F Advanced Learners
Christian-Pagan References

Although a pagan poet may have originally composed and sung the poem, the Christian monk transcribing it probably added Christian elements. Have students find clues that show this dual authorship. [Possible answer: In ll. 90–94 the pagan elements of "old stone gods" are intermixed with references to the devil and hell.]

G Historical Connections
The Geats

The Geats lived in what is today southwestern Sweden. Higlac, king of the Geats and Beowulf's kinsman, was killed in a raid on the Franks in A.D. 521. The complete epic of *Beowulf* forecasts the Geats' defeat by another tribe, the Swedes.

H Elements of Literature
Epic Hero

? What qualities of the epic hero are conveyed by these lines? [Sample answers: He is greater than anyone else in the world; he acts quickly to rescue the helpless.]

RESPONDING TO THE ART

Point out the intricate carvings on the dragon-headed horse collar on p. 22.

Activity. Have students write a paragraph about why people would decorate such an object. [Possible answer: Art was put to practical purposes. The Anglo-Saxons valued useful objects and lovingly decorated bowls, pins, drinking horns, and swords.]

Skill Link

Interpreting the Effects of Historical Context

Many cultures produced poems to celebrate their heroes and to express the values and customs of their civilizations. These poems have been passed down by word of mouth. Thus, repetition of key ideas is essential. As students read *Beowulf,* have them look for repeated key ideas that reveal Anglo-Saxon values.

These ideas might include the following:

- honoring courage over long life
- enjoying feasting, storytelling, and music
- viewing life fatalistically, even within the Christian tradition
- admiring physical strength more than mental acuity
- valuing loyalty to the lord or king above all

Responding to the Art

This illustration from a religious manuscript was produced by monks. To explain the illustration's flat appearance, point out that objects are drawn on top of one another, as if the artist were creating a stack, beginning with fish and ending with rows of boats. (Perspective, the illusion of three dimensions, or depth, was a Renaissance technique, which had not yet been discovered.) Another fascinating aspect of this painting is how the artist shows that the fish are below the water's surface by painting curved bands of color over them.

Activity. Have students describe what is taking place in the scene. [The men are Viking invaders about to do battle. Almost all wield shields, and some have begun to disembark. Note the animal figures on the ships' prows. The boats are crowded with anxious-faced warriors who convey a sense of urgency. Note the bare feet.]

Summary

Beowulf, the hero of the epic, arrives to aid Hrothgar after Herot has suffered for many years. Beowulf is characterized as not only strong and brave but also as wise, just, and noble. Since Grendel uses no weapon, Beowulf asks to face the monster alone in hand-to-hand combat. The grateful Hrothgar accepts Beowulf's offer and hosts a banquet in his honor. *(This summary is continued on p. T27.)*

Ⓐ Elements of Literature

Epic Hero

? How has Beowulf already begun to be glorified? [Possible answers: The king has heard of Beowulf and knows of his noble birth. The king recognizes the peril of Beowulf's journey.]

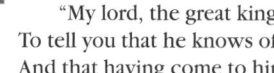

Invasion of Danes under Hinguar (Ingvar) and Hubba. From *Life, Passion, and Miracles of St. Edmund* (c. 1130). England.

The Pierpont Morgan Library, New York.

Beowulf arrives in Denmark and is directed to Herot, the mead-hall of King Hrothgar. The king sends Wulfgar, one of his thanes (or feudal lords), to greet the visitors.

The Arrival of the Hero

4

. . . Then Wulfgar went to the door and addressed
The waiting seafarers with soldier's words:
"My lord, the great king of the Danes, commands me
To tell you that he knows of your noble birth
And that having come to him from over the open

Professional Notes

Critical Comment: "A Man of Archetypal Proportions"

Scholar Alvin A. Lee comments: "Beowulf is not about an individual as such but about a man of archetypal proportions, whose significance, in the broadest and deepest sense, is social. The poem is an imaginative vision of two kinds of human society, one symbolized by generosity, loyalty, and love, the other by monsters of darkness and bloodshed who prey on the ordered, light-filled world man desires and clings to . . . *Beowulf* is not about a complex, individual character whose interior mental processes lead plausibly to certain actions and relations with other people . . . We do not know why, psychologically, Unferth behaves so oddly . . . [The characters in *Beowulf*] are all functionaries playing out their roles as long as *wyrd* (fate) permits, not images of real people but exemplars of human types . . . ."

Sea you have come bravely and are welcome.
Now go to him as you are, in your armor and helmets,
But leave your battle-shields here, and your spears,
Let them lie waiting for the promises your words
May make."
Beowulf arose, with his men
Around him, ordering a few to remain
With their weapons, leading the others quickly
Along under Herot's steep roof into Hrothgar's
Presence. Standing on that prince's own hearth,
Helmeted, the silvery metal of his mail shirt° **B**
Gleaming with a smith's° high art, he greeted
The Danes' great lord:
"Hail, Hrothgar! **C**
Higlac is my cousin° and my king; the days
Of my youth have been filled with glory. Now Grendel's
Name has echoed in our land: Sailors
Have brought us stories of Herot, the best
Of all mead-halls, deserted and useless when the moon
Hangs in skies the sun had lit,
Light and life fleeing together.
My people have said, the wisest, most knowing
And best of them, that my duty was to go to the Danes'
Great king. They have seen my strength for themselves,
Have watched me rise from the darkness of war,
Dripping with my enemies' blood. I drove
Five great giants into chains, chased
All of that race from the earth. I swam
In the blackness of night, hunting monsters
Out of the ocean, and killing them one
By one; death was my errand and the fate
They had earned. Now Grendel and I are called
Together, and I've come. Grant me, then,
Lord and protector of this noble place,
A single request! I have come so far, **D**
Oh shelterer of warriors and your people's loved friend,
That this one favor you should not refuse me—
That I, alone and with the help of my men,
May purge all evil from this hall. I have heard,
Too, that the monster's scorn of men
Is so great that he needs no weapons and fears none.
Nor will I. My lord Higlac
Might think less of me if I let my sword
Go where my feet were afraid to, if I hid
Behind some broad linden shield:° My hands
Alone shall fight for me, struggle for life
Against the monster. God must decide **E**
Who will be given to death's cold grip.
Grendel's plan, I think, will be

139. mail shirt: armored garment made of interlocking metal rings.
140. smith's: metalworker's.

142. cousin: any relative.

172. linden shield: shield made from wood of the linden tree.

B Historical Connections
Armor
The mail shirt was composed of as many as twenty thousand small iron rings riveted or welded shut, creating a mesh-net effect.

C English Language Learners
Understanding Archaic Language
Point out that the word *hail* was once used as a greeting that was like a respectful hello. Although *hail* is now seldom used this way, students may hear it in an expression such as "to hail a taxi." Ask students to make an inference about the meaning of this modern usage of *hail* based on the archaic meaning. Then ask them to use a dictionary, thesaurus, or language database to confirm or refine their inference. [*Hail* means, in this usage, "to summon, call."]

D Struggling Readers
Getting the Main Idea
? Beowulf says he has come to kill Grendel. What proof does he offer that he is up to the task? [He has killed many enemies, chained five giants and chased their race from the earth, and hunted monsters out of the ocean.]

E Reading Skills and Strategies
Making Inferences
? Why do you think Beowulf intends to fight Grendel without a sword? [Possible answers: Beowulf is concerned about Higlac's opinion of him. Since Grendel does not carry a weapon, Beowulf does not wish to have an unfair advantage. If the two engage in hand-to-hand combat, good is pitted against evil on a more elemental level.] Later, in ll. 480–485, readers learn Grendel has put a spell on all weapons to render them useless.

Making the Connections

Cultural Connections: Boasting
Ask students whether they are put off by Beowulf's boasting. [Possible responses: Yes, it seems he is very conceited. No, he is just explaining his past successes.] One *Beowulf* scholar notes that while modern readers often find this boasting offensive, Beowulf also desires to assist others. Ask students what purpose the bragging serves. [Possible answers: The bragging is an implicit promise to help; it is also a presentation of credentials.] Ask students when similar boasting is expected or accepted in our own culture. [Possible answers: Students may boast on college applications; politicians may boast while seeking office.] Finally, explain that boasting was a tradition of epic poetry. Odysseus does it often.

Ⓐ Critical Thinking
Determining the Author's Purpose

? **What do you think the purpose of Part 4 is?** [Sample answers: The purpose is to introduce the character of Beowulf, his proposed deeds, and the Anglo-Saxon concept of fate or *wyrd*. The purpose may also be to include some of the Geats' history.]

Ⓑ Struggling Readers
Deciphering Unusual Syntax

Ask students to tell how they might expect l. 190 to read and why. [Expected word order might be, "Hrothgar, protector of the Danes, replied." This order places the appositive, "protector of the Danes," next to the word it describes, "Hrothgar."] **Point out that this device is used throughout the poem as in l. 233.**

Ⓒ Reading Skills and Strategies
Identifying Cause and Effect

? **What causes Hrothgar to make this speech, reminding Beowulf of the time he helped Beowulf's father?** [Possible answers: Hrothgar wants to explain how he, like Beowulf, was once in a position to restore peace to a troubled land. He may wish to point out that Beowulf is honoring his father's debt to Hrothgar. He wants to show how much the Danes have suffered and are in need of rescue.] **What is the probable effect of these words on Beowulf?** [Possible answers: They increase his determination; or they have no effect because he already knows what he will do.]

Ⓓ Elements of Literature
Alliteration and Kennings

Have students find examples of alliteration and a kenning in these lines. They might also identify places where they hear caesuras. [Sample answers: Alliteration—"How *many* times have *my* *men*", "courage drawn from too many cups"; kenning—"mead-hall"; caesura—"Could stop his madness,/smother his lust"; "With courage drawn/from too many cups"; "and then, in the morning,/ this mead-hall glittering."]

What it has been before, to invade this hall
And gorge his belly with our bodies. If he can,
If he can. And I think, if my time will have come,
There'll be nothing to mourn over, no corpse to prepare
For its grave: Grendel will carry our bloody
Flesh to the moors, crunch on our bones,
And smear torn scraps of our skin on the walls
Of his den. No, I expect no Danes
Will fret about sewing our shrouds,° if he wins.
And if death does take me, send the hammered
Mail of my armor to Higlac, return
The inheritance I had from Hrethel,° and he
From Wayland.° Fate will unwind as it must!"

5

Hrothgar replied, protector of the Danes:
"Beowulf, you've come to us in friendship, and because
Of the reception your father found at our court.
Edgetho had begun a bitter feud,
Killing Hathlaf, a Wulfing warrior:°
Your father's countrymen were afraid of war,
If he returned to his home, and they turned him away.
Then he traveled across the curving waves
To the land of the Danes. I was new to the throne,
Then, a young man ruling this wide
Kingdom and its golden city: Hergar,
My older brother, a far better man
Than I, had died and dying made me,
Second among Healfdane's sons, first
In this nation. I bought the end of Edgetho's
Quarrel, sent ancient treasures through the ocean's
Furrows to the Wulfings; your father swore
He'd keep that peace. My tongue grows heavy,
And my heart, when I try to tell you what Grendel
Has brought us, the damage he's done, here
In this hall. You see for yourself how much smaller
Our ranks have become, and can guess what we've lost
To his terror. Surely the Lord Almighty
Could stop his madness, smother his lust!
How many times have my men, glowing
With courage drawn from too many cups
Of ale, sworn to stay after dark
And stem that horror with a sweep of their swords.
And then, in the morning, this mead-hall glittering
With new light would be drenched with blood, the benches
Stained red, the floors, all wet from that fiend's
Savage assault—and my soldiers would be fewer
Still, death taking more and more.
But to table, Beowulf, a banquet in your honor:

185. shrouds: cloths used to wrap a body for burial.

188. Hrethel: Beowulf's grandfather, former king of the Geats.

189. Wayland: a smith celebrated for his skill in making swords and mail shirts.

194. Wulfing warrior: The Wulfings were a Germanic tribe. Hrothgar's queen might have been a Wulfing.

Taking a Second Look

Review: Summarizing

Summarizing helps students understand and remember what they have read; it also helps them share what they have read with others. A **summary** restates content, but, unlike a paraphrase, it includes only essential information.

Activity

Model your own summary of Part 1, including a description of a monster descended from Cain, who lives in darkness and listens to songs sung by bards about the creation of the world. Have pairs of students summarize one of the other parts they have read. Provide time for pairs who summarized the same part to compare their work. Then pose these questions:

- From what Biblical figure is Grendel descended? [Cain, who slew his brother, Abel]
- Who has come to fight Grendel and what are his qualifications? [Beowulf, a Geat who has hunted and killed many giants and monsters]

Let us toast your victories, and talk of the future."
Then Hrothgar's men gave places to the Geats,
Yielded benches to the brave visitors,
And led them to the feast. The keeper of the mead
Came carrying out the carved flasks,
And poured that bright sweetness. A poet
Sang, from time to time, in a clear
Pure voice. Danes and visiting Geats
Celebrated as one, drank and rejoiced.

Unferth's Challenge

6

Unferth spoke, Ecglaf's son,
Who sat at Hrothgar's feet, spoke harshly
And sharp (vexed by Beowulf's adventure,
By their visitor's courage, and angry that anyone
In Denmark or anywhere on earth had ever
Acquired glory and fame greater
Than his own):
"You're Beowulf, are you—the same
Boastful fool who fought a swimming
Match with Brecca, both of you daring
And young and proud, exploring the deepest
Seas, risking your lives for no reason
But the danger? All older and wiser heads warned you
Not to, but no one could check such pride.
With Brecca at your side you swam along
The sea-paths, your swift-moving hands pulling you
Over the ocean's face. Then winter
Churned through the water, the waves ran you
As they willed, and you struggled seven long nights
To survive. And at the end victory was his,
Not yours. The sea carried him close
To his home, to southern Norway, near
The land of the Brondings, where he ruled and was loved,
Where his treasure was piled and his strength protected
His towns and his people. He'd promised to outswim you:
Bonstan's son° made that boast ring true.
You've been lucky in your battles, Beowulf, but I think
Your luck may change if you challenge Grendel,
Staying a whole night through in this hall,
Waiting where that fiercest of demons can find you."
Beowulf answered, Edgetho's great son:
"Ah! Unferth, my friend, your face

Anglo-Saxon gold buckle (7th century). Sutton Hoo ship treasure.
British Museum, London.

257. Bonstan's son: Brecca.

WORDS TO OWN
vexed (vekst) *adj.:* highly annoyed.

Summary

Unferth, one of Hrothgar's men, accuses Beowulf of boasting. His challenge to the hero reveals additional traits of Beowulf (and the epic hero), such as honesty and self-restraint. Unferth claims that Beowulf was defeated in a swimming match in his youth. Beowulf responds with a tale-within-a-tale, which foreshadows his bravery in the battle with Grendel. Beowulf recalls how he slew nine sea monsters and swam to safety. *(This summary is continued on p. T32.)*

E Advanced Learners

Assessing Motivation

? What is Unferth's motive for challenging Beowulf? [Possible answers: He is jealous of anyone with greater fame and glory than he has. He is suspicious of a foreigner. He is placed here by the storyteller as a complication in the plot, to cause Beowulf to retell some of his previous feats.]

F Elements of Literature

Epic Hero

A challenge to a hero made by a character of inferior status, like Unferth, is a common motif in heroic poetry. When Beowulf meets this challenge, he shows assertiveness as well as restraint and courtesy. Have students hypothesize about some of the things Beowulf might say to such a challenger if his goal were to be impolite or vengeful. [Possible answers: He might get angry at being questioned at all; he might call Unferth a coward for not dealing with Grendel himself.]

G Elements of Literature

Suspense

? How does Unferth's challenge build suspense? [It raises a question in the reader's mind about Beowulf's ability to defeat Grendel.]

Skill Link

Tracing How Word Origins Affect Spelling

Point out some of the common words on this page that are spelled with initial *ch,* such as *change* and *challenge* in l. 259. Encourage students to use their dictionaries to find the origins of these words. [Both came from French words; the French words came from Latin.] Have students note the sound spelled by /ch/ in these words. Also explain that many Old English words or words that have Germanic, not Latin, roots also have the same sound-spelling correspondence, such as *churned* in l. 249. Next, note how the letters *ch* can be used to denote a much different sound, such as that found in *chlorine, chaos,* and *chiropractor.* After students find out where these words come from [Greek], have them predict and then verify the origins of the following words: *monochrome, anchor, cheap, character, chemical,* and *chain.*

Ⓐ Cultural Connections

Odin

Odin, the god of death and war, was also known as Woden. The Vikings believed that if they died as warriors they would enter *Valhalla,* a hall in *Asgard,* Odin's home, where they could dine all night after doing battle. Surprisingly, these warlike people appreciated poetry—so much so that they brought their *skalds,* or court poets, to their battles to read verses for luck and victory.

Ⓑ Appreciating Language

Style

Have students note the conversational tone of this passage. Ask students to identify the grammatical constructions that make it seem as if a person is actually speaking. [Possible answers: Dashes show interruptions—a thought added while speaking. The passage also contains coordinated sentences joined by the conjunctions "and so," which is a natural way for people to talk.]

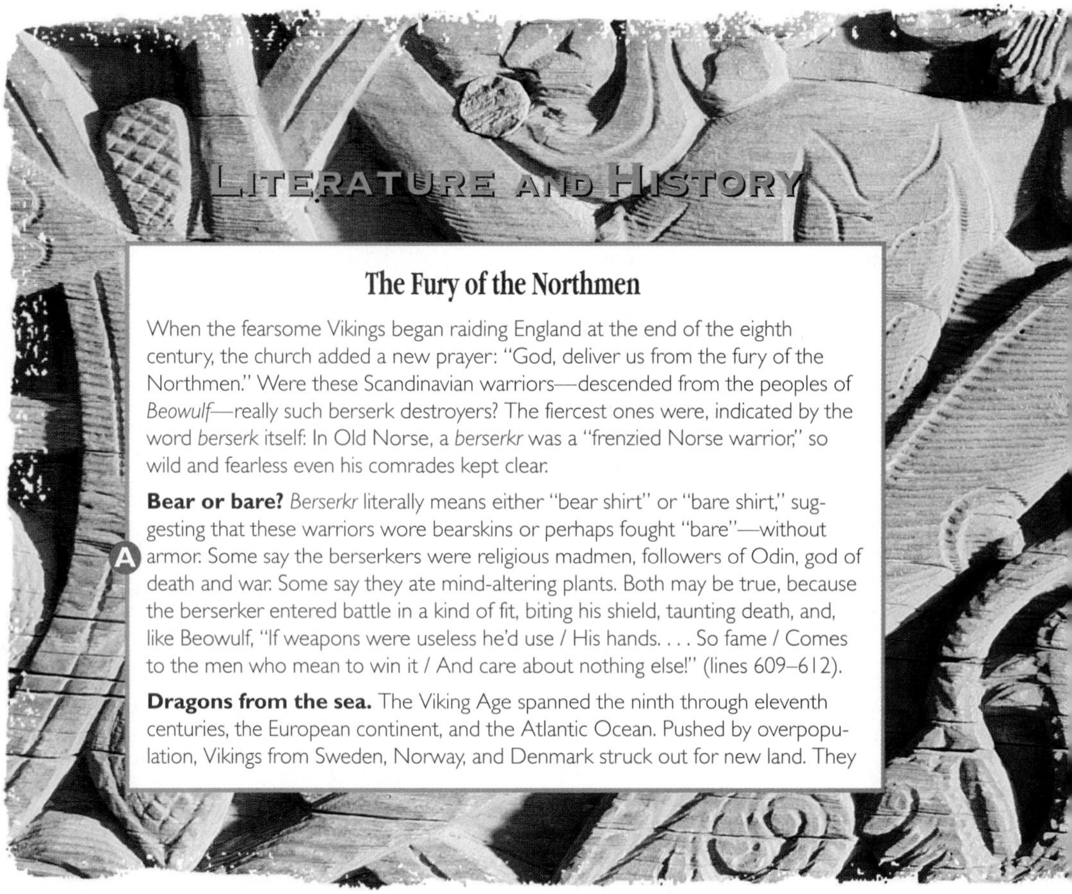

LITERATURE AND HISTORY

The Fury of the Northmen

When the fearsome Vikings began raiding England at the end of the eighth century, the church added a new prayer: "God, deliver us from the fury of the Northmen." Were these Scandinavian warriors—descended from the peoples of *Beowulf*—really such berserk destroyers? The fiercest ones were, indicated by the word *berserk* itself: In Old Norse, a *berserkr* was a "frenzied Norse warrior," so wild and fearless even his comrades kept clear.

Bear or bare? *Berserkr* literally means either "bear shirt" or "bare shirt," suggesting that these warriors wore bearskins or perhaps fought "bare"—without armor. Ⓐ Some say the berserkers were religious madmen, followers of Odin, god of death and war. Some say they ate mind-altering plants. Both may be true, because the berserker entered battle in a kind of fit, biting his shield, taunting death, and, like Beowulf, "If weapons were useless he'd use / His hands. . . . So fame / Comes to the men who mean to win it / And care about nothing else!" (lines 609–612).

Dragons from the sea. The Viking Age spanned the ninth through eleventh centuries, the European continent, and the Atlantic Ocean. Pushed by overpopulation, Vikings from Sweden, Norway, and Denmark struck out for new land. They

Is hot with ale, and your tongue has tried
To tell us about Brecca's doings. But the truth
Is simple: No man swims in the sea
As I can, no strength is a match for mine.
As boys, Brecca and I had boasted—
We were both too young to know better—that we'd risk
Our lives far out at sea, and so
We did. Each of us carried a naked
Sword, prepared for whales or the swift
Sharp teeth and beaks of needlefish.
He could never leave me behind, swim faster
Across the waves than I could, and I
Had chosen to remain close to his side.
I remained near him for five long nights,

Crossing the Curriculum

Geography

Have students research the places where Vikings settled, raided, or traded and have them create a map to show these locations. The type of interaction could be indicated by color coding. (Maps should show Viking settlements in England, France, Germany, Ireland, and what is now the Netherlands. Raiding and trading occurred in Italy, Spain, Russia, parts of the Byzantine Empire, Jerusalem, and even in North Africa.)

Archaeology

Have students research the Sutton Hoo treasure excavated in 1939 (see p. T33). Ask them to focus on one type of discovery, such as the fabulous jewelry or the personal effects of the chieftain, which include the remains of the shield he wore on his left arm as well as his helmet, mask, throwing ax, and coat of mail. Students may draw, model, photocopy, or download pictures of the objects from the Web and explain them to the class in an oral or written presentation.

Science

At this time, the concept of longitude wasn't yet discovered. The Vikings traveled by using the *husan-otra,* which was a stick used for measuring latitude based on the location of the stars. Have students research this and other early methods of navigation. In a short essay, have them evaluate the scientific validity of such methods, including the use of "sun stones" and the practice of gauging the color of the water.

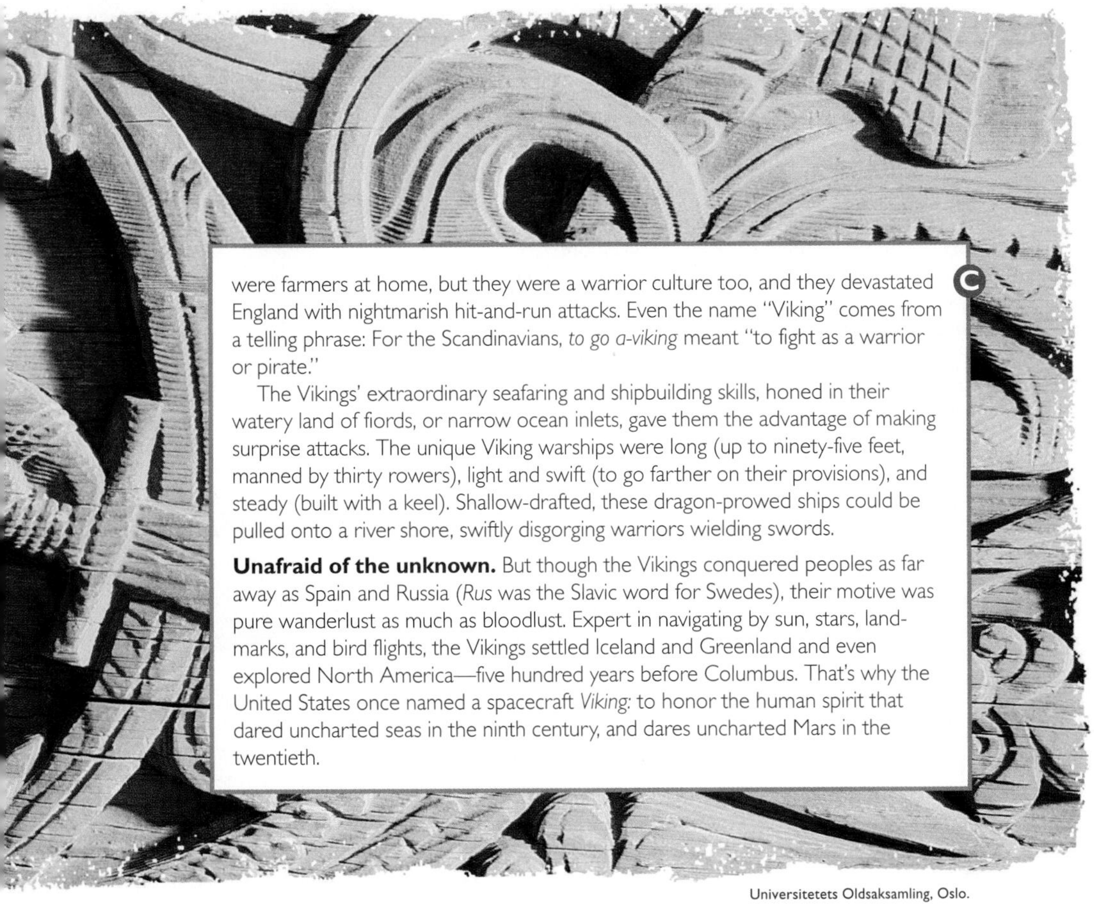

were farmers at home, but they were a warrior culture too, and they devastated England with nightmarish hit-and-run attacks. Even the name "Viking" comes from a telling phrase: For the Scandinavians, *to go a-viking* meant "to fight as a warrior or pirate."

The Vikings' extraordinary seafaring and shipbuilding skills, honed in their watery land of fiords, or narrow ocean inlets, gave them the advantage of making surprise attacks. The unique Viking warships were long (up to ninety-five feet, manned by thirty rowers), light and swift (to go farther on their provisions), and steady (built with a keel). Shallow-drafted, these dragon-prowed ships could be pulled onto a river shore, swiftly disgorging warriors wielding swords.

Unafraid of the unknown. But though the Vikings conquered peoples as far away as Spain and Russia (*Rus* was the Slavic word for Swedes), their motive was pure wanderlust as much as bloodlust. Expert in navigating by sun, stars, landmarks, and bird flights, the Vikings settled Iceland and Greenland and even explored North America—five hundred years before Columbus. That's why the United States once named a spacecraft *Viking*: to honor the human spirit that dared uncharted seas in the ninth century, and dares uncharted Mars in the twentieth.

Universitetets Oldsaksamling, Oslo.

Until a flood swept us apart;
The frozen sea surged around me,
It grew dark, the wind turned bitter, blowing
From the north, and the waves were savage. Creatures
Who sleep deep in the sea were stirred
Into life—and the iron hammered links
Of my mail shirt, these shining bits of metal
Woven across my breast, saved me
From death. A monster seized me, drew me
Swiftly toward the bottom, swimming with its claws
Tight in my flesh. But fate let me
Find its heart with my sword, hack myself
Free; I fought that beast's last battle,
Left it floating lifeless in the sea.

LITERATURE AND HISTORY

Violence and widespread destruction were the hallmarks of a Viking raid. The warriors raped women, slaughtered monks and children, and often killed men by slitting their backbones so their ribs sprang out, exposing their hearts. It is no wonder the Vikings were so feared and hated by the early people of what is now Great Britain. They destroyed monasteries first. The Vikings started with the monastery in Lindisfarne in A.D. 793 and moved quickly onto the church at Jarrow; by A.D. 795 they had also plundered Columba's monastery on Iona. These settlements were preyed upon by the Vikings because the monasteries had accumulated great treasure. To the monks and other people in early Britain these raids brought horror. Up until A.D. 851, most Viking raids were hit-and-run. However, in that year, according to the *Anglo-Saxon Chronicles,* 350 ships destroyed Canterbury and caused more carnage than had ever been heard of. The Vikings even stayed in Canterbury throughout that winter.

C Reading Skills and Strategies

Using Context Clues

? Can you figure out from the context what the word *devastated* means? How? [*Devastated* must mean "badly damaged" or "destroyed," based on its link to the familiar phrases "warrior culture" and "nightmarish raids."]

Skill Link

Using the Thesaurus and Glosses

Call attention to the vivid writing in this epic, achieved in part by the use of exact words, especially active verbs and precise adjectives. Have pairs of students rewrite the following sentences using more vivid verbs and adjectives. Students should use a thesaurus; they may also use some of the Words to Own introduced in this lesson. Sample answers are given.

1. The frozen sea *rose up* around me. [The frozen sea *surged* around me.]
2. A monster *grabbed* me. [A monster *seized* me.]
3. Unferth was *bothered* by Beowulf's courage. [Unferth was *vexed* by Beowulf's courage.]
4. Grendel lived deep in the *dark* cave. [Grendel lived deep in the *murky* cave.]
5. Shrieks of pain *came* from his *tight* throat. [Shrieks of pain *tore* from his *taut* throat.]
6. He had never *seen* a more *disagreeable* beast. [He had never *beheld* a more *loathsome* beast.]

Ⓐ Advanced Learners

Interpreting an Analogy

? In what ways does Beowulf compare his defeat of the sea monsters to a feast? [He serves them his sword for the feast, but they die at the bottom of the sea from eating the "food" he feeds them.]

Ⓑ Reading Skills and Strategies

Connecting with the Text

? Do you agree with Beowulf? Or do you think that his words hold true for his time period only and not in our present day? Why? [Possible responses: Beowulf's words hold true even today. People can "drive away death" by taking steps to protect themselves, such as by wearing seatbelts and not smoking. Or, modern people do not have to fight for their lives as much as the Vikings did; we let fate take its course.]

Ⓒ Elements of Literature

Foil

? In literature, a foil is a character who contrasts with another. How does Unferth serve as a foil to Beowulf? [Possible answer: Unferth is a spiteful, idle boaster who has committed the unpardonable sin of murdering his kinsmen. Beowulf, on the other hand, has earned glory by defending those more helpless than he.]

Ⓓ Cultural Connections

Wergild

Explain to students that even though Beowulf and Unferth seem to inhabit an exceedingly violent world, killing one's relatives or kin was, for the Anglo-Saxon nobility, an unspeakable crime. The Anglo-Saxons had a custom of paying compensation to the relatives of the people they murdered; they even had a word for it: *wergild,* which means "man-payment." If the murdered person was not related to the murderer, then this kind of payment was considered satisfactory by the relatives of the victim. No such way of making amends existed, however, for taking the life of one's own kin.

7

"Other monsters crowded around me,
Continually attacking. I treated them politely,
Offering the edge of my razor-sharp sword.
But the feast, I think, did not please them, filled
Their evil bellies with no banquet-rich food,
Thrashing there at the bottom of the sea;
By morning they'd decided to sleep on the shore,
Lying on their backs, their blood spilled out
On the sand. Afterwards, sailors could cross
That sea-road and feel no fear; nothing
Would stop their passing. Then God's bright beacon
Appeared in the east, the water lay still,
And at last I could see the land, wind-swept
Cliff-walls at the edge of the coast. Fate saves
The living when they drive away death by themselves!
Lucky or not, nine was the number
Of sea-huge monsters I killed. What man,
Anywhere under Heaven's high arch, has fought
In such darkness, endured more misery, or been harder
Pressed? Yet I survived the sea, smashed
The monsters' hot jaws, swam home from my journey.
The swift-flowing waters swept me along
And I landed on Finnish soil. I've heard
No tales of you, Unferth, telling
Of such clashing terror, such contests in the night!
Brecca's battles were never so bold;
Neither he nor you can match me—and I mean
No boast, have announced no more than I know
To be true. And there's more: You murdered your brothers,
Your own close kin. Words and bright wit
Won't help your soul; you'll suffer hell's fires,
Unferth, forever tormented. Ecglaf's
Proud son, if your hands were as hard, your heart
As fierce as you think it, no fool would dare
To raid your hall, ruin Herot
And oppress its prince, as Grendel has done.
But he's learned that terror is his alone,
Discovered he can come for your people with no fear
Of reprisal; he's found no fighting, here,
But only food, only delight.
He murders as he likes, with no mercy, gorges
And feasts on your flesh, and expects no trouble,
No quarrel from the quiet Danes. Now
The Geats will show him courage, soon

Two drinking horns (7th century). Sutton Hoo ship treasure.

© British Museum, London.

WORDS TO OWN

reprisal (ri·prī'zəl) *n.:* punishment in return for an injury.

Reaching All Students

Struggling Readers

Beowulf is a poem that includes rapid shifts in time sequence. Encourage students to keep track of the sequence of events by using a divided time line: one half for the events occurring in Beowulf's present, and the other half for events occurring in his or others' past. Ask students when the events spoken of in this passage occur. [in both Beowulf's past and in Unferth's past] Ask students where they would place these events on a time line. [These events would be placed at the beginning of the time line, or, if the time line is divided into halves, on the first half of the time line.] Ask students what other events, which they have already read about, could be placed on the time line. [Possible answers: Grendel's twelve years of terror; Beowulf's arrival]

He can test his strength in battle. And when the sun
Comes up again, opening another
Bright day from the south, anyone in Denmark
May enter this hall: That evil will be gone!"
Hrothgar, gray-haired and brave, sat happily
Listening, the famous ring-giver sure,
At last, that Grendel could be killed; he believed
In Beowulf's bold strength and the firmness of his spirit.
There was the sound of laughter, and the cheerful clanking
Of cups, and pleasant words. Then Welthow,
Hrothgar's gold-ringed queen, greeted
The warriors; a noble woman who knew
What was right, she raised a flowing cup
To Hrothgar first, holding it high
For the lord of the Danes to drink, wishing him
Joy in that feast. The famous king
Drank with pleasure and blessed their banquet.
Then Welthow went from warrior to warrior,
Pouring a portion from the jeweled cup
For each, till the bracelet-wearing queen
Had carried the mead-cup among them and it was Beowulf's
Turn to be served. She saluted the Geats'
Great prince, thanked God for answering her prayers,
For allowing her hands the happy duty
Of offering mead to a hero who would help
Her afflicted people. He drank what she poured,
Edgetho's brave son, then assured the Danish
Queen that his heart was firm and his hands
Ready:
"When we crossed the sea, my comrades
And I, I already knew that all
My purpose was this: to win the good will
Of your people or die in battle, pressed
In Grendel's fierce grip. Let me live in greatness
And courage, or here in this hall welcome
My death!"
Welthow was pleased with his words,
His bright-tongued boasts; she carried them back
To her lord, walked nobly across to his side.
The feast went on, laughter and music
And the brave words of warriors celebrating
Their delight. Then Hrothgar rose, Healfdane's
Son, heavy with sleep; as soon
As the sun had gone, he knew that Grendel
Would come to Herot, would visit that hall
When night had covered the earth with its net
And the shapes of darkness moved black and silent
Through the world. Hrothgar's warriors rose with him.
He went to Beowulf, embraced the Geats'
Brave prince, wished him well, and hoped

E Elements of Literature

Kennings

Kennings are metaphorical compound words or phrases that indicate a person or thing by a characteristic or quality. What example of a kenning written as a hyphenated compound do you find in these lines? [ring-giver] What does the kenning mean? [king] Point out that Hrothgar is called a ring-giver because he dispenses jewels to his people as symbols of the special tie between him and them.

F Cultural Connections

Anglo-Saxon Women

Welthow exhibits the qualities valued in Anglo-Saxon women, as they are described in the *Exeter Book* (see p. 55): beloved, cheerful, generous, and gracious. Ask students to consider also how well Welthow fits the description of women given in "Women in Anglo-Saxon Culture" (see p. 10).

G Reading Skills and Strategies

Using Context Clues

Use context clues to figure out the meaning of *afflicted* in l. 361. What clues did you use? [*Afflicted* means "suffering," with clues coming from the reference to people needing help.]

H Elements of Literature

Figurative Language

How is the coming of night personified? [Possible answers: Night is capable of covering the earth with a net. Night may be a fisherman with a net; the "shapes of darkness" moving "black and silent" could be fish caught by the fisherman or people caught by night.]

Making the Connections

Cultural Connections

In ll. 364–370, Beowulf expresses an idea that is not all that far from the either-or thinking of Patrick Henry's "Give me liberty or give me death," and Tennyson's "Theirs not to reason why,/Theirs but to do and die." For an Anglo-Saxon warrior, life was an either-or situation: Life without loyalty or courage was worse than death. According to the Anglo-Saxon code of the *comitatus,* warriors must defend their lord to the death. Thus a true hero would worry more about showing fear or being disloyal than about dying. Have students name and discuss modern incarnations of this "do or die" philosophy, which you sometimes hear from extremists championing political causes, as well as from those who compete in sports.

Summary

Suspense builds as Grendel heads toward Herot where, unknown to him, Beowulf and the Geats lie in wait. Grendel breaks down the door and devours one Geat. Next he grabs Beowulf and, in a symbolic battle between good and evil, Beowulf mortally wounds Grendel and hangs his dismembered arm from the rafters. Grendel drags himself off and sinks into the murky waters of his lair. All rejoice at Beowulf's bravery and their deliverance from Grendel's raids. Soon, however, Grendel's vengeful mother attacks Herot and carries off her son's claw. Hrothgar again seeks Beowulf's help. *(This summary is continued on p. T39.)*

Ⓐ Critical Thinking

Speculating

? What does Hrothgar promise Beowulf? [He gives Beowulf command of Herot and promises him treasures.] Why do you think Hrothgar does this? [Possible answers: According to the code of *comitatus,* he is making a promise to reward Beowulf for his loyal service, thereby reaffirming his kingly dignity. Hrothgar is creating a contract, summarizing his own expectations and Beowulf's intentions. The poet may have included these words to build up suspense in the listener/reader about the upcoming battle between Beowulf and Grendel.]

That Herot would be his to command. And then
He declared:
"No one strange to this land
Has ever been granted what I've given you,
No one in all the years of my rule.
Make this best of all mead-halls yours, and then
Keep it free of evil, fight
With glory in your heart! Purge Herot
And your ship will sail home with its treasure-holds full." . . .

The feast ends. Beowulf and his men take the place of Hrothgar's followers and lie down to sleep in Herot. Beowulf, however, is wakeful, eager to meet his enemy.

The Battle with Grendel

8

Out from the marsh, from the foot of misty
Hills and bogs, bearing God's hatred,
Grendel came, hoping to kill
Anyone he could trap on this trip to high Herot.
He moved quickly through the cloudy night,
Up from his swampland, sliding silently
Toward that gold-shining hall. He had visited Hrothgar's
Home before, knew the way—
But never, before nor after that night,
Found Herot defended so firmly, his reception
So harsh. He journeyed, forever joyless,
Straight to the door, then snapped it open,
Tore its iron fasteners with a touch,
And rushed angrily over the threshold.
He strode quickly across the inlaid
Floor, snarling and fierce: His eyes
Gleamed in the darkness, burned with a gruesome
Light. Then he stopped, seeing the hall
Crowded with sleeping warriors, stuffed
With rows of young soldiers resting together.
And his heart laughed, he relished the sight,
Intended to tear the life from those bodies
By morning; the monster's mind was hot
With the thought of food and the feasting his belly
Would soon know. But fate, that night, intended
Grendel to gnaw the broken bones
Of his last human supper. Human
Eyes were watching his evil steps,
Waiting to see his swift hard claws.

Bronze plaque showing a warrior killing a monster.

Statens Historiska Museer, Stockholm.

Assessing Learning

Check Test: True-False

1. Grendel has been attacking Herot Hall for six months. [False]
2. Beowulf requests that Hrothgar allow him to fight Grendel without his weapons. [True]
3. Grendel cannot be harmed because he is protected by God. [False]
4. Hrothgar gives Beowulf command of Herot, promising him treasures if he kills Grendel. [True]

Informal Assessment

Observation Assessment. Use a chart like the following to evaluate students' progress in group-learning situations. Make notes both by observing and by questioning students' performance in these areas:

STUDENT'S NAME:			
Activity:	Always	Sometimes	Never
Participates in discussion			
Completes the assignment with the group			
Supports other group members			
Asks clarifying questions			

Grendel snatched at the first Geat
He came to, ripped him apart, cut
His body to bits with powerful jaws,
Drank the blood from his veins, and bolted
Him down, hands and feet; death
And Grendel's great teeth came together,
Snapping life shut. Then he stepped to another
Still body, clutched at Beowulf with his claws,
Grasped at a strong-hearted wakeful sleeper
—And was instantly seized himself, claws
Bent back as Beowulf leaned up on one arm.
That shepherd of evil, guardian of crime,
Knew at once that nowhere on earth
Had he met a man whose hands were harder;
His mind was flooded with fear—but nothing
Could take his talons and himself from that tight
Hard grip. Grendel's one thought was to run
From Beowulf, flee back to his marsh and hide there:
This was a different Herot than the hall he had emptied.
But Higlac's follower remembered his final
Boast and, standing erect, stopped
The monster's flight, fastened those claws
In his fists till they cracked, clutched Grendel
Closer. The infamous killer fought
For his freedom, wanting no flesh but retreat,
Desiring nothing but escape; his claws
Had been caught, he was trapped. That trip to Herot
Was a miserable journey for the writhing monster!
The high hall rang, its roof boards swayed,
And Danes shook with terror. Down
The aisles the battle swept, angry
And wild. Herot trembled, wonderfully
Built to withstand the blows, the struggling
Great bodies beating at its beautiful walls;
Shaped and fastened with iron, inside
And out, artfully worked, the building
Stood firm. Its benches rattled, fell
To the floor, gold-covered boards grating
As Grendel and Beowulf battled across them.
Hrothgar's wise men had fashioned Herot
To stand forever; only fire,
They had planned, could shatter what such skill had put
Together, swallow in hot flames such splendor
Of ivory and iron and wood. Suddenly
The sounds changed, the Danes started
In new terror, cowering in their beds as the terrible
Screams of the Almighty's enemy sang
In the darkness, the horrible shrieks of pain
And defeat, the tears torn out of Grendel's

Silver and gold brooch with amber ornaments (9th century). Roscrea, County Tipperary.

National Museum of Ireland, Dublin.

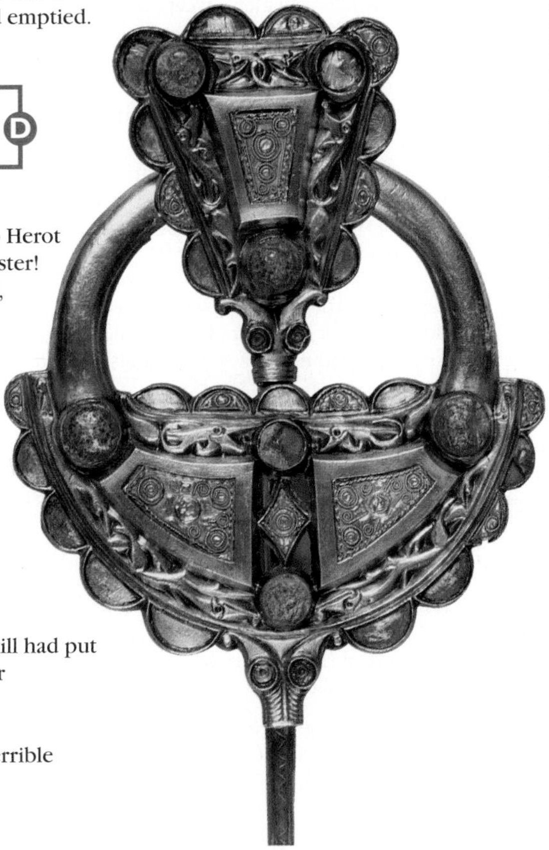

B Reading Skills and Strategies

Making Inferences

? Why do you think Beowulf allows Grendel to slaughter one of the Geats before taking action himself? [Sample responses: Perhaps Beowulf is taking time to formulate a plan of attack. Perhaps Grendel simply moves too quickly for Beowulf to stop him.]

C Elements of Literature

Kennings

? What kennings associate Grendel with evil? [shepherd of evil; guardian of crime] **What form do these kennings take?** [Both these kennings use prepositional phrases.]

D Appreciating Language

Action Verbs

? Beowulf has pledged to kill Grendel with his bare hands. He says, "God will decide who will be given to death's cold grip." What specific verbs are used here to emphasize the fierce grappling of Beowulf and Grendel? [*fastened, cracked, clutched, fought*]

RESPONDING TO THE ART

Brooches were used by the Anglo-Saxons to fasten clothing. One historian calls them "glorified versions of our old friend the safety pin, but with a spring on both sides of the head." The extraordinarily fine brooch shown here appears to be inlaid with amber.

Activity. Have students draw or trace the brooch to experience how detailed it is.

Professional Notes

Critical Comment: Archaeological Finds

Some of the Anglo-Saxon skill and craftsmanship described in ll. 452–464 was confirmed by the 1939 discovery of a burial mound at Sutton Hoo in East Anglia. Believed to be the burial site of a King Raedwald, Sutton Hoo yielded items of silver and gold and thousands of intricately mounted garnets. Prior to this find, scholars had doubted that Anglo-Saxon artisans were capable of creating the magnificent treasures described in *Beowulf*. Yet as Rupert Bruce-Mitford, Keeper of Medieval and Later Antiquities in the British Museum, writes, "the [Sutton Hoo] objects reveal . . . a completely unexpected school of art, and a supreme one. It is pagan Saxon art in its final flower, overloaded, but not decadent. The gold jewelry is brimming with novel and daring ideas. It shows an overflowing exuberance and displays the highest level of craftsmanship, excelling anything known in this medium from the rest of Europe in its era." In addition, because many of the Sutton Hoo treasures—such as a Coptic bronze bowl from Egypt—were not of Anglo-Saxon origin, they indicate that the Anglo-Saxons carried on a much livelier trade than once believed. The description of Herot above has also been confirmed by archaeologists. The building was apparently built of wood held together with iron bands. The gabled roof was overlaid with gold and the floor was inlaid.

A Reading Skills and Strategies

Drawing Conclusions

? How do the actions of Beowulf's men uphold the Anglo-Saxon code of honor? [Possible answer: They are prepared to defend their lord with their lives.]

B Advanced Learners

Christian-Pagan References

? In this passage, what additional evidence do you find of the Christian-pagan tension in this epic? [Possible answers: Grendel is "sin-stained" but also capable of the power to "bewitch" and cast "spells," suggestive of pagan rites. These lines also say Grendel is doomed to hell because he doesn't understand what it is to feud with God.]

C Vocabulary Note

Multiple Meanings

Not all students will readily understand the expression "bound fast." This is because *fast* is a word with many meanings, the most common of which is "quick." Have students jot down some other meanings of *fast.* [Other meanings for the modifier are "firmly fixed," as in *bound fast* or *shut fast;* "firmly loyal," as in *became fast friends;* and "wild," as in a *fast teenager.* The adjective *fast* also can mean "deeply," as in *fast asleep.*]

D Struggling Readers

Getting the Main Idea

Have students read ll. 492–504 and then explain what happens to Grendel in this passage. [Beowulf tears off Grendel's arm and the monster retreats to his den.] If students need help, point out clue words such as "sinews snapped" and "bone split."

Taut throat, hell's captive caught in the arms
Of him who of all the men on earth
Was the strongest.

9

That mighty protector of men
Meant to hold the monster till its life
Leaped out, knowing the fiend was no use
[A] To anyone in Denmark. All of Beowulf's
Band had jumped from their beds, ancestral
Swords raised and ready, determined
To protect their prince if they could. Their courage
Was great but all wasted: They could hack at Grendel
From every side, trying to open
A path for his evil soul, but their points
Could not hurt him, the sharpest and hardest iron
Could not scratch at his skin, for that sin-stained demon
Had bewitched all men's weapons, laid spells
[B] That blunted every mortal man's blade.
And yet his time had come, his days
Were over, his death near; down
To hell he would go, swept groaning and helpless
To the waiting hands of still worse fiends.
Now he discovered—once the afflictor
Of men, tormentor of their days—what it meant
To feud with Almighty God: Grendel
Saw that his strength was deserting him, his claws
[C] Bound fast, Higlac's brave follower tearing at
His hands. The monster's hatred rose higher,
But his power had gone. He twisted in pain,
And the bleeding sinews deep in his shoulder
Snapped, muscle and bone split
[D] And broke. The battle was over, Beowulf
Had been granted new glory: Grendel escaped,
But wounded as he was could flee to his den,
His miserable hole at the bottom of the marsh,
Only to die, to wait for the end
Of all his days. And after that bloody
Combat the Danes laughed with delight.
He who had come to them from across the sea,
Bold and strong-minded, had driven affliction
Off, purged Herot clean. He was happy,
Now, with that night's fierce work; the Danes
Had been served as he'd boasted he'd serve them; Beowulf,

Eagle shield ornament (7th century). Sutton Hoo ship treasure.
British Museum, London.

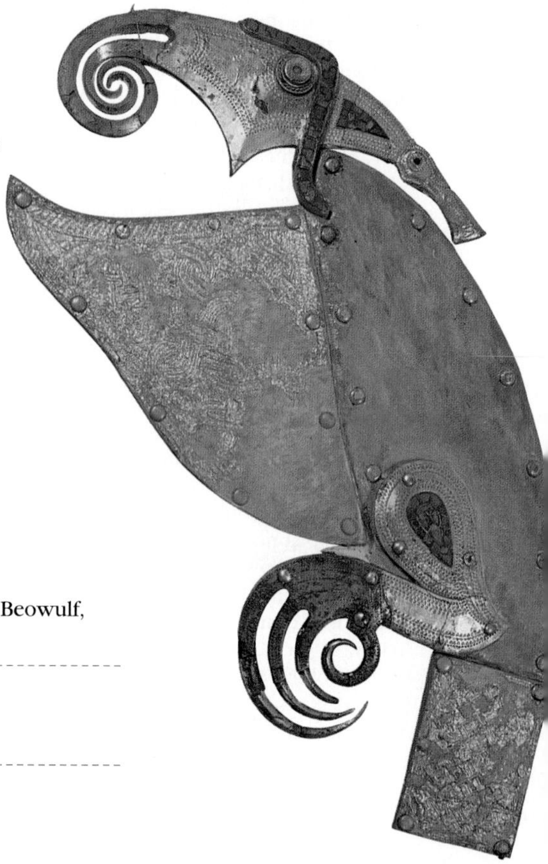

Words to Own

taut (tôt) *adj.:* stretched tight.
sinews (sin′yo͞oz) *n. pl.:* tendons or connective tissues.

Using Students' Strengths

Visual Learners

Many critics think that *Beowulf* may have been sung during three sittings, one for each of the battles. Have students start a three-column chart to compare and contrast Beowulf's battle with Grendel and the two battles that follow it.

Battle with Grendel	Battle with Grendel's Mother	Battle with Dragon

Intrapersonal Learners

Ask students to form small groups and talk about the burdens placed on men to act courageously during this time period. What do students imagine to be the true thoughts and feelings of the warriors who jumped up with their swords raised, "ready to protect their prince"? Students might also talk about whether it was easier to be a man or woman in Anglo-Saxon times. Have them use the background information on p. 10.

Logical/Mathematical Learners

Dragons were highly symbolic in Anglo-Saxon culture. Ask students to speculate on how tales of dragons may have arisen in Anglo-Saxon times. What real-life battles for survival might have prompted storytellers to create fantastic battles like the ones described in *Beowulf?* Students should use the background material on Anglo-Saxon times included in this collection to create logical hypotheses.

A prince of the Geats, had killed Grendel,
Ended the grief, the sorrow, the suffering
Forced on Hrothgar's helpless people
By a bloodthirsty fiend. No Dane doubted
The victory, for the proof, hanging high
From the rafters where Beowulf had hung it, was the monster's **E**
Arm, claw and shoulder and all.

Detail of picture stone from Larbro, Gotland, Sweden.

10

And then, in the morning, crowds surrounded
Herot, warriors coming to that hall
From faraway lands, princes and leaders
Of men hurrying to behold the monster's
Great staggering tracks. They gaped with no sense
Of sorrow, felt no regret for his suffering,
Went tracing his bloody footprints, his beaten
And lonely flight, to the edge of the lake
Where he'd dragged his corpselike way, doomed
And already weary of his vanishing life.
The water was bloody, steaming and boiling
In horrible pounding waves, heat
Sucked from his magic veins; but the swirling **F**
Surf had covered his death, hidden
Deep in murky darkness his miserable
End, as hell opened to receive him.
Then old and young rejoiced, turned back
From that happy pilgrimage, mounted their hard-hooved
Horses, high-spirited stallions, and rode them
Slowly toward Herot again, retelling
Beowulf's bravery as they jogged along.
And over and over they swore that nowhere
On earth or under the spreading sky
Or between the seas, neither south nor north, **G**
Was there a warrior worthier to rule over men.
(But no one meant Beowulf's praise to belittle **H**
Hrothgar, their kind and gracious king!) . . .

Grendel's monstrous mother, in grief for her son, next attacks Herot, and in her dripping claws she carries off one man—Hrothgar's closest friend. The monster also carries off Grendel's arm, which Beowulf had hung high from the rafters. Beowulf is awakened and called for again. In one of

WORDS TO OWN
murky (murk'ē) *adj.:* shadowy.
pilgrimage (pil'grim·ij) *n.:* journey made to a place of religious or historical interest.

E Reading Skills and Strategies
Identifying Cause and Effect

? Why does Beowulf hang Grendel's arm from the rafters of Herot? [Possible answers: Beowulf shows his victory in this way, like a trophy, just as some modern-day hunters hang antlers or stuffed heads on their walls. By displaying Grendel's arm, Beowulf shows that Grendel is defeated and disarmed. Beowulf displays how awful his opponent was and, in so doing, calls attention to his own greatness.] **What effect do you think seeing the arm would have on viewers?** [Possible answers: It would make them honor or stand in awe of Beowulf. It would serve as a warning to other monsters and possible opponents.]

F Elements of Literature
Symbolism

? Reread the description of the lake in which Grendel lies. How is it suggestive of hell? [Possible answers: There is powerful heat in the steaming and boiling waters. The swirling may suggest fires. It is called a "horrible" place and referred to as hell.]

G Elements of Literature
Alliteration

? This passage is a hymn of praise for the conquering hero. What examples of alliteration emphasize the important words in ll. 539–544? [Possible answers: *they, that; spreading sky; warrior, worthier; Beowulf's, belittle; kind, king.*]

H Reading Skills and Strategies
Using Context Clues

? What does *belittle* mean? What context clues did you use to figure this out? [*Belittle* means "to mock, put down," which contrasts with "praise." Another context clue is the word *little* within the word.]

Connections

In his novel *Grendel,* John Gardner tells the basic story of *Beowulf,* but from the monster's point of view. In this excerpt, Grendel tells about his life in the murky swamp where he lives with his mother and he describes one of his attacks on Hrothgar's castle.

Background

Students may be interested to know that Gardner, in addition to being a best-selling novelist, was also a professor of Old and Middle English. Students may note how he creates a few apt alliterations and careful kennings of his own in this piece.

A Critical Thinking

Making Judgments

? According to this selection, is Grendel good or evil? [Possible answers: He is evil because he kills and laughs about having killed. He is just a monster doing what monsters do; he does not have human sensibilities. He is evil because he does show the ability to question and yet does not curb his own hurtful actions.]

B Elements of Literature

Imagery

? What imagery in the description of Grendel's lair associates Grendel with death and darkness? [Possible responses: Images of blackness abound, especially in ll. 545–554. When the wind stirs the waves, the waves are dark and black as they splash toward the sky. The deer and stag prefer to die on the shore rather than attempt to save their lives by jumping into the lake, apparently associating the lake with death.]

Connections — A Novel

In his novel *Grendel* (1971), the contemporary American writer John Gardner (1933–1982) retells part of *Beowulf* from the point of view of the monster. In this excerpt, Grendel tells his own version of one of his raids on Hrothgar's hall.

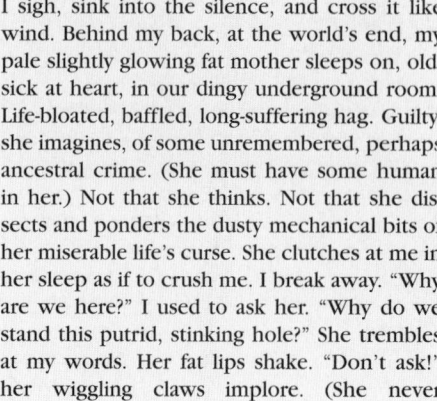

Courtesy of Alfred A. Knopf.

A *from* Grendel

John Gardner

I sigh, sink into the silence, and cross it like wind. Behind my back, at the world's end, my pale slightly glowing fat mother sleeps on, old, sick at heart, in our dingy underground room. Life-bloated, baffled, long-suffering hag. Guilty, she imagines, of some unremembered, perhaps ancestral crime. (She must have some human in her.) Not that she thinks. Not that she dissects and ponders the dusty mechanical bits of her miserable life's curse. She clutches at me in her sleep as if to crush me. I break away. "Why are we here?" I used to ask her. "Why do we stand this putrid, stinking hole?" She trembles at my words. Her fat lips shake. "Don't ask!" her wiggling claws implore. (She never speaks.) "Don't ask!" It must be some terrible secret, I used to think. I'd give her a crafty squint. She'll tell me, in time, I thought. But she told me nothing. I waited on. That was before the old dragon, calm as winter, unveiled the truth. He was not a friend.

And so I come through trees and towns to the lights of Hrothgar's meadhall. I am no stranger here. A respected guest. Eleven years now and going on twelve I have come up this clean-mown central hill, dark shadow out of the woods below, and have knocked politely on the high oak door, bursting its hinges and sending the shock of my greeting inward like a cold blast out of a cave. "Grendel!" they

the most famous verses in the epic, the old king describes where Grendel and his mother live.

11

. . . "They live in secret places, windy
Cliffs, wolf-dens where water pours
From the rocks, then runs underground, where mist
Steams like black clouds, and the groves of trees
Growing out over their lake are all covered
B With frozen spray, and wind down snakelike
Roots that reach as far as the water
And help keep it dark. At night that lake
Burns like a torch. No one knows its bottom,
No wisdom reaches such depths. A deer,

Professional Notes

Critical Comment: Getting to Know Grendel

According to critic Dean McWilliams, Gardner's narrative records Grendel's struggle to understand himself and his world. Students may be interested in McWilliams' account of how Grendel learns about human culture: "[Grendel] hears the Shaper, Hrothgar's court poet. He listens as this artist sings his version of the community's valorous past and its glorious future. Grendel knows this is pure invention, for he has watched the community over the years and knows the truth about the way they live. He also hears the poet tell his fellows that Grendel is their enemy, a son of Cain, cursed by God. Grendel is hurt and angered. . . " Even though Grendel is angered by being thought of in this way, there is still something appealing to him about the Shaper's song. "Drawn by the poet's vision, Grendel tries to join the humans and staggers into their settlement crying, 'Mercy! Peace!' The men meet him with battleaxes, however, and he flees for his life."

squeak, and I smile like exploding spring. The old Shaper, a man I cannot help but admire, goes out the back window with his harp at a single bound, though blind as a bat. The drunkest of Hrothgar's thanes come reeling and clanking down from their wall-hung beds, all shouting their meady, outrageous boasts, their heavy swords aswirl like eagles' wings. "Woe, woe, woe!" cries Hrothgar, hoary with winters, peeking in, wide-eyed, from his bedroom in back. His wife, looking in behind him, makes a scene. The thanes in the meadhall blow out the lights and cover the wide stone fireplace with shields. I laugh, crumple over; I can't help myself. In the darkness, I alone see clear as day. While they squeal and screech and bump into each other, I silently sack up my dead and withdraw to the woods. I eat and laugh and eat until I can barely walk, my chest-hair matted with dribbled blood, and then the roosters on the hill crow, and dawn comes over the roofs of the houses, and all at once I am filled with gloom again.

"This is some punishment sent us," I hear them bawling from the hill.

My head aches. Morning nails my eyes.

"Some god is angry," I hear a woman keen. "The people of Scyld and Herogar and Hrothgar are mired in sin!"

My belly rumbles, sick on their sour meat. I crawl through bloodstained leaves to the eaves of the forest, and there peak out. The dogs fall silent at the edge of my spell, and where the king's hall surmounts the town, the blind old Shaper, harp clutched tight to his fragile chest, stares futilely down, straight at me. Otherwise nothing. Pigs root dully at the posts of a wooden fence. A rumple-horned ox lies chewing in dew and shade. A few men, lean, wearing animal skins, look up at the gables of the king's hall, or at the vultures circling casually beyond. Hrothgar says nothing, hoarfrost-bearded, his features cracked and crazed. Inside, I hear the people praying—whimpering, whining, mumbling, pleading—to their numerous sticks and stones. He doesn't go in. The king has lofty theories of his own.

"Theories," I whisper to the bloodstained ground. So the dragon once spoke. ("They'd map out roads through Hell with their crackpot theories!" I recall his laugh.)

Then the groaning and praying stop, and on the side of the hill the dirge-slow shoveling begins. . . .

Hunted through the woods by packs of hounds,
A stag with great horns, though driven through the forest
From faraway places, prefers to die
On those shores, refuses to save its life
In that water. It isn't far, nor is it
A pleasant spot! When the wind stirs
And storms, waves splash toward the sky,
As dark as the air, as black as the rain
That the heavens weep. Our only help,
Again, lies with you. Grendel's mother
Is hidden in her terrible home, in a place
You've not seen. Seek it, if you dare! Save us,
Once more, and again twisted gold,
Heaped-up ancient treasure, will reward you
For the battle you win!"

Gundestrup cauldron.
National Museum, Copenhagen.

Connecting Across Texts

Connecting with *Beowulf*

Ask students whether learning any part of the story from Grendel's point of view changes how they view the character of Beowulf, the events retold in the poem, or the message of the poem. [Students may say that the Anglo-Saxon creators of Beowulf never intended for Grendel to be anything other than an embodiment of evil, so their interpretations of the character and the poem are untouched by any effort to humanize Grendel. Students may also remark that all struggles change, become more complicated, and include more shades of gray when personal information about the participants is brought to bear. Therefore, Beowulf is slightly diminished, because Grendel is slightly humanized.]

Browsing in the Files

Writers On Writing. John Gardner explains, "Writing a novel is like running grain through a hammermill: one has to get the central action rolling, and then feed in the background, or sprinkle in the larger implications, whenever and wherever one can do it without losing a finger. . . . In a novel like *Grendel,* all the reader needs to know in order to follow the action is that Grendel is a monster; comes from a cave and from a mute, mindless mother; hates his sense of himself as an animal; and feels mysteriously drawn to human beings, whom he hungrily studies, longs to be friends with, and also scorns and occasionally eats." Gardner, who has written extensively about writing, says he wrote the last chapter of *Grendel* (in which Grendel dies) in a kind of altered state or trance. He says that, "When I come out of one of these trance moments, . . . I seem to have been taken over by some muse. Insofar as I'm able to remember what happened, it seems to me it was this: for a moment the real process of our dreams has been harnessed. The magic key goes in, all the tumblers fall at once and the door swings open."

Responding to the Art

The caldron shown here is a product of the highest period of Celtic culture, known as the La Tène culture. As is evident here, these Celts were particularly skilled in metalwork. Much of the art on the caldron depicts the mythology of the Celts. On an inner plate, for example, the figure wearing stag antlers represents the Lord of the Wild Beasts. The significance of many of the figures can only be guessed at. The caldron was used as a kind of kettle for holding warm water or drink. **Activity.** Have students compare this object with the mass-produced cups we use today.

MAKING MEANINGS

(Parts 1–11)

First Thoughts [Respond]

1. Responses might include images of Grendel, Beowulf's battle with Grendel, and the fiery lake.

Shaping Interpretations [Interpret]

2. Herot is a bright hall, a place of drinking, singing, and feasting. Grendel lives in a cold, dark lake so forbidding that hunted deer would rather die than save their lives by plunging into it.

3. The bard's songs are about God's creation of the world, while Grendel is associated with destruction.

4. Darkness is associated with death and destruction—an appropriate time for evil Grendel to prowl. See especially ll. 1–19, 30, 49–50, 82, 112, 392–396, 547–548, and 562.

5. Herot represents order, light—even godliness; Grendel would naturally hate such a symbol. The conflict may suggest the universal struggle between light and dark, good and evil, and life and death.

6. The tale-within-a-tale foreshadows Beowulf's strength and courage in the battles to come. His astonishing feats reveal his superiority over the sea and its monsters, foreshadowing his victory over Grendel.

7. As an epic hero, Beowulf must show superior physical strength, but also high ethics: He must not take unfair advantage of Grendel. Students may suggest that this motif symbolically indicates that the struggle is really on a spiritual level, rather than on a literal, physical level. In other words, the battle against Grendel is really a battle against the forces of evil.

8. If students sympathize, it may be that Gardner helps them see Grendel's perspective; the excerpt also shows Grendel laughing about his evil deeds, which students may interpret as unforgivable.

Connecting with the Text [Synthesize]

9. Possible answers: Beowulf may remind students of Superman, Hercules, Joan of Arc. Students may point out that some of these heroes are strong leaders who espouse social causes. Others are on personal journeys or quests. They differ in the ways they show strength and the causes they champion.

MAKING MEANINGS

First Thoughts

1. What **images** came to your mind as you read this part of the epic? Which image was most vivid?

Shaping Interpretations

2. In what specific ways does Herot **contrast** with the place where Grendel lives?

3. In lines 3–13, the poet describes the bard's songs in Hrothgar's hall. How does the content of the songs **contrast** with Grendel and his world?

Reading Check

a. Why does Herot remain empty for twelve years?

b. Why doesn't Grendel touch King Hrothgar's throne?

c. What do Hrothgar and his council do to try to save his guest-hall?

d. How is Beowulf taunted by the jealous Unferth? How does Beowulf reply?

e. Describe what happens to Grendel when he raids Herot and finds Beowulf in charge.

4. What significance can you see in the fact that Grendel attacks at night? What **images** describing Grendel might associate him with death or darkness?

5. Why do you think Grendel hates Herot? What **symbolic** meaning might underlie the confrontation between Grendel and Hrothgar?

6. Consider the tale-within-a-tale about Beowulf's swimming match with Brecca. What does this story contribute to your understanding of Beowulf's heroic **character** and of his powers?

7. Why do you think it's important to Beowulf and to his image as an **epic hero** that he meet Grendel without a weapon? What **symbolism** do you see in the uselessness of human weapons against Grendel?

8. What do you think of John Gardner's depiction of Grendel in the ***Connections*** on page 36? Do you feel any sympathy for Grendel? Why or why not?

Connecting with the Text

9. Review the notes you made before you read this part of *Beowulf*. Does Beowulf remind you of any heroes from history, current events, books, television, or movies? Who? What similarities do you notice among them? Just as important, how are they different?

Sigurd kills the dragon. Detail of carved portal of Hylestad stave church (12th century).

Universitetets, Oldsaksamling, Oslo.

38

Reading Check

a. Because of Grendel's murderous raids, King Hrothgar's warriors are afraid to gather in their hall.

b. God protects Hrothgar's throne.

c. Hrothgar's men make sacrifices and vows to the pagan gods. Some have also made ineffectual attempts to remain at Herot and ward off the monster.

d. Unferth calls him a boaster and the loser in a swimming match with Brecca. Beowulf replies that after he and Brecca were separated by a storm, Beowulf slew nine sea monsters.

e. After destroying one Geat, Grendel tries to grasp Beowulf, who grips him and tears off his arm. Mortally wounded, Grendel flees.

Connections A News Feature

A Collaboration Across 1,200 Years

D.J.R. BRUCKNER

European noblemen of a thousand years ago had much more exciting and intelligent entertainment than anything to be found now. Anyone who doubts that need only look in on Benjamin Bagby's astonishing performance of the first quarter of the epic poem *Beowulf*—in Anglo-Saxon, no less—tonight at the Stanley H. Kaplan Penthouse at Lincoln Center. . . .

From the moment he strode onstage on Sunday for the opening night, silencing the audience with that famous first word, "Hwaet!" ("Pay attention!"), until hell swallowed the "pagan soul" of the monster Grendel eighty minutes later, Mr. Bagby came as close to holding hundreds of people in a spell as ever a man has. As the epic's warriors argued, boasted, fought, or fell into the monster's maw, there were bursts of laughter, mutters, and sighs, and when Mr. Bagby's voice stopped at the end, as abruptly as it had begun, there was an audible rippling gasp before a thunderclap of applause from cheering people who called him back again and again, unwilling to let him go.

Benjamin Bagby reciting the story of Beowulf in Anglo-Saxon.

©Stephanie Berger. All rights reserved.

Mr. Bagby—a Midwesterner who fell in love with *Beowulf* at twelve . . .—accompanies himself on a six-string lyre modeled on one found in a seventh-century tomb near Stuttgart. This surprisingly facile instrument underscores the meter of the epic verses and is counterpoint to Mr. Bagby's voice as he recites, chants, and occasionally sings the lines.

. . . A translation is handed out to the audience, but after a while one notices people are following it less and just letting the sound of this strange and beautiful language wash over them. Perhaps not so strange, after all—enough phrases begin to penetrate the understanding that one finally knows deep down that, yes, this is where English came from.

—*The New York Times*, July 22, 1997

Carrying the sword Hrunting, Beowulf goes to the lake where Grendel's mother has her underwater lair. Then, fully armed, he dives to the depths of this watery hell.

The Monster's Mother

12

. . . He leaped into the lake, would not wait for anyone's
Answer; the heaving water covered him
Over. For hours he sank through the waves;
At last he saw the mud of the bottom.
And all at once the greedy she-wolf
Who'd ruled those waters for half a hundred
Years discovered him, saw that a creature

Connections

Bruckner reviews a one-man performance of part of *Beowulf.* The actor not only speaks in Anglo-Saxon but accompanies his chanting and singing with a lyre.

FROM THE EDITOR'S DESK

Can students imagine hearing *Beowulf* sung and chanted in Old English? We thought "A Collaboration Across 1,200 Years" would give them a chance to try.

Summary

Armed with the sword Hrunting, Beowulf in full armor dives to the bottom of the lake where Grendel's mother lives. She attacks him but cannot penetrate his chain-mail shirt. Beowulf discovers that his sword is useless against her and continues the fight with his bare hands. Finally, he finds a magic sword, "hammered by giants," and kills Grendel's mother with one fierce blow. Bathed in a symbolic light, Beowulf finds Grendel's body and cuts off his head in revenge for the men he killed. *(This summary concludes on p. T42.)*

Connecting Across Texts

Connecting with *Beowulf*

For hundreds of years, *Beowulf* was strictly performance art. Without brilliant performers reciting *Beowulf,* it may not have reached the ripe old age of 1,200. Use these questions to discuss "A Collaboration Across 1,200 Years."

1. Like Mr. Bagby, how might the early storytellers have held their audience "in a spell"? [They may have used dramatic facial expressions, as well as variations in volume, tone, pauses, gestures, movements, and music.]
2. How are Mr. Bagby's audience and purpose the same as that of early storytellers? How did they differ? [Bagby's listeners are probably familiar with *Beowulf* already, just as early audiences may well have been. Bagby's purpose, like that of the early storytellers, is not just to tell the story but to make it memorable and entertaining. Bagby's listeners, however, do not live in an age where physical courage and loyalty to a king are considered the highest virtues.]

A Struggling Readers

Rereading

Remind students to reread when they lose track of the action or setting. Ask them what setting details they can gather by rereading ll. 590–594. [Beowulf seems to be underwater in a heat-resistant structure with a high-arching roof.]

B Elements of Literature

Epic Hero

? What characteristics of an epic hero does Beowulf display during his fight with Grendel's mother? [Possible answers: Beowulf exhibits superhuman strength. Nothing stops him in his quest to defeat the powers of darkness. He stays focused on "fame," which for him means triumph in a good cause.]

C Reading Skills and Strategies

Visualizing

Have students jot down what saves Beowulf from being killed by Grendel's mother's dagger. Although they will most likely say it was his mail, as the text confirms, they have only to visualize Beowulf lying on the ground, "stretched on his back" to see another possible reason for his being saved. Ask what shape a prostrate body, with outstretched arms, lying on the ground, would take. [the shape of a cross] Ask students how the lines that follow (ll. 628–632) suggest a resurrection. [Possible answers: Holy God sends the victory; Beowulf rises from his near-dead position to fight.]

Responding to the Art

Point out that a warrior's sword and shield were his most precious possessions. A Celtic chief supposedly threw this shield into the Thames as an offering to a river god.

Activity. Ask students to solve the following Anglo-Saxon riddle: "I'm by nature solitary, scarred by spear and wounded by sword, weary of battle. I frequently see the face of war, and fight hateful enemies . . . ." What is this object? [a shield]

From above had come to explore the bottom
Of her wet world. She welcomed him in her claws,
Clutched at him savagely but could not harm him,
Tried to work her fingers through the tight
Ring-woven mail on his breast, but tore
And scratched in vain. Then she carried him, armor
And sword and all, to her home; he struggled
To free his weapon, and failed. The fight
Brought other monsters swimming to see
Her catch, a host of sea beasts who beat at
His mail shirt, stabbing with tusks and teeth
As they followed along. Then he realized, suddenly,
That she'd brought him into someone's battle-hall,
And there the water's heat could not hurt him,
Nor anything in the lake attack him through
The building's high-arching roof. A brilliant
Light burned all around him, the lake
Itself like a fiery flame.
Then he saw
The mighty water witch, and swung his sword,
His ring-marked blade, straight at her head;
The iron sang its fierce song,
Sang Beowulf's strength. But her guest
Discovered that no sword could slice her evil
Skin, that Hrunting could not hurt her, was useless
Now when he needed it. They wrestled, she ripped
And tore and clawed at him, bit holes in his helmet,
And that too failed him; for the first time in years
Of being worn to war it would earn no glory;
It was the last time anyone would wear it. But Beowulf
Longed only for fame, leaped back
Into battle. He tossed his sword aside,
Angry; the steel-edged blade lay where
He'd dropped it. If weapons were useless he'd use
His hands, the strength in his fingers. So fame
Comes to the men who mean to win it
And care about nothing else! He raised
His arms and seized her by the shoulder; anger
Doubled his strength, he threw her to the floor.
She fell, Grendel's fierce mother, and the Geats'
Proud prince was ready to leap on her. But she rose
At once and repaid him with her clutching claws,
Wildly tearing at him. He was weary, that best
And strongest of soldiers; his feet stumbled
And in an instant she had him down, held helpless.
Squatting with her weight on his stomach, she drew
A dagger, brown with dried blood and prepared
To avenge her only son. But he was stretched
On his back, and her stabbing blade was blunted

Battersea shield.
© British Museum, London.

Getting Students Involved

Cooperative Learning

Readers' Theater. Divide the class into groups of three or four, and assign each group one or two sections of *Beowulf*. Ask each group to prepare a Readers' Theater: Have one or two students present a summary of the action to the rest of the class while the other group members act out the scenes, using dialogue from the poem and perhaps some dialogue they write themselves.

Student Teaching. Have students work in pairs to create questions and summaries. After they have read a portion of the text, have one student ask another student questions about the content, about other related lessons or selections, or about style and language. Then, have students reverse the roles. Periodically, stop the reading for students to summarize what they have understood so far.

By the woven mail shirt he wore on his chest.
The hammered links held; the point
Could not touch him. He'd have traveled to the bottom of the earth,
Edgetho's son, and died there, if that shining
Woven metal had not helped—and Holy
God, who sent him victory, gave judgment
For truth and right, Ruler of the Heavens,
Once Beowulf was back on his feet and fighting.

13

Then he saw, hanging on the wall, a heavy
Sword, hammered by giants, strong
And blessed with their magic, the best of all weapons
But so massive that no ordinary man could lift
Its carved and decorated length. He drew it
From its scabbard, broke the chain on its hilt,°
And then, savage, now, angry
And desperate, lifted it high over his head
And struck with all the strength he had left,
Caught her in the neck and cut it through,
Broke bones and all. Her body fell
To the floor, lifeless, the sword was wet
With her blood, and Beowulf rejoiced at the sight.
The brilliant light shone, suddenly,
As though burning in that hall, and as bright as Heaven's
Own candle, lit in the sky. He looked
At her home, then following along the wall
Went walking, his hands tight on the sword,
His heart still angry. He was hunting another
Dead monster, and took his weapon with him
For final revenge against Grendel's vicious
Attacks, his nighttime raids, over
And over, coming to Herot when Hrothgar's
Men slept, killing them in their beds,
Eating some on the spot, fifteen
Or more, and running to his loathsome moor
With another such sickening meal waiting
In his pouch. But Beowulf repaid him for those visits,
Found him lying dead in his corner,
Armless, exactly as that fierce fighter
Had sent him out from Herot, then struck off
His head with a single swift blow. The body
Jerked for the last time, then lay still. . . .

638. scabbard . . . hilt: A scabbard is a case that holds the blade of a sword; a hilt is a sword's handle.

WORDS TO OWN
loathsome (lōth′səm) *adj.:* disgusting.

D Reading Skills and Strategies

Making Predictions

? How will the battle between Grendel's mother and Beowulf end? [Possible answers: Beowulf will win and cut off the arm of Grendel's mother to hang in the mead-hall; Beowulf will die but kill the monster, too.]

E Cultural Connections

Christian Parallels

Critics who trace Christian parallels throughout the epic have commented that Beowulf's immersion into the lair is a kind of baptism by which he is washed clean of sins. Also, the light in l. 646 indicates God's favor.

F Advanced Learners

Word Play

? Is this an example of overkill? Consider the pun on the word *overkill* in your response. [Possible responses: Yes, Beowulf's response to the situation is overdone. The storytellers were not satisfied with a single "kill" in this episode: Two monsters had to be killed, one of which was being killed over again. No, the repeated deaths just heighten the drama.]

Skill Link

Analyzing How Authors Affect Text

As pp. 18–19 indicate, *Beowulf* is a work that evolved over many years and many tellings. Students may explore the complexity of the authorship by rereading those pages as necessary and then, in small groups, discussing the following questions. Sample answers have been provided.

1. What purpose might the first storyteller of this tale have had in telling it? [to provide entertainment and emphasize religious values]
2. What purpose might later storytellers have had? [entertainment as well as a way to explore part of history]
3. How do you think the intended audience—men gathered in mead halls—affected the content of the story? [They may have encouraged the addition of gory details.]
4. If a monk did in fact record *Beowulf,* in what ways do you think he may have changed the story? Consider what he might have taken out as well as what he might have added. [He may have eliminated favorable references to pagan gods and added more references to Christian beliefs.]

After you have given students time to discuss these questions, ask them what questions they still have about how the complex history of *Beowulf's* authorship may have affected its content.

Summary

Many years into his reign as king of the Geats, Beowulf resolves to fight a fire-breathing dragon threatening his people. Fate is no longer on Beowulf's side, however. His sword angers but does not kill the dragon, who advances on Beowulf and lays him low with its steaming breath. A true Anglo-Saxon hero, Beowulf accepts his fate without complaint while all but one of his companions run off in fear. Wiglaf alone remembers the duties due to kinsmen and berates those who run. After Wiglaf and Beowulf kill the dragon, Wiglaf brings the dragon's treasure hoard to the dying king. Beowulf says he willingly gives his life so his people can enjoy the treasure. Beowulf's ashes are placed in a tower by the sea, and twelve loyal followers mourn his loss and praise him for his great deeds.

A Critical Thinking

Analyzing Motivation

? The odds are against Beowulf at this point. Why does he keep fighting? [Sample answers: Beowulf has always done what needs to be done, regardless of the consequences; he remains the same dedicated, determined defender of good against evil. He cannot give up, no matter the cost or the odds.]

B Literary Connections

Have students compare Beowulf with Ulysses, as portrayed in Lord Tennyson's poem of that name (see p. 822).

C Elements of Literature

Epic Hero

? To what extent has Beowulf remained an epic hero? [Possible answers: He has not changed at all. He remains determined to face his enemy. As the leader of his people, it is his ethical responsibility to fight. Beowulf epitomizes the Anglo-Saxon code of honor to the very end.]

Beowulf carries Grendel's head to King Hrothgar and then returns gift-laden to the land of the Geats, where he succeeds to the throne. After fifty winters pass, Beowulf, now an old man, faces his final task: He must fight a dragon who, angry because a thief has stolen a jeweled cup from the dragon's hoard of gold, is laying waste to the Geats' land. Beowulf and eleven warriors are guided to the dragon's lair by the thief who stole the cup. For Beowulf, the price of this last victory will be great.

The Final Battle

14

. . . Then he said farewell to his followers,
Each in his turn, for the last time:
"I'd use no sword, no weapon, if this beast
Could be killed without it, crushed to death
Like Grendel, gripped in my hands and torn
Limb from limb. But his breath will be burning
Hot, poison will pour from his tongue.
I feel no shame, with shield and sword
And armor, against this monster: When he comes to me
I mean to stand, not run from his shooting
Flames, stand till fate decides
Which of us wins. My heart is firm,
My hands calm: I need no hot
Words. Wait for me close by, my friends.
We shall see, soon, who will survive
This bloody battle, stand when the fighting
Is done. No one else could do
What I mean to, here, no man but me
Could hope to defeat this monster. No one
Could try. And this dragon's treasure, his gold
And everything hidden in that tower, will be mine
Or war will sweep me to a bitter death!"
Then Beowulf rose, still brave, still strong,
And with his shield at his side, and a mail shirt on his breast,
Strode calmly, confidently, toward the tower, under
The rocky cliffs: No coward could have walked there!
And then he who'd endured dozens of desperate
Battles, who'd stood boldly while swords and shields
Clashed, the best of kings, saw
Huge stone arches and felt the heat
Of the dragon's breath, flooding down
Through the hidden entrance, too hot for anyone
To stand, a streaming current of fire
And smoke that blocked all passage. And the Geats'
Lord and leader, angry, lowered
His sword and roared out a battle cry,

Dragonesque brooch (2nd century). Romano-British.

© British Museum, London.

Listening to Music

Lament for Beowulf by Howard Hanson, performed by the Eastman-Rochester Symphony Orchestra; and the Mormon Youth Symphony Orchestra and Chorus

It is not surprising that American composer Howard Hanson (1896–1981) wrote a composition inspired by *Beowulf,* for he frequently wrote music that drew on his Scandinavian heritage. Hanson even called his first symphony the "Nordic," as a tribute to his Swedish immigrant parents

Activity

After students read the selection from *Beowulf,* have them listen to Hanson's *Lament for Beowulf* and decide to which event or events in the epic the music best applies. Then ask them to write a paragraph exploring the connections between the music and the poem.

A call so loud and clear that it reached through
The hoary° rock, hung in the dragon's
Ear. The beast rose, angry,
Knowing a man had come—and then nothing
But war could have followed. Its breath came first,
A steaming cloud pouring from the stone,
Then the earth itself shook. Beowulf
Swung his shield into place, held it
In front of him, facing the entrance. The dragon
Coiled and uncoiled, its heart urging it
Into battle. Beowulf's ancient sword
Was waiting, unsheathed, his sharp and gleaming
Blade. The beast came closer; both of them
Were ready, each set on slaughter. The Geats'
Great prince stood firm, unmoving, prepared
Behind his high shield, waiting in his shining
Armor. The monster came quickly toward him,
Pouring out fire and smoke, hurrying
To its fate. Flames beat at the iron
Shield, and for a time it held, protected
Beowulf as he'd planned; then it began to melt,
And for the first time in his life that famous prince
Fought with fate against him, with glory
Denied him. He knew it, but he raised his sword
And struck at the dragon's scaly hide.
The ancient blade broke, bit into
The monster's skin, drew blood, but cracked
And failed him before it went deep enough, helped him
Less than he needed. The dragon leaped
With pain, thrashed and beat at him, spouting
Murderous flames, spreading them everywhere.
And the Geats' ring-giver did not boast of glorious
Victories in other wars: His weapon
Had failed him, deserted him, now when he needed it
Most, that excellent sword. Edgetho's
Famous son stared at death,
Unwilling to leave this world, to exchange it
For a dwelling in some distant place—a journey
Into darkness that all men must make, as death
Ends their few brief hours on earth.
Quickly, the dragon came at him, encouraged
As Beowulf fell back; its breath flared,
And he suffered, wrapped around in swirling
Flames—a king, before, but now
A beaten warrior. None of his comrades
Came to him, helped him, his brave and noble
Followers; they ran for their lives, fled
Deep in a wood. And only one of them
Remained, stood there, miserable, remembering,
As a good man must, what kinship should mean.

703. **hoary** (hôr′ē): ancient.

Viking sword handles, embellished with Viking Age motifs.
Statens Historiska Museer, Stockholm.

D Struggling Readers

Finding Sequence of Events

The events in this section occur in chronological order. To help students follow them, begin a sequence chain. On the chalkboard write the following: (1) Beowulf says goodbye to his followers, and (2) Beowulf heads toward the dragon's cave. Ask students what the next few events in the chain might be. [Possible answers: The dragon rises to meet Beowulf. The battle begins.]

E Cultural Connections

Comitatus

Some critics see the failure of Beowulf's men to come to his aid as an ominous forecast of the demise of the Anglo-Saxons, whose society was built around the code of the *comitatus,* in which a leader who rewarded his loyal followers with riches expected loyalty in return.

F Reading Skills and Strategies

Identifying Cause and Effect

? Why do you think Beowulf's men desert him now? [Possible answers: They see that Beowulf cannot win. They are not epic heroes; they are not as brave as Beowulf; they are not consistently ethical or true to their sense of fate. They are only men while Beowulf, it seems, is something larger and greater.]

Getting Students Involved

Writing

Beowulf's Epitaph. Invite students to write an epitaph for Beowulf, praising his deeds, leadership, bravery, or character. Ask them to include at least one phrase (if not a line or two) from the poem in their epitaph.

Comparing and Contrasting

Epic Heroes. Some students may be interested in comparing and contrasting Beowulf to an epic Greek hero, such as Odysseus, Hercules, or Achilles. They will need to determine points of comparison, such as family background, good deeds, goals, moral values, relationships with followers, accomplishments, and means of death. Students could make charts to display their findings to the class.

Ⓐ Reading Skills and Strategies

Identifying Cause and Effect

? Why does Wiglaf decide to fight side by side with Beowulf? [Possible answers: He believes he owes the good life he has enjoyed to Beowulf. He also remembers swearing to repay Beowulf with his life, if need be.]

Ⓑ English Language Learners

Understanding Idioms

Explain that "had some weight" means, in this case, "had some meaning" or "had some significance." Tell students they may sometimes hear the word *weight* used in a similar way when people talk about a *weighty* matter. Ask them what this expression might mean. [A weighty matter is one that is serious or of great consequence.] Other idioms with weight are *to pull one's weight,* meaning "to do one's share," and *to throw one's weight around,* meaning "to show off one's importance."

Ⓒ Elements of Literature

Alliteration

? What examples of alliteration do you find in these lines? [initial consonants: *butchered, by, beast; swore, swords.*]

Detail of three-ringed gold collar (6th century).
Statens Historiska Museer, Stockholm.

15

His name was Wiglaf, he was Wexstan's son
And a good soldier; his family had been Swedish,
Once. Watching Beowulf, he could see
How his king was suffering, burning. Remembering
Everything his lord and cousin had given him,
Armor and gold and the great estates
Wexstan's family enjoyed, Wiglaf's
Mind was made up; he raised his yellow
Shield and drew his sword. . . .
And Wiglaf, his heart heavy, uttered
The kind of words his comrades deserved:
"I remember how we sat in the mead-hall, drinking
And boasting of how brave we'd be when Beowulf
Needed us, he who gave us these swords
And armor: All of us swore to repay him,
When the time came, kindness for kindness
—With our lives, if he needed them. He allowed us to join him,
Chose us from all his great army, thinking
Our boasting words had some weight, believing
Our promises, trusting our swords. He took us
For soldiers, for men. He meant to kill
This monster himself, our mighty king,
Fight this battle alone and unaided,
As in the days when his strength and daring dazzled
Men's eyes. But those days are over and gone
And now our lord must lean on younger
Arms. And we must go to him, while angry
Flames burn at his flesh, help
Our glorious king! By almighty God,
I'd rather burn myself than see
Flames swirling around my lord.
And who are we to carry home
Our shields before we've slain his enemy
And ours, to run back to our homes with Beowulf
So hard-pressed here? I swear that nothing
He ever did deserved an end
Like this, dying miserably and alone,
Butchered by this savage beast: We swore
That these swords and armor were each for us all!" . . .

Getting Students Involved

Cooperative Learning

Extra! Extra! Read All About It. Have groups of three or four produce a three or four page special edition newspaper about Beowulf. Copy might include news stories on Beowulf's battles, an editorial on respect for elders, a feature story on young Wiglaf, and a Beowulf theme puzzle. Each group member should create at least one story or feature. Other publishing tasks—computer entry, layout, artwork—can be shared by group members.

Beowulf the People's Hero. Ask groups of two or three students to create a comic book version of one of the major events in the story. Groups should plan and devise a storyboard for the comic together, but individual group members can take responsibility for writing the copy and creating the art.

Together, Beowulf and the young Wiglaf kill the dragon, but the old king is fatally wounded. Beowulf, thinking of his people, asks to see the monster's treasure. Wiglaf enters the dragon's cave and finds a priceless hoard of jewels and gold.

16

. . . Then Wiglaf went back, anxious
To return while Beowulf was alive, to bring him
Treasure they'd won together. He ran,
Hoping his wounded king, weak
And dying, had not left the world too soon.
Then he brought their treasure to Beowulf, and found
His famous king bloody, gasping
For breath. But Wiglaf sprinkled water
Over his lord, until the words
Deep in his breast broke through and were heard.
Beholding the treasure he spoke, haltingly:
"For this, this gold, these jewels, I thank
Our Father in Heaven, Ruler of the Earth—
For all of this, that His grace has given me,
Allowed me to bring to my people while breath
Still came to my lips. I sold my life
For this treasure, and I sold it well. Take
What I leave, Wiglaf, lead my people,
Help them; my time is gone. Have
The brave Geats build me a tomb,
When the funeral flames have burned me, and build it
Here, at the water's edge, high
On this spit of land, so sailors can see
This tower, and remember my name, and call it
Beowulf's tower, and boats in the darkness
And mist, crossing the sea, will know it."
Then that brave king gave the golden
Necklace from around his throat to Wiglaf,
Gave him his gold-covered helmet, and his rings,
And his mail shirt, and ordered him to use them well:
"You're the last of all our far-flung family.
Fate has swept our race away,
Taken warriors in their strength and led them
To the death that was waiting. And now I follow them."
The old man's mouth was silent, spoke
No more, had said as much as it could;
He would sleep in the fire, soon. His soul
Left his flesh, flew to glory.

Gilded bronze and ivory casket.
National Museum, Copenhagen.

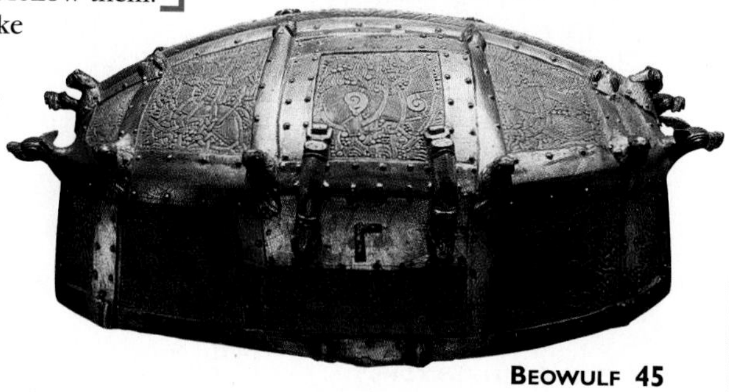

(D) Cultural Connections

Comitatus: The Warrior's Code

Remind students of the importance of dispensing treasure as a symbol of the loyalty between a king and his people in the Anglo-Saxon code. Thus, with his dying words, Beowulf is doing more than equating his life with material possessions. Remind students once again that the entire action of this poem must be placed within the context of the Anglo-Saxon codes of conduct and values rather than within the context of twentieth-century codes and values.

(E) Elements of Literature

Epic Hero

? Is Beowulf an epic hero to the end? Explain your answer. [Possible answers: No, Beowulf fails in his last attempt to slay the dragon. Yes, Beowulf remains courageous until the end; his soul flies "to glory"; he has spent his life fighting evil and has displayed superhuman courage while doing so. He inspires Wiglaf's courage and will be glorified by all who will benefit from the dragon's death.]

Making the Connections

Connecting to the Subject: "Songs of Ancient Heroes"

After students have finished reading the epic, discuss with them the ways in which *Beowulf* is a song. You might discuss the fact that one synonym for *song* is *poem;* you might also talk about the celebratory connotations of the word *song.* This is also a good opportunity to discuss the notion of an epic hero one last time.

Cultural Connections: Viking Burial

Archaeological finds tell us that Vikings loved their ships so much they were often buried in them, together with articles needed in the next life. The coffin in the Sutton Hoo mound was an eighty-six-foot warrior's ship—completely decayed but clearly outlined. There is a passage in *Beowulf* itself (not excerpted here) in which a dead man is placed in his ship and pushed off to sail away into the unknown. On p. 46, students will learn that Beowulf's remains are placed in a tower on land, yet in sight of the sea. This action may represent an alternative Viking burial practice. It may also represent a melding of Viking values into a culture that buried its dead on land, or a later storyteller's need to see such a personage as Beowulf given, in the eyes of his own culture, a proper burial.

A Elements of Literature

Epic Hero

? How do the Geats regard their dead king? [Possible answers: They regard him as the greatest of heroes, the most noble of men. They praise his deeds. They agree that no better man ever lived and that none was "so deserving of praise."]

Responding to the Art

This exquisite and unique gold boat is part of a hoard of gold objects that date back to the third century B.C. They were unearthed by an Irish plowman at Broighter, County Derry. The hoard consists of this model boat, a gold bowl, two chains, and two twisted bracelets. It has been suggested that the hoard was a votive deposit to the Celtic sea god Manannán mac Lir, after whom the Isle of Man came to be named. Gold and other precious objects like this boat have often been turned up in modern Ireland by a plow or discovered entwined in the roots of bog oaks. Some of these objects might have been buried as votive offerings; some were certainly buried centuries later to keep them from the Viking marauders or from Henry VIII's armies. This boat is an example of Celtic art known as La Tène, so named for the site in Switzerland where the style was first recognized.

Activity. Ask students to identify what they notice on this boat. [Note the oars, the seats for the oarsmen, the mast, and the tiny rudder.]

Wiglaf berates the faithless warriors who did not go to the aid of their king. With sorrow, the Geats then cremate the corpse of their greatest king. They place his ashes, along with all of the dragon's treasure, in a huge burial tower by the sea, where it can be seen by voyagers.

17

A
. . . And then twelve of the bravest Geats
Rode their horses around the tower,
Telling their sorrow, telling stories
Of their dead king and his greatness, his glory,
Praising him for heroic deeds, for a life
As noble as his name. So should all men
Raise up words for their lords, warm
With love, when their shield and protector leaves
His body behind, sends his soul
On high. And so Beowulf's followers
Rode, mourning their beloved leader,
Crying that no better king had ever
Lived, no prince so mild, no man
So open to his people, so deserving of praise.

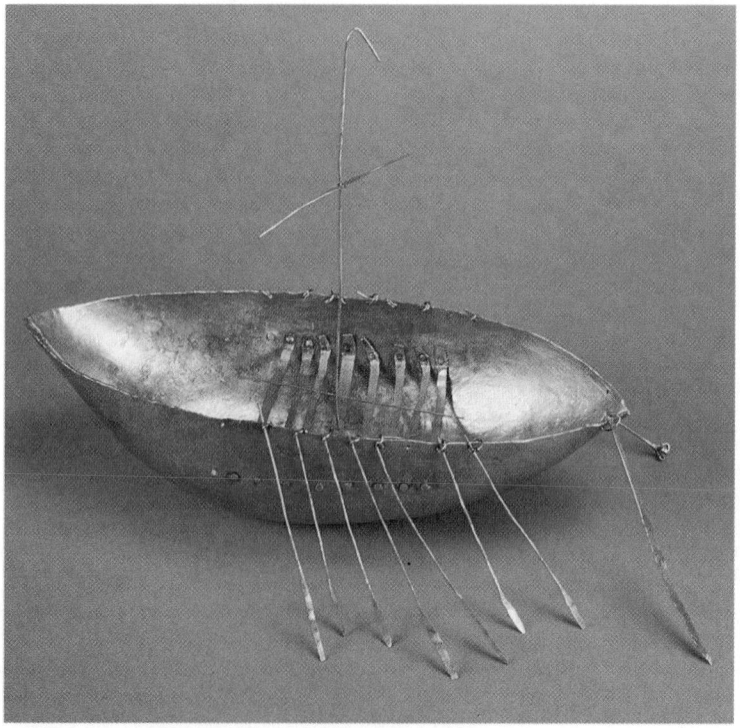

Gold boat (probably 1st century) found at Broighter, County Londonderry, Ireland.

National Museum of Ireland, Dublin.

Resources

Selection Assessment

Formal Assessment

- Selection Test, p. 3

Test Generator (One-Stop Planner)

- CD-ROM

Assessing Learning

Check Test: True-False

1. Using his ancestral sword, Beowulf kills Grendel's mother. [False]
2. Beowulf carries Grendel's head to King Hrothgar and returns home with many fine gifts. [True]
3. Beowulf becomes king of the Geats. [True]
4. After Beowulf's weapons fail him against the dragon, his men rush to help him. [False]
5. Beowulf names Wiglaf as his successor to the throne. [True]

Informal Assessment

Ongoing Assessment. Have students select a project to demonstrate their understanding of the epic. Possibilities include visual or three-dimensional displays, re-enactments, interviews with characters, or literary analyses.

Connections — A Magazine Article

Life in 999: A Grim Struggle

HOWARD G. CHUA-EOAN

Today's world is measured in light-years and Mach speed and sheathed in silicon and alloy. In the world of 999, on the eve of the first millennium, time moved at the speed of an oxcart or, more often, of a sturdy pair of legs, and the West was built largely on wood. Europe was a collection of untamed forests, countless mile upon mile of trees and brush and brier, dark and inhospitable. Medieval chroniclers used the word *desert* to describe their arboreal world, a place on the cusp of civilization where werewolves and bogeymen still lunged out of the shadows and bandits and marauders maintained their lairs.

Yet the forests, deep and dangerous as they were, also defined existence. Wood kindled forges and kept alive the hearths of the mud-and-thatch huts of the serfs. Peasants fattened their hogs on forest acorns (pork was crucial to basic subsistence in the cold of winter), and wild berries helped supplement the meager diet. In a world without sugar, honey from forest swarms provided the only sweetness for food or drink. The pleasures of the serfs were few and simple: earthy lovemaking and occasional dances and fests.

Feudal lords ruled over western Europe, taking their share of the harvests of primitive agriculture and making the forests their private hunting grounds. Poaching was not simply theft (usually punishable by imprisonment) but a sin against the social order. Without the indulgence of the nobility, the peasants could not even acquire salt, the indispensable ingredient for preserving meat and flavoring a culinary culture that possessed few spices. Though a true money economy did not exist, salt could be bought with poorly circulated coin, which the lord hoarded in his castle and dispensed to the poor only as alms.

It was in the lord's castle too that peasants and their flocks sought refuge from wolf packs and barbarian invaders. In 999, however, castles, like most other buildings in Europe, were made of timber, far from the granite bastions that litter today's imagined Middle Ages. The peasants, meanwhile, were relegated to their simple huts, where everyone—including the animals—slept around the hearth. Straw was scattered on the floors to collect scraps as well as human and animal waste. Housecleaning consisted of sweeping out the straw.

Illness and disease remained in constant residence. Tuberculosis was endemic, and so were scabrous skin diseases of every kind: abscesses, cankers, scrofula, tumors, eczema, and erysipelas. In a throwback to biblical times, lepers constituted a class of pariahs living on the outskirts of villages and cities. Constant famine, rotten flour, and vitamin deficiencies afflicted huge segments of society with blindness, goiter, paralysis, and bone malformations that created hunchbacks and cripples. A man was lucky to survive 30, and 50 was a ripe old age. Most women, many of them succumbing to the ravages of childbirth, lived less than 30 years. There was no time for what is now considered childhood; children of every class had to grow up immediately and be useful as soon as possible. Emperors were leading armies in their teens; John XI became Pope at the age of 21.

While the general population was growing faster than it had in the previous five centuries, there was still a shortage of people to cultivate the fields, clear the woodlands, and work the mills. Local taxes were levied on youths who did not marry upon coming of age. Abortion was considered homicide, and a woman who terminated a pregnancy was expelled from the church.

The nobility spent its waking hours battling foes to preserve its prerogatives, the clergy chanting prayers for the salvation of souls, the serfs laboring to feed and clothe everyone. Night, lit only by burning logs or the rare taper, was always filled with danger and terror. The seasons came and went, punctuated chiefly by the occurrence of plentiful church holidays. The calendar year began at different times for different regions; only later would Europe settle on the Feast of Christ's Circumcision, January 1, as the year's beginning.

Thus there was little panic, not even much interest, as the millennium approached in the final months of 999. For what terrors could the apocalypse hold for a continent that was already shrouded in darkness? Rather Europe—illiterate, diseased, and hungry—seemed grimly resigned to desperation and impoverishment. It was one of the planet's most unpromising corners, the Third World of its age.

—from Time

Connections

This article describes life in Europe in A.D. 999. It was a dark, grim, unorganized, and unhealthy existence for most people. At this time, Europe was almost a primitive society.

FROM THE EDITOR'S DESK

"Nothing like a little reality check," remarked one of our editors after she read this article.

B Critical Thinking

Analyzing

? Why might a writer use the concept of speed to define a particular historical age? [Possible answer: The pace of life affects one's perspective on the world. For example, today, people get impatient in a grocery store line that may take five minutes, whereas obtaining food and preparing a meal for two was an entire day's work in A.D. 999.]

C Historical Connections

Salt was so crucial that the original *salary* was the money paid to Roman legionnaires to buy it.

D Reading Skills and Strategies

Connecting with the Text

? How do these facts compare with modern expectations for people in their teens or early twenties? [Possible responses: Today, people of that age are considered young. They may be finishing high school or college; they may be starting their first jobs. They are not expected to lead a country or head a church.]

Connecting Across Texts

Connecting with *Beowulf*

Ask students to summarize the article. After they have done so, you might ask these specific questions:

1. **How does the description of Herot in *Beowulf* compare with the way life is described in this article?** [Possible answer: The richness and beauty of Herot as described in *Beowulf* make it easy to imagine an idyllic castle and fairy-tale existence—unless readers stop to think about the realities of that time. Most people had to scrabble for existence, and life in both castles and huts was primitive and brutish by today's standards.]
2. **How old is Beowulf when he dies? Just how old would he have seemed by the standards of his time?** [Possible answer: Although Beowulf's age is not stated, the poem does say that "fifty winters" passed between his return home and his third battle. If the poet is not exaggerating, Beowulf is likely to be at least sixty-six at the time of his last battle. Because life expectancy at the time was so low, Beowulf's age makes him seem all the more heroic.]

MAKING MEANINGS

(Parts 12–17)

First Thoughts [Respond]

1. Students may say that the themes of loyalty, courage, and good vs. evil, remain relevant.

Shaping Interpretations [Interpret]

2. The dragon, who guards the treasure, is symbolic of death and evil, perhaps even of the devil. One goal of Beowulf's battle with the dragon is to give the captured treasure to the Geats.

3. Details describing the dragon as a serpent, coiled and scaly, occur in ll. 711 and 726; references to the dragon's fiery breath and the smoke surrounding its lair appear in ll. 695–699 and 704–707. The dragon may symbolize death or the devil.

4. In all three battles, the odds seem insurmountable, and Beowulf's victory superhuman. All three battles are dramatically pitched; even for the epic hero, triumph over such dark forces does not come easy. In the first two battles Beowulf fights alone; in the third, he fights almost all alone. Each time he goes to battle, he becomes the symbol of goodness in conflict with evil.

5. Given that Anglo-Saxon society was built on loyalty to a king or protector, the men's failure to help Beowulf is especially ominous. This failure perhaps foreshadows the disintegration of the kingdom after Beowulf's death. The fact that the Geats bury the treasure with Beowulf's ashes may also forecast their downfall.

6. Among the words and images students may mention are those in ll. 831, 839, and 840–841. Students may also mention the somber implication of ll. 834–837.

7. Students may identify the Anglo-Saxon values of courage, loyalty, fighting prowess, and strength (both physical and spiritual). Universal themes include: loyalty and self-sacrifice are admirable traits; good triumphs over evil (but at a painful cost); different members of society have obligations toward one another; and fame can be achieved through good deeds.

Student to Student

A Beowulf Shrinklet

Hrothgar and Grendel could not get along;
the populace thought the killing was wrong.
Beowulf, the hero from o'er the sea,
from monster or dragon he would not flee.
"If treasure I wanteth," the hero thought,
"then I will journey to the great Herot."
Grendel died at the end of the battle.
His mother enraged (and all but little)
wanted revenge for her beloved son,
but the great bold hero ended her fun.
For proof he carried the head and the sword,
and traveled back with troops for a reward.
The great Beowulf returned to his home,
over the oceans on seaweed and foam.
His conscience lived happily as the king.
He died at the hands of another thing.

—Calen Wood
Bakersfield High School
Bakersfield, California

MAKING MEANINGS

First Thoughts

1. Beowulf's story is an ancient one, more than one thousand years old. Did its age make it entirely alien to you, or did you find that it deals with issues or themes that seem relevant in our modern society as well? If so, what are they?

Reading Check

a. Describe how Beowulf manages to kill Grendel's mother.

b. Who comes to Beowulf's aid in his final battle with the dragon? Why does he help Beowulf?

c. What sad scene concludes the epic?

d. What happens to the dragon's hoard?

Shaping Interpretations

2. A hoarded treasure in Old English literature usually **symbolizes** spiritual death or damnation. How does this fact add significance to Beowulf's last fight with the dragon?

3. What details describe the dragon? Keeping those details in mind, explain what the dragon might **symbolize** as Beowulf's final foe.

4. Beowulf battles Grendel, Grendel's mother, and the dragon. What do these battles have in common, and what do they suggest Beowulf and his enemies might represent for the Anglo-Saxons?

5. Given what you know about the structure of Anglo-Saxon society, explain what is especially ominous about the behavior of Beowulf's men during the final battle. What does this suggest about the future of the kingdom?

6. The epic closes on a somber, elegiac note—a note of mourning. What words or **images** contribute to this **tone**?

7. Epic poetry usually embodies the attitudes and ideals of an entire culture. What values of Anglo-Saxon society does *Beowulf* reveal? What universal **themes** does it also reveal?

Extending the Text

8. How would we tell a hero story today? What would the **setting** be, what would the **enemy** be, and what **values** would the hero embody?

9. The ***Connections*** on page 47, "Life in 999: A Grim Struggle," describes daily life in late Anglo-Saxon England. How does this picture of daily life relate to what you've read in *Beowulf*—and to how you live today?

10. In the last episode of the epic, the leader's followers mourn his passing and praise his life. What qualities do we look for in leaders today—are they the same qualities Beowulf's people loved him for?

Challenging the Text

11. What do you think of the way women are portrayed in (or absent from) *Beowulf?*

Reading Check

a. Because his sword is useless against Grendel's mother, Beowulf fights her with his bare hands. At one point, she pins him to the ground and tries to stab him, but Beowulf is protected by his mail shirt and by supernatural or divine aid. He then sees a heavy sword hanging on the wall, and with one stroke he mortally wounds the monster in the neck.

b. The only warrior to come to Beowulf's aid is Wiglaf, who pities Beowulf's suffering and honors his oaths of loyalty.

c. The funeral of Beowulf and the raising of his burial mound conclude the epic.

d. The treasure is buried with Beowulf's ashes.

ELEMENTS OF LITERATURE

Alliteration and Kennings: Taking the Burden off the Bard

The ***Connections*** on page 39 shows that the oral tradition is still alive and still a powerful way of communicating from poet to audience.

The Anglo-Saxon oral poet was assisted by two poetic devices, alliteration and the kenning.

Alliteration. Alliteration is the repetition of sounds in words close to one another. Anglo-Saxon poetry is often called alliterative poetry. Instead of rhyme unifying the poem, the verse line is divided into two halves separated by a rhythmical pause, or **caesura.** In the first half of the line before the caesura, two words alliterate; in the second half, one word alliterates with the two from the first half. Many lines, however, have only two alliterative words, one in each half of the poetic line. Notice the alliterative *g* and the four primary stresses in this Old English line from *Beowulf:*

Gód mid Géatum Gréndles dǽda

Kennings. The kenning, a specialized metaphor made of compound words, is a staple of Anglo-Saxon literature that still finds a place in our language today. *Gas guzzler* and *headhunter* are two modern-day kennings you are likely to have heard.

The earliest and simplest kennings are compound words formed of two common nouns: "sky-candle" for *sun,* "battle-dew" for *blood,* and "whale-road" for *sea.* Later, kennings grew more elaborate, and compound adjectives joined the compound nouns. A ship became a "foamy-throated ship," then a "foamy-throated sea-stallion," and finally a "foamy-throated stallion of the whale-road." Once a kenning was coined, it was used by the singer-poets over and over again.

In their original languages, kennings are almost always written as simple compounds, with no hyphens or spaces between the words. In translation, however, kennings are often written as hyphenated compounds ("sky-candle," "foamy-throated"), as prepositional phrases ("wolf of wounds"), or as possessives ("the sword's tree").

The work of kennings. Scholars believe that kennings filled three needs: (1) Old Norse and Anglo-Saxon poetry depended heavily on alliteration, but neither language had a large vocabulary. Poets created the alliterative words they needed by combining existing words. (2) Because the poetry was oral and had to be memorized, bards valued ready-made phrases. Such phrases made finished poetry easier to remember, and they gave bards time to think ahead when they were composing new poetry on the spot during a feast or ceremony. (3) The increasingly complex structure of the kennings must have satisfied the early Norse and Anglo-Saxon people's taste for elaboration.

Analyzing the text. As you examine these poetic devices, be sure to listen to the way they sound.

1. Read aloud the account of Beowulf's death (lines 791–828), and listen for the effects of the alliteration. Where are **vowels,** rather than consonants, repeated?
2. Look back over lines 233–391 from *Beowulf.* Locate at least two examples of kennings written as **hyphenated compounds,** two examples of kennings written as **prepositional phrases,** and two examples of kennings written as **possessives.** What does each kenning refer to?
3. Compile a list of modern-day kennings, such as *headhunter.*
4. Translators differ dramatically in how they rephrase the Old English to handle alliteration and the kennings. Here is a passage from a translation done many years before the Raffel translation. How does it compare with the corresponding lines (392–398) in Raffel's translation? Which translation sounds more modern? Which do you prefer to listen to?

> Now Grendel came, from his crags of mist
> Across the moor; he was curst of God.
> The murderous prowler meant to surprise
> In the high-built hall his human prey.
> He stalked neath the clouds, till steep before him
> The house of revelry rose in his path,
> The gold-hall of heroes, the gaily adorned.
> —*translated by* J. Duncan Spaeth

ELEMENTS OF LITERATURE

Mini-Lesson: Alliteration and Kennings

Write a line or two from *Beowulf* on the chalkboard. Identify alliteration and kennings one at a time, demonstrating their use in the examples given. Then, after students have read the lesson for themselves, have them work in groups to respond to the listed questions.

1. "*Treasure* they'd won *together*" (l. 793);"Then he *brought* their treasure to *Beowulf*" (l. 796);"Deep in his *breast broke* through" (l. 800); "For *this, this* gold, *these* jewels" (l. 802);"When the *funeral flames* have burned me" (l. 811);"On this *spit* of land, *so sailors* can see" (l. 813). Vowels rather than consonants are sometimes repeated within words.
2. Hyphenated compounds:"sea-paths" (l. 247, the sea) and "gold-ringed" (l. 346, wearing rings). Kennings written as prepositional phrases: "fiercest of demons" (l. 261, Grendel). "shapes of darkness" (l. 380, evil). Kennings written as possessives:"beast's last battle" (l. 290, victory over the beast) and "Heaven's high arch" (l. 309, sky).
3. Sample answers: big bird (airplane), top dog (boss).
4. Spaeth's translation makes the lines even and omits descriptive images, giving mostly narrative facts. The short lines produce an abrupt and unrelenting rhythm. Raffel, on the other hand, retains the power of the verbs and adjectives and lets the line length go as long as necessary for modern English, while maintaining the four-beat line. This is the storyteller's beat, and it produces a conversational rhythm. Raffel's translation probably sounds more modern.

Extending the Text [Synthesize]

8. Possible responses: The hero story would probably be told in prose, perhaps in a novel; the setting could be a battleground on earth, in space, in a sports arena; the enemy might be greed or power; the values of the hero might include hard work, talent, high monetary rewards, good looks, physical prowess, and power.
9. "Life in 999: A Grim Struggle" relates more closely to the story than it does to life today. *Beowulf,* however, paints a rather idealized picture: None of the unsanitary, brutish conditions described in the article are revealed in the poem. Of course, people at the time would not consider their conditions "brutish." That was merely how life was.
10. Beowulf is beloved for his courage, his goodness, and his role as a protector. Students may say that heroes today are revered for their athletic ability, their ability to make money, or their commercial or political influence. People today do not generally expect that leaders will protect them or make sacrifices for them.

Challenging the Text [Evaluate]

11. Most major characters in *Beowulf* are men; only one woman, Welthow, is described. Encourage students to tie their answers to the text and to information about the role of women in society (see p. 10).

Grading Timesaver

Rubrics for each assignment appear on p. 89 in the *Portfolio Management System.*

CHOICES: Building Your Portfolio

1. **Writer's Notebook** You might encourage students to categorize this description of Grendel into details of his appearance and details of his actions. Remind students to save their work. They may use it as prewriting for the Writer's Workshop on p. 67.
2. **Autobiographical Incident** Remind students to choose a situation they would not mind sharing. Invite students to use a who-what-where-when-why organizer or a story map to record prewriting and develop their thinking.
3. **Creative Writing** Have students list the new storyteller's feelings and motives that should be shown in the narration. This activity would be appropriate for either an individual or a group project.
4. **Speaking and Listening** Ask students to work in pairs, sharing comments about ways to dramatize the selection through suspenseful pauses, emphasis of key words, and voice inflections.
5. **Comparing Film and Epic** Brainstorm for a few minutes with the whole class for names of films with heroes who might be compared to Beowulf. Then form groups to work through the activity, focusing on one film of the group's choice.

CHOICES: Building Your Portfolio

Writer's Notebook

1. Collecting Ideas for a Literary Analysis

At the end of this collection, you'll write a literary analysis. When you analyze a literary work, you usually focus on some element in the selection that interests you. You then analyze, or "take apart," the element to see how it works in the text. To start collecting ideas for an analysis, focus now on the **character** of Grendel, the monster. Look back over the passages in *Beowulf* that describe Grendel, and gather evidence on how he is described. Consider these questions: How does the storyteller, in the words he uses to describe the creature, also shape our feelings toward him? What accounts for Grendel's evil? What does Grendel seem to represent in the story? Save your work for later use.

Autobiographical Incident

2. Facing Monsters

Write a brief narrative in which you tell about a time when you, like Beowulf, faced an intense physical challenge, or were taunted over something you said or did, or had to overcome fear to do something that had to be done. Remember that a narrative tells of a series of related events. Give your narrative a strong ending.

Creative Writing

3. It's All in the Point of View

Just as John Gardner tried imagining this story from Grendel's point of view (see ***Connections*** on page 36), you might try retelling an episode from the perspective of one of the other characters, perhaps Grendel, his mother, the dragon, Hrothgar, or Beowulf's detractor, Unferth.

Speaking and Listening

4. Being a Bard

Retell an episode of *Beowulf* for your classmates, or, if it can be arranged, for a grade-school audience. Be faithful to the plot of the story, but feel free to change or adapt the content to fit your audience and your own storytelling talents. (See, for example, the story of *Beowulf* told in shrinklet format on page 48.) Plan an introduction to your story, and try to find ways of involving your listeners. For drama, use gestures, sound effects, and pauses.

Comparing Film and Epic

5. Movies and *Beowulf*

Movies, the cornerstone of American entertainment, often rely on familiar images: Heroes face villains to do battle in all kinds of places—from the ordinary to the strange. In a brief essay, compare and contrast *Beowulf* with some action movie you know well. Use the following questions to guide your comparison:

- Where does each hero come from?
- Who are the hero's trusted aides?
- What role does violence play in the story?
- How does the hero struggle against evil?
- Is the hero an outsider or a part of the community?
- What rewards or glory does the hero receive?

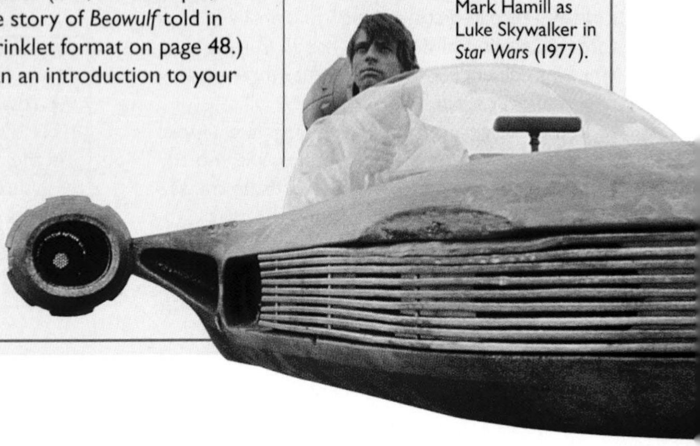

Mark Hamill as Luke Skywalker in *Star Wars* (1977).

Reading Skills and Strategies

VOCABULARY: USING CONTEXT CLUES

Sometimes you can determine the meaning of an unfamiliar word by looking for clues in the **context,** the surrounding words, phrases, and sentences. In fact, you've probably learned many words by using context clues. Below are some of the most useful types of context clues:

Restatement. A difficult word might be rephrased in slightly easier language. Restatements may be signaled by specific words or phrases: *that is, or, in other words.* Look at punctuation—dashes and parentheses also serve as signals. Often a restatement will be an **appositive** set off by commas or an item in a series.

> . . . keeping the bloody feud
> Alive, seeking no peace, offering
> No **truce,** accepting no settlement.
> —*Beowulf,* lines 68–70

A *truce* is something that would end a feud; it's a kind of settlement or a cease-fire.

Comparison. Compare unfamiliar words to familiar words that surround it. Sometimes specific words and phrases may also signal a comparison context clue: *like, as, similar to.*

> . . . but the swirling
> Surf had covered his death, hidden
> Deep in **murky** darkness his miserable
> End.
> —*Beowulf,* lines 530–533

Note all the words that have to do with obscuring from view: *covered, hidden deep, darkness. Murky* means "dark or gloomy, shadowy."

Contrast. An opposition might be set up. Certain key words and phrases signal a contrast context clue: *but, not, although, however, on the other hand.*

> . . . he can come for your people with no fear
> Of **reprisal;** he's found no fighting, here,
> But only food, only delight.
> —*Beowulf,* lines 329–331

Reprisal has to do with resistance, rather than acceptance or encouragement. A *reprisal* is punishment in return for an injury.

Synonym. You might find a word nearby that has the same or nearly the same meaning as the unknown word.

> He murders as he likes, with no mercy, **gorges**
> And feasts on your flesh.
> —*Beowulf,* lines 333–334

Notice the words *feasts on. To gorge* is to glut or to swallow greedily.

Example. Sometimes the text provides an example. Certain words and phrases help you spot example context clues: *such as, including, especially, namely.*

> **Scops,** such as the skilled storytellers who passed down the story of Beowulf, were honored members of Anglo-Saxon society.

Note the key words: *storytellers* and *Anglo-Saxon.* A *scop* is an Old English poet or bard.

Try It Out

Choose any five of the Words to Own from *Beowulf.* For each word, construct a sentence that gives the meaning of the word from its context. Use a different type of context clue for each sentence. To get started, use a chart like the one below. Ask a classmate to find the context clues in your sentences.

Word to Own	Context Clue	Example

A picture stone showing a Viking ship under sail.
Statens Historiska Museer, Stockholm.

Reading Skills and Strategies

This feature focuses on using context clues and is applied whenever possible to *Beowulf.*

Mini-Lesson: Using Context Clues
After the class has read the explanation in the text, list the five kinds of context clues on the chalkboard. Discuss with the class the examples from the text that correspond to each type of context clue. Then, lead students slowly through a passage of the poem, such as ll. 292–391, asking them to look for the clues that help define more difficult vocabulary.

Try It Out

Possible Answers

- Restatement: They wanted *reparation,* but no *payment* could really *compensate for the man's pain.*
- Comparison: The *murky* water, *clouded with the shadows* of the rotting vegetation, revealed nothing about its depths.
- Contrast: He found no *solace,* only repeated accusations and loud demands intruding on his *need to be alone.*
- Synonym: The rope was *taut,* stretched *tightly* across the chasm.
- Example: She felt as if she were on a *pilgrimage* like one made by a believer of Islam to the holy cities of *Mecca and Medina.*

Getting Students Involved

Cooperative Learning

Team Writing. Assign groups of three or four students to work together on Try It Out. Ask each group to develop five sentences, using one of the Words to Own in each sentence. Each sentence should give context clues using one of the five techniques—restatement, comparison, synonym, example, or contrast. Once the sentences are written, have each group exchange their sentences with another group. Then have each group identify the context clues.

OBJECTIVES

1. Read and interpret the episode from an epic poem
2. Recognize distinctive and shared characteristics of cultures
3. Recognize and discuss themes and other literary connections that cross cultures

Summary ■■

Gilgamesh and his close friend Enkidu venture into the forest to chop down a giant cedar. The sound of the falling tree arouses the wrath of Humbaba, the ferocious guardian of the forest. As Humbaba bears down, Gilgamesh seems to lose faith momentarily in the sun god, his divine protector, and begins to feel pity for Humbaba, who is a thankless slave to the gods. When Humbaba strikes Enkidu, however, Gilgamesh wields his ax. To save himself, Humbaba offers to become Gilgamesh's slave. Gilgamesh is tempted, but when Enkidu cries out, he chooses friendship over power.

Background

Uruk is in a part of Mesopotamia that has no lumber. Gilgamesh's journey to the forest and his encounter with Humbaba probably records a real-life event in the larger-than-life manner of epics. It may help students to know that Gilgamesh decided beforehand that he wanted to destroy Humbaba, because the monster was oppressing the people. When Gilgamesh cuts down a cedar, he is felling a sacred tree, but he does so to arouse Humbaba.

Resources

Listening

Audio CD Library

An engaging reading of this poem is provided in the *Audio CD Library:*

- Disc 1, Track 3

WORLD LITERATURE

Mesopotamia

Before You Read

THE HEAD OF HUMBABA

Background

The men and women who lived four thousand years ago would be astounded by the world we live in, and we, very likely, would be astounded by theirs. Obviously, the world has changed in countless ways. Science and technology have transformed the physical world we inhabit, and social and political evolution have altered the way we live. Nations, empires, religions, and languages have come and gone. People now have different beliefs, different worries, different problems.

So you would expect a story four thousand years old to have little to do with you or anything around you today. Your life is so different from the lives of the storyteller and his characters that you might have nothing in common, no shared experience. *Gilgamesh,* for instance, is such an ancient story—a poem, as all stories were in those days. The story was recorded on clay tablets around 2000 B.C. in Sumer, a part of ancient Mesopotamia.

Gilgamesh is the king of Uruk, an ancient Sumerian city. His great friend is Enkidu. Craving an adventure that will bring fame, Gilgamesh convinces Enkidu to journey with him to the cedar forest. There they confront the forest's guardian, the evil giant Humbaba.

Reading Skills and Strategies

Responding to the Text

As you read this adventure from the epic *Gilgamesh*, take notes on a separate piece of paper. Record your responses to what you're reading. Write down any questions you have about the text. Note any details that remind you of *Beowulf*, or of other monster-slaying stories.

Gilgamesh. Relief (8th century B.C.) from Temple of Sargon II. Khorsabad, Iraq.

Louvre, Paris.

(Map) World map by Ptolemy (A.D. 100?–165?). Shaded area indicates general location of Mesopotamia.

Reaching All Students

Struggling Readers

Have students work in pairs to read this selection. Ask them to stop every ten lines or so to sum up the action. Have them identify *who* is in the scene and *what* is happening each time they stop to summarize.

Advanced Learners

Encourage students to gather background information on this epic. They might find a summary or overview of the entire story. In addition, they should find information that will help explain both the action in this excerpt and its significance. Have students present their information to the class.

The Head of Humbaba

from Gilgamesh: A Verse Narrative

retold by **Herbert Mason**

At dawn Gilgamesh raised his ax
And struck at the great cedar.
When Humbaba heard the sound of falling trees,
He hurried down the path that they had seen
But only he had traveled. Gilgamesh felt weak
At the sound of Humbaba's footsteps and called to Shamash°
Saying, I have followed you in the way decreed;
Why am I abandoned now? Suddenly the winds
Sprang up. They saw the great head of Humbaba
Like a water buffalo's bellowing down the path,
His huge and clumsy legs, his flailing° arms
Thrashing at phantoms in his precious trees.
His single stroke could cut a cedar down
And leave no mark on him. His shoulders,
Like a porter's° under building stones,
Were permanently bent by what he bore;
He was the slave who did the work for gods
But whom the gods would never notice.
Monstrous in his contortion, he aroused
The two almost to pity.
But pity was the thing that might have killed.
It made them pause just long enough to show
How pitiless he was to them. Gilgamesh in horror saw
Him strike the back of Enkidu and beat him to the ground
Until he thought his friend was crushed to death.
He stood still watching as the monster leaned to make
His final strike against his friend, unable
To move to help him, and then Enkidu slid
Along the ground like a ram making its final lunge
On wounded knees. Humbaba fell and seemed
To crack the ground itself in two, and Gilgamesh,
As if this fall had snapped him from his daze,
Returned to life

6. Shamash (shä′mäsh′): the sun god. The god has been guiding the hero.

11. flailing: swinging.

15. porter's: A porter is a person who carries things.

go.hrw.com
LEO 12-1

A Literary Connections

Epic Hero

In the epic from which this verse narrative is taken, Gilgamesh is a superhuman hero, two parts god and one part human. As the earliest known epic hero, Gilgamesh may have been the model for many later epic heroes, including Homer's Odysseus. Epic heroes have much in common: They are superior human beings with supernatural strength and spiritual powers, and mighty leaders of their people. Most are a mixture of divine and human birth; we admire their divine, supernatural qualities and sympathize with their weaknesses which remind us of our own.

B Reading Skills and Strategies

Responding to the Text

? Why does Humbaba rush to the scene? What kind of people today might sympathize with him? [Humbaba wants to protect the trees, a goal shared today by environmentalists and others concerned with preserving ancient forests.]

C Elements of Literature

Figurative Language

? What figures of speech are used to describe Humbaba? [Similes are used to compare Humbaba's head to a water buffalo's head and his shoulders to a porter's, weighed down by building stones.] **What characteristics do these comparisons emphasize?** [Humbaba's strength and size]

D Reading Skills and Strategies

Identifying Cause and Effect

? Why does Gilgamesh first feel pity for Humbaba but then quickly change his mind? [Possible answers: Humbaba is a slave to the gods, but the gods never notice him. He seems pitiable to both Enkidu and Gilgamesh, but when Humbaba strikes Enkidu, pity is transformed to rage.]

Making the Connections

Connecting to the Subject: "Songs of Ancient Heroes"

After students have finished reading the selection, ask them to list the similarities and differences between the characters of Beowulf and Gilgamesh. [Similarities might include hero status, supernatural strength, adventuresome spirit, yearning for glory, and a desire to act on behalf of others. Both fight alone, though Gilgamesh travels with a single companion, while Beowulf travels with many. Differences between the two include Gilgamesh's weak faith (see ll. 6–8) and his moments of fear, pity, wavering, or introspection. Beowulf, on the other hand, seems unerringly fixed and focused in his purpose; no decision seems to give him pause. Beowulf is also unwaveringly self-confident.]

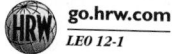

A Reading Skills and Strategies

Responding to the Text

? At this point in the poem, what notes might you make about what is happening? [Possible answers: Humbaba is begging for his life. Humbaba is offering to be Gilgamesh's slave. Gilgamesh is hesitating long enough to let Humbaba plead.] **What questions might you ask?** [Is Gilgamesh showing weakness or a desire for power when he hesitates long enough to let Humbaba plead for his life? Is Humbaba really evil? Does Enkidu show more wisdom in this scene than Gilgamesh?]

B Critical Thinking

Interpreting

? Why does Gilgamesh kill Humbaba even after Humbaba offers to serve him? [Possible answers: Enkidu tells Gilgamesh not to trust Humbaba. Humbaba has tried to kill Enkidu.]

Finding Common Ground

Discuss with students how asking questions, taking notes, and rereading the text can help them to understand it. As students discuss parallels with *Beowulf,* be sure they see the link between Grendel and Humbaba. (Both are monsters who are hostile to human beings.) As students discuss the relevance of the story to their experiences today, be sure they mention the theme of friendship and how the excerpt ends with the peace and solace of companionship.

Responding to the Art

The Sumerian gods each had a spiritual role, such as taking care of the sun or guarding justice. Aby was responsible for the calendar and the seasons.
Activity. Have students speculate on what some of Aby's responsibilities might be.

And stood over Humbaba with his ax
Raised high above his head watching the monster plead
In strangled sobs and desperate appeals
The way the sea contorts under a violent squall.°
I'll serve you as I served the gods, Humbaba said;
I'll build you houses from their sacred trees.
Enkidu feared his friend was weakening
And called out: Gilgamesh! Don't trust him!
As if there were some hunger in himself
That Gilgamesh was feeling
That turned him momentarily to yearn
For someone who would serve, he paused;
And then he raised his ax up higher
And swung it in a perfect arc
Into Humbaba's neck. He reached out
To touch the wounded shoulder of his friend,

And late that night he reached again
To see if he was yet asleep, but there was only
Quiet breathing. The stars against the midnight sky
Were sparkling like mica° in a riverbed.
In the slight breeze
The head of Humbaba was swinging from a tree.

37. **squall:** sudden, brief storm.

53. **mica** (mī′kə): colored, translucent mineral.

Finding Common Ground

Review the notes you took as you read this ancient story. Did you find common ground between yourself and Gilgamesh and his friend? What other responses to the story did you record? Did you have any questions about the story—any details that you did not understand?

Read the story a second time, still taking notes. When you finish the second reading, review your understanding of the story. Are your questions answered? Do you have any different responses?

Now meet with other readers and compare notes.

- Is the text clear?
- Does it remind you of any details in Beowulf's story?
- Have you ever experienced any of Gilgamesh's feelings?
- Does the story have anything to say to people today?

Stone statues of Mesopotamian god Aby and his wife, from Tell Asmar (2600 B.C.).
Iraq Museum, Baghdad.

Assessing Learning

Check Test: True-False

1. Gilgamesh is frightened when he hears Humbaba coming. [True]
2. Humbaba has never been appreciated by the gods he works for. [True]
3. Humbaba attacks Enkidu first. [True]
4. Humbaba offers to serve Gilgamesh instead of the gods. [True]
5. Gilgamesh lets Humbaba escape. [False]

Before You Read
THE SEAFARER

Make the Connection
Has the Time of Heroes Passed?

In the PBS television series *The Power of Myth,* the television journalist Bill Moyers and the mythologist Joseph Campbell talk about heroes. At one point, Campbell says that as a child he had two heroes but now he has none. Here's a bit of the conversation that follows Campbell's comment:

Moyers: *We seem to worship celebrities today, not heroes.*
Campbell: *Yes, and that's too bad. A questionnaire was once sent around to one of the high schools in Brooklyn which asked, "What would you like to be?" Two-thirds of the students responded, "A celebrity." They had no notion of having to give of themselves in order to achieve something.*

Only a thousand years earlier, the poet who wrote "The Seafarer" addressed the same question: Has the time of heroes passed?

Quickwrite
Do you think we "worship celebrities today, not heroes"? And if we do, what effect does that have on what we value and whom we present to children as role models? Freewrite for a few moments to focus your thoughts on this question.

Elements of Literature
The Elegy

The dominant mood in Anglo-Saxon poetry is elegiac. As we have seen in *Beowulf,* this sense of sadness over the grimness and transience of earthly life is found in the heroic epic. It is also found in several Old English fragments and poems in which a bard laments the passing of better days and greater glories.

An **elegy** is a poem that mourns the death of a person or laments something lost.

For more on the Elegy, see page 606 and the Handbook of Literary Terms.

Background
"The Seafarer" is from the so-called Exeter Book, a manuscript of miscellaneous Anglo-Saxon poems dating from around A.D. 940, copied in A.D. 975, and now preserved at Exeter Cathedral in England. Though the manuscript survived the raids and fires of the centuries, the Exeter Book had not been well cared for. There are signs that its cover had been used as a chopping board; its pages had been marked by beer stains; and some had been partly burned. But today its "songs"—copied down by monks—are our chief source of Anglo-Saxon poetry.

The Anglo-Saxons were sea voyagers, and the northern seas were then, as now, especially cruel. The speaker in "The Seafarer" is an old sailor who drifted through many winters on ice-cold seas.

go.hrw.com
LEO 12-1

OBJECTIVES
1. Read and interpret the poem
2. Analyze an elegy
3. Express understanding through writing, speech, and art

SKILLS

Literary
- Analyze an elegy

Writing
- Collect ideas for a literary analysis
- Compare texts
- Write a poem

Speaking/Listening
- Debate a position

Music, Art, Science
- Create a collage

Planning
- **Block Schedule**
  Block Scheduling Lesson Plans with Pacing Guide
- **Traditional Schedule**
  Lesson Plans Including Strategies for English-Language Learners
- **One-Stop Planner**
  CD-ROM with Test Generator

Resources: Print and Media

Reading
- *Graphic Organizers for Active Reading,* p. 2
- *Audio CD Library*
  Disc 1, Track 4

Writing and Language
- *Daily Oral Grammar*
  Transparency 2
- *Grammar and Language Links*
  Worksheet, p. 5
- *Language Workshop CD-ROM*

Assessment
- *Formal Assessment,* p. 5
- *Portfolio Management System,* p. 91
- *Test Generator (One-Stop Planner CD-ROM)*

Summary ■■

The speaker in this elegy is a sailor who has endured many hard winters on the cold northern seas. Yet the sea has a powerful attraction for him, and he prefers its rigors to the comforts of life on land in an age that no longer produces brave and generous heroes. In fact, the sea is used as a powerful metaphor for life itself. The poem ends with a hopeful Christian exhortation to love God.

Ⓐ Elements of Literature

Elegy

? **In what ways do these opening lines suggest an elegy?** [Possible answers: They convey suffering and pain. They may suggest loss of youth and hopefulness.]

Ⓑ Reading Skills and Strategies

Comparing and Contrasting

? **What two ways of life is the poet contrasting?** [He contrasts the lonely, harsh, cold life at sea to the conviviality, warmth, and intimacy of life at home and at the mead hall.]

Ⓒ Reading Skills And Strategies

Analyzing Motivation

? **Why does the seafarer return to the ocean time after time?** [Possible responses: He may feel more at home on the sea than on land. He refers to his excitement at returning to the waves.]

Ⓓ Reading Skills and Strategies

Comparing and Contrasting

Ask students to compare the seafarer's attitude about fate with Beowulf's. [Both take pride in facing danger and accepting what fate brings.]

The Seafarer

translated by **Burton Raffel**

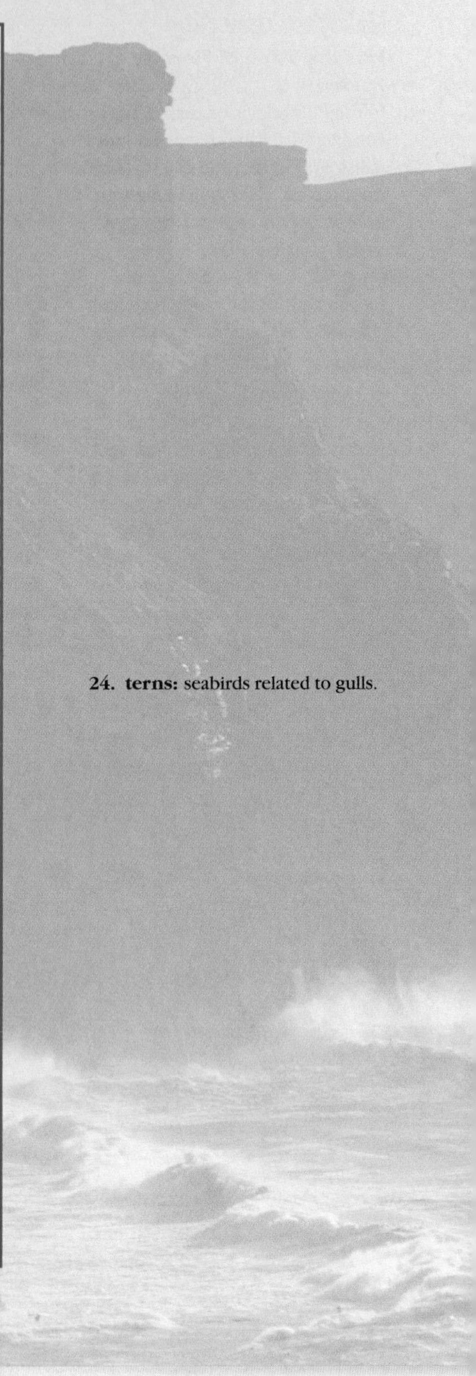

This tale is true, and mine. It tells
How the sea took me, swept me back
And forth in sorrow and fear and pain,
Showed me suffering in a hundred ships,
In a thousand ports, and in me. It tells
Of smashing surf when I sweated in the cold
Of an anxious watch, perched in the bow
As it dashed under cliffs. My feet were cast
In icy bands, bound with frost,
With frozen chains, and hardship groaned
Around my heart. Hunger tore
At my sea-weary soul. No man sheltered
On the quiet fairness of earth can feel
How wretched I was, drifting through winter
On an ice-cold sea, whirled in sorrow,
Alone in a world blown clear of love,
Hung with icicles. The hailstorms flew.
The only sound was the roaring sea,
The freezing waves. The song of the swan
Might serve for pleasure, the cry of the sea-fowl,
The death-noise of birds instead of laughter,
The mewing of gulls instead of mead.
Storms beat on the rocky cliffs and were echoed
By icy-feathered terns° and the eagle's screams;
No kinsman could offer comfort there,
To a soul left drowning in desolation.
    And who could believe, knowing but
The passion of cities, swelled proud with wine
And no taste of misfortune, how often, how wearily,
I put myself back on the paths of the sea.
Night would blacken; it would snow from the north;
Frost bound the earth and hail would fall,
The coldest seeds. And how my heart
Would begin to beat, knowing once more
The salt waves tossing and the towering sea!
The time for journeys would come and my soul
Called me eagerly out, sent me over
The horizon, seeking foreigners' homes.
    But there isn't a man on earth so proud,
So born to greatness, so bold with his youth,
Grown so brave, or so graced by God,
That he feels no fear as the sails unfurl,
Wondering what Fate has willed and will do.
No harps ring in his heart, no rewards,

24. terns: seabirds related to gulls.

Reaching All Students

Struggling Readers

Some students may expect a narrative instead of reflections. Explain that the poem is not a story but a serious look at life from the point of view of someone who has known great hardship and suffering. Read aloud the first page of the poem to students, and ask them to focus on the five Ws: *who* the main character is [the seafarer], *what* the poem is about [sufferings, hardship], *where* [the sea], and *when* it takes place [again and again, over a lifetime], and *why* the speaker returns to the sea [he keeps feeling himself called back].

English Language Learners

Discuss with students the unfamiliar use of familiar words, such as "an anxious *watch*" (meaning "time spent as a lookout") (l. 7) or "the quiet *fairness* of earth," meaning "the safety, beauty, and loveliness of the land" (l. 13). For additional strategies to supplement instruction for English language learners, see

- *Lesson Plans Including Strategies for English-Language Learners*

Advanced Learners

Have students dispute or support the following statement: "The Seafarer" contains both Christian and non-Christian elements. As students prepare their analyses, remind them to use precise words and lines from the poem to support their opinions.

No passion for women, no worldly pleasures,
Nothing, only the ocean's heave;
But longing wraps itself around him.
Orchards blossom, the towns bloom,
Fields grow lovely as the world springs fresh,
And all these admonish° that willing mind
Leaping to journeys, always set
In thoughts traveling on a quickening tide.
So summer's sentinel, the cuckoo, sings
In his murmuring voice, and our hearts mourn
As he urges. Who could understand,
In ignorant ease, what we others suffer
As the paths of exile stretch endlessly on?
And yet my heart wanders away,
My soul roams with the sea, the whales'
Home, wandering to the widest corners
Of the world, returning ravenous° with desire,
Flying solitary, screaming, exciting me
To the open ocean, breaking oaths
On the curve of a wave.
Thus the joys of God
Are fervent° with life, where life itself
Fades quickly into the earth. The wealth
Of the world neither reaches to Heaven nor remains.
No man has ever faced the dawn
Certain which of Fate's three threats
Would fall: illness, or age, or an enemy's
Sword, snatching the life from his soul.
The praise the living pour on the dead
Flowers from reputation: plant
An earthly life of profit reaped
Even from hatred and rancor,° of bravery
Flung in the devil's face, and death
Can only bring you earthly praise
And a song to celebrate a place
With the angels, life eternally blessed
In the hosts of Heaven.
The days are gone
When the kingdoms of earth flourished in glory;
Now there are no rulers, no emperors,
No givers of gold, as once there were,
When wonderful things were worked among them
And they lived in lordly magnificence.
Those powers have vanished, those pleasures are dead.

50. admonish: scold mildly.

61. ravenous: very hungry.

65. fervent: passionate.

75. rancor (raŋ′kər): ill will.

E Reading Skills and Strategies

Monitoring Reading

? What questions or notes might you record at this point in your reading? [Possible answers: Nobody else can understand what it is like for the seafarer to keep being drawn to the sea. It seems like a life in exile. Why does the ocean have such a strong pull on the seafarer? Why do all other pleasures mean nothing in comparison to the ocean?]

F Elements of Literature

Kennings

? What kenning for the sea appears in these lines? [the whales' home] How does this device create a sense of excitement? [It calls up images of the deep and brings home the vastness of the ocean.]

G Literary Connections

The transience of glory is a theme echoed throughout literature. For another ironic lament on this theme, see Shelley's "Ozymandias" (p. 731). For an expression of loss and bewilderment at the close of the nineteenth century, see Tennyson's "Tears, Idle Tears" (p. 804). For an expression of the loss of faith and receding sense of certainty, see Matthew Arnold's "Dover Beach" (p. 848).

H Elements of Literature

Elegy

? What makes this poem an elegy? [Possible answers: Words such as "vanished" and "dead" create a sad tone. The poem mourns what has passed; it mourns what is lost. It reminds readers about the grimness of human existence.]

Using Students' Strengths

Naturalist Learners

The "song of the swan" and the "eagle's screams," as well as the "smashing surf," sound throughout the poem. Invite pairs of students to compare nature imagery in "The Seafarer" and in *Beowulf.* Suggest that they create a chart, showing how the images they find fall into the following categories: weather, the sea, animals, the land. Students might also comment on how much each poet shows awareness of the natural surroundings.

Interpersonal Learners

Have pairs of interpersonal learners prepare an interview or a segment for a talk show with the seafarer. They might question him about some of his journeys, about his inability to stay on land, and about his religious faith. Ask students to perform it live or to videotape their work and play it for the class.

(A) Appreciating Language

Balance and Parallelism

? Part of the beauty of this poem rests in its sentence structure. What examples of balance and parallelism appear in ll. 87–102? [Possible answers: Balanced and parallel constructions are "The weakest survives and the world continues" and "neither its hand nor its brain." "Their faces blanch," "their beards wither," and "they mourn the memory"; and "nothing golden shakes the wrath of God" and "nothing hidden on Earth rises to Heaven."]

(B) Critical Thinking

Interpreting

? How does the poem change here? [Possible answers: The poem starts out in the first person, then seems to shift to the third person. Here, for the first time, the speaker uses the first-person plural. The tone becomes more certain as it departs from individual experience to encompass all people. The speaker begins to make his most definite assertions.]

(C) Reading Skills and Strategies

Finding the Main Idea

? How does the seafarer think that people should act? [Possible answers: They should respect God, live modestly, control pride, and hope for heaven. They should treat the world fairly and seek the grace of God.]

The weakest survives and the world continues,
Kept spinning by toil. All glory is tarnished.
The world's honor ages and shrinks.
Bent like the men who mould it. Their faces
Blanch° as time advances, their beards
(A) Wither and they mourn the memory of friends.
The sons of princes, sown in the dust.
The soul stripped of its flesh knows nothing
Of sweetness or sour, feels no pain,
Bends neither its hand nor its brain. A brother
Opens his palms and pours down gold
On his kinsman's grave, strewing his coffin
With treasures intended for Heaven, but nothing
Golden shakes the wrath of God
For a soul overflowing with sin, and nothing
Hidden on earth rises to Heaven.
We all fear God. He turns the earth,
He set it swinging firmly in space,
Gave life to the world and light to the sky.
Death leaps at the fools who forget their God.
He who lives humbly has angels from Heaven
To carry him courage and strength and belief.
(B) A man must conquer pride, not kill it,
Be firm with his fellows, chaste for himself,
(C) Treat all the world as the world deserves,
With love or with hate but never with harm,
Though an enemy seek to scorch him in hell,
Or set the flames of a funeral pyre°
Under his lord. Fate is stronger
And God mightier than any man's mind.
Our thoughts should turn to where our home is,
Consider the ways of coming there,
Then strive for sure permission for us
To rise to that eternal joy,
That life born in the love of God
And the hope of Heaven. Praise the Holy
Grace of Him who honored us,
Eternal, unchanging creator of earth. Amen.

91. blanch: turn pale.

114. funeral pyre: pile (usually of wood) on which a dead body is burned. See the burial of Beowulf, page 46.

Making the Connections

Connecting to the Subject: "Songs of Ancient Heroes"

Use these questions to help students connect this poem to the subject of the collection.

1. What, if anything, is heroic about this seafarer? [He faces danger and hardship bravely.]
2. In what significant ways does the seafarer compare with Beowulf and Gilgamesh? In what significant ways does he differ from them? [He shares their values but is not a warrior.]
3. The seafarer sees himself as an outsider, a man for whom the "paths of exile stretch endlessly on." How does the condition of being set apart from all others contribute to his "song"? How does it make his song more emotional, more heroic, or more elegiac? [The fact that he is an outsider intensifies the emotional and elegiac qualities of his song.]
4. Which of these heroes, or which of these "songs," is most meaningful to you? Explain your answer. [Answers will vary. Some students will identify more with the loneliness of the seafarer; others, with the prowess of the superheroes.]

PRIMARY **Sources** | A TRANSLATION

The Original Language and the Translator's Task

Here are the opening lines of "The Seafarer" in Old English. Following these lines is a translation by Kevin Crossley-Holland. Burton Raffel, whose very different translation is used on page 56, describes the special demands of verse translation: "Verse translation is a minor art, but a unique one. . . . The translator's only hope is to re-create something roughly equivalent in the new language, something that is itself good poetry and that at the same time carries a reasonable measure of the force and flavor of the original. . . ."

MÆg ic be me sylfum soðgied wrecan,
siþas secgan, hu ic geswincdagum
earfoðhwile oft þrowade,
bitre breostceare gebiden hæbbe,
gecunnad in ceole cearselda fela. . . .

I can sing a true song of myself,
Tell of my travels, of many hard times
Toiling day after day; I can describe
How I have harbored bitter sorrow in
my heart
And often learned that ships are homes
of sadness.

—*translated by* Kevin Crossley-Holland

Making Meanings

First Thoughts

1. What is your first impression of the speaker in this poem? What is his life like? What does he believe in and hope for?

Shaping Interpretations

2. What passages in the poem explain why the seafarer seeks the rigors of the sea rather than the delights of the land? Does he find what he looked for at sea?
3. Lines 58–64 suggest that the poet is beginning to talk about the glories of adventuring at sea, but then he changes direction. What does he turn his attention to over the next sixteen lines?
4. In line 80, the speaker begins to talk about the present state of the world—what does he think of it? How do these thoughts contribute to the poem's **elegiac tone**?
5. The poem ends with a statement of the poet's beliefs. What are they?
6. This short lyric is full of striking **metaphors**—for example, "frozen chains" in line 10. Select three of these metaphors, and explain what is being compared in each one. What emotional effect does each metaphor create?
7. What do you think the seafarer is searching for?

Connecting with the Text

8. In line 88, the poem's speaker says, "All glory is tarnished." Do you think this idea also applies to today's heroes and to present-day life? Explain your response.

Extending the Text

9. Could the sentiments expressed in this poem be applied to the homeless today? Find passages in the poem to support your answer.

Making Meanings

First Thoughts [Respond]

1. The old sailor has had a hard, lonely life. He has traveled in dangerous seas and suffered much from cold, hunger, and exhaustion. He does not identify with the modern world but believes in God and in an eternal home in heaven.

Shaping Interpretations [Interpret]

2. Lines 27–29 imply that the speaker dislikes the false pride of cities. Lines 33–38 and 58–64 suggest his love of journeys and adventures. Yes, he finds what he was looking for but he is not completely satisfied with life at sea either.
3. He begins to focus on the transience of life on earth. Students may say the poet suggests that bravery leads to favor in heaven, or they may interpret this section to mean that bravery is appreciated only in this world, not in heaven.
4. The speaker says the present is a pale reflection of the past. Humans have grown old and weak, and there is no longer any true glory. These thoughts enhance the poem's elegiac tone as they mourn the loss of the world as the sailor has known it in the past.
5. Answers may vary but should be supported with lines from the text. Sample answer: The poet believes that human beings should live according to the ways of God so they will ultimately find joy in heaven, as in ll. 117–122.
6. Possible answers: "Frozen chains" (l. 10) compares ice to chains, which may help readers sense the imprisonment the seafarer feels; "drowning in desolation" (l. 26) compares sadness with drowning, which conveys deep despair; "summer's sentinel" (l. 53) compares a cuckoo to a sentinel: both stand guard to maintain order.
7. The seafarer is searching for home—a port where he can settle down or circumstances that will bring peace to his restless spirit.

Connecting with the Text [Evaluate]

8. Similar feelings expressed today include praise of the past and fears for the present. For example, some glorify our country's founders and feel that there are no leaders of the same caliber in modern politics.

Assessing Learning

Check Test: True-False

1. The narrator claims his tale is true. [True]
2. The narrator states that he has never feared the sea. [False]
3. According to the poem, the seafarer can't resist the lure of the sea for long. [True]
4. The narrator states that the days of glory are gone. [True]
5. According to the narrator, man's goal is to get to heaven. [True]

Extending the Text [Synthesize]

9. Most students will feel that some of the feelings in the poem might apply to the homeless today. For example, the following passages might apply: "No kinsman could offer comfort there,/To a soul left drowning in desolation" (ll. 25–26); "Who could understand,/In ignorant ease, what we others suffer/As the paths of exile stretch endlessly on?" (ll. 55–57).

Grading Timesaver

Rubrics for each assignment appear on p. 91 in the *Portfolio Management System.*

Choices: Building Your Portfolio

1. **Writer's Notebook** As a warm-up for this assignment, you might ask students to say, "Tell me about it" in a number of tones: curious, pleading, angry, sarcastic.
2. **Comparing Texts Across Cultures** Discuss ways to organize this essay. Suggest that students could discuss the poems separately and then point out similarities and differences in a concluding section; or they could organize the essay with one section on similarities and one on differences.
3. **Creative Writing** Give students the option of working alone, in pairs, or in groups for this activity. If necessary, point out kennings and alliteration from the poem such as the "death-noise of birds" (l. 21) or "No passions for women, no worldly pleasures" (l. 45).
4. **Critical Thinking** To help students prepare for the debate, have them develop a chart of arguments for their position statement, support for the position, and possible responses.

Position	Support	Possible Responses

5. **Visual Art** To help students get started, brainstorm with them to find words that represent the speaker's attitude, listing ideas on the chalkboard. Suggest, for example, *powerful sea* or *darkness of life.*

Choices: Building Your Portfolio

Writer's Notebook

1. Collecting Ideas for a Literary Analysis

Earlier in this collection you may have begun collecting ideas for a literary analysis. One of the elements of literature that you can focus on in a literary analysis is tone. **Tone** refers to the writer's or speaker's attitude. Tone is established by word choice. In poetry it can also be established by sound effects. Go through "The Seafarer" and list all the words and phrases and figures of speech that suggest an elegiac or mournful tone. Then read the poem aloud and note sounds that suggest a mournful tone or feeling. Save your work for possible use in the Writer's Workshop on page 67.

Comparing Texts Across Cultures

2. Ancient and Modern

Perhaps the most startling aspect of ancient literature is that it so often deals with emotions and thoughts similar to our own, despite the intervening centuries. Look, for instance, at this short poem by the American poet Robert Frost (1874–1963):

Nothing Gold Can Stay

Nature's first green is gold,
Her hardest hue to hold.
Her early leaf's a flower;
But only so an hour.
Then leaf subsides to leaf.
So Eden sank to grief,
So dawn goes down to day.
Nothing gold can stay.

—Robert Frost

Write a short essay comparing the thoughts expressed here and in "The Seafarer." What sentiments do they share? How do they differ? How do you feel about the main thrust of each poem?

Creative Writing

3. You Are a "Seafarer"

Create a "Seafarer" poem of your own, opening with the line "This tale is true, and mine." Write about your own or someone else's (old or young) aspirations, hopes, joys, and disillusionments. Try to incorporate alliteration and kennings in your poem, in true Anglo-Saxon style.

Critical Thinking

4. No Heroes? A Debate

"There are no heroes today." Do you agree or disagree with this statement? Refer to your responses to the Quickwrite on page 55. Take a position, and then gather evidence to support it—facts, reasons, and examples from life today. Think about what the opposing side might say and how you might respond to their ideas. Hold a debate, with each side allowed three minutes to present its ideas and two minutes to respond to the opposing side's remarks.

Visual Art

5. Depicting a Dilemma

Create a collage that visually represents the speaker's attitudes in "The Seafarer." Working with a partner or a group, put your imaginations to work, and gather images and words from newspapers and magazines. Remember that collages can also contain objects, such as feathers or shells or sand. Be prepared to explain why you included each element in the collage when you present it to your class.

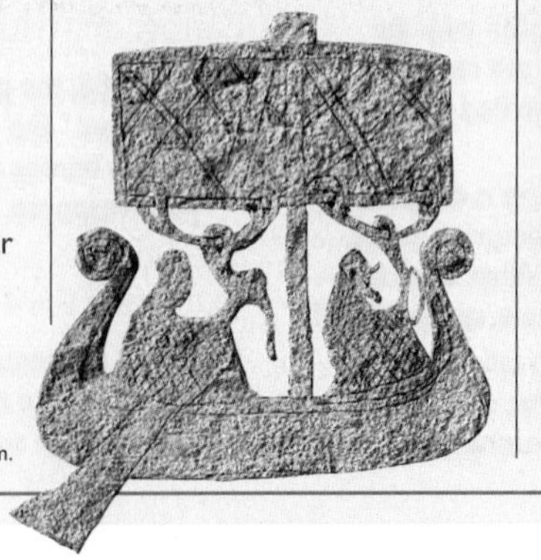

A picture stone showing a Viking ship under sail.
Statens Historiska Museer, Stockholm.

Professional Notes

Critical Comment: Reconciling the Two Parts of the Poem

"The Seafarer" has been the subject of scholarly debate for many years because it seems to shift in tone and subject matter after l. 64. Some critics believe the poem is a dialogue between an experienced mariner and a young man eager to go to sea; others see it as the conflicting emotions of one man. Here, essayist O. S. Anderson discusses his solution:

"The simplest way of uniting [the poem is to assume] that the first part is also in the nature of a homily . . . The cares and sufferings of the poet's earthly existence . . . make him long for the joys of heaven with all his soul . . . This gives a simple and clear connection between the first part of the poem and the second: the earthly life of the poet is full of misery and privation . . . *therefore* the joys of heaven are his only real concern . . . ."

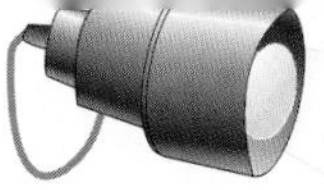

SPOTLIGHT ON

Everyday Poetry: Anglo-Saxon Riddles

translated by **Burton Raffel**

In the Anglo-Saxon period, riddles were "everyday" poetry and intellectual exercises that entertained by puzzling. Like riddles in most cultures, the Anglo-Saxon riddle can be crude; it usually describes some household or farm object or some aspect of ordinary life. Ninety-five riddles are found in the Exeter Book.

The Anglo-Saxons must have whiled away many a long, dark winter evening by repeating riddles like these and having friends guess the answers. The answer to each riddle is below.

32

Our world is lovely in different ways,
Hung with beauty and works of hands.
I saw a strange machine, made (A)
For motion, slide against the sand,
Shrieking as it went. It walked swiftly
On its only foot, this odd-shaped monster,
Traveled in an open country without
Seeing, without arms, or hands,
With many ribs, and its mouth in its middle.
Its work is useful, and welcome, for it loads
Its belly with food, and brings abundance
To men, to poor and to rich, paying
Its tribute year after year. Solve
This riddle, if you can, and unravel its name.

33

A creature came through the waves, beautiful
And strange, calling to shore, its voice
Loud and deep; its laughter froze
Men's blood; its sides were like sword-blades. It swam
Contemptuously along, slow and sluggish,
A bitter warrior and a thief, ripping
Ships apart, and plundering. Like a witch (B)
It wove spells—and knew its own nature, shouting:
"My mother is the fairest virgin of a race
Of noble virgins: She is my daughter
Grown great. All men know her, and me,
And know, everywhere on earth, with what joy
We will come to join them, to live on land!"

47

A worm ate words. I thought that wonderfully
Strange—a miracle—when they told me a crawling
Insect had swallowed noble songs,
A night-time thief had stolen writing
So famous, so weighty. But the bug was foolish (C)
Still, though its belly was full of thought.

Answers: 32. a ship; 33. an iceberg; 47. a bookworm.

Spotlight On

Three Anglo-Saxon riddles describe aspects of nature and human life in verse form. After the class has figured out the riddles given here, ask interested students to research more riddles, either in the *Exeter Book* for more Anglo-Saxon riddles or in the literature of other cultures.

(A) Appreciating Language
Vocabulary

The use of the word *machine* in this context may give students difficulty if they associate a machine only with something that operates on electricity. Remind students that earlier the word was applied to any apparatus used for doing work.

(B) Reading Skills and Strategies
Finding Details

? **What key words help you solve this riddle and why?** [Sample answers: the word "froze" suggests ice, and the words "shore", "waves," and "swam" suggest water.]

(C) Reading Skills and Strategies
Extending the Text

? **Remember that much of Anglo-Saxon poetry was oral rather than written. How does this riddle reflect the Anglo-Saxon love of oral literature?** [Possible response: The riddle calls a bookworm foolish. It makes fun of someone who reads alone, swallowing thought, instead of sharing it in camaraderie with others.]

Resources

Listening
Audio CD Library

For a recording of these Anglo-Saxon Riddles, see the *Audio CD Library:*

- Disc 1, Tracks 5, 6, 7

Professional Notes

Critical Comment: Riddles

In *A Feast of Creatures: Anglo-Saxon Riddle Songs,* Craig Williamson comments on the metaphoric nature of riddles: "The riddles are primitive flower and lyric seed. To us, they offer a world in which there is an eye *(I)* in every other, a charged world where, as Walt Whitman says, there is 'God in every object.'" Ask students to discuss this quotation in relation to the Anglo-Saxon riddles here.

Read On

Portfolio Assessment Options
The following projects can help you evaluate and assess your students' reading accomplishments outside class. Videotapes or photographs of completed projects may be included in students' portfolios.

- **Draw Action Sequences** Invite students to turn the action sequences from a novel they have read into comic-strip sketches. Remind students to return to their novels to find appropriate dialogue to fill the speech or thought balloons of the characters who appear in the sketches. Have students narrate their sketches as they display them for the class.
- **Illustrate the Reading** Have students illustrate one or two of the selections from *Myths and Folk Tales of Ireland.* Illustrations should convey some important aspects of the stories. If possible, show examples of traditional Celtic art to provide students with ideas. Remind students to return to the text to find material for captions that support or define their illustrations.
- **Write a Movie Script** Some students may find that their reading selection lends itself well to a movie interpretation. Suggest that students choose a section of the reading and rewrite it in script form. They should include stage directions, descriptions, and director's notes about camera angles and lighting. If possible, show students a movie script.
- **Give a Testimonial** Have students create an imaginary award they would like to present to a character in the book they have read. They can then write and give a testimonial speech that explains why the character deserves the award. Before they write, students should consider qualities that they want to celebrate. The testimonial should describe the character as well as incidents from the story that illustrate his or her qualities. If there is time, students might design and create the award.

READ ON

A History Mystery

History and fiction merge in Rosemary Sutcliff's *The Eagle of the Ninth* (Farrar, Straus & Giroux). Travel back in time to Roman Britain, where eighteen-year-old Marcus Flavius Aquila, a centurion in the Roman army, attempts to solve the mystery of his father's disappearance and restore the family's honor.

Great Deeds of Ages Past

An exciting blend of narrative, poetry, and drama, *Sundiata* (Dearborn Trade Publishers) is the best-known African epic. It is the story of Sundiata, son of the king of Mali some eight hundred years ago. Passed down by griots, Africa's oral historians, the epic reflects the rich complexity of the ancient civilization of Mali.

Traveling Talk

Some of the most colorful English spoken today comes from a wide range of sources—American, Irish, Caribbean. How did the English language travel around the globe, and what happened to it during those travels? *The Story of English* (Viking Penguin), by Robert McCrum, et al., traces the continuing evolution of our language.

Beyond the Misty Mountains

Full of mythology, magic, and quiet humor, J.R.R. Tolkien's classic fantasy *The Hobbit* (Ballantine and Fawcett) follows the adventures of a comfort-loving Hobbit named Bilbo Baggins. Baggins is tricked by the wizard Gandalf into going on a hazardous quest to recover stolen treasure from the dragon Smaug. *The Lord of the Rings* trilogy continues the saga of Middle Earth.

The Storytelling Tradition of Ireland

The enchanting stories from the ancient oral tradition of Ireland, compiled by Jeremiah Curtin in the 1800s, have been gathered together in *Myths and Folk Tales of Ireland* (Dover). The book includes traditional fairy tales, as well as myths about the fabulous adventures of the great Celtic heroes Cucúlin and Fin MacCumhail.

The English Language

Old English: Where English Came From *by John Algeo*

We have biological ancestors, from whom we inherit the tint of our skin, the shape of our skulls, and everything about our bodies. We also have cultural ancestors, from whom we inherit the society in which we live and especially the language we speak. We in the United States have diverse biological ancestors from whom we get our genes, but as English speakers, we share a common language. So in studying English and its history, we learn more about a legacy that all Americans can share. Ⓐ

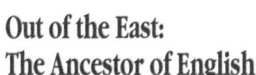

Gold pectoral, or ornamental breastplate (c. 4th–5th century).

Out of the East: The Ancestor of English

Written records of English have been preserved for about 1,300 years. Much earlier, however, a people living in the east, near the Caspian Sea, spoke a language that was to become English. We call their language Proto-Indo-European because at Ⓑ the beginning of recorded history varieties of it were spoken from India to Europe. (*Proto-* means "the first or earliest form of something.")

The speakers of Proto-Indo-European were a vigorous sort who raised cattle and horses. They were fighters, farmers, and herders who used large wagons and built fortresses on hilltops. Eventually, they got the urge to travel and began spreading through Turkey, Iran, India, and most of Europe. In various places their language changed into those we now call Persian, Hindi, Armenian, Greek, Russian, Polish, Irish, Italian, French, Spanish, German, English, Dutch, Norwegian, Swedish, and a good many others. Such languages we call Indo-European.

Wanderlust: The Migrations

Speakers of Indo-European languages eventually wandered all over the earth and were the first human beings to travel into space and reach the moon.

Some early Indo-Europeans lived in what is now southern Denmark and northern Germany. Called Angles and Saxons, they were part of a large group of Germanic peoples living over much of northern Europe. About the middle of the fifth century (the traditional date is A.D. 449), the Anglo-Saxons migrated across the North Sea to the island of Britain and settled very happily in the green and fruitful land they found there.

The British Isles had already been inhabited by some distant Indo-European cousins of the Anglo-Saxons: the Britons, a Celtic people after whom the island was named. They had been

go.hrw.com
LEO 12-English Language

OBJECTIVES

1. Appreciate the development of Old English from its Indo-European roots to its flowering under King Alfred
2. Distinguish key similarities and differences between Old English and our language today

Ⓐ Reading Skills and Strategies

Drawing Upon Background Knowledge

? What events do you already know about that probably influenced the development of the English language? [Sample responses: In this unit, students have read about the Roman occupation of Britain, the invasions of the Angles and Saxons, the conversion of these people to Christianity, and the later invasions of the Vikings. Other influences are the Norman invasion in 1066, the colonization of North America, and the waves of immigrants to the United States and England—any movement of people influences and enriches a language.]

Ⓑ Background

Finding the Roots

The British judge Sir William Jones and the writer Jakob Grimm were the first to note similarities among Indo-European languages and to trace them back to a common origin.

Resources

Viewing and Representing

Videocassette A, Segment 1
English: A Living Language, Part I
Available in English and Spanish.
This segment introduces students to the early history of English. For full lessons plans and worksheets, see the *Visual Connections Teacher's Manual.*

Getting Students Involved

Speaking and Listening

To acquaint students with the sound of Old English, give them information about the pronunciation of Old English words. Ask them to practice reading a short section of *Beowulf* aloud in Old English, and then have them read their passage to the rest of the class. Have listeners try to determine the meaning of each section read. Remind speakers to pause, raise or lower their voices, or slow their reading to help the audience understand the passage.

Ⓐ Background
Danish Influences

One reason that Celtic did not have much influence on English is that the Celts were often either the subjects or the enemies of the Anglo-Saxons. Some Celtic border-chieftains even joined in with the Scandinavians in their raids against the Anglo-Saxons. Ironically, English ended up borrowing more from Danish—the language of the invaders—than it did from the Celts. That is probably because Danish, like English, was a Germanic language and therefore less foreign.

Ⓑ Background
More Words from Latin

The Romans, who had evolved a complex system of laws beginning with the Twelve Tables and extending to the vast codes of Justinian, also gave English many words related to law and government, including *affidavit, agenda, alibi, fiat, posse, propaganda, quorum, verbatim,* and *veto.* Students may enjoy knowing that the Latin words for *senate* and *senator* came from a root meaning "old man."

Ⓒ Background
The Latin Legacy

Other than the examples cited—place words related to government, religion, and learning—English adopted few words directly from Latin. Yet an enormous number of our words can be traced back to Latin roots—because the French that the Normans brought to England in 1066 (see pp. 181–184) is a direct descendant of the Latin language spread by the earlier Roman conquerors of most of Europe.

Ⓓ Background
Language Change

Some language scholars believe that the most significant contribution of the Vikings was the simplification of the system of inflection used in Old English.

conquered by the Romans, who were Indo-Europeans too, so all this jostling for space in the island was just one branch of the family trying to move in on another, rather like relatives from Chicago moving in with their kin in Florida for the winter.

St. Kevin's Monastery (6th century), Glendalough, Ireland.

The Anglo-Saxons got a few words from the Romans in Britain, such as *castra* ("camp"), which can be seen in the names of many English cities (*Chester, Chesterfield, Dorchester, Gloucester, Lancaster, Manchester, Winchester,* and *Worcester*). They also found the cities that the Romans had built, with temples, waterworks, and public baths. They moved into the cities and admired the great buildings, but they never learned to share the Roman passion for bathing.

Meeting the Neighbors

When the Anglo-Saxons first arrived in Britain (which came to be called Engla land, England—the land of the Angles), they had very little to do with the Celts, whom they drove into the west where they still survive today as the Welsh (an Anglo-Saxon word that means "foreigner"). But another group of Celts, the Irish, later sent missionaries to the Angles. About the same time, in A.D. 597, the Roman church sent St. Augustine to do missionary work.

Although there is very little early Celtic influence on the English language—hardly more than a few place names, such as *London* and *Dover*—Latin, the language of the Christian church, was enormously influential. Even while the Anglo-Saxons were still living on the Continent, they had learned some Latin from Roman soldiers and merchants, including words like *mile, street, wall, wine, cheese, butter,* and *dish.* After the Anglo-Saxons settled in England and were converted, they borrowed many other Latin words concerned with religion and learning, such as *school, candle, altar, paper,* and *circle.*

Beginning near the end of the eighth century, other cousins, Northmen or Vikings from Scandinavia, invaded England. They were led by such memorably named worthies as Ivar the Boneless, son of Ragnar Shaggy-britches. It would be a mistake, however, to think of these Vikings as amusingly rough but lovable, like the comic-strip character Hagar the Horrible. They were fierce fighters and very nearly made England into another Scandinavian country. It was the English King Alfred the Great who defeated the Viking invaders and set about assimilating the Northmen into English life.

The influence of the Vikings' Norse language has been very great. Among the words borrowed are such common ones as *get, give, hit, kick, law, sister, skirt, sky, take, window, they, their,* and *them.*

What Tongue Is This?

Despite all the foreign influences, the language of the early English, which we call Old English or Anglo-Saxon, was clearly a Germanic tongue. An example of this language is the following short piece—a text that most readers of this book will know in a modern form:

> Fæder ūre, þū þe eart on heofonum, sī nama gehālgod. Tōbecume þīn rīce. Gewurðe þīn willa on eorðan swā swā on heofonum. Ūrne gedæghwāmlican hlāf syle ūs tō dæg. And forgyf ūs ūre gyltas, swā wē forgyfað ūrum gylltendum. And ne gelǣd þū ūs on costnunge, ac ālȳs ūs of yfele. Sōðlice.

This text is the Lord's Prayer from about the year 1000. It differs from the version we know in many ways. **Words** are different (*costnunge* instead of *temptation,* borrowed later from Latin). **Spellings and pronunciations** are different (*nama,* pronounced "nah-mah," instead of the present-day *name*). **Meanings** are different (*hlāf* in the sense of "bread," surviving today as *loaf*).

Professional Notes

Critical Comment: The Spread of English

The following quotation from *The Story of English,* by Robert McCrum, William Cran, and Robert MacNeil, might interest students: "When Julius Caesar landed in Britain nearly two thousand years ago, English did not exist. Five hundred years later, *Englisc,* incomprehensible to modern ears, was probably spoken by about as few people as currently speak Cherokee . . . Nearly a thousand years later, at the end of the sixteenth century, when William Shakespeare was in his prime, English was the native speech of between five and seven million Englishmen. . . . Between 1600 and the present . . . the speakers of English . . . traveled into every corner of the globe, carrying their language and culture with them. Today, English is used by at least 750 million people. . . . English is more widely scattered, more widely spoken and written, than any other language has ever been. It has become *the* language of the planet, the first truly global language."

And **grammar** is different. Note the word order of *Fæder ūre* for *our Father* and the word ending, or case inflection, *–um* in *on heofonum* ("in heaven").

Old English grammar was different from ours in a number of other ways. For example, all **nouns** were one of three genders—masculine, feminine, or neuter—and the grammatical gender of a noun might have little to do with sex. Thus, of three words for "woman," *hlæfdige* was feminine, *wif* was neuter, and *wifmann* was masculine.

Adjectives had different forms depending on the gender, number, and case of the nouns they modified (*þæt tile wif* but *se tila wifmann,* both meaning "the good woman").

Whereas our **verbs** have two forms in the present tense (for example, *ride, rides*), Old English verbs had four: *ic ride* ("I ride"), *þū ridest* ("you ride"), *hē rideþ* ("he rides"), and *wē ridon* ("we ride").

Like other Indo-European languages, Old English used endings on words to show how they relate to one another and how they are used in a sentence. For example, "The boy killed the dragon" was "Se cnapa slōh þone dracan," while "The dragon killed the boy" was "Se draca slōh þone cnapan." The words for "boy" and "dragon" change their forms, according to whether they are the subject or the object of the verb, and the word for "the" is different, depending on the function of the word it modifies. Today we rely solely on word order to show grammatical differences; Old English relied mainly on changes in word form.

> Beginning near the end of the eighth century, other cousins, Northmen or Vikings from Scandinavia, invaded England. They were led by such memorably named worthies as Ivar the Boneless, son of Ragnar Shaggy-britches.

Anglo-Saxon scribes wrote in a script they learned from Celtic missionaries. It was a pleasant-looking, rounded style of writing, as the sample below shows.

Occasionally, for special purposes, Old English writers used an altogether different alphabet, called the *futhorc,* composed of letters called runes, which they learned from their Germanic cousins while they still lived on the Continent. These runes were probably used by the very early pagan English for magic and for monuments. They were straight, angular letters that were used for carving on wood.

Old English was mainly oral. Because writing was important business, it was usually reserved for Latin, the language of church services, books, education, and contact with other nations. To know Latin was to be learned. Not to know Latin was to be illiterate. It is small wonder that Latin came to have a greater and more lasting influence on English than any other language did.

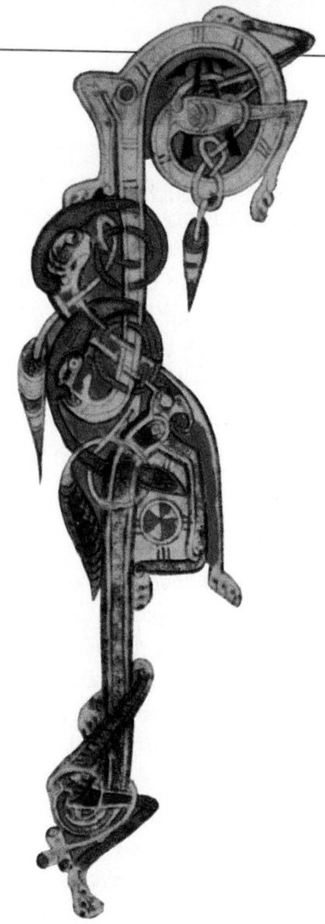

Detail from the Book of Kells (8th century).

The Board of Trinity College, Dublin. Photograph by The Green Studio Ltd, Dublin.

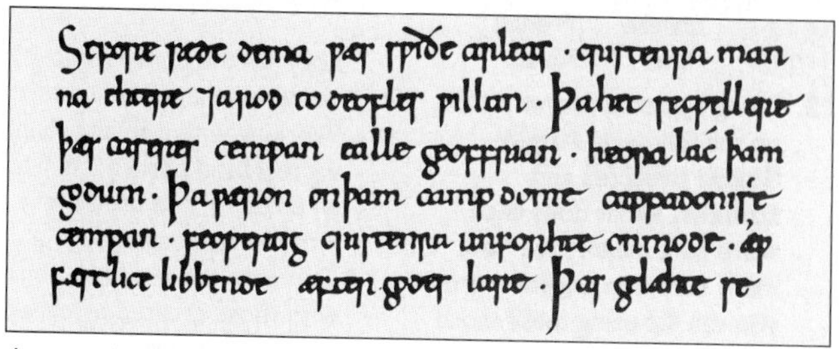

An example of Insular script.

E Reading Skills and Strategies

Making Generalizations

? Just how different is Modern English from Old English? [Possible answer: It is almost entirely different. Modern English no longer has masculine, feminine, and neuter nouns or forms for adjectives that depend on the gender of the noun the adjective is modifying. Modern English no longer uses many inflected verb forms to show the person doing the action, and it no longer uses word endings to show grammatical relationships between nouns. In addition, words, spellings, pronunciations, and meanings can all be different.]

F Advanced Learners

Extending the Text

Ask students to consult a German speaker and prepare a chart showing the inflectional changes that are still used in German nouns to indicate masculine, feminine, and neuter gender.

RESPONDING TO THE ART

The Book of Kells, an illuminated Latin manuscript of the Gospels, richly and intricately ornamented, is the most remarkable book of the Anglo-Saxon period. The chief characteristic of the illuminations is their intricate interlocking patterning of letters and border work. *The Book of Kells,* named for a monastery in Kells, Ireland, was the work of Irish monks and can be seen today in Trinity College, Dublin. A statement made in the twelfth century about an illuminated manuscript, possibly *The Book of Kells* itself, still applies today as we rediscover its beauty: "Examine it carefully, and you will penetrate to the very shrine of art. You will make out intricacies so delicate and subtle, so concise and compact, so full of knots and links, with colors so fresh and vivid, that you might think all this was the work of an angel, not a man."

Crossing the Curriculum

Music

Students interested in music may enjoy researching the types of music prevalent in Britain during the time of the Anglo-Saxons, the countries that may have had influence on that music, and the instruments used.

Art

Invite students to design an elaborate version of a capital letter on heavy paper or poster board, using colorful pens and glitter or gold dusting powder to imitate the fancy lettering monks used to create illuminated manuscripts. Allow students to use the characteristics of early manuscripts (geometric design, flat areas of color, and complicated interweaving of elements) or to experiment with their own styles.

Ⓐ Cultural Connections

High-Tech Jargon

English is still changing, borrowing, and developing. One source of recent change is computer terminology, which has created new words and given some old words new meaning. Here are some examples.

- Give me *input* on this idea. [your opinion]
- This book is *user-friendly*. [easy to understand]

Try It Out

Possible Answers

1. Three languages other than English that are spoken in more than one country include the following:
   - French (France, Ivory Coast, French Guiana)
   - Portuguese (Portugal, Brazil)
   - Dutch (Netherlands, Aruba)
2. These roots and affixes come from older languages and were used in Old English: Roots: *cap*—head; *mis*—send; *miss*—send, *path*—feeling; *ten*—to hold; *tin*—stretch. Prefixes: *in-* —in, not; *mis-* —error, not, wrong; *un-* —not. Suffixes: *-ful*—full of; *-ish*—like; *-hood*—state of; *less*—without; *-ness*—state of. Possible words: capital, dismiss, sympathy, maintenance, procrastination, insincere, mistreat, unlikely, artful, yellowish, selfhood, fearless, sameness
3. belt: Latin *balteus*
   brother: OE *brōthor*
   filly: Old Norse *fylja*
   horse: OE *hors*
   house: OE *hūs*
   night: OE *niht*
   noon: Latin *nōnus*
   pillow: Latin *pulvinus*
   pipe: Latin *pīpāre*
   rug: Old Norse *rugg*
   skin: Old Norse *skinn*
   until: Old Norse *un* + *til*
4. Suggest that students keep their phrases short. Tell them that some letters do not exist in the runic alphabet (*q*, *v*, and *x*) so they will have to use other letters that have similar sounds instead.

Words from Anglo-Saxon

Ⓐ We have come a long way since Anglo-Saxon times—in technology, in society, and in language. But much of the Anglo-Saxons' language, Old English, is still evident in our language.

Although today we have borrowed words from most of the world's languages, our basic vocabulary comes to us from Old English. Words like *heart, foot, head, day, year, earth, father, mother, son, daughter, name, east, full, hound, tooth, eat, weave,* and *sew* are survivals of Old English words (*heorte, fōt, hēafod, dæg, gēar, eorþe, fæder, mōdor, sunu, dohtor, nama, ēast, full, hund, toþ, etan, wefan,* and *siwan*). Indeed, all of those words come to us from Proto-Indo-European; thus, they have been part of our language for thousands of years.

Our **noun plural ending *s*** and **possessive ending *'s*** (as in *hounds, hound's*) come to us from Old English (*hundas, hundes*). So do the endings we use to **compare adjectives,** as in *darker, darkest* (*deorcor, deorcost*). The regular endings for the **past tense and past participle of our verbs,** as in *healed, has healed,* are from Old English (*hǣlde, hæfþ hǣled*), as are the vowel changes in verbs like *sing, sang, sung* (*singan, sang, sungen*). In many other ways, our English is recognizably the same as the oldest English of which we have any record.

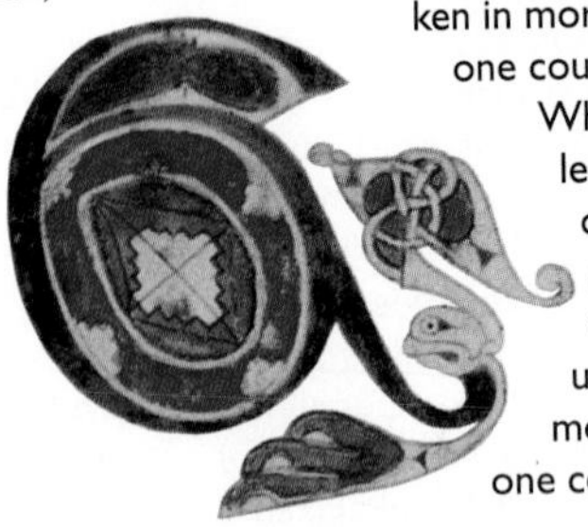

Detail from the Book of Kells (8th century).
The Board of Trinity College, Dublin. Photograph by The Green Studio Ltd, Dublin.

Although we have lost most of the endings from Old English and have borrowed far more words from other languages than we have kept from Old English times, the heart of our speech is still the same. The preceding sentence consists entirely of words that have come to us from Old English, and its grammar would have been understood by an English speaker of the year A.D. 700. Despite its many changes, English has remained basically true to itself.

Try It Out

1. On a map of the world, locate the countries where the following **Indo-European languages** are spoken. Some languages are spoken in more than one country. What are at least three other languages that are used in more than one country?

English	Icelandic
Russian	Irish
German	Spanish
Polish	Portuguese
Danish	French
Hindi	Italian

2. Using a good dictionary, look up the following **Anglo-Saxon prefixes** and **suffixes.** What does each word part mean? See how many common English words you can list using these word parts.

Prefixes	Suffixes
a-	-en
an-	-dom
be-	-hood
for-	-like
mis-	-ness
un-	-ward

3. Four of the following words are native words in **Old English,** four are **Latin** words borrowed into English very early (some while English speakers still lived on the Continent), and four are **Scandinavian** words borrowed as a result of the Norse invasions of England. Which words belong in each group? Check your work by looking at the **etymologies** in a college or unabridged dictionary.

belt	noon
brother	pillow
filly	pipe
horse	rug
house	skin
night	until

4. The Anglo-Saxons sometimes used an alphabet called *futhorc* or *futhark,* comprised of characters called **runes.** The first six letters of the runic alphabet—which spell out the word *futhorc*—looked like this:

ᚠᚢᚦᚩᚱᚳ or ᚠᚢᚦᚨᚱᚲ

Look up the entire runic alphabet in an encyclopedia. Working with a small group, write a brief phrase (such as an epitaph), and translate it into the runic alphabet. Compare your "translations" with those created by other groups in the class.

Assessing Learning

Check Test: True-False

1. English originated as a language 1,300 years ago. [False]
2. The Anglo-Saxons migrated to Britain around the middle of the fifth century. [True]
3. The Anglo-Saxons refused to use any words from the Romans. [False]
4. There is a strong Celtic influence on the English language. [False]
5. Latin influenced English more than any other language because it was the language of the church, education, and diplomacy. [True]

The history
of the written
word is rich a
Page 1

BUILDING YOUR PORTFOLIO

Writer's Workshop

EXPOSITORY WRITING

Analyzing a Literary Work

When you write an analysis of a literary work, you take the work apart to see how it creates meaning. The parts of a literary work that you examine in an analysis are those elements that form its structure. In some analyses you will focus on just one element—character in a short story, for example, or imagery in a poem.

Prewriting

1. **Getting started.** Unless you are assigned a literary work to analyze, your first step will be finding a work that interests you. Your best possibilities are the selections from *Beowulf* and "The Seafarer" in this collection because, presumably, you have read them carefully and talked about them in class. Review the notes you took for the Writer's Notebook assignments in this collection. Do any of your notes especially interest you? Is there some topic here that you can develop?

WORK IN PROGRESS

2. **Focus your analysis.** If you like, you can discuss all the basic elements of your literary work, but you might be better off narrowing your focus to just one or two prominent elements. Here are some possible focuses:
   - The symbolism of Grendel and Herot
   - The Christian elements in Beowulf's story
   - The heroic character of Beowulf as the deliverer of his people
   - The elegiac tone of *Beowulf* and "The Seafarer"
3. **Write a thesis statement.** Next, try out some thesis statements. Your thesis statement must be a sentence; it will be the controlling idea of your essay. You will have to experiment with a thesis statement. As you go along, you might find that a statement is just too broad (maybe it could be the subject of a whole book) or too narrow (you find you just don't have much to say about it).

   Thesis statement: In *Beowulf,* Grendel symbolizes evil while Herot symbolizes goodness.
4. **Gather support.** List all the evidence from the text that explains or supports your thesis statement. Most of your evidence will come from the text itself (this is your **primary source**). You might also want to quote from **secondary sources** that support your thesis statement. Cite specific lines from the text that support your main ideas; then, paraphrase, or state in your own words, what they say. Here is the start of a list of supporting details:

Technology HELP

See Writer's Workshop 2 CD-ROM. *Assignment: Interpretation.*

ASSIGNMENT

Write an essay in which you analyze a literary work or one of its key elements.

AIM

To read carefully to see how a literary element is used in a work, to explain how the element is used to reinforce meaning, and to supply convincing details to support your analysis.

AUDIENCE

Your teacher, classmates, or a literary magazine published by your school or an outside publisher.

MAIN OBJECTIVE

Write an essay analyzing a literary work or one of its key elements

PROCESS OBJECTIVES

1. Use appropriate prewriting techniques to identify and develop a topic
2. Create a first draft
3. Use Evaluation Criteria as a basis for determining revision strategies
4. Revise the first draft incorporating suggestions generated by self- or peer evaluation
5. Proofread and correct errors
6. Create a final draft
7. Choose an appropriate method of publication
8. Reflect on progress as a writer

Introducing the Writer's Workshop

Begin by asking students which of the selections they have read so far is the most interesting to them. Why? Are they drawn more to the people in a story or to the events of the plot? Answers to questions such as these will help students define their interests and develop a topic they can pursue with some enthusiasm.

Planning

- **Block Schedule**
  Block Scheduling Lesson Plans with Pacing Guide
- **One-Stop Planner**
  CD-ROM with Test Generator

Resources: Print and Media

Writing and Language
- *Portfolio Management System*
  - Prewriting, p. 93
  - Peer Editing, p. 94
  - Assessment Rubric, p. 95
- *Workshop Resources*
  - Revision Strategy Teaching Notes, p. 1
  - Revision Strategy Transparencies 1, 2, 3
- *Writer's Workshop CD-ROM*
  - Interpretation

Teaching the Writer's Workshop

Prewriting

- Focus students' attention on the four Prewriting steps outlined on pp. 67–68. Emphasize that a good thesis statement includes ideas or opinions on the topic. Without this, the writer will be reduced to listing facts about the literature, not interpreting it for the reader.
- You may wish to write a simple equation on the board to remind students:

Thesis statement = a subject + your ideas about the subject

Drafting

Encourage the sharing of drafts with other students familiar with the work. Have student reviewers use the Evaluation Criteria to comment and respond.

Evaluating and Revising

As students revise their drafts, suggest that they look closely at the Evaluation Criteria on p. 68. As they revise, ask students to consider whether or not graphic aids could be a way to achieve greater clarity in their analyses.

Proofreading and Publishing

Circulate correct final drafts between groups so that students are reviewing papers about works they did not select. Have students comment on whether or not the analyses spark any interest.

Grading Timesaver

Rubrics for this assignment appear on p. 95 of the *Portfolio Management System.*

Communications Handbook HELP

See Taking Notes and Documenting Sources; Proofreading.

Supporting details, lines 1–29:

Grendel: monster; living in darkness; demon; fiend.

Herot: music; songs about creation; singing heroes; happy people.

Paraphrase: Grendel is associated with all that is not good. He lives underground in darkness. He is called a demon and a fiend. Herot, on the other hand, is a happy place associated with song, creation, pleasure, great warriors.

Drafting

1. **Find a method of organization.** Here are two effective ways to organize your details:

   Chronological order. If you are writing about the development of a main character, you can organize your supporting details in the order in which they occur in the text.

   Order of importance. You might want to start out with a bang and introduce your strongest point first. Or you may reverse that and keep your most powerful point for the very end.

2. **Structure your analysis.** Traditionally, literary analyses take the following simple shape:

   An introduction that states your thesis, or main idea. Here, you must also cite the title and author of your text. You might want to summarize your text briefly. Remember: Do not tell the whole plot in tedious detail. You are writing an analysis, not a summary.

   A body that contains the most persuasive details you can find to support your thesis.

   A conclusion that sums up your main point. Try to find a strong way to conclude your essay.

Evaluating and Revising

1. Skim your text again. Have you cited the best details to support your thesis statement?
2. Check your quotations and the documentation of sources for accuracy. Have you used quotation marks properly?
3. Read your analysis aloud, or ask a peer to evaluate it. Is your ending strong? Do your sentences read smoothly?

Evaluation Criteria

An analysis of a literary work

1. *cites the title and author*
2. *supplies a clear thesis statement*
3. *provides details to support the thesis statement*
4. *quotes accurately from the text, citing page and line numbers and using quotation marks*
5. *cites all secondary sources and uses quotation marks for sources quoted directly*
6. *organizes ideas clearly*
7. *has a strong ending*

Language Workshop HELP

Sentence combining: page 69.

Reaching All Students

Struggling Writers

Encourage students who are analyzing the same work to form a seminar group. Within the group, they can discuss ideas with people familiar with the work. This will help students having difficulty to refine and develop their ideas.

English Language Learners

Students learning English may have difficulty expressing abstract ideas about literature. It may help students to outline their ideas first and then dictate them into a recorder. If possible, listen to the tapes with the students and discuss places where the analysis seems faulty or the support for a point is insufficient.

Language Workshop

Sentence Combining

Read aloud the following sentences. How do they sound?

> Beowulf neared the dragon's cave. He let out a loud battle cry. The dragon rose. The dragon approached Beowulf. It was angry that a man had come to this fearful place. The dragon breathed melting fire and scorching smoke. Beowulf firmly held his sword and shield.

Something holds this scene back, making it stiff: the jerky rhythm of the sentences, which share a basic subject-verb structure. Combining some sentences makes the flow smoother, the action more continuous, and the ideas clearer.

> Beowulf neared the dragon's cave, letting out a loud battle cry. The dragon rose and approached Beowulf, for it was angry that a man had come to this fearful place. While Beowulf firmly held his sword and shield, the dragon breathed melting fire and scorching smoke.

Strategies for Combining Sentences

1. **Turn sentences into phrases.** Often you can turn a short sentence (*He let out a loud battle cry*) into a phrase and insert it into another sentence.

   Beowulf neared the dragon's cave, *letting out a loud battle cry.*

2. **Combine ideas.** When two or more sentences express similar ideas, you may be able to combine subjects, verbs, objects, or entire sentences with conjunctions like *and, but, or, for,* and *yet.*

   The dragon rose *and* approached Beowulf, *for* it was angry that a man had come to this fearful place.

3. **Subordinate ideas.** When two or more sentences express related ideas, create one sentence with a main clause and a subordinate (dependent) clause. To show the relationship between the clauses, you must add a connecting word (such as *although, because, that, who,* or *while*). Placing the subordinate clause first adds even more variety.

   While Beowulf firmly held his sword and shield, the dragon breathed melting fire and scorching smoke.

Writer's Workshop Follow-Up: Revision

Read aloud the essay you wrote for the Writer's Workshop on page 67. Do you hear any short, choppy sentences? Does the writing sound monotonous? Use the sentence-combining techniques you've just practiced to create dynamic action sequences, connect thoughts, and break up monotonous sentences. Read aloud your revisions to a peer reviewer: Do your combined sentences sound better? Do they make relationships between ideas clearer?

Technology HELP

See Language Workshop CD-ROM. *Key word entry: sentence combining.*

Language Handbook HELP

See Sentence Combining: page 1239.

Try It Out

Combine each pair of sentences below into one sentence.

1. The dragon's flaming breath scorched the shield. The shield melted at once.
2. Beowulf swung his sword at the fearsome dragon. Beowulf hit the dragon's impenetrable skin.
3. Then the dragon jumped away. It jumped with flames pouring out of its nostrils.
4. Beowulf faced the monster alone. Beowulf's sword had failed him.

OBJECTIVES

1. Develop strategies for combining sentences
2. Turn short sentences into phrases
3. Combine similar ideas
4. Subordinate ideas to express relationships

Resources

Workshop Resources

- Worksheet, p. 45

Language Workshop CD-ROM

- Sentence Combining

Try It Out

Possible Answers

1. The dragon's flaming breath scorched the shield, melting it at once.
2. Swinging his sword, Beowulf hit the fearsome dragon's impenetrable skin.
3. As the dragon jumped away, flames poured out of its nostrils.
4. Because his sword had failed him, Beowulf faced the monster alone.

Assessing Learning

Quick Check: Sentence Combining

Combine each pair of sentences into one.

1. **Beowulf must go to the mother's den. He will find Grendel's mother there.** [To find Grendel's mother, Beowulf must go to her den.]
2. **Beowulf jumps into the lake. He has all his armor on his back.** [Beowulf jumps into the lake with all his armor on his back.]
3. **He sees Grendel's mother. She is a hideous creature.** [He sees Grendel's mother, a hideous creature.]
4. **His sword does not wound her. It cannot cut through her tough skin.** [Because it cannot cut through her tough skin, his sword cannot wound her.]
5. **Beowulf throws away his useless sword. He wrestles her with his bare hands.** [Beowulf throws away his useless sword and wrestles her with his bare hands.]

Objectives

1. Develop strategies to analyze and evaluate news features
2. Identify the sources of news
3. Recognize the writer's point of view
4. Recognize the writer's motivation
5. Evaluate credibility and context

Using the Strategies

1. The writer's target is the *Los Angeles Times*.
2. The writer wants to convince the reader that her point of view is the only correct one.
3. She appeals to readers' intellects.
4. Possible answers: The tone is critical, sarcastic, and disgruntled.
5. Possible answers: "curiously flaccid"; "gutless form of journalism"; "How much intelligence does it take"; "That'll help."
6. Based on her tone, it seems that the writer is fairly liberal in her politics and supports taxes used to help schools, parks, etc.

Reading for Life

Evaluating a News Feature

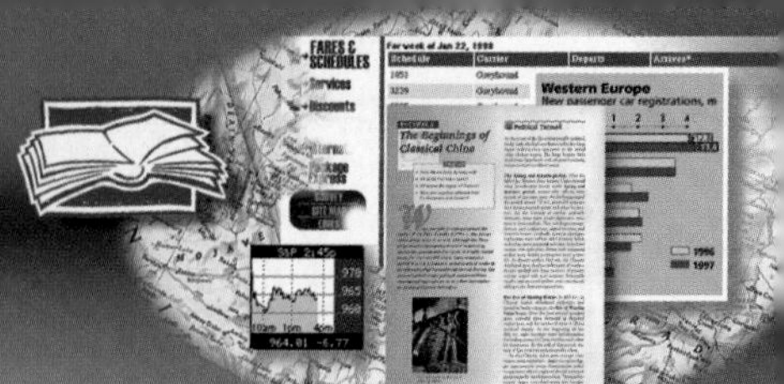

Situation

In the Middle Ages, when people heard any news at all, they heard it randomly, from bards and other travelers. Today we can read many newspapers daily; we can also read electronically transmitted news almost instantaneously on the Internet. As we read news, we should apply analytic and evaluative strategies.

Strategies

What is the source of the news?

- Identify the ownership of the newspaper or the sponsorship of the Web site.

Is the news article signed? If it is, be aware of the writer's stance.

- Does the writer or reporter have a reputation for objectivity, or fairness, or is the writer known as an advocate of a certain political, social, or economic point of view?

Recognize the writer's motivation.

- Does the writer want to inform, entertain, or persuade readers? Does the writer have two or even more purposes?

Evaluate credibility and context.

- If the writer's credentials are not cited, how can you find out who he or she is?
- Does the writer present both sides of an issue? Does the writer present facts that sufficiently support the main ideas and make the opinions believable?
- Does the writer present the information in a logical, convincing way, or does he or she appeal mainly to emotions?

Analyze the tone.

- What is the overall tone? Is it serious, sarcastic, or angry? Analyzing word choices and **connotations** can help you decide.

What California Wrought All Over Itself

MOLLY IVINS

LOS ANGELES— . . . Perhaps I wrong the *Los Angeles Times*, but it seems to me that its recent retrospective on the 20th anniversary of Prop 13, California's original "tax revolt" initiative, was curiously flaccid. It was a throwback to that gutless form of journalism we used to excuse by calling it "objective"; one side said this and the other side says that, therefore we will give them both equal space. The much-maligned *San Francisco Chronicle* actually did a far better job than the august *Times* in its three-part series on the anniversary of Prop 13.

How much intelligence does it take to conclude that Prop 13 has been a disaster for the state? For that matter, how much objectivity does it take? The results of Prop 13 are easily quantified. The state has almost doubled in population since the early '60s. In the last two decades, it has built 20 new prisons but not one new campus of the University of California. Freeways, libraries, parks, and schools (above all the schools) are battered, dilapidated, shrunken. And in the eerie new politics of California that Shrag calls "neopopulist," the voters are about to respond by outlawing bilingual education. That'll help. . . .

—*from the Star-Telegram*
Austin, Texas
May 27, 1998

Proposition 13 was on the ballot in California in 1978. It called for a rollback in property taxes, which are the main source of school financing. The proposition was approved.

Using the Strategies

Use these questions to evaluate the extract from a newspaper column above.

1. Who or what is the writer's target?
2. Does this writer give a balanced presentation of the issues? Or does she want to convince you of *one* point of view?
3. Does the writer appeal mostly to your intellect or to your emotions?
4. How would you describe the writer's tone?
5. What words and phrases indicate the writer's tone?
6. On the basis of the writer's tone, what can you surmise about her politics?

Extending the Strategies

Analyze and evaluate a news article in a local or national newspaper or magazine.

Crossing the Curriculum

Social Studies

Freedom of the press is guaranteed by the Constitution, but the role of the press has grown and changed in the years since the Bill of Rights was ratified. Divide the class into groups to research the role of the journalist in American history. Some possibilities for research include John Peter Zenger, the Muckrakers, William Randolph Hearst, *The Washington Post* during Watergate, and the influence of the Internet today. Groups should prepare a presentation outlining the social and political times and the impact of the journalists' work on changing how the public thinks about and views the world.

Learning for Life

Analyzing Groups

Problem
The early Anglo-Saxons found a sense of community in close-knit kinship groups. How do groups function in your world?

Project
Analyze the way a group that you belong to works. The group might be a family or one that you work with on projects at school. Or it might be a community group of some kind. What is the purpose of the group? How does the group solve problems? How do various people work within the group? What are the advantages and disadvantages of being part of a group?

Preparation
1. From the various groups to which you belong—at home, at school, at work, or through a religious or volunteer organization—choose one that has had a significant effect on you.
2. Determine the purpose of the group.
3. Analyze what the group members have in common, how they recognize and build on one another's strengths, and how their interrelationships affect the group's functioning.

Procedure
1. The next time the group gets together, observe how the members interact. How do they speak to and listen to one another, what roles do different members assume, and how does the group make decisions and work out compromises?
2. Jot down your impressions soon after the meeting. You don't need to use complete sentences—you might even sketch or doodle.

Presentation
Use one of the following formats (or another that your teacher approves):

1. **Say It in Pictures**
   Create a two-page photo-essay about the group for an illustrated magazine. Select photos that show how the group operates (be sure to include yourself in at least one), or take new ones if necessary. Write a caption to accompany each photo, and include a title that will draw readers into the essay. If you have access to desktop-publishing software, produce a camera-ready, or final, version of your photoessay.
2. **A Graphic Presentation**
   Present your analysis in the form of a graphic. (If you were working for a human resources group or a management consultant group, you would probably present your analysis this way.) Here are some possibilities: a flow chart showing how responsibilities are allocated and how projects are completed; a hierarchical chart showing the organization of the group and the responsibilities of various members; a problem-solution chart showing how problems are identified and resolved. Be sure to identify any glitches that you perceive in the ways the group functions.
3. **Talking About Community**
   With three to five other students, present a panel discussion on the various ways in which people build a sense of community. Panel members should represent a variety of groups, such as a family, a neighborhood organization, a sports team, a service club. Meet with the other panel members to phrase a discussion question, prepare a discussion outline, and elect a leader. Hold the discussion in front of an audience, such as the rest of the class or the parent-teacher organization.

Processing
What did you learn from this activity about how you and your classmates feel about groups and group projects? What are some of the needs met by groups in your community? Write a brief reflection for your portfolio.

OBJECTIVES
1. Analyze group structure and dynamics
2. Identify the purpose of a group
3. Recognize problem-solving mechanisms within a group

Resources
Viewing and Representing
HRW Multimedia Presentation Maker
Students may wish to use the *Multimedia Presentation Maker* to create their photo essays.

Grading Timesaver
Rubrics for this Learning for Life project appear on p. 96 of the *Portfolio Management System.*

Developing Workplace Competencies

Preparation	Procedure	Presentation
• Processes information • Reasons • Communicates ideas and information	• Acquires data • Interprets information • Evaluates data	• Thinks creatively • Makes decisions • Designs systems • Applies technology to specific tasks

OBJECTIVES

1. Read literature from the Middle Ages on the subject of "The Gift of Story"
2. Interpret literary elements with special emphasis on ballads, imagery, couplets, and the romance
3. Apply a variety of reading strategies, including determining meanings by analyzing word parts
4. Respond to the literature in a variety of modes
5. Learn and use new words
6. Learn about the evolution and characteristics of Middle English
7. Plan, draft, revise, edit, proof, and publish a compare/contrast essay
8. Identify and correct common agreement problems
9. Demonstrate the ability to analyze a film or play review
10. Evaluate technological advances

Illumination from *Le Roman de Lancelot du Lac* (detail) (early 14th century). Guinevere, queen of Britain, and attendants watching a tournament from a tower. MS 806, fol.262.

The Middle Ages 1066–1485

72

Selection Readability

This Annotated Teacher's Edition provides a summary of each selection in the student book. Following each Summary heading, you will find one, two, or three small icons. These icons indicate, in an approximate sense, the reading level of the selection.

■ One icon indicates that the selection is easy.

■■ Two icons indicate that the selection is on an intermediate reading level.

■■■ Three icons indicate that the selection is challenging.

Responding to the Art

Le Roman de Lancelot du Lac was an early fourteenth-century French manuscript with stunning illuminations on the life of Lancelot, the leading knight at King Arthur's court.

Activity. Have students tell exactly what they *see* in this illustration. Ask them if the illustration represents their previous knowledge of culture and society in the Middle Ages, including social activities, lifestyles, roles of the sexes, dress, and behavior. How does this scene suggest both violence and culture?

Resources

Viewing and Representing

Videocassette A, Segment 4
Available in English and Spanish.
Use the video to introduce students to the culture of chivalry and to explore the history of knighthood. For full lesson plans and worksheets, see the *Visual Connections Teacher's Manual.*

Videocassette A, Segment 1
Available in Spanish and English.
Use the video to introduce students to Middle English. For full lesson plans and worksheets, see the *Visual Connections Teacher's Manual.*

Resources: Print and Media

Viewing and Representing
- *Visual Connections*
  Videocassette A, Segments 1, 4

Assessment
- *Formal Assessment,* p. 15
- *Preparation for College Admission Exams,* p. 5
- *Test Generator (One-Stop Planner CD-ROM)*

Internet
- go.hrw.com (keyword: LE0 12-2)

OBJECTIVES

1. Understand the historical and social forces that shaped the Middle Ages
2. Identify the influence of history on the literary works of the Middle Ages
3. Take notes and discuss the concept of loyalty in today's world
4. Read and understand a time line

Responding to the Quotation

C. S. Lewis (1898–1963) was a great medievalist who taught at Oxford and Cambridge. Students will know him as the author of the Narnia books. You might ask if this description fits our stereotyped image of the Middle Ages. You might also ask what more modern inventions would have appealed to this systematic medieval mind. [computers]

RESPONDING TO THE ART

The Romance of the Rose is one of the most important medieval **allegories** (a story with personified virtues and vices). Written in France, it enjoyed enormous success both there and in England, where Geoffrey Chaucer translated part of it. In this dream-poem, the poet goes to the Garden of Delight, where he meets Rose, his courtly love. Allegorical characters include Idleness, Pleasure, Shame, and Evil Tongue.

Activity. After students have described what they see in this exquisite garden scene, ask them to look for these colors: green, which signified new love, and blue, which symbolized fidelity. The enclosed garden symbolized virginity. Note the fruit on the trees, symbolizing fertility.

The Middle Ages

by David Adams Leeming

At his most characteristic, medieval man was not a dreamer nor a wanderer. He was an organizer, a codifier, a builder of systems. He wanted "a place for everything and everything in the right place." Distinction, definition, tabulation were his delight. Though full of turbulent activities, he was equally full of the impulse to formalize them. War was (in intention) formalized by the art of heraldry and the rules of chivalry; sexual passion (in intention), by the elaborate code of love. . . . There was nothing which medieval people liked better, or did better, than sorting out and tidying up. Of all our modern inventions I suspect that they would most have admired the card index.

—C. S. Lewis

Illumination from a French manuscript of *Romance of the Rose* (15th century).
British Library, London.

go.hrw.com
LEO 12-Middle Ages

Using Students' Strengths

Visual Learners
Have visual learners use the various pieces of art included in this introductory essay to make some generalizations about life in the Middle Ages. You might, however, remind students that art throughout the ages has often been produced by or for those with the greatest advantages and does not always reflect the full range of classes, human activity, or day-to-day life.

Verbal Learners
As they read this collection, have students work in groups of four or five to produce medieval newspapers. Suggest that groups include a news or feature article on the Norman Conquest, feudalism, the plague, Geoffrey Chaucer, chivalry, and heraldry. Students can also include ads for such essential medieval products as longbows, rat poison, books on writing love poetry, or maps of the Holy Land. Remind students to consult the time line for dates.

In October 1066, a daylong battle near Hastings, England, changed the course of history. There, just ten miles from the channel dividing England from France, Duke William of Normandy, France, defeated and killed King Harold of England, the last of the Anglo-Saxon kings. So began the Norman Conquest, an event that radically affected English history, the English character, and the English language. Unlike the Romans, the Normans never withdrew from England.

Who was this William the Conqueror? He was the illegitimate son of the previous duke of Normandy, who was in turn a cousin of the English king called Edward the Confessor. Edward had died childless earlier in 1066, and Harold, the earl of Wessex, had been crowned the following day. But William claimed that the old king had promised the throne to him. Determined to seize what he considered rightfully his, William sailed the English Channel with an enormous army. **A**

William was an efficient and ruthless soldier, but he wanted to rule the Anglo-Saxons, not eliminate them. Today, as a result, rather than a Norman, French-speaking England (and America), we find a culture and a language that combine Norman and Anglo-Saxon elements. To the Anglo-Saxons' more democratic and artistic tendencies, the Normans brought administrative ability, an emphasis on law and order, and cultural unity.

One of William's great administrative feats was an inventory of nearly every piece of property in England—land, cattle, buildings—in the Domesday Book. (The title suggests a comparison between William's judgment of his subjects' financial worth and God's final judgment of their moral worth.) For the first time in European history, people could be taxed based on what they owned. **B**

Although the Normans did not erase Anglo-Saxon culture, they did bring significant changes to England. William and many of his successors remained dukes of Normandy as well as kings of England. The powerful Anglo-Norman entity they molded brought England into mainstream European civilization in a new way. For example, William divided the holdings of the fallen English landowners **C**

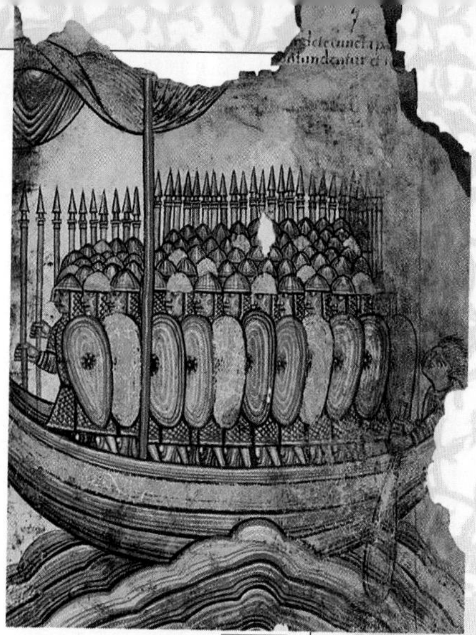

Norman warriors crossing the Channel in 1066, from a French manuscript (11th century). MS N.a. Lat. 1390, fol. 7.

© cliché Bibliothèque Nationale de France, Paris.

October 14, 1066, was one of the decisive days of history. The battle itself was nip and tuck; the shift only of a few elements here or there, a gift of luck could have given the victory to the Anglo-Saxons. If Harold had won at Hastings and had survived, William would have had no choice but to renounce his adventure. There is little likelihood that anyone would have attempted a serious invasion of England during the next millennium—by water, at least. England would have strengthened its bonds with Scandinavia while remaining distrustful of the western Continent—even more distrustful than it is today. The native Anglo-Saxon culture would have developed in unimaginable ways, and William the Conqueror would be dimly known in history only as William the Bastard.

—Morris Bishop

A Exploring the Historical Period

William the Conqueror

William of Malmesbury, one of the greatest English chroniclers, says of William the Conqueror: "He was of just stature, extraordinary corpulence, fierce countenance: his forehead bare of hair; of such strength of arm that it was often a matter of surprise that no one was able to draw his bow which he himself could bend when his horse was on full gallop: he was majestic whether sitting or standing, although the protuberance of his belly deformed his royal person. . . ."

B Exploring the Historical Period

The *Domesday Book*

The work was called a description of England, but the name *Domesday Book,* which means "Doomsday Book," was in general use by the mid-twelfth century. Its name implies not only a judgment of worth but also the fact that all are judged without bias.

C Exploring the Historical Period

Fundamental Political Changes

When William conquered England, he assumed every bit of property was his. All those who had supported King Harold lost their holdings, which William parceled out to two hundred or so Norman lords. As was customary in those times, the lords swore loyalty to William in exchange for the land. This was the beginning of William's centralized government in England. Over time, the power of monarchs in England would diminish as the role of Parliament increased, but the importance of a centralized government would endure.

Professional Notes

Cultural Connections: The *Domesday Book*

This massive survey, written in Latin in red and black ink, was significant because it helped to solidify the feudal system. The survey was managed by seven to eight panels of commissioners who compiled detailed accounts by geographic area of the manors, serfs, huts, mills, fishponds, and streams. Naturally, the nobles resented this survey, but it established a social hierarchy that was recognized for centuries. Today, the *Domesday Book* is on display at the Public Record Office in Chancery Lane, London.

Time Line

This time line shows major events that occurred between the Norman Conquest and the crowning of the first Tudor king of England, Henry VII.

• **1100–1149**

The Epic: A Characteristic Literary Form

Several literary forms were important during the Middle Ages, including the romance and the allegory, but one of the most characteristic early forms was the epic. A long narrative poem on a serious subject, strongly rooted in one society, an **epic** centers on a heroic figure whose actions affect the well-being of an entire group. The greatest of the French epics was *The Song of Roland,* which presents the legends of Charlemagne and his knights. Like the legend of King Arthur and his knights of the Round Table in Britain, it contains exaggerated praise of the past, intervention by supernatural beings, prophetic omens, and a hero who embodies Christian culture.

A Lack of Written Records

Ask students why more of the dates are marked *c.* (*circa,* approximately) in the first half of the time line. [Record keeping became more common and accurate in later time periods.] Students might note that as history moves toward a period of greater historical documentation, so, too, it moves away from the anonymous or group authorship and toward attributed authorship.

• **1100–1249**

Effects of the Crusades

The knights who joined the Crusades had a number of goals. They wanted to free Jerusalem from Turkish control, fight a holy war, and perhaps return with gold and riches. Although they never succeeded completely in their efforts, the Crusades changed European culture in many ways. They helped bring to the West the fruits of Islamic scholarship, technology, and medicine. The Crusades weakened feudalism by causing the deaths of many knights and the destruction of the nobles' holdings at home. The weakening of the nobles increased the power of the kings. Also, the increase in trade stimulated the growth of towns where people could live outside the feudal order.

The Middle Ages, 1066–1485

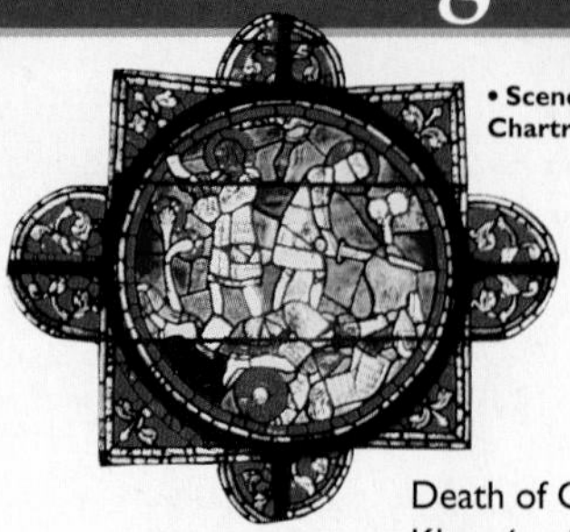

• Scene from the *Story of Roland,* from Chartres Cathedral, France (13th century).

	1066–1099	1100–1149	1150–1199	1200–1249
LITERARY EVENTS		Death of Omar Khayyám, Persian poet and astronomer, 1131 French heroic poem, *Song of Roland,* written, c. 1100	In France, Chrétien de Troyes writes *Lancelot,* c. 1170s In Spain, first mass production of paper, c. 1150	Marie de France, first known European woman to write narrative poetry, dies, c. 1216 Persian poet Saadi born, 1213 Beginnings of German epic poem, the *Nibelungenlied,* c. 1200
CULTURAL/HISTORICAL EVENTS	King Edward the Confessor dies without heir, 1066 Duke of Normandy invades England, 1066 Domesday Book, a record of all land ownership in England, first compiled, 1086 Crusades begin, to free Jerusalem from Turkish control, 1095	Knights Templar, a religious order whose mission was to protect pilgrims to the Holy Land, founded, c. 1119	Construction begins on Cathedral of Notre Dame in Paris, 1163 Thomas à Becket murdered, 1170 Henry II invades Ireland, beginning nearly eight hundred years of British domination, 1171 Minamoto Yoritomo becomes first shogun (military ruler) of Japan, 1192	Mongol leader Genghis Khan invades China, 1211 English barons force King John to sign the Magna Carta, 1215 Pope Gregory IX begins the Inquisition, c. 1232

• A man and his wife on horseback, the wife riding pillion (on a cushioned saddle), from a book of hours (c. 1500).
British Library, London.

Using the Time Line

Have students use a print or nonprint encyclopedia or a database to place the following major events in world history on the time line and to write short descriptions of their significance.

- The Chinese build a mechanical clock. [1090: This early clock, driven by a waterwheel, is a significant advance in the measurement of time.]
- The kingdom of Mali emerges. [About 1235: Sundiata takes over the kingdom of Ghana and trading cities, promotes agriculture, and renews the gold-salt trade.]
- The Model Parliament is held. [1295: When Edward I needs to raise taxes for war against the French, he calls together burgesses and knights from every county to serve as a legislative group. This becomes a "model" for representative government.]

Musée Condé.

• From *Hours of the Duchess of Burgundy* (c. 1450).

Thomas Aquinas writes *Summa Theologica,* 1266–1273

Boccaccio writes the *Decameron,* 1349–1353

Geoffrey Chaucer born, c. 1343

Julian of Norwich, one of the first English women of letters, born, c. 1342

Petrarch crowned poet laureate in Italy, 1341

Development of Japanese Nōh plays, 1300s

Dante Alighieri begins writing the *Divine Comedy,* c. 1307

Chaucer begins *The Canterbury Tales,* c. 1387

Entire Bible translated into English for first time by followers of John Wycliffe, 1380

Legendary hero Robin Hood appears in *Piers Plowman,* c. 1378

Sir Gawain and the Green Knight written, c. 1375

Margery Kempe, author of first autobiography in English, born, c. 1373

Thomas Malory's *Le Morte Darthur* first printed by Caxton, 1485

William Caxton prints first book in English, c. 1475

First book printed with movable type by Gutenberg, 1455

In France, Christine de Pisan writes famous allegory, *Book of the City of Ladies,* 1405

Chaucer dies, 1400

1250–1299	1300–1349	1350–1399	1400–1485

First commoners allowed in British Parliament, c. 1250

Crusades end, 1270

• Marco Polo in Beijing.

Venetian traveler Marco Polo visits court of Kublai Khan in China, 1275

Edward I invades Scotland and declares himself king, 1296

Zimbabwe emerges as major trading empire, 1300s

Aztecs begin to establish empire in Mexico, 1325

Hundred Years' War between England and France begins, 1337

Black Death strikes England, 1348

English language used to open Parliament, 1362

• Chinese porcelain jar (15th century), Hsuan-te (Xuande) period, Ming dynasty.
The Metropolitan Museum of Art. Gift of Robert E. Tod, 1937. (37.191.1). Photograph by Schecter Lee. Photograph © 1986 The Metropolitan Museum of Art.

Ming dynasty begins 300-year rule of China, 1368

Peasants' Revolt in England, 1381

King Richard II deposed, 1399

Benin Kingdom in West Africa flourishes, 1400s

In France, Joan of Arc burned at the stake by the English, 1431

Inca Empire established in Peru, c. 1438

Italian inventor and artist Leonardo da Vinci born, 1452

War between the Houses of York and Lancaster (also called the Wars of the Roses), 1455–1485

Birth of Nicolaus Copernicus, European astronomer, 1473

Martin Luther born in Germany, 1483

First Tudor king, Henry VII, is crowned, 1485

• Wooden helmet of an Aztec warrior.
© British Museum, London.

Using the Time Line

- Osman, whose followers come to be called Ottomans, builds a small state in Anatolia. [1300–1326: This is the beginning of the Ottoman Empire.]
- Ibn Battuta visits most of the countries of the Islamic world. [mid-1300s: Born in Tangier in North Africa, Ibn Battuta becomes an early historian of the African Islamic world.]

- **1250–1299**

Summa Theologica
This work by Thomas Aquinas is hugely important because it applies the reasoning of the ancient Greeks, especially Aristotle, to Christian doctrines.

- **1300–1349**

Dante's *Divine Comedy*
One of the greatest writers of the Middle Ages was Dante Alighieri, whose *Divine Comedy* is ranked with the works of Shakespeare and Homer. It presents a clear and developed medieval world view, including its art, science, religion, and philosophy.

- **1350–1399**

The Rise of the English Language
? What two events on this time line demonstrate that English was beginning to be accepted in England as the language of learning and politics? [English was used to open Parliament in 1362, and the Bible was translated into English in 1380.]

- **1400–1485**

Developments in China
At the beginning of the fifteenth century, an extraordinary young Ming ruler named Yonglo launched great exploratory missions led by a Muslim admiral to learn about the outside world. Yonglo was also the emperor who built the palace known as the Forbidden City, whose nine thousand rooms served as the living quarters of the emperor, his family, and his court. One aspect of its splendor was its mystery: No foreigner or commoner was allowed to enter without special permission.

Joan of Arc and Women of the Middle Ages
As a teenage French girl who commanded troops and led them to victory during the Hundred Years' War, Joan of Arc was scarcely the typical woman of the Middle Ages. Yet she endured a punishment many women suffered: She was tried for witchcraft. Captured by her British enemies, she was given a trial that was probably more political than religious—the British were no doubt embarrassed by the victories of their female opponent.

Ⓐ Exploring the Historical Period

Feudal Loyalty

Oaths of fealty were the backbone of the feudal society. Solemn and unbreakable, these oaths were sworn by a vassal to his chosen lord. The lord, in return, expected faithfulness and service without deception. Often vassals made these pledges over religious relics; or with the vassal's hands between those of his lord, the sacred pledge would be sealed with a kiss. The oath might be similar to this one: "I promise by my faith that from this time forward I will be faithful to Count William and will maintain toward him my homage entirely against every man, in good faith and without any deception."

Ⓑ Background

Feudalism

The basic economic unit of feudalism, as a property system, was the manor. The lord of the manor and the serfs who worked it participated in an economic exchange: The lord provided the serfs with land, simple housing or huts, and protection from the wandering bandits of the Middle Ages. The serfs paid for these things with their services to the lord, which included maintaining his estate and providing him with a portion of what they grew. After paying what they owed to the lord, serfs also had to pay money to the Church. Like slaves, serfs could not leave the land they worked. Unlike slaves, they could not be bought and sold. Theirs was a life of hard labor and no luxury.

Ⓒ Background

The Hauberk

The hauberk was made of small metal discs sewn on linen. It was eventually replaced by chainmail, which was composed of interlocking iron rings.

An attack on a fortress, from a French manuscript (detail) (13th–14th century). MS Fr. 1604, fol. 57v.

© cliché Bibliothèque Nationale de France, Paris.

among his own followers. These men and their families brought to England not only a new language—French—but also a new social system—feudalism—which displaced the old Nordic social structure described in *Beowulf.*

The Anglo-Norman entity that resulted from the Norman Conquest brought England into mainstream European civilization, which included feudalism.

> . . . there was not one hide of land in England that he did not know who owned it, and what it was worth . . .
>
> —*from The Anglo-Saxon Chronicle*

Feudalism and Knighthood: Pyramid Power

Ⓐ Ⓑ More than simply a social system, feudalism was also a caste system, a property system, and a military system. Ultimately, it was based on a religious concept of hierarchy, with God as the supreme overlord. In this sense, even a king held land as a vassal

A CLOSER LOOK

A Terrible Worm in an Iron Cocoon

If we hear the term "medieval period," we inevitably think of knights and their magnificent suits of armor. During the early Middle Ages, armor consisted of a helmet, a shield, and a relatively flexible mail shirt, or hauberk, made of Ⓒ countless riveted or welded iron rings. With the crossbow, however, came the need for more protection, so the knight was forced to compromise flexibility and mobility for self-defense.

Held together by rivets, leather straps, hinges, turning pins, buckles, and pegs, a suit of armor replaced mail as the warrior's chief protection. Knights wore a heavily padded undergarment of leather and a mail shirt under the armor, in addition to plate arm, leg, and foot pieces. Mail covered the neck, elbows, and other joints, and gauntlets constructed of linked plates covered the hands. Some suits of armor weighed 120 pounds and contained 200 custom-fitted iron plates. The knight also carried a variety of weapons: lance, dagger, sword, battle-ax, and club-headed mace.

The threat of death in battle was bad enough, but the armor itself could also be fatal—causing death from suffocation, heart failure, even drowning. Battle during hot weather was particularly difficult. Since small slits in the helmet allowed only a limited line of vision and little ventilation, heatstroke—often deadly for the knight—was common. One anonymous poem describes the armored knight as "a terrible worm in an iron cocoon."

Crossing the Curriculum

Art

The tradition of armorial bearings, or coats of arms, was developed to help make clear who the knight was inside the cocoon of armor. Originally a cloth tunic worn over the armor but also an actual shield, the coat of arms is a highly stylized record of family descent, alliances, property, or profession. The shield, or escutcheon, is divided into nine points or sections and split into a sinister (left) side and a dexter (right) side. In a heraldic emblem, the gentlemen's helmet, mantle, crest, and family motto appear above the shield. Only five colors can be used in heraldry: red, azure, sable, green, and purple. Have students develop a poster illustrating a coat of arms, labeled with the specialized terms and the various colors. Students could also create a coat of arms for themselves as individuals or for the class.

by "divine right." A king as powerful as William the Conqueror could stand firmly at the top of the pyramid. He could appoint certain barons as his immediate vassals, allotting them portions of his land in return for their economic or military allegiance—or both. In turn, the barons could appoint vassals of their own. The system operated all the way down to the landless knights and to the serfs, who were not free to leave the land they tilled.

The feudal system did not always work. Secure in a well-fortified castle, a vassal might choose not to honor his obligations to a weak overlord. The ensuing battles between iron-clad knights around moated castles account for one of the enduring images of the Middle Ages. **D**

> The bond between lord and vassal was affirmed or reaffirmed by the ceremony of homage. The vassal knelt, placed his clasped hands within those of his master, declared, "Lord, I become your man," and took an oath of fealty. The lord raised him to his feet and bestowed on him a ceremonial kiss. The vassal was thenceforth bound by his oath "to love what his lord loved and loathe what he loathed, and never by word or deed do aught that should grieve him."
>
> —Morris Bishop

Yet the feudal system did carry with it a sense of form and manners that permeated the life, art, and literature of the Middle Ages. This sense of formalism came to life most fully in the institution of knighthood and in the related practice, or code, of chivalry. **E**

We cannot think of the medieval period without thinking of knights. Since the primary duty of males above the serf class was military service to their lords, boys were trained from an early age to become warriors. Often, their training took place in houses other than their own, to be sure that the training was strict. When a boy's training was completed,

Only aristocratic knights could afford the huge cost of armor, a war horse, packhorses, a mount to ride when not in battle, and servants. Because of the armor's weight and the complex fittings required to piece it together, a knight couldn't dress himself for battle. In fact, battles were usually scheduled to allow the warring knights time to be dressed. Servants stood by during battle in case the knight was unhorsed. An armored knight on his back was like an upside-down turtle trying to get on its feet. In this position, the knight was vulnerable to his adversary. If he fell into a shallow body of water, he could drown.

During the fifteenth century, the knight and his horse were considered invulnerable. But this role changed dramatically when the longbow and later the musket ball came into warfare. When his armor could no longer protect him in battle, the knight in shining armor became more of a courtier than a combatant. In the last years of their existence, knights participated in exhibitions rather than in warfare.

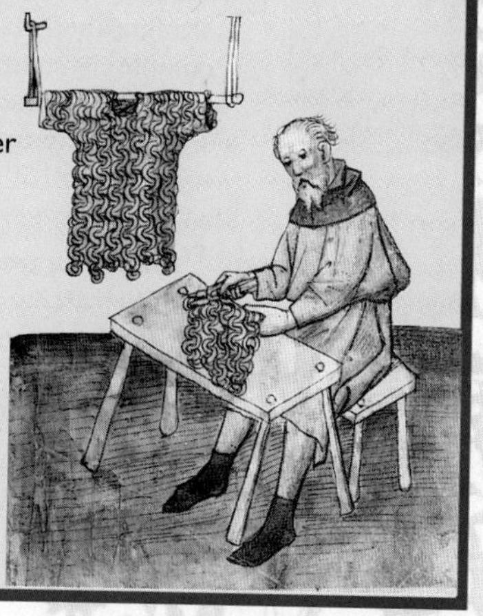

Chain-mail maker.
Stadtbibliothek, Nürnberg.

D Literary Connections

A Voice from Turbulent Times

One of the few female literary voices of the Middle Ages that survived was that of Margaret Paston. The wife of a wealthy noble, Paston wrote letters describing, among other things, ways in which others did not honor feudal obligations, attacks on her own manor, and uncertainty about her future and the safety of her lands and possessions. Her letters have been collected in *Private Life in the Fifteenth Century: Illustrated Letters of the Paston Family.*

E Background

Chivalry

The word *chivalry* comes from French and is related to *cheval,* the word for "horse." In French, a *chevalier* was a knight who rode a horse. In France, as in England, riding was an important skill for any knight, and a common image we preserve today is of knights galloping at full tilt, lance in hand. Yet chivalry was about much more than horseback riding, or even skill in battle. Chivalry was, in fact, a complete code of conduct. The knight's first obligation was to defend his lord, the king, and the Christian faith, but the code also covered how to treat a lady, how to help others, and how to resist the urge to run away if captured.

Getting Students Involved

Cooperative Learning

Social Pyramids. Have students work in groups of three or four to create visual representations of society in the Middle Ages. Each group should create a medieval social pyramid, with serfs at its base, other classes in its middle layers, and the king at the top. For each layer of the pyramid, ask students to create an image or icon. Ask one student to represent the group's work, but ask all students to write a paragraph explaining their individual contributions to the group effort.

Enrichment Activity

Notes from an Armored Knight. Students might enjoy writing a paragraph or more from a knight's point of view. Their writing should explain the process of putting on or the experience of trying to move around in fifty or more pounds of armor.

Ⓐ Exploring the Historical Period

From Boy to Knight

Although there was a great need for knights, not every boy could be one. For one thing, his parents had to be rich enough to buy him a horse, armor, and weapons. Knights were often the sons of nobles. (Chaucer, though born into a middle-class family, was educated as a knight in a noble household.) A knight's education began at approximately age seven, with instruction in good manners and social skills, such as singing, dancing, and playing chess. Young boys also began to learn to use a sword and shield at this time. At about age fourteen, a boy became a squire, a kind of personal servant to a knight. In the Prologue to *The Canterbury Tales,* students will meet a knight traveling with his son, a squire.

Ⓑ Cultural Connections

Women's Status in the Middle Ages

Even the Church viewed women as inferior to men. Women had no authority in the Church and could not serve on the altar. During the Middle Ages, the Church took further steps to diminish women's status by reclaiming convents and monasteries that had been founded or supported by noblewomen.

RESPONDING TO THE ART

Activity. Ask students how, in the three pieces of art on pp. 80–81, the roles of medieval women and men differ. [Possible responses: The women are helping the men prepare for battle, going off to work, and watching a joust. The upper-class women stay out of the fray, but the peasant woman shares the center of the illustration with her husband, who, it must be added, is doing the pushing while his wife sits more or less comfortably holding the wine.]

A medieval knight in armor. MS 42130, fol. 202v.

By permission of the British Library, London.

Ⓐ he was "dubbed," or ceremonially tapped on his shoulder (originally a hard, testing blow). Once knighted, the youth became a man with the title "sir" and the full rights of the warrior caste.

Knighthood was grounded in the feudal ideal of loyalty, and it entailed a complex system of social codes. Breaking any one of those codes would undermine not only the knight's position but also the very institution of knighthood. Thus, in the story of *Sir Gawain and the Green Knight* (page 159), his code of honor binds Gawain to accept a challenge that he believes will bring him certain death.

Feudalism was a pyramid system based on a religious concept of hierarchy. Expected to serve as warriors, males above the serf class were trained as knights.

Women in Medieval Society: No Voice, No Choice

Ⓑ Since they were not soldiers, women had no political rights in a system that was primarily military. A woman was always subservient to a man, whether husband, father, or brother. Her husband's or father's social

Professional Notes

A Critic's Comment: The Middle Ages

J. Huizinga describes life in the Middle Ages: "Illness and health presented a more striking contrast; the cold and darkness of winter were more real evils. Honours and riches were relished with greater avidity and contrasted more vividly with the surrounding misery. We, at the present day, can hardly understand the keenness with which a fur coat, a good fire on the hearth, a soft bed, a glass of wine were formerly enjoyed."

Everything was more pronounced and public: "Lepers sounded their rattles and went about in processions, beggars exhibited their deformity and their misery in churches. Every order and estate, every rank and profession, was distinguished by its costume. The great lords never moved about without a glorious display of arms and liveries, exciting fear and envy."

Off for a day of haying, a peasant pushes his wife to work in a wheelbarrow. MS Lat. 1173, fol. 4v.

© cliché Bibliothèque Nationale de France, Paris.

standing determined the degree of respect she commanded. For peasant women, life was a ceaseless round of childbearing, housework, and hard fieldwork. Women of higher station were occupied with childbearing and household supervision. Such women might even manage entire estates while their men were away on business or at war, but the moment the men returned, the women relinquished their temporary powers.

Women in the Middle Ages had no political rights. A woman's social standing depended completely on her husband's or father's status. (C)

> A woman is a worthy wight:
> She serveth a man both daye and nyght;
> Thereto she putteth all her might,
> And yet she hathe but care and woe.
>
> —Anonymous (fifteenth century)

Chivalry and Courtly Love: Ideal but Unreal

Chivalry was a system of ideals and social codes governing the behavior of knights and gentlewomen. (D) Among its precepts were adhering to one's oath of loyalty to the overlord and observing certain rules of warfare, such as never attacking an unarmed opponent. In addition, adoring a particular lady (not necessarily one's wife) was seen as a means of achieving self-improvement.

Universitätsbibliothek, Heidelberg.

Noblewomen watching a tournament, from a German manuscript (c. 14th century). Cod. Pal. Germ. 848, Codex Manesse, fol. 52v.

(C) Cultural Connections

Women and Power

Women could wield power when the lord of the castle was off fighting somewhere else and their own castle was attacked. In that case, the noblewoman might act as a military commander or even a warrior. At the very least, she might hurl boiling water, hot sand, or stones at the castle's attackers.

(D) Cultural Connections

Chivalry's Lasting Influence

In *The Middle Ages,* Morris Bishop describes how the system of chivalry influences us still: "In time the chivalric code was modified, but it has never died. It set a standard for upper-class behavior, especially in the Victorian era. Our esteem for sentimental love is a medieval relic. 'Women and children come first' is a chivalric motto. When the *Titanic* sank and the gentlemen bowed the ladies into the lifeboats, they were 'verray parfit gentil knights.'"

Making the Connections

Cultural Connections: Feudal Japan and England

Have students compare and contrast Japanese feudal society during the warrior-states era (1467–1568) with English feudal society. Students should discover who was the equivalent of the king (the emperor) and the lords (the daimyo, or warrior-chieftains); how Japanese castles, "knights" on horseback (the samurai), and armor compared with their English feudal counterparts; and how the Japanese code of *bushido* compared with European chivalry. (Alternatively, students might investigate a similar system of feudalism that existed in China during the Zhou Dynasty.)

Ⓐ Exploring the Historical Period

The Middle Ages: A Time of Change

Although the Renaissance is commonly regarded as the period of greatest change in Europe, the Middle Ages was also a time of rebirth or renewal. In fact, the events of the Middle Ages constituted a rebirth of society after the collapse of the Roman Empire. As Brian Wilk and James Hurt write in an essay called "The Middle Ages," the "formidable challenge to the early Middle Ages was to find a mode of social organization to replace the Roman Empire and to weave together the various threads of European culture: the remnants of Latin civilization, Christianity, and the northern, Germanic, 'barbarian' tradition. The solution that gradually emerged over a period of several centuries lay in two institutions, the Roman church and feudalism." They add that "the fixed hierarchy of the medieval church was mirrored in feudalism, the secular social and economic system that gradually emerged to replace the fallen Empire. Feudalism originated in the human need to band together for mutual protection in a lawless and chaotic age. Inhabitants of a particular region placed themselves under the protection of the most powerful local lord and in return for his military protection pledged certain services. Like the church, feudalism echoed certain aspects of the Roman Empire, notably the custom of clients gathering around wealthy patrons, but it also drew heavily upon the Germanic social organization, in which warriors gathered around a powerful chieftain, to whom they were bound by a complex system of obligations and rewards."

> We may still see on illumined screens the knight, with a change of clothing and locale. He has gone Western, but still he is the dextrous cavalier, vaulting to his saddle, the mighty fighter for virtue, ill educated but possessed of a salty wisdom, worshipful, faithful, and tongue-tied in the presence of good women.
>
> —Morris Bishop

The idea that revering and acting in the name of a lady would make a knight braver and better was central to one aspect of chivalry, courtly love. Courtly love was, in its ideal form, nonsexual. A knight might wear his lady's colors in battle, he might glorify her in words and be inspired by her, but the lady always remained pure and out of reach. She was "set above" her admirer, just as the feudal lord was set above his vassel. Since such a concept flew in the face of human nature, it provided built-in drama for poets and storytellers, as the King Arthur sagas illustrate. When Sir Lancelot and Queen Guinevere, for example, cross the line between courtly and physical love, the whole social system represented by Arthur's Round Table collapses. Camelot crumbles.

Chivalry brought about an idealized attitude toward women, but it did little to improve their actual position. A woman's perceived value remained tied to the value of the lands she brought to a marriage. But chivalry did give rise to a new form of literature, the romance (page 167). The greatest English example of the genre is *Sir Gawain and the Green Knight.* Wandering minstrels told many other romances, but most of them were the equivalents of *dum-de-dum* doggerel verse today.

Chivalry led to an idealized attitude toward women and gave rise to a new form of literature, the romance.

The Middle Ages: Four Centuries of Change

Ⓐ These characteristics distinguished the Middle Ages:

- The Norman Conquest of England created a powerful Anglo-Norman entity and brought England into the mainstream of European civilization.
- The feudal system centralized military, political, and economic power in the Crown.
- The Roman Church transcended national boundaries and fostered cultural unity among Europeans.
- The rise of towns and cities freed people to pursue their own commercial and artistic interests.
- The Magna Carta weakened the political power of the Church and laid the groundwork for later English constitutional law.
- Exposure to Eastern civilization as a result of the Crusades broadened Europeans' intellectual horizons.
- The ideals of chivalry improved attitudes toward, but not the rights of, women.
- The rise of the yeoman class paved the way for democracy in England.
- The bubonic plague created a labor shortage that contributed to the end of feudalism and to the passing of the Middle Ages.

The New City Classes: Out from Under the Overlords

For the most part, medieval society centered around the feudal castle, but as the population grew, an increasing number of people lived in towns and cities. Eventually, those population centers would render the feudal system obsolete.

The development of the city classes—lower, middle, and upper-middle—is evident in the works of Geoffrey Chaucer (page 98). Many of his characters make

Crossing the Curriculum

Science/Health

Have students produce posters showing the cycle involved in the spread of plague and on the difference between bubonic, pneumonic, and septicemic plague. Other students could report on brushes with plague in the United States, curbed by quarantines and sanitation measures imposed by the U.S. Public Health Service. Finally, students could report on modern-day infectious diseases that threaten large numbers of people, like AIDS or the Ebola virus.

Fantasy Literature

A number of fantasy writers, such as Anne McCaffrey, in her chronicles of the planet Pern, and Marion Zimmer Bradley, in her stories of Darkover, include aspects of feudalism in their imaginary societies. Have interested students read one or more of their novels and compare the invented social systems to historical English feudalism.

Architecture

The rise of cities saw the rise of urban architecture. Have students report on Durham Cathedral, Winchester Cathedral, the Tower of London, and also on the wooden buildings that housed most of the populace and which eventually fed the Great Fire of London in 1666.

their livings outside the feudal system, and their horizons are defined not by any lord's manor but by such cities as London and Canterbury.

More important, the emerging merchant class had its own tastes in the arts and the ability to pay for what it wanted. Consequently, much medieval art is not aristocratic; it is middle class, even "people's art." The people of the cities were free, tied neither to the land nor to knighthood and chivalry. Their point of view was expressed in the ballads sung in alehouses and at firesides (page 90), in the mystery and miracle plays performed outdoors by the new guilds or craft unions, and even in the great cathedrals and municipal buildings that are synonymous with England to so many tourists today. B

Gradually population centers shifted to the cities, where people lived and worked outside of the feudal system.

The Great Happenings

Against the backdrop of the feudal system imported from the Continent, several specific events radically influenced the course of English history, as well as English literature.

The Crusades: Ho! for the Holy Land. In Chaucer's *Canterbury Tales,* we meet a knight who has fought in "heathen" places—along the Mediterranean Sea and in North Africa. The knight's adventures in the fourteenth

Scene from *Passages d' Outremer* (detail) (15th century), depicting the Crusaders' attack, in 1153, on Ascalon, a Muslim-held city on the coast of the Holy Land. MS Fr. 5594, fol. 157v.

© cliché Bibliothèque Nationale de France, Paris.

Responding to the Art

Ascalon fell to King Baldwin III in 1153, the Franks' last major conquest in the Holy Land. Ascalon, or Ashkelon, located in what is now southwestern Israel, was conquered fifty years after the struggle for the city began. Siege warfare was often used during the Crusades as invaders attempted to destroy a city's protective walls and block off its supplies. In encounters such as the siege of Jerusalem in 1099, moveable towers could be rolled up to the city's walls to raise attackers to the level of the city's defenders.

Activity. Have students speculate on the function of the mantelets shown in the lower right of the painting. [The rectangular boards act as shields through which a battering ram would be propelled against the town's walls. (See below.)]

B Literary Connections

Drama

Although no medieval dramas are included in this collection, students should be encouraged to research and read some of the great medieval plays. Not surprisingly, the dramas began in the Church: In an era when most of the population could not read, plays had enormous value as religious instruction. Typical medieval plays were the miracle plays, based on legends of the saints; the mystery plays, like the partly farcical *The Second Shepherd's Play,* based on biblical history; and the morality plays, allegories like *Everyman,* featuring personified virtues and vices. Among the mystery plays were passion plays, which reenacted events in the last week in the life of Jesus Christ. In England, the presentation of these plays was largely taken over by the trade guilds, which tended to perform the parts of the story that best represented the craft of their members. For example, bakers might reenact the Last Supper, while shipbuilders produced the story of Noah's Ark.

Getting Students Involved

Cooperative Learning

Under Siege. The artwork on this page provides some insight into medieval battle strategy. For example, while attacking a castle or conducting a siege, attackers would often use the protective screen, called a mantelet, that is shown in the lower right-hand corner. Have students form groups of four to investigate one of the following weapons: the trebuchet, the siege tower, the tortoise, the ballista, or the battering ram. Two group members should create a labeled drawing or model of the weapon, while the other two write a short essay explaining its features and use.

A Humanities Connections

Centers of Learning

The capture of rich Islamic cities exposed the Crusaders to a more sophisticated culture than they knew at home. Baghdad and Damascus had well-established public libraries until the thirteenth century, when they were destroyed. About 1340, Cairo was a wealthy city of almost half a million people and an important link in the spice trade. London, by contrast, had only fifty thousand inhabitants in the fifteenth century. Arab universities were also established before their European counterparts. Cairo's Al-Azhar University, founded about 970, is one of the oldest operating universities in the world. Oxford, the oldest university in Great Britain, was established in the twelfth century.

B Exploring the Historical Period

Henry II and Becket

Under Henry II, a system of common law was developed that forms the basis for British common law today. Common law applies to all the people of a country rather than to only certain classes of people. The conflict between Henry and Becket developed when Henry attempted to bring the Church under this common law system. Before this time, Church courts had dispensed mild forms of justice both for clergy and for learned men who claimed "benefit of clergy." Under "benefit of clergy," any person who was able to read could, in theory, commit a crime such as murder, claim the benefit, and receive a minor punishment, such as a jail sentence.

century were really an extension of the Crusades (1095–1270), a series of wars waged by European Christians against the Muslims, with Jerusalem and the Holy Land as the prize. Although the Europeans ultimately failed to hold Jerusalem, they benefited enormously from contact with the higher civilization of the Middle East. This contact with Eastern mathematics, astronomy, architecture, and crafts made possible the rich, varied life we find in Chaucer. If the Crusades produced Chaucer's fairly conventional Knight, they were also at least indirectly responsible for his lively Squire and elegant Prioress.

As a result of the Crusades, Christian Europe was exposed to the Middle East's sophisticated civilization.

The martyrdom of Thomas à Becket: Murder in the cathedral. When Chaucer's pilgrims set out for Canterbury, their goal was the shrine of Saint Thomas à Becket (c. 1118–1170). Thomas, a Norman, had risen to great power as chancellor (prime minister) under his friend King Henry II (reigned 1154–1189). At that time, all Christians belonged to the Catholic Church. Even King Henry was a vassal—of the pope, the head of the Church and God's representative. The pope in those days was enormously powerful and controlled most of the crowned heads of Europe. By appointing his trusted friend Thomas as archbishop of Canterbury (head of the Catholic Church in England), Henry hoped to gain the upper hand in disputes with the Church. But the independent and often combative Thomas took the pope's side more than once, infuriating the king. In December 1170, Henry raged, "Will no one rid me of

Martyrdom of Thomas Becket, from an English psalter (detail) (13th century). MS W34, fol. 15v.

The Walters Art Gallery, Baltimore.

Making the Connections

Cultural Connections: Islamic Contributions

Intellectually, the Middle East led the Middle Ages. The physician Rhazes wrote *Treatise on Smallpox and Measles,* the first accurate study of those infectious diseases. *The Canon of Medicine,* a medical encyclopedia by the physician Avicenna, accurately described many diseases and influenced European medical education for more than six hundred years. In the ninth century, the Baghdad teacher al-Khwarizmi wrote an influential mathematics book that was used as a textbook; the word *algebra* is derived from the Arabic title of his work. Arab astronomers also contributed to knowledge of mathematics as they adapted it to their own field; their contributions added to knowledge of trigonometry.

> Then the third knight inflicted a terrible wound as he lay, by which the sword was broken against the pavement, and the crown which was large was separated from the head; so that the blood white with the brain and the brain red with blood, dyed the surface of the virgin mother Church with the life and death of the confessor and martyr in the colors of the lily and the rose.
>
> —Thomas Grim, an eyewitness to Becket's death

this turbulent priest?" Taking his words literally, four of Henry's knights murdered Becket—right in his own cathedral. Public outrage at the murder led to devotion to St. Thomas the Martyr, and created a backlash against Henry, a significant setback for the monarchy in its power struggles with Rome. **C**

At its worst, this setback led to the kinds of liberties taken by several of the clergymen in *The Canterbury Tales*—corruption that the state was in no position to correct. Thus, Chaucer's Monk lives a life of luxury without regard to the poor, his Friar chases women and money, and his Summoner and his Pardoner blackmail people with threats of eternal damnation. **D**

Yet the medieval Church did have one positive effect: It fostered cultural unity—a system of belief and symbol that transcended the national cultures of Europe. The Church continued to be the center of learning. Its monasteries were the libraries and publishers of the time, and its language, Latin, remained the international language of educated Europeans. Its leader, the pope, was king of all kings—and his "kingdom" had no boundaries.

Public outrage at the political assassination of Thomas à Becket created a backlash against the English monarchy and weakened the king in his power struggle with Rome.

The Magna Carta: Power to (some of) the people. The event that most clearly heralded a return to older, democratic tendencies in England was the signing of the Magna Carta (the "Great Charter") by King John in 1215, at Runnymede. The vicious but pragmatic John was strongly backed by the pope, but the English barons forced him to sign the document. The signing was a defeat for central papal power. As aristocrats writing for aristocrats, the barons had no interest in the rights of the common people. But the Magna Carta later became the basis for English constitutional law, in which such rights as trial by jury and legislative taxation were established. **E**

> No freeman shall be taken, or imprisoned, or outlawed, or exiled, or in any way harmed, nor will we go upon him nor will we send upon him, except by the legal judgment of his peers or by the law of the land.
>
> To none will we sell, to none deny or delay, right or justice.
>
> —Magna Carta, Clauses 39 and 40

In 1215, English barons forced King John to sign the Magna Carta as an effort to curb the Church's power. The document later became the basis for English constitutional law.

C Literary Connections

Becket

T. S. Eliot's poetic drama *Murder in the Cathedral* (1935) is a play about the martyrdom of Becket.

D Critical Reading

Cause and Effect

? **How did the murder of Thomas à Becket lead to corruption within the Church?** [Public outrage caused a backlash against the king; therefore, when there were abuses within the Church, the king, who had lost power in this arena, could not use his influence to correct them.]

E Cultural Connections

King John and the Magna Carta

Students may call to mind images of King John if you tell them that he is portrayed as a prince or king in the Robin Hood films, including an animated version. Legendary for his cowardice and his attempts to squeeze money out of the poor, King John reluctantly safeguarded the nobles' feudal rights because he had almost no choice but to do so. In later years, the English would argue that certain clauses in the Magna Carta applied not just to nobles but to every citizen.

Professional Notes

Historical Connections: The Role of the Clergy

Medieval life was a life of contrasts and contradictions. According to historian J. Huizinga, one startling contradiction was the way people felt about the clergy and the Church. He maintains that throughout the Middle Ages there was an undercurrent of contempt for the clergy that contradicted the great respect shown toward the Church. The average peasant was disgusted by the chaste man who would not fight. Such a man did not fit the popular role model of a champion knight. The worldliness of the higher ranks of the clergy and the corruption of the lower ranks made the situation even worse. Hence, the nobles, merchants, and serfs often made "spiteful jests at the expense of the incontinent monk and the guzzling priest." Ask students to keep this in mind as they read Chaucer's work in this unit.

Ⓐ Exploring the Historical Period

Joan of Arc, Women, and Witchcraft

Perhaps the best-known figure to come out of the Hundred Years' War is the young, illiterate French peasant woman known in English as Joan of Arc (1412–1431). She persuaded the king of France to allow her to lead the French armies to fight the English. For almost two years she was incredibly successful, until she was captured in Burgundy and sold to the English. To escape responsibility for her death, the English turned her over to an ecclesiastical court, which found her guilty of crimes ranging from witchcraft to wearing men's clothes. Joan was burned to death. *Saint Joan,* written by Irish playwright George Bernard Shaw in 1923 and produced three years after Joan's canonization, explores how Joan's ideas were in conflict with the Church and feudal society.

Ⓑ Literary Connections

Agincourt

Shakespeare's play *Henry V* depicts the English yeomen with their longbows battling the French armies at Agincourt. The longbow was a much more flexible weapon than the heavy crossbow. A good archer could fire about twelve arrows from a longbow in the time it took to reload a crossbow. (For more information, see p. 87.)

A CLOSER LOOK

Fleas, Money, and Gunpowder: The End of an Era

The legendary pageantry, the codes of chivalry, the heroic quests undertaken by valiant knights in honor of fair ladies—these images come to mind at the mention of the Middle Ages. But what happened? Why did this period come to an end? Besides the plague's devastating effects, the development of a monetary system and the introduction of gunpowder contributed to changes in medieval England.

Before the eleventh century, few coins existed in England and western Europe. The English upper classes used gold and silver valued by weight, and foreign coins were usually melted down and transformed into ingots. Feudal lords made their own coins for use only on their property, and serfs used a barter system for purchases within the community. But the Crusades brought an economic change, for crusaders needed money that would be accepted in other lands. Silver was heavy, but gold coins were light and already in use throughout trade routes. The use of gold coins improved the peasants' buying and selling power; instead of the barter system, they were now able to earn gold in exchange for their labor or goods. The minting of coins was essential in the revival of England's economy.

Chivalric codes governed hand-to-hand combat during much of the Middle Ages. But the use of guns and gunpowder (and strategic military planning) changed all that. Discovered by the Chinese, gunpowder was introduced into English warfare around 1325. By 1346, warfare in the Western world had changed irreversibly. In

The Hundred Years' War (1337–1453): The arrow is mightier than the armor. What might be called the first national war was waged by England against France. Fought on the Continent, the Hundred Years' War was based on dubious claims to the throne of France by two English kings—Edward III (reigned 1327–1377) and Henry V (reigned 1413–1422). Ⓐ

This long war was militarily unsuccessful for the English. But it was an important factor in the gradual development of a British national consciousness. After the war, the English were no longer best represented by the knight in shining armor, an import from the Continent anyway. Instead, they were more accurately represented by the green-clad yeoman (small landowner) with his longbow. Ⓑ These English yeomen had formed the nucleus of the English armies in France. Their yard-long arrows could fly over castle walls and pierce the armor of knights. These small landowners now became a dominant force in the new society that grew out of the ruins of feudalism. The old ideals of chivalry lived on only in stories, such as the King Arthur tales retold by Sir Thomas Malory.

The English lost the Hundred Years' War with France, but by the war's end the yeomen (small landowners) who had formed the nucleus of the English armies had replaced the knights in armor. With this emergence of the yeoman class, modern, democratic England was born.

Skill Link

Evaluating an Informative Message

After students have finished reading this introductory essay, ask them to evaluate it.

1. Identify the purpose of the essay. [to inform]
2. Brainstorm a list of criteria that might be used to evaluate the introduction, such as accuracy, clarity, completeness, organization, interest level, illustrations, and other features.
3. Have students work in small groups to apply the criteria to the essay. They should provide a specific analysis of each criterion, as well as an overall judgment.

Marble relief (13th century) of mounted knight arrayed in casque and shirt of mail, carrying shield, from the monastery of Poblet, Province of Tarragona, Spain.

The Metropolitan Museum of Art, New York. Dodge Fund. 1913 (13.21).

the landmark battle of Crécy, the French outnumbered the English. The English, aided by the longbow and by explosives, massacred their opponents. Over the next two hundred years, the cannon made the castle—previously impregnable—open to attack. C

The rules of war and class had changed. Chivalry was at an end, and feudal obligation became a thing of the past. As a result, a free and prosperous middle class developed, revolutionizing the country's social and economic systems.

Battle of Crécy, from *Chroniques de Froissart* (detail) (14th century). English longbowmen are depicted overcoming French crossbowmen.

© cliché Bibliothèque Nationale de France, Paris.

C Exploring the Historical Period

The Battle of Crécy

The Battle of Crécy was fought in 1346, during the first decade of the Hundred Years' War. In this conflict, the invading forces of Edward III of England withstood sixteen charges from the cavalry of Philip VI. The French charge was led by Italian mercenaries, Genoese crossbow men paid to fight in Philip's service. Meeting this attack were English archers who fought with six-foot longbows. Crécy proved the superiority of the longbow: More than fifteen hundred French knights and noblemen were killed in the battle. The discipline of English troops who were paid a regular, fixed wage also played an important role in Edward's victory.

RESPONDING TO THE ART

Activity. Have students note that this painting shows how the French, or those fighting for them, were using the heavier crossbow. Point out the Frenchman (or other enemy knight) in the foreground, who is cranking to reload his crossbow. Meanwhile, the English are firing so many arrows from their quick, trusty, and flexible longbows that some French soldiers get shot multiple times, like the poor fellow in the lower left corner sporting two arrows—one in his leg and one in his hip. Also point out how this painting idealizes medieval battle. Warfare during this period was extremely gruesome, but no one in this scene bleeds.

Ⓐ Exploring the Historical Period

The Plague

While the plague resulted in enormous political and social changes, students should also be reminded of its effect on the minds and hearts of those who lived through it. At the very least, the plague heightened awareness of death and the transience of life. At the same time, for some, it fostered a feeling that one might as well seek pleasure, since death was imminent. At the beginning of the *Decameron,* Boccaccio describes the plague's effects on community and family life. Here is just a small part of what he says about the lawlessness, heartlessness, and tragedy of the times: "In this suffering and misery of our city [Florence], the authority of human and divine laws almost disappeared, for, like other men, the ministers and the executors of the laws were all dead or sick or shut up with their families, so that no duties were carried out. Every man was therefore able to do as he pleased. . . . One citizen avoided another, hardly any neighbor troubled about others, relatives never or hardly ever visited each other. Moreover, such terror was struck into the hearts of men and women by this calamity, that brother abandoned brother, and the uncle his nephew, and the sister her brother, and very often the wife her husband. What is even worse and nearly incredible is that fathers and mothers refused to see and tend their children, as if they had not been theirs."

Ⓑ Reading Skills and Strategies

Making Inferences

In the medieval psyche, saints and diseases were linked together. Gout was called Saint Maur's evil, dropsy was St. Eutropius' disease, and so on. The scourge of the plague was so terrible that several saints were called in as protectors, including Saint Sebastian and Saint Christopher. Ask students, given this background, to explain how the epidemic that killed one out of three people might weaken people's faith. [Possible response: When so many died, people might feel the saintly protectors failed.]

Coffin-Making and Burial During the Black Death, from *Annales* (14th century) by Giles de Mussis (10¾″ × 8″).

© Bibliothèque Royale Albert premier, Brussels.

> The character of the pestilence was appalling. The disease itself, with its frightful symptoms, the swift onset, the blotches, the hardening of the glands under the armpit or in the groin, these swellings which no poultice could resolve, these tumors which, when lanced, gave no relief, the horde of virulent carbuncles which followed the dread harbingers of death, the delirium, the insanity which attended its triumph, the blank spaces which opened on all sides in human society, stunned and for Ⓑ a time destroyed the life and faith of the world.
>
> —Winston Churchill

The Black Death. The Black Death, or bubonic plague, which struck England in 1348–1349, delivered another blow to feudalism. Highly contagious and spread by fleas from infected rats, the disease reduced the nation's population by a third—causing a labor shortage and inevitably giving the lower classes more leverage Ⓐ than ever before against their overlords. One long-term result was the serfs' freedom, which knocked out feudalism's last support. By the time King Henry VII's 1486 marriage reconciled the warring Houses of York and Lancaster, the Middle Ages were ending in England. Henry, a strong king, began the Tudor line that would lead to Elizabeth I. England's Renaissance was about to begin.

The Black Death caused a labor shortage, leading to the serfs' freedom and to the end of feudalism.

Quickwrite

Loyalty lay at the heart of the feudal system. The landowners extracted loyalty from their serfs, the lords expected loyalty from their knights, and the king demanded loyalty from everyone. Has loyalty remained as important in today's society? To whom, or to what, are you loyal, and why? Your answer might include institutions, like school or church, but does it also include ideas? Whom do you expect to be loyal to you, and in what ways? Jot down your thoughts on the issue to discuss with others in the class.

(Opposite) A master with his pupils, from the *Chronicles of Hainault* (15th century).

Assessing Learning

Check Test: True-False

1. The Norman Conquest of 1066 radically altered the development of English history, character, and language. [True]
2. Feudalism was a caste system, a property system, a military system, and a system of social behavior. [True]
3. In the feudal system, a woman was considered equal to a man. [False]
4. The Magna Carta, signed in 1215, placed restrictions on democratic tendencies. [False]
5. One long-term result of the Black Death was freedom of the serfs, who were the last support of feudalism. [True]

Collection 2

The Gift of Story

Theme

Stories Give Meaning to Our Lives *Stories, like the ones in this collection, have always been used to entertain us on life's journey and to help us make sense of our experiences.*

Reading the Anthology

Reaching Struggling Readers

The *Reading Skills and Strategies: Reaching Struggling Readers* binder includes a Reading Strategies Handbook that offers concrete suggestions for helping students who have difficulty reading and comprehending text, or students who are reluctant readers. When a specific strategy is most appropriate for a selection, a correlation to the Handbook is provided at the bottom of the teacher's page under the head Struggling Readers. This head may also be used to introduce additional ideas for helping students read challenging texts.

Reading Beyond the Anthology

Read On

Collection 2 includes an annotated bibliography of books suitable for extended reading. The suggested books are related to works in this collection by theme, by author, or by subject. To preview the Read On for Collection 2, please turn to p. T180.

HRW Library

The *HRW Library* offers novels, plays, and short-story collections for extended reading. Each major work in the Library includes thematically or topically related Connections. The Connections are magazine articles, poems, or other pieces of literature. Each book in the *HRW Library* is also accompanied by a Study Guide that provides teaching suggestions and worksheets. The following title is suggested for Collection 2.

READINGS IN WORLD LITERATURE

This collection of readings in world literature provides other famous myths and legends, including stories from ancient Greece, the Norse sagas, and Celtic mythology.

Collection 2 The Gift of Story

Resources for this Collection

Note: All resources for this collection are available for preview on the *One-Stop Planner CD-ROM I with Test Generator.* All worksheets and blackline masters may be printed from the CD-ROM.

Internet Resources
go.hrw.com LE0 12-2

Selection or Feature	Reading and Literary Skills	Vocabulary, Language, and Grammar
Ballads • **Lord Randall** (p. 90) • **Edward, Edward** (p. 92) • **Get Up and Bar the Door** (p. 94) **Connections: Frankie and Johnny** (p. 95) *words by* Boyd Bunch **Elements of Literature: Ballads** (p. 96)	• *Graphic Organizers for Active Reading,* Worksheet pp. 3, 4, 5 • *Literary Elements:* Transparency 3, Worksheet p. 10	• *Grammar and Language Links:* Subject-Verb Agreement, Worksheet p. 7 • *Language Workshop CD-ROM,* Subject-Verb Agreement
from **The Canterbury Tales** (p. 100) Geoffrey Chaucer *translated by* Nevill Coghill • **The Prologue** (p. 103) **Connections:** *from* **The Autobiography of Malcolm X** (p. 126) Malcolm X *with* Alex Haley **Elements of Literature: Imagery** (p. 127) • *from* **The Pardoner's Tale** (p. 129) • *from* **The Wife of Bath's Tale** (p. 138) **Elements of Literature: Couplets** (p. 149)	• *Graphic Organizers for Active Reading,* Worksheet pp. 6, 7, 8 • *Literary Elements:* Transparencies 4, 5, 6, Worksheet pp. 13, 16, 19	• *Words to Own,* Worksheets pp. 3, 4, 5 • *Grammar and Language Links:* Subject-Verb Agreement, Worksheet p. 9; Pronoun-Antecedent Agreement, Worksheet p. 11; Revision Worksheet p. 13 • *Language Workshop CD-ROM:* Subject-Verb Agreement; Pronoun-Antecedent Agreement • *Daily Oral Grammar,* Transparencies 3, 4, 5
World Literature: Italy **Federigo's Falcon** *from the* **Decameron** (p. 153) Giovanni Boccaccio, *translated by* Mark Musa and Peter Bondanella	The World Literature feature offers students the opportunity to explore thematically linked literature from different world cultures. Structured activities called Finding Common Ground are provided in the Pupil's Edition to guide students' explorations of these thematic connections between British and other world literature.	
from **Sir Gawain and the Green Knight** (p. 158) *translated by* John Gardner **Connections: Holding Out for a Hero** (p. 166) *words by* Dean Pitchford **Elements of Literature: Romances** (p. 167)	• *Graphic Organizers for Active Reading,* Worksheet p. 9 • *Literary Elements:* Transparency 7, Worksheet p. 22	• *Words to Own,* Worksheet p. 6 • *Grammar and Language Links:* Pronoun-Antecedent Agreement, Worksheet p. 15 • *Language Workshop CD-ROM,* Pronoun-Antecedent Agreement • *Daily Oral Grammar,* Transparency 6
The Death of Arthur *from* **Le Morte Darthur** (p. 170) Sir Thomas Malory **Spotlight On: The Weaving of Women's Tales** (p. 177)	• *Graphic Organizers for Active Reading,* Worksheet p. 10	• *Daily Oral Grammar,* Transparency 7
The English Language: The Language in Transition (p. 181) John Algeo		
Writer's Workshop: Comparison-Contrast Essay (p. 185)		
Language Workshop: Common Agreement Problems (p. 187)		• *Workshop Resources,* p. 47 • *Language Workshop CD-ROM,* Agreement
Learning for Life: Evaluating Technological Advances (p. 189)		

Other Resources for this Collection

- *Cross-Curricular Activities*, p. 2
- *Portfolio Management System*, Introduction to Portfolio Assessment, p. 1

- *Formal Assessment:*
 Literary Period Introduction
 Test, p. 15
 Literary Period Test, p. 33
- *Test Generator*, Collection Test ◎

Writing	Listening and Speaking Viewing and Representing	Assessment
• *Portfolio Management System*, Rubrics for Choices, p. 97	• *Audio CD Library*, Disc 2, Tracks 2, 3, 4 🎧 • *Portfolio Management System*, Rubrics for Choices, p. 97	• *Formal Assessment*, Selection Test, p. 17 ◎ • *Test Generator (One-Stop Planner CD-ROM)* ◎
• *Portfolio Management System*, Rubrics for Choices, pp. 99, 100, 101	• *Audio CD Library*, Disc 2, Tracks 5, 6, 7, 8 🎧 • *Portfolio Management System*, Rubrics for Choices, pp. 99, 100, 101	• *Formal Assessment*, Selection Tests, pp. 19, 21, 23 • *Test Generator (One-Stop Planner CD-ROM)* ◎ • *Formal Assessment*, Literary Elements Test, p. 31
	• *Audio CD Library*, Disc 2, Track 9 🎧	• *Preparation for College Admission Exams*, p. 7
• *Portfolio Management System*, Rubrics for Choices, p. 103	• *Audio CD Library*, Disc 3, Track 2 🎧 • *Viewing and Representing:* Fine Art Transparency 2 Worksheet p. 8 • *Portfolio Management System*, Rubrics for Choices, p. 103	• *Formal Assessment*, Selection Test, p. 25 • *Test Generator (One-Stop Planner CD-ROM)* ◎
• *Portfolio Management System*, Rubrics for Choices, p. 105	• *Audio CD Library*, Disc 3, Track 3 🎧 • *Portfolio Management System*, Rubrics for Choices, p. 105	• *Formal Assessment*, Selection Test, p. 27
		• *Formal Assessment*, The English Language Test, p. 29
• *Workshop Resources*, p. 7 • *Writer's Workshop 2 CD-ROM*, Expository Writing ◎	• *Viewing and Representing*, HRW Multimedia Presentation Maker	• *Portfolio Management System* • Prewriting, p. 106 • Peer Editing, p. 107 • Assessment Rubric, p. 108
		Portfolio Management System, Rubrics, p. 109

 Transparency CD-ROM Video Audio CD

Collection 2 The Gift of Story

Skills Focus

Selection or Feature	Reading Skills and Strategies	Elements of Literature and Language	Writing	Listening and Speaking	Viewing and Representing
Ballads • **Lord Randall** (p. 90) • **Edward, Edward** (p. 92) • **Get Up and Bar the Door** (p. 94)		Refrain, pp. 90, 96 Ballad, pp. 90, 96 Incremental Repetition, p. 96	Identify Characteristics of a Ballad, p. 97 Research and Write Introductions to American Ballads, p. 97 Write a Folk Ballad, p. 97 Retell a Ballad as a News Story, p. 97 Write a Short Essay Comparing and Contrasting Versions of a Traditional Ballad, p. 97	Give an Oral Performance of a Ballad, p. 96 Sing or Play a Ballad from Another Culture, p. 97	
from **The Canterbury Tales** (p. 100) Geoffrey Chaucer • **The Prologue** (p.103) • *from* **The Pardoner's Tale** (p. 129) • *from* **The Wife of Bath's Tale** (p. 138)	Awareness of Historical Context, p. 150 Pronunciation Guide, p. 102	Vernacular, p. 98 Iambic Pentameter, p. 99 Character, pp. 103, 127, 149 Frame Story, p. 103 Satire, pp. 127, 137 Imagery, p. 127 Personification, p. 137 Symbol, p. 137 Irony, pp. 137, 149 Couplet, p. 149 Half Rhyme, p. 149	Write an Essay Describing a Character, p. 128 Create a Personality Profile for the Pardoner, p. 137 Contrast the Moral Message of the Pardoner's Tale with His Own Character, p. 137 Compare Translations of Chaucer and Create an Original Translation, p. 149 Compare and Contrast the Wife of Bath with a Contemporary Woman, p. 150 Write a Short Essay Analyzing a Character, p. 150 Write a Prologue to an Original Frame Story, p. 150	Prepare and Present a Reading of a Tale, p. 150 Evaluate Song Lyrics Based on *The Canterbury Tales,* p. 150	Use a Chart to Develop Ideas for a Comparison-Contrast Essay, p. 128 Create a Portrait or Collage of a Pilgrim, p. 128 Create an Illuminated Manuscript, p. 150 Evaluate Artistic Interpretations of Chaucer's Pilgrims, p. 150
Reading Skills and Strategies: Analyzing Word Parts (p. 151)	Analyzing Word Parts, p. 151				
World Literature: Italy Federigo's Falcon *from the* **Decameron** (p. 153) Giovanni Boccaccio	Evaluating Historical Context, p. 153	The World Literature feature offers students the opportunity to explore thematically linked literature from different world cultures. Structured activities called Finding Common Ground are provided in the Pupil's Edition to guide students' explorations of these thematic connections between British and other world literature.			
from **Sir Gawain and the Green Knight** (p. 158) *translated by* John Gardner		Romance, pp. 158, 167 Symbolism, p. 167 Images, p. 167 Tone, p. 167 Allegory, p. 167 Quest, p. 167	Compare Gawain to a Modern Hero, p. 168 Write a Plan for a Displaced Version of *Sir Gawain,* p. 168 Write an Essay Agreeing or Disagreeing with the Rules of Courtly Love, p. 168	Group Discussion, p. 168 Panel Discussion of the Roles of Women in *Sir Gawain* and in the Contemporary World, p. 168	
The Death of Arthur *from* **Morte Darthur** (p. 170) Sir Thomas Malory	Using Context Clues, pp. 170, 176 Archaic Words, pp. 170, 176	Romance Hero, pp. 170, 176	Compare Arthur with Beowulf, p. 176 Create a Translation, p. 176		Use a Graphic to Chart Motifs, p. 176 Create a Visual Representation of a Literary Scene, p. 176
The English Language: Middle English: The Language in Transition (p. 181) John Algeo		Schwa, p. 182 Gender. p. 182 Plural Forms, p. 182 Case Endings, p. 183 Borrowed Words, p. 183 Word Origins, p. 184			
Writer's Workshop: Comparison-Contrast Essay (p. 185)			Write a Comparison-Contrast Essay, pp. 185–186		Use a Venn Diagram or Chart, p. 185
Language Workshop: Common Agreement Problems (p. 187)		Agreement, p. 187 • Subject-Verb • Subject Followed by a Parenthetical Phrase • Compound Subject	Revise Sentences to Correct Agreement Problems, p. 187		
Reading for Life: Analyzing a Film or Play Review (p. 188)	Analyze a Review, p. 188 • Elements • Criteria • Tone		Compare a Personal Review to a Review by a Critic, p. 188		
Learning for Life: Evaluating Technological Advances (p. 189)			Write a Job Description, p. 189	Give an Informal Talk, p. 189	Use Graphics, p. 189

Collection 2

THE GIFT OF STORY

Ballads
Chaucer
Boccaccio
from Sir Gawain and the Green Knight
Malory

The stories people tell have a way of taking care of them. If stories come to you, care for them. And learn to give them away where they are needed. Sometimes a person needs a story more than food to stay alive. That is why we put these stories in each other's memory. This is how people care for themselves. One day you will be good storytellers. Never forget these obligations.

—Barry Lopez (American, 1945–   )

OBJECTIVES

1. Read literature from the Middle Ages on the subject of "The Gift of Story"
2. Interpret literary elements with special emphasis on ballads, imagery, couplets, and romance
3. Apply a variety of reading strategies, including determining meanings by analyzing word parts
4. Respond to the literature in a variety of modes
5. Learn and use new words
6. Learn about the development of Middle English
7. Plan, draft, revise, edit, proofread and publish a compare/contrast essay
8. Identify and correct common agreement problems
9. Analyze a film or play review
10. Evaluate technological advances

Responding to the Quotation

American writer Barry Lopez has produced several collections of short stories, as well as a collection of Native American trickster tales, essays, and the fable that this quotation comes from. Elsewhere, Lopez says that when he writes a story, he tries to do so "with a capacity for wonder," so that he can bring something "wonder-full" to the reader. Ask students to summarize what this quotation says about the importance of storytelling. [Possible answers: People need stories to stay alive. Storytelling is so important that people need to lavish care on the telling of stories. Telling stories is a way of caring for others.]

Resources

Viewing and Representing
Videocassette A, Segment 4
Available in Spanish and English.
This video segment explores the history of knighthood. For full lesson plans and worksheets, see the *Visual Connections Teacher's Manual.*

WORK IN PROGRESS

Writing Focus: A Comparison-Contrast Essay

The following **Work in Progress** assignments build to a culminating **Writer's Workshop** at the end of this collection.

• Ballads	Identify characteristics of two ballads (p. 97)
• Prologue to The Canterbury Tales	Use chart to compare characters (p. 128)
• The Pardoner's Tale	Contrast moral message of pardoner's tale with pardoner's character (p. 137)
• The Wife of Bath's Tale	Compare wife of Bath with contemporary woman (p. 150)
• Sir Gawain and the Green Knight	Compare Gawain to a modern hero (p. 168)
• The Death of Arthur	Compare Arthur with Beowulf (p. 176)

Writer's Workshop: Expository Writing / A Comparison-Contrast Essay (p. 185)

OBJECTIVES

Lord Randall / Edward, Edward / Get Up and Bar the Door

1. Read and interpret the ballads
2. Identify and interpret refrains
3. Identify the characteristics of a ballad
4. Express understanding through writing or music

SKILLS

Literary

- Identify and interpret refrains
- Analyze ballads

Writing

- Collect ideas for a compare/contrast essay
- Write introductions to ballads and create a ballad book
- Write a news story
- Compare ballad versions
- Write a ballad

Music

- Perform or play ballads

Planning

- **Block Schedule**
  Block Scheduling Lesson Plans with Pacing Guide
- **Traditional Schedule**
  Lesson Plans Including Strategies for English-Language Learners
- **One-Stop Planner**
  CD-ROM with Test Generator

Before You Read

BALLADS

Make the Connection

The Sensational

THREE DEAD SONS VISIT MOTHER FOR DINNER . . . SLIGHTED WOMAN SPURNS LOVER'S DEATHBED REQUEST . . . MAIDEN HEADED FOR GALLOWS; FAMILY REFUSES HELP. These aren't the latest tabloid headlines or current soap opera summaries; they're the plots of medieval ballads. In the Middle Ages, just as today, certain forms of popular entertainment tended toward the sensational.

Since ballads were the poetry of the people, just as popular music is today, their subjects were predictably popular—domestic tragedy, false love, true love, the absurdity of husband-wife relationships, and the supernatural. Unlike today's music, the ballads were not copyrighted by a singer, but were passed down orally from singer to singer. Using a strong beat and repetition, the ballads were a gift of story passed from performer to performer, from generation to generation.

Quickwrite

Suppose a historian from the future were to analyze today's popular songs. How would the historian describe the music you and your friends enjoy? What subjects dominate the songs? (Are popular songs sensational the way the ballads are?) What inferences would the historian draw about us and our culture from the analysis of the songs and the stories they tell? Record your thoughts on these pop-music questions.

Elements of Literature

The Refrain

In concerts today a singer may invite the audience to "join in on the chorus." It's probable that a single singer sang the narrative portions of a ballad while the audience joined in on the **refrain.** The use of the refrain contributed to the song's rhythm and often reinforced its theme, but there was another practical reason for the refrain: It allowed the singer, who sang from memory and often improvised, time to think of the next verse.

A **refrain** is a repeated word, phrase, line, or group of lines.

For more on Refrain, see the Handbook of Literary Terms.

Background

The word *ballad* is originally derived from an Old French word meaning "dancing song." Although the English ballads' connection with dance has been lost, it is clear from their meter and their structure that the original ballads were composed to be sung to music.

The ballads as we know them today probably took their form in the fifteenth century, but they were not printed until three hundred years later when Sir Thomas Percy, Sir Walter Scott, and others traveled around the British Isles and collected them from the people who still sang them.

Illumination from a French manuscript of *Romance of the Rose* (detail) (15th century).
British Library, London.

go.hrw.com
LEO 12-2

Resources: Print and Media

Reading

- *Graphic Organizers for Active Reading,* pp. 3, 4, 5
- *Audio CD Library*
  Disc 2, Tracks 2, 3, 4

Elements of Literature

- *Literary Elements*
  Transparency 3
  Worksheet, p. 10

Writing and Language

- *Grammar and Language Link*
  Worksheet, p. 7
- *Language Workshop CD-ROM*

Assessment

- *Formal Assessment,* p. 17
- *Portfolio Management System,* p. 97
- *Test Generator (One-Stop Planner CD-ROM)*

Internet

- go.hrw.com (Keyword: LE0 12-2)

This ballad is sung in different versions in several countries. The basic story of the song varies little, but Randall is variously known as Donald, Randolph, Ramsay, Ransome, and Durango. Sometimes his last meal consists of fish, sometimes snakes. The dialect of this version is Scottish. This ballad, like many others, is sung entirely as a conversation.

Lord Randall

"O where hae ye been, Lord Randall, my son?
O where hae ye been, my handsome young man?"
"I hae been to the wild wood; mother, make my bed soon,
For I'm weary wi' hunting, and fain° wald lie down."

"Where gat ye your dinner, Lord Randall, my son?
Where gat ye your dinner, my handsome young man?"
"I din'd wi' my true-love; mother, make my bed soon,
For I'm weary wi' hunting, and fain wald lie down."

"What gat ye to your dinner, Lord Randall, my son?
What gat ye to your dinner, my handsome young man?"
"I gat eels boil'd in broo;° mother, make my bed soon,
For I'm weary wi' hunting, and fain wald lie down."

"What became of your bloodhounds, Lord Randall, my son?
What became of your bloodhounds, my handsome young man?"
"O they swell'd and they died; mother, make my bed soon,
For I'm weary wi' hunting, and fain wald lie down."

"O I fear ye are poison'd, Lord Randall, my son!
O I fear ye are poison'd, my handsome young man!"
"O yes! I am poison'd; mother, make my bed soon,
For I'm sick at the heart, and I fain wald lie down."

4. fain: gladly.
11. broo: broth.

A knight and his lady feeding a falcon, from a German manuscript (detail) (c. 14th century). Cod. Pal. Germ., 848, Codex Manesse, fol. 249v.
Universitätsbibliothek, Heidelberg.

Summary

Told in Scottish dialect, this ballad is in the form of a conversation, or question-and-answer dialogue, between mother and son. Suspense is created through a pattern of incremental repetition. A mother voices suspicions about where her son has been and what has happened to him. In the final stanza she finally admits her fear that he has been poisoned. The son replies that he is poisoned and implies that his "true love" did the deed.

A Elements of Literature

The Ballad

? This question-and-answer format is frequently used in ballads. What is the effect? [Possible answers: It creates suspense; it establishes a conversational rhythm; it invites listeners to speculate about answers.]

B Reading Skills and Strategies

Making Inferences

? What is the connection between the death of the dogs and Lord Randall? [He may be dying of whatever killed the dogs.] **Who poisoned Lord Randall?** [He dined with his true love, which implies that she or someone from her household poisoned him.]

C Elements of Literature

Refrain

? What effect is created by the refrain? [Possible answer: It makes us wonder what is wrong.]

Reaching All Students

Struggling Readers

Help students with the dialect. Begin by rephrasing the first line, "Where have you been, Lord Randall, my son?" Then help students rephrase the fourth line. Point out that an apostrophe can indicate a missing consonant or vowel, as in *wi'* for *with* (l. 4) or *din'd* for *dined* (l. 7). Encourage students to turn dialect into modern English as they read each ballad the first time and then to reread for sense. As needed, help students rephrase the other ballads in this cluster as well.

Advanced Learners

Advanced learners may enjoy exploring all the unanswered questions and implications in these ballads. For example, what motives might Lord Randall's true love have had for poisoning him? Why might Lord Randall have blamed the poisoning on his true love? Why would Edward have killed his father, even if his mother did advise it? Why would she advise it? Invite students to come up with lists of questions to ask each ballad.

Summary ■

Through questions and answers, a son reveals to his mother that he has killed his hawk, his horse, and his father, and now is going away. He is asked what he will leave his wife and children. He declares that they can beg for their bread. To his mother, he leaves a curse for the counsel she gave him, implying that she advised him to murder his father.

Ⓐ Struggling Readers

Using the Glosses

Remind students to paraphrase as they read. Also point out how the glosses can help them. For example, ask how students can tell the meaning of *sae* in l. 4. [The gloss for l. 1 explains that it means *so*.]

Ⓑ Reading Skills and Strategies

Drawing Conclusions

? Why is Edward going away? [Possible answers: He is afraid of punishment. He never wants to see his mother again. He cannot live in the same place now that he is guilty of murder.]

Ⓒ Elements of Literature

Refrain

? Note the use of *O* at the end of each stanza. What effect does it have? [Possible answers: *O* can express regret, shock, or dismay. Its repeated use intensifies the emotional impact.]

"Edward, Edward" is an international ballad, one found across northern Europe and brought to England and Scotland by travelers and sailors. Sir Thomas Percy, who compiled many of the popular ballads in the 1760s, found the same character in a Swedish ballad and also noted that another version of this ballad appeared with the title "Son Davie, Son Davie." Another collector changed the hero's name to Edward.

Edward, Edward

"Why does your brand sae drop wi' blude,°
Edward, Edward?
Why does your brand sae drop wi' blude,
And why sae sad gang ye,° O?"—
"O I hae kill'd my hawk sae gude,°
Mither, mither;
O I hae kill'd my hawk sae gude,
And I had nae mair° but he, O."

"Your hawk's blude was never sae red,
Edward, Edward;
Your hawk's blude was never sae red,
My dear son, I tell thee, O."—
"O I hae kill'd my red-roan steed,
Mither, mither;
O I hae kill'd my red-roan steed,
That erst° was sae fair and free, O."

"Your steed was auld,° and ye hae got mair,
Edward, Edward;
Your steed was auld, and ye hae got mair;
Some other dule ye dree,° O."—
"O I hae kill'd my father dear,
Mither, mither;
O I hae kill'd my father dear,
Alas, and wae is me, O!"

"And whatten penance will ye dree° for that,
Edward, Edward?
Whatten penance will ye dree for that?
My dear son, now tell me, O."—
"I'll set my feet in yonder boat,
Mither, mither;
I'll set my feet in yonder boat,
And I'll fare over the sea, O."

"And what will ye do wi' your tow'rs and your ha',°
Edward, Edward?
And what will ye do wi' your tow'rs and your ha',
That were sae fair to see, O?"—

1. **brand . . . blude:** sword so drip with blood.
4. **gang ye:** go you.
5. **gude:** good.
8. **nae mair:** no more.
16. **erst:** before.
17. **auld:** old.
20. **dule ye dree:** grief you suffer.
25. **whatten . . . dree:** what punishment for sin will you suffer.
33. **ha':** hall; that is, ancestral home.

Using Students' Strengths

Kinesthetic Learners

After students have finished reading the ballads, ask pairs of students to role-play Lord Randall and his mother, Edward and his mother, or the goodman and goodwife. Encourage pairs to assign lines, practice their parts, and then perform the role-play for the class. When students perform, remind them to read the lines as if they were speaking to each other.

Auditory/Musical Learners

Encourage students to explore the school or public musical library to find recordings of sung versions of these or other medieval ballads. If the library collection is extensive enough, students may enjoy comparing several versions of one ballad.

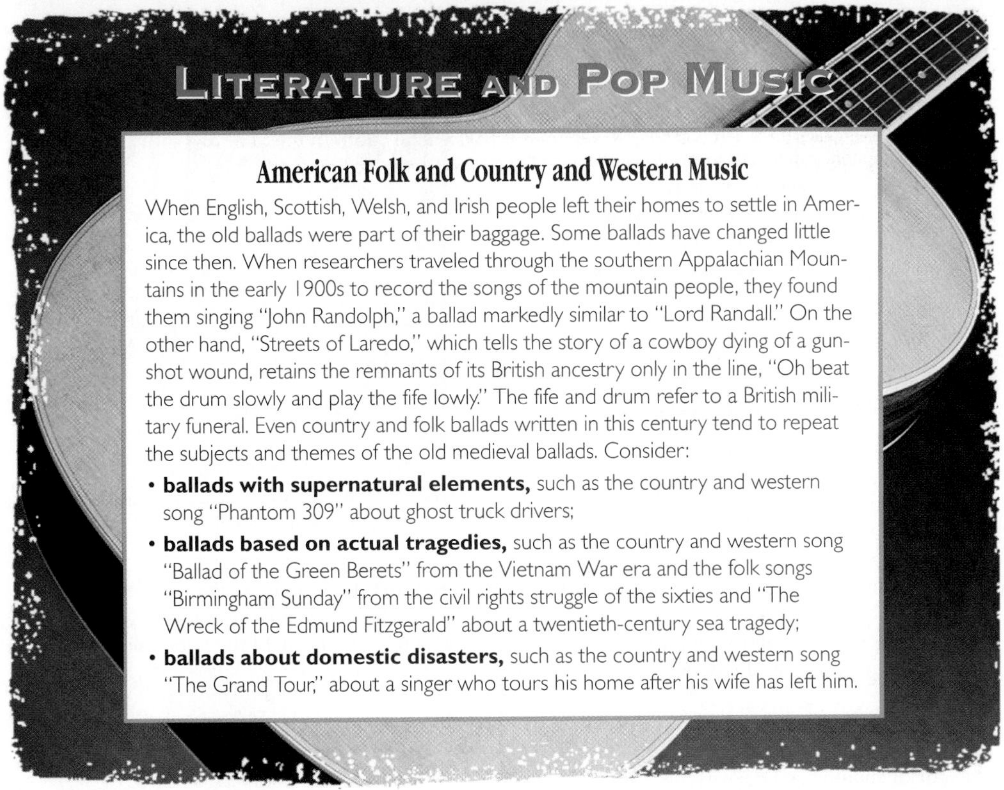

Literature and Pop Music

American Folk and Country and Western Music

When English, Scottish, Welsh, and Irish people left their homes to settle in America, the old ballads were part of their baggage. Some ballads have changed little since then. When researchers traveled through the southern Appalachian Mountains in the early 1900s to record the songs of the mountain people, they found them singing "John Randolph," a ballad markedly similar to "Lord Randall." On the other hand, "Streets of Laredo," which tells the story of a cowboy dying of a gunshot wound, retains the remnants of its British ancestry only in the line, "Oh beat the drum slowly and play the fife lowly." The fife and drum refer to a British military funeral. Even country and folk ballads written in this century tend to repeat the subjects and themes of the old medieval ballads. Consider:

- **ballads with supernatural elements,** such as the country and western song "Phantom 309" about ghost truck drivers;
- **ballads based on actual tragedies,** such as the country and western song "Ballad of the Green Berets" from the Vietnam War era and the folk songs "Birmingham Sunday" from the civil rights struggle of the sixties and "The Wreck of the Edmund Fitzgerald" about a twentieth-century sea tragedy;
- **ballads about domestic disasters,** such as the country and western song "The Grand Tour," about a singer who tours his home after his wife has left him.

"I'll let them stand till they doun fa',
Mither, mither;
I'll let them stand till they doun fa',
For here never mair maun° I be, O."

"And what will ye leave to your bairns° and your wife,
Edward, Edward?
And what will ye leave to your bairns and your wife,
When ye gang owre the sea, O?"—
"The warld's room: let them beg through life,
Mither, mither;
The warld's room: let them beg through life;
For them never mair will I see, O."

"And what will ye leave to your ain° mither dear,
Edward, Edward?
And what will ye leave to your ain mither dear,
My dear son, now tell me, O?"—
"The curse of hell frae me sall ye bear,
Mither, mither;
The curse of hell frae me sall ye bear:
Sic° counsels ye gave to me, O!"

40. **maun:** must.

41. **bairns:** children.

49. **ain:** own.

56. **sic:** such.

LITERATURE AND POP MUSIC

Because ballads deal with the stuff of everyday life—love, murder, violence, low comedy—groups have often opposed them. For example, during early colonial times, Cotton Mather worried that the minds and manners of the country people were being "corrupted" by ballads. (He preferred that they stick to hymns.) Students might find examples of ballads that are *not* focused on sensational violence. These include ballads that developed from American "folk" occupations: lumbering, sailing, riding the range, and mining.

D Critical Thinking

Making Judgments

? What kind of person is Edward? [Possible responses: He is an evil man, guilty of murder and of abandoning his family; or he is mad, as indicated by his killing of the hawk and the horse; or he is impetuous or hot-headed, inflamed by something his mother said and acting without thinking his decision through. Perhaps he would defend himself by saying that his father had done something evil. Guilt over the patricide can still drive Edward to curse his mother for her advice.]

E Appreciating Language

Dialect

? Why didn't the editors decide to print this dialect in modern English? [Possible answers: The ballad would not be authentic. The use of dialect gives insight into the originators of the ballad. Ironically, in dialect, the ballad seems more timeless.]

Making the Connections

Connecting to the Subject: "The Gift of Story"

After students have finished reading all three ballads, ask them to reflect on what makes a ballad more like a story than a lyric poem. You might ask the following questions:

- What literary elements are contained in a story? [character; plot; suspense; climax; resolution]
- What story elements do you find in each of the ballads? [All have characters; all at least suggest some elements of plot, including main events and suspense.]
- What makes these ballads as memorable as any good story? [Possible answers: They relate tragic deeds, including murder and violence. They reveal human relationships. They are slightly mysterious or ambiguous and leave some questions unanswered.]

Summary ■

"Get Up and Bar the Door" is a humorous turn on the age-old theme of the battle of the sexes. A stubborn husband and wife are both unwilling to be the one to get up and bar the door. To end their bickering, they decide to stop talking; the first who breaks the silence will bar the door. When intruders arrive, pull a knife, and threaten to rob and harass them, the man protests. The woman, however, jumps for joy: Her husband has spoken first, so he will have to get up and bar the door.

Ⓐ English Language Learners
Archaic Language

Explain that to *bar* the door means to "lock" it. Tell students that long ago, people would not have said "lock the door" because they used a bar, or piece of wood, placed horizontally across a door, to secure it.

Ⓑ Elements of Literature
The Ballad

? What story elements are introduced in the first three stanzas? [Characters: husband and wife. Setting: at home, before a holiday, when there is plenty to do. Situation: The door needs to be barred. Conflict: The husband and wife are bickering about who will bar the door.]

Ⓒ Critical Thinking
Extending the Text

? What does this pact reveal about the goodman and goodwife? [They are stubborn.]

Ⓓ Historical Connections

The "gentlemen" reveal two facts of life in the Middle Ages: (1) The times were often lawless, and citizens were at the mercy of bandits and thieves; and (2) the upper classes could treat people like the goodman and goodwife however they pleased.

The story in this ballad exists in many versions in Europe, Asia, and the Middle East—perhaps illustrating the universal theme called the battle of the sexes. "Goodwife" and "goodman" are terms once applied to married men and women, something like "Mr." and "Mrs." today.

The story takes place around November 11—Martinmas, or the feast of St. Martin of Tours, which was usually celebrated with a big meal.

The Chef (15th century). Woodcut.

Ⓐ Get Up and Bar the Door

It fell about the Martinmas time,
And a gay time it was then,
When our goodwife got puddings° to make,
And she's boild them in the pan.

The wind sae cauld blew south and north,
And blew into the floor;
Ⓑ Quoth our goodman to our goodwife,
"Gae out and bar the door."

"My hand is in my hussyfskap,°
Goodman, as ye may see;
An° it should nae be barrd this hundred year,
It's no be barrd for me."

They made a paction tween them twa,
Ⓒ They made it firm and sure,
That the first word whaeer should speak,
Should rise and bar the door.

Then by there came two gentlemen,
At twelve o clock at night,
And they could neither see house nor hall,
Nor coal nor candle-light.

Ⓓ "Now whether is this a rich man's house,
Or whether it is a poor?"
But neer a word ane° o them speak,
For barring of the door.

And first they ate the white puddings,
And then they ate the black;
Tho muckle° thought the goodwife to hersel,
Yet neer a word she spake.

Then said the one unto the other,
"Here, man, tak ye my knife;
Do ye tak aff the auld man's beard,
And I'll kiss the goodwife."

"But there's nae water in the house,°
And what shall we do than?"
"What ails ye at the pudding-broo,°
That boils into the pan?"

O up then started our goodman,
An angry man was he:
"Will ye kiss my wife before my een,
And scad° me wi pudding-bree?"°

Then up and started our goodwife,
Gied three skips on the floor:
"Goodman, you've spoken the foremost word,
Get up and bar the door."

3. **puddings:** sausages, the black ones being made with blood.
9. **hussyfskap** (hu'zif·skep): household chores.
11. **an:** if.
23. **ane:** one.
27. **muckle:** much.
33. **but . . . house:** He probably wants water to soften the husband's beard.
35. **what . . . pudding-broo:** What's wrong with using the pudding broth?
40. **scad:** scald. **bree:** broth.

Assessing Learning

Check Test: Short Answers

"Lord Randall"

1. What two places has Lord Randall gone to since he left home? [the woods to hunt and his true love's house for dinner]
2. What has happened to Lord Randall? [His dogs have died, and he has been poisoned.]

"Edward, Edward"

3. What has Edward done? [He has murdered his father.]

"Get Up and Bar the Door"

4. What excuse does the wife give for not being able to bar the door? [She is busy with her household chores.]
5. What causes the husband to speak first? [He is enraged at the fact that the visitors are going to kiss his wife and cut off his beard.]

Connections — A Song

"Frankie and Johnny," one of the most famous of American ballads, comes out of the Midwest and the Mississippi River region. Like most ballads, it tells of love gone wrong.

Frankie and Johnny

words by **Boyd Bunch**

Frankie and Johnny were lovers
Oh, Lordy, how they could love.
They swore to be true to each other,
True as the stars above.
He was her man, but he was doing her wrong.

Frankie she was a good woman
As everybody knows.
Spent a hundred dollars
Just to buy her man some clothes.
He was her man, but he was doing her wrong.

Frankie went down to the corner
Just for a bucket of beer.
Said: "Mr. Bartender,
Has my loving Johnny been here?
He was my man, but he's a-doing me wrong."

"Now I don't want to tell you no stories,
And I don't want to tell you no lies.
I saw your man about an hour ago
With a gal named Nellie Bligh.
He was your man, but he's a-doing you wrong."

Frankie she went down to the hotel,
Didn't go there for fun.
Underneath her kimono
She carried a forty-four gun.
He was her man, but he was doing her wrong.

Frankie looked over the transom
To see what she could spy.
There sat Johnny on the sofa
Just loving up Nellie Bligh.
He was her man, but he was doing her wrong.

Frankie got down from that high stool,
She didn't want to see no more.
Rooty-toot-toot three times she shot
Right through that hardwood door.
He was her man, but he was doing her wrong.

Now the first time that Frankie shot Johnny,
He let out an awful yell.
Second time she shot him
There was a new man's face in hell.
He was her man, but he was doing her wrong.

"Oh, roll me over easy,
Roll me over slow.
Roll me over on the right side,
For the left side hurts me so."
He was her man, but he was doing her wrong.

Sixteen rubber-tired carriages
Sixteen rubber-tired hacks
They take poor Johnny to the graveyard—
They ain't gonna bring him back.
He was her man, but he was doing her wrong.

Frankie looked out of the jailhouse
To see what she could see.
All she could hear was a two-string bow
Crying, "Nearer my God to thee."
He was her man, but he was doing her wrong.

Frankie she said to the sheriff,
"What do you reckon they'll do?"
Sheriff he said, "Frankie,
It's the electric chair for you."
He was her man, but he was doing her wrong.

This story has no moral.
This story has no end.
This story only goes to show
That there ain't no good in men.
He was her man, but he was doing her wrong.

FROM THE EDITOR'S DESK

We included this ballad because it is one of the best known of all American "lowlife" ballads. Carl Sandburg called it a classic and said that Frankie songs may someday be studied as seriously as Moliere or the ballads of Europe.

(A) English Language Learners

Nonstandard Language

"Oh, Lordy," an expression generally not found in standard written English, conveys surprise or strength of feeling. Other nonstandard usages in this poem include many double negatives (as in "don't want to tell you no stories"), double subjects (as in "Frankie she"), and nonstandard verbs and verb forms (such as *a-going, ain't,* and *gonna*). Help students suggest standard substitutes for these usages.

(B) Elements of Literature

Refrain

? How is the refrain used in this ballad? [Possible answers: The refrain focuses attention on the situation, which involves betrayal and infidelity. The repetition suggests Frankie's obsession with her problem.]

(C) Vocabulary Note

Using Context Clues

? What context clues can help you figure out the meaning of the word *transom*? [Possible answers: It is something Frankie can see through. She also stands on a stool to look over it; this suggests it is up relatively high.] A ***transom*** is a window that can be opened above an interior door.

(D) Critical Thinking

Making Inferences

? What has happened to Johnny? [He's dead.]

(E) Critical Thinking

Challenging the Text

? Do you agree with the ballad singer's conclusion? [Answers will vary.]

Connecting Across Texts

Connecting with Medieval Ballads

Ask students what "Frankie and Johnny" has in common with the other three ballads in this collection. [All are stories of relationships gone wrong. All involve the use of force. All involve revenge. (Although this is less the case in "Get Up and Bar the Door," the wife's glee at the end of that ballad suggests she is more concerned with getting the better of her husband than with impending trouble.)]

Ask students how "Frankie and Johnny" differs from the English ballads. [Students may say it is more accessible because it uses American slang. It is also more accessible because of its setting. In the American ballad, it is the man who is the major wrongdoer. In the English ballads, the women all come out looking worse than the men.]

MAKING MEANINGS

First Thoughts [Respond]

1. Possible questions: Why did Lord Randall's true love poison him? Why did Edward kill his father? What "counsels" did his mother give him? What will happen to the goodman and the goodwife?

Shaping Interpretations [Interpret]

2. The variation expresses tragic sadness: Lord Randall is dying, heartbroken by his true love's treachery.
3. In l. 17, Lord Randall's mother tells him that he has been poisoned. In l. 21, Edward reveals that he has killed his father.
4. Edward blames his mother for the tragedy; she seems to have counseled him to kill his father.
5. The gentlemen's threats to kiss the wife and humiliate the husband are menacing. Ironically, the wife is more concerned with the pact of silence than with the danger to her.

Extending the Texts [Connect/ Synthesize]

6. Start by labeling the subjects of the ballads: betrayal in "Lord Randall," a tragic mistake in "Edward, Edward," mindless stubbornness in "Get Up and Bar the Door." Students may name popular singers, like Bob Dylan and Johnny Cash, whose songs imitate traditional ballads. "Frankie and Johnny" is similar to medieval ballads in subject matter (betrayal, a tragic mistake) and in format (it has a refrain and a familiar rhyme scheme).
7. Discuss whether honestly depicting violence is different from glorifying it.

ELEMENTS OF LITERATURE

Ballads

Possible analysis for "Lord Randall":

- Supernatural events: none
- Tragic subject: man poisoned by his lover
- Refrain: final line of each stanza
- Omitted details: reason for the poisoning of Lord Randall
- Incremental repetition: first part of third line of each stanza
- Question and answer: whole ballad
- Conventional phrases: "make my bed soon," "the wild wood"
- Strong beat: throughout, with stronger beat on mother's lines

MAKING MEANINGS

Lord Randall
Edward, Edward
Get Up and Bar the Door

First Thoughts

1. The appeal of the ballads lies partly in what they don't tell you. What questions does each of these songs leave unanswered for you?

Shaping Interpretations

2. What is the emotional effect of the **refrain**'s variation in the fifth stanza of "Lord Randall"?
3. Like many ballads, "Lord Randall" and "Edward, Edward" build up suspense with **incremental repetition:** the repetition of lines with a new element introduced each time to advance the story until a climax is reached. At what point in each ballad does the story reach a climax?
4. What could be the implications of Edward's last response to his mother in the final stanza of "Edward, Edward"?
5. How is the possibility of violence combined with ironic humor in "Get Up and Bar the Door"?

Extending the Texts

6. What popular songs or folk ballads do you know that focus on subjects like the ones in these three famous medieval ballads? Refer to your Quickwrite entry (page 90) for possible ideas.

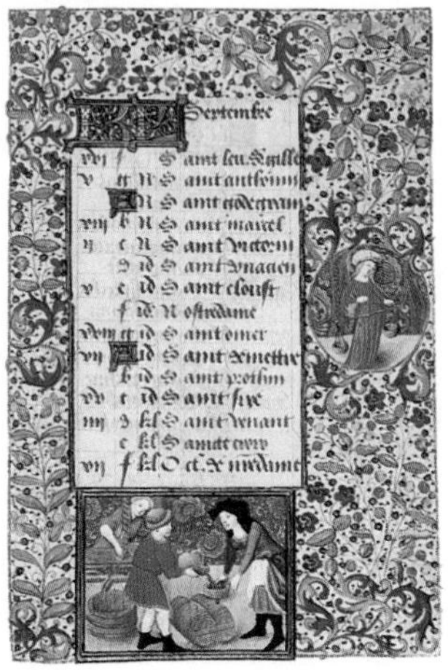

September, calendar page from the Salting Manuscript, *Hours of Margaret de Foix* (c. 1470–1480).
Victoria and Albert Museum, London.

7. People often criticize the media today for glorifying violence. Do you think these ballads, including "Frankie and Johnny" (see ***Connections*** on page 95), glorify violence by singing about it? Why or why not? Is the issue the same? Discuss your responses.

ELEMENTS OF LITERATURE

Ballads: Popular Poetry

Ballads come from an oral tradition, so there are no strict rules dictating their form. However, a number of characteristics have come to be associated with ballads, and every ballad reflects at least some of them: **supernatural events; sensational, sordid, or tragic subject matter;** a **refrain;** and the **omission of details.** The ballad singers also used some of the following conventions:

- **incremental repetition,** to build up suspense. A phrase or sentence is repeated with a new element added each time, until the climax is reached.
- **a question-and-answer format,** in which the facts of a story are gleaned little by little from the answers. Again, this device builds up suspense.
- **conventional phrases,** understood by listeners to have meaning beyond their literal ones. "Make my bed soon" in "Lord Randall" is an example. Whenever a character in a ballad asks someone to make his bed, or to make her bed narrow, it means that the speaker is preparing for death.
- **a strong, simple beat,** with verse forms that are relatively uncomplicated. Ballads were sung for a general, rather than an elitist, audience. Only later, in the era of so-called literary ballads (more sophisticated poems that artfully evoked the atmosphere of the originals), did the rhyme scheme (*abcb*) and meter (a quatrain in which lines of four stresses alternate with lines of three stresses) of the ballad stanza become standard.

Giving an oral performance. With a small group, select a ballad and prepare it for performance. Have an audience **evaluate** your first performance according to **criteria** you all agree on (such as clarity of story, emotional appeal, and so on). Use your audience's evaluations to perfect your final performance.

Choices: Building Your Portfolio

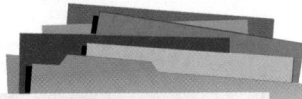

Writer's Notebook

1. Collecting Ideas for a Comparison-Contrast Essay

In the Writer's Workshop on page 185, you'll write an essay in which you compare and contrast two or more pieces of literature or two or more elements in several pieces of literature. These ballads (including the American ballad "Frankie and Johnny") would make excellent subjects for your essay. To gather notes, refer to the ballad characteristics listed on page 96. Make a list of these characteristics and indicate where and how they are used in each ballad. Be sure to take notes on the subjects of the ballads. Save your notes for later use.

Research/Expository Writing

2. A Ballad Book

Find at least four American ballads and present them in a printed form that can be kept in the classroom for future reference. Write a brief introduction to each ballad, telling what you have learned about its origins.

Creative Writing

3. The Saddest Story

Try writing a folk ballad in four-line stanzas on a subject of your choice. Look for possible subjects in the newspaper or on television. Your ballad should tell a brief story, perhaps about some domestic or historic tragedy, and should include at least four ballad characteristics. You might imitate "Lord Randall" and "Edward, Edward," and tell your story in dialogue.

Expository Writing

4. Late-Breaking News!

Take one of the basic situations in these ballads, and retell it as a contemporary news story. Be sure to tell *what* happened, *where* and *when* it happened, *whom* it happened to, *why* it happened, and *how* it happened. Present your news story in print form, complete with headlines, or orally as a segment of a simulated television or radio newscast, complete with a lead.

Research/Comparing Versions

5. The Many Faces of Lord Randall

"Lord Randall" is supposed to have 103 known variations. Find one or two different versions to compare to the original "Lord Randall." (Or select another traditional ballad that exists in several versions.) In a short essay, compare the ballad versions, noting similarities and differences. As part of your essay, try speculating on why certain details in the ballad might have been changed by subsequent singers.

Universitatsbibliothek, Heidelberg.

A musician, from a German manuscript (c. 14th century). Cod. Pal. Germ. 848, Codex Manesse, fol. 312r.

Music/Cultural Comparisons

6. Bringing the Ballads to Life

If you play a musical instrument or sing, try performing some ballads from another culture for your classmates. Or you may collect recordings of the ballads and play them in class. Discuss the ways these ballads are like or unlike the traditional English ballads. For example, do ballads of other cultures have refrains? Do they emphasize feeling over thought?

Grading Timesaver

Rubrics for each Choices assignment appear on p. 97 in the *Portfolio Management System.*

Choices: Building Your Portfolio

1. **Writer's Notebook** Suggest that students use a chart format to take notes.
2. **Research/Expository Writing** Ask students to document their sources for each ballad. You might also require that the introduction to each ballad identify some of its characteristics, such as a question-and-answer format. A classroom book might be compiled with variations of the same ballads.
3. **Creative Writing** Remind students that both "Lord Randall" and "Edward, Edward" record conversations that take place in the wake of tragic incidents. As students prepare to write, ask them to think of conversations that would take place in the aftermath of a tragedy.
4. **Expository Writing** Remind students to create a lead that not only tells the most important information but also immediately creates interest in their article.
5. **Research/Comparing Versions** Encourage students to find ballads by doing a keyword search either in the electronic catalog for their library or online.
6. **Music/Cultural Comparisons** Discuss ways to determine whether a song is a ballad. To be a ballad, a song must tell a story. Point out, however, that many children's songs tell stories, but they are not necessarily ballads. Have students review the list of ballad characteristics before they choose songs to share.

OBJECTIVES

The Prologue

1. Read and interpret the text
2. Identify and analyze characterization
3. Identify and interpret imagery
4. Express understanding through writing or art
5. Understand and use new words

SKILLS

Literary

- Analyze characterization
- Interpret imagery

Writing

- Collect ideas for a compare/contrast essay
- Describe a character

Art

- Create a portrait or collage

Vocabulary

- Use new words

Planning

- **Block Schedule**
  Block Scheduling Lesson Plans with Pacing Guide
- **Traditional Schedule**
  Lesson Plans Including Strategies for English-Language Learners
- **One-Stop Planner**
  CD-ROM with Test Generator

Geoffrey Chaucer

(c. 1343–1400)

Geoffrey Chaucer (1400) by an unknown artist.

By Courtesy of the National Portrait Gallery, London.

Geoffrey Chaucer, often called the father of English poetry, made the English language respectable.

Ordinary people in Chaucer's England spoke the Anglo-Norman composite now called Middle English, a language that became the ancestor of Modern English. But in Chaucer's time the languages of literature, science, diplomacy, and religion were still Latin and French. Before Chaucer it was not fashionable for serious poets to write in English. People felt that English couldn't possibly convey all the nuances and complexities of serious literature. There were, it is true, some exceptions: The so-called Gawain poet (page 158) wrote in a northwestern dialect of English, and, of course, there were the popular ballads.

But the poets who wrote these works lacked the social stature of Chaucer. Chaucer was a well-known government official who served under three kings—Edward III, Richard II, and Henry IV. By composing in the **vernacular**—the everyday language spoken in London and the East Midlands—Chaucer lent respectability to a language that would develop into the medium for one of the world's greatest bodies of literature. In this sense, he was indeed the father of English poetry.

Friends in High Places

Not a great deal is known of Chaucer's life. He was born into a middle-class family in London in the early 1340s, not long after the beginning of the Hundred Years' War. We are told that his father was a wine merchant who had enough money to provide his son with some education. The young Chaucer read a great deal and had some legal training. He became a page to an eminent family from whom he received the finest training in good manners. As he advanced in his government career, he became attached to several noble patrons.

We know, too, that Chaucer was captured in France while serving as a soldier during the Hundred Years' War and that he was important enough to have the king contribute to his ransom. We also know that he married Philippa and had at least two children and that he was on several occasions sent to Europe as the king's ambassador. In 1367, he was awarded the first of several pensions for his services to the Crown. (On April 23, 1374, he was granted the promise of a daily pitcher of wine.) In 1385, he was appointed justice of the peace in the county of Kent, later becoming a member of Parliament. He continued to serve and to enjoy the king's protection.

Writing and Holding a Job

It seems clear that Chaucer was a relatively important government servant and that his work took precedence over his writing. (It would be as if a prominent adviser to the United States president were also a highly acclaimed poet.) Yet he wrote a great deal, and sometimes for personal advancement. In about 1369, for example, he composed his first important poem, *The Book of the Duchess,* in memory of his patron's wife, who had just died of the plague. But Chaucer's writing is just as clearly more than an attempt at political advancement or a passing fancy. Despite his government responsibilities, between 1374 and 1386, Chaucer managed to create several great allegorical poems, including the *House of Fame* and the *Parliament of Fowls,* and his poignant and amusing love story *Troilus and Criseyde.*

go.hrw.com
LEO 12-2

Resources: Print and Media

Reading

- *Graphic Organizers for Active Reading,* p. 6
- *Words to Own,* p. 3
- *Audio CD Library*
  Disc 2, Tracks 5, 6

Elements of Literature

- *Literary Elements*
  Transparencies 4, 6
  Worksheet, pp. 13, 19

Writing and Language

- *Daily Oral Grammar*
  Transparency 3
- *Grammar and Language Link*
  Worksheet, p. 9
- *Language Workshop CD-ROM*

Assessment

- *Formal Assessment,* p. 19
- *Portfolio Management System,* p. 99
- *Test Generator (One-Stop Planner CD-ROM)*

Internet

- go.hrw.com (Keyword: LE0 12-2)

The Italian Connection

In 1372 and 1378, Chaucer traveled in Italy, where he was very likely influenced by the poems of Dante and Petrarch and by the stories of Giovanni Boccaccio (page 152). The connection between Boccaccio's collection of tales called the *Decameron* (c. 1348–1353) and Chaucer's *Canterbury Tales* (c. 1387–1400) is evident. Both use a framing device within which the characters tell their tales, and both include tales based on similar old plots. The framing device in the *Decameron* is a group of people who have fled the plague-ridden city of Florence and tell stories to while away their time in the country. Chaucer's frame is a religious pilgrimage during which each traveler is to tell four stories, two going out and two returning.

Chaucer began writing *The Canterbury Tales* in 1387, during a few years of unemployment when his patron was out of the country. Perhaps because he felt that he had lost his ability to find rhymes, he never completed all the stories. But the collection still must be considered one of the greatest works in the English language. *The Canterbury Tales* alone—even only the Prologue, where each traveler is described—would be sufficient to place Chaucer in the company of Shakespeare and Milton.

The Force of Personality

What is so great about *The Canterbury Tales?* In part, its greatness lies in Chaucer's language. But its greatness also comes from the sheer strength of Chaucer's spirit and personality. John Gardner, one of Chaucer's many biographers, offers a tribute to Chaucer's lasting power:

> In a dark, troubled age, as it seems to us, he was a comfortable optimist, serene, full of faith. For all his delight in irony—and all his poetry has a touch of that—he affirmed this life, to say nothing of the next, from the bottom of his capacious heart. Joy—satisfaction without a trace of sentimental simple-mindedness—is still the effect of Chaucer's poetry and of Chaucer's personality as it emerges from the poems. It is not the simple faith of a credulous man in a credulous age: No poet has ever written better on the baffling complexity of things. But for all the foggy shiftings of the heart and mind, for all the obscurity of God's huge plan, to Chaucer life was a magnificent affair, though sadly transient; and when we read him now, six centuries later, we are instantly persuaded.

In a dark, troubled age, he was a comfortable optimist, serene, full of faith.

The End of the Old Alliterative Anglo-Saxon World

Chaucer used several metrical forms and some prose in *The Canterbury Tales,* but the dominant meter is based on ten syllables, with an unstressed syllable followed by a stressed syllable. We call this meter **iambic pentameter.** It is a rhythm that most closely matches the way English is spoken. You might hear this rhythm if you read aloud this line in Middle English (*swich* means "sweet"):

> ˘ ´ ˘ ´ ˘ ´ ˘ ´ ˘ ´
> And bathed every veyne in swich licour

When we read a line such as this, we experience a version of the meter that was to become the most popular metrical line in English. At a stroke, we have abandoned the old, alliterative world of the Anglo-Saxons and have entered the modern world of Shakespeare, Wordsworth, and even America's Robert Frost.

The Father in the Family Vault

Chaucer died on October 25, 1400, if we are to believe the date on his tombstone (which an admirer erected in Westminster Abbey in 1556). Chaucer was the very first of those many famous English writers who would be gathered into what we know as the Poets' Corner in Westminster Abbey—one of the great tourist sights in London today. "The Father of English poetry," notes Nevill Coghill, "lies in his family vault."

Browsing in the Files

About the Author. As students read *The Canterbury Tales,* they may question whether Chaucer was, as John Gardner asserts, "full of faith." Here is more from Gardner on that topic: "[Chaucer] was religious not only in his palsied old age but all his life: from his first long poem on, he shows his deep and comfortable Christianity, his firm belief in God's love and mercy, and his doubt that acquisitive real-life friars and Popes have much to do with a sinner's reaching heaven. From the beginning to the end of his poetic career, Chaucer's position is clear and unvarying. He defends one virtue, *charity:* the good man's willingness to give the benefit of the doubt, to find some nobility in even the most wretched and deplorable of men; and though he treats many vices, there is only one that he attacks ferociously, again and again, self-righteousness. Chaucer's specific interests change but the theme never changes: God is love, and so is man at his best and evil is non-love, the fear, pride, concupiscence, bigotry, or high doctrine that lead a man to think about no one but himself, forgetting the cornerstone of Christian faith."

Professional Notes

Middle English

The Norman Conquest of 1066 altered the English language forever. Over the generations, the language lost many inflectional endings and much of its Germanic flavor. Although many Old English words, such as *cwene* (queen), *templ* (temple), and *lytel* (little), survived the transition into the average British person's Middle English, many Latin and French words were added to people's vocabulary. Because London was the capital, Chaucer's East Midland dialect was the dialect that eventually evolved into modern English. Thus, students reading *The Canterbury Tales* in the original will be able to recognize many of Chaucer's words, although they may be at a loss as to how to pronounce them.

Ⓐ Historical Connections

Pilgrimages

In Chaucer's day almost everyone from every class made a pilgrimage; many probably went on more than one. According to one Chaucerian scholar, "In one year alone in the early fifteenth century, more than one hundred thousand persons from all over Europe are said to have made the Canterbury pilgrimage."

Ⓑ Historical Connections

Thomas à Becket

Thomas à Becket became a martyr two hundred years before Chaucer's day. In December of 1170, King Henry II became angry when he heard that Becket, then archbishop, had excommunicated bishops who supported Henry's position concerning the rights of the state to try clergy accused of crimes. After four of the king's knights (whether with or without his orders is unknown) murdered Becket at the altar of the cathedral, he was almost immediately named a saint. The Church believed that his body and blood were sacred and had the power to cure; people thus went to Becket's shrine to be healed. They went for other reasons as well. For example, Chaucer suggests that the Knight is on a pilgrimage to give thanks for a successful campaign (see p. 107, ll. 79–80).

Ⓒ Historical Connections

The Route to Canterbury

The pilgrims' way from London to Canterbury was originally a Roman road, known at various times as Cosinge Street and Watling Street. Though one can still travel on this road south from Southwark to Dover, it bears little resemblance to the rural road that passed through hayfields and forests in Chaucer's day. The pilgrims called the road a "slough," or a place with deep mud. In April, the time of this pilgrimage, it was no doubt very muddy.

Ⓓ Historical Connections

Southwark

Southwark was the starting point for pilgrimages not just south to Canterbury but also to holy places to the west of England, such as Salisbury, Glastonbury, and Walsingham.

The Canterbury Tales: Snapshot of an Age

Ⓐ *The Canterbury Tales* gives us a collection of good stories and a snapshot, a picture frozen in time, of life in the Middle Ages. To include the complete range of medieval society in the same picture, Chaucer places his characters on a pilgrimage, a religious journey made to a shrine or holy place. Ⓑ These pilgrims, like a collection of people on tour today, are from many stations and stages of life. Together they travel on horseback from London to the shrine of the martyr Saint Thomas à Becket at Canterbury Cathedral, about fifty-five miles to the southeast.

Ⓒ The *Tales* begin with a General Prologue, the first lines of which establish that this pilgrimage takes place in the spring, the archetypal time of new life and awakening. Fifty-five miles is a long journey by horseback, especially along muddy tracks that would hardly pass as roads today. An inn was always a welcome oasis, even if it provided few luxuries. The poet-pilgrim narrator, whom many consider to be Ⓓ Chaucer himself, starts out at the Tabard Inn in Southwark, a borough in the south of London, where he meets twenty-nine other pilgrims also bound for Canterbury. It is the host of the Tabard who suggests to the pilgrims, as they sit around the fire after dinner, that they exchange tales to pass the time along the way to Canterbury and back to London. The host's suggestion sets up Chaucer's frame story—the main story of the pilgrimage that includes each pilgrim's story.

As the Prologue progresses and we are introduced to the pilgrims, Chaucer's brilliant picture of life in late medieval England comes into focus. Here is what Nevill Coghill, one of Chaucer's translators, says about the Prologue:

Page from *The Canterbury Tales,* from the Ellesmere manuscript (15th century).

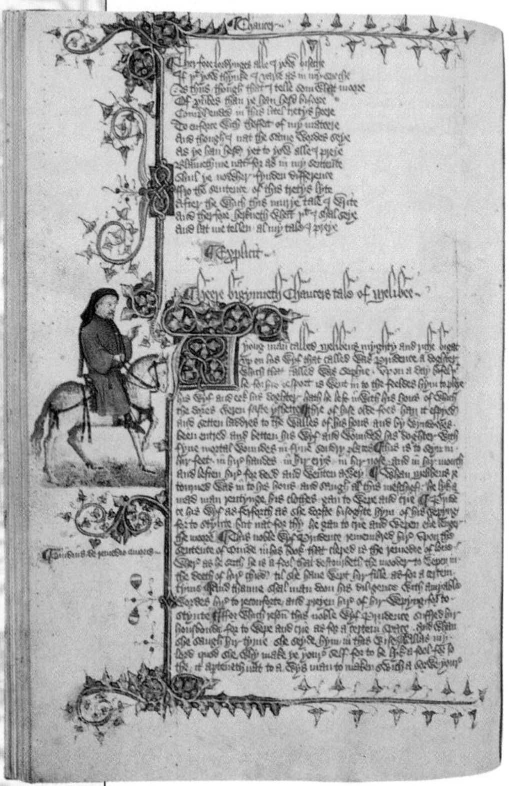

By permission of The Huntington Library, San Marino, California.

Professional Notes

Critical Comment: Few Stories, Great Delight

According to the Host's plan, each pilgrim is to tell two tales on the way to Canterbury and two on the way back—a total of one hundred twenty tales. At a rate of one per month, it would have taken Chaucer ten years to complete *The Canterbury Tales.* In fact, he wrote only twenty-four of the tales in five years. Those stories provide a survey of medieval genres: courtly romance, fabliau (a humorous, satirical, often bawdy tale), pious legend, allegory, beast fable, sermon, and more. They also provide a feast for discussion, exploring, as they do, human frailty and nobility, humor and tragedy, earthly pursuits and spiritual aspirations—in other words, the richness and complexity of the human condition.

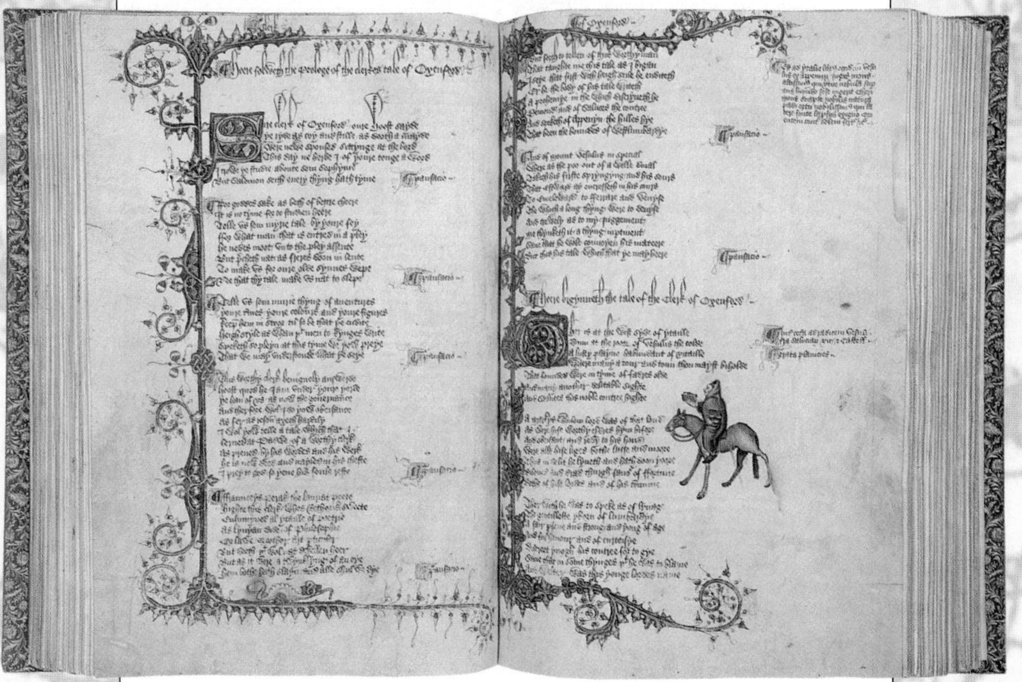

By permission of The Huntington Library, San Marino, California.

Pages from *The Canterbury Tales,* from the Ellesmere manuscript (15th century).

> In all literature there is nothing that touches or resembles the *Prologue.* It is the concise portrait of an entire nation, high and low, old and young, male and female, lay and clerical, learned and ignorant, rogue and righteous, land and sea, town and country, but without extremes. Apart from the stunning clarity, touched with nuance, of the characters presented, the most noticeable thing about them is their normality. They are the perennial progeny of men and women. Sharply individual, together they make a party. **E**

Chaucer, from the Ellesmere manuscript, fol. 153v.

By permission of The Huntington Library, San Marino, California.

At its most basic level, Chaucer's great work possesses an archetypal unity. As a pilgrimage story, it is one of the world's many quest narratives, and it moves appropriately from images of spring and awakening at the beginning of the Prologue to images of penance, death, and eternal life in the Parson's tale at the end of the work. The storytellers themselves are pilgrims, presumably in search of renewal at the Thomas à Becket shrine. Coming as they do from all walks of life, all social classes, they cannot help but represent "everyman," or all of us, on our universal pilgrimage through life. **F**

E Literary Connections

Characterization

Another critic praises Chaucer in this way: "Perhaps the most distinctive of Chaucer's gifts as storyteller is his ability to delineate characters and put them in realistic motion. They come most patently alive in the prologues to the individual tales and in the narrative links (the lively exchanges among the Pilgrims between tales), but most of his people are realized three-dimensionally in the General Prologue as well. The pilgrims make up a human encyclopedia comprehensive and universal but composed of unique individuals."

F Literary Connections

Everyman

Everyman, a drama written in the late fifteenth century, is a morality play in which characters represent abstract ideas, such as Knowledge and Wealth. Everyman is all men, or all people. He is fundamentally good yet drawn by the world of the senses. The play focuses on Everyman's transformation when he must confront death.

Responding to the Art

About ninety manuscripts of *The Canterbury Tales* exist, but not all of them include all the tales. The Ellesmere manuscript, now at the Huntington Library in San Marino, California, is considered the best. Because it was unusual for a secular manuscript to be so elaborately illustrated, scholars assume an aristocrat commissioned this manuscript of Chaucer's masterpiece.

Professional Notes

Critical Comment: Fictional Reporting

While it is true that *The Canterbury Tales* form a remarkable snapshot of an age, E. Talbot Donaldson reminds the reader that the *Tales* are fiction: "I am under the impression that too many readers, too much influenced by Chaucer's brilliant verisimilitude, tend to regard his famous pilgrimage to Canterbury as significant not because it is great fiction, but because it seems to be a remarkable record of a fourteenth-century pilgrimage. A remarkable record it may be, but if we treat it too narrowly as such there are going to be certain casualties among the elements that make up the fiction. Perhaps first among these elements is the fictional reporter, Chaucer the pilgrim, and the role he plays in the Prologue to *The Canterbury Tales* and in the links between them." Donaldson goes on to say Chaucer played different roles in telling his story: He is at times Chaucer the man, Chaucer the pilgrim, and Chaucer the poet.

Ⓐ Literary Connections

The English Language

In *The Story of English*, Robert McCrum, William Cran, and Robert MacNeil write: "From the beginning, English was a crafty hybrid, made in war and peace. It was, in the words of Daniel Defoe, 'your Roman-Saxon-Danish-Norman English.' In the course of one thousand years, a series of violent and dramatic events created a new language which, by the time of Geoffrey Chaucer, is intelligible to modern eyes and ears without the aid of subtitles." After students have read pp. 104–105, ask them if they agree that no "subtitles" are needed. [Many students will feel a translation is absolutely necessary for them to enjoy the work.]

Ⓑ Appreciating Language

Rhymes and Language Change

Rhymes help historians learn how English once sounded. Among poets of Middle English, Chaucer is thought to have been absolutely meticulous about his rhymes. This has enabled linguists to conclude which sound distinctions existed in Chaucer's day, as well as which sound distinctions have appeared or been lost since then.

RESPONDING TO THE ART

William Morris (1834–1896) was a British intellectual who believed that art developed from the love of craft. He founded his own firm to design and manufacture wallpaper and furniture, and his creative efforts ignited the arts and crafts movement. He was a great admirer of the Middle Ages.

Activity. Ask how this title page differs from the title pages of books today. [The pages are highly embellished and the type is artfully chosen to mimic the work of medieval scribes.]

William Morris's edition of *The Works of Geoffrey Chaucer*, published by the Kelmscott Press. C. 43. h. 17.

By permission of the British Library, London.

Chaucer's Middle English is here translated into Modern English by Nevill Coghill. While this version is true to the spirit of Chaucer's original poem, you might attempt at least bits of the *Tales* in the wonderfully musical original.

Brief Pronunciation Guide to Middle English

Vowels

a: *ah,* as in *father.*
ai, ay, ei, ey: a long *a,* as in *pay.*
au, aw: *ow,* as in *house.*
oo: *oh,* as in *oat.*
e: at times, like a long *a,* as in *mate*. When a double *e* is used, it is always long. *Eek* is pronounced āk.
e: at times, like a short *e,* as in *men.*

Ⓐ The final *e* in Middle English is a separate syllable sounded like a final *ah: soote* rhymes with *soda*. But when the final *e* precedes a word that starts with a vowel Ⓑ or an *h,* it is not sounded. In "droghte of March," the final *e* in *droghte* is silent.

Consonants

g: hard *g,* as in *go*, except before *e* or *i* (in words borrowed from French) where it is sounded like *zh,* as in *garage. Pilgrimage* rhymes with *garage.*
gh, ch: like the German *ch,* as in *nicht*. (These sounds are usually silent in Modern English.) *Knight* is pronounced k•nicht′.
–tion, –cial: The *t* and *c* in such words are not blended with the *i* as they are in Modern English (as in the words *condition* and *special*). The *i* is sounded as a separate syllable. *Special* would have three syllables and *condition* four: kon•di•sē•ôn′. (*C* has the sound of *s* when it comes before *i.*)

Preteaching Vocabulary

Words to Own

Have students work in pairs to drill each other on the meanings of words listed at the bottom of the text pages, under the heading, "Words to Own." Students can use the words to complete the following sentences.

1. The [diligent] clerk was promoted to manager.
2. Don't be so [obstinate]; accept the compromise.
3. Don't show off; be [discreet].
4. To save more money, let interest [accrue].
5. They [deferred] the decision until tomorrow.
6. Stop [engendering] confusion!
7. His [guile] certainly tricked me!
8. Be strong; this [adversity] will pass.
9. His [disdainful] sneer revealed his low regard.
10. He is of very tall [stature].
11. She did it under [duress], not voluntarily.
12. The new [statute] will be hard to enforce.
13. A [frugal] buyer watches for sales.
14. He means no harm; his intentions are [benign].
15. Her [personable] ways earn her many friends.

Before You Read

FROM **THE CANTERBURY TALES**

Make the Connection

From Sketch to Portrait

If you went on a tour today, what types of people would you expect to meet? Most of Chaucer's pilgrims are the kinds of people he would have known and perhaps even observed many times riding toward Canterbury on the old pilgrimage road. Here in the *Tales* is a cross section of medieval life: the conservative military man, the talkative and often-married feminist, the lover, the barnyard humorist, the elegant and Frenchified nun, to name a few. Chaucer seems mainly to describe his travelers' appearances in what appear to be mere physical sketches. But a close reading shows that he has cleverly selected details that give us shrewd psychological portraits as well.

Quickwrite

Spend a few minutes describing a real or an imaginary person's appearance, from tip to toe. Try to show how certain details of the person's appearance suggest certain character traits (that she is miserly, that he is vain, that he wants to look like a popular rock star, and so on). Keep your notes.

Elements of Literature

Characterization

To create the portraits of his pilgrim characters—"nine and twenty in a company of sundry folk," Chaucer uses the methods of characterization that writers continue to use to this day. Like his contemporary counterparts, Chaucer reveals his characters

- by telling us directly what the character is like
- by describing how the character looks and dresses
- by presenting the character's words and actions
- by revealing the character's private thoughts and feelings
- by showing how other people respond to the character

Characterization is the process by which the writer reveals the personality of a character.

For more on Character, see the Handbook of Literary Terms.

Background

When Chaucer chooses to have each of his pilgrims tell a story on the way to Canterbury, he is using a popular literary device, the frame story. A **frame story** is a story that includes any number of different narratives. Chaucer uses the outer story of the pilgrimage to unite his travelers' individual tales, and the tales themselves have thematic unity as well. The hundred tales in Boccaccio's *Decameron* (page 154) and the roughly one hundred tales in *The Arabian Nights* are each set within a single fictional frame as well. The frame story is still used today. If you've read Amy Tan's *The Joy Luck Club,* you've read a modern frame story.

Chaucer reciting his poetry. Ms. 61, fr.

The Master and Fellows of Corpus Christi College, Cambridge.

Summary ■■

The prologue introduces the twenty-nine pilgrims who, along with the narrator, are on their way to the shrine of St. Thomas à Becket in Canterbury. The time is April, and the place is The Tabard Inn, just outside London, where the pilgrims are staying overnight. The narrator describes the pilgrims, revealing their personalities through direct and indirect characterization, sharp images, and figurative comparisons. (Chaucer's descriptions of dress and appearance are particularly revealing of psychological traits.) The pilgrims generally fall into the three major divisions of medieval society: the feudal order (like the Knight and his Squire), the church (like the Monk and the Nun), and the merchant or professional class (like the Miller and the Doctor). The narrator then says he will repeat what he has seen and heard, no matter how offensive. Finally, he describes the Host's proposal that each pilgrim tell two tales on the way and two on the return. (The last 22 lines of the Prologue are omitted; they are a lead-in to the Knight's Tale.)

Reaching All Students

Struggling Readers

Pair struggling readers with more proficient readers. As they read the Prologue aloud, have them take notes on each new character. For example, after students meet the Knight, they might write: "The Knight a nobleman, seasoned in battle, brave but not boastful, courteous, and sincere."

English Language Learners

To engage English language learners, have them listen to the description of each pilgrim on the recording in the *Audio CD Library.* Then replay the segment on the CD, listing on the board adjectives that describe the character or verbs that show an action the character has taken. Ask students to describe from these lists their mental pictures of each pilgrim. For other strategies, see

- *Lesson Plans Including Strategies for English-Language Learners*

Advanced Learners

Have advanced learners categorize or classify the pilgrims, using such categories as gender, occupation, style of dress, social class, appearance, attitude toward money, moral character, and personality. (All students will later be asked to classify the pilgrims according to their roles in medieval society; see p. 127, Reading Check item c.)

Ⓐ Appreciating Language

Natural Speech

Play the CD recording of the first eighteen lines of the Prologue in Middle English from the *Audio CD Library,* and ask students for their impressions. Let students know that no matter how archaic Chaucer's East Midland dialect may seem at first glance, it was the colloquial language of his day, the language he heard all around him, on the streets and in the taverns.

Ⓑ Elements of Literature

Rhythm and Rhyme

Chaucer wrote in iambic pentameter, which reflects the natural rhythm of the spoken language. However, he pulled off a tremendous coup: He wrote his tales in rhyming couplets. The couplets do not, however, have an unnatural or singsong quality because they are not end-stopped. The complete thought doesn't end when the couplet ends; instead, a reader has to read beyond the end of a line. This use of "open couplets" creates a highly crafted poetry that sounds entirely natural.

Explore with students the rhymes in the first few lines of both the Middle English and contemporary versions. Have students practice reading both aloud, using punctuation and meaning rather than lines to guide their voices.

Ⓒ Advanced Learners

Analyzing Middle English

Students may enjoy doing a line-by-line comparison of the Middle English and contemporary versions. Direct them to watch for words that have survived unchanged (*that, with, his*), those that have undergone some change (*whan, flour, slepen*), and those the translator had to replace altogether (*soote* to *sweet, swich* to *such, corages* to *heart*). Ask students to form generalizations based on their analyses. [Possible answers: The most common words have survived intact. Verbs, nouns, and adjectives have lost their inflected endings; for example, *slepen* has become *sleep.*]

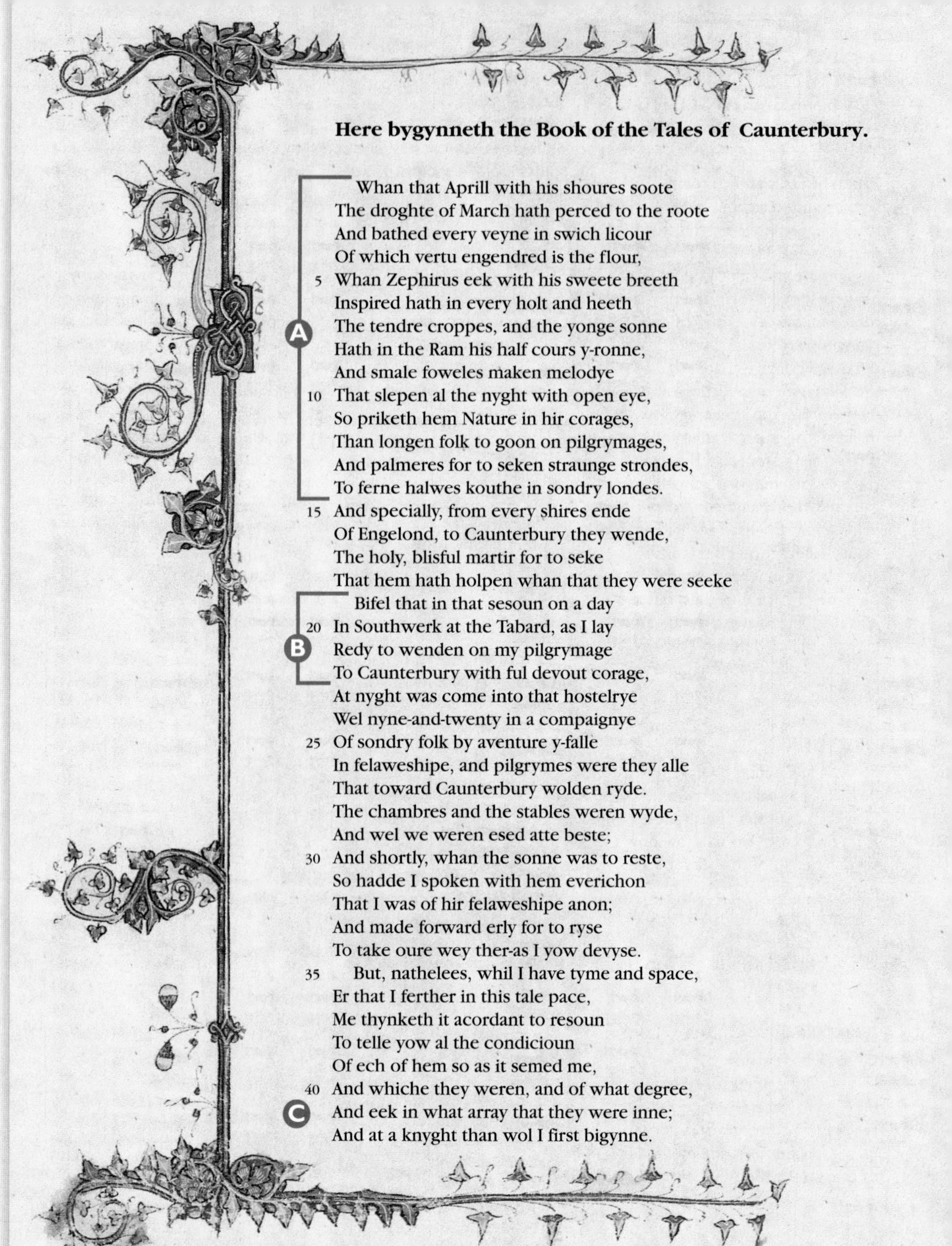

Here bygynneth the Book of the Tales of Caunterbury.

Whan that Aprill with his shoures soote
The droghte of March hath perced to the roote
And bathed every veyne in swich licour
Of which vertu engendred is the flour,
Whan Zephirus eek with his sweete breeth
Inspired hath in every holt and heeth
The tendre croppes, and the yonge sonne
Hath in the Ram his half cours y-ronne,
And smale foweles maken melodye
That slepen al the nyght with open eye,
So priketh hem Nature in hir corages,
Than longen folk to goon on pilgrymages,
And palmeres for to seken straunge strondes,
To ferne halwes kouthe in sondry londes.
And specially, from every shires ende
Of Engelond, to Caunterbury they wende,
The holy, blisful martir for to seke
That hem hath holpen whan that they were seeke
Bifel that in that sesoun on a day
In Southwerk at the Tabard, as I lay
Redy to wenden on my pilgrymage
To Caunterbury with ful devout corage,
At nyght was come into that hostelrye
Wel nyne-and-twenty in a compaignye
Of sondry folk by aventure y-falle
In felaweshipe, and pilgrymes were they alle
That toward Caunterbury wolden ryde.
The chambres and the stables weren wyde,
And wel we weren esed atte beste;
And shortly, whan the sonne was to reste,
So hadde I spoken with hem everichon
That I was of hir felaweshipe anon;
And made forward erly for to ryse
To take oure wey ther-as I yow devyse.
But, nathelees, whil I have tyme and space,
Er that I ferther in this tale pace,
Me thynketh it acordant to resoun
To telle yow al the condicioun
Of ech of hem so as it semed me,
And whiche they weren, and of what degree,
And eek in what array that they were inne;
And at a knyght than wol I first bigynne.

Page from *The Canterbury Tales,* from the Ellesmere manuscript (detail) (15th century).

By permission of The Huntington Library, San Marino, California.

Professional Notes

Critical Comment: Chaucer's Spelling

Students may enjoy this humorous comment on Chaucer's language from Artemus Ward (an American humorist and contemporary of Mark Twain): "Mr. C. had talent, but he couldn't spel. No man has a right to be a lit'rary man onless he knows how to spel. It is a pitty that Chawcer, who had geneyus, was so unedicated. He's the wus speller I know of."

from The Canterbury Tales

Geoffrey Chaucer
translated by **Nevill Coghill**

The Prologue

When in April the sweet showers fall
And pierce the drought of March to the root, and all
The veins are bathed in liquor of such power
As brings about the engendering of the flower,
When also Zephyrus° with his sweet breath
Exhales an air in every grove and heath
Upon the tender shoots, and the young sun
His half-course in the sign of the *Ram*° has run,
And the small fowl are making melody
That sleep away the night with open eye
(So nature pricks them and their heart engages)
Then people long to go on pilgrimages
And palmers° long to seek the stranger strands
Of far-off saints, hallowed in sundry lands,
And specially, from every shire's end
Of England, down to Canterbury they wend
To seek the holy blissful martyr,° quick
To give his help to them when they were sick.
  It happened in that season that one day
In Southwark, at *The Tabard,* as I lay
Ready to go on pilgrimage and start
For Canterbury, most devout at heart,
At night there came into that hostelry
Some nine and twenty in a company
Of sundry folk happening then to fall
In fellowship, and they were pilgrims all
That towards Canterbury meant to ride.
The rooms and stables of the inn were wide:
They made us easy, all was of the best.
And, briefly, when the sun had gone to rest,
I'd spoken to them all upon the trip
And was soon one with them in fellowship,
Pledged to rise early and to take the way
To Canterbury, as you heard me say.
  But none the less, while I have time and space,
Before my story takes a further pace,
It seems a reasonable thing to say

5. Zephyrus (zef'ə·rəs): in Greek mythology, god of the west wind.

8. Ram: Aries, first sign of the zodiac. The time is mid-April.

13. palmers: people who had visited the Holy Land and wore palm fronds to show it.

17. martyr: Saint Thomas à Becket (c. 1118–1170) was martyred at Canterbury, December 29, 1170.

WORDS TO OWN
engendering (en·jen'dər·iŋ) *v.* used as *n.*: creation; production.

D Reading Skills and Strategies

Monitoring Reading

? Point out that ll. 1–18 are all one sentence. After two adverbial clauses beginning with *when* that note the time of year, April, the poet introduces his main point. What is it? [the fact that, according to the poet, people long to go on pilgrimages in the spring] **Why might the urge to go on a pilgrimage hit people in spring?** [Possible answer: Winter is over; it's time for renewal.]

E Struggling Readers

Breaking Down Difficult Text

Students will quickly become aware that many of Chaucer's sentences are very long. Help students break down the long sentences to identify the central idea or event in each. Have them begin with this one, by asking who is at the Inn [the narrator] **and who arrives** [twenty-nine pilgrims]. **Then ask them to state the central idea.** [Central idea: Nine and twenty, or twenty-nine, pilgrims arrive at The Tabard Inn, where the narrator-poet is staying.]

F Elements of Literature

Rhymes and Translation

? Have students compare the rhymes in the translation with those in Chaucer's original. How many rhymes are preserved, even though pronunciations differ today? [Examples: day/lay, hostelry/company, fall/all.]

Professional Notes

Critical Comment: Pilgrimages

According to *The Writer's Guide to Everyday Life in the Middle Ages,* pilgrimages were a popular pastime. People decided to go on one for three possible reasons:

- to improve their chances of salvation
- to gain the healing touch supposedly found in the relics of saints
- to atone for their sins

Historian John Sumption in *Pilgrimage: An Image of Medieval Religion* also argues that people undertook pilgrimages to avoid the shame of publicly confessing their sins at home. Most historians also agree that people often went on pilgrimages just because they wanted to travel, meet new people, and perhaps escape the drudgery of their daily lives. Just as today's tourists have *Fodor's,* pilgrims had a number of guidebooks to help them out, including *Liber Sancti Jacobi* and *Guide for Pilgrims to Saint James.* The pilgrims needed all the help they could get because they were often attacked by thieves and/or swindled by charlatans. These dangers explain why such "sundry folk" or "strange bedfellows" bonded together on these journeys.

Ⓐ Historical Connections

Feudal Wars

The Knight truly is a brave and distinguished man, for the wars in which he fought spanned forty years and fell into three groups: against the Moors at the west end of the Mediterranean, against the Turks at the Mediterranean's east end, and against Lithuanians and Tartars on the Russian border. During this period, the West followed the Church's lead and condemned these enemies as *infidels* or *pagans,* terms applied to those who did not believe in Christ.

Ⓑ Historical Connections

Feudal Order

Point out that the Knight, as Chaucer portrays him here, is an anachronistic figure. The feudal order with its emphasis on chivalry (the knight's code of honor) had all but disappeared by Chaucer's time.

Responding to the Art

Activity. After students have read the Prologue, ask them to assign the names of characters in *The Canterbury Tales* to the people in the illustration. Then ask students to justify their choices by pointing out the details that help to identify the characters.

Miniature of John Lydgate and the Canterbury pilgrims leaving Canterbury, from a volume of Lydgate's poems (early 16th century). MS Royal 18 D II, fol. 148.

British Library, London.

What their condition was, the full array
Of each of them, as it appeared to me,
According to profession and degree,
And what apparel they were riding in;
And at a Knight I therefore will begin.
There was a *Knight,* a most distinguished man,
Who from the day on which he first began
To ride abroad had followed chivalry,
Truth, honor, generousness, and courtesy.
He had done nobly in his sovereign's war
And ridden into battle, no man more,
As well in Christian as in heathen places,

Using Students' Strengths

Auditory/Musical Learners

Ask students to imagine that they, too, have joined the pilgrimage and are riding their horse in the procession. Notice how the steady rhythm of the iambic pentameter suggests the pace of the pilgrimage itself. Ask students to read aloud a section of the Prologue and listen to the rhythm.

Visual Learners

Chaucer delights in visual detail. (He would be the first to point out that someone has a wart on his nose.) As students read, invite them to make a cluster diagram for each character. They should record details about the actions, occupation, dress, physical appearance, and speech of each pilgrim. Some will be inspired to do their own illustrations.

And ever honored for his noble graces.
When we took Alexandria,° he was there.
He often sat at table in the chair
Of honor, above all nations, when in Prussia.
In Lithuania he had ridden, and Russia,
No Christian man so often, of his rank.
When, in Granada, Algeciras sank
Under assault, he had been there, and in
North Africa, raiding Benamarin;
In Anatolia he had been as well
And fought when Ayas and Attalia fell,
For all along the Mediterranean coast
He had embarked with many a noble host.
In fifteen mortal battles he had been
And jousted for our faith at Tramissene
Thrice in the lists, and always killed his man.
This same distinguished knight had led the van
Once with the Bey of Balat, doing work
For him against another heathen Turk;
He was of sovereign value in all eyes.
And though so much distinguished, he was wise
And in his bearing modest as a maid.
He never yet a boorish thing had said
In all his life to any, come what might;
He was a true, a perfect gentle-knight.°
Speaking of his equipment, he possessed
Fine horses, but he was not gaily dressed.
He wore a fustian° tunic stained and dark
With smudges where his armor had left mark;
Just home from service, he had joined our ranks
To do his pilgrimage and render thanks.
He had his son with him, a fine young *Squire,*
A lover and cadet,° a lad of fire
With locks as curly as if they had been pressed.
He was some twenty years of age, I guessed.
In stature he was of a moderate length,
With wonderful agility and strength.
He'd seen some service with the cavalry
In Flanders and Artois and Picardy
And had done valiantly in little space
Of time, in hope to win his lady's grace.
He was embroidered like a meadow bright
And full of freshest flowers, red and white.
Singing he was, or fluting all the day;
He was as fresh as is the month of May.
Short was his gown, the sleeves were long and wide;

WORDS TO OWN
stature (stach′ər) *n.:* height.

51. Alexandria: city in Egypt captured by the Crusaders in 1365. In the next few lines, Chaucer is indicating the knight's distinguished and extensive career.

The Knight, from the Ellesmere manuscript, fol. 10r.

By permission of The Huntington Library, San Marino, California.

74. gentle-knight: In Chaucer's day, *gentle* meant "well bred and considerate."

77. fustian (fus′chən): coarse cloth made of linen and cotton.

82. cadet: soldier.

The Squire, from the Ellesmere manuscript, fol. 115v.

By permission of The Huntington Library, San Marino, California.

C Reading Skills and Strategies

Drawing Conclusions

? What qualities does the Knight possess that are different from those you might expect in a veteran soldier who has been fighting for forty years? [Possible answers: He is modest, considerate, and well-mannered. He is the ideal of chivalry.]

D Elements of Literature

Characterization

? Explain that when Chaucer directly states qualities of the Knight, as in ll. 70–74, he is using direct characterization. On the other hand, ll. 76–78, constitute indirect characterization, because clues help reveal the character. What does the Knight's soiled clothing reveal about him? [The fact that the fustian is coarse and worn suggests a plain, honest, modest man who cares more about thanking God for his blessings than he does about making an impression on others. He might not have much money.]

E Struggling Readers

Using Graphic Aids

There is no gloss for the word *squire,* but there is a clue to the word's meaning in the illustration. Ask students to use the illustration to define *squire* and to compare the Squire with the Knight. [A squire is a knight's attendant. The Squire is younger; his clothing is flashier; his hair is well-coiffed; both he and his horse seem more active, less sedate. Perhaps the Squire also is less knowledgeable or wise.]

F Cultural Connections

The Squire's Clothing

According to Chaucerian expert Muriel Bowden, the Squire's clothing stresses his youthfulness and frivolity: "Short, embroidered gowns and long, wide sleeves were the marks of the ultrafashionable in the late fourteenth century, and pulpit complaints . . . were frequent: short coats were denounced as 'indecent'; embroidery was called unnecessarily expensive (the money so spent should be given to the poor)."

Skill Link

Using Context Clues

Remind students that many words have multiple meanings and that the text often signals the intended meaning. Have students use context clues to determine the intended meaning of each italicized word below. (In some cases, students may need to consult a dictionary to find meanings they may not be familiar with.)

1. "When we *took* Alexandria, he was there." [l. 51]
2. "when Ayas and Attalia *fell,*" [l. 60]
3. "embarked with many a noble *host.*" [l. 62]
4. "and jousted . . . in the *lists* and always killed his man." [ll. 64–65]
5. "He'd seen some *service* with the cavalry" [l. 87]

Also encourage students to use context clues to figure out the meaning of the figurative language used to describe the Squire in ll. 91–92.

Ⓐ Advanced Learners

Close Reading

Have students note the Yeoman's garb. Yeomen once were knights' servants, but later they became landowners and occupied a class just below the gentry. Students may enjoy comparing the descriptions of the characters in the text with the illustrations from the Ellesmere manuscript. Ask what details are omitted from the illustrations.

Ⓑ Historical Connections

Nuns

A nun is a woman who lives in a convent and takes vows of poverty, chastity, and obedience; a prioress is in charge of the nuns. As Mother Superior of a convent, a prioress is under oath not to leave her charges. Have students notice as they read whether this Prioress seems to be a conventional nun. The Prioress's swearing by St. Loy (the patron saint of goldsmiths) is ironic because this saint was known for his refusal to swear.

Ⓒ Elements of Literature

Characterization

? What do these details suggest about the Prioress? [Possible answers: We are told that her French is not good French. She is extremely careful about her table manners, and she consciously eats in a supposedly refined way. She puts on the airs of courtly grace, but to a careful observer like the narrator, her manners are counterfeit. Note: Eglantyne is a kind of rose and also is the name of several romantic heroines. The Prioress herself is a romantic.]

Ⓓ Vocabulary Note

Prefixes and Roots

Point out the word *counterfeit.* Ask students what other words they know that begin with the prefix *counter-* and what the prefix means. [Possible answers: *counterclockwise, counterattack, counterpoint.* The prefix means "against" or "opposite."] Explain that the remainder of the word comes from the Latin word for "to make." A counterfeit is something that is made in imitation of the real thing; it is a fake.

He knew the way to sit a horse and ride.
He could make songs and poems and recite,
Knew how to joust and dance, to draw and write.
He loved so hotly that till dawn grew pale
He slept as little as a nightingale.
Courteous he was, lowly and serviceable,
And carved to serve his father at the table.
  There was a *Yeoman* with him at his side,
No other servant; so he chose to ride.
This Yeoman wore a coat and hood of green,
And peacock-feathered arrows, bright and keen
And neatly sheathed, hung at his belt the while
—For he could dress his gear in yeoman style,
His arrows never drooped their feathers low—
And in his hand he bore a mighty bow.
His head was like a nut, his face was brown.
He knew the whole of woodcraft up and down.
A saucy brace was on his arm to ward
It from the bow-string, and a shield and sword
Hung at one side, and at the other slipped
A jaunty dirk,° spear-sharp and well-equipped.
A medal of St. Christopher° he wore
Of shining silver on his breast, and bore
A hunting-horn, well slung and burnished clean,
That dangled from a baldrick° of bright green.
He was a proper forester, I guess.
  There also was a *Nun,* a Prioress,
Her way of smiling very simple and coy.
Her greatest oath was only "By St. Loy!"°
And she was known as Madam Eglantyne.
And well she sang a service, with a fine
Intoning through her nose, as was most seemly,
And she spoke daintily in French, extremely,
After the school of Stratford-atte-Bowe;°
French in the Paris style she did not know.
At meat her manners were well taught withal;
No morsel from her lips did she let fall,
Nor dipped her fingers in the sauce too deep;
But she could carry a morsel up and keep
The smallest drop from falling on her breast.
For courtliness she had a special zest,
And she would wipe her upper lip so clean
That not a trace of grease was to be seen
Upon the cup when she had drunk; to eat,
She reached a hand sedately for the meat.
She certainly was very entertaining,
Pleasant and friendly in her ways, and straining
To counterfeit a courtly kind of grace,
A stately bearing fitting to her place,

The Canon Yeoman, from the Ellesmere manuscript, fol. 194r.

By permission of The Huntington Library, San Marino, California.

116. dirk: long dagger.

117. St. Christopher: patron saint of travelers.

120. baldrick: belt slung over the shoulder and chest to hold a sword.

124. St. Loy: Saint Eligius, known for his perfect manners.

129. Stratford-atte-Bowe: Benedictine convent near London where inferior French was spoken.

The Prioress, from the Ellesmere manuscript, fol. 148v.

By permission of The Huntington Library, San Marino, California.

Getting Students Involved

Cooperative Learning

On the Road to Canterbury. Have students work in teams of four. Assign each team four pilgrims. Groups should think of ways to create two-dimensional representations of pilgrims that they can place on a road to Canterbury with the other pilgrims. Each pilgrim should be dressed in character; additionally, each should be accompanied by a speech balloon with some characteristic saying. All students in each group should brainstorm ways to represent the pilgrims, but each student should be responsible for creating one pilgrim. When groups have finished their work, have students place their work on a long expanse of paper that represents the road to Canterbury. Have them explain how they decided on the riding order.

And to seem dignified in all her dealings.
As for her sympathies and tender feelings,
She was so charitably solicitous
She used to weep if she but saw a mouse
Caught in a trap, if it were dead or bleeding.
And she had little dogs she would be feeding
With roasted flesh, or milk, or fine white bread. **E**
And bitterly she wept if one were dead
Or someone took a stick and made it smart;
She was all sentiment and tender heart.
Her veil was gathered in a seemly way,
Her nose was elegant, her eyes glass-gray;
Her mouth was very small, but soft and red, **F**
Her forehead, certainly, was fair of spread,
Almost a span° across the brows, I own;
She was indeed by no means undergrown. **G**
Her cloak, I noticed, had a graceful charm.
She wore a coral trinket on her arm,
A set of beads, the gaudies tricked in green,°
Whence hung a golden brooch of brightest sheen **H**
On which there first was graven a crowned A,
And lower, *Amor vincit omnia.*°
Another *Nun,* the secretary at her cell,°
Was riding with her, and *three Priests* as well.
A *Monk* there was, one of the finest sort
Who rode the country; hunting was his sport.
A manly man, to be an Abbott able;
Many a dainty horse he had in stable.
His bridle, when he rode, a man might hear
Jingling in a whistling wind as clear,
Aye, and as loud as does the chapel bell
Where my lord Monk was Prior of the cell.
The Rule of good St. Benet or St. Maur°
As old and strict he tended to ignore;
He let go by the things of yesterday
And took the modern world's more spacious way.
He did not rate that text at a plucked hen
Which says that hunters are not holy men
And that a monk uncloistered is a mere
Fish out of water, flapping on the pier,
That is to say a monk out of his cloister.
That was a text he held not worth an oyster;
And I agreed and said his views were sound;
Was he to study till his head went round
Poring over books in cloisters? Must he toil
As Austin° bade and till the very soil?
Was he to leave the world upon the shelf?
Let Austin have his labor to himself.
This Monk was therefore a good man to horse;

The Nun's Priest, from the Ellesmere manuscript, fol. 179r.

By permission of The Huntington Library, San Marino, California.

159. span: nine inches.

163. a set of beads . . . green: Beads are a rosary, or prayer beads and a crucifix on a string or chain. Every eleventh bead is a gaud, a large bead indicating when the Lord's Prayer is to be said.

166. *Amor vincit omnia* (ä′môr vin′chit ôm′nē·ä′): Latin for "Love conquers all."

167. cell: a small convent connected to a larger one.

177. St. Benet [Benedict] **or St. Maur** [Maurice]: Saint Benedict (c. 480–c. 547) was an Italian monk who founded numerous monasteries and wrote a famous code of regulations for monastic life. Saint Maurice was a follower of Benedict.

190. Austin: Saint Augustine (354–430), bishop of Hippo in North Africa. He criticized lazy monks and suggested they do some hard manual labor.

Using Students' Strengths

Interpersonal Learners

Have students become experts on one well-developed character presented in the Prologue. Then have the "expert" present, or teach, that character to the class.

Intrapersonal Learners

Have students create a diary entry in which they reflect on an imaginary meeting they had with one of the pilgrims. Ask students to record some of their impressions, as well as some of the dialogue that took place.

Verbal Learners

Model reading part of the Prologue aloud to students. As you do so, discuss ways to use pitch, volume, and pauses to achieve fluency and to add dramatic effect. Then read more of the Prologue, and have students identify your use of these skills. Have students work in pairs to practice their own skills on selected passages.

E Critical Thinking
Making Inferences

? Nuns were not supposed to keep pets because the money required for their care was meant for the poor. Based on this bit of information, what can you infer about the Prioress? [She seems more concerned about luxuries than about her responsibilities to her order.]

F Literary Connections

? In Chaucer's time, physical characteristics, such as gap teeth or a white neck, revealed a person's character. Chaucer uses such details to illuminate his characters' inner nature. (See pp. 127–128 for more on this subject.) In the case of the Prioress, the revealing detail is a high forehead, considered a sign of intelligence and good breeding. Note, however, that a nine-inch brow would be most unusual. Why do you think Chaucer exaggerates this feature? [Possible response: He might be exaggerating to gently mock the Prioress for her pretensions to good breeding.]

G Elements of Literature
Understatement

? What effect is created by saying she is "by no means undergrown" rather than saying "She is indeed overgrown"? [Possible answer: The understatement adds to the lightly amusing satire of the Prioress. She must be a bit heavy, or at least very tall.]

H Elements of Literature
Characterization

? In Chaucer's time, coral was considered a defense against worldly temptation, as well as a love charm. Why does he picture the Prioress with a coral trinket on her arm? [Possible answers: It shows she is interested in love, though as a nun, she should not be. Or it shows she is trying to ward off worldly temptation. Since she does not seem to deny herself worldly luxuries, such as a nice veil and cloak, however, it seems possible she also does not deny herself love.]

A Elements of Literature

Characterization

? Like a nun, a monk is a member of a religious order who has taken vows of poverty, chastity, and obedience. How do the details of the Monk's character suggest, without directly saying, that this Monk is not serious about his vocation? [The monk rides a fine horse, hunts hares, wears rich clothes and jewelry, and enjoys good food, such as fat swans (traditionally cooked with their feathers on).]

B Elements of Literature

Irony

? Because peasants in the Middle Ages did not always have enough to eat, obesity was a sign of success and affluence. Why is it ironic that a monk is fat? [Possible response: According to his vow of poverty, a monk is meant to suffer for the world's sins, not enjoy the world's temptations.]

C Elements of Literature

Characterization

? Unlike monks, who lived in monasteries, friars went into the world as beggars to preach, help the poor, and cure the sick. One of a friar's duties was to hear people's confessions and to absolve or forgive them with a penance, or penalty of prayer, or doing good works. How does Chaucer characterize this Friar in these lines? [Possible answer: Chaucer's Friar gives light penances because people pay him. He is more interested in making money than in saving people's souls.]

Greyhounds he had, as swift as birds, to course.°
Hunting a hare or riding at a fence
Was all his fun, he spared for no expense.
I saw his sleeves were garnished at the hand
With fine gray fur, the finest in the land,
And on his hood, to fasten it at his chin
He had a wrought-gold, cunningly fashioned pin;
Into a lover's knot it seemed to pass.
His head was bald and shone like looking-glass;
So did his face, as if it had been greased.
He was a fat and personable priest;
His prominent eyeballs never seemed to settle.
They glittered like the flames beneath a kettle;
Supple his boots, his horse in fine condition.
He was a prelate fit for exhibition,
He was not pale like a tormented soul.
He liked a fat swan best, and roasted whole.
His palfrey° was as brown as is a berry.
  There was a *Friar,* a wanton° one and merry,
A Limiter,° a very festive fellow.
In all Four Orders° there was none so mellow,
So glib with gallant phrase and well-turned speech.
He'd fixed up many a marriage, giving each
Of his young women what he could afford her.
He was a noble pillar to his Order.
Highly beloved and intimate was he
With County folk within his boundary,
And city dames of honor and possessions;
For he was qualified to hear confessions,
Or so he said, with more than priestly scope;
He had a special license from the Pope.
Sweetly he heard his penitents at shrift°
With pleasant absolution, for a gift.
He was an easy man in penance-giving
Where he could hope to make a decent living;
It's a sure sign whenever gifts are given
To a poor Order that a man's well shriven,°
And should he give enough he knew in verity
The penitent repented in sincerity.
For many a fellow is so hard of heart
He cannot weep, for all his inward smart.
Therefore instead of weeping and of prayer
One should give silver for a poor Friar's care.
He kept his tippet° stuffed with pins for curls,
And pocket-knives, to give to pretty girls.

194. course: to cause to chase game.

The Friar, from the Ellesmere manuscript, fol. 76v.

By permission of The Huntington Library, San Marino, California.

211. palfrey: horse.

212. wanton: here, jolly.

213. Limiter: a friar having the exclusive right to beg and preach in an assigned (limited) district.

214. Four Orders: The four orders of mendicant (beggar) friars are the Franciscans, the Dominicans, the Carmelites, and the Augustinians.

225. shrift: confession and absolution.

230. well shriven: well confessed and absolved (or forgiven) of sins.

237. tippet: hood or long sleeve (of his robe).

WORDS TO OWN

personable (pʉr′sən·ə·bəl) *adj.:* attractive in appearance and personality.

Taking a Second Look

Review: Reading Between the Lines

Remind students that writers often use **verbal irony** when they say things that they don't mean. Some readers, unprepared for the humor in Chaucer's work, may take Chaucer's characterizations at face value. Point out, however, that Chaucer will often say one thing while presenting details that indicate the exact opposite. Chaucer's contemporaries would know that monks rose at midnight to say prayers at services called Matins and Lauds, ate a simple dinner, then worked most of the day gardening, farming, and building, then said more prayers at services called Vespers and Complines and then went to bed at eight. Given this strict regimen, they would realize that the monk depicted here does not live up to that ideal. To help students spot Chaucer's verbal irony, encourage them to think about the following:

1. What role or profession does this character play in feudal society?
2. What details does Chaucer present that hint that this person might not fit that role?
3. What seems to concern or occupy this person's thoughts? Is this topic appropriate to his role in life?

Activity

Have students apply these questions to the character of the Friar, depicted in the passage starting l. 212.

And certainly his voice was gay and sturdy,
For he sang well and played the hurdy-gurdy.°
At sing-songs he was champion of the hour.
His neck was whiter than a lily-flower
But strong enough to butt a bruiser down.
He knew the taverns well in every town
And every innkeeper and barmaid too
Better than lepers, beggars and that crew,
For in so eminent a man as he
It was not fitting with the dignity
Of his position, dealing with a scum
Of wretched lepers; nothing good can come
Of commerce with such slum-and-gutter dwellers,
But only with the rich and victual-sellers.°
But anywhere a profit might accrue
Courteous he was and lowly of service too.
Natural gifts like his were hard to match.
He was the finest beggar of his batch,
And, for his begging-district, paid a rent;
His brethren did no poaching where he went.
For though a widow mightn't have a shoe,
So pleasant was his holy how-d'ye-do
He got his farthing° from her just the same
Before he left, and so his income came
To more than he laid out. And how he romped,
Just like a puppy! He was ever prompt
To arbitrate disputes on settling days°
(For a small fee) in many helpful ways,
Not then appearing as your cloistered scholar
With threadbare habit hardly worth a dollar,
But much more like a Doctor or a Pope.
Of double-worsted was the semi-cope°
Upon his shoulders, and the swelling fold
About him, like a bell about its mould
When it is casting, rounded out his dress.
He lisped a little out of wantonness°
To make his English sweet upon his tongue.
When he had played his harp, or having sung,
His eyes would twinkle in his head as bright
As any star upon a frosty night.
This worthy's name was Hubert, it appeared.
There was a *Merchant* with a forking beard
And motley° dress; high on his horse he sat,
Upon his head a Flemish beaver hat
And on his feet daintily buckled boots.

240. hurdy-gurdy: lutelike instrument played by turning a crank.

252. victual-sellers: merchants, especially of food.

261. farthing: British coin worth one fourth of a penny but no longer in circulation.

265. settling days: days on which disputes could be settled out of court by independent negotiators. Though friars often acted as negotiators (for a fee), they were officially forbidden to do so.

270. semi-cope: capelike garment.

274. wantonness: here, pretense.

281. motley: multicolored.

WORDS TO OWN
accrue (ə·kro͞o′) *v.:* increase over time.

D Elements of Literature

Characterization

? What characteristics might a lily-white neck represent? (Refer students to the table of physical characteristics on p. 128.) [Possible answers: The comparison to the lily suggests that the Friar is cowardly, as in the expression "lily-livered coward"; perhaps it means he is loose or immoral.]

E Vocabulary Note

Word Origins and Spellings

Call attention to the word *brethren,* which is the plural of *brother.* Ask what the word refers to here. [all the members of the same society or profession] Call attention to the *-en* ending of this plural word. Note that English has other irregular plurals with this ending. Ask students to name some. [*children, oxen*] Students might be interested to learn that most irregular plurals in English, including those like *teeth* and *mice,* come from Old English, in which plurals were formed in many different ways. Few of these irregular plurals have survived, however. For example, *bees* were once *been, trees* were once *treen,* and *shoes* were once *shoon.*

F Reading Skills and Strategies

Understanding the Author's Attitude

? How does the Friar earn his living? [forgiving sins and settling disputes for a fee] What does his semi-cope reveal about his income? [The Friar's semi-cope is double-worsted, which is expensive, so one can assume he makes a good living selling penances to poor widows.] What is the poet's attitude toward this corruption in the Church? [He disapproves of it greatly.]

G Reading Skills and Strategies

Visualizing

Remind students to visualize as they read each character description. Then ask them to describe in their own words what they see when they visualize the Merchant. [Possible answers: someone sitting far forward on his horse and very erect; someone dressed in motley, which was brightly colored cloth; someone wearing a beaver hat, the latest rage in hats; someone with a beard split down the middle; someone with fancy boots; someone trying to look prosperous.] What secret does the merchant keep hidden? [He is in debt.]

Crossing the Curriculum

Mathematics

Have students find the distance from London to Canterbury. [about 55 miles] Then have them estimate the pilgrims' pace if they were moving "at a slightly faster pace than walking" (ll. 845–846). [perhaps 4–5 mph] Have students allow the pilgrims eight hours of travel each day and two days at the shrine. Ask them to determine how long the trip to Canterbury and back will take. [six days]

Geography

Ask students to locate on a detailed map of England as many of the locations listed in the Prologue as possible. These include Canterbury and Southwark, the pilgrims' destination and point of departure, respectively, as well as Dartmouth, Bath, Norfolk, Baldeswell, Charing Cross, Berwick, and Ware. You might post a sticker on each location explaining its significance in the Prologue.

Ⓐ Advanced Learners

Investigating Textual References

Have students act as editors by creating a gloss for one or more of the unexplained references in the text. For example, students might find out what the Harwich-Holland ranges were or why the Merchant wears a Flemish beaver hat. [Harwich is a port on the southeastern coast of England. A range can be a sea route or direction line. The Merchant thinks there should be police on the sea lanes between Harwich and Holland. His Flemish beaver hat suggests that he trades in English wool in Flanders (Belgium), a region known for its fur market; he wishes to protect his own interests.]

Ⓑ Elements of Literature

Imagery

? How is the Oxford Cleric portrayed? What contemporary stereotype does Chaucer play on? [Both rider and horse are poor and gaunt. Chaucer plays on the stereotype of the starving student.]

Ⓒ Historical Connections

In order to enter a medieval university, students had to join a minor religious order of the Church. Once out of school, they were expected to seek secular employment outside the Church. The Cleric's books would have cost a small fortune, because the printing press had not yet been invented and books were still copied by hand.

Ⓓ Elements of Literature

Characterization

? Explain that a Sarjeant at the Law was one of a select group of lawyers who served as the king's legal advisors. What attitude does the narrator have toward the Sarjeant? [disapproval] **What evidence in the narrative supports your answer?** [Although the narrator calls him "a man to reverence," he finds nothing remarkable in him. The Sarjeant narrow-mindedly and predictably executes his job, and he gives the appearance of being far busier and more knowledgeable than he really is.]

He told of his opinions and pursuits
In solemn tones, he harped on his increase
Of capital; there should be sea-police
(He thought) upon the Harwich-Holland ranges;
He was expert at dabbling in exchanges.
This estimable Merchant so had set
His wits to work, none knew he was in debt,
He was so stately in administration,
In loans and bargains and negotiation.
He was an excellent fellow all the same;
To tell the truth I do not know his name.
  An *Oxford Cleric,* still a student though,
One who had taken logic long ago,
Was there; his horse was thinner than a rake,
And he was not too fat, I undertake,
But had a hollow look, a sober stare;
The thread upon his overcoat was bare.
He had found no preferment in the church
And he was too unworldly to make search
For secular employment. By his bed
He preferred having twenty books in red
And black, of Aristotle's° philosophy,
Than costly clothes, fiddle, or psaltery.°
Though a philosopher, as I have told,
He had not found the stone for making gold.°
Whatever money from his friends he took
He spent on learning or another book
And prayed for them most earnestly, returning
Thanks to them thus for paying for his learning.
His only care was study, and indeed
He never spoke a word more than was need,
Formal at that, respectful in the extreme,
Short, to the point, and lofty in his theme.
A tone of moral virtue filled his speech
And gladly would he learn, and gladly teach.
  A *Serjeant at the Law* who paid his calls,
Wary and wise, for clients at St. Paul's°
There also was, of noted excellence.
Discreet he was, a man to reverence,
Or so he seemed, his sayings were so wise.
He often had been Justice of Assize
By letters patent,° and in full commission.
His fame and learning and his high position
Had won him many a robe and many a fee.
There was no such conveyancer° as he;
All was fee-simple° to his strong digestion,
Not one conveyance could be called in question.
Though there was nowhere one so busy as he,
He was less busy than he seemed to be.

The Clerk of Oxford, from the Ellesmere manuscript, fol. 88r.

By permission of The Huntington Library, San Marino, California.

305. Aristotle's (ar′is·tät′′lz): Aristotle (384–322 B.C.) was a Greek philosopher.
306. psaltery (sôl′tər·ē): stringed instrument that is plucked.
308. stone . . . gold: Alchemists at the time were searching for a stone that was supposed to turn ordinary metals into gold.

320. St. Paul's: London cathedral. Lawyers often met outside it to discuss their cases when courts were closed.

325. letters patent: letters from the king permitting people to act as judges at the Assizes, court sessions held periodically.
328. conveyancer: person who draws up a deed.
329. fee-simple: absolute ownership of real property; in other words, either entirely right or entirely wrong.

Literature and Religion

Places of Pilgrimage

Chaucer's pilgrims are hardly alone in their faith that visiting a holy site will have spiritual benefits. Besides Canterbury, many Christians of Chaucer's time made pilgrimages to Rome and to Jerusalem, both sites that the Wife of Bath, something of a professional pilgrim, had visited. Today, Christian pilgrims still travel to Jerusalem and Rome.

In ancient times, the Jews also made pilgrimages to Jerusalem during three major festivals: Pesah (Passover), Shavuot (Pentecost), and Sukkot (Tabernacles). These pilgrimages, associated with festivals that mark the Jews' escape from Egypt and journey to Israel, were expected of Jewish men.

For a follower of Islam, no place is more sacred than Mecca, located near the Red Sea in western Saudi Arabia. Mecca is the site of the Kaaba, a sacred, cube-shaped building made of stone, around which Muslim pilgrims must walk. Mohammed, the founder of Islam, decreed that all Muslims who are physically and financially able to make the trip must journey to Mecca at least once in their lifetime.

Varanasi, a city on the Ganges River in India and site of fifteen hundred temples, is visited by more than a million Hindu pilgrims each year. The Golden Temple, the main Hindu shrine there, is dedicated to the god Shiva. Pilgrims who worship at the Ganges at Varanasi believe they gain special merit in this life, and Hindus who die in Varanasi believe they are guaranteed release from endless rebirths.

The Grand Shrine of Ise, the most sacred site of Japanese Shinto pilgrimages, is located at Ise in Mie Prefecture, Japan. The shrines there are viewed as the dwelling place of two deities, the sun goddess Amaterasu and the agricultural god Toyuke. The history of Ise shrine dates back some two thousand years, but the actual buildings are always fairly new. By tradition, the shrines must be rebuilt in the same style every twenty-one years.

He knew of every judgment, case, and crime
Ever recorded since King William's time.°
He could dictate defenses or draft deeds;
No one could pinch a comma from his screeds°
And he knew every statute off by rote.
He wore a homely parti-colored° coat,

334. King William's time: William the Conqueror (c. 1027–1087) was king of England from 1066 to 1087.
336. screeds: tiresome, lengthy writings.
338. parti-colored: multicolored.

WORDS TO OWN
statute (stach'o͞ot) *n.:* law.

Literature and Religion

The idea of a religious pilgrimage goes back to ancient times. The Greeks visited the temple of Apollo at Delphi, and Roman temples attracted visitors who hoped for spiritual or physical cures. Since the very early days of the Christian Church, pilgrims have visited the shrines of saints. In fact, by the fourth century, pilgrims were already making the journey to Jerusalem to follow in the footsteps of their Messiah, Jesus Christ. Although Becket's splendid shrine is no longer in Canterbury Cathedral, the grooves in the stone steps reveal the countless numbers of people who traveled to Canterbury seeking salvation or a miracle. Today pilgrims travel to shrines in places like Lourdes, France; Medjugorje, Bosnia-Herzegovina; and to the Basilica of Our Lady of Guadalupe in Mexico. All are believed to be sites of miracles.

Activity. Have students locate on a map the places of pilgrimage listed in the text. You might also ask students to seek out photographs or more complete descriptions of those sites and the rituals performed there, as well as information on current visitor numbers.

Crossing the Curriculum

Geography/History

In what ways was the England of Chaucer's day a country on the move? What were the roads like, who was on them, and where, besides Canterbury, were these travelers headed? In his book *English Wayfaring Life in the Middle Ages,* J. J. Jusserand suggests these categories of wayfarers, among others: herbalists, charlatans, minstrels, jugglers, and tumblers; messengers, merchants, and peddlers; outlaws, wandering workmen, and peasants out of bond; wandering preachers, friars, and pardoners; and pilgrims. Have students investigate any of these classes of travelers, or have them find out about the network of roads and bridges in Chaucer's time, many of which had been constructed during Roman times and were kept in repair in Chaucer's day, theoretically at least, by the tenants of all landed proprietors. As an alternative, students may wish to investigate how pilgrims traveled—by foot, mule, horseback, hand-carried litter, or horse-drawn coach.

A Historical Connections

Medieval Mealtimes

Medieval Britons usually ate only two meals a day: a mid-morning dinner and an early-evening supper. The Franklin, however, also eats sop for breakfast, a mixture of wine, almond milk, ginger, sugar, cinnamon, cloves, and the spice mace poured over good bread.

B Elements of Literature

Characterization

? Is Chaucer using direct characterization, explaining who the Franklin is to the reader? Or is he using indirect characterization, using details to let the reader draw conclusions about the character? [indirect characterization] What inferences can you draw about the Franklin? [Possible answer: Students may say they think the Franklin is a shallow, self-indulgent man who cares too much about eating.]

C Historical Connections

Guilds

Guilds were organizations of tradespeople who taught their trade to apprentices, or trainees. The associations such as the Goldsmiths' Guild or the Fishmongers' Guild, were a powerful economic force, controlling the quality and price of the goods they produced or sold. During this period, members of guilds often wore a special uniform and were upwardly mobile. What do you think the poet thinks of this group and especially their wives? [Possible response: He makes fun of their social climbing and social pretensions.]

Girt with a silken belt of pin-stripe stuff;
Of his appearance I have said enough.
There was a *Franklin*° with him, it appeared;
White as a daisy-petal was his beard.
A sanguine° man, high-colored and benign,
He loved a morning sop of cake in wine.
He lived for pleasure and had always done,
For he was Epicurus'° very son,
In whose opinion sensual delight
Was the one true felicity in sight.
As noted as St. Julian° was for bounty
He made his household free to all the County.
His bread, his ale were finest of the fine
And no one had a better stock of wine.
His house was never short of bake-meat pies,
Of fish and flesh, and these in such supplies
It positively snowed with meat and drink
And all the dainties that a man could think.
According to the seasons of the year
Changes of dish were ordered to appear.
He kept fat partridges in coops, beyond,
Many a bream and pike were in his pond.
Woe to the cook unless the sauce was hot
And sharp, or if he wasn't on the spot!
And in his hall a table stood arrayed
And ready all day long, with places laid.
As Justice at the Sessions° none stood higher;
He often had been Member for the Shire.°
A dagger and a little purse of silk
Hung at his girdle,° white as morning milk.
As Sheriff he checked audit, every entry.
He was a model among landed gentry.
A *Haberdasher,*° a *Dyer,* a *Carpenter,*
A *Weaver,* and a *Carpet-maker* were
Among our ranks, all in the livery
Of one impressive guild-fraternity.
They were so trim and fresh their gear would pass
For new. Their knives were not tricked out with brass
But wrought with purest silver, which avouches
A like display on girdles and on pouches.
Each seemed a worthy burgess,° fit to grace
A guild-hall with a seat upon the dais.
Their wisdom would have justified a plan
To make each one of them an alderman;°
They had the capital and revenue,
Besides their wives declared it was their due.

341. Franklin: well-to-do landowner, but not of the nobility.

343. sanguine: ruddy-complexioned. In Chaucer's day this was considered a sign of a cheerful temperament; today the word signifies optimism.

346. Epicurus' (341–270 B.C.): Epicurus, an ancient Greek philosopher, taught that the goal of life is pleasure, which is achieved through virtue and moderation. Most people came to think of Epicureans as pleasure seekers.

349. St. Julian: patron saint of hospitality.

365. Justice at the Sessions: judge at a periodically held court meeting.

366. Member for the Shire: county representative in Parliament.

368. girdle: belt.

371. Haberdasher (hab′ər·dash′ər): seller of men's clothing and accessories.

379. burgess: citizen.

382. alderman: head of a guild and therefore a town council member.

WORDS TO OWN
benign (bi·nīn′) *adj.:* kind; gracious.

Taking a Second Look

Review: Making Inferences About Character

Remind students that when they make inferences about characters, they use text information and their own knowledge to make an intelligent guess about what characters are like, what their feelings are, and why they behave the way they do.

Activity

Have students form groups of three. Ask each group to work together to identify details of the Franklin's appearance and actions. For instance, they might note that the Franklin is called "high-colored" and that he drinks wine in the morning. What inferences about the Franklin can students draw from these two details? [The poet may suggest that the Franklin's ruddy color comes from his tendency to drink a lot.] Ask students to find other details in the description to confirm these inferences. By thinking about the meaning of the details, students will decide what kind of person the Franklin is and whether they would like to live near him or be in his company on the way to Canterbury. Students might also make predictions about the stories he would tell.

And if they did not think so, then they ought;
To be called *"Madam"* is a glorious thought,
And so is going to church and being seen
Having your mantle carried, like a queen.
  They had a *Cook* with them who stood alone
For boiling chicken with a marrow-bone,
Sharp flavoring-powder and a spice for savor.
He could distinguish London ale by flavor,
And he could roast and seethe and broil and fry,
Make good thick soup, and bake a tasty pie.
But what a pity—so it seemed to me,
That he should have an ulcer on his knee.
As for blancmange,° he made it with the best.
  There was a *Skipper* hailing from far west;
He came from Dartmouth, so I understood.
He rode a farmer's horse as best he could,
In a woollen gown that reached his knee.
A dagger on a lanyard° falling free
Hung from his neck under his arm and down.
The summer heat had tanned his color brown,
And certainly he was an excellent fellow.
Many a draught of vintage, red and yellow,
He'd drawn at Bordeaux, while the trader snored.
The nicer rules of conscience he ignored.
If, when he fought, the enemy vessel sank,
He sent his prisoners home; they walked the plank.
As for his skill in reckoning his tides,
Currents, and many another risk besides,
Moons, harbors, pilots, he had such dispatch
That none from Hull to Carthage was his match.
Hardy he was, prudent in undertaking;
His beard in many a tempest had its shaking,
And he knew all the havens as they were
From Gottland to the Cape of Finisterre,
And every creek in Brittany and Spain;
The barge he owned was called *The Maudelayne.*
  A *Doctor* too emerged as we proceeded;
No one alive could talk as well as he did
On points of medicine and of surgery,
For, being grounded in astronomy,
He watched his patient closely for the hours
When, by his horoscope, he knew the powers
Of favorable planets, then ascendent,
Worked on the images for his dependent.
The cause of every malady you'd got
He knew, and whether dry, cold, moist, or hot;°
He knew their seat, their humor and condition.
He was a perfect practicing physician.
These causes being known for what they were,
He gave the man his medicine then and there.

The Cook, from the Ellesmere manuscript, fol. 47r.

By permission of The Huntington Library, San Marino, California.

397. blancmange (blə·mônzh′): French for "white food." In Chaucer's day this was a sweet dish containing diced chicken, milk, sugar, and almonds.

402. lanyard (lan′yərd): cord.

The Franklin, from the Ellesmere manuscript, fol. 123v.

By permission of The Huntington Library, San Marino, California.

430. dry . . . hot: the four humors, or fluids. People of the time believed that one's physical and mental conditions were influenced by the balance of four major fluids in the body—blood (hot and wet), yellow bile (hot and dry), phlegm (cold and wet), and black bile (cold and dry).

D Elements of Literature

Understatement

? Note that Chaucer does not mention the Cook's open sore until after describing the Cook's delicious specialties. What is the effect? [Possible answers: to entertain readers by horrifying them or by making them laugh; to spoil the reader's appetite.] Note that part of the humorous effect comes from the way the narrator just slips in the disgusting fact in an understated way.

E Historical Connections

Dartmouth

Dartmouth, a coastal shipping town on the English Channel, was known for its piracy and for the brutality of its sailors, a fact that Chaucer's readers would have known.

F Vocabulary Note

Multiple Meanings

? *Nice* has multiple meanings. Here, the word means "subtle; requiring discernment." Why is the use of this meaning ironic, given the Skipper's treatment of his prisoners of war? [Possible response: The distinction between treating prisoners with respect and killing them is not subtle.]

G Cultural Connections

Humors

Doctors in the Middle Ages believed that the twelve signs of the zodiac affected different parts of the body and that the human body contained four kinds of humors, or fluids, also influenced by the stars, that dictated a person's temperament and physical makeup. This explains, in part, Chaucer's attention to physical appearance.

Skill Link

Researching Word Origins

Remind students that knowing word origins can help them learn new words. Discuss with students the information in gloss 430 and note G above, pointing out that our expressions *to be in a good humor* and *to be in a bad humor* (and the adjective forms *good-humored* and *bad-humored*) relate to this historical use of the word. Then have students do research to discover the origin and meaning of the following four words that describe "humorous" temperament:

- *phlegmatic* [dominated by phlegm; dull, sluggish]
- *sanguine* [dominated by blood; ruddy, cheerful]
- *choleric* [dominated by choler, or yellow bile; angry, irritable]
- *melancholic* [dominated by melancholy, or black bile; sad, depressed]

(For further information, see note H on p. T119.) Have students compare *sanguine* and *sanguinary,* which means "bloody" or "bloodthirsty" (a sanguinary battle, to take sanguinary glee). Also, have students check out the now uncommon word *bilious,* the adjective form of *bile,* which can be a synonym of *choleric* but is now more often used to mean "expressing gastric distress." Finally, have students note Chaucer's use of two of these words in ll. 343 and 605, and have them write "humorous" sentences of their own.

Ⓐ Critical Thinking

Determining the Author's Purpose

? How does Chaucer's characterization of the Doctor convey a negative attitude? [Possible answers: Although he says the doctor is a perfect practicing physician, the narrator makes it clear that the Doctor profits from people's illnesses by prescribing drugs that don't work and sharing in the profits with the apothecaries, or pharmacists. Consequently, the doctor is well-dressed and appears to have plenty of money to spend on himself.]

Ⓑ Elements of Literature

Characterization

? What is the Wife of Bath concerned about when she goes to church? What does this suggest about her? [Sample answer: She is concerned that she is the first to the altar and that she is wearing the best clothes. Explain that people approached the altar according to social rank, so her concern suggests she cares more about status than spirituality.]

Ⓒ Historical Connections

Pilgrim Destinations

Jerusalem, Rome, Boulogne (in France), Santiago of Compostela (in Spain), and Cologne (in Germany) were all famous pilgrimage centers. Tell students that Jerusalem was the Christian Holy City, Rome the home of the pope, Santiago of Compostela the resting place of the martyred apostle St. James, and Cologne the site of the largest Gothic church in the Middle Ages. Students should be aware that the Wife of Bath's freedom to travel on pilgrimages was a luxury not available to many women in her time. Pilgrims who had visited Jerusalem, the Holy City, were called palmers because they carried palm fronds, and those who had visited Santiago of Compostela wore a scallop shell in their hat as proof of their visit. Chaucer implies, through his references to "wandering" and "gap teeth," that the Wife of Bath took full advantage of her freedom. (Refer students to p. 127 for more information.)

All his apothecaries in a tribe
Were ready with the drugs he would prescribe
And each made money from the other's guile;
They had been friendly for a goodish while.
He was well-versed in Aesculapius° too
And what Hippocrates and Rufus knew
And Dioscorides, now dead and gone,
Galen and Rhazes, Hali, Serapion,
Averroes, Avicenna, Constantine,
Scotch Bernard, John of Gaddesden, Gilbertine.
In his own diet he observed some measure;
There were no superfluities for pleasure,
Only digestives, nutritives and such.
He did not read the Bible very much.
In blood-red garments, slashed with bluish gray
And lined with taffeta, he rode his way;
Yet he was rather close as to expenses
And kept the gold he won in pestilences.
Gold stimulates the heart, or so we're told.
He therefore had a special love of gold.
  A worthy *woman* from beside *Bath* city
Was with us, somewhat deaf, which was a pity.
In making cloth she showed so great a bent
She bettered those of Ypres and of Ghent.°
In all the parish not a dame dared stir
Towards the altar steps in front of her,
And if indeed they did, so wrath was she
As to be quite put out of charity.
Her kerchiefs were of finely woven ground;°
I dared have sworn they weighed a good ten pound,
The ones she wore on Sunday, on her head.
Her hose were of the finest scarlet red
And gartered tight; her shoes were soft and new.
Bold was her face, handsome, and red in hue.
A worthy woman all her life, what's more
She'd had five husbands, all at the church door,°
Apart from other company in youth;
No need just now to speak of that, forsooth.
And she had thrice been to Jerusalem,
Seen many strange rivers and passed over them;
She'd been to Rome and also to Boulogne,
St. James of Compostella and Cologne,
And she was skilled in wandering by the way.
She had gap-teeth, set widely, truth to say.
Easily on an ambling horse she sat

439. Aesculapius: in Greek and Roman mythology, the god of medicine. The names that follow were early Greek, Roman, Middle Eastern, and medieval medical authorities.

The Physician, from the Ellesmere manuscript, fol. 133r.

By permission of The Huntington Library, San Marino, California.

458. Ypres (ē′pr′) **and of Ghent:** Flemish centers of the wool trade.

463. ground: type of cloth.

470. church door: In Chaucer's day the marriage ceremony was performed at the church door.

WORDS TO OWN
guile (gīl) *n.:* sly dealings.

Well wimpled° up, and on her head a hat
As broad as is a buckler or a shield;
She had a flowing mantle that concealed
Large hips, her heels spurred sharply under that.
In company she liked to laugh and chat
And knew the remedies for love's mischances,
An art in which she knew the oldest dances.
  A holy-minded man of good renown
There was, and poor, the *Parson* to a town,
Yet he was rich in holy thought and work.
He also was a learned man, a clerk,
Who truly knew Christ's gospel and would preach it
Devoutly to parishioners, and teach it.
Benign and wonderfully diligent,
And patient when adversity was sent
(For so he proved in much adversity)
He hated cursing to extort a fee,
Nay rather he preferred beyond a doubt
Giving to poor parishioners round about
Both from church offerings and his property;
He could in little find sufficiency.
Wide was his parish, with houses far asunder,
Yet he neglected not in rain or thunder,
In sickness or in grief, to pay a call
On the remotest, whether great or small,
Upon his feet, and in his hand a stave.°
This noble example to his sheep he gave
That first he wrought, and afterward he taught;
And it was from the Gospel he had caught
Those words, and he would add this figure too,
That if gold rust, what then will iron do?
For if a priest be foul in whom we trust
No wonder that a common man should rust;
And shame it is to see—let priests take stock—
A shitten shepherd and a snowy flock.
The true example that a priest should give
Is one of cleanness, how the sheep should live.
He did not set his benefice to hire°
And leave his sheep encumbered in the mire
Or run to London to earn easy bread
By singing masses for the wealthy dead,
Or find some Brotherhood and get enrolled.°
He stayed at home and watched over his fold
So that no wolf should make the sheep miscarry.

480. wimpled: A wimple is a linen covering for the head and neck.

The Parson, from the Ellesmere manuscript, fol. 206v.

By permission of The Huntington Library, San Marino, California.

505. stave: staff.

517. benefice to hire: He did not hire someone else to perform his duties.

521. find . . . enrolled: He did not take a job as a paid chaplain to a guild.

WORDS TO OWN
diligent (dil′ə·jənt) *adj.:* careful and persistent in work.
adversity (ad·vur′sə·tē) *n.:* trouble; misfortune.

Professional Notes

Critical Comment: A Cornucopia of Characters

There are so many pilgrims and so many details in the Prologue that Chaucer's purpose in presenting them may get lost. What do all these characters and all these separate tales add up to? Paul G. Ruggiers in *The Art of the Canterbury Tales* provides one answer about all these separate characters and "loosely joined episodes": "Whether . . . the subject is marriage, or successful duping, or self-control, or the mystery of fate and fortune, or free will and predestination, or reason and appetite, the variety of subject adds up to a broad examination of the worlds of social, moral, and religious experience." In other words, through each character and each set of details, Chaucer examines nothing less than life itself in all its variety.

D Reading Skills and Strategies
Making Inferences About Character

? Some critics think that the Wife of Bath is based on Chaucer's paternal grandmother, who had three husbands. Based on the description in the text, what words or phrases would you use to describe the Wife of Bath? [Possible answers: a life force; bold; assertive; imposing; earthy; strong; intelligent; frank; stubborn.]

E Reading Skills and Strategies
Making Predictions

? What sort of tale do you think the Wife of Bath will tell? [Possible answers: a tale involving love and marriage, since she has been married five times, or a story about wealth and beauty, since these seem very important to her.] Students can test their predictions when they read her tale.

F Critical Thinking
Hypothesizing

? Chaucer describes the Parson as poor. From what you know of Chaucer's values so far, do you think he will approve or disapprove of the Parson? Why? [Possible answers: He appears to approve of poverty elsewhere in his characterizations and disapprove of wealth and especially greed. He will approve of the Parson because he is "rich in holy thought and work."]

G Historical Connections

Explain that "cursing to extort a fee" refers to the corrupt practice of threatening people with excommunication and damnation unless they paid a fee.

H Advanced Learners
Interpreting Metaphors

Two metaphors are used here to characterize the Parson. One compares him to a shepherd and his parishioners to sheep. The other asks a hypothetical question comparing corruption in priests and men to corroding gold and rusting iron. Have students interpret these metaphors. [Possible answers: The Parson's job is to watch his "sheep," or keep an eye on the spiritual health of his "flock," or the people in his care. The metaphor of gold and iron warns that if gold, a refined metal, corrodes, then iron, a coarse metal, cannot help but rust. This suggests that if a priest sets a poor example, his parish members will follow suit.]

Ⓐ Reading Skills and Strategies

Making Inferences

? What kind of priest is the Parson? [Possible answer: a good one because he stays with his parish instead of going to the city to make money. He is also kind, soft-spoken, modest, and fair and sets a good example for his flock.]

Ⓑ Literary Connections

Piers the Plowman

Chaucer's portrait of the Plowman may refer to the poem *Piers the Plowman,* written in the late 1300s by William Langland. In Langland's poem, the plowman is portrayed as an instrument of salvation to his community. Chaucer may be similarly idealizing his Plowman; this is remarkable, since the writings of Chaucer's contemporaries ridiculed peasants.

Ⓒ Elements of Literature

Allusion

This passage is an allusion to Luke 10:27: "Thou shalt love the Lord thy God with all thy heart, . . . and thy neighbor as thyself."

Ⓓ Reading Skills and Strategies

Comparing/Contrasting

? Chaucer praises the Plowman, the Parson, and the Cleric. What qualities do these men share? [Possible answer: All are generous, spiritual, uninterested in wealth, and full of energy for their work.] In what ways do they differ? [Possible answer: in education and profession.]

He was a shepherd and no mercenary.
Holy and virtuous he was, but then
Never contemptuous of sinful men,
Never disdainful, never too proud or fine,
But was discreet in teaching and benign.
His business was to show a fair behavior
And draw men thus to Heaven and their Savior,
Unless indeed a man were obstinate;
And such, whether of high or low estate,
He put to sharp rebuke, to say the least.
I think there never was a better priest.
He sought no pomp or glory in his dealings,
No scrupulosity had spiced his feelings.
Christ and His Twelve Apostles and their lore
He taught, but followed it himself before.
There was a *Plowman* with him there, his brother;
Many a load of dung one time or other
He must have carted through the morning dew.
He was an honest worker, good and true,
Living in peace and perfect charity,
And, as the gospel bade him, so did he,
Loving God best with all his heart and mind
And then his neighbor as himself, repined
At no misfortune, slacked for no content,
For steadily about his work he went
To thrash his corn, to dig or to manure
Or make a ditch; and he would help the poor
For love of Christ and never take a penny
If he could help it, and, as prompt as any,
He paid his tithes in full when they were due
On what he owned, and on his earnings too.
He wore a tabard smock° and rode a mare.
There was a *Reeve,*° also a *Miller,* there,
A College *Manciple*° from the Inns of Court,
A papal *Pardoner*° and, in close consort,
A Church-Court *Summoner,*° riding at a trot,
And finally myself—that was the lot.
The *Miller* was a chap of sixteen stone,°
A great stout fellow big in brawn and bone.
He did well out of them, for he could go
And win the ram at any wrestling show.
Broad, knotty, and short-shouldered, he would boast
He could heave any door off hinge and post,
Or take a run and break it with his head.

The Miller, from the Ellesmere manuscript, fol. 34v.

By permission of The Huntington Library, San Marino, California.

555. tabard (tab′ərd) **smock:** short jacket.
556. Reeve: serf who was the steward of a manor. He saw that the estate's work was done and that everything was accounted for.
557. Manciple (man′sə·pəl): minor employee whose principal duty was to purchase provisions for a college or law firm.
558. Pardoner: minor member of the Church who bought and sold pardons for sinners.
559. Summoner: low-ranking officer who summoned people to appear in church court.
561. sixteen stone: 224 pounds.

WORDS TO OWN

disdainful (dis·dān′fəl) *adj.:* scornful.
discreet (di·skrēt′) *adj.:* cautious about one's words and actions.
obstinate (äb′stə·nət) *adj.:* unreasonably stubborn.

Professional Notes

Town Life: Shops and Shopkeepers

As a steward or food buyer for a college, the Manciple would have frequented the local shops in town. These shops, which were really workshops, usually had a stall out front where goods were displayed. In most cases, merchants who sold the same type of goods clustered together onto streets called rows, as in Fishmongers' Row. Shopkeepers hung the symbol of their trade outside their store, but there were few written signs, since few shoppers could read. These towns and markets represented the rising middle class during Chaucer's time. Ask students which pilgrims are members of this class. [Possible responses: Merchant; Haberdasher; Dyer; Carpenter; Weaver; Carpet-maker; Cook; the Wife of Bath; Manciple; Miller.]

His beard, like any sow or fox, was red
And broad as well, as though it were a spade;
And, at its very tip, his nose displayed
A wart on which there stood a tuft of hair
Red as the bristles in an old sow's ear.
His nostrils were as black as they were wide.
He had a sword and buckler at his side,
His mighty mouth was like a furnace door.
A wrangler and buffoon, he had a store
Of tavern stories, filthy in the main.
His was a master-hand at stealing grain.
He felt it with his thumb and thus he knew
Its quality and took three times his due—
A thumb of gold, by God, to gauge an oat!°
He wore a hood of blue and a white coat.
He liked to play his bagpipes up and down
And that was how he brought us out of town.
  The *Manciple* came from the Inner Temple;°
All caterers might follow his example
In buying victuals; he was never rash
Whether he bought on credit or paid cash.
He used to watch the market most precisely
And got in first, and so he did quite nicely.
Now isn't it a marvel of God's grace
That an illiterate fellow can outpace
The wisdom of a heap of learned men?
His masters—he had more than thirty then—
All versed in the abstrusest legal knowledge,
Could have produced a dozen from their College
Fit to be stewards in land and rents and game
To any Peer in England you could name,
And show him how to live on what he had
Debt-free (unless of course the Peer were mad)
Or be as frugal as he might desire,
And make them fit to help about the Shire
In any legal case there was to try;
And yet this Manciple could wipe their eye.
  The *Reeve* was old and choleric° and thin;
His beard was shaven closely to the skin,
His shorn hair came abruptly to a stop
Above his ears, and he was docked on top
Just like a priest in front; his legs were lean,
Like sticks they were, no calf was to be seen.
He kept his bins and garners° very trim;
No auditor could gain a point on him.

The Manciple, from the Ellesmere manuscript, fol. 203r.

By permission of The Huntington Library, San Marino, California.

581. thumb . . . oat: In other words, he pressed on the scale with his thumb to increase the weight of the grain.

585. Inner Temple: one of the four legal societies in London comprising the Inns of Court. Only the Inns were permitted to license lawyers.

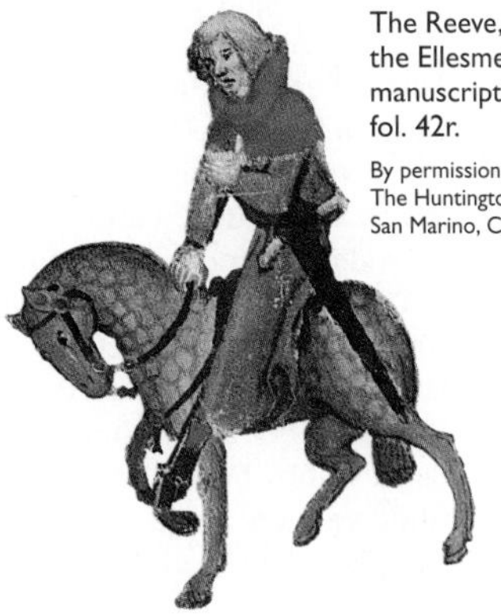

The Reeve, from the Ellesmere manuscript, fol. 42r.

By permission of The Huntington Library, San Marino, California.

605. choleric (käl′ər·ik): having too much choler, or yellow bile, and thus (supposedly) bad-tempered.

611. garners: granaries.

Words to Own
frugal (fro͞o′gəl) *adj.:* thrifty.

E Elements of Literature
Characterization

? Here the Miller is compared to a sow or fox, a spade, a sow's ear, and a furnace door. What do the comparisons suggest about the Miller's character? [Possible answers: They suggest he is rough, uncouth, wild, belligerent, and as ordinary as the most common animal or tool.]

F Cultural Connections

Here Chaucer plays on a medieval saying: "An honest miller has a golden thumb." This expression implies that most millers overcharge their customers by putting their thumbs on the scale.

G Language Note
Idioms

"Could *wipe their eye*" means that the Manciple could make fools of his masters or could defraud them. Here, *wipe* might mean "to swipe, remove, or erase," suggesting that the Manciple could "steal their eyes" or outwit them.

H Cultural Connections
Choler

People in Chaucer's time believed that four bodily fluids, called humors or moistures, caused disease and negatively influenced a person's character when their mixture was out of balance. People associated black bile with depression and delusions, and choler, or yellow bile, with unkindness, instability, and pridefulness. Too much phlegm created sloth, obesity, crooked bodies, and hairless skin. Too much blood made a person sensual or, in older people, caused heart attacks.

Making the Connections

Cultural Connections: Food

As a food buyer, the manciple would have shopped for venison, mutton, or pork, but not horsemeat, which was forbidden by the Church. Seafood included porpoises, whale, haddock, cod, lamprey, tunnies, and eels. Popular vegetables were onions, peas, beans, and cabbage, but not tomatoes, potatoes, or corn, which were not imported from the New World until the 1500s.

Skill Link

Evaluating an Oral Performance

Have students critique and evaluate an oral presentation of the Prologue. First, ask the class to establish a list of criteria they would want an oral presentation of the Prologue to meet. Develop a list of criteria on the chalkboard. You might consider the following:

1. audible voices
2. lively and expressive voices
3. well-paced presentation
4. correct interpretation
5. natural body language
6. good eye contact with the audience

Then, have students develop a rating scale for applying these criteria. Next, have students listen to the Prologue, or a selected part of the Prologue, on the *Audio CD Library* (Disc 2, Track 6). Students can compile data to find out how the class reacted as a whole.

Ⓐ Historical Connections

Reeve

A reeve in the Middle Ages was a manager of an estate, whose job it was to inspect everything and to impose fines on the workers if he found anything wrong.

Ⓑ Elements of Literature

Characterization

? How well does the Reeve do his job? [Possible answer: Chaucer starts out by saying the Reeve does his job well but ends by implying that he is mean to the serfs and has become rich by embezzling from the master.] What does this information tell you about the character of the Reeve? [Possible answers: He is dishonest; he uses people.]

Ⓒ Elements of Literature

Imagery

? In his portrayal of the Summoner, how does Chaucer appeal to the reader's sense of sight? [Possible answer: He enables the reader to see a hideously ugly face, covered with pus-filled pimples, boils, and sores. He lets the reader call to mind other features as well, such as black, scabby eyebrows, narrow eyes, and a scraggly beard.]

Ⓓ Struggling Readers

Adjusting Reading Rate for Enjoyment

There is much to laugh at and enjoy in Chaucer. Yet because there are so many details about each character, students might find themselves reading quickly or reading without reacting to the considerable humor and satire. Ask students what details they might enjoy on this page. [Possible answer: the fun being poked at the Summoner, who drinks till all is "hazy" and whose education is so limited that there are only about two or three Latin phrases that he can recall when he is drunk.]

And he could judge by watching drought and rain
The yield he might expect from seed and grain.
His master's sheep, his animals and hens,
Pigs, horses, dairies, stores, and cattle-pens
Were wholly trusted to his government.
He had been under contract to present
The accounts, right from his master's earliest years.
No one had ever caught him in arrears.
No bailiff, serf, or herdsman dared to kick,
He knew their dodges, knew their every trick;
Feared like the plague he was, by those beneath.
He had a lovely dwelling on a heath,
Shadowed in green by trees above the sward.°
A better hand at bargains than his lord,
He had grown rich and had a store of treasure
Well tucked away, yet out it came to pleasure
His lord with subtle loans or gifts of goods,
To earn his thanks and even coats and hoods.
When young he'd learnt a useful trade and still
He was a carpenter of first-rate skill.
The stallion-cob he rode at a slow trot
Was dapple-gray and bore the name of Scot.
He wore an overcoat of bluish shade
And rather long; he had a rusty blade
Slung at his side. He came, as I heard tell,
From Norfolk, near a place called Baldeswell.
His coat was tucked under his belt and splayed.
He rode the hindmost of our cavalcade.

There was a *Summoner* with us at that Inn,
His face on fire, like a cherubim,°
For he had carbuncles.° His eyes were narrow,
He was as hot and lecherous as a sparrow.
Black scabby brows he had, and a thin beard.
Children were afraid when he appeared.
No quicksilver, lead ointment, tartar creams,
No brimstone, no boracic, so it seems,
Could make a salve that had the power to bite,
Clean up, or cure his whelks° of knobby white
Or purge the pimples sitting on his cheeks.
Garlic he loved, and onions too, and leeks,
And drinking strong red wine till all was hazy.
Then he would shout and jabber as if crazy,
And wouldn't speak a word except in Latin
When he was drunk, such tags as he was pat in;
He only had a few, say two or three,
That he had mugged up out of some decree;
No wonder, for he heard them every day.
And, as you know, a man can teach a jay°
To call out "Walter" better than the Pope.

625. sward (swôrd): lawn.

The Summoner, from the Ellesmere manuscript, fol. 81r.

By permission of The Huntington Library, San Marino, California.

642. cherubim: in medieval art, a little angel with a rosy face.
643. carbuncles (kär′bun′kəlz): pus-filled skin inflammations, something like boils.

650. whelks: pus-filled sores.

660. jay: type of bird.

But had you tried to test his wits and grope
For more, you'd have found nothing in the bag.
Then *"Questio quid juris"*° was his tag.
He was a noble varlet° and a kind one,
You'd meet none better if you went to find one.
Why, he'd allow—just for a quart of wine—
Any good lad to keep a concubine
A twelvemonth and dispense him altogether!
And he had finches of his own to feather:
And if he found some rascal with a maid
He would instruct him not to be afraid
In such a case of the Archdeacon's curse
(Unless the rascal's soul were in his purse)
For in his purse the punishment should be.
"Purse is the good Archdeacon's Hell," said he.
But well I know he lied in what he said;
A curse should put a guilty man in dread,
For curses kill, as shriving brings, salvation.
We should beware of excommunication.
Thus, as he pleased, the man could bring duress
On any young fellow in the diocese.
He knew their secrets, they did what he said.
He wore a garland set upon his head
Large as the holly-bush upon a stake
Outside an ale-house, and he had a cake,
A round one, which it was his joke to wield
As if it were intended for a shield.
He and a gentle *Pardoner* rode together,
A bird from Charing Cross of the same feather,
Just back from visiting the Court of Rome.
He loudly sang *"Come hither, love, come home!"*
The Summoner sang deep seconds° to this song,
No trumpet ever sounded half so strong.
This Pardoner had hair as yellow as wax,
Hanging down smoothly like a hank of flax.
In driblets fell his locks behind his head
Down to his shoulders which they overspread;
Thinly they fell, like rat-tails, one by one.
He wore no hood upon his head, for fun;
The hood inside his wallet had been stowed,
He aimed at riding in the latest mode;
But for a little cap his head was bare
And he had bulging eye-balls, like a hare.
He'd sewed a holy relic on his cap;
His wallet lay before him on his lap,

664. *Questio quid juris* (kwest'ē·ō kwid yo͞o'ris): Latin for "I ask what point of the law [applies]." The Summoner uses this phrase to stall and dodge the issue.
665. varlet (vär'lit): scoundrel.

The Pardoner, from the Ellesmere manuscript, fol. 138r.
By permission of The Huntington Library, San Marino, California.

693. deep seconds: harmonies.

WORDS TO OWN
duress (do͞o·res') *n.:* pressure.

E Cultural Connections

In Chaucer's time, sexual relations outside marriage were cause for excommunication, and the Summoner's job was to track down offenders and deliver them to the Archdeacon for punishment.

F Elements of Literature

Characterization

? How does the Summoner deal with people who keep a mistress? [Possible answer: He ignores offenders if they pay him in money or in wine.] How does the phrase "noble varlet" convey Chaucer's attitude toward the Summoner? [A *varlet* is a scoundrel. The word *noble* in conjunction with *varlet* just means "big" or "complete" scoundrel.]

G Historical Connections

Inns

Medieval inns were identified by holly boughs pinned above their doors or planted and staked in the yard.

H Historical Connections

Chaucer may have modeled the Pardoner on a real pardoner from St. Mary Roncival Hospital, which went through a series of money scandals in the 1380s. Here, *gentle* means that he was of the upper classes, not that his nature was kind.

I English Language Learners

Idioms

Explain that *birds of a feather* is a commonly used expression in English; it refers to people who have quite a bit in common. Ask students to predict what the Pardoner and Summoner may have in common. [Possible answers: They may have the same attitudes toward appearance, drinking, and their professions.]

J Elements of Literature

Characterization

? Long hair was a violation of the rule that men who worked for the Church should wear their hair tonsured (short, with a shaved spot at the top, as a symbol of humility). What other details does Chaucer mention that suggest that the Pardoner is a less-than-savory character? [Possible answers: His hair hangs like rat-tails; he puts on airs by trying to ride in a fashionable style; he has a voice like a goat; he has bulging eyeballs. All are unappealing.]

Getting Students Involved

Cooperative Learning

Bottom of the Barrel, Top of the Heap? Who is the most reprehensible of all the pilgrims? Who is the most noble? Have pairs of students think of their responses, gather written evidence, share their answers and evidence with a partner, and then share their combined thinking with the class.

Rest in Peace. Have students create an obituary for the pilgrim of their choice. Ask them to imagine that he or she died during the pilgrimage to Canterbury. Have students model their obituaries on those commonly found in your local newspaper.

Ⓐ Cultural Connections

Relics

In religious terms, *relics* are the remains (bones, hair, garments, and so on) of a holy person. Saying a prayer with the relic in hand was thought to bring an indulgence, or limited respite from the pains of purgatory after death. Some relics were fake, but believers willingly bought them and provided a steady income to the sellers.

Ⓑ Elements of Literature

Characterization

? Are ll. 730–734 an example of direct or indirect characterization? [They are an example of both. The author directly tells the reader that the Pardoner reads a lesson, tells a story, and sings an Offertory well. He implies that the Pardoner is motivated by greed and sings to "win silver from the crowd."]

Ⓒ Critical Thinking

Challenging the Text

? Has Chaucer told you all about the pilgrims "shortly, in a clause"? [Most students will feel that they have learned a lot about each pilgrim but that Chaucer has not done so "in a clause"; in fact, he has gone on for many pages, in great detail. Others will feel that the Prologue is a fairly short summary, given that so many complex individuals, representative of all walks of life, have been drawn in so few pages.]

Ⓓ Reading Skills and Strategies

Drawing Conclusions

? Who is really the author of these tales? Why do you think the narrator says he is merely recording what other people have said? [Possible answers: Chaucer, of course, invented the characters and their tales, but pretending that he is merely a reporter relieves him of responsibility for the tales' often bawdy content. Also, writing secular poetry was still not a respected profession, and Chaucer, an important government servant and member of the middle class, had his reputation to protect.]

Brimful of pardons° come from Rome, all hot.
He had the same small voice a goat has got.
His chin no beard had harbored, nor would harbor,
Smoother than ever chin was left by barber.
I judge he was a gelding, or a mare.
As to his trade, from Berwick down to Ware
There was no pardoner of equal grace,
For in his trunk he had a pillow-case
Which he asserted was Our Lady's veil.
He said he had a gobbet° of the sail
Saint Peter had the time when he made bold
To walk the waves, till Jesu Christ took hold.
He had a cross of metal set with stones
And, in a glass, a rubble of pigs' bones.
And with these relics, any time he found
Some poor up-country parson to astound,
In one short day, in money down, he drew
More than the parson in a month or two,
And by his flatteries and prevarication
Made monkeys of the priest and congregation.
But still to do him justice first and last
In church he was a noble ecclesiast.°
How well he read a lesson or told a story!
But best of all he sang an Offertory,°
For well he knew that when that song was sung
He'd have to preach and tune his honey-tongue
And (well he could) win silver from the crowd.
That's why he sang so merrily and loud.
  Now I have told you shortly, in a clause,
The rank, the array, the number, and the cause
Of our assembly in this company
In Southwark, at that high-class hostelry
Known as *The Tabard,* close beside *The Bell.*
And now the time has come for me to tell
How we behaved that evening; I'll begin
After we had alighted at the Inn,
Then I'll report our journey, stage by stage,
All the remainder of our pilgrimage.
But first I beg of you, in courtesy,
Not to condemn me as unmannerly
If I speak plainly and with no concealings
And give account of all their words and dealings,
Using their very phrases as they fell.
For certainly, as you all know so well,
He who repeats a tale after a man
Is bound to say, as nearly as he can,
Each single word, if he remembers it,
However rudely spoken or unfit,

707. pardons: small strips of parchment with papal seals attached. They were sold as indulgences (pardons for sins), with the proceeds supposedly going to a religious house. Many pardoners were dishonest, and even loyal church members often ridiculed them.

716. gobbet: fragment.

728. ecclesiast (e·klē′zē·ast): practitioner of church ritual.

730. Offertory: hymn sung while offerings are collected in church.

Making the Connections

Cultural Connections: Relics

Relics were highly valued in medieval society not only by pilgrims but also by the various churches and shrines where the relics were kept. Often one church would steal relics from another in hopes of attracting a larger crowd of pilgrims. Once a pilgrim reached a site, he or she would try to "buy" a relic and bring it home. Relics owned by lay people were traditionally kept in reliquaries shaped as necklaces or rings. The selling of fake relics was, of course, an abuse that Chaucer particularly hated.

Or else the tale he tells will be untrue,
The things pretended and the phrases new.
He may not flinch although it were his brother,
He may as well say one word as another.
And Christ Himself spoke broad in Holy Writ,
Yet there is no scurrility in it,
And Plato says, for those with power to read,
"The word should be as cousin to the deed."
Further I beg you to forgive it me
If I neglect the order and degree
And what is due to rank in what I've planned.
I'm short of wit as you will understand.

Our *Host* gave us great welcome; everyone
Was given a place and supper was begun.
He served the finest victuals you could think,
The wine was strong and we were glad to drink.
A very striking man our Host withal,
And fit to be a marshal in a hall.
His eyes were bright, his girth a little wide;
There is no finer burgess in Cheapside.°
Bold in his speech, yet wise and full of tact,
There was no manly attribute he lacked,
What's more he was a merry-hearted man.
After our meal he jokingly began
To talk of sport, and, among other things
After we'd settled up our reckonings,
He said as follows: "Truly, gentlemen,
You're very welcome and I can't think when
—Upon my word I'm telling you no lie—
I've seen a gathering here that looked so spry,
No, not this year, as in this tavern now.
I'd think you up some fun if I knew how.
And, as it happens, a thought has just occurred
To please you, costing nothing, on my word.
You're off to Canterbury—well, God speed!

774. Cheapside: district of medieval London.

Chaucer, from the Ellesmere manuscript, fol. 153v.

By permission of The Huntington Library, San Marino, California.

E Critical Thinking

Expressing an Opinion

? Do you feel that a writer's or artist's work should be true to life? What arguments can you make for either view? [Sample responses: It does not have to be true to life, because the truth can be boring or painful, and many works of the imagination, including science fiction and fantasy, would never be created by that standard. Or even science fiction and fantasy have to be true to life in the sense that readers must be able to believe what they read; characters, in particular, must be seen as "true to life."]

F English Language Learners

Archaic Language

Students often run into the word *victuals* in literature, but they will not hear it in everyday speech or modern writing. Ask students to use a dictionary to learn what it means. [food or provisions]

G Critical Thinking

Hypothesizing

? What hypotheses can you offer for why the Host proposes his plan for the pilgrims' entertainment? [Possible answers: He may be a playful man; he may do this all the time with groups of pilgrims; he may be bored to death with his usual company; he may have been planning to travel to Canterbury anyway and wishes to be entertained along the way.]

Ⓐ Appreciating Language

Style

Note the use of the open couplet (one that does not in itself express a complete idea). Ask students to identify the rhyme, analyze the placement of the rhyming words, and explain the result. [*Word* rhymes with *deferred,* but the two words are not only in separate sentences but in even separate sections: the Host's speech and the narrator's commentary. The result is a rhyme that sounds conversational and natural, not sing-song.]

Ⓑ Critical Thinking

Speculating

? Why might the pilgrims agree to do as the Host says even before they know what he will propose? [Possible answers: They know the journey will be long. They trust the Host. They know that he is the type of man who will think of something entertaining.]

Ⓒ Critical Thinking

Expressing an Opinion

? Do you agree with the Host that "morality" and "pleasure" define a good story? Why or why not? What does make a good story? [Possible answer: Morality is not necessary for a good story, which does not have to be told to teach anything. Other criteria might include originality, suspense, elements of surprise, action, richly drawn characters, and realistic details.]

Ⓓ Elements of Literature

Characterization

? Is the Host's speech an example of direct or indirect characterization? What does it reveal about him? [It is an example of indirect characterization. The host shows through his own words that he is a man who enjoys people, traveling, and simple entertainment.]

Blessed St. Thomas answer to your need!
And I don't doubt, before the journey's done
You mean to while the time in tales and fun.
Indeed, there's little pleasure for your bones
Riding along and all as dumb as stones.
So let me then propose for your enjoyment,
Just as I said, a suitable employment.
And if my notion suits and you agree
And promise to submit yourselves to me
Playing your parts exactly as I say
Tomorrow as you ride along the way,
Then by my father's soul (and he is dead)
If you don't like it you can have my head!
Hold up your hands, and not another word."
 Well, our opinion was not long deferred,
It seemed not worth a serious debate;
We all agreed to it at any rate
And bade him issue what commands he would.
"My lords," he said, "now listen for your good,
And please don't treat my notion with disdain.
This is the point. I'll make it short and plain.
Each one of you shall help to make things slip
By telling two stories on the outward trip
To Canterbury, that's what I intend,
And, on the homeward way to journey's end
Another two, tales from the days of old;
And then the man whose story is best told,
That is to say who gives the fullest measure
Of good morality and general pleasure,
He shall be given a supper, paid by all,
Here in this tavern, in this very hall,
When we come back again from Canterbury.
And in the hope to keep you bright and merry
I'll go along with you myself and ride
All at my own expense and serve as guide.
I'll be the judge, and those who won't obey
Shall pay for what we spend upon the way.
Now if you all agree to what you've heard
Tell me at once without another word,
And I will make arrangements early for it."
 Of course we all agreed, in fact we swore it
Delightedly, and made entreaty too
That he should act as he proposed to do,
Become our Governor in short, and be
Judge of our tales and general referee,
And set the supper at a certain price.

WORDS TO OWN
deferred (dē·fʉrd′) *v.:* postponed.

Assessing Learning

Check Test: Short Answers

1. **Where are the pilgrims traveling from, and where are they heading?** [from London to Canterbury]
2. **Name three of the pilgrims described by Chaucer.** [Sample answers: the Pardoner, Prioress, Summoner, Wife of Bath, and Knight.]
3. **What month of the year is it?** [April]
4. **What is the pilgrims' mode of transportation?** [horses]
5. **What entertainment does the Host suggest?** [Each pilgrim will tell two stories going and two coming back.]

Informal Assessment

Observation Assessment. As students write and discuss their responses to the Prologue, use the following scale and criteria to assess their performance:

1 = Rarely 2 = Sometimes 3 = Often

_____ 1. Makes personal connections
_____ 2. Notes details of characterization
_____ 3. Uses text to guide interpretation
_____ 4. Monitors reading

We promised to be ruled by his advice
Come high, come low; unanimously thus
We set him up in judgment over us.
More wine was fetched, the business being done;
We drank it off and up went everyone
To bed without a moment of delay.
  Early next morning at the spring of day
Up rose our Host and roused us like a cock,
Gathering us together in a flock,
And off we rode at slightly faster pace
Than walking to St. Thomas' watering-place;
And there our Host drew up, began to ease
His horse, and said, "Now, listen if you please,
My lords! Remember what you promised me.
If evensong and matins will agree°
Let's see who shall be first to tell a tale.
And as I hope to drink good wine and ale
I'll be your judge. The rebel who disobeys,
However much the journey costs, he pays.
Now draw for cut and then we can depart;
The man who draws the shortest cut shall start."

850. if . . . agree: in other words, if you feel the same way in the evening (at evensong, or evening prayers) as you do in the morning (at matins, or morning prayers).

Pigskin binding by Doves Bindery for the Kelmscott *Chaucer* (1896).
Fitzwilliam Museum, University of Cambridge.

E Struggling Readers
Summarizing

Ask students to summarize the bargain that the pilgrims have made with the Host. [Possible answer: The Host has promised to be the judge of the best tale and to give the winner a supper, paid by all, in his tavern, the Tabard Inn. The pilgrims also agree that he can set the price of the supper, as well as standards for judgment. Anyone who refuses to tell a tale must pay the cost of the journey.]

F English Language Learners
Idioms

Tell students that "draw for cut" means the same thing as "draw straws." Have a student familiar with this procedure explain how it works.

Making the Connections

Connecting to the Subject: "The Gift of Story"

The Prologue may be thought of as quite a lovely little gift, but it isn't a story. Help students consider the nature and purpose of the Prologue by asking these questions:

- **What story elements are included in and missing from the Prologue?** [The prologue establishes the setting (both time and place) and the situation and introduces the characters. It lays the groundwork for conflict, but there is as yet no plot and no theme.]
- **In what ways is the Prologue a little like the gift wrapping for *The Canterbury Tales*?** [Like a beautifully wrapped package, the Prologue might make the reader eager to "open" the tales or find out what's inside. It's all part of the presentation.]
- **In what ways is the Prologue itself a kind of "gift of story"?** [It is as entertaining as any story; it is full of details; it reflects life; it recreates a culture; it begs to be retold.]

Connections

Malcolm X describes meeting his Arab guide and seeing the sacred Kaaba inside the Great Mosque of Mecca. At the Great Mosque, he performs a ritual ablution, removes his shoes, walks around the shrine seven times, tries to kiss or touch the Kaaba, prostrates himself, and prays. He drinks from the well of Zem Zem and runs between the two hills of Safa and Marwa. He goes to Mount Arafat and says special prayers.

A Cultural Connections

Pilgrimage to Mecca

Making a hajj, or pilgrimage, to Mecca (if one can afford the journey) is one of the five pillars of Islam. (The others are making a statement of faith, performing five daily prayers, giving to charity, and fasting during the Muslim month of Ramadan.) Within the courtyard of the Great Mosque of Mecca (Al-Haram) is the Kaaba, the holiest shrine of Islam. Tradition says that Abraham and his son Ishmael built the Kaaba to mirror the heavenly house of God, but it has been destroyed and rebuilt many times.

B English Language Learners

Archaic Language

Ablutions refers to washing. The word can often be found in literature of the nineteenth century and earlier. Ask students what special kind of washing is referred to here. [It is a ritual washing or cleansing of the body; Muslims are required to wash before entering a mosque.]

C Vocabulary Note

Prefixes and Roots

Explain that *circumambulate* is derived from the Latin prefix *circum-*, "around," and the Latin word *ambulare*, "to walk." *Circumambulate* is a perfect word here, referring to circling around the Kaaba but also having connotations of ritual movement. Ask students for other words formed with the prefix *circum-* or the root word *ambulare*. [Sample answers: circumnavigate, circumpolar, circumference; ambulatory, ambulance.]

Connections — An Autobiography

A In this passage, Malcolm X describes his first visit to Mecca, the Muslim sacred city.

from The Autobiography of Malcolm X

Malcolm X, with Alex Haley

Mecca, when we entered, seemed as ancient as time itself. Our car slowed through the winding streets, lined by shops on both sides and with buses, cars, and trucks, and tens of thousands of pilgrims from all over the earth were everywhere.

The car halted briefly at a place where a *Mutawaf*[1] was waiting for me. He wore the white skullcap and long nightshirt garb that I had seen at the airport. He was a short, dark-skinned Arab named Muhammad. He spoke no English whatever.

B We parked near the Great Mosque. We performed our ablution and entered. Pilgrims seemed to be on top of each other, there were so many, lying, sitting, sleeping, praying, walking.

My vocabulary cannot describe the new mosque that was being built around the Kaaba. I was thrilled to realize that it was only one of the tremendous rebuilding tasks under the direction of young Dr. Azzam, who had just been my host. The Great Mosque of Mecca, when it is finished, will surpass the architectural beauty of India's Taj Mahal.

C Carrying my sandals, I followed the *Mutawaf.* Then I saw the Kaaba, a huge, black stone house in the middle of the Great Mosque. It was being circumambulated by thousands upon thousands of praying pilgrims, both sexes, and every size, shape, color, and race in the world. I knew the prayer to be uttered when the pilgrim's eyes first perceive the Kaaba. Translated, it is "O God, You are peace, and peace derives from You. So greet us, O Lord, with peace." Upon entering the Mosque, the pilgrim should try to kiss the Kaaba if possible, but if the crowds prevent him getting that close, he touches it, and if the crowds prevent that, he raises his hand and cries out "Takbir!" ("God is great!") I could not get within yards. "Takbir!"

My feeling there in the House of God was a numbness. My *Mutawaf* led me in the crowd of praying, chanting pilgrims, moving seven times around the Kaaba. Some were bent and wizened with age; it was a sight that stamped itself on the brain. I saw incapacitated pilgrims being carried by others. Faces were enraptured in their faith. The seventh time around, I prayed two *Rak'a,* prostrating myself, my head on the floor. The first prostration, I prayed the Koran verse "Say He is God, the one and only"; the second prostration: "Say O you who are unbelievers, I worship not that which you worship. . . ."

As I prostrated, the *Mutawaf* fended pilgrims off to keep me from being trampled.

The *Mutawaf* and I next drank water from the well of Zem Zem. Then we ran between the two hills, Safa and Marwa, where Hajar wandered over the same earth searching for water for her child Ishmael.

Three separate times, after that, I visited the Great Mosque and circumambulated the Kaaba. The next day we set out after sunrise toward Mount Arafat, thousands of us, crying in unison: "Labbayka! Labbayka!" and "Allah Akbar!"... Arriving about noon, we prayed and chanted from noon until sunset, and the *asr* (afternoon) and *Maghrib* (sunset) special prayers were performed.

Finally, we lifted our hands in prayer and thanksgiving, repeating Allah's words: "There is no God but Allah. He has no partner. His are authority and praise. Good emanates from Him, and He has power over all things."

Standing on Mount Arafat had concluded the essential rites of being a pilgrim to Mecca. No one who missed it could consider himself a pilgrim.

1. ***Mutawaf:*** guide for pilgrims visiting Mecca.

Connecting Across Texts

Connecting with *The Canterbury Tales*

Ask students to compare the pilgrimage described by Malcolm X with the one Chaucer narrates:

- Are pilgrimages a thing of the past? [No, they are still popular.]
- What other pilgrimages might people make today? [People visit shrines or temples important to their faith; people also make nonreligious pilgrimages, such as visiting historic places or spots of particular beauty. Visits to the country or the birthplace of a parent, grandparent, or other ancestor are also common.]
- What is important about these rituals? [They provide a time for spiritual renewal and possibly physical and mental renewal. Some pilgrimages put people in touch with their cultural heritage and give them a better understanding of their family's past.]

Making Meanings

First Thoughts

Reading Check

a. When, where, and for what purposes do the pilgrims gather?

b. What plan, which becomes the basis of the frame story, does the Host propose to the pilgrims?

c. Place each pilgrim within one of these three groups that comprised medieval society: the feudal system (related to the land), the Church, and the city (merchants and professionals).

d. In your own words, explain the pilgrim-narrator's plea in lines 745–762.

1. If you were the thirty-first pilgrim, which of your fellow travelers would you choose to travel next to? Which would you definitely try to avoid? Whose story would you be most interested in hearing?

Shaping Interpretations

2. Chaucer is a master at using physical details—eyes, hair, complexion, body type, clothing—to reveal **character.** Tell about at least three pilgrims whose inner natures are revealed by their outer appearances.
3. Clearly, Chaucer **satirizes** the Church of his time. Show how this is true by analyzing two characters connected with the Church. What "good" Church people does Chaucer include to balance his satire?
4. What aspects of society does Chaucer satirize in his portrayals of the Merchant? the Franklin? the Doctor? the Miller?
5. Which pilgrims do you think Chaucer idealizes?
6. In describing the pilgrims, what do you think Chaucer as the pilgrim-narrator has revealed about his own personality, biases, and values?

Extending the Text

7. Which of the pilgrims' professions or trades have survived in society today? Which of Chaucer's character types can still be seen in airports or pulpits, farms or classrooms, city streets or small towns?
8. When would people from all walks of life today travel together in large groups for a common purpose? How do you think the pilgrimage described in *The Autobiography of Malcolm X* (see ***Connections,*** page 126) is similar to, and different from, the journey that Chaucer's pilgrims undertake?

Elements of Literature

Imagery: The Revealing Detail

Chaucer is a master of **imagery,** language that appeals to the senses. Most images are visual, but imagery can also appeal to our senses of hearing, smell, taste, and touch. In a few vivid words, sometimes with a few added figures of speech, Chaucer has created a cast of characters as real to us today as the characters in the latest novel—more real, perhaps, because Chaucer's people exhibit all the essentials of human nature.

With twenty-nine pilgrims to introduce, Chaucer could not develop any character at length. He had to find a few well-chosen details to make immediate impressions. For example, Chaucer devotes only nine lines to the Cook, yet he found just one now-famous image to immortalize the Cook and his unfortunate appearance: The Cook has "an ulcer on his knee," an open sore caused either by a skin disease associated with a bad diet and poor hygiene or by an infectious or communicable disease. With this image in mind, would you be anxious to try the Cook's blancmange, even if it rated "with the best"? How does this detail make you feel about the Cook?

Chaucer also relied upon his readers' knowledge of physiognomy. Based on some of Aristotle's treatises, physiognomy compared varieties of people to animals and asserted that certain physical characteristics revealed one's personality type. Thus, when Chaucer's contemporaries read that the Wife of Bath had "gap-teeth, set widely, truth to say," they knew that the physiognomists believed that a gap between a woman's two front teeth indicated not only that she would travel far but also that she was bold and especially suited for love.

Making Meanings

First Thoughts [Respond]

1. Answers will vary. Students might avoid the Cook but seek out the Wife of Bath. They may be interested in a story from the Knight.

Shaping Interpretations [Interpret]

2. For example, the Knight's stained tunic indicates that he cares little for outward show. Other possibilities include the Pardoner, Squire, Monk, and Miller.
3. Students could analyze the satiric descriptions of the Prioress, Monk, Friar, Summoner, and Pardoner. Chaucer presents favorable pictures of the Oxford Cleric and the Parson.
4. Merchant: "know-it-all" experts in business; Franklin: the pleasure-loving habits of the lesser nobility; Doctor: the greed of the profession; Miller: dishonest businesspeople.
5. He idealizes the Parson, Plowman, Oxford Cleric, and Knight.
6. Chaucer reveals himself as worldly, keenly observant of the appearances and motives of others, even-tempered, good-natured, and intensely curious. He values honesty, modesty, simplicity, and genuine piety. He dislikes hypocrisy and corruption.

Extending the Text [Apply/Synthesize]

7. Surviving occupations include priest, nun, merchant, lawyer, haberdasher, carpenter, cook, ship's captain, and doctor. In some sense all of Chaucer's character types can still be seen, such as rogues, hypocrites, shrewd businesspeople, good soldiers, and book lovers.
8. Religious, political, or cultural events bring people together. Like Chaucer's pilgrims, modern pilgrims would vary greatly in occupation, temperament, and appearance. Today's transportation and topics of conversation would differ from those of Chaucer's pilgrims, and today's group would probably contain a racial mix.

Reading Check

a. The pilgrims meet at an inn, The Tabard, on the night before they head for Canterbury.

b. Each pilgrim will tell two stories on the way to Canterbury and two on the way back.

c. The feudal system: Knight, Squire, Yeoman, Franklin, Plowman, Reeve, Miller; the Church: Prioress, Nun, Priests, Monk, Friar, Parson, Summoner, Pardoner; the city: Merchant, Oxford Cleric, Serjeant at Law, Haberdasher, Dyer, Carpenter, Weaver, Carpet-maker, Cook, Skipper, Doctor, Wife of Bath, Manciple, Poet (Chaucer).

d. The narrator asks permission to re-create the stories exactly as he heard them.

ELEMENTS OF LITERATURE

Imagery

Have students work in groups to find five images from the description of one of the pilgrims in the Prologue. (Give each group a different character, avoiding those with very short descriptions.) Have students identify the sense each of the images appeals to. Ask them to look for at least one image that is not visual. As students share their work, keep track of the senses referred to most often.

Possible Answers

- Ramlike appearance/strength: Miller is capable of powerful physical feats.
- Sowlike appearance/dirtiness: Miller has little regard for social convention.
- Foxlike appearance/slyness: Miller is an expert at stealing grain.
- Goatlike qualities/lechery: Pardoner bleats out love songs.
- Thin, fastidious type/bad temper, irritability: Reeve is choleric.
- Flaring or open nostrils/passion: Miller is a wrangler and a boaster.
- Pus-filled sores/lechery and drunkenness: Summoner is a drinker of strong wine.
- High forehead/intelligence, breeding: Prioress has exaggerated manners and sensitivity.
- White neck/loose or immoral person: Friar is corrupt.

Grading Timesaver

Rubrics for each Choices assignment appear on p. 99 in the *Portfolio Management System*.

CHOICES: Building Your Portfolio

1. **Writer's Notebook** Encourage students to reread the complete description of each character, taking notes in the chart as they do so.
2. **Descriptive Writing** Remind students that details about clothing are also part of appearance.
3. **Art/Character Study** Tell students that collages may also include small objects and textiles.

Analyzing Chaucer's imagery. The table below lists a few physical characteristics and their corresponding physiognomic interpretations. Choose a pilgrim who exhibits each characteristic. How does the physiognomic interpretation reinforce what you already know about the character's nature?

Think of what you know about the animals referred to in the chart. Can you make educated guesses as to why people would associate certain human characteristics with these particular animals?

Think also about this question: How do writers describe characters today? In stories (or movies) do any physical features automatically suggest something about character?

Physical Characteristic	Physiognomic Interpretation
ramlike appearance	strength
sowlike appearance	dirtiness
foxlike appearance	slyness
goatlike qualities	lechery
thin, fastidious type	bad temper, irritability
flaring or open nostrils	passion
pus-filled sores	lechery and drunkenness
high forehead	intelligence, breeding
white neck	looseness or immorality

CHOICES: Building Your Portfolio

Writer's Notebook

1. Collecting Ideas for a Comparison-Contrast Essay

For the Writer's Workshop on page 185, you will be writing an essay of comparison and contrast. Chaucer gives you plenty of characters to compare and contrast. You might find interesting subjects in the Wife of Bath and the Prioress—the only women Chaucer describes at any length. To gather notes for an essay comparing and contrasting these two women, gather information in a chart like the following one. Save your work for possible use later.

Element	Wife of Bath	Prioress
Appearance		
Personality		
Tastes		
Social position		
Life experiences		

Descriptive Writing

2. Creating a Character

Refer to the notes you made for the Quickwrite on page 103. Now that you have read descriptions of Chaucer's characters, you might have many more ideas of how to bring your own character to life. In an essay, describe your character. Remember that Chaucer tells us about such things as appearance, speech, mannerisms, profession, special interests, dislikes. Remember also that Chaucer doesn't necessarily tell us what he *thinks* of his characters; he lets his descriptions speak for themselves. You might want to imagine that your character has joined Chaucer's pilgrims, in a sort of time warp. If you wish, supply a drawing of your character.

Art/Character Study

3. A Canterbury Gallery

Chaucer uses words to create a picture of each pilgrim. Now it's your turn to go from words to pictures by creating a portrait of a pilgrim. Select one pilgrim, and draw an illustration of him or her. Or create a collage showing what you find most memorable and important about the pilgrim. You might want to create a class display of your illustrations or collages.

The story in "The Pardoner's Tale" has roots that are old and widespread. Avarice (or greed) as the root of evil is a theme that appears in stories of many lands. Starting from the Latin saying *"Radix malorum est cupiditas,"* translated loosely as "The love of money is the root of all evil," the Pardoner presents us with an *exemplum,* an anecdote or example inserted into a sermon to teach a moral lesson. As with every tale, Chaucer fits the story to the character of the storyteller.

Chaucer is a master of both **verbal** and **situational irony.** You use both types of irony all the time. You use verbal irony when you say one thing but mean another. For example, when a friend asks how you liked cleaning your room for three hours, you might reply, "It was a blast." Both of you know differently, of course. In situational irony, what actually happens is different from what you expect. You feel situational irony when it rains on the weather forecasters' picnic, or when the police officer's son turns out to be a criminal.

The Pardoner, from the Ellesmere manuscript, fol. 138r.

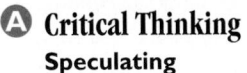

By permission of The Huntington Library, San Marino, California.

from The Pardoner's Tale

Geoffrey Chaucer

translated by **Nevill Coghill**

The Prologue

"But let me briefly make my purpose plain;
I preach for nothing but for greed of gain
And use the same old text, as bold as brass,
Radix malorum est cupiditas.°
And thus I preach against the very vice
I make my living out of—avarice.
And yet however guilty of that sin
Myself, with others I have power to win
Them from it, I can bring them to repent;
But that is not my principal intent.
Covetousness is both the root and stuff
Of all I preach. That ought to be enough.
"Well, then I give examples thick and fast
From bygone times, old stories from the past.
A yokel mind loves stories from of old,
Being the kind it can repeat and hold.
What! Do you think, as long as I can preach
And get their silver for the things I teach,

4. ***Radix malorum est cupiditas*** (ra′diks ma·lō′rum est ko͞o·pi′di·tas): literally, "The root of evil is desire" (1 Timothy 6:10).

Words to Own

avarice (av′ə·ris) *n.:* too great a desire for wealth.
covetousness (kuv′ət·əs·nis) *n.:* the quality of craving wealth or possessions.

Objectives

The Pardoner's Tale

1. Read and interpret the story
2. Express understanding through writing and performance
3. Understand and use new words

Skills

Writing
- Collect ideas for a compare/contrast essay

Speaking/Listening
- Present a dramatization

Vocabulary
- Use new words

Planning

- **Block Schedule** *Block Scheduling Lesson Plans with Pacing Guide*
- **Traditional Schedule** *Lesson Plans Including Strategies for English-Language Learners*
- **One-Stop Planner** *CD-ROM with Test Generator*

A Critical Thinking

Speculating

? Why does the Pardoner admit that he preaches to make a personal profit? [Sample responses: He is so immoral he's proud of his vice; he may be carried away with his own cleverness in using this tale.]

Resources: Print and Media

Reading
- *Graphic Organizers for Active Reading,* p. 7
- *Words to Own,* p. 4
- *Audio CD Library* Disc 2, Track 7

Elements of Literature
- *Literary Elements* Transparency 5 Worksheet, p. 16

Writing and Language
- *Daily Oral Grammar* Transparency 4
- *Grammar and Language Links* Worksheet, p. 11

Assessment
- *Formal Assessment,* p. 21
- *Portfolio Management System,* p. 100
- *Test Generator (One-Stop Planner CD-ROM)*

Internet
- go.hrw.com (keyword: LEO 12-2)

Summary ■■

After a Prologue in which he brazenly brags about his own avarice, the unscrupulous Pardoner tells his tale. As three young men sit in a tavern, a coffin passes, bearing the body of a man who they learn has been murdered by a thief called "Death." The three decide to find Death and kill him. Shortly after they set out, they encounter an old man who tells them that Death awaits under a nearby tree. There they find instead a stash of gold coins, which they decide to steal. While the youngest goes to town for supplies, including wine, the other two decide to kill the third on his return. But, in town, the youngest poisons the wine. When he returns, he is killed, but when his attackers drink the wine, they die, too. (In the original, the Prologue runs 134 lines, the Tale 456 lines, and the Epilogue 50 lines.)

Background

Most of Chaucer's tales are based on older stories or ancient folklore. The earliest known version of the Pardoner's tale is found in the Hindu collection *Vedabbha Jataka.*

Ⓐ Cultural Connections
The Seven Deadly Sins

? In medieval times, people were keenly aware of the seven deadly sins: pride, avarice, lust, anger, gluttony, envy, and sloth. These would bring spiritual death and eternal damnation unless the sinner confessed and obtained pardon. Which of these does the Pardoner acknowledge as his own vices? [avarice, lust, sloth, and perhaps gluttony]

Ⓑ Appreciating Language
Changing Meanings

The word *riot* today is associated with the uprising of a mob, but here the word means "loose living." *Stews* were brothels. *Public-houses* were (and are) places where liquor is sold (*pubs*).

Ⓒ Elements of Literature
Characterization

? What have you learned about the rioters so far? [Possible answers: They are wrongdoers. They are guilty of gluttony, lust, and sloth. They drink, gamble, carouse, and swear.]

That I will live in poverty, from choice?
That's not the counsel of my inner voice!
No! Let me preach and beg from kirk° to kirk
And never do an honest job of work,
No, nor make baskets, like St. Paul, to gain
A livelihood. I do not preach in vain.
There's no apostle I would counterfeit;
I mean to have money, wool and cheese and wheat
Though it were given me by the poorest lad
Or poorest village widow, though she had
A string of starving children, all agape.
No, let me drink the liquor of the grape
And keep a jolly wench in every town!
"But listen, gentlemen; to bring things down
To a conclusion, would you like a tale?
Now as I've drunk a draft of corn-ripe ale,
By God it stands to reason I can strike
On some good story that you all will like.
For though I am a wholly vicious man
Don't think I can't tell moral tales. I can!
Here's one I often preach when out for winning;
Now please be quiet. Here is the beginning."

The Tale

In Flanders once there was a company
Of youngsters haunting vice and ribaldry,°
Riot and gambling, stews and public-houses
Where each with harp, guitar, or lute carouses,
Dancing and dicing day and night, and bold
To eat and drink far more than they can hold,
Doing thereby the devil sacrifice
Within that devil's temple of cursed vice,
Abominable in superfluity,
With oaths so damnable in blasphemy
That it's a grisly thing to hear them swear.
Our dear Lord's body they will rend and tear.° . . .
It's of three rioters I have to tell
Who, long before the morning service bell,
Were sitting in a tavern for a drink.
And as they sat, they heard the hand-bell clink
Before a coffin going to the grave;
One of them called the little tavern-knave
And said "Go and find out at once—look spry!—

21. kirk: Scottish for "church."

42. ribaldry (rib′əl·drē): vulgar language or humor.

52. Our . . . tear: Their oaths refer to "God's arms" and "God's blessed bones."

WORDS TO OWN

carouses (kə·rouz′ez) *v.:* drinks and celebrates noisily.
abominable (ə·bäm′ə·nə·bəl) *adj.:* disgusting; hateful.
superfluity (so͞o′pər·flo͞o′ə·tē) *n.:* excess.
blasphemy (blas′fə·mē′) *n.:* mockery of God.

Preteaching Vocabulary

Words to Own

Have students sort the Words to Own by deciding which have positive, negative, or neutral connotations. To make or support their choices, students might think of contexts in which each word might be used. Then have students complete the exercise below by supplying the word from the Words to Own that is most nearly the synonym or antonym of the word or words given.

Synonyms:
1. strolled [sauntered]
2. forgiveness [absolution]
3. exceed [transcend]
4. greed [avarice]
5. goes on a drinking spree [carouses]

Antonyms:
6. reverence [blasphemy]
7. insufficiency [superfluity]
8. lovable [abominable]
9. rosy complexion [pallor]
10. self-denial [covetousness]

Whose corpse is in that coffin passing by;
And see you get the name correctly too."
"Sir," said the boy, "no need, I promise you;
Two hours before you came here I was told.
He was a friend of yours in days of old,
And suddenly, last night, the man was slain,
Upon his bench, face up, dead drunk again.
There came a privy° thief, they call him Death,
Who kills us all round here, and in a breath
He speared him through the heart, he never stirred.
And then Death went his way without a word.
He's killed a thousand in the present plague,
And, sir, it doesn't do to be too vague
If you should meet him; you had best be wary.
Be on your guard with such an adversary,
Be primed to meet him everywhere you go,
That's what my mother said. It's all I know."
The publican° joined in with, "By St. Mary,
What the child says is right; you'd best be wary,
This very year he killed, in a large village
A mile away, man, woman, serf at tillage,°
Page in the household, children—all there were.
Yes, I imagine that he lives round there.
It's well to be prepared in these alarms,
He might do you dishonor." "Huh, God's arms!"
The rioter said, "Is he so fierce to meet?
I'll search for him, by Jesus, street by street.
God's blessed bones! I'll register a vow!
Here, chaps! The three of us together now,
Hold up your hands, like me, and we'll be brothers
In this affair, and each defend the others,
And we will kill this traitor Death, I say!
Away with him as he has made away
With all our friends. God's dignity! Tonight!"
They made their bargain, swore with appetite,
These three, to live and die for one another
As brother-born might swear to his born brother.
And up they started in their drunken rage
And made towards this village which the page
And publican had spoken of before.
Many and grisly were the oaths they swore,
Tearing Christ's blessed body to a shred;
"If we can only catch him, Death is dead!"
When they had gone not fully half a mile,
Just as they were about to cross a stile,°
They came upon a very poor old man
Who humbly greeted them and thus began,
"God look to you, my lords, and give you quiet!"
To which the proudest of these men of riot
Gave back the answer, "What, old fool? Give place!

67. privy (priv'ē): secretive; furtive.

77. publican: tavern keeper; from *public house,* an inn or tavern.

80. tillage: working the land.

104. stile: steps used for climbing over a wall.

D Historical Connections
The Black Death

? In the mid-fourteenth century, bubonic plague, called the Black Death, spread across Europe. Why would this be an appropriate setting for a story intended to make people repent? [Possible response: The threat of death might spur listeners to seek forgiveness of sins.]

E Critical Thinking
Speculating

? Why do the rioters want to kill Death? [Possible answers: They want to defend themselves against Death. They are so drunk that they set themselves an impossible and ironic task. It is the ultimate act of defiance.]

F Appreciating Language
Specific Meanings

? What does l. 101 mean? [Their cursing involves parts of Christ's body. See ll. 52, 84, and 87.]

G Reading Skills and Strategies
Drawing Conclusions

? Who is this old man? What might he represent, or what purpose might he serve in the story? [Possible answers: He may be Death. He may be an angel or just an old man looking for Death.] **Critics do not agree on an interpretation of this character.**

Reaching All Students

Struggling Readers
Ask students to read the story in segments, stopping to briefly retell the main ideas to a partner. You might suggest they stop after ll. 102, 161, 199, 230, 274, and 290.

English Language Learners
Explain that a pardoner in the Middle Ages traveled around to hear confessions and grant absolution, or forgiveness. While a pardoner was forbidden to accept money, Chaucer implies that many of them did. Point out that in this tale, students will find many discrepancies between what the characters expect to happen and what actually does happen, and between what the Pardoner's tale teaches and the way the Pardoner behaves.

Advanced Learners
Have students formulate a definition of evil and then, as they read, list the evil deeds of the three rioters. [All three get drunk, use profanity, treat the old man rudely, and plan to steal the gold; the two older rioters plan the murder of the youngest; the youngest lies to the apothecary and poisons the wine; the older two stab the youngest.] Finally, have students rank the deeds in their lists and decide which ones are most evil based on their definition of evil.

Ⓐ Elements of Literature
Irony

? What is ironic about the attitudes of the rioters and the old man toward Death? [Sample response: Most people fear Death and try to avoid it, but the old man seeks the ease of Death. The drunken rioters, on the other hand, seek Death out to challenge it. Also, the old man tells the rioters where to find Death, but he cannot die.]

Ⓑ Elements of Literature
Personification

? What personification of Death does the old man offer? What does this image suggest? [He personifies Death as a mother, her house surrounded by a gate (the earth). This image suggests that Death is a comforter or nurturer, providing a home and relief from suffering.]

Ⓒ Struggling Readers
Using Context Clues

Students may not know what is meant by *holy writ.* The word *writ* is related to *write* and can mean "anything written"; it also has a range of related meanings. Ask students to identify the context clues that explain that *holy writ* is scripture. [It is something that can be read; an example from scripture is quoted.]

Ⓓ Elements of Literature
Allusion

The old man is quoting his own variation on the Biblical injunction, "Therefore all things whatsoever ye would that men should do to you, do ye even so to them" (Matthew 7:12).

Ⓔ Critical Thinking
Hypothesizing

? Why does the old man add "if you should live till then"? [Possible responses: He knows for sure what will happen to the rioters; or he can guess, based on his observation of their recklessness; or he may simply be observing that in this time of plague, people cannot count on living to an old age.]

Why are you all wrapped up except your face?
Why live so long? Isn't it time to die?"
The old, old fellow looked him in the eye
And said, "Because I never yet have found,
Though I have walked to India, searching round
Village and city on my pilgrimage,
One who would change his youth to have my age.
And so my age is mine and must be still
Upon me, for such time as God may will.
"Not even Death, alas, will take my life;
So, like a wretched prisoner at strife
Within himself, I walk alone and wait
About the earth, which is my mother's gate,
Knock-knocking with my staff from night to noon
And crying, 'Mother, open to me soon!
Look at me, mother, won't you let me in?
See how I wither, flesh and blood and skin!
Alas! When will these bones be laid to rest?
Mother, I would exchange—for that were best—
The wardrobe in my chamber, standing there
So long, for yours! Aye, for a shirt of hair°
To wrap me in!' She has refused her grace,
Whence comes the pallor of my withered face.
"But it dishonored you when you began
To speak so roughly, sir, to an old man,
Unless he had injured you in word or deed.
It says in holy writ, as you may read,
'Thou shalt rise up before the hoary° head
And honor it.' And therefore be it said,
'Do no more harm to an old man than you,
Being now young, would have another do
When you are old'—if you should live till then.
And so may God be with you, gentlemen,
For I must go whither I have to go."
"By God," the gambler said, "you shan't do so,
You don't get off so easy, by St. John!
I heard you mention, just a moment gone,
A certain traitor Death who singles out
And kills the fine young fellows hereabout.
And you're his spy, by God! You wait a bit.
Say where he is or you shall pay for it,
By God and by the Holy Sacrament!
I say you've joined together by consent
To kill us younger folk, you thieving swine!"
"Well, sirs," he said, "if it be your design
To find out Death, turn up this crooked way

130. shirt of hair: Coarse shirts of woven horsehair were worn as penance. Here, the old man refers to such a shirt used to wrap his body for burial.

137. hoary: white.

WORDS TO OWN
pallor (pal′ər) *n.:* paleness.

Professional Notes

Critical Comment: Christian Imagery

Chaucer scholar Robert P. Miller regards the brothers as "Cain-like" and finds the story illustrative of a vast array of Christian imagery. For example, he notes that Death "lies up the 'crooked way,' the opposite of the straight and narrow; 'in that grove' that is, in the false paradise of cupidity; and 'under a tree' where Adam and Eve lost their true Eden and found Death first. In terms of medieval Christian imagery, this is surely the way to find Death, but not the way to slay him." Miller adds that "the oak tree under which the gold is discovered literally exemplifies the words of [the] text, *Radix malorum est cupiditas.* For this tree may itself be regarded as the tree of evil (or of death) whose root is cupidity symbolized by the golden earthly treasure."

Towards that grove, I left him there today
Under a tree, and there you'll find him waiting.
He isn't one to hide for all your prating.
You see that oak? He won't be far to find.
And God protect you that redeemed mankind,
Aye, and amend you!" Thus that ancient man. (F)
At once the three young rioters began
To run, and reached the tree, and there they found
A pile of golden florins° on the ground,
New-coined, eight bushels of them as they thought.
No longer was it Death those fellows sought, (G)
For they were all so thrilled to see the sight,
The florins were so beautiful and bright,
That down they sat beside the precious pile.
The wickedest spoke first after a while.
"Brothers," he said, "you listen to what I say.
I'm pretty sharp although I joke away.
It's clear that Fortune has bestowed this treasure (H)
To let us live in jollity and pleasure.
Light come, light go! We'll spend it as we ought.
God's precious dignity! Who would have thought
This morning was to be our lucky day?
"If one could only get the gold away,
Back to my house, or else to yours, perhaps—
For as you know, the gold is ours, chaps— (I)
We'd all be at the top of fortune, hey?
But certainly it can't be done by day.
People would call us robbers—a strong gang,
So our own property would make us hang.
No, we must bring this treasure back by night
Some prudent way, and keep it out of sight.
And so as a solution I propose (J)
We draw for lots and see the way it goes;
The one who draws the longest, lucky man,
Shall run to town as quickly as he can
To fetch us bread and wine—but keep things dark—
While two remain in hiding here to mark
Our heap of treasure. If there's no delay,

164. florins: coins worth twenty-four pence. *Pence* is the British plural of *penny*.

The Three Living, The Three Dead, from the *Psalter and Prayer Book of Bonne of Luxembourg, Duchess of Normandy* (14th century), fol. 321v–322r. Grisaille, color, gilt, and brown ink on vellum (4 15/16″ × 3 9/16″). French, Paris.

The Metropolitan Museum of Art.
The Cloisters Collection, 1969 (69.86). Photograph
© 1991 The Metropolitan Museum of Art.

Using Students' Strengths

Logical Learners
Have students construct a flow chart or time line showing the chain of events that lead to the rioters' deaths, beginning with "Rioters decide to kill Death."

Intrapersonal Learners
Provide intrapersonal learners with a photocopy of the tale, on which they can record their own dialogue with the text. Encourage students to record their reactions to as many lines or sections as possible, including their questions, confusion, delight, horror, or judgments.

(F) Struggling Readers
Reading Elliptical Constructions
Explain that in poetry words are often omitted in order to create lines with the correct number of syllables. The construction in l. 161 is particularly troublesome because the order is inverted. Explain that *thus* means "so," and ask students to paraphrase the line. [so the old man] Then ask what part of speech has been omitted that would make this sentence complete. [a verb] Finally, ask what word would make the construction complete. [spoke; said]

(G) Elements of Literature
Irony
? What is ironic about this line? [The young men no longer seek Death to kill him, but they have probably found the instrument of their own Death in the gold coins.]

(H) Elements of Literature
Personification
? What does the capital *F* on *Fortune* tell you? What have the young men forgotten? [Fortune is personified here. The young men have forgotten that they were told Death waited under the tree (Death *is* their Fortune), or they have forgotten that Fortune can be good or bad.]

(I) Appreciating Language
Informal Usage
Chaps, meaning "fellows" or "boys" (today we might say "guys"), is an example of informal language. Although occasionally used in American English, the word is most frequently found in British writings. (The word is the translator's, not Chaucer's.)

(J) Elements of Literature
Characterization
? In this example of indirect characterization, what do the speaker's words reveal about him? [Possible answers: He thinks quickly. He is a schemer. He is greedily protecting his interests.]

Ⓐ Reading Skills and Strategies
Making Predictions

Ask students to predict what they think will happen next. [Possible answer: The youngest rioter will leak the secret of the treasure in town. The remaining rioters will make off with the gold, leaving the youngest with nothing.]

Ⓑ Vocabulary Note
The Prefix *mis-*

Point out the word *miscreants* and its gloss in the margin. Explain that the prefix *mis-* can mean "wrongly," "not," "badly," or "the opposite of." It functions a bit like the prefix *un-*. (The root of the word *miscreant* comes from the Latin word for "creed" or "belief": As the gloss notes, a miscreant is an unbeliever, though it more frequently refers to an evildoer.) Ask students to state other words with the prefix *mis-* and to identify the meanings of the prefix in those words. [Possible answers: *misbehave, misfortune* (opposite of); *misplace, mismanagement* (badly); *misinterpret* (wrongly).]

Ⓒ Critical Thinking
Synthesizing

? All three rioters make frequent references to religion. This is ironic, since they are such evildoers. How do these references to religion connect the rioters thematically to the Pardoner who tells their tale? [Possible answer: Both the Pardoner and the rioters live in a religious society, and they are versed in the religion of their culture, yet none of them allow religion to influence their behavior.]

Ⓓ Cultural Connections

Here the Pardoner describes the consequences of sin. The young man has already fallen into sin because of his drunkenness. As a result, God allows the Devil (Fiend) to lure him further into evil. According to Christian theology, God does not cause evil but allows people to be tempted by it.

When night comes down we'll carry it away,
All three of us, wherever we have planned."
  He gathered lots and hid them in his hand
Bidding them draw for where the luck should fall.
It fell upon the youngest of them all,
And off he ran at once towards the town.
  As soon as he had gone the first sat down
And thus began a parley with the other:
"You know that you can trust me as a brother;
Now let me tell you where your profit lies;
You know our friend has gone to get supplies
And here's a lot of gold that is to be
Divided equally among us three.
Nevertheless, if I could shape things thus
So that we shared it out—the two of us—
Wouldn't you take it as a friendly act?"
  "But how?" the other said. "He knows the fact
That all the gold was left with me and you;
What can we tell him? What are we to do?"
  "Is it a bargain," said the first, "or no?
For I can tell you in a word or so
What's to be done to bring the thing about."
"Trust me," the other said, "you needn't doubt
My word. I won't betray you, I'll be true."
  "Well," said his friend, "you see that we are two,
And two are twice as powerful as one.
Now look; when he comes back, get up in fun
To have a wrestle; then, as you attack,
I'll up and put my dagger through his back
While you and he are struggling, as in game;
Then draw your dagger too and do the same.
Then all this money will be ours to spend,
Divided equally of course, dear friend.
Then we can gratify our lusts and fill
The day with dicing at our own sweet will."
Thus these two miscreants° agreed to slay
The third and youngest, as you heard me say.
  The youngest, as he ran towards the town,
Kept turning over, rolling up and down
Within his heart the beauty of those bright
New florins, saying, "Lord, to think I might
Have all that treasure to myself alone!
Could there be anyone beneath the throne
Of God so happy as I then should be?"
  And so the Fiend, our common enemy,
Was given power to put it in his thought
That there was always poison to be bought,
And that with poison he could kill his friends.
To men in such a state the Devil sends
Thoughts of this kind, and has a full permission

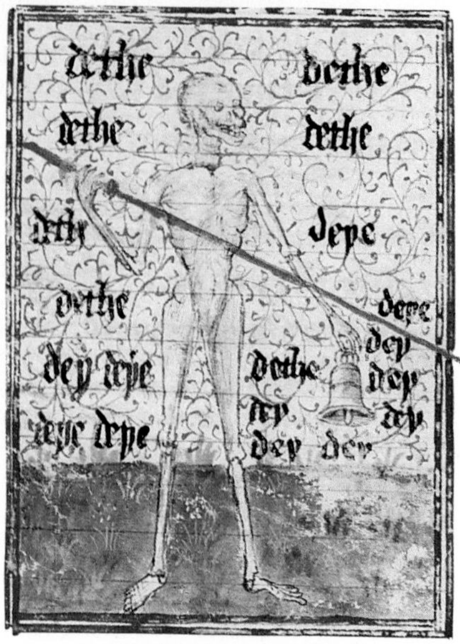

The Bodleian Library, Oxford.

Death with his spear, from *The Pardoner's Tale*. MS Douce 322, fol. 19v.

229. **miscreants** (mis′krē·ənts): criminals; literally, "unbelievers."

Getting Students Involved

Cooperative Learning

Picture This. Assign one of the following sections of "The Pardoner's Tale" to a group of students: ll. 53–93, 94–132, 133–177, 178–217, 218–263, 264–290. Direct students to re-create the story visually on paper; they can work freehand or cut and paste pictures. Also, ask students to add speech balloons, captions, or other text as needed. Groups should divide duties among members but require a written summary of each member's contribution to be handed in with the final product. When all groups are finished, have each group present its section of the tale in order, to the rest of the class. Ask other students to make one positive comment and one suggestion for improvement to each group. Finally, have groups revise their presentations based on the comments. The final product can be displayed on a bulletin board.

To lure them on to sorrow and perdition;°
For this young man was utterly content
To kill them both and never to repent.
  And on he ran, he had no thought to tarry,
Came to the town, found an apothecary°
And said, "Sell me some poison if you will,
I have a lot of rats I want to kill
And there's a polecat too about my yard
That takes my chickens and it hits me hard;
But I'll get even, as is only right,
With vermin that destroy a man by night."
  The chemist answered, "I've a preparation
Which you shall have, and by my soul's salvation
If any living creature eat or drink
A mouthful, ere° he has the time to think,
Though he took less than makes a grain of wheat,
You'll see him fall down dying at your feet;
Yes, die he must, and in so short a while
You'd hardly have the time to walk a mile,
The poison is so strong, you understand."
  This cursed fellow grabbed into his hand
The box of poison and away he ran
Into a neighboring street, and found a man
Who lent him three large bottles. He withdrew
And deftly poured the poison into two.
He kept the third one clean, as well he might,
For his own drink, meaning to work all night
Stacking the gold and carrying it away.
And when this rioter, this devil's clay,
Had filled his bottles up with wine, all three,
Back to rejoin his comrades sauntered he.
  Why make a sermon of it? Why waste breath?
Exactly in the way they'd planned his death
They fell on him and slew him, two to one.
Then said the first of them when this was done,
"Now for a drink. Sit down and let's be merry,
For later on there'll be the corpse to bury."
And, as it happened, reaching for a sup,
He took a bottle full of poison up
And drank; and his companion, nothing loth,°
Drank from it also, and they perished both.
  There is, in Avicenna's° long relation
Concerning poison and its operation,
Trust me, no ghastlier section to transcend
What these two wretches suffered at their end.

244. perdition (pər·dish′ən): damnation.

248. apothecary (ə·päth′ə·ker′ē): druggist. Formerly, apothecaries prescribed drugs.

258. ere: before.

283. loth (lōth): reluctant; unwilling; alternate spelling of *loath*.

285. Avicenna's (av′i·sen′ə): Avicenna (980–1037), a famous Islamic philosopher and doctor, wrote several medical books.

WORDS TO OWN
saunterred (sôn′tərd) *v.:* strolled.
transcend (tran·send′) *v.:* to exceed; surpass.

E Elements of Literature
Irony
? What is ironic about the reason the young man gives for buying poison? [He wants it for "vermin that destroy a man by night." Ironically, the "vermin" he plans to kill are planning to "destroy a man"—him. In addition, he fits his own definition of vermin.]

F Appreciating Language
Style
? Note how relatively short the sentences are in this section. How do these short sentences affect the pace of the story? [They speed up the lines; they reinforce suspense.]

G Elements of Literature
Characterization
Call attention to the words in apposition, "this devil's clay," following the subject. Explain that this is an example of direct characterization, yet it still needs to be interpreted by the reader, for it is essentially a metaphor. Ask students what the author means by "this devil's clay." [Possible answer: The rioter's character was molded, like clay, by the devil. He is, like clay, changeable, easily manipulated, and without inherent form or integrity.]

H Struggling Readers
Rearranging Word Order/Syntax
The usual word order in this sentence is inverted in order to get the rhyming word at the end. Ask students to rearrange the sentence to create an expected word order. [He sauntered back to rejoin his comrades.]

I Elements of Literature
Irony
? What is ironic about the narrator's questions? [The story is, in fact, part of a sermon on avarice.] Remind students that this kind of story within a sermon is called an **exemplum** (see headnote, p. 129).

Assessing Learning

Check Test: Questions and Answers
1. What vice does the Pardoner always preach against? [avarice; greed]
2. What sin does he admit to? [greed]
3. For whom are the three rioters looking? [Death]
4. What do they find in the grove of trees? [a stash of gold coins]
5. How do they eventually find what they are looking for? [They find Death by killing one another to get a larger share of the gold.]

Standardized Test Preparation
For practice in proofreading and editing, see
- *Daily Oral Grammar,* Transparency 4

Ⓐ Reading Skills and Strategies

Recognizing Print Conventions

Call attention to the use of ellipses. See if students know what these print conventions signal. [The ellipses here indicate that a portion of the story is omitted. See also l. 319.] Students should note also that the word *from* is used on p. 129 to indicate that parts of the tale are omitted.

Ⓑ Cultural Connections

Relics

Remind students that holy relics were bits of a saints' bones, hair, nails, or clothing that were believed to have healing powers. Ask students if they think the Pardoner's relics are authentic or fake. [Most students will assume that these relics are fake ones that the Pardoner is selling to make money.]

Ⓒ Appreciating Language

Idioms

Note the use of "ply the spur" (the translator's words, not Chaucer's) and explain that it refers to a rider's digging boot spurs into a horse's haunches while riding. Ask students what we might say today to mean "ride" or "get going." [Possible answers: gun the engine, lay rubber, rev it.] Note "keep the ball in play" in l. 331, a metaphorical way of saying "keep the game going" (also the translator's words).

Ⓓ Elements of Literature

Characterization

? What insights into the characters of the Pardoner, the Host, and the Knight do these lines provide? [Possible answers: The insulting way the Pardoner deals with the Host suggests extreme rudeness. The Host despises the Pardoner. (Some of the omitted lines have the Host expressing in strong language how he feels about the Pardoner.) The Knight seems to function as a superior who intervenes among his inferiors to smooth things over and assuage hard feelings.]

Thus these two murderers received their due,
So did the treacherous young poisoner too. . . .

"One thing I should have mentioned in my tale,
Dear people. I've some relics in my bale
And pardons too, as full and fine, I hope,
As any in England, given me by the Pope.
If there be one among you that is willing
To have my absolution for a shilling°
Devoutly given, come! and do not harden
Your hearts but kneel in humbleness for pardon;
Or else, receive my pardon as we go.
You can renew it every town or so
Always provided that you still renew
Each time, and in good money, what is due.
It is an honor to you to have found
A pardoner with his credentials sound
Who can absolve you as you ply the spur
In any accident that may occur.
For instance—we are all at Fortune's beck°—
Your horse may throw you down and break your neck.
What a security it is to all
To have me here among you and at call
With pardon for the lowly and the great
When soul leaves body for the future state!
And I advise our Host here to begin,
The most enveloped of you all in sin.
Come forward, Host, you shall be the first to pay,
And kiss my holy relics right away.
Only a groat.° Come on, unbuckle your purse!"
"No, no," said he, "not I, and may the curse
Of Christ descend upon me if I do! . . ."

The Pardoner said nothing, not a word;
He was so angry that he couldn't speak.
"Well," said our Host, "if you're for showing pique,
I'll joke no more, not with an angry man."
The worthy Knight immediately began,
Seeing the fun was getting rather rough,
And said, "No more, we've all had quite enough.
Now, Master Pardoner, perk up, look cheerly!
And you, Sir Host, whom I esteem so dearly,
I beg of you to kiss the Pardoner.
"Come, Pardoner, draw nearer, my dear sir.
Let's laugh again and keep the ball in play."
They kissed, and we continued on our way.

296. shilling: coin worth twelve pence.

307. beck: summons; in other words, subject to Fortune's will.

317. groat: silver coin worth four pence.

WORDS TO OWN
absolution (ab′sə·lo͞o′shən) *n.:* forgiveness.

Making the Connections

Connecting to the Subject: "The Gift of Story"

These questions will help students explore the theme:

- In what way is the Pardoner's story about the rioters a gift? That is, what do you receive by reading it? [We are treated to moral instruction and entertainment. The story also increases our knowledge of Chaucer and of his times.]
- In what ways is "The Pardoner's Tale" a story within a story? [It is one of the tales within the frame story of *The Canterbury Tales*. It is also a story within the "story" of the Pardoner himself: It helps to illuminate him.]

Making Meanings

First Thoughts

1. How did you respond to the tale told by the Pardoner? How did you respond to the fact that it was told by a man of the Pardoner's character?

Reading Check

a. How does the Pardoner describe his own character and morals in his Prologue?

b. According to "The Pardoner's Tale," why are the three rioters looking for Death?

c. Where does the old man tell the three rioters to look for Death? How do they treat him?

d. Describe the rioters' plan for the gold and how it proves fatal to all three men.

e. Why do the Pardoner and the Host quarrel at the end of the tale? Who patches up their quarrel?

Shaping Interpretations

2. How do the tavern knave and the publican **personify** Death? What does the rioters' response to the description tell you?
3. What do you think the poor old man may **symbolize**?
4. Irony is a discrepancy between expectations and reality. How many layers of **irony** can you identify in this story?
5. Why is it ironic that the Pardoner preaches a story with this particular moral? How would you account for the psychology of the Pardoner: Is he truly evil, just drunk, or so used to cheating that he does it automatically?
6. What do you think Chaucer is **satirizing** in "The Pardoner's Tale"?
7. What **moral** does the Pardoner want us to draw from his tale? What moral do you think Chaucer wants you to draw from the Pardoner's tale?

Extending the Text

8. Do people with the Pardoner's ethics and tricks still exist today—in any field of life? Explain.
9. How would the Pardoner fill in the following personality profile?

Name: ____________________

Profession: ____________________

Last Book I Read: ____________________

Latest Accomplishment: ____________________

Why I Do What I Do: ____________________

Future Goals: ____________________

Quotation I Like Best: ____________________

Choices: Building Your Portfolio

Writer's Notebook

1. Collecting Ideas for a Comparison-Contrast Essay

WORK IN PROGRESS

You might find ideas for a comparison-contrast essay in "The Pardoner's Tale." (See the assignment in the Writer's Workshop on page 185.) The Pardoner is a clergyman who preaches against the very sins he is guilty of. If a contrast between the Pardoner and his tale interests you, take notes on all the ways the tale and its moral contrast with the Pardoner's own values. Save your notes for later use.

Drama/Pantomime

2. Hamming It Up

Working with a partner or a small group, present a dramatization or a pantomime of "The Pardoner's Tale." To dramatize, write speeches for each character and for a narrator who can fill in the story line. For a pantomime, have one person read Chaucer's text while the others act it out without words.

Reading Check

a. He admits he is corrupt and greedy.

b. They want to kill him.

c. He tells them to look under a nearby oak tree; they treat him with disrespect.

d. The youngest rioter will go to town while the other two stay with the treasure. The two left behind decide to murder the youngest; the youngest forms a plan to kill the other two with poisoned wine. When the youngest returns, the other two kill him, drink the wine, and die.

e. The Host refuses to buy a pardon or kiss the Pardoner's relics. The Knight patches up the quarrel.

Making Meanings

First Thoughts [Respond]

1. Students may judge the Pardoner harshly; some may find his tale amusing. Ask students to use the text to support their answers.

Shaping Interpretations [Interpret]

2. The knave calls Death a "privy thief," and the publican says that Death probably lives near the village where many people have died. The rioters show how foolish they are when they decide to "kill" Death.
3. He may symbolize Death or the futility of trying to overcome death.
4. Ironically, this tale of greed is told by the greedy Pardoner; in the tale, "sworn brothers" should protect, rather than kill, each other. The rioters do find Death under the tree, but they don't kill Death; instead, they die.
5. The Pardoner says that he makes his living through avarice, the very sin he preaches against. Students may contrast the Pardoner's frankness before he tells his tale with his deceit afterward.
6. Chaucer is satirizing greed and pride, as well as clerics who use their offices to deceive the very people they should serve.
7. The Pardoner's moral is that greed can lead to death. Chaucer's moral might be that even a story with a moral can be used for evil purposes.

Extending the Text [Synthesize]

8. Students may refer to real people and to portrayals of tricksters and con artists in films and literature. Some examples include Nanabashu from Navajo myth, Loki from Norse myth, and the Artful Dodger from Dickens.
9. Refer students to the Prologue for specific details of the Pardoner's personality.

Grading Timesaver

Rubrics for each Choices assignment appear on p. 100 in the *Portfolio Management System.*

OBJECTIVES

The Wife of Bath's Tale

1. Read and interpret the story
2. Analyze couplets
3. Determine meanings by using word parts
4. Express understanding through writing, art, drama, and research
5. Understand and use new words

SKILLS

Literary

- Analyze couplets

Reading

- Determine meanings by analyzing word parts

Writing

- Collect ideas for a compare/contrast essay
- Analyze character
- Create a frame for a story

Speaking/Listening

- Bring a pilgrim to life

Music/Art

- Re-create and illustrate a manuscript
- Evaluate artistic interpretations

Vocabulary

- Use new words

Planning

- **Block Schedule**
  Block Scheduling Lesson Plans with Pacing Guide
- **Traditional Schedule**
  Lesson Plans Including Strategies for English-Language Learners
- **One-Stop Planner**
  CD-ROM with Test Generator

Ⓐ Elements of Literature

Irony

? What might be ironic about the Wife of Bath's comment on her views? [Like "The Pardoner's Tale," this tale too may have a serious point; or she will likely focus on marriage.]

No one on the road to Canterbury is more real than the Wife of Bath (a married woman from the city of Bath, west of London). She is Chaucer's most vibrant and irrepressible character. Having outlived five husbands (and possibly looking for a sixth on this pilgrimage), she is witty, intelligent, opinionated, and sensual. The tale she tells belongs to the "marriage group," several tales that explore what men and women want and ought to do in marriage.

from The Wife of Bath's Tale

Geoffrey Chaucer

translated by **Nevill Coghill**

The Wife of Bath, from the Ellesmere manuscript, fol. 72r.
By permission of The Huntington Library, San Marino, California.

The Prologue

The Pardoner started up, and thereupon
"Madam," he said, "by God and by St. John,
That's noble preaching no one could surpass!
I was about to take a wife; alas!
Am I to buy it on my flesh so dear?
There'll be no marrying for me this year!"
"You wait," she said, "my story's not begun.
You'll taste another brew before I've done;
You'll find it doesn't taste as good as ale;
And when I've finished telling you my tale
Of tribulation in the married life
In which I've been an expert as a wife,
That is to say, myself have been the whip.
So please yourself whether you want to sip
At that same cask of marriage I shall broach.
Be cautious before making the approach,
For I'll give instances, and more than ten.
And those who won't be warned by other men,
By other men shall suffer their correction,
So Ptolemy° has said, in this connection.
You read his *Almagest;*° you'll find it there."
"Madam, I put it to you as a prayer,"
The Pardoner said, "go on as you began!
Tell us your tale, spare not for any man.
Instruct us younger men in your technique."
"Gladly," she said, "if you will let me speak,
But still I hope the company won't reprove me
Though I should speak as fantasy may move me,
And please don't be offended at my views;
They're really only offered to amuse." . . .

20. Ptolemy (täl′ə·mē) (A.D. 100?–165?): ancient geographer, astronomer, and mathematician from Alexandria, Egypt.
21. *Almagest:* word meaning "the greatest"; another title for Ptolemy's major work, *Mathematical Composition,* in which he argues that the earth is the center of the universe, a view held in Europe until 1543.

Resources: Print and Media

Reading

- *Graphic Organizers for Active Reading,* p. 8
- *Words to Own,* p. 5
- *Audio CD Library*
  Disc 2, Track 8

Elements of Literature

- *Literary Elements*
  Transparency 5
  Worksheet, p. 16

Writing and Language

- *Daily Oral Grammar*
  Transparency 5
- *Grammar and Language Links*
  Worksheet, p. 13

Assessment

- *Formal Assessment,* p. 23
- *Portfolio Management System,* p. 101
- *Test Generator (One-Stop Planner CD-ROM)*

Internet

- go.hrw.com (keyword: LE0 12-2)

The Tale

When good King Arthur ruled in ancient days
(A king that every Briton loves to praise)
This was a land brim-full of fairy folk.
The Elf-Queen and her courtiers joined and broke
Their elfin dance on many a green mead,°
Or so was the opinion once, I read,
Hundreds of years ago, in days of yore.
But no one now sees fairies any more.
For now the saintly charity and prayer
Of holy friars seem to have purged the air;
They search the countryside through field and stream
As thick as motes° that speckle a sun-beam,
Blessing the halls, the chambers, kitchens, bowers,
Cities and boroughs, castles, courts and towers,
Thorpes,° barns and stables, outhouses and dairies,
And that's the reason why there are no fairies.
Wherever there was wont° to walk an elf
To-day there walks the holy friar himself
As evening falls or when the daylight springs,
Saying his matins° and his holy things,
Walking his limit round from town to town.
Women can now go safely up and down
By every bush or under every tree;
There is no other incubus° but he,
So there is really no one else to hurt you
And he will do no more than take your virtue.
Now it so happened, I began to say,
Long, long ago in good King Arthur's day,
There was a knight who was a lusty liver.
One day as he came riding from the river
He saw a maiden walking all forlorn
Ahead of him, alone as she was born.
And of that maiden, spite of all she said,
By very force he took her maidenhead.°
This act of violence made such a stir,
So much petitioning to the king for her,
That he condemned the knight to lose his head
By course of law. He was as good as dead
(It seems that then the statutes took that view)
But that the queen, and other ladies too,
Implored the king to exercise his grace
So ceaselessly, he gave the queen the case
And granted her his life, and she could choose

35. mead: meadow.

42. motes: dust particles.

45. thorpes: villages.

47. wont (wänt): accustomed.

50. matins (mat′'nz): morning prayers.

54. incubus (in′kyo͞o·bəs): evil spirit believed to descend on a sleeping woman and make her pregnant.

64. maidenhead: virginity.

WORDS TO OWN
implored (im·plôrd′) *v.:* begged.

Background

The Wife of Bath's Prologue is a very long (862 lines) and vigorous defense of women that challenges the medieval view that Eve was responsible for the Fall of man. The small extract here opens with the Pardoner's response to comments made by the Wife of Bath about wanting a sixth husband who will be both her debtor and her slave. The Tale itself is reprinted in its entirety.

Summary ■■

The Wife of Bath tells the story of a "lusty" knight sentenced to death for rape. The queen, however, promises to spare his life if he can discover in a year and a day what women most desire. The knight receives many opinions on this issue. Finally, an ugly old woman promises she will solve the riddle but only if the Knight will grant the first request she makes of him. When he agrees, she explains that women want power over men. All agree that the answer is correct, but, ironically, the knight is still not free because the old woman requires the knight to marry her. Although he complains bitterly of her age, ugliness, and lack of money and noble birth, he does so. The old woman lectures him on what makes a good wife and offers him a choice between a beautiful, fickle wife or an ugly, faithful one. Understanding at last her need for power, he allows her to make the choice. She then rewards him by becoming young, beautiful, *and* faithful.

B Reading Skills and Strategies

Drawing Conclusions

? What is the Wife of Bath's opinion of the friars' getting rid of the fairies? [She says that women are safer from spirits than they used to be but adds at the end, wryly, that the friars also dishonor women. This is a condemnation of the friars, who, even more than other people, are expected to be virtuous.]

C Cultural Connections

Chivalric Code

In the chivalric tradition, violence toward women was not tolerated, and perpetrators were dealt with harshly.

Preteaching Vocabulary

Words to Own

Have students work in groups of two or three to sort the Words to Own into groups of nouns, verbs, and adjectives. Students may suggest words that will modify the nouns, as well as nouns that might follow the adjectives. Then ask students to name the Word to Own most clearly related to each of the following groups of words.

1. asked, begged, pleaded [implored]
2. give in, give up, grant [concede]
3. coerce, shake down, squeeze [extort]
4. is sufficient, satisfies, is adequate [suffices]
5. destruction, epidemic, plague [pestilence]
6. worldly, earthly, at this time [temporal]
7. ancestors, forebears, descendants [lineage]
8. skill, ability, talent [prowess]
9. gift, inheritance, hand-me-down [bequest]
10. empty, hollow, null [void]

Ⓐ Critical Thinking

Making Connections

? What other stories can you name in which a character must solve a riddle in order to save his or her life? [Possible answers: the tale of Rumpelstiltskin; Tolkien's hobbit and Golum; the myth of Oedipus.]

Ⓑ Struggling Readers

Paraphrasing

Lines 78–82 express key ideas in the plot, yet interrupted movement, archaic usage, and unexpected word order may cause confusion. Ask students to paraphrase these lines. [Possible answer: The way things remain, it's not certain that you'll live. You'll live if you can find out what women want most of all, but you'll die if you can't.]

Ⓒ Critical Thinking

Interpreting

? Chaucer has the Wife of Bath break off into a long digression at this point. Here Chaucer is interested not in preserving the integrity of the tale but in accurately depicting the way the Wife of Bath's mind works. Why do you think she temporarily loses track of her story at this point? [Possible responses: She is more interested in the things women want than in the story. Perhaps she wants to create some suspense.]

Ⓓ Reading Skills and Strategies

Analyzing Word Parts

Call attention to the word *ensnares,* and refer students to the information on prefixes on p. 151. Ask them how that information helps them understand the meaning of *ensnares.* [The prefix *en-* means "in," "into," or "within." This word means "catches in a snare, or trap."]

Whether to show him mercy or refuse.
The queen returned him thanks with all her might,
And then she sent a summons to the knight
At her convenience, and expressed her will:
"You stand, for such is the position still,
In no way certain of your life," said she,
"Yet you shall live if you can answer me:
What is the thing that women most desire?
Beware the axe and say as I require.
"If you can't answer on the moment, though,
I will concede you this: You are to go
A twelvemonth and a day to seek and learn
Sufficient answer, then you shall return.
I shall take gages° from you to extort
Surrender of your body to the court."
Sad was the knight and sorrowfully sighed,
But there! All other choices were denied,
And in the end he chose to go away
And to return after a year and day
Armed with such answer as there might be sent
To him by God. He took his leave and went.
He knocked at every house, searched every place,
Yes, anywhere that offered hope of grace.
What could it be that women wanted most?
But all the same he never touched a coast,
Country, or town in which there seemed to be
Any two people willing to agree.
Some said that women wanted wealth and treasure,
"Honor," said some, some "Jollity and pleasure,"
Some "Gorgeous clothes" and others "Fun in bed,"
"To be oft widowed and remarried," said
Others again, and some that what most mattered
Was that we should be cossetted° and flattered.
That's very near the truth, it seems to me;
A man can win us best with flattery.
To dance attendance on us, make a fuss,
Ensnares us all, the best and worst of us.
Some say the things we most desire are these:
Freedom to do exactly as we please,
With no one to reprove our faults and lies,
Rather to have one call us good and wise.
Truly there's not a woman in ten score°
Who has a fault, and someone rubs the sore,
But she will kick if what he says is true;

87. gages: pledges.

Dijon Library, Dijon, France.

A scene from Virgil's *Aeneid* (15th century). MS 493, fol. 74v.

106. cossetted (käs′it·id): pampered.

115. ten score: two hundred. A score is twenty.

Words to Own

concede (kən·sēd′) *v.:* grant.
extort (eks·tôrt′) *v.:* to get by threats or violence.

Reaching All Students

Struggling Readers

To help struggling readers, have them follow along in the text as you read a part of the tale aloud or as they listen to the audio. At the conclusion of each speech, have them summarize the main ideas. Then fill in any missing details or correct any misapprehensions.

English Language Learners

Encourage English language learners to rely on punctuation marks to better understand the meaning across couplets. For additional strategies to supplement instruction for English language learners, see

- *Lesson Plans Including Strategies for English-Language Learners*

Advanced Learners

One critic has stated that the Wife of Bath's story is just another tale with the theme of the transformed ugly or otherwise changed woman, who has to be changed back again by meeting the right man. Do students agree? Ask them to gather evidence and to create and revise their arguments as they read and reread.

You try it out and you will find so too.
However vicious we may be within
We like to be thought wise and void of sin.
Others assert we women find it sweet
When we are thought dependable, discreet
And secret, firm of purpose and controlled,
Never betraying things that we are told.
But that's not worth the handle of a rake;
Women conceal a thing? For Heaven's sake!
Remember Midas?° Will you hear the tale?
Among some other little things, now stale,
Ovid° relates that under his long hair
The unhappy Midas grew a splendid pair
Of ass's ears; as subtly as he might,
He kept his foul deformity from sight;
Save for his wife, there was not one that knew.
He loved her best, and trusted in her too.
He begged her not to tell a living creature
That he possessed so horrible a feature.
And she—she swore, were all the world to win,
She would not do such villainy and sin
As saddle her husband with so foul a name;
Besides to speak would be to share the shame.
Nevertheless she thought she would have died
Keeping this secret bottled up inside;
It seemed to swell her heart and she, no doubt,
Thought it was on the point of bursting out.
Fearing to speak of it to woman or man,
Down to a reedy marsh she quickly ran
And reached the sedge.° Her heart was all on fire
And, as a bittern° bumbles in the mire,
She whispered to the water, near the ground,
"Betray me not, O water, with thy sound!
To thee alone I tell it: It appears
My husband has a pair of ass's ears!
Ah! My heart's well again, the secret's out!
I could no longer keep it, not a doubt."
And so you see, although we may hold fast
A little while, it must come out at last,
We can't keep secrets; as for Midas, well,
Read Ovid for his story;° he will tell.
This knight that I am telling you about
Perceived at last he never would find out
What it could be that women loved the best.
Faint was the soul within his sorrowful breast,

127. Midas: mythical king. Everything he touched turned to gold.

129. Ovid (43 B.C.–C. A.D. 17): Roman poet. Ovid's *Metamorphoses,* a collection of tales, includes one version of the Midas story.

147. sedge: grasslike plant.

148. bittern: type of wading bird.

158. read . . . story: In Ovid's version, it is Midas's barber, not his wife, who tells the secret to a hole in the ground. Reeds grow up in the hole and whisper the secret whenever the wind rustles them.

WORDS TO OWN
void (vɔid) *adj.:* empty.

E Critical Thinking
Making Judgments

? What criticism of women does the Wife of Bath offer? [Women are hypocritical, wanting to do as they please but also wanting to appear virtuous.]

F Elements of Literature
Couplets

? Which rhymes in the translation of these lines seem natural and which seem forced? [Possible answers: Natural: hair, pair; might, sight; knew, too; win, sin; name, shame. Forced: creature, feature.]

G Elements of Literature
Imagery

? What do these images help you visualize? [the reedy marsh; the sedge; Midas's wife with her face close to the ground, whispering]

H Elements of Literature
Irony

? What is the rhetorical purpose of the Wife of Bath's story about Midas? [It seems to support her claim that women cannot keep secrets, but as the sidenote points out, Ovid's version has a man, not a woman, give up the secret, making the reference ironic.]

I Cultural Connections
Chivalric Code

The knight returns to the court even though he can expect to be put to death there. This is in keeping with the chivalric code: A knight must keep his word, even if death is the consequence.

Using Students' Strengths

Musical/Auditory Learners
Have students score a spoken or musical re-creation of the text. Encourage students to mark the text for loudness, softness, crescendo, and decrescendo. If you wish, have students use such terms as *piano* and *forte*. Students might also suggest various tempos, such as 2/4 and 3/4 time.

Kinesthetic Learners
Have pairs or small groups of students choose sections of the story to read dramatically, pantomime, or act out. Provide opportunities for pairs or groups to develop, rehearse, and perform for the class.

Verbal Learners
Verbal learners may enjoy discussions related to the knight's crime and punishment. For example, they might discuss whether the knight was, in fact, punished at all and whether the punishment was commensurate with the crime. They might find motivations for the queen's intervention on his part and for the sympathy of the ladies of the court. They might also discuss the desirability of such a spouse, in Chaucer's day and in ours.

Critical Thinking
Challenging the Text

The four and twenty ladies mysteriously vanish. Do you think this is an irrelevant detail? How would the story be different if the knight simply noticed an old woman sitting at the edge of the wood? [Possible answers: The disappearance of the ladies suggests that something magical or unpredictable is happening. The old woman's ugliness is magnified by contrast with the beautiful vision that disappears. The discouraged knight might not have stopped for the old woman alone.]

English Language Learners
Archaic Language

Point out some of the archaic language on this page that students will encounter again and again as they read literature from earlier times. For example, l. 168 contains *nay*, l. 170 contains *ere*, l. 171 contains *lo*, and l. 181 contains *alack*. Ask students to use context clues to guess the meanings of these words. [*nay*, no; *ere*, before; *lo*, an expression of surprise or wonder; look; *alack*, an expression of dismay; alas]

Appreciating Language
Word Choice

Chaucer says she "rowned" a "pistel" in his ear. *Rowned* means "whispered" and *pistel* means "lesson." What do you think of the translator's word choice? [*Crooned* implies singing and a certain intimacy; *gospel* suggests that the message is what she believes in. Many students may feel the translator has changed the meaning too much.]

Vocabulary Note
Word Origins

Students may also be interested to learn the etymology of *gospel*, which comes from the Old English *godspel*, a combination of the words *god*, meaning "good," and *spell*, meaning "tale or story."

As home he went, he dared no longer stay;
His year was up and now it was the day.
    As he rode home in a dejected mood
Suddenly, at the margin of a wood,
He saw a dance upon the leafy floor
Of four and twenty ladies, nay, and more.
Eagerly he approached, in hope to learn
Some words of wisdom ere he should return;
But lo! Before he came to where they were,
Dancers and dance all vanished into air!
There wasn't a living creature to be seen
Save one old woman crouched upon the green.
A fouler-looking creature I suppose
Could scarcely be imagined. She arose
And said, "Sir knight, there's no way on from here.
Tell me what you are looking for, my dear,
For peradventure° that were best for you;
We old, old women know a thing or two."
    "Dear Mother," said the knight, "alack the day!
I am as good as dead if I can't say
What thing it is that women most desire;
If you could tell me I would pay your hire."
"Give me your hand," she said, "and swear to do
Whatever I shall next require of you
—If so to do should lie within your might—
And you shall know the answer before night."
"Upon my honor," he answered, "I agree."
"Then," said the crone, "I dare to guarantee
Your life is safe; I shall make good my claim.
Upon my life the queen will say the same.
Show me the very proudest of them all
In costly coverchief or jeweled caul°
That dare say no to what I have to teach.
Let us go forward without further speech."
And then she crooned her gospel in his ear
And told him to be glad and not to fear.
    They came to court. This knight, in full array,
Stood forth and said, "O Queen, I've kept my day
And kept my word and have my answer ready."
    There sat the noble matrons and the heady
Young girls, and widows too, that have the grace
Of wisdom, all assembled in that place,
And there the queen herself was throned to hear
And judge his answer. Then the knight drew near
And silence was commanded through the hall.
    The queen gave order he should tell them all
What thing it was that women wanted most.
He stood not silent like a beast or post,
But gave his answer with the ringing word

Medieval knight on horseback.

179. peradventure: perhaps.

194. coverchief . . . caul (kôl): women's headgear. The coverchief covered the entire head; the caul, a small, netted cap, was sometimes ornamented.

Professional Notes

Critical Comment: The Wife of Bath's Heresy

Edwin J. Howard reminds readers of what may well be forgotten as the Wife tells her story: She is on her way to Canterbury to seek salvation. Yet in this story, she is "dealing with a matter of religion: sovereignty in the family; and she [is] utterly heretical in her views, as the Bible very definitely states that woman is to be subject to her husband. All the members of the clergy on the pilgrimage would shudder to hear her bold denial of Holy Writ."

Of a man's voice and the assembly heard:
"My liege° and lady, in general," said he,
"A woman wants the self-same sovereignty°
Over her husband as over her lover,
And master him; he must not be above her.
That is your greatest wish, whether you kill
Or spare me; please yourself. I wait your will."
In all the court not one that shook her head
Or contradicted what the knight had said;
Maid, wife, and widow cried, "He's saved his life!"
And on the word up started the old wife,
The one the knight saw sitting on the green,
And cried, "Your mercy, sovereign lady queen!
Before the court disperses, do me right!
'Twas I who taught this answer to the knight,
For which he swore, and pledged his honor to it,
That the first thing I asked of him he'd do it,
So far as it should lie within his might.
Before this court I ask you then, sir knight,
To keep your word and take me for your wife;
For well you know that I have saved your life.
If this be false, deny it on your sword!"
"Alas!" he said, "Old lady, by the Lord
I know indeed that such was my behest,°
But for God's love think of a new request,
Take all my goods, but leave my body free."
"A curse on us," she said, "if I agree!
I may be foul, I may be poor and old,
Yet will not choose to be, for all the gold
That's bedded in the earth or lies above,
Less than your wife, nay, than your very love!"
"My love?" said he. "By heaven, my damnation!
Alas that any of my race and station
Should ever make so foul a misalliance!"
Yet in the end his pleading and defiance
All went for nothing, he was forced to wed.
He takes his ancient wife and goes to bed.
Now peradventure some may well suspect
A lack of care in me since I neglect
To tell of the rejoicings and display
Made at the feast upon their wedding-day.
I have but a short answer to let fall;
I say there was no joy or feast at all,
Nothing but heaviness of heart and sorrow.
He married her in private on the morrow
And all day long stayed hidden like an owl,
It was such torture that his wife looked foul.
Great was the anguish churning in his head
When he and she were piloted to bed;

213. liege (lēj): lord.

214. sovereignty (säv′rən·tē): power.

235. behest: command; order.

E Elements of Literature

Irony

? Why is it ironic that this should be the answer that saves the knight's life? [He was condemned to death for abusing a woman's sovereignty and assuming he could have mastery over her.]

F Elements of Literature

Couplets

? Which rhymes in the translations of the couplets from ll. 213–248 seem clever and which seem stretched or repetitious? [Possible answers: All are clever and reflect enormous variety, perhaps most especially *behest* and *request*. Or all are clever, but the rhymes *wife* and *life* are repeated, and *it* is used to rhyme with *it*. *Damnation* and *station* are a bit forced.]

G Reading Skills and Strategies

Analyzing Word Parts

? The suffix *-ance* is like the suffix *-ence*: Both suffixes create nouns that suggest a fact, act, or condition. How do the suffixes in *misalliance* and *defiance* help you determine the meaning of those words? [A misalliance is a fact or condition of being misallied, or mismatched. Defiance is an act of defying, or rebelling against.]

H Critical Thinking

Making Judgments

? What is your reaction to the knight's excuses? Do you feel sorry for him, or do you think he is getting what he deserves? [Possible responses: No one should be tricked into marriage. Or he is getting even better than he deserves: He made a deal and should honor it.]

Getting Students Involved

Cooperative Learning

Instant Analysis. Have groups of four students treat the woman's speech on gentleness, poverty, and age as if it were a presidential address. Ask each group to do a TV news "instant analysis" of one of the following sections: ll. 285–308, 309–334, 335–352, 353–366, 367–382, 383–392. In each presentation, have one student report the old woman's actual words, another summarize, another give comments on highlights and key phrases, and another give comments on the possible effect on the knight. Although each member has an individual role in the presentation, all should collaborate during the preparation stages.

Ⓐ Elements of Literature

Characterization

? Is the knight's reaction to the old woman an example of direct or indirect characterization? What does it reveal about his character? [Possible answer: This example of indirect characterization reveals that he is egotistical and shallow. He places too much emphasis on rank and appearance.]

Ⓑ Reading Skills and Strategies

Analyzing Word Parts

? What does the suffix *-ous* tell you about the part of speech of the word *virtuous*? [It is an adjective.] What does the suffix tell you about the meaning of the word? [*Virtuous* means "marked by or given to virtue."] You could ask the same question about *contemptuous* in l. 266.

Ⓒ Struggling Readers

Getting the Main Idea

? The long sermon the crone delivers to her husband on their wedding night, beginning on l. 285, does little to advance the plot. Its inclusion in the tale illustrates how Chaucer was affected by his times: The concept of "gentleness" was central to fourteenth-century courtly life. Etymologically, *gentle* comes from the Old French word for "of noble birth." Tell students that the gist of this sermon appears in the couplet in ll. 293–294. What is the crone's main point about noble birth? [Virtuous conduct—gentleness—is not the result of one's social rank. It is a gift from God to those who will nurture it.]

He wallowed° back and forth in desperate style.
His ancient wife lay smiling all the while;
At last she said "Bless us! Is this, my dear,
How knights and wives get on together here?
Are these the laws of good King Arthur's house?
Are knights of his all so contemptuous?
I am your own beloved and your wife,
And I am she, indeed, that saved your life;
And certainly I never did you wrong.
Then why, this first of nights, so sad a song?
You're carrying on as if you were half-witted
Say, for God's love, what sin have I committed?
I'll put things right if you will tell me how."
"Put right?" he cried. "That never can be now!
Nothing can ever be put right again!
You're old, and so abominably plain,
So poor to start with, so low-bred to follow;
It's little wonder if I twist and wallow!
God, that my heart would burst within my breast!"
"Is that," said she, "the cause of your unrest?"
"Yes, certainly," he said, "and can you wonder?"
"I could set right what you suppose a blunder,
That's if I cared to, in a day or two,
If I were shown more courtesy by you.
Just now," she said, "you spoke of gentle birth,
Such as descends from ancient wealth and worth.
If that's the claim you make for gentlemen
Such arrogance is hardly worth a hen.
Whoever loves to work for virtuous ends,
Public and private, and who most intends
To do what deeds of gentleness he can,
Take him to be the greatest gentleman.
Christ wills we take our gentleness from Him,
Not from a wealth of ancestry long dim,
Though they bequeath their whole establishment
By which we claim to be of high descent.
Our fathers cannot make us a bequest
Of all those virtues that became them best
And earned for them the name of gentlemen,
But bade us follow them as best we can.
"Thus the wise poet of the Florentines,
Dante° by name, has written in these lines,
For such is the opinion Dante launches:
'Seldom arises by these slender branches
Prowess of men, for it is God, no less,

261. wallowed: tossed and turned.

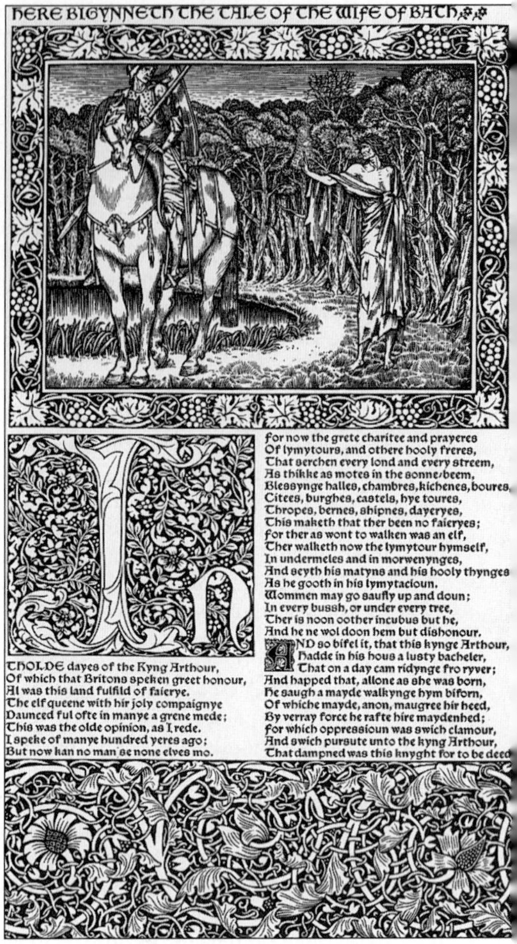

Opening page of the *Tale of the Wife of Bath* (c. 1898) from the Kelmscott *Chaucer.*

Spencer Collection. New York Public Library. Astor, Lenox, and Tilden Foundations.

302. Dante: Dante Alighieri (dän′tā a′lə·gyer′ē) (1265–1321), Italian poet who wrote *The Divine Comedy.* (See page 392.)

WORDS TO OWN

bequest (bē·kwest′) *n.:* gift left by means of a will.
prowess (prou′is) *n.:* outstanding ability.

Taking a Second Look

Review: Comparing Cultures

Remind students that some values cross cultures, while others change over time or are more important in some cultures than others. In this story, ideas about justice, mercy, and the codes of behavior for women and men may offer many contrasts with the ideas of contemporary readers.

Activities

1. Form groups of four to six students. Have each group identify cultural values that are expressed in one of the following text events: the knight is sentenced to death for rape; the knight is viewed with sympathy by the ladies and given a second chance by the queen; the knight honors his promise to the old woman but resents doing so because she is ugly; the knight is rewarded at the end of the tale for letting the woman decide.
2. Have groups then decide whether those cultural values they identify agree with or differ from the values they have acquired.

Wills us to claim of Him our gentleness.'
For of our parents nothing can we claim
Save temporal things, and these may hurt and maim. D
"But everyone knows this as well as I;
For if gentility were implanted by
The natural course of lineage down the line,
Public or private, could it cease to shine
In doing the fair work of gentle deed?
No vice or villainy could then bear seed.
"Take fire and carry it to the darkest house
Between this kingdom and the Caucasus,°
And shut the doors on it and leave it there,
It will burn on, and it will burn as fair
As if ten thousand men were there to see,
For fire will keep its nature and degree,
I can assure you, sir, until it dies.
"But gentleness, as you will recognize,
Is not annexed in nature to possessions.
Men fail in living up to their professions;°
But fire never ceases to be fire.
God knows you'll often find, if you inquire,
Some lording° full of villainy and shame.
If you would be esteemed for the mere name
Of having been by birth a gentleman
And stemming from some virtuous, noble clan,
And do not live yourself by gentle deed
Or take your father's noble code and creed,
You are no gentleman, though duke or earl.
Vice and bad manners are what make a churl.°
"Gentility is only the renown
For bounty that your fathers handed down,
Quite foreign to your person, not your own;
Gentility must come from God alone.
That we are gentle comes to us by grace
And by no means is it bequeathed with place.
"Reflect how noble (says Valerius)°
Was Tullius surnamed Hostilius,°
Who rose from poverty to nobleness.
And read Boethius,° Seneca° no less,
Thus they express themselves and are agreed:
'Gentle is he that does a gentle deed.'
And therefore, my dear husband, I conclude
That even if my ancestors were rude,
Yet God on high—and so I hope He will—
Can grant me grace to live in virtue still,

316. Caucasus (kô′kə·səs): mountain range in southeastern Europe, between the Black Sea and the Caspian Sea; in other words, far away.

324. professions: promises.

327. lording: alternate form of *lord.*

334. churl: ill-mannered person.

341. Valerius (və·lir′ē·əs): first-century A.D. Roman writer who compiled historical anecdotes that public speakers could use.
342. Tullius (tul′ē·əs) **surnamed Hostilius** (hos·til′ē·əs): Tullius Hostilius, legendary king of Rome who rose from humble origins.
344. Boethius (bō·ē′thē·əs) (c. A.D. 480–c. 524): Roman philosopher. In his *Consolation of Philosophy,* he argues that rank is no guarantee of honorable conduct. **Seneca** (sen′i·kə) (c. 4 B.C.–A.D. 65): Roman philosopher whose works were popular in the Middle Ages.

Words to Own
temporal (tem′pə·rəl) *adj.:* limited to this world; not spiritual.
lineage (lin′ē·ij) *n.:* ancestry.

D Reading Skills and Strategies
Making Inferences
? How could "temporal things" "hurt and maim"? [Possible answer: Too many possessions may distract a person from virtue.]

E Struggling Readers
Breaking Down Difficult Text
This lengthy argumentative digression may pose problems for struggling readers. Suggest that students break the text up into manageable chunks, like ll. 310–314. Ask students what strategies they could use. [Possible answers: They could ask and answer questions about it; they could paraphrase it; they could summarize it; they could reread it.]

F Elements of Literature
Couplets
Note that this couplet relies on a slant rhyme or half rhyme. Ask students to find couplets on the page that they regard as outstandingly successful both in terms of sound and sense. [Possible answers: ll. 329–330; 331–332; 333–334.]

G Elements of Literature
Metaphor
? What point is the crone making by comparing men to fire? [Fire remains fire no matter where it is; on the other hand, men do not inherit gentility automatically, no matter what rank in society they belong to.]

H Critical Thinking
Making Judgments
? Apply the old woman's definition of gentility to her own actions. Does she qualify as a gentle person? Explain. [Possible answers: Yes, because she has high standards for virtue and because she saves the knight's life and frets about his unhappiness. No, because she is kind to and worries about a man who has committed a terrible crime. No, because she forces someone to marry her who does not want to.]

Crossing the Curriculum

Mathematics
Have students conduct a survey of at least thirty people on the question "What do women want most?" Ask students to design a standard questionnaire that also asks which of the answers that the knight collected (either the one given in ll. 101–124 or the one given in 214–216) is closest to the truth. In addition, have students collect data on their survey respondents. As a class, tabulate the results, dividing responses by age groups of ten-year spans and by gender and report these results:

1. Bar graph of responses comparing total men and total women.
2. Bar graph of responses within age groups, ignoring gender differences.
3. Bar graph comparing men under twenty-five with men over twenty-five.
4. Bar graph comparing women under twenty-five with women over twenty-five.

Ask students to analyze these graphs.

A Struggling Readers

Paraphrasing

Ask students to paraphrase this rather simple thought about poverty that is expressed in such a complex way. [Possible answer: You may criticize my poverty, but God himself, whom we follow and believe in, and by whom we exist, chose a life of poverty, and every man, woman, and child knows that God would never choose anything shameful.]

B Critical Thinking

Expressing an Opinion

? Do you agree with the old woman's ideas about poverty? [Possible answers: Yes, poverty is a kind of wealth that no one can slander; when you are really poor, you know just who your friends are; the truly poor are those who covet what they cannot have. Or no, poverty does not make you wise or give you "an incentive to livelihood"; instead, it narrows your opportunities and makes you feel shame.]

C Critical Thinking

Classifying

? How would you classify or categorize the types of arguments the old woman makes on the subjects of gentleness, poverty, and age? [Possible answer: She suggests these can all be false arguments against making a marriage, for noble birth and noble actions are not the same, wealth and right attitudes toward money are not the same, and youth and beauty have drawbacks.]

A gentlewoman only when beginning
To live in virtue and to shrink from sinning.
"As for my poverty which you reprove,
Almighty God Himself in whom we move,
Believe, and have our being, chose a life
Of poverty, and every man or wife
Nay, every child can see our Heavenly King
Would never stoop to choose a shameful thing.
No shame in poverty if the heart is gay,
As Seneca and all the learned say.
He who accepts his poverty unhurt
I'd say is rich although he lacked a shirt.
But truly poor are they who whine and fret
And covet what they cannot hope to get.
And he that, having nothing, covets not,
Is rich, though you may think he is a sot.°
"True poverty can find a song to sing.
Juvenal° says a pleasant little thing:
'The poor can dance and sing in the relief
Of having nothing that will tempt a thief.'
Though it be hateful, poverty is good,
A great incentive to a livelihood,
And a great help to our capacity
For wisdom, if accepted patiently.
Poverty is, though wanting in estate,
A kind of wealth that none calumniate.°
Poverty often, when the heart is lowly,
Brings one to God and teaches what is holy,
Gives knowledge of oneself and even lends
A glass by which to see one's truest friends.
And since it's no offense, let me be plain;
Do not rebuke my poverty again.
"Lastly you taxed me, sir, with being old.
Yet even if you never had been told
By ancient books, you gentlemen engage
Yourselves in honor to respect old age.
To call an old man 'father' shows good breeding,
And this could be supported from my reading.
"You say I'm old and fouler than a fen.°
You need not fear to be a cuckold,° then.
Filth and old age, I'm sure you will agree,
Are powerful wardens over chastity.
Nevertheless, well knowing your delights,
I shall fulfill your worldly appetites.
"You have two choices; which one will you try?
To have me old and ugly till I die,
But still a loyal, true, and humble wife
That never will displease you all her life,
Or would you rather I were young and pretty

366. sot: fool.

368. Juvenal (jo͞o′və·n′l) (c. A.D. 60–c. 140): Roman satirist.

376. calumniate (kə·lum′nē·āt′): slander.

389. fen: swamp.

390. cuckold (kuk′əld): man whose wife has been unfaithful to him.

Assessing Learning

Check Test: Questions and Answers

1. **Who assigns the Knight his task?** [the queen]
2. **How long does the knight have to complete his task?** [a year and a day]
3. **Why does he leave the road before he sees the old woman?** [He sees twenty-four dancing maidens.]
4. **When does the old woman tell the knight what she wants from him?** [after he has given the answer to the queen]
5. **What physical change does the old woman undergo at the end of the story?** [She becomes young and beautiful.]

Standardized Test Preparation

For practice in proofreading and editing, see

- *Daily Oral Grammar,* Transparency 5

And chance your arm what happens in a city
Where friends will visit you because of me,
Yes, and in other places too, maybe.
Which would you have? The choice is all your own."
  The knight thought long, and with a piteous groan
At last he said, with all the care in life,
"My lady and my love, my dearest wife,
I leave the matter to your wise decision.
You make the choice yourself, for the provision
Of what may be agreeable and rich
In honor to us both, I don't care which;
Whatever pleases you suffices me."
  "And have I won the mastery?" said she,
"Since I'm to choose and rule as I think fit?"
"Certainly, wife," he answered her, "that's it."
"Kiss me," she cried. "No quarrels! On my oath
And word of honor, you shall find me both,
That is, both fair and faithful as a wife;
May I go howling mad and take my life
Unless I prove to be as good and true
As ever wife was since the world was new!
And if to-morrow when the sun's above
I seem less fair than any lady-love,
Than any queen or empress east or west,
Do with my life and death as you think best.
Cast up the curtain, husband. Look at me!"
  And when indeed the knight had looked to see,
Lo, she was young and lovely, rich in charms.
In ecstasy he caught her in his arms,
His heart went bathing in a bath of blisses
And melted in a hundred thousand kisses,
And she responded in the fullest measure
With all that could delight or give him pleasure.
  So they lived ever after to the end
In perfect bliss; and may Christ Jesus send
Us husbands meek and young and fresh in bed,
And grace to overbid them when we wed.
And—Jesu hear my prayer!—cut short the lives
Of those who won't be governed by their wives;
And all old, angry niggards of their pence,°
God send them soon a very pestilence!

A man and woman on horseback, from *The Devonshire Hunting Tapestries* (detail). Arras 1425–50.

Victoria and Albert Museum, London.

439. niggards (nig′ erdz) **of their pence:** stingy persons.

WORDS TO OWN
suffices (sə·fīs′iz) *v.:* satisfies.
pestilence (pes′tə·ləns) *n.:* plague.

D Elements of Literature
Characterization

? What does this response reveal about the knight? [Possible answers: In the course of the story, he has grown up; he has become less arrogant. Or he is ready to accept his new position.]

E Reading Skills and Strategies
Analyzing Word Parts

Have students use the skill taught on p. 151 to analyze the word *provision* in l. 408. [The prefix *pro-* means "forward," the root *vis* comes from the Latin word for "see," and the suffix *-ion* creates a noun and means "an act or the result of the act." Thus, *provision* means "the result of looking forward."]

F Elements of Literature
Couplets

? What two metaphors are embedded in this couplet? [His heart is bathing and melting in her love.] **Why might the first have been especially striking in Chaucer's time?** [Given the infrequency of bathing, the image of "bathing in a bath of blisses" would have connoted luxury—not a routine chore.] **Also, note the alliteration in l. 429.**

G Critical Thinking
Evaluating

? What makes these lines a perfect ending for the story? [The Wife of Bath is suggesting that Jesus drastically punish husbands who are bossy or stingy. It reminds the reader of the Wife of Bath's purpose in telling the tale. The lines end with biting humor since it is, ironically, a most uncharitable thing for a pilgrim on her way to "salvation" to say.]

Making the Connections

Connecting to the Subject: "The Gift of Story"

Help students evaluate "The Wife of Bath's Tale" with these questions:

- **What effect do you think the Wife of Bath's story had on her listeners?** [Students may say her listeners were very much entertained and also given something to think about. They may also say that some of her listeners may have been quite disturbed by the tale with its rebellious message.]
- **What effect did the Wife of Bath's tale have on you?** [A broad range of answers is possible. Students may say that they were outraged that this criminal knight ended up with a reward. Others may say it gave them insight into Chaucer's life and times. Some may say it was a positive and enjoyable experience to hear a story told from a medieval woman's point of view.]

Ⓐ Elements of Literature

Characterization

? Chaucer creates characters by describing their appearances and actions; this student writer reveals her grandmother's character by describing her hands and what they did. What do the grandmother's hands look like? [They look like leaves. The veins of the hands look like the green veins of leaves. They are rough, wrinkled, worn, bony.] What did those hands do? [worked, knitted, gardened, cooked, scrubbed, toiled, twisted, clenched]

MAKING MEANINGS

First Thoughts [Respond]

1. The Wife of Bath might say that women want power and control over their lives and that men want the same.

Shaping Interpretations [Interpret]

2. It is ironic that a man whose interactions with women were all based on what *he* wanted should have to save his life by finding out what *they* want.
3. She says that being old and ugly will guarantee her faithfulness, that poverty is a virtue, and that gentility is based on how one acts, not on who one's parents are.
4. He gives her the decision, realizing she must choose for herself who she wants to be.
5. She says that friars are too plentiful, women do not like their faults pointed out, women cannot keep secrets, the ideal husband is "meek and young," and women should have power in their marriages. Students may say she is assertive, lustful, and self-aware.
6. Answers will vary. Students might list the proposed answers in order of importance, beginning with power over men and ending, perhaps, with flattery.

Extending the Text [Apply/Synthesize]

7. Responses will vary. Many students may suggest that mutual expectations are common in contemporary relationships.
8. Possible answer: As an assertive woman, she might actively and visibly support contemporary women's causes.

Student to Student

Worn Out

Ⓐ My grandmother's hands
looked like leaves
carved where her veins
stood green.

Her strong fingers were rough.
Her skin gripped her bones,
crinkled and wrinkled,
textured and worn.

Those hands worked.
Ten fingers knitted scarves for the
winter cold,
gardened strawberries and snapdragons
and cooked meals on her old stove
while a blue flame swooned
below the burner's glow.
Her hands scrubbed.
Her calloused hands scrubbed
dusty memories off the walls.

Her hands toiled and twisted
the stubborn lid off the jar of homemade
raspberry jam.
Her fingers clenched the stubborn lid
until her face would seize her bones and cling
while the veins in her hands would jump and
string,
beneath the worn folds of her skin.

Her bones showed from the inside out
pointing up from beneath, supporting her
skin
and revealing the mechanics inside.

Her hands left her behind,
protesting time and clutching will.

—Stephanie Bailey
Taylorsville High School
Salt Lake City, Utah

Portrait of Rembrandt's Mother by Gerard Dou.
Rijksmuseum Foundation.

Connecting Across Texts

Connecting with Chaucer's Characters

In what ways does the character in the poem "Worn Out" connect with a character in the Wife of Bath's story? [This old woman connects with the kind and wise old woman in the tale.]

Be sure to include the beautiful portrait of Rembrandt's mother in your discussion of character.

Making Meanings

First Thoughts

1. What did you think of the Wife of Bath's opinion about what women want most? If she were asked what men want most, how do you suppose she would respond?

Reading Check

a. What were the knight's crime, his original sentence, and his second sentence?
b. What bargain do the knight and the old woman strike?
c. What payment for her help does the old woman demand, and what is the knight's response?
d. What final choice does the old woman offer the knight at the end of the tale? What is his response?

Shaping Interpretations

2. The knight's quest is to find out what women want. What **irony** do you see in this?
3. In lines 276–278, the knight moans about having the old woman for his wife. How does she respond to each objection he raises?
4. How does the knight's response to the choice given him by the old woman show that he's learned his lesson about what women want?
5. What opinions does the Wife of Bath express in the tale? What do all her opinions and her tale itself tell you about her **character**?
6. Look at the various things the Wife of Bath, in her tale, says people think women want. What do you think of those proposed answers?

Extending the Text

7. What do you think contemporary men and women think about what the other wants most out of life or from a relationship? Do you think they would agree, or do they have different wishes and expectations of one another?
8. How would the Wife of Bath fit into contemporary society? What social trends would she support or reject?

Challenging the Text

9. Consider the way this story begins and ends. How does the knight get into trouble, and how do things turn out for him? Does the story satisfy or trouble you, and are there any elements that bother you?

Elements of Literature

Couplets: Sound and Sense

Chaucer's favorite rhyme scheme in *The Canterbury Tales* is the **couplet,** two consecutive lines of poetry that rhyme: "When good King Arthur ruled in ancient *days* / (A king that every Briton loves to *praise*)." (When he was growing old, Chaucer complained that his faculty of rhyming was leaving him, which may be the reason he never finished *The Canterbury Tales*.) Nevill Coghill, the translator of the tales used here, followed Chaucer's rhyme scheme, though he did not always use Chaucer's own rhyming words.

Analyzing Chaucer's rhymes. Look closely at these aspects of Chaucer's rhyme.

1. **Read aloud** parts of the Prologue to see how the couplets animate the survey of the pilgrims. Find some rhymes that are humorous.
2. Find what you think are the equivalents of these words in the Middle English version of the Prologue (page 104): *flower, breath, eye, courage,* and *condition.* The pronunciation of these words has changed since the Middle Ages. According to the words they're rhymed with in the Prologue, how would each of these words have been **pronounced** in Chaucer's day?
3. Identify at least two couplets in the Wife's tale that use **half rhymes** (also called **approximate rhymes**), words that share similar but not identical sounds.

Translating Chaucer. Compare the couplets Coghill uses in his translation of the first forty-two lines of the Prologue with the couplets Chaucer uses in his original. Then try to translate these original lines of the Prologue yourself, perhaps using more of Chaucer's original couplets.

Challenging the Text [Synthesize]

9. Possible answers: The change in the knight's attitude is too sudden. Perhaps the old woman should make the knight suffer instead of giving him bliss. The issue of feminine beauty seems too important in the story.

Elements of Literature

Couplets

1. Both masculine (stressed final syllable: *bat/sat*) and feminine rhymes (stress on syllable prior to final syllable: *middle/fiddle*) are used in the Prologue. Explain that feminine rhymes are usually more humorous than masculine rhymes.
2. *Flower/flour* rhymed with *licour. Breath/breeth* rhymed with *heeth. Eye/eye* rhymed with *melodye. Condition/condicioun* rhymed with *resoun.*
3. Half rhymes in "The Wife of Bath's Tale" include *gentlemen/we can* (ll. 299 and 300) and *capacity/patiently* (ll. 373 and 374).

Translating Chaucer

Students might try translating the couplets from Chaucer's original without preserving the rhyme. Ask what is gained (more accuracy) and what is lost (the music of the verse) with this type of translation.

Reading Check

a. Crime: taking a woman's virginity by force. Original sentence: death. Second sentence: also death, unless he can find out what women most desire.
b. She will tell him the answer to the riddle if he will promise to do the next thing she asks.
c. She demands that he marry her. He responds by pleading with her to ask anything else.
d. She gives him the choice of having her ugly and thus being confident of her fidelity, or having her beautiful and taking his chances on her faithfulness. He says that he wants her to decide.

Grading Timesaver

Rubrics for each Choices assignment appear on p. 101 in the *Portfolio Management System.*

Choices: Building Your Portfolio

WORK IN PROGRESS

1. **Writer's Notebook** Suggest that students jot down line citations from the Prologue or tale as they take notes.
2. **Analyzing Character** Suggest that students create a two-column chart labeled "What sort of person?" on the left and "How do I know?" on the right. In the left column students should write only impressions they have of the character. In the right they should note evidence to support their impressions.
3. **Creative Writing** Tell students they may follow Chaucer's pattern: First, describe the time of year and the characters' reasons for traveling; next, describe the meeting with the other travelers; then, describe each of the travelers.
4. **Visual Art** Good colored pencils or watercolor will give a more authentic look to this project than markers.
5. **Dramatization** Allow students to read excerpts or summaries rather than entire tales. Guide students' choices carefully: "The Miller's Tale" and "The Reeve's Tale" are very bawdy, and others, such as "The Merchant's Tale" and "The Franklin's Tale," have some sexual content. "The Prioress's Tale" is anti-Semitic.
6. **Research: Art/Music** Students may find that these artistic interpretations are most valuable when they shed some light on a facet of a pilgrim's character that students might have otherwise overlooked.

Choices: Building Your Portfolio

Writer's Notebook

1. Collecting Ideas for a Comparison-Contrast Essay

WORK IN PROGRESS

The Wife of Bath is one of Chaucer's most interesting characters. For the comparison-contrast essay you will write for the Writer's Workshop on page 185, you might want to compare the outspoken Wife with a modern-day woman. Take notes on the Wife's opinions, values, and experiences. What does her story reveal about her? How do her opinions, values, and experiences compare with those of a woman today? Is the Wife of Bath a "modern woman" or is she medieval in her outlook? How would today's woman answer the question "What do women want?" You might even take notes on what the Wife of Bath would be doing if she were alive today. Be aware that in this exercise you will be analyzing the influences of a **historical context** on a work. You might find the influences minor. Save your notes.

Analyzing Character

2. Characters to Probe

Whom do you find more interesting, the Pardoner or the Wife of Bath? In an essay of several paragraphs, explain your response to one of these pilgrims and then analyze the person's character. Before you write, review the methods of characterization presented on page 103. Use specific details from the text to support your analysis.

Creative Writing

3. Inventing a Frame

Write a prologue to your own frame story. Begin by deciding what kind of journey or other experience will bring your characters together. Will they meet in a bus station? at an airport? on a summer visit? Maybe your characters are survivors of a storm or accident and are waiting for rescue. List four characters who are sharing this experience. In a prologue, introduce your characters. Describe each character from tip to toe, including details of appearance that suggest each character's traits. (Notice how the student writer of "Worn Out" on page 148 describes her grandmother.) You may write in prose or try your hand at rhymed couplets like Chaucer's. Devote at least six lines to each character. If you are so inspired, provide an illustration of each of your characters.

Visual Art

4. Illustrating

The illuminated manuscript was a popular art form of the Middle Ages. Its pages contained highly decorated initial letters or words or miniature pictures such as those shown on pages 100, 101, and 102. Select a passage from either "The Wife of Bath's Tale" or "The Pardoner's Tale," and write it out with illustrations, as if it were a modern illuminated manuscript.

Dramatization

5. Bring a Pilgrim to Life

Choose a pilgrim other than the Wife of Bath or the Pardoner. Dress as the character, and present a reading of his or her tale to your classmates. At the end of your reading, explain why you chose this character and why you think the tale was suited to its teller.

Research: Art/Music

6. Re-Seeing Chaucer

Artists William Blake (1757–1827) and William Morris (1834–1896) created their own versions of Chaucer's pilgrims, and Nevill Coghill, a translator of Chaucer, also wrote song lyrics for the musical *Canterbury Tales* (1968). Find copies of these works and evaluate them. Do they adhere to the original *Tales* or offer a new interpretation?

Reading Skills and Strategies

VOCABULARY: ANALYZING WORD PARTS

When a word is unfamiliar or difficult to understand, you can often discover its meaning by examining the word's parts. These parts make up the **structure** of the word, which may consist of a **root**, a **prefix**, and a **suffix**.

Roots. Words are built upon a base, or root, which contains the core of the word's meaning. Many words in the English language have Latin or Greek roots. The root *-scribe-* or *-script-*, for instance, comes from Latin and means "to write." Notice that the following words contain this root and that all relate to writing: *inscription, manuscript, postscript, prescribe, scribble, scripture.*

Prefixes. Affixes are word parts that can be attached to a root to modify its meaning. A **prefix** is an affix that is placed *before* the root; it can have a general meaning or several meanings. For instance, *a–*, derived from Old English, means "in, on, of, up, to," as in "ashore." The Latin and Latin-French meaning for *a–* is "from, off, away," as in "averse," and the Greek meaning is "lacking, without," as in "amoral." Here are some examples:

Prefixes	Meanings	Examples
a–, ab–, abs–	from, off, away	abide, absolution
be–	around, about	befall, bequest
co–, col–, com–, con–, cor–, syn–	with, together	concede, synchronize
ex–, e–, ef–	away from, out	exhale, extort
en–, em–, in–	in, into, within	encourage
super–	over, above, extra	superfluity, supervisor

By adding a prefix to a root, a new word is formed with the combined meanings of both. Notice that the word *submarine* is composed of the prefix *sub-*, meaning "below," and the root *-marine-*, meaning "water." Prefixes with different spellings but the same meaning often originate in different languages. In this sentence, the prefixes *quint-* (Latin) and *penta-* (Greek) both mean "five": The *quint*et played in a concert hall shaped like a *penta*gon.

Suffixes. A **suffix** is an affix that is placed *after* the root to modify the root's meaning. The plurals of nouns, tenses of verbs, and comparative and superlative forms of adjectives and adverbs are created by suffixes such as *-ed* or *-s*. A word's meaning and its part of speech can be changed by other suffixes, sometimes called **derivational suffixes**. The word *glory* is a noun. Notice what happens with the addition of various suffixes: glor*ification* (noun); glor*ify* (verb); glor*ious* (adjective); glor*iously* (adverb). Here are some examples:

Suffixes	Meanings	Examples
–ous (adjective)	marked by, given to	efficacious, virtuous
–ic (adjective or noun)	dealing with, caused by	classic, choleric
–ence (noun)	act, condition, fact	pestilence, reverence
–ize (verb)	make, cause to be	energize, sterilize

Try It Out

Each of the following words is from *The Canterbury Tales*. Use a dictionary to determine the root and affix(es) of each word, and show how the structure of each word contributes to the word's meaning.

1. diligent
2. obstinate
3. covetousness
4. superfluity
5. transcend

Silver and gold portable sundial (10th century).
Canterbury Cathedral, Kent.

OBJECTIVES
1. Analyze word parts to determine meaning
2. Recognize common roots, prefixes, and suffixes
3. Apply these skills to determine the meaning of words from *The Canterbury Tales*

Reading Skills and Strategies

Mini-Lesson: Analyzing Word Parts
Point out to the class that the word *inscription* is made up of three parts that contribute to the word's meaning. Write the word on the board, and then, underneath, break it down:

inscription

Prefix	Root	Suffix
in-	*-scrip-*	*-tion*

Explain that the prefix *in-* ("in, into"), the root *-scrip-* ("writing, marking, or script"), and the suffix *-tion* (noun. "state, act, thing") mean "a message or note written in or on something."

Try It Out
Answers may vary, depending on the dictionary used. Students may have to trace roots back through several words. Remind students that they may look up prefixes and suffixes in a dictionary.

1. **diligent** *dis-* ("apart") + *legere* ("to choose") + *-ent* (adj. "that has, shows, or does") = "doing apart from choice; that is, doing something because one must; persevering."
2. **obstinate** *ob-* ("against") + *stare* ("to stand") + *-ate* (adj. "characteristic of") = "characteristic of standing against; not yielding to reason; stubborn."
3. **covetousness** *covet* ("long for with envy") + *-ous* (adj. "marked by, given to") + *-ness* (noun. "state, quality") = "greed; avarice." (Thus, a verb changes to a noun.)
4. **superfluity** *super-* ("over") + *fluere* ("to flow") + *-ity* (noun. "state, quality, condition") = "condition of overflowing; excess."
5. **transcend** *trans-* ("over") + *scandere* ("to climb") = "to climb over; exceed; surpass."

Getting Students Involved

Play the Roots and Affixes Game
Divide the class into groups of five. Begin by reading a root or affix aloud. Give each group two minutes to brainstorm and prepare (without dictionaries) a list of words that contain it. A member from each group should then read its list aloud. Give one point to the group with the shortest list of correct words, two points to the group with the next shortest list, and so on. (Each group earns some points for its efforts.) The group with the longest correct list gets the highest number of points for the round. Continue with different roots and affixes for another four or five rounds. The winning group is the one with the highest overall total.

BROWSING IN THE FILES

About the Author. Boccaccio was a friend of Petrarch, who, among other things, persuaded Boccaccio not to burn some of his earlier works when, in a slump, Boccaccio contemplated doing so. As an illegitimate child, Boccaccio did not have a happy childhood, and he was educated for a career in banking and law that did not suit him. He found some happiness in Naples, where he perhaps met Fiammetta, but in 1340 he was recalled to Florence by his father. Thereafter, Boccaccio faced difficulty but he devoted his life to art.

RESPONDING TO THE ART

Andrea Del Castagno (c.1421–1457) was inspired to become an artist when he met an itinerant painter working in a tabernacle. Legend has it that Castagno started drawing figures on walls and stones. He later painted portraits of the three titans of Italy in the 1300s—Dante, Petrarch, and Boccaccio.
Activity. Ask students what impressions of Boccaccio are suggested by this painting.

Planning

- **Block Schedule**
  Block Scheduling Lesson Plans with Pacing Guide
- **Traditional Schedule**
  Lesson Plans Including Strategies for English-Language Learners
- **One-Stop Planner**
  CD-ROM with Test Generator

WORLD LITERATURE

Italy

Giovanni Boccaccio

(1313–1375)

Giovanni Boccaccio is one of Italy's foremost writers. Raised in Florence, Boccaccio later studied business in Naples, but he soon transferred his ambitions from banking to literature. In his first prose romance, Boccaccio describes meeting a lovely woman named Fiammetta, with whom he falls immediately in love. Scholars have hotly argued about this woman's real identity—and even whether she existed at all. Fiammetta reappears in many of Boccaccio's later works, which often explore the theme of love. It is Fiammetta who tells the story of Federigo's falcon in the *Decameron.*

The two great subjects of the stories in the *Decameron* are love and the corruption of the clergy. Many of the *Decameron's* stories are adaptations of popular folk tales, fables, anecdotes, and even jokes that Boccaccio might have overheard on the bustling streets of medieval Naples. Boccaccio's stories have served as both a source and a model for many writers who followed him, among them Chaucer, Shakespeare, and Milton.

Boccaccio (15th century) by Andrea del Castagno.
Uffizi, Florence.

(Map) Old map showing a portion of the Mediterranean Coast.

go.hrw.com
LEO 12-2

Resources: Print and Media

Reading
- *Audio CD Library*
  Disc 2, Track 9

Assessment
- *Preparation for College Admission Exams,* p. 7

Internet
- go.hrw.com (keyword: LEO 12-2)

Before You Read
FEDERIGO'S FALCON

Make the Connection

The Pain of Love

Few experiences are more painful than falling in love with someone who couldn't care less. We get over it—most of us—and it never—well, almost never—does us serious damage. But while we're suffering, we suffer intensely. It's hard to think about anything else; we can't do our work; food, if we bother to eat, is tasteless; we find ourselves staring into space, missing everything going on around us. Worst of all, we're likely to do something so foolish that we make matters even worse.

But you never know how it will all turn out. In the most painful moments, when you think that things can't possibly get worse, they very well might. Or they might, surprisingly, turn around. . . .

Reading Skills and Strategies

Evaluating Historical Context

As you read this medieval love story, take notes on the ways the characters are like—and unlike—the characters in love stories today, or even the people you know in actual life. Keep movies and TV shows in mind too. Consider the ways in which a work's **historical context** can influence its meaning. Can historical context also be unimportant?

Background

"Federigo's Falcon" is part of the *Decameron,* a collection of tales written in fourteenth-century Italy shortly after a devastating plague struck Florence. The stories are grouped loosely within a frame tale about ten wealthy young Florentines who flee to a villa in the country to escape the plague-ravaged city.

To pass the time, the young people decide that for each of ten days *(decameron* is derived from the Greek words for "ten" and "day") they will elect a king or queen, who, in turn, will choose a theme that the others must use to tell a story. "Federigo's Falcon" is the ninth story told on the fifth day, a day devoted to telling stories with happy endings.

Detail from Frederick II's *Treatise on Falconry.* Ms. Pal. Lat. 1071 fol. 5v.
Apostolic Library, Vatican City, Rome.

OBJECTIVES

1. Read and interpret the story
2. Generate relevant, interesting, and researchable questions
3. Recognize distinctive and shared characteristics of cultures
4. Compare text events with their own experiences
5. Identify the influences of historical context on literature

Summary ■

The nobleman Federigo is so in love with Monna Giovanna, a virtuous married woman, that he impoverishes himself trying to win her and is forced to move to a small farm with only one valuable possession, a falcon. After Monna Giovanna's husband dies, she and her son move to a farm near Federigo's, where the boy grows fond of the falcon. When the son becomes ill, he asks his mother for the bird. Monna Giovanna reluctantly goes to Federigo and offers to dine with him. Deeply honored, Federigo kills the falcon to serve a meal worthy of her. After they have eaten, Monna Giovanna makes her request. The sad irony of the situation is intensified when Monna Giovanna's son dies but is alleviated later when she marries Federigo, whose noble gesture has won her heart.

RESPONDING TO THE ART

Falconry is the art of training hawks to hunt birds and other small game. During the Middle Ages, falconry was the favorite sport of the upper classes. Note the *jesses,* or light strings of leather, attached to the falcon's legs.

Activity. Ask students to speculate on the relationship of the falcon and master. [Most will say it must be close.] Have them recall this image when they read Yeats's "The Second Coming" on p. 923.

Reaching All Students

Struggling Readers

Students may get lost in long sentences, such as the second in the story or the first in paragraph 3. Help students see how semicolons signal major breaks in meaning, while commas signal minor breaks or enclose additional information.

Advanced Learners

Suggest that students read this tale looking for clues to medieval values, such as an emphasis on courtly love and good manners.

Listening to Music

Overture to *Boccaccio* by Franz von Suppé, performed by the Detroit Symphony.

Franz von Suppé's (1819–1895) light opera *Boccaccio,* which premiered in 1879, retells several stories from the *Decameron.*

Activity

Before students read "Federigo's Falcon," have them listen to Suppé's overture or introduction from *Boccaccio.* Then ask students to describe the mood Suppé's overture evokes.

A Reading Skills and Strategies

Evaluating Historical Context

Which details in this first paragraph reflect the medieval time setting? [Federigo's prowess in arms and his courtliness, his participation in jousts and tournaments, and his falcon] **How might these details be updated?** [Federigo could be a sports star known for his graciousness.] **Which details could be retained in a modern story?** [He could still go broke trying to win his love; she could still reject him.]

B Reading Skills and Strategies

Rereading

Upon reading that Monna Giovanna is married, did you reread to see if perhaps you had missed something? If so, did you find any clues? [Possible answer: Although we are not told in the first paragraph that she is married, her virtue plays a part in her refusal to acknowledge Federigo's declarations of love. Also, footnote 2 says that *Monna* means "Madam," a title that suggests marriage.]

C Elements of Literature

Characterization

What have you learned about Federigo so far? [He is so much in love with Monna Giovanna that he has spent all his money trying to win her and now lives in poverty with his prize falcon.]

D Reading Skills and Strategies

Determining Sequence of Events

List the events that lead up to Monna Giovanna's son's request for the falcon. [The boy's father dies; he and his mother move near Federigo's farm; the boy goes hunting with Federigo and admires his falcon.]

E Cultural Connections

Courtly Love

How does Federigo's predicament reflect the medieval conventions of courtly love? [In courtly love stories, a handsome, noble young man falls in love with a beautiful, unattainable older woman, who is often married. The lover suffers agonies because of her refusal to consider him, and he performs noble deeds in her name. Federigo's predicament fits this scenario, except that he has so far performed no noble deeds.]

Federigo's Falcon

from the Decameron

Giovanni Boccaccio

translated by **Mark Musa and Peter Bondanella**

There was once in Florence a young man named Federigo, the son of Messer[1] Filippo Alberighi, renowned above all other men in Tuscany for his prowess in arms and for his courtliness. As often happens to most gentlemen, he fell in love with a lady named Monna[2] Giovanna, in her day considered to be one of the most beautiful and one of the most charming women that ever there was in Florence; and in order to win her love, he participated in jousts and tournaments, organized and gave feasts, and spent his money without restraint; but she, no less virtuous than beautiful, cared little for these things done on her behalf, nor did she care for him who did them. Now, as Federigo was spending far beyond his means and was taking nothing in, as easily happens he lost his wealth and became poor, with nothing but his little farm to his name (from whose revenues he lived very meagerly) and one falcon which was among the best in the world.

More in love than ever, but knowing that he would never be able to live the way he wished to in the city, he went to live at Campi,[3] where his farm was. There he passed his time hawking whenever he could, asked nothing of anyone, and endured his poverty patiently. Now, during the time that Federigo was reduced to dire need, it happened that the husband of Monna Giovanna fell ill, and realizing death was near, he made his last will. He was very rich, and he made his son, who was growing up, his heir, and, since he had loved Monna Giovanna very much, he made her his heir should his son die without a legitimate heir; and then he died.

Monna Giovanna was now a widow, and as is the custom among our women, she went to the country with her son to spend a year on one of her possessions very close by to Federigo's farm, and it happened that this young boy became friends with Federigo and began to enjoy birds and hunting dogs; and after he had seen Federigo's falcon fly many times, it pleased him so much that he very much wished it were his own, but he did not dare to ask for it, for he could see how dear it was to Federigo. And during this time, it happened that the young boy took ill, and his mother was much grieved, for he was her only child and she loved him enormously. She would spend the entire day by his side, never ceasing to comfort him, and often asking him if there was anything he desired, begging him to tell her what it might be, for if it were possible to obtain it, she would certainly do everything possible to get it. After the young boy had heard her make this offer many times, he said:

"Mother, if you can arrange for me to have Federigo's falcon, I think I would be well very soon."

When the lady heard this, she was taken aback for a moment, and she began to think what she should do. She knew that Federigo had loved her for a long while, in spite of the fact that he never received a single glance from her, and so, she said to herself:

"How can I send or go and ask for this falcon of his which is, as I have heard tell, the best that ever

1. **Messer** (mes′ər): title of address similar to *sir.*
2. **Monna** (mō′nə): In Italian, *Monna* is an abbreviation for *Madonna* (mə·dän′ə), a formal title for a woman, similar to *madam.*
3. **Campi** (käm′pē): small town set in the mountains northwest of Florence. *Campi* literally means "fields."

(Above) From an illuminated manuscript (detail) (14th century). MS Bodl. 264, fol. 123v.

The Bodleian Library, Oxford.

Using Students' Strengths

Naturalist Learners

Encourage students to research falcons and falconry in order to understand Federigo's emotions. They might learn who in the Middle Ages engaged in such sport, just how valuable a falcon might be, and why Federigo might have hung on to this one special possession when he had lost all others. Naturalist learners might also like to draw or describe a falcon in flight or demonstrate the various whistles a master might use to call his falcon.

Kinesthetic Learners

After students have finished reading the story, have them work in pairs to act out Monna Giovanna's visit to Federigo's farm. Students should rely on details in the text, but they may also reasonably infer some details, such as Federigo's surprise at finding Monna Giovanna at his door or Federigo's desperation as he looks for food to serve her.

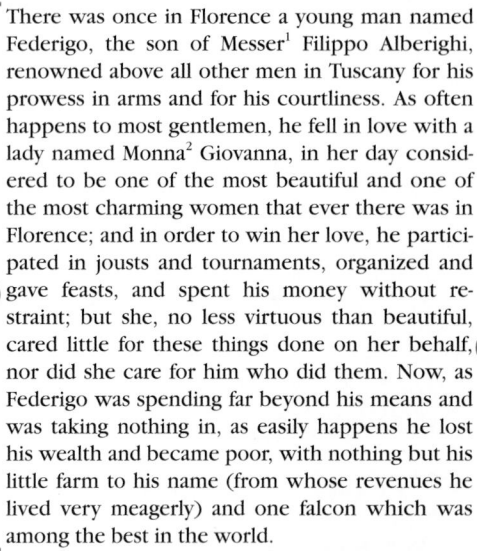

flew, and besides this, his only means of support? And how can I be so insensitive as to wish to take away from this gentleman the only pleasure which is left to him?"

And involved in these thoughts, knowing that she was certain to have the bird if she asked for it, but not knowing what to say to her son, she stood there without answering him. Finally the love she bore her son persuaded her that she should make him happy, and no matter what the consequences might be, she would not send for the bird, but rather go herself for it and bring it back to him; so she answered her son:

"My son, take comfort and think only of getting well, for I promise you that the first thing I shall do tomorrow morning is to go for it and bring it back to you."

The child was so happy that he showed some improvement that very day. The following morning, the lady, accompanied by another woman, as if going for a stroll, went to Federigo's modest house and asked for him. Since it was not the season for it, Federigo had not been hawking for some days and was in his orchard, attending to certain tasks. When he heard that Monna Giovanna was asking for him at the door, he was very surprised and happy to run there. As she saw him coming, she greeted him with feminine charm, and once Federigo had welcomed her courteously, she said:

"Greetings, Federigo!" Then she continued: "I have come to compensate you for the harm you have suffered on my account by loving me more than you needed to; and the compensation is this: I, along with this companion of mine, intend to dine with you—a simple meal—this very day."

To this Federigo humbly replied: "Madonna, I never remember having suffered any harm because of you. On the contrary, so much good have I received from you that if ever I have been worth anything, it has been because of your merit and the love I bore for you; and your generous visit is certainly so dear to me that I would spend all over again that which I spent in the past; but you have come to a poor host."

And having said this, he received her into his home humbly, and from there he led her into his garden, and since he had no one there to keep her company, he said:

"My lady, since there is no one else, this good woman here, the wife of this workman, will keep you company while I go to set the table."

Though he was very poor, Federigo, until now, had never before realized to what extent he had wasted his wealth; but this morning, the fact that he found nothing with which he could honor the lady for the love of whom he had once entertained countless men in the past gave him cause to reflect. In great anguish, he cursed himself and his fortune and, like a man beside himself, he started running here and there, but could find neither money nor a pawnable[4] object. The hour was late and his desire to honor the gracious lady was great, but not wishing to turn for help to others (not even to his own workman), he set his eyes upon his good falcon, perched in a small room; and since he had nowhere else to turn, he took the bird, and finding it plump, he decided that it would be a worthy food for such a lady. So, without further thought, he wrung its neck and quickly gave it to his servant girl to pluck, prepare, and place on a spit to be roasted with care; and when he had set the table with the whitest of tablecloths (a few of which he still had left), he returned, with a cheerful face, to the lady in his garden, saying that the meal he was able to prepare for her was ready.

The lady and her companion rose, went to the table together with Federigo, who waited upon them with the greatest devotion, and they ate the good falcon without knowing what it was they were eating. And having left the table and spent some time in pleasant conversation, the lady thought it time now to say what she had come to say, and so she spoke these kind words to Federigo:

"Federigo, if you recall your past life and my virtue, which you perhaps mistook for harshness and cruelty, I do not doubt at all that you will be amazed by my presumption when you hear what my main reason for coming here is; but if you had children, through whom you might have experienced the power of parental love, it seems certain to me that you would, at least in part, forgive me. But, just as you have no child, I do have one, and I

4. **pawnable:** able to be given as security in return for a loan of money or goods.

F Critical Thinking

Expressing an Opinion

? What conflict does Monna Giovanna face? Do you approve of the way she resolves it? [She is torn between hurting Federigo and granting her son's wish. Most students will defend her choice as the only one a mother could make, but some may believe she should have tried to find an alternative pleasure for her son.]

G Reading Skills and Strategies

Evaluating Historical Context

? How does this exchange reflect the historical context of the story? [It is excessively polite and it follows the conventions of courtly love in that the woman deigns to grant a small favor and the man cherishes his suffering on her account because it ennobles him.]

H Reading Skills and Strategies

Evaluating Historical Context

? What comparisons might you make between this man in love and men or women in love in contemporary stories? [Like people in contemporary stories, this man is desperate. Unlike people in most contemporary love stories, he is willing to give up his dearest possession for his love.]

I Elements of Literature

Irony

? Situational irony occurs when what actually happens is the opposite of what is expected or of what would be appropriate. One example of irony occurs when Monna Giovanna unexpectedly pays a visit to Federigo after he no longer can afford to entertain her. How is this meal an example of situational irony? [Monna Giovanna eats the very falcon which she hopes to receive from Federigo as a gift for her son. The one thing Monna Giovanna wants most right now is the one thing she unwittingly is consuming.]

Getting Students Involved

Cooperative Learning

As the Lovesick Swoon. Refer students to p. 168 for information on courtly love (Choice 3, The Game of Love). Then ask students to work in pairs to illustrate or to act out a situation between two friends discussing one of those rules. (Students may also find their own creative way to present the rule.) Provide time for students to present their interpretations to the class.

Writing an Interior Monologue

What She Really Thought. Students might enjoy writing a humorous or serious interior monologue showing the reactions of Monna Giovanna during various moments of her visit. Students may tell what Monna Giovanna really thought when she first laid eyes on Federigo's run-down farm, when she first realized what she had eaten, and when she realized she would have no falcon to give her beloved son.

Responding to the Art

A Book of Hours was a collection of prayers that were recited at set times of the day and addressed to the Virgin Mary. *The Very Rich Hours,* commissioned from the Limbourg brothers by the Duke of Berry in 1415, is considered the finest illuminated manuscript in existence. The three brothers created illuminations for each month of the year.

Activity. Ask students what they can learn about medieval life from this August scene. [Both men and women from the nobility hunted with falcons; the towns were walled to protect people from their enemies; serfs swam in the river and worked in the fields.]

A Appreciating Language

Dialogue

? How does Monna Giovanna's speech reveal that she has good intentions toward Federigo? [She uses phrases such as "therefore I beg you"; she mentions his nobility; she says he is not obliged in any way. She uses dignified and humble language.]

B Reading Skills and Strategies

Evaluating Historical Context

? What does this scene tell you about the medieval attitude toward crying? [Monna Giovanna does not react negatively to Federigo's tears, and he does not try to check them: Men's tears may not have been considered unmanly.] **Could this scene be included in a contemporary story?** [Possible responses: Yes, Federigo would be seen as sensitive. Or no, he would look like a big baby.]

C Struggling Readers

Breaking Down Difficult Text

This long speech consists of only two sentences. Help students identify each sentence and restate its main idea in their own words. [Possible answers: Fortune has worked against me before, but never so much as now, and I'll tell you why. I have just honored you as best I knew how by feeding you my falcon, and now I am sad.]

August: Departure for the Hunt with Falcons, from the calendar for the *Très riches heures du duc de Berry* by the Limbourg brothers. MS 65 / 1284, fol. 8v.

Musée Condé, Chantilly, France.

cannot escape the common laws of other mothers; the force of such laws compels me to follow them, against my own will and against good manners and duty, and to ask of you a gift which I know is most precious to you; and it is naturally so, since your extreme condition has left you no other delight, no other pleasure, no other consolation; and this gift is your falcon, which my son is so taken by that if I do not bring it to him, I fear his sickness will grow so much worse that I may lose him. And therefore I beg you, not because of the love that you bear for me, which does not oblige you in the least, but because of your own nobility, which you have shown to be greater than that of all others in practicing courtliness, that you be pleased to give it to me, so that I may say that I have saved the life of my son by means of this gift, and because of it I have placed him in your debt forever."

When he heard what the lady requested and knew that he could not oblige her since he had given her the falcon to eat, Federigo began to weep in her presence, for he could not utter a word in reply. The lady, at first, thought his tears were caused more by the sorrow of having to part with the good falcon than by anything else, and she was on the verge of telling him she no longer wished it, but she held back and waited for Federigo's reply after he stopped weeping. And he said:

"My lady, ever since it pleased God for me to place my love in you, I have felt that Fortune has been hostile to me in many things, and I have complained of her, but all this is nothing compared to what she has just done to me, and I must never be at peace with her again, thinking about how you have come here to my poor home where, while it was rich, you never deigned to come, and you requested a small gift, and Fortune worked to make it impossible for me to give it to you; and why this is so I shall tell you briefly. When I heard that you, out of your kindness, wished to dine with me, I considered it fitting and right, taking into account your excellence and your worthiness, that I should honor you, according to my possibilities, with a more precious food than that which I usually serve to other people; therefore, remembering the falcon that you requested and its value, I judged it a food worthy of you, and this very day you had it roasted and served to you as best I could; but seeing now that you desired it in another way, my sorrow in not being able to serve you is so great that I shall never be able to console myself again."

Assessing Learning

Check Test: Short Answer

1. How does Federigo lose his wealth? [He squanders it trying to win Giovanna's love.]
2. What stipulations did Giovanna's husband make before he died? [(1) His son would inherit the fortune. (2) If the son died without an heir, Giovanna would inherit the fortune.]
3. Why does Giovanna want the falcon? [She wants to give it to her ailing son.]
4. Why does Federigo kill the falcon? [He has nothing else to serve as a meal for Giovanna.]

Informal Assessment

Observation Assessment. Tell students you will record how much they participate and what they add to class discussion about the story. Create a five-point scale, with one point given for any related comment and five points awarded for the most thoughtful or useful comments. Use the scale over a period of a week or more. Be sure all students have the opportunity to speak, letting those who have not yet contributed speak first.

And after he had said this, he laid the feathers, the feet, and the beak of the bird before her as proof. When the lady heard and saw this, she first reproached him for having killed such a falcon to serve as a meal to a woman; but then to herself she commended the greatness of his spirit, which no poverty was able or would be able to diminish; then, having lost all hope of getting the falcon and, perhaps because of this, of improving the health of her son as well, she thanked Federigo both for the honor paid to her and for his good will, and she left in grief, and returned to her son. To his mother's extreme sorrow, either because of his disappointment that he could not have the falcon, or because his illness must have necessarily led to it, the boy passed from this life only a few days later.

After the period of her mourning and bitterness had passed, the lady was repeatedly urged by her brothers to remarry, since she was very rich and was still young; and although she did not wish to do so, they became so insistent that she remembered the merits of Federigo and his last act of generosity—that is, to have killed such a falcon to do her honor—and she said to her brothers:

"I would prefer to remain a widow, if that would please you; but if you wish me to take a husband, you may rest assured that I shall take no man but Federigo degli Alberighi."

In answer to this, making fun of her, her brothers replied:

"You foolish woman, what are you saying? How can you want him; he hasn't a penny to his name?"

To this she replied: "My brothers, I am well aware of what you say, but I would rather have a man who needs money than money that needs a man."

Her brothers, seeing that she was determined and knowing Federigo to be of noble birth, no matter how poor he was, accepted her wishes and gave her in marriage to him with all her riches. When he found himself the husband of such a great lady, whom he had loved so much and who was so wealthy besides, he managed his financial affairs with more prudence than in the past and lived with her happily the rest of his days.

Couple, from an illustrated manuscript of the *Decameron* (c. 14th century).

© cliché Bibliothèque Nationale de France, Paris.

Finding Common Ground

Federigo and Monna Giovanna live in fourteenth-century Italy. But we share with them some basic human problems. In your reading notes, you may have commented on some of the lovers' difficulties listed here:

- Federigo loves someone who doesn't love him.
- Giovanna must cope with a dying son's wish.
- Giovanna has to ask a favor of someone she has ignored and rejected.
- Federigo has to deal with the discovery that a noble gesture was actually a terrible mistake.

Try to find some contemporary examples of these lovers' problems. Working with a small group, think about how the lovers in this story might be treated by a contemporary writer or filmmaker. How are the problems faced by Federigo and Monna Giovanna both similar to and different from the problems faced by lovers today? How would their story differ if it were retold—as, say, the story of Joan and Fred—and reset in the world of today? Make a list of the differences and similarities that most intrigue you. What actors would you cast to play Giovanna and Federigo in a movie? Present your findings to other groups in your class.

Connecting Across Texts

Connecting with "The Wife of Bath's Tale"

In "The Wife of Bath's Tale," the old woman argues that gentility is not the result of noble birth but of noble actions. Ask students to consider which characters in "Federigo's Falcon" would agree with her and which would disagree. [Monna Giovanna would agree; she is influenced by Federigo's "last act of generosity." Her brothers, however, while dismayed by Federigo's lack of money, ultimately judge him by his noble birth.]

Finding Common Ground

This feature asks students to explore the links between contemporary lovers and Federigo and Monna Giovanna. To find these links, review recent movies and books to see if lovers today face these same scenarios. Be sure students see that certain human emotions are universal, no matter what era people live in.

D Critical Thinking
Making Connections

? What other stories have you read in which a gift intended to please someone turns out to be exactly what that person does not need or want? [The most famous of such stories is O. Henry's "The Gift of the Magi," in which a wife sells her hair to buy a watch chain for her husband, while he sells his watch to buy decorative combs for her hair. The generosity of their love, however, overshadows the irony.]

E Reading Skills and Strategies
Evaluating Historical Context

? What is significant about this statement? [Monna Giovanna actually prefers not to remarry.] **How does this reflection on Monna Giovanna compare with what you might expect to read in a contemporary love story?** [Possible answers: Women today might also choose not to remarry. Or in a contemporary love story, the man or woman would immediately run into the arms of the waiting lover once he or she was free.]

F Reading Skills and Strategies
Evaluating Historical Context

? What does the role of the brothers suggest about the status of women at this time? [A woman didn't have the freedom to marry whom she wished. Monna Giovanna is obliged to convince her brothers, who serve as her guardians, and they ultimately choose to give her away in marriage.]

G Critical Thinking
Challenging the Text

As the background information on p. 153 explains, this story was meant to have a "happy ending." Students may enjoy debating whether the ending is happy and whether, in most or all ways, the plot is also predictable. Students should support their opinions with details from the text. Some readers might say that the irony in the story was not predictable at all and that it is the irony that makes the tale so enjoyable or sad.

Objectives
1. Read and interpret the text
2. Identify romance
3. Express understanding through expository writing and speaking
4. Use new words

Skills
Literary
- Analyze a romance

Writing
- Collect ideas for a compare/contrast essay
- Analyze story adaptation
- Support an opinion

Speaking
- Take part in a panel discussion

Vocabulary
- Use new words

Viewing/Representing
- Compare depictions of Sir Gawain (ATE)

Planning
- **Block Schedule**
  Block Scheduling Lesson Plans with Pacing Guide
- **Traditional Schedule**
  Lesson Plans Including Strategies for English-Language Learners
- **One-Stop Planner**
  CD-ROM with Test Generator

Before You Read
FROM SIR GAWAIN AND THE GREEN KNIGHT

Make the Connection
Finding a Hero

One of the great works of medieval literature, this story was probably written around 1375, at a time when the old ideals of knightly conduct—courage, loyalty, and courtesy—were beginning to erode. Perhaps, as in our own age, people then were looking forward to the future but were also feeling nostalgic for values that had once defined their lives.

Quickwrite
Are we living in a heroic age? Or do most people feel that there are no genuine heroes today? What do we demand of our heroes today? Do a quick survey of your classmates or of people outside school. Keep your survey results, and think about today's heroes as you read about the severe testing of a hero at King Arthur's court.

Elements of Literature
The Romance

Romances (or at least works with some of the trappings of romances) are still being written today. They take the form of novels, movies, even comic strips. Strictly speaking, a **romance** is a narrative set in a world of pure wish fulfillment, where the ordinary laws of nature are suspended and where idealized and superhuman heroes fight and almost always conquer the forces of evil. The basic narrative pattern of the romance is the **quest,** in which the hero undertakes a perilous journey in search of something of value.

> From the thirteenth century onward, ***romance*** was a term applied to a verse narrative which traced the adventures of a brave knight or other hero who had to overcome danger for love of a noble lady or high ideal.
>
> *For more on the Romance, see page 167 and the Handbook of Literary Terms.*

Background
As *Sir Gawain and the Green Knight* opens, King Arthur and the knights of the Round Table are feasting. Suddenly an enormous green stranger bursts into the hall. King Arthur greets the Green Knight and asks him to state his business. The Green Knight, after a few scornful words about the manliness of King Arthur's knights, says he only wishes to play a New Year's game. He challenges any knight there to agree to "exchange one blow for another"—he will even give that knight his gisarme (gi·zärm′), his two-bladed ax. The stranger says he will stand for the first blow; the knight must agree to let the Green Knight have *his* turn in a year and a day. Gawain accepts the challenge—no other knight except Arthur himself has dared to, and Gawain refuses to let the king give up his life.

Gawain hefts his ax and chops off the giant green head. But the Knight never falters. He picks up his green head, repeats his challenge, and gallops off with the head in his arms.

Just before Christmas the next year, Gawain sadly sets off on the long journey to honor his pledge. One day he comes upon a beautiful castle. The lord of the castle invites him to rest a few days and then suggests an odd "game." The lord says that he will go hunting each day and whatever he wins in the hunt he will give to Gawain. In return, Gawain must give anything he has won that day to the lord.

Each day when the lord goes off hunting, his beautiful young wife tries to seduce Gawain. For two days, Gawain accepts only kisses, and true to his bargain, he gives the lord the kisses when he returns from hunting. But on the morning of the third day, the lady not only kisses Gawain but also makes him accept a magical green girdle, or sash. She says that if he wears the sash, he cannot be killed.

When the lord returns from the hunt, Gawain gives him the kisses but keeps the sash a secret.

Now it's New Year's Day. Gawain sets off to find the Green Chapel and the dreaded Green Knight. Snow and sleet have fallen, and howling winds have piled up drifts of snow. Gawain leaves the castle with the green sash wrapped around his armor. He is certain he is headed for his death.

go.hrw.com
LEO 12-2

Resources: Print and Media
Reading
- *Graphic Organizers for Active Reading,* p. 9
- *Words to Own,* p. 6
- *Audio CD Library*
  Disc 3, Track 2

Elements of Literature
- *Literary Elements*
  Transparency 7
  Worksheet, p. 22

Writing and Language
- *Daily Oral Grammar*
  Transparency 6
- *Grammar and Language Links*
  Worksheet, p. 15
- *Language Workshop CD-ROM*

Viewing and Representing
- *Viewing and Representing*
  Fine Art Transparency 2
  Fine Art Worksheet, p. 8
- *Visual Connections*
  Videocassette A, Segment 4

Assessment
- *Formal Assessment,* p. 25
- *Portfolio Management System,* p. 103
- *Test Generator (One-Stop Planner CD-ROM)*

Internet
- go.hrw.com (keyword: LE0 12-2)

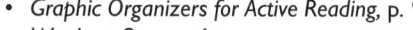

from Sir Gawain and the Green Knight

translated by **John Gardner**

He put his spurs to Gringolet,° plunged down the path,
Shoved through the heavy thicket grown up by the woods
And rode down the steep slope to the floor of the valley;
He looked around him then—a strange, wild place,
And not a sign of a chapel on any side
But only steep, high banks surrounding him,
And great, rough knots of rock and rugged crags
That scraped the passing clouds, as it seemed to him.
He heaved at the heavy reins to hold back his horse
And squinted in every direction in search of the Chapel,
And still he saw nothing except—and this was strange—
A small green hill all alone, a sort of barrow,°
A low, smooth bulge on the bank of the brimming creek
That flowed from the foot of a waterfall,
And the water in the pool was bubbling as if it were boiling.
Sir Gawain urged Gringolet on till he came to the mound
And lightly dismounted and made the reins secure
On the great, thick limb of a gnarled and ancient tree;
Then he went up to the barrow and walked all around it,
Wondering in his wits what on earth it might be.
It had at each end and on either side an entrance,
And patches of grass were growing all over the thing,
And all the inside was hollow—an old, old cave
Or the cleft of some ancient crag, he couldn't tell which
it was.

"Whoo, Lord!" thought the knight,
"Is *this* the fellow's place?
Here the Devil might
Recite his midnight mass.

"Dear God," thought Gawain, "the place is deserted enough!
And it's ugly enough, all overgrown with weeds!
Well might it amuse that marvel of green
To do his devotions here, in his devilish way!
In my five senses I fear it's the Fiend himself

1. **Gringolet:** Gawain's horse.

12. **barrow:** grave mound.

Sir Gawain strikes off the head of the Green Knight in King Arthur's presence, from an English manuscript (c. 15th century). MS Cotton Nero A.X., fol. 94v.
By permission of the British Library, London.

Summary

(Be sure students read Background on p. 158.) When Sir Gawain arrives at the Green Chapel (as he agreed to do a year and a day before), he hears the sound of an ax being sharpened. When the Green Knight bursts forth with a terrible new weapon, Gawain bows his head to take the blow. The Green Knight raises his ax twice, hoping to try Gawain's courage, and with a third blow barely nicks him. Then the Knight reveals himself as the man who gave Gawain hospitality and ordered his wife to tempt Gawain. The Knight accuses Gawain of cheating by accepting the sash from his wife—an accusation that makes Gawain cry with remorse. Finally, the Green Knight concedes that Gawain has repented and spares his life.

Background

On a symbolic level, the Green Knight, as befits his color, can represent the promise of spring, the renewal of life, and the Christian hope of redemption. Gawain, although a hero of extraordinary virtue, can also be seen as a flawed Everyman who must repent and strive to improve himself.

A Elements of Literature

Romance

? Based on the background information, explain why the Green Knight is a romance figure. [He does not conform to the ordinary laws of nature. He is a superhuman figure. Gawain initially associates him with the Devil.]

RESPONDING TO THE ART

The scene here and the one on p. 161 show incidents that occur before Sir Gawain's confrontation with the Green Knight at his chapel.

Activity. Ask students to identify the figures in this illustration. [Sir Gawain at the right, holding a gisarme—the long staff with the crescent-shaped ax at the top; the Green Knight at the left; Arthur and his knights at the table]

Preteaching Vocabulary

Words to Own

Ask students to identify the suffix of each word [*-ed, -ous, -ed*]. Students might work in pairs to compose one long, and perhaps silly, sentence that uses all three words. Then have students answer the following questions. (Possible answers are given.)

1. If a man felt *daunted* by the prospect of a certain challenge, what kind of look might he have on his face? [a discouraged look; a look of hopelessness]
2. If a boxer began to strike a blow but then *feinted*, how might the opponent feel? [probably relieved]
3. If a remedy for the common cold proved to be *efficacious,* how might the researchers who discovered it feel? [proud; triumphant]

Resources

Viewing and Representing

Videocassette: A, Segment 4

Available in English and Spanish.
This segment "To Be a Knight" takes a look at the world of chivalry. For full lesson plans and worksheets, see the *Visual Connections Teacher's Manual.*

Viewing and Representing

Fine Art Transparency

A Fine Art transparency of Juan Wijngaard's illustration for *Sir Gawain and the Green Knight,* showing King Arthur facing the intruder, can be used to pique interest in the story. See the *Viewing and Representing Transparencies and Worksheets*:

- Transparency 2
- Worksheet, p. 8

A Elements of Literature

Romance

? What elements of a romance have you encountered so far in this part of the narrative? (To review the definition of *romance,* refer students to pp. 158 and 167.) [The hero is undertaking a dangerous quest for honor's sake; a nearly perfect hero is facing what appears to be an agent of the Devil.]

B Reading Skills and Strategies

Drawing Conclusions

? Why does the Green Knight keep Gawain waiting? [Possible responses: To keep someone waiting is a way to demonstrate power over that person. It can also be a tactic to make the other person nervous.] In literary terms, it increases suspense for the reader.

Who's brought me to meet him here to murder me.
May fire and fury befall this fiendish Chapel,
As cursed a kirk° as I ever yet came across!"
With his helmet on his head and his lance in hand
He leaped up onto the roof of the rock-walled room
And, high on that hill, he heard, from an echoing rock
Beyond the pool, on the hillside, a horrible noise.
Brrrack! It clattered in the cliffs as if to cleave them,
A sound like a grindstone grinding on a scythe!°
Brrrack! It whirred and rattled like water on a mill wheel!
Brrrrrack! It rushed and rang till your blood ran cold.
And then: "Oh God," thought Gawain, "it grinds, I think,
For me—a blade prepared for the blow I must take
as my right!
God's will be done! But here!
He may well get his knight,
But still, no use in fear;
I won't fall dead of fright!"

And then Sir Gawain roared in a ringing voice,
"Where is the hero who swore he'd be here to meet me?
Sir Gawain the Good is come to the Green Chapel!
If any man would meet me, make it now,
For it's now or never, I've no wish to dawdle here long."
"Stay there!" called someone high above his head,
"I'll pay you promptly all that I promised before."
But still he went on with that whetting noise a while,
Turning again to his grinding before he'd come down.
At last, from a hole by a rock he came out into sight,
Came plunging out of his den with a terrible weapon,
A huge new Danish ax to deliver his blow with,
With a vicious swine of a bit bent back to the handle,
Filed to a razor's edge and four foot long,
Not one inch less by the length of that gleaming lace.
The great Green Knight was garbed as before,
Face, legs, hair, beard, all as before but for this:
That now he walked the world on his own two legs,
The ax handle striking the stone like a walking-stave.°
When the knight came down to the water he would not wade
But vaulted across on his ax, then with awful strides
Came fiercely over the field filled all around
with snow.
Sir Gawain met him there
And bowed—but none too low!
Said the other, "I see, sweet sir,
You go where you say you'll go!

"Gawain," the Green Knight said, "may God be your guard!
You're very welcome indeed, sir, here at my place;

37. kirk: Scottish for "church."

43. scythe (sī*th*): long-handled cutting tool.

Sir Gawain, from *Le Roman de Lancelot du Lac* (detail) (c. 15th century). MS 805, fol. 48.
The Pierpont Morgan Library, New York.

71. walking-stave (stāv): staff.

Reaching All Students

Struggling Readers

Although students are reading only part of the story, the incident here has a strong plot line. Students may find it useful to construct and fill in a plot triangle as they read. They should note the conflict, the main events, the climax, and the resolution. Students can use these triangles to summarize what they have read.

English Language Learners

Students who associate the word *romance* with the popular "love stories" available in paperback on display racks should copy the characteristics of a medieval romance listed on p. 167 and look for examples as they read.

Advanced Learners

As students read, have them consider possible Christian interpretations of this story. Some critics consider Gawain a type, or symbol, of Adam; he has also been regarded as the embodiment of human weakness and fallibility, and, as such, he can be redeemed only by God. Students should form their own opinions about the symbolic message of this tale.

You've timed your travel, my friend, as a true man should.
You recall the terms of the contract drawn up between us:
At this time a year ago you took your chances,
And I'm pledged now, this New Year, to make you my payment.
And here we are in this valley, all alone,
And no man here to part us, proceed as we may;
Heave off your helmet then, and have here your pay;
And debate no more with me than I did then
When you severed my head from my neck with a single swipe."
"Never fear," said Gawain, "by God who gave
Me life, I'll raise no complaint at the grimness of it;
But take your single stroke, and I'll stand still
And allow you to work as you like and not oppose
you here."
He bowed toward the ground
And let his skin show clear;
However his heart might pound,
He would not show his fear.

Quickly then the man in the green made ready,
Grabbed up his keen-ground ax to strike Sir Gawain;
With all the might in his body he bore it aloft
And sharply brought it down as if to slay him;
Had he made it fall with the force he first intended
He would have stretched out the strongest man on earth.
But Sir Gawain cast a side glance at the ax
As it glided down to give him his Kingdom Come,°
And his shoulders jerked away from the iron a little,
And the Green Knight caught the handle, holding it back,
And mocked the prince with many a proud reproof:°
"*You* can't be Gawain," he said, "who's thought so good,
A man who's never been daunted on hill or dale!
For look how you flinch for fear before anything's felt!
I never heard tell that Sir Gawain was ever a coward!
I never moved a muscle when *you* came down;
In Arthur's hall I never so much as winced.
My head fell off at my feet, yet I never flickered;
But you! You tremble at heart before you're touched!
I'm bound to be called a better man than you, then,
my lord."
Said Gawain, "I shied once:
No more. You have my word.
But if my head falls to the stones
It cannot be restored.

Sir Gawain is tempted by the lady of the castle, from an English manuscript (c. 15th century). MS Cotton Nero A.X., fol. 129.

By permission of the British Library, London.

107. his Kingdom Come: life after death.

110. reproof: rebuke; scolding.

WORDS TO OWN
daunted (dônt'ed) *adj.:* intimidated.

C Critical Thinking
Making Connections

? The actual time span was one year and one day. Where else have you read about a similar time span? [In "The Wife of Bath's Tale," this is the same period of time allotted to the Knight to find out what women want.] **Point out that this is a repeated or archetypal element in folklore.**

D Elements of Literature
Characterization

? What do you learn about Gawain from his response to the Green Knight? [He is exceptionally brave.] **What type of characterization is this?** [indirect characterization, implied through the character's words and actions.]

E Critical Thinking
Extending the Text

? How does Gawain react to the Green Knight's taunts? How might real people react? [Though Gawain has indicated that he does not want to be thought a coward, he does not seem particularly upset by the taunts, other than vowing not to flinch again. Real people might dismiss the taunts or react with laughter, fear, anger, or violence. Most people would point out to the Green Knight that he did not flinch a year ago because he knew he had magical powers.]

F Reading Skills and Strategies
Making Predictions

? What will the Green Knight do next? Why do you think so? [Possible answers: The Green Knight will kill Gawain on the next try, for Gawain has just shown some small bit of cowardice. Or the Green Knight will stop his stroke again. It appears that he doesn't want to kill Gawain; instead, he seems to want to test him.]

Skill Link

Analyzing the Protagonist and Antagonist

Explain that a **protagonist** is the central character in a story or a drama, and an **antagonist** is anyone or anything that opposes the protagonist. For example, in *Beowulf,* Beowulf himself is the protagonist, and the antagonist is, at least in part of the story, Grendel.

Activity

Ask students to discuss the following questions with a classmate:

1. Who is the antagonist in this romance? [the Green Knight]
2. Who is the protagonist? [Sir Gawain]
3. What does the antagonist want? [to test or challenge the character of the hero]
4. What does the protagonist want? [to do the honorable thing and honor King Arthur's pledge]

LITERATURE AND ARCHITECTURE

Lighting and heating in early castles was as primitive as the flooring and bedding. Candles made of wax or melted animal fat were either stuck into iron spikes, supported from the walls on brackets, or placed in iron candelabra. Rushes were also burned to give light; one can only imagine the number of fires this must have caused. Early in the Middle Ages, people got heat from an open hearth. The invention of the fireplace, however, represented a great leap forward, for a fireplace not only produced heat but also heated the stones around it. The stones would absorb the heat and slowly release it, even after the fire had ceased burning brightly.

RESPONDING TO THE ART

Jehan Froissart (1337–1410) wrote a famous chronicle of the Hundred Years' War between France and England. This illustration from the *Chronicles* shows how the castles were designed for defense. Archers fired through narrow slitlike windows, called loopholes, that were wider on the inside to make it easier to shoot accurately. Round towers that protruded from the castle's walls made it simpler to pick off soldiers trying to scale the defenses. **Activity.** Based on this art and the feature material on castles, ask if students would like to live in one. Why or why not? [Most students will prefer the amenities of the twenty-first century, but some may favor the romance and excitement of castle life.]

(A) Reading Skills and Strategies

Drawing Conclusions

? Why do you think the Green Knight stops his second blow? [Possible answer: He is trying to wear Gawain down. First, he taunts Gawain about his lack of courage; then he stops his second blow, engaging in a war of nerves with Gawain.]

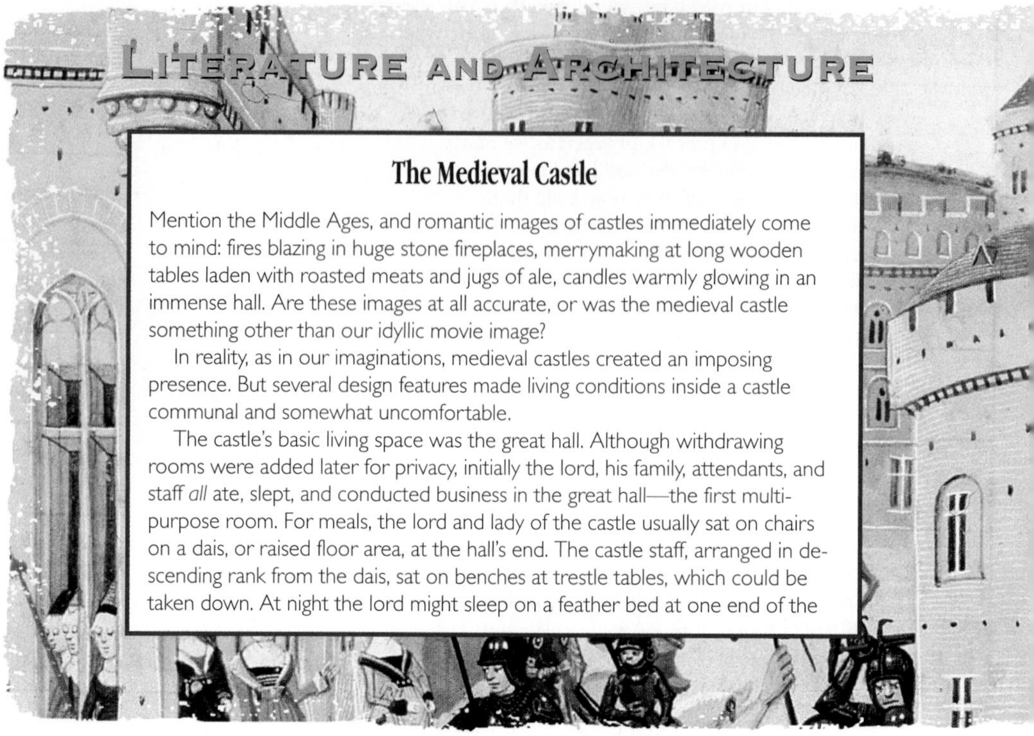

LITERATURE AND ARCHITECTURE

The Medieval Castle

Mention the Middle Ages, and romantic images of castles immediately come to mind: fires blazing in huge stone fireplaces, merrymaking at long wooden tables laden with roasted meats and jugs of ale, candles warmly glowing in an immense hall. Are these images at all accurate, or was the medieval castle something other than our idyllic movie image?

In reality, as in our imaginations, medieval castles created an imposing presence. But several design features made living conditions inside a castle communal and somewhat uncomfortable.

The castle's basic living space was the great hall. Although withdrawing rooms were added later for privacy, initially the lord, his family, attendants, and staff *all* ate, slept, and conducted business in the great hall—the first multipurpose room. For meals, the lord and lady of the castle usually sat on chairs on a dais, or raised floor area, at the hall's end. The castle staff, arranged in descending rank from the dais, sat on benches at trestle tables, which could be taken down. At night the lord might sleep on a feather bed at one end of the

"But be brisk, man, by your faith, and come to the point!
Deal out my doom if you can, and do it at once,
For I'll stand for one good stroke, and I'll start no more
Until your ax has hit—and that I swear."
"Here goes, then," said the other, and heaves it aloft
And stands there waiting, scowling like a madman;
He swings down sharp, then suddenly stops again,
Holds back the ax with his hand before it can hurt,
And Gawain stands there stirring not even a nerve;
He stood there still as a stone or the stock of a tree
That's wedged in rocky ground by a hundred roots.
O, merrily then he spoke, the man in green:
"Good! You've got your heart back! Now I can hit you.
May all that glory the good King Arthur gave you
Prove efficacious now—if it ever can—
And save your neck." In rage Sir Gawain shouted,

WORDS TO OWN

efficacious (ef'i·kā'shəs) *adj.:* effective.

Crossing the Curriculum

Art

Many museums today preserve beautiful examples of arms and armor from medieval times. Among the objects in the Metropolitan Museum of Art's arms and armor collection, for example, are rapiers, halberds, daggers, hunting crossbows, shields, and full sets of armor. Have students present a picture of one of these items to the class and explain what makes it useful or beautiful, or design a weapon, creating their own decorative motifs.

Making the Connections

Cross-Cultural Connections: The Romance

Many romances from France and England are based on the Arthurian legends. In medieval Japan, romances developed around tales of the samurai, a warrior class who, like the medieval knights, were bound by a code of honor to their lord. Encourage students who grew up in other countries to describe romance literature from their homeland's culture.

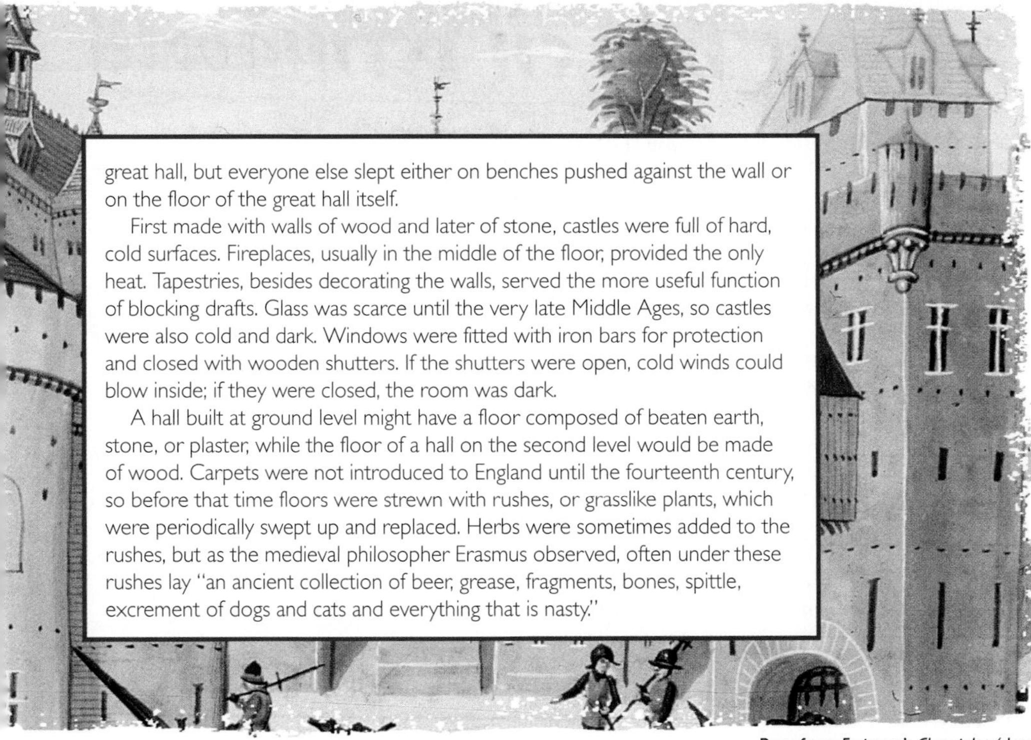

great hall, but everyone else slept either on benches pushed against the wall or on the floor of the great hall itself.

First made with walls of wood and later of stone, castles were full of hard, cold surfaces. Fireplaces, usually in the middle of the floor, provided the only heat. Tapestries, besides decorating the walls, served the more useful function of blocking drafts. Glass was scarce until the very late Middle Ages, so castles were also cold and dark. Windows were fitted with iron bars for protection and closed with wooden shutters. If the shutters were open, cold winds could blow inside; if they were closed, the room was dark.

A hall built at ground level might have a floor composed of beaten earth, stone, or plaster, while the floor of a hall on the second level would be made of wood. Carpets were not introduced to England until the fourteenth century, so before that time floors were strewn with rushes, or grasslike plants, which were periodically swept up and replaced. Herbs were sometimes added to the rushes, but as the medieval philosopher Erasmus observed, often under these rushes lay "an ancient collection of beer, grease, fragments, bones, spittle, excrement of dogs and cats and everything that is nasty."

Page from *Froissart's Chronicles* (detail). MS Fr. 2643, fol. 226v.

© cliché Bibliothèque Nationale de France, Paris.

"*Hit* me, hero! I'm right up to here with your threats!
Is it *you* that's the cringing coward after all?"
"Whoo!" said the man in green, "he's wrathful, too!
No pauses, then; I'll pay up my pledge at once,
I vow!"
He takes his stride to strike
And lifts his lip and brow;
It's not a thing Gawain can like,
For nothing can save him now!

He raises that ax up lightly and flashes it down,
And that blinding bit bites in at the knight's bare neck—
But hard as he hammered it down, it hurt him no more
Than to nick the nape of his neck, so it split the skin;
The sharp blade slit to the flesh through the shiny hide,
And red blood shot to his shoulders and spattered the ground.
And when Gawain saw his blood where it blinked in the snow
He sprang from the man with a leap to the length of a spear;
He snatched up his helmet swiftly and slapped it on,
Shifted his shield into place with a jerk of his shoulders,

B Elements of Literature

Romance

Point out to students that the number three is used in many fairy tales and romances—three brothers, three wishes, three tries. Here, the Green Knight prepares to make the third stroke, signaling the climax of the story.

C Elements of Literature

Romance

? In what ways is the action in this scene characteristic of a romance? [Possible answers: It appears as if good is pitted against evil. Both heroes appear superhuman, and there is life-and-death peril. The hero is tested more than once.]

D Elements of Literature

Alliteration

? What examples of alliteration do you find in these lines? [*b*linding, *b*it, *b*ites, *b*are; *k*night's, *n*eck; *h*ard, *h*e, *h*ammered, *h*urt, *h*im; *n*ick, *n*ape, *n*eck; *s*o, *s*plit, *s*kin]

Skill Link

Analyzing and Responding to a Critical Review

In *The Penguin Short History of English Literature,* Stephen Coote comments on the last scene in the story and compares Gawain to Adam: "Though [the Green Knight] claims to shrive Gawain, Gawain himself now realizes the depth of his guilt. Despite being the flower of chivalry, he is a 'type' or image of Adam—an ordinary man led to forget his trust in the armour of God by the wiles of a woman. Human excellence is marred by original sin and courtly values alone are no protection. Though Gawain can hope to be excused, the girdle itself remains a perpetual reminder of his weakness." Ask students to comment on this interpretation.

A Struggling Readers
Identifying Pronoun Antecedents

? What nouns do the words *he* and *it* refer to? [The first *he* refers to Gawain; the second *he* refers to the Green Knight. *It* refers to Gawain's "staunch and doughty stance."]

B Appreciating Language
Humor

? One aspect of this story that students may miss on a first reading is its humor. In what ways does the Green Knight sound lighthearted here? [Here, and elsewhere, his tone and words seem more suited to a chatty or informal exchange between good friends than to a moment of life and death. For example, the Green Knight speaks "merrily," saying something akin to "Don't be such a jerk!" He also adds that if he had wanted to, he could have taken Gawain's head off, and then, in humorous understatement, says that Gawain could reasonably be "cross" under such circumstances.]

C Reading Skills and Strategies
Identifying Cause and Effect

? To what specific actions of Gawain's does the Green Knight link each of his three strokes of the ax? [The first two strokes are feints because Gawain kept his vow to give his host anything he won during the day. However, on the third day, Gawain kept the Green Knight's sash, thus breaking his vow. The Green Knight nicks Sir Gawain on the third stroke because Gawain lacks only a little in loyalty and took the sash because he loved his life and wanted to protect himself against the magic of the Green Knight, not because he was in love with the Knight's wife.]

And snapped his sword out faster than sight; said boldly—
And, mortal born of his mother that he was,
There was never on earth a man so happy by half—
"No more strokes, my friend; you've had your swing!
I've stood one swipe of your ax without resistance;
If you offer me any more, I'll repay you at once
With all the force and fire I've got—as you
will see.
I take one stroke, that's all,
For that was the compact we
Arranged in Arthur's hall;
But now, no more for me!"

The Green Knight remained where he stood, relaxing on his ax—
Settled the shaft on the rocks and leaned on the sharp end—
And studied the young man standing there, shoulders hunched,
And considered that staunch° and doughty° stance he took,
Undaunted yet, and in his heart he liked it;
And then he said merrily, with a mighty voice—
With a roar like rushing wind he reproved the knight—
"Here, don't be such an ogre on your ground!
Nobody here has behaved with bad manners toward you
Or done a thing except as the contract said.
I owed you a stroke, and I've struck; consider yourself
Well paid. And now I release you from all further duties.
If I'd cared to hustle, it may be, perchance, that I might
Have hit somewhat harder, and then you might well be cross!
The first time I lifted my ax it was lighthearted sport,
I merely feinted and made no mark, as was right,
For you kept our pact of the first night with honor
And abided by your word and held yourself true to me,
Giving me all you owed as a good man should.
I feinted a second time, friend, for the morning
You kissed my pretty wife twice and returned me the kisses;
And so for the first two days, mere feints, nothing more
severe.
A man who's true to his word,
There's nothing he needs to fear;
You failed me, though, on the third
Exchange, so I've tapped you here.

"That sash you wear by your scabbard° belongs to me;
My own wife gave it to you, as I ought to know.
I know, too, of your kisses and all your words
And my wife's advances, for I myself arranged them.

175. staunch (stônch): steadfast. **doughty** (dout'ē): courageous.

199. scabbard (skab'ərd): case that holds the blade of a sword.

WORDS TO OWN
feinted (fānt'id) *v.*: pretended to strike.

Assessing Learning

Check Test: Questions and Answers

1. **How many times does the Green Knight raise his ax over Gawain's head?** [three times]
2. **Why doesn't the Green Knight kill Gawain?** [Gawain is courageous and honorable.]
3. **Why does the Green Knight nick Gawain in the neck?** [He punishes him for his weakness in accepting the green sash.]
4. **What part did the husband play in the temptation of Gawain?** [He arranged it.]
5. **How does Gawain feel about how he has acted?** [He deeply regrets his moment of cowardice.]

It was I who sent her to test you. I'm convinced
You're the finest man that ever walked this earth.
As a pearl is of greater price than dry white peas,
So Gawain indeed stands out above all other knights.
But you lacked a little, sir; you were less than loyal;
But since it was not for the sash itself or for lust
But because you loved your life, I blame you less."
Sir Gawain stood in a study° a long, long while,
So miserable with disgrace that he wept within,
And all the blood of his chest went up to his face
And he shrank away in shame from the man's gentle words.
The first words Gawain could find to say were these:
"Cursed be cowardice and covetousness both,
Villainy and vice that destroy all virtue!"
He caught at the knots of the girdle° and loosened them
And fiercely flung the sash at the Green Knight.
"There, there's my fault! The foul fiend vex it!
Foolish cowardice taught me, from fear of your stroke,
To bargain, covetous, and abandon my kind,
The selflessness and loyalty suitable in knights;
Here I stand, faulty and false, much as I've feared them,
Both of them, untruth and treachery; may they see sorrow
and care!
I can't deny my guilt;
My works shine none too fair!
Give me your good will
And henceforth I'll beware."

At that, the Green Knight laughed, saying graciously,
"Whatever harm I've had, I hold it amended
Since now you're confessed so clean, acknowledging sins
And bearing the plain penance of my point;
I consider you polished as white and as perfectly clean
As if you had never fallen since first you were born.
And I give you, sir, this gold-embroidered girdle,
For the cloth is as green as my gown. Sir Gawain, think
On this when you go forth among great princes;
Remember our struggle here; recall to your mind
This rich token. Remember the Green Chapel.
And now, come on, let's both go back to my castle
And finish the New Year's revels with feasting and joy,
not strife,
I beg you," said the lord,
And said, "As for my wife,
She'll be your friend, no more
A threat against your life."

210. stood in a study: stood thinking deeply.

217. girdle: sash.

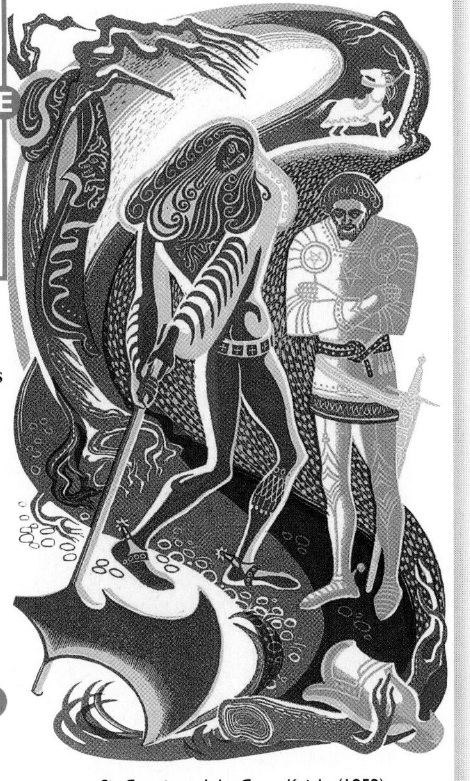

Sir Gawain and the Green Knight (1952) by Dorothea Braby. Golden Cockerel Press.

Rare Books and Manuscripts Division, New York Public Library. Astor, Lenox, and Tilden Foundations.

D Reading Skills and Strategies

Making Inferences

? What do you think is going through Gawain's mind at this point? Why is he now miserable and ashamed? [Possible answers: The Green Knight knows about Gawain's failure of honor and courage, and Gawain is ashamed at having been caught. He is ashamed that even though he has failed, the Green Knight considers him the finest man on earth.]

E Elements of Literature

Romance

? Why does Gawain throw off the sash? [Possible responses: The sash represents his lack of faith in his own courage *and* his failure of honor; to him, therefore, the sash is a reminder that he is not a perfect knight. Or he feels that the sash was deceptively acquired which is anathema to the perfect knight.]

F Literary and Cultural Connections

In the next part of the romance, Gawain refuses the lady's friendship and speaks out against women in general who have tempted men through the ages. He makes Biblical allusions to Adam being tempted by Eve, Solomon by many women, and David by Bathsheba. Nevertheless, Gawain wears the green sash ever after as a reminder of his own failing. The other knights, however, forgive him and wear similar sashes in his honor.

RESPONDING TO THE ART

Dorothea Braby (1909–) is an English wood engraver.
Activity. Have students compare the depictions of Gawain on pp. 159, 160, 161, and 165. Which style do they prefer, and why?

Making the Connections

Connecting to the Subject: "The Gift of Story"

To connect this selection to the uses of storytelling, you might open discussion with the following question:

- What makes this story so entertaining that it is still retold and reprinted today—even as an illustrated children's book? [It contains elements of fantasy (such as the head that reattaches itself and the Green Knight himself); it is suspenseful (such as when Gawain waits for the knight to approach, as well as when he bends under the ax); it contains elements of mystery (the true motive of the temptress is not revealed until the end). It contains humor, and it is highly visual. It is strongly moral.]

Connections

In this song, a modern-day speaker longs for a hero with the qualities traditionally associated with romance heroes: strength, courage, and shrewdeness. The longed-for hero also has elements of the superhuman or the ideal and, although keenly desired, he remains just out of reach.

A Struggling Readers
Summarizing

? How would you sum up this stanza? [Possible answer: The speaker is looking for a modern-day hero but does not know where to find one.]

B English Language Learners
Informal Language

Point out the use of *gotta* in this song. Explain that this is informal usage, common in everyday speech as well as in songs. Ask students what it means. ["got to" or "have to"] Ask students to make a list of the adjectives that follow this word and then sum up the type of hero the speaker wants to find. [He must be strong, fast, fresh from the fight, sure, soon, and larger than life. Possible answer: He is an ideal fantasy.]

C Elements of Literature
Romance

? How is the hero described, in the chorus, like the hero of a romance? [Possible answer: The person has to be very great, ideal, almost superhuman, "larger than life."]

D Elements of Literature
Tone

? What is the tone of this song? [desperate hope]

Connections — A Song

Holding Out for a Hero

words by **Dean Pitchford**

Where have all the good men gone,
And where are all the gods?
A Where's the street-wise Hercules to fight the rising odds?
Isn't there a white knight upon a fiery steed?
Late at night I toss, and I turn, and I dream of what I need.

Chorus:
I need a hero.
I'm holding out for a hero 'til the end of the night.
He's gotta be strong,
And he's gotta be fast,
B *And he's gotta be fresh from the fight.*
I need a hero.
C *I'm holding out for a hero 'til the morning light.*
He's gotta be sure,
And it's gotta be soon,
And he's gotta be larger than life.

Somewhere after midnight,
In my wildest fantasy,
Somewhere just beyond my reach,
D There's someone reaching back for me.
Racing on the thunder and rising with the heat,
It's gonna take a superman to sweep me off my feet.

Chorus

Up where the mountains meet the heavens above,
Out where the lightning splits the sea,
I could swear there is someone somewhere, watching me.

Through the wind and the chill and the rain,
And the storm and the flood,
I can feel his approach
Like a fire in my blood.

Chorus

King Arthur's Wood (c. late 19th century) by Elizabeth Adela Stanhope Forbes.

Connecting Across Texts

Connecting with *Sir Gawain and the Green Knight*

Ask students to apply the definition of the word *hero* in this song to Sir Gawain. [Students may say Gawain is a hero because he is a good man, a "street-wise Hercules" in strength and savvy. They might also say that Gawain is "larger than life" and a "superman" in his deeds and honor.]

Listening to Music

"Sir Lancelot and the Black Knight" by Rick Wakeman. Performed by Rick Wakeman

The legends of King Arthur have inspired all sorts of music, including quite a bit of rock 'n' roll. In 1975, following the success of such British rock "theme" albums as the Beatles' *Sergeant Pepper,* British rock composer Rick Wakeman composed an album called *Myths and Legends of the Round Table.*

Activity

After students read the selection, ask them to listen to Wakeman's rock song about another Arthurian hero, Sir Lancelot. Have them speculate about why Arthurian legends remain so popular, and then have them compare Lancelot's and Gawain's adventures. Finally, ask students why they think so many knights are identified by color. [With all the armor on, it was hard to see their faces.]

MAKING MEANINGS

First Thoughts

1. What do you think of the way the Green Knight and his wife trick and seduce Gawain? Do people today endure similar trials to test their values? Discuss.

> **Reading Check**
> a. Where does Gawain find the Green Knight, and what is the Knight doing?
> b. What happens with the first and second strokes of the Green Knight's ax?
> c. What happens the third time?
> d. Who does the Green Knight turn out to be?
> e. How does the Knight finally evaluate Gawain's character?

Shaping Interpretations

2. "A man who's true to his word, / There's nothing he needs to fear." The Green Knight says this to Gawain after he reveals how Gawain has been tricked. What do you think of this idea?
3. In what ways is Sir Gawain a superhuman **romance hero**? In what ways is he weak or flawed, just as a real person might be?
4. Describe the **symbolic** use of the color green in this story. (Green usually symbolizes hope; it is associated with the appearance of new life in the plant world.)
5. What **images** make the setting of the confrontation seem demonic? Do you think there is any **symbolism** suggested by this setting? Explain.
6. If you read the complete story of Gawain and the Green Knight, you will learn that King Arthur's wicked half sister, Morgan Le Fay, sent the Green Knight to test Gawain. What do you think—did Gawain prove himself to be a good knight or not? Do you think sexual morality is as important in Arthur's court as honesty and courage? Discuss your opinions.
7. How would you describe the writer's **tone** in this story? Is he entirely serious, or do you find moments of humor? Find passages in the story to support your responses.

Extending the Text

8. Do you think people long to find heroes like Gawain today? Do you think the singer of "Holding Out for a Hero" (see ***Connections***, page 166) is thinking of a Gawain type? Why?
9. This story has been read as an **allegory,** or symbolic story, of Christian redemption. From this point of view, who would be the sinner and who would be the Christ figure? What would be the terms of salvation?
10. Compare the romantic triangle in this story—the two men and the woman—with romantic triangles in contemporary fiction or movies.

ELEMENTS OF LITERATURE

Romances: Wishes Fulfilled

Romances are often too incredible for some modern readers, too lacking in the realistic details of life we have come to expect of literature. Yet in *Sir Gawain and the Green Knight,* we feel the gripping reality of sexual temptation and of life in the medieval castle.

The **romance** has a simple, inevitable plot: A hero battles an evil enemy and ultimately wins. As part of the story, the hero undertakes a **quest.** The quest usually has three stages: a dangerous journey, a central test or ordeal to determine if the hero truly has the qualities of a hero, and a return to the point from which the journey began.

> **Elements of Romance**
> - **a near-perfect hero**
> - **an evil enemy**
> - **a quest**
> - **a test of the hero**
> - **supernatural elements**
> - **good vs. evil**
> - **female figures who are usually maidens (in need of rescue), mothers, or crones**

In *Gawain* we have the model of the chivalric hero whose honor is being tested. This is a serious romance whose purpose is clearly to teach a moral lesson. Yet the hero does not have unlimited powers. Gawain is a human being who, like all of us, is limited in his moral and physical strength.

MAKING MEANINGS

First Thoughts [Respond]

1. Students may say that the trickery is unfair, that Gawain was set up. They may think that people today trick one another to get money or power but not to test moral strength.

Shaping Interpretations [Interpret]

2. Answers will vary. Students may say that the story proves this true.
3. Gawain is superhuman in his determination to act honorably and in his resolution to hide his fear. He displays such human qualities as susceptibility to passion, lying, and fear.
4. The Green Knight and the Green Chapel may be symbols of the return of life with each spring or new year. The Green Knight grants renewed life to Gawain.
5. There are thickets, rocks, crags—Gawain is heading *down*ward. There is a gravelike mound, a pool bubbling as if boiling. The place has a cave; it's overgrown with weeds. The setting suggests hell or the underworld.
6. Honesty and courage are certainly important. Some may say that Gawain did prove himself to be a good knight and that it was on the basis of his sexual morality. If he had not refused the wife, it seems certain he would have died. Or would he? On the other hand, he is tested on the basis of honesty, not sexual morality. It was his concealment of the magic sash that doomed him. Ironically, Camelot is eventually destroyed by the illicit affair and resultant duplicity of Sir Lancelot and Queen Guinevere.
7. Although the story is a moral tale, there are moments of humor, such as in the exaggerated grinding of the ax and Gawain's reflection on receiving his "Kingdom Come."

Extending the Text [Evaluate]

8. In some ways a hero like Gawain is needed today: He is courageous, honorable, flawed, and humble. He is also loyal to his king—even willing to give his life for him. The singer of "Holding Out for a Hero" seems to be awaiting a hero like Gawain.
9. Possible answer: Gawain would be the sinner and the Green Knight would be the Christ figure (although an ambiguous one). Salvation depends on a life of honor, admitting cowardice, dishonesty, or sexual transgression and promising atonement.
10. Romantic triangles in contemporary fiction and movies also involve temptation, lying, and rivalry. (They often do not involve redemption and forgiveness.) However, in contemporary fiction the female character is usually more independent and not the tool of her husband. In fact, the female figure may initiate the problem. Of course, contemporary stories tend to deal with more realistic issues and challenges, rather than idealistic tests of character.

> **Reading Check**
> a. Gawain meets the Green Knight at the Green Chapel, where the Knight is sharpening his ax.
> b. The Knight raises the ax twice, but twice he holds it back.
> c. The third time the Green Knight nicks Gawain's neck with the ax.
> d. The Green Knight turns out to have been Gawain's host and the husband of the woman who tempted him.
> e. The Knight judges Gawain to be pure.

Elements of Literature

Romances
Possible Answers

- *Sir Gawain:* flawed hero; a three-part quest; a test; supernatural elements; ambiguously evil enemy; female figure as temptress.
- *Beowulf:* all-good hero; evil enemy; a quest; supernatural elements; good versus evil; no women.
- "The Wife of Bath's Tale": flawed hero; enemy who is actually good; a quest; supernatural elements; no emphasis on good versus evil; female figures including maiden, mother, and crone.

Grading Timesaver

Rubrics for each Choices assignment appear on p. 103 in the *Portfolio Management System.*

Choices: Building Your Portfolio

1. **Writer's Notebook** Suggest that students begin by writing a brief summary or outline of their chosen contemporary story.
2. **Expository Writing** For this activity, suggest that students use realistic, contemporary settings. For example, how would the story be displaced if it were set in a modern large city?
3. **Expository Writing** Remind students to develop their ideas fully, not only by providing examples to prove their points but by fully explaining the relationship of those examples to the points they make.
4. **Critical Thinking/Speaking** Assign students to different groups or panels. Have students discuss the questions informally for a few minutes, examining works in contemporary culture, before assuming roles as "panelists" who adhere to and support only one particular viewpoint.

Romances are still a popular form found in today's novels, movies, television shows, and comics. The *Indiana Jones* movies and the *Star Trek* TV episodes are essentially romances, as are these books, which you may have read: C. S. Lewis's *The Chronicles of Narnia,* many of Lloyd Alexander's books, Brian Jacques's *Redwall* series, J.R.R. Tolkien's *The Lord of the Rings,* and L. Frank Baum's *The Wizard of Oz.*

Romances are traditionally set in the past, which is where the Wife of Bath sets her story: "When good King Arthur ruled in ancient days." Today, romances may also be set in the future, as in the *Star Wars* movies. Through this journey to a remote time or place, the hero learns something of value.

Comparing romances. As part of a group, discuss the Gawain story as a romance. Next, expand your discussion to include other works, using a chart like the one below. Present your ideas to the rest of the class, using specific examples to support your conclusions.

Work	Romance Elements
Sir Gawain	
Beowulf	
"The Wife of Bath's Tale"	
Current movie or TV show	
Novel	

Choices: Building Your Portfolio

Writer's Notebook

1. Collecting Ideas for a Comparison-Contrast Essay

When you write your essay of comparison and contrast for the Writer's Workshop on page 185, you might want to compare one of these medieval stories with a modern story. *Sir Gawain and the Green Knight* would be a good medieval story to use as part of your comparison-contrast. Take notes now on the ways Gawain's experiences are like or unlike the tests that the modern hero must undergo. Be sure to note how each story uses the elements of romance listed on page 167. If your modern story is far from a romance, note how it distorts the romance elements. Save your notes.

Expository Writing

2. Gawain Goes to Hollywood

When the elements of a romance story (or myth) are adapted to a more modern setting, we say that the story has been "displaced." In two or three paragraphs, discuss how *Sir Gawain* might be displaced into a contemporary movie or TV show. Think about the story's **plot, characterization,** and **theme.**

Expository Writing

3. The Game of Love

In the twelfth century, rules governing the "game" of love were actually set down by a court of love in France. Four of the rules are listed below. Do you agree or disagree with these "rules"? Have the rules of love changed? In an essay, explain your position.

iii No one can be bound by a double love.
xiv The easy attainment of love makes it of little value; difficulty of attainment makes it prized.
xvii A new love puts to flight an old one.
xix If love diminishes, it quickly fails and rarely revives.

Critical Thinking / Speaking

4. Roles for Women

In romance literature, women are often represented as (a) maidens, (b) mothers, (c) temptresses, or (d) crones. Is that true in *Sir Gawain?* Do these character roles for women still exist today? Prepare a panel discussion on this issue. Defend your ideas with specific evidence from current fiction and movies, as well as from *Sir Gawain.*

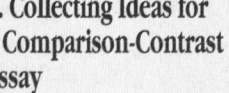

Sir Thomas Malory

(1405?–1471)

The historical identity of Sir Thomas Malory, the author of Britain's most famous work on King Arthur, is almost as uncertain as the identity of the hero of his *Le Morte Darthur.* All we know for sure about Malory is that he was a knight familiar with chivalric romances who was writing in the years 1469–1470. We know this from a sort of postscript that appears in the manuscript of Malory's work that William Caxton printed in 1485. In this postscript, Malory also asks his readers to pray for his deliverance, suggesting that he was in prison during some of the time he was writing his stories about Arthur.

Since the fifteenth century, scholars have been trying to find out more about the actual person who wrote the work Caxton entitled *Le Morte Darthur.* At one time as many as five different "historical" Malorys were proposed. However, most scholars have come to accept the Thomas Malory born in Warwickshire as the most likely author of *Le Morte Darthur.*

This Warwickshire Malory served in France during the Hundred Years' War and apparently fought at the siege of Calais in 1436. A few years later he married a woman named Elizabeth, who bore him a son. Sir Thomas was elected to Parliament at least once and died in 1471, perhaps from the plague.

The record of this aristocratic war hero, however, also contains a series of arrests for theft, burglary, and assault, including the robbing of an abbey in which he supposedly broke eighteen doors and roughed up the monks.

But the charges against Malory were merely accusations, and there is no record of any trials or convictions. The late fifteenth century was a time of great political partisanship and civil disorder, so it is very possible that Malory's imprisonment was politically motivated. He might have backed the wrong side in a political conflict.

The Arthur in Malory's work is not the historical sixth-century general who helped his fellow Britons defend themselves against the invading Saxons. No, Malory's Arthur is a consolidation of later legends that developed in England and on the Continent. Using Celtic and Continental sources, Malory created a mythic Arthur who later became the very embodiment of British values.

Le Morte Darthur, coming as it does at the end of the fifteenth century, serves as a kind of literary swan song to the feudal order of the Middle Ages, with its castles, knights, and chivalric codes. Malory's readers lived in a different world. Cities were growing, and money and competition were replacing the old feudal ways of barter and mutual obligation. Something in the chivalric order that Malory portrayed, however, seems to have answered a longing in his audience for a more orderly world.

In Malory's mythic form, Arthur has the mysterious birth typical of the romance hero. His childhood initiation—pulling a magic sword from a rock—points to his kinship with such mythic and romance heroes as the Greek Theseus and the German Siegfried. His strange death, departure, and promised return also place him among other "once and future kings"—heroes whose return is always hoped for.

The Arthurian tales were carried into the Elizabethan Age. They were resurrected in the nineteenth century by Alfred, Lord Tennyson, in his group of poems called *Idylls of the King* (see pages 802 and 826). Tennyson brought Arthur and his knights back at a time when the English nation, embarked upon empire, needed a reminder of its heroic past and special destiny.

The Arthurian legend was revived yet again in the twentieth century by T. H. White in his best-selling book *The Once and Future King* (1958). Though White's treatment of the Arthurian material is ironic (in keeping with an ironic age), it still inspired the 1960s musical play and movie *Camelot,* which captures the romantic imagination of another generation struggling with disillusion and social disorder.

go.hrw.com
LEO 12-2

Objectives

1. Read and interpret the story
2. Analyze the qualities and actions of a romance hero
3. Use context clues to determine word meaning
4. Express understanding through writing and art

Skills

Literary
- Analyze the qualities and actions of a romance hero

Writing
- Collect ideas for a compare/contrast essay
- Create a translation

Art
- Visually represent a scene

Planning

- **Block Schedule**
  Block Scheduling Lesson Plans with Pacing Guide
- **Traditional Schedule**
  Lesson Plans Including Strategies for English-Language Learners
- **One-Stop Planner**
  CD-ROM with Test Generator

Browsing in the Files

About the Author. Little was known about Malory's life until the 1920s, when a cache of relevant documents was unearthed at the Public Record Office in London. These documents—mostly arrest reports for various minor crimes—revealed, more than anything else, that Malory had quite a knack for getting into trouble.

Resources: Print and Media

Reading
- *Graphic Organizers for Active Reading,* p. 10
- *Audio CD Library*
  Disc 3, Track 3

Writing and Language
- *Daily Oral Grammar*
  Transparency 7

Assessment
- *Formal Assessment,* p. 27
- *Portfolio Management System,* p. 105
- *Test Generator (One-Stop Planner CD-ROM)*

Internet
- go.hrw.com (keyword: LEO 12-2)

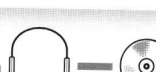

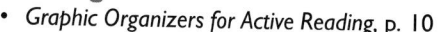

Summary ■■■

The selection opens when, in a dream, Sir Gawain warns King Arthur not to go to war with his illegitimate son and enemy, Mordred. As a treaty between the father and son is about to be arranged, a knight, alarmed by a snake, draws his sword and fighting breaks out. After a fierce battle, only Mordred, Arthur, and the brothers Lucan and Bedivere survive. Angry and impatient, Arthur attacks Mordred. Before succumbing, however, Mordred mortally wounds Arthur. Arthur then orders Bedivere to throw his bejeweled sword into a lake. Twice Bedivere fails to obey because he covets the sword. Finally, shamed by Arthur, he throws the sword into the water. A mysterious hand emerges, shakes the sword three times, and disappears. Arthur then departs for Avilion in a barge piloted by a party of wailing women, perhaps to return at some future time.

Before You Read

THE DEATH OF ARTHUR

Make the Connection

Heroes That Never Die

People have always hated to let go of their heroes. In fact, many cultures tell stories in which the hero promises to return in an hour of need to help the people once again. How do we try to keep our heroes alive? We build statues to them and record their portraits on canvas, coins, and film. But most of all we tell those stories—stories that we hope will keep our heroes and their values alive in the memories of future generations.

Elements of Literature

The Romance Hero

Malory's Arthur is in many ways the archetypal, or typical, romance hero. He is born under mysterious circumstances, grows up in obscurity, and undergoes a childhood initiation involving a magic weapon. In his maturity he fights to defeat evil and promote peace. Throughout his life he is aided by magic weapons and wise mentors. Mysterious events surround his departure from this world, suggesting that he may return when his people need him the most.

If you remember your old myths and fairy tales, you'll recognize these elements of Arthur's story. Even movies and cartoons today use these archetypes of the romance hero. (Check out the story of Superman's origins.)

A **romance hero** is a larger-than-life figure who usually has mysterious origins and in the course of his life performs extraordinary deeds with the aid of magic forces.

Reading Skills and Strategies

Using Context Clues

Malory tells his story of Arthur in the language of the fifteenth century, which is full of archaic expressions. When we say a word is **archaic,** we mean it is not in use. Many of the archaic words in the story are footnoted. When you come across other archaic words that are strange to you, search each word's context—the words surrounding it—to see if you can find a clue to its meaning. It is in part the strangeness of the archaic language that gives this story its magic. "Oddly enough," the American writer John Steinbeck once said of Malory's tales, "I knew the words from whispering them to myself."

Background

Malory's *Le Morte Darthur* contains a series of tales about the birth, education, adventures, and death (or disappearance) of King Arthur. In the early tales, Arthur persuades his knights to unite in the fellowship of the Round Table and dedicate themselves to the chivalric code of honor. For a while, Arthur's vision is realized, and justice prevails in the kingdom. But human frailties, including Arthur's own, gradually corrupt the fellowship of the Round Table. Worst, perhaps, is the betrayal of Lancelot, Arthur's best knight, who falls in love with Queen Guinevere. Arthur and his Round Table become vulnerable to evil forces, personified by Sir Mordred, who is Arthur's illegitimate son.

In the last episode of Malory's manuscript, Arthur meets his wicked son in battle.

Arthur mortally wounded, from *Roman du Saint Graal* (early 14th century). Add. 10294 fol. 93.

British Art Library, London.

Skill Link

Monitoring and Modifying Reading Strategies

Most students will have difficulty reading Malory's prose and will need to employ a variety of reading strategies to comprehend the archaic vocabulary and syntax. Recommend the following step-by-step approach:

1. Read short segments of the text aloud with a partner or in a small group.
2. Adjust your reading rate and the size of the segments to your level of comprehension.
3. After reading each segment, identify any unfamiliar words or unusual sentence structures.
4. Use context, footnotes, and discussions with peers to figure out the meanings of unfamiliar words.
5. Work with others to identify the subject, verb, and object of each sentence.
6. Recast the archaic syntax into more modern structures.

The Death of Arthur
from Le Morte Darthur
Sir Thomas Malory

So upon Trinity Sunday at night king Arthur dreamed a wonderful dream. And in his dream him seemed that he saw upon a chafflet[1] a chair, and the chair was fast to a wheel, and thereupon sat king Arthur in the richest cloth of gold that might be made. And the king thought there was under him, far from him, an hideous deep black water, and therein was all manner of serpents and worms and wild beasts foul and horrible. And suddenly the king thought that the wheel turned up-so-down, and he fell among the serpents, and every beast took him by a limb. And then the king cried as he lay in his bed, "Help! help!" and then knights, squires and yeomen awaked the king, and then he was so amazed that he wist not where he was.

And then so he awaked until it was nigh day, and then he fell on slumbering again, not sleeping nor thoroughly waking. So the king seemed verily that there came sir Gawain unto him with a number of fair ladies with him. So when king Arthur saw him he said, "Welcome, my sister's son, I weened ye had been dead! And now I see thee on live, much am I beholden unto Almighty Jesu. Ah, fair nephew, what been these ladies that hither be come with you?"

"Sir," said sir Gawain, "all these be ladies for whom I have foughten for, when I was man living. And all these are tho[2] that I did battle for in righteous quarrels, and God hath given them that grace at their great prayer, because I did battle for them for their right, that they should bring me hither unto you. Thus much hath given me leave God for to warn you of your death: for and ye fight as to-morn[3] with sir Mordred, as ye both have assigned, doubt ye not ye shall be slain, and the most party of your people on both parties.[4] And for the great grace and goodness that Almighty Jesu hath unto you, and for pity of you and many mo[5] other good men there shall be slain, God hath sent me to you of his special grace to give you warning that in no wise ye do battle as to-morn, but that ye take a treatise[6] for a month day. And proffer you largely,[7] so that to-morn ye put in a delay. For within a month shall come sir Lancelot with all his noble knights, and rescue you worshipfully and slay sir Mordred and all that ever will hold with him."

Then sir Gawain and all the ladies vanished, and anon the king called upon his knights, squires, and yeomen, and charged them wightly[8] to fetch his noble lords and wise bishops unto him. And when they were come the king told them of his avision,[9] that sir Gawain had told him and warned him that and[10] he fought on the morn, he should be slain. Then the king commanded sir Lucan the Butler and his brother sir Bedivere the Bold, with two bishops with them, and charged them in any wise to take a treatise for a month day with sir Mordred: "And spare not. Proffer him lands and goods as much as ye think reasonable."

So then they departed and came to sir Mordred where he had a grim host of an hundred thousand men, and there they entreated sir Mordred long time. And at the last sir Mordred was agreed for to have Cornwall and Kent by king Arthur's days; and after that all England, after the days of king Arthur.

Then were they condescend[11] that king Arthur and sir Mordred should meet betwixt both their hosts, and every of them should bring fourteen persons. And so they came with this word unto Arthur. Then said he, "I am glad that this is done." And so he went into the field.

1. **chafflet:** scaffold.
2. **tho:** those.
3. **for . . . to-morn:** if you fight tomorrow.
4. **most . . . parties:** most part of your people on both sides.
5. **mo:** more.
6. **treatise:** treaty or truce.
7. **proffer you largely:** make generous offers.
8. **wightly:** quickly.
9. **avision:** dream.
10. **and:** if.
11. **condescend:** agreed.

A Struggling Readers
Summarizing

To help students get into the scene, explain that the first paragraph is an account of a dream King Arthur has. Ask students what animals the king imagines attack him. [serpents, worms, and wild beasts] After Arthur is awakened from this nightmare, he falls asleep again and has another dream. Ask students to read the next three paragraphs and summarize the dream. [Possible answer: Arthur imagines that Gawain approaches him with a number of fair ladies and warns him not to fight Mordred.]

B Reading Skills and Strategies
Using Context Clues

? What context clues might you use to figure out the meaning of *weened?* [*Weened* follows the subject *I* and ends in *-ed*, so it is probably a past-tense verb. *Weened* is followed by, roughly, "you were dead," so it may mean "thought." Or it could mean "believed," since it is followed by a sentence that says, "Now I see thee on live" or "Now I see you alive."]

C Elements of Literature
Romance Hero

? How does this passage present Arthur as a romance hero? [He has a dream, or vision, which warns him not only of his death but of future events, such as the coming of Lancelot. Arthur also acts on the basis of this vision, suggesting that he expects supernatural powers to be aligned with his wishes and his well-being.]

Reaching All Students

Struggling Readers
The archaic language in this text will be overwhelming. For this reason, it would be helpful, first, to use the audio disc, and second, to pair readers and to suggest they stop reading at frequent intervals to paraphrase, summarize, or ask and answer questions about what they have read.

English Language Learners
Pair native speakers with students acquiring English. All students should understand that this selection will seem foreign and requires the active use of reading strategies. For other strategies for English language learners, see

- *Lesson Plans Including Strategies for English-Language Learners*

Advanced Learners
Have students analyze sentences that are ungrammatical in terms of today's standards. For example, they might identify sentences with object pronouns used as subjects, or repeated as both subjects and objects. Then have students "translate" the sentences into modern standard English. Students might decide if reading archaic constructions helps take them back to an older time and place. See the Steinbeck remark on p. 170.

A Critical Thinking

Making Judgments

? Why does this battle start the way it does? [Possible answers: It is a tragic mistake. It is an ironic misunderstanding. It is the result of too many people being all too ready to fight. The snake suggests the Garden of Eden and the Fall.]

B English Language Learners

Archaic Grammar

Not only is Malory's vocabulary archaic, but so, too, is his grammar and sentence structure. Here, for example, three negatives are piled up in a single sentence. Ask students how this would be phrased in standard modern English. [Never since that time has there been a more doleful battle in any Christian land . . . .]

C Elements of Literature

Characterization

? What do Arthur's words reveal about him? [Possible answers: He feels compassion for the knights who have been loyal to him and died. He feels the great tragedy of the day's events. He feels the need to avenge the deaths of those loyal to him.]

D Struggling Readers

Getting the Main Idea

To help students follow the action, reread the dialogue here aloud. From just these words alone, students should infer that the king and Mordred are starting hand-to-hand combat. Then encourage them to read on to discover whose helmet is pierced by a sword. [Arthur's]

And when king Arthur should depart he warned all his host that and they see any sword drawn, "look ye come on fiercely and slay that traitor, sir Mordred, for I in no wise trust him." In like wise sir Mordred warned his host "that and ye see any manner of sword drawn, look that ye come on fiercely and so slay all that ever before you standeth, for in no wise I will not trust for this treatise." And in the same wise said sir Mordred unto his host: "for I know well my father will be avenged upon me."

And so they met as their appointment was, and were agreed and accorded thoroughly. And wine was fetched, and they drank together. Right so came out an adder of a little heath bush, and it stung a knight in the foot. And so when the knight felt him so stung, he looked down and saw the adder; and anon he drew his sword to slay the adder, and thought none other harm. And when the host on both parties saw that sword drawn, then they blew bemes,[12] trumpets and horns, and shouted grimly, and so both hosts dressed them[13] togethers. And king Arthur took his horse and said, "Alas, this unhappy day!" and so rode to his party, and sir Mordred in like wise.

And never since was there never seen a more dolefuller battle in no Christian land, for there was but rushing and riding, foining[14] and striking, and many a grim word was there spoken of either to other, and many a deadly stroke. But ever king Arthur rode throughout the battle[15] of sir Mordred many times and did full nobly, as a noble king should do, and at all times he fainted never. And sir Mordred did his devoir[16] that day and put himself in great peril.

And thus they fought all the long day, and never stinted till the noble knights were laid to the cold earth. And ever they fought still till it was near night, and by then was there an hundred thousand laid dead upon the earth. Then was king Arthur wood wroth[17] out of measure, when he saw his people so slain from him. And so he looked about him and could see no mo of all his host and good knights left, no mo on live but two knights: t'one was sir Lucan de Butler and his brother sir Bedivere; and yet they were full sore wounded.

"Jesu mercy!" said the king, "where are all my noble knights become? Alas, that ever I should see this doleful day! For now," said king Arthur, "I am come to mine end. But would to God," said he, "that I wist now where were that traitor sir Mordred that hath caused all this mischief."

Then king Arthur looked about and was ware where stood sir Mordred leaning upon his sword among a great heap of dead men. "Now, give me my spear," said king Arthur unto sir Lucan, "for yonder I have espied the traitor that all this woe hath wrought."

"Sir, let him be," said sir Lucan, "for he is unhappy.[18] And if ye pass this unhappy day ye shall be right well revenged upon him. Good lord, remember ye of your night's dream and what the spirit of sir Gawain told you to-night, and yet God of His great goodness hath preserved you hitherto. And for God's sake, my lord, leave off this, for, blessed be God, ye have won the field. For yet we been here three on live, and with Sir Mordred is not one of live. And therefore if ye leave off now, this wicked day of Destiny is past!"

"Now tide[19] me death, tide me life," said the king, "now I see him yonder alone, he shall never escape mine hands! For at a better avail shall I never have him."

"God speed you well!" said sir Bedivere.

Then the king got his spear in both his hands, and ran toward sir Mordred, crying and saying, "Traitor, now is thy death-day come!"

And when sir Mordred saw king Arthur he ran until him with his sword drawn in his hand, and there king Arthur smote sir Mordred under the shield, with a foin of his spear, throughout the body more than a fathom. And when sir Mordred felt that he had his death's wound he thrust himself with the might that he had up to the burr of king Arthur's spear, and right so he smote his father, king Arthur, with his sword holding in both his hands, upon the side of the head, that the sword pierced the helmet and the tay[20] of the

12. **bemes:** bugles.
13. **dressed them:** prepared to come.
14. **foining:** lunging.
15. **battle:** battalion.
16. **devoir:** knightly duty.
17. **wood wroth:** mad with rage.
18. **unhappy:** unlucky for you.
19. **tide:** betide.
20. **tay:** edge.

Using Students' Strengths

Logical/Mathematical Learners

Have students create a detailed sequence chain showing the events in this story. They might also project the actual amount of time elapsed in each separate scene or action. When they are finished, have students use color coding or shading to identify events that are realistic and events that are unrealistic or fantastic.

Visual Learners

Have students compare and contrast Malory's account of Arthur's death with the account in a movie. Students should consider not only events but also character, mood, theme, language, texture, and overall impact. They should also analyze what is gained and what is lost in each medium. If time permits, allow students to show an excerpt from the film to the class.

brain. And therwith Mordred dashed down stark dead to the earth.

And noble king Arthur fell in a swough to the earth, and there he swooned oftentimes, and sir Lucan and sir Bedivere oft-times hove him up. And so weakly betwixt them they led him to a little chapel not far from the sea, and when the king was there, him thought him reasonably eased.

Then heard they people cry in the field. "Now go thou, sir Lucan" said the king, "and do me to wit[21] what betokens that noise in the field." So sir Lucan departed, for he was grievously wounded in many places. And so as he yode[22] he saw and hearkened by the moonlight how that pillers[23] and robbers were come into the field to pill and to rob many a full noble knight of brooches and bees[24] and of many a good ring and many a rich jewel. And who that were not dead all out, there they slew them for their harness and their riches.

When sir Lucan understood this work he came to the king as soon as he might, and told him all what he had heard and seen. "Therefore by my rede,"[25] said sir Lucan, "it is best that we bring you to some town."

"I would it were so," said the king, "but I may not stand, my head works so. Ah, sir Lancelot!" said king Arthur, "this day have I sore missed thee! And alas, that ever I was against thee! For now have I my death, whereof sir Gawain me warned in my dream."

Then sir Lucan took up the king t'one party and sir Bedivere the other party. And in the lifting up the king swooned, and in the lifting sir Lucan fell in a swoon, that part of his guts fell out of his body, and therewith the noble knight his heart burst. And when the king awoke he beheld sir Lucan, how he lay foaming at the mouth and part of his guts lay at his feet.

"Alas," said the king, "this is to me a full heavy sight, to see this noble duke so die for my sake, for he would have holpen me that had more need of help than I! Alas, that he would not complain him, for his heart was so set to help me. Now Jesu have mercy upon his soul!"

21. **do me to wit:** let me know.
22. **yode:** walked.
23. **pillers:** plunderers.
24. **bees:** bracelets.
25. **rede:** advice.

British Art Library, London.

Bedivere returning Excalibur to the lake upon the death of Arthur, from *Roman du Saint Graal* (early 14th century). Add. 10294 fol. 94.

Then sir Bedivere wept for the death of his brother.

"Now leave this mourning and weeping, gentle knight," said the king, "for all this will not avail me. For wit thou well, and I might live myself, the death of sir Lucan would grieve me evermore. But my time hieth fast," said the king. "Therefore," said king Arthur unto sir Bedivere, "take thou here Excaliber,[26] my good sword, and go with it to yonder water's side. And when thou comest there, I charge thee throw my sword in that water, and come again and tell me what thou seest there."

"My lord," said sir Bedivere, "your commandment shall be done, and lightly[27] bring you word again." So sir Bedivere departed. And by the way

26. **Excaliber:** Arthur's sword, given to him by the mysterious Lady of the Lake.
27. **lightly:** quickly.

E Reading Skills and Strategies
Using Context Clues

? What does the word *swough* mean? [faint; swoon; weak, dizzy state] **How do you know?** [Possible answers: Earlier context revealed that Mordred's sword pierced Arthur's skull, so the reader expects Arthur to swoon or fall. The words "fell . . . to the earth" and "swooned" are also clues.]

F Reading Skills and Strategies
Making Inferences

? Why does Lucan want to take Arthur to "some town"? [Possible answer: Looters are sacking the battlefield. They are even killing the wounded in order to strip them of their valuables. Lucan fears Arthur will be attacked.]

G Vocabulary Note
Word Origins

Guts, meaning "belly" or "intestines," comes from an Old English word meaning "to pour" or "gush out." Today, people tend to use the word *guts* informally; in formal writing, they might use a word like *entrails* or *intestines*. Ask students to name another meaning for *guts* and to speculate on how it might relate to the intestines or belly. [Possible answers: *Guts* means "courage" or "perseverance." It might once have been thought that the seat of bravery or fortitude lay in the guts.]

H Elements of Literature
Romance Hero

Call attention to the gloss explaining Excaliber. Then ask which details suggest a romance hero. [The romance hero is aided by magic weapons. The Lady of the Lake is mysterious; perhaps she has served in the role of wise mentor. There is a mysterious purpose to Arthur's request: He seems to anticipate an unusual result.]

Skill Link

Analyzing Time Frame and Setting

Remind students that a **time frame** is the period of time over which a story takes place. This story begins with dreams and visions that make it hard to determine precise times, but the action then moves rapidly and concretely to the meeting with Mordred, and just as rapidly and concretely into the battle scene.

Activity

Have students work on these questions in small groups.

1. The end of the story returns to the dreamlike and imprecise time frame of the beginning. The exact time of Arthur's death—or even the fact of his death—is impossible to ascertain. How does this add to the appeal of the story?
2. Are any aspects of the setting difficult to visualize or imagine as real? What effect does this have on your feelings about this legend?

(A) Elements of Literature

Romance Hero

? How do these lines suggest that the sword belongs to a romance hero? [This is a mysterious and supernatural event. The sword is shaken three times. Three is a number often found in fairy tales, myths, and lore, and it seems to give some extra special and mystical significance to the event. Arthur seems mysteriously to have known ahead of time that something like this would happen.]

(B) Elements of Literature

Imagery

? What do the details help you see and hear? [A crowded little barge is near the shore; it is filled with women in black hoods, among whom is a queen. They wail—probably a kind of keening for the dead.] **What mood do these images create?** [They create a somber, eerie mood. They raise questions in readers' minds: Where did the women come from? How did they know to come? Who is the queen?]

(C) Critical Thinking

Making Predictions

? What will happen to Arthur? [Possible answers: He will die. Or he will apparently die but not really, for in Avilion he will be "healed of his grievous wound." Or he will disappear now, and no one will ever be certain what became of him. Or he will live only in the imagination of those who loved, served, and, later, wrote or read about him.]

he beheld that noble sword, and the pommel and the haft was all precious stones. And then he said to himself, "If I throw this rich sword in the water, thereof shall never come good, but harm and loss." And then sir Bedivere hid Excaliber under a tree. And so as soon as he might he came again unto the king and said he had been at the water and had thrown the sword into the water.

"What saw thou there?" said the king.

"Sir," he said, "I saw nothing but waves and winds."

"That is untruly said of thee," said the king, "and therefore go thou lightly again, and do my commandment. As thou art to me lief[28] and dear, spare not, but throw it in."

Then sir Bedivere returned again and took the sword in his hand; and yet him thought sin and shame to throw away that noble sword. And so eft[29] he hid the sword and returned again and told the king that he had been at the water and done his commandment.

"What sawest thou there?" said the king.

"Sir," he said, "I saw nothing but waters wap and waves wan."

"Ah, traitor unto me and untrue," said king Arthur, "now hast thou betrayed me twice! Who would ween that thou that hast been to me so lief and dear, and also named so noble a knight, that thou would betray me for the riches of this sword? But now go again lightly; for thy long tarrying putteth me in great jeopardy of my life, for I have taken cold. And but if thou do now as I bid thee, if ever I may see thee, I shall slay thee mine own hands, for thou wouldst for my rich sword see me dead."

(A) Then sir Bedivere departed and went to the sword and lightly took it up, and so he went unto the water's side. And there he bound the girdle about the hilts, and threw the sword as far into the water as he might. And there came an arm and an hand above the water, and took it and cleight it, and shook it thrice and brandished, and then vanished with the sword into the water.

So sir Bedivere came again to the king and told him what he saw. "Alas," said the king, "help me hence, for I dread me I have tarried over long."

(B) Then sir Bedivere took the king upon his back and so went with him to the water's side. And when they were there, even fast by the bank hoved a little barge with many fair ladies in it, and among them all was a queen, and all they had black hoods. And all they wept and shrieked when they saw king Arthur.

"Now put me into that barge," said the king. And so he did softly, and there received him three ladies with great mourning. And so they set them down, and in one of their laps king Arthur laid his head.

And then the queen said, "Ah, my dear brother, why have ye tarried so long from me? Alas, this wound on your head hath caught over much cold!" And anon they rowed fromward the land, and sir Bedivere beheld all tho ladies go froward him. Then sir Bedivere cried and said,

"Ah, my lord Arthur, what shall become of me, now ye go from me and leave me here alone among mine enemies?"

(C) "Comfort thyself," said the king, "and do as well as thou mayest, for in me is no trust for to trust in. For I must into the vale of Avilion[30] to heal me of my grievous wound. And if thou hear nevermore of me, pray for my soul!"

But ever the queen and ladies wept and shrieked that it was pity to hear. And as soon as sir Bedivere had lost the sight of the barge he wept and wailed, and so took[31] the forest and went all that night.

And in the morning he was ware, betwixt two holts hoar,[32] of a chapel and an hermitage. Then was sir Bedivere fain, and thither he went, and when he came into the chapel he saw where lay an hermit groveling on all fours, fast thereby a tomb was new graven. When the hermit saw sir Bedivere he knew him well, for he was but little tofore Bishop of Canterbury that sir Mordred flemed.[33]

"Sir," said sir Bedivere, "what man is there here interred that ye pray so fast for?"

"Fair son," said the hermit, "I wot not verily but by deeming. But this same night, at midnight,

28. **lief:** beloved.
29. **eft:** again.
30. **Avilion:** legendary island, sometimes identified with the earthly Paradise.
31. **took:** took to.
32. **holts hoar:** old thickets.
33. **flemed:** banished.

Assessing Learning

Check Test: True-False

1. Sir Gawain is alive at the beginning of this story. [False]
2. The battle with Mordred begins by accident. [True]
3. The battle has no decisive winner. [True]
4. Sir Bedivere keeps Excaliber for himself. [False]
5. At the end of the selection, Arthur is dead and buried. [False]

here came a number of ladies and brought here a dead corpse and prayed me to inter him. And here they offered an hundred tapers, and they gave me a thousand besants."[34]

"Alas," said sir Bedivere, "that was my lord king Arthur, which lieth here graven in this chapel." Then sir Bedivere swooned. And when he awoke he prayed the hermit that he might abide with him still, there to live with fasting and prayers: "For from hence will I never go," said sir Bedivere, "by my will, but all the days of my life here to pray for my lord Arthur."

"Sir, ye are welcome to me," said the hermit, "for I know you better than ye ween that I do: for ye are sir Bedivere the Bold, and the full noble duke sir Lucan de Butler was your brother." Then sir Bedivere told the hermit all as ye have heard tofore, and so he beleft with the hermit that was beforehand Bishop of Canterbury. And there sir Bedivere put upon him poor clothes, and served the hermit full lowly in fasting and in prayers.

Thus of Arthur I find no more written in books that been authorized, nother more of the very certainty of his death heard I never read. But thus was he led away in a ship wherein were three queens; that one was king Arthur sister, queen Morgan le Fay, the tother was queen of North Wales, and the third was the queen of the Waste Lands. Also there was dame Ninive, the chief lady of the lake, which had wedded sir Pelleas, the good knight; and this lady had done much for king Arthur. And this dame Ninive would never suffer sir Pelleas to be in no place where he should be in danger of his life, and so he lived unto the uttermost of his days with her in great rest.

Now more of the death of king Arthur could I never find, but that these ladies brought him to his grave, and such one was interred there which **D** the hermit bore witness that sometime was Bishop of Canterbury. But yet the hermit knew not in certain that he was verily the body of king Arthur; for this tale sir Bedivere, a knight of the Table Round, made it to be written.

Yet some men say in many parts of England that king Arthur is not dead, but had by the will of our Lord Jesu into another place. And men say that he shall come again, and he shall win the Holy Cross.[35] Yet I will not say that it shall be so, **E** but rather I would say: here in this world he changed his life. And many men say that there is written upon his tomb this verse:

HIC IACET ARTHURUS, REX QUONDAM REXQUE FUTURUS.[36]

And thus leave I here sir Bedivere with the hermit that dwelled that time in a chapel besides Glastonbury, and there was his hermitage. And so they lived in prayers and fastings and great abstinence.

And when queen Guenevere understood that king Arthur was dead and all the noble knights, sir Mordred and all the remnant, then she stole away with five ladies with her, and so she went to Amesbury. And there she let make herself a nun, and weared white clothes and black, and great penance she took upon her, as ever did sinful woman in this land. And never creature could make her merry, but ever she lived in fasting, prayers, and alms-deeds, that all manner of people marvelled how virtuously she was changed.

34. besants: *bezants*, gold coins of Byzantium.

35. Holy Cross: cross on which Jesus was crucified.
36. Latin for "Here lies Arthur, the once and future king."

Head of a Woman (c. 1450) by Pesellino.

Board of Trustees of the National Museums and Galleries on Merseyside (Walker Art Gallery, Liverpool).

RESPONDING TO THE ART

Pesellino (1422–1457), whose real name was Francesco di Stefano and who was also known as Giuochi, was a Florentine artist of the early Renaissance who excelled in small-scale paintings. His works can be seen in the National Gallery of Art in Washington, D.C., the Metropolitan Museum of Art in New York City, and the Museum of Art of Toledo, Ohio.

Activity. This woman's dress is of a later fashion than medieval dress, but traces of the medieval style remain. Ask students to compare this Italian woman's dress with the dress of the women in the illustration on p. 72 or of the Wife of Bath on p. 138.

D Reading Skills and Strategies
Using Context Clues

? What does *interred* mean? [buried] How do you know? [The author is reflecting on the death of Arthur and his grave. He follows *interred* with the word *there,* which refers to a specific place. *Interred* has an ending typical of a past-tense verb, which would fit the context.]

E Elements of Literature
Romance Hero

? What qualities of a romance hero are revealed in this passage? [Arthur's death and future are mysterious; there is a suggestion of his return.]

Making the Connections

Connecting to the Subject: "The Gift of Story"

The Arthurian legend has drawn readers and listeners over the centuries and continues to be retold. Small groups might use these questions to discuss the story's staying power.

- **Why is the story of Arthur so powerful even today?** [He has a mysterious greatness, a noble character, and concern for his people. We all hope for the coming of a leader who can create a just society.]
- **If Malory wrote this story in jail, what do you think attracted him to it?** [The stories of Arthur were old when Malory heard them, and the old ways of feudalism and chivalry were almost dead. A new, changed world was being born. Confined to a cell, Malory might have found imaginative escape in these tales of his country's more heroic past.]

Making Meanings

First Thoughts [Connect]

1. Answers will vary. Students may name heroes like Superman, whose origin is mysterious; they may also name Beowulf, who defeats evil and promotes peace.

Shaping Interpretations [Interpret]

2. Sample answers: Faithful follower—Bedivere. Wise old man—hermit. Dreams—Arthur's dreams of the serpents, wild beasts, and Gawain. Number 3—the hand that comes out of the lake to shake the sword three times. Magic—the hand in the lake. Tests of follower—Bedivere's task to throw the sword in the lake. Betrayal—Mordred's killing of his father.

3. A mysterious barge takes Arthur away. No one actually sees him buried. The inscription on his tomb, together with these details, suggest some mysterious state that is not death, or at least not death everlasting.

Extending the Text [Apply]

4. Answers will vary. The dreamlike elements, as well as the action, remain appealing. The story of loyalty to a great leader who provides moral leadership is still compelling. People today may, however, prefer heroes who accumulate fortunes or who seek to change society.

5. Archaeologists might look for a place not far from water, where there is or was once a chapel, which may be "beside Glastonbury." Opinions about the existence of Arthur will vary.

Grading Timesaver

Rubrics for each Choices assignment appear on p. 105 in the *Portfolio Management System.*

Making Meanings

First Thoughts

1. Does Arthur remind you of any other **romance heroes**—think of your other readings as well as heroes in popular culture. Discuss the connections.

> **Reading Check**
>
> **a.** What does Arthur dream on Trinity Sunday?
>
> **b.** How is the truce between Arthur and Mordred disturbed?
>
> **c.** What is Sir Lucan's advice to Arthur? What does Arthur do?
>
> **d.** What happens between Arthur and Mordred?
>
> **e.** Where does Bedivere take the wounded king? What happens to Bedivere?

Shaping Interpretations

2. Fill in this graphic to show how Malory uses other romance motifs.

Romance Motif	Arthur Story
Faithful follower	
Wise old man	
Dreams	
Number 3	
Magic	
Tests of follower	
Betrayal	

3. What mysterious details surround Arthur's last hours? What possibility do these details and the inscription on Arthur's tomb suggest?

Extending the Text

4. What aspects of this story do you think would appeal to people living at the beginning of the twenty-first century? Or do you think that people need different kinds of heroes today? Why?

5. Many people over the centuries have hunted for Arthur's tomb. According to this story, what should archaeologists look for in their search for Arthur's grave? (Do you think he really existed?)

Choices: Building Your Portfolio

Writer's Notebook

1. Collecting Ideas for a Comparison-Contrast Essay

How does Malory's Arthur, a hero out of medieval romance, compare and contrast with Beowulf, a hero from a different, much older society? Read and review the Anglo-Saxon epic, starting on page 21, and take notes on how the two heroes are both alike and different. Consider each hero's quest, powers, failings, enemies, allies, and achievements or tasks left undone. Save your notes for possible use in the Writer's Workshop on page 185.

Creative Writing

2. Translating Malory

Many writers have translated the stories of Arthur and his knights. Try your hand at translating this story of Arthur's death. You will have to translate the **archaic words** and correct the **archaic punctuation,** but try to keep the power of the story and the excitement of the action. Before you start your translation, decide who your audience will be: children or adults? If you used context clues to guess at the meanings of some of the archaic words as you read, be sure to check your guesses in a dictionary.

Art

3. Arthur in Art

The Arthurian legends have inspired as many visual artists as literary ones. Choose a scene from Malory's account of the death of Arthur, and draw or paint what you see in your mind's eye. Descriptions like that of the hand emerging from the lake or of Arthur being carried off in the barge are particularly suited to visual representation.

Reading Check

a. He has a dream of Sir Gawain, who warns him of his death.

b. A knight who is stung by an adder draws his sword. Others think he is beginning an attack and draw their swords, and the battle begins.

c. Sir Lucan advises Arthur not to pursue Mordred. Arthur vows that Mordred will never escape him and goes after him.

d. Arthur and Mordred fatally wound each other.

e. Bedivere takes Arthur to the water's edge. Later, he dons poor clothes and serves the hermit who buried Arthur.

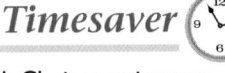

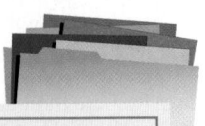

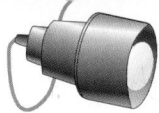

SPOTLIGHT ON

The Weaving of Women's Tales

By God, if women had but written stories . . . (A)

— Geoffrey Chaucer, from *The Wife of Bath's Prologue*

In early Britain, women helped with family and community life, managed estates in their husbands' absence, and pored over books in stone-walled convents. They also composed important works of literature, yet scholars have only recently begun to recognize these women's literary contributions.

The Anglo-Saxon Period: Nameless Voices (B)

Since poems in Anglo-Saxon Britain were composed and transmitted orally, the names of their original authors—whether female or male—have long been obscured. All literary works were generally attributed to the traveling bard (usually male) who recited them. Now, however, many scholars attribute such well-known poems as "The Wife's Lament" and "Wulf and Eadwacer" to women. In these lines from "The Wife's Lament," an anonymous poem, a wife expresses her grief at being banished from her home by her husband (something husbands were permitted to do).

Our lips had smiled to swear hourly
That nothing should split us—save dying—
Nothing else. All that has changed:
It is now as if it had never been,
Our friendship. I feel in the wind
That the man dearest to me detests me. (C)
I was banished to this knoll knotted by woods
To live in a den dug beneath an oak.
Old is this earthen room; it eats at my heart.

—*from* "The Wife's Lament"

No doubt, the names of other women who composed oral works (such as lullabies, elegies, and work songs) were also lost when the works were written down by scribes. One prominent exception to this standard of anonymity was Lioba, a young Wessex nun whose elegant prose was a powerful force in the Church's efforts to convert the Continent.

Anglo-Saxon women also expressed themselves artistically in other (anonymous) ways. Many wove intricate tapestries that recorded the details of their domestic lives amid scenes of men in battle. Others produced beautiful illuminated manuscripts in a few

Timarete painting a portrait, from Giovanni Boccaccio's *De claris mulieribus* (Of famous women), France (2nd half of 15th century). M. 381, fol. 33v.

The Pierpont Morgan Library, New York.

Spotlight On

Because of the focus on the canonical works of the Middle Ages, women writers of this time period are not represented. This feature explains why we know so little about these writers and briefly introduces three of them: the anonymous author of "The Wife's Lament"; Julian of Norwich (c. 1342–?), the nun who wrote about her sixteen visions of God; and Margery Kempe (1373–?), the pilgrim mother of fourteen children who dictated her autobiography to two scribes.

(A) Literary Connections

? In the full text of "The Wife of Bath's Tale," the Wife implies that if women had written stories, they would not tell about the virtue of women, but about the wickedness of men. Is this true? [Some students will be able to cite some women writers who focus on men's wickedness. Others will say that most women writers treat all their characters as individuals—that is, as people with both good and bad traits.]

(B) Struggling Readers

Using Graphic Aids

Remind students that titles, headings, illustrations, and other methods of breaking up text can all signal meaning. Ask what information they might get from this page before reading. [In addition to the title, students should note the subhead and the art. The boxed copy signals information that is somehow different or more important.]

(C) Critical Thinking

Making Connections

As students may be able to infer from this excerpt, the full text of "The Wife's Lament" is extremely emotional and expresses isolation, desperation, and loss. Ask students what this poem has in common with "The Seafarer" on pp. 56–58. [Possible answers: Both share the theme of exile; both have a tone of loss and yearning; both chronicle the extreme suffering of one lonely individual over time.]

Ⓐ Vocabulary Note
Latin Roots

Students may recognize the Latin root *-scrip-* ("write") in *scriptoria*. Ask students what the modern-day equivalent of scriptoria might be. [offices] You might also note that this word is plural; the singular is *scriptorium*. Ask students what other words form plurals in similar ways. [*criterion* and *criteria; datum* and *data; memorandum* and *memoranda*]

Ⓑ Reading Skills and Strategies
Finding the Main Idea

? What is the main idea of this passage? [There were only two ways for a woman to have a chance to write: to be born into a wealthy family or to enter the Church.]

Ⓒ Appreciating Language
Style

? In addition to its presentation of a highly original idea, especially for its time, this passage is also notable for its literary style. Why? [Possible answers: It is poetic. It is rich with balance and parallelism, as in "For where the soul is highest, noblest, most honorable, still it is lowest, meekest, and mildest." It uses repetition dramatically and effectively; notice, for instance, how many sentences begin with "I am. . . ." The language is as elevated and elegant as the subject matter.]

female *scriptoria,* monasteries devoted to copying religious writings. Wealthy women often acted as patrons, commissioning poets and artists to produce works illustrating family history.

The Middle Ages: Court or Cloister

Only two avenues were open to women with literary ambitions in the Middle Ages: the luck to be born into an aristocratic family (girls in such families were sometimes educated alongside their brothers) or service in the Church.

Most women wrote in English rather than in Latin, the formal language used for religious, legal, and political purposes. Women writing in the vernacular wrote mostly about domestic or personal affairs—everyday matters not considered serious or weighty at the time they were written. For both these reasons, few writings by women were preserved in monastery vaults.

For the most part, only in the Church did women have access to the education, economic support, and freedom from family responsibilities necessary for sustained writing. But when women did produce religious writings, they didn't usually fit the accepted mode of orthodox religious works. Women's writings were often more subjective and personal in style. (Today, ironically, we *do* value such personal writing and would probably find the kind of philosophical tract admired in the twelfth century rather dull.)

Julian of Norwich (c. 1342–?)

One of the first English women of letters was a recluse who lived alone in a small cell attached to St. Julian's Church in Norwich. In her only surviving work, *A Book of Showings,* Julian described the sixteen visions of God, or "showings," that she experienced during a critical illness shortly after she turned thirty.

Julian first recorded her revelations in short versions soon after they occurred and in longer versions some twenty years later. Julian's apology to her readers in the short version—"God forbid that you should say or take me for a teacher . . . for I am a woman, ignorant, weak, and frail"— is omitted in the longer version. Perhaps this is a sign that she no longer needed to pretend an inferiority she did not feel.

Julian's visions and reflections revealed a loving, nurturing God. Indeed, the central image in Julian's meditations became "God the Mother."

> As truly as God is our Father, so truly is God our Mother, and he revealed that in everything, and especially in these sweet words where he says: I am he; that is to say: I am he, the power and goodness of fatherhood; I am he, the wisdom and the lovingness of motherhood; I am he, the light and the grace which is all blessed love; I am he, the Trinity; I am he, the unity; I am he the supreme goodness of every kind of thing; I am he who makes you to love; I am he who makes you to long; I am he, the endless fulfilling of all true desires. For where the soul is highest, noblest, most honorable, still it is lowest, meekest, and mildest.
>
> —Julian of Norwich, *from A Book of Showings*

Christine de Pisan, writing, from *The Collected Works of Christine de Pisan* (15th century). French, MS Harley 4431, fol. 4.
By permission of the British Library, London.

Skill Link

Taking Notes and Organizing Information

Suggest that students actively record the information in this Spotlight On by taking notes, creating a chart or charts, or making a graphic organizer. Be sure they share their work in class. The focus of the activity should be to identify the essay's main ideas and supporting details or examples.

Margery Kempe (1373?–?)

The first autobiography in English, *The Book of Margery Kempe,* was dictated by a woman who could probably neither read nor write. Beginning with a religious conversion after the birth of her first child, Margery dictated her lively recollections to two scribes over many years. (The first scribe—thought to be Margery's own son—was nearly illiterate himself, and the work had to be done again with a second.) Although Margery refers to herself almost exclusively as "the creature" rather than "I" (as though to underscore her status as a creation of God), the *Book* projects the voice of a strong-willed, independent personality. In fact, Margery has been compared to Chaucer's vigorous Wife of Bath.

Like Chaucer's pilgrim, Margery was not affiliated with any convent or religious house. At forty, having by this time given birth to fourteen children, Margery made a pact of celibacy with her husband. In the following lines, Margery describes her life of penance.

> She gave herself up to great fasting and great watching; she rose at two or three of the clock, and went to church, and was there at her prayers unto the time of noon and also all the afternoon. Then she was slandered and reproved by many people, because she kept so strict a life. She got a haircloth from a kiln, such as men dry malt on, and laid it in her kirtle as secretly and privily as she might, so **D** that her husband should not espy it. Nor did he, and she lay by him every night in his bed and wore the haircloth every day, and bore children in the time.
>
> —Margery Kempe,
> *from The Book of Margery Kempe*

Dressed entirely in white, Margery traveled extensively in the Holy Land and to shrines in Britain and on the Continent. She made these pilgrimages despite the intolerance and disapproval of her peers. Her plain-spoken declarations of faith and frequent episodes of loud sobbing (she wept daily for fifteen years in sympathy with Christ's suffering) **E** weren't readily understood by others. Indeed, one town even threatened to burn Margery at the stake as a heretic. **F** She also was abandoned—in circumstances risky for a woman traveling alone—by several pilgrimage parties.

Writing a letter, from *Les épitres d'Ovide* (detail) (early 16th century). MS Fr. 875, fol. 23v.

© cliché Bibliothèque Nationale de France, Paris.

Margery's manuscript was widely read in the late Middle Ages but then was lost for centuries before resurfacing in an attic of the British Butler-Bowdon family in 1934. We can only wonder how many other women's writings await a similar rediscovery.

D Struggling Readers
Questioning

Note that Margery Kempe refers to herself as "she" here. Since this passage may not be clear on a first reading, students might slow down and question the text. One question students might ask is why Margery would wear the rough and scratchy haircloth next to her skin. [Hairshirts were commonly worn as penance, as constant reminders to avoid sin and to focus on the spiritual, not on the pleasures of the body.]

E Critical Thinking
Interpreting

? What clues from the story of Margery Kempe indicate that spiritual commitment was valued only to a point in medieval society? [Possible answers: She kept her haircloth a secret from her husband. She was disapproved of and threatened with execution. She was abandoned on several occasions.]

F Critical Thinking
Making Judgments

? What are your impressions of Margery Kempe? [Possible responses: She was a fanatic. She was extremely devout and misunderstood. She marched to the beat of a different drummer. She was persecuted because she was a woman.]

Assessing Learning

Check Test: Short Answer

1. Why don't we know the original authors of poems composed in Anglo-Saxon Britain? [Poems were transmitted orally.]
2. In what two ways could a woman of the Middle Ages pursue a literary life? [She could be born into an aristocratic family or go into the Church.]
3. Why did religious writing by women fail to fit the accepted Church style? [It was too personal and subjective. It was often written in the English vernacular rather than in Latin.]
4. What was Julian of Norwich's radical view of God? [God is both mother and father.]
5. What unusual obstacle did Margery Kempe overcome in recording her autobiography? [It is likely she could neither read nor write.]

Crossing the Curriculum

Art

The beautiful pieces of art in this feature indicate that women of the Middle Ages were just as creative as men were. Have students list what the women are doing. [The art shows women painting on p. 177, writing on p. 178, and carrying on correspondence on p. 179.] Interested students might explore the tales women told in their exquisite tapestries.

Read On

Portfolio Assessment Options

The following projects can help you evaluate and assess students' outside reading. Videotapes or photographs of completed projects might be included in student portfolios.

- **Write and Illustrate a Children's Book**

Students could work together or individually to write and illustrate a children's book (or several books) based on *The Arabian Nights* stories or on the King Arthur stories. Before they start their project, they should examine some children's books to see how they appeal visually to children. The audience's age group should be clearly specified. Research on the stories should be meticulous: The aim is to retell the stories in language children can understand but to remain as true as possible to the originals.

- **A Report on the Hitchhikers as Questers**

Douglas Adams's book is very popular. Have students write an analysis of the book that focuses on its use of quest motifs. The analysis should include plot, characters, themes, and settings. The analysis should conclude with a statement of how the reader feels about the book.

- **A Medieval Woman's Story**

Students who read *Women in the Middle Ages* should be encouraged to write their own essay on women's lives in the Middle Ages, using information from that book and from the literature in this collection. They could focus on education, work, position in society, opportunities, the home, the Church, childbearing, class restrictions, and so on. For the past several years, Workman Publishing has produced beautiful calendars called "Medieval Women." Students might refer to these calendars for information and for art to illustrate their essay. Be sure they document their sources. You might refer them first to an essay by Virginia Woolf on a similar subject; see "Shakespeare's Sister" on p. 1124.

READ ON

Stories That Save a Life

Perhaps you have been entranced by the story of Sindbad's fantastic voyages—just one of the many tales in *The Arabian Nights,* a framework of stories that dates back to the eighth century (translated by Husain Huddawy, W. W. Norton). Princess Scheherazade, whose husband wants to murder her, saves her own life by telling a dazzling variety of tales (fables, fairy tales, romances, and comic and historical anecdotes), stopping each night at the most suspenseful moment. Since her husband wants to hear what happpens next, he cannot bear to kill his gifted storyteller.

Different Lives in a Different Time

What was a woman's life like in the Middle Ages? The answer depends largely on where she lived and what social class she belonged to. In *Women in the Middle Ages* (Barnes & Noble), Frances and Joseph Gies examine the daily lives of women in the nobility, in religious orders, in the emerging trade classes, and in the peasantry.

Pilgrims in Outer Space

Join earthling Arthur Dent and his trusty sidekick from Betelgeuse, Ford Prefect, on a cosmic (and comic) quest through the galaxy. In *The Hitchhiker's Guide to the Galaxy* (Pocket Books), by Douglas Adams, you may "finally learn once and for all the plain and simple answer to all these nagging little problems of Life, the Universe, and Everything!" (First book of a four-volume series.)

A Lasting Hero

Early manuscripts mention a certain Arthur who led the Britons against the Anglo-Saxon invaders. Enlarged through legend, Arthur was eventually transformed into a romantic hero. Many writers have used the Arthurian legend to explore the grand themes of love, loyalty, and betrayal.

Arthur in our time. The English author T. H. White wrote his version of the Arthurian legend, *The Sword in the Stone* (G. P. Putnam's Sons), before World War II, when England once again needed a hero to shore up its national pride. He later expanded this story into a four-part novel, *The Once and Future King,* that explores the problems of war, justice, and national identity. And though White views Arthur's quest as a tragedy, he balances this somber theme with humorous characters and comic fun.

Magical stories made modern. Since his boyhood, the American writer John Steinbeck had been fascinated with Sir Thomas Malory's *Le Morte Darthur.* Realizing that difficult spelling and archaic words repelled modern readers, Steinbeck rewrote Malory's stories in plain, present-day language. In *The Acts of King Arthur and His Noble Knights* (Farrar, Straus and Giroux), the wonder of the original tales shines on.

The English Language

Middle English: The Language in Transition *by John Algeo*

The history of English is divided into three long periods: Old English (before 1066), Middle English (1066–1485), and Modern English (1485 to the present). To be sure, all English speakers did not go to bed on the night of December 31, 1065, speaking Old English and wake up on the morning of January 1, 1066, saying "Let's talk Middle English now!" Language change is slower and subtler than that. And speakers are seldom aware of changes in their own lifetimes.

Some important changes in pronunciation and grammar happened shortly before 1066, however. Then, in 1066, the Normans conquered England, eventually causing extensive changes in vocabulary. The pre-1066 language looks like a foreign tongue, but by the end of the Middle English period it was quite similar to today's English.

What Happened to the Endings?

In Old English, as in the other Germanic languages, people tended to pronounce words with a strong accent on the first syllable but to rush over the following ones. Unstressed vowels consequently lost their distinctive sounds and were pronounced all alike, as a

The Scriptorium in the Tower of the Monastery of Tavara, from a Spanish manuscript (13th century). M. 429, fol. 183.

The Pierpont Morgan Library, New York.

go.hrw.com
LEO 12-English Language

Reaching All Students

Struggling Readers

Assign students to read through this essay to the subhead "Uninvited Guests" on p. 183. Then use the chart below to help students see the actual changes among the three periods of the English language, based on the word *door.* The other words in each sentence are in modern English.

Old English	Middle English	Modern English
The *duru* opened.	The *doore* opened.	The *door* opened.
I opened the *dure.*	I opened the *doore.*	I opened the *door.*
My house has many *dura.*	My house has many *doores.*	My house has many *doors.*

OBJECTIVES

1. Understand the evolution of Old English to Middle English, including the dropping of unstressed vowel sounds at the end of words that often indicated gender, number, and case
2. Appreciate the effects of the Norman conquest on the English vocabulary
3. Research word histories and origins

Resources

Viewing and Representing
Videocassette A, Segment 1
Available in English and Spanish.
For full lesson plans and worksheets, see the *Visual Connections Teacher's Manual.*

A Exploring the Historical Period

Effects of History on Language

? What is the significance of the dates 1066 and 1485? Have students use the time line at the beginning of the unit (pp. 76–77) to identify two key historical events associated with each date. [In 1066, King Edward the Confessor died without an heir, and William of Normandy invaded England. In 1485, the Wars of the Roses ended, and the first Tudor king, Henry VII, was crowned.] Of these four events, the invasion of the Normans had the greatest effect on the language. When students have finished reading, ask them why.

B Appreciating Language

Middle vs. Modern English

Have students look back at the sample of Middle English on p. 104. By comparing this excerpt from *The Canterbury Tales* with its translation on p. 105, students will realize the extent to which Middle English is, indeed, similar to the English we use today. Encourage students to read it aloud, emphasizing the first syllable of words and pronouncing all final vowels as schwas.

Ⓐ Struggling Readers
Summarizing
Suggest that students stop after every section heading in this essay to summarize. For example, have them summarize the section called "What Happened to the Endings?" [Possible summaries: Unstressed vowels lost their original sounds; scribes were unsure how to spell endings of words; or Old English became Middle English when scribes used e to write the unstressed vowels.]

Responding to the Art
The Lindisfarne Gospels are consummate examples of the Irish style of scribal art, noted for intricate interlacing patterns and fantastic animal forms. This manuscript was created in the monastery of Lindisfarne, on an island off England's Northumbrian coast, founded by Irish monks under the direction of a monk named Aidan. The manuscript was written to honor St. Cuthbert, who died in 687. The Lindisfarne monastery was part of the network of Irish-founded monasteries that became centers of art, literature, and philosophy. The beautiful monastery was plundered, burned, and finally destroyed by Viking invaders in 875.
Activity. The Lindisfarne monks created this Latin manuscript in a scriptorium like the one shown in the charming manuscript on p. 181. Have students try to decipher the letters here. The large, ornate letter is *Q* (*Quo*). Some of the words are abbreviated; the lector would recognize the shortened word. See if students can find the scribe's marginal notations.

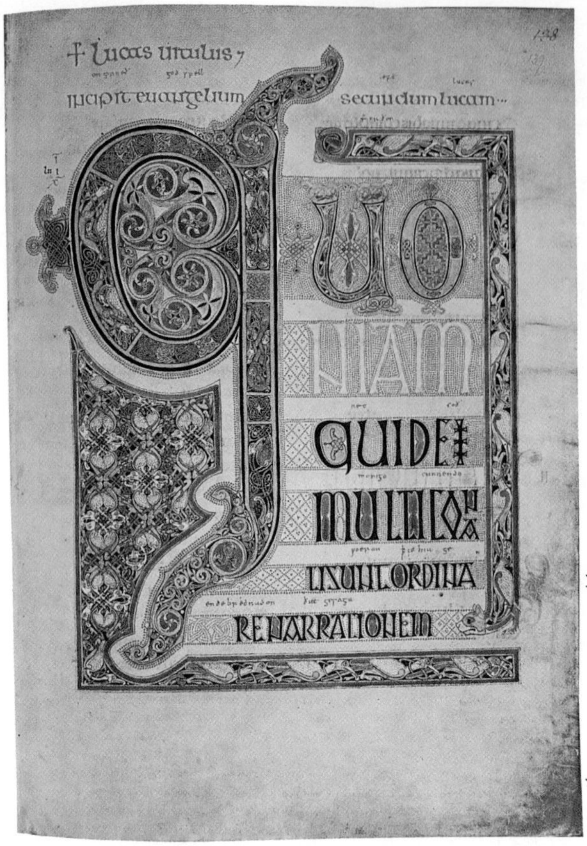

By permission of the British Library, London.

Opening of *St. Luke's Gospel*, from the *Lindisfarne Gospels* (7th century). Cotton MS Nero D.IV, fol. 139.

schwa (ə)—the sound in the last syllable of our word *cola*.

The misspellings that began to turn up in manuscripts show that unstressed vowel sounds merged in late Old English. Ⓐ Scribes sat at their desks all day long, tracing out letter shapes on parchment. About the year 1000, scribes had a great deal of trouble in remembering how the endings of words ought to be spelled. They hesitated about writing *stanas* or *stanes* (stones), *comon* or *coman* (they came). Their indecision shows that the scribes had ceased to pronounce the vowels of those endings differently from one another. Eventually, the scribes gave up trying to spell the endings differently and just used the letter e to write the unstressed vowel: *stanes, comen.* When that happened, the language became what we call Middle English.

Endings and Order

The change in the pronunciation and spelling of vowels had some far-reaching effects on English grammar. Old English nouns had changed their endings to show various things. For example, the Old English word for "door" as the subject of a sentence was *duru,* but as the direct object, it was *dure*. The plural "doors" was *dura.* After the unstressed vowels had fallen together, all three forms became *dore,* with a schwa sound at the end.

The loss of vowel distinctions meant that English speakers had to find other ways of indicating grammatical meanings, or they had to do without such information.

Effects on gender. For gender, Middle English decided to do without. Today almost no one is sorry that English replaced grammatical with natural gender. Instead of talking about "the door . . . she," "the roof . . . he," and "the wife . . . it," we use *he* for males, *she* for females, and *it* for things without gender.

Effects on plural forms. For number, Middle English came to rely on a few plural endings. Old English had many ways of marking the plural of a noun. A few of these survive in Modern English irregular plurals such as *tooth/teeth, ox/oxen,* and *child/children.* Other Old English plural forms, such as *dura* (doors) from *duru* (door), no longer exist. Middle English used the ending *–es* (from Old English *–as*) for most of its plurals. Thus, Old English

Professional Notes

Critical Comment: How New Was Middle English?
In *The Story of English,* authors Robert McCrum, William Cran, and Robert MacNeil agree with John Algeo that Middle English didn't all-of-a-sudden just show up. They write: "Much of what is now called Middle English is no more than a record in writing of what had already happened to spoken Old English. Thus, while spoken Old English had almost certainly lost most of its inflections by the time of the Norman Conquest, it is not until written Middle English that the changes show up in the documents." They also agree that one of the biggest changes between Old English and Middle English was the loss of Old English word endings and note that many of these were replaced by prepositions, such as *by, with,* and *from.*

hund/hundas became Middle English *hound/houndes,* and Old English *dura* was replaced by Middle English *doores.* Today we have only one regular ending, *–s,* as in *hounds* and *doors.*

Effects on case endings. Instead of case endings to show the functions of nouns in a sentence, Middle English came to rely on word order. In Middle English, "The knave slough [killed] the dragon" means something quite different from "The dragon slough the knave"; and that difference is signaled only by the order of the words. The difference from Old English, where word order was much less critical, is profound.

> All English speakers did not go to bed on the night of December 31, 1065, speaking Old English and wake up on the morning of January 1, 1066, saying "Let's talk Middle English now!"

Uninvited Guests

Shortly after the unstressed vowels had come to be pronounced as schwas, a political event occurred that had important consequences for the English language. In 1066, William, duke of Normandy, invaded England with an army of soldiers from France. He defeated the English defenders, led by King Harold, at the Battle of Hastings.

Under William the Conqueror (as he came to be called), French became the language of government, law, education, and upper-class life. English continued to be spoken, of course, by most people: servants, craftsmen, farmers, foresters—the sturdy yeomanry of the land. But French was the language of the rulers. England—once in danger of becoming an outlying part of Scandinavia—now seemed likely to become a province of France. **B**

The two peoples—Vikings from Scandinavia and Normans from France—were in fact related. The Normans were, as their name suggests, not really French, but Scandinavians from the north who had settled in the western regions of France. They acquired the language of their new home, although they never learned to speak it like the native French people. To elegant Parisians, the Normans always sounded strange, foreign, and provincial.

Thus, the conquerors of Anglo-Saxon England were not at all refined emissaries of a higher civilization who brought culture to primitive England. On the contrary, they were a wild bunch only a few generations removed from their piratical ancestors. **C**

In the long run, however, the Norman Conquest was probably a blessing. English was left to itself, to develop and grow without interference by scholars or government officials. The common folk of the early Middle English period were quite untroubled by traditions of spelling or preconceived notions of what their language ought to be like. So they spoke naturally—letting the vowels fall together and giving up the many grammatical endings of Old English, with no sense that they were losing anything of importance. And they were right.

The Battle and the Triumph

For several hundred years, England was a bilingual country. **D** French was spoken by the upper classes among themselves, it was used in law courts and government, and it was used for literature. English was spoken by the lower classes for all the ordinary purposes of daily life—selling grain, buying dishes, scolding children, squabbling with neighbors, and loving the family.

For a time, no one could have said whether French or English would win out as the national language of England. However, several factors tipped the balance to English. Not the least important was the fact that most people spoke English. Also, the Normans in England got into a squabble with France, called the Hundred Years' War. The conflict intensified a feeling of patriotism for things English—especially the English language.

The English language thus gradually reasserted its place in the national life. In the second half of the fourteenth century, about three hundred years after the Conquest, English had again become the primary language in England. This was symbolized by a bill passed in Parliament in 1362 requiring that all law cases be conducted in English instead of in French.

At that time there was no standard English. Instead, people used the English of their native

B Historical Connections

French Rule, French Language

Two hundred years after William's conquest, French was still so often spoken in places of power that Robert of Gloucester wrote in the thirteenth century, "I ween that in all the world there is no country that holds not to her own speech, save England alone." Even in the fourteenth century, accounts of the sitting of Parliament were still recorded in French, and many of the prominent poets continued to write in the language.

C Critical Thinking

Determining the Author's Purpose

? Why do you think the writer includes this information on the history of the Normans? [Part of Algeo's purpose is to be entertaining, and this is interesting information. Algeo includes this information to dispel the idea that the French had the lofty, sophisticated culture, while the English were ignorant.]

D Critical Thinking

Speculating

? How do you think life would have been different had England, and its colonies, remained bilingual? [Possible responses: The culture would have been richer for having two languages. Things would have been too confusing. People in America today would understand other cultures better and would be able to get around the world more easily. There would be intercommunity conflict, as in Canada.]

Resources

Formal Assessment

- English Language Test, p. 29

Skill Link

Understanding Word Order

To help students understand the extent to which word order signals meaning in our language, you might read aloud the first two stanzas of Lewis Carroll's "Jabberwocky." Let students guess at the meanings of the nonsense words.

'Twas brillig, and the slithy toves
Did gyre and gimble in the wabe;
All mimsy were the borogroves,
And the mome raths outgrabe.

"Beware the Jabberwock, my son!
The jaws that bite, the claws that catch!
Beware the Jubjub bird, and shun
The frumious Bandersnatch!"

Ⓐ Vocabulary Note

Words Borrowed from French

In some cases, even though English did borrow a word from French, the English word also remained in the language. This historical fact accounts for a number of synonyms, such as *labor* (from French) and *work* (from English) or *edifice* (from French) and *building* (from English). Students may note that the "fancier"-sounding synonyms come from French.

Reading Skills and Strategies

Mini-Lesson: Outlining

Ask students to produce a simple sentence outline of the section "Both a Borrower and a Lender Be" on this page.

Sample

I. When the English had no word for a concept, they borrowed the word from French.

- A. Borrowed words often came from the fields of law and government.
  - 1. *Chancellor, attorney,* and *court* came from French.
  - 2. *Government, royal,* and *army* came from French.
- B. Borrowed words often came from the world of cuisine. (Example: *venison*)

Try It Out

(Answers for dates may vary according to the dictionary used.) All the words in 1 come from French at some point.

1. *army:* fourteenth century
gentleman: twelfth century
justice: twelfth century
royal: fourteenth century
castle: before twelfth century
guide: fourteenth century
master: before twelfth century
servant: thirteenth century
chief: fourteenth century
herb: fourteenth century
roast: thirteenth century
soldier: fourteenth century

2. a. *chair* (Middle English)
chaise lounge (Modern English, from French)
stool (Old English)
b. *table* (Old English)
tableau (Modern English, from French)
tablet (Middle English)
c. *(wheel)barrow* (Old English)
car (Middle English)
automobile (Modern English)

area. With the reestablishment of English as a language of government, however, the dialect of London (the capital city) quickly became a model to be followed.

In the fourteenth century, literature in English was revitalized. Chaucer, one of our greatest writers, wrote for the English royal court, using the London dialect. The anonymous author of *Sir Gawain and the Green Knight* produced his courtly tale in a northwestern dialect for country gentry. As the language flowered, so did the literature, with the same exuberance and variety.

Both a Borrower and a Lender Be

When English speakers started to use English again to talk about things they had discussed in French for three hundred years, they were literally at a loss for words. They knew no English words for many governmental, legal, military, and artistic things. The simplest thing was to borrow the French terms. And that is just what sensible English speakers did.

Ⓐ Examples of French borrowings are *baron, castle, chancellor, country, duke, government, noble, prince, royal, state; attorney, court, crime, judge, jury, prison; army, captain, corporal, lieutenant, sergeant, soldier; juggler, literature, magic, melody, poetry, sport.* Animals on the hoof looked after by English-speaking workers were, and still are, called by native English names: *cow, hog, sheep, calf, deer.* But when they were slaughtered and served up on the table as food, they were given the French names that the invading nobility used: *beef, pork, mutton, veal, venison.* Thus, our vocabulary continues to echo the English-worker/French-ruler dichotomy of six hundred years ago.

Since the fourteenth century, English has borrowed words from many languages, so English now has one of the richest and most international vocabularies in the world. In turn, English has become a major source of loanwords to other languages. That is another benefit of the Norman Conquest that William and his bully boys could not have imagined or understood.

"Period. New paragraph."

©1998 Carl Rose from cartoonbank.com. All Rights Reserved.

Try It Out

1. First recorded usages. Many new words came into English during the Middle English period. Just before the definition of a word, *Merriam-Webster's Collegiate Dictionary,* Tenth Edition, gives the date or century when the word was first recorded in use. Find that date or century for each of these words. What language did each come from?

army	gentleman	justice
royal	castle	guide
master	servant	chief
herb	roast	soldier

2. Word origins. In each group below, one word was used in Old English, one is a Middle English loan from French, and one is a Modern English loan from French. What origin do you think each word has? Check your guesses in a dictionary.

a. chair, chaise lounge, stool
b. table, tableau, tablet
c. (wheel) barrow, car, automobile

Assessing Learning

Check Test: Questions and Answers

1. What is a schwa sound? [the "uh" sound used in pronunciation of most unstressed vowels in English]

2. What letter did eleventh-century scribes use to represent the schwa sound? [the letter e]

3. How was the difference between subjects and objects indicated in Middle English? [It was indicated by the order of the words in a sentence, just as in Modern English.]

4. What event induced the upper classes to give up speaking French and start speaking English? [the Hundred Years' War against France]

5. Why did speakers of English during this period borrow many words from French? [Old English had no words for certain ideas and objects, so English speakers simply borrowed the French terms for them.]

BUILDING YOUR PORTFOLIO

Writer's Workshop

EXPOSITORY WRITING

A Comparison-Contrast Essay

Every day you look at people, places, experiences, and things and **compare** them (find similarities) and **contrast** them (find differences). Such thinking strategies help you evaluate alternatives and make decisions, ranging from what movie to rent to what college to attend. These skills also help you talk and write about literature. In this workshop you will write a **comparison-contrast essay** analyzing the likenesses or the differences, or both, in two literary works or in selected elements of two literary works.

Prewriting

WORK IN PROGRESS

1. **Check your Writer's Notebook.** You can compare and contrast just about any two texts or elements of texts as long as they are alike or different in at least one significant way. As a topic for your comparison-contrast essay, consider following up on some of the notes you may have saved in your Writer's Notebook. For example, you may have notes on Chaucer's Prioress and Wife of Bath or on Gawain and a modern hero or on King Arthur and Beowulf.
2. **Gather your details.** Once you have decided on the texts you will compare and contrast, go through each text and note similarities and differences. Self-sticking note pads are handy for this. After you have skimmed your texts at least twice to look for details, put the details in some sort of graphic form for easy reference.

   There are many kinds of graphics. One that is commonly used is the **Venn diagram,** like the one shown on the left below, in which the differences between the two texts can be cited in the outer part of the circles and the similarities can be cited where the circles overlap. **Outlines** and **charts** are also useful. The writer who is using the chart on the right below will focus on character. The specific features of a character (perhaps "has magical powers; is heroic, flawed, realistic," and so on) will be listed down the side; the two titles will be listed at the top.

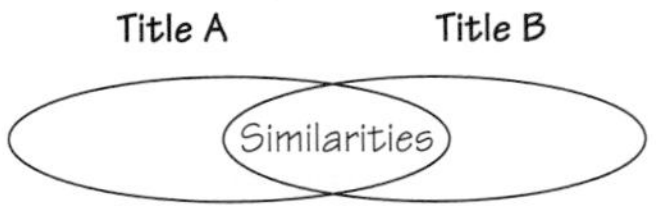

Character	Title A	Title B
Feature 1:		
Feature 2:		
Feature 3:		

Technology HELP

See Writer's Workshop 2 CD-ROM. *Assignment: Expository Writing.*

Assignment

Write an essay comparing and/or contrasting two or more texts or literary elements. The texts may be stories, poems, essays, dramas, or screenplays.

Aim

To inform; to analyze; to evaluate.

Audience

Your teacher, your classmates, or readers of a student literary magazine.

Main Objective

Write a compare/contrast essay

Process Objectives

1. Use appropriate prewriting techniques to identify and develop a topic
2. Create a first draft
3. Use Evaluation Criteria as a basis for determining revision strategies
4. Revise the first draft incorporating suggestions generated by self- or peer evaluation
5. Proofread and correct errors
6. Create a final draft
7. Choose an appropriate method of publication
8. Reflect on progress as a writer

Planning

- **Block Schedule**
  Block Scheduling Lesson Plans with Pacing Guide
- **One-Stop Planner**
  CD-ROM with Test Generator

Introducing the Writer's Workshop

Divide the class into small groups of three or four students. Have each group pick one type of television show they currently watch (situation comedies, news, sports, talk, etc.). Then, have each group identify two particular shows of that type. Have the groups list ways in which the shows are similar and ways in which they are different. Ask students to look beyond the obvious and consider such attributes as the characters of the hosts or actors and the tone and mood of the shows.

Let each group present their lists of similarities and differences to the class. From those presented choose a listing that has both similarities and differences, and construct a Venn diagram on the board with the class's participation.

Resources: Print and Media

Writing and Language

- *Portfolio Management System*
  Prewriting, p. 106
  Peer Editing, p. 107
  Assessment Rubric, p. 108
- *Workshop Resources*
  Revision Strategy Teaching Notes, p. 7
  Revision Strategy Transparencies 4, 5, 6
- *Writer's Workshop 2 CD-ROM*
  Expository Writing

Teaching the Writer's Workshop

Prewriting
Review the Prewriting steps outlined on pp. 185–186. In particular, discuss the two methods of organization outlined on p. 186. If time permits, you may wish to return to the Venn diagram used to introduce the lesson and have students discuss how they might have chosen to develop that topic.

Drafting
Remind students that a clear thesis statement is always important, but it becomes critical when a writer is both comparing and contrasting. If the writer wishes to ensure the reader's comprehension and agreement, then there must be clear statements of intent and conclusion.

Evaluating and Revising
Have students use the Evaluation Criteria provided on p. 186 as a standard for determining needed revisions.

Proofreading
Have students exchange papers and check specifically for errors in agreement. You may wish to complete the Language Workshop on p. 187 before having students proofread their papers.

Publishing and Reflecting
Have students exchange papers and create a Venn diagram based on the paper they receive. They should read the paper carefully and check with the writer to clarify any ambiguities before constructing the diagram. Collate the papers and diagrams, and exchange them across classes. Students' papers should be read and discussed by other groups who may suggest changes to the paper or to the diagram. Return these notes to the student writers. Have each student write a reflection based on what his or her audience seemed to understand or misunderstand about the paper.

Resources

Peer Editing Forms and Rubrics
- *Portfolio Management System,* p. 107

Revision Transparencies
- *Workshop Resources,* p. 7

Communications Handbook HELP

See Taking Notes and Documenting Sources; Proofreading.

3. **Plan your essay.** Decide how you will organize your ideas, and then make an outline. You can present your information using either the **block** or the **point-by-point** method of organization. With the block method you first discuss *all* the relevant features of one subject and then cover the same features of the other subject. With the point-by-point method, you take up *one* feature at a time and discuss it in terms of one subject and then in terms of the other. Here is an example of an outline for each method:

Block Method
Subject 1: Beowulf
- Feature 1: quest
- Feature 2: powers
- Feature 3: achievements

Subject 2: King Arthur
- Feature 1: quest
- Feature 2: powers
- Feature 3: achievements

Point-by-Point Method
Feature 1: quest
- Subject 1: Beowulf
- Subject 2: Arthur

Feature 2: powers
- Subject 1: Beowulf
- Subject 2: Arthur

Feature 3: achievements
- Subject 1: Beowulf
- Subject 2: Arthur

Drafting
1. **Introduce your subjects.** In your **introduction,** be sure to identify the titles and authors of the works you are discussing and give any background information your readers may need. Include a **thesis statement,** which alerts your readers to what you are comparing and/or contrasting and gives some indication of what your analysis has led you to conclude.

> **Thesis statement:** Although both Beowulf and Arthur die bravely, pessimism and disintegration overcome Beowulf's community after his death, whereas there are clear suggestions of rebirth and renewal after Arthur's death.

2. **Support your generalizations.** In the **body** of your essay, present the information you outlined, using the block or point-by-point method of organization. Add specific details, examples, and quotations from the text or from authoritative outside sources to back up your assertions of similarities and differences.
3. **Draw conclusions.** In the last paragraph, write a **conclusion,** summing up your insights, evaluation, or response to your subjects. You may also want to leave your readers with a question or comment, which may motivate them to go back to the works and reevaluate them for themselves.

Evaluation Criteria
A good comparison-contrast essay
1. *identifies what is being compared, gives necessary background information, and includes a thesis statement in the introduction*
2. *compares and/or contrasts at least two features, either by the block or the point-by-point method of organization*
3. *supports general statements with specific examples and quotations from the text or from outside sources*
4. *draws a conclusion from the similarities and/or differences presented*
5. *quotes accurately from the text and documents all quotations carefully*

Evaluating and Revising
Peer evaluation. Working with a classmate who has read your draft, apply each of the criteria in the list at the left to your work, and revise as necessary.

Grading Timesaver

Rubrics for this Writer's Workshop assignment appear on p. 108 of the *Portfolio Management System.*

The history
of the written
word is rich an
Page 1

Language Workshop

Agreement: Common Problems

Here's a draft essay about one character from *The Canterbury Tales.*

The pilgrims who meet by chance at the Tabard Inn is an unlikely collection of travelers. The Friar, along with the similarly well-fed Nun, are among the most outlandish of the pilgrims. Still, the Miller remains my favorite. His knotty shoulders and wart-tipped nose makes quite a vivid picture. Either his wide, black nostrils or his furnace-door mouth are the detail that best suggests the Miller's volatile temper. It's also hard to imagine that a man who can break a door with his head can also play the mournful-sounding bagpipes, but I guess I've just never seen one.

While the writer uses strong, vivid details, she has trouble with some sticky subject-verb combinations. *All* writers, even professionals, encounter the grammatical problems in this paragraph, but these problems can be mastered.

1. *Subject-verb agreement* means that a singular subject takes a singular verb and plural subjects take plural verbs. A subject's number is **not** changed by a following phrase or clause.

   The **pilgrims** who meet by chance at the Tabard Inn **are** an unlikely collection of travelers.

2. In formal usage, a singular subject followed by a parenthetical phrase such as *along with . . . , as well as . . . ,* or *in addition to . . .* remains singular.

   The **Friar,** along with the similarly well-fed Nun, **is** among the most outlandish of the pilgrims.

3. A *compound subject* is two or more subjects having the same verb. A compound subject joined by *and* usually takes a plural verb, even if one subject is singular.

   His knotty **shoulders and** wart-tipped **nose make** quite a vivid picture.

4. When a compound subject is joined by *or* or *nor,* the verb agrees with the subject closer to the verb.

   Either his wide, black **nostrils or** his furnace-door **mouth is** the detail that best suggests the Miller's volatile temper.

Writer's Workshop Follow-Up: Proofreading

Reread the essay you wrote for the Writer's Workshop on page 185, checking for agreement problems. Have you maintained subject-verb agreement in each sentence? After you check for agreement in your essay, ask a peer reviewer to look over your paper for agreement problems; then make any necessary corrections.

Technology HELP

See Language Workshop CD-ROM. *Key word entry: agreement.*

Language Handbook HELP

See Agreement, page 1223.

Try It Out

Choose the word that creates correct agreement in each sentence.

1. Neither the Squire nor the Doctor (seem, seems) as gallant as the Knight.
2. The Nun's rosary beads and brooch (was, were) brightly polished.
3. We wonder how the Oxford Cleric, as well as his twenty volumes of philosophy, (was, were) carried by a horse "thinner than a rake."
4. If any of the pilgrims' character sketches (reveal, reveals) Chaucer himself, the description of the Host is closest.

OBJECTIVES
Determine and use correct subject-verb agreement

Resources

Workshop Resources

- Worksheet, p. 47

Language Workshop CD-ROM

- Agreement

Try It Out

Answers

1. seems; the verb agrees with the subject closer to it in the case of a compound subject joined by *nor*
2. were; a compound subject joined by *and* usually takes a plural verb, even if one subject is singular
3. was; a singular subject followed by a parenthetical phrase remains singular and takes a singular verb
4. reveal; plural subjects (sketches) take plural verbs

Assessing Learning

Quick Check: Agreement

Underline the word that agrees with its subject in each of the following sentences.

1. Our dog, as well as both of our cats, (loves, love) to be held in my lap.
2. Her two sisters and Amy (is, are) fond of chocolate.
3. John or the class officers (have, has) the papers we need.
4. My sisters, my brothers, and my dad (enjoys, enjoy) watching basketball.
5. Neither the garden nor the lawn (is, are) in very good shape right now.

OBJECTIVES
1. Evaluate a review
2. Identify the critic's criteria
3. Determine the critic's attitude and tone

Using the Strategies
Possible Answers

1. authorship, name-recognition, length, lack of surprise, unhappy ending
2. Is the audience interested in William Wallace? Does the movie have sufficient interest to keep an audience's attention for three hours? Does the film have a villain interesting enough to stand against the hero? Given the tone of the film, will the audience be willing to accept the hero's violent death?
3. The author's tone is sarcastic and somewhat flippant. He reduces the message of the film to "Tyranny . . . is a bad thing," a self-evident conclusion. When the author deliberately confuses the words *masochism* and *heroism,* his attitude is obvious, but he states it clearly in the final sentence.
4. Answers will vary. Students who have seen the film may disagree. In particular, readers may wish to challenge the notion that name-recognition is a prerequisite for a movie hero.

Reading for Life

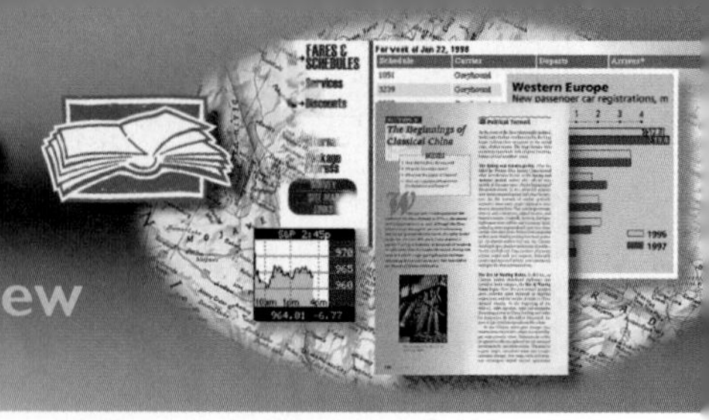

Analyzing a Film or Play Review

Situation
Imagine that you've just seen a videotape of the Oscar-winning film *Braveheart,* about a thirteenth-century Scottish hero, William Wallace. You want to compare your opinion of the film with that of a professional film critic. Here are strategies you should follow.

Another Highland Fling
RICHARD SCHICKEL

Braveheart is too much, too late. Gibson, who directs himself in Randall Wallace's screenplay, starts with certain disadvantages vis-à-vis Rob Roy [another film]: Sir Walter Scott never wrote a novel about William Wallace, and no one named a cocktail after him either. Got a real name-recognition problem here. Got a real length problem too. *Braveheart* runs almost three hours, and though it's full of incident, including several big and expertly staged battle sequences, it really doesn't have enough on its mind to sustain our full attention over that span. Freedom, Wallace keeps telling everyone, is a good thing, worth dying for. Tyranny, on the other hand, is a bad thing. . . .

But we know all that; it's what historical movies have taught us over the years. What you need in this situation is world-class villainy, somebody full of wicked surprise to break up the banalities. This *Braveheart* lacks. . . .

The other problem with *Braveheart* is its unhappy ending. After all that time, you want and expect evil to be confounded. What you get instead is the hero being tortured to death. The suspense is this: Will he crack, cry out in pain, thus robbing posterity of an inspiring example of masochism—sorry, heroism? Come on. That's Mel Gibson the wild horses are trying to pull apart. Of course he's going to die stoically. Everybody knows that a non-blubbering clause is standard in all movie stars' contracts. Too bad there isn't one banning self-indulgence when they direct.

—*from Time,* May 19, 1995

Strategies
Note the title of the review.
- The title may suggest the critic's general opinion and the tone of the review.

Recognize specific elements that the critic evaluates.
- These elements usually include the plot, the screenplay or script, direction, and actors' performances, as well as such elements of film as cinematography, special effects, the soundtrack, and editing.

Recognize the critic's criteria, or standards.
- Critics often compare the elements of one film or play with those of another film or play. They might use a production they consider excellent as a standard by which they judge the production they are reviewing.

Compare the critic's criteria with your criteria.
- Be aware of your own standards of excellence. They may differ from the critic's.

Be aware of the critic's tone.
- Notice the critic's choice of words and how they reveal his or her attitude toward the film.

Evaluate the review.
- Whether or not you agree with the review, decide if it is comprehensive, informative, fair, and convincing.

Using the Strategies
Answer these questions about the review above.

1. What elements of the film does the critic address?
2. What are some of the criteria that the critic uses to assess *Braveheart?*
3. What is the critic's **tone**? What words and phrases contribute to that tone? (Consider the title of the review.)
4. Does the critic convincingly support his opinions? Explain your judgment.

Extending the Strategies
- List the elements that *you* particularly look for when you watch a film.
- Compare your opinion of a film you've seen recently with a professional critic's opinion of that film.

Skill Link

Comparing and Contrasting Media Coverage of Events
This would be a good opportunity to discuss the ways in which movies and world events are reviewed and presented on television (in newscasts, in news analysis shows, and in talk shows), in newspapers, in news magazines, on the radio, and on the Internet. You might have two groups of students work on this project. They should prepare reports on how coverage of a particular event differs from one medium to another. One group should focus on movies; the other group should focus on current events. The groups should report orally on coverage in at least two sources: newspapers, magazines, television newscasts, television news analysis, television talk shows, radio talk shows, and the Internet. Their reports should include a summation of the coverage; an evaluation of the accuracy of the coverage, including possible bias; and a statement of their own evaluation of the event.

Learning for Life

Evaluating Technological Advances

Problem

During the Hundred Years' War, the development of armor-piercing arrows made knighthood obsolete. How will advances in technology affect today's occupations?

Project

Investigate how emerging technology is expected to change an occupation that interests you. How will the demand for workers be affected? How will education and training requirements, as well as job tasks, change?

Preparation

1. Choose an occupation that interests you: one you're thinking of pursuing or simply one you're curious about.
2. Use the *5W-How?* questions (*Who? What? When? Where? Why? How?*) to gather information with a focus.
3. Use print and electronic sources for most of the information you need. You might also consult community groups such as trade or professional organizations.

Procedure

1. To get an overview of the occupation, start with the *Dictionary of Occupational Titles* and the *Occupational Outlook Handbook*. (Both are government publications, and both are available on-line in certain databases.)
2. In addition to using standard sources such as the card catalog and indexes for newspapers, magazines, and databases, consider checking with special-interest newsgroups on the Internet. (Moderated newsgroups are more reliable than unmoderated ones.)
3. Keep in mind that the sources you use should be not only reliable but also relevant, recent, and representative. Remember, too, to document all your sources.

Presentation

Use one of the following formats (or another that your teacher approves):

1. **Traveling Graphics**

   Create a traveling exhibit using hand-drawn or computer-generated **graphics** to display your findings. For example, you could use bar charts to show current and future job openings or qualifications. Include documentation of your sources, and give your exhibit a catchy title. Display your exhibit on Career Day at your school.
2. **Future Expectations**

   Write a job description detailing the tasks and responsibilities an employee in the occupation will be expected to carry out. Use present-tense action verbs (for example, "using an interferometer, a virtual-reality designer measures . . ."), and be as specific as possible. Make your job description accessible to a wider audience by adding a glossary of technical terms arranged in alphabetical order. With classmates who have also chosen this option, compile a booklet of job descriptions, or create a page for your school's database system.
3. **Sharing Interests**

   Give an informal talk reporting your findings to a school- or community-based group that shares your interest in the occupation. For example, students in an earth sciences class might enjoy learning how emerging technology is expected to affect the knowledge and skills required of meteorologists. You may prepare visuals (charts, graphs, and so on) to augment your presentation.

Processing

Did doing this activity confirm or deflate your interest in the occupation? Did it change your views about the kind of education and training you would need, and if so, how? Write a brief reflection for your portfolio.

OBJECTIVES

1. Identify social and economic trends
2. Conduct research
3. Select and prepare a presentation of the research findings

Grading Timesaver

Rubrics for this Learning for Life project appear on p. 109 of the *Portfolio Management System.*

Developing Workplace Competencies

Preparation	Procedure	Presentation
• Identifies general problems • Clarifies problems • Generates related ideas	• Uses resources wisely • Acquires data • Evaluates data • Interprets information	• Processes information • Communicates ideas • Teaches others

OBJECTIVES

1. Read the literature from the Renaissance on the themes of "Love, Death, and Time"; "Under a Hand Accursed"; and "The Power of the Word"
2. Interpret literary elements with special emphasis on poetic meter, sonnets, metaphysical poetry, blank verse, imagery, and figurative language
3. Apply a variety of reading strategies, including determining meanings of words, reading Milton's poetic style, and distinguishing shades of meaning
4. Respond to literature in a variety of modes
5. Learn and use new words
6. Learn about the birth of Modern English, Shakespeare's English, and the growth of Modern English
7. Plan, draft, revise, edit, proofread, and publish an interpretive essay and a cause-and-effect essay
8. Develop skill in using the literary present and making effective transitions
9. Demonstrate the ability to read a consumer report
10. Explore through a variety of projects the characteristics of a Renaissance person

The Renaissance 1485–1660

A Fête at Bermondsey (c. 1570) by J. Hoofnagel. Oil on panel.

Selection Readability

This Annotated Teacher's Edition provides a summary of each selection in the student book. Following each Summary heading, you will find one, two, or three small icons. These icons indicate, in an approximate sense, the reading level of the selection.

- ■ One icon indicates that the selection is easy.
- ■■ Two icons indicate that the selection is on an intermediate reading level.
- ■■■ Three icons indicate that the selection is challenging.

Responding to the Art

As a young man, **Joris Hoofnagel** (1545–1601), the son of a Belgian diamond merchant, traveled through Europe drawing. On their way home, he and his family lost everything to Spanish plunderers and fled to Bavaria. Joris was befriended by a patron, who employed him to illustrate four books on natural history. An engraver as well as a painter, Hoofnagel also made maps, some for a book on world history.

Activity. Ask students to make inferences about the various people shown in this picture: What are they doing? What classes do they come from? How do they live? [Possible responses: They are all heading for a fête, or party; they have a food table set up in an open-air hall, and it looks as if a baker has opened shop. They may be from the upper class, merchant class, or landed class. They are well dressed, some in somber black, and have time for leisure.]

Resources

Viewing and Representing

Videocassette B, Segment 5
Available in English and Spanish.
Use this video to present the life of Queen Elizabeth I.
For full lesson plans and worksheets, see the *Visual Connections Teacher's Manual.*

Videocassette B, Segment 6
Available in English and Spanish.
Use this video as an introduction to Shakespeare's tragedies.
For full lesson plans and worksheets, see the *Visual Connections Teacher's Manual.*

Videocassette A, Segment 1
Available in English and Spanish.
Use the video to introduce students to Renaissance English.
For full lesson plans and worksheets, see the *Visual Connections Teacher's Manual.*

Resources: Print and Media

Viewing and Representing
- *Visual Connections*
  - Videocassette A, Segment 1
  - Videocassette B, Segments 5, 6

Assessment
- *Formal Assessment,* p. 37
- *Preparation for College Admission Exams,* pp. 9, 11
- *Test Generator (One-Stop Planner CD-ROM)*

Internet
- *go.hrw.com* (keyword: *LE0 12-3*)

OBJECTIVES

1. Understand the historical and social forces that shaped the Renaissance
2. Interpret the way historical context influenced literary works in the Renaissance
3. Read and understand a time line
4. Understand the relevance of the Renaissance to our own day
5. Take notes on and discuss the definition of "the good life"

Responding to the Quotation

? These lines are part of the chorus at the end of Act I of *Henry V*. What is Shakespeare saying about England? [Possible answers: He is saying that although England is small in size, it has a large heart, which, in this context, may be interpreted as courage. This relationship of a big heart to a small body is analogous to the relationship of a small country to its "greatness," or importance in the world.]

RESPONDING TO THE ART

This bustling scene of London radiates energy and optimism, even if the foreground is dominated by the squat, dark Tower of London, the prison where enemies of the king were kept. Note the famous arched Traitor's Gate facing the Thames.

Activity. Ask students to list the things taking place in this painting. [People are rowing, shipping goods, riding horseback, writing, leaving on guard detail, conducting a court or business session, and praying.]

The Renaissance

by C. F. Main

O England! model to thy inward greatness,
Like little body with a mighty heart . . .
—*William Shakespeare*

British Library, London.

Tower of London and shipping, with Charles, duke of Orleans, seated in the Tower writing, from the *Poems of Charles Duke of Orleans and Other Works* (c. 1500), Roy 16 F II fol. 73.

go.hrw.com
LEO 12-Renaissance

Reaching All Students

Struggling Readers
Remind students that they are reading an informative essay and might need to adjust their reading rate by slowing down or rereading passages they find confusing the first time. Remind them to look for the summaries printed in bold type, of each section of the essay.

English Language Learners
Before students begin reading on their own, read each of the major headings with them, and tell them what kind of discussion to expect under each. Point out the summary statements, and explain that these will help students focus on and summarize the key ideas in each section.

Advanced Learners
Encourage advanced learners to find a topic in this introduction that they would like to explore and study further. Students may wish, for example, to learn more about Thomas More or Erasmus, or the everyday life of common English people during the Renaissance. Have students share the information they gather.

What do you think people living a hundred years from now will call the age we live in today? Will they say we lived in the Space Age, the Age of Computers, the Age of Anxiety, the Age of Violence? We might be given a label we can't even imagine.

Just as we don't know what people of the future will think of us, the people of Europe living in the 1400s, 1500s, and 1600s didn't know that they were living in the Renaissance. Historical periods—the Middle Ages, the Renaissance, the Romantic period—are historians' inventions, useful labels for complex phenomena. The Middle Ages in England did not end on a certain night in 1485, when King Richard III's naked body, trussed up like a turkey, was thrown in an unmarked grave. And the English Renaissance did not begin the moment a Tudor nobleman was crowned King Henry VII. The changes in people's values, beliefs, and behavior that marked the emerging Renaissance occurred gradually. Much that could be called "medieval" lingered on long after the period known as the Middle Ages was past. Historical periods cannot be rigidly separated from one another, but they can be distinguished.

Beginning in the late 1400s, the English Renaissance marked changes in people's values, beliefs, and behavior.

> Knowledge is power.
> —Francis Bacon, 1597

Rediscovering Ancient Greece and Rome

The term *renaissance* itself is a French word meaning "rebirth." **(A)** It refers particularly to renewed interest in classical learning, which means the writings of ancient Greece and Rome. In the long period of the Middle Ages, most European scholars had forgotten the Greek language, and they used a form of Latin that was very different from the Latin of ancient Rome. Very few ordinary people could read. Those who could read were encouraged to concentrate on texts promoting Church doctrine. But in the Renaissance, people discovered the marvels hidden away in old Greek and Latin classics—books that had been tucked away on the cobwebbed shelves of monasteries for **(B)** hundreds of years. Now people learned to read Greek once more and reformed the Latin that they read, wrote, and spoke.

Some people became more curious about themselves and their world than people in general had been in the Middle Ages, so that gradually there was a renewal of the human spirit—of curiosity and creativity. New energy seemed to be available for creating beautiful things and thinking new, even daring, thoughts. Today we still use the

World map drawn in a fool's head (detail) (1590). Based on *Ortelin's Atlas,* 1570.

© cliché Bibliothèque Nationale de France, Paris.

(A) Humanities Connections

The Term *Renaissance*

The term *Renaissance* was first used in the nineteenth century to characterize the changes that began in the time of Charlemagne and continued through the fifteenth or sixteenth century. Historians now discuss the period as marked by a series of renaissances, rather than one overarching transformation.

(B) Humanities Connections

The Book

Those "books" were actually handwritten manuscripts, preserved by Byzantine and Islamic scholars. With the invention of the printing press in the fifteenth century, however (see p. 198), what we know as the book became a reality and a working tool for scholars. By 1500, printers—particularly Italian printers—had published in book form the works of most of the important Latin authors.

Getting Students Involved

Cooperative Learning

Defining an Age. Students will enjoy discussing the question posed in the first paragraph on p. 193: What label best defines the modern age? Refer students to the boxed list on p. 200, and encourage them to come up with a list of the characteristics of the twentieth century. Students can brainstorm as a group, or they can generate their lists individually and then compile them. Once a master list is available on the chalkboard or on paper, have students work in groups of four or five to accomplish three tasks:

1. Analyze the list, deleting items they believe invalid or unimportant, combining items they believe express similar characteristics, and possibly adding ideas their discussion generates.
2. Rank in order their resulting list of defining characteristics. Include no more than five or six items.
3. Use their list as the basis for a label for the twentieth century.

Time Line

This time line shows major events that occurred both in England and around the world between the time Richard III was killed and the time the English monarchy was restored after Cromwell's death. Note that the time line does not start at the beginning of the Renaissance, which took place in northern Italy around 1300.

• 1485–1515

Age of Exploration

Students may need help making the connection between the age of exploration—which increased knowledge of the world, opened up vast new opportunities for colonization, and created wealth—and the changing world views of the Renaissance.

• 1541–1565

Sonnets

In 1557, the year before Elizabeth became queen, a printer named Richard Tottel put out an important collection of poems entitled *Songs and Sonnets*. The best poems in this book, which is commonly called *Tottel's Miscellany,* had been written some years earlier by Sir Thomas Wyatt and Henry Howard, the Earl of Surrey. Both Wyatt and Surrey were inspired by the Italian scholar and poet Petrarch and were responsible for introducing Petrarch's work into England.

• 1566–1590

Golden Ages in the East

During these years, the Mogul (or Mughal) leader Akbar, the grandson of Babur, was leading a golden age in what is now India. He defended religious freedom and presided over a flowering of culture that can still be seen in India's great miniature paintings and architecture. Meanwhile, beginning in 1587, Shah Abbas was leading the Safavid Empire, in what is now Iran, through a similar period of greatness when both art and industry flourished.

The Renaissance, 1485–1660

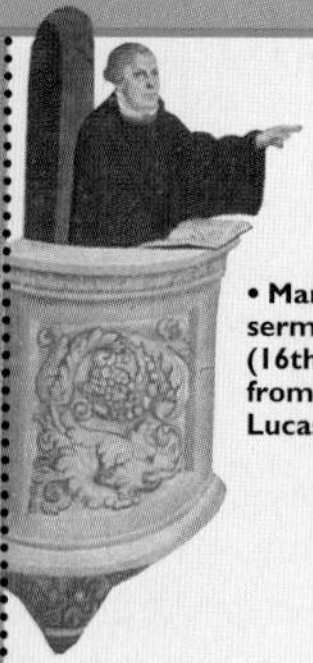

• Martin Luther's sermon (detail) (16th century) from a triptych by Lucas Cranach.

	1485–1515	1516–1540	1541–1565	1566–1590
LITERARY EVENTS	Niccolò Machiavelli's *The Prince* written, 1513	Book licensing laws introduced in England, 1538 Spanish priest Bernardino de Sahagún begins compiling exhaustive Aztec encyclopedia in Mexico, 1529 Thomas More's *Utopia* published, 1516	**William Shakespeare,** the Bard of Avon, born, 1564 *Tottel's Miscellany* (including poems of Wyatt and Surrey) published, 1557	**Edmund Spenser** publishes first three books of *The Faerie Queene,* 1590 **Christopher Marlowe**'s *Doctor Faustus* written, 1588 Okuni, a former priestess, forms first kabuki theater company in Japan (in 1629, Okuni and all other women banned from the kabuki stage), c. 1586 In France, Montaigne begins his *Essais,* 1572
CULTURAL/HISTORICAL EVENTS	Richard III is killed in battle, 1485 John Cabot explores northeast coast of North America, 1497 Vasco da Gama reaches India via Cape of Good Hope, 1498 Leonardo da Vinci paints *Mona Lisa,* c. 1503 Henry VIII crowned king of England, 1509 Balboa crosses Isthmus of Panama and sights Pacific Ocean, 1513	Martin Luther posts his ninety-five theses on church door in Wittenburg, Germany, beginning the Protestant Reformation, 1517 First Africans taken to Americas as slaves, 1517 Magellan leads first expedition to circumnavigate the globe, 1519–1521 Hernando Cortés conquers Mexico, destroying Aztec empire, 1521 In India, Babur conquers Delhi and founds Mogul dynasty, 1526 Henry VIII proclaims himself head of the Church of England, c. 1533	Michelangelo paints *The Last Judgment* on altar wall of the Sistine Chapel, 1534–1541 Polish astronomer Nicolaus Copernicus publishes theory that planets orbit the sun, 1543 Mary Tudor—"Bloody Mary"—reigns, restoring papal authority in England, 1553–1558 Elizabeth I becomes queen of England, 1558	English navy defeats Spanish Armada, 1588

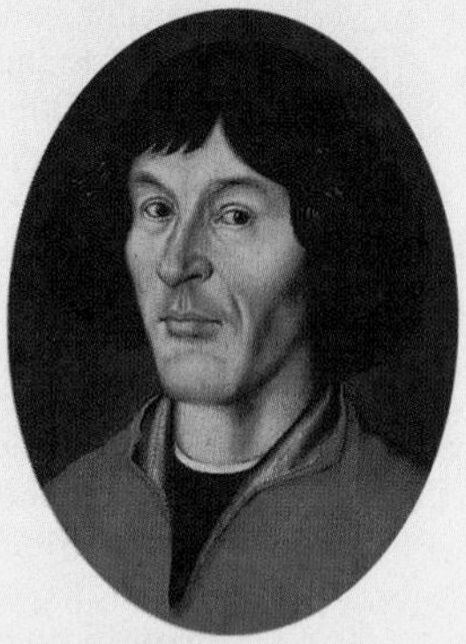

• *Nicolaus Copernicus* (detail) (1575). German School.

• *Mona Lisa* (c. 1503) by Leonardo da Vinci.

• Hernando Cortés (1485–1547), Spanish explorer, meeting Montezuma II (c. 1480–1520), Aztec emperor.

Using the Time Line

Have students use a print or nonprint encyclopedia or a database to place on the time line the following events in history, science, literature, and the arts:

- Botticelli paints *The Birth of Venus.* [c. 1486]
- Leonardo da Vinci draws the human figure in a circle to show proportions. [c. 1485–1490]
- Michelangelo sculpts his marble *David,* seventeen feet tall. [1501–1504]
- Diplomat Baldassare Castiglione publishes *The Courtier,* a book about polite society. [1528]
- Cabeza de Vaca publishes *La Relación,* an account of one of his journeys in the New World. [1542]
- Gerardus Mercator designs a projection of the round earth onto a flat map. [1569]
- Johannes Kepler discovers that the orbits of the planets are elliptical. [1609]

1591–1610

Shakespeare's sonnets published (written c. mid-1590s), 1609

Ben Jonson writes *The Masque of Blackness* and *Volpone*, 1605–1606

Shakespeare writes *King Lear* and *Macbeth*, 1605–1606

Cervantes publishes Part I of *Don Quixote* (Part II published in 1615), 1605

Globe Theatre built in London, 1599

In London, outbreak of plague forces theaters to close, 1593–1594

British East India Company founded for trade with Asia, 1600

Gunpowder Plot, an attempt by Guy Fawkes and others to blow up Parliament and assassinate James I, averted, 1605

First permanent English settlement in North America established at Jamestown, Virginia, 1607

In Italy, Galileo is first to study sky with telescope, 1609

1611–1640

Newspapers first published in London, 1621

Francis Bacon's *Novum Organum* (New Instrument) published, 1620

Aemilia Lanier publishes her book of poetry, *Salve Deus Rex Judaeorum*, 1611

King James Bible published, 1611

John Donne's *Holy Sonnets* written, 1610–1611

• Lithograph showing the arrival of the Pilgrims in Massachusetts Bay (1620).

The *Mayflower* lands at Plymouth Rock, Massachusetts, 1620

English physician William Harvey explains the circulation of blood, 1628

Taj Mahal built near Agra, India, c. 1632–c. 1649

Japan expels all Europeans, 1639

1641–1660

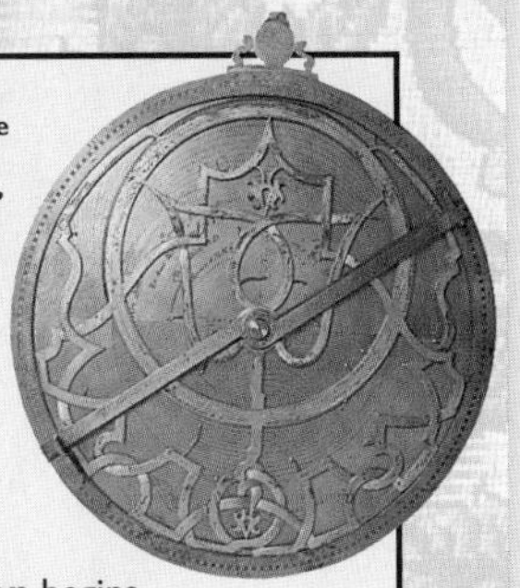

• English astrolabe (1559), a navigational instrument, made for Queen Elizabeth I by Thomas Gemini.

John Milton begins *Paradise Lost*, c. 1658

American poet Anne Bradstreet's *The Tenth Muse Lately Sprung Up in America* published in London, 1650

Puritans close all theaters in England, 1642–1660

English Civil Wars fought, 1642–1651

Manchus proclaim Ch'ing dynasty in China, 1644

• Taj Mahal.

Charles I beheaded, 1649

Dutch establish settlement in South Africa, 1652

Oliver Cromwell rules England as lord protector, 1653–1658

Jews legally readmitted to England (after being expelled in 1290), 1655

Puritan Commonwealth ends; monarchy restored with Charles II, 1660

• The World Map (c. 1540), from the *Portolan Atlas of the World* by Battista Agnese of Venice.

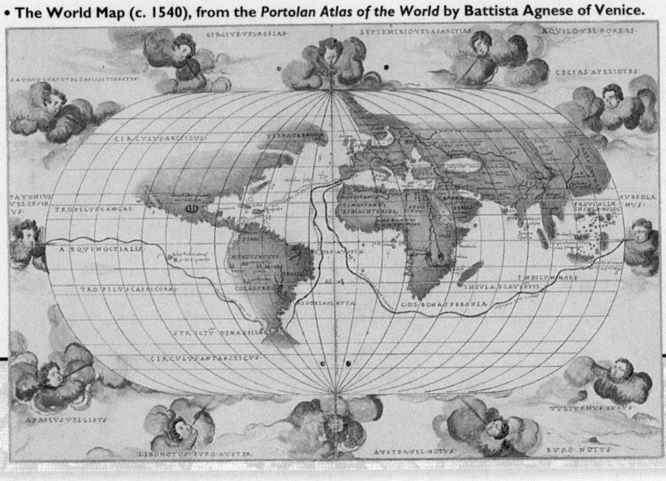

• **1591–1610**

Galileo

Galileo Galilei (1564–1642) made discoveries that challenged the official teachings of the Roman Catholic Church. Galileo's Copernican view that the earth revolved around the sun, rather than the opposite, was denounced by the Church as heresy in 1616 because it contradicted the Bible and displaced humanity as the center of the universe. Galileo was ordered not to spread his theory. In 1632, however, he published *Dialogue on Two Chief World Systems*. He was again summoned by the Church and this time knelt to recant his view publicly. He is said, however, to have muttered on arising, "Eppur si muove" ("But still it [Earth] moves.") He spent the last eight years of his life under house arrest. In 1992, Pope John Paul II officially announced that the Church had been wrong in its condemnation of Galileo.

• **1611–1640**

Francis Bacon and the Scientific Method

Another scientific thinker of the Renaissance was Francis Bacon, who championed the use of experiments, instead of reliance on the conclusions of ancient thinkers. Modern scientific methods are based not only on Bacon's thinking but also on that of René Descartes, a French mathematician of the Renaissance.

Getting Students Involved

Using the Time Line

Ask students to use the time line as a starting point for projects such as the following:

- **Mapping Discoveries**
  Have students identify the entries that refer to voyages of discovery. Then ask them to create a world map tracing the route of each explorer.
- **Going in Depth**
  Ask students to read through the time line and pick an entry that they find intriguing. Then have each student research the significance of the event and give a three-minute oral report.
- **Making Connections**
  Choose an event such as Henry VIII's establishment of the Church of England and create a "focused time line" that traces all the consequences or results of this action. First select events already listed on this time line, and then fill in key related dates from your reading of the period introduction and your research.

Responding to the Art

Paulus Vredeman de Vries (1567–c. 1630), a Flemish painter, continued his famous father's tradition of painting architectural scenes with figures. However elegant this palatial Renaissance interior, we would find it uncomfortable today. Huge, drafty halls such as these were nearly impossible to heat, making several layers of clothing necessary. Garments could not be cleaned in those days—the soap, made from ashes and lye, was far too harsh. Little wonder that there was a brisk trade in perfumes.

Activity. Have students discuss what they see in the painting that reveals something about the customs of the times. They may enjoy creating conversations for some of the couples, particularly the one in the lower left corner, who seem to be having a misunderstanding.

Ⓐ Literary Connections

The Biblical Story of Creation

This version of creation differs a great deal from the story of creation told in the Bible. This passage represents the new thinking of the Renaissance and emphasizes people's freedom to choose. It does not dwell on sin, and it appears to make men and women equal in their capacity to rise and fall.

Ⓑ Exploring the Culture

Renaissance Man: Leonardo da Vinci

Leonardo da Vinci was probably the ultimate Renaissance man. The painter of the *Mona Lisa* (see p. 194) and other important works, he pioneered new artistic techniques such as *sfumato,* a way of softening sharp lines. In addition, he was a scientist who explored everything from the movement of water to human anatomy, as well as an engineer who designed various flying and military machines.

Ⓒ Background

Sources of Renaissance Wealth

Ask students what event on the time line helped open up wealth from the East. [Vasco da Gama's voyage to India in 1498] After this successful journey, the Portuguese began to trade in the Indian Ocean.

Ladies and Gentlemen Dancing in a Sumptuous Interior by Paulus Vredeman de Vries (1567–c. 1630).
Christie's, London.

Ⓐ God made man and woman at the close of the creation, to know the laws of the universe, to love its beauty, and to admire its greatness. He bound his human creatures to no fixed place, to no prescribed form of work, and by no iron necessity, but gave them freedom to will and to love. "I have set thee," says the Creator, "in the midst of the world, that thou mayest the more easily behold and see all that is therein. I created thee a being neither heavenly nor earthly, neither mortal nor immortal only, that thou mightest be free to shape and to overcome thyself. Thou mayest sink into a beast or be born anew to the divine likeness. To thee alone is given a growth and a development depending on thine own free will."

—Pico della Mirandola (1463–1494), *On the Dignity of Humanity*

Ⓑ term "Renaissance person" for an energetic and productive human being who is interested in science, literature, history, art, and other subjects. (In America, Virginia's Thomas Jefferson, author of the Declaration of Independence, is referred to as a "Renaissance man.")

Fifteenth-century scholars rediscovered the writings of ancient Greece and Rome. At this same time, people became more curious about themselves and their world.

It All Began in Italy: A Flourish of Genius

Ⓒ The new energy and creativity were first observable in Italy, where considerable wealth had been generated from banking and trade with the East. The Renaissance began in Italy in the fourteenth century and lasted into the sixteenth. Thinking about just a few of the extraordinary people who flourished in this period—artists such as Leonardo da Vinci and Michelangelo, explorers such as Christopher Columbus, or scientists such as Galileo—reminds us how remarkably rich this period was, and how much we owe to it.

Almost everyone in Europe and Britain at this time was Roman Catholic, in name anyway, so the Church was very rich and powerful, even in political affairs—in ways we would probably object to today. Many of the popes were lavish patrons of artists, architects, and scholars.

Using Students' Strengths

Intrapersonal Learners

Ask students to keep a list of questions and comments that occur to them as they read this essay. When they have finished reading, invite them to write a self-assessment about how well they responded to and understood the essay.

Interpersonal Learners

As students read, or after they finish, have them form small groups to discuss what they might have wanted to be during the Renaissance and where and how they might have lived. Students might also talk about what they would have valued or feared most.

Spatial Learners

Have students create a time line as they read. It should be independent of the time line shown on pp. 194–195 and should reflect the events related in the essay, as well as significant works or moments in the lives of those quoted in the text.

Pope Julius II, for example, commissioned the artist Michelangelo to paint gigantic scenes from the Bible on the ceiling of the Sistine Chapel, a small church in the pope's "city" that was called, as it is today, the Vatican. Lying on his back on a scaffold, Michelangelo painted the Creation, the fall of Man and Woman, Noah's flood, and other Biblical and mythological subjects. His bright, heroic figures, which are still admired by thousands of visitors to Rome each year, show individual human beings who are noble and capable of perfection. This optimistic view of human nature was also expressed by many other Renaissance painters and writers.

The Renaissance began in fourteenth-century Italy, where the Catholic Church financed many intellectual and artistic endeavors.

Humanism: Questions About the Good Life

Refreshed by the classics, the new writers and artists were part of an intellectual movement known as **humanism.** The humanists went to the old Latin and Greek classics to discover new answers to such questions as "What is a human being?" "What is a good life?" and "How do I lead a good life?" Of course, Christianity provided complete answers to these questions, answers that the Renaissance humanists accepted as true. Renaissance humanists found no essential conflicts between the teachings of the Church and those of an ancient Roman moralist like Cicero. They sought instead to harmonize these two great sources of wisdom: the Bible and the classics. Their aim was to use the classics to strengthen, not discredit, Christianity.

The Outdoor Concert (detail) (16th century) by the Italian School.

Hotel Lallemand, Bourges, France.

Some books are to be tasted, others to be swallowed, and some few to be chewed and digested.
—Francis Bacon, 1625

The humanists' first task was to recover accurate copies of these ancient writings. Their searches through Italian monasteries turned up writers and works whose very existence had been forgotten. Their next task was to share their findings. And so they became teachers, especially of the young men who would become the next generation's rulers—wise and virtuous rulers, they hoped. From the Greek writer Plutarch, for instance, these humanist teachers would learn that the aim of life is to attain virtue, not success or money or fame, because virtue is the best possible human possession and the only source of true happiness.

An intellectual movement known as humanism began to use the Latin and Greek classics, combined with traditional Christian thought, to teach people how to live and how to rule.

D Exploring the Culture

The Sistine Chapel

The Sistine Chapel is named after Pope Sixtus IV, who commissioned its construction (1473–81). Unimpressive and unadorned from the outside, the chapel's interior walls feature frescoes depicting events from the life of Christ and Moses, painted by a number of artists. The Old Testament stories on the ceiling and *The Last Judgment* on the wall behind the altar are the work of Michelangelo. During a fifteen-year restoration effort completed in 1994, centuries of dirt, smoke, and varnish were removed. Something close to the gleaming colors the artist originally intended once again illuminate the paintings today.

E Exploring the Culture

Michelangelo

True to the definition of a Renaissance man, Michelangelo excelled in many areas. Not only did he execute the masterwork of the Sistine Chapel, but he created sculptures of monumental proportions that convey the beauty and majesty of the human physique. Michelangelo also became chief architect of St. Peter's Basilica in Rome, one of the most important projects of his time. Although he is less famous for writing, Michelangelo also wrote poetry.

F Humanities Connections

The Humanities

The humanists not only studied the subjects related to a classical education—history, literature, philosophy, and more—but they made these subjects popular again. Hence, the collective term for these subjects became the *humanities*.

G Literary Connections

Milton on Education

The aim of humanistic teaching, as Milton summarized it in his essay "Of Education," was not to produce scholars but to prepare students to "perform justly, skillfully, and magnanimously all the offices both private and public, of peace and war."

Responding to the Art

Jan van der Straet (c. 1523–?), a Belgian by birth, greatly admired the work of Michelangelo.

Activity. Explain to students that this illustration is an engraving. To make an engraving, a sharp instrument called a burin is used to cut a picture or design on the surface of a copper plate. Ink applied with a cloth fills the plate's indentations. After excess ink is removed, the plate, a piece of paper, and a felt blanket are squeezed between the roller of a press, forcing ink onto the paper. Finally, the print is pulled from the page, revealing a copy of the design. Ask students what they can learn from this engraving about sixteenth-century bookmaking.

Printing Shop (1580s) by Jan van der Straet. Engraving.

By permission of The Folger Shakespeare Library, Washington, D.C.

The New Technology: A Flood of Print

The computer has radically transformed how we get information today. Similarly, the printing press transformed the way information was exchanged during the Renaissance. Before this, all books were laboriously written out by hand—you can imagine how difficult and expensive this was and how few books were available.

The inventor of printing with movable type was a German named Johannes Gutenberg (1400?–1468). He printed the first complete book, an immense Latin Bible, at Mainz, Germany, around 1455. From there, the art and craft of printing spread to other cities in Germany, in the Low Countries (the Netherlands, Belgium, and Luxembourg), and in northern Italy. By 1500, relatively inexpensive books were available throughout western Europe. In 1476, printing reached England, then regarded as an

Bookbinder (16th century).

Correr Museum, Venice.

Ⓐ Reading Skills and Strategies

Drawing Conclusions

? Why do you think Gutenberg chose to print the Bible as his first book? [Possible answers: In an age when the vast majority of Europeans shared a common Christian heritage, this was the most widely read and respected book.] The Bible remains a bestseller today and scores of editions and translations are available.

Ⓑ Exploring the Historical Period

The Printing Press

Spain, Hungary, and Poland also had their first printing presses between 1474 and 1476; Denmark and Sweden were equipped by 1482–1483. By 1500, forty thousand titles had been printed, totaling about six million books.

Crossing the Curriculum

Science

The Renaissance was a time of increasing scientific knowledge. For example, Leonardo da Vinci is remembered for his inventions and his analysis of the human body. Have students do oral reports on an English Renaissance scientist, such as the physician William Harvey or the botanists John Parkinson or William Turner.

Music

Encourage students to choose an English composer, such as William Byrd, Thomas Morley, or Thomas Campion, and to find a poem the composer set to music and bring an example of the song to class. Play any recordings they locate, and have students check to see if the lyrics were written by any of the poets in this collection.

island remote from the centers of civilization. In that year, William Caxton (1422?–1491), a merchant, diplomat, and writer who had been living in the Low Countries, set up a printing press in Westminster (now part of London). In all, Caxton's press issued about one hundred different titles, initiating a flood of print in English that is still increasing.

Gutenberg's printing press helped spread the new knowledge, making more books available to more people than ever before.

Erasmus of Rotterdam (detail) (c. 1523) by Hans Holbein the Younger. Oil on wood (42 cm × 32 cm).
Louvre, Paris.

Two Friends—Two Humanists

When you hear people speak of humanism, you may hear the name Erasmus. Desiderius Erasmus (1466?–1536) is today perhaps the best known of all the Renaissance humanists. Erasmus was a Dutch monk, but he lived outside the monastery and loved to travel, visiting many of the countries in Europe, including Italy, France, Germany, and England. He belonged, then, to all Europe. Because he wrote in Latin, he could address his many writings to all the educated people of western Europe.

On his visits to England, Erasmus taught Greek at Cambridge University and became friendly with a number of important people, among them a young lawyer named Thomas More (1477?–1535). More and Erasmus had much in common: They both loved life, laughter, and classical learning, and they both were dedicated churchmen, though they were impatient with some of the Church's corrupt practices at that time.

Like Erasmus, More wrote in Latin—**C** poems, pamphlets, biographies, and his famous treatise on human society, *Utopia* (yo͞o·tō′pē·ə) (1516). This book **D** became immediately popular, and it has been repeatedly translated into English and many other languages. Hundreds of writers have imitated or parodied it, and it has given us a useful adjective for describing impractical social schemes: *utopian*. More himself was far from impractical; he held a number of important offices, rose to the

Sir Thomas More (detail) (16th century) by Hans Holbein the Younger.
© The Frick Collection, New York.

RESPONDING TO THE ART

Hans Holbein the Younger (c. 1497–1543) was a German artist who learned his trade from his father. Because of Holbein's reputation as a master portraitist who could capture lifelike details of skin, clothing, and hair, he was often asked to produce likenesses of royalty. Henry VIII and most of his wives sat for Holbein portraits. The king admired Holbein and pardoned him for pushing down his stairs an Earl who insisted on visiting Holbein's art studio. Holbein died in London during a plague. (For more art by Holbein the Younger, see p. 247.)

Activity. Encourage students to compare Holbein's portraits with others in the book. They could also note what the subjects of these portraits are holding or wearing and why those details are significant. (More is wearing the Seal of the Lord Chancellor.)

C Background

Education for Women

Defying custom, More taught Latin to his daughter Meg; few women in Renaissance Europe were given any kind of higher education.

D Literary Connections

More's *Utopia*

Book I of More's *Utopia* is a dialogue analyzing the social, economic, penal, and moral problems in England. Book II is a narrative describing Utopia. (More coined the word *utopia* from the Greek *ou* meaning "not" and *topos* meaning "place." Etymologically, therefore, it ironically means "nowhere"; the prefatory poem in the book also suggests that it is a pun on *eu-topos*, "good place.") In Utopia, which is nowhere, or nonexistent, poverty, crime, injustice, and other problems do not exist.

Using Students' Strengths

Verbal Learners

Sir Thomas More inspired a new literary genre, the utopian novel, which in fact usually depicts a negative utopia (called *distopia*): a society considered perfect by those in power, but evil or flawed by those not in power. Interested students could give oral summary reports on More's *Utopia* and on two of its most famous twentieth-century descendants, George Orwell's *1984* and Aldous Huxley's *Brave New World*.

Naturalist Learners

Before the Renaissance, gardening was primarily a practical activity. The increased prosperity and scientific curiosity of the Renaissance led to an interest in pleasure gardens. Have students consult a history of gardening to find illustrations of Renaissance gardens that highlight some typical motifs, like mazes, painted statuary, and knot designs (beds separated by low hedges planted in a geometric pattern).

Ⓐ Exploring the Culture

English Humanists

Other English humanists were Sir Thomas Elyot and Roger Ascham, who both wrote in English—yet another sign that Latin would soon cease to be the language of all learned discourse. Elyot's *The Book Named the Governor* (1531) argues that England's leaders need a knowledge of ancient literature, history, and philosophy. Ascham, who was Queen Elizabeth I's tutor, wrote *The Schoolmaster* (1570), which contains "the best advice that was ever given for the study of language" according to Samuel Johnson (1709–1784).

Ⓑ Exploring the Historical Period

The Catholic Reformation

Students should know that this was a time of internal reform in the Church, as well as a time of criticism from those who chose to break away. Pope Paul III, for example, convened the Council of Trent in 1545 to investigate the selling of indulgences, or religious pardons, and other abuses.

Ⓒ Exploring the Historical Period

Protestantism

Luther began the Lutheran church; soon others, including the Anglican, Calvinist, and Anabaptist faiths, sprang up. All of these faiths, and the denominations that developed from them, such as Methodist, Episcopal, and Presbyterian, have come to be called Protestant.

What Was the Renaissance?

Here, reduced to a small list, are the major characteristics of that great era called the Renaissance:

- People expanded their worlds by reading classical Greek and Roman writers rather than only religious writings that promoted Christian doctrine.
- Humanism spread, focusing attention on human life here and now, as well as on eternal life.
- A new technology—printing—made books widely available.
- A growing merchant class, rich with wealth plundered from the Americas, began to challenge the power of the bishops and the pope.
- The spread of scholarly Latin throughout Europe made possible the sharing of ideas.

very top of his profession, was knighted, and, as Lord Chancellor, became one of the king's chief ministers. More continues to fascinate people today. The play *A Man for All Seasons,* by Robert Bolt, later made into a movie (available on videotape), is about More and his tragic standoff with King Henry VIII over a matter of law (see page 202). You might notice that many lawyers and politicians today hang a picture of Thomas More in their offices (the famous Holbein portrait is shown on page 199).

Ⓐ ***Desiderius Erasmus and Thomas More, humanists and close friends, helped shape European thought and history.***

The Reformation: Breaking with the Church

Ⓑ While the Renaissance was going on throughout Europe, there occurred in some countries another important series of events called the **Reformation.** In England these two vast movements were closely related, and their forces were felt by all English writers. Although the exact nature of the Reformation varied from country to country, one feature was common to all Reformers: They rejected the authority of the pope and the Italian churchmen. In England, conflicts with the papacy had occurred off and on over the centuries, but adjustments had always been made on both sides. By the 1530s, an open break with the Roman Church could no longer be avoided.

> Superstition, idolatry, and hypocrisy have ample wages, but truth goes a-begging.
> —Martin Luther, *Table Talk,* published in 1569

By then, a number of circumstances made such a break possible. Strong feelings of patriotism and national identity made the English people resent the financial burdens imposed on them by the Vatican—the pope, after all, was a foreign power in far-off Italy. Moreover, new religious ideas were coming into England from the Continent, especially Ⓒ from Germany. There, a monk named Martin Luther (1483-1546) had founded a new kind of Christianity, based not on what the pope said, but on a personal understanding of the Bible. Like any institution that has

been around for a long time and that has ignored corruption within its ranks, the Church needed reform. Right at home in England, humanists like More and Erasmus were ridiculing old superstitions, as well as the **D** ignorance and idleness of monks and the loose living and personal wealth of priests and bishops.

Strong feelings of patriotism and new ideas coming from the Continent encouraged people to question the authority of the Catholic Church and to object to the financial burdens imposed on them by the pope in Rome.

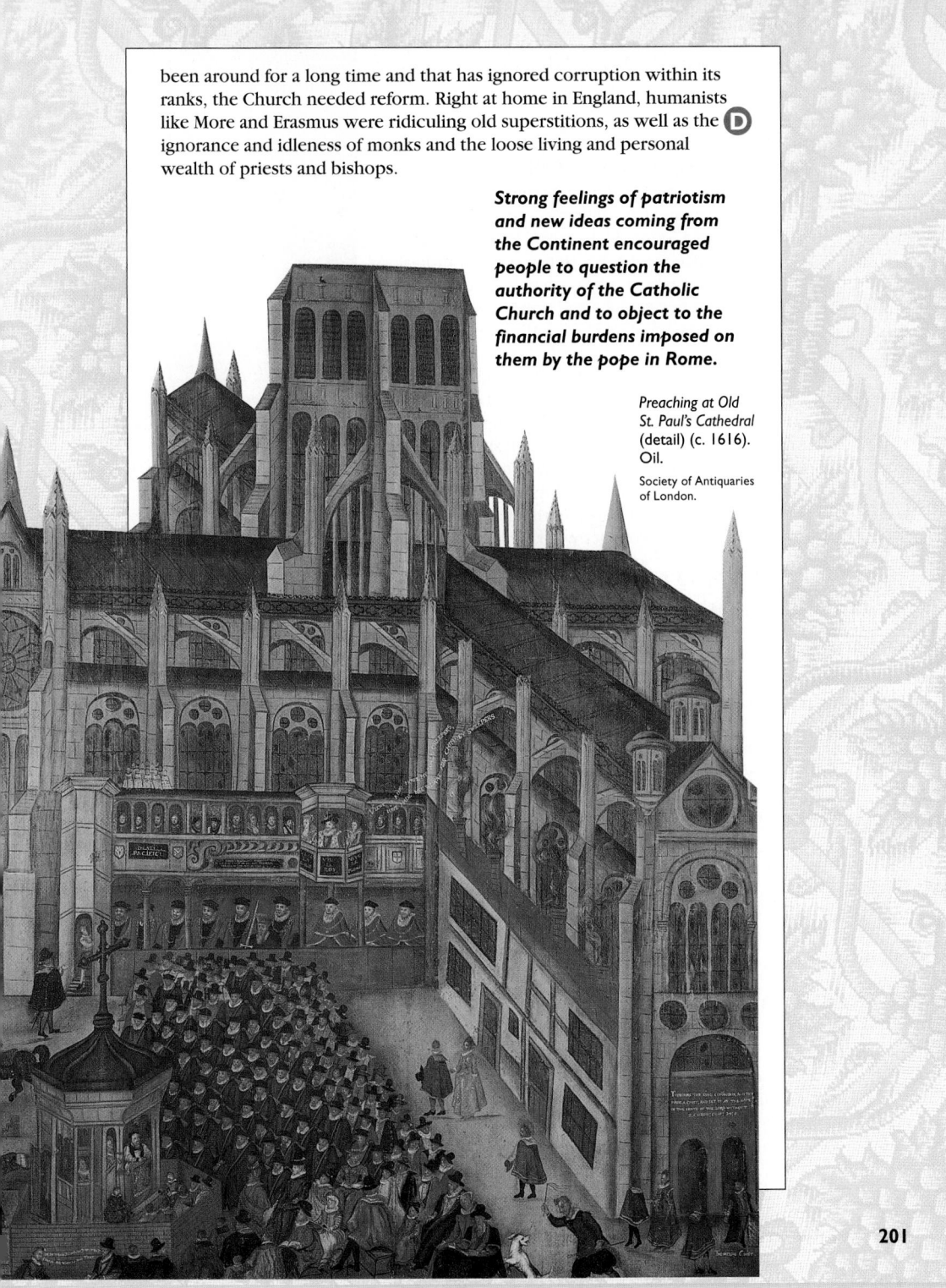

Preaching at Old St. Paul's Cathedral (detail) (c. 1616). Oil.

Society of Antiquaries of London.

D Literary Connections

Erasmus on Ethics

In 1509 Desiderius Erasmus wrote his well-known satire, *The Praise of Folly.* In this book he not only suggested that people return to a simple code of Christian ethics but also made hearty fun of greedy merchants and petty, mincing scholars. Priests and bishops who failed to live a life of poverty and humility were also a special target of his biting wit.

Responding to the Art

Old St. Paul's was under construction from shortly after the Norman conquest until around 1300. The church was the local parish of London and always a center of activity—in fact, a road known as St. Paul's Walk intersected the cathedral. The church, a structure typical of the Gothic period (mid 1100s–1400s), had many spires and flying buttresses.

Today a visitor to Saint Paul's Cathedral in London sees a church very different from the one in this painting. Only a few months after Charles II asked his architect, Christopher Wren, to draw a plan for the restoration of Saint Paul's, the Great Fire of 1666 destroyed most of London, including the cathedral. Wren, one of England's greatest architects, began rebuilding the cathedral in 1675, modeling it after Roman architecture with a great dome inspired by the Pantheon.

Activity. Ask students what they might learn about English society of the period by examining the seating arrangements here. [Possible response: Society is still hierarchical with the nobility sitting in a second-floor gallery.]

Taking a Second Look

Review: Using Text Organizers

Remind students that overview text and headings can help them identify the main ideas and important details in a text. Graphic features like charts and illustrations can serve the same purpose, or they can add new information related to the text.

Activities

1. Have students identify the bold callout text on pp. 200–201 and explain its purpose.
2. Have students explain the purpose of the box at the top of p. 200.
3. Students may have already noticed the text blocks with quotations throughout this essay. Explain that each one is a primary source: It contains the words of a Renaissance figure. Ask students to explain why these quotations appear in the text and what they add to their understanding of the Renaissance.

Ⓐ Literary Connections

Anne Boleyn

This information on King Henry VIII and Anne Boleyn is important background information for reading "Whoso List to Hunt," Sir Thomas Wyatt's poem that appears on p. 215. Be sure students understand how formidable and ruthless Henry VIII could be. Students might also make inferences about what Anne Boleyn's considerable charms must have been.

Ⓑ Reading Skills and Strategies

Making Inferences

? What does the pronoun *this* in the quotation refer to? [More's beard] What does the quotation say about his character? [Possible answers: More was both witty and self-possessed. At the very instant of losing his life, he could respond to the situation with a jab against the king. He did not regret the decision he had made to oppose the king's divorce and supremacy over the Church.]

Ⓒ Humanities Connections

A Faith Born of Protest

The word *Protestant* was first used in April 1529. At that time, it was applied to a number of German protesters who disagreed with the Catholic majority's decision to have Lutheranism condemned. Later, the word came to refer to anyone vocally "*protest*-ant," or those who belonged to a Christian church or sect other than the Catholic or Orthodox Churches.

RESPONDING TO THE ART

Michael Sittou (1469–1525) worked for royalty in Spain, Flanders, London, and Copenhagen, and developed a cosmopolitan painting style.

Activity. Catherine's hair was blonde and long, and as the portrait shows, she was pretty. Her piety and dignity in the face of the humiliation she endured at the hands of her husband earned her the everlasting love of the English people. Ask students to contrast Catherine's portrait with that of her daughter, her only surviving child, on p. 205.

King Versus Pope: All for an Heir

The generations-old conflict between the pope and the king of England came to a climax when Henry VIII wanted to get rid of his wife of twenty-four years. Divorce was not allowed, especially for kings (until recently, that was still true in Britain), so Henry needed a loophole. He asked Pope Clement VII to declare that he, Henry, was not properly married to his Spanish wife, Catherine of Aragon, because she had previously been wedded—for all of five months—to his older brother Arthur, now dead. (It was against Church law to marry a dead sibling's spouse; the Biblical basis for the law is in Leviticus.)

Catherine of Aragon (16th century) by M. Sittou.
Kunsthistorisches Museum, Vienna.

Henry had two motives for wanting to get rid of Catherine. First, although she had borne him a princess, she was too old to give him the male heir that he thought he must have. (Catherine had lost five babies.) What is more, another Ⓐ younger woman had won Henry's dangerous affections: The king now wished to marry Anne Boleyn, who had been his "favorite" for several years. (Henry had earlier seduced Anne's sister.) The pope was not able to grant Henry the annulment of his marriage, even if he had wanted to, because the pope was controlled by Queen Catherine's nephew, the emperor of Spain. And so, upon receiving the pope's refusal in 1533, Henry simply declared himself head of the English Church. He then appointed a new archbishop of Canterbury, who obligingly declared Henry's marriage to Catherine invalid.

> . . . reminding us of a point in astronomy, which is that the longer the days are the farther off is the sun and yet the hotter; so is it with our love, for although by absence we are parted it nevertheless keeps its fervency, at least in my case and hoping the like of yours . . .
>
> —King Henry VIII, in a letter to Anne Boleyn, 1528

With Catherine packed away under house arrest—since she refused to accept the annulment of her marriage—Henry closed all of England's monasteries and sold the rich buildings and lands to his subjects. While the vast majority of his subjects agreed with Henry's changes in the Church, some of them did not. The best known of all those who remained loyal to the pope was Sir Thomas More, now the Lord Chancellor of England. More felt he could not legally recognize his friend Henry as head of the Church. For More's stubbornness, Henry ordered that his Lord Chancellor be beheaded. It wasn't the first—or last—time that Henry executed a friend.

> Ⓑ This hath not offended the king.
>
> —Sir Thomas More, drawing his beard aside as he placed his head on the block, 1535

Ⓒ This was the very beginning of Protestantism in England. Many people were dissatisfied with the new church for reasons just the opposite of More's. They felt that it was not reformed enough, that it was merely a copy of Catholicism, as in

Getting Students Involved

Cooperative Learning

News Live in 1600. Have students work in groups of three or four to choose one Renaissance "news" event and to create a one- or two-minute modern-day newscast based on it. Events can be selected from this essay or from the literature. For example, students could research and present the events surrounding Marlowe's mysterious death; broadcast "live" from the scene of the defeat of the Armada; report on developments in astronomy; or interview Queen Elizabeth on recent events in England, abroad, or at the court. Students may divide the work of researching, writing, practicing, and presenting the event in any way they wish, but each member should write a paragraph detailing his or her own individual contribution to the project.

some respects it was. These dissidents, known as Puritans, Baptists, Presbyterians, Dissenters, and Nonconformists, wanted to get rid of many things they called "popish," such as the bishops, the prayer book, the priest's vestments, and even the church bells and the stained-glass windows. Some of them said that religion was solely a matter between the individual and God. This idea, which is still the foundation of most Protestant churches, is directly traceable to the teachings of those Renaissance humanists who emphasized the freedom of all human beings. **D**

In 1531, refused an annulment by the pope, Henry VIII broke with the Catholic Church in Rome and declared himself head of the English Church. This marked the beginning of the Protestant Reformation in England.

The Great Harry (detail) (1546) from the Anthony Roll manuscript.

The Pepys Library, Magdalene College, Cambridge.

Henry VIII: Renaissance Man and Executioner

The five Tudor rulers of England are easy to remember: They consist of a grandfather, a father, and three children. The grandfather was Henry VII (1457–1509), a Welsh nobleman who seized the throne after England was totally exhausted by the long and bloody struggle called the Wars of the Roses. (Both factions involved used a rose as their emblem, one red, one white.) Henry VII was a shrewd, patient, and stingy man who restored peace and order to the kingdom; without these, there could never have been a cultural Renaissance. **E**

His son Henry VIII (r. 1509–1547) had six wives: After Catherine of Aragon and Anne Boleyn, there were Jane Seymour, Anne of Cleves, Catherine Howard, and Catherine Parr. The fates of these unfortunate women are summarized in a jingle:

> Divorced, beheaded, died,
> Divorced, beheaded, survived.

The sexual intrigues of the court trapped several of Henry's wives: The king could play around, but he couldn't tolerate being suspicious of his wives' fidelity. The price paid by two young wives was heavy. Like Thomas More, Anne Boleyn and Catherine Howard lost their heads on the chopping block.

Despite his messy home life, Henry VIII was a very important figure. He created the Royal Navy, which put a stop to foreign invasions of England and provided the means for this island kingdom to spread its political power, language, and literature all over the globe. If we overlook his use of the sword against his enemies (and friends), Henry VIII himself deserves the title "Renaissance man." He wrote poetry and played many different musical instruments well; he was a champion athlete and a hunter; and he patronized the new humanistic learning. But in his old **F**

D Exploring the Culture

The Source of Protestantism

There is a sixteenth-century saying that "Erasmus laid the egg and Luther hatched it."

E Exploring the Historical Period

Effects of the Wars of the Roses

The Wars of the Roses began in 1455 and were fought by the rival families of York and Lancaster. By the time the struggle ended in 1485, so many baronial families were extinguished that the hierarchy of succession to the throne in England was permanently altered, allowing Henry VII to become king.

F Background

The Ethnocentric English

Henry VIII was a patron of Italian artists, craftsmen, and military engineers. Nevertheless, Henry, like many an Englishman before and after him, was ethnocentric: He believed in the superiority of the English. In *The Civilization of Europe in the Renaissance,* John Hale quotes this Renaissance Italian description of the English: "The English are great lovers of themselves and everything belonging to them; they think there are no other men than themselves, and no other world but England. . . ."

Professional Notes

Critical Comment: Henry VIII's Legacy

What was Henry VIII's greatest accomplishment? According to historian John Burke, it was the creation of what would become the modern Admiralty, or the government department in charge of the navy. Burke writes that Henry VIII also "extended the royal dock yards and encouraged the construction of faster ships with superior fire-power. He laid, as it were, the keels of that future navy which was to thwart the ambitions of one greedy enemy after another." Burke also credits Henry VIII with the creation or development of many beautiful buildings and praises his concern for at least some forms of the law.

RESPONDING TO THE ART

The seated monarch is Henry VIII. Henry hands a sword to the boy king, Edward VI. From the left comes the hated Mary, linked to the Spanish King Philip II—the English always depicted the Spanish in melancholic black. At the far left is the god of war, Mars. At the right is Elizabeth I, who renounces Mary's sword and ushers in Peace and Plenty, at the far right. Elizabeth wears a stiff, inverted-triangle bodice over a bell-shaped skirt. Her extremely white-powdered face is surrounded by reddish hair and a large ruff. (In the queen's later years a wig disguised her scanty hair, a result of smallpox.)

Activity. What details about this scene suggest that it was painted during the reign of Elizabeth I? [The viewer's attention is directed toward Elizabeth as she stands in the foreground dressed in light colors, while all of the others stand behind her in dark clothing.] What might the painting say regarding Elizabeth's attitude toward her reign and the succession of the Tudors? [Elizabeth's position in the painting clearly asserts her place in the succession, as well as her ability to bring peace and plenty (represented here as her attendants) to her country. Henry, in the center of the painting, is a dominant figure; this emphasizes Elizabeth's legitimacy, which had been questioned on various occasions.]

age, Henry was also coarse, dissolute, arrogant, and an unregenerate womanizer. He died without knowing that the child he ignored because she was female would become the greatest ruler England ever had.

Henry VIII's rule was bold and bloody. He increased England's strength and ensured its security by building up the Royal Navy, but those close to the king paid a high price.

An Allegory of the Tudor Succession: The Family of Henry VIII (c. 1589–1595) by the British School, possibly after Lucas de Heere. Oil on panel (45″ × 71¾″).

Yale Center for British Art, Paul Mellon Collection, New Haven.

The Boy King and Bloody Mary

Henry VIII was survived by three children: Mary, daughter of the Spanish princess, Catherine of Aragon; Elizabeth, daughter of Anne Boleyn, a lady-in-waiting at the court; and Edward, son of noblewoman Jane Seymour, who died twelve days after her son's birth. According to the laws of succession, the son had to be crowned first, and so at age nine the son of Henry and Jane Seymour became Edward VI (r. 1547–1553). An intelligent but sickly boy, he ruled in name only while his relatives wielded the actual power.

When Edward died of tuberculosis, he was followed by his half-Spanish half-sister Mary (r. 1553–1558). Mary was a devout, strong-willed Catholic determined to avenge the wrongs done to her mother. She restored the pope's power in England and ruthlessly hunted down Protestants.

Had she lived longer, and had she exercised better judgment, Mary might have undone all her father's accomplishments. But she made a strategic error when she burned about three hundred of her subjects at

the stake. She further lost the support of her people when she married Philip II, king of Spain, a country England was beginning to fear and hate. (Mary was thirty-seven and Philip only twenty-six.) Mary's executions earned her the name "Bloody Mary." When Mary died of a fever, childless, her sister Elizabeth became queen.

Mary Tudor succeeded her father Henry VIII. Immediately, she killed Protestants and reversed her father's policies: She restored the pope's power in England.

Mary Tudor (16th century) by an unknown artist.
Musée Condé, Chantilly, France.

Elizabeth: The Virgin Queen (A)

Elizabeth I (r. 1558–1603) was one of the most brilliant and successful monarchs in history. Since she inherited a kingdom torn by fierce religious feuds, her first task was to restore law and order. She reestablished the Church of England and again rejected the pope's authority, and the pope promptly excommunicated her. To keep Spain appeased, she pretended that she just might marry her widowed brother-in-law, King Philip.

Philip was the first of a long procession of noblemen, both foreign and English, who wanted to wed her. But Elizabeth resisted marriage all her life and officially remained "the Virgin Queen" (thereby giving the American colony Virginia its name). She knew that her strength lay in her independence and her ability to play one suitor off against another. "I am your anointed Queen," she told a group from Parliament who urged her to marry. "I will never be by violence constrained to do anything. I thank God I am endued with such qualities that if I were turned out of the realm in my petticoat, I were able to live in any place in Christendom."

Fain would I climb, yet fear I to fall.
—Sir Walter Raleigh to Elizabeth I, scratched on a windowpane (B)
If thy heart fails thee, climb not at all.
—Elizabeth's reply, scratched underneath

Portrait of Queen Elizabeth I within the Armada Jewel (16th century) by Nicholas Hilliard.
The Victoria and Albert Museum, London.

(A) Exploring the Culture

A Virgin Queen

On the fascinating phenomenon of a virgin queen, Elizabethan expert A. L. Rowse has this to say: "Ordinary mortals, especially at the beginning, could not understand it; they grew to accept it, and in the end to find inspiration in it. Some people, then and since, have thought there was something wrong with her. Those in the best position to know. . . did not think so. Common sense was a sufficient warning as to the danger of child-bearing at the time, and there were the fearful examples of her sister and her mother to bring it home to her. It is fairly clear to a perceptive eye that she did not intend to marry. The Scottish ambassador, Melville, saw well enough that her deepest passion was to rule and that she would never give herself a master—as any sixteenth century woman did by marrying."

(B) Reading Skills and Strategies

Making Inferences

? What do you think this quotation is about? [Sir Walter Raleigh had a love interest in Elizabeth I. He is saying he'd like to approach her, yet he fears doing so, probably because she is queen. She replies, wittily and in verse, that if Raleigh has to wonder about whether he has sufficient courage to woo her, then he shouldn't bother trying.]

Skill Link

Reading to Discover Models for One's Own Writing

Have students consider how they could use elements of this essay as models for their own writing on historical or factual topics.

1. **Ask students to identify aspects of structure and organization they could use.** [They could use headings, or combinations of chronological order and cause-effect analysis with factual exposition.]
2. **Ask students to identify in this model the "extras," especially visual extras, that they could provide in their own writing.** [They could provide illustrations, as well as other visual organizers, such as charts and a time line. They could incorporate and amplify through dramatic placement and design quotations, summaries, and key facts.]
3. **Ask students how they might imitate the style of this piece.** [Students might use a serious style, appropriate to the subject, yet display a witty attitude toward their subject through word choice and phrases such as "With Catherine packed away under house arrest. . . ."]

A Closer Look

This feature explores the extravagances of Renaissance fashion—both the money the upper classes spent on their apparel and the exaggerated styles they preferred. The article describes the men's stuffed doublets that gave them a peascod belly and the women's farthingales (hooped skirts) that made them four feet wide at the hips. The symbolic meaning of various colors and decorative designs or emblems is also discussed.

Ⓐ Vocabulary Note

Multiple Meanings

One of the meanings of *glass* is "mirror." Explain that a mirror was once called a looking glass, just as something to drink from was once more commonly called a drinking glass. Remind students of Lewis Carroll's *Through the Looking Glass,* the sequel to *Alice's Adventures in Wonderland.*

Ⓑ Background

Royal Wardrobes

James I spent an astonishing £36,377 per year on his wardrobe for the five years of his reign. By contrast, Elizabeth I's yearly wardrobe expenses for the last four years of her reign were only £9,535 per year.

Ⓒ Humanities Connections

The Puritan Response

The Puritans strongly condemned what they viewed as excesses and abuses of dress. Phillip Stubbs in *The Anatomie of Abuses* attacks many aspects of culture including fashions such as ruffs. "No pen is able to well to discribe it, as the eye is to vilify it. . . [The ruffs have] three or foure degrees of minor ruffes, placed by degree, step by step, one beneath the others; and all under the Maister devil ruffe; the skyrts, then, of these great ruffes are long and side every way, pleated and crested ful curiously, God wot. Then last of all they are either clogged with golde, silver or silk lace of stately price, wrought all over with needle woork, speckled and sparkled here and there with the sonne, the moone, the stares, and many other antiquities straunge to beholde. Some are wrought with. . . purled lace so cloyed, and other gew gawes. . ."

A CLOSER LOOK

Ⓐ THE GLASS OF FASHION

They displayed their new costumes from ten to twelve o'clock in the morning, strolling up and down the center aisle of St. Paul's Church. Ⓑ They insisted on rich fabrics: velvet, taffeta, gold brocade, and fur. They wore the finest silk stockings and cork platform shoes. They curled their hair, perfumed their gloves, and (if daring) wore makeup. They showed off favorite jewels—pearls, perhaps—in earrings, bracelets, and designs sewn all over their clothes. The men in the Renaissance were peacocks indeed!

Exquisite excess. Women also dressed flamboyantly in the Renaissance. Elizabeth I herself owned eighty wigs and three thousand gowns at her death.

In the 1580s and 1590s, the Renaissance silhouette was ridiculously exaggerated. Ⓒ Starched linen neck ruffs stretched from shoulder to shoulder. Shoulders themselves were extended with "wings" that make even the most exaggerated of today's shoulder pads look like cotton balls. Hoop skirts (called farthingales) could be four feet wide at the hips, and men's full, thigh-length pants were padded to what critics called "monstrous and outrageous greatness."

Women corseted their waists into painful narrowness while men stiffened doublets (an upper garment) with pasteboard and stuffed them with horsehair, rags, or even bran in order to achieve what was called a peascod belly. A man's silhouette was

Portrait of Elizabeth Vernon, countess of Southampton (c. 1610) by an unknown artist.
By permission of the Duke of Buccleuch, Kettering, England.

Portrait of a lady said to be Lady Style (detail) (16th century) by the circle of William Larkin.
Christie's, London.

Portrait of a nobleman said to be the 7th earl of Shrewsbury in garter robes (detail) (16th century) by Paul van Somer.
Christie's, London.

Using Students' Strengths

Kinesthetic Learners

Have students imagine and describe what it would be like to wear one of these costumes. Have them consider how light or heavy, freeing or restricting each would feel. They should think about how the clothes would hang, drag, or pull. They should also consider how easy or hard it would be to perform movements such as ascending and descending steps, reaching, bending, and getting out of carriages.

narrowest at the bottom, where stockings and garters worn above the knee made even shapely legs look better. **D**

Symbols and signals. In the Renaissance, intricate pattern (like poetry's "artificiality") was also a must. Braids, bows, spangles, and lace covered the luxurious fabrics, and slashed sleeves and doublets allowed embroidered underclothes to peek through. Colors were rich and bold—red, gold, black, and white was a favorite combination.

Colors and designs also had symbolic meanings: Green meant love, white and tawny together showed patience in adversity, a pansy represented sadness, a snake flattery, and so on. Queen Elizabeth often wore white and black together—both colors symbolized chastity. Whole treatises were devoted to color and to defining "emblems" such as rainbows, clouds, worms, and flies.

Reading T-shirts. How will historians of dress read the clothes we wear today? Are bodices embroidered with flies so strange when viewed against the sort of printed T-shirts available by the hundreds in any shopping mall? What messages do our clothes send out to the world, and what will they tell the future?

An unknown lady in a masque costume (detail) (c. 1615).

City of Bristol Museum and Art Gallery, Bristol, England.

Lettice Knollys, daughter of Sir Henry Knollys, wife of 4th Lord Paget (detail) (16th century) by the English School.

Manor House, Stanton Harcourt, Oxon, England.

Mary Denton, née Martyn, age 15 in 1573 (detail) (16th century) by the circle of George Gower.

York City Art Gallery, York, England.

***Gilbert Talbot,* 7th earl of Shrewsbury, age 40 (detail) (16th century) by William Seger.**

Christie's, London.

D Cultural Connections

The Big-Belly Look

The peascod belly (or peasecod belly, or goose belly) was a look that began in Spain. The goal was to create a big belly, usually by stuffing horsehair into doublets. Evidently, fat was in for men. (It suggested prosperity.) For women, however, the opposite seems to have been true. Women of the sixteenth century wore bodices called "stomachers," which were often ribbed with bones that pulled the women's bodies into a rigid tightness.

Making the Connections

Cultural Connections

The Elizabethan court was not the only one of its day parading about in rich fabrics and ornate costumes. During this time, the Ming Dynasty (1368–1644) of China displayed its opulence in costume as well. In fact, the silk and textile industry flourished in China, and trade with the far east, across the Silk Route, brought to Europe the growing use of elaborate costumes in richly embroidered silk. In Elizabethan England, a person's costume revealed whether he or she was wealthy or noble, although it did not exactly signify rank. In China during the Ming Dynasty, however, the decoration or embroidery on a robe was clear indication of the wearer's social status or official rank.

Ⓐ Exploring the Historical Period

Mary Stuart

Mary Stuart, Queen of Scots (1542–1587) was Elizabeth's cousin. She should not be confused with "Bloody Mary," who was Mary Tudor (1516–1558), Elizabeth's half sister. Mary Stuart was the daughter of a French mother and Henry VIII's nephew, James V. Married as a young girl to Francis II of France, Mary returned to Scotland in 1560, after her husband's death, to claim the throne of Scotland, which was still independent from England. Mary Stuart's ties to France and Spain through family and religion made her a powerful threat to Elizabeth's England. Elizabeth had her cousin beheaded at Fotheringay on February 8, 1587.

Ⓑ Literary Connections

Maxwell Anderson

American dramatist Maxwell Anderson explored the conflict between the two monarchs in his verse plays *Elizabeth the Queen* (1930) and *Mary of Scotland* (1934).

Scottish National Portrait Gallery, Edinburgh.

Execution of Mary, Queen of Scots (16th century) by an unknown Dutch artist.

Ⓐ A truly heroic person, Elizabeth survived many plots against her life. Several of these plots were initiated by her cousin, another Mary—Mary Stuart, Queen of Scots. As Elizabeth had no children, Mary was heir to England's throne because she, too, was a direct descendant of Henry VII. Ⓑ But Mary, a Catholic, was eventually deposed from her throne in Protestant Scotland. Put under house arrest, she lived as a royal exile in England, carefully watched by her cousin Elizabeth. Elizabeth endured Mary and her plots for twenty years and then, a true daughter of her father, sent her Scottish cousin to the chopping block.

> . . . Then she, lying very still upon the block, one of the executioners holding her slightly with one of his hands, she endured two strokes of the other executioner with an axe, she making very small noise or none at all, and not stirring any part of her from the place where she lay: and so the executioner cut off her head, saving one little gristle, which being cut asunder, he lift up her head to the view of all the assembly and bade God save the Queen. Then, her dress of lawn falling from off her head, it appeared as gray as one of threescore and ten years old, polled very short, her face in a moment being so much altered from the form she had when she was alive, as few could remember her by her dead face. Her lips stirred up and down a quarter of an hour after her head was cut off . . .
>
> —Robert Wynkfielde, an eyewitness to the execution of Mary, Queen of Scots, 1587

Like her father, Elizabeth quickly and efficiently settled disorder both in her kingdom and in her own household. She once again rejected the pope and reestablished the Church of England. Elizabeth's intelligence and independence made her reign one of the most successful in England's history.

The Spanish Armada Sinks: A Turning Point in History

King Philip of Spain, ever watchful for an excuse to hammer at England, used Mary's execution as an excuse to invade England. He assembled a vast fleet of warships for that purpose: the famous Spanish Armada. In 1588, England's Royal Navy, assisted greatly by nasty weather in the Irish Sea, destroyed the Armada. This victory assured England's and all of northern Europe's

(Opposite) *English Ships and the Spanish Armada, August 1588* (detail). English School. Oil.

National Maritime Museum, London.

Crossing the Curriculum

History

The Spanish Armada was one of the largest invading fleets in history, with 130 ships and approximately 27,000 men. When the fleet approached en masse, its firepower was overwhelming. In order to counteract this advantage, the English set fire to eight small ships and let them drift down onto the Armada. The Spanish fleet scattered and then the swifter English vessels were able to assault individual members of the Armada. Since the English boats had better maneuverability, they were able to overcome the superior firepower of the Spanish, who tried to retreat and were then broadsided by storms in the North Atlantic. Of the 130 ships that started out with the Armada, only 60 returned home. Have students who are interested in naval history and tactics do further research on this empire-making battle.

To be a king and wear a crown is more glorious to them that see it than it is pleasure to them that bear it.

—Elizabeth I, 1601

Critical Thinking

Hypothesizing

? Why would Elizabeth I say this?

[Possible answers: People imagine all the glory, honor, and glamour of ruling; but Elizabeth knew better because of her experience; the actual work of being a monarch is not as glamorous or easy as it appears.]

RESPONDING TO THE ART

In this painting, the Spanish Armada, made up of large battleships designed to carry hundreds of infantry for boarding enemy ships, clash with British ships.

Activity. Ask students to examine the painting and tell how the artist conveys the swiftness and maneuverability of the British fleet. How do the flags and pennants contribute to the scene? [By placing the ships at various angles, the artist conveys the naval tactics of the British. The waving pennants and the rolling waves convey a sense of movement, of ships under full sail.]

Crossing the Curriculum

Science

The Renaissance was a time of enormous advances. Nevertheless, the everyday person in England could not afford to get sick. This was an era when even a toothache could prove fatal. Have students investigate medical practices or medical facts of the sixteenth century. Students might look into how few doctors there were (and most of these tended to minister to the nobility), what folk remedies and cures were relied upon, and why smallpox continued to be such a huge health problem at this time. They might also investigate just how little was known about mental health.

History/Architecture

During Tudor times in England (1485–1603), a distinctive style of architecture developed. Ask students to find out what a Tudor house looked like and to determine some of its characteristic features. Students should draw an illustration. They should also speculate on why homes, at least for the upper classes, were becoming so much larger and more comfortable at this time.

Ⓐ Literary Connections

Elizabeth as Literary Symbol

The names *Gloriana, Cynthia,* and *Faerie Queene* come from Edmund Spenser's epic poem *The Faerie Queene*. The name Cynthia was also used by Sir Walter Raleigh in his poem "The Ocean to Cynthia." Cynthia is another name for Diana, the virgin goddess of the moon.

Ⓑ Exploring the Historical Period

James and Jacobean England

James VI of Scotland was the only son of Mary, Queen of Scots, and her second husband, an English nobleman named Lord Darnley. When James succeeded his mother's cousin Elizabeth as sovereign of England, he was called King James I because he was the first James to rule England. The reign of James is called the Jacobean period. (*Jacobus* is the Latin form of *James*.)

independence from the powerful Catholic countries of the Mediterranean. It was a great turning point in history and Elizabeth's finest moment. If Spain had prevailed, history would have been quite different: All of North America, like most of South America, might be speaking Spanish instead of English.

In 1588, the English Royal Navy defeated the Spanish Armada. This stunning sea victory assured England's independence from the powerful Catholic countries of the Mediterranean.

As for her face, it is and appears to be very aged. It is long and thin and her teeth are very yellow and unequal, compared with what they were formerly, so they say, and on the left side less than on the right. Many of them are missing so that one cannot understand her easily when she speaks quickly. Her figure is fair and tall and graceful in whatever she does; so far as may be she keeps her dignity . . .

—André Hurault, French ambassador, writing about Elizabeth I, 1597

A Flood of Literature

What is the connection between these political events and English literature? With their own religious and national identity firmly established, the English started writing as never before. After the defeat of the Armada, Elizabeth became a beloved symbol of peace, security, and prosperity to her subjects, and she provided inspiration to scores of English authors. They represented her mythologically in poetry, drama, and fiction—as Gloriana, Diana, the Faerie Ⓐ Queene, and Cynthia. Literary works that did not directly represent her were dedicated to her because authors knew she was a connoisseur of literature and a person of remarkably wide learning.

Elizabeth encouraged and inspired many writers. With the era of peace and prosperity that followed the defeat of the Spanish Armada, the English started writing as never before.

Decline of the Renaissance: A Dull Man Succeeds a Witty Woman

Elizabeth died childless, so her second cousin, James VI of Scotland, was Ⓑ her successor. James was the son of Elizabeth's cousin Mary whom Elizabeth had beheaded years before. As James I of England (r. 1603–1625), he lacked Elizabeth's ability to resolve (or postpone) critical issues, especially religious and economic ones. James was a spendthrift where Elizabeth had been thrifty; he was thick-tongued and goggle-eyed where she had been glamorous and witty; he was essentially a foreigner where she had been a complete Englishwoman.

James I tried hard. He wrote learned books in favor of the divine right of kings and against tobacco, he patronized Shakespeare, he sponsored a new translation of the Bible, and he was in many respects an admirable man and a benevolent, peaceful ruler. Yet his relationship with many of his subjects, especially with pious, puritanically minded merchants, went from bad to worse.

Professional Notes

Critical Comment: James I on Tobacco

Botanist Charles B. Heiser, Jr., points out that tobacco was an important export crop of the Virginia colony almost from its founding, its use popularized by soldiers and sailors. Back in England, Heiser maintains: "[A]lmost everyone who could afford to took up smoking." However, it was far from universally approved. . . . In the year 1604 appeared the *Counterblasts to Tobacco*, published anonymously but widely known to be the work of James I himself. Why the king was so vehement in his opposition to tobacco is not certain, but his hatred for [Sir Walter] Raleigh, who was an enthusiastic advocate of tobacco, has been suggested as a reason. The *Counterblasts*, a lengthy pamphlet, concludes: "A custome loathsome to the eye, hatefull to the Nose, harmefull to the braine, dangerous to the Lungs, and in the blacke stinking fume thereof, neerest resembling the horrible Stigian smoke of the pit that is bottomelesse."

Others at the time expressed their feelings in verse:

Tobacco, that outlandish weed,
It spends the brain and spoils the seed.
It dulls the sprite, it dims the sight,
It robs a woman of her right.

The difficulties of James's reign became the impossibilities of his son's. Charles I (r. 1625–1649) turned out to be remote, autocratic, and self-destructive. Some of his most powerful subjects had him beheaded in 1649. For the next eleven years, England was ruled by Parliament and the Puritan dictator Oliver Cromwell, not by an anointed king. When Charles's self-indulgent son returned to power eleven years later, in 1660, England had changed in many important ways.

Of course the Renaissance did not end in 1660 as Charles II returned from exile in France, just as it had not begun at any specific date. Renaissance values, which were primarily moral and religious, gradually eroded, and Renaissance energies gradually gave out. The last great writer of the English Renaissance was John Milton, who lived on into an age in which educated people were becoming more worldly in their outlook. Scientific truths were soon to challenge long-accepted religious beliefs.

The English Renaissance was over.

All my possessions for a moment of time.
—Elizabeth I's last words, 1603

The political climate in England began to change after Elizabeth's death. The end of the English Renaissance is usually marked by the return of the exiled king in 1660. By this time, more political and secular values were beginning to challenge the accepted doctrines of religion.

Bird's-eye view of London, from the *Atlas Civitatis Orbis Terrarum* (c. 1574) by Georg Braun. Map L85c #27.

By permission of The Folger Shakespeare Library, Washington, D.C.

C Exploring the Historical Period

Charles and Cromwell

By the time Charles I came to the throne, the Puritans had risen to prominence and their parliamentary party had gained power. By 1642, England was embroiled in civil war that pitted the parliamentary party, led by Oliver Cromwell, against the king's party, or Royalists. Cromwell's followers killed the king, and Cromwell, now considered the foremost military and political strategist of his time, wielded power and asserted England's primacy in world affairs in ways reminiscent of the reign of Elizabeth I.

D Exploring the Historical Period

The Irish Question

The seeds of twentieth-century conflict in Ireland were fertilized during the Renaissance. Henry II had conquered Ireland in 1171, and in succeeding centuries the English seized land, exacted tribute, suppressed Catholicism, prohibited the use of the Irish language, exploited the residents, and plundered the land. Under James I Scottish and English landowners, tenants, and laborers were installed in the northern province of Ulster, a relationship symbolically cemented by changing the name of the historic town of Derry to Londonderry.

In 1707 the Act of Union united England and Scotland into the kingdom of Great Britain, expanded to include Ireland in 1801. The Irish continued to press for independence, however. Great Britain granted dominion status to the Irish Free State in 1921 but did not recognize the Republic of Ireland until 1949. Ulster, or Northern Ireland, heavily Scottish-English and Protestant, remained in the Union. The second half of the twentieth century saw conflict between the unionists on the one hand and Catholic republicans seeking the reunification of Ireland on the other. (For information on Anglo-Irish relations during the eighteenth century, see p. 502.)

Assessing Learning

Check Test: True-False

1. The term *Renaissance* refers to a rebirth of interest in the writings of classical Greece and Rome. [True]
2. New creativity in the arts first appeared during this era in Italy. [True]
3. Renaissance humanists rejected the Bible. [False]
4. The invention of printing helped make classical texts more readily available. [True]
5. In all countries where the Reformation occurred, a key element was the rejection of the authority of the Pope. [True]

A Closer Look

This feature explores the persecution and stereotyping that Jews endured in Europe during the Renaissance.

A Background

Other Restrictions on Jews
Many other restrictions were placed upon Jews. They were not allowed to be high government officials or exert authority over Christians.

B Exploring the Historical Period

Menasseh ben Israel
Menasseh ben Israel is regarded as the founder of the modern Jewish community in England. A Jew living in Holland, he wrote pamphlets to Oliver Cromwell encouraging the readmission of Jews into England. He suggested that Cromwell strike the laws of the deposed monarchs and welcome Jews to the commonwealth, allowing them to worship freely and publicly in their synagogues. By identifying religious persecution with the rule of monarchs, ben Israel may have influenced Cromwell's decision: the granting of an official charter of protection to the Jews of England in 1664. Despite this concession, Cromwell remained intolerant of Catholics and Unitarians.

A CLOSER LOOK

Jewish Life in England: Expulsion and Return

As you read the literature of Renaissance England, you'll notice that many selections use Christian imagery or are about Christian topics. Certainly, all the writers in these collections were Christian. But what about Jewish life in England?

The most famous Jewish character in Renaissance literature is Shylock, the moneylender in Shakespeare's play *The Merchant of Venice* (c. 1596–1598). Shylock is portrayed as cruel and greedy, a man incapable of mercy. In Shakespeare's play, Shylock is a usurer, which means that he lent money at interest, something commonly done by banks today. But charging interest on borrowed money (called usury) was considered sinful by the Christian church. (Many usurers charged exorbitant interest, and a small loan might ruin a poor widow and her family.) **A** Since Jews were usually not allowed to own land, they became the people who handled money.

With Shylock, Shakespeare presents us with a complicated character who is at once a stereotype and a persecuted individual. Stereotypes like this one of the greedy moneylender were used to justify relentless persecution of the Jews. Without a homeland, Jews had been moving for most of their history. Expelled from many European cities and countries, Jewish refugees streamed into cities that already housed more Jews than their rulers wanted. Some cities, such as Venice (the setting for *The Merchant of Venice*), dealt with Jews by segregating them in ghettos and charging them extra taxes.

There were a few Jews in Shakespeare's England, although English Jews had been banished centuries before by King Edward I in 1290—because of controversy over their purchase of land. (Ownership of land by people considered "outsiders" was alarming then, as it still is in some places.) Some individual Jews probably continued to practice their religion in secret, but it wasn't until the middle of the **B** seventeenth century, under the rule of Oliver Cromwell, that Jews were officially allowed to return to England.

***Initial Word-Panel Illumination Showing a Marriage Ceremony,* from the *Hamburg Halakhah Miscellany.* Padua (1467–1477). The Hebrew letters mean "all." Codex Hebrew 337 (Scrin 132) fol. 75v. Vellum (6″ × 4½″).**
Staats und Universitätsbibliothek, Hamburg.

Quickwrite The humanists of the Renaissance were concerned with a question that we still ask ourselves today. "What is a good life?" they wondered. How would you answer this same question? What's the good life for you? Will you have a good life if you're rich, or if you're famous, or if you're able to do some good for someone, or if you have power, or if most of your days are simply happy? Write down your thoughts on this complex question. What do you think has influenced the way you define "the good life"?

Professional Notes

Exploring the Historical Period

Jewish and Muslim Exiles. Jews were expelled from Germany in the 1350s, from France in 1394, from Spain in 1492, from Portugal in 1496, and from the Papal States in 1569. One result of these expulsions was the shifting of Jewish life to Eastern Europe, where in succeeding centuries the Jews would be subject to waves of persecution culminating in the Holocaust. In Spain, the expulsion of the Jews was preceded (and followed) by the infamous Spanish Inquisition, directed against heretics, Jews, Muslims, and apostate converts. The most famous of the Inquisitors was Tomas de Torquemada, who persuaded Queen Isabella that it was her pious duty to expel her 170,000 Jewish subjects. This is the same Isabella who sponsored the voyage of Columbus. Ferdinand and Isabella were also the monarchs who led the final military victories against the Muslims and in 1500 ordered that they too convert or be expelled from Spain. Students may be interested to learn that before the expulsion of the Jews and the Muslims, Spain's multiracial, multireligious composition was unique in Europe and a major factor in the development of its civilization and arts.

Collection 3

Love, Death, and Time

Theme

Eternal Wishes *In all ages, but perhaps especially in the Renaissance, poets use the power of language to express the age-old paradoxes presented by love and faithlessness, by youth and age, by time and our desire to defeat death and live eternally.*

Reading the Anthology

Reaching Struggling Readers

The *Reading Skills and Strategies: Reaching Struggling Readers* binder includes a Reading Strategies Handbook that offers concrete suggestions to help students who have difficulty reading and comprehending text, or students who are reluctant readers. When a specific strategy is most appropriate for a selection, a correlation to the Handbook is provided at the bottom of the teacher's page under the head Struggling Readers. This head may also be used to introduce additional ideas for helping students read challenging texts.

Reading Beyond the Anthology

Read On

At the end of the Renaissance collections, the grade twelve book provides an annotated bibliography of books suitable for extended reading. The suggested books are related to works in these collections by theme, by author, or by subject. To preview the Read On for the Renaissance period, please turn to p. T455.

HRW Library

The *HRW Library* offers novels, plays, and short-story collections for extended reading. Each book in the *Library* includes one or more major works and thematically or topically related Connections. The Connections are magazine articles, poems, or other pieces of literature. Each book in the *HRW Library* is also accompanied by a Study Guide that provides teaching suggestions and worksheets. The two titles shown here will work well to extend the theme of Collection 3.

GREAT EXPECTATIONS
Charles Dickens

Dickens explores the conflicting forces that shape the development of a young boy. In his journey to adulthood, Pip discovers and resolves personal conflicts involving love, pride, and obsession.

ROMEO AND JULIET
William Shakespeare

Shakespeare's classic tale of young love captures the emotional intensity of the Renaissance. Love and death meet on the streets of Verona when the children of two feuding families decide to wed.

Collection 3 Love, Death, and Time

Resources for this Collection

Note: All resources for this collection are available for preview on the *One-Stop Planner CD-ROM I with Test Generator.* All worksheets and blackline masters may be printed from the CD-ROM.

Internet Resources
go.hrw.com LE0 12-3

Selection or Feature	Reading and Literary Skills	Vocabulary, Language, and Grammar
Whoso List to Hunt (p. 214) Sir Thomas Wyatt **Elements of Literature: Poetic Meter** (p. 216)	• *Graphic Organizers for Active Reading,* Worksheet p. 11 • *Literary Elements:* Transparency 8, Worksheet p. 25	• *Daily Oral Grammar,* Transparency 8
from **Amoretti** • **Sonnet 30** (p. 218) • **Sonnet 75** (p. 219) Edmund Spenser **Elements of Literature: Petrarchan and Spenserian Sonnets** (p. 219) **Spotlight On: The Faerie Queene: England Through the Looking Glass** (p. 221)	• *Graphic Organizers for Active Reading,* Worksheet p. 12 • *Literary Elements:* Transparency 9, Worksheet p. 28	• *Daily Oral Grammar,* Transparency 9
Shakespeare's Sonnets: The Mysteries of Love (p. 223) • **Sonnet 18** (p. 224) • **Sonnet 29** (p. 225) • **Sonnet 73** (p. 226) • **Sonnet 116** (p. 228) • **Sonnet 130** (p. 229) William Shakespeare	• *Graphic Organizers for Active Reading,* Worksheets pp. 13, 14 • *Literary Elements:* Poetry Transparencies 1, 2, 3, 4, 5, Teaching Notes p. 91	• *Grammar and Language Links:* Verb Tenses, Worksheet p. 17 • *Language Workshop CD-ROM,* Verb Tenses
The Passionate Shepherd to His Love (p. 231) Christopher Marlowe **The Nymph's Reply to the Shepherd** (p. 235) Sir Walter Raleigh **To the Virgins, to Make Much of Time** (p. 239) Robert Herrick **To His Coy Mistress** (p. 241) Andrew Marvell	• *Graphic Organizers for Active Reading,* Worksheet pp. 15, 16, 17, 18	
• **Song** (p. 245) **Elements of Literature: Metaphysical Poetry** (p. 246) • **A Valediction: Forbidding Mourning** (p. 247) • **Meditation 17** (p. 250) • **Death Be Not Proud** (p. 253) John Donne	• *Graphic Organizers for Active Reading,* Worksheet pp. 19, 20, 21, 22 • *Literary Elements:* Transparency 10, Worksheet p. 31	
• **On My First Son** (p. 257) • **Song: To Celia** (p. 258) Ben Jonson **Connections: Give Us This Day Our Daily Bread** (p. 260) Joseph Papp and Elizabeth Kirkland	• *Graphic Organizers for Active Reading,* Worksheet p. 23	

Other Resources for this Collection

- *Cross-Curricular Activities*, p. 3
- *Portfolio Management System*, Introduction to Portfolio Assessment, p. 1
- *Test Generator*, Collection Test
- *Formal Assessment:* Literary Period Introduction Test, p. 37

Writing	Listening and Speaking Viewing and Representing	Assessment
• *Portfolio Management System*, Rubrics for Choices, p. 110	• *Audio CD Library*, Disc 4, Track 2 • *Portfolio Management System*, Rubrics for Choices, p. 110	• *Formal Assessment*, Selection Test, p. 39 • *Test Generator (One-Stop Planner CD-ROM)*
• *Portfolio Management System*, Rubrics for Choices, p. 111	• *Audio CD Library*, Disc 4, Tracks 3, 4 • *Portfolio Management System*, Rubrics for Choices, p. 111	• *Formal Assessment*, Selection Test, p. 39 • *Test Generator (One-Stop Planner CD-ROM)* • *Formal Assessment*, Literary Elements Test, p. 55
• *Portfolio Management System*, Rubrics for Choices, p. 112	• *Audio CD Library*, Disc 4, Tracks 5, 6, 7, 8 • *Portfolio Management System*, Rubrics for Choices, p. 112	• *Formal Assessment*, Selection Test, p. 41 • *Test Generator (One-Stop Planner CD-ROM)*
• *Portfolio Management System*, Rubrics for Choices, p. 114	• *Audio CD Library*, Disc 4, Tracks 9, 10, 11, 12 • *Viewing and Representing:* Fine Art Transparency 3 Worksheet p. 12 • *Portfolio Management System*, Rubrics for Choices, p. 114	• *Formal Assessment*, Selection Tests, pp. 43, 45 • *Test Generator (One-Stop Planner CD-ROM)*
• *Portfolio Management System*, Rubrics for Choices, p. 116	• *Audio CD Library*, Disc 4, Tracks 13, 14, 15, 16 • *Portfolio Management System*, Rubrics for Choices, p. 116	• *Formal Assessment*, Selection Test, p. 47 • *Test Generator (One-Stop Planner CD-ROM)*
• *Portfolio Management System*, Rubrics for Choices, p. 118	• *Audio CD Library*, Disc 4, Tracks 17, 18 • *Portfolio Management System*, Rubrics for Choices, p. 118	• *Formal Assessment*, Selection Test, p. 49 • *Test Generator (One-Stop Planner CD-ROM)*

Transparency CD-ROM Video Audio CD

Collection 3 Love, Death, and Time

Resources for this Collection

Note: All resources for this collection are available for preview on the *One-Stop Planner CD-ROM I with Test Generator.* All worksheets and blackline masters may be printed from the CD-ROM.

Internet Resources
go.hrw.com LE0 12-3

Selection or Feature	Reading and Literary Skills	Vocabulary, Language, and Grammar
Why So Pale and Wan, Fond Lover? (p. 263) Sir John Suckling **To Lucasta, on Going to the Wars** (p. 264) **To Althea, from Prison** (p. 265) Richard Lovelace	• *Graphic Organizers for Active Reading,* Worksheets pp. 24, 25	• *Words to Own,* Worksheet p. 7
World Literature: Chile **Sonnets** • **Sonnet 17** (p. 268) • **Sonnet 79** (p. 270) Pablo Neruda *translated by* Stephen Tapscott	The World Literature feature offers students the opportunity to explore thematically linked literature from different world cultures. Structured activities called Finding Common Ground are provided in the Pupil's Edition to guide students' explorations of these thematic connections between British and other world literature.	
The English Language: The Birth of Modern English (p. 271) John Algeo		
Writer's Workshop: Interpretive Essay (p. 275)		
Language Workshop: The Literary Present (p. 279)		• *Workshop Resources,* p. 49 • *Language Workshop CD-ROM,* Verb Tenses

Other Resources for this Collection

- *Cross-Curricular Activities,* p. 3
- *Portfolio Management System,* Introduction to Portfolio Assessment, p. 1
- *Test Generator,* Collection Test

Writing	Listening and Speaking Viewing and Representing	Assessment
• *Portfolio Management System,* Rubrics for Choices, p. 120	• *Audio CD Library,* Disc 4, Tracks 19, 20, 21 • *Portfolio Management System,* Rubrics for Choices, p. 120	• *Formal Assessment,* Selection Test, p. 51 • *Test Generator (One-Stop Planner CD-ROM)*
		• *Formal Assessment,* The English Language Test, p. 53
• *Workshop Resources,* p. 13 • *Writer's Workshop 2 CD-ROM,* Interpretation	• *Viewing and Representing,* HRW Multimedia Presentation Maker	• *Portfolio Management System* • Prewriting, p. 121 • Peer Editing, p. 122 • Assessment Rubric, p. 123

Transparency CD-ROM Video Audio CD

Collection 3 Love, Death, and Time

Skills Focus

Selection or Feature	Reading Skills and Strategies	Elements of Literature and Language	Writing	Listening and Speaking	Viewing and Representing
Whoso List to Hunt (p. 214) Sir Thomas Wyatt		Speaker, p. 215 Image, p. 215 Poetic Meter, p. 216	Freewrite in Response to a Poem, p. 216 Write a Paragraph from the Point of View of the Woman Referred to in the Poem, p. 216		
from **Amoretti** • **Sonnet 30** (p. 218) • **Sonnet 75** (p. 219) Edmund Spenser		Paradox, pp. 218, 219 Speaker, p. 219 Image, p. 219 Sonnet, p. 219 Conceit, p. 220 Octave, Sestet, Turn, p. 220 Quatrain, p. 220 Allegory, p. 221 Alexandrine, p. 221 Spenserian Stanza, p. 221	Create a Petrarchan Conceit, p. 220 Write to an Author, p. 220 Create Images of Love, p. 220		
Shakespeare's Sonnets (p. 223) • **Sonnet 18** (p. 224) • **Sonnet 29** (p. 225) • **Sonnet 73** (p. 226) • **Sonnet 116** (p. 228) • **Sonnet 130** (p. 229) William Shakespeare	Paraphrase, p. 227 Repeated Readings, p. 230	Sonnet, pp. 223–224 Turn, pp. 224, 227, 229 Speaker, pp. 227, 229 Metaphor, pp. 227, 229 Image, p. 227 Personification, p. 229 Couplet, p. 229	Collect Ideas for an Essay, p. 230 Compare and Contrast Tones, p. 230 Compare Poems from Different Cultures, p. 230 Write a Response Poem, p. 230	Write a Musical Parody, p. 230 Engage in a Panel Discussion of Contemporary Views of Love, p. 230	Illustrate a Group of Sonnets, p. 230
The Passionate Shepherd to His Love (p. 231) Marlowe **The Nymph's Reply to the Shepherd** (p. 235) Raleigh **To the Virgins to Make Much of Time** (p. 239) Herrick **To His Coy Mistress** (p. 241) Marvell	Paraphrase, p. 242	*Carpe Diem,* p. 231 Pastoral, pp. 233, 236 Tone, p. 236 Image, p. 242 Speaker, p. 242 Hyperbole, Understatement, p. 242	Freewrite in Response to a Poem, p. 242 Compare and Contrast Poems, p. 243 Compare Poems, p. 243 Compare Poems Across Cultures, p. 243 Write a Response to a Poem, p. 243	Write a *Carpe Diem* Song, p. 243 Engage in a Panel Discussion of Gender Traits, p. 243	Create a Collage, p. 243
Song (p. 245) **A Valediction Forbidding Mourning** (p. 247) **Meditation 17** (p. 250) **Death Be Not Proud** (p. 253) John Donne	Using Context Clues, pp. 250, 252 Connotation, p. 250 Main Idea, p. 252	Hyperbole, pp. 245, 246 Speaker, pp. 246, 249 Tone, pp. 246, 252, 254 Metaphysical Poetry, pp. 246–247, 249 Simile, pp. 247, 249 Metaphor, p. 252 Paradox, p. 254	Identify Details that Determine Tone, p. 255 Compare and Contrast Two Valediction Poems, p. 255 Write a Brief Essay Analyzing Donne's Use of Metaphors, p. 255 Create Hyperbolic Statements, p. 255 Write a Valediction Letter, p. 255 Create a High-Tech Conceit, p. 255		Create an Illustration of Death to Accompany "Death Be Not Proud," p. 255
On My First Son (p. 257) **Song to Celia** (p. 258) Ben Johnson	Paraphrase, p. 259	Epigram, p. 257 Irony, p. 259 Epitaph, p. 259	Explain a Response, p. 259 Identify Ideas for Research, p. 259 Elaborate on a Metaphor, p. 259		Identify Details in a Painting, p. 259
Why So Pale and Wan, Fond Lover? (p. 263) Suckling **To Lucasta, on Going to the Wars** (p. 264) / **To Althea, from Prison** (p. 265) Lovelace	Paraphrase, p. 266	Tone, pp. 263, 266 Metaphor, p. 266 Paradox, p. 266 Refrain, p. 266	Paraphrase a Poem, p. 266 Analyze a Poem's Relevance, p. 266 Interview the Cavalier Poets, p. 266 Write a Response from a Modern Lucasta, p. 266		
World Literature: Chile • **Sonnet 17** (p. 268) • **Sonnet 79** (p. 270) Pablo Neruda		Image, p. 270 Metaphor, p. 270	The World Literature feature offers students the opportunity to explore thematically linked literature from different world cultures. Structured activities called Finding Common Ground are provided in the Pupil's Edition to guide students' explorations of these thematic connections between British and other world literature.		
The English Language: The Birth of Modern English (p. 271) John Algeo		Pronunciation and Spelling, pp. 272, 274 Borrowed Words, p. 273	Write Using Another Alphabet, p. 274		
Writer's Workshop: Interpretive Essay (p. 275)			Write an Interpretive Essay, pp. 275–278		
Language Workshop: The Literary Present (p. 279)		Verb Tenses, p. 279 Literary Present, p. 279	Proofread for Tense Correctness and Consistency, p. 279		
Reading for Life: Reading a Consumer Report (p. 280)	Abbreviations, p. 280				

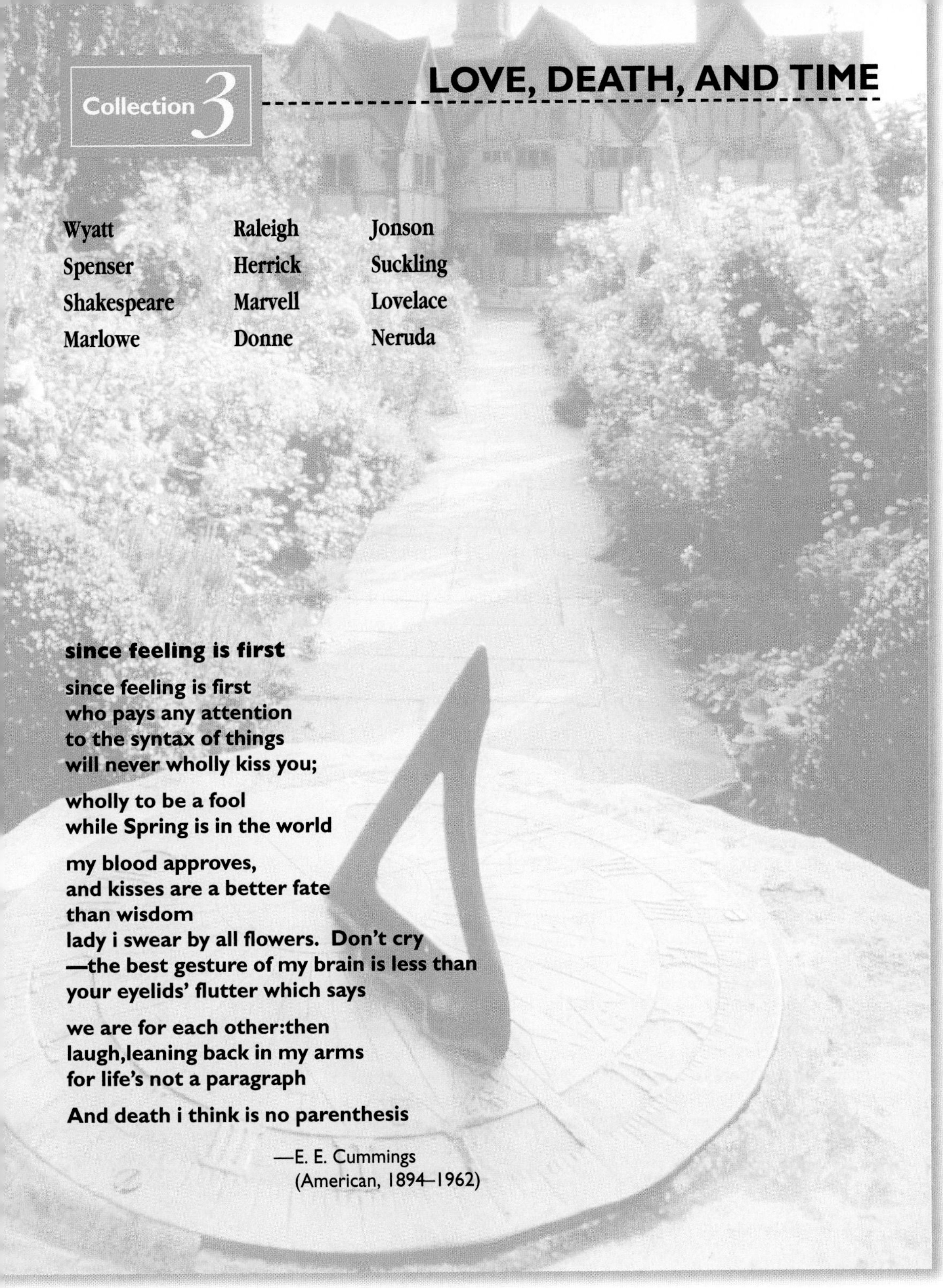

Collection 3

LOVE, DEATH, AND TIME

Wyatt
Spenser
Shakespeare
Marlowe
Raleigh
Herrick
Marvell
Donne
Jonson
Suckling
Lovelace
Neruda

since feeling is first

since feeling is first
who pays any attention
to the syntax of things
will never wholly kiss you;

wholly to be a fool
while Spring is in the world

my blood approves,
and kisses are a better fate
than wisdom
lady i swear by all flowers. Don't cry
—the best gesture of my brain is less than
your eyelids' flutter which says

we are for each other:then
laugh,leaning back in my arms
for life's not a paragraph

And death i think is no parenthesis

—E. E. Cummings
(American, 1894–1962)

OBJECTIVES

1. Read Renaissance literature on the theme of "Love, Death, and Time"
2. Interpret literary elements with special emphasis on sonnets and metaphysical poetry
3. Apply a variety of reading strategies to the literature
4. Respond to the literature in a variety of modes
5. Learn about the development of Early Modern English
6. Plan, draft, revise, proofread, and publish an interpretive essay
7. Develop skill in using the literary present tense
8. Demonstrate the ability to read a consumer report
9. Explore through a variety of projects the characteristics of a Renaissance person

Responding to the Poem

? Many of the poems in this collection (and perhaps most poems in general) reflect on love, death, and time. What is the speaker in this poem saying about these topics? [Possible answers: If you keep trying to find words to express love, you will never feel love; love and spring make fools of us; kisses are better than wisdom; the lover's mere eyelash is better than the gesture of a brain; life is not a rigidly constructed paragraph, and death cannot be restricted to parentheses, that is, an afterthought.] Other features and themes of this poem that students will encounter in this collection: The speaker addresses his "lady"; the speaker wishes to "seize the day" and act now instead of waiting.

Writing Focus: An Interpretive Essay

WORK IN PROGRESS

The following **Work in Progress** assignments build to a culminating **Writer's Workshop** at the end of this collection.

- Shakespeare's sonnets — Take notes on details (p. 230)
- To His Coy Mistress — Freewrite in response to a poem (p. 242)
- Death Be Not Proud — Identify details that determine tone (p. 255)
- Song: To Celia — Take notes on details in piece of art (p. 259)
- To Althea, from Prison — Paraphrase a poem (p. 266)

Writer's Workshop: Expository Writing / An Interpretive Essay (p. 275)

OBJECTIVES

1. Read and interpret the poem
2. Identify poetic meter
3. Express understanding through personal and creative writing

SKILLS

Literary

- Identify poetic meter

Writing

- Explore responses for an interpretive essay
- Write a paragraph from an alternative point of view

Planning

- **Block Schedule**
  Block Scheduling Lesson Plans with Pacing Guide
- **Traditional Schedule**
  Lesson Plans Including Strategies for English-Language Learners
- **One-Stop Planner**
  CD-ROM with Test Generator

BROWSING IN THE FILES

About the Author. Wyatt and the other men suspected of being Anne Boleyn's lovers were imprisoned by Henry VIII. Wyatt's father secured his release.

Sir Thomas Wyatt

(1503–1542)

Sir Thomas Wyatt (16th century) by an unknown artist. Oil on panel (18½" diameter).

By Courtesy of the National Portrait Gallery, London.

Sir Thomas Wyatt was a courtier of Henry VIII and spent much of his life traveling abroad as an ambassador for the king. The life of anyone who worked for the king could be dangerous as well as glamorous: Twice Henry had Wyatt imprisoned on charges that were probably false, and twice Wyatt managed to regain the king's favor. Besides being a diplomat, Wyatt was also a literary innovator who helped to change the nature of English poetry. Up to Wyatt's time, poetry was still essentially medieval in matter and manner, subject and form. Wyatt greatly admired Italian poetry, and he brought a new kind of poem, the love sonnet, to England from Italy. His English sonnets are actually adaptations of Italian sonnets.

Aside from his sonnets, Wyatt wrote many delightful lyrics modeled on English dance-songs, but he never had any of his works printed and publicly distributed. Wyatt had no ambition to be known as a "clerk," or a learned man of letters, the sort of person who published books. As a courtier he was expected to compose songs and verses, just as he was expected to do battle for his king, joust in tournaments, dance, and carry on intrigues with the ladies. And so Wyatt circulated his poems privately among his friends, in handwritten copies. Not until fifteen years after Wyatt's death did most of his poems appear in print. In 1557, an enterprising printer named Richard Tottel published *Songs and Sonnets,* an anthology containing ninety-seven of Wyatt's poems. This book, now called *Tottel's Miscellany,* has a rather bad reputation today because Tottel "improved" the poems by changing many words so that the poems sounded smoother to his ears. To make certain that we read Wyatt's words, rather than Tottel's, scholars had to search out the handwritten copies of the poems that predated their publication.

Before You Read

WHOSO LIST TO HUNT

Make the Connection

Wounded by Love

The battle of the sexes, Cupid's arrow, the thrill of the chase, conquered by love, a good catch: why do so many metaphors for love suggest a contest between hunter and prey? With your classmates, discuss love as a "hunt." Two questions to consider are these: Who inflicts the wounds in love—the pursuer or the pursued? Who is the one conquered?

Quickwrite

What do you think of the idea of love as a "hunt"? Take notes on your responses.

Background

According to traditional gossip, Wyatt wrote this poem about his longing for Anne Boleyn, a beautiful young woman at court. When he noticed that no less a person than King Henry was also attracted to Anne, he gave up the pursuit to whoever else wanted to "hunt" her. Whether or not the story is true, Anne did become the second of Henry's six queens. Wyatt adapted the poem from an Italian sonnet by Francis Petrarch (1304–1374). He also took from Petrarch's commentators the story about Julius Caesar's tame deer (line 13), whose collars were inscribed *Noli me tangere* (Latin for "touch me not"), warning hunters not to molest Caesar's property.

go.hrw.com
LEO 12-3

Resources: Print and Media

Reading

- *Graphic Organizers for Active Reading,* p. 11
- *Audio CD Library*
  Disc 4, Track 2

Elements of Literature

- *Literary Elements*
  Transparency 8
  Worksheet, p. 25

Writing and Language

- *Daily Oral Grammar*
  Transparency 8

Assessment

- *Portfolio Management System,* p. 110
- *Test Generator (One-Stop Planner CD-ROM)*

Internet

- go.hrw.com (keyword: LE0 12-3)

Whoso List to Hunt Ⓐ

Sir Thomas Wyatt

Whoso list° to hunt, I know where is an hind,°
But as for me, alas, I may no more.
The vain travail° hath wearied me so sore
I am of them that farthest cometh behind.
Yet may I, by no means, my wearied mind
Draw from the deer, but as she fleeth afore,
Fainting I follow. I leave off therefore,
Since in a net I seek to hold the wind. Ⓑ

Who list her hunt, I put him out of doubt,°
As well as I, may spend his time in vain.
And graven with diamonds in letters plain
There is written, her fair neck round about, Ⓒ
"Noli me tangere, for Caesar's I am,
And wild for to hold, though I seem tame." Ⓓ

1. list: archaic for "desires." **hind:** female deer (rhymes with *kind*).
3. travail: hard work.
9. put him out of doubt: assure him (that he).

Anne Boleyn (late 16th century) by an unknown artist. Oil on panel (21⅜" × 16⅜").
By Courtesy of the National Portrait Gallery, London.

MAKING MEANINGS

First Thoughts

1. Do you think this poem, specific as it is, describes attitudes and experiences still common in life today? Why or why not?

Shaping Interpretations

2. Given the background information you've just read, who is the hind in this poem and who is Caesar? Who is the **speaker**?
3. What warning does the speaker give potential hunters of the woman?
4. What **image** does the speaker use to show he's finally decided the chase is hopeless?
5. The speaker says the hind may seem tame but is "wild for to hold." Do you think he's referring to the woman herself or to Caesar's claim on her? Explain.

Connecting with the Text

6. If you were King Henry and you came upon this poem, how might you feel about its author? If you were Anne Boleyn, how might you react to the poem?
7. How do you feel about Wyatt's description of love as a hunt or a conquest? (Refer to your Quickwrite notes.)

Summary ■■

This poem uses a hunt metaphor to describe a man pursuing a woman, whom he compares to a deer. The speaker is tired of the chase, and he invites others to take it up. He uses a classical allusion to warn others that their prey (probably Anne Boleyn), like Caesar's deer, is claimed by a powerful ruler (probably Henry VIII). The speaker ends by warning that this woman is wild although she looks tame.

Ⓐ Struggling Readers

Reading Archaic Language

Explain that *whoso* is a pronoun meaning "whoever." Then point out the explanation of the word *list* and ask students to reword the title. ["Whoever Wants to Hunt"]

Ⓑ Elements of Literature

Metaphor

? What do the hunter and hind stand for in this extended metaphor? [The hunter is the speaker, a man in love; the hind is the woman he is pursuing.]

Ⓒ Critical Thinking

Making Inferences

? What does the diamond collar suggest about the woman's role in society? [She is considered a valuable possession; she has had gifts lavished on her.] The words "fair neck," of course, remind the reader that Boleyn's neck was severed by the very man who claimed her.

Ⓓ Historical Connections

? Considering that in 1536 Henry beheaded Boleyn on trumped-up charges of infidelity, how are ll. 13–14 ironic? [Henry had claimed her as his own, but he couldn't be sure she was faithful. She *did* belong to "Caesar" (presumably Henry VIII), so much so that he could kill her if he wished.]

MAKING MEANINGS

First Thoughts [Extend]

1. Possible responses: People today still pursue those who are unattainable and feel frustrated as Wyatt does. Today, however, women may also pursue men. Treating women as possessions is considered disrespectful now.

Shaping Interpretations [Interpret]

2. The hind is Anne Boleyn; Caesar is Henry VIII. The speaker is Wyatt.
3. He gives two warnings: (a) She has already been claimed. (b) Her looks are deceiving; she seems tame but is wild.
4. He uses the image of trying to catch the wind in a net.
5. Possible answers: The speaker is referring to the woman herself—Caesar's claim hasn't altered her wildness or fickleness; or he is referring to the risks involved in pursuing her against Caesar's wishes.

Connecting with the Text [Apply/Evaluate]

6. Possible responses: The king might be glad that the speaker stopped chasing Boleyn, or he might want to punish the speaker for pursuing her in the first place. Boleyn might be flattered, or she might resent being chased.
7. Possible responses: Such metaphors are demeaning; or such metaphors are a poetic convention that work well here.

Elements of Literature

Poetic Meter

Shakespeare usually wrote in iambic pentameter. Write several lines of a Shakespearean sonnet (see pp. 223–229) on the chalkboard, and model scansion for students. Have volunteers read aloud and identify stressed and unstressed syllables. After you have done this, give students a copy of another sonnet, and have them work in pairs to scan it aloud.

Answers

1. **a.** dactyl
   b. iamb
   c. trochee
   d. anapest
2. Many of the lines, including 2, 3, 5, 8, 9, and 10, are in regular iambic pentameter. The first line has eleven syllables and is in iambic pentameter except for the first foot, which is likely anapest. Others have variations due in part to the reader's emphasis and to differences between Elizabethan and modern pronunciation. For additional instruction on poetic meter, see *Literary Elements*
   - Transparency 8
   - Worksheet, p. 25

Grading Timesaver

Rubrics for each assignment appear on p. 110 in the *Portfolio Management System.*

Choices: Building Your Portfolio

1. **Writer's Notebook** Students should select connections to the poem they would not mind sharing with others. At this point, they may choose several key words or phrases.
2. **Creative Writing** Have students try to imagine the thoughts of a strong-willed sixteenth-century woman. Ask them how she might feel about being compared to a hunted deer wearing a collar indicating ownership.

Elements of Literature

Poetic Meter: Giving Form to Feeling

Poetic **meter** is a regular pattern of stressed and unstressed syllables. It is a rhythmic "beat"—like the steady pulse that draws you into dance music. Meter's basic unit is the **foot:** A foot consists of one stressed syllable and one or more unstressed syllables (mú·sĭ·căl). The four basic metrical feet are

1. **iamb** (˘ ´), as in *relief*
2. **trochee** (´ ˘), as in *apple*
3. **anapest** (˘ ˘ ´), as in *introduce*
4. **dactyl** (´ ˘ ˘), as in *broccoli*

Poets also use two other metrical devices: the **spondee** (´ ´), or double stress, and the **caesura** (||), or pause.

The analysis of a poem's meter is called **scansion.** When you scan a poem, you identify the type of foot (or feet) used in each line, and then you count them. **Dimeter** means two feet per line; **trimeter,** three; **tetrameter,** four; **pentameter,** five; and **hexameter,** six. This line from Wyatt's poem is **iambic pentameter** (it has five iambs):

Sĭnce ín ă nét Ĭ séek tŏ hóld thĕ wínd.

Scanning poetry. Few poems are written in a meter that remains exactly regular throughout. The perception of meter may also vary from reader to reader, depending on which parts of phrases or sentences the reader thinks are most heavily stressed. Generally, however, readers can easily identify the dominant metrical pattern used in a poem.

1. Each of the following ordinary phrases uses one type of metrical foot. Identify the metrical foot in each.
   a. Best of all, victory!
   b. I bought a car today.
   c. Look for hidden pitfalls.
   d. in the cool of the night
2. Does Wyatt's "Whoso List to Hunt" show regular iambic pentameter? Scan three or four lines of the poem. What metrical patterns do you identify in these lines? Is the meter irregular in any of these lines? Explain.

Choices: Building Your Portfolio

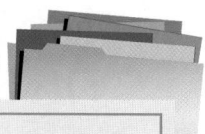

Writer's Notebook

1. Collecting Ideas for an Interpretive Essay

When you write an essay about literature, a good starting point can be your own responses. Reflect on "Whoso List to Hunt" for a few minutes, writing freely about any personal connections you can make to the poem—experiences or feelings that you've had, or perhaps that you've witnessed in others. Try to find the one word or phrase from the poem that most strongly affects your feelings. Save your notes for use in the Writer's Workshop on page 275.

Creative Writing

2. A Woman's Place

What does the concept of love in this poem suggest about the position of women in Wyatt's time? How do you respond to the woman's statement "Caesar's I am"? How do you think *she* feels about her situation? Write a paragraph from the point of view of the "hind," and give her response to the situation described in the poem.

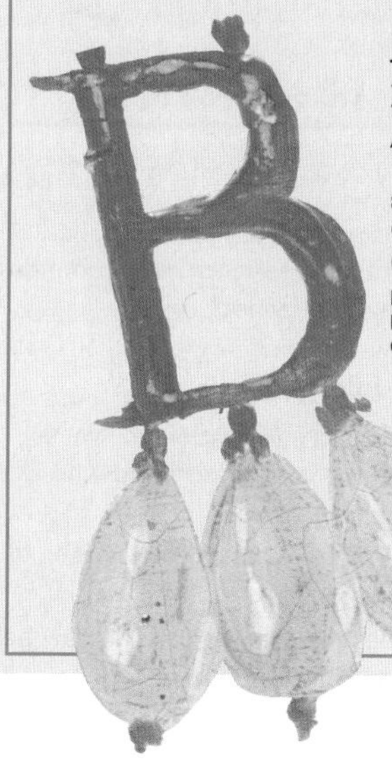

Jewel worn by Anne Boleyn, detail from the portrait *Anne Boleyn* (late 16th century) by an unknown artist. Oil on panel (21⅜″ × 16⅜″).

By Courtesy of the National Portrait Gallery, London.

Edmund Spenser.

The Granger Collection, New York.

Edmund Spenser

(c. 1552–1599)

Spenser—unlike such gentlemanly writers as Wyatt, Surrey, Sidney, and Raleigh—regarded himself primarily as a poet. Upon graduating from Cambridge University, he served as personal secretary to the earl of Leicester, then the favorite of Queen Elizabeth. In Leicester's household, Spenser became acquainted with several other poets and wrote his first book, *The Shepheardes Calender* (1579), a set of twelve pastoral poems, one for each month. Literary historians recognize 1579 as the date when the great age of Elizabethan literature began.

In 1580, Spenser and his new wife went to Ireland in the service of the English government. Except for two or three visits to England, he was to spend the rest of his life in that war-torn country. English troops had invaded and conquered Ireland, but the Irish did not regard themselves as conquered. They particularly resented people like Spenser, who was given an Irish castle and a vast estate in County Cork. Thirty miles away, Sir Walter Raleigh was the proprietor of an even vaster estate than Spenser's. When Raleigh was in Ireland, the two poets met and discussed their works in progress: Raleigh's *The Ocean to Cynthia* and Spenser's *The Faerie Queene*. Raleigh was so impressed with the latter that he persuaded Spenser to accompany him to London in 1589, and there in the following year Books I–III of *The Faerie Queene* were published.

In 1591, Spenser returned to Ireland, where conditions remained very unsettled and dangerous. But he managed to continue work on *The Faerie Queene* and other poems. When his first wife died, Spenser married Elizabeth Boyle, an Anglo-Irish woman living in Cork. Spenser's sonnet sequence *Amoretti* and his marriage hymn *Epithalamion* (both 1595) can be read autobiographically as records of his intense devotion to his wife. In 1596, Books IV–VI of *The Faerie Queene* appeared, along with another marriage song called *Prothalamion.*

As the century drew to a close, the Irish intensified their efforts to expel the English from their land. During one of their raids, Spenser's castle was burned and his infant son killed. Spenser himself escaped to London, where he died suddenly in 1599. He was given a splendid funeral and burial in the part of Westminster Abbey that has become known as the Poets' Corner. He lies near Chaucer, a poet who provided much of his inspiration.

Chaucer, Spenser, and Milton—these three were long regarded as England's greatest nondramatic poets. Of the three, Spenser is perhaps the least highly regarded today. Our age does not itself produce long poems of very high quality, and Spenser's fame depends mainly on the enormously long *Faerie Queene,* which despite its unfinished state runs about 33,000 lines. This poem is such a characteristic product of the Renaissance that some people find it has little to say to our own time. Moreover, Spenser's language is such a hybrid of Chaucerian and Elizabethan English that even when the work was brand new some purists objected to it. The dramatist and poet Ben Jonson, for instance, said Spenser "writ no language." But Spenser's special language is just right for his subject matter, and all the objections to him are easily overlooked by readers who want to lose themselves in the glorious world of imagination. They will always love Spenser.

go.hrw.com
LE0 12-3

OBJECTIVES

Sonnets 30 and 75

1. Read and interpret the sonnets
2. Analyze paradox
3. Distinguish between Petrarchan and Spenserian sonnets
4. Express understanding through critical and creative writing

SKILLS

Literary

- Analyze paradox
- Distinguish between Petrarchan and Spenserian sonnets

Writing

- Imagine a dialogue with Spenser about one of his poems
- Create images of love

Viewing and Representing

- Interpret details in art (ATE)

Planning

- **Block Schedule**
  Block Scheduling Lesson Plans with Pacing Guide
- **Traditional Schedule**
  Lesson Plans Including Strategies for English-Language Learners
- **One-Stop Planner**
  CD-ROM with Test Generator

BROWSING IN THE FILES

About the Author. The son of a clothmaker, Spenser graduated from grammar school as a scholarship student, or "poor boy." Every year the headmaster at the school taught his top students to act so they could put on a play at court. It is likely that Spenser performed as a boy for Queen Elizabeth. Throughout his life, he hoped to return to her court but was unsuccessful.

Resources: Print and Media

Reading

- *Graphic Organizers for Active Reading,* p. 12
- *Audio CD Library*
  Disc 4, Tracks 3, 4

Elements of Literature

- *Literary Elements*
  Transparency 9
  Worksheet, p. 28

Writing and Language

- *Daily Oral Grammar*
  Transparency 9

Assessment

- *Portfolio Management System,* p. 111
- *Test Generator (One-Stop Planner CD-ROM)*

Internet

- go.hrw.com (keyword: LE0 12-3)

Summary ■ ■ ■

The speaker compares his love for a woman to fire and her rejection of his love to ice. However, the speaker is puzzled because if his beloved is like ice and he is like fire, how is it that his desire doesn't melt her coldness but only makes it harder? Also, how is it that his desire isn't cooled by her coldness but instead grows hotter? The sonnet develops this paradox, concluding that in the case of love, the rules of nature are suspended: fire does not melt ice, nor does ice cool fire.

A Critical Thinking

Interpreting

? What do you think the first line means? [The speaker burns with love, but his loved one gives him the cold shoulder.]

B Elements of Literature

Paradox

The use of **paradox**—an internal contradiction for literary effect—was popular with Renaissance poets. Have students restate in their own words the fire-and-ice paradoxes in ll. 2–4, 5–8, and 9–12. [Possible answers: Fire melts ice, but here the ice is frozen harder by the fire; ice cools fire, but here the ice "kindles" the fire.]

C Elements of Literature

Sonnet Couplet

? How does the final couplet answer the paradox? [Love is so powerful it can alter natural laws.]

Responding to the Art

The English artist **Nicholas Hilliard** (1547–1619) painted many tiny portraits, or miniatures, of anonymous courtiers. (For other Hilliard art, see pp. 205, 219, 234, 263, 264, and 265.) **Activity.** Ask students to write an explanation for the flames. How do the flames connect with the poem? [The man is burning with love.]

Before You Read

Sonnets 30 and 75

Make the Connection

The Power of Paradox

Anyone who's been in love understands **paradox:** an apparent contradiction that is somehow true. Love makes you blissful and miserable. It's frightening and healing. It's physical and spiritual. It's incredibly fragile and yet so strong it seems deathless. In short, love is a potent puzzle that we never solve.

Quickwrite

Poets search for images to express the complex experience of falling in and out of love. How would you describe these two feelings: intense desire and loss of interest? Try to find a special image that represents each feeling. (Spenser uses fire and ice.)

Background

Spenser's *Amoretti* ("little love poems") is a sequence of eighty-nine sonnets recording a man's two-year courtship of a woman named Elizabeth (perhaps Spenser's courtship of his bride, Elizabeth Boyle). In Sonnet 30, Spenser uses, in an original way, the convention of the burning man and the icy lady. Sonnet 75 uses another convention, the writer's "eternizing conceit": Submit to my love, and I'll make you famous and even immortal through my writing. But again Spenser gives this old notion a new twist.

from Amoretti

Sonnet 30

Edmund Spenser

A My love is like to ice, and I to fire;
How comes it then that this her cold so great
Is not dissolved through my so hot desire,
But harder grows the more I her entreat?
Or how comes it that my exceeding heat
Is not delayed° by her heart frozen cold,
B But that I burn much more in boiling sweat,
And feel my flames augmented manifold?°
What more miraculous thing may be told
That fire which all thing melts, should harden ice,
And ice which is congealed° with senseless cold,
Should kindle fire by wonderful device?°
C Such is the power of love in gentle mind,
That it can alter all the course of kind.°

6. delayed: tempered.
8. augmented manifold: increased in many ways.
11. congealed: thickened.
12. device: trick.
14. kind: nature.

Unknown Man with Flame Background (16th century) by Nicholas Hilliard.
Ham House, Surrey, England.

Reaching All Students

Struggling Readers

To help students become more organized and specific in their ability to summarize, model a retelling for them. Paraphrase the first four lines of Sonnet 30, then have students take turns summarizing the rest of the poem. In the retellings, make sure students identify and demonstrate an understanding of the main idea and the metaphors that support it.

English Language Learners

At times Spenser inverted usual word orders to maintain the sonnet's rhyme scheme. Work with students to rearrange the words in l. 4 of Sonnet 30 and l. 11 of Sonnet 75. [l. 4: But grows harder the more I entreat her; l. 11: My verse shall eternize your rare virtues.] For more strategies for English language learners, see

- *Lesson Plans Including Strategies for English-Language Learners*

Sonnet 75

Edmund Spenser

One day I wrote her name upon the strand,°
But came the waves and washèd it away;
Again I wrote it with a second hand,
But came the tide, and made my pains his prey.
"Vain man," said she, "that doest in vain assay,°
A mortal thing so to immortalize,
For I myself shall like to this decay,
And eke° my name be wipèd out likewise."
"Not so," quod° I, "let baser things devise°
To die in dust, but you shall live by fame:
My verse your virtues rare shall eternize,
And in the heavens write your glorious name.
Where whenas death shall all the world subdue,
Our love shall live, and later life renew."

1. **strand:** beach.
5. **assay:** try.
8. **eke:** archaic for "also."
9. **quod:** quoth; said. **devise:** plan.

Portrait of an Unknown Lady (16th century) by Nicholas Hilliard.
Victoria and Albert Museum, London.

MAKING MEANINGS

Sonnets 30 and 75

First Thoughts

1. How would you feel if someone in love with you had written these poems? Does your gender affect your response? How?

Shaping Interpretations

2. What **paradoxes** can you find in Sonnet 30? How would you explain them?
3. Fire and ice poems are meant to be clever, but in Sonnet 30, the **speaker** also says something serious about the power of love. What is it?
4. In what sense is the love of the two people in Sonnet 75 still alive today?
5. In Sonnet 75, what **image** does Spenser use for love's impermanence?

Extending the Texts

6. Some attitudes toward love and toward men and women have changed since these sonnets were written. Do you find the speaker's feelings dated or still relevant? Why?

ELEMENTS OF LITERATURE

Petrarchan and Spenserian Sonnets

Renaissance poets wrote with one eye on the past—they made new poems built on older forms and reflecting older themes. Wyatt's sonnets are

Summary

The speaker describes writing his beloved's name in the sand and seeing the waves wash it away twice. When she protests that it is futile to try to immortalize anything mortal, he promises to make her name and their love live forever through his verse.

Background

Spenser was not the only Elizabethan poet to use the eternizing conceit. William Shakespeare and Ben Jonson tried to immortalize in verse what might be lost to death and time.

A Reading Skills and Strategies

Making Inferences

? What does "second hand" mean? [He wrote his beloved's name by hand for a second time.]

B Struggling Readers

Paraphrasing

Point out that the beloved is playing with two meanings of the word *vain* in l. 5 ("proud"; "futile"). Help students paraphrase what it is that the woman feels is useless. [Don't try to immortalize me, for I shall die and my name will disappear like the writing in the sand.]

C Elements of Literature

Eternizing Conceit

? What idea about love does this poem express? [Lovers may die, yet their love can live on in poetry.] Ask students if they believe this conceit.

MAKING MEANINGS

First Thoughts [Respond]

1. Possible response: It would depend on who wrote the poems and on whether the love was reciprocated. Gender may matter; for example, women may dislike being portrayed as cold-hearted.

Shaping Interpretations [Interpret]

2. The poem has two central paradoxes: Ice "kindles" fire, and the fire makes ice colder and harder. The speaker explains that although he is like fire and she is like ice, people in love do not react to each other the way fire and ice do.
3. Love is so powerful it can change the laws of nature.
4. The sonnet preserves their love because people can still read about it.
5. He uses the image of the waves washing away the writing in the sand.

Extending the Texts [Evaluate]

6. Possible responses: The sonnets are dated because they follow the romantic convention that women are cold and men are hot; or they are not dated since people still want to immortalize their loved ones.

Elements of Literature

Petrarchan and Spenserian Sonnets

Have students copy a Petrarchan and a Spenserian sonnet and use different colored markers to indicate the rhyme schemes. Then have them draw boxes around the octave and the sestet (Petrachan) or the quatrains and the couplet (Spenserian).

Answers

1. The turn occurs between the octave and the sestet and shows a logical shift: the octave tells other hunters about the deer; the sestet warns them off.
2. Sonnet 30: *fire/desire; great/entreat/heat/sweat; cold/manifold/told/cold; ice/device; mind/kind;* Sonnet 75: *strand/hand; away/prey/assay/decay; immortalize/likewise/devise/eternize; fame/name; subdue/renew*
3. Conceits will vary. Students might compare love to a sporting event or a loved one's appearance to a constellation or an animal.

Grading Timesaver

Rubrics for each Choices assignment appear on p. 111 in the *Portfolio Management System.*

Choices: Building Your Portfolio

1. **Writer's Notebook** The questions could be literary or personal. Delving into the poems will make them clearer.
2. **Creative Writing** Students might want to vary the beginning, for example, "Love feels like _____."

Resources

Elements of Literature

Formal Assessment

- Literary Elements Test, p. 55

Test Generator *(One-Stop Planner)*

- CD-ROM

adaptations or translations of sonnets written by the Italian Francesco Petrarca (1304–1374), known in English as Francis Petrarch. Petrarch addressed many love poems to a woman identified only as Laura, a proud woman of ideal virtue and beauty who remains totally indifferent to the poet. The poet-lover alternately burns with desire and freezes in Laura's cold disdain.

Sonnets in the Petrarchan manner contain many ingenious comparisons, which in time became known as **Petrarchan conceits.** A **conceit** is a fanciful comparison of two apparently very different things. Love may be compared to a baited hook, for instance, or being in love may be described as plowing water, an obviously futile effort. Petrarchan sonneteers also shape their emotion within a strict structure: fourteen lines of rhymed iambic pentameter, organized in two stanzas, one of eight lines (an **octave**) and one of six lines (a **sestet**). The rhyme in the octave is *abbaabba* and in the sestet usually *cdecde.*

In most Italian sonnets, the octave describes a situation, and the sestet describes a change in the situation. This change is called the **turn.** Sometimes the octave presents a problem and the sestet a solution or even another viewpoint. Sometimes the sestet intensifies the octave's problem with no solution. The possibilities are endless.

Two **English sonnet** forms—the Spenserian and Shakespearean sonnets—originated in the Renaissance. Like the Petrarchan sonnet, both forms use iambic pentameter, but they both differ from the Petrarchan sonnet in having three 4-line stanzas (**quatrains**) and a concluding couplet. The rhyme scheme of the *Amoretti* sonnets is original with Spenser: *abab bcbc cdcd ee.* Since it demands four words for two of the rhymes, only a clever rhymer can manage it.

Analyzing sonnets. Look back now at the sonnets by Wyatt and Spenser.

1. In what line is the **turn** of Wyatt's "Whoso List to Hunt" (page 215)? Does the turn show a logical or an emotional shift?
2. Identify the **rhyming words** in Spenser's Sonnets 30 and 75.
3. Make up your own **Petrarchan conceit** for the experience of love or for a loved one's appearance.

Choices: Building Your Portfolio

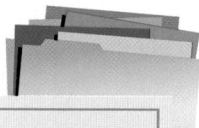

Writer's Notebook

1. Collecting Ideas for an Interpretive Essay

If you could talk to Spenser about one of these sonnets (whether to praise, challenge, argue, or just question), which would you focus on? Choose one, and then jot notes as you reread it carefully. Speak to Spenser directly about his ideas, words, feelings, sounds—anything. Save your dialogue for possible use with the Writer's Workshop assignment on page 275.

Creative Writing

2. Images of Love

In Sonnet 30, what images suggest desire and indifference? In Sonnet 75, what images suggest love's impermanence? Make a love's listing of your own, of the things that love, in all its variations, can be compared to. You could open your lines like this:

Love's passion is like _____ .

Be sure to check the images you jotted down in your Quickwrite notes before you read Spenser's poems.

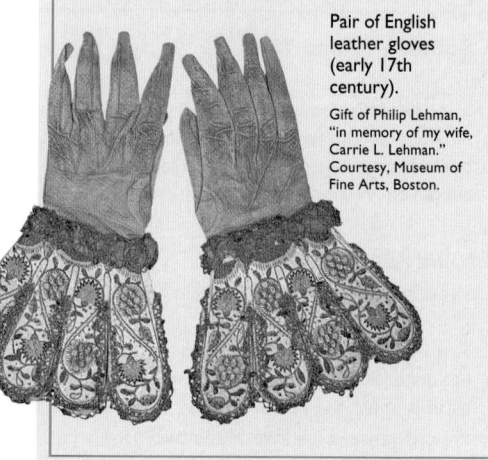

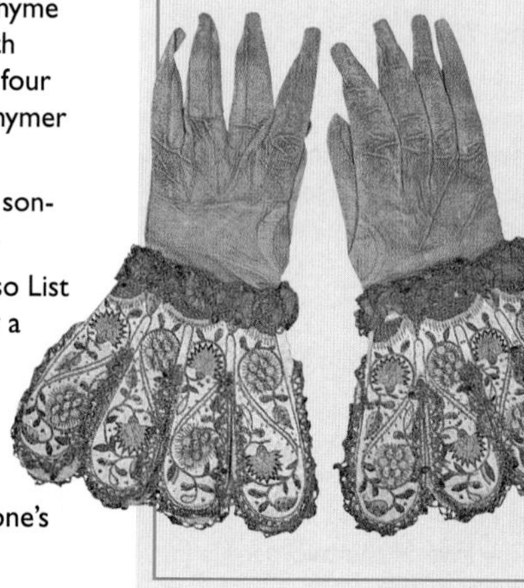

Pair of English leather gloves (early 17th century).

Gift of Philip Lehman, "in memory of my wife, Carrie L. Lehman." Courtesy, Museum of Fine Arts, Boston.

Crossing the Curriculum

Science

Students might want to examine Sonnet 30 from a scientific point of view. Have them discuss the properties of water in both a liquid and solid state, as well as the effects of fire on liquids or frozen substances. Students might comment on whether the cause and effect relationships stated by the speaker are, under any circumstances, scientifically possible.

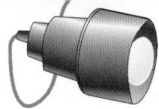

SPOTLIGHT ON

The Faerie Queene: England Through the Looking Glass

In Spenser's long, complex, and unfinished poem *The Faerie Queene,* the word *faerie* does not mean a wee, airy creature dancing among the flowers. Rather, *faerie* suggests grand, heroic beings whose superhuman powers come from their own virtue and piety. The Faerie Queene herself (who does not even appear in the existing poem) is Gloriana, an idealized portrait of Queen Elizabeth, and her realm is at once the England that Spenser loved and a strange, imaginary country. **A**

The poem is a romantic or chivalric **epic.** Unlike the classical epics of Virgil and Homer, romantic epics have an open form, with multiple characters and multiplying plots spreading out in all directions. The marvels, knights, ladies, battles, tournaments, enchantments, dragons, giants, dwarfs, and demons derive from the medieval romances of chivalry, such as the tales of King Arthur.

But its lively stories are only the surface of *The Faerie Queene*. Spenser's moral purposes are especially evident. In a letter to Raleigh, Spenser said that he intended his work to be an **allegory:** Each leading character in the twelve projected books was to embody one virtue or quality; taken together, they would characterize a truly noble person. The heroes or heroines of the six completed books exemplify holiness, temperance, chastity, friendship, justice, and courtesy. **B**

The poem is a tremendous feat of rhyming: Each nine-line iambic stanza has only three rhymes—*ababbcbcc*. The last line's extra foot makes it hexameter. This line, called an **alexandrine,** often sums up a stanza or finishes it off with a striking image. This verse form, which Spenser created for *The Faerie Queene,* is now called the **Spenserian stanza.**

Trying to experience Spenser's immense poem by reading only a few verses is like trying to experience the ocean by looking at a teacup of sea water. However, the three stanzas that follow, describing the hideous Duessa, show Spenser's delight in heroic violence and the gusto with which he describes ugliness.

The Rainbow Portrait of Queen Elizabeth (16th century) by Federico Zuccaro.

Hatfield House, Hertfordshire, England.

Spotlight On

The Faerie Queene is far too long an epic to include in an anthology. This feature introduces students to Spenser's masterpiece and explains it within both historical and literary contexts.

A Historical Connections

Spenser dedicated this poem to Queen Elizabeth, who liked it very much. Returning the honor in a unique way, she paid Spenser a life pension of £50 a year—a considerable sum that was more than double the rent on his sizeable estate of three thousand acres.

B Background

One of the allegorical figures is the Redcross Knight, who represents both mankind and England. He tries to travel toward what is good, but even with Una (Truth) at his side, he sometimes fails. Because the Redcross Knight cannot distinguish between appearance and reality, he sometimes takes up with Falsehood (Duessa). There are other allegorical characters whom students will not encounter in this excerpt: Sansloy (Lawlessness and Force), Abessa (Superstition), and Corceca (Ignorance). Besides symbolizing truth, Una is also the daughter of Adam and Eve, as well as the representation of the Christian faith and the Anglican Church. She wants to save mankind; therefore, she has to deal with those in league with the devil, such as Duessa.

Using Students' Strengths

Auditory/Musical Learners

To give students more practice with meter, have them tap or clap the rhythms in *The Faerie Queene* stanzas. Ask them if they can identify the lines that are perfect iambic pentameter.

Interpersonal Learners

Encourage students to share their reactions to the details they read and the mental images they create. Students might also discuss their responses to the rather graphic details Spenser has created for his readers.

BROWSING IN THE FILES

A Critic's Comment. Spenser's love of Chaucerian language and his concern for moral values has made him the great mediator between the Middle Ages and the modern poets. According to C. S. Lewis, he is "the man who saved us from the catastrophe of too thorough a renaissance."

Summary ■■■

This excerpt from Canto VIII of Book I of *The Faerie Queene* tells of a knight who has been rescued from the evil clutches of Duessa, or Falsehood. The knight's traveling companion, Una, or Truth, orders him to disrobe Duessa. The knight does so and sees Falsehood's hideous characteristics. In the end, Una and the knight decide to let Duessa go free.

(A) English Language Learners

Archaic Language

All students should use the glosses that appear in the margins of this excerpt, but you should assure English language learners that the language of this poem is difficult for all readers. Help students paraphrase, and clarify as needed. In the first line, explain that *bad* is pronounced *bade,* and is an archaic word for "commanded."

(B) Humanities Connections

The ugliness of this allegorical description of "Falsehood exposed" may have been suggested by the following lines from Revelation 17:16: "These shall hate the whore, and shall make her desolate and naked."

(C) Elements of Literature

Imagery

? Why does Spenser create such a hideous picture of Duessa? [Possible answer: In Spenser's day there would have been nothing pleasing or even neutral about Falsehood. Falsehood would be imagined as something hideous and incomparably ugly. People needed to be afraid to behold it.] **How do we feel about lies today?** [Most students will probably agree that lies are generally unacceptable.]

As this part of the story from Canto VIII of Book I opens, a knight has been rescued from the clutches of a foul female creature called Duessa, or Falsehood. The knight is ordered by his traveling companion, Una, or Truth, to disrobe Duessa—not a tempting prospect.

Oral reading. Reading aloud will immediately help solve most of the problems posed by Spenser's unusual spellings. Pronounce the words more or less exactly as they are spelled. Paying attention to the rhymes will help.

"The Fowle Duessa"

from The Faerie Queene

Edmund Spenser

(A) So as she bad, that witch they disaraid,
And robd of royall robes, and purple pall,°
And ornaments that richly were displaid;
Ne sparèd they to strip her naked all.
Then when they had despoild her tire and call,°
Such as she was, their eyes might her behold,
That her misshapèd parts did them apall:
A loathly, wrinckled hag, ill favoured, old,
Whose secret filth good manners biddeth not be told.

Her craftie head was altogether bald,
And as in hate of honorable eld,°
Was overgrowne with scurfe and filthy scald;°
(B) Her teeth out of her rotten gummes were feld,°
And her sowre breath abhominably smeld;
Her drièd dugs,° like bladders lacking wind,
(C) Hong downe, and filthy matter from them weld;°
Her wrizled° skin as rough, as maple rind,°
So scabby was, that would have loathd all womankind. . . .

Which when the knights beheld, amazd they were,
And wondred at so fowle deformèd wight.
"Such then," said Una, "as she seemeth here,
Such is the face of falsehood, such the sight
Of fowle Duessa, when her borrowed light
Is laid away, and counterfesaunce° knowne."
Thus when they had the witch disrobèd quight,
And her filthy feature° open showne,
They let her goe at will, and wander wayes unknowne.

2. **pall:** mantle.
5. **tire and call:** attire and headgear.
11. **eld:** old age.
12. **scald:** scabs.
13. **feld:** fallen.
15. **dugs:** breasts.
16. **weld:** ran.
17. **wrizled:** wrinkled. **rind:** bark.
24. **counterfesaunce:** hypocrisy.
26. **feature:** appearance.

Listening to Music

"Greensleeves" (traditional), performed by Alfred Deller

Fantasia on Greensleeves by Ralph Vaughan Williams, performed by London Festival Orchestra

Fantasy is an important element in *The Faerie Queene* and also an important element in British music. In the twentieth century the traditional tune "Greensleeves" inspired the *Fantasia* on *Greensleeves* by British composer Ralph (räf) Vaughan Williams (1872–1958). His elaboration on "Greensleeves" takes the form of a fantasia, or fantasy, which in music refers to a composition with a free structure determined by the composer's own imagination.

Activity

Have students listen to the traditional rendition of "Greensleeves" and to Vaughan Williams's famous fantasia. Then ask them to choose one of the sonnets by Spenser or Wyatt and write a "word fantasia" in which they expand the poem into a free verse or prose composition that elaborates on lines, images, and ideas from the original sonnet.

Shakespeare's Sonnets: The Mysteries of Love

Shakespeare. The name calls to mind characters in the great plays, who have come to life on stages around the world: *Hamlet, Macbeth, Romeo and Juliet, King Lear, Othello.* Yet had Shakespeare written no plays at all, he would still have an immense reputation as a poet for his *Sonnets* (1609). There are 154 sonnets altogether, their speaker is male, and their chief subject is love. Beyond these three points, however, there is little agreement, only questions:

Is the sonnets' speaker a dramatic character invented by Shakespeare, like Romeo, Macbeth, or Hamlet, or is he the poet himself? The speaker does call himself Will a few times, and he does make puns on his name, but is there any evidence that Will is the speaker in all the sonnets? If the sonnets are about the real man Shakespeare, then who are the real people behind the characters the sonnets mention: the rival poet, the beloved young man who may be the subject of many of the first 126 sonnets, or the beautiful and exciting dark-complexioned woman of some later sonnets?

Maids and winged hearts (detail) from *Emblèmes et Devises d'Amour* (early 16th century) by Pierre Sala. Stowe 955 fol. 12b–13.
British Library, London.

Is the order in which the sonnets were originally published (probably without Shakespeare's consent) the correct or the intended sequence? Could they be arranged to tell a more coherent story? *Should* they be so arranged?

And in the 1609 publication, who is the "Mr. W. H." mentioned as the "only begetter" of the sonnets: the young man? someone else?

These and dozens of other questions about the sonnets have been asked and answered over and over again—but never to everybody's satisfaction. We have hundreds of conflicting theories, but no absolutely convincing answers.

About the individual sonnets, though, if not the whole sequence, agreement is perfect: They are among the supreme utterances in English. They say profound things about important human experiences, and they say them with great art.

OBJECTIVES

Sonnets 29, 73, 116, 130

1. Read and interpret the sonnets
2. Express understanding through writing, speaking and listening, and art

SKILLS

Writing
- Collect ideas for an interpretive essay through repeated readings
- Compare and contrast tones
- Compare poems across cultures
- Write a response to Sonnet 130
- Write a parody

Speaking/Listening
- Engage in a panel discussion

Art
- Illustrate the sonnets

Viewing and Representing
- Discuss a painting's title (ATE)

Planning

- **Block Schedule**
  Block Scheduling Lesson Plans with Pacing Guide
- **Traditional Schedule**
  Lesson Plans Including Strategies for English-Language Learners
- **One-Stop Planner**
  CD-ROM with Test Generator

Resources: Print and Media

Reading
- *Graphic Organizers for Active Reading,* pp. 13, 14
- *Audio CD Library*
  Disc 4, Tracks 5, 6, 7, 8
- *Literary Elements:* Poetry Transparencies 1–5, p. 93; Teaching Notes p. 91

Writing and Language
- *Grammar and Language Links*
  Worksheet, p. 17
- *Language Workshop CD-ROM*

Assessment
- *Formal Assessment,* p. 41
- *Portfolio Management System,* p. 112
- *Test Generator (One-Stop Planner CD-ROM)*

Internet
- go.hrw.com (keyword: LE0 12-3)

Ⓐ Historical Connections

Renaissance Calendar

The Julian calendar, which set May in summer, not spring, was in use when Shakespeare wrote this sonnet. This explains his reference to a "summer's day" in May.

Ⓑ Literary Connections

Conceits

Explain that this is an example of the eternizing conceit that students read about on p. 218. This concept states that the sonnet itself immortalizes, or "eternizes," earthly, human love. Students will learn more about conceits on p. 247, when they are introduced to metaphysical conceits in the poems of John Donne. For now, however, you might refer students back to the text about Petrarchan conceits on p. 220. Explain that Shakespeare lost patience with reading the same old Petrarchan conceits repeatedly and, in response, created some new ones of his own.

The Sonnets' Form

Each of Shakespeare's sonnets has its formal organization established by the rules of the sonnet form. Each sonnet also has a logical organization of ideas, also established by the sonnet form. Here is how Shakespeare structured Sonnet 18 to make these two organizations cooperate in a way that seems natural, not forced.

Logical organization	Sonnet 18		Formal organization
A question and tentative answers	Shall I compare thee to a summer's day?	a	First quatrain
	Thou art more lovely and more temperate.	b	
	Ⓐ Rough winds do shake the darling buds of May,	a	
	And summer's lease hath all too short a date.	b	
	Sometime too hot the eye of heaven shines,	c	Second quatrain
	And often is his gold complexion dimmed;	d	
	And every fair from fair sometime declines,	c	
	By chance, or nature's changing course untrimmed.	d	
The turn	But thy eternal summer shall not fade,	e	Third quatrain
	Nor lose possession of that fair thou owest,	f	
	Nor shall Death brag thou wander'st in his shade	e	
	When in eternal lines to time thou grow'st.	f	
A final answer	Ⓑ So long as men can breathe, or eyes can see,	g	Couplet
	So long lives this, and this gives life to thee.	g	

In the English sonnet form known as the **Shakespearean sonnet,** the fixed requirements are fourteen iambic pentameter lines divided into three quatrains and a couplet, with the rhyme scheme *ababcdcdefefgg.* (See page 219 for Spenserian and Petrarchan forms.)

The logical organization of ideas, of course, varies from sonnet to sonnet. Here in Sonnet 18, the first line's question is followed by negative answers: The speaker's beloved does have some resemblances to a summer's day, but only superficial ones. The first two quatrains concentrate on the summer day's imperfections rather than on the loved one.

Then comes the **turn,** a shift in focus or thought. Here the speaker turns from the faulty summer's day to the beloved, and by the end of the third quatrain, the speaker has entirely abandoned the opening comparison. Like most literary terms, the word *turn* is a metaphor; the speaker, figuratively speaking, is "turning" from one thing to another.

In an Italian sonnet, divided into an eight-line octave and six-line sestet, the turn usually occurs after the octave. Sonnet 18, with its turn after line 8, follows this pattern, but in an English sonnet, the final couplet is often a second turn of great impact: a final summary or explanation of all that came before. In this sonnet, the couplet says, perhaps with some exaggeration, that by being addressed in this poem, the beloved person has become immortal.

(For Shakespeare's biography, see page 289.)

Assessing Learning

Check Test: True-False

1. Love is the main subject of Shakespeare's sonnets. [True]
2. Sonnets have ten lines. [False]
3. Shakespearean sonnets have a rhymed couplet at the end. [True]
4. The "turn" in a sonnet is a shift in focus or thought. [True]
5. Shakespearean and Italian sonnets have the same rhyme scheme and structure. [False]

Professional Notes

Critical Comment: Literary Research

Scholars hope to someday know the story behind the sonnets. As recently as January 1995, Vassar College professor Donald Foster announced the discovery of what many believe to be a Shakespearean funeral elegy. He and others are studying this work to see what light it sheds on the shadowy figures behind the sonnets. In the meantime, new criticism such as Helen Vendler's *The Art of Shakespeare's Sonnets* asserts that "the sonnets will remain intelligible, moving, and beautiful."

Before You Read

SONNETS 29, 73, 116, 130

Make the Connection

The Heart of the Matter

Earlier (page 212), we asked the humanist's question, "What is the good life?" A related question may be equally difficult, and that is "What is the happy life?" What is it that makes us happy, that lets us look back over years receding into the past, and ahead to the inevitable conclusion, without sorrow or despair? Wealth hasn't answered the question satisfactorily for many people. Power always seems to dwindle away or be wrenched out of our hands in an instant. Fame evaporates faster than the early morning fog. If there is any answer to this question, for many people it is love. Time passes and death is inescapable, but love, if we are fortunate enough to find it or create it, sustains us through it all.

In these four sonnets, Shakespeare speculates about what love is, and what it does to us and for us.

Quickwrite

People warn you not to confuse infatuation with love: Having stars in your eyes makes for a wonderful glow but blurry vision. Eventually, a warm glow comes up against a reality check—and sometimes it doesn't pass. What distinguishes love from infatuation? Write freely for a few minutes trying to identify a few qualities of each, or of the people you've seen enjoying—or suffering from—each.

go.hrw.com
LEO 12-3

In this sonnet, the speaker describes how he rids himself of such ugly emotions as envy, self-pity, self-hatred, and the dismal feeling of certainty that everybody else is luckier than he is.

Sonnet 29

William Shakespeare

When, in disgrace° with Fortune and men's eyes,
I all alone beweep my outcast state,
And trouble deaf heaven with my bootless° cries, (A)
And look upon myself and curse my fate,
Wishing me like to one more rich in hope,
Featured like him, like him° with friends possessed,
Desiring this man's art,° and that man's scope,°
With what I most enjoy contented least;
Yet in these thoughts myself almost despising, (B)
Haply° I think on thee, and then my state, (C)
Like to the lark° at break of day arising
From sullen° earth, sings hymns at heaven's gate; (D)
  For thy sweet love remembered such wealth brings
  That then I scorn to change my state with kings.

1. disgrace: out of favor.
3. bootless: useless; futile.
6. one . . . him . . . him: three different men whom the speaker envies.
7. art: literary ability. **scope:** power.
10. haply: by chance.
11. lark: English skylark, a bird whose song seems to pour down from the sky.
12. sullen: gloomy.

Henry Percy, 9th earl of Northumberland.
Rijksmuseum, Amsterdam.

Summary ■■

In the first eight lines, the speaker bemoans his lack of looks, ability, prospects, and powerful friends. In the tenth line, however, there is a turn. The speaker recalls the richness that love has bestowed on him and declines to change his place with kings.

(A) Elements of Literature

The Complaint

? A **complaint** is a plaintive poem. Many of the sonnets in the major sonnet sequences of Edmund Spenser and Shakespeare are complaints, the laments and pleas of unrequited lovers. Shakespeare begins this sonnet with a complaint but ends it unexpectedly. In ll. 1–4, what are some of the speaker's complaints? [Possible response: He says he's unlucky, disliked, alone, and discouraged.]

(B) Reading Skills and Strategies

Understanding Syntax

Tell students that understanding the syntax of a poem can help them grasp its meaning. Point out that the poem is all one sentence: The first introductory clause in the poem begins with *When* in l. 1 and goes through l. 8; the second introductory clause begins with *Yet*, meaning *But*, and is in l. 9. The main clause starts at the beginning of l. 10 and is accompanied by a major shift in tone.

(C) Critical Thinking

Interpreting

? What causes the speaker's spirits to rise? [Possible response: the thought of his beloved's love.]

(D) Elements of Literature

Simile

? To what does the speaker compare his rising spirits? [His spirits are like a lark singing at the break of day.]

Reaching All Students

English Language Learners

Ask students if they've heard the expression, "I'd give anything to be in your place." Explain that the speaker in Shakespeare's sonnet is wishing he could change places with a series of other people. Urge students to read to find out why he's unhappy with his lot in life and how he feels at the end of the sonnet about changing places with others. For other ideas, see

- *Lesson Plans Including Strategies for English-Language Learners*

Professional Notes

Critical Comment: Conflict

Shakespearean scholar Helen Vendler explains that this poem presents the conflict between two kinds of reality in the Renaissance world: the social hierarchy and the natural world. The beginning of the poem is about the social world: It pits the speaker's "outcast state" against the state of men in political favor. The sonnet then turns to the natural world, with the soaring image of a lark singing as the sun rises.

Summary

Through metaphors of autumn, twilight, and glowing embers, the speaker conveys his advancing age and weakening hold on life. In a turn at the end of the poem, the speaker acknowledges that his beloved recognizes his frailties, yet loves him all the more because he'll soon be gone.

A Elements of Literature

Poetic Meter

Have students identify the meter of the sonnet. [The sonnet is written in Shakespeare's characteristic iambic pentameter.] You should explain that *mayst* (l. 1) is read as one syllable and that *perceivest* (l. 13), in the final couplet, is read as two syllables.

B Advanced Learners

Parallel Structures

? What parallel structure introduces each of the three metaphors? [words that say, in effect, "You see in me . . ."] What effect does the parallelism have on the poem? [Possible answer: The parallelism makes the poem more haunting by linking the three metaphors that suggest old age and death.]

C Critical Thinking

Interpreting

? How does the speaker's advancing age affect his beloved? [The beloved loves him more because of his mortality.]

RESPONDING TO THE ART

John Atkinson Grimshaw (1836–1893) was an English landscape painter who used a camera to project images onto his canvas. (For other Grimshaw art, see pp. 756 and 814.)

Activity. Invite students to look up the meaning of the word *afterglow* and discuss how it fits as the title of the painting and the poem. [The word conveys the glow of a dying fire, the glow of light at the end of the day, and the glow of love at the end of life.]

In several sonnets, the speaker emphasizes the difference between his age and his beloved's: He is much older, and so presumably will die first. In Sonnet 73, the speaker dwells on his advanced years. This sonnet is rich in striking metaphors, with each quatrain developing a single metaphor.

Sonnet 73

William Shakespeare

A That time of year thou mayst in me behold
When yellow leaves, or none, or few, do hang
Upon those boughs which shake against the cold,
Bare ruined choirs° where late the sweet birds sang.
B In me thou see'st the twilight of such day
As after sunset fadeth in the west,
Which by and by black night doth take away,
Death's second self, that seals up all in rest.
In me thou see'st the glowing of such fire,
That on the ashes of his youth doth lie
As the deathbed whereon it must expire,
Consumed with that which it was nourished by.°
C This thou perceivest, which makes thy love more strong,
To love that well which thou must leave ere long.

4. choirs: parts of a church or cathedral in which services are held. The landscape of Shakespeare's England was dotted with church ruins resulting from Henry VIII's abolition of monasteries.

12. consumed . . . nourished by: choked by the ashes of the wood that once fed its flame.

An October Afterglow (detail) (19th century) by John Atkinson Grimshaw.
Christie's, London.

Reaching All Students

Struggling Readers

Renaissance poetry will be difficult for struggling readers, but once they have figured out the vocabulary, the sentiments will appeal to them. Have students read aloud the poem at least twice. Discuss tough words or phrasings. Have them list images of autumn, death, or transitory things. Discuss how these words help create the tone and the theme of the poem. Have students retell the poem in their own words.

Professional Notes

Critical Comment: Metaphor

Literary scholar Helen Vendler says this sonnet contains three models of life: a season, a day, and a fire. A season and a day fade, but a fire burns, providing a glow. So, too, the love the speaker invokes in the final couplet does not fade but glows and grows stronger as the end approaches.

Making Meanings

Sonnets 29 and 73

First Thoughts

1. Obviously, the **speakers** in these two sonnets are in love, but what other emotions do you hear in their voices? Do you hear joy, sorrow, or something else?

Shaping Interpretations

2. Like many of the sonnets, Sonnet 29 is actually a single sentence. In the long introductory clause, what does the speaker say he envies?
3. The main clause of Sonnet 29 begins the **turn.** Where is it? How does the speaker's **tone,** or attitude, change after the turn?
4. In Sonnet 73, what four **metaphors** does the speaker use to describe himself? What contrast is implied between the speaker and his beloved?
5. Find the **turn** of Sonnet 73. What is its logical relationship to what comes before?
6. How do the seasonal and daily **images** in Sonnet 73 contribute to the poem's **tone**?
7. In Sonnet 73, the idea of line 12 is somewhat compressed. **Paraphrase** it in your own words, after you have thought about what originally fed ("nourished") the speaker's fires—fires that are now choked ("consumed").

Extending the Texts

8. If you wrote a contemporary version of Sonnet 29 ("When I failed the quiz and left my lunch at home . . ."), what would you replace Shakespeare's complaints with? Look at his list of problems, and see if you can come up with a contemporary version.
9. What people today could you imagine being the speakers of these sonnets?

Challenging the Text

10. In Sonnet 29, what do you think is the effect of devoting so many lines to the speaker's mental problems and so few to their cure?

Making Meanings

Sonnets 29 and 73

First Thoughts [Interpret]

1. Students may hear regret, sorrow, joy, melancholy.

Shaping Interpretations [Interpret]

2. He envies anyone who has reason to hope, is handsome, has many friends, or has ability and power.
3. The turn begins at l. 9. In l. 10, the tone changes from self-pity to delight.
4. The metaphors compare the speaker to a bare tree in autumn, the ruins of a church, the twilight after sunset, and the glowing embers of a dying fire. The beloved is young, and the speaker is old.
5. The turn occurs in l. 13. Earlier the speaker says he is growing old and must die soon. The couplet suggests that his beloved will love him more now because she will soon be without him.
6. They emphasize the passing of time, making the sonnet poignant and reinforcing its melancholy tone.
7. Possible answer: Because life itself fed the fire (as wood feeds a real fire), a paraphrase might be, "I am consumed by the life that I have lived—I have used up my time."

Extending the Texts [Synthesize]

8. Students might wish to be like others who have greater ability in sports, or an easier time getting good grades.
9. Possible answers: Sonnet 29—a young, unsuccessful person; Sonnet 73—an older man married to a younger woman.

Challenging the Texts [Evaluate]

10. The numerous complaints suggest the extent of the speaker's unhappiness. The unexpected shift in l. 10 shows how quickly love can uplift one's spirits. This quick shift increases the emotional impact of the poem.

Making the Connections

Connecting to the Theme: "Love, Death, and Time"

All the themes suggested by the title are found in Sonnet 73. To emphasize their interconnection, try these activities:

1. On the chalkboard, list with students the images that suggest the passage of time. Then ask students how these images also show the passage of life to death. [Possible answers: Day leads to night; autumn to winter; sunset to night.]

2. Then point out the turn. Ask students the following questions. How does the turn at the end of the poem also suggest death? [It talks about leaving "ere long."] How does the turn suggest the passing of time? [Time is suggested by the same reference to death: leaving "ere long."] How does the turn praise love? [Love continues and is strengthened despite the approach of death.]

Summary

This sonnet tells what love is and what it is not. Love is not changeable, but fixed and unalterable. Love is also not "Time's fool": It doesn't change as time passes or when beauty fades. In the final couplet, the speaker claims that if he's wrong about love, then he "never [wrote]" and no one "ever loved."

Ⓐ Reading Skills and Strategies
Finding the Main Idea

? Which lines in the poem define love by telling what it is not? [ll. 2–4, 9, 11] Which lines define it by telling what it is? [ll. 5–8, 12]

Ⓑ Advanced Learners
Synecdoche

Explain that **synecdoche** is a figure of speech in which a part of something represents the whole. Have students find the synecdoche in this sonnet and explain why it is used. [Rosy lips and cheeks: They represent health and youth, which are subject to the ravages of time.]

Ⓒ Struggling Readers
Understanding Allusions

Explain that the poet is alluding to the medieval image of time as the "Grim Reaper" who cuts off life with a sweep of a sickle, a blade for cutting crops.

Ⓓ Critical Thinking
Interpreting

? Do you think the speaker is describing love as it is, or as it should be? Explain. [Optimistic students will argue that the speaker is describing love as it is; the more cynical will say love as it should be.]

Ⓔ Reading Skills and Strategies
Making Connections

Ask students to compare Sonnet 116's idea of what will endure with the ideas expressed in Spenser's Sonnet 75. [Possible answer: Both sonnets note that the body will decay and love will live on. Sonnet 75 claims that the speaker's verse will last—and it has.]

Perhaps the most famous of Shakespeare's sonnets, Sonnet 116 defines true love metaphorically as a "marriage of true minds." Such love is completely firm against all "impediments," a word taken from the priest's remarks to those attending a Church of England wedding: "If any of you know cause or just impediment why these persons should not be joined together . . ."

Sonnet 116

William Shakespeare

Let me not to the marriage of true minds
Admit impediments. Love is not love
Which alters when it alteration finds,
Or bends with the remover to remove.
Oh no! It is an ever-fixèd mark°
That looks on tempests and is never shaken.
It is the star to every wandering bark,°
Whose worth's° unknown, although his height be taken.°
Love's not Time's fool, though rosy lips and cheeks
Within his bending sickle's compass° come.
Love alters not with his brief hours and weeks,
But bears it out° even to the edge of doom.°
  If this be error and upon me proved,
  I never writ, nor no man ever loved.

5. mark: seamark; a prominent object on shore that serves as a guide to sailors.
7. bark: boat.
8. worth's: value's. **height be taken:** altitude measured to determine a ship's position.
10. compass: range; reach.

12. bears it out: survives. **doom:** the Last Judgment; the final judgment at the end of the world.

The Bradford Table Carpet, detail of scenes of rural life (late 16th century). Embroidered on linen canvas with colored silks. English.
Victoria and Albert Museum, London.

Reaching All Students

English Language Learners

To improve students' comprehension, work with them to change the negative sentences to positive constructions. For example, the first sentence might read: "I will not allow anything to stand in the way of true love"; the second sentence might read, "True love is changeless and loyal. . . ." For additional strategies for English language learners, see

- *Lesson Plans Including Strategies for English-Language Learners*

Assessing Learning

Check Test: True-False

Sonnet 29

1. The speaker finds comfort in riches. [False]

Sonnet 73

2. The speaker compares himself to autumn, twilight, and a dying fire. [True]

Sonnet 116

3. This sonnet presents an ideal picture of love that is steady and persevering. [True]

This sonnet ridicules the fashionable, exaggerated metaphors some of Shakespeare's fellow poets were using to describe the women they loved: Your eyes are suns that set me on fire, your cheeks are roses, your breasts are snowballs. Such metaphors, known as **conceits,** are traceable to Petrarch, but by 1600 they had become, through overuse, tiresome or laughable. (Note that the word *mistress* in this poem simply meant "girlfriend" in the Renaissance.)

Sonnet 130

William Shakespeare

My mistress' eyes are nothing like the sun,
Coral is far more red than her lips' red.
If snow be white, why then her breasts are dun,°
If hairs be wires, black wires grow on her head.
I have seen roses damasked,° red and white,
But no such roses see I in her cheeks.
And in some perfumes is there more delight
Than in the breath that from my mistress reeks,°
I love to hear her speak, yet well I know
That music hath a far more pleasing sound.
I grant I never saw a goddess go,°
My mistress, when she walks, treads on the ground.
　And yet, by Heaven, I think my love as rare
　As any she belied° with false compare.°

3. **dun:** brown.

5. **damasked:** streaked.

8. **reeks:** is exhaled.

11. **go:** walk.

14. **belied:** misrepresented. **compare:** comparison.

Making Meanings

Sonnets 116 and 130

First Thoughts

1. Do you agree with Sonnet 116's definition of love? Why or why not?
2. In Sonnet 130, how do you picture the speaker's mistress?

Shaping Interpretations

3. What **metaphors** does Sonnet 116 use to describe the steadiness of love? How is time **personified** in this poem?
4. In Sonnet 116, between which lines does the **turn**—the change in **moods**—occur? How would you speak these lines to convey the change in mood?
5. What does the final **couplet** add to the message of Sonnet 116?
6. Sonnet 130 could have been written by someone who had read too many Petrarchan sonnets. How does the **speaker** poke fun at them?
7. Do you think the speaker's mistress in Sonnet 130 is actually unattractive? Why or why not?
8. Why is the **couplet** in Sonnet 130 absolutely necessary to keep the sonnet from being misunderstood?
9. If you came upon these two sonnets without knowing they were by the same writer, would you infer, from the attitudes expressed, that they were by one writer or two? Why?

Extending the Texts

10. Which of these four Shakespearean sonnets do you think could be read at a wedding? Could any of them be part of a funeral service? Explain.

Summary

With humor and audacity, the speaker describes his beloved, who he says is nothing like the red-lipped, rosy-cheeked, sweet-voiced damsels of typical love poetry; instead, she is an ordinary mortal. Yet, the speaker makes it clear that it is not his love who disappoints, but rather gushing poetry with conventional sentiments about beauty.

A Critical Thinking

Analyzing

? When the speaker talks about his beloved, how does he first surprise and then reconfirm your expectations? [He surprises readers by saying his love is not beautiful but then confirms their expectations by saying he loves her anyway.]

B Reading Skills and Strategies

Determining the Author's Purpose

? Why, in your opinion, did the poet write this sonnet? [Shakespeare wants to amuse readers by making fun of trite conceits; he also wants to affirm that love exists between real—not idealized—men and women.]

C Critical Thinking

Challenging the Text

? Is the poem's parody successful, in your opinion? Why or why not? [Sample responses: Yes, it's clever and funny; or no, he's unkind to the woman he professes to love and is not very funny.]

Making Meanings

Sonnets 116 and 130

First Thoughts [Respond]

1. Possible responses: Yes, love should be steady, and unchanging. No, everyone accepts that people change with time, so love must change too.
2. She has pale lips; dust-colored breasts; black, wiry hair; and colorless cheeks.

Shaping Interpretations [Interpret]

3. Love is as steady as a seamark (ll. 5–6) or the North Star (ll. 7–8). Time is a grim reaper who cuts down youth (ll. 9–10).
4. The turn occurs between ll. 13 and 14. Possible responses: They might be spoken emphatically or ironically.
5. The couplet emphasizes the poem's message, showing how strongly the speaker believes what he is saying.
6. The speaker reverses the conventional romantic conceits by using unflattering comparison and understatement.
7. No, he is mocking the convention; or yes, she is, but her beloved doesn't mind.
8. It affirms his love for his mistress and his dislike of overused conceits.
9. The sonnets seem to be by different people: a cynic (130) and an idealist (116).

Extending the Texts [Evaluate]

10. Sonnets 29, 116, and 130 focus on love and could be read at a wedding. Sonnet 73 could be read at a funeral.

Grading Timesaver

Rubrics for each assignment appear on p. 112 in the *Portfolio Management System.*

CHOICES: Building Your Portfolio

1. **Writer's Notebook** Have students write down one question they have about the poem.
2. **Comparing and Contrasting Tones** **Tone** is the attitude a writer takes toward the reader, a subject, or a character. One possibility might be to compare the radically different tones of Sonnets 116 and 130.
3. **Comparing Poems Across Cultures** Before students begin writing, check their charts to see if they have noted historical and cultural influences.
4. **Creative Writing** As an alternative, let students begin their answers in their own way. Students might work in pairs. Boys might imagine what a girl would say if Sonnet 130 had been written about her.
5. **Creative Writing** To get students started, have them suggest various song titles. Write them on the chalkboard. Some examples include "Love Me Tender," "I Just Called to Say I Love You," and "I Will Always Love You."
6. **Visual Art** Suggest students work in a variety of mediums such as colored tissue paper, paint, or photography. Students may also wish to use computer graphics.
7. **Panel Discussion** Have students bring in magazine ads and lists of television commercials and films to form the basis for discussion. Ask students to identify the messages about love that the media projects. Do students think there is too much of a link between buying a product and finding love? If possible, it might be useful to compare messages from different decades.

CHOICES: Building Your Portfolio

Writer's Notebook

1. Collecting Ideas for an Interpretive Essay

When you write about literature, repeated readings are a basic step in finding new insights and writing topics. Choose the sonnet that you're most drawn to, and read it again, slowly. Then try reading it aloud, and copy it out on a piece of paper. For each reading, make notes on the words and ideas that affect you most strongly. For each reading, note at least one new detail you didn't see before. (You might want to highlight passages with a different color marker for each reading.) Save your work for possible use with the Writer's Workshop on page 275.

Comparing and Contrasting Tones

2. What Makes Tone?

Identify two sonnets in which you detect tones or moods. Compare and contrast the sonnets by focusing on each speaker's tone. Discuss how word choice, figurative language, imagery, and sound effects work together to create a very specific tone for each poem.

Comparing Poems Across Cultures

3. Love's the Same?

Look back at the modern love poem by the American poet E. E. Cummings on page 213. Write a brief essay in which you compare that poem with one of Shakespeare's sonnets. Do you think the poems reflect different cultures and historical contexts? Before you write, you might gather the details for your comparison in a chart like the following:

	Poem 1	Poem 2
Message		
Figurative language		
Form		
Tone		

Creative Writing

4. The Mistress Answers Back

Sonnet 130 is written from the male speaker's point of view. But how would his mistress reply? Write your own sonnet (or just a few verses) to a boyfriend, using this as a beginning: "My boyfriend's eyes are . . . "

Creative Writing

5. Mocking Modern Love

Sonnet 130 is a witty parody of love poems popular in Shakespeare's day. Write your own parody of modern love songs expressed in one style of popular music: country, heavy metal, alternative rock, and so on. Listen to several examples of the style first, paying attention to melody, rhythm, story line, imagery, and tone.

Visual Art

6. Being Moody

Create an emotionally suggestive illustration for each sonnet, using only two colors and one visual image in each illustration. The image may be a real object, such as a lark, or an abstract pattern, such as a heart shape. Combine colors and image creatively to convey the feelings you find in the poem.

Panel Discussion

7. Love in Our Time

In our own time—in art, entertainment, and ads—romantic love is exalted as a pinnacle of human happiness (especially, in the media, love with someone gorgeous, trim, and trendy). But what of people who never find a partner—or a perfect one? Are they losers? Is romantic love essential for happiness? In a panel discussion, critique our culture's messages about love, using examples. Be sure to look back at your Quickwrite notes (page 225) for your ideas about what true love is.

Before You Read

The Passionate Shepherd
The Nymph's Reply
To the Virgins
To His Coy Mistress

Make the Connection

Love's Logic

You have heard it before. On the radio or in a music video, a lead singer appeals passionately to a woman to be his love, although the specific lyrics vary. What you may not know is that people have heard this message for centuries. The "invitation to love" is an old poetic tradition. It was especially common in Renaissance England. Along with descriptions of all the delights that await a hesitant young woman, the Renaissance poet pressures her with what may really be the oldest "line" in the world: "We are all going to die, so take your pleasures now."

Quickwrite

What current love songs can you think of—in any popular music style? Look for songs sung by an impatient suitor to a specific lover who hasn't quite committed herself or himself—or not in the way the singer wants. If you can, find the words, or transcribe them. Listen to the songs as closely as you can. How is love treated in popular music today? Take notes on all your reflections.

Elements of Literature

Carpe Diem

The poems that follow reflect an ancient theme the Romans called *carpe diem* (kär′pe dē′em), meaning "seize the day." *Carpe diem* is a call to live life to the fullest right now: "Let us eat and drink, for tomorrow we die," as the Roman poet Horace said. *Carpe diem* poems are the literary counterpart of the human skull that was sometimes part of the decor at wild Roman parties—a grisly reminder of the fate none of us can escape.

Carpe diem, literally "seize the day," is a literary theme that urges living in the present moment, especially in pleasurable pursuits.

For more on Carpe Diem, *see the Handbook of Literary Terms.*

Embroidered picture of a woman, possibly personifying Summer (detail) (late 17th century). Satin embroidered with silk, metal thread, and beads. English.

By Courtesy of the Board of Trustees of the Victoria and Albert Museum, London.

OBJECTIVES

The Passionate Shepherd/ The Nymph's Reply/To the Virgins/To His Coy Mistress

1. Read and interpret the poems
2. Recognize and interpret the use of *carpe diem*
3. Express understanding through writing, music, art, speaking and listening

SKILLS

Literary
- Recognize and explore the use of *carpe diem*

Writing
- Collect ideas on a *carpe diem* poem
- Compare and contrast *carpe diem* poems
- Compare "The Bait" with "The Passionate Shepherd"
- Compare a Dorothy Parker poem to a *carpe diem* poem
- Write a reply to "To the Virgins" or "To His Coy Mistress"

Speaking/Listening
- Engage in a panel discussion

Music
- Write a *carpe diem* song

Art
- Create a collage

Viewing and Representing
- Speculate about a figure (ATE)
- Analyze use of color (ATE)

Planning

- **Block Schedule**
  Block Scheduling Lesson Plans with Pacing Guide
- **Traditional Schedule**
  Lesson Plans Including Strategies for English-Language Learners
- **One-Stop Planner**
  CD-ROM with Test Generator

Resources: Print and Media

Reading
- *Graphic Organizers for Active Reading,* pp. 15, 16, 17, 18
- *Audio CD Library*
  Disc 4, Tracks 9, 10, 11, 12

Viewing and Representing
- *Viewing and Representing*
  Fine Art Transparency 3
  Fine Art Worksheet, p. 12

Assessment
- *Portfolio Management System,* p. 114
- *Test Generator (One-Stop Planner CD-ROM)*

Internet
- go.hrw.com (keyword: LE0 12-3)

Browsing in the Files

About the Author. Many of the theories about Marlowe's death are conspiracy theories. One critic has suggested that Marlowe staged his own death by substituting the corpse of a sailor for his own body in order to escape to Europe. Others have maintained that the dramatist was killed to prevent him from testifying against an important figure in Queen Elizabeth's government who was involved in her spy network.

A Critic's Comment. Did Renaissance artists ever go platinum? Evidently, in terms of his own era, Marlowe came close. When set to music in the 1580s, Marlowe's famous pastoral poem "The Passionate Shepherd to His Love" may have been as big—relatively speaking—as any song ever recorded by the Rolling Stones or Elvis Presley. One critic called it one of the rages of the 1580s, adding that it resulted in great commercial acclaim for its author.

Summary ■

"Come live with me," urges the shepherd in "The Passionate Shepherd to His Love." He describes some of the pleasures of the country that he and his love will enjoy and lists the things he will make for her, including a cap of flowers and slippers with gold buckles. He promises that shepherds will dance and sing for her delight each May morning.

Christopher Marlowe

(1564–1593)

Reputed portrait of Christopher Marlowe (1585). French School. Oil.

The Master and Fellows of Corpus Christi College, Cambridge, England.

Marlowe belonged to the first generation of Elizabethan dramatists. His career ended about the time Shakespeare's began, although he was only two months older than Shakespeare. The son of a shoemaker in Canterbury, Marlowe won scholarships to the King's School in Canterbury and then to Cambridge University. While still a student, he translated some love poems by Ovid, the Roman poet. The poems were declared too erotic by the Bishop of London, who had the books burned.

After completing his studies, Marlowe apparently became a spy. Elizabeth's government maintained an elaborate espionage system to keep track of Roman Catholics, but just what spying Marlowe did for the government remains uncertain. It *is* certain that Marlowe had only six more years to live when, at twenty-three, he came down to London from Cambridge. He also associated with a number of other recent university graduates living near the London theaters and supporting themselves by writing plays and pamphlets. Excitement and danger were part of their lives. Marlowe himself was jailed for his involvement in a street fight that ended with one man murdered.

Another brush with the law came when Marlowe's roommate, a fellow dramatist named Thomas Kyd, accused him of making scandalous, seditious, and atheistic speeches. Marlowe was arrested. A few days before the case was to be heard, he went with some rather shady characters down the Thames to a tavern in Deptford. After supper the men got into a violent fight over the bill; Marlowe was stabbed above the eye and died instantly. The court acquitted his assailant on the grounds of self-defense, though it is very possible that all the testimony in this case was fabricated and that Marlowe was assassinated for reasons not yet discovered. Theories about Marlowe's life and death are abundant; there are even a few people today who believe, without any evidence, that Marlowe wasn't murdered but lived on to write all of Shakespeare's plays for him.

All of Marlowe's dramatic poems are tragedies: *Dido, Queen of Carthage* (written with Thomas Nashe); *Tamburlaine; The Jew of Malta; The Massacre at Paris; Edward II;* and *Doctor Faustus.* Marlowe's greatest tragic heroes have been called "overreachers": self-driven, power-hungry men who refuse to recognize either their limitations as human beings or their responsibilities to God and their fellow creatures. Tamburlaine seeks power through military conquest; Barabbas, the Jew of Malta, through money; Faustus, through knowledge. They all want to be more than mere men, and only death can put an end to their monstrous ambitions. To express these grandiose themes, Marlowe created wild and soaring poetry, like nothing ever heard before on the stage. Although Marlowe did not write Shakespeare's plays, he showed Shakespeare what was possible in dramatic poetry.

go.hrw.com
LEO 12-3

Reaching All Students

Struggling Readers

As students read the poem on p. 233, ask them to answer the following questions after each stanza: "What is the main idea?" "What does the shepherd want?" "What does he offer?"

English Language Learners

Explain that during the Renaissance, people used the intimate pronoun *thou* meaning "you" when speaking directly to people they loved. *Thee* and *thy* are forms of *thou.*

Getting Students Involved

Charting Pastoral Pleasures

Have students make a chart listing the senses of hearing, sight, smell, and touch. As they read Marlowe's famous pastoral on p. 233, have them list under each heading the details that appeal to each of the senses. Their charts might include these details, among others:

Hearing	Sight	Smell	Touch
shallow rivers	gowns	roses	rocks
waterfalls	gold buckle	fragrant posies	finest wool
birds	rocks		lined slippers

This poem is part of two literary traditions. It is part of the *carpe diem* tradition, and it is a **pastoral,** from *pastor,* the Latin word for "shepherd." Pastoral works are set in an idealized countryside, and their characters are often blends of the naive and the sophisticated. The most famous of English pastorals, Marlowe's poem has often been set to music, and several poets have written answers or sequels to it.

The Passionate Shepherd to His Love

Christopher Marlowe

Come live with me, and be my love,
And we will all the pleasures prove°
That valleys, groves, hills, and fields,
Woods, or steepy mountain yields.

And we will sit upon the rocks,
Seeing the shepherds feed their flocks
By shallow rivers, to whose falls
Melodious birds sing madrigals.°

And I will make thee beds of roses,
And a thousand fragrant posies,
A cap of flowers, and a kirtle,°
Embroidered all with leaves of myrtle.

A gown made of the finest wool
Which from our pretty lambs we pull,
Fair linèd slippers for the cold,
With buckles of the purest gold.

A belt of straw and ivy buds,
With coral clasps and amber studs,
And if these pleasures may thee move,
Come live with me, and be my love.

The shepherd swains° shall dance and sing
For thy delight each May morning.
If these delights thy mind may move,
Then live with me, and be my love.

2. prove: experience.

8. madrigals: complicated songs for several voices.

11. kirtle: dress, gown, or skirt.

21. swains: young boys.

Shepherd and Shepherdess with Cupid in Pastoral Landscape (detail) (17th century). Embroidered textile. Colored silk and isinglass on canvas (10¼″ × 14″).

The Metropolitan Museum of Art. Gift of Irwin Untermyer, 1964. (64. 101. 1313). Photograph ©1977 The Metropolitan Museum of Art.

Resources

Viewing and Representing

Fine Art Transparency

Students can decide whether *The Hireling Shepherd* by William Holman Hunt presents an idealized or a realistic view of a shepherd's life. See the *Viewing and Representing* booklet:

- Transparency 3
- Worksheet, p. 12

A Advanced Learners

Pastoral Poetry

Have students read the headnote with this poem. Ask them what makes this poem a pastoral. [Possible answer: It portrays none of the hardships of farm life: work, bad weather, dirt, lost or sick sheep, poor housing, little leisure, and loneliness.]

B Elements of Literature

Carpe Diem

? In what way is the speaker offering the suggestion to "seize the day"? [He is offering many "delights" to tempt his love in the hope that she will spontaneously go with him.]

C Elements of Literature

Refrain

? A **refrain** is a repeated line used for emphasis or effect. What is the effect of repeating l. 1 in ll. 20 and 24? [The repetition gives the poem a songlike effect and suggests the speaker's urgency.]

D Reading Skills and Strategies

Responding to the Text

? Would you be persuaded by the speaker's arguments? Why or why not? [Possible responses: No, because he couldn't possibly fulfill all his promises; or yes, the speaker is sensitive and passionate, and life with him would be full of pleasures.]

Crossing the Curriculum

Music

The sweet madrigals of the English Renaissance complement the themes in this poem. Students might find examples of the songs and airs of Renaissance composers such as Thomas Tallis, Orlando Gibbons, John Dowland, and William Byrd, and explain how the words, the sounds of the characteristic musical instruments (such as the lute and viol), and the tunes evoke the atmosphere expressed by Marlowe.

Connecting Across Texts

Connecting with *Utopia*

Remind students that the Renaissance was an age of extraordinary optimism. One of its premier writers was Sir Thomas More, who wrote *Utopia,* the story of an imaginary island with peace-loving inhabitants. Have students research additional information about More's Utopia, and compare it with the life suggested in this poem. [More's Utopia has no war, corruption, or crime; land is owned in common. Unlike the pastoral idyll of Marlowe's poem, however, all people have to work.]

Summary ▪

In "The Nymph's Reply to the Shepherd," the clever nymph says that not every shepherd tells the truth. She then responds to the pleasures and gifts the shepherd offers by painting a realistic view of each one. For example, she says rivers rage and flowers fade. She ends by saying that she might be moved to be the shepherd's love if youth and love lasted forever.

Browsing in the Files

About the Author. Raleigh was considered quite good-looking, and as biographer Robert Lacey writes, "he was one of the most handsome men at court." Scholars A. D. Wraight and Virginia F. Stern note that "Raleigh always cut a splendid figure at Court in his subtle satins and brocades, a single jewel in his ear. . . ." Lacey also notes that "his charms did not go unnoticed by members of the fair sex," including Queen Elizabeth herself. This man with so many gifts and accomplishments could not save himself from death, but he could go nobly to his fate. When it came time for him to be executed, he checked the ax to see if it was sharp (he was originally condemned to the hideous death of being drawn, hanged, and quartered). When asked how he would like to lie on the block, he replied, "So the heart be right, it is no matter which way the head lieth."

Responding to the Art

Nicholas Hilliard (1547–1619) was an Elizabethan portrait painter with an eye for detail. (For other Hilliard art, see pp. 205, 218, 219, 263, 264, and 265.)
Activity. Students might enjoy speculating about what Raleigh would say about today's fashions.

Sir Walter Raleigh

(1552?–1618)

Sir Walter Raleigh (16th century) by Nicholas Hilliard.
By Courtesy of the National Portrait Gallery, London.

Raleigh is one of the most colorful figures of a very colorful age. A handsome, expensively dressed, and probably arrogant man, at the peak of his success he was Queen Elizabeth's confidential secretary and captain of her guard. He fought brilliantly for England in France, Spain, Ireland, and America. He was passionately devoted to the cause of colonizing the Americas, and to advertise its products he became one of the first bold Englishmen to smoke tobacco and grow potatoes.

In his rise to power, Raleigh made many enemies, some of whom saw their chance to destroy him when the queen died. They poisoned King James's mind against him, and—on trumped-up evidence—he was convicted of treason. Raleigh was sentenced to death in 1603, though his execution was not carried out until 1618.

Imprisoned in the Tower of London during this long interval, he conducted chemical experiments and wrote a *History of the World* that runs from Adam and Eve to the establishment of the Roman Empire. He also dreamed of another expedition to Guiana, on the northern coast of South America; he had explored Guiana earlier in his life and believed it contained vast hoards of gold and jewels. In 1617, still under a death sentence, he was allowed to undertake his last voyage to Guiana. It turned out to be a disaster. The English obtained no treasure, and the Spanish killed many of Raleigh's men, including his beloved son. Very ill with fever, Raleigh sailed home to face a certain and shameful death. But according to the verdict of history, the shame is King James's, not Raleigh's. Raleigh was sacrificed to satisfy the Spanish, who were clamoring for his death as a condition for maintaining peaceful relations with England. The English, who hated and feared the Spanish, had not forgotten Raleigh when they deposed and beheaded James's son, King Charles I, in 1649.

In his speech on the scaffold, Raleigh described himself as "a seafaring man, a soldier, and a courtier." Although he did publish his *History,* he did not think of himself as a writer. He was carefree with his poems; only about thirty-five of them have survived, and they have been slowly assembled by literary researchers through the past four centuries. His most ambitious poem is *The Ocean to Cynthia,* one of the hundreds of literary works that Queen Elizabeth's subjects wrote to express their love and devotion. It survives only in fragments. This is unfortunate, because Raleigh's poems have considerable merit. They are powerful, outspoken, even blunt, and suffused with the courage of a man who was always ready to accept without self-pity whatever life might bring him. He could have been thinking of himself when he wrote in his *History,* "There is no man so assured of his honor, of his riches, health, or life, but that he may be deprived of either or all, the very next hour or day to come."

go.hrw.com
LEO 12-3

Reaching All Students

English Language Learners
To help students understand the content, have them retell the poems in prose, replacing unfamiliar words with easier synonyms.

Advanced Learners
Have students analyze the structure, rhyme scheme, and meter in both poems to see how good a parody Raleigh's poem is. [They have the same structure (six quatrains), meter (iambic tetrameter), and rhyme scheme (aabb).]

Getting Students Involved

Drafting a Reply
Before students begin reading Raleigh's "The Nymph's Reply," ask them how *they* would respond to the shepherd. What counterarguments might they use? Ask them to draft a quick reply in their journals. Then have them read Raleigh's poem and compare their arguments with his.

Here is Raleigh's reply to Marlowe's "Passionate Shepherd." Elizabethan London was a small place, and Raleigh's and Marlowe's paths must have crossed more than once. Other poets, including John Donne and Robert Herrick, replied to Marlowe, but Raleigh wrote the best answer. His speaker is identified as a "nymph," which means a young woman. Like her creator, she has a strong character. A

The Nymph's Reply to the Shepherd

Sir Walter Raleigh

If all the world and love were young,
And truth in every shepherd's tongue,
These pretty pleasures might me move
To live with thee and be thy love.

But Time drives flocks from field to fold,°
When rivers rage and rocks grow cold,
And Philomel° becometh dumb;
The rest complains of cares to come.

The flowers do fade, and wanton° fields
To wayward winter reckoning yields; B
A honey tongue, a heart of gall° C
Is fancy's spring, but sorrow's fall.

Thy gowns, thy shoes, thy beds of roses,
Thy cap, thy kirtle, and thy posies.
Soon break, soon wither, soon forgotten,
In folly ripe, in reason rotten.

Thy belt of straw and ivy buds,
Thy coral clasps and amber studs,
All these in me no means can move D
To come to thee and be thy love.

But could youth last and love still breed,
Had joys no date, nor age no need,
Then these delights my mind might move E
To live with thee and be thy love.

5. fold: pen where sheep are kept in winter.

7. Philomel: the nightingale.

9. wanton: luxuriant.

11. gall: a bitter substance.

Embroidered wall hanging of the Morell family, Constanz, East Switzerland (detail) (1601).
Schweizerisches Landesmuseum, Zurich.

A Vocabulary Note

Multiple Meanings

As the headnote explains, *nymph* means "young woman," but Raleigh was no doubt aware of its other meanings. The word *nymph* comes from the Greek word for "bride," and in Greek and Roman mythology, a nymph was a nature spirit. After students have read the poem, ask them how these meanings apply. [Sample response: Coming from an "enraptured" bride or a nature spirit, these cynical ideas are ironic.]

B Reading Skills and Strategies

Comparing/Contrasting

? How does the nymph's view of life differ from the shepherd's? [Sample responses: The shepherd envisions an ideal life, focusing on positive things such as youth and spring and summer; the nymph points out all the flaws in this vision, focusing on negatives such as age and fall and winter.]

C Vocabulary Note

Antonyms

Notice how the poet uses antonyms in ll. 11, 12, and 16, to contrast the sweet promises of the shepherd with the bitter realities of life. [He uses three sets of antonyms: honey and gall, spring and fall, folly and reason.]

D Struggling Readers

Paraphrasing

? How might this stanza be paraphrased? [Possible answer: All these wonderful things that you are offering cannot convince me to be your love.]

E Elements of Literature

Carpe Diem

? How does the poet satirize the *carpe diem* theme? [Possible answer: He makes the shepherd's offers seem unrealistic, impossible, and ridiculous.]

MAKING MEANINGS

The Passionate Shepherd
The Nymph's Reply

First Thoughts [Respond]

1. Possible responses: Shepherd, 4: charming in his infatuation but lacking in logic; or shepherd, 10: enthusiastic and optimistic in his love. Nymph, 10: logical, realistic, and clever; or nymph, 2: too hardhearted and cynical.

Shaping Interpretations [Interpret]

2. The speaker envisions a life of carefree pleasure. The speaker will make his beloved beds of flowers, a cap of flowers, a gown embroidered with myrtle leaves, a gown of finest wool, lined slippers with gold buckles, a belt of straw and ivy buds decorated with coral and amber. The couple will sit on rocks watching shepherds dance and sing.
3. The summer weather, their unfettered free time, and their ability to buy gold buckles, amber studs, and coral clasps seem unrealistic. The hard work, hazards, and lonely life of the shepherd play no part in this idealized world.
4. The nymph points out that winter replaces spring, rivers rage, rocks grow cold, birds stop singing, flowers fade, and pretty clothes "break." She would be his love if youth and joy could last forever.
5. Possible answers: The tone is cynical, realistic, ironic, sarcastic.

Extending the Texts [Synthesize]

6. Possible response: A modern woman might be too savvy to take him seriously, and she might laugh at him; or she might be swept off her feet by such a romantic approach.
7. Students may mention advertisements for cruise ships or vacation and honeymoon spots, as well as movies, novels, and television shows with impossibly happy or unrealistic endings.

MAKING MEANINGS

The Passionate Shepherd to His Love
The Nymph's Reply to the Shepherd

First Thoughts

1. Rate the shepherd and the nymph on the persuasiveness of their arguments, using a scale of 0 to 10 (with 10 being most persuasive). Be ready to justify your ratings.

Shaping Interpretations

2. Describe the life that the shepherd envisions with his love. How will they be dressed? How will they spend their time?
3. In **pastoral** writing, the harsh realities of country life do not exist. Which details of the shepherd's description seem distinctly idealistic? What realistic, gritty details of a shepherd's life can you imagine?
4. In her reply, what flaws does the nymph find in the shepherd's idyllic vision? What are her conditions for living with him?
5. What is the **tone** of the nymph's reply?

Extending the Texts

6. How do you think a modern young woman would respond to the shepherd's invitation?
7. Idyllic escape with a loved one still has a strong appeal, whether the retreat is a remote island or a mountaintop hideaway. How is this romantic escape motif used today in literature, television, movies, and advertising?

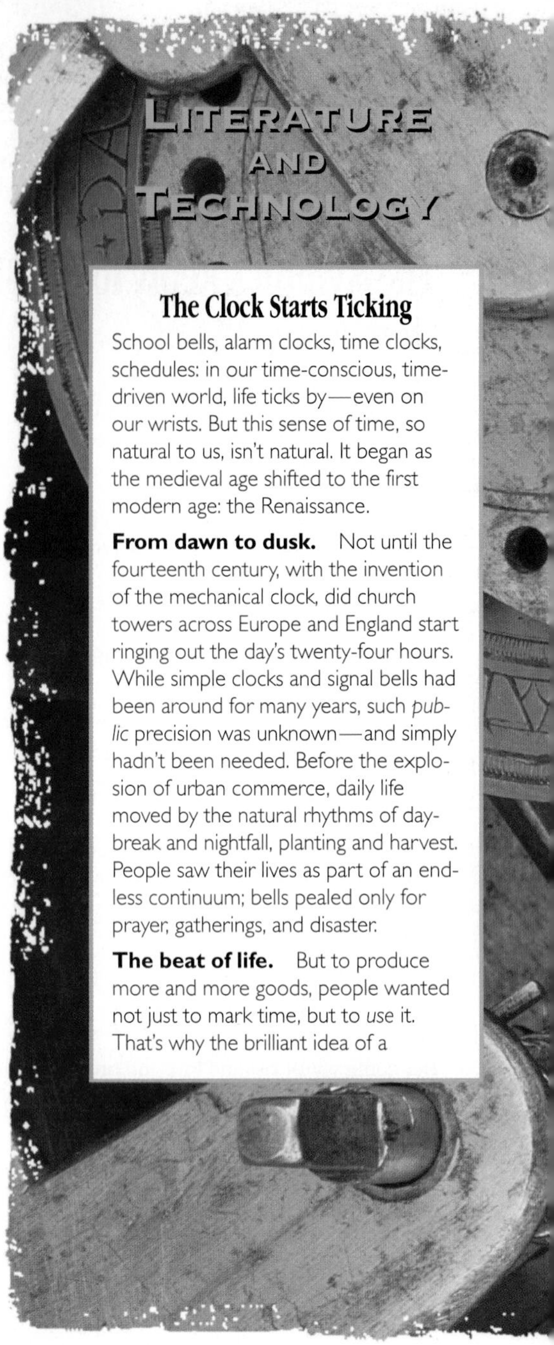

LITERATURE AND TECHNOLOGY

The Clock Starts Ticking

School bells, alarm clocks, time clocks, schedules: in our time-conscious, time-driven world, life ticks by—even on our wrists. But this sense of time, so natural to us, isn't natural. It began as the medieval age shifted to the first modern age: the Renaissance.

From dawn to dusk. Not until the fourteenth century, with the invention of the mechanical clock, did church towers across Europe and England start ringing out the day's twenty-four hours. While simple clocks and signal bells had been around for many years, such *public* precision was unknown—and simply hadn't been needed. Before the explosion of urban commerce, daily life moved by the natural rhythms of daybreak and nightfall, planting and harvest. People saw their lives as part of an endless continuum; bells pealed only for prayer, gatherings, and disaster.

The beat of life. But to produce more and more goods, people wanted not just to mark time, but to *use* it. That's why the brilliant idea of a

Using Students' Strengths

Naturalist Learners

Have students list the joys of nature that the nymph refuses. Some of the details might interest students in further research. For example, they could research the appearance and song of the nightingale, so beloved of English poets. They might learn more about myrtle, called the "flower of the gods," and other wildflowers that grow in England. Students might find out which flowers have value as food or medicine.

Getting Students Involved

Performing a Dramatic Reading

Pair boys.and girls together and ask the pairs to read the poems: Marlowe's first, then Raleigh's. Readers should try to imagine themselves as the characters and to ask themselves these questions: Does the shepherd really think he can convince the nymph with his argument? Does the nymph think that the shepherd believes she would be convinced? The answers should help students determine the tone they will use for reading the poems aloud.

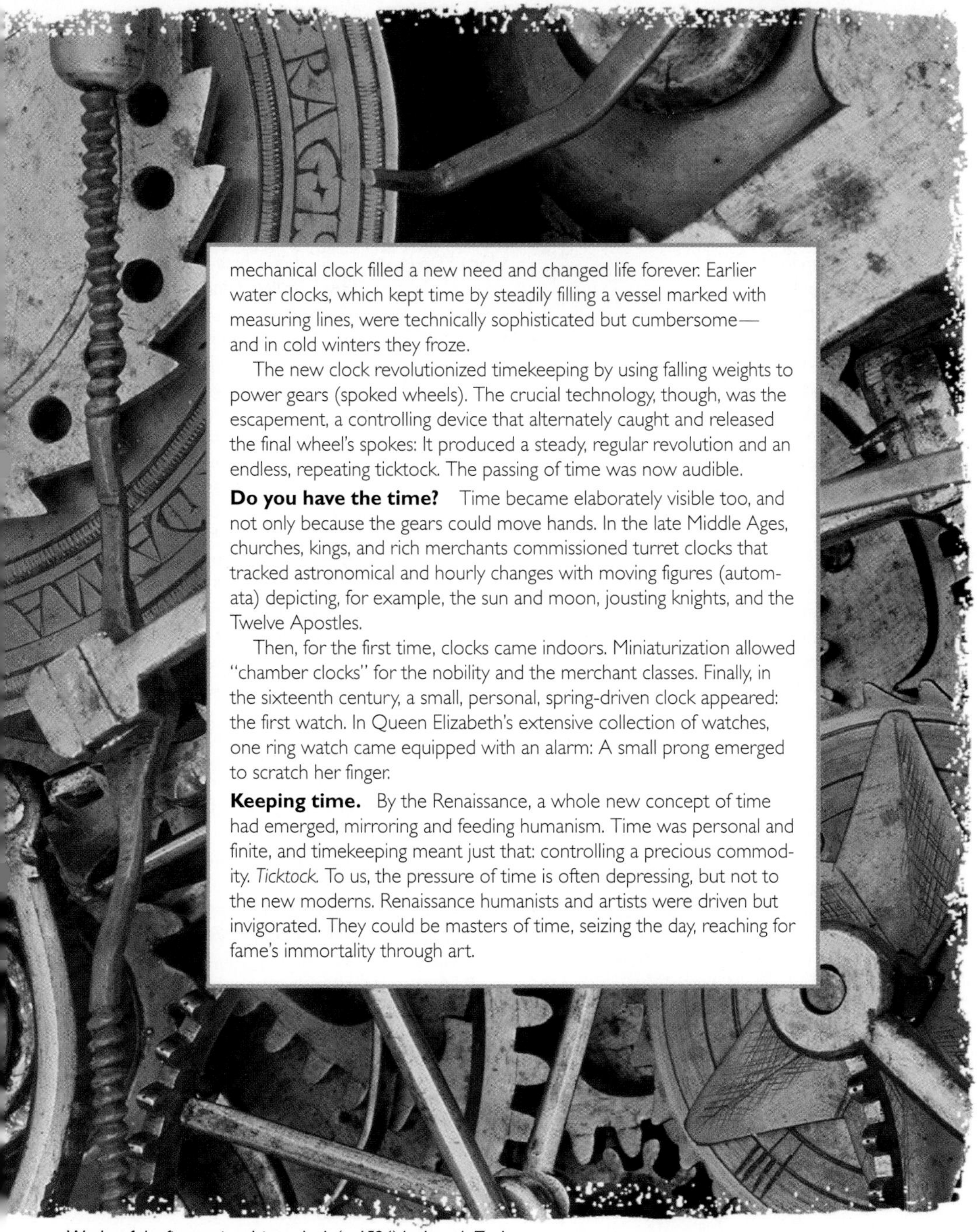

mechanical clock filled a new need and changed life forever. Earlier water clocks, which kept time by steadily filling a vessel marked with measuring lines, were technically sophisticated but cumbersome—and in cold winters they froze.

The new clock revolutionized timekeeping by using falling weights to power gears (spoked wheels). The crucial technology, though, was the escapement, a controlling device that alternately caught and released the final wheel's spokes: It produced a steady, regular revolution and an endless, repeating ticktock. The passing of time was now audible.

Do you have the time? Time became elaborately visible too, and not only because the gears could move hands. In the late Middle Ages, churches, kings, and rich merchants commissioned turret clocks that tracked astronomical and hourly changes with moving figures (automata) depicting, for example, the sun and moon, jousting knights, and the Twelve Apostles.

Then, for the first time, clocks came indoors. Miniaturization allowed "chamber clocks" for the nobility and the merchant classes. Finally, in the sixteenth century, a small, personal, spring-driven clock appeared: the first watch. In Queen Elizabeth's extensive collection of watches, one ring watch came equipped with an alarm: A small prong emerged to scratch her finger.

Keeping time. By the Renaissance, a whole new concept of time had emerged, mirroring and feeding humanism. Time was personal and finite, and timekeeping meant just that: controlling a precious commodity. *Ticktock.* To us, the pressure of time is often depressing, but not to the new moderns. Renaissance humanists and artists were driven but invigorated. They could be masters of time, seizing the day, reaching for fame's immortality through art.

Works of the first spring-driven clock (c. 1524) by Joseph Zech.
Society of Antiquaries of London.

LITERATURE AND TECHNOLOGY

Few inventions in the West were as public as the clock. Clocks first appeared in town centers—usually in church towers. There they not only announced themselves visually but also clanged out the hour. As individuals sought to use time to regulate their lives, however, clocks became privately owned possessions. At first people were content with a household clock, and then, as with the telephone in our own times, a timepiece became something that everybody needed to wear or carry. How did this timely trend catch on? As the writer Daniel Boorstin notes in *The Discoverers,* "The first advertisement for the clock was the clock itself, performing for new publics all over Europe." As the clock proliferated, so did references in literature to time and timekeeping. References to time and clocks in other Renaissance works are found in *Julius Caesar, Macbeth,* Marvell's poem "The Garden," and Shakespeare's Sonnet 12.

Assessing Learning

Check Test: True-False

"The Passionate Shepherd"

1. The shepherd woos his love by telling her how beautiful she is. [False]
2. It was possible for the shepherd to give his love all that he promises her. [False]

"The Nymph's Reply"

3. The nymph points out some aspects of life that the shepherd neglected to mention. [True]
4. The nymph eventually agrees to marry the shepherd. [False]

Browsing in the Files

About the Author. Herrick doesn't sound like a traditional man of the cloth, and that held true in other aspects of his life as well. He called Devonshire "dull" and "loathèd," and admitted to being bored there. He kept a tame pig and taught it to drink from a tall drinking mug. He once threw his sermon at a congregation that had the audacity to look bored.

Summary ■

Herrick's lyric "To the Virgins, to Make Much of Time" may be the most famous of all *carpe diem* poems, and its first line is a **coda,** or summary, of the "live for today" philosophy. The speaker warns that time flies and youth fades. For these reasons, he says, young women should marry quickly before they lose the chance.

Robert Herrick

(1591–1674)

Robert Herrick (18th century) by Schiavonetti.

By Courtesy of the National Portrait Gallery, London.

We first hear of Herrick as an apprentice to his uncle, a London goldsmith and jeweler; it is pleasant to think that the future poet may have acquired his taste for small, beautiful things in his uncle's workshop. Herrick apparently lacked ambition and drive, since he did not enter the university until he was twenty-two, a very late age in those days, and he did not leave it until he was twenty-nine. For the next few years, he had no regular occupation, but enjoyed himself in London as a member of Ben Jonson's circle of young friends. At some point, he was ordained a priest, but the serious part of Herrick's life did not begin until he was thirty-nine.

Herrick was then called to a parish in Dean Prior, in Devonshire, far from London, in the West Country, which Londoners habitually regarded as wretched and barbaric. According to some of Herrick's poems, this was an intolerable exile; according to others, it was heaven on earth. At any rate, Herrick's stay in Dean Prior came abruptly to an end in 1647 with the arrival of the Parliamentary Army, which deprived him of his parish and substituted in his place a clergyman of a more puritanical stripe. (It would not be easy to find a less puritanical priest than Herrick.) When the king was restored some thirteen years later, so was Herrick, and he lived on at Dean Prior until he died at the age of eighty-three.

While deprived of his parish and living in London, Herrick published a fat little volume containing about 1,400 poems. The book was called *Hesperides, or the Works Both Human and Divine of Robert Herrick, Esq.* (1648). Less than a fourth of the poems fit into the "divine" category, and these are mainly witty verses on Biblical characters and events. All the rest of the poems are definitely "human," though the book's last line—"Jocund his Muse was; but his Life was chaste"—shows that Herrick's life was a bit less lively than his poetry. The word *Hesperides* in the title is borrowed from classical mythology; it is the collective name for the nymphs who live in a garden where they watch over a tree that bears golden apples. The title implies that Herrick's book is a garden full of precious things.

Herrick borrowed more than his title from classical antiquity. He was so steeped in Latin poetry that he frequently wrote his poems as if he were an ancient Roman, imposing pagan customs, creeds, and rituals on the English countrypeople and his own household. He imitated the Latin love poets, especially Catullus, when he addressed poems to beautiful women with such classical names as Julia, Corinna, Perilla, Anthea, and Electra.

Herrick also wrote about his small house, his spaniel named Tracy, the royal family in far-off London—whatever came into his mind. Altogether, his poems give us a picture of "Merrie England," which is not so much the England of any particular time or place, but an ideal, pastoral state where sadness is momentary and pleasure innocent.

go.hrw.com
LEO 12-3

Reaching All Students

Struggling Readers

To do a Read, Rate, Reread exercise, have students divide a piece of paper into four columns. After they read the poem for the first time, ask them to rate their comprehension on a scale from 1 to 10, 1 being the lowest level and 10 being the highest. Next, have them write questions about the meaning of the text at the points where their understanding broke down. In their rereading, they should try to answer these questions, and then they should rate their comprehension once again. Have them repeat this process until all four readings have been completed. For additional help, see p. 59 of the *Reading Strategies Handbook* in the *Reading Skills and Strategies* binder.

English Language Learners

Your students' cultural backgrounds will affect their attitudes toward this poem. Girls raised in traditional cultures such as India, where marriages often occur at a young age, may react in one way, while girls raised in cultures where marriages are postponed until later, may react in another way. Encourage students to respect each other's opinions in class discussion.

Advanced Learners

Compare and contrast the *carpe diem* theme of "To the Virgins" with the world view expressed in the following political epigram from Herrick.

Moderation

In things a moderation keep,
Kings ought to shear, not skin, their sheep.

The first line of this little lyric, Herrick's most popular poem, has been a metaphorical part of our language ever since the nineteenth century, when Herrick was "discovered" by people interested in Renaissance literature. Instead of courting one woman, as in most *carpe diem* poems, Herrick addresses all "virgins," or young women. As you read, remember that Herrick was a priest.

To the Virgins, to Make Much of Time

Robert Herrick

Gather ye rosebuds while ye may, **A**
Old Time is still a-flying;
And this same flower that smiles today,
Tomorrow will be dying.

The glorious lamp of heaven, the sun, **B**
The higher he's a-getting,
The sooner will his race be run,
And nearer he's to setting.

That age is best which is the first,
When youth and blood are warmer;
But being spent, the worse, and worst
Times still° succeed the former.

Then be not coy,° but use your time; **C**
And while ye may, go marry:
For having lost but once your prime,
You may forever tarry.°

12. still: always.

13. coy: cold; inaccessible; aloof.

16. tarry: delay; linger.

Spring (detail) (1595) by Lucas van Valkenborch.
Christie's, London.

A Elements of Literature

Carpe Diem

The Latin poet Catullus originated the theme *carpe diem.* Although the phrase is usually translated as "seize the day," *carpo* in Latin means "reap" and can refer to picking, plucking, or gathering flowers or fruit. Ask how this meaning fits with Herrick's imagery. [He refers to gathering rosebuds.]

B Advanced Learners

Understanding Allusion

The second stanza is a classical allusion to the story of the sun god Helios. Have students look up the myth and use it to interpret the allusion. [Helios crossed the heavens each day in a fiery chariot, "rising" high at noon, and "setting" at night.]

C Critical Thinking

Interpreting

? How does the last stanza reflect the *carpe diem* philosophy? [It urges the virgins to seize the opportunity to marry while they are young and beautiful and still have the chance.]

RESPONDING TO THE ART

Flemish artist **Lucas van Valkenborch** (c. 1535–1597) was part of a family of landscape and genre painters.

Activity. Ask students to write a paragraph describing exactly what they *see* in the painting, beginning with the woman in the center. Then have them imagine what is "happening" in this scene.

Using Students' Strengths

Auditory Learners

Have students read Herrick's poem aloud, so they can feel its bouncy, songlike rhythm. Point out that its meter differs from that of other poems in this collection. Be sure to play the recording of the poem in the *Audio CD Library,* Disc 4, Track 11.

Visual Learners

Herrick's text has three stanzas of persuasive reasoning with a conclusion in the fourth stanza. Have students use a flow chart like the one on the right to identify the reasoning, summarizing each stanza in their own words.

stanza 1 [ ]
+
2 [ ]
+
3 [ ]
↓
4 [ ]

Browsing in the Files

About the Author. In his last years Marvell's hatred of Charles II grew so pronounced that some people began to dread being near Marvell, for fear he would get them in trouble with the king. Because Marvell had many political foes, a popular rumor arose that he was poisoned—although it is more likely that he died during a fever from lack of medical care.

The first edition of *Miscellaneous Poems* (1681) included a certificate from "Mary Marvell" designed to prove the authenticity of the poems. The document, signed on October 15, 1680, asserted that the poems "are printed according to the exact Copies of my late dear Husband, under his own Hand-Writing. . . ." Some scholars think that if the woman claiming to be his wife had not devised this scheme, Marvell's lyrics might have been lost forever.

Summary ■

The speaker uses hyperbole at the beginning of the poem to describe the extreme lengths to which he would go to express his love if only there were time enough to do so. In the middle of the poem he employs the famous image of a "winged chariot hurrying near" to remind his mistress of death and decay. In the final lines, the speaker uses a challenging and defiant tone to urge his mistress "therefore" to "tear our pleasures" from life, for time will never stand still.

Andrew Marvell

(1621–1678)

Andrew Marvell (c. 1655–1660) by an unknown artist. Oil on canvas (23½″ × 18½″).

By Courtesy of the National Portrait Gallery, London.

Marvell, whose very English name should be accented on its first syllable, like *marvelous,* was the son of a clergyman, who sent him to Cambridge University. There he must have received an excellent education, because the poet John Milton, who was not easily impressed by other men's learning, said that Marvell was "well read in the Greek and Latin classics." After receiving his B.A., he traveled for several years to Holland, France, Italy, and Spain. There is, surprisingly, no record of Marvell's having been involved in the great upheaval of the 1640s. He seems to have survived the Civil Wars without allying himself with either the Royalists or the Parliamentarians. About 1650, he became a tutor to Mary Fairfax, an heiress and a daughter of Sir Thomas Fairfax, who had served as lord general of the Parliamentary armies. The Fairfaxes had several large estates, one of them at a place called Nun Appleton, and there Marvell wrote a remarkable long poem, "Upon Appleton House." But he did not publish this or any of the other poems that are so highly regarded today. In the best Renaissance fashion, he wrote only for his friends' and his own entertainment.

After leaving the Fairfax household, where presumably he wrote his best poems, Marvell became tutor to a ward of Oliver Cromwell, the lord protector and virtual dictator of England in the 1650s. Then, in 1657, he became assistant to John Milton, who needed help in carrying out his duties as Latin secretary to the Council of State because he was blind. Marvell became active in politics, serving as member of Parliament for his native city, Hull, from 1659 until his death. When King Charles II was restored and the Commonwealth government dissolved in 1660, Marvell somehow had enough influence with the Royalists to save Milton's life. At this point in his career, Marvell began to publish verse satires against his political opponents and prose pamphlets on issues of the day. But his lyric poems remained in manuscript until after his death, when his housekeeper, calling herself Mary Marvell and claiming to be his wife, sold them to a publisher, who brought them out.

Marvell's posthumous volume, called *Miscellaneous Poems,* made little impression when it appeared in 1681. Styles in poetry had changed after 1660, so that Marvell's witty, ingenious metaphors must have seemed old-fashioned to readers who admired the lucid, rational poems of the Restoration writers. Today we are in a better position to appreciate Marvell. To many judicious critics, his poems seem to sum up much that is admirable in Renaissance lyric poetry. Like Jonson, he is a master craftsman, always in control of his materials. His poems have the precision, urbanity, and lightness of touch associated with the "sons of Ben." Many of Marvell's poems are also, under their graceful surfaces, deep and thoughtful, like Donne's. No wonder that Marvell is sometimes called the "most major" of the minor poets in English.

go.hrw.com
LEO 12-3

Reaching All Students

Struggling Readers

Help less able readers by telling them there are three divisions of the speaker's argument: (1) If we had time enough, we could (and should) court each other for an eternity (ll. 1–20); (2) but time is short and old age and death come very soon (ll. 21–32); (3) therefore, let us make the most of the time we have in which to be happy (ll. 33–46). Stop at the end of each section and have students tell what happens in their own words. Explain difficult references such as *make our sun stand still* (a Biblical allusion to Joshua 10:13, in which the Lord made the sun stop for the children of Israel).

Advanced Learners

Encourage students to consider this poem in light of the fact that Marvell never married. In your opinion, what was his purpose in writing this poem? To promote the institution of marriage? To entertain? To assuage his own regrets for never marrying? To express life's fleeting nature?

Crossing the Curriculum

Social Studies

The concern in Renaissance poetry over marrying early might make students wonder about marriage customs of the times. Students may want to do research on these customs. Was the implied threat in the last two lines of Herrick's poem realistic? Note that Anne Boleyn was 33 when she married Henry VIII and Elizabeth I never married. You might suggest Antonia Fraser's *The Wives of Henry VIII* (1992) for fascinating information on marriage customs.

This poem is the most famous "invitation to love" in English. Nobody has ever assumed that Marvell, a bachelor, was writing to a particular woman. But the poem is a much deeper poem than others of its kind. Its speaker dwells on the details of human mortality with morbid exactitude, to make his beloved feel that even immoral behavior while alive is preferable to being good but dead. The title could be rephrased as "To his cold, standoffish girlfriend"; at the time, *mistress* did not mean a sexual partner.

To His Coy Mistress (A)

Andrew Marvell

Had we but world° enough, and time,
This coyness,° Lady, were no crime.
We would sit down, and think which way
To walk, and pass our long love's day.
Thou by the Indian Ganges' side
Shouldst rubies find; I by the tide
Of Humber° would complain.° I would
Love you ten years before the Flood,°
And you should, if you please, refuse
Till the conversion of the Jews.°
My vegetable° love should grow
Vaster than empires and more slow;
An hundred years should go to praise
Thine eyes, and on thy forehead gaze;
Two hundred to adore each breast,
But thirty thousand to the rest;
An age at least to every part,
And the last age should show your heart.
For, Lady, you deserve this state,°
Nor would I love at lower rate.
But at my back I always hear
Time's wingèd chariot hurrying near;
And yonder all before us lie
Deserts of vast eternity.
Thy beauty shall no more be found,
Nor, in thy marble vault, shall sound
My echoing song; then worms shall try
That long-preserved virginity,
And your quaint honor turn to dust,
And into ashes all my lust:
The grave's a fine and private place,
But none, I think, do there embrace.
Now therefore, while the youthful hue
Sits on thy skin like morning dew,
And while thy willing soul transpires°
At every pore with instant fires,

1. world: geographical space.
2. coyness: reluctance to make a commitment.
7. Humber: muddy river in Marvell's hometown of Hull; here, ironically compared to the grand Ganges in India. **complain:** utter complaints about not being loved.
8. Flood: Noah's flood, described in Genesis.
10. conversion of the Jews: Christians once believed that all Jews would be converted to Christianity immediately before the Last Judgment.
11. vegetable: plantlike; having the power to grow very large, like oak trees.
19. state: ceremony.
35. transpires: breathes out.

Two Lovers (detail) (15th century) from an Italian slipware plate.

© British Museum, London.

(A) Vocabulary Note

Word Origins

The word *coy* comes from the Latin word *quietus* and once meant "shy." Ask students to discuss the extent of this mistress' reticence. [Possible answer: She is extremely quiet; we don't hear a single word from her.] *Coy* has undergone changes over the years; it now suggests a certain deliberate flirtatiousness.

(B) Reading Skills and Strategies

Getting the Main Idea

? How does the speaker use the first stanza to argue that he and his mistress do not have time to waste? [Possible answers: He uses hyperbole to emphasize how great his love is, but his examples, such as finding rubies by the Ganges and spending one hundred years to praise his love's eyes, would all require absurd delays. The extreme contrast between the speaker's intense love and the time he is willing to take to express it, suggests an exaggeration.]

(C) Elements of Literature

Personification

? How is time personified? What role does time play in the speaker's argument? [Time is presented as a charioteer chasing the speaker. Time becomes the enemy in the poem because it overtakes the lovers, destroying their beauty, song, honor, and love.]

(D) Elements of Literature

Carpe Diem

? What tells you this is a *carpe diem* poem? [It warns that there is not time to "languish," delay pleasure, or miss opportunities. It emphasizes the fading of beauty, the inevitability of death, and the vastness of eternity.]

Professional Notes

Critical Comment: Images

Among the many critics who have admired this poem is T. S. Eliot, who praises the "variety and order" of Marvell's images, noting the "high speed, the succession of concentrated images," and the way each image magnifies the original idea. Even without his complimentary words, however, it is quite clear that Eliot liked the poem, for he took Marvell's words "Let us roll all our strength and all/Our sweetness up into one ball" (ll. 41–42) and used something very much like them in his own poem, "The Love Song of J. Alfred Prufrock." There Eliot also rolled "all" up into a "ball," writing, "To have squeezed the universe into a ball/To roll it toward some overwhelming question."

Making Meanings

To the Virgins . . .
To His Coy Mistress

First Thoughts [Respond/Interpret]

1. The speaker in "To His Coy Mistress" is addressing one woman. He wants only her and knows he can do nothing without her agreement. The speaker in "To the Virgins" is trying to persuade women in general to be less hesitant. Both talk about the passing of time and making the most of youth.

Shaping Interpretations [Interpret]

2. In "To the Virgins" the sun shows the passage of time and emphasizes the speaker's point that one must act before it is too late. Marvell uses the sun in a similar way but makes it active by having it chase the young lovers. The last two lines say that the lovers cannot stop time, but they can make time run after them.
3. In Herrick's poem, time brings death and the likelihood that girls will not be able to marry in later years. In Marvell's poem, time brings death, loss of beauty, and decay of the body. Marvell compares time to a winged chariot. Students may see a charioteer crossing the sky pulled by magnificent horses.
4. Herrick says that young women should get married while they have the chance. Marvell's speaker does not mention marriage, which suggests his focus is freedom and pleasure.
5. The first section contains many examples of hyperbole (ll. 7–10, 11–12). An example of understatement occurs in ll. 31–32. These add wit and a wry note to the poem.
6. The exaggeration in ll. 8–19 is a mockery of love poems. You can hear echoes of Sonnet 130 in the speaker's proposal to take hundreds of years to praise parts of his love's anatomy.

Extending the Texts [Synthesize]

7. Some students may feel that the poem and the media value only youth and pleasure. Others may feel that the media values marriage.

Challenging the Texts [Synthesize]

8. Students may challenge the ideas that women are only attractive when they are young or that their lives are worthless without a man.

Now let us sport us while we may,
And now, like amorous birds of prey,
Rather at once our time devour
Than languish in his slow-chapped° power.
Let us roll all our strength and all
Our sweetness up into one ball,
And tear our pleasures with rough strife
Through the iron gates of life;
Thus, though we cannot make our sun
Stand still, yet we will make him run.

40. slow-chapped: slow-jawed. Time is seen as consuming life.

Making Meanings

To the Virgins, to Make Much of Time
To His Coy Mistress

First Thoughts

1. Herrick and Marvell have similar objectives but different approaches. How do you react to the two poems and poets? Is one more persuasive than the other? How are their arguments both similar and different?

Shaping Interpretations

2. The sun appears in both "To the Virgins" (line 5) and "To His Coy Mistress" (line 45). How does each poet use the sun? How would you **paraphrase** the last two lines of Marvell's poem to his coy mistress?
3. What does each poet say about time and its effects on youth and beauty? A famous **image** of time appears in couplet form in Marvell's poem, in lines 21–22. What does he compare time to? What does this image make you see?
4. What does the **speaker** in "To the Virgins" say about marriage? How do you think the speaker in Marvell's poem feels about marriage?
5. Marvell's poem contains both **hyperbole** (see page 245) and **understatement.** Find examples of each rhetorical device. What does each device contribute to the poem's effect on the reader?
6. Where in his poem does Marvell seem to be making fun of certain kinds of love poems? Where do you spot echoes of Shakespeare's Sonnet 130 (page 229)?

Extending the Texts

7. Do you think there are echoes of Herrick's poem in contemporary media? Does the **speaker** in this poem hold any values that are shared by modern advertisements, television shows, or popular songs? What are they?

Challenging the Texts

8. What do these two poems imply about the relationship between men and women? Would a modern woman (or man) be likely to challenge any assumptions apparently held by the writer, or by the speaker in each poem? What might they challenge, what might they agree with, and why?

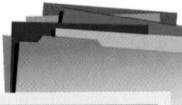

Choices: Building Your Portfolio

Writer's Notebook

1. Collecting Ideas for an Interpretive Essay

WORK IN PROGRESS

Choose a *carpe diem* poem that you would like to write about. Before you start to analyze the poem, read it aloud at least once. Freewrite briefly about your initial reaction to the poem. Then try to state its theme in your own words. Now read it again, this time looking for other elements to focus on—perhaps figures of speech, imagery, or sound effects. Make notes on these elements of the poem, and their effects on you. Save your notes for

Assessing Learning

Check Test: True-False

"To the Virgins . . ."

1. Herrick's poem is about picking flowers and maintaining a garden. [False]
2. The speaker in Herrick's poem wishes to marry all the virgins. [False]

"To His Coy Mistress"

3. The speaker says he has enough time to praise his love. [False]
4. The speaker says that to avoid being at the mercy of time, he and his lover must outrun time. [True]

possible use with the Writer's Workshop on page 275.

Comparing and Contrasting Poems

2. Probing Poems

In an essay, compare and contrast at least two of the *carpe diem* poems by Marlowe, Raleigh, Herrick, and Marvell. You might collect your data in a chart like the following one:

Element	Poem 1	Poem 2
Personal reaction Theme Images Figures of speech Sounds Tone		

Comparing Poems

3. Donne Answers Back

The poet John Donne (1572–1631) wrote "The Bait," a poem that was clearly inspired by Marlowe's "Passionate Shepherd." Locate Donne's poem (it's commonly found in poetry anthologies). In a brief essay, explain whether this poem is an answer to Marlowe's poem, an imitation of it, or neither. Remember to provide specific references to both poems.

Comparing Poems Across Cultures

4. The Moment Passes

In a brief essay, compare the following poem by the American poet Dorothy Parker (1893–1967) to one of the *carpe diem* poems you've just read.

Unfortunate Coincidence

By the time you swear you're his,
  Shivering and sighing,
And he vows his passion is
  Infinite, undying—
Lady, make a note of this:
  One of you is lying.

—Dorothy Parker

Creative Writing

5. Silent No More

Write an answer to either (a) the speaker of "To the Virgins," taking the point of view of an older woman, or (b) the speaker of "To His Coy Mistress," beginning your answer with the words "Had we but world enough and time." Your response may be poetry or prose, but give it a title.

Music/Literature

6. Seize the Song

Write your own *carpe diem* song in any musical style. You might write songs that can be paired, as Marlowe's and Raleigh's are. You might try to imitate the melancholic, romantic tone of some of the poems you've read, or you might adopt the more modern style of today's songs, which are sometimes romantic, sometimes plaintive, sometimes humorous. You might also refer to the Quickwrite notes you made for the exercise on page 231.

Art/Literature

7. Picturing a Poem

Create a collage to illustrate one of the poems you've just read. Find elements for your collage that pick up images in the poem. Be sure to add to your collage the phrase in the poem you think is most important.

Panel Discussion

8. As Time Goes By

Hold a panel discussion in which you exchange views on the gender traits you infer were characteristic of the sixteenth century. Compare these traits with gender traits you find in modern novels, movies, and TV shows. Have things changed in the relations between men and women? Or are these relations in many ways the same? You might also address this question: Are gender traits fixed by genes, or are they learned? Can they be changed?

Grading Timesaver

Rubrics for each Choices assignment appear on p. 114 in the *Portfolio Management System.*

CHOICES: Building Your Portfolio

1. **Writer's Notebook** One example of an element to note might be the sprightly rhythm in Herrick's poem, which contributes to the pleasure-loving tone of the speaker.
2. **Comparing and Contrasting Poems** Show students how they might use the chart by starting one on the chalkboard.

Element	Poem 1 Marlowe	Poem 2 Marvell
images	roses, waterfalls, fields, gold buckles	marble vault, worms, dust, ashes, morning dew

3. **Comparing Poems** Encourage students to draft a basic paraphrase first, keeping the language simple. This should help them compare the two works.
4. **Comparing Poems Across Cultures** Ask students to paraphrase Parker's poem, as well as to characterize the more modern tone and point of view, before they begin writing.
5. **Creative Writing** Students may begin by determining the tone of their answer. Will it be direct, ironic, parodic? How much of the original will be quoted or transformed? How will it end?
6. **Music/Literature** Tell students that some songwriters start by writing the music; others, the lyrics. Encourage them to decide how they will begin, and then discuss how this decision will affect their process.
7. **Art/Literature** Students can add other words to their collages, perhaps romantic-sounding place names or descriptive adjectives.
8. **Panel Discussion** Urge students to consider the influence of society on relationships between the sexes.

Making the Connections

Connecting to the Theme: "Love, Death, and Time"

Now that students have read a number of *carpe diem* poems, ask them to state the general theme of the poems using the theme words of this collection: love, death, and time. [Possible answer: These *carpe diem* poems urge people to take advantage of love now rather than later, because time is fleeting and death awaits.]

OBJECTIVES

Song/A Valediction . . ./ Meditation 17/ Death Be Not Proud

1. Read and interpret the poems and meditation
2. Analyze metaphysical poetry
3. Interpret metaphysical conceits
4. Use context clues to determine word meanings
5. Express understanding through writing, art, and technology

SKILLS

Literary
- Analyze metaphysical poetry
- Interpret metaphysical conceits

Reading
- Figure out meaning from context clues

Writing
- Collect details that support an interpretation of tone
- Compare and contrast poems
- Analyze metaphors
- Use literature as a model for creative writing

Art
- Illustrate a poem

Technology
- Create a high-tech conceit about love

Viewing and Representing
- Make inferences about an artwork (ATE)

Planning

- **Block Schedule**
  Block Scheduling Lesson Plans with Pacing Guide
- **Traditional Schedule**
  Lesson Plans Including Strategies for English-Language Learners
- **One-Stop Planner**
  CD-ROM with Test Generator

John Donne
(1572–1631)

John Donne (c. 1595) by an unknown artist.
Private Collection.

Donne (a Welsh name pronounced "dun") wrote learned, passionate, argumentative poetry, most of which he never published, since he was never ambitious to be known publicly as a poet. His first aim in life was to be "courtier"—that is, a member of the queen's government. But he had a serious handicap: He was born into a prominent Roman Catholic family, being descended from no less a person than Sir Thomas More, the Lord Chancellor whom Henry VIII had beheaded in 1535.

When Donne was only eleven years old, he was already studying at Oxford. Catholic boys went to the university very young, to avoid the oath of allegiance to the queen, whom the pope had excommunicated. Barred from taking a degree because of his religion, Donne returned to his native city of London and in his late teens became a law student at Lincoln's Inn, one of the Inns of Court where lawyers were trained. He had no financial worries since his father, a prosperous iron merchant, had died when Donne was four and left him some money. He now became "Jack" Donne, a handsome, well-dressed youth who devoted his mornings to heavy reading in philosophy and foreign literature and his afternoons to circulating in society. A friend described him as being "a great visitor of ladies, a great frequenter of plays, a great writer of conceited verses."

After various adventures, such as taking part in two naval expeditions against Spain, Donne became private secretary to Sir Thomas Egerton, lord keeper of the great seal. This was an important post, the starting point of a brilliant career in government, for by now Donne had abandoned his Catholicism and spent his inheritance. But he blasted all his hopes and ambitions when, in 1601, he secretly married seventeen-year-old Anne More (no relation). Marriage with a minor, without her father's consent, was then a serious crime against both church and state. As soon as Anne's father heard about it, he had Donne arrested, jailed, and dismissed from his position. In jail, Donne wrote his shortest poem:

> John Donne,
> Anne Donne,
> Undone.

Though he was not kept in prison long, Donne never did recover his position, and for years he and Anne had to live off the bounty of friends and relatives. They certainly needed help since they eventually had twelve children, five of whom died in infancy.

In the early 1600s, Donne continued to read voraciously and to write poetry for private circulation and prose for public consumption. He wrote against the Church of Rome so effectively that he became known as an important defender of the Church of England. And so the new king, James I, persuaded Donne to become a clergyman in 1615. His brilliant, theatrical sermons immediately won him advancement in the Church, and he rose to be dean of St. Paul's, the principal cathedral of England, in London.

Thus, Jack Donne became the Reverend Dr. John Donne. He preached outdoors before the cathedral, and he preached at court before the king, always with great effect, for he put into his sermons the same passion and inventiveness that he put into his poems. He died full of years and honors, and a portrait showing how he looked in his death shroud can still be seen in St. Paul's.

go.hrw.com
LEO 12-3

Resources: Print and Media

Reading
- *Graphic Organizers for Active Reading,* pp. 19, 20, 21, 22
- *Audio CD Library*
  Disc 4, Tracks 13, 14, 15, 16

Elements of Literature
- *Literary Elements*
  Transparency 10
  Worksheet, p. 31

Assessment
- *Formal Assessment,* p. 47
- *Portfolio Management System,* p. 116
- *Test Generator (One-Stop Planner CD-ROM)*

Internet
- go.hrw.com (keyword: *LEO 12-3)*

Before You Read
SONG

Make the Connection
Love's Illusions
Unlike the multitude of Renaissance songs idealizing women, the following song satirizes women, using **hyperbole** (hī·pur′bə·lē), or extreme exaggeration. Imagine a lover who has fallen hard for the Perfect Woman once too often—and now takes a hard view of perfection.

Quickwrite
Think about songs popular today. Do most of them celebrate faithfulness and joy in a loved one, or do most complain about infidelity and betrayal? Jot down your general impression of today's popular love songs and their lyrics. You might begin by thinking of one or two songs you know fairly well and discussing them with examples.

Background
Donne's love poems are collectively known as his "Songs and Sonnets," but the title is misleading: Most of the poems are too intellectually demanding to be called songs, and none is a sonnet by formal definition. The following poem was indeed a song, however, because one manuscript includes musical accompaniment.

Song
John Donne

Go, and catch a falling star,
    Get with child a mandrake° root,
Tell me, where all past years are,
    Or who cleft° the devil's foot,
Teach me to hear mermaids° singing, **A**
Or to keep off envy's stinging,
        And find
        What wind
Serves to advance an honest mind.

If thou be'st born to strange sights,
    Things invisible to see,
Ride ten thousand days and nights,
    Till age snow white hairs on thee,
Thou, when thou return'st, wilt tell me
All strange wonders that befell thee,
        And swear
        Nowhere **B**
Lives a woman true, and fair.

If thou find'st one, let me know,
    Such a pilgrimage were sweet;
Yet do not, I would not go,
    Though at next door we might meet,
Though she were true, when you met her,
And last, till you write your letter,
        Yet she **C**
        Will be
False, ere I come, to two, or three.

2. mandrake: plant whose forked root is said to resemble a human being's torso and legs.
4. cleft: split.
5. mermaids: the sirens of Greek mythology. The song of these sea nymphs lured sailors to crash their ships on rocky shores.

Summary ■■■
Using a series of commands, the speaker challenges his listener to find a true and beautiful woman. He uses fantastic imagery and hyperbole to make it clear that he thinks the task is impossible. The speaker closes by saying that even if a seemingly loyal and fair woman were found, she would soon prove untrue.

A Critical Thinking
Classifying
? How would you classify or describe the commands made in the first stanza? [All are ridiculous, absurd, or impossible.]

B Reading Skills and Strategies
Getting the Main Idea
? The speaker's main idea is expressed in ll. 16–18. What is it? [A woman who is faithful and fair does not exist.]

C Elements of Literature
Hyperbole
? Everything in this poem is exaggerated: the tasks, the length of the journey, and the generalizations about women's behavior. What outrageous exaggeration appears in the last six lines? [Even if a woman had been pure before the speaker's friend met her and stayed faithful long enough for him to inform the speaker, by the time the speaker met her—even if she lived next door—she would have betrayed two or three other men.]

Reaching All Students

Struggling Readers
The message of the poem will interest all students. To get students into the poem, have them copy the first stanza and underline the imperative verbs that begin each impossible command: *Go, Get, Tell, Teach, keep,* and *find.* Guide students through the first stanza, indicating where each command begins and ends. Once they have paraphrased each command, they should be able to spot the exaggeration in all of them.

English Language Learners
Explain to students that the form *'st* in *be'st, return'st,* and *find'st* is a contraction of the verb form *est,* an archaic form of the present tense. To find the meaning of the word, tell students to ignore the *'st* ending and focus on the verb alone. For other strategies to engage English language learners with the literature, see
- *Lesson Plans Including Strategies for English-Language Learners*

Connecting Across Texts

Male-Female Stereotypes
This poem is a witty expression of the theme of love that uses a sharp-edged stereotype to make its point. Have students discuss some of the other male and female stereotypes in this collection. ["hot" men and "cold" women; women who hesitate and men who urge them on; and women—such as the nymph—who have no trouble saying no to men]

MAKING MEANINGS

First Thoughts [Respond]

1. Possible responses: It reflects the bitterness of a man who has had troubles in love, not an indictment of all women; or it is funny because it is so witty and exaggerated; or it is offensive because it insults women.

Shaping Interpretations [Interpret]

2. Possible answers: a friend or men in general. An unhappy romance might have prompted the poem.

3. No such woman exists.

4. He will not go to see the "true, fair" woman if his friend finds her because even if she lives next door, she will be false to other men before he gets there.

5. The commands in stanza 1; "ten thousand days and nights" (l. 12); the exaggeration in ll. 25–27.

6. Possible answers: The tone might be cynical, offensive, dramatic. A statement that reveals a cynical or offensive tone is "Nowhere/Lives a woman true, and fair." Words that reveal a fanciful or dramatic tone include *mermaids, mandrake root,* and *ten thousand days*. Maybe the speaker is only exaggerating for effect, but even jokes have an implied meaning.

Connecting with the Text [Respond]

7. Possible responses: outrage; laughter; arguments.

Extending the Text [Apply]

8. Titles that might help students get started include "My Heart Will Go On," "How Am I Supposed to Live Without You?" and "You're My Everything." Students may say that although they contain hyperbole, love songs today are more positive than this poem. Be sure to have them check that out.

Challenging the Text [Apply]

9. Possible answer: Yes; change all female references to male.

MAKING MEANINGS

First Thoughts

1. What is your reaction to this poem: Is it offensive to women, funny, both, or something else?

Shaping Interpretations

2. To whom is this **speaker** talking? What do you think might have occasioned the poem?

3. In the second stanza, what does the speaker say his listener will discover about a woman both "true and fair"?

4. In the last stanza, what does the speaker say he will not do? Why?

5. What **hyperbole** does the speaker use to make his points?

6. How would you describe the speaker's **tone**? List at least three words that reveal his attitude. Do you think he is being serious?

Connecting with the Text

7. How would you respond to Donne's challenge in this poem?

Extending the Text

8. What examples of **hyperbole** do you see in love songs, whether modern or from other times? How do the sentiments in Donne's song compare with those in love songs? (Refer to your Quickwrite notes for ideas.)

Challenging the Text

9. Could this poem be revised slightly to be about the faithlessness of men? How?

ELEMENTS OF LITERATURE

Metaphysical Poetry

In the nineteenth century, Samuel Coleridge described Donne's inventiveness as a "forge and fireblast" that could twist "iron pokers into true-love knots." In the 1590s, when Donne started writing, this blazing poetic style was truly revolutionary. Most poets then aimed for sweet, smooth, musical-sounding verse. But Donne would have none of it. "I sing not siren-like, to tempt, for I am harsh," he says in one poem. The new style he forged came to be called, by later critics, **metaphysical poetry**—a term that reflected its intensity of intellect, its self-conscious invention, and its bold emotion.

For the most part, Donne based the rhythm and sounds of his poems on colloquial—that is, spoken—English. "For God's sake hold your tongue and let me love," he begins one poem. The speaker in his poems frequently sounds blunt and angry, or he broods to himself, or he seems to be thinking out loud. At times the speaker almost seems to be lecturing the woman he is addressing.

Whatever his tone, Donne's speaker is always using his brains and bringing into the poems ideas from books, especially books of philosophy and theology. He also brings in images from everyday activities and trades and from learned disciplines like law, medicine, and science. Reading a metaphysical poem is frequently like figuring out the solution to a riddle—or trying to untangle a complicated knot.

To their critics, metaphysical poets were show-offs. They were accused of writing poems just to display their learning and wit.

Responding to the metaphysical poets. The seventeenth-century poet and critic John Dryden, who disliked it, said metaphysical poetry "perplexed the minds of the fair sex with nice speculations of philosophy." How do you feel about this kind of intellectual poetry? Can you see a connection between the metaphysical poets' imagery and the art by Escher, below?

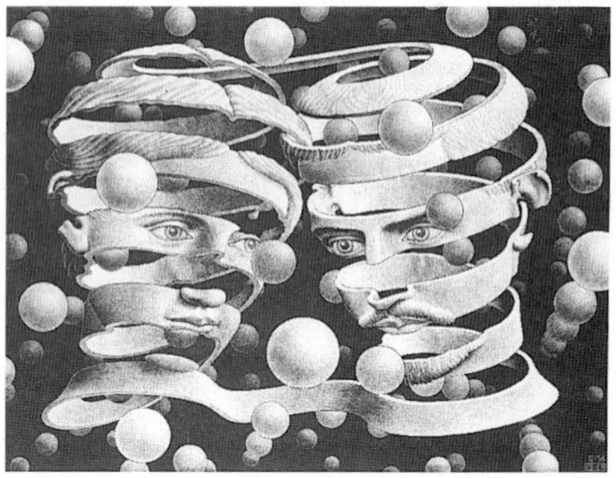

Private Collector.

Bond of Union (1956) by Maurits Cornelius Escher.

ELEMENTS OF LITERATURE

Metaphysical Poetry

Possible answers: Most students will consider Dryden's view antiquated, pointing out that people of both sexes enjoy philosophical speculation and intellectual challenges. They may comment on the highly unusual merging of human heads and mathematical spirals in the M. C. Escher art. The imagery in the art and in the metaphysical poetry explores love through complex, analytical, almost scientific mathematical comparisons.

Before You Read

A Valediction: Forbidding Mourning

Make the Connection

Hard Partings

Leaving someone you love for a long time is never easy, but if this poem is autobiographical—as Izaak Walton, Donne's friend and biographer, claimed—Donne was trying to ease a parting of great pain. The poem is typical of Donne's poetry in having a dramatic occasion, a particular situation, on which the poem is spoken. Here, the speaker, a man about to take a long journey, says goodbye ("valediction") to the woman he loves, telling her not to cry or feel sad ("forbidding mourning").

Quickwrite

If you were leaving for a long time, what would you say to someone you love who is left behind? If you were the one left, what would you want to hear? Take notes on your thoughts.

Elements of Literature

Metaphysical Conceits

This poem contains the most famous of all **metaphysical conceits.** These are odd and surprising figures of speech in which one thing is compared with another thing that is very much unlike it. The metaphysical poets—as their name suggests—used such conceits for an analytic and psychological investigation of love and life. Here are some examples of these unusual conceits: A lover's tears are newly minted coins; the king's court is a bowling alley; a man is a world; lovers are holy saints. In this poem, the lovers are said to be the two prongs of a compass, the kind used to draw circles in geometry.

Mrs. Pemberton (16th century) by Hans Holbein the Younger.
The Victoria and Albert Museum, London.

> **Metaphysical conceits** are especially complex and ingenious figures of speech that make surprising connections between two seemingly dissimilar things.
>
> *For more on Conceit, see the Handbook of Literary Terms.*

Background

Walton said Donne wrote the poem for his wife when he left for a diplomatic mission to France. She urged him not to go because she was pregnant and unwell, but he felt obligated to the mission's leader, Sir Robert Drury. Two days after arriving in Paris, Donne had a vision which he described to Sir Robert: "I have seen my dear wife pass twice by me through this room, with her hair hanging about her shoulders, and a dead child in her arms." A messenger sent back to England returned with the news that "Mrs. Donne . . . after a long and dangerous labor . . . had been delivered of a dead child" on the very day Donne had the vision.

In reading the poem, notice that the entire first stanza is a **simile** introduced by *As* and followed by *So.* The dying men in the stanza are not part of the dramatic situation, but only offered as an analogy to the lovers' separation.

Summary ■■■

In this beautiful poem of farewell, addressed by a husband to his wife, the husband forbids his wife to mourn his leaving on a journey. The first eight lines urge the wife to behave with quiet dignity when they part, just as virtuous people die without drama or display. The speaker uses elegant metaphysical imagery to describe their relationship as a union of souls so complete that distance cannot separate them.

Background

Lines 9–16 of "A Valediction: Forbidding Mourning" reflect the cosmology, or world view, held by many Christians in the 1600s. The view held that Earth was the center of the universe, and the other heavenly bodies encircled it in concentric spheres. Perfection existed only in the heavenly spheres beyond the moon. Life on Earth was "sublunary"—beneath the sphere of the moon—and was considered inferior.

Responding to the Art

Hans Holbein the Younger (1497–1543) was a talented German portrait painter who pleased even the demanding Henry VIII. (For other works by Holbein, see p. 199.)

Activity. Ask students how they can tell that this portrait is meant to be worn. [It has jewels on it and a ring at the top for a chain.] Then ask them how we remember loved ones today.

Reaching All Students

Struggling Readers

To understand this complex poem, students need to know how a compass works. Borrow one and demonstrate its use. Make sure students see how the fixed foot and the moving foot are related and how a circle is made. Then ask students to suggest ways in which the movement of a compass might sum up the relationship of two people: one who remains in place, and the other who goes away but thinks of the other as his or her "center."

English Language Learners

Because of the difficulty of this poem, pair English language learners with advanced learners. Go over the glosses with each pair to be sure they understand them. Then preteach these idioms and archaic expressions:

l. 1: *pass away*—die
l. 3: *whilst*—while
l. 7: *'twere*—it were
l. 10: *reckon*—guess, figure out
l. 31: *hearkens*—listens attentively

Advanced Learners

Donne expected his readers to enjoy dissecting a difficult text. Have students identify three challenging stanzas, lines, or metaphors in the poem and offer their own interpretations of them.

Ⓐ Critical Thinking
Interpreting

? Why does the speaker urge his wife to part from him quietly? [It would spoil the sacredness of their love to display their feelings publicly.]

Ⓑ Elements of Literature
Simile

? What comparison does Donne use to express the separation of the lovers' souls in the sixth stanza? [The souls are compared to a lump of gold beaten thinner than paper. Their separation does not resemble a division but instead an expansion into a thin golden foil.]

Ⓒ Elements of Literature
Metaphysical Conceit

Lines 25–28 contain the classic metaphysical conceit in the poem. Ask students to explain what is being compared and why it is a conceit. [These lines compare the husband and wife to the two legs of a compass, suggesting that one point remains fixed, while the other circles around, always in relation to it. It is a conceit because it is a clever, complex, original comparison.]

Ⓓ Appreciating Language
Word Choice

? What makes the use of the word *circle* such a perfect choice at the end of this poem? [Like perfect love, a circle has no beginning and no end: It is continuous and everlasting. As the gloss notes, it is also a symbol of perfection. The circle not only harkens back to the compass image, but also to the orbit of heavenly bodies which Donne referred to earlier.]

A Valediction: Forbidding Mourning

John Donne

As virtuous men pass mildly away,
And whisper to their souls, to go,
Whilst some of their sad friends do say,
The breath goes now, and some say, no:

So let us melt, and make no noise,
No tear-floods, nor sigh-tempests move,
'Twere profanation° of our joys
To tell the laity° our love.

Moving of th' earth° brings harms and fears,
Men reckon what it did and meant,°
But trepidation of the spheres,°
Though greater far, is innocent.°

Dull sublunary° lovers' love
(Whose soul° is sense°) cannot admit
Absence, because it doth remove
Those things which elemented° it.

But we by a love, so much refined,
That ourselves know not what it is,
Interassurèd of the mind,
Care less eyes, lips, and hands to miss.

Our two souls therefore, which are one,
Though I must go, endure not yet
A breach,° but an expansion,
Like gold to airy thinness beat.

If they be two, they are two so
As stiff twin compasses are two,
Thy soul the fixed foot, makes no show
To move, but doth, if th' other do.

And though it in the center sit,
Yet when the other far doth roam,
It leans, and hearkens after it,
And grows erect, as that comes home.

Such wilt thou be to me, who must
Like th' other foot, obliquely° run;
Thy firmness° makes my circle just,°
And makes me end, where I begun.

7. **profanation:** lack of reverence.
8. **laity:** laypersons; here, those unable to understand the "religion" of true love.
9. **moving of th' earth:** earthquake.
10. **meant:** "What does it mean?" was a question ordinarily asked of any unusual phenomenon.
11. **trepidation of the spheres:** irregularities in the movements of remote heavenly bodies.
12. **innocent:** unobserved and harmless compared to earthquakes.
13. **sublunary:** under the moon, therefore subject to change.
14. **soul:** essence. **sense:** the body with its five senses; that is, purely physical rather than spiritual.
16. **elemented:** comprised; composed.
23. **breach:** break; split.
34. **obliquely:** off course.
35. **firmness:** fidelity. **just:** perfect. A circle symbolizes perfection, hence wedding rings.

Getting Students Involved

Oral Reading
Have students take turns reading one verse each. Make sure they pay attention to punctuation and that they read with the appropriate expressions. Have them refer to the side margin for definitions of unfamiliar words.

Using Students' Strengths

Kinesthetic Learners
Have pairs of students act out the Donnes' farewell. They should base their interpretation on the background information on p. 247 as well as on details in the poem.

Making Meanings

First Thoughts

1. Were your reactions to this poem different in any way from your reactions to the preceding *carpe diem* poems? If so, how, and why?

Shaping Interpretations

2. How would you paraphrase the **simile** in lines 1–8?
3. The **speaker** tells his wife that their love is different from that of other couples. What difference does he see, and how does he express it?
4. Why do you think Donne refers to irregular events on earth and in the spheres in lines 9–12? What kind of event is like the separation of lovers?
5. How would you explain the **conceit** Donne uses in lines 25–36? What does it suggest about the nature of love?
6. Why does the speaker insist that the lovers—obviously two people—are actually one?
7. What impression did you form of the writer as you read and discussed this poem? What sort of man is he?
8. Do you think this poem comforted Mrs. Donne? Why, or why not?

Challenging the Text

9. Samuel Johnson, writing in the eighteenth century, disapproved of metaphysical conceits as "the discovery of occult resemblances in things apparently unlike. . . . The most heterogeneous ideas are yoked by violence together." Do you agree or disagree with Johnson? Do the conceits in this poem work well for you? Why, or why not?

Portrait of a lady with a large ruff, an armillary sphere in the background (16th century), by the English School.
Johnny van Haeften Gallery, London.

Making Meanings

First Thoughts [Respond]

1. Possible response: Yes, this poem about parting evokes different feelings than poems about seizing the opportunity for love. It is a moving expression of love and attachment.

Shaping Interpretations [Interpret]

2. Virtuous men die peacefully and silently, so let us part without tears and rely on the strength of our sacred love.
3. Their love is deeper than the love of the body—they are two souls joined together. They are unlike ordinary lovers whose love disappears when they physically part.
4. The reference to earthquakes underscores the trauma that lovers feel during separation. The separation of the speaker and his wife is like "trepidation of the spheres," movements in the cosmos that go unnoticed on Earth.
5. The speaker compares himself and his wife to the two legs of a compass. She leans toward him when he moves away, but he always returns to her at her fixed position in the center of his life. The nature of love, as defined by this conceit, is constant even as it allows for movement and physical separation.
6. He does so to emphasize their union, harmony, and trust.
7. Possible answers: He is passionate and intellectual.
8. Possible responses: Most women probably would be consoled and feel secure in being loved so greatly. The dangers of his journey, however, are still present.

Challenging the Text [Evaluate]

9. Be sure students understand the levels of meaning in these conceits, before they judge them. Johnson was a rationalist, not a poet.

Making the Connections

Connecting to the Theme: "Love, Death, and Time"

Use these discussion points and questions to connect the poem to the theme.

1. According to the speaker, what is unique about the love he shares with his beloved?
2. How do ideals of love expressed in this poem compare with the ideals expressed in other poems in this unit?
3. Compare the idea of love expressed in this poem with the idea of love expressed by Shakespeare as "an ever-fixèd mark."
4. Compare the ideal of love expressed in this poem with the shepherd's offer. Also compare the nymph's attitude toward the speaker, with the woman's probable attitude toward the speaker in this poem.

Summary ■ ■ ■

This deeply religious meditation on the meaning of death and suffering begins with a Latin quotation that sums up Donne's main idea: A funeral bell tolling for one person is a reminder to all of us that we will die. Donne uses a series of extended analogies to illustrate the interconnectedness of all human beings as creatures of God: People are part of a book authored by God; they are part of a continent which is diminished by the loss of any one person. Finally, referring to a Christian belief, Donne equates affliction with treasure that can secure the sufferer a place in heaven.

Responding to the Art

Activity. Have students discuss the feelings the painting evokes. They should focus on what they see. Encourage individual interpretation. [Students may cite the somber colors, the indistinct landscape, the solitary church and stark trees, the huddled posture of the figures who may or may not be heading into the sunset.] Ask students to evaluate the use of the painting with "Meditation 17." [Possible response: The lonely, somber mood of the painting connects to the theme of death. The word *evening* also seems appropriate. The two people appear to be leaning on each other.] See if anyone notes a significance in the bright sky.

Before You Read
Meditation 17

Make the Connection
Last Partings

There is one valediction that everyone must make: one parting and passage that time holds in store for all of us, whether we prepare ourselves for the journey or not. In 1624, prompted by a serious illness, Donne wrote a series of meditations. The opening of this one refers to the practice, in Donne's time, of ringing church bells to announce the death of a parish member.

Reading Skills and Strategies
Using Context Clues

Donne's meditation will probably contain words that are unfamiliar to you. In many cases, using **context clues** will help you guess at the meanings of these words. For example, if you did not know precisely what the word *toll* means, you would be able to make a pretty good guess, from the first sentence, that it has to do with ringing a bell. (You would be able to figure, also from context, that it does not mean the payment due for using bridges and tunnels and highways.) Always check your guesses on word meanings in a dictionary. The word *toll*, for example, does mean "to ring a bell," but it also has strong **connotations** associated with death. For instance, we would not say a bell *tolled* for a wedding. (Even the sound of the verb *toll* is mournful.)

A Wooded Landscape at Evening (detail) (19th century) by Carl Bondel.
Bonhams, London.

Listening to Music

Lamentations of Jeremiah, part 1, by Thomas Tallis, performed by the King's Singers

The most influential composer of the Tudor era, Thomas Tallis (1505–1585) served as organist for four English monarchs beginning with Henry VIII. In this stormy period in England's religious history, it is a testament to Tallis's talent (as well as to Elizabeth's tolerance when not provoked) that although he remained a Roman Catholic, he was not demoted from his position when England returned to the Protestant faith after Queen Mary died and her half sister, Elizabeth, ascended to the throne. As a composer, Tallis is noted for sacred choral music. *The Lamentations of Jeremiah,* inspired by the Biblical book of *Jeremiah,* which is a lament for the fall of Jerusalem, is considered one of his finest works.

Activity

After students read Donne's religious verse, have them listen to Part 1 of Tallis's *Lamentations of Jeremiah.* Then ask them to write a paragraph or two comparing the spirit and fervor of Donne's verse with the emotions expressed in Tallis's composition.

Meditation 17

John Donne

Nunc lento sonitu dicunt, Morieris.	Now, this bell tolling softly for another, says to me, Thou must die.

Perchance he for whom this bell tolls, may be so ill, as that he knows not it tolls for him; and perchance I may think myself so much better than I am, as that they who are about me, and see my state, may have caused it to toll for me, and I know not that. The Church is catholic, universal, so are all her actions; all that she does belongs to all. When she baptizes a child, that action concerns me; for that child is thereby connected to that Head[1] which is my Head too, and engrafted into that body, whereof I am a member. And when she buries a man, that action concerns me: All mankind is of one Author, and is one volume; when one man dies, one chapter is not torn out of the book, but translated[2] into a better language; and every chapter must be so translated; God employs several translators; some pieces are translated by age, some by sickness, some by war, some by justice; but God's hand is in every translation; and his hand shall bind up all our scattered leaves[3] again, for that Library where every book shall lie open to one another: As therefore the bell that rings to a sermon, calls not upon the preacher only, but upon the congregation to come; so this bell calls us all: but how much more me, who am brought so near the door by this sickness. There was a contention as far as a suit[4] (in which both piety and dignity, religion and estimation,[5] were mingled), which of the religious orders should ring to prayers first in the morning; and it was determined, that they should ring first that rose earliest. If we understand aright the dignity of this bell that tolls for our evening prayer, we would be glad to make it ours, by rising early, in that application, that it might be ours, as well as his, whose indeed it is. The bell doth toll for him that thinks it doth; and though it intermit[6] again, yet from that minute, that that occasion wrought upon him, he is united to God. Who casts not up his eye to the sun when it rises? but who takes off his eye from a comet when that breaks out?[7] Who bends not his ear to any bell, which upon any occasion rings? but who can remove it from that bell, which is passing a piece of himself out of this world? No man is an island, entire of itself; every man is a piece of the continent, a part of the main;[8] if a clod be washed away by the sea, Europe is the less, as well as if a promontory were, as well as if a manor of thy friends or of thine own were; any man's death diminishes me, because I am involved in mankind; and therefore never send to know for whom the bell tolls; it tolls for thee. Neither can we call this a begging of misery or a borrowing of misery, as though we were not miserable enough of ourselves, but must fetch in more from the next house, in taking upon us the misery of our neighbors. Truly it were an excusable covetousness if we did; for affliction[9] is a treasure, and scarce any man hath enough of it. No man hath affliction enough that is not matured, and ripened by it, and made fit for God by that affliction. If a man carry treasure in bullion, or in a wedge of gold, and have none coined into current monies, his treasure will not defray[10] him as he travels. Tribulation is treasure in the nature of it, but it is not current money in the use of it, except we get nearer and nearer our home, Heaven, by it. Another man may be sick too, and sick to death, and this affliction may lie in his bowels, as gold in a mine, and be of no use to him; but this bell, that tells me of his affliction, digs out, and applies that gold to me; if by this consideration of another's danger I take mine own into contemplation, and so secure myself by making my recourse[11] to my God, who is our only security.

1. **Head:** Christ.
2. **translated:** spiritually carried across from one realm to another.
3. **leaves:** pages.
4. **contention . . . suit:** argument that went as far as a lawsuit.
5. **estimation:** self-esteem.
6. **intermit:** cease.
7. **comet . . . out:** Comets were regarded as signs of disaster to come.
8. **main:** mainland.
9. **affliction:** suffering.
10. **defray:** pay for.
11. **making my recourse:** turning for aid.

A Humanities Connections

Biblical Allusion

The idea that all Christians are members of the same body can be found in First Corinthians 12:12–27.

B Advanced Learners

Extended Metaphor

? Donne says humanity is a book and God is its author. How does Donne extend, or develop, this metaphor? [Each person is a chapter. When a person dies, his or her chapter is translated into a "better language," the afterlife, by one of God's many translators—age, sickness and war, or justice. God both oversees the translation and rebinds the pages for final opening in the Library, or heaven.]

C Reading Skills and Strategies

Using Context Clues

? What context clues could you use to help you determine the meaning of the word *clod?* [The context says that a clod can be washed away. It is also clear that a clod is smaller than a promontory, which is a kind of headland. From these clues you could guess that a *clod* is a clump of earth.]

D Humanities Connections

Biblical Allusion

This idea is related to the Beatitudes in the Gospels, in which Christ tells people that those who mourn with others will be blessed.

E Elements of Literature

Theme

? According to Donne, how can people profit from the suffering of others? [They can see suffering as a reminder that pain and death will also come to them. Suffering can give them an opportunity to turn to God.]

Skill Link

Using Study Strategies

One way students can understand the text better is by outlining it as they read. This study strategy will enable them to clearly see the progression of main ideas and supporting details throughout the meditation. Begin an outline for students, and have them finish it on their own.

I. All people are connected.
   A. The church is universal.
      1. One birth links us all.
      2. Each death affects everyone, as if we are all part of one book.
         a. Death is like a translation into a "better language," the afterlife.
         b. Eventually, God will gather us (our pages) together (into the same book).

MAKING MEANINGS

First Thoughts [Respond]

1. Students may be puzzled by the idea that affliction is a treasure because most people do not welcome suffering.

Shaping Interpretations [Interpret]

2. People form part of a body that has Christ as its head; pages in a book whose translation God oversees; pieces of the continent. These metaphors imply that God joins everyone together in society.
3. Affliction is a treasure because it helps people get nearer to God. Like money, tribulation has little worth when hoarded, but is valuable when used to help others turn to God.
4. He is saying that everyone must die and that another's death should remind people of their own mortality.
5. We are interconnected; must die; must welcome suffering, for it helps us get to heaven. Students must agree with the fact that everyone must die, but may argue about humanity's interdependence, the role of suffering, and belief in an afterlife.
6. The tone might be described as dignified and optimistic, characterized by profound religious values, including belief in an afterlife and in divine mercy.

Extending the Text [Synthesize]

7. Possible response: "Any man's death diminishes me, because I am involved in mankind" and "no man is an island" seem appropriate to the world today.
8. Students might predict the book is about a death that has a great effect on others, or about great suffering. (Its setting is the Spanish Civil War.) Other good titles might be "No Man Is an Island," "A Wedge of Gold," or "As Gold in a Mine."

MAKING MEANINGS

First Thoughts

1. Are there any ideas in Donne's meditation that you find puzzling or hard to accept or understand? Why?

Shaping Interpretations

2. Several of Donne's **metaphors** suggest something about the relationship of people to one another. Look at those metaphors—what do they imply about society?
3. Why does the speaker feel that affliction is a treasure? In what ways is tribulation like money?
4. How would you explain what Donne means by saying "the bell . . . tolls for thee"?
5. What do you think Donne's **main ideas** are in this meditation? Do you agree with them all?
6. How would you describe the speaker's **tone:** depressed, angry, resigned, or something else? What beliefs and values do you think account for the tone?

Extending the Text

7. Which lines from Meditation 17 do you think are particularly relevant to life today: in your community, in the United States, or in the "global community"?
8. Ernest Hemingway found a title for a novel in Donne's meditation. What would you predict *For Whom the Bell Tolls* (1940) is about? Can you find two or three other phrases in the meditation that would make good titles? Which ones?

READING SKILLS AND STRATEGIES

Using Context Clues

Context clues can be found in several places: (1) The unfamiliar word might be defined in an appositive; (2) the sentences surrounding the unfamiliar word might give you a clue to its meaning; (3) the structure of the word itself might help you figure out what it means. (See also Reading Skills and Strategies on page 51.)

Locate where Donne uses the following words. Use context clues to help you guess at what Donne uses each word to mean. Check all your guesses in a dictionary.

perchance	promontory	covetousness
catholic	aright	bullion
engrafted	wrought	

The Ruins of Holyrood Chapel (c. 1824) by Louis Jacques Mandé Daguerre.

READING SKILLS AND STRATEGIES

Possible Answers

perchance—"possibly" ("maybe" is a clue); *catholic*—"universal" (note how "universal" is used in sentence); *engrafted*—"implanted" (*graft* should be a clue); *promontory*—"headland" (see contrast clue, with "clod"); *aright*—"correctly" ("right" is a clue); *wrought*—"worked, formed" (the intensity of the bell's impact should be a clue); *covetousness*—"greed" (clues are complex, but the context is about the desire for suffering, as if affliction were gold we are greedy for); *bullion*—"ingots of gold" (gold is mentioned in the same sentence).

Before You Read
DEATH BE NOT PROUD

Make the Connection

Defeat or Triumph?

Although death is inescapable, it is not, for everyone, an invincible victor. For those who believe in immortality—as Donne firmly did—death is merely an episode in the progress of the soul, the moment of its delivery from the confines of the body to eternal life.

Quickwrite

Use the words *Defeats* and *Triumphs* as two headings. Under each head, write down the ways you think some deaths could be seen as triumphs and others as defeats.

Background

In Donne's collected poems, which are grouped by type, "Death Be Not Proud" is one of nineteen "Holy Sonnets" included in the category of "Divine Poems." Because Donne never published the "Holy Sonnets," and because they are arranged in different ways in contemporary manuscripts and in books printed after his death, we do not know the order in which he wanted us to read them.

Board of Trustees of the National Museums and Galleries on Merseyside (Walker Art Gallery), Liverpool.

Death Be Not Proud Ⓐ

John Donne

Death be not proud, though some have callèd thee
Mighty and dreadful, for thou art not so,
For those whom thou think'st thou dost overthrow,
Die not, poor Death, nor yet canst thou kill me.
From rest and sleep, which but thy pictures° be,
Much pleasure,° then from thee, much more must flow,
And soonest our best men with thee do go,
Rest of their bones, and soul's delivery.°
Thou art slave to fate, chance, kings, and desperate men,
And dost with poison, war, and sickness dwell,
And poppy,° or charms° can make us sleep as well,
And better than thy stroke; why swell'st° thou then?
One short sleep past, we wake eternally,
And death shall be no more; Death, thou shalt die. Ⓒ

Ⓑ

5. pictures: images. A sleeping person can resemble a dead person.
6. much pleasure: That is, rest and sleep give much pleasure.
8. rest . . . delivery: Death gives the body rest and delivers the soul from the bondage of the body.
11. poppy: opium. **charms:** magic; hypnotism.
12. swell'st: swell with pride.

Summary ■■■

In this sonnet the speaker taunts Death, asserting that Death does not kill and that Death itself will die—because Death is the soul's deliverance into eternal life. Death is also the slave of "fate, chance, kings, and desperate men." Therefore, Death can inflict only a temporary "sleep"; the soul will awaken, live eternally, and defeat Death.

Ⓐ Elements of Literature

Apostrophe

? An **apostrophe** is a direct address to an absent or dead person, to an abstract quality, or to an object, as if it were present and capable of responding. To whom is this sonnet addressed? [Death]

Ⓑ Critical Thinking

Speculating

? Why doesn't death actually kill those whom it thinks it kills? [Possible answers in terms of this poem: There is an afterlife; death is a transitional state; the spirit of a person goes on living.] What evidence does the speaker give to prove that Death is not as mighty as it thinks? [Death itself is subject to other forces: fate, chance, kings, and desperate men, who command Death to do their bidding.]

Ⓒ Elements of Literature

Sonnets

? Is this poem a Shakespearean or Petrarchan sonnet? How do you know? [It is a Shakespearean sonnet because of its rhyme scheme and its structure, three quatrains and a concluding couplet.]

Reaching All Students

Struggling Readers

Students will find the direct address and the imperative voice in the title confusing. Add a comma after *Death* and explain that Death is being addressed, as if it is a person. Then ask students to supply a modern translation of "be not." [don't be] If necessary, you can model a paraphrase of the title such as "Death, don't think you're so great."

English Language Learners

Encourage students to rearrange and substitute words as they read. For example, for "nor yet canst thou kill me," students might read, "you still can't kill me."

For other strategies for engaging English language learners with the literature, see

- *Lesson Plans Including Strategies for English-Language Learners*

MAKING MEANINGS

First Thoughts [Respond]

1. Students may or may not find their own ideas in the poem. Surprising taunts include the claim that Death is a slave and will die.

Shaping Interpretations [Interpret]

2. Death does not kill anyone. He serves fate, chance, kings, and desperate men.
3. In sleep, the body is motionless and gives the appearance of death; in sleep, as in death, a person rises renewed, freed from pain and worldly cares.
4. The paradox is resolved by the assumption that there is eternal life.
5. Possible response: The tone is defiant. Words that reveal the tone include "[you are not] mighty and dreadful" and "Death, thou shalt die."

Connecting with the Text [Respond]

6. Responses will vary depending on students' experiences. Donne's response might seem brave or full of bluster. His comments must be read from a traditional Christian perspective.

Extending the Text [Synthesize]

7. Gunther's *Death Be Not Proud* is a moving recollection of his son's brave fight against a terminal illness. Gunther's son was only seventeen when he died of a brain tumor. His father believes that his son's spirit and courage triumphed over death.

MAKING MEANINGS

First Thoughts

1. Did you find any of your Quickwrite ideas in Donne's poem? Did any of his taunts to Death seem surprising or highly original to you? If so, which ones?

Shaping Interpretations

2. According to the poem, why shouldn't Death be proud? Whom must Death serve as a slave?
3. Explain how rest and sleep are the "pictures" of Death (line 5).
4. How does the sonnet resolve its **paradoxes,** or seeming contradictions: that those who die do not die and that Death itself will die?
5. What is the speaker's **tone** in this poem—how does he feel toward Death? What words reveal his attitude?

Connecting with the Text

6. How would you respond to Donne's mockery of Death?

Extending the Text

7. John Gunther used this poem's opening words as the title of a book he wrote about the death of his teenage son. What attitude toward this personal tragedy does the father's choice of title suggest?

Still Life—Vanitas (1623) by Pieter Claesz. Oil on wood.

The Metropolitan Museum of Art, Rogers Fund, 1949 (49.107). Photograph ©1979 The Metropolitan Museum of Art.

Assessing Learning

Check Test: Multiple Choice

"Song"

1. The speaker in "Song" (a) feels foolish because everything he wants is impossible to obtain; (b) wants to go on a pilgrimage to worship the most beautiful woman in the world; (c) believes that finding a woman true and fair is as impossible as catching a falling star. [c]

"A Valediction: Forbidding Mourning"

2. The speaker says that he and the woman to whom he speaks share a love that (a) makes their two souls one; (b) is great because she is obedient to him; (c) makes them travel together. [a]

"Meditation 17"

3. Donne says that all human lives are interconnected because (a) we are all descendants of the first woman; (b) we are all made by God; (c) we all live on the same earth. [b]
4. Donne says that "tribulation is treasure" because (a) it can be hidden; (b) we carry it with us; (c) it can urge us to turn to God. [c]

"Death Be Not Proud"

5. In "Death Be Not Proud," the speaker argues that (a) death is only mighty and dreadful to those who are not Christians; (b) when all have died and awakened in eternal life, death will be no more; (c) if we could rid the world of poison, war, sickness, and desperate men, then death would no longer exist. [b]

CHOICES: Building Your Portfolio

Writer's Notebook

1. Collecting Ideas for an Interpretive Essay

In questions following Donne's "Song," Meditation 17, and "Death Be Not Proud," you were asked to interpret the speaker's **tone.** Take one of these works, and look for at least three details that support your interpretation of tone. Look for word choice, sound effects, and direct statements. Save your work for possible use in the Writer's Workshop on page 275.

Comparing and Contrasting Poems

2. Thinking About Goodbyes

Richard Lovelace's "To Lucasta, on Going to the Wars" (page 264) is also a valediction poem addressed to a beloved woman. Read Lovelace's poem. Then, in an essay, compare and contrast Lovelace's farewell with Donne's "A Valediction: Forbidding Mourning." Focus on the consoling arguments that the speakers use to comfort the one left behind.

Analyzing Metaphors

3. Meditating on Metaphors

In a brief essay, take two of the metaphors in Meditation 17, and show how Donne uses them to make his points. Be sure to explain the terms of each metaphor and to show how Donne extends them.

Creative Writing

4. Stretching the Truth

Imitate the first stanza of Donne's "Song" by constructing some hyperbolic statements of your own to show the impossibility of something. You might want to respond to the points Donne raises in "Song."

Creative Writing

5. Just Before Parting

Suppose that you, like Donne, are leaving a loved one behind for a long, possibly dangerous journey. Write your own "valediction" in a brief letter. Be sure to refer to the opinions you expressed in the Quickwrite on page 247.

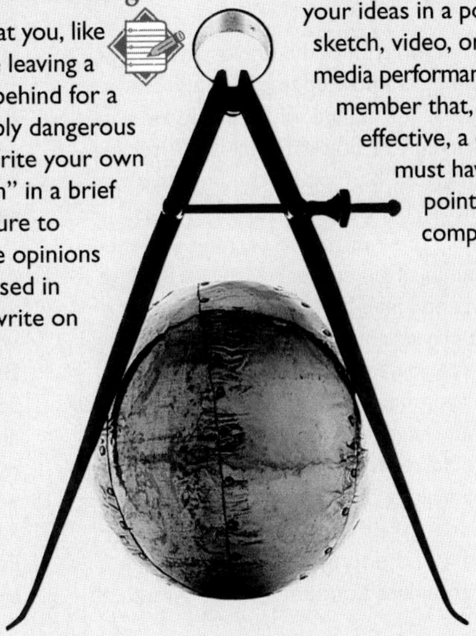

Art and Literature

6. Picturing Death

In "Death Be Not Proud," Donne forcefully personifies Death. How do you picture Death from his words and images? Draw or paint an illustration of Death to accompany Donne's poem.

Technology

7. Love in a High-Tech World

If Donne were writing today, he might have chosen a computer and modem, rather than a geometer's compass, as a conceit for the "connectedness" of lovers. Think of a high-tech conceit you could use to express a love relationship. Collaborate with one or two classmates, and express your ideas in a poem, sketch, video, or mixed-media performance. Remember that, to be effective, a conceit must have apt points of comparison.

Grading Timesaver

Rubrics for each assignment appear on p. 116 in the *Portfolio Management System.*

CHOICES: Building Your Portfolio

1. Suggest that imagery can provide a good basis for interpreting tone.

2. Before beginning this activity, students could complete Making Meanings items 3, 4, and 5 (p. 266) for Lovelace's poem.

3. and 4. Have students create a chart that lists, defines the terms of, and identifies the point Donne makes with each metaphor or hyperbole.

5., 6., and 7. Have students brainstorm a list of ideas and images before they begin their letter, artwork, or technological conceit project.

RESPONDING TO THE ART

Pieter Claesz (c. 1597–1661) was a Dutch still life painter.

Activity. Tell students that in a Dutch still life, objects take on symbolic meanings. This painting in particular, implies that because we all will die, it is useless to become attached to material objects. What specific reminders or symbols of death do students find in the painting on p. 254? [The reminders are the skull, the spilled wine glass, and the abandoned writing materials.]

Getting Students Involved

Using Graphic Organizers

Students can use a graphic organizer like the one that follows to order their points for Choices activity #2. Remind them that they can use various logical structures to organize their essay. For example, they can list all the points about one poem and then all the points about the other, or they can move back and forth from one poem to the other for each point they make.

	"Valediction"	"Lucasta"
Tone Metaphors Separation Consolation		

Objectives

On My First Son/Song: To Celia

1. Read and interpret the poems
2. Identify epigrams
3. Express understanding through critical and creative writing and music

Skills

Literary

- Identify epigrams

Writing

- Take notes for an interpretive essay on a piece of art
- Write a paragraph responding to the poet's resolution to stop loving so much
- Analyze a work and note relevant questions for further study
- Elaborate on or create a definition

Music

- Write a love song

Planning

- **Block Schedule**
  Block Scheduling Lesson Plans with Pacing Guide
- **Traditional Schedule**
  Lesson Plans Including Strategies for English-Language Learners
- **One-Stop Planner**
  CD-ROM with Test Generator

Browsing in the Files

Writers on Writing. Jonson was cynical about being a writer: "Poetry in this latter Age hath prov'd but a mean Mistress, to such as have addicted themselves to her."

Ben Jonson

(1572?–1637)

Benjamin Jonson (early 17th century) after Abraham van Blyenberch. Oil on canvas (18½″ × 16½″).

By Courtesy of the National Portrait Gallery, London.

Although Jonson was christened Benjamin, he was, and is, always known as Ben. He was probably born in the same year as his friend John Donne, and if his friend William Shakespeare had never existed, Jonson would probably be regarded as the chief dramatist of the age.

Ben's father died before he was born. His stepfather, a bricklayer, intended to make him into a bricklayer too, but while still a boy, Jonson became acquainted with William Camden, scholar and headmaster of the superb Westminster School. Camden enrolled young Ben in his school and educated him at his own expense.

Jonson never attended a university, but he had an immense knowledge of Latin literature and a small acquaintance with Greek. He was no mere pedant or bookish recluse. After leaving Westminster, Ben joined the English army and fought against the Spanish in Flanders. There, while the two massed armies watched, he engaged in single combat with the Spanish champion and killed him. Back in England, he became a playwright and an actor, specializing in loud and roaring parts. He had two brushes with the law: once when he killed a fellow actor in a duel and escaped hanging by demonstrating that he could read, and once when he went to prison for making derogatory remarks about Scotland in a play. In short, Jonson was very much a part of the tough, violent life of the time—a complete Londoner, holding forth at the Mermaid Tavern, where his witty combats with Shakespeare and others are mentioned in contemporary writings.

Gradually, Jonson became known as a dramatist. He was particularly good at devising masques (elaborate, expensively mounted productions) for the court of King James. Jonson also wrote tragedies and comedies for the public theaters.

Jonson's attitude toward his writing was different from Donne's and Shakespeare's; Jonson was more like today's writers, who are, for the most part, eager for public notice. In 1616, Jonson astonished the reading public by publishing a number of his plays and poems under the title *Works*, a label traditionally reserved for more intellectual subjects, such as theology and history. But Jonson believed that poems and plays *are* serious works of art, as serious in their own way as history and theology, and as worthy of high regard.

At the height of his career, Jonson was a sort of literary dictator in London—opinionated and crusty but admired by a number of younger writers, who became known as the "tribe of Ben" or the "sons of Ben." They stood by Jonson in his old age, when he was sick and poor and neglected because his blunt and forthright manner had made him many enemies. Jonson was buried near Chaucer in Westminster Abbey, in what later became known as the Poets' Corner. His inscription required only four words: "O rare Ben Jonson."

go.hrw.com
LEO 12-3

Resources: Print and Media

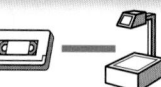

Reading

- *Graphic Organizers for Active Reading,* p. 23
- *Audio CD Library*
  Disc 4, Tracks 17, 18

Assessment

- *Formal Assessment,* p. 49
- *Portfolio Management System,* p. 118
- *Test Generator (One-Stop Planner CD-ROM)*

Internet

- go.hrw.com (keyword: LE0 12-3)

Before You Read

ON MY FIRST SON

Make the Connection

The Bonds of Love

When you hear the word *love,* do you first think of romantic love? If you do, this is a natural response. But the ties of love also bind us powerfully to family, to friends, even to pets. And one of love's ironies is that a strong bond of love, so strengthening and fulfilling, also opens us to heartache when it is cut.

Quickwrite

What does the word *bond* mean to you? With a few classmates, brainstorm meanings, connotations, and associations (don't think only of love). You may want to create a cluster diagram to show your ideas. Afterward, look up *bond* in the dictionary, and compare what you find with your brainstormings.

Elements of Literature

The Epigram

Both of Jonson's poems you will read were published in his *Epigrams* (1616), a classical form Jonson favored in contrast to both Elizabethan romanticism and metaphysical complexity. For the ancients, an **epigram** was written to give permanence to an event or observation; it was pointed, polished, and striking—like engraving on a monument. Jonson's epigrams (which are short poems) often show a two-part structure, the first part establishing the mood or the event, the second making a pithy point.

Background

This poem is about Jonson's son, Benjamin, who died of the plague on his seventh birthday. (Jonson and his wife also lost a daughter, Mary, in infancy.) The name *Benjamin* in Hebrew means "a child of the right hand" and, ironically, connotes "a lucky, clever child."

On My First Son

Ben Jonson

Farewell, thou child of my right hand, and joy; **A**
  My sin was too much hope of thee, loved boy:
Seven years thou wert lent to me, and I thee pay,° **B**
  Exacted° by thy fate, on the just° day.
Oh, could I lose all father° now! for why
Will man lament the state he should envy—
To have so soon 'scaped world's and flesh's rage, **C**
  And if no other misery, yet age?
Rest in soft peace, and asked, say, "Here doth lie
  Ben Jonson his best piece of poetry; **D**
For whose sake henceforth all his vows be such
  As what he loves may never like too much."

3. thee pay: pay thee back.
4. exacted: forced. **just:** exact. Loans were often made for exactly seven years.
5. father: sense of fatherhood; the need to mourn like a father.

Portrait of a boy (16th century) by Robert Peake the Elder.

Christie's, London.

Summary ■

Beginning with a farewell to his dead son, the speaker regrets having forgotten that his child was merely loaned to him by God. He consoles himself with the thought that his son is now free of the pains of living and growing old. In the last lines, the speaker offers an epitaph for his son, calling him "his best piece of poetry." He concludes with a vow never again to "like" or cling "too much" to what he loves.

A Critical Thinking

Interpreting

? Why do you suppose the speaker calls hope a sin? [Possible answers: Perhaps he feels that his son's death is God's punishment for his caring too much about his child; or perhaps he has such high hopes for his son that he forgets how fragile life is.]

B Historical Connections

Seven-Year Loans

Tell students that in Elizabethan times large loans were made for a term of seven years. Ask students how Jonson uses this idea as a metaphor. [Possible response: He compares his son to a loan from God that came due after seven years.]

C Critical Thinking

Making Connections

? How does the view expressed in these lines relate to those expressed in "Death Be Not Proud" (see p. 253)? [Donne and Jonson would agree that heaven is the goal of life. Donne's ll. 7–8 in "Death Be Not Proud" suggest that we all must die eventually and that in death, we all enter a state we aspire to. Despite these assurances, Jonson's pain still comes through very clearly.]

D Elements of Literature

Epigram

Samuel Taylor Coleridge defined an epigram like this: "What is an epigram? A dwarfish whole/Its body brevity, and wit its soul." Consider this definition and the one in the text, and discuss why this poem is an epigram. [Possible answers: It memorializes the death of Jonson's son; its language is pointed and brief; its essence is witty; it has no conceits.]

Skill Link

The Epigram

To help students understand the epigram, introduce this poem written by Sarah Cleghorn in 1917:

The Golf Links

The golf links lie so near the mill
That almost every day
The laboring children can look out
And see the men at play.

Note how economically the author expresses the irony of men at play and children at work; note, too, how just four lines speak volumes.

Activity

Ask students to answer the following question about the preceding epigram:

- What "pithy point" does the poet want to make about society? [A society that allows children to work while men play has questionable values.]

Summary ■■

In this verse, a man addresses the woman from whom he wants a pledge of love. He so loves her that he prefers her kiss to wine. He so loves her that he would not exchange her kiss for a drink of Jove's nectar (which would make him immortal). His lover has even the power to bestow life and her own beauty on a faded wreath.

A Vocabulary Note

Multiple Meanings

Pledge means more than "to promise." It also means "to drink to the health of" or "to salute." Have students explain how both meanings work in the poem. [The speaker is talking both about making a promise of love and about raising a glass in tribute to his love.]

B English Language Learners

Understanding Archaic Language

Explain that *doth* means "does" and that *sup* (related to *sip*) means "to take a mouthful." Help students paraphrase ll. 5–8. [Possible answer: The thirst that rises from the soul/Asks for a divine drink/But even if I could sip Jove's nectar/I would not trade it for yours.] Note also that late in l. 9 means "lately," "recently," and that when in l. 15 could be read as "then."

RESPONDING TO THE ART

Activity. This little piece is a reminder that "Song: To Celia" has been set to music. A **motet** is a musical composition for a choir and is usually sung without instrumental accompaniment. Compare this clever circular musical notation to the way music is usually written.

Before You Read

SONG: TO CELIA

Make the Connection

Love's Tributes

Part of loving is telling—acting on that burning desire to reveal your heart's devotion. In this short lyric, the speaker addresses Celia, telling her—exuberantly—how much he loves her.

Quickwrite

It isn't easy to find ways to talk about love. How do characters in movies and television shows manage it? Think of one or two characters, and try to recall how each expresses, explains, or describes his or her feelings. Jot down some of those contemporary expressions of love.

Background

Jonson once said that he always wrote out his poems in prose before turning them into verse, just as his master Camden had taught him to. At times, it must be admitted, the prose that he versified was not his own but someone else's. Jonson crafted this poem out of five different prose passages that he found in the *Epistles* of the Greek philosopher Philostratus (A.D. 170?–245). This poem has a very famous tune that many people still know.

Throughout his life, Jonson's enemies taunted him for once being a bricklayer. In a sense, he remained a bricklayer all his creative life, a builder whose tiniest construction, like this song, is solid and seamless.

Song: To Celia

Ben Jonson

Drink to me only with thine eyes,
And I will pledge with mine;
Or leave a kiss but in the cup,
And I'll not look for wine.
The thirst that from the soul doth rise
Doth ask a drink divine;
But might I of Jove's nectar° sup,
I would not change° for thine.
I sent thee late a rosy wreath,
Not so much honoring thee
As giving it a hope, that there
It could not withered be.
But thou thereon didst only breathe,
And sent'st it back to me;
Since when it grows, and smells, I swear,
Not of itself but thee.

7. Jove's nectar: Jove, more commonly called Jupiter, is the supreme god in Roman mythology. Nectar was the drink that kept the gods immortal.
8. change: exchange.

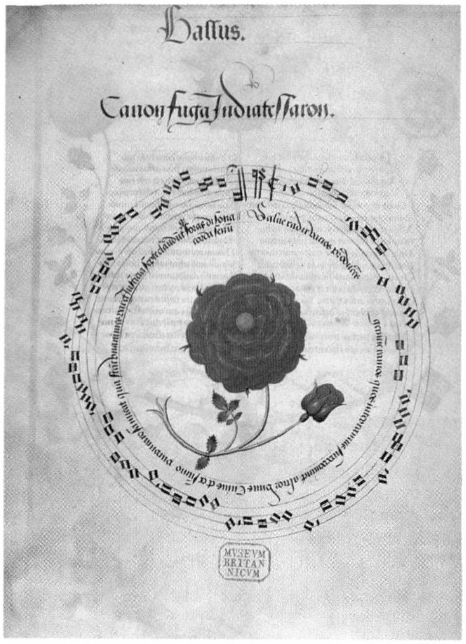

Motets (16th century) by Richard Sampson. Roy 11 E XI fol. 2v Canon, with circular staves and rose at center.

British Library, London.

Crossing the Curriculum

History

On p. 257 it is noted that Jonson's beloved son died of plague. During the 1590s, the plague wreaked havoc in London. Encourage students to research the history of the plague in the city from 1518 to 1636. Students might be interested to learn that doctors recommended hollowing out a large onion and filling it with fig, rue, and Venice treacle as a way to avoid the plague, or that homes struck by the plague were marked by a red wooden cross nailed to the door.

Music

Thomas Arne (1710–1778), who also composed the British national anthem "Rule, Britannia," created music for Jonson's poem and called it "Drink to Me Only with Thine Eyes." This song is a classic, which can be found in old songbooks. Encourage students to find the music and listen to the song before they compose their own music for the selection in the Choices activity #5.

MAKING MEANINGS

On My First Son
Song: To Celia

First Thoughts

1. What to you is the most important single line in each of Ben Jonson's poems? Why? Does your response to each poem relate to what you wrote for your Quickwrites before you read each poem? How?

Shaping Interpretations

2. In "On My First Son," why can the early death of a boy named Benjamin be regarded as **ironic**?
3. In "On My First Son," what comfort does Jonson suggest is possible in lines 7–8? Do you feel he's comforted?
4. In "To Celia," what do you think it means to "drink" and "pledge" with the eyes?
5. What does "thine" refer to in line 8 of "To Celia"?
6. How would you **paraphrase** lines 9–16 of "To Celia"?
7. These two poems are about two very different situations. Is there, nonetheless, anything that they share—any attitudes or beliefs? If you didn't know they were both by Jonson, would there be any reason to believe that they were written by the same person?
8. Jonson borrowed some of the features of "On My First Son" from Latin works: the direct address to the dead boy in line 9 and the first three words of the **epitaph,** or inscription, "Here doth lie . . . ." But the idea that his son is his best poem is original with Jonson. What do you think of this statement?

Connecting with the Text

9. What seemingly insignificant object—like the wreath returned by the speaker's beloved in "To Celia"—is nevertheless priceless to you because of the associations it evokes? Why is it priceless to you?

CHOICES: Building Your Portfolio

Writer's Notebook

1. Collecting Ideas for an Interpretive Essay

Suppose you want to interpret a piece of art in this collection (perhaps the unusual painting on page 254). Your first step is to take notes on all the details you *see* in the painting: specific objects, colors, movement, a story perhaps. Look closely and write freely. Save your notes for the Writer's Workshop on page 275.

Explaining a Response

2. Rebutting Jonson

In "On My First Son," Jonson resolves never again to love so strongly, because his loss is unbearable. What do you think of Jonson's resolution? What effect could it have on him? In a paragraph, answer these questions.

Explaining a Response

3. Everyday Living

In one or two paragraphs, explain how the hard existence described in "Give Us This Day Our Daily Bread" (see ***Connections*** on page 260) corresponds to your previous notion of life in the late 1500s. Conclude by noting some aspects of Renaissance life you'd like to research.

Creative Writing

4. What Is Love?

In "To Celia," Jonson implicitly defines love as the soul's thirst (line 5). Elaborate on this definition in a paragraph (or a poem, if you like), or create a different definition based on your own metaphor.

Music

5. Crooning About Love

Write a love song of your own that begins with Jonson's first two lines in "To Celia."

MAKING MEANINGS

On My First Son
Song: To Celia

First Thoughts [Respond]

1. Possible responses: "Here doth lie Ben Jonson his best piece of poetry"; or the first line of "Song: To Celia." These lines deliver the poems' emotional impact. Encourage students to share their Quickwrites about expressions of love and the meanings of the word *bond.*

Shaping Interpretations [Interpret]

2. It is ironic because the name Benjamin suggests luck. Also, he died the day he turned seven, which is considered a lucky number.
3. His son is free from the cares of the world and physical decay. Students may feel that the speaker is not really comforted but is trying to rationalize his loss.
4. Traditionally, the meeting of lovers' eyes can convey much more than spoken words. Here they pledge their faithfulness.
5. It refers to the lady's nectar, or by extension, her love.
6. Possible answer: I recently sent you a wreath in the hope that it would not die. You sent it back alive, growing, and covered with your scent.
7. Possible answer: They are both about love. Yes, the passion in both poems could indicate that they have the same author. They both use simple diction and songlike rhythms. Their messages are simple—not metaphysical.
8. Certainly the statement is humble and moving, suggesting that none of his works are as wonderful as this boy was.

Connecting with the Text [Synthesize]

9. Students will probably choose something that reminds them of a happy time. Be sure they choose something they would not mind sharing with others.

Grading Timesaver

Rubrics for each assignment appear on p. 118 in the *Portfolio Management System.*

CHOICES: Building Your Portfolio

1. Have students try to include everything they see. They'll be surprised at what is there.
2. **and 3.** Remind students to support their opinions with details from the text.
4. Ask students for elaboration, especially descriptive details.
5. Suggest that they imitate Jonson's meter.

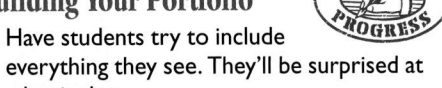

Connections

The authors transport the reader back in time to experience what life was like in sixteenth century England. Poverty, squalor, and injustice were widespread and only became worse as the population grew. Starvation was the grim outcome for many as jobs and food grew scarce.

Joseph Papp was a well-known theater impressario in New York City. For years he directed productions of Shakespeare in the Park and ran the Public Theater. Papp brought the world *A Chorus Line* and *Hair*. He died in 1991.

A Allusions

Explain that the title of this essay alludes to the Lord's Prayer, recited by both Catholics and Protestants.

B Outlining

Point out that the first sentence of each paragraph is also the topic sentence. Students can see the progression of these ideas clearly if they outline the text. The following is an example of the format they might follow:

I. Lifestyle
   A. You are barely surviving.
   B. Your father could be a farmer or a husbandman.
II. Contradictions
   A. Queen Elizabeth rules the country.
   B. Men rule within families.

[etc.]

C Historical Connections

Mercantilism

The depletion of the population of Europe that resulted from the plague in the fourteenth century influenced the rise of mercantilism, a doctrine that was popular from the sixteenth to the eighteenth centuries. Mercantilism included the notion that a large and growing population was a necessary attribute of a wealthy and powerful nation. While many mercantilists recognized that larger populations would keep wages down, they were not concerned about the harmful results of population growth. They did not consider that life became insupportable when food supplies dwindled, wages fell in comparison to prices, or crop failure produced famine.

Connections — A HISTORY

Three Peasants (detail) (16th or 17th century) by Albrecht Dürer. Oil on panel.
Kunsthistorisches Museum, Vienna.

Had he not crossed paths with the scholar William Camden, Ben Jonson might have spent his life laying brick rather than composing poetry. Most young people of the age—those who didn't come from wealthy families or didn't acquire generous patrons—had difficult, exhausting lives. For them, witty conceits praising adored ladies were as foreign as the moon—and life was consumed with making ends meet.

A Give Us This Day Our Daily Bread

Joseph Papp and Elizabeth Kirkland

B You are living in England in the late years of the sixteenth century. Like most people, you live with your family in the countryside, eking out a meager existence as best you can. If you're lucky, your father is a yeoman farmer who owns enough land to support his family, or a "husbandman" who has less property but supplements his income by wage earning.

The land you live in is full of contradictions. A woman, Queen Elizabeth, rules the nation, while within the family, men still rule women. A highly educated elite enjoys the fruits of literature, while many people can't even read. The government invests huge sums of money in voyages of exploration and wars with other nations, while science and medicine remain in an appallingly primitive state. In London, the royal court glitters with jewels and finery, while misery reigns in rural hovels. Rich young men wander around Europe for fun, while in England, thousands of homeless people wander from parish to parish, begging and stealing to survive.

The gap between the rich and the poor seems to have widened in the 1570s and 1580s; wealth and power are concentrated in the hands of the few, and many people can't even find a job.

You come from a family of laborers. You don't have much land at all, hardly even a vegetable garden you can call your own, and you are completely dependent on whatever wages you can get by harvesting other people's crops and doing odd jobs around the village. There is no money for such "extras" as education or nice clothes or red meat. In fact, your father's daily income, even when combined with yours, barely covers the cost of feeding you and your brothers and sisters; thank goodness your mother is able to bring in a few extra pennies from her spinning.

Your dependent status as a tenant makes your perch in life still more precarious. To an unjust and unscrupulous landlord, profit is more important than principles, and yours feels no obligation to look out for your best interests. If he decides to "enclose" the land—to stop using it for farming and turn it into grazing pastures for sheep—he has endless means of forcing you out: He might make you give up your lease, or renew it only at great expense, or, most commonly, charge you exorbitant rent.

C While your family has been struggling against these odds and worrying about how to make ends meet from day to day, larger forces have been at work that are going to affect you drastically. First, England has been undergoing a huge increase in population. The two-and-a-half million English people who were alive when your grandparents were

born will practically have doubled by the time your grandchildren die. This unprecedented population growth is already being translated into inflated prices, as too many people chase after scarce resources. It also means that wages stay unacceptably low; with so many laborers on the job market, farmers and other employers can easily find people willing to work for the pathetically low wages they offer if you're not interested.

Getting and spending have been a constant (D) battle, and staying on the winning side has depended on plentiful harvests, which bring the twofold benefit of jobs and low grain prices. But in recent years the battle has become a losing one: The heavy rains of the last two summers have ruined the harvests, the population has been growing faster than the crops, and famine has begun to cast its long, thin shadow across your life.

Grain—whether you eat the oatmeal cakes of northern England or the coarse wheat bread of the southerners—is a staple of your diet and, if you have no land and have to buy all (E) your grain on the market, your single biggest expense. When prices shoot up, as they do in bad harvest years, it spells disaster for many a citizen; the Carriers in Shakespeare's *Henry IV Part 1* remember a comrade who "never joyed since the price of oats rose. It was the death of him." You try to find cheaper kinds of grain than your usual wheat, supplementing your diet with stomach-filling peas and beans—but even the prices of these are rising now, and you begin to realize, horrifying though it is, that there aren't many alternatives. Starvation seems inevitable.

You wonder how you and your family are going to cope with the steady advance of such hunger, the hair falling out and the skin turning gray and the bleak prospect of watching (F) your fellow villagers "starving and dying in our streets and in the fields [because] of lack of bread," as a contemporary in the northern town of Newcastle writes.

To make matters worse, there has been an economic recession too, mainly because of a slump in the cloth trade that your mother had been depending on for her livelihood. Many people rely on the cloth and wool trades for their living, and now, "the deadness of that trade and want of money is such that they are for the most part without work, and know not how to live," as an official of one parish reports.

—*from Shakespeare Alive!*

Summer (detail) (16th century) by Jorg Breu the Elder.

(D) Literary Connections

"Getting and spending" alludes to Wordsworth's sonnet "The World Is Too Much with Us" (see p. 671), in which the speaker laments the effects of materialism. Writing approximately 250 years after the time discussed here, Wordsworth idealized the rural setting in which many people suffered in the late 1500s.

(E) Critical Thinking

Evaluating

? Why is "Give Us This Day Our Daily Bread" a good title for this essay? How does it connect to the essay's main idea? [It's a good title because bread is about all some people had, and if they didn't get it, they would starve. People seemed desperate enough to pray for mere bread. In this essay, the line from the prayer is not metaphorical; it is literal and reminds us of the basic level of need and survival emphasized in this essay.]

(F) Reading Skills and Strategies

Responding to the Text

? The writers use the second person in this essay, saying "you this" and "you that." How did that affect you as you read? [The use of *you* draws the reader into the essay. It puts the reader into the time and place and asks him or her to mentally experience the hardships of daily life.]

Connecting Across Texts

Connecting with Jonson's Poems

Papp and Kirkland describe another side of the world into which Ben Jonson was born. Jonson did spend a short time as a workman, but because he was educated, because he lived in the city, and because his stepfather was a tradesman, he did not live with the same threats to his survival as the rural laborers described in this essay. (Many of those laborers would not have had the time or even the skills to read or contemplate Jonson's verse.)

Ask students how the picture of life presented in this essay compares with the picture of life presented by Jonson in his poem "Song: To Celia." [Possible answer: When Jonson writes a love song to Celia, for example, he seems as far away from the facts in this essay as Earth is from Pluto. Drinking, toasting, making allusions to Roman gods and their nectar, and imagining the luxury of a rosy wreath are light years away from the suffering and privation depicted in this essay.]

OBJECTIVES

Why So Pale and Wan/ To Lucasta/To Althea

1. Read and interpret the poems
2. Analyze tone
3. Express understanding through critical and creative writing

SKILLS

Literary

- Analyze tone

Writing

- Write a paraphrase of one of the poems by a Cavalier poet
- Evaluate a literary work for its relevance
- Write talk-show interview questions
- Write a modern Lucasta's response to her lover

Planning

- **Block Schedule**
  Block Scheduling Lesson Plans with Pacing Guide
- **Traditional Schedule**
  Lesson Plans Including Strategies for English-Language Learners
- **One-Stop Planner**
  CD-ROM with Test Generator

Sir John Suckling

(1609–1642)

Richard Lovelace

(1618–1657)

Sir John Suckling (detail) (17th century) by an unknown artist. Oil on panel (34.3 cm × 28.6 cm).

By Courtesy of the National Portrait Gallery, London.

It is convenient to consider these two poets together because they were Royalists; that is, they supported King Charles in the Civil Wars of the 1640s. Because of their politics, they are sometimes called Cavalier poets, "Cavalier" being the nickname for a supporter of the king, as "Roundhead" is for a supporter of Parliament. But these poets had more than politics in common; they shared a common literary goal, which was to write poems that sound like elegant conversation. In the next century, Alexander Pope, looking back at the work of the poets of the mid–seventeenth century, referred to them as "the mob of gentlemen who wrote with ease." Pope should have said that they *seemed* to write with ease, because he knew better than most people how hard it is to make any kind of writing, and especially poetry, sound easy and at the same time be technically accomplished.

John Suckling was born rich, but he gambled away his money and spent a lot of it on extravagant clothes. Suckling's military career included service as a gentleman soldier on the Continent and as the commander of a troop of cavalry fighting in Scotland for King Charles. He plotted unsuccessfully to deliver one of the king's chief advisers from the Tower of London; then he fled to France. There, at the age of thirty-three, he died—by suicide or murder (accounts vary). Suckling's poems, which were mostly published after his death, tend to be lighthearted, as was his life. Dryden praised him, saying that he had "the conversation of a gentleman." He is said to be the inventor of cribbage, a card game.

Lovelace (pronounced "love-less"), besides being very handsome, was altogether a more serious person than the playboy Suckling. Like his fellow Cavalier poets, he was very rich, at least at the beginning of his life. He was also a connoisseur of music, painting, and horsemanship. While still a student at Oxford, he made such an impression on King Charles and Queen Henrietta Maria, who were visiting the university, that the royal couple ordered the authorities to confer on him the Master of Arts degree at once. Lovelace became an ardent Royalist, and when the Civil Wars broke out, he fought bravely for King Charles. The Roundheads caught him twice and imprisoned him both times. His last days were sad, his health and fortune ruined in the service of a lost cause.

Richard Lovelace (detail) (17th century) by Wenceslaus Hollar.

By Courtesy of the National Portrait Gallery, London.

go.hrw.com
LEO 12-3

Resources: Print and Media

Reading

- *Graphic Organizers for Active Reading,* pp. 24, 25
- *Words to Own,* p. 7
- *Audio CD Library*
  Disc 4, Tracks 19, 20, 21

Assessment

- *Formal Assessment,* p. 51
- *Portfolio Management System,* p. 120
- *Test Generator (One-Stop Planner CD-ROM)*

Internet

- go.hrw.com (keyword: LE0 12-3)

Before You Read

WHY SO PALE AND WAN
TO LUCASTA
TO ALTHEA

Make the Connection

Knights Ride Again

Cavalier, cavalry, chivalry: the common root of all three words is the Latin word for "horse," *caballus.* All three also share, in their earliest uses, the dual meanings of "horseman" and "knightly behavior." Thinking about these two ideas gives you a way of understanding the Cavalier poets, who saw themselves as modern-day knights. They adopted the chivalrous code of intense loyalty to a leader, to God, and to one beloved woman. But they were also boisterously masculine, pleasure-loving, worldly, and cynical.

Quickwrite

After you read each poem, write out your immediate responses. If you could ask each poet one question, what would it be? What idea would you challenge each poet about?

Elements of Literature

Tone

The Cavalier poets' attitudes toward women, warfare, honor, and the other matters that concerned them shaped the tone of their poetry vividly. In these three poems, you'll hear the tone of voice strongly, and it will let you know how each poet feels about his subject. Try to read these poems as if you were listening to someone speaking aloud.

> **Tone** is the attitude a writer takes toward the reader, a subject, or a character.
>
> *For more on Tone, see the Handbook of Literary Terms.*

In Renaissance literature, young men suffer horribly from unrequited love. Part of the convention is that the women whom the men admire show no pity. In fact, they ignore pleas for attention so firmly that the men become "pale and wan"—that is, sickly looking—like the young fellow whom the speaker of this poem is so irritated with.

Why So Pale and Wan, Fond Lover?

Sir John Suckling

Why so pale and wan, fond lover? (A)
Prithee, why so pale?
Will, when looking well can't move her,
Looking ill prevail?
Prithee, why so pale? (B)

Why so dull and mute, young sinner?
Prithee, why so mute?
Will, when speaking well can't win her,
Saying nothing do't?
Prithee, why so mute?

Quit, quit, for shame; this will not move,
This cannot take her.
If of herself she will not love,
Nothing can make her:
The devil take her! (C)

An Unknown Youth Leaning Against a Tree Among Roses (16th century) by Nicholas Hilliard.
Victoria and Albert Museum, London.

Summary ■

The speaker addresses a man who is pining for the love of a woman who is indifferent to him. In a series of rhetorical questions, the speaker advises the young man to drop his futile suit. The speaker's tone progresses from lighthearted teasing to angry impatience, ending with a mild curse on the cold lady.

(A) Vocabulary Note

Archaic Words

? *Fond* in Suckling's era meant "foolish." How does that meaning affect your reading of the title? [It immediately establishes the lover as deluded.]

(B) Elements of Literature

Tone

? What tone do you hear in these rhetorical questions? [The tone is teasing and cynical. If looking good can't win the lady, looking so sickly certainly won't!]

(C) Advanced Learners

Identifying the Person Addressed

While this poem is generally viewed as one man speaking to another, it is possible the poet is talking to himself. Is it possible even, that the speaker is a woman? Ask students to make a case for any of these interpretations. [The speaker could be addressing himself because "The devil take her" shows a strong emotional involvement; or the speaker could be an older man giving advice to a younger man; or the speaker could be an older woman telling a young man to "shape up."]

BROWSING IN THE FILES

About the Authors. When Suckling was twenty-five he came into his inheritance; in that same year he gambled a great deal, squandering most of his money. He hoped to recoup his losses by marrying an heiress, but his courtship proved unsuccessful.

Lovelace is best known for his two poems reprinted here. Holding true to his ideals, he spent the last years of his life living on charity and died in poverty.

Professional Notes

Critical Comment: Careless Elegance

Someone once said that Cavalier poetry sounds as if it had been written while falling off a horse. This remark isn't completely unfair; the Cavalier poets did try to give the impression of having dashed off flawless poems with little effort. Inspired by the inherited code of the gentleman, the Cavaliers emphasized *sprezzatura,* or fine, careless elegance.

After students have read Suckling's poem, ask them which word and sound is most often picked up. ["her"]

Summary ■

A man addresses his beloved directly and explains why he must leave her and go to war. His metaphors connect love and war, and he offers the paradox that his infidelity is really faithfulness, since she could not count on his keeping faith with her if he failed to honor his other commitments.

Ⓐ Appreciating Language

Pun

? Which word in this line has multiple meanings and can be read as a pun? [*Arms* can mean a woman's arms or an army's weapons.]

Ⓑ Elements of Literature

Tone

? What tones do you hear in the second and third stanzas? [resolution; affection; regret; a bit of pomposity]

Ⓒ Elements of Literature

Paradox

Paraphrase the paradox stated in the last two lines. [It is only because I love something more than you that I can love you as much as I do.]

RESPONDING TO THE ART

Here is another exquisite portrait by **Nicholas Hilliard** (1547–1619). (For other Hilliard art, see pp. 205, 218, 219, and 234.)

Activity. Have students describe what they see in the portraits on pp. 263, 264, and 265. What is the tone or mood of each portrait? (Students may wish to speculate on whose hand the man in the portrait on p. 265 is holding.)

The English Civil Wars are the backdrop to this poem. Like John Donne's "A Valediction: Forbidding Mourning" (page 248), the poem takes the form of a lover's goodbye to his beloved. Unlike Donne's, Lovelace's speaker is full of noble sentiments. It is tempting to identify Lovelace himself with this speaker, for the poet was an idealist about king and country, ready to sacrifice his happiness, fortune, and life in their service.

To Lucasta, on Going to the Wars

Richard Lovelace

Tell me not, sweet, I am unkind,
  That from the nunnery°
Of thy chaste breast and quiet mind
Ⓐ To war and arms I fly.

True, a new mistress now I chase,
  The first foe in the field;
And with a stronger faith embrace
Ⓑ A sword, a horse, a shield.

Yet this inconstancy is such
  As you too shall adore;
I could not love thee, dear, so much,
Ⓒ Loved I not honor more.

2. **nunnery:** literally, a convent for nuns; here, a metaphor for a pure, safe place.

George Clifford, 3rd earl of Cumberland (16th century) by Nicholas Hilliard.
National Maritime Museum, London.

Getting Students Involved

Cooperative Learning

Choral Reading. Choral reading may be used as a subtle way of providing support for less able readers by giving them a model to follow. When doing choral reading, make sure each group has at least one strong reader who feels confident with the material. Take time to examine punctuation and plan pauses and breathing. In reading "To Althea, from Prison," on p. 265, for example, students may plan to make a full stop after the first four lines of each stanza because in each case there is either a semicolon or period (indicating a longer pause). Remind students that when there is **enjambment,** or a run-on line, they should simply continue on to the next line with no pause. Make sure that students have adequate time and a place to practice where they can hear themselves.

Like "To Lucasta, on Going to the Wars," this poem follows the fashion, set by Sir Philip Sidney and Ben Jonson, of giving the women in poems classical names. Whether real women are hidden behind the names Lucasta and Althea, we do not know, nor does it matter, for there is little or no connection between having a love affair and the ability to write a good poem. We do know that Lovelace was imprisoned during the Civil Wars, and it seems likely that a man as attractive as he was would be visited by a female admirer.

To Althea, from Prison

Richard Lovelace

When Love with unconfinèd wings
  Hovers within my gates,
And my divine Althea brings
  To whisper at the grates; **A**
When I lie tangled in her hair **B**
  And fettered to her eye,
The gods° that wanton° in the air
  Know no such liberty.

When flowing cups run swiftly round,
  With no allaying Thames,°
Our careless heads with roses bound,
  Our hearts with loyal flames;
When thirsty grief in wine we steep,
  When healths and drafts go free,
Fishes that tipple in the deep
  Know no such liberty. **C**

When, like committed linnets,° I
  With shriller throat shall sing
The sweetness, mercy, majesty,
  And glories of my King;°
When I shall voice aloud how good
  He is, how great should be,
Enlargèd° winds that curl the flood°
  Know no such liberty.

Stone walls do not a prison make,
  Nor iron bars a cage:
Minds innocent and quiet take
  That for an hermitage.° **D**
If I have freedom in my love,
  And in my soul am free,
Angels alone, that soar above,
  Enjoy such liberty.

A Man Holding a Hand from a Cloud (miniature) (16th century) by Nicholas Hilliard.
Victoria and Albert Museum, London.

7. gods: In many seventeenth-century versions of this poem, "gods" is replaced by "birds." **wanton:** frolic.

10. allaying Thames (temz): That is, the wine is not diluted with water from the Thames River.

17. committed linnets: caged birds.

20. my King: Charles I, king of England from 1625 to 1649.

23. enlargèd: released. **flood:** sea.

28. hermitage: holy refuge.

Summary ■■

This speaker talks of the nature of confinement versus liberty and asserts that, although he is in jail, presumably for political reasons, he is spiritually and imaginatively free. He sums up his situation in the famous paradox at the beginning of the last stanza. The refrain ending each stanza also emphasizes the triumph of freedom of the mind over physical confinement.

Ⓐ Reading Skills and Strategies

Diction

Find two words in the first stanza that refer to freedom, and two words that refer to imprisonment. [*unconfinèd, liberty; tangled, fettered*] Lovelace uses these words to set up the paradox in his poem.

Ⓑ Elements of Literature

Tone

? What tone do you hear in this first stanza? [longing; joy; passion]

Ⓒ Critical Thinking

Comparing/Contrasting

? Why does the speaker compare and contrast himself with fishes and the winds? [Both have the freedom to go where they wish, which the speaker lacks. Both, however, lack freedoms that the speaker has: The fish cannot experience camaraderie; the winds cannot commit to a principle.]

Ⓓ Critical Thinking

Expressing Your Opinion

? Do you agree with the opinion expressed in the famous last stanza? Why or why not? [Sample responses: Some students will agree that we can be imaginatively free anyplace; others will disagree saying that peoples' physical surroundings can break their spirits and minds.]

Assessing Learning

Check Test: Multiple Choice

"Why So Pale and Wan, Fond Lover?"

1. The speaker scolds his friend for (a) being interested in a woman who is indifferent to him; (b) courting a woman in an outdated fashion; (c) stealing the woman the speaker loved. [a]

"To Lucasta, on Going to the Wars"

2. The speaker argues that (a) Lucasta should go to a nunnery; (b) his new mistress is more beautiful than Lucasta; (c) if he did not honor his commitment to serve in the army, he would not be an honorable lover. [c]

"To Althea, from Prison"

3. The speaker finds freedom (a) when he escapes from prison; (b) in his books; (c) in his mind even though his body is in a cell. [c]

Making Meanings

Why So Pale and Wan . . ., To Lucasta . . ., and To Althea . . .

First Thoughts [Synthesize]

1. They might agree that pride and honor must come before love, and disagree on what to sacrifice for freedom and honor.

Shaping Interpretations [Interpret]

2. He tells the lover that the woman cannot be made to love him, and to forget her: The tone goes from caring to annoyed to disgusted. In "To Lucasta," the tone is confident, high-minded; in "To Althea," calm acceptance.

3. He uses *mistress* to refer to the army; *chase* for his battlefield foe; *embrace* for his allegiance to the military; and *inconstancy* for his departing from Lucasta for the field of battle. Possible answer: It omits the ugly horrors of war.

4. The paradoxes are resolved in ll. 11–12. He is saying that a man cannot be loyal to a woman if he does not honor his other commitments.

5. Most students will point to l. 10, although the reader has only the speaker's words to trust, not Lucasta's.

6. He compares himself to others who seem to have more liberty but actually have less. In the last stanza he says only the angels are as free as he is.

7. The speaker is held captive by Althea's eyes.

8. Stone walls and iron bars cannot imprison a mind. He feels free because he can still love Althea and praise his king.

9. The poem implies that shackles on one's mind create a prison far more confining than a jail. Students may argue that some jails are worse than this speaker could imagine.

Extending the Texts [Synthesize]

10. Answers will vary, but encourage careful thought. Would different women have different responses?

Grading Timesaver

Rubrics for each assignment appear on p. 120 in the *Portfolio Management System.*

Making Meanings

Why So Pale and Wan, Fond Lover?
To Lucasta, on Going to the Wars
To Althea, from Prison

First Thoughts

1. Imagine Suckling and Lovelace discussing their conceptions of love. What would they agree and disagree on?

Shaping Interpretations

2. In "Why So Pale and Wan, Fond Lover?" what advice does the speaker give the pale lover? What is his **tone,** and how does it differ from Lovelace's in "To Lucasta" and "To Althea"?
3. In "To Lucasta," how does the speaker use **metaphors** of love to describe war? What do you think of these romantic ways of talking about war?
4. The speaker in "To Lucasta" implies two **paradoxes:** that his inconstancy (line 9) is really constancy and that to be loyal he must be disloyal. According to the speaker, how could these seemingly contradictory statements be true?
5. What evidence can you find in "To Lucasta" for believing that Lucasta has the same values as the speaker and will therefore not whine or scold him for losing her?
6. In "To Althea," what comparison is made in each stanza's final two-line **refrain**? What is different about the last comparison?
7. How would you explain line 6 in "To Althea"?
8. In "To Althea," what is the famous **paradox** stated in lines 25–26? What makes the jailed speaker free?
9. What does "To Althea" imply about what *does* make a prison? Do you agree or disagree?

Extending the Texts

10. Again, we have three poems either addressed to women or about a woman's treatment of a man. But the women's feelings are unknown. What do you imagine a modern woman's response would be to each speaker?

Choices: Building Your Portfolio

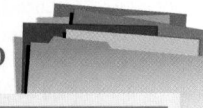

Writer's Notebook

1. Collecting Ideas for an Interpretive Essay

Paraphrasing is a useful technique for preparing to write about any literary work. To **paraphrase,** you put a literary text into your own words. Paraphrasing helps you to check your own understanding of the work, particularly your understanding of metaphors or paradoxes, and your reading of any unusual syntax. Paraphrasing helps you identify places where your understanding is solid, or places where you need to think more about the text's meaning. Paraphrase any one of the three poems by the Cavalier poets. Save your work for possible use in the Writer's Workshop on page 275.

Analyzing a Poem's Relevance

2. The Poem Across Time

Does "To Althea, from Prison"—a poem about liberty and bondage—have any relevance to late-twentieth-century life? In a brief essay, give your opinion, referring to actual world conditions or events and citing specific passages from the poem to support your views.

Challenging the Texts

3. Face to Face

Suppose you could face these poets, say on a talk show. In a brief essay, list the questions you would ask. What challenges would you make to the poets' ideas or values? Be sure to refer to the notes you made in the Quickwrite on page 263.

Creative Writing

4. A Modern Lucasta

Write out a modern Lucasta's answer to a man who delivered this poem to her as he set off to war.

Choices: Building Your Portfolio

1. One of the essential aspects of a good paraphrase is the rephrasing of figures of speech in nonmetaphorical language.

2. and 3. Remind students to be specific in their opinions and questions and to support them with details.

4. Make sure students address the issues in the poem.

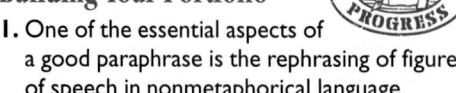

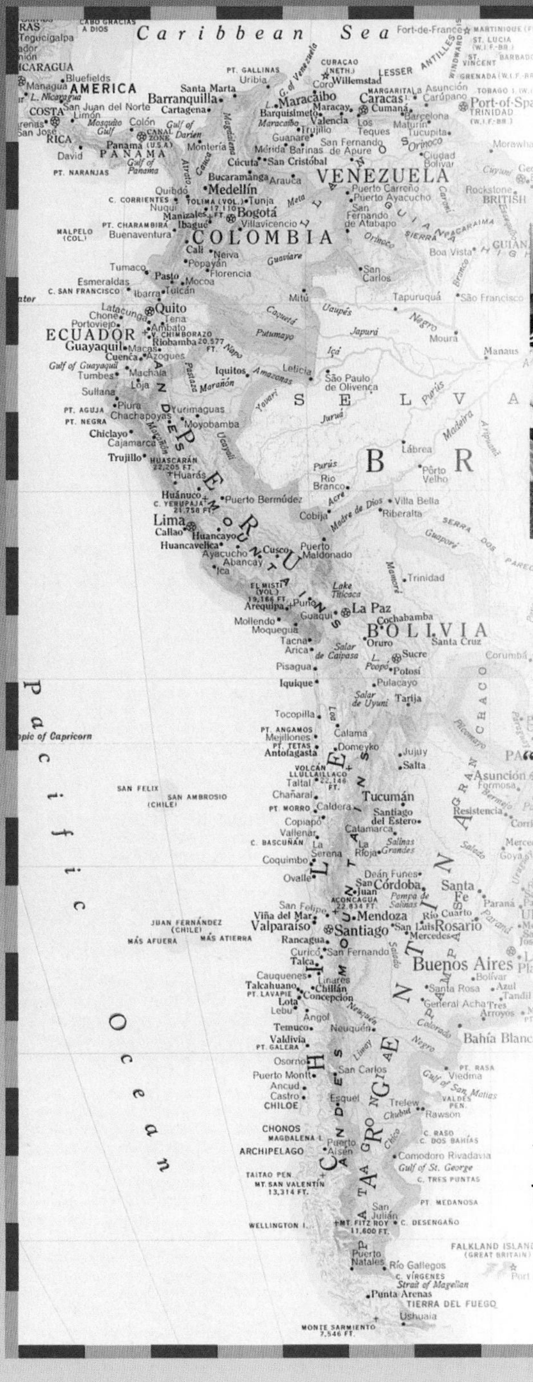

Chile

WORLD LITERATURE

Pablo Neruda campaigning in Chile (1969).

Pablo Neruda

(1904–1973)

"I have lived singing and defending them," Pablo Neruda said of the Chilean people. Neruda had two passions in his life: poetry and politics.

Neruda was writing poetry seriously by the age of ten. At fourteen, he was literary editor of a newspaper. He published a hugely popular collection of love poems at twenty, and finally, in 1971, he won the Nobel Prize in literature.

Neruda was equally fervent about government service and human rights activism—concerns that often put his life in danger. In 1948, Neruda's anti-censorship writings forced him to cross the Andes and flee his beloved Chile, but by 1952 he returned a hero. Even at the end of his life, Neruda faced possible exile. Just twelve days before Neruda died, Marxist President Salvador Allende—whom Neruda helped elect—was overthrown and possibly murdered in a bloody revolt by right-wing military leaders.

(Map) ©Rand McNally R. L. #98-S-116.

Browsing in the Files

About the Author. When he was thirteen or fourteen, Neftalí Reyes Basoalto changed his name to Pablo Neruda, a name that was to become one of the most famous in the history of Latin American letters. Here the poet explains why he changed his name: "I remember that my father, out of the best possible motives, objected to my becoming a writer, because he thought it would ruin the family and me personally, and in particular that I should end by doing nothing at all. . . . And one of the first defensive measures I adopted was changing my name."

Writers on Writing. The interviewer Rita Guibert asked Neruda whether he would continue to write if he were elected president of Chile. He responded, "Writing is like breathing to me. I couldn't live without breathing, nor could I live without writing."

Planning

- **Block Schedule**
  Block Scheduling Lesson Plans with Pacing Guide
- **Traditional Schedule**
  Lesson Plans Including Strategies for English-Language Learners
- **One-Stop Planner**
  CD-ROM with Test Generator

Reaching All Students

English Language Learners

Both poems are presented in Spanish and English and are available in both languages in the *Audio CD Library,* Disc 4, Tracks 22, 23, 24 and 25. Students who know both Spanish and English should be encouraged to read the poems in both languages and compare their responses to each of them.

Discuss with students the difficulty of translating poetry, which is rooted in sound as well as sense. Spanish-speaking students can evaluate these translations. For additional strategies for English language learners, see

- *Lesson Plans Including Strategies for English-Language Learners*

OBJECTIVES

Sonnets 17 and 79

1. Read and interpret sonnets
2. Connect text themes with students' own experience and that of others
3. Recognize distinctive and shared characteristics of cultures
4. Recognize and discuss themes and connections that cross cultures

Background

One Hundred Love Sonnets, the collection from which these poems come, was one of Neruda's later works. In it, he celebrates the great love of his last years, Matilde Urrutia. Although written primarily in free verse, Neruda's sonnets have much in common with Renaissance sonnets. They contain fourteen lines; they passionately celebrate love and beauty; and they describe that profound union of two separate souls, which is also found in Donne.

RESPONDING TO THE ART

David Alfaro Siqueiros (1896–1974) was one of the most famous Mexican mural painters of the 1920s and 1930s. The Mexican muralists usually focused on political themes, and as shown here, painted with intense emotion. In this painting, Siqueiros uses bold, vigorous brush strokes to paint two lovers who seem to be growing out of the very rock on which they stand.

Activity. Ask students what message they think Siqueiros is conveying about the love between this man and woman. [Possible answers: It is deep, as if drawn from the earth itself. It is as strong as rock, built on rock, or part of the very rock on which it stands. The man and woman are one with the earth and one with each other because the earth and both lovers are made of the same colors and textures.]

Before You Read

SONNETS 17 AND 79

Make the Connection

Mention the Renaissance poets, and the word *love* comes to mind almost immediately. Their sonnets resonate with the passion born of true love. But the Renaissance does not hold exclusive rights to this often mysterious emotion. Poets in modern times have also explored the experience of love.

The sonnets you are about to read were originally written in Spanish by the famous Chilean poet Pablo Neruda. You may not have had the experience Neruda describes in his sonnets. The speaker and his beloved are mature; they have probably been intimately connected for a long time.

Be sure to listen to these sonnets read aloud in Spanish to hear the special music they create in their original language.

Quickwrite

How does the love of older people differ from youthful love? Or does it? Take notes on your responses.

The Lover's Rock (1963) by David Alfaro Siqueiros. Mixed media on masonite (80 cm × 60 cm).

Private Collection. Courtesy of Galería Arvil, Mexico City, Mexico. Reproduction authorized by: Instituto Nacional de Bellas Artes y Literatura, Mexico. © Estate of David Alfaro Siqueiros/ SOMAAP Mexico/Licensed by permission of the British Library.

go.hrw.com LEO 12-3

Using Students' Strengths

Auditory Learners

Have a Spanish reader and an English reader alternate readings of Neruda's sonnets. Ask students to compare the sounds and to decide if the Spanish and English versions evoke similar or different feelings.

Intrapersonal Learners

Have students use their journals to reflect on and record their responses to the intense emotions expressed in these poems.

Kinesthetic Learners

Sonnet 79 on p. 270 is filled with images of things that can be touched. Students can identify these images and discuss how each might *feel.* (rough, smooth, hard, soft, cool, warm, etc.) [Possible answers: wall—rough, damp; flame—hot; rock—cool, hard; swan—soft; key—cold.]

Sonnet 17

Pablo Neruda

translated by **Stephen Tapscott**

I do not love you as if you were salt-rose, or topaz, (A)
or the arrow of carnations the fire shoots off.
I love you as certain dark things are to be loved,
in secret, between the shadow and the soul.

I love you as the plant that never blooms (B)
but carries in itself the light of hidden flowers;
thanks to your love a certain solid fragrance,
risen from the earth, lives darkly in my body.

I love you without knowing how, or when, or from where.
I love you straightforwardly, without complexities or pride; (C)
so I love you because I know no other way

than this: where *I* does not exist, nor *you,*
so close that your hand on my chest is my hand, (D)
so close that your eyes close as I fall asleep.

Soneto 17

No te amo como si fueras rosa de sal, topacio
o flecha de claveles que propagan el fuego:
te amo como se aman ciertas cosas oscuras,
secretamente, entre la sombra y el alma.

Te amo como la planta que no florece y lleva
dentro de sí, escondida, la luz de aquellas flores,
y gracias a tu amor vive oscuro en mi cuerpo
el apretado aroma que ascendió de la tierra.

Te amo sin saber cómo, ni cuándo, ni de dónde,
te amo directamente sin problemas ni orgullo:
así te amo porque no sé amar de otra manera,

sino así de este modo en que no soy ni eres,
tan cerca que tu mano sobre mi pecho es mía,
tan cerca que se cierran tus ojos con mi sueño.

Summary ■■■

This sonnet explores the theme of romantic love through a speaker who says he does not love as if the beloved were an object; instead, he loves in a way that is more deep, mysterious, and profound. The speaker says he loves as if the loved one were actually part of him.

(A) Critical Thinking

Hypothesizing

? How might the speaker love a salt-rose, topaz, or ember? [The speaker could love these things the way people appreciate or even love objects for their value or beauty.]

(B) Advanced Learners

Relating Literature and Art

Challenge students to find precise words and images in the poem that they can relate to the painting on p. 268. [The dark colors suggest the love of "certain dark things"; the facelessness of the lovers suggests something shared "in secret" and perhaps also shared "between the shadow and the soul." The use of the same brown color for both the rock and the lovers suggests that the same "fragrance risen from the earth" could live in both of their bodies. The figures also seem "so close" as to be nearly one.]

(C) Elements of Literature

Sonnet

? How is Neruda's form different from the form of other sonnets? [The others had either an octave and a sestet or three quatrains and a couplet. This, like Petrarch's sonnets, has two quatrains and then, unlike the other forms, a divided sestet or two triplets.]

(D) Reading Skills and Strategies

Finding the Main Idea

? How would you paraphrase the poem's main idea? [Love has made the beloved so much a part of the speaker that they share a single body.]

Assessing Learning

Check Test: True-False

1. Neruda lived in the fifteenth century. [False]
2. Neruda wrote in Spanish. [True]
3. Neruda won the Nobel Prize in Literature. [True]
4. Neruda was Argentinean. [False]
5. These sonnets are about politics. [False]

Summary ■ ■ ■

The speaker begins the poem by asking his love to "tie" her heart to his. He goes on to evoke, by means of surreal images, the fearful mystery of night and sleep and suggests that love, or his love specifically, can tie him "to a purer motion": one that answers questions and unlocks doors.

Ⓐ Critical Thinking

Interpreting

? What does this speaker fear? [Possible answers: The speaker expresses fear of night, fear of darkness. The speaker says that fear can overtake the loveless person with all the dark punctuality of a train by night.] **How does the speaker say that such fear can be overcome?** [Possibly through love or by becoming one with another person.]

Finding Common Ground

What is love? What does it do for us? You might have students use the discussion questions in the text to make a chart listing all the properties of love. They should base their list on the love poems in this collection.

Love
Unites people
Conquers fear
Conquers time
Conquers distance
Conquers death
Etc.

Sonnet 79

Pablo Neruda

translated by **Stephen Tapscott**

By night, Love, tie your heart to mine, and the two
together in their sleep will defeat the darkness
like a double drum in the forest, pounding
against the thick wall of wet leaves.

Night travel: black flame of sleep
that snips the threads of the earth's grapes,
punctual as a headlong train that would haul
shadows and cold rocks, endlessly.

Because of this, Love, tie me to a purer motion,
to the constancy that beats in your chest
with the wings of a swan underwater,

so that our sleep might answer all the sky's
starry questions with a single key,
with a single door the shadows had closed.

Soneto 79

De noche, amada, amarra tu corazón al mío
y que ellos en el sueño derroten las tinieblas
como un doble tambor combatiendo en el bosque
contra el espeso muro de las hojas mojadas.

Nocturna travesía, brasa negra del sueño
interceptando el hilo de las uvas terrestres
con la puntualidad de un tren descabellado
que sombra y piedras frías sin cesar arrastrara.

Por eso, amor, amárrame al movimiento puro,
a la tenacidad que en tu pecho golpea
con las alas de un cisne sumergido,

para que a las preguntas estrelladas del cielo
responda nuestro sueño con una sola llave,
con una sola puerta cerrada por la sombra.

Finding Common Ground

Before you discuss these poems, check your Quickwrite notes. Even if, after listening to the poems' speakers, you did not say, "Those could be *my* words," you may have said "Yes!" to some ideas, moods, feelings, and images. Then again, you may have some arguments to pick with Neruda or his speakers: Your ideas about love may not always mesh with theirs. What is your reaction? Here are some other questions you might want to discuss:

- What do you think Sonnet 17 means about love being dark and secret?
- What do you think of the ideas that love completes people and that it unites them so that they seem as one person? Have you encountered that idea in other poems in this collection? Where?
- Could you relate to the fear of night in Sonnet 79? Do you think love is the answer?
- What was your favorite **image** in each poem?
- Does Neruda use complex **metaphors** that remind you of the metaphysical poets' love of complex and unusual comparisons? Point out one or two examples.
- Do Neruda and the Renaissance poets hold similar notions about love, or are they very different?
- Do you find in Neruda's poems a conviction that love conquers time—as you find in Renaissance poetry?
- Where do your thoughts on love fall—close to Neruda or to the Renaissance poets?

Use your notes to discuss with classmates what you think romantic love is, what it means to people today, and what it has meant in ages past.

The English Language

The Birth of Modern English

by John Algeo

The Modern English period can be dated from 1485, when Henry VII, the first Tudor king of England, came to the throne. The House of Tudor brought peace to the land, introduced the Reformation and Renaissance to England, helped to promote a pride in things English, and began the spread of our language all over the world. Just ten years before, in 1475, William Caxton had printed the first book in English. That event **A** might also be taken as marking the beginning of the Modern period, for printed books were to help unify and spread English **B** and make the opportunity to read and write readily available to all English-speaking people.

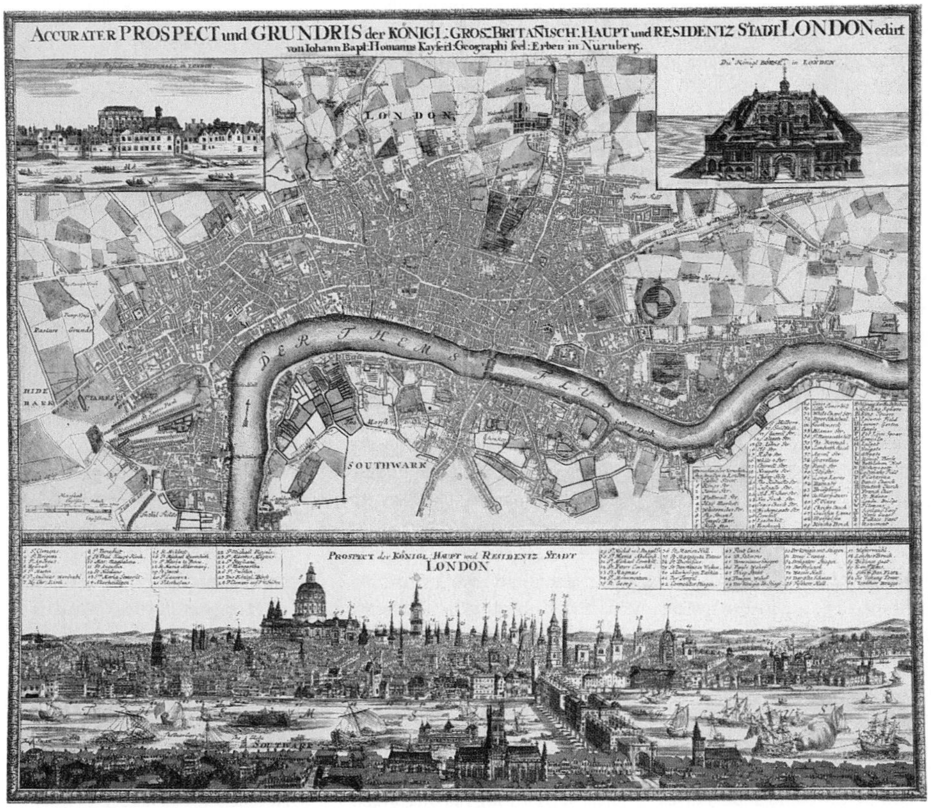

ACCURATER PROSPECT und GRUNDRIS der KÖNIGL: GROS: BRITANISCH: HAUPT und RESIDENTZ STADT LONDON edirt
von Johann Bapt: Homanns Kayserl: Geographi seel: Erben in Nurnberg.
SOUTHWARK
PROSPECT der KÖNIGL HAUPT und RESIDENTZ STADT LONDON

British Library, London.

Aerial map and view across the Thames from the South Bank, with St. Paul's and London Bridge (c. 1730) by J. B. Homans.

OBJECTIVES

1. Understand how English developed from Middle English to Early Modern English, especially through the Great Vowel Shift
2. Appreciate the effect of the printing press on the evolution of spelling and structure in Modern English
3. Appreciate the influence of other languages on Modern English

A Exploring the Culture

Books and Literacy

When William Caxton (c. 1422–1491) set up his press at Westminster, he began a great communications revolution. Before 1500, a total of only thirty-five thousand books had been printed throughout Europe, mostly in Latin. Between 1500 and 1640, in England alone, more than twenty thousand new items were printed in English. Literacy rose accordingly: By 1600, nearly half the people in towns and cities had minimal literacy.

B Exploring the Culture

Books and Protestantism

Printed books, particularly the Bible, helped the spread of Protestantism (see p. 200), since a key tenet of the "protests" was that individuals could learn the will of God themselves by reading the Scriptures, rather than relying on religious authorities.

Resources

Viewing and Representing

Videocassette A, Segment 1

Available in English and Spanish.
For full lesson plans and worksheets, see the *Visual Connections Teacher's Manual.*

Assessment

Formal Assessment

- English Language Test, p. 53

Reaching All Students

Struggling Readers

Review the changes in word endings by recording them on the chalkboard and modeling the sound shifts.

English Language Learners

Students may enjoy citing additional examples of words that have come to English from their cultures. Encourage students to include cognates, words with a slight difference in spelling or pronunciation (such as the French *liberté* and the English *liberty).*

Advanced Learners

Challenge students to consult reference works to compile a list of Latin phrases adopted whole into English. Start students off with these examples: *ex officio, caveat emptor, sub rosa, ex libris, vox populi.*

Ⓐ Background

Shifting Vowels

The change in vowel sounds may look haphazard, but in fact, it is very regular and patterned. Each of the "long" or tense vowels came to be pronounced with the tongue a little higher in the mouth. The two that were originally highest turned into diphthongs (combinations of two vowels pronounced together). The Great Vowel Shift probably began late in the fourteenth century, shortly before Chaucer's death, and was completed during the first years of the Early Modern English period.

Ⓑ Reading Skills and Strategies

Comparing/Contrasting

Read aloud the different pronunciations of the sentence *See the same old moon in the cloudy sky.* Ask students who have studied modern French, Spanish, or German how the vowels in this sentence sound compared with the vowel sounds they have heard in these modern languages. [Middle English vowels sound much like the vowels in these modern European languages.]

Ⓒ Background

Vowel Sounds and Spelling

Caxton adopted Middle English spelling. Post–Great Vowel Shift, however, the sounds originally represented by the five vowel letters became quite different. Because English adopted a pre–Great Vowel Shift spelling for post–Great Vowel Shift sounds, English today uses the five vowel letters in a way that is different from that of other European languages that did not undergo a vowel shift.

The Language Changes That Made Modern English

When William Caxton printed the first books in English, he tried to make them look as much like handwritten manuscripts as he could. The shapes of the letters in his type font, the spellings he used, his choice of words and sentence structures—all suggested the manuscript writing of an earlier time. Because printing was a newfangled invention, Caxton wanted his printed books to look as much as possible like the manuscripts that people were familiar with. Yet, despite his efforts, it is clear that the language of the late 1400s and early 1500s was a new form of English.

English during the first part of the Modern period, when it still resembled Middle English in some ways and had not yet reached the form we recognize as our own, is known as Early Modern English. That term embraces English from about 1485 through the mid-1700s.

Grammatical differences between Middle and Modern English were not very great. Middle English had already lost many of the inflections of Old English. The few it kept and passed on to Early Modern English are mainly ones we still have today: the plural ending *–s* and the possessive ending *–'s* for nouns; the comparative and superlative endings *–er* and *–est* for adjectives; and the verb endings for the past tense (*–ed*), past participle (*–ed* or *–en*), present participle (*–ing*), and the third-person singular of the present tense (*–s*). In place of that *–s,* Early Modern English also had an ending we no longer use, *–eth,* and in addition one for the second-person singular, *–est* (as in "he thinketh" and "thou thinkest").

> Because British explorers, merchants, and settlers had an itch to travel, and scratched it vigorously, the English language has never been the same.

Shifting Vowels

Ⓐ The greatest change between Middle and Early Modern English was in the pronunciation of the "long" or tense vowels, illustrated by these words (given in their present-day spellings): *bite, feet, cane, mouse, boot, load.* In Middle English times, the vowels of these words had been pronounced as follows: *bite* like "beet," *feet* like "fate," *cane* like "khan" or "con," *mouse* like "moose," *boot* like "boat," and *load* like "laud" or "(out–)lawed." Ⓑ The sentence *See the same old moon in the cloudy sky* would have sounded in Middle English something like "Say the sahm awld moan in the cloody skee."

If we could go back to Chaucer's London by a time-travel machine, our first impression would be that some language other than English was being spoken. After a while, however, we would probably get used to it and decide that it was English after all, although pronounced very oddly.

No one knows why these changes (called the Great Vowel Shift) happened—many such big changes in language are inexplicable. However, something rather similar is going on in some varieties of English today. In New York City, Philadelphia, and various other places, especially in the middle part of the East Coast and westward from there, words like *bad, cab,* and *fan* sound something like "behd," "kehb," and "fehn." If that kind of change should become general and extend to other words and other parts of the country, two hundred years from now, people may be pronouncing *See the same old moon in the cloudy sky* something like "Sigh the seem oold mown in the clawdy skay." Stranger things have happened in the history of languages, and that change is no more improbable than was the Great Vowel Shift five hundred years ago.

Lagging Spelling

Ever since 1475, when books were first printed in English, we have had a tendency to keep our spelling unchanged, whatever happens to our pronunciation. Therefore, our spelling tends to become further and further out of line with the way Ⓒ we say words. When Caxton started printing books, he used a spelling for English that was already old-fashioned; and we have done little to modernize it since.

Ever since English first began to be printed, people have worried about the failure of our spelling to match our pronuncia-

Professional Notes

Critical Comments: Spelling

In *The Story of English,* Robert McCrum, William Cran, and Robert MacNeil explain that not only are the vowel sounds in English spelled in various and unpredictable ways, but there are also some unique vowel sounds as well as consonant sounds with highly unpredictable spellings: "There are some very rare and difficult vowels [in English; for example] the vowel sound in *bird* and *nurse* occurs in virtually no other language. There are no fewer than thirteen spellings for *sh: shoe, sugar, issue, mansion, mission, nation, suspicion, ocean, conscious, chaperon, schist, fuchsia,* and *pshaw.* An old bit of doggerel for foreign students advises:

> Beware of *heard,* a dreadful *word*
> That looks like *beard* and sounds like *bird,*
> And *dead:* it's *said* like *bed,* not *bead*—
> For goodness' sake, don't call it *deed!*"

To the long list of reasons for English's many strange spellings, Jean Fargo adds this one in *Discovering Words: The Stories Behind English:* "As writing became more of a business . . . scribes did not always stick to the rules. Sometimes when they were paid by the inch, they added extra letters to make words longer."

tion. Many proposals have been made to reform English spelling, ranging from simply omitting silent letters, as in *tho* for *though* and *thru* for *through,* to more thorough reforms: "Wun sistem uv spelling wood seek tu eeliminaet awl iregguelarity." There have been even more radical suggestions, such as abandoning the Latin alphabet altogether and adopting a new one. One example is called the Shaw alphabet, designed for a contest set up by the twentieth-century writer George Bernard Shaw in his will. An example of the Shaw alphabet follows.

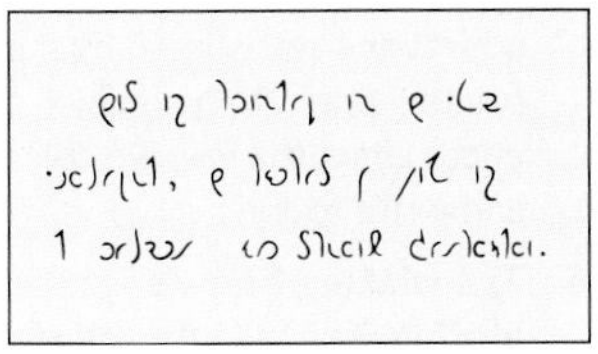

Serious spelling reform has little chance of success. English speakers have been remarkably faithful to the spellings that were decided upon during the Early Modern English period. We seem unlikely to change them now.

O Brave New World: The Spread of English and Foreign Influences

The reign of Queen Elizabeth I saw the beginning of the extension of English to the far corners of the world. The British established colonies in North America—in a land they called Virginia after the Virgin Queen and later in New England and many other places. Exploration, settlement, and commerce all led to the borrowing of words from many other languages.

French contributed *bigot, bombast, duel, explore, jaunty, moustache, shock,* and *vogue.* From Italian came *balcony, cameo, design, duo, fugue, grotto, portico, stanza, trill,* and *violin;* from Spanish or Portuguese, *alligator, apricot, banana, brocade, corral, hammock, renegade,* and *tobacco;* from Indian languages of Central America and the Caribbean, by way of Spanish, *avocado, cannibal, chocolate, maize, potato,* and *tomato;* from Dutch, *cruise, deck, freight, keel, skipper, smuggle, yacht, duffel, spool, knapsack, easel, etch,* and *landscape.*

The adventures of British explorers, merchants, and settlers during the Early Modern English period enriched our vocabulary immensely. Because they had an itch to travel, and scratched it vigorously, the English language has never been the same.

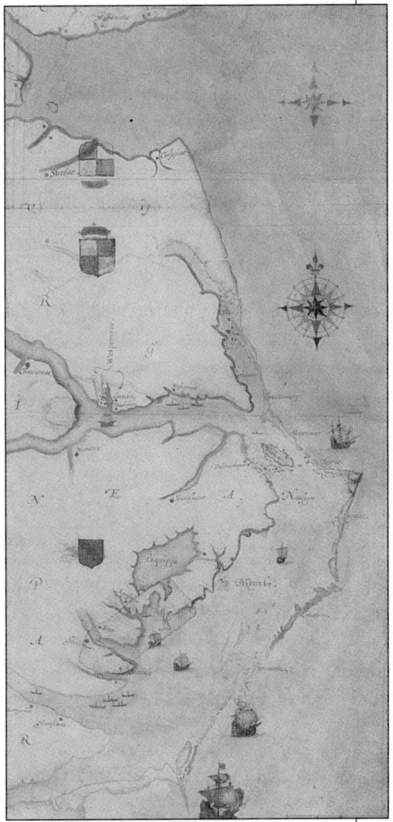

Manuscript map of Raleigh's Virginia (c. 1585) by John White.

© British Museum, London.

The New Learning: Classical Influences

While English was picking up words from languages abroad, it did not neglect the classical languages, Latin and Greek. The literature, art, philosophy, history, and culture of Rome and Athens were taken as ideals during the Renaissance. Naturally, modern European languages, including English, also borrowed words from Latin and Greek.

Among many other words, English borrowed from Latin *abdomen, area, compensate, delirium, editor, gradual, imitate, janitor, medium, orbit, peninsula, quota, series, strict, superintendent, ultimate, urban,* and *urge.* From Greek, usually by way of Latin and sometimes other intermediate languages, came *aristocracy, barbarous, chaos, comedy, cycle, drama, epoch, history, mystery, rhythm, theory, tragedy,* and *zone.*

D Background

Spelling Reform

This says, "Our system of spelling would seek to eliminate all irregularity." Note, however, how irregular the words *eliminate* and *irregularity* seem when they are made "regular"! Have students discuss spelling reforms they might wish to make. Also suggest that they try spelling their own names phonetically or apply their ideas about spelling reform to their names.

E Background

Modern Spelling

Advertising seems to have made at least a few inroads in changing modern spelling. For example, the word *lite,* usually used to describe a diet product, is used regularly. Other common spelling changes include *tho* for *though* and *thru* for *through.* You might ask students to name others that seem both recent and popular.

F Elements of Literature

Allusion

The phrase *O brave new world* in this subhead is an allusion to a line in Shakespeare's play *The Tempest* (V.1.182–183): "O brave new world, / That has such people in it!" Twentieth-century British author Aldous Huxley used the phrase as the title and the whole line as the epigraph of his distopian novel. Huxley invents slang and new words for his futuristic world; advanced students may enjoy reading this novel or Anthony Burgess's *A Clockwork Orange,* which also makes use of invented words.

Using Students' Strengths

Auditory Learners

Play an audio or video recording of the scenes in *My Fair Lady* or *Pygmalion* (by George Bernard Shaw), in which Henry Higgins first meets Eliza Doolittle, comments on her language, and subsequently gives her lessons. You can do this for the sheer enjoyment of the scenes, or you could ask students to listen for and chart differences in the pronunciation of the two characters. In either case, discuss how the scenes relate to the information in this essay.

Skill Link

Outlining

Outlining is a tool for establishing the form of a piece of writing. The idea of outlining is to divide articles containing factual information into main ideas, subtopics, and details. One good way to start to look for main ideas is to examine the headings in an article. For instance, in this essay, the writer explains the differences between Middle and Early Modern English. An outline of the first two subsections on p. 274 might look like the following:

I. Few grammatical changes from Middle to Early Modern English
II. Big changes in pronunciation of vowels
  A. Cause unknown
  B. Similar shift occurring today
    1. Shift only in middle of East Coast
    2. *Eh* sound replacing short-*a* sound

Activity

Ask students to outline the entire essay or an assigned portion of it.

Ⓐ Exploring the Historical Period

The Rise of Standard Language

Old English was developing into a standard language in the interval between the Norse and Norman invasions, but its full development was cut short by the conquest of 1066. Thereafter, since French was used as the language of government, no variety of English had the opportunity to develop into a standard. During the Early Modern English period, however, such a standard did arise, and has existed ever since.

Try It Out

1. brooch (brōch, bro͞och)
   creek (krēk; *often* krik)
   garage (gə•räzh′, -räj′; *Brit.:* gar′ äzh′, -ij)
   mature (mə•to͝or′, -cho͝or′, -tyo͝or′)
   roof (ro͞of, ro͝of)
   which (which, wich)
2. Some answers will depend on the dictionary a student has. Some dictionaries may provide no answer for particular words.
   adviser/advisor
   cater-cornered/cater-corner
   collectible/collectable
   cozy/cosy
   descendant/descendent
   finicky/finicking
   mama/mamma/momma
   parakeet/parrakeet
3. *balcony*—Italian
   brocade—Spanish or Portuguese
   canoe—Spanish
   catastrophe—Greek
   landscape—Dutch
   mustache—French
   scientific—Latin
   volcano—Italian
4. Possible answers: television, films, radio, and perhaps the Internet.
5. "This is printed in the Shaw alphabet, the purpose of which is to reform our spelling completely."

The Rise of Standard English

Ⓐ Languages come in many varieties. A standard language is one that is used widely throughout a country and enjoys the respect of both those who use it and those who do not. It is typically the language of government and education.

The Early Modern English standard language was the result of several influences. The law clerks who recorded the proceedings of courts and who maintained the legal archives of England set a pattern of language usage that others followed. Especially important was the usage of the Court of Chancery, presided over by the Lord High Chancellor of England: Consequently, the widely used and prestigious form of Early Modern English is sometimes called Chancery Standard.

The introduction of the printing press, as already noted, helped to spread the new standard written language throughout England, making it available to all literate English speakers. Literacy was also increasing at this time. English people were reading the Book of Common Prayer (first published during the reign of Queen Elizabeth's brother and predecessor, King Edward VI) and the Authorized Version of the Bible (popularly known as the King James Bible because it was published during the reign of Elizabeth's successor, King James I). The phrases and rhythms of those two books, prayer book and Bible, were powerful influences in shaping the ideal of language to which English speakers looked during the Renaissance and for centuries after.

Try It Out

1. **Pronouncing words.** The fact that some words are pronounced in more than one way today is a sign that our language is still in the process of change. How do you pronounce the following words? Look in a dictionary to see if other pronunciations are listed.

brooch	garage	roof
creek	mature	which

2. **Investigating spellings.** Although our spelling is more consistent than that of the Renaissance, some words still have more than one possible spelling. What other spellings can the following words have?

adviser	descendant
cater-cornered	finicky
collectible	mama
cozy	parakeet

3. **Locating etymologies.** During the Renaissance, English borrowed words from many foreign languages. From what language does each of the following words come? Look up the words in a dictionary that gives **etymologies,** or word origins.

balcony	landscape
brocade	mustache
canoe	scientific
catastrophe	volcano

4. **Analyzing influences on English.** The standard English of the Renaissance was based on the language used by the government in law courts and was spread by the printing press. What influences affect the way we talk and write today?
5. **Translating Shaw's alphabet.** Using the following key, write the passage in the Shaw alphabet on page 273 in conventional spelling.

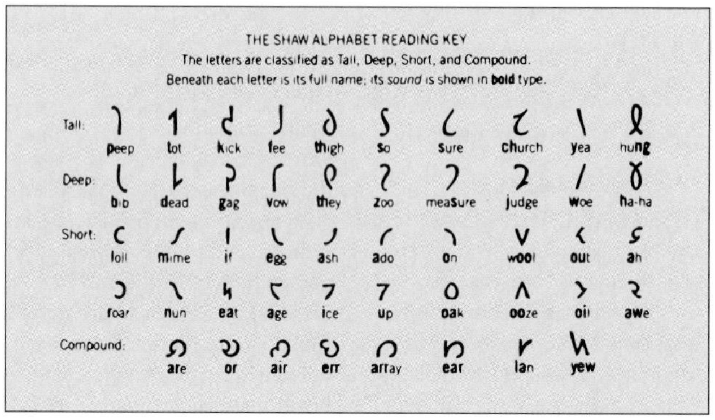
THE SHAW ALPHABET READING KEY
The letters are classified as Tall, Deep, Short, and Compound.
Beneath each letter is its full name; its *sound* is shown in **bold** type.
Tall:
peep
tot
kick
fee
thigh
so
sure
church
yea
hung
Deep:
bib
dead
gag
vow
they
zoo
measure
judge
woe
ha-ha
Short:
loll
mime
if
egg
ash
ado
on
wool
out
ah
roar
nun
eat
age
ice
up
oak
ooze
oil
awe
Compound:
are
or
air
err
array
ear
Ian
yew

Assessing Learning

Check Test: True-False

1. The most important change that brought English into the modern period was the Great Vowel Shift. [True]
2. Printers like William Caxton tried to make printed books look less like handwriting. [False]
3. Some people worry about the failure of English spelling to match the pronunciation. [True]
4. English has borrowed words from only five other languages. [False]
5. Two books with a powerful impact on the English language were the book of Common Prayer and the King James Bible. [True]

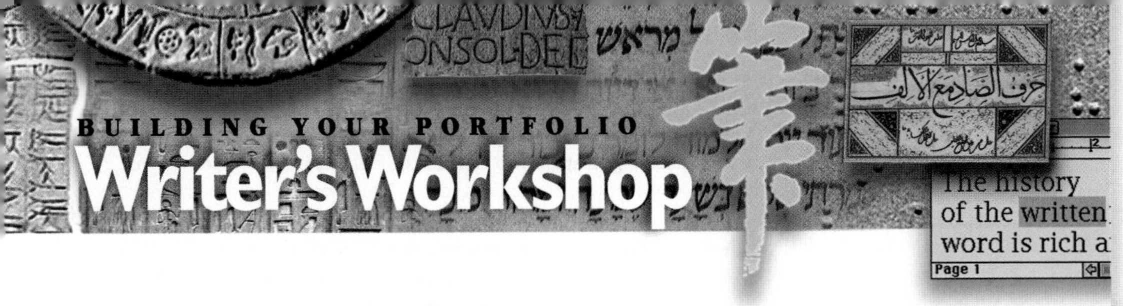

BUILDING YOUR PORTFOLIO

Writer's Workshop

EXPOSITORY WRITING

AN INTERPRETIVE ESSAY

One way you can make sense of any experience, including the experiences of reading literature, viewing movies, and looking at art, is by **interpreting** it—explaining its meaning in your own words. In this Writer's Workshop, you'll write an interpretive essay about a work of literature, film, or art.

Prewriting

1. **Check your Writer's Notebook.** By doing the Writer's Notebook activities in this collection, you may have already done much of the prewriting for an interpretive essay. Check back over your Writer's Notebook entries. You can add to or change what you did in your Writer's Notebook, or you can proceed with the prewriting activities that follow.

WORK IN PROGRESS

2. **Act and react.** If you still don't have a subject, go to a library, bookstore, or video store and find a work that's new to you and that you won't mind reading or viewing more than once. You might instead choose two different works, or two versions of a work (for example, a novel and its movie adaptation), to **compare and contrast.** Read or view each work carefully.

   Usually, your first reaction to a work is a personal one: delight or dismay, liking or loathing. Take a few minutes to take notes on your response, and don't worry about whether your response is "correct": No two people are likely to respond to any work in precisely the same way.

3. **Dig deeper.** To interpret the work for your readers, you need to move beyond personal response to **analysis**—reading (or viewing) the work critically to determine what its parts, or elements, are and how they work together to express some meaning about experience. The charts below show the elements to look for in poetry and in art.

Elements of Poetry

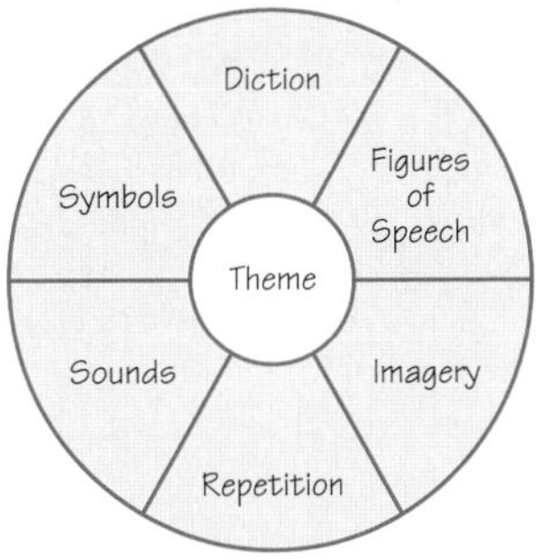

Elements of Art

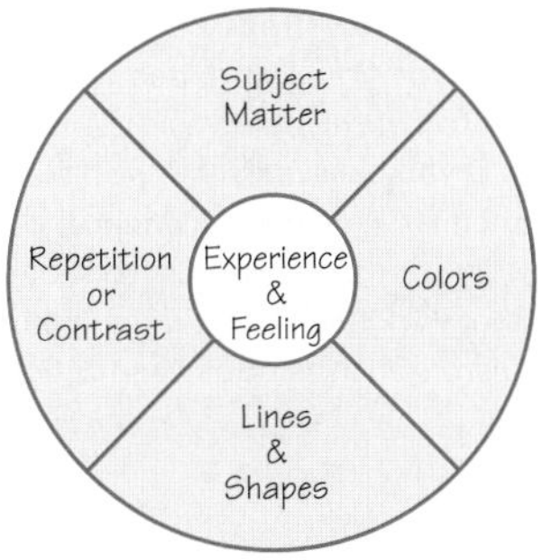

Technology HELP

See Writer's Workshop 2 CD-ROM. *Assignment: Interpretation.*

ASSIGNMENT
Write an essay interpreting a literary work, a movie, or a piece of art.

AIM
To inform; to explain; to persuade.

AUDIENCE
Your classmates or members of reading, film, or art groups.

Try It Out

Working with a partner or a small group, identify the literary elements used in one of the following:

1. an episode of a TV sitcom or soap opera
2. a popular song

MAIN OBJECTIVE

Write an essay interpreting a literary work, a movie, or a piece of art

PROCESS OBJECTIVES

1. Use appropriate prewriting techniques to identify and develop a topic
2. Create a first draft
3. Use Evaluation Criteria as a basis for determining revision strategies
4. Revise the first draft, incorporating suggestions generated by self- or peer-evaluation
5. Proofread and correct errors
6. Create a final draft
7. Choose an appropriate method of publication
8. Reflect on progress as a writer

Planning

- **Block Schedule**
  Block Scheduling Lesson Plans with Pacing Guide
- **One-Stop Planner**
  CD-ROM with Test Generator

Try It Out
Possible Answers

1. Students may find motif, climax, hyperbole, foil, protagonist, setting, and suspense, among other literary elements.
2. Students may find refrain, tone, symbol, assonance, and alliteration, among other literary elements.

Resources: Print and Media

Writing and Language

- *Portfolio Management System*
  Prewriting, p. 121
  Peer Editing, p. 122
  Assessment Rubric, p. 123
- *Workshop Resources*
  Revision Strategy Teaching Notes, p. 13
  Revision Strategy Transparencies 7, 8
- *Writer's Workshop 2 CD-ROM*
  Interpretation

Introducing the Writer's Workshop

Remind students that we often try to determine why someone did or said something. When we try to understand motives or real meanings, we are engaging in interpretation. Since human nature is central to literature and art, we can interpret these forms of expression in much the same way as we interpret the human behavior we experience every day.

Teaching the Writer's Workshop

Prewriting

- Ask students to use the Elements of Poetry or the Elements of Art pie charts on p. 275 to analyze the work they have chosen. Students should fill in the sections of the chart as they read or view the work. Remind them to include basic information as well as any unusual or interesting things they notice under each category.
- Remind students that meaningful elaboration comes from an engaged reading or viewing of the work. Review with students the chart on p. 276, and stress the point that a writer must be intimately familiar with a piece of literature or art in order to interpret it fairly.

Strategies for Elaboration: Analyzing a Work

Use the following strategies to analyze the elements of the work you've chosen.

- Read or view the work again, noting things you missed the first time. New insights may occur to you on a second reading or viewing.
- If you are writing about a piece of art, take notes on these elements: colors, details emphasized, overall tone or mood. Do you "read" a story into the painting? If you are writing about a portrait, look closely at what the person is wearing or holding. What background has the artist given the subject? What has the artist omitted from the portrait? If there are several people in a painting, what are their relationships (are they, for example, indifferent to one another, or are they warm and loving)?
- Freewrite on the connection you see between the work and its title.
- For a short written work, make a copy for yourself and use different colors of markers to highlight the various literary elements.
- Compare your ideas about the work with the ideas of others who are familiar with it. Their interpretations may differ from yours, but their ideas may help you clarify your own thinking.

The Elements of Film

See Film as Literature, pages 1012-1016.

4. **Find a focus.** In the space of a short essay, it would be difficult to analyze all the elements of a work. To make your interpretation manageable, look back at your personal response and your critical-reading notes. Which elements struck you most strongly? How do those elements help bring out the theme or the writer's or artist's meaning? Choose the ones that seem most significant to you. (More than three may prove unwieldy.) For example, you might focus on how diction and imagery help develop the theme of a poem or on how point of view affects the theme of a short story or on how color affects the feeling you have for a painting.

5. **Stake your claim.** In a sentence or two, state your opinion about the relationship between the elements you've chosen and the work's theme or meaning. This preliminary thesis statement will make a useful guide for planning your paper. Keep in mind, though, that you may decide to change it as you gather information to support your opinion and begin drafting your paper.

Communications Handbook HELP

See Evaluating the Credibility of Sources; Taking Notes and Documenting Sources.

6. **Search for support.** Since your thesis is an opinion, not a cut-and-dried fact, your readers expect you to back it up with reasons and evidence. Your reasons, which serve as the major points or claims of your essay, explain *why* you believe each of the elements you've chosen helps reveal the work's theme or meaning. Evidence for each of your reasons consists of ideas, quotations, and details from or about the work. Most evidence comes from the work itself (the *primary source*), but some may come from *secondary sources* such as books and articles about the work or its author.

Using Students' Strengths

Auditory Learners

Some students will find it easier to analyze and interpret shorter literary works if they are able to hear the works read aloud. Options include having students work in small groups on the same literary work and reading the work aloud or providing students with headphones and a commercially or student-produced recorded reading of the work.

Crossing the Curriculum

Historical Interpretation

Some students may prefer to interpret a historical document, such as Abraham Lincoln's Gettysburg Address or the Preamble to the Constitution. Ask them to approach their chosen document as they would a literary work. Students should recognize that literary elements such as tone, point of view, diction, and figurative language are as likely to be found in the great historical documents as they are in poetry or fiction.

Model

Thesis Statement: In Sonnet 30, Edmund Spenser's imagery underscores his theme—that the speaker and his love are in direct opposition to each other.

Major Point: Spenser uses images of fire and ice, of hot and cold.

Evidence to Prove Major Point: In line 1, Spenser says, "My love is like to ice, and I to fire." In lines 5–6, he says, "Or how comes it that my exceeding heat / Is not delayed by her heart frozen cold."

Strategies for Elaboration: Gathering Support

Use the following strategies to gather the information you'll need to support your thesis statement.

- Read or examine the work again with your thesis statement and major points in mind.
- Be sure to copy quotations exactly. For a written work, include the page numbers for quotations from a work of fiction or the line numbers for quotations from a work of poetry.
- If you draw on secondary sources, avoid plagiarism by noting the author, title, and date and place of publication so that you can credit your sources.
- Review your notes to make sure that all your evidence is directly related to your thesis statement.

7. **Get organized.** The easier your ideas are to follow, the more likely your readers will accept them. To organize your material, look again at your thesis statement and your main points. Assessing the kinds of details you've chosen to support your thesis can help you choose a sensible order for your ideas.
   - If you're focusing on diction and imagery, you might group related ideas in **logical order,** with points about diction in one group and points about imagery in a second group.
   - For a thesis on character, you might arrange examples in **chronological order** to show how a character changes during the story. Or you could use **order of importance,** moving from your most important point to your least important one (or vice versa).
   - If you're **comparing and contrasting** two works, you could treat each of the elements of one work first and then turn to those of the other work, or you could alternate between the works as you discuss each element.

Communications Handbook HELP

See Proofreading.

Evaluation Criteria

An effective interpretive essay

1. *includes an introduction that identifies the title and author (or artist or director) of the work and gives necessary background information about it*
2. *includes a clear and precisely worded thesis statement*
3. *identifies major points that support the thesis*
4. *for each major point, gives ample, specific, and relevant supporting evidence*
5. *is clearly and consistently organized*
6. *has a conclusion that reinforces the thesis of the essay*

Drafting

- Before students write their first drafts, they should review all seven points covered under Prewriting on pp. 275–277.
- Use models to demonstrate the elements of an effective interpretive essay, such as thesis statement, major points of evidence, and restatement of thesis.
- Remind students to use only every other line when they write their drafts. They should also leave extra space in the right margin for comments and editing marks.

Crossing the Curriculum

Viewing and Representing

Elements of Art. Bring in a photograph or poster of an abstract work of art that contains forms and shapes. With the whole class, identify elements such as color, shape, texture, and composition, the arrangement of objects in relation to one another. Then ask students to select one of these elements and jot down ideas about how the element they selected contributes to the theme, or meaning, of the picture. Encourage students to develop personal interpretations of the artwork and share these with the class.

Evaluating and Revising

Model for the class the process of evaluating an essay. Then have students use the Evaluation Criteria provided here to review their drafts and determine needed revisions.

Proofreading

Have students proofread their own papers first and then exchange them with other students. Remind students to be particularly careful to check for the correct use of the literary present tense. If time permits, the final copy should be put aside for at least a day before it is proofread for the final time by the author.

Publishing

Encourage students to share their interpretive essays with the members of community literary or art groups as well as classmates and friends.

Reflecting

Have students write and date a brief reflection for their portfolio on the experience of writing an interpretive essay. Guiding questions might include the following:

- Did the process of interpreting a literary work, film, or piece of art help you develop new insights into the work? Did it change your ideas about what's involved in creating a literary work, film, or piece of art? Explain your responses.
- Which was harder for you, developing a thesis or building a convincing case for it? Why?
- Which part, or parts, of the writing process will you approach differently the next time you write an interpretive essay? Why?

Resources

Peer Editing Forms and Rubrics

- *Portfolio Management System,* p. 122

Revision Transparencies

- *Workshop Resources,* p. 13

Language Workshop HELP

Literary present: *page 279.*

Revision STRATEGIES

Does your conclusion round out your essay smoothly? If not, add a sentence or two using different forms of the key words in your thesis statement. Ask a writing partner to give feedback on your conclusion.

Drafting

1. **The introduction: setting the stage.** In your introduction, identify the work's title and author or artist (for a film, the title and either the director or the leading actor or both), and state your thesis. Provide just enough background information about a story or poem or movie so that your readers will be able to follow your ideas, but avoid summarizing the entire work. Remember that your readers are primarily interested in your insights about the work. If you are interpreting a piece of art, describe carefully in your introduction exactly what you see in the painting. Help your reader see the work too.
2. **The body: building your case.** As you develop the body of your essay, take one or more paragraphs to state each of your major points and to present the evidence that supports it. Use quotations from a literary work where they help you make a point especially well.
3. **The conclusion: wrapping it up.** Create a satisfying conclusion by stepping back once again to the focused overview you presented in your introduction. Don't just summarize your major points; instead, restate your thesis in a way that echoes the ideas in your introduction and provides your essay with a satisfying, forceful closure.

Evaluating and Revising

As you read your or your partner's draft, evaluate these points:

- Is there enough background information about the work so that the reader can follow the ideas?
- Does the thesis statement make the focus clear?
- Is there enough evidence to make the thesis convincing? Are the supporting details directly related to the thesis?
- Does the ending tie the ideas together and reinforce the thesis?

Grading Timesaver

Rubrics for this Writer's Workshop assignment appear on p. 123 of the *Portfolio Management System.*

Language Workshop

Sense Through Tense: The Literary Present

When you talk or write about literature or film or art, you should use what is called the **literary present.** Thus, do not say "In Act V Lady Macbeth tried to wash the blood from her hands." Instead, say

"In Act V Lady Macbeth **tries** to wash the blood from her hands."

The present tense is used because, in the world of literature, Lady Macbeth is forever and always washing that blood from her hands. In the same way, you would not say of the beautiful miniature on page 218: "The young man sat amid devouring flames." Instead you would say

"The young man **sits** amid devouring flames."

Forever and always, that young man will be staring out from the burning flames. When you write about a writer's purpose or technique, you don't say "In Sonnet 75, Spenser's speaker asserted the eternal nature of his love." Instead, because the speaker in the sonnet will forever be asserting the nature of his love, you write

"In Sonnet 75, Spenser's speaker **asserts** the eternal nature of his love."

Here's an important distinction to keep in mind: When you quote directly from a work, use the same tense the author uses, whatever it may be. However, when you paraphrase the writer's ideas or draw your own conclusions about the work, use the literary present.

ORIGINAL *(past tense)*	One day I **wrote** her name upon the strand, But **came** the waves and **washèd** it away. —Edmund Spenser, Sonnet 75
PARAPHRASE *(literary present)*	The speaker in Edmund Spenser's Sonnet 75 **writes** his beloved's name in the sand, but the waves **erase** it.
CONCLUSION *(literary present)*	In line 5 of Sonnet 75, Spenser **uses** the word *vain* in two different senses: *conceited* and *fruitlessly.*

Writer's Workshop Follow-Up: Proofreading

Look back at the interpretive essay you wrote for the Writer's Workshop beginning on page 275. Have you used the literary present correctly? Check to make sure that in direct quotations you've used the same tense the writer used. Then, check again, changing any verbs in your paraphrases of the work and in your own conclusions to the literary present. You might begin by focusing on one or two paragraphs: Circle each verb, and determine whether its tense is correct in that context.

Technology HELP

See Language Workshop CD-ROM. *Key word entry: verb tenses.*

Language Handbook HELP

See Tenses and Their Uses, pages 1225–1226.

Try It Out

Change the verbs that should be in the literary present in the following sentences.

1. The speaker in Spenser's Sonnet 75 proposed to immortalize his beloved's virtues.
2. Twice the speaker had written her name in the sand, and twice the waves erased her name.
3. Protesting, the woman pointed out that she herself "shall like to this decay."
4. The speaker insisted that the woman "shall live by fame."

OBJECTIVES

1. Use the literary present tense correctly when analyzing literature, film, or art works
2. Use the same tense the author uses when quoting directly from a work

Resources

Workshop Resources

- Worksheet, p. 49

Language Workshop CD-ROM

- Verb Tense

Try It Out

Answers

1. The speaker in Spenser's Sonnet 75 [proposes] to immortalize his beloved's virtues.
2. Twice the speaker [writes] her name in the sand, and twice the waves [erase] her name.
3. Protesting, the woman [points] out that she herself "shall like to this decay."
4. The speaker [insists] that the woman "shall live by fame."

Assessing Learning

Quick Check: Literary Present

Decide which verbs in the following sentences should be in the literary present tense, and change the ones that should be.

1. The speaker in Christopher Marlowe's "The Passionate Shepherd to His Love" made promises to his love. [makes]
2. He offered to make her comfortable with cushions of flowers. [offers]
3. He also said she will have a beautiful embroidered skirt. [says]
4. In Sir Walter Raleigh's poem, the young woman replied to Marlowe's shepherd. [replies]
5. Her answer, based in reality, is a firm refusal. [Correct]

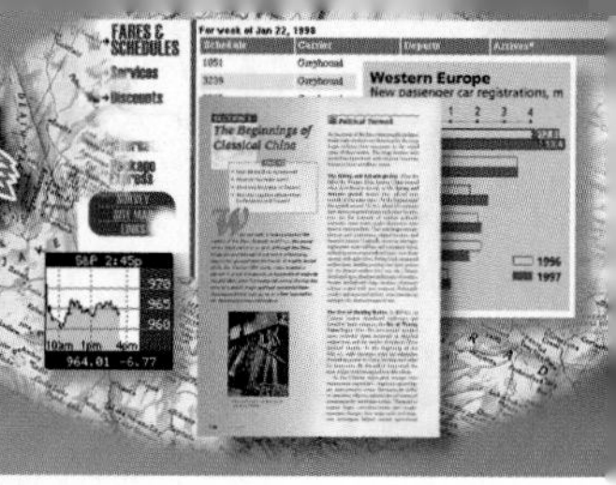

OBJECTIVES

1. Understand how to read a consumer report
2. Recognize criteria used in the evaluation of consumer products
3. Interpret standard abbreviations
4. Understand the value of comparative reviews

Teaching the Lesson

This may be a good time to ensure that all students know how to read common consumer documents such as a unit price statement, a warranty, a hazard warning, etc. The winter holidays are a good time to collect an assortment of these documents, which can be grouped and examined by students.

Using the Strategies

Answers

1. The criteria are: fit, features, construction, claimed volume, and books held.
2. S=small, M=medium, L=large
3. There is no absolute correlation between quality and price, but generally, the lower priced backpacks are of poorer quality.
4. Possible answers: either Eagle's Peak Sierra models (Key nos. 6 and 10)
5. Possible answer: RAYtote (Key no. 1; $48; 2200 cu. in.)

Reading for Life

Reading a Consumer Report

Situation

A Renaissance person might have written a sonnet for someone he or she loved, but you've decided to give a practical gift. You want to make sure you get the best quality at a price you can afford, so you consult a product review in a magazine or on-line. As you read, apply these strategies in order to **evaluate the data** and **make a decision.**

Strategies

Notice how the report is presented.

- It may consist of running text, a chart or other graphic display, or both.

Recognize the criteria used in the evaluation.

- If there is a chart, the criteria may be indicated in the title as well as in the column headings.
- Consider other criteria— your special requirements or those of the person you're buying the gift for.

Interpret abbreviations.

- Some abbreviations may be self-explanatory (such as *P* for "poor" and *E* for "excellent"). Others may be explained in footnotes.

Recognize the structure of the comparison.

- Notice how the items are arranged—for example, from best to worst or from most expensive to least expensive.

Key no.	Brand	Price	Score 0 P F G VG E 100	Fit	Features	Construction	Claimed volume	Books held
1	RAYtote	$48	▬▬▬	■ (M,L)	■	■	2200 cu. in.	59
2	Lugger	45	▬▬▬	■ (S,M,L)	■	▭	1670	49
3	Rugged Gear	50	▬▬▬	▭ (M,L)	▭	▭	2200	48
4	Mountain Climber	42	▬▬▬	■ (M,L)	▭	▭	1700	52
5	Alpine Able	29	▬▬	⊡ (S,M)	▭	■	1875	52
6	Eagle's Peak Sierra with Lining	50	▬▬	⊡ (S,M)	▭	■	1500	49
7	Heavy Hiker	48	▬▬	■ (S,M)	▭	■	1874	50
8	Total Tote	38	▬▬	⊡ (S,M)	⊡	■	1586	47
9	Trail Tough	33	▬▬	⊡ (S,M)	▭	■	1910	53
10	Eagle's Peak Sierra	40	▬▬	⊡ (S,M)	▭	■	1500	49

■ Excellent ▭ Very good ⊡ Good ▨ Fair ▢ Poor

Check other sources.

- In stores, read information provided by the manufacturer. Also read product descriptions in other print and electronic sources. Take notes and compare this information with what you find in a consumer report.

Using the Strategies

Answer these questions about the chart above.

1. In this chart from a product review of backpacks, what are the criteria for comparison?
2. What do the abbreviations S, M, and L stand for?
3. What can you conclude about quality in relation to price?
4. Which product would be a good choice if you were looking for a compact but sturdy pack for short hikes?
5. Which product presumably gives you the most room at the lowest price?

Extending the Strategies

- Identify a product you are interested in purchasing, and investigate it in a consumer report. Describe specific criteria you want your purchase to meet.
- Identify other specific sources of information you might check before choosing a particular product.

280 THE RENAISSANCE

Reaching All Students

Struggling Readers

Students will be more engaged if this exercise deals with some product in which they have a genuine interest: TVs, cars, skis, CD players, etc. If possible, bring in many different product review magazines such as *Consumer Reports* and *Car and Driver.* After finishing the practice exercise, have students use the magazines to complete the Extending the Strategies activity.

Collection 4

Under a Hand Accursed

Theme

A Tragic View of Life *In Shakespeare's tragedies, the great questions about human existence are addressed: What is evil, and what drives men and women to commit deeds of darkness? What are the consequences of our freedom to make choices in life?*

Reading the Anthology

Reaching Struggling Readers

The *Reading Skills and Strategies: Reaching Struggling Readers* binder includes a Reading Strategies Handbook that offers concrete suggestions to help students who have difficulty reading and comprehending text, or students who are reluctant readers. When a specific strategy is most appropriate for a selection, a correlation to the Handbook is provided at the bottom of the teacher's page under the head Struggling Readers. This head may also be used to introduce additional ideas for helping students read challenging texts.

Reading Beyond the Anthology

Read On

At the end of the Renaissance collections, the grade twelve book includes an annotated bibliography of books suitable for extended reading. The suggested books are related to works in these collections by theme, by author, or by subject. To preview the Read On for the Renaissance period, please turn to p. T455.

HRW Library

The *HRW Library* offers novels, plays, and short-story collections for extended reading. Each book in the Library includes one or more major works and thematically or topically related Connections. The Connections are magazine articles, poems, or other pieces of literature. Each book in the *HRW Library* is also accompanied by a Study Guide that provides teaching suggestions and worksheets. The following titles are recommended for Collection 4.

OTHELLO
William Shakespeare

Renaissance Venice is the setting for Shakespeare's tale of the Moorish general who "lov'd not wisely but too well." This tragic story of love and betrayal explores the destructive powers of jealousy and ambition.

HAMLET
William Shakespeare

Hamlet, prince of Denmark, is tormented by the need to avenge his father's death. His decision to seek justice, regardless of the consequences, sets in motion a fatal chain of events.

Collection 4 Under a Hand Accursed

Resources for this Collection

Note: All resources for this collection are available for preview on the *One-Stop Planner CD-ROM I with Test Generator.* All worksheets and blackline masters may be printed from the CD-ROM.

Internet Resources
go.hrw.com LE0 12-4

Selection or Feature	Reading and Literary Skills	Vocabulary, Language, and Grammar
The Tragedy of Macbeth (p. 297) William Shakespeare **Connections: On the Knocking at the Gate in *Macbeth*** (p. 330) Thomas De Quincey **Critical Comments:** • **Macbeth's Porter** (p. 332) • **The King's Evil** (p. 367) • **Hecate: Queen of the Night** (p. 368) • **Soliloquies and Asides** (p. 383) • **The Mystery of Evil** (p. 384) **Connections: Macbeth and the Witches** (p. 386) Richard Armour **Elements of Literature: Imagery and Figurative Language** (p. 389)	• *Graphic Organizers for Active Reading,* Worksheet pp. 26, 27, 28, 29, 30 • *Literary Elements:* Transparency 11 Worksheet p. 34	• *Words to Own,* Worksheet p. 9 • *Grammar and Language Links:* Active and Passive Voice, Worksheet p. 19; Revision Worksheet p. 21 • *Language Workshop CD-ROM,* Voice • *Daily Oral Grammar,* Transparencies 10, 11
World Literature: Italy Canto 34 *from* **The Inferno of Dante** (p. 393) Dante Alighieri *translated by* Robert Pinsky	The World Literature feature offers students the opportunity to explore thematically linked literature from different world cultures. Structured activities called Finding Common Ground are provided in the Pupil's Edition to guide students' explorations of these thematic connections between British and other world literature.	
The English Language: Shakespeare's Language (p. 399) John Algeo		

Collection Planner

Other Resources for this Collection

- *Cross-Curricular Activities,* p. 4
- *Portfolio Management System,* Introduction to Portfolio Assessment, p. 1
- *Test Generator,* Collection Test

Writing	Listening and Speaking Viewing and Representing	Assessment
• *Portfolio Management System,* Rubrics for Choices, p. 124	• *Visual Connections:* Videocassette B, Segment 6 • *Audio CD Library,* Disc 5, Tracks 2, 3, 4 • *Viewing and Representing:* Fine Art Transparency 4 Worksheet p. 16 • *Portfolio Management System,* Rubrics for Choices, p. 124	• *Formal Assessment,* Selection Tests, pp. 57, 59, 61, 63, 65 • *Test Generator (One-Stop Planner CD-ROM)* • *Preparation for College Admission Exams,* p. 15
	• *Audio CD Library,* Disc 5, Track 5	
		• *Formal Assessment,* The English Language Test, p. 67

Transparency CD-ROM Video Audio CD

Collection 4 Under a Hand Accursed

Skills Focus

Selection or Feature	Reading Skills and Strategies	Elements of Literature and Language	Writing	Listening and Speaking	Viewing and Representing
The Tragedy of Macbeth (p. 297) William Shakespeare	Reading Blank Verse, pp. 318, 385 • Iamb • Pentameter	Tragedy, p. 300 Paradox, p. 318 Character, pp. 318, 333, 351, 369, 388 Conflict, p. 318 Resolution, pp. 318, 389–390 Contrast, p. 318 Irony, p. 318 Foreshadow, pp. 333, 388 Suspense, p. 333 Mood, p. 333 Images, pp. 333, 384, 389 Symbol, pp. 333, 369 Comic Relief, p. 333 Soliloquy, pp. 351, 383 Metaphor, p. 351 Turning Point, pp. 351, 390 Dumb Show, p. 369 Asides, p. 383 Meter, p. 385 Parody, pp. 386, 389 Climax, pp. 388, 390 Tragic Heroes, pp. 388–390 Themes, p. 388 Internal Conflict, p. 389 External Conflict, p. 389 Figurative Language, p. 389 Context, p. 389 Protagonist, p. 390 Antagonist, p. 390 Rising Action, p. 390 Falling Action, p. 390 Complication, p. 390	Identify Language Used to Create Effects, p. 390 Analyze the Character of Lady Macbeth, p. 390 Analyze the Author's Purpose, p. 390 Write an Essay Analyzing the Structure of *Macbeth,* p. 390 Rewrite the Banquet Scene in a Contemporary Setting, p. 390	Create an Oral Interpretation of a Soliloquy, p. 390	Make a Sketch of Proposed Set and Costume Designs for One Scene in *Macbeth,* p. 390
Reading Skills and Strategies: Determining Meanings (p. 391)	Word Mapping, p. 391 Context Clues, p. 391 Multiple Meanings, p. 391				
World Literature: Italy Canto 34 *from* **The Inferno of Dante** (p. 393) Dante Alighieri	The World Literature feature offers students the opportunity to explore thematically linked literature from different world cultures. Structured activities called Finding Common Ground are provided in the Pupil's Edition to guide students' explorations of these thematic connections between British and other world literature.				
The English Language: Shakespeare's Language (p. 399) John Algeo		Shakespeare's Pronunciation, p. 399 Shakespeare's Grammar, p. 400 Connotations, p. 400 Shakespeare's Words, p. 402			

Collection 4

UNDER A HAND ACCURSED

Shakespeare

Dante

> Fate has given this man a spirit
> Which is always pressing onwards, beyond control,
> And whose mad striving overleaps
> All joys of the earth between pole and pole.
> Him shall I drag through the wilds of life
> And through the flats of meaninglessness,
> I shall make him flounder and gape and stick
> And to tease his insatiableness
> Hang meat and drink in the air before his watering lips;
> In vain he will pray to slake his inner thirst,
> And even had he not sold himself to the devil
> He would be equally accursed.
>
> —Johann Wolfgang von Goethe, *from Faust*
> (German, 1749–1832)

(Background) Orson Welles in his film production of *Macbeth* (1948).

Objectives

1. Read Renaissance literature on the theme of "Under a Hand Accursed"
2. Interpret literary elements with special emphasis on imagery and figurative language
3. Apply a variety of reading strategies, particularly determining meanings through mapping
4. Respond to the literature in a variety of modes
5. Understand and use new words
6. Learn about Shakespeare's English

Introducing the Theme

The two classic works of literature in this collection (*Macbeth* and Canto 34 from *The Divine Comedy*) explore the mystery of evil and the consequences of our freedom to make choices.

Responding to the Quotation

? According to Goethe's lines, what causes human beings to be "accursed"? [Possible response: Humans become accursed by always wanting and being tempted by what is beyond their reach.]

Writing Focus: Analyzing Causes and Effects

The following **Work in Progress** assignment builds to a culminating **Writer's Workshop** at the end of Collection 5.

- The Tragedy of Macbeth — Exploring causes of emotional effects (p. 390)

Writer's Workshop: Expository Writing / Analyzing Causes and Effects (p. 459)

Objectives

1. Understand the development of drama in Britain
2. Identify a miracle play, a mystery play, a morality play, and an interlude
3. Appreciate the history and development of the Renaissance theater
4. Read and understand a diagram of the Globe Theater

Responding to the Art

David Vinckboons (1575–1629) is known for his landscape paintings that focus on commonplace objects and occurrences. Vinckboons often depicts peasant scenes and everyday life, such as this street scene at a fair.
Activity. Ask students to describe the activities taking place in this picture. [buying, selling, talking, dancing, herding animals] What modern events are like this fair? [state fairs, carnivals, street fairs, farmers' markets]

The Renaissance Theater

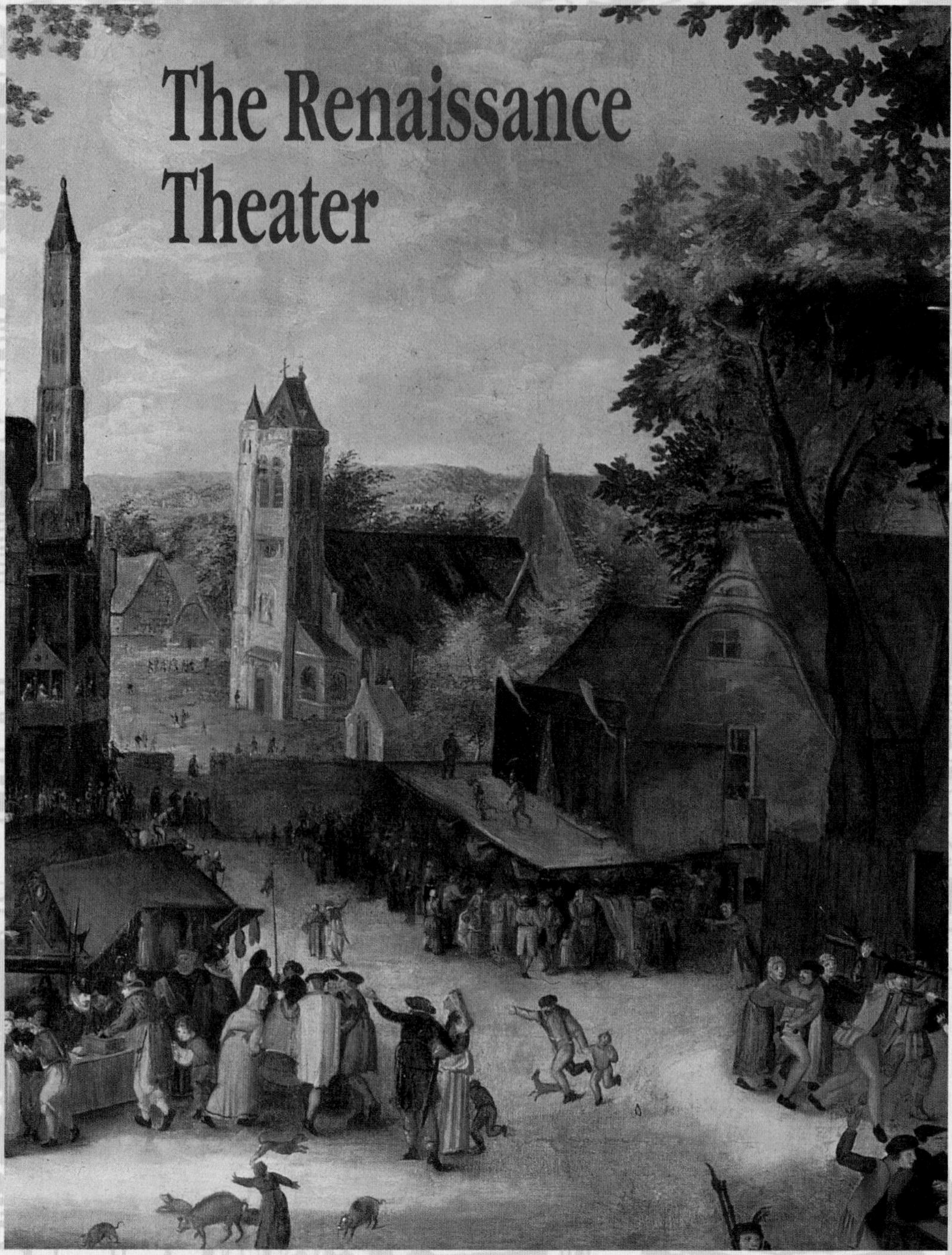

A Flemish Fair (detail) (late 16th to early 17th century) by David Vinckboons.

Cheltenham Art Gallery & Museums, Gloucestershire, England.

Reaching All Students

Struggling Readers

Provide students with a study guide that leads them through the essay with questions that follow the order in which the information is presented. Provide one main-idea question for each paragraph. Here is one sample guide question for the opening section of the essay: Section 1: What were the forerunners of the Renaissance theater? [church dialogue songs, miracle and mystery plays, morality plays, and interludes]

English Language Learners

To help students establish a context before reading this information, assign them to small groups to discuss experiences they have had seeing plays or participating in dramas or class skits. Ask them to describe the theater, audience, play, costumes, and scenery. As they discuss, review the related vocabulary. Ask them to look at the picture of the Globe (p. 284) and compare it with their knowledge of theaters.

Advanced Learners

After students have read the essay, have them do further research on the forerunners of Renaissance drama, especially the plays *Everyman* and *The Second Shepherd's Play.*

Drama as Teacher: The Forerunners

Even before the Renaissance, the English had been writing and performing plays for several centuries. Some scholars believe that medieval drama evolved from church ceremonies such as the dialogue songs performed at Easter Eve services. In these tiny playlets, three women would appear at a door representing the tomb of Christ and guarded by an angel. The angel would ask in Latin, "Whom do you seek?" and then he would announce the Resurrection. **A**

Globe Playhouse (detail) (c. 1599–1613) by C. Walter Hodges.

From this obscure beginning, drama moved out of the churches and into the marketplaces of towns. There, in the 1300s and 1400s, various workers' guilds cooperated in staging cycles of plays that dramatized the whole history of the human race as then understood: its creation by God, its fall through the wiles of Satan, its life in Old Testament times, its redemption by Christ, and its final judgment at the end of the world. **B** Parts of four cycles of these plays have been preserved, and they are named after the towns where they probably originated: York, Chester, Coventry, and Wakefield. Gradually, the plays became less religious, often relying on *deus ex machina* (an artificial device arbitrarily used to resolve a plot), and comedy was incorporated into them. The wife of Noah, for instance, makes a great fuss about entering the ark and is carried kicking and screaming aboard. Comic scenes like this one provide an early example of English skill in mixing the comic with the serious in drama. The most notable play of the period just before the Renaissance is *Everyman,* based on a Dutch original (see page 451).

Representation of a Mystery Play (detail) (1825) by David Jee.

By permission of the British Library, London.

Several kinds of plays, then, were written and produced before the Renaissance: **miracle** and **mystery plays** that taught people stories from the Bible and saints' legends; **moralities** that taught people how to live and die; and, starting in the early 1500s, a new kind of play called an **interlude.** **C** Interludes were one-act plays, some of them indistinguishable from moralities, others rowdy and farcical. With the interludes the playwrights stopped being anonymous. Even before the new humanist learning came in, there were strong dramatic traditions that the great Renaissance playwrights knew about. **D**

go.hrw.com
LEO 12-4

A Background

Easter Dialogue Song

The three women were representations of the three Marys who visited Christ's empty tomb on the first Easter morning. Although their dress indicated they were women, these roles were played by choirboys. The angel was played by a priest in a white robe. When the Marys state that they are seeking Jesus, the angel responds, "He is not here, he has risen again as foretold. Go, announce that he is risen from the dead."

B Exploring the Culture

Guild Plays

A guild was like a trade union combined with a club. There was one for each trade, and each had its own play to perform in the cycle, which might contain as many as forty-eight plays. Although these performances were given outdoors and had no single stage, those responsible for the production were able to include many amazing effects. Existing records show stars and clouds, burning altars, and fireworks devices; temples were set ablaze and angels were lowered from the sturdier scaffolds.

C Humanities Connections

Pre-Renaissance Plays

The mystery play was a Bible history play, based on stories from both the Old and New Testaments. Examples of mystery plays include *The Second Shepherd's Play* and the York play of *The Crucifixion of Christ.* The miracle play differed from the mystery play in that it dramatized stories not in the Bible, such as lives of the saints. The morality play, which did not appear until the fifteenth century, presented human characters as representations of virtues and vices. *Everyman* is a morality play.

D Exploring the Culture

Humanists

In a 1998 biography of Thomas More, Peter Ackroyd defines a humanist as a student of classical learning in the related fields of grammar, rhetoric, and literature (p. 199). More was also a devoted churchman, as was Erasmus, though both deplored superstition and corruption in the Church.

Using Students' Strengths

Spatial Learners

Before students begin reading, visit the school auditorium or a local theater that contains a proscenium stage. If possible, also visit a theater in the round. Encourage students to contrast the physical settings of the two and to imagine how the cast might interact differently with the audience in each setting. Assign students to small groups and have them stage two versions of the same scene—one for a proscenium stage and one for theater in the round.

Visual Learners

Use the videocassette segment "Shakespeare's Tragic Heroes" from the *Visual Connections Program* to help students appreciate some of the staging difficulties early playwrights faced. After looking at a scene on the video, examine the diagram on p. 284 and discuss how Shakespeare might have staged the same scene at the Globe.

Ⓐ Exploring the Culture

Rowdy Audiences

Theaters built in the suburbs escaped the demands of profit-sharing innkeepers and the rancor of city authorities, who claimed, with some justification, that the boisterous crowds gathered in inn yards (especially on Sundays) occasioned a danger not just of "ungodliness" and licentiousness but also of fire, riot, accident, crime, and the spread of plague. Invite students to identify a contemporary parallel. [Possible answer: the problems with crowds at rock concerts.]

Ⓑ Exploring the Historical Period

Lenten Dispensation

Although theater companies were commanded not to perform on Sundays or during the weeks of Lent (the six weeks preceding Easter), these ordinances were frequently ignored, and by 1616, it was possible to obtain an official Lenten Dispensation—for forty-four shillings.

Ⓒ Background

Building the Globe

After the death of James Burbage, his sons Richard and Cuthbert were unable to renew the lease on the land on which the Theater stood. Although they had lost the lease, the brothers' interpretation of the law was that the Theater still belonged to them. So arming themselves with axes, Shakespeare and his companions began the Theater's demolition under the direction of carpenter Peter Street. They carried the wood and timber over London Bridge to Bankside, where Street built the Globe on the marshy ground opposite the Rose. The name of the Globe was inspired by the burden Hercules was often depicted bearing on his shoulders. Building the Globe from the demolished Theater could well have seemed a Herculean feat to Shakespeare and his friends.

Old Traditions, New Theaters

By the mid-sixteenth century, the art of drama in England was three centuries old, but the idea of housing it in a permanent building was new. Even after theaters had been built, plays were still regularly performed in improvised spaces when acting companies toured the provinces or presented their plays in the large houses of royalty and nobility.

Ⓐ Ⓑ In 1576, James Burbage, the father of Shakespeare's partner and fellow actor Richard Burbage, built the first public theater and called it, appropriately, the Theater. Shortly thereafter, a second playhouse, called the Curtain, was erected. Both of these were in a northern suburb of London, where they would not offend the staid residents of London proper. Then came the Rose, the Swan, the Fortune, the Globe, the Red Bull, and the Hope—far more public theaters than in any other European capital.

The Globe: "This Wooden O"

The Globe is the most famous of the public theaters because the company that Shakespeare belonged to owned it. Many of his Ⓒ plays received their first performances there. It was built out of timbers salvaged from the Theater, which was demolished in 1599. Unfortunately, the plans for the Globe have not survived, though there still exist old, panoramic drawings of London in which its exterior is pictured. But the most important sources of information about the theater's structure are the plays themselves, with their stage directions and other clues.

Most scholars now accept as accurate the reconstruction of the Globe published by C. Walter Hodges, whose drawing appears on this page. Notice that the theater has three main parts: the building proper, the stage, and the tiring house, or backstage area, with the flag flying from its peak to indicate that there will be a performance that day.

KEY

a	Main entrance
b	The yard
c	Entrance to lowest gallery
d	Entrance to staircase and upper galleries
e	Corridor serving the different sections of the middle gallery
f	Middle gallery ("Twopenny Rooms")
g	"Gentlemen's Rooms" or "Lords' Rooms"
h	The stage
j	The hanging being put up round the stage
k	The "hell" under the stage
l	The stage trap, leading down to the hell
m	Stage doors
n	Curtained "place behind the stage"
o	Gallery above the stage, used as required sometimes by musicians, sometimes by spectators, and often as part of the play
p	Backstage area (the tiring house)
q	Tiring-house door
r	Dressing rooms
s	Wardrobe and storage
t	The hut housing the machine for lowering enthroned gods, etc., to the stage
u	The "heavens"
w	Hoisting the playhouse flag

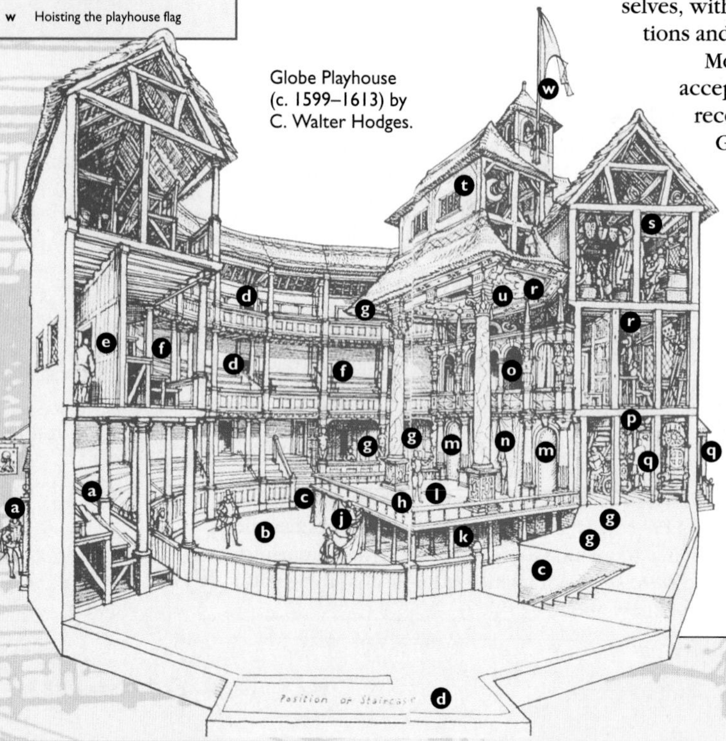

Globe Playhouse (c. 1599–1613) by C. Walter Hodges.

Skill Link

Using Text Organizers: Diagrams

Ask students to study the drawing on this page of the Globe Playhouse by C. Walter Hodges. Point out that the letters in black circles were not part of Hodges's original sketch but were superimposed on the drawing in order to create a diagram. The purpose of the diagram is to illustrate the physical layout of the Globe and to indicate how some theatrical effects were achieved. The key above the drawing identifies each part of the Playhouse indicated by a letter. If students wish to learn the name of any lettered section of the drawing or to study the relationship of the various parts of the Globe Playhouse, they should consult the text next to the appropriate letter(s) in the key.

Activity

After students have read this essay, have them use the information they have learned and this diagram of the Globe to answer these questions:

A wooden structure three stories high, the building proper surrounded a spacious inner yard open to the sky. It was probably a sixteen-sided polygon. Any structure with that many sides would appear circular, so it is not surprising that Shakespeare referred to the Globe as "this wooden O" in his play *Henry V.* There were probably only two entrances to the building, one for the public and one for the theater company. But there may have been another public door used as an exit, because when the Globe burned down in 1613, the crowd escaped quickly and safely.

General admission to the theater cost one penny; this entitled a spectator to be a groundling, which meant he or she could stand in the yard. Patrons paid a little more to mount up into the galleries, where there were seats and a better view of the stage. The most expensive seats were chairs set right on the stage along its two sides. People who wanted to be conspicuous rented them, though they must have been a great nuisance to the rest of the audience and the actors. A public theater held a surprisingly large number of spectators—three thousand, according to two contemporary accounts. Since the spectators must have been squeezed together, it is no wonder that the authorities always closed the theaters during plague epidemics.

Up Close and Personal

The stage jutted halfway out into the yard, so that the actors were in much closer contact with the audience than actors are in modern theaters. Thus, every tiny nuance of an actor's performance could affect the audience. The actors were highly trained, and they could sing, dance, declaim, wrestle, fence, clown, roar, weep, and whisper. Large, sensational effects were also plentiful. Spectators loved to see witches or devils emerge through the trapdoor in the stage, which everybody pretended led down to Hell, just as everybody pretended that the ceiling over part of the stage was the Heavens. This ceiling was painted with elaborate suns, moons, and stars, and it contained a trapdoor through which angels, gods, and spirits could be lowered on a wire and even flown over the other actors' heads.

Behind the Scenes

The third part of the theater was the tiring (from *tire,* an archaic form of "attire") house, a tall building that contained machinery and dressing rooms and that provided a two-story back wall for the stage. Hodges's drawing of the Globe shows that this wall contained a gallery above and a curtained space below. The gallery had multiple purposes, depending on what play was being performed: Spectators could sit there, musicians could perform there, or parts of the play could be acted there—as if on balconies, towers, hills, and the like. The curtained area below the gallery was used mainly for "discoveries" of things prepared in advance and hidden from the audience until the proper time. In Shakespeare's *Merchant of Venice,* for example, the curtain is drawn to reveal three small chests, one of which hides the heroine's picture. Apparently, this curtained area

D Background

Rebuilding the Globe

The fire in the Globe occurred in June 1613 during the first scenes of a new play by Shakespeare called *Henry VIII.* The company lost not just the building, costumes, properties, and scripts, but also the advice of their leading playwright who ended his London career that year (see pp. 293–294, "The Last Years: Continued Diversity"). The Globe was rebuilt in 1614; it was closed by the Puritans in 1642 and razed in 1644 to make room for residences. The only marker indicating its location is a plaque on a brewery wall.

Sam Wanamaker, an American, began a drive in 1970 to rebuild the Globe. Wanamaker, a respected actor, producer, and director of stage and screen, zealously raised funds and coaxed the British into rebuilding the theater. He chose a site two hundred yards from the old theater, and construction started in 1989. The new theater's first season opened in June 1997 with a nostalgic production of *Henry V.* (See p. 288.)

E Exploring the Historical Period

The Plague

Because of the plague, London theaters were closed from 1592 to 1594, 1603, and 1609. During these three epidemics, fifty thousand of London's two hundred thousand residents died. This highly infectious disease, called *Pasteurella pestis,* is transmitted to humans by fleas from infected rats. It is characterized by high fever, chills, delirium, and painful festering of the lymph glands called "buboes" (hence, "bubonic plague"). Death could come in three or four days. The worst recorded epidemic, in the fourteenth century, is estimated to have killed up to three-fourths of the people in Asia and Europe in less than twenty years.

F Background

The Stage

The contrast between Renaissance and modern theaters refers to the modern proscenium stage, which is often elevated and set back from the audience.

Skill Link

Using Text Organizers (con't.)

1. If you looked at the [W] section of the Playhouse known as the peak and saw no flag flying, what would you know? [there would be no performance today]
2. If there were a malfunction in the hut, which character in *Macbeth* would be most likely to be affected: the flying witches, Lady Macbeth, Macduff? [the flying witches]
3. If you wished to have the best seats in the house, what lettered section would you sit in? [h—the stage]
4. If you were a musician hired to play one of Shakespeare's songs during a performance, where might you sit? [o—in the gallery]
5. If you were a groundling, where would you sit? [b—in the yard]

A Background

Props

The Renaissance theaters had a variety of properties, today commonly known as "props." Some props were so cumbersome that they were set on the main stage, where they remained throughout the play. The actors ignored them until they were relevant to the action.

B Exploring the Culture

Acting Techniques

Because of the lack of scenery, the focus was on the actors and the playwrights' words. To help with their characterizations, Renaissance actors used certain recognized stylistic movements to portray traditional dramatic emotions, such as rage, fear, and desperation. Thus what appeared to Renaissance audiences as natural probably included formalized gestures and grandiloquent delivery of lines that would seem artificial to modern audiences.

Globe Theater at Bankside (detail) (17th century). Watercolor.

© British Museum, London.

was too small, too shallow, and too far out of the sight of some spectators to be used as a performance space. If a performer were "discovered" behind the curtains (as Marlowe's Dr. Faustus is discovered in his study), he would quickly move out onto the stage to be seen and heard better. **A** When large properties such as thrones, beds, desks, and so on were pushed through the curtains onto the stage, the audience would know at once that the action was taking place indoors. When the action shifted to the outdoors, the property could be pulled back behind the curtain.

The Power of Make-Believe

Renaissance audiences took for granted that the theater cannot show "reality": Whatever happens on the stage is make-believe. When the people in the audience saw actors carrying lanterns, they knew it was night, even though the sun was shining brightly overhead. Often, instead of seeing a scene, they heard it described, as when Shakespeare has a character exclaim over a sunrise,

> But look, the morn in russet mantle clad
> Walks o'er the dew of yon high eastward hill.
>
> —*Hamlet,* Act I, Scene 1, lines 166–167

When a forest setting was called for, there was no painted scenery imitating real trees, bushes, flowers, and so on. Instead, a few bushes and small trees might be pushed onto the stage, and then the actors spoke lines that evoked images in the spectators' minds. In *As You Like It,* Rosalind simply looks around and announces, "Well, this is the forest of Arden." **B** As the theatrical historian Gerald Bentley put it, Renaissance drama was "a drama of persons, not a drama of places."

Crossing the Curriculum

Social Sciences

Students may wish to look up examples of morality plays and find out what virtues and vices were the most popular choices for representation. Ask students to create a pie chart showing their findings or to perform an excerpt from one of the plays, either with actors or as a puppet show.

Architecture

Ask students to study different artists' renderings of the Globe and to analyze their accuracy in light of the information presented in this article and of students' own knowledge of Shakespeare's plays.

Pomp and Pageantry

The scenery may have been kept to a minimum, but the theaters themselves were ornate. The interiors were painted brightly, with many decorations, and the space at the rear of the stage could be covered with colorful tapestries or hangings. Costumes were rich, elaborate, and expensive. The manager-producer Philip Henslowe once paid twenty pounds (then an enormous sum) for a single cloak for one of his actors to wear. Henslowe's lists of theatrical properties mention chariots, fountains, dragons, beds, tents, thrones, booths, and wayside crosses, among other things.

The audience also enjoyed the processions—religious, royal, military—that occurred in many plays. These would enter the stage from one door, cross the stage, and then exit by the other door. A few quick costume changes as the actors passed through the tiring house could double and triple the apparent number of people in a procession.

Lady Masquer (detail) (c. 1610) by Inigo Jones.

Devonshire Collection, Chatsworth. Reproduced by permission of the Chatsworth Settlement Trustees.

Music Most Eloquent

When people went to the London theater, they expected not only to see a tragedy or comedy acted but also to hear music, both vocal and instrumental. Trumpets announced the beginning of the play and important arrivals and departures within the play. High up in the gallery, musicians played between acts and at other appropriate times during the performance. And scattered throughout most of the plays, especially the comedies, were songs.

The songs in Shakespeare's plays are the best of this kind that have come down to us, for Shakespeare excelled in lyric and in dramatic poetry. He included a great variety of songs in his plays: sad, happy, comic, thoughtful songs, each one adapted to the play and scene in which it occurs and to the character who performs it. Some of the songs advance the dramatic action, some help establish the mood of a scene, and some reveal character. Like this invitation to love (from the comedy *Twelfth Night*), all of these songs are fresh and spontaneous, not contrived and artificial.

O mistress mine, where are you roaming?
O, stay and hear, your true love's coming,
  That can sing both high and low.
Trip no further, pretty sweeting;
Journeys end in lovers meeting,
  Every wise man's son doth know . . .

What is love? 'tis not hereafter;
Present mirth hath present laughter;
  What's to come is still unsure.
In delay there lies no plenty;
Then come kiss me, sweet and twenty;
Youth's a stuff will not endure.

Getting Students Involved

Enrichment Activities

Shakespeare On-line. Have students conduct Web searches for information about Shakespeare. (See if they can find the Shakespeare Insult server, an interesting way to bring Elizabethan language to life.) Students may also exchange e-mail with Shakespeare scholars on related listservs. *(You may want to preview Internet activity that you suggest to students. Because these resources are sometimes public forums, their content can be unpredictable.)*

Staging a Court Masque. Point out that the costume above was created by the great theatrical designer Inigo Jones for a court masque. A masque, or royal entertainment, was performed by amateurs and included elaborate settings and fantastic costumes. Ben Jonson, Shakespeare's contemporary, collaborated with Inigo Jones on many masques for James I. Ask students to research the dancing and music associated with masques. Then challenge them to design a masque of their own.

C Background

Philip Henslowe

Philip Henslowe owned the Rose, the Fortune, and the Hope theaters. His stepdaughter married Edward Alleyn, a great Renaissance actor. Alleyn inherited his father-in-law's papers, which included a diary that served as a priceless source of information on the Renaissance theater. Henslowe's papers relate information about the company called Lord Strange's Men and later Lord Chamberlain's Men. Christopher Marlowe (see p. 232) wrote for Henslowe's troupe.

D Exploring the Culture

Theatrical Music

Like Shakespeare's other plays, *Macbeth* demands musical flourishes—trumpets, drums, "alarums" (clamor and martial sounds—clanking swords, galloping hoofs, shouting voices), cannons, and thunder. Available musical instruments included viols and virginals, the recorder (a flutelike instrument), the cornet (a trumpet-like cylinder of ivory or wood with finger holes like those on a recorder), the sackbut (an early trombone), and a double-reed instrument called the hautboy (hoʹ boiʹ), or oboe.

E Humanities Connections

Davenant's *Macbeth*

After the Puritans' temporary closure of the theaters (1642–1660), *Macbeth* was brought back to the stage in a version adapted by William Davenant. John Downes, who served as the prompter for the company, described the version as follows: "The tragedy of *Macbeth* alter'd by *Sir William Davenant;* being drest in all it's Finery, as new Cloath's, new Scenes, Machines, as flying for the Witches; with all the singing and Dancing in it: THE first Compos'd by *Mr. Lock,* the other by *Mr. Channell* and *Mr. Joseph Priest;* it being all Excellently perform'd, being in the nature of an Opera, it Recompenc'd double the Expence; it proves still a lasting Play." Ask students to note the changes Davenant made to the play.

F Elements of Literature

Carpe Diem

? Why is this poem a *carpe diem* poem? [It urges a young woman to "seize the day" and stay to meet her lover.]

Ⓐ Exploring the Historical Period

Court Performances

In England, players formed part of the royal household and plays were usually performed at court on feast days. Professional actors were called on to perform. Shakespeare's *Twelfth Night* may have been presented at court before it appeared in public.

Ⓑ Background

Status of Actors

Richard Burbage (see p. 284) had acquired the right to lease Blackfriars Hall earlier, but wealthy neighbors refused to accept adult actors in their midst. Even prominent actors like Burbage were not considered respectable by London's upper class, so the hall was leased to a company of boy actors. By 1608 Shakespeare had a coat of arms, and his company had acquired considerable status; the council was happy to turn Blackfriars over to the now-respectable adult professionals.

Ⓒ Exploring the Culture

Repertory Companies

In Shakespeare's day, actors formed what we call repertory companies. Instead of signing up to perform a single play for a long run, they were members of an acting company that performed a number of plays on consecutive days. (Henslowe's company may hold the record, with fifty-five new or recently revised plays performed in 126 weeks.) These companies filled the roles in each play with members of their own group. The actors shared in the company profits, and boys were apprenticed as they would have been in a guild. Boys acted the women's roles until their voices changed, which accounts for the lack of older women's roles in plays (such portrayals would have been difficult for boys) and the number of women characters disguised as men. Many Shakespearean repertory groups exist today in the United States and other countries. The Shakespearean Festival at Ashland, Oregon, uses a Globe-like theater in its annual summer repertory performances. Also, Minneapolis has the Tyrone Guthrie Theater, which was designed in the Shakespearean manner but with a closed roof and modern lighting and machinery.

The movie *Shakespeare in Love* (1998) includes a great deal of detail on the Elizabethan theaters (though the historical premise of the story itself is false).

Unfortunately, most of the original music for Shakespeare's songs has been lost. But just as the plays themselves have inspired many composers of music for opera, orchestra, and ballet, so have the songs from the plays been set to music right up to the present.

Varying the Venue

Ⓐ The acting companies performed in two other kinds of spaces: in the great halls of castles and manor houses, and in indoor, fully covered theaters in London.

For performances in a great hall, a theater company must have had a portable stage. In these buildings, the usual entertainment was a bear being attacked by dogs. The bear pits were vile places, but their temporary stages could easily accommodate any play except for scenes requiring the use of Heavens overhanging the stage.

Ⓑ Something like this stage may also have been used in private theaters like the Blackfriars, which Shakespeare's company, the King's Men, acquired in 1608. One great advantage of the Blackfriars—a disused monastery that was entirely roofed over—was that the company could perform there in cold weather and, since artificial lighting always had to Ⓒ be used, at night. Thus, the King's Men could put on plays all during the year, increasing profits for the shareholders, among them Shakespeare.

Groundlings Get Close Look

LONDON June 12, 1997—Attending Shakespeare's Globe means pondering seemingly impertinent questions: As you're deciding what seats to buy, box office personnel ask, "Would you like to be a groundling?"

Excuse me? Soon, you learn that the word comes from Elizabethan theater. Groundlings were grimy, snaggle-toothed creatures who stood on the ground without seats, eating, picking pockets.

At the Globe, groundlings still get away with a lot. They prop their elbows on the lip of the stage for the ultimate front-row seat. Moshing is not yet outlawed. Only when you pull out a camera do ushers discreetly intervene.

At last Thursday's *Henry V*, people in the seats seemed so drawn in that they moved down to stand among the groundlings. That's not surprising: The lack of the usual theatrical artifice makes you want to get closer to the play.

—*from USA Today*

(Below) Aerial view of the new Globe Theatre on London's South Bank.

(Below) A 1997 production of Shakespeare's *Henry V* at the new Globe Theatre, London.

288

Assessing Learning

Check Test: True-False

1. The first public theater was built in the sixteenth century. [True]
2. Many of Shakespeare's plays were performed at the Globe Theater. [True]
3. The scenery in the Renaissance theater was elaborate and detailed, imitating reality precisely. [False]
4. Music was an important part of the performance of a Renaissance play. [True]
5. Blackfriars was a monastery where players went to pray before important performances. [False]

William Shakespeare

(1564–1616)

Every literate person has heard of Shakespeare, the author of more than 36 remarkable plays and more than 150 poems. Over the centuries, these literary works have made such a deep impression on the human race that all sorts of fancies, legends, and theories have been invented about their author. There are even those who say that somebody other than Shakespeare wrote the works that bear his name, although these deluded people cannot agree on who, among a dozen candidates, this other author actually was. Such speculation is based on the misconception that little is known about Shakespeare's life; in fact, Shakespeare's life is better documented than the life of any other dramatist of the time except perhaps for Ben Jonson, a writer who seems almost modern in the way he publicized himself. Jonson was an honest, blunt, and outspoken man who knew Shakespeare well; for a time the two dramatists wrote for the same theatrical company, and Shakespeare even acted in Jonson's plays. Often niggardly in his judgments of other writers, Jonson published a poem praising Shakespeare, asserting that he was superior to all Greek, Roman, and English dramatists, predicting that he would be "not of an age, but for all time." Jonson's judgment is now commonly accepted, and his prophecy has come true. **D**

The Years in Stratford-on-Avon

Shakespeare was born in Stratford-on-Avon, a historic and prosperous market town in Warwickshire, and was christened in the parish church there on April 26, 1564. **E** His father was John Shakespeare, a merchant once active in the town government; his mother—born Mary Arden—came from a prominent family in the county. Presumably, for seven years or so, William attended the Stratford grammar school, where he obtained an excellent education in Latin, the Bible, and English composition. (The students had to translate Latin works into English and then turn them back into Latin.) After leaving school, he may have been apprenticed to a butcher, but because he shows in his plays very detailed knowledge of many different crafts and trades, speculators have proposed a number of different occupations that he could have had. At eighteen, Shakespeare married Anne Hathaway, the twenty-six-year-old daughter of a farmer living near Stratford. They had three children, a daughter named Susanna and twins named Hamnet and Judith.

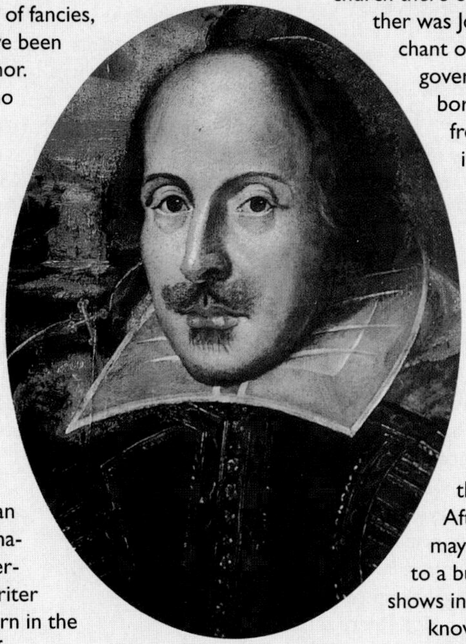

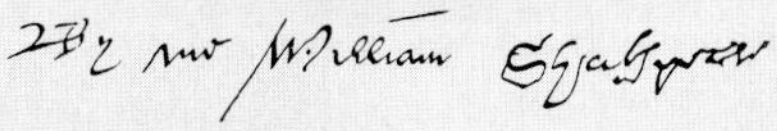

Flower Portrait of William Shakespeare (detail) by an unknown artist. Oil.

From the Royal Shakespeare Company Collection with the permission of the Governors of the Royal Shakespeare Theater, London.

RESPONDING TO THE ART

The Flower Portrait, so called because Mrs. Charles Flower donated it to the Shakespeare Memorial in the nineteenth century, bears the inscription "William Shakespeare 1609." Some critics believe that it is the only surviving portrait made during Shakespeare's lifetime. Another portrait with an old but now challenged claim to authenticity is the expertly executed Chandros oil. Like the Flower Portrait, it shows a man with receding (though blacker) hair, but it adds a gold earring in the left ear and a beard.

D Background

Ben Jonson

Shakespeare had already established a reputation when Jonson came to London in hope of pursuing a career in the theater. The two men probably met in late 1596 or early 1597. In 1598 Shakespeare acted in Jonson's *Every Man in His Humour*.

E Exploring the Historical Period

Stratford-on-Avon

The development of agriculture was key to the prosperity of Stratford in medieval times. In 1196 King John granted the town a market, which is still held twice a week. One of the markets was for cattle, known as *rother* in Old English. This word was used to name one of the main thoroughfares of the town. Under Edward VI, Stratford became an independent township and continued to flourish. An important craft and trading center, Stratford became known for its great fairs. Various companies of London players performed at Stratford when on tour.

Using Students' Strengths

Visual Learners

Ask students to make a KWL chart to help them through the essay. Have them record what they already know (K) about Shakespeare in the left column, what they want (W) to know in the center, and what they learn (L) as a result of their reading in the right column.

K	W	L

Ⓐ Exploring the Historical Period

The Lost Years

Little is known about Shakespeare from 1585, when his twins were christened, until his emergence in London in 1592. Some scholars refer to this period as the "Lost Years." To fill the void, myths sprang up, such as the following tale by Samuel Johnson: "Many came on horseback to the play, and when *Shakespear* fled to London from the terror of a criminal prosecution, his first expedient was to wait at the door of the playhouse, and hold the horses of those who had no servants. . . . *Shakespear* finding more horses put into his hand than he could hold, hired boys to wait under his inspection. . . . In time *Shakespear* found higher employment, but as long as the practice of riding to the play-house continued, the waiters that held the horses retained the appellation of *Shakespear's Boys.*"

Ⓑ Background

Chettle's Apology

In his pamphlet *Kind-Hart's Dream,* Chettle wrote, "I am sorry as if the originall fault a had been by [my?] fault, because my selfe haue seene his [Shakespeare's] demeanor no less ciuill than he exelent in the qualities he professes: Besides, diuers of worship, haue reported, his vprightness of dealing, which argues his honesty, and his facetious grace in writting, that aprooves his Art."

Ⓒ Exploring the Culture

The Clown

The clown, an actor who specialized in comic roles, was an important part of the acting company. In addition to being a genius at embellishing comic roles, William Kemp was a master jigger. Jigs, a main attraction at the playhouses, were often performed at the end of the play. Toward the end of the century, the popularity of the clown began to wane. Kemp was with Shakespeare's company from 1594 to 1599. Among his performances were Dogberry in *Much Ado About Nothing* and Peter in *Romeo and Juliet.*

Anne Hathaway's cottage in Shottery, a mile outside Stratford.

We don't know how the young Shakespeare supported his family, but according to tradition, he taught school for a few years. The two daughters grew up and married; the son died when he was eleven.

Off to London

How did Shakespeare first become interested in the theater? Presumably, by seeing plays. We know that traveling acting companies frequently visited Stratford, and we assume that he attended their performances and that he also went to the nearby city of Coventry, where a famous cycle of religious plays was put on every year. But to be a dramatist, one had to be in London, where the theater was flourishing in the 1580s. Exactly when Shakespeare left his family and moved to London (there is no evidence that his wife was ever in the city) is uncertain; scholars say that he probably arrived there in 1587. It is certain that he was busy and successful in the London theater by 1592, when a fellow dramatist named Robert Greene attacked him in print and ridiculed a passage in his early play *Henry VI.* Greene, a down-and-out Cambridge graduate, warned other university men then writing plays to beware of this mere actor who was writing plays—an "upstart crow beautified with our feathers." Greene died of dissipation just as his ill-natured attack was being published, but a friend of his named Henry Chettle immediately apologized in print to Shakespeare and commended Shakespeare's acting and writing abilities and his personal honesty.

From 1592 on, there is ample documentation of Shakespeare's life and works. We know where he lived in London, at least approximately when his plays were produced and printed, and even how he spent his money. From 1594 until his retirement in about 1613, he was a member of one company, which also included the great tragic actor Richard Burbage and the popular clown Will Kemp. Although actors and others connected with the theater had a very low status legally, in practice they enjoyed the patronage of noblemen and even royalty. It is a mistake to think of Shakespeare as an obscure actor who somehow wrote great plays; he was well known even as a young man. He first became famous as the author of a best-seller, an erotic narrative poem called *Venus and Adonis* (1593). This poem, as well as the more serious poem *The Rape of Lucrece* (1594), was dedicated to a rich and extravagant young nobleman, the earl of Southampton. The dedication of *Lucrece* suggests that Shakespeare and his wealthy patron were on very friendly terms.

Emma Thompson (left) in Kenneth Branagh's film production of *Much Ado About Nothing* (1993).

Shakespeare's Early Plays: Variety and Prosperity

Among Shakespeare's earliest plays are the following, with the generally but not universally

Skill Link

Developing Workplace Competencies

Ask students to imagine they are twenty-three years old and have three children to support and have arrived empty-handed in the city of London today. What plan could they come up with to make money? Why was Shakespeare's alleged scheme to hold the horses of theatergoers a sound idea for a business? Ask students to list the reasons.

[(1) There was a perceived need for this service; (2) the service was not difficult or expensive; (3) there was a pool of young boys (labor) eager to work; (4) there was no competition; (5) Shakespeare could get to know the wealthy patrons who attended the theater. Wealthy patrons could eventually help him move into other areas of the theater.]

accepted dates of their first performances: *Richard III* (1592–1593), a chronicle or history play about a deformed usurper who became king of England; *The Comedy of Errors* (1592–1593), a rowdy farce about mistaken identity, based on a Latin play; *Titus Andronicus* (1593–1594), a blood-and-thunder tragedy full of rant and atrocities; *The Taming of the Shrew, The Two Gentlemen of Verona,* and *Love's Labor's Lost* (all 1593–1595), three agreeable comedies; and *Romeo and Juliet* (1594–1595), a poetic tragedy about ill-fated lovers—the Shakespeare play still most frequently taught in schools. The extraordinary thing about these plays is not so much their immense variety—each one is quite different from all the others—but the fact that they are all regularly revived and performed on stages all over the world today.

Richard Easton and Hal Holbrook in *King Lear* (1993).

Years of Prosperity

By 1596, Shakespeare was beginning to prosper. He had his father apply to the Heralds' College (D) for a coat of arms that the family could display, signifying that they were "gentlefolk," or people of high social standing. On Shakespeare's family crest is a falcon shaking a spear. To support this claim to gentility, Shakespeare bought New Place, a handsome house and grounds in Stratford, a place so commodious and elegant that the queen of England once stayed there after Shakespeare's daughter Susanna inherited it. Shakespeare also, in 1599, joined with a few other members of his company, now called the Lord Chamberlain's Men, to finance a new theater—the famous Globe—on the south side of the Thames. The "honey-tongued Shakespeare," as he was called in a book about English literature published in 1598, was now earning money as a playwright, an actor, and a shareholder in a theater. By 1600, Shakespeare was regularly associating with members of the aristocracy, and six of his plays had been given command performances at (E) the court of Queen Elizabeth.

During the last years of Elizabeth I's reign, Shakespeare completed his cycle of plays about England during the Wars of the Roses: *Richard II* (1595–1596), both parts of *Henry IV* (1596–1597), and *Henry V* (1599). Also in this period he wrote the tragedy *Julius Caesar* (1599)—and the comedies that are most frequently performed today: *A Midsummer Night's Dream* (1595–1596), *The Merchant of Venice* (1596–1597), *Much Ado About Nothing* (1598–1599), *As You Like It* (1598–1600), and *Twelfth Night* (1600–1601). (F) And finally at this time he wrote or rewrote *Hamlet* (1600–1601), the tragedy that, of all his tragedies, has provoked the most varied and controversial interpretations from critics, scholars, and actors. Shakespeare indeed prospered under Queen Elizabeth; according to an old tradition, she asked him to write *The Merry Wives of Windsor* (1600–1601) because she

Mel Gibson and Helena Bonham-Carter in Franco Zeffirelli's film production of *Hamlet* (1990).

D Exploring the Culture

Social Mobility

Although Elizabethan society revolved around a class system, there was some room for social mobility. As an actor, Shakespeare would have been classified in the Queen's statutes along with "rogues, vagabonds, and sturdy beggars." However, a prosperous and prominent actor could buy a degree of respectability by obtaining a coat of arms. The attitude was as follows: "who can live idly and without manual labor, and will bear the port, charge and countenance of a gentlemen, he shall be called master and taken for a gentleman."

E Exploring the Historical Period

The Court of Elizabeth I

As a female ruler, Elizabeth I recognized the importance of maintaining a royal image that made her the focus of loyalty and power. To this end, her court became the social and political center of the realm. Various activities at court promoted the concept of loyal subjects in the service of their queen. These activities included religious ceremonies, dances, and, of course, plays. Every royal Christmas included a play. In the 1580s Elizabeth had her own company, and in later years the Lord Chamberlain's Men often performed at her court.

F Exploring the Culture

Masques

It is likely that Shakespeare wrote *Twelfth Night* for Queen Elizabeth's Christmas revel. The traditional time for royal entertainments was the Christmas period, which concluded with a Twelfth Night play or masque. The masque was an elaborate dramatic presentation characterized by great spectacle, music, poetry, and dancing. The script for a masque usually included several songs and two hundred lines of dialogue in verse. Many of the most extravagant masques were written by Ben Jonson.

Crossing the Curriculum

History

If you are English or of English descent, you can claim a coat of arms if you can prove you are descended on the male side from someone whose coat is registered at the College of Arms. If you are not, you may apply for a coat of arms and pay a fee. Students might be interested in researching the Herald's College and what the process involves. Students may present their findings to the class in a brief oral report.

Music

Ask students to use a music encyclopedia or other source to find musical works based on Shakespeare's plays. (Examples: Tchaikovsky's *Romeo and Juliet,* Verdi's *Otello*) Students could present either brief oral summaries describing the literary and musical works or taped excerpts from a musical work with their own commentary.

Ⓐ Exploring the Historical Period

Death of a Queen

After ruling for almost a half century, Elizabeth was suffering from the infirmities of old age. The court moved to Richmond on January 21, 1603. On February 2, the Lord Chamberlain's Men traveled ten miles upriver in the bitter cold to perform one last time before their queen. It may be that *Hamlet* was the last play that Elizabeth saw. She died March 24 after naming James of Scotland her successor.

Ⓑ Exploring the Culture

Grooms of the Chamber

Becoming grooms of the royal chamber meant that the players were considered members of the royal household. This position did not guarantee them a fixed salary, as they were not usually in attendance. However, each man did receive four and a half yards of scarlet-red cloth for his livery from Sir George Home, Master of the Great Wardrobe. The costume was probably worn by the King's Men on public occasions. In addition, James rewarded the players generously at each performance. No troupe gave more performances before James than his own men. According to one calculation, they performed almost two hundred times between the issuance of the patents and the year of Shakespeare's death.

Ⓒ Literary Connections

Tragedies

Shakespeare was not the only writer to turn to tragedy at this time: Jonson wrote *Sejanus;* George Chapman was writing a series of French histories; Henslowe produced Chettle's *The Tragedy of Hoffman.*

Ⓓ Background

Edmund Shakespeare

Edmund was probably Shakespeare's youngest brother. He died in December, most likely of plague, and was buried in the church of St. Saviour's, a few hundred yards from the Globe.

Christopher Walken (top) and Raul Julia in *Othello,* New York Shakespeare Festival (1991).

wanted to see the merry, fat old knight Sir John Falstaff (of the Henry plays) in love.

Shakespeare prospered even more under Elizabeth's successor, King James of Scotland. Fortunately for Shakespeare's company, as it turned out, James's royal entry into London in 1603 had to be postponed for several months because the plague was raging in the city. While waiting for the epidemic to subside, the royal court stayed in various palaces outside London. Shakespeare's company took advantage of this situation and, since the city theaters were closed, performed several plays for the court and the new king. Shakespeare's plays delighted James, for he loved literature and was starved for pleasure after the grim experience of ruling Scotland for many years. He immediately took the company under his patronage, renamed them the King's Men, gave them patents to perform anywhere in the realm, provided them with special clothing for state occasions, increased their salaries, and appointed their chief members, including Shakespeare, to be grooms of the royal chamber. All this patronage brought such prosperity to Shakespeare that he was able to make some very profitable real estate investments in Stratford and London.

Shakespeare's "Tragic Period": Beyond Experience

In the early years of the seventeenth century, while his financial affairs were flourishing and everything was apparently going very well for him, Shakespeare wrote his greatest tragedies: *Hamlet* (already mentioned), *Othello* (1601–1602), *King Lear* (1605), *Macbeth* (1605–1606), and *Antony and Cleopatra* (1606–1607). Because these famous plays are so preoccupied with evil, violence, and death, some critics feel that Shakespeare must have been unhappy and depressed when he wrote them. Moreover, such critics find even the comedies he wrote at this time more sour than sweet: *All's Well That Ends Well* (1602–1603) and *Measure for Measure* (1604). And so, instead of paying tribute to Shakespeare's powerful imagination, which is everywhere evident, these critics invent a "tragic period" in Shakespeare's biography, and they search for personal crises in his private life. When they cannot find these agonies, they invent them. To be sure, in 1607, an actor named Edmund Shakespeare, who may well have been William's younger brother, died in London. But by 1607, Shakespeare's alleged "tragic period" was almost over.

It is quite wrong to assume a one-to-one

Glenn Close and Alan Bates in Franco Zeffirelli's film production of *Hamlet* (1990).

Skill Link

Creating Charts

Samuel Johnson (see p. 570), in his preface to his 1765 edition of Shakespeare's plays, identified Shakespeare as a realistic dramatist, mingling tragedy and comedy, laughter and tears. Nevertheless, for convenience' sake, Shakespeare's works are often classified as tragedies, comedies, or histories. You might ask a small group of students to prepare a master chart for the class, listing the plays in each category along with a one- or two-sentence summary of each play. Another group could use a film guide to chart which plays have been filmed, along with the date of production and a critic's rating of each film.

correspondence between writers' biographies and their works, because writers must be allowed to imagine whatever they can. It is especially wrong in the case of a writer like Shakespeare, who did not write to express himself but to satisfy the patrons of the theater that he and his partners owned. Shakespeare must have repeatedly given the audience just what it wanted; otherwise, he could not have made so much money from the theater. To insist that he had to experience and personally feel everything that he wrote about is absurd. He wrote about King Lear, who cursed his two monstrous daughters for treating him very badly; in contrast, what evidence there is suggests that he got along very well with his own two daughters. And so, instead of "tragic" we should think of the years 1600–1607 as glorious, because in them Shakespeare's productivity was at its peak. It seems very doubtful that a depressed person would write plays like these. In fact, they would likely make their creator feel exhilarated rather than sad. E

Denzel Washington in Kenneth Branagh's film production of *Much Ado About Nothing* (1993).

The Last Years: Continued Diversity

In about 1610, Shakespeare decided that, having made a considerable sum from his plays and theatrical enterprises, he would retire to his handsome house in Stratford, a place he had never forgotten, though he seems to have kept his life there rather separate from his life in London. His retirement was not complete, for the records show that after he returned to Stratford he still took part in the management of the King's Men and their two theaters: the Globe, an octagonal building opened in 1599 and used for performances in good weather, and the Blackfriars, acquired in 1608 and used for indoor performances. Shakespeare's works in this period show no signs of diminished creativity, except that in some years he wrote one play instead of the customary two, and they continue to illustrate the great diversity of his genius. Among them are the tragedies *Timon of Athens* (1607–1608) and *Coriolanus* (1607–1608) and five plays that have been variously classified as comedies, romances, or tragicomedies: *Pericles* (1607–1608), *Cymbeline* (1609–1610), *The Winter's Tale* (1610–1611), *The Tempest* (1611–1612), and *The Two Noble Kinsmen* (1612). His last English history play, *Henry VIII* (1613), contained a tribute to Queen Elizabeth—a somewhat tardy tribute, because, unlike most of the other poets of the day, Shakespeare did not praise her in print when she died in 1603. (Some scholars argue, on very little evidence, that he was an admirer of the earl of Essex, a former intimate of Elizabeth whom she had beheaded for rebellion.) F During the first performance of *Henry VIII,* in June of 1613, the firing of the cannon at the end

Kenneth Branagh in his film production of *Henry V* (1989). G

E Reading Skills and Strategies

Finding the Main Idea

Ask students to identify the main point the writer is making in this section. [Shakespeare's works are not a reflection of his private life but of his genius and desire to please his audience.]

F Exploring the Historical Period

Essex's Rebellion

Actually Shakespeare would have been more influenced by the fate of the Earl of Southampton, his patron. In 1601 Southampton was involved in Essex's treasonous plot to dethrone Elizabeth. Essex and Southampton were both tried and sentenced to death. However, Elizabeth was persuaded to commute Southampton's sentence to life imprisonment. He remained in prison for the duration of Elizabeth's reign.

G Background

Kenneth Branagh

Respected British actor Kenneth Branagh has produced and starred in film versions of several of Shakespeare's classics. These include *Henry V, Much Ado About Nothing,* and *Hamlet.* In these productions, Branagh has shared the screen with popular actors such as Denzel Washington and Michael Keaton.

Getting Students Involved

Cooperative Learning

Shakespeare on Magazine TV. Have students form small groups to produce and present a feature piece on William Shakespeare for a primetime magazine television show. Ask students to imagine that they can go back in time so they can interview Shakespeare and his contemporaries for their show. Each group may use this essay as a foundation and do additional research as necessary. They may choose to focus on one or more aspects of Shakespeare's life. Each person in the group should have one or more functions to perform as a member of the team. For example, one member might be a researcher as well as a performer. After the features have been completed, ask each group to present their piece to the class, either in person or on videotape.

Ⓐ Exploring the Culture

The Ballad of the Globe Fire

In Shakespeare's time, a **ballad** was any short verse piece, usually focusing on a single dramatic situation. A few days after the fire at the Globe, a ballad-maker gave the following account:

Out run the knights, out run the lords,
And there was great ado;
Some lost their hats, and some their swords,
Then out run Burbage, too.
The reprobates, though drunk on Monday,
Prayed for the fool and Henry Con-day [Condell, an actor].
O sorrow, pitiful sorrow, and yet all is true.

Ⓑ Background

Shakespeare's Monument

Within a few years of Shakespeare's death, a stone bust was sculpted and placed on the north wall of the chancel of Holy Trinity, a few yards from his grave. Pen in hand, the playwright looks up as he pauses in his writing.

Ⓒ Critical Thinking

Interpreting

Ask students to explain what McCarthy means by this simile. [Possible responses: Shakespeare does not reveal himself in his plays; rather he reveals universal truths about human nature.]

Ⓐ of Act I set the Globe on fire (it had a thatched roof), and it burned to the ground. Only one casualty is recorded: A bottle of ale had to be poured on a man whose breeches were burning. Fortunately, the company had the Blackfriars in which to perform until the Globe could be rebuilt and reopened in 1614.

Shakespeare's last recorded visit to London was made with his son-in-law Dr. John Hall in November 1614, though he may have gone down to the city afterward because he continued to own property there, including a building very near the Blackfriars Theater. Probably, though, he spent most of the last two years of his life at New Place, with his daughter Susanna Hall (and his granddaughter Elizabeth) living nearby. Ⓑ He died on April 23, 1616, and was buried under the floor of Stratford Church, with this epitaph warning posterity not to dig him up and transfer him to the graveyard outside the church—a common practice in those days to make room for newer corpses:

Good friend, for Jesus' sake forbear
To dig the dust enclosèd here!
Blest be the man that spares these stones,
And curst be he that moves my bones.

Patrick Stewart and Anjanue Ellis in *The Tempest,* New York Shakespeare Festival (1995).

Shakespeare's Genius: Imagination and "Soul"

What sort of man was Shakespeare? This is a very hard question to answer because he left no letters, diaries, or other private writings containing his personal views; instead, he left us plays, and in a good play the actors do not speak for the dramatist but for the characters they are impersonating. We cannot, then, say that Shakespeare approved of evil because he created murderers or advocated religion because he created clergymen; we cannot say that he believed in fatalism because he created fatalists, or admired flattery because he created flatterers. All these would be naive, contradictory reactions to the plays. Shakespeare's characters represent such a vast range of human behavior and attitudes that they must be products of his careful observation and fertile imagination rather than extensions of himself. Ⓒ A critic named Desmond McCarthy once said that trying to identify Shakespeare the man in his plays is like looking at a very dim portrait under glass: The more you peer at it, the more you see only yourself.

Trying to identify Shakespeare the man in his plays is like looking at a very dim portrait under glass: The more you peer at it, the more you see only yourself.

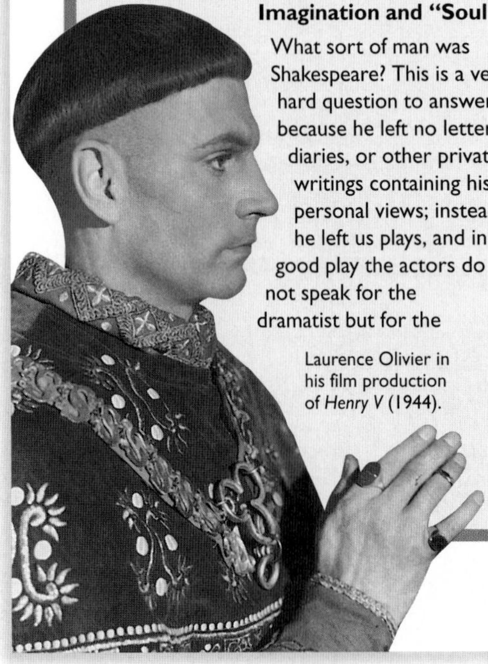

Laurence Olivier in his film production of *Henry V* (1944).

A Complete Man of the Theater

One thing is certain: Shakespeare was a complete man of the theater who created works specifically for his own acting company and his own stage. He had, for instance, to provide good parts in every play for the principal performers in the company, including the come-

Skill Link

Analyzing and Responding to a Critical Review

Read aloud this comment by Samuel Taylor Coleridge and ask students to discuss how it relates to the essay: "In the plays of Shakespeare every man sees himself, without knowing that he does so: as in some of the phenomena of nature, in the mist of the mountain, the traveller beholds his own figure, but the glory round the head distinguishes it from a mere vulgar copy. . . . So in Shakespeare: every form is true, everything has reality for its foundation; we can all recognize the truth, but we see it decorated with such hues of beauty, and magnified to such proportions of grandeur, that, while we know the figure, we know also how much it has been refined and exalted by the poet."

Mel Gibson in Franco Zeffirelli's film production of *Hamlet* (1990).

dians acting in tragedies. Since there were no actresses, he had to limit the number of female parts in his plays and create them in such a way that they could readily be taken by boys. For instance, although there are many fathers in the plays, there are very few mothers: While boys could be taught to flirt and play shy, acting maternally would be difficult for them. Several of Shakespeare's young women characters disguise themselves as young men early in Act I— an easy solution to the problem of boys playing girls' parts. Shakespeare also had to provide the words for songs because theatergoers expected singing in every play; furthermore, the songs had to be devised so that they would exhibit the talents of particular actors with good voices. Since many of the plays contain many characters, and since there were a limited number of actors in the company, Shakespeare had to arrange for doubling and even tripling of roles: That is, a single actor would have to perform more than one part. Since, of course, an actor could impersonate only one character at a time, Shakespeare had to plan his scenes carefully, so that nobody would ever have to be on stage in two different roles at the same time. A careful study of the plays shows that Shakespeare handled very masterfully all these technical problems of dramaturgy.

Never Out of Print

Although the plays are primarily performance scripts, from earliest times the public has wanted to read them as well as see them staged. In every generation, people have felt that the plays contain so much wisdom, so much knowledge of human nature, so much remarkable poetry that they need to be pondered in private as well as enjoyed in public. Most readers have agreed with what the poet John Dryden said about Shakespeare's "soul": The man who wrote the plays may be elusive, but he was obviously a great genius whose lofty imagination is matched by his sympathy for all

Dear Miss Disdain (Beatrice from *Much Ado About Nothing*) (late 18th to early 19th century) by Louise Jopling.

D Exploring the Historical Period

Women on Stage

Records indicate that a woman played Desdemona in *Othello* by late 1660. After this, women's roles slowly began to be played by actresses rather than boys. By the end of the seventeenth century, actresses such as Nell Gwyn, Katherine Corey, and Elizabeth Barry had established themselves as masterful interpreters of major theatrical roles.

E Background

Multiple Roles

Shakespeare's company was thought to have had about twelve adult members and four boy apprentices. For *King Richard III,* with a cast of more than forty, the actors certainly had their work cut out for them.

F Cultural Connections

Reading vs. Seeing

Most readers today need annotated editions of the plays to help them with Shakespeare's use of now-archaic vocabulary, elevated language, and words whose definitions have changed. For some people, these problems are at least partially resolved when they watch a good performance, since the actor's gestures, phrasing, and intonation help convey the meaning. (Students may benefit from studying "Shakespeare's Language," pp. 399–402, before reading *Macbeth.*)

G Critical Thinking

Making Connections

Ask students how Dryden's point of view mirrors the one expressed by Desmond McCarthy on p. 294. [McCarthy believes that instead of revealing himself in his plays, Shakespeare reveals universal truths about nature. Here Dryden also indicates that the man himself is "elusive," but his "sympathy for all kinds of human behavior" is obvious.]

Ⓐ Exploring the Culture

Publishing Plays

This secrecy surrounding the scripts was well founded: Even without printed versions, some of Shakespeare's plays were pirated, including *King Henry VI* and *King Henry V*. However, the pirated versions, recorded by imperfect memory, in no way lived up to the originals.

Ⓑ Background

Quartos

A quarto, about nine by twelve inches, is one quarter the size of a standard printing sheet. The first of Shakespeare's plays to be printed in quarto size was *Titus Andronicus* in 1594, and by his death, about half of his plays had been published as quartos. Unfortunately, some contained significant printing errors and were thus called "bad quartos." One bad quarto of *Hamlet* called Polonius "Corambis" and produced this faulty version of Hamlet's famous soliloquy:

> To be, or not to be, I there's the point,
> To die, to sleep, is that all? I all:
> No, to sleepe, to dreame, I mary there it goes . . .

Ⓒ Background

The First Folio

This collection was assembled by actors John Hemings and Henry Condell and printed in the summer of 1623 at William Jaggard's busy shop. Jaggard printed a thousand copies of the attractive volume, of which two hundred have survived. The first folio is considered the most reliable text for the thirty-six plays it includes. (A folio—the word is related to the word *fold*—is one half the size of a standard printing sheet.)

Glenn Close and Mel Gibson in Franco Zeffirelli's film production of *Hamlet* (1990).

kinds of human behavior. Reading the plays, then, is a rewarding experience in itself; it is also an excellent preparation for seeing them performed on stage or on film.

Shakespeare's contemporaries were so eager to read his plays that enterprising publishers did everything possible, including stealing them, to make them available. Of course, the company generally tried to keep the plays unpublished because they did not want them performed by rival companies. Even so, eighteen plays were published in small books called quartos before Shakespeare's partners collected them together and published them after his death. This collection, known as the "first folio" because of its large size, was published in 1623. Surviving copies of this folio are regarded as valuable treasures today. But, of course, the general reader need not consult any of the original texts of Shakespeare because his works never go out of print; they are always available in many different languages and many different formats. The plays that exist in two different versions (one in a quarto and one in the folio) have provided scholars with endless matter for speculation about what Shakespeare actually intended the correct text to be. Indeed, every aspect of Shakespeare has been, and continues to be, thoroughly studied and written about by literary and historical scholars, theater and film people, experts in many fields, and amateurs of every stripe. No wonder that he is mistakenly regarded as a great mystery.

JOSEPH PAPP PRESENTS
RICHARD III
AUGUST 3–SEPTEMBER 2, 1990
DELACORTE THEATER CENTRAL PARK

Poster featuring Denzel Washington in *Richard III* at the New York Shakespeare Festival (1990).

Laurence Olivier and Anna Calder-Marshall in the Mobil Showcase Network production of *King Lear* (1984).

Assessing Learning

Check Test: Questions and Answers

1. Where was Shakespeare born? [Stratford-on-Avon]
2. Who were the two monarchs of England before whom Shakespeare's company performed? [Elizabeth I and James I]
3. What step did Shakespeare take to become one of the "gentlefolk"? [He had his father obtain a coat of arms.]
4. What did the second monarch do for Shakespeare and his company? [He gave them patents to perform anywhere in the realm and made them grooms of the royal chamber.]
5. What kinds of plays did Shakespeare write? [tragedies, comedies, and histories]

The Tragedy of Macbeth: The Sources of the Play

D Orson Welles in his film production of *Macbeth* (1948).

RESPONDING TO THE ART

Orson Welles's movie *Macbeth* is full of powerful visual images. **Activity.** Ask students to discuss the face in this photograph. In what ways could it show "a man in time and timelessness"? [Possible answer: The face could be from any century and conveys emotions that are universal, yet the man is dressed in a style that indicates a particular time.]

D Background

Orson Welles's *Macbeth*

An unorthodox and innovative actor, Orson Welles made a name for himself in radio drama and the theater during the 1930s. His first film, *Citizen Kane* (1941), is considered by many to be a cinematic masterpiece. In 1998 the film placed number one on the American Film Institute's list of the top one hundred American movies. For his film version of *Macbeth,* Welles used many stylized, melodramatic effects. His concept of the play's theme, presented at the beginning of the movie, was that it presents the "agents of Chaos, priests of hell and magic" manipulating human ambition against "Christian law and order." To highlight this concept, Welles created a new character, a monk, to act as a foil for the witches. Welles took many liberties with Shakespeare's script—giving the newly created monk lines borrowed from Ross and other minor characters, rearranging scenes, and cutting dialogue to speed up the action. Welles called the film a "violently sketched drawing of a great play."

Skill Link

Analyzing and Responding to a Critical Review

Critic Edgar Stoll offers the following thoughts about the changes Shakespeare made: "If . . . Shakespeare had . . . followed Holinshed—made more of Macbeth's grievances, dilated on Duncan's unfitness and his own fitness to rule, without bringing on his head the blood of an old man, asleep, his benefactor and guest! If he had not dwelt on reasons for committing instead of not committing the crime! And if afterwards he had expressed the psychologically natural or appropriate opinions upon his own conduct, excusing or palliating it, perhaps even justifying it! If in short Macbeth . . . had acted more like the human beings we know of; why, then we should have had decidedly less of contrast and excitement, of imagination and emotional power generated and discharged, of poetry and drama." Ask students if they agree with this opinion.

A Literary Connections

Additional Sources

Some critics believe that Shakespeare consulted Buchanan's *History of Scotland* because elements of Macbeth's characterization are more similar to this account than they are to Holinshed's. Other possible sources include Seneca's *Medea* and Aeschylus's *Agamemnon*.

B Exploring the Historical Period

The Gunpowder Plot

An account by Nicolo Molin in the Venetian State Papers tells how the Gunpowder Plot was discovered: "About two months ago Lord Salisbury received anonymous letters from France, warning him to be on his guard, for a great conspiracy was being hatched by priests and Jesuits. . . . Lord Mounteagle read the letter and, in great astonishment took it to the Earl of Salisbury, who at once carried it to the King. . . . Meantime, the King read the letter and in terrified amaze he said 'I remember that my father died by gunpowder. I see the letter says the blow is to be struck on a sudden. Search the basements of the meeting place.'"

C Critical Thinking

Making Connections

Ask students to think of modern movie thrillers that could be comparable in atmosphere to *Macbeth*.

[Answers will vary, depending on the movies that are popular when students read the play.]

RESPONDING TO THE ART

There have been many great Shakespearean actresses. A theatergoer once said of Sarah Kemble Siddons's Lady Macbeth: "Well, sir, I smelt blood! I swear that I smelt blood." Ellen Terry was a famous British actress of the nineteenth century, who started at the age of eight in a theatrical performance of a Shakespeare play.

Activity Compare this Lady Macbeth with the one on p. 370.

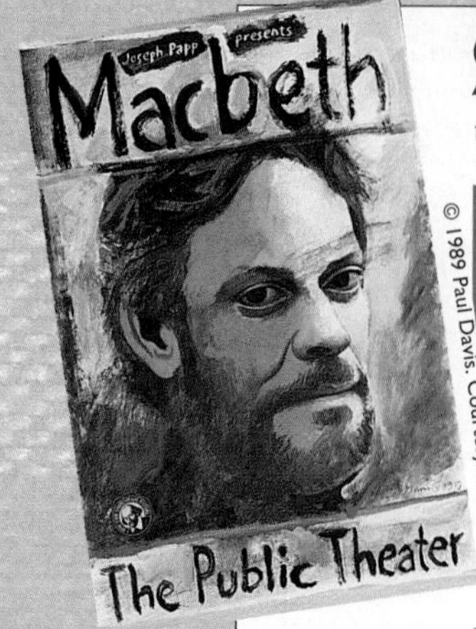

Joseph Papp presents
Macbeth
The Public Theater

© 1989 Paul Davis. Courtesy of the artist.

Poster for *Macbeth*, featuring Raul Julia, at the Public Theater, New York (1990).

Shakespeare's play *Macbeth* conforms to the general rule of Renaissance tragedies, in which the drama had to be about real people whose deeds are recorded in history. (Renaissance comedies, on the other hand, concerned the imaginary doings of fictitious characters.) Shakespeare took the main events of Macbeth's career as king of Scotland (1040–1057) from Raphael Holinshed's *Chronicles of England, Scotland, and Ireland* (1577), the book that provided Shakespeare with historical material for many of his plays. But there are striking differences between his account of Macbeth and Holinshed's. The historical A Macbeth had a much more legitimate claim to King Duncan's throne than Shakespeare's Macbeth did. The historical Macbeth gained the throne with the help of other nobles dissatisfied with King Duncan, and he ruled rather successfully. In contrast, Shakespeare's Macbeth has no supporters except his wife, whose strong and ambitious nature Shakespeare develops from a brief statement in the history. And in the play, the reign of Macbeth and his wife brings nothing but violence and disaster to Scotland.

A witch placing a crown on Macbeth's head in the Faux-Real production of *Htebcam* (1994) ("Macbeth" spelled backward).

One explanation for these changes to Holinshed's story is that Shakespeare wanted to explore—from a safe distance—the events and attitudes of his own time. Contemporary audiences have all but lost sight of the scandal that was a backdrop for the play: the Gunpowder Plot of 1605, in B which several Catholic zealots plotted to blow up King James I and his Protestant Parliament. Garry Wills, a professor and political columnist, says that for its Elizabethan audience, *Macbeth* was a C thriller. (For Wills, the Gunpowder Plot would compare to a plan to bomb the U.S. Capitol building during a presidential address.) The threat to an anointed king, and the perceived evil behind it, was relived in Macbeth's complete threat to the social order in a Scotland of the distant past.

Shakespeare altered his source text, in ways both small and large, in order to pay homage to his own king and country; his changes were

Ellen Terry as Lady Macbeth (detail) (1888–1889) by John Singer Sargent. Tate Gallery, London.

Crossing the Curriculum

History

Have students brainstorm questions they would like to ask about the real Macbeth and Duncan. The questions might include: Why were the nobles dissatisfied with Duncan's rule? What had the real Duncan done to Macbeth's father and Lady Macbeth's grandfather, brother, and first husband? What was Macbeth's claim to the throne? What kind of ruler was he? How did his reign end? Students should report their findings to the class.

Dramatic Arts

Have students work in small groups to select and research a twentieth-century, tragic political event in order to write a short play about it. Each group will need researchers, script writers, actors, and a director. The play should be a tragic thriller, as *Macbeth* was to the Renaissance audience. Have each group perform its play for the class.

The three witches in Roman Polanski's film production of *Macbeth* (1971).

intended for an audience of his *particular* moment in history. If he ever saw it, *Macbeth* must have pleased King James, the patron of Shakespeare's company. Since James had recently survived the Gunpowder Plot, he was especially interested in attacks on kings. James always defended the idea that he ruled by divine right. Moreover, he was a Scot and claimed to be a direct descendant of Banquo, to whom the third witch says, "Thou shalt get kings, though thou be none." For these reasons, scholars have for a long time thought of *Macbeth* as a play written for a command performance at court, though there is absolutely no proof that it was. James refused to sit through long plays, and this royal shortcoming has even been used to explain the fact that *Macbeth* is one of Shakespeare's shortest plays.

We can also say that Shakespeare made many changes in Holinshed's story because he was much more interested in psychological truth than in historical fact. And in this sense, *Macbeth* is also about *real* people, men and women tempted by ambition and power, caught up in a web of wants and needs. In playing out these real feelings and desires, Shakespeare's Macbeth transcends the historical Macbeth and gives us a portrait and a play for all times. As the critic Sylvan Barnet notes, "When one reads or sees *Macbeth,* one cannot help feeling that one is experiencing a re-creation or representation of what a man is, in the present, even in the timeless."

The Banquet (detail) by an unknown artist, from Act III, Scene 4, of *Macbeth* at London's Princess Theatre (1853).

Victoria and Albert Museum, London.

D Background

King James, the Writer

King James I, for whom *Macbeth* may have been written, was a writer himself. Two of his favorite subjects were his own ancestry and witchcraft, both of which play a prominent part in the play.

E Background

Inspiration for *Macbeth*

During a visit to Oxford in August 1606, King James saw a show that featured three sibyls reciting Latin verses containing prophesies to Banquo, James's forebear and the founder of the house of Stuart. The entertainment greatly pleased James. About six weeks later, Shakespeare and his company came to Oxford. Some scholars believe that Shakespeare heard of the king's favorable reaction to the entertainment and decided to write a play about Macbeth and Banquo to please his new monarch.

F Exploring the Historical Period

Lady Macbeth

The historical Lady Macbeth's first name, as reported in the 1909 British Isles edition of *The Dictionary of National Biography,* was Gruach.

Professional Notes

Aristotle on Tragedy

Basing his analysis of tragedy on Greek drama of the fifth century B.C., Aristotle wrote, "Tragedy is an imitation of some action that is important, entire, and of a proper magnitude, by language embellished and rendered pleasurable, . . . in the way not of narration, but of action, effecting through pity and terror the refinement of such passions."

OBJECTIVES

1. Read and interpret the drama
2. Analyze tragedy
3. Identify and analyze imagery and figurative language
4. Identify and interpret blank verse
5. Determine meanings through mapping
6. Express understanding through writing, oral interpretation, and art

SKILLS

Literary
- Analyze tragedy
- Analyze imagery and figurative language

Reading
- Identify and interpret blank verse
- Determine meanings through mapping

Writing
- Collect ideas for a cause-and-effect essay
- Analyze a character
- Analyze the writer's purpose
- Analyze tragedy
- Update a scene

Speaking/Listening
- Perform a soliloquy

Art
- Sketch the set and costumes for one or more scenes

Planning

- **Block Schedule**
  Block Scheduling Lesson Plans with Pacing Guide
- **Traditional Schedule**
  Lesson Plans Including Strategies for English-Language Learners
- **One-Stop Planner**
  CD-ROM with Test Generator

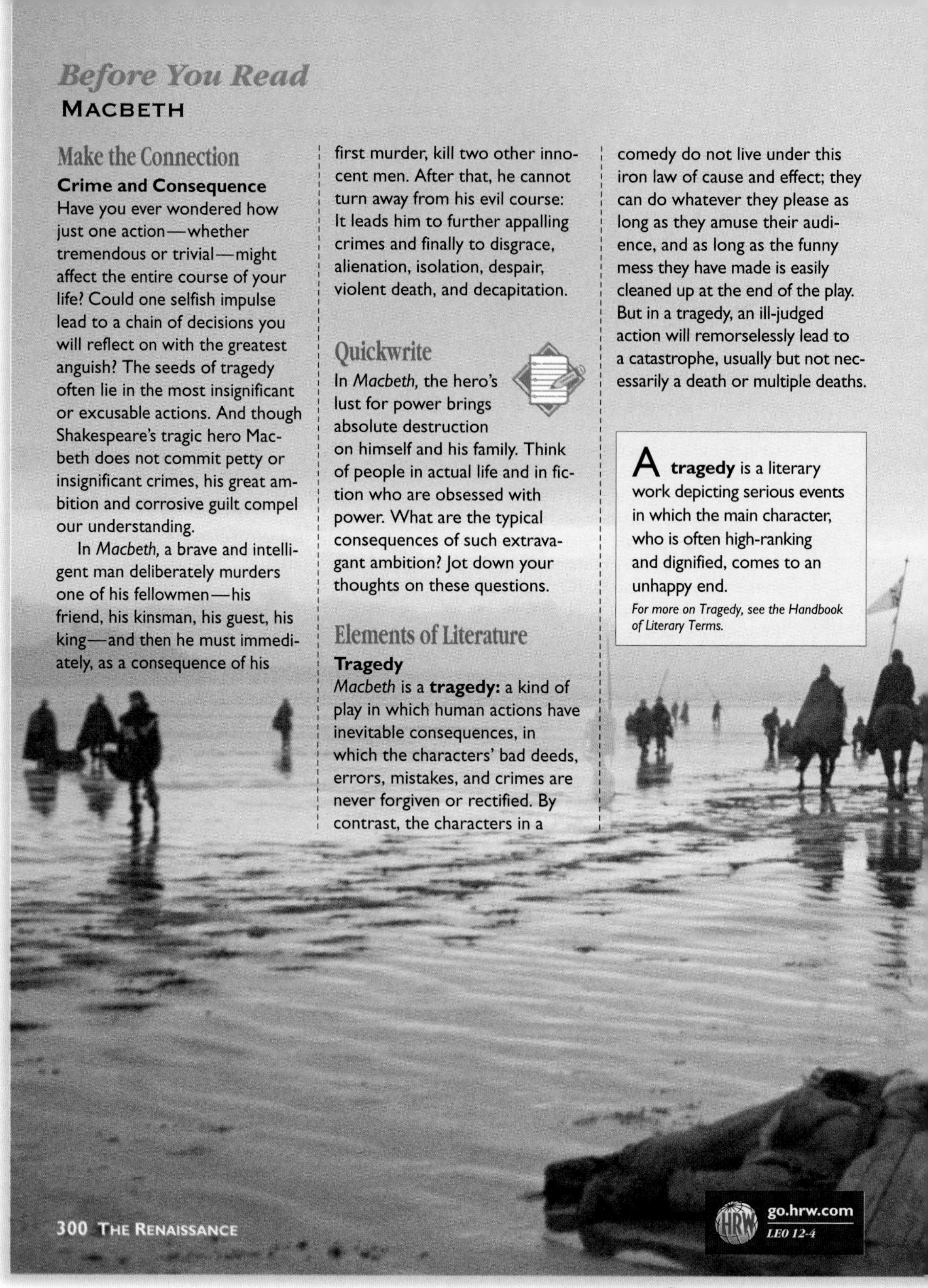

Before You Read
MACBETH

Make the Connection
Crime and Consequence

Have you ever wondered how just one action—whether tremendous or trivial—might affect the entire course of your life? Could one selfish impulse lead to a chain of decisions you will reflect on with the greatest anguish? The seeds of tragedy often lie in the most insignificant or excusable actions. And though Shakespeare's tragic hero Macbeth does not commit petty or insignificant crimes, his great ambition and corrosive guilt compel our understanding.

In *Macbeth,* a brave and intelligent man deliberately murders one of his fellowmen—his friend, his kinsman, his guest, his king—and then he must immediately, as a consequence of his first murder, kill two other innocent men. After that, he cannot turn away from his evil course: It leads him to further appalling crimes and finally to disgrace, alienation, isolation, despair, violent death, and decapitation.

Quickwrite
In *Macbeth,* the hero's lust for power brings absolute destruction on himself and his family. Think of people in actual life and in fiction who are obsessed with power. What are the typical consequences of such extravagant ambition? Jot down your thoughts on these questions.

Elements of Literature
Tragedy

Macbeth is a **tragedy:** a kind of play in which human actions have inevitable consequences, in which the characters' bad deeds, errors, mistakes, and crimes are never forgiven or rectified. By contrast, the characters in a comedy do not live under this iron law of cause and effect; they can do whatever they please as long as they amuse their audience, and as long as the funny mess they have made is easily cleaned up at the end of the play. But in a tragedy, an ill-judged action will remorselessly lead to a catastrophe, usually but not necessarily a death or multiple deaths.

A **tragedy** is a literary work depicting serious events in which the main character, who is often high-ranking and dignified, comes to an unhappy end.

For more on Tragedy, see the Handbook of Literary Terms.

go.hrw.com
LEO 12-4

Resources: Print and Media

Reading
- *Graphic Organizers for Active Reading,* pp. 26, 27, 28, 29, 30
- *Words to Own,* p. 9
- *Audio CD Library*
  Disc 5, Tracks 2, 3, 4

Elements of Literature
- *Literary Elements*
  Transparency 11
  Worksheet, p. 34

Writing and Language
- *Daily Oral Grammar*
  Transparencies 10, 11
- *Grammar and Language Links*
  Worksheets, pp. 19, 21

Viewing and Representing
- *Viewing and Representing*
  Fine Art Transparency 4
  Fine Art Worksheet, p. 16
- *Visual Connections*
  Videocassette B, Segment 6

Assessment
- *Formal Assessment,* pp. 57, 59, 61, 63, 65
- *Portfolio Management System,* p. 124
- *Preparation for College Admission Exams,* p. 15
- *Test Generator (One-Stop Planner* CD-ROM*)*

Internet
- go.hrw.com (keyword: LEO 12-4)

The Tragedy of Macbeth

William Shakespeare

CHARACTERS

Duncan, king of Scotland
Malcolm, **Donalbain** — his sons
Macbeth, **Banquo**, **Macduff**, **Lennox**, **Ross**, **Menteith**, **Angus**, **Caithness** — noblemen of Scotland
Fleance, son to Banquo
Siward, earl of Northumberland, general of the English forces
Young Siward, his son
Seyton, an officer attending on Macbeth
Son to Macduff
An English Doctor
A Scottish Doctor
A Porter
An Old Man
Three Murderers
Lady Macbeth
Lady Macduff
A Gentlewoman attending on Lady Macbeth
Hecate
Witches
Apparitions
Lords, Officers, Soldiers, Attendants, and Messengers

Setting: Scotland; England

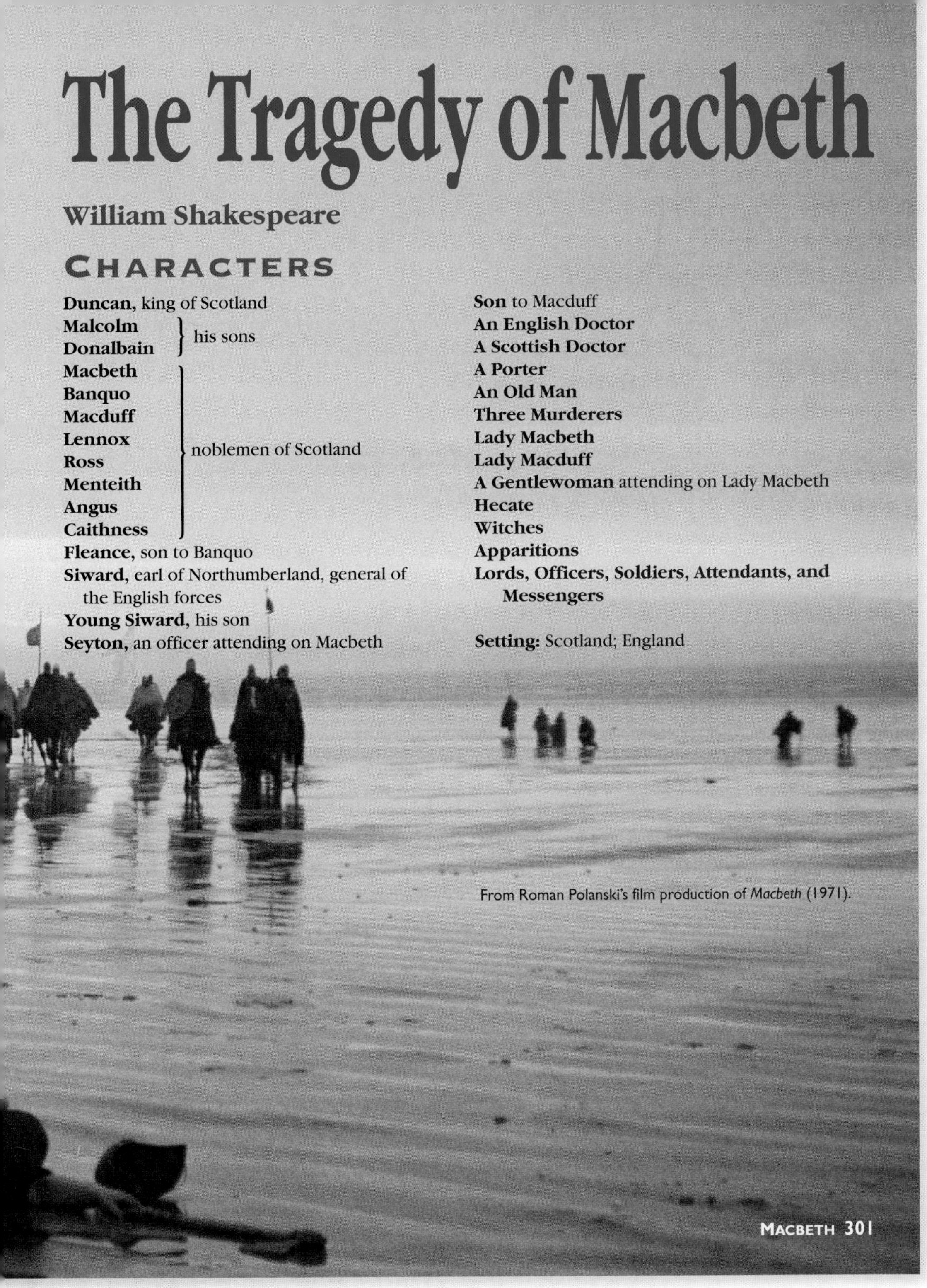

From Roman Polanski's film production of *Macbeth* (1971).

Summary ■■■

Overview: As the play begins, Macbeth is a noble and valiant captain who loyally serves King Duncan of Scotland. However, Macbeth's ambition soon makes him hunger for greater power. Provoked by his equally ambitious wife and encouraged by the prophecies of three witches, Macbeth murders Duncan and becomes king. Macbeth kills his former comrade-in-arms, Banquo, because he fears that Banquo suspects what he has done. Macbeth attempts to scare another perceived threat, Macduff, by slaughtering the nobleman's family. Driven mad by guilt, Lady Macbeth commits suicide, while Macbeth continues desperately along a course of destruction. Macduff and his supporters successfully besiege Macbeth's castle. After Macduff slays Macbeth, Duncan's son Malcolm is proclaimed king.

Background

Basing his work on Greek drama of the fifth century B.C., Aristotle noted the elements necessary to a tragedy, which in turn, influenced the Elizabethan interpretation of tragedy. Aristotle wrote that tragedy centers on a hero, generally of high status, who possesses a weakness, or tragic flaw, that ultimately causes the character's downfall. The catastrophe and its resolution leave the audience with a sense of catharsis, or cleansing.

Summary

Scene 1: Three cackling witches plan to meet Macbeth on the heath as he returns from battle.

Scene 2: A captain reports to King Duncan of Scotland that Macbeth has killed the traitor Macdonwald in battle. Another lord reports that Macbeth and Banquo have forced the invading Norwegians to surrender. Unknown to Macbeth, Duncan condemns to death the present Thane of Cawdor for treason and awards Macbeth his title.

Resources

Viewing and Representing

Videocassette B, Segment 6

Available in English and Spanish

This segment presents excerpts from plays that illustrate the classic tragic hero. For full lesson plans and worksheets, see *Visual Connections Teacher's Manual.*

Fine Art Transparency

The transparency of the 1911 poster for *Macbeth* by Edmund Dulac captures the dark, foreboding atmosphere of the play. See the *Viewing and Representing Transparencies and Worksheets:*

- Transparency 4
- Worksheet, p. 16

A Elements of Literature

Theme

? This rhymed couplet is the witches' most famous utterance. What theme does it introduce? [Appearances are deceiving; good and evil become blurred.]

Answers to Margin Questions

Line 2. They might gesture threateningly, cackle sinisterly, and wear ragged costumes and hideous makeup.

Line 7. The captain would gasp from weakness but speak urgently to convey the good news.

ACT I **Scene 1.** *An open place.*

Thunder and lightning. Enter three WITCHES.

First Witch.
When shall we three meet again?
In thunder, lightning, or in rain?

Second Witch.
When the hurlyburly's done,
When the battle's lost and won.

Third Witch.
That will be ere the set of sun.

First Witch.
Where the place?

Second Witch. Upon the heath.

Third Witch.
There to meet with Macbeth.

First Witch.
I come, Graymalkin.°

Second Witch.
Paddock° calls.

Third Witch. Anon!°

All.
Fair is foul, and foul is fair.
Hover through the fog and filthy air. [*Exeunt.*]

Scene 2. *A camp.*

Alarum within.° *Enter* KING DUNCAN, MALCOLM, DONALBAIN, LENNOX, *with* ATTENDANTS, *meeting a bleeding* CAPTAIN.

King.
What bloody man is that? He can report,
As seemeth by his plight, of the revolt
The newest state.

Malcolm. This is the sergeant
Who like a good and hardy soldier fought
'Gainst my captivity. Hail, brave friend!
Say to the king the knowledge of the broil°
As thou didst leave it.

Captain. Doubtful it stood,
As two spent swimmers, that do cling together
And choke their art.° The merciless Macdonwald—
Worthy to be a rebel for to that
The multiplying villainies of nature
Do swarm upon him—from the Western Isles°
Of kerns and gallowglasses° is supplied;
And Fortune, on his damnèd quarrel smiling,
Showed like a rebel's whore: but all's too weak:
For brave Macbeth—well he deserves that name—
Disdaining Fortune, with his brandished steel,

? **2.** *This scene, played against thunder and lightning, sets the mood of the play. The witches might have made their appearance through the trapdoor on the stage. Thunder would have been produced by rolling cannonballs in the area above the stage. How could these actresses (actors in Shakespeare's day) convey a sense of menace?*

8. Graymalkin: the witches' attendant, a gray cat.

9. Paddock: toad. **Anon!:** Soon!

Alarum within: trumpets offstage.

6. broil: quarrel.

? **7.** *The captain is bloody and could be carried in or supported by others. How would he speak his lines?*

9. choke their art: hinder each other's ability to swim.

12. Western Isles: a region of West Scotland comprising the Outer Hebrides.

13. kerns and gallowglasses: lightly armed Irish soldiers and heavily armed soldiers.

Reaching All Students

Struggling Readers

To help students gain an understanding of the plot, have them do a retelling of each scene. Make sure their summaries include the main events and characters. Events should be presented in chronological order. Model a retelling of the first scene to help students understand the strategy. For help in applying this strategy, see the *Reading Strategies Handbook,* p. 69, in the *Reading Skills* and *Strategies* binder.

English Language Learners

Students may benefit from reading the essay "Shakespeare's Language" (pp. 399–402) before reading *Macbeth.* For other strategies for engaging English language learners with the literature, see

- *Lesson Plans Including Strategies for English-Language Learners*

Advanced Learners

As students read the play, ask them to compare it to other plays, stories, or movies in which ambition leads a character astray. Have students consider the following: the nature of the ambition, the actions taken by the character to satisfy this ambition, the influence of other characters, the outcome, and the underlying theme.

From the Stratford Festival production of *Macbeth* (1983).

"What bloody man is that?"

Which smoked with bloody execution, **B**
Like valor's minion° carved out his passage
Till he faced the slave;
Which nev'r shook hands, nor bade farewell to him, **C**
Till he unseamed him from the nave to th' chops,°
And fixed his head upon our battlements.

King.
O valiant cousin! Worthy gentleman!

Captain.
As whence the sun 'gins his reflection°
Shipwracking storms and direful thunders break,
So from that spring whence comfort seemed to come **D**
Discomfort swells. Mark, King of Scotland, mark:
No sooner justice had, with valor armed,
Compelled these skipping kerns to trust their heels
But the Norweyan° lord, surveying vantage,°
With furbished arms and new supplies of men,
Began a fresh assault. **E**

King. Dismayed not this
Our captains, Macbeth and Banquo?

19. minion: favorite.

22. unseamed . . . chops: split him from navel to jaws.

? **23.** *Notice how this horrible action is described by a messenger, not shown on stage. What did Macbeth do to the rebellious Macdonwald?*

25. 'gins his reflection: rises.

31. Norweyan: Norwegian. **surveying vantage:** seeing an opportunity.

B Elements of Literature

Imagery

Blood is mentioned more than one hundred times in the play. As they read, ask students to think about its significance as an image and to consider whether it has different meanings at different points in the drama.

C Elements of Literature

Tragedy

? In what way does the description of Macbeth and his deeds conform to the definition of a tragic hero? [Macbeth is loyal, courageous, and overcomes great odds in battle.]

D Elements of Literature

Paradox

A **paradox** is an apparent contradiction that on closer inspection is actually true. Ask how this paradox relates to the witches' statement "Fair is foul, and foul is fair" in I.1.10. [The witches' statement is also a paradox: What is seemingly good turns out to be bad. The paradox in I.1.27–28 indicates that a place of comfort actually breeds discomfort.]

E Reading Skills and Strategies

Making Predictions

? Based on what you know about Macbeth so far, how do you think he will react to the new assault? [Possible responses: He will be unfazed; or, he may be hesitant but will fight anyway.]

Answer to Margin Question

Line 23. Macbeth slashed Macdonwald from navel to jaws, beheaded him, and stuck the head on top of the castle wall.

Skill Link

Understanding Textual References

Review the elements of a play script, such as the cast of characters, stage direction, and dialogue, and point out where each appears on the page. Explain that plays are often divided into acts and scenes and that line numbers may appear in script margins to help orient readers. Then, open to the first page of *Macbeth* and point out the act and scene labels and line numbers. Explain that when a line of dialogue appears directly after the speaker's name, not on a separate line, it is called a split line and is not counted as a separate line. Next, tell students they can write the act, scene, and line numbers in a kind of abbreviation when referring to specific lines or scenes in their writing and discussions. In these abbreviated references, the act number always appears first (in capital Roman numerals); the scene number, second (in Arabic numerals in this text, though lowercase Roman numerals are used in some texts); and the line number(s), third (in Arabic numerals).

Read aloud the following references. Ask students to locate each reference and copy the line of dialogue.

I.1.10 ["Fair is foul, and foul is fair."]
I.2.67 ["What he hath lost, noble Macbeth hath won."]
I.7.46–47 ["I dare do all that may become a man/Who dares do more is none."]

Now, ask students to write the abbreviated references for the king's first line on this page. [I.2.24, stands for Act I, Scene 2, Line 24.]

A Reading Skills and Strategies
Responding to the Text

? What are your first impressions of Macbeth? [Sample responses: He is a brave and intimidating soldier who is defending Scotland from rebellion and invasion; or, he is a barbaric soldier whose vicious tactics are disturbing.]

B Appreciating Language
Word Choice

? In what way does the word choice in these lines highlight the mood? [Possible response: Each of the lines ends with a forbidding phrase—*terrible numbers, disloyal traitor, dismal conflict*—that serves to increase the ominous mood in this scene.]

C Reading Skills and Strategies
Drawing Conclusions

? Why does Duncan give the title Thane of Cawdor to Macbeth? [Macbeth has just taken the lead role in saving the country from internal and external attack. A new title is an appropriate reward.]

D Critical Thinking
Making Connections

? How might this line relate to I.1.4? [A title has been both lost and won in the battle.]

Answers to Margin Questions

Line 35. Possible responses: The captain is speaking ironically and is saying that Macbeth and Banquo were *not* daunted by the new assault; or, he is speaking in an admiring tone.

Line 44. Students may come to see Duncan as overly trusting and naive.

Line 67. Possible response: Enthusiastically; the king is proud to bestow this honor on Macbeth.

Captain. Yes;
As° sparrows eagles, or the hare the lion.
If I say sooth,° I must report they were
As cannons overcharged with double cracks;
So they doubly redoubled strokes upon the foe.
Except° they meant to bathe in reeking wounds,
Or memorize another Golgotha,°
I cannot tell—
But I am faint; my gashes cry for help.

King.
So well thy words become thee as thy wounds;
They smack of honor both. Go get him surgeons.
[*Exit* CAPTAIN *attended.*]

[*Enter* ROSS *and* ANGUS.]

Who comes here?

Malcolm. The worthy Thane° of Ross.

Lennox.
What a haste looks through his eyes! So should he look
That seems to° speak things strange.

Ross. God save the king!

King.
Whence cam'st thou, worthy thane?

Ross. From Fife, great king;
Where the Norweyan banners flout the sky
And fan our people cold.
Norway himself,° with terrible numbers,
Assisted by that most disloyal traitor
The Thane of Cawdor, began a dismal conflict;
Till that Bellona's bridegroom,° lapped in proof,°
Confronted him with self-comparisons,°
Point against point, rebellious arm 'gainst arm,
Curbing his lavish° spirit: and, to conclude,
The victory fell on us.

King. Great happiness!

Ross. That now
Sweno, the Norways' king, craves composition;°
Nor would we deign him burial of his men
Till he disbursèd, at Saint Colme's Inch,°
Ten thousand dollars to our general use.

King.
No more that Thane of Cawdor shall deceive
Our bosom interest:° go pronounce his present° death,
And with his former title greet Macbeth.

Ross.
I'll see it done.

King.
What he hath lost, noble Macbeth hath won. [*Exeunt.*]

35. As: No more than.

? 35. *This line can be delivered in several ways. How do you imagine the captain speaks it?*

36. sooth: truth.

39. Except: unless.

40. memorize another Golgotha: make the place as memorable as Golgotha, where Christ was crucified.

? 44. *Duncan can be played in several ways: as a strong but aging king; as a frail old man; as a kind but foolish old man who doesn't understand what's going on. As the play goes on, decide how you interpret Duncan's character.*

45. Thane: Scottish title of nobility.

47. seems to: seems about to.

51. Norway himself: that is, the king of Norway.

54. Bellona's bridegroom: Bellona is the goddess of war. Macbeth, who is a great soldier, is called her mate. **lapped in proof:** clad in armor.

55. self-comparisons: countermovements.

57. lavish: insolent; rude.

59. composition: peace terms.

61. Saint Colme's Inch: island off the coast of Scotland.

64. bosom interest: heart's trust. **present:** immediate.

? 67. *As you read, notice how later events relate to the king's words. How would you have him say these lines?*

Skill Link

Using Context Clues

Context often provides clues to the meaning of unfamiliar words: (1) the unfamiliar word might be defined in an appositive, as in "Sweno, the Norway's king"; (2) words with similar or contrasting meanings might point to the word's definition, as in "fair is foul, and foul is fair"; (3) the sentences surrounding the unfamiliar word might give a clue.

Activity

Ask students to choose three words from Act I whose meaning they are unsure of and to use the context to guess at the meaning of each. Have them check their guesses in a dictionary.

Scene 3. *A heath.*

Thunder. Enter the three WITCHES.

First Witch.
Where hast thou been, sister?
Second Witch.
Killing swine.
Third Witch.
Sister, where thou?
First Witch.
A sailor's wife had chestnuts in her lap,
And mounched, and mounched, and mounched. "Give me,"
quoth I.
"Aroint thee,° witch!" the rump-fed ronyon° cries.
Her husband's to Aleppo gone, master o' th' *Tiger:*
But in a sieve° I'll thither sail,
And, like a rat without a tail,
I'll do, I'll do, and I'll do.
Second Witch.
I'll give thee a wind.
First Witch.
Th' art kind.
Third Witch.
And I another.
First Witch.
I myself have all the other;
And the very ports they blow,°
All the quarters that they know
I' th' shipman's card.°
I'll drain him dry as hay:
Sleep shall neither night nor day
Hang upon his penthouse lid;°
He shall live a man forbid:°
Weary sev'nights nine times nine
Shall he dwindle, peak,° and pine:
Though his bark cannot be lost,
Yet it shall be tempest-tossed.
Look what I have.
Second Witch.
Show me, show me.
First Witch.
Here I have a pilot's thumb,
Wracked as homeward he did come.

[*Drum within.*]

Third Witch.
A drum, a drum!
Macbeth doth come.

6. Aroint thee: begone.
rump-fed ronyon: fat-rumped, scabby creature.

8. But . . . sieve: Witches were believed to have the power to sail in sieves.

15. ports they blow: harbors they blow into.

17. card: compass.

20. penthouse lid: eyelid.
21. forbid: cursed.

23. peak: grow pale.

Summary

Scene 3: Macbeth and Banquo meet the three witches, who make three predictions: that Macbeth will be Thane of Cawdor; that Macbeth will be king; and that Banquo will beget kings. Ross and Angus, two noblemen, arrive to tell Macbeth he has been made Thane of Cawdor. The news causes Macbeth to take the witches' prophecies seriously, and he begins to consider murdering King Duncan.

E Historical Connections

Witchcraft

In the seventeenth century, many European Christians believed in witchcraft. James I of England became convinced of the existence of witches when the alleged North Berwick witches claimed responsibility for a storm that nearly sank his honeymoon ship. He executed hundreds of accused witches in his native Scotland for acts similar to those described by the witches in this scene.

F Reading Skills and Strategies

Connecting with the Text

? These lines introduce the theme of sleeplessness in the play. What can cause sleeplessness? [Possible responses: disturbing experiences; worry; guilt.]

G Elements of Literature

Figurative Language

A *bark* is a word for a ship. However a bark in a tempest is often used as a metaphor for a soul in turmoil. Ask students what "his bark cannot be lost" suggests about the witches' powers. [Possible response: The metaphor suggests that the witches do not have ultimate control over people's lives or decisions. They cannot take the sailor's life and soul unless he surrenders to evil.]

H Historical Connections

Witchcraft

According to superstition, the body parts of people who had suffered violent deaths were very powerful in working black magic. In this case, the pilot died when he was "wracked," or shipwrecked, on his way home.

Skill Link

Speaking and Listening: Evaluating a Dramatic Reading

Discuss with students the differences between merely reading aloud and giving a dramatic reading, focusing on characterization through speech. Introduce elements of dramatic speech such as pitch, tone, articulation, accent, and pace. Assign specific passages to students, and have them practice on their own before giving a dramatic reading in class. Encourage them to try out different pitches, paces, and tones until they are satisfied with their presentations. Deliver I.2.35 in two ways to model the difference between a quick, witty, ironic reading and a slow, awe-struck interpretation. After each student performs his or her passage, ask the class to evaluate the performance. Students should consider how well the speaker used the elements of dramatic speech.

Ⓐ Reading Skills and Strategies

Responding to the Text

? These lines are an incantation, or magic spell, recited as the witches spin nine times. How do you react to this incantation? [Possible response: The choral chanting and dancing suggest a frightening and mysterious ritual.]

Ⓑ Vocabulary Note

Word Origins

? *Weird* derives from the Old English word *wyrd,* meaning "fate" or "destiny." *The Oxford English Dictionary* notes that one use of the word, in its plural form, refers to "The Fates, three goddesses that determined the course of human life." In addition, it points out that "the evolution of the forms found in Shakespeare's *Macbeth* was from *weyrd* to *weyard* (retained in Acts III and IV in the First Folio) and *weyward* (used in Acts I and II); the latter was no doubt due to association with *wayward,* a word used many times by Shakespeare. . . . In several passages the prosody clearly requires the word to be pronounced as two syllables . . . ." Considering this information, what conclusions can you draw about spelling and usage at the time *Macbeth* was written? [Possible responses: Spelling was not standardized. Shakespeare seems to have used words in new ways, and sometimes a word was used to convey various meanings.]

Answers to Margin Questions

Line 38. Macbeth has not heard these lines before but is unknowingly echoing the witches' comment (I.1.10). He may be referring to the terrible thunder, lightning, and fog and the wonderful victory, or he may mean that the killing of Macdonwald and the butchery of Sweno's forces were foul, but having succeeded has made the day fair.

Line 39. Banquo might step back and reach for his sword or raise his hand to ward them off. He might gasp or sound surprised as he completes his casual question only to be confronted by the strange trio.

All.
The weird sisters, hand in hand,
Posters° of the sea and land,
Thus do go about, about:
Thrice to thine, and thrice to mine,
And thrice again, to make up nine.
Peace! The charm's wound up.

[*Enter* MACBETH *and* BANQUO.]

Macbeth.
So foul and fair a day I have not seen.

Banquo.
How far is't called to Forres?° What are these
So withered, and so wild in their attire,
That look not like th' inhabitants o' th' earth,
And yet are on't? Live you, or are you aught
That man may question? You seem to understand me,
By each at once her choppy° finger laying

33. Posters: travelers.

? **38.** *What words is Macbeth echoing here? Why, given the weather, does Macbeth think the day is "fair"?*

39. Forres: a town in northeast Scotland and site of King Duncan's castle.

? **39.** *What should Banquo do as he sees the witches? How should his voice change between the words* Forres *and* What?

44. choppy: chapped; sore.

"All hail, Macbeth! Hail to thee, Thane of Glamis!"

From the Stratford Festival production of *Macbeth* (1983).

Getting Students Involved

Cooperative Learning

Trace the Imagery. Shakespeare's use of imagery in *Macbeth* is brilliant, commenting on and reinforcing character, plot, atmosphere, and theme. Divide the class into five groups, letting each group choose one of the following motifs:

- blood
- clothing
- light and darkness
- sickness and health
- unnatural events in nature that mirror human evil

Have each group follow its motif through the play, identifying pertinent lines. Once they have compiled their list, have them analyze how the images contribute to the atmosphere, foreshadow or echo plot events, and reveal the characters' inner feelings. If students want a challenge, they can identify other motifs in *Macbeth* and follow them through the play.

Upon her skinny lips. You should° be women,
And yet your beards forbid me to interpret
That you are so.

Macbeth. Speak, if you can: what are you?

First Witch.
All hail, Macbeth! Hail to thee, Thane of Glamis!

Second Witch.
All hail, Macbeth! Hail to thee, Thane of Cawdor!

Third Witch.
All hail, Macbeth, that shalt be king hereafter!

Banquo.
Good sir, why do you start, and seem to fear
Things that do sound so fair? I' th' name of truth,
Are ye fantastical, or that indeed
Which outwardly ye show? My noble partner
You greet with present grace and great prediction
Of noble having and of royal hope,
That he seems rapt withal:° to me you speak not.
If you can look into the seeds of time,
And say which grain will grow and which will not,
Speak then to me, who neither beg nor fear
Your favors nor your hate.

First Witch. Hail!

Second Witch. Hail!

Third Witch. Hail!

First Witch.
Lesser than Macbeth, and greater.

Second Witch.
Not so happy,° yet much happier.

Third Witch.
Thou shalt get° kings, though thou be none.
So all hail, Macbeth and Banquo!

First Witch.
Banquo and Macbeth, all hail!

Macbeth.
Stay, you imperfect° speakers, tell me more:
By Sinel's death I know I am Thane of Glamis;
But how of Cawdor? The Thane of Cawdor lives,
A prosperous gentleman; and to be king
Stands not within the prospect of belief,
No more than to be Cawdor. Say from whence
You owe° this strange intelligence?° Or why
Upon this blasted heath you stop our way
With such prophetic greeting? Speak, I charge you.

[WITCHES *vanish.*]

Banquo.
The earth hath bubbles as the water has,
And these are of them. Whither are they vanished?

45. should: must.

? **51.** *Banquo's words give a clue as to how Macbeth reacts to the witches. What is Macbeth doing? When Banquo asks, "Are ye fantastical," whom is he addressing?*

57. rapt withal: entranced by it.

? **61.** *What does Banquo ask the witches?*

66. happy: lucky.

67. get: beget.

70. imperfect: incomplete.

? **71.** *Sinel is Macbeth's father. What do you think Macbeth's tone is here? Is he overeager? or just casually curious?*

76. owe: own; have. **intelligence:** information.

? **Stage direction.** *The witches on Shakespeare's stage would have vanished through the trapdoor. Is Banquo, in his next speech, intrigued or disturbed? How does Macbeth feel?*

C Critical Thinking

Speculating

? Why might Macbeth "start" and "seem to fear"? [Possible answer: Since he is a close kinsman of Duncan's, perhaps he has already had the idea that he will one day be king. Given the brutal way he treated Macdonwald, perhaps he has secretly thought of killing the king.]

D Elements of Literature

Paradoxes

? How could these paradoxes be true? [Possible answers: Banquo could be lesser in rank than Macbeth but greater in personal honor or achievement; or, Banquo could be dissatisfied with his rank but happier about himself as a person.] Prophecies from Greek mythology were often cloaked in paradox in order to subtly foreshadow dramatic events in the story. The witches' puzzling paradoxes come out of a long soothsaying tradition.

E Elements of Literature

Imagery

? How does this bubble image (perhaps of mineral or sulfur hot springs) contribute to the mood of the scene? [Possible answers: It suggests mysterious forces at work; or, it may also suggest foulness, as bubbling sulfur springs often have a strong, unpleasant odor.]

Answers to Margin Questions

Line 51. Macbeth is startled. He might show fear in different ways, perhaps by his facial expressions or gestures of surprise. Banquo is addressing the witches, asking them if they are real.
Line 61. Banquo asks the witches to foretell his future, too, if they can.
Line 71. Macbeth's tone might be puzzled, intrigued, or entranced—or perhaps all three.
Stage Direction. Possible answer: Banquo seems to be puzzled and dismisses the witches as fantasies. Macbeth is eager to hear more.

Ⓐ Reading Skills and Strategies

Comparing and Contrasting Characters

? Compare and contrast Banquo's and Macbeth's reactions to the witches. [Possible answer: Both men are serious. Banquo, however, tries to explain their presence, wondering if he and Macbeth were hallucinating. Macbeth seems to accept their authority and wants them to explain their prophecies.]

Ⓑ English Language Learners

Understanding Archaic Language

To help students understand the meaning of the archaic language used in the passage, have them make a chart listing each archaic word they come across and its modern translation.

Archaic Form	Modern Translation
hath	has
o'er	over
afeard	afraid
didst	did

Ⓒ Historical Connections

Witchcraft

In his book *Daemonologie,* published in 1597, James I asserts that witches are "agents of the devil." Here Banquo echoes James's belief.

Ⓓ Elements of Literature

Figurative Language

? A **metaphor** is a comparison between two seemingly unlike things without a connective word such as *like* or *as*. This metaphor is one of many clothing metaphors in the play. How would you rephrase it? [Possible answer: Why are you calling me by someone else's name or title?]

Macbeth.
Into the air, and what seemed corporal° melted
As breath into the wind. Would they had stayed!

Banquo.
Were such things here as we do speak about?
Or have we eaten on the insane root°
That takes the reason prisoner?

Macbeth.
Your children shall be kings.

Banquo. You shall be king.

Macbeth.
And Thane of Cawdor too. Went it not so?

Banquo.
To th' selfsame tune and words. Who's here?

[*Enter* ROSS *and* ANGUS.]

Ross.
The king hath happily received, Macbeth,
The news of thy success; and when he reads°
Thy personal venture in the rebels' fight,
His wonders and his praises do contend
Which should be thine or his. Silenced with that,
In viewing o'er the rest o' th' selfsame day,
He finds thee in the stout Norweyan ranks,
Nothing afeard of what thyself didst make,
Strange images of death.° As thick as tale
Came post with post,° and every one did bear
Thy praises in his kingdom's great defense,
And poured them down before him.

Angus. We are sent
To give thee, from our royal master, thanks;
Only to herald thee into his sight,
Not pay thee.

Ross.
And for an earnest° of a greater honor,
He bade me, from him, call thee Thane of Cawdor;
In which addition,° hail, most worthy thane!
For it is thine.

Banquo. What, can the devil speak true?

Macbeth.
The Thane of Cawdor lives: why do you dress me
In borrowed robes?

Angus. Who was the thane lives yet,
But under heavy judgment bears that life
Which he deserves to lose. Whether he was combined
With those of Norway, or did line° the rebel
With hidden help and vantage, or that with both
He labored in his country's wrack, I know not;
But treasons capital,° confessed and proved,
Have overthrown him.

81. corporal: corporeal (bodily, physical).

84. insane root: henbane, believed to cause insanity.

90. reads: considers.

97. Nothing . . . death: killing, and not being afraid of being killed.

98. post with post: messenger with a message.

104. earnest: pledge.

106. addition: title.

112. line: support.

115. capital: deserving death.

Crossing the Curriculum

Social Studies

How much did Shakespeare stray from his historical sources to add political correctness and dramatic impact to his play? Have students locate the English chronicler Raphael Holinshed's account of Macbeth or use *The Arden Shakespeare,* which contains a large portion of Holinshed's version of events as an appendix. After reading, they can compare Holinshed's account with the play. Students can use a graphic organizer to represent the similarities and differences they find.

Art

In ancient Greek theater, all the actors wore huge, exaggerated masks. Although no one in *Macbeth* wears an actual mask, one motif running throughout the play is that of masking one's true feelings behind a pleasing face. Have students research the different kinds of masks that were used in Greek drama, specifically tragedy. What purpose did they serve? If masks were to be used in a production of *Macbeth,* in what ways could they be implemented effectively?

Architecture

Have students research Scottish castles and their locales, particularly Inverness, Dunsinane, Cawdor, and Glamis. Students should seek information about the current castles and their uses, as well as evidence of older castles that previously existed on the sites. If possible, students should provide pictures of an eleventh-century castle. (All of the castles mentioned here are more recent structures, usually built on older foundations.)

Macbeth (*aside*). Glamis, and Thane of Cawdor:
The greatest is behind. (*To* ROSS *and* ANGUS.) Thanks for your pains.
(*Aside to* BANQUO.) Do you not hope your children shall be kings,
When those that gave the Thane of Cawdor to me
Promised no less to them?

Banquo (*aside to* MACBETH). That, trusted home,°
Might yet enkindle you unto the crown,°
Besides the Thane of Cawdor. But 'tis strange:
And oftentimes, to win us to our harm,
The instruments of darkness tell us truths,
Win us with honest trifles, to betray 's
In deepest consequence.
Cousins,° a word, I pray you.

Macbeth (*aside*). Two truths are told
As happy prologues to the swelling act
Of the imperial theme.—I thank you, gentlemen.—
(*Aside.*) This supernatural soliciting
Cannot be ill, cannot be good. If ill,
Why hath it given me earnest of success,
Commencing in a truth? I am Thane of Cawdor:
If good, why do I yield to that suggestion
Whose horrid image doth unfix my hair
And make my seated heart knock at my ribs,
Against the use of nature? Present fears
Are less than horrible imaginings.
My thought, whose murder yet is but fantastical,
Shakes so my single° state of man that function
Is smothered in surmise, and nothing is
But what is not.°

Banquo. Look, how our partner's rapt.

Macbeth (*aside*).
If chance will have me king, why, chance may crown me,
Without my stir.

Banquo. New honors come upon him,
Like our strange° garments, cleave not to their mold
But with the aid of use.

Macbeth (*aside*). Come what come may,
Time and the hour runs through the roughest day.

Banquo.
Worthy Macbeth, we stay upon your leisure.

Macbeth.
Give me your favor.° My dull brain was wrought
With things forgotten. Kind gentlemen, your pains
Are registered where every day I turn
The leaf to read them. Let us toward the king.
(*Aside to* BANQUO.) Think upon what hath chanced, and at more time,

? **117.** *"Behind" here means "to follow." How should this important aside be spoken? What is Macbeth's mood?*

120. trusted home: trusted all the way.

121. enkindle . . . crown: arouse in you the ambition to become king.

? **126.** *How does this speech show Banquo as part of the conscience of the play?*

127. Cousins: This word is used frequently by Shakespeare to mean "fellows" or "kindred friends" of some sort.

? **Stage direction.** *When a character is delivering an aside, the director or the playwright must arrange for the others on stage to be involved in some way so that it would be natural for them not to notice the character delivering the aside. Where should Macbeth go on stage to deliver this important aside? What do you think he meant by the "swelling act" in line 128? Where are Banquo, Angus, and Ross?*

? **137.** *What do you suppose Macbeth is thinking of that makes his seated (fixed) heart knock at his ribs in an unnatural way?*

140. single: unaided; weak.

142. nothing . . . not: Nothing is real to me except my imaginings.

? **142.** *What might Macbeth do as Banquo notices him brooding?*

145. strange: new.

? **145.** *What does Banquo compare Macbeth and his new honors to? Is Banquo's mood different from Macbeth's?*

149. favor: pardon.

E Elements of Literature

Aside

? An **aside** consists of private words spoken by a character to the audience or to another character. These asides let the audience know Macbeth's and Banquo's thoughts without other characters being aware of them. What might Ross and Angus think if they heard Macbeth and Banquo? [that they are traitors]

F Struggling Readers

Paraphrasing

Have students paraphrase Banquo's comments about what the witches' motives might be. [Banquo suggests that the "instruments of darkness" often tell a small truth to lure people into evil.] Remind students that the witches are not meant to be benevolent, and their motives should seem questionable.

G Elements of Literature

Tragedy

? What are the two ways Macbeth imagines he could become king? [by murdering Duncan or by waiting to see if chance brings him to the throne] What hint is there of his tragic flaw? [the "horrid image" absorbing him]

Answers to Margin Questions

Line 117. He might sound eager, exultant, or determined. His mood might be one of glee or wonder.
Line 126. He warns Macbeth that the witches may be trying to harm him.
Stage Direction. Macbeth might come downstage and face the audience, while the other characters remain upstage, engaged in conversation. The "swelling act" suggests the stately music that heralds a king.
Line 137. Macbeth may be imagining murdering Duncan to become king.
Line 142. He might continue to stare off or look up.
Line 145. He compares Macbeth's honors to new clothes, not yet broken in. Banquo's mood is calm because he dismisses the witches' comments; Macbeth's mood is excited because he believes the witches.

Skill Link

Comparing and Contrasting

Writers often reveal characters' natures by contrasting them with those of other characters. In Act I, both Macbeth and Banquo encounter the witches. Although they are both curious about the witches, their reactions are very different. Ask students to use a Venn diagram to compare the similarities and differences of the two characters' reactions to the witches. After they finish the diagram, ask for conclusions about Macbeth and Banquo's attitudes.

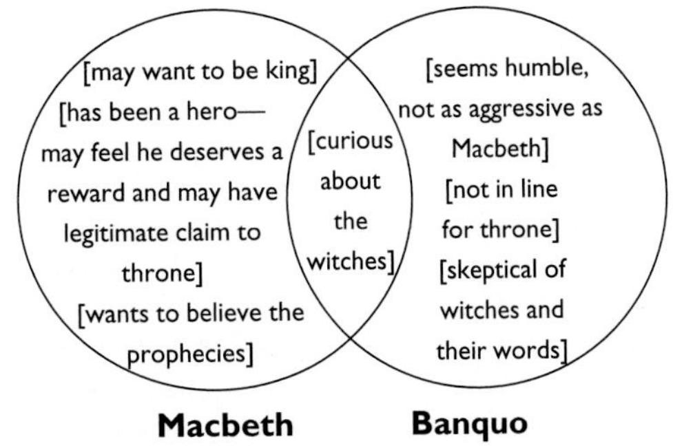
[may want to be king]
[has been a hero—may feel he deserves a reward and may have legitimate claim to throne]
[wants to believe the prophecies]
[curious about the witches]
[seems humble, not as aggressive as Macbeth]
[not in line for throne]
[skeptical of witches and their words]
Macbeth
Banquo

Summary

Scene 4: At his palace, Duncan proclaims his son Malcolm heir to the throne. Macbeth acknowledges that Malcolm is an obstacle in his path to the throne and that "black and deep desires" stir in him.

Ⓐ Elements of Literature

Theme

? A **theme** is a central idea in a play. How do these lines reflect a major theme of *Macbeth?* [Possible answer: Duncan is unable to distinguish appearance from reality; he cannot read people's characters.]

Ⓑ Reading Skills and Strategies

Making Inferences

? What might Macbeth make of these words? [Sample response: With his imagination so worked up, he might construe this as a promise of the throne; or, he might appreciate Duncan's deep gratitude.]

Answers to Margin Questions

Line 8. Possible answer: The way he died was the finest thing he ever did. This might be taken at face value—praise for his courage in confessing and facing death without fear—or it could be construed as an ironic comment on the quality of his life.

Line 12. Duncan has revealed his weak spot—he is too trusting and not a good judge of character. Ironically, even as Duncan is acknowledging his mistake about the previous Thane of Cawdor, he is making the same mistake about Macbeth.

Line 32. Some students may hope that Macbeth, hearing the king's praise, will remain honorable; others may be suspicious of his sincerity. The king hugs Banquo, but he gives Macbeth the honor of being Thane of Cawdor and speaks of him with greater admiration and respect. Macbeth might feel that Duncan is treating him more as an equal and Banquo more as a friend.

The interim having weighed it, let us speak
Our free hearts each to other.

Banquo. Very gladly.

Macbeth.
Till then, enough. Come, friends. [*Exeunt.*]

Scene 4. *Forres. The palace.*

Flourish.° *Enter* KING DUNCAN, LENNOX, MALCOLM, DONALBAIN, *and* ATTENDANTS.

King.
Is execution done on Cawdor? Are not
Those in commission yet returned?

Malcolm. My liege,
They are not yet come back. But I have spoke
With one that saw him die, who did report
That very frankly he confessed his treasons,
Implored your highness' pardon and set forth
A deep repentance: nothing in his life
Became him like the leaving it. He died
As one that had been studied in his death
To throw away the dearest thing he owed°
As 'twere a careless trifle.

Ⓐ **King.** There's no art
To find the mind's construction in the face:
He was a gentleman on whom I built
An absolute trust.

[*Enter* MACBETH, BANQUO, ROSS, *and* ANGUS.]

O worthiest cousin!
The sin of my ingratitude even now
Was heavy on me: thou art so far before,
That swiftest wing of recompense is slow
To overtake thee. Would thou hadst less deserved,
That the proportion° both of thanks and payment
Ⓑ Might have been mine! Only I have left to say,
More is thy due than more than all can pay.

Macbeth.
The service and the loyalty I owe,
In doing it, pays itself.° Your highness' part
Is to receive our duties: and our duties
Are to your throne and state children and servants;
Which do but what they should, by doing everything
Safe toward° your love and honor.

King. Welcome hither.
I have begun to plant thee, and will labor
To make thee full of growing. Noble Banquo,
That hast no less deserved, nor must be known
No less to have done so, let me enfold thee
And hold thee to my heart.

Flourish: of trumpets.

? **8.** *What does this famous line mean: "nothing in his life / Became him like the leaving it"?*

10. owed: owned.

? **12.** *What irony would you feel here? What does Duncan fail to realize about another face?*

19. proportion: greater amount.

23. pays itself: is its own reward.

27. safe toward: safeguarding.

? **32.** *You know Macbeth's thoughts. How do you feel about him as the king lavishes praise on him? Is the king's reception of Banquo even warmer? How might Macbeth react here?*

Professional Notes

Critical Comment: Macbeth's Temptation

Alfred Harbage of Harvard University comments on the weird sisters: "In the play they are Elizabethan witches, their prescriptive powers subtly curtailed; they predict, abet, and symbolize damnation but do not determine it. Any sense that Macbeth is a helpless victim, his crime predestined, his will bound, is canceled as the play proceeds. We may seem to see in the encounter on the heath the very inception of his lethal designs, but we should ask with Banquo,

Good sir, why do you start and seem to fear
Things that sound so fair?

Nothing in the witches' prophecies would have suggested to an untainted mind that to 'be king hereafter' meant to be a murderer first." Ask students whether they agree with this assessment of Macbeth. Was he or was he not entertaining treasonous thoughts before he saw the witches?

"We will establish our estate upon
Our eldest, Malcolm."

From Roman Polanski's film production of *Macbeth* (1971).

Banquo. There if I grow,
The harvest is your own.
King. My plenteous joys,
Wanton in fullness, seek to hide themselves
In drops of sorrow. Sons, kinsmen, thanes,
And you whose places are the nearest, know,
We will establish our estate upon
Our eldest, Malcolm, whom we name hereafter (C)
The Prince of Cumberland: which honor must
Not unaccompanied invest him only,
But signs of nobleness, like stars, shall shine
On all deservers. From hence to Inverness,°
And bind us further to you.
Macbeth.
The rest is labor, which is not used for you.°
I'll be myself the harbinger,° and make joyful
The hearing of my wife with your approach; (D)
So, humbly take my leave.
King. My worthy Cawdor!
Macbeth (*aside*).
The Prince of Cumberland! That is a step
On which I must fall down, or else o'erleap,
For in my way it lies. Stars, hide your fires;
Let not light see my black and deep desires:
The eye wink at the hand;° yet let that be
Which the eye fears, when it is done, to see. [*Exit.*]
King.
True, worthy Banquo; he is full so valiant,
And in his commendations° I am fed;
It is a banquet to me. Let's after him,
Whose care is gone before to bid us welcome. (E)
It is a peerless kinsman. [*Flourish. Exeunt.*]

? 35. *There's a clue in this line that shows how moved the king is. What is the king doing at the words "drops of sorrow"?*

42. **Inverness:** Macbeth's castle.

? 43. *Who is to inherit Duncan's crown?*

44. **The rest . . . you:** When rest is not used for you, it is labor.

45. **harbinger:** sign of something to come.

52. **wink . . . hand:** be blind to the hand's deed.

? 53. *Where in this speech do we begin to hear Macbeth talk in terms of darkness?*

55. **his commendations:** praises of him.

(C) Historical Connections

Tanistry and Laws of Succession

Apparently this announcement is not as innocent as it seems. Duncan was violating two laws by naming Malcolm his successor: first, a law prohibiting a minor from succeeding to the throne; second, the law of tanistry, in effect from A.D. 843 to 1058 (coinciding with the end of Macbeth's reign) that said no son of a king on the throne could succeed his father directly. Tanistry required that the first ranking adult of the nearest branch of the family be elected to succeed the king, acting as military leader of all the king's forces (as Macbeth does in the play). Then succession would revert to the original branch of the family, so that the line of succession alternated between the branches of the royal family.

(D) Elements of Literature

Imagery

Have students contrast the two celestial images in the scene. [Sample response: Duncan states that nobleness will shine like a star on those who deserve it, while Macbeth asks that the stars not illumine his "black and deep desires." Duncan welcomes the light, while Macbeth calls for darkness.]

(E) Struggling Readers

Making Predictions

Ask students where everyone is going to spend the night. [Inverness, the site of Macbeth's castle] Then ask them to guess what might happen there. [Duncan might further reward Banquo and Macbeth; Macbeth might give way to his dark desires.]

Answers to Margin Questions

Line 35. Wiping away tears of joy.
Line 43. His son Malcolm.
Line 53. In l. 50, Macbeth speaks of literal darkness (telling the stars to hide their light), and in l. 51, he speaks of the darkness in his heart.

Connecting Across Texts

Connecting with "The Glass of Fashion"

Ask students to review "The Glass of Fashion" (pp. 206–207) to help them visualize how the audience who attended the premiere of *Macbeth* would have dressed. *Macbeth* itself, however, was set in an earlier period, the eleventh century. As the play mentions, cloaks were popular in that era. Cloaks were semicircular, worn long, and fastened by a cord or brooch. Breeches, or drawstring pants with stirrup feet, were in vogue for men. Direct interested students to an illustrated history of fashion to find other examples of clothing from the eleventh century that the characters might have worn. Have them use these as ideas for original costumes for several characters and display students' designs on the bulletin board.

Summary

Scene 5: At Inverness, Lady Macbeth reads a letter from Macbeth relaying the witches' prophecies. Fearing Macbeth is too soft-hearted to do what he must to become king, she resolves to use her power over him to steel his will. When she learns the king will visit their castle that night, Lady Macbeth sees it as the perfect opportunity to murder him.

Ⓐ Reading Skills and Strategies
Blank Verse

Ask students to consider why there is a shift from the measured rhythms of blank verse in the previous scene to rapid prose in this letter. [Possible response: Rapid prose is better suited to a hastily written letter than iambic pentameter.]

Ⓑ Reading Skills and Strategies
Making Inferences

? How does Macbeth feel about the prophecy that he will be king? [Possible answer: He is delighted and cannot wait to tell his wife, whom he calls his "dearest partner of greatness." He seems to believe the prophecy will come true.]

Ⓒ Critical Thinking
Evaluating

? Do you agree with Lady Macbeth's interpretation of Macbeth's character? Why or why not? [Possible answer: Her characterization of him as too kind does not seem to fit the man who slit in half and beheaded Macdonwald and now plots murder to become king.]

Answers to Margin Questions

Stage Direction. Encourage students to discuss movement, pauses, and reactions. She may be pacing, reading lines with varying emphasis, using facial expressions to show emotions, such as joy, upon hearing the words "Thane of Cawdor."

Line 13. Lady Macbeth may clutch the letter to her breast or tuck it into the bodice of her dress. She is addressing the absent Macbeth. Students may associate the phrase with caring or sensitive feelings, like the tenderness of a mother nursing her infant.

Scene 5. *Inverness. Macbeth's castle.*

Enter Macbeth's wife, LADY MACBETH, *alone, with a letter.*

Lady Macbeth (*reads*). "They met me in the day of success; and I have learned by the perfect'st report they have more in them than mortal knowledge. When I burned in desire to question them further, they made themselves air, into which they vanished. Whiles I stood rapt in the wonder of it, came missives° from the King, who all-hailed me 'Thane of Cawdor'; by which title, before, these weird sisters saluted me, and referred me to the coming on of time, with 'Hail, king that shalt be!' This have I thought good to deliver thee, my dearest partner of greatness, that thou mightst not lose the dues of rejoicing, by being ignorant of what greatness is promised thee. Lay it to thy heart, and farewell."

Glamis thou art, and Cawdor, and shalt be
What thou art promised. Yet do I fear thy nature;
It is too full o' th' milk of human kindness
To catch the nearest way. Thou wouldst be great,
Art not without ambition, but without
The illness° should attend it. What thou wouldst highly,
That wouldst thou holily; wouldst not play false,
And yet wouldst wrongly win. Thou'dst have, great Glamis,
That which cries, "Thus thou must do" if thou have it;
And that which rather thou dost fear to do

? **Stage direction.** *As you picture Lady Macbeth reading this letter, try to imagine what she would be doing on stage and what her mood would be, especially at the words "Thane of Cawdor."*

6. missives: messengers.

? **13.** *What does Lady Macbeth do with the letter? Whom is she addressing here with "thou" and "thy"? How would you explain "th' milk of human kindness"?*

18. illness: wickedness; evil nature.

"My dearest love, / Duncan comes here tonight."

From the Stratford Festival production of *Macbeth* (1983).

Making the Connections

Cultural Connections: Witchcraft

Shakespeare was writing about witches for an audience obsessed by witchcraft. People of the time believed that witches were linked to the devil and they preyed not only on people's souls but also on dead bodies not buried in consecrated ground. Today, certain cultures still believe in beings who use supernatural powers for wicked ends.

Discuss with students how other writers and film directors have portrayed witches, such as those in fairy tales or in movies like *The Wizard of Oz* or *The Crucible.* Ask how these portrayals compare with that of the three witches in *Macbeth.*

Than wishest should be undone. Hie thee hither,
That I may pour my spirits in thine ear,
And chastise with the valor of my tongue
All that impedes thee from the golden round
Which fate and metaphysical° aid doth seem
To have thee crowned withal.

[*Enter* MESSENGER.]

What is your tidings?

Messenger.
The king comes here tonight.

Lady Macbeth. Thou'rt mad to say it! **D**
Is not thy master with him, who, were't so,
Would have informed for preparation?

Messenger.
So please you, it is true. Our thane is coming.
One of my fellows had the speed of him,°
Who, almost dead for breath, had scarcely more
Than would make up his message.

Lady Macbeth. Give him tending;
He brings great news. [*Exit* MESSENGER.]
The raven himself is hoarse
That croaks the fatal entrance of Duncan
Under my battlements. Come, you spirits
That tend on mortal° thoughts, unsex me here,
And fill me, from the crown to the toe, top-full
Of direst cruelty! Make thick my blood,
Stop up th' access and passage to remorse,
That no compunctious visitings of nature°
Shake my fell° purpose, nor keep peace between **E**
Th' effect and it! Come to my woman's breasts,
And take my milk for gall,° you murd'ring ministers,°
Wherever in your sightless° substances
You wait on nature's mischief! Come, thick night,
And pall° thee in the dunnest° smoke of hell,
That my keen knife see not the wound it makes,
Nor heaven peep through the blanket of the dark,
To cry "Hold, hold!"

[*Enter* MACBETH.]

Great Glamis! Worthy Cawdor!
Greater than both, by the all-hail hereafter!
Thy letters have transported me beyond
This ignorant present, and I feel now
The future in the instant.

Macbeth. My dearest love,
Duncan comes here tonight.

Lady Macbeth. And when goes hence?

Macbeth.
Tomorrow, as he purposes. **F**

? **26.** *What do you guess the "golden round" is?*

27. metaphysical: supernatural.

33. had . . . him: had more speed than he did.

? **36.** *Who is the raven she refers to as being hoarse? Why does she call him a raven?*

39. mortal: deadly.

43. compunctious . . . nature: natural feelings of compassion.

44. fell: savage.

46. gall: a bitter substance; bile. **murd'ring ministers:** agents of murder.

47. sightless: invisible.

49. pall: cover with a shroud, a burial cloth. **dunnest:** darkest.

? **52.** *How has Lady Macbeth reinforced the witches' statement: "Fair is foul, and foul is fair . . ."?*

? **57.** *Is their passion for each other as great as their passion for power? If you feel it is, how might a director illustrate it here?*

D Critical Thinking

Interpreting

? **Why is Lady Macbeth so shocked by the messenger's statement?** [Sample responses: Duncan's arrival has come upon her suddenly; she fears she may not have time to prepare. The messenger's reference to Duncan may seem to echo her thoughts, making her think he can read her mind; or she has been imagining Macbeth as king and thinks the messenger is referring to him.]

E Elements of Literature

Tragedy

? What role do you think Lady Macbeth will play in Macbeth's downfall? [Possible response: Lady Macbeth calls on spirits to "unsex" her and fill her with cruelty. She is steeling herself to participate in the murder of Duncan. Like the witches, she will provoke Macbeth into doing the evil deed that will lead to his tragic downfall.]

F Advanced Learners

Defending an Interpretation

Ask students to discuss as many interpretations of this line as possible. [Possible answers: Macbeth's line could imply that Duncan plans to leave tomorrow but Macbeth and his wife will prevent it. Lady Macbeth follows up on this idea with her metaphorical statement that "Never shall sun that morrow see," implying that Duncan will not be alive the following day. Students may also interpret Macbeth's line as an innocent statement, in which case Lady Macbeth is the first to suggest the murder.] Then have students judge which interpretation is most likely in light of all that has taken place. Pairs of students with differing views can debate the point.

Answers to Margin Questions

Line 26. The king's crown.

Line 36. She may be speaking figuratively of the raven as a symbol of death, or she may be referring to the breathless messenger who brings the news that bodes ill for Duncan.

Line 52. She has prayed that her finest qualities be made foul.

Line 57. Macbeth's greeting suggests real passion. A director might have Macbeth and Lady Macbeth embrace or gaze into each other's eyes.

A Critical Thinking

Making Connections

? How does this line relate to Duncan's statement, "There's no art/To find the mind's construction in the face" (I.4.11–12)? [Possible answer: It supports Duncan's comment by suggesting that the face can be used as a mask to conceal evil thoughts.]

B Critical Thinking

Interpreting

? What does Lady Macbeth think will happen after Duncan's murder? [She assumes Macbeth will be king.] Note that neither Macbeth nor Lady Macbeth has mentioned killing Malcolm, and this fact suggests that Malcolm has a less legitimate claim to the throne than Macbeth.

Summary

Scene 6: King Duncan arrives at Macbeth's castle. The king comments with dramatic irony on the pleasant atmosphere surrounding Macbeth's home. Lady Macbeth graciously welcomes the king while plotting his murder.

C Elements of Literature

Imagery

Have students contrast the image of the martlet with that of the bird Lady Macbeth imagined in Act I, Scene 5, ll. 36–38. [Possible response: Lady Macbeth imagined a "hoarse raven," while the noble Banquo sees the "temple-haunting martlet."] In Christian folklore the raven is often associated with prophecy, the devil, and death. The martlet, or swallow, on the other hand, is noted for nesting in church steeples.

Answers to Margin Questions

Line 69. Macbeth is impressed by her fervor; eager to pursue the enterprise; eager for reassurances that all will be well.

Line 9. Though readers know evil lurks within (Macbeth and his wife plan to kill Duncan), the visitors remark how pleasant the castle is. This dramatic irony illustrates the paradox "Fair is foul, and foul is fair." Lady Macbeth probably pretends to be pleased and flattered by the royal visit.

Lady Macbeth. O, never
Shall sun that morrow see!
Your face, my thane, is as a book where men
May read strange matters. To beguile the time,°
Look like the time; bear welcome in your eye,
Your hand, your tongue: look like th' innocent flower,
But be the serpent under't. He that's coming
Must be provided for: and you shall put
This night's great business into my dispatch;°
Which shall to all our nights and days to come
Give solely sovereign sway and masterdom.

Macbeth.
We will speak further.

Lady Macbeth. Only look up clear.°
To alter favor ever is to fear.°
Leave all the rest to me. [*Exeunt.*]

61. beguile the time: deceive people of the day.

66. dispatch: management.

? 69. *How is Macbeth feeling?*

69. clear: undisturbed.

70. To alter . . . fear: To show an altered face is dangerous.

Scene 6. *Before Macbeth's castle.*

Hautboys° and torches. Enter KING DUNCAN, MALCOLM, DONALBAIN, BANQUO, LENNOX, MACDUFF, ROSS, ANGUS, *and* ATTENDANTS.

King.
This castle hath a pleasant seat;° the air
Nimbly and sweetly recommends itself
Unto our gentle senses.

Banquo. This guest of summer,
The temple-haunting martlet,° does approve°
By his loved mansionry° that the heaven's breath
Smells wooingly here. No jutty,° frieze,
Buttress, nor coign of vantage,° but this bird
Hath made his pendent bed and procreant° cradle.
Where they most breed and haunt, I have observed
The air is delicate.

[*Enter* LADY MACBETH.]

King. See, see, our honored hostess!
The love that follows us sometime is our trouble,
Which still we thank as love. Herein I teach you
How you shall bid God 'ield° us for your pains
And thank us for your trouble.

Lady Macbeth. All our service
In every point twice done, and then done double,
Were poor and single business to contend
Against those honors deep and broad wherewith
Your majesty loads our house: for those of old,
And the late dignities heaped up to them,
We rest your hermits.°

King. Where's the Thane of Cawdor?
We coursed° him at the heels, and had a purpose

Hautboys: oboes.

1. seat: situation; setting.

4. martlet: a bird that builds nests in churches. **approve:** prove.

5. mansionry: nest (dwelling).

6. jutty: projection.

7. coign of vantage: advantageous corner (of the castle).

8. procreant: breeding.

? 9. *This scene contrasts strongly with the previous one. Again, what irony do you feel as Duncan admires the castle? How do you imagine Lady Macbeth acts as she now enters to greet her guests?*

13. 'ield: reward.

20. We rest your hermits: We'll remain dependents who will pray for you.

21. coursed: chased.

Using Students' Strengths

Kinesthetic Learners

Students should appreciate the fact that Lady Macbeth values the art of acting. In keeping with her instructions, have students perform a pantomime of one of the shorter scenes of the play. (Act I, Scene 5 would be a good choice.) Volunteers should take the parts of the various characters and work on appropriate gestures and facial expressions.

Auditory/Musical Learners

Traditional Scottish musical instruments include the drumlike *tympanum,* the flutelike *cuisie,* and the familiar bagpipes. Have groups of students collaborate to find audio recordings of music featuring these instruments (or modern ones resembling them) that can be used as background music for one of the scenes in the play. Have each group play their selection for the class as students silently reread the chosen scene.

"See, see, our honored hostess!"
From Roman Polanski's film production of *Macbeth* (1971).

To be his purveyor:° but he rides well,
And his great love, sharp as his spur, hath holp° him
To his home before us. Fair and noble hostess,
We are your guest tonight.

Lady Macbeth. Your servants ever
Have theirs, themselves, and what is theirs, in compt,°
To make their audit at your highness' pleasure,
Still° to return your own.

King. Give me your hand.
Conduct me to mine host: we love him highly,
And shall continue our graces toward him.
By your leave, hostess. [*Exeunt.*]

22. purveyor: advance man.
23. holp: helped.
26. in compt: in trust.
28. Still: always.
31. *How do you imagine the scene ends?*

Scene 7. *Macbeth's castle.*

Hautboys. Torches. Enter a SEWER,° *and diverse* SERVANTS *with dishes and service, and pass over the stage. Then enter* MACBETH.

Sewer: butler.

Macbeth.
If it were done when 'tis done, then 'twere well
It were done quickly. If th' assassination
Could trammel up the consequence, and catch,
With his surcease,° success; that but this blow
Might be the be-all and the end-all—here,
But here, upon this bank and shoal of time,

1. *This is one of Shakespeare's great soliloquies, in which Macbeth voices his indecision and possibly his conscience. What are his conflicts?*
4. his surcease: Duncan's death.

D Elements of Literature
Irony

What does Duncan say spurred Macbeth homeward? [Macbeth's love for his wife] **What is Duncan's tone? What irony is the audience aware of?** [Duncan is probably speaking affectionately, unaware that Lady Macbeth plans to urge Macbeth to murder him.]

E Elements of Literature
Character

Ask students to summarize what they know of Duncan's character. [Students may mention positive qualities such as appreciativeness, kindness, courtesy, and generosity. They may also include negative traits such as foolishness and gullibility.]

Summary

Scene 7: Macbeth speaks his first important soliloquy, explaining how his ambition has led him to thoughts of murder. He is joined by Lady Macbeth, who taunts him to show his manliness by killing Duncan.

Answers to Margin Questions

Line 31. Perhaps Duncan and Lady Macbeth join hands and move offstage, or the king may kiss her hand.
Line 1. 1) He is afraid of the consequences of the murder. 2) He has obligations as Duncan's kinsman, subject, and host. 3) He is afraid that Duncan's death might outrage people.
4) He is motivated by ambition, not by hatred of Duncan or dissatisfaction with his rule as king.

Assessing Learning

Check Test: Questions and Answers

1. In Act I, Scene 2, why does King Duncan give Macbeth a new title? [to reward him for his brave service]
2. What do the witches predict for Macbeth and Banquo? [Macbeth will become Thane of Cawdor and king; Banquo will father kings.]
3. When the audience first meets Lady Macbeth, what is she doing? [reading a letter from Macbeth]
4. Whom does Duncan name as Prince of Cumberland? [his son Malcolm]
5. In the final scene of this act, what is the conflict between Lady Macbeth and Macbeth? [whether or not to kill Duncan]

Informal Assessment

On-Going Assessment. Use the following criteria to rank students' oral responses on a scale of one (low) to three (high) as they answer questions or participate in discussion:

1. Student uses important words from the play (especially theme words about sleeplessness, time, blood, guilt, etc.).
2. Student quotes lines from the play when appropriate.
3. Student uses citations correctly.

Ⓐ Elements of Literature

Figurative Language

? What comparison is Macbeth making in ll. 25–28? [Possible answer: He compares his intent to commit murder to a horse; his ambition to a spur. But like an inept rider, he may overleap or vault over the horse and fall to the other side.]

Ⓑ Elements of Literature

Figurative Language

? In this passage, Lady Macbeth says that Macbeth had clothed himself in hope. How does she then personify hope? [Possible response: She says that hope was inebriated, has since slept it off, and now wakes "green and pale."] What is she trying to achieve through this personification? [Possible answer: She is trying to goad Macbeth into action by accusing him of being sickly and pale—or in other words, weak.] To help students hear the figurative language in this scene, play Disc 5 Track 2 from the Audio CD Library.

Ⓒ Critical Thinking

Making Judgments

? How appropriate do you think the word *coward* is to describe Macbeth if he does not kill Duncan? Explain. [Possible responses: The word is not appropriate at all: a person who refrains from killing someone is rational and civilized, not a coward. The word is appropriate because in Macbeth's time the definition of manliness probably involved using force to take what one felt one deserved.]

Answer to Margin Question

Line 26. Students may say yes; without ambition there is no reason for Macbeth to kill Duncan; or no, Lady Macbeth provides a spur.

We'd jump° the life to come. But in these cases
We still have judgment here; that we but teach
Bloody instructions, which, being taught, return
To plague th' inventor: this even-handed° justice
Commends° th' ingredients of our poisoned chalice
To our own lips. He's here in double trust:
First, as I am his kinsman and his subject,
Strong both against the deed; then, as his host,
Who should against his murderer shut the door,
Not bear the knife myself. Besides, this Duncan
Hath borne his faculties° so meek, hath been
So clear° in his great office, that his virtues
Will plead like angels trumpet-tongued against
The deep damnation of his taking-off;°
And pity, like a naked newborn babe,
Striding the blast, or heaven's cherubin horsed
Upon the sightless couriers° of the air,
Shall blow the horrid deed in every eye,
That° tears shall drown the wind. I have no spur
To prick the sides of my intent, but only
Vaulting ambition, which o'erleaps itself
And falls on th' other——

[*Enter* LADY MACBETH.]

How now! What news?

Lady Macbeth.
He has almost supped. Why have you left the chamber?

Macbeth.
Hath he asked for me?

Lady Macbeth. Know you not he has?

Macbeth.
We will proceed no further in this business:
He hath honored me of late, and I have bought
Golden opinions from all sorts of people,
Which would be worn now in their newest gloss,
Not cast aside so soon.

Lady Macbeth. Was the hope drunk
Wherein you dressed yourself? Hath it slept since?
And wakes it now, to look so green° and pale
At what it did so freely? From this time
Such I account thy love. Art thou afeard
To be the same in thine own act and valor
As thou art in desire? Wouldst thou have that
Which thou esteem'st the ornament of life,°
And live a coward in thine own esteem,
Letting "I dare not" wait upon° "I would,"
Like the poor cat i' th' adage?°

Macbeth. Prithee, peace!
I dare do all that may become a man;
Who dares do more is none.

7. jump: risk. (Macbeth knows he will be condemned to hell for the sin of murder.)

10. even-handed: impartial.

11. Commends: offers.

17. faculties: powers.

18. clear: clean.

20. taking-off: murder.

23. sightless couriers: winds.

25. That: so that.

? **26.** *Macbeth says he has no spur to prick the sides of his intent. Is that true?*

37. green: sickly.

42. ornament of life: crown.

44. wait upon: follow.

45. poor . . . adage: saying about a cat who wants fish but won't wet its paws.

Skill Link

Recognizing Faulty Modes of Persuasion

When reading persuasive text, students should be on the lookout for fallacies that indicate illogical thinking. The following are five common types of fallacies:

1. **Begging the Question** Something presented as true that in fact needs to be proven
2. **False Analogy** An illogical, trivial, or misleading comparison
3. **Attacking the Person** Name-calling
4. **Either-Or Reasoning** Allowance of only two extreme alternatives
5. **Hasty Generalization** A conclusion that is based on insufficient evidence or that ignores exceptions

Ask students to identify the fallacies in the arguments Lady Macbeth uses in Scene 7 to convince Macbeth to murder Duncan. [Sample responses: She begs the question of why Macbeth should be king. She illogically links his sense of purpose to his love for her. She attacks him and his manhood, calling him a coward. She presents him with an either-or choice: Kill Duncan or live in shame the rest of his life. She makes the hasty generalization that murder will be easy and without any negative consequences.]

Lady Macbeth. What beast was't then
That made you break° this enterprise to me?
When you durst do it, then you were a man;
And to be more than what you were, you would
Be so much more the man. Nor time nor place
Did then adhere,° and yet you would make both.
They have made themselves, and that their fitness now
Does unmake you. I have given suck, and know
How tender 'tis to love the babe that milks me:
I would, while it was smiling in my face,
Have plucked my nipple from his boneless gums,
And dashed the brains out, had I so sworn as you
Have done to this.
Macbeth. If we should fail?
Lady Macbeth. We fail?
But° screw your courage to the sticking-place,°
And we'll not fail. When Duncan is asleep—
Whereto the rather shall his day's hard journey
Soundly invite him—his two chamberlains
Will I with wine and wassail° so convince,°
That memory, the warder of the brain,
Shall be a fume, and the receipt of reason
A limbeck only:° when in swinish sleep
Their drenchèd natures lie as in a death,
What cannot you and I perform upon
Th' unguarded Duncan, what not put upon
His spongy officers, who shall bear the guilt
Of our great quell?
Macbeth. Bring forth men-children only;
For thy undaunted mettle° should compose
Nothing but males. Will it not be received,
When we have marked with blood those sleepy two
Of his own chamber, and used their very daggers,
That they have done't?
Lady Macbeth. Who dares receive it other,
As we shall make our griefs and clamor roar
Upon his death?
Macbeth. I am settled, and bend up
Each corporal agent to this terrible feat.
Away, and mock the time° with fairest show:
False face must hide what the false heart doth know.
[*Exeunt.*]

48. break: disclose; reveal.

52. adhere: suit.

54. *How does Lady Macbeth try to intimidate her husband in this speech? Watch what she says about herself in the next lines. There has been some question as to whether "We fail?" (line 59) should be a question. How does the meaning change if the line is spoken as a statement?*

60. But: only. **sticking-place:** the notch in a crossbow.

64. wassail: drinking. **convince:** overcome.

67. the receipt . . . only: The reasoning part of the brain would become like a **limbeck** (or still), distilling only confused thoughts.

72. *"Quell" is murder. What are Lady Macbeth's plans?*

73. mettle: spirit.

81. mock the time: deceive the world.

81. *Should Macbeth pause here? How should these key words be spoken?*

82. *How is this yet another echo of the witches' words in Scene 1?*

D Historical Connections

Macbeth's Children

Many people have puzzled over Lady Macbeth's children, especially in light of Macduff's line in IV.3.216, "He had no children," which seems to refer to Macbeth. Critic Elizabeth Nielson says that the historical Lady Macbeth had a son by a former husband who was killed in battle; this might explain why the fictional Lady Macbeth refers to having children although none are mentioned in the play.

E Critical Thinking

Recognizing Bias

What cultural stereotype is behind Macbeth's comment about male children? [Possible response: He believes that only men are capable of hard decisions and violence. Lady Macbeth's strength astounds him.]

F Reading Skills and Strategies

Making Inferences

Why does Macbeth ask the question in ll. 74–77? [Possible answer: It is a rhetorical question, not a true inquiry. He is leaning toward accepting Lady Macbeth's arguments and is talking himself into murder.]

G Critical Thinking

Making Connections

Compare Macbeth's words about a "false face" to Lady Macbeth's words in I.5.61–64. What do you think of the similarity? [Possible response: Macbeth is becoming more evil—he has taken Lady Macbeth's advice so seriously that now he says virtually the same thing as she does.]

Answers to Margin Questions

Line 54. She challenges Macbeth's manliness and makes murder sound easy. "We fail?" could be spoken with irony, disbelief, or ridicule. If the line were a statement, it would express the idea that the outcome was fated.

Line 72. She plans to get Duncan's chamberlains so drunk that they pass out; she and Macbeth will murder Duncan and frame the servants.

Line 81. He should pause and speak grimly or with determination.

Line 82. This line echoes "Fair is foul, and foul is fair" in that the mask of a fair face conceals the foul heart.

Resources

Selection Assessment

Formal Assessment

- Selection Test, p. 57

Test Generator (One-Stop Planner)

- CD-ROM

MAKING MEANINGS

Act I

First Thoughts [Respond]

1. Possible responses: She seems conniving, ambitious, evil, and clever. She and Macbeth seem close because of the way they greet each other; she may be the stronger one in the relationship, judging by the way she manipulates him.

Shaping Interpretations [Interpret]

2. Scene 1 suggests a stormy, violent play in which supernatural elements and treachery play a part. The thunder and lightning, fog, and filthy air suggest hidden evils.

3. Possible answer: Their foreknowledge of his new title tempts him to commit murder to make the prophecy come true.

4. Students may guess that Banquo will prove to be a better person than Macbeth even if he never wins the crown.

5. While Macbeth "start[s], and seem[s] to fear," Banquo maintains his poise. Banquo is skeptical and wary of the witches, but Macbeth, who commands them to speak, seems superstitious and credulous.

6. He weighs his aversion to murder against his desire to be king; he wonders whether to wait and see what happens or to make the prophecy come true. Duncan's naming of Malcolm as his heir causes Macbeth to consider violence as a resolution.

7. Possible answers: Lady Macbeth is ruthless and strong in her resolve to murder Duncan. Macbeth is open to persuasion, sensitive, easily impressed by the witches. Lady Macbeth wins; Macbeth is persuaded.

8. Dramatic irony—Duncan praises the place where he will be murdered.

Extending the Text [Synthesize]

9. It could be explained if Macbeth has secretly yearned to become king. Possible evidence: I.3.51—he may start because of a guilty conscience; I.3.134–137—he immediately thinks of murder, though the witches have said nothing about that option. The witches could also represent the potential for evil in every person.

MAKING MEANINGS

Act I

First Thoughts

1. What are your impressions of Lady Macbeth at the end of Act I? What is her relationship with Macbeth (beyond being his wife)? What details in this act support your impressions?

> **Reading Check**
>
> **a.** In Scene 1, where do the witches plan to meet again, and why?
>
> **b.** What news about Macbeth does the bloodstained captain bring to the king in Scene 2?
>
> **c.** What does the king determine to do for Macbeth? Why?
>
> **d.** What do the witches tell Macbeth and Banquo in Scene 3?
>
> **e.** In what lines do you discover Lady Macbeth's plans for Duncan when he visits the castle?

Shaping Interpretations

2. In the very first scene of a play, a dramatist must tell the audience what kind of play they are about to see. What does the brief opening scene of *Macbeth* reveal about the rest of the play? How does the weather reflect the human passions revealed in the rest of the act?

3. How does the witches' prophecy of Macbeth's coming greatness act as a temptation for him?

4. Explain the **paradox,** or the apparently contradictory nature, of the witches' greeting to Banquo in Scene 3: "Lesser than Macbeth, and greater." How is this paradox true?

5. How does Banquo's reaction to the witches differ from Macbeth's? What do you think Macbeth's reaction suggests about his **character**?

6. One of the most interesting parts of any serious play is what goes on in the characters' minds. What **conflict** rages in Macbeth after he hears the witches' prophecy? What **resolution** to this conflict does Macbeth express in his aside, in Scene 4, lines 48–53?

7. Find details in the play that point to temperamental **contrasts** between Macbeth and his wife. Who is more single-minded and logical? Who is more argumentative and sensitive? Which one wins the argument?

8. What **irony** would the audience feel as they watch Duncan enter the castle and hear him praise its peacefulness?

Extending the Text

9. One critic has said that the witches are "in some sense representative of potentialities within" Macbeth. How could that statement be explained? Is there any evidence in this act that Macbeth has wanted to be king before? Explain your answer.

READING SKILLS AND STRATEGIES

The Melody of Language: Blank Verse

Almost all of *Macbeth* is written in **blank verse,** or unrhymed iambic pentameter, a form of poetry that comes close to imitating the natural rhythms of English speech. An **iamb** is a metrical foot that has one unstressed syllable followed by one stressed syllable. (Each of the following is an iamb: *Macbeth, success, to win.*) **Pentameter** means that each line of verse has five feet, so one line of iambic pentameter has five iambs. Read this line aloud to hear the meter:

Banquo: Go͝od sír, wh̆y dó yŏu stárt, ănd seém tŏ feár . . .

Examining blank verse. Some lines in *Macbeth* are irregular, with fewer feet or with feet that are not iambs. The play even has a few prose passages, indicated by lines that are set full measure.

1. Scan one major speech by Macbeth and one by Lady Macbeth anywhere in Act I. What variations in iambic pentameter do you find? Why do you think these variations exist—how do sound and sense relate to each other?

2. Do the witches speak in blank verse? Why do you suppose Shakespeare wrote their speeches in this way?

3. Find a prose passage in Act I. Why do you think Shakespeare chose to use prose in this passage?

> **Reading Check**
>
> **a.** They plan to meet Macbeth on the heath and prophesy his fate.
>
> **b.** Macbeth has beheaded Macdonwald and joined Banquo to fight.
>
> **c.** To give Cawdor's title to Macbeth as a reward for saving the nation.
>
> **d.** They name Macbeth Thane of Glamis and Cawdor and "king hereafter." They tell Banquo he will "get kings, though [he] be none."
>
> **e.** Scene 5, ll. 39, 44, 46, 50, 58–59

READING SKILLS AND STRATEGIES

1. The meter in Macbeth's speeches is less regular than Lady Macbeth's; his dialogue sounds more erratic, hers is calmer. Macbeth's speech mirrors his conflicted thoughts, while Lady Macbeth's speech reflects her calculating will.

2. No. (They speak in tetrameter.) It separates their speech from that of more earthly characters and emphasizes its incantation-like nature.

3. There is only one (Scene 5, ll. 1–12), a quotation from a letter Macbeth wrote in prose.

ACT II Scene 1. *Inverness. Court of Macbeth's castle.*

Enter BANQUO, *and* FLEANCE, *with a torch before him (on the way to bed).* (A)

Banquo.
How goes the night, boy?
Fleance.
The moon is down; I have not heard the clock.
Banquo.
And she goes down at twelve.
Fleance. I take't, 'tis later, sir.
Banquo.
Hold, take my sword. There's husbandry° in heaven.
Their candles are all out. Take thee that too.
A heavy summons° lies like lead upon me,
And yet I would not sleep. Merciful powers,
Restrain in me the cursèd thoughts that nature
Gives way to in repose!

[*Enter* MACBETH, *and a* SERVANT *with a torch.*]

Give me my sword!
Who's there?
Macbeth.
A friend.
Banquo.
What, sir, not yet at rest? The king's a-bed: (B)
He hath been in unusual pleasure, and
Sent forth great largess to your offices:°
This diamond he greets your wife withal,
By the name of most kind hostess; and shut up°
In measureless content.
Macbeth. Being unprepared,
Our will became the servant to defect,°
Which else should free have wrought.
Banquo. All's well.
I dreamt last night of the three weird sisters:
To you they have showed some truth.
Macbeth. I think not of them. (C)
Yet, when we can entreat an hour to serve,
We would spend it in some words upon that business,
If you would grant the time.
Banquo. At your kind'st leisure.
Macbeth.
If you shall cleave to my consent, when 'tis,°
It shall make honor for you.
Banquo. So° I lose none
In seeking to augment it, but still keep
My bosom franchised° and allegiance clear,°
I shall be counseled.

? **Stage direction.** *Who is Fleance? What would you remember of the witches' prophecy when you see him here? Do we know if Macbeth and his wife have any children?*

4. husbandry: economizing.

6. summons: call to sleep.

14. largess to your offices: gifts to your servants' quarters.

16. shut up: concluded.

18. to defect: to insufficient preparations.

? **24.** *This is the second time Macbeth has suggested he and Banquo talk. Do you think he might want to confide in Banquo? Does he want to get Banquo on his side? How would you characterize his motives?*

25. cleave . . . 'tis: join my cause, when the time comes.

26. So: provided that.

28. franchised: free (from guilt). **clear:** clean.

Summary

Scene 1: Macbeth comes upon Banquo and Banquo's son Fleance after midnight as they make their way to bed. Macbeth and Banquo talk of the witches' predictions, and Macbeth again suggests a private talk with Banquo. After they leave, Macbeth imagines a blood-covered dagger before him. When the bell sounds, Macbeth steals away to commit the murder.

(A) Historical Connections

Lighting

? Theaters in Shakespeare's time did not have elaborate lighting and stage effects. What clues in the stage directions and dialogue would alert audiences that the time was after midnight? [Possible answers: references to the torch; the moon being down; the hour being past twelve o'clock; the stars out like unlit candles; Fleance's comment that "'tis later."]

(B) Vocabulary Note

The Prefix [*a*-]

People now say someone is "in bed," not "a-bed." But there are a few forms that are still used with the introductory *a* that means "on" or "in," such as *aloft*. Ask students to think of other examples. [Possible responses: *atop, aboard, aflutter.*]

(C) Reading Skills and Strategies

Responding to the Text

? Do you think Macbeth is telling the truth? [Sample responses: Yes, having taken things into his own hands, he is concentrating less on the prophecy; or, no, he is trying not to arouse Banquo's suspicions.]

Answers to Margin Questions

Stage Direction. Fleance is Banquo's son. Earlier, the witches told Banquo that he would beget kings—perhaps this son. The play gives no indication if Macbeth and Lady Macbeth have children other than Lady Macbeth's reference to having nursed a baby.

Line 24. He may wish to find out if Banquo would support his claim if Duncan died naturally, to feel Banquo out as a possible accessory, or to find out in general what Banquo is thinking. Students might say Macbeth's motives are self-serving.

Getting Students Involved

Cooperative Learning

Looking Back in History. Divide the class into groups to research and share information about specific historical references in *Macbeth*. Possible topics are the family trees of Macbeth and Lady Macbeth, showing their relationship to royalty; maps of or specific information on the locations mentioned in the text; or the actual chronology of historical events, such as the Scottish wars during the rule of Edward the Confessor. Have the groups produce a particular collaborative project—such as a family tree, map, or oral presentation—to share with the class. Designated roles could include the following: a leader to guide the group; researchers to gather information; synthesizers to put the information together into a final format; and presenters to explain the completed project.

Ⓐ Struggling Readers

Breaking Down Difficult Text

To help students comprehend this important soliloquy, which extends through l. 64, read it aloud or have students listen to the recording. Then, guide the group in a line-by-line analysis, asking students to paraphrase every few lines. Encourage students to discuss what they learn about Macbeth's state of mind. [Possible response: His anxiety about the murder he plans to commit is making him unbalanced.]

Ⓑ Elements of Literature

Theme

? In what way does this soliloquy reflect the theme of appearance versus reality? [Possible response: Macbeth's hallucination shows how appearance and reality have become interchangeable in his crazed condition. The two states have become blurred.]

Ⓒ Critical Thinking

Making Connections

? How does Macbeth's attitude toward wicked dreams differ from Banquo's in ll. 7–9? [Possible answer: Banquo deliberately stays awake to avoid bad dreams; Macbeth seems to revel in them.]

Answers to Margin Questions

Line 32. The bell signals the murder of Duncan.

Line 41. He draws his own dagger to compare it to the imaginary one. Some students may say that an imaginary dagger is more effective; others, that an actual dagger would clearly show the power of Macbeth's vivid imagination.

Macbeth. Good repose the while!

Banquo.
Thanks, sir. The like to you!

[*Exit* BANQUO, *with* FLEANCE.]

Macbeth.
Go bid thy mistress, when my drink is ready,
She strike upon the bell. Get thee to bed.

[*Exit* SERVANT.]

Is this a dagger which I see before me,
The handle toward my hand? Come, let me clutch thee.
I have thee not, and yet I see thee still.
Art thou not, fatal vision, sensible°
To feeling as to sight, or art thou but
A dagger of the mind, a false creation,
Proceeding from the heat-oppressèd brain?
I see thee yet, in form as palpable°
As this which now I draw.
Thou marshal'st me the way that I was going;
And such an instrument I was to use.
Mine eyes are made the fools o' th' other senses,
Or else worth all the rest. I see thee still;
And on thy blade and dudgeon° gouts° of blood,
Which was not so before. There's no such thing.
It is the bloody business which informs°
Thus to mine eyes. Now o'er the one half-world
Nature seems dead, and wicked dreams abuse°
The curtained sleep; witchcraft celebrates

? **32.** *What is to happen upon the ringing of the bell?*

36. sensible: perceptible to the senses.

40. palpable: obvious.

? **41.** *What does Macbeth do at this moment? If you were directing the play, would you suspend a dagger in front of Macbeth during this speech? Why or why not?*

46. dudgeon: hilt. **gouts:** large drops.

48. informs: gives shape.

50. abuse: deceive.

"Is this a dagger which I see before me,
The handle toward my hand?"

From the Stratford Festival production of *Macbeth* (1983).

Using Students' Strengths

Intrapersonal Learners

Although the play may deemphasize the murder of Duncan by placing it offstage, remind students that Macbeth is about to take a human life. Ask them to think about Duncan, who is about to be murdered in his sleep, and to jot down a few notes about the feelings they have about him as a king and as a human being. Ask students to share their ideas with the class.

Auditory Learners

Macbeth and Lady Macbeth are speaking in hushed tones in a darkened castle. In these scenes, sounds fuel the imagination. The ringing of the bell, the screaming of the owl, the crickets' crying, the muttered utterances of disturbed sleep, and the knocking at the gate move the plot forward. Read aloud these scenes, letting students create the sound effects.

Pale Hecate's° offerings; and withered murder,
Alarumed° by his sentinel, the wolf,
Whose howl's his watch, thus with his stealthy pace,
With Tarquin's° ravishing strides, towards his design
Moves like a ghost. Thou sure and firm-set earth,
Hear not my steps, which way they walk, for fear
Thy very stones prate of my whereabout,
And take the present horror from the time,
Which now suits with it.° Whiles I threat, he lives:
Words to the heat of deeds too cold breath gives.

[*A bell rings.*]

I go, and it is done: the bell invites me.
Hear it not, Duncan, for it is a knell
That summons thee to heaven, or to hell. [*Exit.*]

Scene 2. *Macbeth's castle.*

Enter LADY MACBETH.

Lady Macbeth.
That which hath made them drunk hath made me bold;
What hath quenched them hath given me fire. Hark! Peace!
It was the owl that shrieked, the fatal bellman,
Which gives the stern'st good-night.° He is about it.
The doors are open, and the surfeited grooms
Do mock their charge with snores. I have drugged their possets,°
That death and nature do contend about them,
Whether they live or die.

Macbeth (*within*). Who's there? What, ho?

Lady Macbeth.
Alack, I am afraid they have awaked.
And 'tis not done! Th' attempt and not the deed
Confounds° us. Hark! I laid their daggers ready;
He could not miss 'em. Had he not resembled
My father as he slept, I had done't.

[*Enter* MACBETH.]

My husband!

Macbeth.
I have done the deed. Didst thou not hear a noise?

Lady Macbeth.
I heard the owl scream and the crickets cry.
Did not you speak?

Macbeth. When?

Lady Macbeth. Now.

Macbeth. As I descended?

Lady Macbeth. Ay.

52. Hecate's: Hecate (hek′it), goddess of sorcery.

53. Alarumed: called to action.

55. Tarquin's: Tarquin was a Roman tyrant who raped a woman named Lucrece.

60. now suits with it: now seems suitable to it.

? **64.** *Trace in this soliloquy a vision, a call to action, and a leave-taking. What should you be feeling as an audience as Macbeth exits?*

? **3.** *What sound would you hear here? In this soliloquy, who are the "them" and who is "He"?*

4. stern'st good-night: The owl's call is supposed to portend death. The bellman was a person who rang a bell outside a condemned person's cell the night before his execution, to warn him to confess his sins.

6. possets: bedtime drinks.

11. Confounds: ruins.

? **13.** *How should Lady Macbeth say this last line, which reveals why the plans have changed? Do you think she is beginning to show remorse?*

D Critical Thinking

Defending Interpretations

? Shakespearean critic G. Wilson Knight points out that Shakespeare includes Christian imagery throughout *Macbeth,* depicting the murder as a conflict between grace and evil. If the play is interpreted in this way, how does Macbeth, in this soliloquy, reject grace and turn himself over to the powers of evil? [He rejects his good reasons for not killing Duncan. As he approaches Duncan's chamber, Macbeth imitates Tarquin's stealth and knowingly embraces evil.]

E Elements of Literature

Tragedy

? In what way does the bell toll not only for Duncan but also for the tragic hero? [Possible response: The bell that summons the king to heaven or hell also announces Macbeth's journey to damnation.]

Summary

Scene 2: Lady Macbeth drugged Duncan's guards but has been unable to murder Duncan because of his resemblance to her father. Macbeth murders Duncan offstage and reenters, deeply troubled and dazed. Lady Macbeth scolds him and places the bloody daggers beside the sleeping grooms, whom she smears with blood.

F Critical Thinking

Expressing an Opinion

? Why do you think Shakespeare chose not to show Duncan's murder? [Sample response: It might detract from the still-unfolding suspense of the scene.]

Answers to Margin Questions

Line 64. Vision: ll. 33–49; call to action: ll. 50–61; leave-taking: ll. 62–64. Possible feelings: horror; revulsion; suspense.

Line 3. You would hear an owl shrieking. The grooms are "them" and Macbeth is "He."

Line 13. She might speak with remorse, tenderness, or surprise at her own inability to overcome her emotions. If she is not feeling remorse, she at least shows a more vulnerable side of her character.

Skill Link

Making Inferences About Character

When you make an inference about a character, you make an intelligent guess about his or her personality, feelings, and behavior based on evidence in the text. When making inferences about a character, pay attention to the character's speech, appearance, thoughts, and actions. It is important to also pay attention to what other characters say and think about the character.

Activities

1. As students complete each act, ask them to make inferences about Macbeth. What is he really like? What motivates him to act the way he does? What are his true feelings?
2. After students complete the play, have them write a character analysis of Lady Macbeth. What are her strengths? her weaknesses? What do those around her think about her? What is her relationship with her husband?

Ⓐ English Language Learners
Supplying Missing Words
Students might have difficulty with the construction of this sentence. Point out that this is a shortened version of "It is a foolish thought to say that this is a sorry sight."

Ⓑ Reading Skills and Strategies
Comparing and Contrasting
? How is killing Duncan different from killing Macdonwald? How are they similar? [Possible answers: Killing on the battlefield to defend one's country against a traitor is acceptable, whereas the assassination of the king for personal, selfish gain is not. Students may say, however, that the brutal way in which Macbeth kills Macdonwald shows a side of Macbeth's nature that will emerge more fully in the murder of Duncan. They may point out that Macbeth believes he is justified in committing both murders.]

Ⓒ Elements of Literature
Irony
? What is ironic about Macbeth's desire for a blessing? [It is ironic that he desires a blessing when he has just broken a religious commandment by killing the king, a person who supposedly rules by divine right.]

Answer to Margin Question
Line 33. Possible answers: Yes, the words "must not" and "make us mad" suggest that she is fighting to control a troubled soul; or, no, she is just trying to calm Macbeth.

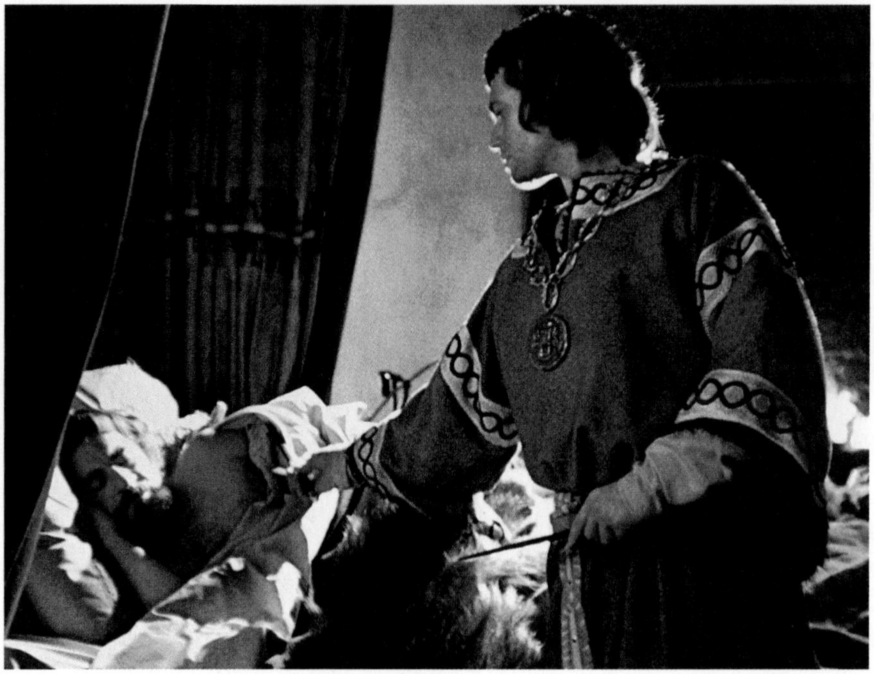

Macbeth pointing the dagger at Duncan in Roman Polanski's film production of *Macbeth* (1971).

Macbeth. Hark!
Who lies i' th' second chamber?
Lady Macbeth. Donalbain.
Macbeth. This is a sorry sight.
Lady Macbeth.
A foolish thought, to say a sorry sight.
Macbeth.
There's one did laugh in 's sleep, and one cried "Murder!"
That they did wake each other. I stood and heard them.
But they did say their prayers, and addressed them
Again to sleep.
Lady Macbeth. There are two lodged together.
Macbeth.
One cried "God bless us!" and "Amen" the other,
As they had seen me with these hangman's hands:
List'ning their fear, I could not say "Amen,"
When they did say "God bless us!"
Lady Macbeth. Consider it not so deeply.
Macbeth.
But wherefore could not I pronounce "Amen"?
I had most need of blessing, and "Amen"
Stuck in my throat.
Lady Macbeth. These deeds must not be thought
After these ways; so, it will make us mad.

? **33.** *Is Lady Macbeth fighting for control here?*

Macbeth.
Methought I heard a voice cry "Sleep no more!
Macbeth does murder sleep"—the innocent sleep,
Sleep that knits up the raveled sleave° of care, **D**
The death of each day's life, sore labor's bath,
Balm of hurt minds, great nature's second course,°
Chief nourisher in life's feast——

Lady Macbeth. What do you mean?

Macbeth.
Still it cried "Sleep no more!" to all the house:
"Glamis hath murdered sleep, and therefore Cawdor
Shall sleep no more: Macbeth shall sleep no more."

Lady Macbeth
Who was it that thus cried? Why, worthy thane,
You do unbend your noble strength, to think
So brainsickly of things. Go get some water,
And wash this filthy witness from your hand.
Why did you bring these daggers from the place?
They must lie there: go carry them, and smear
The sleepy grooms with blood.

Macbeth. I'll go no more.
I am afraid to think what I have done;
Look on 't again I dare not.

Lady Macbeth. Infirm of purpose!
Give me the daggers. The sleeping and the dead
Are but as pictures. 'Tis the eye of childhood
That fears a painted devil. If he do bleed,
I'll gild the faces of the grooms withal, **E**
For it must seem their guilt. [*Exit. Knock within.*]

Macbeth. Whence is that knocking?
How is't with me, when every noise appalls me?
What hands are here? Ha! They pluck out mine eyes!
Will all great Neptune's ocean wash this blood
Clean from my hand? No; this my hand will rather
The multitudinous seas incarnadine,°
Making the green one red.

[*Enter* LADY MACBETH.] **F**

Lady Macbeth.
My hands are of your color, but I shame
To wear a heart so white. (*Knock.*) I hear a knocking
At the south entry. Retire we to our chamber.
A little water clears us of this deed:
How easy is it then! Your constancy
Hath left you unattended.° (*Knock.*) Hark! more knocking.
Get on your nightgown, lest occasion call us
And show us to be watchers.° Be not lost
So poorly in your thoughts.

36. raveled sleave: tangled thread.

38. second course: sleep (the less substantial first course is food).

? **41.** *Who else complained about sleep? In what way has Glamis "murdered sleep"?*

? **46.** *What is the "filthy witness"? What actions are the couple engaged in here? In the next line, Lady Macbeth discovers the daggers. Why is she so alarmed at seeing them in her husband's hands? How could Macbeth have been carrying them so they weren't visible before?*

? **55.** *What will Lady Macbeth do to the grooms if Duncan bleeds enough?*

61. incarnadine: make red.

? **63.** *Based on this speech, what does Lady Macbeth look like?*

68. Your . . . unattended: Your firmness has deserted you.

70. watchers: that is, up late.

? **71.** *What is Macbeth acting like?*

D Elements of Literature

Figurative Language

Identify the metaphors that describe sleep. [a knitter who untangles the threads of care; the death of the life of each day; a bath that soothes a laborer; an ointment that heals the mind; the body's greatest need after food] **What effect do these metaphors suggest that sleep has on people?** [It comforts, heals, and nourishes them.]

E Appreciating Language

Puns

? When one puts gold leaf on something, it is then *gilt,* a homophone of *guilt.* How does this pun reflect the theme of appearance versus reality? [While appearances (gilt) might conceal reality, they are only a superficial layer barely covering what is truly inside (guilt).]

F Elements of Literature

Imagery

? How does the imagery concerning blood and water in Macbeth's speech contrast with that in Lady Macbeth's speech? [He believes that "all great Neptune's ocean" could not clean his hands, while she claims "a little water clears us of this deed."] What is the significance of this difference? [Lady Macbeth is practical—water washes away blood. Macbeth is speaking on a metaphorical level. He believes his sin will contaminate the oceans of the world.]

Answers to Margin Questions

Line 41. Banquo decides not to sleep in order to avoid evil dreams (II.1.6–9). Since first imagining Duncan's murder, Macbeth has been stuck in time, at the moment of the murder. Without sleep to make the transition to a new day, he may continue to relive that moment. The murder has put an end to sleep and an end to the passage of time for Macbeth.

Line 46. It is Duncan's blood. They are cleaning up after the murder. She is probably shocked that Macbeth removed the murder weapons, which could implicate him. They may have been in his belt or sleeve.

Line 55. She will smear the blood on their faces.

Line 63. Possible answer: Her hands are bloody, but she appears confident.

Line 71. Possible answer: He is acting lost and dazed.

Professional Notes

Critical Comment: Murdering Sleep

The critic Mark Van Doren points out that nothing could be more horrible than Macbeth's act of murdering sleep, for in Shakespeare's plays, sleep "is ever the privilege of the good and the reward of the innocent. If it has been put to death, there is no goodness left. One of the witches knows how to torture sailors by keeping sleep from their penthouse lids [1.3.19–20], but only Macbeth can murder sleep itself." The loss of sleep is the loss of hope; Macbeth's world is beginning to disintegrate. Ask students how they react to this motif of insomnia. What often results from the inability to sleep? [hallucinations; illness; irrationality; depression]

(A) Elements of Literature
Tragedy

? In what way does this line convey the message that Macbeth knows the depth of evil to which he has sunk? [If he fully acknowledges the horror of his deed, he will be unable to bear knowing he committed it.]

(B) Critical Thinking
Making Judgments

? How serious is Macbeth when he says he wishes Duncan could be awakened by the knocking? Explain. [Possible responses: He is serious because he is genuinely horrified by his deed; or, he is not serious because he knows it is impossible.]

Summary

Scene 3: A drunken porter responds to Macduff's and Lennox's knocking at the gate. Lennox describes strange upheavals in nature the previous night as Macduff discovers Duncan's body. When Macbeth says that he killed Duncan's grooms because they had murdered Duncan, Lady Macbeth faints. Duncan's sons Malcolm and Donalbain flee the country fearing for their lives.

(C) Historical Connections
Gunpowder Plot of 1605

This play would have held great interest for James I, who lived through the discovery of the Gunpowder Plot in November 1605. Some critics believe that the porter's speech is filled with references to the Jesuit priest Father Henry Garnett, who was implicated in the plot and hanged as a traitor. Garnett used the assumed name "Farmer" and defended equivocation as just. (For more on this plot, see Professional Notes below.)

Answers to Margin Questions
Stage direction. Possible responses: He might wish it could awaken his soul or conscience; or, he might wish he could awaken to a state of grace.

Stage direction. The porter might stagger, fumble with the gates or keys, pantomime the people he is imagining, put his hands over his ears, or pretend to do his own knocking.

"My hands are of your color, but I shame
To wear a heart so white."

From the Stratford Festival production of *Macbeth* (1983).

(A) **Macbeth.**
To know my deed, 'twere best not know myself.

[*Knock.*]

(B) Wake Duncan with thy knocking! I would thou couldst!
[*Exeunt.*]

Scene 3. *Macbeth's castle.*

Enter a PORTER. *Knocking within.*

Porter. Here's a knocking indeed! If a man were porter of hell gate, he should have old° turning the key. (*Knock.*) Knock, knock, knock! Who's there, i' th' name of Beelzebub?° (C) Here's a farmer, that hanged himself on th' expectation of plenty. Come in time! Have napkins enow° about you; here you'll sweat for 't. (*Knock.*) Knock, knock! Who's there, in th' other devil's name? Faith, here's an equivocator,° that could swear in both the scales against either scale; who committed treason enough for God's sake, yet could not equivocate to heaven. O, come in, equivocator. (*Knock.*) Knock, knock, knock! Who's there? Faith, here's an English tailor come hither for stealing out of a French hose:° come in, tailor. Here you may roast your goose.° (*Knock.*) Knock,

? **Stage direction.** *In the theater, this sharp, loud knocking is frightening. In the next line, what might Macbeth wish the knocking could awake in himself?*

? **Stage direction.** *Note that the porter is drunk. What would he be doing during this long speech while the knocking persists?*

2. have old: grow old.

3. Beelzebub: the Devil.

5. enow: enough.

7. equivocator: The porter means a Jesuit (who allegedly used false arguments in his zeal for souls).

12. French hose: tightfitting stocking.

13. goose: iron used by a tailor for pressing.

Professional Notes

The Gunpowder Plot of 1605
In his book *Witches & Jesuits,* historian Gary Wills outlines the basic facts of the Gunpowder Plot of 1605. This plot greatly shocked Protestants of the time. "A cell of papists—the 'enemy within' of that time, directed from Rome by skulking Jesuits—had trundled keg after keg of gunpowder into a vault under Parliament. A munitions expert named Guy Fawkes was discovered with the detonating materials, ready to ignite the fuse (train) when the King was addressing his Parliament, in presence of the Prince his heir and all leading members of his court. The Parliament—all the Lords Spiritual and Temporal, the leading justices, and members of Commons—would be consumed in a particularly horrible way."

knock; never at quiet! What are you? But this place is too cold for hell. I'll devil-porter it no further. I had thought to have let in some of all professions that go the primrose way to th' everlasting bonfire. (*Knock.*) Anon, anon! (*Opens an entrance.*) I pray you, remember the porter.

[*Enter* MACDUFF *and* LENNOX.]

Macduff.
Was it so late, friend, ere you went to bed,
That you do lie so late?

Porter. Faith, sir, we were carousing till the second cock:° and drink, sir, is a great provoker of three things.

Macduff. What three things does drink especially provoke?

Porter. Marry, sir, nose-painting, sleep, and urine. Lechery, sir, it provokes and unprovokes; it provokes the desire, but it takes away the performance: therefore much drink may be said to be an equivocator with lechery: it makes him and it mars him; it sets him on and it takes him off; it persuades him and disheartens him; makes him stand to and not stand to; in conclusion, equivocates him in a sleep, and giving him the lie, leaves him.

Macduff. I believe drink gave thee the lie° last night.

Porter. That it did, sir, i' the very throat on me: but I requited him for his lie, and, I think, being too strong for him, though he took up my legs sometime, yet I make a shift to cast° him.

Macduff. Is thy master stirring?

[*Enter* MACBETH.]

Our knocking has awaked him; here he comes.

Lennox.
Good morrow, noble sir.

Macbeth. Good morrow, both.

Macduff.
Is the king stirring, worthy thane?

Macbeth. Not yet.

Macduff.
He did command me to call timely° on him:
I have almost slipped the hour.

Macbeth. I'll bring you to him.

Macduff.
I know this is a joyful trouble to you;
But yet 'tis one.

Macbeth.
The labor we delight in physics° pain.
This is the door.

Macduff. I'll make so bold to call,
For 'tis my limited service.° [*Exit* MACDUFF.]

Lennox.
Goes the king hence today?

21. second cock: about 3 A.M.

32. gave thee the lie: pun meaning "called you a liar" and "stretched you out, lying in bed."

35. cast: here, a pun meaning "to cast in plaster" and "to vomit" (cast out).

? **36.** ***All the time this humorous bantering is going on, what do we know these king's men are about to discover?***

40. timely: early.

44. physics: cures.

46. limited service: appointed duty.

D Struggling Readers

Say Something

At several designated points in the porter's speech, have students pause and say something to a partner about what they've just read. Encourage them to start a dialogue by asking each other what explicit details in the speech might support the idea that the castle is hell. ["Porter of hell gate," "Beezelbub," etc.] For help in applying this strategy, see the *Reading Strategies Handbook,* p. 85, in the *Reading Skills and Strategies* binder.

E Critical Reading

Making Judgments

? Why do you think the porter appears in this act? [Possible responses: He provides comic relief, lessening the tension of the events in the act; or, his description of Macbeth's castle as hell underscores the horrible deed that has taken place there and builds suspense about its consequences.]

F Elements of Literature

Irony

? What is ironic about Macduff's use of the word *timely?* [Macduff's arrival is not "timely" but too late to save the king.]

Answer to Margin Question
Line 36. The body of Duncan and the bloodied grooms.

Crossing the Curriculum

Social Studies
From King Arthur to Prince William, the English have always worried about succession. Review with students the laws of succession discussed on p. 311. Have students research the laws of succession in England today and report on debates concerning those statutes and the status of the monarchy itself. Students should create a chart comparing the rules then and now, as well as the reasons behind the differences.

Science
Read aloud Lennox's first speech on p. 326 and have students brainstorm in groups to provide natural explanations for the unnatural occurrences mentioned there and in II.4.1–18. Ask each group to write a brief report outlining their speculations. [For example, an earthquake could cause chimneys to crumble and the earth to shake. However, how often does Scotland experience earthquakes?]

Ⓐ Elements of Literature

Theme

Lennox reports an instance of nature mirroring unnatural events in society. Although such theories are rejected today, Elizabethans firmly believed that when people committed horrible acts, darkness, storms, earthquakes, and unnatural occurrences, such as deformed births, followed. (See Professional Notes below.)

Ⓑ English Language Learners

Supplying Missing Letters

Shakespeare often uses unfamiliar contractions. For example, *o'* means "of," *th'* means "the," and *is't* means "is it." Students should make a list of such contractions and their meanings as they read.

Ⓒ Reading Skills and Strategies

Comparing and Contrasting

? Compare this passage to II.1.49–64. How are Macbeth's and Macduff's purposes similar? How is the bell used in each passage? [Both characters are trying to find words that are adequate for the situation—Macbeth to work himself up to commit murder; Macduff to express horror at the evil that has been done. Ironically, the earlier bell signaled the time for Macbeth to commit murder, but here it rings to announce that murder.]

Answers to Margin Questions

Line 47. Macbeth must be sick with anxiety. As he says the first two words, he realizes they are a lie, so he amends his statement. His correction could make him appear nervous.

Line 54. Unnatural winds and voices, screeching owls, and earthquakes parallel the unnatural death of Duncan.

Line 55. The line is ironic because the night was rough for reasons that Macbeth knows but Lennox does not. Macbeth might speak as if he were simply agreeing with Lennox but with a sidelong glance at his wife. His tone might indicate a trace of fatigue or remorse.

Line 63. Macduff speaks of the king as if he were a sacred building, or temple, that is a sacrilege to attack. This image reflects the Elizabethan belief that kings were divinely anointed.

Macbeth. He does: he did appoint so.

Lennox.
The night has been unruly. Where we lay,
Our chimneys were blown down, and, as they say,
Lamentings heard i' th' air, strange screams of death,
And prophesying with accents terrible
Of dire combustion° and confused events
New hatched to th' woeful time: the obscure bird
Clamored the livelong night. Some say, the earth
Was feverous and did shake.

Macbeth. 'Twas a rough night.

Lennox.
My young remembrance cannot parallel
A fellow to it.

[*Enter* MACDUFF.]

Macduff.
O horror, horror, horror! Tongue nor heart
Cannot conceive nor name thee.

Macbeth and Lennox. What's the matter?

Macduff.
Confusion now hath made his masterpiece.
Most sacrilegious murder hath broke ope
The Lord's anointed temple,° and stole thence
The life o' th' building.

Macbeth. What is't you say? The life?

Lennox.
Mean you his majesty?

Macduff.
Approach the chamber, and destroy your sight
With a new Gorgon:° do not bid me speak;
See, and then speak yourselves. Awake, awake!

[*Exeunt* MACBETH *and* LENNOX.]

Ring the alarum bell. Murder and treason!
Banquo and Donalbain! Malcolm! Awake!
Shake off this downy sleep, death's counterfeit,
And look on death itself! Up, up, and see
The great doom's image! Malcolm! Banquo!
As from your graves rise up, and walk like sprites,
To countenance° this horror. Ring the bell.

[*Bell rings. Enter* LADY MACBETH.]

Lady Macbeth.
What's the business,
That such a hideous trumpet calls to parley°
The sleepers of the house? Speak, speak!

Macduff. O gentle lady,
'Tis not for you to hear what I can speak:

? 47. *How must Macbeth be feeling?*

52. **combustion:** tumult; uproar.

? 54. *In Elizabethan times, people often believed that nature mirrored terrible things happening to human beings, especially to kings. How did this weather mirror what was happening to the king in Macbeth's castle?*

? 55. *A single line, but full of irony. How would Macbeth say it?*

62. **Lord's anointed temple:** body of the king.

? 63. *How would you explain Macduff's metaphors?*

66. **Gorgon:** creature from Greek mythology whose face could turn an onlooker to stone.

74. **countenance:** be in keeping with.

76. **parley:** conference of war.

Professional Notes

The Elizabethan World

The Elizabethans thought the universe extended in a great chain beginning with God and extending down to the lowliest insects and worms. Everything in this chain had a place, reflecting a natural order. Harmony in heaven mirrored harmony in nature and in the political and social world. When this order was disrupted, the structure of the universe broke down. Audiences therefore were probably not surprised when Duncan's killing led to natural disturbances.

The repetition, in a woman's ear,
Would murder as it fell.

[*Enter* BANQUO.]

O Banquo, Banquo!
Our royal master's murdered.

Lady Macbeth. Woe, alas!
What, in our house?

Banquo. Too cruel anywhere.
Dear Duff, I prithee, contradict thyself,
And say it is not so.

[*Enter* MACBETH, LENNOX, *and* ROSS.]

Macbeth.
Had I but died an hour before this chance,
I had lived a blessèd time; for from this instant
There's nothing serious in mortality:°
All is but toys. Renown and grace is dead,
The wine of life is drawn, and the mere lees°
Is left this vault° to brag of.

[*Enter* MALCOLM *and* DONALBAIN.]

Donalbain.
What is amiss?

Macbeth. You are, and do not know't.
The spring, the head, the fountain of your blood
Is stopped; the very source of it is stopped.

Macduff.
Your royal father's murdered.

Malcolm. O, by whom?

Lennox.
Those of his chamber, as it seemed, had done't:
Their hands and faces were all badged° with blood;
So were their daggers, which unwiped we found
Upon their pillows. They stared, and were distracted.
No man's life was to be trusted with them.

Macbeth.
O, yet I do repent me of my fury,
That I did kill them.

Macduff. Wherefore did you so?

Macbeth.
Who can be wise, amazed, temp'rate and furious,
Loyal and neutral, in a moment? No man.
The expedition° of my violent love
Outrun the pauser, reason. Here lay Duncan,
His silver skin laced with his golden blood,
And his gashed stabs looked like a breach in nature
For ruin's wasteful entrance: there, the murderers,
Steeped in the colors of their trade, their daggers

? **82.** *The emphasis on Lady Macbeth's gentleness and fairness when we know the foulness underneath might well merit a snicker from the audience. The snicker might be expected to grow into a laugh when she says, "What, in our house?" These are difficult moments to act. How do you think Lady Macbeth should be behaving?*

87. mortality: life.

89. lees: dregs.

90. vault: pun on "wine vault" and the "vault of heaven."

? **94.** *Macbeth and Lady Macbeth might well look at each other at this moment. Does Lennox draw the conclusion they wanted him to draw: that the servants killed Duncan?*

96. badged: marked.

104. expedition: haste.

D Appreciating Language

Style

? How does the style of Macbeth's and Macduff's announcements of Duncan's death to the king's sons differ? [Macbeth speaks in metaphors; Macduff is straightforward.]

E Critical Thinking

Making Judgments

? What has Macbeth done that was not in the plan? Was this wise? [Sample responses: He killed the two grooms. No, there was no reason to complicate the situation with more murders; or yes, Lennox appears to believe Macbeth's story, and the grooms cannot protest.]

F Elements of Literature

Imagery

? Why does Macbeth use such extravagant imagery to describe Duncan's death? [Possible responses: His pretentious eloquence is meant to cover up his insincerity. His anxiety and guilt make him ramble on inappropriately.] **Point out that Macbeth says that Duncan had "silver skin" and "golden blood," implying Duncan's royal and saintly qualities.**

Answers to Margin Questions

Line 82. Possible answer: She must play the part seriously, expressing the surprise and horror that such a deed merits.

Line 94. Some students may say that "as it seemed" suggests that Lennox is not fully convinced. Others may argue that Lennox's line "No man's life was to be trusted with them" is as good as an indictment.

Reaching All Students

Struggling Readers

Have students do a Sketch to Stretch exercise, drawing images that relate to an assigned passage to help them visualize the events. Have them share their drawings with the class and discuss the thematic links, conclusions, generalizations, or cause-and-effect relationships that the images help them see. For help in applying this strategy, see the *Reading Strategies Handbook,* p. 101, in the *Reading Skills and Strategies* binder.

English Language Learners

Have students choose words to include on working English vocabulary lists. Check the lists to help students focus on more common words rather than obscure, archaic, or high-level words. For other strategies for engaging English language learners with the literature, see

- *Lesson Plans Including Strategies for English-Language Learners*

Advanced Learners

Have students rewrite a small portion of the play in prose form. They should make archaic sentence structures more modern by changing inverted word orders and adding missing letters to contractions. Students can read their prose versions aloud and the rest of the class can guess which passages in the play have been rewritten.

A Critical Thinking
Interpreting

? What causes Lady Macbeth to cry out? [Possible answers: She follows her own suggestion in I.7.78, and makes her "griefs and clamor roar." She is trying to draw attention away from Macbeth's absurd and unnatural speech by pretending to faint; or, she is shocked by the murder of the grooms, begins to fall apart, and actually faints.]

B Elements of Literature
Imagery

? What does the image of Banquo standing in "the great hand of God" suggest about his intent? [He intends to stand on the side of righteousness in fighting the "treasonous malice" that killed Duncan. It also suggests that he does not believe that the murder has been avenged yet—in other words, he fears that the grooms were not guilty.]

C Critical Thinking
Interpreting

? What does each of the following characters seem to think of the evidence: Lennox, Banquo, Macduff, Lady Macbeth, Macbeth, Malcolm, and Donalbain? [Sample responses: Most students may think that Lennox believes the grooms are guilty. Banquo is not sure but may be suspicious of Macbeth because of what he knows from Act I. Macduff appears to agree with Banquo. Lady Macbeth may think that Macbeth reveals too much with the murder of the grooms and his cover-up speech; or, she may applaud his deception. Macbeth is starting to act on his own, which may mean that he feels confident that the evidence points away from him. Malcolm and Donalbain may not suspect anyone in particular—they just fear for their lives and want to flee.]

D Reading Skills and Strategies
Drawing Conclusions

? What does Donalbain's parting comment mean? [Those closest to the crown or in line for it are in the most danger of being killed.]

Unmannerly breeched with gore.° Who could refrain,°
That had a heart to love, and in that heart
Courage to make 's love known?

A **Lady Macbeth.** Help me hence, ho!

Macduff.
Look to the lady.

Malcolm (*aside to* DONALBAIN). Why do we hold our tongues,
That most may claim this argument for ours?°

Donalbain (*aside to* MALCOLM).
What should be spoken here,
Where our fate, hid in an auger-hole,°
May rush, and seize us? Let's away:
Our tears are not yet brewed.

Malcolm (*aside to* DONALBAIN). Nor our strong sorrow
Upon the foot of motion.°

Banquo. Look to the lady.

[LADY MACBETH *is carried out.*]

And when we have our naked frailties hid,°
That suffer in exposure, let us meet
And question° this most bloody piece of work,
To know it further. Fears and scruples° shake us.
B In the great hand of God I stand, and thence
Against the undivulged pretense° I fight
Of treasonous malice.

Macduff. And so do I.

All. So all.

Macbeth.
Let's briefly° put on manly readiness,
And meet i' th' hall together.

All. Well contented.

[*Exeunt all but* MALCOLM *and* DONALBAIN.]

C **Malcolm.**
What will you do? Let's not consort with them.
To show an unfelt sorrow is an office°
Which the false man does easy. I'll to England.

Donalbain.
To Ireland, I; our separated fortune
Shall keep us both the safer. Where we are
D There's daggers in men's smiles; the near in blood,
The nearer bloody.

Malcolm. This murderous shaft that's shot
Hath not yet lighted, and our safest way
Is to avoid the aim. Therefore to horse;
And let us not be dainty of° leave-taking,
But shift away. There's warrant° in that theft
Which steals itself° when there's no mercy left.

[*Exeunt.*]

110. unmannerly breeched with gore: unbecomingly covered with blood, as if wearing red trousers. **refrain:** check oneself.

114. That . . . ours: who are the most concerned with this topic.

116. auger-hole: unsuspected place.

119. Our tears . . . motion: We have not yet had time for tears, nor to express our sorrows in action.

120. naked frailties hid: poor bodies clothed.

122. question: discuss.

123. scruples: suspicions.

125. undivulged pretense: hidden purpose.

127. briefly: quickly.

130. office: function.

138. dainty of: fussy about.

139. warrant: justification.

140. steals itself: steals oneself away.

Scene 4. *Outside Macbeth's castle.*

Enter ROSS *with an* OLD MAN.

Old Man.
Threescore and ten I can remember well:
Within the volume of which time I have seen
Hours dreadful and things strange, but this sore° night
Hath trifled former knowings.°

Ross. Ha, good father,
Thou seest the heavens, as troubled with man's act,
Threatens his bloody stage. By th' clock 'tis day,
And yet dark night strangles the traveling lamp:°
Is't night's predominance,° or the day's shame,
That darkness does the face of earth entomb,
When living light should kiss it?

Old Man. 'Tis unnatural,
Even like the deed that's done. On Tuesday last
A falcon, tow'ring in her pride of place,°
Was by a mousing° owl hawked at and killed.

Ross.
And Duncan's horses—a thing most strange and certain—
Beauteous and swift, the minions° of their race,
Turned wild in nature, broke their stalls, flung out,°
Contending 'gainst obedience, as they would make
War with mankind.

Old Man. 'Tis said they eat° each other.

Ross.
They did so, to th' amazement of mine eyes,
That looked upon't.

[*Enter* MACDUFF.]

Here comes the good Macduff.
How goes the world, sir, now?

Macduff. Why, see you not?

Ross.
Is't known who did this more than bloody deed?

Macduff.
Those that Macbeth hath slain.

Ross. Alas, the day!
What good could they pretend?°

Macduff. They were suborned:°
Malcolm and Donalbain, the king's two sons,
Are stol'n away and fled, which puts upon them
Suspicion of the deed.

Ross. 'Gainst nature still.
Thriftless° ambition, that will ravin up°
Thine own life's means!° Then 'tis most like
The sovereignty will fall upon Macbeth.

3. sore: grievous.
4. trifled former knowings: made trifles of former experiences.

7. traveling lamp: sun.
8. predominance: astrological supremacy.

12. tow'ring . . . place: soaring at her summit.
13. mousing: normally mouse-eating.

15. minions: darlings.
16. flung out: lunged wildly.

18. eat: ate.

24. pretend: hope for. **suborned:** bribed.

28. Thriftless: wasteful. **ravin up:** greedily devour.
29. own life's means: parent.

Summary

Scene 4: Ross and an Old Man speak of wild and unnatural events that were observed during the night and the day following Duncan's murder. Macduff reveals that Duncan's sons are suspected of murdering their father and that Macbeth has gone to Scone to be installed as king. Macduff will not attend Macbeth's coronation, and he voices doubts about the new king's reign.

E Elements of Literature

Theme

? How does the dialogue between the Old Man and Ross compare to Lennox's speech in II.3.48–54? [Like Lennox, Ross and the Old Man present evidence that disorders in nature are mirroring the unnatural death of the king, supporting the Elizabethan idea that the murder is a disruption of natural law.]

F Elements of Literature

Figurative Language

? Here, Ross presents an image of Duncan's horses gone wild and cannibalizing each other. How are the horses a metaphor for Macbeth? [Possible answer: Macbeth, too, has been the minion of his race as the savior of his country. He, too, has turned wild, broken out of his rank, and destroyed one of his own.]

G Critical Thinking

Speculating

? Macduff could appear to be speaking plainly. How would the meaning change if you assume that he is speaking ironically? Why would he not speak his thoughts openly? [Possible answer: He could be insinuating that there was a plot. He might not speak openly if he lacks proof of a plot, does not trust Ross, or fears being implicated in the serious crimes.]

H Elements of Literature

Irony

? What is ironic about Ross's comment on the motive for the murder? [He has the correct motive but the wrong perpetrator.]

Skill Link

Applying Meanings of Roots

Explain that knowing the meanings of frequently used roots can help unlock the meanings of new words. For example, the root *vestire* in *invested* means "to clothe." This knowledge can help reveal the meaning of *invested* (II.4.32), which here means "clothed and crowned as king." Ask students to look up each of the following words from Act II in a dictionary. Have them tell what the root means and how it relates to the meaning of the word.

1. surfeited (II.2.5)	[facere—"to do"—to do more than]
2. infirm (II.2.51)	[firmus—"hold, support"—not firm, weak]
3. provoker (II.3.22)	[vocare—"to call"—to call forth]
4. beauteous (II.4.15)	[bellus—"pretty"—full of beauty]

Connections

Thomas De Quincey argues that an audience must feel a "sympathy of comprehension" for Macbeth and Lady Macbeth in order for the play to be effective. He does not intend or expect the audience to applaud them for their murderous actions but rather to try to understand the feelings of the characters. The knocking at the gate is a call to the audience to come back to reality, back from the depths of evil in Macbeth's hellish world. The knocking has a jarring effect on the audience, summoning them into the everyday world, so they can become keenly aware of the gravity and horror of the actions of Macbeth and his wife.

A Reading Skills and Strategies

Responding to the Text

? What were your own impressions of the section of *Macbeth* that De Quincey refers to? [Students who say that the knocking did not strike them as odd may acknowledge that a stage production would make the action more impressive. Other students may say that they found the knocking a strange intrusion—until they read of its effect on Macbeth and Lady Macbeth.]

B Reading Skills and Strategies

Finding the Main Idea

? Explain De Quincey's point in this paragraph. [Possible answer: The audience must feel some interest in or "sympathy of comprehension" for the murderer and want to understand him, or they will lose interest in the plot.]

C Historical Connections

Scottish kings were crowned on the Stone of Destiny—supposedly Jacob's pillow, as mentioned in Genesis 28:10–13. This stone was stolen and taken to Westminster Abbey by King Edward the Confessor in 1296.

Connections AN ESSAY

from On the Knocking at the Gate in *Macbeth*

Thomas De Quincey

From my boyish days I had always felt a great perplexity on one point in *Macbeth*. It was this: The knocking at the gate which succeeds to the murder of Duncan produced to my feelings an effect for which I never could account. The effect was that it reflected back upon the murderer a peculiar awfulness and a depth of solemnity; yet, however obstinately I endeavored with my understanding to comprehend this, for many years I never could see *why* it should produce such an effect.

. . . At length I solved it to my own satisfaction; and my solution is this: —Murder, in ordinary cases, where the sympathy is wholly directed to the case of the murdered person, is an incident of coarse and vulgar horror; and for this reason—that it flings the interest exclusively upon the natural but ignoble instinct by which we cleave to life: an instinct which, as being indispensable to the primal law of self-preservation, is the same in kind (though different in degree) amongst all living creatures. This instinct, therefore, because it annihilates all distinctions, and degrades the greatest of men to the level of "the poor beetle that we tread on," exhibits human nature in its most abject and humiliating attitude. Such an attitude would little suit the purposes of the poet. What then must he do? He must throw the interest on the murderer. Our sympathy must be with *him* (of course I mean a sympathy of comprehension, a sympathy by which we enter into his feelings, and are made to understand them—not a sympathy of pity or approbation). In the murdered person, all strife of thought, all flux and reflux of passion and of purpose, are crushed by one overwhelming panic; the fear of instant death smites him "with its petrific mace."[1] But in the murderer, such a murderer as a poet will condescend to, there must be raging some great storm of passion—jealousy, ambition, vengeance, hatred—which will create a hell within him; and into this hell we are to look.

In *Macbeth,* for the sake of gratifying his own enormous and teeming faculty of creation, Shakespeare has introduced two murderers: and, as usual in his hands, they are remarkably discriminated: but—though in Macbeth the strife of mind is greater than in his wife, the tiger spirit not so awake, and his feelings caught chiefly by contagion from her—yet, as both were finally involved in the guilt of murder, the

1. **petrific mace:** stone club. This is an allusion to Milton's *Paradise Lost* (Book X, line 294), in which Death wields a "mace petrific."

Macduff.
He is already named,° and gone to Scone°
To be invested.°
Ross. Where is Duncan's body?
Macduff.
Carried to Colmekill,°
The sacred storehouse of his predecessors
And guardian of their bones.
Ross. Will you to Scone?
Macduff.
No, cousin, I'll to Fife.

31. named: elected. **Scone** (skōōn).
32. invested: installed as king.
33. Colmekill: Iona Island, the ancient burying place of Scottish kings. (It was founded by St. Colm.)

Assessing Learning

Check Test: Questions and Answers

1. How does Duncan die? [Macbeth stabs him.]
2. Why doesn't Lady Macbeth murder Duncan? [The sleeping Duncan reminds her of her father.]
3. What does Lady Macbeth do to make others seem guilty? [She smears blood on the grooms.]
4. Immediately after Duncan dies, Macbeth hears a voice cry out. What does it say Macbeth has murdered? [sleep]
5. Who flees the castle in fear? [Duncan's sons, Malcolm and Donalbain]

Informal Assessment

Observation Assessment. As students discuss the play, note whether they are making specific references to the text. The following scale (three being the highest) may help you evaluate students quantitatively.

1 point: Speaks generally with little mention of acts, scenes, and lines
2 points: Refers to acts, scenes, and lines without citing specific references
3 points: Frequently cites specific references to acts, scenes, and lines

murderous mind of necessity is finally to be presumed in both. This was to be expressed; and, on its own account, as well as to make it a more proportionable antagonist to the unoffending nature of their victim, "the gracious Duncan," and adequately to expound "the deep damnation of his taking off," this was to be expressed with peculiar energy. We were to be made to feel that the human nature—i.e., the divine nature of love and mercy, spread through the hearts of all creatures, and seldom utterly withdrawn from man—was gone, vanished, extinct, and that the fiendish nature had taken its place. And, as this effect is marvellously accomplished in the *dialogues* and *soliloquies* themselves, so it is finally consummated by the expedient under consideration; and it is to this that I now solicit the reader's attention. If the reader has ever witnessed a wife, daughter, or sister in a fainting fit, he may chance to have observed that the most affecting moment in such a spectacle is *that* in which a sigh and a stirring announce the recommencement of suspended life.

. . . All action in any direction is best expounded, measured, and made apprehensible, by reaction. Now, applying this to the case in *Macbeth:* Here, as I have said, the retiring of the human heart and the entrance of the fiendish heart was to be expressed and made sensible. Another world has stepped in; and the murderers are taken out of the region of human things, human purposes, human desires. They are transfigured: Lady Macbeth is "unsexed"; Macbeth has forgot that he was born of woman; both are conformed to the image of devils; and the world of devils is suddenly revealed. But how shall this be conveyed and made palpable? (D) In order that a new world may step in, this world must for a time disappear. The murderers and the murder must be insulated—cut off by an immeasurable gulf from the ordinary tide and succession of human affairs—locked up and sequestered in some deep recess; we must be made sensible that the world of ordinary life is suddenly arrested, laid asleep, tranced, racked into a dread armistice; time must be annihilated, relation to things without abolished; and all must pass self-withdrawn into a deep syncope[2] and suspension of earthly passion. Hence it is that, when the deed is done, when the work of darkness is perfect, then the world of darkness passes away like a pageantry in the clouds: The knocking at the gate is heard, and it makes known audibly that the reaction has commenced; the human has made its reflux upon the fiendish; the pulses of life are beginning to beat again; and the reestablishment of the goings-on of the world in which we live first makes us profoundly sensible of the awful parenthesis that had suspended them. (E)

2. **syncope** (siŋ′kə·pē): unconsciousness.

Ross. Well, I will thither.

Macduff.
Well, may you see things well done there. Adieu, (F)
Lest our old robes sit easier than our new! (G)

Ross.
Farewell, father.

Old Man.
God's benison° go with you, and with those
That would make good of bad, and friends of foes! (H)
[*Exeunt omnes.*]

40. **benison:** blessing.

(D) Elements of Literature

Tragedy

? How does Macbeth's transfiguration confirm his role as the tragic hero? [Possible response: Destructive ambition leads Macbeth down a diabolical path and fundamentally changes his personality. He casts aside his humanity and becomes evil. Despite his rank, Macbeth seems to be on a path to an inevitable downfall.]

(E) Struggling Readers

Finding the Main Idea

Ask students what De Quincey's main point is. Help them determine this by pointing out topic sentences and supporting details that lead to the main idea. [Possible answer: The knocking represents the intrusion of the ordinary, everyday world on the devil's world that has reigned at Dunsinane since Duncan's murder.]

(F) Vocabulary Note

Foreign Words in English

Adieu comes from Old French and means "I commend you to God." According to *The Oxford English Dictionary,* however, it was used in English as early as Chaucer's time. Shakespeare used it in the sense of "formal leave-taking" in *Antony and Cleopatra, All's Well That Ends Well,* and here, in *Macbeth.*

(G) Elements of Literature

Figurative Language

? What warning does Macduff convey using the clothing metaphor? [He hints that with Macbeth as king instead of Duncan, their new situations ("robes") may not suit them as well as their old ones did.]

(H) Critical Thinking

Challenging the Text

? Is this line an appropriate end for this bloody act? Explain. [Sample responses: The Old Man's words may foreshadow events or warn that, by attending the coronation, Ross and other Macbeth supporters are opportunistic or hypocritical—trying to "make good of bad, and friends of foes." The line is appropriate not only because the Old Man is disturbed by recent events, but also because it reinforces the theme of reversal, of "fair is foul."]

Connecting Across Texts

Connecting with *Macbeth*

De Quincey presents an argument explaining the reasons for including the knocking at the gate in the play. After students read De Quincey's essay and "Macbeth's Porter" (p. 332), have them use the following chart to summarize and evaluate their own and the critic's theories for including the knocking and the porter scenes. (The critic's theories have been filled in.)

Purpose of the Knocking at the Gate and Porter Scenes

	What Is Gained	What Is Lost
Knocking	brings audience and Macbeths back to reality	immediacy of the horror inside Dunsinane
Porter	comic relief	suspense and intensity because of comic element

Critical Comment

This critic debunks the theories that Shakespeare created the porter's role in order to provide a part for everyone in his acting company or to lessen the tension of the scene through comic relief. Instead, he asserts that the porter's role is essential to the play and in fact increases tension and suspense by delaying the discovery of Duncan's body.

Ⓐ Literary Connections

Actors and Roles

In Shakespeare's theater, the problem often was not to find parts for everyone but to arrange the many roles so that a handful of actors could cover them. Actors were known to play multiple roles in a single production by deftly changing their costumes and appearances.

Ⓑ Literary Connections

The Porter's Scene

Not all critics, however, agree with this assessment. One argument for cutting the scene was given by the English poet Samuel Taylor Coleridge: "This low soliloquy of the Porter, and his few speeches afterwards, I believe to have been written for the mob by some other hand, perhaps with Shakespeare's consent; and that finding it take, he with the remaining ink of a pen otherwise employed, just interpolated the words 'I'll . . . bonfire' [ll. 15–17]. Of the rest not one syllable has the ever-present being of Shakespeare."

Resources

Selection Assessment

Formal Assessment

- Selection Test, p. 59

Test Generator (One-Stop Planner)

- CD-ROM

Critical Comment

Macbeth's Porter

Why does Macbeth's comic porter—speaking a gross, drunken rigmarole—appear in Scene 3, right after the murder of Duncan? Is this not a monstrous interruption?

Ⓐ One way to account for the scene is to remind ourselves that Shakespeare was writer-in-residence to a company of actors and therefore bound to provide parts for every member in every play—even a part for the chief comedian in a tragedy. But this is not a satisfactory explanation because it was not characteristic of Shakespeare merely to do what was expected of him as a professional writer; he always did something more, almost making a virtue out of theatrical necessity. And so, as a second explanation of the porter's scene, some critics have argued that it is designed to provide **comic relief** from the tense aftermath of Duncan's murder. But this also is not a convincing reason, because the scene actually increases tension rather than relieves it. As Macbeth and his wife stand whispering about the evil thing they have done, they—and the audience—are startled to hear a loud and totally unexpected knocking on the main gate of the castle. Even a hardened criminal would be startled by the coincidence of these events, and Macbeth and his wife are mere beginners in crime. While they hastily retreat into their bedroom, the porter (a word meaning "door tender") shuffles on stage to answer the knocking at his leisure, thus prolonging the interval between the murder and its discovery and greatly increasing suspense. And, after all, suspense is what makes drama interesting.

Theatergoers in Shakespeare's day were accustomed to comic porters; they were familiar figures in miracle plays, in which they kept the gates of hell. They were expected to be droll and at the same time sinister. "Who's there, i' th' name of Beelzebub?" asks Macbeth's porter, referring to one of the chief devils and implying that the castle is a place the Devil occupies. And indeed it already has become hell, which is as much a state of mind as a particular place. Lady Macbeth has called for the "smoke of hell" in Act I, and Macbeth has been unable Ⓑ to say "Amen" when Duncan's men cried "God bless us!" in Act II. To cut out the porter's scene, as many directors have done (and also many editors of school texts), is to weaken the fabric of the play.

Mervyn Blake as the porter in the Stratford Festival production of *Macbeth* (1983).

Reading Check

a. He promises Banquo honor if Banquo will stand by him. Banquo agrees to support Macbeth if he can maintain his integrity.
b. Macbeth sees a bloody dagger in the air foreshadowing the murder of Duncan.
c. Lady Macbeth hears an owl scream and crickets cry. Macbeth hears Malcolm and Donalbain cry out "Murder," "God bless us," and "Amen." He hears a voice saying he has murdered sleep.
d. The sleeping Duncan resembles her father. She plans, lays the daggers ready, returns the daggers, smears the grooms.
e. He says it will never wash off—it will stain all the waters of the world.
f. He pretends that he is the porter to hell.
g. He comes to wake the king.
h. He did it out of love for Duncan.
i. Malcolm goes to England and Donalbain goes to Ireland.
j. Macduff says that Malcolm and Donalbain are guilty (ll. 24–27), but skips Macbeth's coronation, possibly because he suspects him.

Making Meanings

Act II

First Thoughts

1. What was your reaction to the murder of Duncan? Why do you think Shakespeare decided to murder Duncan and his guards offstage?

Reading Check

a. In Scene 1, Macbeth asks Banquo to meet him later for "some words." What incentive does he offer Banquo? How does Banquo reply?

b. Describe the vision that Macbeth has at the end of Scene 1. What details foreshadow the action to come?

c. In Scene 2, as Macbeth kills Duncan, what does Lady Macbeth hear? What does Macbeth hear?

d. Why, according to Lady Macbeth, was she unable to kill Duncan herself? Which tasks related to the murder does she perform?

e. In Scene 2, how does Macbeth respond to Lady Macbeth's suggestion that he go wash the "filthy witness" from his hands?

f. In Scene 3, what is the porter pretending as he goes to open the gate?

g. Why has Macduff come?

h. What reason does Macbeth give for killing Duncan's two guards?

i. Where do Duncan's sons decide to go?

j. In Scene 4, whom does Macduff suspect of Duncan's murder?

Shaping Interpretations

2. Though Macbeth encounters no actual opposition until long after Duncan is murdered, Shakespeare must **foreshadow** some trouble for him and, to build up **suspense,** must start one character edging toward suspicion of Macbeth. Who is this character, and what inkling does he give of his dissatisfaction with Macbeth?

3. In Act I, Scene 7, Lady Macbeth seemed to be planning to murder Duncan herself. But at the last moment, in Act II, Scene 2, she is unable to wield her dagger. Consider the reason she gives, and decide what her actions and explanation reveal about her **character.**

4. In Scene 3, when Duncan's corpse is discovered, Macbeth utters a hypocritical lament beginning, "Had I but died. . . ." But is it really hypocritical? The critic A. C. Bradley argues that, although the speech is meant to be a lie, it actually contains "Macbeth's profoundest feelings." Explain this apparent contradiction. How does Macbeth feel about having murdered Duncan? What clues tell you how he feels?

5. Lady Macbeth's fainting spell, like everything else she has done so far, has a purpose. What message do you think she wants her fainting spell to convey?

6. Macduff becomes an important character in the three remaining acts. Describe how Shakespeare **characterizes** him in Scenes 3 and 4.

7. What would you say is the **mood** of Act II? What **images** and actions help to create this mood? Why might images of blood and water appear in Scene 2? What do they **symbolize**?

Extending the Text

8. A terrible murder is committed in this act. How do various characters respond to the violence? How would people today, say, react to the news that a ruler has been assassinated in cold blood and that a nation is in political chaos?

Challenging the Text

9. Review De Quincey's interpretation of the porter's scene in the ***Connections*** on page 330; review also the Critical Comment on page 332. What purpose do you see for this scene? Is it just for **comic relief**, or does it have other dramatic functions? Give reasons for your interpretation.

10. In some productions of *Macbeth,* Scene 4 is cut. Why would this be done? Is there any dramatic purpose for keeping it? Why do you think the Old Man is included in the scene?

Making Meanings

Act II

First Thoughts [Respond]

1. Possible Responses: The murder is awful, especially since Duncan put his trust in Macbeth. The murders may be offstage because they are too bloody and upsetting; seeing the murders would take the focus off Macbeth and arouse more sympathy for Duncan.

Shaping Interpretations [Interpret]

2. Macduff, in II.3.101, questions Macbeth's killing of the grooms and, in II.4.36, skips Macbeth's coronation.
3. Perhaps she is not as detached as she would like to be or appear to be.
4. It could be intended as a lie, but it is more likely an ambiguous sentiment. It may be true that Macbeth will never again feel that anything is worthwhile, that he has ruined his own life in taking Duncan's. In this case the speech would be true, but not as the hearers understand it, as a lament for Duncan. Macbeth is nervous about discovery (II.3.47) and feels guilty (II.3.55), though not guilty enough to confess.
5. She might want to divert attention from Macbeth's rambling explanation of why he had murdered the grooms and create an impression of shock and grief.
6. Macduff is courteous, dutiful, loyal, sensitive, poetic, discerning, bold, wary, and impulsive.
7. The mood is sinister and violent. It is set by the dagger vision and what follows (II.1.33–61); the image of Duncan dead (II.3.105–108); the cannibal horses (II.4.14–18). Blood and water may symbolize death and life or guilt and repentance; they appear here because characters, such as Macbeth, face grave consequences for their actions.

Extending the Text [Synthesize]

8. Possible answers: Macduff is horrified; Malcolm and Donalbain fear for their own lives; Lennox seems overwhelmed. Today, too, most people would be horrified. Others, desensitized by so much violence around them and in the media, might accept it cynically.

Challenging the Text [Evaluate]

9. Possible answers: The porter's ramblings provide comic relief from the tension caused by Duncan's murder. In another sense, however, the scene increases tension: The audience must wait to discover if Macbeth will get away with his dreadful deed.
10. Possible answers: The beginning of the scene is jarring; or, the scene reinforces the mood of suspicion and hellish evil. Perhaps the Old Man represents wisdom or serves to show that even those who are not part of the royal court sense trouble.

Summary

Scene 1: Banquo reveals that he now suspects Macbeth murdered Duncan. To maintain normal appearances, Macbeth invites Banquo to a banquet at court. Out of fear, Macbeth hires assassins to kill Banquo and his son Fleance to ensure that Banquo's descendants cannot inherit the throne.

A Reading Skills and Strategies

Making Inferences

? What does Banquo think of Macbeth now? [He suspects that Macbeth killed Duncan.]

B English Language Learners

Pronoun Usage

? Here and elsewhere, students may note the use of the pronoun *which* where we would use a form of *who.* How would this line read in modern English? [Possible answer: "Let your highness, to *whom* my duties are tied forever, command me."]

C Struggling Readers

Making Inferences

Help students make inferences by creating an It Says... I Say chart on which they can combine their own thoughts with text information. The chart should have four columns labeled as follows: Question, It Says, I Say, And So. Begin with the question of why Macbeth is so curious about Banquo's plans. Have students fill in what the text says, followed by their own opinions and then by the answer [Macbeth is plotting against Banquo.] based on the combination of information on the chart. For help in applying this strategy, see the *Reading Strategies Handbook,* p. 25, in the *Reading Skills and Strategies* binder.

D Critical Thinking

Speculating

? Do you think people would believe that Malcolm and Donalbain were guilty? Why or why not? [Sample responses: Yes, because Malcolm was to inherit the throne and because they both ran away; or no, because they were loving sons who respected their father.]

Answer to Margin Question

Line 10. Banquo is troubled and thoughtful; he is suspicious that Macbeth has helped the prophecies along; yet, because they did come true, he is hopeful about the witches' prediction concerning him and his descendants.

ACT III Scene 1. *Forres. The palace.*

Enter BANQUO.

Banquo.
Thou hast it now: king, Cawdor, Glamis, all,
As the weird women promised, and I fear
Thou play'dst most foully for't. Yet it was said
It should not stand° in thy posterity,
But that myself should be the root and father
Of many kings. If there come truth from them—
As upon thee, Macbeth, their speeches shine—
Why, by the verities on thee made good,
May they not be my oracles as well
And set me up in hope? But hush, no more!

[*Sennet° sounded. Enter* MACBETH *as king,* LADY MACBETH, LENNOX, ROSS, LORDS, *and* ATTENDANTS.]

Macbeth.
Here's our chief guest.
Lady Macbeth. If he had been forgotten,
It had been as a gap in our great feast,
And all-thing° unbecoming.
Macbeth.
Tonight we hold a solemn supper, sir,
And I'll request your presence.
Banquo. Let your highness
Command upon me, to the which my duties
Are with a most indissoluble tie
For ever knit.
Macbeth.
Ride you this afternoon?
Banquo. Ay, my good lord.
Macbeth.
We should have else desired your good advice
(Which still° hath been both grave and prosperous°)
In this day's council; but we'll take tomorrow.
Is't far you ride?
Banquo.
As far, my lord, as will fill up the time
'Twixt this and supper. Go not my horse the better,°
I must become a borrower of the night
For a dark hour or twain.
Macbeth. Fail not our feast.
Banquo.
My lord, I will not.
Macbeth.
We hear our bloody cousins are bestowed°
In England and in Ireland, not confessing

4. stand: continue.

? **10.** *What would you say Banquo's mood is? Is he envious or thoughtful and troubled?*

Sennet: trumpet.

13. all-thing: altogether.

21. still: always. **grave and prosperous:** weighty and profitable.

25. Go not my horse the better: unless my horse goes faster than I expect.

29. are bestowed: have taken refuge.

Skill Link

Using Graphic Organizers

Encourage students to use graphic organizers to chart important ideas, facts, and details from a text. Two types of graphic organizers are time lines and Venn diagrams. A **time line** lists events in chronological order. **Venn diagrams** consist of two intersecting circles used to compare and contrast information.

Activities

1. To help students focus on the plot, have them keep a time line of the key events that take place. Pause periodically to review with the class what has happened in the play so far.
2. Have students use a Venn diagram to compare and contrast the characters of Macbeth and Lady Macbeth. (For an example of a Venn diagram, see p. T309.)

Their cruel parricide, filling their hearers
With strange invention.° But of that tomorrow,
When therewithal we shall have cause of state
Craving us jointly.° Hie you to horse. Adieu,
Till you return at night. Goes Fleance with you?

Banquo.
Ay, my good lord: our time does call upon 's.

Macbeth.
I wish your horses swift and sure of foot,
And so I do commend you to their backs.
Farewell. [*Exit* BANQUO.]
Let every man be master of his time
Till seven at night. To make society
The sweeter welcome, we will keep ourself
Till supper-time alone. While° then, God be with you!

[*Exeunt* LORDS *and all but* MACBETH *and a* SERVANT.]

Sirrah, a word with you: attend° those men
Our pleasure?

Attendant.
They are, my lord, without the palace gate.

Macbeth.
Bring them before us. [*Exit* SERVANT.]
To be thus° is nothing, but° to be safely thus—
Our fears in Banquo stick deep,
And in his royalty of nature reigns that
Which would be feared. 'Tis much he dares;
And, to° that dauntless temper° of his mind,
He hath a wisdom that doth guide his valor
To act in safety. There is none but he
Whose being I do fear: and under him
My genius is rebuked,° as it is said
Mark Antony's was by Caesar. He chid the sisters,
When first they put the name of king upon me,
And bade them speak to him; then prophetlike
They hailed him father to a line of kings.
Upon my head they placed a fruitless crown
And put a barren scepter in my gripe,
Thence to be wrenched with an unlineal hand,
No son of mine succeeding. If't be so,
For Banquo's issue have I filed° my mind;
For them the gracious Duncan have I murdered;
Put rancors° in the vessel of my peace
Only for them, and mine eternal jewel°
Given to the common enemy of man,°
To make them kings, the seeds of Banquo kings!
Rather than so, come, fate, into the list,°
And champion me to th' utterance!° Who's there?

32. invention: lies.

34. us jointly: our joint attention.

35. *Macbeth has asked three important questions in this scene. What are they? How do you think he would ask them?*

42. *Notice that Macbeth uses the "royal we"; that is, he speaks of himself as "we," as a representative of all the people. Why do you think he wants to be alone?*

43. While: until.

44. attend: await.

48. thus: king. **but:** unless.

52. to: added to. **temper:** quality.

56. genius is rebuked: guardian spirit is cowed.

63. *What is an "unlineal hand"? What is a "barren scepter"? What is eating at Macbeth now?*

65. filed: defiled; dirtied.

67. rancors: bitter enmity.

68. eternal jewel: immortal soul.

69. common enemy of man: Satan.

71. list: battle.

72. champion me to th' utterance: fight against me till I give up.

72. *Why exactly is Macbeth so angry? What has he given up in order to make Banquo's sons kings?*

E Critical Thinking
Making Judgments

In the historical writings of Holinshed, Banquo shares guilt in the murder of Duncan. In the play, however, this is not the case. (Shakespeare wanted to flatter James I, who was a descendant of Banquo.) Why has Banquo done nothing about his suspicions of Macbeth, despite his vow to fight against malice in II.3.120–126? [Sample response: Perhaps Banquo suspects Macbeth but cannot prove anything, so he thinks it best to play along with him. However, in III.1.36, his disgust for Macbeth is apparent in his desire to leave quickly.]

F Critical Thinking
Interpreting

Why does Macbeth fear Banquo? [Possible response: Macbeth fears Banquo's honesty, loyalty, courage, and intellect. He fears that Banquo will eventually turn against him. He also fears that Banquo's sons may claim the throne as predicted by the witches.]

G Elements of Literature
Tragedy

How do these lines underscore Macbeth's role as the tragic hero? [Possible response: Macbeth is fully aware that by killing Duncan he has lost his eternal soul; he has done so because of his tragic flaw—ambition.]

Answers to Margin Questions

Line 35. Macbeth asks if Banquo is going riding, how far he is going, and if Fleance will accompany him. He would probably try to speak casually.
Line 42. He probably wants others to think he will be alone so they don't suspect that he has set up a secret meeting.
Line 63. Both terms refer to the idea of a king without offspring. Macbeth is upset that Banquo's sons will inherit Macbeth's throne.
Line 72. He is angry that he has sold his own soul so that another man's sons can become kings.

Getting Students Involved

Cooperative Learning

Question and Answer. Assign pairs of students to read a passage aloud. One student should ask questions that arise during the reading, and the other should answer as many of them as possible. Have them reverse roles after an assigned number of lines. At the end of each scene, both students should summarize what they understand in a short paragraph and list their unanswered questions.

Macbeth's Psychological Profile. In groups of four or five, students should analyze Macbeth's thoughts and motivations in Act III. Have one member of the group record these observations. Then, have students collaborate to write a psychological profile of Macbeth, answering the following questions: Is guilt causing him to hallucinate, or does he really see things others do not? Why does he plot additional murders? (Students should cite specific lines to support their theories.)

A English Language Learners

Identifying Pronoun Referents

? Pronoun referents do not always precede the pronoun. Read this section aloud. What is the pronoun referent for *he* in l. 77? [*Banquo,* from l. 84]

B Reading Skills and Strategies

Making Inferences

? What is the point of Macbeth's extended comparison of men and dogs? [Possible answer: He says, in effect, that the word *men* does not distinguish among the different types of men any more than the word *dog* distinguishes among the different breeds of dogs he names. He implies that these murderers are curs and wants to know if they are capable of the job.]

C Elements of Literature

Irony

? What is ironic about Macbeth's words in ll. 107–108? [Possible response: It is ironic that Macbeth thinks he will be restored to perfect health through the murder of his friend.]

D Reading Skills and Strategies

Responding to the Text

? What do you think the murderers mean in ll. 108–114? [Sample responses: They are probably poor and out of work and are willing to take chances. They are disillusioned and eager to "spite the world."] Do you feel any sympathy for the two murderers? Why or why not? [Sample responses: Yes, they seem gullible, and Macbeth is just using them; or, no, whatever their situation is, murder is not acceptable.]

Answers to Margin Questions

Line 74. Answers will vary. After students have read the scene, return to the question. Based on ll. 110–111, few students will suggest that these men are officers who bear Banquo a personal grudge.

Line 91. Macbeth convinces the murderers that Banquo is to blame for their troubles. He attacks their manhood by accusing them of being the lowest type of dog, similar to the way Lady Macbeth attacked him.

[*Enter* SERVANT *and two* MURDERERS.]

Now go to the door, and stay there till we call.

[*Exit* SERVANT.]

Was it not yesterday we spoke together?

Murderers.
It was, so please your highness.

Macbeth. Well then, now
Have you considered of my speeches? Know
That it was he in the times past, which held you
So under fortune,° which you thought had been
Our innocent self: this I made good to you
In our last conference; passed in probation° with you,
How you were borne in hand,° how crossed; the instruments,°
Who wrought with them, and all things else that might
To half a soul° and to a notion° crazed
Say "Thus did Banquo."

First Murderer. You made it known to us.

Macbeth.
I did so; and went further, which is now
Our point of second meeting. Do you find
Your patience so predominant in your nature,
That you can let this go? Are you so gospeled,°
To pray for this good man and for his issue,
Whose heavy hand hath bowed you to the grave
And beggared yours forever?

First Murderer. We are men, my liege.

Macbeth.
Ay, in the catalogue ye go for° men;
As hounds and greyhounds, mongrels, spaniels, curs,
Shoughs, water-rugs° and demi-wolves, are clept°
All by the name of dogs: the valued file°
Distinguishes the swift, the slow, the subtle,
The housekeeper, the hunter, every one
According to the gift which bounteous nature
Hath in him closed,° whereby he does receive
Particular addition, from the bill°
That writes them all alike: and so of men.
Now if you have a station in the file,
Not i' th' worst rank of manhood, say't,
And I will put that business in your bosoms
Whose execution takes your enemy off,
Grapples you to the heart and love of us,
Who wear our health but sickly in his life,°
Which in his death were perfect.

Second Murderer. I am one, my liege,
Whom the vile blows and buffets of the world
Hath so incensed that I am reckless what
I do to spite the world.

? **74.** *What do you imagine the murderers would be like: the all-too-common "hit men" of contemporary movies? Or could they simply be officers who have a grudge against Banquo? (They have been portrayed in many ways.)*

78. held you / So under fortune: kept you from good fortune.

80. probation: review.

81. borne in hand: deceived. **instruments:** tools.

83. soul: brain. **notion:** mind.

88. gospeled: so meek from reading the Gospel (of Jesus).

? **91.** *What techniques is Macbeth using on the murderers? Does it remind you of the way Lady Macbeth goaded him into killing Duncan?*

92. go for: pass as.

94. Shoughs, water-rugs: shaggy dogs and long-haired water dogs. **clept:** called.

95. valued file: classification by valuable traits.

99. closed: enclosed.

100. bill: list.

107. who wear . . . life: who are "sick" while he (Banquo) still lives.

Getting Students Involved

Enrichment Activity

The Art of Name-calling. "Dunghill groom," "serpent's egg," "valiant flea," and "false caterpillar" are just a few of the insults that Shakespeare's characters hurled at one another. Shakespeare was a master in the art of name-calling. He often used dog imagery in his insults, as he does in this scene with the murderers. Here are some additional dog curses Shakespeare used in other plays: "common cry of curs," "butcher's cur," "cut-throat dog," "thou mongrel beef-witted lord," "puppy-headed monster," and "false hound." As students read the rest of the play, ask them to keep a list of the insults used by various characters. You might want to play Disc 5, Track 3 from the Audio CD Library, which covers various parts of Act III.

Activity

Choose an insult from the play and analyze why it is effective in its context. Take into account how the recipient of the insult reacts to it.

From Roman Polanski's film production of *Macbeth* (1971).

"It is concluded: Banquo, thy soul's flight,
If it find heaven, must find it out tonight."

First Murderer. And I another
So weary with disasters, tugged with fortune,
That I would set° my life on any chance,
To mend it or be rid on't.
Macbeth. Both of you
Know Banquo was your enemy.
Both Murderers. True, my lord.
Macbeth.
So is he mine, and in such bloody distance°
That every minute of his being thrusts
Against my near'st of life:° and though I could
With barefaced power sweep him from my sight **E**
And bid my will avouch° it, yet I must not,
For° certain friends that are both his and mine, **F**
Whose loves I may not drop, but wail his fall
Who I myself struck down: and thence it is
That I to your assistance do make love,
Masking the business from the common eye
For sundry weighty reasons.

113. set: risk.

116. distance: quarrel.

118. near'st of life: vital spot.

120. avouch: justify.

121. For: because of.

? **126.** *How is Macbeth justifying to the murderers the fact that he has to ask them to do the job of killing Banquo?*

E Struggling Readers

Summarizing

To make summarizing less overwhelming, have students summarize this passage within the framework of a "Somebody Wants But So" strategy. Step by step have them identify who the *somebody* is [Macbeth], what the somebody *wants* [to murder Banquo himself], *but* what happens to prevent it [he can't for political reasons], and *so* how the situation works out [he hires murderers to do the job for him]. For help in applying this strategy, see the *Reading Strategies Handbook,* p. 111, in the *Reading Skills and Strategies* binder.

F Advanced Learners

Extending the Text

Ridding oneself of political opponents is a common tactic of tyrants. Ask students to research and report on how some twentieth-century tyrants, such as Stalin, dealt with opposition and how even democratic leaders can abuse power to achieve their own ends (such as Richard Nixon's "enemies list").

Answer to Margin Question

Line 126. Macbeth argues that for political reasons he must appear unblemished and retain the goodwill of his and Banquo's mutual friends.

Using Students' Strengths

Verbal Learners

After students have finished Act III, have groups trace different strands of imagery throughout the play thus far and read their favorite passages aloud. As students read various lines from the play, they should be able to identify similarities, differences, changes over time, echoes, and repetitions in Shakespeare's use of various images.

Logical/Mathematical Learners

Have students work in groups of three or four to create Character Sociograms—graphics with symbols and words that show the relationships between characters. Challenge students to include all the significant characters that have appeared in the play up to this point and to be creative in the kind of symbols they produce to show how each character relates to the others.

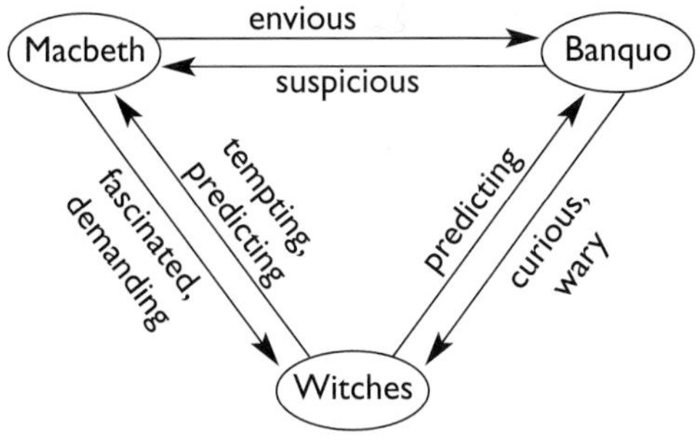

Ⓐ Reading Skills and Strategies

Summarizing

Have students summarize Macbeth's final instructions. [Possible answer: Within the next hour, he will tell the murderers the place and time for killing Banquo. The murder must be done at some distance from the palace and in such a way that Macbeth cannot fall under suspicion. Fleance must also be killed.]

Ⓑ Elements of Literature

Tragedy

? In what way has Macbeth's view of murder changed since he killed Duncan? [Possible response: Macbeth was horrified and upset both before and after killing Duncan. Now he is very casual about killing Banquo and Fleance.] What does this suggest about his downfall as the tragic hero? [Possible response: He is ignoring his conscience and is surrendering to evil.]

Answer to Margin Question

Line 140. Macbeth has arranged to give them the details of carrying out the murder. He is calculating and controlled. Lady Macbeth has no part in the arrangements.

Second Murderer. We shall, my lord,
Perform what you command us.

First Murderer. Though our lives——

Macbeth.
Your spirits shine through you. Within this hour at most
I will advise you where to plant yourselves,
Acquaint you with the perfect spy° o' th' time,
The moment on't; for't must be done tonight,
And something° from the palace; always thought°
That I require a clearness:° and with him—
To leave no rubs° nor botches in the work—
Fleance his son, that keeps him company,
Whose absence is no less material to me
Than is his father's, must embrace the fate
Of that dark hour. Resolve yourselves apart:°
I'll come to you anon.

Murderers. We are resolved, my lord.

Macbeth.
I'll call upon you straight. Abide within.

130. perfect spy: exact information.

132. something: some distance. **thought:** remembered.

133. clearness: freedom from suspicion.

134. rubs: flaws.

138. apart: alone (make up your minds by yourselves).

? 140. *What has Macbeth arranged with the murderers? What is his mood here? Does Lady Macbeth have any part in arranging these next murders?*

"Gentle my lord, sleek o'er your rugged looks."

From Roman Polanski's film production of *Macbeth* (1971).

Crossing the Curriculum

Social Studies

Students may note that as of III.1.10, Banquo has not yet acted on his suspicions of Macbeth. What evidence should Banquo have before he brings an accusation? Students can explore the standards of probable cause required for an arraignment and the proof required for an actual conviction. Given these laws, ask students whether Banquo should act now or wait.

Performing Arts

In Shakespeare's day, Banquo's ghost entered through a trapdoor in the rear of the stage. Today, Banquo's ghost presents directors with some interesting staging challenges. Assign students to groups of four or five, and have them stage the banquet scene in which Banquo's ghost appears to Macbeth. Remind students that techniques used in film often will not work in live performances.

It is concluded: Banquo, thy soul's flight,
If it find heaven, must find it out tonight. C *[Exeunt.]*

Scene 2. *The palace.*

Enter LADY MACBETH *and a* SERVANT.

Lady Macbeth.
Is Banquo gone from court?

Servant.
Ay, madam, but returns again tonight.

Lady Macbeth.
Say to the king, I would attend his leisure
For a few words.

Servant. Madam, I will. *[Exit.]*

Lady Macbeth. Nought's had, all's spent,
Where our desire is got without content:
'Tis safer to be that which we destroy
Than by destruction dwell in doubtful joy. D

[Enter MACBETH.*]*

How now, my lord! Why do you keep alone,
Of sorriest fancies your companions making,
Using those thoughts which should indeed have died
With them they think on? Things without° all remedy
Should be without regard: what's done is done.

Macbeth.
We have scorched° the snake, not killed it:
She'll close° and be herself, whilst our poor malice°
Remains in danger of her former tooth.
But let the frame of things disjoint,° both the worlds° suffer,
Ere we will eat our meal in fear, and sleep
In the affliction of these terrible dreams
That shake us nightly: better be with the dead,
Whom we, to gain our peace, have sent to peace,
Than on the torture of the mind to lie
In restless ecstasy.° Duncan is in his grave;
After life's fitful fever he sleeps well.
Treason has done his worst: nor steel, nor poison,
Malice domestic,° foreign levy,° nothing,
Can touch him further. E

Lady Macbeth. Come on.
Gentle my lord, sleek° o'er your rugged° looks;
Be bright and jovial among your guests tonight.

Macbeth.
So shall I, love; and so, I pray, be you:
Let your remembrance apply to Banquo;°
Present him eminence,° both with eye and tongue:
Unsafe the while, that we must lave°
Our honors in these flattering streams

? **7.** *What reversal of attitudes is taking place here?*

11. without: beyond.

? **12.** *This scene can be played in several ways. Is Lady Macbeth hostile to her husband and angry with him? Or can she be shown to have some tenderness in this scene?*

13. scorched: slashed.

14. close: heal. **malice:** enmity; hatred.

16. frame of things disjoint: universe collapse. **worlds:** heaven and earth.

22. ecstasy: frenzy.

25. Malice domestic: domestic war (civil war). **foreign levy:** exaction of tribute by a foreign country.

? **26.** *What do you picture the couple doing in this scene? Are they sitting together? Are they close, or is there a distance between them?*

27. sleek: smooth. **rugged:** furrowed.

30. Let . . . Banquo: That is, focus your thoughts on Banquo.

31. eminence: honors.

32. lave: wash.

C Critical Thinking

Making Connections

? How is this couplet like the closing couplet of Act II, Scene 1? [Possible answer: Both show Macbeth's resolve to commit murder, and both warn the intended victims—first Duncan, then Banquo and Fleance—that the end is near and that their souls will face final judgment that night.]

Summary

Scene 2: Lady Macbeth expresses her discontent and then scolds Macbeth for brooding about Duncan's murder. Macbeth responds that he envies Duncan, who no longer needs to worry about treachery. He then admits that he fears Banquo and his children and that a "deed of dreadful note" will soon be accomplished. However, he does not specify that the deed will be the murder of Banquo and Fleance.

D Critical Thinking

Speculating

? Why is Lady Macbeth unhappy? [Sample responses: She seems to be growing apart from her husband—she doesn't even know about his plans to murder Banquo and Fleance; or, she has discovered that the throne is not worth the price of murder.]

E Elements of Literature

Theme

? How is the motif of sleeplessness highlighted in these lines? [Macbeth sleeps fitfully and has terrible dreams, while Duncan is at peace. This reinforces the idea that Macbeth "murdered sleep" (II.2.40–42).]

Answers to Margin Questions

Line 7. Realizing that they must now live with fear and suspicion, Lady Macbeth is beginning to believe that the throne is not worth the price of murder.

Line 12. She may be sympathetic, pleading, cajoling, or scolding.

Line 26. If Macbeth and his wife are seen as being emotionally close, they may touch each other as they move about. But if they are understood to be drifting apart—Lady Macbeth complains that he keeps to himself—they may avoid touching or stand far apart.

Professional Notes

Critical Comment: Public and Private

According to the critic J. L. Styan, "Shakespeare's *Macbeth* is another play, touching the opposition of the public and the private world and the consequent horrors of a divided mind." Ask students to examine the play in terms of Macbeth's separation of the public and private.

[Possible answer: In his mind, Macbeth knows the evil he has done, but publicly he tries to hide his deeds and true feelings in order to maintain his position. This struggle between his inner reality and his outer, superficial demeanor adds to the anguish he already feels for murdering Duncan.]

LITERATURE AND COMPUTERS

Encourage students to use search engines to find Web sites devoted to Shakespeare or to *Macbeth*. Also invite students to discover how Shakespeare is taught in England by locating e-mail addresses of peers in the United Kingdom and exchanging correspondence on the topic. Ask students to share their findings with the whole class.

Ⓐ Elements of Literature
Theme

? How do Macbeth's words play on the "Fair is foul, and foul is fair" theme? [Possible response: Macbeth and Lady Macbeth will appear jovial and nonchalant at the night's banquet to mask their true feelings: what appears to be fair is really foul.]

Ⓑ Elements of Literature
Imagery

? What atmosphere do these references to bats and beetles convey? [Sample responses: sinister; evil; dark; foreboding.]

Ⓒ Critical Thinking
Analyzing

? How have Lady Macbeth and Macbeth changed? [Possible answer: Lady Macbeth was calm and decisive as she planned the murder of Duncan; now she is fearful and uncertain. Macbeth was more hesitant about murdering Duncan; however, once he had committed the deed, he was able to murder the grooms on the spur of the moment without consulting his wife. Now he has calmly directed additional murders without involving her. Some students may think that he has become more evil than she.]

Answer to Margin Question
Line 35. Lady Macbeth speaks with urgency and fear. She is worried about Macbeth's state of mind.

LITERATURE AND COMPUTERS

The Bard and the Database

In literary circles it's known as the "Authorship Question": Did William Shakespeare, the actor from Stratford-on-Avon, really write the greatest poetry the world has ever known?

This question has been around since the 1700s, and over the years people have proposed as many as fifty-eight various writers as possible authors of Shakespeare's plays and poems, ranging from Sir Francis Bacon to Sir Walter Raleigh to Queen Elizabeth I herself.

Matching Shakespeare. Hoping to apply some twentieth-century computer technology to this seventeenth-century problem, Professor Ward Elliott of Claremont McKenna College near Los Angeles created a database of Renaissance literature, including the King James Bible, all of Shakespeare's poetry, and material from twenty-seven of the most promising candidates, and embarked upon his "Matching Shakespeare" study. Elliott's plan was first to identify Shakespeare's unique style

Ⓐ And make our faces vizards° to our hearts,
Disguising what they are.
Lady Macbeth. You must leave this.
Macbeth.
O, full of scorpions is my mind, dear wife!
Thou know'st that Banquo, and his Fleance, lives.
Lady Macbeth.
But in them nature's copy's not eterne.°
Macbeth.
There's comfort yet; they are assailable.
Then be thou jocund. Ere the bat hath flown
His cloistered flight, ere to black Hecate's summons
Ⓑ The shard-borne° beetle with his drowsy hums
Hath rung night's yawning peal, there shall be done
A deed of dreadful note.
Lady Macbeth. What's to be done?
Ⓒ **Macbeth.**
Be innocent of the knowledge, dearest chuck,°
Till thou applaud the deed. Come, seeling° night,
Scarf up° the tender eye of pitiful day,
And with thy bloody and invisible hand
Cancel and tear to pieces that great bond

34. vizards: masks.

? **35.** *With what degree of urgency must Lady Macbeth say this line?*

38. nature's copy's not eterne: That is, they won't live forever.

42. shard-borne: carried on scaly wings.

45. chuck: chick (a term of endearment).
46. seeling: eye-closing; blinding.
47. Scarf up: blindfold.

through computer analysis and then to compare this to the styles of various writers to see if any matched up.

Elliott's "Matching Shakespeare" study applied dozens of different linguistic tests, but five conventional tests and a powerful new one proved most accurate. The conventional tests measured features like the number of relative clauses and hyphenated compound words and length of words and sentences, and the new test used a pattern recognition technique.

And the real Shakespeare is. What have the tests shown? Did Shakespeare write Shakespeare? Based on his studies, Elliott believes that he has been able to eliminate all the principal candidates. Every writer failed at least one of the conventional tests, with some failing four or five. On the other hand, Shakespeare's writings all fell within a consistent profile. Although the study does not definitively prove that it was Shakespeare himself who wrote the works attributed to him, Elliott (along with most reputable scholars) feels that it does demonstrate that one individual *did* write them all.

Why has such a fuss been made about the authorship of Shakespeare's works? In part, it's because people cannot believe that someone who led such a seemingly ordinary life could have been such a genius. Shakespeare still confounds all the scholarly detectives who continue to debate the "Authorship Question."

Which keeps me pale! Light thickens, and the crow
Makes wing to th' rooky° wood.
Good things of day begin to droop and drowse,
Whiles night's black agents to their preys do rouse.
Thou marvel'st at my words: but hold thee still; **D**
Things bad begun make strong themselves by ill:
So, prithee, go with me. *[Exeunt.]*

Scene 3. *Near the palace.*

Enter three MURDERERS.

First Murderer.
But who did bid thee join with us? **E**

Third Murderer. Macbeth.

Second Murderer.
He needs not our mistrust; since he delivers
Our offices and what we have to do
To the direction just.°

First Murderer. Then stand with us.
The west yet glimmers with some streaks of day.
Now spurs the lated° traveler apace

51. rooky: full of rooks, or crows.

? **1.** *The identity of the Third Murderer is not made clear. Whom would you name as possible suspects?*

4. He needs . . . just: We need not mistrust him (the Third Murderer) since he describes our duties according to our exact directions.

6. lated: belated.

D Elements of Literature

Imagery

Shakespeare ends this scene with two couplets followed by a tag, instead of the usual single couplet. Again, he seems to be invoking the evil of night to mask a murder scene, as in Act II, Scene 1, when Macbeth prepares to kill Duncan.

Summary

Scene 3: Three murderers set upon Banquo and Fleance as the two approach Macbeth's palace. They kill Banquo, but Fleance escapes.

E Reading Skills and Strategies

Drawing Conclusions

There has been a great deal of speculation about the identity of the third murderer. One popular answer is that the murderer is Macbeth himself. As students continue to read, ask them to look for evidence that Macbeth is in fact *not* the third murderer. [Possible responses: He is with his banquet guests as one of the murderers reports back to him (III.4.10). Also, his shock upon hearing Fleance escaped (III.4.20–25) seems genuine.]

Answer to Margin Question

Line 1. Perhaps he is a messenger sent by Macbeth or one of Macbeth's officers. He cannot be Macbeth himself (see annotation E, above). Other explanations suggest that the way Shakespeare's plays were performed and printed may account for the additional character. Perhaps Shakespeare needed to give an actor a part, or perhaps the number of murderers was consistent in some copies of the script but not in the one used for the First Folio.

Skill Link

Questioning as a Study Strategy

Put up a large sheet of paper on which students can write questions for other students to answer. Periodically check to make sure that misconceptions are cleared up. Leave some time at the beginning or end of class to discuss the posted questions and answers and to allow students to add or answer questions. In a different colored ink, write "Anything New?" next to interpretations that may change as students encounter additional information in the text. Remind them that as new clues surface, they must rethink or expand their interpretations. (For example, speculation about Lady Macbeth's children must also take into account IV.3.216, which students have not yet read.)

Ⓐ English Language Learners

Identifying Pronoun Referents

? To whom do the pronouns *he* (l. 9) and *his* (l. 12) refer? [Banquo] How do you know? [The murderers are waiting for Banquo's arrival, his voice is heard offstage, and he soon enters.]

Ⓑ Reading Skills and Strategies

Making Inferences

? What can you infer about the third murderer from these lines? [Possible response: He is very familiar with the comings and goings of the palace, indicating that he is no stranger to the court.]

"O, treachery! Fly, good Fleance, fly, fly, fly!"

From Roman Polanski's film production of *Macbeth* (1971).

To gain the timely inn, and near approaches
The subject of our watch.

Third Murderer. Hark! I hear horses.

Banquo (*within*). Give us a light there, ho!

Second Murderer. Then 'tis he. The rest
That are within the note of expectation°
Already are i' th' court.

First Murderer. His horses go about.

Third Murderer.
Almost a mile: but he does usually—
So all men do—from hence to th' palace gate
Make it their walk.

[*Enter* BANQUO *and* FLEANCE, *with a torch.*]

Second Murderer.
A light, a light!

Third Murderer. 'Tis he.

First Murderer. Stand to't.

10. within . . . expectation: on the list of expected guests.

Banquo.
It will be rain tonight.

First Murderer. Let it come down.

[*They set upon* BANQUO.] **C**

Banquo.
O, treachery! Fly, good Fleance, fly, fly, fly! **D**

[*Exit* FLEANCE.]

Thou mayst revenge. O slave! [*Dies.*]

Third Murderer.
Who did strike out the light?

First Murderer. Was't not the way?°

Third Murderer.
There's but one down; the son is fled.

Second Murderer.
We have lost best half of our affair.

First Murderer.
Well, let's away and say how much is done. [*Exeunt.*]

? 19. *What would the murderers be doing as the light goes out?*

19. way: thing to do.

? 21. *Disposal of bodies is always a problem for directors of Shakespeare's plays. How would you have Banquo's body carried off? By whom?*

? 22. *This scene, so necessary to the play, is often called the play's turning point or technical climax. What have been Macbeth's good fortunes so far?*

Scene 4. *The palace.*
Banquet prepared. Enter MACBETH, LADY MACBETH, ROSS, LENNOX, LORDS, *and* ATTENDANTS.

Macbeth.
You know your own degrees;° sit down:
At first and last, the hearty welcome.

Lords.
Thanks to your majesty.

Macbeth.
Oneself will mingle with society°
And play the humble host.
Our hostess keeps her state,° but in best time
We will require° her welcome.

Lady Macbeth.
Pronounce it for me, sir, to all our friends,
For my heart speaks they are welcome.

[*Enter* FIRST MURDERER.]

Macbeth.
See, they encounter° thee with their hearts' thanks.
Both sides are even: here I'll sit i' th' midst:
Be large in mirth; anon we'll drink a measure°
The table round. (*Goes to* FIRST MURDERER.) There's blood upon thy face.

Murderer.
'Tis Banquo's then.

Macbeth.
'Tis better thee without than he within.°
Is he dispatched?

1. degrees: ranks.

? 2. *This crucial scene is often called the dramatic climax of the play; it is tremendously exciting when staged well. Notice where Macbeth's subjects become aware of his capacity for irrational behavior.*

4. society: the company.

6. keeps her state: remains seated in her chair of state.

7. require: request.

10. encounter: meet.

12. measure: goblet.

15. thee . . . within: outside you than inside him.

Getting Students Involved

Enrichment Activity

Who Is the Third Murderer? The Third Murderer also has been identified as a supporter of Banquo and his sons. This camp argues that Fleance—especially on foot—would never have been able to escape three grown men without "insider" help. The Third Murderer is the one who accuses the others of blowing out the torch, so perhaps he really is Fleance's secret helper. Ask students to reread this section and express their opinion of this theory.

C Critical Thinking

Challenging the Text

? The deaths of the traitors (Macdonwald and Cawdor) and the first three murders (Duncan and the two grooms) are all committed offstage. Should this one occur onstage? Why or why not? [Possible responses: The violent nature of the play would not be as evident if every death were simply reported by the characters. Seeing the dying Banquo saving his son makes the audience more sympathetic to him and less to Macbeth.]

D Elements of Literature

Tragedy

? Why is this a turning point for Macbeth? [Possible answer: Even though we do not know how things will end, Fleance's escape means that the prophecy about Banquo can still come true. Moreover, this is the first time that Macbeth has been openly thwarted, so it may foreshadow a reversal of momentum in the play.]

Summary

Scene 4: The banquet is underway when one of the murderers calls Macbeth aside to tell him that Banquo is dead, but Fleance has escaped. Lady Macbeth urges Macbeth to join the table. Macbeth, however, envisions Banquo's ghost taking his seat at the banquet table and speaks to the ghost, causing the guests to think he is unstable. Lady Macbeth at first says that her husband is ill and then, fearing what he might reveal, she dismisses the guests. Macbeth closes the scene by saying that he will send for Macduff and revisit the witches.

Answers to Margin Questions

Line 19. As the light goes out, the murderers might be attacking Banquo.
Line 21. Shakespeare's plays were written for theater in the round. Since the curtains could not be drawn, one option would be to have the murderers move the body.
Line 22. Macbeth has acquired Cawdor and the throne, and although he has aroused suspicion, he is apparently without open opposition. Fleance's escape is his first clear failure.
Line 2. The subjects become aware around III.4.48–58.

A Vocabulary Note

The Prefix *non-*

Explain that the prefix *non-* means "not" or "opposite of." The word *nonpareil* is a combination of the prefix *non-*, meaning "not," and the French word *pariel*, meaning "parallel." *Nonpariel* means someone or something having no parallel or being without equal.

B Critical Thinking

Expressing an Opinion

? Do you agree with Macbeth's claim that he would have been "perfect" if only Fleance had been killed? Why or why not? [Sample response: No, it is the nature of obsessively ambitious people never to be satisfied.]

C Elements of Literature

Irony

? Why is the line "But Banquo's safe?" ironic? [It might sound as if he is asking if Banquo is well, but he is actually asking if Banquo was safely dispatched—that is, murdered.]

D Elements of Literature

Figurative Language

? Who or what is the serpent? [Banquo, now dead] Who is "the worm that's fled"? [Fleance has fled and may pose a threat in the future. However, he is not dangerous yet, perhaps because of his youth.] Have students connect this line to III.2.13 in which Macbeth calls Banquo a snake.

Answer to Margin Question

Line 20. He would act surprised, horrified, or angry.

"Never shake / Thy gory locks at me."
From the Stratford Festival production of *Macbeth* (1983).

Murderer. My lord, his throat is cut;
That I did for him.
Macbeth. Thou are the best o' th' cutthroats.
Yet he's good that did the like for Fleance;
[A] If thou didst it, thou art the nonpareil.
Murderer.
Most royal sir, Fleance is 'scaped.
Macbeth (*aside*).
[B] Then comes my fit again: I had else been perfect,
Whole as the marble, founded° as the rock,
As broad and general as the casing air:°
But now I am cabined, cribbed,° confined, bound in
[C] To saucy° doubts and fears.—But Banquo's safe?
Murderer.
Ay, my good lord: safe in a ditch he bides,
With twenty trenchèd° gashes on his head,
The least a death to nature.
Macbeth. Thanks for that.
[D] (*Aside.*) There the grown serpent lies; the worm° that's fled
Hath nature that in time will venom breed,
No teeth for th' present. Get thee gone. Tomorrow
We'll hear ourselves° again. [*Exit* FIRST MURDERER.]

? 20. *How would Macbeth react to this line?*

22. **founded:** firmly based.
23. **broad . . . casing air:** unconfined as the surrounding air.
24. **cribbed:** penned up.
25. **saucy:** insolent.
27. **trenchèd:** trenchlike.
29. **worm:** serpent.
32. **hear ourselves:** talk it over.

Professional Notes

Critical Comment: Staging the Scene

The critic G. Wilson Knight suggests this simple stage set for Act III, Scene 4:

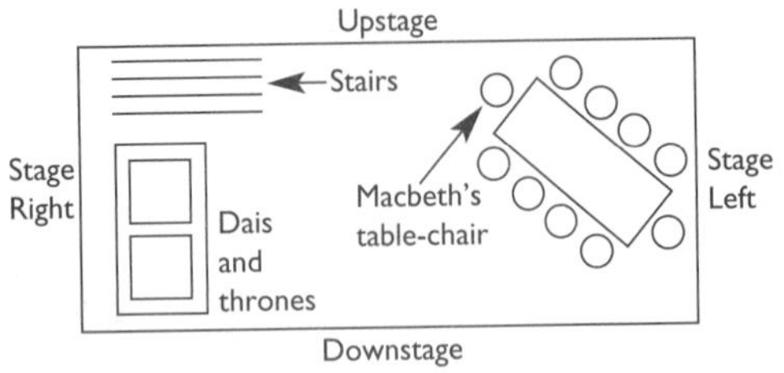

He suggests staging Scene 4 as follows: It begins with Macbeth and Lady Macbeth sitting on their thrones, with the guests at the banquet table. Macbeth goes to the stairs to speak aside to the murderer; he returns down right. The ghost of Banquo enters, walks stately down the stairs, and takes Macbeth's chair at the table. Lady Macbeth leads Macbeth downstage right to calm him. The ghost exits behind the thrones. The ghost next walks directly to the dais and sits in Macbeth's throne, the place Macbeth most fears to associate with Banquo. Macbeth approaches the ghost and banishes it; the ghost again exits into upstage shadow. The guests go off both right and left, Macbeth sinks onto the dais, and Lady Macbeth kneels before him. Finally, the couple laboriously climbs the stairs hand in hand, stopping halfway for Macbeth's final lines.

Lady Macbeth. My royal lord,
You do not give the cheer.° The feast is sold
That is not often vouched, while 'tis a-making,
'Tis given with welcome. To feed were best at home;°
From thence, the sauce to meat° is ceremony;
Meeting were bare without it.

[*Enter the* GHOST OF BANQUO, *and sits in Macbeth's place.*]

Macbeth. Sweet remembrancer!°
Now good digestion wait on appetite,
And health on both!

Lennox. May't please your highness sit.

Macbeth.
Here had we now our country's honor roofed,°
Were the graced person of our Banquo present—
Who may I rather challenge for unkindness
Than pity for mischance!°

Ross. His absence, sir,
Lays blame upon his promise. Please't your highness
To grace us with your royal company?

Macbeth.
The table's full.

Lennox. Here is a place reserved, sir.

Macbeth.
Where?

Lennox.
Here, my good lord. What is't that moves your highness?

Macbeth.
Which of you have done this?

Lords. What, my good lord?

Macbeth.
Thou canst not say I did it. Never shake
Thy gory locks at me.

Ross.
Gentlemen, rise, his highness is not well.

Lady Macbeth.
Sit, worthy friends. My Lord is often thus,
And hath been from his youth. Pray you, keep seat.
The fit is momentary; upon a thought°
He will again be well. If much you note him,
You shall offend him and extend his passion.°
Feed, and regard him not.—Are you a man?

Macbeth.
Ay, and a bold one, that dare look on that
Which might appall the devil.

Lady Macbeth. O proper stuff!
This is the very painting of your fear.
This is the air-drawn dagger which, you said,
Led you to Duncan. O, these flaws° and starts,
Imposters to° true fear, would well become

33. cheer: sense of cordiality.

35. The feast . . . home: The feast seems sold (not given) when the host fails to welcome the guests. Mere eating is best done at home.

36. meat: food.

? 37. *Lady Macbeth has summoned her husband to her area of the stage. What mood is she in?*

? **Stage direction.** *The ghost is crucial to this scene. From what you read here, should the ghost be imagined? Or should it actually appear on stage? How should it look, if so?*

37. remembrancer: reminder.

40. our . . . roofed: our nobility under one roof.

43. Who . . . mischance: whom I hope I may reprove because he is unkind rather than pity because he has encountered an accident.

? 46. *When Macbeth says this line, what does he see?*

? 49. *How should Macbeth ask this question? Whom should he be talking to?*

? 51. *According to Macbeth's speech here, what is the ghost doing? Does anyone else see the ghost? How should the others be acting?*

? 53. *Do you think this is true? Or is Lady Macbeth desperately trying to cover for her husband?*

55. upon a thought: as quick as a thought.

57. extend his passion: lengthen his fit.

? 58. *Where do you think Lady Macbeth has taken her husband so that she can whisper this intimidating line?*

63. flaws: gusts; outbursts.

64. to: compared with.

E Appreciating Language

Puns

Point out the pun on the homophones *meat* and *meet.* Explain that Lady Macbeth is saying that meeting (and dining) without ceremony is like eating meat without sauce. Point out other puns in the play, such as the ones spoken by the porter in II.3.11–13, and ask students to explain them.

F Elements of Literature

Tragedy

? In what way does this scene mark the beginning of Macbeth's actual deterioration? [Macbeth's evil deeds and guilty conscience take tangible form. His bizarre behavior bewilders his guests and marks the climax of the play.]

G Struggling Readers

Interpreting

? To whom is Macbeth talking in l. 50? In what way are his words true? [His protest to the ghost is literally true—he did not strike the fatal blow—but he is the instigator of the crime and therefore responsible.] Make sure students are aware of the setting and what is occurring there before they answer this question.

H Reading Skills and Strategies

Making Inferences

? What does Lady Macbeth think is causing Macbeth to cry out? [his tortured imagination] How do you know? [She says the ghost is a "painting," or image, of what Macbeth fears—not the real thing.]

Answers to Margin Questions

Line 37. She may be alarmed, concerned, or irritated.
Stage direction. An imagined ghost could heighten the audience's sense of Macbeth's disturbed mental state, but if the actor who plays Banquo appears on stage, Macbeth's vision could seem as real to the audience as it does to him. The ghost could appear with gashes on his head or throat.
Line 46. Macbeth sees Banquo's ghost occupying his seat.
Line 49. He is angry or horrified. He is speaking to his guests.
Line 51. Perhaps the ghost is shaking its head. No one else sees the ghost. The guests could act embarrassed or frightened.
Line 53. No specific illness has ever been mentioned. She is covering for him.
Line 58. She has pulled him away from the guests.

Getting Students Involved

Cooperative Learning

Hot Seat. At any appropriate point in the play, such as the end of an act, students can assume the persona of a character. Divide the class into groups of four or five. Then, ask each group member to select a different character. Students should be given two minutes to respond "in character" to questions posed by other members of the group.

Rewriting a Scene. Invite students to work in groups of four or five to translate a scene from the play into modern English. Encourage students not to lose any of the characterization or dramatic impact in their translation. When all the translations are complete, ask the groups to perform their scenes for the class.

(A) Reading Skills and Strategies

Making Inferences

? Lady Macbeth has resumed her earlier goading role, taunting Macbeth for being womanly or acting weakly. What is her motivation? [Possible answer: She is afraid Macbeth will either reveal too much and condemn himself or be thought mad. In either case, they risk losing their position of power if he does not regain his composure.]

(B) Elements of Literature

Imagery

? How does this horrible image of the risen dead reflect Macbeth's evil deeds? [Possible answer: As a consequence of the unnatural deaths of Duncan and Banquo, even the dead are not following the normal course of nature by remaining dead, or so Macbeth thinks. Macbeth is referring to Banquo who had twenty stab wounds in his head.]

(C) Critical Thinking

Evaluating

? Other editions put the ghost's entry after the first sentence in l. 91. Why would this change be effective? [Possible answer: The ghost would seem to come when summoned by Macbeth.]

Answers to Margin Questions

Line 68. He might glower at Macbeth, shake his head, or make threatening gestures.

Line 70. He is pointing to the ghost, possibly turning to Lady Macbeth for confirmation of what he sees. Perhaps he speaks in a despairing tone or in a mocking manner.

Line 75. He seems to be talking to himself. He is clearly not talking to the ghost, who has exited.

Line 85. He has resumed playing the host with apologies for his behavior, which he attributes to an illness. Notice his momentary strength in ll. 84–92 as he dismisses the frightening vision of Banquo's ghost.

Line 93. Macbeth is addressing Banquo's ghost, who stares accusingly at him.

A woman's story at a winter's fire,
Authorized° by her grandam. Shame itself!
Why do you make such faces? When all's done,
You look but on a stool.

Macbeth. Prithee, see there!
(A) Behold! Look! Lo! How say you?
Why, what care I? If thou canst nod, speak too.
If charnel houses° and our graves must send
Those that we bury back, our monuments
Shall be the maws of kites.° [*Exit* GHOST.]

Lady Macbeth. What, quite unmanned in folly?

Macbeth.
If I stand here, I saw him.

Lady Macbeth. Fie, for shame!

Macbeth.
Blood hath been shed ere now, i' th' olden time,
Ere humane statute purged the gentle weal;°
Ay, and since too, murders have been performed
Too terrible for the ear. The time has been
That, when the brains were out, the man would die,
And there an end; but now they rise again,
(B) With twenty mortal murders on their crowns,°
And push us from our stools. This is more strange
Than such a murder is.

Lady Macbeth. My worthy lord,
Your noble friends do lack you.

Macbeth. I do forget.
Do not muse at me, my most worthy friends;
I have a strange infirmity, which is nothing
To those that know me. Come, love and health to all!
Then I'll sit down. Give me some wine, fill full.

(C) [*Enter* GHOST.]

I drink to th' general joy o' th' whole table,
And to our dear friend Banquo, whom we miss;
Would he were here! To all and him we thirst,°
And all to all.°

Lords. Our duties, and the pledge.

Macbeth.
Avaunt! and quit my sight! Let the earth hide thee!
Thy bones are marrowless, thy blood is cold;
Thou hast no speculation° in those eyes
Which thou dost glare with.

Lady Macbeth. Think of this, good peers,
But as a thing of custom; 'tis no other.
Only it spoils the pleasure of the time.

Macbeth.
What man dare, I dare.
Approach thou like the rugged Russian bear,
The armed rhinoceros, or th' Hyrcan° tiger;

---

66. Authorized: vouched for.

? **68.** *What could the actor playing Banquo do here in mockery of Macbeth?*

? **70.** *What action is Macbeth engaged in here? What is his tone?*

71. charnel houses: vaults containing bones.

73. our . . . kites: Our tombs shall be the bellies of rapacious birds.

? **75.** *Whom is Macbeth talking to?*

76. purged . . . weal: cleansed the state and made it gentle.

81. mortal . . . crowns: deadly wounds on their heads.

? **85.** *What impression is Macbeth trying to create?*

91. thirst: desire to drink.

92. all to all: Let everybody drink to everybody.

? **93.** *Whom is Macbeth talking to now? According to this speech, what might the ghost be doing?*

95. speculation: sight.

101. Hyrcan: of Hyrcania (near the Caspian Sea).

Crossing the Curriculum

Art

Have students use the descriptions in the stage directions to design a set for one of the scenes in the play. They can use the stage set on p. 344 as a model. Remind them that the set must provide entrances, exits, and acting space for the players. Ask them to sketch their set design on a large sheet of drawing paper.

Social Sciences

Stage a philosophical debate in your classroom. Have students take sides on the question, "Does history repeat itself?" Encourage students to locate events in the play that have occurred in history. Divide the students on each side into smaller groups for developing supporting arguments. Have each group's spokesperson present one supporting argument to the class.

Take any shape but that, and my firm nerves°
Shall never tremble. Or be alive again,
And dare me to the desert° with thy sword.
If trembling I inhabit then, protest me
The baby of a girl.° Hence, horrible shadow!
Unreal mock'ry, hence! [*Exit* GHOST.]
Why, so: being gone,
I am a man again. Pray you, sit still.

Lady Macbeth.
You have displaced the mirth, broke the good meeting,
With most admired° disorder.

Macbeth. Can such things be,
And overcome us° like a summer's cloud,
Without our special wonder? You make me strange
Even to the disposition that I owe,°
When now I think you can behold such sights,
And keep the natural ruby of your cheeks,
When mine is blanched with fear.

Ross. What sights, my lord?

Lady Macbeth.
I pray you, speak not: he grows worse and worse;
Question enrages him: at once, good night.
Stand not upon the order of your going,°
But go at once.

Lennox. Good night; and better health
Attend his majesty!

Lady Macbeth. A kind good night to all!

[*Exeunt* LORDS.]

Macbeth.
It will have blood, they say: blood will have blood.
Stones have been known to move and trees to speak;
Augurs and understood relations° have
By maggot-pies and choughs and rooks brought forth°
The secret'st man of blood. What is the night?°

Lady Macbeth.
Almost at odds with morning, which is which.

Macbeth.
How say'st thou, that Macduff denies his person
At our great bidding?

Lady Macbeth. Did you send to him, sir?

Macbeth.
I hear it by the way,° but I will send:
There's not a one of them but in his house
I keep a servant fee'd.° I will tomorrow,
And betimes° I will, to the weird sisters:
More shall they speak, for now I am bent° to know
By the worst means the worst. For mine own good
All causes° shall give way. I am in blood
Stepped in so far that, should I wade no more,

102. nerves: sinews.

104. desert: lonely place.

106. If . . . girl: If then I tremble, proclaim me a baby girl.

? **108.** *How "brave" should Macbeth appear to be with all the "brave" talk in these lines? What is his mood when he says "I am a man again"?*

110. admired: amazing.

? **110.** *Lady Macbeth and her husband converse in private again. What would the other guests be doing?*

111. overcome us: come over us.

113. You . . . owe: You make me wonder what my nature is.

? **117.** *What clue here would tell the actor playing Macbeth how he is to be behaving?*

119. Stand . . . going: Do not insist on departing in your order of rank.

? **122.** *Read this speech carefully, and decide how Macbeth would deliver it: Slow? Fast? What is his mood?*

124. Augurs . . . relations: auguries (omens) and comprehended reports.

125. By . . . forth: by magpies, crows, and rooks (telltale birds) revealed.

126. What . . . night: What time of night is it?

? **127.** *Is the old fire still present in Lady Macbeth? Or is she suddenly tired and broken?*

130. by the way: incidentally.

132. fee'd: that is, paid to spy.

133. betimes: quickly.

134. bent: determined.

136. causes: considerations.

D Elements of Literature

Theme

? The "overthrow of order" might be considered a theme in *Macbeth.* At the opening of the banquet scene, Macbeth says, "You know your own degrees" [the assertion of order], and at its end Lady Macbeth says, "Stand not upon the order of your going." This degeneration of order is symbolic not only of Macbeth's mental state but also of the state of Scotland. What other lines might be seen as building on this theme? [Possible answers: Students might cite III.2.16; lines that refer to the "fair is foul" theme, such as I.1.10; or Lady Macbeth's speech in I.5.38–52.]

E Cultural Connections

Just as in II.1.56–58, here Macbeth is worried about nature revealing his actions. In Shakespeare's time, many people believed that a murdered victim could identify his or her murderer. King James, in his *Daemonologie,* says, "for as in a secret murther, if the dead carkasse bee at any time thereafter handled by the murtherer, it will gush out of bloud, as if the bloud were crying to the heauen for reunge of the murtherer, God hauing appoynted that secret supernaturall signe, for tryall of that secrete vnnaturall crime."

F Reading Skills and Strategies

Drawing Conclusions

? What conclusion is Macbeth drawing about Macduff? [Sample response: This is the second time that Macduff has refused to attend a ceremony (the first was Macbeth's coronation). Macbeth must realize by now that Macduff suspects him of Duncan's murder.]

Answers to Margin Questions

Line 108. He is brave enough to plant his feet firmly on the floor, though he is shaking and terrified. His mood is one of relief once the ghost exits.

Line 110. whispering in subdued tones; glancing at Macbeth

Line 117. He could be babbling because "he grows worse and worse."

Line 122. The speech could be spoken slowly in a weary, resigned manner.

Line 127. Lady Macbeth is exhausted; her fire is spent.

Making the Connections

Connecting to the Theme: "Under a Hand Accursed"

The phrase "Under a Hand Accursed" is a specific quotation from the play (III.6.49), in which Lennox refers to Scotland as suffering under a ruler who has committed murder. Perhaps the phrase refers to the curses of the witches, suggesting that Macbeth's actions were fated, or to the curse of heaven, suggesting that Macbeth is damned for his sins.

Ⓐ English Language Learners

Supplying Missing Words

Point out that the verb *go* is missing from the sentence "Come, we'll [go] to sleep." Show students how to recognize elliptical sentences and use context clues to mentally provide the missing words.

Ⓑ Elements of Literature

Tragedy

? What do these lines about being a beginner suggest regarding Macbeth's descent into evil? [Possible response: He considers himself a mere novice, or beginner, at committing evil deeds, suggesting that he will continue on his destructive path.]

Answers to Margin Questions

Line 140. Students may cite the word "tedious" or the lines in which Lady Macbeth points out that Macbeth is exhausted by lack of sleep. Others may disagree, saying that ll. 139–140 and 143–144 suggest he is motivated to continue.

Line 144. She may shake her head in sorrow and dismay.

Scene 5. The lines here differ markedly from the blank verse (unrhymed iambic pentameter) of most of the play. It is written, starting at l. 2, in rhymed couplets. Students may argue that this suggests the work of another author.

Summary

Scene 5: Hecate, queen of the witches, berates the weird sisters for leaving her out of their previous encounters with Macbeth. She promises to marshal magic forces to ensure Macbeth's ruin.

From the Stratford Festival production of *Macbeth* (1983).

"Come, let's make haste; she'll soon be back again."

Returning were as tedious as go o'er.
Strange things I have in head that will to hand,
Which must be acted ere they may be scanned.°

Lady Macbeth.
You lack the season of all natures,° sleep.

Macbeth.
Ⓐ Come, we'll to sleep. My strange and self-abuse°
Ⓑ Is the initiate fear that wants hard use.°
We are yet but young in deed. [*Exeunt.*]

Scene 5. *A witches' haunt.*

Thunder. Enter the three WITCHES, *meeting* HECATE.

First Witch.
Why, how now, Hecate! you look angerly.

Hecate.
Have I not reason, beldams° as you are,
Saucy and overbold? How did you dare
To trade and traffic with Macbeth
In riddles and affairs of death;

? **140.** *Does the prospect of a new adventure animate Macbeth? Or is he spent and exhausted?*

140. may be scanned: can be examined.

141. season . . . natures: seasoning (preservative) of all living creatures.

142. self-abuse: delusion.

143. initiate . . . use: beginner's fear that lacks hardening practice.

? **144.** *How might Lady Macbeth react to this last line?*

? **Scene 5.** Macbeth *was published in the first folio in 1623, seven years after Shakespeare had died. Some people think that this scene was written by someone else because the play was short and needed fleshing out. After you read the scene, decide if you think it "sounds" like the rest of the play.*

2. beldams: hags.

Using Students' Strengths

Auditory/Musical Learners

Ask students to rewrite Hecate's speech (ll. 2–35) as a rap song. Have them pay particular attention to their word choice and rhythm. After students have a chance to share their songs aloud, ask them to return to the original speech and to analyze its word choices and rhythm, noting the downbeats that give it a singsong feel.

Interpersonal Learners

At any logical point, such as the end of an act, have students stage a mock talk show featuring characters from the play. A volunteer should serve as the talk show host. Other volunteers should play the roles of guests, while the rest of the class acts as the audience. The host sets the stage by giving the audience background information and introducing the guests. Then the audience asks the guests questions. Remind students to focus on important themes and events in the play.

And I, the mistress of your charms,
The close contriver° of all harms,
Was never called to bear my part,
Or show the glory of our art?
And, which is worse, all you have done
Hath been but for a wayward son,
Spiteful and wrathful; who, as others do,
Loves for his own ends, not for you.
But make amends now: get you gone,
And at the pit of Acheron°
Meet me i' th' morning: thither he
Will come to know his destiny.
Your vessels and your spells provide,
Your charms and everything beside.
I am for th' air; this night I'll spend
Unto a dismal and a fatal end:
Great business must be wrought ere noon.
Upon the corner of the moon
There hangs a vap'rous drop profound;°
I'll catch it ere it come to ground:
And that distilled by magic sleights°
Shall raise such artificial sprites°
As by the strength of their illusion
Shall draw him on to his confusion.°
He shall spurn fate, scorn death, and bear
His hopes 'bove wisdom, grace, and fear:
And you all know security°
Is mortal's chiefest enemy. [*Music and a song.*]
Hark! I am called; my little spirit, see,
Sits in a foggy cloud and stays for me. [*Exit.*]

[*Sing within,* "Come away, come away," *etc.*]

First Witch.
Come, let's make haste; she'll soon be back again.
[*Exeunt.*]

Scene 6. *The palace.*

Enter LENNOX *and another* LORD.

Lennox.
My former speeches have but hit your thoughts,°
Which can interpret farther. Only I say
Things have been strangely borne.° The gracious Duncan
Was pitied of Macbeth: marry, he was dead.
And the right-valiant Banquo walked too late;
Whom, you may say, if't please you, Fleance killed,
For Fleance fled. Men must not walk too late.
Who cannot want the thought,° how monstrous
It was for Malcolm and for Donalbain
To kill their gracious father? Damnèd fact!°

7. close contriver: secret inventor.

15. Acheron: river of Hades.

24. profound: heavy.

26. sleights: arts.

27. artificial sprites: spirits created by magic arts.

29. confusion: ruin.

32. security: overconfidence.

1. My . . . thoughts: My recent words have only coincided with what you have in your mind.

3. borne: managed.

8. cannot . . . thought: cannot help but think.

10. fact: evil deed.

C Reading Skills and Strategies

Making Inferences

? Why is Macbeth "wayward" in Hecate's eyes? [Possible answer: He is not devoted to the cause of evil but rather does evil out of self-interest.]

D Elements of Literature

Tragedy

? What draws Macbeth "on to his confusion"? [his tragic flaw—ruthless ambition] What will cause him to continue down his destructive path? [overconfidence]

Summary

Scene 6: Lennox expresses his suspicions of Macbeth to an unnamed lord. The lord reports that Macduff, who refused to answer Macbeth's summons, has gone to England to obtain the aid of King Edward and Lord Siward in order to remove the tyrant Macbeth and restore the Scottish crown to Malcolm.

E Critical Thinking

Analyzing Tone

? What is Lennox's tone here? What does he now think about Duncan's murder? Why? [Sample responses: He seems to be sarcastic and suspicious—he thinks Macbeth was responsible, perhaps because of the things Macbeth said and did at the banquet; or, he seems perplexed, questioning how these sons—Malcolm, Donalbain, and now Fleance—could be so evil as to kill their fathers.]

Assessing Learning

Check Test: Questions and Answers

1. Why is Macbeth determined to have Banquo killed? [so that Banquo's sons will never rule]
2. Whom else does Macbeth mark for death? [Banquo's son Fleance]
3. What event have Macbeth and Lady Macbeth planned for the evening of the murder? [a banquet]
4. What does Macbeth see at this event? [the ghost of Banquo]
5. What are Macduff and Malcolm doing in England? [securing an army to overthrow Macbeth]

Informal Assessment

Self-Assessment. Ask students to evaluate their use of each of the following reading strategies, using a scale of one (low) to three (high): **1.** visualizing scenes; **2.** rereading for specific references to support their points; **3.** using their reading notes to answer questions. Hold short conferences with students to discuss their self-assessments.

A Struggling Readers

Reading Aloud

To help students think about how they interpret a text as they read, have them pause at several points in this passage and think aloud. They can predict, make comparisons, identify comprehension problems, or visualize the text as they read. Make sure you model this strategy for them before they begin, using another passage from the play. Then, if students need extra assistance allow them to work on the lord's speech with a partner. One person can think aloud while the other records the comments that are made. For help in applying this strategy, see the *Reading Strategies Handbook,* p. 135, in the *Reading Skills and Strategies* binder.

B Elements of Literature

Theme

Point out that this line is the source of the collection title.

Answers to Margin Questions

Line 24. Lennox has spoken with some doubt on previous occasions, as when reporting the death of the blood-smeared grooms in II.3.95–99. In part of this speech, however, he speaks in a sarcastic tone. Read the speech aloud to the class, or coach a student to read it to express the distaste for Macbeth that Lennox now feels.

Line 49. The lords have grown so suspicious about Macbeth's motive for silencing the grooms and placing blame on those who have fled, that Malcolm and Macduff are working in England to raise an army against the king.

How it did grieve Macbeth! Did he not straight,
In pious rage, the two delinquents tear,
That were the slaves of drink and thralls° of sleep?
Was not that nobly done? Ay, and wisely too;
For 'twould have angered any heart alive
To hear the men deny't. So that I say
He has borne all things well: and I do think
That, had he Duncan's sons under his key—
As, an 't° please heaven, he shall not—they should find
What 'twere to kill a father. So should Fleance.
But, peace! for from broad words,° and 'cause he failed
His presence at the tyrant's feast, I hear,
Macduff lives in disgrace. Sir, can you tell
Where he bestows himself?

Lord. The son of Duncan,
From whom this tyrant holds the due of birth,°
Lives in the English court, and is received
Of the most pious Edward° with such grace
That the malevolence of fortune nothing
Takes from his high respect.° Thither Macduff
Is gone to pray the holy king, upon his aid°
To wake Northumberland° and warlike Siward;°
That by the help of these, with Him above
To ratify the work, we may again
Give to our tables meat, sleep to our nights,
Free from our feasts and banquets bloody knives,
Do faithful homage and receive free° honors:
All which we pine for now. And this report
Hath so exasperate the king that he
Prepares for some attempt of war.

Lennox. Sent he to Macduff?

Lord.
He did: and with an absolute "Sir, not I,"
The cloudy° messenger turns me his back,
And hums, as who should say "You'll rue the time
That clogs° me with this answer."

Lennox. And that well might
Advise him to a caution, t' hold what distance
His wisdom can provide. Some holy angel
Fly to the court of England and unfold
His message ere he come, that a swift blessing
May soon return to this our suffering country
Under a hand accursed!

Lord. I'll send my prayers with him.

[*Exeunt.*]

13. thralls: slaves.

19. an 't: if it.

21. for . . . words: because of frank talk.

? **24.** *Lennox is sometimes called the "ironic" character of the play. Do you agree? What tone would he use in this speech?*

25. due of birth: birthright.

27. Edward: Edward the Confessor (reigned 1042–1066).

29. nothing . . . respect: does not diminish the high respect in which he is held.

30. upon his aid: to aid him (Malcolm).

31. To wake Northumberland: that is, to arouse the people in an English county near Scotland. **Siward:** earl of Northumberland.

36. free: freely granted.

41. cloudy: disturbed.

43. clogs: burdens.

? **49.** *This is basically an "information" scene. Can you summarize what it tells you about the plot?*

MAKING MEANINGS

Act III

First Thoughts [Synthesize]

1. Sample titles: "Botches in the Work" or "A Deed of Dreadful Note" (taken from quotations).

Shaping Interpretations [Interpret]

2. Possible response: Perhaps he wanted to show a change in Macbeth's character—to show him not only growing accustomed to murder but becoming more devious in his actions and arranging the crimes so that his denial would be technically true (an equivocation).
3. Possible answers: Some changes involve role reversal—she plans the first murder, but he plans Banquo's murder without consulting her. They are very close as they plan and carry out Duncan's murder and now she is not even in his confidence. Perhaps their feelings of guilt and their growing distrust of others have eroded their trust in each other.
4. Possible answers: In the literal sense, Macbeth's words indicate the time in which the scene takes place, probably dusk—the time in which there is a blurring between light and dark. In a metaphorical sense, his words comment on the blurring between good and evil. In Scene 4, ll. 78–83 are directed literally at the ghost, but could also metaphorically mean that past misdeeds continue to haunt a person.
5. It is the first time that Macbeth's plans have gone awry, and it leaves open the possibility that Banquo's descendants will be kings.
6. Possible answer: The scene plays upon the frightening possibility of madness. It leaves open the question of whether the ghost is real or Macbeth's hallucination. This blurring also occurs in the witches' scenes and in the descriptions of the natural world's response to Duncan's murder.

MAKING MEANINGS

Act III

First Thoughts

1. What title would you give to Act III?

Reading Check

a. In the short **soliloquy** that opens Scene 1, what does Banquo reveal that he knows about Macbeth? What does he decide to do?
b. How and why does Macbeth arrange Banquo's murder? How is Lady Macbeth involved in the murder?
c. In Scene 3, who escapes the murderers?
d. Describe what happens in Scene 4 when Ross, Lennox, and the other lords invite Macbeth to share their table. What does Macbeth do? What does Lady Macbeth do?
e. Macduff does not appear at all in Act III. Where is he, and why?
f. By Scene 6, what opinion do Lennox and the other lord hold of Macbeth?

Shaping Interpretations

2. Why do you suppose Shakespeare did not have Macbeth kill Banquo with his own hands, as he killed Duncan and his two guards? What can you infer about Macbeth's changing **character** after seeing how he engages in this complex plan involving professional murderers?
3. The relationship between Macbeth and Lady Macbeth has changed in several ways since they became rulers of Scotland. Find details in this act that reveal some of these changes. What reasons can you suggest for these changes?
4. In Scene 2, Macbeth describes his surroundings by saying, "Light thickens, and the crow / Makes wing to th' rooky wood." How can these remarks also be seen as a **metaphorical** commentary on the events of the play? What other remarks by Macbeth function in this way?
5. In Shakespeare's tragedies, a **turning point** usually occurs in the third act. At this moment, something happens that moves the action ever downward to its tragic conclusion. How is Fleance's escape a **turning point** in this play?
6. How does the banquet scene blur the clear-cut and common-sense distinction that most of us make between the real and the imaginary? In what other scenes has this distinction also been blurred?
7. At the beginning of Scene 2, Lady Macbeth quietly tells herself, "Nought's had, all's spent, / Where our desire is got without content." What does she mean? At this point, would her husband agree?
8. Nobody except Macbeth sees Banquo's ghost. In some productions of the play, the ghost does not appear onstage; in others it does. If you were the director, which would you choose? What effect is created by having Banquo appear at the banquet, made up as a ghost? What is gained by having it appear as though no person motivates Macbeth's terrifying behavior?

Extending the Text

9. After his vision of Banquo's ghost in Scene 4, Macbeth finally accepts that "blood will have blood." What does this phrase mean? Is it relevant to today's world? How?

Challenging the Text

10. Shakespeare never reveals the identity of the Third Murderer, introduced in Scene 3. Who do you think the murderer is? Do you think the introduction of this Third Murderer is a flaw in the play? Explain your response.

Shaping Interpretations (cont'd)

7. She realizes they have committed a terrible crime and fulfilling their ambitions has not made them happy. Macbeth thinks it is still possible to achieve peace, if only he can kill Banquo and Fleance.
8. Staging options: Have an actor play the ghost; use technology to project a ghost; use strong light to suggest the ghost's presence; or do not represent the ghost on stage in order to suggest it is a figment of Macbeth's imagination. Having Banquo's ghost on stage blurs the distinction between the real and the imaginary and shows the strong influence murder can have on the mind of the murderer. Having no ghost emphasizes that Macbeth is hallucinating.

Extending the Text [Synthesize]

9. Those guilty of taking a life will be found out and will pay with their own lives. The line is relevant to a debate about the death penalty.

Challenging the Text [Evaluate]

10. The third murderer may be one of Macbeth's trusted men, one of the witches, or one of Banquo's followers making sure Fleance escapes so the prophecy can come true. His inclusion is not a flaw—it adds to the horror of the crime; or, it is a flaw because it distracts the audience's attention from other more important issues.

Resources

Selection Assessment

Formal Assessment

- Selection Test, p. 61

Test Generator (One-Stop Planner)

- CD-ROM

Reading Check

a. Banquo suspects that Macbeth murdered Duncan, but he decides not to voice his suspicions.
b. Macbeth sees Banquo as a threat. He hires murderers and convinces them that Banquo wronged them. Lady Macbeth is not involved.
c. Fleance escapes the murderers.
d. Only Macbeth sees Banquo's ghost and speaks to him. Lady Macbeth tries to cover for Macbeth by saying that he customarily has fits; she then hurriedly dismisses the guests.
e. He has gone to the court of Edward, King of England, to ask for an army to help overthrow Macbeth.
f. They believe he is guilty of the murders of Duncan and Banquo and feel he is a tyrant.

Summary

Scene 1: As the three witches concoct a foul brew and chant over their caldron, Macbeth enters and demands to know the future. The witches show him three apparitions: An armed head tells him to "beware Macduff"; a bloody child says that no one born of a woman will hurt him; and a child wearing a crown and holding a branch tells him he will not be conquered until Birnam Wood comes to Dunsinane. A final apparition shows a line of eight kings, including Banquo, with the last figure holding a mirror to indicate the continuation of Banquo's royal line. The witches vanish and Lennox appears, revealing that Macduff has fled to England. As the scene ends, Macbeth resolves to murder Lady Macduff and her children.

A Cultural Connections

? The ingredients the witches use probably reflect beliefs prevalent in Elizabethan England. Why else might this disgusting recipe be appropriate? [Possible response: The witches are in league with evil, and the recipe reflects their wickedness.]

B Advanced Learners

Identifying Assonance

Point out the repetition of this couplet. (ll. 10–11 and ll. 20–21) Have students note the use of **assonance,** the repetition of vowel sounds, in the accented syllables of *double, trouble,* and *bubble.* Ask students to come up with their own couplet that mimics that of the witches. Make sure students use assonance in their couplets.

Answer to Margin Question

Stage Direction. Possible responses: The witches might act gleeful, focused, or serious.

ACT IV Scene 1. *A witches' haunt.*

Thunder. Enter the three WITCHES.

First Witch.
Thrice the brinded° cat hath mewed.

Second Witch.
Thrice and once the hedge-pig° whined.

Third Witch.
Harpier° cries, 'Tis time, 'tis time.

First Witch.
Round about the caldron go:
In the poisoned entrails throw.
Toad, that under cold stone
Days and nights has thirty-one
Swelt'red venom sleeping got,°
Boil thou first i' th' charmèd pot.

All.
Double, double, toil and trouble;
Fire burn and caldron bubble.

A

Second Witch.
Fillet° of a fenny° snake,
In the caldron boil and bake;
Eye of newt and toe of frog,
Wool of bat and tongue of dog,
Adder's fork° and blindworm's° sting,
Lizard's leg and howlet's° wing,
For a charm of pow'rful trouble,
Like a hell-broth boil and bubble.

All.
B
Double, double, toil and trouble;
Fire burn and caldron bubble.

? **Stage direction.** *This scene usually begins in darkness. In Shakespeare's day, the caldron might have risen through the trapdoor. How would you have the witches act: gleeful? lamenting?*

1. **brinded:** brindled.
2. **hedge-pig:** hedgehog.
3. **Harpier:** an attendant spirit like Graymalkin and Paddock in Act I, Scene 1.

8. **Swelt'red . . . got:** venom sweated out while sleeping.

12. **Fillet:** slice. **fenny:** from a swamp.

16. **fork:** forked tongue. **blindworm's:** legless lizard's.
17. **howlet's:** owl's.

"I conjure you, by that which you profess, Howe'er you come to know it, answer me."

From the Stratford Festival production of *Macbeth* (1983).

Using Students' Strengths

Kinesthetic Learners

Divide the class into two teams. Each team should prepare and then pose in five tableaux, or "frozen scenes," from the play. If the other team guesses the scene being represented on the first try, the presenting team gets five points; on the second try, two points; and on the third try, one point. The team with the most points wins. Remind students to present scenes the audience actually sees. They should not, for example, show Duncan being murdered.

Verbal Learners

Ask students to choose a soliloquy or a portion of a scene to memorize. Have them recite their speeches to the class while you videotape them, if possible. Interested students could create an appropriate backdrop for their scene.

Third Witch.
Scale of dragon, tooth of wolf,
Witch's mummy,° maw and gulf°
Of the ravined° salt-sea shark,
Root of hemlock digged i' th' dark,
Liver of blaspheming Jew,
Gall of goat, and slips of yew
Slivered in the moon's eclipse,
Nose of Turk and Tartar's lips,
Finger of birth-strangled babe
Ditch-delivered by a drab,°
Make the gruel thick and slab:°
Add thereto a tiger's chaudron,°
For th' ingredients of our caldron.

All.
Double, double, toil and trouble;
Fire burn and caldron bubble.

Second Witch.
Cool it with a baboon's blood,
Then the charm is firm and good.

[*Enter* HECATE *and the other three* WITCHES.]

Hecate.
O, well done! I commend your pains;
And every one shall share i' th' gains:
And now about the caldron sing,
Like elves and fairies in a ring,
Enchanting all that you put in.

[*Music and a song:* "Black Spirits," *etc.*]

[*Exeunt* HECATE *and the other three* WITCHES.]

Second Witch.
By the pricking of my thumbs,
Something wicked this way comes:
Open, locks,
Whoever knocks!

[*Enter* MACBETH.]

Macbeth.
How now, you secret, black, and midnight hags!
What is't you do?

All. A deed without a name.

Macbeth.
I conjure you, by that which you profess,
Howe'er you come to know it, answer me:
Though you untie the winds and let them fight
Against the churches; though the yesty° waves
Confound° and swallow navigation up;

23. Witch's mummy: mummified flesh of a witch. **maw and gulf:** stomach and gullet.

24. ravined: ravenous.

31. drab: harlot.

32. slab: slimy.

33. chaudron: entrails.

? *This exciting scene has five major sections, each with its own intensity. See if you can identify them when you're finished.*

? **48.** *How has Macbeth's attitude toward the witches changed since his earlier encounters with them?*

53. yesty: foamy.

54. Confound: destroy.

C Elements of Literature

Imagery

? How is the state of the kingdom under Macbeth's rule reflected in the images of dismemberment? [Possible response: The kingdom is torn by dissension because of Macbeth's evil deeds.]

D Literary Connections

Book Titles from *Macbeth*

? Mystery writer Agatha Christie used l. 44 as the title of a book, and science fiction writer Ray Bradbury used l. 45 as the title of a novel. Why might mystery and science fiction writers allude to this play? [Possible reponse: The play is about murder and the mysterious, supernatural forces of evil.]

E Elements of Literature

Tragedy

? In what way do these lines indicate the extent to which Macbeth has degenerated? [Possible answer: The witches talk about him in dehumanizing terms— "something wicked"—suggesting he is as evil as the witches themselves.]

F Struggling Readers

Finding Details

? What catastrophic events does Macbeth mention in ll. 52–60? [Winds destroy churches; the sea swallows ships; crops are destroyed; castles and pyramids crumble; seeds are destroyed.] **What point is he making with this list?** [Possible response: Macbeth is determined to get an answer from the witches no matter what damage occurs.]

Answers to Margin Questions

Scene sections. Possible divisions are 1) caldron scene, 2) Macbeth's appearance, 3) the three apparitions, 4) the show of eight kings, and 5) Macbeth's talk with Lennox.

Line 48. Macbeth is no longer awed by the witches; he conjures them up and scorns them.

Professional Notes

Critical Comment: Ultimate Rebellion

In his essay "The Story of Night: *Macbeth,*" John Holloway maintains that in IV.1.50 Macbeth deliberately conjures up the witches, "even at the cost of universal destruction. In effect these lines come near to a curse upon the whole of Nature. Rebellion has been taken to its full extent." As students read Act IV, ask them to keep this interpretation in mind. Do they think Macbeth displays his ultimate wickedness here? Explain. [Possible responses: Macbeth is as evil as he can become in this scene because he purposely invites dark forces into his world and ignores any possible consequences. No, Macbeth is rapidly becoming more sinister, and he will probably commit even more evil acts.]

A Critical Thinking

Interpreting

? What might the sow symbolize? [Possible response: Macbeth. Like the sow that has consumed her young, the king, who should protect his people, has instead murdered innocent subjects. Students may cite ll. 64–67 to reinforce this interpretation.]

B Elements of Literature

Tragedy

? What is Macbeth's only interest now? [His only interest is his own personal gain.]

C Elements of Literature

Theme

? To fulfill his ambition, Macbeth has upset the social order by killing Duncan. What is he unable to control? [the supernatural world of spirits] Where in the play was this previously demonstrated? [in his inability to make the witches elaborate on their prophecies, or to get rid of Banquo's ghost]

D Critical Thinking

Defending an Interpretation

Critic Cleanth Brooks feels that the bloody (l. 77) and crowned (l. 90) apparitions of children that Macbeth sees are symbols of "the future which Macbeth would like to control." Other critics feel the apparitions represent certain people, specifically Macduff and Malcolm. Ask students to propose and defend their own interpretations of these apparitions. [Answers will vary.]

Answers to Margin Questions

Line 61. Students who recall Hecate's lines in Act III, Scene 5 may say that Macbeth is not a full participant in evil. Students who focus on Act IV, Scene 1 may say that the witches now identify him as "something wicked."

Line 67. They are tossing ingredients into the boiling caldron and muttering incantations while speaking with Macbeth.

Line 71. Perhaps the apparition speaks to warn Macbeth that Macduff could defeat him. The helmet suggests that the defeat might occur in battle.

Though bladed corn be lodged° and trees blown down;
Though castles topple on their warders' heads;
Though palaces and pyramids do slope°
Their heads to their foundations; though the treasure
Of nature's germens° tumble all together,
Even till destruction sicken,° answer me
To what I ask you.

First Witch. Speak.

Second Witch. Demand.

Third Witch. We'll answer.

First Witch.
Say, if th' hadst rather hear it from our mouths,
Or from our masters?

Macbeth. Call 'em, let me see 'em.

First Witch.
A Pour in sow's blood, that hath eaten
Her nine farrow;° grease that's sweaten°
From the murderer's gibbet° throw
Into the flame.

All. Come, high or low,
Thyself and office° deftly show!

[*Thunder.* FIRST APPARITION: *an Armed Head.*°]

Macbeth.
Tell me, thou unknown power——

First Witch. He knows thy thought:
Hear his speech, but say thou nought.

First Apparition.
Macbeth! Macbeth! Macbeth! Beware Macduff!
Beware the Thane of Fife. Dismiss me: enough.

B [*He descends.*]

Macbeth.
Whate'er thou art, for thy good caution thanks:
Thou hast harped° my fear aright. But one word more——

First Witch.
C He will not be commanded. Here's another,
More potent than the first.

D [*Thunder.* SECOND APPARITION: *a Bloody Child.*]

Second Apparition.
Macbeth! Macbeth! Macbeth!

Macbeth.
Had I three ears, I'd hear thee.

Second Apparition.
Be bloody, bold, and resolute! Laugh to scorn
The pow'r of man, for none of woman born
Shall harm Macbeth. [*Descends.*]

55. bladed . . . lodged: grain in the ear be beaten down.

57. slope: bend.

59. nature's germens: seeds of all life.

60. sicken: sicken at its own work.

? **61.** *These exchanges are spoken rapidly. Do the witches now see Macbeth as a participant in evil?*

65. farrow: young pigs.
sweaten: sweated.

66. gibbet: gallows.

? **67.** *What are the witches doing all during this scene?*

68. office: function.

Armed Head: helmeted head.

? **71.** *Why does the helmeted head deliver this message? How does the form of the apparition support the warning the apparition gives?*

74. harped: hit upon; struck the note of.

Reaching All Students

Struggling Readers

Have students do a "Save the Last Word for Me" strategy. Have them choose a section of the play that makes a strong impact on them, and ask them to write down their thoughts about it on a note card. Then, have students share their passages and comments in small groups. For help in applying this strategy, see the *Reading Strategies Handbook*, p. 77, in the *Reading Skills and Strategies* binder.

English Language Learners

One approach to engaging English language learners is to ask them to listen to the recording of the portions of *Macbeth* included in the *Audio CD Library*. Encourage them to take notes and question any words or lines they do not understand. Ask them if listening to the spoken words helps them better understand the written words.

Macbeth.
Then live, Macduff: what need I fear of thee?
But yet I'll make assurance double sure,
And take a bond of fate.° Thou shalt not live;
That I may tell pale-hearted fear it lies,
And sleep in spite of thunder.

[*Thunder.* THIRD APPARITION: *a Child Crowned, with a tree in his hand.*]

What is this,
That rises like the issue° of a king,
And wears upon his baby-brow the round
And top of sovereignty?°

All. Listen, but speak not to't.

Third Apparition.
Be lion-mettled, proud, and take no care
Who chafes, who frets, or where conspirers are:
Macbeth shall never vanquished be until
Great Birnam Wood to high Dunsinane Hill
Shall come against him. [*Descends.*]

Macbeth. That will never be.
Who can impress° the forest, bid the tree
Unfix his earth-bound root? Sweet bodements,° good!
Rebellious dead, rise never, till the Wood
Of Birnam rise, and our high-placed Macbeth
Shall live the lease of nature,° pay his breath
To time and mortal custom.° Yet my heart
Throbs to know one thing. Tell me, if your art
Can tell so much: shall Banquo's issue ever
Reign in this kingdom?

All. Seek to know no more.

Macbeth.
I will be satisfied.° Deny me this,
And an eternal curse fall on you! Let me know.
Why sinks that caldron? And what noise° is this?

[*Hautboys.*]

First Witch. Show!
Second Witch. Show!
Third Witch. Show!
All.
Show his eyes, and grieve his heart;
Come like shadows, so depart!

[*A show of eight* KINGS *and* BANQUO, *last* KING *with a glass° in his hand.*]

Macbeth.
Thou art too like the spirit of Banquo. Down!
Thy crown does sear mine eyelids. And thy hair,

? 82. *Macbeth takes the child's message to mean he need not fear Macduff. Nonetheless, why should the second apparition's message be approached with caution?*

84. take . . . fate: get a guarantee from fate (that is, he will kill Macduff and thus will compel fate to keep its word).

87. issue: offspring.

89. round . . . sovereignty: that is, crown.

? 93. *What does the third apparition prophesy? What must be Macbeth's mental state at this point?*

95. impress: conscript; draft.

96. bodements: prophecies.

99. lease of nature: natural life span.

100. mortal custom: natural death.

? 102. *What is Macbeth's mood? How might his tone change when he asks about Banquo's issue, or children?*

104. satisfied: that is, fully informed.

106. noise: music.

? **Stage direction.** *A parade of eight Stuart kings passes before Macbeth. These are the kings of Banquo's line. The last king holds up a mirror (**glass**) to suggest an infinite number of descendants. Banquo appears last. According to the next speech, how does Banquo act toward Macbeth?*

E Reading Skills and Strategies
Drawing Conclusions

? Why will Macbeth kill Macduff despite the prophecy that no man "born of woman" can harm him? [Possible response: He will kill Macduff to ensure that fate cannot trick him. Perhaps he does not completely trust the apparition.]

F Appreciating Language
Poetry

? Macbeth suddenly starts to speak entirely in rhymed couplets, whereas previously he used them mainly to end a scene. What might account for this change? [Possible answer: Macbeth is so influenced by the witches that he begins to speak in rhyme as they do.]

G Critical Thinking
Speculating

? Why might the witches initially refuse to answer his question and then give in? [Possible answers: They refuse because it is something he should not know, and they want to make sure that he takes full responsibility for asking for the knowledge; or, they are just tempting him more by refusing.]

Answers to Margin Questions

Line 82. The message seems to mean no one can harm Macbeth, but the wording is unusual and may be some sort of riddle.
Line 93. Macbeth will not be defeated until Birnam Wood marches on his castle at Dunsinane. Since the second and third prophecies seem impossible to fulfill, Macbeth must feel untouchable and hence be exultant.
Line 102. Macbeth is consumed by the desire to know whether Banquo's descendants will inherit his throne. His tone might change from exultation to desperate determination.
Stage direction. He smiles at Macbeth and gestures to indicate that the eight kings are his descendants.

Professional Notes

Critical Comment: The Parade of Kings

Critic G. Wilson Knight suggests that the parade of eight kings in Act IV, Scene 1, be played "with deliberation and ceremony." He would have the kings pause as they pass Macbeth and then group themselves around a throne as if posing for a photograph, waiting for Banquo's ghost. Banquo actually seats himself on the throne to illustrate his truly royal spirit, as contrasted with the hypocrisy of Macbeth. Ask a small group of students to demonstrate this staging and then their own alternative. The class can discuss the effectiveness of each.

Ⓐ Historical Connections

Critic Kenneth Muir says, "The twofold balls are usually taken to refer to the double coronation of James at Scone and Westminster. . . . The treble scepters are the two used for investment in the English coronation and the one used in the Scottish coronation."

Ⓑ Critical Thinking

Speculating

? Review Lennox's speech in Act III, Scene 6. Why do you think he is still attending Macbeth? [Sample responses: He is afraid to leave; he is waiting for more substantial proof; or he is a spy in Macbeth's castle.]

Ⓒ Elements of Literature

Irony

? Why are these lines ironic? [Macbeth himself trusts the witches, so he is damning himself.]

Answers to Margin Questions

Line 124. Banquo still has bloody gashes. Macbeth must be furious and confused that despite the three promising prophecies, Banquo will win in the end.

Line 136. Lennox's entrance marks the sudden return of reality and sanity. It changes the focus of suspense, redirecting the audience's attention to the thanes' increasing suspicions. Lennox tells Macbeth that Macduff has fled to England to raise an army to fight against him.

Thou other gold-bound brow, is like the first.
A third is like the former. Filthy hags!
Why do you show me this? A fourth! Start,° eyes!
What, will the line stretch out to th' crack of doom?°
Another yet! A seventh! I'll see no more.
And yet the eighth° appears, who bears a glass
Which shows me many more; and some I see
That twofold balls and treble scepters° carry:
Horrible sight! Now I see 'tis true;
For the blood-boltered° Banquo smiles upon me,
And points at them for his.° What, is this so?

First Witch.
Ay, sir, all this is so. But why
Stands Macbeth thus amazedly?
Come, sisters, cheer we up his sprites,°
And show the best of our delights:
I'll charm the air to give a sound,
While you perform your antic round,°
That this great king may kindly say
Our duties did his welcome pay.

[*Music. The* WITCHES *dance, and vanish.*]

Macbeth.
Where are they? Gone? Let this pernicious hour
Stand aye accursèd in the calendar!
Come in, without there!

[*Enter* LENNOX.]

Lennox. What's your grace's will?

Macbeth.
Saw you the weird sisters?

Lennox. No, my lord.

Macbeth.
Came they not by you?

Lennox. No indeed, my lord.

Macbeth.
Infected by the air whereon they ride,
And damned all those that trust them! I did hear
The galloping of horse.° Who was't came by?

Lennox.
'Tis two or three, my lord, that bring you word
Macduff is fled to England.

Macbeth. Fled to England?

Lennox.
Ay, my good lord.

Macbeth (*aside*).
Time, thou anticipat'st° my dread exploits.
The flighty purpose never is o'ertook
Unless the deed go with it.° From this moment

116. Start: that is, from the sockets.

117. crack of doom: blast (of a trumpet) at Doomsday.

119. eighth: King James I of England (the present king).

121. twofold . . . scepters: coronation emblems.

123. blood-boltered: matted with blood.

124. his: his descendants.

? **124.** *What does Banquo look like? What must be Macbeth's mental state now?*

127. sprites: spirits.

130. antic round: grotesque, circular dance.

? **136.** *How would the mood on stage change as Lennox appears? What crucial information does he give Macbeth?*

140. horse: horses (or horsemen).

144. anticipat'st: foretold.

146. The flighty . . . it: The fleeting plan is never accomplished unless an action accompanies it.

Crossing the Curriculum

Art

Ask students what prop or piece of scenery has captured their imagination: the witches' caldron, the castle, or the banquet room? Then, have students work in groups of four to create this prop or piece of scenery for the play. Assign each student a role: an artist (to design the piece), a production manager (to oversee the collection of necessary building materials), and workers (to build, paint, and erect the prop or piece).

Psychology

Have interested students write a short essay exploring Macbeth's transformation from a loyal soldier into a cold-blooded murderer. Encourage them to explain Macbeth's sightings of the bloody dagger, Banquo's ghost, and the series of apparitions in Act IV as symptoms of his descent into madness. Have students address the connection between Macbeth's visions and his mental deterioration.

The very firstlings of my heart° shall be
The firstlings of my hand. And even now,
To crown my thoughts with acts, be it thought and done:
The castle of Macduff I will surprise;°
Seize upon Fife; give to th' edge o' th' sword
His wife, his babes, and all unfortunate souls
That trace him in his line.° No boasting like a fool;
This deed I'll do before this purpose cool:
But no more sights!—Where are these gentlemen?
Come, bring me where they are. [*Exeunt.*]

147. firstlings . . . heart: that is, first thoughts, impulses.

150. surprise: attack suddenly.

153. trace . . . line: are of his lineage.

? **156.** *By this speech, how does Macbeth show he has fallen ever deeper into evil? How different is Macbeth now from the reluctant murderer of the first part of the play? Why does Macbeth want to murder Macduff's children?*

? **Stage direction.** *In many productions, the mood of this scene contrasts dramatically with the previous scenes of horror. How would you stage this domestic scene to suggest the vulnerability of Lady Macduff and her children?*

Scene 2. *Macduff's castle.*

Enter Macduff's wife LADY MACDUFF, *her* SON, *and* ROSS.

Lady Macduff.
What had he done, to make him fly the land? (E)

Ross.
You must have patience, madam.

Lady Macduff. He had none:
His flight was madness. When our actions do not,
Our fears do make us traitors.

Ross. You know not
Whether it was his wisdom or his fear.

Lady Macduff.
Wisdom! To leave his wife, to leave his babes,
His mansion and his titles,° in a place
From whence himself does fly? He loves us not;
He wants the natural touch:° for the poor wren,
The most diminutive of birds, will fight,
Her young ones in her nest, against the owl.
All is the fear and nothing is the love;
As little is the wisdom, where the flight
So runs against all reason.

Ross. My dearest coz,°
I pray you, school° yourself. But, for your husband,
He is noble, wise, judicious, and best knows
The fits o' th' season.° I dare not speak much further:
But cruel are the times, when we are traitors
And do not know ourselves; when we hold rumor
From what we fear,° yet know not what we fear,
But float upon a wild and violent sea
Each way and move. I take my leave of you.
Shall not be long but I'll be here again.
Things at the worst will cease,° or else climb upward
To what they were before. My pretty cousin,
Blessing upon you!

Lady Macduff.
Fathered he is, and yet he's fatherless.

7. titles: possessions.

9. wants . . . touch: that is, lacks natural affection for his wife and children.

14. coz: cousin.

15. school: control.

17. fits . . . season: disorders of the time.

? **17.** *How could Ross show his fear in line 17?*

20. hold . . . fear: believe rumors because we fear.

24. cease: cease worsening.

(D) Literary Connections

Paradise Lost and *Macbeth*

The critic A. C. Bradley connects this passage to the quotation by Satan in Milton's *Paradise Lost,* "For only in destroying I find ease/ To my relentless thoughts" (Book IX, ll. 129–130), saying that this idea may have been inspired by Macbeth.

Summary

Scene 2: At Macduff's castle, Ross tells Lady Macduff that Macduff has gone to England. She cannot understand why her husband left without explanation and accuses him of betraying his marriage vows. When Ross exits, mother and son exchange tender words, interrupted first by a messenger urging them to flee for their lives and then by murderers who stab the son and pursue Lady Macduff offstage.

(E) Reading Skills and Strategies

Responding to the Text

? What do you think Lady Macduff is feeling? Why might Macduff have fled without telling her? [Sample responses: She is feeling betrayed, worried, or angry. Macduff might have fled without telling her so that anyone trying to find out where he was would be unable to get any information from her; or, he may have put his duty to his country before his family.]

Answers to Margin Questions

Line 156. At first Macbeth was indecisive and reluctant about killing Duncan. He now, however, has grown so evil that he can order a murder without a second thought. Students may say that Macbeth has gone from a reluctant murderer to a cold-blooded one; other students may see little difference since the outcome of his actions is always the same—someone dies. Possible response: Macbeth wants to murder Macduff's family to avenge Macduff for escaping to England where Macbeth suspects that Macduff will plot against him.

Stage direction. Answers will vary. The scene might take place in a bedroom or living room to make the ensuing violence more personal and wrenching.

Line 17. He might extend his hands as if pleading. He might lower his voice or look over his shoulder.

Professional Notes

Critical Comment: Macbeth's Imagination

By rejecting "sights" (l. 155), Macbeth may be expressing his dismay at what he has learned from the apparitions or rejecting the bloody figments of his imagination that have haunted him throughout the play. In his introduction to *Macbeth,* critic Harold Bloom says, "His imagination is so strong . . . that we can see that it *is* imagination, rather than ambition or the witches, that victimizes and destroys Macbeth." Explore this point of view with students. Some may find it convincing; others may argue that Macbeth's fall is brought on by a combination of imagination, ambition, the witches, and susceptibility to Lady Macbeth's persuasion.

Ⓐ Humanities Connections

The Bible

Macduff's son may be referring to Jesus's statement about trusting in God: "Look at the birds in the sky. They neither sow nor reap nor gather into barns: yet your heavenly Father feeds them. Are you not worth much more than they are?" (Matthew 6:26)

Ⓑ Elements of Literature

Imagery

? In what ways is a bird a fitting image for Macduff's son? [Possible responses: The image of the innocent, trapped bird makes the boy seem defenseless and vulnerable. It is also a reminder that Macbeth has resolved to trap Macduff's family in their home.]

Ⓒ Reading Skills and Strategies

Responding to the Text

? How do you feel about Lady Macduff and her son? [Students will probably find relief in these two guiltless characters and admire their close relationship. Some may enjoy their witty banter but worry about their safety.]

Ⓓ Elements of Literature

Suspense

? What is the point of having this messenger arrive to warn of danger? [Possible answer: It increases suspense; the audience knows of the impending danger, realizes it is near, and hopes the mother and son will escape.]

Answers to Margin Questions

Line 30. He might kiss Lady Macduff's cheek or hand and tousle the boy's hair. Answers about Ross's age will vary.
Line 31. She might act betrayed by her husband's flight and afraid of the general chaos, or, she might conceal her fear for her son's sake.

Ross.
I am so much a fool, should I stay longer,
It would be my disgrace° and your discomfort.
I take my leave at once. [*Exit* ROSS.]

Lady Macduff. Sirrah,° your father's dead:
And what will you do now? How will you live?

Son.
As birds do, mother.

Lady Macduff. What, with worms and flies?

Son.
With what I get, I mean; and so do they.

Lady Macduff.
Poor bird! thou'dst never fear the net nor lime,°
The pitfall nor the gin.°

Son.
Why should I, mother? Poor birds they are not set for.
My father is not dead, for all your saying.

Lady Macduff.
Yes, he is dead: how wilt thou do for a father?

Son. Nay, how will you do for a husband?

Lady Macduff. Why, I can buy me twenty at any market.

Son. Then you'll buy 'em to sell° again.

Lady Macduff.
Thou speak'st with all thy wit, and yet, i' faith,
With wit enough for thee.°

Son.
Was my father a traitor, mother?

Lady Macduff. Ay, that he was.

Son. What is a traitor?

Lady Macduff. Why, one that swears and lies.°

Son. And be all traitors that do so?

Lady Macduff. Every one that does so is a traitor, and must be hanged.

Son. And must they all be hanged that swear and lie?

Lady Macduff. Every one.

Son. Who must hang them?

Lady Macduff. Why, the honest men.

Son. Then the liars and swearers are fools; for there are liars and swearers enow° to beat the honest men and hang up them.

Lady Macduff. Now, God help thee, poor monkey! But how wilt thou do for a father?

Son. If he were dead, you'd weep for him. If you would not, it were a good sign that I should quickly have a new father.

Lady Macduff. Poor prattler, how thou talk'st!

[*Enter a* MESSENGER.]

Messenger.
Bless you, fair dame! I am not to you known,
Though in your state of honor I am perfect.°

29. It . . . disgrace: That is, I would weep.

? **30.** *In taking his leave, how would Ross show affection for Lady Macduff and her young son? Would you have Ross be younger or older than Lady Macduff?*

30. Sirrah: here, an affectionate address to a child.

? **31.** *How would you have Lady Macduff act in this scene? Frightened? Bitter? Loving? Resigned?*

34. lime: birdlime (smeared on branches to catch birds).

35. gin: trap.

41. sell: betray.

43. for thee: for a child.

47. swears and lies: takes an oath and breaks it.

55. enow: enough.

62. in . . . perfect: That is, I am fully informed of your honorable rank.

Getting Students Involved

Cooperative Learning

Defining a Traitor. Have students work in groups of four or five to define the word *traitor.* They might wish to use a graphic organizer, such as a cluster map, to organize their thoughts. Then, have them debate the following question: How might someone be a traitor to his or her country? Before students read Scene 2, ask the groups to speculate on how Lady Macduff will feel about her husband's leaving Scotland. After they read the scene, have the groups discuss whether they accept Lady Macduff's definition of a traitor as someone "who swears and lies." Is Macduff a traitor or is there another explanation for his behavior? Finally, have students compare the behavior of Macduff and Macbeth. Who is more of a traitor? Why?

I doubt° some danger does approach you nearly:
If you will take a homely° man's advice,
Be not found here; hence, with your little ones.
To fright you thus, methinks I am too savage;
To do worse to you were fell° cruelty,
Which is too nigh your person. Heaven preserve you!
I dare abide no longer. [*Exit* MESSENGER.]

Lady Macduff. Whither should I fly?
I have done no harm. But I remember now
I am in this earthly world, where to do harm
Is often laudable, to do good sometime
Accounted dangerous folly. Why then, alas,
Do I put up that womanly defense,
To say I have done no harm?—What are these faces?

[*Enter* MURDERERS.]

Murderer.
Where is your husband?

Lady Macduff.
I hope, in no place so unsanctified
Where such as thou mayst find him.

Murderer. He's a traitor.

Son.
Thou li'st, thou shag-eared° villain!

Murderer. What, you egg!

[*Stabbing him.*]

Young fry° of treachery!

Son. He has killed me, mother:
Run away, I pray you! [*Dies.*]

[*Exit* LADY MACDUFF, *crying* "Murder!" *followed by* MURDERERS.]

Scene 3. *England. Before the king's palace.*

Enter MALCOLM *and* MACDUFF.

Malcolm.
Let us seek out some desolate shade, and there
Weep our sad bosoms empty.

Macduff. Let us rather
Hold fast the mortal° sword, and like good men
Bestride our down-fall'n birthdom.° Each new morn
New widows howl, new orphans cry, new sorrows
Strike heaven on the face, that° it resounds
As if it felt with Scotland and yelled out
Like syllable of dolor.°

Malcolm. What I believe, I'll wail;
What know, believe; and what I can redress,

63. doubt: fear.
64. homely: plain.
67. fell: fierce.

? **69.** *Some readers think that this messenger has been sent by Lady Macbeth. Is there any support for this theory? Would it be within her character? What must Lady Macduff do when she hears this terrible message?*

? **75.** *What would Lady Macduff and her son do as they see the murderers enter the room?*

79. shag-eared: hairy-eared.
80. fry: spawn.
3. mortal: deadly.
4. Bestride . . . birthdom: protectively stand over our native land.
6. that: so that.
8. Like . . . dolor: similar sound of grief.

E Elements of Literature

Theme

? How do Lady Macduff's words reflect the "Fair is foul, and foul is fair" theme? [Possible response: There is no escape in a world where evil acts are rewarded and good acts are overlooked.]

F Critical Thinking

Evaluating

? What is your opinion of Scene 2? [Some students will say this is a strong scene because it clearly shows the extent of Macbeth's cruelty. It is also a very touching scene in the midst of violent acts. Others may contend that the banter between mother and son is unnaturally lively, although their defiance of the murderers at the end is admirable. Most students will be touched by the fact that Macduff's son, who is just a boy, tries to save his mother as he dies. Some students may be troubled by the death of the young boy on stage.]

Summary

Scene 3: Macduff attempts to secure Malcolm's aid in fighting Macbeth, but Malcolm first tests Macduff's loyalty to Scotland. After Macduff proves his integrity, Malcolm tells him an army is ready to attack Macbeth's forces. Ross enters and tells Macduff that his wife, children, and servants have been murdered. Turning his shock and grief to anger, Macduff prays to meet Macbeth in battle.

Answers to Margin Questions

Line 69. No, since she does not know of the plans. Lady Macbeth has been upset by Macbeth's mood swings, wild imagination, and emotional distance from her. However, there has been no evidence that she has initiated any action, so she probably has not sent the messenger. Lady Macduff looks for some way to flee and asks what she has done. She soon recalls, however, that under Macbeth's rule innocence and goodness are of no value.

Line 75. The lines suggest that the boy might try to protect his mother—perhaps he steps in front of her to shield her. Lady Macduff might try to block her son from the murderer's path. Perhaps they both back away.

Professional Notes

Critical Comment: The Murder of Lady Macduff

Read students the following critical comment by G. Wilson Knight: "The murder of Lady Macduff can be best done before simple curtains. Generally it gets laughter. It is, however, not meant to hold any grandeur of action. Macbeth's exploits get less and less dignified and more mad. They are meant to. Duncan's murder was tragically grand; Banquo's melodramatic; and this is almost ludicrous. The producer must bring out its quality of ghoulish horror fearlessly and no one will laugh. He must avoid a lot of screams at the end." Ask students to share their reactions to Knight's interpretation. Have them discuss how they might stage the scene to bring out its quality of "ghoulish horror."

Ⓐ Reading Skills and Strategies

Identifying Cause and Effect

? Why is Malcolm wary? [Possible response: Macduff was once a good friend of Macbeth and, so far as Malcolm knows, has not been injured by him. Thus, Malcolm is worried that Macduff, possibly in league with Macbeth, has been sent to trick or kill him.]

Answer to Margin Question

Line 14. Neither Malcolm nor Macduff knows that Macbeth has already had Macduff's family killed.

As I shall find the time to friend,° I will.
What you have spoke, it may be so perchance.
This tyrant, whose sole° name blisters our tongues,
Was once thought honest:° you have loved him well;
He hath not touched you yet. I am young; but something
You may deserve of him through me;° and wisdom°
To offer up a weak, poor, innocent lamb
T' appease an angry god.

Macduff.
I am not treacherous.

Malcolm. But Macbeth is.
A good and virtuous nature may recoil
In° an imperial charge. But I shall crave your pardon;
That which you are, my thoughts cannot transpose:°

10. to friend: to be friendly, favorable.

12. sole: very.

13. honest: good.

? **14.** *What great irony would the audience feel upon hearing this line, given what has just taken place in the previous scene?*

15. deserve . . . me: that is, earn by betraying me to Macbeth. **wisdom:** it may be wise.

20. recoil / In: give way under.

21. transpose: transform.

"He has killed me, mother."

From the Stratford Festival production of *Macbeth* (1983).

Using Students' Strengths

Verbal Learners

Have students choose one of the main characters in the play and write a brief character sketch. Students should use at least three of the following methods to show what their character is like.

- his/her appearance
- his/her actions
- his/her words
- the reaction of others to him/her

Then have students present their character sketches to the class. They should deliver their sketches in the manner that their chosen characters would speak.

Angels are bright still, though the brightest° fell:
Though all things foul would wear° the brows of grace,
Yet grace must still look so.°

Macduff. I have lost my hopes.

Malcolm.
Perchance even there where I did find my doubts.
Why in that rawness° left you wife and child,
Those precious motives, those strong knots of love,
Without leave-taking? I pray you,
Let not my jealousies° be your dishonors,
But mine own safeties. You may be rightly just°
Whatever I shall think.

Macduff. Bleed, bleed, poor country:
Great tyranny, lay thou thy basis° sure,
For goodness dare not check° thee: wear thou thy wrongs;
The title is affeered.° Fare thee well, lord:
I would not be the villain that thou think'st
For the whole space that's in the tyrant's grasp
And the rich East to boot.

Malcolm. Be not offended:
I speak not as in absolute fear of you.
I think our country sinks beneath the yoke;
It weeps, it bleeds, and each new day a gash
Is added to her wounds. I think withal°
There would be hands uplifted in my right;°
And here from gracious England° have I offer
Of goodly thousands: but, for° all this,
When I shall tread upon the tyrant's head,
Or wear it on my sword, yet my poor country
Shall have more vices than it had before,
More suffer, and more sundry ways than ever,
By him that shall succeed.

Macduff. What should he be?

Malcolm.
It is myself I mean, in whom I know
All the particulars° of vice so grafted°
That, when they shall be opened,° black Macbeth
Will seem as pure as snow, and the poor state
Esteem him as a lamb, being compared
With my confineless harms.°

Macduff. Not in the legions
Of horrid hell can come a devil more damned
In evils to top Macbeth.

Malcolm. I grant him bloody,
Luxurious,° avaricious, false, deceitful,
Sudden,° malicious, smacking of every sin
That has a name: but there's no bottom, none,
In my voluptuousness:° your wives, your daughters,
Your matrons and your maids, could not fill up

22. the brightest: Lucifer, the angel who led the revolt of the angels and was thrown out of heaven; Satan.

23. would wear: desire to wear.

24. so: like itself.

26. rawness: unprotected condition.

29. jealousies: suspicions.

30. rightly just: perfectly honorable.

32. basis: foundation.

33. check: restrain.

34. affeered: legally confirmed.

? **37.** *This speech might present a problem for the actor playing Macduff because it does not clearly relate to what has gone before it. It seems too grand and philosophical at this point in the play. How would you have the actor deliver this speech?*

41. withal: moreover.

42. in my right: on behalf of my claim.

43. England: the king of England.

44. for: despite.

51. particulars: special kinds. **grafted:** engrafted.

52. opened: in bloom (that is, revealed).

55. confineless harms: unbounded evils.

? **57.** *How has Macduff responded to this speech?*

58. Luxurious: lecherous.

59. Sudden: violent.

61. voluptuousness: lust.

B Reading Skills and Strategies

Drawing Conclusions

? **What is Macduff about to do? Why?** [Possible response: He is preparing to leave. He sees that Malcolm does not trust him, so he thinks there is no hope of saving Scotland now. There cannot be an alliance between the thanes who oppose Macbeth and the rightful king (Malcolm) because Malcolm is too nervous to trust anyone.]

C Elements of Literature

Imagery

? **What imagery is used to portray Scotland?** [Scotland is depicted as a stabbed woman sinking "beneath the yoke," weeping and bleeding, and suffering a new wound every day.] **What scene does this image recall?** [the murder of Lady Macduff]

D Critical Thinking

Getting the Main Idea

? **What comparison does Malcolm make between himself and Macbeth?** [Possible response: Malcolm says that his sins are so great that Macbeth would seem pure and innocent in comparison.]

E Historical Connections

Malcolm

In keeping with Holinshed's *Chronicle,* Shakespeare has Malcolm charge himself with lust, avarice, and deceit. "Shakespeare is showing the nature of royalty by describing the opposite," says critic Kenneth Muir.

Answers to Margin Questions

Line 37. Depending upon the interpretation of Malcolm, the actor might play the role as if he were disheartened, resigned, offended, or angry.

Line 57. Macduff says that no one, not even a devil from hell, is worse than Macbeth.

Ⓐ Struggling Readers
Rereading

❓ Suggest that students reread this paragraph, stopping to paraphrase each sentence. Then, ask them how Macduff responds to Malcolm's self-accusation. [Possible response: He implies that Malcolm could keep his uncontrolled lust secret. This flaw in a king is preferable to Macbeth's ruthless rule.]

Ⓑ Critical Thinking
Hypothesizing

❓ Why do you suppose Macduff reacts as he does to Malcolm's confessions? [Sample response: Macduff is a political realist who can tolerate imperfections in a king and does not expect a saint. Here, he rationalizes Malcolm's confessed faults as preferable to Macbeth's violence and irrationality.]

Ⓒ Reading Skills and Strategies
Drawing Conclusions

❓ Why can't Macduff tolerate Malcolm's last confession, although he has accepted Malcolm's previous flaws? [Sample response: Although lust and avarice might exist in men who are otherwise sufficiently moral to rule, Malcolm, in his last statement, denies that he has any moral virtues and suggests that his rule would cause chaos and strife. To Macduff, this probably sounds too much like Macbeth's rule.]

Answers to Margin Questions

Line 66. Ask this question after students have read through l. 139. By discussing his imaginary vices, Malcolm can see what and how much Macduff will tolerate. Malcolm seems to be trying to see whether Macduff is loyal to Scotland or loyal to Macbeth.

Line 84. Ask this question after students have read through l. 139. Malcolm must convince Macduff that all these allegations about himself are true, yet somehow let the audience know that he is merely testing Macduff. An ironic delivery might not convince Macduff; a serious delivery might elicit a more concerned response.

The cistern of my lust, and my desire
All continent° impediments would o'erbear,
That did oppose my will. Better Macbeth
Than such an one to reign.

Macduff. Boundless intemperance
In nature° is a tyranny; it hath been
Th' untimely emptying of the happy throne,
And fall of many kings. But fear not yet
To take upon you what is yours: you may
Convey° your pleasures in a spacious plenty,
And yet seem cold, the time° you may so hoodwink.
We have willing dames enough. There cannot be
That vulture in you, to devour so many
As will to greatness dedicate themselves,
Finding it so inclined.

Malcolm. With this there grows
In my most ill-composed affection° such
A stanchless° avarice that, were I king,
I should cut off the nobles for their lands,
Desire his jewels and this other's house:
And my more-having would be as a sauce
To make me hunger more, that I should forge
Quarrels unjust against the good and loyal,
Destroying them for wealth.

Macduff. This avarice
Sticks deeper, grows with more pernicious root
Than summer-seeming° lust, and it hath been
The sword of our slain kings.° Yet do not fear.
Scotland hath foisons to fill up your will
Of your mere own.° All these are portable,°
With other graces weighed.

Malcolm.
But I have none: the king-becoming graces,
As justice, verity, temp'rance, stableness,
Bounty, perseverance, mercy, lowliness,
Devotion, patience, courage, fortitude,
I have no relish of° them, but abound
In the division of each several crime,°
Acting it many ways. Nay, had I pow'r, I should
Pour the sweet milk of concord into hell,
Uproar° the universal peace, confound
All unity on earth.

Macduff. O Scotland, Scotland!

Malcolm.
If such a one be fit to govern, speak:
I am as I have spoken.

Macduff. Fit to govern!
No, not to live. O nation miserable!
With an untitled° tyrant bloody-sceptered,

64. continent: restraining.

❓ 66. *Why do you think Malcolm is drawing attention to his vices? What could he hope to accomplish?*

67. nature: man's nature.

71. Convey: secretly manage.

72. time: here, people.

77. ill-composed affection: evilly compounded character.

78. stanchless: never-ending.

❓ 84. *How do you imagine Malcolm delivering this speech? How could his delivery affect Macduff's response?*

86. summer-seeming: youthful, or transitory.

87. sword . . . kings: the cause of death to our kings.

89. foisons . . . own: enough abundance of your own to satisfy your covetousness. **portable:** bearable.

95. relish of: taste for.

96. division . . . crime: variations of each kind of crime.

99. Uproar: put into a tumult.

104. untitled: having no right to the throne.

Skill Link

Applying Meanings of Prefixes

Knowing the meanings of frequently used prefixes can help unlock the meanings of new words. For example, knowing that the prefix *con-* means "with" can help us to understand *concord* (l. 98) and *confound* (l. 99). *Concord* comes from the root *cor,* meaning "heart," and the prefix *con-,* meaning "with." Explain how these two word parts may have evolved into the word *concord,* meaning "peace:" When your heart is with someone, you're at peace. Repeat this modeling process with the word *confound.* Then, ask students to look up each of the following words from Act IV to discover its meaning by investigating its prefix and root word.

1. conspirers [IV.1.91] [*con*—"with"—people who plot]
2. discomfort [IV.2.29] [*dis*—"away"—upset]
3. unsanctified [IV.2.77] [*un*—"not"—not holy]
4. redress [IV.3.9] [*re*—"back"—pay back]

When shalt thou see thy wholesome days again,
Since that the truest issue of thy throne
By his own interdiction° stands accursed,
And does blaspheme his breed?° Thy royal father
Was a most sainted king: the queen that bore thee,
Oft'ner upon her knees than on her feet,
Died° every day she lived. Fare thee well!
These evils thou repeat'st upon thyself
Hath banished me from Scotland. O my breast,
Thy hope ends here!

Malcolm. Macduff, this noble passion,
Child of integrity, hath from my soul
Wiped the black scruples,° reconciled my thoughts
To thy good truth and honor. Devilish Macbeth
By many of these trains° hath sought to win me
Into his power; and modest wisdom° plucks me
From over-credulous haste: but God above
Deal between thee and me! For even now
I put myself to° thy direction, and
Unspeak mine own detraction;° here abjure
The taints and blames I laid upon myself,
For° strangers to my nature. I am yet
Unknown to woman, never was forsworn,
Scarcely have coveted what was mine own,
At no time broke my faith, would not betray
The devil to his fellow, and delight
No less in truth than life. My first false speaking
Was this upon myself. What I am truly,
Is thine and my poor country's to command:
Whither indeed, before thy here-approach,
Old Siward, with ten thousand warlike men,
Already at a point,° was setting forth.
Now we'll together, and the chance of goodness
Be like our warranted quarrel!° Why are you silent?

Macduff.
Such welcome and unwelcome things at once
'Tis hard to reconcile.

[*Enter a* DOCTOR.]

Malcolm.
Well, more anon. Comes the king forth, I pray you?

Doctor.
Ay, sir. There are a crew of wretched souls
That stay° his cure: their malady convinces
The great assay of art;° but at his touch,
Such sanctity hath heaven given his hand,
They presently amend.°

Malcolm. I thank you, doctor.

[*Exit* DOCTOR.]

107. interdiction: curse; exclusion.

108. breed: ancestry.

111. Died: that is, prepared for heaven.

? **114.** *How might the tone change here? How has Macduff proved himself?*

116. scruples: suspicions.

118. trains: plots.

119. modest wisdom: prudence.

122. to: under.

123. detraction: slander.

125. For: as.

135. at a point: prepared.

137. the chance . . . quarrel: May our chance of success equal the justice of our cause.

? **137.** *Where should Malcolm pause in this line? Should he act puzzled, or matter-of-fact?*

142. stay: await.

143. convinces . . . art: defies the efforts of medical science.

145. presently amend: immediately recover.

D Reading Skills and Strategies
Comparing and Contrasting Characters

? **What difference between Malcolm and Duncan does this scene highlight?** [Sample responses: By lying about himself, Malcolm tests Macduff, shows that he knows the "art/to find the mind's construction in the face" (I.4.11–12), and uses it to discern Macduff's true character. Duncan, on the other hand, was deceived twice by traitors.]

E Elements of Literature
Character

? **How does Malcolm characterize himself now?** [He says he is chaste, honest, uninterested in possessions, faithful, loyal, and truthful.]

F Struggling Readers
Finding Details

? **What good news has Malcolm been withholding?** [Siward and ten thousand men are ready to march on Macbeth.] **Remind students that Malcolm is on Macduff's side and wants to join forces to defeat Macbeth.**

G Historical Connections
Edward the Confessor

These lines refer to the special ability Edward the Confessor supposedly possessed. (See "The King's Evil," p. 367.)

Answers to Margin Questions

Line 114. Malcolm drops his sinful, arrogant air and speaks in his normal, gentle tone. Macduff has shown that he is completely loyal to Scotland, disgusted by Macbeth's actions, and repulsed by the vices that Malcolm claimed to have possessed.

Line 137. There should be a fairly sharp break before "Why are you silent?" Most students will feel he is probably matter-of-fact because he realizes that he has stunned Macduff.

Skill Link

Inferring Cause and Effect

A cause makes something happen. An effect is what happens as a result of that cause. Although an author may state the cause and its effect, more often the reader must infer the probable cause or the probable effect. To do this, readers use information in the text in addition to prior knowledge and experience of how things happen.

Activities

1. As students read the play, ask volunteers to write cause questions about characters' actions on index cards, such as, "Why does Macbeth have Macduff's family killed?" Collect the cards and read each question to the entire class. As students suggest possible answers, write them on the board.
2. Encourage students to use a graphic organizer, such as a story map, to identify as many effects as possible resulting from Macbeth's murder of Duncan. In some cases students may indicate a chain reaction where an effect becomes a cause that leads to yet another effect. For example, the death of Duncan leads to Macbeth's becoming king, which leads to dissension among the people of Scotland.

Ⓐ Elements of Literature

Foil

? A **foil** is a character that sets off another character by strong contrast. How is Edward the Confessor a foil for Macbeth in this scene? [Possible answer: Not only does Edward the Confessor's touch heal instead of harm, but he also can foresee the future. The people under his rule enjoy many blessings instead of murders and crimes.]

Ⓑ Struggling Readers

Getting the Main Idea

Remind readers that Scotland was previously compared to a woman who had been stabbed. Ask students what Ross now says Scotland is. ["our grave"] Why is he so negative? [Macbeth is killing many innocent people.]

Ⓒ Appreciating Language

Double Meanings

? In these lines Macduff and Ross seem to have a coherent conversation, yet the words they use have various meanings. Here, *well* means to Macduff that his family is alive and healthy, while to Ross *well* means that Macduff's family is at peace in death, beyond the reach of more evil. Where in the play is there another example of this type of wordplay? [Possible answer: the words "Banquo's safe" in III.4.25.]

Answers to Margin Questions

Stage direction. Students may guess that Ross relates the news that Macduff's family has been murdered.

Line 176. He would probably look away, aware of the profound grief he must cause with his report.

Macduff.
What's the disease he means?
Malcolm. 'Tis called the evil:°
A most miraculous work in this good king,
Which often since my here-remain in England
I have seen him do. How he solicits heaven,
Himself best knows: but strangely visited° people,
All swoll'n and ulcerous, pitiful to the eye,
The mere° despair of surgery, he cures,
Hanging a golden stamp° about their necks,
Put on with holy prayers: and 'tis spoken,
To the succeeding royalty he leaves
The healing benediction. With this strange virtue°
He hath a heavenly gift of prophecy,
And sundry blessings hang about his throne
That speak° him full of grace.

[*Enter* ROSS.]

Macduff. See, who comes here?
Malcolm.
My countryman; but yet I know him not.
Macduff.
My ever gentle° cousin, welcome hither.
Malcolm.
I know him now: good God, betimes° remove
The means that makes us strangers!
Ross. Sir, amen.
Macduff.
Stands Scotland where it did?
Ross. Alas, poor country!
Almost afraid to know itself! It cannot
Be called our mother but our grave, where nothing°
But who knows nothing is once seen to smile;
Where sighs and groans, and shrieks that rent the air,
Are made, not marked;° where violent sorrow seems
A modern ecstasy.° The dead man's knell
Is there scarce asked for who, and good men's lives
Expire before the flowers in their caps,
Dying or ere they sicken.
Macduff. O, relation
Too nice,° and yet too true!
Malcolm. What's the newest grief?
Ross.
That of an hour's age doth hiss the speaker;°
Each minute teems° a new one.
Macduff. How does my wife?
Ross.
Why, well.
Macduff. And all my children?

146. evil: scrofula, called "the king's evil" because it allegedly could be cured by the king's touch.

150. strangely visited: oddly afflicted.

152. mere: utter.

153. stamp: coin.

156. virtue: power.

159. speak: proclaim.

? **Stage direction.** *Ross is Macduff's countryman. What news do you anticipate he brings with him?*

161. gentle: noble.

162. betimes: quickly.

166. nothing: no one.

169. marked: noticed.

170. modern ecstasy: ordinary emotion.

174. relation / Too nice: tale too accurate.

175. That . . . speaker: The report of the grief of an hour ago is hissed as stale news.

176. teems: gives birth to.

? 176. *Does Ross look at Macduff on this line, or does he turn away?*

Crossing the Curriculum

Health

Many people in the Middle Ages believed that God could strike them with an illness. They, therefore, turned to God's representatives for healing—specifically to monks and divinely anointed kings. The practice of "the king's touch," in which sick people sought healing from kings, was popular around the time of Macbeth's rule. Students should research "the king's touch" and the disease scrofula (tuberculosis of the lymphatic glands) and report to the class.

History

Edward the Confessor (1003–1066) was raised at a monastery in Normandy and retained his interest in religion throughout his reign. He was said to have had a thin frame, a delicate complexion, feminine hands, blue eyes, and golden hair. According to historian J. R. Green, legends abound about his "pious simplicity, his blitheness and gentleness of mood." Have students find out more about his reign and his effect on both England and Scotland.

Ross. Well too.
Macduff.
The tyrant has not battered at their peace?
Ross.
No; they were well at peace when I did leave 'em.
Macduff.
Be not a niggard of your speech: how goes't?
Ross.
When I came hither to transport the tidings,
Which I have heavily° borne, there ran a rumor
Of many worthy fellows that were out;°
Which was to my belief witnessed° the rather,
For that I saw the tyrant's power° afoot.
Now is the time of help. Your eye in Scotland
Would create soldiers, make our women fight,
To doff their dire distresses.
Malcolm. Be't their comfort
We are coming thither. Gracious England hath
Lent us good Siward and ten thousand men;
An older and a better soldier none
That Christendom gives out.°
Ross. Would I could answer
This comfort with the like! But I have words
That would° be howled out in the desert air,
Where hearing should not latch° them.
Macduff. What concern they?
The general cause or is it a fee-grief
Due to some single breast?°
Ross. No mind that's honest
But in it shares some woe, though the main part
Pertains to you alone.
Macduff. If it be mine,
Keep it not from me, quickly let me have it.
Ross.
Let not your ears despise my tongue forever,
Which shall possess them with the heaviest sound
That ever yet they heard.
Macduff. Humh! I guess at it.
Ross.
Your castle is surprised;° your wife and babes
Savagely slaughtered. To relate the manner,
Were, on the quarry° of these murdered deer,
To add the death of you.
Malcolm. Merciful heaven!
What, man! Ne'er pull your hat upon your brows;
Give sorrow words. The grief that does not speak
Whispers the o'er-fraught heart,° and bids it break.
Macduff.
My children too?

? **179.** *What is the double meaning of this line?*

182. heavily: sadly.
183. out: up in arms.
184. witnessed: attested.
185. power: army.
192. gives out: reports.
194. would: should.
195. latch: catch.
197. fee-grief . . . breast: that is, personal grief belonging to an individual.

? **203.** *Macduff's pain becomes visible. How should we see it?*

204. surprised: suddenly attacked.
206. quarry: heap of slaughtered game.
210. Whispers . . . heart: whispers to the overburdened heart.

? **211.** *How full, or soft, a voice would you have Macduff use in this line?*

D Cultural Connections
Women Warriors
Holinshed reports that it was customary for women of Scotland to join men on the battlefield: "In these daies also the women of our countries were of no lesse courage than the men; for all stout maidens and wiues (if they were not with child) marched as well in the field as did the men. . . . When they saw their owne bloud run from them in the fight, they waxed neuer a whit astonished with the matter, but rather doubling their courage with more egernesse they assailed their enimies."

E Elements of Literature
Figurative Language
? Point out that this is an example of **synecdoche**—the use of part of something to stand for the whole. What does "your ears" stand for? [you] "My tongue?" [me] What is the literal meaning of this line? [Please don't hate me for what I am about to tell you.]

F Critical Thinking
Expressing an Opinion
? What do you think of the way Ross breaks the bad news to Macduff? [Sample responses: It is similar to the way Macduff gently tried to break the news of Duncan's death to Lady Macbeth in Act II, except that she not only already knew about it but had planned it. Here, Macduff deserves the sensitivity Ross uses. Even though Ross lied earlier, it is easy to understand why it was hard for him to tell the truth. His reluctance to deliver the news also builds suspense and increases the pathos of the scene.]

Answers to Margin Questions
Line 179. For Macduff, "peace" means that his family is well. For Ross, it means the peace that comes with death.
Line 203. By the look of grief on his face and the tone of his voice.
Line 211. He might whisper. He could cry out in distress or try to master his feelings by speaking in a controlled, normal tone.

Skill Link

Comparison and Contrast: Conflicts
Have students compare and contrast several of the internal and external conflicts in *Macbeth,* such as Macbeth's debate about whether to kill Duncan versus Lady Macbeth's determination to commit the murder; or, Lady Macbeth's inner turmoil after Duncan's death versus Macbeth's increasing ease with murder, as evidenced by his reactions to the deaths of Banquo and Macduff's family. Then, have interested students compare and contrast these conflicts with conflicts found in other Shakespearean plays they have read. Students should write a brief essay discussing their conclusions.

Ⓐ Reading Skills and Strategies
Drawing Conclusions

? To whom is Macduff referring when he says "He"? [Possible responses: He could be referring to Malcolm, implying that Malcolm—who presumably does not yet have children—cannot understand the grief Macduff feels. It is more likely, however, that Macduff is referring to Macbeth, suggesting that he can never take adequate revenge (since Macbeth has no children) or that only a man without children could have committed such crimes.]

Ⓑ Critical Thinking
Making Connections

? How do Lady Macbeth, Malcolm, and Macduff differ in their definitions of manhood? [Possible responses: Lady Macbeth believes a man takes advantage of opportunity no matter whom he hurts or at what cost. Malcolm feels a man must be strong and not give in to grief. Although Macduff maintains that a man must be strong, he also believes that a man must express the pain that grief brings.]

Answers to Margin Questions

Line 216. If students think Macduff refers to Macbeth, they might say he speaks with pain and scorn. If he refers to Malcolm, he might be reminding himself of the reason for Malcolm's lack of understanding, and his tone might be less harsh.

Line 220. Malcolm urges Macduff to act on his feelings. At the beginning of the scene, Malcolm's desire to grieve for his father suggests that he would not criticize Macduff for his desire to grieve.

Ross. Wife, children, servants, all
That could be found.
Macduff. And I must be from thence!
My wife killed too?
Ross. I have said.
Malcolm. Be comforted.
Let's make us med'cines of our great revenge,
To cure this deadly grief.
Macduff.
He has no children. All my pretty ones?
Did you say all? O hell-kite!° All?
What, all my pretty chickens and their dam°
At one fell swoop?
Malcolm.
Dispute° it like a man.
Macduff. I shall do so;
But I must also feel it as a man.
I cannot but remember such things were,
That were most precious to me. Did heaven look on,
And would not take their part? Sinful Macduff,

? **216.** *How would Macduff say this line: "He has no children"?*

217. hell-kite: hellish bird of prey.

218. dam: mother.

220. Dispute: counter.

? **220.** *Is Malcolm being critical or encouraging here?*

"Bring thou this fiend of Scotland and myself;
Within my sword's length set him."

From the Stratford Festival production of *Macbeth* (1983).

Assessing Learning

Check Test: Fill-in-the-Blank

1. When the Second Witch says, "Something wicked this way comes," she is referring to ______. [Macbeth]
2. The Second Apparition says Macbeth cannot be harmed by ______. [anyone born of woman]
3. A line of eight kings descended from ______ passes before Macbeth. [Banquo]
4. To punish Macduff, Macbeth hires assassins to kill ______. [Macduff's wife and children]
5. Malcolm tests ______ loyalty to Scotland by pretending to be more evil and ruthless than Macbeth. [Macduff's]

Informal Assessment

Written Assessment. To determine whether students are aware of some of the themes that recur throughout the play, ask them to write a one-page paper identifying and explaining one of the recurring themes of the play. Students should discuss any symbols associated with that theme and refer to dialogue or scenes that reflect the theme.

The following scale will help you score these assignments:

1 point: Theme is not well defined or supported.
2 points: Theme is stated; needs clearer support.
3 points: Theme is defined; support is adequate.
4 points: Theme is precisely defined; support is thorough.

They were all struck for thee! Naught° that I am,
Not for their own demerits but for mine
Fell slaughter on their souls. Heaven rest them now! C

Malcolm.
Be this the whetstone of your sword. Let grief
Convert to anger; blunt not the heart, enrage it.

Macduff.
O, I could play the woman with mine eyes,
And braggart with my tongue! But, gentle heavens,
Cut short all intermission;° front to front°
Bring thou this fiend of Scotland and myself;
Within my sword's length set him. If he 'scape,
Heaven forgive him too!

Malcolm. This time goes manly.
Come, go we to the king. Our power is ready;
Our lack is nothing but our leave.° Macbeth
Is ripe for shaking, and the pow'rs above
Put on their instruments.° Receive what cheer you may.
The night is long that never finds the day. E *[Exeunt.]*

D

225. Naught: wicked.

232. intermission: interval. **front to front:** forehead to forehead (that is, face to face).

237. Our lack . . . leave: We need only to take our leave.

239. Put . . . instruments: arm themselves.

Critical Comment

The King's Evil

In Act IV, Scene 3, Malcolm and Macduff, exiled from Scotland, discuss the characteristics of a good king and praise King Edward, who has given them political asylum in England. Edward, a saintly monarch known to history as "the Confessor," was believed to have the gift of healing any of his subjects who suffered from an ailment known as the king's evil, a kind of scrofula or tuberculosis of the lymphatic glands and primarily a disease of children. Long before Shakespeare's time, the custom of being touched by the king was abandoned, but King James revived the practice and his successors continued it for a century or so. The eighteenth-century writer Samuel Johnson, scrofulous as a child, was one of the last English people to receive the royal touch.

The National Gallery, London.

Edward the Confessor (detail of the Wilton Diptych).

The conversation between Malcolm and Macduff not only compliments King James indirectly, but also implicitly condemns Macbeth, a kingly killer rather than a healer of children. Edward cures evil; Macbeth *is* evil.

C Historical Connections

Laws Against Profanity

Critic Kenneth Muir suggests that "Heaven" may have replaced "May God," "Then God," or "God, God" in the original manuscript in order to sidestep the penalties levied by an Act of Parliament that prohibited profanity on the stage. The act read: "For the preventing and avoiding of the great abuse of the holy Name of God, in Stage-playes, Enter-ludes, May-games, Shews, and such-like . . . if . . . any person do or shall in any Stage-play . . . jestingly or prophanely speak, or use the holy Name of God, or of Jesus Christ, or of the Holy Ghost, or of the Trinity . . . [that person] shall forfeit for every such offence . . . ten pounds . . . ." Muir writes, "I suspect that 'God' . . . was what Shakespeare wrote."

D Elements of Literature

Tragedy

? In what way is Macbeth "ripe for shaking"? [Possible answer: As the tragic hero, Macbeth is headed for a downfall. His crimes have become so egregious that the time for action against him has come.]

E Appreciating Language

Aphorism

? This line reads like an **aphorism,** a concise statement expressing a principle or truth. What does it mean, both literally and in a larger sense? [Possible response: Just as night must give way to day, the darkness of Macbeth's reign will end and peace will return. Natural rhythms will be restored.] Note too, how the line echoes the motif of nightmares and sleeplessness associated with Macbeth and his wife since Duncan's murder.

Critical Comment

This feature provides information on King Edward and King James who were both known as healers of "the king's evil"—the disease scrofula. The conversation in Act IV, Scene 3 between Malcolm and Macduff sheds a positive light on James and also shows Macbeth to be evil.

Professional Notes

Critical Comment: Dramatic Purpose

After the swift-moving action of previous scenes, students sometimes feel that Scene 3 adds little to the story. Critic Mark Van Doren observes, however, that the scene does not interrupt the play; rather, "it is one of its essential parts, glancing forward as it does to a conclusion wherein Macduff can say, 'The time is free' (V.8.55) and wherein Malcolm can promise . . . deeds of justice." Ask students to recall how bloody and dangerous a place Macbeth's Scotland has become. From this scene, Van Doren says readers can get a sense that there is "another country to the south where a good king works miracles with his touch." Stormy, chaotic Scotland is but a small part of a larger, more peaceful world.

Critical Comment

Hecate is a character from Greek mythology, whereas the witches were based on actual women in Elizabethan society who were outcasts and believed to be witches. Many scholars believe that Hecate's scenes were added to the play by Thomas Middleton, a contemporary of Shakespeare.

Ⓐ Literary Connections

Hecate's Scenes

Because the characterization of Hecate in Middleton's play is so vastly different from that in Shakespeare's, some critics actually think that Middleton is the least likely person to have written the scene.

Resources

Selection Assessment

Formal Assessment

- Selection Test, p. 63

Test Generator (One-Stop Planner)

- CD-ROM

Critical Comment

Hecate: Queen of the Night

Hecate (here pronounced in two syllables, with the accent on the first: hek´it) is a figure from Greek mythology, a queen of the night and protector of witches and enchanters. This character comes from books, unlike the witches, who were based on older, usually widowed women, whose solitary lives placed them at the margins of Scottish society. Every theatergoer would find the witches believable, and every educated person would know that King James had written an important treatise called *Daemonologie,* asserting that witches "are channels through which the malignity of evil spirits might be visited upon human beings."

Most Shakespearean scholars believe that the scenes involving Hecate (Act III, Scene 5; Act IV, Scene 1) were written by somebody other than Shakespeare and introduced into *Macbeth* at some time before 1623, when the play was first printed. This other writer has never been positively identified, although Ⓐ some people think he was Thomas Middleton (d. 1627), a contemporary of Shakespeare and a fellow writer for the King's Men. Two songs, the first beginning with the words "Come away" (Act III, Scene 5) and the second with "Black Spirits" (Act IV, Scene 1), were also added to the Hecate scenes, and these songs are indeed by Middleton, the complete texts of them occurring in his thriller *The Witch.*

And so the practice of adding things to *Macbeth* began very early, and it has continued throughout most of the play's long stage history. The supernatural elements seem to invite directors to devise spectacles and take liberties, especially with the witches, who have been flown on wires in some productions and whose parts have been played by ballet dancers in others.

Macbeth holding out his hand to the three witches.

From the Stratford Festival production of *Macbeth* (1983).

Reading Check

a. A toad that has sweated out venom; a slice of snake; a newt's eye; a frog's toe; a bat's wool; a dog's tongue; an adder's forked tongue; a blindworm's sting; a lizard's leg; an owl's wing; dragon scales; a wolf's tooth; a witch's mummy; the gullet and stomach of a shark; a hemlock root; a Jew's liver; a goat's gall; slips of yew; a Turk's nose; a Tartar's lips; a murdered baby's finger; a tiger's entrails; and a baboon's blood. This shows just how evil the witches are.

b. The witches stop him from voicing his questions, but he wants to know if he will remain in power and if Banquo's heirs will rule. The witches let the apparitions answer with prophecies and show him a procession of eight kings who are Banquo's descendants.

c. A helmeted head warns him about Macduff, a bloody child says, "none of woman born/Shall harm Macbeth," and a crowned child prophesies that Macbeth will not be conquered until Birnam Wood comes to Dunsinane.

d. Macduff; Macduff has fled to England.

e. Macbeth vows to kill Macduff's family. Lady Macduff and her son are murdered.

f. Scotland has fallen on hard times, with many new widows, orphans, and sorrows.

g. He claims to be lustful, greedy, and determined to use power to create chaos.

h. Macduff says that the first two (lust and avarice) can be accepted, but he denounces Malcolm after the last confession (the deliberate intent to create chaos).

MAKING MEANINGS

Act IV

First Thoughts

1. What effect did the brutal murders of Lady Macduff and her son have on you? Have your feelings for Macbeth changed from the opening of the play until now? How do you account for your reactions?

Reading Check

a. What ingredients go into the witches' stew? What **symbolic** purpose does this vile concoction serve?

b. What has Macbeth come to ask the witches, and how do they answer?

c. Describe the three apparitions Macbeth sees when he visits the witches. What does each apparition tell him?

d. Which nobleman does Macbeth plan to murder after talking with the witches? How is his plan foiled?

e. At the end of Scene 1, what does Macbeth vow? How is his vow carried out in Scene 2?

f. According to the conversation between Malcolm and Macduff in Scene 3, what has happened to Scotland during Macbeth's reign?

g. What faults does Malcolm claim to have?

h. How does Macduff respond to each of Malcolm's three "confessions"?

Shaping Interpretations

2. In this act, Macbeth seeks out the witches, just as they initiated the encounter in Act I. How has Macbeth's situation changed since he last talked with the witches? How has his moral **character** deteriorated? Find lines and actions that support your interpretation.

3. Do you think the witches have caused any of these changes, directly or indirectly? Explain your reasons for thinking as you do.

4. In Scene 1, the eight kings appear in what was called in Shakespeare's day a **dumb show**—an interpolated brief scene in which nothing is said. What is the point of this particular dumb show?

5. In Scene 2, the lines spoken by Macduff's wife and son illustrate Shakespeare's great skill at **characterization.** Using only a few words, he brings the woman and the child to life. How would you describe Lady Macduff? How would you describe the boy?

6. Both the murderer and Lady Macduff herself call Macduff a traitor. In what sense does each mean it? Do you think Macduff is a traitor, in either sense?

7. In Scene 3, Malcolm deliberately lies to Macduff. What does this behavior, and the reason for it, reveal about Malcolm?

Extending the Text

8. In Scene 3, Malcolm and Macduff decry the chaos that Macbeth's rule has brought to Scotland, as if Macbeth's disorder has become Scotland's. Does that happen today—does the weakness or the evil of a nation's leader become that of a nation itself? Explain your response.

Challenging the Text

9. The murder of Macduff's small son is one of the most pitiful and shocking scenes in Shakespeare. Do you think it might have been better to have it reported after the fact rather than to have shown the carnage on stage? What would be lost and what would be gained by this change?

4. It shows Macbeth that Banquo's descendants will provide the country with a succession of kings.

5. Possible answers: Lady Macduff is loyal, good, protective, worried, and loving. However, she might also be quick to judge—she drew the wrong conclusion about her husband. The boy is clever, loyal, witty, and brave.

6. Lady Macduff means it in the sense that she thinks her husband has abandoned his family. The murderer calls him a traitor to the king (Macbeth). Most students will probably agree that Macduff is not a traitor in either sense.

7. Malcolm tests Macduff's loyalty because he is prudent and wary, not naive as his father was.

Extending the Text [Apply]

8. Some students will say that a leader's character often reflects the character of the nation as a whole; or that a nation will blindly follow its ruler. Other students will say, however, that the nation cannot be held accountable for the deeds of one individual.

Challenging the Text [Evaluate]

9. Possible answers: No, this murder puts Macbeth beyond redemption; it should be seen and acknowledged. Yes, it should be left to the audience's imagination. Without the onstage murder, there would be less distress for the audience, but the play might lose its immediacy, and the audience might be less involved in the upcoming struggle to depose Macbeth.

MAKING MEANINGS

Act IV

First Thoughts [Respond]

1. Possible response: The brutal murders are appalling and shocking. Macbeth evoked some pity at the beginning, but now he commands none. He has sunk to the lowest depths of evil.

Shaping Interpretations [Interpret]

2. When the witches first met him, he was a hero returning from battle, having saved his nation from a traitor. Now, the first prophecies have been fulfilled, but he has become a murderer and traitor himself—he has betrayed his country and his honor (Line references will vary).

3. Possible responses: Yes, the witches are responsible for setting in motion a chain of evil events. Macbeth resists as best he can, but fate overcomes him; or, no, Macbeth chooses to act of his own free will. There is no evidence that he has been forced into action.

Summary

Scene 1: A lady-in-waiting and a doctor discuss Lady Macbeth's sleepwalking. As they are speaking, Lady Macbeth enters, walking in her sleep. She rubs her hands repeatedly to rid them of the blood that she imagines stains them. From Lady Macbeth's words, the onlookers infer that she and Macbeth murdered Duncan, but the doctor is afraid to speak of his suspicions.

Ⓐ Appreciating Language

Prose

Point out that this scene is almost entirely in prose in contrast to the blank verse used in most of the play. As students read, have them consider why Shakespeare switches to prose in this scene. [Possible response: The shift from blank verse to prose emphasizes Lady Macbeth's inner turmoil.]

Ⓑ Elements of Literature

Theme

? The link between unnatural acts and unusual events in nature is one of the themes of the play. Why does the doctor call Lady Macbeth's sleepwalking "a perturbation of nature"? [Because sleepwalking is an ambiguous state between sleeping and waking, the doctor thinks it is unnatural. He believes that Lady Macbeth's sleepwalking is an outward sign of an inner disturbance.] What other lines focus on this theme? [Possible answers: II.3.48–55; II.4.4–20; IV.1.50–60]

ACT V Scene 1. *Dunsinane. In the castle.*

Enter a DOCTOR *of physic and a waiting* GENTLEWOMAN.

Ⓐ **Doctor.** I have two nights watched with you, but can perceive no truth in your report. When was it she last walked?

Gentlewoman. Since his majesty went into the field, I have seen her rise from her bed, throw her nightgown upon her, unlock her closet,° take forth paper, fold it, write upon't, read it, afterwards seal it, and again return to bed; yet all this while in a most fast sleep.

Ⓑ **Doctor.** A great perturbation in nature, to receive at once the benefit of sleep and do the effects of watching!° In this slumb'ry agitation, besides her walking and other actual performances,° what, at any time, have you heard her say?

5. **closet:** chest.

9. **effects of watching:** deeds of one awake.

11. **actual performances:** deeds.

"Out, damned spot! Out, I say!"

From the Stratford Festival production of *Macbeth* (1983).

Using Students' Strengths

Interpersonal Learners

Ask students how the tabloids today would treat the story of Macbeth. Then have students work in groups to write a newspaper article about the incidents in *Macbeth.* Remind students to use quotations from the play. Students may want to add features such as captioned pictures or editorials.

Visual Learners

As students consider the decision-making process that leads to Macbeth's downfall, have them complete an Options Tree. Starting with the decision of whether to believe the witches' initial predictions, they should trace the path Macbeth follows from one decision to another. Ask students to speculate in their reading notes about how Macbeth's fate might have differed if, for example, he had decided not to murder Duncan.

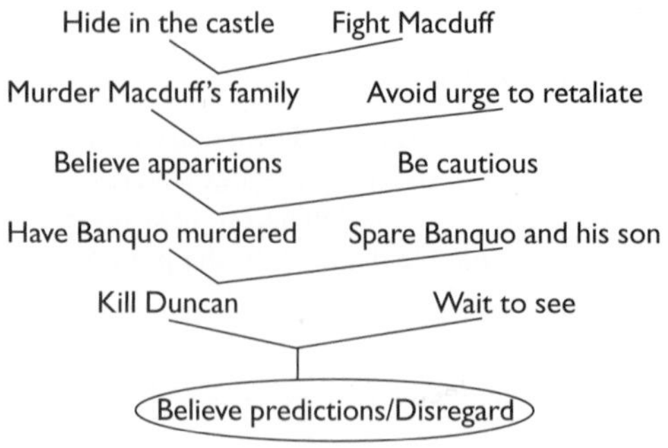

Gentlewoman. That, sir, which I will not report after her.

Doctor. You may to me, and 'tis most meet° you should.

Gentlewoman. Neither to you nor anyone, having no witness to confirm my speech.

[*Enter* LADY MACBETH, *with a taper.*]

Lo you, here she comes! This is her very guise,° and, upon my life, fast asleep! Observe her; stand close.°

Doctor. How came she by that light?

Gentlewoman. Why, it stood by her. She has light by her continually. 'Tis her command.

Doctor. You see, her eyes are open.

Gentlewoman. Ay, but their sense° are shut.

Doctor. What is it she does now? Look, how she rubs her hands.

Gentlewoman. It is an accustomed action with her, to seem thus washing her hands: I have known her continue in this a quarter of an hour.

Lady Macbeth. Yet here's a spot.

Doctor. Hark! she speaks. I will set down what comes from her, to satisfy° my remembrance the more strongly.

Lady Macbeth. Out, damned spot! Out, I say! One: two: why, then 'tis time to do't. Hell is murky. Fie, my lord, fie! A soldier, and afeard? What need we fear who knows it, when none can call our pow'r to accompt?° Yet who would have thought the old man to have had so much blood in him?

Doctor. Do you mark that?

Lady Macbeth. The Thane of Fife had a wife. Where is she now? What, will these hands ne'er be clean? No more o' that, my lord, no more o' that! You mar all with this starting.

Doctor. Go to,° go to! You have known what you should not.

Gentlewoman. She has spoke what she should not, I am sure of that. Heaven knows what she has known.

Lady Macbeth. Here's the smell of the blood still. All the perfumes of Arabia will not sweeten this little hand. Oh, oh, oh!

Doctor. What a sigh is there! The heart is sorely charged.°

Gentlewoman. I would not have such a heart in my bosom for the dignity° of the whole body.

Doctor. Well, well, well——

Gentlewoman. Pray God it be, sir.

Doctor. This disease is beyond my practice.° Yet I have known those which have walked in their sleep who have died holily in their beds.

Lady Macbeth. Wash your hands; put on your nightgown; look not so pale! I tell you yet again, Banquo's buried. He cannot come out on 's° grave.

Doctor. Even so?

Lady Macbeth. To bed, to bed! There's knocking at the gate.

13. meet: suitable.

16. guise: custom.

17. close: hidden.

? **20.** *Why must Lady Macbeth have light by her continually?*

22. sense: powers of sight.

? **28.** *After setting down the taper on a table, what does Lady Macbeth do with her hands?*

30. satisfy: confirm.

34. to accompt: into account.

? **35.** *What does she think is still on her hands?*

? **37.** *Who is the Thane of Fife?*

40. Go to: an exclamation.

? **43.** *What action is suggested by this line?*

45. charged: burdened.

47. dignity: worth; rank.

50. practice: professional skill.

55. on 's: of his.

? **55.** *Whom does she think she is speaking to here?*

C Elements of Literature

Theme

? Here again is the sleep motif. What does Lady Macbeth's disturbed sleep represent? [Possible answers: Students will probably guess that she is racked by guilt. Her sleeplessness may reflect the idea that Macbeth's stabbing of Duncan "murdered sleep."]

D Reading Skills and Strategies

Comparing and Contrasting

? Reread II.2.66–67. How are Lady Macbeth's assumptions in Act II proved incorrect here? [Possible answer: She assumed it would be easy to clean up after the murder because it is physically easy to wash the blood off one's hands. She did not take into account the psychological effects of the murder, such as the obsessive hand washing she is now exhibiting.] Washing one's hands to remove guilt is a ritualistic act that has a long history. For instance, in the New Testament Pontius Pilate, the Roman governor of Judea, washed his hands before he released Jesus to the Romans to be crucified.

E Reading Skills and Strategies

Making Inferences

? To which events and people does Lady Macbeth refer? What clues let you know? [Duncan—"old man"; Macduff's family—"The Thane of Fife had a wife. Where is she now?"; possibly Banquo—"starting," which may reflect on Macbeth's startled reaction in III.4.63]

F Critical Thinking

Hypothesizing

? The doctor and the gentlewoman express pity for Lady Macbeth. Why do you think Shakespeare has them do so? [Possible response: He wants the audience to pity the guilt-torn sleepwalker and not view her as completely evil.]

Answers to Margin Questions

Line 20. She fears the dark, perhaps associating it with murder or with hell, which she calls "murky" in l. 32.

Line 28. She checks them and upon finding an invisible spot of blood, tries to wash it off.

Line 35. Duncan's blood

Line 37. Macduff

Line 43. She sniffs an imaginary spot on one hand.

Line 55. Macbeth

Crossing the Curriculum

Health

We are only just beginning to understand what happens when sleep is disturbed, as it is during a sleepwalking episode. Sleepwalking usually occurs about one to four hours after falling asleep when the sleeper is coming out of stage IV non-REM (Rapid Eye Movement) sleep. Sleepwalking episodes average from five to twenty minutes and are usually, though not always, calm. Occasionally, sleepwalking is combined with sleeptalking, as in the case of Lady Macbeth. Generally, sleepwalking, especially in children, is not an indication of any emotional or psychological problem. However, in adults, sleepwalking occasionally can signal a serious disturbance. Have students research the main causes of sleepwalking and current methods of dealing with it. Ask them to share their findings with the class.

Ⓐ Elements of Literature

Imagery

? Point out the images of illness used to represent evil. What does the doctor mean when he talks about "infected minds"? [guilty consciences] Why do these "infected minds" eventually "discharge their secrets"? [Possible response: The feelings of guilt become so great that a confession must burst forth sooner or later in order to clear one's conscience.]

Summary

Scene 2: In the country near Dunsinane, the Scottish lords prepare to join forces with an approaching English army to fight against Macbeth. The lords discuss their plans and Macbeth's reported state of mind.

Ⓑ Critical Thinking

Making a Judgment

? What is your opinion of Macbeth: Is he mad or does he possess a "valiant fury"? [Possible responses: He is mad, as evidenced by his hallucinations and the pointless murders he has committed; or, he possesses a valiant desire to keep the throne at all costs.]

Answers to Margin Questions

Line 59. She thinks she hears knocking at the gate, as in Act II, Scene 2. She leaves the stage in frantic haste.

Line 70. They know the truth about Duncan's murder but realize they would endanger their lives by speaking out.

Line 5. The third apparition (IV.1.92–94) said, "Macbeth shall never vanquished be until/ Great Birnam Wood to high Dunsinane Hill/ Shall come against him."

Come, come, come, come, give me your hand! What's done
cannot be undone. To bed, to bed, to bed!
[*Exit* LADY MACBETH.]

Doctor. Will she go now to bed?
Gentlewoman. Directly.
Doctor.
Foul whisp'rings are abroad. Unnatural deeds
Do breed unnatural troubles. Infected minds
To their deaf pillows will discharge their secrets.
More needs she the divine° than the physician.
God, God forgive us all! Look after her;
Remove from her the means of all annoyance,°
And still° keep eyes upon her. So good night.
My mind she has mated° and amazed my sight:
I think, but dare not speak.
Gentlewoman. Good night, good doctor.
[*Exeunt.*]

? **59.** *Once again there is a sudden dramatic change. What echo from the past brings it about? How do you think Lady Macbeth leaves the stage?*

65. divine: priest.

67. annoyance: injury.

68. still: continuously.

69. mated: baffled.

? **70.** *What do the doctor and gentlewoman know? Why won't they speak out?*

Scene 2. *The country near Dunsinane.*

Drum and colors. Enter MENTEITH, CAITHNESS, ANGUS, LENNOX, SOLDIERS.

Menteith.
The English pow'r° is near, led on by Malcolm,
His uncle Siward and the good Macduff.
Revenges burn in them; for their dear° causes
Would to the bleeding and the grim alarm°
Excite the mortified° man.
Angus. Near Birnam Wood
Shall we well meet them; that way are they coming.
Caithness.
Who knows if Donalbain be with his brother?
Lennox.
For certain, sir, he is not. I have a file°
Of all the gentry: there is Siward's son,
And many unrough° youths that even now
Protest° their first of manhood.
Menteith. What does the tyrant?
Caithness.
Great Dunsinane he strongly fortifies.
Some say he's mad; others, that lesser hate him,
Do call it valiant fury: but, for certain,
He cannot buckle his distempered° cause
Within the belt of rule.°
Angus. Now does he feel
His secret murders sticking on his hands;
Now minutely revolts upbraid° his faith-breach.
Those he commands move only in command,
Nothing in love. Now does he feel his title

1. pow'r: army.

3. dear: heartfelt.

4. alarm: call to arms.

5. mortified: half dead.

? **5.** *Where have you heard about Birnam Wood before?*

8. file: list.

10. unrough: beardless.

11. Protest: assert.

15. distempered: swollen with disease.

16. rule: self-control.

18. minutely revolts upbraid: rebellions every minute rebuke.

Skill Link

Analyzing and Responding to a Critical Review

Focusing on ll. 20–22, in which Macbeth's title is likened to a giant's robe on a dwarfish thief, critic Caroline F. E. Spurgeon writes, "This imaginative picture of a small, ignoble man encumbered and degraded by garments unsuited to him, should be put against the view emphasized by some critics (notably Coleridge and Bradley) of the likeness between Macbeth and Milton's Satan in grandeur and sublimity." Explore with students whether they judge Macbeth as "small and ignoble" or full of "grandeur and sublimity." After students have read "The Fall of Satan" (p. 441), ask them what similarities Coleridge and Bradley might have seen between Macbeth and Satan.

Hang loose about him, like a giant's robe
Upon a dwarfish thief.

Mentieth. Who then shall blame
His pestered° senses to recoil and start,
When all that is within him does condemn
Itself for being there?

Caithness. Well, march we on,
To give obedience where 'tis truly owed.
Meet we the med'cine° of the sickly weal,°
And with him pour we, in our country's purge,
Each drop of us.°

Lennox. Or so much as it needs
To dew° the sovereign° flower and drown the weeds.
Make we our march towards Birnam.
[Exeunt, marching.]

Scene 3. *Dunsinane. In the castle.*

Enter MACBETH, DOCTOR, *and* ATTENDANTS.

Macbeth.
Bring me no more reports; let them fly all!
Till Birnam Wood remove to Dunsinane
I cannot taint° with fear. What's the boy Malcolm?
Was he not born of woman? The spirits that know
All mortal consequences° have pronounced me thus:
"Fear not, Macbeth; no man that's born of woman
Shall e'er have power upon thee." Then fly, false thanes,
And mingle with the English epicures.
The mind I sway° by and the heart I bear
Shall never sag with doubt nor shake with fear.

[Enter SERVANT.]

The devil damn thee black, thou cream-faced loon!°
Where got'st thou that goose look?

Servant.
There is ten thousand——

Macbeth. Geese, villain?

Servant. Soldiers, sir.

Macbeth.
Go prick thy face and over-red° thy fear,
Thou lily-livered boy. What soldiers, patch?°
Death of° thy soul! Those linen° cheeks of thine
Are counselors to fear. What soldiers, whey-face?

Servant.
The English force, so please you.

Macbeth.
Take thy face hence. *[Exit* SERVANT.]
Seyton!—I am sick at heart,
When I behold—Seyton, I say!—This push°

23. **pestered:** tormented.

27. **med'cine:** that is, Malcolm. **weal:** commonwealth.

29. **Each . . . us:** that is, every last drop of our blood.

30. **dew:** bedew; water (and thus make grow). **sovereign:** royal; also, remedial.

? **31.** *The "falling action" of a Shakespearean play is usually swift. How does this scene show that the hero's enemies are now rallying to crush him? What group is shown in this scene?*

3. **taint:** become infected.

5. **mortal consequences:** future human events.

9. **sway:** move.

11. **loon:** fool.

? **12.** *Macbeth is in an extreme state of agitation. Which of the apparitions' prophecies is he relying on? How would you stage his treatment of the servant, which follows?*

14. **over-red:** cover with red.

15. **patch:** fool.

16. **of:** upon. **linen:** pale.

20. **push:** effort.

C Elements of Literature

Tragedy

? Here the Scottish thanes talk of joining forces with Malcolm. Is Macbeth's impending fall that of a tragic hero, or is he a villain? [Possible responses: He is a tragic hero in that although he starts out as a brave general loyal to his King, he possesses a character flaw that takes over his personality and causes his downfall; or, he is too ruthless to be a true hero, as he is easily persuaded to kill Duncan and keeps killing to maintain his powerful position. He is not noble in any way.]

Summary

Scene 3: Because of the witches' prophecies, Macbeth feels confident that he is invincible inside his castle. A servant brings news of the approaching army.

D Struggling Readers

Finding Details

? Macbeth refers to two of the prophecies uttered by the apparitions, but he appears to forget the third. What prophecy does he neglect to mention? ["Beware Macduff!"] Remind students that the prophecies are in Act IV, Scene 1.

E Elements of Literature

Imagery

? After King Duncan's murder, Lady Macbeth chided her husband for wearing "a heart so white." What similar imagery does Macbeth now use to rebuke his servant? ["lily-livered boy;" "linen cheeks;" "whey-face"] How do Macbeth's insulting remarks reveal his character? [Possible responses: His rude remarks may be an attempt to mask his own fears; they reveal his estrangement from his own supporters.]

Answers to Margin Questions

Line 31. A number of the thanes of Scotland are now openly against Macbeth and are marching toward Dunsinane. They report that English forces, along with Malcolm and Macduff, are on the way to join them.

Line 12. He relies on the prophecies that he cannot be defeated until Birnam Wood comes to Dunsinane and that "no man . . . born of woman" can defeat him. He treats his servant scornfully, standing proud while the servant cowers in fear.

Skill Link

Analyzing Meter

Remind students that **meter** is a regular pattern of stressed and unstressed syllables. Meter's basic unit is the **foot,** consisting of one stressed syllable and one or more unstressed syllables. The metrical foot used most by Shakespeare is the **iamb,** which has an unstressed syllable followed by a stressed syllable, as in the word *relief.* To scan poetry, identify the type of foot (or feet) in a single line and then count the number of feet.

Tetrameter means four feet per line; **pentameter** means five. To help students hear the meter, have them try the following approach: 1) Figure out whether a line is iambic pentameter or tetrameter. 2) Read the line as if it were true to the meter, noting where the regular accents on the words come out wrong. 3) Correct the reading for accents. Once they have practiced, let students read their favorite speech to the class.

Ⓐ Critical Thinking

Making Connections

Ask students to read Shakespeare's Sonnet 73, on p. 226, and to compare the poem with this speech of Macbeth's. [Possible answer: The imagery of yellow leaves implies the "fall" of someone's life in both passages; however, Macbeth expresses dissatisfaction, while the speaker of the sonnet seems accepting of death and comforted by the strong love of someone close to him.]

Ⓑ Historical Connections

According to *Shakespeareana Genealogica,* "The Setons of Touch were (and are still) hereditary armor-bearers to the kings of Scotland; there is thus a peculiar fitness in the choice of this name."

Ⓒ Appreciating Language

Punctuation

? How do the dashes in this speech show Macbeth's state of mind? [They indicate that the speech is disjointed and that Macbeth is very agitated.]

Ⓓ Elements of Literature

Figurative Language

? To what "disease" is Macbeth referring? What is ironic about his metaphor? [He calls the rebellious thanes and their English allies a disease and recommends purging the land. Ironically, the audience knows, even if Macbeth does not, that he is the sickness in the land and that he is calling for his own demise.]

Answers to Margin Questions

Line 22. Answers will vary. Students may be confused by the contradiction between l. 21, in which Macbeth seems to think there is a possibility his cause may succeed and l. 22, in which he sounds defeated, and perhaps fatalistic.
Line 37. Lady Macbeth
Line 56. Some possibilities are disgust, irritation, arrogance, self-pity, concern for the country, and whimsy.

Will cheer me ever, or disseat° me now.
I have lived long enough. My way of life
Is fall'n into the sear,° the yellow leaf,
And that which should accompany old age,
As honor, love, obedience, troops of friends,
I must not look to have; but, in their stead,
Curses not loud but deep, mouth-honor, breath,
Which the poor heart would fain deny, and dare not.
Seyton!

[*Enter* SEYTON.]

Seyton.
What's your gracious pleasure?
Macbeth. What news more?
Seyton.
All is confirmed, my lord, which was reported.
Macbeth.
I'll fight, till from my bones my flesh be hacked.
Give me my armor.
Seyton. 'Tis not needed yet.
Macbeth.
I'll put it on.
Send out moe° horses, skirr° the country round.
Hang those that talk of fear. Give me mine armor.
How does your patient, doctor?
Doctor. Not so sick, my lord,
As she is troubled with thick-coming fancies
That keep her from her rest.
Macbeth. Cure her of that.
Canst thou not minister to a mind diseased,
Pluck from the memory a rooted sorrow,
Raze out° the written troubles of the brain,
And with some sweet oblivious° antidote
Cleanse the stuffed bosom of that perilous stuff
Which weighs upon the heart?
Doctor. Therein the patient
Must minister to himself.
Macbeth.
Throw physic° to the dogs, I'll none of it.
Come, put mine armor on. Give me my staff.
Seyton, send out.—Doctor, the thanes fly from me.—
Come, sir, dispatch.° If thou couldst, doctor, cast
The water° of my land, find her disease
And purge it to a sound and pristine health,
I would applaud thee to the very echo,
That should applaud again.—Pull't off, I say.—
What rhubarb, senna, or what purgative drug,
Would scour these English hence? Hear'st thou of them?

21. disseat: unthrone (with wordplay on *cheer,* pronounced *chair*).

? **22.** *What mood is Macbeth in now?*

23. sear: withered.

35. moe: more. **skirr:** scour.

? **37.** *Who is the doctor's patient?*

42. Raze out: erase.

43. oblivious: causing forgetfulness.

47. physic: medical science.

50. dispatch: hurry.

51. cast/The water: literally, analyze the urine.

? **56.** *Lines 47–56 contain almost a roller coaster of emotions. Can you cite some?*

Getting Students Involved

Enrichment Activity

Researching Medieval Medicine. Although some doctors in the Middle Ages were well-trained and had studied the writings of such Greek physicians as Hippocrates, the majority relied on folk remedies. Various herbs and poultices were an essential part of the practice. For instance, egg whites were used to relieve digestive problems and marigolds to reduce fever. Purgative drugs, or drugs designed to cleanse the system, included dandelions, rhubarb, and senna. When Lady Macbeth becomes ill, Macbeth calls a doctor and encourages him to use these folk remedies on her. Ask students to investigate medical practices in the mid-eleventh century. What training did doctors need? What ailments were they most often called upon to treat? How effective were their treatments?

Doctor.
Ay, my good lord; your royal preparation
Makes us hear something.

Macbeth. Bring it° after me.
I will not be afraid of death and bane°
Till Birnam Forest come to Dunsinane.

Doctor (*aside*).
Were I from Dunsinane away and clear, E
Profit again should hardly draw me here. [*Exeunt.*]

58. **it:** the armor.
59. **bane:** destruction.

? 60. *Is Macbeth truly courageous here? Or would you suggest that he is merely coasting on a kind of false bravery lent to him by the witches' prophecies?*

Scene 4. *Country near Birnam Wood.*

Drum and colors. Enter MALCOLM, SIWARD, MACDUFF, *Siward's son* YOUNG SIWARD, MENTEITH, CAITHNESS, ANGUS, *and* SOLDIERS, *marching.*

Malcolm.
Cousins, I hope the days are near at hand
That chambers will be safe.°

Menteith. We doubt it nothing.°

Siward.
What wood is this before us?

Menteith. The Wood of Birnam.

Malcolm.
Let every soldier hew him down a bough
And bear't before him. Thereby shall we shadow F
The numbers of our host, and make discovery°
Err in report of us.

Soldiers. It shall be done.

Siward.
We learn no other but° the confident tyrant
Keeps still in Dunsinane, and will endure°
Our setting down before't.

Malcolm. 'Tis his main hope,
For where there is advantage to be given°
Both more and less° have given him the revolt,
And none serve with him but constrainèd things
Whose hearts are absent too.

Macduff. Let our just censures
Attend the true event,° and put we on
Industrious soldiership.

Siward. The time approaches,
That will with due decision make us know
What we shall say we have and what we owe.°
Thoughts speculative their unsure hopes relate, G
But certain issue strokes must arbitrate:°
Towards which advance the war.° [*Exeunt, marching.*]

2. **That . . . safe:** that a man will be safe in his bedroom. **nothing:** not at all.

? 5. *Stop and describe what the soldiers are to do here and why.*

6. **discovery:** Macbeth's scouts.

? 7. *Malcolm seems to have more authority at this point in the play. Can you find specific instances where his new authority could be dramatized?*

8. **no other but:** nothing but that.
9. **endure:** allow.
11. **advantage . . . given:** afforded an opportunity.
12. **more and less:** high and low.
15. **just . . . event:** true judgments await the actual outcome.
18. **owe:** own. The contrast is between "what we shall say we have" and "what we shall really have."
20. **certain . . . arbitrate:** The definite outcome must be decided by battle.
21. **war:** army.

E Critical Thinking

Speculating

? The doctor does not help Lady Macbeth and does not satisfy Macbeth. What do you think is the purpose of having him appear in the play? [Possible answer: Through him the audience finds out that Lady Macbeth is not immune to the emotional consequences of committing murder. She is sick with guilt, unlike her husband who callously continues to order murders.]

Summary

Scene 4: Malcolm orders the soldiers gathered near Birnam Wood to camouflage themselves with branches as they advance toward Macbeth's castle.

F Reading Skills and Strategies

Visualizing

? As the camouflaged forces move on Dunsinane, how will they look to an observer on the battlements of the castle? [Possible answer: Birnam Wood will appear to be moving toward Dunsinane.]

G English Language Learners

Rearranging Word Order

Students may have a difficult time understanding sentences like this one that do not follow contemporary patterns. Two things make this sentence difficult: 1) the adjective *speculative* follows the noun it modifies; 2) the subject *thoughts* is far removed from the verb *relate*. Ask students to translate this sentence into standard word order. [Speculative thoughts relate their unsure hopes.] Explain that Siward is saying that "strokes," or fighting, will settle the issues that the thanes and Malcolm are speculating about now.

Answers to Margin Questions

Line 60. He seems to be fortifying his failing courage with false hopes based on the enigmatic words of the apparitions.
Line 5. Each soldier is to cut a leafy branch and carry it in front of him as camouflage so that Macbeth's scouts will not see the advancing army.
Line 7. He might lead the troops or give orders. Others could show that they defer to and protect him through their actions.

Summary

Scene 5: In his castle, Macbeth awaits the approaching army. An offstage cry is heard, and Seyton enters with news that Lady Macbeth is dead. Depressed by the news, Macbeth delivers his famous "Tomorrow" soliloquy, declaring that life "is a tale told by an idiot, full of sound and fury,/Signifying nothing." When a messenger brings news that Birnam Wood is approaching the castle, Macbeth realizes that the witches have tricked him and that he is likely to be defeated.

A Reading Skills and Strategies

Finding Details

? What strategy is Macbeth planning to use? [Possible answer: Macbeth is putting his faith in the witches and their prophecies and in the strength of his castle. He is planning to stay in the castle and outlast the siege.]

B Elements of Literature

Imagery

? What food imagery does Macbeth use in this passage? ["taste of fears" and "supped full with horrors"] What is he saying? [Possible answer: He has done so many horrible deeds and has worried so much about their consequences that his senses are numb, preventing him from feeling fear.]

Answer to Margin Question

Line 7. In contrast to Malcolm's calm forcefulness and determination, Macbeth could act bitter and scornful and show false bravery.

"Tomorrow, and tomorrow, and tomorrow
Creeps in this petty pace from day to day,
To the last syllable of recorded time."

From Orson Welles's film production of *Macbeth* (1948).

Scene 5. *Dunsinane. Within the castle.*

Enter MACBETH, SEYTON, *and* SOLDIERS, *with drum and colors.*

Macbeth.
Hang out our banners on the outward walls.
The cry is still "They come!" Our castle's strength
Will laugh a siege to scorn. Here let them lie
Till famine and the ague° eat them up.
Were they not forced° with those that should be ours,
We might have met them dareful,° beard to beard,
And beat them backward home.

[*A cry within of women.*]

What is that noise?

Seyton.
It is the cry of women, my good lord. [*Exit.*]

Macbeth.
I have almost forgot the taste of fears:
The time has been, my senses would have cooled
To hear a night-shriek, and my fell° of hair
Would at a dismal treatise° rouse and stir
As life were in't. I have supped full with horrors.
Direness, familiar to my slaughterous thoughts,
Cannot once start° me.

4. **ague:** fever.
5. **forced:** reinforced.
6. **met them dareful:** that is, met them on the battlefield boldly.

? 7. *Macbeth should contrast with Malcolm now. How should he be acting?*

11. **fell:** pelt.
12. **treatise:** story.
15. **start:** startle.

Professional Notes

Critical Comment: The Witches

Critic Willard Farnham discusses the role of the witches: "Before we make up our minds about the guilt of the hero and, finally, the meaning of the tragedy, we must first decide what power these beings [witches] wield over the actions and fortunes of the hero. They are witches having the forms of repulsive old women, but they are not mortal witches, such as the law might get its hands upon and put to death in the England or Scotland of Shakespeare's day. They are 'weird sisters,' but the word 'weird' as applied to them cannot mean that they have control of Macbeth's destiny and compel him to do all that he does. Macbeth is certainly no mere puppet moving under their manipulation. Nothing is clearer than that Shakespeare writes of Macbeth as of a man who has free will so far, at least, as the choice of good or evil is concerned, and who in choosing evil creates for himself physical misfortune and a spiritual hell on earth. In what they do the witches show themselves to have a power over Macbeth that is limited, however strong it may be. They are supernatural agents of evil, and in working to make fair into foul they reveal both the capacities and the incapacities that the Christian tradition has attributed to devils. They tempt Macbeth to do evil, and tempt him with great subtlety. They cannot force him to do it."

[*Enter* SEYTON.]

Wherefore was that cry?

Seyton.
The queen, my lord, is dead.

Macbeth.
She should° have died hereafter;
There would have been a time for such a word.°
Tomorrow, and tomorrow, and tomorrow
Creeps in this petty pace from day to day,
To the last syllable of recorded time;
And all our yesterdays have lighted fools
The way to dusty death. Out, out, brief candle!
Life's but a walking shadow, a poor player
That struts and frets his hour upon the stage
And then is heard no more. It is a tale
Told by an idiot, full of sound and fury,
Signifying nothing.

[*Enter a* MESSENGER.]

Thou com'st to use thy tongue; thy story quickly!

Messenger.
Gracious my lord,
I should report that which I say I saw,
But know not how to do't.

Macbeth. Well, say, sir.

Messenger.
As I did stand my watch upon the hill,
I looked toward Birnam, and anon, methought,
The wood began to move.

Macbeth. Liar and slave!

Messenger.
Let me endure your wrath, if't be not so.
Within this three mile may you see it coming;
I say a moving grove.

Macbeth. If thou speak'st false,
Upon the next tree shalt thou hang alive,
Till famine cling° thee. If thy speech be sooth,°
I care not if thou dost for me as much.
I pull in resolution,° and begin
To doubt° th' equivocation of the fiend
That lies like truth: "Fear not, till Birnam Wood
Do come to Dunsinane!" And now a wood
Comes toward Dunsinane. Arm, arm, and out!
If this which he avouches° does appear,
There is nor flying hence nor tarrying here.
I 'gin to be aweary of the sun,
And wish th' estate° o' th' world were now undone.
Ring the alarum bell! Blow wind, come wrack!
At least we'll die with harness° on our back. [*Exeunt.*]

17. should: inevitably would.
18. word: message.

? 28. *A scene that began in defiance changes with the great speech beginning "She should have died hereafter." What is Macbeth's new mood? Does Macbeth speak only for himself here, or for the general human condition?*

? 35. *What is Macbeth thinking of now?*

40. cling: wither. **sooth:** truth.
42. pull in resolution: restrain confidence.
43. doubt: suspect.

47. avouches: asserts.
50. th' estate: the orderly condition.
52. harness: armor.

? 52. *Macbeth ends the scene in a state of great emotion. How would you characterize his mental state?*

Crossing the Curriculum

Music
Have students work in groups to locate recorded music that creates an appropriate mood for each act of the play. Remind students to go back and review the major events in each act to help them identify music that reflects the atmosphere of each act. Have students share their musical selections with the class and explain why they chose them.

Social Studies
Some students may wish to explore the military strategies in the text and in Holinshed's *Chronicles*. They might explore the use of camouflage, siege tactics, castle defense, various armor and weapons, or even the use of bagpipes and trumpets for military battle calls. Ask students to research their topic and give an oral report on their findings. Interested students can compare and contrast battle tactics in Macbeth's time with those used today.

C Critical Thinking
Interpreting

? There is a great deal of critical debate about the meaning of this line. Popular interpretations include these: 1) like all humans, she would inevitably die sometime; and 2) at a different time, Macbeth could have paid more attention to her death. What do you think Macbeth means, and why? [Possible responses: Macbeth rationalizes his grief by putting it within the context of human mortality; or, he is so self-absorbed that the emotional impact of Lady Macbeth's death doesn't fully register.]

D Critical Thinking
Interpreting

? How does Macbeth feel about his life as king now? [Possible responses: He realizes the pointlessness of his ambition and the insignificance of his struggles.]

E Elements of Literature
Figurative Language

? What metaphors does Macbeth use for life? ["A walking shadow," "a poor player," and "a tale told by an idiot" all refer to life.] To which major theme of the play do these images relate? [the theme of false appearances]

F Literary Connection
The Sound and the Fury

William Faulkner wrote a novel called *The Sound and the Fury*, part of which is narrated by Benjy, a man of low intelligence who might fit Macbeth's definition of an idiot.

G Elements of Literature
Tragedy

? What admirable quality does Macbeth display here? [Possible answer: Even though he knows he is doomed, he remains the courageous soldier, ready to die in battle.]

Answers to Margin Questions
Line 28. Macbeth is pensive, showing philosophical resignation to the brevity and meaninglessness of life. He laments the human condition.
Line 35. He recalls the prophecy about Birnam Wood advancing on Dunsinane.
Line 52. Macbeth is near despair. Realizing that it matters little whether he remains in the castle or goes out, he resolves to die fighting.

Summary

Scene 6: Upon reaching the front of Macbeth's castle, Malcolm orders his troops to throw down their camouflage and attack. Siward and his son are to lead, with Malcolm and Macduff in reserve.

Ⓐ Appreciating Language

Word Choice

Point out that the words *worthy* and *noble* emphasize how just the soldiers' cause is and how strongly these men contrast with Macbeth. No one uses such words to describe him anymore.

Ⓑ Elements of Literature

Figurative Language

? In what way are the trumpets "clamorous harbingers of blood and death"? [Possible response: The trumpets lead the soldiers into battle, where the men face shedding their blood and possibly dying.]

Scene 6. *Dunsinane. Before the castle.*

Drum and colors. Enter MALCOLM, SIWARD, MACDUFF, *and their* ARMY, *with boughs.*

Malcolm.
Now near enough. Your leavy° screens throw down,
Ⓐ And show like those you are. You, worthy uncle,
Shall, with my cousin, your right noble son,
Lead our first battle.° Worthy Macduff and we°
Shall take upon 's what else remains to do,
According to our order.°

Siward. Fare you well.
Do we° but find the tyrant's power° tonight,
Let us be beaten, if we cannot fight.

Macduff.
Make all our trumpets speak; give them all breath,
Ⓑ Those clamorous harbingers of blood and death.
[*Exeunt. Alarums continued.*]

1. **leavy:** leafy.

4. **battle:** battalion. **we:** Malcolm uses the royal "we."

6. **order:** plan.

7. **Do we:** if we do. **power:** forces.

"Make all our trumpets speak; give them all breath,
Those clamorous harbingers of blood and death."
From the Stratford Festival production of *Macbeth* (1983).

Listening to Music

"Mi si affaccia un pugnal?"; "Schiudi, inferno"; "Ah! la paterna mano"; and "Una macchia è qui tuttora" from *Macbeth* by Giuseppe Verdi Performed by the New York Metropolitan Opera Company

Giuseppe Verdi (jyōō-sep'ā vâr'dē) (1813–1901) revolutionized Italian opera with masterpieces such as *Aida, Rigoletto, Il Trovatore,* and *La Traviata.* An admirer of Shakespeare's plays, he drew on them for inspiration for his fine operas: *Otello, Falstaff,* and *Macbeth.* Verdi's *Macbeth* is famous in the music world for its rousing choruses, strong characterization, and high drama—the last two qualities are not at all a surprise, given the source. *Macbeth* premiered in Florence, Italy, in 1847.

Activity

After students have finished reading *Macbeth,* play these highlights from Verdi's opera and have students guess, based on the mood of the music, which of the following scenes or incidents Verdi is attempting to capture:

- "Mi si affaccia un pugnal?" ("Is this a dagger appearing before me?")—Macbeth's dagger scene
- "Schiudi, inferno" ("Open your maw, O Hell!")—chorus mourning Duncan's murder
- "Ah! la paterna mano" ("Ah, this is father's hand")—Macduff mourns his family's murder
- "Una macchia è qui tuttora" ("A stain is still here")—Lady Macbeth's sleepwalking scene

Scene 7. *Another part of the field.*

Enter MACBETH.

Macbeth.
They have tied me to a stake; I cannot fly,
But bearlike I must fight the course.° What's he
That was not born of woman? Such a one
Am I to fear, or none.

[*Enter* YOUNG SIWARD.]

Young Siward.
What is thy name?

Macbeth. Thou'lt be afraid to hear it.

Young Siward.
No; though thou call'st thyself a hotter name
Than any is in hell.

Macbeth. My name's Macbeth.

Young Siward.
The devil himself could not pronounce a title
More hateful to mine ear.

Macbeth. No, nor more fearful.

Young Siward.
Thou liest, abhorrèd tyrant; with my sword
I'll prove the lie thou speak'st.

[*Fight, and* YOUNG SIWARD *slain.*]

Macbeth. Thou wast born of woman.
But swords I smile at, weapons laugh to scorn,
Brandished by man that's of a woman born. [*Exit.*]

[*Alarums. Enter* MACDUFF.]

Macduff.
That way the noise is. Tyrant, show thy face!
If thou be'st slain and with no stroke of mine,
My wife and children's ghosts will haunt me still.
I cannot strike at wretched kerns,° whose arms
Are hired to bear their staves.° Either thou, Macbeth,
Or else my sword, with an unbattered edge,
I sheathe again undeeded.° There thou shouldst be;
By this great clatter, one of greatest note
Seems bruited.° Let me find him, Fortune!
And more I beg not. [*Exit. Alarums.*]

[*Enter* MALCOLM *and* SIWARD.]

Siward.
This way, my lord. The castle's gently rend'red:°
The tyrant's people on both sides do fight;
The noble thanes do bravely in the war;
The day almost itself professes° yours,

2. course: bout; round. (He has in mind an attack of dogs or men upon a bear chained to a stake.)

? **4.** *What is Macbeth desperately clinging to now?*

17. kerns: foot soldiers (contemptuous).

18. staves: spears.

20. undeeded: that is, having done nothing.

22. bruited: reported.

24. gently rend'red: surrendered without a struggle.

27. itself professes: declares itself.

Summary

Scene 7: On the field, Macbeth kills Young Siward. Macbeth exits with Macduff in pursuit. Old Siward informs Malcolm that Macbeth's castle has fallen, barely defended by his disaffected subjects.

C Elements of Literature

Figurative Language

? This bear-baiting comparison would have been familiar to Shakespeare's audience (See note, l. 2). In that bloody sport, the bear, however valiant, has no real chance. What does Macbeth's use of this image reveal about his state of mind? [Possible answer: He feels utterly trapped, like the bear whose chain limits its movements and prevents it from using its strength to its advantage.]

D Critical Thinking

Interpreting

? Why does Macbeth still believe that no man born of woman can harm him—especially after seeing how the first prophecy came true? [Possible answer: Macbeth is so desperate at this point that he clings to false hope rather than face defeat.]

E Reading Skills and Strategies

Comparing and Contrasting Characters

? How does Macduff's motivation to fight contrast with Macbeth's? [Possible answer: Macduff wants to avenge his family and kill only Macbeth; Macbeth's motivation to murder is selfishness and ambition for power.]

Answer to Margin Question

Line 4. Macbeth clings to the prophecy, which he interprets as meaning no living person can harm him since everyone is born of a woman.

Skill Link

Analyzing and Responding to a Critical Review

Ask students to discuss this analysis by Terry Eagleton: "*Macbeth* centers around a single action—the murder of Duncan—which . . . is seen as self-defeating. The whole structure of the play makes this clear: Scotland moves from health to sickness and back into health. Malcolm replaces Duncan, and the wheel comes full circle without Macbeth having made any permanent achievement. The energy he expends in trying to secure his position contrasts ironically with his lack of attainment: his actions are canceled out by the circular movement of the play, and he becomes a momentary aberration in Scotland's history, an aberration without lasting consequence: the history rights itself and continues." [Students may agree that Macbeth himself recognizes this when he speaks of "a tale told by an idiot, signifying nothing."]

Summary

Scene 8: Macduff confronts Macbeth, who at first refuses to fight him, warning Macduff that no one born of woman can harm him. Macduff explains that he was not born of woman but by Caesarean section. Macbeth again refuses to fight, but Macduff goads him by vowing to place him in a cage and display him as a fallen tyrant. Their fight begins and continues offstage. Ross reports to Siward that Young Siward has died bravely. Macduff returns with the head of Macbeth and proclaims Malcolm king of Scotland. Malcolm promises to restore peace and order to the land.

A Literary Connections

Classical Allusions

Macbeth is saying that he does not wish to die like the Roman leaders Brutus and Cassius, who killed themselves with their own swords rather than face defeat.

B Critical Thinking

Interpreting

? What motivates Macbeth to say, "My soul is too much charged/With blood of thine already"? [He now feels guilty about murdering Macduff's family.]

And little is to do.
Malcolm. We have met with foes
That strike beside us.°
Siward. Enter, sir, the castle.
[Exeunt. Alarum.]

Scene 8. *Another part of the field.*

Enter MACBETH.

A
Macbeth.
Why should I play the Roman fool, and die
On mine own sword? Whiles I see lives,° the gashes
Do better upon them.

[*Enter* MACDUFF.]

Macduff. Turn, hell-hound, turn!
B
Macbeth.
Of all men else I have avoided thee.
But get thee back! My soul is too much charged°
With blood of thine already.

29. That . . . us: that is, who deliberately miss us.

2. Whiles . . . lives: so long as I see living men.

5. charged: burdened.

"I have no words: / My voice is in my sword, thou bloodier villain / Than terms can give thee out!"

From Roman Polanski's film production of *Macbeth* (1971).

Reaching All Students

Struggling Readers

To help students understand the differences and similarities between characters in the play, have them use a scale or comparison grid to rate characters on their traits, such as deciding who is more loyal, Macbeth or Macduff. For a more complete explanation of this strategy as well as information on the use of other scales, see the *Reading Strategies Handbook,* p. 93, in the *Reading Skills and Strategies* binder.

Advanced Learners

Have interested students choose a character from *Macbeth* and write an introduction, as if they were introducing that character as the guest speaker at a banquet. Remind students that introductions can be serious or humorous. Have students deliver their introductions in a formal manner. Encourage them to dramatize their brief speech with appropriate pauses, inflection, and enunciation.

Macduff. I have no words:
My voice is in my sword, thou bloodier villain
Than terms can give thee out!° [*Fight. Alarum.*]
Macbeth. Thou losest labor:
As easy mayst thou the intrenchant° air
With thy keen sword impress° as make me bleed:
Let fall thy blade on vulnerable crests;°
I bear a charmèd life, which must not yield
To one of woman born.
Macduff. Despair° thy charm,
And let the angel° whom thou still hast served
Tell thee, Macduff was from his mother's womb
Untimely ripped.
Macbeth.
Accursèd be that tongue that tells me so,
For it hath cowed my better part of man!°
And be these juggling fiends no more believed, **C**
That palter° with us in a double sense;
That keep the word of promise to our ear,
And break it to our hope. I'll not fight with thee.
Macduff.
Then yield thee, coward,
And live to be the show and gaze o' th' time:°
We'll have thee, as our rarer monsters° are,
Painted upon a pole,° and underwrit,
"Here may you see the tyrant."
Macbeth. I will not yield,
To kiss the ground before young Malcolm's feet,
And to be baited° with the rabble's curse.
Though Birnam Wood be come to Dunsinane,
And thou opposed, being of no woman born,
Yet I will try the last. Before my body
I throw my warlike shield. Lay on, Macduff;
And damned be him that first cries "Hold, enough!" **D**
[*Exeunt, fighting. Alarums.*]

[*Reenter fighting, and* MACBETH *slain. Exit* MACDUFF, *with* MACBETH. *Retreat and flourish.° Enter, with drum and colors,* MALCOLM, SIWARD, ROSS, THANES, *and* SOLDIERS.]

Malcolm.
I would the friends we miss were safe arrived.
Siward.
Some must go off;° and yet, by these I see,
So great a day as this is cheaply bought.
Malcolm.
Macduff is missing, and your noble son.
Ross.
Your son, my lord, has paid a soldier's debt:
He only lived but till he was a man; **E**
The which no sooner had his prowess confirmed

8. terms . . . out: words can describe you.

9. intrenchant: incapable of being cut.

10. impress: make an impression on.

11. vulnerable crests: heads that can be wounded.

13. Despair: despair of.

14. angel: that is, fallen angel; fiend.

? **16.** *What is the meaning of lines 15–16? How do they relate to the prophecy?*

18. better . . . man: manly spirit.

20. palter: equivocate.

24. gaze . . . time: spectacle of the age.

25. monsters: freaks.

26. Painted . . . pole: pictured on a banner set by a showman's booth.

29. baited: assailed (like a bear by dogs).

Retreat and flourish: trumpet call to withdraw, and fanfare.

36. go off: die (theatrical metaphor).

C Critical Thinking

Synthesizing

? Why might it be fitting for Macbeth to be tricked by "palter[ing] . . . in a double sense"? [Possible answer: Since Macbeth used this technique to escape detection as Duncan's murderer, it seems right that his own trick is used to deceive him.]

D Elements of Tragedy

Tragedy

? A tragedy must arouse pity for a fallen hero. To do this, the playwright must remind the audience of the hero's potential for greatness. In what way do these lines do this? [Possible response: Even though he knows he is doomed, Macbeth vows to fight to the death, displaying his courage.]

E Critical Thinking

Expressing an Opinion

? Compare Ross's speech here to Siward's on p. 382 (ll. 46–49). Note that both are delivering brief, moving eulogies on a fallen soldier. Do you agree with these sentiments? Why or why not? [Some students will think it is good to praise soldiers who fight bravely and are willing to sacrifice their lives for a cause. Others may say that making heroes of dead soldiers simply glorifies the dirty business of war.]

Answer to Margin Question
Line 16. As the prophecy predicts, Macduff was not "of woman born" in the natural way but was delivered by Caesarean section.

Making the Connections

Connecting to the Theme: "Under a Hand Accursed"

When students have finished the play, have them reexamine the collection theme. In what sense was Macbeth's "hand accursed"? Were Macbeth's actions fated? Or were his actions totally under his control? Encourage students to suggest other characters from literature, movies, or real life who could be said to have a "hand accursed." In what ways are these figures like Macbeth? In what ways are they different?

Cultural Connections: Investment Ceremonies

Have students work in pairs to learn how various countries celebrate a government leader's taking office. Assign one country to each pair, and have them find answers to the following questions: What title does the head of state use? Where is the inauguration ceremony held? Who attends? Who presides? What promises, if any, does the new officeholder make? Ask each pair to report its findings to the class.

A Reading Skills and Strategies

Comparing and Contrasting

? What earlier event in the play does this mirror? [Possible answer: The beheading of Macdonwald by Macbeth (the traitor beheaded by the loyal Scot). Also, the murder of a king (Macbeth) in order to restore order mirrors the murder of a king (Duncan), an action that has destroyed order.]

B Elements of Literature

Tragedy

? Review with students the elements of a classic tragedy. (See Background, p. T301.) Given the definitions, is Macbeth the typical tragic hero? Why? [Possible answers: Yes, because he is an honorable nobleman who falls as a result of a tragic flaw; or no, because he is a brutal person from the start and a "butcher," as Malcolm calls him.]

Answers to Margin Questions

Line 53. Malcolm exhibits great concern for each missing man and promises posthumous honor for young Siward. Old Siward, satisfied his son died bravely facing the enemy, says no further honor is necessary.

Stage direction. Relieved; gracious; moved; jubilant.

Line 75. Answers will vary. Students may suggest that Malcolm lead the way and that the others follow in order of rank.

In the unshrinking station° where he fought,
But like a man he died.

Siward. Then he is dead?

Ross.
Ay, and brought off the field. Your cause of sorrow
Must not be measured by his worth, for then
It hath no end.

Siward. Had he his hurts before?

Ross.
Ay, on the front.

Siward. Why then, God's soldier be he!
Had I as many sons as I have hairs,
I would not wish them to a fairer death:
And so his knell is knolled.

Malcolm. He's worth more sorrow,
And that I'll spend for him.

Siward. He's worth no more:
They say he parted well and paid his score:°
And so God be with him! Here comes newer comfort.

A [*Enter* MACDUFF, *with Macbeth's head.*]

Macduff.
Hail, king! for so thou art: behold, where stands
Th' usurper's cursèd head. The time is free.°
I see thee compassed° with thy kingdom's pearl,
That speak my salutation in their minds,
Whose voices I desire aloud with mine:
Hail, King of Scotland!

All. Hail, King of Scotland!

[*Flourish.*]

Malcolm.
We shall not spend a large expense of time
Before we reckon with your several loves,°
And make us even with you. My thanes and kinsmen,
Henceforth be earls, the first that ever Scotland
In such an honor named. What's more to do,
Which would be planted newly with the time°—
As calling home our exiled friends abroad
That fled the snares of watchful tyranny,
Producing forth the cruel ministers°
B Of this dead butcher and his fiendlike queen,
Who, as 'tis thought, by self and violent hands°
Took off her life—this, and what needful else
That calls upon us,° by the grace of Grace
We will perform in measure, time, and place:°
So thanks to all at once and to each one,
Whom we invite to see us crowned at Scone.

[*Flourish. Exeunt omnes.*]

42. unshrinking station: that is, place at which he stood firmly.

52. parted . . . score: departed well and settled his account.

? **53.** *What character traits does Malcolm show in this scene? How is old Siward like a military man to the end?*

? **Stage direction.** *Macduff enters with Macbeth's head on a pole. A great shout goes up. What is Macduff's tone in the next speech?*

55. The time is free: The world is liberated.

56. compassed: surrounded.

61. reckon . . . loves: reward the devotion of each of you.

65. What's . . . time: What else must be done that should be newly established in this age.

68. ministers: agents.

70. self . . . hands: her own violent hands.

72. calls upon us: demands my attention.

73. in . . . place: fittingly, at the appropriate time and place.

? **75.** *Scone (skōōn) is a village in Scotland. For centuries, all Scottish kings were crowned in Scone on the Stone of Destiny. The stone was taken to England in 1296 and was returned to Scotland, to Edinburgh Castle, in 1996. How would you have the characters exit? Who would exit last?*

Assessing Learning

Check Test: Questions and Answers

1. Name two important actions that Lady Macbeth performs while sleepwalking. [Possible answers: She rubs her hands as if washing them; she writes a letter; she speaks, implicating herself and Macbeth in the murders of Duncan, Banquo, and Lady Macduff.]
2. Macbeth has been planning to let the English besiege his castle, but after the report that Birnam Wood is moving, how do his plans change? [He decides to go out and fight.]
3. What choice does Macduff give Macbeth? [to fight or to yield, which would lead to imprisonment and exposure to public mockery]
4. Who becomes the new king of Scotland? [Malcolm]

Informal Assessment

Peer Evaluation. As students complete group activities, ask them to rate their group's performance, on a scale of one (low) to three (high), on each of the following criteria:

1. Focuses on the purpose of the activity.
2. Supports ideas with quotations from the text.
3. Makes connections between different parts of the text.

Critical Comment

Soliloquies and Asides

Renaissance playwrights had two useful devices for revealing to an audience or reader a dramatic character's inmost thoughts and feelings: soliloquies and asides.

A **soliloquy** is a meditative kind of speech in which a character, usually alone on stage and pretending that the audience is not present, thinks out loud. Everybody understands that the speaker of a soliloquy tells the truth freely and openly, however discreditable that truth may be. For instance, in his famous soliloquy beginning "To be or not to be," Shakespeare's Hamlet admits to the audience that he is thinking of committing suicide.

Asides are much shorter than soliloquies, but just as truthful. **Asides** are a character's private comments on what is happening at a given moment in a play. They are spoken out of the side of the mouth, so to speak, for the benefit of the audience; the other characters on stage pretend that they do not hear them. For example, Macbeth's asides in Act I, Scene 3, tell us that he cannot put the witches' prophecies out of his mind.

Macbeth's tragic decline can be best traced in his solo speeches—his asides and soliloquies. The most important of these, which are what make the play so interesting psychologically, occur as follows:

Act I, Scene 3, lines 130–142
Act I, Scene 4, lines 48–53
Act I, Scene 7, lines 1–28
Act II, Scene 1, lines 33–64
Act III, Scene 1, lines 48–72
Act IV, Scene 1, lines 144–156
Act V, Scene 3, lines 19–29
Act V, Scene 5, lines 9–15

The early soliloquies show Macbeth's indecision and his fierce inner conflict; then, after he succumbs to evil, they show the terror in his soul and his inability to recover his lost innocence. At times they even show that he is reconciled to his murderous career, especially after the second set of prophecies gives him a false sense of security. But finally the soliloquies show his despair and loss of feeling about, and interest in, life itself. All these changing states of mind are expressed in powerful images that help the audience share Macbeth's suffering. In contrast, we see Lady Macbeth mainly from the outside, though an attentive reader can find speeches in which she also reveals feelings. In *Macbeth,* the inner spiritual catastrophe parallels the outer physical catastrophe.

Nicholas Pennell as Macbeth in the Stratford Festival production of *Macbeth* (1983).

Critical Comment

This feature sheds light on the use of soliloquies and asides as dramatic devices by Renaissance playwrights. Macbeth's soliloquies and asides give the audience insight into his psyche and show the evolution of his tragic downfall.

A Critical Thinking

Expressing an Opinion

? Do you agree that Macbeth's soliloquies and asides are helpful to the reader? Why or why not? [Sample responses: Yes, because if these were left out of the play, readers would not become aware of Macbeth's shift in attitude about the murder; or, no, because it is evident from Macbeth's actions what is going on in his mind.]

B Reading Skills and Strategies

Comparing and Contrasting

Ask students to compare the changes Macbeth goes through with those experienced by Lady Macbeth. [Possible response: Lady Macbeth, like her husband, experiences a decline. Earlier in the play, in contrast to her husband, she is decisive and has no qualms about killing Duncan. After the murder, she is almost gleeful, while her husband is consumed by guilt. However, after becoming queen, she slowly deteriorates. As Macbeth becomes increasingly comfortable with his evil deeds, she becomes distraught. Finally she is driven mad by guilt. Like Macbeth, she sinks into despair.]

Skill Link

Using a Chart to Organize Information

After they have read "Soliloquies and Asides," ask students to give an example from the play of each kind of speech and to tell what purpose each one serves. Have them record this information on a chart like the one that follows.

Term	Example	Purpose
aside	I.3.130–142	to show Macbeth's vivid imagination and feelings of fear
soliloquy	I.7.1–28	to give us insight into Macbeth's thoughts about murdering Duncan

After students complete their charts, have them share with the class their examples and their theories about the specific purpose of the selected soliloquies and asides.

Critical Comment

This feature explores the use of evil in Shakespeare's great tragedy, *Macbeth*. Images of darkness, night, and blood enhance the atmosphere of mystery and wickedness that pervades *Macbeth*. These images help the audience see and feel Macbeth's steady deterioration after he kills Duncan. Shakespeare wants us to see Macbeth's character as tragic, not contemptible—he wants us to be immersed in evil, yet remain sympathetic.

Ⓐ Critical Thinking

Challenging the Text

? Do you agree with this critic's analysis of Shakespeare's goals and purposes? Support your opinion with references to the text. [Sample responses: Yes, Shakespeare wants us to at least empathize with Macbeth, which is why he does not show all the murders onstage and allows us to see Macbeth's uneasiness concerning Duncan's murder. No, Shakespeare does not want us to sympathize with Macbeth or think of him as good. The playwright shows us the utter evil of Macbeth by having him heartlessly order the murder of Macduff's family.]

Ⓑ Struggling Readers

Summarizing

Discuss this section from the Critical Comment with your students and then have them summarize what the author is saying about evil. [Possible answer: Since evil is by nature mysterious, it cannot be explained.]

Critical Comment

The Mystery of Evil

Macbeth fascinates us because it shows, perhaps more clearly than any of Shakespeare's other tragedies, how a character can change as a result of what he does. *Macbeth* also shows that crime does not pay, but that smug cliché is not very relevant to the play: Macbeth is "caught" as soon as he understands the witches' prophecy, and his mental anguish begins before he commits any crimes.

At the start of the play, the mere thought of committing a murder terrifies Macbeth, although he is no novice at carving up men in battle. But it is one thing to fight openly, quite another to kill stealthily. His wife says her great warrior-husband Macbeth is "too full o' th' milk of human kindness." Shakespeare apparently wants us to think of Macbeth as a good man and to feel sympathetic toward him even after he becomes a murderer. When Duncan's body is found, Macbeth does not feel excited about becoming king; instead, he mutters to himself, "The wine of life is drawn." He can't enjoy his kingly state; he is too terrified by what he is doing. "Full of scorpions is my mind," he says to his wife. He lives in such constant terror that by the end of the play he is numb to all feeling—even to the death of his beloved wife. A "dead butcher," Malcolm calls him: an automatic killer.

Lady Macbeth's deterioration is different from her husband's but just as dramatic. Legally, she is only an accomplice, never an actual murderer. But she is the first to decide that Duncan must die; Macbeth wavers right up to the last moment. After the first murders, she exerts immense self-control over herself while he surrenders to his nerves. But she does eventually crack under the strain. Malcolm might not have called her a "fiendlike queen" after her death had he known how much she suffered from pangs of conscience. Both Macbeth and his wife are moral beings who excite our pity rather than our contempt or disgust.

But why do they commit their crimes? The customary answer to this question—that they are ambitious—leads only to another question: Why are they so ambitious that they are willing to commit such crimes? Ultimately, these questions are unanswerable, because evil is as mysterious as it is real. Shakespeare makes no attempt to solve the mystery; instead, in *Macbeth,* he uses language to make it even more mysterious. The world of *Macbeth* is filled, from beginning to end, with mysterious and repulsive images of evil.

The Imagery: Darkness, Night, Blood

First of all, there are the witches. The play opens with the three witches performing their sinister rites and chanting, "Fair is foul, and foul is fair," blurring the differences between these opposites. Macbeth's first speech joins the same opposites, as though they were synonyms: "So foul and fair a day I have not seen." Macbeth's speech thus establishes a connection between himself and the witches even before he meets them.

Shakespeare's audience would have immediately recognized the witches as embodiments of evil in league with Satan himself. Several times they refer to themselves as the "weird sisters"—*weird* here meaning maliciously and perversely supernatural, possessing harmful powers given them by evil spirits in the form of nasty pet animals such as old gray tomcats and toads. English and Scottish witches are not to be regarded as the Fates of Greek mythology whose baleful influence could not be resisted. Rather, they are tempters of a kind that Shakespeare's contemporaries believed they should always avoid. One of the witches seems to foretell Macbeth's future by saying, "All hail, Macbeth, that shalt be king hereafter!" After an inner struggle, and under the influence of his wife's goading, Macbeth chooses to make

Making the Connections

Cultural Connections: Abuses of Power

Just as the murder of Duncan and the events surrounding it cause political upheaval in the play, the murder of contemporary political leaders can also cause civil uprisings and unrest.

Have students discuss the effects of revolution, assassination, and abuses of power in modern times. Have them cite current examples and explore the political ramifications of each.

"hereafter" happen immediately. Nowhere in the play do the witches *cause* Macbeth to make this wicked decision. Rather, he voluntarily surrenders himself, following a visionary dagger—a manifestation of his decision—that leads him into Duncan's bedroom. Having once given in to evil, Macbeth is thereafter under the control of evil forces stronger than his own moral sense.

Shakespeare expresses these evil forces in images of darkness, night, and blood. He has Banquo call the weird sisters "instruments of darkness," linking them to the thick gloom that pervades the whole play and provides a cover under which evil can do its work. Even in daylight Macbeth and his wife invoke the night: "Come, thick night," Lady Macbeth cries as part of her prayer asking evil spirits to "unsex" her. Macbeth also calls for night to come, to blindfold "the tender eye of pitiful day" so that the killers he has hired can safely murder innocent Banquo and his son.

By setting many of the violent scenes at night and by making the scenes in *Macbeth* "murky," full of "fog and filthy air," and pierced by the cries of owls, Shakespeare suppresses all the pleasant associations night might have, especially as the time for refreshing sleep. Just as he commits his first murder, Macbeth thinks he hears a horrible voice crying, "Macbeth does murder sleep"; thereafter, he becomes an insomniac and his wife a sleepwalker. Darkness, voices, ghosts, hallucinations—these are used to express Macbeth's and his wife's surrender to evil and their subsequent despair.

Evil in *Macbeth* takes the form of violence and bloodshed. Right after the opening scene with the witches, a man covered with gashes appears before King Duncan, who asks, "What bloody man is that?" Between this scene and the final one, in which Macbeth's bleeding and "cursèd" head is displayed on a pike, human blood hardly stops running. Images of blood appeal not only to our sense of sight but also to our sense of touch (Macbeth's bloody and secret murders are "sticking on his hands" in the last act), and even to our sense of smell ("Here's the smell of the blood still," Lady Macbeth moans in Act V as she holds out her "little hand"). Such imagery is designed to make us feel moral revulsion, not just physical disgust: Bloodshed leads only to more bloodshed.

The Poetry: Expressing the Dark Night

All this imagery reminds us that *Macbeth* is a poem as well as a play—a dramatic poem sharing many of the characteristics of lyric poetry. The most obvious of these is **meter**, here the unrhymed iambic pentameter or **blank verse** that Shakespeare's predecessor Christopher Marlowe established as the appropriate medium for tragedy. Poetry is to tragedy as singing is to opera: It elevates and enhances the emotional impact of the experience being communicated. Indeed, without the poetry there could be no tragedy, because without it Shakespeare could not have expressed the dark night into which Macbeth's soul sinks. And a tragic poet is much more concerned with states of mind and feeling than with physical action. Macbeth shares with Shakespeare's other great tragic heroes—Hamlet, Lear, Othello—the ability to express in eloquent, moving language whatever he is feeling. One of the most famous speeches of this kind occurs when, near the end of his bloody career, Macbeth sums up what life means to him:

Out, out, brief candle!
Life's but a walking shadow, a poor player
That struts and frets his hour upon the stage
And then is heard no more. It is a tale
Told by an idiot, full of sound and fury,
Signifying nothing.

—Act V, Scene 5, lines 23–28

The bitter nihilism of these metaphors suggests that Macbeth is already dead in spirit, although his body must undergo a last battle. By murdering Duncan, he has murdered more than sleep: He has destroyed himself.

C Critical Thinking
Challenging the Text

? Do you agree with this critic's interpretation? [Sample responses: Yes, because it seems that the witches cast a spell over Macbeth, or he has been fated to follow the course he takes. No, Macbeth is susceptible to suggestions by Lady Macbeth and to the witches' prophecies, but he has a choice about whether or not to commit these murders.]

D Reading Skills and Strategies
Drawing Conclusions

? Why is it important that the reader feel "moral revulsion" in addition to "physical disgust"? [Possible response: The death of the traitor Macdonwald made the reader feel physical disgust but not moral revulsion, since the death could be viewed as justifiable. In order to recognize the extent of evil in the play, the reader must be repulsed by the immorality of Macbeth's later actions.]

E Appreciating Language
Blank Verse

Remind students that blank verse mimics the rhythms of natural, spoken English and that the speeches in the play are delivered as sentences, not as lines of poetry.

F Reading Skills and Strategies
Finding the Main Idea

? What is the main point the author is making here? [Possible answer: Poetry is well suited for Shakespeare's tragedies because through poetry, the tragic hero can eloquently express his state of mind.]

Skill Link

Identifying Main Idea and Supporting Details

Remind students that a **main idea** is a message, insight, or lesson that is the focus or key idea in a piece of writing. A selection usually contains more than one main idea. **Supporting details** are the facts and ideas that the writer includes to further develop, explain, or illustrate the main idea. One way to try to find main ideas in a critical essay is to look at the subheads. For instance, under the subhead *The Imagery: Darkness, Night, Blood,* five paragraphs appear, each of which has a main idea (usually found in the first sentence), followed by supporting details that help elaborate on the broader topic indicated by the subhead.

Activity

Ask students to record the main ideas and supporting details of each paragraph under this subhead, using a graphic organizer like the one on the right. Then, have students use their charts to write a concise summary of the section.

Paragraph	Main Idea	Supporting Details
1		
2		
3		
4		
5		

Connections

This feature focuses on **parody,** or the imitation of a work of literature, art, or music for amusement or instruction. Richard Armour parodies the first and third scenes of the play in which the witches predict great things for Macbeth and Banquo.

A Elements of Literature
Tone

? The tone in Armour's opening paragraph is quite different from Shakespeare's. How would you characterize the tone? What creates it? [Sample responses: References to a picnic and to the Edinburgh Ugly Contest create a humorous or playful tone.]

B Appreciating Language
Puns

? Shakespeare uses clever puns to add wit to the conversation in *Macbeth.* What puns does Armour use? What is the effect? [Possible answer: *Blowing* is used to refer to "forcibly pushing air out of the mouth" and "blowing up with an explosive." The idea of secretly planting bagpipes—a harmless Scottish musical instrument—in the enemy's camp is amusing.]

C Appreciating Language
Anachronism

? An **anachronism** is a reference to an object or word not in use at the time of the story. What is the effect of Armour's anachronisms? [References to sports and occupations that did not yet exist contribute to the humor.]

Resources
Listening

Audio CD Library

A recording of this short selection is provided in the *Audio CD Library:*

- CD 5, Track 4

Connections — A Parody

Nothing is impervious to **parody,** not even the high seriousness of a play like Shakespeare's *Macbeth.* In the following piece from *Twisted Tales from Shakespeare,* Richard Armour presents another view of the three weird sisters. You and your classmates might want to write a parody of your own.

Macbeth and the Witches

Richard Armour

A Three witches, extremely weird sisters, are having a picnic amidst thunder and lightning somewhere in Scotland. Judging from their appearance, they were placed one-two-three in the Edinburgh Ugly Contest.

"When shall we three meet again in thunder, lightning, or in rain?" asks one of them. They hate nice weather and are happiest when they are soaking wet and their hair is all stringy.

"When the hurly-burly's[1] done, when the battle's lost and won," another replies. A battle is going on between the forces of Duncan, the King of Scotland, and some Norwegians, assisted by the rebel Thane of Cawdor. At the moment it's looking good for Duncan, because B two of his generals, Macbeth and Banquo, have cunningly put bagpipes into the hands of the enemy, who are blowing their brains out.

The witches hear some dear friend[2] calling and depart. "Fair is foul, and foul is fair," they C comment philosophically as they leave. This must have been pretty upsetting to any moralists, semanticists, or baseball umpires who chanced to overhear them.

Shortly afterward, the battle having been won by Macbeth and the weather having turned bad enough to be pleasant, the witches meet again.

"Where hast thou been, Sister?" asks one.

"Killing swine," the second replies. All three of them have been busy doing similar diverting things, and one of them happily shows the others the thumb of a drowned sailor which she is adding to her thumb collection.[3]

1. See also hurdy-gurdy, hunky-dory, and okey-dokey.

2. A cat and a toad. Witches have to make friendships where they can.

3. In a comedy, this would be considered tragic relief.

The three witches and Lady Macbeth (in front) from the Faux-Real production of *Htebcam* (1994).

Connecting Across Texts

Connecting with *Macbeth*

Be sure that students know the definition of **parody:** the imitation of a work of literature, art, or music for amusement or instruction. Have students discuss why *Macbeth* is a good subject for parody. [It is a well-known classic. The language allows for many types of wordplay. It is such a somber piece of work that an amusing imitation seems all the more humorous. It is easy to make fun of many of the situations because they are so bizarre.] You might have students work in small groups to write a parody of another section of *Macbeth.* Suggest that they use techniques similar to those used by Richard Armour in his parody: changes of tone, puns, anachronisms, various types of wordplay, and amusing footnotes. When the parodies are complete, have each group read their parody to the entire class.

Macbeth and Banquo come by at this point, on their way to inform the King that they have defeated the rebels. They would rather tell him in person than render a report in triplicate.

"Speak, if you can," says Macbeth boldly to the hags. "What are you?" He rather thinks they are witches but would like to hear it from their own skinny lips.

The witches start hailing.[4] They hail Macbeth as Thane of Glamis and Thane of Cawdor and say he will be King Hereafter. Not to leave Banquo out, they hail him as "lesser than Macbeth, and greater." (The witches are masters of gobbledyspook.) He won't be a king, they say, but he'll beget kings, and now they have to begetting along.

Macbeth knows he is Thane of Glamis, but has no idea (or didn't have until now) of becoming Thane of Cawdor or King Hereafter. "Stay, you imperfect speakers, tell me more," he commands. But the witches, perhaps not liking the way he refers to their elocution, vanish into thin air, making it slightly thicker.

While Macbeth is meditating about what the witches have forecast for him, a couple of the King's henchmen, straight from a busy day of henching, ride up. They bring word that Duncan is liquidating the Thane of Cawdor and giving his title to Macbeth, it being an inexpensive gift. (Duncan, as King of Scotland, was Scotcher than anybody.)

"Look how our partner's rapt," remarks Banquo, noticing that Macbeth, stunned with all the good news, acts as if he has been struck on the noggin. But Macbeth is only lost in thought and will find his way out presently. Thus far the witches have been batting 1,000, and Macbeth is beginning to take more than a casual interest in Duncan's health.[5]

4. Until now it has been raining.
5. Henceforth, when he says "How are you?" to the King, it will be a bona fide question.

[These are Richard Armour's footnotes.]

Making Meanings

Act V

First Thoughts

1. How do you feel about what happens to Macbeth's body after he is dead?

Reading Check

a. Why, according to the doctor, is Lady Macbeth walking in her sleep?
b. In Scene 2, what opinion of Macbeth do the Scottish lords now hold?
c. When does Lady Macbeth die?
d. What is Macbeth's plan for dealing with the attacking troops? Why has he been forced to choose this plan?
e. What changes in his personality does Macbeth describe in Scene 5, lines 9–15?
f. In the speech in Scene 5 that begins "Tomorrow, and tomorrow, and tomorrow . . ." (lines 19–28), how does Macbeth describe life? What metaphors does he use?
g. How are the prophecies proclaimed by the three apparitions in Act IV, Scene 1, fulfilled in Act V?
h. At the end of the play, what has become of Macbeth? Who becomes King?

Shaping Interpretations

2. Theatrically, the spectacle of Lady Macbeth walking in her sleep is one of the most striking scenes in the play. It is entirely Shakespeare's invention, not found or suggested in his source. Why do you suppose Shakespeare has her walk in her sleep? How is this scene related to the remarks that Macbeth makes about sleep in Act II, Scene 2, just after he kills Duncan?
3. In the sleepwalking scene, Lady Macbeth refers to many of her waking experiences. For example, the words "One: two" may refer to the moment in Act II, Scene 1, when she struck the bell

Making Meanings

Act V

First Thoughts [Respond]

1. Students may pity Macbeth and be repulsed by the violence; or, they may feel he deserves such a death.

Shaping Interpretations [Interpret]

2. Lady Macbeth's sleepwalking reveals how she has changed. Intially she had been the cool planner, protecting Macbeth from betraying himself, and now she is wracked by guilt and betrays herself and her husband without realizing it. Her sleepwalking, like Macbeth's insomnia, reinforces the theme of Macbeth "murdering sleep."
3. (Some critics think "one: two" is the clock striking and not a reference to Duncan's death.) The washing of the hands and the command to put on the nightgown refer to her actions on the night of Duncan's murder. The Thane of Fife's wife refers to the murder of Lady Macduff. The burial of Banquo picks up on Macbeth's strange behavior at the banquet, where he thinks he sees Banquo's ghost .
4. Night and day may stand for tyranny and freedom, or evil and good. The remark foreshadows the outcome because it hints that Macbeth will be defeated.
5. Possible answers: The climax occurs with Macbeth's death; or, the climax occurs when Macduff reveals the details of his birth, and Macbeth realizes that he is doomed.
6. Possible answers: the "Tomorrow" soliloquy because it shows his resignation; or, the "I will not yield" speech, before he fights Macduff because it shows that he wants to face death bravely.

Reading Check

a. Her mind is "infected" with evil; she has a guilty conscience.
b. They think Macbeth has either gone mad or has become a cruel, violent tyrant.
c. She dies in Scene 5 as the enemy approaches.
d. In V.5.2–7, Macbeth plans to let the attackers besiege the castle and drive them off after they wear themselves out. He has been forced to adopt this plan because many of his troops have defected to help Malcolm. In V.5.51–52, Macbeth learns that Birnam Wood has come to Dunsinane, and he feels betrayed by the prophecies. Instead of yielding, however, he decides to fight and kill as many people as possible.
e. He has forgotten what it is like to fear; he is numb to horror.
f. He describes life as brief, dreary, and meaningless. Life is like a brief candle, a poor player strutting for a short time upon the stage, a story told by an idiot—noisy but without meaning.
g. Birnam Wood comes to Dunsinane, as the army uses branches to disguise its advance. Macduff is not "born of woman," since he was delivered by Caesarean section. Macbeth does fear Macduff, especially when Macbeth learns Macduff was not born naturally.
h. Macbeth is beheaded by Macduff. As planned by Duncan, Malcolm takes the throne.

Connecting with the Text [Apply]

7. Possible responses: Students may agree that an individual's life is trivial and leaves no lasting mark. Others may disagree, arguing that human life has meaning and that individuals can make a difference.

Challenging the Text [Evaluate]

8. Possible answers: It might make the other ghosts seem more real because Macbeth would not be the only person to see a ghost. It might focus too much attention on Lady Macbeth, or, it might add to the audience's understanding of her demise. Such a scene, however, might seem undignified or distract audiences with its unintentional humor.

The Play as a Whole

Shaping Interpretations [Interpret]

1. Like the first Thane of Cawdor, Macbeth oppresses the nation with his tyrannical rule. In effect, he does his country a service by dying. But Macbeth never begged pardon like Cawdor did, and he threw away his good name, honor, and integrity. In real life, convicted murderers sometimes repent.

2. Possible answers: No, the ending of the play shows the closing of the circle: Malcolm becomes king and order is restored; justice triumphs and good overcomes evil. Yes, the play shows that evil, as manifested in Macbeth, can overcome good.

3. Possible answers: Yes, the reader feels sorry that he gives in to murderous impulses because he has the potential to be good; or, no, the reader can feel no sympathy for such a brutal person. Many students will have lost sympathy when Macbeth killed Duncan, or if not then, later in the play when he has Lady Macduff and her son killed.

4. Macbeth turns his strengths—courage in battle, ambition, imagination—to evil use. He values the opinions of others; this quality serves him honorably (I.7.32–35), but also leads him to be swayed by Lady Macbeth's opinions (in the same scene).

5. Possible responses: One of the grooms awakens in time to avert the murder of Duncan; Banquo warns the king about the witches' prophecies and puts him on his guard. Either of these might have thwarted Macbeth's plans and perhaps have saved him from himself.

6. Internal conflicts such as ambition versus morality, loyalty versus treachery, and honesty versus deception relate to the murder of Duncan and Banquo. External conflicts occur between Macbeth and Banquo, as Macbeth worries that Banquo's descendants will dethrone him, and between Macbeth and Macduff, as Macduff grows to distrust him. In the end, Macbeth and his wife have guilty consciences due to internal conflicts. Macduff kills Macbeth.

(continued on p. T389)

Resources

Selection Assessment

Formal Assessment

- Selection Test, p. 65

Test Generator (One-Stop Planner)

- CD-ROM

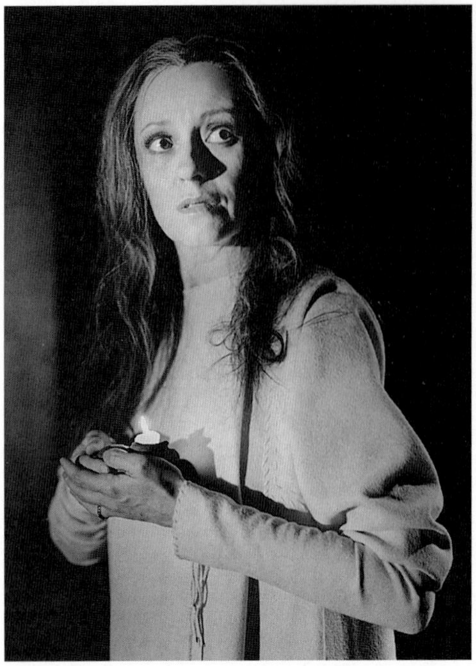

Lady Macbeth holding a candle in a dark hallway.
From the Stratford Festival production of *Macbeth* (1983).

signaling Macbeth to go kill Duncan. Find traces of other experiences in what she says while sleepwalking.

4. At the end of Act IV, Malcolm says, "The night is long that never finds the day." In what metaphorical sense does he use the terms *night* and *day*? How does his remark **foreshadow** the outcome of the play?

5. The last act of *Macbeth* contains the play's **climax**—the most emotional and suspenseful part of the action—the moment when the characters' conflict is finally resolved. Which part of Act V do you consider the climax? Explain.

6. Shakespeare gave most of his **tragic heroes** an impressive dying speech in which they say something significant about their own life and death. Although he did not write such a speech for Macbeth, which speech of Macbeth's do you think serves in the play as his dying speech? Why do you select this speech rather than some other one?

Connecting with the Text

7. What are your reactions to the idea expressed by Macbeth that life "is a tale / Told by an idiot, full of sound and fury, / Signifying nothing" (Scene 5, lines 26–28)? Explain your response.

Challenging the Text

8. Sometime shortly after 1660, a playwright named William Davenant (who claimed to be a natural son of Shakespeare) added another sleepwalking scene to *Macbeth:* He had the ghost of Duncan chase Lady Macbeth about the stage. How might this scene change the way audiences perceive Lady Macbeth's character? Might it make the other ghosts in the play seem any more or less real? What might the scene add to the play, and what might it take away?

The Play as a Whole

Shaping Interpretations

1. "Nothing in his life / Became him like the leaving it," says Malcolm in Act I, referring to the traitorous Thane of Cawdor. Malcolm also says that this Thane of Cawdor threw away the dearest thing he owned. How might these two statements also apply to Macbeth? Could these lines apply to any people in actual life?

2. One of the **themes** of *Macbeth* centers on evil, which Shakespeare saw as a force beyond human understanding. Do you think Shakespeare also saw evil as stronger than the forces of good? Support your answer with events from the play.

3. The philosopher Aristotle argued that a bad man cannot be the principal character of a tragedy. Does Shakespeare keep you from losing all sympathy for Macbeth in spite of Macbeth's increasing viciousness? Was there a point at which you lost sympathy for Macbeth? If so, where?

4. One critic has observed that part of Macbeth's tragedy is the fact that many of his strengths are also his weaknesses. Explain this apparent contradiction in Macbeth's **character.** What are his strengths? Which ones also work against him?

5. Think of a single event, at any time during the course of the play, that could have averted Macbeth's tragic end. What would this event be?

How could it have come about? How would it affect the outcome of the play?

6. **Internal conflicts** rage within Macbeth, as well as **external conflicts** with other characters. Explain some of the play's main conflicts, and trace their **resolution.**

Extending the Text

7. What modern figure, real or fictional, had a downfall, like Macbeth's, that came after an attempt to gain great power? How is this modern figure like Macbeth, and how different? Would this modern figure make a good **tragic hero**? Refer to your Quickwrite notes (see page 300) as you answer this question.

Challenging the Text

8. Think about the quotation from Goethe on page 281. Do you think Macbeth himself has the free will to control his own destiny? Or is he controlled by fate?
9. Do you think people should **parody** a great tragic play like *Macbeth,* the way Richard Armour does in "Macbeth and the Witches" (see ***Connections*** on page 386)? Why or why not?

ELEMENTS OF LITERATURE

Imagery and Figurative Language

Macbeth's poetry is rich in imagery and figurative language that help to create atmosphere and reveal character and theme.

1. Powerful images in the play contrast the natural and the unnatural, as in Lady Macbeth's speech in Act I, Scene 7, lines 54–59:

. . . I have given suck, and know
How tender 'tis to love the babe that milks me:
I would, while it was smiling in my face,
Have plucked my nipple from his boneless gums,
And dashed the brains out, had I so sworn as you
Have done to this.

a. What unnatural sounds and events are reported in Act II, Scenes 2–4? Look at the **context** of these images. What mood do they create?

b. Look at the witches' scenes. What would you say is the emotional effect of each scene? Besides the witches themselves, what unnatural images occur in these scenes?

2. We hear about sleep and sleeplessness throughout the play. How is sleep described in these figures of speech?

a. **First Witch.** . . . I'll drain him dry as hay:
Sleep shall neither night nor day
Hang upon his penthouse lid; . . .

—Act I, Scene 3, lines 18–30

b. **Macbeth.** Methought I heard a voice cry "Sleep no more!
Macbeth does murder sleep"—the innocent sleep,
Sleep that knits up the raveled sleave of care,
The death of each day's life, sore labor's bath,
Balm of hurt minds, great nature's second course,
Chief nourisher in life's feast—

—Act II, Scene 2, lines 34–39

3. Choose one of the following images, and find three speeches (from different scenes in the play) in which the image occurs:

blood   darkness   disease   planting

Look back at the **context** of each speech (what happens just before and after): What is the emotional effect of each one?

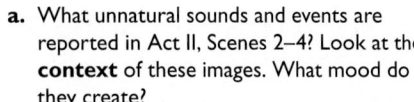

Francesca Annis and Jon Finch in Roman Polanski's film production of *Macbeth* (1971).

Extending the Text [Synthesize]

7. Students may mention a variety of modern tyrants and dictators: Adolf Hitler, Joseph Stalin, Ferdinand Marcos, Manuel Noriega, or Pol Pot. Such leaders may be like Macbeth in their methods and motivations but unlike him in circumstances. Students may say that some of these figures would make tragic heroes because they had the potential for greatness but also flaws that precipitated their descent into evil. Some students may see these figures as fully evil and completely unworthy of the label "tragic hero."

Challenging the Text [Synthesize and Evaluate]

8. Possible answers: Macbeth's fate is merely foretold by the witches; he is the one who kills Duncan, conspires against Banquo, and has Macduff's family murdered; or, Macbeth is under the spell of the witches who plant the seeds of murder in his head, create the brew that draws him into their conspiracy, and trick him into believing that he is invincible. Students may argue that Shakespeare deliberately left the witches' roles ambiguous.
9. Possible answers: Yes, parody is a good reminder not to take ourselves or our literary idols too seriously; or, no, writers should not make fun of a well-written piece of literature that teaches worthwhile lessons about human nature.

Resources

Elements of Literature
Imagery and Figurative Language
For additional instruction on imagery and figurative language, see *Literary Elements*:

- Transparency 11
- Worksheet, p. 34

ELEMENTS OF LITERATURE

Imagery and Figurative Language
Possible Answers

1. a. In Scene 2, Macbeth reports that someone cried out "Murder" while asleep and that he heard a voice accusing him of "murdering sleep." Scene 3 includes the knocking that unnerves Macbeth and Lady Macbeth. Lennox's speech (II.3.48–55) chronicles the night's unusual weather and events, as does the dialogue between Ross and the Old Man (II.4.1–20). These images create an eerie mood suitable for the unnatural act of murder.

b. Students may say that the scenes are creepy, disturbing, or strange. Unnatural images include the attending toad, the strange comments regarding sailing in a sieve, the taking of a pilot's thumb, the witches' appearances and disappearances into thin air, and the horrific ingredients for the brew.

2. a. Sleep is something that weighs on the eyelid.

b. Sleep is an untangler, the death of the day, a bath, a balm, and food.

3. Possible answers:
Blood: II.1.46–47; II.3.105–110; III.4.122–126.
Darkness: I.5.48–52; II.4.6–10; III.2.46–53
Disease: IV.3.141–145; V.1.62–64; V.3.37–45
Planting: I.4.28–29; IV.1.58–61; V.8.64–69.
Answers regarding the emotional effects of each scene will vary.

Grading Timesaver

Rubrics for each Choices assignment appear on p. 124 in the *Portfolio Management System.*

CHOICES: Building Your Portfolio

1. **Writer's Notebook** Remind students that an effect can have multiple causes. Encourage them to be thorough in their search of the text.
2. **Analyzing a Character** Ask students to cite specific references to speeches by Lady Macbeth, discuss why Shakespeare might have included particular wording or actions, and tell what these words or actions suggest.
3. **Analyzing the Writer's Purpose** Before students begin writing, have them review Macbeth's speeches to look for places in the play in which he uses the same techniques as the witches (equivocation, or deceit through ambiguity). This will allow students to see the question in a broader perspective.
4. **Analyzing Tragedy** As a prewriting exercise, suggest that students organize information on a chart. They should write the elements of tragedy across the top of the chart. Below each, they should give examples of how *Macbeth* either meets or does not meet each criterion.
5. **Creative Writing** Remind students that although the setting is modernized, the characters must retain the personalities that Shakespeare created. To pinpoint a character's key traits, students may want to create a word cluster.
6. **Oral Interpretation** Suggest that students experiment with various readings to find the most effective pitch, tempo, volume, and pace. Ask them to recopy the speech in large, readable letters and to make notations, indicating where pauses for emphasis would be effective.
7. **Art** Suggest that students research the type of furniture and clothing used in Scotland in the mid-eleventh century.

CHOICES: Building Your Portfolio

Writer's Notebook

1. Collecting Ideas for a Cause-Effect Essay

With cause and effect, we often work backward: We are first aware of the effect and then we search for the cause(s). For Thomas De Quincey, the porter scene in *Macbeth* produced a certain effect, "a peculiar awfulness and a depth of solemnity." In the ***Connections*** essay on page 330, De Quincey explores the cause of this increased tension. What scenes in *Macbeth* had a strong emotional effect on you? Go back to the play and find the words and actions that caused this effect. Save your work for the Writer's Workshop on page 459.

Analyzing a Character

2. Monster or Not?

Lady Macbeth is sometimes regarded as a monster, ruthlessly ambitious and fiendishly cruel. What clues can you find in the play suggesting that Shakespeare did not want us to judge her so severely? In an essay, analyze her character as it is revealed through her words and actions and her relationship with Macbeth.

Analyzing the Writer's Purpose

3. Probing Shakespeare's Mind

When Macbeth discovers how Macduff entered the world (Act V, Scene 8), he also discovers that the witches are "juggling fiends" who have given him a false sense of security. Why do you think Shakespeare shows Macbeth taken in by their prophecies? What might Shakespeare be implying about Macbeth's **character**? about the witches' powers? Is he suggesting that Macbeth might be a victim of mysterious evil forces? Write your answer in one or two paragraphs.

Analyzing Tragedy

4. A Tragic Structure

Traditionally, critics have thought of the following as the classic elements of a Shakespearean tragedy: (a) a **protagonist, the tragic hero,** a man of high estate, whose desires or conflicts set the action in motion; (b) an **antagonist** who blocks this protagonist; (c) a **rising action** in which **complications** develop, leading in the third act to a **turning point**; (d) a **falling action** that inexorably leads to a tragic **climax;** (e) a **resolution,** in which the social order that had been torn asunder by the action is restored. In an essay, analyze *Macbeth*, showing how the play does or does not follow this tragic pattern.

Creative Writing

5. Macbeth Today

Rewrite the banquet scene (Act III, Scene 4), when Macbeth sees Banquo's ghost. Change the setting to a modern time and place, and let the characters speak in today's language. For example, Lady Macbeth might explain that Macbeth is suffering from stress. The Scottish lords might be cabinet members. Provide a list of characters that includes a phrase describing each character.

Oral Interpretation

6. Say the Soliloquy

With a small group, select one of Macbeth's soliloquies and "perform" it in the way a choir interprets a song: Vary voice pitches, volume, tempo, rhythm, meter, and tone. Repeat key lines as a refrain, and use echoing words, vocal sound effects, harmony, and chanting to accentuate and enhance the words.

Art

7. Bring a Scene to Life

Sketch the set and costumes you would provide for at least one scene of *Macbeth.* In set design, you must indicate placement of furniture and describe lighting. Costume sketches must describe materials and colors.

Reading Skills and Strategies

Vocabulary: Mapping Meanings

If you draw on your own personal knowledge and experience when learning a new word, the word more readily becomes a part of your working vocabulary. **Mapping** is a vocabulary-building strategy that encourages active participation. Mapping works like this: First, you see a new word used in a sentence. Before you look up the dictionary definition, you use **context clues** to guess at the word's meaning. After you look the word up in the dictionary, you use the word in a sentence of your own and become familiar with its different forms. Here's an example of mapping:

corporal →

Banquo: Whither are they vanished?
Macbeth: Into the air, and what seemed **corporal** melted
As breath into the wind.

Your guess: Something solid. **Context** suggests corporal is something that doesn't melt like breath. Corpse, a dead body, is a word that sounds similar. Perhaps there's some relation.

Definition: of the body; bodily.

Your sentence: Corporal punishment in schools has often been the subject of heated debates.

Other forms: corporally (adv.)

Here are some helpful suggestions for using mapping as one of your vocabulary-building strategies:

1. Have you heard the word before? Maybe you've heard a word that sounds similar to it.
2. Are there any context clues in the sentence?
3. Try substituting your guess for the word. Does it make sense in the context?
4. Many words have **multiple meanings.** When you look up the word in the dictionary, make sure you read all the definitions. Select the one that fits best; make sure that it's the right part of speech. *Corporal,* for example, can also refer to an officer in the army. But that definition doesn't work here, and, besides, it's a noun. You're looking for an adjective in this context.
5. Think about the other forms of the word for a few moments. You might also want to use them in some sentences.

Try It Out

In each sentence below, the vocabulary word is given in boldface. Using the mapping example for the word *corporal* as a guide, draw your own map for each of the following words.

1. **Macbeth.** . . . Thou sure and firm-set earth,
Hear not my steps, which way they walk, for fear
Thy very stones **prate** of my whereabout,
And take the present horror from the time,
Which now suits with it.
—Act II, Scene 1, lines 56–60

2. **Lady Macbeth. Infirm** of purpose!
Give me the daggers. The sleeping and the dead
Are but as pictures. 'Tis the eye of childhood
That fears a painted devil.
—Act II, Scene 2, lines 51–54

3. **Macbeth.** . . .Will all great Neptune's ocean wash this blood
Clean from my hand? No; this my hand will rather
The **multitudinous** seas incarnadine,
Making the green one red.
—Act II, Scene 2, lines 59–62

4. **Macduff.** Confusion now hath made his masterpiece.
Most **sacrilegious** murder hath broke ope
The Lord's anointed temple, and stole thence
The life o' th' building.
—Act II, Scene 3, lines 60–63

Reading Skills and Strategies

This feature explains the strategy of mapping to help determine word meanings and applies it to *Macbeth.*

Mini-Lesson: Mapping

Begin by having a class discussion about how students treat an unknown word in a text they are reading. Do they try to use context clues to unlock the meaning? Do they stop to look it up in the dictionary? Or do they just read on? Discuss the benefits and problems resulting from each strategy. Then have students read the explanation in the text on how to use mapping to determine word meaning. When they have finished, lead them through the mapping process with a new word from the play, modeling this process on the board.

Try It Out

As students prepare to do the Try It Out exercises, explain that when they create sentences with unfamiliar words, the results may sound stiff or unnatural. For example, words like *prate* may not fit smoothly into a modern English sentence. Because these unfamiliar words may be difficult for some students to use, have students work in pairs so that they can concentrate on the process of mapping. Students may not be able to find other forms for some of the words.

Possible Answers

1. prate: to talk idly; chatter (v); foolish or trivial talk (n)
2. infirm: weak; irresolute (adj); infirmity (n)
3. multitudinous: very numerous (adj); multitude (n)
4. sacrilegious: disrespectful of something sacred (adj); sacrilege (n)

Using Students' Strengths

Spatial Learners

Some students may wish to include a pictorial element in their word mapping, associating an image with each word.

Verbal Learners

Suggest that some students include etymologies in their maps.

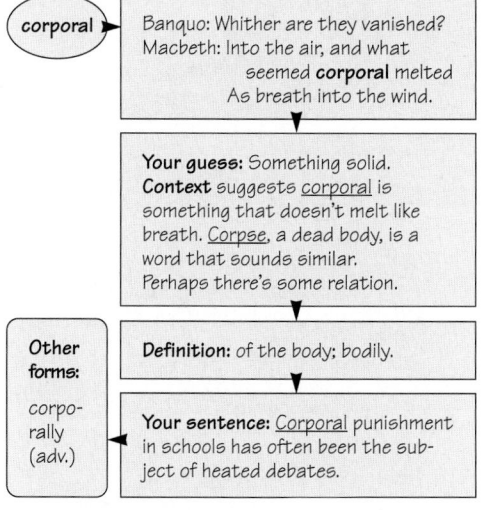

OBJECTIVES

1. Read and interpret the epic poem excerpt
2. Generate relevant, interesting, and researchable questions
3. Recognize distinctive and shared characteristics of cultures
4. Compare text events with contemporary experiences and values

SKILLS

Viewing/Representing

- Analyze details in paintings (ATE)

Planning

- **Traditional Schedule**
  Lesson Plans Including Strategies for English-Language Learners
- **One-Stop Planner**
  CD-ROM with Test Generator

RESPONDING TO THE ART

Domenico di Michelino (1414–1491) (born Domenico di Francesco) took his name from his teacher, a carver of bone and ivory. Domenico's sole surviving work is *Dante Reading from the Divine Comedy,* a detail of which is shown here. He painted it for the Florence Cathedral in six months, receiving a bonus of fifty percent for his fine work.

Activity. Ask students to look carefully at the details of this painting. At the left, a figure laboriously climbs one of the tiers of the underworld (perhaps Purgatory). Dante is crowned with laurel, the classic tribute to victors. The book of poems he holds emits a beatific light. A city is seen in the background to the right, with a beast rising above it.

WORLD LITERATURE

Italy

Dante Alighieri

(1265–1321)

Dante Alighieri (dän′tā a′lə·gyer′ē) decided to write his masterpiece, *The Divine Comedy,* in Italian rather than in Latin, and thus became the father of Italian literature. Dante was born in Florence, but his involvement in the violent politics of his city led to his banishment for life—Dante was warned that he would be burned at the stake if he were ever found in Florence again.

The Divine Comedy, completed during Dante's exile, is the supreme and culminating work of medieval thought. Many people consider this complex, symbolic poem to be the greatest poem ever written in any language. In three sections, Dante tells of an imaginary journey that takes him through Hell, Purgatory, and Heaven. In the course of his journey, Dante gives expression to nearly every major intellectual conception achieved in the Middle Ages.

Dante and His Poems (detail) (1465) by Domenico di Michelino.
Duomo, Florence.

(Map) Old map showing the Mediterranean Coast.

Resources

Listening

Audio CD Library

For a recording of this canto, see

- Disc 5, Track 5

Before You Read

FROM **THE INFERNO OF DANTE**

Background

If you had to name the three most evil people of all time, who would be on your list? The sinner at the pit of Hell in Dante's *Inferno* is Judas Iscariot, who suffers the greatest torment of all because he betrayed Jesus Christ to the Romans. The other two "worst" sinners whom Dante puts in the very jaws of Satan may come as a surprise—although you have probably met them in Shakespeare: Brutus and Cassius, the conspirators of ancient Rome who plotted the assassination of Julius Caesar. Another surprise is Dante's description of the worst part of Hell: Instead of a burning pit of fire and brimstone, the bottom of Hell is a ghastly, windswept lake of ice.

Dante's journey to Hell takes place in the first part of his long epic poem, *The Divine Comedy.* (The epic is a comedy in the sense that it has a happy ending.) Led by the poet Virgil, who, for Dante, symbolized human reason, Dante travels to the Inferno down through a kind of deep funnel that bores into the center of the earth. Around this abysmal cavity run nine ledges, or circles, which grow ever narrower as the cavity bores deeper into the earth. On each circle a certain kind of sin is punished. The sins of the flesh are on the upper circle, where punishment is mildest. Sins of anger are in the middle, and sins against reason are on the lowest circles, where torment is greatest.

Dante in the Valley of Terrors (late 19th to early 20th century) by William Frank Calderon.

From the Inferno, Dante ascends gradually through Purgatory. Then Virgil turns his traveler over to a woman named Beatrice ("blessed") who leads Dante into Paradise, where he is granted a blissful vision of God and salvation. What Dante learns of sin from visiting the agonies of Hell, of renunciation in witnessing the trials in Purgatory, and of joy in sharing the glories of Paradise will turn him from error forever.

As this part of *The Inferno* opens, Dante and his guide approach the last circle of Hell. It is dominated by the gigantic winged figure of Satan, frozen in ice.

Quickwrite

How do you envision Hell? Freewrite a description of what you think Hell might be like.

go.hrw.com
LEO 12-4

Summary ■■■

This Canto is extremely difficult but the struggle to read it will pay off. *The Divine Comedy* has been called the greatest poem in the world, and senior-level students should have some awareness of what the great epic is all about. They will be helped if they can visualize the setting of the Inferno: nine ledges which grow ever narrower as they bore into the center of the earth. Students will be interested in the colossal figure of Satan, frozen in ice at the bottom of the pit, his leathery wings so huge that the pilgrims mistake them for the arms of a windmill. They will also be intrigued by the idea of hell being an icy realm.

In this canto, Dante and his guide, Virgil, descend into Judecca, the innermost part of hell and the center of the earth. There they encounter Satan's frozen, gigantic, three-faced head, each face with a mouth that chews and tortures a sinner: Judas Iscariot, Brutus, and Cassius, all of whom committed acts of betrayal. Virgil leads Dante away from Satan's head and guides him up Satan's legs to the outside world. The canto ends just before dawn on Easter morning, with the two men glimpsing stars in the heavens.

Background

Dante's concept of various levels of punishment in hell somewhat parallels a theory known as the Great Chain of Being, popular during the Renaissance. This theory proposes that the universe is an infinite series of stations, ranging from the lowest level of existence, to the most perfect, which is God.

RESPONDING TO THE ART

Tell students that these wild beasts in Dante's path represent particular sins: the Leopard of Malice and Fraud, the Lion of Violence and Ambition, and the She-Wolf of Incontinence.

Activity. Ask students to think of various symbols that represent sins or evils or dangers today.

Professional Notes

Critical Comment: Virgil Leads the Way

Generally regarded as the greatest of the classical Roman poets, Virgil (70–19 B.C.) had enormous influence on Western thought and English literature. His greatest work is the *Aeneid,* which describes the founding of Rome and the city's attempts to conquer the world. Also influential are Virgil's *Eclogues,* ten pastoral poems that celebrate rural life and mourn the loss of farms. During the Middle Ages, some people saw the fourth *Eclogue* as a prophecy of the birth of Christ and the *Aeneid* as an expression of near-Christian values. Dante's reverence for Virgil is evident in the *Divine Comedy,* where Virgil appears as Dante's spiritual guide.

Ⓐ Critical Thinking

Making Connections

? In the complete work from which this selection is taken, Dante explains that the Ninth Circle is the place for those who commit "Sins of Fraud which Break Special Obligations." This Circle has several rings. The First Ring contains "Betrayers of Relatives"; the Second Ring, "Betrayers of their Country"; the Third Ring, "Betrayers of Guests"; and the Fourth Ring, "Betrayers of the Redeemer and Emperor." In which ring would you place Macbeth? Why? [Possible response: Macbeth fits appropriately in all four rings. By slaying Duncan, Macbeth defrauds the country of its rightful ruler and in the process betrays his friends Banquo, Macduff, and Malcolm, who is also his cousin, and guest.]

Ⓑ Elements of Literature

Theme

? In what way does Satan reflect the "Fair is foul, and foul is fair" motif of *Macbeth?* [Possible response: Satan, the epitome of evil, was at one time a beautiful angel.]

Ⓒ Reading Skills and Strategies

Making Inferences

? Why is it important for Dante to "arm" himself "with the quality of fortitude"? [Possible answer: Dante will need all the courage he possesses to face Satan.]

Answer to Margin Question

Lines 7–18. The immense figure of Satan looks like a mill, his wings like blades. The ice-covered dead look like straw sheathed in glass; the body of one is bent like a bow.

from The Inferno of Dante

Dante Alighieri

translated by **Robert Pinsky**

Ⓐ Canto 34

"And now, *Vexilla regis prodeunt*
Inferni°—therefore, look," my master said
As we continued on the long descent,

"And see if you can make him out, ahead."
As though, in the exhalation of heavy mist
Or while night darkened our hemisphere, one spied

A mill—blades turning in the wind, half-lost
Off in the distance—some structure of that kind
I seemed to make out now. But at a gust

Of wind, there being no other shelter at hand,
I drew behind my leader's back again.
By now (and putting it in verse I find

Fear in myself still) I had journeyed down
To where the shades were covered wholly by ice,°
Showing like straw in glass—some lying prone,

And some erect, some with the head toward us,
And others with the bottoms of the feet;
Another like a bow, bent feet to face.

When we had traveled forward to the spot
From which it pleased my master to have me see
Ⓑ That creature° whose beauty once had been so great,

He made me stop, and moved from in front of me.
Ⓒ "Look: here is Dis," he said, "and here is the place
Where you must arm yourself with the quality

Of fortitude." How chilled and faint I was
On hearing that, you must not ask me, reader—
I do not write it; words would not suffice:

I neither died, nor kept alive—consider
With your own wits what I, alike denuded
Of death and life, became as I heard my leader.

2. *Vexilla regis prodeunt / Inferni:* Latin for "The banners of the king of Hell advance." These words perversely echo a well-known Latin hymn.

14. where . . . ice: This is Judecca (jo͞o · dek′ə), the final division of Cocytus (kō · sīt′əs) and the innermost part of Hell. Judecca is named for Judas Iscariot, who betrayed Jesus.

? **7–18.** *What comparisons does Dante use to help you visualize what the narrator sees?*

21. creature: Satan. Dante also calls him by the names Lucifer, Beelzebub, and Dis. Before Satan rebelled against God and was cast down from Heaven, he was an angel of tremendous beauty.

Reaching All Students

Struggling Readers

Many students will not know enough about Catholicism to understand the symbolism in Dante. Briefly explain (or have students familiar with Catholicism explain) the ideas of Heaven, Purgatory, and Hell. The concept of such a stratified afterlife may be new to some students. The selection itself will be challenging for all readers. Listening to it read on audiotape will aid comprehension.

English Language Learners

Students will need help understanding the progression of the poem. As students read, have them work with a partner dividing the text into sections and summarizing each part in a few short sentences. For other strategies for English language learners, see

- *Lesson Plans Including Strategies for English-Language Learners*

Advanced Learners

Ask students to explore and report on the concepts of "hell" in various religions. In brief, students will find that Judaism, Christianity, and Islam conceive of a fiery realm (though the details vary and a sinner's stay there is not necessarily eternal), while Hinduism and Buddhism hold to multiple, escapable "hells." As students read, urge them to contrast these ideas with Dante's concept of hell.

The emperor of the realm of grief protruded
From mid-breast up above the surrounding ice.
A giant's height, and mine, would have provided

Closer comparison than would the size
Of his arm and a giant. Envision the whole
That is proportionate to parts like these.

If he was truly once as beautiful
As he is ugly now, and raised his brows
Against his Maker—then all sorrow may well

Come out of him. How great a marvel it was
For me to see three faces° on his head:
In front there was a red one; joined to this,

Each over the midpoint of a shoulder, he had
Two others—all three joining at the crown.
That on the right appeared to be a shade

Of whitish yellow; the third had such a mien
As those who come from where the Nile descends.
Two wings spread forth from under each face's chin,

Strong, and befitting such a bird, immense—
I have never seen at sea so broad a sail—
Unfeathered, batlike, and issuing three winds

That went forth as he beat them, to freeze the whole
Realm of Cocytus that surrounded him.
He wept with all six eyes, and the tears fell

Over his three chins mingled with bloody foam.
The teeth of each mouth held a sinner, kept
As by a flax rake: thus he held three of them

In agony. For the one the front mouth gripped,
The teeth were as nothing to the claws, which sliced
And tore the skin until his back was stripped.

"That soul," my master said, "who suffers most,
Is Judas Iscariot; head locked inside,
He flails his legs. Of the other two, who twist

With their heads down, the black mouth holds the shade
Of Brutus: writhing, but not a word will he scream;
Cassius is the sinewy one on the other side.

31. *Who is the "emperor of the realm of grief"?*

41. three faces: grotesque perversion of the Trinity.

Inscription over Hell Gate (late 18th to early 19th century) by William Blake.
Tate Gallery, London.

D Reading Skills and Strategies

Making Inferences

Why do you think Satan has three faces? Why are they different colors? [Sample responses: Three is an important number in Christian theology because it signifies the Christian Trinity of the father, son, and Holy Ghost. The triple-faced image of Satan is a parody—or grotesque perversion—of this concept. Perhaps the various colors of his faces represent the different races of human beings, indicating that no race is free of evil.]

E Critical Thinking

Extending the Text

Virgil describes the three men whom Dante considers the worst sinners (betrayers) or criminals in history. What kinds of people are considered the world's worst criminals now? [Sample responses: serial killers; leaders, such as Hitler or Pol Pot, who commit genocide; people who hurt children; terrorists]

F Literary Connections

The Tragedy of Julius Caesar

Why are Brutus and Cassius in the Ninth Circle of hell? [Brutus and Cassius not only conspire against their leader, Julius Caesar, but they also kill him.] **How are their sins like those of Judas?** [Judas, too, betrayed his leader and friend, Jesus, to the Romans who crucified him.]

Answer to Margin Question
Line 31. Satan.

Responding to the Art

William Blake (1757–1827), who was nearly penniless at the time of his death, was working on a cycle of drawings based on Dante's work. The inscription Dante says appears over the gate to hell is "Abandon all hope, you who enter!"

Activity. Ask students to point out the details and color Blake uses in his painting to portray Hell as a terrible place.

Using Students' Strengths

Auditory/Musical Learners

To help students appreciate the mood and rhythm of the poem, have them locate appropriate background music for the canto. You might suggest exploring liturgical music or some modern atonal pieces. Students should bring a recording of the music they choose to play for the class. Students can read the canto while the music is playing.

Kinesthetic Learners

Invite groups of students to act out the poem. Have them assume the roles of the narrator, Dante, and Virgil. The students playing Dante and Virgil can read the dialogue; the narrator can read the rest. Emphasize that Virgil and Dante should not merely recite their lines but should use gestures and facial expressions to convey the action. (Note that the auditory and kinesthetic learners could work together, the first group providing the music for the reading by the second.)

Ⓐ Elements of Literature

Allegory

? How might Virgil's words apply to more than the task at hand? [Possible answer: He is talking about climbing up the legs of Satan but also about the difficulty of turning away from evil in general.]

Answer to Margin Question
Lines 40–68. Satan's.

Responding to the Art

Pieter Bruegel (1525/30–1569) is considered the greatest Dutch painter of his time. He depicted political and social, allegorical, and Biblical subjects. His paintings, with titles such as *The Blind Leading the Blind, Avarice,* and *Triumph of Death* (featured here), seem to indicate that Bruegel had a pessimistic and tragic view of humanity.

Activity. Ask students to describe all the things they see happening in this painting. Can they locate the people fighting Death, who is mounted on a horse in the center of the painting, wielding a scythe? Have them note also people being ferried across the River Styx at the left.

But night is rising again, and it is time
  That we depart, for we have seen the whole."
  As he requested, I put my arms round him,

And waiting until the wings were opened full
  He took advantage of the time and place
  And grasped the shaggy flank, and gripping still,

From tuft to tuft descended through the mass
  Of matted hair and crusts of ice. And then,
  When we had reached the pivot of the thighs,°

Just where the haunch is at its thickest, with strain
  And effort my master brought around his head
  To where he'd had his legs: and from there on

He grappled the hair as someone climbing would—
  So I supposed we were heading back to Hell.
  "Cling tight, for it is stairs like these," he sighed

? **40–68.** *Reread the description of this "emperor of grief" and try to draw what you see. After you read lines 69–80, stop and explain whose wings and flank and hair the narrator is referring to.*

75. pivot of the thighs: This midpoint of Satan's body is also the center of the earth. At this spot Virgil turns himself upside down because henceforth the travelers must journey *up* Satan's legs in order to reach the surface of the Southern Hemisphere.

The Triumph of Death (c. 1562) by Pieter Bruegel the Elder. Oil on panel. Prado, Madrid.

Crossing the Curriculum

Social Studies

Have students research the Great Chain of Being, the concept of metaphysical and natural hierarchy popular during the Renaissance. You might also have them look into the doctrine of correspondences, in which the highest-ranking members of one group correspond to the highest-ranking members of another group. For instance, the lion, the greatest of the animals, corresponds to the king, the greatest of the humans, causing one often to be used as a symbol for the other. Ask students to create a poster comparing the levels suggested by one of these Renaissance theories to the levels of hell in Dante's epic poem. Students should share their posters with the class.

Art

Have students create a diorama of the innermost circle of hell. Ask them to base their artwork on details given in Dante's text.

Like one who is exhausted, "which we must scale
To part from so much evil." Then he came up
Through a split stone, and placed me on its sill,

And climbed up toward me with his cautious step.
I raised my eyes, expecting I would see
Lucifer as I left him—and saw his shape

Inverted, with his legs held upward. May they
Who are too dull to see what point I had passed **B**
Judge whether it perplexed me. "Come—the way

Is long, the road remaining to be crossed **C**
Is hard: rise to your feet," the master said,
"The sun is at mid-tierce."° We had come to rest

In nothing like a palace hall; instead
A kind of natural dungeon enveloped us,
With barely any light, the floor ill made.

"Before I free myself from the abyss,
My master," I said when I was on my feet,
"Speak, and dispel my error: where is the ice?

And how can he be fixed head-down like that?
And in so short a time, how can it be
Possible for the sun to make its transit

From evening to morning?" He answered me,
"You imagine you are still on the other side,
Across the center of the earth, where I

Grappled the hair on the evil serpent's hide
Who pierces the world. And all through my descent,
You were on that side; when I turned my head

And legs about, you passed the central point
To which is drawn, from every side, all weight.
Now you are on the opposite continent

Beneath the opposite hemisphere to that **D**
Which canopies the great dry land therein:
Under the zenith of that one is the site

Whereon the Man was slain° who without sin
Was born and lived; your feet this minute press
Upon a little sphere whose rounded skin

? **90.** *Can you infer what point it is that they have just passed?*

93. mid-tierce: Formerly, tierce was the period from 6:00 to 9:00 A.M. (the first third of the day), so mid-tierce is about 7:30 A.M. In Hell, the sun is never consulted in telling time, but now that Dante and Virgil have emerged from Hell, the sun is used for that purpose.

115. Under the zenith . . . slain: Under the zenith, or highest point, of the Northern Hemisphere's sky—a point reached directly through the earth and thus "opposite" where Dante and Virgil now stand—is the city of Jerusalem, the site where Jesus Christ, "the Man," was slain.

B Appreciating Language

Terza Rima

Point out that Dante used a rhyme scheme called *terza rima,* which consists of sequences of *tercets,* three lines of interlocking rhyme. The rhyme scheme is *aba bcb ded* and so on. The advantage of *terza rima* is that in three lines the poet can express a thought in such a way that it can stand on its own, while, at the same time, be a part of the whole. Although much of Dante's rhyme has been lost in translation, students can see evidence of it in this stanza. What two words rhyme in this tercet? [they/way]

C Elements of Literature

Allegory

? What might the road stand for in a more general sense? [Possible answer: The road might stand for the "path" humans must take away from sin and toward goodness.] Why is it hard to cross? [It is hard to cross because humans are always tempted to do evil.]

D English Language Learners

Comparing/Contrasting

? Make sure that students understand the difference between the two hemispheres that Virgil describes for Dante. How does Virgil characterize each hemisphere? [Possible answer: One realm is identified with Satan, the source of evil; the other with Jesus Christ, the son of God and source of all good.]

Answer to Margin Question

Line 90. Still within the earth, they have crossed from the northern to the southern hemisphere, climbing toward Purgatory.

Making the Connections

Connecting to the Theme: "Under a Hand Accursed"

When students have finished the canto, ask them to discuss the following question: If you assume that, as Dante states, Satan is the source of all evil, how would that affect your understanding of Macbeth's actions as being "under a hand accursed"? [Possible answer: Belief in Satan may make the witches' role in Macbeth's actions more significant.]

Cultural Connections

Humanism was a movement in Italy during the late Middle Ages that advocated turning to Greek and Latin writers as a source of inspiration and guidance. In the Early Renaissance (from the eleventh to the end of the fourteenth century), cultured men like Dante, Boccaccio, Petrarch, and Salutati sought moral lessons in the classics. This is sometimes referred to as Moral Humanism. Have students research this topic further and discuss the effects of Moral Humanism in Dante's epic poem.

Critical Thinking

Interpreting

? What fanciful geological theory does Virgil offer? [Where the travelers stand was once the surface of the earth, which, "impelled by fear" and by the force of Satan's fall, either became covered with water and issued forth on the other side of the world, or rose up here into the Mount of Purgatory that Dante must now climb.]

Answer to Margin Question

Line 140. The stars symbolize hope. The image of "the beautiful things that Heaven bears" contrasts sharply with the bleak, horrifying scene in hell.

FINDING COMMON GROUND

As its name suggests, this feature requires students to discover, through lively discussion, areas of agreement about something related to the themes or about controversial issues in the literature.

- Discuss the behavior of Judas, Brutus, and Cassius, and pinpoint their common error. [All were traitors to their leaders or country, and their treasonous actions brought death, war, and chaos.] All of this, of course, reflects Dante's own politics and his bitterness at those who seized power in Florence and sentenced him to exile.
- Ask students to consider the following questions: What type of "sins" does Macbeth commit? How are his sins similar to those of Judas? to Brutus and Cassius? How would Dante categorize Macbeth, and what punishment might he allot to him?
- Allow students to work in pairs to brainstorm the sins they feel are prevalent today. Require them to explain how they have devised the punishments appropriate to each crime and remind them to refer to Dante for guidance.
- You might suggest that students compare Robert Frost's "Fire and Ice" to Dante's view of what hell is like.

Forms the Judecca's other, outward face.
Here it is morning when it is evening there;
The one whose hair was like a ladder for us

Is still positioned as he was before.
On this side he fell down from Heaven; the earth,
Which till then stood out here, impelled by fear

Veiled itself in the sea and issued forth
In our own hemisphere. And possibly,
What now appears on this side° fled its berth

And rushing upward left a cavity:
This hollow where we stand." There is below,
As far from Beelzebub as one can be

Within his tomb, a place one cannot know
By sight, but by the sound a little runnel°
Makes as it wends the hollow rock its flow

Has worn, descending through its winding channel:
To get back up to the shining world from there
My guide and I went into that hidden tunnel;

And following its path, we took no care
To rest, but climbed: he first, then I—so far,
Through a round aperture I saw appear

Some of the beautiful things that Heaven bears,
Where we came forth, and once more saw the stars.

126. What now appears on this side: The island of Mount Purgatory, the pinnacle at which a sinner makes a total renunciation of sin, is apparently formed out of the inner earth displaced by Lucifer's fall. Climbing this peak will be the next leg of Dante's journey.

131. runnel: stream. This rivulet may derive from the river Lethe, the river of forgetfulness in classical mythology.

? **140.** *As he does in the* Purgatorio *and* Paradiso, *Dante ends the* Inferno *with the word* stars. *What do you think the stars symbolize? How does the end of this Canto contrast with the other sights the travelers have seen?*

FINDING COMMON GROUND

Evil has fascinated artists and poets of every age. Certainly, of the three sections of *The Divine Comedy,* Hell is by far the most fascinating place—for readers, that is. Discuss Dante's particular vision of Hell with other students, and see if you can arrive at a consensus on this question: "What acts deserve the worst torments of Hell?" (Review your Quickwrite notes before you begin.)

- What do you think Judas, Brutus, and Cassius may have in common? What sins did all three commit?
- Brutus and Cassius have leading roles in Shakespeare's *Julius Caesar,* but Dante clearly did not regard them as heroes (and neither did Shakespeare). What do you think Dante's attitude would have been toward Shakespeare's Macbeth? Do you think Macbeth would have occupied a place in Dante's Hell? Cite support from the play to explain your answer.
- In a memorable line, Dante describes his terror in the lowest depths of Hell by saying "I neither died, nor kept alive" (line 28). What do you think he means in this verse? Why would such a fate be especially terrifying?
- Suppose Dante were writing today: What categories of "sin" would he find especially prevalent in the modern world? Keep in mind the kinds of sins he felt merited the worst punishment. What kinds of punishments would be especially suitable for the offenders?

Assessing Learning

Check Test: True-False

1. The first thing Dante notices about hell is that it is unbearably hot. [False]
2. Satan has two heads. [False]
3. Brutus and Macbeth are in Satan's mouths. [False]
4. According to this poem, Lucifer was once a beautiful angel. [True]
5. Dante's climb up Satan's legs symbolizes his turning away from sin. [True]

Informal Assessment

Self-Assessment

Ask students to use the following criteria to rate their own reading on a scale of 1 to 5, one being the lowest.

- Amount of attention paid while reading.
- Effort made to predict events while reading.
- Effort made to understand the narrative.

The English Language

Shakespeare's Language

by John Algeo

OBJECTIVES

1. Understand the pronunciation, grammar, and vocabulary of Shakespeare's English
2. Identify examples of forms commonly used by Shakespeare: contractions, forms of possessive and personal pronouns, forms of verbs, negative constructions, archaic words, and inkhorn terms.

Shakespeare's language is an early form of Modern English, basically the same kind of English we speak. But we need glosses, or explanations, for some words and phrases because English has changed during the past four hundred years.

Louvre, Paris.

Lady Macbeth Sleepwalking (late 18th to early 19th century) by Henry Fuseli.

Speaking the Speech: Shakespeare's Pronunciation

The actors who pronounced Shakespeare's lines on the stage of the Globe Theater would not have sounded like modern actors, American or British. We need not be concerned with the details of their pronunciation, but some differences are obvious even from the written text of the plays. For example, Shakespeare's contemporaries, like English speakers today, used a great many contractions. But they contracted words in different ways than we do. **B**

Shakespeare liked to contract the pronouns that begin with vowels (*us* and *it*), as the following examples show:

. . . we / Shall take upon's what else remains to do . . .

. . . To mend it, or be rid on't [of it].

. . . for't must be done to-night.

What is't that moves your Highness?

Shakespeare also frequently omitted unstressed syllables from the middle of words (as we still do in words like *fam'ly*):

. . . o'er the rest . . .

. . . will these hands ne'er be clean?

. . . my near'st [nearest] of life . . .

Thou marvel'st at my words . . .

RESPONDING TO THE ART

Born in Zurich, **Henry Fuseli** (1741–1825) was commissioned to paint eight illustrations of various Shakespearean plays for a book of engravings entitled *Shakespeare Gallery.* For *Macbeth,* a play that appealed strongly to Fuseli's imagination, he included this illustration of Lady Macbeth sleepwalking. (For other art by Fuseli, see p. 401.)

Activity. Have students compare and contrast this painting with the photograph on p. 370. [Both present a dark, eerie scene with light revealing a distraught Lady Macbeth and startled viewers looking on. In this painting, the wind blowing her hair and the demonic figure in the background contribute to a sense of mystery.]

B Exploring the Culture

Current Contractions

Nowadays we favor the contraction of *not* into *n't,* as in "She isn't"; and the contraction of verbs, as in "She's here," "They've gone," and "We'll try," where *'s, 've, and 'll* represent *is, have,* and *will,* respectively.

Using Students' Strengths

Verbal Learners

When students first study French or Spanish, one of the most common stumbling blocks is the fact that these languages have two words for *you.* Have students research these and other languages that have different forms for *you* and share their findings about how and when each form of the pronoun is used. [*Tu* (intimate singular) and *vous* (formal singular; plural) in French; *tú* (familiar singular) and *usted* (formal singular; plural) in Spanish]

Auditory/Musical Learners

Ask students if they have ever sung the following song lyrics: "My country 'tis of thee, sweet land of liberty, of thee I sing" and "I can't get no satisfaction." Point out that these lines prove that modern songwriters use archaic forms, double negatives, and unusual word order to maintain a certain rhythm or create emphasis just as Shakespeare did. Have students find other examples of song lyrics that use these devices and share what they find with the class.

Resources

Viewing and Representing

Videocassette A, Segment 1: "English: A Living Language," Part 1

Available in Spanish and English. This video explores the development of the English language during the Renaissance.

(A) Appreciating Language

Personal Pronouns

Students may have noticed Shakespeare's use of the pronoun *it* for humans, instead of personal pronouns such as *he, she,* or *who.*

(B) Exploring the Culture

Social Classes

It is not surprising that the English of Shakespeare's time used different pronoun forms to distinguish between social equals and those who were not on equal terms. Elizabethan society was a hierarchy with distinct social classes. The society valued birth and lineage, as evidenced by coats-of-arms. People's fashions and behavior had to be suited to their rank. This social hierarchy was believed to reflect the natural order God had built into the universe.

(C) Critical Thinking

Speculating

? How do you think Macbeth would have reacted if Banquo had used the *th-* form to his face? [Possible responses: Macbeth would have had an excuse to arrest Banquo; Macbeth might have viewed it as one more reason to kill Banquo.]

A whole syllable could be omitted from the beginning of a word if it was unstressed (as in the use of *'cause* for *because,* an omission we still make today):

> . . . 'cause he fail'd . . .
>
> Point against point, rebellious arm 'gainst arm . . .
>
> . . . 'Twixt this and supper.
>
> . . . if he 'scape . . .
>
> I 'gin to be aweary of the sun . . .

Some of Shakespeare's words are stressed on different syllables from those we would now accent. For example, in "Stop up th' access and passage to remorse," the iambic rhythm of the line shows us that Shakespeare pronounced "acCESS," rather than "ACcess," as we would.

Other words have changed their forms in various ways since Shakespeare's day. In *Macbeth,* we find *murther* for *murder, afeard* for *afraid, aweary* for *weary,* and *alarum* for *alarm.*

Shakespeare's Grammar

Although Shakespeare's grammar is essentially the same as ours, it differs in numerous minor ways.

(A) Shakespeare could use *which* where we use *who* to refer to a person: ". . . the slave / Which ne'er shook hands." He could also use *the which,* especially with broad or unstated antecedents: "He only liv'd but till he was a man; / The which [his manhood] no sooner had his prowess confirm'd, . . . / But like a man he died." Shakespeare could also use the pronoun *who* in an indefinite sense, for which we use *the one who:* "Who was the thane, lives yet."

In present-day English, we use *mine* as a pronoun and *my* to modify a noun: "It's mine" but "It's my book." Shakespeare used both forms to modify nouns: *mine* before words beginning with a vowel, and *my* before words beginning with a consonant, just as we use *an* and *a* today ("an orange," "a lemon"): "Ha! they pluck out *mine* eyes. / Will all great Neptune's ocean wash this blood / Clean from *my* hand?"

> In some respects, Shakespeare's vocabulary was more complex than ours.

(B) Today, we generally use only a single pronoun for the person or people we talk to: *you* (with its possessives *your* and *yours*). Shakespeare had a choice between *th-* forms (*thou, thee, thy, thine*) and *y-* forms (*ye, you, your, yours*). *Thou* and *ye* were subject forms, like *I; thee* and *you* were object forms, like *me.*

(C) *Th-* forms were used in talking to one person with whom the speaker was intimate (wife, husband, bosom buddy) or to whom the speaker was socially superior (child, servant, subject). *Y-* forms were used in talking to several persons, or to one person who was a social equal but not an intimate friend, or who was a superior (parent, boss, king). In the singular, *th-* forms showed intimacy or superiority; *y-* forms showed equality or servility.

Shakespeare made careful use of the different **connotations** of *th-* and *y-* forms. When Macbeth and Banquo meet the weird sisters (Act I, Scene 3), they address the witches with *y-* forms because the two soldiers are in awe of these supernatural women; the witches, however, use *th-* forms for Macbeth and Banquo, thereby asserting their superiority over the mere mortals.

Macbeth and Banquo normally address one another with *y-* forms because, though equals, they are not intimates. At the beginning of Act III, however, when Banquo is thinking about the foul deeds that Macbeth has obviously used to come to the throne, he uses *th-* forms for Macbeth, since he regards Macbeth's murderous actions as having made a moral inferior of him. Banquo can think what he wants, but when Macbeth actually appears, Banquo addresses him with *y-* forms again. For Banquo to have called King Macbeth *thou* to his face would have been an insulting breach of etiquette.

The verb in Shakespeare's day had a special ending, *–st,* to go with *thou* as a subject, thus: "thou know'st," "thou didst," and "thou hast." It also had an alternative ending, *–th,* for the third-person singular ending, *–s,* that we still use today. Shakespeare could use "he knows" or "knoweth," "he does" or "doth," and "he has" or "hath." The two forms meant the same thing, although the *–s* ending was more common, and the *–th* probably sounded rather formal or old-fashioned even in Shakespeare's day. Sometimes Shakespeare used the two together—"The

Getting Students Involved

Cooperative Learning

Macbeth's Eulogy. Invite students to write a eulogy for Macbeth in Shakespearean English. Have them work in small groups to develop several lines of blank verse, using some of the language devices explained in this essay. They should pay attention to diction, dropped syllables, contractions, pronoun forms, and helping and other verb forms, especially the unemphatic *do.* Give volunteers an opportunity to read their eulogies to the class.

Speaking and Listening

What Did He Say? Have students work in pairs, taking turns reading aloud and then rephrasing examples from *Macbeth* that illustrate the language devices Algeo discusses. Have one student select and read a line in Shakespearean English and then ask the listener to translate the line into informal Modern English.

earth hath bubbles, as the water has"—with no apparent difference in meaning.

Shakespeare could omit the helping verb *do* in questions and negative sentences where we must have it:

> Live you? [Do you live?]
>
> Ride you this afternoon? [Do you ride this afternoon?]
>
> Fail not our feast. [Don't fail (to be at) our feast.]
>
> He loves us not. [He doesn't love us.]

On the other hand, Shakespeare could use an unstressed *do* where we cannot:

> . . . swimmers, that do cling together . . .
>
> . . . such things here as we do speak about . . .
>
> His wonders and his praises do contend . . .
>
> . . . the earth / Was feverous, and did shake.

Shakespeare had a wider choice of past participles than we do in standard English today, although some of Shakespeare's forms have survived even today in nonstandard speech:

> I have spoke. [for *spoken*]
>
> And his great love . . . hath holp him. [for *has helped*]

Shakespeare could use forms of *be* instead of *have* to make a perfect tense of verbs indicating motion: "They *are* not yet *come* back."

Where we would say "Come on, *let's go* to the king," Shakespeare has simply "Come, *go we* to the King." Shakespeare's *go we* is an old first-person command that is more direct than the *let's go* form we now prefer.

In both Shakespeare's English and ours, noun phrases may consist of a determiner (like *the, a, my*), an adjective, and a noun: *the old house*. However, in short expressions used to address a person, Shakespeare could put the adjective first: "Gentle my Lord" [for "My gentle Lord"] and "Gracious my Lord" [for "My gracious Lord"].

Some of what we consider "mistakes" today are also found in Shakespeare. They are actually old ways of using English that have fallen out of favor in standard English; for example:

> There's daggers in men's smiles . . . [There *are* daggers]
>
> Who I myself struck down . . . [*Whom* I myself struck down]
>
> . . . ask'd for who . . . [for *whom*]

Macbeth and the Witches (late 18th to early 19th century) by Henry Fuseli.
Petworth House, Petworth, Sussex, England.

Ⓓ Appreciating Language

The Functional *Do*

Today, we make a sentence negative by contracting the adverb *not* with the first auxiliary verb, such as "They aren't trying." We make a statement into a question by changing the order of the subject and the first auxiliary verb: "They are trying" to "Are they trying?" If there is no auxiliary verb (as in "They try"), we have to add an otherwise meaningless *do* as a filler for negative sentences ("They don't try") and questions ("Do they try?"). Shakespeare did not have to use the filler *do*. He could say "They try not" and "Try they?" which are not used in our language today when spoken formally.

Ⓔ Appreciating Language

The Unemphatic *Do*

We cannot use *do* as an auxiliary in unemphatic affirmative statements. We can say "They *do* try" with emphasis on *do* if we want to contradict someone who has suggested that they do not try, but in the United States, it seems stilted to say "They do try" without emphasis on *do*. Shakespeare could and did use this. For him, "They try" and "They do try" (with unstressed *do*) were simply alternate ways of saying the same thing.

RESPONDING TO THE ART

Swiss-born painter **Henry Fuseli** (1741–1825) greatly admired Shakespeare. (See p. 399.)
Activity. Encourage students to identify details in this painting that build an eerie mood. [Possible responses: The ghastly light on the witches and the faces of Banquo and Macbeth; the devillike helmet worn by Macbeth; Macbeth's bloody sword juxtaposed against the black earth.]

Making the Connections

Cross-Cultural Connections

***Macbeth* in Japanese Film.** Japanese director Akira Kurosawa filmed an acclaimed adaptation of *Macbeth* entitled *Throne of Blood* (1957). The film moved the story to sixteenth-century Japan and adapted it to a samurai setting. Because the Japanese culture has no witches, the supernatural is represented by an old woman of the woods, a traditional Japanese evil spirit, who delivers the prophesies.

Ⓐ Appreciating Language

"Fire-New" from Shakespeare

Shakespeare was, in his own phrase, "a man of fire-new words." New words in the sixteenth century that appeared in his works were *armada, demonstrate, dire, emphasis, prodigious,* and *vast.* Other words that first appeared in print in his First Folio were *accommodation, assassination, dexterously, dislocate, indistinguishable, reliance,* and *submerged.* Shakespeare's works also contain numerous original phrases familiar today but once fresh from his pen: "It was Greek to me" (*Julius Caesar*); "salad days" (*Anthony and Cleopatra*); "green-ey'd jealousy" (*The Merchant of Venice*); "the crack of doom" (*Macbeth*); and so on. Finally, a word like *multitudinous* is a reminder that Shakespeare had one of the largest vocabularies of any English writer—some thirty thousand words. (Estimates vary, but an educated person today probably has a vocabulary of only fifteen thousand words.)

Try It Out

a. Sonnet 73, l. 5, "see'st"
b. Sonnet 116, l. 2, "impediments"; Sonnet 130, l. 5, possible "damasked"
c. Because this requires judgment calls that students may feel hesitant to make, you may want to answer this question together in class. In Sonnet 116, l. 5, "fixèd" is a certain example because of the accent.
d. Sonnet 73, l. 13, "thy"
e. Sonnet 29, l. 10, "thee"; Sonnet 73, l. 14, "thou"
f. Sonnet 73: l. 1, "mayst"; l. 13, "perceivest"; l. 10, "doth"; l. 6 "fadeth"
g. Sonnet 116, l. 11, "love alters not"
h. Sonnet 73, l. 2, "do hang"
i. Sonnet 116, l. 14, "writ"
j. Sonnet 130, l. 5, "damasked"

Shakespeare's Words

Ⓐ In some respects, Shakespeare's vocabulary was more complex than ours. We commonly use three words for location: *here, there,* and *where.* Shakespeare had nine, because in addition to those three, six others were available that are now rare, if not archaic: *hence, thence, whence* ("from here, from there, from where") and *hither, thither, whither* ("to here, to there, to where"):

> Whence cam'st thou, worthy Thane? [Where did you come from?]
>
> I will thither. [I will go (to) there.]
>
> Whither should I fly? [Where should I fly to?]

Shakespeare uses other words that are now rare or obsolete:

> I say sooth . . . [I tell the truth; we still have *sooth* in the form *soothsayer* ("truth teller").]
>
> This diamond he greets your wife withal [with] . . .
>
> Send out moe [more] horses. [In Early Modern English, *moe* referred to number, *more* to size.]

In Shakespeare's plays, some of the words that strike us as "fancy" were fancy even when he used them. They were "inkhorn terms"—words borrowed from the classical languages and used for their mouth-filling and impressive sounds, as well as for their subtleties of meaning. Just after he has stabbed King Duncan, Macbeth says that his hand will never be clean again, but will rather

> The multitudinous seas incarnadine . . .

"But the script says, 'Lay on Macduff.'"

He means that the blood on his hands would "make the many seas red," but the word *multitudinous* seems to mean far more than the short word *many,* and the literal meaning of *incarnadine* ("to turn into the blood-red color of raw flesh") is especially appropriate to Macbeth's actions and state of mind. Shakespeare was using fancy words—but for a purpose.

The trickiest words in Shakespeare, however, are those that look familiar but have different meanings than their present-day versions. They are false friends that make us think we understand what the language means, while in fact indicating something different from what we expect. Here are a few examples:

> Sweno, the Norways' king, craves composition [agreement, peace terms] . . . .
>
> Are ye fantastical [illusory, imaginary], or that indeed / Which outwardly ye show [seem, appear]?
>
> Say from whence / You owe [own, have] this strange intelligence [information].
>
> Sleep, that knits up [straightens out] the raveled sleave [tangled thread] of care. . . . [The image of reknitting the sleeve of a sweater that has unraveled makes sense, but is wrong.]

Because of differences like these between Shakespeare's English and ours, it takes some effort for us to read his plays and poetry. What we can get from the reading, however, is well worth the effort.

Try It Out

Find an example in Shakespeare's sonnets (pages 225–229) of each of the following:

a. A contraction that we would not use today
b. An "inkhorn term"
c. A word pronounced differently from the way we pronounce it today
d. *Thy* where we would use *your*
e. *Thou, thee,* or *thine* (notice who is talking to whom)
f. The *–th* and *–st* forms of verbs
g. A negative like "They try not" (instead of "They don't try")
h. An unemphatic statement like "They do try" (instead of "They try")
i. An unusual form of a verb (like "I have spoke")
j. A word we no longer have or no longer use with the same meaning

(Opposite) *St. Jerome* (detail) (15th century) by Domenico Ghirlandaio. Chiesa di Ognissanti, Florence.

Assessing Learning

Check Test: True-False

1. Shakespeare uses various means to delete a syllable from a line to keep the blank verse intact. [True]
2. Shakespeare could choose from multiple pronoun forms, third-person singular verb forms, and past participles. [True]
3. The *th-* and *y-* forms of pronouns in Shakespeare's time were interchangeable. [False]
4. Rather than say "let's go," Shakespeare might have said "go we." [True]
5. An "inkhorn term" is a word that looks familiar but has a meaning different from its present-day version. [False]

Collection 5

The Power of the Word

Theme

Words to Live By *Language helps us understand the human condition. One use of language has always been to embody the words of our sages and prophets, to tell us who we are and where we are going.*

Reading the Anthology

Reaching Struggling Readers

The *Reading Skills and Strategies: Reaching Struggling Readers* binder provides materials coordinated with the Pupil's Edition (see the Collection Planner, p. T402B) to help students who have difficulty reading and comprehending text, or students who are reluctant readers. The binder for twelfth grade is organized around ten individual skill areas and offers the following options:

- **MiniRead** MiniReads are short, easy texts that give students a chance to practice a particular skill and strategy before reading selections in the Pupil's Edition. Each MiniRead Skill Lesson can be taught independently or used in conjunction with a Selection Skill Lesson.
- **Selection Skill Lessons** Selection Skill Lessons allow students to apply skills introduced in the MiniReads. Each Selection Skill Lesson provides reading instruction and practice specific to a particular piece of literature in the Pupil's Edition.

Reading Beyond the Anthology

Read On

At the end of the Renaissance collections, the grade twelve book provides an annotated bibliography of books suitable for extended reading. The suggested books are related to works in these collections by theme, by author, or by subject. To preview the Read On for the Renaissance period, please turn to p. T455

HRW Library

The *HRW Library* offers novels, plays, and short-story collections for extended reading. Each book in the Library includes one or more major works and thematically or topically related Connections. The Connections are magazine articles, poems, or other pieces of literature. Each book in the *HRW Library* is also accompanied by a Study Guide that provides teaching suggestions and worksheets. The title shown here will work well to extend the theme of Collection 5.

PYGMALION
George Bernard Shaw
Shaw's great play is based on the legend of the sculptor who brought a statue to life by the power of love. Professor Higgins, the main character of Shaw's play, uses language to transform a young Cockney girl into an elegant society woman, with unexpected results.

Collection 5 The Power of the Word

Resources for this Collection

Note: All resources for this collection are available for preview on the *One-Stop Planner CD-ROM I with Test Generator.* All worksheets and blackline masters may be printed from the CD-ROM.

Internet Resources
go.hrw.com LE0 12-5

Selection or Feature	Reading and Literary Skills	Vocabulary, Language, and Grammar
• **Of Studies** (p. 405) • **Axioms** *from the* **Essays** (p. 407) Sir Francis Bacon **Spotlight On: The Example of a Queen: Elizabeth I** (p. 410) Katharina M. Wilson	• *Reading Skills and Strategies: Reaching Struggling Readers* • MiniRead Skill Lesson, p. 13 • Selection Skill Lesson, p. 19 • *Graphic Organizers for Active Reading,* Worksheet p. 31	
from **The King James Bible** (p. 413) • *from* **Genesis 1-3** (p. 415) **Connections: A Beam of Protons Illuminates Gutenberg's Genius** (p. 419) Malcolm W. Browne **Psalms: Worship Through Poetry** (p. 421) • **Psalm 23** (p. 422) • **Psalm 137** (p. 423) • **The Parable of the Good Samaritan** (p. 425)	• *Graphic Organizers for Active Reading,* Worksheets pp. 32, 33, 34, 35	• *Grammar and Language Links:* Prepositions and Prepositional Phrases, Worksheet p. 23 • *Language Workshop CD-ROM,* Prepositions • *Daily Oral Grammar,* Transparency 12
World Literature: Worlds of Wisdom • **Night** *from the* **Koran** (p. 428) • **Shell-Neck, Slim, and Grim** *from* **The Panchatantra** (p. 430) • **Zen Parables** (p. 431) • **Sayings of Saadi** (p. 432) • **Taoist Anecdotes** (p. 433) • *from* **Analects of Confucius** (p. 433) • **Jabo Proverbs** (p. 434)	The World Literature feature offers students the opportunity to explore thematically linked literature from different world cultures. Structured activities called Finding Common Ground are provided in the Pupil's Edition to guide students' explorations of these thematic connections between British and other world literature.	
from **Paradise Lost** (p. 438) **The Fall of Satan** (p. 440) John Milton **Spotlight On: Allegory** (p. 451)	• *Reading Skills and Strategies:* Reaching Struggling Readers • MiniRead Skill Lesson, p. 23 • Selection Skill Lesson, p. 29 • *Graphic Organizers for Active Reading,* Worksheet p. 36	• *Grammar and Language Links:* Gerunds and Gerund Phrases, Worksheet p. 25 • *Language Workshop CD-ROM,* Verbals and Verbal Phrases • *Daily Oral Grammar,* Transparency 13
The English Language: The Growth of Modern English (p. 456) John Algeo		
Writer's Workshop: Analyzing Causes and Effects (p. 459)		
Language Workshop: Effective Transitions (p. 463)		• *Workshop Resources,* p. 51 • *Language Workshop CD-ROM,* Transitions
Learning for Life: A New Curriculum (p. 465)		

Other Resources for this Collection

- *Cross-Curricular Activities,* p. 5
- *Portfolio Management System,* Introduction to Portfolio Assessment, p. 1
- *Formal Assessment:*
  Literary Period Test, p. 83
  Literary Elements Test, p. 81
- *Test Generator,* Collection Test

Writing	Listening and Speaking Viewing and Representing	Assessment
• *Portfolio Management System,* Rubrics for Choices, p. 126	• *Audio CD Library,* Disc 6, Tracks 2, 3 • *Portfolio Management System,* Rubrics for Choices, p. 126	• *Formal Assessment,* Selection Test, p. 69 • *Test Generator (One-Stop Planner CD-ROM)* • *Preparation for College Admission Exams,* p. 17
• *Portfolio Management System,* Rubrics for Choices, p. 127	• *Audio CD Library,* Disc 6, Tracks 4, 5, 6, 7 • *Viewing and Representing:* Fine Art Transparency 5 Worksheet p. 20 • *Portfolio Management System,* Rubrics for Choices, p. 127	• *Formal Assessment,* Selection Tests, pp. 71, 73, 75 • *Test Generator (One-Stop Planner CD-ROM)* • *Preparation for College Admission Exams,* p. 19
	• *Audio CD Library,* Disc 6, Tracks 8, 9, 10, 11, 12, 13, 14	
• *Portfolio Management System,* Rubrics for Choices, p. 129	• *Audio CD Library,* Disc 6, Tracks 15, 16 • *Viewing and Representing:* Fine Art Transparency 6 Worksheet p. 24 • *Portfolio Management System,* Rubrics for Choices, p. 129	• *Formal Assessment,* Selection Test, p. 77 • *Test Generator (One-Stop Planner CD-ROM)*
		• *Formal Assessment,* The English Language Test, p. 79
• *Workshop Resources,* p. 17 • *Writer's Workshop 2 CD-ROM,* Cause and Effect	• *Viewing and Representing,* HRW Multimedia Presentation Maker	• *Portfolio Management System,* • Prewriting, p. 131 • Peer Editing, p. 132 • Assessment Rubric, p. 133
		• *Portfolio Management System,* Rubrics p. 134

Transparency CD-ROM Video Audio CD

Collection 5 The Power of the Word

Skills Focus

Selection or Feature	Reading Skills and Strategies	Elements of Literature and Language	Writing	Listening and Speaking	Viewing and Representing
Of Studies (p. 405) **Axioms** *from the* **Essays** (p. 407) Sir Francis Bacon	Main Idea, pp. 405, 409 Key Statements, p. 405 Details, p. 409	Parallel Structure, pp. 405, 409 Paradox, p. 409	Speculate on the Effects of Technology on Books and Reading, p. 409 Analyze a Writer's Attitude, p. 409 Write an Essay in Response to Bacon, p. 409		
from **The King James Bible** (p. 413) • *from* **Genesis** (p. 415) **Psalms** (p. 421) • **Psalm 23** (p. 422) • **Psalm 137** (p. 423) • **The Parable of the Good Samaritan** (p. 425)	Respond to the Text, pp. 415, 420	Imagery, pp. 415, 424 Foreshadow, p. 420 Symbol, p. 420 Psalm, p. 421 Metaphor, p. 424 Parable, pp. 425–426 Irony, p. 426 Repetition, p. 427 Parallel Structure, p. 427	Identify Character Traits, p. 427 Create a Contemporary Parable, p. 427 Write an Essay Comparing Translations of Psalm 23, p. 427	Perform an Oral Recital of a Psalm, p. 427 Research, Write, and Present an Oral Report on an Invention from the Renaissance, p. 427	
World Literature: Worlds of Wisdom	Connect with Texts, pp. 428, 434	The World Literature feature offers students the opportunity to explore thematically linked literature from different world cultures. Structured activities called Finding Common Ground are provided in the Pupil's Edition to guide students' explorations of these thematic connections between British and other world literature.			
from **Paradise Lost** (p. 438) **The Fall of Satan** (p. 440) John Milton **Spotlight On: Allegory** (p. 451)	Monitor Reading Strategies, p. 440 Context Clues, p. 440 Glossary, p. 440 Read Aloud, p. 440 Analogies, p. 449 Read Irregular Syntax, p. 450 Read Blank Verse, p. 450	Elegy, p. 435 Blank Verse, p. 438 Images, p. 449 Purpose, p. 449 Paradox, p. 449 Dramatic Irony, p. 449 Epic Similes, p. 449 Iamb, p. 450 Subject, Verb, Direct Object, p. 450 Allegory, p. 451	Identify Causes and Effects of Contemporary Evils, p. 450 Write a Prose Paraphrase of a Speech in *Paradise Lost,* p. 450 Write a Brief Essay Analyzing Milton's Characterization of Satan, p. 450 Rewrite the Opening of *Paradise Lost* as a Dramatic Dialogue, p. 450		Draw Comparative Sketches of Milton's and Dante's Visions of Hell, p. 450
Reading Skills and Strategies: Multiple Meanings of Words (p. 454)	Multiple Meanings of Words, p. 454 Word Origins, p. 454 Contexts, p. 454				
The English Language: The Growth of Modern English (p. 456) John Algeo		Grammars and Dictionaries, p. 456 Ornate vs. Plain Style, p. 456 Inkhorn Terms, p. 457 Euphuism, p. 457 Metaphysical Conceit, p. 457 Elements of Style, p. 457			
Writer's Workshop: Analyzing Causes and Effects (p. 459)			Write an Essay Analyzing the Causes and/or Effects of an Event, Situation, or Trend, pp. 459–462		Create a Cause-and-Effect Map, p. 460
Language Workshop: Effective Transitions (p. 463)			Use Effective Transitions, p. 463 Revise Sentences to Improve Transitions, p. 463		
Reading for Life: Analyzing and Creating Graphics (p. 464)	Analyze Data, p. 464				Choose an Appropriate Graphic to Display Data, p. 464
Learning for Life: A New Curriculum (p. 465)			Write a Proposal for Revising a School's Curricula, p. 465	Stage a One-Person Show, p. 465	Create a Collage, p. 465

Bacon
from The King James Bible
Worlds of Wisdom
Milton

A word is dead
When it is said,
Some say.
I say it just
Begins to live
That day.

—Emily Dickinson
(American,
1830–1886)

Writing Focus: Analyzing Causes and Effects

WORK IN PROGRESS

The following **Work in Progress** assignments build to a culminating **Writer's Workshop** at the end of this collection.

• Of Studies	Speculate on effects of technology (p. 409)
• King James Bible	Speculate on causes of character traits (p. 427)
• Paradise Lost	Identify causes and effects of contemporary evils (p. 450)

Writer's Workshop: Expository Writing / Analyzing Causes and Effects (p. 459)

OBJECTIVES

1. Read literature of the Renaissance on the theme of "The Power of the Word"
2. Interpret literary elements with special emphasis on allegory
3. Apply a variety of reading strategies to the literature, particularly distinguishing multiple meanings of words
4. Respond to the literature in a variety of modes
5. Understand and use new words
6. Learn about the growth of Modern English
7. Plan, draft, and revise an expository essay analyzing causes and effects
8. Use transitional expressions effectively
9. Demonstrate the ability to create and read graphics
10. Explore through a variety of projects the creation of a new educational curriculum

Responding to the Quotation

? According to Dickinson's poem, what makes a word "live" and have power? [Possible response: When people use a word to communicate and express feeling, the word comes alive for the speaker/writer and the audience.]

RESPONDING TO THE ART

The work of Florentine painter **Domenico Ghirlandaio** (1449–1494), one of Michelangelo's teachers, is noted for its expressive feeling and historical detail. Ghirlandaio's life ended before he could realize his dream of painting allegorical pictures on all the walls of Florence.

Activity. Encourage students to list items that this scholar probably found indispensable. The subject of the painting is St. Jerome (c. A.D. 347–c. A.D. 420), who translated the Bible from the Hebrew to Latin. Jerome is often shown in the desert or in a study. Here he is placed in a rich Renaissance setting.

OBJECTIVES
1. Read and interpret the essay
2. Analyze parallel structure
3. Identify the main idea
4. Express understanding through critical and creative writing

SKILLS
Literary
- Analyze parallel structure

Reading
- Identify the main idea

Writing
- Predict and analyze effects of technology on reading
- Analyze the writer's attitude
- Write an original essay

Viewing/Representing
- Respond to a photograph (ATE)

Planning
- **Block Schedule**
  Block Scheduling Lesson Plans with Pacing Guide
- **Traditional Schedule**
  Lesson Plans Including Strategies for English-Language Learners
- **One-Stop Planner**
  CD-ROM with Test Generator

BROWSING IN THE FILES
About the Author. Bacon intended to write an encyclopedia, but he completed only part of it. In *New Atlantis,* a short utopian fantasy, he describes an assembly of scholars devoted to scientific study and research. This concept inspired the chartering of the British scientific academy known as the Royal Society in 1660, more than thirty years after Bacon's death. Although this intellectual institution was later satirized by Jonathan Swift in *Gulliver's Travels* (1726), it boasts a distinguished history and remains in existence today.

Sir Francis Bacon
(1561–1626)

Sir Francis Bacon, Viscount of St. Albans (detail) (late 16th to early 17th century) by Paul van Somer. Oil.
Private Collection.

From his earliest days, Francis Bacon knew that he was an important person. When he was about nine, Queen Elizabeth asked him how old he was, and he is said to have replied, "Two years younger than your Majesty's happy reign." A boy who speaks like this will go far, and Bacon went far. He rose in his chosen profession, the law, until he reached the very top and became Lord Chancellor of England and lord keeper of the great seal, an office that his father, Sir Nicholas Bacon, had also held. He was elevated to the peerage, the British nobility who could govern as members of the House of Lords, and he amassed a large fortune, though he was often in debt because of his extravagant lifestyle. At the height of his political career, he was found guilty of taking bribes and banished to his country estate, where he devoted himself full time to thinking and writing about new ways to discover knowledge.

Bacon once wrote a now-famous letter to his uncle, Lord Burghley, Elizabeth's secretary of state, in which he said, "I have taken all knowledge to be my province." Of course, he did not master all knowledge, but he did make important contributions to many different branches of knowledge: political science, economics, biology, physics, music, architecture, botany, constitutional law, industrial development, philosophy, religious thought, mythology, astronomy, chemistry, landscape gardening, and literature.

But he is most famous for his vision of humanity's future, when knowledge would be based on verifiable experimentation, and science would be separate from theology.

Bacon's best-known literary works, the *Essays,* are intended to help people get ahead in life. Bacon was the first Englishman to use the word *essay* to designate a brief discourse in prose. He took the word from the French writer Montaigne (män·tān′). But, whereas Montaigne's delightful *essais* are mainly about a fascinating person, Montaigne himself, Bacon writes instead about humanity in general.

Bacon had embarked on a new career as a practicing scientist when death overtook him. One wintry day, he descended from his carriage carrying a dead chicken, to freeze it in the snow and thereby test the preservative powers of cold. Today this seems like a painfully obvious thing to do, but nobody had tried it in a systematic way before 1626. Suddenly, in the midst of the experiment, Bacon took a chill. His servants carried him into nearby Highgate, the house of the earl of Arundel. In poor health most of his life, Bacon died there of complications resulting from exposure.

In all his works, Bacon's aim was to make the world better. As the destroyer of old Aristotelian ways of thinking and as the stimulator of "modern" ones, Bacon has no equal.

go.hrw.com
LEO 12-5

Resources: Print and Media
Reading
- *Reading Skills and Strategies*
  MiniRead Skill Lesson, p. 13
  Selection Skill Lesson, p. 19
- *Graphic Organizers for Active Reading,* p. 31
- *Audio CD Library*
  Disc 6, Tracks 2, 3

Assessment
- *Formal Assessment,* p. 69
- *Portfolio Management System,* p. 126
- *Preparation for College Admission Exams,* p. 17
- *Test Generator (One-Stop Planner CD-ROM)*

Internet
- go.hrw.com (keyword: LEO 12–5)

Before You Read
OF STUDIES

Make the Connection
Why Read?
Two popular sayings present contrasting points of view about the relationship of books and learning to life. According to one axiom, "Knowledge is power." According to the other, more cynical saying, "It's not *what* you know but *whom* you know." Bacon himself coined the first saying, but he would probably have agreed with both views, since he was extremely learned and also very well connected to powerful people.

Elements of Literature
Parallel Structure
Bacon's sentences have been studied for centuries as models of **parallel structure**—the repetition of words, phrases, or sentences that have the same grammatical structure. Parallelism makes a passage rhythmic and memorable. Bacon also uses it to present contrasting ideas. Reading aloud and paying attention to punctuation and parallel structure will help you make sense of Bacon's long, complex sentences.

Reading Skills and Strategies
Identifying the Main Idea
Bacon's essay is only one paragraph in length, but it is packed with ideas. As you read, take notes. Jot down statements that seem important to you. Often you will find **key statements** at the beginning and end of essays like this one. Those key statements often contain the main idea of the essay.

A Still Life with Books (detail) (17th century) by Charles E. Bizet d'Annonay.
Musée de l'Ain, Bourg-en-Bresse, France.

Summary ■■■

Of Studies
This essay is about the proper purposes for reading and studying. Bacon argues that although reading has many subsidiary purposes, its main aim is to train the reader to think clearly and judge wisely. The tone is pragmatic, worldly-wise, and authoritative. The style is measured, balanced, and rational, making much use of parallel structure and figurative comparisons.

Axioms from the *Essays*
These **axioms**, or seemingly self-evident truths, are short statements presented without reasons to support their conclusions. The titles of the essays from which the statements are excerpted follow each axiom. Bacon's concerns are wide-ranging, and his self-confident assertions offer his audience concise advice on the best ways to live wisely and well.

Background

Bacon's essays are highly polished, finished works, despite the fact that the root meaning of the word *essay* is "trial" or "attempt." The number of Bacon's essay collections grew over the years: By 1597, he had written ten; by 1613, thirty-nine; and by 1625, fifty-eight.

Professional Notes

Acquaint students with the once hotly debated allegation that Bacon wrote some or all of Shakespeare's plays. This claim was made by Delia Bacon, a descendant of the philosopher, and is now dismissed by most serious scholars.

A Reading Skills and Strategies

Identifying the Main Idea

A topic or subject may be expressed in one word or phrase (as in a title), but a **main idea** states an attitude or point of view on a topic and is usually expressed in a sentence or two. Suggest that students start with the topic (studies) and then formulate one statement summarizing Bacon's attitude toward studies.

B Elements of Literature

Parallel Structure

Note that here Bacon uses both parallel subjects—"Crafty men," "simple men," and "wise men"—as well as parallel predicates—"contemn," "admire," and "use." Point out to students that Bacon avoids a boring sameness throughout the essay by varying the grammatical elements that he makes parallel.

C Critical Thinking

Interpreting

? To what does Bacon compare books? What does this comparison tell you about his attitude toward the importance of books in one's life? [Possible response: He compares books to food, suggesting that books are essential to life itself, with some books containing more intellectual "nutrients" than others.]

D Struggling Readers

Using Graphic Aids

To help students understand Bacon's structure, have them list the parallel grammatical elements in various sentences, such as "wise," "witty," "subtle," "deep," "grave," and "able to contend" in this sentence.

A Of Studies

Sir Francis Bacon

Studies serve for delight, for ornament, and for ability. Their chief use for delight is in privateness and retiring;[1] for ornament, is in discourse; and for ability, is in the judgment and disposition of business. For expert men can execute, and perhaps judge of particulars, one by one; but the general counsels, and the plots and marshalling of affairs, come best from those that are learned. To spend too much time in studies is sloth;[2] to use them too much for ornament is affectation;[3] to make judgment wholly by their rules is the humor[4] of a scholar. They perfect nature and are perfected by experience; for natural abilities are like natural plants that need pruning by study; and studies themselves do give forth directions too much at large, except they be bounded in by experience. (B) Crafty men contemn[5] studies; simple men admire[6] them; and wise men use them: For they teach not their own use; but that is a wisdom without them[7] and above them, won by observation. Read not to contradict and confute;[8] nor to believe and take for granted; nor to find talk and discourse; but to weigh and consider. (C) Some books are to be tasted, others to be swallowed, and some few to be chewed and digested: That is, some books are to be read only in parts; others to be read, but not curiously;[9] and some few to be read wholly, and with diligence and attention. Some books also may be read by deputy, and extracts made of them by others; but that would be only in the less important arguments, and the meaner sort of books; else distilled books are like common distilled waters,[10] flashy[11] things. Reading maketh a full man; conference[12] a ready man; and writing an exact man. And therefore, if a man write little, he had need have a great memory; if he confer little, he had need have a present wit;[13] and if he read little, he had need have much cunning, to seem to know that[14] he doth not. (D) Histories make men wise; poets witty;[15] the mathematics subtle; natural philosophy deep; moral grave; logic and rhetoric able to contend. *Abeunt studia in mores.*[16] Nay, there is no stond[17] or impediment in the wit but may be wrought[18] out by fit studies: like as diseases of the body may have appropriate exercises. Bowling is good for the stone and reins;[19] shooting for the lungs and breast; gentle walking for the stomach; riding for the head; and the like. So if a man's wit be wandering, let him study the mathematics; for in demonstrations, if his wit be called away never so little, he must begin again: If his wit be not apt to distinguish or find differences, let him study the Schoolmen;[20] for they are *cymini sectores:*[21] If he be not apt to beat over[22] matters, and to call one thing to prove and illustrate another, let him study the lawyers' cases; so every defect of the mind may have a special receipt.[23]

1. **privateness and retiring:** privacy and leisure.
2. **sloth:** laziness.
3. **affectation:** artificial behavior designed to impress others.
4. **humor:** whim.
5. **contemn:** despise.
6. **admire:** archaic for "marvel at."
7. **without them:** separate from them; outside them.
8. **confute:** dispute.
9. **curiously:** carefully.
10. **common distilled waters:** homemade concoctions.
11. **flashy:** superficial; vapid.
12. **conference:** conversation; discussion.
13. **present wit:** ability to think fast.
14. **that:** what.
15. **witty:** imaginative.
16. ***Abeunt . . . mores:*** Latin for "Studies help form character," from Ovid's (43 B.C.–C. A.D. 17) *Heroides.*
17. **stond:** stoppage.
18. **wrought:** worked.
19. **stone and reins:** archaic for "kidney stones and the kidneys."
20. **schoolmen:** medieval philosophers.
21. ***cymini sectores:*** Latin for "hairsplitters"; literally, "dividers of cumin seed."
22. **beat over:** thoroughly discuss.
23. **receipt:** remedy.

Reaching All Students

Struggling Readers

Identifying the Main Idea was introduced on p. 405. For a lesson directly tied to this selection that teaches students to identify main ideas using strategies called Read, Rate, Reread, and Most Important Word, see the *Reading Skills and Strategies* binder:

- MiniRead Skill Lesson, p. 13
- Selection Skill Lesson, p. 19

English Language Learners

As students listen to the essay read aloud, ask them to pay attention to the regular rhythm created by the parallel grammatical elements. The repetition at the heart of Bacon's parallel structures should help students identify the author's main ideas. For additional strategies to supplement instruction, see

- *Lesson Plans Including Strategies for English-Language Learners*

Advanced Learners

Have students formulate a contemporary axiom that captures a piece of practical wisdom in a few words. The axiom should respond in some way to an idea in Bacon's essay or to one of his axioms. Students may present their axioms in the form of bumper stickers or T-shirt designs, and display their work in the classroom.

Bacon's essays are written in a terse, compressed style that demands a reader's full attention. For the most part, Bacon does not develop his ideas in paragraphs. Instead, he writes a sentence containing one idea, then follows it with a sentence containing another idea. While the sentences are all related to the topic of the essay, they are related in different ways—and they could be rearranged without much damage to the whole. The effect is like a string of beads all the same size.

Many of the sentences contain nuggets of wisdom known as axioms or adages. Like proverbs, axioms do not argue or explain, but merely make positive statements. What do the axioms in this selection suggest about Bacon's values?

Axioms *from the* Essays

Sir Francis Bacon

Men fear death as children fear to go in the dark; and as that natural fear in children is increased with tales, so is the other. **E**

—"Of Death"

Revenge is a kind of wild justice, which the more man's nature runs to, the more ought law to weed it out.

—"Of Revenge"

The virtue of prosperity is temperance; the virtue of adversity is fortitude.

—"Of Adversity"

He that hath wife and children hath given hostages to fortune. **F**

—"Of Marriage and Single Life"

There was never proud man thought so absurdly well of himself as the lover doth of the person loved: And therefore it was well said, *That it is impossible to love and to be wise.*

—"Of Love"

They that deny a God destroy man's nobility, for certainly man is of kin to the beasts by his body, and if he be not of kin to God by his spirit, he is a base and ignoble creature.

—"Of Atheism"

A principal fruit of friendship is the ease and discharge of the fullness and swellings of the heart.

—"Of Friendship"

A man's own observation, what he finds good of, and what he finds hurt of, is the best physic [medicine] to preserve health.

—"Of Regiment of Health"

As the baggage is to an army, so is riches to virtue. **G**

—"Of Riches"

No man prospers so suddenly as by others' errors.

—"Of Fortune"

There is no excellent beauty that hath not some strangeness in the proportion.

—"Of Beauty"

God Almighty first planted a garden. And indeed it is the purest of human pleasures.

—"Of Gardens"

Men in great place are thrice servants: servants of the sovereign or state, servants of fame, and servants of business.

—"Of Great Place"

It were better to have no opinion of God at all than such an opinion as is unworthy of him.

—"Of Superstition"

E Elements of Literature

Parallel Structure

Axioms are intended to be memorable, and the use of parallel structure is a very effective way to make an axiom easy to remember. Have students identify the parallel structures in the first, third, ninth, and thirteenth axioms.

F Critical Thinking

Extending the Text

The words following the axiom from "Of Marriage and Single Life" are these: "for they are impediments to great enterprises, either of virtue or mischief." Ask students if they think marriage keeps a person from being all he or she can be in life. [Most students will probably agree that a person can have both marriage and success.]

G Critical Thinking

Making Connections

? How does this axiom compare with the following from the Bible: "It is easier for a camel to go through the eye of a needle than for a rich man to enter into the Kingdom of God" (Matthew 19:24)? [Possible answers: They are very similar: As the weight of baggage hinders an army from achieving its goal, so riches impede virtuous behavior.]

Resources

Selection Assessment

Formal Assessment

- Selection Test, p. 69

Test Generator (One-Stop Planner)

- CD-ROM

Making the Connections

Connecting to the Theme: "The Power of the Word"

People across the ages have expressed ideas in short memorable statements. These statements provide powerful support in times of crises and indecision. Have students brainstorm a list of sayings that their friends or family use when talking about love, death, chance, or other serious topics. Give them an example to get them started, such as "Love conquers all."

Assessing Learning

Check Test: True-False

1. According to Bacon, you can feel secure if you make judgments based only on what you have studied. [False]
2. Bacon says you do not need to read every book thoroughly. [True]
3. In Bacon's view, mental pursuits are superior to physical ones, such as walking and riding. [False]
4. According to Bacon, study offers a cure for each weakness of the intellect. [True]

Student to Student

This student poem praises the boundless power and inventiveness of the human mind. Words and writing are also celebrated as products of the world-shaping mind.

A Critical Thinking

Making Connections

? Would Bacon agree with this statement? [Possible responses: Bacon would probably agree. He says, ". . .there is no . . . impediment to the wit, but it may be wrought out by studies." He believes that the mind must be honed by reading, writing, and conversation. On the other hand, as a writer, Bacon may have been painfully aware of the limitations of language.]

B Elements of Literature

Metaphor

? What metaphor does the poet use to emphasize the creativity of the human mind? [The mind is the sculptor of Earth.] **Discuss why you think this is an effective or an ineffective metaphor.** [Possible responses: The metaphor is effective because, in some way, we all create our dwelling places; or it is ineffective because Earth and nature have such power over us.]

C Critical Thinking

Making Connections

? How does this idea relate to the collection theme, "The Power of the Word"? [Possible answer: Words shape our lives. To be so powerful, their source, the mind, also must be awe-inspiring.]

RESPONDING TO THE ART

American photographer **Jerry Uelsmann** (1934–) often combines several negatives to convey different levels of reality simultaneously.

Activity. Ask students what is surreal about this photo. [Instead of a ceiling, the study has a sky overhead. There is a tiny person walking on the manuscript on the writing table.] Ask how this photo connects with details in "Mind."

Student to Student

Mind

A The mind knows no boundaries,
words no obstacles.
Every problem, a wall
in a maze of society.
And creativity, the rubberband,
leads us out,
but always manages to bring us back
ever so quickly.
Imagination is the tiny cave
in this maze that we hide in
for a moment of rest.
Thoughts, the last hope
of serenity and peace.
The mind surrounds this society.
B It molds this sculpture we call Earth.
Whoever said the pen is mightier than the sword
was correct.
C Writing comes from words,
from thoughts,
from the strongest
thing ever built.
The Mind.

—Andrea D. Marzullo
Bellevue East Senior High School
Bellevue, Nebraska

Untitled (1976) by Jerry Uelsmann.

© 1976 by Jerry Uelsmann.

Connecting Across Texts

Connecting to "Of Studies"

Ask students to name some of the similarities and differences between the poem "Mind" and the essay "Of Studies." [Possible answers: Both works focus on the mind and its enormous abilities; they both express optimism about human beings and the power of their minds. The works differ in their literary forms; also, Bacon does not address imagination as the student does, but the student does not allude to memory.]

Making Meanings

First Thoughts

1. Bacon says that only a few books are to be "chewed and digested." What books would be on your list in this category? Why would you include them?

Reading Check

In no more than three sentences, state what you think is Bacon's **main idea** in "Of Studies." Then quote **details** from the essay that support your statement of its main idea.

Shaping Interpretations

2. Bacon says that too much studying is laziness. Do you agree? Explain how this **paradox,** or seeming contradiction, can be true.
3. Bacon had the reputation of being a hard, ambitious man, and his essays are frequently said to be cynical and lacking in warmth. Find remarks in "Of Studies" that could support this view. How did *you* feel about the person behind this essay?
4. Bacon's fondness for **parallel structure** and balanced sentences is apparent in "Of Studies." For example: "Some books are to be tasted, others to be swallowed, and some few to be chewed and digested." Find and read aloud other examples of Bacon's parallelism and balance.

Connecting with the Text

5. Why do *you* read? Compare your reasons with Bacon's arguments for reading. How do you feel about the ideas expressed in "Mind" on page 408?

Extending the Text

6. What passages in "Of Studies" do you think could apply especially well to today's arguments about the value of education?

Challenging the Text

7. "Of Studies" was written almost four hundred years ago. Are any of its points dated? Do you disagree with anything Bacon says?

Choices: Building Your Portfolio

Writer's Notebook

WORK IN PROGRESS

1. Collecting Ideas for a Cause-Effect Essay

Bacon's essay upholds the value of books and of reading—but with a seventeenth-century perspective. What effects do you think modern technology has on our use of books and on the reading process itself? Think about CD-ROMs, computer databases, and the video images that constantly engulf us. Do you think people will still read books in the near future? Will they still use books in their studies? Save your notes to use with the Writer's Workshop on page 459.

Analyzing the Writer's Attitude

2. Having Much Cunning

Bacon maintains that a person who reads little needs to "have much cunning, to seem to know" what he actually doesn't know. Analyze this part of "Of Studies" to determine Bacon's attitude toward such a pretense. Does he speak strongly against it, or does he imply that it is not a serious failing? Explore your findings in a short essay of your own.

Creative Writing

3. Talking Back to Bacon

Write an essay of your own in response to Bacon's reflections on studies. You might focus on the entire essay or on just one statement. Your response to Bacon might be anything—from total disagreement to total approval of all he says, though that's not likely. In your opening statement, tell what the topic of your own essay will be. Be sure to bring in examples and experiences from real life today to support or refute Bacon. Give your essay a title that uses the word "On."

Reading Check

Possible response: Studies are a vital element of human experience, enabling people to develop their natures fully. They should be balanced with engagement in the real world and performed for a purpose. Studies improve the mind in specific ways, depending upon the subject studied—such as science, mathematics, or poetry.

Making Meanings

First Thoughts [Respond]

1. Possible responses: Students might mention classic literature or books about religion or philosophy since these books require reflection and leave a lasting impression.

Shaping Interpretations [Interpret]

2. Bacon means that excessive studying at the expense of practical action is self-indulgent. The paradox is that someone can study too much, acquiring knowledge in the abstract and not putting it to work in the real world. Most students will probably agree with Bacon's thought, but some may feel that knowledge does not need to have an immediate application in order to be valuable.
3. Examples include sentences beginning "So if a man's wit" and "If he be not apt." Students' opinions of Bacon will vary. Some may see him as cynical, others as realistic.
4. Students may cite the sentences beginning "To spend too much time," "Crafty men contemn studies," and "Reading maketh a full man."

Connecting with the Text [Synthesize]

5. Comparisons should clearly articulate students' own reasons and demonstrate an understanding of Bacon's reasons. Students will probably agree with the ideas in the student poem, especially regarding the mind's power.

Extending the Text [Analyze]

6. Students might cite passages beginning "For expert men can execute"; "Reading maketh a full man"; and "Nay, there is no stond."

Challenging the Text [Evaluate]

7. Answers will vary. Most students will agree that Bacon's fundamental points are still valid.

Grading Timesaver

Rubrics for each Choices assignment appear on p. 126 in the *Portfolio Management System.*

Spotlight On

This feature describes the education of upper-class women in Renaissance England, focusing on Elizabeth I. To illustrate the breadth of her intellectual accomplishments, two of her works appear in boxes within the feature: a love poem, "On Monsieur's Departure," full of witty conceits, and a political speech, designed to rouse the English people to defend their country against a possible Spanish invasion.

A Background

Humanists

Sir Thomas More (c. 1477–1535) was a scholar and author in addition to serving as chancellor of England. More, who eventually became a religious martyr, presented a new vision of human society in *Utopia* (1516). (For further information on More, see p. 199 in Collection 3.)

Desiderius Erasmus (c. 1466–1536), the renowned Dutch cleric and brilliant humanist scholar, set forth imaginative and progressive views on education. He urged that Latin be taught to children at home through conversation even before grammar was taught in school, that corporal punishment be restrained, and that a strong emphasis be placed on motivating students to connect with their studies. (For further information on Erasmus, see p. 199 in Collection 3.)

B Exploring the Historical Period

Anne Boleyn

Elizabeth's mother, Anne Boleyn, was the second of Henry VIII's six wives and the second who failed to give him the male heir he wanted. Henry had Anne Boleyn beheaded before Elizabeth was three years old.

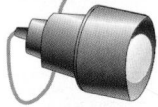

SPOTLIGHT ON

The Example of a Queen: Elizabeth I

by **Katharina M. Wilson**

It is your shame (I speak to you all, you young gentlemen of England) that one maid should go beyond you all in excellency of learning and knowledge of diverse tongues.

—Roger Ascham, tutor to the future Queen Elizabeth I

New Opportunities

With the advent of humanism, Renaissance women of upper-class birth enjoyed great opportunities for artistic and intellectual growth. Education, especially classical learning, was no longer restricted to the clergy. Women as well as men of privileged classes were now expected to seek personal fulfillment by studying a wide array of subjects. **A** Sir Thomas More and Desiderius Erasmus—leading humanists of the day—argued that education would make women better wives and mothers (especially since women had traditionally directed the early education of their children), but that their role should remain a private rather than a public one.

Most advocates of women's education also linked its desirability to the growth of moral virtue. Their intent, especially in Protestant countries, was to allow women to participate more fully in religious life. Men *and* women were encouraged to read and understand God's word. Not surprisingly, many English Renaissance works penned by women have a religious or devotional nature.

King Henry VIII, an enlightened monarch who was quite interested in the new philosophy, appointed humanist scholars to tutor both his son Edward and his daughter Elizabeth. Henry's last wife, Catherine Parr, herself a learned woman and an author (she composed a religious treatise, *A Lamentation or Complaint of a Sinner*), encouraged the king's daughter to study and to translate Latin and French texts into English. Many aristocratic families followed the example set by the royal court, taking great pains to employ scholars as tutors for their children.

A Most Extraordinary Pupil

The studious young girl in the royal family eventually became Queen Elizabeth I (1533–1603), the most influential of England's learned women. During her reign, she dazzled the ambassadors at court with her superb literary training, knowledge of the classics, and political and diplomatic skills. Countless poets and dramatists—Shakespeare, Spenser, and Raleigh among them—praised her learning and grace.

Elizabeth Tudor's early childhood was spent happily in the royal household. But following the execution of **B** her mother, Anne Boleyn, in 1536, she was declared illegitimate. Still, her father continued to

Portrait of a Girl (16th century), possibly Queen Elizabeth, by an English School artist.
Victoria and Albert Museum, London.

Using Students' Strengths

Interpersonal Learners

Have students work with a partner to create a chart that compares their education with Elizabeth's. Students should list the subjects they have studied (in and out of school), and then list Elizabeth's studies. Ask students to compare the lists, with one student noting similarities and another differences. They can then collaborate on preparing a summary statement of similarities and differences.

My Studies	Elizabeth's Studies
[geography	[geography
biology	mathematics
basketball]	needlepoint]

Visual Learners

Ask students to create a design that might be used on a stamp, plate, T-shirt, or other commemorative object honoring Elizabeth I. To generate ideas, students might research some of the designs created to honor Diana, Princess of Wales. On the back of the design, students can explain how their design appropriately highlights one of Elizabeth's attributes.

Musical Learners

Have students demonstrate their understanding of Elizabeth's poem on p. 412 by setting it to music. Students might sing, play instruments, or combine the two. Ask students to explain how the mood and rhythm of their musical creations reflect the meaning of the poem.

A Procession of Queen Elizabeth I (c. 1600) attributed to Robert Peake the Elder.

provide for her education, and her tutors Sir John Cheke and Roger Ascham left us a record of her early training. Her daily schedule was rigorous. Every day she would study Greek (classical authors such as Sophocles and Demosthenes) and Latin (Roman authors like Cicero and Livy, as well as the Scriptures). In studying languages, Elizabeth followed the methods advocated by Renaissance educators: First, she read the Greek or Latin texts; then she translated them into polished English prose; and finally, she retranslated the texts into the original languages, attempting to approximate her source as well as she could.

In addition to Greek and Latin, Elizabeth spoke and read French, Italian, Spanish, Flemish, Welsh, and German. Like most upper-class girls, she also received lessons in riding, music, astronomy, geography, philosophy, mathematics, and needlepoint. In fact, the original manuscript of Elizabeth's translation (done at age eleven, no less) of Queen Marguerite de Navarre's *The Mirror of the Sinful Soul* is enclosed in an elaborately embroidered silk cover that is most likely her own work. Little wonder, then, that as queen she was highly acclaimed for her learning and talents.

Expressions of Love and Duty

After the death of Elizabeth's staunchly Catholic half-sister, Mary Tudor, Elizabeth herself was crowned queen in 1558. She returned England to Protestantism and ruled with great prudence for the next forty-five years. Often urged to marry, Elizabeth had the political skill to recognize the dangers of such an act. She rejected many proposals of marriage because she had "already joined [her]self in marriage to a husband, namely, the kingdom of England."

This is not to say, however, that Elizabeth didn't entertain the attentions of several suitors who came to woo her. She is thought to once have been deeply in love with Robert Dudley, a member of her court. Later, Elizabeth grew attached to the earl of Essex, an alleged traitor whom she, however regretfully, ordered executed. She wrote the following poem as a going-away gift for still another suitor, the much younger duke of Alençon, whom she affectionately called "Monsieur" and rebuffed because of public hostility to the match. Written in the poetic style practiced by her countrymen Spenser and Wyatt, Elizabeth's poem describes the paradoxes and pangs of love.

C Background

Accomplishments

English Renaissance humanist and scholar Roger Ascham wrote about Elizabeth, "Her perseverance is equal to that of a man, and her memory long keeps what it quickly picks up. She talks French and Italian as well as she does English. When she writes Greek and Latin, nothing is more beautiful than her handwriting. She delights as much in music as she is skillful in it."

D Exploring the Historical Period

Religious Conflict

Turmoil between Catholics and Protestants intensified in England during this time. When Mary Tudor became queen, she made Catholicism the state religion, supplanting the Protestant Church of England founded by her father Henry VIII. (Mary was embittered because her own mother had been cruelly banished by Henry.) Because Mary suspected Elizabeth of plotting with the Protestants to gain the throne, Mary had Elizabeth imprisoned in the Tower of London for two months. To prevent Elizabeth from taking the throne, Mary had her charged with adultery, complicity to rebel, and other crimes; however, Elizabeth's opponents failed to prove anything against her. When Elizabeth became queen, she took the religious middle ground, restoring the Protestant Church of England while retaining many Catholic features. Throughout her reign, however, many Catholics continued to oppose her, and toward the end of her reign, Elizabeth permitted the persecution of Catholics.

RESPONDING TO THE ART

Explain to students that a procession is a parade of people who move forward in an orderly or formal way. (For more art by Peake, see p. 257.)

Activity. Ask students to find details in the painting that suggest order or formality.

Making the Connections

Connecting to the Theme: "The Power of the Word"

After students have read the Spotlight On Elizabeth I, discuss with them the value and emphasis placed on education in Elizabeth's time. Ask them to compare and contrast the power of the written word in Elizabethan times with the power of scientific, technological, or computer literacy in our own time.

Crossing the Curriculum

Film Studies

The character of Elizabeth I has been dramatized in many film productions, among them *Fire Over England* (1936) and *The Sea Hawk* (1940) with Flora Robson, *Elizabeth and Essex* (1939) and *The Virgin Queen* (1955) with Bette Davis, and *Elizabeth* (1998) with Cate Blanchett. Ask students to view one of these productions and then hold a panel discussion, comparing and contrasting the film character with the historical figure.

A Humanities Connection

Strength at the Helm

When Elizabeth came to the throne, England needed a strong leader. War and religious conflict had weakened the country, the treasury was depleted, and the rulers of both Spain and France wanted to conquer England. By the end of Elizabeth's reign, England was rich, secure, and enjoying its greatest literary period. English ships ruled the seas, and England had begun to establish itself as a world power.

B Exploring the Historical Period

Sea Power

England's ongoing problems with Spain intensified after English privateers began capturing Spanish ships carrying treasure from the American colonies. Philip II's decision to invade England came after Elizabeth knighted Francis Drake for sailing around the world, thereby challenging Spanish dominance in the Americas. Spain's "invincible" Armada was made up of 130 ships carrying more than 30,000 men. These mighty ships, however, were no match for the speed, maneuverability, and firepower of England's coastal vessels. With the defeat of the Armada, England took Spain's place as master of the world's seas.

C Literary Connections

The Rise of English

Although at the beginning of the period it was doubted that English would ever replace Latin as the language of scholarship and literature, by its end, Spenser, Shakespeare, and Jonson had all written masterworks in English.

On Monsieur's Departure

I grieve, and dare not show my discontent;
I love, and yet am forced to seem to hate;
I do, yet dare not say I ever meant;
I seem stark mute, but inwardly do prate;
  I am and not; I freeze and yet am burn'd;
  Since from myself, my other self I turn'd;

My care is like my shadow in the sun,
Follows me flying, flies when I pursue it,
Stands and lies by me, doth what I have done;
His too familiar care doth make me rue it:
  No means I find to rid him from my breast
  Till by the end of things it be surpress'd.

Some gentler passions slide into my mind,
For I am soft and made of melting snow;
Or be more cruel, Love, and so be kind—
Let me or float or sink, be high or low,
  Or let me live with some more sweet
    content,
  Or die and so forget what love ere meant.

—Elizabeth I

Aside from writing poems, letters, prayers, sermons, and translations (not to mention governing the country, conducting foreign policy, fostering the arts, and dedicating herself fervently to the new religion), Queen Elizabeth also wrote masterful speeches and political addresses. One of her best-known orations is the "Tilbury Speech." Given in 1588, before news of the Spanish Armada's destruction had reached England, Elizabeth's speech was meant to rouse her land forces to defend England against Spanish invasion. Here, the English queen powerfully demonstrates her identification with—and pride in—her nation.

My loving people: We have been persuaded by some that are careful of our safety to take heed how we commit ourself to armed multitudes for fear of treachery, but I assure you I do not desire to live to distrust my faithful and loving people. Let tyrants fear. I have always so behaved myself that, under God, I have placed my chiefest strength and safeguard in the loyal hearts and goodwill of my subjects. And therefore I am come amongst you, as you see, at this time, not for my recreation and disport, but being resolved in the midst and heat of the battle to live or die amongst you all, to lay down for my God, and for my kingdom, and for my people, my honor and my blood, even in the dust. I know I have the body but of a weak and feeble woman, but I have the heart and stomach of a king—and of a king of England too—and think foul scorn that Parma, or Spain, or any prince of Europe should dare to invade the borders of my realm. To which, rather than any dishonor shall grow by me, I myself will take up arms, I myself will be your general, judge, and rewarder of every one of your virtues in the field. I know already for your forwardness you have deserved rewards and crowns, and we do assure you, in the word of a prince, they shall be duly paid you.

—Elizabeth I

And what do we know of those women who were less fortunate than Elizabeth or her aristocratic countrywomen? The literacy rate among them (as among Renaissance men neither nobly born nor affiliated with the Church) is almost impossible to estimate. Many people who could read could not write, and thus could not sign their names to county rolls—one of the standard tools for measuring literacy. Still, judging by the sheer number of books printed and translations produced in this period, we can safely assume that reading for moral improvement and personal pleasure had finally entered the humble home.

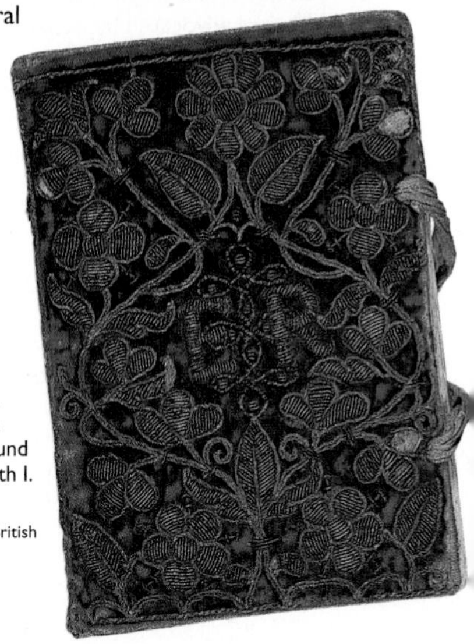

Copy of the New Testament (1603), bearing the initials E. R., probably bound for Queen Elizabeth I. H.D. 37.

By permission of the British Library, London.

Skill Link

Analyzing Persuasive Messages

Have a volunteer read aloud the excerpt from Elizabeth's "Tilbury Speech." As they listen to the speech, ask students to jot down adjectives describing Elizabeth's character and her message. Have students work in small groups, using their notes and other information from the Spotlight On to informally discuss the queen's character. Later, groups can present a more formal character analysis.

Assessing Learning

Check Test: True-False

1. Some humanists believed education would lead women to become better wives and mothers. [True]
2. The type and scope of Elizabeth's education was typical of that received by all young women in Renaissance England. [False]
3. Elizabeth would not tolerate the invasion of England by any other European country. [True]
4. During Elizabeth's time the masses began to read for moral instruction and personal pleasure. [True]

The King James Bible (1611): A Masterpiece by a Committee

One of the first acts of James I after he was crowned king of England was to sponsor a new translation of the Bible. There were many translations of the Bible available, but the king, like others, disliked the interpretive comments included in the existing translations. Moreover, Renaissance scholarship had made people more historically minded and sensitive to textual inaccuracies. The new translation would be checked against the most authoritative Hebrew and Greek texts available.

To produce the translation, the king appointed a team of fifty-four learned clergymen. They broke up into groups, each with a section of the Scriptures to translate and each with a pair of scholars to check the work. Seven years later, after a committee of bishops gave it a final review, the new translation was published. It has become known variously as the "King James Bible" because James sponsored it; as the "Authorized Version" because the Anglican Church authorized its use; and simply as the "English Bible" because it has been so important to the civilization and literature of all English-speaking countries.

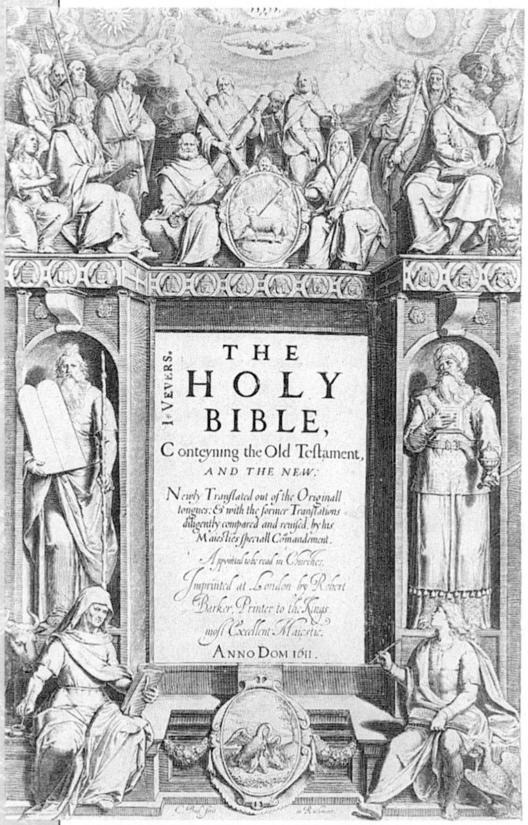

Title page of the Holy Bible (1611). Printed by Robert Barker, London.

The Pierpont Morgan Library, New York. PML 5460.

go.hrw.com
LEO 12-5

OBJECTIVES

1. Read and interpret selections from the King James Bible
2. Identify and analyze imagery
3. Monitor comprehension
4. Express understanding through creative and critical writing, oral interpretation, and research

SKILLS

Literary
- Analyze imagery

Reading
- Monitor comprehension through dialoguing with the text

Writing
- Collect ideas for a cause-and-effect essay
- Write an original parable
- Write a comparison-contrast essay

Speaking/Listening
- Present an oral interpretation of psalms
- Research and present an oral report on Renaissance inventions

Viewing/Representing
- Interpret a painting (ATE)

Planning

- **Block Schedule**
  Block Scheduling Lesson Plans with Pacing Guide
- **Traditional Schedule**
  Lesson Plans Including Strategies for English-Language Learners
- **One-Stop Planner**
  CD-ROM with Test Generator

BROWSING IN THE FILES

Writers on Writing. The Biblical writers were aware of the power and limits of language and interested in the art and craft of writing, as the following excerpts illustrate.
- "My tongue is the pen of a ready writer." (from Psalm 45:1)
- "A word fitly spoken is like apples of gold in pictures of silver." (Proverbs 25:11)
- "Of making many books there is no end." (Ecclesiastes 12:12)

Resources: Print and Media

Reading
- *Graphic Organizers for Active Reading,* p. 32
- *Audio CD Library*
  Disc 6, Track 4

Writing and Language
- *Daily Oral Grammar*
  Transparency 12
- *Grammar and Language Links*
  Worksheet, p. 23

Assessment
- *Formal Assessment,* p. 71
- *Preparation for College Admission Exams,* p. 19
- *Test Generator (One-Stop Planner CD-ROM)*

Internet
go.hrw.com (keyword: LEO 12–5)

A Literary Connections

Biblical Vocabulary

The King James Bible has been a major force in stabilizing the English language since the seventeenth century. Part of its effectiveness lies in its limited vocabulary. In contrast to the thirty-thousand-word vocabulary of Shakespeare's First Folio, the King James Bible uses only eight thousand words. Some seventeenth-century religious dissenters even attempted to limit their vocabulary to those eight thousand words. This idea was destined to fail, since additional words were needed for a great many things unheard of in Biblical times, such as *parliament* and the names of North American plants and animals.

Background

Make sure students know that there are reference books, called *concordances*, for locating Biblical passages. These Biblical concordances index phrases in the same manner as the index at the back of *Bartlett's Familiar Quotations*. The only difference is that a Bible is needed to look up the quotations in full. Two widely used concordances for the King James Bible are *Strong's Exhaustive Concordance of the Bible* and *Young's Analytical Concordance*.

RESPONDING TO THE ART

Note the eagle at the writer's inkwell. In Biblical iconography (visual symbolism), an eagle represents John the Evangelist.

Title page of the Holy Bible (detail) (1611). Printed by Robert Barker, London.

The Pierpont Morgan Library, New York. PML 5460.

If English-speaking people living before our time read anything, they read the English Bible. And if they read nothing themselves, they regularly heard the Bible read in Church. For nearly four centuries, most writers in English have been influenced, consciously or unconsciously, by the English Bible. They have quoted it, echoed it, paraphrased it, alluded to it, imitated it, and retold its fascinating stories over and over.

A Everyday English speech is full of words and phrases from the English Bible: "loving kindness," "tender mercy," "long suffering." We "cast pearls before swine" and "wait until the eleventh hour" before acting. We speak of the "wisdom of Solomon" and the "patience of Job." Many Biblical words (such as *scapegoat*) are by now so embedded in our language that we use them without knowing we are using Biblical language.

But even when the King James Bible was first published, its language sounded old-fashioned. The translators had preserved much of the style of William Tyndale, a Bible translator who had been dead for more than seventy years—years in which the language had changed rapidly. In 1611, English people were beginning to address each other as "you," but the new Bible kept the archaic verb forms and the old second-person pronouns *thou, thy, thine,* and *thee*.

Over the years, the language of the King James Bible has become even more distant from ordinary English. For some readers, this remoteness makes it more moving and evokes more sublime feelings than does a Bible in the vernacular. The King James Bible stands with Shakespeare as an exemplar of English when the language was, as many people believe, more flexible and eloquent than at any other time, and more capable of stirring people's hearts and minds.

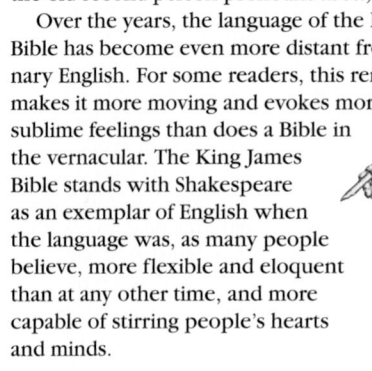

Title page of the Holy Bible (detail) (1611). Printed by Robert Barker, London.

The Pierpont Morgan Library, New York. PML 5460.

Skill Link

Evaluating Informative Messages

In an introductory statement, the translators of the King James Bible directly address their audience. They identify their purposes, admit their problems, and give the reasons behind many of their stylistic decisions. At one point, they use vivid figurative language and Biblical diction to praise the noble act of translation itself, another example of the power of the word.

Read aloud the following quotation from the translators' preface and elicit students' responses. Students may also want to comment on the value and quality of other translations they have read.

> "Translation it is that openeth the window, to let in the light; that breaketh the shell, that we may eat the kernel; that putteth aside the curtain, that we may look into the most holy place; that removeth the cover of the well, that we may come by the water; even as Jacob rolled away the stone from the mouth of the well, by which means the flocks of Laban were watered. Indeed without translation into the vulgar tongue, the unlearned are but like children at Jacob's well (which was deep) without a bucket or something to draw with . . . ."

Before You Read

FROM **GENESIS**

Make the Connection

How and Why

The first book of the Bible is called Genesis, which means "coming into being." Genesis opens with two accounts of creation: Chapter 1 emphasizes the cosmos or universe; Chapter 2 looks at the earth and humanity. Although Moses is traditionally thought of as the author of Genesis, many Biblical scholars now say that two different writers recorded these two creation accounts, which may well be regarded as complementary. Both narratives are very spare and simple but elevated in style.

Besides telling us how the physical universe we know came into being, the first chapters of Genesis deal with how and why human beings were created, and especially, in Chapter 3, why individual members of the human race must suffer and die, and why the history of the whole race has been so bloody and troubled.

Elements of Literature

Imagery

The ancient writers of the Bible were addressing an unsophisticated people. To appeal to their audience, they used a pictorial style rich in **imagery** to tell the story of the primordial origins of the whole human race. Through the centuries, many artists have interpreted scenes from Genesis.

Reading Skills and Strategies

Responding to the Text

As you read this selection from Genesis, and other Biblical selections here, keep a piece of paper handy. Record questions, responses, even memories evoked by these old texts. You might be reading these texts for the first time, or you might have read them or heard them many times in your childhood. Whatever your past experiences with the Bible, you'll find some of these passages striking strong emotional and intellectual responses.

Creation of Adam (detail) (1508–1512) by Michelangelo. Fresco.
Sistine Chapel, Vatican Palace, Rome.

Summary

This selection presents the first three chapters of Genesis, the first book of the Old Testament in the King James version published in 1611. Chapter 1 deals mainly with the creation of the cosmos; Chapter 2 with the creation of earth, animals, and human beings; and Chapter 3 with Adam and Eve's temptation and fall.

The first two chapters are creation narratives, and most Biblical scholars now believe that the two narratives had different authors, although together they constitute a unified vision of the divine creation. Both accounts have a spare yet eloquent style, seemingly simple and straightforward but with symbolic resonances of great depth and suggestiveness. The powerfully evocative images of God, of the first human beings, and of the Edenic Paradise have profoundly influenced the values, literature, and art of all Judeo-Christian societies. Like the creation stories of other cultures, the Genesis accounts ask and answer eternal human questions about where we came from, how we must live, and why we suffer and die. The stories also testify to the power of the word, since most of creation is summoned into existence by God's command, and Adam's power over nature is signified by God's giving him responsibility for naming the creatures of the earth.

RESPONDING TO THE ART

Michelangelo Buonarroti (1475–1564) always insisted that he was primarily a sculptor. However, the Italian artist was also a painter, an architect, and a poet—a true Renaissance genius. Commissioned by the Pope to paint the Sistine Chapel in the Vatican in Rome, he labored for four years on this arduous task.

Activity. Ask students to interpret what is happening in the painting. Have them begin by identifying the two major figures: Adam, with his almost lifeless outstretched hand, on the left, waits to be given life by the finger of God, on the right.

A Vocabulary Note

Word Origins

In Hebrew the words used here are *tohu* and *bohu*: "trackless waste" and "emptiness." The images imply the concept of creation *ex nihilo*, or "creation from nothing."

B Elements of Literature

Imagery

? What image or images does this description bring to mind? [Possible responses: A snapshot-like sequence of a variety of plants that are mature and ready to reproduce; an image of growing plants in a nature documentary, with seeds becoming plants and plants blossoming and giving fruit, as in time-lapse photography.]

C Vocabulary Note

Word Origins

The common name for God in Hebrew is *Elohim*, a plural form. The plural here might be the use of the royal "We."

D Critical Thinking

Interpreting

? Regarding humanity's relationship with nature, what do you think God's words mean here? [Possible response: People rule the earth and all its living things and may use them however they see fit.]

from Genesis

In the beginning God created the heaven and the earth. And the earth was without form, and void; and darkness was upon the face of the deep. And the spirit of God moved upon the face of the waters.[1] And God said, "Let there be light": And there was light. And God saw the light, that it was good: And God divided the light from the darkness. And God called the light Day, and the darkness he called Night. And the evening and the morning were the first day.

And God said, "Let there be a firmament[2] in the midst of the waters, and let it divide the waters from the waters." And God made the firmament, and divided the waters which were under the firmament from the waters which were above the firmament: And it was so. And God called the firmament Heaven. And the evening and the morning were the second day.

And God said, "Let the waters under the heaven be gathered together unto one place, and let the dry land appear": And it was so. And God called the dry land Earth; and the gathering together of the waters called he Seas: And God saw that it was good. And God said, "Let the earth bring forth grass, the herb[3] yielding seed, and the fruit tree yielding fruit after his kind, whose seed is in itself, upon the earth": And it was so. And the earth brought forth grass, and herb yielding seed after his kind,[4] and the tree yielding fruit, whose seed was in itself, after his kind: And God saw that it was good. And the evening and the morning were the third day.

And God said, "Let there be lights in the firmament of the heaven to divide the day from the night; and let them be for signs, and for seasons, and for days, and years: And let them be for lights in the firmament of the heaven to give light upon the earth": And it was so. And God made two great lights; the greater light to rule the day, and the lesser light to rule the night: He made the stars also. And God set them in the firmament of the heaven to give light upon the earth, and to rule over the day and over the night, and to divide the light from the darkness: And God saw that it was good. And the evening and the morning were the fourth day.

And God said, "Let the waters bring forth abundantly the moving creature[5] that hath life, and fowl that may fly above the earth in the open firmament of heaven." And God created great whales, and every living creature that moveth, which the waters brought forth abundantly, after their kind, and every winged fowl after his kind: And God saw that it was good. And God blessed them, saying, "Be fruitful, and multiply, and fill the waters in the seas, and let fowl multiply in the earth." And the evening and the morning were the fifth day.

And God said, "Let the earth bring forth the living creature after his kind, cattle, and creeping thing, and beast of the earth after his kind": And it was so. And God made the beast of the earth after his kind, and cattle after their kind, and everything that creepeth upon the earth after his kind: And God saw that it was good. And God said, "Let us make man in our[6] image, after our likeness: And let them have dominion[7] over the fish of the sea, and over the fowl of the air, and over the cattle, and over all the earth, and over every creeping thing that creepeth upon the earth." So God created man in his own image, in the image of God created he him; male and female created he them. And God blessed them, and God said unto them, "Be fruitful, and multiply, and replenish the earth, and subdue it: And have dominion over the fish of the sea, and over the fowl of the air, and over every living thing that moveth upon the earth." And God said, "Behold, I have given you every herb bearing seed, which is upon the face of all the earth, and every tree, in the which is the fruit of a tree yielding seed; to you it shall be for meat.[8]

1. **waters:** Only water existed before the Creation began.
2. **firmament:** sky. Since the sky is blue, it is natural to suppose that there are waters above it. Where, otherwise, would the rain come from?
3. **herb:** vegetation.
4. **his kind:** its nature. *Its* is a word that came into common use late in the seventeenth century.
5. **creature:** created beings; an old plural without the *s*.
6. **our:** my. God refers to himself as "we" to indicate his authority.
7. **dominion:** power to rule.
8. **meat:** food. What we call meat, the Bible calls *flesh*.

Reaching All Students

Struggling Readers

Suggest that students write the numbers 1–7 in a vertical column in their notebooks before they start reading. Then as they read, have them summarize what God did on each of the seven days of Creation. Also ask them to look for clues, such as "And God saw that it was good," that signal the end of one day's activity.

English Language Learners

One way of engaging English language learners is to have them listen to the recording of the selection in the *Audio CD Library.* For additional strategies to supplement instruction, see

- *Lesson Plans Including Strategies for English-Language Learners*

The Creation of the Animals by a Flemish School artist. Oil.
Navarra Museum, Pamplona, Spain.

And to every beast of the earth, and to every fowl of the air, and to everything that creepeth upon the earth, wherein there is life, I have given every green herb for meat": And it was so. And God saw everything that he had made, and, behold, it was very good. And the evening and the morning were the sixth day.

Thus the heavens and the earth were finished, and all the host[9] of them. And on the seventh day God ended his work which he had made; and he rested on the seventh day from all his work which he had made. And God blessed the seventh day, and sanctified[10] it: because that in it he had rested from all his work which God created and made.

These are the generations of the heavens and of the earth when they were created, in the day that the LORD God made the earth and the heavens, and every plant of the field before it was in the earth, and every herb of the field before it grew: For the LORD God had not caused it to rain upon the earth, and there was not a man to till the ground. But there went up a mist from the earth, and watered the whole face of the ground. And the LORD God formed man of the dust of the ground, and breathed into his nostrils the breath of life; and man became a living soul. And the LORD God planted a garden eastward in Eden; and there he put the man whom he had formed. And out of the ground made the LORD God to grow every tree that is pleasant to the sight, and good for food; the tree of life also in the midst of the garden, and the tree of knowledge of good and evil. And a river went out of Eden to water the garden; and from thence it was parted, and became into four heads.[11] The name of the first is Pison:[12] That is it which compasseth the whole land of Havilah, where there is gold; and the gold of that land is good: There is bdellium[13] and the onyx[14] stone. And the name of the second river is Gihon: The same is it that compasseth the whole land of Ethiopia. And the name of the third river is Hiddekel: That is it which goeth toward the east of Assyria. And the fourth river is Euphrates. And the LORD God took the man, and put him into the garden of Eden to dress it and to keep it. And the LORD God commanded the man, saying, "Of every tree of the garden thou mayest freely eat: But of the tree of the knowledge of good and evil, thou shalt not eat of it: For in the day that thou eatest thereof thou shalt surely die."

And the LORD God said, "It is not good that the man should be alone; I will make him an help meet[15] for him." And out of the ground the LORD God formed every beast of the field, and every fowl of the air; and brought them unto Adam to see what he would call them: And whatsoever Adam called every living creature, that was the name thereof. And Adam gave names to all cattle, and to the fowl of the air, and to every beast of the field; but for Adam there was not found an help meet for him. And the LORD God caused a deep sleep to fall upon Adam, and he slept: And he took one of his ribs, and closed up the flesh instead thereof; and the rib, which the LORD God had taken from man, made he a woman, and

9. **host:** multitude.
10. **sanctified:** made holy.
11. **heads:** A head is the beginning, or source, of a river.
12. **Pison:** This and the other geographical names (except for Ethiopia, for which modern translations say *Cush*) locate the Garden of Eden in Mesopotamia (modern Iraq).
13. **bdellium** (del′ ē · əm): precious substance, either a stone or a resin.
14. **onyx:** gemstone.
15. **help meet:** suitable helper.

E Cultural Connections

The concept of the Sabbath (from the Hebrew *shabbat*, or "rest") has its origin in the divine rest described here. Jews consider Saturday the seventh day, their day of rest. Most Christians set aside Sunday, and Muslims, Friday, as their weekly day of rest and worship.

F Reading Skills and Strategies

Comparing/Contrasting

? How does the creation of man differ from God's other acts of creation? [Possible responses: God uttered words to bring the other elements of creation into existence, but He carefully formed man out of dust; God also breathed life into man alone, giving him a living soul.]

G Elements of Literature

Allusion

The title of John Steinbeck's novel *East of Eden* is a reference to this passage.

H Critical Thinking

Interpreting

? What does the manner of Eve's creation imply about the relationship of Adam and Eve? [Possible responses: God formed Eve from Adam so that they would be of the same bones and flesh, implying a powerful bond; or Eve, being formed of Adam's rib, is meant to be subordinate to him.]

Using Students' Strengths

Visual Learners

To capitalize on the powerful imagery of Genesis, have students create an illustrated time line on which they represent chronologically the events in the selection. They should start with the period when the earth was without form and end with the creation of Eve. Have them include details about each day's activities, using both words and visual images.

Skill Link

Analyzing Text Structures

Transitions. Point out that in the King James translation of Genesis, many sentences begin with *and*—a stylistic choice that keeps the narrative flowing. Today, prose writers use a variety of transitional expressions to ensure coherence and to indicate relationships among ideas:

- To add similar ideas: *and, moreover, in addition, besides*
- To link opposite ideas: *however, yet, on the other hand, in spite of*
- To indicate reasons: *because, since*
- To indicate results: *consequently, then*
- To indicate time: *at once, finally*

Have students work in groups to write a modern version of a Genesis incident, using appropriate transitional expressions. Encourage groups to read their work aloud and compare their use of transitions.

A Critical Thinking
Analyzing Persuasion

? How does the serpent tempt Eve, and why do you think he is effective? [Possible responses: The serpent argues that Adam and Eve will not die if they eat the fruit but will gain the knowledge of good and evil and will "be as gods." The temptation to be like God proves too much for Eve and she gives in. She reveals a common human desire for knowledge and power.]

B Background

At no time is the forbidden fruit identified as an apple, even though it is commonly represented as such. All that is said in the text is that the fruit is pretty, looks good to eat, and holds a promise of wisdom.

C English Language Learners
Interpreting Idioms

Point out that "the eyes of them both were opened" does not mean that Adam and Eve were physically blind. In this idiom, which is still used today, "opening the eyes" means becoming aware of a truth.

D Reading Skills and Strategies
Making Generalizations

? What familiar human tendency is presented here? [Possible response: the tendency to blame others for our own failings.]

E Reading Skills and Strategies
Responding to the Text

? How do you feel toward Adam and Eve when God decides to drive them out of Eden? [Possible responses: Students may feel sympathy for the pair or may feel that Adam and Eve freely chose to disobey God and therefore must endure the consequences of their actions.]

brought her unto the man. And Adam said, "This is now bone of my bones, and flesh of my flesh: She shall be called Woman, because she was taken out of Man." Therefore shall a man leave his father and his mother, and shall cleave[16] unto his wife: And they shall be one flesh. And they were both naked, the man and his wife, and were not ashamed.

Now the serpent[17] was more subtil[18] than any beast of the field which the LORD God had made. And he said unto the woman, "Yea, hath God said, 'Ye shall not eat of every tree of the garden'?" And the woman said unto the serpent, "We may eat of the fruit of the trees of the garden: But of the fruit of the tree which is in the midst of the garden, God hath said, 'Ye shall not eat of it, neither shall ye touch it, lest ye die.'" And the serpent said unto the woman, "Ye shall not surely die: For God doth know that in the day ye eat thereof, then your eyes shall be opened, and ye shall be as gods, knowing good and evil." And when the woman saw that the tree was good for food, and that it was pleasant to the eyes, and a tree to be desired to make one wise, she took of the fruit thereof, and did eat, and gave also unto her husband with her; and he did eat. And the eyes of them both were opened, and they knew that they were naked; and they sewed fig leaves together, and made themselves aprons. And they heard the voice of the LORD God walking in the garden in the cool of the day: And Adam and his wife hid themselves from the presence of the LORD God amongst the trees of the garden. And the LORD God called unto Adam, and said unto him, "Where art thou?" And he said, "I heard thy voice in the garden, and I was afraid, because I was naked; and I hid myself." And he said, "Who told thee that thou wast naked? Hast thou eaten of the tree, whereof I commanded thee that thou shouldest not eat?" And the man said, "The woman whom thou gavest to be with me, she gave me of the tree, and I did eat." And the LORD God said unto the woman, "What is this that thou hast done?" And the woman said, "The serpent beguiled me, and I did eat." And the LORD God said unto the serpent, "Because thou hast done this, thou art cursed above all cattle,[19] and above every beast of the field; upon thy belly shalt thou go, and dust shalt thou eat all of the days of thy life: And I will put enmity[20] between thee and the woman, and between thy seed and her seed; it shall bruise thy head, and thou shalt bruise his heel." Unto the woman he said, "I will greatly multiply thy sorrow and thy conception;[21] in sorrow thou shalt bring forth children; and thy desire shall be to thy husband, and he shall rule over thee." And unto Adam he said, "Because thou hast hearkened unto[22] the voice of thy wife, and hast eaten of the tree, of which I commanded thee, saying, 'Thou shalt not eat of it': Cursed is the ground for thy sake; in sorrow shalt thou eat of it all the days of thy life; thorns also and thistles shall it bring forth to thee; and thou shalt eat the herb of the field; in the sweat of thy face shalt thou eat bread, till thou return unto the ground; for out of it wast thou taken: For dust thou art, and unto dust shalt thou return." And Adam called his wife's name Eve; because she was the mother of all living. Unto Adam also and to his wife did the LORD God make coats of skins, and clothed them.

And the LORD God said, "Behold, the man[23] is become as one of us, to know good and evil: and now, lest he put forth his hand, and take also of the tree of life,[24] and eat, and live forever": Therefore the LORD God sent him forth from the garden of Eden, to till the ground from whence he was taken. So he drove out the man; and he placed at the east of the garden of Eden cherubims,[25] and a flaming sword which turned every way, to keep the way of[26] the tree of life.

—Genesis 1–3

16. **cleave:** be faithful.
17. **serpent:** traditionally understood to be the form assumed by Satan to tempt Eve. Satan is also identified with the angel Lucifer, who revolted against God and was expelled from Heaven.
18. **subtil:** subtle.
19. **cattle:** animals.
20. **enmity:** hostility.
21. **conception:** pains in childbearing.
22. **hearkened unto:** listened and obeyed.
23. **man:** both man and woman.
24. **tree of life:** the first indication that the tree granting everlasting life is prohibited to humanity.
25. **cherubims:** large, fierce angels, quite unlike the modern idea of a cherub.
26. **keep the way of:** prevent access to.

Making the Connections

Cultural Connections: Creation Accounts

The Genesis account of creation is a key to the beliefs of Jews, Muslims, and Christians. Other religions and cultures have their own creation accounts. Encourage students to discover (through interviews or library research) some creation narratives from other cultures. Have them share what they find with the class and discuss what questions each account raises and answers.

Assessing Learning

Check Test: Questions and Answers

1. What does God do on the first day of creation? On the seventh? [On the first day, God creates light, separates it from darkness, and names the two Day and Night. On the seventh day, having finished the work of creation, God rests.]
2. Why does God create Eve? [It is "not good" for Adam to be alone.]
3. With what does the serpent tempt Eve? [with the forbidden fruit; with the promise that she and Adam will become like gods]
4. How does God punish Adam and Eve? [Adam is condemned to a life of unremitting work and certain death; Eve will experience sorrow and pain in childbirth and will be under Adam's dominion.]

Connections — A Newspaper Article

A Beam of Protons Illuminates Gutenberg's Genius

MALCOLM W. BROWNE

The birth of modern printing four centuries ago is cloaked in obscurity, but with the help of the cyclotron used to develop the atomic bomb, scientists are wresting long-forgotten secrets from Gutenberg Bibles and other antique documents to reconstruct the technology of the Renaissance.

In cooperation with scholars at New York City's Pierpont Morgan Library and elsewhere, a group of researchers at the Davis campus of the University of California has learned that Johann Gutenberg of Mainz, Germany, was an even greater inventor and innovator **F** than historians had known. At Davis, physicists and historians have pioneered a technique capable of probing the atoms making up paper, parchment, and ink, thereby opening a new dimension of history to exploration.

The German invention of movable type around 1450 is one of the farthest-reaching technological achievements in history. Movable type, which could be assembled rapidly and put on a printing press, **G** permitted the mass production of books and documents. Literacy, traditionally reserved to churchmen, scholars, scribes, and aristocrats, spread swiftly to the masses and forever changed the nature of society.

Paradoxically, however, the earliest printers left no written descriptions of their monumental achievement. According to Paul Needham, curator of printed books and bindings at the Morgan Library (which owns three Gutenberg Bibles), no one knows what Gutenberg's printing press looked like.

But Dr. Needham and the cyclotron team at Davis have learned a great deal about how Gutenberg and his associates worked and what materials they used.

Directing the cyclotron analyses of old documents is Thomas A. Cahill, head of the Crocker Nuclear Laboratory at Davis. "One of the most remarkable things we discovered in our five-year study," Dr. Cahill said in an interview, "was that Gutenberg's genius extended to the formulation of inks as well as the development of movable type. Other printers of the late 15th century and printers even today tend to use inks based on oils and carbon black. But for Gutenberg, nothing but the best would do. We found within a few seconds of our first analysis of his ink that it is unusually rich in compounds of lead and copper. Lead and copper were Gutenberg's signature, and their presence in the ink on a document is as convincing a sign of his agency as his own hand would be."

Dr. Cahill believes the high levels of copper and lead in Gutenberg's inks account for the fact that the printing in his books remains as fresh, glossy, and black as it was when it came off his press. Bibliographers regard the Gutenberg Bible, printed between 1454 and 1456, as one of the most perfectly printed books ever, rarely matched in quality even in modern times.

H Gutenberg's most famous work is his "forty-two-line Bible," so called because nearly every column of type in its 1,286 pages is forty-two lines long. Some of the forty-two-line Bibles were printed on paper and others on vellum, but experts regard the workmanship in all of them as superb. The left and right margins of each of the two columns on each page are perfectly squared off, and Gutenberg avoided hyphenation by inconspicuously squeezing his type together or spreading it out.

Dr. Cahill and Richard N. Schwab, a history professor at Davis, began applying the cyclotron to historical problems in the early 1980s as an outgrowth of the Crocker Laboratory's work on air pollution. The cyclotron accelerates a narrow beam of protons that pierces a sample, and protons collide with some of the atoms in the sample along the way. When this happens, the atoms emit X-rays, whose varying energies match the specific types of atoms from [which] they were emitted. A detector measures these energies, and with this data a computer can determine the types and quantities of the elements present in the substance being studied.

The analysis of Gutenberg documents required still subtler techniques, Dr. Cahill said. Although the signatures of Gutenberg inks depend on their copper and lead content, the quantities of these and other metals varied appreciably from one batch of ink to another. Gutenberg's workers evidently compounded their inks according to a general recipe but may have been sloppy in their measuring. Similarly, the cyclotron can detect differences among the atomic signatures of various batches of paper (often bearing different watermarks) that Gutenberg used. A single Bible often contains pages from several

Connections

This newspaper article reports how contemporary scientists are using atomic technology to reconstruct how Gutenberg printed his Bibles. As a result of their analysis, these scholars have developed a deeper understanding and appreciation of Gutenberg's achievement, and they are refining a method that can be used to study other early documents.

F Reading Skills and Strategies

Finding the Main Idea

In accordance with standard journalistic style, the main points of this article are presented near the beginning. After students have read the article, have them return to the second paragraph and identify the main ideas. [The main ideas are that Gutenberg was "an even greater inventor and innovator" than had been thought and that the cyclotron technology used in the study of the Gutenberg Bibles holds great promise for other historical research projects.]

G Reading Skills and Strategies

Connecting with the Text

? How do you think the invention of movable type has affected your life? [Possible responses: It has made available at low cost a wide variety of reading material for both educational and recreational purposes, thus making possible the education of a great many people.]

H Critical Thinking

Making Inferences

? What does the "workmanship" of which Browne speaks suggest about Gutenberg's character? [Possible responses: He was a perfectionist; his respect for the Bible led him to pay close attention to its visual presentation.]

Connecting Across Texts

Connecting to Genesis

The article about Gutenberg's methods deals specifically with the first printed Bibles. The article sheds light on the part technology played in the widespread dissemination of the creation narrative—as well as of the entire Bible.

The availability of printed copies of the Bible encouraged greater consistency in religious quotation and teaching because the text of the Bible became more uniform and reliable.

Making Meanings

First Thoughts [Respond]

1. Most will say that Eden, with its easy abundance, was a great loss. There, humans did not have to face the tragedies of suffering and death.

Shaping Interpretations [Interpret]

2. God's supreme authority and power; holiness, justice, and benevolence; infinite variety

3. The Sabbath is the day on which God stopped working. God's blessing on the Sabbath indicates the importance of setting aside a day for rest and contemplation.

4. Humans have a special status since they are formed by God. Genesis emphasizes our purpose of caring for the earth and enjoying a personal relationship with the Creator.

5. Adam's creation from dust foreshadows the return of his body to dust after death.

6. People now know good and evil. Women must suffer in childbirth and be ruled by men. Men must labor for food. Everyone must die.

7. Some students may feel that by eating the fruit, Adam and Eve share in the knowledge that had been reserved for God alone. This could mean that, like God, they now are capable of knowing both good and evil and that they have lost their primal innocence. In this sense, the tree opens their minds, with all the problems and advantages that knowledge brings.

8. Paradise is pictured as beautiful, peaceful, and abundant, supplying humanity's every need.

9. Students' responses may vary, but many will reflect on the origins of the earth and of the human race, on the relationship between the human and the divine, and on the sources of good and evil.

Extending the Text [Evaluate]

10. Possible response: Characteristic traits include ambition and curiosity, traits that persist today. The drive for knowledge and power can be both bad and good, depending upon the means people use to achieve their aims.

---

different batches of paper that were printed at separate times.

By calculating how various inks and papers were combined in each volume, Dr. Cahill and his associates were able to reconstruct Gutenberg's manufacturing process step by step. "There were times when we could almost hear Gutenberg's press creaking," Dr. Cahill said.

This led to the realization that Gutenberg's workshop was much more sophisticated than many scholars had supposed, he said. The shop evidently employed a team of typesetters, all working simultaneously on separate batches of pages, carefully calculating space and text to make certain the assembled volume would come out exactly right.

These separately composed sections fit together almost seamlessly, but there are a few exceptions. One of the rare visible flaws occurs in the middle of Psalm 79, according to Dr. Needham of the Morgan Library.

"The compositor setting the type up to that point was probably sitting next to the compositor who was setting subsequent pages," he said. "One can see that the planning was not quite perfect, because the first compositor found himself in trouble on his last page, stuck with too much space and too little text. He eliminated abbreviations and stretched out his lines, but even so he came up short, and that page has only forty-one lines."

—*from The New York Times*, May 12, 1987

Page from Johann Gutenberg's 42-line Latin Bible (1453–1456) printed at Mainz.

The Granger Collection, New York.

Making Meanings

First Thoughts

1. How do you feel about the world that was lost when Adam and Eve sinned?

Shaping Interpretations

2. What characteristics or qualities of God does the Genesis narrative emphasize? (In your answer, consider the phrases "and it was so" and "it was good.")

3. How does this narrative explain the Sabbath—the day of rest?

4. How does this narrative view God's human creations? According to Genesis, what is our purpose on earth?

5. The name Adam relates to the Hebrew *adamah,* meaning "of the soil." How does Adam's creation from dust **foreshadow** his ultimate fate?

6. What aspects of the human condition does the story of Adam and Eve account for?

7. Scholars have speculated about the meaning of the tree of knowledge of good and evil. Read the text carefully, and decide what you think this tree **symbolizes** and exactly what happened as a result of Adam and Eve's eating of its fruit.

8. How does the writer of Genesis picture Paradise? In *your* imagination, what would a paradise be like?

9. What responses and questions did you note as you read Genesis? If you wish, share your notes in class.

Extending the Text

10. According to Genesis, what traits are characteristic of the human creation? Do you think these traits are still manifested in human life today? Are they totally negative traits, positive traits, or a mixture?

Listening to Music

The Creation, H21, no. 2, by Joseph P. Haydn, performed by Herbert von Karajan and the Berlin Philharmonic

The Creation (1798), composed by Joseph Haydn (1732–1809), is the composer's most famous and influential oratorio. An instrumental and choral tour-de-force, *The Creation* is an infinitely descriptive work, telling the creation story recounted in the Book of Genesis through virtually every conceivable solo and choral vocal form: arias, duets, trios, and full choruses.

Activity

The Creation is above all a highly descriptive piece of music. Have students create webs of descriptive words and phrases that each musical excerpt calls to mind. Have students compare their word webs. Then discuss ways in which Haydn's work captures the images and events of the Genesis creation story.

salms: Worship Through Poetry

A The Bible is full of poetry. Every book of it contains poems or fragments of poems inserted into the prose text, and much of the prose itself is highly rhythmical. One book, the Psalms, consists entirely of poems, some of which were set to music and sung during worship services in the ancient temple in Jerusalem. The book of Psalms preserves 150 of these songs, a fraction of the total number that the ancient Hebrews knew and sang. Psalms were used as hymnals and included songs appropriate for many types of worship: thanksgiving, lament, praise, and devotion. Modern scholars now agree that the psalms were written by many authors over many centuries, but seventy-three of the psalms are said to be "for David" or "concerning David," the heroic Hebrew king.

B In English, a collection of psalms is called a psalter (the *p* is silent as in the word *psalm* itself). (In Hebrew, the name for the collection is *Tehillim,* **C** or "songs of praise.") There have been dozens of English psalters besides the one in the King James Bible, but none of them has lasted so well and so long. King James's translators did not try to impose rhyme on their versions because there is no rhyme in the originals. Instead, they imitated such Hebrew poetic devices as **repetition** and **parallel structure** (the use of sentences or phrases similar in structure):

Let the floods clap their hands,
Let the hills be joyful together.
—Psalm 98:8

The psalmists were fond of saying essentially the same thing twice, in different words ("thy rod and thy staff" in Psalm 23). The King James Bible uses the numbering of the ancient Hebrew manuscripts; some other Bibles use a different numbering derived from a Greek translation of the Hebrew, and these Bibles have an extra psalm, number 151.

Biblical poetry, then, is much like modern free verse in that it does not have rhyme and meter but it does have other patterns of repetition, balance, antithesis, and parallelism. Metaphors and similes abound, and so do images drawn from nature and everyday experience:

My God, in him will I trust.
Surely he shall deliver thee from the snare of the fowler,
And from the noisome pestilence.
He shall cover thee with his feathers,
And under his wings shalt thou trust:
His truth shall be thy shield and buckler.
Thou shalt not be afraid for the terror by night;
Nor for the arrow that flieth by day;
Nor for the pestilence that walketh in darkness;
Nor for the destruction that wasteth at noonday.
—Psalm 91:2–6

(Above left) Illuminated "P" (detail) (c. 1500) from a Flemish Bible.
Victoria and Albert Museum, London.

Objectives

Psalms 23 and 137/ Parable of the Good Samaritan

1. Read and interpret psalms and a parable
2. Express understanding through creative writing, comparing translations, oral interpretations, research, and speaking

Skills

Literary
- Interpret psalms
- Understand a parable

Writing
- Collect ideas for a cause-and-effect essay
- Create a parable
- Compare psalm translations

Speaking/Listening
- Recite psalms
- Deliver an oral report

Planning

- **Block Schedule**
  Block Scheduling Lesson Plans with Pacing Guide
- **Traditional Schedule**
  Lesson Plans Including Strategies for English-Language Learners
- **One Stop Planner**
  CD-ROM with Test Generator

Browsing in the Files

Poetry in the Bible. Other books of the Bible that are essentially prose also contain poetic expression (such as David's lament for Saul and Jonathan in 2 Samuel 1:19–27 and Mary's "Magnificat" in Luke 1:46–55). In addition, much of the wisdom literature (Job, Proverbs, the Song of Solomon, and Ecclesiastes) and prophetic literature (Isaiah, Jeremiah) of the Bible is also lyrical. Historically, the Psalms and the Gospels have been the books of the Bible most often published as separate volumes. *The Bay Psalm Book* (1640) was the first book published in America.

Resources: Print and Media

Reading
- *Graphic Organizers for Active Reading,* pp. 33, 34, 35
- *Audio CD Library*
  Disc 6, Tracks 5, 6, 7

Viewing and Representing
- *Viewing and Representing*
  Fine Art Transparency 5
  Fine Art Worksheet, p. 20

Assessment
- *Formal Assessment,* pp. 73, 75
- *Portfolio Management System,* p. 127
- *Test Generator (One-Stop Planner CD-ROM)*

Summary ■■

The Hebrew **psalms**, hymns to or about God, are collected in the Book of Psalms in the Old Testament. The speaker of Psalm 23, a lyric poem, uses two extended metaphors: the first compares God with a shepherd and the second with a generous host. The figurative language creates a picture of a benevolent God who guides, comforts, and provides for those in His care. The idea that life is a dangerous journey with human beings as pilgrims is also implied. The tone of the poem is serene and trusting, an equilibrium created as much by the rhythmic repetition of words and parallel grammatical elements as by the imagery. Images, such as "green pastures," are concrete and natural, echoing the pastoral, or sheep-herding, way of life of the Hebrew people for whom the songs were originally written.

Ⓐ Reading Skills and Strategies

Finding the Main Idea

After students have read Psalm 23, have them come back to this line. Ask how the idea in this sentence surfaces again and again in the psalm's details. [Possible response: At first the speaker's soul is restored because he can trust God to supply his needs and to deal kindly with him. Then his soul is restored because it inhabits "the paths of righteousness." Its final restoration comes in the promise of "goodness and mercy" throughout life and in a place "in the house of the Lord forever."]

Ⓑ Reading Skills and Strategies

Responding to the Text

? What kinds of experiences do you think people would describe as "walk[ing] through the valley of the shadow of death"? [Possible responses: dealing with a life-threatening illness or accident; living with depression; being a victim of violent crime.]

Before You Read

PSALM 23

Make the Connection

The Lord Is . . .

This song of trust, affirming the speaker's faith and confidence in God, is probably the best-known religious poem in the Western world. The opening verses, comparing God to a shepherd, use the kind of pastoral imagery found throughout the Bible. Then the metaphors in the psalm change, and the Lord becomes a host providing a banquet for the speaker, whose enemies watch him enviously as he eats, not daring to harm him. Among the rich and varied images of the poem, there is also a suggestion of the speaker as a pilgrim traveling through a dangerous world.

Quickwrite

This song was sung by a pastoral people, so the comparison of the Lord to a shepherd is appropriate. The world is very different for most people today. What metaphors would you use to describe the comforting presence of God?

Shepherds. Bas-relief on the lintel over the west portal of Chartres Cathedral.

Cathedral, Chartres, France.

Psalm 23

The Lord is my shepherd; I shall not want.
He maketh me to lie down in green pastures:
He leadeth me beside the still waters.
Ⓐ He restoreth my soul:
He leadeth me in the paths of righteousness for his name's sake.°
Ⓑ Yea, though I walk through the valley of the shadow of death,
I will fear no evil: For thou art with me;
Thy rod and thy staff they comfort me.
Thou preparest a table before me in the presence of mine enemies:
Thou anointest my head with oil; my cup runneth over.
Surely goodness and mercy shall follow me all the days of my life:
And I will dwell in the house of the Lord forever.

5. **his name's sake:** That is, he will live up to his name as shepherd.

Reaching All Students

Struggling Readers

Have students do a Text Reformulation in which they rewrite one of the psalms in prose form. This exercise will help students make inferences and identify main ideas and themes. For additional help with this strategy, see p. 127 of the *Reading Strategies Handbook* in the *Reading Skills and Strategies* binder.

English Language Learners

To help students struggling with the archaic language, have them work with others to rewrite the psalm in the language of today. Divide the class into small groups, and have each group put its version on the chalkboard for discussion. For additional strategies to supplement instruction, see

- *Lesson Plans Including Strategies for English-Language Learners*

Before You Read
PSALM 137

Make the Connection
Captivities
This is a song of entreaty on the occasion of a national catastrophe: Many Israelites are being held captive in Babylon. This lament over a remembered home has been recited by many captives in the thousands of years since it was first sung in ancient Babylon.

Quickwrite
What other experiences in the history of the world might have inspired people to beg for release from captivity or even to seek vengeance on their captors? Take notes on your thoughts.

Background
In the sixth century B.C., Nebuchadnezzar, king of Babylonia, conquered Jerusalem and deported most of the Israelites to Babylon, a great ancient city, which is now a ruin, on the Euphrates River south of Baghdad. The speaker of Psalm 137 is a captive Israelite, bitterly lamenting his people's exile. The Babylonians have asked their captives to sing to entertain them, but what do the captives have to sing about?

Psalm 137

By the rivers of Babylon, there we sat down, yea, we wept,
When we remembered Zion.°
We hanged our harps
Upon the willows in the midst thereof. **C**
For there they that carried us away captive required of us a song;
And they that wasted us required of us mirth,
Saying, "Sing us one of the songs of Zion."
How shall we sing the LORD's song
In a strange land?
If I forget thee, O Jerusalem,
Let my right hand forget her cunning.
If I do not remember thee,
Let my tongue cleave° to the roof of my mouth;
If I prefer not Jerusalem above my chief joy.
Remember, O LORD, the children of Edom° in the day of Jerusalem;
Who said, "Raze it,° raze it, even to the foundation thereof."
O daughter of Babylon,° who art to be destroyed;
Happy shall he be, that rewardeth thee
As thou hast served us.
Happy shall he be, that taketh
And dasheth thy little ones against the stones. **D**

2. Zion: a hill in Jerusalem that is often a symbol for the whole of Israel.

13. cleave: adhere; stick.
15. children of Edom: The Edomites, neighbors of the Israelites, rejoiced when the Israelites' kingdom was conquered and most of its population deported.
16. Raze it: Level it to the ground.
17. daughter of Babylon: the Babylonian people.

Summary

The speaker of Psalm 37 is a Hebrew who was taken captive by foreign conquerors, the Babylonians, and forced to leave his beloved Jerusalem. The tone is progressively mournful, resolute, angry, and vengeful. The natural images of water and willows suggest weeping, loss, and longing, and the setting is "a strange land" far from home. Singing and laughter are unnatural for a people in exile. Memories of home and the hope of destroying the destroyers sustain the displaced speaker. Words here have the power to preserve the past in memory and to conjure up a future in which the tables will be turned on the speaker's enemies.

C Elements of Literature
Imagery
? What kinds of feelings are being expressed by the image "harps/Upon the willows"? How do those feelings relate to the singer's situation? [Possible responses: a feeling of displacement, or not belonging, because the singer is a displaced person in Babylon; depression and a sense of uselessness, because the speaker longs for his homeland.]

D Reading Skills and Strategies
Reading Aloud
? Read this line so that *thy* is emphasized. Does the emphasis help you to understand the singer any better? Explain. [Possible responses: Yes, it suggests that the singer has seen his or her own babies dashed to death by the captors. It also better illustrates ll. 18–19, which suggest that Babylon's retribution will resemble the wrongs it has dealt the Hebrews.]

Crossing the Curriculum

Music
Psalm 23 and Psalm 137 express markedly different feelings. How might these psalms have sounded when sung? Pairs or groups of students may begin to explore the question by finding one or more pieces of music that they feel capture the essence of each psalm. As they play their selections for the class, have them explain their choices.

Social Studies
Offer these activities to interested students, and have them present their findings in a format of their own choosing:

- For Psalm 23: Find out more about sheepherding around the world in the past and present. Try to discover what characteristics would make some shepherds more effective than others.
- For Psalm 137: Do some research to learn why the city of Jerusalem is so important to the singer. Speculate on what the city meant to him in the past and why it occupies his thoughts in the present.

MAKING MEANINGS

First Thoughts [Respond]

1. Possible responses: Psalm 23 might remind the singer of Psalm 137 that God, the divine Shepherd, could guide the Hebrews out of captivity and bring them again to their own land. It also stresses God's provision for all, even for the needs of a captive, and hints that the singer's enemies would see this and be amazed.

Shaping Interpretations [Interpret]

2. The speaker describes the metaphorical "green pastures" and "still waters" to which God will lead him (sheep will not drink from rapidly moving water); he speaks of the comforting presence of the Shepherd's rod and staff.

3. The speaker describes the Host's graciousness in preparing a table for him and providing an overflowing cup.

4. Homesickness is conveyed strongly in ll. 1–2 and 10–14, as is revenge in ll. 15–21. Reactions to the final line will vary, but could include horror, fear, or understanding.

Connecting with the Text [Synthesize]

5. The psalm might remind survivors of God's love for them; the images of the "valley of the shadow" and "the house of the Lord" are easily applied to death and to the hope that the departed will be welcomed into heaven.

6. Possible responses: Psalm 23 evokes pictures of green fields, pools of water, a frightening valley, and a welcoming table. Psalm 137 evokes visions of people weeping by a river and sorrowfully hanging their harps on willows, as well as bitter memories of burning cities and murdered children.

Extending the Text [Analyze]

7. Psalm 137 would have meaning and relevance for any group facing literal or figurative captivity; it might also be appropriate for times of warfare. Its continuing relevance resides in the emotions expressed—love for homeland, lament over exile, and a desire to see wrongs avenged.

Jeremiah Lamenting over Jerusalem.

MAKING MEANINGS

Psalms 23 and 137

First Thoughts

1. How do you think Psalm 23 could be used to provide solace to the singer of Psalm 137?

Shaping Interpretations

2. In Psalm 23, how does the singer extend the **metaphor** comparing God to a shepherd?
3. The second metaphor in Psalm 23 compares God to a generous host. (In the ancient Middle East, it was a sign of hospitality to anoint a guest's head and dusty feet with oil.) How does the speaker extend this metaphor of God as a gracious host and the singer as his guest?
4. The speaker in Psalm 137 is both homesick and vengeful. Which lines convey these emotions most vividly to you? How did you react to the final line?

Connecting with the Text

5. Psalm 23 is often read at funerals or memorial services. Why do you think people find it consoling? (Refer to your Quickwrite notes for page 422.)
6. Both psalms are full of vivid **imagery.** What pictures does each song put in your mind?

Extending the Text

7. On what occasion might Psalm 137 be sung? What relevance does this lament have for people today? (You might want to refer to your Quickwrite notes for page 423.)

Listening to Music

Psalm 23, set to music by Franz Schubert, performed by the King's College Choir

Over the centuries, many composers have set psalms to music. Among them is Franz Schubert (1797–1828), the Austrian Romantic composer who began his musical career as a singer in the choir of the School of the Imperial and Royal Court Chapel in Vienna. Schubert is especially known for his *lieder,* or German art songs, of which he wrote over six hundred. He is also known for his Symphony No. 8 (the "Unfinished Symphony").

Activity

After students have read Psalm 23, let them listen to Schubert's musical setting of the psalm and comment on the feelings it evokes. Interested students might research some contemporary settings of the psalms, such as English composer John Rutter's version of Psalm 23 (from *Requiem*). Pop/rock versions of Psalm 137 may be found in Don McLean's 1971 album *American Pie* ("Babylon") and Manfred Mann's Earth Band 1976 album *The Roaring Silence* ("The Road to Babylon").

Before You Read

THE PARABLE OF THE GOOD SAMARITAN

Make the Connection

Profound Truths

A **parable** is a very short anecdote that teaches a moral or religious lesson. In the Christian Bible, instead of speaking abstractly and philosophically, Jesus often teaches his followers by means of parables. On the surface, parables seem to be simple stories. Looked at closely, they concern the profound truths and moral laws on which human happiness depends. Perhaps you know some parables from other traditions.

Quickwrite

To test your Biblical knowledge, write down quickly what you think a Good Samaritan is.

Background

To understand this parable, you have to know that it is set in a totally Jewish context. According to Jewish law, the priest and the Levite (a member of the priestly tribe) would be considered legally unclean if they touched a dead person. Samaritans were people from Samaria who had a mixed ancestry and a mixed religion. They used the Torah of the Hebrew Bible as their scriptures, but the Israelites to the south frowned on the Samaritans' mixed religious practices. The lawyer is questioning Jesus.

The Parable of the Good Samaritan

And, behold, a certain lawyer stood up, and tempted him, saying, "Master, what shall I do to inherit eternal life?" He said unto him, "What is written in the law? how readest thou?" And he answering said, "Thou shalt love the Lord thy God with all thy heart, and with all thy soul, and with all thy strength, and with all thy mind; and thy neighbor as thyself." And he said unto him, "Thou hast answered right: This do, and thou shalt live." But he, willing to justify himself, said unto Jesus, "And who is my neighbor?" And Jesus answering said, "A certain man went down from Jerusalem to Jericho, and fell among thieves, which stripped him of his raiment,[1] and wounded him, and departed, leaving him half dead. And by chance there came down a certain priest that way: And when he saw him, he passed by on the other side. And likewise a Levite, when he was at the place, came and looked on him, and passed by on the other side. But a certain Samaritan, as he journeyed, came where he was: And when he saw him, he had compassion on him, and went to him, and bound up his wounds, pouring in oil and wine,[2] and set him on his own beast, and brought him to an inn, and took care of him. And on the morrow when he departed, he took out two pence, and gave them to the host, and said unto him, 'Take care of him; and whatsoever thou spendest more, when I come again, I will repay thee.' Which now of these three, thinkest thou, was neighbor unto him that fell among the thieves?" And he said, "He that showed mercy on him." Then said Jesus unto him, "Go, and do thou likewise."

—Luke 10:25–37

1. **raiment:** clothing.
2. **oil and wine:** ancient medicine.

Summary ■■

This excerpt from the Gospel of St. Luke in the New Testament contains a parable. The main characters of the frame story are a lawyer, symbolizing the letter of the law, and Jesus, who represents the spirit of love and compassion. The setting is Palestine in the time of Jesus when observance of Jewish religious law was the standard by which Jews judged one another and others. In order to answer the lawyer's question "Who is my neighbor?" Jesus tells of a man who was robbed and left to die on the roadside. Two upright Jews, obeying the letter of the law which forbids them to touch the dead, pass the victim by, but a Samaritan, an outsider and a heretic, selflessly helps the dying man. Jesus's original Jewish audience would see the irony in the least likely man being the source of compassion. The moral lesson of inclusiveness suggests that true neighborliness can transform social relations.

A Historical Connections

A lawyer was an expert in the Mosaic law, not an attorney in the modern sense. The word *tempted* here means *tested*, and it identifies the lawyer as one of those critics who often challenged Jesus by trying to trap him with difficult questions.

B Reading Skills and Strategies

Making Inferences

? What do you infer from the sequence in which passersby encounter the victim? [Possible responses: First is the priest, whose calling would make him the most likely rescuer. Then comes the Levite, not as important as a priest but, as a person dedicated to service in the Temple, someone who might be expected to help. Last is the Samaritan, the actual rescuer—not a religious leader, and even to some extent an outsider. The sequence implies that anyone can be a neighbor, even those one might least expect.]

Using Students' Strengths

Auditory Learners

Because the parable is short, students can read it aloud. Have them read the parable only, or, to emphasize the story within a story, have one student read the parable and another read the introductory and closing material that form the framework.

Assessing Learning

Check Test: True-False

1. The parable is Jesus' answer to the question, "Who is my neighbor?" [True]
2. A priest and a Levite did not stop to help the victim. [True]
3. The Samaritan not only took care of the victim's wounds but also paid his expenses. [True]
4. Jesus ends the parable with a command to go and act like the Samaritan. [True]
5. The parable has no meaning or application outside its time and place. [False]

MAKING MEANINGS

First Thoughts [Respond]

1. Anyone could be a neighbor. A neighbor is actually someone who lives next door or nearby.

Shaping Interpretations [Interpret]

2. The law says that to achieve eternal life, one must love God with all one's strength and love others as one loves oneself.
3. The lawyer wants to prove that he has a good reason for questioning Jesus, and he may want to test Jesus further.
4. The traveler was attacked by thieves, robbed, beaten, and left for dead.
5. The audience would have expected the priest and the Levite to be sensitive to the demands of charity, even if it meant defiling themselves. But the Samaritan, who is not only an outsider but a heretic, is the only one who has compassion for the victim.

Extending the Text [Synthesize]

6. Students might name a famous person, such as Mother Teresa, or someone they know personally. The closest parallel to the Good Samaritan would be a person who willingly gives assistance without thought of reward.

Challenging the Text [Evaluate]

7. Possible response: The attack by thieves may not need modifying, but the Levite might become a doctor or social worker.
8. Some students may believe that contemporary life is much more complex; more prejudice exists, and people have more excuses to avoid helping a victim. Other students may suggest that—for these same reasons—the parable is more relevant today than ever.

The Good Samaritan (1633) by Rembrandt van Rijn.

©Rijksmuseum–Stichting, Amsterdam.

MAKING MEANINGS

First Thoughts

1. According to the **parable,** how are you supposed to answer the question "Who is my neighbor?" In actuality, how would you answer the question?

Shaping Interpretations

2. Jesus asks the lawyer at the beginning what the law says about eternal life. What does the law say?
3. Why does the lawyer press on and ask another question: Who is my neighbor?
4. According to the parable, what happened to the man who journeyed from Jerusalem to Jericho?
5. Why is it **ironic** that the priest and the Levite ignore the wounded man, but the Samaritan helps him?

Extending the Text

6. What Good Samaritans do you know of in the world today? How does your response compare with the notes you took for the Quickwrite on page 425?

Challenging the Text

7. If you were writing an updated version of this parable, which details would you change to make it relevant to life in our society today?
8. Do you think this parable makes a point that is still important today? Talk about its relevance at the end of the twentieth century.

Making the Connections

Cultural Connections

Jesus implies that even an enemy who rescues you is your neighbor. The parable's context is the clash between Hebrews and Samaritans. Have students name other historical and contemporary conflicts and persons to which Jesus's parable could apply.

CHOICES: Building Your Portfolio

Writer's Notebook

1. Collecting Ideas for a Cause-Effect Essay

The effects of disobedience are the focus of the opening chapters of Genesis. This tendency to disobedience is one of many characteristics fundamental to human nature. Jot down some notes about another human trait, such as loyalty or ambition. You could ask yourself why: Why are some people loyal or ambitious? Or you could ask yourself what if: What if all competition were removed from society so that ambition was stifled? Save your notes to use in the Writer's Workshop on page 459.

Creative Writing

2. A Parable for Today

Try writing your own parable to illustrate a practical lesson about life today. First, identify the moral or spiritual truth you want to illustrate. Then, think of an everyday event that happened to you or someone you know that could illustrate this lesson. The parables in the Christian Bible find lessons in a poor woman who loses a coin, a dishonest employee who cheats his boss, bridesmaids who are asleep when the wedding party arrives, and a father who welcomes back a son who has been so wasteful he becomes the Biblical equivalent of a homeless person.

Comparing Translations

3. Same Psalm, Different Words

The version of Psalm 23 below appeared in a psalter translated by the Massachusetts Puritans and published in the *Bay Psalm Book* (1640). Write an essay comparing it to the version in the King James Bible. Tell which version you prefer and why.

Oral Interpretation

4. Making a Psalm Sing

Prepare a group of the psalms for oral recitation. As you prepare for your presentation, pay particular attention to the way the psalms use **repetition** and **parallel structure** to create rhythm. How many speakers will you assign to each psalm? The psalms were originally sung to the accompaniment of a harp. Will you provide any background music to dramatize your interpretations?

Research / Speaking

5. The Inventive Renaissance

In the ***Connections*** article "A Beam of Protons Illuminates Gutenberg's Genius" (page 419), you read about Gutenberg's innovations. What other remarkable inventions or technological innovations date from the Renaissance? Who are the people behind these creations? Select one person or invention to write about, and present your findings in a brief oral report.

Psalm 23

The Lord to me a shepherd is; want therefore shall not I.
He in the folds of tender grass doth cause me down to lie.
To waters calm me gently leads, restore my soul doth he;
He doth in paths of righteousness for his name's sake lead me.
Yea, though in valley of death's shade I walk, none ill I'll fear,
Because thou art with me; thy rod and staff my comfort are.
For me a table thou hast spread in presence of my foes;
Thou dost anoint my head with oil; my cup it overflows.
Goodness and mercy surely shall all my days follow me.
And in the Lord's house I shall dwell so long as days shall be.

Grading Timesaver

Rubrics for each Choices assignment appear on p. 127 in the *Portfolio Management System.*

CHOICES: Building Your Portfolio

1. **Writer's Notebook** Have students brainstorm a list of possible traits before they begin writing.
2. **Creative Writing** Invite students to gain experience as oral historians by interviewing people and asking them to share experiences from which they learned valuable lessons. Students may change their subjects' names and other details but should keep the narratives simple. Have students share their efforts. If two or more parables teach a similar lesson, have the class discuss how the stories differ.
3. **Comparing Translations** Encourage students to use a two-column response journal. As they compare the two versions verse by verse, have them make one note about each version in the appropriate column. When they have finished, students will find enough common positive and negative comments to help them form an overall evaluation.
4. **Oral Interpretation** Background music, if used, should reflect the general tone of the psalm. Encourage students to experiment with recitation techniques, including the following:
   - working not only with chorus and soloists but with duets and trios;
   - splitting a group to reflect parallel expressions of thought;
   - repeating key words for echo effect (as with the last word of Psalm 23).
5. **Research/Speaking** Encourage students to research various inventions and their creators on the Internet. Make sure they document their sources appropriately.

Assessing Learning

Informal Assessment

Peer Assessment. Ask students to write two sentences explaining what they think is the central message conveyed by "The Parable of the Good Samaritan." Then have students trade papers and write two-sentence comments, assessing whether each writer captured the essential meaning of the parable.

OBJECTIVES

1. Read and interpret wisdom texts from a variety of world cultures
2. Connect text themes with students' own experience and that of others
3. Recognize distinctive and shared characteristics of cultures
4. Recognize and discuss themes and connections that cross cultures

Planning

- **Block Schedule**
  Block Scheduling Lesson Plans with Pacing Guide
- **Traditional Schedule**
  Lesson Plans Including Strategies for English-Language Learners
- **One-Stop Planner**
  CD-ROM with Test Generator

Background

Confucianism. The wisdom literature collected as the *Analects* of Confucius (c. 551–c. 479 B.C.) was intimately connected with one of the most powerful political philosophies in history. Used by the rulers of the Chinese empire to maintain obedience and social harmony, Confucianism taught that a prosperous and cohesive society must be tightly structured with the members' roles and mutual obligations clearly defined.

Resources

Viewing and Representing

Fine Art Transparency

A Fine Art transparency of Chou Chi Ch'ang's *Arhats Bestowing Alms upon Beggars* can be used with *Sayings of Saadi* as a prereading motivator.

See the *Viewing and Representing Transparencies and Worksheets:*

- Transparency 5
- Worksheet, p. 20

WORLD LITERATURE

Worlds of Wisdom

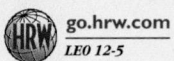

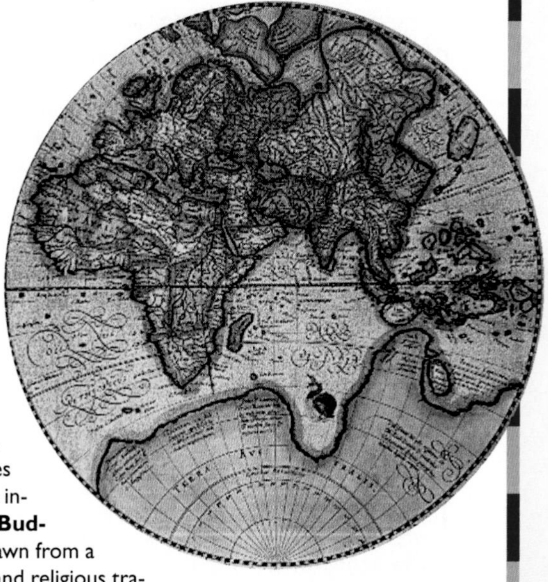

Before You Read

Background

From age to age, from culture to culture, human beings have wrestled with the same problems and questions: How should we live? How can we be happy? What is justice?

Although the pieces of world wisdom that follow come from a wide variety of sources in Africa and Asia, they have two features in common. First, the forms represented here—prophecy, fable, parable, anecdote, and proverb—all spring from the oral tradition. Second, just as with the wisdom literature in the Hebrew Bible, many of these pieces have religious contexts.

The **Koran,** the holy book of Islam, contains God's revelation to Mohammed by the angel Gabriel. The text was first written down in Arabic in the middle of the seventh century.

The text of ***The Panchatantra,*** the most famous Sanskrit collection of fables from ancient India, probably dates from 100 B.C. to around A.D. 400. According to tradition, this anthology was created as a practical manual in statecraft for young princes.

The parables illustrating the insights of **Zen Buddhism** are drawn from a philosophical and religious tradition within Buddhism that originated in China and then flowered in Japan starting in the twelfth century.

The poet **Saadi,** whose real name was Musharrif Od-Din Muslih Od-Din, lived in thirteenth-century Persia (now Iran). As a follower of Sufism, a mystical sect of Islam, he believed in the holiness of all creation. His witty, practical sayings and lush lyrics made him one of Persia's best-loved poets.

Taoism (dou'iz'əm), another Eastern tradition of religion and philosophy, developed in China shortly after the time that Buddhism first began in India, during the last centuries B.C.

Confucius, the founder of yet another Chinese philosophical system, left no written works. After his death in around 479 B.C., his disciples gathered his sayings in a collection known as the *Analects.*

For many centuries, the **Jabo** people of Liberia in West Africa have relied on proverbs in many key aspects of their social life and legal proceedings.

Reading Skills and Strategies

Connecting with the Texts

As you read the pieces that follow, jot down notes on the ones that connect with something in your own background or in today's world. (You might also copy down quotes that you especially like.)

(Map) The world, from Mercator's *Atlas* (c. 1595).

go.hrw.com LEO 12-5

Reaching All Students

English Language Learners

Assign English language learners to small groups of students with varied degrees of English proficiency. Ask each group to concentrate on the wisdom literature of just one culture. If possible, have a student from that culture in the group. Encourage students to formulate questions about the culture and to discuss how they can find answers to their questions.

Advanced Learners

Invite students to choose a theme such as love of neighbor and investigate how the theme is handled in the wisdom literature of several cultures. They may present their findings in an oral report.

Night
from the Koran

translated by **N. J. Dawood**

In the Name of Allah, the Compassionate, the Merciful

By the night, when she lets fall her darkness, and by the radiant day! By Him that created the male and the female, your endeavors have different ends!

For him that gives in charity and guards himself against evil and believes in goodness, We shall smooth the path of salvation; but for him that neither gives nor takes and disbelieves in goodness, We shall smooth the path of affliction. When he breathes his last, his riches will not avail him. (A)

It is for Us to give guidance. Ours is the life of this world, Ours the life to come. I warn you, then, of the blazing fire, in which none shall burn save the hardened sinner, who denies the truth and gives no heed. But the good man who purifies himself by almsgiving[1] shall keep away from it: and so shall he that does good works for the sake of the Most High only, not in recompense[2] for a favor. Such men shall be content.

1. **almsgiving:** performing deeds of charity.
2. **recompense:** repayment.

Leaf from a Koran (11th century) in Kufic calligraphy. Iranian. Ink, colors, gold on paper.

The Metropolitan Museum of Art, Rogers Fund, 1940 (40.164.2a). Photograph ©1989 The Metropolitan Museum of Art.

Summary ▪▪

This excerpt is from the *Koran*, the holy book of the Islamic faith. Muslims believe that God revealed every word of this holy book to Mohammed in Arabic in the seventh century. The excerpt begins with a personification of night as a woman loosening her dark hair and with an acknowledgment of God as the creator of all. It then goes on to give moral directives to humanity on how to live a holy life. The speaker in the last two paragraphs appears to be God himself (or God's representative) who promises salvation to those who practice charity and believe in goodness. Affliction and "blazing fire" are promised to those who fail to give and believe. According to the speaker, worldly riches will save no one at the hour of death; contentment will come only to those who do good for God's sake alone.

Background

Translated literally, the Arabic word *Koran* (Qur'an) means "The Recital," attesting once again to the power of the word.

(A) Critical Thinking

Drawing Conclusions

? According to the text, what kind of life should a person live? What will happen to those who live otherwise? [Possible responses: A person should live a good, charitable life. Those who do not will be punished, and no amount of money will save them.]

Resources

Listening

Audio CD Library

For a recording of this selection see the *Audio CD Library:*

- Disc 6, Track 8

Making the Connections

Connecting to the Theme: "The Power of the Word"

"In the beginning was the Word. . . ." (John 1:1) This striking statement about the power of the word comes from the New Testament. Ask students how this message applies to the wisdom texts reprinted here. [Possible responses: They express the foundations of societies; they embody people's definitions of themselves. These powerful words tell individuals not only how to behave but also who they are at their core.]

Summary

This brief story, with animal characters whose actions illustrate a practical lesson, is from a collection of Hindu fables called *The Panchatantra*, dating from about 100 B.C. to A.D. 400. The plot involves a turtle, Shell-Neck, and two ganders, Slim and Grim. The setting is a lake which is drying out due to drought. When ganders plan to fly to another lake, their friend, the turtle, begs them to carry him off on a stick placed between their bills. The ganders warn the turtle that if he opens his mouth to speak he will fall to his death, foreshadowing his fate. When the sound of human voices distracts the turtle, Shell-Neck opens his mouth to speak and falls to the ground. The moral—to heed advice from well-meaning friends—is stated explicitly in a short stanza of verse. In this story, ill-timed words have the power to destroy.

A Elements of Literature

Foreshadowing

? The storyteller inserts a warning. What do you think will happen? [Possible response: The turtle won't follow his own plan.]

B Elements of Literature

Irony

? Why is it ironic that the sound of people chattering causes the turtle to lose his grip on the stick? [Possible response: Even though he vowed silence, the turtle's fascination with words undoes him.]

C Reading Skills and Strategies

Connecting with the Text

? If this fable were written to give advice to young people today, what message do you think it would convey? [Possible response: When a trusted friend gives you advice, follow it.]

Resources

Listening

Audio CD Library

For a recording of this selection see the *Audio CD Library:*

- Disc 6, Track 9

Shell-Neck, Slim, and Grim
from The Panchatantra

translated by **Arthur W. Ryder**

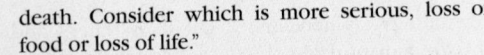

A Pair of Wild Fowls (detail) (1600–1625) attributed to Manṣūr, Imperial Mughal.
Collection Navin Kumar, New York.

In a certain lake lived a turtle named Shell-Neck. He had as friends two ganders whose names were Slim and Grim. Now in the vicissitudes[1] of time there came a twelve-year drought, which begot ideas of this nature in the two ganders: "This lake has gone dry. Let us seek another body of water. However, we must first say farewell to Shell-Neck, our dear and long-proved friend."

When they did so, the turtle said: "Why do you bid me farewell? I am a water dweller, and here I should perish very quickly from the scant supply of water and from grief at loss of you. Therefore, if you feel any affection for me, please rescue me from the jaws of this death. Besides, as the water dries in this lake, you two suffer nothing beyond a restricted diet, while to me it means immediate death. Consider which is more serious, loss of food or loss of life."

But they replied: "We are unable to take you with us since you are a water creature without wings." Yet the turtle continued: "There is a possible device. Bring a stick of wood." This they did, whereupon the turtle gripped the middle of the stick between his teeth, and said: "Now take firm hold with your bills, one on each side, fly up, and travel with even flight through the sky, until we discover another desirable body of water."

(A) But they objected: "There is a hitch in this fine plan. If you happen to indulge in the smallest conversation, then you will lose your hold on the stick, will fall from a great height, and will be dashed to bits."

"Oh," said the turtle, "from this moment I take a vow of silence, to last as long as we are in heaven." So they carried out the plan, but while the two ganders were painfully carrying the turtle over a neighboring city, the people below noticed the spectacle, and there arose a confused buzz of talk as they asked: "What is this cartlike object that two birds are carrying through the atmosphere?"

(B) Hearing this, the doomed turtle was heedless enough to ask: "What are these people chattering about?" The moment he spoke, the poor simpleton lost his grip and fell to the ground. And persons who wanted meat cut him to bits in a moment with sharp knives.

(C) "And that is why I say:

To take advice from kindly friends
Be ever satisfied:
The stupid turtle lost his grip
Upon the stick, and died."

1. **vicissitudes:** unpredictable changes.

Professional Notes

Critical Comment

Arthur W. Ryder, translator, offers these comments on *The Panchatantra*: "*The Panchatantra* is a *niti-shastra*, or textbook of *niti*. The word *niti* means roughly 'the wise conduct of life.' . . . It can be practiced only by a social being, and represents an admirable attempt to answer the insistent question how to win the utmost possible joy from life in the world of men. . . . Granted security and freedom from worry, then joy results from three occupations—from resolute, yet circumspect, use of the active powers; from intercourse with like-minded friends; and above all, from worthy exercise of the intelligence. . . One must have at one's disposal all valid results of scholarship, yet one must not be a scholar. . . . One must command a wealth of detailed fact, ever alert to the deceptiveness of seeming fact. . . . One must understand that there is no substitute for judgment, and no end to the reward of discriminating judgment."

Zen Parables

compiled by **Paul Reps**

The Moon Cannot Be Stolen

Ryokan, a Zen master, lived the simplest kind of life in a little hut at the foot of a mountain. One evening a thief visited the hut only to discover there was nothing in it to steal.

Ryokan returned and caught him. "You may have come a long way to visit me," he told the prowler, "and you should not return empty-handed. Please take my clothes as a gift."

The thief was bewildered. He took the clothes and slunk away.

Ryokan sat naked, watching the moon. "Poor fellow," he mused, "I wish I could give him this beautiful moon."

Temper

A Zen student came to Bankei and complained: "Master, I have an ungovernable temper. How can I cure it?"

"You have something very strange," replied Bankei. "Let me see what you have."

"Just now I cannot show it to you," replied the other.

"When can you show it to me?" asked Bankei.

"It arises unexpectedly," replied the student.

"Then," concluded Bankei, "it must not be your own true nature. If it were, you could show it to me at any time. When you were born, you did not have it, and your parents did not give it to you. Think that over."

The Gates of Paradise

A soldier named Nobushige came to Hakuin, and asked: "Is there really a paradise and a hell?"

"Who are you?" inquired Hakuin.

"I am a samurai," the warrior replied.

"You, a soldier!" exclaimed Hakuin. "What kind of ruler would have you as his guard? Your face looks like that of a beggar."

Nobushige became so angry that he began to draw his sword, but Hakuin continued: "So you have a sword! Your weapon is probably much too dull to cut off my head."

As Nobushige drew his sword, Hakuin remarked: "Here open the gates of hell!"

At these words the samurai, perceiving the master's discipline, sheathed his sword and bowed.

"Here open the gates of paradise," said Hakuin.

Courtesy of Museum of Fine Arts, Boston. Edward Sylvester Morse Collection.

Square dish (Edo period, early 18th century) by Ogata Kenzan and Ogata Korin. Stoneware with underglaze and enamel decoration.

The First Principle

When one goes to Obaku temple in Kyoto, he sees carved over the gate the words "The First Principle." The letters are unusually large, and those who appreciate calligraphy[1] always admire them as being a masterpiece. They were drawn by Kosen two hundred years ago.

When the master drew them he did so on paper, from which workmen made the larger carving in wood. As Kosen sketched the letters, a bold pupil was with him who had made several gallons of ink for the calligraphy and who never failed to criticize his master's work.

"That is not good," he told Kosen after the first effort.

"How is that one?"

"Poor. Worse than before," pronounced the pupil.

Kosen patiently wrote one sheet after another until eighty-four First Principles had accumulated, still without the approval of the pupil.

Then, when the young man stepped outside for a few moments, Kosen thought: "Now is my chance to escape his keen eye," and he wrote hurriedly, with a mind free from distraction: "The First Principle."

"A masterpiece," pronounced the pupil.

1. **calligraphy:** the art of beautiful handwriting.

Connecting Across Texts

Connecting to English Literature

Throughout this anthology, literary characters appear who could benefit from the practical and philosophical advice offered in the selections in the Worlds of Wisdom. Have students choose one of the following characters (or any other that appeals to them) and offer that character one of the messages given in Worlds of Wisdom:

- Beowulf, Grendel, or The Seafarer
- The Wife of Bath or Gawain
- Macbeth or Lady Macbeth

Students may retell a tale in their own words or create a new narrative. Encourage them to make the moral message explicit. (If students have read the selection from *Paradise Lost* in this collection, they may want to offer some words of wisdom to Milton's Satan or to Adam and Eve.)

Summary

These four parables are from the Zen Buddhist tradition which began in China and matured in Japan in the twelfth century. Zen Buddhist principles stress detachment from worldly goods and desires in favor of a simple life of disciplined self-mastery and inner peace. Zen parables often have two characters, a master or teacher and a student or ordinary person who receives instruction from the master. The lesson the master teaches frequently involves an ironic twist or a paradox meant to make listeners examine their assumptions and rethink the way they are living.

D Reading Skills and Strategies

Interpreting Connotations

? What does the word *slunk* suggest about the thief's behavior? [Possible response: He knew that what he was doing was wrong, but he did it anyway.]

E Critical Thinking

Interpreting

? What does the master mean by this remark? [Possible responses: The moon cannot be taken or given, yet one can still enjoy it and share one's enjoyment with others. Awareness of beauty has more value than material possessions.]

F Critical Thinking

Evaluating

? What life message do you get from this parable? Do you agree with it? [Possible response: Attitudes and actions, like a temper, are learned and can be changed.]

G Critical Thinking

Interpreting

? What is Hakuin telling the samurai? [Possible responses: Anger and violence are hell. A peaceful, disciplined life is paradise.]

H Reading Skills and Strategies

Connecting with the Text

? What message do you get from this parable? [Possible responses: Use one's natural talent and be oneself; don't try so hard to please others.]

Resources

Listening

Audio CD Library

For a recording of this selection see the *Audio CD Library:*

- Disc 6, Track 10

Summary ■■

These five selections are among the didactic works of the thirteenth-century Persian poet Saadi. The poet was a Sufi, a follower of a mystical strain in Islam that stresses the unity of all creation. This theme is illustrated in the first saying, in which the speaker makes the moral point that one person's suffering should be felt by all. The remaining sayings give clever advice on how to survive and prosper in a competitive world. The lessons are delivered with wit and humor. The last selection is a fable with animal antagonists.

Background

Little is known of Saadi's life, and the available autobiographical information is not considered reliable. However, it is known that he spent much of his life traveling through Asia Minor, Syria, and Egypt. He may also have visited India and been captured and imprisoned by Crusaders.

Ⓐ Reading Skills and Strategies

Connecting with the Text

? Based on this saying, what advice do you think Saadi would offer students if he were speaking at a contemporary high school graduation ceremony? [Possible responses: Learn from your experiences—education is not complete without them.]

Ⓑ Critical Thinking

Interpreting

? What do you think Saadi is trying to tell readers here? [Possible responses: Taking dangerous chances has its rewards, but if you prefer quiet and safety, stay put. If you want to achieve success, you must take risks.]

Resources

Listening

Audio CD Library

For a recording of this selection see the *Audio CD Library:*

- Disc 6, Track 11

Sayings of Saadi

translated by **Idries Shah**

Portrait of a dervish (early 17th century), Turkish. Colors on paper (8⅝″ × 4³⁄₁₆″).

The Metropolitan Museum of Art, New York. The Cora Timken Burnett Collection of Persian Miniatures and Other Persian Art Objects. Bequest of Cora Timken Burnett, 1956 (57.51.30). Photograph ©1978 The Metropolitan Museum of Art.

The Unfed Dervish

When I see the poor dervish[1] unfed
My own food is pain and poison to me.

Information and Knowledge

Ⓐ However much you study, you cannot know
without action.
A donkey laden with books is neither an
intellectual nor a wise man.
Empty of essence, what learning has he—
Whether upon him is firewood or book?

The Elephant Keeper

Make no friendship with an elephant keeper
If you have no room to entertain an elephant.

Safety and Riches

Ⓑ Deep in the sea are riches beyond compare.
But if you seek safety, it is on the shore.

The Fox and the Camels

A fox was seen running away in terror. Someone asked what was troubling it. The fox answered: "They are taking camels for forced labor." "Fool!" he was told, "the fate of camels has nothing to do with you, who do not even look like one." "Silence!" said the fox, "for if an intriguer were to state that I was a camel, who would work for my release?"

1. **dervish:** Muslim monk dedicated to a life of poverty.

Getting Students Involved

Cooperative Learning

Have students discuss how the selections in Worlds of Wisdom apply to modern life. To encourage them to become effective members of a cooperating group, have them write about how well they do each of the following:

- contributing to the discussion
- encouraging others to speak
- assisting with organization
- taking/sharing responsibility for progress

Laozi (detail) from *Homage to the First Principle*, a Yüan dynasty wall painting.

Courtesy of the Royal Ontario Museum, Toronto.

Taoist Anecdotes

translated and edited by **Moss Roberts**

Gold, Gold

Many, many years ago there was a man of the land of Ch'i who had a great passion for gold. One day at the crack of dawn he went to the market—straight to the gold dealers' stalls, where he snatched some gold and ran. The market guards soon caught him. "With so many people around, how did you expect to get away with it?" a guard asked.

"When I took it," he replied, "I saw only the gold, not the people." **C**

—Lieh Tzu

A Clever Judge

In the days when Ch'en Shu-ku was a magistrate in Chienchou, there was a man who had lost an article of some value. A number of people were arrested, but no one could discover exactly who the thief was. So Shu-ku laid a trap for the suspects. "I know of a temple," he told them, "whose bell can tell a thief from an honest man. It has great spiritual powers."

The magistrate had the bell fetched and reverently enshrined in a rear chamber. Then he had the suspects brought before the bell to stand and testify to their guilt or innocence. He explained to them that if an innocent man touched the bell it would remain silent, but that if the man was guilty it would ring out. **D**

Then the magistrate led his staff in solemn worship to the bell. The sacrifices concluded, he had the bell placed behind a curtain, while one of his assistants secretly smeared it with ink. After a time he took the suspects to the bell and had each one in turn extend his hands through the curtain and touch the bell. As each man withdrew his hands, Shu-ku examined them. Everyone's hands were stained except for those of one man, who confessed to the theft under questioning. He had not dared touch the bell for fear it would ring.

—Chang Shih-nan

from The Analects of Confucius

translated and annotated by **Arthur Waley**

The Master said, "Yu, shall I teach you what knowledge is? When you know a thing, to recognize that you know it, and when you do not know a thing, to recognize that you do not know it. That is knowledge." **E**

The Master said, "Even when walking in a party of no more than three I can always be certain of learning from those I am with. There will be good qualities that I can select for imitation and bad ones that will teach me what requires correction in myself."

Tzu-kung asked, saying, "Is there any single saying that one can act upon all day and every day?" The Master said, "Perhaps the saying about consideration: 'Never do to others what you would not like them to do to you.'" **F**

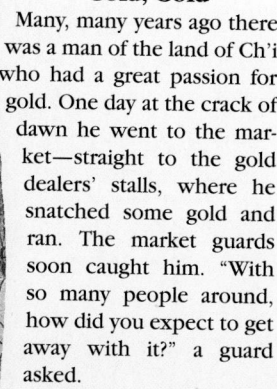

Portrait of Confucius based on ancient traditions. Relief from the stele in the Pei Lin de Siganfou.

Summary ■■

These examples of wisdom literature come from two different traditions of ancient Chinese thought, Taoism and Confucianism, the latter named after a Chinese philosopher who died around 479 B.C. The two Taoist anecdotes are concerned with the psychology of thieves, illustrating by means of a simple story how the actions of criminals are affected by their obsessions and their fear of exposure.

In contrast to the Taoist selections, the three excerpts from Confucian teaching are concerned with abstract subjects: the nature of knowledge, the possibility of learning from others, and the search for a single ethical principle upon which to base all action. As in the Zen parables, a master is quoted as an authority.

C Reading Skills and Strategies

Finding the Main Idea

? What do you think is the lesson taught in this anecdote? [Possible response: The thief's obsession with gold so blinded him that he failed to see the consequences of his action.]

D Critical Thinking

Speculating

? Why do you think the magistrate has the suspects testify in front of the bell? [Possible response: He uses the bell to make the true thief reveal himself.]

E Struggling Readers

Paraphrasing

Ask students to put Confucius's thoughts about knowledge in their own words. [Possible responses: Knowledge is knowing what you do and do not know.]

F Cultural Connections

Confucius's thought is similar to the Golden Rule, the precept stated by Jesus in the Sermon on the Mount: "Always treat others as you would like them to treat you." This ethical principle has also been espoused by ancient Hebrew writers, by the Greek philosophers Plato and Aristotle, and by the Roman statesman Seneca.

Using Students' Strengths

Visual Learners

Have students draw cartoons, paint pictures, or create sculptures or collages depicting any one of the moral or life lessons presented in the wisdom literature. Encourage them to search in today's world for modern visual parallels to the traditional wisdom texts.

Interpersonal Learners

Have students write, then read aloud, advice column letters about modern personal and social problems. Have volunteers reply to each letter by citing appropriate quotations from Worlds of Wisdom.

Musical Learners

Invite students to bring in recordings of wisdom literature that have been set to music or to play an appropriate recording as they read a wisdom text in class.

Resources

Listening

Audio CD Library

For recordings of these selections, see the *Audio CD Library:*

- Disc 6, Tracks 12, 13

Summary ■■

These **proverbs**, or short wise sayings, are from the Jabo people of Liberia in West Africa. They come out of an oral tradition and their wisdom reflects the shared experience of the community. Brief and pointed, so they can be remembered easily, the proverbs also make use of images and metaphors that link humans and nature. In the first proverb, the power of words is communicated by comparing their scope to the vastness of the sky. The proverbs embody the ethical system of the people who created and preserved them.

Ⓐ Elements of Literature

Metaphor

Ask students to explain this metaphor. [Possible responses: The spoken word has great influence; it extends over the entire earth and no one remains unaffected by it.]

Ⓑ Reading Skills and Strategies

Connecting with the Text

Ask students to rephrase these proverbs in their own words or to relate them to modern sayings they know. [Possible responses: Timing is everything; talk is cheap; his bark is worse than his bite; if you talk the talk, you have to walk the walk.]

Finding Common Ground

To help students better grasp the literal and implied meanings of the selections, have them work in pairs. Students should freely express any problems or dilemmas they have with the ideas, any connections to real-life experience, and any judgments they make on a lesson's usefulness or relevance to them. Remind students to discuss only experiences they feel comfortable sharing.

Resources

Listening

Audio CD Library

For a recording of this selection see the *Audio CD Library:*

- Disc 6, Track 14

Jabo Proverbs

translated by **George Herzog**

Ⓐ As the sky extends over all, so do words that have been spoken.

Ⓑ One doesn't throw the stick after the snake has gone.

Daring talk is not strength.

It is not the person who looks at you with sparkling eyes when you speak who understands your words; but the one who bends his head down, he is the one who really understands.

Grebo face mask from the Ivory Coast. Wood, paint (27½″ high).

The Metropolitan Museum of Art, New York. The Nelson A. Rockefeller Collection.

Finding Common Ground

You probably recognized some ways you could apply these insights to life today. Looking over your reading notes and thinking back over the selections, jot down some responses to the following questions, or talk about them with a small group.

- How could these insights be applied to life today? Are any of them hopelessly outdated? Why?
- Wisdom literature often uses **metaphor** and conveys its moral or message indirectly. Did you understand what all these bits of wisdom mean? Talk about the advice that you found difficult or obscure.
- These selections cover a wide range of topics, including good works, greed, foolishness, self-discipline, anger, guilt, prudence, true knowledge, friendship, and practical foresight. Did you disagree with any of this worldly wisdom? Why?

Assessing Learning

Check Test: Questions and Answers

1. According to the Koran, what must people do to avoid "the blazing fire"? [Give alms (money, food, clothing) without expecting anything in return.]
2. What happens to Shell-Neck in the fable from *The Panchatantra* and why? [The turtle dies because he forgets his friends' advice.]
3. What is the message in the Zen story of the samurai? [Embracing violence opens the gates of hell.]
4. In the Taoist story of the magic bell, how does the judge discover the thief? [The judge announces that a certain bell can detect a thief so the guilty one reveals himself by failing to touch the bell.]
5. In the Jabo proverbs, why are spoken words compared to the sky? [because both cover the world]

John Milton

(1608–1674)

John Milton (c. 1650) by Robert Streater. Oil on canvas (27¼" × 21½").

The Metropolitan Museum of Art, New York. Gift of Mrs. Wheeler Smith, 1908 (08.237.1). Photograph ©1978 The Metropolitan Museum of Art.

Early in his life, John Milton resolved to be a great poet. His teachers and his parents encouraged him in this ambition because they believed, as Milton said later in his life, that he "might perhaps leave something so written to aftertimes as they should not willingly let it die." Time has confirmed his parents' and his teachers' confidence in him: Milton's *Paradise Lost,* his major epic, is one of the most brilliant achievements in English poetry and perhaps the richest and most intricately beautiful poem in the world. Posterity has not let *Paradise Lost* die.

Milton was fortunate in his parents. His father, a musician and prosperous businessman, had Milton educated at St. Paul's School (which he loved) and Cambridge University (which he hated). Indulged in every way by his parents, Milton spent the next eight years after college (1632–1640) continuing his education by himself, since he firmly believed that a poet must be a person of learning, familiar with ancient and contemporary philosophy, history, languages, and literatures. He made a leisurely tour of Italy, whose language and culture he had long admired, and there he visited many interesting people, including the astronomer Galileo. Throughout this period, he wrote poems in English, Latin, Greek, and Italian. Some of these he collected and published in 1645. It has become customary to refer to them as Milton's "Minor Poems," but they would not be minor if anyone else had written them.

An Early, Brilliant Career

The two outstanding poems of Milton's early career are known today by their short titles: *Comus* and *Lycidas*. *Comus* is a masque, an elaborate pageant of the sort that Ben Jonson was famous for writing. *Comus* was presented at Ludlow Castle in 1634, for and by the earl of Bridgewater's family. It opens with two brothers and a sister—played by the earl's children—lost in a forest. The sister, separated from her brothers, is invited by a flashy magician named Comus to join his troupe and live a life of pleasure. But the girl is able to resist all his seductions because her heart is pure. *Comus* gave Milton an early opportunity to dramatize an idea he firmly believed in: Human beings have been given the ability and freedom to choose between good and evil, and so long as they choose the good they will remain strong and free.

Just as *Comus* surpasses all other Renaissance masques by the beauty of its language and the depth of its thought, so does *Lycidas* surpass all other pastoral elegies written in English. An **elegy** celebrates the memory of a dead person; this poem remembers Edward King, a fellow student of Milton's who was shipwrecked and drowned in the Irish Sea in 1637. The elegy is called pastoral because it imitates some ancient elegies by using imagery of shepherds and their flocks. Milton and Edward King (renamed Lycidas), both of whom had been preparing for careers in the Church, are the young shepherds feeding their flock. Milton changed his mind about the Church, and King—a most promising youth—was killed. To lament this loss, Milton harmonizes the classical and Christian views of death, in a way characteristic of Christian humanists. But the poem is more about life than death because it celebrates a human being's capacity to create something significant, even in a short lifetime.

OBJECTIVES

1. Read and interpret the poem
2. Monitor reading strategies
3. Analyze epic similes, irregular syntax, and blank verse
4. Express understanding through creative writing, paraphrasing a text, analyzing a character, and comparing texts
5. Draw a visual representation of the text

SKILLS

Reading

- Monitor reading strategies
- Analyze epic similes, irregular syntax, and blank verse

Writing

- Collect ideas for a cause-and-effect essay
- Paraphrase a poetic text
- Write an essay analyzing a character
- Write an original dramatic dialogue
- Compare Satan and hell in Milton and Dante

Art

- Draw a visual representation of the text

Viewing/Representing

- Analyze visual responses to the text (ATE)

Planning

- **Block Schedule**
  Block Scheduling Lesson Plans with Pacing Guide
- **Traditional Schedule**
  Lesson Plans Including Strategies for English-Language Learners
- **One-Stop Planner**
  CD-ROM with Test Generator

Resources: Print and Media

Reading

- *Reading Skills and Strategies*
  MiniRead Skill Lesson, p. 23
  Selection Skill Lesson, p. 29
- *Graphic Organizers for Active Reading,* p. 36
- *Audio CD Library,* Disc 6, Tracks 15, 16

Writing and Language

- *Daily Oral Grammar,* Trnsp. 13
- *Grammar and Language Links* Worksheet, p. 25

Viewing and Representing

Viewing and Representing
Fine Art Transparency 6
Fine Art Worksheet, p. 24

Assessment

- *Formal Assessment,* p. 77
- *Portfolio Management System,* p. 129
- *Test Generator (One-Stop Planner* CD-ROM)

Internet

go.hrw.com (keyword: LE0 12-5)

RESPONDING TO THE ART

English painter **Robert Streater** (1624–1679) created murals, landscapes, and portraits. His allegorical ceiling painting, *The Triumph of Truth and the Arts,* can still be seen in an Oxford theater.

Activity. Milton lived during the ascendancy of the Puritan faction. Compare his dress with that of the royalist Raleigh on p. 234.

Browsing in the Files

About the Author. Milton has been described as a man who suffered many hardships in his personal life. In June 1642, he married a young girl, Mary Powell, who left him within six weeks and did not return until 1645. Subsequently, she bore him three daughters and a son who died in infancy. She herself died in 1652. In 1656, Milton married Katherine Woodcock, who died in childbirth in 1658. In 1663, Milton—now blind, poor, and discredited—married Elizabeth Minshul, who survived him by many years.

Exploring the Historical Period

Escaping the Plague

Milton was completing *Paradise Lost* in April 1665 when the plague erupted in London. Estimates vary, but by the late summer and fall, as many as ten thousand people a week were reported to be dying of the highly contagious pestilence. In *A Journal of the Plague Year,* (pp. 558–564), Daniel Defoe vividly describes the crowded death carts and huge burial pits where scores of corpses were dumped in haste. One of those mass burial grounds—the "great pit in Finsbury"—was located near Milton's residence. The poet (whose images of hell are so vivid) must have seen or at least heard of the sick and crazed victims who threw themselves into the burial pits before they were dead. Milton and his daughters, however, had an alternative: They fled the city.

Responding to the Art

Hungarian painter **Michaly von Munkacsy** (1844–1900) lived and worked in Paris. He died in an asylum, a drawing pencil in his hand.

Activity. Milton had trouble with his daughters; he seems to have been a hard man to live with. How is this aspect of his personality suggested in the painting?

Milton's Political Activity: Intelligent Devotion

In the 1640s, an ongoing struggle between King Charles and his Parliament came to a head. Milton, believing that a poet must be active in the life of his time, entered the paper warfare that accompanied the conflict and started publishing prose works—some of them very elaborate and a few of them very insulting—in support of the Parliamentary Party. For this reason, some people have referred to Milton as a Puritan, but this is a label that has only limited application to a person of Milton's stature. If he shared some of the Puritans' ideas and attitudes, such as their extreme dislike of kings and bishops, he also differed greatly from them in other important ways. For instance, he advocated divorce for incompatible married couples, and he argued that the press should be free from government censorship and interference. Although we take these freedoms for granted, most people in the seventeenth century, particularly most Puritans, considered them dangerously radical.

During part of this period, Milton served in the government of England under Oliver Cromwell, who, with the title of lord protector, ruled England after the Parliamentary Party had won the Civil Wars and executed King Charles. As Latin secretary to the Council of State, Milton was responsible for all correspondence with foreign countries, Latin then being the language of diplomacy.

But Milton's eyesight was gradually failing. By 1652, he could only distinguish day from night; otherwise, by the age of forty-four, before he had finished his life's work, Milton was totally blind. Among the few poems he wrote during this time is the following sonnet about the calamity of his middle age:

On His Blindness

When I consider how my light is spent
 Ere half my days in this dark world and wide,
 And that one talent which is death to hide
 Lodged with me useless, though my soul more bent
To serve there with my Maker, and present
 My true account, lest He returning chide,
 "Doth God exact day-labor, light denied?"
 I fondly ask. But Patience, to prevent
That murmur, soon replies, "God doth not need
 Either man's work or His own gifts. Who best
 Bear His mild yoke, they serve Him best. His state
Is kingly: Thousands at His bidding speed,
 And post o'er land and ocean without rest;
 They also serve who only stand and wait."

The Blind Milton Dictating Paradise Lost *to His Daughters* (19th century) by Michaly von Munkacsy. Oil.

Collection of the New York Public Library, New York. Astor, Lenox, and Tilden Foundations.

go.hrw.com
LEO 12-5

All for Nothing

To Milton, the ideal government was a republic in which the most capable, intelligent, and virtuous men would serve as leaders. To establish and maintain such a government in England, he had devoted most of his intelligence and energy for twenty years. Then suddenly, in 1660, the cause for which he had worked so hard became totally discredited; the English recalled their dead king's son from exile and crowned him as King Charles II. Overnight, Milton found himself stripped of his possessions and under arrest as a traitor. Fortunately, influential friends, including the poet Andrew Marvell, intervened, and Milton was allowed to go into retirement rather than to the scaffold. From then on, he lived in seclusion with his three daughters and his third wife, his first two wives and only son having died. By reading aloud to him, his daughters enabled him to carry on the studies he thought necessary for a poet.

Adam and Eve are the heroes of Milton's epic, and they represent us all.

Milton's Great Epic: *Paradise Lost*

Being a poet, in Milton's view, meant imitating the great writers of antiquity, the epic poets Homer and Virgil and the Greek dramatists Aeschylus, Sophocles, and Euripides. Because those writers chose subjects drawn from their own nation's history, Milton first pondered various English subjects for his works, especially King Arthur and the knights of the Round Table. But finally, after years of thinking and reading, Milton decided that King Arthur's exploits were mainly fictitious, and so he settled on subjects drawn from the Bible. Milton thought the Bible alone contained everything people needed to know for the practice of true religion; he rejected not only the Roman Catholic Church and the Church of England, but also all the sects—Puritan or otherwise—that had sprung up in England since the Reformation began. While the Christian religion was the most important matter in his life, to Milton religion involved only God, God's Word (the Bible), and each individual human being.

Milton published *Paradise Lost* twice: first in a ten-book version in 1667 and then in twelve books in 1674, the year of his death. It's no exaggeration to say that Milton in one way or another worked on this epic all his life. He made many different plans and even once thought of it as a tragedy with Satan, the fallen archangel transformed into the chief devil, as its protagonist. In the finished poem, Satan is still very conspicuous. The first two books are devoted mainly to him, he appears frequently in Books III through X, and Milton lavishes on him some of his most glorious writing. It's not surprising, then, that many readers have regarded Satan as the secret hero of the poem, especially since he receives no such grand treatment in the Bible. Milton was "of the Devil's party without knowing it," asserted the poet and artist William Blake. But this argument is convincing only to those who concentrate on certain parts of the poem and ignore the rest of it. Moreover, in literary works, evil frequently seems more interesting than good, and if any part of *Paradise Lost* fails from a literary point of view, it is Milton's portrayal of God.

In *Paradise Lost,* Milton took relatively few verses from the Bible, mainly from Genesis, and developed them into a 10,565-line poem. He used the conventions and devices of the classical epic to make the poem a work of art; he used his great learning and wide experience of human affairs to make the poem profound. Although the poem ranges back and forth between Hell and Heaven, the most important action takes place on Earth, where the first human beings, Adam and Eve, are given the choice of obeying or disobeying God. They choose, as everybody knows, to disobey, and having done so, they accept their punishment and make the best of the life that is left to them. They are the heroes of Milton's epic, and they represent us all.

Browsing in the Files

About the Author. One of the most reliable of the early biographies of Milton is that written by Edward Phillips, Milton's nephew, pupil, and literary executor. Phillips visited Milton's household frequently and later used his firsthand experience in writing his *Life of John Milton* (1694). Phillips' comments on Milton's daughters (quoted below) are especially revealing, indicating that reading to their brilliant, blind father was far from an idyllic experience.

"Yet excusing only the eldest daughter by reason of her bodily infirmity, and difficult utterance of speech (which to say truth I doubt was the principal cause of excusing her), the other two were condemned to the performance of reading, and exactly pronouncing of all the languages of whatever book he should at one time or another think fit to peruse; viz., the Hebrew (and I think the Syriac), the Greek, the Latin, the Italian, Spanish, and French. All which sorts of books to be confined to read, without understanding one word, must needs be a trial of patience, almost beyond endurance; yet it was endured by both for a long time; yet the irksomeness of this employment could not always be concealed, but broke out more and more into expressions of uneasiness; so that at length they were all (even the eldest also) sent out to learn some curious and ingenious sorts of manufacture that are proper for women. . . , particularly embroideries in gold and silver."

Professional Notes

Critics' Comments

Two of the best-known remarks about Milton's epic come from the eminent eighteenth-century critic Samuel Johnson (see p. 570) and the essayist Charles Lamb (1775–1834). Johnson admired the achievement of *Paradise Lost* and recognized its power and greatness, but he believed that "nobody ever wished it longer." Lamb, taking an enthusiastic step further, wrote:

"'We read the *Paradise Lost* as a task,' says Dr. Johnson. Nay, rather as a celestial recreation, of which the dullard mind is not at all hours alike recipient. 'Nobody ever wished it longer';—nor the moon rounder, he might have added. Why, 'tis the perfectness and completeness of it, which makes us imagine that not a line could be added to it, or diminished from it, with advantage."

Ⓐ Literary Connections

Homer's *Iliad* begins, "Sing, goddess, the anger of Peleus's son Achilles . . . ." The *Odyssey* begins, "Sing in me, Muse, and through me tell the story . . . ." Ask interested students to read the complete opening invocations of the *Iliad* and the *Odyssey* and compare and contrast them with Milton's invocation. They may also want to read the opening lines of Virgil's *Aeneid* and Dante's *Divine Comedy* for parallels and contrasts with Milton's opening lines.

Ⓑ Elements of Literature

Iambic Pentameter

Have students scan the first few lines of "The Fall of Satan." Except for the very first line, with the five-syllable word *disobedience* in the middle, the first five lines are regular iambic pentameter. This is a good opportunity to review the rules of meter with students. (See Poetic Meter in Collection 3, p. 216.)

Paradise Lost: Milton's Epic

At the very beginning of *Paradise Lost,* Milton describes the content of his epic as "things unattempted yet in prose or rhyme" (line 16). His allusions to Homer, Virgil, Dante, and a host of lesser epic poets leave no doubt that Milton wanted *Paradise Lost* to sum up and also surpass all previous epics. The quality that would set Milton's epic apart, of course, was that it dealt with great deeds on a cosmic scale at the dawn of Creation—rather than with earthly matters.

Ⓐ There is a formal, set way to begin an epic. At the outset, an epic poet does two things: The speaker invokes the Muse (one of the nine Greek goddesses who inspire poets and other practitioners of the arts and sciences) to speak or sing through the poet; and the speaker states the subject of the poem. Milton does both these things in the first, complicated sentence (lines 1–16) of *Paradise Lost.* Grammatically, this sentence begins in line 6 with the command "Sing, Heavenly Muse." "Sing," says Milton, and now we move back to line 1, "Of man's first disobedience," which is Adam and Eve's first act of disobedience against God, who has forbidden them to eat the fruit of a particular tree in Eden (see the selection from Genesis, page 416). The result, or "fruit," of their disobedience is expulsion from and loss of Paradise, another name for the Garden of Eden. Yet all is not lost, because a "greater Man" (line 4), Jesus Christ, has restored the possibility of Paradise to the human race.

Milton calls this argument "great" (line 24), for he is attempting to resolve a dilemma that has puzzled many people throughout the ages. On the one hand, we are told that through his Eternal Providence (line 25) God takes loving care of creation; on the other hand, we know that there are many very bad things in the world, such as war, crime, poverty, disease, oppression, and injustice. In *Paradise Lost,* Milton asserts that God is not responsible for these evils; instead, Adam and Eve's disobedience to God "Brought death into the world, and all our woe" (line 3). God gave Adam and Eve the freedom to choose between good and evil, and the strength to resist evil; yet they chose evil, and their offspring—all of us—have suffered the effects of their choice ever since.

This explanation is not original to Milton; many Christians have accepted it for centuries. Yet a reader need not accept this traditional explanation of the evil in the world in order to enjoy and admire the poem. (Indeed, some readers have found evidence in the poem that Milton himself did not really believe it.) The poem is rich enough to provide support for many different interpretations.

Reading *Paradise Lost*

Ⓑ Milton decided to write his epic in his native language and in Shakespeare's meter, which is **blank verse,** or unrhymed iambic pentameter. Though blank verse was the usual meter in dramatic poetry, it was not used at all for nondramatic poems in Milton's day and for long after. Most of Milton's sentences are long, and many of them are not in normal word

Connecting Across Texts

Milton and Shakespeare

Paradise Lost is an epic that also contains elements of tragedy, and Milton's characters share some of the traits of Shakespeare's heroes. Critic Harold Bloom makes these observations: "*Paradise Lost* is magnificent because it is persuasively tragic as well as epic; it is the tragedy of the fall of Lucifer into Satan . . . . In another sense of 'the tragic,' *Paradise Lost* is the tragedy of Eve and Adam, who like Satan have their inevitably Shakespearean qualities and yet seem somewhat less persuasive representations than Satan, who is granted more of a Shakespearean growing inner self."

As they read, ask students to compare and contrast Adam, Eve, Satan, and Macbeth.

order (subject-verb-object). Also, his vocabulary includes words not used in ordinary prose today. (Unfamiliar proper nouns are explained in the notes, but they still have to be understood in their context.)

In Milton's heroic, optimistic view of life, goodness was not goodness unless it resulted from a struggle to overcome evil. God purposely let Satan escape from Hell and establish himself on Earth, not only so that Satan's deeds would damn him further but also so that human beings would have something to fight against—and with God's help triumph over. In one of his prose tracts, *Areopagitica* (1644), Milton describes life as a race in which good must compete with bad. Virtue, he says, is not virtue unless it is won in the "dust and heat" of the conflict with evil. And so, when Adam and Eve lose Paradise, they also gain something: the opportunity to prove themselves in the real world. The Archangel Michael, who comes to dispossess them of their perfect garden, tells them how to live in the new, imperfect world. Practice good deeds, he says, and patience, temperance, faith, and love, and

then wilt thou be not loath
To leave this Paradise, but shalt possess
A Paradise within thee, happier far.

—*Paradise Lost,* Book XII, lines 585–587

Tate Gallery, London.

The Fallen Angels Entering Pandemonium, from *Paradise Lost,* Book I, by John Martin (exhibited 1841).

RESPONDING TO THE ART

English painter **John Martin** (1789–1854), an eccentric Romantic known as Mad Martin, is often remembered more for his extravagant plans to improve London's sanitation system than for his paintings. The intensity of his personal life, however, is also reflected in such artworks as *The Fallen Angels Enter Pandemonium,* in which the angels are practically obscured by the dramatic grandeur of Pandemonium. In his paintings of burning cities and natural disasters, Martin strove for physical immensity on the canvas. Eventually, the public tired of his colossal spectacles. (For other art by Martin, see p. 735.) In Milton's epic, Pandemonium is the capital of hell, established by Satan. The word comes from *pan,* meaning "all," and *daimon,* meaning "demon."

Activity. Compare this depiction of hell with Dante's (p. 394) and Bruegel's (p. 396). Note the lake of fire. What does *pandemonium* mean today? [wild disorder and confusion]

Making the Connections

Connecting to the Theme: "The Power of the Word"

In his pamphlet *Areopagitica,* Milton wrote of the power of books. He said books "are not absolutely dead things, but do contain a potency of life in them to be as active as that soul was whose progeny they are; nay, they do preserve as in a vial the purest efficacy and extraction of that living intellect that bred them." Therefore, he concluded, "who kills a man kills a reasonable creature, God's image; but he who destroys a good book kills reason itself, kills the image of God, as it were, in the eye."

Summary ■ ■ ■

This excerpt is from the beginning of John Milton's epic poem *Paradise Lost*. Milton's purpose in writing this monumental work of over 10,000 lines of blank verse was to answer the question of why God permits His human creations to suffer and die, or, in Milton's words in l. 26, to "justify the ways of God to men." Milton also intended to write an epic that was at least equal in gravity and grace to the epics of Homer and Virgil. To that end, he followed many of the conventions of the classical epics, such as beginning with an invocation to the Muse of poetry and with a statement of his subject. The events of his narrative, however, are drawn from the Bible, and his thesis that good will eventually overcome evil is essentially Christian.

Milton begins with an account of how Satan and his angels rose up against God and were thrust from heaven. He stresses the pride and willfulness that were Satan's motives for rebellion. In fact, the portrait he paints of Satan's character is so fascinating that some critics consider Satan, not Adam, the epic's hero, or main focus. Milton paints vivid pictures of two settings: heaven and hell, using imagery of light and dark to contrast heaven's glory with hell's horror. In a dialogue between Satan and Beelzebub, another fallen angel, Satan vows to avenge himself on God by tempting Adam and Eve to do evil and thus disrupt God's plans for His creation. Beelzebub, less audacious than Satan, wonders whether even in hell the fallen angels are the subjects of God, but Satan adamantly rejects this view. Using similes and classical allusions, Milton describes Satan as a giant in chains, an image that conveys both Satan's enormous will and his subordinate status. In Milton's view, Satan cannot win his cosmic conflict with God because his will to do evil is permitted by God and ultimately serves God's ends.

Before You Read
THE FALL OF SATAN

Make the Connection

Evil on an Epic Scale

Why does evil exist? What is the source of its power to fascinate? The struggle of good versus evil is central to *Paradise Lost*—in this case, the conflict exists on a truly epic scale, as Satan first rebels (in Book I) against God and then (in Book IX) ensnares Adam and Eve to do likewise. In Milton's epic, and in the Bible, this original choice of evil over good explains the burdens of humanity and our fateful tendency to misuse our reason and freedom to let pride override fear of God.

Reading Skills and Strategies

Monitor Your Reading Strategies

Milton wrote in the 1600s, and on first reading, you may be daunted by his style. As you read Milton, you will find it helpful to identify areas of difficulty and apply strategies to deal with them. For example, Milton often **omits words** and **inverts syntax,** wrenching some of his sentences out of the usual subject-verb-complement order. If you are having problems finding the **subject and verb** in one of his long or inverted sentences, reread it until you can locate these core sentence parts. If you are stalled by an unfamiliar word, try using **context clues** to figure it out. Make use of the **glossary** printed at the right of the poem. Answer the **side questions** to help you summarize key ideas as you go along. Above all, **read the text aloud** and pay attention to the pauses signaled by the punctuation.

Milton is challenging—just as many good things are. But when you have solved the puzzles posed by Milton's style, you should be hooked by this exciting story of the primal battle between the forces of good and the forces of evil.

The Angel of Divine Presence (late 18th to early 19th century) by William Blake. Watercolor.
Fitzwilliam Museum, University of Cambridge.

The Fall of Satan
from Paradise Lost
John Milton

Of man's first disobedience, and the fruit
Of that forbidden tree, whose mortal taste
Brought death into the world, and all our woe, **A**
With loss of Eden, till one greater Man°
Restore us, and regain the blissful seat,
Sing, Heavenly Muse,° that on the secret top
Of Oreb, or of Sinai,° didst inspire
That shepherd,° who first taught the chosen seed°
In the beginning how the Heavens and Earth
Rose out of Chaos; or if Sion hill°
Delight thee more, and Siloa's brook° that flowed
Fast by the oracle of God, I thence
Invoke thy aid to my adventurous song,
That with no middle flight intends to soar
Above the Aonian mount,° while it pursues
Things unattempted yet in prose or rhyme.
And chiefly thou, O Spirit,° that dost prefer
Before all temples the upright heart and pure,
Instruct me, for thou know'st; thou from the first
Wast present, and with mighty wings outspread
Dove-like sat'st brooding on the vast abyss
And mad'st it pregnant: what in me is dark
Illumine, what is low raise and support;
That to the height of this great argument
I may assert Eternal Providence, **B**
And justify the ways of God to men.
 Say first, for Heaven hides nothing from thy view,
Nor the deep tract of Hell, say first what cause
Moved our grand parents° in that happy state,
Favored of Heaven so highly, to fall off
From their Creator, and transgress his will
For one restraint,° lords of the world besides?°
Who first seduced them to that foul revolt?
The infernal Serpent;° he it was, whose guile,
Stirred up with envy and revenge, deceived
The mother of mankind, what time his pride
Had cast him out from Heaven, with all his host
Of rebel angels, by whose aid aspiring
To set himself in glory above his peers,°
He trusted to have equaled the Most High,
If he opposed; and with ambitious aim
Against the throne and monarchy of God,
Raised impious war in Heaven and battle proud

? **1–6.** *After you finish this invocation to the Muse, sum up what the subject of Milton's story will be.*

4. one greater Man: Christ.

6. Heavenly Muse: Urania, the muse of astronomy and sacred poetry. Milton hopes to be inspired by Urania, just as Moses was divinely inspired to receive and interpret the word of God for the Hebrews.
7. Oreb . . . Sinai: alternative names for the mountain where Moses received heavenly inspiration.
8. shepherd: Moses. **chosen seed:** the Hebrews.
10. Sion hill: Zion, a hill near Jerusalem on which the Temple was built.
11. Siloa's brook: stream that flowed past the Temple, "the oracle of God," on Sion hill.
15. Aonian mount: in Greek mythology, Mount Helicon, the home of the Muses. Milton intends to write an epic greater than those of the classical Greek poet Homer and the classical Roman poet Virgil.
17. Spirit: the Holy Spirit; divine inspiration.

? **26.** *According to this line, what is Milton's purpose? How would you paraphrase this purpose?*

29. grand parents: Adam and Eve.

32. one restraint: the command not to eat of the fruit of the tree of knowledge. **besides:** in every other way.
34. Serpent: Milton anticipates Satan's final form.

39. peers: equals; the other archangels.

Resources

Viewing and Representing

Fine Art Transparency

A Fine Art transparency of William Blake's *The Ancient of Days* can be used with this lesson as a prereading motivator. See the *Viewing and Representing Transparencies and Worksheets:*

- Transparency 6
- Worksheet, p. 24

A Reading Skills and Strategies

Monitoring Reading Strategies

The first sentence of Milton's epic does not follow standard subject-verb-object order. Note that the subject *(you)* is understood, that the verb is *sing,* and that the opening prepositional phrase, "Of man's first disobedience," precedes the verb. Have students rewrite this part of the sentence in conventional word order. ["Heavenly Muse, sing of man's first disobedience . . . ."]

B Critical Thinking

Making Connections

? How does reading the account from Genesis on pp. 416–418 help you to understand Milton's invocation? [Possible response: Milton takes part of his plot from the account of the Garden of Eden and makes references to the void/abyss, making light out of darkness, and the spirit of God.]

Answers to Margin Questions

Lines 1–6. The subject will be humanity's first crime against God, the fall from innocence that made humans subject to suffering and death, and the salvation of humanity by Jesus Christ.
Line 26. Milton's purpose is to state the reasons behind God's actions.

Reaching All Students

Struggling Readers

Monitor Your Reading Strategies was introduced on p. 440. For a lesson directly tied to this selection that teaches students to monitor their reading using a strategy called Say Something, see the *Reading Skills and Strategies* binder:

- MiniRead Skill Lesson, p. 23
- Selection Skill Lesson, p. 29

English Language Learners

Students will require assistance in understanding the progression of the poem. As they read, they should work with a partner, dividing the text into sections and summarizing the development of each section in a few short sentences. Be sure to have them answer the margin questions.

A Elements of Literature

Alliteration

? How does alliteration make this statement vivid to the reader? [Possible response: The repeated *h* sound—*Him, Hurled headlong, hideous*—emphasizes the sudden explosive quality of the event.]

B Reading Skills and Strategies

Making Predictions

? What kind of speech would you expect from a person filled with "obdurate pride and steadfast hate"? [Possible responses: self-justification; repetitious complaints about injuries; threats; refusals to listen to reason.] Have students look for those characteristics in the words of Satan (beginning on l. 84).

C Elements of Literature

Allusion

This description echoes the inscription over the entrance to hell in Dante's *Inferno:* "All hope abandon ye who enter here."

D Vocabulary Note

Word Origins

Beelzebub is described in Matthew's gospel as "the prince of the devils," but the literal translation of his name is "lord of the flies" or "lord of filth," specifically, excrement. (Students may be familiar with William Golding's 1954 novel, *Lord of the Flies.*)

Answers to Margin Questions

Lines 28–44. He asks why Adam and Eve disobeyed and who lured them into doing so. He answers that Satan tricked them out of envy, revenge, and thwarted pride.

Lines 54–56. Satan is tormented by the thought of lost happiness and eternal pain.

Lines 61–74. Possible responses: flames, torture, sorrow, darkness, hopelessness, absence of God.

Line 91: Once bright and glorious, he is now ruined and miserable.

With vain attempt. Him the Almighty Power
Hurled headlong flaming from the ethereal sky
With hideous ruin and combustion down
To bottomless perdition,° there to dwell
In adamantine° chains and penal° fire,
Who durst° defy the Omnipotent to arms.
Nine times the space that measures day and night
To mortal men, he with his horrid crew
Lay vanquished, rolling in the fiery gulf,
Confounded though immortal. But his doom
Reserved him to more wrath; for now the thought
Both of lost happiness and lasting pain
Torments him; round he throws his baleful eyes,
That witnessed huge affliction and dismay
Mixed with obdurate° pride and steadfast hate.
At once as far as angels ken° he views
The dismal situation waste and wild:
A dungeon horrible on all sides round
As one great furnace flamed, yet from those flames
No light, but rather darkness visible
Served only to discover sights of woe,
Regions of sorrow, doleful shades, where peace
And rest can never dwell, hope never comes
That comes to all; but torture without end
Still urges,° and a fiery deluge, fed
With ever-burning sulfur unconsumed:
Such place Eternal Justice had prepared
For those rebellious, here their prison ordained
In utter darkness, and their portion set
As far removed from God and light of Heaven
As from the center thrice to the utmost pole.°
O how unlike the place from whence they fell!
There the companions of his fall, o'erwhelmed
With floods and whirlwinds of tempestuous fire,
He soon discerns, and weltering° by his side
One next himself in power, and next in crime,
Long after known in Palestine, and named
Beelzebub.° To whom the Arch-Enemy,
And then in Heaven called Satan,° with bold words
Breaking the horrid silence thus began:
"If thou beest he—but O how fallen! how changed
From him, who in the happy realms of light
Clothed with transcendent brightness didst outshine
Myriads though bright—if he whom mutual league,
United thoughts and counsels, equal hope
And hazard in the glorious enterprise,
Joined with me once, now misery hath joined
In equal ruin: into what pit thou seest
From what height fallen! so much the stronger proved
He with his thunder;° and till then who knew

? **28–44.** *What questions does Milton ask, and how does he answer them?*

47. perdition: damnation.

48. adamantine (ad′ə·man′tin): unbreakable. **penal:** punishing.

49. durst: dared.

? **54–56.** *What torments Satan in Hell?*

58. obdurate: stubborn; unrepentant.

59. ken: can see.

? **61–74.** *Here starts a description of Hell. As you read, note the details as Milton describes them. Which aspect of Hell would be the hardest to bear?*

68. still urges: always afflicts.

74. center . . . pole: three times the distance from Earth, or "center," to the outermost point in the universe. In Milton's cosmos, Earth is the center of ten concentric spheres.

78. weltering: rolling about.

81. Beelzebub (bē·el′zə·bub′): next in power to Satan; described as prince of the devils in Matthew 12:24.

82. Satan: Hebrew for "adversary" or "opposer."

? **91.** *How has Beelzebub, Satan's former comrade, changed?*

93. He . . . thunder: God.

Taking a Second Look

Review: Context Clues

Remind students that using context clues means figuring out the meaning of an unfamiliar word by examining the words or sentences surrounding it. Milton often embeds synonyms and appositives in his sentences—words and phrases which explain or define other words.

Activity

Have students use context clues to arrive at the meaning of *baleful* in l. 56. Have students list the words in the sentence that describe Satan's mental and emotional state (*wrath, pain, torments, affliction, dismay, hate*) and then speculate on what the eyes of such a person would look like.

The force of those dire arms? Yet not for those,
Nor what the potent Victor in his rage
Can else inflict, do I repent or change,
Though changed in outward luster, that fixed mind
And high disdain, from sense of injured merit,
That with the Mightiest raised me to contend,
And to the fierce contention brought along
Innumerable force of spirits armed
That durst dislike his reign, and, me preferring,
His utmost power with adverse power opposed
In dubious battle on the plains of Heaven,
And shook his throne. What though the field be lost?
All is not lost; the unconquerable will,
And study° of revenge, immortal hate,
And courage never to submit or yield:
And what is else not to be overcome?
That glory never shall his wrath or might
Extort from me. To bow and sue for grace
With suppliant knee, and deify his power
Who from the terror of this arm so late
Doubted° his empire, that were low indeed,
That were an ignominy° and shame beneath
This downfall; since by fate the strength of gods
And this empyreal substance° cannot fail,
Since through experience of this great event,
In arms not worse, in foresight much advanced,
We may with more successful hope resolve
To wage by force or guile eternal war
Irreconcilable to our grand Foe,
Who now triumphs, and in the excess of joy
Sole reigning holds the tyranny of Heaven."
So spake the apostate° Angel, though in pain,
Vaunting° aloud, but racked with deep despair;
And him thus answered soon his bold compeer:°
"O Prince, O Chief of many thronèd Powers,
That led the embattled Seraphim° to war
Under thy conduct, and in dreadful deeds
Fearless, endangered Heaven's perpetual King,
And put to proof his high supremacy,
Whether upheld by strength, or chance, or fate;
Too well I see and rue the dire event,°
That with sad overthrow and foul defeat
Hath lost us Heaven, and all this mighty host
In horrible destruction laid thus low,
As far as gods and heavenly essences
Can perish: for the mind and spirit remains
Invincible, and vigor soon returns,
Though all our glory extinct, and happy state
Here swallowed up in endless misery.
But what if he our Conqueror (whom I now

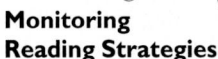

Rare Books and Manuscript Division. The New York Public Library, New York.

Illustration from *Paradise Lost* (17th century). Engraving.

107. study: pursuit.
114. doubted: archaic for "feared for."
115. ignominy (ig′nə·min′ē): dishonor.
117. empyreal (em·pir′ē·əl) **substance:** heavenly—and therefore indestructible—substance of which all angels (including Satan) are made.

? ***93–124.*** *What details in Satan's speech show that he feels that he and God are opposing generals of two armies? Does Satan admit defeat?*

125. apostate: guilty of abandoning one's beliefs. Satan is an apostate.
126. vaunting: boasting.
127. compeer: companion; equal. Now Beelzebub speaks.
129. Seraphim: highest order of angels.

134. event: archaic for "outcome."

E Critical Thinking

Analyzing Character

? **How does Satan begin this speech?** [by expressing sympathy for Beelzebub] **What is he talking about now?** [himself, and his determination not to "repent or change"] **What does this rapid change in subject suggest about Satan's personality?** [Possible response: He cares only for himself and is obsessed with anger.]

F Elements of Literature

Theme

Here Satan introduces "the unconquerable will," a theme that colors his speeches throughout the poem. Suggest that students keep a running list of what Satan says about the power of the will. Ask what Satan suggests about God's will compared to his own. [Possible response: God's will is not as strong as Satan's, for God was shaken (Satan believes) and doubted the outcome of the battle in Heaven.]

G Reading Skills and Strategies

Monitoring Reading Strategies

Lines 128–142 constitute one sentence. Have students read the sentence aloud and break down the difficult passages. Help them understand that the first six lines are a direct address to Satan, the main idea of the sentence is packed into l. 134, and in ll. 139–140 Beelzebub seems to agree with Satan—before going on to question his fate.

Answer to Margin Question

Lines 93–124. Satan refers to God as the "Victor," with His "innumerable force of spirits armed," after the two "powers" opposed "in dubious battle." He speaks of heaven as a lost "field"; however, he speaks of God as a "grand Foe" in an "eternal War," suggesting that he does not concede that his defeat is final.

Skill Link

Evaluating a Persuasive Speech

Tell students that the highly polished rhetoric and powerful speechmaking skills displayed by Satan are one of his most attractive qualities. The reader may abhor Satan's ideas but still be impressed by the magnificent way he conveys them.

Activities

1. Have students read aloud Satan's rousing speech (ll. 84–124), dividing it into sections, varying pace and volume from section to section.
2. Ask students which section of the speech they find most impressive, and why.
3. Ask students why they think Satan can sometimes be persuasive, despite the evil or emptiness of his ideas.

LITERATURE AND SOCIETY

Historically, censorship has been the rule rather than the exception, existing in such times and places as fifth-century Athens (the "Golden Age" of classical Greece), thirteenth-century Spain, Russia both before and after the Communist revolution, and the United States in war time. Currently, according to a study by Freedom House, about two billion people live in countries where the strictest forms of censorship govern their daily lives. Roughly the same number of people live in countries where free speech and a free press are the cornerstones of civil liberty. Have interested students find examples of censorship in action in today's world and research organizations that combat it.

Answer to Margin Question

Lines 128–155. Beelzebub thinks that, although defeated, the rebel angels maintain their spirit; however, he wonders whether God has deliberately left them their spirit so that they might suffer all the more. He does not have Satan's utterly invincible pride and ego.

LITERATURE AND SOCIETY

Censoring the Word

Most of us tend to associate censorship with either foreign dictatorships or the issue of obscenity. For the authorities of seventeenth-century England, however, the power of the word was great—potentially so great that freedom of speech and freedom of the press were unknown. Newspapers, books, and pamphlets were all subject to strict censorship.

Keeping a wary eye. Even in Elizabethan times, the government had kept a wary eye on literary activity, especially on drama. Plays and players had to be licensed, and playwrights were careful to avoid offending the powerful. For example, in his play *Henry IV*, Shakespeare changed the name Sir John Oldcastle to Sir John Falstaff to avoid offending the Oldcastle family, friends of Queen Elizabeth.

Government control of the press had its origins in the rise of newspapers and journalism early in the seventeenth century. Oliver Cromwell, a Puritan and the lord protector of England, banned all unofficial periodicals in 1655. After the Restoration of King Charles II in 1660, so-called licensing laws were regularly enacted by Parliament. The laws forbade publishing any material contrary to the doctrine of the Church of England or scandalous to the government. Penalties were stiff: fines, imprisonment, and sentencing to the pillory, where the offender was fastened to a wooden board with holes for the head and hands.

A censor's who's who. The list of writers who ran afoul of the licensing laws reads like a "who's who" of seventeenth-century literature.

In 1605, Ben Jonson was arrested and in danger of having his nose and ears slit for his coauthorship of *Eastward Hoe*. The play contained disrespectful remarks

Of force° believe almighty, since no less
Than such could have o'erpowered such force as ours)
Have left us this our spirit and strength entire
Strongly to suffer and support our pains,
That we may so suffice° his vengeful ire,
Or do him mightier service as his thralls°
By right of war, whate'er his business be,
Here in the heart of Hell to work in fire,
Or do his errands in the gloomy deep?
What can it then avail,° though yet we feel
Strength undiminished, or eternal being
To undergo eternal punishment?"
Whereto with speedy words the Arch-Fiend replied:

144. of force: of necessity.

148. suffice: archaic for "satisfy."

149. thralls: slaves.

153. avail: be of help or advantage.

? **128–155.** *What does Beelzebub think of their situation? How is Beelzebub different from Satan?*

Getting Students Involved

Cooperative Learning

Debating Censorship. Have groups of students take opposing (or at least different) sides of a censorship issue. Censorship of student writing is an issue on which students usually have strong opinions. Encourage them to debate this or another issue; make it the topic of a panel discussion; or create some form of persuasive presentation, such as a radio or television commercial.

Each group should list and divide the tasks necessary to prepare and present their side of the issue. One list for planning a debate might look like this:

- Research past and present incidents of censorship
- Identify causes and effects of censorship, both specific and general
- Prepare visual aids
- Organize and set up the debate or discussion (time, place, rules, etc.)
- Choose speakers to be in the debate or on the panel

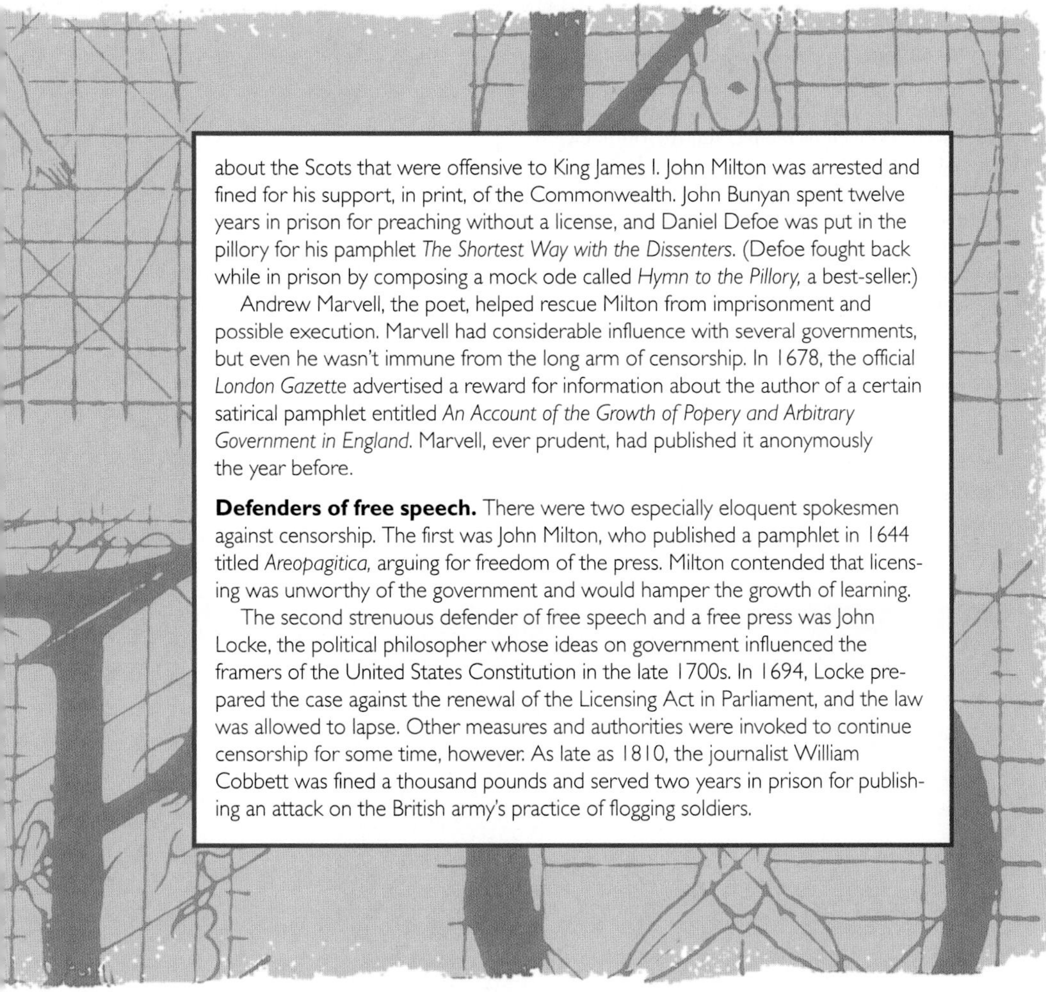

about the Scots that were offensive to King James I. John Milton was arrested and fined for his support, in print, of the Commonwealth. John Bunyan spent twelve years in prison for preaching without a license, and Daniel Defoe was put in the pillory for his pamphlet *The Shortest Way with the Dissenters.* (Defoe fought back while in prison by composing a mock ode called *Hymn to the Pillory,* a best-seller.)

Andrew Marvell, the poet, helped rescue Milton from imprisonment and possible execution. Marvell had considerable influence with several governments, but even he wasn't immune from the long arm of censorship. In 1678, the official *London Gazette* advertised a reward for information about the author of a certain satirical pamphlet entitled *An Account of the Growth of Popery and Arbitrary Government in England.* Marvell, ever prudent, had published it anonymously the year before.

Defenders of free speech. There were two especially eloquent spokesmen against censorship. The first was John Milton, who published a pamphlet in 1644 titled *Areopagitica,* arguing for freedom of the press. Milton contended that licensing was unworthy of the government and would hamper the growth of learning.

The second strenuous defender of free speech and a free press was John Locke, the political philosopher whose ideas on government influenced the framers of the United States Constitution in the late 1700s. In 1694, Locke prepared the case against the renewal of the Licensing Act in Parliament, and the law was allowed to lapse. Other measures and authorities were invoked to continue censorship for some time, however. As late as 1810, the journalist William Cobbett was fined a thousand pounds and served two years in prison for publishing an attack on the British army's practice of flogging soldiers.

"Fallen Cherub, to be weak is miserable,
Doing or suffering:° But of this be sure,
To do aught° good never will be our task, **A**
But ever to do ill our sole delight,
As being the contrary to his high will
Whom we resist. If then his providence
Out of our evil seek to bring forth good,
Our labor must be to pervert that end,
And out of good still° to find means of evil;
Which ofttimes may succeed, so as perhaps
Shall grieve him, if I fail not, and disturb
His inmost counsels from their destined aim. **B**
But see the angry Victor° hath recalled

158. doing or suffering: whether active or passive.
159. aught: anything whatever.

? **159–162.** *What does Satan vow? Would you say this is the essence of evil? Explain.*

165. still: always.

169. angry Victor: God.

A Reading Skills and Strategies
Monitoring Reading Strategies

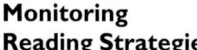

Lines 159–160 offer a fine example of the way form and content mesh. Just as Satan juxtaposes his own evil against God's goodness, he emphasizes this opposition with a mirror-like sentence made of two opposing statements. Ask students to paraphrase the sentence. [Possible response: It will never be our task to do good, but it will always be our delight to do evil.] Encourage students to be alert for other parallel structures in which Satan sets himself in opposition to God.

B Reading Skills and Strategies
Making Predictions

? How do you suppose Satan will "disturb / His inmost counsels from their destined aim," or inflict havoc on God's designs? [Possible responses: He will introduce evil into the world. He will tempt Adam and Eve.] Note that in the council of demons that follows this excerpt, God's plan to create a world—a plan that was spoken of in heaven before the rebellion—is brought up. The demons quickly agree that the best revenge is to ruin that creation. Students may check their predictions against ll. 215–220.

Answer to Margin Question

Lines 159–162. Possible response: Satan vows to do only evil forever and to always oppose God. Since God is the essence of goodness, Satan is the essence of evil.

Crossing the Curriculum

Music
In this part of Milton's epic, Satan presents himself as king of hell. Ask pairs of students to find recorded music that expresses Satan's character. Some of the more sinister pieces in the soundtracks of John Williams's *The Empire Strikes Back* and *Raiders of the Lost Ark* are possibilities. Have one partner play the recording while the other reads an appropriate excerpt from the text.

Architecture
Book I closes with the building of Pandaemonium ("the place of all daemons"), a citadel to serve as the capital of hell. Have students sketch a design for this building, keeping in mind Satan's lust for glory and stated goal to "reign in hell." If possible, have students read Milton's description in ll. 678–768 of the full-length poem.

Science
Line 74 of this selection offers a clue to Milton's view of the cosmos. Ask students to find out about the state of astronomical knowledge at the time Milton was writing (c. 1650). Invite them to share their findings with the class by making posters or giving an oral presentation with chalkboard drawings. Together, discuss how Milton's comment reflects or contradicts the thinking of his day.

Ⓐ Struggling Readers

Finding Details

? What does Satan's description indicate about the way in which his troops left heaven? [Possible response: They were driven over the edge of heaven and fell to hell, chased by "sulfurous hail" and "thunder / Winged with red lightning."] **Now that the moment has passed, what does Satan seem to believe about the power that God displayed?** [Possible answer: God has stopped showing His rage and power because He is worn out.]

RESPONDING TO THE ART

William Blake not only rejected the neoclassical literary style of the eighteenth century but also defied contemporary conventions in the visual arts in both his choice of materials and his artistic philosophy. He refused to paint in oil, believing that oils lacked precision. Instead, he chose watercolors and, sometimes, tempera, a medium that results in a dull finish. Blake hated the academic rules of painting, stressed imagination over reason, and constructed his ideal forms from inner visions, not from observations of the natural world. See p. 645 for more biographical information on the artist. (For more art by Blake, see pp. 395, 440, 448, 451, 623, 638, 646, 647, 648, 649, 651, 654.)

Activity. Ask students what religious symbol appears in this painting. [the cross mounted on the globe] Then have them discuss the effect of including that symbol. [Possible response: It underscores all that Satan loses when he falls from grace.]

His ministers of vengeance and pursuit
Back to the gates of Heaven; the sulfurous hail
Shot after us in storm, o'erblown hath laid
The fiery surge, that from the precipice
Of Heaven received us falling, and the thunder,
Winged with red lightning and impetuous rage,
Perhaps hath spent his shafts, and ceases now
To bellow through the vast and boundless deep.
Let us not slip° the occasion, whether scorn
Or satiate° fury yield it from our Foe.
Seest thou yon dreary plain, forlorn and wild,
The seat of desolation, void of light,
Save what the glimmering of these livid flames
Casts pale and dreadful? Thither let us tend
From off the tossing of these fiery waves,
There rest, if any rest can harbor there,
And reassembling our afflicted powers,
Consult how we may henceforth most offend
Our Enemy, our own loss how repair,
How overcome this dire calamity,

178. slip: lose.

179. satiate: satisfied.

Satan in His Original Glory (late 18th to early 19th century) by William Blake.

Tate Gallery, London.

Skill Link

Analyzing and Responding to Critical Reviews

In *A Reader's Guide to John Milton*, Marjorie Nicholson says, "the character of Satan is one of the greatest creations in any language. The greatness lies not only—indeed, not primarily—in the depiction of the majestic character of Books I and II, but in the slow and steady degeneration of an angel who once stood next to God Himself in Heaven. As we read *Paradise Lost* we watch the subtlety of Milton's art as the character gradually diminishes from grandeur and magnificence to baseness and final degradation, so that we are inevitably alienated from admiration."

Ask students what comments from or about Satan suggest that he may have further to fall.

Writing of Satan's "sense of injured merit," the author and critic C. S. Lewis notes: "No one had in fact done anything to Satan. . . . In the midst of a world of light and love, of song and feast and dance, he could find nothing to think of more interesting than his own prestige."

Ask students whether Lewis's view seems justified at this point in the poem.

What reinforcement we may gain from hope,
If not, what resolution from despair."
  Thus Satan talking to his nearest mate
With head uplift above the wave, and eyes
That sparkling blazed; his other parts besides,
Prone on the flood, extended long and large,
Lay floating many a rood,° in bulk as huge
As whom the fables name of monstrous size,
Titanian or Earth-born, that warred on Jove,
Briareos or Typhon,° whom the den
By ancient Tarsus held, or that sea-beast
Leviathan,° which God of all his works
Created hugest that swim the ocean stream:
Him haply slumbering on the Norway foam,
The pilot of some small night-foundered° skiff,
Deeming some island, oft, as seamen tell,
With fixèd anchor in his scaly rind
Moors by his side under the lee, while night
Invests° the sea, and wishèd morn delays:
So stretched out huge in length the Arch-Fiend lay
Chained on the burning lake; nor ever thence
Had risen or heaved his head, but that the will
And high permission of all-ruling Heaven
Left him at large to his own dark designs,
That with reiterated crimes he might
Heap on himself damnation, while he sought
Evil to others, and enraged might see
How all his malice served but to bring forth
Infinite goodness, grace, and mercy shown
On man by him seduced, but on himself
Treble confusion, wrath, and vengeance poured.
  Forthwith upright he rears from off the pool
His mighty stature; on each hand the flames
Driven backward slope their pointing spires, and rolled
In billows, leave in the midst a horrid vale.
Then with expanded wings he steers his flight
Aloft, incumbent° on the dusky air
That felt unusual weight, till on dry land
He lights, if it were land that ever burned
With solid, as the lake with liquid fire;
And such appeared in hue, as when the force
Of subterranean wind transports a hill
Torn from Pelorus,° or the shattered side
Of thundering Etna,° whose combustible
And fueled entrails thence conceiving fire,
Sublimed° with mineral fury, aid the winds,
And leave a singèd bottom all involved°
With stench and smoke: such resting found the sole
Of unblest feet. Him followed his next mate,
Both glorying to have scaped the Stygian° flood

? **169–191.** *Satan thinks of himself merely as a defeated general. What does he now propose?*

196. rood: an old unit of measure varying locally from about six to eight yards.

198–200. Titanian . . . Typhon: In an epic simile, Milton compares Satan to the Titans and Giants of Greek mythology. Briareos, a hundred-handed Giant, helped Zeus (Jove) battle the Titans. Typhon, a hundred-headed serpent-monster from Cilicia (near Tarsus), attacked heaven and was imprisoned by Zeus.
201. Leviathan: Biblical sea monster, either a reptile or a whale.
204. night-foundered: overtaken by night.
208. invests: covers.

? **209–220.** *What are God's plans for Satan?*

226. incumbent: lying.

? **230–238.** *Read this important epic simile carefully. Notice the natural forces that Satan is compared with. How does this description of Satan contrast with Blake's image on page 446?*
232. Pelorus: headland in Sicily, Italy; now called Cape Faro.
233. Etna: volcano in Sicily, Italy.

235. sublimed: vaporized.
236. involved: enveloped.
239. Stygian (stij′ē·ən): of or like the river Styx; infernal, hellish. In Greek mythology, the river Styx encircles the underworld.

B Reading Skills and Strategies
Monitoring Reading Strategies

? Milton paints remarkable visual images. As you reread this passage, imagine how Satan might look in a film version of this scene. How does Milton seem to shift the reader's visual vantage point as he begins this new section? [Possible responses: We have been focusing on Satan's head as he talks to Beelzebub. Now we are asked to take a longer view—to be reminded of Satan's size and to see the other fallen angels around him.]

C Elements of Literature
Epic Simile

? Does the comparison to the Leviathan/island add to the description of Satan, or is it a distraction? [Possible responses: Perhaps the detail that the sailors were fooled by the beast's size is a subtle reminder of Satan's own deceptive (and self-deceptive) abilities. Or, this epic simile seems more like a digression.]

D Reading Skills and Strategies
Drawing Conclusions

? Why do you think Milton intrudes into the story in such an omniscient fashion here? [Possible response: Perhaps he realized that some readers would be attracted to the image of Satan, and he wanted to put the character in perspective.]

Answers to Margin Questions

Lines 169–191. Satan now proposes that the rebels rest, reassemble, take council, repair their losses, and take on new resolve.
Lines 209–220. God plans to see that humanity is showered with grace while allowing Satan to continue to damn himself by hatching more evil plans, thereby remaining eternally crushed by God's vengeance.
Lines 230–238. While Blake's painting glows with a gold and ivory light, Milton's image suggests the black and red of an exploding volcano.

Using Students' Strengths

Visual Learners

A graphic device—such as a series of wide, upward-pointing arrows—might help students understand Satan's speeches. In each wide arrow, have students note in their own words one threat or accusation that Satan makes against God (such as "I will bring evil out of God's plan for good"). Encourage individuals or groups to compare arrows and look for shared statements.

Interpersonal Learners

Have students form small groups and work together to list possible answers to one of the following questions:

- Why would a person want to put an end to someone else's happiness?
- Why do some people who seemingly have "the good life" ruin it for themselves?

Have the groups compare lists and discuss which answers might be given by Satan, Adam, and Eve.

A Reading Skills and Strategies

Monitoring Reading Strategies

As students continue to monitor their reading strategies, remind them that being aware of personal responses to a text is a vital part of reading well. Ask students to jot down their reactions to Satan and his belligerent declarations. If necessary, prompt them with questions such as: Why is Satan so proud to possess the "infernal world"? [Possible response: He believes he is God's equal.]

B Elements of Literature

Repetition and Irony

Point out to students that "Be it so" echoes the refrain "And it was so" in Genesis. Ask students how Milton makes the phrase ironic. [Possible response: By putting it in Satan's mouth, Milton twists it into a declaration of destruction and rebellion.]

C Critical Thinking

Making Connections

? How does the proverb "misery loves company" apply here? [Possible responses: Satan is eager to rally his forces so that they may "share with us their part / In this unhappy mansion." He needs support to seek revenge against God; he may also believe that sharing the torment with others will alleviate his own pain.]

Answers to Margin Questions

Lines 254–255. Possible response: It doesn't matter where you are physically; the mind can create a wonderful or miserable place for you to dwell in mentally.

Line 263. Possible response: Satan reasserts his enormous pride, tries to convince himself that evil is good (an obvious contradiction), and plans to rule an empire of evil.

As gods, and by their own recovered strength,
Not by the sufferance° of supernal° power.
"Is this the region, this the soil, the clime,"
Said then the lost Archangel, "this the seat
That we must change for Heaven, this mournful gloom
For that celestial light? Be it so, since he
Who now is sovereign can dispose and bid
What shall be right: farthest from him is best,
Whom reason hath equaled, force hath made supreme
Above his equals. Farewell, happy fields,
Where joy forever dwells! Hail, horrors! hail,
Infernal world! and thou, profoundest° Hell,
Receive thy new possessor; one who brings
A mind not to be changed by place or time.
The mind is its own place, and in itself
Can make a Heaven of Hell, a Hell of Heaven.
What matter where, if I be still the same,
And what I should be, all but less than he
Whom thunder hath made greater? Here at least
We shall be free; the Almighty hath not built
Here for his envy, will not drive us hence:
Here we may reign secure, and in my choice
To reign is worth ambition, though in Hell:
Better to reign in Hell than serve in Heaven.
But wherefore let we then our faithful friends,
The associates and copartners of our loss,
Lie thus astonished° on the oblivious° pool,
And call them not to share with us their part
In this unhappy mansion, or once more
With rallied arms to try what may be yet
Regained in Heaven, or what more lost in Hell?"

241. sufferance: permission. **supernal:** heavenly.

251. profoundest: lowest; deepest.

? **254–255.** *Satan and Beelzebub land in Hell. How would you paraphrase what the proud Satan says in these lines? Do you agree?*

? **263.** *What do you make of this declaration? What do you predict Satan will do next?*

266. astonished: dazed. **oblivious:** causing forgetfulness.

The Fall of Satan (1825) (detail) by William Blake. Illustration for *The Book of Job.*
Tate Gallery, London.

Assessing Learning

Check Test: True-False

1. Satan had been one of God's favored angels. [True]
2. Satan was very ugly, with red skin and horns. [False]
3. When Satan says "[F]arthest from him is best" (l. 247), he means that the rebels can do as they please when away from God. [True]
4. Satan rebels because God made him a slave. [False]

Informal Assessment

Observation Assessment. Note students' responses in class discussion, group work, and written comments. Rate them as follows:
1=Rarely 2=Sometimes 3=Never

___ **1.** Makes connections with other texts
___ **2.** Shows knowledge of poetic devices
___ **3.** Considers multiple levels of meaning
___ **4.** Makes personal connections
___ **5.** Challenges the text

MAKING MEANINGS

First Thoughts

1. How did you react to Milton's portrait of Satan? What **images** describing Satan or words spoken by Satan made the greatest impression on you?

> **Reading Check**
>
> a. Whom does Milton call upon at the outset (lines 1–16)? What question does he ask about Adam and Eve (lines 27–33)?
>
> b. What is Milton's **purpose** in writing this epic story?
>
> c. Why was Satan cast out of Heaven?
>
> d. In his first speech, what does Satan tell Beelzebub that he will never do? What course does he favor instead?
>
> e. According to Milton in lines 210–220, who allows Satan the freedom to pursue his evil intentions?
>
> f. In his last speech, what does Satan claim are the advantages of life in Hell?

Shaping Interpretations

2. According to Milton, how is the rebellion of Satan and the angels against God connected with "man's first disobedience" and the origin of evil in the world? How does Milton explain the existence of evil in a world created by a loving God?
3. Reread Milton's first description of Hell (lines 53–74). How is hell both a psychological state and a physical place? What do you make of the poet's use of **paradox** in the phrase "darkness visible" (line 63)?
4. In his opening speech, Satan vows never to "repent or change" (line 96). Nevertheless, do you catch any hint of longing in this speech for the angels' former state? How might this yearning be related to Milton's mention of "the thought . . . of lost happiness" in lines 54–55?
5. Beelzebub reminds Satan that even in Hell the evil angels may be unwittingly serving God's purposes. How does Satan reply to this objection in lines 157–168?
6. In lines 210–220, Milton offers a solemn assurance that despite all Satan's power and grandeur, the devil is still subject to God's purposes. How do these lines contribute a level of **dramatic irony** to Satan's ringing assertion of freedom in his final speech (lines 242–270)?
7. Discuss why some people see Milton's Satan as a heroic figure. How do you feel about this heroic depiction of Satan?
8. What **images** in the story helped you to see and smell Hell?

Connecting with the Text

9. Perhaps the most famous verses of this passage are in Satan's last speech (lines 254–255):

   The mind is its own place, and in itself
   Can make a Heaven of Hell, a Hell of
   Heaven.

   In your experience, is this an accurate description of what the mind can do?

Extending the Text

10. Do people today use the arguments and rationalizations used by Satan and his old crony Beelzebub in their dialogue (lines 143–168)? If so, how?

READING SKILLS AND STRATEGIES

Reading Milton's Poetic Language

Analyzing epic similes. The word *as* in Milton's epic tells us that a simile is coming, an elaborate **epic simile,** in which something in the poem is compared to something quite outside the poem—often an animal, sometimes a human being or human action. These epic similes allowed Milton to bring into his epic a variety of non-Biblical material. Note the **analogies,** or similarities between two unlike things, that the similes are based on.

1. What epic similes are used to describe Satan's bulk in lines 196–208? What is compared to what? How are these things alike?
2. What epic simile describes Satan's landing on dry land in lines 230–237? What is compared to what? How are these things alike?

MAKING MEANINGS

First Thoughts [Respond]

1. Students may be surprised at the depiction of Satan. Satan is evil, but his audacity and persuasiveness are charismatic. Compelling images include his blazing eyes and his immense size (ll. 193–202).

Shaping Interpretations [Interpret]

2. Out of revenge, Satan (ll. 157–168) plans to corrupt God's original creation (humans). According to Milton, God allows evil to exist in order to have good come from it.
3. Possible responses: Hell is a place of physical torment; "Lost happiness" (l. 55) and "dismay" (l. 57) suggest psychological pain as well. "Darkness visible" is a state incomprehensible to the human senses. Hell's flames give no light, yet the darkness is visible—a paradox only God can understand.
4. Satan's tone is mournful as he laments Beelzebub's lost glory. His greatest sorrow, however, is losing his status and happiness in heaven, which stokes his revenge and prevents his repentance.
5. Satan rejects that possibility, saying that his angels will devote themselves to subverting any of God's plans.
6. Satan's assertions of independence contrast sharply with Milton's statement that his actions are allowed by "high permission of all-ruling Heaven." Lines 214–215 suggest that Satan increases his own torment by opposing God.
7. Satan's intensity, persuasiveness, and pride strike some people as heroic; however, students may suggest that "heroic" can never apply to someone who is evil.
8. Possible responses: "fiery gulf" (l. 52), "ever-burning sulfur" (l. 69), "floods and whirlwinds of tempestuous fire" (l. 77).

Connecting with the Text [Evaluate]

9. The human imagination is capable of transforming reality—of finding happiness even in misery, of finding sorrow even in the midst of joy.

Extending the Text [Apply]

10. Possible responses: Yes; Satan's assertions of hell's advantages resemble the rationalizations that many people use to excuse their failures.

Reading Check

a. The Heavenly Muse; he asks why Adam and Eve violated God's one restriction on their freedom.

b. His purpose is to affirm God's benevolence and to explain God's treatment of humanity (ll. 25-26).

c. He led a rebellion of angels (l. 43).

d. He will never "repent or change" (l. 96). He seeks revenge by thwarting God's plans and mounting another attack against Heaven.

e. "All-ruling Heaven," or God

f. He and his angels are assured control there.

READING SKILLS AND STRATEGIES

Reading Milton's Poetic Style: Analyzing Epic Similes

1. Satan's body is compared to the bodies of the Greek mythological giants Briareos and Typhon and of the biblical sea creature Leviathan. All of these creatures are alike in their vast size and their terrifying appearance and power.

2. Satan's landing is compared to the smashing of a hill or to a volcano torn from its original site by a subterranean blast and carried by the wind. These explosive actions are alike in their enormous force.

Reading Irregular Syntax

1. *He/discerns/companions.* To clarify, repeat the verb or supply a synonym. (He discerns his companions and sees Beelzebub weltering by his side.)

2. Possible answer: Fallen Cherub, weakness is miserable. Let us be strong in avoiding good; let us delight in acting contrary to God.

Reading Blank Verse

1. Infernal world! and thou,
profoundest Hell, / Receive thy new
possessor, one who brings / A mind
not to be changed by place or time.
(Note variance in l. 253.)

2. Milton varies meter, putting a preposition or relative pronoun in a stressed position. For example, in ll. 27–29:

"Say first, for Heaven hides
nothing from thy view, / Nor the
deep tract of Hell, say first what
cause / Moved our grand parents in
that happy state."

Grading Timesaver

Rubrics for each Choices assignment appear on p. 129 in the *Portfolio Management System.*

Reading irregular syntax. To accommodate the demands of his meter, Milton often uses irregular syntax in which the sentences do not follow the normal subject-verb-complement order. In addition, Milton's sentences are long, and often words are omitted which have to be supplied by the reader.

1. In lines 76–78, what are the **subject,** the **verb,** and the **direct object**? What additional words should be supplied in lines 78–81 to make sense of the rest of this sentence?
2. Using normal English syntax, how would you rephrase lines 157–162?

Reading blank verse. Milton uses **blank verse,** or unrhymed iambic pentameter, to give his epic an exalted tone. Iambic pentameter means that each line of the poem has ten syllables, with five strong stresses alternating with five weaker stresses (the lines begin with an unstressed syllable and end with a stressed one). An **iamb** is an unstressed syllable followed by a stressed one, as in the word *rĕfér.*

1. Scan lines 251–253 to show that they are written in iambic pentameter.
2. Choose a passage to read aloud so that you can hear the beat of the iambs. Where does Milton vary the meter to give his verse variety and to prevent a singsong rhythm?

CHOICES: Building Your Portfolio

Writer's Notebook

1. Collecting Ideas for a Cause-Effect Essay

WORK IN PROGRESS

In *Paradise Lost,* Milton argues that God is not responsible for the evils of our world. Rather, Adam and Eve's disobedience, their misuse of reason and freedom, caused these evils. What do you think is one of the biggest evils that exists in the world today? What are its causes? What are its effects? As you note your ideas, draw from your own experience, but also consider other sources, such as historical evidence. Save your work to use in the Writer's Workshop on page 459.

Paraphrasing a Text

2. Paraphrasing Milton

Choose one of the long speeches in this excerpt from *Paradise Lost*: for example, lines 84–124 (Satan), 128–155 (Beelzebub), 157–191 (Satan), or 242–270 (Satan). Write a prose paraphrase of the speech you select. You'll have to supply words that Milton omits and use normal English syntax.

Analyzing a Character

3. Analyzing the Arch-Fiend

In a brief essay, discuss Milton's characterization of Satan. Examine Satan's appearance, his actions, his words, and his effect on others. Where does Milton directly characterize Satan? Is Satan a heroic figure from any perspective? Open with a general statement summing up the character of the Arch-Fiend.

Creative Writing

4. A Fallen Angel Dialogue

Milton originally planned *Paradise Lost* as a drama. Working with a small group, try recreating the opening scene of the poem as a dramatic dialogue between Satan and Beelzebub. Start by compressing the two characters' speeches. How will you incorporate Milton's background narration and descriptive details into your dialogue?

Comparing Texts/Art

5. Two Hells

Another famous description of Hell and its overlord appears in the selection from *The Inferno of Dante* on page 394. Prepare two lists, one for Milton and one for Dante, and compare their images of Satan and his infernal domain. If you wish, draw the two underworlds—they are dramatically visual.

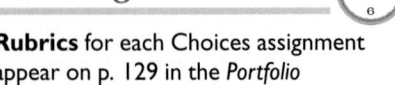

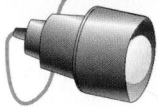

SPOTLIGHT ON

Allegory: Telling Two Stories at Once

Modern photographers sometimes create striking effects by superimposing one image on another to produce a double exposure. In the same way, writers sometimes use the literary form known as **allegory** to tell two stories at once. Allegories are usually used for teaching. In an allegory, characters, settings, and events stand for abstract ideas. Allegories thus have two meanings: a literal meaning and a symbolic one.

Allegories were especially popular during the Middle Ages. Around 1509, an enduringly relevant play called *Everyman* used the techniques of allegory to teach people the value of good deeds. Everyman (who stands for exactly what his name indicates) is summoned by Death to give an account of his life. Everyman asks his friends, who have allegorical names such as Fellowship, Beauty, and Strength, to go with him, but only Good Deeds stays with him to the end. *Everyman* is periodically dusted off and revived for the stage today. It still gets good reviews.

The Renaissance produced two masterly allegories. Edmund Spenser's *The Faerie Queene* is a long, rich allegory about the adventures of characters who embody such things as holiness, chastity, truth, falsehood, hypocrisy, and despair. (See page 221.) John Bunyan's allegorical novel *The Pilgrim's Progress from This World to That Which Is to Come* (1678), commonly called *The Pilgrim's Progress,* was such a success that, like many filmmakers today, he produced a second part. (B)

The Perils of Piety

The narrator of *The Pilgrim's Progress* is a dreamer. Asleep, he dreams about a man called Christian who lives with his family in a city called Destruction. Besides living in a city with this appalling name, Christian has another problem: On his back he bears an immense burden that he cannot get rid of. It is like a part of himself. And so he decides to leave home and go on a "progress," or journey, to a wonderful place that he has heard of called the Celestial City. On this trip, described through most of the book, he has a few pleasant experiences, (A) such as his visit to House Beautiful and the Delectable Mountains, but most of his adventures are unpleasant and even dangerous. He falls into the Slough (a mudhole; rhymes with "cow") of Despond, he climbs the Hill Difficulty, he fights a dragonlike monster called Apollyon, and he is arrested and unjustly punished in a place called Vanity Fair. His most insidious encounters are with characters who try to distract him from his progress: Mr. Worldly Wiseman, Talkative, Little-Faith, and Ignorance. Finally, all these obstacles overcome, Christian enters the Celestial City, where he will dwell eternally in bliss and where he is eventually joined by his wife,

©The Frick Collection, New York.

Christian Reading in His Book
(late 18th or early 19th century)
by William Blake.

Spotlight On

This feature provides an overview of the genre of allegory, giving summaries of two famous examples: the medieval play *Everyman* and Edmund Spenser's *The Faerie Queene.* The feature goes on to explore in detail John Bunyan's 1678 allegory of salvation, *The Pilgrim's Progress,* including an excerpt in which the main character Christian and his friend Hopeful are imprisoned in the dungeon of the Giant Despair. With Hopeful's help, Christian chooses to bear his hardships and await God's help rather than take his own life as the Giant urges him to do.

(A) Elements of Literature
Allegory

The word *allegory* comes from two Greek words: *allos,* or "other," and *agoreuein,* "to speak in assembly." The word has close ties with *agora,* or "marketplace." An allegory, then, is meant for public sharing—either with a viewing audience (as in the case of the play *Everyman*) or with a reading audience (as in the case of *The Pilgrim's Progress*).

(B) Background
John Bunyan

Born near Bedford, England, John Bunyan (1628–1688) served in the Parliamentary army from 1644 to 1646. Some time after his marriage in 1649, Bunyan underwent a great spiritual struggle. As a result, he left the Church of England and joined a Baptist congregation at Bedford. Since Bunyan became a lay preacher at a time when nonconformist preaching was banned, he was arrested for preaching and was imprisoned from 1660 to 1672. From the Bedford jail, he wrote nine books. When finally released from prison, Bunyan became the pastor of the Bedford Baptist congregation. In 1675, however, he was imprisoned again, and it was during this time that he completed the first part of *The Pilgrim's Progress.*

Using Students' Strengths

Visual Learners

One of the most effective attributes of allegory is its conversion of abstract ideas into vivid, concrete images that have an immediate appeal to the senses. Have students draw, paint, or create a collage of their own personal visions of Christian, the Giant Despair, Doubting Castle, the Celestial City, or any other person or place in the selection that appeals to them. Alternatively, students might create concrete visual images that represent such ideas as hope, strength, good deeds, truth, hypocrisy, despair, and holiness. Remind them that to be effective as allegory their images need to be literal and realistic while at the same time suggesting the ideas for which they stand.

RESPONDING TO THE ART

See p. 645 and pp. T395 and T446 for information on Blake.
Activity. Invite students to think about what literal and figurative burden Christian might be carrying.

A Background

Christian's Tone

The travelers' imprisonment is partly their own fault because Christian persuaded Hopeful to take an ostensibly easier path, not knowing that this course would force them to cross Giant Despair's property. As a result, a tone of self-recrimination colors Christian's speeches in this excerpt.

B Humanities Connections

The Wizard of Oz

Certainly *The Wizard of Oz*—both the book by L. Frank Baum and the Hollywood movie—was intended more to entertain than to instruct. Nevertheless, readers and viewers of Dorothy's adventures on the way to the Emerald City usually sense its allegorical dimensions. After all, the lost and confused Dorothy is a kind of Everyperson on a journey, beset by evildoers (witches and goblins) and accompanied by three friends—a Scarecrow who needs a brain, a Tin Man who needs a heart, and a Lion who needs courage. Ask students if they can think of other allegorical aspects of *The Wizard of Oz*.

C Literary Connections

Echo of a Psalm

Most students will recognize this reference to Psalm 23 (see p. 422). They may surmise from the comparison that Christian survived the Valley of the Shadow of Death by being protected by God.

Title page of *The Pilgrim's Progress* by John Bunyan.

Christiana, and their children. Bunyan describes their journey in the second part of *The Pilgrim's Progress*.

In the following excerpt, Christian and his companion, Hopeful, have been imprisoned in the dungeon of Giant Despair's Doubting Castle. Goaded by his wife, Diffidence, the giant has starved them, beaten them mercilessly, and urged them to kill themselves. Christian and Hopeful talk about what to do.

Christian: "Brother," said Christian, "what shall we do? The life that we now live is miserable. For my part I know not whether it is best to live thus, or to die out of hand. 'My soul chooseth strangling rather than life,'[1] and the grave is more easy for me than this dungeon. Shall we be ruled by the Giant?"

Hopeful: "Indeed our present condition is dreadful, and death would be far more welcome to me than thus forever to abide; but yet let us consider, the Lord of the country to which we are going hath said, 'Thou shalt do no murder': no, not to another man's person; much more then are we forbidden to take his counsel to kill ourselves. Besides, he that kills another can but commit murder upon his body; but for one to kill himself is to kill body and soul at once. And moreover, my brother, thou talkest of ease in the grave; but hast thou forgotten the hell whither for certain the murderers go? For 'no murderer hath eternal life,'[2] etc. And let us consider again that all the law is not in the hand of Giant Despair. Others, so far as I can understand, have been taken by him, as well as we; and yet have escaped out of his hand. Who knows but that God that made the world may cause that Giant Despair may die? Or that at some time or other he may forget to lock us in? Or but he may in short time have another of his fits before us, and may lose the use of his limbs? And if ever that should come to pass again, for my part, I am resolved to pluck up the heart of a man,[3] and to try my utmost to get from under his hand. I was a fool that I did not try to do it before; but however, my brother, let's be patient, and endure a while. The time may come that may give us a happy release; but let us not be our own murderers." With these words Hopeful at present did moderate the mind of his brother; so they continued together (in the dark) that day, in their sad and doleful condition.

Well, toward evening the Giant goes down into the dungeon again, to see if his prisoners had taken his counsel; but when he came there he found them alive; and truly, alive was all; for now, what for want of bread and water, and by reason of the wounds they received when he beat them, they could do little but breathe. But, I say, he found them alive, at which he fell into a grievous rage, and told them that, seeing they had disobeyed his counsel, it should be worse with them than if they had never been born.

At this they trembled greatly, and I think that Christian fell into a swoon; but coming a little to himself again, they renewed their discourse about the Giant's counsel; and whether yet they had best to take it or no. Now Christian again seemed to be for doing it, but Hopeful made his second reply as followeth:

Hopeful: "My brother," said he, "rememberest thou not how valiant thou hast been heretofore? Apollyon could not crush thee, nor could all that thou didst hear, or see, or feel, in the Valley of the Shadow of Death. What hardship, terror, and amazement hast thou already gone through, and art thou now nothing but

1. **My soul . . . life:** quotation from Job 7:15.
2. **no murderer . . . life:** quotation from 1 John 3:15.
3. **pluck . . . man:** be brave.

Connecting Across Texts

Connecting with "Allegory: Telling Two Stories at Once"

John Bunyan and John Milton were contemporaries, and both wrote about religious faith. However, there is a world of difference in their writing styles. Have students compare this excerpt from *The Pilgrim's Progress* to the excerpt from Book I of *Paradise Lost* (see pp. 441–448). Ask them to identify at least three stylistic differences, supporting their statements with examples from the texts. Students may use a chart similar to the following to organize and present their material.

Style Differences

	Bunyan	Milton
vocabulary	simple	heightened
syntax	plain	irregular
literary elements	allegory	epic simile

fear? Thou seest that I am in the dungeon with thee, a far weaker man by nature than thou art; also this Giant has wounded me as well as thee, and hath also cut off the bread and water from my mouth; and with thee I mourn without the light. But let us exercise a little more patience; remember how thou playedst the man[4] at Vanity Fair, and wast neither afraid of the chain, nor cage, nor yet of bloody death. Wherefore let us (at least to avoid the shame that becomes not a Christian to be found in) bear up with patience as well as we can."

Now night being come again, and the Giant and his wife being in bed, she asked him concerning the prisoners, and if they had taken his counsel. To which he replied, "They are sturdy rogues, they choose rather to bear all hardship than to make away themselves." Then said she, "Take them into the castle yard tomorrow, and show them the bones and skulls of those that thou hast already dispatched, and make them believe, ere a week come to an end, thou also wilt tear them in pieces, as thou hast done their fellows before them."

So when the morning was come, the Giant goes to them again, and takes them into the castle yard, and shows them, as his wife had bidden him. "These," said he, "were pilgrims as you are once, and they trespassed in my grounds, as you have done; and when I thought fit, I tore them in pieces, and so within ten days I will do you. Go, get you down to your den again"; and with that he beat them all the way thither. They lay therefore all day on Saturday in a lamentable case, as before. Now when night was come, and when Mrs. Diffidence and her husband the Giant were got to bed, they began to renew their discourse of their prisoners; and withal the old Giant wondered that he could neither by his blows nor his counsel bring them to an end. And with that his wife replied, "I fear," said she, "that they live in hope that some will come to relieve them, or that they have picklocks about them, by the means of which they hope to escape." "And sayest thou so, my dear?" said the Giant; "I will therefore search them in the morning."

Well, on Saturday about midnight they began to pray, and continued in prayer till almost break of day.

Now a little before it was day, good Christian, as one half-amazed, brake out in this passionate speech: "What a fool (quoth he) am I, thus to lie in a stinking dungeon, when I may as well walk at liberty! I have a key in my bosom called Promise, that will (I am persuaded) open any lock in Doubting Castle." Then said Hopeful, "That is good news, good brother; pluck it out of thy bosom and try." Then Christian pulled it out of his bosom, and began to try at the dungeon door, whose bolt (as he turned the key) gave back, and the door flew open with ease, and Christian and Hopeful both came out. Then he went to the outward door that leads into the castle yard, and with his key opened that door also. After, he went to the iron gate, for that must be opened, too; but that lock went damnable hard, yet the key did open it. Then they thrust open the gate to make their escape with speed, but that gate, as it opened, made such a creaking that it waked Giant Despair, who, hastily rising to pursue his prisoners, felt his limbs to fail, for his fits took him again, so that he could by no means go after them. Then they went on and came to the King's highway, and so were safe because they were out of his jurisdiction. . . .

—John Bunyan, *from The Pilgrim's Progress*

Next to the Bible, *The Pilgrim's Progress* has been the most widely read of all English books. What accounts for Bunyan's enormous appeal? He wrote for people who believed that every human being is engaged in a continuous battle against forces of evil that, while powerful, are not as powerful as God. And so Bunyan told his readers what they most wanted to hear: how, with God's help, they could defeat evil and attain eternal life. He expressed his message in language familiar to his readers, drawn from their daily experiences and from the Bible, folk tales, and popular literature. In Bunyan's literary double exposure, his readers recognized their own lives made surprising and interesting.

4. **thou playedst the man:** you were brave.

D Background

Christian's Companions

During the events at Vanity Fair, Hopeful was not yet Christian's companion. There, Christian suffered with his friend Faithful, who ultimately was executed for his fidelity. Hopeful, a citizen of that town, was converted through the power of their example and took Faithful's place on the journey.

E Literary Connections

Vanity Fair

William Makepeace Thackeray published a novel in 1847–48, using Bunyan's term for a corrupt and worldly place, Vanity Fair, as the title for his portrait of a venal and materialistic society.

F Background

The Promise

It is no accident that the travelers' escape from prison comes on a Sunday morning—the day and time when, Christians believe, Christ arose from the prison of the grave. A hope in Christ's resurrection may represent the essence of the "Promise" that secures the captives' release.

G Humanities Connections

The Puritans

The Pilgrim's Progress was one of the first books brought by the Puritans to America.

H Literary Connections

Students may be interested in hearing Huckleberry Finn's comment (from *The Adventures of Huckleberry Finn* by Mark Twain) on *The Pilgrim's Progress*, a book he finds at the home of a family who takes him in.

"There was some books, too, piled up perfectly exact, on each corner of the table. One was a big family Bible full of pictures. One was *Pilgrim's Progress*, about a man that left his family, it didn't say why. I read considerable in it now and then. The statements was interesting, but tough."

Assessing Learning

Informal Assessment

Ongoing Assessment. One way to make a rough evaluation of students' grasp of the material is to take a yes/no vote on the following statements, following up with small-group discussions.

1. Allegory is intended primarily to appeal to an unsophisticated audience.
2. If an allegorical figure has a clear symbolic value, it need not also be literally convincing.
3. In the excerpt from *The Pilgrim's Progress*, Giant Despair represents forces that tempt Christians to reject their beliefs.
4. Readers are intended to see in the allegorical character Hopeful the importance of remembering the power of God.

Remind students that arguments can be made for either response. After the small groups have discussed the rationales for their responses, have them report to the class.

Reading Skills and Strategies

Mini-Lesson: Vocabulary
Distinguishing Multiple Meanings of Words

This lesson focuses on words with multiple meanings in the selections by Bacon and Milton and explains how students can use a dictionary to distinguish the meanings and origins of such words.

Try It Out

Possible Answers

1. (a) light: noun (Greek, *leukos*—"white"; Latin, *lux* and *lumen*—"light") As the daylight waned, Eva turned on the *light.* (b) light: adjective (Greek, *elaphros*; Latin, *levis*—"having little weight") Imagine such a small, *light* fruit carrying the weight of humanity's first sin.
2. (a) mind: noun (Greek, *menos*—"spirit"; Latin, *mens*—"mind") Satan will not change his *mind.* (b) mind: transitive and intransitive verbs have the same origin as the noun. (intransitive) Most politicians *mind* how they are portrayed by the press. (transitive) He did not *mind* the heat.
3. (a) bear: transitive verb (Latin, *ferre*; Greek, *pherein*; Sanskrit, *bharati*—"to carry," "bring") Adam and Eve *bear* the responsibility for their exile from Eden. Eve would *bear* children with pain. (b) bear: noun (Old English, *bera*; Indo-European, *bheros*—"brown animal") Adam named all the animals, including the *bear.*
4. (a) arm: noun (Old English, *earm*; Latin, *armus*; Old High German, *arm*) They walked *arm* in *arm* down the path. (b) arm: noun or transitive/intransitive verb (Old French, *armes*; Latin, *arma*—"implements," "weapons") Satan *armed* himself with wits and wiles.
5. (a) fast: adjective (Old English, *faest*, akin to German *fest*—"firm," "stable") The Good Samaritan held *fast* to his principles. (b) fast: intransitive verb (Middle English *fasten*, akin to Germen *fasten*—"hold fast") Some people *fast* on the Sabbath.

Reading Skills and Strategies

VOCABULARY: DISTINGUISHING MULTIPLE MEANINGS OF WORDS

Many words have, over time, accumulated more than one meaning. One word that has developed more than one meaning is *humor:*

> To spend too much time in studies is sloth . . . to make judgment wholly by their rules is the **humor** of a scholar.
>
> —Sir Francis Bacon, *from* "Of Studies"

Bacon uses the word *humor* to mean a person's general disposition or temperament. But if we say "My sister has a great sense of humor," we are referring to her ability to appreciate what is funny or amusing. These two definitions are related, however; they share the same origin and so are found under the same entry in the dictionary.

Using the dictionary. Arrangements of definitions may vary from dictionary to dictionary. In some dictionaries, the most frequently encountered meaning appears as the first definition, specialized senses follow, and rare, archaic, and obsolete senses are listed at the end. In other dictionaries, definitions are arranged in order from the oldest sense to the most recent.

Distinguishing word origins. Some words not only have different meanings but also have different origins. The fact that such words are spelled identically is an accident. Take the word *mean,* for example:

> Some books also may be read by deputy, and extracts made of them by others; but that would be only in the less important arguments, and the **meaner** sort of books . . .
>
> —Sir Francis Bacon, *from* "Of Studies"

The following chart shows the different meanings and **etymologies,** or origins, of *mean.*

Word	Origin	Present Meanings
1. mean	Old English *mænan:* to mean, tell, complain	to have in mind; intend; propose
2. mean	Old English *(ge)mæne:* plentiful, common	low in value; poor; inferior; stingy; miserly; bad-tempered
3. mean	Latin *medius:* middle	halfway between extremes; medium; average

Sometimes two meanings of the word can be used with different, but equally strong and relevant effects:

> . . . the thought
> Both of lost happiness and lasting pain
> Torments him; round he throws his **baleful** eyes,
> That witnessed huge affliction and dismay
> Mixed with obdurate pride and steadfast hate.
>
> —John Milton, *Paradise Lost,* Book I, lines 54–58

Baleful can mean "wretched" as well as "evil." Milton uses the multifaceted nature of language to complicate our image of Satan.

Try It Out

Using a dictionary, look up the **origin** and different **meanings** of each word listed below. Then use each word in two different **contexts** to illustrate two of the word's different meanings.

1. light **2.** mind **3.** bear **4.** arm **5.** fast

Reaching All Students

Struggling Readers

To help students become aware that some words have one meaning in slang usage and another in standard speech, ask volunteers to write on the chalkboard a list of slang words they commonly use, for example, *chill* or *lame.* Then have them use each word in a sentence, one sentence showing the word's slang meaning and the other its meaning in standard English. If necessary, students should refer to a dictionary for standard meanings.

English Language Learners

To develop students' competence with the vocabulary words presented in Try It Out, have them use multiple meanings of the same word in a short paragraph. Pair up students with different abilities and ask them to work together to illustrate at least two meanings of one of the exercise words in their paragraph. Afterward, have students share their work with the rest of the class.

READ ON

Love and War

The filmmaker Kenneth Branagh has brought a lively new perspective to some of Shakespeare's plays. *Henry V* (1989), about the warrior-king who led the attack on Agincourt in the early fifteenth century, is packed with action and adventure. The confused lovers in *Much Ado About Nothing* (1993), played by Branagh and Emma Thompson, spar and spark against a sunny Italian landscape. Both films are available on video.

Motorcycle Meditations

Part travelogue, part meditation, part rambling discourse, Robert Pirsig's *Zen and the Art of Motorcycle Maintenance* (Bantam Books) is above all an inquiry into human values. While taking an extended motorcycle trip, Pirsig pursues the same questions that intrigued Francis Bacon, John Milton, and the writer(s) of Genesis: What is the nature of the universe, and what is our place in it? How should we conduct our lives?

The Bard's Background and Playground

People flocked to Renaissance London in droves, where the theater was a major attraction. Shakespeare was an integral part of this world, but there's been a tendency to divorce the man from his background. *Shakespeare of London* (Penguin) by Marchette Chute and *Shakespeare Alive!* (Bantam Books) by Joseph Papp and Elizabeth Kirkland help bring the legend back to life, placing Shakespeare in the theatrical and social context where he thrived.

A Crisis of Conscience

Scholar, ambassador, Lord Chancellor, family man—Sir Thomas More had it all. But then King Henry VIII changed everything by deciding to divorce his wife, which meant breaking with the pope—an action More opposed. More's decision to follow his personal beliefs rather than his political interests serves as the basis for Robert Bolt's play, *A Man for All Seasons* (Vintage/Random House), also a 1966 film starring Paul Scofield and Orson Welles, as well as a 1988 made-for-television movie with Charlton Heston, John Gielgud, and Vanessa Redgrave. (Both versions are available on videotape.)

Love Is . . .

In *The Love Poems of Robert Herrick and John Donne* (Barnes & Noble), the works of two of the most well-known Renaissance poets come gloriously together. Even though both poets write about love, their ideas and style differ. The editor, Louis Untermeyer, notes that "Donne plunges the reader into emotion with nervous desperation," while Herrick "is all delicacy and delight." Donne's metaphysical passion and Herrick's spirited banter make this collection a complete exploration of the power of love.

READ ON

This feature provides suggestions for further reading and viewing of works by and about Renaissance authors and about the themes and values which were important to them.

Portfolio Assessment Options

The following projects can help you evaluate and assess your students' reading accomplishments outside of class. Videotapes or audiotapes of completed projects may be included in students' portfolios.

- **Write a Review**
  Have students write a film review of Kenneth Branagh's rendering of Shakespeare. They might even write a comparison with a stage version they have seen or with Lawrence Olivier's film version of *Henry V.*
- **Create a Museum Exhibit**
  Have students set up a museum exhibit depicting the life and times of Shakespeare, More, Bacon, or Milton. Students might build a mechanical model of the Globe Theater, for example, as well as display photographs and original art work which present a picture of the writer and his times.
- **Act Out a Scene**
  Have a group of students prepare to act out a scene from *A Man for All Seasons* for the class. Individuals can take responsibility for props, music, and costumes. A narrator might set up the scene by speaking directly to the audience. When students are ready, they may enjoy having their performance videotaped.
- **Create an Anthology**
  Have students create a collection of their favorite poems, passages of dialogue, and prose passages from the works they have read by Renaissance authors. They may add captions that reflect their own feelings or thoughts about each selection. If they wish, students can also include drawings and create an original cover for their book.

OBJECTIVES

1. Learn about the first grammars and dictionaries
2. Distinguish ornate and plain styles of English
3. Identify and understand different styles of English today

Ⓐ Humanities Connections
Greek Language Study

The Greek tradition of language study, which focused on grammar, logic, and rhetoric, still shapes language study today. Greek scholars in Alexandria developed the formal system we know as grammar. In *The Art of Letters* (c. 100 B.C.), Dionysus Thrax writes about how sentences, words, syllables, and letters, coalesce in recognizable patterns to express thought.

Ⓑ Background
Early Dictionaries

In 1623, Henry Cockeram published his *English Dictionarie*, the first book of definitions to be given the name dictionary. In 1656, Thomas Blount published *Glossographia*, which included about nine thousand words with full definitions and etymologies.

Ⓒ Humanities Connections
Webster's Dictionary

The Webster's *Third New International Dictionary* (considered the most comprehensive English-language dictionary currently published in the United States) is a descendant of Noah Webster's *An American Dictionary of the English Language,* first published in 1828. When the 1961 edition of Webster's Dictionary was published, it created considerable controversy. Some critics regarded its "permissiveness" as a failure on the part of the dictionary's editors to foster the use of good English. Among other things, the dictionary was criticized for including slang and nonstandard words such as "ain't."

Ⓓ Literary Connections
Unrest and Writing

This social and political unrest resulted in the publication of more than twenty thousand books and pamphlets on political and religious issues.

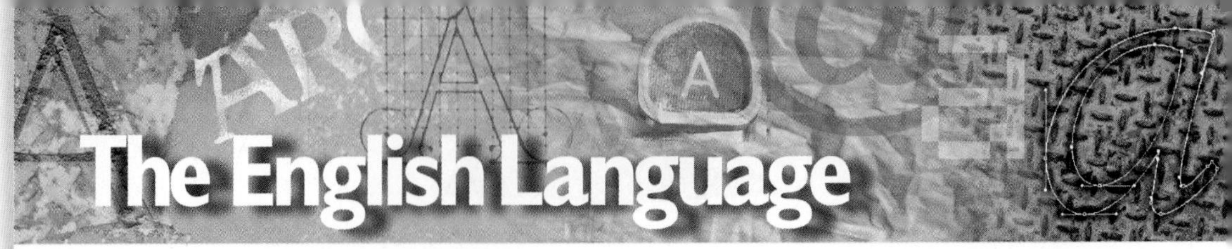

The English Language

The Growth of Modern English

by John Algeo

Ⓐ During the seventeenth century, interest in the English language grew rapidly. English scholars vigorously studied the grammar, vocabulary, and style of written English.

The First Grammars and Dictionaries

The first grammars of English appeared shortly before the end of the sixteenth century. These small books imitated widely used Latin grammars and were intended to help English-speaking students learn Latin and foreigners learn English. The first such grammar was William Bullokar's *Pamphlet for Grammar* (1586). Although it would not compare well with the best grammars of our language written today, four hundred years later, it was no small achievement for its day. To write a grammar of a language for which there were no other grammar books was an accomplishment.

By the end of the seventeenth century, a great many grammar books had been written, and more continued to appear through the eighteenth and nineteenth centuries. Difficult as it may be for some of us to understand today, English speakers were fascinated by grammars of their language. Popular as grammar books were, however, readers and writers of English were even more interested in dictionaries.

The first English dictionary appeared at the beginning of the seventeenth century. In 1604, Robert Cawdrey published *A Table Alphabeticall . . . of Hard Usuall English Wordes.* As that title suggests, the earliest dictionaries made no effort to list all the words in the English language. Rather they were simply lists of "hard" words—learned, often borrowed words—that a reader might come across but that would be difficult for the ordinary person to understand.

The first dictionaries gave only a familiar synonym for each hard word. Gradually, dictionaries began to expand the number of words they listed and the kinds of information they included about each word. Definitions increased from single-word synonyms to fuller descriptions of meaning. In the eighteenth century, efforts were made to include all the words of the language and to define all their uses. New sorts of information added to the entry for a word included its etymology (origin and history), its part of speech, quotations illustrating its use, and its pronunciation.

Ⓑ As English dictionaries increased the number of words they included and the information they gave about each word, they became better and better. Today, English has the best dictionaries of any language on earth. The greatest of English dictionaries is the *Oxford English Dictionary* in twenty large volumes. It attempts to trace the history of all English words from their first appearance in the language until today. Ⓒ The biggest dictionary a high school student is likely to need is one like the *Webster's Third New International Dictionary,* and for most ordinary uses, smaller desk dictionaries serve very well.

The Battle of Styles: Ornate vs. Plain

Ⓓ The seventeenth century was an age of social unrest. In England, the Cavaliers, who supported the king and the established Anglican church, were opposed by the Puritans, who supported Parliament and a congregational form of church. The Cavaliers dressed elegantly, ate with gusto, attended the theater, and generally lived a high life. Puritans, on the other hand, dressed and ate plainly, thought the theater was wicked, and generally lived sober, God-fearing, dull lives. There was bound to be trouble between them. And so there was, with

go.hrw.com
LEO 12-English Language

Using Students' Strengths

Visual Learners

Have students design posters that express the message and meaning of one or more of the quotations in Try It Out #2 on p. 458.

Musical Learners

Have students listen to recordings of English folk songs or carols from the Renaissance period and update the lyrics into modern English.

Auditory Learners

Call on volunteers to read aloud sentences and passages from *Paradise Lost* or "Of Studies" that they consider to be written in ornate style. Have other students restate the passage using plain-style English. Emphasize that plain style does not necessarily include slang or colloquialisms.

the Puritans eventually gaining control of Parliament, executing the king, closing the theaters, and establishing a military and church dictatorship in England.

The difference in lifestyles between the Cavaliers and the Puritans was echoed in a difference in language styles: an ornate style versus a plain style. However, there was by no means a simple equivalence between Cavaliers and ornate style on the one hand and Puritans and plain style on the other. Indeed, in some cases, it was the other way around.

Popular as grammar books were, readers and writers of English were even more interested in dictionaries.

The ornate style used many words borrowed from foreign languages and learned words, thus creating what were scornfully called "inkhorn terms." An inkhorn was a container made from the horn of an animal and was used to hold ink for writing with a quill pen. **Inkhorn terms** were words that scholars might use in writing, but that seemed out of place in ordinary conversation. It was such inkhorn terms that were listed in the dictionaries of "hard" words.

Another aspect of the ornate style was called **euphuism** (after Euphues, a character in two books by John Lyly, who used alliteration, balanced expressions, antitheses, fantastic similes, mythological allusions, and other verbal tricks to create an artificial elegance of language). An example is the following sentence, in which Euphues cites some proverbs against rash and excessive action: "The vine watered with wine is soon withered, the blossom in the fattest ground is quickly blasted, the goat the fatter she is the less fertile she is; yea, man the more witty he is the less happy he is."

Still another aspect of the ornate style was the **metaphysical conceit,** an extended and exaggerated metaphor, such as that in Donne's poem "A Valediction: Forbidding Mourning."

Plain style, on the other hand, valued simplicity and clarity. It came to be favored especially by those with scientific interests, something that is natural enough. If you are going to describe a scientific experiment or observation, you are less interested in having people admire your cleverness with language than in having them understand what you did or saw. Scientists try not to intrude personally into the object of study. Their work and their language are supposed to be impersonal and public.

In the metaphysical or euphuistic ideal, on the other hand, the reader sees the world through the highly personal eyes of the writer. The aim is to surprise the reader by revealing the world in a fresh way. Thus, the two styles, contrasting sharply in their aims, contrast also in their techniques.

The plain style was promoted especially through the work of the Royal Society. Founded in the second half of the seventeenth century, the Royal Society is one of the oldest organizations in Europe for "improving natural knowledge," that is, promoting scientific study. Members of the Society did much to combat the excesses of ornate style. As a result of their work and example, today the plain style is the unchallenged ideal for good prose.

What Is Style?

Although a plain style is our ideal today, we still find other kinds of style in use. What makes a style?

When we talk or write, we have a choice of ways to express our meaning. For example, if we want to mention our male parent, we can call him father, dad, papa, sire, pater, pop, my old man, or various other names. Obviously, those words, although they all mean the same thing in that they can all refer to the same person, are very different from one another in how they are used. If you are filling out an employment questionnaire, you are not going to be asked, "What is your daddy's name?" If you are telling a friend why you can't use the family car tonight, you are probably not going to say, "My sire is using it."

The options we take in talking or writing determine the style of our language. **Style** is the choice we make among alternative ways of saying the same thing. Among the elements that make up a style are options like these:

1. Short and simple versus long and complex

E Literary Connections

Inkhorn Terms

Inkhorn terms were referred to as far back as 1553 when Thomas Wilson observed in *Art of Rhetorique*: "Among all other lessons this should first be learned, that wee never affect any straunge ynkehorne termes, but to speake as is commonly received. . . ." Among his examples of inkhornisms are the following: *revoluting; ingent affabilitie; ingenious capacity; magnifical dexteritie; dominicall superioritie;* and *splendidious*.

F Background

The Royal Society

Founding members of the Royal Society included architect Christopher Wren, chemist Robert Boyle, and Bishop John Wilkins. Isaac Newton would later serve as president of the society. In the beginning, it was largely a Puritan venture whose purpose was to discuss scientific matters in the spirit of Francis Bacon. The journal *Philosophical Transactions of the Royal Society*, begun in 1665, was one of the world's earliest periodicals.

Resources

Formal Assessment

- English Language Test, p. 79

Reaching All Students

Struggling Readers

To help students grasp the differences between plain and ornate styles, have them list these differences in separate columns as they reread this feature.

Advanced Learners

Have students research government publications and political speeches to find examples of wordy, puffed-up language. Students should then present a brief oral report on one document, identifying its purpose and analyzing its language. Students may discuss whether they believe the language is an intentional attempt to fool or mislead the public.

Ⓐ Literary Connections

Ornate Style

In *The Elements of Style*, Strunk and White advise: "Rich, ornate prose is hard to digest, generally unwholesome, and sometimes nauseating. If the sickly-sweet word, the overblown phrase are a writer's natural form of expression, as is sometimes the case, he will have to compensate for it by a show of vigor and by writing something as meritorious as Solomon's 'Song of Songs'."

Try It Out

1. **Using a Dictionary.** Students might list etymology, synonyms, technical definitions, sample sentences, parts of speech, and levels of usage.
2. **Recognizing Allusions.** Possible answers:
   - **a.** responsible for another's welfare
   - **b.** someone in an unfamiliar situation
   - **c.** a delightful place that offers all that is needed
   - **d.** excessive self-love often brings about a defeat or loss
   - **e.** prepare oneself for the inevitable, such as death
   - **f.** have a close call; survive in spite of poor odds
   - **g.** humble, pious people will outlast the wicked and unjust
   - **h.** show kindness without expecting a reward
   - **i.** forsake war and adopt the ways of peace
   - **j.** a character flaw
3. **Comparing Styles.** Most students will agree that "A Valediction: Forbidding Mourning" uses an ornate style with complex figures of speech and long, involved, indirect statements; "Song: To Celia" has a plain style, using short and simple statements. Milton's *Paradise Lost* is written in ornate style, using long sentences and many adjectives and adverbs; the King James version of the Bible uses a plain style with ordinary words and short sentences.

sentences. A sequence of short, simple sentences is likely to seem childish or simple-minded, but many long, complex ones are likely to seem confused.

2. **Active versus passive verbs,** as in "The Puritans chopped off King Charles's head" (active) versus "King Charles's head was chopped off" (passive). Passive verbs are especially useful for telling that something happened without telling who did it. They are favorites of scientific and bureaucratic writers, but many other people find them mealy-mouthed.
3. **Direct versus qualified statements.** Direct statements tell the facts just as they are. Qualified statements add words like *perhaps, possibly, it seems, it would appear, it is likely that, generally, make an effort to,* and so on. Writers may think that using qualifications will get them off the hook if they say something wrong. But readers find the result wishy-washy.
4. **Noun- versus verb-centeredness.** We can *agree* on something, or *reach an agreement* about it. We can *wash* the car, or *give* it *a wash.* We can *decide* to go, or *come to a decision* to do so. We can *promise* our friends something, or *make a promise to* them *about* it. When we put the main meaning into the verb, we have a more direct and forceful sentence, but putting the main meaning into a noun after the verb lets us emphasize it.
5. **Plain versus fancy words.** Plain words like *newspaper, home, watery,* and *to run* are more comfortable than fancy words like *periodical, domicile, aqueous,* and *to course.* There are times, to be sure, when we want our language to be fancy. The danger in using fancy words, however, is that we will use them not quite right, and the result will be, not fancy, but unintentionally funny. Ⓐ

Try It Out

1. **Using a dictionary.** The English dictionary began its development during the seventeenth century with lists of "hard" words and their meanings. Look at the entry for a word in a modern desk dictionary. You may choose any word you like, but the following are suggestions:

atom	dwarf	hopefully
map	sphinx	learn

   What different kinds of information does the entry give you about the word? To start off, you will find the spelling and pronunciation of the word. What else? (You will find somewhat different kinds of information in the entries for various words and for the same word in various dictionaries.)
2. **Recognizing allusions.** Allusions, or references, to the King James Bible and the Book of Common Prayer abound in the English language. What do the following expressions mean? Find the passage in which each expression was originally used (it is indicated in parentheses).
   - **a.** My brother's keeper (Genesis 4:9)
   - **b.** A stranger in a strange land (Exodus 2:22)
   - **c.** A land flowing with milk and honey (Exodus 3:8)
   - **d.** Pride goes before a fall. (Proverbs 16:18)
   - **e.** Put one's house in order (2 Kings 20:1; Isaiah 38:1)
   - **f.** Escape by the skin of one's teeth (Job 19:20)
   - **g.** The meek shall inherit the earth. (Psalm 37:11)
   - **h.** Cast your bread upon the waters (Ecclesiastes 11:1)
   - **i.** Beat swords into plowshares (Isaiah 2:4)
   - **j.** Feet of clay (Daniel 2:33)
3. **Comparing styles.** Compare the style either of John Donne's "A Valediction: Forbidding Mourning" (page 248) and Ben Jonson's "Song: To Celia" (page 258), or of the King James account of the temptation and fall of Adam and Eve (page 416) and Milton's account of the fall of Satan in *Paradise Lost* (page 441). Note differences in vocabulary, length and complexity of sentences, repeated versus varied patterns of language, simple and direct statements versus involved and indirect ones, and the use of descriptive adjectives and adverbs. Which work is in plain style? Which is ornate?

Assessing Learning

Check Test: Multiple Choice

1. English grammar books first appeared shortly before the end of the (a) fifteenth century, (b) sixteenth century, (c) seventeenth century, (d) eighteenth century. [b]
2. English dictionaries appeared at the beginning of the (a) fifteenth century, (b) sixteenth century, (c) seventeenth century, (d) eighteenth century. [c]
3. The plain style is likely to include (a) inkhorn terms, (b) clear terms, (c) euphemisms, (d) metaphysical conceits. [b]
4. Members of the Royal Society favored (a) plain style, (b) Latin-based language, (c) ornate style, (d) combination of plain and ornate style. [a]
5. Style can best be defined as (a) ability to write a poem, (b) command of the English language, (c) use of figurative language, (d) characteristic use of words. [d]

Writer's Workshop

The history of the written word is rich a...

Page 1

EXPOSITORY WRITING

ANALYZING CAUSES AND EFFECTS

Thomas De Quincey wondered for years why the knocking at the gate after Duncan's murder had such a solemnly awful effect, and playgoers debate to this day what drove Macbeth and Lady Macbeth to such bloody abandon. Analysis of **causes** and **effects** in both literature and life is never ending.

Prewriting

1. **Checking your Writer's Notebook.** By doing the Writer's Notebook activities on pages 390, 409, 427, and 450, you may have already completed the prewriting for an essay that analyzes causes and effects. Check back over your Writer's Notebook entries. You can repeat any activity to add to or improve what you've already done, or you can proceed with the prewriting activities that follow.

2. **Finding a topic.** The two questions that cause-and-effect writing answers are *Why?* and *What's the result?* You do not have to answer both in your essay, though you may—for example, De Quincey explains why Shakespeare "invented" the knocking at the gate and also describes its emotional and theatrical effect (page 330). To find a topic to write about, consider

 - **events:** occurrences, such as Macduff's leaving his family in *Macbeth*

 - **situations,** or **phenomena:** ongoing conditions, such as increasing vandalism in a community

 - **trends:** changes over time, such as the availability of CD-ROM technology

3. **Literature or life?** Like De Quincey, you may want to explain something that intrigues (or irritates or moves) you in a poem or play: *Why does Macduff leave his family? What are the effects of this event, in the play or on the audience?* You may also pose a "What if?" question and predict plausible results: *What if Lady Macbeth had not gone mad?* Or you might extend a literary work: *How will Banquo's son react when Malcolm is crowned?*

 For a real-life topic, you'll write best about something that concerns you or stirs your curiosity: *Why are daytime talk shows so popular? What will happen when your TV is also a computer? Why is your advanced math class three-fourths male?*

Technology HELP

See Writer's Workshop 2 CD-ROM. *Assignment: Cause and Effect.*

ASSIGNMENT
Write an essay analyzing the causes and/or effects of an event, situation, or trend.

AIM
To explain causes, effects, or both; to persuade your readers.

AUDIENCE
Your classmates or people affected by the subject.

MAIN OBJECTIVE
Write an essay analyzing the causes and/or effects of an event, situation, or trend

PROCESS OBJECTIVES
1. Use appropriate prewriting techniques to identify and develop a topic
2. Create a first draft
3. Use Evaluation Criteria as a basis for determining revision strategies
4. Revise the first draft, incorporating suggestions generated by self- or peer-evaluation
5. Proofread and correct errors
6. Create a final draft
7. Choose an appropriate method of publication
8. Reflect on progress as a writer

Planning

- **Block Schedule**
 Block Scheduling Lesson Plans with Pacing Guide

- **One-Stop Planner**
 CD-ROM with Test Generator

Introducing the Writer's Workshop

Ask for two volunteers to role-play a discussion between a parent and a child about why the child came home late last night. Have the volunteers leave the room for five minutes to organize. After the discussion, have the other students list the causes and effects that each role-play volunteer uses to make his or her point. Conclude the activity by discussing the relationship between the causes and effects stated by each player in the role-play.

Resources: Print and Media

Writing and Language
- *Portfolio Management System*
 - Prewriting, p. 131
 - Peer Editing, p. 132
 - Assessment Rubric, p. 133
- *Workshop Resources*
 - Revision Strategy Teaching Notes, p. 17
 - Revision Strategy Transparencies 9, 10

- *Writer's Workshop 2 CD-ROM*
 - Cause and Effect

Teaching the Writer's Workshop

Prewriting

- To help students select topics, have the class compile a list of questions that intrigue them about the literature they have read. A reader may, for example, be interested in speculating about Lady Macbeth's childhood. The list of questions can be broadened to include events in the world today which relate to the literature. Why, for example, has the Middle East had such a bloody history?
- As students work on their cause-effect maps, encourage them to include citation information in their drafts. For example, if they are writing about a literary work, such as *Macbeth,* they should write down act, scene, and line numbers for any quotations they intend to cite. Keeping this record will save them time and frustration when they write the final versions of their essays.

Strategies for Elaboration

Piling Up Proof
For some topics, support will come from outside sources, not just your logic and experience. Recognize your many options for sufficient and accurate evidence:
- Facts, data, historical evidence
- Similar situations (analogies)
- Literary quotations, imagery, and paraphrases
- Expert opinions
- Anecdotes
- Eyewitness accounts
- Personal experience
- Responses to opponents

Notice that your topic may have a broad or a personal focus. Also consider more abstract speculation. For example, *Macbeth* brings up the traits of ambition, leadership, and dominance, suggesting topics such as *What creates a good leader? What are the effects of friendship with a bold, dominant person?*

4. **Mapping the possibilities.** A visual map of ideas can open your mind to many perspectives. One technique is to begin by writing and circling a statement of your topic (the event, situation, or trend). Analyze it. What produced it? What happened (or might happen) because of it? Then write down *any* possibilities, showing the connections with arrows. You might discover a chain of causes and effects: *A* causes *B, B* causes *C,* and so on. Stimulate your thinking with the Strategies for Elaboration on the left.

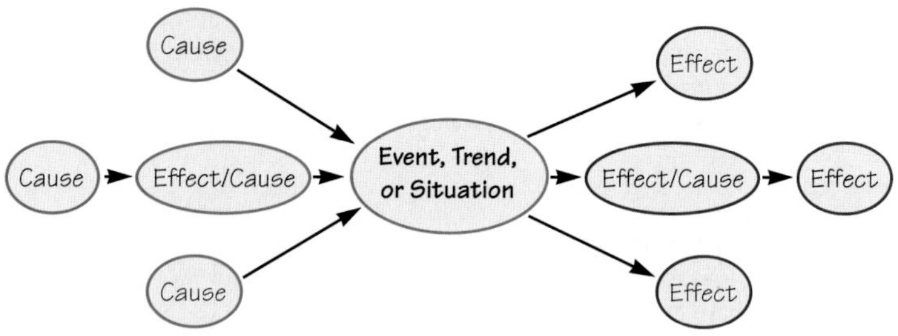

5. **Identifying a thesis.** After generating ideas, assess them. First, have you mapped out the situation or event to your satisfaction? If not, you need more ideas or another topic. Next, decide on a thesis for your essay: a statement of your topic that clearly indicates if you'll discuss causes, effects, or both.
6. **The evidence, please.** In this paper, you are conjecturing, or advancing an explanation. You must convince your readers that the causes or effects you propose are *plausible and likely*—and that means providing solid evidence or support. Stating your opinion isn't enough.

FoxTrot *by* Bill Amend

FOXTROT ©1994 Bill Amend. Reprinted with permission of UNIVERSAL PRESS SYNDICATE. All rights reserved.

Using Students' Strengths

Visual Learners

The body of a cause-effect essay can be arranged in several different ways. Some students may benefit from seeing different arrangements illustrated in charts. You might put the following examples on the chalkboard or on a poster.

BODY: Situation, cause, cause, cause, effect, effect, effect.
BODY: Situation, effect, effect, effect, cause.
BODY: Situation, cause, effect, cause, effect, cause, effect.

To compile your evidence, you might use a two-column chart. On the left, write the causes or effects you've chosen from your map. To the right of each one, write all your ideas for evidence, as well as objections and counterarguments.

Model

Topic: Why do Donalbain and Malcolm keep silent and flee in fear right after their father's murder?

Causes	Supporting Evidence
shock	They feel "strong sorrow" but tears aren't "brewed" yet—too soon. **Objection?** They're thinking pretty well for being in shock. **Counterargument:** Yes, but shock suspends horror; people function "normally," and then they collapse.
suspicion	Macduff raised the question of why Macbeth killed the guards. Malcolm: Fake grief is easy if there's a motive.

7. **Being believable.** Choosing evidence also means considering who's reading it. What support will your audience find compelling, thought-provoking, or in line with its interests? And no matter who your readers are, you must come across as reasonable and trustworthy. You don't have to be stiffly serious; you might even be funny about the effects of forbidding off-campus lunches, for example. Your **tone,** however, must convey assurance and conviction.

Drafting

1. **The introduction.** Your essay should open in a way that will capture your readers' attention, while also quickly getting to what you're explaining. Always describe or define the situation clearly, in as much detail as your readers need. Classmates will need minimal scene setting for Malcolm and Donalbain's escape in *Macbeth*, but if your topic is the potential effects of televising court proceedings, readers will need sufficient data and information to see and understand current and past court situations. Also include your thesis statement.
2. **The body.** Redraw your cause-effect map to use as a good guide for writing. Take the causes or effects you've settled on, determine their order, number them, and redraw the map with numbers included. Refer to this map as you write your draft. Here are some general rules and tips for organizing the body of your essay:
   - Discuss causes before effects.
   - Use chronological order for cause-effect chains and for some topics spread out over time.
   - Otherwise, choose an arrangement that's easy to follow and persuasive: least/most important, least/most familiar, personal/social concerns, concrete/abstract explanations.

Communications Handbook HELP

See Taking Notes and Documenting Sources.

Try It Out

With a small group, brainstorm at least three causes and three effects for the topics below. Then, suggest possible evidence (or where to find it) for each cause and each effect.

1. high salaries of professional athletes or rock stars
2. Banquo's murder
3. computer technology for home use

Try It Out

Possible Answers

1. Causes: importance of entertainment to Americans; value of sports as a rallying point for people; desire to obtain the very best players possible; willingness of people to spend money on tapes and CDs.
   Effects: Sports figures and entertainers are held up as models; sports figures and entertainers may have greater status than they deserve; sports figures and entertainers lose touch with the people they entertain.
2. Causes: Macbeth is jealous of Banquo; Macbeth fears Banquo will father more children, thus increasing the likelihood that the witches' prophecy will come true; Macbeth is psychologically disturbed and out of control.
   Effects: The Thanes begin to mistrust Macbeth more than before; Macbeth's guilt increases; Macbeth adds to the chaos in Scotland.
3. Causes: Technology is relatively inexpensive; people see its value for work and entertainment; people want to keep up with the modern world.
   Effects: technological literacy among children; more efficient work at home; increased sources of information in the home.

Drafting

After students have written their first drafts, have them work with a partner to read the opening paragraphs and check for

- a clear thesis statement
- an interesting opening
- sufficient background information

Partners should offer constructive criticism and ideas for improvements.

Reaching All Students

Struggling Writers

Ask students having difficulty writing their drafts to write each of their causes and effects on separate index cards. Remind them to include supporting facts or evidence for each. Then, students can arrange the index cards on their desks until they find an effective order. Finally, they can use the arranged cards to begin drafting paragraphs.

Advanced Learners

Arrange students in groups of four, and ask them to consider the following scenario: A rich graduate has donated five million dollars to the school. The only restriction is that the money must be used to improve students' learning. Ask students to brainstorm a list of possible causes of the donor's generosity and the effects a gift of this sort would have on their school. Have a spokesperson from each group present the group's ideas to the class.

Evaluating and Revising
In addition to cautioning students about oversimplification and the *post hoc* fallacy, warn those who are writing about real-life topics to avoid using hypothetical effects. Sometimes writers, in an effort to make their cases stronger, predict dire hypothetical effects that are not based in reality and tend to weaken arguments. Another practice to warn students against is the use of unspecified research. The signs of this problem are expressions such as "Studies show . . . ," "Research proves . . . ," and "The evidence indicates . . . ," which are not backed up with a citation to any source.

Proofreading
Encourage students to wait a day or two between finishing the final version of their essay and proofreading it. A waiting period often helps writers see errors that they may miss if they proofread as soon as they have finished writing.

Publishing
Ask students who chose real-life topics to consider sending their essays to a newspaper's op-ed page or a club's newsletter. If students wrote personal essays, ask them to share their essays with friends, family, or teen magazines. Ask students who wrote about literary topics to read their essays to the class to see if others challenge or applaud their insights.

Reflecting
Ask students to explain which aspect of the writing process they found most challenging when they analyzed the causes and effects of a situation or event for their essay.

Resources
Peer Editing Forms and Rubrics
- *Portfolio Management System,* p. 132

Revision Transparencies
- *Workshop Resources,* p. 17

Grading Timesaver
Rubrics for this Writer's Workshop assignment appear on p. 133 of the *Portfolio Management System.*

Language Workshop HELP

Effective transitions: page 463.

Evaluation Criteria

An effective essay that analyzes causes and effects
1. *clearly describes the event, situation, or trend*
2. *clearly focuses on causes and/or effects and discusses them thoroughly*
3. *presents convincing arguments and refutes counterarguments*
4. *presents causes or effects in an effective order*
5. *presents sufficient and accurate evidence*
6. *uses an authoritative tone*
7. *opens engagingly and concludes decisively*

Revision STRATEGIES

To improve your opening and closing, read them together. (Skip everything else.) Could you link them in some way? Is one stronger or clearer than the other? Why? If necessary, add or cut details.

Communications Handbook HELP

See Proofreading.

- Answer objections to a cause or effect along with the cause or effect.
- Bring up alternative explanations either before or after your own. ("Before" gets them out of the way; "after" lets you refer to your better ideas.)

3. **The conclusion.** Write a conclusion that sums up your explanation of causes and/or effects. You might also refer to your introduction.

Evaluating and Revising
1. **Peer review.** Read like a skeptic, someone who's tough to convince and itching to find a legitimate flaw. (But when the explanation's good, admit it and point out why.) Look for sound logic. Beware of
   - **oversimplification:** having too few causes or effects to explain the situation, or mistaking a contributing cause for a necessary one
   - **the *post hoc, ergo propter hoc* fallacy ("after this, therefore because of this"):** assuming that if A preceded B, then A must have caused B
2. **Self-evaluation.** If you do get objections from reviewers, answer them calmly. Put a check mark on your paper by each spot where you include one of the features given in the Evaluation Criteria to the left. Then go back and revise your paper to include any of the features you didn't find.

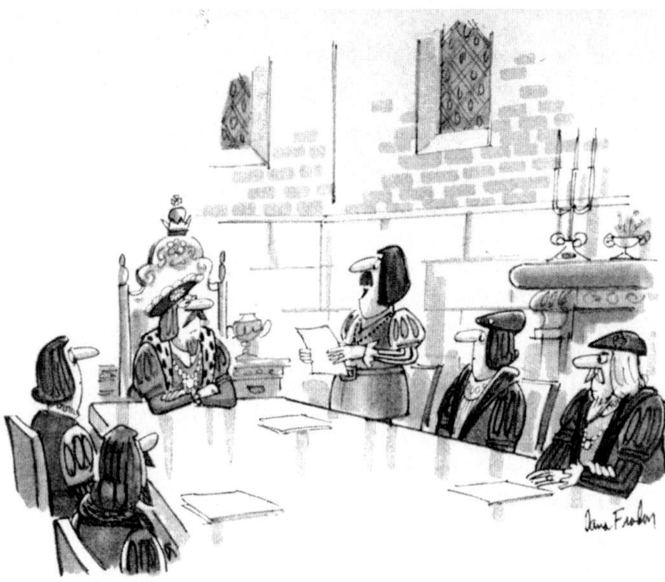

Dana Fradon ©1980 from THE NEW YORKER COLLECTION. All rights reserved.

"Your Majesty, according to our study the shoe was lost for want of a nail, the horse was lost for want of a shoe, and the rider was lost for want of a horse, but the kingdom we lost because of overregulation."

Skill Link
Using Suggestions of Others to Improve Communication
If students choose to read their essays aloud to the class, review with them some important elements of speech first, such as pitch, tone, articulation, and pace. Have students practice reading on their own before they read their essays to the class. After each student reads his or her essay, ask the class to evaluate the performance based on the following criteria:
- clear enunciation
- sufficient volume
- natural rhythm
- appropriate tone
- variety of points of emphasis

The history
of the written
word is rich and
Page 1

Language Workshop

Objectives

1. Use effective transitions to connect ideas
2. Use transitional expressions to express relationships of cause and effect, time, and importance

Effective Transitions: Connecting Ideas

An essay that speculates about causes and effects delves into relationships. When you write, you're leading readers not just to see the facts or events *X, Y, Z,* but exactly how *X, Y,* and *Z* are connected. If readers must labor to understand the links, you won't be very convincing. Thus, **transitions,** ways to connect ideas, are extremely important in cause-effect writing. Notice how the boldface words in the following paragraph make it easy to follow; they create coherence both by connecting words and thoughts and by stating relationships.

> Immediately after their father's murder, Malcolm and Donalbain don't even cry. **The two brothers** speak to no one and hastily leave Scotland in fear—**even though** the obvious murderers are dead. Are **they two** cold, uncaring **children**? Or are there **other explanations** for **this behavior**? One **explanation** is simple: shock. Malcolm himself asks, "Why do we hold our tongues . . . ?," **so** we know he is not just **upset and confused.**

Techniques for Creating Effective Transitions

1. Use a pronoun, noun, or synonym to refer to a word or phrase used earlier. Notice how *the two brothers* and *children* refer to Malcolm and Donalbain and how *this behavior* and *upset and confused* are related.
2. Repeat a word used earlier. For example, *they two* refers to "the two brothers," and *explanation* refers to "other explanations."
3. Use transitional expressions that express relationship. In the paragraph above, *even though* and *so* link ideas. Here are some other examples of transitional expressions:
   - cause-effect: *as a result, because, consequently, since, therefore*
   - time: *after, eventually, finally, immediately, meanwhile, next, then*
   - importance: *first, last, mainly, most important, primarily*

Writer's Workshop Follow-Up: Revision

Take another look at the cause-effect essay you wrote for page 459. Have you implied a link that you need to state directly? Have you signaled to the reader what is important or in what sequence events occurred? Have you used pronouns and nouns to add variety and to refer to previous words and ideas? Working with a writing partner, underscore the transitions you've used. Then, go back and add transitions to make your sentences and paragraphs flow as clearly and smoothly as possible.

Technology HELP

See Language Workshop CD-ROM. *Key word entry: transitions.*

Try It Out

Turn these sentences into a clear paragraph by inserting logical, effective transitions. You may combine sentences, add words and phrases, and replace words and phrases with better ones.

For three years now the Panthers have made it all the way to state championships. And they have lost in the first round. The Panthers have obviously been good. Why do they keep losing here? One explanation leaps out when you study the stats. In each game either three or four fouled out in the first half. The best are on the bench, not on the floor. First, that's simply demoralizing for others. The opposing team gets more free shots.

Resources

Workshop Resources

- Worksheet, p. 51

Language Workshop CD-ROM

- Transitions

Try It Out

Possible Answers

For three years now the Panthers have made it all the way to the state championships, and every year they have lost in the first round. As this record shows, the Panthers have obviously been good, but why do they keep losing in the first round? One explanation leaps out when you study the Panthers' stats. In each first-round game, three or four players fouled out in the first half. When this happens, the best players are on the bench, not on the floor. First, that fact is simply demoralizing for other players. Second, it means the opposing team gets more free shots.

Assessing Learning

Quick Check: Effective Transitions

Underline the transitional words in the following paragraph. [Answers are underlined.]

Shakespeare wrote historical plays, tragedies, comedies, and sonnets. His tragic works include *Julius Caesar, Romeo and Juliet, Hamlet,* and *Macbeth.* When *Hamlet* was published, Shakespeare had already produced *Romeo and Juliet* and *Julius Caesar.* Even though the latter was created before *Macbeth,* both plays appeared for the first time in the posthumously published First Folio in 1623. Shakespeare never saw the first collection of his plays; nevertheless, he had a very full life in the theater, producing his works at the Globe theater and before royalty.

> **OBJECTIVES**
> 1. Analyze data, and choose an appropriate kind of graph or table in which to display it
> 2. Understand the varied purposes and forms of line graphs, bar graphs, pie graphs, and statistical tables

Teaching the Lesson

You may wish to have students bring in samples of the various types of charts and graphs from other textbooks, newspapers, or magazines. Have students examine these in small groups, determining why a particular type of visual was chosen in each situation.

Using the Strategies

Possible Answers

1. bar graph and statistical table
2. at increments of 10%
3. Answers may vary, but in general the most accurate depiction would be in a statistical table. However, if the overall purpose is to show trends, then a bar graph would be a good choice.
4. Possible answers: In a statistical table, it is possible to include additional columns; in a bar graph, the population information could become the vertical axis with the percentage of people reading shown as a shaded section of the bar.

Reading for Life

Analyzing and Creating Graphics

Situation

You've been impressed by the power of the word and have volunteered to tutor students in reading. In an effort to motivate your students, you want to show them rates of literacy in various parts of the world. You've gathered information and have decided to display it in a graph or table.

Strategies

Analyze your data, and choose an appropriate kind of graph or table in which to display it.

- Make sure you know exactly what your data show. All data on a single subject should be displayed in the same format.
- Choose a **line graph, bar graph, pie graph,** or **statistical table.** A **line graph** shows changes in one or more entities across time. A **bar graph** compares two or more entities in relation to quantity and time. For example, a bar graph might show population figures for several countries over two years. A **pie graph** shows percentages of a whole. A pie graph might show the percentages of people in a single country who practice different religions. In a **statistical table,** similar kinds of data are displayed in columns. A statistical table might show the populations of various cities within a country.

```
Rates of Literacy for Various Countries,
   1985 and 1998, in percentages

Democratic Republic of Congo (formerly Zaire):
   1985, 40%; 1998, 72%
India: 1985, 36%; 1998, 52%
Indonesia: 1985, 64%; 1998, 86.3%
Japan: 1985, 99%; 1998, 99.9%
Kenya: 1985, 40%; 1998, 69%
People's Republic of China: 1985, 75%; 1998, 73%
Saudi Arabia: 1985, 15%; 1998, 65%
South Africa: 1985, 77%; 1998, 76%
Sudan: 1985, 20%; 1998, 32%
United Kingdom: 1985, 99%; 1998, 99%
United States: 1985, 99%; 1998, 97.9%
```

Graph the information.

- Find a line, bar, or pie graph or a statistical table to use as a model. For a line or bar graph you'll need to create a horizontal axis that shows periods of time and a vertical axis that shows numbers or percentages. For a pie graph you'll need to scale segments of the graph to the quantities you're displaying. For a statistical table you'll need to label the columns.

Label the graph or table.

- Arrange data in a logical order, and label every part of the graph so that readers can recognize the information and interpret its meaning. Provide a title for the entire graph, and if necessary, provide a key that explains any special symbols, colors, or abbreviations.

Using the Strategies

1. Which two kinds of graphic formats would best display the data in the box above?
2. At what increments would you mark the percentages of literacy rates on a bar graph?
3. How could you best display the growth in literacy in each country for the two periods?
4. If you also had data on the population of each country, how could you change your graph or table to include that information?

Extending the Strategies

- Create a graph or table to display information about people in your community, state, or nation, such as their ethnic identification, level of education, or religious affiliation.
- Find and interpret graphic displays of information on a subject that interests you.

Graph the Information: Sample Responses

	1985	1998
China	75%	73%
Congo	40%	72%
India	36%	52%
Indonesia	64%	86%
Japan	99%	100%
Kenya	40%	69%
Saudia Arabia	15%	65%
South Africa	77%	76%
Sudan	20%	32%
UK	99%	99%
USA	99%	98%

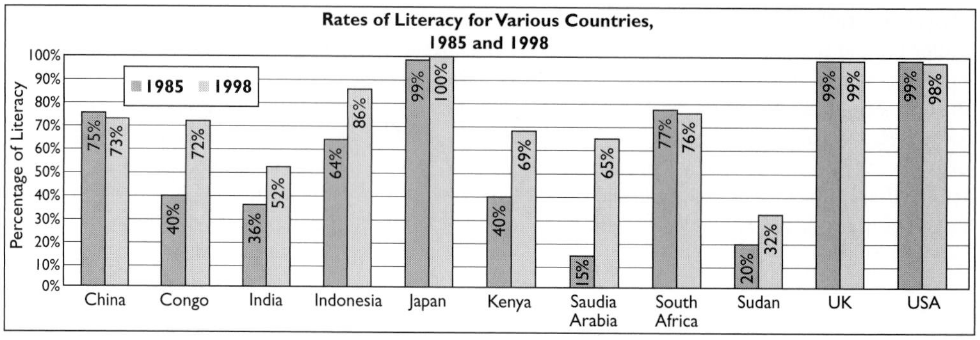

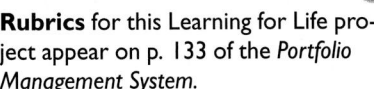

Learning for Life

A New Curriculum

OBJECTIVES

1. Identify the characteristics of a new curriculum
2. Conduct research
3. Choose and complete a project incorporating research information

Problem

The term *Renaissance person* is still used to describe someone who is skilled and knowledgeable in many areas—the arts and the sciences. Thomas Jefferson, the third president of the United States, was called a Renaissance man. Jefferson was a skilled writer, statesman, musician, inventor, architect, and philosopher. What would a person need to *know* and be able to *do* to be considered a Renaissance person today? How should we educate children to be "Renaissance people"?

Project

Identify a real person, or create an imaginary one, who exemplifies the characteristics of a modern-day Renaissance person. Suggest educational innovations to produce "Renaissance people."

Preparation

1. Working with a small group, brainstorm to generate a list of the areas in which a person of the twenty-first century should be skilled and knowledgeable.
2. Taking each area in turn, work together to establish the criteria necessary to qualify as a new Renaissance person. Be as specific as you can. If one area is languages, for example, should the person be able to speak, read, and write more than one language? Are two languages sufficient? Make it a group decision.
3. Review the curricula in all major subject areas in your school. Form a committee to study them, and make recommendations.

Procedure

1. Decide whether you'll develop your presentation around a real person or create an imaginary character. If you decide on a real person, someone may come to mind immediately, or you may need to do some research. To create an imaginary character, you can draw on the methods of direct and indirect characterization you've studied in this book, and in your composition text.
2. Think, too, about whether you'll approach this activity straightforwardly or handle it with humor. Deciding now which mode of presentation you'll use (see below) can help you choose the approach you prefer.

Presentation

Use one of the following formats (or another that your teacher approves):

1. **Write a Proposal**
   Focus on your study of the school's curricula, and write a proposal for revised curricula for all major areas. Open with an overview of your proposal and a summation of your recommendations. Describe in your introduction the kind of learning a Renaissance person of the twenty-first century will require.
2. **Coming to Life**
   Stage a one-person show depicting the Renaissance person you've chosen or created. Your production can be as simple or elaborate as you like. Present your show live, or arrange to have a friend videotape it to show at a schoolwide assembly or a school-board meeting.
3. **Images and Essences**
   Create a collage that conveys the multifaceted characteristics of a Renaissance person of today. Combine various objects and materials such as photographs, scraps of material, words—anything you find meaningful—using shapes, colors, and textures to capture the person's essence.

Processing

Did doing this activity change your ideas about what should be taught in the schools? Did it make you want to be a modern-day Renaissance person? Write a reflection for your portfolio.

Resources

Viewing and Representing
HRW Multimedia Presentation Maker
Students may wish to use the *Multimedia Presentation Maker* to present the main points of their proposals.

Grading Timesaver

Rubrics for this Learning for Life project appear on p. 133 of the *Portfolio Management System.*

Developing Workplace Competencies

Preparation	Procedure	Presentation
• Works on teams • Generates ideas • Makes inferences • Ranks alternatives	• Thinks creatively • Processes information • Interprets information • Acquires data	• Communicates information and ideas • Draws conclusions • Exhibits self-esteem • Uses self-management skills

The Restoration and the Eighteenth Century 1660-1800

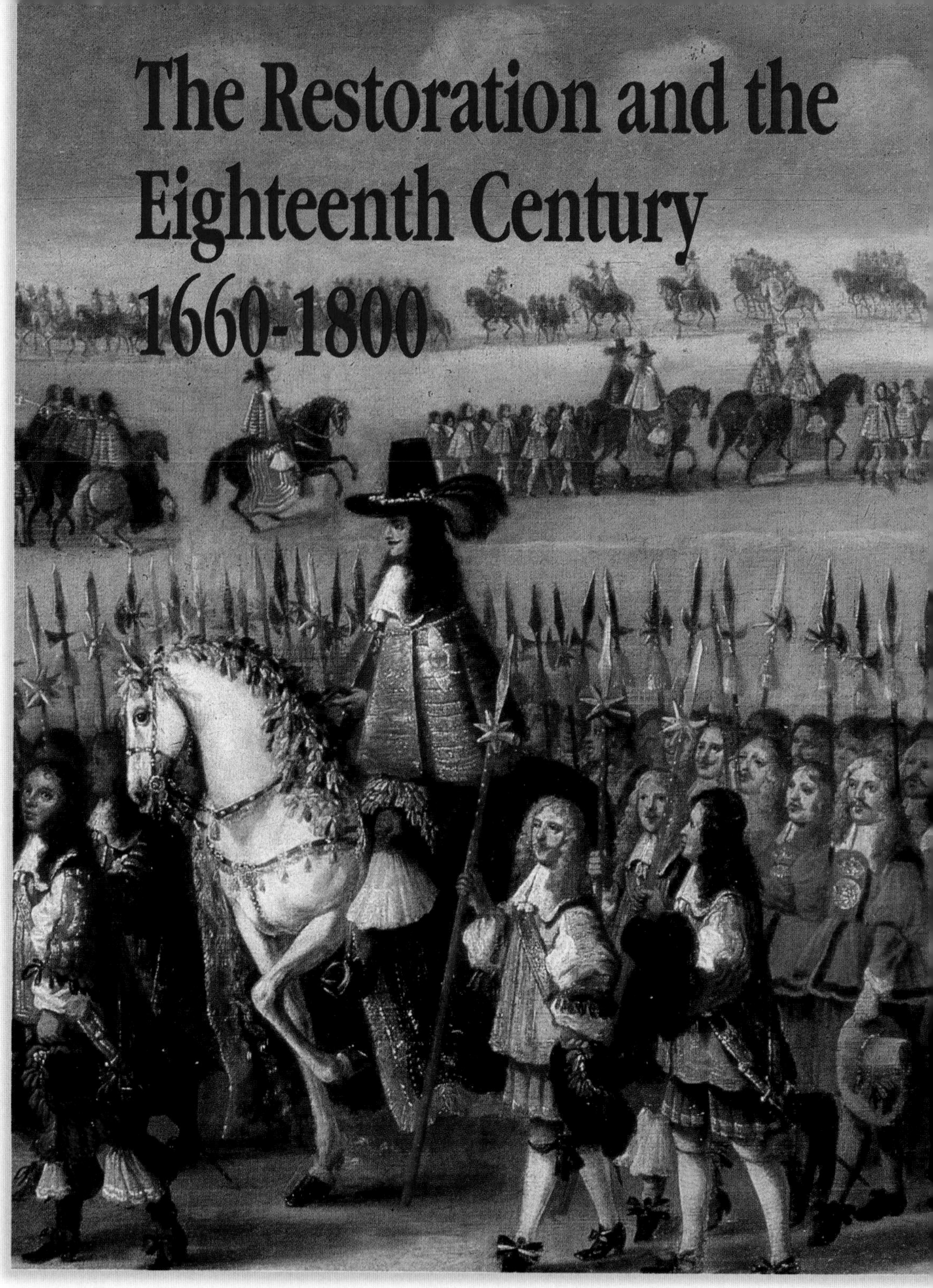

OBJECTIVES

1. Read literature from the Restoration and the eighteenth century on the themes "The Sting of Satire" and "An Appetite for Experience"
2. Interpret literary elements with special emphasis on satire, wit, style, and the elegy
3. Apply a variety of reading strategies to literature of the Restoration and the eighteenth century, with special emphasis on distinguishing shades of meanings
4. Respond to literature in a variety of modes
5. Learn and use new words
6. Learn how correcting and preserving the English language was emphasized in the eighteenth century
7. Plan, draft, revise, edit, proofread, and publish a persuasive essay
8. Write and revise sentences to achieve parallelism
9. Investigate local employment resources

Selection Readability

The Annotated Teacher's Edition provides a summary of each selection in the student book. Following each Summary heading, you will find one, two, or three small icons. These icons indicate, in an approximate sense, the reading level of the selection.

■ One icon indicates that the selection is easy.

■■ Two icons indicate that the selection is on an intermediate reading level.

■■■ Three icons indicate that the selection is challenging.

Coronation Procession of Charles II to Westminster from the Tower of London (detail) (1661) by Dirck Stoop.

Responding to the Art

Dutch painter **Dirck Stoop** (c. 1610–1686) often painted scenes of cavalry engagements, hunting, and seaports. He also captured several important events in the life of King Charles II, including the restoration of the king to the British throne.

Activity. Call attention to the way Stoop gives his painting depth by making the horses and people in the background smaller and smaller. (The use of such linear perspective was a Renaissance innovation in Western art.) In what ways is Stoop's portrayal of this momentous occasion highly idealized? [The procession is orderly and seems to move through an empty and stylized cityscape; there are no spectators, which would have been highly unlikely.]

Resources

Viewing and Representing
Videocassette B, Segment 7
Available in Spanish and English. This video shows life in the big, burgeoning city of London with its growing population and huge class differences.

Resources: Print and Media

Viewing and Representing
- *Visual Connections*
  Videocassette B, Segment 7

Assessment
- Formal Assessment, p. 87
- *Test Generator (One-Stop Planner CD-ROM)*

Internet
- *go.hrw.com* (keyword: *LEO 12-6*)

OBJECTIVES

1. Understand the historical and social forces that shaped the Restoration and the Eighteenth Century
2. Interpret the way historical context influenced literary works in the Restoration and the Eighteenth Century
3. Read and understand a time line
4. Understand the relevance of the Restoration and the Eighteenth Century to our day
5. Take notes on and discuss the changes students have seen in their lifetime

Responding to the Quotation

Ask students what conclusions they can draw about English society based on this quotation. [Possible response: An enormous gap still exists between the rich and the poor, but now there are more gradations in between, including three groups that might be considered middle class.] Prompt students to compare this description with American society today.

RESPONDING TO THE ART

English artist **William Hogarth** (1697–1764) described his own work as "modern moral subjects . . . similar to representations on the stage." In some of his paintings, he tries to steer people toward middle class values by presenting examples of horrid behavior. He wanted to be a social critic, yet he also cultivated the aristocracy to enhance both his artistic stature and his purse. No one was above Hogarth's barbs, not even the prime minister. (For other art by Hogarth, see pp. 473, 478, 480, and 580.)

Activity. Have students list the details of eighteenth-century life they can see in this painting.

The Restoration and the Eighteenth Century

by **C. F. Main**

There are seven groups in English society
1. *The Great, who live profusely.*
2. *The Rich, who live very plentifully.*
3. *The Middle Sort, who live well.*
4. *The Working Trades, who labor hard, but feel no want.*
5. *The Country People, Farmers, etc., who fare indifferently.*
6. *The Poor, that fare hard.*
7. *The Miserable, that really pinch and suffer want.*

—Daniel Defoe

Southwark Fair (18th century) by William Hogarth.
Tate Gallery, London.

Reaching All Students

Struggling Readers

Encourage students to preview the essay using headings and illustrations. Remind students that the boldfaced sentences at the end of each section of text can help them summarize and find main ideas. Explain that the chart on p. 477 is useful for getting a quick overview of key events in the arts and sciences during this period.

English Language Learners

For strategies to use with English language learners, see

- *Lesson Plans Including Strategies for English-Language Learners*

From 1660 to 1800, people from England and Europe were pouring into North America. These eager voyagers not only sought freedom from religious and political persecution; they also saw money to be made in the American continent's rich lands and forests—in furs, tobacco, and logs for British sailing ships. They also began transporting Africans for use as slave labor in the Americas. In 1775, these Colonies rebelled against British rule and eventually won their freedom. The United States was a raw, vigorous, brand-new nation. Across the Atlantic, things were very different.

In 1660, England was utterly exhausted by nearly twenty years of civil war. By 1700, it had lived through a devastating plague and a fire that left more than two thirds of Londoners homeless. By the middle of the eighteenth century, however, England had settled into a period of calm and order, at least among the upper classes. Despite the loss of the American Colonies, the reinvigorated British military forces established new settlements around the globe. And though life for many was wretched, the middle class grew. Throughout this long period in a very old nation with tastes much more refined than raw, British men and women also produced many brilliant works of philosophy, art, and literature.

This long period of time in England—from 1660 to 1800—has been given several labels: the Augustan Age, the Neoclassical period, the Enlightenment, and the Age of Reason. Each of these labels applies to some characteristics of these 140 years, but none applies to all.

We, therefore, the Representatives of the United States of America, in General Congress, Assembled, . . . do, in the Name, and by Authority of the good People of these Colonies, solemnly Publish and Declare, . . . that all political Connection between them and the State of Great-Britain, is and ought to be totally dissolved. . . .

—Declaration of Independence, July 4, 1776, Philadelphia

Nothing of importance happened today.

—Diary entry reportedly made by King George III, July 4, 1776

I would have been glad to have lived under my woodside, and to have kept a flock of sheep, rather than to have undertaken this government.

—Oliver Cromwell, speaking to Parliament, 1658

In contrast to the vital Colonies of North America, England was exhausted by war and disease in 1660. But by the end of the eighteenth century, England had transformed itself.

Augustan and Neoclassical: Comparisons with Rome

Many people liked to find similarities between England in this period and ancient Rome, especially during the reign of the emperor Octavian (63 B.C.–A.D. 14). When he became emperor, Octavian was given the high-sounding name *Augustus,* meaning "the exalted one." Augustus restored peace and order to Rome after Julius Caesar's assassination. Similarly, the Stuart monarchs of England restored peace and order to England after the civil wars that led up to the execution of King Charles I in 1649, and that continued even after the king was dead.

The Execution of King Charles I at Whitehall, London, January 30, 1649. Woodcut.

The Granger Collection, New York.

go.hrw.com
LEO 12-Restoration

A Exploring the Historical Period

The Growth of the United States

The restoration in 1660 of the Anglican Church as the official Church of England and the continued struggle between Catholics and Protestants caused many English to emigrate to the New World. In 1607, the Jamestown colonists had numbered about 100. By 1753, the Colonial population was around 1,300,000. By 1783, at the end of the eighteenth century, there were over 3 million people in the United States.

B Exploring the Historical Period

The Atlantic Slave Trade

A massive business enterprise, and a triangular trade exchanged manufactured goods, crops, raw materials, and human beings between Africa, the Americas, and Europe. Although Portugal and Spain at first led the way in this trade, England dominated it from 1690 to 1807, when the slave trade was abolished.

C Humanities Connections

Neoclassical Music

The balanced, elegant qualities of the music of the Neoclassical Period—for example, compositions by Henry Purcell (1659–1695) and George Frederic Handel (1685–1759)—are consistent with the style of the period's literature and philosophy. Both Purcell and Handel turned to classical motifs for inspiration. Examples are Purcell's opera *Dido and Aeneas* and Handel's *Julius Caesar* and *Xerxes.*

D Background

Augustus

Augustus reigned during the golden age of Roman literature and architecture. He boasted that he had "found Rome brick and left it marble." After his death, the Romans worshipped him as a god.

Professional Notes

Cultural Connections: The Fall of Puritanism

In 1660, after the Civil War in Britain, the common people not only welcomed back the Stuart family in the person of Charles II but also relished the return of the merry English pastimes of bull-baiting, bear-baiting, horse-racing, cock-fighting, may-pole dancing, decking the halls with holly and ivy for Christmas, and eating mince pie. The Puritan enthusiasm for religious devotion had exhausted itself and even Cromwell's sons were indifferent to it.

Time Line

This time line shows major events between the time Charles II was proclaimed king of England and Napoleon rose to the head of the revolutionary government of France in 1799.

- **1660–1669**

Molière

Molière's plays, such as *The Misanthrope,* satirized the upper class and the new rich, setting the standard for European comedies: witty, urbane, fast-paced plays that depicted relationships between men and women.

- **1670–1689**

The Test Acts

The Test Acts passed by Parliament in 1673 and 1678 restricted activities of people who were not members of the Anglican church. The law required that all people holding civilian or military positions swear allegiance to the English Crown and take communion in the Church of England. A series of laws passed between 1828 and 1871 finally repealed the Test Acts.

- **1690–1709**

Coffee

Coffeehouses became the social centers for middle- and upper-class Londoners. For an example of the social significance of coffee, see Alexander Pope's *The Rape of the Lock,* Canto III, ll. 33–48 (pp. 528–529).

Peter the Great

At a time when England was beginning to enjoy a constitutional monarchy, Peter the Great was increasing the power of the czar in Russia. However, he is also credited with westernizing Russia and introducing important reforms in administration, industry, commerce, and culture.

Isolation in the East

At this time, Japan was almost completely off limits to Europeans (only the port of Nagasaki remained open) and trading with China was limited mostly to the Dutch, who were more adept at cross-cultural exchanges than the English.

The Restoration and the Eighteenth Century, 1660–1800

LITERARY EVENTS

1660–1669

In France, Jean-Baptiste Molière's *The Misanthrope* first performed, 1666

London theaters reopen; actresses appear on stage for the first time in England, 1660s

Samuel Pepys begins his diary, 1660

1670–1689

Aphra Behn publishes *Oroonoko,* an early anti-slavery novel, 1688

Poems of Bashō help popularize haiku poetry in Japan, 1680s

John Dryden's *All for Love, or The World Well Lost* first produced, 1678

John Bunyan publishes *The Pilgrim's Progress,* Part 1 (Part 2 appears in 1684), 1678

1690–1709

First issue of **Addison** and **Steele**'s *The Tatler* printed (*The Spectator* is begun in 1711), 1709

In Mexico, Sor Juana Inés de la Cruz publishes *Respuesta a Sor Filotea* (Reply to Sister Philotea), a defense of women's intellectual rights, 1691

1710–1739

Swift publishes *A Modest Proposal,* protesting English treatment of Irish poor, 1729

Jonathan Swift publishes *Gulliver's Travels,* 1726

Daniel Defoe publishes *Robinson Crusoe,* 1719

Alexander Pope writes *The Rape of the Lock,* 1712

CULTURAL/HISTORICAL EVENTS

1660–1669

Charles II proclaimed king of England (crowned in 1661), 1660

In Massachusetts, John Eliot translates the Bible into Algonquian, 1661

Plague claims more than 68,000 people in London, 1665

Great Fire destroys much of London, 1666

• *The Great Fire of London* (1666) by an unknown artist.

1670–1689

Ashanti empire formed in Africa, c. 1670s

English Test Act bans Roman Catholics from public office, 1673

James II, king of England, 1685–1688, tries to re-establish Catholic Church

Newton publishes *Philosophiae Naturalis Principia Mathematica* (Mathematical Principles of Natural Philosophy), 1687

"Glorious Revolution": James II succeeded by Protestant rulers William and Mary, 1688

1690–1709

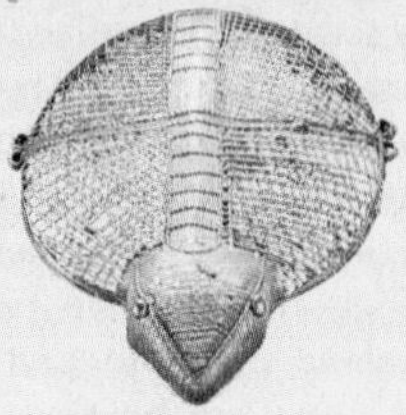

• Turtle-shaped Ashanti emblem (17th or 18th century) from Ghana. Gold.

John Locke publishes *An Essay Concerning Human Understanding,* 1690

English Parliament enacts Penal Laws, depriving Irish Catholics of civil rights, 1695

England, Wales, and Scotland politically unified as Great Britain, 1707

1710–1739

George I, a German who could not speak English, becomes king of England, 1714

In England, Lady Mary Wortley Montagu introduces Turkish practice of inoculation against smallpox, 1718

• Newton's reflecting telescope (1688). Royal Society, London.

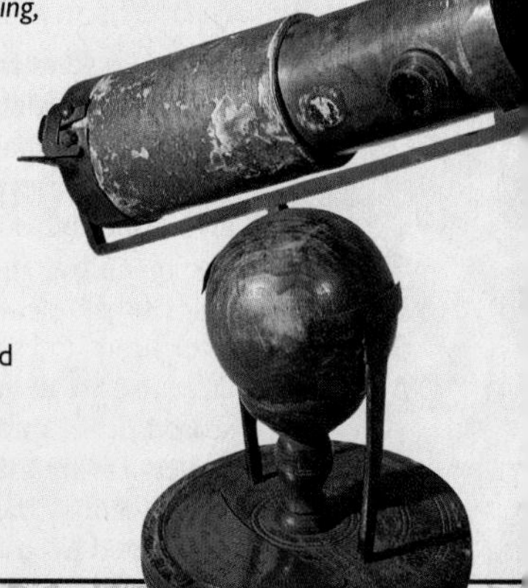

Using the Time Line

Have students use a print or nonprint encyclopedia or a database to place the following events on the time line.

- William and Mary sign the English Bill of Rights, transferring some royal powers to the elected members of Parliament. [1689]
- Parliament passes the *Habeas Corpus Act,* which keeps prisoners from being thrown into jail for opposing the king and languishing there without a trial. [1679]
- The British Museum is founded in London. [1753]
- Adam Smith publishes *The Wealth of Nations.* [1776]
- Mozart composes *The Marriage of Figaro.* [1786]
- The Swedish inventor Anders Celsius invents the centigrade thermometer. [1742]
- James Hargreaves invents the spinning jenny, which spurs the Industrial Revolution. [1764]

• Frontispiece of Phillis Wheatley's *Poems on Various Subjects, Religious and Moral* (1773).

In France, **Voltaire** publishes *Candide,* 1759

Samuel Johnson publishes his *Dictionary of the English Language,* 1755

Thomas Gray publishes "Elegy Written in a Country Churchyard," 1751

Samuel Richardson publishes *Pamela, or Virtue Rewarded,* 1740

African American poet Phillis Wheatley's *Poems on Various Subjects, Religious and Moral* published in London, 1773

Oliver Goldsmith publishes *The Vicar of Wakefield,* 1766

Wordsworth and **Coleridge** publish *Lyrical Ballads,* 1798

Mary Wollstonecraft publishes *A Vindication of the Rights of Woman,* 1792

James Boswell's *The Life of Samuel Johnson* published, 1791

Olaudah Equiano, once held in slavery in Colonial America, publishes his autobiography in Britain, 1789

1740–1764

George III, crowned king of England, 1760, becomes known as the king who lost the American Colonies

In France, Denis Diderot begins work on the *Encyclopédie,* 1747

Benjamin Franklin invents the lightning rod, 1752

Catherine II ("Catherine the Great") becomes czarina of Russia, 1762

• *Catherine the Great* (1762–1769) by Vigilius Erichsen.

1765–1779

British Parliament passes Stamp Act for taxing American Colonies, 1765

Mozart writes *Symphony No. 1* at age nine, 1765

• Teapot reading "Stamp Act Repeal'd" (English, 1766).

Boston Tea Party protests tax on tea, 1773

American Revolution begins, 1775

1780–1800

James Watt develops the steam engine, 1780s

• French Revolution button (c. 1789–1793) translating to "Liberty or Death." Brass with miniatures painted on ivory.

French Revolution begins with storming of the Bastille, 1789

British crush Irish nationalist rebellion led by Theobald Wolfe Tone, 1798

Rosetta stone (key to deciphering Egyptian hieroglyphics) found in Egypt, 1799

Napoleon heads revolutionary government in France, 1799

Using the Time Line (cont.)

- Louis XIV commissions the building of the Palace at Versailles. [1661]

Ask students to think about the following questions.

1. What relationship can students infer between James II's attempts to reestablish the Catholic Church and the ascension of William and Mary in 1688? [The English wished to maintain the Protestant status quo.]
2. How might the Penal Laws of 1695 have contributed to the writing of Swift's *A Modest Proposal?* [Swift saw the sufferings of the Irish firsthand.]
3. What event might have led Equiano to publish his autobiography in England rather than America in 1789? [England had an anti-slavery tradition begun by Aphra Behn.]
4. What work or works laid the foundation for the storming of the Bastille in 1789? [Locke's "An Essay Concerning Human Understanding"]

• **1740–1764**

The Seven Years' War

The Seven Years' War actually began in 1754 in North America (where it is called the French and Indian War) with disputes between the British and French over territories on that continent. The war expanded to include most of Europe, where Britain's ally Prussia did most of the fighting against France and its allies Austria and Russia. Meanwhile, Great Britain carried on the war in North America and India. As a result of this war, the British took almost all French territory in Canada and all French possessions east of the Mississippi River except New Orleans. It also gained dominion over India.

Catherine II of Russia

Catherine II (1729–1796), a German princess, became empress of Russia when she overthrew her husband Peter (who was later murdered). She became interested in the liberal ideas of the Age of Reason and promoted European culture in Russia. Personally extravagant, she nevertheless also spent money building schools and hospitals. While teachers, scientists, writers, artists, and actors enjoyed freedoms and a golden age, however, Catherine brutally suppressed peasant revolts.

• **1780–1800**

Lyrical Ballads

William Wordsworth (1770–1850) and Samuel Taylor Coleridge (1772–1834) collaborated on *Lyrical Ballads,* now considered the foundation of English Romantic poetry. In this work they announced that they were attempting to eschew the specialized formal language of eighteenth-century poetry, for language, Wordsworth said, that was "really used by men."

Jean-Jacques Rousseau

Many of the philosophical underpinnings of the French Revolution lay in the writings of Jean-Jacques Rousseau (1712–1778), one of the most influential thinkers of the Age of Reason. For example, he advocated government by common consent and a legal system that expresses the general will of the people, and proposed that humans in their natural state are good but become evil because they must live in society, which brings out aggression and selfishness.

A Closer Look

This feature discusses the fashions and leisure-time activities of the upper class.

A Exploring the Historical Period

The Restoration

One reason Charles II was restored to power was that things had gone awry during Cromwell's rule. Cromwell began with democratic strides: He abolished the monarchy and the House of Lords, he instituted the commonwealth (a republican form of government), and he oversaw the drafting of a constitution for England. Beset with problems, however, Cromwell soon ripped up the constitution and lapsed into rule as a military dictator. He also instituted a strict Puritan morality, which made leisure-time activities such as going to the theater against the law.

B Literary Connections

Shakespeare and Classical Sources

Remind students that in an earlier generation, Shakespeare had been heavily influenced by the Latin classics, especially works by Terence, Ovid, and Seneca.

C Explaining the Historical Period

Reason and Enlightenment

Francis Bacon, Lord Chancellor of England (1561–1626), was the first to endorse the slow careful process of examining physical evidence, performing experiments, and evaluating various hypotheses against the results of these experiments. His writings set the stage for the growth in scientific knowledge that occurred in the mid-1600s.

King Charles II of England (c. 1675) by (school of) Nicholas Dixon. Vellum.

Fitzwilliam Museum, University of Cambridge, England.

The people of both Rome and England were weary of war, suspicious of revolutionaries and radicals, and ready to settle down, make money, and enjoy life. The Roman Senate had hailed Augustus as the second founder of Rome; in 1660, the English people brought back the son of Charles I from his exile in France, crowned him as King Charles II, and hailed him as their savior. As a warning to revolutionaries, they dug up the corpse of Oliver Cromwell, who had ruled England between Charles I and Charles II, and cut off its head. The monarchy was restored without shedding a drop of blood.

In this age, many English writers consciously modeled their works on the old Latin classics, which they had studied in school and university. These writings that imitate Latin works were called neoclassical—"new classical." The classics, it was generally agreed, were valuable because they represented what was permanent and universal in human experience. All educated people knew the Latin classics better than they knew their own English literature.

With the restoration of the king, England likened itself to Augustan Rome: Both had entered a period of calm and order after an era of political turmoil.

Reason and Enlightenment: Asking "How?"

Labels like the "Age of Reason" and the "Enlightenment" reveal how people were gradually changing their view of themselves and the world. For instance, Shakespeare, the greatest writer of the Renaissance, expressed a commonly held view when he described the unusual events that preceded the assassination of Julius Caesar—"a tempest dropping fire" and "blue lightning." These unnatural events, says a character in the play *Julius Caesar,* are "instruments of fear and warning." For centuries people had believed that before a great public disaster

A CLOSER LOOK

Life Among the "Haves" . . .

According to the law, all men were equal. But some were more equal than others, especially England's wealthy, during the Restoration and the eighteenth century. Famous for its excesses, this artificial age offered extreme luxuries to those known as "quality" or "polite" society—the rich.

Greatly influenced by the French in manners, dress, furniture, gardens, and recreation, the elite gathered regularly at London's fashionable coffeehouses—numbering three thousand by the early eighteenth century. These centers of news, gossip, and gambling were places to see and to be seen in. Another meeting place, the city's formal gardens, offered illuminated groves, dining, and fireworks.

Whatever their haunt, both men and women devoted themselves to colorful and extravagant fashion. Men carried snuffboxes and wore velvet or satin coats, lace ruffles, silk knee breeches, high-heeled shoes with gold or silver buckles, and broad-brimmed hats decorated with feathers. Women wore low-cut silk dresses with hoops made from whalebones. Their elaborate petticoats were fashioned from colorful silk, velvet, or chintz, often quilted or trimmed with silver.

Professional Notes

Critical Comment: Pathetic Fallacy

The phrases quoted from Shakespeare above are examples of the **pathetic fallacy,** an overly emotional or portentous view of nature. The term was introduced by English writer and critic John Ruskin (1819–1900), in a discussion of these lines: *They rowed her in across the rolling foam the cruel, crawling foam.* "The foam is not cruel," wrote Ruskin, "neither does it crawl. The state of mind which attributes to it these characters of a living creature is one in which the reason is unhinged by grief. All violent feelings have the same effect. They produce in us a falseness in all our impressions of external things, which I would generally characterize as the 'pathetic fallacy.'" Note that *pathetic* in Ruskin's phrase means "relating to feeling," not "deserving of pity." The fallacy lies in "the difference between the ordinary, proper, and true appearance of things to us; and the extraordinary, or false appearances, when we are under the influence of emotion of contemplative fancy."

like the assassination of a ruler, the earth and sky gave warnings. People believed that unusual events such as earthquakes, comets, and even babies born with malformations had some kind of meaning, and that they were sent as punishment for past misdoings or as warning of future troubles. People did not ask, "*How* did this unusual event take place?" but "*Why* did this unusual event take place, and what does it *mean*?"

Gradually, during the Enlightenment, people stopped asking "Why?" questions and started asking "How?" questions, and the answers to those questions—about everything from the workings of the human body to the laws of the universe—became much less frightening and superstitious.

A Scene from "The Beggar's Opera" (c. 1728) by William Hogarth. Oil.
Collection of Paul Mellon, National Gallery, Washington.

By 1664, wigs and makeup were the rage for men and women. Powdered and stuffed with horsehair, women's headdresses grew to enormous proportions. Jewels, flowers, ribbons, plumage, and even fruit decorated these monstrous structures—reaching two to three feet in height. Men also wore their hair in pigtails—tied with a bow and powdered. In 1795, a tax was created to generate income from the rich—a guinea on every powdered head. Cosmetics were made from ingredients such as borax, vinegar, bread, eggs, and pigeon wings. Black patches, or fake beauty marks, were an important fashion accessory.

The wealthy divided the year between London, country estates, and health resorts. A whirlwind of masked balls, dances, and formal dinner parties, known as the London season, ended by the first week in June. Summers were often spent in seaside towns and at freshwater springs. Daniel Defoe described one trendy health resort: "[The attendants] present you with a little floating dish like a basin, in which the lady puts her handkerchief and a nosegay, of late the snuffbox is added, and some patches; through the bath occasioning a little perspiration, the patches do not stick as kindly as they should."

It was a careless, pleasure-seeking time centered on dancing, dining, drinking, theatergoing, card playing, and gambling. As is always the case with fashion, change was inevitable. By the end of the eighteenth century, the lifestyle of the wealthy leaned toward simplicity and sobriety.

Embroidered casket (c. 1665).
Lady Lever Art Gallery, Port Sunlight, England.

D Exploring the Historical Period

The Growing Popularity of Science

Charles II was himself a good chemist and was interested in methods of navigation. His interest led to the founding of the Royal Society of London (see p. 474) and to the fact that science became the thing to do among the courtiers of the day.

E Exploring the Culture

Charles II on Pleasure

Charles II's quotation further illustrates the prevailing attitude of the "haves": "God will never damn a man for allowing himself a little pleasure."

RESPONDING TO THE ART

William Hogarth (see p. T468) was commissioned to do this painting of "The Beggar's Opera," an attack on the fashionable excess of Italian opera. (For other art by Hogarth, see pp. 468, 478, 480, and 580.)

Activity. Ask students to comment on the two women kneeling in the foreground and the men to whom they kneel. What difference in class do students see? On whom is the most attention focused? [the man in red]

Using Students' Strengths

Logical/Mathematical Learners

Ask students if they have seen a comet. Some students might recall Hale-Bopp in 1998, for instance. Then have students read the first paragraph on p. 474. When they are finished, have volunteers research and explain the mathematical principles behind Halley's calculations of parabolic orbits.

Visual Learners

Have students who are interested in fashion and style create a collage showing eighteenth-century styles and their "echoes," or imitations, throughout history. For example, students could show the powdered headdresses of this era next to a photograph of a 1960's "beehive" hairdo. Another idea would be to juxtapose the powdered ponytail of the eighteenth-century gentleman with that of the 1960's hippie.

Ⓐ Exploring the Historical Period

Robert Hooke

Robert Hooke (1635–1703) was one of the great scientific minds of the seventeenth century. Like Leonardo da Vinci, however, he made more discoveries than he actually carried to completion. For example, he anticipated some of the ideas about gravity that Sir Isaac Newton would go on to formulate. Known for his study of elasticity as well as for his work on watches and clocks, Hooke made contributions to many fields of science. Students can view some of his biological drawings on pp. 509–510.

Ⓑ Humanities Connections

The Royal Society

Among the prominent, early members of the Royal Society were the scientists Robert Hooke and Robert Boyle (considered the founder of modern chemistry), the architect Christopher Wren (who designed much of London after the Great Fire including St. Paul's Cathedral), and the poet and playwright John Dryden.

Ⓒ Reading Skills and Strategies

Summarizing

? How would you summarize the characteristics of modern English prose? [Possible answers: straightforward; precise; efficient; simple rather than elaborate; accessible; concise.]

Ⓓ Exploring the Culture

Deism

Deism, a product of the Age of Enlightenment, was a religious belief based on reason and the observation of nature. The philosophers Rousseau and Voltaire of France and Germany's Immanuel Kant embraced Deism, strains of which also appear in the U.S. Declaration of Independence. ("They are endowed by their creator with certain inalienable rights.") The contents of this document were influenced by leading colonial Deists, including Benjamin Franklin, Thomas Jefferson, and Thomas Paine.

For instance, the astronomer Edmond Halley (1656–1742) took the terror out of celestial phenomena by calculating when they were going to occur. He computed, with "immense labor," he said, the orbit of the comet that still bears his name. He predicted it would appear in 1758, 1834, 1910, and 1986—and it did. And how did he know it would reappear at seventy-six-year intervals? Because that was the time it took to complete its orbit. Such a reasonable, mathematical explanation made no connection at all between the comet and human affairs.

> The truth is, the science of Nature has been already too long made only a work of the brain and the fancy: It is now high time that it should return to the plainness and soundness of observations on material and obvious things.
>
> —Robert Hooke

Natural phenomena were increasingly explained by scientific observation as people began to ask how things happened in the natural world.

The Birth of Modern English Prose: Stripping Down

In 1662, to answer questions about the universe, King Charles II chartered a group of philosophers: the Royal Society of London for the Promotion of Natural Knowledge. Among other things, its members called for a kind of writing that was precise, exact, and not decorated with the elaborate metaphors or odd allusions of their predecessors. Above all, these new scientists wanted to shorten the endless sentences of their predecessors. And so in this age was born what we think of as modern English prose.

While the Royal Society affected the course of English prose, the "founder and first true master" of modern English prose was John Dryden (1631–1700), an all-around man of letters. Because of his influence, the era in which Dryden lived is often referred to as the "age of Dryden." In the *Essay of Dramatic Poesy* (1668), a major critical work, Dryden sought to "vindicate the honor of our English writers." He also wrote comedies, as well as the best tragedy of the day, *All for Love* (1677), a neoclassical version of Shakespeare's *Antony and Cleopatra*. Among Dryden's achievements in poetry were perfecting the technique of English poetry, regularizing meter, and making diction precise. He was a master of explaining ideas, of reasoning in verse. Dryden set the standards that most of the poets of the next century aspired to.

Under the influence of the Royal Society and John Dryden, English prose became more precise, exact, and plain.

Changes in Religion: More Questions

The new scientific and rational explanations of phenomena gradually began to affect some people's religious views. If comets were not sent by God to warn people, perhaps God didn't interfere at all in human affairs. Perhaps the universe was like an immense piece of clockwork, set in motion by a Creator who more or less withdrew from this perfect mechanism and let it run by itself. Such a view, part of a complex of ideas known as Deism, could make people feel self-satisfied and complacent,

Professional Notes

Cultural Connection: The Royal Society

Although historian J. R. Greene maintains that "wits and fops" flocked to the Royal Society, it led the way to ground-breaking discoveries: Willis was the first to explore the composition of the brain; Woodward founded the science of mineralogy; John Ray established zoology as a science; and Sir Isaac Newton (1642–1727) discovered the laws of gravity and principles governing the movement of the planets.

Interior of Henry VII's Chapel, Westminster Abbey (c. 1750) by Canaletto.

Museum of London.

especially if they believed, as Alexander Pope noted in his long poem *Essay on Man* (page 524), that "Whatever is, is right." Some philosophers even argued that "In this best of all possible worlds, . . . all is for the best"—a view that the French writer Voltaire ridiculed in his novel *Candide* (1759). (See page 538.) But, other than a tiny minority of "enlightened" rationalists and materialists, most people, including great philosophers and scientists like Sir Isaac Newton (1642–1727) and John Locke (1632–1704), remained religious. Christianity in its various forms continued to exercise an undiminished power over almost all Europeans in this period, just as it had in the Middle Ages and the Renaissance.

E

> Nature and Nature's laws lay hid in night:
> God said, Let Newton be! and all was light.
>
> —Alexander Pope, epitaph intended for Sir Isaac Newton

The new science influenced religion: A movement called Deism viewed the universe as a perfect mechanism, which God had built and left to run on its own.

RESPONDING TO THE ART

The real name of Italian painter **Canaletto** (1697–1768) was Giovanni Antonio Canal. Known for his scenes of Venice, here Canaletto captures the soaring verticality of Westminster Abbey's nave.

Activity. Westminster Abbey is the most famous church in England. Ask students to speculate on what attitude Canaletto takes toward the prime symbol of Christianity in England based on the details in this painting. [The light that illuminates the soaring Gothic arches reveals Canaletto's attitude of awe and reverence toward the Abbey.]

E Humanities Connections

Rationalism and Materialism

Rationalism emphasizes the authority of human reason. In the seventeenth century, philosophical rationalism held that reason is more powerful than sensory experience and that, through reason, humans can understand the nature of reality. In the eighteenth century, cultural rationalism emphasized reason over faith in explaining human destiny. Thomas Paine, author of *The Age of Reason* (1793), was a prominent figure in this movement.

Materialism holds that everything is a state of matter. Even human consciousness, this theory argues, is caused by chemical reactions. Materialism can be traced to the fifth century B.C., when the Greek philosophers Leucippus and Democritus developed *atomism,* the notion that indivisible particles (atoms) make up everything that exists. Because of the spread of Christianity and its emphasis on spirituality, interest in materialism waned for several centuries. However, the rise of modern science during the 1600s renewed discussion of materialism among philosophers.

Crossing the Curriculum

Architecture

St. Paul's Cathedral is considered to be the quintessential combination of neoclassical and baroque architecture. Have students work in a small group to find, create, and display, one of the following: pictures, slides, photographs, drawings, or a model of Wren's masterpiece. Ask students to use their visual representations to point out specific features that are characteristic of the two major architectural styles.

Music

Ask a small group of students to set up a radio station for broadcasting the music of this time period. Programming should include a playlist, introductory comments, commercials, and interviews with composers and musicians. Encourage students to consider folk or popular music of the time as well as classical pieces. Students could present a fifteen- or thirty-minute tape of musical selections and their interpolations.

A Exploring the Historical Period

Religious Intolerance

The outlawing of these various religious groups was largely a reaction against the revolutionary fervor of the ultra-conservative Oliver Cromwell and his followers.

B Exploring the Historical Period

Anti-Catholic Sentiment

One infamous act that inspired such rumors was the Gunpowder Plot of 1605, in which the Catholic Guy Fawkes was convicted of attempting to blow up the Houses of Parliament when King James I and government officials were scheduled to be there. The plot was discovered, the assassination averted, and the conspirators killed, but anti-Catholic hostility remained strong for more than a century. Today, English people still hold a festival on the anniversary of the event (November 5) and burn Guy Fawkes in effigy. To commemorate the plot, the vaults beneath the Houses of Parliament are searched before a new session begins.

C Exploring the Historical Period

The Glorious Revolution

James II was adamantly Catholic. He violated English law by appointing several Catholics to high office.

Responding to the Art

Little is known about **Balthasar Nebot**, an English painter possibly of Spanish origin. He is best known for two series of garden views and did several versions of paintings on Covent Garden.

Activity. Invite students to compare this market to contemporary farmers' markets. [both are in the open air; farmers' markets today often have covered booths; this market is large]

Covent Garden with St. Paul's Church (detail) (18th century) by Balthasar Nebot.

Guildhall Art Gallery, London.

Religion and Politics: Repression of Minority Sects

Religion determined people's politics in this period. Charles II reestablished the Anglican Church as the official church of the country, which it continues to be in England to this day. (In the United States, this denomination is called the Episcopal Church.) With the approval of Parliament, the king attempted to outlaw all the various Puritan and Independent sects—dozens of them, all happily disagreeing among themselves—that had caused so much uproar during the preceding thirty years. Persecution of these various sects continued throughout the eighteenth century.

> A brave world, sir, full of religion, knavery, and change: We shall shortly see better days.
>
> —Aphra Behn

When Charles II reestablished the Anglican Church as the official church of the country, other sects were outlawed and persecuted.

The Bloodless Revolution: Protestants from Now On

Charles II had a number of illegitimate children, but no legal heir. When he died in 1685, he was succeeded by his brother James II, a practicing Roman Catholic. Most English people were utterly opposed to James. After all, it was widely believed that Roman Catholics had not only set fire to London and caused other disasters, but were actively plotting to hand the country over to the pope. When James's queen produced a little boy—a Catholic heir—pressure on the royal family became so great that, in 1688, they suddenly fled to France. Thus, the so-called Glorious (bloodless) Revolution (1688) was accomplished. James II was succeeded by his Protestant daughter, Mary, and her Dutch husband,

William of Orange. Ever since, the rulers of England have been, at least in name, Anglicans. **D**

During the "Glorious Revolution," Charles's Roman Catholic successor was forced into exile, and Protestant rule resumed with the ascension of William of Orange and Mary to the throne.

Addicted to the Theater

For more than twenty years, while the Puritans held power, the theaters in England were closed. During the exile of the royal court in France, Charles had become addicted to theatergoing, so one of the first things he did after regaining his throne was to repeal the ban on play performances, imposed in 1642.

The Restoration and the Eighteenth Century

After the reestablishment of the monarchy, these major events occurred in the arts and sciences:

- With King Charles II's return to the throne and a period of increased stability, writers drew on the "new classical" style of Roman, Greek, and Latin models. **E**
- Thinkers in this Age of Reason emphasized logic, scientific observation, and factual explanation. These rational explanations affected some people's religious views.
- Literary tastes turned to wit and satire to expose excesses and moral corruption.
- In journalism, the periodical essay developed, commenting on public manners and values.
- To satisfy the reading tastes of a developing middle class, writers began to experiment with long fictional narratives called novels.
- Theaters closed by the Puritans reopened, and female actors were now included on the stage; drama during the Restoration was witty, bawdy, and cynical.
- By the end of the period, the excesses of the rich and the onset of industrialization turned people's taste to an appreciation of nature and simplicity.

The First Opera House in the Haymarket (18th century) by William Capon.
Guildhall Library. Corporation of London.

RESPONDING TO THE ART

William Capon (1757–1827) practiced his talents in a variety of genres. He learned portrait painting from his father, but he later became a scene painter for the Italian Opera and the Drury Lane Theater. He also worked as an architect, building a theater in Kildare, Ireland. Later he was appointed draftsman to the Duke of York. He produced numerous watercolor paintings of London scenes.

Activity. Ask students how Capon's interest in architecture is evident in this painting. Looking at the shadows, they may wish to speculate on the time of day depicted.

D Exploring the Culture

Church and State

Point out that Queen Elizabeth II is the titular head of the Church of England.

E Humanities Connections

Neoclassicism

Neoclassicism, or "new classicism," replaced the baroque, a highly ornate and decorative style. By contrast, neoclassical style offered simpler, more elegant lines reminiscent of past grandeur.

Getting Students Involved

Cooperative Learning

Good Morning, Restoration England. Have students work in small groups to create and perform a TV talk show interview with one of the historical figures mentioned in this essay. Students might choose anyone from Voltaire to King Charles II, the scientist Sir Isaac Newton to the actress Nell Gwyn (see p. 478) who was one of Charles II's paramours. After the students have done enough preliminary research to decide on an interesting subject, one person should take responsibility for in-depth research, another for writing, two for performing the interview, and a final member for directing it. After the interview has been performed, suggest that each student write a self-assessment of his or her contribution to the group project.

Ⓐ Literary Connections

John Bunyan

Among these writers was John Bunyan. Bunyan's life and religious works, such as *The Pilgrim's Progress,* strongly contrast with the frivolity associated with the age.

A Closer Look

This feature describes the appalling life of the poor in this elegant and ostentatious age. The essay particularly focuses on the overcrowding and filth the poor suffered in the city of London.

Ⓑ Exploring the Historical Period

Debtors' Prison

At this time, debt was a serious offense. Anyone in debt could suddenly be taken off to prison at a moment's notice and kept there for years (where, of course, there was no possibility of paying off what was owed). In general, crimes against property were much more brutally punished than they are now, and people could hang for as small an offense as stealing a rabbit.

Ⓒ Exploring the Historical Period

Medical Science

Remind students that until the work of Louis Pasteur in the mid-1800s, germs were not known to cause disease.

RESPONDING TO THE ART

(See p. 468 for information on Hogarth.)

Activity. Invite students to describe everyday scenes of the times depicted in Hogarth's artwork. Elicit suggestions on what the people holding the lantern might tell their family when they finally make it home through the hazardous streets. Ask students what actions reform-minded Londoners may have advocated after seeing this picture.

Charles and his brother James patronized companies of actors. Boys and men no longer acted the female roles. The new theater had real actresses, like the famous Nell Gwyn, and the new plays emphasized the sexual relations of men and women in very unsentimental and unromantic ways. The great, witty comedies produced during this period (such as William Wycherly's *The Country Wife* and William Congreve's *The Way of the World*) reflected the life of the rich and leisured people of that time—the Frenchified, pleasure-loving upper classes—and their servants and hangers-on. In addition to dramatists, a large number of prose and verse Ⓐ writers, many of them Dissenters, did not cater to the tastes of sophisticated people but wrote solely for ordinary readers.

Upon his return from France, Charles II reopened the London theaters. For the first time, female actors acted in the witty, urbane comedies written by Restoration dramatists.

A CLOSER LOOK

. . . AND LIFE AMONG THE "HAVE-NOTS"

For the poor, life is always hard, but during the Restoration and the eighteenth century, the poor lived in deplorable conditions, without the aid of doctors or police, and beyond the reach of education, religion, and charity. As if that were Ⓑ not enough, the poor also lived under the threat of debtors' prisons where torture was common.

Overcrowding in London's tenements and workhouses reached an all-time high during the period. Entire families lived together in one-room garrets or cellars infested with rats, lice, snails, and bedbugs. Unhealthy conditions worsened with the institution of a window tax in 1696. In order to avoid the tax, many blocked up their windows, creating stagnant air and cutting off light. Space and air seemed luxuries that only the rich could afford. Adding to the filth and discomfort, household garbage and human waste were thrown out into the streets. Butcher shops and slaughterhouses matter-of-factly tossed bloody remnants into open drains that intersected with streets and walkways.

Night (18th century) by William Hogarth.

Although medical science had begun to develop, superstition still marked the treatment of the sick in the early part of the eighteenth century. For example, smallpox was commonly treated with a black powder made by burning thirty to forty live toads. Bleeding served as a Ⓒ remedy for most ailments. As odd as it might seem today, the connection between dirt and disease hadn't been made by the medical profession. And since physicians practiced medicine almost

Connecting Across Texts

Connecting with *Pilgrim's Progress*

Although England had rejected Puritanism as a form of government, the general public loved John Bunyan's *Pilgrim's Progress,* an allegory about a Christian Pilgrim traveling from the City of Destruction through the Slough of Despond and Doubting Castle to the Heavenly City. The work was praised for the simplicity of its language and the childlike earnestness of its message. J. R. Greene writes, "in its sunny kindliness, unbroken by one bitter word, 'Pilgrim's Progress' is among the noblest of English poems."

The Age of Satire: Attacks on Immorality and Bad Taste

Today, Alexander Pope and Jonathan Swift are regarded as the most accomplished literary artists of the early eighteenth century. And though their era became known as the "age of Pope," both men had a profound influence on succeeding writers. During their own lifetimes, however, Pope and Swift were frequently out of harmony with the values of the age, and both often criticized it severely.

Although Pope addressed his works exclusively to the educated and leisured classes, he also attacked the members of these classes for their immorality and their bad taste, two failings that were usually associated in Pope's mind. Pope loved order, discipline, and craftsmanship; both he and Swift were appalled by the squalor and shoddiness—in art, manners, and morals—that underlay the polished surfaces of Augustan life. This violent and filthy underside of eighteenth-century life is illustrated in the

exclusively with the upper classes, they knew little of the ailments of the poor. Personal hygiene, or the lack of it, certainly contributed to the general state of health. One observer described a pauper woman's petticoats as "standing alone with dirt."

During the first part of the eighteenth century, the overall death rate surpassed the birthrate. In the worst years, more than 74 percent of London's children died before the age of five. Many of those children who did survive were forced to work for a living as soon as physically able, and sometimes sooner. Often, they suffered abuse by their guardians, supervisors, or employers. **D**

It's no wonder that many sought comfort and warmth in inexpensive alcohol. Starting in 1720 and for the next thirty years, cheap gin was readily available in the capital. The poor were especially susceptible to the disastrous effects of gin—high crime and death rates throughout most of the century. In fact, during a two-year period, 12,000 people out of London's population of 800,000 were convicted of illegally selling gin. Not until the Act of 1751, when alcohol was highly taxed, did the death rate fall dramatically. **E**

Eventually, improvements in agriculture created a demand for manure, and a use for street filth was found. That, coupled with the Paving Acts of 1762, did much to clean up London's streets. In 1769, a dispensary movement provided free advice and medicine for the underprivileged. Only then was the belief dispelled that the London poor owed their illnesses to vice and foolishness.

The Old Fleet Prison (closed 1844) by an unknown artist.

D Exploring the Historical Period

London

Historian Peter Gay writes this about London in *Age of Enlightenment*: "Although glittering mansions were rising to house urbanized aristocrats and merchants, London remained a city of dirt, disease, and crime. Along the dimly lit streets footpads and pickpockets flourished. Over the rooftops hung a thick haze darkened by coal fumes. Bad air was not the only peril; smallpox alone killed 1 in 13 and in 1740 London burials outnumbered baptisms 2 to 1."

E Exploring the Historical Period

Gin Mania and Other Social Problems

Historian R. K. Webb notes in *Modern England* that "drunkenness was endemic as a means of escape from squalor and frustration and in the early eighteenth century it grew worse, as some little surplus accrued to the poor in good times and found its way into purchasing the oblivion of gin, made cheaper by newly lowered duties and by the efficiency of the burgeoning distilling industry. The Gin Mania of the thirties and forties was a cultural fact of the first order and a factor of no mean importance in keeping down the increase in population. Gambling was another outlet . . ."

Taking a Second Look

Review: Analyzing Word Parts

Remind students that, in addition to using context clues, they can analyze word parts to determine the meanings of unfamiliar words. The word parts that make up a word can include a root, a prefix, and a suffix. A **root** is the base that contains the core of the word's meaning. A **prefix** is a word part placed before the root that combines with the root. The **suffix** is a word part that comes after the root.

Activity

Each of the following words appears on this page. Ask students to use a dictionary to determine the roots, prefixes, and suffixes of each word. Ask them to explain how understanding the structure of each word contributes to their understanding of its meaning.

1. influence [*in* (in) + *fluere* (to flow) + *ence* (act, condition, fact)]
2. succeeding [*sub* (under, after) + *cedere* (to go) + *ing* (act or process of)]
3. immorality [*im* (not) + *moralis* (moral) + *ity* (state of)]
4. contributed [*con* (with, together) + *tribute* (pay) + *ed* (past tense)]
5. surpassed [*sur* (over, beyond) + *passer* (pass) + *ed* (past tense)]
6. susceptible [*sus* (under) + *capere* (to take) + *ible* (capable of)]
7. dispensary [*dis* (out) + *pendere* (to weigh) + *ary* (a place for)]

Ⓐ Literary Connections

New Readers, New Tastes

? The number of people who could read was increasing during this age. As new readers emerged, however, they came from lower levels of society, and their education and tastes differed from those of readers a century ago. A new demand emerged for political and domestic gossip. How does Sheridan satirize this human and enduring taste for the lurid and sensational? [The speaker pretends never to look at the papers but obviously reads enough to know what's in them.]

Ⓑ Literary Connections

The New Journalists

Journals of this period included Daniel Defoe's *Review*, Joseph Addison and Richard Steele's *The Tatler,* and Addison's *The Spectator,* which he published with some help from Steele and also occasional help from other literary lights such as Jonathan Swift. The most famous of these was *The Spectator*, though it was extremely short-lived. Published between 1711 and 1712, *The Spectator* was briefly revived in 1714. Its fine essays, which provided lessons in learning and life, continue to endure. For more on Defoe, Addison, and Steele, see pp. 556–569.

RESPONDING TO THE ART

(See p. 468 for information on Hogarth.)

Activity. Ask students to examine each face in the audience and guess which vice Hogarth is satirizing.

The Laughing Audience (1733) by William Hogarth.

> It is an age, indeed, which is only fit for satire, and the sharpest I have shall never be wanting to lance its villainies. . . .
>
> —John Dryden, *from* Dedication to his *Life of Plutarch,* 1683

paintings and engravings of William Hogarth (1697–1764). Swift shared many of Pope's attitudes and ideals, and in his exposure of the mean and sordid in human behavior, Swift's works resemble Hogarth's art. Neither Swift nor Pope felt smug or satisfied with the world, as many English people did. Both writers deplored the corrupt politics of the time and the growing commercialism and materialism of the English people.

Pope and Swift both used satire to expose the moral corruption and crass commercialism of eighteenth-century England.

Journalism: A New Profession

In contrast with Swift and Pope and their aristocratic values, a writer named Daniel Defoe (1660–1731) stood for values that we think of as being middle class: thrift, prudence, industry, and respectability. Defoe had no interest in polished manners and social poise. Swift and Pope looked down their noses at him. "Defoe has written a vast many things," Pope once said, "and none bad, though none excellent."

> Ⓐ The newspapers! Sir, they are the most villainous—licentious—abominable—infernal—Not that I ever read them—no—I make it a rule never to look into a newspaper.
>
> —Richard Sheridan, *from The Critic*

Ⓑ Defoe, like the essayists Joseph Addison and Sir Richard Steele, followed a new profession: journalism. Eighteenth-century journalists did not merely describe contemporary political and social matters; they also saw themselves as reformers of public manners and morals. Journalists today—using both print and video—still see themselves in reformer roles.

As the middle class grew, journalists—and the reforms they advocated—became increasingly important.

Public Poetry: Conceived in Wit

Today when we think of great poetry, we think of great lyrics: the sonnets of Shakespeare, Keats, and Wordsworth, the religious poems of Donne and Eliot, the private poems of Emily Dickinson, and the lyrics

of such twentieth-century poets as William Butler Yeats, Robert Frost, and Elizabeth Bishop. These poets reveal in their poems their innermost thoughts and feelings, their honest and original responses to life. "Genuine poetry," said Matthew Arnold, a nineteenth-century poet and critic, "is conceived and composed in the soul."

Later critics like Matthew Arnold put down the poetry of people such as Alexander Pope because, he said, it was conceived and composed in their "wits"—that is, in their minds, not their souls. But these so-called Augustan poets did not define poetry in Arnold's way and so should not be judged by his standards. They had no desire to expose their souls; they thought of poetry as having a public rather than a private function.

Augustan poets would write not merely a poem, but a particular kind of poem. They would decide in advance the kind of poem, much as a carpenter decides on the kind of chair to make. The best Augustan poems are like things artfully made for a particular purpose, usually a public purpose. Many of the popular kinds of poetry were inherited from classical antiquity.

If, for instance, a grand person such as a general or a titled lady died, the poets would celebrate that dead person in **elegies,** the appropriate kind of poem for the occasion. Augustan elegies did not tell the truth about a dead person, even if the truth could be determined; rather, they said the very best things that the poet could think of saying.

At the opposite extreme, a poet might decide that a certain type of behavior, or even a certain conspicuous person, should be exposed to public ridicule. The poet would then write a **satire,** a kind of writing that does not make a just and balanced judgment of people and their behavior but rather says the worst things about them that the poet can think of saying.

Mr. and Mrs. William Chase (18th century) by Joseph Wright of Derby.
Agnew & Sons, London.

Responding to the Art

Joseph Wright of Derby (1734–1797) began his career as a portraitist, but became known for experimenting with unusual lighting effects. His early portraits noted the play of light over a subject's details—a sleeve or a sword hilt, for example. He later produced a series of paintings that explored the technique of *chiaroscuro,* dramatic contrasts of light and shadow. His paintings were known as "candlelight" pictures because many times they restricted light to a single source, often a candle.

Activity. Ask students what they learn about the people shown in this painting and how they learn it. Have them note the bird and the musical instrument and speculate whether the painter or the Chases chose to include them and why. Ask students what items they would want included in their own portraits.

C Literary Connections

Popular Taste

Like journalists of the day, writers like Pope and Swift aimed at reforming and educating their readers. Pope in particular, however, was much too formal and classical in his style to draw a wide readership. These readers, instead, flocked to the novel.

Professional Notes

Critical Comment: Wit

Wit in the Augustan Age was by no means commonplace: Pope was not only its most notable practitioner but often the *only* name associated with this literary phenomenon. Defining wit, as employed by Pope, has challenged critics ever since. Pope himself called it "invention" in his Preface to the *Iliad*. But that's not the only meaning he gave it: He used the word forty-six times in his *Essay on Criticism*, and the various contexts ascribe to it a whole range of meanings. Critic William K. Wimsatt Jr., takes this stab at a definition: "Wit in its favorable connotation is a kind of mental alertness to resemblances . . . and also a kind of verbal smartness, a meaning compressed and pointed in a juncture of words . . . Wit is the quality of Pope's poetry." For more on wit, see pp. 533–534.

Ⓐ Literary Connections

The Ode

The classical model for the ode comes from the Greek poet Pindar (c. 522–438 B.C.), whose poems celebrated victors of the ancient Olympic games.

Ⓑ Literary Connections

The Novel

One might say a novel is anything that is long and fictional. Its earliest ancestors are the epic of ancient times and the romance of the Middle Ages: Both are long tales of highly fictionalized (if not totally imaginative) adventures. Over time and across cultures, other kinds of long stories developed, including the picaresque story, in which the many adventures of some happy rascal are chronicled and, usually, satirized. Yet none of these forms had either the plot structure (problem, rising action, climax, and resolution) or the kind of character development associated with the novel today.

Ⓐ Another important kind of poem was the **ode**—an ambitious, often pompous poetic utterance expressing a public emotion, like the jubilation felt after a great naval victory.

Regardless of its kind, every poem had to be carefully and artificially constructed; every poem had to be dressed in exact meter and rhyme. Poems were not to sound like spontaneous and impromptu utterances, just as people were not to appear in public except in fancy dress. Those who could afford it adorned themselves with vast wigs, ribboned and jeweled clothing, and red shoes with high heels. People's movements were dignified and stately in public. Nothing was what we would today call natural—neither dress nor manners nor poetry.

Poetry of the period was not private, intimate, or spontaneous; rather, it was highly artificial and carefully crafted for public occasions.

Ⓑ The First English Novels

By the mid-eighteenth century, people were writing—and others, including women, were eagerly buying (or borrowing)—long fictional narratives called **novels** ("something new"). These novels, which were a development of the middle class, were often broad and comical—the adventures, for example, of a handsome ne'er-do-well or lower-class beauty, frequently recounted in endless episodes or through a series of letters. Authorities disagree as to whether *Robinson Crusoe* and Defoe's other fictional narratives are true novels, but many agree that the novel began either with Defoe or with the writers of the next generation.

Robinson Crusoe and Friday leaving the island. Illustration for Daniel Defoe's *Robinson Crusoe.*

Making the Connections

Cross-Cultural Connections: The First (?) Novel

The first novel in world literature is generally thought to be *The Tale of Genji,* written about A.D. 1000 by Murasaki Shikibu, a lady-in-waiting to the Japanese empress Akito. A vast chronicle of court life, the work had enormous impact on later literature and is called the greatest single work in Japanese literature. Sometimes called the first English novel, sometimes a "proto-novel," Lady Aphra Behn's *Oroonoko, or the History of the Royal Slave* (1688) combines fiction, history, and travelogue into a realistic account of the British slave trade with South American colonies. *Robinson Crusoe* (1719–20) gets the nod from some because it does have a plot—the story of the courage and ingenuity of a castaway and his Man Friday—but that plot is more a sequence of events than something which influences character. Samuel Richardson's *Pamela* (1740–42) has definite character development. *Pamela* is an epistolary novel in two parts, *Aggressive Chastity* and *Provocative Prudence.* In a series of letters to her parents, young Pamela describes going into service with a wealthy woman whose son pursues her with base intentions. Her resistance is rewarded: He marries her and is reformed.

Tom Jones Refused Admittance by the Nobleman's Porter (18th century) by Thomas Rowlandson. Illustration for Henry Fielding's *Tom Jones*.

The novels of one of the most prominent eighteenth-century novelists, Henry Fielding (1707–1754), are literally crammed with rough and rowdy incidents, and though Fielding does manage to make his characters seem good, they are never soft or sentimental. Fielding's rollicking novel *Tom Jones* has even been made into an Oscar-winning movie, proof that his high-spirited characters are still fresh and funny today. Samuel Richardson (1689–1761) was perhaps the first novelist to explore in great detail the emotional life of his characters, especially his heroines (in *Pamela* and *Clarissa*). The novels of Laurence Sterne (1713–1768) are experimental and whimsical—and still unique despite the efforts of many imitators to copy them. All these novels tell us something of what life at this time was like. They also help us understand the humor and disappointments of human experience in all ages.

Novels, so named because they were "new," became popular during the mid-eighteenth century. Women were among the most eager readers.

The Commanding Figure of Johnson

Along with all the other labels given to parts of this long period in English history, some people refer to the last part of the eighteenth century as the "age of Johnson." Even today, Samuel Johnson remains a commanding figure who speaks with authority about many of the things that matter to men and women. Johnson's views of humanity were conservative and traditional. He criticized the popular belief in progress (the belief that things are getting better and better) and the assumption that men

C Literary Connections

Tom Jones

Tom Jones (1749), a masterpiece of British literature, chronicles the life of a foundling, Tom, raised with a squire's son who is always trying to get Tom into trouble. When the two become rivals for the attentions of the daughter of a neighboring squire, Tom is banished and finds himself in a series of picaresque adventures, some bawdy. Lord Byron called Tom "an accomplished blackguard."

D Literary Connections

The Epistolary Novel

Richardson's works illustrate the genre of the epistolary novel, a story composed as a collection of serialized letters. Letters provide an intimate, immediate account of a character's emotions and activities; this is what Fielding ruthlessly mocks in his fictional parodies of Richardson's works, *Shamela* and *Joseph Andrews*.

E Literary Connections

Tristram Shandy

Laurence Sterne's major work is *Tristram Shandy* (1759–1767), a novel in multiple volumes that ostensibly chronicles Tristram's life from conception to adulthood, but never gets beyond age two or three. Most of the prose consists of reflections on a multitude of topics and about a number of people in Tristram's life. According to Sterne, his one rule was to be spontaneous; the result is an eccentric work, sprinkled with one-sentence chapters, unfinished sentences, and a generous use of dots, dashes, and asterisks.

F Humanities Connections

The Age of Johnson

The phrases "age of Johnson" or "age of sensibility" are used to describe the transitional period in which aesthetic tastes turned away from the wit and technical brilliance of Neoclassicism. The age of Romanticism would usher in an interest in the Middle Ages, a love of gothic horror, and a delight in primitive art and architecture antithetical to Augustan ideals.

Ⓐ Exploring the Historical Period

Luddites

Because the Industrial Revolution began in Great Britain, its people were the first to experience the disruptive changes of urbanization and environmental pollution. Workers whose jobs were eliminated by industrial improvements often rioted and wrecked the equipment in protest. It was claimed that in 1779, a man named Ned Lud wrecked two frames belonging to his Leicestershire employer. Workers who followed in his footsteps were known as Luddites.

Quickwrite

Help students to identify examples of major cultural changes they have witnessed. Then ask them to construct time lines of their own lives. Have students place events on the time line from the subject areas mentioned in this essay (religion, science, fashion, art, literature, theater, music, architecture, and politics) as well as other areas they feel are culturally important or important to them as individuals. Encourage students to incorporate visual as well as verbal entries. For example, they might choose to use photographs or drawings to show the changes they have observed. They might also compile an auditory time line to exemplify changing musical or spoken-language trends, or an audiovisual time line revealing changes in television programming (for instance, examples of children's educational programs over time). Students may enjoy sharing their results with the class.

and women are naturally good (that is, the notion that if society is reformed, people will automatically do what is right).

> Johnson's conversation was by much too strong for a person accustomed to obsequiousness and flattery; it was *mustard in a young child's mouth*!
>
> —Hester Lynch Thrale Piozzi, Johnson's friend

The commanding figure at the end of the eighteenth century was Dr. Samuel Johnson, a man of conservative and traditional beliefs. He questioned the optimistic assumption that the future would be better than the past.

Searching for a Simpler Life

Ⓐ By the time of Johnson's death in 1784, the world was changing in disturbing and profound ways. The Industrial Revolution was turning English cities and towns into filthy, smoky slums. Across the English Channel, the French were about to murder a king and set their whole society on a different political course. The eighteenth century was closing, and—just as at the end of the twentieth century, people sensed that a new era was about to begin—people in England knew that the age of elegance, taste, philosophy, and reason was over.

As a reflection of all this change, writers were developing new interests. Appalled at the industrial blight, they were turning to external nature and writing about the effect of the natural landscape on the human psyche. Disgusted with the excessive focus on the upper classes and "good taste," they were looking back at the past and searching out the simple poems and songs composed by nameless, uneducated folk poets. They were even becoming interested in the literary possibilities of the humble life and were trying to enter into the consciousness of the poor and simple. Nothing could be less Augustan than these tendencies. In short, a new literary age was already beginning during the lifetime of the last great representative of the older age.

At the end of the century, as industrialization mushroomed, writers returned to nature and folk themes for inspiration.

Quickwrite

During the eighteenth century, there was a great shift in the way most people thought about the world. Natural phenomena were more and more being explained by the new method of rational, scientific observation. The Renaissance love of the pastoral was abandoned, in favor of eighteenth-century tastes in fashion and art that ran to the artificial and highly formal. What are the prevailing philosophies and tastes in your world? What changes in people's thinking—about religion, science, fashion, art, politics, the environment, or anything else—have you seen during your lifetime?

(Opposite) *"Well-a-day! Is this my son Tom!"* (detail) (18th century) by Samuel Hieronymous Grimm.

British Library, London.

Assessing Learning

Check Test: True-False

1. There was a tendency in this age to model writing on the works of Latin writers. [True]
2. English prose lost some of its tendency to fanciness and decoration. [True]
3. Most people rejected Christianity and turned to Deism and other Enlightenment ideas. [False]
4. Catholics and all Protestants, except Anglicans, met with tolerance. [False]
5. The new journalists of this period saw themselves as reformers as well as writers. [True]

Collection 6

The Sting of Satire

Theme

A World of Rascals *When society fails to live up to its values, writers turn to satire. Using the tools of exaggeration, irony, and ridicule, satirists show us what is wrong with our world and what we should do to correct it.*

Reading the Anthology

Reaching Struggling Readers

The *Reading Skills and Strategies: Reaching Struggling Readers* binder provides materials coordinated with the Pupil's Edition (see the Collection Planner, p. T484B) to help students who have difficulty reading and comprehending text, or students who are reluctant readers. The binder for twelfth grade is organized around ten individual skill areas and offers the following options:

- **MiniRead** MiniReads are short, easy texts that give students a chance to practice a particular skill and strategy before reading selections in the Pupil's Edition. Each MiniRead Skill Lesson can be taught independently or used in conjunction with a Selection Skill Lesson.
- **Selection Skill Lessons** Selection Skill Lessons allow students to apply skills introduced in the MiniReads. Each Selection Skill Lesson provides reading instruction and practice specific to a particular piece of literature in the Pupil's Edition.

Reading Beyond the Anthology

Read On At the end of the Restoration and Eighteenth Century collections, the grade twelve book includes a Read On, an annotated bibliography of books suitable for extended reading. To preview the Read On for this period, please turn to p. T608.

HRW Library The *HRW Library* offers novels, plays, and short-story collections for extended reading. Each book in the Library includes a major work and thematically or topically related Connections. Each book in the *HRW Library* is also accompanied by a Study Guide that provides teaching suggestions and worksheets. The two titles shown here will work well to extend the theme of Collection 6.

THE IMPORTANCE OF BEING EARNEST
Oscar Wilde

Can a young man found in a handbag in Victoria Station grow up to marry a member of the aristocracy? Love does conquer all in Wilde's play, a witty satire of Victorian pretensions.

PRIDE AND PREJUDICE
Jane Austen

Can a middle class girl find love with a handsome aristocrat, particularly one who is wealthy and proud? Jane Austen uses her hero and heroine to present a subtle but fierce satire of English society.

Collection 6 The Sting of Satire

Resources for this Collection

Note: All resources for this collection are available for preview on the *One-Stop Planner CD-ROM I with Test Generator.* All worksheets and blackline masters may be printed from the CD-ROM.

Internet Resources
go.hrw.com LE0 12-6

Selection or Feature	Reading and Literary Skills	Vocabulary, Language, and Grammar
from **Gulliver's Travels** Jonathan Swift • *from* **Part 1: A Voyage to Lilliput** (p. 487) **Critical Comment: Under the Guise of Lilliput** (p. 495) • *from* **Part 2: A Voyage to Brobdingnag** (p. 497) **Elements of Literature: Satire** (p. 500) **A Modest Proposal** (p. 502) Jonathan Swift **Connections: Top of the Food Chain** (p. 509) T. Coraghessan Boyle **Spotlight On: Women Writers of the Restoration and the Eighteenth Century** (p. 516) C. F. Main	• *Reading Skills and Strategies: Reaching Struggling Readers* • MiniRead Skill Lesson, p. 33 • Selection Skill Lesson, p. 40 • *Graphic Organizers for Active Reading,* Worksheet pp. 37, 38 • *Literary Elements:* Transparency 12 Worksheet p. 37	• *Words to Own,* Worksheet pp. 11, 12, 13 • *Grammar and Language Links:* Participles and Participial Phrases, Worksheet p. 27 • *Language Workshop CD-ROM,* Verbals and Verbal Phrases • *Daily Oral Grammar,* Transparency 14
Heroic Couplets (p. 521) *from* **An Essay on Man** (p. 524) **Elements of Literature: Poetic Form and Meter** (p. 525) *from* **The Rape of the Lock** • **Canto III** (p. 526) • **Canto V** (p. 530) Alexander Pope **Elements of Literature: Wit** (p. 533)	• *Graphic Organizers for Active Reading,* Worksheet pp. 39, 40, 41 • *Literary Elements:* Transparency 13 Worksheet p. 40	• *Grammar and Language Links:* Infinitives and Infinitive Phrases, Worksheet p. 29 • *Language Workshop CD-ROM,* Verbals and Verbal Phrases • *Daily Oral Grammar,* Transparencies 15, 16
World Literature: France *from* **Candide** (p. 537) Voltaire *translated by* Richard Aldington	• *Literary Elements:* Transparency 14 Worksheet p. 43	The World Literature feature offers students the opportunity to explore thematically linked literature from different world cultures. Structured activities called Finding Common Ground are provided in the Pupil's Edition to guide students' explorations of these thematic connections between British and other world literature.

Other Resources for this Collection

- *Cross-Curricular Activities,* p. 6
- *Portfolio Management System,* Introduction to Portfolio Assessment, p. 1
- *Test Generator,* Collection Test
- *Formal Assessment* Literary Period Introduction Test, p. 87

Writing	Listening and Speaking Viewing and Representing	Assessment
• *Portfolio Management System,* Rubrics for Choices, p. 135	• *Audio CD Library,* Disc 7, Tracks 2, 3, 4 • *Viewing and Representing:* Fine Art Transparency 7 Worksheet p. 28 • *Portfolio Management System,* Rubrics for Choices, p. 135	• *Formal Assessment,* Selection Tests, pp. 89, 91, 93 • *Test Generator (One-Stop Planner CD-ROM)* • *Preparation for College Admission Exams,* p. 21
• *Portfolio Management System,* Rubrics for Choices, p. 137	• *Audio CD Library,* Disc 8, Tracks 2, 3, 4, 5 • *Viewing and Representing:* Fine Art Transparency 8 Worksheet p. 32 • *Portfolio Management System,* Rubrics for Choices, p. 137	• *Formal Assessment,* Selection Tests, pp. 95, 97 • *Test Generator (One-Stop Planner CD-ROM)*
	• *Audio CD Library,* Disc 8, Track 6	• *Preparation for College Admission Exams,* p. 23

Transparency CD-ROM Video Audio CD

Collection 6 The Sting of Satire

Skills Focus

Selection or Feature	Reading Skills and Strategies	Elements of Literature and Language	Writing	Listening and Speaking	Viewing and Representing
from **Gulliver's Travels** • *from* **Part 1: A Voyage to Lilliput** (p. 487) • *from* **Part 2: A Voyage to Brobdingnag** (p. 497) **A Modest Proposal** (p. 502) Jonathan Swift	Identify a Writer's Stance, pp. 487, 496 Recognize Persuasive Techniques, pp. 502, 513 • Logical • Emotional • Ethical Interpret Connotations, p. 513	Tone, pp. 487, 496, 500 Irony, pp. 487, 496, 500–501, 513–514 • Verbal • Situational • Dramatic Satire, pp. 495–496, 500–502, 513 Allegory, p. 495 Parody, p. 496 Symbol, p. 496 Characterization, p. 500 Exaggeration/Hyperbole, p. 500 Understatement, p. 501 Sarcasm, p. 501 Author's Purpose, p. 513 Diction, p. 513 Tall Tale, p. 514 Stance, p. 514	Choose a Topic Suitable for Persuasive Writing, p. 514 Write a First-Person Narrative, p. 514 Write an American Tall Tale Based on *Gulliver's Travels,* p. 514 Summarize and Compare the Work of Two Satirists, p. 514 Write a Contemporary Version of *A Modest Proposal,* p. 514 Write an Alternative Version of *A Modest Proposal* from a Different Point of View, p. 514	Research, Write, and Present an Oral Report on the Works of William Hogarth, p. 514	Identify Satiric Elements in the Works of William Hogarth, p. 514
Reading Skills and Strategies: Distinguishing Shades of Meaning (p. 515)	Distinguish Shades of Meaning, p. 515 • Denotation • Connotation • Synonym • Antonym • Thesaurus • Context				Use a Graphic Organizer, p. 515
Heroic Couplets (p. 521) *from* **An Essay on Man** (p. 524) *from* **The Rape of the Lock** • **Canto III** (p. 526) • **Canto V** (p. 530) Alexander Pope	Responding to the Text, pp. 521, 523, 535 Paraphrase, pp. 523, 525 Summarize, pp. 525, 533, 535 Compare, p. 525 Using Reference Materials, p. 526 Context, p. 526 Glosses, p. 526 Story Map, p. 533 Main Events, p. 533 Chronological Order, p. 533 Reflecting on Reading Process, p. 535	Pastoral, p. 520 Antithesis, pp. 521, 523, 525 Heroic Couplet, pp. 522, 525 Iambic Pentameter, p. 522 Triplet, pp. 522, 525 Closed Couplet, p. 522 Sentence, p. 525 Epigram, p. 525 Rhyme, p. 525 Assonance, p. 525 Alliteration, p. 525 Allusion, p. 526 Mock Epic, p. 526 Cantos, p. 527 Epic Simile, p. 533 Satire, p. 533 Irony, p. 533 Wit, p. 533	Identify Contemporary Topics for Persuasive Writing, p. 535 Write an Essay Identifying the Targets of Pope's Satire and Describing His Use of Satiric Devices, p. 535 Write an Essay Comparing *The Rape of the Lock* to a True Epic, p. 535 Write a Contemporary Mock Epic, p. 535 Write a Mock-Heroic Description of a Common Activity, p. 535 Write an Essay Describing the Process of Reading Pope's Works, p. 535	Prepare and Present an Oral Reading, p. 525 Prepare a Rebuttal for One of Pope's Sayings About Human Nature, p. 535	Identify the Attributes of Baroque Art, p. 532
World Literature: France *from* **Candide** (p. 537) Voltaire *translated by* Richard Aldington	Connecting Text to Current Events, pp. 537, 540	Parody, p. 540	The World Literature feature offers students the opportunity to explore thematically linked literature from different world cultures. Structured activities called Finding Common Ground are provided in the Pupil's Edition to guide students' explorations of these thematic connections between British and other world literature.		

Collection 6

THE STING OF SATIRE

Swift
Pope
Voltaire

Satire is a sort of glass, wherein beholders do generally discover everybody's face but their own.

—Jonathan Swift,
Preface to *The Battle of the Books*

Writing Focus: An Essay on a Controversial Issue

The following **Work in Progress** assignments build to a culminating **Writer's Workshop** at the end of Collection 7.

• A Modest Proposal	Choose a topic (p. 514)
• The Rape of the Lock	Brainstorm issues (p. 535)

Writer's Workshop: Persuasive Writing / An Essay on a Controversial Issue (p. 612)

OBJECTIVES

1. Read literature of the Restoration and the eighteenth century on the theme of "The Sting of Satire"
2. Interpret literary elements with special emphasis on satire, poetic meter, and wit
3. Apply a variety of reading strategies to the literature including distinguishing shades of meaning, recognizing the writer's stance, and recognizing persuasive techniques
4. Respond to the literature in a variety of modes
5. Learn and use new words
6. Learn about the eighteenth-century emphasis on correcting and preserving the English language
7. Plan, draft, revise, proofread, and publish a persuasive essay

RESPONDING TO THE ART

Samuel Hieronymous Grimm (1733–1794) was known for his caricatures and for his illustration of William Shakespeare's work. Describing Grimm's technique, naturalist Gilbert White explained: "He first of all sketches his scrapes with a lead-pencil, then he pens them all over, as he calls it, with Indian ink, rubbing out the superfluous pencil strokes; then he gives a charming shading with a brush dipped in Indian ink; and last he throws a light tinge of watercolours over the whole." **Activity.** Ask students what is being caricatured, or exaggerated, here. Students might enjoy relating how fashions and fads of their own times have provoked similar comments from parents and other adults.

Responding to the Quotation

Ask students to paraphrase this quotation. [Possible answer: When you look in the mirror of satire, you see everyone but yourself.]

Objectives

1. Read and interpret the story
2. Identify and analyze irony
3. Identify and analyze satire
4. Identify writer's stance
5. Identify persuasive techniques
6. Express understanding through writing, art, or speaking
7. Understand new words

Skills

Literary
- Analyze satire
- Interpret irony

Reading
- Identify the writer's stance
- Identify persuasive techniques
- Interpret connotations
- Distinguish shades of meaning

Writing
- Collect ideas for a persuasive essay
- Write a first-person narrative
- Write a tall tale
- Compare satires
- Write a "modest proposal"
- Use a different point of view

Speaking/Listening
- Present research findings

Vocabulary
- Demonstrate understanding of new words

Viewing/Representing
- Analyze and interpret various works of fine art (ATE)

Planning

- **Block Schedule**
  Block Scheduling Lesson Plans with Pacing Guide
- **Traditional Schedule**
  Lesson Plans Including Strategies for English-Language Learners
- **One-Stop Planner**
  CD-ROM with Test Generator

Jonathan Swift

(1667–1745)

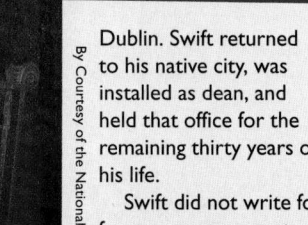

By Courtesy of the National Portrait Gallery, London.

Jonathan Swift (c. 1718) by Charles Jervas. Oil on canvas (48½″ × 38¼″).

Jonathan Swift is the principal prose writer of the early eighteenth century and England's greatest satirist. He was an Anglo-Irishman, a label applied to people who live in Ireland but who regard themselves as more English than Irish. Swift was born in Dublin of English parents, seven months after the death of his father, a lawyer. His mother returned to England when Swift was three years old, and the boy was looked after by his uncle Godwin.

Although Swift was poor, his prosperous uncle paid for his education. Hoping to advance himself, Swift went to England and became secretary to Sir William Temple, a distant relative—a writer, a wealthy country gentleman, and a statesman. The job gave Swift the opportunity to mingle with public figures, read, and look about for a more important and permanent position. Unfortunately, nothing came of Temple's patronage. After several years of disappointment, Swift took his life into his own hands, obtained a master's degree from Oxford University, and was ordained a priest in the Church of Ireland, a counterpart to the Church of England.

Swift seemed fated to live in Ireland, although he desperately wanted a career in England. Now, as a priest, he was assigned to remote parishes in the Irish countryside. To Swift, Ireland seemed a cultural desert, inhabited mainly by Roman Catholic natives and Scottish Presbyterian immigrants—people whom Swift neither admired nor respected. And so he escaped to England whenever possible. Swift hoped to be made an English bishop, but his political friends fell from power, and the only appointment he could obtain was back in Ireland, as the dean of St. Patrick's Cathedral in Dublin. Swift returned to his native city, was installed as dean, and held that office for the remaining thirty years of his life.

Swift did not write for fame or money; most of his books and pamphlets were published anonymously. Nor did he write simply to divert or entertain, though most of his works are marked by his powerful imagination and many of them are amusing. Swift's aim in writing was to improve human conduct, to make people more decent and humane. His first important book, *A Tale of a Tub* (1704), is a lively, outspoken exposure of "gross corruptions in religion and learning," to quote Swift's own words. It scandalized many respectable readers when they discovered that a clergyman had written it, because it seemed to treat sacred matters irreverently. *Gulliver's Travels* (1726) attacks many different varieties of human misbehavior, vice, and folly. Swift even became an Irish patriot in his pamphlets, defending the Irish against the oppressive policies of their English rulers. The most famous of his pamphlets is *A Modest Proposal* (1729). In a letter to Pope, Swift justified these pro-Irish writings: "What I do is owing to perfect rage and resentment, and the mortifying sight of slavery, folly, and baseness about me, among which I am forced to live."

As the years passed, Swift made fewer and fewer visits to London, though he continued to correspond with Alexander Pope and with many other friends. His last days were sad: He suffered from a disease of the inner ear which made him dizzy, deaf, and disoriented. He was buried in his cathedral in Dublin, where troops of tourists now pause every day of the year to read his epitaph, which ends: "Go, traveler, and imitate, if you can, one who strove with all his strength to champion liberty."

go.hrw.com
LEO 12-6

Resources: Print and Media

Reading
- *Reading Skills and Strategies*
  MiniRead Skill Lesson, p. 33
  Selection Skill Lesson, p. 40
- *Graphic Organizer for Active Reading,* pp. 37, 38
- *Words to Own,* pp. 11, 12, 13
- *Audio CD Library*
  Disc 7, Tracks 2, 3, 4

Elements of Literature
- *Literary Elements*
  Transparency 12
  Worksheet, p. 37

Writing and Language
- *Daily Oral Grammar*
  Transparency 14
- *Grammar and Language Links*
  Worksheet, p. 27
- *Language Workshop CD-ROM*

Viewing and Representing
- *Viewing and Representing*
  Fine Art Transparency 7
  Fine Art Worksheet, p. 28

Assessment
- *Formal Assessment,* pp. 89, 91, 93
- *Portfolio Management System,* p. 135
- *Preparation for College Admission Exams,* p. 21
- *Test Generator (One-Stop Planner CD-ROM)*

Internet
- *go.hrw.com (keyword: LEO 12-6)*

Before You Read

FROM GULLIVER'S TRAVELS

Make the Connection

Reforming the World

The way some people see it, the world stands in urgent and constant need of reform. Some would-be reformers write editorials or preach sermons. Others use a different weapon to stress the need for change: the stinging criticism of satire. What do you see in today's society that you think should be reformed?

Reading Skills and Strategies

Identifying the Writer's Stance

As you read Swift's story and essay, keep in mind that he is a reformer, a person who believes there is something seriously wrong with people and institutions as they are. As you read, take notes. Note the objects of his disapproval. Jot down words, phrases, and situations he uses to convey his feelings. Look for instances where he **overstates** or **underplays** details in order to make a point. After your reading, use your notes as you discuss how Swift's urge to reform affects the **tone** of his writing.

Elements of Literature

Irony

Swift, like all satirists, wants to make his readers recognize the gap between things as they are and things as they ought to be. To get his audience to feel this contrast, Swift constantly resorts to **irony** to sharpen the sting of his satire.

> **Irony** is a pointed contrast between reality and expectations. There are three types of irony: **Verbal irony** is a contrast between what is said and what is actually meant; **situational irony** is a contrast between what is expected to happen and what actually does happen; and **dramatic irony** is a contrast between what a character knows and what the reader or audience knows.
>
> *For more on Irony, see the Handbook of Literary Terms.*

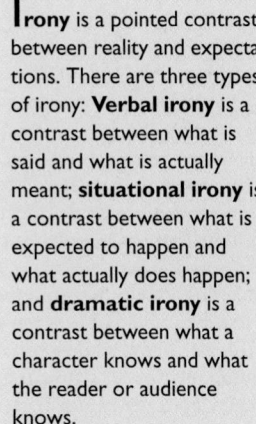

Lilliputians examining the man-mountain's possessions. Illustration from *Gulliver's Travels* (1726).

Summary

The first excerpt begins as Gulliver awakens from a deep sleep to find himself tied to the ground by a race of people less than six inches tall. These Lilliputians attack him when he first attempts to move but then give him food and drink when he pantomimes his desires. Over time, he wins over the Lilliputians and learns about their tiny world, which is beset with problems not unlike those in the England of Swift's day.

Preteaching Vocabulary

Words to Own

Ask students to work in pairs to find the meanings of each word and to use each in a sentence. Then ask them to work together to discuss and complete the following analogies.

1. drawing : sketched :: guess : [conjectured]
2. flattered : complimented :: claimed : [alleged]
3. issue : warning :: proclaim : [edict]
4. joyous : sad :: beneficial : [pernicious]
5. vague : ambiguous :: sticky : [viscous]
6. charming : alluring :: offensive : [odious]
7. elephant : huge :: mite : [diminutive]
8. fire : extinguish :: riot : [quelled]
9. defeat : lost :: victory : [prevailed]
10. foolish : wise :: scanty : [copious]

A Reading Skills and Strategies

Getting the Main Idea

? Whom has Swift chosen to narrate this story, and where has he placed this character? [Swift is using a traveler named Gulliver, who, at the moment, is lying on his back, tied down and "able to see nothing but the sky."] **Why did Swift choose to start the episode in this way?** [Possible answer: Gulliver has no idea what has happened to him; like the reader, he must figure out where he is and what his relationship is to the place where he has ended up.]

B Elements of Literature

Irony

? What is ironic about the fact that Gulliver's captors are armed? [Possible answers: Their tiny bows and arrows are fairly useless against such a huge enemy. Also, Gulliver seems harmless enough, yet the first impulse of his captors seems to be one of distrust and violence.]

C Elements of Literature

Satire

? Remind students that **satire** is criticism mixed with humor. **What is humorous so far?** [Possible answers: The presence of a huge Gulliver and impossibly tiny Lilliputians is ridiculous and laughable; so too is the way Gulliver is tied down and shot at. The made-up language is also silly.]

The full title that Swift gave his most famous book is *Travels into Several Remote Nations of the World. In Four Parts. By Lemuel Gulliver, First a Surgeon, and then a Captain of Several Ships.* Immediately upon publication, it was a sensational success. It seemed so convincing that some readers went about claiming that they had heard of, or even met, its author. But Gulliver is, of course, a figment of Swift's imagination.

The book seems to be a true account of actual adventures because Swift includes many realistic-sounding details and even maps of the places Gulliver visits. The first part, describing the visit to Lilliput, opens with an account of Gulliver's early life: his birth, parentage, and schooling. After studying medicine, Gulliver becomes a ship's doctor and embarks on a long voyage; when the ship breaks up in a storm, he manages to swim ashore and, exhausted, falls into a deep sleep. What could be more convincing?

from Gulliver's Travels

from Part 1: A Voyage to Lilliput

Jonathan Swift

I lay down on the grass, which was very short and soft, where I slept sounder than ever I remember to have done in my life, and, as I reckoned, above nine hours; for when I awaked, it was just daylight. I attempted to rise, but was not able to stir: For as I happened to lie on my back, I found my arms and legs were strongly fastened on (A) each side to the ground; and my hair, which was long and thick, tied down in the same manner. I likewise felt several slender ligatures[1] across my body, from my armpits to my thighs. I could only look upward; the sun began to grow hot, and the light offended my eyes. I heard a confused noise about me, but in the posture I lay, could see nothing except the sky.

In a little time I felt something alive moving on my left leg, which advancing gently forward over my breast, came almost up to my chin; when bending my eyes downward as much as I could, I perceived it to be a human creature not six inches high, with a bow and arrow in his hands, and a (B) quiver at his back. In the meantime, I felt at least forty more of the same kind (as I conjectured) following the first. (C) I was in the utmost astonishment, and roared so loud, that they all ran back in a fright; and some of them, as I was afterward told, were hurt with the falls they got by leaping from my sides upon the ground. However, they soon returned, and one of them, who ventured so far as to get a full sight of my face, lifting up his hands and eyes by way of admiration, cried out in a shrill, but distinct voice, *Hekinah degul*:[2] The others repeated the same words several times, but then I knew not what they meant. I lay all this while, as the reader may believe, in great uneasiness: At length, struggling to get loose, I had the fortune to break the strings, and wrench out the pegs that fastened my left arm to the ground; for, by lifting it up to my face, I discovered the methods they had taken to bind me, and at the same time with a violent pull, which gave me excessive pain, I a little loosened the strings that tied down my hair on the left side, so that I was just able to turn my head about two inches. But the creatures

1. **ligatures:** ties or bonds.

2. ***Hekinah degul:*** This and other examples of the Lilliputian (lil′ə·pyo͞o′shən) tongue are mainly nonsense words. Swift was very fond of puns, pig Latin, and other kinds of word games.

WORDS TO OWN

conjectured (kən·jek′chərd) *v.:* reasoned; guessed.

Reaching All Students

Struggling Readers

Identifying the Writer's Stance was introduced on p. 487. For a lesson directly tied to this selection that teaches students to identify writer's stance using a strategy called Think-Aloud, see the *Reading Skills and Strategies* binder:

- MiniRead Skill Lesson, p. 33
- Selection Skill Lesson, p. 40

English Language Learners

Students may benefit from translating Swift's highly visual language into a series of sketches or cartoon panels of the following scenes: armed Lilliputians moving cautiously over Gulliver; Lilliputians giving him food and drink; trusting Lilliputian boys and girls playing hide and seek in his hair. For additional strategies, see

- *Lesson Plans Including Strategies for English-Language Learners*

Advanced Learners

Invite students to read and report on the full novel or a summary of the novel. Students will find that in addition to Lilliput and Brobdingnag, Gulliver also visits Laputa, a flying island that is home to a race of foolish philosophers, and Houhynhynm land (pronounced "whinnimland"), home of wise, virtuous horses, and Yahoos, an inferior, human-like race.

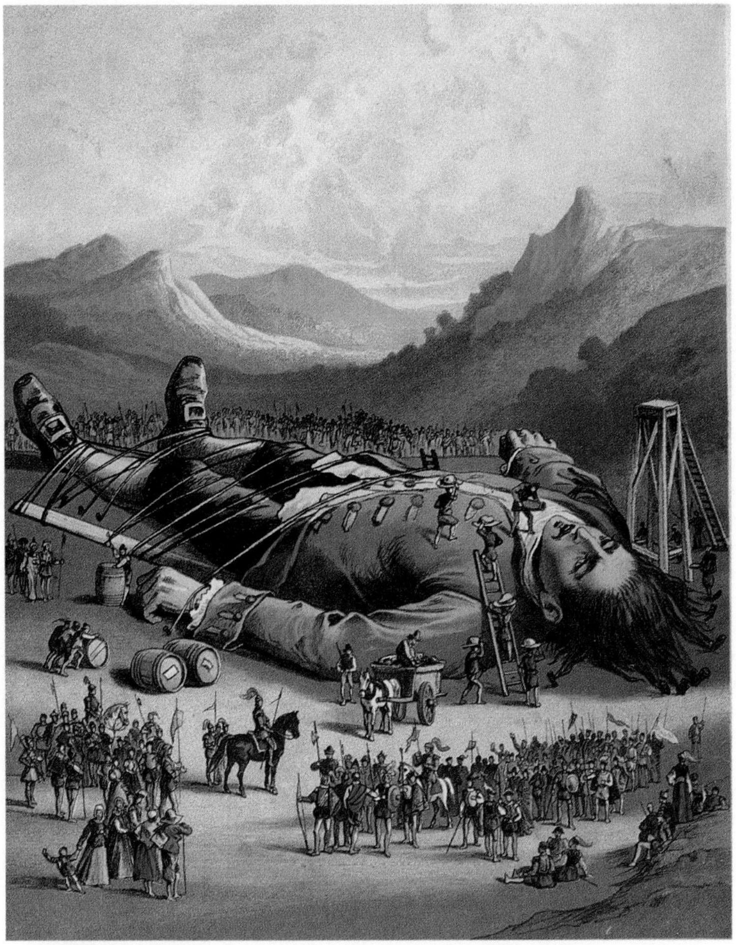

Gulliver awakens in Lilliput (c. 1880), illustration by an unknown artist.

ran off a second time, before I could seize them; whereupon there was a great shout in a very shrill accent, and after it ceased, I heard one of them cry aloud, *Tolgo phonac;* when in an instant I felt above an hundred arrows discharged on my left hand, which pricked me like so many needles; and besides, they shot another flight into the air, as we do bombs in Europe, whereof many, I suppose, fell on my body (though I felt them not), and some on my face, which I immediately covered with my left hand. When this shower of arrows was over, I fell a-groaning with grief and pain, and then striving again to get loose, they discharged another volley larger than the first, and some of them attempted with spears to stick me in the sides; but, by good luck, I had on me a buff jerkin,[3] which they could not pierce. I thought it the most prudent method to lie still, and my design was to continue so till night, when, my left hand being already loose, I could easily free myself: And as for the inhabitants, I had reason to believe I might be a match for the greatest armies they could bring against me, if they were all of the same size with him that I saw. But fortune disposed otherwise of me.

When the people observed I was quiet, they discharged no more arrows; but, by the noise increasing, I knew their numbers were greater; and about four yards from me, over against my right ear, I heard a knocking for above an hour, like that of people at work; when turning my head that way, as well as the pegs and strings would permit me, I saw a stage erected, about a foot and a half from the ground, capable of holding four of the inhabitants, with two or three ladders to mount it: From whence one of them, who seemed to be a person of quality, made me a long speech, whereof I understood not one syllable. But I should have mentioned, that before the principal person began his oration, he cried out three times, *Langro dehul san* (these words and the former were afterward repeated and explained to me). Whereupon

3. **buff jerkin:** short, closefitting leather jacket, often without sleeves.

D Elements of Literature
Satire

? Here Swift compares the flurry of random arrows to bombs. What is he satirizing by means of this comparison? [Possible answers: By comparing the Lilliputian arrows to bombs, he is mocking Europe's willingness to go to war over the slightest pretext and then to escalate that war for no apparent reason. He believes that countries generally overreact when threatened and then ignore the suffering of the defeated. Ironically, however, "war" does not really stop the violence.]

E Critical Thinking
Interpreting

? What details lead Gulliver to conclude that this character is the "principal person"? [Possible answers: He speaks from a stage and gives a long speech; the Lilliputians respond to his directions by cutting some of the strings; he is taller than his attendants; one attendant carries his train.] **What type of leader might Swift be spoofing?** [Possible answers: This leader could represent an absolute ruler or leader who relies on the trappings of power.] **Remind students to think of the target of Swift's satire at every opportunity.**

F Reading Skills and Strategies
Identifying the Writer's Stance

? What attitude might Swift have toward the "principal person"? [Possible answers: He seems to find the very idea of a principal person absurd. He seems to think this person should be satirized.]

Making the Connections

Cultural Connections: Nonverbal Communication

Lead a class discussion to identify the various nonverbal methods Gulliver uses to communicate with the Lilliputians and to interpret their messages. Speculate with students on how he might have ended up in trouble if he had used cues differently—and perhaps offensively—in Lilliput. Point out, for instance, that the A-OK sign, with the thumb and forefinger shaping a circle, has a different meaning depending on the culture in which it is used. A French person would interpret the gesture as meaning "worthless," or "no good"; a Japanese person would think it was a symbol for money; a Latin American would consider the gesture an insult.

Discuss with students what kinds of nonverbal communication and messages are fairly universal and which are culturally determined. To explore universal messages, ask three groups of students to make presentations on gestures, facial expressions, and nonverbal sounds. Each group should present several examples within their category, with the class interpreting them.

To explore cultural differences, ask a fourth group to research and report on nonverbal communication that varies across cultures.

Ⓐ Reading Skills and Strategies

Identifying the Writer's Stance

? What is the author's attitude toward the leader's or king's speech? How do you know? [Possible answers: Swift is criticizing or making fun of the speech, which seems to include a whole range of emotions and messages (and, therefore, probably says not much at all). It seems more important for the king or leader to act "every part of an orator" than to actually say something meaningful.]

Ⓑ Reading Skills and Strategies

Visualizing

Remind students to form pictures in their minds as they read this selection, which is full of visual detail. Ask them what they see as they read this passage. [Possible answer: Gulliver is using the gesture of touching his fingers to his lips to show that he wants food.] **Also remind students that Gulliver is still lying on his back; the illustration on this page shows Gulliver at a different moment in the story.**

Ⓒ Elements of Literature

Irony

? What is ironic about this situation? [Possible answers: Gulliver has been treated as an enemy, tied down, and shot at. But now that he is hungry, the Lilliputians are generously rushing to serve him.]

immediately about fifty of the inhabitants came and cut the strings that fastened the left side of my head, which gave me the liberty of turning it to the right, and of observing the person and gesture of him who was to speak. He appeared to be of a middle age, and taller than any of the other three who attended him, whereof one was a page who held up his train, and seemed to be somewhat longer than my middle finger; the other two stood one on each side to support him. He acted every part of an orator, and I could observe many periods of threatenings, and others of promises, pity, and kindness.

I answered in a few words, but in the most submissive manner, lifting up my left hand, and both my eyes to the sun, as calling him for a witness; and being almost famished with hunger, having not eaten a morsel for some hours before I left the ship. I found the demands of nature so strong upon me, that I could not forbear showing my impatience (perhaps against the strict rules of decency) by putting my finger frequently on my mouth, to signify that I wanted food. The *Hurgo*[4] (for so they call a great lord, as I afterward learnt) understood me very well. He descended from the stage, and commanded that several ladders should be applied to my sides, on which above an hundred of the inhabitants mounted and walked toward my mouth, laden with baskets full of meat,[5] which had been provided and sent thither by the King's orders, upon the first intelligence[6] he received of me. I observed there was the flesh[7] of several animals, but could not distinguish them by the taste. There were shoulders, legs, and loins, shaped like those of mutton, and very well dressed, but smaller than the wings of a lark. I ate them by two or three at a mouthful, and took three loaves at a time, about the bigness of musket bullets. They supplied me as fast as they could, showing a thousand marks of wonder and astonishment at my bulk and appetite.

I then made another sign that I wanted drink. They found by my eating, that a small quantity would not suffice me; and being a most ingenious

Reprinted by permission of Philomel Books from *Gulliver's Travels in Lilliput*, retold by Ann Keay Beneduce, illustrations ©1993 by Gennady Spirin.

Gulliver in Lilliput, illustration by Gennady Spirin.

4. ***Hurgo:*** This Lilliputian word is perhaps a partial anagram (a word formed by rearranging the letters of another word) of the English word *rogue.* It would be characteristic of Swift to call a "great lord" a rogue.
5. **meat:** archaic for "food."
6. **intelligence:** news.
7. **flesh:** meat.

Crossing the Curriculum

Geography/Art

Explain that detailed maps lend authenticity to Swift's original edition of *Gulliver's Travels.* If possible, bring in a facsimile of an original edition so students can look at the maps. Otherwise, invite students to draw their own maps of Lilliput, noting where various text events may occur.

Science

Throughout *Gulliver's Travels* Swift combines fantasy elements with the latest technological developments and scientific understandings of the era. In order to prove this point, have students go through the selection looking for scientific facts, principles, or technologies that play a part in the story. Students can then create a posterboard illustrating the scientific principle or technology that Swift describes.

people, they slung up with great dexterity one of their largest hogsheads,[8] then rolled it toward my hand, and beat out the top; I drank it off at a draft, which I might well do, for it hardly held half a pint, and tasted like a small wine of Burgundy, but much more delicious. They brought me a second hogshead, which I drank in the same manner, and made signs for more, but they had none to give me. When I had performed these wonders, they shouted for joy, and danced upon my breast, repeating several times as they did at first, *Hekinah degul.* They made me a sign that I should throw down the two hogsheads, but first warned the people below to stand out of the way, crying aloud, *Borach mivola,* and when they saw the vessels in the air, there was an universal shout of *Hekinah degul.* I confess I was often tempted, while they were passing backward and forward on my body, to seize forty or fifty of the first that came in my reach, and dash them against the ground. But the remembrance of what I had felt, which probably might not be the worst they could do, and the promise of honor I made them, for so I interpreted my submissive behavior, soon drove out those imaginations. Besides, I now considered myself as bound by the laws of hospitality to a people who had treated me with so much expense and magnificence. However, in my thoughts, I could not sufficiently wonder at the intrepidity of these diminutive mortals, who durst venture to mount and walk on my body, while one of my hands was at liberty, without trembling at the very sight of so prodigious a creature as I must appear to them.

After some time, when they observed that I made no more demands for meat, there appeared before me a person of high rank from his Imperial Majesty. His Excellency, having mounted on the small of my right leg, advanced forward up to my face, with about a dozen of his retinue. And producing his credentials under the Signet Royal,[9] which he applied close to my eyes, spoke about ten minutes, without any signs of anger, but with a kind of determinate resolution; often pointing forward, which, as I afterward found, was toward the capital city, about half a mile distant, whither it was agreed by his Majesty in council that I must be conveyed. I answered in few words, but to no purpose, and made a sign with my hand that was loose, putting it to the other (but over his Excellency's head for fear of hurting him or his train) and then to my own head and body, to signify that I desired my liberty. It appeared that he understood me well enough, for he shook his head by way of disapprobation, and held his hand in a posture to show that I must be carried as a prisoner. However, he made other signs to let me understand that I should have meat and drink enough, and very good treatment. Whereupon I once more thought of attempting to break my bonds; but again, when I felt the smart of their arrows, upon my face and hands, which were all in blisters, and many of the darts still sticking in them, and observing likewise that the number of my enemies increased, I gave tokens[10] to let them know that they might do with me what they pleased. Upon this, the *Hurgo* and his train withdrew, with much civility and cheerful countenances.

Soon after I heard a general shout, with frequent repetitions of the words, *Peplom selan,* and I felt great numbers of people on my left side relaxing the cords to such a degree, that I was able to turn upon my right, and to ease myself with making water; which I very plentifully did, to the great astonishment of the people, who conjecturing by my motions what I was going to do, immediately opened to the right and left on that side, to avoid the torrent which fell with such noise and violence from me. But before this, they had daubed my face and both my hands with a sort of ointment very pleasant to the smell, which in a few minutes removed all the smart of their arrows. These circumstances, added to the refreshment I had received by their victuals and drink, which were very nourishing, disposed me to sleep. I slept about eight hours, as I was afterward assured; and it was no wonder, for the physicians, by the Emperor's order, had mingled a sleeping potion in the hogshead of wine. . . .

8. **hogsheads** (hôgz′hedz′): barrels.
9. **Signet Royal:** royal seal; the seal used as a signature to mark documents as official.

10. **gave tokens:** signaled.

WORDS TO OWN
diminutive (də·min′yo͞o·tiv) *adj.:* very small.

D Struggling Readers

Finding Sequence of Events

Encourage students to list events in a sequence chain or other organizer. Suggest that students record only the most important events, such as "Gulliver awakens," "the Lilliputians give Gulliver wine to drink," and "Gulliver is carried to the capital city."

E Reading Skills and Strategies

Identifying the Writer's Stance

? Here Gulliver evidently experiences mixed emotions about how he should treat the Lilliputians: He imagines hurting them but restrains himself. Why do you think Swift includes these details? What point might he be making? [Possible answers: He might be suggesting that it is human nature to want to strike back at those who have hurt or harmed you, but that the impulse should be restrained. He may be saying that if people would think for a moment before choosing violence, a lot of needless pain could be avoided.]

F Critical Thinking

Challenging the Text

? Do you find Gulliver's ability to communicate through sign language and gestures convincing? Why or why not? [Possible answers: Communicating hunger and thirst is convincing because the nonverbal messages for that seem fairly universal. Communicating more abstract thoughts, such as sincerity, is less convincing: There are no universal gestures for these, and Gulliver is a complete stranger to Lilliputian culture.]

Getting Students Involved

Cooperative Learning

Explore Alternatives. Have students suppose that Gulliver devises an escape plan and that their mission is to assist him. Assign groups of five to brainstorm, gather information from the text, and invent a way for Gulliver to leave Lilliput. Encourage students to be as specific about their schemes as possible by writing them as a series of steps, as a flow chart, or as some other type of schematic. For example, picking up on text clues about Lilliputian etiquette, students could detail techniques Gulliver might use to win the confidence of his captors and thus regain his freedom. Have students share their escape plans with the class. When students are finished, invite them to assess how well they worked as a group, including how fairly each member contributed to the project.

Ⓐ Appreciating Language

Humor

? What is funny about this description? [The idea of the tiny Lilliputians dancing on Gulliver's hands and playing hide and seek in his hair seems ludicrous.] **What is the effect of this humor?** [Possible answers: These details show the innocence on both sides. Both Gulliver and the Lilliputians are playful, and some trust has developed between them.]

Ⓑ Elements of Literature

Satire

? What might Swift be satirizing by presenting the details of this rope-dancing ritual? [Possible answers: courtly behavior; the English court of his time; the things people will do to please the king or to be in favor; the irrelevance of the test to the position; the absurdity of such political "games"; the ridiculousness of political favoritism.]

Ⓒ Historical Connections

Historical Figures

The Emperor may be a spoof on George I. Flimnap is probably a caricature of Sir Robert Walpole, the Whig Prime Minister, and Reldresal is perhaps Lord Townshend.

Ⓓ Appreciating Language

Pun

? What double meaning does the word *fall* have here? [Possible answer: an actual fall or a fall from favor or grace.]

Ⓔ Elements of Literature

Satire

? What is Swift poking fun at or criticizing? [Possible answers: He is criticizing "leaping and creeping," or low-down or side-stepping behaviors that people perform for the sake of ingratiating themselves or advancing themselves politically. The "agility" he is mocking is a kind of political agility, in which people will do any kind of "fancy footwork" to get what they want.]

My gentleness and good behavior had gained so far on the Emperor and his court, and indeed upon the army and people in general, that I began to conceive hopes of getting my liberty in a short time. I took all possible methods to cultivate this favorable disposition. The natives came by degrees to be less apprehensive of any danger from me. I would sometimes lie down, and let five or six of them dance on my hand. And at last the boys and girls would venture to come and play at hide-and-seek in my hair. I had now made a good progress in understanding and speaking their language. The Emperor had a mind one day to entertain me with several of the country shows, wherein they exceed all nations I have known, both for dexterity and magnificence. I was diverted with none so much as that of the rope dancers,[11] performed upon a slender white thread, extended about two foot, and twelve inches from the ground. Upon which I shall desire liberty, with the reader's patience, to enlarge a little.

This diversion is only practiced by those persons who are candidates for great employments, and high favor, at court. They are trained in this art from their youth, and are not always of noble birth, or liberal education. When a great office is vacant, either by death or disgrace (which often happens), five or six of those candidates petition the Emperor to entertain his Majesty and the court with a dance on the rope, and whoever jumps the highest without falling, succeeds in the office. Very often the chief ministers themselves are commanded to show their skill, and to convince the Emperor that they have not lost their faculty. Flimnap, the Treasurer, is allowed to cut a caper on the straight rope, at least an inch higher than any other lord in the whole empire. I have seen him do the summerset[12] several times together upon a trencher[13] fixed on the rope, which is no thicker than a common packthread[14] in England. My friend Reldresal, principal Secretary for Private Affairs, is, in my opinion, if I am not partial, the second after the Treasurer; the rest of the great officers are much upon a par.

These diversions are often attended with fatal accidents, whereof great numbers are on record. I myself have seen two or three candidates break a limb. But the danger is much greater when the ministers themselves are commanded to show their dexterity; for, by contending to excel themselves and their fellows, they strain so far, that there is hardly one of them who hath not received a fall, and some of them two or three. I was assured that a year or two before my arrival, Flimnap would have infallibly broke his neck, if one of the King's cushions, that accidentally lay on the ground, had not weakened the force of his fall.

There is likewise another diversion, which is only shown before the Emperor and Empress, and first minister, upon particular occasions. The Emperor lays on the table three fine silken threads of six inches long. One is blue, the other red, and the third green. These threads are proposed as prizes for those persons whom the Emperor hath a mind to distinguish by a peculiar mark of his favor. The ceremony is performed in his Majesty's great chamber of state, where the candidates are to undergo a trial of dexterity very different from the former, and such as I have not observed the least resemblance of in any other country of the Old or the New World. The Emperor holds a stick in his hands, both ends parallel to the horizon, while the candidates advancing one by one, sometimes leap over the stick, sometimes creep under it backward and forward several times, according as the stick is advanced or depressed. Sometimes the Emperor holds one end of the stick, and his first minister the other; sometimes the minister has it entirely to himself. Whoever performs his part with most agility, and holds out the longest in leaping and creeping, is rewarded with the blue-colored silk; the red is given to the next, and the green to the third, which they all wear girt[15] twice round about the middle; and you see few great persons about this court, who are not adorned with one of these girdles. . . .

One morning, about a fortnight after I had obtained my liberty, Reldresal, principal Secretary (as they style him) of Private Affairs, came to my house attended only by one servant. He ordered his coach to wait at a distance, and desired I would give him an hour's audience; which I readily consented to, on account of his quality and personal

11. **rope dancers:** tightrope dancers.
12. **summerset:** somersault.
13. **trencher:** wooden platter usually used for serving food.
14. **packthread:** twine.
15. **girt:** encircled.

Professional Notes

Critical Comment: Awards of Honor

Historian David Nokes points out that the colors of the silks awarded to those who perform with greatest agility "are the colours of the three highest British orders of honour, the Garter (blue), the Bath (red), and the Thistle (green)." The Most Noble Order of the Garter was founded by King Edward III in 1348; one story has it that it was meant to resemble King Arthur's court, where a lady might give a knight her garter as a token. The Most Ancient and Most Noble Order of the Thistle was founded by King James II in 1687, but is likely a continuation of a medieval chivalric order in Scotland. A larger order, The Most Honourable Order of the Bath was founded by George I in 1725 as a reward for military or civilian service, but it too has more ancient roots, perhaps in the bathing rituals of medieval knights.

Gulliver is measured by the tailors (c. late 19th to early 20th century), illustration by Arthur Rackham.

merits, as well as of the many good offices he had done me during my solicitations at court. I offered to lie down, that he might the more conveniently reach my ear; but he chose rather to let me hold him in my hand during our conversation. He began with compliments on my liberty, said he might pretend to some merit in it; but, however, added, that if it had not been for the present situation of things at court, perhaps I might not have obtained it so soon. "For," said he, "as flourishing a condition as we appear to be in to foreigners, we labor under two mighty evils: a violent faction at home, and the danger of an invasion by a most potent enemy from abroad. As to the first, you are to understand, that for about seventy moons past there have been two struggling parties in this empire, under the names of *Trameck-san* and *Slamecksan,* from the high and low heels on their shoes, by which they distinguish themselves. It is alleged indeed, that the high heels are most agreeable to our ancient constitution: But however this be, his Majesty hath determined to make use of only low heels in the administration of the government, and all offices in the gift of the Crown, as you cannot but observe; and particularly, that his Majesty's Imperial heels are lower at least by a *drurr* than any of his court; (*drurr* is a measure about the fourteenth part of an inch). The animosities between these two parties run so high, that they will neither eat nor drink, nor talk with each other. We compute the *Tramecksan,* or High-Heels, to exceed us in number; but the power is wholly on our side. We apprehend his Imperial Highness, the Heir to the Crown, to have some tendency toward the High-Heels; at least we can plainly discover one of his heels higher than the other, which gives him a hobble in his gait. Now, in the midst of these intestine[16] disquiets, we are threatened with an invasion from the island of Blefuscu, which is the other great empire of the universe, almost as large and powerful as this of his Majesty. For as to what we have heard you affirm, that there are other kingdoms and states in the world inhabited by human creatures as large as yourself, our philosophers are in much doubt, and would rather conjecture that you dropped from the moon, or one of the stars; because it is certain, that an hundred mortals of your bulk would, in a short time, destroy all the fruits and cattle of his Majesty's dominions. Besides, our histories of six thousand moons make no mention of any other regions, than the two great empires of Lilliput and Blefuscu. Which two mighty powers have, as I was going to tell you, been engaged in a most obstinate war for six and thirty moons past. It began upon the following

16. **intestine:** internal.

WORDS TO OWN

alleged (ə·lejd′) *v.:* declared or asserted, often without proof.

RESPONDING TO THE ART

The charming, fanciful work of English illustrator and watercolorist **Arthur Rackham** (1867–1939) has enlivened many literary works.

Activity. Pose this question to students: Since the people of Lilliput are described as about six inches tall, about how tall is Gulliver in this painting?

F Historical Connections

The Anglican Perspective

Assuming that Swift is referring to life in England here, the "two mighty evils" that exist from an Anglican point of view are the domestic threat of Roman Catholicism and the international threat of France, England's traditional enemy.

G Elements of Literature

Satire

? Does Swift diminish the philosophical division between the two factions in England? [Possible answers: He parodies them, using nearly identical but nonsensical names; he indicates that their violent differences are based on something as insignificant as the height of the heels of their shoes.]

H Advanced Learners

Satire

Invite students to determine whom Swift is satirizing. [Possible answers: Given the historical context, Swift might be satirizing the Anglicans and the Roman Catholics, the nobility and the common people, the nobility and the bureaucrats, the Royalists and the Parliamentarians, or the Whigs and the Tories.]

I Reading Skills and Strategies

Identifying the Writer's Stance

? What purpose might the author have for telling the reader that the heir walks with "a hobble"? [Possible answers: Swift is suggesting that the heir is hobbled by indecision; or that the heir repeatedly tries to straddle both sides of an issue.]

Using Students' Strengths

Kinesthetic Learners

Students may enjoy acting out some of the nonverbal communication that occurs in this story. This activity might take the format of charades, in which students draw from a hat a particular scene or part of what happens in a scene, act it out, and continue to provide nonverbal clues until their audience guesses what they are communicating.

Visual Learners

In a caricature or visual satire, the artist distorts the appearance of the subject in order to convey a quality and to make a point. Ask students to compile a collection of political cartoons, categorize them by subject, and analyze the techniques of caricature used by the artists. Encourage students to create their own satirical cartoons, based on politics or on some issue of current interest in your school.

A Reading Skills and Strategies

Identifying the Writer's Stance

? In this passage, what is the object of Swift's disapproval? [Possible answers: He is showing his scorn for narrow-minded appeals to scripture to justify prejudice; using obscure references that are difficult to refute; arguing fine points that cannot be settled.]

B Humanities Connections

Individual Choice

Many of the Enlightenment thinkers stressed the notion that people have the ability to choose for themselves, rather than to have a government, ruler, or church choose for them. Rousseau, for example, championed the notion that people were born free yet "everywhere" living "in chains" because government or society usurped their choices.

C Elements of Literature

Irony

? What is ironic about this comment? [Possible answers: Gulliver knows he should not get involved in petty politics, yet he rationalizes his decision to do the expedient thing by saying he'll just defend the Lilliputians.]

Responding to the Art

Grandville (1803–1847) is the pseudonym of a French illustrator who used a witty blend of human and animal features in his caricatures of public figures.

Activity. Ask students to identify the Big-Endians and the Little-Endians in the battle of the eggs and to describe how Grandville shows the wounded warriors. Students might recognize Swift's theme as similar to the one in Dr. Seuss's *The Butter Battle Book,* in which those who butter the top of their slices of bread war with those who favor the opposite approach.

occasion. It is allowed on all hands, that the primitive way of breaking eggs[17] before we eat them, was upon the larger end: But his present Majesty's grandfather, while he was a boy, going to eat an egg, and breaking it according to the ancient practice, happened to cut one of his fingers. Whereupon the Emperor his father published an edict, commanding all his subjects, upon great penalties, to break the smaller end of their eggs. The people so highly resented this law, that our histories tell us there have been six rebellions raised on that account; wherein one Emperor lost his life, and another his crown. These civil commotions were constantly fomented by the monarchs of Blefuscu; and when they were quelled, the exiles always fled for refuge to that empire. It is computed, that eleven thousand persons have, at several times, suffered death, rather than submit to break their eggs at the smaller end. Many hundred large volumes have been published upon this controversy: But the books of the Big-Endians have been long forbidden, and the whole party rendered incapable by law of holding employments. During the course of these troubles, the emperors of Blefuscu did frequently expostulate by their ambassadors, accusing us of making a schism[18] in religion, by offending against a fundamental doctrine of our great prophet Lustrog, in the fifty-fourth chapter of the Brundrecal (which is their Alcoran).[19] This, however, is thought to be a mere strain upon the text, for the words are these: *That all true believers shall break their eggs at the convenient end;* and which is the convenient end, seems, in my humble opinion, to be left to every man's conscience, or at least in the power of the chief magistrate to determine. Now the Big-Endian exiles have found so much credit in the Emperor of Blefuscu's court, and so much private assistance and encouragement from their party here at home, that a bloody war has been carried on between the two empires for six and thirty moons with various success; during which time we have lost forty capital ships, and a much greater number of smaller vessels, together with thirty thousand of our best seamen and soldiers; and the damage received by the enemy is reckoned to be somewhat greater than ours. However, they have now equipped a numerous fleet, and are just preparing to make a descent upon us; and his Imperial Majesty, placing great confidence in your valor and strength, has commanded me to lay this account of his affairs before you."

I desired the Secretary to present my humble duty to the Emperor, and to let him know, that I thought it would not become me, who was a foreigner, to interfere with parties; but I was ready, with the hazard of my life, to defend his person and state against all invaders.

17. **way of breaking eggs:** The English eat a boiled egg by standing it up in an egg cup, cutting off one end with a knife, and scooping out the contents with a spoon.

Lilliput (19th century), illustration by Grandville.

18. **schism:** division.
19. **Alcoran:** archaic English name for the Koran, Islam's sacred book.

WORDS TO OWN
edict (ē′dikt′) *n.:* official order.
quelled (kweld) *v.:* subdued.

Skill Link

Analyzing and Responding to a Critical Review

Allan Bloom calls Swift's travelogue an "amazing rhetorical achievement. It is the classic children's story and it is a rather obscene tale. Swift was able to charm innocence and amuse corruption, and this is a measure of his talent. . . . Swift had not only the judgment with which to arrive at a reasoned view of the world, but the fancy by means of which he could recreate that world in a form which teaches where argument fails and which satisfies all while misleading none." Ask students how the travelogue "teaches where argument fails." [Possible answer: Swift shows rather than tells; his symbolic use of size implies that power is relative; conversations, rather than lectures, lead readers to Swift's conclusions.]

Critical Comment

Under the Guise of Lilliput

Swift's contemporaries immediately understood that Swift was doing two things in this part of *Gulliver's Travels.* Under the pretense of describing politics in Lilliput, he was indirectly referring to politicians and political events in his own country. Swift's first readers were quick to identify the actual statesmen lurking behind such made-up names as Reldresal and Flimnap, and they saw parallels between events in Lilliput and events in England.

While it is interesting to know something about the real political background of *Gulliver's Travels,* it is much more important to understand that Swift is **satirizing** certain characteristics to be found in the political struggles of all countries at all times in history. For instance, in the imaginary Lilliput there are two major parties, distinguished by a trivial detail: the height of the heels on the shoes they wear. Similarly, in many actual countries there are also two major parties that struggle for power. Swift wants us to think about what distinguishes such real political parties from each other. Are the issues important or minor? **D**

Later in this section, Gulliver discovers another characteristic that distinguishes the two parties: the way they eat their eggs. The Big-Endians always cut open the big end of the boiled egg, and the Little-Endians always cut open the little end. These parties have had a long and bitter history: One emperor has lost his life, another his throne, and many Lilliputians have had to go live in another country, Blefuscu. All these details suggest that Swift was thinking of specific events in English history, and these events determined what he said about Lilliput. **E** It is even possible to identify the parallels between Swift's fictions and historical facts. Lilliput, for example, represents England; and Blefuscu represents France, where some English Catholics lived in exile. The Big-Endians are people loyal to Catholicism, England's old religion, and the Little-Endians are those loyal to Anglicanism, England's new religion. The emperor who lost his life can be identified with Charles I; the one who lost his throne is James II.

Any narrative incorporating parallels of this kind is called an **allegory** (see page 451). But again, knowing how to interpret the allegory in a particular way is much less important than understanding the general meaning of the satire, which is directed against follies and excesses wherever they are found.

George III, as the King of Brobdingnag, inspects Napoleon, as Gulliver (c. 1803) by James Gillray.

Critical Comment

This feature points out that although Swift was satirizing specific political events in England at the time, it is more important for readers to realize that the satire can apply to any society in any time period.

D Critical Thinking

Extending the Text

? In your opinion, could any part of Swift's text be applied to the two major political parties in this country? Why or why not? [Possible answers: Yes, because the differences between Republicans and Democrats don't seem all that great at times, and their agendas can appear to be motivated more by the desire for power than the common good. No, because the United States has an entirely different type of government, and its parties differ on significant issues, such as the power of the states in relation to the power of the federal government.]

E Historical Connections

Whigs vs. Tories

Part of the political conflict reflected in Swift's story is the opposition of the Whig and Tory parties. Associated with the country gentry, Tories sought the return of the Catholic Stuart heirs to the British throne. Whigs, whose interests were those of the wealthy middle classes, supported the limited constitutional monarchy of Protestant rulers.

Assessing Learning

Check Test: True-False

1. Gulliver's captors provide him with both food and drink. [True]
2. Gulliver eventually learns that his captors have put a sleeping potion in his drink. [True]
3. Gulliver says government offices are filled by rope dancers. [True]
4. The principal Secretary for Private Affairs says there are no opposing parties in the kingdom. [False]
5. He also says some citizens did not abide by a new law regarding the breaking of eggs. [True]

MAKING MEANINGS

First Thoughts [Respond]

1. Students will probably find the mockery of corruption, political parties, court life, and bureaucracy very funny. The serious point underlying the satire is the need to reform these institutions.

Shaping Interpretations [Interpret]

2. Like the travel books he parodies, Swift uses fantastic lies such as the Lilliputians' remarkable social order, politics, and court life. Swift also includes trivial details about drinking, eating, sleeping, body positions, and attempts at communication.
3. Officials are expected to rope-dance nimbly; and to leap over or creep under a stick held by the king or the first minister. These activities satirize the qualifications of office-holders. Some students may note that the Lilliputians think they are important (big), although they are actually small and their values petty and meaningless.
4. Yes, the smallness of the Lilliputians suggests their pettiness.
5. Swift's satire plays with the idea that size indicates moral character. Chaucer emphasizes that his pilgrims' true characters do not match the images they project.
6. The careful reader can hear Swift's mockery conveyed through detail and word choice. For example, when Swift writes, "It is computed, that eleven thousand persons have, at several times, suffered death, rather than submit to break their eggs at the smaller end," the reader can sense the jeering judgment.
7. Swift seems to think these differences are often overstated. He suggests, for example, the need to hire officials on merit rather than politics, to eliminate court ceremony, and to reevaluate the importance of philosophical differences.
8. Some students may say that bitterness toward certain people doesn't necessarily lead to misanthropy. Others may say that Swift's hope of reforming human society proves he is not a misanthrope.

Extending the Text [Synthesize]

9. Students may draw parallels to two-party systems, religious schisms, feuding, and awarding of government positions for reasons other than merit.

MAKING MEANINGS

First Thoughts

1. What do you think is the funniest part of Gulliver's adventures in Lilliput? What serious point, if any, do you see beneath the surface of the humor?

Reading Check

a. How large are the Lilliputians? Why doesn't Gulliver seize and harm the Lilliputians who come close to him?

b. What test do the candidates for high office in Lilliput have to undergo? What disaster almost happened to Flimnap?

c. Describe the two evils that threaten Lilliput, according to Reldresal.

d. Explain how the war between Lilliput and Blefuscu began.

Shaping Interpretations

As you answer these questions, refer to your reading notes.

2. The travel books of Swift's time were famous for fantastic lies about exotic places and trivial details about the traveler's daily life there. How does this selection **parody,** or imitate and make fun of, these travel books?
3. Swift also uses the travel book as a medium for **satire.** He expects his readers to find similarities between what happens in Lilliput and what goes on at home. What qualifications are the officials of Lilliput expected to have in order to hold high office? How does Swift use **irony** in his description of the Lilliputian officials?
4. Is there any relationship between the physical size of the Lilliputians and the way Swift wants us to evaluate their behavior? Does their size **symbolize** some other kind of "smallness"? Explain.
5. Compare the way Swift **characterizes** the Lilliputians with the way Chaucer characterizes the pilgrims in the Prologue to *The Canterbury Tales* (page 105). How does each writer **satirize** the moral failings of his characters?
6. How would you describe Swift's **tone**—his attitude toward the Lilliputians? What words or passages support your answer?
7. The institutions for which Swift urges reform here include politics and religion. What does he think of the differences that divide people into factions and sects? What other aspects of Lilliputian (and by implication English) life does Swift suggest are ripe for reform?
8. Because of the bitterness of his satire, some readers have concluded that Swift despaired of true reform and was really a confirmed misanthrope, or hater of humanity. Do you think someone as bitter about life as Swift is has to be a misanthrope? Explain your answer.

Extending the Text

9. The Critical Comment on page 495 explains how Lilliputian politics paralleled British politics of Swift's time. What parallels can you detect between Lilliput and what you know of modern politics, in either this country or some other one?

Gulliver tows the enemy's ships to Lilliput. Illustration from a 19th-century edition of *Gulliver's Travels.*

The Granger Collection, New York.

Reading Check

a. The Lilliputians are "not six inches high." Gulliver is first deterred from harming them by their arrows and later by his sense of honor.

b. The candidates must rope-dance. Flimnap would have broken his neck had he not fallen on a cushion.

c. The two evils are "a violent faction at home" and the threat of invasion.

d. The Emperor of Lilliput commanded his subjects to break eggs at the small end, but some rebelled and Blefescu gave them sanctuary.

On his second voyage, Gulliver finds himself marooned in Brobdingnag. Here everything—people, animals, buildings—is twelve times larger than in England or anywhere else in the known world. The situation in Part I is now completely reversed, and Gulliver discovers what it is like to be an insignificant, timid midget among giants. He also learns that nothing is either big or little except by comparison. All sorts of humiliating accidents happen to him: A baby picks him up and tries to suck on his head; a monkey stuffs him with food and carries him up onto a roof; he is almost drowned in a bowl of cream; a farmer exhibits him for money, as though he were a trained flea. Finally he goes to live at court, where he tries to impress the king and queen with his importance, and especially with the importance of England and its civilization, which nobody in Brobdingnag has ever heard of.

Although its inhabitants look like immense and ugly brutes, Brobdingnag is a kind of utopia, a model civilization with an enlightened and benevolent king. Notice how the king treats Gulliver in spite of his opinion of Gulliver's size and civilization. Continue to take notes as you read.

from Part 2: A Voyage to Brobdingnag

Jonathan Swift

It is the custom that every Wednesday (which, as I have before observed, was their Sabbath) the King and Queen, with the royal issue of both sexes, dine together in the apartment of his Majesty, to whom I was now become a favorite; and at these times my little chair and table were placed at his left hand, before one of the saltcellars.[1] This prince took a pleasure in conversing with me, inquiring into the manners, religion, laws, government, and learning of Europe; wherein I gave him the best account I was able. His apprehension was so clear, and his judgment so exact, that he made very wise reflections and observations upon all I said. But, I confess, that after I had been a little too copious in talking of my own beloved country, of our trade, and wars by sea and land, of our schisms in religion, and parties in the state; the prejudices of his education prevailed so far, that he could not forbear taking me up in his right hand, and stroking me gently with the other, after an hearty fit of laughing, asked me, whether I were a Whig or a Tory.[2] Then turning to his first minister, who waited behind him with a white staff, near as tall as the mainmast of the *Royal Sovereign,*[3] he observed how contemptible a thing was human grandeur, which could be mimicked by such diminutive insects as I. "And yet," said he, "I dare engage, those creatures have their titles and distinctions of honor, they contrive little nests and burrows, that they call houses and cities; they make a figure in dress and equipage;[4] they love, they fight, they dispute, they cheat, they betray." And thus he continued on, while my color came and went several times, with indignation to hear our noble country, the mistress of arts and arms, the scourge of France, the arbitress of Europe, the seat of virtue, piety, honor, and truth, the pride and envy of the world, so contemptuously treated.

But as I was not in a condition to resent injuries, so, upon mature thoughts, I began to doubt whether I were injured or no. For, after having

1. **saltcellars:** dishes of salt.
2. **Whig . . . Tory:** the two chief political parties of eighteenth-century Great Britain.
3. ***Royal Sovereign:*** one of the largest British warships of Swift's age. A white staff is the symbol of the office of the British treasurer.
4. **equipage** (ek′wi·pij′): carriage and horses with attendant servants.

WORDS TO OWN

copious (kō′pē·əs) *adj.:* wordy; profuse.
prevailed (prē·vāld′) *v.:* predominated; held sway.

Summary ■

Gulliver takes a second journey and lands in Brobdingnag, another fantastic setting, where everything is on a gigantic scale and Gulliver is a mere midget in comparison. He meets the king, who is curious, intelligent, and generous, but also condescending toward Gulliver's earnest account of events in England.

A Reading Skills and Strategies

Identifying the Writer's Stance

? What is the writer's attitude toward this prince? [Possible answers: Gulliver says the prince is a person of great wisdom and extreme courtesy, but the writer portrays him as a person who is curious, intelligent, and generous but also mocking and insensitive.]

B Elements of Literature

Satire

? How does the prince belittle Gulliver and England? [Possible answers: He calls Gulliver an insect and remarks on the ridiculousness of the intrigue and bickering in such a small, insignificant country as England. He makes the English sound like ants or little rodents that make their nests and scurry about mindlessly.]

C Elements of Literature

Irony

? What is ironic about Gulliver's reference to his "noble country"? [Possible answers: He loves a country filled with wars, schisms, and party politics; he does not understand the perspective of the king (twelve times larger), who views England as tiny and unimportant.]

Using Students' Strengths

Logical/Mathematical Learners

Have students create a visual chart showing the relative sizes of a Lilliputian, a human being and a Brobdingnagian. Students should begin with a human being and then use textual information and ratio to determine what size the other two will be on their charts. Students may want to go a step further and include a few animals or items of furniture from each country, all in scale.

Verbal Learners

Have students find, read, and report on the old nursery tale "Tom Thumb." Popular in the sixteenth century, the tale was published in the seventeenth century and frequently reproduced later in children's books and collections of fairy tales. Ask students to compare Tom's experiences and reflections with Gulliver's in Brobdingnag.

RESPONDING TO THE ART

Richard Redgrave (1804–1888) worked on a national art education project in England and was engaged as Inspector of the Queen's pictures. He and his brother Samuel were co-authors of a respected reference book on English art.

Activity. Ask students to identify objects in the painting that give clues to Gulliver's height. [the post against the wall] Have them describe how the artist has emphasized the farmer's amazement at what he is seeing.

A Elements of Literature
Satire

? What human follies and weaknesses does Swift mock in these lines? [people's obsession with fashion, courtly manners, and empty speech]

B Reading Skills and Strategies
Identifying the Writer's Stance

? Why does Swift include the passage about the enormous flies? [Possible answers: to show the relativity of size to bravery; to emphasize Gulliver's small size and vulnerability; to describe scientific detail on a near-microscopic level; to entertain the reader]

C Reading Skills and Strategies
Responding to the Text

? How do you react to the many specific details that describe these flies? [Possible responses: The flies are disgusting. Thinking about their excrement and spawn is repulsive.]

Victoria and Albert Museum, London.

Gulliver Exhibited to the Brobdingnag Farmer (19th century) by Richard Redgrave.

been accustomed several months to the sight and converse of this people, and observed every object upon which I cast my eyes, to be of proportionable magnitude, the horror I had first conceived from their bulk and aspect was so far worn off, that if I had then beheld a company of English lords and ladies in their finery and birthday clothes,[5] acting their several parts in the most courtly manner, of strutting, and bowing, and prating;[6] to say the truth, I should have been strongly tempted to laugh as much at them as this King and his grandees[7] did at me. Neither indeed could I forbear smiling at myself, when the Queen used to place me upon her hand toward a looking glass, by which both our persons appeared before me in full view together; and there could be nothing more ridiculous than the comparison; so that I really began to imagine myself dwindled many degrees below my usual size. . . .

I was frequently rallied[8] by the Queen upon account of my fearfulness, and she used to ask me whether the people of my country were as great cowards as myself. The occasion was this: The kingdom is much pestered with flies in summer; and these odious insects, each of them as big as a Dunstable lark, hardly gave me any rest while I sat at dinner, with their continual humming and buzzing about my ears. They would sometimes alight upon my victuals, and leave their loathsome excrement or spawn behind, which to me was very visible, though not to the natives of that country, whose large optics were not so acute as

5. **birthday clothes:** new outfits worn on a royal's birthday.
6. **prating:** talking pompously.
7. **grandees** (gran·dēz′): important persons; from *grande,* Spanish and Portuguese for "a nobleman of the highest rank."

8. **rallied:** teased.

WORDS TO OWN
odious (ō′dē·əs) *adj.:* hateful; offensive.

Connecting Across Texts

Connecting with "A Voyage to Lilliput"

Discuss with students the satirical point made by the juxtaposition of Gulliver's voyages to Lilliput and Brobdingnag: During the first he looks down on the inhabitants, but during the second he is looked down upon. Swift's point is that importance or value, like size, is relative: It shifts depending on the perspective of the one doing the evaluating. You might also want to refer students to T. H. White's *The Once and Future King,* in which Merlin educates young Arthur, the future king, by turning him into a fish, an ant, a goose and a badger. Arthur's perceptions from these points of view are amusing and thought-provoking.

mine in viewing smaller objects. Sometimes they would fix upon my nose or forehead, where they stung me to the quick, smelling very offensively, and I could easily trace that viscous matter, which our naturalists tell us enables those creatures to walk with their feet upward upon a ceiling. I had much ado to defend myself against these detestable animals, and could not forbear starting when they came on my face. It was the common practice of the dwarf to catch a number of these insects in his hand, as schoolboys do among us, and let them out suddenly under my nose, on purpose to frighten me, and divert the Queen. My remedy was to cut them in pieces with my knife as they flew in the air, wherein my dexterity was much admired. . . .

He [the King] was perfectly astonished with the historical account I gave him of our affairs during the last century, protesting it was only an heap of conspiracies, rebellions, murders, massacres, revolutions, banishments; the very worst effects that avarice, faction, hypocrisy, perfidiousness, cruelty, rage, madness, hatred, envy, lust, malice, and ambition, could produce.

His Majesty, in another audience, was at the pains to recapitulate the sum of all I had spoken; compared the questions he made with the answers I had given; then taking me into his hands, and stroking me gently, delivered himself in these words, which I shall never forget, nor the manner he spoke them in. "My little friend Grildrig,[9] you have made a most admirable panegyric upon your country. You have clearly proved that ignorance, idleness, and vice, are the proper ingredients for qualifying a legislator: that laws are best explained, interpreted, and applied by those whose interest and abilities lie in perverting, confounding, and eluding them. I observe among you some lines of an institution, which in its original might have been tolerable, but these half erased, and the rest wholly blurred and blotted by corruptions. It doth not appear from all you have said, how any one perfection[10] is required toward the procurement of any one station among you; much less that men are ennobled on account of their virtue, that priests are advanced for their piety or learning, soldiers for their conduct or valor, judges for their integrity, senators for the love of their country, or counselors for their wisdom. As for yourself (continued the King), who have spent the greatest part of your life in traveling, I am well disposed to hope you may hitherto have escaped many vices of your country. But by what I have gathered from your own relation, and the answers I have with much pains wringed and extorted from you, I cannot but conclude the bulk of your natives to be the most pernicious race of little odious vermin that nature ever suffered to crawl upon the surface of the earth."

9. **Grildrig:** the Brobdingnagians' name for Gulliver.
10. **perfection:** virtue.

Private Collection.

Gulliver in Brobdingnag (c. late 19th to early 20th century). Original watercolor illustration by Arthur Rackham for *Gulliver's Travels*.

WORDS TO OWN

viscous (vis′kəs) *adj.:* having the form of a sticky fluid.
pernicious (pər·nish′·əs) *adj.:* wicked; extremely harmful.

D Vocabulary Note

Latin Roots

? Point out the word *conspiracies* and explain that the Latin root *spirare* means "to breathe" and the prefix *con-* means "together" or "with." Ask students to explain why conspirators might be regarded as people who breathe together. [Possible answer: They work closely and usually in secret toward a common goal. Their physical proximity, for the sake of secrecy, may make them seem as if they inhabit one body.]

E Elements of Literature

Irony

? What type of irony do you find in this passage? [Verbal irony: The king's summary is the opposite of the image Gulliver was trying to convey and the image the British hold of their government.]

F Elements of Literature

Satire

? Why is this conclusion satirical? [Possible answers: It is extremely critical; it employs gross exaggeration; it is humorous in a bitter way; it is sarcastic.]

G Critical Thinking

Making Judgments

? Does this criticism of the English apply as well to other societies? [Sample responses: Yes, many societies are troubled by vice, corruption, and hypocrisy. Or no, the king assumes the worst about the English due to Gulliver's account; his conclusions are not well founded.]

Assessing Learning

Check Test: True-False

1. Swift depicts the Brobdingnags as very narrow minded and stupid. [False]
2. Gulliver and the king have many conversations about manners, religion, government, and other matters. [True]
3. The queen holds Gulliver in her hand to compare their sizes in a mirror. [True]
4. Gulliver is frightened by the flies in the kingdom. [True]
5. The king decides Gulliver's countrymen are admirable people. [False]

Making the Connections

Connecting to the Theme: "The Sting of Satire"

Who is stung by this satire, and why? Explain to students that without a specific target, satire loses its punch. Using a graphic organizer like the following, record on the chalkboard students' opinions about the target or targets of this selection's satire. Be sure students link their answers to appropriate passages in the text.

Text Reference	Who	Why

MAKING MEANINGS

First Thoughts [Respond]

1. Many students may see the royal family as benevolent, while some might see them as condescending and patronizing. They might be considered arrogant, cruel in their humor, and judgmental. Some possible virtues are kindness, sympathy, encouragement, inquisitiveness, and cleverness.

Shaping Interpretations [Interpret]

2. The king implies that the distinction between the two is silly, although it is important to the British.

3. Possible answer: He sees himself next to the queen in the mirror; to him the flies are as large as larks; he is the subject of ridicule.

4. The king's speeches indicate that he is intelligent and perceptive, perhaps even cynical. The king's gentle treatment of Gulliver may mean he is kind, or it may also imply condescension.

5. One example is Gulliver's indignation that the king sullies England's reputation, although the king is going by Gulliver's account. Another instance occurs when the king says that "ignorance, idleness, and vice" are the qualifications of officials in England.

6. Gulliver is sickened by the oversized flies of the kingdom, and the king is disgusted by the pettiness of Gulliver's people.

7. Gulliver reacts indignantly to the king's comparison of human beings with insects. After his experiences in Lilliput, he should understand the relationship of perspective to individual interpretation of reality. Students might also bring up Gulliver's naïve defense of England.

8. Swift's tone is somewhere between serious and objective and incredulous. For example, the narrator says "as I was not in a condition to resent injuries, so, upon mature thoughts, I began to doubt whether I were injured or no." He also mentions how the king was "perfectly astonished," mirroring the astonishment of the narrator at the king's response.

Extending the Text [Apply]

9. One point is political corruption: "they love, they fight, they dispute, they cheat, they betray."

MAKING MEANINGS

First Thoughts

1. What do you think of the Brobdingnagian royal family? What faults and virtues do you see in them?

Reading Check

a. To what form of life does the king first compare Gulliver?
b. In comparison, what do English people think of themselves, according to Gulliver?
c. What feat of dexterity can Gulliver perform that impresses the Brobdingnagians?
d. From Gulliver's defense of England, the king evaluates English officials and institutions. According to the king, what are the qualifications for English legislators?

Shaping Interpretations

As you answer these questions, be sure to refer to your reading notes.

2. Explain why the king roars with laughter when he asks if Gulliver is a Whig or a Tory.
3. Why does Gulliver begin to think of himself as small?
4. How does Swift **characterize** the king of Brobdingnag? Which actions show the king's personality traits?
5. Where does Swift use **verbal irony** to make his points?
6. What connections can you make between Gulliver's experience with the Brobdingnagian flies and the king's dismissal of humanity as "little odious vermin"?
7. What evidence suggests that Gulliver is learning little from his experiences in Brobdingnag?
8. How would you describe Swift's **tone** as he tells about the Brobdingnags? Find words or passages to support your answer.

Extending the Text

9. Find at least one passage in the Brobdingnag episode that could apply to politics in the United States today.

ELEMENTS OF LITERATURE

Satire: Bitter Laughter

A **satire** is any piece of writing designed to make its readers feel critical—of themselves, of their fellow human beings, of their society. Some satires are intended to make us laugh at human foolishness and weakness; others make us angry and indignant at human vices and crimes. In *The Rape of the Lock* (page 527), Alexander Pope provides many examples of the good-natured, laughable kind of satire. Like Pope's, Swift's satire also provokes laughter, but often laughter of a bitter kind.

While satire is usually directed at humanity in general, or at stereotyped groups of people such as clumsy surgeons or greedy lawyers, it can also be aimed at a particular person. In *Gulliver's Travels,* for instance, Swift satirizes the prime minister Sir Robert Walpole, whom he believed to be corrupt, calling him "Flimnap."

Satirists are dissatisfied with things as they are, and they want to make them better. Instead of giving constructive advice, though, they emphasize what is wrong with the world and its inhabitants. They don't say "Be good!" "Obey the Golden Rule!" "Put others before yourself." Instead, they make fun of vicious, selfish, mean-spirited people in the hope that we will see ourselves in such people and mend our ways. Satirists perform an important function in society when they expose errors and absurdities that we no longer notice because custom and familiarity have blinded us to them.

One of the devices that satirists use to make folly and vice appear ridiculous, and therefore unattractive, is **exaggeration.** We must not expect satirists to be objective, to give both sides of a question, to show the good as well as the bad traits of a character. Instead, satirists are likely to exaggerate by picturing all politicians as corrupt, all members of the clergy as hypocritical, all teachers as pedantic, all young adults as irresponsible. They realize that such generalizations cannot be 100 percent accurate, but for satirical purposes exceptions do not count. Wildly extravagant exaggeration, or **hyperbole,** is conspicuous in popular magazines such as *Mad*—though *Mad*'s satire lacks the moral purposes and subtlety of Swift's and Pope's satire.

Reading Check

a. The king compares Gulliver to an insect.
b. According to Gulliver, English people think of themselves as noble, creative, powerful, virtuous, and honorable.
c. He uses his knife in midair to kill the huge flies that annoy him.
d. According to the king, the qualifications for English legislators are ignorance, idleness, and vice.

The great satirists expect their readers to be alert and intelligent enough to detect the presence of satire even when there is no exaggeration. For instance, Swift once wrote, without any explanation at all, "Last week I saw a woman flayed, and you will hardly believe how much it altered her appearance for the worst." Since to "flay" a person is to peel off the skin (a common form of capital punishment in those days), Swift's remark is a complete **understatement**—the opposite of an exaggeration. By making the statement sound shockingly casual and offhanded, Swift implies that such cruelty is common but that people do not become upset by it and instead pretend to have no concern at all.

Understatement is a form of **irony,** the device of saying one thing and meaning just the opposite. When irony is particularly cruel or cutting, it can come close to **sarcasm.** "Great!" we say sarcastically, when we actually mean "Terrible!" In literature, irony is extended far beyond mere sarcasm. In his *Directions for Servants,* for instance, Swift, under the pretense of telling servants how to behave, actually tells them how to misbehave—and in great detail. Here is how he advises servants to respond to a request for a drink.

> When you carry a glass of liquor to any person who hath called for it, do not bob him on the shoulder, or cry, "Sir, or madam, here's the glass!" That would be unmannerly, as if you had a mind to force it down one's throat. But stand at the person's left shoulder and wait his time; and if he strikes it down with his elbow by forgetfulness, that was his fault and not yours.

Ironic advice of this sort is more amusing and much more memorable than straightforward, sincere advice.

A writer who habitually uses irony runs the risk of being misunderstood. As an ironist, Swift earned a reputation for being scandalous, irresponsible, and even irreligious. Yet he claimed he never wrote anything "without a moral view."

Brobdingnag (detail) (c. 1800) drawn by R. Corbould, engraved by C. Warren, from *Cooke's Pocket Edition of Select Novels.*

Looking at satire. Swift's novel is almost two hundred years old. Look closely at the relevance of his satire to today's world.

1. According to Swift, what is basically wrong with the world and its inhabitants? How do you feel about his stance on morality?
2. Where do you see the techniques of Swiftian satire put to use today? What are some of the specific targets of contemporary satire?
3. Swift's novel is highly visual, and many artists and even political cartoonists have been inspired by Gulliver and his travels. If you like to draw, you might try to illustrate one of Gulliver's adventures. If you see parallels between Swift's satiric book and politics today, draw a cartoon based on an incident or character from *Gulliver's Travels.* (In about 1803, an English cartoonist lampooned Napoleon—whom the English detested—by showing him as the tiny Gulliver being inspected by George III as the king of Brobdingnag. See page 495.)

ELEMENTS OF LITERATURE

Mini-Lesson: Satire

Ask students to name the various ways in which they responded to Swift's satire. [Possible answers: amusement, disgust, laughter, judgment, curiosity, reflection.] Create a cluster diagram on the board. Put the word *satire* in the center and record the various ways in which students respond. Point out that satire can arouse many responses, and that the way the reader responds can be related to how close he or she is to the target of the satire. Thus, students may find this satire more amusing than pointed because it criticizes a society, a time, and a place that is not their own.

1. Students may say that the two things wrong with the world and its inhabitants are corruption and pettiness. Some students may feel Swift is too strict and unrealistic in his expectations of moral behavior, while others might support his implied standards of honesty, integrity, and reluctance to enter into conflict.
2. Students will most likely mention examples from electronic media, particularly comedy skits, sitcoms, animated cartoons, or movies. Other examples might be magazine features, novels, comic strips, and editorial cartoons. There are many popular targets, including politicians, celebrities, and social behavior.
3. Encourage students to use visual exaggeration, perhaps through caricature, size, or incongruous activity.

Summary ■

Swift makes an outrageous proposal that he ironically calls "modest." He suggests that Irish babies be slaughtered and sold to the gentry as food, relieving their parents of a financial burden while adding variety to the tables of the nobility. He also discusses the possibility of using older children as food, but reluctantly dismisses the idea as impractical.

Swift's six reasons for making the proposal are:

1. It would greatly lessen the number of Papists (a derogatory term for Catholics).
2. Landlords can seize the Irish children in payment for rents.
3. The nation's wealth will be increased because there are so many children (and a new dish will be added to the nation's tables).
4. The breeders will sell their children and will not have to support them.
5. The business of taverns will be increased (with the introduction of a new food).
6. The plan would be a great inducement to marriage. Women would be well treated when pregnant—just as mares and cows and sows are.

Ⓐ Reading Skills and Strategies

Distinguishing Shades of Meaning

Have students define the word *modest* here. Students may think of *modest* only in relation to decency or shyness about one's body. Ask them to use the dictionary to find other meanings. [not bold; limited in size, amount, or scope.] The word, of course, as used here, drips with irony.

Ⓑ Critical Thinking

Extending the Text

? Considering this was written more than two centuries ago, there are striking similarities to modern society. What contemporary social issues are detailed in this paragraph? [Possible answers: hunger, homelessness, poverty.]

Before You Read

A MODEST PROPOSAL

Background

This essay, Swift's best and most famous pamphlet, describes the desperate conditions in Ireland and protests the English treatment of the Irish. For three years before Swift published this pamphlet in 1729, the Irish harvests had been so poor that little remained for the farmers, after selling their crops, to pay the rents demanded by their English landlords. Beggars and starving children were everywhere. Money was in short supply. Swift argued that most of the money was shipped off to England, where the landlords lived, and little remained in Ireland to be spent on Irish goods. England's policies kept the Irish poor.

In *A Modest Proposal,* Swift offers an outrageous solution to these problems of human misery—perhaps the most outrageous solution ever offered. But there is nothing outrageous about Swift's manner. In this pamphlet, he assumes the role of a "practical" economic planner, pretending to be objective, full of common sense, even benevolence. It is this difference between its straightforward style and its appalling content that gives the pamphlet its force.

Ultimately, Swift is protesting against a purely statistical view of humanity—a view that would reduce people to breeders and babies to meat. Swift risks appearing as a monster himself in order to expose the monstrous behavior of others.

Reading Skills and Strategies

Recognizing Persuasive Techniques

Swift's essay is perhaps the most famous and most skilled example of **persuasive writing** used for the purpose of **satire.** As you read, take notes, locating examples of the following persuasive techniques: **logical appeals** (supporting a position with evidence, such as facts or statistics); **emotional appeals** (passages that use words that arouse strong feelings); and **ethical appeals** (passages that establish the writer as sincere and qualified to make the remarks). The questions alongside key paragraphs can be used as a guide to your reading.

A starving, orphaned Irish child (detail).

National Library of Ireland, Dublin.

Ⓐ A Modest Proposal

Jonathan Swift

FOR PREVENTING THE CHILDREN OF POOR PEOPLE IN IRELAND FROM BEING A BURDEN TO THEIR PARENTS OR COUNTRY, AND FOR MAKING THEM BENEFICIAL TO THE PUBLIC

Ⓑ It is a melancholy object to those, who walk through this great town,[1] or travel in the country, when they see the streets, the roads, and cabin doors, crowded with beggars of the female sex, followed by three, four, or six children, all in rags, and importuning every passenger for an alms.[2] These mothers instead of being able to work for their honest livelihood, are forced to employ all their time in strolling, to beg sustenance for their helpless infants, who, as they grow up either turn thieves for want[3] of work, or leave their

1. **town:** Dublin.
2. **importuning . . . alms:** asking passersby for a handout.
3. **want:** lack; need.

WORDS TO OWN

sustenance (sus′tə·nəns) *n.:* food or money to support life.

Preteaching Vocabulary

Words to Own

Have students work in groups of two or three to sort the words in any way they wish. They may sort by parts of speech; they may determine which of the Words to Own relate to social interactions or attitudes; they may determine which of the words relate to meeting or fulfilling needs. Then ask students to name the Word to Own most clearly related to each of the following groups of words.

1. briefness, shortness [brevity]
2. overfull, more than satisfied [glutted]
3. careful, precise [scrupulous]
4. obtain, get [procure]
5. hatreds, hostilities [animosities]
6. criticize strongly, blame, condemn [censure]
7. veered from the topic, wandered [digressed]
8. respect, courteous yielding [deference]
9. food, support [sustenance]
10. convenient, useful [expedient]

dear native country to fight for the Pretender[4] in Spain, or sell themselves to the Barbadoes.[5]

I think it is agreed by all parties, that this prodigious number of children, in the arms, or on the backs, or at the heels of their mothers, and frequently of their fathers, is in the present deplorable state of the kingdom, a very great additional grievance; and therefore whoever could find out a fair, cheap, and easy method of making these children sound and useful members of the commonwealth would deserve so well of the public, as to have his statue set up for a preserver of the nation.

But my intention is very far from being confined to provide only for the children of professed beggars; it is of a much greater extent, and shall take in the whole number of infants at a certain age, who are born of parents in effect as little able to support them, as those who demand our charity in the streets.

> **?** *What problem does the narrator propose to solve? In the next paragraph, look for the first statement of his proposal.*

As to my own part, having turned my thoughts, for many years, upon this important subject, and maturely weighed the several schemes of other projectors,[6] I have always found them grossly mistaken in their computation. It is true a child, just dropped from its dam,[7] may be supported by her milk, for a solar year[8] with little other nourishment, at most not above the value of two shillings, which the mother may certainly get, or the value in scraps, by her lawful occupation of begging, and it is exactly at one year old that I propose to provide for them, in such a manner, as, instead of being a charge upon their parents, or the parish, or wanting food and raiment[9] for the rest of their lives, they shall, on the contrary, contribute to the feeding and partly to the clothing of many thousands.

There is likewise another great advantage in my scheme, that it will prevent those voluntary abortions, and that horrid practice of women murdering their bastard children, alas! too frequent among us, sacrificing the poor innocent babes, I doubt,[10] more to avoid the expense, than the shame, which would move tears and pity in the most savage and inhuman breast.

The number of souls[11] in Ireland being usually reckoned one million and a half, of these I calculate there may be about two hundred thousand couples whose wives are breeders, from which number I subtract thirty thousand couples, who are able to maintain their own children, although I apprehend there cannot be so many under the present distresses of the kingdom, but this being granted, there will remain an hundred and seventy thousand breeders. I again subtract fifty thousand for those women who miscarry, or whose children die by accident, or disease within the year. There only remain an hundred and twenty thousand children of poor parents annually born: The question therefore is, how this number shall be reared, and provided for, which, as I have already said, under the present situation of affairs, is utterly impossible by all the methods hitherto proposed, for we can neither employ them in handicraft,[12] or agriculture; we neither build houses (I mean in the country) nor cultivate land: They can very seldom pick up a livelihood by stealing until they arrive at six years old, except where they are of towardly parts,[13] although, I confess they learn the rudiments much earlier, during which time, they can however be properly looked upon only as probationers,[14] as I have been informed by a principal gentleman in the county of Cavan,[15] who protested to me, that he never knew above one or two instances under the age of six, even in a part of the kingdom so renowned for the quickest proficiency in that art.[16]

I am assured by our merchants, that a boy or girl, before twelve years old, is no saleable com-

4. **the Pretender:** James Edward (1688–1766), son of England's last Catholic king, the deposed James II (1633–1701); James Edward made several attempts to gain the English throne.
5. **sell . . . Barbadoes:** go to the West Indies and work as indentured servants to pay off their passage.
6. **projectors:** speculators; schemers.
7. **dam:** mother (ordinarily used only of animals).
8. **solar year:** from the first day of spring in one year to the last day of winter in the next.
9. **raiment** (rā′mənt): clothing.
10. **doubt:** suspect.
11. **souls:** people.
12. **handicraft:** manufacturing.
13. **of towardly parts:** exceptionally advanced or mature for their age.
14. **probationers:** apprentices.
15. **Cavan:** inland county in Ireland that is remote from Dublin.
16. **that art:** stealing.

Resources

Viewing and Representing

Fine Art Transparency

A fine art transparency of Thomas Gainsborough's *A Cottage Girl with Dog and Pitcher* can be used as a prereading motivator. See the *Viewing and Representing Transparencies and Worksheets:*

- Transparency 7
- Worksheet, p. 28

C Reading Skills and Strategies

Interpreting Connotations

? Why has the author chosen to use the phrase "dropped from its dam" instead of simply saying "born"? [Swift is making the poor parents and their children seem like animals rather than people.]

D Reading Skills and Strategies

Recognizing Persuasive Techniques

? What type of appeal is the writer making in this passage? [Possible answers: An ethical appeal— his plan will eliminate abortion and infanticide. Students may also reasonably interpret this as an emotional appeal.]

E Elements of Literature

Irony

? How are these remarks about stealing ironic? [Possible answers: Because most people want their children to grow up and get good jobs, it is ironic to train people to steal as a profession; the remarks mock the English stereotype of the Irish as dishonest.]

Answer to Boxed Question

The narrator proposes to solve the problem of the "prodigious" number of poverty-stricken Irish children.

Reaching All Students

English Language Learners

English language learners benefit from knowing how information is connected. Encourage them to write the word *proposal* at the center of a web, and to take notes as they read on the details of this proposal. Encourage students to add subcategories to their web as they go along: For example, they might detail information on who will benefit from the proposal and how.

Advanced Learners

Ask students to find out how this essay was received once it was published in 1729. (Many readers took Swift seriously and accused him of cannibalism.) Invite students to share what they learn with the class.

Ⓐ Elements of Literature
Satire

? What methods of satire are used in this passage about the market value of children? [Possible answers: understatement (the idea of pricing a child); verbal irony (the author's proposal is not "modest" but instead outrageous); situational irony (the very idea of selling a child for food is a reversal of all that we value); and parody (mimicking the language of business).]

Ⓑ Reading Skills and Strategies
Interpreting Connotations

? Why does Swift choose to use the word *devoured*? [Possible answers: Not only does it refer to eating, it also refers to the idea that the rich landlords have already consumed the resources of the parents' rents. It has connotations of both greed and gluttony.]

Ⓒ Elements of Literature
Satire

? What attitudes toward Catholics are being satirized? [Possible answers: Swift is satirizing the attitude that deems a Catholic child less valuable or desirable than a Protestant one. He is also satirizing Protestants who want to get rid of Catholics. Swift may also be mocking Catholics themselves, for his narrator makes fun of the fact that so many children are born nine months after Lent, a time supposedly devoted to fasting and other religious abstinence.]

Ⓓ Reading Skills and Strategies
Recognizing Persuasive Techniques

? In discussing the economics of his proposal, what kind of appeal is the writer making? [a logical appeal]

Ⓔ Elements of Literature
Irony

? What kind of irony is present in this logical appeal? [Verbal irony: The facts and figures are marshaled in defense of an indefensible proposal; the writer does not mean what he is saying but means the opposite.]

Answers to Boxed Questions
He is proposing that children be sold as meat. He believes Catholics contribute to their poverty by having too many children.

---

modity, and even when they come to this age, they will not yield above three pounds, or three pounds and half a crown at most on the exchange, which cannot turn to account[17] either to the parents or the kingdom, the charge of nutriment and rags having been at least four times that value.

I shall now therefore humbly propose my own thoughts, which I hope will not be liable to the least objection.

I have been assured by a very knowing American[18] of my acquaintance in London, that a young healthy child well nursed is at a year old a most delicious, nourishing, and wholesome food, whether stewed, roasted, baked, or boiled, and I make no doubt that it will equally serve in a fricassee,[19] or ragout.[20]

> **?** *Here the narrator offers his "modest" proposal. What horrible plan is he actually proposing?*

I do therefore humbly offer it to public consideration, that of the hundred and twenty thousand children, already computed, twenty thousand may be reserved for breed, whereof only one-fourth part to be males, which is more than we allow to sheep, black cattle, or swine, and my reason is that these children are seldom the fruits of marriage, a circumstance not much regarded by our savages; therefore one male will be sufficient to serve four females. That the remaining hundred thousand may at a year old be offered in sale to the persons of quality, and fortune, through the kingdom, always advising the mother to let them suck plentifully in the last month, so as to render them plump, and fat for a good table. A child will make two dishes at an entertainment for friends, and when the family dines alone, the fore or hind quarter will make a reasonable dish, and seasoned with a little pepper or salt will be very good boiled on the fourth day, especially in winter.

I have reckoned upon a medium, that a child just born will weigh twelve pounds, and in a solar year if tolerably nursed increaseth to twenty-eight pounds.

I grant this food will be somewhat dear,[21] and therefore very proper for landlords, who, as they have already devoured[22] most of the parents, seem to have the best title to the children.

Infant's flesh will be in season throughout the year, but more plentiful in March, and a little before and after, for we are told by a grave author,[23] an eminent French physician, that fish being a prolific diet, there are more children born in Roman Catholic countries about nine months after Lent, than at any other season, therefore reckoning a year after Lent, the markets will be more glutted than usual, because the number of popish[24] infants, is at least three to one in this kingdom, and therefore it will have one other collateral advantage by lessening the number of papists among us.

> **?** *Reread this paragraph carefully. What bias does the narrator reveal?*

I have already computed the charge of nursing a beggar's child (in which list I reckon all cottagers,[25] laborers, and four-fifths of the farmers) to be about two shillings per annum,[26] rags included, and I believe no gentleman would repine to give ten shillings for the carcass of a good fat child, which, as I have said will make four dishes of excellent nutritive meat, when he hath only some particular friend, or his own family to dine with him. Thus the squire will learn to be a good landlord, and grow popular among his tenants, the mother will have eight shillings net profit, and be fit for work until she produceth another child.

Those who are more thrifty (as I must confess the times require) may flay[27] the carcass; the skin of which, artificially[28] dressed, will make ad-

17. **turn to account:** be profitable.
18. **American:** To Swift's readers, this label would suggest a barbaric person.
19. **fricassee** (frik′ə·sē′): stew with a light gravy.
20. **ragout** (ra·go͞o′): highly flavored stew.
21. **dear:** expensive.
22. **devoured:** made poor by charging high rents.
23. **grave author:** François Rabelais (frän·swȧ′ rab′ə·lā′) (c. 1483–1553), French satirist; his work is comic, not "grave."
24. **popish:** Roman Catholic; a derogatory term.
25. **cottagers:** tenant farmers.
26. **per annum:** Latin for "by the year"; annually.
27. **flay:** remove the skin of.
28. **artificially:** with great artifice; that is, skillfully.

WORDS TO OWN
glutted (glut′id) *v.:* overfilled.

Using Students' Strengths

Intrapersonal Learners
Encourage intrapersonal learners to keep a journal or log of their responses to this essay as they read. Ask them to record their thoughts not only about the proposal but their reactions to and conjectures about the personality and motives of this "proposer."

Courtesy of the National Library of Ireland, Dublin.

Images of Ireland (18th century). Hand-colored pastel drawings used for engraving in Mr. and Mrs. S. C. Hail's *Ireland* (1841–1843).

mirable gloves for ladies, and summer boots for fine gentlemen.

As to our city of Dublin, shambles[29] may be appointed for this purpose, in the most convenient parts of it, and butchers we may be assured will not be wanting, although I rather recommend buying the children alive, and dressing them hot from the knife, as we do roasting pigs. F

A very worthy person, a true lover of his country, and whose virtues I highly esteem, was lately pleased, in discoursing on this matter, to offer a refinement upon my scheme. He said, that many gentlemen of this kingdom, having of late destroyed their deer, he conceived that the want of venison might be well supplied by the bodies of young lads and maidens, not exceeding fourteen years of age, nor under twelve, so great a number of both sexes in every country being now ready to starve, for want of work and service:[30] and these to be disposed of by their parents if alive, or otherwise by their nearest relations. But with due deference to so excellent a friend, and so deserving a patriot, I cannot be altogether in his sentiments, for as to the males, my American acquaintance assured me from frequent experience, that their flesh was generally tough and lean, like that of our schoolboys, by continual exercise, and their taste disagreeable, and to fatten them would not answer the charge. Then as to the females, it would, I think with humble submission,[31] be a loss to the public, because they soon would become breeders themselves: And besides it is not improbable that some scrupulous people might be apt to censure such a practice (although in-

29. **shambles:** slaughterhouses.
30. **service:** employment as servants.

31. **with humble submission:** with all due respect to those who hold such opinions.

Words to Own

deference (def′ər·əns) *n.:* respect.
scrupulous (skro͞o′pyə·ləs) *adj.:* extremely careful and precise in deciding what is right or wrong.
censure (sen′shər) *v.:* to condemn.

Responding to the Art

These are rare pastels drawn from life in eighteenth-century Ireland. Refer students also to the little watercolor that opens the essay, on p. 502.
Activity. Ask students what these pictures tell them about life in Ireland in Swift's time. [Note the beggars, the poverty, the creels or handmade baskets, the way the people are dressed. Note the all-too familiar image of the starving child, in an orphanage, with the caption "Oh some of them are too naked to stand up."]

F Reading Skills and Strategies

Distinguishing Shades of Meaning

? When the narrator suggests "dressing" children "hot from the knife" what does he mean? What effect does he expect his word choice to have? [The narrator is suggesting that the children be "dressed" or stuffed when they are freshly killed. He expects that this advice will horrify his readers.]

Professional Notes

Scholar C. F. Main writes that "Swift has always been a controversial figure to his biographers, who have attacked him, defended him, and speculated wildly about his life, especially about his relationships with women. Some biographers have claimed that he was married to Esther Johnson, a friend whom Swift always called Stella. Fourteen years younger than he, Stella was just a child when Swift first met her at Sir William Temple's house and began to supervise her education. Eventually they became so deeply attached to each other—though there was always a third person present whenever they met—that at Swift's suggestion she moved to Dublin, where she lived with a Mrs. Dingley, who had also been a member of Temple's household. There is no evidence at all that Swift and Stella ever married. However odd their relationship may appear, many letters, journals, and poems exist to prove that it was a very satisfactory one for both Swift and Stella."

Ⓐ English Language Learners

Archaic Language

Explain that while we usually use the word *abroad* to mean "outside the country," the expression *to go abroad* was once more commonly used simply to mean "to go out" or "to go outdoors," as it does here.

Ⓑ Reading Skills and Strategies

Distinguishing Shades of Meaning

? What meaning does the word *reasonably* have in this passage? [It suggests, ironically, that Swift's readers expect a certain class of people to perish by hideous means.]

Ⓒ Historical Connections

Here Swift gets more personal by attacking Protestants who live in England and do not support the Church of Ireland, in which he was a priest.

Ⓓ Historical Connections

Tenant Farms

Direct students' attention to the final observation that English landlords have already seized the tenants' corn, cattle, and money. Remind students of Britain's rigid class structure, which enriched the ruling class at the expense of the working class. The tenant farm system in Ireland could permanently impoverish and indebt an individual or a family to a landowner. A farmer could work all year and owe more than was made on the farm.

Ⓔ Historical Connections

"Colonial" Ireland

During this period, England treated Ireland like a colony, plundering it for resources and exploiting the Irish by selling them the goods made from those resources. During Swift's time, important goals for Ireland were to circulate money within its borders and to grow and manufacture its own goods.

Answers to Boxed Questions

He wants readers to be repulsed and angry. The problem of the "aged, diseased, or maimed" is also taken up. Swift dismisses that as a problem, saying that they are dying every day from cold, famine, filth, and vermin and will soon be no problem as they will be dead.

deed very unjustly) as a little bordering upon cruelty, which, I confess, hath always been with me the strongest objection against any project, how well soever intended.

> ? *The narrator claims to be sensitive to charges of cruelty. How do you think Swift wants you to feel about the narrator?*

But in order to justify my friend, he confessed that this expedient was put into his head by the famous Sallmanaazor,[32] a native of the island Formosa, who came from thence to London, above twenty years ago, and in conversation told my friend, that in his country when any young person happened to be put to death, the executioner sold the carcass to persons of quality, as a prime dainty, and that, in his time, the body of a plump girl of fifteen, who was crucified for an attempt to poison the emperor, was sold to his imperial majesty's prime minister of state, and other great mandarins[33] of the court, in joints[34] from the gibbet,[35] at four hundred crowns. Neither indeed can I deny, that if the same use were made of several plump young girls in this town, who, without one single groat to their fortunes, cannot stir abroad (A) without a chair,[36] and appear at the playhouse, and assemblies in foreign fineries, which they never will pay for; the kingdom would not be the worse.

(B) Some persons of a desponding spirit are in great concern about that vast number of poor people, who are aged, diseased, or maimed, and I have been desired to employ my thoughts what course may be taken, to ease the nation of so grievous an encumbrance. But I am not in the least pain upon that matter, because it is very well known, that they are every day dying, and rotting, by cold, and famine, and filth, and vermin,[37] as fast as can be reasonably expected. And as to the younger laborers they are now in almost as hopeful[38] a condition. They cannot get work, and consequently pine away for want of nourishment, to a degree, that if at any time they are accidentally hired to common labor, they have not strength to perform it, and thus the country and themselves are in a fair way[39] of being soon delivered from the evils to come.

> ? *What other problem does the narrator take up? What is his solution, and how is it similar to his main proposal?*

I have too long digressed, and therefore shall return to my subject. I think the advantages by the proposal which I have made are obvious and many as well as of the highest importance.

For first, as I have already observed, it would greatly lessen the number of papists, with whom we are yearly overrun, being the principal breeders of the nation, as well as our most dangerous enemies, and who stay at home on purpose with a (C) design to deliver the kingdom to the Pretender, hoping to take their advantage by the absence of so many good Protestants,[40] who have chosen rather to leave their country, than stay at home, and pay tithes[41] against their conscience, to an idolatrous Episcopal curate.

(D) (E) Secondly, the poorer tenants will have something valuable of their own, which by law may be made liable to distress,[42] and help to pay their landlord's rent, their corn and cattle being already seized, and money a thing unknown.

Thirdly, whereas the maintenance of an hundred thousand children, from two years old, and upwards, cannot be computed at less than ten

32. **Sallmanaazor:** George Psalmanazar (c. 1679–1763), a Frenchman who pretended to be from Formosa, an old Portuguese name for Taiwan; his writings were fraudulent.
33. **mandarins** (man′də·rinz): officials. The term comes from *mandarim,* the Portuguese word for high-ranking officials in the Chinese empire, with which the Portuguese traded.
34. **joints:** large cuts of meat, including the bone.
35. **gibbet** (jib′it): gallows.
36. **chair:** sedan chair; a covered seat carried by servants.
37. **vermin:** pests such as lice, fleas, and bedbugs.
38. **hopeful:** actually, hopeless. Swift is using the word with intentional irony.
39. **are in a fair way:** have a good chance.
40. **good Protestants:** that is, in Swift's view, bad Protestants, because they object to the Church of Ireland's bishops and regard them as "idolatrous."
41. **tithes** (tīthz): monetary gifts to the church equivalent to one tenth of each donor's income.
42. **liable to distress:** That is, the money from the sale of their children may be seized by their landlords.

Words to Own

expedient (ek·spē′dē·ənt) *n.:* convenient means to an end.
digressed (di·grest′) *v.:* wandered off the subject.

Skill Link

Recognizing Logical, Deceptive, and Faulty Modes of Reasoning

Remind students of some of the pitfalls of argument, such as manipulating statistics to lead to invalid conclusions, slanting an argument, and suggesting a false cause.

Ask students to determine the faulty modes of reasoning that underlie the following arguments, paraphrased from *A Modest Proposal:*

1. There is no reason to worry about the conditions of older, sick, or disabled people: They are dying as fast as can be expected.
2. There is no reason to worry about young laborers: They can't get work, so they will probably starve to death.
3. The cost of rearing children will be eliminated.
4. The profits gained by selling children will result in a better economy for everyone.
5. Because mothers will profit from selling their children, they will be more loving toward them.

shillings apiece per annum, the nation's stock will be thereby increased fifty thousand pounds per annum, besides the profit of a new dish, introduced to the tables of all gentlemen of fortune in the kingdom, who have any refinement in taste, and the money will circulate among ourselves, the goods being entirely of our own growth and manufacture.[43]

Fourthly, the constant breeders, besides the gain of eight shillings sterling per annum, by the sale of their children, will be rid of the charge of maintaining them after the first year.

Fifthly, this food would likewise bring great custom to taverns, where the vintners[44] will certainly be so prudent as to procure the best receipts[45] for dressing it to perfection, and consequently have their houses frequented by all the fine gentlemen, who justly value themselves upon their knowledge in good eating, and a skillful cook, who understands how to oblige his guests will contrive to make it as expensive as they please.

Sixthly, this would be a great inducement to marriage, which all wise nations have either encouraged by rewards, or enforced by laws and penalties. It would increase the care and tenderness of mothers toward their children, when they were sure of a settlement for life to the poor babes, provided in some sort by the public to their annual profit instead of expense, we should soon see an honest emulation[46] among the married women, which of them could bring the fattest child to the market, men would become as fond of their wives, during the time of their pregnancy, as they are now of their mares in foal, their cows in calf, or sows when they are ready to farrow,[47] nor offer to beat or kick them (as is too frequent a practice) for fear of a miscarriage.

> **?** *The narrator states the specific advantages of his proposal. Who profits from these "advantages," and who suffers?*

Many other advantages might be enumerated. For instance, the addition of some thousand carcasses in our exportation of barreled beef. The propagation of swine's flesh, and improvement in the art of making good bacon, so much wanted among us by the great destruction of pigs, too frequent at our tables, which are no way comparable in taste, or magnificence to a well-grown, fat yearling child, which roasted whole will make a considerable figure at a Lord Mayor's feast, or any other public entertainment. But this, and many others I omit being studious of brevity.

Supposing that one thousand families in this city, would be constant customers for infants' flesh, besides others who might have it at merry meetings, particularly weddings and christenings, I compute that Dublin would take off annually about twenty thousand carcasses, and the rest of the kingdom (where probably they will be sold somewhat cheaper) the remaining eighty thousand.

I can think of no one objection, that will possibly be raised against this proposal, unless it should be urged that the number of people will be thereby much lessened in the kingdom. This I freely own, and it was indeed one principal design in offering it to the world. I desire the reader will observe, that I calculate my remedy for this one individual kingdom of Ireland, and for no other that ever was, is, or, I think, ever can be upon earth. Therefore let no man talk to me of other expedients:[48] *Of taxing our absentees*[49] *at five shillings a pound; of using neither clothes, nor household furniture, except what is of our own growth and manufacture; of utterly rejecting the materials and instruments that promote foreign luxury; of curing the expensiveness of pride, vanity, idleness, and gaming*[50] *in our women; of introducing a vein of parsimony,*[51]

43. **own growth and manufacture:** home-grown, edible children, not imported ones.
44. **vintners** (vint′nərz): wine merchants.
45. **receipts:** old-fashioned for "recipes."
46. **emulation** (em′yo͞o·lā′shən): competition.
47. **farrow** (far′ō): to produce piglets.

48. **other expedients:** At one time or another, Swift had advocated all these measures for the relief of Ireland, but they were all ignored by the government. This section was italicized in all editions printed during Swift's lifetime to indicate that Swift made these proposals sincerely rather than ironically.
49. **absentees:** English landowners who refused to live on their Irish property.
50. **gaming:** gambling.
51. **parsimony** (pär′sə·mō′nē): thriftiness; economy.

WORDS TO OWN
procure (prō·kyoor′) *v.:* to obtain; get.
brevity (brev′ə·tē) *n.:* being brief.

F Reading Skills and Strategies
Recognizing Persuasive Techniques

? What type of appeal is this? [another logical appeal, based on statistics]

G Elements of Literature
Irony

? What do you find to be the most ironic aspect of this paragraph? [Possible answer: The idea that people would feast on children at weddings and even worse, at christenings, is brutally ironic.]

H Struggling Readers
Breaking Down Difficult Text

This begins a list of ideas that Swift actually regards as reasonable but doubts will be implemented. Ask students to determine where each separate idea begins. [The semicolon marks off each idea.]

I Critical Thinking
Recognizing Bias

Although Swift is searing in his condemnation of the English and their prejudices against the Irish, he expresses a few prejudices of his own and of his time. Ask students to identify them. [Possible answers: He expresses a prejudice against women; he regards his culture as superior to those in Lapland and Brazil; he reflects the prejudice of his time against Jews; he looks down on and condemns shopkeepers.]

Answer to Boxed Question

He claims that society as a whole, including the Protestants, the landlords, the tavern owners and wine merchants, and the poor themselves will benefit. In truth, the poor would suffer horrendously.

Assessing Learning

Check Test: True-False

1. Swift's proposal takes into account only the children of beggars. [False]
2. Swift says that children born to poor parents in Ireland could become useful, wage-earning citizens if they were well fed. [False]
3. The proposal recommends that the majority of children would be saved for breeding purposes. [False]
4. Swift points out that one advantage of the proposal would be an increase in marriages. [True]
5. Swift recommends against exporting the new commodity. [True]

Standardized Test Preparation

For practice with ACT and SAT formats see
- *Preparation for College Admission Exams,* p. 21

For practice in proofreading and editing, see
- *Daily Oral Grammar,* Transparency 14

Ⓐ Critical Thinking

Determining the Author's Purpose

? What clues in this passage reveal the true, rather than ironic, purpose of Swift's essay? [The reference to "visionary" thoughts hints that Swift favors the solutions suggested previously. Swift seems to believe that society lacks the unity and determination to implement these suggestions for improving the lives of the poor, and he seems weary and frustrated by this fact.]

Ⓑ Critical Thinking

Evaluating

? This is information about the cycle of poverty in Ireland, discussed earlier. Why does Swift not only repeat the information but also place it so near the end of the essay? [These are the problems that must be solved, that require radical solutions (though eating children's flesh is not one of them). Swift reminds his reader of just how intolerable life is for some people.]

Ⓒ Reading Skills and Strategies

Recognizing Persuasive Techniques

? With what kinds of appeals does Swift close his essay? [As earlier, Swift relies almost exclusively on logical appeals, however ironic.]

Answer to Boxed Question

First, the politicians do not have a solution to the problem. How would they feed and clothe a hundred thousand useless people? Second, the poor would probably say they would rather have been eaten when they were a year old, rather than have suffered as they have.

prudence, and temperance; of learning to love our country, wherein we differ even from Laplanders, and the inhabitants of Topinamboo;[52] *of quitting our animosities, and factions,*[53] *nor act any longer like the Jews, who were murdering one another at the very moment their city*[54] *was taken; of being a little cautious not to sell our country and consciences for nothing; of teaching landlords to have at least one degree of mercy toward their tenants. Lastly of putting a spirit of honesty, industry, and skill into our shopkeepers, who, if a resolution could now be taken to buy only our native goods, would immediately unite to cheat and exact*[55] *upon us in the price, the measure, and the goodness, nor could ever yet be brought to make one fair proposal of just dealing, though often and earnestly invited to it.*

Therefore I repeat, let no man talk to me of these and the like expedients, till he hath at least a glimpse of hope, that there will ever be some hearty and sincere attempt to put them in practice.

Ⓐ But as to myself, having been wearied out for many years with offering vain, idle, visionary thoughts, and at length utterly despairing of success, I fortunately fell upon this proposal, which as it is wholly new, so it hath something solid and real, of no expense and little trouble, full in our own power, and whereby we can incur no danger in disobliging[56] England. For this kind of commodity will not bear exportation, the flesh being of too tender a consistence, to admit a long continuance in salt, although perhaps I could name a country,[57] which would be glad to eat up our whole nation without it.

After all I am not so violently bent upon my own opinion, as to reject any offer, proposed by wise men, which shall be found equally innocent, cheap, easy, and effectual. But before something of that kind shall be advanced in contradiction to my scheme, and offering a better, I desire the author, or authors will be pleased maturely to consider two points. First, as things now stand, how they will be able to find food and raiment for a hundred thousand useless mouths and backs. And secondly, there being a round million of creatures in human figure, throughout this kingdom, whose whole subsistence[58] put into a common stock would leave them in debt two millions of pounds sterling, adding those who are beggars by profession to the bulk of farmers, cottagers, and laborers, with their wives and children, who are beggars in effect; I desire those politicians, who dislike my overture, and may perhaps be so bold to attempt an answer, that they will first ask the parents of these mortals, whether they would not at this day think it a great happiness to have been sold for food at a year old, in the manner I prescribe, and thereby have avoided such a perpetual scene of misfortunes, as they have since gone through, by the oppression of landlords, the impossibility of paying rent without money or trade, the want of common sustenance, with neither house nor clothes to cover them from inclemencies of weather, Ⓑ and the most inevitable prospect of entailing[59] the like, or great miseries, upon their breed forever.

> **?** *What two points support the narrator's proposal?*

Ⓒ I profess in the sincerity of my heart that I have not the least personal interest in endeavoring to promote this necessary work, having no other motive than the public good of my country, by advancing our trade, providing for infants, relieving the poor, and giving some pleasure to the rich. I have no children, by which I can propose to get a single penny; the youngest being nine years old, and my wife past childbearing.

52. Topinamboo: Swift is referring to a region of Brazil in which reside various native peoples collectively called the Tupinambá. Here, Swift suggests that if Brazilian peoples and Laplanders can love their seemingly inhospitable lands, the Irish should love Ireland.
53. factions: political groups that work against the interests of other such groups or against the main body of government.
54. their city: Jerusalem, which the Roman emperor Titus (A.D. 39–81) destroyed in A.D. 70, while Jewish factions fought one another.
55. exact: force payment.
56. disobliging: offending.
57. a country: England.
58. whole subsistence: all their possessions.
59. entailing: passing on to the next generation.

WORDS TO OWN
animosities (an′ə·mäs′ə·tēz) *n. pl.:* hostilities; violent hatreds or resentments.

Making the Connections

Connecting with the Theme: "The Sting of Satire"

Discuss with students why the sting of this particular satire is so sharp. Students might consider the following:

- What do you learn about the relationship of the English to the Irish at this point in history?
- What do you learn about the condition of the poor in Ireland?
- What do you learn about the cultural differences between the Irish and English?
- What injustices are revealed?
- Who, in particular, might be the target of this criticism?
- What true course of action is recommended?

Connections — A Short Story

Top of the Food Chain

T. Coraghessan Boyle

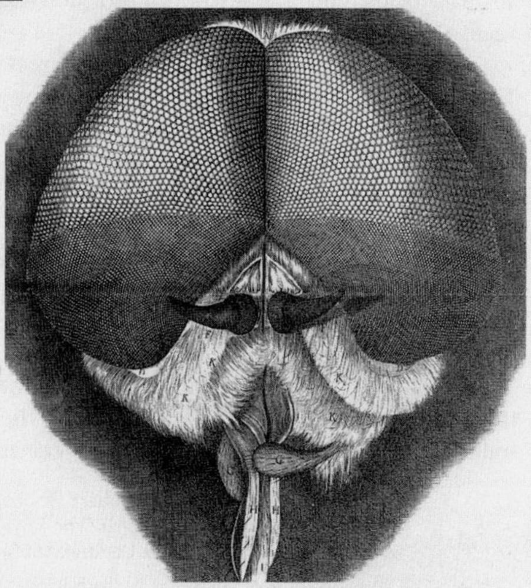

Eye of a Fly (1665) by Robert Hooke, from *Micrographia* (The Royal Society, London, 1665).
Rare Books and Manuscripts Division. The New York Public Library. Astor, Lenox and Tilden Foundations.

The thing was, we had a little problem with the insect vector[1] there, and believe me, your tamer stuff, your Malathion and pyrethrum and the rest of the so-called environmentally safe products,[2] didn't begin to make a dent in it, not a dent, I mean it was utterly useless—we might as well have been spraying Chanel No. 5 for all the good it did. (D) And you've got to realize these people were literally covered with insects day and night—and the fact that they hardly wore any clothes just compounded the problem. Picture if you can, gentlemen, a naked little two-year-old boy so black with flies and mosquitoes it looks like he's wearing long johns, or the young mother so racked with the malarial shakes she can't even lift a Diet Coke (E) to her lips—it was pathetic, just pathetic, like something out of the Dark Ages . . . Well, anyway, the decision was made to go with DDT.[3] In the short term. Just to get the situation under control, you understand.

Yes, that's right, Senator, *DDT:* Dichlorodiphenyltrichloroethane.

Yes, I'm well aware of that fact, sir. But just (F) because *we* banned it domestically, under pressure from the bird-watching contingent and the hopheads down at the EPA, it doesn't necessarily follow that the rest of the world—especially the developing world—was about to (G) jump on the bandwagon. And that's the key word here, Senator: developing. You've got to realize this is Borneo we're talking about here, not Port Townsend or Enumclaw. These people don't know from square one about sanitation, disease control, pest eradication. It rains a hundred and twenty inches a year, minimum.[4] They dig up roots in the jungle. They've still got headhunters along the Rajang River, for god's sake.

And please don't forget they *asked* us to come in there, practically begged us—and not only the World Health Organization but the Sultan of Brunei and the government in Sarawak too. We did what we could to accommodate them and reach our objective in the shortest period of time and by the most direct and effective means. We went to the air. Obviously. And no one could have foreseen the consequences, no one, not even if we'd gone

1. **vector:** bearer or carrier of disease.
2. **Malathion** (mal′ə·thī′än′) **and pyrethrum** (pī·reth′rəm) **. . . safe products:** Malathion and pyrethrum are insecticides made from organic substances. Though they are less toxic than synthetic, or human-made, insecticides, their safety is still debated.
3. **DDT:** a synthetic compound first discovered to be an insecticide in 1939. Widely used during World War II, DDT was later found to cause such toxic effects in other animal populations that its use was severely restricted in the United States in 1972.
4. **hundred and twenty inches . . . minimum:** In comparison, the average yearly rainfall in most of the United States is less than half this figure.

Reaching All Students

Struggling Readers

Because much of this story is implied, have students work in pairs to make the inferences that will fill in the blanks. For instance, the satire opens in mid-conversation. The speaker is responding to an implied question about why his group was in Borneo in the first place. As students read on they need to decide to whom pronouns refer. In other cases, they will need to decide what question was just asked that the speaker is now answering.

English Language Learners

Read aloud the first sentence in a conversational tone. Point out that the narrator uses informal idioms and refers to western products such as the perfume Chanel No. 5. English language learners may enjoy being paired with native speakers who can help them interpret the word choices as well as the tone they create.

Connections

Using the weapon of understatement, this satire lays out the damaging environmental effects of the American decision to spray DDT on the rain forests of Borneo. The speaker blandly chronicles a chain reaction of environmental disasters that he claims could never have been foreseen. He ends with a cliché, saying there is a silver lining in every cloud and things could have turned out worse.

D Struggling Readers

Identifying Pronoun Antecedents

This story begins in the middle of a congressional hearing and never introduces either the speaker or the audience. Ask students to consider who *we, me,* and *you* might be. ["We" includes the narrator and a group probably operating under the authority of the U.S. government. "Me" (or "I") is the leader of, or spokesperson for, that group. "You" are members of the subcommittee investigating what happened.]

E Elements of Literature

Irony

? What is ironic about comparing the inability to lift a Diet Coke can to one's lips to living in the Dark Ages? [It suggests that lifting a Diet Coke can to one's lips is an enlightened or civilized act. It seems to define the ability to drink Diet Coke as a benchmark of our civilization.]

F Advanced Learners

Evaluating

? What is the effect of hearing only the speaker's voice? [The reader must infer not only the questions but the tone of voice in which they are asked. The reader is also free to imagine ways in which the speaker may be skirting questions, as well as his effect upon his listeners.]

G Reading Skills and Strategies

Distinguishing Shades of Meaning

? What does the speaker's use of the word *developing* imply? [He thinks the country is uncivilized; he thinks only scientific advances can help the country. He thinks he knows better than the inhabitants what is best for their country.]

Ⓐ Elements of Literature

Irony

? Why is it ironic that local village headmen wear running shorts? [This shows ways in which the West has infiltrated and changed local Iban culture: In this case, the effect is somewhat humorous, and certainly in contrast to what the reader expects these people might wear. It makes the natives seem a bit absurd because their lives are such a mixture of their traditional ways and influences from the West.]

Ⓑ Reading Skills and Strategies

Interpreting Connotations

? What does the use of the verb *shrug* reveal about the narrator's attitude? [Possible answers: He is acting cool and cavalier; he is indifferent.]

Ⓒ Critical Thinking

Determining the Author's Purpose

By this point in the story, students may be able to predict (especially if they have looked at the illustrations) a whole chain of disastrous events resulting from the use of DDT. Ask students to decide what the author's purpose might have been in creating this fictional scenario. [Possible answers: He is criticizing the ways Americans respond to problems in foreign countries; he is criticizing the use of DDT or other chemicals; he is criticizing ethnocentric attitudes.]

out and generated a hundred environmental impact statements—it was just one of those things, a freak occurrence, and there's no defense against that. Not that I know of, anyway . . .

Caterpillars? Yes, Senator, that's correct. That was the first sign: caterpillars.

But let me backtrack a minute here. You see, out in the bush they have these roofs made of thatched palm leaves—you'll see them in the towns too, even in Bintulu or Brunei—and they're really pretty effective, you'd be surprised. A hundred and twenty inches of rain, they've got to figure a way to keep it out of the hut, and for centuries, this was it. Palm leaves. Well, it was about a month after we sprayed for the final time and I'm sitting at my desk in the trailer thinking about the drainage project at

Blue Fly (1665) by Robert Hooke, from *Micrographia* (The Royal Society, London, 1665).

Rare Books and Manuscripts Division. The New York Public Library. Astor, Lenox and Tilden Foundations.

Kuching, enjoying the fact that for the first time in maybe a year I'm not smearing mosquitoes all over the back of my neck, when there's a knock at the door. It's this elderly gentleman, tattooed from head to toe, dressed only in a pair of running shorts—they love those shorts, by the way, the shiny material and the tight machine stitching, the whole country, men and women both, they can't get enough of them. . . . Anyway, he's the headman of the local village and he's very excited, something about the roofs—*atap,* they call them. That's all he can say, *atap, atap,* over and over again.

It's raining, of course. It's always raining. So I shrug into my rain slicker, start up the 4 × 4, and go have a look. Sure enough, all the *atap* roofs are collapsing, not only in his village but throughout the target area. The people are all huddled there in their running shorts, looking pretty miserable, and one after another the roofs keep falling in, it's bewildering, and gradually I realize the headman's diatribe has begun to feature a new term I was unfamiliar with at the time—the word for caterpillar, as it turns out, in the Iban dialect. But who was to make the connection between three passes with the crop duster and all these staved-in roofs?

Our people finally sorted it out a couple weeks later. The chemical, which, by the way, cut down the number of mosquitoes exponentially, had the unfortunate side effect of killing off this little wasp—I've got the scientific name for it somewhere in my report here, if you're interested—that preyed on a type of caterpillar that in turn ate palm leaves. Well, with the wasps gone, the caterpillars hatched out with nothing to keep them in check and chewed the roofs to pieces, which was unfortunate, we admit it, and we had a real cost overrun on replacing those roofs with tin . . . but the people were happier, I think, in the long run, because, let's face it, no matter how tightly you weave those palm leaves, they're just not going to keep the water out like tin. Of course, nothing's perfect, and we had a lot of complaints about the rain drumming on the panels, people unable to sleep, and what-have-you . . .

Yes, sir, that's correct—the flies were next.

Well, you've got to understand the magnitude of the fly problem in Borneo, there's nothing like it here to compare it with, except maybe a garbage strike in New York. Every minute of every day you've got flies everywhere, up your nose, in your mouth, your ears, your eyes, flies in your rice, your Coke, your Singapore sling, and your gin rickey. It's enough to drive you to distraction, not to mention the diseases these things carry, from dysentery to typhoid to cholera and back round the loop again. And once the mosquito population was down, the flies seemed to breed up to fill in the gap—Borneo wouldn't

Skill Link

Reading to Take Action

Explain that one of the purposes a reader may have for reading satire, in addition to being informed about a subject and entertained, is to learn enough to take action. Ask students what course of future action might be planned on the basis of the following information.

1. A chemical that is outlawed in the United States, DDT, was used in a foreign country, by an American aid group.
2. The group from the U.S. decided to reach "its objective" in the shortest possible amount of time and by the most direct means.
3. The use of DDT had disastrous results, including deaths among the native population.
4. Each "remedy" undertaken had unforeseen results.
5. The whole operation was costly in every way, including financially.

Professional Notes

Rachel Carson and DDT

DDT was used during World War II to kill body lice and fleas and after the war as a crop insecticide. Concern emerged in the 1950s, however, about the fact that the insecticide accumulated in the bodies of birds and fish, a problem documented by Rachel Carson in *Silent Spring* (1962), a seminal work in awakening environmental consciousness. The U.S. government restricted the domestic use of DDT in 1972, but permitted its sale abroad.

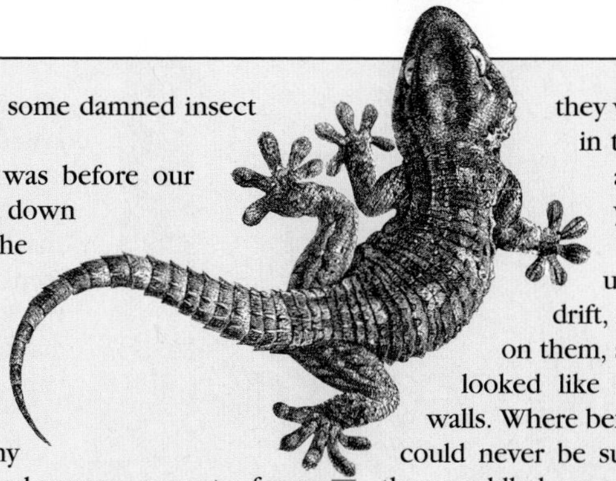

be Borneo without some damned insect blackening the air.

Of course, this was before our people had tracked down the problem with the caterpillars and the wasps and all of that, and so we figured we'd had a big success with the mosquitoes, why not a series of ground sweeps, mount a fogger in the back of a Suzuki Brat, and sanitize the huts, not to mention the open sewers, which as you know are nothing but a breeding ground for flies, chiggers, and biting insects of every sort. At least it was an error of commission rather than omission. At least we were trying.

I watched the flies go down myself. One day they were so thick in the trailer I couldn't even *find* my paperwork, let alone attempt to get through it, and the next they were collecting on the windows, bumbling around like they were drunk. A day later they were gone. Just like that. From a million flies in the trailer to none . . .

Well, no one could have foreseen that, Senator.

The geckos ate the flies, yes. You're all familiar with geckos, I assume, gentlemen? These are the lizards you've seen during your trips to Hawaii, very colorful, patrolling the houses for roaches and flies, almost like pets, but of course they're wild animals, never lose sight of that, and just about as unsanitary as anything I can think of, except maybe flies.

Yes, well don't forget, sir, we're viewing this with twenty-twenty hindsight, but at the time no one gave a thought to geckos or what they ate—they were just another fact of life in the tropics. Mosquitoes, lizards, scorpions, leeches—you name it, they've got it. When the flies began piling up on the windowsills like drift, naturally the geckos feasted on them, stuffing themselves till they looked like sausages crawling up the walls. Where before they moved so fast you could never be sure you'd seen them, now they waddled across the floor, laid around in the corners, clung to the air vents like magnets—and even then no one paid much attention to them till they started turning belly-up in the streets. Believe me, we confirmed a lot of things there about the buildup of these products[5] as you move up the food chain and the efficacy—or lack thereof—of certain methods, no doubt about that . . .

The cats? That's where it got sticky, really sticky. You see, nobody really lost any sleep over a pile of dead lizards—though we did tests routinely and the tests confirmed what we'd expected, that is, the product had been concentrated in the geckos because of the number of contaminated flies they consumed. But lizards are one thing and cats are another. These people really have an affection for their cats—no house, no hut, no matter how primitive, is without at least a couple of them. Mangy-looking things, long-legged and scrawny, maybe, not at all the sort of animal you'd see here, but there it was: They loved their cats. Because the cats were functional, you understand—without them, the place would have been swimming in rodents inside of a week.

You're right there, Senator, yes—that's exactly what happened.

You see, the cats had a field day with these feeble geckos—you can imagine, if any of you have ever owned a cat, the kind of joy these animals must have experienced to see their nemesis, this ultra-quick lizard, and it's just barely creeping across the floor like a bug.

5. **these products:** insecticides.

D Reading Skills and Strategies

Recognizing Persuasive Techniques

? Many of the details included in this story by a prominent American writer are horrifying and revolting. Why does the author include them? [Details such as the unhealthy conditions of the sewers are part of the emotional appeal of the story. Although the narrator recounts them in a very matter-of-fact way, the reader gains insight into the enormity and horror of the problems.]

E Elements of Literature

Satire

? Why is the reference to Hawaiian trips satirical? [It implies that while the countries they are supposedly helping are suffering, the senators are off on vacation.]

F English Language Learners

Colloquial Language

Tell students that this use of the word *sticky* is colloquial. Ask students to use context clues to decide what it means. [troublesome, difficult to deal with]

G Reading Skills and Strategies

Predicting

? What do you think happens next? [Possible answers: The cats die from eating the poisoned geckos. Rats overrun the area and become the next problem.]

Connecting Across Texts

Connecting with "A Modest Proposal"

If T. Coraghessan Boyle could sit down and have a chat with Jonathan Swift, chances seem good that the two men would agree that humans sometimes don't deserve to be at the top of the food chain. They might also agree that human interests often run contrary to nature. To stimulate discussion about how these two pieces of literature overlap, consider asking these questions:

- **What devices do both Swift and Boyle use to create their satires?** [Both propose outrageous solutions to serious problems. Both use exaggeration and understatement, as well as biting barbs that condemn those whom the authors believe to be at fault.]
- **In what ways are both works highly persuasive?** [Swift's essay argues against the inhumane conditions in which the poor Irish live and very effectively uses ironic logical appeals. Boyle's story argues against ethnocentrism and shortsightedness in response to environmental problems; it effectively uses ironic emotional appeals.]
- **Which satire do you find more effective and why?** [Boyle's satire of modern American attitudes is more immediate, and so more humorous; or Swift's audacious proposal is a masterpiece that showcases the range and power of satire.]

A Reading Skills and Strategies

Recognizing Persuasive Techniques

? How does this outcome make the ultimate argument against the course of action undertaken by the narrator? [It shows its disastrous result, which is bubonic plague, the great killer of Medieval Europe. It also understates the effects of the plague in a barbaric way ("we lost a few").]

B Critical Thinking

Evaluating

? Do you think this is an example of effective persuasive writing? [Possible answers: No, it is only fiction, and it succeeds more in disturbing people than calling them to action. Yes, it shows clearly that one society does not necessarily know what is best for another.]

Well, to make a long story short, the cats ate up every dead and dying gecko in the country, from snout to tail, and then the cats began to die . . . which to my mind would have been no great loss if it wasn't for the rats. Suddenly there were rats everywhere—you couldn't drive down the street without running over half-a-dozen of them at a time. They fouled the grain supplies, fell in the wells and died, bit infants as they slept in their cradles. But that wasn't the worst, not by a long shot. No, things really went down the tube after that. Within the month we were getting scattered reports of bubonic plague, and of course we tracked them all down and made sure the people got a round of treatment with antibiotics, but still we lost a few and the rats kept coming . . . **A**

It was my plan, yes. I was brainstorming one night, rats scuttling all over the trailer like something out of a cheap horror film, the villagers in a panic over the threat of the plague and the stream of nonstop hysterical reports from the interior—people were turning black, swelling up and bursting, that sort of thing—well, as I say, I came up with a plan, a stopgap, not perfect, not cheap, but at this juncture, I'm sure you'll agree, something had to be implemented.

We wound up going as far as Australia for some of the cats, cleaning out the SPCA facilities and what-have-you, though we rounded most of them up in Indonesia and Singapore—approximately fourteen thousand in all. And yes, it cost us—cost us upfront purchase money and aircraft fuel and pilots' overtime and all the rest of it—but we really felt there was no alternative. It was like all nature had turned against us.

And yet still, all things considered, we made a lot of friends for the U.S.A. the day we dropped those cats, and you should have seen them, gentlemen, the little parachutes and harnesses we'd tricked up, fourteen thousand of them, cats in every color of the rainbow, cats with one ear, no ears, half a tail, three-legged cats, cats that could have taken pride of show in Springfield, Massachusetts, and all of them twirling down out of the sky like great big oversized snowflakes . . .

It was something. It was really something.

Of course, you've all seen the reports. There were other factors we hadn't counted on, adverse conditions in the paddies and manioc fields[6]—we don't to this day know what predatory species were inadvertently killed off by the initial sprayings, it's just a mystery—but the weevils[7] and whatnot took a pretty heavy toll on the crops that year, and by the time **B** we dropped the cats, well—the people were pretty hungry, and I suppose it was inevitable that we lost a good proportion of them right then and there. But we've got a CARE program going there now and something hit the rat population—we still don't know what, a virus, we think—and the geckos, they tell me, are making a comeback.

So what I'm saying is it could be worse, and to every cloud a silver lining, wouldn't you agree, gentlemen?

6. **paddies and manioc fields:** Paddies, or rice paddies, are small, flooded fields used to grow rice in eastern and southern Asia. Manioc, also called cassava, is a kind of tuber cultivated in tropical areas.

7. **weevils:** snouted beetles extremely destructive to rice and grain crops.

Reading Check

a. The narrator says the landlords should have the first claim on the flesh of the children, since they have already figuratively devoured the parents.

b. The narrator says males are too tough and their taste is disagreeable. Females would be a loss to the breeding population. Also, some people think the practice borders on cruelty. He says old people are already dying as quickly as can be reasonably expected.

c. According to the narrator, his plan (1) reduces the number of Catholics, (2) gives the poor a tangible asset, (3) aids the economy and introduces a new food, (4) decreases the time "breeders" have to raise children, (5) improves tavern business and (6) encourages marriage.

d. The proposal, if carried out, would diminish the population.

e. Swift does not begin to reveal his proposal until the ninth paragraph. The main idea is that impoverished children be sold to and eaten by the rich.

MAKING MEANINGS

First Thoughts

1. Do you think Swift goes too far in *A Modest Proposal*? Why or why not?

Shaping Interpretations

2. Why does the narrator express the hope that his plan "will not be liable to the least objection" just before he introduces it? What is **ironic** in Swift's use of the word *modest* to describe his proposal?
3. How would you state the **purpose** of this essay? Whom or what is Swift trying to reform?
4. Describe the narrator's real meaning when he asserts that England will not mind if Ireland kills and eats its babies. What element of **satire** is evident here?
5. Near the end of the pamphlet, the speaker lists "other expedients" that might help lessen the present distress in Ireland. Some of these options are very constructive. Why, then, does the narrator brush these ideas for reform aside?
6. Find sentences in which the speaker uses **ethical appeals** by describing himself favorably and claiming to possess virtues that—considering the nature of his proposal—he could not possibly have. (Check your reading notes.)

Reading Check

a. Why does the narrator think the food he proposes is "very proper for landlords"?
b. Why does the narrator reject the idea of selling and eating the twelve- to fourteen-year-olds? Why is he unconcerned about old people suffering from sickness, poverty, and neglect?
c. About midway in the pamphlet, the narrator lists the advantages of his proposal. What are the six principal advantages?
d. Describe the one objection that the narrator anticipates to his proposal.
e. Where does Swift tell what his "modest" proposal is? How would you **sum up** his proposal's **main idea**?

7. Find places in the proposal where the speaker uses **logical appeals** to support his suggestions. (Be sure to check your reading notes.)

Extending the Text

8. What other human disasters resulting from bureaucratic incompetence around the world could be targets for another "modest proposal"?

READING SKILLS AND STRATEGIES

Interpreting Connotations: Emotional Appeals

Diction, or word choice, is especially important in **persuasive writing.** Swift is particularly skillful in choosing words with strong **connotations**—that is, words loaded with strong feelings, associations, or even judgments. Some of Swift's loaded words follow. (Check your reading notes to see if you spotted more.)

savages	beggars	filth
male and female	rags	idolatrous
popish infants	breeders	carcasses

In each instance, another word or term could have been chosen to create a different, less harsh effect. For example, *male* and *female*—as opposed to *man* and *woman*—make us think of animals, not human beings, which is Swift's intention.

1. Find the places in the text where the words listed above are used. What is the emotional effect of each word choice?
2. What other tamer or more positive words could have been used to create different emotional effects?

MAKING MEANINGS

First Thoughts [Respond]

1. Students might believe that any response to injustice, no matter how extreme, is justified; or they might feel that Swift's proposal is too graphic and that his irony might be lost on some readers.

Shaping Interpretations [Interpret]

2. Without the irony, readers might take the proposal seriously. Both the expression of the hope and the description of the proposal as "modest" are ironic, given the outlandish character of the proposal.
3. Swift is drawing attention to the predicament of the Irish by recommending extreme and ridiculous solutions. He hopes to reform English landlords, ineffective political leaders, and "rational" social planners.
4. One interpretation is that the narrator is criticizing the cruelty and insensitivity of the English. He purposely overstates the case, using exaggeration to call attention to hardships in Ireland.
5. By mentioning reasonable solutions, Swift emphasizes Britain's failure to design and implement constructive programs to improve the miserable conditions in Ireland. Swift brushes these proposals aside just as England has in the past.
6. Among claims of the narrator's virtues are paragraph 4, sentence 1; paragraph 8, sentence 1; last paragraph, sentence 1.
7. Logical appeals appear throughout the essay, including in the sixth and seventh paragraphs.

Extending the Text [Apply/Synthesize]

8. Responses will vary. Students might use the themes of world hunger, outbreaks of epidemics, or environmental degradation.

READING SKILLS AND STRATEGIES

1. Possible emotions associated with each word are: savages—contempt; male and female—debasement; popish infants—prejudice; beggars—contempt; rags—pity; breeders—dehumanizing; filth—disgust; idolatrous—self-righteous judgment; carcasses—repugnance.
2. Possible replacements are: savages—the Irish; male and female—men and women; popish infants—Catholic children; beggars—the poor; rags—inadequate clothing; breeders—parents; filth—lack of proper sanitation; idolatrous—relating to a different faith; carcasses—bodies.

Grading Timesaver

Rubrics for each Choices assignment appear on p. 135 in the *Portfolio Management System.*

CHOICES: Building Your Portfolio

1. **Writer's Notebook** Spending five minutes on a class brainstorming session will also generate numerous ideas.
2. **Creative Writing** To prompt brainstorming, list a few possible scenarios on the chalkboard, including the ones below, and invite students to freewrite about them in their journals.
   - Imagine being transported through time, waking one hundred years from now.
   - Imagine awakening on another planet.
3. **Creative Writing/Speaking** Tell students that, in addition to superhuman size and strength, heroes of American tall tales often have other superhuman abilities. For example, they may stop a blizzard, lift an ox, or carve out valleys with their footfalls.
4. **Comparing Satires** Suggest that students work together to compare the two authors' works. Students can gather examples from Swift's or Boyle's text. Then the pairs can share their examples and examine the points that the authors make through satire.
5. **Persuasive Writing** In order to choose a topic, have students review their answers for Making Meanings #8. After they have drafted their essays, have them review the discussion of Shades of Meaning on p. 515 and go through their essays with an eye to sharpening word choice.
6. **Creative Writing** Students may express their views in a straightforward or satirical way. Remind them that it is more important to establish a clear and unwavering point of view than to be ironic, sarcastic, or satirical.
7. **Research/Speaking** Display posters or photographs of some Hogarth paintings. Call attention to any exaggeration used.

CHOICES: Building Your Portfolio

Writer's Notebook

1. Collecting Ideas for a Persuasive Essay

The passion that drove Swift is the right starting point for persuasion. To write a good persuasive essay, you have to *care.* Think about the contemporary issues raised in Extending the Text (pages 496, 500, and 513). If some fire your passion, quickly jot down what you feel about them, and *why.* If none does, find your "hot-button" issue by freewriting about these phrases: *What really makes me angry is* _______, or *If I had the power, I would change* _______. Save your notes for the Writer's Workshop on page 612.

Creative Writing

2. Slumberers Awake

Many characters in literature, like Gulliver, awaken from a deep sleep to find themselves in strange, new circumstances. Rip Van Winkle, for example, wakes to find he's been sleeping for twenty years and that his country is no longer a British colony. The hero of Franz Kafka's *The Metamorphosis* wakes to find he has become a horrible bug. Imagine that overnight some fantastic change happens to you. Write a first-person narrative describing what happened, where and when it happened, and why it happened.

Creative Writing/ Speaking

3. Tell the Tale

With its humorous exaggeration and outlandish plot, *Gulliver's Travels* has some of the characteristics of a **tall tale,** a type of folk literature particularly associated with Mark Twain and the American West. Retell one of Gulliver's adventures in the form of a tall tale, one that cowboys might have told to amuse themselves around a campfire. Make Gulliver an American character.

Comparing Satires

4. Two Satirists

What similarities do you notice between Swift's satire in *A Modest Proposal* and Boyle's satire in the ***Connections*** story "Top of the Food Chain" (page 509)? In a brief essay, explore how each writer uses satirical devices. At the start of your essay, briefly **summarize** the main points presented in each text.

Persuasive Writing

5. A New Modest Proposal

Attack an evil you see in society today by writing an **ironic** "modest proposal" for its solution—so outrageously horrifying that readers will see at once the tragedy of the situation. Remember: As Swift was, you might be attacked for insensitivity. Your moral outrage must be made clear by gross exaggeration.

Creative Writing

6. Shift the Stance

Swift approached the subjects of corruption in England and poverty in Ireland from the point of view of a reformer. In *A Modest Proposal* he ironically takes the stance of a benevolent humanitarian, something like a modern social worker. Imagine an essay on the Irish problem written by someone with an entirely different **stance,** or position. For example, suppose that the writer is an Irish parent with hungry children or Sir Robert Walpole, lord of the Treasury, or King George II of England. Take a stand other than Swift's, and write an essay expressing your views.

Research/Speaking

7. Artistic Barbs

Research the paintings of William Hogarth (1697–1764), an English artist who, like Swift, was a powerful critic of eighteenth-century English life. Present your findings to your class in an oral report. Show pictures of Hogarth's work if you can.

Reading Skills and Strategies

VOCABULARY: DISTINGUISHING SHADES OF MEANING

Our language is rich and varied, in part because many words communicate various shades of meaning. Even words that have very similar definitions have subtly different meanings, emotional overtones, and associations, including associations with their opposite meanings.

Denotation and connotation. The dictionary definition, or explicit meaning of a word, is called its **denotation.** The denotation of *odious* as it is used in the following quotation from *Gulliver's Travels* is "causing or deserving loathing or disgust."

> I cannot but conclude the bulk of your natives to be the most pernicious race of little **odious** vermin that nature ever suffered to crawl upon the surface of the earth.

However, words can communicate more than ideas; they can also convey attitudes and emotions. These associated attitudes and emotional overtones that are communicated by words are called **connotations.** For example, while both *odious* and *hateful* mean "causing or deserving loathing," most people associate different emotions with each word. *Odious* is associated with a particular, loathsome quality in a thing or person that causes feelings of disgust. On the other hand, *hateful* is associated with a more general unpleasantness of character that causes feelings of strong dislike and aversion.

Synonyms and antonyms. Words that have similar meanings are called **synonyms.** *Odious* and *hateful* are synonyms. Dictionaries usually give one or more synonyms for each word. You can also find synonyms in a **thesaurus,** a dictionary of synonyms.

When choosing a synonym or figuring out the meaning of a word from a synonym, you need to be sure its meaning suits the **context.** For example, *hateful* is a synonym for *odious* when it means "causing or deserving loathing." However, it is not a synonym for *odious* when it means "showing or feeling hate."

1. Everyone at court disliked and avoided the **hateful** young queen.
2. His long illness had made the old king so **hateful** that he no longer loved his own children.

Words that have opposite or almost opposite meanings are called **antonyms.** *Odious* and *lovable* are antonyms. *Attractive* and *appealing* are also antonyms for *odious.* Dictionaries sometimes list antonyms at the end of the entry for a word.

Try It Out

On your own paper, draw a chart like the following one, excluding the example *odious.* In the appropriate column beside each of the other five Words to Own from *Gulliver's Travels,* write the denotation as it is used in the selection, the connotations, a synonym, and an antonym. Use a dictionary and a thesaurus for reference as necessary.

Word to Own	Denotation	Connotations	Synonym	Antonym
odious	causing loathing	loathsome quality, disgust	hateful	lovable
diminutive				
quelled				
copious				
prevailed				
pernicious				

Skill Link

Determining Shades of Meaning

Have students find synonyms for the underlined words that would alter the reader's perceptions of the statement.

1. The *mayor* greeted her *constituents.* [politician, leader; fans, electorate, voters]
2. The state decided to monitor car *emissions.* [exhaust, pollution]
3. The *disappointed* pitcher watched the *rain* on game day. [pouting, disgruntled, sad; downpour, drizzle]
4. The attorney *encouraged* the witness. [prodded, badgered, coaxed]
5. Someone *purchased* the *well-worn* sofa at the garage sale. [acquired, bargained for; stained, shabby, threadbare]

OBJECTIVES

1. Distinguish shades of meaning in words
2. Distinguish between denotative and connotative meanings
3. Understand synonyms and antonyms
4. Use references such as a dictionary and a thesaurus to determine precise shades of meaning

Reading Skills and Strategies

Mini-Lesson: Identifying Shades of Meaning

The study of denotations, connotations, synonyms, and antonyms involves using a dictionary and a thesaurus. Review the traditional thesaurus, the newer dictionary format, and the digital version. If possible, demonstrate to students ways to access a computerized thesaurus, using either a computer or a transparency of a screen printout that shows appropriate entries.

Try It Out

Word: *diminutive*
Denotation: smaller than average
Connotation: condescension (possibly)
Synonym: tiny, small
Antonym: huge

Word: *quelled*
Denotation: put an end to, crushed, quieted
Connotation: forcefulness
Synonym: stopped
Antonym: encouraged

Word: *copious*
Denotation: very plentiful
Connotation: generous, abundant
Synonym: abundant
Antonym: scanty

Word: *prevailed*
Denotation: won
Connotation: suggests triumph
Synonym: succeeded
Antonym: failed

Word: *pernicious*
Denotation: causing injury
Connotation: evil, wicked
Synonym: destructive
Antonym: harmless

Spotlight On

Relative to the time periods before it, and even to several years that would follow, the eighteenth century was a period of remarkable opportunity for women writers. This feature introduces students to a few of the era's most important women writers.

A Exploring the Culture

More Women Writers

Several factors contributed to the increasing number of women writers: the rise of the middle class, which meant the average family had more money to buy books; more education and more leisure time, which resulted in more interest in literature. To meet the demand, publishers needed more material and more writers.

B Literary Connections

Roman à Clef

This kind of a novel, which thinly disguises society people or celebrities as characters, is called a *roman à clef* ("novel with a key"), alluding to the keys that unlock the true identities of the characters.

C Humanities Connections

Gothic Motifs

Gothic architecture is characterized by immense edifices that reach to the sky with flamboyant (literally "flamelike") patterns, often decorated with gargoyles. Their complex and sometimes grotesque ornamentation is echoed in the plot structures of Gothic novels, which twist and turn to reveal dark secrets.

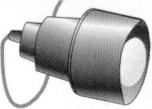

SPOTLIGHT ON

Women Writers of the Restoration and the Eighteenth Century

by **C. F. Main**

For now that Aphra Behn had done it, girls could go to their parents and say, You need not give me an allowance; I can make money by my pen.

—Virginia Woolf, *from A Room of One's Own*

Living by the Pen

Samuel Johnson once said that a woman who issued her opinions to the public was something like a dog walking on its hind legs. "It is not done well; but you are surprised to find it done at all," he quipped. Had he looked around, Johnson might have been surprised indeed. During his lifetime the number of women writers in England increased enormously. Of course, there had always been many women who wrote letters, kept journals and diaries, and recorded in notebooks their recipes, prayers, poems, and private thoughts. But eighteenth-century women—fortuitously aided by the explosion of the middle class and emergence of a literary marketplace—were increasingly able to have their work published, even able to earn a living by writing. They no longer needed a well-to-do family or patron, as Renaissance women writers had; in this new era, if a woman's work was likely to appeal to readers, a printer was bound to print it.

The variety of these women's writings is astonishing. In the mid-1600s, Katherine Philips—who called herself Orinda, and whom admirers took to calling "the Matchless Orinda"—became England's first famous woman writer. Her rather traditional poems, mostly on the theme of friendship, were addressed to a circle of confidants, mainly but not entirely women, to whom she gave such fancy names as Lucasia, Rosania, Cratander, and Silvander.

Illustration (detail) from an 1803 edition of Ann Radcliffe's Gothic romance *The Mysteries of Udolpho.*

By the late eighteenth century, the Minerva Press was flooding the bookstalls with popular fiction written mostly by women. Scandalous romances and satirical novels, with characters who were often thinly disguised society folk, became a staple. Also popular were the new Gothic novels, in which frightening and apparently supernatural events took place in remote castles. In fact, the best-selling novels of Ann Radcliffe (1764–1823), the most famous writer of eighteenth-century Gothics, are recognizable ancestors of today's horror fiction.

Using Students' Strengths

Interpersonal Learners

Students may enjoy reading the feature aloud with a partner and pausing occasionally to comment on interesting points of view—especially Samuel Johnson's comment about women. Have partners take notes on their consultations, which they can later share in class discussion.

Visual Learners

Encourage students to think of different ways to organize the information given in the article into a graphic. For example, students might want to construct a chart that compares the featured writers or place the contributions of writers on a time line. Emphasize that students' graphics should reinforce the main ideas of the article.

Auditory/Musical Learners

Students may enjoy coming up with a "theme song" or selection of program music that would characterize each of the major writers or one of her works. For example, for Lady Mary Wortley Montagu, they might choose typical Turkish music or something evocative of travels in exotic places. Provide time for students to play and explain their choices to the class.

Women also publicly commented—as journalists, advocates, and critics—on the most important and controversial issues of the day. Early feminists like Mary Astell (1666–1731) and Lady Mary Chudleigh (1656–1710) wrote that marriage laws enslaved women, making them little more than their husbands' property. (In contrast, Margaret Cavendish [1623–1674], duchess of Newcastle, took it for granted that marriage was an arrangement ordained by God, and published a huge biography of her husband the duke, whom she presented as a paragon.) Hannah More (1745–1833), an early British voice for the abolition of slavery, produced many widely circulated tracts about the moral education of women and the poor.

Aphra Behn (1640–1689)

Aphra Behn, born Aphra Johnson to working-class parents in Kent, was the first English woman to earn her living by writing. She was a free spirit, the sort of woman who used to be called an adventuress, and she had the luck to write in the era when women were at last permitted to work in the theater as actors, playwrights, and producers. In her lifetime, both she and her writings were very well known, but during the two hundred years after her death, her works and her life came to be regarded as outrageous and were forgotten.

Consequently, at this late date it is impossible to recover many details of her biography. She perhaps spent most of her early years in Guiana, she married a Mr. Behn (usually pronounced "bane") who died in 1666, possibly a casualty of the Great Plague of 1664–1665, and she was a spy for her country during a war against the Dutch. Beyond these bare facts lies much interesting speculation. What is certain is that she left an impressive literary legacy. For nearly ten years in a row, her plays, comedies for the most part, were successively produced in London. In *The Rover* (1677–1681), her best-known play, three young Spanish women, who are curious about sex, encounter three young traveling Englishmen during carnival time in Spain.

Behn also published several collections of translations and poems, as well as a dozen short novels, one of which is her masterpiece *Oroonoko* (1688). Its hero is an African prince, a powerful man with a noble mind and body, who has been tricked into slavery and transported to the island of Surinam.

Aphra Behn.

Behn's genius makes him seem very real to the reader, who is bound to be moved by his suffering.

In the following speech, Oroonoko, who has been renamed Caesar by his slave master, exhorts his fellow slaves to fight the unjust rule of the English.

> "And why," said he, "my dear friends and fellow sufferers, should we be slaves to an unknown people? Have they vanquished us nobly in fight? Have they won us in honorable battle? And are we, by the chance of war, become their slaves? This would not anger a noble heart, this would not animate a soldier's soul. No, but we are bought and sold like apes, or monkeys, to be the sport of women, fools, and cowards, and the support of rogues, renegades that have abandoned their own countries for raping, murders, thefts, and villainies. Do you not hear every day how they upbraid each other with infamy of life, below the wildest savages, and shall we render obedience to such a degenerate race, who have no one human virtue left to distinguish them from the vilest creatures? Will you, I say, suffer the lash from such hands?" They all replied with one accord, "No, no, no; Caesar has spoke like a great captain, like a great king."
>
> —Aphra Behn, *from Oroonoko*

D Background
Aphra Behn
Behn sought favor at Charles II's court and worked as a secret agent in the Netherlands during the Second Dutch War (1665–1667). Her code name, Astraea, became her nickname among her literary colleagues. She was not paid for spying, however, and served a term in debtors' prison when she returned to England.

E Literary Connections
Restoration Humor
Filled with wit, Behn's plays were as ribald as those of any male writer during the Restoration, a literary era known for its bawdiness.

F Literary Connections
Prose Fiction
This narrative about a slave revolt led by an African prince influenced the development of prose fiction in England and presaged some of the work of Daniel Defoe. Behn's work was hugely popular during her lifetime, and her lasting contributions to English literature and culture were later recognized when she was buried in Westminster Abbey.

Getting Students Involved

Cooperative Learning

Book Jackets. Ask students to form groups of four. Challenge each group to create a book jacket for one of the works mentioned in this feature. Groups should divide among themselves the tasks of creating cover art, the author's biography, the synopsis, the critical reviews for the back cover, and the general design and layout. Somewhere in the synopsis and the reviewer's comments, students should include the following information: genre, characters, setting, and theme. They should also make a statement about the work's overall literary significance. Have students present their finished products to the class. As a final step, each group should summarize the process they went through to create the book jacket, noting individual contributions made by each group member.

Ⓐ Exploring the Historical Period

Smallpox Vaccine

Today, Montagu is universally acknowledged as the person who introduced the smallpox vaccine into Britain. She had observed its use during her travels in Turkey.

Ⓑ Reading Skills and Strategies

Drawing Conclusions

? What does this passage reveal about the behavior of many society women in Montagu's day? [Possible answers: They were impolite, conformist, judgmental, hierarchical, and obsessed with fashion.]

Ⓒ Critical Thinking

Speculating

? Why do you think readers enjoyed this kind of writing? [Possible answers: It provides a taste of an exotic world. Montagu was herself an interesting person who not only traveled to fascinating places but was able to record an experience other women could only dream about.]

RESPONDING TO THE ART

Joseph Highmore (1692–1780), an English historical and portrait painter, was sent by his father to work for an attorney. Highmore disliked the work and spent all his off hours drawing. To learn about anatomy, he went to medical school lectures. His big opportunity came when the Order of the Bath revived in 1725, and he was asked to paint pictures of several knights. Highmore's best work is considered to be his series of a dozen pictures to accompany Richardson's book *Pamela.*

Activity. Tell students that the full title of Richardson's book is *Pamela, or Virtue Rewarded,* and that Mr. B. is a suitor who tries to take advantage of the teenage maidservant. The book takes the form of letters between the characters, and of Pamela's journal, which Mr. B. reads without her permission. Invite students to make up dialogue for Mr. B. and Pamela to accompany this painting.

Lady Mary Wortley Montagu (1689–1762)

Though she had a more privileged upbringing than Aphra Behn, Lady Mary Wortley Montagu also educated herself, spending much of her childhood buried among the books in her father's vast library. From an early age, she was known as clever and daring. At twenty-three, she eloped on horseback with Edward Wortley Montagu, flouting her family's wish that she marry for money. After a serious bout with smallpox, she championed smallpox inoculations in Britain. Later, she dared to refuse the romantic attentions of her one-time good friend, Alexander Pope, who then tried, unsuccessfully, to destroy her in his satires.

Although she was herself a talented poet, her fame now rests on her letters, which were published in four volumes immediately after her death. They are still a valuable source of information about eighteenth-century life in England, France, and even Turkey, where she lived for a time while her husband was the English ambassador to Constantinople.

In the following passage, taken from a letter written to a friend in 1717, Lady Montagu describes a trip to the women's public baths in the Turkish city of Sofia (now the capital of Bulgaria).

> I was in my traveling habit, which is a riding dress, and certainly appeared very extraordinary to them, yet there was not one of 'em that showed the least surprise or impertinent curiosity, but received me with all the obliging civility possible. I know no European court where the ladies would have behaved themselves in so polite a manner to a stranger. I believe in the whole there were two hundred women and yet none of those disdainful smiles or satiric whispers that never fail in our assemblies when anybody appears that is not dressed exactly in fashion. They repeated over and over to me, "Uzelle, pek uzelle," which is nothing but, "Charming, very charming." The first sofas were covered with cushions and rich carpets, on which sat the ladies, and on the second their slaves behind 'em, but without any distinction of rank by their dress, all being in the state of nature, that is, in plain English, stark naked. . . .
>
> The lady that seemed the most considerable amongst them entreated me to sit by her and would fain have undressed me for the bath. I excused myself with some difficulty, they all being so earnest in persuading me. I was at last forced to open my skirt and show them my stays, which satisfied 'em very well, for I saw they believed I was so locked up in that machine that it was not in my own power to open it, which contrivance they attributed to my husband.
>
> —Lady Mary Wortley Montagu

Montagu spent the last twenty years of her life living alone in a villa in Italy. The letters to her daughter that survive from this period provide a record of Montagu's continuing curiosity about the world; her pride in her granddaughter's scholarly bent, which she encourages her daughter to nourish; and her own deep sense of self-reliance.

Fanny Burney (1752–1840)

Fictionalized letters, as funny and reflective as those of the prolific Lady Montagu, soon found their way into print as epistolary novels, or novels composed of letters.

One of the first and most important epistolary novels is *Evelina* (1778), by Frances "Fanny" Burney, the daughter of well-known musicologist Charles Burney. The heroine of this novel, Burney's first, is a beautiful, intelligent girl who must overcome many obstacles in order to win the man she loves, a good man whose wealth and social position are well beyond her own. Due to a misunderstanding, her father has abandoned her, and most of her other relatives are eccentric and socially awkward.

Frances d'Arblay Burney (1785) by Edward Francis Burney.

By Courtesy of the National Portrait Gallery, London.

Professional Notes

Lady Mary on Women's Education

These excerpts are from a letter Lady Mary Montagu wrote to her daughter: "No entertainment is so cheap as reading, nor any pleasure so lasting. She will not want new fashions nor regret the loss of expensive diversions or variety of company if she can be amused with an author in her closet." Later in the letter, Lady Mary offers a warning: "The second caution to be given her (and which is most absolutely necessary) is to conceal whatever learning she attains, with as much solicitude as she would hide crookedness or lameness. . . . The use of knowledge in our sex (beside the amusement of solitude) is to moderate the passions and learn to be contented with a small expense, which are the certain effects of a studious life and, it may be, preferable even to that fame which men have engrossed to themselves and will not suffer us to share."

But they are also quite funny. Burney had a real gift for comedy, which is a distinguishing feature of the English novel. The plot twists in *Evelina* and the odd behavior of the characters hold the reader's attention right up to the inevitable happy ending.

Burney had a keen eye and ear for the hypocrisy—and humor—of social relations in her day. Her work was praised by such notables as Samuel Johnson and David Garrick, and she was accepted into the Bluestocking Circle, a group of prominent women who shared literary and scholarly interests. **D** Burney was also appointed to a position in the queen's household (which she found dreadfully boring and only escaped when she became quite ill). **E**

This praise and prominence implies Burney had a brilliant education. However, like Behn and Montagu before her, she was largely self-taught. She also had qualms about the propriety of a writing career. At fifteen, thinking that her already voluminous work was inconsequential, Burney made a great bonfire of the pages, including the beginnings of *Caroline Evelyn,* a novel that she later rewrote as *Evelina*. Indeed, Burney was so insecure about her writing that she published *Evelina* anonymously at first; its great success finally encouraged her to put her name on the title page.

In the following passage from her diary, Burney announces the publication of *Evelina* with an endearing mock grandeur.

> This year was ushered in by a grand and most important event! At the latter end of January, the literary world was favored with the first publication of the ingenious, learned, and most profound Fanny Burney! I doubt not but this memorable affair will, in future times, mark the period whence chronologers will date the zenith of the polite arts in this island! . . .
>
> My little book, I am told, is now at all the circulating libraries. **F** I have an exceeding odd sensation when I consider that it is now in the power of *any* and *every* body to read what I so carefully hoarded even from my best friends, till this last month or two; and that a work which was so lately lodged, in all privacy, in my bureau, may now be seen by every baker and butcher, cobbler and tinker, throughout the three kingdoms, for the small tribute of threepence.
>
> —Fanny Burney

Yet the thought that she might be identified as *Evelina*'s author (a fact known by few but her sisters Susanna and Charlotte) sends Burney into a panic.

> My aunt and Miss Humphries being settled at this time at Brompton, I was going thither with Susan to tea, when Charlotte acquainted me that they were then employed in reading *Evelina* to the invalid, my cousin Richard.
>
> This intelligence gave me the utmost uneasiness—I foresaw a thousand dangers of a discovery—I dreaded the indiscreet warmth of all my confidants. In truth, I was quite sick with apprehension, and was too uncomfortable to go to Brompton, and Susan carried my excuses. **G**
>
> Upon her return, I was somewhat tranquilized, for she assured me that there was not the smallest suspicion of the author, and that they had concluded it to be the work of a *man*!
>
> —Fanny Burney

Despite the assumption of Burney's relatives, and the reading public in general, that most published works were authored by men, eighteenth-century Britain was relatively open to women writers. In fact, for a brief period, women writers were in the ascendancy, and some male writers resorted to using female pseudonyms to get their work into print. Yet this freedom didn't last. By the mid-1800s, when a woman's sphere had again narrowed to home and hearth, women with literary aspirations once more faced enormous obstacles.

Mr. B. Finds Pamela Writing (18th century), illustration by Joseph Highmore from Samuel Richardson's *Pamela*.
Victoria and Albert Museum, London.

D Background
Bluestockings

David Garrick, one of Samuel Johnson's pupils, became the greatest actor and theatrical entrepreneur of the age and a frequent guest of the Bluestocking Circle. Burney herself recounts how the group got its name: A gentleman who declined an invitation to speak, saying he did not have the proper clothes, was told by a member to come "in his blue stockings," the ordinary worsted hose he was wearing at the time. When he did so, his stockings became the group's nickname. The term *bluestocking*, incidentally, was often used derisively to mock women intellectuals.

E Background
Fanny Burney

Burney was Keeper of the Robes, which sounds boring indeed. She performed this role for Queen Charlotte from 1786 to 1791.

F Exploring the Historical Period
Libraries

A "golden age" of libraries occurred during the seventeenth and eighteenth centuries, when the first state-supported libraries were opened and many private libraries still in existence today were founded.

G Critical Thinking
Hypothesizing

? Why would Burney have been so reluctant to be known as an author? [Possible answers: She was worried about revealing through her characters something about herself or her ideas; she was reluctant, as a woman, to be in the limelight; she was a shy person who did not want to draw attention to herself.]

Getting Students Involved

Writing a Historical Diary Entry

Have students write a diary entry from the point of view of a woman writer during this time. Try to imagine the woman's concerns and triumphs. Students should also mention briefly any fears of discovery or problems with money that a female writer might encounter. Students can use Burney's entry as a model for their own writing and should draw additional material from the text.

Professional Notes

Fanny Burney

When Fanny Burney's novel *Evelina* was first published, the market was filled with novels of "mawkish mediocrity" according to critic Austin Dobson. Burney herself was surprised at the novel's success, telling a friend "I thought *Evelina's* only admirers would be schoolgirls, and destined her to no nobler inhabitation than a circulating library." Burney was proved wrong, however, and the shy, retiring, nearsighted girl, who was nicknamed 'old lady' became a sensation.

OBJECTIVES

1. Read and interpret the heroic couplets and the poems
2. Identify antithesis
3. Analyze poetic form and meter
4. Interpret a mock epic
5. Interpret the use of wit
6. Respond to the text
7. Use reference materials to understand allusions
8. Express understanding through writing and speaking

SKILLS

Literary
- Analyze antithesis
- Analyze poetic form and meter
- Interpret a mock epic
- Interpret the use of wit

Reading
- Respond to the text
- Use reference materials

Writing
- Collect ideas for a persuasive essay
- Analyze satire
- Compare epics
- Write a mock epic
- Write about an everyday event in mock-epic style
- Analyze the reading experience

Speaking
- Deliver a rebuttal to Pope

Viewing/Representing (ATE)
- Analyze and interpret paintings

Planning

- **Block Schedule**
  Block Scheduling Lesson Plans with Pacing Guide
- **Traditional Schedule**
  Lesson Plans Including Strategies for English-Language Learners
- **One-Stop Planner**
  CD-ROM with Test Generator

Alexander Pope

(1688–1744)

Alexander Pope, the most important poet of the early eighteenth century, was a child prodigy. As a very little boy, he later admitted, he "lisped in numbers." That is, he could speak in meter even before he could pronounce English properly. Such a talented youth would ordinarily be educated at Cambridge or Oxford. But Pope's family was Roman Catholic and therefore prohibited from attending these universities, as well as from voting, from holding public office, and even from practicing their religion.

Pope's father, a retired linen merchant, could afford to educate his son at home, which was perhaps the best place for Pope since his health was very delicate. Early in life he contracted a kind of tuberculosis that stunted his growth and disfigured his body, so that eventually his servants had to lace him into a canvas brace before he could sit upright. Since he continually suffered pains in his head, bones, and joints, it is no wonder he spoke of his life as "this long disease."

In spite of all of this, Pope led a remarkably busy and productive life. When he was sixteen, he began his poetic career, as the Roman poet Virgil did, by writing **pastorals**—poems describing the countryside. When he was twenty-three, he published *An Essay on Criticism,* a poem inspired in part by the Latin poet Horace's *Art of Poetry.* At twenty-four, he published a miniature classical epic, *The Rape of the Lock.* During his thirties he translated into English two enormous Greek epics, Homer's *Iliad* and, with the help of two assistants, Homer's *Odyssey.* In these works, Pope was not at all limited by his classical models, but used them to make works that were fresh and original. For this reason, he is sometimes referred to as a neoclassical (that is, new classical) poet.

Alexander Pope and Dog Bounce (detail) (c. 1718) attributed to Jonathan Richardson.
Hagley Hall, Worcestershire, England.

Pope's early, brilliant successes inspired envy in lesser writers, who lampooned and ridiculed him. To defend himself he turned to satire, a kind of writing highly congenial to his temperament. The great satires of Pope's maturity include *The Dunciad* (1728, enlarged and revised in 1742), which attacks dull, uninteresting writers of all kinds and shows the forces of stupidity, ignorance, and folly taking over the world, and the *Moral Essays* (1731–1735), which pass judgment on certain immoral men and women as well as on very rich people who lack common sense and good taste. Finally, *An Epistle to Dr. Arbuthnot* (1735) contains both a defense of Pope's career as a writer and attacks on his literary enemies.

As a man Pope was, and still is, both loved and hated. In his lifetime and long after, he had a reputation for cruelty, malice, and ill nature. It now seems clear that he had none of these bad qualities but could appear to have them when provoked—as a caged tiger would have them when poked with a stick. We now realize that he was often goaded into writing satire, but that does not necessarily prove that Pope himself was peevish and mean. On the contrary, Pope had a large circle of friends, men and women, including some of the best writers of the day, who found him good-natured, generous, and brilliant in conversation. His agreeable manners, his large expressive eyes, and his way of dressing elegantly in bright colors charmed his friends. At his beautiful estate on the river Thames below London, he entertained important writers, artists, and political figures of the day. Pope became rich and famous; as for the people who raged against him, most of them are remembered today only because they disliked Alexander Pope.

go.hrw.com LEO 12-6

Resources: Print and Media

Reading
- *Graphic Organizers for Active Reading,* pp. 39, 40, 41
- *Audio CD Library*
  Disc 8, Tracks 2, 3, 4, 5

Elements of Literature
- *Literary Elements*
  Transparency 13
  Worksheet, p. 40

Writing and Language
- *Daily Oral Grammar*
  Transparencies 15, 16
- *Grammar and Language Links*
  Worksheet, p. 29
- *Language Workshop CD-ROM*

Viewing and Representing
- *Viewing and Representing*
  Fine Art Transparency 8
  Fine Art Worksheet, p. 32

Assessment
- *Formal Assessment,* pp. 95, 97
- *Portfolio Management System,* p. 137
- *Test Generator (One-Stop Planner* CD-ROM)

Internet
- *go.hrw.com* (keyword: *LEO 12-6*)

Before You Read

HEROIC COUPLETS

FROM AN ESSAY ON MAN

Make the Connection

Quotable Wisdom

For the writers of Pope's time, the purpose of poetry was to combine the pleasing with the useful. The clarity, elegance, and compression of Pope's own style ensured that his works would more than fulfill this ideal. With the exception of Shakespeare, Pope is the most widely quoted writer in all of English literature, perhaps because he often wrote in heroic couplets, in which a memorable thought is expressed in a pair of rhyming lines. What sources do we quote from today?

Reading Skills and Strategies

Responding to the Text

As you read Pope, keep your notebook handy. You might record your responses in the form of a double-entry journal: a quote that catches your attention on the left and your response to it on the right.

Pope Quote	My Response

Elements of Literature

Antithesis

Pope habitually expresses himself in antitheses (an·tith′ə·sēz′). An **antithesis** uses parallel structures to present a balanced contrast: "Give me liberty, or give me death." ("Give me liberty, or kill me" fails as an antithesis because it isn't parallel or balanced.) By compressing elements of similarity and difference, antithesis helps to make a statement more forceful and (often) more memorable.

Antithesis is a contrast of ideas expressed in a grammatically balanced statement.

For more on Antithesis, see the Handbook of Literary Terms.

Title page of Pope's *An Essay on Man*, designed by Pope.

Summary ■■

This selection of heroic couplets and one triplet has been drawn from Pope's longer works. Pope praises the artistry of music (#1); encourages deep, rather than superficial learning (#2); counsels moderation in accepting new ideas (#3); comments on writing as a skill (#4); espouses quickness in offering praise (#5) and forgiveness (#6); notes the endurance of hope (#7) and the power of education (#8); notes how readily evil people can find the means to act (#9); and declares how carefully he chooses targets for his satires (#10).

BROWSING IN THE FILES

About the Author. Critic J. V. Guerinot says this about Pope: "Pope was an appealing, even if dangerous, man. He made the best of the times in which he lived and out of the rag and bone heap that fate had given him for a body. He was interested in everything—the classics, the latest books of his friends, cooking, painting and architecture, his garden and house, the gardens and houses (both much larger) of his friends, his poetry, his grotto. From modest beginnings as the son of a well-to-do linen draper, he raised himself by his own abilities to become the greatest poet of his age, friend of the noblest and richest and most exciting men in England. This he did despite being (as a Roman Catholic) denied university enrollment and penalized by harsh laws and despite being (as a hunchbacked dwarf four and a half feet high) almost never free from pain."

Reaching All Students

Struggling Readers

Encourage students to work with a partner to discuss the meaning of each couplet before deciding on a response.

English Language Learners

Help students to identify the subject, verb, and main clause in each couplet. Once they understand this "core," ask them to decide how it is explained, qualified, or added on to.

Advanced Learners

Have students find one of these couplets in context (except 9, which they will encounter in *The Rape of the Lock*) and to determine how the context leads up to and away from the excerpted couplet. Provide students with an opportunity to share what they discover.

A Reading Skills and Strategies

Responding to the Text

? Do you agree with Pope? Why or why not? [Possible answers: Yes, because only geniuses can create true masterpieces; no, there are some methods for teaching the average person to appreciate and write both music and poetry.]

B Humanities Connections

Pope's Allusions

This allusion to the Pierian spring, said in antiquity to have inspired the nine Muses, is typical of Pope's style. Remind students that Pope wrote for a highly educated, upper-class audience, who considered such classical allusions elegant.

C Critical Thinking

Interpreting

? What type of figurative language is used here? [simile] To what is the ability to write easily compared? [to dancing] What aspects of writing lend themselves to this comparison? [Students may say that both are difficult artistic performances that require talent and work, and that both rely on the use of rhythm.]

Responding to the Art

Jean Rigaud (1700–?), a French painter, did several English landscapes.

Activity. Ask if any students can explain the significance of Greenwich in geography. [Greenwich, a borough of London, is the site of an imaginary line designated as zero longitude. All other longitudes—and the world's time zones—are calculated from this line.]

Pope is the greatest master of the **heroic couplet,** so-called because both he and his predecessor John Dryden used this form in their translations of the epic poems of antiquity. Each heroic couplet consists of two rhymed lines of **iambic pentameter.** (For variety, Pope occasionally introduces a **triplet.**) Many express a thought in a complete sentence: Such a couplet is called **closed:**

> Trust not yourself; but your defects to know,
> Make use of every friend—and every foe.

Although this couplet from *An Essay on Criticism* is part of a long and carefully organized explanation, it still makes good sense when it is plucked out of its context and allowed to stand by itself. Yet removing couplets from the poems in which they are embedded is dangerous, because it may lead us to think of the poems as strings of beads that can be easily broken apart. In reality, Pope's couplets are so carefully arranged into verse paragraphs that they are more like the forged links of an iron chain than separable units.

Heroic Couplets

Alexander Pope

A
1 Music resembles poetry: in each
Are nameless graces[1] which no methods[2] teach,
And which a master hand alone can reach.
—*An Essay on Criticism,* lines 143–145

B
2 A little learning is a dangerous thing;
Drink deep, or taste not the Pierian[3] spring.
—*An Essay on Criticism,* lines 215–216

3 Be not the first by whom the new are tried,
Nor yet the last to lay the old aside.
—*An Essay on Criticism,* lines 335–336

C
4 True ease in writing comes from art, not chance,
As those move easiest who have learned to dance.
—*An Essay on Criticism,* lines 362–363

1. **nameless graces:** pleasing passages that cannot be explained.
2. **methods:** instruction books showing how to write poems.
3. **Pierian** (pī·ir′ē·ən): an allusion to the Muses, Greek goddesses of the arts and literature. The Muses were said to live in a district of Greece called Pieria.

Making Meanings

First Thoughts [Respond]

1. Students may feel that, despite the difficult language, the messages are timeless. Some may feel that Couplet 10 is irrelevant.

Shaping Interpretations [Interpret]

2. a. Couplet 3; b. Verse 1; c. Couplet 7; d. Couplet 3 might be construed as doing so; e. Couplet 8; f. Couplet 6; g. Couplet 4.

3. Possible answers: Someone who knows little about medicine decides on an ill-advised self-treatment plan; an amateur chemist causes a blast.

4. He suggests that *art* is purposeful and carefully practiced, while *chance,* or luck, relies on fortune.

5. Possible paraphrase for Couplet 5: Praise merit when you see it; your praise is meaningless if you wait until everyone else is giving it. By being concise, Pope makes his couplets memorable.

(Continued on p. T523)

5 Be thou the first true merit to befriend;
His praise is lost, who stays till all commend.

—*An Essay on Criticism,* lines 474–475

6 Good nature and good sense must ever join;
To err is human, to forgive, divine.

—*An Essay on Criticism,* lines 524–525

7 Hope springs eternal in the human breast:
Man never is, but always to be blest.

—*An Essay on Man,* Epistle I, lines 95–96

8 'Tis education forms the common mind,
Just as the twig is bent, the tree's inclined.

—*Moral Essays,* Epistle I, lines 149–150

9 But when to mischief mortals bend their will,
How soon they find fit instruments of ill!

—*The Rape of the Lock,* Canto III, lines 125–126

10 Satire's my weapon, but I'm too discreet
To run amuck, and tilt[4] at all I meet.

—*Imitations of Horace, Satire I,* Book II, lines 69–70

4. **tilt:** charge at or thrust a weapon toward an opponent.

View Across Greenwich Park Towards London (detail) (18th century) by Jean Rigaud.
Roy Miles Gallery, London.

Making Meanings

First Thoughts

1. Share the responses to the couplets you recorded in your reading notebook. Do you find the advice in the couplets useful, or does it seem out-of-date? Why?

Shaping Interpretations

2. Tell in which of the couplets Pope does each of the following:
   a. Advocates a mean between two extremes.
   b. Suggests that geniuses are born, not made.
   c. Explains why people are never satisfied with what they have.
   d. Compares writing to putting on clothes.
   e. Shows how important education is for the young.
   f. Advises critics to be generous.
   g. Suggests that good writing results from practice and skill, not luck or accident.
3. Give some examples showing how a little learning can be dangerous (Couplet 2).
4. Read the couplet on true ease in writing, and explain the difference between what is suggested by the words *art* and *chance.*
5. Pope compresses a large amount of meaning into the twenty or so syllables of each of his couplets. Try **paraphrasing,** or expressing in your own words, the idea expressed in any couplet that you find hard to understand. What does Pope gain by compressing his meaning?
6. Pope habitually uses **antithesis** to focus and clarify his meaning. List all the antitheses you can find in these couplets.

Extending the Text

7. Does any couplet particularly connect with life today—in politics, education, or the arts? Explain the connection as you see it.

Challenging the Text

8. Do you take issue with any of these pronouncements? How would you rephrase any of them to get at a different point altogether?

D Elements of Literature

Antithesis

? Why is this an example of antithesis? [Possible answer: Opposing ideas are presented using a parallel structure. Human frailty and divine compassion are opposites; both are expressed through the parallel and balanced use of infinitives—"to err" and "to forgive."]

E Appreciating Language

Style

? What is the purpose of the comma in the second line? [Possible answer: It indicates a pause and emphasizes the antithesis between actually being "blest" and hoping to be "blest."]

F Humanities Connections

A Midsummer Night's Dream

People's ability to use their talents in negative ways is a common literary theme. Shakespeare's *A Midsummer Night's Dream,* for example, is a lighthearted yet satiric treatment of mischief makers and the mayhem they create. Remind students that Shakespeare predated Pope by a century.

G Reading Skills and Strategies

Responding to the Text

? In the first line, Pope uses a metaphor to compare satire to a weapon. Is the comparison effective? Why or why not? [Sample responses: Yes, because words can be sharp; words can "cut." No, because the comparison seems like a cliché.]

Writers on Writing

Pope knew the effect his writing could have. He once wrote the following about the bite of his satire: "Yes I am proud; I must be proud to see Men, not afraid of God, afraid of me."

(Continued from p. T522)

6. Possibilities are Verse 1: "which no methods teach,/And which a master hand alone can reach"; and Couplet 6: "To err is human, to forgive, divine."

Extending the Text [Apply]

7. One example: Couplet 6 might apply to those who continually criticize a public figure for past mistakes rather than giving the person a chance to learn and lead. The variety of responses should show students that each couplet might be interpreted in several ways.

Challenging the Text [Evaluate/Synthesize]

8. Students may disagree with any of the couplets. Possible rephrasing of Couplet 9: "When to goodness mortals bend their mind,/How soon they find fit reasons to be kind."

Summary ■■■

This excerpt, written in heroic couplets, is rich in antithesis as Pope explores his paradoxical view of humanity, which he says is the "glory, jest, and riddle of the world."

Ⓐ Elements of Literature
Epigrams

? What might Pope mean by this couplet? [Rather than speculating about God, people should spend time learning about humanity by studying history and the fine arts.]

Ⓑ Appreciating Language
Word Choice

? Why is the word *isthmus* especially appropriate here? [An isthmus is a small strip of land connecting two larger bodies of land and bordered on both sides by water. Through this comparison, Pope is saying that human beings form a link between the spiritual world of heaven above and the physical world of the animals below.]

Ⓒ Elements of Literature
Antithesis

? Why is this an example of antithesis? ["Darkly wise" and "rudely great" are grammatically and structurally parallel: Both consist of two-syllable *-ly* adverbs preceding single-syllable adjectives. Each phrase also offers contrasts: We associate wisdom with light, not darkness, and greatness with refinement not rudeness.]

RESPONDING TO THE ART

See p. 520 for information on Pope.

Activity. Remind students that Pope had a spinal deformity and was less than five feet tall. Ask students to point out the line in Pope's essay that fits with the shattered statue in the painting. ["Created half to rise, and half to fall."]

An Essay on Man is Pope's long (1,304 lines) philosophical poem, published when he was forty-five. A lifetime of reading, in both English and foreign languages, contributed to its composition. The poem is concerned not only with "man," by which Pope means the whole human race, but with the entire universe as well. It's important to know that the ideas in the poem are not merely the private notions of Pope and his friends, but that they come from many authors, including Plato, Aristotle, St. Thomas Aquinas, Dante, Erasmus, Shakespeare, Bacon, and Milton.

In the following lines from the *Essay,* Pope generalizes about the human race. Pope's "man" is all of us. Do you agree that everyone has the characteristics Pope describes?

from An Essay on Man

Alexander Pope

Ⓐ Know then thyself,° presume not God to scan;°
The proper study of mankind is man.
Ⓑ Placed on this isthmus of a middle state,°
Ⓒ A being darkly wise, and rudely great:
With too much knowledge for the skeptic° side,
With too much weakness for the Stoic's pride,°
He hangs between; in doubt to act, or rest;
In doubt to deem himself a god, or beast;
In doubt his mind or body to prefer;
Born but to die, and reasoning but to err;
Alike in ignorance, his reason such,
Whether he thinks too little, or too much:
Chaos of thought and passion, all confused;
Still° by himself abused, or disabused;°
Created half to rise, and half to fall;
Great lord of all things, yet a prey to all;
Sole judge of truth, in endless error hurled:
The glory, jest, and riddle of the world!

1. Know . . . thyself: a moral precept of Socrates and other ethical philosophers. **scan:** pry into; speculate about.
3. middle state: that is, having the rational intellect of angels and the physical body of beasts.
5. skeptic: The ancient Skeptics doubted that humans can gain accurate knowledge of anything. They emphasized the limitations of human knowledge.
6. Stoic's pride: The ancient Stoics' ideal was a calm acceptance of life and an indifference to both pain and pleasure. Stoics are called proud because they refused to recognize human limitations.
14. still: always; continually. **disabused:** undeceived.

Alexander Pope (18th century). Self-portrait. Oil.
Bryn Mawr College, Bryn Mawr, Pennsylvania.

Getting Students Involved

Pope's Poetics

Have students complete the following activity individually or in pairs.

1. Where does alliteration lend emphasis in the excerpt from *An Essay on Man*? [l. 1, "then–thyself"; l. 2, "mankind is man"; l. 5, "skeptic side"; l. 8, "doubt to deem"; l. 12, "too. . .too"; l. 15, "half. . .half."]
2. Find an example of a rhymed triplet. [Verse 1 on p. 522.]
3. Find examples of pauses within the lines of the heroic couplets on pp. 522–523. [Verse 1, l. 1; couplet 2, l. 2; Couplet 4, l. 1; Couplet 5, l. 2; Couplet 6, l. 2.]
4. Find an example in the heroic couplets on pp. 522–523 of a line that moves along quickly. What words create the effect? [Couplet 3, ll. 1–2: one-syllable words and alliteration speed the rhythm. Couplet 9, l. 2: assonance—the repetition of the short *i* sound—speeds this line.]

Making Meanings

First Thoughts

1. What one word would you use to **summarize** the human condition as Pope describes it?

Shaping Interpretations

2. In almost every sentence of this passage, Pope says something flattering about the human race, only to follow it with something insulting. What characteristics does he think we should be proud of? What characteristics should we be ashamed of?
3. How many **sentences** are in this verse?
4. In what ways do you think human beings could be seen as the "glory" of this world? as its "jest"? as its "riddle"?
5. How does the wording of lines 5–6 and lines 15–16 exhibit **antithesis**? Try **paraphrasing** each of these couplets in your own words.
6. These couplets from the *Essay* are like variations on a single theme, in that each one presents a paradoxical view of humanity. Which couplet do you think is the most interesting and true?

Challenging the Text

7. Discuss your opinion of Pope's opening couplet.
8. **Compare** Pope's view of humanity with the view expressed by William Shakespeare's Hamlet in the following lines: "What a piece of work is a man! how noble in reason! how infinite in faculties! in form and moving how express and admirable! in action how like an angel! in apprehension how like a god! the beauty of the world, the paragon of animals!" (*Hamlet,* Act II, Scene 2). Whose view do you accept?

Elements of Literature

Poetic Form and Meter

Heroic couplets. Although heroic couplets follow a rigid metrical pattern, Pope takes pains to keep them from being monotonous. For instance, he varies the location of the main pause within a line, as in this quotation from "Elegy to an Unfortunate Lady" (note the position of the commas).

> Poets themselves must fall, like those they sung;
> Deaf the praised ear, and mute the tuneful tongue;
> Even he, whose soul now melts in mournful lays,
> Shall shortly want the generous tear he pays.

Some lines move fast, and some are slow—as these lines from "Windsor-Forest" show.

> See the bold youth strain up the threatening steep,
> Rush through the thickets, down the valleys sweep,
> Hang o'er their coursers' heads with eager speed,
> And earth rolls back beneath the flying steed.

In the first line of this passage, Pope uses language that imitates the effort of riding a horse uphill; in the second, the speed of riding downhill. For variety, Pope occasionally introduces **triplets**—three rhymed lines instead of two.

Epigrams. Pope had a dog named Bounce, one of whose puppies he gave to his friend Frederick, Prince of Wales, who lived in Kew. Pope had an epigram engraved on the puppy's collar. An **epigram** is a short poem, often satirical, that ends in a witticism or clever turn of thought. To whom do you think the epigram is addressed? (Don't say, "the prince," because surely the prince knows his own dog.)

> **Epigram Engraved on the Collar of a Dog**
> I am his Highness' dog at Kew;
> Pray tell me, sir, whose dog are you?

Read aloud: A Pope performance. Present "Two Minutes of Pope" to the class. Read a selection of couplets aloud to feel the effect of **pauses, rhymes, assonance,** and **alliteration.** Be sure to experiment with alternative readings before you make your presentation.

Making the Connections

Connecting with the Subject: "The Sting of Satire"

Students may not immediately sense the "sting" of Pope's writing. Use the following questions to stimulate discussion.

- For whom, do you think, is Pope writing?
- Whom, do you think, is Pope criticizing?
- In general, what kinds of things would Pope think of as superior or inferior?
- What is Pope's general impression of humanity?

Making Meanings

First Thoughts [Respond]

1. Possible responses: Ambiguous, paradoxical, contradictory. Humans are this way because they are ignorant and knowledgeable, strong and weak at the same time.

Shaping Interpretations [Interpret]

2. Positive qualities include wisdom, knowledge, and judgment. Negative traits include weakness, doubt, error, ignorance, arrogance, passion, and confusion.
3. Pope writes only two sentences, the first two lines in one and the remainder of the poem (sixteen lines) in the second.
4. Possible answers: "glory"—human accomplishments, such as knowledge and fine arts; "jest"—foibles, such as aggression, greed; "riddle"—the ambiguity of human behavior (for example, our ability to help and hurt others, to gain knowledge and choose ignorance).
5. The wording is parallel, yet the lines contrast nearly opposite human qualities. Possible paraphrase: People have too much knowledge to accept limitations on human knowledge, but they are too weak to adopt the stoic stance that human knowledge is unlimited. (ll. 5–6). Humans succeed and fail; they control their world but remain vulnerable to its perils (ll. 15–16).
6. Students may like ll. 15–16, which focus on human glory and vulnerability.

Challenging the Text [Synthesize]

7. Students may agree that humans should know themselves; however, many will take exception to the notion that people should not explore spiritual issues.
8. Students will probably agree that, taken out of context, Hamlet's view of mankind is more positive than Pope's. Students should support their own views of humanity with examples.

Elements of Literature

The epigram may be addressed to other dogs, to anyone who might find the prince's dog should it get lost, or to status-conscious people in general.

Summary ■■■

By Canto III of this **mock epic** (a parody of a true epic) the fair Belinda has joined friends at a gathering at Hampton Court. There, she and others of wealth and leisure, including the Baron, sip coffee, gossip, flirt, and play cards. Throughout these proceedings, the Baron schemes to shear a lock of Belinda's hair and does so despite the efforts of sylphs (nymphs) gathered to defend it. Using a volley of snuff and a hairpin as weapons, the outraged Belinda and the Baron engage in battle. When the Baron shows no remorse, Belinda is forced to concede. Her consolation, the speaker suggests, is that her lock of hair will join the other stars in heaven, an absurd parody of the typical metamorphoses of classical literature.

Background

Here students will read **cantos** (sections of a long poem) written in heroic couplets to which they have just been introduced. These couplets, with their strong antitheses, help contrast the truly "epic" world of *Beowulf* and the *Odyssey* with the mock-epic, pretentious world of Belinda and the Baron.

Before You Read

FROM THE RAPE OF THE LOCK

Make the Connection

A Tempest in a Teapot

If you notice the newspapers and magazines at a supermarket checkout counter, you'll probably agree that ordinary Americans like to read about rich and famous people—those in politics, sports, show business, and society. Many readers find it especially interesting to learn about the trivial problems or petty quarrels of prominent people. *The Rape of the Lock* tells the story of a petty quarrel among the eighteenth-century English nobility. After you've read the first part of the poem, see if you don't agree that some tastes in reading haven't changed very much since Pope's day.

Reading Skills and Strategies

Using Reference Materials

Because Pope's subject is based on a contemporary incident, his poem contains **allusions,** references to people, places, and events that were well known to readers in his day but are probably unfamiliar to you. Sometimes you can understand an allusion by studying its **context.** You can also consult the information under Background on this page and in the side notes, or **glosses,** that accompany the poem.

Elements of Literature

Mock Epic

A poem like *The Rape of the Lock* is called a **mock epic.** The comedy of a mock epic arises from the discrepancy between a subject and its treatment: The subject is trivial, while its treatment is grandiose. In mock epics, fleas become elephants, and cracked teacups become major catastrophes. Pope used the traditional epic devices in a comic way, and his educated contemporaries had the pleasure of recognizing many similarities between *The Rape of the Lock* and serious epics like Homer's *Iliad,* Virgil's *Aeneid, Beowulf,* and Milton's *Paradise Lost.* For instance, the classical epics all have gods and goddesses who intervene in human affairs. Following these models, Pope includes some tiny, airy spirits called sylphs, who try in vain to prevent the "rape" from taking place. Readers would also recognize the epic device of the warning dream: Such a dream comes to Belinda from a supernatural being. Since epics always include battles, Pope includes a card game in his poem as well as a screaming match after Belinda loses her curl. In the complete poem of 794 lines (158 of which appear here), there are many such parallels to serious epics.

A **mock epic** is a comic narrative poem that parodies the epic by treating a trivial subject in a lofty, grand manner. A mock epic uses dignified language, elaborate figures of speech, and supernatural intervention.

For more on the Mock Epic, see the Handbook of Literary Terms.

Background

When Pope wrote about people, he wrote mainly about the rich, perhaps because the general public found it more interesting to read about the rich than about the poor. The chief characters in *The Rape of the Lock* all belong to the leisure classes, and they spend their time amusing themselves rather than working for a living.

The title of Pope's comic masterpiece means "the violent theft of a lock of hair." The poem is based on a real incident. The lock in question belonged to a certain rich and fashionable young lady named Arabella Fermor. The theft in question was committed by a certain rich and fashionable young man named Robert, Lord Petre. When Robert snipped a curl from Arabella's hairdo, he set off a quarrel between the Fermor and the Petre families. Had the two families been less sensible, their row might have escalated into bitter hatred. As it turned out, the feud subsided into laughter—thanks to Alexander Pope.

At the suggestion of a friend of the two families and patron of Pope's, Pope composed *The Rape of the Lock,* changing the name of Arabella to Belinda and calling Robert "the Baron." To make the warring families realize how trivial the "rape" actually was, Pope treated it very, very seriously. He dressed his poem in all the trappings of heroic poetry, as though he were Homer or Virgil writing an epic of the fall of Troy.

Reaching All Students

Struggling Readers

Assure students that many modern readers have problems understanding the mock-serious language of this eighteenth-century poem. Since Pope is making fun of the lifestyle of the upper classes, he assumes the reader has a lot of background knowledge. For instance, "gave the ball" in l. 12 refers to holding a social dance, "Indian screen" in l. 14 denotes a fire screen made in India, often used to protect ladies from sparks, the "board" in l. 33 is an archaic word for dining table, a "nosegay" in l. 69 is a corsage, and "peer" in l. 75 means nobleman. Have students work in pairs to find references they do not understand, and as a class help clarify these confusing passages.

English Language Learners

Prepare a brief glossary of archaic language in the poem and give it to English language learners as a resource. Include *dost, hither, oft, thou, lo, o'er, ere, 'tis,* and similar words.

Pope's poem is divided into five sections called **cantos.** Canto I begins like a proper epic, with a statement of the subject and an invocation to the Muse—a female deity who was supposed to inspire poets and other artists. Pope, however, clearly signals his comic intentions in the very first couplet:

What dire offense from amorous causes springs,
What mighty contests rise from trivial things,
I sing—

In Canto II, Belinda and her friends take a boat up the river Thames to a party. All who see her admire the two beautiful curled locks that hang down her back. And despite the small army of sprites (spirits) assigned to protect Belinda's beautiful hair, the Baron resolves to possess these locks.

from The Rape of the Lock

Alexander Pope

Canto III

Close by those meads, forever crowned with flowers,
Where Thames with pride surveys his rising towers,
There stands a structure° of majestic frame,
Which from the neighboring Hampton takes its name.
Here Britain's statesmen oft the fall foredoom
Of foreign tyrants, and of nymphs° at home;
Here thou, great Anna!° whom three realms obey,
Dost sometimes counsel take—and sometimes tea. **(A)**
Hither the heroes and the nymphs resort,
To taste awhile the pleasures of a court;
In various talk th' instructive hours they passed,
Who gave the ball, or paid the visit last;
One speaks the glory of the British queen,
And one describes a charming Indian screen; **(B)**
A third interprets motions, looks, and eyes;
At every word a reputation dies.
Snuff,° or the fan,° supply each pause of chat,
With singing, laughing, ogling, and all that.
Meanwhile, declining from the noon of day,
The sun obliquely shoots his burning ray;
The hungry judges soon the sentence sign,
And wretches hang that jurymen may dine. . . . **(C)**
Belinda now, whom thirst of fame invites,
Burns to encounter two adventurous knights,
At omber° singly to decide their doom;
And swells her breast with conquests yet to come. . . .
The nymph exulting fills with shouts the sky;
The walls, the woods, and long canals reply.
Oh thoughtless mortals! ever blind to fate,
Too soon dejected and too soon elate.

3. structure: Hampton Court, a royal residence on the river Thames, upstream from London.

6. nymphs: young ladies.

7. Anna: Queen Anne (1665–1714), who ruled England, Ireland, and Scotland.

17. snuff: powdered tobacco product sniffed or rubbed on the teeth and gums. **fan:** standard equipment for a lady.

25. omber: a card game for three players, popular in the eighteenth century.

Resources

Viewing and Representing

Fine Art Transparency

Use the fine art transparency of "The Honorable Mrs. Graham" by Thomas Gainsborough to help students visualize the setting of this poem and its drawing-room atmosphere.

- Transparency 8
- Worksheet, p. 32

Elements of Literature

Mock-Epic

For additional instruction on mock-epic, see *Literary Elements:*

- Transparency 13
- Worksheet, p. 40

(A) Appreciating Language

The Zeugma

? What is the double meaning of the verb *take,* as it is used in this line? [It means both to accept (advice) and to drink (tea).] Explain that this figure of speech is called *zeugma* (zyoog′mə), from Greek for "yoke." Zeugma occurs when a verb has two subjects or objects, or an adjective modifies two nouns, yet the two contexts have significantly different connotations. What is the effect of this figure of speech here? [Possible response: By elevating taking tea to the level of holding a royal consul, Pope establishes the comic tone of the mock epic.]

(B) Elements of Literature

Mock Epic

? How is the epic form mocked in ll. 11–16? [Pope glorifies the small talk and gossip of court life as if it were on the level of "the glory of the British queen." These petty aristocrats are a far cry from the kings of old, the usual heroes of epics.]

(C) Elements of Literature

Wit

? What do these two lines mean? [Judges and jurymen get hungry around dinner time, so they quickly finish up their work, signing papers that will result in hangings, so they can rush home to eat on time.] Why is this an example of wit? [It expresses a truth about human nature in an elegant way. These clever lines have been quoted for centuries.]

Crossing the Curriculum

Architecture

Have students research Hampton Court to find out what it looked like, both inside and outside. Students can draw, copy, or download pictures, or they can create an architectural drawing of the building or the gardens, which include a sunken pond laid out by Henry VIII, as well as William III's formal garden. (They might include in their sketch the challenging maze that adjoins the Lions Gate.)

Social Studies

Students may also research the significance of Hampton Court in history from the time of Henry VIII through the Stuart kings to George III. For example, Henry VIII and Sir Thomas More are said to have spent an uneasy time together in the gallery there as they discussed the king's proposed divorce. This gallery is now called the Haunted Gallery because it is allegedly the home of the spirit of Catherine Howard, one of Henry's beheaded wives.

Ⓐ Elements of Literature

Mock Epic

? In what ways is this treatment of coffee characteristic of a mock epic? [Possible answers: It takes a trivial thing, coffee, and goes into great detail about the way it is prepared and served. It makes a silly subject lofty.]

Ⓑ Vocabulary Note

The Prefix *pro-*

? The prefix *pro-* can have several meanings, including "forward." In what way is the word *prolong* a combination of the meanings "forward" and "long"? [Possible answer: To prolong something is to make it longer: When *long* goes "forward," it gets longer.]

RESPONDING TO THE ART

Charles Robert Leslie (1794–1859) was born in England to American parents. After being an art professor at the U. S. Military Academy at West Point, he returned to London and the Royal Academy of Art. Most of his paintings depict scenes from famous plays and novels, including Alexander Pope's *The Rape of the Lock,* Laurence Sterne's *Tristram Shandy,* Jonathan Swift's *Gulliver's Travels,* and Miguel de Cervantes' *Don Quixote.* An art critic of the time called Leslie's work "masterly in every respect . . . except their coloring, in which a dull red or burnt sienna tint is too prevalent."

Activity. Have students study the painting to identify Belinda, the Baron, and Sir Plume. Invite them to make up conversations for the group of men at the door and the group of women around Belinda. Have them also note the two private, whispered conversations going on, and imagine how these dialogues might have differed from the louder talk.

Sudden, these honors shall be snatched away,
And cursed forever this victorious day.
   For lo! the board with cups and spoons is crowned,
The berries° crackle, and the mill° turns round;
On shining altars of Japan° they raise
The silver lamp; the fiery spirits blaze:
From silver spouts the grateful liquors glide,
While China's earth° receives the smoking tide.°
At once they gratify their scent and taste,
And frequent cups prolong the rich repast.
Straight hover round the fair her airy band;
Some, as she sipped, the fuming liquor fanned,

34. berries: coffee beans. **mill:** coffee grinder.
35. altars of Japan: small lacquered tables.

38. China's earth: china cups, made of earthenware. **smoking tide:** coffee.

Sir Plume Demands the Restoration of the Lock (1854) by C. R. Leslie. Oil.
Private Collection.

Using Students' Strengths

Visual Learners

Invite students to illustrate scenes from the poem, using as many text details as they can. Encourage students to reread the poem looking for visual details such as rich brocades, silver coffee urns, and diamond earrings. Students can present their drawings to the class with a brief discussion of the scenes. Alternatively, students may wish to storyboard the action conveyed in the excerpt provided. Display students' work around the room.

Verbal Learners

Students may take special interest in the poem's many puns. Have them keep a list as they read. In columns beside their lists, students should explain how each pun relates to the context and how it succeeds as humor. Have students work in small groups to compare their lists after they have read the poem.

Some o'er her lap their careful plumes displayed,
Trembling, and conscious of the rich brocade.
Coffee (which makes the politician wise,
And see through all things with his half-shut eyes)
Sent up in vapors to the Baron's brain
New stratagems, the radiant lock to gain.
Ah, cease, rash youth! desist ere 'tis too late,
Fear the just gods, and think of Scylla's fate!°
Changed to a bird, and sent to flit in air,
She dearly pays for Nisus' injured hair!
  But when to mischief mortals bend their will,
How soon they find fit instruments of ill!
Just then, Clarissa drew with tempting grace
A two-edged weapon from her shining case:
So ladies in romance assist their knight,
Present the spear, and arm him for the fight.
He takes the gift with reverence, and extends
The little engine° on his fingers' ends;
This just behind Belinda's neck he spread,
As o'er the fragrant steams she bends her head.
Swift to the lock a thousand sprites repair,
A thousand wings, by turns, blow back the hair;
And thrice they twitched the diamond in her ear;
Thrice she looked back, and thrice the foe drew near.
Just in that instant, anxious Ariel° sought
The close recesses of the virgin's thought;
As on the nosegay in her breast reclined,
He watched th' ideas rising in her mind,
Sudden he viewed, in spite of all her art,
An earthly lover lurking at her heart.°
Amazed, confused, he found his power expired,
Resigned to fate, and with a sigh retired.
  The peer now spreads the glittering *forfex*° wide,
T' enclose the lock; now joins it, to divide.
Even then, before the fatal engine closed,
A wretched sylph too fondly interposed;
Fate urged the shears, and cut the sylph in twain,
(But airy substance soon unites again).
The meeting points the sacred hair dissever
From the fair head, forever, and forever!
  Then flashed the living lightning from her eyes,
And screams of horror rend th' affrighted skies.
Not louder shrieks to pitying Heaven are cast,
When husbands, or when lapdogs breathe their last;
Or when rich china vessels fallen from high,
In glittering dust, and painted fragments lie!
  "Let wreaths of triumph° now my temples twine,"
The victor cried, "the glorious prize is mine!
While fish in streams, or birds delight in air,
Or in a coach and six the British fair,

50. Scylla's fate: In Greek mythology, Scylla is turned into a seabird by the gods after she betrays her father Nisus by cutting off his purple lock of hair, on which his life and kingdom depend.

60. engine: instrument.

67. Ariel: chief of the heavenly sprites sent to protect Belinda.

72. earthly lover . . . heart: If in her heart Belinda wants the Baron to succeed, the sprites cannot protect her.

75. *forfex:* Latin for "scissors."

89. wreaths of triumph: like the ones worn by athletic and military heroes in ancient times.

C Reading Skills and Strategies

Using Reference Materials

Point out that there are many allusions in the poem that draw on mythology or classical writings. Remind students to use the glosses to help them. Then, modeling your own use of the gloss and paraphrases, work with students to supply an interpretation of these lines. [These lines warn the Baron: "Stop before it's too late." They remind the reader that Scylla was changed into a seabird because she cut her father's hair.]

D Elements of Literature

Wit

? Why is this particular couplet—already encountered on p. 523—a good example of wit? [It expresses a truth about human nature: that people have a tendency to make mischief or do harm, and that it is an all-too-easy goal to achieve. This idea is expressed with economy and elegance.]

E Elements of Literature

Antithesis

? In ll. 75–76, what is particularly clever about the use of antithesis in the description of the scissors? [The Baron spreads the scissors to enclose the lock of hair; he joins the scissors to separate the lock from Belinda's head—the verbs name contradictory actions but work together to produce a unified description.]

Professional Notes

Critical Comment: Pope to "Belinda"

Share with students this passage from a letter Pope wrote to Arabella Fermor: "As to the following cantos, all the passages of them are as fabulous as the vision at the beginning, or the transformation at the end (except the loss of your hair, which I always mention with reverence). The human persons are as fictitious as the airy ones; and the character of Belinda as it is now managed, resembles you in nothing but in beauty." Ask students to comment on the purpose and tone of this letter. [Some students may find the letter a straightforward explanation of his work, with a bit of flattery thrown in. Some may see the letter as an attempt to forestall Arabella's anger and the flattery as insincere. Others may detect a note of gentle mockery.]

Ⓐ Reading Skills and Strategies

Drawing Conclusions

? How long will the Baron's reputation last? [It will live only a short time. No one travels around in a coach with six horses anymore; no one now reads *Atalantis*; few people pay visits on holy days; few people use candles in large numbers; and few people believe in nymphs.]

Ⓑ Elements of Literature

Mock Epic

Explain that "to arms" is a rallying cry that would usually be called out when an army is attacked. Here the call to arms is an element of the mock epic: In this battle between Belinda and the Baron, the arms will not be real arms, and the fighting will not be serious fighting.

Ⓒ Elements of Literature

Mock Epic

? How does Belinda revenge herself on the Baron? [She throws snuff in his face to make him sneeze; she embarrasses him and threatens him with a bodkin.] How are these actions in line with the purposes of a mock epic? [They are silly, not valiant. These flighty, comical actions are in stark contrast to the actions of a classical epic.]

As long as *Atalantis*° shall be read,
Or the small pillow grace a lady's bed,
While visits shall be paid on solemn days,
When numerous wax lights in bright order blaze,
While nymphs take treats, or assignations give,
So long my honor, name, and praise shall live!
What time would spare, from steel receives its date,°
And monuments, like men, submit to fate!". . .

93. *Atalantis:* *The New Atalantis* (1709), a fashionable novel by Mrs. Delarivière Manley (1663–1724), which thinly disguised some contemporary scandals.

99. date: destruction.

In Canto IV, Pope describes an incident that occurs in all proper epics: a descent into the underworld. Just as Virgil had Aeneas travel down to Hades, Pope has Umbriel, a "melancholy sprite," fly down to a dismal, imaginary place called the Cave of Spleen. (Spleen *was the eighteenth century's name for what we call depression; rich, idle people were particularly subject to spleen in Pope's day.) In the cave, Umbriel obtains a vial of "soft sobs, melting griefs, and flowing tears," as well as an immense bag full of "sighs, sobs, and passions," which somewhat resembles the bag of unfavorable winds in Homer's* Odyssey, *given to Odysseus to keep tightly closed so his ship won't be blown off course. Umbriel then returns to the earth's surface and empties the contents of the bag and vial over Belinda and her girlfriend, who is even angrier than Belinda. The canto ends with Belinda lamenting to the Baron:*

> *"O, hadst thou, cruel! been content to seize*
> *Hairs less in sight, or any hairs but these!"*

The others in Belinda's tea-party audience shed tears of pity, but the Baron ignores her pleas: "Fate and Jove had stopped the Baron's ears."

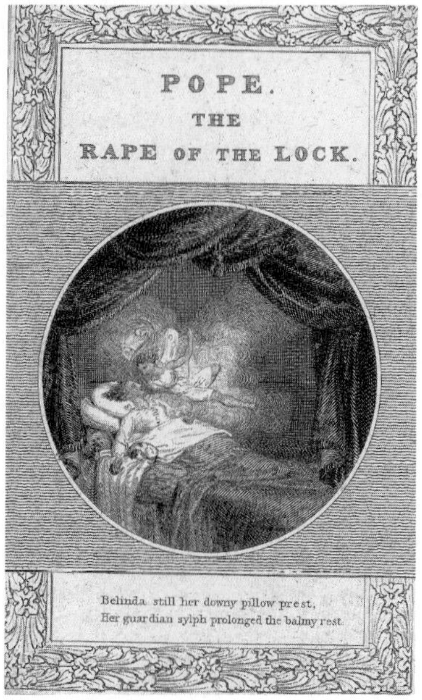

"Belinda still her downy pillow prest . . ."

Canto V

"To arms, to arms!" the fierce virago° cries,
And swift as lightning to the combat flies.
All side in parties, and begin th' attack;
Fans clap, silks rustle, and tough whalebones° crack;
Heroes' and heroines' shouts confus'dly rise,
And bass and treble voices strike the skies.
No common weapons in their hands are found,
Like gods they fight, nor dread a mortal wound.°. . .
    See, fierce Belinda on the Baron flies,
With more than usual lightning in her eyes:
Nor feared the chief th' unequal fight to try,
Who sought no more than on his foe to die.
But this bold lord with manly strength endued,

1. virago: ferocious woman; here, Belinda's girlfriend, who leads the attack on the Baron and his friends.

4. whalebones: used to shape and stiffen women's clothing.

8. like gods . . . mortal wound: Like gods, who are immortal and have no fear of physical wounds, these fighters do not fear the wounds inflicted by words.

Getting Students Involved

Cooperative Learning

Character Talk Show. Have five students play the parts of the characters of Belinda, the Baron, Clarissa, Ariel, and Belinda's friend (the "virago" of Canto V, l. 1) in a round-table discussion of the plot of the poem. A sixth student should interview the five characters at various times during the story. Encourage students to consider how their real-life analogues during Pope's day would have reacted to seeing themselves represented in his mock epic. Give the group a time limit for their discussion. Later students might engage in a second round-table discussion for the purposes of self-assessment.

Professional Notes

Critical Comment: Swift Praises Pope

Writing about his friend Pope, whose wit he admired, Swift remarked:

> In POPE, I cannot read a Line,
> But with a Sigh, I wish it mine;
> When he can in one Couplet fix
> More Sense than I can do in Six:
> It gives me such a jealous Fit,
> I cry, Pox take him, and his Wit.
>
> —*Jonathan Swift*
> *On the Death of Dr. Swift*

She with one finger and a thumb subdued:
Just where the breath of life his nostrils drew,
A charge of snuff the wily virgin threw;
The gnomes direct, to every atom just,
The pungent grains of titillating dust.
Sudden with starting tears each eye o'erflows,
And the high dome re-echoes to his nose.
"Now meet thy fate," incensed Belinda cried,
And drew a deadly bodkin° from her side. . . .
"Boast not my fall," he cried, "insulting foe!
Thou by some other shalt be laid as low.
Nor think, to die dejects my lofty mind:
All that I dread is leaving you behind!
Rather than so, ah, let me still survive,
And burn in Cupid's flames—but burn alive."
"Restore the lock!" she cries; and all around
"Restore the lock!" the vaulted roofs rebound.
Not fierce Othello° in so loud a strain
Roared for the handkerchief that caused his pain.
But see how oft ambitious aims are crossed,
And chiefs contend till all the prize is lost!
The lock, obtained with guilt, and kept with pain,
In every place is sought, but sought in vain:
With such a prize no mortal must be blessed,
So Heaven decrees! with Heaven who can contest?
Some thought it mounted to the lunar sphere,
Since all things lost on earth are treasured there.
There heroes' wits are kept in ponderous vases,
And beaux'° in snuffboxes and tweezer cases.
There broken vows and deathbed alms are found,
And lovers' hearts with ends of riband bound. . . .
But trust the Muse—she saw it upward rise,
Though marked by none but quick, poetic eyes: . . .
A sudden star, it shot through liquid air,
And drew behind a radiant trail of hair.°. . .
Then cease, bright nymph! to mourn thy ravished hair,
Which adds new glory to the shining sphere!
Not all the tresses that fair head can boast,
Shall draw such envy as the lock you lost.
For, after all the murders° of your eye,
When, after millions slain, yourself shall die;
When those fair suns shall set, as set they must,
And all those tresses shall be laid in dust,
This lock, the Muse shall consecrate to fame,
And midst the stars inscribe Belinda's name.

22. bodkin: long, ornamental hairpin, shaped like a dagger.

31. Othello: Shakespeare's tragic hero Othello gave his wife a handkerchief, which his enemy stole and then used as evidence of the wife's unfaithfulness.

42. beaux': fashionable gentlemen's.

48. trail of hair: the word *comet* derives from a Greek word for "long-haired."

53. murders: Just as Belinda's eyes are said to "eclipse the day" (Canto I, line 14), here they are said to murder the young men who admire her. Both compliments are ancient and trite in love poetry.

D Reading Skills and Strategies

Using Reference Materials

Ask students to use the gloss to explain why Pope compares Belinda's cries to those of Othello. [He equates in mockery Belinda's feelings about her snipped hair with Othello's anguish at his wife's supposed betrayal.]

E Critical Thinking

Interpreting

What do you think Pope is saying about the intelligence of beaux in ll. 41–42? [Possible answers: Pope implies that the gentlemen are unintelligent (since their wits fit into such small boxes); or the society that develops such elaborate cases must be vain and frivolous.]

F Advanced Learners

Making Connections

Point out what happens to Belinda's lock in this passage. Challenge students to find the conclusion to Ovid's *Metamorphoses* and to determine the literary parallel. [The recently assassinated Julius Caesar is transformed into a comet, as is Belinda's hair.]

G Elements of Literature

Mock Epic

What does Pope describe in ll. 51–58? [Belinda's old age and death] Why are these humorous? [The suggestion that Belinda will "slay" millions with her beautiful eyes and then achieve eternal greatness among the stars is so ridiculously exaggerated it is humorous.]

Assessing Learning

Check Test: True-False

1. The Baron is determined to have a lock of Belinda's hair. [True]
2. After the Baron cuts off the lock, Belinda faints. [False]
3. A sprite pours a bag of sobs, grief, and tears over Belinda and her friend. [True]
4. Belinda tells the Baron she would have given him the lock if he'd asked for it. [False]
5. The poet concludes by telling Belinda to stop mourning the loss of her lock of hair. [True]

Standardized Test Preparation

For practice in proofreading and editing, see

- *Daily Oral Grammar,* Transparencies 15, 16

Literature and the Arts

Perhaps the best-known Baroque music is that composed by Johann Sebastian Bach and George Frideric Handel. Bach wrote cantatas, chorales, concertos, suites, solo pieces, masses, and even fingering exercises for his students. Among Bach's works that Pope, a coffee addict, might have found amusing is his *Coffee Cantata,* in which a musical dialogue between a young girl and her father explores ideas about drinking the popular new beverage of the day. Handel is best known for his oratorios and suites, including his *Messiah* and *Water Music.*

Activity. Expose students to representative art, architecture, and music of the Baroque period. Ask students to research and present examples from the work of artists Rubens, Van Dyck, and Hogarth; the architect Wren; and the composer Purcell.

Literature and the Arts

The Storm Before the Calm: Baroque Art

The Renaissance did not pass serenely into the order, balance, and cool reason of the neoclassic age. In between—and often coexisting with neoclassicism in England—was the Baroque: a style and culture born of conflict, crisis, and quest.

Colonnades and swirling clouds. What typified the Baroque, a style that developed in seventeenth-century Italy and lasted in Europe and the Americas into the eighteenth century? The **Baroque** was marked by massive colonnaded cathedrals where interior walls seemed alive with sculpture; brightly painted ceilings that tricked the eye into a blue sky of swirling clouds and angels; opera that joined melodic music, elaborate costumes, dance, and melodrama; dramatic religious paintings so naturalistic they shocked; and intimate portraits of common people.

Baroque, a term adopted by later detractors, means "irregular, distorted," but the emphasis of the Baroque was really energy, sensuous appeal, and imaginative synthesis of art forms and ideas. There was, indeed, much to balance: Catholicism and Protestantism, monarchy and democracy, God and science, human genius and human insignificance.

With English restraint. Like the Renaissance, the Baroque Era came later to England than to continental Europe and, tempered by Protestantism, was more restrained. Both **Peter Paul Rubens** (1577–1640) and **Sir Anthony Van Dyck** (1599–1641), two great Baroque artists from Catholic Flanders, painted in England for Charles I. But Van Dyck's elegant, realistic portraits had a greater influence on English portraiture than Rubens's robust, writhing, heroically scaled figures. Later, **William Hogarth** created sensitive portraits of the English middle class, and his satirical series (depicting, for example, a marriage contract) convey a theatrical quality and a sly insistence that appearance is rarely reality.

In architecture, the Baroque shows itself in the restrained but fluid grandeur of the design for St. Paul's Cathedral by **Sir Christopher Wren** (1632–1723) and also in Wren's ambitious, unrealized scheme for rebuilding London after the Great Fire in 1666. Wren's plan was a spatial and aesthetic synthesis of streets, squares, shops, public buildings, and churches, all culminating in St. Paul's.

In Baroque music, elements we take for granted were startlingly new: writing attuned to individual instruments and voices, melody played against a bass line, chordal harmonies, and a solo voice or instrument against an orchestra. While English audiences rejected the flamboyance of Italian and French opera, they acclaimed the composer **Henry Purcell** (1659–1695) and his inventive uses of the new forms—including a brilliant, brief opera, *Dido and Aeneas.*

Baroque art was the natural successor of the High Renaissance. It embraced the complexities, contrasts, and challenges of a new world—and could be neither simple nor still.

Background: Baroque Abbey of Wilhering in Linz, Austria.

Listening to Music

"Hornpipe" from Suite II of *Water Music* by George Frideric Handel, performed by the New York Philharmonic

Background

The son of the court barber for the duke of Saxony, German-born composer George Frideric Handel (1685–1759) first came to London in 1710 and soon won the patronage of Queen Anne. Already well known in Hanover, Germany, he remained in royal favor in London when the elector of Hanover succeeded Anne as England's George I. Handel composed his famous *Water Music* for a celebratory boat ride that the new king and his courtiers made in 1717 and *Music for the Royal Fireworks* for a later celebration. In the area of choral music, Handel's masterpiece is the oratorio *Messiah.* (An *oratorio* is a dramatic but unstaged musical retelling of a religious story.)

Activity

Have students listen to "Hornpipe" from Suite II of *Water Music.* Note that the music was written to celebrate a royal event in the same era as Pope's poem and that the audience to which Handel catered was from the same social rank as Pope's characters. Then have students freewrite about this society based on the music and on their reading of the poetry.

Making Meanings

First Thoughts

1. Who, if anyone, do you think is victorious by the end of the action? Cite examples to support your response.

> **Reading Check/ Summary**
>
> Get together with two or three classmates, and devise a **story map** that will **summarize** the **main events** of the poem in **chronological order.** Compare your story outlines in class to see if you all agree on the main events that lead up to and follow the "rape."

Shaping Interpretations

2. In the satirical passage that opens Canto III (lines 1–18), what seems to be Pope's **tone**—his attitude toward the queen and her courtiers? Is he scornful or amused? How can you tell?
3. In Canto III, line 86, Pope juxtaposes—that is, places side by side—dying husbands and dying lapdogs. What is the effect of this juxtaposition? Find other juxtapositions in the poem.
4. A mock epic amusingly parodies the style and conventions of the epic. Since Homer, one epic hallmark has been the elaborate **epic simile,** or extended comparison between two unlike things. What comparisons are the basis of the extended similes in Canto III (lines 57–58 and 85–88) and Canto V (lines 31–32)?
5. In the complete poem, Pope frequently makes **satirical** remarks about the world outside the privileged ranks to which Belinda and her friends belong. Two examples of such remarks occur in Canto III, lines 21–22 and lines 45–46. Who or what are Pope's targets in these couplets?
6. The world outside the poem and the world inside it come together in Canto III, lines 7–8. What is the effect of the three words after the dash?
7. Belinda's victory at cards (Canto III, lines 23–28) and her cries of triumph are ironic because her happiness is so momentary; it's about to be shattered by the rape of her lock. **Irony** always involves a discrepancy of some kind. Explain why Belinda's victory over the Baron (Canto V, lines 13–22) also might be considered ironic.
8. Based on the extracts you have read, how would you state Pope's **theme** in this mock epic?

Extending the Text

9. Do you think any of the satire in Pope's poem could be applied to aspects of contemporary life? If so, how? Cite specific passages from Pope that could serve as satiric commentaries on people's behavior in the late twentieth century.

Elements of Literature

Wit: Ne'er So Well Expressed

Pope and his contemporaries admired a quality they called **wit.** Writers and other people who possessed wit were intellectually brilliant. Their ability to detect resemblances enabled them to write in images, similes, metaphors, and other figures of speech. Their language was polished and exact; their manner, cool and controlled.

The opposite of wit was dullness. Pope ridiculed the dull writers of his day, calling them dunces, in a long, brilliant, and insulting poem called the *Dunciad.* The chief dunce of the first version of the *Dunciad* (1728) was Lewis Theobald (pronounced "tibbald"), an editor of Shakespeare whom Pope called "piddling" because he was so concerned with the minute details of Shakespeare's texts. In 1742, when Pope reissued the *Dunciad,* Theobald was replaced as chief dunce by Colley Cibber, an actor and playwright who promoted his own career by publishing an egotistical biography. Theobald and Cibber lacked wit; Pope and such friends of his as Jonathan Swift and John Gay had wit.

Wit, then, meant cleverness. But it also meant something more serious:

> True wit is Nature to advantage dressed:
> What oft was thought, but ne'er so well
> expressed.

Making Meanings

First Thoughts [Respond]

1. Although some students may see the Baron as victorious in acquiring the lock, most will agree that the narrator implies that Belinda wins because she will have undying fame. Some students may feel no one wins because both people are made to look ridiculous.

Shaping Interpretations [Interpret]

2. Most students will agree that Pope is tolerantly amused. His humor is especially evident in the juxtaposition of important and utterly trivial elements in many of the couplets (for example, the mention of counsel and tea in l. 8). If he had wanted to create a more scornful tone, he might have used harsher words and imagined more serious consequences to the fight.
3. The effect of the juxtaposition in this line is humorous: Because lapdogs are often the pets of women, Pope's comparison actually belittles the husbands. Other examples are the British queen versus an Indian screen (Canto III, ll. 13–14), and the heroes' wits versus the little wits of the beaux (Canto V, ll. 41–42).
4. In Canto III, ll. 57–58, Pope compares the frivolous characters of the poem with ladies and their knights preparing for battle. In Canto III, ll. 85–88, Pope sets up a contrast between true tragedy (mourning a mate's death) and mock tragedy (lamenting the breakage of a household item). In Canto V, ll. 31–32, Pope alludes to a classic tragedy (betrayal and murder) by mentioning Othello's handkerchief, but the effect is humorous because the "death" of the lock is insignificant compared to Othello's betrayal.
5. In Canto III, ll. 21–22, students might see a criticism of judges and juries who are so irresponsible they rush to sentence defendants just so they can eat dinner on time. In Canto III, ll. 45–46, students may interpret Pope's target as leaders who think they see the whole situation when they see only what they want.
6. Most students will see that the effect is to deflate the solemnity of royal councils with the mention of an everyday activity—drinking tea. Others may think the lines humanize a powerful monarch.
7. Her victory is ironic because, in the scuffle between the two, the lock disappears. Another irony is Pope's use of lofty language to describe a silly fight, which consists of throwing snuff (the weapon) and the Baron's resulting sneeze (the wound).
8. Some students will cite secondary themes (such as criticism of the English judicial system), but most will agree that the major theme comments on the petty disputes that preoccupy people.

Extending the Text [Apply]

9. Students may note ridiculous feuds, cagey politicians, and a questionable judicial system in contemporary life. Have them cite specific lines to support their comparisons.

ELEMENTS OF LITERATURE

Mini-Lesson: Wit

Reinforce the ideas in the feature by drawing diagrams like the following on the chalkboard. Working with the class, write words that Pope associates with witty and dull people in the area between the inner and middle circles on the appropriate diagrams. In the outer rings record Pope's examples of witty and dull literature or sayings about wit.

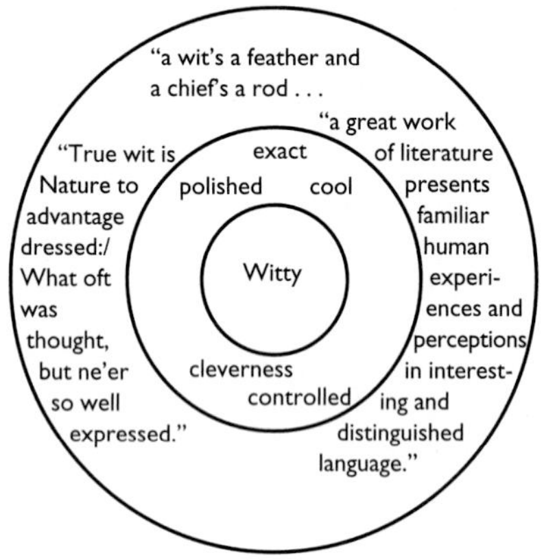

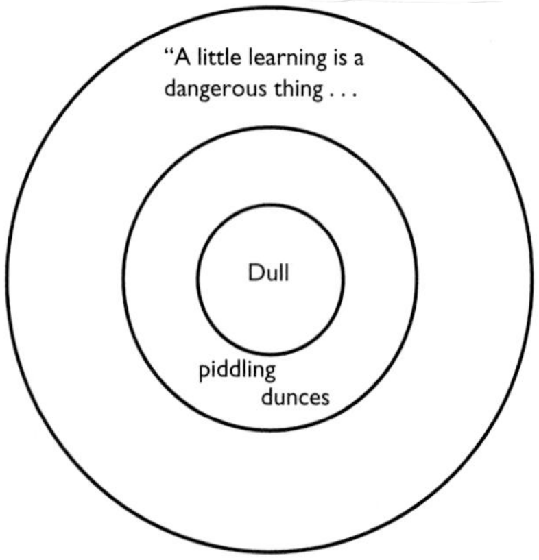

Possible Answers

1. Examples include the cleverness of the play on "take" (l. 8) or the glorified details of ceremonial coffee-drinking (ll. 34–38) in *The Rape of the Lock,* Canto III, or witty couplets like Couplet 10.
2. Truths about human nature are found in Couplets 2, 4, and 6 or in lines from *An Essay on Man.*
3. Wit is expressed through satiric television comedies, popular songs, editorials, comedy acts, and cartoons that lampoon human nature. Students might mention cartoonists Gary Larson *(The Far Side)* and Scott Adams *(Dilbert),* columnist Dave Barry, or comedians Damon Wayans or Jerry Seinfeld.

In this couplet from *An Essay on Criticism* (lines 97–98), Pope describes something he calls "true wit." The nearest modern equivalent of true wit is what we think of as great literature, or the classics. According to Pope, these great works express ideas that people have always accepted as true ("what oft was thought"). In great works, these familiar thoughts are not expressed in dull language, but are "to advantage dressed." The term *Nature* in this couplet refers not only to what we now think of as nature—the great outdoors with its birds, beasts, trees, plants, oceans, deserts—but also to human nature and the experiences of human beings.

The couplet on true wit might be summarized as follows: "A great work of literature presents familiar human experiences and perceptions in interesting and distinguished language. A great work reminds us, in an exciting and memorable way, of what we already know about the universe and its inhabitants."

But Pope did not regard wit as the most important quality a person can have:

> A wit's a feather and a chief's a rod;
> An honest man's the noblest work of God.

In this couplet, from Pope's *An Essay on Man* (Epistle IV, lines 247–248), the word *wit* is used as the name of a person, a writer. The writer is compared with a chief (a great leader, such as a general, king, or president) and with an honest man. Of the three, Pope gives first place to the honest man, God's noblest work. In comparison with this virtuous person, a wit is a mere "feather"—a light and flighty decoration—and a great man of action is a mere "rod"—a defender and corrector of society. Pope came to believe that virtue and morality are more important than intellectual brilliance (though he always was inclined to feel that second-rate writing was a kind of immorality, because a bad writer defrauds the reading public). Pope spoke his final words on morality while lying on his deathbed, when he said to the attending priest, "There is nothing that is meritorious but virtue and friendship, and indeed friendship itself is only part of virtue."

Though Pope thought it important to be a wit, he thought it more important to be a virtuous person.

Where is wit? Examine Pope's wit, and think about where wit is found today.

1. Find at least two examples from *The Rape of the Lock* that illustrate wit in the sense of "cleverness."
2. Now find an example of Pope's wit in its deeper sense: the elegant expression of a truth about human nature.
3. How would you define "wit" in today's world? Is there anyone on the contemporary scene whom you admire as an exponent of wit?

Pope's Villa, Twickenham by Samuel Scott.
Ackermann and Johnson Ltd., London.

Reading Check

Students should mention at least the following events in chronological order:

- The socialites gossip.
- The group has coffee, and the Baron gets the idea of snipping the lock.
- Clarissa gives the Baron a pair of scissors.
- He cuts the lock and gloats.
- Belinda throws snuff at him to make him sneeze.
- Belinda and the Baron trade words, and a melee ensues.
- The lock is lost, and the narrator contends it has become a comet.

CHOICES: Building Your Portfolio

Writer's Notebook

1. Collecting Ideas for a Persuasive Essay

Why not, like Pope, use the rich, the famous, and even the trivial to find controversial issues and values to write about in a persuasive essay? Scan TV programs about celebrities, print and TV ads in which celebrities endorse products or causes, and newspaper photos and stories of athletes and stars. Jot down brief descriptions (who, what, and why). Then react imaginatively. Brainstorm *issues*—perhaps of censorship, privacy, morality, sexism, elitism, or wealth. Save your ideas for the Writer's Workshop on page 612.

Analyzing Satire

2. Targeting Pope's Targets

In an essay, identify the targets of Pope's satire in *The Rape of the Lock*, and describe the devices Pope uses to ridicule these targets. To discover Pope's satirical targets, be sure to use the reference sources mentioned on page 526. Consider what Pope says about social role-playing and about the foolishness of human behavior in general.

Comparing Epics

3. From *Beowulf* to Pope

Compare Pope's mock epic with a serious epic: *Beowulf*, or, if you know it well, Homer's *Iliad* or *Odyssey*. Consider these elements of the epic in your discussion: invocations to the Muse, statement of subject, intervention of gods and goddesses, epic battles, a hero or heroine who reflects the values of a particular society, and use of elevated language.

Creative Writing

4. Mocking Modern Life

Write a mock epic about some event in contemporary life that's blown out of proportion: two teenage girls wearing the same dress at a school dance, two teenage boys who show up for a date with the same girl at the same time, a school mascot that gets lost, and so on. Be sure to include these devices: an **invocation to the Muse, intervention by the gods,** an **epic battle,** and a **warning dream.**

Creative Writing

5. Your Mock-Heroic Style

In Canto III of *The Rape of the Lock,* Pope describes making and drinking coffee in rich, elevated, and roundabout language (lines 33–40). This mock-heroic writing style breaks the elementary rule which says that writers must try to use simple, direct language when describing simple activities. As an exercise in mock-heroic writing, write a prose description of a common activity (such as riding a bicycle or cooking and eating a hamburger), using inflated language and rich images.

Speaking / Listening

6. Talking Back to Pope

Which one of Pope's sayings about human nature do you disagree with? Prepare for oral delivery a lighthearted rebuttal of the poet's position, starting with a sentence such as the following: "Resolved: That Alexander Pope erred when he claimed that . . . " Support your rebuttal with specific examples and incidents.

Analyzing Your Reading Process

7. Reading Reflections

Think back over your reading of Pope's poetry, and consult your reading notes. Which of his works did you find easiest to understand, and why? Which was most difficult, and why? How did the heroic couplets affect your reading? **Summarize** your reading experience in a brief essay analyzing the strategies you used to get at Pope's meaning. Conclude your essay by describing your general response to Pope's style.

Grading Timesaver

Rubrics for each Choices assignment appear on p. 137 in the *Portfolio Management System.*

CHOICES: Building Your Portfolio

1. **Writer's Notebook** After students complete an individual search for topics, they may enjoy a class brainstorming session in which they pool ideas.
2. **Analyzing Satire** To help students notice the targets and devices in *The Rape of the Lock*, encourage them to log references as they reread the poem.
3. **Comparing Epics** Students can use a checklist like the following to compare the epic form with Pope's mock epic. Ask students to include a brief description of each element.

Elements	True Epic	Mock Epic
Invocation to the muse	______	______
Statement of subject	______	______
Serious subject	______	______
Superhuman intervention	______	______
Battles	______	______
Representative hero/heroine	______	______
Elevated language	______	______
Wordplay	______	______
Satiric devices	______	______
Target(s) of criticism	______	______

4. **Creative Writing** Students may wish to complete this assignment in groups. They may also prefer acting out the epic to presenting it solely as a written composition.
5. **Creative Writing** Suggest that students keep a journal to record their observations.
6. **Speaking/Listening** Have students work with partners to review Pope's statements. The partners should invite each other to react to specific statements that seem controversial or daring.
7. **Analyzing Your Reading Process** To help students prewrite and draft, you might review and name common reading strategies.

OBJECTIVES

1. Read and interpret the satire
2. Generate relevant, interesting, and researchable questions
3. Recognize distinctive and shared characteristics of cultures
4. Compare text events with students' own experience and that of others
5. Recognize and discuss how satire might apply across cultures

Planning

- **Block Schedule**
  Block Scheduling Lesson Plans with Pacing Guide
- **Traditional Schedule**
  Lesson Plans Including Strategies for English-Language Learners
- **One-Stop Planner**
  CD-ROM with Test Generator

BROWSING IN THE FILES

About the Author. Voltaire's collected works fill fifty-two volumes and his published letters fill one hundred seven volumes. And all this came from a man who devoted himself, at least during the last twenty years of his life, more to politics, philosophy, and religious controversy than to literature. Voltaire spent part of his enormous energy on writing, part of it on getting rich (he was one of the richest writers of all time, though born to only a middle-class family), and part of it being jailed and exiled. At the age of twenty-two, he was exiled for his political satires; a year later he was imprisoned in the Bastille; nine years later he was again imprisoned in the Bastille and then exiled to England. Regarded as a great dramatist and philosopher, Voltaire is also credited with writing the first modern history and was the official historiographer of France.

WORLD LITERATURE

France

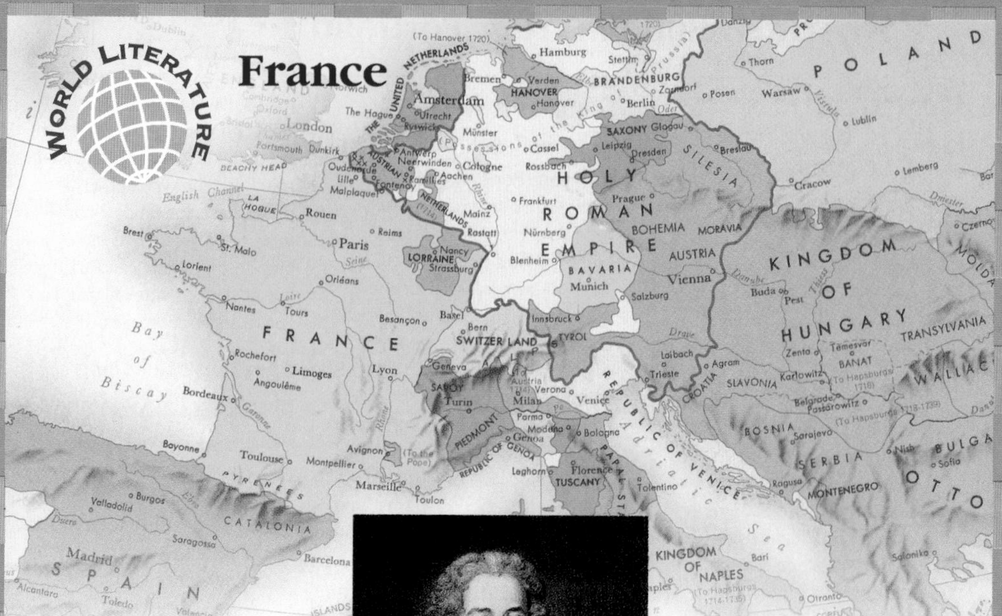

Voltaire

(1694–1778)

Voltaire (1833) engraved by James Mollison from an original by Nicolas de Largillière.

François-Marie Arouet (är·we), better known by his pen name, Voltaire, is remembered chiefly for his lifelong fight against injustice. Throughout his life, he implored his fellow philosophers to "Crush the infamous," by which he meant all things inhumane and oppressive. As a satirist, philosopher, historian, dramatist, and poet, Voltaire continually criticized the wastefulness of war, the intolerance of organized religion, and the plight of the poor.

Born in Paris to middle-class parents, Voltaire studied law for a time but soon gave it up to become a writer. His early reputation was based on his classical tragedies and his lampoons of the government. Yet Voltaire's celebrity did not prevent his being brutally beaten at the hands of an offended nobleman, imprisoned in the Bastille, and exiled to England in 1726.

In London, Voltaire met Jonathan Swift and Alexander Pope and was deeply influenced by the works of Bacon, Newton, and Locke, which emphasize the experimental method in science. When he returned to Paris, Voltaire wrote philosophical essays and historical studies that reflect this influence—he avoided the abstract in favor of a concrete focus on the way people actually lived and worked according to their beliefs. Many of these writings, collected under the title *Philosophical Letters,* were considered heretical and burned by the French parliament in 1734. Voltaire lived much of his later life near the Swiss border with France. He died during a rare visit to Paris, taken at age eighty-three to see his last play produced. Initially refused a Christian burial, Voltaire's remains were interred in Paris with great ceremony thirteen years later, following the revolution so greatly influenced by his ideas for reform.

(Map) Europe in 1721. Map ©Rand McNally R.L. #98-S-116.

go.hrw.com
LEO 12-6

Resources: Print and Media

Reading
- *Audio CD Library*
  Disc 8, Track 6

Elements of Literature
- *Literary Elements*
  Transparency 14
  Worksheet, p. 43

Assessment
- *Preparation for College Admission Exams,* p. 23

Internet
- *go.hrw.com* (keyword: *LEO 12-6*)

Before You Read

FROM **CANDIDE**

Background

In the tumultuous social climate of eighteenth-century Europe, writers, scientists, and philosophers questioned the "settled truths" of society as they never had before. Yet direct challenges to authority can be dangerous, in the eighteenth century or in any age. Satire—with its indirect criticism and deflating humor—thus became the weapon of choice for many eighteenth-century thinkers.

Voltaire used the device of the travel book, as Jonathan Swift did in *Gulliver's Travels,* to satirize everything—the Church, the state, and the mindless optimism of some eighteenth-century philosophers. Voltaire's hero Candide is an innocent who has been schooled by the repellent Doctor Pangloss to believe that everything that happens in the world happens for the best. The convictions of sweet-tempered Candide are severely tested in a series of outrageous and hilarious adventures. And, just as Swift's use of the name "Gulliver" may suggest the adjective "gullible," Voltaire's choice of "Candide"—punning on "candor, candid"—points to the qualities of childlike honesty, trust, and naiveté.

King Frederick II Comes to See Voltaire (c. 1750) drawn by Mousiau, engraving by P. Baquoy.

In the opening chapters of the novel, Voltaire singles out for his wicked satire some of the most important social institutions of eighteenth-century Europe. When Candide presumes to court the Baron's daughter, he is tossed out of the castle in short order. No sooner does he become the hero of the Bulgarians than he is thrown into chains and flogged. (Master of the humorous overstatement, Voltaire has his hero thrashed a ridiculous four thousand times.) Candide's experiences, however funny, reveal that the worlds of both the castle and the army are deeply flawed by snobbery, hypocrisy, and brutality.

Another target for the author's stinging criticism is the complacency of the philosopher Doctor Pangloss, whose name means "all tongue." Throughout the increasingly wretched events of *Candide,* Pangloss blithely mouths the theories of the German philosopher Gottfried Leibniz, who believed that an utterly rational God made a rational world in which everything, including evil, has a place and a purpose. Like Leibniz, Doctor Pangloss's perpetual slogan is "In this best of all possible worlds, . . . all is for the best."

Reading Skills and Strategies

Connecting Text to Current Events

Think about how Voltaire's satire might apply to aspects of today's world. Jot down notes as you read.

Summary ▪

In this excerpt from the first two chapters of *Candide,* the reader meets the main character, Candide, who is growing up on the estate of the noble Baron Thunder-ten-tronck. When Candide is caught expressing amorous interest in the baron's daughter, Cunegonde, he is expelled from the estate. At first he wanders aimlessly, but is soon captured by the Bulgarians, impressed into military service, and severely punished after his attempt at desertion.

Background

Written as an account of the travels of an impressionable young man in eighteenth-century Europe, *Candide* is actually a vehicle for satire of the social, philosophical, political, and religious institutions of Voltaire's day. The characters are exaggerations: Candide is naïve and trusting to the point of absurdity; Doctor Pangloss, his teacher, is a caricature of the rational, optimistic philosopher who sees a good reason for everything that exists and tortures logic rather than admit that anything could be amiss in "this best of all possible worlds."

Skill Link

Analyzing and Responding to a Critical Review

Ben Ray Redman, editor of *The Portable Voltaire,* writes, "[Voltaire] was, obviously not a great creative writer. . . He created no characters, he filled no scenes with bustling life, he explored no depths of human nature, he exposed and manipulated no psychological subtleties. In other words, he was not a great modern novelist, for the good and sufficient reason that in his day the modern novel had not yet been born; and he was no originator, no pioneer in literature. *Candide* is, indeed, a masterpiece, the origins and elements of which have been traced to *The Thousand and One Nights* [and] *Gulliver's Travels.* It is, in short, the tale at its highest level. But, even at its highest, this form is not one which is capable of bearing burdens that other literary forms can bear; not one in which the experience of life can find its fullest, most profound, and most affecting expression." Ask students whether they agree with this evaluation. Allow them to debate the evaluation's specific points: Is Candide a character or a caricature? What incidents stand out? Does *Candide* have emotional content? What literary traditions does Voltaire incorporate in *Candide*?

A Appreciating Language
Word Choice

? The word *candide* is French for "candid." What does the word *candid* mean, and what would you expect from a character named "Candid"? [Possible answers: The word *candid* means "open, frank, and naïve." The reader would expect this character to be naïve about people and their intentions toward him.]

B Elements of Literature
Satire

? What is satirical about the Baron's name? [Possible answers: With so many syllables, it seems overblown. The word *thunder* suggests a loud, large, unpleasant person. It is a very German name, which is apparently no compliment in this case, since the gloss explains that Voltaire disdained Westphalia.]

C Reading Skills and Strategies
Connecting Text to Current Events

? Which of these details has a parallel in our modern world? [Possible answers: Some people still object to marriages on the basis of social, cultural, and economic reasons, such as religion, race, socioeconomic background, and ethnicity. Rich people still sometimes command more respect than the poor even if they have nothing but their wealth to recommend them. Some people still keep dogs for hunting, and members of the clergy still dispense charity.]

D Reading Skills and Strategies
Finding the Main Idea

? What are the key ideas in Pangloss's philosophy? [There is no effect without cause; there are no accidents; everything has a purpose, which is to serve human needs.] **What main idea do these ideas support?** ["In this, the best of all possible worlds, . . . all is for the best."]

A *from* Candide

Voltaire

translated by **Richard Aldington**

Chapter I

How Candide was brought up in a noble castle and how he was expelled from the same

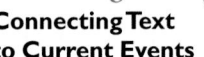

Le Baron....voyant cette cause & cet effet, chassa Candide du Château à grands coups de pied dans le derriere;
Candide Chap. 1er

"The Baron . . . observing this cause and effect, expelled Candide from the castle by kicking him in the backside frequently and hard."

The New York Public Library, General Research Division. Astor, Lenox, and Tilden Foundations.

In the castle of Baron Thunder-ten-tronckh in Westphalia[1] there lived a youth, endowed by Nature with the most gentle character. His face was the expression of his soul. His judgment was quite honest and he was extremely simple-minded; and this was the reason, I think, that he was named Candide. Old servants in the house suspected that he was the son of the Baron's sister and a decent honest gentleman of the neighborhood, whom this young lady would never marry because he could only prove seventy-one quarterings,[2] and the rest of his genealogical tree was lost, owing to the injuries of time. The Baron was one of the most powerful lords in Westphalia, for his castle possessed a door and windows. His Great Hall was even decorated with a piece of tapestry. The dogs in his stableyards formed a pack of hounds when necessary; his grooms were his huntsmen; the village curate was his Grand Almoner.[3] They all called him "My Lord," and laughed heartily at his stories. The Baroness weighed about three hundred and fifty pounds, was therefore greatly respected, and did the honors of the house with a dignity which rendered her still more respectable. Her daughter Cunegonde,[4] aged seventeen, was rosy-cheeked, fresh, plump, and tempting. The Baron's son appeared in every respect worthy of his father. The tutor Pangloss[5] was the oracle of the house, and little Candide followed his lessons with all the candor of his age and character. Pangloss taught metaphysico-theologo-cosmolonigology.[6] He proved admirably that there is no effect without a cause and that in this best of all possible worlds, My Lord the Baron's castle was the best of castles and his wife the best of all possible Baronesses. "'Tis demonstrated," said he, "that things cannot be otherwise; for, since everything is made for an end, everything is necessarily for the best end. Observe that noses were made to wear spectacles; and so we have spectacles. Legs were visibly instituted to be breeched, and we have breeches.

1. **Westphalia** (west·fā′lē·ə): region in western Germany, noted for its excellent ham. In a letter to his niece, Voltaire described Westphalia as "vast, sad, sterile, detestable."
2. **quarterings:** divisions on a coat of arms or family tree. Seventy-one is an absurdly high number, tracing a person's genealogy back over 2,000 years.
3. **Grand Almoner:** member of a noble household responsible for allotting charity to the poor.
4. **Cunegonde** (kyo͞o′nä·gônd′).
5. **Pangloss:** Greek for "all tongue."
6. **metaphysico-theologo-cosmolonigology:** This nonsense term is a satirical poke at the philosopher Leibniz and his followers, especially the embedded syllable *-nig-*, a shortened form of *nigaud,* which is French for "simpleton."

Reaching All Students

Struggling Readers

Assign each student a single passage to concentrate on, and ask students to take notes on what they learn from their assigned passage. For example, they may learn that the Baron is powerful because his castle has windows and a door; they might also infer from that passage that Westphalia must be relatively primitive and poor. Later, as the class discusses the selection, students can share insights on their selected passage.

Advanced Learners

Have students etymologically analyze both Pangloss's name and his brand of philosophy: metaphysico-theologo-cosmolonigology. Ask students to share with the class their conjectures not only about these matters but about Pangloss's role in the selection as a whole.

Stones were formed to be quarried and to build castles; and My Lord has a very noble castle; the greatest Baron in the province should have the best house; and as pigs were made to be eaten, we eat pork all the year round; consequently, those who have asserted that all is well talk nonsense; they ought to have said that all is for the best." Candide listened attentively and believed innocently; for he thought Mademoiselle Cunegonde extremely beautiful, although he was never bold enough to tell her so. He decided that after the happiness of being born Baron of Thunder-ten-tronckh, the second degree of happiness was to be Mademoiselle Cunegonde; the third, to see her every day; and the fourth to listen to Doctor Pangloss, the greatest philosopher of the province and therefore of the whole world. One day when Cunegonde was walking near the castle, in a little wood which was called The Park, she observed Doctor Pangloss in the bushes, giving a lesson in experimental physics to her mother's waiting-maid, a very pretty and docile brunette. Mademoiselle Cunegonde had a great inclination for science and watched breathlessly the reiterated experiments she witnessed; she observed clearly the Doctor's sufficient reason, the effects and the causes, and returned home very much excited, pensive, filled with the desire of learning, reflecting that she might be the sufficient reason of young Candide and that he might be hers. On her way back to the castle she met Candide and blushed; Candide also blushed. She bade him good morning in a hesitating voice; Candide replied without knowing what he was saying. Next day, when they left the table after dinner, Cunegonde and Candide found themselves behind a screen; Cunegonde dropped her handkerchief, Candide picked it up; she innocently held his hand; the young man innocently kissed the young lady's hand with remarkable vivacity, tenderness, and grace; their lips met, their eyes sparkled, their knees trembled, their hands wandered. Baron Thunder-ten-tronckh passed near the screen, and, observing this cause and effect, expelled Candide from the castle by kicking him in the backside frequently and hard. Cunegonde swooned; when she recovered her senses, the Baroness slapped her in the face; and all was in consternation in the noblest and most agreeable of all possible castles.

Chapter II

What happened to Candide among the Bulgarians

Candide, expelled from the earthly paradise, wandered for a long time without knowing where he was going, turning up his eyes to Heaven, gazing back frequently at the noblest of castles which held the most beautiful of young Baronesses; he lay down to sleep supperless between two furrows in the open fields: It snowed heavily in large flakes. The next morning the shivering Candide, penniless, dying of cold and exhaustion, dragged himself toward the neighboring town, which was called Waldberghoff-trarbk-dikdorff. He halted sadly at the door of an inn. Two men dressed in blue noticed him. "Comrade," said one, "there's a well-built young man of the right height."[7] They went up to Candide and very civilly invited him to dinner. "Gentlemen," said Candide with charming modesty, "you do me a great honor, but I have no money to pay my share." "Ah, sir," said one of the men in blue, "persons of your figure and merit never pay anything; are you not five feet five tall?" "Yes, gentlemen," said he, bowing, "that is my height." "Ah, sir, come to table; we will not only pay your expenses, we will never allow a man like you to be short of money; men were only made to help each other." "You are in the right," said Candide, "that is what Doctor Pangloss was always telling me, and I see that everything is for the best." They begged him to accept a few crowns,[8] he took them and wished to give them an IOU, they refused to take it, and all sat down to table. "Do you not love tenderly . . ." "Oh, yes," said he. "I love Mademoiselle Cunegonde tenderly." "No," said one of the gentlemen. "We were asking if you do not tenderly love the King of the Bulgarians." "Not a bit," said he, "for I have never seen him." "What! He is the most charming of kings, and you must drink his health." "Oh, gladly, gentlemen." And he drank. "That is sufficient," he was told. "You are now the support, the aid, the defender, the hero of the Bulgarians, your fortune is made, and your glory assured." They immediately put

7. **height:** Voltaire is making fun of the recruiting practices of the "King of the Bulgarians"—Voltaire's satiric name for King Frederick the Great of Prussia—who chose and organized soldiers according to their height.
8. **crowns:** units of money.

E Elements of Literature
Satire

? How does Voltaire satirize the attempts of his age to apply reason to all situations? [Possible answers: By showing that it can result in ridiculous conclusions: The shape of noses and legs necessitates the existence of spectacles and breeches; stones are in the world so that castles can be built; if the meat of the pig is edible, it should be eaten all year long; if Pangloss is the greatest philosopher of Westphalia, then he is the greatest philosopher in the world.] **Why is the passage ironic?** [The conclusions are presented as logical, but readers can see that they are illogical.]

F Elements of Literature
Allusion

? What biblical story does this incident allude to? [It alludes to the expulsion of Adam and Eve from the Garden of Eden. They were expelled for eating the fruit of knowledge and then realizing their own nakedness.]

G Critical Thinking
Making Judgments

? Do you think the soldier is sincere when he says that "men were only made to help each other"? Why or why not? [Possible answers: The comment is suspicious; the comment is probably made ironically; the man may want to help Candide, but he may not be capable of living up to his own noble sentiments.] **What might this passage foreshadow?** [Possible answers: It may foreshadow the fact that someone will not help him but will take advantage of him.]

Assessing Learning

Check Test: True-False
1. Candide is a deceptive person who tries to outwit the Baron. [False]
2. The Baron is a powerful person. [True]
3. Because Candide falls in love with the Baroness, he is sent away forever. [False]
4. Candide volunteers to serve in the Bulgarian army. [False]
5. Candide survives four thousand strokes as he runs the gauntlet. [True]

Standardized Test Preparation
For practice with ACT and SAT formats see
- *Preparation for College Admission Exams,* p. 23

Ⓐ Elements of Literature

Satire

? How is satire used in this passage? [Possible answers: Voltaire satirizes the notion of liberty, or free will, in a situation in which a person must choose between evils. He also employs comic exaggeration in details such as running the gauntlet thirty-six times, gathering a regiment of two thousand men, and surviving four thousand strokes.]

Ⓑ Reading Skills and Strategies

Connecting Text to Current Events

? What modern-day equivalents can you name for actions such as these? [Possible answers: Powerful leaders retain the power to pardon crimes. Some doctors still use outmoded or suspect methods of healing. Wars are eternal.]

Finding Common Ground

So students might easily refer to their notes when answering the questions, suggest that they use graphic organizers like the following to record their thoughts. For the third set of questions, encourage students to brainstorm as a class for elements of the popular romance or adventure narrative.

Modern "Candide"

What he would be taught today	
Modern attitudes	
Modern corruptions	
Platitudes tested	

Modern "Panglosses"

In education	
In politics	
In religion	
Other	

Modern Entertainment

Qualities of popular entertainment	Parodied in Candide?

irons on his legs and took him to a regiment. He was made to turn to the right and left, to raise the ramrod and return the ramrod, to take aim, to fire, to march double time, and he was given thirty strokes with a stick; the next day he drilled not quite so badly, and received only twenty strokes; the day after, he only had ten and was looked on as a prodigy by his comrades. Candide was completely mystified and could not make out how he was a hero. One fine spring day he thought he would take a walk, going straight ahead, in the belief that to use his legs as he pleased was a privilege of the human species as well as of animals. He had not gone two leagues[9] when four other heroes, each six feet tall, fell upon him, bound him, and dragged him back to a cell. He was asked by his judges whether he would rather be thrashed thirty-six times by the whole regiment or receive a dozen lead bullets at once in his brain. Ⓐ Although he protested that men's wills are free and that he wanted neither one nor the other, he had to make a choice; by virtue of that gift of God which is called *liberty,* he determined to run the gauntlet[10] thirty-six times and actually did so twice. There were two thousand men in the regiment. That made four thousand strokes which laid bare the muscles and nerves from his neck to his backside. As they were about to proceed to a third turn, Candide, utterly exhausted, begged as a favor that they would be so kind as to smash his head; he obtained this favor; they bound his eyes and he was made to kneel down. Ⓑ At that moment the King of the Bulgarians came by and inquired the victim's crime, and as this King was possessed of a vast genius, he perceived from what he learned about Candide that he was a young metaphysician[11] very ignorant in worldly matters, and therefore pardoned him with a clemency which will be praised in all newspapers and all ages. An honest surgeon healed Candide in three weeks with the ointments recommended by Dioscorides.[12] He had already regained a little skin and could walk when the King of the Bulgarians went to war with the King of the Abares.[13]

9. **leagues:** A league is a unit of distance equal to about three miles.
10. **run the gauntlet:** run between two rows of soldiers who strike the victim with clubs or other weapons.
11. **metaphysician** (met′ə·fə·zish′ən): philosopher who studies the nature of reality and the origin and structure of the universe.
12. **Dioscorides** (dī′əs·kôr·ə·dēz′): Greek army physician who wrote a treatise on medicine in the first century A.D. Even in Voltaire's day, Dioscorides' work was out-of-date.
13. **Abares** (a·bär′): that is, the French, who fought against the "Bulgarians," or Prussians, in the Seven Years' War (1756–1763).

Finding Common Ground

The disasters that befall the innocent Candide—including expulsion from the Baron's castle and impressment into a foreign army—are presented with such deft wit that readers often laugh out loud. Yet Voltaire's humor never obscures his deeper point, that humanity and social institutions are in need of reform. The need for reform, as well as admonitions couched in satire, may continue to be found in our world.

Thinking back over the story, jot down some brief notes in response to the following questions:

- If a "Candide" were created today, what would he be taught? What attitudes and corruptions in society would a modern Candide face, testing all those platitudes he'd learned about life?
- Are there "Panglosses" in the world today—in education, politics, or religion? Where and why do you still hear people saying things like "It's all for the best"?
- Is *Candide* a **parody** of the popular adventures or romances on today's best-seller lists or in the movies? Why do the kind of romances *Candide* makes fun of continue to appeal to us?

Take a moment to reflect on your responses and the notes you've already made; then, get together with a few classmates for a discussion of *Candide* and its satiric intent. Be sure your agenda includes discussion of whether or not Voltaire's underlying message against intolerance, cruelty, and smugness still has some timely applications in today's world. After your group has finished its discussion, share your findings with the class.

(Opposite) *Astronomy, 1750* by Richard Houston. Museum of the History of Science, Oxford.

Connecting Across Texts

Connecting with *The Rape of the Lock*

Use the following questions to help students make connections across selections:

- What are the goals of each satire? How are they alike, and how are they different? [Pope's goal appears to be more to amuse, in a witty, critical way, than to change the world. While Voltaire appears to want to entertain his readers, he also wishes to expose society's ills.]
- How are the two satires alike in the characters they portray? How are they different? [Both focus on the upper class; both take pot shots at, among others, a baron. Both caricature the people in their works, although Voltaire does this to a far greater extent than Pope.]

Collection 7

An Appetite for Experience

Theme

This Great, Wide World *The Restoration and the eighteenth century were times of great intellectual curiosity. Writers of the period began recording public events through the private lens of the journal and diary, and through biography. Public life is the stuff of most of the literature here, not the private and personal.*

Reading the Anthology

Reaching Struggling Readers The *Reading Skills and Strategies: Reaching Struggling Readers* binder includes a Reading Strategies Handbook that offers concrete suggestions to help students who have difficulty reading and comprehending text, or students who are reluctant readers. When a specific strategy is most appropriate for a selection, a correlation to the Handbook is provided at the bottom of the teacher's page under the head Struggling Readers. This head may also be used to introduce additional ideas for helping students read challenging texts.

Reading Beyond the Anthology

Read On At the end of the Restoration and Eighteenth Century collections, the grade twelve book includes an annotated bibliography of books suitable for extended reading. The suggested books are related to works in these collections by theme, by author, or by subject. To preview the Read On for this period, please turn to p. T608.

HRW Library The *HRW Library* offers novels, plays, and short-story collections for extended reading. Each book in the Library includes one or more major works and thematically or topically related Connections. The Connections are magazine articles, poems, or other pieces of literature. Each book in the *HRW Library* is also accompanied by a Study Guide that provides teaching suggestions and worksheets. The following title is recommended for Collection 7.

THE TIME MACHINE and THE WAR OF THE WORLDS
H. G. Wells
These two classics of science fiction influenced the genre throughout the twentieth century. More than mere tales of scientific gadgetry, the stories show the effect of technology on people's lives.

Collection 7 An Appetite for Experience

Resources for this Collection

Note: All resources for this collection are available for preview on the *One-Stop Planner CD-ROM 2 with Test Generator.* All worksheets and blackline masters may be printed from the CD-ROM.

Internet Resources
go.hrw.com LE0 12-7

Selection or Feature	Reading and Literary Skills	Vocabulary, Language, and Grammar
from **The Diary of Samuel Pepys** (p. 543) Samuel Pepys **Connections: On Keeping a Notebook** (p. 552) Joan Didion	• *Graphic Organizers for Active Reading,* Worksheet p. 42	• *Words to Own,* Worksheet p. 14 • *Grammar and Language Links:* Appositives and Appositive Phrases, Worksheet p. 31 • *Language Workshop CD-ROM,* Appositives and Appositive Phrases • *Daily Oral Grammar,* Transparency 17
from **A Journal of the Plague Year** (p. 557) Daniel Defoe **Spotlight On: Joseph Addison and Sir Richard Steele** (p. 567)	• *Graphic Organizers for Active Reading,* Worksheet p. 43	• *Words to Own,* Worksheet p. 15 • *Grammar and Language Links:* Clauses, Worksheet p. 33 • *Language Workshop CD-ROM,* Independent and Subordinate Clauses • *Daily Oral Grammar,* Transparency 18
• *from* **A Dictionary of the English Language** (p. 571) • **Letter to Lord Chesterfield** (p. 575) Samuel Johnson **Elements of Literature: Style** (p. 578) **Spotlight On: In Support of Shakespeare** (p. 580) (Dryden and Johnson)	• *Graphic Organizers for Active Reading,* Worksheet pp. 44, 45 • *Literary Elements:* Transparency 15 Worksheet p. 46	• *Words to Own,* Worksheet p. 16 • *Daily Oral Grammar,* Transparencies 19, 20
from **The Life of Samuel Johnson** (p. 583) James Boswell	• *Graphic Organizers for Active Reading,* Worksheet p. 46	• *Words to Own,* Worksheet p. 17 • *Daily Oral Grammar,* Transparency 21
World Literature: Germany *from* **Faust, Part I** (p. 591) Johann Wolfgang von Goethe *translated by* Louis MacNeice	The World Literature feature offers students the opportunity to explore thematically linked literature from different world cultures. Structured activities called Finding Common Ground are provided in the Pupil's Edition to guide students' explorations of these thematic connections between British and other world literature.	
Elegy Written in a Country Churchyard (p. 600) Thomas Gray **Elements of Literature: The Elegy** (p. 606)	• *Graphic Organizers for Active Reading,* Worksheet p. 47 • *Literary Elements:* Transparency 16 Worksheet p. 49	• *Daily Oral Grammar,* Transparency 22
The English Language: Decorum and Order (p. 609) John Algeo		
Writer's Workshop: Essay on a Controversial Issue (p. 612)		
Language Workshop: The Power of Parallelism (p. 617)		• *Workshop Resources,* p. 53 • *Language Workshop CD-ROM,* Parallel Structure
Learning for Life: Locating Information and Resources (p. 619)		

Other Resources for this Collection

- *Cross-Curricular Activities,* p. 7
- *Portfolio Management System,* Introduction to Portfolio Assessment, p. 1
- *Formal Assessment:*
  Literary Period Test, p. 113
  Literary Elements Test, p. 111
- *Test Generator,* Collection Test

Writing	Listening and Speaking Viewing and Representing	Assessment
• *Portfolio Management System,* Rubrics for Choices, p. 140	• *Audio CD Library,* Disc 9, Track 2 • *Portfolio Management System,* Rubrics for Choices, p. 140	• *Formal Assessment,* Selection Test, p. 99 • *Test Generator (One-Stop Planner CD-ROM)* • *Preparation for College Admission Exams,* p. 25
• *Portfolio Management System,* Rubrics for Choices, p. 142	• *Audio CD Library,* Disc 9, Track 3 • *Viewing and Representing:* Fine Art Transparency 9 Worksheet p. 36 • *Portfolio Management System,* Rubrics for Choices, p. 142	• *Formal Assessment,* Selection Test, p. 101 • *Test Generator (One-Stop Planner CD-ROM)*
• *Portfolio Management System,* Rubrics for Choices, p. 144	• *Audio CD Library,* Disc 10, Tracks 2, 3 • *Portfolio Management System,* Rubrics for Choices, p. 144	• *Formal Assessment,* Selection Test, p. 103 • *Test Generator (One-Stop Planner CD-ROM)*
• *Portfolio Management System,* Rubrics for Choices, p. 146	• *Audio CD Library,* Disc 10, Track 4 • *Portfolio Management System,* Rubrics for Choices, p. 146	• *Formal Assessment,* Selection Test, p. 105 • *Test Generator (One-Stop Planner CD-ROM)* • *Preparation for College Admission Exams,* p. 27
	• *Audio CD Library,* Disc 10, Track 5	
• *Portfolio Management System,* Rubrics for Choices, p. 147	• *Audio CD Library,* Disc 10, Track 6 • *Portfolio Management System,* Rubrics for Choices, p. 147	• *Formal Assessment,* Selection Test, p. 107 • *Test Generator (One-Stop Planner CD-ROM)*
		• *Formal Assessment,* The English Language Test, p. 109

• *Workshop Resources,* p. 21
• *Writer's Workshop 2 CD-ROM,* Controversial Issues
	• *Viewing and Representing,* HRW Multimedia Presentation Maker	• *Portfolio Management System*
		  • Prewriting, p. 149
		  • Peer Editing, p. 150
		  • Assessment Rubric, p. 151

		• *Portfolio Management System,* Rubrics, p. 152

Transparency CD-ROM Video Audio CD

Collection 7 An Appetite for Experience

Skills Focus

Selection or Feature	Reading Skills and Strategies	Elements of Literature and Language	Writing	Listening and Speaking	Viewing and Representing
from **The Diary of Samuel Pepys** (p. 543) Samuel Pepys	Monitor Your Reading, p. 543 • Archaic Words • Sentence Structure • Allusions Reading Seventeenth-Century Language, p. 554	Diary, pp. 543, 554 Primary Source, p. 554	Identify Issues Relevant to Contemporary Life in Pepys's Diary, p. 555 Write a Character Study of Pepys, p. 555 Write Contemporary Diary Entries Modeled on Pepys or Didion, p. 555 Write a Story or Poem Based on an Event Recorded in Pepys's *Diary*, p. 555		Create a Time Line, p. 554
from **A Journal of the Plague Year** (p. 557) Daniel Defoe	Evaluate Sources of Information, p. 557	Journal, p. 557 Journalists, p. 557 Image, p. 565 Tone, p. 565	Identify Potential Topics for Writing, p. 566 Compare and Contrast Disaster Reports, p. 566 Write an Essay Supporting an Opinion, p. 566 Write a First-Person Narrative Describing a Natural Disaster, p. 566	Have a Round-Table Discussion of Defoe's Credibility and a Writer's Responsibility, p. 566	
from **A Dictionary of the English Language** (p. 571) **Letter to Lord Chesterfield** (p. 575) Samuel Johnson		Dictionary, p. 571 Tone, pp. 575, 578 Irony, pp. 578–579 Style, pp. 578–579 Adage/Proverb, p. 578 Metaphor, p. 578	Freewrite a Letter of Protest, p. 579 Write a Paragraph Analyzing the Character of Johnson, p. 579 Write an Essay Analyzing an Author's Tone, p. 579 Write Twenty Original Dictionary Entries, p. 579 Rewrite the "Letter to Lord Chesterfield" in Contemporary Language and Style, p. 579		
from **The Life of Samuel Johnson** (p. 583) James Boswell		Biography, p. 583	Identify a Position, Supporting Points, and Counterarguments, p. 589 Write a Biographical Sketch , p. 589 Research and Report on the Membership of the Literary Club, p. 589		Analyze Artistic Representations of Johnson and Compare with Boswell's, p. 589
World Literature: Germany *from* **Faust, Part I** (p. 591) Johann Wolfgang von Goethe	The World Literature feature offers students the opportunity to explore thematically linked literature from different world cultures. Structured activities called Finding Common Ground are provided in the Pupil's Edition to guide students' explorations of these thematic connections between British and other world literature.				
Elegy Written in a Country Churchyard (p. 600) Thomas Gray	Reading Inverted Sentences, p. 600 Analyzing Word Choice and Word Order, pp. 606–607 Paraphrase, p. 607 Generalization, p. 606	Image, p. 605 Personify, p. 605 Stereotype. p. 606 Theme, pp. 606, 607 Elegy, p. 606 Pastoral, p. 606 Gothic, p. 606 Setting, p. 606 Speaker, p. 607 Tone, p. 607	Write Two Thesis Statements for Possible Persuasive Topics, p. 607 Write a Brief Essay Comparing Two Elegies, p. 607 Write an Epitaph from the Point of View of One of the Characters Mentioned in Gray's "Elegy," p. 607 Write a Contemporary Meditation, p. 607	Prepare and Present an Oral Reading of Gray's "Elegy," p. 607	
The English Language: Decorum and Order (p. 609) John Algeo		Adapted, Coined, and Borrowed Words, p. 609 Dictionaries, p. 610 Pronunciation, p. 610 Homophones, p. 610 New Words, p. 610	Compare Entries from Johnson's *Dictionary* with Those in a Modern Dictionary, p. 611 Investigate New Words, p. 611 Identify Usage Problems, p. 611		
Writer's Workshop: Essay on a Controversial Issue (p. 612)			Write an Essay on a Controversial Issue, pp. 612–616		
Language Workshop: The Power of Parallelism (p. 617)		Parallel Structures, p. 617	Revise Sentences to Correct Faulty Parallelism, p. 617		
Reading for Life: Using Text Organizers (p. 618)	Locate and Catetgorize Information, p. 618				
Learning for Life: Locating Information and Resources (p. 619)	Identify Sources of Information for Dislocated Workers, p. 619			Prepare and Produce a Thirty-Second PSA, p. 619	Publish a Brochure, p. 619 Design and Produce a Promotional Poster, p. 619

Collection 7

AN APPETITE FOR EXPERIENCE

Pepys | Johnson | Goethe
Defoe | Boswell | Gray

He who neglects to drink of the spring of experience is likely to die of thirst in the desert of ignorance.

—Ling Po (Chinese, 701–762)

OBJECTIVES

1. Read literature of the Restoration and eighteenth century on the subject of "An Appetite for Experience"
2. Interpret literary elements with special emphasis on style and the elegy
3. Apply a variety of reading strategies particularly analyzing word choice and word order
4. Respond to the literature in a variety of modes
5. Learn and use new words
6. Learn about language change and the role of dictionaries
7. Plan, draft, and revise a persuasive essay on a controversial issue
8. Write sentences using parallel elements correctly
9. Demonstrate the ability to use text organizers
10. Locate information resources through a variety of projects

Responding to the Quotation

? Supply the implied parts of Ling Po's metaphor. If experience is a spring (water source) and ignorance is a desert, where is the spring located? [Possible responses: in an oasis, a garden, a fertile place.] What does thirst represent? [our desire for knowledge; our need to learn about life] Encourage students to reflect on and discuss how experience shapes a person's intellectual and personal development.

RESPONDING TO THE ART

Richard Houston (1721–1775) was born in Ireland and settled in London. The Houston etching on this page represents the Age of Reason. Young scientists are studying the universe by means of telescopes, globes, and other instruments.

Activity. Ask students to discuss what the young men in the etching are studying and what the objects of their study reveal about the age in which they lived.

WORK IN PROGRESS

Writing Focus: An Essay on a Controversial Issue

The following **Work in Progress** assignments build to a culminating **Writer's Workshop** at the end of this collection.

- Diary of Samuel Pepys — Take notes on controversial issues (p. 555)
- A Journal of the Plague Year — Identify potential topics (p. 566)
- Letter to Lord Chesterfield — Freewrite ideas on topics for protest (p. 579)
- The Life of Samuel Johnson — Focus on counterarguments (p. 589)
- Elegy Written in a Churchyard — Write thesis statements (p. 607)

Writer's Workshop: Persuasive Writing / An Essay on a Controversial Issue (p. 612)

Objectives

1. Read and interpret the diary
2. Analyze the diary form
3. Monitor comprehension of seventeenth-century language
4. Express understanding through critical and creative writing, research, and speaking
5. Learn and use new words

Skills

Literary
- Analyze the diary form

Reading
- Monitor comprehension of seventeenth-century language

Writing
- Collect issues for a persuasive essay
- Analyze a character
- Write a diary entry
- Create an original story or poem

Research/Speaking
- Research and present an oral report on a topic from Pepys's diary

Vocabulary
- Learn and use new words

Planning

- **Block Schedule**
  Block Scheduling Lesson Plans with Pacing Guide
- **Traditional Schedule**
  Lesson Plans Including Strategies for English-Language Learners
- ***One-Stop Planner***
  CD-ROM with Test Generator

Samuel Pepys

(1633–1703)

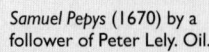

Samuel Pepys (1670) by a follower of Peter Lely. Oil.
The Pepys Library, Magdalene College, Cambridge.

For nine years—1660 to 1669—Samuel Pepys, whose name is pronounced "peeps," kept a secret diary which, when published long after his death, made him very famous. Pepys was not a writer but an official in the government office that maintained the Royal Navy and provided it with ships and supplies. Although a cousin helped Pepys obtain his first appointment in the Navy Office, it was Pepys's own diligence and skill that accounted for his rapid advancement. He did much to increase the honesty and efficiency of naval supply and maintenance.

Along with his public career, Pepys's private affairs also prospered. Starting humbly in life as the son of a tailor who managed to send him to Cambridge University, Pepys became so rich that when he was forced to retire in 1688 for political reasons, he could live the rest of his life like a gentleman, in leisure, comfort, and elegance.

Pepys had an insatiable appetite for experience, a vast capacity for pleasure, and an immense desire for learning—languages, literature, science, and everything connected with his naval occupation. Small things delighted him. When he heard "a fellow whistle like a bird exceeding well," he resolved to take lessons in bird whistling. Of a new watch he said, "I could not forbear carrying it in my hand and seeing what o'clock it was a hundred times." His house was full of creatures: cats, two dogs, a whistling blackbird, canaries, even for a time an eagle. He owned many books, carpenters' tools, maps and charts, a telescope, and several musical instruments that he could play—a flageolet, a lute, a flute, and a small harpsichord (which he never mastered). He composed a few songs that are still regarded as singable, he was proud of his dancing, and he liked expensive clothes and oil paintings. In everything he sought pleasure, and he usually found it. Whenever his head ached from business or his wife was angry at him for flirting with other women, he took refuge in the theater. He saw so many plays and recorded his impressions of them so accurately that the *Diary* is now regarded as an important document for theater history.

Historians of all kinds find the *Diary* useful because Pepys was a firsthand observer of public events and contemporary life. In 1660, he was one of the Englishmen who went to bring exiled King Charles II back to England. He witnessed joyous occasions like Charles's coronation in 1661 and national disasters like the plague of 1665 and the Great Fire of 1666. These important public happenings he recorded in his *Diary* along with trivial personal ones. For instance, on one occasion he records something that happened at the theater:

> I went to Mr. Crew's house and thence to the theater, where I saw again *The Lost Lady,* which doth now please me better than before. And here, I sitting behind in a dark place, a lady spat backward upon me by a mistake, not seeing me. But after seeing her to be a very pretty lady, I was not troubled at all.

According to the *Diary,* Pepys's life was full of unexpected little events like this one. Reading the *Diary* over Pepys's shoulder, we see the lively panorama of Restoration London—and in many of his observations, we also see ourselves.

go.hrw.com
LEO 12-7

Resources: Print and Media

Reading
- *Graphic Organizers for Active Reading,* p. 42
- *Words to Own,* p. 14
- *Audio CD Library*
  Disc 9, Track 2

Writing and Language
- *Daily Oral Grammar*
  Transparency 17
- *Grammar and Language Links*
  Worksheet, p. 31
- *Language Workshop CD-ROM*

Viewing and Representing
- *Visual Connections*
  Videocassette B, Segment 7

Assessment
- *Formal Assessment,* p. 99
- *Portfolio Management System,* p. 140
- *Preparation for College Admission Exams,* p. 25
- *Test Generator (One-Stop Planner CD-ROM)*

Internet
- go.hrw.com (keyword: LEO 12-7)

Before You Read

FROM THE DIARY OF SAMUEL PEPYS

Make the Connection

Capturing the Moment

Many people kept detailed diaries in the seventeenth century, and a surprisingly large number of these diaries have survived. The pious people we now call Puritans used their diaries to analyze their moral behavior and record their spiritual progress. In contrast, Pepys in his *Diary* pays little attention to the state of his soul, though he almost always mentions going to church on Sunday, often with disparaging comments ("a sorry, silly sermon"). But Pepys was not an introspective person; his *Diary* is interesting because it tells us what he saw and heard and said and did. Many people today keep diaries and journals. What do you think their motives are?

Reading Skills and Strategies

Monitoring Your Reading

Many aspects of Pepys's seventeenth-century usage might give you trouble. Some **archaic words, sentence structures,** and **allusions** will be strange to you. As you read these diary entries, monitor your comprehension. If you are having trouble with archaic words and unfamiliar allusions, the footnotes will help you. If some words still puzzle you, you can refer to the glossary at the back of the book or to a dictionary. Keep notes on your reading process.

Elements of Literature

Diary

Pepys's *Diary* is so detailed, wide-ranging, and frank that it has become a byword for this form of writing. Each page of this vivid chronicle reveals Pepys's curious eye, candid opinions, and clear relish for life in the great city.

A **diary** is a daily, personal account of feelings, impressions, and events. Unlike journals, which are usually less personal records of events often written with another reader in mind, most diaries are quite intimate and written only for the owner's private reference and pleasure.

For more on the Diary, see the Handbook of Literary Terms.

Background

Pepys's diary was truly a secret one. He wrote it only for his own use and in a kind of shorthand that had recently been invented. He doubly safeguarded the most intimate details of his life by recording them in a private foreign language that appears to mix together Latin, French, and Spanish words. Yet, since he did not destroy the *Diary* at the end of his life but bequeathed it along with his other books to Cambridge University, he must have recognized its value as literature and history. He must, in other words, have imagined people reading it. But not until the 1970s was it possible to read everything in the *Diary* because earlier editors could not bring themselves to transcribe and print the more personal entries. And though it covers only nine years, the *Diary* is immense; in the 1970s and 1980s it was published—along with notes, commentaries, and indices—in eleven fat volumes.

When he began the *Diary,* in 1660, Pepys was twenty-seven, married to twenty-year-old Elizabeth St. Michel, and in the service of Edward Montagu. Until recently, he and his wife had been living in a turret room in Whitehall Palace, without servants or proper facilities for washing and cooking. Nine years later, when he stopped keeping the *Diary* because of eye trouble, Pepys and his family had their own handsome townhouse, one of a complex of buildings that made up the Navy Office. Their household was not much like most modern ones because they had several live-in servants who did most of their work: three housemaids, a waiting woman for Elizabeth, a footboy for Samuel, and a coachman to drive and look after their coach and horses. Although Pepys and his wife had no children, their house was always full of people.

Summary ■■■

These five dated entries are from the multivolume diary written by Samuel Pepys from 1660 to 1669. Through hard work and good connections, Pepys rose in government service to become a wealthy man with access to the politically powerful and socially prominent figures of his day. Therefore, his diary, which records both his public and private experiences, provides not only an insider's view of life among Restoration London's middle and upper classes but also a revelation of the character of Samuel Pepys himself. In the first entry, the royalist Pepys reports, with satisfaction, on the drawing and quartering of a man involved in the overthrow of Charles I. In the second entry, he offers an eyewitness account of the 1661 coronation of Charles II. Here Pepys gives not only a vivid description of the ceremony itself but also reveals his personal irritation at being too far back in the crowd. His account of the terrible Fire of London is detailed, immediate, and compelling. He puts the reader at the scene as skillfully, if not as succinctly, as any modern journalist. Taken as a whole, the five entries show Pepys to be a keenly observant, sociable, pleasure-loving man, both humane and frankly aware of his shortcomings.

Preteaching Vocabulary

Words to Own

Have students, working in pairs or small groups, jot down the five Words to Own listed at the bottom of the selection pages and note their meanings. Ask each pair or group to collaborate and write a five- or six-sentence description of a present-day social occasion, such as a party, wedding, or dance. (They may use *cavalcade* figuratively, or change it to the more modern *motorcade.*) Have a volunteer from each group read the description aloud to the class. Give feedback on how well each group was able to use the words in context.

Resources

Listening

Audio CD Library

A recording of these *Diary* entries is provided in the *Audio CD Library*:

- Disc 9, Track 2

Viewing and Representing

Videocassette B, Segment 7

Available in English and Spanish. The *Visual Connections Segment* "London Life" examines the bustling city that forms the backdrop of Pepys's *Diary*. For full lesson plans and worksheets, see the *Visual Connections Teacher's Manual*.

A Historical Connections

Capital Punishment

Public execution was commonplace in seventeenth-century Europe, and hanging, as well as drawing and quartering (eviscerating and dividing the corpse into four parts), was a widely accepted method of punishment.

B Reading Skills and Strategies

Monitoring Your Reading

Work with students to paraphrase these sentences in modern English. They will need to infer from the context in what sense Pepys uses "chance." Ask students what the author's point is in mentioning the earlier execution. [He feels fortunate to have witnessed both of these historic events.]

C Elements of Literature

Character

? What do we learn about Samuel Pepys's personality when we read this candid sentence? [Possible responses: He has a quick temper. He takes out his anger on objects rather than on people. He notices and analyzes his own behavior.]

D Reading Skills and Strategies

Connecting with the Text

Have students list popular present-day events that draw thousands who are willing to wait in discomfort for hours for a chance to see for themselves. Discuss the aspect of human nature we share with Pepys that makes us want to be eyewitnesses, even in our own age of live-TV broadcasts and widespread video recording.

from The Diary of Samuel Pepys

Samuel Pepys

October 13, 1660
A Public Execution, A Private Explosion

To my Lord's[1] in the morning, where I met with Captain Cuttance. But my Lord not being up, I went out to Charing Cross to see Major General Harrison[2] hanged, drawn, and quartered—which was done there—he looking as cheerfully as any man could do in that condition. He was presently cut down and his head and his heart shown to the people, at which there was great shouts of joy. It is said that he said that he was sure to come shortly at the right hand of Christ to judge them that now have judged him. And that his wife doth expect his coming again.[3]

Thus it was my chance to see the King beheaded at Whitehall and to see the first blood shed in revenge for the blood of the King at Charing Cross. From thence to my Lord's and took Captain Cuttance and Mr. Sheply to the Sun tavern and did give them some oysters. After that I went by water home, where I was angry with my wife for her things lying about, and in my passion kicked the little fine basket which I bought her in Holland and broke it, which troubled me after I had done it.

Within all the afternoon, setting up shelves in my study. At night to bed.

April 23, 1661
The Coronation of Charles II

. . . About four in the morning I rose. And got to the Abbey,[4] where I followed Sir J. Denham the surveyor with some company that he was leading in. And with much ado, by the favor of Mr. Cooper his man, did get up into a great scaffold across the north end of the Abbey—where with a great deal of patience I sat from past four till eleven before the King came in. And a pleasure it was to see the Abbey raised in the middle, all covered with red and a throne (that is a chair) and footstool on the top of it. And all the officers of all kinds, so much as the very fiddlers, in red vests.

At last comes in the Dean and Prebends[5] of Westminster with the Bishops (many of them in cloth-of-gold copes[6]); and after them the nobility all in their Parliament robes, which was a most magnificent sight. Then the Duke[7] and the King with a scepter (carried by my Lord of Sandwich) and sword and mond[8] before him, and the crown too.

The King in his robes, bareheaded, which was very fine. And after all had placed themselves—there was a sermon and the service. And then in the choir at the high altar he passed all the ceremonies of the coronation—which, to my very great grief, I and most in the Abbey could not see. The crown being put upon his head, a great shout begun. And he came forth to the throne and there passed more ceremonies: as, taking the oath and having things read to him by the Bishop,[9] and his Lords (who put on their caps as soon as the King put on his crown) and Bishops came and kneeled before him.

And three times the King-at-arms went to the three open places on the scaffold and proclaimed that if anyone could show any reason why Ch. Steward [Charles Stuart] should not be King of England, that now he should come and speak.

And a general pardon also was read by the Lord Chancellor; and medals flung up and down by my

1. **my Lord's:** Edward Montagu (1625–1672), earl of Sandwich; he was a cousin of Pepys and his superior at the Naval Office.
2. **Harrison:** Thomas Harrison (1606–1660), one of the people responsible for the execution of King Charles I in 1649.
3. **coming again:** with Christ, on Christ's return to earth.
4. **Abbey:** Westminster Abbey, the church in London where all monarchs of England are crowned and where many of them are buried.
5. **Prebends** (prē′bəndz): prebendaries; clergy who receive a prebend, or salary paid from the church's revenues.
6. **copes:** ceremonial robes.
7. **Duke:** James II (1633–1701), duke of York and the king's brother.
8. **mond:** golden globe and cross; a symbol of royal power.
9. **Bishop:** bishop of London. (The archbishop of Canterbury, who ordinarily would have officiated, was too ill to do so.)

Reaching All Students

Struggling Readers

Monitoring Your Reading was introduced on p. 543 under Reading Skills and Strategies. One good strategy to use to monitor comprehension is Think Aloud. For information on using this strategy, see p. 135 of the *Reading Strategies Handbook* in the *Reading Skills and Strategies* binder.

English Language Learners

Pair these students with more proficient speakers and have them read aloud to one another and paraphrase selected passages. Encourage English language learners to listen to the recording of the selection in the *Audio CD Library* while following the printed text. For additional strategies, see:

- *Lesson Plans Including Strategies for English-Language Learners.*

Lord Cornwallis—of silver;[10] but I could not come by any.

But so great a noise, that I could make but little of the music; and indeed, it was lost to everybody. But I had so great a list to piss, that I went out a little while before the King had done all his ceremonies and went round the Abbey to Westminster Hall, all the way within rails, and 10,000 people, with the ground covered with blue cloth—and scaffolds all the way. Into the hall I got—where it was very fine with hangings and scaffolds, one upon another, full of brave ladies. And my wife in one little one on the right hand.

Charles II's entry into London at his restoration, 1660. Engraving.

Here I stayed walking up and down; and at last, upon one of the side stalls, I stood and saw the King come in with all the persons (but the soldiers) that were yesterday in the cavalcade; and a most pleasant sight it was to see them in their several robes. And the King came in with his crown on and his scepter in his hand—under a canopy borne up by six silver staves, carried by Barons of the Cinque Ports—and little bells at every end.

And after a long time he got up to the farther end, and all set themselves down at their several tables—and that was also a rare sight. And the King's first course carried up by the Knights of the Bath. And many fine ceremonies there was of the heralds leading up people before him and bowing; and my Lord of Albemarles going to the kitchen and eat a bit of the first dish that was to go to the King's table.

But above all was these three Lords, Northumberland and Suffolk and the Duke of Ormond, coming before the courses on horseback and staying so all dinner-time; and at last, to bring up Dymock, the King's Champion, all in armor on horseback, with his speare and target carried before him. And a herald proclaim that if any dare deny Ch. Steward to be lawful King of England, here was a champion that would fight with him; and with those words the champion flings down his gauntlet;[11] and all this he doth three times in his going up toward the King's table. At last, when he is come, the King drinks to him and then sends him the cup, which is of gold; and he drinks it off and then rides back again with the cup in his hand.

I went from table to table to see the Bishops and all others at their dinner, and was infinite pleased with it. And at the Lords' table I met with Wll. Howe and he spoke to my Lord for me and he did give him four rabbits and a pullet; and so I got it, and Mr. Creed[12] and I got Mr. Michell to give us some bread and so we at a stall eat it, as everybody else did what they could get.

I took a great deal of pleasure to go up and down and look upon the ladies—and to hear the music of all sorts; but above all, the twenty-four violins.

About six at night they had dined; and I went up to my wife and there met with a pretty lady

10. **medals . . . of silver:** coronation badges.

11. **gauntlet:** leather glove covered with metal plates to protect the hand during combat.

12. **Howe . . . Creed:** Pepys's fellow workers in the Navy Office.

WORDS TO OWN

cavalcade (kav′əl·kād′) *n.:* parade of horses and carriages.

E Vocabulary Note

Old and New Meanings

Explain that even though we usually think of a champion as someone who competes for self (or team), in this even older sense of the word, a champion defends another person.

F Appreciating Language

Literal and Figurative Meanings

Have the students look up *gauntlet* in the dictionary. Discuss how the literal medieval meaning of "throwing down (and taking up)" a part of the knight's armor has evolved into the figurative, modern meaning of "giving and accepting a challenge." Stress that the connotative meaning of the modern idiom retains its old combative flavor.

Using Students' Strengths

Mathematical/Logical Learners

One striking characteristic of Samuel Pepys that his *Diary* reveals is his astonishing energy; his days are packed with activity and frequent movement around the city of London. To illustrate this, have students make a time line that shows the hour-by-hour activities of one day in the author's life.

Interpersonal Learners

Have students, working in pairs, assume the roles of Samuel Pepys and an interviewer, such as a newspaper reporter or talk-show host. The subject of the interview should be the important events Pepys has witnessed, and his replies should reflect his character as revealed by his diary.

Auditory/Musical Learners

Pepys mentions several different musical instruments in the diary entries included here (violin, lute, harpsichord). Encourage students to locate recordings that feature these instruments—ideally compositions that Pepys might have heard in his day—and play the recordings for the class.

Ⓐ Reading Skills and Strategies

Making Inferences

? Why does Pepys think it is "foolery, to take too much notice of such things"? [Possible responses: He is more influenced by science than by religion. He is contemptuous of people who attribute natural occurrences to God's will.]

Ⓑ Struggling Readers

Finding Sequence of Events

Point out that the author often begins paragraphs with "And" or "At last." Ask students to skim through all the entries, jotting down the opening words of paragraphs. Emphasize that Pepys frequently signals the passage of time (and sometimes a change of place) with transitional words and phrases like these. Urge students to use these verbal signals to follow the sequence of events as they read.

LITERATURE AND SCIENCE

Mad for Science

Whether in computers, audio equipment, laser surgery, or virtual reality, dizzying scientific change greets us daily. *New!* shifts to *Obsolete!* at warp speed, so our age seems more scientifically turbulent than any before. Yet today's innovations, in many ways, are a small blip on the screen compared to the scientific revolution taking off in the seventeenth and eighteenth centuries.

From alchemy to method. This new science was a defiant break with the past, with "science" that was really metaphysical philosophy or magical alchemy. Instead, the Enlightenment's "natural philosophy" (physical science) insisted on observation, hypothesis, testing, and mathematical analysis—in short, the scientific method you learn in lab class today.

Geniuses, experiments, and arguments. Dominated by the genius of Isaac Newton (1642–1727), seventeenth-century England was truly ablaze with brilliant scientific minds, avid amateur experimenting, and passionate public quarrels (which Newton's nasty temper inflamed). Robert Boyle (1627–1691) founded modern chemistry. Edmond Halley (1656–1742) accurately predicted a comet's appearance centuries in the future. William Harvey (1578–1657) outlined our blood's circulation. Robert Hooke (1635–1703), a typical encyclopedist, coined the word *cell,* invented a watch spring, built a calculator, and first posed Kepler's planetary-motion laws in mechanical terms.

(Mrs. Frankelyn, a doctor's wife, a friend of Mr. Bowyers) and kissed them both—and by and by took them down to Mr. Bowyers's. And strange it is, to think that these two days have held up fair till now that all is done and the King gone out of the hall; and then it fell a-raining and thundering Ⓐ and lightning as I have not seen it do some years—which people did take great notice of God's blessing of the work of these two days—which is a foolery, to take too much notice of such things. . . .

At Mr. Bowyers's, a great deal of company; some I knew, others I did not. Here we stayed upon the leads[13] and below till it was late, expecting to see the fireworks; but they were not performed tonight. Only, the City had a light like a glory round about it, with bonfires.

Ⓑ At last I went to King Street; and there sent Crockford[14] to my father's and my house to tell them I could not come home tonight, because of the dirt and a coach could not be had.

And so after drinking a pot of ale alone at Mrs. Harper's, I returned to Mr. Bowyers's; and after a little stay more, I took my wife and Mrs. Frankelyn (who I proffered the civility of lying with my wife at Mrs. Hunt's tonight) to Axe Yard. In which, at

13. **leads:** rooftop; from the sheets of lead used to cover a roof.

14. **Crockford:** apparently a servant.

WORDS TO OWN

proffered (präf′ərd) *v.:* offered; proposed.
civility (sə·vil′ə·tē) *n.:* courtesy.

Taking a Second Look

Review: Using Context Clues

Several words appear in the passage on p. 547 that may be unfamiliar to students or are used in an unfamiliar, archaic sense. These include the following: *dirt, pot (of ale,) tipple, yeoman, sparks, foxed.* The Literature and Science feature also uses vocabulary that may be unfamiliar, such as *obsolete, turbulent, metaphysical, alchemy,* and *prototype.* Have students identify synonyms and antonyms within the text that will help them discover the meanings of the words as well as infer the definitions from the overall meaning of the sentences or paragraphs. They should write the words and their contextual definitions in their reading notes.

Newton (awing even Queen Anne, who knighted him) explained the world's mysteries as never before—partly because he invented a tool to do it: calculus. Among Newton's other stunning achievements were discovering that white light contains all colors, formulating the three laws of motion (every physicist's bedrock), and defining universal gravitation. Newton realized, as no one else had, that gravitational pull accounts both for orbiting planets and for falling apples.

Promoting natural knowledge. But even without Newton's genius, there were so many new ideas and inventions—the vacuum pump, barometer, compound microscope—that a group of Londoners created the "Invisible College," essentially a science club that evolved into the Royal Society of London for the Promotion of Natural Knowledge. While never a government body (its brash motto was *Nullius verba,* "at the dictation of no one"), the Royal Society was chartered by Charles II in 1662. Dedicated both to hands-on experimenting and to publishing journal articles, it was a prototype information highway, giving scientists across Europe new knowledge—faster than ever before.

Newton served as Royal Society president, but so did the nonscientist Samuel Pepys, showing the age's fascination with natural curiosities and cutting-edge thought. While some of the Society's experiments were crackpot and cruel to animals—as satirized by both Joseph Addison and Jonathan Swift—the Society was, and still is centuries later, one of the world's most prestigious and influential scientific groups.

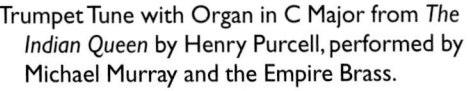

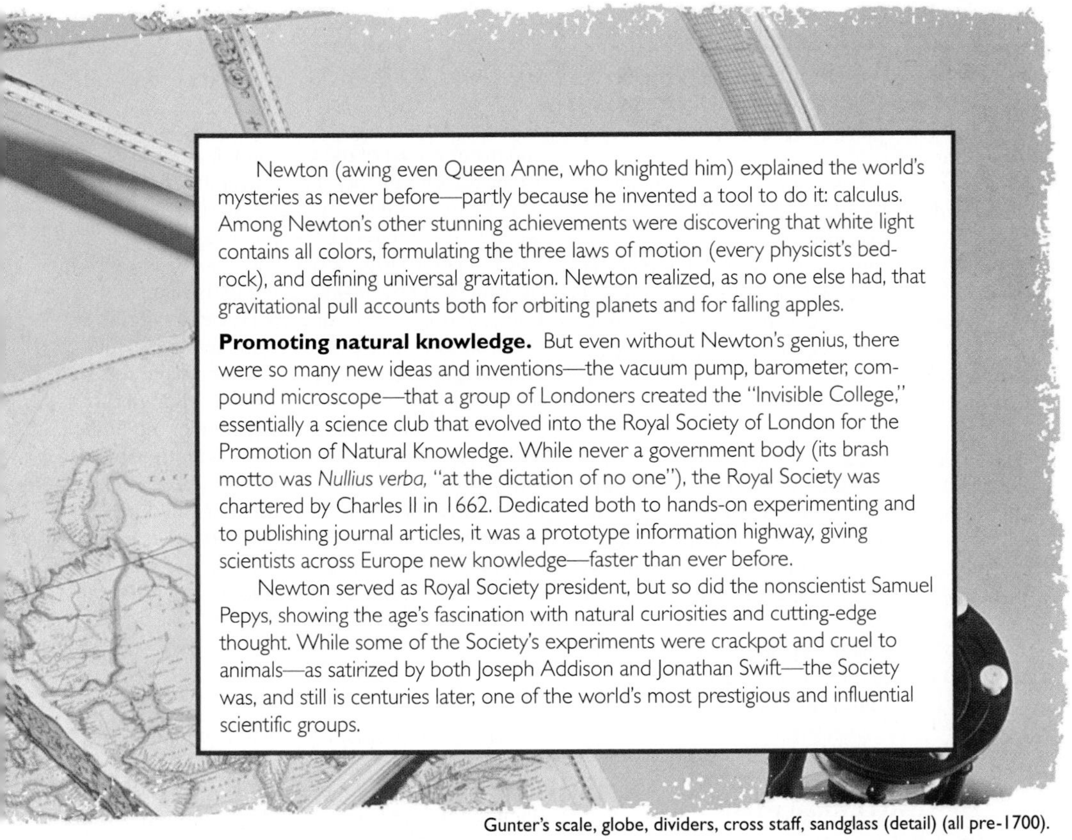

Gunter's scale, globe, dividers, cross staff, sandglass (detail) (all pre-1700).
National Maritime Museum, London.

the further end, there was three great bonfires and a great many great gallants,[15] men and women; and they laid hold of us and would have us drink the King's health upon our knee, kneeling upon a fagot;[16] which we all did, they drinking to us one after another—which we thought a strange frolic. But these gallants continued thus a great while, and I wondered to see how the ladies did tipple.

At last I sent my wife and her bedfellow to bed, and Mr. Hunt and I went in with Mr. Thornbury (who did give the company all their wines, he being yeoman of the wine cellar to the King) to his house; and there, with his wife and two of his sisters and some gallant sparks that were there, we drank the King's health and nothing else, till one of the gentlemen fell down stark drunk and there lay spewing. And I went to my Lord's pretty well. But no sooner a-bed with Mr. Sheply but my head begun to turn and I to vomit, and if ever I was foxed it was now—which I cannot say yet, because I fell asleep and sleep till morning—only, when I waked I found myself wet with my spewing. Thus did the day end, with joy everywhere; and blessed be God, I have not heard of any mischance to anybody through it all, but only to Serjeant Glynne,[17] whose horse fell upon him

15. **gallants:** merrymakers.
16. **fagot:** bundle of twigs or sticks used to make a bonfire. The toast of loyalty was often drunk while kneeling.

17. **Serjeant Glynne:** The title is legal rather than military. Sir John Glynne and Sir John Maynard were unpopular because they had been prominent judges during the Commonwealth period.

LITERATURE AND SCIENCE

To help students appreciate the historic development of science and technology, ask them to imagine that they live in an earlier time, before the discovery of some piece of scientific knowledge that we now take for granted—that the sun rises and sets because the earth is revolving or that infections are caused by microorganisms. How would they explain the sun's apparent motion or the occurrence of disease? How would they go about attempting to test or verify their explanations? Discuss the long-term significance of the scientific method that emerged during the seventeenth century. Encourage students also to discuss current directions in the development of technology and examples of technological changes they have witnessed in their own lifetimes. What sorts of scientific laws and technological inventions do they think future generations will take for granted? [Possible responses: laws of quantum theory; inventions such as microchips; the interface of television and telephone.]

Listening to Music

Trumpet Tune with Organ in C Major from *The Indian Queen* by Henry Purcell, performed by Michael Murray and the Empire Brass.

Often named as England's first great composer, Henry Purcell (1659–1695) was a brilliant musician who before the age of twenty-one was already playing the organ at London's Westminster Abbey. A versatile composer, he produced church music, theater music, and all manner of ceremonial music for Charles II, James II, and William and Mary. Today, Purcell is probably most famous for his stirring trumpet voluntaries (introductions), fanfares (loud flourishing of trumpets), and other trumpet tunes, often accompanied by organ, like the Trumpet Tune in C Major that originally appeared in his 1695 theater production *The Indian Queen.*

Activity

Before students read the section of Pepys's diary that chronicles the coronation of Charles II (pp. 544–545), have them listen to Purcell's trumpet tune from *The Indian Queen.* Ask them to jot down adjectives predicting the kind of society likely to produce such music. Then tell students to read Pepys's description of the coronation to see if their predictions are correct.

A Reading Skills and Strategies

Monitoring Your Reading

Since the Coronation Day entry is a long and detailed one, students should pause at this point to review their notes and check their comprehension. Making an hour-by-hour time line of the events of the day would be a good way to summarize what they have read. Another strategy would be to create an outline of the day's events, distinguishing the major and minor details.

B Elements of Literature

Character

? What do these matter-of-fact details show about Pepys's character? [Possible responses: He acknowledges his mistakes; he is physically vigorous and resilient; he keeps his obligations faithfully, even when he feels ill.]

C Vocabulary Note

Archaic Words

Hither and *thither* are adverbs synonymous with "here" and "there." They are usually used with verbs of motion, as Pepys uses them here.

D Reading Skills and Strategies

Monitoring Your Reading

Students should notice a change in level of difficulty and modify their reading rate to increase comprehension. "Two Ordinary Days" are indeed ordinary and easy to understand. "A Bad Night," on the other hand, includes more archaic vocabulary and syntax (*wenches, lest, gagged, design, by which the thieves meant to try what looking there would [be] after them and know our company*). Context clues and questioning techniques will help students understand this colorful description of the author's exaggerated fears.

yesterday and is like to kill him; which people do please themselves with, to see how just God is to punish that rogue at such a time as this—he being now one of the King's Serjeants and rode in the cavalcade with Maynard, to whom people wished the same fortune.

There was also this night, in King Street, [a woman] had her eye put out by a boy's flinging of a firebrand into the coach.

Now after all this, I can say that besides the pleasure of the sight of these glorious things, I may now shut my eyes against any other objects, or for the future [not] trouble myself to see things of state and show, as being sure never to see the like again in this world.

Waked in the morning with my head in a sad taking through the last night's drink, which I am very sorry for. So rise and went out with Mr. Creed to drink our morning draft, which he did give me in chocolate to settle my stomach. And after that to my wife, who lay with Mrs. Frankelyn at the next door to Mrs. Hunt's.

And they were ready, and so I took them up in a coach and carried the lady to Paul's and there set her down; and so my wife and I home—and I to the office.

October 28–29, 1661
Two Ordinary Days

At the office all the morning, and dined[18] at home; and so to Paul's churchyard to Hunt's,[19] and there find my theorbo done. Which pleases me very well, and costs me 26*s* to the altering—but now he tells me it is as good a lute as any is in England, and is worth well 10£. Hither I sent for Captain Ferrers to me, who comes with a friend of his and they and I to the theater and there saw *Argalus and Parthenia;*[20] where a woman acted Parthenia and came afterward on the stage in man's clothes, and had the best legs that I ever saw; and I was very well pleased with it. Thence to the Ringo alehouse, and thither sent for a belt maker and bought of him a handsome belt for second mourning,[21] which cost me 24*s* and is very neat. So home and to bed.

This day I put on my half-cloth black stockings and my new coat of the fashion, which pleases me well; and with my beaver[22] I was (after office was done) ready to go to my Lord Mayor's feast,[23] as we are all invited; but the Sir Wms.[24] were both loath to go because of the crowd, and so none of us went; and I stayed and dined with them, and so home; and in the evening, by consent, we met at the Dolphin, where other company came to us and would have been merry; but their wine was so naught[25] and all other things out of order, that we were not so; but stayed long at night and so home and to bed. My mind not pleased with the spending of this day, because I had proposed a great deal of pleasure to myself this day at Guildhall.

This Lord Mayor, it seems, brings up again the custom[26] of Lord Mayors going the day of their installment to Paul's,[27] and walking round about the cross and offering something at the altar.

July 11, 1664
A Bad Night

. . . Home, weary; and not being very well, I betimes[28] to bed.

And there fell into a most mighty sweat in the night, about eleven o'clock; and there, knowing what money[29] I have in the house and hearing a noise, I begin to sweat worse and worse, till I melted almost to water. I rung, and could not in half an hour make either of the wenches hear me; and this made me fear the more, lest they might be gagged; and then I begin to think that there

18. **dined:** Dinner was eaten at midday.
19. **Hunt's:** Hunt, a musical instrument maker, repaired and altered Pepys's theorbo, or lute.
20. ***Argalus and Parthenia:*** an old play by Henry Glapthorne (c. 1610–c. 1643). In the revival Pepys saw, female actors played the women's roles rather than boy actors, as had been customary.
21. **second mourning:** period of less solemn mourning following the deep mourning Pepys had been observing for his uncle Robert, who had died three months earlier.
22. **beaver:** hat made of beaver fur.
23. **Lord Mayor's feast:** an annual event held at the Guildhall.
24. **Sir Wms.:** Sir William Penn (1621–1670) and Sir William Batten (?–1667), both officials in the Navy Office.
25. **naught:** worthless.
26. **custom:** These ceremonies had not been observed during the Commonwealth period.
27. **Paul's:** St. Paul's Cathedral. A huge cross stood in the square before the cathedral.
28. **betimes:** archaic for "early."
29. **money:** about £1,000—a very large sum.

Getting Students Involved

Cooperative Learning

Creating a 1660s London Newspaper. Assign students to groups of four or five, aiming for a mix of abilities and motivation levels in each group. Provide a list of newspaper features to be included in the 1660s newspaper they will work together to create:

- news story (or stories) with headline(s)
- editorial with headline
- advice column featuring a letter from Samuel Pepys or his wife and a response to it
- advertisement(s) featuring products of the day and places to buy them

Have each group choose one of the *Diary* dates included in the text and write articles for one issue of a daily newspaper based on the information Pepys provides, as well as the students' inferences and background knowledge about London in the 1660s. Each group needs to decide who will write each article. Then, they can brainstorm to provide each writer with ideas for the assigned article. When the articles are completed, display each group's efforts on the bulletin board. Embellishments might include artwork and a name and logo for the newspaper. (An alternate approach to this activity is to have the entire class create one newspaper. In this approach, each group collaborates to write one of the articles for the class newspaper.)

was some design in a stone being flung at the window over our stairs this evening, by which the thieves meant to try what looking there would [be] after them and know our company. These thoughts and fears I had, and do hence apprehend the fears of all rich men that are covetous and have much money by them. At last Jane[30] rose and then I understand it was only the dog wants a lodging and so made a noise. So to bed, but hardly slept; at last did, and so till morning.

September 2, 1666
The First Day of the Great Fire of London

Lord's Day. Some of our maids sitting up late last night to get things ready against our feast today, Jane called us up, about three in the morning, to tell us of a great fire they saw in the City.[31] So I rose, and slipped on my nightgown and went to her window, and thought it to be on the backside of Mark Lane at the furthest; but being unused to such fires as followed, I thought it far enough off, and so went to bed again and to sleep. About seven rose again to dress myself, and there looked out at the window and saw the fire not so much as it was, and further off. So to my closet[32] to set things to rights after yesterday's cleaning. By and by Jane comes and tells me that she hears that above three hundred houses have been burned down tonight by the fire we saw, and that it was

30. Jane: Jane Birch, the Pepyses' servant.

31. City: London. The Great Fire started in a bakery, raged for four days and four nights, and destroyed some 13,000 residences. It leveled four fifths of the City and left about 100,000 people homeless.

32. closet: private room.

The Great Fire of London (17th century).

E Elements of Literature

Diary

? **Bringing together all the clues the diary has provided so far about the character of Samuel Pepys, do you think that he is glad or sorry to be able to compare his own fears with those of "all rich men"?** [Possible responses: He is glad because he enjoys material possessions. Or, he is sorry and having second thoughts about his own covetousness.]

Reaching All Students

English Language Learners

Pepys frequently omits the subject, predicate, or both from his sentences. This could be confusing for English language learners, who rely on predictable sentence structures. Help them fill in the missing elements in these sentences to aid their comprehension and to give them needed practice in choosing tense forms and maintaining subject-verb agreement. Possible answers are indicated.

1. [I stayed] [w]ithin all the afternoon, setting up shelves in my study (p. 544).
2. The King [appeared] in his robes, bare headed, which was very fine (p. 544).
3. But [there was] so great a noise, that I could make but little of the music (p. 545).
4. At Mr. Bowyers's, [I found] a great deal of company; some I knew, others I did not (p. 546).
5. . . . and so my wife and I [went] home—and I [went] to the office (p. 548).
6. So [I hurried] home and [went] to bed (p. 548).
7. My mind [was] not pleased with the spending of this day, because I had proposed a great deal of pleasure to myself this day at Guildhall (p. 548).
8. So [I ran] down, with my heart full of trouble . . . (p. 550).

Responding to the Art

The pages of Pepys's *Diary* reproduced here are a reminder of how basic his writing tools were: paper, a pen, a container of ink.

Activity. Ask students to compare their own writing tools and processes. Does the medium affect the length, style, or other features of the finished product? Do they prefer one method over the other? If Samuel Pepys had possessed a computer, how might it have affected his writing and revising?

A Elements of Literature

Character

? What aspect of Pepys's nature does this statement reveal? [Possible response: He has concern for others, even his social inferiors.]

B Reading Skills and Strategies

Drawing Conclusions

The term "lamentable fire" and the description of the "poor pigeons" typify the author's language throughout this entry. Encourage students to note Pepys's use of descriptive language and small details to depict the scene and convey his horror.

C Critical Thinking

Interpreting

? At this point, Samuel Pepys goes to the King's quarters, where he is welcomed and given a command to carry out. What does this indicate about the change in his status since the coronation? [Possible responses: Pepys has gained political power. He has joined the royal inner circle and serves as an advisor to the King and Lord Mayor. He is using the fire as an opportunity to gain the King's favor.]

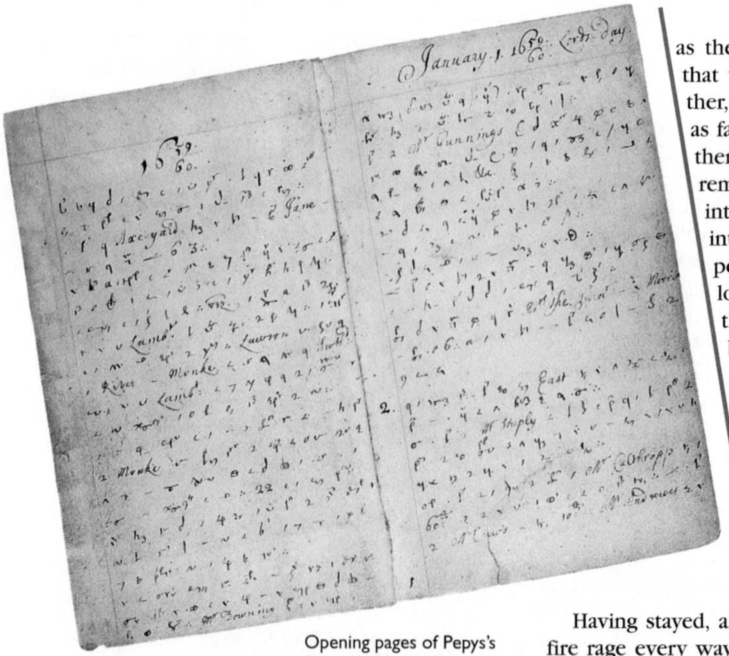

Opening pages of Pepys's *Diary* (1659–1660).
The Pepys Library, Magdalene College, Cambridge.

now burning down all Fish Street by London Bridge. So I made myself ready presently, and walked to the Tower[33] and there got up upon one of the high places, Sir J. Robinson's little son going up with me; and there I did see the houses[34] at that end of the bridge all on fire, and an infinite great fire on this and the other side the end of the bridge—which, among other people, did trouble me for poor little Michell and our Sarah[35] on the bridge. So down, with my heart full of trouble, to the Lieutenant of the Tower, who tells me that it begun this morning in the King's baker's house in Pudding Lane, and that it hath burned down St. Magnes Church and most part of Fish Street already. So I down to the waterside and there got a boat and through bridge, and there saw a lamentable fire. Poor Michell's house, as far as the Old Swan,[36] already burned that way and the fire running further, that in a very little time it got as far as the Steelyard while I was there. Everybody endeavoring to remove their goods, and flinging into the river or bringing them into lighters[37] that lay off. Poor people staying in their houses as long as till the very fire touched them, and then running into boats or clambering from one pair of stair by the waterside to another. And among other things, the poor pigeons I perceive were loath to leave their houses, but hovered about the windows and balconies till they were some of them burned, their wings, and fell down.

Having stayed, and in an hour's time seen the fire rage every way, and nobody to my sight endeavoring to quench it, but to remove their goods and leave all to the fire; and having seen it get as far as the Steelyard, and the wind mighty high and driving it into the City, and everything, after so long a drought, proving combustible, even the very stones of churches, and among other things, the poor steeple by which pretty Mrs. —— lives, and whereof my old schoolfellow Elborough is parson, taken fire in the very top and there burned till it fall down—I to Whitehall with a gentleman with me who desired to go off from the Tower to see the fire in my boat—to Whitehall, and there up to the King's closet in the chapel, where people came about me and I did give them an account dismayed them all; and word was carried in to the King, so I was called for and did tell the King and Duke of York what I saw, and that unless his Majesty did command houses to be pulled down, nothing could stop the fire. They seemed much troubled, and the King commanded me to go to my Lord Mayor from him and

33. **Tower:** Tower of London, a short walk from Pepys's house.
34. **houses:** Shops and dwellings were built on London Bridge.
35. **Sarah:** maid whom Mrs. Pepys discharged on December 5, 1662. Pepys wrote: "The wench cried, and I was ready to cry too."
36. **Michell's house . . . Old Swan:** Betty Michell, a former sweetheart of Pepys, lost her house in the fire. The Old Swan was a tavern on Thames Street, near London Bridge.
37. **lighters:** large, open barges.

Crossing the Curriculum

Geography

An understanding of the location of various places mentioned in the diary will help students visualize the progress of the fire. Have volunteers find a map of London from Pepys's time and use it as a model to sketch one of their own. (The map on p. 271 may be helpful.) Then, have students see how much of the path of the Great Fire they can trace. Be sure they identify as many of the landmarks Pepys mentions as possible.

Social Studies

Have students work in groups to study the history and culture of Pepys's time. After they have completed their research, have them set up panels to present their findings. Sample topics include the following:

- food and drink of the seventeenth century
- the Barons of the Cinque Ports, the Knights of the Bath, and other orders of nobility
- Whitehall
- the English monarch's royal treasures
- the social practice of drinking chocolate
- coinage and money of the time
- London Bridge
- how the Great Fire spurred the architectural career of Christopher Wren

command him to spare no houses but to pull down before the fire every way. The Duke of York bid me tell him that if he would have any more soldiers, he shall; and so did my Lord Arlington afterward, as a great secret. Here meeting with Captain Cocke, I in his coach, which he lent me, and Creed with me, to Paul's; and there walked along Watling Street as well as I could, every creature coming away loaden with goods to save—and here and there sick people carried away in beds. Extraordinary good goods carried in carts and on backs. At last met my Lord Mayor in Canning Street, like a man spent, with a hankercher about his neck. To the King's message, he cried like a fainting woman, "Lord, what can I do? I am spent. People will not obey me. I have been pull[ing] down houses. But the fire overtakes us faster than we can do it." That he needed no more soldiers; and that for himself, he must go and refresh himself, having been up all night. So he left me, and I him, and walked home—seeing people all almost distracted and no manner of means used to quench the fire. The houses too, so very thick thereabouts, and full of matter for burning, as pitch and tar, in Thames Street—and warehouses of oil and wines and brandy and other things. Here I saw Mr. Isaccke Houblon,[38] that handsome man—prettily dressed and dirty at his door at Dowgate, receiving some of his brothers' things whose houses were on fire; and as he says, have been removed twice already, and he doubts (as it soon proved) that they must be in a little time removed from his house also—which was a sad consideration. And to see the churches all filling with goods, by people who themselves should have been quietly there at this time.

By this time it was about twelve o'clock, and so home and there find my guests, which was Mr. Wood and his wife, Barbary Shelden, and also Mr. Moone—she mighty fine, and her husband, for aught I see, a likely man. But Mr. Moone's design and mine, which was to look over my closet and please him with the sight thereof, which he hath long desired, was wholly disappointed, for we were in great trouble and disturbance at this fire, not knowing what to think of it. However, we had an extraordinary good dinner, and as merry as at this time we could be.

While at dinner, Mrs. Batelier came to inquire after Mr. Woolfe and Stanes (who it seems are related to them), whose houses in Fish Street are all burned, and they in a sad condition. She would not stay in the fright.

As soon as dined, I and Moone away and walked through the City, the streets full of nothing but people and horses and carts loaden with goods, ready to run over one another, and removing goods from one burned house to another—they now removing out of Canning Street (which received goods in the morning) into Lumbard Street and further; and among others, I now saw my little goldsmith Stokes receiving some friend's goods, whose house itself was burned the day after. We parted at Paul's, he home and I to Paul's Wharf, where I had appointed a boat to attend me; and took in Mr. Carcasse and his brother, whom I met in the street, and carried them below and above bridge, to and again, to see the fire, which was now got further, both below and above, and no likelihood of stopping it. Met with the King and Duke of York in their barge, and with them to Queenhithe[39] and there called Sir Rd. Browne to them. Their order was only to pull down houses apace, and so below bridge at the waterside; but little was or could be done, the fire coming upon them so fast. Good hopes there was of stopping it at the Three Cranes[40] above, and at Buttolph's Wharf below bridge, if care be used; but the wind carries it into the City, so as we know not by the waterside what it doth there. River full of lighter[s] and boats taking in goods, and good goods swimming in the water; and only, I observed that hardly one lighter or boat in three that had the goods of a house in, but there was a pair of virginals[41] in it. Having seen as much as I could now, I away to Whitehall by appointment, and there walked to St. James's Park, and there met my wife and Creed and Wood and his wife and walked to my boat, and there upon the water again, and to the fire up and down, it still

38. Houblon: Houblon and others mentioned in the following paragraphs were prominent Londoners, all friends or acquaintances of Pepys.

39. Queenhithe (kwēn · hīth′): harbor off Thames Street. *Hithe* is archaic for "port" or "haven."

40. Three Cranes: name for a set of stairs that led down to the river.

41. virginals: small, sixteenth-century stringed instruments; harpsichords.

D Reading Skills and Strategies

Making Inferences

Point out to students that the rare inclusion of a direct quotation makes this entry more like a report intended for a reading audience. Ask students to look for other features that distinguish this entry from earlier ones and which may suggest that Pepys consciously viewed this particular account as a potential historical document. [Possible responses: Richness of detail; colorful, descriptive language; frequent mention by name of people he met and spoke to during the crisis.]

E Elements of Literature

Character

? What do you infer about Pepys's character from the fact that he hosts a dinner party and remarks on the quality of the meal while the fire rages nearby? [Possible responses: He is insensitive to the suffering of others. He believes in carrying on bravely during a crisis.]

Getting Students Involved

Cooperative Learning

Setting Priorities During the Great Fire. Pepys saw goods floating in the river and open barges (lighters) packed with belongings. Ask students to imagine that they are fleeing the fire and to set their own priorities for loading their barges. Small groups should discuss and rank the items from the list that follows, deciding which items they would load and which they would leave behind, and for what reasons.

List of Goods

__ book collection	__ crate of food
__ family mementos	__ clothes trunk
__ harpsichord	__ riding horse
__ silverware	__ important papers
__ oil paintings	__ pets

Suggest that students use the following process of elimination: (1) Select the two or three most important items; (2) select the two or three least important items; (3) rank the top two or three in order of significance; (4) rank the bottom two or three in order of insignificance. This process will lead students to determine the most and least important items (and the values they represent) and to reach a consensus on how to make decisions about the items that fall in between. Have students display their charts, compare their rankings, and explain their rationales.

Connections

In this excerpt, Joan Didion explains how little she is concerned about the accuracy of the facts she records in her notebooks. She is aiming for a different kind of truth, a fidelity to her emotional experience.

BROWSING IN THE FILES

About the Author. Joan Didion is highly regarded as a writer of fiction, nonfiction, and screenplays. In addition to *Slouching Toward Bethlehem*, her books include the nonfiction work *After Henry* (1993) and the novel *The Last Thing He Wanted* (1997).

Ⓐ Cultural Connections

As students prepare to compare Samuel Pepys's approach to diary writing with Joan Didion's it will help them to appreciate an important difference between the world views of people in the twentieth century and people in the seventeenth century. In the seventeenth century, for one belief to be "right," conflicting beliefs were necessarily "wrong." Ask students to contrast this mentality to present-day American pluralism—a climate in which people are more accustomed to tolerate the existence of a wide variety of beliefs and ideas. These culturally conditioned views of the world certainly helped shape Pepys's emphasis on facts and Didion's emphasis on personal perception.

Connections — An Essay

Ⓐ The American writer Joan Didion (1934–) explains her reasons for keeping a notebook in this excerpt from her collection of essays *Slouching Towards Bethlehem* (1968). While not secret like Pepys's diaries, Didion's notebooks nonetheless serve as a storehouse of her experiences.

On Keeping a Notebook

Joan Didion

. . . So the point of my keeping a notebook has never been, nor is it now, to have an accurate factual record of what I have been doing or thinking. That would be a different impulse entirely, an instinct for reality which I sometimes envy but do not possess. At no point have I ever been able successfully to keep a diary; my approach to daily life ranges from the grossly negligent to the merely absent, and on those few occasions when I have tried dutifully to record a day's events, boredom has so overcome me that the results are mysterious at best. What is this business about "shopping, typing piece, dinner with E, depressed"? Shopping for what? Typing what piece? Who is E? Was this "E" depressed, or was I depressed? Who cares?

In fact I have abandoned altogether that kind of pointless entry; instead I tell what some would call lies. "That's simply not true," the members of my family frequently tell me when they come up against my memory of a shared event. "The party was *not* for you, the spider was *not* a black widow, *it wasn't that way at all.*" Very likely they are right, for not only have I always had trouble distinguishing between what happened and what merely might have happened, but I remain unconvinced that the distinction, for my purposes, matters. The cracked crab that I recall having for lunch the day my father came home from Detroit in 1945 must certainly be embroidery, worked into the day's pattern to lend verisimilitude; I was ten years old and would not now remember the cracked crab. The day's events did not turn on cracked crab. And yet it is precisely that fictitious crab that makes me see the afternoon all over again, a home movie run all too often, the father bearing gifts, the child weeping, an exercise in family love and guilt. Or that is what it was to me. Similarly, perhaps it never did snow that August in Vermont; perhaps there never were flurries in the night wind, and maybe no one else felt the ground hardening and summer already dead even as we pretended to bask in it, but that was how it

increasing and the wind great. So near the fire as we could for smoke; and all over the Thames, with one's face in the wind you were almost burned with a shower of firedrops—this is very true—so as houses were burned by these drops and flakes of fire, three or four, nay five or six houses, one from another. When we could endure no more upon the water, we to a little alehouse on the bankside over against the Three Cranes, and there stayed till it was dark almost and saw the fire grow; and as it grew darker, appeared more and more, and in corners and upon steeples and between churches and houses, as far as we could see up the hill of the City, in a most horrid malicious bloody flame, not like the fine flame of an ordinary fire. Barbary and her husband away before us. We stayed till, it being darkish, we saw the fire as only one entire arch of fire from this to the other side the bridge, and in a bow up the hill, for an arch of above a mile long. It made me weep to see it. The churches, houses, and all on fire and

WORDS TO OWN

malicious (mə·lish′əs) *adj.:* intentionally mischievous or harmful; spiteful.

Connecting Across Texts

Connecting with *The Diary of Samuel Pepys*

Pair students and have them create an imaginary dialogue between Samuel Pepys and Joan Didion on the subject of keeping a diary. Students may find it useful to take up the roles in oral dialogue. They should address the following questions:

- Do you keep a diary for yourself or for others to read?
- Are the routine events of daily life interesting? Why, or why not?
- How important is it to report events accurately in your diary?
- Is your diary about you, about the people you meet, or a mix of the two?

[Possible responses: Both Pepys and Didion keep a diary as a private chronicle, one not intended for others to read. Pepys uses a secret code to insure the privacy of his diary. The two writers disagree on the importance of routine events. Pepys likes to record them faithfully while Didion finds them boring. Pepys prefers to record facts as exactly as possible; Didion, on the other hand, is deliberately impressionistic. She says explicitly that her diary is about herself. Pepys would probably say that his diary is about other people. Careful readers will have noticed, however, that Pepys reveals much about himself and his feelings.]

felt to me, and it might as well have snowed, could have snowed, did snow.

How it felt to me: that is getting closer to the truth about a notebook. I sometimes delude myself about why I keep a notebook, imagine that some thrifty virtue derives from preserving everything observed. See enough and write it down, I tell myself, and then some morning when the world seems drained of wonder, some day when I am only going through the motions of doing what I am supposed to do, which is write—on that bankrupt morning I will simply open my notebook and there it will all be, a forgotten account with accumulated interest, paid passage back to the world out there: dialogue overheard in hotels and elevators and at the hatcheck counter in Pavillon (one middle-aged man shows his hat check to another and says, "That's my old football number"); impressions of Bettina Aptheker and Benjamin Sonnenberg and Teddy ("Mr. Acapulco") Stauffer; careful *aperçus* about tennis bums and failed fashion models and Greek shipping heiresses, one of whom taught me a significant lesson (a lesson I could have learned from F. Scott Fitzgerald, but perhaps we all must meet the very rich for ourselves) by asking, when I arrived to interview her in her orchid-filled sitting room on the second day of a paralyzing New York blizzard, whether it was snowing outside.

I imagine, in other words, that the notebook is about other people. But of course it is not. I have no real business with what one stranger said to another at the hatcheck counter in Pavillon; in fact I suspect that the line "That's my old football number" touched not my own imagination at all, but merely some memory of something once read, probably "The Eighty-Yard Run." Nor is my concern with a woman in a dirty crepe de Chine wrapper in a Wilmington bar. My stake is always, of course, in the unmentioned girl in the plaid silk dress. *Remember what it was to be me:* That is always the point. . . .

Joan Didion.

flaming at once, and a horrid noise the flames made, and the cracking of houses at their ruin. So home with a sad heart, and there find everybody (B) discoursing and lamenting the fire; and poor Tom Hater came with some few of his goods saved out of his house, which is burned upon Fish Street Hill. I invited him to lie at my house, and did receive his goods: but was deceived in his lying there, the noise coming every moment of the growth of the fire, so as we were forced to begin to pack up our own goods and prepare for their removal. And did by moonshine (it being brave, dry, and moonshine and warm weather) carry much of my goods into the garden, and Mr. Hater and I did remove my money and iron chests into my cellar—as thinking that the safest place. And got my bags of gold into my office ready to carry (C) away, and my chief papers of accounts also there, and my tallies into a box by themselves. So great was our fear, as Sir W. Batten had carts come out of the country to fetch away his goods this night. We did put Mr. Hater, poor man, to bed a little; but

WORDS TO OWN
discourcing (dis·kôrs′iŋ) *v.* used as *adj.:* talking.

(B) Reading Skills and Strategies

Connecting with the Text

? Have you ever experienced a destructive disaster such as a fire, earthquake, or devastating storm? If not, have you ever imagined the experience as you watched a news report of such a disaster on TV? Were your feelings like the ones Samuel Pepys expresses? [Responses will vary.]

(C) Elements of Literature

Diary

? How does the author's choice of details here fit with your perception of him so far? [Possible responses: He has often shown his interest in money. There are other places in the diary where his mood changes within one paragraph, as it does here.]

Making the Connections

Connecting to the Subject: "An Appetite for Experience"

Point out to students that the selection ends with Pepys missing a night of sleep. In this case, the crisis of the fire keeps him awake. Ask them to review the entries and note how frequently the author stays up very late, rises early, or remains awake all night. Discuss what this indicates about his "appetite for experience" and what other indicators of that appetite the *Diary* entries provide.

Assessing Learning

Check Test: True-False

1. Pepys witnesses the hanging of a man involved in the execution of King Charles. [True]
2. According to Pepys, women were not allowed to attend the coronation. [False]
3. Pepys advises the King to stop the fire in London by pulling down houses. [True]
4. Pepys, distressed by the destruction he has seen during the Great Fire, cannot eat. [False]
5. Pepys states he is lucky he does not have to move his goods out of his house. [False]

Standardized Test Preparation

For practice with ACT and SAT formats, see
- *Preparation for College Admission Exams,* p. 25

For practice in proofreading and editing, see
- *Daily Oral Grammar,* Transparency 17

Making Meanings

First Thoughts [Evaluate]

1. Pepys is brutally honest when he records his outburst of temper (Oct. 13, 1660), describes his drunkenness (Apr. 23, 1661), records his own irrational fears (Jul. 11, 1664). Pepys states openly what he thinks of people and situations. He likes the ladies but is disappointed with his seat. He seems pleased that Serjeant Glynne is seriously injured (Apr. 23, 1661).

Shaping Interpretations [Interpret]

2. Possible responses: Pepys probably does not want to dwell morbidly on the execution; at the time, much must have been written and said about it, so perhaps he did not feel the need to record it in his diary.

3. Similarities: Both include formality, ceremony, tradition; both install a new head of state; both figures recite an oath; both are witnessed by large crowds and are followed by all-night celebrations.
Differences: coronation includes much religious ritual, while inauguration includes little; king serves by divine right, while president has been elected.

4. Pepys's *Diary* would be of great use to historians because Pepys was an eyewitness who included useful details, such as the fire's source, its extent, and its effect on the inhabitants of London. These details could be compared with other eyewitness reports to piece together an accurate account of the fire.

5. Pepys does not seem to take any more interest in his wife than he does in other people he knows. In fact, his passing remarks seem to indicate that their relationship is not a particularly close or devoted one.

Extending the Text [Apply]

6. Possible responses: Similarities: We are fond of money and possessions; we get excited about public spectacles, such as the Olympics; we are vulnerable to natural disasters. Differences: We live in a democracy, Pepys in a monarchy; our daily routines are not very flexible, while Pepys seems to come and go at will; our social conventions dictate that we downplay our physical appetites, whereas Pepys seems unrestrained in that respect.

7. Pepys's account is like present-day reporting because, as an eyewitness, he provides extensive details of the event. His account differs because he did not write it with an audience in mind, he concentrated on his own experience, and he did not write as succinctly as modern journalists.

8. Some students may prefer Pepys's direct and simple accounts, while others may like Didion's more expressive and personal style.

Reading Check
Major Events
1. Execution of Major General Harrison, October 13, 1660
2. Coronation of Charles Stuart, April 23, 1661
3. The Great Fire of London, September 2, 1666

---

he got but very little rest, so much noise being in my house, taking down of goods.

About four o'clock in the morning, my Lady Batten sent me a cart to carry away all my money and plate[42] and best things to Sir W. Rider's at Bednall Green; which I did, riding myself in my nightgown in the cart; and Lord, to see how the streets and the highways are crowded with people, running and riding and getting of carts at any rate to fetch away thing[s]. I find Sir W. Rider tired with being called up all night and receiving things from several friends. His house full of goods—and much of Sir W. Batten and Sir W. Penn's. I am eased at my heart to have my treasure so well secured. Then home with much ado to find a way. Nor any sleep all this night to me nor my poor wife.

42. **plate:** gold- or silver-plated dishes, eating utensils, and the like.

Making Meanings

First Thoughts

1. Do you think Pepys is totally honest when recording details of his life? Cite entries to support your evaluation.

Reading Check
Trace, day by day, the **major events** covered in these diary entries. You might record the events in the form of a **time line.**

Shaping Interpretations

2. Pepys gives very few details in the *Diary* about the execution that he witnessed. Why do you suppose he doesn't devote much space to it?
3. How is the inauguration of a U.S. president both like and unlike the king's coronation?
4. Of what use would Pepys's account of the Great Fire be as a **primary source** for a later historian?
5. From Pepys's references to his wife, Elizabeth, what can you conclude about their relationship?

Extending the Text

6. How is Pepys's life like or unlike your own? Do you think the values of seventeenth-century life, as Pepys describes them, are similar to or different from those of your own time? Explain.
7. Today, reporting like Pepys's description of the fire would be done by the media. How does Pepys's account compare with reporting today?
8. Which style of keeping a **diary** appeals to you: Pepys's detailed method or Joan Didion's impressionistic approach (described in the ***Connections*** on page 552)? Why?

Reading Skills and Strategies

Reading Seventeenth-Century Language

These extracts from Pepys's *Diary* have been modernized for ease of reading. That is, the **archaic spellings** have been brought up to date. For example, in the first entry, the words *abbey, followed, surveyor, chair, footstool,* and *fiddlers* are spelled *abby, fallowed, surveyour, chaire, footstoole,* and *fidlers* by Pepys. **Capitalization** has also been modernized; Pepys tended to capitalize indiscriminately, especially nouns.

1. Here are some other words from these entries (including a surname), spelled as Pepys spelled them. How would each word be spelled today? From these and other **archaic spellings,** what inferences can you make about how some words might have been pronounced in Pepys's day?

bonefyres	turne	alter
musique	themselfs	noyse
frolique	shewe	loaden
tiple	Frankelyn	ruine

2. Look over the diary entries, and find examples of **archaic syntax**—sentence structures that would not be used in formal English today.
3. Find examples of **verb forms** that are different from standard verb forms used today.

Did any other examples of seventeenth-century usage give you difficulty? What strategies did you use to solve your problems? Be sure to check your reading notes.

Choices: Building Your Portfolio

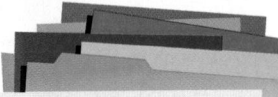

Writer's Notebook

1. Collecting Ideas for a Persuasive Essay

Personal records can suggest many controversial issues. Embedded in Pepys's *Diary,* for example, are questions about capital punishment and civil disaster planning. Review these diary entries, and list all the other issues they raise in your mind. Evaluate your list, and jot down notes on issues that you have strong feelings about. Save your notes for the Writer's Workshop on page 612.

Analyzing Character

2. Pepys: What Manner of Man?

Using the *Diary* excerpts as evidence, evaluate Pepys's character: What kind of man does he seem to be—socially, politically, religiously, and personally? Present your conclusions in an essay, using citations from the *Diary* to support your statements. Be sure to open your character study with a thesis statement.

Research/Speaking

3. Find Out More

Pepys's *Diary* is rich in topics for further research. Scan the entries again and find a topic that you would like to know more about—perhaps the public execution of King Charles I in 1649. Using the library and the Internet, prepare material for a brief presentation to the class. You could even work with other students to organize a broad-ranging seminar on seventeenth-century London.

Creative Writing

4. Dear Diary

Write several days' entries for a diary of your own that could serve as a record of the life of an American teenager in the early years of the twenty-first century. As Pepys did, include specific dates, events, and names, or write entries more like those Joan Didion wrote. If you follow Didion, you will write more about what it feels like to live your life.

Creative Writing

5. Opening Up the Diary

More and more writers of fiction are going to historical records, such as diaries and letters, for story ideas. You may have read "The Dog of Pompeii" by Louis Untermeyer, in which the writer imagines what happened to a young boy and his dog when Mount Vesuvius rained fire and ash down on the city of Pompeii in A.D. 79. Take an event from Pepys's *Diary* (perhaps the fire of London) and open it up. In other words, use it as the basis for a story or poem of your own. Put your readers at the scene by including descriptive details—if they are not in the *Diary,* you will have to imagine them.

Leather bucket used in the Great Fire of London (17th century).
London Museum, London.

Objectives

1. Recognize archaic spellings, vocabulary, and syntax
2. Develop strategies to interpret archaic usage
3. Make inferences about archaic pronunciations

Reading Skills and Strategies

Answers

1. bonfires, music, frolic, tipple, turn, themselves, show, Franklin, altar, noise, laden, ruin. (Remind students that Pepys wrote before the introduction of dictionaries and standardized spelling.) Answers on pronunciation will vary. In general, Pepys's language appears to have more long vowels and extended word endings.
2. Possible examples: ". . . it fell a-raining and thundering and lightning as I have not seen it do some years . . . " (p. 546) and "So I down to the waterside and there got a boat and through bridge, and there saw a lamentable fire" (p. 550).
3. Some verb forms are *doth* and *hath* for *does* and *have* and *is come* instead of *has come.*

Grading Timesaver

Rubrics for each Choices assignment appear on p. 140 in the *Portfolio Management System.*

Choices: Building Your Portfolio

1. **Writer's Notebook** Encourage students to look back in their own diaries (if they keep them) for ideas.
2. **Analyzing Character** Students may wish to organize their information in chart form and then debate the conclusions they draw with a partner or group before they finalize the arguments for their essays.
3. **Research/Speaking** For additional research ideas, read to students the Social Studies note on p. T550 under Crossing the Curriculum.
4. **Creative Writing** Allow students to fictionalize reality in Didion's manner, even if the style they adopt is the more matter-of-fact one used by Pepys.
5. **Creative Writing** Suggest that students begin by choosing the event and writing down an impressionistic list of words, phrases, and images.

OBJECTIVES

1. Read and interpret the journal
2. Identify and analyze the journal form
3. Evaluate sources of information
4. Express understanding through critical and creative writing and discussion
5. Learn and use new words

SKILLS

Literary
- Identify and analyze the journal form

Reading
- Evaluate the credibility of information sources

Writing
- Chart ideas for a persuasive essay
- Compare and contrast two works
- Support an opinion
- Write a narrative about a natural disaster

Speaking/Listening
- Discuss and evaluate an author's credibility

Vocabulary
- Learn and use new words

Planning

- **Block Schedule**
  Block Scheduling Lesson Plans with Pacing Guide
- **Traditional Schedule**
  Lesson Plans Including Strategies for English-Language Learners
- ***One-Stop Planner***
  CD-ROM with Test Generator

BROWSING IN THE FILES

About the Author. Defoe was apparently held in low regard by some of his contemporaries. Jonathan Swift wrote in 1708, "there is no enduring him," and in 1713 Joseph Addison called him "a false, shuffling, prevaricating rascal—unqualified to give his testimony in a Court of Justice."

Daniel Defoe

(1660–1731)

Daniel Defoe (detail) (17th century). Engraving. London Library.

Daniel Foe—he added the aristocratic prefix *De* to his name when he was about thirty-five—attended an excellent academy where he studied history, law, economics, geography, and natural science. Defoe's family were Dissenters, Protestants who did not approve of the Church of England, and so he was barred from attending either Oxford or Cambridge. When he was around twenty, he set himself up as a merchant, trading in haberdashery, brandy, wool, real estate, and eventually civet cats. He married when he was twenty-four. Meanwhile, he began publishing books and pamphlets.

Throughout his long life, Defoe was a very busy person, sometimes successful in business, sometimes bankrupt and hiding from his creditors. He often traveled about the country as a spy, even performing such services for his favorite monarch, King William III. And he constantly wrote and wrote and wrote—altogether over five hundred different works, in prose and verse, including a news pamphlet, *The Review,* which he put out three times a week for over seven years. He touched on every conceivable subject: the choice of a wife, the history of the devil, the manufacture of glass.

Defoe's innumerable writings might be roughly classified into four groups. A large number are concerned with political and religious controversies. His pamphlet *The Shortest Way with the Dissenters* (1702) called for the punishment of the Dissenters—Defoe's own party—and confiscation of their property. When the Church of England party discovered, to their anger, that the pamphlet was ironic, Defoe was arrested, exposed in the pillory three times, and indefinitely jailed. He was released on the condition that he become a spy and a writer for the very government that had locked him up because of his satire.

A second, didactic group of writings advises people on how to become virtuous as well as rich. A third group is made up of journalistic accounts of sensational events, such as "A True Relation of the Apparition of one Mrs. Veal" (1706), a remarkable ghost story based on the alleged reappearance of a real Mrs. Veal who had died, and *A Journal of the Plague Year* (1722). The fourth group contains Defoe's fiction, including the novels *Robinson Crusoe* (1719) and *Moll Flanders* (1722).

The story of Robinson Crusoe is well known in a general way: A sailor is shipwrecked on a tropical island and for many years manages to lead a more or less civilized life there, without human companionship, until he meets a young native of the island whom he saves from certain death at the hands of "cannibals" and names Friday. This classic book has an almost universal appeal because it portrays a single, strong individual who, all alone, triumphs over his desolate, hostile surroundings.

Many people believe that Defoe modeled Robinson Crusoe on an actual person, a Scottish sailor named Alexander Selkirk, who had written a memoir of his experiences as a castaway. But it was only the *idea* of a marooned man that Defoe used. Though he presents Crusoe's experiences as true autobiography, they are entirely Defoe's own invention; the episodes in the book have nothing to do with Selkirk or with anyone else. It is a tribute to Defoe's skill that many readers have assumed the tale to be true. An irony of literary history becomes apparent when one realizes that, in spite of his voluminous contributions to literature, Defoe is usually remembered as the author of only this one book.

go.hrw.com LEO 12-7

Resources: Print and Media

Reading
- *Graphic Organizers for Active Reading,* p. 43
- *Words to Own,* p. 15
- *Audio CD Library*
  Disc 9, Track 3

Writing and Language
- *Daily Oral Grammar*
  Transparency 18
- *Grammar and Language Links*
  Worksheet, p. 33
- *Language Workshop CD-ROM*

Viewing and Representing
- *Viewing and Representing*
  Fine Art Transparency 9
  Fine Art Worksheet, p. 36

Assessment
- *Formal Assessment,* p. 101
- *Portfolio Management System,* p. 142
- *Test Generator (One-Stop Planner CD-ROM)*

Internet
- go.hrw.com (keyword: LE0 12-7)

Before You Read

FROM **A JOURNAL OF THE PLAGUE YEAR**

Make the Connection

The Contagion of Fear

The events were grim indeed. When the London plague was at its worst, in August and September of 1665, it may have killed as many as ten thousand people every week—an enormous toll in a city whose total population was less than half a million. During the plague, people who could afford to leave London did so, in large numbers. Wherever they went, to outlying villages and towns, they terrified the local inhabitants, who believed that they could become infected from any city dweller, sick or well. Inside London, if any family member came down with the plague, the whole family was confined by law to its dwelling.

Quarantines of this kind were totally ineffective. Although everybody in those days assumed that the plague could be caught from another person, modern medical research tells us that it is primarily transmitted from rat to rat and from rat to person by fleas. Fleas prefer to bite rats, but when rats become scarce (because they die of plague), the fleas bite people. When the last rat has died of plague, then people stop dying. Since Defoe and his contemporaries did not understand how the plague was communicated, the disease seemed not only horrible, but also mysterious and irrational, as though an angry God were punishing them for their wrongdoings. What contemporary events have confused and frightened people so much that they began talking about divine punishment?

Elements of Literature

Journal

Defoe was a practical man, and he realized that the materials of history might be a source of profit. Thus, *A Journal of the Plague Year* illustrates the form of the **journal**—but at one remove from an actual eyewitness account. This work is, in effect, a semi-fictional reconstruction of an authentic, contemporaneous record, ingeniously written to make readers feel that the narrator was really an eyewitness to the events—when, in fact, he wasn't.

By blending a nonfiction form with made-up details, Defoe became one of the first writers to fuel a debate that continues into our own time. How far can **journalists** (note the formation of the word from *journal*) go in stretching the literal truth in order to re-create a real event?

A **journal** is a record of events, kept daily or on a regular basis, by a person who is an eyewitness or a participant. A journal is usually less personal and intimate than a diary.

For more information on the Journal, see the Handbook of Literary Terms.

Background

This work, which Defoe published in 1722, pretends to be a firsthand account of an epidemic of bubonic plague that had ravaged London fifty-seven years before, in 1665, when Defoe was five years old. To tell the story, Defoe invented a narrator called "H. F.," who may be Henry Foe, an uncle of Defoe's who may have lived in London during the epidemic and who may have told Defoe about it. "H. F." is said to be a saddler, one who manufactures, repairs, or sells horses' saddles—in other words, an ordinary citizen.

Altogether, Defoe had four kinds of materials to aid his powerful imagination: his own childhood memories; the reminiscences of his uncle Henry and other older people; city records; and printed matter such as pamphlets, books, and sermons about the plague. He worked these materials into a convincing narrative that seems to be related by somebody who is actually experiencing, from day to day, the grim events that he describes.

Reading Skills and Strategies

Evaluating Sources of Information

As you read Defoe's account of the plague, keep in mind what you have just learned about the sources of his information. Remember that he did not observe firsthand the events he describes. Jot down details that you think make his account believable. Note also any details that seem exaggerated or sensationalized.

Summary ■■

These excerpts are from Daniel Defoe's retrospective account of the bubonic plague that ravaged London in 1665, killing tens of thousands and instilling in survivors a terror of contagion. Writing fifty-seven years after the actual plague, Defoe presents his narrative in the form of a journal, written in the first person by a narrator whom Defoe identifies as H. F. The initials probably refer to Henry Foe, Daniel's uncle, who may have shared his memories of the plague with his nephew. Of course, Defoe would have had additional primary sources available to him, including other eyewitness accounts and official records and pamphlets. Perhaps relying more on his imagination than on historical sources, however, Defoe makes his account seem immediate and reliable by including exact place names, quoting from victims, and describing the awful course and treatment of the disease. But beyond capturing events, Defoe, like a novelist, creates characters (the man who breaks quarantine and the drunken piper who gets tossed into the death cart) and puts them in compelling life-and-death situations. Defoe's tone is both serious and curious, with his curiosity sometimes bordering on a relish for the sensational.

Preteaching Vocabulary

Words to Own

Have students fill the blanks in the following sentences, using the Words to Own listed at the bottom of the selection pages.

1. The runner consumed a [prodigious] amount of carbohydrates before the race.
2. The little boy was constantly [importuning] his grandmother for treats.
3. The singer had an [inimitable] style.
4. The starving artist works in a [garret].
5. The clown [diverted] the children's attention.
6. In their haste, they threw away useful items [promiscuously].
7. Her bold new ideas were condemned as [lunacy].
8. The wound proved to be a [mortal] one.
9. The storm had [calamitous] results.
10. People cheered when the fire [abated].

Resources

Listening

Audio CD Library

A recording of these excerpts from *A Journal of the Plague Year* is provided in the *Audio CD Library*:

- Disc 9, Track 3

Viewing and Representing

Fine Art Transparency

A fine art transparency of Mrs. Alexander Farmer's *An Anxious Hour* may be used with this lesson as a prereading motivator. (Note: Students will have to have read Thomas Gray's "Elegy Written in a Country Churchyard" on p. 601 in order to complete the worksheet.) See the *Viewing and Representing Transparencies and Worksheets*:

- Transparency 9
- Worksheet, p. 36

(A) Vocabulary Note

Used in this sense, the word *visitation* means a disaster perceived as "a punishment sent by God."

(B) Elements of Literature

Journal

? From what point of view is Defoe writing? [first person] Why does he assume this viewpoint even though he was not an eyewitness? [Possible response: He wants to make the journal seem convincing and personal.]

(C) Reading Skills and Strategies

Evaluating Sources of Information

? Does the description of the screaming woman seem true to life or exaggerated? Why? [Possible responses: It seems true to life because people in a crisis behave wildly. It seems exaggerated because the woman's repetition of "death" is dramatic and poetic.]

(D) Critical Thinking

Speculating

? Why does Defoe hide the identity of the merchant? [Possible responses: because suicide was considered a disgrace and a sin; because he wants to make his narrator seem kind and humane.]

(E) Historical Connections

It is a sad irony of the plague that it made many Londoners wealthy. With so many fatalities, the wealth of the prosperous city was inherited by the relatively few people who survived.

from A Journal of the Plague Year

Daniel Defoe

1. The Infection Spreads

Here the opinion of the physicians agreed with my observation afterward, namely, that the danger was spreading insensibly, for the sick could infect none but those that came within reach of the sick person; but that one man who may have really received the infection and knows it not, but goes abroad and about as a sound person, may give the plague to a thousand people, and they to greater numbers in proportion, and neither the person giving the infection or the persons receiving it know anything of it, and perhaps not feel the effects of it for several days after.

For example, many persons in the time of this (A) visitation never perceived that they were infected till they found to their unspeakable surprise, the tokens come out upon them; after which they seldom lived six hours; for those spots they called the tokens were really gangrene spots, or mortified flesh[1] in small knobs as broad as a little silver penny, and hard as a piece of callus or horn; so that, when the disease was come up to that length, there was nothing could follow but certain death; and yet, as I said, they knew nothing of their being infected, nor found themselves so much as out of order, till those mortal marks were upon them. But everybody must allow that they were infected in a high degree before, and must have been so some time, and consequently their breath, their sweat, their very clothes, were contagious for many days before. . . .

2. Dismal Scenes

(B) I had some little obligations, indeed, upon me to go to my brother's house, which was in Coleman Street[2] parish and which he had left to my care, and I went at first every day, but afterward only once or twice a week.

In these walks I had many dismal scenes before my eyes, as particularly of persons falling dead in the streets, terrible shrieks and screechings of women, who, in their agonies, would throw open their chamber windows and cry out in a dismal, surprising manner. It is impossible to describe the variety of postures in which the passions of the poor people would express themselves.

Passing through Tokenhouse Yard, in Lothbury, of a sudden a casement[3] violently opened just over my head, and a woman gave three frightful (C) screeches, and then cried, "Oh! death, death, death!" in a most inimitable tone, and which struck me with horror and a chillness in my very blood. There was nobody to be seen in the whole street, neither did any other window open, for people had no curiosity now in any case, nor could anybody help one another, so I went on to pass into Bell Alley.

Just in Bell Alley, on the right hand of the passage, there was a more terrible cry than that, though it was not so directed out at the window; but the whole family was in a terrible fright, and I could hear women and children run screaming about the rooms like distracted, when a garret window opened and somebody from a window on the other side the alley called and asked, "What is the matter?" upon which, from the first window, it was answered, "Oh Lord, my old master has hanged himself!" The other asked again, "Is he quite dead?" and the first answered, "Ay, ay, quite dead; quite dead and cold!" This person was (D) a merchant and a deputy alderman, and very rich. I care not to mention the name, though I knew his name too, but that would be an hardship to the (E) family, which is now flourishing again.

1. **gangrene . . . flesh:** decay of soft tissues from a blockage of blood flow.
2. **Coleman Street:** This place and other places Defoe names are all within the old City of London, unless otherwise noted.
3. **casement:** hinged window.

WORDS TO OWN

mortal (môr′təl) *adj.:* fatal.
inimitable (in·im′i·tə·bəl) *adj.:* difficult or impossible to imitate.
garret (gar′it) *n.:* attic.

Skill Link

Analyzing the Characteristics of Clear Text

After students have read the journal excerpts, have them go back and identify and analyze elements that help clarify the text. First, ask them to find concise sentences. [Example: The first sentence in the second paragraph on p. 562 succinctly conveys Defoe's feelings.] Next, ask them to find examples of parallel sentence structure. [Possible response: Parallelism in the first paragraph on p. 564 helps clarify the effects of the plague.] Finally, ask students to determine whether Defoe exhibits completeness of ideas and covers his subject thoroughly. [Possible response: Defoe has explained, in great detail, the emotional and physical impact of the plague on himself and others.]

The Granger Collection, New York.

Lord, have mercy on London. Woodcut.

But this is but one; it is scarce credible what dreadful cases happened in particular families every day. People in the rage of the distemper, or **F** in the torment of their swellings, which was indeed intolerable, running out of their own government,[4] raving and distracted, and oftentimes laying violent hands upon themselves, throwing themselves out at their windows, shooting themselves, etc.; mothers murdering their own children in their lunacy, some dying of mere grief as a passion, some of mere fright and surprise without any infection at all, others frighted into idiotism and foolish distractions, some into despair and lunacy, others into melancholy madness.

The pain of the swelling was in particular very violent, and to some intolerable; the physicians and surgeons may be said to have tortured many **G** poor creatures even to death. The swellings in some grew hard, and they applied violent drawing plasters or poultices[5] to break them, and if these did not do they cut and scarified[6] them in a terrible manner. In some those swellings were made hard partly by the force of the distemper and partly by their being too violently drawn, and were so hard that no instrument could cut them, and then they burnt them with caustics,[7] so that many died raving mad with the torment, and some in the very operation. In these distresses, some, for want of help to hold them down in their beds, or to look to them, laid hands upon

4. **out of their own government:** unable to control themselves.

5. **drawing plasters or poultices** (pōl′tis·iz): hot packs used to soften sores and draw infection to the skin's surface.

6. **scarified:** punctured.

7. **caustics:** chemicals that can burn or eat away flesh.

WORDS TO OWN

lunacy (lo͞o′nə·sē) *n.:* madness. This word is derived from *luna,* Latin for "moon." People once believed that the phases of the moon could affect the human mind.

RESPONDING TO THE ART

This woodcut was created in London during the plague.

Activity. Ask students to study the woodcut carefully. Have them select three elements of the composition—one verbal message, one large visual feature, and one small visual feature—and write a sentence or two describing the feeling or idea each element conveys. Then have them share their impressions with the class.

F Historical Connections

Theories of Illness

Seventeenth-century physiology attributed health to a balance in the body of four fluids called "humors" or "tempers": blood, phlegm, yellow bile (choler), and black bile (melancholy). Illness was thought to result from an imbalance of these fluids, or a "distemper." The word *distemper* survives in modern English to describe emotional disturbance in humans and infection in animals.

G Reading Skills and Strategies

Evaluating Sources of Information

? What sources would Defoe have used in order to describe these medical procedures? [Possible responses: city records, doctors' notes, and other documents from the plague years; information from his uncle and others who remembered the epidemic.] How does his use of these sources affect the credibility of his *Journal*? [Primary sources help to make the *Journal* more credible.]

Reaching All Students

Struggling Readers

Encourage students to write down text organizers, such as subheadings, in their reading notes and to include the major details of each section of the *Journal* under its corresponding subheading. This informal outline of the *Journal* may later be used as a guide to write a summary of the selection.

English Language Learners

Read sections of the *Journal* aloud as students follow along in their books. Before reading a section, point out any idiomatic expressions and new vocabulary words in that section and explain them. For additional strategies to supplement instruction, see

- *Lesson Plans Including Strategies for English-Language Learners*

Advanced Learners

Discuss with students the ways in which today's print and broadcast media blend news-reporting with entertainment. Ask students for specific examples. Encourage them to reflect on how this blending of elements affects our perceptions of news events. Then ask them to compare the strategies Defoe uses in his *Journal* with those they have observed in contemporary media.

Ⓐ Critical Thinking

Making Judgments

Remind students that quarantine is based on the idea that individual liberties must sometimes be limited in order to protect the welfare of the whole community. Encourage them to think of examples where individual liberties are limited in present-day life. [highway speed limits, for instance] Ask students if they think it was right or wrong for the man to violate quarantine and lie to the innkeepers. [Possible responses: He was wrong because he put other people at risk of infection. He was right because everyone should have the freedom to travel wherever he or she wishes.]

themselves as above. Some broke out into the streets, perhaps naked, and would run directly down to the river if they were not stopped by the watchman or other officers, and plunge themselves into the water wherever they found it.

It often pierced my very soul to hear the groans and cries of those who were thus tormented, but of the two this was counted the most promising particular in the whole infection, for if these swellings could be brought to a head, and to break and run, or, as the surgeons call it, to digest, the patient generally recovered; whereas those who, like the gentlewoman's daughter, were struck with death at the beginning, and had the tokens come out upon them, often went about indifferent easy till a little before they died, and some till the moment they dropped down, as in apoplexies[8] and epilepsies is often the case. Such would be taken suddenly very sick, and would run to a bench or bulk,[9] or any convenient place that offered itself, or to their own houses if possible, as I mentioned before, and there sit down, grow faint, and die. This kind of dying was much the same as it was with those who die of common mortifications,[10] who die swooning, and, as it were, go away in a dream. Such as died thus had very little notice of their being infected at all till the gangrene was spread through their whole body; nor could physicians themselves know certainly how it was with them till they opened their breasts or other parts of their body and saw the tokens.

3. Escape from Quarantine

Ⓐ I remember one citizen who, having thus broken out of his house in Aldersgate Street or thereabout, went along the road to Islington;[11] he attempted to have gone in at the Angel Inn, and after that the White Horse, two inns known still by the same signs, but was refused; after which he came to the Pied Bull, an inn also still continuing the same sign. He asked them for lodging for one night only, pretending to be going into Lincolnshire,[12] and assuring them of his being very sound and free from the infection, which also at that time had not reached much that way.

They told him they had no lodging that they could spare but one bed up in the garret, and that they could spare that bed for one night, some drovers being expected the next day with cattle; so, if he would accept of that lodging, he might have it, which he did. So a servant was sent up with a candle with him to show him the room. He was very well dressed, and looked like a person not used to lie in a garret; and when he came to the room he fetched a deep sigh, and said to the servant, "I have seldom lain in such a lodging as this." However, the servant assuring him again that they had no better, "Well," says he, "I must make shift; this is a dreadful time; but it is but for one night." So he sat down upon the bedside, and bade the maid, I think it was, fetch him up a pint of warm ale. Accordingly the servant went for the ale, but some hurry in the house, which perhaps

8. **apoplexies** (ap′ə·plek′sēz): strokes.
9. **bulk:** low stall projecting from a wall or storefront.
10. **mortifications:** early term for gangrene.
11. **Islington:** suburb north of London.
12. **Lincolnshire:** county on the east coast of England.

Londoners fleeing into the countryside to escape the plague. Woodcut.

The Granger Collection, New York.

Skill Link

Using Context Clues and Reference Materials

Defoe often uses unfamiliar and archaic words. Encourage students to use context clues to discover word meanings and the overall meaning of sentences and paragraphs. If they cannot find a meaning from context, they may also refer to the glossary or a dictionary. Then, have them complete the following matching exercise:

1. easy	[e]	**a.**	animal herder
2. swoon	[f]	**b.**	accept
3. drover	[a]	**c.**	release
4. make shift	[b]	**d.**	reason
5. bade	[h]	**e.**	relaxed
6. rug	[g]	**f.**	faint
7. sexton	[j]	**g.**	blanket
8. sermon	[i]	**h.**	ordered
9. score	[d]	**i.**	lesson
10. vent	[c]	**j.**	caretaker

employed her other ways, put it out of her head, and she went up no more to him.

The next morning, seeing no appearance of the gentleman, somebody in the house asked the servant that had showed him upstairs what was become of him. She started. "Alas!" says she, "I never thought more of him. He bade me carry him some warm ale, but I forgot." Upon which, not the maid, but some other person was sent up to see after him, who, coming into the room, found him stark dead and almost cold, stretched out across the bed. His clothes were pulled off, his jaw fallen, his eyes open in a most frightful posture, the rug of the bed being grasped hard in one of his hands, so that it was plain he died soon after the maid left him; and 'tis probable, had she gone up with the ale, she had found him dead in a few minutes after he sat down upon the bed. The alarm was great in the house, as anyone may suppose, they having been free from the distemper till that disaster, which, bringing the infection to the house, spread it immediately to other houses round about it. . . . **B**

4. Burial Pits and Dead-Carts

There was a strict order to prevent people coming to those pits, and that was only to prevent infection. But after some time that order was more necessary, for people that were infected and near their end, and delirious also, would run to those pits, wrapped in blankets or rugs, and throw themselves in, and, as they said, bury themselves. . . .

This may serve a little to describe the dreadful condition of that day, though it is impossible to say anything that is able to give a true idea of it to those who did not see it, other than this, that it was indeed very, very, very dreadful, and such as no tongue can express. **C**

I got admittance into the churchyard[13] by being acquainted with the sexton who attended; who, though he did not refuse me at all, yet earnestly persuaded me not to go, telling me very seriously (for he was a good, religious, and sensible man) that it was indeed their business and duty to venture, and to run all hazards, and that in it[14] they might hope to be preserved; but that I had no apparent call to it but my own curiosity, which, he said, he believed I would not pretend was sufficient to justify my running that hazard. I told him I had been pressed in my mind to go, and that perhaps it might be an instructing sight, that might not be without its uses. "Nay," says the good man, "if you will venture upon that score, name of God go in; for, depend upon it, 'twill be a sermon to you, it may be, the best that ever you heard in your life. 'Tis a speaking sight," says he, "and has a voice with it, and a loud one, to call us all to repentance," and with that he opened the door and said, "Go, if you will."

His discourse had shocked my resolution a little, and I stood wavering for a good while, but just at that interval I saw two links[15] come over from the end of the Minories, and heard the bellman,[16] and then appeared a dead-cart, as they called it, coming over the streets; so I could no longer resist my desire of seeing it, and went in. There was nobody, as I could perceive at first, in the churchyard, or going into it, but the buriers and the fellow that drove the cart, or rather led the horse and cart; but when they came up to the pit they saw a man go to and again, muffled up in a brown cloak, and making motions with his hands under his cloak, as if he was in great agony, and the buriers immediately gathered about him, supposing he was one of those poor delirious or desperate creatures that used to pretend, as I have said, to bury themselves. He said nothing as he walked about, but two or three times groaned very deeply and loud, and sighed as he would break his heart.

When the buriers came up to him they soon found he was neither a person infected and desperate, as I have observed above, or a person distempered in mind, but one oppressed with a dreadful weight of grief indeed, having his wife and several of his children all in the cart that was just come in with him, and he followed in an agony and excess of sorrow. He mourned heartily, as it was easy to see, but with a kind of masculine grief that could not give itself vent by tears; and calmly defying the buriers to let him alone, said he would only see the bodies thrown in and go **D**

13. **churchyard:** location of the cemeteries.
14. **in it:** in doing it (going up to the rim of the pits).
15. **links:** torches.
16. **bellman:** bell ringer who accompanied the dead-cart.

B Reading Skills and Strategies

Identifying Cause and Effect

? Based on your knowledge of how the bubonic plague actually spread, is it likely that the traveler really caused the outbreak in this community? Why or why not? [Possible response: No, because the real agents were rats and fleas.]

C Elements of Literature

Journal

? Why does Defoe's narrator pause here to comment that the horror was too great for words to express? [Possible responses: Defoe was truly shocked by what he had heard and read. This is one more way to make the journal seem immediate and personal.]

D Reading Skills and Strategies

Comparing and Contrasting

Have students compare Defoe's description of the grief-stricken man with Pepys's descriptions of some of the victims of the great fire. (There are several on p. 551.) [They will notice that Defoe's description includes more details and puts more emphasis on the emotions of the character, whereas Pepys's descriptions say little about the feelings of the people he mentions.]

Getting Students Involved

Cooperative Learning

Becoming Experts. Place students in groups of three or four that include a mix of ability and motivation levels. Each student will become an expert on one section of Defoe's *Journal* and then report on that section to the group. Each report should include responses to the following:

1. What facts are provided in this section of the *Journal*?
2. What images does the narrator use to make the facts seem real and dramatic?
3. What source material did Defoe probably use to create this section: documents from the 1660s, eyewitness accounts from his uncle and others, his imagination?

Students may use chart paper and colored markers to outline their responses before presenting reports to their groups.

Ⓐ Cultural Connections

Burial Practices

Disposing of bodies in a solemn and dignified fashion is a concern of cultures throughout the world. Although the specifics differ widely, the customs of every culture combine sanitary precautions (burial, entombment, cremation) with rituals that soothe and reassure the mourners. In contrast, the most terrible disasters—war, plague, genocide—bring about the breakdown of these important cultural rituals, making the disaster all the more devastating for survivors.

Ⓑ Reading Skills and Strategies

Making Inferences

? Why does Defoe make John Hayward the source of the piper's story? [Possible responses: It makes the narrative more convincing; perhaps a real John Hayward was the true source of the anecdote.] **What is the effect of mentioning details that John Hayward contradicts?** [Possible response: This reminds the reader that Defoe's narrator is strongly committed to factual reporting.]

away, so they left importuning him. But no sooner was the cart turned round and the bodies shot into the pit promiscuously, which was a surprise to him, for he at least expected they would have been decently laid in, though indeed he was afterward convinced that was impracticable; I say, no sooner did he see the sight but he cried out aloud, unable to contain himself. I could not hear what he said, but he went backward two or three steps and fell down in a swoon. The buriers ran to him and took him up, and in a little while he came to himself, and they led him away to the Pie Tavern over against the end of Houndsditch, where, it seems, the man was known, and where they took care of him. He looked into the pit again as he went away, but the buriers had covered the bodies so immediately with throwing in earth, that though there was light enough, for there were lanterns, and candles in them, placed all night round the sides of the pit, upon heaps of earth, seven or eight, or perhaps more, yet nothing could be seen.

This was a mournful scene indeed, and affected me almost as much as the rest; but the other was awful and full of terror. The cart had in it sixteen or seventeen bodies; some were wrapped up in linen sheets, some in rags, some little other than naked, or so loose that what covering they had fell from them in the shooting out of the cart, and they fell quite naked among the rest; but the matter was not much to them, or the indecency much to any one else, seeing they were all dead, and were to be huddled together into the common grave of mankind, as we may call it, for here was no difference made, but poor and rich went together; there was no other way of burials, neither was it possible there should, for coffins were not to be had for the prodigious numbers that fell in such a calamity as this.

5. A Poor Piper

. . . John Hayward . . . was at that time undersexton of the parish of St. Stephen, Coleman Street. By undersexton was understood at that time gravedigger and bearer of the dead. This man carried, or assisted to carry, all the dead to their graves which were buried in that large parish, and

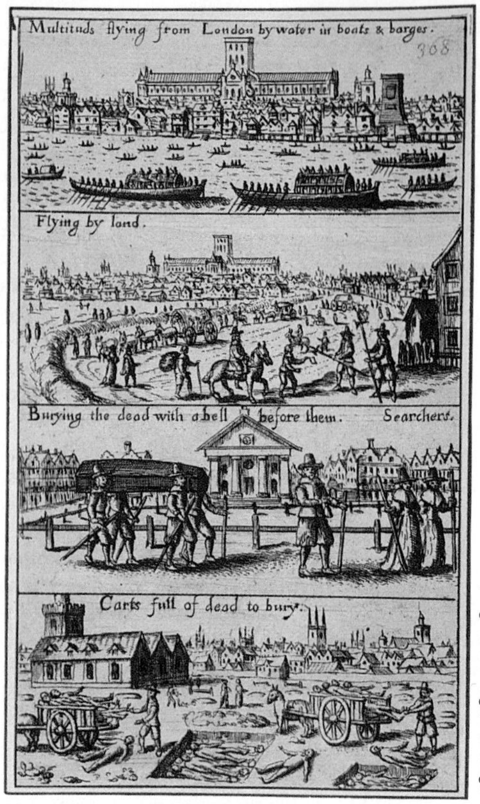

Plague of London (1665). Woodcut.

Master and Fellows, Magdalene College, Cambridge.

who were carried in form;[17] and after that form of burying was stopped, went with the dead-cart and the bell to fetch the dead bodies from the houses where they lay. . . .

It was under this John Hayward's care, and within his bounds, that the story of the piper,[18] with which people have made themselves so merry, happened, and he assured me that it was true. It is said that it was a blind piper; but, as John told me, the fellow was not blind, but an ignorant, weak, poor man, and usually walked his

17. **in form:** according to the customary burial rites.
18. **piper:** bagpiper.

Words to Own

importuning (im′pôr·to͞on′iŋ) *v.* used as *n.*: making repeated demands of.
promiscuously (prə·mis′kyo͞o·əs·lē) *adv.*: casually.
prodigious (prō·dij′əs) *adj.*: huge.

Using Students' Strengths

Mathematical/Logical Learners

A popular, present-day technique for presenting statistics is exemplified by this statement: "Every Y minutes, this disease claims another victim." Have students research the London plague statistics in order to express the death toll in this fashion. (They should divide the number of minutes in one year by the number of fatalities per year.) After researching statistics on twentieth-century causes of death (auto accidents, heart disease, cancer, etc.) students may likewise express the death statistics in terms of minutes.

By constructing a chart or graph that shows these in descending order, students will be able to compare the plague with contemporary threats to life.

rounds about ten o'clock at night and went piping along from door to door, and the people usually took him in at public houses[19] where they knew him, and would give him drink and victuals, and sometimes farthings;[20] and he in return would pipe and sing and talk simply, which diverted the people; and thus he lived. It was but a very bad time for this diversion while things were as I have told, yet the poor fellow went about as usual, but was almost starved; and when anybody asked how he did he would answer, the dead-cart had not taken him yet, but that they had promised to call for him next week. **C**

It happened one night that this poor fellow, whether somebody had given him too much to drink or no—John Hayward said he had not drink in his house, but that they had given him a little more victuals than ordinary at a public house in Coleman Street—and the poor fellow, having not usually had a bellyful for perhaps not a good while, was laid all along upon the top of a bulk or stall, and fast asleep, at a door in the street near London Wall, towards Cripplegate; and that upon the same bulk or stall the people of some house, in the alley of which the house was a corner, hearing a bell which they always rang before the cart came, had laid a body really dead of the plague just by him, thinking, too, that this poor fellow had been a dead body, as the other was, and laid there by some of the neighbors. **D**

Accordingly, when John Hayward with his bell and the cart came along, finding two dead bodies lie upon the stall, they took them up with the instrument they used and threw them into the cart, and all this while the piper slept soundly.

From hence they passed along and took in other dead bodies, till, as honest John Hayward told me, they almost buried him alive in the cart; yet all this while he slept soundly. At length the cart came to the place where the bodies were to be thrown into the ground, which, as I do remember, was at Mount Mill; and as the cart usually stopped some time before they were ready to shoot out the melancholy load they had in it, as soon as the cart stopped the fellow awaked and struggled a little to get his head out from among the dead bodies, when, raising himself up in the cart, he called out, "Hey! where am I?" This frighted the fellow that attended about the work; but after some pause John Hayward, recovering himself, said, "Lord, bless us! There's somebody in the cart not quite dead!" So another called to him and said, "Who are you?" The fellow answered, "I am the poor piper. Where am I?" "Where are you?" says Hayward. "Why, you are in the dead-cart, and we are going to bury you." "But I an't dead though, am I?" says the piper, which made them laugh **E** a little—though, as John said, they were heartily frighted at first; so they helped the poor fellow down, and he went about his business.

I know the story goes he set up his pipes in the cart and frighted the bearers and others so that they ran away; but John Hayward did not tell the story so, nor say anything of his piping at all; but that he was a poor piper, and that he was carried away as above I am fully satisfied of the truth of. . . .

6. A Violent Cure

I heard of one infected creature who, running out of his bed in his shirt in the anguish and agony of his swellings, of which he had three upon him, got his shoes on and went to put on his coat; but the nurse resisting, and snatching the coat from him, he threw her down, ran over her, ran downstairs and into the street, directly to the Thames in his shirt, the nurse running after him, and calling to the watch to stop him; but the watchman, frighted at the man, and afraid to touch him, let him go on; upon which he ran down to the Stillyard stairs, threw away his shirt, and plunged into the Thames, and, being a good swimmer, swam **F** quite over the river; and the tide being coming in, as they call it (that is, running westward) he reached the land not till he came about the Falcon stairs, where landing, and finding no people there, it being in the night, he ran about the streets there, naked as he was, for a good while, when, it being by that time high water,[21] he takes the river again, and swam back to the Stillyard,

19. **public houses:** taverns.
20. **farthings:** small British coins (no longer in use) worth one quarter of a penny.

21. **high water:** high tide.

WORDS TO OWN
diverted (də·vurt'id) *v.:* amused.

C Reading Skills and Strategies
Connecting with the Text

? Think of people you know who make jokes in the face of misfortune. Share a few specific examples. What does a person's reaction to misfortune tell you about the person? [Possible responses: The person is foolish, courageous, optimistic, nervous, eager to reassure others.]

D Reading Skills and Strategies
Visualizing

Point out the subtle but compelling imagery of this scene. Although it is not as dramatic as many other scenes in the *Journal*, the casual act of putting a body out for collection—like trash at the curb—makes it in some ways more horrifying.

E Critical Thinking
Interpreting

? What makes the piper's question funny? [Possible response: It creates a strong contrast with the grim setting, relieving the tension of the mortifying mistake.]

F Elements of Literature
Tone

Although Defoe portrays this section of the *Journal* as a serious description, the image of the half-naked man pursued by his nurse seems deliberately comic. Encourage students to analyze the effect of this mixture of comic and serious elements.

Reaching All Students

Struggling Readers

Section 6, "A Violent Cure," consists of one long compound-complex sentence. Ask students to notice how Defoe uses commas and semicolons to punctuate the sentence. Have them copy out a few of the imbedded independent clauses, writing them as sentences. Then ask them to identify the subject, verb, and other elements that each one contains. In some cases, a word will need to be supplied. Students may need help, but the following, simpler example should get them started: "He ran down to the Stillyard stairs, threw away his shirt, and plunged into the Thames." [He ran down to the Stillyard stairs. He threw away his shirt. He plunged into the Thames.]

Responding to the Art

This is the title page of a document that contains the names of those who died in the year 1665. **Activity.** Ask students to comment on visual details, such as the winged hourglass at the top and the other icons in the border. Ask them to contrast these icons to ones we use today on sympathy cards and cemetery monuments to commemorate the dead. What might the differences in imagery reflect about the respective attitudes of the two eras toward death? [Possible responses: The seventeenth-century images suggest a more direct and harsh look at death than contemporary images, which seek to offer comfort and hope.]

A Vocabulary Note

The Prefix *mal-*

Ask students to look up *malignity* in the dictionary or infer its meaning from context clues. Note its similarity to the word *malicious,* which was one of the Words to Own in Samuel Pepys's *Diary.* Ask students to brainstorm a list of words that share this common prefix, taking care to distinguish between words with the *mal-* prefix and others that simply begin with the same three letters (like *malt* and *mall*).

B Reading Skills and Strategies

Drawing Conclusions

? What does Defoe mean by "lessen the value of it"? Would describing the joy make the joy seem less important, or the grief seem less important? [The pronoun "it" is ambiguous; this sentence is a good subject for open-ended discussion.]

landed, ran up the streets again to his own house, knocking at the door, went up the stairs and into his bed again; and that this terrible experiment cured him of the plague, that is to say, that the violent motion of his arms and legs stretched the parts where the swellings he had upon him were, that is to say, under his arms and his groin, and caused them to ripen and break; and that the cold of the water abated the fever in his blood. . . .

7. The Plague Diminishes

. . . The contagion despised all medicine; death raged in every corner; and had it gone on as it did then, a few weeks more would have cleared the town of all, and everything that had a soul. Men everywhere began to despair; every heart failed them for fear; people were made desperate through the anguish of their souls, and the terrors of death sat in the very faces and countenances of the people.

In that very moment when we might very well say, "Vain was the help of man,"—I say, in that very moment it pleased God, with a most agreeable surprise, to cause the fury of it to abate, even (A) of itself; and the malignity declining, as I have said, though infinite numbers were sick, yet fewer died, and the very first weeks' bill[22] decreased 1,843; a vast number indeed!

It is impossible to express the change that appeared in the very countenances of the people that Thursday morning when the weekly bill came out. It might have been perceived in their countenances that a secret surprise and smile of joy sat on everybody's face. They shook one another by the hands in the streets, who would hardly go on the same side of the way with one another before. Where the streets were not too broad they would open their windows and call from one house to another, and ask how they did, and if they had heard the good news that the plague was abated. Some would return, when they said good news, and ask, "What good news?" and when they answered that the plague was abated and the bills decreased almost two thousand, they would cry out, "God be praised!" and would weep aloud for joy, telling them they had heard nothing of it; and such was the joy of the people that it was, as it were, life to them from the grave. (B) I could almost set down as many extravagant things done in the excess of their joy as of their grief; but that would be to lessen the value of it. . . .

22. **bill:** count of the dead that was published every week so long as the plague raged.

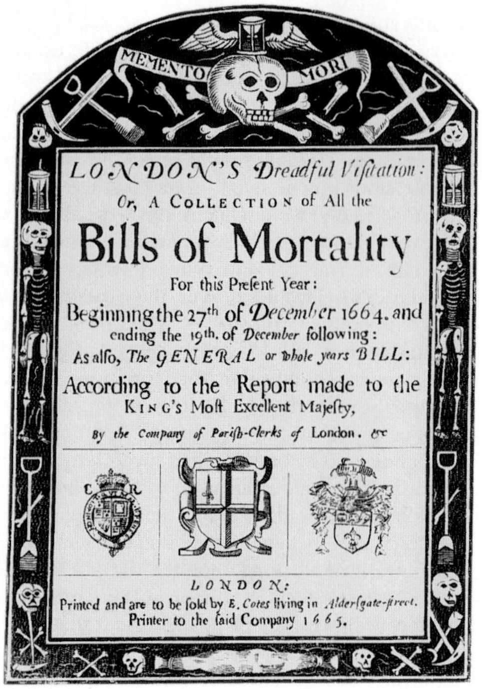

Title page of *A Collection of All the Bills of Mortality* (1665).

8. I'm Alive!

. . . I shall conclude the account of this calamitous year . . . with a coarse but sincere stanza of my own, which I placed at the end of my ordinary memorandums the same year they were written:

A dreadful plague in London was
  In the year sixty-five,
Which swept an hundred thousand souls
  Away; yet I alive!

H. F.

Words to Own

abated (ə·bāt′id) *v.:* lessened.
calamitous (kə·lam′ə·təs) *adj.:* bringing great trouble.

Making the Connections

Connecting to the Subject: "An Appetite for Experience"

Have students review the entire selection, looking specifically for passages where Defoe apparently wants to provoke the following responses in the reader: disgust, pity, amusement, curiosity, intellectual interest, moral enlightenment. (This may be an activity for small groups, each group looking at the text for a particular reader response.) What seems to be Defoe's purpose in writing *A Journal of the Plague Year*? What type of experience is he offering his readers? What appetites is he hoping to satisfy? (Remind students that the *Journal* was written many years after the plague.)

Assessing Learning

Check Test: True-False

1. The effects of the plague showed up immediately on an infected person. [False]
2. If tokens (buboes) were opened and drained, people often recovered. [True]
3. People were allowed to go to the burial pits, since the plague could not be spread by corpses. [False]
4. Even after the plague had diminished, people were afraid to touch or even talk to each other. [False]

Making Meanings

First Thoughts

1. What did you feel was the strongest **image** in this account of an urban epidemic? Why?

> **Reading Check**
>
> a. Where does Defoe let the reader know his *Journal* is being written long after the plague took place? How does he explain this change in form?
>
> b. Who are the four characters whom the narrator features? How does each of their situations differ?
>
> c. What were the symptoms of the disease?
>
> d. What attempts were made to cure people?

Shaping Interpretations

2. What seems to be the **tone** of the *Journal*—the attitude of the writer toward the events he is recounting? Do you think the tone would have been different if the *Journal* really had been written during the plague?
3. What techniques does Defoe use to make his journal seem authentic?
4. Why does Defoe, or his narrator, say that the manner of burial makes no difference to a dead person? To whom do you think the manner of burial *does* make a difference?
5. Why would the story of the piper be improved if it contained the bit about his playing the pipes while he was in the dead-cart? Why, then, does the narrator refuse to include this bit?
6. Why does H. F. call his little poem "coarse"?

Connecting with the Text

7. How do you think experiencing a plague of this sort would change a person's attitude toward life and death?

Extending the Text

8. What is meant by the expression "morbid curiosity"? Where does this kind of curiosity appear in contemporary life, and how do you account for it?
9. Few words in English have the shock value of *plague*. Can you think of anything in your own world that is described as a plague? How does the plague Defoe describes compare to the "plagues" of today?

Defoe in the Pillory (detail) (17th century), from a chapbook edition of *Jure Divino*.

By permission of the British Library, London.

Making Meanings

First Thoughts [Respond]

1. Answers will vary. Students should be encouraged to expand on reasons why they found a particular image compelling.

Shaping Interpretations [Interpret]

2. The tone is serious, sorrowful, grave. The tone may have been more hysterical or frightened if the journal had been written during the epidemic.
3. Defoe uses the first-person point of view. He includes detailed descriptions of people and places. His narrator insists that the facts are true.
4. He wants to stress the finality of death and to remind the reader that the dead person knows and feels nothing. The manner of burial matters to the mourners.
5. It would make the piper's grim experience more comical, his incongruous cheerfulness more striking. The narrator refuses to include this bit because it is not proven, and he likes to remind the reader that he includes only factual information.
6. *Coarse* means "rude" or "inappropriate." The narrator uses a serious, mournful tone in the *Journal*. In contrast, the short rhyme does not sound serious. It belittles the suffering of those who died in the plague.

Connecting with the Text [Evaluate]

7. Answers will vary. The experience might dull the emotions and diminish the value placed on human life, or it might cause a greater appreciation of life and health.

Extending the Text [Synthesize]

8. "Morbid curiosity" is the desire to observe and learn about death and suffering. There are abundant examples in contemporary life ("rubbernecking" at auto wrecks, TV journalists' interviewing relatives of victims). There are also many ways to account for it: desire for vicarious excitement; the feeling of good fortune that we, like H. F., have been spared misfortune.
9. Responses will vary. Probable answers include drug and alcohol abuse as well as a variety of infectious diseases. Many students will say the plague of 1665 was worse than modern "plagues."

> **Reading Check**
>
> a. Defoe's use of the past tense and phrases like "I remember" indicate that the *Journal* was written years later. The story of the piper makes the impression stronger. The final sentence, "ordinary memorandums the same year" is the clearest statement. He does not explain the delay.
>
> b. The four featured characters are the man who died in the garret of the inn, the man whose wife and children were in the dead cart, the poor piper, and the man who was cured by swimming. They represent the ways that the plague affected individual lives, both directly and indirectly, and a variety of possible outcomes.
>
> c. Some victims experienced no symptoms until "tokens" of gangrene appeared when the disease was advanced. Others experienced painful swellings.
>
> d. Physicians applied plasters and poultices and attempted to lance or burn the swellings in order to drain them.

Grading Timesaver

Rubrics for each Choices assignment appear on p. 142 in the *Portfolio Management System.*

CHOICES: Building Your Portfolio

1. **Writer's Notebook** Encourage students to make thorough brainstorming charts before they begin writing.
2. **Comparing Journals** To help students arrive at a conclusion about Defoe's success at imitating a journal, ask them if Defoe's account of the plague is as believable—if it sounds as authentic—as Pepys's account of the Great Fire. Ask them to explain their answer. Suggest that it may be possible that Defoe's fiction seems more authentic than Pepys's eyewitness account. Ask students to give reasons why they agree or disagree with this possibility.
3. **Supporting an Opinion** Bring copies of several daily newspapers, both national and local, to the classroom, or direct students to read them in the library or on the Internet. Using the 5W-How? questions (who, what, when, where, why, and how), they should record the major details of disasters.
4. **Creative Writing** Have students begin to organize their details for their narratives with a 5W-How? chart. Have students list the facts of *what, who, where, when, why,* and *how* that relate to their topic. They may check their graphic organizers for details as they write.
5. **Discussion/Evaluating Credibility** After students have reviewed the Background on p. 557, help them to break the task into parts: first, analysis of the *reliability* of Defoe's sources; second, analysis of the *credibility* of Defoe's account; third, *evaluation* of a writer's responsibility to readers.

CHOICES: Building Your Portfolio

Writer's Notebook

1. Collecting Ideas for a Persuasive Essay

Defoe uses officials (the sexton, for example) to make his journal account more convincing—a strategy also important in persuasion. If you are arguing the issue that germ warfare is so dangerous to the survival of human life that all experimentation with biological weapons should cease, support for your opinion may come from an interview with an expert in the field. Make a three-column chart headed *Public Disasters, Issues,* and *Experts.* Then, for each column, brainstorm ideas for persuasive essays (TV and newspaper stories can help). Save your notes for the Writer's Workshop on page 612.

Comparing Journals

2. Charting Pepys and Defoe

In an essay, compare and contrast Defoe's *A Journal of the Plague Year* and Pepys's diary entry about the Great Fire of London (page 549). (Remember that Pepys's *Diary* is a nonfiction account, unlike Defoe's *Journal.*) Gather information

Elements of Comparison	*Pepys's Diary*	*Defoe's Journal*
Tone		
Point of view		
Use of details		

for your essay by filling out a chart like the one above. Conclude your essay by deciding how good (or bad) a job Defoe does of imitating a personal journal.

Supporting an Opinion

3. Forgetting or Confronting?

Some people argue that life itself is often very disagreeable—so why should we have to read about dreadful, depressing events in books like Defoe's? Wouldn't it be better just to forget calamities, atrocities, and disasters, and remember only the pleasant things that have happened? How do you feel about this point of view? Using the events in the *Journal* as support, write an essay in which you either defend or attack this position.

Creative Writing

4. You Are There!

Examine several accounts (from newspapers, magazines, or television or radio) of a recent natural disaster. Then, write a narrative of the event as though you were an observer or a participant. Use either the format of a newspaper article or that of a TV news documentary. Include the details that will make your story believable: names, dates, places, times, causes, effects, motives, and so on.

Discussion / Evaluating Credibility

5. Do You Believe Him?

Reread the Background material on page 557 that describes Defoe's sources of information. Review also the notes you took while reading the selection. Then, form a group for a round-table discussion of Defoe's sources and how he used them. Consider which of his sources was the most reliable and which the least, and decide how much or how little he may have used each one. Then, discuss the credibility of Defoe's account. Does it stand up most credibly as history, journalism, or fiction? Finally, consider any writer's responsibility in writing a book that claims to be a firsthand account but is not. (Are any such books written today?) At the conclusion of your discussion, present a summation of your group's views.

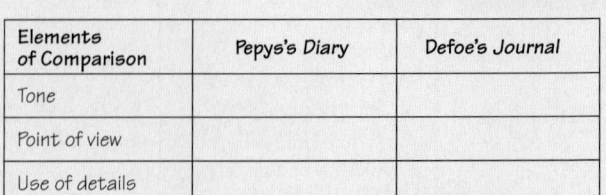

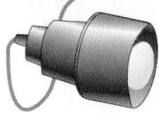

Joseph Addison and Sir Richard Steele

Wit, morality, and coffeehouse gossip. Ⓐ In the early eighteenth century, London's thriving coffeehouse scene provided politicians, actors, and aristocrats a place to meet, to read newspapers, and to gossip. Coffeehouse conversations reflected the nation's commercial, cultural, and political life to such an extent that they were called "the penny universities" because one could receive a complete education there for the price of a newspaper.

Sir Richard Steele and Joseph Addison's contribution to this intellectual scene was the periodical essay, a forerunner of modern newspapers and magazines. This publication consisted of a single printed sheet, issued at least once a week and usually containing a single piece of writing. Steele and Addison are often paired because of their work on

By Courtesy of the National Portrait Gallery, London.

Joseph Addison (detail) (before 1717) by Sir Godfrey Kneller. Oil on canvas (36″ × 28″).

By Courtesy of the National Portrait Gallery, London.

Sir Richard Steele (1711) by Sir Godfrey Kneller. Oil on canvas (36″ × 28″).

two enormously popular periodicals, *The Tatler,* which appeared three times a week from April 1709 to January 1711, and *The Spectator,* which appeared daily except Sunday from March 1, 1711, to December 6, 1712. Both publications elevated the periodical essay to an art form.

Two very different talents. Sir Richard Steele (1672–1729), born of English parents in Dublin and orphaned early, was educated in London at a privately endowed school, the Charterhouse. There he met his future collaborator Joseph Addison, a brilliant student who was the son of an English clergyman. Steele followed him to Oxford two years later but left the university before graduating and

Spotlight On

This feature provides an overview of two great eighteenth-century essayists and includes three excerpts from the periodicals they founded. The first excerpt from *The Spectator* emphasizes the superiority of language over pageantry to evoke the imagination. The two excerpts from *The Tatler* offer an amusing dialogue between Adam and Eve on who was at fault in the Garden of Eden.

RESPONDING TO THE ART

Sir Godfrey Kneller (1646–1723), appointed court painter in 1680, produced portraits of six English monarchs, from Charles II to George I, as well as members of their courts. He satisfied his patrons with flattering portraits, although many were finished in assembly-line fashion by his assistants.

Activity. Invite students to point out the similarities in the two portraits.

Ⓐ Appreciating Language

Evolving Meanings

The literary meaning of the word *wit* has evolved over the centuries. In the Renaissance, it described a writer's ability to create metaphor by discovering similarities between apparently dissimilar things. By 1700, it had taken on the added meaning of the ability to express ideas elegantly. Alexander Pope defines *wit* in his *Essay on Criticism* (1711) as "What oft was Thought but ne'er so well Exprest."

Reaching All Students

Struggling Readers

Have students preview this feature, looking particularly at the subheadings of its three sections. Ask them to create prereading questions based on the subheadings and to write the questions in their reading notes. They should leave room after each question for a response based on their reading. Encourage them to generate two or more questions for each heading.

English Language Learners

English language learners will benefit from taking turns reading all or part of the feature aloud in class. For more instructional strategies for English language learners, see

- *Lesson Plans Including Strategies for English-Language Learners.*

Advanced Learners

After students have read the brief excerpts from *The Spectator* and *The Tatler*, ask them to speculate about Addison and Steele's perceptions of their readers, and to do the same for Daniel Defoe. Have them contrast these writers' views of their reading public and notice how their views of their audiences affect the writers' content and style.

Ⓐ Humanities Connections

After the accession of King George I, one of Steele's interesting posts was that of supervisor of the famed Drury Lane Theater, where David Garrick later made his reputation as an actor.

Ⓑ Reading Skills and Strategies

Connecting with the Text

? Who among your friends has a temperament that is the opposite of yours? [Most students will be able to provide an example.] Why might people with dissimilar personalities enjoy each other's company and work well together? [Possible responses: We all admire in others qualities we lack; dissimilar people complement each other.]

Ⓒ Literary Connections

Samuel Johnson praised Addison in his *Lives of the Poets* (1781), saying "Whoever wishes to attain an English style . . . must give his days and nights to the volumes of Addison." In contrast, Alexander Pope condemned him through the character of Atticus in *An Epistle to Dr. Arbuthnot* (1735). As a critic, Atticus would

Damn with faint praise, assent with civil leer.
And without sneering, teach the rest to sneer.
Willing to wound, and yet afraid to strike,
Just hint at fault, and hesitate dislike;
Alike reserved to blame or to commend,
A timorous foe and a suspicious friend.

returned to London, where he became an officer in the Life Guards, the royal escort unit, and a young man about town. After serving in the army at home and abroad, Steele devoted himself to politics, journalism, and managing a theater. He even became a member of Parliament, and for a time edited the *London Gazette*, the government's official newspaper. A warmhearted, jovial, impulsive man, and a devoted husband, Steele was often short of money. Ⓐ Being knighted by George I in 1715 did not make him any richer. In debt and suffering from a stroke, he was thoroughly miserable during the last years of his life.

Ⓑ Joseph Addison (1672–1719) was a different sort of man, with a reputation for being cold and haughty. After receiving bachelor's and master's degrees from Oxford, he wrote poems and dedicated them to various statesmen in hopes of advancing his career in government. Eventually his talents were noticed, and he was elected to Parliament, finally becoming secretary of state. Both Steele and Addison wrote plays, but Steele's, characteristically, were comedies. Addison's most successful play, *Cato*—an immensely successful tragedy first performed in 1713—was a history of Rome Ⓒ that referred to contemporary politics. In politics and literature Addison was successful, but his final years were as troubled as Steele's. Addison quarreled with, and died without being reconciled to, his partner Steele and his good friends Jonathan Swift and Alexander Pope.

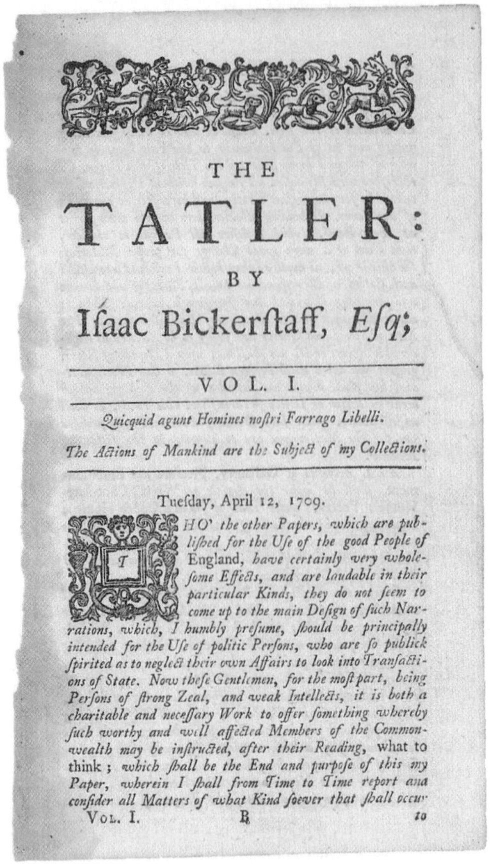
THE

TATLER:

BY

Iſaac Bickerſtaff, *Eſq;*

VOL. I.

Quicquid agunt Homines noſtri Farrago Libelli.

The Actions of Mankind are the Subject of my Collections.

Tueſday, April 12, 1709.

T*HO' the other Papers, which are publiſhed for the Uſe of the good People of* England, *have certainly very wholeſome Effects, and are laudable in their particular Kinds, they do not ſeem to come up to the main Deſign of ſuch Narrations, which, I humbly preſume, ſhould be principally intended for the Uſe of politic Perſons, who are ſo publick ſpirited as to neglect their own Affairs to look into Tranſactions of State. Now theſe Gentlemen, for the moſt part, being Perſons of ſtrong Zeal, and weak Intellects, it is both a charitable and neceſſary Work to offer ſomething whereby ſuch worthy and well affected Members of the Commonwealth may be inſtructed, after their Reading,* what to think; *which ſhall be the End and purpoſe of this my Paper, wherein I ſhall from Time to Time report and conſider all Matters of what Kind ſoever that ſhall occur*

VOL. I. B *to*

Opening page of *The Tatler*, volume I (1709).

A brief but remarkable partnership. Addison and Steele wrote more than nine hundred essays during their partnership; these essays remain the pair's most enduring work. The first issue of *The Tatler* promised current reports from reliable sources. For example, they claimed that new poetry would come straight from Will's Coffeehouse; St. James's Coffeehouse would provide current events; accounts of "gallantry, pleasure, and entertainment" would be obtained from White's Chocolate House. In other words, the paper promised the city's best gossip in a single printed sheet. In the first issue of *The Tatler*, Steele said, "The general purpose of this paper is to expose the false arts of life, to pull off the disguises of cunning, vanity, and affectation, and to recommend a general simplicity in our dress, our discourse, and our behavior." And in issue Number 10 of *The Spectator*, Addison said, "I shall endeavor to enliven morality with wit and temper wit with morality."

Addison and Steele were both ardent Whigs, a political party that supported reforms opposed by the conservative Tories. However, their periodicals practiced moderation when commenting on public affairs. Their essays sought to educate the new reading public of upper-class women and prosperous merchants on matters of taste, style, and politics. In Addison's words, *The Spectator*'s goal was to bring "philosophy out of the closets and libraries, schools and colleges, to dwell in clubs and assemblies, at tea tables and in coffeehouses."

One way Addison made philosophy more accessible was by critiquing entertainment. He reviewed popular stage productions, asking why "the

Using Students' Strengths

Interpersonal Learners

Have students work in small groups to create dialogue for a dramatic scene set in a present-day coffeehouse or meeting place. They may model their coffeehouse on the ones frequented by Addison and Steele or on a meeting place to which students go to talk. They should create an informal script in which participants use wit and critical intelligence as they discuss a topic of current interest. Have each group enact its scene for the class.

Intrapersonal Learners

Have students write letters to the authors in which they demonstrate their knowledge of the historical period by mentioning literary and historical facts that they have acquired through their reading. The letters may also include questions directed to Addison and Steele about the authors' lives, times, and writing careers.

ordinary method of making a hero is to clap a huge plume of feathers upon his head." "One would believe," reasons *The Spectator,* "that we thought a great man and a tall man the same thing." The essay urged readers to look beyond scenery and costume and to explore the power of their own imagination:

> A good poet will give the reader a more lively idea of an army or a battle in a description, than if he actually saw them drawn up in squadrons and battalions, or engaged in the confusion of a fight. Our minds should be opened to great conceptions and inflamed with glorious sentiments by what the actor speaks, more than by what he appears. Can all the trappings or equipage of a king or hero give Brutus half that pomp and majesty which he receives from a few lines in Shakespeare?
>
> —from *The Spectator*

Addison and Steele's original combination of satire and sentiment resulted in playful essays such as *The Tatler's* Number 217. This essay comments on marital relations with a clever "translation" of Milton's *Paradise Lost:* In Addison and Steele's version, Adam upbraids Eve by complaining:

> Madam, if my advices had been of any authority with you when that strange desire of gadding possessed you this morning, we had still been happy: But your cursed vanity and opinion of your own conduct . . . has ruined both yourself, and me who trusted you.
>
> —from *The Tatler*

Eve's rebuttal protests:

(D)

> Was I to have been always at your side, I might as well have continued there, and been but your rib still: But if I was so weak a creature as you thought me, why did you not interpose your sage authority more absolutely? . . . Had you not been too easy, neither you or I had now transgressed.
>
> —from *The Tatler*

The editors gently, wryly show their readers the folly of domestic strife while advising a moderate path that will avoid "conjugal enmity." Their essays could ridicule bad puns or ponder the nature of true literary "genius." The only constant in their coverage was an intolerance for vanity and excess.

Steele and Addison's collaboration in *The Tatler* and *The Spectator* expanded the genre of the periodical essay with a blend of humor and instruction. In addition, the partnership left a detailed literary record of eighteenth-century society and thought. Their essays are models of insight, wit, and common sense that compel readers of any age.

Stockjobbers Extraordinary (18th century), satirical sketch by Robert Dighton.
Guildhall Library. Corporation of London.

RESPONDING TO THE ART

Robert Dighton (1752–1814) was a painter, caricaturist, and writer who gained fame by creating caricatures of famous people. In this caricature, he makes fun of a profession—stockbroking. (*Stockjobber* is British slang for "stockbroker.")

Activity. What features and behaviors of these men does the artist choose to exaggerate in his caricature? [Possible responses: their sour frowns, their large hands, their intense absorption in money and news, their plumpness.] How does the tone of Dighton's art fit with that of the writing of Addison and Steele? [Possible response: Like the cartoonist, Addison and Steele use wit and satire.]

(D) Critical Thinking

Synthesizing

? Review the story of the fall of man in Genesis (p. 418). How does Eve explain her mistake? [Possible response: She blames the serpent.] How does Adam explain his mistake? [Possible response: He blames Eve.] How does this compare with the exchange of accusations that Addison and Steele include in *The Tatler?* [Possible response: Adam and Eve blame one another.] Struggling Readers may need help paraphrasing the *Tatler* exchange between Adam and Eve. This discussion may be broadened for all students by introducing Milton's version of the exchange of accusations in *Paradise Lost*, Book IX, ll. 1134–1161.

Getting Students Involved

Cooperative Learning

Writing a Periodical Essay. Prepare a series of topic sheets, each with a topic of current interest and a list of questions that might be asked about it. Create groups of three to four students with a mix of learning styles in each group and randomly distribute the topic sheets. Each group can create their own issue of *The Spectator* or *The Tatler* centered on the topic they have been assigned. Encourage the inclusion of artwork and original cartoons.

Assessing Learning

Check Test: Questions and Answers

1. What form did most of Addison and Steele's work take? [essay form]
2. Where was their work usually published? [in *The Spectator* and *The Tatler*]
3. How did the temperaments of the two writers differ? [Steele was warm and friendly; Addison, cold and calculating.]
4. What was their stated writing purpose? [to teach morality in an amusing way]
5. What other accomplishments did the two writers have? [Each wrote individual works and held public positions.]

OBJECTIVES

From *A Dictionary . . .* / Letter to Lord Chesterfield

1. Read and interpret the dictionary entries and letter
2. Identify and analyze the author's style
3. Express understanding through critical and creative writing
4. Learn and use new words

SKILLS

Literary
- Identify and analyze style

Writing
- Analyze character
- Analyze tone
- Create dictionary definitions
- Rewrite a letter by Johnson

Vocabulary
- Learn and use new words

Viewing/Representing
- Analyze a painting (ATE)

Planning

- **Block Schedule**
  Block Scheduling Lesson Plans with Pacing Guide
- **Traditional Schedule**
  Lesson Plans Including Strategies for English-Language Learners
- **One-Stop Planner**
  CD-ROM with Test Generator

BROWSING IN THE FILES

Writers on Writing. Johnson once said, "The only end of writing is to enable the readers better to enjoy life, or better to endure it." He was clearly aware of the fragile relationship between language and the reality it aims to represent, for he wrote in the preface to his *Dictionary,* "I am not so lost in lexicography as to forget that words are the daughters of earth and that things are the sons of heaven."

Samuel Johnson

(1709–1784)

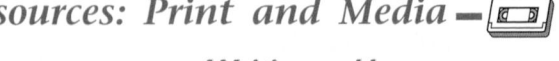

Samuel Johnson (detail) (1756) by an unknown artist.
Private Collection.

Samuel Johnson was the dominant literary figure in England during the latter part of the eighteenth century. Johnson is famous not for one or two masterpieces, but for a great variety of writings and for three large projects: *A Dictionary of the English Language* (1755); an edition of Shakespeare's plays (1765) with an important critical preface and useful notes; and *The Lives of the Poets* (1779–1781) in ten volumes, a series of biographical-critical introductions. A wise man, a moralist, a talker, an eminent writer and critic, a beloved friend of people rich, poor, young, and old, Johnson became in his own day an English institution. Even today, his personality is vivid because so many of his contemporaries recorded their impressions of him. We think of him as a large, imposing person of untidy appearance and odd mannerisms, very fond of drinking tea and of discoursing with his friends on just about every subject that concerns human beings.

Of course, he was not always like that. Johnson's beginnings were humble and unpromising. The son of an unsuccessful bookseller in the small city of Lichfield, he was a puny, weak infant who suffered from the effects of smallpox and scrofula, an infection of the lymph glands of the neck, which made him blind in one eye and deaf in one ear.

Despite his early weaknesses, Johnson grew into a sturdy youth, gradually exhibiting the qualities that characterized him as an adult: vigor, courage, pride, bossiness, and dedication to learning. He had to leave Oxford after only one year because he lacked money to continue; after that, he was spectacularly unsuccessful as a teacher in a private school. In 1737, Johnson moved to London with his wife, Elizabeth Porter, a widow twenty years his senior, whom he called Tetty and loved passionately.

While Johnson was struggling for recognition as a writer, he became addicted to the city life in London and began to disparage life in the countryside and provincial cities. "There is in London," he once said, "all that life can afford"; and "When a man is tired of London, he is tired of life."

Gradually Johnson's days of poverty and obscurity came to an end. In 1750, a series of essays called *The Rambler* made him famous as "a teacher of moral and religious wisdom," to quote his biographer, James Boswell. Meanwhile, his remarkable *Dictionary* had been published. And in 1762, in recognition of his services to literature, Johnson received a life pension from King George III—an English monarch that most Americans have heard of.

Johnson shared his prosperity with others, for he was always a devout man and his religion required him to be charitable. He also could not stand to be alone, with no one to talk to. He numbered among his intimates the painter Sir Joshua Reynolds, the statesman Edmund Burke, the historian Edward Gibbon, the musicologist Dr. Charles Burney, and his fellow writer Oliver Goldsmith.

Unlike most habitual talkers, Johnson attracted people because he talked so well. He also liked to be asked questions, so that his talk was never a monologue. His words came out in beautifully rounded sentences, just as though he were writing. Many people offered him their hospitality, especially Henry and Hester Thrale, a rich brewer and his wife. After Johnson's death, Mrs. Thrale published her *Anecdotes* about him, in which she said "No man loved laughing better."

go.hrw.com LEO 12-7

Resources: Print and Media

Reading
- *Graphic Organizers for Active Reading,* pp. 44, 45
- *Words to Own,* p. 16
- *Audio CD Library*
  Disc 10, Tracks 2, 3

Elements of Literature
- *Literary Elements*
  Transparency 15
  Worksheet, p. 46

Writing and Language
- *Daily Oral Grammar*
  Transparencies 19, 20

Assessment
- *Formal Assessment,* p. 103
- *Portfolio Management System,* p. 144
- *Test Generator (One-Stop Planner CD-ROM)*

Internet
- go.hrw.com (keyword: LE0 12-7)

Before You Read

FROM A DICTIONARY OF THE ENGLISH LANGUAGE

Background

Johnson's *Dictionary*—the first comprehensive and authoritative one in English—contains about 40,000 words and many, many definitions. The verb *to take,* for instance, has one hundred thirteen different meanings, and *to set,* sixty-six. Most of these definitions Johnson wrote himself; those he took from the wordbooks of his predecessors he is careful to identify. Before Johnson's time, academies of scholars in France and in Italy had produced large dictionaries of French and Italian, but there was no such academy in England. Therefore, Johnson took on the job himself; England must have its own dictionary, and Johnson was the man to write it!

How did he do it? First, he read an enormous number of literary, religious, philosophical, scientific, and technical books, most of them borrowed from friends. As he read, he marked passages and underlined a key word in each passage; this was the word he intended to define. Next, his copyists—he had six of them, all Scotsmen except one—copied out the marked passages on slips of paper and filed each slip alphabetically according to the key word. The slips were pasted into eighty large notebooks. Finally, using the passages, Johnson wrote definitions of the key words. There were originally about 240,000 passages—too many to be printed. When the *Dictionary* was finally put out in 1755 by a combination of five publishing firms, it contained about 114,000 illustrative passages in two volumes.

Johnson's *Dictionary* was, and is, a prodigious accomplishment. Forty members of the French Academy worked for forty years on the French dictionary; Johnson and his six copyists worked for about nine years on the English one. The *Dictionary* made Johnson's name familiar to every literate person in England and the American Colonies. It was the basis of all subsequent English dictionaries, including those of the American Noah Webster (1758–1843), who did little else in his lifetime except compile dictionaries that contained thousands of definitions and illustrative quotations taken without acknowledgment from Johnson. Johnson's *Dictionary* was not completely superseded until 1928, when the last of the ten volumes of *A New English Dictionary* was published. This work, revised in twenty volumes, is now called *The Oxford English Dictionary* (*OED*).

Although more comprehensive dictionaries have since been produced, Johnson's *Dictionary* lives on because it reflects its author's interesting character and sense of humor. None of the selections given here is a complete entry; there are no etymologies or origins of the words, no definitions reflecting the various shades of meaning, and few illustrative quotations. For an example of a complete definition, see the entry below for the words *giggle* and *giggler.*

To GI'GGLE. *v. n.* [*gichgelen,* Dutch.] To laugh idly; to titter; to grin with merry levity. It is retained in Scotland.
GI'GGLER. *n. ſ.* [from *giggle.*] A laugher; a titterer; one idly and fooliſhly merry.

A ſad wiſe valour is the brave complexion,
That leads the van, and ſwallows up the cities:
The *giggler* is a milk-maid, whom infection,
Or the fir'd beacon, frighteth from his ditties. *Herbert.*

We ſhew our preſent, joking, *giggling* race;
True joy conſiſts in gravity and grace. *Garrick's Epilogue.*

Summary

These definitions are from the first comprehensive dictionary of English, which was compiled over a nine-year period by Samuel Johnson and six assistants. Published in 1755, Johnson's dictionary defined about 140,000 words and included parts-of-speech designations, etymologies, variant meanings, and illustrative examples from professional writers. Unlike the anonymous committees who compile today's dictionaries, Johnson reveals his character and expresses his opinions in his dictionary. His definitions have a personal, idiosyncratic tone, often revealing his political preferences (see *pension*) and social prejudices (see *mushroom*), as well as his wit, humor, and erudition. Johnson also feels free to designate a word as "low" or "cant," based on his own sensibilities, whereas modern lexicographers would rely on community usage patterns, not on their own judgment, to rate a word's acceptability. Precisely because of its subjectivity, Johnson's dictionary provides a window on his personality and on the age in which he lived, revealing the strengths and limitations of both.

Resources

Listening

Audio CD Library

A recording of this selection is provided in the *Audio CD Library:*

- Disc 10, Track 2

Ⓐ Critical Thinking

Interpreting

? Based on this entry, do you think Samuel Johnson truly admires athletic people? [Possible responses: Yes, because of the positive adjectives he includes in the definition. No, because the quotation he includes from Dryden calls them brutes.]

Ⓑ Vocabulary Note

Word Origins

Students may easily infer how Johnson's understanding of this word relates to our modern medical definition of *autopsy.*

Ⓒ Vocabulary Note

Latin Roots

Companion is from the Latin prefix *com-* ("with") and *panis* ("bread"). Sharing bread with someone is a token of friendship; Johnson chose an unlikely citation and an unexpected definition.

Ⓓ Cultural Connections

Language and Gender

? Why does the author call this "a woman's word?" [Possible response: perhaps it was used most often by women.] **Do men and women use distinct vocabularies in our own times?** [Responses will vary. Examples of differences may include jargon and slang.]

Ⓔ Elements of Literature

Echoic Words/Onomatopoeia

As Samuel Johnson recognizes, *hiss* is an example of what modern lexicographers call an echoic word. Writers, especially poets, choose such words to create the sound effect called onomatopoeia.

from A Dictionary of the English Language

Samuel Johnson

alligator. The crocodile. This name is chiefly used for the crocodile of America, between which, and that of Africa, naturalists have laid down this difference, that one moves the upper, and the other the lower jaw; but this is now known to be chimerical,[1] the lower jaw being equally moved by both.

to apricate. To bask in the sun.

Ⓐ **athletick.** Strong of body; vigorous; lusty; robust.

> Science distinguishes a man of honor from one of those *athletick* brutes, whom undeservedly we call heroes.
>
> —Dryden.

Ⓑ **autopsy.** Ocular demonstration; seeing a thing oneself.

balderdash. Anything jumbled together without judgment; rude mixture; a confused discourse.

bedpresser. A heavy lazy fellow.

> This sanguine coward, this *bedpresser,* this horseback-breaker, this huge hill of flesh.
>
> —Shakespeare, *Henry IV,* Part 1.

to blab. To tell what ought to be kept secret.

board. A piece of wood of more length and breadth than thickness.

to budge. To stir; to move off the place: a low word.

catsup. A kind of pickle, made from mushrooms.

Ⓒ **companion.** A familiar term of contempt; a fellow.

> I scorn you, scurvy *companion*! What? you poor, base, rascally, cheating, lack-linen mate: Away, you moldy rogue, away.
>
> —Shakespeare, *Henry IV,* Part 2.

cough. A convulsion of the lungs, vellicated by some sharp serosity. It is pronounced *coff.*

dedication. A servile address to a patron.

den. A cavern or hollow running horizontally, or with a small obliquity, underground; distinct from a hole, which runs down perpendicularly.

dull. Not exhilarating; not delightful; as, *to make dictionaries is* dull *work.*

eel. A serpentine, slimy fish that lurks in mud.

essay. A loose sally of the mind; an irregular indigested piece; not a regular and orderly composition.

excise. A hateful tax levied upon commodities, and adjudged not by the common judges of property, but wretches hired by those to whom excise is paid.

favorite. One chosen as a companion by his superior; a mean wretch whose whole business is by any means to please.

fillip. A jerk of the finger let go from the thumb.

Ⓓ **frightfully.** Disagreeably; not beautifully. A woman's word.

fun. (A low cant[2] word.) Sport; high merriment; frolicsome delight.

gambler. (A cant word, I suppose, for *game* or *gamester.*) A knave whose practice it is to invite the unwary to game and cheat them.

goose. A large waterfowl proverbially noted, I know not why, for foolishness.

gravy. The serous juice that runs from flesh not much dried by the fire.

> They usually boil and roast their meat until it falls almost off from the bones; but we love it half raw, with the blood trickling down from it, delicately terming it the *gravy,* which in truth looks more like an ichorous or raw bloody matter.
>
> —Harvey, *On Consumptions.*

Ⓔ **to hiss.** To utter a noise like that of a serpent and some other animals. It is remarkable, that this word cannot be pronounced without making the noise which it signifies.

1. **chimerical** (kī·mer′i·kəl): fanciful.

2. **cant:** a word Johnson uses to describe language he disapproves of because he perceives it to be of base origins.

Reaching All Students

Struggling Readers

Remind students that Johnson's entries appear without some of their components, including the part of speech. Have students supply the part of speech for words that are in current use and then check their accuracy in an up-to-date dictionary. They will notice that some words (for example *board* and *excise*) are designated in today's dictionaries as more than one part of speech.

English Language Learners

Help students identify entries in Johnson's *Dictionary* that live on as familiar words in present-day English. Have them look up the current meanings in their dictionaries and compare and contrast them with Johnson's definitions. For additional strategies to supplement instruction, see

- *Lesson Plans Including Strategies for English-Language Learners*

Advanced Learners

Ask students to write in their reading notes some examples of slang terms that have declined in popularity in the course of their experience, as well as examples of the newest popular slang. Encourage them to speculate about how slang vocabulary originates and how it declines. Ask them to relate these ideas to entries Johnson identifies as "low" and "cant" words.

immaterial. (1) Incorporeal; void of matter. (2) Unimportant; without weight; impertinent; without relation. This sense has crept into the conversation and writings of barbarians; but ought to be utterly rejected.

jogger. One who moves heavily and dully.

lexicographer. A writer of dictionaries; a harmless drudge, that busies himself in tracing the original, and detailing the signification of words.

to lift. To rob; to plunder.

lingo. Language; tongue; speech. A low cant word.

lunch, luncheon. As much food as one's hand can hold.

merrythought. A forked bone on the body of fowls; so called because boys and girls pull in play at the two sides, the longest part broken off betokening priority of marriage.

mouth. (1) The aperture in the head of any animal at which the food is received. . . . (4) A speaker; a rhetorician; the principal orator. In burlesque language.

> Every coffeehouse has some particular statesman belonging to it, who is the *mouth* of the street where he lives.
>
> —Addison.

mushroom. An upstart; a wretch risen from the dunghill; a director of a company.

network. Anything reticulated or decussated, at equal distances, with interstices between the intersections.

osprey. The sea-eagle, of which it is reported, that when he hovers in the air, all the fish in the water turn up their bellies, and lie still for him to seize which he pleases.

parody. A kind of writing, in which the words of an author or his thoughts are taken, and by a slight change adapted to some new purpose.

pastern. The knee of a horse.

pat. Fit; convenient; exactly suitable either as to time or place. This is a low word, and should not be used but in burlesque writings.

Dr. Samuel Johnson's house, City of London.
The house was designed by Johnson in the 18th century.

patron. One who countenances, supports, or protects. Commonly a wretch who supports with insolence, and is paid with flattery.

pension. An allowance made to anyone without an equivalent. In England it is generally understood to mean pay given to a state hireling for treason to his country.

to period. To put an end to. A bad[3] word.

pompous. Splendid; magnificent; grand.

rhinoceros. A vast beast in the East Indies armed with a horn in his front.

river. A land current of water bigger than a brook.

romance. A tale of wild adventures in war and love.

3. **bad:** low; vulgar.

F Reading Skills and Strategies

Making Inferences

? What does this entry tell us about the character of Samuel Johnson? [Possible responses: He is humble; he is making a joke at his own expense; he encourages his readers to be skeptical about the authority of the *Dictionary*.] Which other entry has a similar impact? [*dull*]

G English Language Learners

Idiom

Point out that *merrythought* is a colorful British equivalent for what Americans call the *wishbone*. English language learners may need to have the custom of pulling apart wishbones explained in more detail. Invite volunteers to describe wishing customs in their native cultures.

H Reading Skills and Strategies

Making Generalizations

? In which other entries does Johnson give implausible or questionable information about animals? [Possible responses: alligator, eel, torpedo, whale.] What does this tell us about his education and background? [Possible responses: This is an area of weakness in his vast storehouse of knowledge. It also is indicative of the low level of scientific knowledge in his time.]

I Critical Thinking

Recognizing Bias

? What does Samuel Johnson think of patrons (those who use their wealth to support artists and writers)? [Patrons act for selfish reasons. Patrons turn those they support into flatterers.] In which other entries is a similar bias revealed? [Possible responses: *dedication, favorite, pension*.] Johnson himself hesitated to accept a pension from King George III in 1762.

Using Students' Strengths

Logical/Mathematical Learners

Forty French scholars took forty years to produce the French dictionary; Johnson and his six assistants took nine years and developed 240,000 passages. Have students use the statistics provided to work out a probable work schedule for Johnson and his team. How many books might Johnson have read? How many entries per day might he have written?

Kinesthetic Learners

Divide the class into teams for a game of charades. Write selected terms from Johnson's *Dictionary* on slips of paper. Choose entries that lend themselves to pantomime, such as *romp*. Have students from one team draw a slip at random and act out the designated term, according to Johnson's definition. Have members of the opposing team identify the term being enacted.

Verbal/Linguistic Learners

Before students finish reading the selection, provide them with a list of the words included in the excerpt, without Johnson's definitions. Ask them to predict the definitions Johnson will provide. After reading the selection, have them check their predictions against the actual *Dictionary* entries.

A Critical Thinking

Making Connections

? What writers would be likely to disagree with Johnson when he writes that the sonnet is unsuitable to English? [Possible responses: Spenser, Shakespeare, Milton.]

B Critical Thinking

Interpreting

? What comparison between England and Scotland is Johnson implying? [Possible responses: People in Scotland are poor; people in Scotland are inferior and eat food fit only for horses.]

MAKING MEANINGS

First Thoughts [Respond]

1. Responses will vary. Encourage students to explain their answers in detail.

Shaping Interpretations [Interpret]

2. Possible responses: *alligator, catsup, companion, essay, jogger, mushroom, osprey, to sneeze, torpedo, whale.*
3. Possible response: He considers people who use such words inferior.
4. Possible responses: Johnson's personality emerges through his opinionated and humorous definitions. Many entries show playful or sardonic humor, such as those for *hiss, lunch,* and *osprey.* Political and religious preferences are shown in the entries for *excise, oats, tory,* and *whig.*
5. Possible responses: Language changes with popular use. Words may gain acceptance as more people use them, such as *fun,* which is no longer considered slang. Words, such as *lunch,* may change as customs and habits change.

Connecting with the Text [Synthesize]

6. Many entries, including *autopsy, companion, essay, favorite, jogger,* and *vivacious,* have changed drastically.

Challenging the Text [Evaluate]

7. Students' responses will vary but should demonstrate the understanding that an entire society—not individual people—maintains and changes language. New dictionaries require years of work by many contributors.

to romp. To play rudely, noisily, and boisterously.

> A stool is the first weapon taken up in a general *romping* or skirmish.
>
> —Swift, *Rules to Servants.*

smoke. The visible effluvium, or sooty exhalation from anything burning.

to sneeze. To emit wind audibly by the nose.

A **sonnet.** A short poem consisting of fourteen lines, of which the rhymes are adjusted by a particular rule. It is not very suitable to the English language, and has not been used by any man of eminence since Milton.

soup. Strong decoction[4] of flesh for the table.

stammel. Of this word I know not the meaning.

suds. A lixivium[5] of soap and water.

tiny. Little; small; puny. A burlesque word.

tittletattle. Idle talk; prattle; empty gabble.

torpedo. A fish which while alive, if touched even with a long stick, benumbs the hand that so touches it, but when dead is eaten safely.

tory. (A cant term, derived, I suppose, from an Irish word signifying a savage.) One who adheres to the ancient constitution of the state, and the apostolical hierarchy of the Church of England, opposed to a whig.

to traipse. (A low word, I believe, without any etymology.) To walk in a careless or sluttish manner.

tree. A large vegetable rising, with one woody stem, to a considerable height.

unkindly. Unnatural; contrary to nature.

vivacious. Long-lived.

whale. The largest of fish.

whig. The name of a faction.

to worm. To deprive a dog of something, nobody knows what, under his tongue, which is said to prevent him, nobody knows why, from running mad.

zed. The name of the letter *z.*

4. **decoction** (dē·käk′shən): extract made by boiling a substance down to its essence.
5. **lixivium** (liks·iv′ē·əm): mixture; solution.

B **OATS.** *n. ſ.* [aten, Saxon.] A grain, which in England is generally given to horſes, but in Scotland ſupports the people.

MAKING MEANINGS

First Thoughts

1. Which definition surprised or interested you the most? Explain your answer.

Shaping Interpretations

2. Which definitions contain what we would regard as errors of fact?
3. What is Johnson's attitude toward slang, which he calls "low words" or "cant"?
4. How does Johnson's personality come through in the voice of the *Dictionary*? Which definitions show the writer's sense of humor? Which show his political bias and religious preferences?
5. Based on your own experiences and the answers you gave to the preceding questions, what inferences can you make about language, especially about the way it changes? Cite examples from the *Dictionary* to support or illustrate your answers.

Connecting with the Text

6. How do these entries compare with entries for the same words in your current dictionary?

Challenging the Text

7. Who, in your opinion, should decide what a word means and how it is pronounced?

Assessing Learning

Check Test: True-False

1. Johnson's *Dictionary* was the first comprehensive English dictionary. [True]
2. Johnson derived most of his definitions from earlier dictionaries. [False]
3. Johnson read extensively in order to choose words and find definitions. [True]
4. Johnson's *Dictionary* was never imitated. [False]
5. Johnson colored many definitions with his own opinions. [True]

Standardized Test Preparation

For practice in proofreading and editing, see

- *Daily Oral Grammar,* Transparency 19

Before You Read

LETTER TO LORD CHESTERFIELD

Background

Long before Johnson completed work on his dictionary, he put out a pamphlet titled *Plan of a Dictionary of the English Language* (1747). The pamphlet was dedicated, at his publisher's suggestion, to Philip Dormer Stanhope, fourth earl of Chesterfield—an accomplished, rich, elegant, and learned nobleman. The publisher, Robert Dodsley, wanted Chesterfield's patronage, or financial support, of Johnson's *Dictionary,* a very expensive venture. But nothing came of the attempt to capture the great man's interest. Johnson even called on Chesterfield a few times, but he was denied entrance at least once. He received only a token contribution from Chesterfield: ten pounds.

In 1755, just before the finished dictionary actually appeared, Dodsley again approached Chesterfield, who by this time had probably forgotten all about the *Plan* and its dedication to him. After all, Chesterfield was a very busy and important man. This time he did respond, though not by giving money. Without ever having seen the dictionary, Chesterfield published two letters praising it in a weekly newspaper.

Johnson, not knowing that Dodsley had again approached Chesterfield, read the two generous letters with surprise and indignation. They could easily be misconstrued; the public might conclude that Chesterfield had given what today would be called a "grant" to Johnson. The letters put Johnson in an embarrassing position because he had asserted in the preface to the *Dictionary* that he had received no "patronage of the great." And so he wrote Chesterfield a letter that has since become famous. The letter's language is very formal; how would you describe its **tone**?

Dr. Johnson in the Anteroom of Lord Chesterfield Waiting for an Audience (1748) by Edward Matthew Ward.
Tate Gallery, London.

Make the Connection

Pride and Protest

Do wealthy and influential people today help struggling writers, artists, and scientists? What do they expect to gain, if anything, from such patronage?

Quickwrite

How would you feel if a wealthy person praised some work you had labored over, but he or she had never responded to your requests for help when you needed it? Jot down some notes on how you might respond.

Summary ■■■

As the Background on the pupil page explains, this letter was written to Philip Dormer Stanhope, Lord Chesterfield, who had ignored Johnson's repeated appeals for financial backing for the *Dictionary*, yet who, upon publication, created the impression that he had supported Johnson. Chesterfield's opportunistic letters of commendation naturally angered Johnson. In his response, Johnson therefore adopts a tone of dignified outrage, using irony and the metaphor of a drowning man to characterize Lord Chesterfield's endorsement as too little, too late. Although Johnson's style is restrained and elegant, the letter is clearly the rebuke of a man who had worked too long and too hard to share the credit for his solitary labor.

RESPONDING TO THE ART

Edward Matthew Ward (1816–1879), an English painter, specialized in what were known as "historical anecdotes." This is one of several he did that feature Dr. Johnson.

Activity. Ask students to identify Johnson in the painting and note details that suggest his personality and status in the group.

Preteaching Vocabulary

Words to Own

Have students locate the Words to Own and their definitions on the selection pages and copy them into their reading notes. Then ask them to work in pairs and use the words in informal narratives. (Suggest military or sports themes as good subjects for this group of words.) In a chart like the one at the right, ask students to fill in a synonym and an antonym for each of the vocabulary words.

Word	Synonym	Antonym
contending	[battling]	[agreeing]
repulsed	[rebuffed]	[attracted]
encumbers	[handicaps]	[aids]
impart	[give]	[withhold]
cynical	[doubting]	[trusting]

Resources

Listening

Audio CD Library

A recording of this selection is provided in the *Audio CD Library:*

- Disc 10, Track 3

Elements of Literature

Style: A Personal Mark

For additional instruction on style, see *Literary Elements:*

- Transparency 15

A Elements of Literature

Irony

? What is the difference between what Dr. Johnson writes in this first paragraph and what we know he actually thinks and feels? [Possible responses: He does not feel honored by Lord Chesterfield's writings. He knows exactly how he will answer, as the rest of the letter shows.]

B Elements of Literature

Allusion

Johnson's allusions to Nicolas Boileau and later to Virgil seem intended to offset Johnson's exaggerated humility and to remind Lord Chesterfield subtly of their intellectual equality.

C Vocabulary Note

Archaic Language

Point out to students that *suffer* here means "allow."

D Elements of Literature

Style

? What is the effect of this short, simple sentence after so much complex syntax? [Possible responses: It gets the reader's attention. It stresses Johnson's indignant tone and adds an ironic note of sadness.]

Letter to Lord Chesterfield

Samuel Johnson

To the Right Honorable the Earl of Chesterfield

February 7, 1755

My Lord:

A *I have been lately informed by the proprietor of the World,*[1] *that two papers, in which my Dictionary is recommended to the public, were written by your Lordship. To be so distinguished is an honor which, being very little accustomed to favors from the great, I know not well how to receive, or in what terms to acknowledge.*

B *When, upon some slight encouragement, I first visited your Lordship, I was overpowered, like the rest of mankind, by the enchantment of your address;*[2] *and could not forbear to wish that I might boast myself le vainqueur du vainqueur de la terre;*[3] *that I might obtain that regard for which I saw the world* ***contending****; but I found my attendance so little encouraged that neither pride nor modesty would* **C** *suffer me to continue it. When I had once addressed your Lordship in public, I had exhausted all the art of pleasing which a retired and uncourtly scholar can possess. I had done all that I could; and no man is well pleased to have his all neglected, be it ever so little.*

Seven years, my Lord, have now passed since I waited in your outward rooms, or was ***repulsed*** *from your door, during which time I have been pushing on my work through difficulties of which it is useless to complain, and have brought it, at last, to the verge of publication without one act of assistance, one word of encouragement, or one smile of favor.* **D** *Such treatment I did not expect, for I never had a patron before.*

The shepherd in Virgil[4] *grew at last acquainted with Love, and found him a native of the rocks.*

1. ***World:*** name of the newspaper in which Chesterfield (1694–1773) published his letters praising Johnson's *Dictionary*.

2. **address:** conversational manner or skill.

3. ***le vainqueur . . . terre:*** French for "the conqueror of the conqueror of the world." Chesterfield would have recognized that Johnson is quoting a famous line of a poem by the French poet Nicolas Boileau (1636–1711).

4. **the shepherd in Virgil:** In a pastoral poem by the Roman poet Virgil (70–19 B.C.), a shepherd discovers that love is unkind; Johnson similarly discovered that patrons are unkind.

Words to Own

contending (kən·tend′iŋ) *v.* used as *adj.:* competing; struggling.

repulsed (ri·pulst′) *v.:* driven away.

Reaching All Students

Struggling Readers

Call on a student to read aloud, stopping at the end of an independent clause (marked by a period or semicolon.) Then call on another student to paraphrase the sentence or clause just read. Give assistance and explanation as needed. When the whole letter has been read in this way, ask students to summarize its overall meaning orally. Then have them record their summaries in their reading notes.

English Language Learners

English differs from many other languages in its forms of negation. Johnson's angry tone prompts him to use negations liberally. Before reading the letter, have students review the negative elements in English by identifying them in the following sentences and rewriting the sentences to say the same thing without using any negative elements. In sentences 3 and 4, point out the effects of the double negatives.

1. **My sister has not finished sixth grade.** [not: My sister has yet to finish sixth grade.]
2. **The man was unaware of the flat tire.** [un-: The man believed he had good tires.]
3. **The two books are not dissimilar.** [not, dis-: The two books are similar.]
4. **She had no money for unnecessary items.** [no, un-: She had money for necessary items only.]
5. **None of their homework is difficult.** [None: Their homework is easy.]

Is not a patron, my Lord, one who looks with unconcern on a man struggling for life in the water, and, when he has reached ground, encumbers him with help? The notice which you have been pleased to take of my labors, had it been early, had been kind; but it has been delayed till I am indifferent, and cannot enjoy it; till I am solitary,[5] and cannot impart it; till I am known, and do not want[6] it. I hope it is no very cynical asperity[7] not to confess obligations where no benefit has been received, or to be unwilling that the public should consider me as owing that to a patron, which Providence has enabled me to do for myself. **E**

Having carried on my work thus far with so little obligation to any favorer of learning, I shall not be disappointed though I should conclude it, if less be possible, with less; for I have been long wakened from that dream of hope, in which I once boasted myself with so much exultation, my Lord, **F**

Your Lordship's most humble,
most obedient servant,

Sam. Johnson

5. **solitary:** Johnson's wife had been dead for three years.
6. **want:** need.
7. **asperity:** bitterness.

Words to Own

encumbers (en·kum′bərz) *v.:* burdens or hinders.
impart (im·pärt′) *v.:* share; tell.
cynical (sin′i·kəl) *adj.:* mistrustful.

Dr. Johnson, Mrs. Johnson, Mr. Garrick, and others assembled for a play performed by Samuel Richardson (1748) at The Pantiles, Tunbridge Wells. Engraving by Thomas Loggan.

E Reading Skills and Strategies
Reading Elliptical Constructions

Ask students to paraphrase ". . . had it been early, had been kind" with the omitted words supplied. [If it had been early, then it would have been kind.]

F Reading Skills and Strategies
Summarizing

? In your own words, summarize Johnson's opinions regarding patrons, as stated in this conclusion. [Possible responses: Do not rely on patrons; depend on yourself; it's better to achieve less than to owe somebody too much.]

Professional Notes

Johnson on Chesterfield

There is abundant evidence that Samuel Johnson was both deeply hurt and keenly angered by Lord Chesterfield's casual dismissal of the *Dictionary.* Johnson remarked at the time, "I have sailed a long and painful voyage round the world of the English language; and does he now send out two cockboats to tow me into harbor?" This sailing metaphor is similar to the drowning metaphor he employs in his letter.

MAKING MEANINGS

First Thoughts [Respond]

1. Possible responses: Writing the letter would make one feel powerful, courageous; it would provide a release for anger.

Shaping Interpretations [Interpret]

2. Possible response: Johnson's primary purpose was to set the record straight, although the pleasure of rebuking Chesterfield may have been a big factor.

3. Johnson uses irony in describing the "honor" he has been paid and in his definition of a patron. His tone is one of dignified reproach.

4. An "uncourtly scholar" is intelligent, curious, and studious but lacks important social and political connections.

5. Possible responses: Lord Chesterfield was humbled by Johnson's accusation; he admired the eloquence of the letter; he was a very fair-minded person; he enjoyed the connection with the newly famous Johnson.

Connecting with the Text [Apply]

6. Responses will vary. Encourage students to justify their chosen methods of protest and explain why the response they have chosen best fits the hypothetical situation.

> **Reading Check**
>
> **a.** Johnson stopped because the earl did not respond to his requests.
>
> **b.** Johnson ironically defines a patron as someone who offers help after it is no longer needed.
>
> **c.** He gives credit to Providence and his own hard work.
>
> **d.** He says that hope was a dream and implies that self-reliance is more valuable.

MAKING MEANINGS

First Thoughts

1. If you had been in Johnson's position, what kind of satisfaction would writing this letter have given you?

> **Reading Check**
>
> **a.** Johnson says that he had asked the earl for help, but then stopped. Why did he stop?
>
> **b.** How does Johnson define a patron?
>
> **c.** To whom does Johnson give credit for his accomplishment?
>
> **d.** What does Johnson say about hope at the letter's end?

Shaping Interpretations

2. What, apparently, was Johnson's motive in writing the letter? To set the record straight? To annoy Chesterfield? To rebuke him? To gloat over him?

3. Where in the letter does Johnson use **irony**? How would you describe the letter's **tone**?

4. Johnson refers to himself as an "uncourtly scholar." What traits does such a person typically possess?

5. Chesterfield did not take offense at the letter, but kept it lying on a table in his office where any visitor might read it. Why do you suppose he didn't become angry?

Connecting with the Text

6. Review your Quickwrite notes. What kind of complaint would you make to someone who had failed to help you when you needed it or had praised you for work he or she had once refused to support? Would you write a letter, as Johnson did, or would your protest take another form? Explain your answer.

ELEMENTS OF LITERATURE

Style: A Personal Mark

Like most important writers, Johnson developed an individual style, a way of writing and speaking like nobody else's. Johnson's style is more complicated than the plain, simple style of Swift. Johnson ordinarily wrote long but carefully constructed sentences, like this one from the preface to his *Dictionary:*

> Such is the exuberance of signification which many words have obtained, that it was scarcely possible to collect all their senses; sometimes the meaning of derivatives must be sought in the mother term, and sometimes deficient explanations of the primitive may be supplied in the train of derivation.

This sentence illustrates Johnson's fondness for

1. longish **words of Latin derivation:** *exuberance, signification, derivatives, deficient, explanations.*
2. **parallel structure:** the two clauses beginning *sometimes.*
3. **exact expression:** The words *exuberance of signification* may sound strange, but they say exactly what Johnson means.

Like Sir Francis Bacon in the Renaissance, Johnson could also sum up an idea in a very few words so that it has the sound of an **adage** or **proverb:**

> If you are idle, be not solitary; if you are solitary, be not idle.

Notice how the first part of this sentence is both balanced against and contrasted with the second. Here are two more sentences by Johnson in which the contrasts are held in balance:

> Let me smile with the wise, and feed with the rich.
>
> Marriage has many pains, but celibacy has no pleasures.

But at times Johnson could be pompous and wordy. Instead of saying "Charity begins at home," he would say, "A man should first relieve those who are nearly connected to him, by whatever tie; and

ELEMENTS OF LITERATURE

Possible Responses

1. From the *Dictionary* definition of *network*: *reticulated* and *decussated.*

2. From the letter: "The notice which you have been pleased to take of my labors, had it been early, had been kind; but it has been delayed till I am indifferent, and cannot enjoy it; till I am solitary, and cannot impart it; till I am known, and do not want it."

3. From the letter: *cynical asperity.*

4. From the *Dictionary*: "**romance.** A tale of wild adventures in war and love."

5. From the letter: "Is not a patron, my Lord, one who looks with unconcern on a man struggling for life in the water, and, when he has reached ground, encumbers him with help?"

Making the Connections

Connecting to the Subject: "An Appetite for Experience"

On p. 573, students will find a photograph of Samuel Johnson's London home, which he himself designed. His career included a wide range of activities—social, political, scholarly, and literary—that reflect an appetite for experience. Ask students to discuss whether or not they think Johnson lived up to his own dictum: "It is better to live rich than to die rich."

then, if he has anything to spare, may extend his bounty to a wider circle."

And finally, like all great writers, Johnson is a master **inventor of metaphors.** During a conversation about Shakespeare and a forgotten minor writer, for instance, Johnson remarked, "We must not compare the noise made by your teakettle here with the roaring of the ocean."

Analyzing Johnson's style. Look at the *Dictionary* and the "Letter to Lord Chesterfield." Find at least one example of Johnson's use of

1. long, Latin-based words
2. parallel structure and balance in sentences
3. unusual, but exact, expressions
4. concise statements of ideas
5. strong metaphors

CHOICES: Building Your Portfolio

Writer's Notebook

1. Collecting Ideas for a Persuasive Essay

In his "Letter to Lord Chesterfield," Johnson uses **irony** to protest the unfair treatment he has received at the hands of a powerful person. What behavior of the rich or powerful would you like to protest, perhaps in a letter to the editor? You may want to develop the ideas you discussed in responding to question 6 on page 578. Freewrite ideas on how you might express your protest. Save your work for the Writer's Workshop on page 612.

Analyzing Character

2. The Man Behind the Pen

Study Johnson's definitions and his letter to Lord Chesterfield, and write a long paragraph in which you analyze the character of the man who wrote them. Consider these questions: What are his values? What are his likes and dislikes and biases? Is he proud? Is he capable of laughing at himself? Is he ever modest? Cite details from the *Dictionary* excerpts and the letter to illustrate your points.

Analyzing Tone

3. Killed with Kindness

Johnson's "Letter to Lord Chesterfield" is a masterpiece of the polite put-down. While Johnson's tone appears civilized and restrained, he is slyly savaging Lord Chesterfield. In a short essay, use quotations from the letter to illustrate how Johnson condemns Lord Chesterfield without appearing to utter an angry word.

Creative Writing

4. Imitating Johnson

Make your own dictionary of twenty words. In each entry, first give the part of speech; second, give at least one common definition; last, write a complete sentence that illustrates how the word is used. The only rule for this activity is that you can't look in a dictionary until after your definitions are finished. You might include these in your list of twenty: *apple, door, growl, nose, song, turtle.*

Creative Writing

5. Modernizing the Master

Johnson was a master of both written and oral language, and his "Letter to Lord Chesterfield" illustrates his formal writing style. Use a less formal, more contemporary style to rewrite Johnson's letter, retaining all of his meaning. You may restructure his sentences, but try to make your letter flow smoothly and sound pleasant to the ear.

Grading Timesaver

Rubrics for each Choices assignment appear on p. 144 in the *Portfolio Management System.*

CHOICES: Building Your Portfolio

1. **Writer's Notebook** Point out to students that irony is a formal, serious form of sarcasm. Encourage them to experiment with irony in their freewriting.
2. **Analyzing Character** Have students list answers to the questions, and then go to the texts in search of material to support their answers.
3. **Analyzing Tone** It will be helpful for students to begin by listing the various polite forms of address and formal compliments that Johnson includes in the letter.
4. **Creative Writing** Have students use a four-column graphic organizer when choosing their entries, with a column for the word, its part of speech, its definition, and a sentence demonstrating its use.
5. **Creative Writing** Students will find it useful to write a summary of Johnson's letter, clarifying each section, before they attempt to paraphrase it.

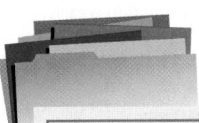

Spotlight On

This feature examines the evaluation of Shakespeare by two great English men of letters: John Dryden and Samuel Johnson. In excerpts from their critical writings, both men, writing in different centuries, extol Shakespeare's universality and fidelity to nature.

After discussing the feature, encourage interested students to do further research on related topics, including the neoclassical movement in France and England, the life and work of John Dryden, and the popularity of Shakespeare's plays over the centuries.

A Literary Connections

The pettiness of some of Shakespeare's critics is epitomized by Thomas Rymer (1641–1713) in *A Short View of Tragedy* (1693). Rymer criticized Othello's jealousy as improperly motivated and remarked that the lesson provided by the episode with Desdemona's handkerchief was that "ladies should look to their linen." Johnson called such censure "the petty cavils of petty minds."

B Literary Connections

Neoclassicism

Following the rediscovery of Aristotle's *Poetics* in the sixteenth century, admiration for and imitation of ancient Greek and Roman writers came to dominate European and British literature. The principles of neoclassicism dictated that the style should fit the subject matter and that art must both delight and instruct.

RESPONDING TO THE ART

William Hogarth (1697–1764) was an engraver and art critic as well as a painter. Tell students that *Richard III* relates the story of a man so determined to force his way onto the throne that he kills all his rivals, including his two young nephews. (For more art by Hogarth, see pp. 468, 473, 478, and 480.)

Activity. Ask students their opinions on why Hogarth chose to downplay Richard III's deformed back in this painting. Have each student select three specific details from Hogarth's painting and freewrite about their probable significance. Then discuss these in class.

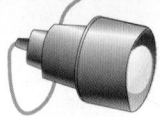

SPOTLIGHT ON

In Support of Shakespeare

Literature, like certain styles of clothing and music, moves in and out of fashion, and no less a writer than William Shakespeare fell victim to the trend toward neoclassical standards of order and taste. But two key writers of the age, John Dryden and Samuel Johnson, saw beyond contemporary fashion and helped reestablish Shakespeare's reputation with influential critical essays.

Dryden's case for Shakespeare. John Dryden (1631–1700)—poet, dramatist, critic, and translator of foreign works into English—was an all-around "man of letters," perhaps the first Englishman to deserve that title. Samuel Johnson himself called Dryden "the father of English criticism." Dryden's literary career spanned the last forty years of the seventeenth century, and he cast a long shadow into the eighteenth.

Dryden's lasting reputation is based on his critical writings, and the centerpiece of these is *Of Dramatic Poesy: An Essay* (1668), a work that includes his comments on Shakespeare. (The word *poesy* means "literature.") In order to appreciate Dryden's observations, remember that Shakespeare had been dead only fifty years when Dryden wrote this piece. Shakespeare's plays were not being studied in nearly every English-speaking school, read in translation all over the world, and constantly performed by profes-

David Garrick as Richard III (1745) by William Hogarth.

Board of Trustees of the National Museum and Galleries on Merseyside. Walker Art Gallery, Liverpool, England.

Using Students' Strengths

Verbal/Linguistic Learners

Have students look in local and national newspapers and magazines for examples of present-day criticism, including reviews of movies, plays, books, and musical recordings. Encourage them to look for reviews of works about which they have already formed their own opinions. Ask them to analyze the evidence reviewers use to praise or criticize the work.

Auditory Learners

Have students select short speeches or scenes from Shakespeare's plays that reflect the feeling and passion that Dryden and Johnson praise. (Alternatively, you can make the selections and assign them to students.) Ask students to rehearse their scenes and then present them to the class, attempting to portray the human feeling that Shakespeare reveals.

sionals and amateurs everywhere—as they are today. Shakespeare was then only one of the many dramatists of the preceding age and far from the most popular one. When Dryden praised Shakespeare highly, he was not echoing a commonly held opinion; he was advancing a new idea—that Shakespeare's genius is his ability to represent nature as it really is. (*Nature* here includes human nature as well as the natural universe.) In his trademark lucid prose, Dryden makes the case for Shakespeare in the passage below. C

> To begin, then, with Shakespeare: He was the man who, of all modern and perhaps ancient poets, had the largest and most comprehensive soul. All the images of nature were still [always] present to him, and he drew them not laboriously, but luckily; when he describes anything, you more than see it, you feel it too. Those who accuse him to have wanted [lacked] learning give him the greater commendation: He was naturally learned; he needed not the spectacles of books to read nature; he looked inwards, and found her there.
>
> —John Dryden, *from Of Dramatic Poesy: An Essay*

David Garrick in four of his principal tragic roles: Lear, Macbeth, Richard III, and Hamlet (detail) by an unknown artist.

Victoria and Albert Museum, London.

Johnson: defending the Bard. Nearly a century after Dryden argued for Shakespeare's universal appeal, Samuel Johnson published his now-famous *Preface to Shakespeare* in 1765. Following Dryden, Johnson also praises Shakespeare for his ability to render nature truthfully:

> Shakespeare is, above all writers, at least above all modern writers, the poet of nature; the poet that holds up to his readers a faithful mirror of manners and of life. His characters are not modified by . . . the accidents of transient fashions or temporary opinions: They are the genuine progeny of common humanity, such as the world will always supply and observation will always find. His persons act and speak by the influence of those general passions and principles by which all minds are agitated and the whole system of life is continued in motion. In the writings of other poets a character is too often an individual: In those of Shakespeare it is commonly a species. D
>
> —Samuel Johnson, *from Preface to Shakespeare*

Convinced of Shakespeare's preeminence as a dramatic poet, Johnson also refutes charges that Shakespeare took too many liberties with the three dramatic unities. These unofficial rules limited dramatists to representing only those events that occur in a single day at a single location, and forbade them to combine elements of tragedy and comedy in a single play. E Because he believed so strongly in the value of common sense and experience, Johnson contends that the "unities are not essential to a just drama," and that, especially in Shakespeare's case, "they are always to be sacrificed to the nobler beauties of variety and instruction."

Both Dryden and Johnson left considerable legacies to English literature. Perhaps, though, they are best remembered not just as writers but as eloquent speakers for an entire community of readers.

C Historical Connections

Restoration England

Although Shakespeare did not enjoy great popularity in Dryden's time, the London theater in general flourished in the years after 1660. Drama had been banned under the Puritans but was restored by Charles II. The lavish productions of the period were mainly enjoyed by aristocratic audiences. Principal writers included Dryden himself, George Etherege, William Wycherley, and William Congreve.

D Reading Skills and Strategies

Finding the Main Idea

Ask students to restate Johnson's words in simple, contemporary English and record their paraphrases in their reading notes. Have the class compare and discuss the kernels of meaning that individuals discover. Encourage students to add to their reading notes any additional insights they get from class discussion.

E Literary Connections

Aristotle's Unities

The principle of the three unities is derived from Aristotle's *Poetics* (fourth century B.C.). However, Aristotle actually insists only on unity of action (the avoidance of subplots). He mentions unity of time casually and writes nothing about unity of place. The insistence on the three unities is a contrivance of sixteenth- and seventeenth-century writers.

Assessing Learning

Check Test: Short Answers

1. Who were two of Shakespeare's earliest advocates? [John Dryden and Samuel Johnson]
2. How did Johnson assess Dryden's role in English literature? [He called Dryden "the father of English criticism."]
3. How long after Shakespeare's death did Dryden publish his critical work? [fifty years]
4. About how long after Dryden's work did Johnson publish his *Preface to the Plays of William Shakespeare*? [one hundred years]
5. What did both Dryden and Johnson find valuable in Shakespeare? [the truth to nature, or realism, and the universal appeal of his characters]

OBJECTIVES

1. Read and interpret the biography
2. Identify and evaluate biography
3. Express understanding through writing, analyzing art, research, and history
4. Learn and use new words

SKILLS

Literary
- Identify and evaluate biography

Writing
- Create a biographical sketch

Research/History
- Carry out historical and literary research

Vocabulary
- Learn and use new words

Viewing/Representing
- Analyze and compare portraits

Planning

- **Traditional Schedule**
  Lesson Plans Including Strategies for English-Language Learners
- **One-Stop Planner**
  CD-ROM with Test Generator

RESPONDING TO THE ART

George Willison (17??–1797), a Scots portrait painter, acquired a fortune in India, leaving him free to paint.

Activity. Invite students' comments on the artist's possible reasons for including the owl in the background.

James Boswell (1740–1795)

James Boswell was a Scotlander, the heir to a large fortune, and eldest son of Lord Auchinleck (pronounced aff-leck), a strait-laced judge who expected his son to settle down in Scotland and carry on the family profession of law. Young Boswell had other plans. While studying law and classics at Glasgow and Edinburgh, he yearned to travel, to write, to visit great cities, to know famous people and become famous himself, to frequent taverns, and to pursue beautiful women. Boswell's father was totally unsympathetic to these desires, but finally, in 1762, he capitulated and allowed his twenty-two-year-old son to escape to London.

There, a year later, Boswell met Samuel Johnson, then age fifty-three and famous for his *Dictionary.* Gradually Boswell discovered a serious purpose for his life: He would become familiar with Johnson, study his character and personality, record his ideas and opinions, and eventually write his biography—one of the greatest biographies in English—*The Life of Samuel Johnson* (1791). Boswell published only two other books: *An Account of Corsica* (1768) and *Journal of a Tour to the Hebrides* (1785).

Johnson advised Boswell not only to read in the literal sense of the word, but also to "read diligently the great book of mankind." This Boswell did, not only in Scotland and England and while studying law in Holland, but also on a leisurely tour of Germany, Switzerland, France, and Italy. Wherever he went, Boswell kept a written record of his own and other people's behavior and conversation. To avoid taking notes in public, he trained his memory to recall the exact details of an event and the exact words of a conversation. These he later wrote down in private. During his lifetime he accumulated an immense number of journals, memoranda to himself, and letters—thousands of pages of personal writing.

Although he used some of this material in his three books, he died with most of it unpublished. For about 125 years, Boswell's papers were stored in such places as an old croquet box and the loft over a stable until—between 1920 and 1949—they were purchased from Boswell's heirs and deposited in the Yale University Library. Now that many of them have been published, we perhaps have available more firsthand written information on Boswell than on any other person, living or dead. The youthful journals, *Boswell's London Journal* and *Boswell on the Grand Tour,* are particularly frank and interesting reading.

"Good Heaven! What is Boswell?" he once asked in a letter to a friend. The journals show that he was a person full of contradictions and contrasts, as all people are to some degree. Eventually he became a family man and followed his father's legal profession in Edinburgh and, later, in London. But after an evening of highly moral conversation, he would prowl for the rest of the night in the more disreputable parts of the city, often behaving in a loud and brash manner. Once, before the beginning of a play, he entertained a theater audience by mooing like a cow. Often he could not restrain himself from "effusions of ludicrous nonsense and intemperate mirth." No wonder to some of his contemporaries he seemed to be an uncouth buffoon. We know better.

Scottish National Portrait Gallery, Edinburgh.

James Boswell (1765) by George Willison. Oil.

go.hrw.com
LEO 12-7

Resources: Print and Media

Reading
- *Graphic Organizers for Active Reading,* p. 46
- *Words to Own,* p. 17
- *Audio CD Library*
  Disc 10, Track 4

Writing and Language
- *Daily Oral Grammar*
  Transparency 21

Viewing and Representing
- *Visual Connections*
  Videocassette B, Segment 7

Assessment
- *Formal Assessment,* p. 105
- *Portfolio Management System,* p. 146
- *Preparation for College Admission Exams,* p. 27
- *Test Generator (One-Stop Planner CD-ROM)*

Internet
- go.hrw.com (keyword: LE0 12-7)

Before You Read

FROM **THE LIFE OF SAMUEL JOHNSON**

Make the Connection

Looking Back

When James Boswell sat down to write his great biography of Johnson in 1785, his subject was already dead. Yet Boswell didn't have to rely on his memory alone. He had a wealth of material to work from: voluminous letters and notes, every scrap of information Johnson's friends could provide, and—most important—his own vivid and detailed journals. Countless other writers have also followed Boswell's method, rereading and transforming their own journal entries into polished pieces of biography, journalism, even fiction.

Quickwrite

Take a few quick notes on a person whose biography you might like to write. The person must be someone you know well and admire very much. Save your notes for further development after you have read Boswell on Johnson.

Elements of Literature

Biography

In his *Life of Samuel Johnson,* Boswell was not only a recorder of facts, but also a master storyteller with an eye for the rich details that make an incident interesting. Boswell brings to life the whole Johnson household: the wretched Dr. Levett, whom Johnson supported; the blind Miss Williams, who made her home with Johnson and who, when she poured tea, put her finger in the cup to tell when it was full; the black servant Francis Barber, who was Johnson's friend and heir—even the cat Hodge, who loved oysters. Thanks to Boswell, we know of Johnson's deep attachments to women: first to his wife and then, after her death, to others, especially Hester Thrale, who disappointed him so bitterly by marrying a music teacher.

Throughout the biography, we often see Boswell provoking Johnson to speak out on a topic, or manipulating the conversation for dramatic effect, in much the same way a playwright manages the dialogue of his or her characters. Perhaps the most brilliant parts of the *Life* are the civilized conversations it records.

It is precisely this detail—the large number of actual conversations he reports—that sets Boswell's *Life* apart from other biographies. We have more of Johnson's ordinary talk than that of any other person who lived before the invention of tape recorders. Of course, Johnson's talk was never "ordinary"; it was original, forthright, vigorous, astonishing, and well worth preserving.

A **biography** is an account of a person's life written or told by another person.

For more on Biography, see the Handbook of Literary Terms.

Background

To call Boswell a successful biographer is to say that he possessed several literary talents. He was, first of all, an accurate historian. *The Life of Samuel Johnson* was based on a great mass of journals, records, letters, notes, and memoranda, and condensed to produce a reliable account not only of Johnson but of the whole age as well. Johnson had circles of friends from all walks of life, but Boswell emphasized his relations with people whose names are still well known: among many others, the painter Joshua Reynolds, the actor David Garrick, the statesman Edmund Burke, the musicologist Charles Burney, and the novelist and dramatist Oliver Goldsmith. All study of the artistic and intellectual life of the times begins with Boswell's biography.

Boswell also aimed to show his subject "more completely than any man who has ever yet lived." To do so, he had to be a "psychologist" in the popular sense of that word, a person who listens to, understands, and feels deep sympathy for other people. Boswell appreciated Johnson's sudden outbursts of anger, his fits of depression, his morbid fear of madness and death, just as he appreciated Johnson's cheerfulness, cleverness, and fatherly feelings toward himself. What is more important, Boswell's literary talent enabled him to capture in words all the inconsistency and astonishing humanity of Samuel Johnson.

Summary

These excerpts are from the biography of Samuel Johnson, written by his younger friend and admirer James Boswell. At the age of twenty-two, Boswell met Johnson, who was fifty-three and already famous for his *Dictionary* and his conversation. Boswell both admired and liked the great man and decided early in their relationship to make his life's work a complete account of Johnson's life and ideas. With that purpose in mind, Boswell took voluminous notes and kept a detailed journal, which he later used as source material when he began writing the biography after Johnson's death. Published in 1791, *The Life of Samuel Johnson* is amazing for its wealth of detail and its record of verbatim conversations between Johnson, Boswell, and other associates. These dialogues reveal both Boswell's skill in drawing Johnson out and Johnson's originality and wit. Boswell also brings Johnson to life in all his eccentricity. For example, he describes Johnson's slovenly appearance, his tendency to talk to himself, and his weakness for superstitious rituals, as well as his love of company and argument. The portrait of Johnson is also a portrait of the intellectual landscape of late eighteenth-century England, which Johnson completely dominated.

Preteaching Vocabulary

Words to Own

Have students copy into their reading notes the Words to Own and their definitions listed on the selection pages. Then, ask them to use the words orally in sentences of their own creation. Finally, have them use the words appropriately in the following cloze activity.

A [noxious] odor [deterred] the woman from going into her son's room. She feared that his [slovenly] habits and [aversion] to cleaning were the cause of the problem, but he reassured her that his advanced science project was producing the smell. She thanked him for his [candor].

Resources

Listening

Audio CD Library

A lively recording of "*from* The Life of Samuel Johnson" is provided in the *Audio CD Library:*

- Disc 10, Track 4

Viewing and Representing

Videocassette B, Segment 7

Available in English and Spanish. This segment examines life in London during this time period. For full lesson plans and worksheets, see the *Visual Connections Teacher's Manual.*

A Reading Skills and Strategies

Generating Questions

Ask students to look over the subheadings included in the selection and to skim the selection itself, noting key words and phrases. Have them predict what information each section of the selection will provide and record questions in their reading notes that they expect will be answered in the biography.

B Connecting Across Texts

Remind students of Johnson's definition of *oats,* which they recently read in the *Dictionary*; it gives evidence of his opinion of the Scots.

C Reading Skills and Strategies

Connecting with the Text

? Have you ever met a very important and intimidating person? How did you feel? How did you behave? [Many students will have anecdotes to relate; some, like Boswell, will probably have been embarrassed.]

from The Life of Samuel Johnson

James Boswell

A Boswell's First Meeting with Johnson, 1763

This is to me a memorable year; for in it I had the happiness to obtain the acquaintance of that extraordinary man whose memoirs I am now writing; an acquaintance which I shall ever esteem as one of the most fortunate circumstances in my life. Though then but two-and-twenty, I had for several years read his works with delight and instruction, and had the highest reverence for their author, which had grown up in my fancy into a kind of mysterious veneration, by figuring to myself a state of solemn elevated abstraction, in which I supposed him to live in the immense metropolis of London. . . .

Mr. Thomas Davies the actor, who then kept a bookseller's shop in Russel Street, Covent Garden, told me that Johnson was very much his friend, and came frequently to his house, where he more than once invited me to meet him; but by some unlucky accident or other he was prevented from coming to us. . . .

At last, on Monday the 16th of May, when I was sitting in Mr. Davies's back parlor, after having drunk tea with him and Mrs. Davies, Johnson unexpectedly came into the shop; and Mr. Davies having perceived him through the glass door in the room in which we were sitting, advancing toward us—he announced his awful[1] approach to me, somewhat in the manner of an actor in the part of Horatio, when he addresses Hamlet on the appearance of his father's ghost, "Look, my Lord, it comes." I found that I had a very perfect idea of Johnson's figure, from the portrait of him painted by Sir Joshua Reynolds soon after he had published his *Dictionary,* in the attitude of sitting in his easy chair in deep meditation, which was the first picture his friend did for him, which Sir Joshua very kindly presented to me, and from which an engraving has been made for this work. Mr. Davies mentioned my name, and respectfully introduced me to him. I was much agitated; and recollecting his prejudice against the Scotch, of which I had heard much, I said to Davies, "Don't tell where I come from."—"From Scotland," cried Davies roguishly. "Mr. Johnson (said I), I do indeed come from Scotland, but I cannot help it." I am willing to flatter myself that I meant this as light pleasantry to soothe and conciliate him, and not as an humiliating abasement at the expense of my country. But however that might be, this speech was somewhat unlucky; for with that quickness of wit for which he was so remarkable, he seized the expression "come from Scotland," which I used in the sense of being of that country, and, as if I had said that I had come away from it, or left it, retorted, "That, Sir, I find, is what a very great many of your countrymen cannot help." This stroke stunned me a good deal; and when we had sat down, I felt myself not a little embarrassed, and apprehensive of what might come next. He then addressed himself to Davies. "What do you think of Garrick?[2] He has refused me an order for the play for Miss Williams, because he knows the house will be full, and that an order would be worth three shillings." Eager to take any opening to get into conversation with him, I ventured to say, "O, Sir, I cannot think Mr. Garrick would grudge such a trifle to you." "Sir (said he, with a stern look), I have known David Garrick longer than you have done: and I know no right you have

Samuel Johnson (18th century) by an unknown artist. From *The Life of Samuel Johnson* by James Boswell.

1. **awful:** producing awe; now more commonly "awesome."

2. **Garrick:** the English actor David Garrick (1717–1779), a former pupil of Johnson.

Reaching All Students

Struggling Readers

The first section contains a number of words that may be unfamiliar, such as *veneration, abstraction, roguishly, conciliate, abasement,* and *discomfited.* Remind students to look for context clues—synonyms, antonyms, and restatements—to help define unfamiliar words. Later, they can check their understanding of these and other difficult words in the glossary or a dictionary as needed.

English Language Learners

One approach to engaging English language learners is to ask them to listen to the recording of the selection in the *Audio CD Library.* For additional strategies to supplement instruction for English language learners, see

- *Lesson Plans Including Strategies for English-Language Learners*

Advanced Learners

Have students compare the style and tone of Boswell's biography of Johnson with any other biography that they have read. Encourage them to notice how the choice of language and details reveals the biographer's attitude toward the subject and in turn affects the reader's response to the subject.

to talk to me on the subject." Perhaps I deserved this check; for it was rather presumptuous in me, an entire stranger, to express any doubt of the justice of his animadversion[3] upon his old acquaintance and pupil. I now felt myself much mortified, and began to think that the hope which I had long indulged of obtaining his acquaintance was blasted. And, in truth, had not my ardor been uncommonly strong, and my resolution uncommonly persevering, so rough a reception might have deterred me forever from making any further attempts. Fortunately, however, I remained upon the field not wholly discomfited. . . .

I was highly pleased with the extraordinary vigor of his conversation, and regretted that I was drawn away from it by an engagement at another place. I had, for a part of the evening, been left alone with him, and had ventured to make an observation now and then, which he received very civilly; so that I was satisfied that though there was a roughness in his manner, there was no ill nature in his disposition. Davies followed me to the door, and when I complained to him a little of the hard blows which the great man had given me, he kindly took upon him to console me by saying, "Don't be uneasy. I can see he likes you very well." **D**

Boswell's First Visit to Johnson

A few days afterward I called on Davies, and asked him if he thought I might take the liberty of waiting on Mr. Johnson at his Chambers in the Temple.[4] He said I certainly might, and that Mr. Johnson would take it as a compliment. So upon Tuesday the 24th of May, . . . I boldly repaired to Johnson. His Chambers were on the first floor of No. 1, Inner-Temple-lane, and I entered them with an impression given me by the Reverend Dr. Blair,[5] of Edinburgh, who had been introduced to him not long before, and described his having "found the Giant in his den," an expression, which, when I came to be pretty well acquainted with Johnson, I repeated to him, and he was diverted at this picturesque account of himself. . . .

He received me very courteously; but, it must be confessed, that his apartment, and furniture, and morning dress, were sufficiently uncouth. His brown suit of clothes looked very rusty; he had on a little old shriveled unpowdered wig, which was too small for his head; his shirtneck and knees of his breeches were loose; his black worsted stockings ill drawn up; and he had a pair of unbuckled shoes by way of slippers. **E** But all these slovenly particularities were forgotten the moment that he began to talk. Some gentlemen, whom I do not recollect, were sitting with him; and when they went away, I also rose; but he said to me, "Nay, don't go." "Sir (said I), I am afraid that I intrude upon you. It is benevolent to allow me to sit and hear you." He seemed pleased with this compliment, which I sincerely paid him, and answered, "Sir, I am obliged to any man who visits me." I have preserved the following short minute[6] of what passed this day:

"Madness frequently discovers itself merely by unnecessary deviation from the usual modes of the world. My poor friend Smart[7] showed the disturbance of his mind, by falling upon his knees, and saying his prayers in the street, or in any other unusual place. Now although, rationally speaking, it is greater madness not to pray at all, than to pray as Smart did, I am afraid there are so many who do not pray, that their understanding is not called in question."

Concerning this unfortunate poet, Christopher Smart, who was confined in a madhouse, he had, at another time, the following conversation with Dr. Burney:[8] BURNEY. "How does poor Smart do, Sir; is he likely to recover?" JOHNSON. "It seems as if his mind had ceased to struggle with the disease; for he grows fat upon it." BURNEY. "Perhaps, Sir, that may be from want of exercise." JOHNSON. "No, sir; he has partly as much exercise as he used to have, for he digs in the garden. Indeed, before

3. **animadversion** (an'i·məd·vur'zhən): critical comment.
4. **Temple:** area in London where lawyers and other professional people lived and worked.
5. **Blair:** Hugh Blair (1718–1800), a Presbyterian clergyman and writer.

6. **minute:** note; memo.
7. **Smart:** Christopher Smart (1722–1771), a poet.
8. **Dr. Burney:** Charles Burney (1726–1814), a musicologist and father of the novelist Fanny Burney (1752–1840).

WORDS TO OWN
deterred (dē·turd') *v.:* prevented.
slovenly (sluv'ən·lē) *adj.:* untidy.

D Elements of Literature
Point of View

? What point of view has Boswell chosen? [Boswell writes in the first person.] **How does it affect his portrayal of Samuel Johnson?** [Possible responses: It makes the biography intimate and personal; it helps to show how Johnson interacted with other people; it adds humor, especially because of the difference in their ages.]

E Elements of Literature
Imagery

? Pick out the many concrete details that Boswell includes in this physical description of Dr. Johnson. Why does Boswell create this unflattering image of his subject? [Possible responses: He wants the biography to be realistic; he wants to show the contrast between Johnson's sharp mind and his sloppy appearance, as the next sentence shows: ". . . all these slovenly particularities were forgotten the moment he began to talk."]

Using Students' Strengths

Visual Learners

Encourage students to create their own drawings or caricatures of Samuel Johnson, based on Boswell's description. They will want to refer to the whole selection for descriptions of eccentricities and mannerisms, as well as for details about his clothing and wig.

Auditory/Interpersonal Learners

Have the students assume the roles of Johnson and Boswell and read aloud the dialogues in the selection. They may also expand on the dialogues by adding additional comments and statements that they think the speakers might have made.

Assessing Learning

Check Test: True-False

1. Johnson is completely gracious and polite when Boswell first meets him. [False]
2. Boswell finds Johnson's clothes, his furniture, and his apartment shabby and unkempt. [True]
3. When quizzed by Boswell, Johnson states he would never have anything to do with raising a child. [False]
4. Johnson always made serious efforts to avoid argument or contradiction. [False]

Ⓐ Critical Thinking

Expressing an Opinion

Samuel Johnson asserts that Christopher Smart should not have been confined to the madhouse because his behavior was not harmful to society. This is a question we face today: Should mentally ill people be welcome in the community or live apart in institutions? Ask students to express their opinions and support them with reasons.

Ⓑ Appreciating Language

Puns

A play on the multiple meanings of a word (such as *coddle*) may be informal or literary, humorous or serious. (See the *Handbook of Literary Terms* for an example of a serious pun created by Shakespeare.) Boswell enjoyed puns and writes elsewhere in the *Life of Samuel Johnson* that ". . . a good pun may be admitted among the smaller excellencies of lively conversation."

Ⓒ Cultural Connections

Both Johnson and Boswell were probably aware of the ideas of John Locke, (1632–1704), whose *Essay Concerning Human Understanding* (1690) had a profound effect on English philosophy. Locke also expressed strong ideas about child development. For example, he advocated exposing children to rigorous living conditions so they would grow strong and healthy.

Oliver Goldsmith, James Boswell, and Samuel Johnson (left to right).

his confinement, he used for exercise to walk to the alehouse; but he was *carried* back again. I did not think he ought to be shut up. His infirmities were not noxious to society. He insisted on people praying with him; and I'd as lief[9] pray with Kit Smart as anyone else. Another charge was, that he did not love clean linen; and I have no passion for it." Johnson continued. "Mankind have a great aversion to intellectual labor; but even supposing knowledge to be easily attainable, more people would be content to be ignorant than would take even a little trouble to acquire it.". . .

Boswell Quizzes Johnson

I know not how so whimsical a thought came into my mind, but I asked, "If, Sir, you were shut up in a castle, and a newborn child with you, what would you do?" JOHNSON. "Why, Sir, I should not much like my company." BOSWELL. "But would you take the trouble of rearing it?" He seemed, as may well be supposed, unwilling to pursue the subject: but upon my persevering in my question, replied, "Why yes, Sir, I would; but I must have all conveniences. If I had no garden, I would make a shed on the roof, and take it there for fresh air. I should feed it, and wash it much, and with warm water to please it, not with cold water to give it pain." BOSWELL. "But, Sir, does not heat relax?" JOHNSON. "Sir, you are not to imagine the water is to be very hot. I would not *coddle*[10] the child. No, Sir, the hardy method of treating children does no good. I'll take you five children from London, who shall cuff[11] five Highland children. Sir, a man bred in London will carry a burden, or run, or wrestle, as well as a man brought up in the hardiest manner in the country." BOSWELL. "Good living, I suppose, makes the Londoners strong." JOHNSON. "Why, Sir, I don't know that it does. Our chairmen[12] from Ireland, who are as strong men as any, have been brought up upon potatoes. Quantity makes up for quality." BOSWELL. "Would you teach this child that I have furnished you with, anything?" JOHNSON. "No, I should not be apt to teach it." BOSWELL. "Would not you have a pleasure in teaching it?" JOHNSON. "No, Sir, I should *not* have a pleasure in teaching it." BOSWELL. "Have you not a pleasure in teaching men? *There* I have you. You have the same pleasure in teaching men, that I should have in teaching children." JOHNSON. "Why, something about that.". . .

Johnson's Eccentricities

. . . Talking to himself was, indeed, one of his singularities ever since I knew him. I was certain that he was frequently uttering pious ejaculations; for fragments of the Lord's Prayer have been distinctly overheard. His friend Mr. Thomas Davies, of whom Churchill[13] says, "That Davies hath a very pretty wife," when Dr. Johnson muttered "lead us not into temptation," used with waggish and gallant humor to whisper [to] Mrs. Davies, "You, my dear, are the cause of this."

He had another particularity, of which none of his friends ever ventured to ask an explanation. It appeared to me some superstitious habit, which he had contracted early, and from which he had never called upon his reason to disentangle him. This was his anxious care to go out or in at a door or passage by a certain number of steps from a

9. **lief** (lēf): willingly.
10. **coddle:** cook in hot water. Johnson is having fun with the two distinct meanings of the word, the other being "treat tenderly."
11. **cuff:** win a fight or a scuffle with.
12. **chairmen:** porters who transported people through the London streets in sedan chairs (covered seats).
13. **Churchill:** Charles Churchill (1731–1764), author of satirical and comic poems.

WORDS TO OWN
noxious (näk′shəs) *adj.:* harmful.
aversion (ə·vur′zhən) *n.:* dislike.

Skill Link

Breaking Down Difficult Text

Boswell's (and Johnson's) syntax alternates between short, simple sentences and longer, more complex constructions. Have students break down the following complex sentences into their component independent and dependent clauses, as well as clarify pronoun and modifier references. Then have them paraphrase the sentences in contemporary English.

1. "Though then but two-and-twenty, I had for several years read his works with delight and instruction, and had the highest reverence for their author, which had grown up in my fancy into a kind of mysterious veneration, by figuring to myself a state of solemn elevated abstraction, in which I supposed him to live in the immense metropolis of London. . . ."
2. "'Mankind have a great aversion to intellectual labor; but even supposing knowledge to be easily attainable, more people would be content to be ignorant than would take even a little trouble to acquire it. . . .'"
3. "I am fully aware how very obvious an occasion I here give for the sneering jocularity of such as have no relish of an exact likeness; which to render complete, he who draws it must not disdain the slightest strokes."

certain point, or at least so as that either his right or his left foot (I am not certain which) should constantly make the first actual movement when he came close to the door or passage. Thus I conjecture: For I have, upon innumerable occasions, observed him suddenly stop, and then seem to count his steps with a deep earnestness; and when he had neglected or gone wrong in this sort of magical movement, I have seen him go back again, put himself in a proper posture to begin the ceremony, and, having gone through it, break from his abstraction, walk briskly on, and join his companion. A strange instance of something of this nature, even when on horseback, happened when he was in the Isle of Skye.[14] Sir Joshua Reynolds has observed him to go a good way about rather than cross a particular alley in Leicesterfields;[15] but this Sir Joshua imputed to his having had some disagreeable recollection associated with it.

That the most minute singularities which belonged to him, and made very observable parts of his appearance and manner, may not be omitted, it is requisite to mention, that while talking or even musing as he sat in his chair, he commonly held his head to one side toward his right shoulder, and shook it in a tremulous manner, moving his body backward and forward, and rubbing his left knee in the same direction, with the palm of his hand. In the intervals of articulating he made various sounds with his mouth, sometimes as if ruminating, or what is called chewing the cud, sometimes giving a half whistle, sometimes making his tongue play backward from the roof of his mouth, as if clucking like a hen, and sometimes protruding it against his upper gums in front, as if pronouncing quickly under his breath, *too, too, too:* all this accompanied sometimes with a thoughtful look, but more frequently with a smile. Generally when he had concluded a period, in the course of a dispute, by which time he was a good deal exhausted by violence and vociferation, he used to blow out his breath like a whale. This I supposed was a relief to his lungs; and seemed in him to be a contemptuous mode of expression, as if he had made the arguments of his opponent fly like chaff before the wind.

I am fully aware how very obvious an occasion I here give for the sneering jocularity of such as have no relish of an exact likeness; which to render complete, he who draws it must not disdain the slightest strokes. But if witlings[16] should be inclined to attack this account, let them have the candor to quote what I have offered in my defense. . . .

14. **Isle of Skye:** largest of the Inner Hebrides, a group of islands off the west coast of Scotland.
15. **Leicesterfields** (les′tər·fēldz): square in London.

16. **witlings:** people who think they're witty.

WORDS TO OWN
candor (kan′dər) *n.:* honesty.

D Elements of Literature

Biography

? What does Boswell mean when he writes that "the most minute singularities . . . may not be omitted"? [Possible responses: He does not want to leave out the smallest detail; he believes that a complete description is very important.] **What is the effect of the particular details that follow?** [Possible responses: They create a comical image of Johnson; they make Johnson seem odd.] **What is Boswell's message to people who laugh?** [He insists that the biographer must include everything, "must not disdain the slightest strokes."]

An Early London Coffeehouse (detail) (c. 1705) signed A. S.
British Museum, London.

Making the Connections

Connecting to the Subject: "An Appetite for Experience"

Ask students to comment on what they know of Boswell from the biographical sketch on p. 582 and what they have inferred from reading the selection. It is clear that his appetite for experience was hearty, and his journals reveal that he was able to satisfy it in many ways. Ask students to reflect and comment on the implications of Boswell's journal writing for their own lifelong writing habits.

Crossing the Curriculum

Geography

Have students create a map display that identifies the birthplaces of both Johnson and Boswell and traces Boswell's travels before he settled in London. The display may also include a map of eighteenth-century London that identifies specific locations mentioned in Boswell's biography (Covent Garden, the Temple, Leicesterfields), as well as others mentioned by Pepys and Defoe.

Making Meanings

First Thoughts [Respond]

1. Strengths might include his wit and intellect; weaknesses might include his temper, his appearance, and his superstitions.

Shaping Interpretations [Interpret]

2. Boswell learns that Johnson is a down-to-earth person with sloppy personal habits and a sense of humor.
3. Possible response: Many people today would consider Johnson's behavior unconventional because our society values neat appearance and polite manners. Boswell didn't try to change Johnson because he liked him the way he was and because he was the younger and less influential person in the relationship.
4. In some instances recorded by Boswell, Johnson seems conscious of his own greatness. However, Boswell also depicts Johnson as refreshingly informal, warm, and friendly.
5. Boswell claims it is the biographer's job to give an accurate, complete description. Some students may agree, while others will argue for a more flattering, less comprehensive portrayal.
6. Encourage students to begin by examining the basis on which a judgment of "rude" is made before they evaluate Johnson's manners. Responses will vary.
7. Responses will vary. Readers learn more about Johnson's personality because they see him in relationship with Boswell. On the other hand, a more objective portrayal might give a clearer picture of other aspects of Johnson's life.

Extending the Text [Synthesize]

8. Responses will vary. Some students may see the difference as a simple matter of degree. Others may argue that eccentricity is chosen, whereas insanity is involuntary.
9. Johnson would be less interesting if he were more conventional. Eccentricity is important to society because it constantly challenges norms we take for granted. Our society values conformity in some areas and applauds eccentricity in others. Encourage students to provide specific examples of both.

Johnson's Love of Argument

. . . I mentioned a new gaming club,[17] of which Mr. Beauclerk[18] had given me an account, where the members played to a desperate extent. JOHNSON. "Depend upon it, Sir, this is mere talk. *Who* is ruined by gaming? You will not find six instances in an age. There is a strange rout made about deep play: Whereas you have many more people ruined by adventurous trade,[19] and yet we do not hear such an outcry against it." THRALE. "There may be few people absolutely ruined by deep play; but very many are much hurt in their circumstances by it." JOHNSON. "Yes, Sir, and so are very many by other kinds of expense." I had heard him talk once before in the same manner; and at Oxford he said, "he wished he had learnt to play at cards." The truth, however, is, that he loved to display his ingenuity in argument; and therefore would sometimes in conversation maintain opinions which he was sensible were wrong, but in supporting which, his reasoning and wit would be most conspicuous. He would begin thus: "Why, Sir, as to the good or evil of card playing—" "Now (said Garrick), he is thinking which side he shall take." He appeared to have a pleasure in contradiction, especially when any opinion whatever was delivered with an air of confidence; so that there was hardly any topic, if not one of the great truths of religion and morality, that he might not have been incited to argue, either for or against. . . .

17. **gaming club:** gambling club.
18. **Beauclerk:** Topham Beauclerk (1739–1780), a fashionable gentleman descended from King Charles II.
19. **trade:** business.

Making Meanings

First Thoughts

1. Judging from these accounts, what do you think was Johnson's greatest strength as a person? What was his greatest fault?

Shaping Interpretations

2. Before meeting Johnson, Boswell thought that he lived in "a state of solemn elevated abstraction." Explain how the actual experience of meeting and talking with Johnson differed from Boswell's expectations.
3. Do you consider any of Johnson's behavior unconventional? Would others agree with you? Why, do you suppose, didn't Boswell ask Johnson about his eccentricities or attempt to make him more conventional?
4. By the time of their first meeting, Johnson was already a very famous man. Does Boswell show him as conscious of his own greatness, or is Boswell's picture refreshingly informal on the whole? Discuss your opinions.
5. What defense does Boswell offer for describing Johnson's eccentricities in the *Life*? Do you think the defense is valid?
6. Was Johnson an impolite person, or did he only seem rude? Explain your answer.
7. In this biography, Boswell often mentions himself—his own feelings, impressions, and conclusions about Johnson. Do you think these references contribute significantly to Boswell's work, or should he have been more detached and objective in your view? Explain your answer.

Extending the Text

8. What do we mean when we call someone "eccentric"? How is *eccentricity* different from *insanity*?
9. Do you think Johnson would have been more or less interesting had his behavior been more conventional? Why is eccentricity of behavior important to society? How is eccentricity regarded in our society today?

Reading Check

a. How did Boswell feel as he was about to meet Johnson?
b. How was Johnson dressed when Boswell first visited him in his study?
c. What superstitious habit did Johnson have?
d. Describe the peculiar mannerisms Johnson exhibited when he was talking.
e. Why, according to Boswell, did Johnson sometimes express opinions that he did not really believe?

Reading Check

a. Boswell felt awe-struck and nervous.
b. Johnson's clothes were old and needed ironing. His wig was too small, his shoes unbuckled.
c. He counted his steps whenever he passed through a doorway.
d. He held his head on one side, rocked his body while rubbing his knee, and made a series of sounds with his tongue. When he concluded, he blew out a noisy breath.
e. According to Boswell, Johnson enjoyed contradicting others, especially if they were very sure of themselves; he liked to debate and didn't care which side he took.

CHOICES: Building Your Portfolio

Writer's Notebook

1. Collecting Ideas for a Persuasive Essay

Johnson's enjoyment in arguing "either for or against" a position is a good lesson for persuasive writers. To make your position convincing, you must foresee *counterarguments:* opposing points. Which of these subjects in Boswell's remembrance most intrigues you—gambling, childrearing, mental illness, national prejudice? Think of any controversial issue, and state a position you could support ("Our state lottery should be abolished"). Quickly write two possible supporting points. Then disagree with yourself, and write one opposing point. Save your notes for the Writer's Workshop on page 612.

Creative Writing

2. Becoming a Boswell

Refer to your Quickwrite notes about a person you might choose as a subject for a biography, and write a two- or three-page **biographical sketch** of that person. Include an account of your first meeting. As Boswell does, record some of your subject's conversations or sayings, and incorporate them into your sketch as dialogue. How will you present yourself?

Analyzing Art

3. Johnson in Pictures

Look carefully at the illustrations of Johnson on pages 584 and 586 and at the one below. What do you see in each illustration? What does each suggest about Johnson's character and activities? Do they echo Boswell's admiring description of Johnson, or are any of them satirical? Write a paragraph in which you analyze these illustrations. If details in the pictures puzzle you, ask questions about them.

Research/History

4. Johnson and His Cronies

Together with a number of his friends, Johnson founded a social group called the Literary Club in 1764. The club met at a tavern called the Turk's Head in the London neighborhood of Soho. Research the membership of the club. See if you can come up with thumbnail biographical sketches as well as pictures of at least three of its famous members besides Boswell, who was elected to membership in 1773.

Samuel Johnson with James Boswell (18th century).

Grading Timesaver

Rubrics for each Choices assignment appear on p. 146 in the *Portfolio Management System*.

CHOICES: Building Your Portfolio

1. **Writer's Notebook** Brainstorm as a class to come up with a list of possible topics.
2. **Creative Writing** Before students begin writing, discuss with them the range of choices they have in representing themselves as biographers. They may choose an intimacy like Boswell's, a complete third-person objectivity, or an intermediate position. Encourage them to consider how this choice will affect the portrayal of their subject.
3. **Analyzing Art** Have students work in threes so that they can open their books to all three portraits simultaneously. Have students discuss each question in the prompt and take notes for use in their paragraphs.
4. **Research/History** Students may research the membership of the Literary Club by consulting an encyclopedia or by skimming Boswell's *The Life of Samuel Johnson* for information on the members. Instruct students to put their thumbnail sketches in a context, perhaps a meeting between the three members at the Turk's Head.

Assessing Learning

Standardized Test Preparation

For practice with ACT and SAT formats, see
- *Preparation for College Admission Exams,* p. 27

For practice in proofreading and editing, see
- *Daily Oral Grammar,* Transparency 21

OBJECTIVES

1. Read and interpret the verse drama
2. Recognize distinctive and shared characteristics of cultures
3. Compare text events with students' own experience and that of others
4. Recognize and discuss themes that cross cultures

RESPONDING TO THE ART

Johann Heinrich Tischbein (1751–1829) was the best known of a family of German painters. A friend of Goethe, he painted the writer's portrait several times.
Activity. Ask students to discuss why painting a picture of a friend might be easier in some ways and harder in others than painting a stranger. Have them point out details that suggest this painting may have been done in Italy, where Goethe went to nurse his wounds after a painful love affair.

Resources

Audio CD Library
A dramatic reading of this selection is available in the *Audio CD Library:*
- Disc 10, Track 5

Germany

WORLD LITERATURE

Johann Wolfgang von Goethe (1749–1832)

Johann Wolfgang von Goethe (gö′tə), born in Frankfurt, Germany, is one of the towering giants in world literature. Goethe had a huge intellectual appetite and was accomplished in several fields. Indeed, when Napoleon, the supreme egotist, met Goethe in 1808, he exclaimed, *"Voilà un homme!"* ("There is a man!"). During his long and prolific career (his published works run to 133 volumes), Goethe made significant contributions to politics, science, and philosophy. As a writer, he is ranked with Shakespeare, Dante, Homer, and Virgil.

Goethe in the Countryside (late 18th to early 19th century) by Johann Heinrich Tischbein.

Staedelsches Kunstinstitut, Frankfurt.

Early in Goethe's career he became a leader of the *Sturm und Drang* (Storm and Stress) movement. This movement, which opposed the Enlightenment's emphasis on cool reason and promoted use of the imagination and spontaneous expression, heralded the start of German Romanticism. In 1774, publication of his romantic novel *The Sorrows of Young Werther,* the story of a sensitive young man engaged in an unhappy love affair, gave Goethe international recognition. One year later and for the next decade, he was a cabinet minister at the court of Saxe-Weimar, the cultural center of Germany.

Like many of his characters, Goethe was inspired from youth to old age by a series of love affairs. Bettina von Arnim-Brentano, perhaps the most influential woman in Goethe's life, also loved Ludwig van Beethoven.

Goethe was also an accomplished musician. "I can always work better after I have been listening to music," he wrote. But he was so extremely sensitive to noise that the sound of a barking dog or an orchestra's kettledrums was torture to him.

(Map) Europe in 1810, at the height of Napoleon's power. Map ©Rand McNally R.L. #98-S-116.

go.hrw.com
LEO 12-7

Before You Read

FROM **FAUST**

Background

The selection you are about to read is based on the life of an actual sixteenth-century magician, Georg Faust. Legend has it that this magician sold his soul to the devil in return for comprehensive knowledge about magic. Tales of Faust's exploits circulated widely in the late 1500s. These tales, though crudely narrated and full of clodhopping humor, inspired the English playwright and poet Christopher Marlowe to write his own version, *The Tragical History of Doctor Faustus* (1604). Marlowe invests Faust with a tragic dignity not seen in the earlier folk tales. Centuries later, the German novelist Thomas Mann (1875–1955) created in *Doktor Faustus* a modern composer who sells his soul in exchange for musical genius. The French composer Charles Gounod (1818–1893) also used the legend in his famous opera *Faust.*

Presented as a Romantic hero, Goethe's Faust is unique among all versions of the tragic story. At the end of his long sufferings, this Faust is granted salvation as others are dragged off to Hell.

As this excerpt from Goethe's play opens, Faust is overwhelmed with despair. He feels he doesn't understand the meaning of existence. Scholarship is not enough for him; he wants to *experience* life fully. Distracted from his suicidal thoughts by the sound of church bells, Faust sets out on a walk through the countryside. He is soon soothed by the beauty of spring and concludes that he might be able to accept his own limitations and simply enjoy living. But when he returns to his study, Mephistopheles, a demon, plays the devil's advocate.

Quickwrite

To what lengths would you go to get something that you are passionate about? Write down what you would sacrifice or trade to get what you desire. Then write down your limits—what you would *not* sacrifice or trade for any amount of money or fame.

Faust and Marguerite watched by Mephistopheles.

Summary

This excerpt is from a translation of Goethe's two-part German verse drama. A herald of the Romantic movement, Goethe reconceived the legendary Faust, creating the prototype of the Romantic hero, a seeker who devalues intellectual knowledge in favor of direct emotional experience. Faust and the demon Mephistopheles strike a bargain in which Faust agrees to be Mephistopheles' slave in the next world in return for the chance to experience all aspects of existence in this world. Through the dialogue, Faust is characterized as a proud, humorless, dissatisfied man who cannot accept the limitations of being human. Mephistopheles, in contrast, is a joking, off-hand, essentially devious character who panders to Faust's unrealistic strivings in order to entrap him for eternity. Faust signs a contract in blood, symbolizing his willingness to barter away his life. In a soliloquy, Mephistopheles reveals that Faust's insatiable appetite for experience beyond what is permitted to humans would damn him even without his making a pact with the devil.

Background

Sturm und Drang (Storm and Stress) is part of the title of a play (1776) by Friedrich von Klinger, and it became the name of a literary movement in Germany, which flourished from the 1760s to the 1780s. The movement rejected the rigidity of neoclassicism, valuing creative individuality instead. In drama, *Sturm und Drang* gave rise to violently individualistic heroes like Faust; its effects were seen in fiction and poetry as well. Since many of the movement's writers mellowed in their later years, the term has become synonymous with adolescent exuberance.

A **Elements of Literature**

Simile

? What feelings does Mephistopheles' comparison bring out? [Possible responses: fear, horror, disgust.]

B **Vocabulary Note**

Idioms

Explain that this idiom should not be taken literally. *In the same coin* means "in the same type of payment."

C **Critical Thinking**

Connecting Across Texts

? Compare the ideas Faust expresses here with the ideas expressed by the speaker in Andrew Marvell's poem *To His Coy Mistress* (p. 241). Do either Faust or Marvell's speaker believe in life after death? [Possible response: Faust is uncertain, or unwilling, to consider it. Marvell's speaker implies that death is final.] What are the striking similarities between them? [Possible response: Both use violent language in describing their desires. Both are eager for immediate experience.]

from Faust, Part I

Johann Wolfgang von Goethe

translated by **Louis MacNeice**

Mephistopheles.
A Stop playing with your grief which battens°
Like a vulture on your life, your mind!
The worst of company would make you feel
That you are a man among mankind.
Not that it's really my proposition
To shove you among the common men;
Though I'm not one of the Upper Ten,°
If you would like a coalition
With me for your career through life,
I am quite ready to fit in,
I'm yours before you can say knife.
I am your comrade;
If you so crave,
I am your servant, I am your slave.
Faust.
And what have I to undertake in return?
Mephistopheles.
Oh it's early days to discuss what that is.
Faust.
No, no, the devil is an egoist
And ready to do nothing gratis°
Which is to benefit a stranger.
Tell me your terms and don't prevaricate!
A servant like you in the house is a danger.
Mephistopheles.
I will bind myself to your service in this world,
To be at your beck and never rest nor slack;
When we meet again on the other side,
B In the same coin you shall pay me back.
Faust.
C The other side gives me little trouble;
First batter this present world to rubble,
Then the other may rise—if that's the plan.
This earth is where my springs of joy have started,
And this sun shines on me when broken-hearted;
If I can first from them be parted,
Then let happen what will and can!
I wish to hear no more about it—
Whether there too men hate and love
Or whether in those spheres too, in the future,
There is a Below or an Above.

1. **battens:** grows fat.

7. **Upper Ten:** aristocracy; upper ranks. The phrase is short for "upper ten thousand."

18. **gratis** (grat′is): for free.

Reaching All Students

Struggling Readers

Have students read the dialogue aloud, taking turns in the roles of Faust and Mephistopheles. Explain that they should pause at the end of a line only when punctuation (a period or semicolon) signals a full stop. Encourage students to experiment with change of emphasis and tone of voice to alter shades of meaning. Have them repeat difficult sections as needed.

English Language Learners

Faust and Mephistopheles discuss their agreement in this excerpt. To monitor students' comprehension of the plot, have them work together to create, in today's language, a written contract that directly states the terms of the character's agreement. Encourage students to provide as much detail as possible.

Advanced Learners

Encourage students to research the life and work of Goethe's friend and fellow writer Johann Christoph Friedrich von Schiller (1759–1805), who is considered second only to Goethe in literary achievements in this period of world literature.

Faust and Mephistopheles (1826–1827) by Eugène Delacroix.
Wallace Collection, London.

Responding to the Art

French painter **Eugène Delacroix** (1798–1863) exemplifies nineteenth-century Romanticism. Since he kept a daily journal from the age of twenty-three, art historians possess a rich trove of details about his life and work. His technique of applying contrasting colors with small brushstrokes influenced the Impressionists of the 1860s. A lover of books, Delacroix illustrated literature by Shakespeare and Sir Walter Scott, in addition to Goethe's *Faust.* Goethe remarked that the image of Faust created by Delacroix fit perfectly with the one in his own mind.

Activity. Invite students to study the posture of Mephistopheles and of Faust and imagine what they might be saying to each other and feeling inwardly. Or invite students to look closely at the shelf above the two men for symbols of death and disorder.

Mephistopheles.
With such an outlook you can risk it.
Sign on the line! In these next days you will get
Ravishing samples of my arts;
I am giving you what never man saw yet.

Faust.
Poor devil, can *you* give anything ever?
Was a human spirit in its high endeavour
Even once understood by one of your breed?
Have you got food which fails to feed?
Or red gold which, never at rest,
Like mercury runs away through the hand?
A game at which one never wins?
A girl who, even when on my breast,
Pledges herself to my neighbour with her eyes?
The divine and lovely delight of honour
Which falls like a falling star and dies?

D Reading Skills and Strategies
Making Inferences

? What does Faust feel at this point in the dialogue? [Possible responses: distrust, contempt, skepticism.]

E Critical Thinking
Classifying

? Faust gives five illustrations of how the demon's promises may disappoint him. What five pleasures of life do they represent? [food, wealth, recreation, romance, fame]

Getting Students Involved

Enrichment Activity

Temptations of Today. Ask students to gather examples of advertisements from various media: magazines, newspapers, radio, and television. For the broadcast media, they may record the ad on either audiotape or videocassette or simply transcribe the verbal message. Encourage them to collect ads for a wide range of products—you might suggest cars, beauty products, or beverages. In class, discuss the methods of persuasion the advertisers use. These will probably include exaggerated promises; associating the product with pleasure, beauty, success, and fame; suggestions that the buyer seek immediate gratification ("buy now, pay later"). Have students compare the methods used in today's advertisements with the methods used by Mephistopheles, particularly in ll. 16, 37–40, 54–55, 78–81, 100–103, 126–130, and 182–201. The similarities will highlight for students aspects of Faust's character that are common to people in all times and places.

Ⓐ Elements of Literature

Parallel Structure

Point out to students the way in which the repetition of "if ever" adds drama and emphasis and helps build the tension that explodes in Faust's final, short line, "That's my wager!"

Ⓑ Elements of Literature

Aside

? Imagine this line delivered two ways: spoken to Faust by Mephistopheles or spoken as an aside. How does the method of delivery affect the demon's character? [Possible response: He seems more devious if the line is spoken as an aside.] Why does he use "we"? [Possible responses: It is the editorial "we" for exaggerated formality. He means the devil and himself.]

Ⓒ Elements of Literature

Tone and Irony

? What word would you use to describe Mephistopheles's tone in these lines? [Possible responses: offhand, casual, matter-of-fact, flippant.] How is the tone ironic? [The bargain he is making with Faust is very serious, but his tone is light.]

Ⓓ Reading Skills and Strategies

Drawing Conclusions

? What does Faust mean when he makes this statement? [Possible responses: A promise is only as good as the man who makes it; written contracts have no value; written contracts corrupt the pledge they are supposed to guarantee.]

Show me the fruits which, before they are plucked, decay
And the trees which day after day renew their green!

Mephistopheles.
Such a commission° doesn't alarm me,
I have such treasures to purvey.
But, my good friend, the time draws on when we
Should be glad to feast at our ease on something good.

Faust.
If ever I stretch myself on a bed of ease,
Then I am finished! Is that understood?
If ever your flatteries can coax me
To be pleased with myself, if ever you cast
A spell of pleasure that can hoax me—
Then let *that* day be my last!
That's my wager!

Mephistopheles.
Done!

Faust.
Let's shake!
If ever I say to the passing moment
'Linger a while! Thou art so fair!'
Then you may cast me into fetters,
I will gladly perish then and there!
Then you may set the death-bell tolling,
Then from my service you are free,
The clock may stop, its hand may fall,
And that be the end of time for me!

Mephistopheles.
Think what you're saying, we shall not forget it.

Faust.
And you are fully within your rights;
I have made no mad or outrageous claim.
If I stay as I am, I am a slave—
Whether yours or another's, it's all the same.

Mephistopheles.
I shall this very day at the College Banquet°
Enter your service with no more ado,
But just one point—As a life-and-death insurance
I must trouble you for a line or two.

Faust.
So you, you pedant,° you too like things in writing?
Have you never known a man? Or a man's word? Never?
Is it not enough that my word of mouth
Puts all my days in bond for ever?
Does not the world rage on in all its streams
And shall a promise hamper *me*?
Yet this illusion reigns within our hearts
And from it who would be gladly free?
Happy the man who can inwardly keep his word;
Whatever the cost, he will not be loath to pay!

54. commission: authorization to perform duties.

Frontispiece of Christopher Marlowe's *Dr. Faustus* (1636).

78. College Banquet: dinner given by a successful candidate for the Ph.D. degree.

82. pedant (ped′'nt): overly precise scholar.

Listening to Music

"The Kermesse Waltz" ("*Ainsi que la brise*") from *Faust* by Charles Gounod, performed by the Paris Opera.

Mephisto Waltz No. 2 by Franz Liszt, performed by the Boston Pops.

"Menuet des follets" from *The Damnation of Faust* by Hector Berlioz, performed by the Hungarian State Orchestra.

There have been as many musical adaptations of the *Faust* legend as literary ones. The most famous is the opera by France's Charles Gounod (1818–1893), in which the catchy "Kermesse Waltz" captures the gaiety of a village fair after Mephistopheles is sent away. From Hungary's Franz Liszt (1811–1886) comes *Mephisto Waltz No. 2,* a symphonic poem in which Mephistopheles (Mephisto) and Faust turn a village wedding into a manic music exhibition. From France's Hector Berlioz (1803–1869) comes the opera *The Damnation of Faust* with its "*Menuet des follets*" ("Minuet of the Will-o'-the Wisps"), in which Mephisto invokes evil spirits to encircle the home of Faust's beloved Marguerite.

Activity

After students read the *Faust* excerpt, have them listen to as many musical compositions on the Faust theme as possible. From these compositions, have them choose background music for a film adaptation of the excerpt. Students can simply explain how they would use the music or can create an actual tape.

But a parchment, duly inscribed and sealed,
Is a bogey° from which all wince away.
The word dies on the tip of the pen
And wax and leather lord it then.
What do you, evil spirit, require?
Bronze, marble, parchment, paper?
Quill or chisel or pencil of slate?
You may choose whichever you desire.

Mephistopheles.
How can you so exaggerate
With such a hectic rhetoric?
Any little snippet is quite good—
And you sign it with one little drop of blood.

Faust.
If that is enough and is some use,
One may as well pander to your fad.°

Mephistopheles.
Blood is a very special juice.

Faust.
Only do not fear that I shall break this contract.
What I promise is nothing more
Than what all my powers are striving for.
I have puffed myself up too much, it is only
Your sort that really fits my case.
The great Earth Spirit has despised me
And Nature shuts the door in my face.
The thread of thought is snapped asunder,
I have long loathed knowledge in all its fashions.
In the depths of sensuality
Let us now quench our glowing passions!
And at once make ready every wonder
Of unpenetrated sorcery!
Let us cast ourselves into the torrent of time,
Into the whirl of eventfulness,
Where disappointment and success,
Pleasure and pain may chop and change
As chop and change they will and can;
It is restless action makes the man.

Mephistopheles.
No limit is fixed for you, no bound;
If you'd like to nibble at everything
Or to seize upon something flying round—
Well, may you have a run for your money!
But seize your chance and don't be funny!

Faust.
I've told you, it is no question of happiness.
The most painful joy, enamoured hate, enlivening
Disgust—I devote myself to all excess.
My breast, now cured of its appetite for knowledge,
From now is open to all and every smart,

93. bogey: evil spirit.

105. pander to your fad: go along with your frivolous request.

E Elements of Literature
Symbol

? **What does the drop of blood symbolize?** [Possible response: Blood symbolizes life. Faust is signing over his life with his blood.]

F Reading Skills and Strategies
Drawing Conclusions

? **What is the implied object of "chop and change" in ll. 123 and 124?** [The object is the person, the man.] **What is Faust saying?** [Possible responses: Pleasure and pain shape a man's personality; without experience of pleasure and pain, manhood is not possible.]

G Vocabulary Note
Idiom

The idiom *run for your money* originated in horse-racing slang.

H Elements of Literature
Oxymoron

? **An oxymoron is a figure of speech that combines apparently contradictory or incongruous ideas. What examples can you find here?** ["painful joy," "enamored hate," "enlivening disgust"] **Why does Faust use these contradictions?** [Possible responses: He is confused and excited; he wants to express a wide range of experience; he wants to point to extremes.]

Taking A Second Look

Review: Using Context Clues

A number of words in this selection that are not footnoted will probably be unfamiliar to students. Remind them to use the context, or the surrounding lines, to infer the meanings of these unfamiliar words. They can also use the glossary and a dictionary as needed. In the quoted sentences from *Faust* at right, have students infer the meanings of the underlined words, looking at the larger context in the selection as necessary.

1. "Tell me your terms, and don't <u>prevaricate</u>!" (l. 20) [lie]
2. "Such a commission doesn't alarm me, / I have such treasures to <u>purvey</u>." (ll. 54–55) [give]
3. "Then you may cast me into <u>fetters</u>, / I will gladly perish then and there!" (ll. 67–68) [chains]
4. "Whatever the cost, he will not be <u>loath</u> to pay!" (l. 91) [reluctant]
5. "Grasping the highest and lowest with my spirit, / piling men's <u>weal</u> and woe upon my neck." (ll. 138–139) [well-being]
6. "In vain he will pray to <u>slake</u> his inner thirst . . . ." (l. 216) [satisfy]

Ⓐ Critical Thinking

Connecting Across Texts

? Compare this exchange between Faust and Mephistopheles with their recollections of Satan in Milton's *Paradise Lost* (pp. 438–448). In ll. 254–255, Satan declares: "The mind is its own place, and in itself/can make a Heaven of Hell, a Hell of Heaven." Would Mephistopheles agree? Would Faust? [Possible answers: The demon seems less likely to agree; he views experience as limited and limiting. Faust is more likely to agree, based on what he says here.]

Ⓑ Elements of Literature

Metaphor

? What are the "iron rations"? [the endless punishment the devil and demons must endure]

Ⓒ Reading Skills and Strategies

Drawing Conclusions

? What does Mephistopheles suggest a poet might be able to do for Faust? [Possible responses: grant all his wishes; turn him into a man who combines both passion and reason.] How would you describe the tone of ll. 167–168? [sarcastic]

Ⓓ Critical Thinking

Expressing an Opinion

? Mephistopheles makes a generalization about humans: "You are in the end . . . what you are." Do you agree that a person is incapable of change or growth? Are we all limited in our potential? [Responses will vary.]

And what is allotted to the whole of mankind
That will I sample in my inmost heart,
Grasping the highest and lowest with my spirit,
Piling men's weal and woe upon my neck,
To extend myself to embrace all human selves
And to founder in the end, like them, a wreck.

Ⓐ **Mephistopheles.**

O believe *me,* who have been chewing
These iron rations many a thousand year,
Ⓑ No human being can digest
This stuff, from the cradle to the bier.°
This universe—believe a devil—
Was made for no one but a god!
He exists in eternal light
But *us* he has brought into the darkness
While *your* sole portion is day and night.

Faust.

I will all the same!

Mephistopheles.

That's very nice.
There's only one thing I find wrong;
Time is short, art is long.
You could do with a little artistic advice.
Confederate with one of the poets
And let him flog his imagination
To heap all virtues on your head,
A head with such a reputation:
Ⓒ Lion's bravery,
Stag's velocity,
Fire of Italy,
Northern tenacity.
Let *him* find out the secret art
Of combining craft with a noble heart
And of being in love like a young man,
Hotly, but working to a plan.
Such a person—*I'd* like to meet him;
'Mr. Microcosm'° is how I'd greet him.

Faust.

What am I then if fate must bar
My efforts to reach that crown of humanity
After which all my senses strive?

Mephistopheles.

You are in the end . . . what you are.
You can put on full-bottomed wigs° with a million locks,
Ⓓ You can put on stilts instead of your socks,
You remain for ever what you are.

Faust.

I feel my endeavours have not been worth a pin
When I raked together the treasures of the human mind,
If at the end I but sit down to find

145. bier (bir): platform on which a coffin or corpse is placed.

168. Mr. Microcosm (mī'krō·kä'zəm): that is, representing the microcosm, or essence, of the world.

173. full-bottomed wigs: wigs that cover the back and shoulders. Popular among men and women in seventeenth-century Europe, such wigs were considered signs of upper-class status.

Using Students' Strengths

Verbal/Linguistic Learners

In ll. 159–162, Goethe uses condensed forms of stereotypical similes to reinforce the images of four personality traits. Ask students to list other personality traits and supply some of the most common similes for them. Encourage them also to create their own original similes for human qualities. Discuss the usefulness, in prose and poetry, of both familiar and original comparisons.

Interpersonal Learners

Have students work in pairs to rehearse and stage the excerpt or portions of it. Have the class critique the various performances; provide specific guidelines or criteria for the class evaluation. A successful presentation should bring out Faust's arrogance and self-absorption in contrast to Mephistopheles's off-handed humor and devious nature.

No new force welling up within.
I have not a hair's breadth more of height,
I am no nearer the Infinite.

Mephistopheles.

My very good sir, you look at things
Just in the way that people do;
We must be cleverer than that
Or the joys of life will escape from you.
Hell! You have surely hands and feet,
Also a head and you-know-what;
The pleasures I gather on the wing,
Are they less mine? Of course they're not!
Suppose I can afford six stallions,
I can add that horse-power to my score
And dash along and be a proper man
As if my legs were twenty-four.
So good-bye to thinking! On your toes!

E

Mephistopheles appearing to Faust, by Alexander Mayer.

E Elements of Literature

Carpe Diem Theme

Remind students that the Latin term *carpe diem* ("seize the day") is used to describe the idea of living life to the fullest in the present. These lines are particularly explicit in their expression of this theme. Ask students to identify other parts of this selection in which the *carpe diem* theme is apparent and to recall other works that reveal this theme. [Possible responses: Marlowe's "The Passionate Shepherd to His Love"; Marvell's "To His Coy Mistress"; Herrick's "To the Virgins, to Make Much of Time."]

RESPONDING TO THE ART

Activity. Encourage students to compare the paintings of Faust and Mephistopheles that accompany this verse drama and tell which one they think captures the character of their relationship most effectively.

Assessing Learning

Check Test: True-False

1. Mephistopheles is a demon. [True]
2. Mephistopheles offers to be Faust's slave. [True]
3. Mephistopheles's offer carries a high price. [True]
4. Faust says that when he is tired of searching for the Infinite, he will know it is time to die. [True]
5. Mephistopheles decides to let Faust break their contract. [False]

Ⓐ Reading Skills and Strategies
Drawing Conclusions

? These are Mephistopheles' final words to Faust in this selection (the viewpoint shifts next from second person to third person). Restate in your own words what the demon is telling Faust. Does Mephistopheles wait deliberately for Faust to leave before saying this, or is Faust in such a hurry that he misses the words? [Responses will vary.]

Ⓑ Reading Skills and Strategies
Making Inferences

? Why does Mephistopheles say that Faust would be "equally accursed" even without their bargain? [Possible responses: because Faust was unhappy before they met; because Faust is not capable of change, he "is what he is"; because Faust's appetite for experience is too strong.]

Finding Common Ground

Arrange students in groups of four or five of mixed background and motivation, so each group will have an ample pool of diverse ideas. Have them work together to brainstorm lists of fictional characters and real people; then have them narrow their lists to five or six individuals for comparison purposes. They should use a graphic organizer like the following to record their ideas.

	qualities	others' reactions	positive/ negative?
name			
name			
name			
name			
name			

The world's before us. Quick! Here goes!
I tell you, a chap who's intellectual
Is like a beast on a blasted heath
Driven in circles by a demon
While a fine green meadow lies round beneath.

Faust.
How do we start?

Mephistopheles.
We just say go—and skip.
But please get ready for this pleasure trip.
[*Exit Faust.*]
Only look down on knowledge and reason,
The highest gifts that men can prize,
Only allow the spirit of lies
To confirm you in magic and illusion,
And then I have you body and soul.
Fate has given this man a spirit
Which is always pressing onwards, beyond control,
And whose mad striving overleaps
All joys of the earth between pole and pole.
Him shall I drag though the wilds of life
And through the flats of meaninglessness,
I shall make him flounder and gape and stick
And to tease his insatiableness
Hang meat and drink in the air before his watering lips;
In vain he will pray to slake his inner thirst,
And even had he not sold himself to the devil
He would be equally accursed.

Faust's covenant with Mephistopheles (detail) by Franz Strassen.

Finding Common Ground

Working with a small group, discuss plays, movies, novels, or television shows in which a character has wanted—passionately—what he or she could not have. Then, think of people in actual life who have sold out in some way to possess something of great value to them. (Also think about your own Quickwrite entry.) Consider the following questions:

- Do these people have any qualities in common? If so, what are they?
- How do those around these people regard them—fearfully? respectfully? with envy? Why do such people give rise to these responses?
- Can such striving ever have positive effects? Or is it always destructive?

Compare your group's conclusions with those of other groups. What do you agree on? On what issues do you remain divided?

Making the Connections

Connecting to the Subject: "An Appetite for Experience"

Point out to students that Faust represents the appetite for experience carried to the extreme. Fiction makes it possible for writers like Goethe to create characters who embody such extremes. Ask students to discuss whether they believe Faust is a tragic hero in the classic sense. Do his arrogant pride (*hubris*) and appetite for experience cause his downfall?

Thomas Gray
(1716–1771)

Thomas Gray is perhaps the best lyric poet of the mid-eighteenth century, an age that is not known for its great lyric poets. The son of a London merchant, he spent nine years at one of the great English "public" schools, Eton College, which is neither public nor a college. (It is the equivalent of a prep school for boys who expect to go to Cambridge or Oxford.) At eighteen, Gray entered Cambridge University, where he lived for the remaining thirty-seven years of his life, reading literature in a variety of languages; studying archaeology, law, history, botany, and zoology; painting landscapes; playing the harpsichord; and growing geraniums in his window boxes. In a quiet, inconspicuous way, he became very learned. These years were interrupted only briefly by a grand tour of France, Switzerland, and Italy with Horace Walpole, a friend from Eton and son of England's prime minister, who paid the expenses.

The great crisis of Gray's life came when Richard West, his best friend from Eton, died of tuberculosis at the age of twenty-four. Gray sought consolation in writing poetry. He was always reluctant to publish his verses; although he carefully and fastidiously revised and rewrote them, they never seemed to him to be quite finished. Moreover, he was painfully shy and, unlike most writers, he really did not want the world's applause. Imagine his distress when his "Elegy Written in a Country Churchyard" made him famous. Gray's other poems—only thirteen of which he published during his lifetime—were also widely admired. Most of them are elegant, gloomy, and artificial: exactly what midcentury taste demanded. Few of these other poems are of much interest today except to historians of English poetry, who find that in several ways Gray anticipated the Romantic Age to come.

Thomas Gray (1747–1748) by John Giles Eccardt. Oil on canvas (15⅞″ × 12⅞″).

By Courtesy of the National Portrait Gallery, London.

Gray led a quiet, frugal, low-key existence. Unlike everybody else in his century, he was never on the back of a horse. Although he was made a professor of history at Cambridge, he never delivered any lectures, which is all that a professor did in those days. He spent his vacations in London, reading in the British Museum (now the British Library), or in the Lake District (a picturesque part of northern England made famous by the poets of the next age), or in Stoke Poges, a village where his mother and aunt lived. There he is buried, beside his mother, in the cemetery that he immortalized in his "Elegy."

go.hrw.com
LE0 12-7

OBJECTIVES

1. Read and interpret the poem
2. Identify and interpret a pastoral elegy
3. Read and understand inverted sentences
4. Analyze word choice and word order
5. Express understanding through critical and creative writing or performance

SKILLS

Literary
- Identify and interpret a pastoral elegy

Writing
- Gather ideas for an essay on a controversial issue
- Compare and contrast two elegies
- Create a monologue
- Write an elegy

Reading
- Read and understand inverted sentences
- Analyze word choice and word order

Listening/Speaking
- Perform and critique spoken poetry

Viewing/Representing
- Interpret works of art (ATE)

Planning

- **Block Schedule**
  Block Scheduling Lesson Plans with Pacing Guide
- **Traditional Schedule**
  Lesson Plans Including Strategies for English-Language Learners
- ***One-Stop Planner***
  CD-ROM with Test Generator

Resources: Print and Media

Reading
- *Graphic Organizers for Active Reading,* p. 47
- *Audio CD Library*
  Disc 10, Track 6

Elements of Literature
- *Literary Elements*
  Transparency 16
  Worksheet, p. 49

Writing and Language
- *Daily Oral Grammar*
  Transparency 22

Assessment
- *Formal Assessment,* p. 107
- *Portfolio Management System,* p. 147
- *Test Generator (One-Stop Planner CD-ROM)*

Internet
- go.hrw.com (keyword: LE0 12-7)

Summary ■ ■ ■

Gray's rhyming iambic pentameter lines (*abab*) have the expected somber, pensive tone and rhythm typical of an **elegy,** a poem about death. The setting is a country churchyard, or cemetery, at dusk, where the speaker is musing on the obscure lives of country people who are buried there. By contrasting pastoral images of nature with those of sophisticated pomp and power, the speaker expresses the central theme of the poem: Rich and poor, famous and humble, share a common end—the grave. He also makes use of polished generalizations, such as "The paths of glory lead but to the grave" and poetic personifications of abstract qualities or states like Ambition and Knowledge. In keeping with the attitude of respect for common people characteristic of the Romantic movement, the speaker asserts that it is only circumstances, not any inherent deficiency, that keep ordinary people from making their mark on the world. At the end, the speaker (whom most readers take to be Gray himself) offers his own epitaph, portraying himself as an obscure, generous, and melancholy soul trusting in God's mercy.

Responding to the Art

George Stubbs (1724–1806), a self-taught English artist, was most highly regarded for his paintings of horses. He studied the anatomy of horses in minute detail; sometimes he even carried a horse carcass up two or three flights of stairs to his dissecting room. In contrast to this calm scene of haycarting, some of Stubbs's paintings are graphically violent.

Activity. Have students discuss what this painting shows about life in the country for eighteenth-century men and women.

Before You Read

Elegy Written in a Country Churchyard

Make the Connection

Ordinary People

Have you ever wondered about the hidden lives of ordinary people—or about the dashed hopes that might lie behind the name on a roadside mailbox or a worn tombstone? If fate had been different, could one of those names have been that of a great writer, president of the United States, or maybe the scientist who will discover the cure for cancer? Gray was one of the first writers in English to believe that the lives of ordinary people are suitable subjects for serious poetry.

Haycarting
(18th century)
by George Stubbs.

Board of Trustees of the National Museums and Galleries on Merseyside (Lady Lever Art Gallery, Port Sunlight, England).

Reading Skills and Strategies

Reading Inverted Sentences

Gray wrote his elegy in 1751, so it is not surprising that he uses many **archaic words**—such as *lea* instead of the modern *meadow.* You'll find many of these archaic words defined in the side notes. A greater challenge to the modern reader is Gray's frequent use of **inverted sentence structures.** The normal word order in an English sentence is subject-verb-complement. But to accommodate his meter or rhyme scheme, Gray often inverts, or twists, these sentence elements so that they are out of order. Thus, in line 14, for example, instead of writing "Where the turf heaves" (subject-verb), Gray writes, "Where heaves the turf" (verb-subject). As you read the poem, look for the subject and verb of each sentence; the more you read, the less awkward the inversions will seem.

Background

Gray had this poem published anonymously in 1751—only because a copy of it had fallen into the hands of an unscrupulous magazine editor who threatened to print it with Gray's name on it. The poem immediately became a great favorite of readers, a position it still maintains because it sounds so beautiful and because what it says about death is so true. Everybody dies: The famous people of the earth are no different from the rest of us in that respect. We all eventually come to the same dusty end. Painfully obvious truths of this kind are called *truisms,* and a poet can be forgiven his truisms only if he utters them memorably. Gray's "Elegy" exemplifies Pope's definition of true wit: "What oft was thought but ne'er so well expressed."

Gray wanted this poem printed without any spaces between stanzas "because the sense is in some places continued beyond them." The fact that it is almost never printed in this way perhaps justifies Gray's misgivings about publishers and makes the reading of lines 61–73 a bit more difficult than it should be.

Elegy Written in a Country Churchyard

Thomas Gray

The curfew tolls the knell of parting day,
The lowing herd wind slowly o'er the lea,°
The plowman homeward plods his weary way,
And leaves the world to darkness, and to me. (A)

Now fades the glimmering landscape on the sight,
And all the air a solemn stillness holds;
Save where the beetle wheels his droning flight,
And drowsy tinklings lull the distant folds.

Save that from yonder ivy-mantled tower
The moping owl does to the moon complain (B)
Of such, as wand'ring near her secret bower,
Molest her ancient solitary reign.

Beneath those rugged elms, that yew tree's shade,
Where heaves the turf in many a mold'ring heap,
Each in his narrow cell forever laid,
The rude° forefathers of the hamlet sleep.

The breezy call of incense-breathing morn,
The swallow twitt'ring from the straw-built shed,°
The cock's shrill clarion, or the echoing horn,°
No more shall rouse them from their lowly bed.

(C)

For them no more the blazing hearth shall burn,
Or busy housewife ply her evening care:
No children run to lisp their sire's return,
Or climb his knees the envied kiss to share.

Oft did the harvest to their sickle yield,
Their furrow oft the stubborn glebe° has broke;
How jocund did they drive their team afield!
How bowed the woods beneath their sturdy stroke!

Let not Ambition mock their useful toil,
Their homely joys and destiny obscure; (D)
Nor Grandeur hear with a disdainful smile,
The short and simple annals of the poor.

The boast of heraldry,° the pomp of power,
And all that beauty, all that wealth e'er gave, (E)
Awaits alike th' inevitable hour.
The paths of glory lead but to the grave.

2. lea: meadow.

16. rude: uneducated; unpolished.

18. shed: nest.
19. horn: hunting horn.

26. glebe: soil.

33. boast of heraldry: pride in one's ancestry. Heraldry is the study of family coats of arms.

(A) Elements of Literature

Tone

? Why does the speaker associate himself with the darkness? [Possible responses: It makes him seem sad; it establishes a gloomy tone.]

(B) Elements of Literature

Imagery

? What is the effect of the images of the owl and the moon? [Possible responses: They are scary; sinister; mysterious.]

(C) Critical Thinking

Interpreting

? Why does the speaker combine cheerful images (breezes, birds) with the repeated words "no more"? [Possible response: The combination stresses the contrast between life and death.]

(D) Elements of Literature

Personification

Point out Gray's use of personification in this stanza. Encourage students to notice the many instances throughout the poem in which abstract ideas are given human qualities.

(E) Reading Skills and Strategies

Connecting with the Text

? What implications might this idea have for how we choose to live our lives? [Possible responses: It makes ambition seem pointless; it suggests that arrogant people should become humble.]

Resources

Listening

Audio CD Library

A recording of this poem is provided in the *Audio CD Library:*

- Disc 10, Track 6

Skill Link

Analyzing Rhythm and Rhyme

Ask students to identify the rhyme scheme of Gray's four-line stanzas. [*abab*] Remind them that an *iamb* is a metrical foot containing one unstressed and one stressed syllable, and that a line of iambic pentameter contains five iambic feet. This meter closely resembles the rhythms of normal English speech. Ask students to scan the following lines and decide whether or not they are in iambic pentameter.

1. "Ye whose hearts are fresh and simple" (Longfellow, "The Song of Hiawatha") [no]
2. "These waters, rolling from their mountain springs" (Wordsworth, "Lines Composed a Few Miles Above Tintern Abbey") [yes]
3. "Well, they are gone and here must I remain" (Coleridge, "This Lime-Tree Bower My Prison") [yes]
4. "Cannon to the right of them" (Tennyson, "The Charge of the Light Brigade") [no]

Responding to the Art

Jasper Cropsey (1823–1900), an American painter, built a model house that won an award in New York City when he was only fourteen. He took up painting later, when ill health prevented him from working as an architect. His landscapes were favorably compared to those of the English painters J. M. W. Turner and John Constable. During the Civil War, he painted a view of the Gettysburg battlefield.

Activity. Encourage students to match descriptions in Gray's poem with details in Cropsey's painting.

Ode to a Country Churchyard (Gray's Elegy) (1883) by Jasper F. Cropsey. Oil on canvas (13 ½″ × 25 ⅕″).
The Newington-Cropsey Foundation, Hastings-on-Hudson, New York.

Nor you, ye proud, impute to these the fault,
If Mem'ry o'er their tomb no trophies° raise,
Where through the long-drawn aisle and fretted vault°
The pealing anthem swells the note of praise.

Can storied urn° or animated° bust
Back to its mansion call the fleeting breath?
Can Honor's voice provoke° the silent dust,
Or Flatt'ry soothe the dull cold ear of Death?

Perhaps in this neglected spot is laid
Some heart once pregnant with celestial fire,
Hands that the rod of empire might have swayed,
Or waked to ecstasy the living lyre.

But Knowledge to their eyes her ample page
Rich with the spoils of time did ne'er unroll;
Chill Penury° repressed their noble rage,°
And froze the genial current° of the soul.

Full many a gem of purest ray serene,
The dark unfathomed caves of ocean bear:
Full many a flower is born to blush unseen,
And waste its sweetness on the desert air.

38. trophies: monuments.

39. fretted vault: elaborately ornamented church ceiling.

41. storied urn: an urn with an inscription on it. **animated:** lifelike.

43. provoke: evoke; call forth.

51. penury: poverty. **rage:** emotion; feeling.

52. genial current: warm impulses.

A Reading Skills and Strategies

Reading Inverted Sentences

Ask students to identify the subjects, verbs, complements, and modifiers of the sentences contained in this stanza and to rearrange them in conventional word order. [Perhaps some heart, once pregnant with celestial fire, is laid in this neglected spot, hands that might have swayed the rod of empire, or that might have waked the living lyre to ecstasy.]

B Elements of Literature

Figurative Language

? In context, what might the "spoils of time" be? [Possible response: knowledge of history, art, music, literature, science.]

C Critical Thinking

Challenging the Text

? Do you agree with Gray's use of the verb "waste"? If a talent or virtue does not find an audience, is it wasted? [Responses will vary. Encourage students to use examples and illustrations from their own experience.]

Using Students' Strengths

Naturalist Learners

Encourage students to research some of the birds and plants that Gray includes in the "Elegy." What flowers, for example, bloom in the desert (l. 56)? Why does he write that the beech tree "wreathes its old fantastic roots so high" (l. 102)? Have them present their findings to the class, preferably using visual aids as well as oral explanations.

Visual Learners

In l. 33, Gray uses "The boast of heraldry" to sum up the pride in family history that has been important to the British aristocracy and that has left its mark on American life as well. Encourage students to research the history of coats of arms and to illustrate and explain some of the symbols associated with them. Students may also create their own heraldic emblems adapted to the values of modern life.

Some village Hampden° that with dauntless breast
The little tyrant of his fields withstood;
Some mute inglorious Milton here may rest, **E**
Some Cromwell° guiltless of his country's blood. **D**

Th' applause of list'ning senates to command,
The threats of pain and ruin to despise,
To scatter plenty o'er a smiling land,
And read their hist'ry in a nation's eyes

Their lot forbade: nor circumscribed alone
Their growing virtues, but their crimes confined;
Forbade to wade through slaughter to a throne,
And shut the gates of mercy on mankind,

The struggling pangs of conscious° truth to hide,
To quench the blushes of ingenuous° shame,
Or heap the shrine of Luxury and Pride
With incense, kindled at the Muse's flame.°

Far from the madding° crowd's ignoble strife, **F**
Their sober wishes never learned to stray;
Along the cool sequestered vale of life
They kept the noiseless tenor° of their way. **G**

Yet ev'n these bones from insult to protect
Some frail memorial° still erected nigh,
With uncouth° rhymes and shapeless sculpture decked,
Implores the passing tribute of a sigh.

Their name, their years, spelt by th' unlettered muse,°
The place of fame and elegy supply:
And many a holy text around she strews, **H**
That teach the rustic moralist to die.

For who to dumb Forgetfulness a prey,
This pleasing anxious being e'er resigned,
Left the warm precincts of the cheerful day,
Nor cast one longing ling'ring look behind?

On some fond breast the parting soul relies,
Some pious drops° the closing eye requires;
Ev'n from the tomb the voice of Nature cries,
Ev'n in our ashes live their wonted fires.

For thee,° who mindful of th' unhonored dead
Dost in these lines their artless tale relate;
If chance, by lonely Contemplation led,
Some kindred spirit shall inquire thy fate, **I**

57. village Hampden: an obscure person who, with opportunity, might have been famous like John Hampden (1594–1643), an English statesman who defied the king over unjust taxation shortly before the English Civil Wars.
60. Cromwell: Lord Protector Oliver Cromwell, who ruled England from 1653 to 1658.

69. conscious: guiltily aware; conscientious.
70. ingenuous: naively innnocent.

72. incense . . . flame: tributes paid to them by poets.

73. madding: frenzied.

76. tenor: course.

78. frail memorial: modest tombstone, in contrast to the elaborate tombs inside the church.
79. uncouth: unsophisticated; artless.
81. unlettered muse: humble engraver of the tombstone.

90. drops: mourners' tears.

93. thee: Gray himself.

D Elements of Literature
Parallelism
The three lines beginning with "Some" unify the description of rural people begun in l. 46. Point out to students that "some" here denotes one among many and thus emphasizes the great number of such people. This is a subtle way in which the poet generalizes.

E Elements of Literature
Allusion
? What sort of person is a "mute inglorious Milton"? [Possible responses: a potentially great poet who has no opportunity to write; a poet whose words no one can hear because they are unpublished.]

F Literary Connections
In an allusion to Gray's "Elegy," British novelist and poet Thomas Hardy (1840–1928) called his first successful novel *Far from the Madding Crowd* (1874). Hardy's novels take place in lonely rural settings similar to Gray's churchyard.

G Critical Thinking
Interpreting
? What do these lines convey about the lives of country people? [Their lives are peaceful; they are fortunate not to get caught up in "ignoble strife."]

H Vocabulary Note
Archaic Phrases
Let students know that "to supply the place" means "to be a substitute," and that "teach . . . to die" means "teach a proper moral attitude about dying."

I Critical Thinking
Hypothesizing
? Who might the "kindred spirit" be? [Possible responses: another poet; a curious person; another lonely, melancholy person.]

Reaching All Students

Struggling Readers
Reading Inverted Sentences was introduced on p. 600. For a lesson directly tied to this poem that teaches students to read inverted sentences using a strategy called Text Reformulation, see the *Reading Skills and Strategies* binder p. 127.

English Language Learners
The combination of inverted sentence structure, archaic vocabulary, and elliptical constructions in Gray's "Elegy" make it a challenge for these readers. Let students work in small groups or with partners, and assign each group or pair a few stanzas to paraphrase and interpret. Remind them to use context clues, questioning strategies, and reference materials.

Advanced Learners
Encourage students to compare and contrast Gray's "Elegy Written in a Country Churchyard" with Milton's elegy "Lycidas." Tell them that both poets were moved to write by the loss of a young friend and that both employ conventional pastoral elements. Ask them to pay particular attention to the word choice, imagery, and metrical patterns of each poem.

A Elements of Literature

Point of View

? Why does Gray give the poem a new speaker for the last eight stanzas? [Possible responses: This gives a voice to one of the obscure people the poem describes. The first speaker has died.]

B Critical Thinking

Interpreting

? What sort of person does this description portray? [Possible responses: lonely, sad, troubled.]

C Elements of Literature

Personification

? What is the effect of giving Earth a lap, Science a frown (or smile), and Melancholy the ability to mark? [Possible responses: Seeming more like people, they evoke sympathy. They seem to be in close relationship with the young poet.]

MAKING MEANINGS

First Thoughts [Respond]

1. Responses will vary. Some students will be struck by pastoral imagery, such as the "lowing herd," while others will recall gothic images, such as the "moping owl."

Shaping Interpretations [Interpret]

2. The poet warns Ambition and Grandeur not to mock the simple country people. There are more than a dozen other instances of personification, including Memory (l. 38), Knowledge (l. 49), Pride (l. 71), and Misery (l. 123).
3. The humble gravestones show names and dates as well as verses, sculpture, and quotations from the Bible, all intended to remind the living of those who are buried there.
4. Most students will agree that it is not necessary to make that assumption in order to understand the poem. The assumption is appealing because we know that Gray led a shy, quiet life like the poet in his poem and because he creates the voice of the old man to describe the young poet.
5. The epitaph describes the poet as educated, generous, sincere, and devout.
6. The stereotype does not fit the lives of many well-known poets who participated in public life, had diverse careers, and did not exhibit the tendency to be melancholy.

(Answers continue on p. T605.)

(A) Haply° some hoary-headed swain° may say,
"Oft have we seen him at the peep of dawn
Brushing with hasty steps the dews away
To meet the sun upon the upland lawn.

"There at the foot of yonder nodding beech
That wreathes its old fantastic roots so high,
His listless length at noontide would he stretch,
And pore upon the brook that babbles by.

(B) "Hard° by yon wood, now smiling as in scorn,
Mutt'ring his wayward fancies he would rove,
Now drooping, woeful wan, like one forlorn,
Or crazed with care, or crossed in hopeless love.

"One morn I missed him on the customed hill,
Along the heath, and near his fav'rite tree;
Another came; nor yet beside the rill,°
Nor up the lawn, nor at the wood was he.

"The next with dirges due in sad array
Slow through the churchway path we saw him borne.
Approach and read (for thou canst read)° the lay,
Graved on the stone beneath yon aged thorn."°

The Epitaph

(C) *Here rests his head upon the lap of Earth*
A youth to Fortune and to Fame unknown:
Fair Science frowned not on his humble birth,°
And Melancholy marked him for her own.

Large was his bounty, and his soul sincere,
Heaven did a recompense as largely send:
He gave to Mis'ry all he had, a tear:
He gained from Heaven ('twas all he wished) a friend.

No farther seek his merits to disclose,
Or draw his frailties from their dread abode,
(There they alike in trembling Hope repose)
The bosom of his Father and his God.

97. haply: perhaps. **hoary-headed swain:** white-haired countryman.

105. hard: close.

111. rill: brook.

115. thou canst read: The "swain" who is speaking is apparently illiterate.

116. thorn: hawthorn bush.

119. fair . . . birth: He was educated—*science* meant learning in general—despite his modest beginnings.

Reading Check

a. The speaker is in the cemetery of a country church at nightfall. He hears the buzz of a beetle, the bells of sheep, and the hoot of an owl.

b. They will never again experience the swallow's song, the cock's crow, the sound of the hunting horn, the blazing hearth, supper, their children's greetings, farm work.

c. They might have become national leaders, musicians, poets. The gems and flowers are symbols of the unrealized potential and talent of the people buried in the churchyard.

d. Their "lot" kept them from holding high political office and being remembered in history. It also prevented them from becoming tyrants, murderers, and lovers of luxury.

e. The old man might remember him as a familiar figure in the neighborhood, quiet and melancholy.

Student to Student

Searching for a Future in the Dusk

In the dusk of a soft summer's eve,
Crushing the cool, prickly lawn,
I lie stretched out
And gaze at the dome sky
like the tip of an enormous egg
Polished to a shiny blue.

I can feel myself soaring **D**
Up, up,
Until I reach out
And touch the thin shell
Of my prison.

The light fades
And my wall drains of color,
Like finger paints in the rain, **E**
Until I can see through it
To the universe beyond;
The purple sea
With a thousand lighthouses
Sprinkling its surface like glitter.

I imagine then,
If I broke the shell,
How far I would tumble
Into my future,
Where I could ride the fireflies
Of possibility
Into the heavens
Of the me to come.

And I wonder,
If I might glance back,
For a moment,
To the shadowing past, **F**
And long
For the prickle of a lawn
At dusk.

—Melynn Minson
Hillcrest High School
Midvale, Utah

Making Meanings

First Thoughts

1. What did you feel was the strongest **image** in this poem? Why?

Reading Check

a. Where is the speaker, and what time of day is it? What, according to the **images** in stanzas 2 and 3, does he hear?

b. In the fourth through eighth stanzas, the speaker describes the ordinary people in the churchyard. Name the various things they will never again experience.

c. What does the speaker imagine these humble people might have become if they'd had the chance (lines 45–60)? What do the details in lines 53–56 have to do with this idea?

d. What did their "lot," or place in life, forbid the poor people to experience, according to lines 61–72?

e. What does the speaker imagine an old man (the "hoary-headed swain") might say of him one day (lines 98–116)?

Shaping Interpretations

2. The poet **personifies** ambition and grandeur in lines 29 and 31. What does he warn them not to do? What other examples of **personification** can you find in the poem?

3. According to lines 77–92, what evidence on their gravestones shows that humble, ordinary people also wish to be remembered?

4. Many readers of the "Elegy" have assumed that Gray himself is the poet whose epitaph is given in the final lines. Is it necessary to make this assumption to understand the poem? Why does the assumption seem attractive?

5. Suppose that Gray is being autobiographical. What defense does he give of his life? Would *you* be happy with such an epitaph—or would you wish to be remembered differently?

6. From Gray's time almost to the present, many people have thought of poets as possessing the

Connecting Across Texts

Connecting with "Elegy Written in a Country Churchyard"

Have students compare and contrast Gray's "Elegy" with "Searching for a Future in the Dusk." They should use a graphic organizer and list such elements as imagery, tone, and theme. Encourage them to look for gothic and pastoral elements in Minson's poem and to comment on which of the two poems reveals a more enthusiastic appetite for experience.

Making Meanings

(Continued from p. T604.)

7. Both quotations reinforce the idea that life is fleeting for everyone and that even achieving glory is made insignificant by the finality of death.

8. Gray includes elements in the "Elegy" that achieve both purposes. His generalizations and use of personification clearly aim at conveying ideas about mortality. At the same time, his use of imagery successfully expresses emotion.

Extending the Text [Synthesize]

9. Gray's poem expresses many timeless feelings, including the dread of death, sorrow at the unfair distribution of wealth and opportunity, the comfort to be found in remembering the dead and hoping one day to be remembered. The student poem, however, sees a beginning in the evening sky where Gray saw only an ending.

Student to Student

In this lyric poem, the speaker anticipates breaking out of a comfortable present into an exciting future of infinite possibility. The optimistic tone is in sharp contrast to Gray's elegiac meditation on death.

D Elements in Literature

Metaphor

? What process does the poet suggest with the image of an egg as a prison? [Possible responses: a baby bird hatching; the process of birth.]

E Elements of Literature

Simile

Ask students to notice this simile and identify others in the poem. Have them discuss how the poet's references to light and color contribute to the optimistic tone of the poem.

F Reading Skills and Strategies

Connecting with the Text

? Do you ever look back with longing on a secure, safe time or place when you were younger and less experienced? [Most students will be able to describe such an experience.]

ELEMENTS OF LITERATURE

Possible Responses

1. Many details are pastoral, such as the herd, the tinkling bell, the birds and plants, the heath, and the rill.

2. Gothic details include the yew (traditional symbol of mourning), the "mold'ring heap" and the "narrow cell."

3. Lines 31–32: "[Don't let] Grandeur hear with a disdainful smile, / The short and simple annals of the poor"; ll. 55–56: "Full many a flower is born to blush unseen,/And waste its sweetness on the desert air"; ll. 73–74: "Far from the madding crowd's ignoble strife,/Their sober wishes never learned to stray."

characteristics described in lines 98–112. Gray established here a **stereotype** that the public long accepted as genuine. Does this stereotype fit any of the poets you have studied so far in this book? (Think particularly of Chaucer, Shakespeare, Donne, Milton, Pope, and Swift.)

7. The poem contains at least two statements that are still frequently quoted:

a. "The paths of glory lead but to the grave." (line 36)

b. "Full many a flower is born to blush unseen, And waste its sweetness on the desert air." (lines 55–56)

How do these lines relate to the poem's **theme**?

8. In one sense, most neoclassical writers thought the purpose of literature was to convey ideas. Most Romantic writers, by contrast, thought the purpose of literature was to convey emotions. Judging by his "Elegy," in which group do you think Gray seems to fit?

Extending the Text

9. What ideas in this old poem still relate to our lives and feelings today? Do you think the student who wrote the poem on page 605 shared any of Gray's feelings?

ELEMENTS OF LITERATURE

The Elegy

The term **elegy** originally referred to a poem written in a particular meter; in Roman literature, elegies are frivolous and sensual. By Gray's time the term *elegy* was applied to longish, serious poems reflecting on death—either death in general or the death of a particular person. Gray ends his "Elegy" with an epitaph—a poem short enough to be inscribed on a particular person's tombstone.

Gray's "Elegy" combines elements from several literary traditions. First of all, it is a **pastoral** elegy. Like Milton's famous elegy *Lycidas,* its setting is outdoors in a beautiful summery landscape. The poet keeps a certain distance from the dirt and bad smells of actual country life. His rural people are not individuals but types: the weary plowman, the busy housewife, the hoary-headed swain. These figures are idealized; oafs and boors do not appear. Rural life in a pastoral is always placid and civilized.

Another element in the "Elegy" is the **Gothic,** which supplies the "moping" owl, the graveyard, and the general gloominess. But unlike most Gothic writers, Gray isn't interested in giving his readers shivers and thrills; he is trying instead to create an atmosphere.

Finally, like many other writers of his time, Gray decorates his poem with polished **generalizations** about life and death: "The paths of glory lead but to the grave." These generalizations give the elegy the solidity of classical architecture.

1. What are five details of **setting** that Gray uses to idealize the **pastoral** landscape in the poem?

2. What are the **Gothic** details that contribute to the atmosphere in lines 13–16?

3. Find at least three additional examples of Gray's use of polished **generalizations.**

READING SKILLS AND STRATEGIES

Analyzing Word Choice and Word Order

Many words in this poem were regarded—until the twentieth century—as particularly "poetic." Examples of such words are *oft* (line 25), *e'er* (line 34), and *ye* (line 37).

1. List three other "poetic" words you find in the elegy. What words would be used in their place today?

2. What effect do such words have on your reading of this poem?

In many of Gray's sentences, the normal word order of English (subject-verb-complement) is violated. Gray writes "The air a solemn stillness holds" instead of "The air holds a solemn stillness."

3. Find other examples of **inverted word order** in the poem. How would you rephrase them so that they conform to normal English word order?

4. Put your reworded sentences back in the poem. What happens to the meter or rhyme?

Perhaps the most difficult lines to sort out syntactically are lines 61–72. The following outline might help to clarify the **syntax** of these lines:

READING SKILLS AND STRATEGIES

Possible Responses

1. "o'er" (l. 63), *over;* "thee" (l. 93), *you;* "yon" (l. 105), *that* or *yonder.*

2. The words make the poem sound formal and give it the ring of antiquity.

3. "Oft did the harvest to their sickle yield" (l. 25): The harvest often yielded to their sickle; "Some pious drops the closing eye requires" (l. 90): The closing eye requires some pious drops.

4. The stress pattern doesn't always conform to iambic pentameter and the end rhyme is lost.

5. Their circumstances did not let them command the applause of officials, ignore everyday worries, give large amounts to charity, or become famous. Nor has their poverty kept them simply from doing good, but also it has kept them from doing harm. Their situation also did not allow them to kill to gain a throne, to ignore the needs of others, to lie, to hide their feelings of shame, or to become conceited because poets praised them.

"Their lot forbade" them
"to command" "the applause of list'ning senates"
"to despise" "the threats of pain and ruin"
"to scatter plenty o'er a smiling land,
And read their hist'ry in a nation's eyes."

"Nor" has their lot ever
"circumscribed alone
Their growing virtues, but their crimes confined."

Their lot also forbade them
"To hide" "the struggling pangs of conscious truth"
"To quench the blushes of ingenuous shame,
Or heap the shrine of Luxury and Pride
With incense, kindled at the Muse's flame."

5. Try now to **paraphrase** lines 61–72 using conventional syntax and as many sentences as you need.

Choices: Building Your Portfolio

Writer's Notebook

1. Collecting Ideas for a Persuasive Essay

When Thomas Gray writes "the paths of glory lead but to the grave," you have a clear idea of his stance: Despite fame, one inevitable destination awaits us all. Effective persuasive writing also relies on conveying a clear stance—in a thesis statement giving the writer's position on an issue. Review the controversial issues you've explored in your other Writer's Notebook entries. Which issues grab your interest? Select two issues; then write a thesis statement that conveys your position on each issue. Working with a partner, discuss your thesis statements. How can you make your stance clearer or stronger? Save your work for the Writer's Workshop on page 612.

Comparing Elegies

2. Elegies Across the Centuries

In a brief essay, discuss the similarities and differences between Gray's "Elegy" and another famous elegy, "The Seafarer," on page 56. Consider the elements of **speaker, theme,** and **tone.**

Creative Writing

3. Talking Back to the Poet

Suppose one of the villagers was allowed to speak his or her epitaph. Write out what he or she might say to the poet. You might consider these characters: the busy housewife; the children's sire; the person once full of "celestial fire"; the person who might have ruled an empire; the person who might have "waked" the lyre; the village Hampden; the mute inglorious Milton; the Cromwell; the hoary-headed swain.

Creative Writing

4. Graveyard Meditations

Suppose you were standing in a graveyard today. Write a brief meditation about the experience, including a description of the place, of the imagined lives of the people buried there, and of your feelings about death. Be sure to describe the time of day, the weather, and the sounds you hear. (If you don't want to use yourself as the speaker, make up a speaker.)

Performance

5. Gray Alive!

Prepare the elegy for a group performance. You might want to have a group of male readers, a group of female readers, and several solo parts. Give each reader a copy of the poem so that he or she can take notes on how the assigned lines should be read. Rehearse your performance, and consider asking several student critics to analyze and critique your oral interpretation of the poem.

Grading Timesaver

Rubrics for each Choices assignment appear on p. 147 in the *Portfolio Management System.*

Choices: Building Your Portfolio

1. **Writer's Notebook** Remind students of the elements of a thesis statement.
2. **Comparing Elegies** Have students list evidence of tone, theme, and speaker for each of the elegies, and then organize the information from their lists on a Venn diagram. This will help them highlight similarities and differences and plan their paragraphs before they begin writing their critical essay.
3. **Creative Writing** Discuss with the class the various characters the poem provides: the housewife; the farmer; the potential statesman, musician, or poet; the old man. Encourage them to be creative in composing an epitaph, possibly using meter, rhyme, or figurative language that fits the character they have chosen.
4. **Creative Writing** Ask students to describe cemeteries they have visited and to compare the sensory details they recall with those in Gray's "Elegy." Encourage them to find present-day equivalents for the pastoral and gothic images in Gray's poem.
5. **Performance** Establish groups of four or five students, and provide ample time for planning and preparation. Tell the groups that they may take creative liberties with the poem, using repetition for emphasis or even adding lines for some characters. They should aim to bring out the sentiments the elegy evokes rather than simply turning it into a stage play. Provide them with a checklist of criteria for a successful presentation, which they can use while planning and again when they evaluate other groups' performances.

Read On

Students should be encouraged to choose additional readings that will enrich their understanding of the historical period and of the literary, social, and cultural concepts that have been introduced in class.

Portfolio Assessment Options

The following projects will enable students to demonstrate understanding of what they read. Videotapes and audiotapes as well as original artwork reinforce a variety of learning styles and diversify portfolio contents.

- **Be a Boswell** Ask students to write a biographical anecdote about a person they have been reading about. They should pretend that they are a friend or acquaintance, as Boswell was of Dr. Johnson, and should write in the first person.
- **Film at Eleven** Students can plan and stage a hypothetical interview, in the style of a TV news-magazine show, with a person from one of the selections. Working with a partner, they may make an audiotape or a videotape of the interview.
- **In the Interest of Science** Have students draw up a scientific proposal for submission to the Royal Society of London. The proposal should outline a new experiment including the hypothesis to be tested, the procedures to be followed, and perhaps the anticipated results. Charts, diagrams, and illustrations may accompany the proposal.
- **The Screenplay** Students may choose a significant or emotionally charged scene from the literature and write a screenplay that includes dialogue, stage directions, camera angles, and so on. Working with a small group, they may videotape the scene using the screenplay and the directions it includes.
- **Classic Comics** Using all or part of a work of literature, have students re-create the action and dialogue in comic-book format.

READ ON

Diary of a Castaway

Since its publication in 1719, Daniel Defoe's *Robinson Crusoe* has spawned countless imitations, adaptations, and even a TV sitcom (*Gilligan's Island,* which remains popular decades after its debut in the 1960s). Perhaps the story contained in Crusoe's fictional autobiography has endured because it poses an age-old question: How might *we* react if plucked from our ordinary lives and set on a barren island? Could we face the physical hardships and mental isolation of such an extraordinary new life?

An "Ordinary" Day

As it did in Daniel Defoe's *A Journal of the Plague Year,* the raw material of life serves as a basis for fiction in *One Day in the Life of Ivan Denisovich* (Penguin). Aleksandr Solzhenitsyn took firsthand materials—his own eight years in a Stalinist labor camp—and reworked these personal experiences into a narrative related by an everyman character dubbed Ivan (Russian for John).

Down on the Farm

Like Pope and Swift, George Orwell uses satire to reveal the absurdities of human nature. In his 1945 novel *Animal Farm* (Harcourt Brace), Orwell satirizes the problems of a supposedly equal society. The animals of Manor Farm revolt against their incompetent owner and install the "Seven Commandments of Animalism," which the sheep simply remember as "four legs good, two legs bad." But when the pigs Napoleon and Snowball disagree about the future of the farm, a rivalry for power ensues. (This novel is available in the HRW Library.)

The Mad Monarch

King George III (r. 1760–1820) lost the American Colonies for good, and his mind for a brief spell. His suffering transforms him from a distant, public figure in control of others to a person of flesh and blood, at the mercy of nature and those around him. Nigel Hawthorne stars in *The Madness of King George,* a 1995 film directed by Nicholas Hytner and based on Alan Bennett's play *The Madness of George III.*

A Scientific Star

Scientific activity flourished in the second half of the seventeenth century, with London as an important center. Isaac Newton was the first notable hero of modern science, the man who brought the heavenly bodies down to earth with his theory of gravitation. But did an apple *really* fall on his head? Find out in *Physics: From Newton to the Big Bang* (Franklin Watts), Albert and Eve Stwertka's interesting history of modern physics.

The English Language

Decorum and Order

by John Algeo

In the eighteenth century, some English speakers believed that the English language had become as good as it could be. Therefore, they should try to prevent any more changes, which could only lead to the degeneration of the language. It was a foolish opinion, but some people today still hold it. Only, they think that English has reached perfection in *our* time, so any change from the way *we* talk and write will lead to the death of our language.

Change Is Growth

A language does not die or degenerate simply because it changes. A language dies only when nobody speaks it. The oft-predicted death of English is like that of Mark Twain, who read his own obituary in an American newspaper while he was in England. He cabled the newspaper: "The reports of my death are greatly exaggerated." So are reports of the "death" of English.

Throughout its history, English has grown in the number of its speakers and the uses it is put to. Today, English is the most widely distributed language in the world and is used for more purposes—scientific, technical, commercial, and personal—than any other language. Far from being in danger of degenerating or dying, English is among the most vital of all human languages. [A]

Change in language is natural. It is, moreover, a good thing, for without change a language would indeed die. Change in language has many causes. When English speakers first settled North America, they found animals, plants, land formations, and other things for which they had no names. To talk about these unfamiliar things, they had to **adapt old words, coin new words,** or **borrow words from other languages.** [B]

Americans have done all three things. English sailors had used the word *bluff* as an adjective to mean "broad and flat"; Americans adapted it as a noun to mean "cliff," of which they encountered a good many. To name the action of reorganizing an election district for the unfair advantage of one party, Americans coined the word *gerrymander* (from Elbridge *Gerry,* a nineteenth-century governor of Massachusetts, who helped carve out an election district that looked like a *salamander*). In the Southwest, English-speaking cowboys learned from their Spanish-speaking counterparts how to catch horses and cattle with a long rope that had a loop with a slipknot at one end. They borrowed the Spanish name for the rope: *lasso.*

Another cause of change is a natural drift in the way we use language. As each new generation learns English, it introduces little changes. And so over the generations, a language gradually changes, until one day we realize that some very big and important changes have happened over a thousand years, although none of the thirty generations who lived during that time was aware of using language very differently from those who came before or after them.

Change in language, far from being a sign of degeneracy, is the way language adapts to new conditions. It is the way language stays alive. Change is not degeneration; it is growth. All living things must grow

> Change in language, far from being a sign of degeneracy, is the way language adapts to new conditions. It is the way language stays alive.

OBJECTIVES

1. Understand and appreciate how language changes
2. Trace the development of dictionaries
3. Compare dictionary entries
4. Investigate new words
5. Identify usage problems

A Cultural Connections

Mandarin Chinese is the only language spoken by more people in the world today than English.

B Background

Of the estimated 750,000 words in English, about half are of Germanic origin, and the next largest group is of Latin origin—either from Latin itself or from one of the Romance languages. Examples of words borrowed or derived from other languages include these: *psychology* (Greek), *coffee* (Turkish), *pajamas* (Hindi), *bazaar* (Persian), *vodka* (Russian), *robot* (Czech). Native American languages also contributed important words, including *toboggan* and *skunk*.

Resources

Viewing and Representing

Videocassette A, Segment 2

Available in English and Spanish.

This segment explores the development of the English language and literature from the Restoration through the twentieth century. For full lesson plans and worksheets, see the *Visual Connections Teacher's Manual.*

Reaching All Students

Struggling Readers

Before they read the selection, have students use the title of the selection as well as the subheadings to create questions they expect the author to answer. They should record the questions in their reading notes, leaving room to fill in answers as they read. Encourage them to create more than one question for each section.

English Language Learners

Ask students to list English words that have been derived or directly borrowed from their native languages. Likewise, make lists of English words that have been incorporated into their native languages. For additional strategies to supplement instruction for English language learners, see

- *Lesson Plans Including Strategies for English-Language Learners*

Advanced Learners

Encourage students to consider in more depth the social, cultural, and political implications of language. They might research related topics, such as the movement to make English the official language of the United States or the history of efforts to suppress Native American or other indigenous languages.

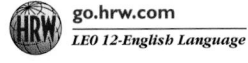

Ⓐ Cultural Connections

In 1994, the French legislature passed the French Language Law, imposing stiff fines for the public use of English words and phrases. Among the popular terms being outlawed were "Walkman," "joystick," and "weekend." This effort to arrest change in the French language has been largely unsuccessful, and portions of the law have since been repealed.

Ⓑ Historical Connections

In 1604, Robert Cawdrey, a teacher, assembled the first English dictionary, which he called *The Table Alphabeticall of Hard Words*. The book defined about 3,000 English words that had been taken from other languages. Later in the century, more extensive dictionaries were published. In 1721, Nathan Bailey produced a dictionary containing 60,000 words, an early attempt to define all words rather than just the difficult ones.

Ⓒ Background

Computers and information technology have brought about the introduction of countless new words, including many that are compounds of existing words (such as *laptop* and *database*). Literally hundreds of specialized dictionaries have been published to help readers keep up with these new vocabularies—some with apt titles, such as *Cyberspeak: An Online Dictionary* (Andy Ihnatko, 1996.)

through change. Languages are no exception.

Stop the Changes!

Some English speakers today are obsessed with the fear that the changes they notice in English mean the language is about to slip into incoherence and to disintegrate, unless we do something about it—and fast. That obsession first became a large-scale concern of English speakers during the eighteenth century.

Jonathan Swift was one of the writers of this period who was concerned about the well-being of English and the dangers he saw it facing. He especially disliked the idea that a language should be "perpetually changing." So Swift wrote *A Proposal for Correcting, Improving, and Ascertaining the English Tongue* (1712), in which he suggested that a group of persons should take the responsibility on themselves of overseeing the language, improving it, unifying it, and above all stabilizing it so that it would stop changing. A number of other countries in Ⓐ Europe had established or were to develop such groups, usually called "academies": Italy, France, and Spain are examples.

The idea of an English Academy never caught on, however. One reason for its failure was the individualism of many English speakers, who were unwilling to let anybody else tell them how they ought to talk. Another reason was the rapid development of English Ⓑ dictionaries, which became "authorities" for English speakers who were insecure about their own usage and wanted advice about what to say and write.

The Dictionary

The tradition of making English dictionaries reached a high point with Samuel Johnson, who in 1755 published his two-volume *Dictionary of the English Language*. In the United States, Noah Webster produced a dictionary that came to fill the place in U.S. life that Johnson's dictionary filled in Great Britain. Webster wanted to produce a dictionary that would record the English of the United States, not just that of the mother country.

Webster's dictionary was so successful that today many dictionaries use *Webster* in their titles, but none of them preserve anything from old Noah's book. *Webster* in a dictionary's title is no guarantee of anything—it is only an advertising technique to take advantage of the fact that people associate Webster with dictionaries. With dictionaries, you can't always tell a book by its cover.

In the nineteenth century, a group of English scholars began to work on a dictionary to replace Johnson's, which had become very outdated. Their work eventually developed into the greatest dictionary in the world: *The Oxford English Dictionary*. Recently this dictionary has been expanded to twenty volumes and also put into electronic form as a compact disc.

Samuel Johnson composed his dictionary single-handedly and by candlelight. Today, teams of lexicographers cooperate in producing dictionaries using the latest computer techniques. As the language changes, so do the ways we keep up with it.

Changes Are Happening Today

Jonathan Swift was not able to stop English from changing, however much he wanted to. Nor can anyone else. The nature of language is to change, and we can see change going on around us today.

Pronunciation is constantly changing. Not long ago, many Americans pronounced the words *horse* and *hoarse* or *morning* and *mourning* differently from each other; now most pronounce them alike. Today most Americans still pronounce the words *cot* and *caught* or *pond* and *pawned* differently, but increasingly many of us are pronouncing them alike. In a hundred years or so, it is likely that such pairs will be **homophones** (words that sound the same, but are different in meaning and spelling) for the majority of our fellow citizens. *Forehead* used to be generally pronounced to rhyme with *horrid;* today, it usually rhymes with *more bread.*

The very words we use are also changing. We make up **new** Ⓒ **words** out of elements already in English, like *to eyeball, feedback,* and *minibike.* We **borrow words from foreign languages,** like *karate* from Japanese, *klutz* from Yiddish, and *macho* from Spanish. Words also change their meaning, or disappear altogether if we stop using them, often because

Using Students' Strengths

Auditory Learners

Have students sample some differences in pronunciation. Begin by having them pronounce the example words listed under Pronunciation above. Then, select words from the dictionary for them to pronounce. Look for words such as *tomato* and *harass,* for which the dictionary provides two pronunciations. Call attention to any differences in pronunciation among members of the class and discuss the reasons for these differences.

Intrapersonal/Interpersonal Learners

Before students read the selection, have them freewrite about why they think people resist language change. Encourage them to include examples from their own experience. After they have read the essay, arrange them in small groups to discuss and compare what they wrote and what they learned from their reading.

Verbal/Linguistic Learners

Form teams to play the "dictionary game." Using the dictionary, each team writes a specified number of unfamiliar words and their definitions on slips of paper. They invent one imaginary word and its definition and include it with the real words. Their opponents must determine, without checking the dictionary, which is the imaginary word.

the things they name have changed or disappeared. For example, people used to preserve food by keeping it in a chest with blocks of ice; such a chest was called an *icebox.* When gas and electric refrigerators were invented, some people continued to use the old word for them, thus changing the meaning of *icebox.* But gradually the word has been disappearing; it is rare today and soon will probably drop out of the language altogether.

We also change our **grammar.** For example, the older past tense of the verb *dive* is *dived.* But today we use a new past form, *dove,* invented by analogy with irregular verbs like *drive,* whose past tense is *drove.* D

The words we use, the way we use them, and the way we say them are all changing constantly. Often, when a change begins, many people do not like it. It sounds odd, sloppy, or mistaken. And new uses do often begin as mistakes. But whether the new use has been deliberately introduced or has slipped into the language as an error, if many people adopt it, it becomes part of the language—just one more option we have for expressing ourselves. When a change is new or has not yet been widely accepted, we need to be careful about using it, because some people will be so distracted by the way we are talking that they will fail to hear what we are saying.

What Is Good English?

Good English is English that communicates the ideas and effects we want to get across. Bad English is language that does not communicate successfully. Bad English may be ambiguous: "Mike lost his textbook, but somebody found it and put it in his locker." Whose locker did the book go in, Mike's or somebody's? Bad English may actually be clear, but distracting: "Everybody should have his own textbook." Is everybody male? Aren't there any females around? If we say, "Everybody should have their own textbook," someone will object that *everybody* is singular, whereas *their* is plural, so the two don't go together. If we say, "Everybody should have his or her own textbook," someone else will object that the statement sounds too awkward.

Each of the choices above is likely to distract someone who hears or reads it. All of them may interfere with communication, and therefore all of them are, to that extent, bad English. The best English in such cases avoids the problem by rewording the statement: "Everybody should have a textbook" or "All students should have their own textbooks." Good English does not get in the way; it does not call attention to itself and away from the message. Good English communicates just what we want to communicate and nothing else.

Try It Out

1. **Comparing dictionary entries.** Compare the sample entry for the word *giggle* in Johnson's *Dictionary* (page 571) with the entry for that word in a modern dictionary. What kinds of information does the modern dictionary give that Johnson's does not? How do the meanings Johnson gives compare with those in the modern dictionary?
2. **Investigating new words.** The following words and expressions are all relatively new to the English language. How many of them are familiar to you? Which of them are listed in the dictionary you use?

   Catch-22
   ego trip
   laptop
   schlep
   in-line skates
   CD-ROM
   play hardball
   ten-speed
3. **Identifying usage problems.** People disagree about the correct usage of the following words. Do you know what the disagreement is? Look up these words in at least two dictionaries to see what is said about them.

   impact (verb)
   hopefully
   data
   irregardless

D Background

A familiar example is the evolving past participle of *sneak.* Traditionally, it is *sneaked,* but *snuck* is gradually gaining acceptance. *Snuck* appeared in the *Oxford English Dictionary* for the first time in the 1986 Supplement; several citations are included. The 1980 *Oxford American Dictionary* cautions, "The past form *snuck* is only acceptable when the writer is attempting to portray regional dialect." The 1991 *American Heritage Dictionary* labels it "nonstandard." Yet *snuck* is heard with greater and greater frequency and will probably gain legitimacy over time.

Try It Out
Possible Responses

1. The modern dictionary gives the pronunciation and the tense forms for the verb. Most soft-cover modern dictionaries no longer include the derivation of the word. Modern dictionaries are neutral in their definitions and do not mention Scotland.
2. Responses will vary, depending on students' experience and the dictionaries they consult.
3. Many maintain that *impact* is a noun and should not be used as a verb. Many also regard *hopefully* as an adverb and object to its use to mean "it is hoped." *Data* is technically the plural of *datum*, but *data* is now often treated as singular. *Irregardless* is technically a double negative, since both the prefix *ir-* and the suffix *-less* negate *regard.*

Resources

Assessment
Formal Assessment

- The English Language Test, p. 109

Assessing Learning

Check Test: Short Answers

1. When does a language die? [when no one speaks it anymore]
2. How do people name new things and ideas? [They borrow from other languages, coin new words, and adapt existing words.]
3. Why does language change? [to adapt to new conditions]
4. What is the purpose of a dictionary? [It is a source of information on definitions, pronunciations, and derivations.]
5. What is good English? [English that communicates clearly]

MAIN OBJECTIVE
Write a persuasive essay on a controversial issue

PROCESS OBJECTIVES
1. Use appropriate prewriting techniques to identify and develop a topic
2. Create a first draft
3. Use Evaluation Criteria as a basis for determining revision strategies
4. Revise the first draft incorporating suggestions generated by self- or peer-evaluation
5. Proofread and correct errors
6. Create a final draft
7. Choose an appropriate method of publication
8. Reflect on progress as a writer

Planning

- **Block Schedule**
  Block Scheduling Lesson Plans with Pacing Guide
- **One-Stop Planner**
  CD-ROM with Test Generator

BUILDING YOUR PORTFOLIO
Writer's Workshop

Technology HELP

See Writer's Workshop 2 CD-ROM. *Assignment: Controversial Issue.*

ASSIGNMENT
Write a persuasive essay on a controversial issue.

AIM
To persuade; to inform and explain.

AUDIENCE
People who disagree on the issue or are undecided; readers of your school or local newspaper.

PERSUASIVE WRITING
AN ESSAY ON A CONTROVERSIAL ISSUE

Both Jonathan Swift and Alexander Pope were attuned to the **controversial issues** of their day, and they didn't shy away from addressing those issues and trying to win others to their way of thinking. When you care deeply about a controversial issue, it's only natural to take a stand on it and to defend your position against objections. That's the essence of writing a persuasive essay. Persuasive writing will force you to draw on a wide range of writing skills: analyzing causes and effects, comparing and contrasting details, reporting information, and evaluating points for refuting objections to your arguments.

Prewriting

WORK IN PROGRESS

1. **Checking your Writer's Notebook.** By completing the Writer's Notebook activities in Collections 6 and 7, you may have already completed some of the prewriting for a persuasive essay on a controversial issue. Check your entries for usable material, and then proceed with the prewriting activities that follow.
2. **Exploring possible issues.** Today, no less than in Swift's and Pope's time, our society is confronted with controversial social and political issues that responsible people feel compelled to think out for themselves. To find an issue that intrigues you, try the strategies for elaboration that follow.

Strategies for Elaboration: Exploring Issues

- Watch or listen to TV or radio news programs and talk shows. They'll give you ideas about current controversies.
- Look through recent newspapers and magazines, noting the issues raised in articles, editorials, editorial cartoons, and news photos.
- Read through your Writer's Notebooks for entries dealing with issues and controversies.
- Brainstorm with friends, classmates, and family members about possible controversial issues.
- Draw up a series of "Should . . . ?" questions. One example: "Should failing students be allowed to participate in school-sponsored extracurricular activities?"

Resources: Print and Media

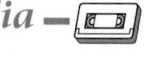

Writing and Language
- *Portfolio Management System*
  Prewriting, p. 149
  Peer editing, p. 150
  Assessment Rubric, p. 151
- *Workshop Resources*
  Revision Strategy Teaching Notes, p. 21
  Revision Strategy Transparencies 11, 12, and 13
- *Writer's Workshop 2 CD-ROM*
  Controversial Issue

The history
of the written
word is rich and
Page 1

3. **Choosing an issue.** After you've explored possible issues, you'll have to select one for your essay. To choose one issue to write about, use these guidelines:
   - Do you really care? You'll write more convincingly about an issue that you feel strongly about.
   - Is the issue arguable? Make sure the issue is one that reasonable people may disagree on. For instance, you'd have a hard time finding anyone to argue that citizens *shouldn't* vote.
   - Is it truly a controversial issue, not merely a matter of taste? You may believe that Broadway musicals are the ultimate American musical form, but you won't convince jazz buffs that jazz is inferior. It's a personal preference.
4. **Taking a stand.** Begin your exploration of the issue by spending a few minutes freewriting about it. Then state your opinion on the issue in one or two sentences. Even if your mind's not completely made up yet, writing a preliminary **thesis statement**—also known as a **proposition** or **position statement**—will guide you as you gather information. Remember that you can always change the wording of your proposition once you've reached a final conclusion.
5. **Targeting your audience.** Even more than other types of writing, persuasive writing is audience-centered. To convince readers that your opinion has merit (even if they don't agree with it), you need to know and understand their views and values. Adopting a formal, serious tone will help you create a favorable impression and make readers inclined to take your ideas seriously, as will approaching them with appeals tailored to their needs and interests.
   - **Tap into their feelings. Emotional appeals** stir readers' feelings. Used sparingly, such appeals can help personalize the issue for readers. If you're advocating the use of "signers" to translate sports events for students with hearing disabilities, try to let your audience know how it *feels* to be unable to participate fully in school activities. Words with strong **connotations** (ones with powerful positive *or* negative overtones) can be particularly effective in tapping into people's emotions.
   - **Reason with them. Logical appeals** engage your readers' reasoning skills, their ability to think clearly. Readers expect you to offer sound reasons for your position (statements that explain *why* you hold your opinion

Introducing the Writer's Workshop

- Pass out copies of back issues of a national news magazine.
- Ask students to find the advertisement that they think is the most persuasive.
- Ask volunteers to explain why they chose the ads they did.
- Encourage students to think about what the regular readers of the magazine are probably like.
- Point out that to be effective, persuasive writing needs to target a particular audience.
- Remind students that although they do not write persuasive material every day, they are the targets of persuasion every day.

Teaching the Writer's Workshop

Prewriting

- Remind students that if the purpose of their writing is to persuade, they must consider their audience as well as their arguments. As they select a topic, they must also be considering the nature of their intended audience.
- Have students read and discuss the prewriting information included on pp. 612–616. In particular, have them work on organizing their papers according to one of the methods shown on pp. 615–616.

Reaching All Students

Struggling Writers

Students having trouble with the concept of targeting specific audiences may need to see some examples of different approaches for different audiences. Give students a controversial issue, such as requiring students to wear uniforms, and two distinct hypothetical audiences—high school students and board-of-education members. Put students into small groups to analyze their two audiences and compose a one-paragraph argument for each. Then, have students list and discuss specific differences in approach, vocabulary, tone, and style for each audience.

Prewriting

- When students are selecting topics, you might want to encourage them to select issues about which they have some firsthand knowledge. Suggest that they consider topics related to an issue at school or in the community.
- Encourage students to avoid abstract topics like "parents and teenagers should communicate more with one another." These topics tend not to be controversial, and they produce hypothetical examples that are rarely persuasive.

Try It Out

Answers

1. Circular reasoning; "Sixteen-year-olds are mature enough to vote and should be allowed to do so."
2. Hasty generalization; "A dress code might be a partial solution to our problems."
3. Either-or reasoning; "The crime rate may decline if we build more prisons."

on the issue) and to back up your reasons with solid evidence, or proof. Appropriate factual evidence may consist of statistics, examples, and anecdotes (brief stories based on personal experience)—all of which can be verified by testing, by drawing on personal observations, or by consulting reliable sources. Expert testimony (statements by recognized authorities on the issue) also qualifies as evidence.

Try It Out

Identify the logical fallacy in each of the following sentences. Then revise the fallacy to make the statement logical.

1. The voting age should be lowered to sixteen because sixteen-year-olds are mature enough to vote.
2. Our school needs a dress code because a dress code is the solution to our problems.
3. Unless the state builds more prisons, the crime rate will continue to rise.

Strategies for Elaboration: Avoiding Fallacies

In listing reasons for your position, take care to avoid these **fallacies,** or mistakes in logic.

- **Hasty generalization**—basing a conclusion on insufficient evidence or overlooking exceptions: *No local merchants will suffer if the proposed chain store is approved.*
- **Attacking the person** (in Latin, *ad hominem,* meaning "to the person"; informally, "name-calling")—attacking people who support the issue: *Hunters just enjoy killing animals.*
- **False authority**—quoting an expert in one field as an authority in an unrelated field: *According to former state Supreme Court Justice Eldon Bates, the state's annual vehicle inspections are a waste of taxpayers' time and money.*
- **Circular reasoning**—offering as a reason a statement that's actually a restatement of an opinion: *The City Council should build more bike paths because our community needs bike paths.*
- **Either-or reasoning**—assuming that an issue has only two possible sides: *Either we abolish the welfare system or we foster perpetual dependence on government handouts.*
- **Non sequitur** (Latin for "It does not follow")—presenting unrelated ideas as though one were the logical consequence of the other: *Our city's rapid population growth demands a higher speed limit.*

- **Earn their trust. Ethical appeals** invoke your readers' sense of fair play, establishing your credibility and character. Demonstrating that you're knowledgeable, reasonable, sincere, and trustworthy helps win respect for you and, in turn, for your ideas.

  One way to establish your trustworthiness is to consider different sides of an issue, to acknowledge the most significant **counterarguments** (opposing points). By **conceding,** or accommodating, opposing points that do have merit, you establish common ground without sacrificing your principles. Then you can concentrate on **refuting,** or providing conclusive evidence against, those counterarguments that you consider invalid.

6. **Coping with counterarguments.** Once you've listed possible reasons in support of your position, get together with a partner or a small group to brainstorm for likely counterarguments. Think about the kinds of evidence that will convince your particular audience to rethink their counterarguments. You may find it helpful to chart the most significant counterarguments and possible refutations for them, as in the following example.

Skill Link

Recognizing Logical, Deceptive, and Faulty Modes of Persuasion

Some examples of faulty arguments follow. After discussing in class why the arguments are faulty, have students prepare more examples of faulty reasoning and keep the examples in the classroom for reference.

1. Joe failed his Regents so he will never get into college. [generalization]
2. The human body is like a machine. Every problem can be traced to some faulty mechanism. [false analogy]
3. Everyone agrees that lowering taxes is a good idea. [begging the question]
4. The Republicans lost because very few women voted. [cause-and-effect fallacy]
5. If we don't balance the budget, we will destroy social security. [either-or fallacy]
6. People who don't read aren't very intelligent. [stereotype]

Model

Proposition: The City Council should approve the construction of a sports stadium proposed for the city's south side.

Counterarguments	Refutations
• Taxpayer dollars should not be directed to building this facility.	• Tax revenues generated by the new facility will balance out any expenditures.
• Property taxes will increase city-wide to pay for construction.	• Construction of the new facility will be paid for by a bond issue and by funds from the professional sports teams that will use the facility.
• The new facility will disturb residents in the area.	• Traffic and sound-pollution control measures are a fundamental part of construction plans.

7. **Organizing your material: deduction or induction?** As you begin to organize your material, decide whether you'll present your argument **deductively** (moving from your proposition to your reasons and evidence) or **inductively** (moving from your reasons and evidence to your proposition). These two different approaches can be thought of as a pair of pyramids, one upside-down and the other right-side up.

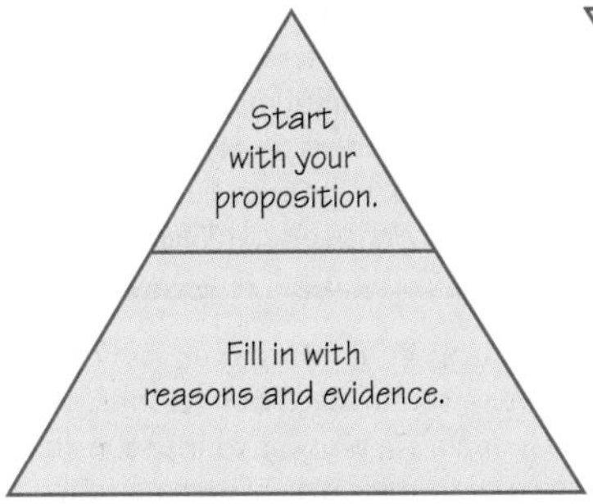

Deductive Reasoning

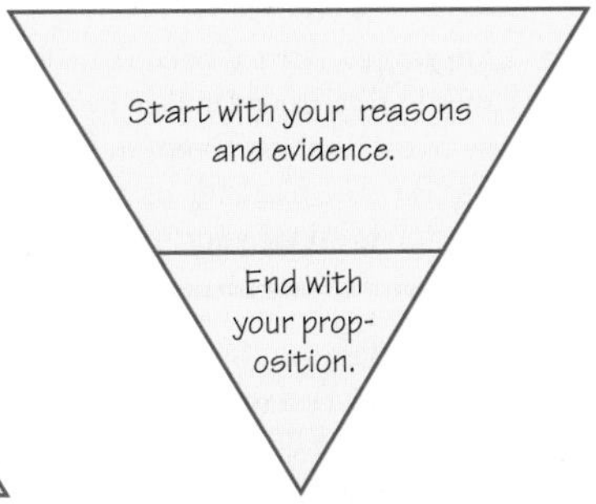

Inductive Reasoning

Think, too, about how you'll work in the counterarguments you've chosen to concede or refute—before, after, or along with your own argument. Three basic types of organizational patterns can work well for a persuasive essay:

- **Order of importance**—beginning or ending with the appeal likely to have the strongest impact on your audience.
- **Chronological order**—proposing (or attacking) a course of action in the order events occurred or would occur.

Communications Handbook HELP

See Taking Notes and Documenting Sources.

Using the Model

Remind students that while it is very important to have counterarguments and refutations clearly outlined, it is equally important that the counterarguments and refutations be supported by strong evidence. Have students assume the role of the writer of this chart and evaluate the supporting evidence:

- ? Do I have projected tax revenues for the new facility? Is the source reliable?
- ? Do I have evidence to support my contention that the facility will be paid for by a bond issue and by funds from the professional teams that will use the facility?
- ? Do I have reliable evidence that the construction plans are sound?

Crossing the Curriculum

Debate

Have students debate with a partner the controversial issues they chose to write about. The first partner should present his or her arguments in favor of the position, and the second student should offer objections and counterarguments. The partners should then switch roles. Students can take notes during the debates to use later in addressing counterarguments in their own essays.

Drafting

Remind students to use only every other line when they write their drafts. They should also leave extra space in the right margin. These blank spaces will be used for comments and editing marks.

Evaluating and Revising

Have students use the Evaluation Criteria provided here to review their drafts and determine needed revisions.

Proofreading

Have students proofread their own papers first and then exchange them with another student. Encourage students to look for strong, parallel phrasing and to edit sentences for use of parallel structure. The Language Workshop on p. 617 includes models and practice in parallel structure.

If time permits, the edited copy should be put aside for at least a day before it is proofread for the final time by the author.

Resources

Peer Editing Forms and Rubrics

- *Portfolio Management System,* p. 149

Revision Transparencies

- *Workshop Resources,* p. 21

Evaluation Criteria

An effective persuasive essay

1. *focuses on a controversial issue*
2. *defines the issue clearly*
3. *provides sufficient background information*
4. *includes a clearly worded position statement*
5. *supports the position with relevant, convincing reasons and evidence*
6. *concedes or refutes counterarguments*
7. *conveys a knowledgeable and sincere tone*
8. *concludes by underscoring the writer's position on the issue*

Language Workshop HELP

Parallel structure: page 617.

Communications Handbook HELP

See Proofreading.

Revision STRATEGIES

Is your tone assertive rather than arrogant, reasonable rather than derisive? Working with a partner, circle any words in your draft that seem arrogant or derisive. Then, replace them with words less likely to offend.

- **Logical order**—comparing and contrasting opposing positions and your refutations, either by grouping all objections and following them with all your refutations or by alternating opposing positions and refutations.

Drafting

1. **The introduction: defining the issue.** Before readers can begin to follow your line of reasoning, they need to know precisely what the issue is. Get them involved immediately with a vivid image, a startling statistic, an engaging anecdote, or a rhetorical question (one asked merely for effect). Define the issue clearly, provide any necessary background, and (if you've reasoned deductively) state your proposition succinctly.
2. **The body: developing your argument.** As you present each of your reasons, buttress it with evidence drawn from your investigation of the issue. Emphasize your most compelling reason by devoting the most space to it. In arguing your case and accommodating or refuting counterarguments, remember to keep your tone reasonable and confident.

Strategies for Elaboration: Drafting Persuasively

Focus on the following strategies to develop your persuasive essay:

- **Repetition.** Focus attention on key terms and core ideas by arranging them in parallel structure.
- **Rhythm.** Create a rhythmic flow of sound by using words or syllables with similar vowel or consonant sounds, by varying the length and structure of sentences, and by beginning some sentences with a phrase, a clause, or a one-word modifier instead of the subject.
- **Language.** Formal needn't be forbidding, nor must serious language be stuffy. In fact, using familiar, everyday language is a subtle but effective way of establishing common ground with your readers. A persuasive essay isn't the place for using slang and sentence fragments, but it *is* the place for speaking your mind directly, forcefully, and self-confidently.

3. **The conclusion: driving the message home.** To bring your essay to an effective end, restate your opinion forcefully, summarize your reasons, or issue a call to action. If you've reasoned inductively, present your proposition so that it seems the natural outgrowth of everything that has led up to it.

Evaluating and Revising

As you read your or your partner's draft, evaluate these points:

- Is the issue clearly defined? Is it arguable? Has enough background information been provided?
- Is the proposition clearly stated? Is its placement effective?
- Are the reasons and evidence relevant and convincing?
- Is the tone knowledgeable, reasonable, and appropriate for the issue and the audience?

Grading Timesaver

Rubrics for this Writer's Workshop assignment appear on p. 151 of the *Portfolio Management System.*

Language Workshop
The history
of the written
word is rich and
Page 1

Effective Sentences: The Power of Parallelism

One way to create a sense of urgency about a persuasive issue is to focus attention on key terms and core ideas by using **parallel structure.**

Parallel structure is the use of matching *forms* for sentence elements that have the same *function.* Pairing adjectives with adjectives, prepositional phrases with prepositional phrases, noun clauses with noun clauses (and so on) emphasizes the relationship between the elements. You can use parallel structure to link coordinate ideas, to compare or contrast ideas, and to link ideas with correlative conjunctions (such as *both . . . and, either . . . or*).

Compare the awkwardness of these examples of faulty parallelism with the clarity of Jonathan Swift's phrasing in *A Modest Proposal:*

FAULTY **To tax** our absentees at five shillings a pound; **of using** neither clothes, nor household furniture, except what is of our own growth and manufacture. . . . [infinitive paired with prepositional phrase]

PARALLEL **Of taxing** our absentees at five shillings a pound; **of using** neither clothes, nor household furniture, except what is of our own growth and manufacture. . . . [prepositional phrase paired with prepositional phrase]

—*from A Modest Proposal*

FAULTY . . . I rather recommend **buying the children alive,** and **to dress them hot from the knife.** . . . [gerund phrase paired with infinitive phrase]

PARALLEL . . . I rather recommend **buying the children alive,** and **dressing them hot from the knife.** . . . [gerund phrase paired with gerund phrase]

—*from A Modest Proposal*

Writer's Workshop Follow-up: Proofreading

Look at the persuasive essay you wrote for the Writer's Workshop on page 612. What key terms or ideas do you want to emphasize? Where could you use parallel structure to stress your ideas? Working with a writing partner, put a check mark next to any sentences where the use of parallel structure would strengthen your essay. Then, revise these sentences to incorporate parallel structures. Also, look for sentences where you have not used parallel structure correctly, and revise these sentences so the grammatical elements are parallel.

Technology HELP

See Language Workshop CD-ROM. *Key word entry: parallel structure.*

Language Handbook HELP

See Using Parallel Structure, page 1237.

Try It Out

Correct the faulty parallelism in each of the following sentences.

1. The narrator of *A Modest Proposal* considers his solution fair, cheap, and being easy.
2. He refutes the suggestion of selling and eating twelve- to fourteen-year-olds, arguing that the males' flesh would be too tough and the females to be lost as breeders.
3. His ideas are horrifying, not only because they are vulgar, but also for their cruelty.

OBJECTIVES

1. Use parallel structure to write effective sentences
2. Recognize the use of matching forms for sentence elements that have the same function

Resources

Workshop Resources

- Worksheet, p. 53

Language Workshop CD-ROM

- Parallel Structure

Try It Out

Possible Answers

1. The narrator of *A Modest Proposal* considers his solution fair, cheap, and easy.
2. He refutes the suggestion of selling and eating twelve- to fourteen-year-olds, arguing that the males' flesh would be too tough and the females would be lost as breeders.
3. His ideas are horrifying, not only because they are vulgar but also because they are cruel.

Assessing Learning

Quick Check: Parallel Structure

Correct the faulty parallelism in each of the following sentences.

1. When my younger brother, Jerry, was a little boy, his favorite activities were singing for his friends and to pretend to play the piano. [When my younger brother, Jerry, was a little boy, his favorite activities were singing for his friends and pretending to play the piano.]
2. Our parents decided to buy a piano and on hiring a music teacher. [Our parents decided to buy a piano and to hire a music teacher.]
3. Jerry was more interested in playing by ear than to take lessons. [Jerry was more interested in playing by ear than in taking lessons.]
4. Jerry went on to become as successful at writing music as he was as a performer. [Jerry went on to become as successful at writing music as he was at performing it.]

Reading for Life

Using Text Organizers

Objectives

1. Develop strategies for locating and categorizing information in texts
2. Recognize varied types of text organizations
3. Use headings and index
4. Identify graphic features

Teaching the Lesson

You may wish to borrow several U.S. history books from the library and have students work through the strategies listed here, using a different book in each of several small groups. Then, have the class compare the organizations of the books they have reviewed.

Using the Strategies

Possible Answers

1. The Revolutionary War
2. "Continuing Unrest"
3. The Tea Act of 1773; The Intolerable Acts of 1774
4. The import rates for British goods in relation to repressive acts of the British government
5. A statement summary follows the section on the Tea Act of 1773.

Situation

In this collection you've read about some extraordinary events in seventeenth-century England. Suppose you wanted to find out what was occurring in America at the same time. You might consult a book about American history and make use of the following strategies to **locate** and **categorize information.**

Strategies

Notice how the text is organized.

- Scan the table of contents to get a general idea of the scope of information covered.
- Look at chapter openings and look for overviews that summarize each chapter's content. Summaries may also appear periodically within chapters.
- Notice the structure of the headings. Textbooks often use headings of different sizes to rank information according to major topics and subtopics.

Use headings and the index.

- You can use headings or the index to locate specific information if you don't want to read everything in every chapter. You can also use headings to create an outline or to structure your notes.

Notice graphic features.

- Features may include charts, graphs, time lines, tables, photographs, boxed text, and bulleted or numbered lists.

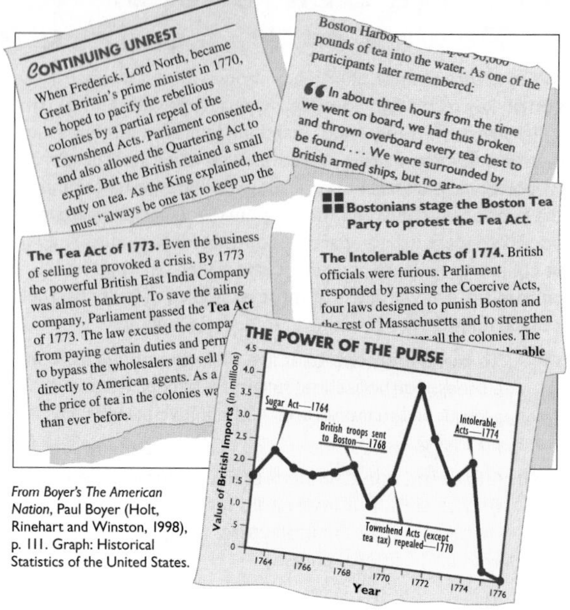

From Boyer's The American Nation, Paul Boyer (Holt, Rinehart and Winston, 1998), p. 111. Graph: Historical Statistics of the United States.

Using the Strategies

Answer these questions about the section of a page from the American history textbook that is shown above.

1. Which text heading indicates the start of a major section?
2. Which of the headings indicate subsections?
3. What relationship is illustrated by the graph?
4. Can you find a chapter or section summary?
5. Does the book include first-hand quotations?

Extending the Strategies

- Identify and evaluate the text organizers in one of the collections in this volume of *Elements of Literature.*
- Check the indices in the back of this book to see what information they provide.
- Examine a print or electronic text. Make suggestions on how the text might be reorganized to make it easier to locate information. What additional features would make the text more useful to you?

Reaching All Students

Struggling Readers

Some students might profit by thinking of boldfaced heads, subheads, words, phrases, and sentences as the publisher's way of highlighting the main ideas in a chapter of a textbook. Point out that the questions that come at the end of a division of a textbook are also keys to main ideas.

Advanced Learners

Provide your advanced learners with a photocopy of a chapter of a textbook with all the heads and subheads deleted. Have them study the text and supply the heads and subheads they think would be helpful to organize the information for the reader.

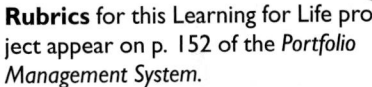

Learning for Life

Locating Information and Resources

Problem

The poet John Dryden was one of many people put out of work as a result of the political upheavals that took place between 1649 and 1660. What resources exist today for people in your community who lose their jobs through downsizing or layoffs?

Project

Investigate what services are available locally through federal, state, and city or county offices for dislocated workers in need of job-search and placement assistance or retraining. Who is eligible to receive the services, and how does a person go about obtaining them?

Preparation

1. Use brainstorming or clustering to determine what you already know about the topic. Have you seen or heard advertisements about such services? Has anyone you know used one of the services?
2. Plan your strategy for conducting research. What print and nonprint sources will you check? Use the library, but don't overlook such possible sources as the telephone book, the Internet, on-line databases, and the student services offices of the local community college, university, or vocational-technical center.

Procedure

1. As you identify the various services and gather information on them, keep a record of your findings and their sources. If you interview someone, for example, take careful notes, or ask permission to tape-record the interview for later review.
2. Look for ways to personalize the information for your intended audience—those who have lost their jobs through no fault of their own. Facts and figures are important, but an anecdote about someone who found a new job through one of the services might go even further to motivate unemployed workers to use the services available.

Presentation

Use one of the following formats (or another that your teacher approves):

1. **Modern-Day Pamphleteering**
   Design a brochure that details the services available and eligibility requirements and that lists addresses, telephone numbers, and hours of operation. If you have access to desktop publishing software, use it to produce and publish your brochure. Obtain permission to place copies of the brochure where many people will see it—for example, at the public library or at a supermarket, shopping mall, or neighborhood center.
2. **Poster Promotion**
   Design a poster that promotes the services and that motivates people to take advantage of them. Briefly highlight all necessary information (services offered, eligibility requirements, addresses, telephone numbers, and hours of operation), and consider including tear-off strips that people can take with them for later reference. Obtain permission to display the poster at one of the sites suggested.
3. **Going on the Radio**
   Prepare a thirty-second public service announcement (PSA) promoting one of the services for broadcast by a local radio station. To ensure that your PSA is in keeping with the station's format, consider the kind of programming it features (news, sports, music, or a mixture) and the demographics (age, sex, income, and so on) of its intended audience. Ask the station manager to schedule air time for your PSA.

Processing

What is your opinion about the number and variety of services available to dislocated workers? Write a brief reflection for your portfolio.

OBJECTIVES

1. Identify government services available to dislocated workers in need of assistance
2. Conduct research
3. Select and complete a project designed to present research results

Resources

Viewing and Representing

HRW Multimedia Presentation Maker

Students may wish to use the *Multimedia Presentation Maker* to create a multimedia promotion.

Grading Timesaver

Rubrics for this Learning for Life project appear on p. 152 of the *Portfolio Management System.*

Developing Workplace Competencies

Preparation	Procedure	Presentation
• Uses self-management skills • Determines relevant information • Makes inferences • Locates resources	• Organizes and maintains files for data • Compares similarities and differences • Interprets information • Recognizes relationships	• Synthesizes information • Communicates information and ideas • Demonstrates individual responsibility • Exhibits self-esteem

OBJECTIVES

1. Read literature from the Romantic period on the themes of "The Power of Imagination" and "The Quest for Beauty"
2. Interpret literary elements with special emphasis on romantic lyrics and apostrophe
3. Apply a variety of reading strategies to the literature, including reading archaic words and distinguishing words that sound or look alike
4. Respond to the literature in a variety of modes
5. Learn about the variety of English dialects
6. Plan, draft, revise, and edit a research paper
7. Develop skill in varying style, voice, tone, and diction
8. Research and interpret labor and population trends

The Romantic Period 1798–1832

Selection Readability

This Annotated Teacher's Edition provides a summary of each selection in the student book. Following each Summary heading, you will find one, two, or three small icons. These icons indicate, in an approximate sense, the reading level of the selection.

■ One icon indicates that the selection is easy.

■■ Two icons indicate that the selection is on an intermediate reading level.

■■■ Three icons indicate that the selection is challenging.

The Curfew (19th century) by Samuel Palmer.
Agnew and Sons, London.

621

Responding to the Art

English painter **Samuel Palmer** (1805–1881) had his first exhibit at age fourteen. He painted mainly landscapes and said that he loved the "raving-mad splendor of orange twilight glow." A friend of William Blake, Palmer adopted Blake's mystical, imaginative style. Neglected for years after his death, Palmer's work was rediscovered by the Neo-Romantics, who saw in it overtones of surrealism.

Activity. Explain to students that in the Middle Ages *curfew* (literally "cover fire") was the time when a bell was rung to signal townspeople to extinguish candles and cooking fires for the night. By the nineteenth century, *curfew* had come to refer to the bell itself. You might have students return to this painting after they have read the introduction The Romantic Period. How does this painting reveal some of the characteristics of Romanticism, as listed on p. 630? [Note the emphasis on the beauty of the natural world; the solitary thinker; the simple pastoral scene; the emphasis on emotion; the lack of any industrialization in the scene; the way nature mirrors the contemplative pose of the human figure.]

Resources

Viewing and Representing

Videocassette B, Segment 8

Available in English and Spanish.
This video explores Romantic ideas about nature and the imagination. For full lesson plans and worksheets, see the *Visual Connections Teacher's Manual.*

Formal Assessment

- Literary Period Introduction Test, p. 117

OBJECTIVES

1. Understand the historical and social forces that shaped the Romantic period
2. Interpret the way historical context influenced literary works in the Romantic period
3. Read and understand a time line
4. Understand the relevance of the Romantic period to our day
5. Examine the artwork of the Romantic period and the ways Romantic artists perceived the world

Responding to the Quotation

The quotation is from a letter written by Blake. Ask students if they agree that the imagination forms the "real world" and the visible world is just a shadow. [Some students may agree that imagination can be richer and more "real" than reality, but other students will probably regard the statement as exaggerated. To them, the real world is the material, "vegetable universe."]

RESPONDING TO THE ART

Because he was constantly sketching, **Sir John Gilbert** (1817–1897) had an abundance of visual memories. These enabled him to draw accurately from memory no matter where he happened to be. He is known for his Romantic treatment of English landscapes.

Activity. Point out the train that moves across the landscape. Tell students that the train was a new invention that boomed in popularity at the end of the Romantic era. Ask students to consider how this painting explores the convergence of nature, growing industrialization, and city life that occurred during the Romantic period.

The Romantic Period

by **Harley Henry**

The divine arts of imagination: imagination, the real & eternal world of which this vegetable universe is but a faint shadow.

—William Blake

Worcester (detail) (19th century) by Sir John Gilbert.
Guildhall Art Gallery, Corporation of London.

go.hrw.com
LEO 12-Romanticism

Reaching All Students

Struggling Readers

Before students begin reading the historical introduction, play the *Visual Connections* segment on the Romantic period to give students a visual overview. Make the point that the Romantic movement affected not only literature but also art and music. We can see its influence in the landscapes of J.M.W. Turner and John Constable and hear its rhythms in the symphonies of Ludwig van Beethoven.

Advanced Learners

Invite students to research the roots of Romantic thought in the work of Johann Wolfgang von Goethe (1749–1832) and Jean-Jacques Rousseau (1712–1778). How did Goethe's *Sturm und Drang* (Storm and Stress) movement influence the development of Romanticism in England? How did Rousseau's lyrical descriptions of nature, his concept of "the noble savage," and his belief in individual liberty influence William Wordsworth and Samuel Taylor Coleridge?

During the spring of 1798, two young English poets, aged 27 and 25, sold some of their poems to raise money for a trip to Germany. Each had published books of poetry, but a new joint work was to be anonymous. As Samuel Taylor Coleridge, the younger of the pair, told the printer: "Wordsworth's name is nothing . . . mine *stinks*." A

Soon after they left England, their book, *Lyrical Ballads, with a Few Other Poems,* appeared. Among the "few other poems" was Coleridge's long narrative *The Rime of the Ancient Mariner* (page 684) and a last-minute addition, Wordsworth's "Lines Composed a Few Miles Above Tintern Abbey" (page 658). Both of these works are now among the most important poems in English literature.

So began what is now called the "Romantic period" in England. Literary historians have found other momentous events to mark its beginning and end, but we should remember the casual, modest appearance of *Lyrical Ballads* as we consider the Romantic period and the writers associated with it.

The Pierpont Morgan Library, New York.

Frontispiece of *America: A Prophecy* (1793) by William Blake.

The publication of a collection of poems called* Lyrical Ballads, *a collaboration between William Wordsworth and Samuel Taylor Coleridge, began the Romantic period in England.

Turbulent Times, Bitter Realities

Another way to date the Romantic period is to say that it started with the French Revolution in 1789 and ended with the Parliamentary reforms of 1832 that laid the political foundations for modern Britain. The era was dominated by six poets: Three (William Blake, William Wordsworth, and Samuel Taylor Coleridge) were born before the period began and lived through most or all of it, while three others (the "second generation" of Percy Bysshe Shelley, John Keats, and George Gordon, Lord Byron) began their short careers in the second decade of the new century but died before 1825. It was a turbulent, revolutionary age, one in which England changed from an agricultural society to an industrial nation with a large and restless working class concentrated in the teeming mill towns.

We think about this era in terms of some important historical events. Beginning in America in 1776, an age of revolution swept across

It was the best of times, it was the worst of times, it was the age of wisdom, it was the age of foolishness, it was the epoch of belief, it was the epoch of incredulity, it was the season of Light, it was the season of Darkness, it was the spring of hope, it was the winter of despair, we had everything before us, we had nothing before us, we were all going direct to Heaven, we were all going direct the other way. . . .

—Charles Dickens, *from A Tale of Two Cities*

RESPONDING TO THE ART

William Blake (1757–1827), an English poet, engraver, and painter, believed that his work was influenced by archangels visiting from another world. Much of his work has religious themes.

Activity. Explain to students that the larger figure in the painting is Urizen, a character in a personal mythology that Blake spent his life creating. Urizen is God or Jehovah, but he is also a symbol of humanity in bondage to reason. Humanity can only be freed by union with Los (the imagination) or Luvah (passion). Ask students to speculate about what Blake may have had in mind when he included Urizen in this painting and what prophecy he may be making about America. [Possible response: Like many Romantics, Blake may have been depressed by the rationalism that dominated American thought.]

A Background

Samuel Taylor Coleridge

Samuel Taylor Coleridge said his name "stinks" in England because he was a radical at a time when the British feared radical influences from the French Revolution. The penniless Coleridge was about to become a Unitarian minister, a post he did not anticipate with enthusiasm, when he received a grant from the wealthy Wedgwood family, giving him a life income of 150 pounds a year so that he could explore his talents. This surprising windfall from the china manufacturing family enabled Coleridge to make a much-desired trip to Germany and to devote the rest of his life to literature.

Getting Students Involved

Enrichment Activity

A Tale of Two Cities. The boxed quotation above is the opening passage of Charles Dickens's novel about the French Revolution called *A Tale of Two Cities* (available in the HRW Library). The two cities in the title are, of course, Paris and London. Dickens's novel has a colorful cast of characters, including the unforgettable Madame Defarge, a revolutionary fanatic who encodes the names of aristocrats in her knitting. However, the novel centers on two look-alike friends, the honorable French aristocrat Charles Darnay and the cynical, dissolute Englishman, Sydney Carton. Both love Lucie Manette, but Darnay wins her. When Darnay returns to France to rescue a former servant, he is betrayed by Madame Defarge and condemned to death. Because of Lucy's love for Darnay, Carton rescues the Frenchman and takes his place on the guillotine. After students have read this essay, ask them to return to the boxed quotation to discuss the relevance of the paradoxes to the age.

Time Line

This time line shows major events that occurred in the Romantic Period between the French Revolution and the abolition of slavery in the British Empire.

• 1786–1793
The French Revolution
The revolutionaries who overthrew the Bastille limited the power of King Louis XVI, established the 1789 *Declaration of the Rights of Man,* and set up a constitutional monarchy. By September 1792, however, the more radical Jacobins were in control and were calling for the King's head.

• 1794–1801
Napoleon Bonaparte
Napoleon Bonaparte (1769–1821) rose to power in France in an astonishingly short period of time because of his brilliant military strategy and ruthless opportunism. In 1785, the young Napoleon was a new army officer; by 1799, he was the military dictator of France by virtue of a coup. Shortly after, he had himself crowned emperor, and by 1810, he ruled most of Europe. After France's defeat at Waterloo, he was exiled to the island of St. Helena, where he died in 1821.

• 1809–1813
The Brothers Grimm
Jacob Ludwig Carl Grimm (1785–1863) and Wilhelm Carl Grimm (1786–1859) were German-born brothers whose collections of folk songs and folk tales, led almost single handedly to the birth of folklore as a science. Realists in a Romantic era, the Grimms gave up plans for legal careers to pursue scholarly research. The work of Jacob in particular has had a lasting and significant impact on philology and etymology.

• 1809–1813
The Luddites
The Luddites, named after the probably mythical Ned Ludd, were a group of artisans who attacked weaving machines throughout northern England. They felt that the new technology was threatening their livelihoods. In 1812, many Luddites were shot under orders of a factory owner named Horsfall (who was murdered in reprisal). The movement dissolved in 1813 after many of its members were hanged in York. The word *Luddite* survives today to denote someone who opposes the development and spread of technology.

The Romantic Period, 1798–1832

LITERARY EVENTS

1786–1793

Mary Wollstonecraft critiques female educational restrictions in *A Vindication of the Rights of Woman,* 1792

William Blake publishes *Songs of Innocence,* 1789

Robert Burns publishes *Poems, Chiefly in the Scottish Dialect,* 1786

1794–1801

Maria Edgeworth's *Castle Rackrent,* the first historical novel in English, satirizes absentee landowners in Ireland, 1800

William Wordsworth and **Samuel Taylor Coleridge** publish *Lyrical Ballads,* 1798

Ann Radcliffe's *The Mysteries of Udolpho* popularizes the Gothic novel, 1794

1802–1808

Johann Wolfgang von Goethe publishes Part I of *Faust,* 1808

Charles and Mary Lamb publish *Tales from Shakespeare,* 1807

1809–1813

Jane Austen publishes *Pride and Prejudice,* 1813

Brothers Grimm begin to publish *Grimm's Fairy Tales,* 1812

Charles Dickens born, 1812

Lord Byron publishes first two cantos of *Childe Harold's Pilgrimage,* 1812

CULTURAL/HISTORICAL EVENTS

1786–1793

Corbis-Bettmann

• Drawing (late 18th century) by Jacques-Louis David of Marie Antoinette, queen of France, being led to execution.

French Revolution begins with storming of Bastille, 1789

King Louis XVI of France beheaded, 1793

France declares war on England, 1793

1794–1801

Thomas Jefferson elected U.S. president, 1800

Napoleon conquers parts of Italy, 1800

Act of Union creates United Kingdom of Great Britain and Ireland, 1801

• *Napoleon I in Royal Garb* (1806) by Jean Auguste Dominique Ingres. Musée de l'Armée, Paris.

1802–1808

Workday of pauper children limited to 12 hours in England, 1802

United States purchases Louisiana Territory from France, 1803

Napoleon crowns himself emperor in France, 1804

Egypt gains independence from Ottoman Turks, 1805

Lord Nelson defeats Napoleon's navy at Battle of Trafalgar, 1805

Construction begins on Arc de Triomphe in Paris, 1806

United States bans importation of slaves from Africa, 1808

1809–1813

Simón Bolívar begins series of South American rebellions against Spain, 1810

Venezuela declares independence from Spain, 1811

English artisans called Luddites riot and destroy textile machines, fearing that industrialism threatens their livelihoods, 1811

Napoleon invades Russia, 1812

United States declares war on Great Britain, 1812

Mexico declares its independence from Spain, 1821

Using the Time Line

Ask students to choose five familiar events or publications from the time line. Have students pool what they know about the events or publications, looking for connections among them that may reveal something about the Romantic period. Encourage students to speculate about the spirit of the times and to consider how they might have felt if they had lived in the Romantic era. Students can use a chart like the following to organize their observations and ideas.

Event or Publication	What I Know	Its Relation to Others	Spirit of the Time?
[Children's workday limited to 12 hrs.]	[Eventually child labor became illegal.]	[Dickens wrote about this.]	[People began to see that child labor was harsh.]

• Natty Bumppo, from James Fenimore Cooper's *The Last of the Mohicans.*

• *Scarlet Ibis* by John James Audubon. Collection of New-York Historical Society.

Mary Shelley, daughter of Mary Wollstonecraft, publishes *Frankenstein,* 1818

Noted actor Edmund Kean debuts as Shylock in Shakespeare's *The Merchant of Venice,* 1814

Sir Walter Scott publishes *Ivanhoe,* 1819

John Keats writes his greatest poems between January and September, 1819

Noah Webster publishes *An American Dictionary of the English Language,* 1828

John James Audubon begins publishing *The Birds of America,* 1827

James Fenimore Cooper publishes *The Last of the Mohicans,* 1826

Alexander Pushkin begins his novel in verse, *Eugene Onegin,* 1823

Victor Hugo publishes *The Hunchback of Notre Dame,* 1831

Emily Dickinson born in Amherst, Massachusetts, 1830

1814–1818

British forces burn Washington, D.C., 1814

Allied British, Dutch, and German forces defeat Napoleon at Waterloo, 1815

German confederation created to replace Holy Roman Empire, 1815

• *Se-Quo-Yah* (19th century), lithograph printed by Lehman and Duval after a painting by Charles Bird King (1785–1862). Given by Miss William Adger/ Philadelphia Museum of Art, Philadelphia.

1819–1821

One of a series of ineffective Factory Acts prohibits employment of all children under 9 years of age, 1819

First steamship, the *Savannah,* crosses the Atlantic in 29 days, 1819

Antarctica sighted by Russian, British, and American ships, 1820

George III, mentally unstable since 1810, dies, 1820

Cherokee system of writing created by Sequoyah, 1821

1822–1828

Liberia founded as home for former U.S. slaves, 1822

Rosetta stone deciphered, allowing Egyptian hieroglyphics to be read, 1822

In the U.S., Monroe Doctrine closes the Americas to further European colonization, 1823

First labor unions permitted in Great Britain, 1824

• Rosetta stone (detail) (196 B.C.), Egypt. British Museum, London.

1829–1833

Catholic Emancipation Act allows British Roman Catholics to hold public office, 1829

Charles Darwin serves as naturalist on HMS *Beagle* during expedition along coast of South America, 1831

• *Horrid Massacre in Virginia* (detail) (early 1830s). Virginia Historical Society, Richmond.

Nat Turner leads slave rebellion in Virginia, 1831

Reform Act extends voting rights in Britain to upper-middle-class men, 1832

Slavery abolished in British Empire, 1833

• **1814–1818**

Frankenstein

At first glance, Mary Shelley's *Frankenstein* seems to suggest a criticism of science: A scientist tries to imitate God and create life. However, one of the novel's many ironies is that the creation turns out to be not only monstrous but also somehow more human than its creator. For more on Mary Shelley, see p. 728.

• **1819–1821**

Sir Walter Scott

Sir Walter Scott (1771–1832) was already a famous poet when he began publishing novels anonymously. By 1827, he had written more than twenty-five books, including the medieval romance *Ivanhoe,* which is still read by high-school students today. The popularity of Scott's exotic settings was an indication of the strength of the Romantic movement.

• **1829–1833**

Charles Darwin

Charles Darwin (1809–1882) spent five years as a naturalist aboard H.M.S. *Beagle* on its voyage along the coast of South America on the way to the Galapagos Islands. After he returned to England, he took another twenty years to assimilate all that he had observed and to develop his theories of evolution. When he finally published his theories in *On the Origin of Species by Means of Natural Selection* (1859), they had a very powerful impact on nearly every area of Western thought.

The Right to Vote

The Reform Bill of 1832 was the beginning of changes in voting rights in Britain that would continue for one hundred years and result finally, in suffrage, by 1918, for about three-quarters of Britain's population. As a start, the Reform Bill gave some well-to-do middle-class men the right to vote. It also changed the formula for districts for electing members of Parliament, giving more democratic weight to new industrial cities such as Manchester.

Using the Time Line

Critical Thinking

Ask students to answer these questions:

1. **What political upheavals occurred during the Romantic era?** [Possible responses: the French Revolution; Egypt rebelled against the Turks; Simon Bolivar against Spain; Venezuela against Spain; Nat Turner against slavery.] **What generalizations can you draw from these events?** [Possible responses: The Romantic era raised hopes of freedom for many; it was a time of social unrest.]
2. **Name two social reforms in Britain aimed at improving the lot of the working person.** [The Factory Acts of 1819 tried to prohibit the employment of children under age nine. The first labor unions were formed in 1824.] **What inference can you draw from these events?** [Possible response: During this era, friction between workers and owners grew as reformers tried to improve workers' quality of life and conservative owners became more reactionary as the violence in France escalated.]

Ⓐ Exploring the Historical Period

The French Revolution

Tell students that the French Revolution was one of the critical turning points of the era. Among other things, the optimism of the Enlightenment, which had fostered the revolution, was shattered as France spiraled into a bloody Reign of Terror and then into dictatorship.

Ⓑ Humanities Connections

Thomas Carlyle

Thomas Carlyle was a Scottish essayist and historian, as well as an important social critic of his day. A lifelong friend of the American essayist Ralph Waldo Emerson, he is remembered as a critic of material wealth and of the class society that condemned British workers to live in poverty. A political conservative, however, Carlyle must have been horrified by the French Revolution.

Ⓒ Literary Connections

"Bliss . . . to be alive"

? These ecstatic words about the French Revolution are from William Wordsworth's *The Prelude,* Book XI. Wordsworth further writes: "France standing on the top of golden hours/ and human nature seeming born again." Why, in light of future developments, are these comments ironic? [The French Revolution soon proved to be far from humanity's "golden hour."]

Storming of the Bastille (18th century) by an unknown artist.

Versailles, France.

western Europe, releasing political, economic, and social forces that produced, during the next century, some of the most radical changes ever experienced in human life.

The American Revolution had lost for England her thirteen colonies. This was a great economic loss, but it was also a loss of prestige and of confidence. The more radical revolution in France, which started with the storming of the prison called the Bastille on July 14, 1789, had far more serious repercussions. For the ruling classes in England, the French Revolution came to represent their worst fears: the overthrow of an anointed king by a democratic "rabble." To English conservatives, the French Revolution meant the triumph of radical principles, and they feared that the revolutionary fever would spread across the Channel.

> The Executioners, desperate lest themselves be murdered . . . seize the hapless Louis: six of them desperate, him singly desperate, struggling there; and bind him to their plank. Abbé Edgeworth, stooping, bespeaks him: "Son of Saint Louis, ascend to Heaven." The Axe clanks down; a King's Life is shorn away.
>
> —Thomas Carlyle, describing the execution of Louis XVI on January 21, 1793

But democratic idealists and liberals like Wordsworth felt exhilarated by the events in France. During the revolution's early years, they even made trips to France to view the "new regime" at first hand, as if it were a tourist attraction like the Acropolis in Greece. Wordsworth later wrote, "Bliss

Using Students' Strengths

Auditory/Musical Learners

Have students find a recording of or sheet music for "La Marseillaise," the French national anthem, and play or sing it for the class. Written in 1792 as a marching song for French troops battling Austria, it became immensely popular at revolutionary gatherings. Originally named "War Song of the Army of the Rhine," it was renamed "La Marseillaise," when soldiers from Marseilles sang it as they entered Paris. The Convention accepted it as the national anthem in 1795, but it was banned as too revolutionary in 1815. It was permanently reinstated in 1879. Students should also listen for this song in Schumann's composition "The Two Grenadiers" and Tchaikovsky's "1812 Overture." Ask them to consider which lines in the song reflect the spirit of Romanticism.

was it in that dawn to be alive, / But to be young was very heaven!"

Even Wordsworth became disillusioned, however, when in 1792 the "September massacre" took place in France. Hundreds of French aristocrats—some with only the slightest ties to the regime of King Louis XVI—had their heads severed from their bodies by a grisly new invention, the guillotine.

And that wasn't the end of it. In the midst of the blood and turmoil and calls from France for worldwide revolution, control of the French government changed hands again. Napoleon Bonaparte, an officer in the French army, emerged first as dictator and then, in 1804, as emperor of France. In the end, Napoleon—whose very name today suggests a tyrant—became as ruthless as the executed king himself. **D**

Musée Carnavelet/Photo Bulloz.

Fin Tragique de Louis XVI (Tragic End of Louis XVI) (18th century) by an unknown artist.

All of these bewildering changes in western Europe made conservatives in England more rigid than ever. England instituted severe repressive measures: They outlawed collective bargaining and kept suspected spies or agitators in prison without a trial. In 1803, England began a long war against Napoleon. English guns first defeated Napoleon's navy at the Battle of Trafalgar and, finally, in 1815, with the help of allies, sent his army packing at Waterloo, Belgium. **E**

The conservatives in England felt they had saved their country from a tyrant and from chaos; the early supporters of the revolution, like Wordsworth, felt betrayed. For them, Waterloo was simply the defeat of one tyrant by another.

London, 1802

Milton! thou shouldst be living at this hour;
England hath need of thee; she is a fen
Of stagnant waters: altar, sword, and pen,
Fireside, the heroic wealth of hall and bower,
Have forfeited their ancient English dower
Of inward happiness. We are selfish men;
Oh! raise us up, return to us again;
And give us manners, virtue, freedom, power.
Thy soul was like a star, and dwelt apart;
Thou hadst a voice whose sound was like the sea;
Pure as the naked heavens, majestic, free,
So didst thou travel on life's common way,
In cheerful godliness; and yet thy heart
The lowliest duties on herself did lay. **F**

—William Wordsworth

Political upheaval in France and the United States touched England as well. Conservative economic and political measures and a lengthy war against Napoleon consolidated the power of the rich.

D Exploring the Historical Period

Napoleon: Good and Bad

To his credit, Napoleon did make some improvements in French life. He restored order, got the economy going again, weeded out corruption, and even established public schools. He also created the Napoleonic code, a comprehensive set of laws. Among his many errors, however, is one of the worst real estate deals of all time: the sale of the Louisiana Territory for a mere fifteen million dollars.

E Appreciating Language

Idioms

The expression "to meet your Waterloo" comes from this event and means "to be completely, finally defeated."

F Literary Connections

Wordsworth and Milton

This sonnet is not only addressed to Milton, but it borrows heavily from him. It opens with a direct address, and its octave (rhymed *abbaabba*) runs right into the sestet with no change of emphasis. To Wordsworth, Milton was a voice of integrity and selflessness. Wordsworth wrote the sonnet immediately after his return from France in 1802, where he was reunited with Annette Vallon and their child, Caroline, whom he had not seen for nearly ten years. He was struck with the vanity he saw in England, as contrasted with the desolation that the revolution had produced in France. The sonnet is an outcry against undisturbed wealth. As a contrast in mood, read the sonnet Wordsworth wrote while on his way to France, p. 669.

Skill Link

Using Reference Material to Explore Eponyms

Explain to students that **eponyms** are words that come from people's names. *Guillotine* is an example; it is named after Joseph-Ignace Guillotin, a French physician who promoted a 1789 law requiring executions by "means of a machine." In his view this machine would be more efficient and humane. Dubbed "the widow" by the French underworld, the guillotine was used up until the twentieth century.

English has derived other words from French names. Divide the class into five groups, and have each group use dictionaries or other reference works on word origins to discover the eponymous sources of one of the following pairs of words, the meaning of each word, and the approximate date it was first used.

1. *napoleon* and *chateaubriand*
2. *chauvinism* and *martinet*
3. *pasteurize* and *nicotine*
4. *daguerreotype* and *silhouette*

Take a few minutes at the beginning or end of a class period to have groups report on their discoveries.

Ⓐ Exploring the Historical Period

The Industrial Revolution

The *Oxford Illustrated History of Britain* documents these staggering changes in the British economy: "Coal output doubled between 1750 and 1800 as steam pumps enabled deeper and more productive seams to be mined, and horse-worked railways bore coal ever-greater distances to water transport. Iron production, boosted by war demand [and] by the use of coal instead of charcoal for smelting, . . . rose by two hundred percent between 1788 and 1806."

Ⓑ Exploring the Historical Period

Conditions in Cities

Historian Christopher Harvie writes that factory towns were squalid, that they "smoked and stank," and that "they were expensive both in terms of rent and of human life. . . . If housing was bad, sanitation was worse. Better-off citizens could combine to create commissions, to provide water and sewerage, light the streets, and provide some sort of policing, but if anything, this worsened the plight of their poorer neighbors. A middle-class area's new water-closets all too often drained into the working class's water supply."

Ⓒ Literary Connections

Adam Smith

Adam Smith wrote *The Wealth of Nations* in 1776. In it he incorporated the idea of *laissez faire,* which had already been developed by French economic philosophers of the Enlightenment. This work became the philosophical basis of capitalism and served as a justification for ignoring the suffering of millions.

The Tyranny of Laissez Faire

Ⓐ At the same time, the Industrial Revolution was bringing about other changes in English life. Previously, goods had been made by hand, at home. Now, production switched to factories, where machines worked many times faster than human beings could work by hand. Ⓑ Since factories were in cities, the city populations increased, causing desperate living conditions that would appall even the most hardened social worker today.

In addition, the communal land once shared by small farmers was taken over by individual owners. Some of these rich owners transformed the fields into vast private parks, generously stocked with deer for their own Christmas hunts. Others divided the land neatly into privately held fields. Whatever happened to the land, it was no longer communally owned. This resulted in large numbers of landless people. Just as some unemployed and homeless do today, these landless people migrated to cities in search of work. Or they went on the dole, or welfare.

> Ⓒ Every man, as long as he does not violate the laws of justice, is left perfectly free to pursue his own interest his own way, and to bring both his industry and capital into competition with those of any other man or order of men.
>
> —Adam Smith, *from The Wealth of Nations*

The economic philosophy that kept all this misery going was a policy called laissez faire (les′ā fer′), "let (people) do (as they please)." According to this policy, economic forces should be allowed to operate freely without government interference. The result of

A Surrey Cornfield (19th century) by George Vicat Cole.

RESPONDING TO THE ART

George Vicat Cole (1833–1893) was a follower of both J.M.W. Turner and John Constable, the foremost landscape artists of the period.

Activity. Encourage students to make a generalization about how crops were harvested in the early nineteenth century, based on details in this painting. [Most of the work was done by hand.]

Professional Notes

Critical Comment: The Enclosure Movement

Although the enclosure movement was good for agricultural production because it allowed modern ideas such as crop rotation, crop diversification, and animal husbandry to flourish, it was undeniably hard on the poor. Those who had lost their land or property due to enclosure acts were rightly suspicious of government. Their dissatisfaction is conveyed in the following popular ditty of the period:

> They hang the man and flog the woman
> That steals the goose from off the common
> But leave the greater criminal loose
> That steals the common from the goose.

Encourage students to reread the section of the text on enclosures and then discuss the quatrain.

laissez faire was that the rich grew richer, and the poor suffered even more. The system, of course, had its most tragic effects on the helpless, especially the children. Small children of the poor were often used like beasts of burden. In the coal pits, for example, very small children were even harnessed to carts for dragging coal, just as if they had been small donkeys. D

Frustrated by England's resistance to political and social change that would improve conditions, the Romantic poets turned from the formal, public verse of the eighteenth-century Augustans to a more private, spontaneous, lyric poetry. These lyrics expressed the Romantics' belief that imagination, rather than mere reason, was the best response to the forces of change. Wordsworth spoke of imagination this way:

Bedlam Furnace, Madeley Dale, Shropshire (1803) by Paul Sandby Munn.
Private Collection.

. . . spiritual love acts not nor can exist
Without imagination, which, in truth,
Is but another name for absolute power E
And clearest insight, amplitude of mind,
And Reason in her most exalted mood.

—*from The Prelude*

The poets of the Romantic period responded to social and economic changes caused by rapid industrialization and to governmental policies that ignored the problems of the poor.

Children pushing a coal cart through a mine shaft (1842).

RESPONDING TO THE ART

Paul Sandby Munn (1773–1845) was an English watercolorist who painted landscapes.

Activity. Explain to students that the factory in the background may be a steel foundry. Ask them what they think living conditions might have been like in Madeley Dale and what the artist's purpose might have been in choosing this subject. [Possible response: The artist was probably trying to show how factories had blasted and burned the landscape. The white steam and sulfur fumes rising from the furnace seem to envelop the tiny figures, struggling to pursue their lives.]

D Exploring the Historical Period

Child Labor

William Blake criticizes child labor in his chimney sweeper poems (pp. 652–653). Indeed, there was much to criticize about this harsh practice, in which small children were pushed with poles or pins or even scorched with fire to make them crawl into narrow black channels filled with soot. Many children, after years of such horrors, were crippled or chronically ill.

E Literary Connections

Blake and Wordsworth

Ask students how Wordsworth's ideas compare with those of Blake as expressed in the quotation on p. 622. [Possible answer: The two poets seem to agree that real power lies in the imagination.]

Crossing the Curriculum

Science

Of all the discoveries that changed England and other nations as they industrialized, the most pivotal was probably James Watt's 1765 invention of the steam engine. Encourage students to draw a diagram showing how a steam engine works. Minimally, the diagrams should show the coal conveyor and mill, the source of incoming air and water, the steam drum, and the flue and chimney through which the gases escape.

Social Studies

Although Josiah Tucker had called the city of London "no better than a wen," or wart, under the Georges, London was a playground for the rich. Ballooning was popular. Puppet shows, waxwork museums, and music halls attracted large audiences. The most popular entertainment, however, was boxing. (Lord Byron himself was taught to box by Gentleman Jackson, one of the leading fighters of the day.)

The art of silhouetting was in vogue, and most families, whether aristocratic or common, had their portraits done. The upper class shopped at the new shopping arcades, especially the Burlington Arcade in Picadilly. In short, life in London was full of exciting diversions for the rich. Ask students to choose one of these entertainments and give a brief oral report on it.

Ⓐ Vocabulary Note

Word Origins

Romance comes from the Old French word *romans*, which refers to the act of writing in *Roman,* or Latin, which was a common language for the educated classes in most of Europe for centuries.

Ⓑ Struggling Readers

Using Graphic Aids

Ask what purpose this chart serves and tell students how they might use it to learn more about the Romantic period. [Possible answers: This chart defines key concepts; it summarizes information in the text.] Suggest that students read the essay first, then go to the chart and take up each feature one by one, and then return to the essay to find support for each characteristic.

RESPONDING TO THE ART

Sir Edward Burne-Jones (1833–1898), an English painter, designer, and illustrator, was inspired by Arthurian romances and Greek myths. Burne-Jones, whose paintings had a dreamlike quality, also designed stained-glass windows and illustrated a book on Geoffrey Chaucer. In explaining his work, he said, "I mean by a picture, a beautiful romantic dream of something that never was, never will be in a better light than any light that ever shone in a land that no one can define or remember, only desire. . . ."

Activity. Ask students to point out details in this painting that make it part of the Romantic tradition. To help them get started, ask them to name ways in which a realistic painting of the same subject might be different.

The Sleeping Princess (19th century) by Sir Edward Burne-Jones.

Ⓑ What Was Romanticism?

Romanticism is characterized by these general features:

- Romanticism turned away from the eighteenth-century emphasis on reason and artifice. Instead, the Romantics embraced imagination and naturalness.
- Romantic-era poets rejected the public, formal, and witty works of the previous century. They preferred poetry that spoke of personal experiences and emotions, often in simple, unadorned language.
- The Romantics each used the lyric as the form best suited to expressions of feeling, self-revelation, and the imagination.
- Wordsworth urged poets to adopt a democratic attitude toward their audiences; though endowed with a special sensibility, the poet was always "a man speaking to men."
- Many Romantics turned to a past or an inner dream world that they felt was more picturesque and magical than the ugly industrial age they lived in.
- Most Romantics believed in individual liberty and sympathized with those who rebelled against tyranny.
- The Romantics thought of nature as transformative; they were fascinated by the ways nature and the human mind "mirrored" the other's creative properties.

What Does "Romantic" Mean?

Ⓐ The word *romantic* comes from the term *romance,* one of the most popular genres of medieval literature. (See page 167.) Later, Romantic writers self-consciously used the elements of romance in an attempt to go back beyond the refinements of neoclassical literature to older types of writing that they saw as more "genuine." The romance genre also allowed writers to explore new, more psychological and mysterious aspects of human experience.

Today, the word *romantic* is often a negative label used to describe sentimental writing, particularly those best-selling paperback "romances" about love—a subject that many people mistakenly think the Romantic poets popularized. As a historical term, however, *romantic* has at least three useful meanings, all of them relevant to the Romantic poets.

First, the term *romantic* signifies a fascination with youth and innocence, with "growing up" by exploring and learning to trust our emotions and our sense of will and identity. Second, the term *romantic* is applied to a stage in the cyclical development of societies: This is the stage when people

need to question tradition and authority in order to imagine better—that is, happier, fairer, and healthier—ways to live. *Romantic* in this sense is associated with idealism. (The 1966–1975 period in the United States might be called a romantic era.) And third, in the so-called Romantic period of the first half of the nineteenth century (up to the Civil War in America), Western societies reached the conditions necessary for industrialization. This demanded that people acquire a stronger and stronger awareness of change and that they try to find ways to adapt to it. In this sense, we still live with the legacy of the Romantic period.

The term romantic signifies a fascination with youth and innocence, a questioning of authority and tradition for idealistic purposes, and an adaptation to change.

Poetry, Nature, and the Imagination

Lyrical Ballads did not remain unnoticed or anonymous for long. In 1800, with Coleridge looking over his shoulder, Wordsworth composed a Preface for the expanded collection. In it he declared that he was writing a new kind of poetry that he hoped would be "well adapted to interest mankind permanently. . . ." The subject matter would be different from that of earlier giants of poetry—like Dryden and Pope—who used

Private Collection.

Autumn Leaves (20th century) by Daniel Sherrin.

C Background

William Godwin

English Romantics who wished to reform society, which William Wordsworth in "London 1802" called "a fen/of stagnant waters," turned to a work entitled *An Enquiry Concerning Political Justice* (1793) by William Godwin. The work criticized the existing social structure and proposed an ideal solution, based on the human rights of individuals. One representative of the English government was so outraged by what he saw as Godwin's radical ideas that he labeled Godwin a disease, not a man.

D Literary Connections

Lyrical Ballads

In his introduction to the *Lyrical Ballads,* David Perkins writes, "[T]he poems are designed to reveal the psychology of the human mind and heart—to disclose, as Wordsworth says, 'the primary laws of our nature,' 'the essential passions of the heart.' "

RESPONDING TO THE ART

Daniel Sherrin (c. 1865–c. 1940) was a landscape painter inspired by Romantic ideals.

Activity. Notice the white light that serves as the focal point of the painting. What might the light suggest? [Possible response: The white light seems to draw the viewer toward a better world.]

Professional Notes

Critical Comment: Romantic vs. Augustan

One of the ways in which earlier critics distinguished the Romantic age from the Augustan age was by calling the Romantic age the age of poetry and the Augustan age the age of prose. Brian Wilkie and James Hurt explain that, "[T]he Neoclassic period created functional modern prose, the syntax and diction, say, of our better magazines. . . ." However, people also needed poetry and "the spiritual adventure symbolized by the word" and the Romantics gave them that. The two visions of the world—the adventure of Romanticism and the sane order of Neoclassical prose—complement one another. After students have studied this period, have them return to this quotation and discuss whether or not they feel Wilkie and Hurt's distinction between the two ages is valid.

Getting Students Involved

Writing

Nature Essays. In addition to Romantic poets, essayists past and present have explored, reveled in, and extolled nature, sometimes for its own sake, sometimes in relation to human beings. Many anthologies of nature writing have been published in recent years, including collections of historical pieces and volumes of new essays. Have students seek out one of these anthologies, find an essay they particularly like, and, in a brief report, both summarize and evaluate it.

Ⓐ Literary Connections

Lyrical Ballads

The first edition of Wordsworth and Coleridge's *Lyrical Ballads* had a shorter preface, titled "Advertisement." Wordsworth called the poems "experiments" to see "how far the language of conversation in the middle and lower classes of society is adapted to the purposes of poetic pleasure."

Ⓑ Reading Skills and Strategies

Responding to the Text

Ask students to paraphrase this quotation. Do they agree with Coleridge? Why or why not? [Answers may vary, but students should note that Coleridge presents an objective, empirical criterion for defining the best in poetry.]

A Closer Look

This feature discusses George Gordon, Lord Byron's life and his creation of the Byronic hero and its influence on American culture. Marlon Brando and James Dean were American film stars of the 1950s who epitomized the ill-fated Byronic hero.

Ⓒ Literary Connections

Byron Blasts Wordsworth

One of the many reasons for calling Byron "mad" and "bad" is his disrespect for established and venerable writers, among which, in his own day, was Wordsworth himself. Byron never hesitated to poke fun at Wordsworth. Here, he makes fun of the excessive length and, according to Byron, absurd complexity of Wordsworth's poetry:

And Wordsworth, in a rather long
Excursion
(I think the quarto holds five hundred pages),
Has given a sample from the vasty version
Of his new system to perplex the sages;
'Tis poetry at least by his assertion,
and may appear so when the Dog Star rages
And he who understands it would be able
To add a story to the Tower of Babel.

For more irreverence from Byron on the subject of Wordsworth, see p. 661.

poetry to satirize, or to persuade the reader with argumentative techniques. For Wordsworth, good poetry was "the spontaneous overflow of powerful feelings." Ⓐ And such poetry should use simple, unadorned language to deal with commonplace subjects for a particular purpose. The form is often a lyric that lends itself to spontaneity, immediacy, a quick burst of emotion, and self-revelation. Furthermore, Wordsworth focused on rural life instead of city life, because in the country "the passions of men are incorporated with the beautiful and permanent forms of Nature." Wordsworth found hope in "certain inherent and indestructible qualities of the human mind, and likewise . . . certain powers in the great and permanent objects that act upon it, which are equally inherent and indestructible." In other words, there is nature, and there are human beings to experience nature.

> Ⓑ Not the poem we have *read,* but that to which we *return,* with the greatest pleasure, possesses the genuine power, and claims the name of *essential poetry.*
>
> —Samuel Taylor Coleridge

A CLOSER LOOK

An Irresistible Bad Boy: The Byronic Hero

> Ⓒ "Mad, bad, and dangerous to know."
>
> —Lady Caroline Lamb, speaking of George Gordon, Lord Byron

"A man proud, moody, cynical, with defiance on his brow, and misery in his heart, a scorner of his kind, implacable in revenge, yet capable of deep and strong affection." This model of reckless, wounded manhood described by Thomas Babington Macaulay (1800–1859) became known as the Byronic hero. Both in his life and in his poetry, George Gordon, Lord Byron (1788–1824) gave his name to a type of hero who was devastatingly attractive yet fatally flawed.

Byron's personal charms and poetic talents offset a physical disability (a clubfoot), which embarrassed him terribly, and the complicated romantic entanglements that made him a social outcast. His heroes, whom he often invited his readers to identify with himself, were also passionate yet flawed individualists: intellectually searching, incapable of compromise, forever brooding over some mysterious past sin, painfully yet defiantly alone.

Byron, 6th Baron (detail) (1835) by Thomas Phillips.

By Courtesy of the National Portrait Gallery, London.

Heroes for an unheroic age. The immense popularity of the Byronic hero and the Romantic-age celebration of his prototypes—Cain, Faust, Prometheus, and Napoleon—wasn't hard to understand. These were rash rebels, hailed or resurrected in reaction to a neoclassical world in which order and restraint ruled the day. Most of these daring figures, whose ambitions were doomed from the start, also embodied the deep pessimism of early nineteenth-century life. The failure of the French Revolution had dampened idealism throughout Europe. And the

Getting Students Involved

Enrichment Activity

Comparing Wordsworth and Coleridge. Although Wordsworth and Coleridge achieved, with *Lyrical Ballads,* one of the greatest collaborations in English literature, they were very different personalities. Here is how critic Martin Gardner describes them: "Coleridge and Wordsworth were a study in contrast. Coleridge: outgoing, impulsive, emotional, unstable, weak-willed, impractical, helpless, careless; at times a liar and a hypocrite, but always fun-loving and lovable. Wordsworth: cool, rational, industrious physically as well as intellectually, cautious, reserved, grim. . . . Yet the two men had much in common: a Protestant outlook, a love of nature, a love of poetry, enormous talent, and, it must also be said, a common conviction that Wordsworth was potentially the greatest poet in England." Have students create a Venn diagram comparing and contrasting the two great poets. Students can begin by analyzing the quotations from the poets on this page.

> I think Poetry should surprise by a fine excess and not by Singularity—it should strike the Reader as a wording of his own highest thoughts, and appear almost a Remembrance.
>
> —John Keats, in a letter written February 27, 1818

The Romantics are often called nature poets. This description is misleading if it suggests that their poetry is full of charming scenes of forests, mountains, and streams—like the scenic overlooks on highways or the pictures on travel brochures. **D**

The Romantics prized experiences of the beauty and majesty of nature. They did not think of nature as hostile, but they had a strong sense of its mysterious forces, and they were intrigued by the ways that nature and the human mind act upon each other. In the Preface, Wordsworth says that the poet "considers man and nature as essentially adapted to each other, and the mind of man as naturally a mirror of the fairest and most interesting properties of nature." **E**

Each of the Romantic poets had his own special view of the creative power of the imagination and of the ways in which the human mind is

labyrinthine restrictions of state, church, and society allowed no suitable outlets for the outsized energy of creative young men like Byron and his fictional heroes.

Marlon Brando in Laslo Benedek's film *The Wild One* (1954).

The American heirs. The model of a sensitive rebel continues to be an engaging one for popular heroes of recent time: In post–World War II America, for example, as society had settled into a bland conformity, several searching, sensitive malcontents arrested the attention of moviegoers everywhere.

One version of the Byronic bad boy was played by Marlon Brando, who popularized motorcycles, leather jackets, and a sullen demeanor in his 1954 film *The Wild One*. The leader of a motorcycle gang, Brando is asked, "What are you rebelling against?" His response: "What have you got?" The actor James Dean personified youthful rebellion in both his brief film career and his tragically short life. In *Rebel Without a Cause* (1955), Dean's portrayal of Jim Stark, an alienated character searching for the meaning of manhood, made him a cult hero.

Like all Byronic heroes, these modern characters beckon their admirers to explore personal freedoms and to reject confining conventions. Because this freedom is achieved only by questioning accepted social behavior, these heroes are invariably lonely and misunderstood. And because this freedom often compels them to perform dangerous acts, the lives of these heroes can be much too short. Lord Byron died of a fever at age thirty-six, while fighting for Greek independence. James Dean died in an automobile accident at age twenty-four. **F**

James Dean in Nicholas Ray's film *Rebel Without a Cause* (1955).

Crossing the Curriculum

Art

Ask students to preview examples of artwork from the Romantic period in this essay and in Collections 8 and 9. Students should examine the works for their subject matter as well as for the ways in which the subjects are treated. Then, ask students to choose the work which seems most "Romantic" to them, based on their understanding of the term so far. Have them give reasons for their choice.

Film and Popular Culture

Have students examine contemporary books and films to find modern examples of Byronic heroes. Have them share their findings in a class discussion. How do the rebellious but sensitive heroes they discover compare and contrast to Byron's heroes? If they find no Byronic figures, what do they think that reveals about the times?

D Literary Connections

Romantic Poetry and Nature

One reason the Romantics have been viewed mistakenly as mere nature poets derives from the enormous popularity of some of Wordsworth's lyrics. For example, most people know or recognize these lines:

I wandered lonely as a cloud
That floats on high o'er vales and hills,
When all at once I saw a crowd,
A host, of golden daffodils . . . .

Because of this poem, Wordsworth was often mockingly, sometimes seriously, called the daffodil poet. It is important to make the point that Wordsworth never wrote just simply about nature; he wrote about nature and its effect on the human mind.

E Advanced Learners

Romantic vs. Transcendental Views of Nature

Students may associate the Romantic concept of nature with the transcendentalist view as defined by Ralph Waldo Emerson and Henry David Thoreau. Point out that both the English Romantics and the American Transcendentalists believed that a direct contemplation of nature led to spiritual knowledge and inspiration. Wordsworth felt that the interaction of the mind and nature, mediated by the imagination, produced spiritual insights. Emerson felt that nature and the individual were one and that intuition would lead people to visions of this oneness, which he called the Over-Soul.

F Historical Connections

The Byronic Hero

Other examples of the Romantic or Byronic hero can be found in history; one example is T. E. Lawrence (1888–1935), known as Lawrence of Arabia for his legendary efforts against the Ottoman Turks on the Arabian Peninsula during World War I. Lawrence was unconventional, sometimes shocking his superiors and the society in which he lived. Never fully comfortable with his fame and never able to shake the sense of guilt and despair that haunted him, he died at age forty-six, after a motorcycle accident.

Ⓐ Vocabulary Note

Word Origins

It is interesting in this context to go back to the etymology of *imagination,* which derives from the word *image*. (One meaning of *image* as a verb is "to reflect" or "to mirror.") Furthermore, the word *image* comes from the Latin *imago,* which may be akin to the Latin *imitare* meaning "to imitate." One can only wonder whether Wordsworth turned to this etymology as he created his theory.

RESPONDING TO THE ART

Explain to students that the exponents of Romanticism, in "the Age of Sensibility," preferred feeling and sympathy over reason and the formalities of courtly society. In the art world, Romanticism was a reaction against the Rococo movement, its lavish, decorative, and extravagant predecessor. Sentimental and emotional subjects were the focus of Romantic paintings, such as this one by **Henry Fuseli (Johann Heinrich Fussli),** in which a woman sits on the floor cradling herself as if overcome by sleep or strong emotion. Here, the artist omits the excesses of ornamentation of previous art movements and presents emotion as he imagines it is felt by the subject.

Activity. Invite students to compare this painting to another by the same artist on p. 399.

adapted to nature. You will notice that the poems usually present imaginative experiences as very powerful or moving. This suggests that, in addition to being a special faculty of the mind, the imagination is also a kind of desire, a motive that drives the mind to learn and to know things Ⓐ it cannot learn by rational and logical thinking. So, although the mind is naturally a "mirror" of nature, as Wordsworth thought, the imagination actually moves the mind in mysterious ways to imitate (without being sacrilegious) the powers of its Maker. The purpose of this imitation is to create new realities in the mind and (as a result) in poetry.

In the Romantic period, poetry was no longer used to make complex arguments in a witty, polished style. Romantic poets used unadorned language to explore the significance of commonplace subjects, the beauty of nature, and the power of the human imagination.

Das Schweigen (*Silence*) (detail) (1799–1801) by Johann Heinrich Füssli. Oil on canvas (63.5 cm × 51.5 cm).

Kunsthaus, Zurich. © 2000 by Kunsthaus Zurich. All rights reserved.

Taking a Second Look

Review: Recognizing Cause and Effect

Students may find this passage on the Romantic theory of the imagination challenging. To help them, point out that the argument consists of a series of causes and effects. You might create a cause-and-effect chain as follows:

Cause: Imagination drives the mind to learn.
Effect: The mind moves in mysterious ways.
Cause: The mind moves in mysterious ways.
Effect: The mind imitates the powers of its maker.
Cause: The mind imitates the powers of its maker.
Effect: The mind creates new realities in itself.
Cause: The mind creates new realities in itself.
Final Result: These new realities become poetry.

Encourage students to look for the hidden structure within difficult text. By a process of elimination, they should be able to uncover the hidden logic in the text.

Activity

As students read the essay, encourage them to try looking for the underlying structure of other difficult passages.

The Idea of the Poet

In 1802, in order to clarify his remarks about poetry, Wordsworth added to his Preface a long section on the question, *What is a poet?* His answer began: "He is a man speaking to men."

If this seems strange, consider what happens in a good many of the poems in the following collections. There is a person in the poem—we will call him the "speaker" to distinguish him from the poet—who is "speaking to" someone or something else: a young Highland girl, a baby asleep in a cottage, a skylark, even a Greek vase or a season of the year.

Each poem of this type not only asks us to imagine (pretend) that the "speaking" is taking place, but also makes us consider what *kind* of speaking is taking place. Is the speaker praising or confessing or complaining or worshipping or expressing envy? That is, what is the speaker doing by "speaking"?

> I will not Reason & Compare: my business is to Create.
>
> —William Blake

B

The speaking in lyric poetry is not the Augustan reasoning in verse. It is a more emotional, passionate speaking from the heart. It has been said that we do not *hear* lyric poetry so much as *overhear* it—as if (using our imagination again) we are eavesdropping on a private conversation or on someone talking to himself or herself out loud. The Romantic lyric, then, speaks in what has been called the true voice of feeling or the language of the heart. In writing this way, the Romantics created a kind of poetry that poets today continue to use. C

For lyric poetry to be successful, the speaker and the speaking must be convincing. Thus, the poet must create an artful illusion of the voice of the speaker that conveys certain truths or ideas. Though they did not reason in verse like the Neoclassic poets, the Romantics were deeply concerned with the truths of the heart and the imagination—with truth, as Wordsworth said, "carried alive into the heart by passion." Or, as Keats once wrote to a friend, "What the imagination seizes as beauty must be truth whether it existed before or not." D

Wordsworth's deceptively simple definition of the poet as "a man speaking to men" was thus a revolutionary concept in a number of ways. If we think of the speaker (not the poet) as an ordinary person, then it is a very democratic definition. Poetry is to be about human experience, about the fundamental relationship between the mind (including the heart and the imagination) and other people and other things. The speaking should be convincing so that it can seem a genuine and sincere account of that experience, no matter how special or extravagant the experience may appear to be.

The speakers in Romantic poetry speak in the language of feelings, or of the heart. This exploration of the emotional experiences of ordinary people was revolutionary.

B Literary Connections

T. S. Eliot on Blake

If students think Blake sounds like a man who had a mind of his own, T. S. Eliot agrees. He says Blake "approached everything with a mind unclouded by current opinions. . . . This makes him terrifying."

C Cultural Connections

Augustans vs. Romantics

? The Augustan poets wrote in an age when order had just been restored to a society badly in need of it. Naturally enough, the Augustans celebrated order, hierarchy, and enlightened rule. The Romantics, on the other hand, lived in a society badly in need of social change, even of revolution. How did the Romantics rebel? [Possible responses: They wanted to write about personal feelings; they supported individual rights; they used common, everyday language.]

D Literary Connections

Wordsworth on Poetry

The context of Wordsworth's comment is this: "[People] talk of poetry as of a matter of amusement and idle pleasure; who will converse with us as gravely about a taste for poetry, as they express it, as if it were a thing as indifferent as a taste for rope-dancing, or Frontiniac or sherry. Aristotle, I have been told, hath said that poetry is the most philosophic of all writing; it is so: its object is truth, not individual and local, but general, and operative; not standing upon external testimony, but carried alive into the heart by passion; truth which is its own testimony, which gives strength and divinity to the tribunal to which it appeals, and receives them from the same tribunal. Poetry is the image of man and nature."

Getting Students Involved

Cooperative Learning

Visual Representation of the Romantic Era. Invite small groups of students to create a visual representation of the Romantic era. One possibility is a words-only or images-only collage. Another is a series of links for a Romantic-era video game. A third option might be an MTV-style video with music and poetry interfused. Whatever students wish to create, suggest the following plan: Gather to brainstorm ideas and adopt a plan of action. Put half the team in charge of research and half in charge of development. Have students return to work as a group to revise and fine-tune the final product. Have two members of the group be responsible for presenting the project to the class while the remaining members create a written assessment.

A Closer Look

This feature describes the origins and development of the Gothic style from Horace Walpole's idiosyncratic castle Strawberry Hill to Ann Radcliffe's Gothic novel *The Mysteries of Udolpho.*

A Literary Connections

The Gothic Romance

Other highlights of the Gothic romance include Ann Radcliffe's *Italian* (1797), Matthew Gregory Lewis's *The Monk* (1796), William Beckford's *Vathek* (1786), and Charles Robert Maturin's Irish version of the Faust legend, *Melmoth the Wanderer* (1820).

B Literary Connections

Modern Gothic Writers

? Modern practitioners of the Gothic include Stephen King, Clive Barker, Ira Levin, Whitley Strieber, Anne Rice, William Peter Blatty, and Dean Koontz. How popular is this style of novel today among teenagers? [Answers will vary depending on the tastes of the class.]

C Literary Connections

Ann Radcliffe

Ann Radcliffe never visited the countries where her stories took place, yet *The Mysteries of Udolpho* was one of the most popular novels in England in its time. The novel is set in the eerie atmosphere of a haunted castle high in the Apennines in Italy. The main character, Emily St. Aubert, is imprisoned by her evil guardians until freed by her lover. Among Radcliffe's admirers were Christina Rossetti, Samuel Taylor Coleridge, and Lord Byron.

D Literary Connections

Gothic Romances Redux

Radcliffe's novels and the more powerful novel by Charlotte Brontë, *Jane Eyre* (1847), ultimately spawned a whole category of twentieth-century fiction. Today's Gothic romance novel almost invariably features a mysterious, brooding mansion; an even more mysterious, brooding hero; and a poor but plucky heroine who saves the day and wins the man. Do students feel these novels provide a "delicious melancholy" and "awaken our best and purest feelings"? Why or why not?

The Romantic Poet

In saying that the poet is "a man speaking to men," Wordsworth did not mean that the poet is just a man. In the Preface, it is clear that the poet is a special person, "endowed with more lively sensibility, more enthusiasm and tenderness . . . a greater knowledge of human nature, and a more comprehensive soul, than are supposed to be common among mankind." Though the word *supposed* (meaning *thought*) may suggest that Wordsworth thought his fellow citizens had too low an estimate of much of humankind, all of the Romantic poets described the poet in such lofty terms.

. . . what we have loved,
Others will love, and we will teach them how;
Instruct them how the mind of man becomes
A thousand times more beautiful than the earth
On which he dwells, above this frame of things
(Which, 'mid all revolution in the hopes
And fears of men, doth still remain unchanged)
In beauty exalted, as it is itself
Of quality and fabric more divine.

—William Wordsworth,
from The Prelude

A CLOSER LOOK

THE LURE OF THE GOTHIC

Literature of the Romantic period is filled with examples of the eerie and supernatural: Samuel Coleridge's haunted *The Rime of the Ancient Mariner* and Mary Shelley's famously horrible *Frankenstein.* The Romantics' taste for terror grew from a sensibility called "Gothic" that set stories in gloomy medieval castles. The intention of the Gothic? To make readers' blood run cold. (A)

A "little gothick Castel." Much credit for the popularity of the Gothic style must go to a dramatically unorthodox construction project. In 1747, Horace Walpole (1717–1797) began building what he called a "little gothick Castel." A more conventional choice by the son of wealthy, powerful Prime Minister Robert Walpole (1676–1745) would have been a mansion in the popular neoclassical style. Neoclassical architecture—like the White House in the United States—is inspired by ancient Roman and Greek models and emphasizes balance and symmetry. In stark contrast, the Gothic revels in rustic irregularity: quirky battlements (medieval-style fortifications with openings for defenders) or overgrown landscaping. Walpole's home, named Strawberry Hill, was designed to be gloriously imperfect; when its odd, medieval battlements collapsed, the ruin only enhanced its charm and intensified its melancholy atmosphere.

Making monsters. Walpole had constructed a Gothic ruin; in 1764, he filled it with monsters. His novel *The Castle of Otranto* uses ghosts, living statues, and an eerie forest cave to illustrate a royal family's collapse. With this terrifying, imaginative story, Walpole created the first Gothic novel, a genre of horror tales that we recognize today. (B)

The effects of Walpole's creations were far-reaching. The model of his crumbling house and of stories that provoked violent emotions helped begin the Romantic period's love affair with all things Gothic. Contemporary tastes thought that Gothic architecture reflected the wild, unpredictable aspects of nature; its ruins reflected human aspirations and failures. A melancholy painting or a desolate landscape could enhance spiritual awareness. Ann Radcliffe (1764–1823), one of the best-known Gothic novelists, describes this ideal awareness in *The Mysteries of Udolpho* (1794). In twilight gloom, a character finds "that delicious melancholy which no person, who had felt it once, would resign for the gayest pleasures. They awaken our best and purest feelings; disposing us to benevolence, pity, and friendship." (C) (D)

Exploring unseen "evils." The turn from rational enlightenment to Gothic sensationalism indicated

For William Blake, for example, the poet was the bard, an inspired revealer and teacher. The poet, wrote Coleridge, "brings the whole soul of man into activity" by employing "that synthetic and magical power . . . the imagination." Shelley called poets "the unacknowledged legislators of the world." Keats wrote that a poet is a "physician" to all humanity and "pours out a balm upon the world." Nothing, wrote Wordsworth in *The Recluse,*

> . . . can breed such fear and awe
> As fall upon us often when we look
> Into our Minds, into the Mind of Man—
> My haunt, and the main region of my song.

The poet, in sum, is someone human beings cannot do without.

The Romantic poets found a way through the imagination to fulfill the poet's traditional role as "prophet, priest, and king" in a time of change. E

more than just a fad for terrifying tales and quirky architecture. The Gothic was one way in which people of the age expressed a sense of helplessness about forces beyond their control: frightening revolutions in Europe and industrialization's unsettling economic changes. The familiar, sensational trappings of the Gothic novel that we know today were less important than its ability to let readers, if only for a moment, share their fears about the age's suffering, injustice, and other unseen "evils."

Two Men Contemplating the Moon (1819) by Caspar David Friedrich.

Staatliche Kunstsammlungen Dresden, Gemäldegalerie Neue Meister.

E Critical Thinking

Challenging the Text

Ask students to explain this summary statement and to evaluate its applicability today. Students may or may not be able to name contemporary poets who fit the bill, but they will surely know songwriters who do. Ask students which of these "poets" inspire worthy feelings and deeds, which simply record their world, and which offer a dangerous vision.

RESPONDING TO THE ART

Caspar David Friedrich (1774–1840) was a German painter best known for his landscapes and seascapes, which contain both literal and allegorical elements. In explaining one of his paintings, Friedrich said that the mountains stood for faith and the fir trees for hope. His work caused controversy, since he often depicted humans as powerless before the forces of nature. In summing up his version of the Romantics' philosophy, Friedrich said, "The artist's feeling is his law."

Activity. Ask students if the place depicted in the painting seems inviting or threatening. Encourage them to talk about the elements that set the mood, such as the tree branches, the relative sizes and positions of the people, and the phases of the moon. Students might also discuss the predominant choice of color and how it helps set the mood.

Assessing Learning

Check Test: Short Answer

1. The publication of which book started the Romantic era in England? [*Lyrical Ballads, with a Few Other Poems* by William Wordsworth and Samuel Taylor Coleridge]
2. What economic transformation was England undergoing during the Romantic era? [It was changing from an agricultural society to an industrial nation.]
3. What does *laissez faire* mean, and what was it in the context of this period? [It means "let people do as they please"; it was an economic philosophy that discouraged interfering with market forces.]
4. What did the Romantics emphasize about human experience? [They emphasized imagination, emotions, common bonds between people, and humanity's relationship with nature.]
5. Who were the Gothic writers of the Romantic period? [Samuel Taylor Coleridge, Mary Shelley, Horace Walpole, Ann Radcliffe]

Responding to the Art

In **William Blake**'s grim prophecy for Europe, famine strikes. In this visionary engraving, a dead baby (presumably Europe) lies before a black pot of boiling liquid from which evil-looking steam pours. Two women surround the baby—one appears defeated while the other gazes above the smoke.

Activity. Ask students to note the face raised upward and to contrast it with the upper half of the painting, in which a fire blazes and an appalling blackness looms. Why might Blake have such negative feelings about Europe's future? [Possible response: Most of Europe was under the control of kings who had little concern for the plight of the common people.]

Quickwrite

One way to help students respond to the art of this period is by asking them to chart information about it. For each painting they might record the title, subject, dominant images, and mood or feelings evoked. After students have studied the art piece by piece, encourage them to focus on just one painter or painting and draw up a list of questions for further research.

Europe: A Prophecy: Famine (detail) (1794) by William Blake. Relief etching with white line engraving, watercolor.

Private Collection

Quickwrite This introduction to the great Romantic period in English literature is illustrated with pieces of fine art, many of them painted by famous Romantic artists of England and continental Europe. Look over these paintings and take notes on their subjects. (Note their titles.) What exactly does each one make you see? What emotions does each evoke? Do any of the paintings seem mysterious? Which of these paintings or painters might provide material for further research?

(Opposite) *Donati's Comet over Balliol College* (19th century) by William of Oxford (circle of).

The Maas Gallery, London.

Getting Students Involved

Enrichment Activity

Romanticism Today. The Romantic movement is still a strong part of America's cultural heritage. Think about the essay and try to trace how the thoughts and ideas that were popular in England from 1798 to 1832 might still influence us today. For instance, the environmental movement is in large part an outgrowth of Romanticism. Another Romantic influence might be the continued use in poetry and prose of the everyday speech of the common people. Ask students if, for example, they think the language of rap might be an outgrowth of Wordsworth's emphasis on using the language of people "on the street." Have students continue this activity on their own, extending the discussion into fields such as music, art, and dance.

Collection 8

The Power of Imagination

Theme

Since Feeling Is First *Rejecting the emphasis on reason, the Romantic lyric poets express belief in the power of the imagination and the superiority of feeling. Focusing on ordinary people (not the nobility), on country life (not the court), and on the natural world (not cities), the Romantics look to the individual to remake the world by the light of intuition.*

Reading the Anthology

Reaching Struggling Readers

The *Reading Skills and Strategies: Reaching Struggling Readers* binder includes a Reading Strategies Handbook that offers concrete suggestions to help students who have difficulty reading and comprehending text, or students who are reluctant readers. When a specific strategy is most appropriate for a selection, a correlation to the Handbook is provided at the bottom of the teacher's page under the head Struggling Readers. This head may also be used to introduce additional ideas for helping students read challenging texts.

Reading Beyond the Anthology

Read On

At the end of the Romantic Period collections, the grade twelve book includes an annotated bibliography of books suitable for extended reading. The suggested books are related to works in these collections by theme, by author, or by subject. To preview the Read On for the Romantic Period, please turn to p. T769

HRW Library

The *HRW Library* offers novels, plays, and short-story collections for extended reading. Each book in the Library includes a major work and thematically or topically related Connections. Each book in the *HRW Library* is also accompanied by a Study Guide that provides teaching suggestions and worksheets. The two titles shown here will work well to extend the theme of Collection 8.

A MIDSUMMER NIGHT'S DREAM
William Shakespeare

Shakespeare's most popular comedy is the tale of three sets of lovers loose in the forest. Confusion reigns when Puck, a meddlesome sprite, decides to fix the lovers' complicated problems with the help of a love potion.

WUTHERING HEIGHTS
Emily Brontë

Emily Brontë used her prodigious imagination to write one of literature's most passionate love stories. Heathcliff, a young foundling, is raised at Wuthering Heights on the wild Yorkshire Moors and falls in love with the daughter of the house, Catherine.

Collection 8 The Power of Imagination

Resources for this Collection

Note: All resources for this collection are available for preview on the *One-Stop Planner CD-ROM 2 with Test Generator.* All worksheets and blackline masters may be printed from the CD-ROM.

Internet Resources
go.hrw.com LE0 12-8

Selection or Feature	Reading and Literary Skills	Vocabulary, Language, and Grammar
To a Mouse (p. 641) Robert Burns	• *Graphic Organizers for Active Reading,* Worksheet p. 48	• *Daily Oral Grammar,* Transparency 23
Blake's Poems (p. 646) • **The Tyger** (p. 647) **Primary Sources: "Blake is a real name . . ."** (p. 648) Charles Lamb • **The Lamb** (p. 650) • **The Chimney Sweeper: Innocence** (p. 652) • **The Chimney Sweeper: Experience** (p. 653) • **A Poison Tree** (p. 654) William Blake **Elements of Literature: Parallelism** (p. 655)	• *Graphic Organizers for Active Reading,* Worksheet pp. 49, 50, 51, 52	• *Daily Oral Grammar,* Transparency 24
• **Lines Composed a Few Miles Above Tintern Abbey** (p. 657) • **Strange Fits of Passion Have I Known** (p. 663) • **She Dwelt Among the Untrod-den Ways** (p. 664) • **A Slumber Did My Spirit Seal** (p. 664) • *from* **Ode: Intimations of Immortality I, II, V** (p. 667) • **Composed upon Westminister Bridge** (p. 669) • **The World Is Too Much with Us** (p. 671) William Wordsworth **Elements of Literature: Romantic Lyrics** (p. 672)	• *Graphic Organizers for Active Reading,* Worksheet pp. 53, 54, 55, 56, 57 • *Literary Elements:* Transparencies 17, 18, 19 Worksheet pp. 52, 55, 58	• *Grammar and Language Links:* Parallel Structure, Worksheet p. 35 • *Language Workshop CD-ROM,* Writing Clear Sentences
World Literature: Russia **I Have Visited Again** (p. 675) Alexander Pushkin	The World Literature feature offers students the opportunity to explore thematically linked literature from different world cultures. Structured activities called Finding Common Ground are provided to guide students' explorations of these thematic connections between British and other world literature.	
• **Kubla Khan** (p. 679) **Primary Sources: Dorothy Wordsworth Describes Coleridge** (p. 682) • **The Rime of the Ancient Mariner** (p. 683) Samuel Taylor Coleridge **Primary Sources: Coleridge Describes His Addiction** (p. 703) **Connections:** *from* **In Patagonia** (p. 704) Bruce Chatwin	• *Graphic Organizers for Active Reading,* Worksheet pp. 58, 59	• *Grammar and Language Links:* Revision Worksheet, p. 37

Other Resources for this Collection

- *Cross-Curricular Activities,* p. 8
- *Portfolio Management System,* Introduction to Portfolio Assessment, p. 1
- *Test Generator,* Collection Test
- *Words to Own,* Worksheet p. 18
- *Formal Assessment,* Literary Period Introduction Test, p. 117

Writing	Listening and Speaking Viewing and Representing	Assessment
• *Portfolio Management System,* Rubrics for Choices, p. 153	• *Audio CD Library,* Disc 11, Track 2 • *Portfolio Management System,* Rubrics for Choices, p. 153	• *Formal Assessment,* Selection Test, p. 119 • *Test Generator (One-Stop Planner CD-ROM)*
• *Portfolio Management System,* Rubrics for Choices, p. 154	• *Audio CD Library,* Disc 11, Tracks 3, 4, 5, 6, 7 • *Viewing and Representing:* Fine Art Transparency 10 Worksheet p. 40 • *Portfolio Management System,* Rubrics for Choices, p. 154	• *Formal Assessment,* Selection Tests, pp. 120, 121, 122, 123 • *Test Generator (One-Stop Planner CD-ROM)*
• *Portfolio Management System,* Rubrics for Choices, p. 156	• *Audio CD Library,* Disc 11, Tracks 8, 9, 10, 11, 12, 13, 14, 15, 16 • *Portfolio Management System,* Rubrics for Choices, p. 156	• *Formal Assessment,* Selection Tests, pp. 124, 126, 127, 128, 129 • *Test Generator (One-Stop Planner CD-ROM)*
	• *Audio CD Library,* Disc 11, Track 17	
• *Portfolio Management System,* Rubrics for Choices, p. 158	• *Audio CD Library,* Disc 11, Tracks 18, 19 • *Portfolio Management System,* Rubrics for Choices, p. 158	• *Formal Assessment,* Selection Tests, pp. 130, 131 • *Test Generator (One-Stop Planner CD-ROM)* • *Preparation for College Admission Exams,* pp. 29, 31

Transparency CD-ROM Video Audio CD

Collection 8 The Power of Imagination

Skills Focus

Selection or Feature	Reading Skills and Strategies	Elements of Literature and Language	Writing	Listening and Speaking	Viewing and Representing
To a Mouse (p. 641) Robert Burns	Using Context and Glosses, p. 641	Dialect, pp. 641, 644 Speaker, p. 644 Tone, p. 644 Alliteration, p. 644	Identify Potential Research Topics, p. 644 Write an Essay Responding to the Poem, p. 644 Write an Alternative Version of "To a Mouse," p. 644 Write a Reply from the Mouse, p. 644		
Blake's Poems (p. 646) **The Tyger** (p. 647) **The Lamb** (p. 650) **The Chimney Sweeper: Innocence** (p. 652) **The Chimney Sweeper: Experience** (p. 653) **A Poison Tree** (p. 654) William Blake	Paraphrase, p. 653	Symbol, pp. 647, 651 Image, pp. 648, 655 Speaker, pp. 648, 651 Narrator, p. 651 Moral Lesson, p. 653 Tone, p. 653 Theme, p. 654 Parallelism, p. 655 Poetic Structure, p. 655	Generate Research Questions Based on Blake's Biography and Art, p. 655 Write a Brief Essay Comparing an Early Draft of "The Tyger" with the Final Version, p. 655 Write an Essay Explaining the Religious Issues Raised by Blake in "The Tyger" and "The Lamb," p. 655 Write the Opening or Closing Paragraphs of a Prose Narrative, p. 655	Select Background Music to Accompany an Oral Reading of "A Poison Tree," p. 655	Create an Original Illustration for a Blake Poem, p. 655
Lines Composed a Few Miles above Tintern Abbey (p. 657) **Strange Fits of Passion Have I Known** (p. 663) **She Dwelt Among the Untrodden Ways** (p. 664) **A Slumber Did My Spirit Seal** (p. 664) *from* **Ode: Intimations of Immortality** (p. 667) **Composed Upon Westminister Bridge** (p. 669) **The World Is Too Much with Us** (p. 671) William Wordsworth	Recognize Patterns of Organization, pp. 657, 662 Run-on Lines, p. 662 Main Idea, p. 662 Paraphrase, p. 666	Blank Verse, pp. 657, 662, 672 Iambic Pentameter, p. 657 Image, pp. 662, 673 Figures of Speech, p. 666 Epigraph, p. 668 Paradox, pp. 668, 670 Mood, p. 668 Personification, pp. 669–670 Romantic Lyrics, p. 672 Sonnet, p. 672 Ode, p. 672 Apostrophize, p. 672 Meditative Poem, p. 672 Speaker, p. 672 Tone, p. 672 Theme, pp. 672, 673	Identify Possible Research Topics in the Life of Dorothy Wordsworth, p. 673 Write an Essay Tracing a Theme in Wordsworth, p. 673 Write an Essay Identifying Romantic Themes and Images in Wordworth's Poetry, p. 673 Write an Essay Comparing Texts Across Cultures, p. 673 Rewrite "She Dwelt Among the Untrodden Ways" from the Point of View of a Woman, p. 673 Write a Prose Description that Personifies a City or Town, p. 673	Create a Talk Show, p. 673	
World Literature: Russia **I Have Visited Again** (p. 675) Alexander Pushkin	The World Literature feature offers students the opportunity to explore thematically linked literature from different world cultures. Structured activities called Finding Common Ground are provided in the Pupil's Edition to guide students' explorations of these thematic connections between British and other world literature.				
Kubla Khan (p. 679) **The Rime of the Ancient Mariner** (p. 683) Samuel Taylor Coleridge	Respond to the Text, p. 679 Read Archaic Words, p. 707 Synonyms, p. 707	Image, p. 682 Rhyme Scheme, pp. 682–683 Meter, pp. 682–683, 706, 708 Alliteration, pp. 682, 706, 708 Speaker, p. 682 Symbol, pp. 682, 708 Ballad, p. 683 Internal Rhyme, pp. 683, 706, 708 Assonance, pp. 683, 706, 708 Narrator, p. 706 Figurative Language, p. 706 Simile, p. 706 Metaphor, p. 706 Personification, p. 706 Ballad Stanza, p. 706 Allegory, p. 708	Identify Potential Topics for a Research Paper, p. 708 Write an Essay Analyzing a Theme, p. 708 Write an Essay Analyzing the Effect of Sound Structures on Meaning, p. 708 Write an Essay Analyzing Unanswered Questions in "The Rime of the Ancient Mariner," p. 708 Write an Essay Exploring the Allegorical Meaning of "The Rime of the Ancient Mariner," p. 708 Write a Prose Summary of a Conclusion for "Kubla Khan," p. 708 Write a Brief Narrative in Which the Ancient Mariner Finds Peace, p. 708		Sketch Three or Four Drawings of Xanadu for a Dream Journal, p. 708

Collection 8

THE POWER OF IMAGINATION

Burns
Blake
Wordsworth
Pushkin
Coleridge

The poet's eye, in a fine frenzy rolling,
Doth glance from heaven to earth, from earth to heaven;
And, as imagination bodies forth
The forms of things unknown, the poet's pen
Turns them to shapes, and gives to airy nothing
A local habitation and a name.

—William Shakespeare, *from A Midsummer Night's Dream*

OBJECTIVES

1. Read literature from the Romantic period on the theme of "The Power of Imagination"
2. Interpret literary elements with special emphasis on romantic lyrics
3. Apply a variety of reading strategies to the literature with special emphasis on patterns of organization and reading archaic words
4. Respond to the literature in a variety of modes
5. Plan, draft, revise, and edit a research paper

Responding to the Quotation

Ask students what the quotation suggests about the power of imagination. [Possible responses: A poet can use imagination to create anything. A poet can make imaginary things real. The imagination can link heaven and earth.] All these answers suggest the transcendent, creative power of the imagination. Also, point out to students that the passage is written in blank verse, or unrhymed iambic pentameter. Students will read more about blank verse on p. 657.

Resources

Viewing and Representing
Videocassette B, Segment 8
Available in Spanish and English. This video explores Romantic ideas about nature and the imagination. For full lesson plans and worksheets, see the *Visual Connections Teacher's Manual.*

WORK IN PROGRESS

Writing Focus: The Research Paper

The following **Work in Progress** assignments build to a culminating **Writer's Workshop** at the end of Collection 9.

• To a Mouse	Identify potential research topics (p. 644)
• Blake's poems	Generate research questions based on biography and art (p. 655)
• Wordsworth's poems	Generate questions about Dorothy Wordsworth (p. 673)
• The Rime of the Ancient Mariner	Find topics in history (p. 707)

Writer's Workshop: Expository Writing / The Research Paper (p. 773)

Objectives

1. Read and interpret the poem
2. Identify the dialect
3. Use context and glosses to determine meaning
4. Express understanding through analytical and creative writing

Skills

Literary
- Interpret dialect

Reading
- Use context and glosses

Writing
- Collect ideas for a research paper
- Analyze the reading response
- Create a new speaker and audience
- Create a different point of view

Viewing/Representing
- Analyze and interpret fine art (ATE)

Planning

- **Block Schedule**
  Block Scheduling Lesson Plans with Pacing Guide
- **Traditional Schedule**
  Lesson Plans Including Strategies for English-Language Learners
- **One-Stop Planner**
  CD-ROM with Test Generator

Robert Burns

(1759–1796)

In 1786, a Scottish farmer thrust himself into the Scottish and English literary worlds. The farmer was Robert (Robby) Burns, and the book that catapulted him out of the barnyard was *Poems, Chiefly in the Scottish Dialect.*

Within a year, Burns had left his native Ayrshire (in southwestern Scotland) for the first time and become the toast of Edinburgh. He seized the moment to issue a new edition of his poems (1787) with an Edinburgh publisher. In a new preface to this edition, he proclaimed, "The poetic genius of my country found me . . . at the plow; and threw her inspiring mantle over me. . . . I tuned my wild, artless notes, as she inspired."

Burns was certainly eager to cultivate an audience among the literati of Edinburgh, but he also consciously reinforced his image as an untutored rustic inspired by Scotland itself. He was fully aware that his fame would probably be temporary, and it was. After this auspicious beginning, Burns's stature declined. He actually wrote relatively little poetry afterward. Instead, he devoted himself to collecting, editing, rewriting, and creating over three hundred Scottish folk songs; most of the lyrics he wrote he set to traditional airs. This is the work that established Burns's most enduring reputation. Scottish immigrants to North America and elsewhere took his song collections with them, and they sang Burns's words to remember their homeland. Even now, many people mark the New Year by singing "Auld Lang Syne," one of Burns's lyrics.

Only ten years after his first success, Burns died of heart disease. Though his reputation includes credible legends of heavy drinking, it is clear that poor nutrition and the long-term physical hardships of farming led to his early death.

By the early nineteenth century, Burns was well on the way to becoming the single most important symbol of Scottish literature. Burns was an extraordinary poet in part because

Robert Burns (c. 1792) by Alexander Nasmyth. Oil on canvas (12½″ × 9½″).

By Courtesy of the National Portrait Gallery, London.

Scottish culture, both popular and refined, seems to have spoken through him. He grew up in the folk culture of small isolated Scottish villages and farms, where the few pleasures were all the more precious. Much of what Wordsworth noted as the "presence of human life" in Burns's work comes from his immersion in the lives of ordinary human beings. The pleasure we take from his poetry comes in part from our recognition of things common and enduring in human experience.

At the same time, Burns himself was quite aware of the tradition of Scottish literature, which was undergoing a studied revival in the eighteenth century. Burns had the benefit of some excellent (though short-lived) formal education before he was needed full time for farm labor, and he was well read in English authors. The apparent artlessness of what he wrote and the simple pose he adopted as a humble plowman mask a mastery of literary forms. Burns, in fact, could write perfectly well in the literary English of his time as well as in a range of Scottish, from heavy dialect to a beautiful blending of folk idioms and literary language.

go.hrw.com
LEO 12-8

Resources: Print and Media

Reading
- *Graphic Organizers for Active Reading,* p. 48
- *Audio CD Library*
  Disc 11, Track 2

Writing and Language
- *Daily Oral Grammar*
  Transparency 23

Assessment
- *Formal Assessment,* p. 119
- *Portfolio Management System,* p. 153
- *Test Generator (One-Stop Planner CD-ROM)*

Internet
- go.hrw.com (keyword: LEO 12-8)

Before You Read
To a Mouse

Make the Connection
The Persistence of the Unforeseen
Here a plowman speaks to a mouse whose nest he has overturned—a seemingly insignificant event. But the speaker also recognizes his own human dilemma in the sudden disruption of the mouse's shelter, carefully constructed against the cruel winter—what the British writer Thomas Hardy was to call "the persistence of the unforeseen."

Elements of Literature
Dialect
Dialect is speech native to a particular geographical area or to a social or political group. People brought up speaking a dialect sometimes know no other kind of speech and need no other to communicate within their community. However, when government transactions, the law, and the business of educated society are conducted in another language, speakers of dialect can be at a disadvantage. This was the case among the rural population of nineteenth-century Scotland, where English was the official language.

Dialect is speech characteristic of a particular region or group.
For more on Dialect, see the Handbook of Literary Terms.

Reading Skills and Strategies
Using Context and Glosses
When used as thickly and consistently as Robert Burns uses it here, Scottish dialect sounds like a foreign language. Yet while Burns's poems seem to call for translation, they also contain some easy-to-read passages that will help you understand others that are not easy to grasp. The meanings of some words can be figured out by their sounds or their context in a phrase or line. Others are so deeply rooted in their Scottish origins that you will have to consult the side glosses. When you have finished reading, jot down your reactions to the dialect.

Background
As an educated and well-read man, Burns had the option of using either Scottish dialect or the king's English. Depending on the subject or occasion of a poem, he proceeded to use both. But there is little question that, if it were not for his poems in dialect, he would figure in literary history as no more than a pleasant poet who accepted the genteel conventions of his time and its sentimental distortions of "the simple life."

The difficulties of poems in dialect have caused some people to attempt to translate them into contemporary language. But attempts to render dialect poetry into plain English often fail. This is simply because the logic of a poem is only part of what it means to convey. When sound is divorced from sense, the qualities of rhythm, music, and color are diminished, and meaning becomes prosaic.

To enjoy and relish the music, rhythm, and lilting Scottish dialect of "To a Mouse," listen to it read aloud on audiotape.

Robert Burns's Birthplace (19th century) by George Washington Brownlow.

Summary

The speaker, a farmer who has turned up a mouse's nest with his plow, pities the creature and sympathizes with its humble ways. He compares his own lot in life with that of the mouse and considers the mouse more fortunate because the mouse worries only about the present, while the speaker regrets the past and fears the future.

Browsing in the Files
About the Author. Burns was not only a man of great intellect but also of great physical strength, as this quotation by Allan Cunningham suggests: "He was strong, and proud of his strength. I saw him one evening match himself with a number of masons; and out of five-and-twenty practised hands, the most vigorous young men in the parish, there was only one that could lift the same weight as Burns."
Writers on Writing. Burns said "I never had the least thought or inclination of turning Poet till I got once heartily in love and then rhyme and song were, in a manner, the spontaneous language of my heart."

Reaching All Students

Struggling Readers
Display the additional glosses listed under English Language Learners on the board and share them with the group. Then have students work in pairs. Ask them to try reading the poem line by line and rewriting each line of the poem as they read. Encourage pairs to check the glosses when they encounter troublesome words.
If a word is not glossed, have them consult a dictionary.

English Language Learners
Provide English language learners with the following additional glosses: *tim'rous* (timorous, fearful); *panic's* (panic is); *breastie* (breast); *wad* (would); *rin* (run); *an'* (and); *wi'* (with); *na* (not); *'s a sma* (is a small); *'t* (it); *wee-bit* (small); *housie* (house); *win's* (winds); *ane* (one); *o'* (of); and whatever additional words you wish to include.

Advanced Learners
Encourage students to read more of Burns's work, perhaps exploring one category, such as ballads, folk tunes, or poems addressed to Highland Mary. She was a sweetheart of Burns, named Mary Campbell, and the subject of "O, Highland Mary" and "My Highland Lassie," among other works.

Ⓐ Reading Skills and Strategies

Responding to the Text

? What might you or someone else you know do if you uncovered a mouse while plowing? [Possible responses: Many people would just keep going; some would try to rescue it; some people might even try to kill it; very few would stop to have a conversation.]

Ⓑ Reading Skills and Strategies

Using Context and Glosses

Tell students that *cowran* here means "cowering," a word that describes a cringing posture adopted by those who are fearful. For instance, a dog usually *cowers* in front of a man with a stick. Once students are clear on the meaning of this word, ask them to use context clues and the glosses to paraphrase the first line. [little, sleek, cowering, timorous beast]

Ⓒ Critical Thinking

Making Connections

? How do ll. 7–8 display a typical Romantic concern? [Possible answers: The speaker worries that humanity and nature are at odds; or that humanity has disturbed or is destroying the balance of nature.]

Ⓓ Struggling Readers

Getting the Main Idea

? Read ll. 19–23 and find time clues. Based on these clues, why can't the mouse build another house? [The winds are strewing the grasses of her old nest, and the green moss has died. The bitter, keen winds of December are coming shortly.]

Highland Landscape, Scotland (late 19th or early 20th century) by Charles Stuart.
Private Collection.

To a Mouse

Ⓐ **Robert Burns**

On Turning Her Up in Her Nest, with the Plow, November, 1785.

Ⓑ
Wee, sleeket,° cowran, tim'rous beastie,
O, what a panic's in thy breastie!
Thou need na start awa sae hasty,
Wi' bickering brattle!°
I wad be laith° to rin an' chase thee,
Wi' murd'ring pattle!°

Ⓒ
I'm truly sorry man's dominion
Has broken Nature's social union,
An' justifies that ill opinion,
Which makes thee startle
At me, thy poor, earth-born companion,
An' fellow mortal!

I doubt na, whyles,° but thou may thieve;
What then? poor beastie, thou maun° live!
A daimen-icker in a thrave°
'S a sma request:
I'll get a blessin wi' the lave,°
An' never miss 't!

Ⓓ
Thy wee-bit housie, too, in ruin!
It's silly wa's° the win's are strewin!
An' naething, now, to big° a new ane,
O' foggage° green!
An' bleak December's winds ensuin,
Baith snell° an' keen!

1. **sleeket:** sleek.

4. **bickering brattle:** skirmishing, rattling sounds.
5. **laith:** loath; unwilling.
6. **pattle:** plow staff.

13. **whyles:** sometimes.
14. **maun:** must.
15. **daimen-icker in a thrave:** occasional ear of grain out of a bundle.
17. **lave:** remainder.

20. **silly wa's:** feeble walls.
21. **big:** build.
22. **foggage:** moss.

24. **snell:** bitter.

Using Students' Strengths

Naturalist Learners

Invite students to comment on details about nature that are included in the poem, such as whether or not mice actually nest outdoors in winter in climates such as that of Scotland. Students might also gather details about the size, composition, and appearance of mouse nests and whether those nests are used in winter for warmth or for raising young.

Thou saw the fields laid bare an' wast,
An' weary winter comin fast,
An' cozie here, beneath the blast,
Thou thought to dwell,
Till crash! the cruel coulter° past
Out thro' thy cell.

That wee-bit heap o' leaves an' stibble,
Has cost thee monie a weary nibble!
Now thou's turn'd out, for a' thy trouble,
But° house or hald,°
To thole° the winter's sleety dribble,
An' cranreuch° cauld!

But Mousie, thou art no thy-lane,°
In proving foresight may be vain:
The best laid schemes o' mice an' men
Gang aft agley,°
An' lea'e us nought but grief an' pain,
For promis'd joy!

Still, thou art blest, compar'd wi' me!
The present only toucheth thee:
But och! I backward cast my e'e,
On prospects drear!
An' forward, tho' I canna see,
I guess an' fear!

29. coulter: plow blade.

34. but: without. **hald:** land.

35. thole: endure.

36. cranreuch: hoarfrost.

37. no thy-lane: not alone.

40. gang aft agley: go often amiss.

Ploughing (detail) (late 19th or early 20th century) by Aldin Cecil.

E Elements of Literature

Dialect

? What is the effect of the repetition of *wee* and *wee-bit* in ll. 1, 19, and 31? [Possible answers: The repetition emphasizes the difference in size between the mouse and man; *wee* is also a word with endearing connotations, so it colors readers' perceptions of the speaker and his relationship to the mouse.]

F Advanced Students

Making the Connections

Encourage students to learn how the plot of John Steinbeck's novel *Of Mice and Men* relates to this poem. [Possible answer: Retarded, innocent Lennie plans to live "on the fatta the lan's" but in the end is flushed from hiding in the brush and killed.]

G Elements of Literature

Dialect

? How would this poem be different if the Scottish dialect were replaced with Modern English? [Possible answers: It would be easier to read; the poem would lose its colloquial flavor and individuality; the reader would be less likely to want to read the poem aloud or hear it read; it would lose its lilt.]

Making the Connections

Cultural Connections: A Celebration of Burns

Every January 25, Scots around the world gather to celebrate Scottish culture and Robert Burns's birthday. The evening's entertainment includes a banquet of traditional foods such as haggis (a mixture of sheep's or calf's heart, lungs, and liver combined with suet, onions, oatmeal, and seasoning), the recitation of a number of Burns's poems, and perhaps the singing of a few of his songs. Burns is more than just a favorite son of Scotland; he is a national symbol. In his time, Scotland was struggling to maintain its national identity. The Act of Union in 1707 brought Scotland under direct British rule, and, in 1745, the attempts by Scottish Jacobites to overthrow the English government were crushed. The English punished Scotland by charging tariffs and by outlawing tartan cloth and bagpipes. The revival of Scotland's literature, of which Burns was a central figure, provided a way for Scots to regain their individuality and national pride. Other poets, besides Burns, wrote in the Lowlands Scottish dialect, called Lallan, but Burns's added attention to the techniques of English poetry as well as the traditions of the Scottish folk song made him a success at home and abroad.

MAKING MEANINGS

First Thoughts [Respond]

1. The speaker's mood is contemplative, playful, sympathetic, compassionate, and then melancholy. Students may have had similar feelings in situations in which they witnessed a small tragedy.

Shaping Interpretations [Interpret]

2. The tone changes by l. 37, becoming more melancholy. The speaker says his past is dreary, and he can only guess at the future and fear it.
3. *Dominion* may refer to human rule over the earth, *union* to the fact that in nature animals of all types share the earth and usually coexist without destroying each other's homes. The words imply that humans are part of nature, but their need for dominion destroys nature's delicate balance.
4. Things do not always turn out as planned for both mice and people. The mouse, however, deals only with the present while humans contemplate past failures and worry about the future.
5. Comical sound effects include "bickering brattle" in l. 4 and "till crash! I the cruel coulter past" in l. 29.

Connecting with the Text [Respond]

6. Students may agree that humans do not have total control over their lives. Students may share past experiences when their plans went awry.

Extending the Text [Apply/Evaluate]

7. Students should cite specific contemporary examples, such as films set in Ireland or Jamaica or urban rap songs. Dialect adds to a work's realism and anchors it firmly in the time and place it is meant to re-create. Some students may enjoy dialect, while others may say it slows their reading down too much.

Grading Timesaver

Rubrics for each Choices assignment appear on p. 153 in the *Portfolio Management System.*

MAKING MEANINGS

First Thoughts

1. How would you describe the **speaker's** mood? Do you ever feel the same? When?

Shaping Interpretations

2. Where does the speaker's **tone** change? What does the speaker imply in the last stanza about his own past and his prospects for the future?
3. When you paraphrase the second stanza, what are the meanings of the words *dominion* and *union* here, in your view? What attitude about people and nature does the use of these words imply?
4. What comparisons between the mouse and himself does the speaker make in the last two stanzas?
5. Read aloud some uses of **alliteration** in the poem. Are any of the poem's sound effects comical?

Connecting with the Text

6. How do you feel about the philosophy of the future expressed in lines 39–40 (the best-known lines of the poem)? How does your own experience reflect or contradict these lines? (Do you recognize in these lines the title of a novel by John Steinbeck?)

Extending the Text

7. Burns's use of **dialect** was a great departure from the elegant language of most eighteenth-century poets. What dialects are used in drama, songs, films, and fiction today? How do you feel about the use of dialect for realism?

CHOICES: Building Your Portfolio

Writer's Notebook

1. Collecting Ideas for a Research Paper

You might find an interesting topic for further research in the biography of Burns on page 640. Jot down questions you have about the life of Robert Burns, about his works, or about the political situation of Scotland in the late eighteenth century. Save your notes for the Writer's Workshop on page 773.

Monitoring Your Reading Process

2. Frankly Speaking

Write an essay explaining your response to this poem, including any difficulty you had with the dialect. Be as frank as you want to be, but support your response with specific reasons and quotations from the poem. (Be sure to consult your reading notes.)

Creative Writing

3. Creature Connections

Have another speaker address another creature—fly, cockroach, spider, moth. Imitate Burns, and imagine what the creature is thinking of the encounter. What connection does the speaker see between the creature and himself?

Creative Writing

4. From the Mouse's Mouth

What does the mouse think as her wee bit of leaves and stubble is ruined by the plow? Write the mouse's reply to her fellow mortal. Use dialect if you wish.

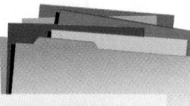

William Blake

(1757–1827)

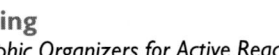

By Courtesy of the National Portrait Gallery, London.

William Blake (detail) (1807) by Thomas Phillips. Oil on canvas (35 ¼″ × 17 ¼″).

William Blake's life is not as "romantic" or "poetic" as the lives of Coleridge, Shelley, and Keats were. By all accounts, he was somewhat happily married to the same woman for much of his life. He never traveled, and he lived outside London for only three years (1800–1803). He began his artistic training at ten, when his father, a London shopkeeper, sent him to one of the best drawing schools. Apprenticed to an engraver at fourteen, Blake worked steadily at his craft as an engraver and as a professional artist throughout a long life, in good times and bad.

During his lifetime, Blake's work received very little attention, and a great deal of his poetry was never published in the sense of being "public." When his work was noticed, readers and viewers too often decided that it, and therefore Blake himself, was weird, confused, or mad. What we really know of Blake—from the enormous energy and variety of his poetry, paintings, drawings, and engravings—is that he was quite simply a great artist in the fullest sense.

A woman at a gathering is said to have asked Blake *where* he had come upon the scene he had just vividly described to her. "*Here,* madam," he said, pointing his finger at his forehead. To paraphrase Blake, if we see with imagination, we see all things in the infinite. But if we see only with reason, we see only ourselves. "I know that this world is a world of imagination & vision," he wrote.

> I see everything I paint in this world, but everybody does not see alike. To the eyes of a miser, a guinea [a coin] is more beautiful than the sun, & a bag worn with the use of money has more beautiful proportions than a vine filled with grapes. . . . But to the eyes of the man of imagination nature is imagination itself. As a man is, so he sees. . . . To me this world is all one continued vision of fancy or imagination.

One of the purposes of Blake's art was to change the way people "see" and thus to open up new worlds to them—"one continued vision" of what had once been ordinary and commonplace, but would become "imagination itself." One of Blake's most famous statements about his art (in the prophetic poem *Jerusalem*) is "I must create a system or be enslaved by another man's." But in creating the "system" for his own works, Blake was also aware that he himself could be trapped by it. The line that follows the one above is "I will not Reason & Compare: my business is to Create."

The history of Blake the poet cannot really be separated from that of Blake the visual artist. Not only did he provide illustrations for most of his poems, but he also printed much of his poetry himself (and sometimes only for himself), using engraving methods he himself had created. According to Blake's nineteenth-century biographer Alexander Gilchrist, "the poet and his wife did everything in making the book [*Songs of Innocence* (1789)]—writing, designing, printing, engraving—everything except manufacturing the paper; the very ink, or color rather, they did make. Never before surely was a man so literally the author of his own book."

A good deal of what Blake wrote other than his poems is cryptic and needs illumination from his art. But one characteristic of the man himself shines through clearly—the optimism sustained by his continuous joy in the "one continued vision" of his art. As one acquaintance described Blake, "He was a man without a mask; his aim single, his path straightforward, and his wants few; so he was free, noble, and happy."

go.hrw.com
LE0 12-8

Objectives

The Tyger / The Lamb / The Chimney Sweeper / A Poison Tree

1. Read and interpret the poems
2. Identify parallelism
3. Express understanding through writing, music, and art

Skills

Literary
- Identify parallelism

Writing
- Collect ideas for a research paper
- Compare and contrast drafts
- Analyze structure and imagery
- Create a prose narrative

Music
- Find background music
- Listen to and analyze music

Viewing/Representing
- Illustrate a poem (ATE)
- Analyze and interpret fine art (ATE)

Planning

- **Block Schedule**
  Block Scheduling Lesson Plans with Pacing Guide
- **Traditional Schedule**
  Lesson Plans Including Strategies for English-Language Learners
- **One-Stop Planner**
  CD-ROM with Test Generator

Resources: Print and Media

Reading
- *Graphic Organizers for Active Reading,* pp. 49, 50, 51, 52
- *Audio CD Library*
  Disc 11, Tracks 3, 4, 5, 6, 7

Writing and Language
- *Daily Oral Grammar*
  Transparency 24

Viewing and Representing
- *Viewing and Representing*
  Fine Art Transparency 10
  Fine Art Worksheets, p. 40

Assessment
- *Formal Assessment,* pp. 120, 121, 122, 123
- *Portfolio Management System,* p. 154
- *Test Generator (One-Stop Planner* CD-ROM)

Internet
- go.hrw.com (keyword: LE0 12-8)

Browsing in the Files

About the Author. William Blake is honored as much for his painting as for his poetry. Regarded as one of the greatest artists England has ever produced, Blake earned his living as an engraver. His engraving technique (which he claimed had been revealed to him by his dead brother in a dream) influenced his highly original painting, with its bold outlines and vigorous modeling. Yet despite, or maybe because of, the originality of his genius, Blake and his wife often existed at a near-poverty level, eating cold scraps and moving from one cheap rental to another. That Blake had any time at all to produce his fine painting and poetry is due to the generosity and dedication of a handful of friends, patrons, and collectors.

Writers on Writing. In William Blake's copy of a volume of poetry by William Wordsworth, Wordsworth's explanation of the poetic process begins, "The powers requisite for the production of poetry are, first, those of observation and description. . . . 2dly, Sensibility." The marginal note in Blake's handwriting reads, "One Power alone makes a Poet: Imagination, The Divine Vision." Blake's poetry is certainly visionary, and he makes no apologies for locating its source in the divine. "I am not ashamed, afraid, or averse to tell you what Ought to be Told," he writes in one letter, "That I am under the direction of Messengers from Heaven, Daily & Nightly."

Blake's Poems: Exploring Contraries

William Blake first published the *Songs of Innocence* in 1789. In 1794, these songs and the *Songs of Experience* were issued together in one volume, the title page promising a demonstration of "the two Contrary States of the Human Soul."

Blake conceived the first of these states, "Innocence," as a state of genuine love and naive trust toward all humankind, accompanied by unquestioned belief in Christian doctrine. Though a firm believer in Christianity, Blake thought that its doctrines were being used by the English Church and other institutions as a form of social control: to encourage among the people passive obedience and acceptance of oppression, poverty, and inequality. Recognition of this marks what Blake called the state of "Experience," a profound disillusionment with human nature and society. One entering the state of "Experience" sees cruelty and hypocrisy only too clearly but is unable to imagine a way out. Blake also conceived of a third, higher state of consciousness he called "Organized Innocence," which is expressed in his later works. In this state, one's sense of the divinity of humanity coexists with oppression and injustice, though involving continued recognition of and active opposition to them.

When reading the *Songs of Innocence* and, to a lesser extent, the *Songs of Experience,* it is important to remember that Blake intended them not as simple expressions of religious faith. The poems are demonstrations of viewpoints that are necessarily limited or distorted by each narrator's or speaker's state of consciousness.

The Ghost of Samuel Appearing to Saul (1800) by William Blake. Pen and ink with watercolor over graphite (12 9/16″ × 13 1/2″).

Rosenwald Collection, © 1998 Board of Trustees, National Gallery of Art, Washington, D.C.

Responding to the Art

According to the Bible, Samuel (c. 1050 B.C.) was the last judge of Israel. Saul was the first king of Israel, anointed by Samuel. But King Saul disobeyed the Lord. Just before a crucial battle the ghost of Samuel, in the form of an old man, appeared to Saul. Samuel said that the Lord would deliver the king into the hands of the enemy. Saul and his sons perished in battle the next day.

Reaching All Students

Struggling Readers

Before students read "The Tyger" on their own, go over the first stanza with them. Make sure they understand that the speaker is addressing the tiger in an apostrophe, as if the two were face to face. Ask students to focus on the questions the speaker asks the tiger and the answers he imagines. Be sure students see that Blake is concerned about the relationship between good and evil, innocence and experience.

Advanced Learners

Blake's biographer Peter Ackroyd has suggested that the "ludicrously comic" tiger in the illustration (p. 647) has that silly grin on its face because it is amused at critics who have produced "such a bewildering confusion of explanations" of this poem. Invite students to find two of these explanations and to tell how they support or contradict one another.

Before You Read

THE TYGER

Make the Connection

More Than Meets the Eye

While almost everyone agrees that "The Tyger" is one of the most powerful of Blake's *Songs of Experience,* there has been much disagreement about the meaning of the poem's central **symbol**, the tiger itself. One possibility is that the tiger represents a strong revolutionary energy that can enlighten and transform society—a positive but dangerous force Blake believed was operating in the French Revolution. The poem's speaker, at any rate, cannot comprehend such a startling energy, and can only wonder whether it is demonic or godlike.

Quickwrite

What will the tiger in Blake's poem mean to you? Spend two minutes free-writing whatever comes into your mind when you think about the word *tiger.*

Background

To William Blake, who saw visions and devoted his life to worshiping God with his poetry and art, the world was filled with symbols. He believed that every object and event on earth had a mystical or spiritual meaning. He gave each symbol a rich assortment of meanings that even his contemporaries could not fully understand.

The Tyger *from* Songs of Experience

William Blake

Tyger! Tyger! burning bright
In the forests of the night, (A)
What immortal hand or eye
Could frame thy fearful symmetry?

In what distant deeps or skies
Burnt the fire of thine eyes?
On what wings dare he aspire? (B)
What the hand dare seize the fire? (C)

And what shoulder, and what art,
Could twist the sinews of thy heart?
And when thy heart began to beat,
What dread hand? and what dread feet?

What the hammer? what the chain?
In what furnace was thy brain?
What the anvil? what dread grasp
Dare its deadly terrors clasp? (D)

When the stars threw down their spears,°
And watered heaven with their tears,
Did he smile his work to see?
Did he who made the Lamb make thee?

Tyger! Tyger! burning bright
In the forests of the night,
What immortal hand or eye,
Dare frame thy fearful symmetry?

17. stars . . . spears: a reference to the angels who fell with Satan and threw down their spears after losing the war in heaven.

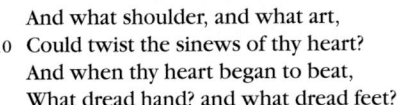

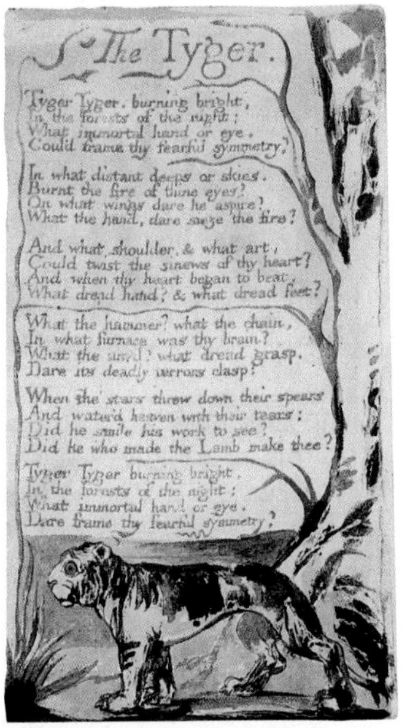

The Tyger (1793) by William Blake from his book *Songs of Experience.* Hand-colored etching.

Library of Congress, Washington, D.C.

Summary ■

In this famous apostrophe to a tiger, the speaker asks who could have made such a fearsome creature and how. The questions remain unanswered, and the poem ends almost exactly as it began, in awe of the tiger's "fearful symmetry."

Resources

Viewing and Representing

Fine Art Transparency

A Fine Art transparency of Morris Hirshfield's *Tiger* can be used for discussion and contrast. See the *Viewing and Representing Transparencies and Worksheets:*

- Transparency 10
- Worksheet, p. 40

(A) Elements of Literature

Imagery

? What images do you see in your mind's eye when you read these first two lines? [Possible answer: The flame-like color of the tiger's stripes through the trees of a dark forest.]

(B) Struggling Readers

Identifying Pronoun Antecedents

After you have made sure students understand the meaning of *aspire,* [soar; hope to succeed] ask who *he* is. [*He* is the creator of the tiger.] Have students read on to find the different possible answers suggested in stanzas two through five.

(C) Struggling Readers

Reading Elliptical Constructions

Point out that l. 7 omits words. Ask how it might be stated in full. [Possible answer: On what wings does the creator dare to rise up or hope to create such a creature as the tiger?] Line 8 adds a word: *the.* Ask students to restate this line without the first *the.* [What hand dares to create such a creature?]

(D) Elements of Literature

Parallelism

? What questions in this stanza have a similar structure? ["What the hammer? what the chain?" "What the anvil?"] These parallel constructions quicken the pace and lend dramatic urgency to the poem.

Skill Link

Analyzing and Responding to a Critical Review

The meaning of the central symbol of the tiger is open to much interpretation. Critics have suggested it might represent the destructive forces of nature; creative or artistic power; or revolutionary violence. During the period when Blake was working on this poem, the revolutionaries of France were being compared to beasts. Scholar Peter Ackroyd quotes the following references to tigers: "After the Paris massacres of 1792, an English statesman declared, 'One might as well think of establishing a republic of tigers in some forest of Africa,' and there were newspaper references to 'the tribunal of tigers.' At a later date, the bloodthirsty revolutionary leader Marat was said to have eyes that resembled 'those of the *tiger cat.*' "

Have students evaluate Ackroyd's and other interpretations.

MAKING MEANINGS

First Thoughts [Respond]

1. Students may say that the tiger's "burning" appeals to them the most, as it is a powerful image that conjures up the tiger's markings as well as its glowing eyes.

Shaping Interpretations [Interpret]

2. The speaker repeatedly asks the tiger who created it, implying that the creator is even more daring and powerful, and perhaps even more dangerous, than the tiger itself.

3. God as creator is suggested in ll. 3 and 20. A demonic creator is implied in ll. 5–12 and 17–18. The fourth stanza suggests a blacksmith.

4. Enlightenment is suggested by the images of "deeps or skies," the symmetrical build of the tiger, and the reference to wings—perhaps of angels or of God. Violence is suggested by the tiger's "burning" coat and eyes, the allusion to the fallen angels, and finally the tiger's association with a dread creator who twists the sinews of the heart.

5. The phrase could describe the animal's symmetrical markings, its graceful movement, or the perfect match of a tiger's form to its function as predator.

6. The change from *could* to *dare* suggests that the creation of the tiger was a dangerous or forbidden act.

7. The speaker is in awe of the tiger's power and fascinated by its deadly beauty, but he is also fearful of its destructive capability. The speaker also seems fascinated by the idea of a powerful and dread creator.

8. Students may say that the tiger represents a powerful natural force that is both beautiful and destructive.

Connecting with the Text [Synthesize]

9. Students may suggest fire, volcanoes, or sharks, which also embody fierce but beautiful power.

Extending the Text [Evaluate]

10. The poem's simple meter and rhyme and its vivid description appeal to younger readers, who often see tigers as exciting and deliciously scary.

MAKING MEANINGS

First Thoughts

1. Which of the poem's **images** appeals most strongly to you? Why do you think it does?

Shaping Interpretations

2. What question does the poem's **speaker** ask the tiger over and over? What answer is implied?

3. Where in the poem does the speaker wonder if the tiger may have been created by God? What **imagery** tells us that the speaker also suspects that the tiger could be a demonic creation? What images suggest a human creator—like a blacksmith or a goldsmith?

4. What **imagery** suggests that the tiger could be a force of enlightenment? of violence?

5. What do you think is meant by the tiger's "fearful symmetry"? (Picture the tiger's stripes.)

6. The last stanza of the poem virtually repeats the first. In your view, what is the significance of the one word changed in the last stanza?

7. How does the poem testify to the simultaneous attraction to and repulsion from evil?

8. Review your Quickwrite notes. What do you think is the meaning of the poem's central **symbol,** the tiger?

Connecting with the Text

9. If you had to choose your own **symbol** for all the things represented by Blake's tiger, what would your symbol be? Why?

Extending the Text

10. Why do you think this poem has always appealed to children as well as to adults? What qualities might the word *tiger* connote to a young child?

PRIMARY Sources — A LETTER

Charles Lamb (1775–1834), perhaps the most accomplished Romantic essayist, uses a letter to sing his praises of William Blake.

"Blake is a real name . . ."

To Bernard Barton

Blake is a real name, I assure you, and a most extraordinary man, if he be still living. He is the Robert [William] Blake, whose wild designs accompany a splendid folio edition of the *Night Thoughts,* which you may have seen, in one of which he pictures the parting of soul and body by a solid mass of human form floating off, God knows how, from a lumpish mass (facsimile to itself) left behind on the dying bed. He paints in watercolors marvelous strange pictures, visions of his brain, which he asserts that he has seen. They have great merit. He has *seen* the old Welsh bards on Snowden—he has seen the beautifulest, the strongest, and the ugliest man, left alone from the massacre of the Britons by the Romans, and has painted them from memory (I have

Elohim Creating Adam (1795–1805) by William Blake.

Tate Gallery, London.

The Agony in the Garden (c. 1799–1800) by William Blake.
Tate Gallery, London.

seen his paintings), and asserts them to be as good as the figures of Raphael and Angelo, but not better, as they had precisely the same retrovisions and prophetic visions with himself. The painters in oil (which he will have it that neither of them practiced) he affirms to have been the ruin of art, and affirms that all the while he was engaged in his water paintings, Titian was disturbing him, Titian the Ill Genius of Oil Painting. His pictures—one in particular, the Canterbury Pilgrims (far above Stothard's)—have great merit, but hard, dry, yet with grace. He has written a catalogue of them with a most spirited criticism on Chaucer, but mystical and full of vision. His poems have been sold hitherto only in manuscript. I never read them; but a friend at my desire procured the Sweep Song. There is one to a tiger, which I have heard recited, beginning:

Tiger, Tiger, burning bright,
Thro' the desarts of the night,

which is glorious. But, alas! I have not the book; for the man is flown, whither I know not, to Hades or a madhouse—But I must look on him as one of the most extraordinary persons of the age.

—Charles Lamb

Primary Sources

Charles Lamb is known both as an essayist and as a man who had a wide circle of literary friends, including Samuel Taylor Coleridge. He held Wednesday evening meetings with a number of these literary people—meetings which became deservedly famous and at which Lamb himself exhibited his eloquence and wit. A Romantic essayist, Lamb did not, like essayists in the past, try to cover a subject fully, but instead, wrote to re-create a particular feeling, character, or moment. This letter is written in the same easy, intimate style that characterizes his essays. Blake's comments on his own painting ability, as paraphrased in this letter, were actually stated this way: "I do not pretend to Paint better than Rafael or Mich. Angelo or Julio Romano or Alb. Durer, but I do Pretend to Paint finer than Rubens or Rembt. or Correggio or Titian."

A Cultural Connections

Giants of Renaissance Painting

Raphael (1483–1520) is especially known for his many paintings of the Madonna and child, in which the figures glow with both humanity and serene holiness. Michelangelo (1475–1564), one of the greatest and most influential artists of all time, painted the ceiling and a wall of the Sistine Chapel (see p. 197) and created magnificent sculptures of *David* and the *Pieta*. Titian (c. 1477–1576) was a master of color, whose many works include explorations of mythic characters, religious subjects, and portraits.

RESPONDING TO THE ART

Activity. Ask students to explain what these works have in common. [Both show powerful, otherworldly figures (God on p. 648; an angel on p. 649) with outstretched arms. One is creating Adam, and the other is comforting Christ in the garden of Gethsemane just before he is to be arrested by Roman soldiers. *Elohim* is a Hebrew name for God.]

Getting Students Involved

Dramatic Reading

The Tone Tells It. As a speaking and listening activity, invite students to practice reading selected portions of this letter aloud, trying to re-create its exact tone. Urge them to try to convey through the spoken word the same sense of awe and admiration for Blake that Lamb achieves with his written words.

Writing

Blake and the Romantics. Blake's poetry and artwork are essentially religious. He was a firm believer in Christianity and rejected the philosophies of rationalism and deism, popular among Romantic thinkers of the period. After students have read his poems, ask them to write a short paragraph on why Blake should or should not be included among the Romantics.

Summary ■

As in "The Tyger," the speaker asks the Lamb who made it, but this time answers the question: The creator made the Lamb; Christ the Redeemer made the Lamb. When the speaker identifies himself as a child, he links the Lamb and Christ to his own innocence.

A Elements of Literature
Tone

? **What is the tone of the first two lines?** [Possible answers: It is innocent, childlike, gentle; it suggests a child's voice, or a parent talking to a child.] **How is this tone different from the tone of "The Tyger"?** [Possible answer: The two are opposites. The tone of "The Tyger" is urgent and immediate, the voice loud or insistent; this tone is gentle and calm, the voice soft and soothing.]

B English Language Learners
Archaic Language

Point out "bid thee." Explain that *bid* means "to command or order." Ask students what "bid thee" means here. [commanded you] **Also, ask students what words they know that contain the root word *bid*.** [Possible answers: *forbid, forbidding,* and *bidding*.]

C Reading Skills and Strategies
Using Context and Glosses

Point out to students that the word *mead* is glossed. What context clues might help students confirm this definition? [Possible answers: A *mead* is a place where lambs graze; it is a geographical feature like a stream.]

D Elements of Literature
Parallelism

? **What examples of parallelism do you find in these lines?** ["He is meek, and He is mild" and "I a child, and thou a lamb."] **How does this parallelism serve to draw the speaker and the lamb together?** [Possible response: The parallelism emphasizes the innocence of the creator, the child speaker, and the lamb itself.]

Before You Read
THE LAMB

Make the Connection
The Balance of Contraries

William Blake's poetry and art reflect his fascination with the Bible and his struggles to find answers to questions that profoundly disturbed him: Why do human beings do evil? Why do evil people sometimes prosper? Why does God allow innocent children to suffer?

One of Blake's early conclusions about the problem of good and evil is his idea that "Without contraries is no progression." "The Lamb" and "The Tyger" reflect what Blake termed "two contrary states of the human soul," both of which are as essential to humanity as joy and sadness, innocence and experience.

Quickwrite

If *tiger* connotes fierceness, mystery, and awe, what qualities does *lamb* suggest? Jot down some words and images that come to mind when you visualize a lamb.

Background

One of the *Songs of Innocence,* this poem has often been read as a statement of Christian faith. However, we know that Blake's other writings show Christ as an active fighter against injustice, not the "meek" and "mild" lamb—a common symbol for Christ—with which this innocent speaker identifies. The speaker's viewpoint is thus an incomplete representation of Blake's beliefs.

The Lamb
from Songs of Innocence
William Blake

Little Lamb, who made thee?
Dost thou know who made thee?
Gave thee life, and bid thee feed
By the stream and o'er the mead,°
Gave thee clothing of delight,
Softest clothing, wooly, bright;
Gave thee such a tender voice,
Making all the vales° rejoice?
Little Lamb, who made thee?
Dost thou know who made thee?

Little Lamb, I'll tell thee,
Little Lamb, I'll tell thee:
He° is called by thy name,
For He calls himself a Lamb.
He is meek, and he is mild;
He became a little child.
I a child, and thou a lamb,
We are called by his name.
Little Lamb, God bless thee!
Little Lamb, God bless thee!

4. mead: meadow.
8. vales: valleys.
13. He: Christ.

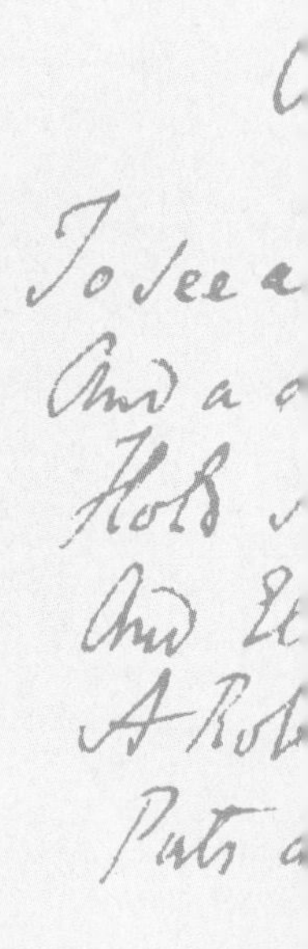

Making the Connections

Cultural Connections: The Lamb as Symbol

The lamb is an important symbol for both Jews and Christians. The Jewish holiday of Passover commemorates the night, just before the exodus from Egypt, when the Israelites smeared the blood of a lamb on their doorposts so the angel of God would "pass over" their homes and not slay their firstborn sons (Exodus 12). Both Christians and Jews treasure Psalm 23 ("The lord is my shepherd"), and Christians recount the parable of the lost sheep (Matthew 18:10–14). Christians also identify Jesus as "the lamb of God" (John 1:29) and as a triumphant lamb who appears at the last days (Revelation 14:1). "Paschal lamb" is a traditional symbol among Jews at Passover. Capitalized, "Paschal Lamb" refers to Jesus.

"Auguries of Innocence" by William Blake (transcribed c. 1807) from the Pickering or Ballads Manuscript.

The Pierpont Morgan Library/Art Resource, New York.

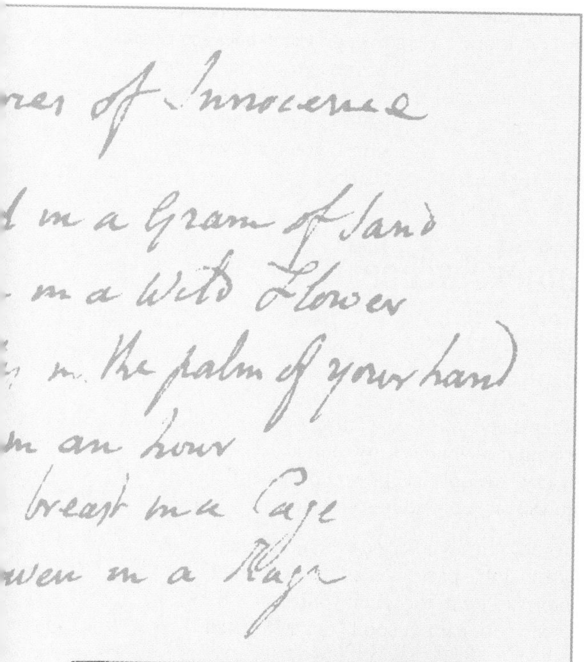

Making Meanings

First Thoughts

1. Look back at your Quickwrite notes. How do your associations with the word *lamb* relate to the associations suggested in this poem?

Shaping Interpretations

2. What did its creator do for the lamb in the first stanza?
3. How does the second stanza respond to the question posed in the first?
4. What do you know about the **speaker** of the poem?
5. How is the lamb both a literal object and a **symbol** in this poem?
6. Christ called himself a lamb because, like the Passover lamb slain to save the people of Israel, he sacrificed himself for the people. What might this imply about the fate of the young **speaker** in this poem?
7. How do you think the voice of the speaker in "The Lamb" is different from the voice of the speaker in "The Tyger"? Why do you think the questions in "The Lamb" get answers?

Connecting with the Text

8. How would you represent innocence? How would you represent experience? Why?

Challenging the Text

9. Blake wrote a two-line poem called "An Answer to the Parson" in which the parson (or preacher) asks, "Why of the sheep do you not learn peace?" The **narrator** replies, "Because I don't want you to shear my fleece." How would the narrator of this poem disagree with the narrator of "The Lamb"?

The Lamb (c. 1789–1794) by William Blake from his book *Songs of Innocence and of Experience.* Relief etching finished in pen and watercolor.

Fitzwilliam Museum, University of Cambridge, Cambridge, England.

Making Meanings

First Thoughts [Respond]

1. Students will probably say that the poem fulfilled their expectations by portraying a lamb as a sweet, meek creature.

Shaping Interpretations [Interpret]

2. The creator gave the lamb life, grass for grazing, clothing (its fleece), and a gentle bleet.
3. The speaker says that Christ made the lamb.
4. The speaker says he is a child.
5. The lamb is an animal in the literal sense, but it is also a symbol of meekness and innocence.
6. The speaker may have to be sacrificed for the sins of others.
7. The speaker in "The Lamb" is more sentimental, more childlike. Because this is a poem of innocence, answers seem easy to find, although they may seem oversimplified to some.

Connecting with the Text [Apply]

8. Students may suggest that babies or children, dolls or teddy bears, or flowers represent innocence. Experience may be represented by eye glasses or graying hair, by ancient trees or mighty rivers.

Challenging the Text [Extend]

9. The narrator of "An Answer to the Parson" would object to this poem's simplicity and say the narrator of "The Lamb" is naïve and inexperienced.

Using Students' Strengths

Visual Learners

Have students work in groups of three to design a stamp or poster that honors the balance of contraries in Blake's work. Ask one student to be in charge of researching and presenting images, a second to suggest the text (perhaps a short quotation from or about Blake), and the third to execute the final design. All students should confer on how the elements will be arranged and work together to create sketches of the layout.

Auditory/Musical Learners

Have students work in groups to prepare musical evocations of the tiger and the lamb. The music may be original, or it may come from any classical or popular source. Tell students to be sure of the feeling, mood, or image they associate with their animal before selecting or creating the music. Also encourage them to create two themes that complement each other as innocence and experience and good and evil do in Blake's philosophy. Encourage students to share their musical presentations in class.

Summary ■■

The speaker is a young boy whose father sold him to work as a chimney sweeper. The child speaker innocently tries to cheer himself and his fellow chimney sweep, Tom Dacre, with a vision of God as a loving father who will reward them with endless joy in heaven if they do their duty here and now. The discrepency between the speaker's naïve tone and his desperate plight forms the basis of the poem's ironic power.

(A) Historical Connections

The Plight of the Poor

During William Blake's lifetime, the population and the cost of living in England doubled while the average wage increased by only one half. In this new age, the wife and children often earned the larger part of a family's poverty-level income. Before Parliament outlawed the use of children as chimney sweeps in 1832, children as young as four or five were forced to crawl down dangerously narrow chimneys. The smaller the child, and therefore the younger, the better.

(B) Elements of Literature

Symbol

? What do you think the "coffins of black" in l. 12 suggest, besides literal death? [Possible answers: They may symbolize the dark confines of the chimney; the sense of suffocation and terror of being forced into a small space, especially for a young child; or the death of innocence and childhood.]

(C) Elements of Literature

Dramatic Irony

? The innocent child expresses optimism about how things will turn out if "all do their duty," but the adult reader knows better. What does the adult reader know, and how does this knowledge make the final lines sting? [Possible answers: The adult knows there is probably only suffering ahead for this child, that doing one's duty is no guarantee of earthly reward, that death is probably the only release for this child. The lines sting because of their dramatic irony: The reader knows what the speaker does not.]

Before You Read

THE CHIMNEY SWEEPER (INNOCENCE/EXPERIENCE)

Make the Connection

Cold Comfort

In these two poems, one from *Songs of Innocence* and the other from *Songs of Experience,* Blake speaks for the poor children of his day who were forced to do backbreaking labor. In Blake's London, buildings were heated by coal or wood-burning fireplaces, so every house had at least one chimney that had to be cleaned regularly. Poor children were often used to do this dirty work because they could fit easily into the narrow chimney passages. In fact, some poor parents were so desperate that they sold their children to "masters" who managed crews of young sweepers. The work was dangerous, and the children were badly treated by masters concerned only with profits.

Quickwrite

If you could cry out against an evil of our day—and get people to listen—which social problem would you choose?

Background

In the late 1700s, prices increased sharply, and work became scarce. William Blake saw starving people rooting through garbage, homeless families sleeping in doorways, and children begging on the streets or working at backbreaking jobs. Most members of the upper class believed that they deserved their worldly success, and that the poor must be innately evil, deserving the hunger and appalling conditions that they endured.

Blake was said to be mad, not only because he saw visions, but also because his poems cry out against the social problems he saw all around him: the growing division between classes, the wretched working conditions, and child labor. No one should go hungry, he said, in a land as green and wealthy as England.

The Chimney Sweeper

from Songs of Innocence

William Blake

(A)
When my mother died I was very young,
And my father sold me while yet my tongue
Could scarcely cry "'weep! 'weep! 'weep! 'weep!"°
So your chimneys I sweep, and in soot I sleep.

There's little Tom Dacre, who cried when his head,
That curled like a lamb's back, was shaved: so I said
"Hush, Tom! never mind it, for when your head's bare
You know that the soot cannot spoil your white hair."

And so he was quiet, and that very night,
As Tom was a-sleeping, he had such a sight!—
That thousands of sweepers, Dick, Joe, Ned, and Jack,
(B) Were all of them locked up in coffins of black.

And by came an Angel who had a bright key,
And he opened the coffins and set them all free;
Then down a green plain leaping, laughing, they run,
And wash in a river, and shine in the Sun.

Then naked and white, all their bags left behind,
They rise upon clouds and sport in the wind;
And the Angel told Tom, if he'd be a good boy,
He'd have God for his father, and never want° joy.

And so Tom awoke; and we rose in the dark,
And got with our bags and our brushes to work.
Though the morning was cold, Tom was happy and warm;
(C) So if all do their duty they need not fear harm.

3. 'weep . . . 'weep: the child's attempt at the chimney sweepers' cry of "Sweep! Sweep!"
20. want: lack.

Listening to Music

Cockaigne Overture, Opus 40 ("In London Town"), by Sir Edward Elgar

Celebrated composer Sir Edward Elgar (1857–1934) grew up outside Worcester, England, where his father ran a music shop and played the organ at Worcester Cathedral. Surrounded by music, the young Elgar studied law for a year but at age fifteen left to become a music teacher, performer, arranger, and finally composer.

Activity

Have students decide which of the two chimney sweepers that Blake portrays on pp. 652–653 would be more likely to dwell in the London that Elgar suggests in this musical selection.

Background

Unlike the sweeper in *Songs of Innocence,* this sweeper does not accept oppression and poverty because he believes he will be rewarded in heaven. This little speaker recognizes that the people who pray for him (his parents) are the same ones who sold him into a life of hard labor.

The first three lines are spoken by an adult who finds the child. The rest of the poem is the bitter response of the child.

The Chimney Sweeper

from Songs of Experience

William Blake

A little black thing among the snow
Crying "'weep, 'weep," in notes of woe!
"Where are thy father & mother? say?"
"They are both gone up to the church to pray.

"Because I was happy upon the heath,
And smil'd among the winter's snow; (A)
They clothed me in the clothes of death, (B)
And taught me to sing the notes of woe.

"And because I am happy, & dance & sing,
They think they have done me no injury,
And are gone to praise God & his Priest & King,
Who make up a heaven of our misery."

MAKING MEANINGS

First Thoughts

1. Did these poems remind you of any tragedies in modern life involving the treatment of young children? (Consult your Quickwrite notes.) Discuss your responses.

Shaping Interpretations

2. What details of the speaker's history do you learn in the first poem? What is his present life like?

3. In the first poem, how does the angel reassure Tom Dacre in his dreams? What **moral lesson** does the speaker in the first poem draw from Tom's dream?

4. How does Tom Dacre's dream contrast with the actual conditions of his daily life?

5. How does the speaker of the first poem feel about his situation? How do you feel about it?

6. In the second poem the young chimney sweeper is asked where his parents are. What is the boy's answer? What do you think are his "clothes of death"?

7. How would you **paraphrase** the last two lines of the second poem?

8. How would you describe the **tone** of the second poem? How does this sweeper's attitude toward his life and his parents contrast with the attitude of the speaker in the first poem?

9. In each poem, what is the emotional effect of the child's mispronunciation of the chimney sweepers' cry?

Extending the Text

10. Do people today sometimes take the attitude expressed by the speaker of the first poem: If you are good, if you do your duty, you need not fear harm? Expand on your responses.

Summary ■

A chimney sweeper weeps in the snow while his parents are at church. He says they made him a sweep because he was happy, and now, because he still appears happy, they think they have not hurt him. The system, he says, rationalizes his misery and creates a heaven out of his suffering.

(A) Elements of Literature

Imagery

? How does Blake use colors to suggest innocence and experience? [Possible answer: The little sweeper, blackened not only by soot but also by experience, was once as clean and white, as innocent, as the snow.]

(B) Reading Skills and Strategies

Drawing Conclusions

? Whom does the chimney sweep blame for his misery? [Possible answers: He blames his parents; he also seems to blame the whole system of God, priest, and king that allows his exploitation.]

MAKING MEANINGS

First Thoughts [Respond]

1. Students may name any situation in which children are made to assume more responsibility or are subjected to more experiences than they are ready for.

Shaping Interpretations [Interpret]

2. The speaker's mother died when he was young, and his father sold him off as a chimney sweeper. His present life is one of fear and drudgery.

3. The angel promises Tom that if he is good, he will have God as his father and will always be happy. The lesson is that if Tom performs his duties, he will eventually be rewarded.

4. In the dream, Tom is clean and carefree. In reality, he lives in filthy conditions.

5. The speaker innocently accepts his position, protecting himself with the hope that, somehow, being a good child will save him. Students may consider this position naïve.

6. The parents are in church. The "clothes of death" are the black clothes he wears to sweep chimneys or his future as a chimney sweeper.

7. Possible answer: His parents have gone to praise the very system that subjects him and his friends to such evils.

8. The tone of the second poem is bitter. While the first speaker is accepting or even forgiving, the second understands and resents the harm he has been done.

9. The cry reminds the reader that the children are so young they cannot properly pronounce *sw.* It also becomes a command to the audience—'weep!'

Extending the Text [Apply]

10. Students may say that young children often hear such promises, although they often reject them as untrue as they grow older.

Summary ■■

The speaker relates how he hides his anger from an enemy and secretly cultivates it. The anger grows into a tree that bears a poisonous apple, which the speaker's foe steals and eats. When the apple causes the foe to die, the speaker is glad. It appears he, too, has been poisoned by his secret anger.

Ⓐ Elements of Literature
Parallelism

? What is the effect of the series of sentences all beginning with *I*? [Possible answer: The sentences seem emphatic and perhaps childish in their repetitive simplicity.] Are there other examples of parallel structure later in the poem? If so, what are they? [Yes, the sentences starting with *And* are parallel.]

Ⓑ Critical Thinking
Expressing an Opinion

? Do you agree with the poet's implication in l. 4 about the danger of repressed anger? Why or why not? [Sample responses: Yes, the only way to get rid of your anger is to express it. No, angry words can cause pain or spark more angry words; it is often better to wait until your anger cools.]

Ⓒ Struggling Readers
Reading Elliptical Constructions

Ask students to fill in the missing words in this statement. [Possible answer: In the morning, I was glad to see that my foe was stretched out (dead) beneath the tree.]

Making Meanings

First Thoughts [Respond]

1. Students may say they would emphasize the last line, because it contains an important twist.

Shaping Interpretations [Interpret]

2. The two methods are expressing anger or suppressing it, thereby letting it grow. The speaker's foe eats the poisoned apple and dies.
3. The poison tree is the symbol of the speaker's growing anger.
4. The speaker's foe is the victim, although the speaker is one as well because he allows his anger to fester and possess him.
5. The speaker is good in expressing anger to the friend but evil in allowing the anger for the foe to grow.
6. The theme is that repressed anger can poison both the enemy and the person who harbors it.
7. Blake is alluding to the fruit tree that figured in the temptation of Adam and Eve in the Garden of Eden.

Connecting with the Text [Respond]

8. Students may have noted that built-up anger can lead to tragedy.

Before You Read
A Poison Tree

Make the Connection
The Fruits of Anger

What happens to anger that is allowed to grow and fester, anger that is nurtured with our own deceit? In this poem, one of Blake's *Songs of Experience,* the speaker describes what happens when anger is left unresolved. As you read, think about how anger is symbolized in the poem—and about other ways it's portrayed.

Quickwrite
Jot down some notes describing the ways anger can be destructive, not only to the object of the anger, but also to the person feeling it.

A Poison Tree
from Songs of Experience
William Blake

Ⓐ I was angry with my friend:
I told my wrath, my wrath did end.
I was angry with my foe:
Ⓑ I told it not, my wrath did grow.

And I watered it in fears,
Night and morning with my tears;
And I sunned it with smiles,
And with soft deceitful wiles.°

And it grew both day and night,
Till it bore an apple bright;
And my foe beheld it shine,
And he knew that it was mine,

And into my garden stole
When the night had veiled the pole:
Ⓒ In the morning glad I see
My foe outstretched beneath the tree.

8. **wiles:** cunning tricks.

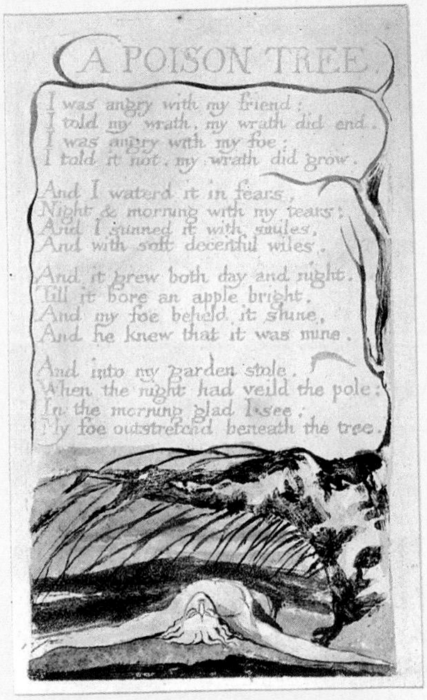

Private Collection.

A Poison Tree (1794) by William Blake from his book *Songs of Experience.* Relief etching with watercolor and pen additions.

Making Meanings

First Thoughts

1. If you were reading this poem aloud, which part of the last stanza would you emphasize? Why?

Shaping Interpretations

2. What two ways of handling anger are mentioned in the poem? What actually happens to the speaker's foe in the last stanza?
3. What is the "poison tree"?
4. Who are the victims in the poem?
5. How is the speaker both good and evil?
6. What do you see as the **theme** of the poem?
7. What do you make of Blake's allusion to forbidden fruit in the third stanza?

Assessing Learning

Check Test: Short Answer

1. Which poems are joyful or awe-struck? [The Tyger, The Lamb]
2. Which poems are sad or bitter? [Chimney Sweepers, Poison Tree]
3. What is one target of Blake's criticism? [child labor]

Connecting with the Text

8. Does the poem describe ways in which anger can be destructive that are similar to the ways you wrote about in your Quick-write notes? Explain your response.

Elements of Literature

Parallelism

When words are arranged in balanced, similar structures, they are said to be **parallel.** Blake was especially fond of parallelism, and the use of this device contributes to the childlike simplicity on the surface of his poems. You'll become aware of the rhythmic effects of parallelism if you read Blake's poems aloud.

Much of "The Tyger" consists of questions that start with the word *what.* Sometimes the questions occupy one or two full verses; occasionally, Blake varies them so that one verse is split into two or three questions.

1. What examples of parallelism can you find in "The Lamb"?
2. How does Blake use parallelism in "The Chimney Sweeper" poems?
3. How does "A Poison Tree" use parallelism to link ideas from stanza to stanza?

Choices: Building Your Portfolio

Writer's Notebook

1. Collecting Ideas for a Research Paper

Skim Blake's biography, and jot down topics that you would be interested in pursuing, including social conditions in London in the late eighteenth century. Then, review the reproductions of Blake's art. (Be sure to look back through the introduction to the Romantic period.) What questions do you have about his paintings? Save your notes for the Writer's Workshop on page 773.

Comparing/Contrasting Drafts

2. Second-Guessing Blake

In an early draft of "The Tyger," Blake inserted the following lines after the third stanza:

Could fetch it from the furnace deep
And in thy horrid ribs dare steep
In the well of sanguine wee
In what clay and in what mold
Were thy eyes of fury rolled

This early version also lacked the fifth stanza of the final version. In a brief essay, compare and contrast the early draft and the final version of "The Tyger," commenting on why you think Blake made the changes he did.

Analyzing Structure and Imagery

3. Below the Surface

In a brief essay, explain how both "The Tyger" and "The Lamb," although they seem to be simple lyrics, are concerned with very profound questions of religion. Comment on the **structure** and **imagery** of the two poems.

Creative Writing

4. Down the Chimney

Based on details in "The Chimney Sweeper," write the opening or closing paragraphs of a prose narrative that tells about the childhood of a chimney sweeper in Blake's London. You may want to write in the first person, as if for an autobiography.

Music

5. To Read By

With a small group, find a piece of classical or popular music that would serve as background for a reading of "A Poison Tree."

Art

6. Be Like Blake

Part of Blake's genius is the illustrations he created for his poems. Be like Blake: Create an illustration for any one of Blake's poems you've read.

Elements of Literature

Answers

1. The use of couplets and two stanzas as a call-and-response; the repetition of questions (ll. 1–2, 9–10) and answers (ll. 11–12, 19–20); and the identification between the speaker, lamb, and creator are all examples of parallelism in "The Lamb."
2. In the first poem, parallelism includes the use of couplets, the inclusion of contrasting settings, and the division of lines at their midpoints grammatically or typographically (ll. 5–7, 9–11, 13–24). In the second poem, instances of parallelism include sentences beginning with *They* and *And.*
3. The ideas in "A Poison Tree" are linked between stanzas by the balance of logical constructions, expansion on a theme (stanzas 1 and 2), and cause and effect (stanzas 2 and 3 and 3 and 4).

Choices: Building Your Portfolio

1. Encourage students to include questions with each topic.
2. Direct students to consider the effect of each change separately and then the overall impact of each.
3. Suggest that students organize their essays around the questions about good and evil which they discover, supporting their comments with references to the structure and imagery of the poems.
4. In order to add punch to the opening, have students do some research on London's poor at this time.
5. Ask groups to share their musical selections with the class.
6. Students do not need to mimic Blake's style.

Grading Timesaver

Rubrics for each Choices assignment appear on p. 154 in the *Portfolio Management System.*

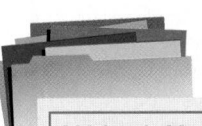

OBJECTIVES

...Tintern Abbey / Strange Fits ... / She Dwelt ... / A Slumber ... / Intimations ... / ...Westminster Bridge / The World ...

1. Read and interpret the poems
2. Identify and analyze blank verse
3. Analyze the use of personification
4. Interpret romantic lyrics
5. Recognize verse paragraphs as patterns of organization
6. Express understanding through expository, analytical, and creative writing, as well as through technology

SKILLS

Literary
- Identify and analyze blank verse
- Analyze the use of personification
- Interpret romantic lyrics

Reading
- Recognize verse paragraphs as patterns of organization

Writing
- Collect ideas for a research paper
- Trace a theme across cultures
- Identify Romantic themes and images
- Compare texts
- Rewrite a poem
- Personify a city

Media/Speech
- Create a talk show

Music
- Compare literary and musical interpretations of a theme

Viewing/Representing
- Analyze and interpret fine art (ATE)

William Wordsworth

(1770–1850)

William Wordsworth (1842) by Benjamin Robert Haydon. Oil on canvas (49″ × 39″).

By Courtesy of the National Portrait Gallery, London.

Surveying Wordsworth's life can be like walking around a large statue, awed by its presence and puzzled by its apparent importance. Sometimes Wordsworth must have felt the same way. As he thought about his early life and re-created it in his autobiographical poem *The Prelude*, Wordsworth said he felt as if he were "two consciousnesses"—one remembering, the other one remembered.

When Wordsworth's mother died in 1778, he and his three brothers were sent to school at Hawkshead in the Lake District. His sister, Dorothy, aged seven, had to live with relatives. When their father died in 1783, the children were placed under the guardianship of two uncles. William managed to get a degree from Cambridge in 1791, but had little interest in the few careers open to him—the main one being the Church—as an educated man with no title, wealth, or head for business. In late 1791, he went to France to learn the language and, as it turned out, discovered the bliss of being young in that time of birth and rebirth known as the French Revolution. Thus began a decade of painful growth, as he searched for and eventually found his vocation as a poet.

After he returned from France in 1792, Wordsworth was sickened by the war between France and England that began in 1793, and he gradually became deeply disillusioned about his hopes for change. Late that year he went on a long walking tour. This experience—and the collapse of his radical hope of perfecting society—drove him back to poetry.

In 1795, his fortunes began to change. He was reunited with his sister, Dorothy, who became a constant companion and inspiration. When he inherited some money from a friend, he and Dorothy took up residence in a rent-free cottage, and the poet Samuel Taylor Coleridge suddenly burst upon their lives. By June 1797, when he and Dorothy moved to a country house four miles from the village where Coleridge lived, Wordsworth had produced a good deal of new poetry, none yet published, including a play and some stark narratives. Coleridge and Wordsworth quickly became powerful influences on each other's work. *Lyrical Ballads* (1798) was the fruit of their friendship and mutual influence. During the following decade, Wordsworth wrote most of his best poetry.

But sometime after 1805, Wordsworth's poetic powers began to decline. By the time he was in his forties, his life was centered on his family; on his duties as a minor government official in the land of his boyhood, the Lake District, where he settled for good in 1799; and on his unflagging diligence as a poet. As his writing lost its energy and his political opinions grew more conservative, he became a kind of literary monument.

By the Victorian era, Wordsworth was the poet laureate (1843), a cartoon image of an old gentleman delighting in daffodils and butterflies while wandering about the Lake District. This image endured in part because the family suppressed the fact that in 1792 Wordsworth had fathered a child in France with a young woman he never married.

The distinguishing quality of Wordsworth's best lyric poetry comes from his simple delight in the nature of experience itself and in the mind's capacity to shape everyday experience into something lasting and poetic. Poetry, he wrote in the preface to *Lyrical Ballads,* is the "spontaneous overflow of powerful feelings"; but, he added, poems of lasting value are produced only by someone who has "thought long and deeply." The marriage of feeling and thought, as Coleridge recognized, made Wordsworth "the best poet of the age."

go.hrw.com
LEO 12-8

Planning

- **Block Schedule**
  Block Scheduling Lesson Plans with Pacing Guide
- **Traditional Schedule**
  Lesson Plans Including Strategies for English-Language Learners
- **One-Stop Planner**
  CD-ROM with Test Generator

Resources: Print and Media

Reading
- *Graphic Organizers for Active Reading,* pp. 53, 54, 55, 56, 57
- *Audio CD Library*
  Disc 11, Tracks 8, 9, 10, 11, 12, 13, 14, 15, 16

Elements of Literature
- *Literary Elements*
  Transparencies 17, 18, 19
  Worksheets, pp. 52, 55, 58

Writing and Language
- *Grammar and Language Links*
  Worksheet, p. 35
- *Language Workshop CD-ROM*

Assessment
- *Formal Assessment,* pp. 124, 126, 127, 128, 129
- *Portfolio Management System,* p. 156
- *Test Generator (One-Stop Planner CD-ROM)*

Internet
- go.hrw.com (keyword: LE0 12-8)

Before You Read

Lines Composed a Few Miles Above Tintern Abbey

Make the Connection

Nature's Power

William Wordsworth loved nature in all of its forms, and he believed that nature made him a better person. Loving nature, he writes in this poem, quiets his mind, lightens his mood, guides him to kind acts, and brings him closer to God.

Elements of Literature

Blank Verse

Wordsworth composed poetry in his head while he walked, "his jaws working the whoal time," recalled a country person who observed him. He spoke the words aloud to memorize them and to get the rhythm right. When Wordsworth was a child, under the direction of his father, he had memorized and recited long passages in **blank verse** from the works of Shakespeare and Milton. In "Tintern Abbey," Wordsworth uses for the first time a less formal, "conversational" blank verse that he had learned from Coleridge. The words and phrases he repeats give his poetry the flowing rhythm of natural speech.

> **Blank verse** is poetry written in unrhymed **iambic pentameter.** Each line contains five iambs; each iamb, or metrical foot, is an unstressed syllable followed by a stressed syllable.
>
> *For more on Blank Verse, see the Handbook of Literary Terms.*

Reading Skills and Strategies

Recognizing Patterns of Organization

Before you read this poem aloud, look for the end punctuation and the indents that signal the end of one stanza and the beginning of another. (How many stanzas are in the poem?) Then, as you read, make notes on how Wordsworth used these stanzas to organize his ideas.

Background

"Tintern Abbey" (which refers to the ruined abbey mentioned only in the title) is one of the most important short lyric works in English literature. A major step forward in Wordsworth's writing and a definitive statement of some of the Romantics' ideas, it has inspired and guided many poets since. The ease with which Wordsworth wrote it is therefore even more astonishing.

In July 1798, Wordsworth and his sister, Dorothy, went on a vigorous walking tour in southern Wales. Shortly after leaving the Wye River valley, Wordsworth, by his own account, began to compose this poem about revisiting the valley, concluding it "just as I was entering Bristol in the evening after a ramble of four or five days. . . . Not a line of it was altered, and not any part of it written down till I reached Bristol. It was published almost immediately after."

Wordsworth had previously written two long descriptive poems and a few other descriptive lyrics, but nothing quite like this. He had been hard at work on the narrative ballads that make up *Lyrical Ballads* when he went on his tour. But he had learned something important from two poems by Coleridge, "This Lime-Tree Bower My Prison" and "Frost at Midnight": the use of a flowing blank verse and the easy maneuvering of the meditative poem.

This style was explored and refined in the many poems Coleridge and Wordsworth termed "conversation poems." First perfected by Coleridge, the conversation poem is usually a deeply personal meditation, seemingly spoken to a silent listener or to a loved one who is absent or asleep.

The apparent ease of its composition hides the art of "Tintern Abbey," evident even in the title, which asks us to imagine that these lines were poured out at the time the speaker returned to the Wye Valley after five years' absence. The many days of composition on the way back to Bristol were spent creating a poem in which we seem to hear the easy, immediate utterance of what is going on in the heart and mind of the speaker.

Summary ■ ■ ■

This lyric poem is a meditation on what the Wye River Valley in Wales, which stands for all of nature, has meant to the speaker. He first describes the physical beauty of the valley, seen after a five-year absence, and then explains how his youthful, passionate response has given way to a deeper, more contemplative appreciation. He celebrates that he no longer has to be physically present in nature to receive its healing powers; his memory of these beautiful sights can lift his spirits and inspire him to acts of kindness at any time or place. Finally, the speaker addresses his sister, saying her presence makes the landscape even more precious to him.

Background

Remind students that Wordsworth composed this poem and memorized it during a five-day walking tour of Wales. Have students try reading portions of this poem as they walk, coordinating the iambic pentameter with their footfalls. After they have practiced, invite volunteers to demonstrate their coordination of the two.

Reaching All Students

Struggling Readers

Students at first may find Wordsworth's poetry overwhelming. To help them get started, remind them that Wordsworth was tired of the kind of poetry that was witty, satirical, and intellectual. He wanted to break free of the Neoclassical conventions and write spontaneously about his personal feelings. Although his ideas do not seem revolutionary to modern-day readers, they were new enough in his day to launch a literary movement.

Advanced Learners

William Vaughn Moody and Robert Morse Lovett, in *A History of English Literature,* say that Wordsworth is special because of his sensitivity to nature, his sense of truth, his treatment of human nature, and his mysticism—his belief in a spirit that affects all things. When students have finished reading and responding to his poems, ask them to use their notes to write an introduction to Wordsworth's poetry that could be included in this collection.

Ⓐ Elements of Literature

Blank Verse

Ask students to count the syllables in the first two lines. Then, note that the lines do not rhyme. Remind students that this is blank verse which, though seemingly artless, is a carefully controlled, rhythmic form.

Ⓑ Appreciating Language

Sound and Sense

? What words suggest the sounds the speaker hears? [*Rolling, soft,* and *murmur* all describe the sound of falling water. Even the word *waters* itself has a flowing sound.] What mood do these sounds create? [Possible response: a peaceful, tranquil mood.]

Ⓒ Elements of Literature

Imagery

? What images does Wordsworth use to "paint" this scene he loves? [the dark sycamore, plots around cottages, green orchard thickets, hedgerows, green farms, and smoke wreaths]

Ⓓ Struggling Readers

Paraphrasing/Rearranging Syntax

Remind students to stop and break down confusing sentences. Start them out with this one:" "Even though I've been gone a long time . . ." and ask them to supply the remainder. [Possible answer: I could still see these beautiful sights in my mind's eye.]

Responding to the Art

J. M.W. Turner (1775–1851), a contemporary of Wordsworth, is perhaps the most famous English watercolorist of all time.

Activity. Ask students to look at the interplay of light and sky with the gothic arches and columns. Next, have them note how the colors of the sky are echoed in the marble of the church. What is the tone of this painting—that is, what feeling for the abbey does it create? [perhaps religious awe; note the effect of the golden light, as if casting a blessing on the ruins]

Lines Composed a Few Miles Above Tintern Abbey

On Revisiting the Banks of the Wye During a Tour. July 13, 1798

William Wordsworth

Five years have past; five summers, with the length
Of five long winters! and again I hear
These waters, rolling from their mountain springs
With a soft inland murmur.—Once again
Do I behold these steep and lofty cliffs,
That on a wild secluded scene impress
Thoughts of more deep seclusion; and connect
The landscape with the quiet of the sky.
The day is come when I again repose
Here, under this dark sycamore, and view
These plots of cottage ground, these orchard tufts,
Which at this season, with their unripe fruits,
Are clad in one green hue, and lose themselves
'Mid groves and copses.° Once again I see
These hedgerows,° hardly hedgerows, little lines
Of sportive wood run wild: these pastoral farms,
Green to the very door; and wreaths of smoke
Sent up, in silence, from among the trees!
With some uncertain notice, as might seem
Of vagrant dwellers in the houseless woods,
Or of some Hermit's cave, where by his fire
The Hermit sits alone.
These beauteous forms,
Through a long absence, have not been to me
As is a landscape to a blind man's eye:
But oft, in lonely rooms, and 'mid the din
Of towns and cities, I have owed to them
In hours of weariness, sensations sweet,
Felt in the blood, and felt along the heart;
And passing even into my purer mind,
With tranquil restoration:—feelings too
Of unremembered pleasure: such, perhaps,
As have no slight or trivial influence
On that best portion of a good man's life,
His little, nameless, unremembered acts
Of kindness and of love. Nor less, I trust,
To them I may have owed another gift,
Of aspect more sublime; that blessed mood,
In which the burden of the mystery,

14. copses: areas densely covered with shrubs and small trees.
15. hedgerows: rows of bushes, shrubs, and small trees that serve as fences.

Tintern Abbey (1834) by J.M.W. Turner.
British Museum, London.

Listening to Music

Symphony No. 6 in F (*Pastoral*), first movement, by Ludwig van Beethoven

Of all the composers who have created pastorals, none is more famous than the German Romantic Ludwig van Beethoven (1770–1827), who composed some of his greatest works after going deaf. The *Pastoral Symphony* is one of the great program works in music history. An ode to nature, this cheerful, melodic movement is labeled "The Awakening of Joyful Feelings upon Arrival in the Country."

Activity

Have students listen to the first movement of Beethoven's *Pastoral Symphony* and discuss how it captures the mood of its title. After students have read Wordsworth's poems, ask them to write a journal entry that Wordsworth might have written expressing his reaction to Beethoven's musical homage to nature.

In which the heavy and the weary weight
Of all this unintelligible world,
Is lightened:—that serene and blessed mood,
In which the affections° gently lead us on,—
Until, the breath of this corporeal° frame
And even the motion of our human blood
Almost suspended, we are laid asleep
In body, and become a living soul:
While with an eye made quiet by the power
Of harmony, and the deep power of joy,
We see into the life of things.
If this
Be but a vain belief, yet, oh! how oft—
In darkness and amid the many shapes
Of joyless daylight; when the fretful stir
Unprofitable, and the fever of the world,
Have hung upon the beatings of my heart—
How oft, in spirit, have I turned to thee,
O sylvan° Wye! thou wanderer through the woods,
How often has my spirit turned to thee!
And now, with gleams of half-extinguished thought,
With many recognitions dim and faint,
And somewhat of a sad perplexity,
The picture of the mind° revives again:
While here I stand, not only with the sense
Of present pleasure, but with pleasing thoughts
That in this moment there is life and food
For future years. And so I dare to hope,
Though changed, no doubt, from what I was when first
I came among these hills; when like a roe°
I bounded o'er the mountains, by the sides
Of the deep rivers, and the lonely streams,
Wherever nature led: more like a man
Flying from something that he dreads, than one
Who sought the thing he loved. For nature then
(The coarser pleasures of my boyish days,
And their glad animal movements all gone by)
To me was all in all.—I cannot paint
What then I was. The sounding cataract°
Haunted me like a passion: the tall rock,
The mountain, and the deep and gloomy wood,
Their colors and their forms, were then to me
An appetite; a feeling and a love,
That had no need of a remoter charm,°
By thought supplied, nor any interest
Unborrowed from the eye.—That time is past,
And all its aching joys are now no more.
And all its dizzy raptures. Not for this
Faint° I, nor mourn nor murmur; other gifts

42. affections: feelings.
43. corporeal: bodily.
56. sylvan: associated with the forest or woodlands.
61. picture of the mind: primarily the picture in the mind, but also the picture the individual mind has of itself.
67. roe: deer.
76. cataract: waterfall.
81. remoter charm: appeal other than the scene itself.
86. faint: become weak; lose heart.

E Critical Thinking
Interpreting

As Wordsworth recalls these scenes of the Wye Valley while working " 'mid the din of towns and cities," how have these memories affected him? [Possible response: They have restored his balance; made him a kinder, more generous person; and led him to a transcendent state in which he almost mystically gains insight into the meaning of life.]

F Reading Skills and Strategies
Recognizing Patterns of Organization

Stanzas of fixed length are not required in blank verse. What visual clue signals a stanza break? [An indentation shows when one stanza, or "verse paragraph," ends, and another begins.] **How does the focus or emphasis change when the stanza changes?** [The poet now addresses the river directly in an apostrophe—"O sylvan Wye! Thou wanderer. . . ."]

G Critical Thinking
Interpreting

How does the speaker describe his past relationship with the landscape? [In his youth, he loved the natural world with a passion and did lots of hiking, but he accepted what he saw at face value. He says he was more like a man fleeing something he dreads than like one seeking the things he loves.] **How does he relate to the land now?** [Instead of the "dizzying rapture" of long ago, he senses something sublime in nature that interfuses with the mind of man.]

Taking a Second Look

Review: Monitoring Reading Strategies

Remind students that monitoring reading strategies involves rereading; using resources, such as dictionaries and glosses; and questioning.

Activity

Have students name one or more strategies they might employ to improve their comprehension after reading each of the following lines or groups of lines:

1. **Lines 41–46** [Possible answers: Reread slowly; use the glosses; ask what state these words describe perhaps a state of suspended animation or a trancelike state.]
2. **Lines 49–55** [Possible answers: Reread slowly; use a dictionary to find the meanings of such words as *vain* and *fretful*; ask what the word *this* refers to (the belief that nature soothes, heals, and gives insights).]
3. **Lines 58–65** [Possible answers: Reread slowly; use the glosses and dictionary if needed; ask what the speaker means by "half-extinguished thought" or "the recognitions dim and faint" (dim recollections and unformed insights).]

A Reading Skills and Strategies

Drawing Conclusions

? What change in the speaker's attitude toward nature do ll. 88–93 describe? [Possible answer: He is no longer recklessly passionate. He now has a deeper understanding of both nature and himself.]

B Appreciating Language

Famous Poetic Line

? Line 91 is often quoted. What makes it memorable? [Possible answers: It resonates with wisdom and sadness through the alliteration in "still, sad"; it captures a limitation of the human condition through the mournful paradox of "still music."]

C Critical Thinking

Summarizing

? How does the poet see his senses, mind, and conscience as interrelated? [Possible response: Sensory experiences are central to his being; they anchor his thoughts and his moral decisions.]

D Reading Skills and Strategies

Recognizing Patterns of Organization

? What shift takes place in this final verse paragraph? [The poet addresses his "dear friend," his sister Dorothy.]

E Elements of Literature

Blank Verse

? Wordsworth's blank verse has an informal quality. What makes these lines conversational? [Possible answers: He uses the first person and allows his lines to run on like an ongoing conversation; sometimes he seems to be talking to himself.]

Have followed; for such loss, I would believe,
Abundant recompense.° For I have learned
To look on nature, not as in the hour
Of thoughtless youth; but hearing oftentimes
The still, sad music of humanity,
Nor harsh nor grating, though of ample power
To chasten and subdue. And I have felt
A presence that disturbs me with the joy
Of elevated thoughts; a sense sublime
Of something far more deeply interfused,
Whose dwelling is the light of setting suns,
And the round ocean and the living air,
And the blue sky, and in the mind of man:
A motion and a spirit, that impels
All thinking things, all objects of all thought,
And rolls through all things. Therefore am I still
A lover of the meadows and the woods,
And mountains; and of all that we behold
From this green earth; of all the mighty world
Of eye, and ear—both what they half create,
And what perceive; well pleased to recognize
In nature and the language of the sense
The anchor of my purest thoughts, the nurse,
The guide, the guardian of my heart, and soul
Of all my moral being.
Nor perchance,
If I were not thus taught, should I the more
Suffer° my genial° spirits to decay:
For thou art with me here upon the banks
Of this fair river; thou my dearest Friend,°
My dear, dear Friend; and in thy voice I catch
The language of my former heart, and read
My former pleasures in the shooting lights
Of thy wild eyes. Oh! yet a little while
May I behold in thee what I was once,
My dear, dear Sister! and this prayer I make,
Knowing that Nature never did betray
The heart that loved her; 'tis her privilege,
Through all the years of this our life, to lead
From joy to joy: for she can so inform
The mind that is within us, so impress
With quietness and beauty, and so feed
With lofty thoughts, that neither evil tongues,
Rash judgments, nor the sneers of selfish men,
Nor greetings where no kindness is, nor all
The dreary intercourse° of daily life,
Shall e'er prevail against us, or disturb
Our cheerful faith, that all which we behold
Is full of blessings. Therefore let the moon

88. recompense: repayment.

113. suffer: allow.
genial: creative.

115. my dearest Friend: Wordsworth's sister Dorothy.

131. intercourse: dealings; social contacts.

(Opposite) *Landscape* (detail) (19th century) by Patrick Nas
Roy Miles Gallery, London.

Skill Link

Recognizing Distinctive and Shared Cultural Characteristics

Images like "steep and lofty cliffs" and streams with "a soft inland murmur" indicate that Wordsworth had a specific scene in mind when he wrote. This is what is called "a sense of place" by both literary and environmental writers. Every section of the United States offers its own sense of place: The dry hills of Texas are nothing like the stream-cut mountains of North Carolina; the plains of Kansas are unlike the maple forests of Vermont.

Activities

1. Have students in groups of three go through "Tintern Abbey" line by line, noting images of the sky, trees, water, air, prevailing winds, geological features, such as cliffs, and so on. Then, have students brainstorm images for natural features in their own region or state.
2. Have students use their individual lists to write a poem or a short prose account of what their area means to them.
3. Variation for urban dwellers: Have students focus on the natural features within their city such as its parks, lakes, hills, or valleys.

Shine on thee in thy solitary walk;
And let the misty mountain winds be free
To blow against thee: and, in after years,
When these wild ecstasies shall be matured
Into a sober pleasure; when thy mind
Shall be a mansion for all lovely forms,
Thy memory be as a dwelling place
For all sweet sounds and harmonies; oh! then,
If solitude, or fear, or pain, or grief,
Should be thy portion, with what healing thoughts
Of tender joy wilt thou remember me,
And these my exhortations!° Nor, perchance—
If I should be where I no more can hear
Thy voice, nor catch from thy wild eyes these gleams
Of past existence—wilt thou then forget
That on the banks of this delightful stream
We stood together; and that I, so long
A worshipper of Nature, hither came
Unwearied in that service: rather say
With warmer love—oh! with far deeper zeal
Of holier love. Nor wilt thou then forget
That after many wanderings, many years
Of absence, these steep woods and lofty cliffs,
And this green pastoral° landscape, were to me
More dear, both for themselves and for thy sake!

146. exhortations: strong advice.

158. pastoral: relating to herds or flocks, pasture land, and country life.

F Critical Thinking

Evaluating

? Acting as an older brother, the speaker gives his younger sister some passionate advice. If you were the sister, would you pay attention to the speaker's "exhortations"? Why or why not? [Possible answers: Yes, the speaker's passionate feelings affect the reader so that he or she, like the sister, is given a new, powerful view of nature; or no, the sentences become longer and more complicated, and they are broken up by lots of dashes, which make them less effective than the clearer, simpler images that came earlier.]

G Elements of Literature

Romantic Lyrics

? This poem is an example of a typical Romantic lyric, the meditation (see p. 672). What does *meditation* mean? Why does that label apply to this poem? [Possible answer: In a meditation, a person contemplates something in a religious or devotional way. A Romantic meditation is a poem in which the speaker muses seriously on a topic. Here, Wordsworth meditates on nature, attributing to it divine or transcendental powers.]

H Elements of Literature

Blank Verse

? Note that the poet does not lapse into rhyme for the sake of closure here. Why not? [Possible answers: No rhyme is needed. The thoughts themselves achieve a sense of finality or closure. Rhyme would spoil the ending by giving it a singsong quality.]

RESPONDING TO THE ART

Patrick Nasmyth (1787–1831) was born in Scotland and worked in London mainly as a landscape painter.

Activity. Point out that this landscape is a detail from a larger work, and have students note how tiny the human figures are. Ask students what feelings about nature are conveyed by making people (and the things they construct) so relatively small. [Possible response: It enhances nature's sublime powers.]

Professional Notes

Critical Comment: *Lyrical Ballads*

The critical reception of *Lyrical Ballads* was lukewarm at best. In 1799, the Reverend Charles Burney wrote that "Tintern Abbey" was ". . . poetical, beautiful, and philosophical: but somewhat tinctured with gloomy, narrow, and unsociable ideas of seclusion from the commerce of the world: as if men were born to live in woods and wilds, unconnected with each other."

Byron Mocks the Verse Paragraph

Byron couldn't resist poking fun at Wordsworth, and he even took a pot shot at verse paragraphs. Here are two lines from the middle of a poem criticizing Wordsworth (and by implication others):

> [Wordsworth]
> Who, both by precept and example, shows
> That prose is verse, and verse is merely prose . . .

Making Meanings

First Thoughts [Respond]

1. Possible responses: a picture of the young poet's enthusiasm, his current meditative view of the landscape, or his excitement at his sister's excitement.

Shaping Interpretations [Interpret]

2. It refers to the mystery of an "unintelligible world" that often confounds and puzzles people.

3. The stages are his boyhood days, later youth, and present maturity.

4. The gifts are understanding and maturity. He continues to perceive nature with joy, though not with the rapture of the past. He now sees nature as a moral guide that is "half-created" by the person viewing it.

5. The poet has felt despair; he has seen enough of life to know its sadness.

6. The speaker sees his youthful self in his sister. Her presence deepens his love of the Wye Valley and the memories of this trip will sustain him in the future.

7. On this visit, the speaker tranquilly recalls his former, more passionate emotions.

8. The speaker views his past with a mixture of awe and regret, his present with a meditation on his losses and gains, and his future with hope for the consoling and healing power of his memories of nature.

9. The speaker realizes that the scene means even more to him now than it did in the past because of his deeper appreciation of nature and the presence of his sister, and he hopes she will also remember this visit and his advice. Students may share personal losses and means of coping with such losses.

Connecting with the Text [Evaluate]

10. Some students may agree with Wordsworth that they would be less excited and energetic but more calmly appreciative and wiser.

Making Meanings

First Thoughts

1. What single **image,** feeling, or idea in this poem do you think you will remember longest? Why?

Reading Check

a. What does the speaker hear and see in the first verse paragraph (lines 1–22)?

b. Why are these "beauteous forms" not, for the speaker, "As is a landscape to a blind man's eye" (line 24)?

c. What has the speaker lost since he first "came among these hills" (line 67)?

d. What does the speaker see in his "dear Sister" that makes him more aware of what he "was once" (line 120)?

e. Scan the **meter** of the poem. Find three examples of **run-on lines** that keep the poem from sounding mechanical and singsong.

Shaping Interpretations

2. What do you think is meant by "the burden of the mystery" (line 38)?

3. What three stages of his growing up does the speaker describe (lines 73–111)?

4. What "gifts" (line 86) and "abundant recompense" (line 88) does the speaker believe he has received for his "loss" (line 87)?

5. What do you think the speaker means when he says in lines 88–91 that he has heard "the still, sad music of humanity"?

6. What role does the speaker's sister play in this poem?

7. How is this poem an example of Wordsworth's idea that poetry "takes its origin from emotion recollected in tranquility"?

8. What would you say is Wordsworth's attitude toward his past, his present, and his future?

9. Summarize and comment on the significance of the speaker's conclusion, beginning with line 102. Have you ever had to come to terms with losing part of your past? How did you resign yourself to its loss?

Connecting with the Text

10. Imagine that you were away for five years from a place you loved, just as Wordsworth was away from Tintern Abbey. How do you think you might have changed in that time?

Reading Skills and Strategies

Patterns of Organization: Verse Paragraphs

Wordsworth's **blank verse** is best read aloud in the long, rolling movements of his verse paragraphs, or groups of lines that develop a main idea. These verse paragraphs mark five major transitions of thought in "Tintern Abbey." Review your reading notes to see what you wrote about these transitions from one idea to another.

In the first paragraph (lines 1–22), the poet unifies his long clauses by repeating the word *again* in lines 4, 9, and 14. The function of the paragraph is to establish the time interval between the speaker's visits to the Wye (five years) and to describe the scene. In the second paragraph (lines 22–49), Wordsworth makes his thought easier to follow by repeating a phrase ("blessed mood," lines 37 and 41).

Slowly and carefully read aloud another verse paragraph of "Tintern Abbey," observing the punctuation and **run-on lines.** Then, write a few sentences stating whether or not you think that the verse paragraph you have chosen is unified by one **main idea.** If so, state the main idea.

The ruins of Tintern Abbey today.

Reading Check

a. He hears the river and sees cliffs, a quiet sky, a sycamore tree, orchard tufts, and hedgerows.

b. Unlike a blind man, the speaker has seen and been affected by the landscape.

c. He has lost his innocence. He is older and more contemplative now.

d. He sees passion in her eyes (ll. 118–119)—her spontaneous joy in nature.

e. The meter is unrhymed iambic pentameter. Run-on lines include ll. 3, 9, 17, 34, 39, 45, 47.

Reading Skills and Strategies

Possible Answers

Main Idea: The second verse paragraph is unified by the description of the value of the speaker's memories. The third describes how often the speaker relies on these memories. The fourth gives the history of the speaker's responses to nature. The fifth returns to the presence of the speaker's sister and to the landscape as experienced through her.

Before You Read

STRANGE FITS OF PASSION HAVE I KNOWN
SHE DWELT AMONG THE UNTRODDEN WAYS
A SLUMBER DID MY SPIRIT SEAL

Make the Connection

Lucy—Love and Loss

These lyrics, written during Wordsworth's stay in Germany in 1799, are three of five poems called the Lucy poems that were published together in 1800 in the expanded *Lyrical Ballads.* As in other "literary mysteries," where we suspect a hidden connection between the writer's life and his work, there has been much speculation about who Lucy was. "She lived unknown," but because Wordsworth had immortalized her in his poems, Lucy became famous throughout nineteenth-century England as an enduring symbol of the universal experience of love and loss.

Quickwrite

Alfred, Lord Tennyson, who was Wordsworth's contemporary, wrote that it is ". . . better to have loved and lost / Than never to have loved at all." What do you think? Write a brief response to Tennyson's words.

Strange Fits of Passion Have I Known

William Wordsworth

(A)

Strange fits of passion have I known:
And I will dare to tell,
But in the Lover's ear alone,
What once to me befell.

When she I loved looked every day
Fresh as a rose in June,
I to her cottage bent my way,
Beneath an evening moon.

Upon the moon I fixed my eye,
All over the wide lea;°
With quickening pace my horse drew nigh
Those paths so dear to me.

And now we reached the orchard-plot;
And, as we climbed the hill,
The sinking moon to Lucy's cot°
Came near, and nearer still.

(B)

In one of those sweet dreams I slept,
Kind Nature's gentlest boon!
And all the while my eyes I kept
On the descending moon.

(C)

My horse moved on; hoof after hoof
He raised, and never stopped:
When down behind the cottage roof,
At once, the bright moon dropped.

What fond and wayward thoughts will slide
Into a Lover's head!
"O mercy!" to myself I cried,
"If Lucy should be dead!"

10. lea (lē): meadow.
15. cot: cottage.

Summary ■■

In the first five quatrains of this poem, the speaker tells of riding horseback one evening to the cottage of his beloved and watching the moon sink ever lower as he approaches. In the last two quatrains, the pace quickens, and the tone turns ominous. The moon suddenly drops behind the cottage, and the speaker is overcome with fear that his beloved has died.

(A) Struggling Readers

Rearranging Word Order

Ask students to rearrange the title to create an expected word order. [I have known strange fits of passion.] Now ask students to rearrange ll. 2–4. [And I will dare to tell only the Lover what once happened to me.] Remind students to rearrange examples of unusual word order into more familiar patterns as they read.

(B) Elements of Literature

Romantic Lyrics

? What structure and rhyme scheme does this Romantic lyric employ? [The poem has seven four-line quatrains with an *abab* rhyme scheme.]

(C) Critical Thinking

Synthesizing

? What are some of the contrasts you find in this poem? [day and night (stanza 2), activity and stillness (stanzas 3 and 5), ascent and descent (stanza 4)] How do the contrasts contribute to the theme of love and loss? [Possible answer: When a person loves deeply, he or she fears the loss of love or the death of the loved one. The natural contrasts of day and night, movement and stillness, ascent and descent build up to the central contrast of love and loss.]

Professional Notes

Wordsworth as Poet Laureate

The position of poet laureate was created in 1616, when James I appointed Ben Jonson and gave him a pension. William Wordsworth was appointed to the post by Queen Victoria in 1843, at a time when his poetic powers had declined but his popularity was at its height. By then many critics regarded Wordsworth as a traitor to the Romantic cause because of his waning imagination and increasingly conservative political views. He was mocked as a sentimental "Daddy Wordsworth," but he still exerted some influence. Twenty years before Tennyson took the post of poet laureate, Wordsworth heralded the emerging power of his eventual successor, remarking to a friend, "We have also a respectable show of blossom in poetry, two brothers of the name of Tennyson, in particular one not a little promising."

Summary

"She Dwelt . . ." uses images from nature to express appreciation for a woman whose artless beauty and inner purity make her rare and memorable. The mood turns to sadness, however, when the speaker reveals that the death of this woman has touched him profoundly.

Ⓐ English Language Learners

Archaic Language

As a verb, *tread* has an irregular past *trod* and an irregular and rarely used past participle *trodden.* Based on this information, ask students what "untrodden ways" are. [Possible answers: Places where others have not walked or gone; or, metaphorically, unusual ways of being or living.]

Ⓑ Critical Thinking

Synthesizing

? How might Lucy be a representation of the Romantic ideal of womanhood? [Possible response: She lives a solitary life close to nature and far from the corrupting influences of the city. She is neither rich, famous, nor widely admired, but she is fair and pure.]

She Dwelt Among the Untrodden Ways

William Wordsworth

She dwelt among the untrodden ways
  Beside the springs of Dove,°
A Maid whom there were none to praise
  And very few to love:

A violet by a mossy stone
  Half hidden from the eye!
—Fair as a star, when only one
  Is shining in the sky.

She lived unknown, and few could know
  When Lucy ceased to be;
But she is in her grave, and, oh,
  The difference to me!

2. **Dove:** river in central England.

When Coleridge read the following poem, he called it an epitaph, which underscores the fact that it is death that the speaker meditates on in each of these "Lucy" poems. Coleridge also thought Wordsworth might have written the poem "in some gloomier moment," when he "fancied the moment when his sister might die."

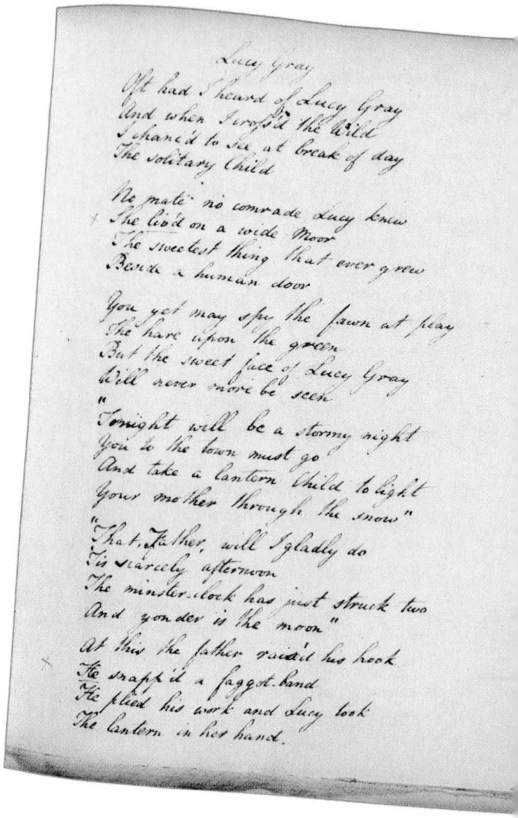

Lucy Gray

Oft had I heard of Lucy Gray
And when I cross'd the Wild
I chanc'd to see at break of day
The solitary Child

No mate no comrade Lucy knew
She liv'd on a wide Moor
The sweetest thing that ever grew
Beside a human door

You yet may spy the fawn at play
The hare upon the green
But the sweet face of Lucy Gray
Will never more be seen

"Tonight will be a stormy night
You to the town must go
And take a lantern Child to light
Your mother through the snow"

"That, Father, will I gladly do
'Tis scarcely afternoon
The minster-clock has just struck two
And yonder is the moon"

At this the father rais'd his hook
He snapp'd a faggot-band
He plied his work and Lucy took
The lantern in her hand.

Manuscript of "Lucy Gray" by William Wordsworth. Though about a girl named Lucy, this poem is not one of the "Lucy" poems.

The Wordsworth Trust, Dove Cottage.

A Slumber Did My Spirit Seal

William Wordsworth

A slumber did my spirit seal;
  I had no human fears:
She seemed a thing that could not feel
  The touch of earthly years.

No motion has she now, no force;
  She neither hears nor sees;
Rolled round in earth's diurnal° course,
  With rocks, and stones, and trees.

7. **diurnal** (dī·ʉr′nəl): daily.

(Opposite) *Young Girl at Window* (1875) by Winslow Homer. Watercolor on paper mounted on masonite (6¼″ × 4¾″).

From the collection of the New Britain Museum of Art, Connecticut. Harriet Russell Stanley Fund. Photograph by E. Irving Blomstrann.

Getting Students Involved

Cooperative Learning

A Lucy Scrapbook. Have students work in small groups to create a Lucy scrapbook. The scrapbooks should contain the Lucy poems, in the order in which Wordsworth wrote them. Scrapbooks may also contain items that students find or create, such as the following: journal entries reflecting Wordsworth's thoughts on the poems, introductions to each poem, visual images of love and loss associated with Lucy, critical comments on the poems, selected responses from students in the class, and other items of the group's choosing. Invite students to create a title page as well as an author page, detailing each group member's contribution to the project. Display the completed scrapbooks in the classroom.

Summary ■■

In "A Slumber . . ." the speaker's beloved is dead, though she seemed a timeless creature. Now, the speaker's own spirit is sealed; his fears are stilled since his beloved has become a fixed part of the eternal cycle of nature.

C Appreciating Language

Word Choice

Point out the words *slumber* and *seal*. Ask students what connotations each word has. [Possible responses: Students may associate *slumber* with sleep and sleep with death; they may associate *seal* with the closing of a tomb or with putting something away for a long time or forever.]

D Reading Skills and Strategies

Making Inferences

? What is the state of the speaker, and what is the state of his beloved? [Possible answer: The speaker and his beloved are both dead in some way: The speaker is deadened to feeling; the woman is physically dead and beyond feeling. Both are invulnerable; both are "sealed" off from the living.]

E Advanced Learners

Paradox

Invite students to explore the paradox of motionless stillness and stillness in motion presented in this poem. [Possible answer: Death is the ultimate "stillness" yet the dead "are rolled round in earth's diurnal course"; the processes of nature continue.]

Responding to the Art

Winslow Homer (1836–1910) was an American painter with a passionate love of nature.
Activity. Invite students to notice the dreamlike quality in the gaze of the woman at the window. Ask students what they imagine this young woman might be thinking.

Literature and Geography

Wordsworth grew up delighting in the blue lakes and rainbows of the Lake District, enjoying nutting expeditions, ice skating, kite flying, fishing, and long walks. As Wordsworth recalls in *The Prelude,* "Fair seed-time had my soul, and I grew up/Fostered alike by beauty and by fear."

Activity. Have students create a map of the Lake District, showing not only its geography but also the places of literary interest to which tourists flock today.

Making Meanings

First Thoughts [Respond]

1. While the power of the poems does not hinge on Lucy's identity, students may say that the possibility of Wordsworth's basing the poem on an actual romantic experience influences their reading.

Shaping Interpretations [Interpret]

2. In each poem, Lucy has died or is feared to be dead. The speaker reacts to these possibilities with terror, horror, sadness, numbness, and an overwhelming sense of loss. The speaker may be trying to prepare himself for the inevitable separation that death brings to all lovers.

3. The speaker is addressing the Lover, that is, someone who will empathize with his tale. The strange fit of passion is a sudden fear that a loved one might be dead.

4. The moon's disappearance behind the cottage sparks the speaker's "wayward thoughts" about Lucy's death.

5. Lucy is identified as a violet and compared to a star. One is shy and obscure, the other brilliant and striking. The speaker suggests that this woman embodies all possibilities for him.

6. Possible answer: His spirit was deadened; he had nothing more to fear.

Connecting with the Text [Synthesize]

7. Responses will vary but most students will feel that the speakers of these poems would agree with Tennyson.

Literature and Geography

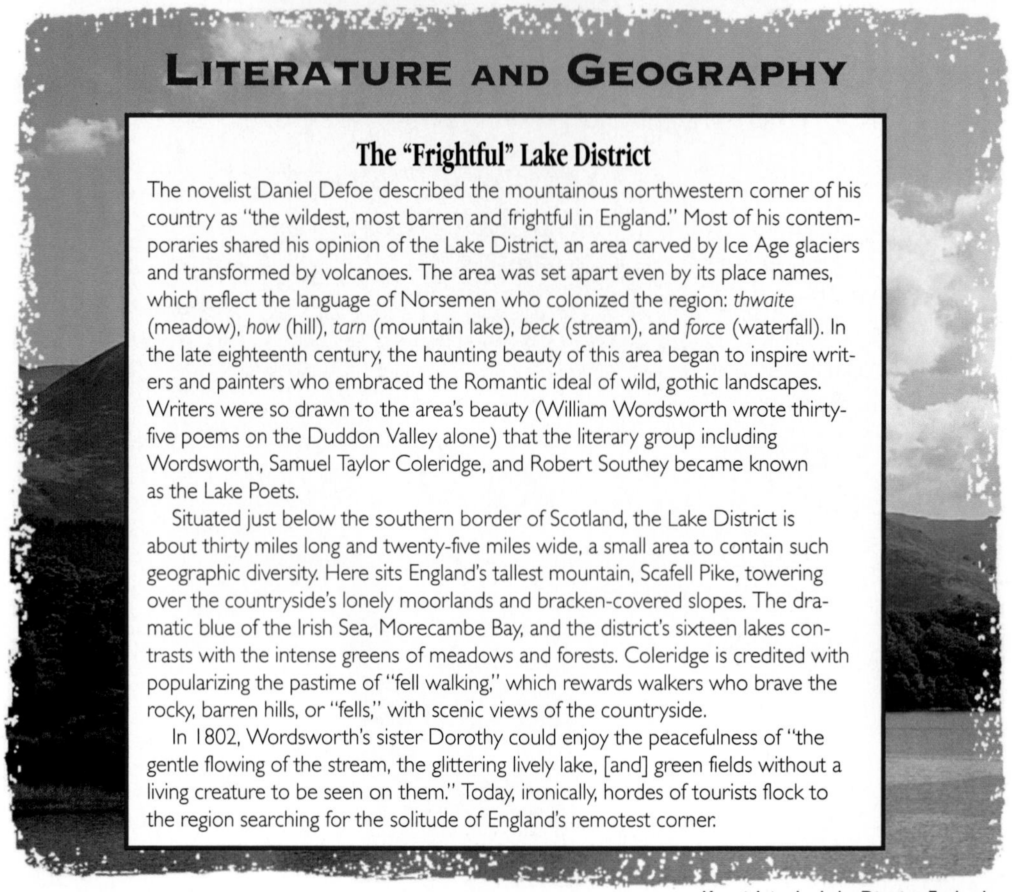

The "Frightful" Lake District

The novelist Daniel Defoe described the mountainous northwestern corner of his country as "the wildest, most barren and frightful in England." Most of his contemporaries shared his opinion of the Lake District, an area carved by Ice Age glaciers and transformed by volcanoes. The area was set apart even by its place names, which reflect the language of Norsemen who colonized the region: *thwaite* (meadow), *how* (hill), *tarn* (mountain lake), *beck* (stream), and *force* (waterfall). In the late eighteenth century, the haunting beauty of this area began to inspire writers and painters who embraced the Romantic ideal of wild, gothic landscapes. Writers were so drawn to the area's beauty (William Wordsworth wrote thirty-five poems on the Duddon Valley alone) that the literary group including Wordsworth, Samuel Taylor Coleridge, and Robert Southey became known as the Lake Poets.

Situated just below the southern border of Scotland, the Lake District is about thirty miles long and twenty-five miles wide, a small area to contain such geographic diversity. Here sits England's tallest mountain, Scafell Pike, towering over the countryside's lonely moorlands and bracken-covered slopes. The dramatic blue of the Irish Sea, Morecambe Bay, and the district's sixteen lakes contrasts with the intense greens of meadows and forests. Coleridge is credited with popularizing the pastime of "fell walking," which rewards walkers who brave the rocky, barren hills, or "fells," with scenic views of the countryside.

In 1802, Wordsworth's sister Dorothy could enjoy the peacefulness of "the gentle flowing of the stream, the glittering lively lake, [and] green fields without a living creature to be seen on them." Today, ironically, hordes of tourists flock to the region searching for the solitude of England's remotest corner.

Keswick in the Lake District, England.

Making Meanings

Strange Fits of Passion Have I Known
She Dwelt Among the Untrodden Ways
A Slumber Did My Spirit Seal

First Thoughts

1. Read the poems as if Lucy were the speaker's sister. Then, read them as if she were a young woman he loved romantically. Do you think that the identity of Lucy makes a difference in the way you read the poems?

Shaping Interpretations

2. What has happened to Lucy in each of these poems? What is the speaker feeling in each poem?

3. Whom is the speaker addressing in "Strange Fits of Passion"? What *is* the speaker's strange fit of passion?

4. What is the role of the moon in "Strange Fits of Passion"?

5. What two contrasting **figures of speech** does the speaker use to describe Lucy in "She Dwelt Among the Untrodden Ways"? How could one woman be like both of these things?

6. How would you **paraphrase** the first two lines of "A Slumber Did My Spirit Seal"?

Connecting with the Text

7. Review your Quickwrite notes. Do you think the speaker of any of these poems would agree with what you wrote?

Before You Read

FROM ODE: INTIMATIONS OF IMMORTALITY

Make the Connection

Clouds of Glory

When we speak of the immortality of the soul, we are usually referring to the idea that the soul lives on after death. In this poem, however, Wordsworth is musing about the state of the soul *before* birth and for a short time after. He remembers how luminous the world appeared to him when he was a young child and how the brightness faded as he grew older. These memories give him a vague sense, or *intimation,* that prior to birth his soul was in a state of bliss and that some of that heavenly joy remained with him through early childhood.

Quickwrite

Do you ever feel that the kind of joy you experienced as a child has changed now that you are grown up? Or do you think you feel joy just as intensely as an adult? Jot down some notes about the special feelings of joy you might have had as a child.

Background

This ode is called Wordsworth's finest short poem (for more on the traditional ode, see page 672; Wordsworth's ode is irregular). Only three of its eleven stanzas are printed here, and the interested student is urged to read the entire poem. Wordsworth says that the poem was inspired by feelings he had as a child—that it was difficult for him to believe that his body would ever die. He used to think that no matter what happened to other people, he would somehow be taken directly up to heaven, as the prophet Elijah was. The sentiments in the ode, suggesting the existence of a prior life, offended some people, and Wordsworth took pains to say that he did not mean to change, or even to challenge, anyone's beliefs. Remember that what you are reading is only a portion of the entire poem. In this part of the ode, Wordsworth traces the origins of joy and how our sense of joy changes as we grow up. These portions of the ode contain some of Wordsworth's most famous lines.

Age of Innocence (1788) by Sir Joshua Reynolds.
Tate Gallery, London.

from Ode (A)

Intimations of Immortality from Recollections of Early Childhood

William Wordsworth

The Child is Father of the Man;
And I could wish my days to be
Bound each to each by natural piety. (B)

1

There was a time when meadow, grove, and stream,
The earth, and every common sight,
To me did seem
Apparelled in celestial light,
The glory and the freshness of a dream.
It is not now as it hath been of yore;— (C)
Turn wheresoe'er I may,
By night or day,
The things which I have seen I now can see no more. (D)

Summary

After stating that the child is father of the man, the speaker recalls the celestial light and glory of childhood. In the first two stanzas, his mood is elegiac, but it grows more philosophical in the fifth stanza, where he equates birth with a sleep in which we almost forget our heavenly origins although we are "trailing clouds of glory." As the child grows up, this glory fades "into the light of common day."

(A) Elements of Literature

Romantic Lyrics

? An **ode** usually is a long lyric poem with a serious subject and an elaborate stanza structure. What appears "elaborate" about the structure of this poem? [Possible answers: The arrangement of the lines is complicated. Long and short lines alternate in ones and twos, and some lines are aligned left while others are centered.]

(B) Elements of Literature

Paradox

? What might this paradox mean? [Possible answers: What happens to us in childhood determines our adult selves.] **How do the next two lines relate to this concept?** [The speaker hopes that he will be as reverent of nature as an adult as he was as a child.]

(C) English Language Learners

Archaic Language

Invite students to use context clues and familiarity with modern equivalents to determine the meanings of *hath, yore,* and *wheresoe'er.* [*Hath*—"has"; *yore*—"long ago"; *wheresoe'er*—"wherever"]

(D) Reading Skills and Strategies

Finding the Main Idea

? What is the main idea of this stanza? [Possible answer: All is changed. The world was once clothed in light, but now it no longer is. Once the speaker could see things he cannot see now.]

RESPONDING TO THE ART

Sir Joshua Reynolds (1723–1792) is one of England's most important painters. Experimental painting methods left some of his work poorly preserved.
Activity. Ask students how this image relates to Wordsworth's ode.

Reaching All Students

Struggling Readers

Build as much background for students as possible by reading them the summary and asking them to put themselves in the place of the speaker who is looking back on his childhood. Then, put selected lines on the board and talk about what they mean with students before they read the whole selection.

A Reading Skills and Strategies

Comparing and Contrasting

? What stays the same and what changes in stanza two? [Possible answer: Nature changes, and yet it stays the same. Even though the rainbow, for example, comes and goes and the moon changes its phase, their patterns are eternal, and their beauty returns. For the speaker, however, the change is permanent: The glory is gone.]

B Reading Skills and Strategies

Drawing Conclusions

? What might the "vision splendid" be? [Possible answers: a vision of heaven; faith in God; hope.]

C Elements of Literature

Rhythm

? What is the rhythm of this poem? Is it blank verse? [The rhythm is strongly iambic, but the poem is not blank verse because it rhymes and the number of iambs in each line varies.] **What is the effect of the rhythm?** [It makes the poem sound very "poetic," rather than conversational.]

2

The Rainbow comes and goes,
And lovely is the Rose,
The Moon doth with delight
Look round her when the heavens are bare,
Waters on a starry night
Are beautiful and fair;
The sunshine is a glorious birth;
But yet I know, where'er I go,
That there hath passed away a glory from the earth.

5

Our birth is but a sleep and a forgetting:
The Soul that rises with us, our life's Star,
Hath had elsewhere its setting,
And cometh from afar:
Not in entire forgetfulness,
And not in utter nakedness,
But trailing clouds of glory do we come
From God, who is our home:
Heaven lies about us in our infancy!
Shades of the prison-house begin to close
Upon the growing Boy,
But He beholds the light, and whence it flows,
He sees it in his joy;
The Youth, who daily farther from the east
Must travel, still is Nature's Priest,
And by the vision splendid
Is on his way attended;
At length the Man perceives it die away,
And fade into the light of common day.

Making Meanings

First Thoughts

1. Do these three stanzas remind you in any way of your own feelings about childhood and adulthood? Check your Quickwrite notes, and compare your responses with those of other readers.

Shaping Interpretations

2. The **epigraph,** or opening quotation, of Wordsworth's poem presents a **paradox,** an apparent contradiction. What can childhood experiences teach us as adults?
3. In stanza 1, what did the speaker once have but has now lost? What does the image "apparelled in celestial light" make you see?
4. According to stanza 2, how does the speaker feel now when he looks on nature?
5. What **mood,** or feeling, do the first two stanzas create for you? (Pay particular attention to the closing lines of each stanza.)
6. In stanza 5, how does the speaker see "birth" as "a sleep and a forgetting"? What does he say we forget after we are born?
7. How does stanza 5 go on to describe infancy, boyhood, and adulthood?

Challenging the Text

8. In these stanzas, Wordsworth offers his explanation for the intense joys of childhood that later disappear. How do you feel about his conclusions? What arguments could you present to challenge the poet's explanations for these emotional shifts from childhood to maturity?
9. Wordsworth describes growing up as "shades of the prison-house begin[ning] to close." Can you think of actual life experiences that either support or challenge that view? Explain your responses to Wordsworth's views.
10. Wordsworth had a happy childhood. How about someone who had an unhappy childhood—would Wordsworth's ideas hold up for that person? Explain.

Making Meanings

First Thoughts [Respond]

1. Students may look back nostalgically on childhood, or they may say their joys have grown deeper as they grow older.

Shaping Interpretations [Interpret]

2. Students may say that childhood can teach adults to respond to life in original ways, unencumbered by what others think or by past experiences.
3. The speaker has lost his fresh, new way of looking at the world. Among other things, the image may suggest holiness, purity, or eternity.
4. The speaker feels that what he sees now is but a shadow of what he once saw.
5. The mood is elegiac; the theme is loss; the images convey diminishment.
6. Birth is a sleep between two states of being, a forgetting of our heavenly origin. When we sleep, we nearly, but not entirely, forget our waking state. In childhood, we nearly, but not entirely, forget our former home in heaven.
7. The fifth stanza is an extended metaphor, comparing the journey of the soul (from heaven to infancy to childhood to adulthood) to the daily journey of the sun. Like the sun, we rise into a bright dawn (infancy), the morning light of childhood lengthens into afternoon shadows (adulthood), and finally the light darkens as evening approaches.

Challenging the Text [Apply/Evaluate]

8. Students may agree with Wordsworth or see an opposite process: As people mature, the light of wisdom shines more steadily upon them, or they get closer to rather than further away from their mortality.
9. Possible answers: As a person grows up, he or she must assume much more responsibility. Growing up means ever-widening experiences and opportunities.
10. Students may say that neglected or abused children grow up trailing dark clouds. For them, growing up may mean release from suffering or greater freedom.

Before You Read

COMPOSED UPON WESTMINSTER BRIDGE

Make the Connection

The Effect of Imagination

Wordsworth chose to spend most of his time in the English countryside, especially in the beautiful Lake District where, he believed, Nature had made him a poet. First published in 1807, this sonnet shows that Wordsworth, the nature lover, could be moved not only by mountains and waterfalls, but also by the majesty of a sleeping city, in this case London. But this is clearly a different London from the one where Blake's chimney sweeper lived and from the one known as the "great wen [boil]" that shocked many of Wordsworth's contemporaries because of its filth and poverty. It is London seen from a distance, and by a man happily journeying to see his daughter in France. Here, London's filth and poverty are disguised and transfigured by the poet's imagination.

Quickwrite

What are your impressions of a city at the start of the day? Freewrite on your ideas about a wakening cityscape.

Elements of Literature

Personification

Wordsworth breathes life into his sonnet by using **personification,** a kind of metaphor in which a nonhuman thing is talked about as if it were human. Look for details that personify the city, the sun, the river, even the houses of London.

Composed upon Westminster Bridge

September 3, 1802

William Wordsworth

Earth has not anything to show more fair:
Dull would he be of soul who could pass by (A)
A sight so touching in its majesty:
This City now doth, like a garment, wear (B)
The beauty of the morning; silent, bare,
Ships, towers, domes, theaters, and temples lie (C)
Open unto the fields, and to the sky;
All bright and glittering in the smokeless air.
Never did sun more beautifully steep
In his first splendor, valley, rock, or hill;
Ne'er saw I, never felt, a calm so deep!
The river glideth at his own sweet will:
Dear God! the very houses seem asleep;
And all that mighty heart is lying still!

Westminster Bridge, London (detail) (late 19th or early 20th century) by Louis H. Grimshaw.

Summary

This Italian sonnet praises the quiet, shimmering beauty of London in the early morning light. In the octet, the city is personified as wearing the beauty of the morning "like a garment," and its buildings are seen as "bright and glittering." In the sestet, the sun, the river, and the houses also are personified, contributing to the paradoxical picture in the last line of a powerful city peacefully at rest.

Be sure students read the sonnet on p. 627.

(A) Critical Thinking

Determining the Speaker's Attitude

? What is the speaker's attitude toward the city? [Possible answer: The speaker is enthralled with the city and glorifies it by describing it as majestic.]

(B) Elements of Literature

Personification

? How does Wordsworth personify the city in ll. 4–5? [He suggests it wears the beauty of the morning like a garment or piece of clothing.]

(C) Critical Thinking

Interpreting

? What impression of London does this list of city features create? [Possible response: It reveals the vast size of the city.]

RESPONDING TO THE ART

Louis H. Grimshaw (1870–c. 1934) specialized in moonlit city views. Note the ships on the Thames and Big Ben silhouetted against the sky.

Activity. Ask students what details in the poem are echoed in the painting. [Students might cite particular phrases like "silent, bare" or "bright and glittering" or clauses like "the river glideth" or "the very houses seem asleep."]

Reaching All Students

Struggling Readers

Remind students that Wordsworth believed that poetry should present an "overflow of powerful feelings." Ask students to find examples of such extravagant emotional outpourings in this poem: Give them this start—"Earth has nothing better to show."

Advanced Learners

Invite students to find Blake's poem "London" in *Songs of Innocence and Experience* and to contrast the view of the city that Blake presents in that poem with the one presented here.

MAKING MEANINGS

First Thoughts [Respond]

1. Students may say that the city's "glittering" or its "calm" most appeals to them; they may be surprised by the reference to the "still heart" of the city.

Shaping Interpretations [Interpret]

2. The speaker notices the city's skyline—its ships, towers, domes, theaters, and temples, as well as the smokeless air, the river, houses, and the calm silence.
3. The city wears beauty "like a garment"; the houses sleep; the city's heart is still.
4. A heart cannot be alive and still at the same time.
5. The city's majesty and calm move the speaker most.

Connecting with the Text [Apply]

6. Students' comparisons will vary but should refer to specific details, such as the city's beauty, its quiet, and its features.

RESPONDING TO THE ART

The mosaic showing the Tritons, Nereids, and sea-antelope is overlaid on **Gustave Courbet's** (1819–1877) moody painting of waves and a stormy sky.

Activity. Why do you think people liked to imagine that gods lived in the sea and sky and controlled nature's many moods? [It's appealing to the imagination and comforting to think of the world as full of the divine and of mystery, of nature controlled by gods who can be placated. The Romantics would not be interested in a purely scientific explanation for these waves and clouds.]

MAKING MEANINGS

First Thoughts

1. What feature of the city described in the poem appeals to you most? Does any detail in the poem surprise you? Why? Compare your responses with another reader's.

Shaping Interpretations

2. What details and features of the city are noticed by the speaker?
3. What details **personify** the city?
4. What **paradox,** or seeming contradiction, do you find in the poem's last line?
5. What quality or characteristic of the scene seems to move the speaker most deeply?

Connecting with the Text

6. Compare the city that you know best, either from personal experience or from reading, with the London described in this poem. Be sure to check your Quickwrite notes.

Mosaic of Tritons, Nereids, and sea-antelope (1st century) from Ostia, Italy.
Museo Ostiense, Ostia, Italy.

The Wave (19th century) by Gustave Courbet.
Pushkin Museum, Moscow.

Assessing Learning

Check Test: Short Answer

"...Tintern Abbey..."

1. How have the speaker's attitudes toward nature changed since youth? [He is calmer and not as passionate but as an adult sees deeper meanings in nature now.]

"Strange Fits..." / "She Dwelt..." / "A Slumber..."

2. What is the state of Lucy in these poems? [She is dead or feared dead.]

"She Dwelt Among the Untrodden Ways"

3. To what is the woman compared? [a violet and a star]

"Composed upon Westminster Bridge"

4. What is the attitude of the speaker toward the city? [The speaker praises the city's beauty.]

"The World Is Too Much with Us"

5. What is the "world"? [commerce, industry, urban living]

Before You Read

THE WORLD IS TOO MUCH WITH US

Make the Connection

Out of Tune

The "world" is usually thought of as the world of material objects—the world of money and status symbols, the world of power, competition, and ambition. In seeking out the pleasures of this material world, what could a person lose?

Quickwrite

Do you ever feel "out of tune" with the world you live in? Freewrite for a few minutes about times when you have felt that modern life was taking you away from something you cherished or toward something you felt was wrong.

Background

Wordsworth wrote this sonnet in 1807 at a time when he realized that his imaginative powers were beginning to fail. Although he continued to compose new works and to edit *The Prelude,* a long poem published after his death, he knew he was no longer responding to nature with the youthful passion that had inspired his earlier poems.

This sonnet also counterattacks the ferocious criticism that Wordsworth was receiving from conservative reviewers, especially Francis Jeffrey in the *Edinburgh Review.* Jeffrey accused Wordsworth of using unpoetic language, but, even more, of conspiring against society, brooding needlessly over problems "instead of contemplating the wonders and pleasures which civilization has created for mankind." A critic considered Wordsworth an enemy of progress because of his "idle discontent with the existing institutions of society" and his yearning for an earlier, less civilized time when people lived in harmony with nature.

The World Is Too Much with Us

William Wordsworth

The world is too much with us; late and soon,
Getting and spending, we lay waste our powers:
Little we see in Nature that is ours;
We have given our hearts away, a sordid boon!° **A**
This Sea that bares her bosom to the moon;
The winds that will be howling at all hours,
And are upgathered now like sleeping flowers;
For this, for everything, we are out of tune;
It moves us not.—Great God! I'd rather be
A Pagan suckled in a creed outworn;
So might I, standing on this pleasant lea,°
Have glimpses that would make me less forlorn; **B**
Have sight of Proteus° rising from the sea;
Or hear old Triton° blow his wreathèd horn.

4. **sordid boon:** foul gift. That is, the act of giving our hearts away is shameful.

11. **lea:** meadow.
13. **Proteus** (prō′tē·əs): in Greek mythology, a sea god who can change shape at will.
14. **Triton** (trī′tən): in Greek mythology, a sea god who controls the waves by blowing a conch shell. (See the mosaic on page 670.)

Summary ■■

This sonnet laments the tendency to get caught up in material considerations (the "world") at the expense of the soul, or deeper self. In the first nine lines, the speaker's tone is one of restrained disapproval as he states his theme that "we are out of tune" with nature. In the middle of the ninth line, however, the tone changes, (signaled by the expletive, "Great God!") and the speaker passionately proclaims he would rather revert to paganism than remain cut off from life's meaning.

Ⓐ Reading Skills and Strategies

Identifying Cause and Effect

? What is the cause of people being "out of tune" as indicated in l. 8? [Possible answers: They spend too much time "getting and spending," that is, making a living and acquiring goods. Materialism has diminished people's capacity to value nature.]

Ⓑ Critical Thinking

Interpreting

? Why, according to the speaker, might it be better to be a "pagan"? [Possible answer: As a "pagan," one would see one's gods in nature, that is, one might find meaning in life by looking at nature.] Point out that so-called pagan gods were associated with natural phenomena, such as lightning and rain. In pagan times, too, there were not as many material goods to lure people away from fear or reverence for nature.

Making the Connections

Connecting with the Theme: "The Power of Imagination"

You might prompt discussion with these questions:

- Lucy may well be a completely imaginary woman. What power does she have over the speaker? [The speaker loves Lucy so much that her death is imagined, feared, and deeply lamented.]
- How does Wordsworth take a single view of London and transform it through the power of imagination? [London at this time was a dirty, teeming city, belching the fumes of the industrial revolution. Yet Wordsworth transforms it to a "smokeless," or unclouded, vision of calm beauty and grandeur.]
- How does Wordsworth best use his imaginative powers? [Students may say that he uses these powers best to remind his readers of nature.]

Making Meanings

First Thoughts [Respond]

1. Students may feel that ll. 1–4 or 9–10 are most important, since these lines contain direct statements of the main ideas.

Shaping Interpretations [Interpret]

2. By the "world," the speaker means the materialistic, commercial world. He thinks people have given up their "hearts," the essential things of life, for material things. Students may or may not agree, depending on their own views on materialism.
3. The speaker believes that pagans understood the significance of nature in human life, as evidenced by their worship of the divine in nature.
4. The sonnet is divided in half by the dash in the middle of the ninth line. The first part is stately, restrained, mournful; the second is angry, exasperated, demonstrative.
5. Possible answer: Humanity has given up its most important gift, nature, in return for the so-called progress of civilization.

Connecting with the Text [Synthesize]

6. If students disagree with Wordsworth, they should refer to specific lines where they feel his argument fails; for example, they may take issue with l. 4. If they agree with Wordsworth, they should outline why a connection to nature is so important to human happiness; for example, they may point out how rejuvenating it is to the human spirit simply to watch the ocean or a sunrise.

Extending the Text [Apply/Evaluate]

7. Many students may argue that America at the turn of the twenty-first century is more materialistic and success-driven than ever.

Making Meanings

First Thoughts

1. What do you think is the most important line in this poem? Explain your choice.

Shaping Interpretations

2. What does the speaker mean by the "world"? What do you think the speaker means when he says "We have given our hearts away" (line 4)? Do you agree with the speaker?
3. Why does the speaker think he would "rather be / A Pagan"?
4. What are the two parts of this sonnet? How is the **tone** of the second part different from the tone of the first part?
5. Write one sentence that, in your opinion, states the **theme** of the poem.

Connecting with the Text

6. What is your first reaction to the speaker's attack on modern life? Do you agree with Wordsworth that if people were "in tune" with nature they would be happier and less materialistic? Why or why not?

Extending the Text

7. How are the ideas about materialism and progress expressed in this poem relevant to today's world? (Think about your Quickwrite notes.)

Elements of Literature

Romantic Lyrics

The poems in this section represent a number of lyric forms—from variations of traditional sonnet schemes and experiments with the ode to the distinctive Romantic lyric form, the "meditative poem."

The **sonnet** was popular in Romantic poetry as a traditional type of occasional poem written on an important subject, public or private. Milton, for example, had used the sonnet in this way. But for the Romantics the sonnet was also used for experimentation. Coleridge's early sonnets, called "effusions" to excuse their looseness, helped him create the meditative poem. Keats's sonnets shaped the stanza forms for his odes. The main sonnet form was the **Italian,** or **Petrarchan,** sonnet, composed of an octave (eight lines) and a sestet (six lines). But the Romantics also used the **Shakespearean** sonnet of three quatrains and a couplet.

The Romantic **ode** was a self-conscious use of a classical form that had been brought into English literature in the seventeenth and eighteenth centuries by the writers John Dryden and Thomas Gray. The structure of the Romantic ode was certainly influenced by the Romantic meditative poem. Sometimes a poem in the manner of an ode was called a "hymn." A traditional ode has two distinctive features: (1) It uses heightened, impassioned language, and (2) it addresses some object. The ode may speak to, or **apostrophize,** objects (an urn), creatures (a skylark, a nightingale), and presences or powers (intellectual beauty, autumn, the west wind). The speaker invokes the object and then creates a relationship with it, through praise or prayer.

The Romantics developed the **meditative poem** and passed it on to later generations of poets. It is the best example of the "artful illusion" of the lyric in which we are to imagine a person speaking. The prototype of the form—Wordsworth's "Tintern Abbey"—is in a flowing **blank verse** in which the stanzas are the equivalent of paragraphs, beginning and ending where sense, rather than strict form, dictates. The tone of these lyrics is much easier and more colloquial than the tone of the odes. Coleridge called one of his meditative lyrics a "conversation poem."

Recognizing speakers and tone. Reread Wordsworth's lyrics aloud, paying attention to the voices you hear.

1. As you read, think about the speakers: the bard or prophet who speaks about matters of great concern; the wanderer who happens upon something that turns out to be revealing; the traveler who returns from far-off lands with his tale to tell; and the aesthete or lover of poetic experiences who finds beauty in all the details of life. Which of these **speakers** do you see in each of Wordsworth's poems?
2. What are examples of a colloquial **tone** in "Tintern Abbey"?

Elements of Literature

Possible Answers

1. Students may name any of the types mentioned; they may also hear a nature lover, a back-to-the-earth convert, a lonely person pining for his love, or a social healer. Ask students to match speakers and poems.
2. A colloquial tone is found wherever the speaker adopts an honest, self-critical attitude; in run-on lines such as ll. 3, 9, and 34; and in conversational words and phrases such as *perhaps* (l. 31) and *I trust* (l. 35).

CHOICES: Building Your Portfolio

Writer's Notebook

1. Collecting Ideas for a Research Paper

Because of space limitations, very little mention is made here of Dorothy Wordsworth, the poet's sister. Dorothy, who was separated from her four brothers when she was only seven years old and was not reunited with William until she was twenty-three, became the poet's devoted companion. Her journals reveal that she also had a strong influence on her brother's poetry. Do some preliminary research on Dorothy Wordsworth. Write down two or three questions about her life that you would like to find answers to. Save your notes for possible use in the Writer's Workshop on page 773.

Tracing a Theme

2. Nature as Teacher

The last two lines of "Ode: Intimations of Immortality" are among Wordsworth's most famous:

> To me the meanest flower
> that blows can give
> Thoughts that do often lie
> too deep for tears.

In an essay, show how this sentiment could be seen as a theme that runs throughout this collection of poems by Wordsworth. Be sure to quote lines from the poems to support your topic. Explain as fully as you can what you think these lines mean.

Analyzing Wordsworth as a Romantic

3. Typecasting

In an essay, identify the **themes** and **images** of Wordsworth's poems that you would classify as typically Romantic. Use at least one example from each of the poems you have read.

Comparing Texts Across Cultures

4. Clouds of Glory?

Wordsworth said that the account of the fall of Adam and Eve in Genesis is similar to his account of the source and loss of joy in "Ode: Intimations of Immortality." In an essay, compare Wordsworth's ideas in "Ode" with the account from Genesis (page 416). Consider this line from "Ode": "there hath passed away a glory from the earth." Does it connect the two texts?

Creative Writing

5. Changing the Gender

Rewrite "She Dwelt Among the Untrodden Ways" with a woman as the speaker, writing about a man she has loved and lost. Keep the meter and tone of the poem, and some of the original words if you like. What title will you give your poem?

Creative Writing

6. A City as a Person

Write a prose description of a city or town that a speaker is seeing from afar. Use personification to characterize your city or town. You might open with Wordsworth's first line: "Earth has not anything to show more fair."

Media and Literature

7. Wordsworth Live!

Imagine that Wordsworth, through the miracle of time travel, is a talk show guest in our century. With others, create a radio talk program in which one student plays the part of Wordsworth, answering callers' questions about humanity's relationship to nature. Have another student act as the show's host and others in the class act as callers.

Grading Timesaver

Rubrics for each Choices assignment appear on p. 156 in the *Portfolio Management System.*

CHOICES: Building Your Portfolio

1. **Writer's Notebook** Students could begin with an encyclopedia biography, but also direct their attention to the letter written by Dorothy Wordsworth on p. 682.
2. **Tracing a Theme** Encourage students to begin by discussing the lines or freewriting about them. A second step might be for students to gather supporting evidence from the poems before beginning to write.
3. **Analyzing Wordsworth as a Romantic** Have students organize their notes in a list. In the left-hand column, students may write the characteristics of Romanticism. (If they have difficulty beginning, tell them to review the boxed summary on p. 630.) In the right-hand column students can note examples of Wordsworth's poetry that fit each characteristic.
4. **Comparing Texts Across Cultures** Students may wish to work in pairs to discuss and explore the connections before they write.
5. **Creative Writing** Ask groups to begin by brainstorming qualities that a female Romantic poet would praise in a man. Would she admire a Byronic hero, as described on pp. 632–633? Group members should rewrite the poem individually and then rejoin their groups to compare their efforts.
6. **Creative Writing** Students might also open by stating the opposite of Wordsworth's claim about London.
7. **Media and Literature** Have students prepare their programs beforehand, meeting as a group to decide on questions and answers for their "guest." Each group should choose one member to act the role of Wordsworth and one member to play the host of the talk program. The other members of the group may join the audience and "call in" their questions to Wordsworth when the host gives them their cue.

OBJECTIVES

- Read and interpret the poem
- Explore cultural diversity
- Analyze themes that cross cultures
- Express understanding through group discussion

Planning

- **Block Schedule**
  Block Scheduling Lesson Plans with Pacing Guide
- **Traditional Schedule**
  Lesson Plans Including Strategies for English-Language Learners
- **One-Stop Planner**
  CD-ROM with Test Generator

BROWSING IN THE FILES

About the Author. Biographer Henri Troyat makes great claims for the importance of Pushkin to Russian literature. He says that "the whole of Russian literature proceeded from [Pushkin's] genius." Over the years, many have agreed with him. In 1880, a monument to Pushkin was unveiled in Moscow. Both Dostoyevsky and Turgenev, leading writers of the day and among the immortals of Russian literature, made speeches for Pushkin "of such impassioned conviction that their listeners were moved to tears." Indeed, Dostoyevsky honored Pushkin as "universal and all-human" and noted his "spiritual affinity with other people." It is for this universal spirit that Pushkin is chiefly known.

Resources

Audio CD Library
A dramatic reading of this selection is available in the *Audio CD Library:*

- Disc 11, Track 17

Alexander Pushkin

(1799–1837)

The Russians revere, reread, and quote Pushkin as the English do Shakespeare. A master of verse, drama, and fiction, Pushkin is usually called the father of modern Russian literature. Even in his early works, influenced in style by the Russian Romantics and French neoclassicists, he focused on Russian settings and folk tales. As his genius matured, he developed a new realism in characterization and a vigorous, simple, and natural language unlike any in Russian literature. Born into an old aristocratic (though not wealthy) family in Moscow, Pushkin had an African great-grandfather—Abram Hannibal, a general under Peter the Great—whose ancestry he cherished.

Through both his father's extensive library and his beloved nurse's old tales, Pushkin steeped himself in imaginative literature. He gained fame early and took a government post, but his radical political verse and wild living resulted in years of exile from St. Petersburg—and the beginning of his masterwork, *Eugene Onegin,* a verse novel. Pushkin, like one of his own Romantic characters, was fatally wounded in a duel over his wife's honor, fought under circumstances that remain partly mysterious today. While his wife was a great flirt, the evidence against her came in anonymous letters that some thought were motivated by a political vendetta against Pushkin.

Alexander Pushkin (19th century) by W. Troponin.

(Map) Europe in 1815, after the Treaty of Vienna.
Map ©Rand McNally R.L. #98-S-116.

Reaching All Students

Struggling Readers
Read the first stanza aloud so students understand that the speaker is revisiting the country house to which he had been exiled earlier. Then, have students read the next two stanzas to identify the scenes the speaker sees now and the past events which these scenes bring to mind. Finally, explain that the scene in the last two stanzas turns the speaker's thoughts away from the past and into the future.

English Language Learners
Be sure students understand the word *exiled* before they begin. Be sensitive to some students who may consider themselves exiled. Remind them, however, that the poem is not just a recollection of scenes from the speaker's past but is also a meditation on his current life and his hopes for the future.

Before You Read
I Have Visited Again

Background

Though Alexander Pushkin was only in his mid-thirties when he wrote this poem, he had already led a tumultuous, often disappointing, yet brilliant life in nineteenth-century Russia. Like Wordsworth revisiting Tintern Abbey, Pushkin is returning to a dearly remembered place: his ancestral home near Pskov. Some dark memories hover too, however, for his previous visit was enforced—a two-year exile from St. Petersburg because of his revolutionary sympathies. Partly because Pushkin was a literary hero, Czar Nicholas I ended the exile—but not the close surveillance and censorship of Pushkin. As Pushkin writes this poem, he is again a "free" man working in the government in St. Petersburg, but now he hates court social life (which his young wife loves). He wants only to live in the country and write, but his repeated requests to leave have been denied.

Quickwrite

Project yourself ten years into the future, living in another place. What one setting from your life now, or from your childhood, would you be drawn to revisit? Describe it briefly, and explain why it has meaning for you.

An Autumn Lane (detail) (late 19th or early 20th century) by Edward Wilkins Waite.

By Courtesy of Burlington Paintings, London.

go.hrw.com
LEO 12-8

Summary ■■

In this lyric poem, the speaker returns to his childhood home in the Russian countryside. The dilapidated cottage reminds him of his childhood and a beloved nurse, and the wooded slopes of a less happy period in adulthood when he was exiled for political reasons. The speaker suggests his theme through a personification in ll. 30–37, in which pine trees murmur a welcome to him. In the last stanza, his melancholy at the changes he sees in himself and in his old home gives way to hope as he imagines his grandson coming to the same spot and receiving the same welcoming murmur from the next generation of pines. The speaker clearly sees nature as a timeless source of consolation and renewal in a decaying world.

Background

Pushkin was exiled, in his own words, for "one line of one silly letter." In fact, he had written a number of epigrams and some revolutionary poems. One, called "Ode to Liberty," cried out, "Rise up, dull slaves!/It was law, not nature, tyrants,/Put the crown upon your head;/You may be over the people,/But the law is over you." The czar might have sent Pushkin to Siberia; instead, he exiled him first to the southern provinces and then he put him in his father's care. A letter written by a government official and approved by the czar said this: ". . . by removing him from St. Petersburg for a time, giving him some work to do, and putting good examples before him, he may yet become an excellent servant of the state."

Using Students' Strengths

Intrapersonal Learners

Invite students to think about a time when they returned to a place that had been meaningful to them in the past. Encourage students not only to describe the experience in their journals but also to recall the emotions it evoked. If the landscape was a factor in their memories, ask them to explain how it fit in.

Naturalist Learners

Pushkin's pine trees, of course, were in Russia, but pines grow in most parts of the United States. Ask students to research which species of pine grow in your area, what their life cycle is, what other plants and animals cohabit pine woods, and what use human beings make of the trees.

A Reading Skills and Strategies
Making Inferences

? What does the phrase "obedient to life's law" reveal about the changes in the speaker since he was last at this place? [Possible answers: The phrase suggests that the law of life is change; or that he has undergone physical aging; or that he has achieved greater emotional acceptance and wisdom.]

B Reading Skills and Strategies
Responding to the Text

? What do you think it might be like to return one day to the place where you grew up and find it changed? [Possible responses: It would be sad or interesting; it would be a reminder of the passage of time and of mortality; it would awaken old memories, especially of loved ones; it would cause reflections on times past and perhaps the present and future as well.]

C Elements of Literature
Symbol

? What do you think the poet is suggesting by referring to the fisherman dragging "an ancient net" to the bottom of "a fathomless" lake? [Possible answers: The lake is like memory; it goes very deep: it may even be fathomless; looking into the past is a bit like fishing for just a few details out of the many that are in that deep "lake" of memory; the phrase "ancient net" may refer to human beings' deep-seated need to recollect.]

RESPONDING TO THE ART

Born in south Russia, **Arkhip Kuindzhi** (c. 1842–1910) was mostly a self-taught painter.
Activity. Ask students to use a piece of paper to cover the two leaning trees in the center of the painting and to notice how different the painting would be without those diagonal elements.

I Have Visited Again

Alexander Pushkin

translated by **D. M. Thomas**

. . . I have visited again
That corner of the earth where I spent two
Unnoticed, exiled years. Ten years have passed
Since then, and many things have changed for me,
(A) And I have changed too, obedient to life's law—
But now that I am here again, the past
Has flown out eagerly to embrace me, claim me,
And it seems that only yesterday I wandered
Within these groves.

(B) Here is the cottage, sadly
Declined now, where I lived with my poor old nurse.
She is no more. No more behind the wall
Do I hear her heavy footsteps as she moved
Slowly, painstakingly about her tasks.

Here are the wooded slopes where often I
Sat motionless, and looked down at the lake,
Recalling other shores and other waves . . .
It gleams between golden cornfields and green meadows,
A wide expanse; across its fathomless waters
(C) A fisherman passes, dragging an ancient net.

Birch Trees by Arkhip Kuindzhi.
Tretyakov Gallery, Moscow.

Getting Students Involved

Enrichment Activity

Dear Diary I. Point out that Pushkin was sensitive to the details of his beloved landscape. What detail does he notice about the windmill? [It is so crooked it barely turns.] Challenge students to recast Pushkin's poem into a diary entry for the day of his visit to his old home and place of exile. Encourage students to return to the text of the poem for details to include in the entry, such as particular landmarks or the emotions Pushkin expresses.

Dear Diary II. Have students write a diary entry as themselves, beginning, "I've been thinking about [a place where I once lived]." Students should try to conjure up concrete details about the place and their specific reactions to it. Give students who have lived in one place all their lives a choice: They can write about that place or about some place they long to visit. Invite all students to personify one or more aspects of their chosen place.

Along the shelving banks, hamlets are scattered
—Behind them the mill, so crooked it can scarcely
Make its sails turn in the wind . . .
On the bounds
Of my ancestral acres, at the spot
Where a road, scarred by many rainfalls, climbs
The hill, three pine trees stand—one by itself,
The others close together. When I rode
On horseback past them in the moonlit night,
The friendly rustling murmur of their crowns
Would welcome me. Now, I have ridden out
Upon that road, and seen those trees again.
They have remained the same, make the same murmur—
But round their aging roots, where all before
Was barren, naked, a thicket of young pines
Has sprouted; like green children round the shadows
Of the two neighboring pines. But in the distance
Their solitary comrade stands, morose,
Like some old bachelor, and round its roots
All is barren as before.
I greet you, young
And unknown tribe of pine trees! I'll not see
Your mighty upward thrust of years to come
When you will overtop these friends of mine
And shield their ancient summits from the gaze
Of passersby. But may my grandson hear
Your welcome murmur when, returning home
From lively company, and filled with gay
And pleasant thoughts, he passes you in the night,
And thinks perhaps of me . . .

D

E

Finding Common Ground

Only one speaker appears in Pushkin's poem, but the lovely landscape he describes becomes practically a second character. The narrator greets new pine trees, recalls past encounters with wooded hills, and imagines his own grandchild engaging in the same conversations with nature. Working with a small group and referring to your Quickwrite notes, respond to Pushkin's description of his particular "corner of the earth." Here are some ideas you might focus on.

- Can an urban landscape evoke the kinds of feelings that Pushkin describes? Why or why not?
- In the Romantic period, many writers looked to nature to explain complex feelings about themselves or their culture. With a group of classmates, review the responses to nature in Percy Bysshe Shelley's "Ode to the West Wind" (page 734), John Keats's "Ode to a Nightingale" (page 755), or William Wordsworth's "Tintern Abbey" (page 658). How does Pushkin's relationship with nature compare with these?

Connecting Across Texts

Connecting with British Romantic Poetry

Students may be interested to know that Pushkin not only read the British Romantics but also was tremendously influenced by them, especially Byron. Students may be reminded of this connection when they read Byron in Collection 9, especially the excerpt from *Don Juan*. Pushkin echoed its theme and character types in his work *The Prisoner of the Caucasus*.

D Elements of Literature

Personification

? What does the speaker personify in ll. 28–31? [Possible answers: The speaker personifies the pine trees by speaking of their welcoming murmur.] **How do the characters of the trees differ?** [The pair of trees is like a couple, with little saplings like children around their roots. The solitary tree is a "bachelor," and the ground around its roots is bare.] **Do you expect the speaker to identify with the pair of pines or the single tree? Why?** [Possible answers: The single pine because he feels exiled; or the pair of pines because he seems to approve of the "green children," the baby pines.]

E Critical Thinking

Evaluating the Text

? How does the speaker's final wish bring a fitting end to the poem? [Possible answer: By ending the poem with the wish that the murmur of the young pines might remind his grandson of the speaker, he provides a fitting end to his meditation on mortality and the effects of a cherished landscape on the human heart.]

Finding Common Ground

This feature asks students to discover similarities among the Romantic poets' view of nature. To prepare students, have them consider the following issues:

- **The use of apostrophe to address aspects of nature** [Possible response: All the Romantics use apostrophe, but Pushkin's use of this device seems the most casual and conversational.]
- **The power of the imagination and its relationship with nature** [Possible answers: Blake believes in the power of the imagination but relates it to God not nature; Wordsworth and other Romantics put great faith in the power of the imagination but view nature as its source; in ll. 15–17 Pushkin says that this place lets him imagine other places; in the last few lines after looking at the baby pines, the speaker shares an imaginative journey into the future. Thus Pushkin, like other Romantics, considers nature an inspiration.]

OBJECTIVES

Kubla Khan / The Rime of the Ancient Mariner

1. Read and interpret the poems
2. Interpret a literary ballad
3. Respond to the text
4. Express understanding through critical and creative writing, and art

SKILLS

Literary
- Interpret a literary ballad

Reading
- Respond to the text

Writing
- Collect ideas for a research paper
- Analyze a theme
- Analyze sound devices
- Analyze a plot
- Interpret symbols
- Write new endings

Music
- Use musical interpretation to understand literature
- Compare literary and musical ballads

Viewing/Representing (ATE)
- Analyze and interpret fine art
- Create art to interpret literature

Planning

- **Block Schedule**
  Block Scheduling Lesson Plans with Pacing Guide
- **Traditional Schedule**
  Lesson Plans Including Strategies for English-Language Learners
- **One-Stop Planner**
  CD-ROM with Test Generator

By Courtesy of the National Portrait Gallery, London.

Samuel Taylor Coleridge (1792) by Peter Vandyke. Oil on canvas (21½″ × 17½″).

Samuel Taylor Coleridge

(1772–1834)

He was "the most wonderful man that I have ever known," said Wordsworth. The two poems that follow are only sketches in comparison with the full portrait of Coleridge, a man who was unquestionably a genius.

The youngest child of a village parson, Coleridge began his classical education at home. When he arrived at Cambridge University in 1792, he already had a reputation for insatiable curiosity and wide reading in "out-of-the-way" books.

He left the university in 1794 without a degree but with a commitment to a utopian colony in America. The experiment never materialized, but Coleridge gave radical lectures and married one of the prospective utopians. In 1796, he moved to a village in Somerset, with one book of poetry published but no prospects of a career. The next twenty months, which ended when he and Wordsworth went to Germany to study, were a time of miracles. In 1798, *Lyrical Ballads* was published, and by then English Romanticism had begun.

Wordsworth and Coleridge became catalysts for each other, and the friendship helped Coleridge write most of his best poems. But convinced that Wordsworth was "the best poet of the age," the poet in Coleridge hid in the giant's shadow. After the year in Germany, Wordsworth returned in late 1799 to his native Lake District. Coleridge abandoned his own roots and followed (as he told a friend) "a great, a true poet, I am only a kind of metaphysician."

Despite this characteristic modesty, Coleridge was, if only in brief periods, a "true poet" and, moreover, a profound philosopher. The middle period of his life, from 1800 to 1818, produced great achievements, most notably his lectures on Shakespeare and the *Biographia Literaria,* a work on philosophy and criticism. These writings laid the foundations of twentieth-century literary theory.

But for Coleridge this period was also a time of pain and despair, memorialized in "Dejection: An Ode" (1802) and played out in the collapse of his marriage, his increasing addiction to opium (prescribed for painful attacks of arthritis), and his inability to discipline his wonderful mind.

By 1816, Coleridge had put himself under the care of a kindly physician, Dr. James Gillman. Despite the effect he had on others, Coleridge himself was lonely. The loneliness came from a lifelong need for affection and support—a need that made the isolation of the writer's life often unbearable for him. His addiction to laudanum (a mixture of alcohol and opium), which began before he was thirty, was not controlled until his residence with the Gillmans.

Living at a time when common pains are easily relieved by aspirin, we may find it difficult to imagine the need for a painkiller like laudanum, which was commonly used in Coleridge's time—even given to infants. Little was known then about withdrawal symptoms. Coleridge's addiction was made worse by the laudanum he took to relieve the discomforts he suffered when he tried to stop using the drug. Although scholars disagree about the destructive effect of opium on his achievements, there is no question that he was badly addicted.

Coleridge was truly magnanimous, generous of his intellect and spirit and devoted to the good of his fellow human beings. The full portrait of Coleridge, however, is too great for anyone to master. Anyone, that is, except someone like Coleridge himself.

go.hrw.com
LEO 12-8

Resources: Print and Media

Reading
- *Graphic Organizers for Active Reading,* pp. 58, 59
- *Audio CD Library*
  Disc 11, Tracks 18, 19

Writing and Language
- *Grammar and Language Links*
  Worksheet, p. 37

Assessment
- *Formal Assessment,* pp. 130, 131
- *Portfolio Management System,* p. 158
- *Preparation for College Admission Exams,* pp. 29, 31
- *Test Generator (One-Stop Planner CD-ROM)*

Internet
- go.hrw.com (keyword: LE0 12-8)

Before You Read
KUBLA KHAN

Make the Connection
Dream World
The poem you are about to read may challenge the limits of your imagination. Fantastical and strange, it is like a vivid yet incomprehensible dream. Coleridge, in fact, suggested that the poem came to him in a dream. And like a dream, the poem contains allusions to the deepest human desires—for pleasure, order, beauty, awe, even chaos and war. It also holds within it the moment when—upon awaking—the vividness and logic of the dream are suddenly, perhaps forever, lost to the dreamer. As you read, think about how dreams work and how the poem may imitate or reproduce that process.

Reading Skills and Strategies
Responding to the Text
Take notes as someone reads this poem aloud to you or as you listen to it on an audiotape. After the reading is over, describe at least one image that remains vividly in your mind. Jot down at least one question you'd like to ask the poet.

Background
An enchanting poem, "Kubla Khan" has a lyrical tone and manner that resemble a meditative ode. Full of mystery and dread, "Kubla Khan" was composed at about the same time (late 1797 or early 1798) as *The Rime of the Ancient Mariner.*

"Kubla Khan" has always intrigued readers, including Byron, who, after reading it in manuscript, apparently prevailed on Coleridge to publish it in 1816. At the time, Coleridge added a prose introduction that offered a rational account of the poem's origins. He claimed it was written in a reverie brought on by opium taken after he read a provocative passage in a seventeenth-century travel book. Coleridge contended that he woke from his dream and was interrupted by a visitor while composing the poem. Only a fragment of his original vision could be reproduced, he claimed.

Kubla Khan (1216–1294) was the grandson of Genghis Khan and was the Mongol conqueror of China.

Kublai Khan (Yüan Dynasty, China).

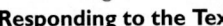

National Palace Museum, Taipei, Taiwan, Republic of China.

Summary ■■

In "Kubla Khan," Coleridge asserts the supremacy of the imagination. His speaker states that Kubla Khan built a majestic pleasure dome in Xanadu with gardens, forests, and winding streams. Deep in a chasm a fountain or geyser burst forth, sending the sacred river Alph into a lifeless ocean. Amid the noise of the geyser, Khan hears voices prophesying war. The speaker then turns his attention to a vision of an Abyssinian maiden. He claims that if he could recapture her music, he could rebuild the pleasure dome at Xanadu, arousing people's fear and awe as if he were a god.

BROWSING IN THE FILES

Writers on Writing. Coleridge explains how he came to write "Kubla Khan": "In consequence of a slight indisposition, an anodyne had been prescribed, from the effect of which he fell asleep in his chair at the moment that he was reading the following sentence . . . 'Here the Kubla Khan commanded a palace to be built, and a stately garden thereunto: and thus ten miles of fertile ground were inclosed with a wall.' The author continued for about three hours in a profound sleep . . . during which time he has the most vivid confidence that he could not have composed less than two to three hundred lines . . . On awakening, he appeared to himself to have a distinct recollection of the whole, and taking his pen, ink, and paper, instantly and eagerly wrote down the lines that are here preserved."

Reaching All Students

Struggling Readers
Remind students that Coleridge is trying to capture dreams or visions in this poem. Students should focus on feeling the mood of the poem rather then interpreting every image and symbol exactly. Students should remember that Coleridge considered literature a magical mixture of thought and emotions that should expand, not limit, human experience. The poet would therefore welcome various interpretations.

Advanced Learners
The concept of a pleasure dome captivated Georgian society. In fact, huge pleasure halls, such as Vauxhall Pleasure Gardens and Ranelagh Gardens, were at the center of London social life. There, visitors enjoyed the ornamental gardens, concerts, cream teas, and grottoes. Perhaps, Coleridge's Xanadu was inspired by these real-life gardens. Encourage students to research one of these "pleasure domes" and compare it to Coleridge's Xanadu.

(A) Historical Connections

Kubla Khan (1215–1294) was the emperor of China from 1271–1294. *Khan* is from a Turkic word meaning "prince" or "ruler." Xanadu, however, is an imaginary place.

(B) Reading Skills and Strategies

Responding to the Text

? What images strike you as you read these lines? [Sample answer: The pleasure dome, the sacred river, the measureless caverns, and the sunless sea are vivid and fantastic.]

(C) Critical Thinking

Making Judgments

? Do the measurements given in l. 6 make this poem's setting a realistic place? Why or why not? [Possible answers: No, places like measureless caverns are too fantastic to be part of a realistic setting; the measurement of "twice-five" has a folkloric feel; or yes, specific measurements lend realism to the text.]

(D) Struggling Readers

Rereading

A change in tone occurs in ll. 14–16. Encourage students to reread ll. 12–16 and determine what that change is. [Possible answers: The images suddenly become haunting, or even demonic; the tone becomes sinister.]

Kubla Khan

Samuel Taylor Coleridge

(A) In Xanadu did Kubla Khan
A stately pleasure-dome decree:
(B) Where Alph,° the sacred river, ran
Through caverns measureless to man
Down to a sunless sea.
(C) So twice five miles of fertile ground
With walls and towers were girdled round:
And there were gardens bright with sinuous rills,°
Where blossomed many an incense-bearing tree;
And here were forests ancient as the hills,
Enfolding sunny spots of greenery.

But oh! that deep romantic chasm which slanted
Down the green hill athwart a cedarn cover!°
A savage place! as holy and enchanted
(D) As e'er beneath a waning moon was haunted
By woman wailing for her demon-lover!

3. Alph: probably a reference to the Greek river Alpheus, which flows into the Ionian Sea, and whose waters are fabled to rise up again in Sicily.

8. sinuous (sin′yo͞o·əs) **rills:** winding streams.

13. athwart a cedarn cover: crossing diagonally under a covering growth of cedar trees.

Palace of Kublai Khan at Peking (14th century).
Miniature from the *Livre des Merveilles*. Ms. Fr. 2810, fol. 37.
© cliché Bibliothèque Nationale de France, Paris.

Listening to Music

The Pleasure Dome of Kubla Khan, Opus 8, by Charles Tomlinson Griffes

Born in Elmira, New York, the innovative American composer Charles Tomlinson Griffes (1884–1920) became interested in music while recovering from typhoid at age eleven. He later studied music in Berlin, and he was influenced by nineteenth-century German Romanticism and by Oriental art. His interest in Asian culture inspired his 1917 ballet *Sho-jo.*

Activity

Have students listen to Griffes's tone poem after they read Coleridge's "Kubla Khan." Ask them to keep the images in the poem in mind as they listen to the tone poem and to draw the scene that the words and music evokes.

And from this chasm, with ceaseless turmoil seething,
As if this earth in fast thick pants were breathing,
A mighty fountain momently° was forced:
Amid whose swift half-intermitted burst
Huge fragments vaulted like rebounding hail,
Or chaffy grain beneath the thresher's flail:°
And 'mid these dancing rocks at once and ever
It flung up momently the sacred river.
Five miles meandering with a mazy° motion
Through wood and dale the sacred river ran,
Then reached the caverns measureless to man,
And sank in tumult to a lifeless ocean:
And 'mid this tumult Kubla heard from far
Ancestral voices prophesying war!
The shadow of the dome of pleasure
Floated midway on the waves;
Where was heard the mingled measure°
From the fountain and the caves.
It was a miracle of rare device,
A sunny pleasure-dome with caves of ice!

A damsel with a dulcimer°
In a vision once I saw:
It was an Abyssinian° maid,
And on her dulcimer she played,
Singing of Mount Abora.°
Could I revive within me
Her symphony and song,
To such a deep delight 'twould win me,
That with music loud and long,
I would build that dome in air,
That sunny dome! those caves of ice!
And all who heard should see them there,
And all should cry, Beware! Beware!
His flashing eyes, his floating hair!
Weave a circle round him thrice,
And close your eyes with holy dread,
For he on honeydew hath fed,
And drunk the milk of Paradise.

19. momently: at each moment.

22. thresher's flail: heavy, whiplike tool used to thresh, or beat, grain in order to separate the kernels from their chaff, or husks.

25. mazy: like a maze; having many turns.

33. measure: rhythmic sound.

37. dulcimer: musical instrument that is often played by striking the strings with small hammers.

39. Abyssinian: Ethiopian. Ethiopia is in northeast Africa.

41. Mount Abora: probably a reference to John Milton's (1608–1674) *Paradise Lost,* in which Mount Amara, in Ethiopia, is a mythical, earthly paradise.

E Advanced Learners

Figurative Language

? What image of the earth is conveyed by the figurative language in ll. 18–22? [Possible answer: The comparisons to panting breath, "rebounding hail," and "grain beneath the thresher's flail" show the earth in violent turmoil.]

F Appreciating Language

Word Choice

? An inexplicable conflict arises in this part of the poem, reflected in the use of words with contrary connotations, such as *pleasure* and *war* in ll. 30–31. What other words have contradictory connotations in the first two stanzas? [Possible answers: *Stately, sacred, bright,* and *holy* seem to conflict with *sunless, savage, enchanted,* and *haunted.*] **How would you explain this conflict?** [Possible response: The poem describes a dream, and dreams are often full of contradictions.]

G Exploring the Historical Period

Romanticism

? To what characteristic Romantic interest does the setting of Xanadu and the character of the Abyssinian girl appeal? [Possible response: the interest in the exotic.]

H Struggling Readers

Questioning

? What question might you ask at this point in the poem? [Possible answers: What change has just occurred? What is the speaker describing here? How has the emphasis or focus changed?] **Here the speaker stops relating the story of Kubla Khan and starts to describe a personal vision.**

I Critical Thinking

Synthesizing

? In ll. 45–46, how is the speaker's desire to build a dome with music like the poet's creation of the poem? [Sample responses: The poet uses the music of poetry to create a magical land; the poem seems incomplete, just as the dome is as yet incomplete; both dreams and music are vivid and real, yet ethereal.]

Making the Connections

Connecting with the Theme: "The Power of Imagination"

Whether Coleridge's account of the poem's composition is true, the poem definitely has the feel of a dream or vision. Ask students what gives the poem this quality. [Students may mention the strange allusions in the poem, its many contradictions, its exotic setting, its quick shifts, and its multiple visions.]

Crossing the Curriculum

Social Studies

In 1211, the Mongols under their leader Genghis Khan stormed into China with 100 thousand horsemen. By 1279, all of China was at their feet. They also expanded their empire into Russia, Eastern Europe, and the Middle East. The Mongols used their dominance to promote trade with the west over the Silk Road. Kubla Khan is chiefly famous for hosting the Venetian merchant Marco Polo for 17 years. Have students do further research on Kubla Khan's rule in China.

Primary Sources

In this excerpt from a letter she wrote to a friend, Dorothy Wordsworth describes Coleridge in glowing terms.

Ⓐ Reading Skills and Strategies

Finding the Main Idea

Remind students that in good descriptions, details combine to form one dominant impression. Ask students to name the dominant impression that Dorothy Wordsworth creates of Coleridge here. [Sample answer: Coleridge's great mind and spirit, which are apparent when he speaks, cause a listener immediately to forget the irregularity of his features.]

Ⓑ Elements of Literature

Allusion

? Dorothy Wordsworth is quoting a passage on the role of the poet from *A Midsummer Night's Dream* by William Shakespeare. To see the quotation in context turn to the collection opener on p. 639. What compliment is she paying Coleridge? [Possible response: She is saying his imagination embodies forms in a creative frenzy.]

Making Meanings

First Thoughts [Respond]

1. Striking images include the sacred river, the floating dome, the damsel with a dulcimer, and the speaker's flashing eyes.

Shaping Interpretations [Interpret]

2. Within the chasm, turmoil seethes, and a fountain or geyser spews from the earth. In l. 30, ancestral voices warn of war.
3. He sees a damsel with a dulcimer. He imagines himself recreating the pleasure dome in the air.
4. The rhyme scheme in the first stanza is *abaabccdbdb;* it varies in later stanzas. The meter is iambic with varying numbers of feet in each line. Line 25 contains alliteration of the sound *m* in "*m*iles *m*eandering with a *m*azy *m*otion," invoking the lazy course of the river. Lines 19, 27, and 50 also provide examples of alliteration.

Primary Sources — A Letter

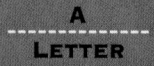

Silhouette of Dorothy Wordsworth (1806) by an unknown artist.

© Wordsworth Trust, Grasmere, England.

Dorothy Wordsworth, William Wordsworth's sister, wrote this letter to Mary Hutchinson, the woman who would later become William's wife. Coleridge, by the way, returned Dorothy's admiration.

Dorothy Wordsworth Describes Coleridge

Racedown, June, 1797

Ⓐ . . . You had a great loss in not seeing Coleridge. He is a wonderful man. His conversation teems with soul, mind, and spirit. Then he is so benevolent, so good tempered and cheerful, and, like William, interests himself so much about every little trifle. At first I thought him very plain, that is, for about three minutes: he is pale and thin, has a wide mouth, thick lips, and not very good teeth, longish loose-growing half-curling rough black hair. But if you hear him speak for five minutes you think no more of them. His eye is large and full, not dark but gray, such an eye as would receive from a heavy soul the dullest expression; but it speaks every emotion of his animated Ⓑ mind; it has more of the "poet's eye in a fine frenzy rolling" than I ever witnessed. He has fine dark eyebrows, and an overhanging forehead. . . .

Making Meanings

First Thoughts

1. What **image** in the poem do you remember most vividly? (Check your reading notes.)

Shaping Interpretations

2. Why is the "deep romantic chasm" of line 12 called a "savage place"? What ominous note is introduced in the second stanza?
3. What does the speaker see in a vision in the third stanza? How does the speaker imagine himself in this stanza?
4. Describe the **rhyme scheme** and **meter** of the poem. What examples of **alliteration** add to the poem's music?
5. Who is the **speaker** of the poem? Compare him with Kubla Khan. Why is the "damsel with a dulcimer" important to the speaker?
6. How could the speaker "build that dome in air"? What do you think the dome **symbolizes**?
7. Where does the poet use contrasting **images**? In your view, does he offer any synthesis of these images in the concluding stanza?
8. Many ancient cultures regarded poets as seers who had a special relationship with the gods and thus were to be treated with special reverence. How may Coleridge be alluding to such beliefs in the closing lines of the last stanza?

Challenging the Text

9. Does the poem seem to you to bear out Coleridge's own description of it as a fragment? Or do you think that these lines were all the poet really intended to write? Why?

---

5. The speaker is an artist who wants to create beauty, just as Kubla Khan created the pleasure dome. The damsel represents imagination, the power or "song" by which the speaker may rebuild the dome.
6. The speaker can rebuild the dome in the "air" out of words and imagination. It represents mysterious, miraculous creation.
7. Examples occur in ll. 14, 28, 47. The contrast is still unresolved in l. 47, but the tone changes to a celebration of the opposites instead of a conflict between them.
8. The people use magic ritual to protect themselves against the prophetic poet (l. 51) and regard the poet with fear and awe, because he has "drunk the milk of Paradise."

Challenging the Text [Evaluate]

9. Students may say the poem is a dream fragment, as it seems surreal and unfinished. Or, they may be skeptical of the poet's explanation; the "fragment" has an intensity that would be difficult to sustain in a longer work.

Before You Read

THE RIME OF THE ANCIENT MARINER

Make the Connection

Crime and Confession

Have you ever done something on impulse, knowing even while you were doing it that you would regret it forever? The Ancient Mariner's strange tale turns on just such an action. And the dreadful consequences of his impulsive deed are as hypnotizing to us as they are to the Mariner's spellbound listener. As you read, try to chart your responses to the Mariner's story. When do you feel sympathy for the Mariner—or sorrow or horror or fear? When do you feel his story is true, and when is it hopelessly distorted by his own guilt?

Quickwrite

Jot down a few ideas about what confession means to you. What purpose does confession have for the teller and the listener? Is a listener even necessary? Why do you think the act of confession plays such an important part in law and religion?

Elements of Literature

The Literary Ballad

Coleridge's **literary ballad** imitates the traditional **folk ballad** in both subject matter and form. Like the old folk ballads, his sensational narrative blends real with supernatural events. Coleridge was a skilled poet, and to avoid monotony, he often varies his **meter** and **rhyme scheme.** He also uses sophisticated sound devices like **internal rhyme** ("The guests are *met,* the feast is *set*") and **assonance** ("'Tis sweeter far to *me*"). To give his ballad an archaic sound, he uses language that was even old-fashioned in his own time.

> **A literary ballad,** a songlike poem that tells a story, is written in imitation of the folk ballad, which springs from a genuine oral tradition.
>
> *For more on the Literary Ballad, see the Handbook of Literary Terms.*

Background

Coleridge wrote *The Rime of the Ancient Mariner* as part of the collaboration with Wordsworth in 1797–1798 that culminated in *Lyrical Ballads.* Twenty years later, in the *Biographia Literaria,* Coleridge recalled that he and Wordsworth had made a poetic division of labor based on their interest in the two powers of poetry: (1) to represent ordinary events and objects in an unfamiliar way so as to make them fresh and interesting and (2) to make believable the unfamiliar and strange.

Coleridge's task was to write about "persons and characters supernatural, or at least romantic; yet so far as to transfer from our inward nature a human interest and semblance of truth sufficient to procure for these shadows of imagination that willing suspension of disbelief for the moment, which constitutes poetic faith." "With this view," he said, "I wrote the *Ancient Mariner.*" The poem was the first item in the 1798 edition of *Lyrical Ballads.* But partly because of Wordsworth's discomfort with the incongruity between it and the rest of the poems in the volume, Coleridge modernized many of the deliberately old-fashioned words he had used. The marginal notes were added in 1817 and need to be viewed as "modern" and rational comments on the Mariner's tale.

Coleridge's poem no doubt reflects his avid reading of travelers' accounts of strange lands. It was apparently Wordsworth who suggested the use of the albatross. It is helpful in reading this hypnotic narrative to keep in mind three things. First, there is no explanation for the killing of the albatross. The results of the act, rather than the act itself, are important. Second, the moral of the story, pronounced by the Mariner at the end, is, as Coleridge later observed, too much and too little; that is, it is too obtrusive and yet not adequate. Finally, the poem must be seen in the light of Coleridge's own more settled religious convictions, which contrast with the spiritual despair of the Mariner:

Alone on a wide wide sea:
So lonely 'twas, that God
 himself
Scarce seemed there to be.

Summary ■■

This literary ballad is a harrowing exploration of the torments that guilt can inflict on the human soul. The principal characters are the ancient Mariner and the Wedding Guest to whom the Mariner tells his tale. The Mariner begins by describing how his square-masted ship set sail under a good wind and traveled toward the South Pole. On the way, he committed the senseless crime of killing an albatross that the sailors believed was a good omen. The Mariner describes the punishments that rained down on him, including the death of his shipmates, the haunting of the ship by supernatural forces, and his having to wander the earth retelling his tale to passing strangers for the rest of his life.

Background

Coleridge had never been to sea when he wrote this poem, and some critics have complained that the poem lacks verisimilitude. Furthermore, Coleridge appears not to have known much about albatrosses. Realism, however, was never his objective. Students should be urged to suspend their disbelief and have, as Coleridge suggests, "poetic faith."

Reaching All Students

Struggling Readers

Help students read Coleridge's poem by assigning them a specific purpose for reading. For example, you might ask them to keep track of realistic and supernatural events. Consider giving students blank transparency overlays on which to mark these events as they read.

English Language Learners

Point out the marginal notes that Coleridge provided. Explain that, in most cases, these notes help sum up the action. (One notable exception occurs on p. 688.) Tell students that they can rely in a general way on these notes to check their own comprehension of the plot as they read. Students may also use these notes as an aid to summarizing the action. In fact, you could encourage students to create additional margin notes to summarize other passages.

Advanced Learners

Coleridge's criticism and philosophy have been just as influential as his poetry. Have students read excerpts from *Biographia Literaria* (1817), perhaps chapter 13 (on imagination) and chapter 14 (on defining prose and poetry), which are included in *The Portable Coleridge* (Viking, 1977). Students can share insights about Coleridge at appropriate points during the class discussion of the ballad.

Ⓐ Reading Skills and Strategies
Archaisms

You might tell students that the original version of the poem printed in *Lyrical Ballads* in 1798 was titled *The Rime of the Ancyent Marinere*. These archaic spellings reflected Coleridge's original intent to write the poem in the style of Middle English.

Ⓑ Critical Thinking
Determining the Author's Purpose

? The introductory Argument is a summary. **What purpose do you think it serves?** [Possible answers: It sets the scene. It suggests that the plot will be less important than the psychological elements in the poem; it helps lead readers into a poem that would otherwise seem to start out too abruptly; it lends credence to the Mariner's account.]

RESPONDING TO THE ART

Gustave Doré (1833–1883), a French engraver, created the illustrations on these pages. A renowned nineteenth-century illustrator, Doré also illustrated many classics, including the Bible, Milton's *Paradise Lost,* Alfred, Lord Tennyson's *Idylls of the King,* and Dante's *Divine Comedy.* Doré is best known for the bizarre and grotesque scenes that dominate much of his work.

Activity. Ask students to preview the illustrations for the ballad (in particular the illustration of an albatross on p. 707) and record predictions about what will happen based on this preview.

Ⓐ The Rime of the Ancient Mariner

Samuel Taylor Coleridge

Argument

Ⓑ How a Ship having passed the Line was driven by storms to the cold Country toward the South Pole; and how from thence she made her course to the tropical Latitude of the Great Pacific Ocean; and of the strange things that befell; and in what manner the Ancient Mariner came back to his own Country.

"It is an ancient Mariner, / And he stoppeth one of three."

Getting Students Involved

Writing

Creating a Ship's Log. After students have finished the poem, invite them to rewrite the events of the poem in the form of a ship's log kept by the ancient Mariner. Remind them to be true to the chronology and events of the poem, but encourage creativity in the wording and in the addition of observations to the log.

Part I

It is an ancient Mariner,
And he stoppeth one of three.
"By thy long gray beard and glittering eye,
Now wherefore stopp'st thou me? **C**

An ancient Mariner meeteth three Gallants bidden to a wedding feast, and detaineth one.

The Bridegroom's doors are opened wide,
And I am next of kin;
The guests are met, the feast is set:
May'st hear the merry din."

He holds him with his skinny hand,
"There was a ship," quoth he.
"Hold off! unhand me, gray-beard loon!"
Eftsoons° his hand dropt he.

12. **eftsoons:** archaic for "at once."

He holds him with his glittering eye— **D**
The Wedding Guest stood still,
And listens like a three years' child:
The Mariner hath his will.

The Wedding Guest is spellbound by the eye of the old seafaring man, and constrained to hear his tale.

The Wedding Guest sat on a stone:
He cannot choose but hear;
And thus spake on that ancient man, **E**
The bright-eyed Mariner.

"The ship was cheered, the harbor cleared,
Merrily did we drop
Below the kirk,° below the hill, **F**
Below the lighthouse top.

23. **kirk:** church.

The Sun came up upon the left,
Out of the sea came he!
And he shone bright, and on the right
Went down into the sea.

The Mariner tells how the ship sailed southward with a good wind and fair weather, till it reached the Line.

Higher and higher every day,
Till over the mast at noon°—"
The Wedding Guest here beat his breast,
For he heard the loud bassoon.

30. **over . . . noon:** The ship has reached the equator, here called the Line.

The bride hath paced into the hall, **G**
Red as a rose is she;
Nodding their heads before her goes
The merry minstrelsy.°

The Wedding Guest heareth the bridal music; but the Mariner continueth his tale.

36. **minstrelsy** (min′strəl·sē): group of musicians.

The Wedding Guest he beat his breast,
Yet he cannot choose but hear;
And thus spake on that ancient man,
The bright-eyed Mariner.

Professional Notes

Critical Comment: Wordsworth's Contributions to the Ballad

These are William Wordsworth's words on his contribution to this ballad: "Much the greatest part of the story was Mr. Coleridge's invention, but certain parts I suggested; for example, some crime was to be committed which should bring upon the Old Navigator, as Coleridge afterwards delighted to call him, the spectral persecution, as a consequence of that crime and his own wanderings. . . . 'Suppose,' said I, 'you represent him as having killed one of these [albatrosses] on entering the South Sea, and that the tutelary spirits of these regions take upon them to avenge the crime.' . . . I also suggested the navigation of the ship by the dead men, but do not recollect that I had anything more to do with the scheme of the poem."

C Elements of Literature

Literary Ballad

Ballads contain story elements. Ask students what story element(s) they encounter here. [Possible answers: The scene is set; the reader meets the characters, the ancient Mariner and the Wedding Guest; the wedding feast may or may not be the principal setting.]

D Elements of Literature

Literary Ballad

? Like prose narratives, ballads are about characters. What do you learn about the Mariner through his words, appearance, and actions so far? [Possible answers: The Mariner is grizzled and gray-haired; he appears to be obsessed with telling his tale; he appears to detain a total stranger with his "glittering eye."]

E Cultural Connections

Mesmerizers

In the 1800s, Franz Anton Mesmer developed a method of hypnotism that he claimed was caused by some magnetic force that penetrated the human nervous system. Many people believed that mesmerizers could "fix" a victim and immobilize him with an "evil eye." Mesmerizers played on the Romantics' love of the Gothic and were popular attractions in theaters in both England and America.

F Elements of Literature

Imagery

? What does the imagery in ll. 22–24 describe? [Possible answers: It describes the ship's departure; it shows how the ship seems to "drop" from view because of the curvature of the earth's surface; it adds a sense of mystery or doom to the departure.]

G Critical Thinking

Evaluating

? What is the effect of interrupting the Mariner's account with a loud bassoon and the revelry of the wedding feast in ll. 31–36? [Sample answers: The interruption creates suspense; the joy of the celebration contrasts with the somber tone of the Mariner's tale.]

Ⓐ Elements of Literature

Personification

? How does Coleridge personify the ship caught up in the stormy blast? [Possible response: He compares the ship to a person who is leaning forward as he pursues his enemy.]

Ⓑ Literary Connections

Coleridge's Sources

Many of the sight and sound images of the ice and snow have been traced to travel books Coleridge read about the Antarctic regions. Although Coleridge appears to suggest elsewhere that these sailors are headed around the cape of Africa, these details may come from reports of those who traveled through the Strait of Magellan at the southern tip of South America. See pp. 704–705 for more information.

Ⓒ Reading Skills and Strategies

Reading Archaic Words

Point out the word *thorough*. Ask students what modern word is meant. [through] Explain that Coleridge revised this poem considerably after its first publication. In response to criticism, he took out many of the more archaic words, expressions, and spellings, but this one remains.

Ⓓ Critical Thinking

Speculating

? Why are the sailors happy to see the albatross? [Possible response: After being at sea with no living thing in sight, they are happy to see a bird because usually such a sighting is a sign of land.] Point out the Christian references associated with the bird: The albatross "crossed" the ship; the sailors greeted it as if it had a Christian soul; the bird ate the sailor's food as in the sacrament of communion.

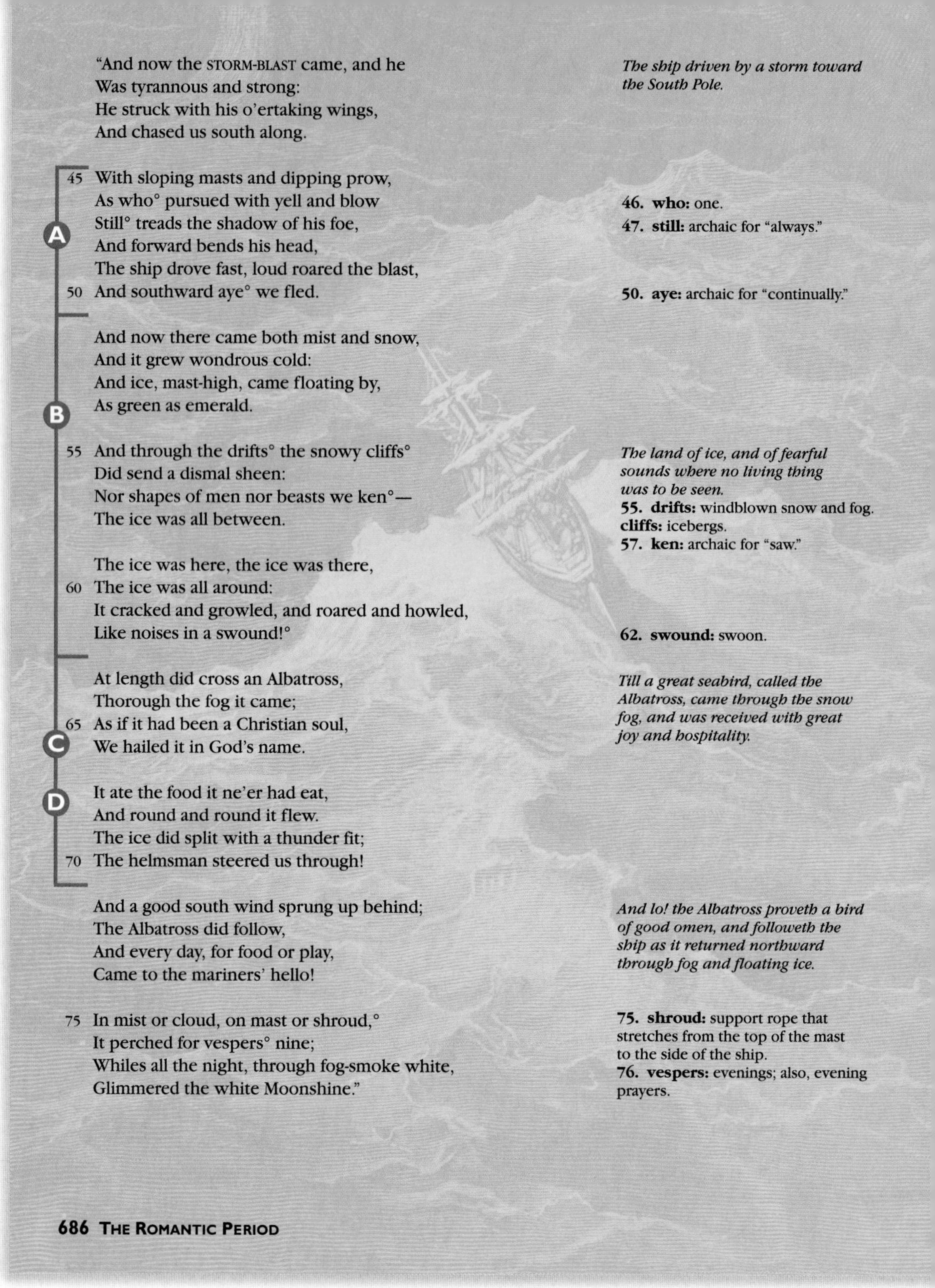

"And now the STORM-BLAST came, and he
Was tyrannous and strong:
He struck with his o'ertaking wings,
And chased us south along.

The ship driven by a storm toward the South Pole.

With sloping masts and dipping prow,
As who° pursued with yell and blow
Still° treads the shadow of his foe,
And forward bends his head,
The ship drove fast, loud roared the blast,
And southward aye° we fled.

46. **who:** one.
47. **still:** archaic for "always."
50. **aye:** archaic for "continually."

And now there came both mist and snow,
And it grew wondrous cold:
And ice, mast-high, came floating by,
As green as emerald.

And through the drifts° the snowy cliffs°
Did send a dismal sheen:
Nor shapes of men nor beasts we ken°—
The ice was all between.

The land of ice, and of fearful sounds where no living thing was to be seen.

55. **drifts:** windblown snow and fog. **cliffs:** icebergs.
57. **ken:** archaic for "saw."

The ice was here, the ice was there,
The ice was all around:
It cracked and growled, and roared and howled,
Like noises in a swound!°

62. **swound:** swoon.

At length did cross an Albatross,
Thorough the fog it came;
As if it had been a Christian soul,
We hailed it in God's name.

Till a great seabird, called the Albatross, came through the snow fog, and was received with great joy and hospitality.

It ate the food it ne'er had eat,
And round and round it flew.
The ice did split with a thunder fit;
The helmsman steered us through!

And a good south wind sprung up behind;
The Albatross did follow,
And every day, for food or play,
Came to the mariners' hello!

And lo! the Albatross proveth a bird of good omen, and followeth the ship as it returned northward through fog and floating ice.

In mist or cloud, on mast or shroud,°
It perched for vespers° nine;
Whiles all the night, through fog-smoke white,
Glimmered the white Moonshine."

75. **shroud:** support rope that stretches from the top of the mast to the side of the ship.
76. **vespers:** evenings; also, evening prayers.

Crossing the Curriculum

Psychology

Why did Coleridge set this tale at sea? On one level, the sea is a source of mystery and has been a traditional setting for tales of the supernatural. On another level, many writers of the Romantic period—from the American Herman Melville to Coleridge—believed that human beings have an elemental attraction to the sea. In the words of Rachel Carson, a historian of the sea: "All at last return to the sea, to Oceanus, the ocean river, like the ever-flowing stream of time, the beginning and the end." Encourage students to comment on this theory that we are attracted to the sea because it represents a beginning and an end for us.

"God save thee, ancient Mariner!
From the fiends, that plague thee thus!—
Why look'st thou so?"—With my crossbow
I shot the ALBATROSS.

The ancient Mariner inhospitably killeth the pious bird of good omen.

Part II

The Sun now rose upon the right:
Out of the sea came he,
Still hid in mist, and on the left
Went down into the sea.

And the good south wind still blew behind,
But no sweet bird did follow,
Nor any day for food or play
Came to the mariners' hello!

And I had done a hellish thing,
And it would work 'em woe:
For all averred,° I had killed the bird
That made the breeze to blow.
Ah wretch! said they, the bird to slay,
That made the breeze to blow!

His shipmates cry out against the ancient Mariner for killing the bird of good luck.

93. averred (ə·vurd′): asserted; claimed.

Nor dim nor red, like God's own head,
The glorious Sun uprist:°
Then all averred, I had killed the bird
That brought the fog and mist.
'Twas right, said they, such birds to slay,
That bring the fog and mist.

But when the fog cleared off, they justify the same, and thus make themselves accomplices in the crime.

98. uprist: archaic for "rose."

The fair breeze blew, the white foam flew,
The furrow° followed free;
We were the first that ever burst
Into that silent sea.

The fair breeze continues; the ship enters the Pacific Ocean, and sails northward, even till it reaches the Line.

104. furrow: ship's wake.

Down dropt the breeze, the sails dropt down,
'Twas sad as sad could be;
And we did speak only to break
The silence of the sea!

The ship hath been suddenly becalmed.

All in a hot and copper sky,
The bloody Sun, at noon,
Right up above the mast did stand,
No bigger than the Moon.

Day after day, day after day,
We stuck, nor breath nor motion;
As idle as a painted ship
Upon a painted ocean.

E Critical Thinking

Speculating

? **As in other ballads, not every detail is explained. Why do you think the Mariner shoots the albatross?** [Possible answers: He is bored; he is showing off; he is annoyed or unhinged by the bird's presence; "the fiends" cause him to do it.] **Point out that his lack of motive adds mystery to the poem.**

F Struggling Readers

Ask students to summarize the events in Part I. [A Mariner stops a Wedding Guest and tells him how he and his shipmates sailed to the South Pole. On the trip, the boat was followed by an albatross, which the Mariner shot with his crossbow.]

G Struggling Readers

Identifying Cause and Effect

? **Why does the shipmates' opinion of the Mariner change in ll. 93–102?** [Possible answer: They worry that the albatross's death will cause a calm, so they are angry at the Mariner for killing the bird. Yet when the day dawns fair and the breeze blows, they decide they are glad he killed the albatross and now blame the bird for causing the previous snow, fog, and mist.]

H Elements of Literature

Literary Ballad

? **Part of what makes this ballad literary is the use of devices such as internal rhyme. Find three examples of internal rhyme in these lines.** [*averred/bird* (l. 93); *red/head* (l. 97); *they/slay* (l. 101)] **How do these affect the meaning?** [The internal rhyme focuses attention on the issue the sailors are debating: Was it right to kill the albatross?]

I Elements of Literature

Repetition

? **How does Coleridge use repetition to reinforce the poem's meaning?** [Possible response: By repeating the phrase *day after day* and the word *painted,* the poet brings home the helpless, entrapped feeling the sailors have when the ship is becalmed.]

Crossing the Curriculum

Science

Students may wonder what kind of albatross Coleridge wrote about. Some may know, for example, that albatrosses cannot perch because their webbed toes have no backward extension that would make perching possible. Invite students to research the different species of albatrosses and suggest which kind Coleridge may have had in mind. (Possibilities include the Royal Albatross, the Sooty Albatross, and the Wandering Albatross.)

Geography

As students read, ask them to think about the probable route of the Mariner's ship. Then have students work in pairs or small groups to create a rough map, showing the route and noting those places where key events occurred. Again, students should use textual references to support their speculations. For instance, the word *kirk,* Scottish in origin, suggests that the voyage begins in Scotland.

A Appreciating Language
Famous Poetic Lines

? Why do you think these lines have been quoted so often? [Possible answers: The internal repetition makes them easy to remember; it is an enormous irony to be dying of thirst while surrounded by water.]

B Literary Connections
Shakespearean Allusion

? You may recognize this borrowing from *Macbeth,* I.3.32–34 (see p. 306). Just after the witches pronounce a curse on a sailor, sending a storm to shipwreck him, the text reads:

The weird sisters, hand in hand,
Posters of the sea and land,
Thus do go about, about.

What mood does this allusion help to build? [Possible response: a foreboding and ominous mood.]

C Appreciating Language
Idiom

In reality, an albatross is too large to be hung around a person's neck. The phrase "an albatross around the neck," however, is often used to describe a burden someone must bear.

D Struggling Readers
Summarizing

Ask students to summarize Part II. [After the Mariner shot the albatross, the crew decided he had done the right thing because a good breeze blew the ship into the Pacific Ocean and back up to the Equator. Suddenly, however, the ship was becalmed and the sailors grew thirsty. They then turned on the Mariner, blaming him for their situation, and they hung the dead bird around his neck.]

And the Albatross begins to be avenged.

(A)
Water, water, everywhere,
And all the boards did shrink;
Water, water, everywhere,
Nor any drop to drink.

The very deep did rot: O Christ!
That ever this should be!
Yea, slimy things did crawl with legs
Upon the slimy sea.

A Spirit had followed them; one of the invisible inhabitants of this planet, neither departed souls nor angels; concerning whom the learned Jew, Josephus, and the Platonic Constantinopolitan, Michael Psellus, may be consulted. They are very numerous, and there is no climate or element without one or more.

(B)
About, about, in reel and rout°
The death-fires° danced at night;
The water, like a witch's oils,
Burnt green, and blue and white.

And some in dreams assurèd were
Of the Spirit that plagued us so;
Nine fathom deep he had followed us
From the land of mist and snow.

And every tongue, through utter drought,
Was withered at the root;
We could not speak, no more than if
We had been choked with soot.

The shipmates, in their sore distress, would fain throw the whole guilt on the ancient Mariner: in sign whereof they hang the dead seabird round his neck.

Ah! welladay!° what evil looks
(C) Had I from old and young!
Instead of the cross, the Albatross
About my neck was hung.

(D)
Part III

There passed a weary time. Each throat
Was parched, and glazed each eye.
A weary time! a weary time!
How glazed each weary eye,
When looking westward, I beheld
A something in the sky.

The ancient Mariner beholdeth a sign in the element afar off.

At first it seemed a little speck,
And then it seemed a mist;
It moved and moved, and took at last
A certain shape, I wist.°

A speck, a mist, a shape, I wist!
And still it neared and neared:
As if it dodged a water sprite,
It plunged and tacked and veered.°

127. reel and rout: violent, whirling movement.
128. death-fires: a firelike, luminous glow that is said to be seen over dead bodies.
139. welladay: archaic for "alas," an exclamation of sorrow.
152. wist: archaic for "knew."
156. tacked and veered: turned toward and then away from the wind.

Crossing the Curriculum

Science

Explain that many of the strange phenomena the Mariner recounts have scientific explanations. The "death-fires" in l. 128 are known as St. Elmo's fire. These electrical fields sometimes appear on a ship's rigging, and sailors often view them as omens of disaster. The water that looks like "witch's oils" is probably caused by plankton, tiny cell-like creatures that float in massive drifts in ocean currents. Some plankton are bioluminescent and glow white and green in the dark. Polychaete worms may be an explanation for the slimy creatures that are described in ll. 123–126. Have students research any of these phenomena in depth and present their findings to the class.

"Through utter drought all dumb we stood!"

With throats unslaked,° with black lips baked,
We could not laugh nor wail;
Through utter drought all dumb we stood!
I bit my arm, I sucked the blood,
And cried, A sail! a sail!

With throats unslaked, with black lips baked,
Agape° they heard me call:
Gramercy!° they for joy did grin,
And all at once their breath drew in,
As they were drinking all.

See! see! (I cried) she tacks no more!
Hither to work us weal;°
Without a breeze, without a tide,
She steadies with upright keel!

The western wave was all aflame.
The day was well-nigh done!
Almost upon the western wave
Rested the broad bright Sun;
When that strange shape drove suddenly
Betwixt us and the Sun.

At its nearer approach, it seemeth him to be a ship; and at a dear ransom, he freeth his speech from the bonds of thirst.
157. unslaked: unrelieved of thirst.

163. agape: with mouths wide open in wonder or fear.
A flash of joy.
164. gramercy (grə·mur′sē): from Middle French *grand merci,* an exclamation of great thanks.

And horror follows. For can it be a ship that comes onward without wind or tide?
168. work us weal: do us good.

RESPONDING TO THE ART

This engraving shows crew members massed at the ship's prow, looking at the oncoming vessel. Activity. Ask students to identify realistic and unrealistic elements in this illustration. [It is unrealistic to think so many crew members, especially in their dehydrated state, would be so far forward. On the other hand, the ship and its rigging are realistically conveyed, and some crew members in the foreground do look either "dumb" from thirst or desperate for rescue.]

E Elements of Literature

Foreshadowing

? What clues in ll. 169–170 does Coleridge provide to suggest that this is a supernatural vessel? [Possible answer: A sailing ship cannot tack or steady itself without a breeze or a tide.] **What might the ship's position in ll. 175–176 foreshadow?** [Possible answers: The eclipse of the sun by the ship suggests that it will bring the sailors doom; the eclipse itself could be a general omen of doom.]

Taking a Second Look

Review: Inverted Sentences

Remind students that understanding inverted sentences involves rearranging the words to create an order that makes sense and seems natural. Often this involves moving the verb so that it follows the subject; it may also involve moving the direct object or other complement to follow rather than precede the verb.

Activities

1. As a class, read l. 159, which is also the caption for the illustration. Talk about why this is an example of inverted word order. Ask a volunteer to recast the sentence in a more usual word order.
2. Ask students to find another example of inverted word order on this page (l. 164). Have one volunteer explain why this line represents inverted word order and then ask a volunteer to recast the sentence.
3. Have students work in pairs to find and recast other examples of inverted word order on pp. 690–691.
4. Invite students to construct inverted sentences of their own about the poem. [Sample responses: This story a Mariner tells; cursed is the Mariner for what he has done.]

A Reading Skills and Strategies
Visualizing

? **What do these lines enable you to see or to think you see?** [Possible response: Like the Mariner, the reader may visualize the illusion of a skeleton ship in which there are two figures: a Specter Woman and Death.] **Who does the woman turn out to be?** [Nightmare Life-In-Death]

B Elements of Literature
Literary Ballad

? **What aspects of a literary ballad are evident in these lines?** [Possible answers: There is internal rhyme (*done/won*) in l. 197. The real blends with the supernatural.]

C Appreciating Language
Descriptive Detail

? **What does the expression "looked sideways up" convey?** [Possible answer: It shows fear: The crew is too scared to look straight up.] **Note how this descriptive detail is both economical and masterfully expressive because it enables the reader to visualize motion and facial expressions.**

D Reading Skills and Strategies
Interpreting Analogies

? **The word *lifeblood* is still used metaphorically, as in "Water is the lifeblood of a ship." Here, however, Coleridge uses the word in the same way we use the word *blood* today. What is effective about this usage?** [Possible answer: Here, Coleridge creates an analogy: Fear drains life itself (as expressed by *lifeblood*) in the same way a drinker drains a cup.]

E Struggling Readers
Summarizing

Ask students to sum up the action in Part III. [The crew of the becalmed ship suffer torments of thirst and then encounter a haunted vessel sailed by Death and Nightmare Life-in-Death. When a star-dogged moon rises, the crew falls dead, except the Mariner.]

And straight the Sun was flecked with bars,
(Heaven's Mother send us grace!)
As if through a dungeon grate he peered
With broad and burning face.

It seemeth him but the skeleton of a ship.

Alas! (thought I, and my heart beat loud)
How fast she nears and nears!
Are those *her* sails that glance in the Sun,
Like restless gossameres?°

And its ribs are seen as bars on the face of the setting Sun.

184. gossameres: filmy cobwebs.

Are those *her* ribs through which the Sun
Did peer, as through a grate?
And is that Woman all her crew?
Is that a DEATH? and are there two?
Is DEATH that woman's mate?

The Specter Woman and her Deathmate, and no other onboard the skeleton ship.

Her lips were red, *her* looks were free,
Her locks were yellow as gold:
Her skin was as white as leprosy,
The Nightmare LIFE-IN-DEATH was she,
Who thicks man's blood with cold.

Like vessel, like crew!

The naked hulk alongside came,
And the twain were casting dice;
"The game is done! I've won! I've won!"
Quoth she, and whistles thrice.

Death and Life-in-Death have diced for the ship's crew, and she (the latter) winneth the ancient Mariner.

The Sun's rim dips; the stars rush out:
At one stride comes the dark;
With far-heard whisper, o'er the sea,
Off shot the specter bark.°

No twilight within the courts of the Sun.

202. specter bark: ghost ship.

We listened and looked sideways up!
Fear at my heart, as at a cup,
My lifeblood seemed to sip!
The stars were dim, and thick the night,
The steersman's face by his lamp gleamed white;
From the sails the dew did drip—
Till clomb° above the eastern bar
The hornèd° Moon, with one bright star
Within the nether tip.°

At the rising of the Moon,

209. clomb (klōm): archaic for "climbed."
210. hornèd: crescent.
210–211. star . . . tip: A star dogging, or following, the moon is believed by sailors to be an evil omen.

One after one, by the star-dogged Moon,
Too quick for groan or sigh,
Each turned his face with a ghastly pang,
And cursed me with his eye.

One after another,

Four times fifty living men,
(And I heard nor sigh nor groan)
With heavy thump, a lifeless lump,
They dropped down one by one.

His shipmates drop down dead.

Making the Connections

Cultural Connections: Games of Dice

During the reign of the Georges, gambling was a popular pastime in England. One of the most popular games of chance was called E. O. (Even and Odd), which was played with dice. People have played with dice since the dawn of civilization. Probably, the earliest dicelike objects were made from sheep anklebones. Although the Greek historian Herodotus maintains the Lydians invented dice during a famine in the reign of King Atys, dice are mentioned in the *Rig Veda* and probably come from Asia. Dice are also found in Egyptian tombs built before 2000 B.C. In ancient Greece, dice, or *astragalos,* made from sheep anklebones, were associated with the fickleness of Fate. Ask students why a game of dice would be an appropriate way for Death and Death-in-Life to decide the Mariner's punishment for his misdeed.

The souls did from their bodies fly,—
They fled to bliss or woe!
And every soul, it passed me by,
Like the whizz of my crossbow!

But Life-in-Death begins her work on the ancient Mariner.

Part IV

"I fear thee, ancient Mariner!
I fear thy skinny hand!
And thou art long, and lank, and brown,
As is the ribbed sea sand.

The Wedding Guest feareth that a Spirit is talking to him;

I fear thee and thy glittering eye,
And thy skinny hand, so brown."—
Fear not, fear not, thou Wedding Guest!
This body dropt not down.

Alone, alone, all, all alone,
Alone on a wide wide sea!
And never a saint took pity on
My soul in agony.

But the ancient Mariner assureth him of his bodily life, and proceedeth to relate his horrible penance.

The many men, so beautiful!
And they all dead did lie:
And a thousand thousand slimy things
Lived on; and so did I.

He despiseth the creatures of the calm,

I looked upon the rotting sea,
And drew my eyes away;
I looked upon the rotting deck,
And there the dead men lay.

And envieth that they should live, and so many lie dead.

I looked to heaven, and tried to pray;
But or° ever a prayer had gusht,
A wicked whisper came, and made
My heart as dry as dust.

245. or: before.

I closed my lids, and kept them close,
And the balls like pulses beat;
For the sky and the sea, and the sea and the sky
Lay like a load on my weary eye,
And the dead were at my feet.

The cold sweat melted from their limbs,
Nor rot nor reek did they:
The look with which they looked on me
Had never passed away.

But the curse liveth for him in the eye of the dead men.

F Critical Thinking

Making Judgments

? Do the Wedding Guest's suspicions that he is talking to a spirit (ll. 224–231) seem reasonable? Why or why not? [Yes, after such a tale, the idea that the Mariner is a ghost is not far-fetched; or no, he would have to be slightly unhinged to doubt that the man in front of him is not human.]

G Elements of Literature

Literary Ballad

? How does Coleridge use repetition to emphasize that the Mariner is now cut off from the rest of humanity? [Possible answers: By repeating the word *alone*, the poet makes it clear that because of his guilt the Mariner will suffer a different fate from his colleagues.]

H Critical Thinking

Interpreting

? Some critics see this poem as a tale of sin and Christian redemption. How might the Mariner's physical isolation reflect his spiritual condition? [Because he alienated himself from nature by killing the albatross, he is now alone on the ship. This physical isolation mirrors his spiritual isolation from his fellow crewmates and from God.]

I Elements of Literature

Literary Ballad

? How do supernatural and realistic elements work together in this stanza? [Possible answer: Realistically, the bodies should begin to decompose; yet moisture evaporates from them, and they keep the expressions of hatred they held at the moment of death.]

Getting Students Involved

Cooperative Learning

Talk It Through. To help the class interpret this ballad, divide the class into small groups of four to six students. Assign, or have each group choose, one of the following five categories of response: structure (including the division into parts and the use of the frame); meaning (including theme or moral); symbolism (including the albatross); use of the supernatural; or literary devices (including imagery, rhyme, and sound devices). Ask each member of the group to generate at least one significant question that will open up discussion about that category. Then, have the group as a whole discuss possible answers to each question in preparation for a ten-minute panel discussion in front of the class. After each panel discussion, ask for comments or questions from the audience before another group takes its turn. When all groups have finished, ask each one to complete its own self-assessment.

Ⓐ Elements of Literature

Imagery

? What visual images does Coleridge create in this stanza? [Possible answer: He suggests beams of light from the moon falling on the sea, forming a hoary or frostlike pattern on its surface, except in the area where the ship casts its shadow, where the water is a "still and awful red."]

Ⓑ Critical Thinking

Interpreting

? What does the Mariner notice in these stanzas? [the beauty of the water snakes] **How does he feel toward them?** [He feels love for them.]

Ⓒ Reading Skills and Strategies

Reading Archaic Words

The word *selfsame* is used today, though infrequently. It comes from the Middle English *selve same*. Ask students to tell what it means [same] **and how it is like *lifeblood*.** [Like *lifeblood*, its shortened form does the exact job that the longer word does.]

Ⓓ Reading Skills and Strategies

Identifying Cause and Effect

? Why does the albatross drop from the Mariner's neck at this point? [Possible answers: Because he blesses living things, even though he does so "unaware," or unintentionally, he is able to pray; because of its enormous weight and/or state of putrefaction.]

An orphan's curse would drag to hell
A spirit from on high;
But oh! more horrible than that
Is the curse in a dead man's eye!
Seven days, seven nights, I saw that curse,
And yet I could not die.

In his loneliness and fixedness he yearneth toward the journeying Moon, and the stars that still sojourn, yet still move onward; and everywhere the blue sky belongs to them, and is their appointed rest, and their native country and their own natural homes, which they enter unannounced, as lords that are certainly expected and yet there is a silent joy at their arrival.

The moving Moon went up the sky,
And nowhere did abide:
Softly she was going up,
And a star or two beside—

Her beams bemocked the sultry main,°
Like April hoarfrost° spread;
But where the ship's huge shadow lay,
The charmèd water burnt alway°
A still and awful red.

267. main: archaic for "open sea."
268. hoarfrost: crystalline deposits from freezing dew; frost.
270. alway: archaic for "always."

By the light of the Moon he beholdeth God's creatures of the great calm.

Beyond the shadow of the ship,
I watched the water snakes:
They moved in tracks of shining white,
And when they reared, the elfish light
Fell off in hoary° flakes.

276. hoary: white or gray.

Within the shadow of the ship
I watched their rich attire:
Blue, glossy green, and velvet black,
They coiled and swam; and every track
Was a flash of golden fire.

Their beauty and their happiness.

O happy living things! no tongue
Their beauty might declare:
A spring of love gushed from my heart,
And I blessed them unaware:
Sure my kind saint took pity on me,
And I blessed them unaware.

He blesseth them in his heart.

The spell begins to break.

The selfsame moment I could pray;
And from my neck so free
The Albatross fell off, and sank
Like lead into the sea.

Part V

Oh sleep! it is a gentle thing,
Beloved from pole to pole!
To Mary Queen the praise be given!
She sent the gentle sleep from Heaven,
That slid into my soul.

Crossing the Curriculum

Science

What are the actual scientific explanations for some of the phenomena Coleridge cites? How accurate is his use of such references? Page 692 includes references to red waters (which may suggest red tides), to water snakes, and possibly to the Aurora Australis, or the Southern Lights. Have students investigate these phenomena and decide if Coleridge's use of them is scientifically accurate. Explain that red tides are discolorations of the sea caused by invasions of red dinoflagellates that kill fish and other organisms by releasing poison. Then, suggest that students find out where and why red tides occur. Or explain that water snakes can be both fresh and salt water creatures. Suggest that students research how far out in the ocean water snakes can live. You might also suggest they investigate what causes the Aurora Australis and whether it is visible at the probable latitude of the Mariner's ship.

Invite students to choose one or more of these areas of investigation and to share what they learn with the class.

The silly° buckets on the deck,
That had so long remained,
I dreamt that they were filled with dew;
And when I awoke, it rained.

My lips were wet, my throat was cold,
My garments all were dank;
Sure I had drunken in my dreams,
And still my body drank.

I moved, and could not feel my limbs:
I was so light—almost
I thought that I had died in sleep,
And was a blessèd ghost.

And soon I heard a roaring wind:
It did not come anear;
But with its sound it shook the sails,
That were so thin and sere.°

The upper air burst into life!
And a hundred fire flags sheen,
To and fro they were hurried about!
And to and fro, and in and out,
The wan stars danced between.°

And the coming wind did roar more loud,
And the sails did sigh like sedge;°
And the rain poured down from one black cloud;
The Moon was at its edge.

The thick black cloud was cleft,° and still
The Moon was at its side:
Like waters shot from some high crag,
The lightning fell with never a jag,
A river steep and wide.

By grace of the holy Mother, the ancient Mariner is refreshed with rain.

297. silly: simple; plain.

He heareth sounds and seeth strange sights and commotions in the sky and the element.

312. sere: archaic for "worn."

313–317. The upper . . . danced between: apparently describes the shifting lights of an aurora, which sometimes resemble waving, luminous folds of fabric.

319. sedge: reedy plants.

322. cleft: split.

"I dreamt that they were filled with dew;
And when I awoke, it rained."

E Critical Thinking

Interpreting

? Point out that in this stanza the long drought is broken. How might this incident be interpreted metaphorically? [Possible response: Once the Mariner begins to see beauty in the world, absolution, like rain, pours down on him.]

F Reading Skills and Strategies

Reading Archaic Words

? In addition to *sere,* what other archaic word appears in this stanza? [anear] Tell students that the prefix *a-,* as in *afar* or *aflame,* was commonly used in the standard written English of earlier times.

G Struggling Readers

Summarizing

? What events are described on this page? [Possible answer: It finally rains and the Mariner drinks the fresh water and wonders if he might be a ghost. He hears the wind shaking the sails and sees an aurora; he witnesses a flash of lightning.]

Skill Link

Evaluating Oral Literary Performance

The tremendous oral power of the poetry in this collection makes it ideal for honing students' speaking ability. Try this process with students:

1. Elicit from students a list of the qualities that mark an oral presentation: volume, pronunciation, enunciation, inflection, pacing, pitch, eye contact, facial expression, and body language. Now, model a short reading for students, perhaps doing it several times, each time with a "poor" performance on one or more criteria. Have students critique your performance.
2. After you approve their choices, have students memorize a passage of five to twenty lines. Students should practice with an assigned partner, each evaluating the other on criteria they have developed and offering suggestions for improvement.
3. Provide class time for each performance. For every speaker, appoint two other students to act as evaluators, providing written comments to the speaker. (You may want to review evaluators' comments before passing them on to the speaker.)

Ⓐ Elements of Literature

Literary Ballad

? What supernatural element appears here? [The dead men groan and rise.] Explain to students that folk stories about ships navigated by dead sailors are entrenched in the oral tradition of the sea.

Ⓑ English Language Learners

Shortened Forms of Words

? What does *'gan* mean? [began] Explain that common words like this are often shortened for poetic purposes.

Ⓒ Advanced Learners

Analyzing Detail

? Why is this detail included about the Mariner's nephew? [Possible answer: It intensifies the horror by suggesting that the dead are not just strangers but loved ones.]

Ⓓ Elements of Literature

Literary Ballad

A literary ballad uses evocative language to create its effects. Point out the use of internal rhyme here [*around/sound*], and mention that it is characteristic of this literary ballad. Ask students to find examples of alliteration in the lines that follow, which evoke the sweet sounds of dead souls singing. [Possible answer: "Sometimes a-dropping from the sky/I heard a skylark sing."]

The bodies of the ship's crew are inspired and the ship moves on.

The loud wind never reached the ship,
Yet now the ship moved on!
Beneath the lightning and the Moon
The dead men gave a groan.

They groaned, they stirred, they all uprose,
Nor spake, nor moved their eyes;
It had been strange, even in a dream,
To have seen those dead men rise.

The helmsman steered, the ship moved on;
Yet never a breeze up-blew;
The mariners all 'gan work the ropes,
Where they were wont° to do;
They raised their limbs like lifeless tools—
We were a ghastly crew.

338. wont (wänt): accustomed.

The body of my brother's son
Stood by me, knee to knee:
The body and I pulled at one rope,
But he said nought to me.

"I fear thee, ancient Mariner!"
Be calm, thou Wedding Guest!
'Twas not those souls that fled in pain,
Which to their corses° came again,
But a troop of spirits blest:

But not by the souls of the men, nor by demons of earth or middle air, but by a blessed troop of angelic spirits, sent down by the invocation of the guardian saint.

348. corses: archaic for "corpses."

For when it dawned—they dropt their arms,
And clustered round the mast;
Sweet sounds rose slowly through their mouths,
And from their bodies passed.

Around, around, flew each sweet sound,
Then darted to the Sun;
Slowly the sounds came back again,
Now mixed, now one by one.

Sometimes a-dropping from the sky
I heard the skylark sing;
Sometimes all little birds that are,
How they seemed to fill the sea and air
With their sweet jargoning!°

362. jargoning: archaic for "twittering."

And now 'twas like all instruments,
Now like a lonely flute;
And now it is an angel's song,
That makes the heavens be mute.

Skill Link

Analyzing and Responding to Critical Reviews

Here are some interpretations of the poem's symbolism for students to consider and evaluate.

1. **Death and Rebirth.** Critic Maud Bodkin sees the poem as an archetypal story, that is, a narrative that is found in all cultures. She believes its theme explores death and rebirth. There are many powerful images of death and rebirth in the poem: sleep and waking, winter and spring, night and day.
2. **Crime and Punishment.** In *The Romantic Imagination*, Cecil M. Bowra suggests that readers might ask why there is "all this pother about a bird." Bowra goes on to say, "The poem is a myth of a guilty soul and marks in clear stages the passage from crime through punishment to such redemption as is possible in this world." Some critics suggest the Mariner's crime represents original sin.

It ceased; yet still the sails made on
A pleasant noise till noon,
A noise like of a hidden brook
In the leafy month of June,
That to the sleeping woods all night
Singeth a quiet tune.

Till noon we quietly sailed on,
Yet never a breeze did breathe:
Slowly and smoothly went the ship,
Moved onward from beneath.

Under the keel nine fathom deep,
From the land of mist and snow,
The spirit slid: and it was he
That made the ship to go.
The sails at noon left off their tune,
And the ship stood still also.

The lonesome Spirit from the South Pole carries on the ship as far as the Line, in obedience to the angelic troop, but still requireth vengeance.

The Sun, right up above the mast,
Had fixed her° to the ocean:
But in a minute she 'gan stir,
With a short uneasy motion—
Backwards and forwards half her length
With a short uneasy motion.

384. fixed her: seemed to hold the ship motionless.

Then like a pawing horse let go,
She made a sudden bound:
It flung the blood into my head,
And I fell down in a swound.

How long in that same fit I lay,
I have not to declare;
But ere my living life returned,
I heard and in my soul discerned
Two voices in the air.

The Polar Spirit's fellow demons, the invisible inhabitants of the element, take part in his wrong; and two of them relate, one to the other, that penance long and heavy for the ancient Mariner hath been accorded to the Polar Spirit, who returneth southward.

"Is it he?" quoth one, "Is this the man?
By him who died on cross,
With his cruel bow he laid full low
The harmless Albatross.

The spirit who bideth by himself
In the land of mist and snow,
He loved the bird that loved the man
Who shot him with his bow."

The other was a softer voice,
As soft as honeydew:
Quoth he, "The man hath penance done,
And penance more will do."

E Struggling Readers
Rearranging Syntax

Providing help as needed, ask students to rearrange and paraphrase the first three lines of this stanza to create a more usual word order. [Possible answer: We sailed quietly on till noon. Although no breeze ever blew, the ship moved slowly and smoothly, pushed on from underneath the water.]

F Critical Thinking
Interpreting

? What is moving the ship? [The spirit from the polar region is moving the ship from below.]

G Reading Skills and Strategies
Reading Archaic Words

? What does *swound* mean? Why might Coleridge have chosen this word? [Possible answers: Coleridge is suggesting a "swoon," or a faint; he is creating consonance and assonance with *down* and *swound*; he is making one of his deliberately archaic word choices; he is adding interest and drama through the use of an unusual word; or he just needed a good rhyme for *bound*.]

H Elements of Literature
Literary Ballad

? Remember that a ballad, above all, tells a story. What characteristics of popular storytelling appear in these stanzas? [Possible answers: Dialogue moves the action along; the phrase "And penance more will do" creates suspense by foreshadowing an ominous fate for the Mariner.]

A Struggling Readers

Summarizing

Before students read Part VI, have them summarize Part V. [After the albatross falls from his neck, the Mariner sleeps. When rain falls, he drinks and sees strange phenomena, such as the aurora, lightning, and a strong wind. Although the wind never reaches the ship, the polar spirit that loved the albatross pushes the vessel northward. The ship is sailed by the animated bodies of the dead crew. When the ship stops, the Mariner faints and hears two voices discussing his penance.]

B Struggling Readers

Rereading/Reading On

? What should you do if you do not know who these two speakers are? [Possible answers: Go back and reread. Read on to find out what the text reveals.] **Explain that these voices belong to unidentified characters, perhaps friends of the polar spirit or the moon and ocean themselves.**

C Elements of Literature

Allusion

? The swift, magical movement of the ship while the Mariner is in a trance parallels Odysseus's homeward journey in Homer's *Odyssey* (Book 13), in which the gods put Odysseus in a trance while they speed his ship home. What is the effect of this allusion? [Possible answers: It suggests a similarity between the two men; it suggests that this is an archetypal journey that is both physical and spiritual; it gives the poem a classical flavor; it confirms the poem as a literary ballad.]

A Part VI

FIRST VOICE

"But tell me, tell me! speak again,
Thy soft response renewing—
What makes that ship drive on so fast?
What is the ocean doing?"

SECOND VOICE

"Still as a slave before his lord,
The ocean hath no blast;°
His great bright eye most silently
Up to the Moon is cast—

If he may know which way to go;
For she guides him smooth or grim.
See, brother, see! how graciously
She looketh down on him."

415. blast: wind.

FIRST VOICE

"But why drives on that ship so fast,
Without or wave or wind?"°

The Mariner hath been cast into a trance; for the angelic power causeth the vessel to drive northward faster than human life could endure.

423. without . . . wind: with neither wave nor wind.

SECOND VOICE

"The air is cut away before,
And closes from behind.

Fly, brother, fly! more high, more high!
Or we shall be belated:
For slow and slow that ship will go,
When the Mariner's trance is abated."°

429. abated: lessened.

I woke, and we were sailing on
As in a gentle weather:
'Twas night, calm night, the Moon was high;
The dead men stood together.

The supernatural motion is retarded; the Mariner awakes, and his penance begins anew.

All stood together on the deck,
For a charnel dungeon° fitter:
All fixed on me their stony eyes,
That in the Moon did glitter.

435. charnel (chär′nəl) **dungeon:** burial vault.

The pang, the curse, with which they died,
Had never passed away:
I could not draw my eyes from theirs,
Nor turn them up to pray.

Skill Link

Analyzing and Responding to a Critical Review

Coleridge confessed in his *Biographia Literaria* that he had written the following epigram, which had been anonymously published earlier.

To the Author of the Ancient Mariner
Your poem must eternal be,
Dear sir! It cannot fail,
For 'tis incomprehensible,
And without head or tail.

Activities

Ask students to do the following:

1. Paraphrase Coleridge's "review" of his ballad, noting the qualities he ascribes to it.
2. Compare Coleridge's opinion with their own response to the ballad. For example, students may indeed find the ballad eternal, but not in the way Coleridge means.
3. Invite students to discuss their points of agreement and disagreement with Coleridge's witty self-assessment.

And now this spell was snapt: once more
I viewed the ocean green,
And looked far forth, yet little saw
Of what had else° been seen—

The curse is finally expiated [removed, after penance is done].

445. had else: would have otherwise.

Like one, that on a lonesome road
Doth walk in fear and dread,
And having once turned round walks on,
And turns no more his head;
Because he knows, a frightful fiend
Doth close behind him tread.

But soon there breathed a wind on me,
Nor sound nor motion made:
Its path was not upon the sea,
In ripple or in shade.

It raised my hair, it fanned my cheek
Like a meadow gale of spring—
It mingled strangely with my fears,
Yet it felt like a welcoming.

Swiftly, swiftly flew the ship,
Yet she sailed softly too:
Sweetly, sweetly blew the breeze—
On me alone it blew.

Oh! dream of joy! is this indeed
The lighthouse top I see?
Is this the hill? is this the kirk?
Is this mine own countree?

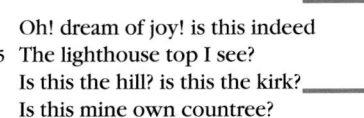

"And on the bay the moonlight lay,
And the shadow of the Moon."

And the ancient Mariner beholdeth his native country.

We drifted o'er the harbor bar,
And I with sobs did pray—
O let me be awake, my God!
Or let me sleep alway.

The harbor bay was clear as glass,
So smoothly it was strewn!°
And on the bay the moonlight lay,
And the shadow of the Moon.

473. strewn: stretched out; calmed.

The rock shone bright, the kirk no less,
That stands above the rock:
The moonlight steeped in silentness
The steady weathercock.°

479. weathercock: rooster-shaped weather vane.

D Reading Skills and Strategies

Using Glosses

This marginal note not only contains Coleridge's own words about the curse but explains the meaning of the word *expiated.* Remind students that they can use these glosses in three ways: (1) to provide clues to meaning; (2) to confirm their own ideas about what they've read; or (3) to correct their ideas.

E Critical Thinking

Synthesizing

? How did the sea appear to the Mariner earlier? [It was rotting.] Why does he see it now as green? [Possible answer: Green is the color of birth or, in this use, rebirth. Just as the expiation of sin is a rebirth for the Mariner, the sea is transformed from death to life.]

F Elements of Literature

Literary Ballad

? What literary devices does Coleridge use to convey the joy the Mariner feels at being wafted home? [Possible answer: The alliteration of the *s* sound and the assonance in *sweetly, breeze,* and *me* all mimic the soft wind, creating a sense of harmony and joy at speeding home.]

G Advanced Learners

Parallelism

? How do these lines mirror some of the opening lines? (If needed, refer students to ll. 22–24.) [Possible answers: They return to the ship's starting place, where the poet noted the disappearance of the same landmarks; they bring the reader full circle; they show the joy of returning to the familiar.]

H Reading Skills and Strategies

Reading Archaic Words

Ask students to identify the archaic usage and spelling. [*Mine* is archaic for *my; countree* is an archaic spelling for *country.*] At one time, *mine* preceded words beginning with vowels, while *my* preceded words beginning with consonants.

Getting Students Involved

Cooperative Learning

The Mariner on Trial. Have students hold a mock trial for the ancient Mariner upon his return to shore. Choose two teams of five, one group holding the Mariner accountable for the deaths of his crewmates and one contending that he is a victim, unjustly condemned for an act that is not even a legal crime. Each team should gather textual evidence, logical arguments, and any ethical and environmental arguments that students think are appropriate. They should then present their case with visual aids and/or use themselves as witnesses. Appoint one student to act as trial judge, taking responsibility for the orderly conduct of the trial. After both teams have made their presentations, ask the class as a whole to determine which side made the stronger case.

Ⓐ Struggling Readers

Getting the Main Idea

? What is happening now? [Possible answer: The Mariner sees a seraph on the body or "corse" of every sailor. Each seraph is waving a hand and shining like a beacon to the land.]

Ⓑ Cultural Connections

Choirs of Angels

In Christian theology, the nine choirs of angels are, in descending order, Seraphim, Cherubim, and Thrones in the first circle; Dominions, Virtues, and Powers in the second; and Principalities, Archangels, and Angels in the third. The word *angel* comes from the Greek *angelos,* meaning "messenger." Some of the orders are named from references in the New Testament (Ephesians 1:21 and Colossians 1:16).

Ⓒ Elements of Literature

Literary Ballad

? What elements of a literary ballad can you identify in this stanza? [Possible answers: internal and end rhyme; alliteration, assonance, and consonance; also supernatural elements in the seraphs whose silence is like music.]

Responding to the Art

This illustration shows the seraphs on the bay.

Activity. Ask students to tell what they think is distinctively Romantic about this illustration. [Possible answers: The angels are themselves fantastic and mysterious; they emerge from a shadowy world and seem to multiply and take clearer form as they approach; their wings even seem to beat; the moon and the nighttime setting are also eerily evocative; no human presence appears in the illustration.]

And the bay was white with silent light,
Till rising from the same,
Full many shapes, that shadows were,
In crimson colors came.

The angelic spirits leave the dead bodies,

A little distance from the prow
Those crimson shadows were:
I turned my eyes upon the deck—
Oh, Christ! what saw I there!

And appear in their own forms of light.

Each corse lay flat, lifeless and flat,
And, by the holy rood!°
A man all light, a seraph man,°
On every corse there stood.

This seraph band, each waved his hand:
It was a heavenly sight!
They stood as signals to the land,
Each one a lovely light;

This seraph band, each waved his hand,
No voice did they impart—
No voice; but oh! the silence sank
Like music on my heart.

But soon I heard the dash of oars,
I heard the Pilot's cheer;
My head was turned perforce away
And I saw a boat appear.

The Pilot and the Pilot's boy,
I heard them coming fast:
Dear Lord in Heaven! it was a joy
The dead men could not blast.

489. rood: crucifix.

490. seraph man: angel of the highest rank.

"Full many shapes, that shadows were,
In crimson colors came."

Making the Connections

Connecting with the Legend: Wagner and Scott

Choice 7 on p. 708 likens the *Rime* to the legend of the Flying Dutchman, a story from the European maritime tradition about a spectral ship doomed to wander forever because of the captain's rash pledge to sail around the Cape of Good Hope in a storm. In his 1843 opera *The Flying Dutchman (Der Fliegende Hollander)*, Richard Wagner offers the captain salvation: The curse is lifted when a Norwegian maiden agrees to marry him. Interested students could choose an orchestral piece or song from Wagner's opera to play for the class.

Another version of the legend puts the ship in the North Sea. Sir Walter Scott uses this setting in his 1813 narrative poem *Rokeby*, in which murder and plague doom a ship to be banned from every harbor. Interested students could compare these works with Coleridge's *Rime*.

I saw a third—I heard his voice:
It is the Hermit good!
He singeth loud his godly hymns
That he makes in the wood.
He'll shrieve° my soul, he'll wash away
The Albatross's blood.

512. shrieve (shrēv): archaic for "after hearing confession, release from guilt."

Part VII

The Hermit of the Wood,

This Hermit good lives in that wood
Which slopes down to the sea.
How loudly his sweet voice he rears!
He loves to talk with marineres
That come from a far countree.

He kneels at morn, and noon, and eve—
He hath a cushion plump:
It is the moss that wholly hides
The rotted old oak stump.

The skiff boat° neared: I heard them talk,
"Why, this is strange, I trow!°
Where are those lights so many and fair,
That signal made but now?"

523. skiff boat: rowboat.
524. trow: archaic for "believe."

Approacheth the ship with wonder.

"Strange, by my faith!" the Hermit said—
"And they answered not our cheer!
The planks looked warped! and see those sails,
How thin they are and sere!
I never saw aught° like to them,
Unless perchance it were

531. aught: anything.

Brown skeletons of leaves that lag°
My forest brook along;
When the ivy tod° is heavy with snow,
And the owlet whoops to the wolf below,
That eats the she-wolf's young."

533. lag: drift; move more slowly than the current.
535. ivy tod: clump of ivy.

"Dear Lord! it hath a fiendish look—
(The Pilot made reply)
I am afeared"—"Push on, push on!"
Said the Hermit cheerily.

The boat came closer to the ship,
But I nor spake nor stirred;
The boat came close beneath the ship,
And straight° a sound was heard.

545. straight: straightaway; at once.

D Critical Thinking

Evaluating

? Is the shift in focus to the Hermit effective? Why or why not? [Sample responses: Yes, the Hermit might represent all that the Mariner should be: pious, wholesome, joyful. His presence is explained; or no, the Hermit seems unrelated to the story, a distraction.] **The presence of the Hermit, a stock figure in medieval literature, is one of the many clues that suggests the Mariner's tale is set in the Middle Ages.**

E Struggling Readers

Summarizing

Ask students to summarize the events in Part VI. [Possible response: A supernatural force drives the ship homeward. When the Mariner is able to look at the sea and not at his dead companions, a gentle breeze blows only on him. When the ship gets into the harbor, an angel stands over every corpse and sends a beacon to the land. The beacons are answered by a boat rowed by a Pilot, the Pilot's son, and a Hermit.]

F Reading Skills and Strategies

Finding Sequence of Events

? What has led up to this point? [The Pilot's boat, containing the Pilot, the Pilot's boy, and the Hermit, is approaching the Mariner's ship. When the Pilot is afraid of moving closer, the Hermit says to keep going, so the boat approaches the gunwales.]

Listening to Music

"The Great Silkie" (also called "Silkie," "The Great Silkie of Sule Skerry," "Grey Silkie," etc.) (Traditional), performed by Judy Collins and Joan Baez.

Among the many supernatural legends of seafaring peoples are the tales of silkies (also spelled *selkies* and *selchies,* and sometimes called Finns or roane), enchanted creatures who are seals at sea but take on human form when on land. Number 113 of Francis Child's famous collection of British ballads tells the dramatic story of one such creature, "The Great Silkie of Sule Skerry." (A skerry is a small, rocky isle.) Originating in the Orkney or Shetland islands between Scotland and Norway, the ballad has several variants.

Activity

Have students listen to the folk ballad after reading *The Rime of the Ancient Mariner* and consider what the two works have in common. Remind students that folk ballads are anonymously composed and passed on in the oral tradition; Coleridge's poem is a literary ballad, consciously written to imitate a folk-ballad style.

Have students work in pairs to condense Coleridge's poem to manageable length and set it to original music or music borrowed from another folk song.

Ⓐ Struggling Readers

Summarizing

Providing help as needed, ask students to summarize what unexpected event happens in these stanzas. [Possible answer: The ship sinks, but the Mariner is saved by being taken into the Pilot's boat.]

Ⓑ Elements of Literature

Literary Ballad

? What elements of popular ballads do you find here? [Possible answers: Because the rowboat is caught in the maelstrom or whirlpool of the sinking ship, there is a feeling of doom. The shrieking, praying, and insane laughter of those in the boat accelerates the action. The Mariner is assumed to be the devil, a stock character in folk ballads. There is both suspense and a sense of the unpredictable and the uncanny.]

Responding to the Art

The illustrations on these pages show the rapid sequence of events surrounding the sinking of the Mariner's ship.

Activity. Ask students to decide which elements are most dramatic in these illustrations. [Sample responses: The human figure in the first or third illustrations; the whirl of the sea; the near-verticality of the pitched boat in the last illustration; the eeriness of clouds, shore, and mist.]

Under the water it rumbled on,
Still louder and more dread:
It reached the ship, it split the bay;
The ship went down like lead.

The ship suddenly sinketh.

Stunned by that loud and dreadful sound,
Which sky and ocean smote,°
Like one that hath been seven days drowned
My body lay afloat;
But swift as dreams, myself I found
Within the Pilot's boat.

The ancient Mariner is saved in the Pilot's boat.

551. smote: struck.

Upon the whirl, where sank the ship,
The boat spun round and round;
And all was still, save that the hill
Was telling of the sound.

I moved my lips—the Pilot shrieked
And fell down in a fit;
The holy Hermit raised his eyes,
And prayed where he did sit.

I took the oars: the Pilot's boy,
Who now doth crazy go,
Laughed loud and long, and all the while
His eyes went to and fro.
"Ha! ha!" quoth he, "full plain I see,
The Devil knows how to row."

And now, all in my own countree,
I stood on the firm land!
The Hermit stepped forth from the boat,
And scarcely he could stand.

"It reached the ship, it split the bay;
The ship went down like lead."

Professional Notes

Critical Comment: Coleridge

Critic Martin Gardner says that Coleridge was a compulsive talker. The essayist Charles Lamb once imagined himself button-holed by Coleridge and forced to escape by snipping off the button. Five hours later, he returned, found Coleridge, eyes closed, still holding the button and talking eloquently. Ask students how this portrait of Coleridge connects with the character of the ancient Mariner.

"O shrieve me, shrieve me, holy man!"
The Hermit crossed° his brow.
"Say quick," quoth he, "I bid thee say—
What manner of man art thou?" **C**

The ancient Mariner earnestly entreateth the Hermit to shrieve him; and the penance of life falls on him.

575. crossed: made the sign of the cross.

Forthwith° this frame of mine was wrenched
With a woeful agony,
Which forced me to begin my tale;
And then it left me free. **D**

578. forthwith: at once.

Since then, at an uncertain hour,
That agony returns:
And till my ghastly tale is told,
This heart within me burns. **E**

And ever and anon throughout his future life an agony constraineth him to travel from land to land;

"Upon the whirl, where sank the ship,
The boat spun round and round."

"'Ha! ha!' quoth he, 'full plain I see,
The Devil knows how to row.'"

C Reading Skills and Strategies

Reading Archaic Words

Although the words *shrieve* and *shrift* are still in use, they are rare and students may not know them. Encourage students to use a dictionary or other resource to find out what the Mariner requests. [He wants absolution for sin, which generally follows confession but precedes penance.]

D Elements of Literature

Literary Ballad

? Like a prose narrative, a literary ballad usually has a climax. Where and what is the climax here? [In l. 581 the Mariner realizes that telling the tale brings some peace.]

E Struggling Readers

Paraphrasing

Ask students to paraphrase this important stanza. [Sample answer: At unpredictable moments, a feeling of agony grips the mourner and will not go away until he tells his tale.]

Assessing Learning

Check Test: Short Answer

1. Who is the narrator of the story? [the Mariner]

2. To whom does the Narrator tell his story? [the Wedding Guest]

3. What does the Mariner do that appears to cause suffering for the crew? [He kills an albatross.]

4. Who "wins" in the game of dice? [Life-in-Death; the woman on the skeleton ship]

5. What is the effect of the story on the Wedding Guest? [At times he is fearful, but he feels compelled to listen. Overall, he is "a sadder and a wiser man."]

Informal Assessment

Observation Assessment. Use the following checklist to assess students' comprehension and communication as they discuss the story.

1 = Rarely 2 = Sometimes 3 = Often

___ Takes part in discussion
___ Demonstrates independent reasoning
___ Processes others' remarks and ideas
___ Cites textual support for ideas
___ Relates the text to personal experience
___ Makes connections between ideas
___ Challenges the text

A Elements of Literature

Literary Ballad

? In some ways, this stanza suggests why the ballad persists as an element of folk culture. Why? [Possible answers: Some tales just beg to be retold. It is as if there is some kind of strange destiny in the retelling of some tales. Some tales embody the kinds of universal messages that must be shared.]

B Reading Skills and Strategies

Reading Archaic Words

? What three archaic or lesser-known words do you find in this passage? What more modern words might you substitute for them? [Bower-arbor; vesper-evening prayer; biddeth-calls]

C Elements of Literature

Theme/Moral

? What is the moral of the ballad? [Students will probably say that it is to love all creatures great and small.] **Point out that these words echo the first stanza of a Protestant hymn by C. F. Alexander composed in 1848:**

All things bright and beautiful
All creatures great and small
All things wise and wonderful
The Lord God made them all.

D Critical Thinking

Expressing an Opinion

? How relevant is this moral to readers today? [Possible response: The moral is a lesson that humanity must learn over and over—that we must respect all life.]

I pass, like night, from land to land;
I have strange power of speech;
That moment that his face I see,
I know the man that must hear me:
To him my tale I teach.

What loud uproar bursts from that door!
The wedding guests are there:
But in the garden bower the bride
And bridemaids singing are:
And hark the little vesper bell,
Which biddeth me to prayer!

O Wedding Guest! this soul hath been
Alone on a wide wide sea:
So lonely 'twas, that God himself
Scarce seemed there to be.

O sweeter than the marriage feast,
'Tis sweeter far to me,
To walk together to the kirk
With a goodly company!—

To walk together to the kirk,
And all together pray,
While each to his great Father bends,
Old men, and babes, and loving friends
And youths and maidens gay!

Farewell, farewell! but this I tell
To thee, thou Wedding Guest!
He prayeth well, who loveth well
Both man and bird and beast.

He prayeth best, who loveth best
All things both great and small;
For the dear God who loveth us,
He made and loveth all.

The Mariner, whose eye is bright,
Whose beard with age is hoar,
Is gone: and now the Wedding Guest
Turned from the bridegroom's door.

He went like one that hath been stunned,
And is of sense forlorn:°
A sadder and a wiser man,
He rose the morrow morn.

"The Mariner, whose eye is bright,
Whose beard with age is hoar,
Is gone."

And to teach, by his own example, love and reverence to all things that God made and loveth.

623. **forlorn:** deprived.

Making the Connections

Connecting with the Theme: "The Power of Imagination"

Students will have little trouble seeing the imaginative power of *The Rime of the Ancient Mariner;* now ask them to see how this work reflects its age. Have students turn to the list of the characteristics of Romanticism on p. 630 and evaluate whether each is reflected in Coleridge's poem, and if so, how. Students may successfully work on this task in small groups. Each group could then choose a spokesperson for a panel discussion of this question: How does Coleridge's imagination reflect the Romantic era?

PRIMARY **Sources** A LETTER

Joseph Cottle was a close friend of the poet and the first publisher of *Lyrical Ballads.*

Coleridge Describes His Addiction

TO JOSEPH COTTLE

April 26, 1814

You have poured oil in the raw and festering wound of an old friend's conscience, Cottle! but it is *oil of vitriol*! I but barely glanced at the middle of the first page of your letter, and have seen no more of it—not from resentment, God forbid! but from the state of my bodily and mental sufferings, that scarcely permitted human fortitude to let in a new visitor of affliction.

The object of my present reply is to state the case just as it is—first, that for ten years the anguish of my spirit has been indescribable, the sense of my danger staring, but the conscience of my GUILT worse, far worse than all! I have prayed with drops of agony on my brow, trembling not only before the justice of my Maker, but even before the mercy of my Redeemer. "I gave thee so many talents. What hast thou done with them?" Secondly, overwhelmed as I am with the sense of my direful infirmity, I have never attempted to disguise or conceal the cause. On the contrary, not only to friends have I stated the whole case with tears, and the very bitterness of shame; but in two instances, I have warned young men, mere acquaintances, who had spoken of having taken laudanum, of the direful consequences, by an ample exposition of its tremendous effects on myself.

Thirdly, though before God I cannot lift up my eyelids, and only do not despair of his mercy, because to despair would be adding crime to crime, yet to my fellow men I may say, that I was seduced into the ACCURSED habit ignorantly. I had been almost bedridden for many months with swelling in the knees. In a medical journal I unhappily met with an account of a cure performed in a similar case, or what appeared to me so, by rubbing in of laudanum, at the same time taking a given dose internally. It acted like a charm, like a miracle! I recovered the use of my limbs, of my appetite, of my spirits, and this continued for near a fortnight. At length, the unusual stimulus subsided, the complaint returned—the supposed remedy was recurred to—but I cannot go through the dreary history. Suffice it to say, that effects were produced, which acted on me by terror and cowardice of PAIN and sudden death, not (so help me God!) by any temptation of pleasure, or expectation, or desire of exciting pleasurable sensations. On the very contrary, Mrs. Morgan and her sister will bear witness so far, as to say that the longer I abstained, the higher my spirits were, the keener my enjoyments—till the moment, the direful moment arrived, when my pulse began to fluctuate, my heart to palpitate, and such a dreadful falling abroad, as it were, of my whole frame, such intolerable restlessness and incipient bewilderment, that in the last of my several attempts to abandon the dire poison, I exclaimed in agony, what I now repeat in seriousness and solemnity, "I am too poor to hazard this!" Had I but a few hundred pounds, but £200, half to send to Mrs. Coleridge, and half to place myself in a private madhouse, where I could procure nothing but what a physician thought proper, and where a medical attendant could be constantly with me for two or three months (in less than that time, life or death would be determined) then there might be hope. Now there is none! O God! how willing would I place myself under Dr. Fox in his establishment; for my case is a species of madness, only that it is a derangement, an utter impotence of the volition, and not of the intellectual faculties. You bid me rouse myself: go, bid a man paralytic in both arms to rub them briskly together, and that will cure him. "Alas," he would reply, "that I cannot move my arms is my complaint and my misery."

Your affectionate, but most afflicted,

S. T. Coleridge

Primary Sources

In this letter to his publisher, Coleridge describes how he became addicted to laudanum and his futile efforts to overcome the problem. Coleridge scholar Martin Gardner says this about Coleridge's addiction: "The older Coleridge became, the heavier he used opium. It was a habit he could not shake, and a never-ceasing source of misery, both physical and spiritual. His nightmares became more frequent, more severe. He felt himself approaching madness. One of his letters to Dr. James Gillman, a physician and friend, was a heart-rending plea for escape from 'the terror that haunts my mind.' The final eighteen years of his sad, slovenly life were spent in Dr. Gillman's home, at Highgate, where his opium doses could be carefully kept to a minimum." In Coleridge's own epitaph, he said he found "death in life." This may allude to his addicted state. Of course, this was also the name of a character in his famous *Rime*.

E Appreciating Language

Idioms

"Oil of vitriol" is another name for sulfuric acid. It is sometimes used in metaphoric exaggerations—not just pouring acid on a wound, but *oil of vitriol.*

F Critical Thinking

Making Judgments

? What fear does Coleridge express here? [Because of his addiction, he is wasting his talent.] Was this a realistic fear? [Yes, addiction dims one's talents and consumes one's time and attention.] Note the allusion to the New Testament parable of the talents (Matthew 25:1–30).

G Critical Thinking

Extending the Text

? In what forums do addicts today provide such warnings? [in organizations like Alcoholics Anonymous]

Skill Link

Evaluating Sources of Information

Ask students how the picture Coleridge presents of himself in this letter differs from the description provided by Dorothy Wordsworth (p. 682) and the biographical information on p. 678. Have students organize their inquiry by means of a chart. In this chart, students should record not only facts and details gathered from these sources, but their assessment of each writer's motivation and objectivity. As a final step in this process, ask students to form questions for further research or study, based on contradictions or missing information in the sources.

Connections

In this excerpt from a modern travel book, Bruce Chatwin tells of a dreadful 1593 voyage by John Davis that resembles the one in *The Rime of the Ancient Mariner* in many respects. An account of this voyage appeared in Hakluyt's book, which Coleridge was reading at about the time he wrote his famous poem.

A Historical Connections

Navigation

The Strait of Magellan is a narrow passageway of water between the southernmost mainland of South America and the islands of Tierra del Fuego. Before the opening of the Panama Canal, this waterway was part of the shortest route between the Atlantic and Pacific oceans. The strait was named for the Portuguese explorer, Ferdinand Magellan, who led the first European expedition through the passage in his quest to sail around the world in 1520.

B Struggling Readers

Summarizing

Invite struggling readers to summarize what they have read so far. [Possible answer: Davis, the commander of the *Desire,* had begun a journey with Cavendish's fleet. He became separated from Cavendish near Port Desire; his captain, Cavendish, then took off, thinking Davis had deserted him.]

C Historical Connections

Navigation

Only in recent centuries have developments in navigational techniques allowed ships to determine accurately the positions of known islands. At one time, even if a sailing ship sighted land, it might wait three weeks for favorable winds and then not be able to find suitable anchorage.

D Critical Thinking

Making Connections

? How does this action compare with what happened on the ship of the ancient Mariner? [Possible answers: The Mariner and these men engage in senseless killing; both the Mariner and these men kill innocent birds; there is no connection: The Mariner kills the albatross for no reason—these men kill the penguins to provision their ship and survive.]

Connections — A Travel Book

In this passage from his classic travel book, the writer Bruce Chatwin (1940–1989) tells a chilling story. Before this extract opens, Chatwin has said: "Albatrosses and penguins are the last birds I'd want to murder." He had been describing the penguin colony in Patagonia, on the south coast of Argentina. Now he flashes back to 1593.

from In Patagonia

Bruce Chatwin

On October 30, 1593, the ship *Desire,* of 120 tons, limping home to England, dropped anchor in the river at Port Desire, this being her fourth visit since Thomas Cavendish named the place in her, his flagship's, honor, seven years before.

The captain was now John Davis, a Devon man, the most skilled navigator of his generation. Behind him were three Arctic voyages in search of the Northwest Passage. Before him were two books of seamanship and six fatal cuts of a Japanese pirate's sword.

Davis had sailed on Cavendish's Second Voyage "intended for the South Sea." The fleet left Plymouth on August 26, 1591, the Captain-General in the galleon *Leicester;* the other ships were the *Roebuck,* the *Desire,* the *Daintie,* and the *Black Pinnace*. . . .

Cavendish was puffed up with early success, hating his officers and crew. On the coast of Brazil, he stopped to sack the town of Santos. A gale scattered the ships off the Patagonian coast, but they met up, as arranged, at Port Desire.

A The fleet entered the Magellan Strait with the southern winter already begun. A sailor's frostbitten nose fell off when he blew it. Beyond Cape Froward, they ran into northwesterly gales and sheltered in a tight cove with the wind howling over their mastheads. **B** Reluctantly, Cavendish agreed to revictual in Brazil and return the following spring.

On the night of May 20, off Port Desire, the Captain-General changed tack without warning. At dawn, the *Desire* and the *Black Pinnace* were alone on the sea. Davis made for port, thinking his commander would join him as before, but Cavendish set course for Brazil and thence to St. Helena. One day he lay down in his cabin and died, perhaps of apoplexy, cursing Davis for desertion: "This villain that hath been the death of me."

Davis disliked the man but was no traitor. The worst of the winter over, he went south again to look for the Captain-General. Gales blew the two ships in among some undiscovered islands, now known as the Falklands.

C This time, they passed the Strait and out into the Pacific. In a storm off Cape Pilar, the *Desire* lost the *Pinnace,* which went down with all hands. Davis was alone at the helm, praying for a speedy end, when the sun broke through the clouds. He took bearings, fixed his position, and so regained the calmer water of the Strait.

He sailed back to Port Desire, the crew scurvied and mutinous and lice lying in their flesh, "clusters of lice as big as peason, yea, and some as big as beans." He repaired the ship as best he could. The men lived off eggs, gulls, baby seals, scurvy grass, and the fish called *pejerrey.* On this diet they were restored to health.

D Ten miles down the coast, there was an island, the original Penguin Island, where the sailors clubbed twenty thousand birds to death. They had no natural enemies and were unafraid of their murderers. John Davis ordered the penguins dried and salted and stowed fourteen thousand in the hold. . . .

As they came up to the Equator, the penguins took their revenge. In them bred a "loathsome worme" about an inch long. The

Connecting Across Texts

Connecting to *The Rime of the Ancient Mariner*

Is it possible that Coleridge used John Davis's voyage as the basis for his tale? What are the similarities between these accounts, and, just as important, what are the differences? Ask students to work in pairs to compare and contrast the works. They might focus on these criteria and add more of their own:

- Setting
- Types of horrors, who suffers, dies, and how
- Characteristics of the survivors
- The role of crime, punishment, and redemption

Then ask students to work on their own to write a short persuasive essay on whether Coleridge may have been either familiar with or used the elements of this tale.

worms ate everything, iron only excepted—clothes, bedding, boots, hats, leather lashings, and live human flesh. The worms gnawed through the ship's side and threatened to sink her. The more worms the men killed, the more they multiplied.

Around the Tropic of Cancer, the crew came down with scurvy. Their ankles swelled and their chests, and their parts swelled so horribly that "they could neither stand nor lie nor go."

The Captain could scarcely speak for sorrow. Again he prayed for a speedy end. He asked the men to be patient; to give thanks to God and accept his chastisement. But the men were raging mad, and the ship howled with the groans and curses of the dying. Only Davis and a ship's boy were in health, of the seventy-six who left Plymouth. By the end there were five men who could move and work the ship.

And so, lost and wandering on the sea, with topsails and spritsails torn, the rotten hulk drifted, rather than sailed, into the harbor of Berehaven on Bantry Bay on June 11, 1593. The smell disgusted the people of that quiet fishing village. . . .

"The Southern Voyage of John Davis" appeared in Hakluyt's edition of 1600. Two centuries passed and another Devon man, Samuel Taylor Coleridge, set down the 625 controversial lines of *The Ancient Mariner,* with its hammering repetitions and story of crime, wandering, and expiation.

John Davis and the Mariner have these in common: a voyage to the Black South, the murder of a bird or birds, the nemesis which follows, the drift through the tropics, the rotting ship, the curses of dying men. Lines 236–239 are particularly resonant of the Elizabethan voyage:

> The many men, so beautiful!
> And they all dead did lie:
> And a thousand thousand slimy things
> Lived on; and so did I.

In *The Road to Xanadu,* the American scholar John Livingston Lowes traced the Mariner's victim to a "disconsolate Black Albitross" shot by one Hatley, the mate of Captain George Shelvocke's privateer in the eighteenth century. Wordsworth had a copy of this voyage and showed it to Coleridge when the two men tried to write the poem together. . . .

Lowes demonstrated how the voyages in Hakluyt and Purchas fueled Coleridge's imagination. "The mighty great roaring of ice" that John Davis witnessed on an earlier voyage off Greenland reappears in line 61: "It cracked and growled, and roared and howled." But he did not, apparently, consider the likelihood that Davis's voyage to the Strait gave Coleridge the backbone for his poem.

Engraving (1875) by Gustave Doré for Coleridge's *The Rime of the Ancient Mariner.*

E Reading Skills and Strategies

Responding to the Text

? What effects do these details have on you? [Possible response: These details are horrifying. They make it clear that the men did not just die; instead, they endured absolute horror and misery before dying.]

Reading Check

a. The poem begins with an omniscient narrator, but from l. 41 on, the narrator is the ancient Mariner, speaking to the Wedding Guest. The Mariner kills an albatross—the embodiment of love and good fortune. Because of his act of irrational destruction, the Mariner is punished with a life of permanent alienation. The crew dies but continues to sail the ship, and the Mariner's journey continues as he does penance for his sin. Eventually, he returns home, but he is fated always to travel and retell his story, thereby reliving his horrors and shame.

b. The ship is becalmed; the Mariner and crew suffer from heat and thirst.

c. A woman (Life-in-Death) and Death are the occupants. The crewmen die, leaving the Mariner the last living occupant of the ship.

d. A "wicked whisper" makes his heart "as dry as dust." When he turns his attention away from himself and blesses the water snakes, he is able to pray.

e. The Mariner says he is destined to travel from land to land, telling his tale as penance for his sin. His lesson is to respect all living things.

(Answers continue on p. T706.)

MAKING MEANINGS

First Thoughts [Respond]

1. Possible response: People should have compassion for living things. [Answers will vary.]

Shaping Interpretations [Interpret]

2. The wedding is mentioned at the beginning, in the middle (ll. 345–346), and at the end of the poem. The joy of the wedding party (a celebration of love) contrasts with the Mariner's grim tale (a lack of love).
3. The Mariner begins by seeing himself as cursed and his surroundings as ugly. When he recognizes the beauty of the water snakes and blesses them, he begins to love, and the albatross falls from his neck. The changes are believable because in his isolation he can recognize his need for other living beings.
4. Shame focuses on the self; it is the concern that one has lost respect. Guilt focuses on the victims of one's actions; it is a feeling of self-reproach for having done something unethical. The Mariner experiences shame after he kills the albatross. He feels guilt when he acknowledges the great harm he caused the bird and his crew.
5. The Mariner's immediate penance is to suffer alone on the ship. His lifetime penance is to be an outcast, wandering and telling his story to relieve his agony. Students may say that, literally, the penance makes little sense, for the Mariner only shot a bird; allegorically, however, the penance is fitting, for the albatross is a symbol of all living creatures.
6. One who loves generously and completely will live happily and well. To the Mariner, this moral is sufficient, but students may have various suggestions for enhancing the ending.
7. The guest is sad because he has heard a tragic story and wiser because he has learned the importance of loving others. Kubla Khan hears ancestral voices prophesying war.
8. The notes help summarize the plot. They do not alter the meaning of the poem but do add a critical or scholarly voice. Students may feel the notes are part of the poem and should be consulted, or they may feel the original poem should stand alone; in either case, students should explain and support their views.

MAKING MEANINGS

First Thoughts

1. Do you think that this poem tells us something significant about human conduct? Why or why not? If so, would it apply to most people?

> **Reading Check**
>
> a. Who is presented as the **narrator** of the ballad? To whom is he telling his story? In a **time line,** summarize the main events of the Mariner's story.
>
> b. According to Part II, what consequences follow the Mariner's killing of the albatross?
>
> c. Who are the occupants of the strange ship that appears in Part III? What results from their appearance?
>
> d. In Part IV, why is the Mariner unable to pray? What happens that enables him to pray?
>
> e. At the end of the ballad, how does the Mariner describe his current life? What lesson does he draw for the Wedding Guest from this tale?

Shaping Interpretations

2. Where in the poem is the wedding mentioned? How does this context for the ballad affect your response to it?
3. Describe in detail the changing states of the Mariner in Part IV. Given the circumstances, are these changes believable?
4. After he shoots the albatross, the Mariner experiences both shame and guilt. What is the difference between these two emotions? Where in the poem does he experience each emotion?
5. What is the Mariner's "penance" (line 408)? What penance does he have left to do? Does it seem fair to you that he should have to do any sort of penance? Why? (Refer to your Quickwrite notes for ideas.)
6. Explain in your own terms the Mariner's **moral** (lines 612–617). Does the story indicate that he ought to have added something to his moral conclusion? Explain.
7. Why is the Wedding Guest sadder but wiser after hearing the Mariner's tale? What other figures in Coleridge's poems in this collection are also listening to a speaker?
8. What do you think of Coleridge's side notes to the poem? Do you think reading them alters the meaning of the poem? Should they be consulted in a careful reading of the poem? Why or why not?
9. This ballad is famous for its use of vivid **figurative language** and memorable sound devices. What do you think are several especially effective examples of **simile, metaphor, personification, alliteration, assonance,** and **internal rhyme**?
10. For the most part, the form of the poem is the regular **ballad stanza.** Occasionally, however, Coleridge varies the **meter** of the lines and the length of the stanzas. Read aloud several examples of such variations.
11. What differences do you notice between Coleridge's tale of the Ancient Mariner and the story described in Bruce Chatwin's *In Patagonia*? (See ***Connections*** on page 704.)

Extending the Text

12. There was a time in American history when almost every schoolchild could recite parts of *The Rime of the Ancient Mariner.* Find some stanzas that strike you as particularly quotable. What situations in contemporary life could you apply the lines to?

Challenging the Text

13. Coleridge once said that he would have preferred to write *The Rime of the Ancient Mariner* as a work of "pure imagination." He believed that it had "too much" of a moral, and that the moral was stated too openly. Do you agree or disagree with Coleridge about the message in his poem? Why?

9. In ll. 33–34, a simile likens the bride's beauty to that of a rose. In ll. 195–199, a metaphor describes Death and Life-in-Death, casting dice for the Mariner's life. Lines 41–44 personify the storm to show its power. In ll. 171–173, the repetition of *w* sounds speeds up the poem's rhythm and suggests the absent breeze. Assonance occurs in ll. 521–522 to emphasize the stump and enhance the lyrical quality of the stanza. Internal rhyme of "noon" and "tune" slows l. 381 to reflect the sudden stopping of the ship.
10. Lines 45–50, 248–252, and 586–588 exemplify breaks in the pattern. These shifts call attention to the events described and help avoid a singsong quality.
11. Possible response: In Coleridge's version, the bird is a single albatross, rather than thousands of penguins, and there is only one boat rather than several.

Reading Skills and Strategies

Reading Archaic Words

To give his ballad an antique flavor, Coleridge used many words that were **archaic,** or out of date, even at the time of his writing.

1. Here is a list of some of the archaic words in the poem. Note what each one means, and then substitute a modern **synonym** in the poem for each one. How does the flavor of the ballad change?

- **a.** *eftsoons* (line 12)
- **b.** *uprist* (line 98)
- **c.** *wist* (line 152)
- **d.** *Gramercy* (line 164)
- **e.** *clomb* (line 209)
- **f.** *wont* (line 338)
- **g.** *corses* (line 348)
- **h.** *rood* (line 489)
- **i.** *shrieve* (line 512)
- **j.** *trow* (line 524)

2. Are any forms of those words still in use today? Which ones?

3. Sometimes the archaic meaning of a word gives us a clue to the history of a word in current use. Look at the use of the word *jargoning* in line 362. What does the word *jargon* mean today? How is contemporary jargon like a bird twittering? (Check the etymology of the word in a dictionary.)

"With my crossbow / I shot the ALBATROSS."

Reading Skills and Strategies

This feature focuses on reading archaic language, which is applied to *The Rime of the Ancient Mariner.*

Possible Answers

1. a. at once, quickly; rapidly
b. rose up, came up; emerged
c. knew, understood; thought
d. an expression of gratitude; thank goodness
e. climbed, went up, rose; ascended
f. accustomed, used to; habituated to
g. corpses; bodies
h. crucifix; cross
i. release from guilt, forgive; absolve
j. believe, think; say

2. Forms still in use are risen *(uprist),* mercy *(Gramercy),* climb *(clomb),* wont *(wont),* corpses *(corses),* and shrive *(shrieve).*

3. The word *jargon* today can connote an unintelligible language or a language that is specific to a certain professional group. Contemporary jargon is like a bird twittering in that to anyone who is not part of the group, jargon is meaningless, empty noise.

Extending the Text [Synthesize/Evaluate]

12. Students' responses will vary but may include ll. 115–118 for its vivid simile and ll. 284–291, which express the relief of overcoming a terrible burden and rediscovering happiness.

Challenging the Text [Evaluate]

13. Some students may agree that the moral is unsuited to the tale or seems out of place when so baldly stated; others may say that if the poem were a work of "pure imagination," it would be impossible to understand and frustrating to read. Have students support their answers.

Grading Timesaver

Rubrics for each Choices assignment appear on p. 158 in the *Portfolio Management System.*

CHOICES: Building Your Portfolio

1. **Writer's Notebook** Other possible starting points are the route of the Mariner's ship, the sea creatures he encounters, even wedding customs of an earlier age.
2. **Analyzing a Theme** Recommend that students consider each focus point in turn—powers, dangers, and limits—and scan the text for images, events, or symbols that suggest this focus.
3. **Analyzing the Melodies of Language** Encourage students to consider how sound affects the pacing of the poem as well as the reader's emotional response.
4. **Analyzing the Plot** Another question students might consider is why the Wedding Guest listened at all.
5. **Interpreting Symbolism** To help students determine the elements of the allegory, direct them to write down the events that illustrate the moral of the tale. Then, have students name the symbolic purpose of the characters, setting, and plot as they refer to these significant events.
6. **Creative Writing** Suggest students brainstorm to list questions unanswered by the poem. Then, students can choose one or more questions to explore in their individual prose summaries.
7. **Creative Writing** Encourage students to link the Mariner's peace to the method by which he gains this temporary respite: confession. Students should review their narrative to make sure their solutions do not contradict the poem.
8. **Art** Students may create their art using a computer-drawing software program.

CHOICES: Building Your Portfolio

Writer's Notebook

1. Collecting Ideas for a Research Paper

The writer Bruce Chatwin did research to see if a real incident might have been the source of Coleridge's story of crime and punishment. (See ***Connections*** on page 704.) Chatwin's article or Coleridge's ballad might have raised some interesting questions in your mind that could be the subject of a research paper. Review the poem and the article, and jot down topics that you would like to know more about. You might start with expeditions to Patagonia or with John Davis's expedition of 1593. Save your notes.

Analyzing a Theme

2. Imagination Probing

There is general agreement that one of the major themes of "Kubla Khan" concerns the power of imagination. In a brief essay, analyze how Coleridge develops this theme in the poem. What symbolic hints does he provide about the powers, dangers, and limits of the human imagination? At the end of your essay, explain your own views of Coleridge's theme.

Analyzing the Melodies of Language

3. Sound and Sense

Listen to "The Rime of the Ancient Mariner" on an audiotape, or read it aloud yourself. Take notes on the sound effects: **meter, rhyme, alliteration,** and **assonance.** In an essay, analyze the effects of sound on the meaning of the poem. How does Coleridge use sound effects to create a mood and to evoke feelings? Cite specific lines from the poem to illustrate your points.

Analyzing the Plot

4. Asking Why

Like the old ballads, this strange story of the Ancient Mariner leaves some questions unanswered. For example, how could the Mariner tell that the Wedding Guest was a fit audience for this tale? Why did the Mariner shoot the albatross? How can the Mariner's punishment be regarded as fitting his crime? In a brief essay, analyze these or other questions that you think are unsatisfactorily resolved by the ballad.

Interpreting Symbolism

5. A Symbolizing Tale

An **allegory** is a prose or verse tale in which the characters, actions, and settings are **symbolic;** that is, they have both a literal and a figurative meaning. Could Coleridge's ballad be regarded as an allegory? If so, what do the various elements in the ballad symbolize? How may the tale as a whole be interpreted on an allegorical level? In a brief essay, explain your answers.

Creative Writing

6. Finishing Out the Khan

Suppose that we take Coleridge at his word and assume that "Kubla Khan" is really an unfinished fragment. Basing your idea on the existing lines, write a summary in prose of how the poem might be completed. Specify what you imagine the story line might be.

Creative Writing

7. Finding Peace

The Ancient Mariner has much in common with other legendary figures, such as the Flying Dutchman, who are condemned to wander the world in a quest for atonement or redemption. Imagine that the Mariner ultimately finds peace. Describe in a brief narrative how this might occur.

Art

8. Dreaming, Drawing, Remembering

Suppose that Coleridge kept a dream journal, and that he drew pictures in it to remind him of what he had seen in the dream that resulted in "Kubla Khan." Sketch three or four drawings that he might have used to help him recall the images he saw in his dream.

Assessing Learning

Standardized Test Preparation

For practice with ACT and SAT formats, see

- *Preparation for College Admission Exams,* p. 31

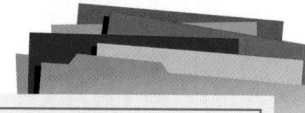

Collection 9

The Quest for Beauty

Theme

Realms of Gold *The Romantic poets embrace all aspects of existence in their quest for beauty and meaning in art and in life—the sublime and the ordinary, the passionate and the serene, the transitory and the permanent.*

Reading the Anthology

Reaching Struggling Readers

The *Reading Skills and Strategies: Reaching Struggling Readers* binder includes a Reading Strategies Handbook that offers concrete suggestions to help students who have difficulty reading and comprehending text or students who are reluctant readers. When a specific strategy is most appropriate for a selection, a correlation to the Handbook is provided at the bottom of the teacher's page under the head Struggling Readers. This head may also be used to introduce additional ideas for helping students read challenging texts.

Reading Beyond the Anthology

Read On

At the end of the Romantic Period collections, the grade twelve book includes an annotated bibliography of books suitable for extended reading. The suggested books are related to works in these collections by theme, by author, or by subject. To preview the Read On for the Romantic Period, please turn to p. T769.

HRW Library

The *HRW Library* offers novels, plays, and short-story collections for extended reading. Each book in the Library includes a major work and thematically or topically related Connections. Each book in the *HRW Library* is also accompanied by a Study Guide that provides teaching suggestions and worksheets. The title shown here will work well to extend the theme of Collection 9.

FRANKENSTEIN
Mary Shelley
This great Romantic novel is about the discovery of the secret of creation. In Mary Shelley's novel, the imagination turns demonic, and the new creation turns against its creator. A quintessential romantic story, *Frankenstein* is also recommended for Collection 11, The Paradox of Progress.

Collection 9 The Quest for Beauty

Resources for this Collection

Note: All resources for this collection are available for preview on the *One-Stop Planner CD-ROM 2 with Test Generator.* All worksheets and blackline masters may be printed from the CD-ROM.

Internet Resources
go.hrw.com LE0 12-9

Selection or Feature	Reading and Literary Skills	Vocabulary, Language, and Grammar
• **She Walks in Beauty** (p. 711) • **The Destruction of Sennacherib** (p. 712) • *from* **Don Juan, Canto II** (p. 714) • *from* **Childe Harold's Pilgrimage, Canto IV** (p. 721) George Gordon, Lord Byron **Primary Sources: Byron Writes to Shelley** (p. 724) **Spotlight On: Women Writers in the Romantic Period** (p. 726)	• *Graphic Organizers for Active Reading,* Worksheets pp. 60, 61, 62, 63	• *Grammar and Language Links:* Adverb Clauses, Worksheet p. 39 • *Language Workshop CD-ROM,* Types of Subordinate Clauses • *Daily Oral Grammar,* Transparency 25
• **Ozymandias** (p. 730) • **Ode to the West Wind** (p. 734) **Critical Comment: Shelley and the Ode** (p. 737) **Elements of Literature: Apostrophe** (p. 738) • **To a Skylark** (739) Percy Bysshe Shelley	• *Graphic Organizers for Active Reading,* Worksheets pp. 64, 65, 66 • *Literary Elements:* Transparency 20 Worksheet p. 61	• *Daily Oral Grammar,* Transparency 26
World Literature: China **Jade Flower Palace** (p. 744) Tu Fu	The World Literature feature offers students the opportunity to explore thematically linked literature from different world cultures. Structured activities called Finding Common Ground guide students' explorations of thematic connections between British and other world literature.	
• **On First Looking into Chapman's Homer** (p. 746) • **When I Have Fears** (p. 748) **Primary Sources: Keats's Last Letter** (p. 749) • **La Belle Dame sans Merci** (p. 750) • **Ode to a Nightingale** (p. 754) **Connections: O sweet spontaneous** (p. 758) E. E. Cummings **Critical Comment: Dialogue with the Soul** (p. 759) **Elements of Literature: Imagery** (p. 759) • **Ode on a Grecian Urn** (p. 760) John Keats **Critical Comment: The Arc of Experience** (p. 763)	• *Graphic Organizers for Active Reading,* Worksheets pp. 67, 68, 69, 70, 71	• *Grammar and Language Links:* Adjective Clauses, Worksheet p. 41 • *Language Workshop CD-ROM,* Types of Subordinate Clauses
World Literature: China • **Question and Answer Among the Mountains** (p. 767) • **Word-Pattern** (p. 767) • **To Tan-Ch'iu** (p. 767) Li Po	The World Literature feature offers students thematically linked literature from different world cultures. Structured activities called Finding Common Ground are provided to guide students' explorations of these thematic connections between British and other world literature.	
The English Language: Variety in Language (p. 770) John Algeo		
Writer's Workshop: Research Paper (p. 773)		
Language Workshop: Aspects of a Writer's Style (p. 777)		• *Workshop Resources,* p. 55
Learning for Life: Labor and Population Trends (p. 779)		

Other Resources for this Collection

- *Cross-Curricular Activities,* p. 9
- *Portfolio Management System,* Introduction to Portfolio Assessment, p. 1
- *Formal Assessment:*
  Literary Period Test, p. 150
  Literary Elements Test, p. 148
- *Test Generator,* Collection Test
- *Words to Own,* Worksheet p. 20

Writing	Listening and Speaking Viewing and Representing	Assessment
• *Portfolio Management System,* Rubrics for Choices, p. 160	• *Audio CD Library,* Disc 12, Tracks 2, 3, 4, 5 • *Portfolio Management System,* Rubrics for Choices, p. 160	• *Formal Assessment,* Selection Tests, pp. 133, 134, 135, 137 • *Test Generator (One-Stop Planner CD-ROM)* • *Preparation for College Admission Exams,* p. 33
• *Portfolio Management System,* Rubrics for Choices, p. 162	• *Audio CD Library,* Disc 12, Tracks 6, 7, 8 • *Viewing and Representing:* Fine Art Transparency 11 Worksheet p. 44 • *Portfolio Management System,* Rubrics for Choices, p. 162	• *Formal Assessment,* Selection Tests, pp. 138, 139, 140 • *Test Generator (One-Stop Planner CD-ROM)* • *Preparation for College Admission Exams,* p. 35
	• *Audio CD Library,* Disc 12, Track 9	
• *Portfolio Management System,* Rubrics for Choices, p. 163	• *Audio CD Library,* Disc 12, Tracks 10, 11, 12, 13, 14 • *Visual Connections:* Videocassette B, Segment 8 • *Portfolio Management System,* Rubrics for Choices, p. 163	• *Formal Assessment,* Selection Tests, pp. 141, 142, 143, 144, 145 • *Test Generator (One-Stop Planner CD-ROM)*
• *Audio CD Library,* Disc 12, Tracks 15, 16, 17		
		• *Formal Assessment,* The English Language Test, p. 146
• *Workshop Resources,* p. 27 • *Writer's Workshop 2 CD-ROM,* Informative Report	• *Viewing and Representing,* HRW Multimedia Presentation Maker	• *Portfolio Management System* • Prewriting, p. 166 • Peer Editing, p. 167 • Assessment Rubric, p. 168
		• *Portfolio Management System,* Rubrics, p. 169

Transparency CD-ROM Video Audio CD

Collection 9 The Quest for Beauty

Skills Focus

Selection or Feature	Reading Skills and Strategies	Elements of Literature and Language	Writing	Listening and Speaking	Viewing and Representing
She Walks in Beauty (p. 711) **The Destruction of Sennacherib** (p. 712) *from* **Don Juan, Canto II** (p. 714) *from* **Childe Harold's Pilgrimage, Canto IV** (p. 721) George Gordon, Lord Byron	Dialogue with the Text, pp. 712–713 Dialogue with the Text, p. 714	Anapestic Rhythm, p. 712 Simile, p. 713 Personification, p. 713 Image, p. 713 Meter, p. 713 Couplet, p. 713 Ottava Rima, pp. 714, 720 Figures of Speech, pp. 720, 725 Satire, pp. 720, 725 Irony, p. 725 Tone, p. 725 Spenserian Stanza, p. 725 Apostrophe, p. 725	Identify Possible Research Questions, p. 725 Write a Response to a Poem from Another Point of View, p. 725 Write an Essay Comparing *Don Juan* with *The Rape of the Lock*, p. 725 Analyze a Verse Form, p. 725 Write a Sequel to Don Juan, p. 725 Write a Prose Apostrophe, p. 725		
Ozymandias (p. 730) **Ode to the West Wind** (p. 734) **To a Skylark** (p. 739) Percy Bysshe Shelley	Identify Speakers, pp. 730, 732 Hearing the Music of Poetry, p. 739	Apostrophe, p. 738 Terza Rima, p. 738 Sonnet, p. 738 Onomatopoeia, pp. 738, 742 Alliteration, pp. 738, 742 Analogue, p. 739 Symbol, pp. 739, 742 Simile, p. 742 Assonance, p. 742 Rhyme, pp. 738, 742 Parody, p. 742 Theme, p. 742 Tone, p. 742	Create a Survey and Summarize the Results, p. 742 Write an Essay on Shelley's Use of Sound Effects, p. 742 Compare and Contrast "Ozymandias" with a Renaissance Sonnet, p. 742 Write a Parody of Shelley, p. 742		
World Literature: China **Jade Flower Palace** (p. 744) Tu Fu	The World Literature feature offers students the opportunity to explore thematically linked literature from different world cultures. Structured activities called Finding Common Ground are provided in the Pupil's Edition to guide students' explorations of these thematic connections between British and other world literature.				
On First Looking into Chapman's Homer (p. 746) **When I Have Fears** (p. 748) **La Belle Dame sans Merci** (p. 750) **Ode to a Nightingale** (p. 754) **Ode on a Grecian Urn** (p. 760) John Keats	Read Inverted Syntax, pp. 746, 747 Paraphrase, p. 747 Recognize Motifs, p. 750 Dialogue with the Text, pp. 754, 759 Images, pp. 760, 763	Sonnet, pp. 746–747, 764 Turn, pp. 746, 749, 764 Image, pp. 747, 753, 759 Simile, pp. 747, 749 Tone, p. 749 Ballad, pp. 750, 753 Speakers, p. 753 Meter, p. 753 Mood, pp. 754, 759 Synaesthesia, p. 759 Metaphor, p. 763	Identify Potential Research Topics Connected to Keats's Life, p. 764 Write an Essay Comparing Two Odes, p. 764 Write an Essay Comparing and Contrasting Text Elements in Two Poems, p. 764 Write an Essay Analyzing Text Structure in "Ode on a Grecian Urn," p. 764 Write a Personal Letter to the Speaker in "When I Have Fears," p. 764 Write an Explanation of What Ails the Knight in "La Belle Dame sans Merci," p. 764	Improvise a Musical Setting for "La Belle Dame sans Merci," p. 764	Select Images to Illustrate, p. 759 Illustrate a cartoon version of "La Belle Dame sans Merci," p. 764 Write a Prose Response to a Work of Art, p. 764
Reading Skills and Strategies: Homonyms, Homophones, and Homographs (p. 765)	Homonyms, Homophones, and Homographs, p. 765				
World Literature: China **Question and Answer Among the Mountains** (p. 767) **Word-Pattern** (p. 767) **To Tan-Ch'iu** (p. 767) Li Po	The World Literature feature offers students the opportunity to explore thematically linked literature from different world cultures. Structured activities called Finding Common Ground are provided in the Pupil's Edition to guide students' explorations of these thematic connections between British and other world literature.				
The English Language: Variety in Language (p. 770) John Algeo	Dialectical Meanings, p. 772	Dialects, p. 770			
Writer's Workshop: Research Paper (p. 773)			Write a Research Paper, pp. 773–776		
Language Workshop: Aspects of a Writer's Style (p. 777)		Voice, Tone, Diction, p. 777	Revise Sentences to Achieve an Appropriate Tone, p. 777		
Reading for Life: The Credibility of Sources (p. 778)	Sources, p. 778				
Learning for Life: Labor and Population Trends (p. 779)			Write an Editorial Based on Research, p. 779	Speech Based on Research, p. 779	Graphic Display of Data, p. 779

Collection 9

THE QUEST FOR BEAUTY

Byron
Shelley
Tu Fu
Keats
Li Po

A thing of beauty is a joy forever:
Its loveliness increases; it will never
Pass into nothingness.
—John Keats, *from Endymion*

Night (detail) (late 19th or early 20th century) by Edward Robert Hughes.

Writing Focus: The Research Paper

The following **Work in Progress** assignments build to a culminating **Writer's Workshop** at the end of this collection.

- Byron's poems — Ask questions to find topic (p. 725)
- Shelley's poems — Take a survey (p. 742)
- Keats's poems — Find a subject in literature (p. 764)

Writer's Workshop: Expository Writing / The Research Paper (p. 773)

OBJECTIVES

1. Read literature of the Romantic period on the theme "The Quest for Beauty"
2. Interpret literary elements with special emphasis on apostrophe, terza rima, and the sonnet
3. Apply a variety of reading strategies including using homonyms, homophones, and homographs
4. Respond to the literature in a variety of modes
5. Learn and use new words
6. Learn about variety in language
7. Plan, draft, and revise a research paper
8. Develop skill in choosing an appropriate writing style
9. Demonstrate an ability to evaluate the credibility of sources
10. Research labor and population trends through a variety of projects

Responding to the Quotation

? Do you agree with this statement? Why or why not? [Possible responses: Yes, a work of art could survive over millennia. Or no, most types of beauty, such as physical beauty, fade in time.]

RESPONDING TO THE ART

Edward Robert Hughes (1851–1914) was a nineteenth-century British painter who began his career as a member of the Pre-Raphaelites (a school of artists who wished to return to what they believed was the less artificial style of painting that preceded the work of the Italian painter Raphael). Hughes later broke away from the strictures of the Pre-Raphaelite school and began to create more subjective and symbolic works.

Activity. Ask students to discuss what they see in this painting that they consider beautiful and how it might relate to the quotation from Keats.

Objectives

She Walks . . . / . . . Sennacherib/ Don Juan/Childe Harold's . . .

1. Read and interpret the poems
2. Identify and analyze anapestic rhythm and ottava rima
3. Monitor comprehension
4. Express understanding through critical and creative writing

Skills

Literary

- Identify and analyze anapestic rhythm and ottava rima

Reading

- Monitor comprehension by dialoguing with the text

Writing

- Collect ideas for a research paper
- Respond to a poem from another point of view
- Compare two poems
- Analyze verse form
- Write a sequel
- Write a prose apostrophe

Viewing and Representing

- Make inferences about an artwork by analyzing visual details (ATE)

Planning

- **Block Schedule**
  Block Scheduling Lesson Plans with Pacing Guide
- **Traditional Schedule**
  Lesson Plans Including Strategies for English-Language Learners
- **One-Stop Planner**
  CD-ROM with Test Generator

George Gordon, Lord Byron

(1788–1824)

Byron, 6th Baron (late 18th to early 19th century) by Richard Westall.

Until one fateful day in 1794, George Gordon Byron seemed destined to grow up confined by the harsh Calvinism of Scotland. On that day, Byron's cousin was killed in battle and young George became first in line to be the sixth Baron Byron of Rochdale. Byron assumed the title when he was ten years old.

Byron's literary elevation came no less suddenly. In 1812, the midpoint of the Romantic period, Byron became a celebrity with the publication of the first two cantos of a poem called *Childe Harold's Pilgrimage,* based on his recent travels to Europe and Asia Minor. Byron "awoke one morning," as he later said, "and found myself famous."

Like his father (a sea captain, a psychopath, and a spender of women's fortunes), Byron seems to have had an obsessive determination to prove himself in every way. Extraordinarily handsome, he was born with a clubfoot, and in compensation he learned swimming, boxing, and horse riding. His life style aggravated a glandular problem and a tendency toward grotesque obesity, so he would periodically go on brutal binge diets.

The shocking aspects of Byron's private life have become legendary as a result of his literary fame, not the reverse. But they are shocking, nevertheless—and sometimes rather sad. Scandal concerning his sexual affairs (including a relationship with his half sister Augusta), his scandalous separation from his wife, and his radical, pro-French political views made life in England uncomfortable. Byron left for the Continent in 1816, never to return.

Byron's literary career had begun modestly in 1807 with a small collection of short lyric pieces that was harshly reviewed by the *Edinburgh Review.* In response, Byron wrote the satire *English Bards and Scotch Reviewers* (1809), which reveals the vein of wit that helped cast Byron as a rebellious mocker of established conventions. His target in this satire was not only the *Edinburgh Review;* he also took on such Romantic icons as Wordsworth and Coleridge.

When Byron left England in 1816, he was drawn into contact with Percy Shelley and his wife, Mary, in Switzerland. Because of the association with Shelley, Byron's writing life now began in earnest. It intensified when he moved to Italy. The Byron we glimpse in these years, despite the debauchery and the circuslike menagerie he kept about him in Venice, is a man who works very hard at his writing. His wildness and aristocratic ease obscure what was, in fact, a period of great literary productivity.

As a poet, Byron was not a "Romantic" in style. His masters, in fact, were the neoclassical writers whose wit and precision he admired. Yet throughout the nineteenth century he was regarded as the incarnation of "Romantic." His premature death seemed to reinforce this image. Byron set sail for Greece in July 1823 to support the Greek nationalists in their struggle for independence from Turkey. In a marshy town in Greece called Missolonghi, he came down with fevers that took his life only a few months after his thirty-sixth birthday.

go.hrw.com
LEO 12-9

Resources: Print and Media

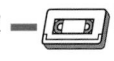

Reading

- *Graphic Organizers for Active Reading,* pp. 60, 61, 62
- *Audio CD Library*
  Disc 12, Tracks 2, 3, 4

Writing and Language

- *Daily Oral Grammar*
  Transparency 25
- *Grammar and Language Links*
  Worksheet, p. 39
- *Language Workshop CD-ROM*

Viewing and Representing

- *Visual Connections*
  Videocassette B, Segment 8

Assessment

- *Formal Assessment,* pp. 133, 134, 135
- *Portfolio Management System,* p. 160
- *Test Generator* (*One-Stop Planner CD-ROM*)

Internet

- go.hrw.com (keyword: LE0 12-9)

SHE WALKS IN BEAUTY

Make the Connection
The Eye of the Beholder
No matter how often we hear that beauty is only skin deep, we all know the mysterious attraction of a beautiful person. Beauty moves us. We want to believe that outer appearances express inner qualities.

Quickwrite

If a man compares a woman's beauty to night, what qualities do you expect he sees in her? Write down what you think.

Background
"She Walks in Beauty," one of Byron's most famous poems, was supposedly inspired by Lady Wilmot Horton, a beautiful woman whom Byron saw at a ball, perhaps in the spring of 1814. Lady Horton was in mourning and, in the fashion of the times, was wearing a black dress decorated with glittering spangles.

She Walks in Beauty

George Gordon, Lord Byron

She walks in beauty, like the night
 Of cloudless climes° and starry skies;
And all that's best of dark and bright
 Meet in her aspect° and her eyes:
5 Thus mellowed to that tender light
 Which heaven to gaudy day denies.

One shade the more, one ray the less,
 Had half impaired the nameless grace
Which waves in every raven tress,
10 Or softly lightens o'er her face;
Where thoughts serenely sweet express
 How pure, how dear their dwelling place.

And on that cheek, and o'er that brow,
 So soft, so calm, yet eloquent,
15 The smiles that win, the tints that glow,
 But tell of days in goodness spent,
A mind at peace with all below,
 A heart whose love is innocent!

2. **climes:** atmospheres; climates.
4. **aspect:** face; look.

MAKING MEANINGS

First Thoughts
1. How does Byron respond to this "dark" beauty? (Compare his response with your Quickwrite notes.)

Shaping Interpretations
2. What in the woman's appearance does the speaker praise? What conclusions does he draw about her character and personality?
3. What does the speaker imply about day when he calls it "gaudy"?

4. "Dark and bright" (line 3) suggests a balance of opposites. How is this idea developed?
5. What do you think the speaker means by "below" in line 17?

Challenging the Text
6. This poem has been criticized as sentimental and dependent on clichés. Tell whether or not you agree and why.
7. Do you think that inward nature can be revealed by outward appearances? Explain.

GEORGE GORDON, LORD BYRON 711

Reaching All Students

Struggling Readers
Some students may have difficulty with Byron's metered verse. Have them work in groups of three to read and interpret the poem one stanza at a time. Each member should take a turn reading a stanza aloud to the group. The members can then discuss what the stanza means and work together to write a paraphrase or summary of each stanza after their discussion.

English Language Learners
To prepare students for the poem's theme, arrange them in small groups with learners of varied proficiencies to explore this question: "What makes someone or something beautiful?" Then have them share their ideas and develop a list of the characteristics the group agrees make someone or something beautiful.

Summary ■■

The speaker describes a beautiful woman he sees at a ball. She has the best aspects of everything that is "dark and bright," and projects sweetness, purity, innocence, and peacefulness.

Ⓐ Elements of Literature
Imagery
❓ What is the focus of the imagery? [the contrast between dark and light]

Ⓑ Critical Thinking
Synthesizing
❓ How does the description in ll. 11–12 relate the woman's attractiveness to an inner beauty? [Possible response: The woman's face reveals her beautiful thoughts.]

Ⓒ Reading Skills and Strategies
Finding the Main Idea
❓ What is the main idea expressed in this stanza? [Possible response: The woman's external appearance reflects the nature of her soul.]

MAKING MEANINGS

First Thoughts [Respond]
1. Byron responds passionately; he seems to be in awe.

Shaping Interpretations [Interpret]
2. The speaker praises the meeting of darkness and light in the woman's appearance. The balance suggests her peacefulness and goodness.
3. Daylight is garish compared to the soft light of night.
4. The pairing occurs again in ll. 7 and 9–10. See also ll. 13–14.
5. Possible response: "Below" could refer to earthly concerns. The woman's innocence gives her peace amid earthly strife.

Challenging the Text [Evaluate and Analyze]
6. Possible response: The poet's praise is clichéd, but the poem's startling and original images transcend conventional sentiment.
7. Possible responses: Yes, a person's facial expression and body language can give clues to his or her inner nature. Or no, physical beauty alone does not indicate that a person is either happy or good.

Summary ■■

The speaker recounts the Biblical tale of the Israelites escaping a murderous invasion by King Sennacherib's Assyrian army. According to the story, the Angel of Death takes the lives of the invaders as they sleep.

Browsing in the Files

About the Author. When Byron went to the aid of the Greek nationalists who were fighting for independence from the Turks, he acted on the principles of liberty and independence which he celebrated in his poetry. He died fighting in the Greek cause and, as a result, attention was focused on the struggles for freedom of other subjugated national groups throughout Europe. Sir Herbert Grierson remarked that "when he [Byron] went to Greece, it was not only a man and an English peer who went but a Power in Europe." Throughout the nineteenth century, Byron remained a symbol of a new spirit in European culture and politics.

A Elements of Literature

Anapestic Rhythm

? What does the rhythm of ll. 1–2 suggest? [Possible responses: The anapestic rhythm mimics the sound of pounding horses' hooves. The regular stressed third beat of the meter suggests a steady drumbeat or heartbeat.]

B Reading Skills and Strategies

Dialogue with the Text

? What picture does Byron create for you in ll. 5–8? [Possible response: The Assyrians begin their attack fresh and full of vigor, like summer leaves. The next morning, they are scattered and strewn on the battlefield like crumpled autumn leaves blown by the wind.]

Before You Read

THE DESTRUCTION OF SENNACHERIB

Make the Connection

Old Tales of Miracles

The Romantics loved old stories, old ballads, tales of heroism and fantasy—like this Biblical story of the miraculous deliverance of the Israelites from the Assyrian army. Watch for the images that romanticize the conflict—that glorify the victor and demonize the enemy. Can you think of ways in which people demonize their enemies today?

Reading Skills and Strategies

Dialogue with the Text

Be sure to read this poem aloud. After the first stanza, jot down a few notes about the picture Byron is creating. Then, as you continue to read, make notes on how the picture changes.

Elements of Literature

Anapestic Rhythm

Byron skillfully uses the bouncy **anapestic rhythm** (˘˘′), which was quite popular in the nineteenth century but has seldom been used by serious poets since.

Background

In both Kings and Chronicles, the Bible tells the story of the attempt of the Assyrian king Sennacherib (sə•nak′ər•ib) to capture and enslave Jerusalem. With his mighty army about to descend on the city, "the Angel of Death"—in the form of a sudden pestilence or plague—killed man and beast alike, yet spared the king. In the Biblical account, Sennacherib's failure so disgraced "Ashur" (Assyria) that his own sons murdered him on his return. This poem and "She Walks in Beauty" are from a collection called *Hebrew Melodies,* lyrics that were to be set to music.

Cavalryman Fording a Stream. Fragment of a wall relief (8th–7th century B.C.) from the palace of Sennacherib at Nineveh, Assyria.

The Metropolitan Museum of Art, New York. Gift of John D. Rockefeller, Jr., 1932. Photograph ©1981 The Metropolitan Museum of Art.

Reaching All Students

Struggling Readers

Before students read the poem, ask them to imagine a city that has succumbed to a plague. If they were to walk around in that city, what do they think they would see, hear, or smell? Ask students to write down their responses and share them with a partner. Suggest that they record their thoughts so that later they can compare their mental images with Byron's choice of images in the poem.

English Language Learners

Pair English language learners with partners who are more proficient in the language. Have pairs use reciprocal teaching strategies to assist their comprehension. First they can read the poem aloud, pausing after each stanza. Then one student can summarize the stanza and discuss with the other any questions that arose while reading. The two can then trade roles for the next stanza. After pairs go through the poem in this way, have each one reread it silently from start to finish.

The Destruction of Sennacherib

George Gordon, Lord Byron

The Assyrian came down like the wolf on the fold,
And his cohorts were gleaming in purple and gold; [A]
And the sheen of their spears was like stars on the sea,
When the blue wave rolls nightly on deep Galilee.°

Like the leaves of the forest when summer is green,
That host° with their banners at sunset were seen: [B]
Like the leaves of the forest when autumn hath blown,
That host on the morrow lay withered and strown.

For the Angel of Death spread his wings on the blast,
And breathed in the face of the foe as he passed;
And the eyes of the sleepers waxed deadly and chill,
And their hearts but once heaved, and forever grew still!

And there lay the steed with his nostril all wide,
But through it there rolled not the breath of his pride; [C]
And the foam of his gasping lay white on the turf,
And cold as the spray of the rock-beating surf.

And there lay the rider distorted and pale,
With the dew on his brow, and the rust on his mail:° [D]
And the tents were all silent, the banners alone,
The lances unlifted, the trumpet unblown.

And the widows of Ashur are loud in their wail,
And the idols are broke in the temple of Baal;°
And the might of the Gentile,° unsmote° by the sword, [E]
Hath melted like snow in the glance of the Lord!

4. Galilee: Sea of Galilee, a lake north of Jerusalem.

6. host: the army; also, a great number.

18. mail: kind of body armor made of linked metal rings.

22. Baal (bā′əl): the Assyrian god.
23. Gentile: Sennacherib and the Assyrians (non-Israelites).
unsmote: not destroyed.

MAKING MEANINGS

First Thoughts

1. What do you think killed the Assyrians?

Shaping Interpretations

2. What are the Assyrians doing in the first stanza, and what has happened in the second? What **similes** describe the changing scenes? (Look at your reading notes for ideas.)
3. How is death **personified** in stanza 3?
4. What **images** and **similes** in the last three stanzas help you see the aftermath of the defeat?
5. Read aloud to hear the poem's **meter.** How does it help reinforce the poem's action? How do you think this meter would suit a modern battle poem?
6. Who is the hero of this battle?

Challenging the Text

7. Do you think Byron demonizes the Assyrians in this poem? Explain.
8. Read the poem aloud again and listen to the **couplets.** How do you feel about Byron's use of rhyme?

Crossing the Curriculum

Art

Encourage students to compare the verbal descriptions of mass death in the poem with a visual image of war. For example, they might compare and contrast the scene in the fourth stanza with the image of a horse in Picasso's painting *Guernica*. Encourage students to write brief summaries of their conclusions and to share these with the class, or have them create their own visual image of war's destruction.

Making the Connections

Connecting to the Theme: "The Quest for Beauty"

Ask students to discuss why this poem belongs in a collection called "The Quest for Beauty." [Possible responses: "By means of his extraordinary imagery and use of figurative language, Byron has made it possible to see beauty in a frightening tableau of menace and death. The enemy is dazzling as well as deadly, and the battle that never takes place has a haunting spiritual beauty.]

C Struggling Readers

Visualizing

Have students detail how they visualize the horse described in ll. 13–16? [Possible response: The lifeless horse is lying on the ground with open nostrils but not breathing. White saliva like sea spray on rocks has spilled onto the ground from its mouth.]

D Appreciating Language

Diction

? What words in ll. 17–20 emphasize the scene's stillness? [Possible responses: "Lay" and "dew" suggest a gentle setting; "unlifted" and "unblown" emphasize actions left undone.]

E Critical Thinking

Interpreting

? What do ll. 22–24 tell you about the Lord's might? [Possible responses: It is like the sun's rays. Or it is powerful and capable of destruction.]

MAKING MEANINGS

First Thoughts [Respond]

1. Possible responses: The Angel of Death represents some sudden calamity such as a lethal contagious illness or a deadly natural disaster.

Shaping Interpretations [Interpret]

2. The Assyrians attack in the first stanza; in the second, they lie dead. The leaf simile unites the two events by contrasting summer and autumn foliage.
3. Death is personified as an angel who breathes on the faces of the sleeping soldiers.
4. The dead horse and rider, and the wails of the Assyrian women show the effects of the plague.
5. Possible response: The anapestic tetrameter evokes the charging hoof beats of the horses; this meter would not suit a description of a modern motorized battle.
6. Possible response: There is no human hero; the Assyrians have been defeated by a supernatural intervention ("the glance of the Lord").

Challenging the Text [Evaluate]

7. Possible response: Yes, because they are described as wolves attacking weaker and milder prey.
8. Possible response: The rhymed couplets contribute to the quick pace and air of inevitability that characterize the poem.

Summary ■■

At twilight, Haidee, the daughter of a pirate, walks along the beach with Don Juan. They kiss passionately. Afterward, as Don Juan sleeps, Haidee watches over her beloved, and the speaker comments on the constancy of women and the treachery of men, perhaps foreshadowing the couple's fate. At the moment, however, the lovers' affection unites and pleases them.

Background

Explain that the reader must resist the temptation to look for the "real" Byron in the characters and voices in his poetry. For example, some readers have been tempted to find Byron in the narrator of *Don Juan,* but the "real" Byron is more likely revealed in the wit, humor, and inventiveness displayed throughout his work rather than in any single character or voice.

Resources

Viewing and Representing

Videocassette B, Segment 8

Available in English and Spanish. This segment explores the Romantic Movement. For full lesson plans and worksheets, see the *Visual Connections Teacher's Manual.*

FROM THE EDITOR'S DESK

Don Juan is a timeless archetype that never ceases to capture the imagination. We suggest that you encourage students to research and discuss classic and modern interpretations of the archetype, such as the title characters of Mozart's opera *Don Giovanni* and of the film *Don Juan De Marco.*

Before You Read

FROM **DON JUAN**

Make the Connection

Chasing a Dream

The legendary Don Juan (in Spanish, hwän) is a notorious seducer of women, the greatest lover in history, a man whose passion for women drove him from one affair to another—with narrow escapes in between. But Byron's Don Juan (jo͞o′ən) is different from other versions. His hero is an innocent who becomes involved in many amorous adventures simply because he is, like Byron, so handsome and irresistible. However, the narrator (also like Byron) is not innocent, and that makes for lively satire. As women chase the innocent beauty of Don Juan around the world, the narrator shows us another fruitless quest: for pure beauty and love in a hypocritical world.

Reading Skills and Strategies

Dialogue with the Text

Some things in this excerpt are sure to catch you off guard. Label a column in your notebook "Surprises." Every time Byron or his lively speaker catches you with something unexpected—a joke, a change of tone, a funny rhyme, an odd detail, a "modern" idea—make a quick note, with line numbers.

Elements of Literature

Ottava Rima

The eight-line stanza form of *Don Juan* is based on the Italian ottava rima (ō·tä′və rē′mə). While Byron adheres strictly to the demands of the form, his **tone** is loosely conversational, colloquial, and continually punctuated by digressions. One of the poem's charms is that it moves at a pace appropriate to the narrator's quick shifts of attention. He is confident that the reader will stay with him when, every now and then, he slows down and dawdles over something he sees from the corner of his eye.

> **Ottava rima,** in its English form, is eight lines of iambic pentameter, rhyming *abababcc.*
>
> *For more on Ottava Rima, see the Handbook of Literary Terms.*

Background

Don Juan is the longest satirical poem in English literature. Left unfinished at Byron's death, it comprises sixteen long divisions (cantos) and part of a seventeenth. The form the poem would take came to Byron late in his comparatively brief life. But once Byron mastered it, he found it accommodated everything he wanted to say about the world he knew. The result was a poem of enormous popularity and scandalous interest, since Byron's own erotic exploits lay behind it. In contrast with the solemn lyricism of his contemporaries, Byron hearkened back to poets like Alexander Pope, with their penchant for wit as both social grace and weapon against folly. This extract comes from the early part of *Don Juan,* where the hero finds himself shipwrecked on a Greek island. Haidee, the daughter of a pirate, falls in love with Don Juan. To enjoy the fun, read the poem aloud.

Sunset on the Yorkshire Coast (c. 1885) by Richard Weatherill.

Chris Beetles Ltd., London.

Reaching All Students

Struggling Readers

Students may have difficulty with the poem's fluid point of view and changes of tone. Ask them to read the poem together in small groups, discussing the main idea of each stanza as they read. They can then reflect on the poem's themes and organization before rereading it to improve their comprehension.

English Language Learners

This excerpt from *Don Juan* is quite long and contains language that might prove daunting to English language learners. Read the poem aloud as students follow along in their texts. Pause frequently to monitor comprehension by asking students to summarize the section just read and to relate it to their own experience.

Advanced Learners

Encourage students to look for changes in tone and point of view as they read the poem. Ask students to keep track of such changes and to try to discern the purpose behind them. Students may use their notes in a discussion of Byron's narrative voice as compared to that of other Romantic poets such as Wordsworth or Coleridge.

from Don Juan, Canto II

George Gordon, Lord Byron

It was a wild and breaker-beaten coast,
With cliffs above, and a broad sandy shore,
Guarded by shoals and rocks as by an host,°
With here and there a creek, whose aspect wore
A better welcome to the tempest tost;°
And rarely ceased the haughty billow's roar,
Save on the dead long summer days, which make
The outstretched ocean glitter like a lake.

. . . .

The coast—I think it was the coast that I
Was just describing—Yes, it *was* the coast— **A**
Lay at this period quiet as the sky,
The sands untumbled, the blue waves untost, **B**
And all was stillness, save the seabird's cry,
And dolphin's leap, and little billow crost
By some low rock or shelf, that made it fret
Against the boundary it scarcely wet.

And forth they° wandered, her sire being gone,
As I have said, upon an expedition;
And mother, brother, guardian, she had none,
Save Zoe, who, although with due precision
She waited on her lady with the sun,
Thought daily service was her only mission, **C**
Bringing warm water, wreathing her long tresses,
And asking now and then for castoff dresses.

It was the cooling hour, just when the rounded
Red sun sinks down behind the azure° hill,
Which then seems as if the whole earth it bounded,
Circling all nature, hushed, and dim, and still, **D**
With the far mountain crescent half surrounded
On one side, and the deep sea calm and chill
Upon the other, and the rosy sky,
With one star sparkling through it like an eye.

And thus they wandered forth, and hand in hand,
Over the shining pebbles and the shells,
Glided along the smooth and hardened sand,
And in the worn and wild receptacles **E**
Worked by the storms, yet worked as it were planned,
In hollow halls, with sparry° roofs and cells,
They turned to rest; and, each clasped by an arm,
Yielded to the deep twilight's purple charm.

3. host: army.

5. tempest tost: storm tossed.

17. they: Haidee and Don Juan.

26. azure: sky-blue.

38. sparry: made of shiny rock.

A Reading Skills and Strategies

Determining the Author's Purpose

? What do you think is the purpose of this comment on the narrator's wandering attention? [Possible response: The effect is a comic contrast with the serious narration.]

B Appreciating Language

Diction

? What do the adjectives in l. 12 have in common, and what effect does this similarity create? [Possible response: They both begin with the prefix *un-*, a fact that emphasizes the scene's stillness.]

C Critical Thinking

Making Judgments

? What is the narrator's view of servants as expressed in ll. 21–24? [Possible response: The narrator views servants as having only small hopes and ambitions of their own, such as a desire for cast-off clothing.] **How would you describe this point of view?** [Possible responses: satiric, aristocratic, possibly condescending.]

D Reading Skills and Strategies

Comparing and Contrasting

? How does the tone in ll. 25–32 contrast with that of the preceding stanza? [Possible response: The tone shifts from informal, to satiric social commentary to a highly poetic appreciation of nature.]

E Elements of Literature

Ottava Rima

? Ask students to mark the stanza's *abababcc* rhyme scheme. How does this format affect the poem? [Possible responses: Rhyming words such as *hand, sand,* and *planned* help carry the reader through the stanza. The final couplet (*arm, charm*) helps mark the stanza's ending.]

Using Students' Strengths

Auditory/Musical Learners

Encourage students to notice the stanzas' witty endings. Have volunteers read the stanzas aloud and then paraphrase them in prose. Then ask students to discuss how the rhythm and rhyme of the verse contribute to the humorous tone. Then students can experiment with various oral interpretations of the poem, varying their voice quality and inflection to emphasize the wit and humor of the lines.

Interpersonal Learners

Ask students to play the roles of Haidee and Don Juan ten years after the events described in the selection as the couple discuss their memories of the night on the moonlit beach. Remind students that they will first have to decide what happened to the couple and their relationship in the intervening years. Urge them to base their characterizations and their predictions on details and suggestions offered in the poem.

A Elements of Literature

Tone

? What is the tone of the final couplet in ll. 55–56? [Possible responses: The couplet has a tongue-in-cheek tone that undercuts the more passionate, conventionally romantic diction that precedes it.]

B Reading Skills and Strategies

Dialogue with the Text

? What do you find surprising in ll. 55–58? [Possible response: The narrator doesn't seem to take the lovers' passion very seriously. He seems detached and even amused by their mutual absorption.]

C Critical Thinking

Evaluating

? How would you characterize the metaphor in ll. 63–64? [Possible responses: strained, excessive, absurd.] **In what way is such a metaphor appropriate to Byron's purpose?** [Possible response: Since the poem is openly satirical and flouts some Romantic conventions, the absurdity of the metaphor may serve to reflect the characters' impossible-to-sustain love for each other.]

D Elements of Literature

Satire

? What is the subject of the narrator's satire in ll. 81–84? [Possible responses: The narrator indirectly mocks women's demands for constancy from their lovers and men's reputation for infidelity; he contrasts Haidee's innocence with real-life problems women face when men are unfaithful.]

They looked up to the sky, whose floating glow
  Spread like a rosy ocean, vast and bright;
They gazed upon the glittering sea below,
  Whence the broad moon rose circling into sight;
They heard the wave's splash, and the wind so low,
  And saw each other's dark eyes darting light
Into each other—and, beholding this,
Their lips drew near, and clung into a kiss;

A long, long kiss, a kiss of youth and love,
  And beauty, all concentrating like rays
Into one focus, kindled from above;
  Such kisses as belong to early days,
Where heart, and soul, and sense, in concert° move,
  And the blood's lava, and the pulse a blaze,
Each kiss a heart quake—for a kiss's strength,
I think, it must be reckoned by its length.

By length I mean duration; theirs endured
  Heaven knows how long—no doubt they never reckoned;
And if they had, they could not have secured
  The sum of their sensations to a second:
They had not spoken; but they felt allured,
  As if their souls and lips each other beckoned,
Which, being joined, like swarming bees they clung—
Their hearts the flowers from whence the honey sprung.

They were alone, but not alone as they
  Who shut in chambers think it loneliness;
The silent ocean, and the starlight bay,
  The twilight glow, which momently° grew less,
The voiceless sands, and dropping° caves, that lay
  Around them, made them to each other press,
As if there were no life beneath the sky
Save theirs, and that their life could never die.

They feared no eyes nor ears on that lone beach,
  They felt no terrors from the night, they were
All in all to each other: Though their speech
  Was broken words, they *thought* a language there—
And all the burning tongues the passions teach
  Found in one sigh the best interpreter
Of nature's oracle°—first love—that all
Which Eve has left her daughters since her fall.

Haidee spoke not of scruples, asked no vows,
  Nor offered any; she had never heard
Of plight° and promises to be a spouse,
  Or perils by a loving maid incurred;
She was all which pure ignorance allows,
  And flew to her young mate like a young bird;
And, never having dreamt of falsehood, she
Had not one word to say of constancy.

53. in concert: together.

68. momently: at each moment.

69. dropping: dripping.

79. oracle: revelation.

83. plight: promise of marriage.

Taking a Second Look

Review: Identifying the Author's Stance

Remind students that the **author's stance** is his or her attitude or point of view toward the subject at hand. The author's stance can be a result of a political viewpoint, a personal belief, or an intense feeling about a topic or an issue.

Activities

1. Divide students into small groups of four or five. After they have read the poem several times, ask them to discuss the narrator's view of Don Juan and Haidee's love. Remind them to point to specific lines from the poem to support their interpretation. Then have the groups share their opinions and come to some consensus as a class on a word or phrase that best describes Byron's stance.
2. Next, discuss with students how Byron's stance on romantic love affects the structure and tone of the poem. How might this stance have affected Byron's decision to use the ottava rima form? What is the overall tone of the poem and how appropriate is it to convey Byron's stance? How do other aspects of the poem, such as figurative language and imagery, help to convey the author's point of view?

Night and Sleep (1888)
by Simeon Solomon.
Pencil and chalk (349 mm × 286 mm).
Birmingham Museums & Art Gallery, Birmingham, England.

She loved, and was beloved—she adored, **E**
  And she was worshipped; after nature's fashion,
Their intense souls, into each other poured,
  If souls could die, had perished in that passion,—
But by degrees their senses were restored,
  Again to be o'ercome, again to dash on;
And, beating 'gainst *his* bosom, Haidee's heart
Felt as if never more to beat apart.

Alas! they were so young, so beautiful,
  So lonely, loving, helpless, and the hour
Was that in which the heart is always full,
  And, having o'er itself no further power,
Prompts deeds eternity can not annul,° **F**
  But pays off moments in an endless shower
Of hellfire—all prepared for people giving
Pleasure or pain to one another living.

Alas! for Juan and Haidee! they were
  So loving and so lovely—till then never,
Excepting our first parents, such a pair
  Had run the risk of being damned forever; **G**
And Haidee, being devout as well as fair,

101. annul: cancel.

Responding to the Art

Simeon Solomon (1840–1905) came from an English family of eight children, three of whom became artists. Lively and precocious, Solomon, at age fifteen, formed a sketching club with three colleagues. At first an adherent of the Pre-Raphaelite school, he later turned to classical models, especially to the work of Leonardo da Vinci.

Activity. What relationship is being depicted in the drawing? How does it relate to Haidee and Don Juan? [Possible response: It depicts a man and a woman in an intimate embrace in which one lover is sleeping and the other is lovingly watching or guarding the sleeping partner, as Haidee watches over the sleeping Don Juan.]

E Vocabulary Note

The Prefix *be-*

? Explain that the prefix *be-* is very versatile, having many meanings. When prefixed to verbs, *be-* can be used as an intensifier, with the general meanings of "completely," "thoroughly," or "excessively." *Beloved* means "completely or dearly loved." What other words make use of this meaning of the prefix? [Possible responses: *bedeck, besmear, bewitch.*]

F Reading Skills and Strategies

Comparing and Contrasting

? How does the perspective change in ll. 97–104? [Possible response: The nostalgic narrator initially praises the lovers' passion, but he ends with a jaded view of the pain lovers bring to each other.]

G English Language Learners

Biblical Allusions

Not all students will recognize this allusion to the Genesis story of Adam and Eve. Either briefly recount the Biblical story to the class or have a student do so. Then help students see that Byron is using the allusion to contrast the couple's innocence and perfection with the possible terrible consequences of their deed.

Crossing the Curriculum

Journalism

Have students look for examples of gossip, satire, and opinion on a current romance in a newspaper or magazine. Ask each student to share an example with the class and to write a paragraph drawing a parallel between the item and an incident, detail, or comment in the poem. You may want to provide issues of local and national newspapers and magazines for students to use as resources.

Music

Ask volunteers to research and listen to Mozart's opera *Don Giovanni.* Have them prepare a plot summary and share it with the class along with selected portions from an audio or video recording of the opera (with translations if possible). Encourage the class to discuss how the opera differs from Byron's poem. Students should refer to specific musical passages in their comments.

A Reading Skills and Strategies

Dialogue with the Text

? Students might find it surprising that Byron brings up hell and purgatory in the middle of his tale about the two lovers. What might ll. 110–112 foreshadow? [Possible response: The lines indicate that the affair will end badly, perhaps with Don Juan leaving Haidee disgraced and with a broken heart.]

B Struggling Readers

Finding Details

? What does Haidee do and feel as Don Juan sleeps? [With his head on her bosom, she looks up to heaven and then down at him, full of passionate love and willingness to surrender to her feelings.]

C Elements of Literature

Repetition

? What is the effect of the repetition of comparisons in ll. 121–128? [Possible response: The repetition creates suspense and emphasizes the bounty of the lovers' joy.]

Responding to the Art

Frank Dicksee (1853–1928), an English painter, produced several works featuring literary characters. This painting depicts a character from Shakespeare's play *The Tempest*. In the play, Miranda and her father, Prospero, live on an enchanted island. Young and innocent, Miranda falls in love with Ferdinand, a handsome young man who is shipwrecked on the island after a storm. (For other art by Dicksee, see p. 750.)

Activity. If students are familiar with *The Tempest*, ask them to find parallels between Haidee and Miranda that would explain the use of Miranda's image here. [Possible responses: Both Haidee and Miranda live on an island under the care of a father. Both are young and innocent. Both fall in love with a man who is shipwrecked on their island.]

Had, doubtless, heard about the Stygian river,°
And hell and purgatory—but forgot
Just in the very crisis she should not.

. . . .

And when those deep and burning moments passed,
And Juan sunk to sleep within her arms,
She slept not, but all tenderly, though fast,°
Sustained his head upon her bosom's charms;
And now and then her eye to heaven is cast,
And then on the pale cheek her breast now warms,
Pillowed on her o'erflowing heart, which pants
With all it granted, and with all it grants.

An infant when it gazes on a light,
A child the moment when it drains the breast,
A devotee when soars the Host° in sight,
An Arab with a stranger for a guest,
A sailor when the prize has struck in fight,°
A miser filling his most hoarded chest,
Feel rapture; but not such true joy are reaping
As they who watch o'er what they love while sleeping.

110. Stygian river: the river Styx. In Greek mythology, the Styx encircles Hades (hā′dēz′), the underworld.

115. fast: firmly.

123. Host: the Eucharistic wafer that is lifted up during the Anglican or Catholic Mass. Devout church members believe it is the Body of Christ.

125. prize . . . fight: captured enemy ship that has lowered its flag in surrender.

Miranda (1878) by Sir Frank Dicksee.
The Maas Gallery, London.

Getting Students Involved

Cooperative Learning

Satirical Newspaper. Arrange students in groups to construct a satirical newspaper. Each paper should discuss a single topic and include a mock-serious editorial, a humorous essay, and several cartoons. After deciding on a focus, each group should compare ideas and divide up the tasks so that they are not duplicating one another's work. After the groups have finished their newspaper, have them pass out copies of their work to another group. Students can evaluate the newspaper by analyzing how well each contribution furthered the aims of the newspaper as a whole. They can then assess their own contribution to the general purpose. Finally, allow group members to compare their experiences of working on the project.

For there it lies so tranquil, so beloved,
All that it hath of life with us is living;
So gentle, stirless, helpless, and unmoved,
And all unconscious of the joy 'tis giving;
All it hath felt, inflicted, passed, and proved,
Hushed into depths beyond the watcher's diving;
There lies the thing we love with all its errors
And all its charms, like death without its terrors.

The lady watched her lover—and that hour
Of Love's, and Night's, and Ocean's solitude,
O'erflowed her soul with their united power;
Amidst the barren sand and rocks so rude°
She and her wave-worn love had made their bower,°
Where nought upon their passion could intrude,
And all the stars that crowded the blue space
Saw nothing happier than her glowing face.

Alas! the love of women! it is known
To be a lovely and a fearful thing;
For all of theirs upon that die° is thrown,
And if 'tis lost, life hath no more to bring
To them but mockeries of the past alone,
And their revenge is as the tiger's spring,
Deadly, and quick, and crushing; yet, as real
Torture is theirs, what they inflict they feel.

They are right; for man, to man so oft unjust,
Is always so to women; one sole bond
Awaits them, treachery is all their trust;°
Taught to conceal, their bursting hearts despond°
Over their idol, till some wealthier lust
Buys them in marriage—and what rests beyond?
A thankless husband, next a faithless lover,
Then dressing, nursing, praying, and all's over.

Some take a lover, some take drams° or prayers,
Some mind their household, others dissipation,°
Some run away, and but exchange their cares,
Losing the advantage of a virtuous station;
Few changes e'er can better their affairs,
Theirs being an unnatural situation,
From the dull palace to the dirty hovel:°
Some play the devil, and then write a novel.

Haidee was Nature's bride, and knew not this;
Haidee was Passion's child, born where the sun
Showers triple light, and scorches even the kiss
Of his gazelle-eyed daughters; she was one
Made but to love, to feel that she was his
Who was her chosen: What was said or done
Elsewhere was nothing—She had nought to fear,
Hope, care, nor love beyond, her heart beat *here.*

140. rude: rough.
141. bower: rustic dwelling place.
147. die: one of a pair of dice.
155. treachery . . . trust: Treachery is the only thing women can count on getting from men.
156. despond: despair.
161. drams: shots of liquor.
162. dissipation: riotous, wild living.
167. hovel: open shed or hut; miserable dwelling.

D Critical Thinking
Challenging the Text
? What sense, if any, can you make of the poet's comparison of the object of one's love to "death without its terrors" (l. 136)? [Possible responses: Don Juan is asleep, which is like a death that is not frightening; or, the comparison makes no sense since it is hard to imagine death as a positive thing.]

E Elements of Literature
Satire
? What attitude toward women does the narrator express in ll. 145–152? [Possible response: He satirizes them as entirely depending on love, causing their lovers to grow bored, and quickly seeking revenge when their lover leaves them.]

F Elements of Literature
Tone
? What is the tone of the narrator's comments on marriage in ll. 153–160? [Possible response: cynical and hopeless.]

G Historical Connections
In 1816, Lady Caroline Lamb published a novel, *Glenarven,* that was based on her scandalous affair with Byron. The novel included a letter that Byron wrote to break off the relationship.

Professional Notes

Critical Comment: Byron's Style
According to critics Ernest J. Lovell, Jr., and John Clubbe, Byron's style differs greatly from that of other Romantic poets because Byron "was an author but not an intellectual. He alone among the major Romantic poets could write, 'I liked the Dandies—they were always very civil to *me*—though in general they disliked literary people'; or, 'in general I do not draw well with Literary men . . . I never know what to say to them after I have praised their last publication.'"

Assessing Learning

Check Test: Questions and Answers
1. Who are the lovers in the poem? [Haidee and Don Juan]
2. Why is Haidee alone with Don Juan? [Her father is on an expedition.]
3. What is the speaker's attitude toward the lovers? [by turns idealizing and mocking, sometimes cynical]
4. How are the two characters married? [by expressing their love to each other]

Standardized Test Preparation
For practice in proofreading and editing, see
- *Daily Oral Grammar,* Transparency 25

Ⓐ Elements of Literature

Climax

? Lines 177–184 bring a climax to the lovers' relationship that results in their "marriage" in the next stanza. What is the effect of the final couplet on this climax? [Possible response: The climax is deflated by the satiric humor and political allusion in the couplet.]

Making Meanings

First Thoughts [Respond]

1. Possible responses: Readers today would find the poem's scandal unremarkable. Or, today's readers would still find the theme of sexual passion to be controversial.

Shaping Interpretations [Interpret]

2. Haidee does not know of falsehood and so is "ignorant" of evil.
3. The two lovers are alone in a natural paradise. Byron compares their innocence and impending downfall to Adam and Eve's in l. 107.
4. Examples include the star "eye" in l. 32, "blood's lava" in l. 54, and the comparison of the lovers to "swarming bees" in l. 63. Exaggeration balances the idyllic scenes with humor and advances Byron's satirical purpose.
5. Humorous final couplets include ll. 23–24, 167–168, and 183–184.
6. Possible responses: It is satirical and exaggerated, yet indulgent and sentimental.
7. Some of Byron's targets are Lady Caroline Lamb, Castlereagh, and conventional morality and religion. The poem satirizes the exaggerated sincerity and sentimentality of the Romantic tradition.

Connecting with the Text [Apply]

8. Possible response: The biggest surprise was the political commentary in the climactic description of the couple's love in l. 184.
9. Possible response: Both Byron's condemnation of the "conventional" women of his day and his idealization of the innocent, natural Haidee are outdated. See notes E and F on p. T719. See also ll. 161–168.

Ⓐ
And oh! that quickening of the heart, that beat!
    How much it costs us! yet each rising throb
Is in its cause as its effect so sweet,
    That Wisdom, ever on the watch to rob
Joy of its alchemy,° and to repeat
    Fine truths, even Conscience, too, has a tough job
To make us understand each good old maxim,
So good—I wonder Castlereagh° don't tax 'em.

And now 'twas done—on the lone shore were plighted
    Their hearts; the stars, their nuptial torches, shed
Beauty upon the beautiful they lighted:
    Ocean their witness, and the cave their bed,
By their own feelings hallowed° and united,
    Their priest was Solitude, and they were wed:
And they were happy, for to their young eyes
Each was an angel, and earth paradise.

181. alchemy (al′kə·mē): chemistry (here, miraculous power to change things).

184. Castlereagh: British foreign secretary from 1812 to 1822, much disliked by radicals, including Byron and Shelley.

189. hallowed: made holy.

Making Meanings

First Thoughts

1. Though Byron insisted it was a moral poem, *Don Juan* was the focus of scandalous interest when it was published. How would readers today respond to the supposed "scandalous" passages?

> **Reading Check**
>
> a. What is the **setting**?
>
> b. Who is Haidee's only companion (besides Don Juan), and why?
>
> c. In what ways is Haidee, lines 81–88, described as totally innocent? Why doesn't she ask her lover for a vow of constancy?
>
> d. According to lines 145–168, what do women do when they lose love? Why?
>
> e. Describe the nuptials that Haidee and Juan celebrate in lines 185–190.

Shaping Interpretations

2. What do you think the speaker means by linking Haidee with "pure ignorance" (line 85)?
3. In what way could this story be analogous to the story of Adam and Eve (page 416)? Where does Byron suggest the association directly?
4. Find at least three exaggerated **figures of speech,** and discuss Byron's intended effects.
5. Where does Byron use the final couplet in the **ottava rima** for comic effect?
6. What is the speaker's **tone** when he describes Don Juan and Haidee falling in love?
7. If *Don Juan* is in part witty **satire,** who or what are Byron's targets? Where do you find some barbs directed at the whole Romantic tradition, as exemplified by Wordsworth and Coleridge?

Connecting with the Text

8. Discuss your reading notes in class. What was your favorite or biggest "surprise" in the poem?
9. What do you think of Byron's attitude toward women?

> **Reading Check**
>
> a. The setting is a rocky coast with cliffs and a sandy shore.
>
> b. Haidee's maid Zoe; her father is on an expedition.
>
> c. Haidee cannot imagine falsehood or betrayal. She does not ask for promises because she does not see the need for them.
>
> d. Women seek revenge. Some take lovers, drink, or pray; some run away. They want revenge because without love, life becomes meaningless to them.
>
> e. The priest was solitude; the nuptial torches were stars; the witness was the ocean, and their bed was the cave.

Before You Read

FROM CHILDE HAROLD'S PILGRIMAGE

Make the Connection

The Journey Out—and In
A quest may have a goal, but if the journey is long enough, the traveler may discover that in the quest itself lies the prize. What is explored, all alone on a journey, is the lonely self. That may be true even when the pilgrim, like Byron's Childe Harold, cuts a spirited path through exotic lands. And it is especially true when the pilgrim is alone in vast, glorious, but heartless nature.

Quickwrite

Briefly freewrite about your strongest memory or mental image of the ocean. How do you feel about the sea?

Background

This long poem—which made Byron suddenly famous—appeared in sections (cantos) from 1812 to 1818. It is a thinly disguised autobiographical account of Byron's own journeys. Its pilgrim, Childe Harold, became the prototype for the moody, dashingly handsome character type who would eventually be dubbed the "Byronic hero." (In medieval times, *child* likely meant a young noble awaiting knighthood; Byron uses it as a title, like Lord or Sir, for a youth of "gentle" birth.) In this excerpt from the final canto, the speaker addresses the ocean. The last two verses are Byron's personal conclusion to the whole poem. By this time, Byron said, he had ceased trying to separate himself from the figure of Childe Harold.

The Wanderer over the Sea of Clouds (1818) by Caspar David Friedrich.
Hamburger Kunsthalle, Hamburg, Germany.

Summary ■■■

The speaker expresses a love for nature, especially for the ocean; he notes that his poetic abilities are declining but hopes that his readers will remember some of his writing.

Background

The first two cantos of the poem, which parallel Byron's own pilgrimage from Lisbon to Athens, set the theme of the Romantic traveler destined to be disillusioned by his failure to fulfill his youthful hopes for endless pleasure, originality, and adventure. The same theme continues throughout the third canto, which reflects Byron's own personal disillusionment with fame and love (he had separated from his wife). In the fourth canto, the one from which this selection was excerpted, the anguished eloquence of Romantic melancholy reaches its highest pitch.

RESPONDING TO THE ART

Caspar David Friedrich (1774–1840), who specialized in landscapes and seascapes, was one of Germany's most highly regarded Romantic painters. (For more information, see p. 637.)

Activity. Ask students to answer the following questions:

1. What is the man in the painting doing? [He is standing on a mountain top looking down at clusters of clouds and the tops of other mountains.]
2. How do you think the man in the painting feels about what he is viewing? [awed, overwhelmed, euphoric]
3. What is romantic about this image? [the solitary figure in a swirling, turbulent natural setting; the identification of the human wanderer with the voyaging clouds]

Resources: Print and Media

Reading
- *Graphic Organizers for Active Reading,* p. 63
- *Audio CD Library*
  Disc 12, Track 5

Assessment
- *Formal Assessment,* p. 137
- *Portfolio Management System,* p. 160
- *Preparation for College Admission Exams,* p. 33
- *Test Generator (One-Stop Planner CD-ROM)*

Internet
- go.hrw.com (Keyword: LE0 12-9)

Ⓐ Elements of Literature
Spenserian Stanza

? **This poem is in Spenserian stanzas, nine lines with an *ababbcbcc* rhyme scheme. The first eight lines are in iambic pentameter and the last line, an alexandrine, is in iambic hexameter. In what way does this intricate form fit the subject?** [Possible response: The complex form reflects the seriousness of Byron's concerns and the depth of his feelings.]

Ⓑ Elements of Literature
Apostrophe

? **How does the apostrophe in l. 10 add power to the description of the ocean?** [Possible response: The speaker urges the sea to "roll on," which both depicts the sea's action and suggests the strength of its motion.]

Ⓒ Appreciating Language
Word Choice

? **What is the effect of Byron's choice of three adjectives that begin with the prefix *un-* in l. 18?** [Possible response: The repetition of *un-* stresses how insignificant humans are in the face of the power of nature.]

Ⓓ Critical Thinking
Classifying

? **How would you characterize the speaker's feelings for the ocean as expressed in ll. 19–27? Support your response with evidence from the text.** [Possible response: He expresses happy, playful, and loving feelings. The speaker talks of the ocean as a mother ("on thy breast/to be borne") in whom he has placed his trust.]

Ⓔ Reading Skills and Strategies
Making Connections

? **What has the speaker decided to do in ll. 28–32?** [He has decided to stop writing.] **What are some real-life situations in which people might make a similar decision?** [Possible responses: An athlete decides to retire before his waning skills become evident; a singer stops performing because her voice is no longer what it once was.]

from Childe Harold's Pilgrimage, Canto IV

George Gordon, Lord Byron

1

There is a pleasure in the pathless woods,
There is a rapture on the lonely shore,
There is society, where none intrudes,
By the deep sea, and music in its roar:
I love not man the less, but Nature more,
From these our interviews, in which I steal°
From all I may be, or have been before,
To mingle with the Universe, and feel
What I can ne'er express, yet cannot all conceal.

2

Roll on, thou deep and dark blue Ocean—roll!
Ten thousand fleets sweep over thee in vain;
Man marks the earth with ruin—his control
Stops with the shore; upon the watery plain
The wrecks are all thy deed, nor doth remain
A shadow of man's ravage, save his own,
When, for a moment, like a drop of rain,
He sinks into thy depths with bubbling groan,
Without a grave, unknelled,° uncoffined, and unknown.

3

And I have loved thee, Ocean! and my joy
Of youthful sports was on thy breast to be
Borne, like thy bubbles, onward: From a boy
I wantoned° with thy breakers—they to me
Were a delight; and if the freshening° sea
Made them a terror—'twas a pleasing fear,
For I was as it were a child of thee,
And trusted to thy billows far and near,
And laid my hand upon thy mane—as I do here.

4

My task is done, my song hath ceased, my theme
Has died into an echo; it is fit
The spell should break of this protracted dream.
The torch shall be extinguished which hath lit
My midnight lamp—and what is writ, is writ;
Would it were worthier! but I am not now

6. steal: remove myself.

18. unknelled (un·neld′): without the traditional ringing of a church bell to announce his death.

22. wantoned: frolicked; played happily.
23. freshening: becoming rough as the wind comes up.

Crossing the Curriculum

Art
Have each student find a picture that reflects a lonely or meditative aspect of nature. Encourage students to browse in art books or to look for other works by artists whose illustrations and paintings have accompanied material in this textbook. Students may share their findings in an informal discussion, focusing on the mood of each piece and its vision of nature.

Using Students' Strengths

Naturalist Learners
Have small groups of students discuss how they commune with nature. Do they go bird-watching, take hikes in the woods, or go for long walks by the ocean? Encourage students to explain what they gain from their experience and how it compares to the speaker's. In what ways are their feelings about nature the same as his? In what ways do they differ?

That which I have been—and my visions flit
Less palpably° before me—and the glow
Which in my spirit dwelt is fluttering, faint, and low. F

35. **palpably:** clearly.

5

Farewell! a word that must be, and hath been—
A sound which makes us linger;—yet—farewell!
Ye! who have traced the Pilgrim to the scene G
Which is his last, if in your memories dwell
A thought which once was his, if on ye swell
A single recollection, not in vain
He wore his sandal shoon and scallop shell;°
Farewell! with *him* alone may rest the pain,
If such there were—with *you,* the moral of his strain.° H

43. **sandal shoon . . . shell:** *Shoon* is archaic for "shoes." Sandals and a scallop shell worn on a hat were traditional emblems of pilgrims. The scallop shell is a symbol of St. James, whose shrine in Spain was a great attraction to pilgrims.
45. **strain:** passage of poetry or song.

Wreckers off the Brittany Coast (1911) by Georges P. C. Maroniez.
Bonhams, London.

F Reading Skills and Strategies

Making Inferences

? What do you think is the "glow" that is "fluttering, faint, and low" in ll. 35–36? [Possible responses: the speaker's creative spark, his passion for his writing, his youthful exuberance.]

G Vocabulary Note

Word Origins

Students might be interested to know that the word *pilgrim* comes from the Middle English word *pelegrim,* meaning "foreigner." Ask students what they associate with the word *pilgrim.* [Possible responses: Puritans seeking religious freedom in North America, characters in Chaucer's *Canterbury Tales,* a devout person journeying to a holy place.]

H Critical Thinking

Speculating

? Why might the speaker make such a final wish for the reader as in ll. 44–45? [Possible responses: The speaker hopes that the pain and misadventures he has recounted do not cause the reader pain; or, the speaker gallantly suggests that the reader might painlessly learn the main character's own hard-won lessons.]

Assessing Learning

Check Test: Questions and Answers

1. **What is the speaker's attitude toward humanity's treatment of the earth?** [He thinks humans destroy it.]
2. **How does the speaker remember his first experiences with the ocean?** [happily; with a "pleasing fear"]
3. **How does the setting suddenly change in the fourth stanza?** [After describing the joys of nature, the speaker reflects on his own spirit and on ending the poem.]
4. **How does the speaker describe the main character of the poem?** [as a pilgrim]

Primary Sources

Byron's letter refers to his contemporary, the Romantic poet John Keats, and to the Neoclassical poet Alexander Pope. Unlike most of his contemporaries, Byron admired the technical brilliance of the Neoclassical poets. He claimed the innovations of Romantics such as Wordsworth, Coleridge, and Keats were "all in the wrong, one as much as another . . . we are upon a wrong revolutionary poetical system." Shelley's elegy for Keats, *Adonais* (1821), mistakenly attributed Keats's illness to a scathing review of *Endymion* ("killed off by one critique," railed Byron in *Don Juan,* "snuffed out by an article"). In fact Keats died of tuberculosis, which he contracted while nursing his brother Tom.

If students read this letter carefully, they can gain much information about the poetry and personalities of Keats, Shelley, and Byron. Divide the class into small groups. Invite each group to find information about the three writers, revealed either directly or indirectly in the letter. Encourage students to organize their comments in a three-column chart. Afterward, invite the group to share their charts with the entire class.

PRIMARY **Sources** A LETTER

The poet John Keats had died of tuberculosis in Rome on February 23, 1821. Here is Byron's rather self-centered response to the news. (He thinks bad critical reviews hastened Keats's death.) The child mentioned in the first sentence is Allegra, the daughter Byron had with Claire Clairmont, Mary Shelley's stepsister. Allegra would not live long.

Byron Writes to Shelley

Ravenna, April 26, 1821

The child continues doing well, and the accounts are regular and favorable. It is gratifying to me that you and Mrs. Shelley do not disapprove of the step which I have taken, which is merely temporary.

I am very sorry to hear what you say of Keats—is it *actually* true? I did not think criticism had been so killing. Though I differ from you essentially in your estimate of his performances, I so much abhor all unnecessary pain, that I would rather he had been seated on the highest peak of Parnassus than have perished in such a manner. Poor fellow! though with such inordinate self-love he would probably have not been very happy. I read the review of *Endymion* in the *Quarterly.* It was severe—but surely not so severe as many reviews in that and other journals upon others.

. . . I have published a pamphlet on the Pope controversy, which you will not like. Had I known Keats was dead—or that he was alive and so sensitive—I should have omitted some remarks upon his poetry, to which I was provoked by his *attack* upon *Pope,* and my disapprobation of *his own* style of writing.

You want me to undertake a great poem—I have not the inclination nor the power. As I grow older, the indifference—*not* to life, for we love it by instinct—but to stimuli of life, increases. Besides, this late failure of the Italians has latterly disappointed me for many reasons—some public, some personal. My respects to Mrs. S.

Yours ever,
B.

P. S.—Could not you and I contrive to meet this summer? Could not you take a run here *alone?*

Byron Among the Ancient Ruins (early 19th century). Steel engraving.
The Granger Collection, New York.

Making the Connections

Cultural Connections: Letters

In the early nineteenth century, letters were the main form of long-distance communication. In England, postage was billed on the basis of the number of miles the letter traveled. Many people kept their letters short because use of a second sheet of note paper doubled the charge. Envelopes were not widely used until the 1840s. Single sheet letters were folded and then sealed. Gentlemen at times carried seals on a chain hanging from their waistcoat. These were dipped in beeswax that was melted with a desk taper and then applied to the letter. Red sealing wax was used for business correspondence, various other colors for social missives, and black for messages of mourning.

Using Students' Strengths

Interpersonal Learners

Arrange students in groups of four or five, and have them consider this line from Byron's letter: "As I grow older, the indifference—*not* to life, for we love it by instinct—but to stimuli of life, increases." What is the difference between "life" and its "stimuli"? Ask each group to use Byron's work and the letter to form an answer, and then have the groups share their conclusions.

Making Meanings

First Thoughts

1. Think about your Quickwrite notes. How do your memories and feelings about the sea compare with the speaker's?

Shaping Interpretations

2. In stanza 2, what does the speaker say man does to earth? What can man do to the sea—or the sea do to him?
3. In stanza 3, what **figure of speech** describes the sea as a horse?
4. What single aspect of the ocean does the speaker repeatedly emphasize?
5. In spite of the ocean's destructive aspects, the speaker professes that he loves it passionately. What does this tell you about his personality?
6. What link does the speaker imply between the pilgrim and himself in the final two stanzas?
7. From this brief excerpt, what would you guess the pilgrim was searching for?

Extending the Text

8. How can the fierce identification and rapture experienced by this speaker in the presence of nature be felt today? Which of the poem's lines strike you as being particularly **ironic,** from the vantage point of this century? Why?

Choices: Building Your Portfolio

Writer's Notebook

1. Collecting Ideas for a Research Paper

Byron's visit to the Shelleys in Switzerland resulted in a famous novel, *Frankenstein,* written by Shelley's young wife. Several topics for research might be found in the life of Mary Wollstonecraft Shelley (see page 728). Byron's letter about Keats's death might also inspire research (see page 724). Research begins with questions. What questions are raised by the information on Mary Shelley or by Byron's letter? Save your notes for the Writer's Workshop on page 773.

Another Point of View

2. Answering Byron

Write a response to one of Byron's poems from another point of view. You might speak as the dark beauty, the Assyrian, Haidee, or even the ocean. Try to answer in rhyme.

Comparing Poems

3. Wit Across Centuries

In an essay, compare Byron's *Don Juan* and Alexander Pope's *The Rape of the Lock* (page 527). Consider each work's narrative and at least two of these elements: **verse form, tone, satirical targets,** and use of **irony.**

Analyzing Verse Form

4. From Spenser to Byron

Byron's verse form in *Childe Harold's Pilgrimage* is the **Spenserian stanza** (page 221). Describe the technical requirements of the form, and discuss how Byron uses it.

Creative Writing

5. Don Juan Lives On

Using Byron's hints in the selection, write a brief sequel, in poetry or prose, about Don Juan and Haidee's future. How will he treat her, and she him? You might also include some satirical jabs at popular romance novels that top the best-seller lists today.

Creative Writing

6. Speaking to Nature

In stanzas 2 and 3 of *Childe Harold,* the speaker uses an **apostrophe** (see page 738) to address the sea. Write a prose apostrophe, or address, to some element of nature—sea, wind, fire, snow, rain. Use stanzas 2 and 3 as a model.

Making Meanings

First Thoughts [Respond]

1. Students may have experienced a similar love and "pleasing fear" when swimming. Others may have feared the ocean totally and kept their distance.

Shaping Interpretations [Interpret]

2. Man destroys the earth but cannot destroy the sea, which has the power to wreck ships and drown sailors.
3. Metaphor: a horse's mane.
4. The ocean's boundlessness.
5. It reveals the speaker's love of nature, especially its more powerful and expansive aspects, a central characteristic of the Romantic spirit.
6. The two are about to embark on the final journey toward death.
7. Possible response: The pilgrim was searching for self-knowledge or meaning and beauty in life.

Extending the Text [Synthesize]

8. Possible responses: Nature's wonders have not changed and can provoke a similar reaction today. Lines 12–13 are ironic because oceans are now polluted.

Choices: Building Your Portfolio

1. Encourage students to use various sources to assist them in their research, including the Internet.
2. Before students begin writing, have them reread the chosen poem and choose specific lines to which they can respond.
3. Students may use a three-column graphic organizer to outline their essays.
4. Students may also wish to explain how this verse form is different from others.
5. Encourage students to imitate Byron's verse form if they choose to write their sequel as a poem.
6. Students may wish to address some aspect of nature that they have personally dealt with, such as a hurricane or a flood.

Grading Timesaver

Rubrics for each Choices assignment appear on p. 160 in the *Portfolio Management System.*

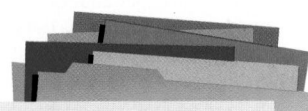

Spotlight On

This feature concentrates on two female novelists of the Romantic period whose work both reflected and challenged the Romantic tenets of their time. A selection from *Pride and Prejudice* reveals Jane Austen's capacity for wit and satire and an excerpt from *Frankenstein* demonstrates Mary Shelley's command of Gothic horror.

After students have read the feature, ask them to make generalizations about the women writers of the Romantic era and to compare and contrast them with the male Romantic writers whose work they have been studying. Urge interested students to do additional research on Jane Austen or Mary Shelley, or to investigate other female writers of the era.

A Background

For many years, Mary Wollstonecraft worked for the London publisher James Johnson, who later published *A Vindication of the Rights of Woman.* Wollstonecraft left England for Paris in 1792 and witnessed the French Revolution. When she returned in 1795, she joined the intellectual circle that gathered at William Godwin's home, a group that included Thomas Paine, William Blake, and William Wordsworth. She married Godwin in 1797.

B Literary Connections

Horace Walpole

Horace Walpole was a writer and collector who helped launch the English Gothic style in literature and architecture. His medieval horror story *The Castle of Otranto* (1765) had many admirers and emulators, as did the turreted Gothic house he built on Strawberry Hill. The poet Thomas Gray was one of Walpole's many friends and Walpole printed Gray's *Odes of 1757* on his private printing press.

C Humanities Connections

William Godwin's social philosophy had a tremendous influence on the Romantic movement. He advanced ideas of anarchism, atheism, and radical personal freedom. His most famous work is *An Enquiry Concerning Political Justice and Its Influence on General Virtue and Happiness* (1793).

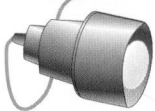

SPOTLIGHT ON

Women Writers in the Romantic Period

Critics and historians may continue to quibble over the dates and definitions of Romanticism, but all agree that the period 1798–1832 in England was characterized by profound social change and unprecedented literary productivity. These phenomena altered the position that women occupied in society and brought about new opportunities and new problems for women writers. As the major male Romantic writers (the so-called Big Six) solidified their claim to poetry as the genre that represented the highest literary achievement, women writers turned to the novel. Two of these writers, Mary Shelley and Jane Austen, can be said to be Romantics; however, their social position as women writers prevented them from simply adopting their male contemporaries' philosophies and literary styles.

Mary Wollstonecraft (late 18th century) by John Opie.

Tate Gallery, London.

Romantic writers embraced certain elements of Enlightenment philosophy; for example, they applauded Enlightenment philosophers' idealism and faith in the perfectibility of human beings. However, these writers deplored the insistence on reason over emotion, and an emphasis on science that discounted the spiritual and supernatural. As a result, male writers increasingly incorporated qualities associated with women—such as extreme emotional sensitivity—into their own work. Inspired by Mary Wollstonecraft's *A Vindication of the Rights of Woman* (1792), literary women, on the other hand, countered the prevailing Romantic trends by writing books that portrayed women as rational as well as sensitive creatures, possessing both sense *and* sensibility, to borrow the title of one of Jane Austen's novels.

As encouraging as Wollstonecraft's *Vindication* must have been to some women of the day, it produced quite the opposite reaction in most male, and many female, members of society: The novelist Horace Walpole (1717–1797) called her "a hyena in petticoats." The resulting backlash, which had been simmering since the publication of *Vindication* in 1792, reached full boil when William Godwin published *Memoirs of the Author of a "A Vindication of the Rights of Woman"* (1798), a tribute to his late wife that scandalized the public with its accounts of her illicit love affairs. In this climate, women who challenged the conventional views of marriage and women's roles were ridiculed. Those who spoke their minds in print risked being publicly renounced and having their work rejected by publishers.

Jane Austen (1775–1817)

Jane Austen was already practicing her craft when Mary Shelley was born. The daughter of an Anglican minister, Austen grew up in a respectable family with social status but little money. What few resources they had were spread thin among two

Using Students' Strengths

Interpersonal Learners

Arrange students in small groups to take turns reading each of the three sections of the feature. Ask them to stop periodically to discuss what they find interesting or controversial about the ideas presented. Encourage students to share their own knowledge and opinions about the topics covered and to make lists of further information they would like to obtain about the lives and careers of the writers profiled.

Kinesthetic Learners

Ask students to give a dramatic reading of each of the boxed excerpts from the work of Austen and Shelley. Ask for volunteers to play the roles of the narrator and the speaking characters in the Austen excerpt and for a narrator to read and actors to mime what the narrator sees in the excerpt from *Frankenstein*. Each excerpt will involve three performers.

Jane Austen (late 18th or early 19th century). Engraving.
New York Public Library. Miriam and Ira D. Wallach Division of Art, Prints, and Photographs. Astor, Lenox and Tilden Foundations.

daughters and five sons, with the largest expenses being devoted, as was common practice, to the formal education of the boys. Jane and her sister received an education typical for girls of the gentry: two years at a boarding school and lessons at home in the female accomplishments of drawing, music, and needlework. Jane also must have made good use of her father's library. D

In an era when being known as a lady novelist was often more a stigma than an honor, it is not surprising that Austen published all her novels anonymously, despite the fact that critics generally agreed her stories would not harm young female readers' moral development. Careful readers, however, could see Austen's subtle but fierce satire of the social and educational status quo. Austen's novels about the social habits, marriage conventions, and manners of the English gentry quietly insist that women are rational creatures, much the same assertion that brought so much scorn upon the writer of *A Vindication of the Rights of Woman.* E Furthermore, Austen's exquisitely rendered descriptions of her characters are often cloaked in an irony detectable only to those sympathetic to her critique of society's constraints on women. The opening sentences of her most famous novel, *Pride and Prejudice,* illustrate her trademark irony and humor: F

> It is a truth universally acknowledged that a single man in possession of a good fortune must be in want of a wife.
>
> However little known the feelings or views of such a man may be on his first entering a neighborhood, this truth is so well fixed in the minds of the surrounding families that he is considered as the rightful property of some one or other of their daughters.
>
> "My dear Mr. Bennet," said his lady to him one day, "have you heard that Netherfield Park is let at last?"
>
> Mr. Bennet replied that he had not.
>
> "But it is," returned she; "for Mrs. Long has just been here, and she told me all about it."
>
> Mr. Bennet made no answer.
>
> "Do not you want to know who has taken it?" cried his wife impatiently.
>
> "*You* want to tell me, and I have no objection to hearing it."
>
> This was invitation enough.
>
> "Why, my dear, you must know, Mrs. Long says that Netherfield is taken by a young man of large fortune from the north of England. . . ."
>
> "Is he married or single?"
>
> "Oh! single, my dear, to be sure! A single man of large fortune . . . What a fine thing for our girls!"
>
> "How so? how can it affect them?"
>
> "My dear Mr. Bennet," replied his wife, "how can you be so tiresome! You must know that I am thinking of his marrying one of them."
>
> "Is that his design in settling here?"
>
> "Design! nonsense, how can you talk so! But it is very likely that he *may* fall in love with one of them, and therefore you must visit him as soon as he comes."
>
> —Jane Austen, *from Pride and Prejudice*

The Austen family remained so protective of their daughter's reputation (and presumably their own as well) that when Jane Austen died at the age of forty-one, the headstone made for her grave G made no mention of the six novels that, to this day, have never been out of print. Instead, it praised "the benevolence of her heart, the sweetness of her temper, and the extraordinary endowments of her mind."

D Background

George Austen, Jane's father, was a notable classical scholar with a distinguished library. As a result, Jane had easy access to a wealth of knowledge. Her reading included the novels of Henry Fielding and Samuel Richardson, volumes of the periodical, *The Spectator,* Oliver Goldsmith's *History of England,* and the poems of William Cowper. In fact, Jane's entire family loved books, and reading aloud in the evenings was a popular Austen activity.

E Exploring the Culture

Married Women

Once married, a woman in nineteenth-century England lost control over any property she possessed. Everything she owned became her husband's property to do with as he wished. The one exception was a wife's land. Her husband could not sell or mortgage it, but he could collect any income derived from it.

F Background

Pride and Prejudice

Pride and Prejudice was published on January 29, 1813 in an edition of about fifteen hundred copies. Miss Annabella Milbanke, who was to marry Lord Byron in 1815, wrote to her mother that she thought the novel "a very superior work . . . the most probable fiction I have ever read." Many others must have felt the same because the first edition was sold out by July and a second one was published in November.

G Background

Jane Austen's Death

In an article in the *British Medical Journal,* Zachary Cope diagnosed Jane Austen as having a form of Addison's disease, which, due to failure of the adrenal glands, causes anemia, weakness, and low blood pressure. In 1817, the year of her death, the disease was unidentified and thus untreatable. Jane died in her sister Cassandra's arms on Friday, July 18. She was buried in Winchester Cathedral the following Thursday. It is interesting to note that neither her sister Cassandra nor her mother attended Jane's funeral, as it was not the custom for women to do so in nineteenth-century England.

Crossing the Curriculum

Health

Jane Austen probably succumbed to Addison's disease. Encourage students to find out more about this illness. When and how was it identified? What are the symptoms? What is the treatment? What is the prognosis for someone suffering from the disease today? Have students present their findings in a brief oral report.

Humanities

Have students work in pairs to research the contributions of women to all the arts, including painting and music, during the Romantic period. Encourage students to take notes and summarize their information on a time line. Afterward they can compare time lines and discuss which areas of artistic expression were more or less open to nineteenth-century women and what limitations were placed on their participation.

A Background

When Mary told her father she loved Shelley, Godwin ordered her not to see the young poet again. The situation was complicated by the fact that Shelley was about to lend Godwin, who was on the brink of financial ruin, a considerable sum of money. Shelley, however, would not be deterred in his pursuit; he even threatened suicide if Mary did not run off with him. She finally gave in, and the couple eloped to France after declaring their love at the graveside of Mary Wollstonecraft, Mary Shelley's mother.

B Literary Connections

Mary Wollstonecraft Shelley's first published work, entitled *History of a Six Weeks Tour* (1817), was a record of her tour of Europe with Percy Bysshe Shelley after their elopement.

C Background

Frankenstein

Frankenstein was first published on March 11, 1818. Since Percy Shelley felt that Mary's gender, name, and youth would hinder the novel's chances of success, the work was presented to publishers as written by a friend of Percy Shelley who wished to remain anonymous. After publication, most people assumed that Shelley himself had written the novel. Even after its true authorship was revealed, some people still believed that Percy Shelley had written most of it. Mary Shelley remarked in 1837, "There is nothing to which contemporaries are more prone, than to discover that an author does not write his own works."

RESPONDING TO THE ART

Richard Rothwell (1800–1868) was born in Ireland and lived in London, Paris, and Rome. He was chief assistant to Sir Thomas Lawrence, the most successful portrait painter of the time. Upon Lawrence's death, Rothwell was entrusted with the task of completing already-commissioned portraits, but he failed to live up to the reputation of his predecessor.
Activity. Ask students what qualities this portrait of Mary Shelley emphasizes.

Mary Wollstonecraft Shelley (1797–1851)

Mary Wollstonecraft Shelley, child of two of the most influential writers of the period, grew up in an unconventional and intellectual household frequented by leading artists and writers of the day. Her famous mother had died a few days after giving birth, and William Godwin remarried a woman who was everything Mary Wollstonecraft was not: dull and conventional. Because her stepmother tried to force her into domesticity, the young girl escaped by reading in her father's library and engaging in stimulating adult conversation with the artists and intellectuals who considered themselves students of William Godwin's philosophy. One of these guests was a brilliant young poet named Percy Bysshe Shelley, with whom Mary went on to share a brief eight years of passion, intellectual partnership, adventure, and tragedy. (A)

In 1814, a teenage Mary Wollstonecraft Godwin eloped with Shelley (who was married at the time), and in 1816 she married him after the death of his legal wife. The couple endured the deaths of three of their four children, and in 1822, Shelley drowned in a boating accident in Italy. Mary Shelley never remarried, and when she died at age fifty-three she was survived by her son, Percy Florence Shelley, and by a literary legacy of six novels, volumes of essays, poems, travel narratives, and a comprehensive journal. (B) Whatever her other accomplishments, however, the reputation of Mary Shelley is forever linked to her first novel, *Frankenstein,* which she began when she was just nineteen.

Mary Shelley (1840) by Richard Rothwell. Oil on canvas (29″ × 24″).

By Courtesy of the National Portrait Gallery, London.

(C) The Author's Introduction to the 1831 edition explains the origins of this most famous book. The Shelleys spent the summer of 1816 at Lake Geneva with Mary Shelley's stepsister Claire and Lord Byron. Since the weather had been cold and rainy, the group decided that for amusement and an exercise in composition, each one of them would make up a ghost story. Frustrated during the daylight hours by her lack of inspiration, Mary Shelley was visited in her dreams by a vision that would become the subject of the most enduring horror story in English literature.

> I saw—with shut eyes, but acute mental vision—I saw the pale student of unhallowed arts kneeling beside the thing he had put together. I saw the hideous phantasm of a man stretched out, and then, on the working of some powerful engine, show signs of life and stir with an uneasy, half-vital motion. . . . He would hope that, left to itself, the slight spark of life which he had communicated would fade, that this thing which had received such imperfect animation would subside into dead matter, and he might sleep in the belief that the silence of the grave would quench forever the transient existence of the hideous corpse which he had looked upon as the cradle of life. He sleeps; but he is awakened; he opens his eyes; behold, the horrid thing stands at his bedside, opening his curtains and looking on him with yellow, watery, but speculative eyes.
>
> —Mary Wollstonecraft Shelley, *from Frankenstein*

With the story of Victor Frankenstein's monstrous, motherless creation, Mary Shelley could examine her own fears of motherhood and her own orphaned condition; in addition, she could vent an anger and violence considered especially unfeminine in her day.

For today's readers, poetry dominates the literary landscape of the Romantic period; however, novelists such as Mary Shelley and Jane Austen remind us of women's participation in a flourishing genre. In the fantasies of Gothic novels, in the privacy of letters and journals, or in very public and forceful essays, women writers recorded their perspectives on the events of a turbulent age.

Assessing Learning

Check Test: Questions and Answers

1. Who wrote *A Vindication of the Rights of Women?* [Mary Wollstonecraft]
2. Jane Austen influenced the direction of what genre of writing? [the novel]
3. Who did Mary Wollstonecraft Godwin marry? [Percy Bysshe Shelley]
4. Where was Mary Shelley when she was inspired to write *Frankenstein* and whom was she with? [at Lake Geneva in Switzerland with her stepsister, husband, and Lord Byron]
5. What is "unfeminine" about the novel *Frankenstein?* [It is angry and violent.]

Percy Bysshe Shelley

(1792–1822)

When young Percy Shelley arrived at Oxford in 1810, his father introduced him to that bookish town's most important bookseller: "My son here," he said, "has a literary turn; he's already an author . . . do pray indulge him in his printing freaks." By spring, one of those "freaks"—an unsigned pamphlet on atheism—got Percy expelled and started a lifelong quarrel with his father. It was the first of many upheavals in the short, ill-fated life of an "author" who followed his "literary turn" wherever it led. In his own time, though, Shelley was better known for his shocking domestic life and opinions than for his impressive body of writing.

Shelley was convinced that human thought and expression had the power to change life for the better. Neither the upheavals of his personal life nor the strenuous reaching of his imagination toward a cosmic vision ever subverted his energies or optimism.

At nineteen, already estranged from his family, Shelley embarked on a career of courting the unconventional. To "rescue" her from a tyrannical father, he eloped with sixteen-year-old Harriet Westbrook, a classmate of his sisters'. Three years later he abandoned Harriet and ran away with seventeen-year-old Mary Godwin, the daughter of two of the most important radicals of the 1790s, Mary Wollstonecraft and William Godwin. Godwin was a rationalist who had once been Percy's intellectual idol. Percy's alliance with Mary also involved responsibility for Mary's fifteen-year-old stepsister, Jane Clairmont (she soon changed her name to Claire), who accompanied the pair on their elopement to Switzerland. Claire's brief affair with Byron brought Shelley and Byron together in Switzerland in 1816 in one of the age's most important literary relationships.

Shortly after their return to England after a second trip to Switzerland, Mary's older half sister, Fanny, committed suicide. Then Harriet, only twenty-one, drowned herself in a pond in London's Hyde Park. Percy was now free to wed Mary, but was denied custody of his two children with Harriet.

Shelley and Mary now fled their debts and notoriety in England and returned to the Continent. The next four years were Shelley's most productive, with one inspired work following another. The year 1821 saw the publication of his great elegy on the death of Keats, *Adonais.*

In 1822, when he was not yet even thirty, Shelley and a companion, Edward Williams, drowned when their sailing boat, the *Ariel,* sank in a storm off the northwestern coast of Italy. Almost two weeks later, Shelley's body washed ashore, a copy of Sophocles in one pocket and of Keats in the other. The body was burned in a pyre on the beach while friends (including Byron) stood by, and Shelley's ashes were buried in the Protestant cemetery in Rome. The epitaph on Shelley's gravestone, composed by his friend and fellow poet Leigh Hunt, read *Cor Cordium,* Latin for "heart of hearts."

Shelley's literary career, though obscured by the soap-opera character of his life, is all the more remarkable because of it. His literary productivity was, with but a few slow periods, unceasing. As his father recognized, Shelley was certainly an "author."

It is said that the Italian sailors who encountered Shelley's boat in the storm on July 8, 1822, offered in vain to take Shelley and Williams on board. When this offer was refused, the sailors pleaded with the Englishmen to furl their sails lest they be lost. As Williams tried to do so, Shelley seized his arm and stopped him. We must certainly regret Shelley's untimely death, but at the same time, we can't help but wonder at his power to capture, and be captured by, the great dark forces that so fascinated him.

Shelley Composing Prometheus Unbound (detail) (1845) by Joseph Severn.
Keats-Shelley Memorial House, Rome.

go.hrw.com
LEO 12-9

OBJECTIVES

Ozymandias/West Wind/Skylark

1. Read and interpret the poems
2. Identify apostrophe
3. Interpret a symbol
4. Analyze terza rima in a sonnet
5. Identify speaker
6. Appreciate music of language
7. Express understanding through critical and creative writing

SKILLS

Literary
- Identify apostrophe
- Interpret a symbol
- Analyze terza rima in a sonnet

Reading
- Identify speakers
- Appreciate music of language

Writing
- Collect ideas for a research paper
- Analyze sound effects
- Compare and contrast sonnets
- Write a parody

Viewing and Representing
- Make inferences about an artwork (ATE)

Planning

- **Block Schedule**
  Block Scheduling Lesson Plans with Pacing Guide
- **Traditional Schedule**
  Lesson Plans Including Strategies for English-Language Learners
- **One-Stop Planner**
  CD-ROM with Test Generator

Resources: Print and Media

Reading
- *Graphic Organizers for Active Reading,* pp. 64, 65, 66
- *Audio CD Library*
  Disc 12, Tracks 6, 7, 8

Elements of Literature
- *Literary Elements*
  Transparency 20
  Worksheet, p. 61

Writing and Language
- *Daily Oral Grammar*
  Transparency 26

Viewing and Representing
- *Viewing and Representing*
  Fine Art Transparency 11
  Fine Art Worksheet, p. 44

Assessment
- *Formal Assessment,* pp. 138, 139, 140
- *Portfolio Management System,* p. 162
- *Preparation for College Admission Exams,* p. 35
- *Test Generator* (*One-Stop Planner CD-ROM*)

Internet
- go.hrw.com (keyword: LEO 12-9)

Summary ■ ■

Shelley's sonnet is a haunting reflection on the transience of earthly power. The first speaker quotes a desert traveler who came upon the ruins of a monument to Ozymandias, a pharaoh of ancient Egypt. The traveler, in turn, quotes the ruler's boastful inscription on the monument's pedestal. Amid the ruins, the inscription becomes an ironic comment on the vanity of human ambition. The only powerful thing that remains is the expression the sculptor captured on the statue's face, but even that the sand and wind are in the process of destroying. The last line suggests this irony: "The lone and level sands" will eventually erase the artist's, as well as the pharaoh's, bid for immortality.

Background

Tell students that in the Great Hall at Karnak, the greatest colonnaded hall ever erected, one hundred men could stand on the capital of each column. In light of this fact, what kind of monument to himself would they expect Ozymandias to build? Write students' ideas on the chalkboard, and have students review them after reading the poem.

Resources

Viewing and Representing

Use the aura of mystery in the Fine Art Transparency *Pyramids of Giza—Sunset Afterglow* by Thomas Seddon to capture students' imaginations. See the *Viewing and Representing: Transparencies and Worksheets:*

- Transparency 11
- Worksheet, p. 44

Before You Read

OZYMANDIAS

Make the Connection

The Test of Time

All human beings, and all human beauty, must perish. But can't our works survive us? We leave, but isn't what we leave behind proof that our passage matters? Like the poets of another restless age, the Renaissance, the Romantic poets posed these questions.

Reading Skills and Strategies

Identifying Speakers

As you read the poem, think about who is speaking to you. Be aware of clues in the text that indicate a change in speaker. Jot down notes on who the speakers are and when their speeches start and stop.

Background

Shelley wrote relatively few sonnets, and this is certainly one of his best. It is all the more interesting because it was written as part of a friendly and informal poetry competition with Keats in 1817. Their poetic topic was Egypt: Some extraordinary fragments from the empires of several Egyptian kings named Ramses had recently been put on display at the British Museum in London. Ozymandias is the Greek name for Ramses II (ruled c. 1290–1224 B.C.), who left monuments all over Egypt, including the temples of Karnak and Luxor. This Ramses is thought to be the pharaoh who contended with Moses at the time of the Hebrews' exodus from Egypt.

Reaching All Students

Struggling Readers

Read aloud ll. 1–8 of the poem. Stop and ask students what remains of the monument to Ozymandias. [Just two legs without a body and a shattered face wearing a sneering expression] Now read the rest of the poem aloud. Afterward, have students contrast the words of the inscription with the ruins of the monument.

English Language Learners

One approach to engaging English language learners is to ask them to listen to the recording of the selection in the *Audio CD Library.* For additional strategies to supplement instruction for English language learners, see

- *Lesson Plans Including Strategies for English-Language Learners*

Ozymandias

Percy Bysshe Shelley

I met a traveler from an antique land
Who said: Two vast and trunkless legs° of stone
Stand in the desert . . . Near them, on the sand,
Half sunk, a shattered visage° lies, whose frown,
And wrinkled lip, and sneer of cold command,
Tell that its sculptor well those passions read
Which yet survive, stamped on these lifeless things,
The hand that mocked them, and the heart° that fed:
And on the pedestal these words appear:
"My name is Ozymandias, king of kings:
Look on my works, ye Mighty, and despair!"
Nothing beside remains. Round the decay
Of that colossal wreck, boundless and bare
The lone and level sands stretch far away.

2. trunkless legs: that is, the legs without the rest of the body.

4. visage: face.

8. hand . . . heart: the hand of the sculptor who, with his art, derided the passions to which Ozymandias gave himself wholeheartedly.

Fallen colossus, Ramesseum, Thebes, Egypt. Photograph (1857) by Francis Frith.
Private Collection.

A Critical Thinking

Speculating

? Why do you think Shelley never names the traveler? [Sample responses: The traveler's name is irrelevant to the poem's message; or the mystery of the traveler's identity adds to the poem's drama.]

B Struggling Readers

Deciphering Difficult Syntax

As students look carefully at the poet's use of commas in ll. 4–8, lead them to see that the main clause is "a shattered visage lies." Then read this paraphrase of the subsequent clauses to the class: The face's frown, wrinkled lip, and sneer prove that its sculptor accurately captured the ruler's arrogant emotions—emotions that have survived both the sculptor who copied them in stone and the ruler who felt them in his heart. Ask students to find the phrase that is omitted from this paraphrase. [stamped on these lifeless things] What word does this phrase modify? [passions]

C Reading Skills and Strategies

Drawing Inferences from Textual Evidence

? What inferences can you make about Ozymandias based on the statue's expression and the inscription on its base? [Most students will say the pharaoh was cruel and proud.]

D Elements of Literature

Irony

? How does the setting described in ll. 12–14 add to the irony of this inscription? [The barren sands reinforce the irony that the king's great works have disappeared.]

Crossing the Curriculum

History

Tell students that Shelley wrote a poetic version of the following inscription recorded by an ancient Greek historian: "I am Ozymandias, king of kings; if anyone wishes to know what I am and where I lie, let him surpass me in some of my exploits." And Ramses II did have exploits! He reigned for sixty-seven years, fought many battles, and had fifty-two sons. Encourage students to learn more about Ramses II and his role in Egyptian and Hebrew history.

Architecture

Ask students to research a monument from any area of the world and write a few paragraphs about it. Tell them to consider the aspects of the work that make it monumental and to decide if the monument achieves its purpose. If students instead want to design a monument of their own, have them write a proposal that explains their intent and includes a sketch of the structure.

Making Meanings

First Thoughts [Respond]

1. The ruler's passions probably include greed, egomania, and contempt for others.

Shaping Interpretations [Interpret]

2. Speakers include the original I who narrates the poem, a traveler, and Ozymandias.
3. The king boasted of his mighty works, but they have all but disappeared.
4. The speaker shows that pride is a passing vanity and that even art is destroyed by time. [Possible response: the message is for all who seek immortality through art.]

Extending the Text [Apply]

5. Students will probably point to boastful dictators such as Saddam Hussein or to deposed or discredited figures such as General Marcos of the Philippines and Stalin in Russia, whose monuments were toppled at the end of the Cold War.

From the Editor's Desk

We realize how hard it is sometimes for students to imagine that poetry is written by flesh-and-blood people. That's why we thought your students would enjoy seeing the original manuscript pages from Shelley's "Ozymandias," especially the one with the doodles and crossouts.

Making Meanings

First Thoughts

1. What do you think are the passions that the sculptor captured in Ozymandias's "visage"?

Shaping Interpretations

2. Even in the brief space of a sonnet, Shelley suggests a number of narrative frames. How many **speakers** do you hear in this poem? (Be sure to check your reading notes.)
3. **Irony** is a discrepancy between expectations and reality. Explain the fundamental irony in the sonnet.
4. Discuss what you think is the speaker's **message** about pride—and whom you think the message is for.

Extending the Text

5. Could this poem apply to any contemporary figures who wield political power? Explain.

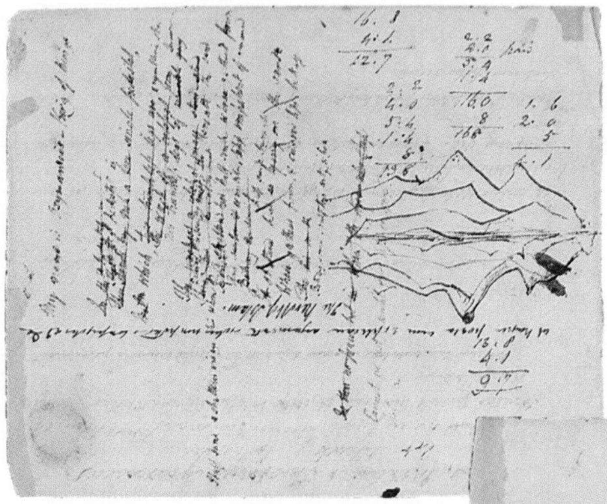

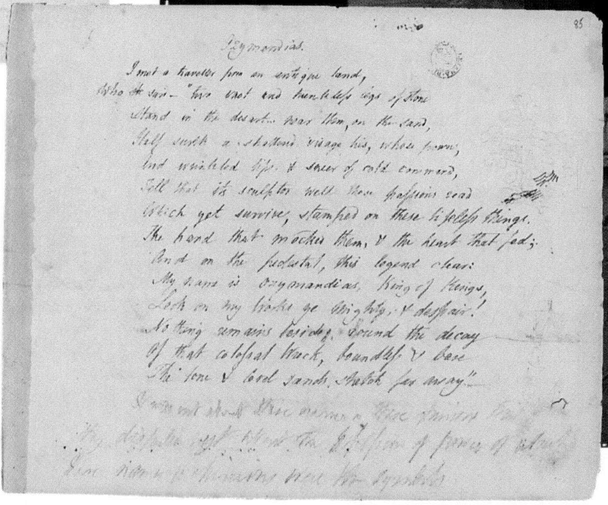

Manuscript pages from "Ozymandias" by Percy Bysshe Shelley. MS. Shelley e. 4, fol. 85 recto and verso.

The Bodleian Library, Oxford.

Using Students' Strengths

Interpersonal Learners

Creating monuments to famous people can be a risky business. Students might enjoy role-playing a scene between Ozymandias and the sculptor as the sculptor is called in to design the monument and engrave its inscription. Have them consider how Ozymandias might speak to the sculptor and whether the sculptor would argue with the king or try to please him. As an alternative, students might role play a scene between a contemporary world leader and an artist commissioned to paint the ruler's portrait or sculpt a monument to him or her.

Musical/Auditory Learners

Students might compose or choose background music that suits the mood of the poem and then read the poem aloud accompanied by their choice of music.

Literature and Archaeology

A Glimpse of an Antique Land

In 1807, the poet Robert Southey complained about a new British fad. "Everything now must be Egyptian," he said. "The ladies wear crocodile ornaments and you sit on a sphinx in a room hung round with mummies." General Napoleon Bonaparte, later emperor of France, started this craze when he invaded Egypt in 1798. Bonaparte's campaign was unusual because his troops were accompanied by a small army of geographers, astronomers, geologists, meteorologists, and artists. The general wanted information about his new territory, and scholars' pictures and reports on Egyptian culture fascinated Western audiences. In England, the people who decorated their homes in Egyptian style wanted more information on the vanished culture of ancient Egypt, with its immense wealth and knowledge. The carefully preserved bodies of ancient pharaohs, a religion that stressed a belief in the afterlife, the tales of fantastic temples buried in desert sand—all these fed Romantic appetites for the occult, the exotic, and the mysterious.

Poster (19th century) advertising Professor Pepper at Egyptian Hall.

The Hulton Deutsch Collection.

Looking for loot. When Napoleon returned to France, he took his wife, Josephine, seven small antiquities. That tiny collection began a plundering of Egypt's art that eventually filled museums around the world. Soon collectors were producing a steady stream of antiquities: immense appendages—arms, feet, heads—that had been broken from larger statues; elaborate stone tombs called sarcophagi; and tapered pillars, called obelisks, that represented the holy rays of the sun and guarded the tombs of kings. These, in turn, were incorporated into the Romantic imagination as they were painted by artists and described by poets—for example, the "two vast and trunkless legs of stone" in Percy Bysshe Shelley's "Ozymandias."

Art collecting or grave robbing? One of the best-known collectors was the Italian adventurer Giovanni Battista Belzoni (1778–1823). Many of his findings were sold to the British Museum. In 1815, he described a bust of Ramses II as lying on the sand "apparently smiling at me, at the thought of being taken to England." The success of collectors like Belzoni, however, ensures that today many Egyptian treasures can be seen only in museums in London, Paris, and New York. Before the discovery of King Tutankhamen's tomb in 1922, explorers were thought to be the rightful owners of Egypt's historical artifacts. In the controversy surrounding that excavation, a member of the British Parliament questioned the fairness of this policy when he asked the prime minister "if he has received any request from Egyptian citizens for permission to ransack the tombs of British kings and queens in Westminster Abbey." Governments and archaeologists now have a heightened awareness of the importance of a nation's treasures, and removing such important artifacts would be impossible today. King Tut's body remains in its grave, and most of the magnificent artifacts from his tomb are housed in the Egyptian Museum, in Cairo.

Edfu Temple, Egypt.

Literature and Archaeology

Ramses II was a military pharaoh who ruled from c.1304–c.1237 B.C. To mark his victories against the Hittites and the Libyans, he inscribed numerous monuments with his name and likeness, many of which survive today. One of Ramses' best-known works is found at Abu Simbel, a temple cut into a sandstone cliff that includes four sixty-seven-foot figures of the pharaoh. When the Egyptian government built the Aswan High Dam in the 1960s, the Nile's waters threatened to submerge Ramses' temple. From 1964 to 1966, a team of engineers worked to disassemble the site and cut it away from the cliff. The temple Ramses dedicated to the gods of the sun is now safely reconstructed two hundred feet from the river.

Making the Connections

Cultural Connections

Point out to students that issues of "collecting" versus "grave robbing" still exist today. One example involves the digging up of ancient human remains on lands considered sacred to Native American peoples. Have students research and read newspaper and magazine articles on this subject. Ask them to compare a current situation to the one described in the feature above and to form teams to debate the merits of arguments on both sides of the issue.

Professional Notes

Critical Comment: Art Acquisition

In 1816, Shelley and his friend Lord Byron probably discussed the controversy surrounding the Elgin Marbles, the ancient Greek statues that Lord Elgin, the British ambassador to Turkey, had brought to London. Back in 1645, when Turkey ruled Greece, the Acropolis of Athens was used as a Turkish garrison. Gunpowder kept at the temple exploded and damaged much of the ancient sculpture there. During Elgin's tour of duty, priceless sculpture still littered the ground around the Acropolis. The French ambassador convinced the Turkish authorities to allow him to collect antiquities, and Elgin quickly followed suit. In London experts appraised the Elgin Marbles as among the finest, if not the finest, works of classical art in existence. Some critics, including Byron, called the sculptures "Lord Elgin's robberies." The debate still continues over whether the sculptures should be returned to Greece.

Summary ■■

Shelley's long ode, consisting of five sonnets with a terza rima rhyme scheme, is an extended apostrophe addressed to the powerful West Wind. After simply addressing the wind and describing its powerful effects: blowing fallen leaves; scattering clouds; and roiling the ocean, Shelley uses a paradox to characterize the wind as "Destroyer and preserver." Shelley then concludes by asking the wind to share its power with him so that his words may spark new life in the world as the wind rekindles "ashes and sparks" in a dying fire.

Writers on Writing

In his famous essay "A Defense of Poetry," Shelley describes how poetry is created by a divine, imaginative spirit: "Poetry is not like reasoning," he argues, "a power to be exerted according to the determination of will. A man cannot say, 'I will compose poetry.' The greatest poet even cannot say it; for the mind in creation is as a fading coal, which some invisible influence, like an inconstant wind, awakens to transitory brightness."

Ⓐ Elements of Literature

Apostrophe

? Throughout the poem, Shelley personifies the wind and addresses it directly. What examples of apostrophe can you find in the first line? ["O wild West Wind, thou breath...."] What effect does this figure of speech have? [Possible response: It makes the wind seem alive and powerful.]

Before You Read

Ode to the West Wind

Make the Connection

Swept Away

The faces of nature range from pacifying to terrifying, all of which the Romantics explored. Yet what so often attracted them in nature was the aspect philosophers call the sublime: the wildness, immensity, terror, and awesome grandeur of natural phenomena like the Alps or violent storms. To grasp nature's power suddenly—whether just by seeing Niagara Falls or by living through a hurricane—is, while terrible, also exhilarating, even transporting. When you read this poem, consider why people find such power (and fear) thrilling. Why would Shelley shout to the wind, "Be thou me . . . !"?

Quickwrite

Have you ever experienced the sublime aspect of nature? When? Freewrite for a few minutes, describing the scene and your emotions.

Background

This major lyric, written in late October 1819, was provoked by Shelley's watching an oncoming storm near Florence, Italy, where he was living. It marks, in his creative life, a temporary note of exaltation after a period of intense grief over the death of his three-year-old son, William. The ode demands to be read aloud.

Ode to the West Wind

Percy Bysshe Shelley

I

Ⓐ O wild West Wind, thou breath of Autumn's being,
Thou, from whose unseen presence the leaves dead
Are driven, like ghosts from an enchanter fleeing,

Yellow, and black, and pale, and hectic° red,
Pestilence-stricken multitudes: O thou,
Who chariotest to their dark wintry bed

The winged seeds, where they lie cold and low,
Each like a corpse within its grave, until
Thine azure° sister of the Spring shall blow

Her clarion° o'er the dreaming earth, and fill
(Driving sweet buds like flocks to feed in air)
With living hues and odors plain and hill:

Wild Spirit, which art moving everywhere;
Destroyer and preserver; hear, oh, hear!

4. **hectic:** relating to the feverish flush caused by wasting diseases such as tuberculosis.

9. **azure:** sky-blue.

10. **clarion:** type of trumpet.

(Opposite) *The Bard* (1817) by John Martin.
Laing Art Gallery, Newcastle-upon-Tyne, England (Tyne & Wear Museums).

Reaching All Students

Struggling Readers

Students may find this extended apostrophe difficult to interpret. Explain that in sections I, II, and III, the speaker begins by addressing the wind directly (l. 1: "O wild West Wind"; l. 15: "Thou"; l. 29: "Thou"). (Be sure students understand that "thou" is an archaic form of the word *you*.) The speaker then goes on to describe the effects of the wind on the seeds, leaves, clouds, and sea. At the end of each section, he asks the wind to hear him. Have students read to answer this question: What request do you think the speaker wants to make of the wind?

Advanced Learners

Ask students to consider how Shelley suggests in this poem the archetypal cycle of death and rebirth in both the natural world and the world of the poet.

RESPONDING TO THE ART

John Martin (1789–1854) loved sweeping landscapes and dramatic narrative. His painting, *The Bard,* illustrates the Romantic idea of the *sublime,* the fascination with strong emotion and awe-inspiring natural beauty. Martin's painting draws on an ode by Thomas Gray that memorializes King Edward I's tradition of having bards, or singers, put to death. In the painting, a small figure with a lyre can be seen ready to hurl himself from a precipice. Below, the king's army is retreating.

Activity. Ask students to answer the following questions:

1. Why might the king want to eliminate the bards? [Possible responses: They might oppose his authority; they might record his failures in battle; they might stir up the people against him.]
2. "Ode to the West Wind" is, in part, about the role of the poet or bard in society. What does the painting reveal about that role? [Possible response: Bards were so important they were often put to death because of their songs.]

Using Students' Strengths

Auditory Learners

Remind students that Shelley was inspired to write this poem by a "tempestuous wind" that preceded a hail and rainstorm over the Arno River. Then play the recording from the *Audio CD Library* of Sections I and II of the poem. What effect is created by Shelley's long lines and rapid-fire images of ghosts, pestilence, corpses, and sepulchers? [Possible responses: The long lines create a breathless feeling; the images of death create a sense of gloom.]

Ⓐ Struggling Readers

Breaking Down Difficult Text

Tell students that while the first section of the poem describes the wind's effects on leaves and seeds, the second section describes its effects on clouds. Help students find Shelley's comparisons for the windswept clouds by looking for the clue word *like:*

(1) In ll. 16–17 the clouds are shook from Heaven *like* decaying leaves are shed from tree boughs;

(2) in ll. 18–21 the clouds become "Angels of rain and lightning" spread over the sky *like* the hair of a frenzied dancer.

Ask students what effect these comparisons have on the reader. [Possible responses: They convey a sense of impending doom; of frantic hysteria.]

Ⓑ Elements of Literature

Apostrophe

? **In ll. 14 and 28, the speaker talks directly to the wind. What request does he keep making?** [He wants the wind to "hear" his words.] **What do you think the speaker wants to say?** [At this point in the poem, answers will vary.]

Ⓒ Elements of Literature

Imagery

? **How does the poet describe the wind's effect on the sea?** [By blowing up huge waves, the wind creates chasms in the Atlantic. The wind's cry also frightens the underwater forests of seaweed.]

Ⓓ Reading Skills and Strategies

Making Connections

? **How do ll. 43-45 link the first three sections of the poem?** [Each line reintroduces the imagery from a previous section.]

II

Thou on whose stream, mid the steep sky's commotion,
Loose clouds like earth's decaying leaves are shed,
Shook from the tangled boughs of Heaven and Ocean,

Angels of rain and lightning: there are spread
On the blue surface of thine aery° surge,
Like the bright hair uplifted from the head

Of some fierce Maenad,° even from the dim verge
Of the horizon to the zenith's height,
The locks of the approaching storm. Thou dirge°

Of the dying year, to which this closing night
Will be the dome of a vast sepulcher,
Vaulted with all thy congregated might

Of vapors, from whose solid atmosphere
Black rain, and fire, and hail will burst: oh, hear!

III

Thou who didst waken from his summer dreams
The blue Mediterranean, where he lay,
Lulled by the coil of his crystalline streams,

Beside a pumice° isle in Baiae's bay,°
And saw in sleep old palaces and towers
Quivering within the wave's intenser day,

All overgrown with azure moss and flowers
So sweet, the sense faints picturing them! Thou
For whose path the Atlantic's level powers

Cleave° themselves into chasms, while far below
The sea-blooms and the oozy woods which wear
The sapless foliage of the ocean, know

Thy voice, and suddenly grow gray with fear,
And tremble and despoil° themselves: oh, hear!

IV

If I were a dead leaf thou mightest bear;
If I were a swift cloud to fly with thee;
A wave to pant beneath thy power, and share

The impulse of thy strength, only less free
Than thou, O uncontrollable! If even
I were as in my boyhood, and could be

The comrade of thy wanderings over Heaven,
As then, when to outstrip thy skiey° speed
Scarce seemed a vision; I would ne'er have striven

19. aery: archaic for "airy"; unsubstantial; seen only in the mind.

21. Maenad (mē′nad′): in Greek mythology, a woman who performs frenzied dances in the worship of Dionysus, the Greek god of wine and crops.

23. dirge: slow, solemn poem or song that expresses grief or mourning.

32. pumice: light, porous volcanic stone. **isle . . . bay:** in the Bay of Naples where pumice is found. These islands were once summer resorts for Roman nobility and, in Shelley's time, were notable for their ruins of ancient villas and monumental baths.

38. cleave: divide.

42. despoil: strip.

50. skiey: like the sky; also, coming from the sky.

Taking a Second Look

Review: Paraphrasing

Remind students that paraphrasing involves restating the ideas of a text in their own words. Paraphrasing is a good way for students to check their understanding of what they read.

Activity

Use the Breaking Down Difficult Text annotation above to help students paraphrase section II of the poem. Now form groups of three or four students each and assign each group to work together on a paraphrase of either section III, IV, or V of the poem. Afterward, have each group read aloud their assigned section and then their paraphrase of it. Then discuss how paraphrases can help readers understand a poem but cannot substitute for the experience of reading the original language.

As thus with thee in prayer in my sore need.
Oh, lift me as a wave, a leaf, a cloud!
I fall upon the thorns of life! I bleed! E

A heavy weight of hours has chained and bowed
One too like thee: tameless, and swift, and proud.

V

Make me thy lyre,° even as the forest is:
What if my leaves are falling like its own!
The tumult of thy mighty harmonies

Will take from both a deep, autumnal tone,
Sweet though in sadness. Be thou, Spirit fierce, F
My spirit! Be thou me, impetuous° one!

Drive my dead thoughts over the universe
Like withered leaves to quicken a new birth!
And, by the incantation of this verse,

Scatter, as from an unextinguished hearth°
Ashes and sparks, my words among mankind!
Be through my lips to unawakened earth

The trumpet of a prophecy! O, Wind,
If Winter comes, can Spring be far behind? G

57. lyre: the Aeolian (ē·ō′lē·ən) harp, a stringed instrument that emits sound when the wind blows across its strings.

62. impetuous: forceful; rushing.

66. unextinguished hearth: from "A Defense of Poetry": "The mind in creation is as a fading coal, which some invisible influence, like an inconstant wind, awakens to transitory brightness. . . ."

Critical Comment

Shelley and the Ode

This ode is both an expression of Shelley's sense of purpose as a public poet, and a personal meditation on the role. In what a biographer calls a moment of both "triumph and defiance," Shelley copied a Greek phrase from the dramatist Euripides in his notebook after finishing the poem: "By virtuous power, I, a mortal, vanquish thee, a mighty god." H

A genuine **ode** in its overall style and arrangement, the form of this poem is special. It consists of five sonnets in **terza rima,** with each section ending, as a Shakespearean **sonnet** does, with a couplet. Each group of three lines picks up the rhyme of the second line of the preceding three lines.

Shelley's admirers have been a little embarrassed by the exaggerated self-dramatization of "I fall upon the thorns of life! I bleed!" (line 54). But the poem is full of such heightened effects. They are consistent with the manner of the ode, with its large scale—the earth, the air, and the sea—with its imagery, and with the situation of the speaker, who is striving in "sore need" in prayer with a higher power.

"Ode to the West Wind" expresses Shelley's fascination with power and with those forces—both destroyers and preservers—that inspire the same powers within the poet.

E Critical Thinking

Expressing an Opinion

? **In l. 54, the speaker refers to the "thorns of life." What is he talking about?** [He is referring to life's problems. (Perhaps the poet was thinking of his son's death.)] **This line is often quoted either to defend Shelley as the most Romantic of the Romantic poets or to make fun of him. What is your opinion of the line?** [Sample responses: The line seems overly dramatic; or the line fits the impassioned tone of the poem in which the speaker is speaking as if in prayer.]

F Elements of Literature

Apostrophe

? **What requests does the speaker make of the wind in section V?** [He wants to be the wind's instrument—its lyre or trumpet; he wants to be fierce, powerful, and impetuous like the wind, scattering his poems like ashes and sparks to reawaken hope in humankind.]

G Reading Skills and Strategies

Comparing and Contrasting

? **How does the speaker's view of himself change in section V?** [Possible response: The speaker moves from thinking of himself as a passive object of the wind, as in section IV, to seeing himself as a lyre or even a trumpet sounding to the world.]

H Literary Connections

Euripides (c. 480–406 B.C.) was the last of ancient Greece's three great tragedians, after Aeschylus and Sophocles. He took no part in public affairs, preferring instead to sit in a cave and look out to sea. His behavior earned him the reputation of an unsociable eccentric. His plays, of which nineteen survive, are famous for their psychological and moral insight.

Skill Link

Analyzing and Responding to a Critical Review

Shelley once wrote, "When my brain gets heated with thought, it soon boils and throws off images and words faster than I can skim them off." John Stuart Mill compared Shelley's imagery to Wordsworth's, finding that "Never did a fancy so teem with sensuous imagery as Shelley's. Wordsworth economizes an image, and detains it until he had distilled all the poetry out of it, and it will not yield a drop more: Shelley lavishes his with a profusion which is unconscious because it is inexhaustible. [The one, like a thrifty housewife, uses all his materials and wastes none: the other scatters them with a reckless prodigality of wealth of which there is perhaps no similar instance.]" Ask students to comment on Shelley's and Mill's comments, referring to specific images in their answers.

Making Meanings

First Thoughts [Respond]

1. Students may be moved by the images of nature's power, or they may be struck by the final lines' message of hope.

Shaping Interpretations [Interpret]

2. The images are blowing leaves, fleeting clouds, and the sea.
3. In the final sections, the speaker asks for the wind's power, rather than describing its effects.
4. The wind scatters leaves (l. 2), but it also drops seeds to the earth (ll. 6–7).
5. He sees himself as "swift, and proud" (l. 56) as the wind, and he longs to be as free as it is.
6. A smoldering hearth contains both dead ashes and living sparks. Words can contain the weariness of death and the prophecy of life. Words can also go unheeded and later spark interest in readers.
7. The speaker asks the wind to give him the voice of prophecy and power of expression. If winter (grief, silence) comes, he asserts that spring (poetry, rebirth) will soon return.
8. Lines 1–54. The speaker asks the wind (Nature) to revive his crushed spirit.

Connecting with the Text [Apply]

9. Students may suggest images of power, such as the force of the sea, or images of beauty, such as a bird's song.

Challenging the Text [Evaluate]

10. Some students will agree with the interpretation, while others will argue that creative powers are not an "outside force" but an inner one.

Making Meanings

First Thoughts

1. Which lines of this poem do you think are most important or have the most beautiful sounds?

Shaping Interpretations

2. What is the central **image** of each of the first three sections?
3. How are sections IV and V different in approach and emphasis from the first three?
4. How can the wind be both "destroyer and preserver" (line 14)? Cite lines to support your ideas.
5. Why do you think the speaker identifies with the wind so intensely?
6. How do you explain the **paradox** that words are like "ashes and sparks" (line 67)?
7. What do you think lines 68–70 mean?
8. What lines of this ode can you connect with the grief of a parent who has just seen a child die? What comfort does the parent find?

Connecting with the Text

9. What aspect of nature would you choose to represent the sublime? Refer to your Quickwrite notes for ideas.

Challenging the Text

10. To some, this ode argues that poetry is created only when the poet is inspired by an outside, greater force. Explain whether you agree.

Elements of Literature

Apostrophe: Throwing Words to the Wind

An **apostrophe** is a figure of speech in which a writer directly addresses a person (usually absent), a personified inanimate object, or an abstract idea. Shelley's opening invocation "O wild West Wind" is an apostrophe, with the device recurring repeatedly. In fact, this poem, like several of Shelley's might be called an **extended apostrophe.**

Perhaps the origins of the apostrophe lie in the repeated invocations of prayer, when the faithful call upon God to hear them. Indeed, not only is the apostrophe a favorite Romantic device, but many Romantic poems are also titled or described as "hymns."

Analyzing apostrophe. The apostrophe also has an interesting relation to Romantic "empathy," or deep sympathy or identification with a person or object. Shelley, for example, closes "Ode to the West Wind" with an ecstatic prayer to *be* or *become* what he apostrophizes. In what lines of "Ode to the West Wind" does Shelley directly address the wind? (How many direct addresses can you find?)

Terza Rima and the Sonnet

In "Ode to the West Wind," Shelley adapts a rhyme scheme called **terza rima** to the sonnet form. Terza rima consists of sequences of three lines of interlocking rhyme. As a technician, Shelley adjusts sound to sense in passages of chiming, onomatopoeic beauty; as a thinker, he dramatizes cycles of death and rebirth.

Analyzing the ode's structure. Take Shelley's great ode apart to see how it works.

1. Identify Shelley's **rhyme scheme** in each fourteen-line section. Are the schemes all the same?
2. Each section is also a **sonnet.** Review sonnet forms (pages 219 and 223), and tell how Shelley has adapted them. Explain whether Shelley's sonnets have **turns.**

Working in groups, prepare each section of the ode for choral reading. When you prepare your scripts, be sure to note passages that use **onomatopoeia** and **alliteration.**

Elements of Literature

Apostrophe

Outline on the chalkboard the three types of apostrophe mentioned in the selection, and provide an example of each. Possibilities include (1) absent people: "Milton! thou shouldst be living at this hour" from Wordsworth's "London, 1802"; (2) objects: "Thou still unravished bride of quietness," from Keats's "Ode on a Grecian Urn" p. 761; and (3) ideas: "Death be not proud," from Donne's poem by the same name, p. 253.

Analyzing Apostrophe

Shelley addresses the wind in ll. 1–2, 5, 9, 13–14, 15, 19, 23, 26, 28, 29, 36, 41–42, 43–57, 59, and 61–70.

Many natural elements are depicted in Shelley's poem. You may want to ask students to choose one element (other than the wind) and write an apostrophe to it.

Analyzing the Ode's Structure

1. *ababcbcdcdedee;* yes
2. Shelley has no octave, sestet, or quatrain, using only terza rima for the first twelve lines of each section. Final couplets suggest the English sonnet form. Shelley varies his subject, tone, and manner of address, but there are no turns that answer questions or indicate a climax.

Before You Read

TO A SKYLARK

Make the Connection

Sky-Drunk, Earthbound

The singing bird is a favorite romantic comparison or *analogue* for the poet: The human singer yearns to capture the ethereal beauty of the bird's song but feels, as Shelley does here, that a human being can never produce pure song. (See also John Keats's "Ode to a Nightingale," page 755.)

While the Romantic poets loved nature, they were not interested in making exact and detailed observations of natural phenomena. To them, nature often represented a higher realm of being, harmony, and even divinity. Shelley composed this poem in June 1820 at his summer residence on the northwestern coast of Italy.

Reading Skills and Strategies

Hearing the Music

Be sure to listen to this poem read aloud. As you listen, follow the text and note the lines that help you imagine the skylark's song.

Elements of Literature

Symbol

Shelley's skylark is used in the poem as a **symbol**—it is a skylark, but at the same time, it stands for something much larger than itself. As you read, think about what the skylark symbolizes to the poet, and then consider how appropriate the comparison is. The lark is a small bird resembling a sparrow. It seldom lights in trees or shrubs but soars high above the ground, singing. Often the skylark soars so high it cannot be seen—only its song can be heard. There are no skylarks in the United States.

The Skylark (c. 1792–1797) by Thomas Bewick.

Iain Bain Collection, Hertfordshire, England.

To a Skylark

Percy Bysshe Shelley

Hail to thee, blithe° Spirit!
  Bird thou never wert,
That from Heaven, or near it,
  Pourest thy full heart
In profuse° strains of unpremeditated° art. (A) (B)

Higher still and higher
  From the earth thou springest
Like a cloud of fire;
  The blue deep thou wingest,
And singing still dost soar, and soaring ever singest.

In the golden lightning
  Of the sunken sun,
O'er which clouds are bright'ning,
  Thou dost float and run;
Like an unbodied joy whose race is just begun.

1. **blithe:** joyful; carefree.

5. **profuse:** abundant. **unpremeditated:** unplanned; done without forethought.

Summary ■■

In this ode, another extended apostrophe, the speaker addresses a skylark. The speaker first emphasizes the ethereal, or otherworldly, quality of the bird and its song. He then compares the skylark to an unknown poet, a lovelorn maiden, a glow-worm, and a rosebud. The speaker next inquires about the source of the bird's joy and finally asks the skylark to teach him "half the gladness" it knows so he can captivate readers with his poems in the same way the skylark captivates him with its song.

Background

Mary Shelley recalls the incident that inspired this poem: "It was on a beautiful summer evening, while wandering among the lanes whose myrtle hedges were the bowers of fireflies, that we heard the caroling of the skylark which inspired one of the most beautiful of Shelley's poems"

(A) Elements of Literature

Symbol

? How does the poet explain in ll. 2–5 his assertion that the skylark was never a bird? [He claims the skylark is a heavenly spirit.] Why would the poet make such a claim? [Possible responses: He idealizes the skylark; the skylark's song symbolizes art and pure beauty to the poet and as such, transcends physical or material form.]

(B) Reading Skills and Strategies

Analyzing Language Choices

After students have read the gloss on the word *unpremeditated,* point out that the word reflects an important Romantic ideal. Ask students why the speaker seems to admire the skylark's *unpremeditated,* or spontaneous flow of song. [Possible responses: The speaker thinks this flow is beautiful; he wishes he could write poetry with the spontaneity of the skylark.]

Resources

Assessment

Formal Assessment

- Literary Elements Test, p. 148

Reaching All Students

Struggling Readers

Before asking students to analyze the poem, play the CD recording for them. Of the three Shelley poems in this cluster, "To a Skylark" is probably the easiest for students to appreciate for its sheer musicality. Since the joyful music of the skylark and of poetry itself is the theme of the poem, students will begin to appreciate the message of the work without having to understand every word of it.

Advanced Learners

These students will notice that "To a Skylark," "Ode to the West Wind," and "Ozymandias" all deal with the artist's sources of inspiration and role in society. Encourage students to compare the messages of the various poems on these key questions.

Ⓐ Reading Skills and Strategies
Connecting with the Text

? Here the speaker asks the skylark a question. The next four stanzas provide four possible answers to this question. How would you answer the question? [Answers will vary. Students should cite objects or experiences they consider pure and lovely.]

Ⓑ Critical Thinking
Speculating

? What is the speaker suggesting about himself as a poet? [Possible response: He is hinting that he feels ignored and unappreciated but hopes someday that the world will recognize him.]

Ⓒ Critical Thinking:
Expressing an Opinion

? Which of the four similes in ll. 36–55 best helps you to understand the speaker's feelings about the skylark? Why do you find that simile more effective than the others? [Answers will vary. Students should justify their choices by explaining the way the simile connected with their personal experiences or their sense of beauty.]

The pale purple even°
  Melts around thy flight;
Like a star of Heaven,
  In the broad daylight
Thou art unseen, but yet I hear thy shrill delight,

Keen as are the arrows
  Of that silver sphere,°
Whose intense lamp narrows
  In the white dawn clear
Until we hardly see—we feel that it is there.

All the earth and air
  With thy voice is loud,
As, when night is bare,
  From one lonely cloud
The moon rains out her beams, and Heaven is overflowed.

What thou art we know not;
  What is most like thee?
From rainbow clouds there flow not
  Drops so bright to see
As from thy presence showers a rain of melody.

Like a Poet hidden
  In the light of thought,
Singing hymns unbidden,
  Till the world is wrought
To sympathy with hopes and fears it heeded not:

Like a high-born maiden
  In a palace-tower,
Soothing her love-laden
  Soul in secret hour
With music sweet as love, which overflows her bower:°

Like a glow-worm golden
  In a dell° of dew,
Scattering unbeholden
  Its aereal hue
Among the flowers and grass, which screen it from the view!

Like a rose embowered°
  In its own green leaves,
By warm winds deflowered,
  Till the scent it gives
Makes faint with too much sweet those heavy-wingèd thieves:

Sound of vernal° showers
  On the twinkling grass,
Rain-awakened flowers,
  All that ever was
Joyous, and clear, and fresh, thy music doth surpass:

16. even: archaic for "evening."

22. silver sphere: "a star of Heaven" (line 18).

45. bower: archaic for "boudoir," a woman's bedroom, dressing room, or private sitting room.

47. dell: small valley.

51. embowered: enclosed; sheltered.

56. vernal: occurring in the spring.

Skill Link

Analyzing an Ode

Tell students that an ode is a poetic form that has changed so often it is difficult to define. Share with students some generally accepted characteristics of odes.

- An ode is usually a long, stately poem that uses impassioned language to pay tribute to a subject.
- An ode often uses apostrophe, invoking an object, creature, or power and then meditating on that subject.
- Since the word ode originally meant "song" in Greek, most odes use musical sound effects such as rhyme, rhythm, alliteration, and assonance to express a wide range of emotions.

There are three types of English odes: Pindaric, Horatian, and Irregular. The Pindaric ode has very complicated rhythmic and stanzaic patterns; the Horatian ode follows one stanza pattern throughout the entire poem, and the Irregular ode allows for freedom and variations.

Activity

Ask students to discuss these questions in pairs.

1. What type of ode is "Ode to the West Wind? [Horatian]
2. What characteristics of an ode does "To a Skylark" possess? [all of them except numbered sections]

Teach us, Sprite or Bird,
What sweet thoughts are thine:
I have never heard
Praise of love or wine
That panted forth a flood of rapture so divine.

Chorus Hymeneal,°
Or triumphal chant,
Matched with thine would be all
But an empty vaunt,°
A thing wherein we feel there is some hidden want.

What objects are the fountains
Of thy happy strain?°
What fields, or waves, or mountains?
What shapes of sky or plain?
What love of thine own kind? what ignorance of pain?

With thy clear keen joyance°
Languor° cannot be:
Shadow of annoyance
Never came near thee:
Thou lovest—but ne'er knew love's sad satiety.°

Waking or asleep,
Thou of death must deem
Things more true and deep
Than we mortals dream,
Or how could thy notes flow in such a crystal stream?

We look before and after,
And pine for what is not:
Our sincerest laughter
With some pain is fraught;
Our sweetest songs are those that tell of saddest thought.

Yet if we could scorn
Hate, and pride, and fear;
If we were things born
Not to shed a tear,
I know not how thy joy we ever should come near.

Better than all measures
Of delightful sound,
Better than all treasures
That in books are found,
Thy skill to poet were, thou scorner of the ground!

Teach me half the gladness
That thy brain must know,
Such harmonious madness
From my lips would flow
The world should listen then—as I am listening now.

66. chorus Hymeneal: wedding song. *Hymeneal* is derived from Hymen, the Greek god of marriage.

69. vaunt: boast.

72. strain: melody.

76. joyance: archaic for "rejoicing."

77. languor: indifference; lack of spirit or interest.

80. satiety: feeling of weariness due to overfulfillment of appetite or desire.

Nature's Glory (c. 1860s) by John Wainwright.
Courtesy Christopher Cole, Beaconsfield, England.

D Critical Thinking: Interpreting

? Why does the speaker want to learn the skylark's "sweet thoughts"? [Possible answers: He wants to experience the same joy as the skylark; he wants to be inspired to produce beautiful poems as the skylark is inspired to produce beautiful songs.]

E Reading Skills and Strategies: Analyzing Language Choices

? Why does the poet choose to use a string of rhetorical questions in this section? [He wants to show that the speaker is grasping for answers to the skylark's source of joy and inspiration.]

F Reading Skills and Strategies: Extending the Text

? Do you agree with these comments that human nature can never be satisfied; that human happiness always involves some sadness? [Sample responses: Yes, because even a completely pleasurable experience does not last; or no, sorrow does not taint every happy experience we have.]

G Reading Skills and Strategies: Hearing the Music

? What words or phrases in the last two stanzas help you to imagine the skylark's song? [delightful, sound; gladness; harmonious madness]

H Critical Thinking: Making Inferences

? How has the world come to listen, as the speaker desired? [Sample response: People are reading this poem, which reflects some of the pure and beautiful qualities of the skylark's song.]

Getting Students Involved

Choral Reading

The short lines and short stanzas of the poem make it a good choice for reading aloud in groups. Divide the class into three groups and assign seven stanzas to each group. After the reading, have students point out examples of rhymes and repeated consonant sounds they enjoyed reading. Ask which stanza is their favorite and why.

Crossing the Curriculum

Science

Challenge students to think of other creatures that could represent Romantic qualities. Have them research one such animal in an encyclopedia or on the Internet. Then have them write both a brief factual description of the animal and a Romantic appreciation of the animal. In a class discussion, compare the two ways of viewing the subject.

MAKING MEANINGS

First Thoughts [Respond]

1. Students may say the speaker envies the skylark's spontaneous joy.

Shaping Interpretations [Interpret]

2. The speaker asks the bird the inspiration for its song (ll. 71–75) and how it sings so purely (ll. 81–85). He asks the bird to teach him its thoughts (ll. 61–62) and its gladness (ll. 101–105)

3. Responses include ll. 1–5, 10, 20, 35, 38, 45, 56, 65–67, 76, 85, 97 and 103. Words include "joyous," "spontaneous," and "free."

4. The speaker compares the skylark to an unappreciated poet, a maiden in a tower, an unseen glow-worm, and a rose in a bower. These similes show that the speaker feels isolated and neglected and hopes to win the world's attention by creating beautiful songs.

5. The speaker has to be free from hate, pride, fear, and sorrow.

6. Students may point to ll. 63–65 or 76–77 to say that the bird represents joy, beauty, and purity.

7. Passages include ll. 1–5, 36–40, 46–50, and 61–65.

8. The phrases reinforce the idea that the skylark is idealized, free, soaring to new poetic heights, and untouched by the world.

Connecting with the Text [Synthesize]

9. Students should be able to recall situations when they regretted something in the past or longed for something in the future. They should be able to think of situations, such as going away to camp, in which happiness is tinged with sorrow.

Challenging the Text [Analyze]

10. Possible response: On the objective, scientific level, a bird's song carries no message for human beings; its messages are directed to others of its own species. The skylark's song, though beautiful to human ears, cannot speak as movingly and relevantly to us as can the voice of a human singer.

MAKING MEANINGS

First Thoughts

1. What, in your opinion, does the speaker most envy about a skylark?

Shaping Interpretations

2. What questions does the speaker ask the bird, and what does he ask the bird to teach him?

3. As you listened to the poem read aloud, which words helped you to imagine (and hear) the skylark's song? What one word would you use to sum up the bird's special music? (Refer to your reading notes.)

4. How are the four **similes** in lines 36–55 related, and what do you think they show about the skylark and about the speaker?

5. What, according to lines 91–95, would be necessary for "harmonious madness" to flow from the speaker of the poem?

6. In your opinion, what does this skylark **symbolize** to the speaker? What lines support your interpretation?

7. What passages in the poem seem to reflect the Romantics' esteem for spontaneity in poetry?

8. How do you interpret these phrases: "unbodied joy" (line 15), "ignorance of pain" (line 75), "ne'er knew love's sad satiety" (line 80), "scorner of the ground" (line 100), "harmonious madness" (line 103)?

Connecting with the Text

9. Lines 86–90 are among the most quoted in English poetry. Do you see these lines reflected in your life? If so, how?

Challenging the Text

10. Even one of the greatest lyrics in the English language can be challenged! Look closely at what Shelley says to the skylark. What might a scientist say to Shelley's request to "Teach us . . . What sweet thoughts are thine"? Do you feel that in some ways the songs of humans are more transporting than the song of the skylark? (How are they different?) Discuss your challenges to the text.

CHOICES: Building Your Portfolio

Writer's Notebook

1. Collecting Ideas for a Research Paper

Suppose you wanted to do a research paper on how people today feel about nature. One way to gather information is to give ten people copies of "Ode to the West Wind" and "To a Skylark," along with a questionnaire that explores their attitudes toward nature. Work with a partner to develop the survey questions, and write up a summary of the responses. Keep your notes for the Writer's Workshop on page 773.

Responding to Language Melodies

2. Turning Words into Music

Shelley's poetry is marked by sound effects (**alliteration, onomatopoeia, assonance,** and **rhyme**) that create a musical quality. In a brief essay, cite outstanding examples of these sound effects in "Ode to the West Wind" and "To a Skylark." Conclude your essay with a statement of your response to Shelley's style.

Comparing and Contrasting Sonnets

3. Shelley's Renaissance Ancestors

Compare and contrast the **structure, subject, theme,** and **tone** of "Ozymandias" with those of any Renaissance sonnet you read in Collection 3.

Creative Writing

4. I Bleed! I Swoon! I Parody!

The Romantics, like all great writers, have been objects of parody. **Parody** is an amusing imitation of a work's style or subject matter. Try your hand at a parody of one of Shelley's great poems. You might get a start by using one of Shelley's first lines. If you're artistic, try a cartoon sequence parodying one of the poems.

Grading Timesaver

Rubrics for each Choices assignment appear on p. 162 in the *Portfolio Management System.*

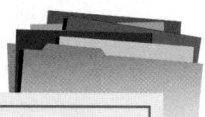

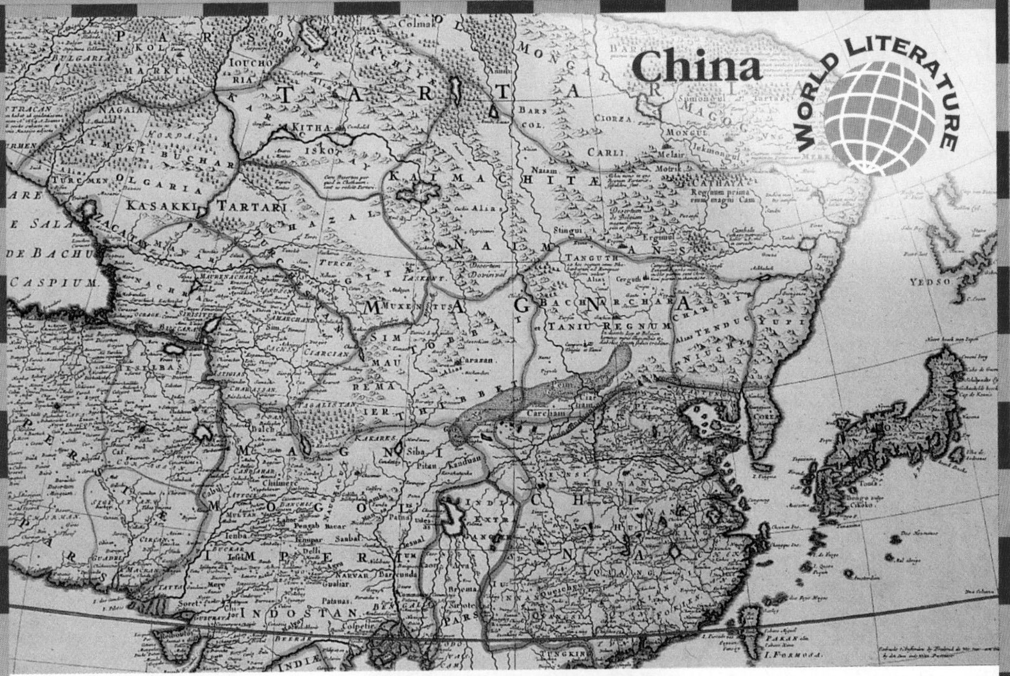

China

WORLD LITERATURE

Tu Fu

(712–770)

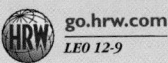

Portrait of Tu Fu (Ch'ing dynasty). Rubbing from a Chinese carving, from *Travels of a Chinese Poet* by Florence Ayscough (London: Jonathan Cape, 1934).

New York Public Library, General Research Division. Foundations. Photographer: Robert Rubic.

In a poem, Tu Fu (do͞o fo͞o) wrote, "I shall not die in peace until I have found words that will startle the readers." At once an unequaled innovator and a master of exacting *lü-shih* (lyo͞o′shi), or "regulated verse," Tu Fu indeed changed Chinese poetry forever. Unlike earlier poets, he did not restrict a poem to a single subject, setting, or mood; he mixed private and public concerns; and he wrote honestly—even bitterly and blackly—about current events. Yet he could see humor even in his own poverty, and his striking images show how nature nourished him. Tu Fu's difficult life began when he failed the imperial writing exams. Thereafter, he took minor government positions (he eventually passed a special exam), constantly moving throughout China to support a large family he cherished.

In 759, he bravely left official service without any financial support. Though Tu Fu barely eked out a living from patrons, he wrote nearly 80 percent of his elegant, objective poetry in his last years. Along with his friend Li Po (page 766), Tu Fu was one of the most brilliant poets of the High T'ang. During Tu Fu's life, his reputation never matched Li Po's, but now Tu Fu is often called China's greatest poet.

(Above) Map of Mongolia showing Japan and China (c. 1680) by Frederick de Wit.

go.hrw.com
LEO 12-9

OBJECTIVES

1. Read and respond to the poem
2. Compare and contrast poems that cross cultures
3. Connect poem with students' own experience
4. Write a poem on a similar theme

Planning

- **Block Schedule**
  Block Scheduling Lesson Plans with Pacing Guide
- **Traditional Schedule**
  Lesson Plans Including Strategies for English-Language Learners
- **One-Stop Planner**
  CD-ROM with Test Generator

BROWSING IN THE FILES

About the Author. Tu Fu's poetry brought an objective realism to Chinese literature that was so unprecedented that he has been called the "poet-historian." Tu Fu's personal crisis was a loss of faith in Confucianism, which can be felt in much of his poetry. Like the English Romantics, Tu Fu felt a strong connection with nature and an abiding love for the common people. As he once said, he found a "goodness" in the poor that sustained him and inspired him to make in his economic poverty an artistic wealth.

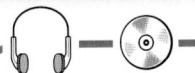

Resources: Print and Media

Reading
- *Audio CD Library*
  Disc 12, Track 9

Internet
- go.hrw.com (keyword: LE0 12-9)

Summary ■

The speaker describes the scene around the ruins of an old palace. The building is alive with memories and hints of past glory. The speaker wants to write a poem but is overcome by sad thoughts of the transience of all things.

Ⓐ Struggling Readers

Summarizing

? As described in ll. 3–14, what has happened to the palace? [It has crumbled into ruins over time.]

Ⓑ Elements of Literature

Tone

? What is the speaker's attitude toward his subject? [Possible response: Overcome by the ravages of time and the impermanence of all human endeavor, he is serious, sad, and unsettled.] What is implied about the speaker's attitude toward his writing? [Possible response: His realization that everything disappears in time fills him with sadness and makes it hard for him to write since neither the past nor the future can be relied upon.]

Ⓒ Critical Thinking

Challenging the Text

? Do you think the final question is an effective way to end the poem? Why or why not? [Possible responses: No, because it shifts the focus of the poem too abruptly from the past to the future; or, yes, because the question is a logical progression which expands the poem from a contemplation of the past to a meditation on time itself.]

Finding Common Ground

Challenge students to think of contemporary displays of power, pride, or even beauty that have already crumbled or been destroyed, such as deactivated nuclear power plants or public buildings or sculpture defaced by graffiti or other vandalism. Students can use these and other examples as springboards to the discussion topics. Help them see that the speaker of "Jade Flower Palace" expresses a more personal sense of sadness, loss, and uncertainty than does the more detached and philosophical speaker of "Ozymandias." Students can write their poems individually and then rejoin their groups to discuss each other's work.

Before You Read

Jade Flower Palace

Background

Two intense quests informed Tu Fu's troubled life: to write poetry and to obtain a high government position. The combination could have been glorious, for Tu Fu lived during the eighth century, part of China's T'ang era: a peak of cultural and artistic achievement. Although Tu Fu showed great brilliance, in 736 (at twenty-four) he failed the imperial examinations and lost all chance at an exalted office. For a Confucian who saw service to the emperor as life's greatest good, the blow cut deeply. An even sharper and sadder blow—but one that produced great poetry—was Tu Fu's disillusionment with imperial wisdom and power. In a 755 rebellion that Tu Fu witnessed, 36 million of China's 53 million people were killed or driven from their homes. His own son died of starvation. During this period, Tu Fu wrote "Jade Flower Palace."

Quickwrite

"Who can say what the years will bring?" Write your thoughts on Tu Fu's question.

By permission of the British Library, London.

A Keepsake from the Cloud Gallery (1750). Chinese. ADD Ms. 22689.

Jade Flower Palace

Tu Fu

translated by **Kenneth Rexroth**

The stream swirls. The wind moans in
The pines. Gray rats scurry over
Broken tiles. What prince, long ago,
Built this palace, standing in
Ruins beside the cliffs? There are
Green ghost fires in the black rooms.
The shattered pavements are all
Washed away. Ten thousand organ
Pipes whistle and roar. The storm ⒶⒶ
Scatters the red autumn leaves.
His dancing girls are yellow dust.
Their painted cheeks have crumbled
Away. His gold chariots
And courtiers are gone. Only
A stone horse is left of his
Glory. I sit on the grass and
Start a poem, but the pathos of Ⓑ
It overcomes me. The future
Slips imperceptibly away.
Ⓒ Who can say what the years will bring?

Finding Common Ground

The similarities between this poem and Shelley's "Ozymandias" (page 731) are striking. Like these eighth- and eighteenth-century observers, you can also ponder the ruins of power.

- With one or more classmates, compare your Quickwrite notes on the passing of time.
- Working with a partner or small group, explore the differences and similarities between "Jade Flower Palace" and "Ozymandias."
- To write a poem on the same theme today, what physical site would you choose? (It might be an abandoned site, not necessarily a destroyed one.) What objects would you focus on? Work with a partner or a small group to write a poem on Tu Fu's theme.

Reaching All Students

English Language Learners

To help students empathize with the speaker's mood and experience, have them examine photographs of ruins of formerly beautiful places and discuss their feelings about the changes.

Advanced Learners

Invite students to evaluate the imagery in the poem as they read. Challenge them to come up with other images that Tu Fu might have used to help the reader visualize the scene.

Making the Connections

Connecting to the Theme: "The Quest for Beauty"

Have students discuss how Tu Fu's solitary reflections relate to the collection's theme. [Possible responses: The poet examines the ephemeral quality of beauty and yearns for a beauty that will endure.]

John Keats

(1795–1821)

John Keats by Charles Armitage Brown.

By courtesy of the National Portrait Gallery, London.

It is surprising that Keats became a poet at all, and surely a wonder that, when he died at the age of twenty-five, he had accomplished enough to become one of our major poets.

John Keats's short life was plagued with troubles, and he lacked most of the advantages a poet often needs to get started. His father, who ran a London livery stable, died when Keats was eight. His mother died of tuberculosis when he was fourteen, leaving the family finances tied up and inaccessible to the Keats children. After four years in a school where his literary interests were encouraged, he was apprenticed at the age of fifteen to learn medicine. Keats saw something of his own country as a young man, but his only foreign travel was a desperate trip to Italy when he was dying, enduring what he called a "posthumous existence." He had friends and supporters who recognized his poetic genius, but he never enjoyed a close collaborative relationship with another poet. A man of small stature (he was barely over five feet tall), he lived in close acquaintance with death and the fragile nature of human life.

In 1816, not yet twenty-one, Keats completed his medical studies at Guy's Hospital in London. Before he could be legally licensed as a surgeon, he made the momentous decision to become a poet. Some harsh reviews of his first book of poetry (1817) stung him and added to the periodic doubts that made his dedication to poetry sometimes seem an awful burden. Now much of Keats's time was spent nursing his brother Tom, who was dying of tuberculosis.

After Tom's death in December 1818, Keats had a little more than two years to make what he could of his determination to lead a "literary life." Great passages and nearly perfect poems poured from him in that miraculous time. Already in failing health, he never knew the greatness of his achievements, which might have given him at least the consolation of literary success. He had also fallen in love—her name was Fanny Brawne—but his poor health and money problems kept him from marrying. "I am three and twenty," he wrote despairingly in March 1819, "with little knowledge and middling intellect. It is true that in the height of enthusiasm I have been cheated into some fine passages, but that is not the thing."

In the next six months, he wrote some of his most glorious poems. Yet, he lamented in a November letter to his brother George (who had immigrated to Kentucky in 1817), "Nothing could have in all circumstances fallen out worse for me than the last year has done, or could be more damping to my poetical talent." Three months later he coughed up blood. His medical training and the nursing of Tom made the truth obvious: "That drop of blood is my death warrant." His only chance, a slim one, was to live in a warmer climate.

After declining an invitation from the Shelleys to join them in Pisa, Italy, Keats and his friend Joseph Severn, an artist, settled in Rome in late 1820. There Keats died in February 1821 and was buried in the Protestant cemetery—that "camp of death," as Shelley called it in *Adonais,* his powerful elegy for Keats.

The stark sadness of Keats's life heightens our awareness of the qualities of his poems—not bleak, subdued, or heavy with resignation, but rich in sensuous detail and exciting representations of intense emotional experiences, full of courageous hope for what the imagination can seize and enjoy in life. Above all, they show us what Keats was able to wrest from his troubled life by singlemindedly working at the art of poetry.

OBJECTIVES

. . . Chapman's Homer / When I Have Fears / La Belle Dame . . . / . . . Nightingale / . . . Grecian Urn

1. Read and interpret the poems
2. Identify and analyze sonnet and ballad form
3. Recognize and connect imagery
4. Understand inverted syntax
5. Recognize common motifs
6. Track speaker's mood
7. Construct images based on text
8. Express understanding through writing, art, or music

SKILLS

Literary
- Identify and analyze sonnet and ballad form
- Recognize and connect imagery

Reading
- Understand inverted syntax
- Recognize common motifs
- Track speaker's mood
- Construct images based on text

Writing
- Collect ideas for a research paper
- Analyze text structures
- Compare two odes
- Compare and contrast text elements
- Write a personal letter
- Write an explanation
- Write an apostrophe to a painting

Art
- Illustrate poem in cartoon form

Music
- Improvise and perform a musical setting for the poem

Viewing and Representing
- Make inferences about artworks (ATE)

Resources: Print and Media

Reading
- *Graphic Organizers for Active Reading,* pp. 67, 68, 69, 70, 71
- *Audio CD Library*
  Disc 12, Tracks 10, 11, 12, 13, 14

Writing and Language
- *Grammar and Language Links* Worksheet, p. 41
- *Language Workshop CD-ROM*

Viewing and Representing
- *Visual Connections*
  Videocassette B, Segment 8

Assessment
- *Formal Assessment,* pp. 141, 142, 143, 144, 145
- *Portfolio Management System,* p. 163
- *Test Generator (One-Stop Planner CD-ROM)*

Internet
- go.hrw.com (keyword: LE0 12-9)

Planning

- **Block Schedule**
  Block Scheduling Lesson Plans with Pacing Guide
- **Traditional Schedule**
  Lesson Plans Including Strategies for English-Language Learners
- **One-stop Planner**
  CD-ROM with Test Generator

Summary ■■

The speaker recalls how a reading of Homer's *Iliad*, in a translation by the Elizabethan poet George Chapman, ignited his sympathetic imagination. He could perceive the experience described in the poetry so intensely that the moment matches the discovery and excitement explorers feel when gazing upon a planet or an ocean they have never seen before.

BROWSING IN THE FILES

Writers on Writing. In Keats's discussions with friends over the hostile tone of his preface to *Endymion,* his first published poem, he remarked: "I never wrote one single Line of Poetry with the least Shadow of public thought." What Keats did listen to, in his own words, was "the eternal Being, the Principle of Beauty—and the Memory of great Men."

RESPONDING TO THE ART

Activity. Tell students that Apollo is the Greek god of poetry, music, sunlight, and prophecy. Invite them to discuss what these realms have in common. Then ask them to discuss what they see in the painting and how these images relate to Keats.

Before You Read
ON FIRST LOOKING INTO CHAPMAN'S HOMER

Make the Connection
The Wonder of Words

For all the Romantics, poetry was the true adventure. Imagination opened whole worlds; the best poetry opened thrilling vistas of absolute newness—as Keats says here.

Reading Skills and Strategies
Reading Inverted Syntax

Keats, like many other poets of his time, often inverts the syntax of his sentences to meet the demands of meter and rhyme. The word order of a traditional English sentence is subject-verb-complement. If you have trouble with Keats's syntax, look for the subject and verb of each sentence.

Elements of Literature
The Sonnet

Sonnets usually have two parts, no matter what the stanzaic structure is. The first part may present a problem, question, or idea that the second part resolves, answers, or emphasizes. The **turn** begins the second part. Keats wrote this sonnet in the Italian form, using an eight-line octave and a six-line sestet. Keats's next sonnet, "When I Have Fears" (page 748), marks a change to the Shakespearean form. (See pages 219 and 223.)

Background

In 1816—just before his twenty-first birthday—Keats wrote this poem, his first mature work, in a few hours. Keats once said that "if poetry comes not as naturally as the leaves to a tree, it had better not come at all."

This poem was connected with an exciting literary experience. Keats's favorite teacher, Charles Cowden Clarke, had invited him to spend an evening reading a translation of Homer's *Iliad* by George Chapman, a contemporary of Shakespeare. They stayed up all night. Keats went home at dawn and by ten that morning sent Clarke this sonnet.

The Chariot of Apollo (late 19th or early 20th century) by Odilon Redon.
Louvre, Paris.

go.hrw.com
LEO 12-9

Reaching All Students

Struggling Readers
Reading inverted sentences was introduced on p. 600. One strategy to use with inverted sentences is Text Reformulation. For information on using this strategy, see p. 127 of the Reading Strategies Handbook in front of the *Reading Skills and Strategies* binder.

English Language Learners
Ask students to recall an experience in which they read a story or saw a film for a second time and suddenly discovered meaning that had totally escaped them before. Have them share these experiences and explain how Keats's poem describes a similar discovery.

Advanced Readers
Have students analyze the rhyme scheme *(abbaabbacdcdcd)* and meter (iambic pentameter with variations) of Keats's sonnet and compare it with other sonnets they know.

On First Looking into Chapman's Homer

John Keats

Much have I traveled in the realms of gold, **A**
  And many goodly states and kingdoms seen;
  Round many western islands have I been
Which bards in fealty to Apollo° hold.
Oft of one wide expanse had I been told
  That deep-browed Homer ruled as his demesne;°
  Yet did I never breathe its pure serene°
Till I heard Chapman speak out loud and bold: **B**
Then felt I like some watcher of the skies
  When a new planet swims into his ken;° **C**
Or like stout Cortez° when with eagle eyes
  He stared at the Pacific—and all his men
Looked at each other with a wild surmise— **D**
  Silent, upon a peak in Darien.

4. bards in fealty to Apollo: poets in loyal service (as feudal tenants to their lord) to Apollo, the Greek god of poetry.
6. demesne (di·mān′): domain.
7. serene: archaic for "clear air."
10. ken: range of vision.
11. Cortez: sixteenth-century Spanish explorer. In this now famous mistake, Keats confuses Cortez with Balboa, another Spanish explorer. Balboa was actually the first European to see the eastern shore of the Pacific Ocean from the heights of Darien in Panama.

MAKING MEANINGS

First Thoughts

1. Which **image** from the poem can you still see?

Shaping Interpretations

2. **Paraphrase** this poem line by line, reordering Keats's inverted syntax. Do any lines still give you difficulty?
3. How would you sum up each of the two parts of this **sonnet**?
4. What does the speaker say he had already experienced before he read Homer? How does he say he felt on reading Homer?
5. What could "realms of gold" (line 1) be?
6. Look at the two famous **similes** in lines 9–14. What is Keats telling you about how he felt on reading Homer? By implication, what is he comparing the experience of reading poetry to?

Extending the Text

7. Keats could not have dreamed of film, computers, and virtual reality. What do you think of their powers, as compared with those of poetry?

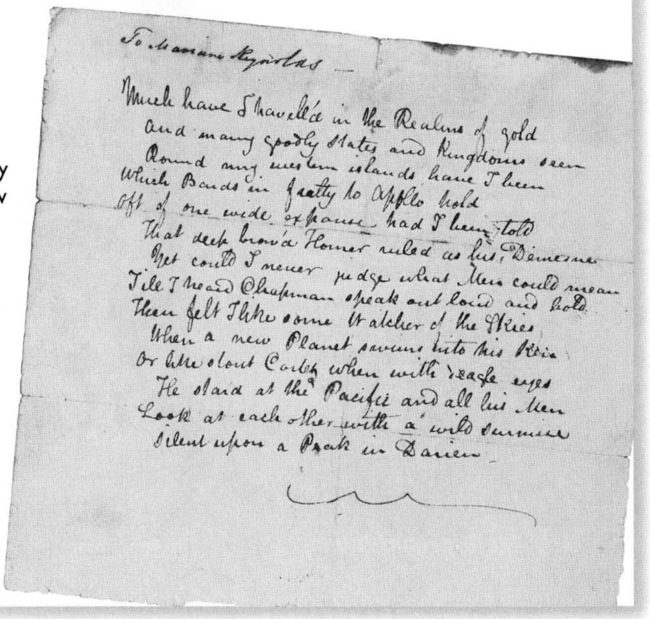
Much have I travell'd in the Realms of gold
and many goodly States and Kingdoms seen
Round many western islands have I been
Which Bards in fealty to Apollo hold
Oft of one wide expanse had I been told
That deep brow'd Homer ruled as his Demesne
Yet could I never judge what Men could mean
Till I heard Chapman speak out loud and bold
Then felt I like some Watcher of the Skies
When a new Planet swims into his Ken
Or like stout Cortez when with eagle eyes
He star'd at the Pacific and all his Men
Look at each other with a wild surmise
Silent upon a Peak in Darien

Manuscript of "On First Looking into Chapman's Homer" by John Keats.
Victoria and Albert Museum, London.

Getting Students Involved

Enrichment Activity

Oral Reading. Have students working in pairs find and read various translations of Homer's epic poems. Encourage them to read sections aloud to one another and decide which translation they find most interesting and readable. Then have them choose a passage from that translation and prepare an oral reading for presentation to the class.

Crossing the Curriculum

Science

Encourage interested students to find out more about William Herschel's discovery of the planet Uranus. Then have pairs of students role-play an interview, with one taking the role of Herschel and the other taking the role of an eighteenth-century news reporter seeking information about the discovery.

A Reading Skills and Strategies

Inverted Syntax

Ask students to reword these two lines using traditional word order. [I have traveled much in the realms of gold and seen many goodly states and kingdoms.]

B Elements of Literature

Sonnet

? Where does the turn occur in this sonnet? [between ll. 8 and 9]

C Historical Connections

Explain that l. 10 may refer to the then relatively recent discovery of the planet Uranus by William Herschel in 1791.

D Appreciating Language

Diction

? What do the words "wild surmise" in l. 13 suggest about the actions and expressions of Cortez's men? [Possible response: The words illustrate men silenced with amazement, barely daring to guess that they have reached a new sea.]

MAKING MEANINGS

First Thoughts [Respond]

1. Possible responses: "Deep-browed Homer," the astronomer, or perhaps the final image of men silent on the mountain peak.

Shaping Interpretations [Interpret]

2. Students should write paraphrases that demonstrate understanding of the content and use traditional word order.
3. Part 1, ll. 1–8, recounts the speaker's past literary experience and prepares the ground for the second part; part 2, ll. 9–14, describes his awe upon reading Chapman.
4. He had already read many great poets. On reading Homer, he felt like the discoverer of a new planet.
5. Possible response: imaginary lands.
6. Keats's similes describe the thrill of discovery. The comparison implies that poetry can reveal new truths to readers.

Extending the Text [Synthesize]

7. Possible response: While film, computers, and virtual reality effectively present information and simulate real experience, they do not tap the imagination as well as the written word.

Summary

The speaker worries that an early death may prevent him from fulfilling his artistic promise and may separate him from his beloved. These thoughts of death cause him to question the ultimate importance of fame and love.

Resources

Viewing and Representing

Videocassette B, Segment 8

Available in English and Spanish. This segment explores the Romantics. For full lesson plans and worksheets, see the *Visual Connections Teacher's Manual.*

A Elements of Literature

Imagery

? What images are used to describe the speaker's potential works? ["rich garners," "full-ripened grain"] How are they appropriate to a poem about death? [Possible responses: These are agricultural images of the harvest, which signal the coming of winter; also death frequently is referred to as "the grim reaper."]

B Critical Thinking

Interpreting

? Point out that a change in the speaker's attitude occurs at the sonnet's turn in l. 12. Why do you think the speaker's thoughts on death change his attitude toward love and fame? [Possible response: Thinking of death puts all earthly experience into perspective.]

RESPONDING TO THE ART

John Callcott Horsley (1817–1903), English artist, painted mostly historical subjects. When he turned to more contemporary subjects, his colleagues teased him by saying the ingredients for these paintings were merely "sunshine and pretty women."

Activity. Ask students to study the images in the painting and tell a partner what they think is going on between the man and woman. [Possible response: The man is writing love poetry and giving it to the woman to read, but he is distracted from his composition and his beloved by more philosophical thoughts.]

Before You Read

WHEN I HAVE FEARS

Make the Connection

The End in Sight

An intense creative mission may be both a blessing and a burden: It focuses life but increases time's pressure. In Keats's case, the fears he expressed in this poem are even more poignant because we know that his death at age twenty-five confirmed them. His aspirations to both love and fame were frustrated. John Keats did "cease to be" within three years of writing this sonnet.

Quickwrite

If you knew your time on earth was short, what would you most regret not being able to do or experience? Jot down your thoughts.

Background

By 1820, shortly before he died, Keats had published his new poems in "one of the richest volumes in the history of English poetry." He also hoped to nurture his "little dramatic skill" by writing a few more narrative poems to "nerve me up to the writing of a few fine plays—my greatest ambition." He longed to follow Shakespeare into "the fierce dispute/Betwixt damnation and impassioned clay."

Our tragedy is that he could not. Our wonder must be that none of the great poets who came before him—Chaucer, Spenser, Shakespeare, Milton, Pope, or Wordsworth—would be found in this book if they had died at twenty-five.

When I Have Fears

John Keats

When I have fears that I may cease to be
    Before my pen has gleaned my teeming brain,
Before high-pilèd books, in charact'ry,°
A   Hold like rich garners the full-ripened grain;
When I behold, upon the night's starred face,
    Huge cloudy symbols of a high romance,
And think that I may never live to trace
    Their shadows, with the magic hand of chance;
And when I feel, fair creature of an hour,
    That I shall never look upon thee more,
Never have relish in the fairy° power
B   Of unreflecting love!—then on the shore
Of the wide world I stand alone, and think
Till Love and Fame to nothingness do sink.

3. charact'ry: the characters of the alphabet.
11. fairy: supernatural; unearthly.

The Poet's Theme (19th century) by John Callcott Horsley.

Reaching All Students

Struggling Readers

Have students read this poem twice, once aloud with a partner and once silently. Urge them to focus on the speaker's feelings and to talk about their own responses after each reading.

English Language Learners

This poem is essentially one long sentence. Suggest students break it down and read it as follows: two lines at a time through l. 10; ll. 11 and 12 to the exclamation point; and then from there to the end.

Advanced Learners

Keats rightly feared that his life would be a short one. Ask students to reflect on the experiences that Keats's poem predicts will be cut short if he dies young. Then, challenge them to write a requiem in the form of a chant, song, or poem that expresses both Keats's thoughts on mortality and the reader's own knowledge of what Keats achieved. Encourage students to share their requiems with the class.

PRIMARY Sources — A LETTER

Keats's Last Letter

Rome, 30 November 1820

My dear Brown,

'Tis the most difficult thing in the world to me to write a letter. My stomach continues so bad, that I feel it worse on opening any book, yet I am much better than I was in quarantine. Then I am afraid to encounter the pro-ing and con-ing of anything interesting to me in England. I have an habitual feeling of my real life having passed, and that I am leading a posthumous existence. God knows how it would have been—but it appears to me—however, I will not speak of that subject. I must have been at Bedhampton nearly at the time you were writing to me from Chichester—how unfortunate—and to pass on the river too! There was my star predominant! I cannot answer anything in your letter, which followed me from Naples to Rome, because I am afraid to look it over again. I am so weak (in mind) that I cannot bear the sight of any handwriting of a friend I love so much as I do you. Yet I ride the little horse, and, at my worst, even in quarantine, summoned up more puns, in a sort of desperation, in one week than in any year of my life. There is one thought enough to kill me; I have been well, healthy, alert, etc., walking with her, and now—the knowledge of contrast, feeling for light and shade, all that information (primitive sense) necessary for a poem, are great enemies to the recovery of the stomach. There, you rogue, I put you to the torture; but you must bring your philosophy to bear, as I do mine, really, or how should I be able to live? Dr. Clark is very attentive to me; he says, there is very little the matter with my lungs, but my stomach, he says, is very bad. I am well disappointed in hearing good news from George [Keats's brother], for it runs in my head we shall all die young. I have not written to Reynolds yet, which he must think very neglectful; being anxious to send him a good account of my health, I have delayed it from week to week. If I recover, I will do all in my power to correct the mistakes made during sickness; and if I should not, all my faults shall be forgiven. Severn is very well, though he leads so dull a life with me. Remember me to all friends, and tell Haslam I should not have left London without taking leave of him, but from being so low in body and mind. Write to George as soon you receive this, and tell him how I am, as far as you can guess; and also a note to my sister—who walks about my imagination like a ghost—she is so like Tom. I can scarcely bid you goodbye, even in a letter. I always made an awkward bow.

God bless you!
John Keats

MAKING MEANINGS

First Thoughts

1. How do the feelings you recorded in your Quickwrite notes compare with the ones Keats expresses in this poem?

Shaping Interpretations

2. What **simile** describes the books the speaker hopes to write?

3. Whom does the speaker address, and what line tells you?

4. Where is this sonnet's **turn**?

5. Describe the speaker's **tone.** Do you think it is constant or does it change? Explain.

Connecting with the Text

6. What do you think the last line means? How does it make you feel about the speaker and what is soon to happen to him?

Primary Sources

Already very ill, Keats planned to go to Italy to benefit from the warm climate. He had hoped that his good friend Charles Brown might go with him; Brown learned of the plan too late and just missed Keats, who sailed for Italy on September 17, 1820, accompanied by another friend, Joseph Severn. Once in Italy, Keats kept in contact with Brown through letters. This letter to Brown was the last one written by Keats before he died on February 23, 1821. (Brown's sketch of Keats is shown on p. 745.)

Ask students to imagine they are writing what may be their last letter to their best friend. What would they want to tell their friend? What images, ideas, and feelings would they like to record in a last letter? Have students freewrite on the subject for a few minutes, and then ask them to share their ideas. After the discussion, turn their attention to Keats's last letter: What are Keat's concerns? Have students compare the content of Keats's letter with the ideas they came up with for their own last letters.

MAKING MEANINGS

First Thoughts [Respond]

1. Like Keats, students will probably include lost opportunities and lost love among their regrets.

Shaping Interpretations [Interpret]

2. The simile of the harvest describes the act of writing poetry.

3. The speaker is addressing his lover; this is revealed in ll. 9–10.

4. In the middle of l. 12, the poem shifts from a consideration of regrets to the effects of that meditation.

5. The tone is anxious, melancholy, regretful. The end of the poem becomes more calm and sad.

Connecting with the Text [Apply]

6. Possible responses: The last line tells how in the face of death, love and fame no longer matter. The line reveals the speaker's despair and creates empathy for him.

Using Students' Strengths

Visual Learners

As students read Keats's letter, they should take note of pairs of complementary or contradictory words, images, and ideas. These can be organized into two columns on a chart. Ask students to compare their charts and discuss what the pairs suggest about the author's state of mind.

Getting Students Involved

Cooperative Learning

Who Are These People? Have students work in groups of three or four to find out more about the people mentioned in Keats's letter and the types of relationships he had with them. These include Charles Brown, Dr. Clark, John Hamilton Reynolds, Joseph Severn, William Haslam, George Keats, and Fanny Keats (John Keats's sister). Each group may choose one person, with each group member assigned to research a different aspect of that person's life.

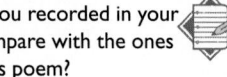

Summary

The speaker hears a melancholy knight tell a strange tale of falling in love with a beautiful lady and following her to a cave where, lulled to sleep, the knight dreams. In his dream, noblemen warn him that *"la belle dame sans merci"* ("the beautiful woman without pity") is bewitching him. Waking, he discovers himself free, but alone and depressed.

Background

The French poet Alain Chartier was born in Bayeux in 1385. An active member of the royal court of Charles VII, today Chartier is considered more of a political figure than a literary one. In his time, however, he was highly regarded as a love poet. "La Belle Dame sans Merci" (1424) was his most famous poem. The title most likely appealed to Keats because it recalls the courtly ballads of the troubadours, which evoke another place and time, and adds an air of mystery to his poem.

Browsing in the Files

About the Author. Keats wrote "La Belle Dame sans Merci" on April 21, 1819. A second version was printed in the newspaper *Indicator* on May 10, 1820. Unfortunately, Keats made some changes in the second version that did not improve the poem. In the first line, he changed "knight-at-arms" to "wretched wight," thus relinquishing chivalric associations; the lady's magical powers diminish with the replacing of "And there she lulled me asleep" (l. 33) with "And there we slumber'd on the moss." The original version prevailed over time and it is reprinted here.

Responding to the Art

See p. T718 for artist information. **Activity.** Invite students to match details from the poem with those in the painting. Draw students' attention to the posture of the knight. Ask: How does it fit with the description of the lady as "without pity"?

Before You Read

La Belle Dame sans Merci

Make the Connection

Under Beauty's Spell

The figure of woman as temptress—irresistibly beautiful, but emotionally cold—is ancient. Indifferent to the fate of those who come under her spell, she vanishes as swiftly and mysteriously as she arrives, leaving her victim spiritless, deprived of his manhood—and forever obsessed with the unobtainable. Let your reading of this poem move on two levels: How does the woman so captivate the speaker? What is it about the tale that so captivates Keats, the Romantic poet?

Reading Skills and Strategies

Recognizing Common Motifs

Before you read, jot down examples of beautiful, heartless women from books, movies, television, folk tales, or any other source. Why are these women able to bend men to their will?

Elements of Literature

Ballad

Like many of Wordsworth's ballads, this songlike **ballad** has a seemingly direct simplicity. Like Coleridge's story of the ancient Mariner, it re-creates the medieval ballad's air of mystery and enchantment. The poem looks back to older literature, but the story it tells is still heard in today's folk music repertoire.

Background

"La Belle Dame sans Merci" (The Beautiful Woman Without Pity) repeats the title of a poem by the fifteenth-century French poet Alain Chartier. Keats, who was fascinated with the self-destroying experiences of intense passion, wrote his poem in the spring of 1819.

Bristol Museums and Art Gallery.

La Belle Dame sans Merci (late 19th or early 20th century) by Sir Frank Dicksee.

Reaching All Students

English Language Learners

Students may find it difficult to read the poem because much of the vocabulary is no longer in use. Preview the side glosses carefully to help students.

Advanced Learners

Encourage students to locate and read an English translation of Chartier's poem. Then they can compare and contrast it with Keats's ballad.

La Belle Dame sans Merci

John Keats

O, what can ail thee, knight-at-arms,
Alone and palely loitering?
The sedge° has withered from the lake,
And no birds sing.

O, what can ail thee, knight-at-arms, **A**
So haggard and so woebegone?
The squirrel's granary° is full,
And the harvest's done.

I see a lily on thy brow,
With anguish moist and fever dew, **B**
And on thy cheeks a fading rose
Fast withereth too.

I met a lady in the meads,°
Full beautiful—a fairy's child, **C**
Her hair was long, her foot was light,
And her eyes were wild.

I made a garland for her head,
And bracelets too, and fragrant zone;°
She looked at me as she did love, **D**
And made sweet moan.

I set her on my pacing steed,
And nothing else saw all day long,
For sidelong would she bend and sing
A fairy's song. **E**

She found me roots of relish sweet,
And honey wild, and manna dew,°
And sure in language strange she said
"I love thee true."

She took me to her elfin grot,°
And there she wept and sighed full sore,
And there I shut her wild wild eyes
With kisses four.

And there she lulled me asleep,
And there I dreamed—Ah! woe betide!
The latest° dream I ever dreamed
On the cold hill side.

I saw pale kings and princes too,
Pale warriors, death-pale were they all; **F**
They cried, "La Belle Dame sans Merci
Hath thee in thrall!"°

3. sedge: reedy plants.

7. granary: place for storing grain.

13. meads: archaic for "meadowlands."

18. zone: archaic for "belt" or "girdle."

26. manna dew: the sweet juice exuded by the European ash tree and by certain other plants. Also, in Exodus 16:13-36, manna is the food God miraculously provides for the Israelites.

29. grot: archaic for "cave" or "grotto."

35. latest: archaic for "last."

40. in thrall: archaic for "enslaved."

A Elements of Literature
Ballad

? **What is the effect of repeating the first line of the poem in l. 5?** [Possible response: The repetition is characteristic of ballads, and it gives the poem a song-like quality.]

B Elements of Literature
Metaphor

? **Remind students that a metaphor is an implied comparison. What do the "lily" and "fading rose" of ll. 9 and 11 suggest?** [Possible responses: The knight's paleness; they are ghostly or sickroom images.]

C Reading Skills and Strategies
Recognizing Common Motifs

? **What images in ll. 13–16 suggest that the lady may not be a mere mortal?** ["A fairy's child," "eyes were wild"] **What does this imply about her ability to bend men to her will?** [Possible response: It implies that she has a mysterious, otherworldly power over men that cannot be easily explained or dispelled.]

D Appreciating Language
Dual Meaning

? **How does the meaning of l. 19 change if the word *as* is read as meaning *as if* instead of as meaning *while?*** [Possible response: The reader would be more uncertain of the lady's honesty. The lady might take on a sinister quality.]

E Reading Skills and Strategies
Drawing Conclusions

? **What is the effect of the shorter length and different rhythm of l. 24 compared to the other lines in the stanza?** [Possible response: The variation makes the line stand out and gives the lady's "fairy song" a mysterious sound.]

F Critical Thinking
Analyzing

? **What do the details in ll. 37–42 suggest about the men's appearances?** [Possible responses: They resemble skeletons, ghosts, or images of death.] **Who might these men be?** [Possible response: Other men who fell under the fatal spell of a woman.]

Crossing the Curriculum

Social Sciences
Keats's poem draws on many elements of folklore. Ask students to research folklore sources in the library and find another example of a story featuring a woman with extraordinary powers. Or students can ask family and friends to share stories they were told as children featuring witches or fairy godmothers. During one class period, have students share the folk tales they have discovered and discuss the powerful woman in each.

Music
Have students research the traditions of the French troubadours in Medieval and Renaissance times. Ask each student to find an example of a troubadour love song and to sing it or play a recording for the class. Some students may want to create and perform their own courtly love ballad.

(A) Critical Thinking

Interpreting

? What does the knight realize has happened to him when he awakens? [Possible responses: The knight has died; or he has been brought close to death; or he has been robbed of his youth and power by the lady.]

RESPONDING TO THE ART

Frank Cadogan Cowper (1877–1958) painted portraits as well as historical and fantasy scenes. He was influenced by pre-Raphaelite ideas, which he carried into the twentieth century. Cowper was honored with a commission to paint six murals for the Houses of Parliament in London. Poppies, such as those depicted in the painting, became closely associated with World War I battlefield casualties after John McCrae wrote a poem in 1915 that begins "In Flanders fields the poppies blow/Between the crosses, row on row."

Activity. Ask students to explore the following questions:

1. What do you think has happened to the knight? [Since he is so motionless and does not hear the woman, he is probably dead or in a deep sleep.] Invite discussion on why the woman seems so indifferent to the knight's condition. [Possible responses: She knows he is not really harmed; she enjoys the power she holds over him.]
2. Compare Cowper's depiction of the woman with Dicksee's on p. 750. Which do you think is closer to Keats's creation and why?

(A)

I saw their starved lips in the gloam,°
  With horrid warning gaped wide,
And I awoke, and found me here,
  On the cold hill's side.

And this is why I sojourn° here,
  Alone and palely loitering,
Though the sedge is withered from the lake,
  And no birds sing.

41. gloam: archaic for "twilight."

45. sojourn: visit.

La Belle Dame Sans Merci (1926) by Frank Cadogan Cowper.
Private Collection/Bridgeman.

Making the Connections

Connecting to the Theme: "The Quest for Beauty"

Ask students what this poem suggests about the possible consequences of a quest for beauty. [Possible responses: An immoderate or obsessive quest for beauty may result in disaster for the lover or poet who cannot let go of his ideal.]

Assessing Learning

Check Test: True-False

1. The first speaker in the poem is the knight. [False]
2. The lady is described as having long hair and wild eyes. [True]
3. The knight tells the lady that he loves her. [False]
4. The men in the knight's dream warn him that the lady has enslaved him. [True]
5. The knight awakes in his own room. [False]

Student to Student

A Poem Within a Poem

Once I was pensive, very pensive
watching a mysterious, melancholic poet
writing a poem

All that he was writing
was just a poem within a poem: **B**

A dark night of bitterness,
the song of a bird,
the solitude of the Aurora,
the smell of a rose
make a poem within a poem

Take this poem to a poet
who remembers a beloved who does not come—
Take it to a disconsolate poet who wants to reach Diana
Take it to a singer who wants the moon to fall in love
To a man who feels the sadness of being alone
To Neruda who once wrote the sad verses of the night
To the passionate poet
who writes what comes from his heart.

—Arnulfo J. López
James Madison High School
Vienna, Virginia

MAKING MEANINGS

First Thoughts

1. What to you is the most important word in the descriptions of the woman, and why?

Shaping Interpretations

2. Who are the poem's two **speakers,** and where does one stop speaking and the other begin?
3. How do the poem's **images** help you visualize the knight and the time of year?
4. How do you interpret the dream in stanza 10?
5. Where does Keats vary each stanza's **meter,** and what is the effect of the rhythmic change?

Extending the Text

6. How does the poem above relate to the poems by Keats and the other Romantic poets?
7. How does Keats's literary **ballad** compare with the old folk ballads on pages 91–95?
8. Compare Keats's La Belle Dame with the seducers you listed in your reading notes. Why do you think this character type is so prevalent across cultures? Is it fair to women? What is the comparable male type?

Connecting Across Texts

Connecting with "La Belle Dame sans Merci"

Ask students to work in pairs to compare aspects of "A Poem Within a Poem" with those of "La Belle Dame sans Merci." Encourage students to use a graphic organizer such as the one that follows.

	"A Poem"	"La Belle Dame"
Tone		
Language		
Poet's Desire		
Objects Praised or Admired		
Theme		

Student to Student

This student poem ponders the nature of poetry, of poets, and of the experiences that move poets to write.

B Reading Skills and Strategies

Responding to the Text

? What do you think is the "poem within a poem"? [Possible responses: The author may mean that a thing of beauty is a poem itself.]

MAKING MEANINGS

First Thoughts [Respond]

1. Possible responses: *Wild,* because the word is repeated often and suggests that the woman is like a force of nature; or, *beautiful,* because that is what attracts the knight.

Shaping Interpretations [Interpret]

2. The first speaker (stanzas 1–3) is the narrator. The second speaker (stanzas 4–12) is the knight. The shift occurs when the knight responds to the narrator's questions.
3. The images of the knight's loneliness, pallor, aimlessness, fatigue, and feverishness help the reader see his sickness and loss. The withered sedge and harvest show that the season is late fall.
4. Possible response: The dream suggests that the woman is some sort of force that enchants and then enslaves men.
5. The meter varies in the last line of each stanza. The change arrests the reader's progress and breaks the flow of the first three lines.

Extending the Text [Synthesize]

6. The poem mentions several themes common to Romantic poets: melancholy, passion, and loss.
7. Keats's ballad contains the question-and-answer format, supernatural events, and tragic subject matter common to traditional ballads.
8. Students may feel that the character type is prevalent in the history of literature because it presents the male perspective of the struggle between the sexes. Some students may see it as a sexist stereotype which is unfair to women. Comparable male types include Don Juans who seduce women and then leave them, or handsome gigolos who deceive women for money.

Summary ■ ■ ■

The speaker becomes intoxicated with a nightingale's song and the images it evokes in his mind. He wishes for poetic inspiration and for the freedom to fly like the bird away from the suffering that time and change inflict. He imagines that composing poetry could free him from his distress and that death would be a sweet release if the bird could sing him to his rest. As the last notes of the bird's song fade, the speaker returns to ordinary consciousness, wondering if his extraordinary experience was only a dream.

Background

During the late spring and early summer of 1819, Keats wrote five odes—to Psyche, to a nightingale, on a Grecian urn, on melancholy, and on indolence. A sixth ode, "To Autumn," was written in September 1819. The phrase "great odes" is sometimes applied to all of the 1819 odes and sometimes to only three or four of them, since they vary in quality. "Ode to a Nightingale" was probably written early in May. On May 3, 1819, Keats wrote of the "delightful forwardness" of spring in his journal and mentioned a remark which, although changed, is reflected in ll. 47–49 of "Ode to a Nightingale": "the violets are not withered, before the peeping of the first rose."

Before You Read

ODE TO A NIGHTINGALE

Make the Connection

Dark Mysteries

From the first lines of this poem, you realize the speaker is passing into an altered state, a reverie not wholly of the waking world. He is sharing an intense experience of extremes, a searching flight of the mind at once joyful and despairing, spiritual yet startlingly concrete. If you let yourself take this daring journey with Keats (as unfamiliar as it may seem at first), you will find yourself in a mysterious realm. Keats is not afraid of the dark.

Reading Skills and Strategies

Dialogue with the Text

Track the speaker's **mood,** or emotional state. After each stanza, quickly write down one word or phrase describing his mood.

Background

When Keats was twenty-three, he spent a few months at the Hampstead home of his friend Charles Brown, who remembered: "In the spring of 1819 a nightingale had built her nest near my house. Keats felt a tranquil and continual joy in her song, and one morning he took his chair from the breakfast table to the grass plot under a plum tree, where he sat for two or three hours. When he came into the house, I perceived he had some scraps of paper in his hand, and these he was quietly thrusting behind the books. On inquiry, I found those scraps, four or five in number, contained his poetic feeling on the song of our nightingale." There are no nightingales in North America. Their unearthly, sad, sweet song can only be heard in the British Isles and in central and western Europe.

The Nightingale, published in *Harper's Monthly* (1866). Woodcut.

Reaching All Students

Struggling Readers

If possible, introduce students to the poem by playing the CD recording and pausing after each stanza for a discussion of difficult vocabulary and syntax. Then have students in small groups slowly reread each stanza aloud, pausing frequently to paraphrase and summarize what has happened and discuss how the speaker feels about his experience.

English Language Learners

The language and syntax of this poem might prove very difficult for students not proficient in English. Students will benefit from active interaction with what they are reading. Place a blank transparency over "Ode to a Nightingale," and have students use colored markers to highlight sections they are having difficulty understanding. Review these sections with students to ensure comprehension.

Advanced Learners

Keats's "Ode to a Nightingale" is famous for its lush imagery. Ask students to review the poem and pick out images they find particularly effective. Then, have students describe how each image helps set the mood of the poem and paint a picture for the reader. Students might also discuss what makes these images so effective and memorable.

Ode to a Nightingale

John Keats

1

My heart aches, and a drowsy numbness pains
My sense, as though of hemlock° I had drunk,
Or emptied some dull opiate to the drains°
One minute past, and Lethewards° had sunk:
'Tis not through envy of thy happy lot,
But being too happy in thine happiness—
That thou, light-wingèd Dryad° of the trees,
In some melodious plot
Of beechen° green, and shadows numberless,
Singest of summer in full-throated ease.

2

O, for a draft of vintage!° that hath been
Cooled a long age in the deep-delvèd earth,
Tasting of Flora° and the country green,
Dance, and Provençal° song, and sunburnt mirth!
O for a beaker full of the warm South,
Full of the true, the blushful Hippocrene,°
With beaded bubbles winking at the brim,
And purple-stainèd mouth;
That I might drink, and leave the world unseen,
And with thee fade away into the forest dim:

3

Fade far away, dissolve, and quite forget
What thou among the leaves hast never known,
The weariness, the fever, and the fret
Here, where men sit and hear each other groan;
Where palsy° shakes a few, sad, last gray hairs,
Where youth grows pale, and specter-thin, and dies;
Where but to think is to be full of sorrow
And leaden-eyed despairs,
Where Beauty cannot keep her lustrous eyes,
Or new Love pine at them beyond tomorrow.

4

Away! away! for I will fly to thee,
Not charioted by Bacchus and his pards,°
But on the viewless wings of Poesy,°
Though the dull brain perplexes and retards:
Already with thee! tender is the night,

2. hemlock: poison made from the hemlock plant.
3. drains: dregs.
4. Lethewards (lē′thē·wərds): toward Lethe. In Greek and Roman mythology, Lethe is the river of forgetfulness that flows through the underworld.
7. Dryad (drī′ad′): in Greek mythology, nature goddess associated with trees.
9. beechen: archaic for "pertaining to beech trees."

11. vintage: wine.

13. Flora: the richness of flowers. Flora is the Roman goddess of flowers.
14. Provençal (prō′vän·säl′): from Provence, a region in southern France known in the Middle Ages for its troubadours singing love songs.
16. blushful Hippocrene (hip′ō·krēn′): wine, which he would drink for inspiration. In Greek mythology, Hippocrene is the Muses' fountain, whose waters inspire the poets who drink from it.

25. palsy: a disease of the nervous system that causes partial paralysis and involuntary shaking.

32. not . . . pards: not by getting drunk. Bacchus, the Roman god of wine, was sometimes pictured in a chariot pulled by leopards, shortened here to "pards."
33. on . . . Poesy: on the invisible wings of poetry; that is, by using his poetic imagination.

A Reading Skills and Strategies

Dialogue with the Text

? How does the speaker feel in the opening lines of the poem? What effect do these lines have on you? [Possible responses: melancholy, heartbroken, and numb. The reader may be intrigued, puzzled, or made sad by the opening lines.]

B Critical Thinking

Interpreting

? What is the speaker wishing for here? [The speaker wants a glass of wine to remind him of the warm Southern sun where the grapes are grown.]

C Reading Skills and Strategies

Identifying Cause and Effect

? What does the speaker hope will be the effect of drinking the wine? [He hopes it will allow him to escape his present cares and low spirits.] Why might he hope for this effect? [Possible response: He is finding his life difficult and disappointing.]

D Critical Thinking

Determining the Author's Point of View

? How does the speaker feel about human life? [Possible response: It is full of pain, suffering, and loss.]

E Historical Connections

Keats's younger brother Tom died of tuberculosis several months before Keats wrote this poem. It could be that the poet was thinking of him when writing l. 26.

F Elements of Literature

Tone

? How does the tone of the poem change in ll. 31–33? [The speaker begins to have hope and courage to escape his pain with poetry.]

Skill Link

Monitoring Reading Comprehension

Remind students that it is important for them to pay attention to their level of comprehension while reading. If they have trouble understanding a passage, they can use strategies, such as asking questions to help them focus on what they do not understand. For example, after reading each stanza, students might ask: "How does the speaker feel about the nightingale?" "How does the speaker feel about himself?"

1. Divide students into small groups of four or five. Have a member of each group read one stanza at a time. Then have the other group members frame questions about the speaker's feelings or what is happening in the poem. Students can suggest answers to these questions or frame new ones.
2. Have students continue to take turns reading the poem aloud, one stanza at a time. Ask them to repeat the questioning strategy at the end of each stanza, generating new questions when necessary.
3. After students finish reading, have the groups get together to discuss as a class how asking and answering their own questions helped them to understand the poem.

A Reading Skills and Strategies

Comparing and Contrasting

? How does the image of the moon and stars contrast with that of the earthly world below? [Possible response: The imaginative depiction of the moon as an enthroned queen surrounded by fairy stars is contrasted with a dark, gloomy, twisting, and mossy world below.]

Responding to the Art

See artist information on p. T226.
Activity. Ask students to describe the mood of the painting and then to determine exactly what elements of the painting create that mood. They should mention the solitary figure who looks very tiny on the wooded path. They should also note the golden color of the painting, the lengthening shadows that suggest evening time, and the bare branches that suggest autumn or winter. The figure itself appears to be a farmer, walking, probably slowly, alongside his loaded cart.

And haply the Queen-Moon is on her throne,
    Clustered around by all her starry Fays;°
        But here there is no light,
Save what from heaven is with the breezes blown
    Through verdurous° glooms and winding mossy ways.

37. **Fays:** fairies.

40. **verdurous** (vʉr′jər·əs): full of green foliage.

Christopher Wood Gallery, London.

Forge Valley, Scarborough (19th century) by John Atkinson Grimshaw.

Skill Link

Analyzing and Responding to a Critical Review

The critics Cleanth Brooks and Robert Penn Warren offer the following interpretation of "Ode to a Nightingale": "This poem is essentially a reverie induced by the poet's listening to the song of the nightingale. In the first stanza, the poet is just sinking into the reverie; in the last stanza, he comes out of the reverie and back to a consciousness of the actual world in which he and all other human beings live. The first lines of the poem and the last, therefore, constitute a sort of frame for the reverie proper. . . . The poet has chosen to present his reverie largely in terms of imagery—imagery drawn from nature, the flowers and leaves, etc., actually associated with the bird physically, and imagery drawn from myth and literature. . . . The images are elaborate and decorative and the poet dwells upon them lovingly and leisurely, developing them in some detail as pictures. . . . The loving elaboration and slowed movement resembles the slowed movement of meditative trance, or dream, and therefore is appropriate to the general tone of this poem."

After students have finished reading the poem, ask them to comment on the critics' analysis.

5

I cannot see what flowers are at my feet,
Nor what soft incense hangs upon the boughs,
But, in embalmèd° darkness, guess each sweet
Wherewith the seasonable month endows
The grass, the thicket, and the fruit tree wild;
White hawthorn, and the pastoral eglantine;°
Fast fading violets covered up in leaves;
And mid-May's eldest child,
The coming° musk rose, full of dewy wine,
The murmurous haunt of flies on summer eves.

6

Darkling° I listen; and, for many a time
I have been half in love with easeful Death,
Called him soft names in many a musèd rhyme,
To take into the air my quiet breath;
Now more than ever seems it rich to die,
To cease upon the midnight with no pain,
While thou art pouring forth thy soul abroad
In such an ecstasy!
Still wouldst thou sing, and I have ears in vain—
To thy high requiem° become a sod.°

7

Thou wast not born for death, immortal Bird!
No hungry generations tread thee down;
The voice I hear this passing night was heard
In ancient days by emperor and clown:
Perhaps the selfsame song that found a path
Through the sad heart of Ruth,° when, sick for home,
She stood in tears amid the alien corn;°
The same that ofttimes hath
Charmed magic casements,° opening on the foam
Of perilous seas, in fairy lands forlorn.

8

Forlorn! the very word is like a bell
To toll me back from thee to my sole self!
Adieu! the fancy° cannot cheat so well
As she is famed to do, deceiving elf.
Adieu! adieu! thy plaintive° anthem fades
Past the near meadows, over the still stream,
Up the hillside; and now 'tis buried deep
In the next valley glades:
Was it a vision, or a waking dream?
Fled is that music:—Do I wake or sleep?

43. embalmèd: perfumed.

46. eglantine (eg′lən·tīn′): kind of rose.

49. coming: soon to bloom.

51. darkling: archaic for "in the dark."

60. requiem (rek′wē·əm): Mass or song for the dead. **sod:** piece of topsoil held together by the matted roots of living grasses.

66. Ruth: in the Bible, a young widow who left her own people to go with her mother-in-law to a strange land.
67. corn: British generic term for grain.
69. casements: windows. Images of open windows intrigued Keats.

73. fancy: imagination.

75. plaintive: sad; mournful.

B Elements of Literature

Imagery

? How do the descriptions of the vegetation in ll. 41–45 evoke smells without describing their sources? [The speaker uses words such as *incense, embalmed,* and *sweet,* as well as giving suggestive details such as the presence of fruit trees.]

C Reading Skills and Strategies

Dialogue with the Text

? How would you characterize the speaker's mood in ll. 51–56? What is your attitude toward his reflections? [Possible responses: Morose, dispirited, passive. Some may sympathize with the speaker's weary response to life's difficulties. Others may see him as indulging in self-pity or lacking in will or drive.]

D Struggling Readers

Interpreting Details

? Although he is "half in love with easeful Death," the speaker sees a flaw in that solution in ll. 59–60. What is this flaw? [If he is dead, he will no longer hear the nightingale's song.]

E Critical Thinking

Drawing Conclusions

? What does the speaker mean when he refers to the bird as immortal? [The nightingale's song has been heard through the ages.] **What do you think the bird might symbolize for the speaker?** [Possible responses: enduring art, the eternal beauty of nature.]

F Appreciating Language

Transitions

? What key word links the last stanza of the poem to the stanza that precedes it? [forlorn] **Why is the repetition of this word appropriate to the subject?** [Possible responses: because the author's mood throughout the poem is forlorn; the repetition echoes the sound of the tolling bells which Keats mentions.]

G Elements of Literature

Tone

? How would you describe the tone at the end of the poem? [Possible responses: reflective, resigned.]

Crossing the Curriculum

Music

Have students play a song or piece of music for the class that has a strong emotional effect on them. Then ask them to compare the effect of that music on them to the effect of the nightingale's song on the poem's speaker. Have them identify and analyze specific elements of the music that appeal to them or move them. Encourage students to use verbal images to express the emotional effect the music has on them.

Using Students' Strengths

Visual Learners

The lush images in this poem paint mental pictures for the reader. Have students choose a section of the poem to illustrate. They can draw or paint their own illustrations, or they can seek out works of art that aptly convey images in the poem.

Connections

Cummings's poem celebrates the pure nonrational creativity of nature that eludes all attempts to categorize or explain it.

A Elements of Literature
Apostrophe

? Point out that both of Keats's odes in this collection use apostrophe. Who or what does the speaker address in this poem? [the earth]

B Critical Thinking
Synthesizing

? How does the poem's unconventional use of punctuation and line division reflect the theme of the poem? [Possible responses: The theme of the poem is nature's wild creativity that cannot be understood or tamed by science or philosophy; the poem's flouting of conventional form mirrors the inexplicable exuberance the speaker sees in the earth's perennial renewal.]

C Appreciating Language
Diction

? What is the effect of the poet's use of *thee, thy,* and *thou?* [Possible responses: The language reflects the Romantic poets' worship of the sublime in nature. Cummings's use of such formal, almost Biblical, address may show that his respect for nature also borders on religious reverence.]

D Critical Thinking
Making Connections

? How is Cummings's characterization of death like Keats's in stanza 6 of "Ode to a Nightingale? [Possible response: Neither view death as wholly negative: Keats says he is "half in love with easeful Death," and Cummings calls death the "rhythmic lover."]

E Reading Skills and Strategies
Drawing Conclusions

? How can spring be earth's answer to philosophers and scientists? [Possible responses: Philosophers and scientists look to the earth for rational answers to the meaning of life, but the burst of life and beauty that is spring shows that nature cannot be summed up in a logical system.]

Connections — A Poem

The American poet E. E. Cummings (1894–1962) uses his unique style to praise both nature's mystery and its capacity to elude our scientific probings.

O sweet spontaneous

E. E. Cummings

O sweet spontaneous
earth how often have
the
doting

          fingers of
prurient philosophers pinched
and
poked

thee
,has the naughty thumb
of science prodded
thy

     beauty   .how
often have religions taken
thee upon their scraggy knees
squeezing and

buffeting thee that thou mightest conceive
gods
       (but
true

to the incomparable
couch of death thy
rhythmic
lover

        thou answerest

them only with

                    spring)

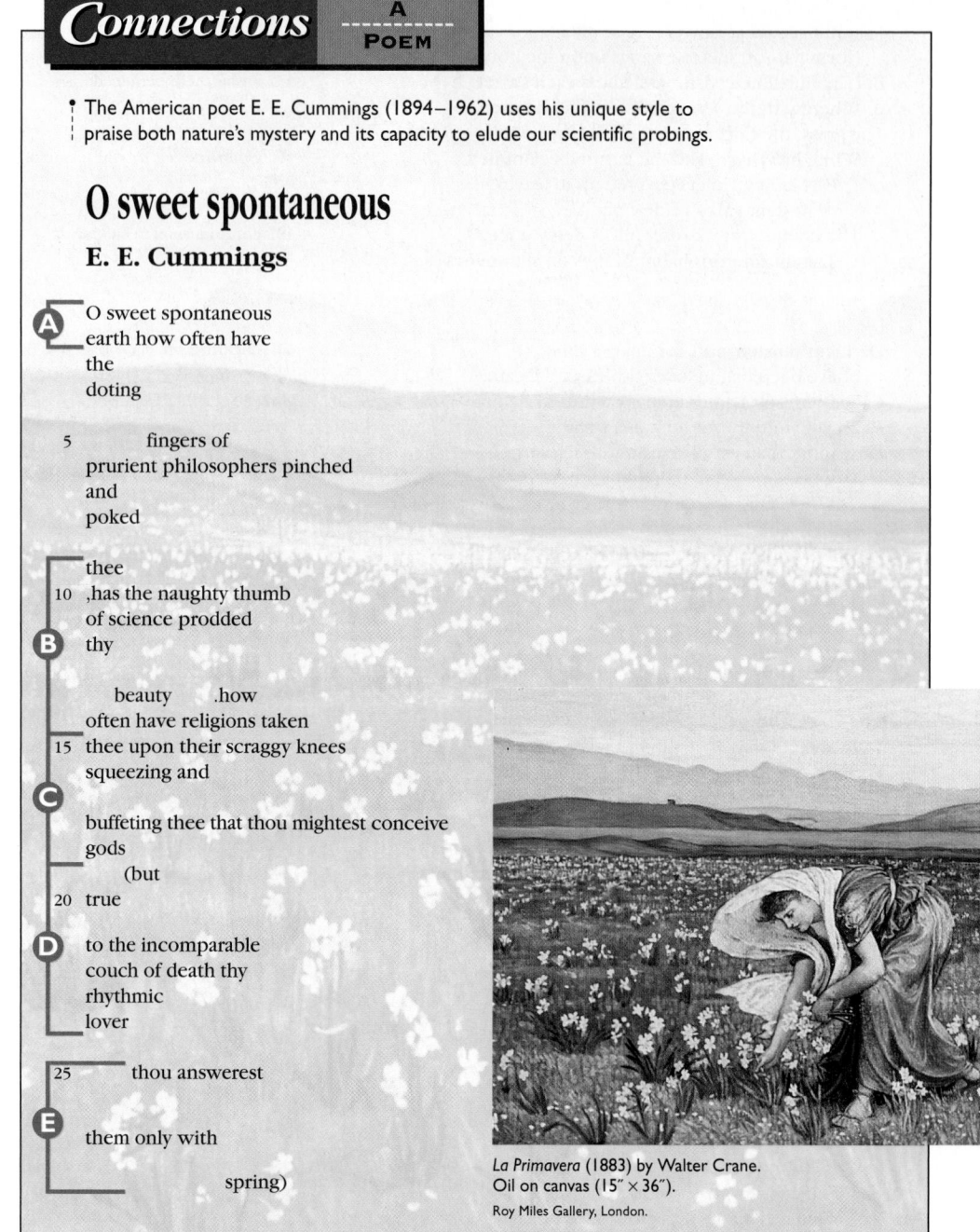

La Primavera (1883) by Walter Crane. Oil on canvas (15″ × 36″).
Roy Miles Gallery, London.

Connecting Across Texts

Connecting to "Ode to a Nightingale"

Point out that both "Ode to a Nightingale" and "O sweet spontaneous" sing the praises of nature. However, Keats and Cummings use very different forms to convey similar ideas. Ask students to use a Venn diagram to compare and contrast the two poems. Suggest they consider elements such as imagery, diction, form (including meter and rhyme), and tone. After they complete the diagrams, ask for general conclusions about the two poems.

Critical Comment

Dialogue with the Soul

Keats's completed poem is not "about" or "on" the nightingale but, as the title tells us, "to" the nightingale. The speaker seems, as the poem opens, to have already passed beyond the limit of ordinary experience and become "too" happy in the experience conveyed in the nightingale's song. The poem consists of a series of propositions, each containing its own rejection as to how the speaker might imitate the "ease" of the song he hears—wine, poetry, even death are considered. Each time, the speaker in his humanness is drawn back to his "sole self," to a preference for poetry as a celebration, not of "summer" but of human life as a process of soul making. **F**

Making Meanings

First Thoughts

1. When you finish Keats's poem, what **image** is strongest in your mind?

Shaping Interpretations

2. Describe the **setting** of the poem—its time and place.
3. Why do you think the speaker wants to capture the nightingale's "ease," and why is he "too happy in [its] happiness" (stanza 1)?
4. Describe the changing desires and ideas that the speaker passes through in stanzas 2–3, 4–5, and 6–7. How does he resolve each one?
5. What differences are emphasized between the realm (or experience) of the nightingale and that of the speaker?
6. What do you think the speaker realizes by the end of the poem?
7. Review your reading notes, and explain whether you feel the speaker's **mood** is more, or less, exalted at the poem's end than at its beginning.

Connecting with the Text

8. How would you answer the speaker's final question? Explain your response.

Extending the Text

9. How would you compare Keats's response to nature with Cummings's "O sweet spontaneous" (see *Connections* on page 758)?
10. Can you think of any experience a person today might have that compares with Keats's—say, a city person? Explain your response.

Elements of Literature

Imagery: Poets' Conjurings

This poem is famous for its lush imagery. Several of its images, in fact, have been used by other writers as titles. (The American novelist F. Scott Fitzgerald called one of his tragic love stories *Tender Is the Night*.)

1. What concrete **images** in the poem conjure up quite different historical or mythological periods?
2. In the poetic device called **synaesthesia,** one sense experience (such as smell) is described in terms of another (such as touch): "soft incense" (line 42). Find other examples of **synaesthesia** in Keats's ode.
3. If you were going to illustrate this poem, which images would you focus on?

F Critical Comment

Expressing an Opinion

? Do you agree that the speaker in "Ode to a Nightingale" ends up seeing poetry as a means of celebrating "human life as a process of soul making?" Why or why not? [Possible responses: Yes, he has acknowledged life's difficulties, and he sees poetry as a way of transcending and transforming them. No, the speaker remains unsure of the meaning of his vision at the end of the poem. The nightingale has fled and he is again alone with his "sole self."]

Making Meanings

First Thoughts [Respond]

1. Possible responses: the images of a nightingale singing pale, dying youth or of a peaceful summer evening.

Shaping Interpretations [Interpret]

2. The setting is a garden in summer.
3. Possible responses: The speaker wants the bird's "ease" for his worldly troubles. He is "too happy" because the beauty of the bird's song cannot give him any permanent solution to his human problems.
4. In stanza 2, the speaker wants to join the bird by drinking, but in stanza 3 he thinks of the woes of mortals. In stanza 4, he connects with the bird through poetry. His mood calms in stanza 5 as he hears the song. In stanza 6, he contemplates death; in stanza 7, he takes comfort from the immortality of the bird's song.
5. The speaker's realm is that of time and decay; the nightingale's realm is one of eternity.
6. Possible response: The speaker is inspired by his encounter with ideal beauty, but he realizes that there is no way to escape his "sole self."
7. Possible responses: Since he has had a taste of "ease" he can never achieve, the speaker's mood is less exalted at the poem's end. Or, because of his experience with the nightingale, his mood is more hopeful since he sees poetry as a means of creating enduring beauty in a human context.

Elements of Literature

Imagery

Possible Answers

1. The images are the Biblical character of Ruth and classical Roman deities such as Bacchus.
2. "Leaden-eyed" (l. 28) combines sight and touch; "embalmed darkness" (l. 43) combines smell and sight.
3. Students might focus on visual images such as the Queen-Moon "clustered around by all her starry Fays" (ll. 36–37).

Connecting with the Text [Apply]

8. Students may feel that the nightingale's song was not a dream, but the speaker's personal experiences and reactions were dream-like.

Extending the Text [Synthesize]

9. Both poems acknowledge the inevitability of death and celebrate nature's vital beauty.
10. Possible response: A city person might hear a bird singing or view a beautiful sunset, resulting in the same questions and conclusions about the human condition.

Summary ■■■

In this ode, the speaker addresses an antique Greek vase upon which two scenes are painted. In the first, gods or men pursue maidens in a forest setting while musicians play. In the second scene, a crowd of people and a priest lead an animal toward a "green altar" for a ritual sacrifice. The mood here is solemn and mournful in contrast with the feverish excitement of the first scene. In the final stanza, the speaker celebrates the urn as a symbol of art, imagination, eternity, and idealized beauty, and imagines that the urn tells us the only thing it knows: that "Beauty is truth, truth beauty."

FROM THE EDITOR'S DESK

Tell students that this ode contains what is probably Keats's most memorable and enigmatic line: "Beauty is truth, truth beauty." We suggest you ask students what they think it means and have them give some examples from their own lives to illustrate their interpretations. They may also want to explore a possible source for this line in Plato's *Symposium*, which proposes that the true essence of love lies in the balance of truth and beauty.

Before You Read

ODE ON A GRECIAN URN

Make the Connection

Unheard Melodies

This poem is a work of art about the contemplation of a work of art—a Grecian urn, or jar. That means the ode is both concrete (descriptive) and contemplative (philosophical). It moves from rich images to abstract ideas about art versus life, permanence versus change, and body versus spirit.

Reading Skills and Strategies

Constructing Images

Stop after reading stanzas 1–3 aloud and then after stanza 4, and describe the urn's pictures as you see them. Make sketches if you like.

Background

Antique Greek vases are usually black with reddish painting, often depicting mythological subjects. Many vases show gods, goddesses, heroes, and mortals entangled in adventures. Traditionally, urns have been used for planting or burial. No one knows exactly what urn Keats had in mind when he wrote this ode. Probably it is an imaginative combination of several vases he had seen, including two in the British Museum. The vase Keats describes has a series of scenes going around it, something like the one on page 762.

Youth singing and playing the kithara, attributed to the Berlin Painter. Terra-cotta amphora (c. 490), said to be from Nola.

The Metropolitan Museum of Art, New York. Fletcher Fund, 1956. (56.171.38). Photograph ©1989 The Metropolitan Museum of Art.

Reaching All Students

Struggling Readers

Read the poem to the class, stopping to explain unfamiliar vocabulary and classical allusions. Then have students do a close stanza-by-stanza reading of the poem with a partner. Be sure to remind students to make use of the marginal glosses. Provide each pair with a copy of the poem on which they can write questions. Then have all the pairs get together to ask their questions and discuss possible answers.

English Language Learners

Point out that when speaking directly to the urn the speaker uses the archaic form *thou* to mean "you." Explain that *thy* is a form of *thou,* as in "thou (you) canst not leave thy (your) song." You might also wish to explain other archaic forms used in the poem: *ye* meaning "you" or "your"; the *-st* and *-t* endings on verbs, such as *canst, hast,* and *wilt.*

Advanced Learners

Before students begin to read "Ode on a Grecian Urn," have them reflect on the technique of apostrophe. On a sheet of paper, have them list the technique's advantages and limitations. Ask students to use these notes after they have read the poem to discuss how effectively Keats makes use of apostrophe.

Ode on a Grecian Urn

John Keats

1

Thou still unravished bride of quietness,
  Thou foster child of silence and slow time, (A)
Sylvan° historian, who canst thus express
  A flowery tale more sweetly than our rhyme:
What leaf-fringed legend haunts about thy shape
  Of deities or mortals, or of both,
    In Tempe or the dales of Arcady?°
  What men or gods are these? What maidens loath?° (B)
What mad pursuit? What struggle to escape?
  What pipes and timbrels?° What wild ecstasy?

2

Heard melodies are sweet, but those unheard
  Are sweeter; therefore, ye soft pipes, play on; (C)
Not to the sensual ear, but, more endeared,
  Pipe to the spirit ditties° of no tone:
Fair youth, beneath the trees, thou canst not leave
  Thy song, nor ever can those trees be bare;
    Bold Lover, never, never canst thou kiss,
Though winning near the goal—yet, do not grieve;
    She cannot fade, though thou hast not thy bliss,
  Forever wilt thou love, and she be fair! (D)

3

Ah, happy, happy boughs! that cannot shed
  Your leaves, nor ever bid the Spring adieu;°
And, happy melodist, unwearied,
  Forever piping songs forever new; (E)
More happy love! more happy, happy love!
  Forever warm and still to be enjoyed,
    Forever panting, and forever young;
All breathing human passion far above,
  That leaves a heart high-sorrowful and cloyed,°
    A burning forehead, and a parching tongue.

4

Who are these coming to the sacrifice?
  To what green altar, O mysterious priest,
Lead'st thou that heifer lowing° at the skies,
  And all her silken flanks° with garlands dressed?

3. sylvan: of the forest. (The urn is decorated with a rural scene.)

7. Tempe (tem′pē) **. . . Arcady** (är′kə·dē): valleys in ancient Greece; ideal types of rural beauty.
8. loath: reluctant.
10. timbrels: tambourines.

14. ditties: short, simple songs.

22. adieu (à·dyö′): French for "goodbye."

29. cloyed (kloid): satiated; wearied with excess.

33. lowing: mooing.
34. flanks: sides between the ribs and the hips.

(A) Elements of Literature

Metaphor

? What do each of the metaphors in the first lines tell you about the urn? [Possible response: They describe the urn as undamaged by time, lasting for centuries, and preserving history.]

(B) Reading Skills and Strategies

Constructing Images

? What is the scene depicted on the urn as described in ll. 5–10? [In a pastoral setting, men and gods are shown chasing fleeing maidens, while musicians play.]

(C) Critical Thinking

Expressing an Opinion

? What is your opinion of the speaker's assertion that "unheard" melodies, imagined experiences, are "sweeter" than real ones? [Possible responses: Imagination can often conjure up something better, "sweeter," than what one experiences in reality. Or, imagination can't take the place of actual living experience, which we can perceive with our senses.]

(D) Reading Skills and Strategies

Identifying Main Ideas

? How does l. 20 sum up a main idea of the poem? [The line refers to the unchanging scene on the urn: The youth and girl will always remain as they are; art can preserve beauty, love, and youth, whereas in life they will fade and die.]

(E) Appreciating Language

Repetition

? What words are repeated often in ll. 21–27? [happy, forever] **What is the effect?** [Possible response: The words emphasize that the happiness depicted on the urn will endure; the repetition exhibits the speaker's enthusiasm for the enduring quality of art.]

Crossing the Curriculum

Social Sciences

Ask students to imagine what a person in the future would think upon finding a relic from modern times, such as a computer or a cellular phone. Have students indicate the person's response to the artifact either in an interview, a personal letter, or a newspaper report. Be sure to make clear what conclusions the person draws about who we are and how we live.

Art

Have students study the decoration of ancient Greek vases from photographs in books. Ask them to discuss how the decoration relates to the function of the urns. Ask them also what stories they find presented in the decoration. They may compare their readings of the urns with that of Keats.

Ⓐ Reading Skills and Strategies

Constructing Images

? Stanza 4 (ll. 31–40) describes another scene depicted on the urn. What does the speaker see? [people going to present a sacrifice; a priest leading a heifer to slaughter] What does the speaker imagine? [The speaker imagines a town, still and empty.]

Ⓑ Critical Thinking

Interpreting

? What effect does viewing the urn have on the speaker as described in ll. 44–45? [Possible responses: Because the urn has lasted so long, it seems immortal, and viewing it is like contemplating eternity; the result is that the speaker is saddened by thinking of the passage of time and of his own brief life.]

Ⓒ Historical Connections

Two years before writing "Ode on a Grecian Urn," Keats wrote the following lines to a friend: "I am certain of nothing but of the holiness of the Heart's affections, and the truth of the imagination. What the Imagination seizes as Beauty must be truth—whether it existed before or not—for I have the same idea of all our passions as of love: They are all in their sublimity, creative of essential beauty."

Ⓓ Cultural Connections

Discuss with students how the idea of beauty is relative to a specific culture and time period. Taking the quotation above into account, ask students what kind of universal absolutes the poet could be referring to in ll. 49–50.

What little town by river or seashore,
Or mountain-built with peaceful citadel,°
Is emptied of this folk, this pious morn?
And, little town, thy streets forevermore
Will silent be; and not a soul to tell
Why thou art desolate, can e'er return.

5

O Attic° shape! Fair attitude!° with brede°
Of marble men and maidens overwrought,°
With forest branches and the trodden weed;
Thou, silent form, dost tease us out of thought
As doth eternity: Cold Pastoral!°
When old age shall this generation waste,
Thou shalt remain, in midst of other woe
Than ours, a friend to man, to whom thou say'st,
"Beauty is truth, truth beauty,"—that is all
Ye know on earth, and all ye need to know.

36. citadel (sit′ə·del′): fortress.

41. Attic: Athenian; classically elegant. **attitude:** disposition or feeling conveyed by the postures of the figures on the urn. **brede:** interwoven design.
42. overwrought: decorated to excess; also, in reference to the men and maidens, overexcited.
45. pastoral: artwork depicting idealized rural life.

Attic vase painting showing transport of amphoras.
Louvre, Paris.

Making the Connections

Connecting to the Theme: "The Quest for Beauty"

Ask students what "Ode on a Grecian Urn" suggests about the positive and negative sides of the quest for beauty. [Possible responses: The quest is positive in that the contemplation of ideal beauty gives us an experience of the eternal or timeless. However, the very same contemplation reminds us of the transience of our own earthly life.] Does Keats find the quest worth the effort? Explain. [Possible response: Yes, because without an experience of ideal beauty, there is no comfort or consolation for our mortal woes.]

Cultural Connections

Have students work in pairs to research ancient Greek culture to find out the prevailing concept of beauty in that time and place. After each pair reports its findings, using illustrations of ancient Greek artifacts, sculpture, and architecture, challenge students to compare classical Greek standards of beauty with those of Keats's day or of our own.

Critical Comment

The Arc of Experience

This poem depicts a beautiful curve of emotion and engagement that begins and ends with detachment. At its center, it abandons all restraints, including those of art itself, to live in that world which is "happy" and "forever." By itself, the third stanza seems "overwrought" (a word used in the more detached fifth stanza)—so much so that we feel that all controls have been lost. But this is precisely the nature of the speaker's experience. Bit by bit, a miniature world of human passions comes alive, only to remind us that it is as dead as the clay on which it is represented. Keats has shown us that in the midst of change, art seems to provide the only truth. Yet this is a truth that depends not on sensory experience, but on the human imagination. E

MAKING MEANINGS

First Thoughts

1. What passages in this poem do you think are most important, and why?

Shaping Interpretations

2. Discuss your understanding of the three **metaphors** for the urn in lines 1–3.
3. Describe the details and actions "frozen" on the vase. Be sure to refer to your reading notes.
4. How do you interpret lines 28–30?
5. Why do you think "unheard" melodies (line 11) are "sweeter" to the speaker? How would you relate this idea to Romanticism?
6. If the urn could "tease us out of thought" (line 44), what state would we be in, and would it be better than thinking? Explain.
7. What do lines 46–50 mean to you?
8. According to stanza 5, what will happen to the urn when the speaker is dead? What message does the urn give to people?

Challenging the Text

9. Some critics complain that stanza 3 is badly written because Keats used "happy" and "forever" too many times. How would you respond to this criticism? Explain.
10. A famous textual difficulty surrounds the poem's last two lines. Based on the manuscript, some scholars enclose the entire couplet within quotation marks. Explain how this could change the meaning. (Would the sentiments expressed in the couplet be the urn's or the poet's?)

E Critical Thinking

Speculating

? According to this interpretation, would the urn still be beautiful if there were no humans to view it? Explain. [Possible response: No, the beauty of the urn is dependent on the truth that the human imagination sees in it; without the human imagination, the artwork on the urn is "as dead as the clay on which it is represented."]

MAKING MEANINGS

First Thoughts [Respond]

1. Students may say that the most important passages are the first four lines or the last two.

Shaping Interpretations [Interpret]

2. Possible responses: "Still unravished bride of quietness" describes the urn's intact survival; "foster child of silence and slow time" indicates that the urn has survived for centuries by being hidden; and "sylvan historian" relates how the decorations on the urn tell a pastoral story from the past.
3. The frozen actions are men and gods chasing young women, youths making music under the trees, and people in a procession to a sacrifice.
4. Possible response: They describe the results of the emotional excess described in the lines preceding it.
5. The "unheard" melodies depend on the imagination not on the senses and thus transcend time and decay. Romantic elements include the tension between timelessness in an ideal world and change in the actual world, and the suggestion that imagination may overcome time.
6. Possible response: "Out of thought" would be a state of lifeless limbo—the opposite of the vivacity the speaker sees in the urn. The state is not better than thought because it is cold, death-like, and lacking passion.
7. Possible responses: Beauty is an ideal that never fades: It is truth in the sense that it cannot be questioned or changed.
8. The urn will survive the speaker, reminding future generations that "beauty is truth."

Challenging the Text [Evaluate/Synthesize]

9. Possible responses: The criticism is warranted: "Happy" is repeated six times; "forever" five times. Or, the repetition is effective because it emphasizes the speaker's unbridled enthusiasm for the urn's beauty and the passion it represents.
10. If the entire couplet is enclosed in quotation marks, the urn speaks for itself; if only the phrase is quoted, the conclusion is the poet's.

Grading Timesaver

Rubrics for each Choices assignment appear on p. 163 in the *Portfolio Management System.*

Choices: Building Your Portfolio

1. **Writer's Notebook** Students might consider looking for information in Keats's letters to friends and relatives.
2. **Analyzing Text Structure** Direct students to identify the rhyme scheme and meter of the Shakespearean sonnet and evaluate the sonnet's turn. Students can then apply their notes to a sonnet by Keats.
3. **Comparing Odes** Students may begin their comparisons by paraphrasing the poet's statements on inspiration.
4. **Comparing and Contrasting Text Elements** For subject, encourage students to characterize the bird as well as the setting of the poem. Have them examine the symbolism of the bird's song. For tone and theme, students can think about the author's situation and emotions, focusing on his message to the reader.
5. **Analyzing Text Structure** Students might find it useful to summarize each stanza in order to identify the speaker's ambiguity and its resolution.
6. **Art** Students might wish to use a story map to identify the important events of the plot.
7. **Creative Writing** Students might begin by making a simple list of the fears indicated in the poem.
8. **Creative Writing** Be sure students understand they have the option of writing their explanation in poetry or prose.
9. **Creative Writing** Advise students to choose a painting that stimulates their imagination as the urn excited Keats's.
10. **Music** Encourage students to create a melody that reflects the mood of the poem or choose an appropriate piece from classical or popular music.

Choices: Building Your Portfolio

Writer's Notebook

1. Collecting Ideas for a Research Paper

These poems by Keats and the tragic details of his life could provide you with many subjects for further research. You might want to focus on the plague of tuberculosis; on Keats's stay in Rome, in a small house near the Spanish Steps that is a museum today; on Keats's family and what happened to his brothers and sister; on Fanny Brawne, of whom Keats wrote, "I can bear to die—I cannot bear to leave her." You might start your research with W. Jackson Bate's biography *John Keats.*

Analyzing Text Structure

2. Taking a Turn

Choose one of Keats's **sonnets** (pages 747 and 748), and show how it follows the structure of the Shakespearean sonnet. Be sure to identify where the shift in focus or attention, the **turn,** occurs.

Comparing Odes

3. Poets on Poets

Both Keats's "Ode to a Nightingale" and Shelley's "Ode to the West Wind" (page 734) are concerned, at least partially, with the subject of poetic inspiration. In a brief essay, write a comparison of these two odes. Focus on how each poem treats the subject.

Comparing and Contrasting Text Elements

4. Poets on Birds

Like Keats, Shelley addresses a poem to a bird—a skylark. In an essay, compare and contrast Shelley's "To a Skylark" (page 739) with Keats's "Ode to a Nightingale." Consider **subject, symbolism** of the bird, **theme,** and **tone.**

Analyzing Text Structure

5. Life for Art's Sake

Many of Keats's odes portray the speaker in a state of tension or ambiguity that is explored and then tentatively resolved. In a brief essay, trace this structure in "Ode on a Grecian Urn." What positive and negative aspects of human art are explored in this ode?

Art

6. "La Belle Dame" Illustrated

Illustrate "La Belle Dame sans Merci" in the form of a cartoon. First, block out the plot of the story. Then, decide whether you will include dialogue in cartoon bubbles or use quotations from the poem as captions for the frames of your cartoon.

Creative Writing

7. If You Have Fears . . .

From your perspective—nearly two hundred years after this sonnet was written—write a personal letter to the speaker of "When I Have Fears," and respond to his fears.

Creative Writing

8. The Knight Talks Back

Are you satisfied with the knight's explanation of his problem in "La Belle Dame sans Merci"? Create your own explanation of what "ails" the knight in Keats's poem.

Creative Writing

9. Copying Keats

Select a painting in this book, and, like Keats in "Ode on a Grecian Urn," directly address it. In a paragraph, tell what is happening in the painting, pose questions about what will never happen, and describe your feelings.

Music

10. Being a Balladeer

Try to improvise a musical setting for "La Belle Dame sans Merci." Write a melody for the poem, and perform your song.

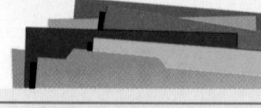

Reading Skills and Strategies

Vocabulary: Homonyms, Homophones, and Homographs

Some words cause reading, spelling, and pronunciation problems because they either are spelled *or* sound like other words or they are spelled *and* sound like other words. These homonymous words have different origins and different meanings. Therefore, they have separate entries in the dictionary. As a group, homonymous words are sometimes simply called homonyms. However, this may seem somewhat confusing because one of the three specific classes of words in this group is also called homonyms. The other two kinds are classified as homophones and homographs.

Homonyms. Two or more individual words that have the same spelling and the same pronunciation are called **homonyms.** Notice how Wordsworth uses the word *roe* in the following excerpt.

> when like a **roe**
> I bounded o'er the mountains, by the sides
> Of the deep rivers, and the lonely streams,
> Wherever nature led. . . .
>
> —William Wordsworth, *from* "Tintern Abbey"

Roe, as Wordsworth uses it, means "deer." However, *roe,* meaning "eggs of a fish," has the same pronunciation as well as the same spelling. Thus, *roe* and *roe* are homonyms.

Homophones. You are probably most familiar with this category. **Homophones** are two or more words that sound alike but have different spellings, such as *soar* and *sore.* In the following passages, *soar* means "to fly upward"; *sore* means "extreme."

> The blue deep thou wingest,
> And singing still dost **soar,** and soaring ever singest.
>
> —Percy Bysshe Shelley, *from* "To a Skylark"

> I would ne'er have striven
> As thus with thee in prayer in my **sore** need.
>
> —Percy Bysshe Shelley, *from* "Ode to the West Wind"

Homographs. Two or more words that have the same spelling but are pronounced differently are **homographs.** In the following lines, Shelley uses the word *desert* (dez′ərt), meaning "arid geographical region."

> I met a traveler from an antique land
> Who said: Two vast and trunkless legs of stone
> Stand in the **desert** . . .
>
> —Percy Bysshe Shelley, *from* "Ozymandias"

The meaning of the word *desert* (dez′ərt), as Shelley uses it, may be the one you most often associate with the word's spelling. However, *desert* (di·zurt′) means "deserved punishment or reward." For example, a criminal who receives punishment is said to receive his just *deserts* (di·zurts′). A second homograph for *desert* (dez′ərt) is the verb *desert* (di·zurt′), which has the same etymology as the noun *desert* but means "to abandon" or "forsake."

Classification	Homonymous Word	Meaning
Homonyms	host host host	an army one who entertains a guest the Eucharist wafer
Homophones	holy wholly	sacred completely
Homographs	wind (wind) wind (wīnd)	air movement to coil

Try It Out

Using a dictionary. Find a homonym, homophone, or homograph for each of the words listed below. Remember that the words you look up will be separate dictionary entries. On your own paper, write each word, and indicate whether it is a homonym, homophone, or homograph. Then, use each homonym, homophone, or homograph in a sentence.

1. slay **2.** bark **3.** fair **4.** bow **5.** bare

Objectives

1. Recognize ways of making meaning from a text
2. Understand the use of homonyms, homophones, and homographs

Reading Skills and Strategies

This feature focuses on the strategy of understanding and using homonyms, homophones, and homographs, which is illustrated, whenever possible, by selections from texts that appear in this anthology.

Mini-Lesson: Homonyms, Homophones, and Homographs

After the students have read the explanation in the text, write the three kinds of homonymous words—Homonyms, Homophones, and Homographs—as headings across the chalkboard as you discuss them. In your discussion, give the class the examples from the text that correspond to each type. Then ask students to come up with their own examples, and list each under the correct heading.

Try It Out

1. Homophone: Sleigh; We rode the *sleigh* through the snow. Did David *slay* Goliath?
2. Homonym: Bark; The chihuahua's *bark* is worse than its bite. The *bark* on this tree feels rough.
3. Homonym: Fair (celebration; beautiful; not stormy; honest; according to the rules). We had fun at the state *fair*. The knight rescued the *fair* maiden. The weather will be *fair* today. The judge was a *fair* man. Everyone should play *fair*. Homophone: Fare; We paid the *fare* for the bus. We would have walked if the weather were *fair*.
4. Homograph: Rhymes with *go* or *prow;* I like the *bow* on your hair. After the dance, he made a *bow*. Homonyms: Bow (a curve or arch; an instrument that propels arrows; a decorative knot; a device used in playing a stringed instrument). Look at the *bow* of the rainbow. Robin was deft with the *bow* and arrow. Put this *bow* on the gift box. The violinist picked up his *bow* and began to play.
5. Homonym: Bare (naked or unadorned; to make open or view). The table was clean and *bare*. I will *bare* my arm for the doctor to give me a shot. Homophone: Bear; The circus *bear* wore a vest, but his head was *bare*.

OBJECTIVES

Question and Answer . . . / Word-Pattern/To Tan-Ch'iu

1. Read and interpret the poems
2. Compare text elements with students' own experiences and those of others
3. Recognize and discuss themes and connections that cross cultures

Planning

- **Block Schedule**
  Block Scheduling Lesson Plans with Pacing Guide
- **Traditional Schedule**
  Lesson Plans Including Strategies for English-Language Learners
- **One-Stop Planner**
  CD-ROM with Test Generator

BROWSING IN THE FILES

About the Author. The friendship between Li Po and Tu Fu is the most famous in Chinese poetry. Although they had very different personalities and outlooks (for one, Li Po was a Taoist instead of a Confucian), they wrote poems to each other frequently. A Chinese saying distinguishes them by describing Tu Fu as a poet's poet and Li Po as a poet of the people. Both poets often wrote in a form called *lü-shih,* which is the Chinese sonnet. A *lü-shih* has eight lines and it emphasizes parallelism. In a *lü-shih,* each of the words of a line corresponds with the words of certain other lines in the poem. There are some twenty-eight categories that parallel words can fall under, from animals to times and seasons to clothing and ornaments.

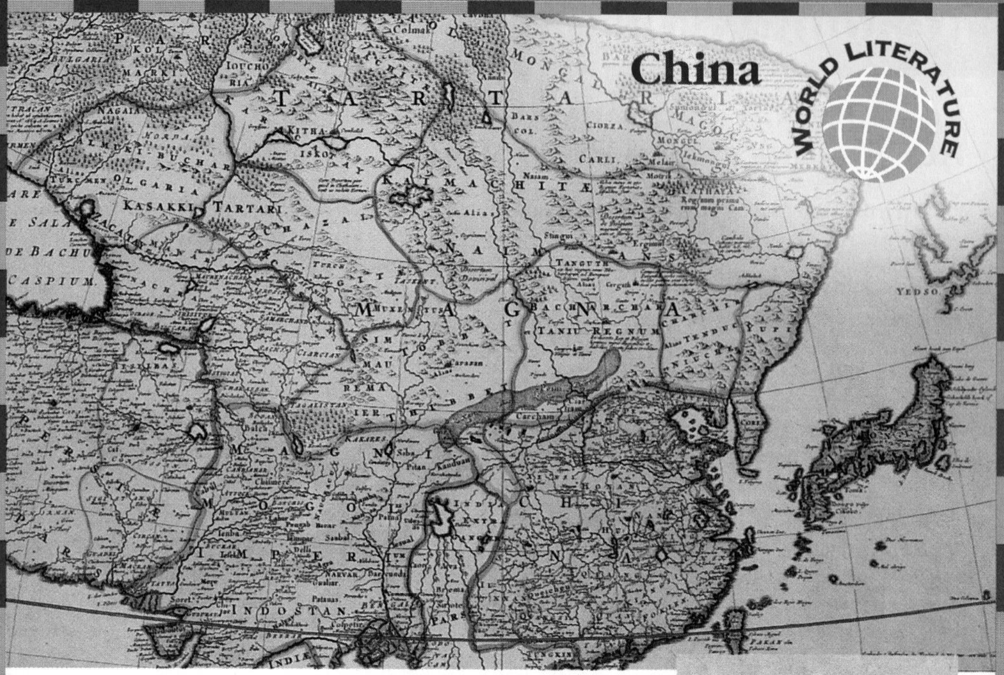

Li Po

(701–762)

A wandering, pleasure-loving poet, Li Po (lē bō) embodies for many the creative spirit of the T'ang dynasty (618–906) at its peak. Unlike the age's other great poet, Tu Fu (page 743), Li Po had no desire for government service or advancement. Reared in a wealthy family in Szechwan province, he chose life as a hermit-poet, drifting where his spirit took him. Walking, writing, marrying (four times), and socializing with poets, peasants, and leaders, Li Po became famous and was eventually invited to the emperor's court. With his unconventional behavior, he was dismissed after only three years.

While an excellent poetic technician, Li Po favored looser folk forms, which he adapted for his original, bold, and sometimes ecstatic language. In a legend appropriate to a nature mystic, Li Po supposedly drowned while trying to embrace the moon's reflection in water. In fact, he may have died from mercury poisoning. Like other Taoists, he took alchemical potions believed to guarantee immortality.

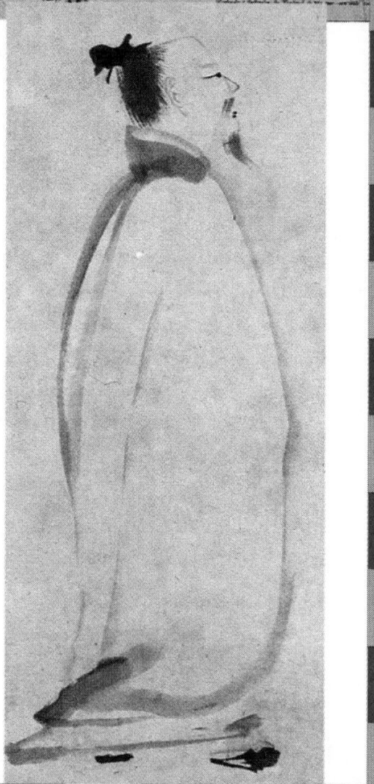

Li Po Chanting in Stroll (southern Sung dynasty, 13th century) by Liang Kai. Tokyo National Museum.

(Map) Mongolia showing Japan and China (c. 1680) by Frederick de Wit.

go.hrw.com
LEO 12-9

Resources: Print and Media

Reading
- *Audio CD Library*
  Disc 12, Tracks 15, 16, 17

Internet
- go.hrw.com (keyword: LE0 12-9)

Before You Read

QUESTION AND ANSWER AMONG THE MOUNTAINS
WORD-PATTERN
TO TAN-CH'IU

Background

Li Po believed in the Taoist philosophy and religion, in which nature—spontaneous, creative, uncomplicated by will—shows life's essence. The conventional human world, on the other hand, debased and deformed by ambition and materialism, is not true reality. Li Po was a social man who had many friends, but for spiritual and poetic renewal, he retreated reclusively to nature.

Quickwrite

Would your ideal life include frequent solitary retreats into nature? Why or why not?

Fragment of Chinese wallpaper (18th century).
Victoria and Albert Museum, London.

Question and Answer Among the Mountains

Li Po

translated by **Robert Kotewall** *and* **Norman L. Smith**

You ask me why I dwell in the green mountain;
I smile and make no reply for my heart is free of care.
As the peach-blossom flows down stream and is gone into **A**
 the unknown,
I have a world apart that is not among men. **B**

Word-Pattern

Li Po

translated by **Florence Ayscough** *and* **Amy Lowell**

The Autumn wind is fresh and clear;
The Autumn moon is bright.
Fallen leaves whirl together and scatter.
The jackdaws, who have gone to roost, are startled again.
We are thinking of each other, but when shall we see each other? **C**
Now, tonight, I suffer, because of my passion.

To Tan-Ch'iu

Li Po

translated by **Arthur Waley**

My friend is lodging high in the Eastern Range,
Dearly loving the beauty of valleys and hills.
At green Spring he lies in the empty woods,
And is still asleep when the sun shines on high.
A pine-tree wind dusts his sleeves and coat; **D**
A pebbly stream cleans his heart and ears.
I envy you, who far from strife and talk
Are high-propped on a pillow of blue cloud. **E**

Summary ■

In "Question and Answer Among the Mountains," the speaker explains why he lives in a remote natural setting. He praises the freedom he enjoys far from human society. In "Word-Pattern," he paints an autumn scene and expresses longing for an absent love. In "To Tan-Ch'iu," the speaker envies a friend's peaceful life in the beautiful and remote eastern mountains.

A Critical Thinking

Interpreting

? What do you think the blossom flowing in the stream's current might symbolize? [Possible response: The blossom mirrors the speaker's own free-spirited wandering in nature.]

B Reading Skills and Strategies

Making Inferences

? What does the speaker imply by the phrase "a world apart"? [Possible responses: Nature is beyond human control. Nature is a deeper, more meaningful reality than the affairs of humankind.]

C Critical Thinking

Challenging the Text

? Does the speaker's conclusion complete the picture he is creating, or does it seem sudden and out of place? Explain. [Possible responses: The conclusion suits the rest of the poem because the earlier autumnal images are also lonely and sad. Or it is too abrupt because the beautiful autumn images have nothing to do with someone who is pining for an absent love.]

D Appreciating Language

Word Choice

? What is the effect of the poet describing the wind as a "pine-tree wind"? [Possible response: The phrase makes efficient use of a few words to give a picture of wind blowing through pine trees.]

E Elements of Literature

Imagery

? What does the image of the speaker's friend "propped on a pillow of blue cloud" suggest to you? [Possible responses: The friend's eyes are on the sky; his spirit is lifted by the sky's beauty and is resting in comfort.]

Reaching All Students

Struggling Readers

Encourage students to read these poems aloud. The structures are straightforward and should present less difficulty than those of many other poems in this collection. The ideas expressed, however, are neither simple nor commonplace. Ask students to pay attention to line breaks and punctuation and to let their voices fall naturally when periods signify the end of a sentence. After reading each poem, have students discuss the various moods of the speaker.

Finding Common Ground

As its name suggests, this feature requires students, through lively discussion, to discover areas of agreement between their experience and the subject matter or theme of literature from another culture. Brainstorm with the class on how Li Po's poems may be considered Romantic. Encourage students to consider in their comparisons the poet's techniques, tone, subject matter, and language. Write students' ideas on the chalkboard. [Students may point out elements such as the use of everyday language and heightened emotion, the emphasis on natural images, and the focus on being alone and communing with nature.]

When students experiment with Li Po's verse by changing specific words and images, direct them also to pay attention to the subtle changes in connotation, mood, and tone. Suggest that they make a three-column chart, with a list of the original words and images in Li Po's verse in the first column and, in the second and third columns, a list of their changes and the consequences of those changes both in literal meaning and in the feel of the poem.

The Emperor Ming Huang Traveling in Shu (T'ang dynasty, A.D. 618–906) by an unknown artist.

Collection of the National Palace Museum, Taiwan, Republic of China.

Finding Common Ground

These terse poems may seem very different from those of the English Romantics. And yet, in Li Po's poems, the same profound communion with nature is present. Their subject is not just nature, but what nature means to human life.

- How does nature affect you? In a small group, try to pinpoint a significant personal experience (not necessarily dramatic or earth-shattering) linked to a natural setting.
- Now, focus on Li Po's poems with these questions: What do you think the last line of "Question and Answer Among the Mountains" means? What does the image in the third line suggest to you? Try changing any sensory word in "Word-Pattern" to another, and notice the effect. What is changed or lost? Which images in "To Tan-Ch'iu" evoke the qualities of remoteness, pleasure, and peace?
- If you were planning a poetry anthology, which of Li Po's poems would you pair with Keats's "Ode to a Nightingale"? Why? Discuss in your group the similarities and differences you see in the two poets. Which one do most readers prefer?

Making the Connections

Connecting with the Theme: "The Quest for Beauty"

Ask how Li Po shares the Romantic poets' quest for beauty in nature. [In the poems, the speaker tries to find beauty and tranquillity by being alone in a natural setting and escaping the corrupting influences of human society, as do Wordsworth, Byron, Shelley, and Keats in many of their poems.] Have students analyze how Li Po's poems show some of the same elements that are found in the poetry of the Romantic period. For their comparison, students may use a chart similar to the one that follows.

Romantic Characteristics	Elements in Li Po's Poetry
Nature	wind and moon in autumn
emotions	Loneliness of absent lover

READ ON

Revolutionary Fever

The revolution that occurred in France at the end of the eighteenth century had enormous repercussions on the other side of the English Channel. *A Tale of Two Cities,* one of Charles Dickens's most popular (and shortest) novels, examines the period that "was the spring of hope" as well as "the winter of despair." (This novel is available in the HRW Library.)

Share in the Terror

Mary Shelley said of *Frankenstein* (Penguin) that she wanted to write a story that "would speak to the mysterious fears of our nature and awaken thrilling horror." She succeeded, writing what many consider to be the first science fiction novel as well as a vivid version of the Romantic mythology of the self. The 1931 film, which made Boris Karloff a star, is the best of the film versions.

The Evil That Men Do

In his classic novel *The Strange Case of Dr. Jekyll and Mr. Hyde,* Robert Louis Stevenson advances the genre Mary Shelley began. When his experiments succeed and the utterly evil Mr. Hyde emerges, Dr. Jekyll's problems begin—and multiply. (Also available on videotape in several classic versions.)

Tinkering with Nature

Like the Romantic poets, Annie Dillard turns to nature for inspiration and reflection. In *Pilgrim at Tinker Creek* (Harper's Magazine Press), her collection of essays, Dillard muses about her past, her present, and her environment while describing the interplay among the plants and animals of Virginia's Tinker Creek. For Dillard, life at the creek reflects "the intricacy of beauty, the pressure of fecundity, the elusiveness of the free, and the flawed nature of perfection."

Love and Marriage

Originally published in 1813, Jane Austen's novel *Pride and Prejudice* (Norton) is about five husband-hunting sisters in nineteenth-century England and the delicate tangles of love and courtship they ensnare themselves in. What struck people then, and strikes us now, is Austen's ability to make commonplace people and events interesting. The superficially trivial content is deceptive; it masks a deeper irony that exposes the manners and mores of the period. (This novel is available in the HRW Library.)

READ ON

Portfolio Assessment Options

The following projects can help you evaluate your students' outside reading. Consider recording projects for students' portfolios.

- **Evaluate Accuracy** Have students work in small groups to evaluate the historical accuracy of *A Tale of Two Cities*. Suggest they begin by listing significant period details from Dickens's novel and then verifying them in at least two historical accounts of the French Revolution. Social studies teachers may be able to suggest reliable references.
- **Create a Newspaper** Have students work together to create a newspaper covering events related to one of the books. Suggest they include editorials, news stories, and even advertisements and cartoons. Display the finished products.
- **Write a Poem** Students may write a poem reflecting a theme they have encountered in a book they have read. Ask them to write in the style of one of the poets in this collection.
- **Be a Dramaturge** Have students prepare a theatrical presentation inspired by one of the books. They may design sets, write soliloquies, or do preproduction work. They should be able to discuss how their creations relate to the themes of the book.

OBJECTIVES

1. Understand and appreciate variety in language
2. Distinguish dialects of English, particularly American regional English
3. Use a dictionary to determine meaning and usage

Ⓐ Literary Connections

Robert Burns's best known and most appreciated poems are in Scottish dialect. William and Dorothy Wordsworth were also interested in the dialect of the people of the Scottish Highlands. (See, for example, William Wordsworth's "The Solitary Reaper.")

Ⓑ Background

You may want to emphasize that standard English is considered proper or desirable not because it is intrinsically better than other dialects but because it provides the common ground necessary to make communication easier and more reliable.

The English Language

Variety in Language

by John Algeo

William Wordsworth wrote a preface to *Lyrical Ballads,* in which he talked about the kind of poetry he and Samuel Taylor Coleridge tried to produce, especially about its subjects and its language. He said that their subject matter was to be "incidents and situations from common life" and that their language was to be that "really used" by ordinary people. One aspect of the Romantic movement was its fascination with common, especially rural, life and customs; with earthiness; and with simple people and their language.

Ⓐ The study of dialect was encouraged by a Romantic conviction that the simple country life was better than the complex city life. As a result, we often think of dialect as a form of language spoken by uneducated rural people. But, in fact, it is far more than that.

What Are Dialects?

We have seen that language has many ways of saying the same thing. How we talk depends partly on where we come from, what ethnic or social group we belong to, whether we are male or female, what education we have had, and how old we are. Such kinds of variation are called **dialects.** Dialects are the various forms in which a language exists, not some peculiar or quaint versions of it.

A language is like ice cream; it comes in various flavors. If you want ice cream, you ask for chocolate, vanilla, butter pecan, peppermint, or a lot of other flavors. But it would make no sense to say, "I just want plain ice cream—none of those flavors, just the real stuff." Ice cream only comes in flavors; apart from its flavors, no ice cream exists. In the same way, a language only comes in dialects; apart from its dialects, no language exists.

Many of us think that the way we talk is real English, whereas the way others talk is some odd dialect. However, we all talk dialects, none intrinsically odder (or better) than any of the others.

Many of us think that the way we talk is real English, whereas the way others talk is Ⓑ some odd dialect. However, we all talk dialects, none intrinsically odder (or better) than any of the others.

How Odd That You Should Say That

Dialects differ among themselves in the words that are used, the way words are pronounced, and the way words are put together.

Vocabulary. Depending on where you come from, a *porch* may be a *gallery, piazza, stoop,* or *veranda.* A *dragonfly* may be a *darning needle, mosquito hawk, snake doctor,* or *snake feeder. Pancakes* may be *batter cakes, flannel cakes, fritters,* or *hot cakes.*

In most parts of the United States, *rubber band* is the term for an elastic loop that holds things together; but if you are from the Minneapolis–St. Paul area, you may call it a *rubber binder. Soft drink* is what most of us call a flavored carbonated beverage; it may also be *soda, pop,* or *soda pop;* an old-fashioned term is *phosphate.* If you are from New England, you may call it *tonic,* which means something more specific (quinine water) in the rest of the country.

Pronunciation. Most Americans pronounce *fog, hog,* and *log* as "fawg," "hawg," and "lawg," with the same vowel they use in *law, paw,* and *raw.* But they use a different vowel sound in *lock, pot,* and *top.* In parts of New York and the north central states, however, *fog, hog,* and *log* have the same vowel as *lock, pot,* and *top,* whereas *law, paw,* and

go.hrw.com
LEO 12-English Language

Reaching All Students

English Language Learners

While they are reading this feature, encourage students to take time to pronounce aloud each dialect word as it is mentioned in the text. Reading words aloud will help students listen to examples carefully and gain a better understanding of the various American regional dialects.

Advanced Learners

Challenge students to come up with equivalent dialect terms for some of the italicized examples in the essay itself or in the lists of words under Try It Out on p. 772. Write students' suggestions on the chalkboard and have them provide a definition for each word and a sentence using the word in context.

raw have a different sound. In eastern New England and in western Pennsylvania and some places to the west, including most of the Far West, all of those words may be pronounced with the same vowel (either an "aw"-like or an "ah"-like sound).

Those who come from the southern United States tend to pronounce *greasy* as "greazy," whereas those from the northern states tend to make it sound like "greassy." TV ads for dishwasher detergents generally use the northern pronunciation, which seems to be gaining ground. Some people, having heard both pronunciations, use them both, but may develop special meanings for the two ways of saying the word. They may think that "greassy" means literally "coated with grease," while using "greazy" as a metaphor meaning "untrustworthy, disagreeable." In this way, two pronunciations of the same word may eventually turn into different words, as happened long ago with *shade* and *shadow, of* and *off,* and *flour* and *flower.*

Regional usage. Prepositions are especially subject to dialect variation. Whether you are sick *to, at, in,* or *on* your stomach depends mainly on where you learned to talk. So also does how you tell time—whether you say a quarter *of, till,* or *to* the hour. In most of the United States, people stand *in line,* but in New York City, they stand *on line.* Most Americans, when they are not away, are *at home,* but some are *to home.*

C For a long time, English has had a problem with the second person pronoun *you.* We make one word do double duty—for both the singular and the plural, for talking to one person and for talking to many. Some dialects, however, have tried to distinguish between the singular and plural forms. In certain parts of the North, especially in cities, some people say *youse* or *yuzz* for the plural; in the Appalachian Mountain region, some people say *you'uns.* But neither of those forms has ever made much headway in educated use. Throughout the South, however, the plural form *y'all* is widely used by the best-educated speakers, only, however, when referring to more than one person. Another new plural form that is gaining ground, especially in informal speech, is *you guys.*

American Regional Dialects D

The first English settlers in America brought with them the dialects that they spoke in the British Isles. As soon as they settled into their new country, however, they began to develop new dialects.

Today, regional dialect boundaries are clearest along the eastern coast of the United States, where English speakers first settled. There are three main dialect areas: Northern, Midland, and Southern.

Nowadays, some of the traditional differences among these regions are disappearing as our life styles change and become more uniform. What used to be called a *skillet* in the South and a *spider* in parts of the North is now almost everywhere a *frying pan* or a *frypan.* When horses pulled wagons, the horizontal wooden bar by which the wagon was attached to the animals' harness was called a *singletree* or *swingletree* in the South and a *whippletree* or *whiffletree* in the North. But now the object is foreign to the experience of most of us, so we have no name whatever for it.

New dialect terms, however, will doubtless come into existence. For example, we might expect dialect variation in the terms we use for limited-access highways, for the rest areas along them, and for the center

"A host? You call that a host! Why, back in the States . . ."

Cartoon by Mike Williams. © Punch. Courtesy Rothco.

C Appreciating Language

Diction

Point out to students that many languages (including English at an earlier time) have a way to differentiate between a familiar and a polite form of *you.* (The choice of which form to use depends on the degree of intimacy or formality the speaker wishes to convey to the person being addressed.) Remind students of the difference between Shakespeare's use of *you* and *thou.*

D Reading Skills and Strategies

Outlining

Ask students to find the main idea of each subsection of the essay and to identify the details that support it. Tell them that the heads introducing each subsection may give them clues to what is covered there, and that examples usually serve to support a main idea or generalization. They may record their findings in classic outline form, with main ideas indicated by Roman numerals. Or they may want to use another kind of graphic organizer such as main idea boxes or a cluster diagram.

Resources

Viewing and Representing

Videocassette A, Segment 2

The visual connections segment contains information on using and appreciating dialects. See also the *Visual Connections Teacher's Manual.*

Assessment

Formal Assessment

- The English Language Test, p. 146

Using Students' Strengths

Interpersonal Learners

Have students who speak similar dialects of English work in pairs to study the characteristics of their particular dialect. Urge them to list examples of vocabulary, syntax, and pronunciations that are characteristic of their peers, family, or people in their geographic area. Ask the pairs to share their lists with the class and have the class discuss the varieties of English spoken in their classroom and distinguish a few important characteristics of each variety.

Auditory Learners

Ask students to listen to a recording of a story or poem written in a distinctive dialect, such as a selection from the novel *Adventures of Huckleberry Finn* by Mark Twain or "Tam o' Shanter" by Robert Burns. After students have listened to the recording several times, ask them to consider questions like these: How does the dialect affect the telling of the story? How would the selection be different if it were written in standard English?

Ⓐ Critical Thinking

Making Connections

Ask students what terms they use for each of the places or objects described here and at the bottom of p. 771. [Possible responses: *freeways, rest stops, islands, bodega,* and *sandal.*]

Try It Out

Possible Answers

1. If students' answers differ, encourage them to compare the places where they have lived in the United States. Possible additions to the lists include *tennis shoe, sneaker, village, town.*
2. *acknowledge the corn:* a chiefly Midwestern phrase meaning "to admit to being drunk" (the word corn is short for "corn liquor") or "to admit to any mistake."
   Adam's off-ox: Midwest, South, and Southwest, meaning "a person or thing one does not know and cannot identify" or "a person that is especially slow, poor, or stubborn."
   all in: chiefly, Northern old-fashioned, meaning "exhausted" or "uncomfortable."
   bayou: around Louisiana, meaning "a creek or small river with a sluggish current"; in the West, meaning "a dry watercourse," "a body of still water," or "a small lake or pond."
   bismarck: upper Midwest, meaning "a deep-fried cake."
   blinky: chiefly Plains States, meaning "sour," especially in regard to milk.
   chill bumps: South, the equivalent of "gooseflesh" or "goosebumps."
3. The way people speak reflects the changes around them, so interest in both dialects and change in life is not unusual. In contemporary life, the connection may be used to trace peoples' concerns and attitudes in a fast-changing world.

Ⓐ barrier that divides the two directions of traffic. In addition, there will be varied terms for a small neighborhood store that is open early and late hours, or for an informal kind of open shoe that has a strap between the big toe and the other toes. Such objects have many names.

American Ethnic Dialects

Another important kind of dialect is ethnic speech. People who share a common cultural heritage tend to talk alike. Almost every immigrant group has its own ethnic dialect. Among the larger are Yiddish English, spoken by many Jews; Hispanic English of several kinds, spoken by Latinos, Cuban Americans, and Puerto Ricans; and black English, a mixture of African influences, Southern dialect, and features that developed in the African American community.

Among the features of black English (which are, however, by no means found in the speech of all African Americans) are the following: In pronunciation, final clusters of consonants are simplified, usually by dropping all except the first consonant: *most* becomes "mose," and *find* becomes "fine." *Nice* and *mine* become something like "nahs" and "mahn." The article *a* is used instead of *an* before words beginning with a vowel: *a orange, a apple.* These features are typical of the Southern dialect too.

Other features, although often found in Southern speech, are much more common in black English. The ending *–s* is frequently omitted from verbs, possessive nouns, and plural nouns that have a number before them: "He work hard," "my brother car," "four ticket." The verb *be* is either omitted altogether or used in the unchanged form of *be,* rather than *am, is, are.* These two uses, however, mean different things: "She here" means "She is here right now," while "She be here" means "She is usually or regularly here."

Black English also has distinctive words, some of which have become a part of general English vocabulary: *chigger* (sand flea), *goober* (Southern and Midland for peanut), *gumbo, jazz, juke (box), nitty-gritty,* and *zombie.* Other uses are known outside the black-English-speaking community as slang, such as *bad* pronounced with a long, drawn-out vowel ("baaaad"), meaning "very good."

As new influences come to bear on the life and language of the nation, new dialects are likely to arise. Language changes continually, but in different ways among different groups—and that is why dialects exist.

Try It Out

1. **Connecting to your experience.** Which of the following groups contains words that seem most familiar to you?
   a. pail, quarter of, angleworm, mud wasp, fussbudget, brook
   b. bucket, quarter till, fishing worm, mud dauber, fussbutton, run
   c. bucket, quarter to, wiggler, dirt dauber, fussbox, branch

   The first group is of predominantly Northern words, the second of Midland words, and the third of Southern words. Name at least two other words that are part of your regional dialect, and then locate their equivalents in at least one other regional dialect. (Classmates or neighbors from different parts of the country might be good resources.)
2. **Using the dictionary.** Here are some terms with special meanings in dialect use. Look up these words in the *Dictionary of American Regional English* (or some other dialect dictionary) to find out where they are used and what they mean.

acknowledge the corn	bayou
	bismarck
Adam's off-ox	blinky
all in	chill bumps

3. **Connecting past and present.** The Romantics were concerned with change in life and society. Some of them were also concerned with varieties of dialects. How are these two concerns connected? How could these concerns also be important in contemporary life?

Assessing Learning

Check Test: Questions and Answers

1. With what kind of language were the Romantics fascinated? [common everyday language]
2. What is a dialect? [the manner of a person's speech, which is influenced by where the person is from, what social or ethnic group the person belongs to, and his or her education, gender, and age]
3. How do dialects differ? [in the words and pronunciation that are used and in the way the words are put together in sentences]
4. Which pronoun differs greatly among American dialects of English? [the second-person pronoun *you*]
5. Where are American regional dialects clearest? [on the Atlantic coast]

EXPOSITORY WRITING
THE RESEARCH PAPER

Much of the writing you encounter every day—in the magazines and newspapers you read, the textbooks you study, and the Web sites you browse—has an informative purpose. **Expository** (or informative) **writing** is also the kind of writing you will be asked to do most often in your school and working life. When you write a research paper, your goal is to inform, and your task is to collect, organize, and present information that will expand your readers' knowledge and understanding of your topic.

Prewriting

WORK IN PROGRESS

1. **Find a topic.** Whether you choose the topic yourself or a teacher or editor assigns a general subject area, you should begin by brainstorming to find topics that interest you. Make a list of potential topics. Your Writer's Notebook jottings from Collections 8 and 9 may already contain ideas for topics. Highlight a few of the strongest possibilities. Decide which topic most intrigues you, and be sure it will also appeal to your readers. For example, you may want to find out more about Lord Byron's scandalous life. You may want to learn about the nationalist revolutions that the Romantic poets championed or the scourge of the nineteenth century—tuberculosis.
2. **Narrow your topic, and freewrite about it.** In most cases, the first topic you come up with will be too broad to handle effectively in a research paper. Your next step, then, will be to narrow the focus—from Lord Byron's reputation, for example, to the specific reasons why he left England in 1816.
   Once you have narrowed your topic, freewrite what you already know about it, and then generate questions you want to answer.
3. **Be sure the topic can be researched.** The questions you decide to explore should be ones you can find answers to in available research sources. You will need at least five or six good sources of information, either **print sources,** such as books or magazine articles that you find in a library, or **nonprint sources,** such as Web sites or personal interviews.
4. **Anticipate your audience's needs.** Before you start to write, think about the people who will read your paper. To anticipate your audience's needs, ask yourself the following questions:
   - What will my readers already know about the topic?
   - What more will they need to know to understand the topic?
   - What will they be curious about? What will interest them the most?

Technology HELP

See Writer's Workshop 2 CD-ROM. *Assignment: Informative Report.*

ASSIGNMENT
Write a research paper on a topic of interest to you and your readers.

AIM
To gather, organize, and present ideas for the purpose of informing readers.

AUDIENCE
Your teacher, classmates, or others interested in learning more about your topic.

Try It Out
With a partner or a small group, review the introduction to "The Romantic Period" (pages 622–638). On the basis of that introduction, brainstorm a list of topics that you might like to research and write about.

go.hrw.com
LEO Research Paper

MAIN OBJECTIVE
Write a research paper

PROCESS OBJECTIVES
1. Use appropriate prewriting techniques to identify and develop a topic
2. Create a first draft
3. Use Evaluation Criteria as a basis for determining revision strategies
4. Revise the first draft incorporating suggestions generated by self- or peer-evaluation
5. Proofread and correct errors
6. Create a final draft
7. Choose an appropriate method of publication
8. Reflect on progress as a writer

Planning

- **Block Schedule**
  Block Scheduling Lesson Plans with Pacing Guide
- **One-Stop Planner**
  CD-ROM with Test Generator

Resources: Print and Media

Writing and Language
- *Portfolio Management System*
  Prewriting, p. 166
  Peer Editing, p. 167
  Assessment Rubric, p. 168
- *Workshop Resources*
  Revision Strategy Teaching Notes, p. 27
  Revision Strategy Transparencies 14, 15, 16
- *Writer's Workshop 2 CD-ROM*
  Informative Report

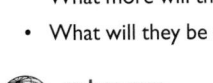

Introducing the Writer's Workshop

Bring to class the nonfiction best-seller list from *The New York Times, Time, Publisher's Weekly,* or a similar source. List the titles on the board and give students a brief one-sentence summary of each. Discuss what possible role research played in helping each author to produce a best seller. Generally, at least one or two books are on the list from these categories:

biography/autobiography
science
psychology/sociology
history
personal experience/dramatic event
personal finance

The research on which these books are based ranges from the very simple—verifying names, dates, places, and events—to the very complex—clinical studies and complicated computer modeling. In this discussion, stress the writer's duty to the reader to ensure that the appropriate research has been carefully done and that conclusions are based on an objective consideration of the facts.

Teaching the Writer's Workshop

Prewriting

Review the Prewriting steps outlined in the student's book, pp. 773–775, and define for students your expectations for the research and for the final paper. If possible, define a schedule linked to interim goals. This is particularly vital for students who have trouble getting started or difficulty monitoring their own performance.

Strategies for Evaluating Sources

To decide which of your sources are most useful, apply the four Rs:

1. How **relevant** to your topic is the information in the source?
2. How **reliable** are the facts found in the source?
3. How **recent** is the source?
4. How **representative** of different sides of the issue is the source?

5. **Research your topic.** Though general reference books will help you get an overview of your topic, specialized reference books, such as biographical dictionaries and encyclopedias on particular subjects, will provide more detailed information. Check a library catalog for books on your topic, and consider whether sources such as the *Readers' Guide to Periodical Literature,* indices to major newspapers, and an Internet search engine might direct you to useful information. You might also contact experts at a government office, museum, or historical society.

   As you do your research, be aware of the need to strike a balance between primary and secondary sources. A **primary source** is original, firsthand information: letters, journal entries, autobiographies, historical documents such as marriage records. A **secondary source** is information about or derived from primary sources: critical writings, reviews, encyclopedia entries, biographies. Secondary sources are usually readily available, but you should not, if possible, rely on them exclusively. Be sure to evaluate all sources for accuracy. Take notes on index cards or in a computer file.

Guidelines for Doing Research

- Start with a list of major topics and questions to look up.
- Write down definitions of key terms you discover as you do your research. You may need to define some of these terms in your paper.
- To ensure the accuracy of all quotations, copy the words exactly. Also keep a precise record of the source so that you can double-check the quote and document it correctly.

6. **State your controlling idea.** Reread your notes, and summarize your **controlling idea,** or **thesis,** in a brief statement. In a research paper, the controlling idea is an objective statement of your main concern; it defines the boundaries of your topic and the approach you are taking. Here are two thesis statements:
   - Lord Byron was less a typical Romantic figure in his poetry than in his life; he defied contemporary social conventions, but he was conservative in his literary expressions.
   - The American poet Walt Whitman echoed the values of the Romantics, including their emphasis on lyricism, self-expression, and individual freedom.

7. **Organize.** Present your information in a logical sequence. You can create a framework for organizing a research paper by using one of these methods:
   - **Order of importance.** Go from your most important point to your least important, or vice versa.
   - **Chronological.** Organize your events in time order.
   - **Block comparison and contrast.** Examine several aspects of one subject; then, examine the same aspects in the same order for a second subject, and so on.
   - **Point-by-point comparison and contrast.** Examine one aspect for the first subject; then, examine the same aspect for the second subject, and so on.
   - **Cause and effect.** Organize your details according to their causal relationships.

Reaching All Students

Struggling Writers

To keep this assignment within the reach of struggling writers, begin by helping them to narrow their topics to a manageable size. Be sure also, that they have selected a topic for which there is research material available within their reading range. If students are very interested in areas such as sports or computer games, help them to find topics related to these interests. Research will be easier for students if they are familiar with the vocabulary associated with the topic.

Encourage struggling writers to do some preliminary research before constructing outlines, but require outlines very early in the process. Without the framework of an outline, struggling writers may end the research phase with a loose collection of facts that points to nothing in particular. Encourage students who have difficulty reading to include media sources in their early research.

8. **Outline.** List the major aspects of your topic as main headings, using an order that reflects your approach to the subject. Your preliminary outline may change during the drafting and revising processes. For now, consider making separate piles of index cards—or printouts of the notes in your computer file—to represent your major headings. Within each pile, cluster information under subheadings. Look for holes—aspects that haven't been fully explored and relevant questions that haven't been answered. Do additional research to fill in the holes.

Drafting

1. **Begin forcefully.** The introductory paragraph of a research paper has two purposes: to define the topic clearly and to get the reader interested. Try to accomplish both purposes in one stroke by defining your topic in an engaging way. You might begin with one of the following: a surprising fact or statistic that has a bearing on your thesis, a quotation from an expert, a question that highlights different views of the subject. Describing a scene or narrating an anecdote is another effective way to open a research paper.

2. **Develop your points.** Follow your outline. Check off each item as you cover it to be sure you don't omit essential information. As you write your draft, however, you may find yourself reworking the outline as you revise your understanding of what is important about your topic.

3. **Define your terms.** Define the terms that your readers might not understand. Do not define terms they already know. For example, if you were writing an article for historians on the Greek fight for independence from Turkey in the nineteenth century, you would not have to define *nationalism,* but you would have to do so if you were writing a paper on the same topic for a general audience.

4. **Support your points.** Back up generalizations with specific details. If space permits, use anecdotes. Try to use concrete words rather than abstract ones. Use facts and figures to demonstrate the validity of your statements, and provide all necessary background information.

5. **Use quotations for forcefulness.** The exact words from expert sources can add interest and authority to a research paper, but you should avoid overusing direct quotations. In general, use quotations when they are strong. Otherwise, **summarize** or **paraphrase**—but be sure to use your own words and sentence structure. In other words, don't **plagiarize**—don't pass off another writer's words or ideas as if they were yours.

6. **Maintain an authoritative stance.** When you write, keep your tone consistent and confident, to assure your audience that you know your subject. Use language that is more or less formal, depending upon your audience. Most research papers assigned in class should be written in the third person and in relatively formal language, with a serious and objective tone.

7. **Wrap it up neatly.** The ending of a research paper usually restates the main point or points in a different way. It might also put the subject in a larger context or suggest related topics that could be explored further.

Model Outline

Title: Tuberculosis in the Nineteenth Century

Thesis statement: In the nineteenth century, tuberculosis was a widespread and deadly disease that could be neither cured nor prevented.

I. Causes of disease
  A. Medical understanding
  B. Popular understanding
II. Course of disease
  A. Symptoms
  B. Treatments
    1. Rest cure
    2. Change of climate
  C. Mortality
III. Failure to prevent contagion
  A. Inadequate quarantine
  B. Poor ventilation

Language Handbook HELP

See Quotation Marks, page 1247.

Drafting

Before students begin to draft their papers, review the information on parenthetical citations on p. 776. You may wish to review with students the types of information for which citations are essential.

Remind students that they may wish to begin by working on the body of the paper. The introduction can be done later, and perhaps more easily, once the direction and tone of the paper have been firmly set.

Models of research papers on a variety of topics are available on the HRW Website (Keyword: research paper). These may be downloaded and reproduced for use in class.

Reaching All Students

English Language Learners

Students learning English may be handicapped by their inability to read research materials available only in English. In this situation, there are a number of options. Have students do a survey of materials available in their native languages. Guide them to choose topics based on the materials available. Help students to select a topic for which original research (surveys, opinion polls, experiments, etc.) can be partially substituted for reading research. Supplement reading research with audio and video sources. Team English learners with students researching similar topics. The native speaker can help with vocabulary and difficult passages.

Evaluating and Revising

Have students set up in teams of three to review each other's papers, using the guide questions and the Evaluation Criteria provided on this page as basic tools. One evaluator should read for sense: Does the author state a clear thesis and does the paper develop and support this thesis? The other evaluator should read for documentation: Are quotations, statistics, etc. used effectively to support major points? Are sources properly documented? While the two evaluators are reading, the author of the paper should be available to answer questions.

Proofreading and Publishing

Have students work with a peer to proofread each other's papers. Focus on correct documentation. Completed papers may be exchanged with other classes.

Reflecting

Have students respond to questions on their research process:

- Did you begin your research early enough?
- Did you keep adequate track of the sources you were using?
- Did you always clearly indicate direct quotations in your notes?
- How would you organize your research differently next time?

Resources

Peer Editing Forms and Rubric

- *Portfolio Management System*, p. 167

Revision Transparencies

- *Workshop Resources*, p. 27

Grading Timesaver

Rubrics for this Writer's Workshop assignment appear on p. 168 of the *Portfolio Management System.*

Communications Handbook HELP

See Research Strategies; Evaluating the Credibility of Sources; Model Research Paper.

Revision STRATEGIES

Clear transitions guide your reader from subtopic to subtopic, from idea to idea. If you are dealing with the development of a subject over time, transitions such as first, then, next, last, *and* finally *will be important. For discussions of cause and effect, consider transitions such as* therefore, thus, so, *and* because.

Evaluation Criteria

A good research paper

1. *contains an identifiable controlling idea, or thesis, which is clearly stated early in the report*
2. *tailors the tone and level of the language to the audience*
3. *presents facts objectively*
4. *supports the points adequately*
5. *documents all sources correctly*
6. *conveys a consistent, authoritative tone*

Documenting Sources: Parenthetical Citations and Works Cited

It is crucial, when writing a research paper, to decide which information you need to *document* (cite the source for). Use these guidelines to determine which pieces of information need documentation:

- In general, don't document information that is readily available in several reference books, such as the basic facts of Byron's life.
- Document unusual, little-known facts or facts and statistics that your readers might question.
- Document all direct quotations and paraphrases.
- Document theories or opinions that are not your own.
- Document any data from surveys, experiments, or research studies.

When you document a source, you provide the information in two places: a parenthetical citation within the body of the paper and the works cited list at the end of the paper.

Parenthetical citations appear in parentheses immediately after material from a particular source. In most cases, all you need to cite is the author's last name and a page number. For example, here's a parenthetical citation for a report on Byron:

> According to one critic, the "main pleasure of reading Byron is the contact with a singular personality" (West, 111).

That parenthetical citation shows that the writer has used a quotation from a work by West. Here's how the entry for the same source will look in the **works cited** list:

> West, Paul. Byron and the Spoiler's Art. New York: Lumen Books, 1992.

The works cited list contains full bibliographic information on all the works cited in the paper so that readers can locate the sources. For more complete information on documenting sources, consult the *MLA Handbook for Writers of Research Papers,* fourth edition.

Evaluating and Revising

Exchange papers with a partner, and discuss these questions:

- Do you need more or stronger evidence to support your thesis statement?
- Have you presented your ideas in a logical sequence?
- Have you punctuated direct quotations correctly?
- Have you documented your sources clearly and completely?

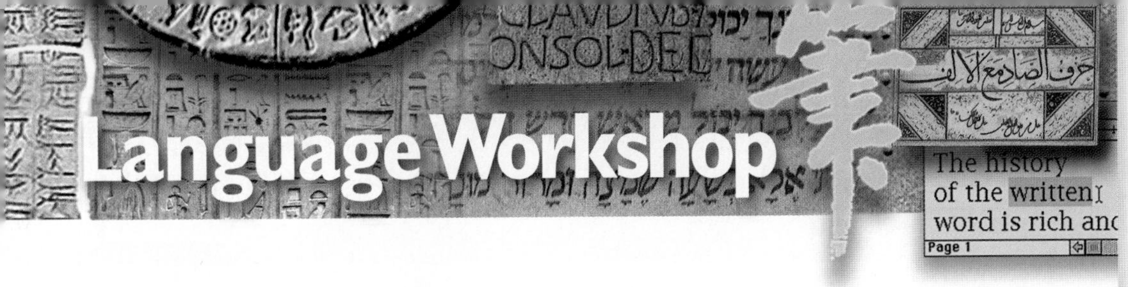
The history
of the written
word is rich and
Page 1

Language Workshop

Aspects of a Writer's Style

The Romantic poets drew upon the expressive power of ordinary speech and rejoiced in the uniqueness of each writer's **voice.** As a result, the **style** of Romantic poetry differs from that of eighteenth-century poetry. Style and voice are closely related elements of poetry. Two other elements that contribute to the overall effect of a work are **tone** and **diction.** These four elements come together like the threads of a fabric, each woven into the others. Technically, they can be defined in this way:

- **Style** is the way a writer uses and adapts language to express ideas. Writers adapt their language to the situation much as people adapt their dress to the occasion: formal for formal occasions, casual for casual occasions—and a whole range of choices in between. Style is a matter of making choices about sentence structure, punctuation, and diction.
- **Voice** is the unique sound and rhythm of the writer's language—the writer's personal way of communicating. In other words, the writer sounds like himself or herself, no matter what the situation, just as the writer would be recognizable in formal wear or in jogging clothes.
- **Tone** is the attitude the writer takes toward his or her subject. A writer's voice is capable of more than one tone. For instance, a writer may sound both angry and sarcastic or both sad and sentimental.
- **Diction,** the writer's choice of words, is an element of style and helps to establish both voice and tone.

Sentences that are formal in style can become informal with a few changes.

EXAMPLE Earth has not anything to show more fair . . .
—William Wordsworth, *from* "Composed upon Westminster Bridge"

Nothing on earth is more beautiful.

Tone can be changed by substituting synonyms with different connotations.

EXAMPLE It is an ancient Mariner. . . .
—Samuel Taylor Coleridge, *from The Rime of the Ancient Mariner*

It is a doddering old sailor.

Writer's Workshop Follow-Up: Revision

Reread the research paper you wrote for the Writer's Workshop on page 773. Is your overall style relatively formal? Do you communicate a serious and objective attitude? Is your tone consistently authoritative? Examine your diction. For words that seem imprecise, substitute more exact words. For words loaded with emotional connotations, substitute synonyms that convey a more balanced stance.

Try It Out

Rank the words in each group below, identifying them as most formal, formal, somewhat formal, or least formal. Then discuss your choices with some classmates.

1. rationalization, excuse, alibi, cop-out
2. hit, strike, percuss, wallop
3. knowledge, erudition, know-how, learning
4. soil, earth, dirt, alluvium

OBJECTIVES
Understand the basic elements of style: voice, tone, and diction

Resources

Workshop Resources
- Worksheet, p. 55

Try It Out

Possible Answers
(Answers are ordered from most to least formal.)
1. rationalization, alibi, excuse, cop-out
2. percuss, strike, hit, wallop
3. erudition, knowledge, learning, know-how
4. alluvium, soil, earth, dirt

Assessing Learning

Quick Check: Style

Identify the most formal word in the groups of words below. (Answers are set in brackets.)
1. teacher, guide, mentor [mentor]
2. draft, configuration, outline [configuration]
3. ask, question, inquire [inquire]
4. rough, bumpy, irregular [irregular]
5. hasten, hurry, rush [hasten]

OBJECTIVES

1. Evaluate the credibility of sources
2. Distinguish between primary and secondary sources
3. Evaluate electronic and video sources

Using the Strategies

Possible Answers

1. "Frankenstein's Progeny" and *Frankenstein* because they have little to do with Mary Shelley's life, and "A Frankenstein FAQ" because it is not from a reliable site.
2. *The Letters of Mary Wollstonecraft Shelley* and *Mary Shelley's Journal*
3. *Mary Shelley: A Biography*
4. "The Mary Shelley Page," because it is from an educational site

Reading for Life

Evaluating Credibility of Sources

Situation

The human-made monster! It's now a fixture in literature, movies, and television, but it began with Mary Wollstonecraft Shelley's novel *Frankenstein.* You're curious to know how a nineteen-year-old woman of the Romantic era could have invented such a fantastic and original story. To learn about the author's life, you've gathered some sources; now you want to evaluate their **credibility,** or reliability.

Sources

1. Mary Wollstonecraft Shelley, The Letters of Mary Wollstonecraft Shelley, ed. Betty T. Bennett. 3 vols. Baltimore: Johns Hopkins University Press, 1988.
2. Muriel Spark, Mary Shelley: A Biography. New York: New American Library, 1987.
3. Mary Wollstonecraft Shelley, Mary Shelley's Journal, ed. Frederick L. Jones. Norman: University of Oklahoma Press, 1947.
4. Linda Badley, "Frankenstein's Progeny," in Film, Horror, and the Body Fantastic. Greenwich, Conn.: Greenwood Press, 1995.
5. Arthur Penn Patterson, "A Frankenstein FAQ [Frequently Asked Question]: Question 7," Watershed Online, August 1, 1998. <http://www.watershed.winniped.mb.ca/MS7.html>.
6. "The Mary Shelley Page," San Antonio College LitWeb, March 9, 1998. <http://www.accd.edu/sac/english/bailey/mshelley/htm>.
7. James Whale, director, Frankenstein, starring Boris Karloff, Colin Clive, Mae Clarke, and John Boles. Universal Pictures, 1931.

Strategies

For information on a well-known figure, look for primary sources.

- Primary sources include letters, journals, diaries, and autobiographies written by the subject and his or her contemporaries.

Select secondary sources on your subject (books and articles by experts).

- Check the writer's credentials. Is he or she knowledgeable on the subject? For example, has the writer written other works on the same or a related topic?
- Evaluate the writer's motivation. Is it to inform, persuade, or entertain? How might the purpose affect the presentation?
- Be alert to any ideological bias that might interfere with the writer's objectivity.
- Evaluate the publisher. Does it publish reputable, highly regarded works, such as scholarly journals or academic books?
- Check the publication dates. Recent sources may be more comprehensive and more accurate, but older sources may provide important historical details.

Evaluate electronic and video sources carefully.

- Government (*gov*) and non-profit *(org)* Web sites are more often reliable than commercial (*com*) sites.
- Documentaries are more reliable than true stories that have been fictionalized.

Using the Strategies

1. Which sources listed in the box above would you eliminate without investigating further? Why?
2. What two primary sources would you select?
3. Which secondary source would you choose?
4. Which seems to be the most promising Internet site? Why?

Extending the Strategies

- Compile a list of credible sources of information on the life and works of one of your favorite writers.
- Compare a film version of a novel with the novel itself.

Learning for Life

Researching Labor and Population Trends

Problem

During the Romantic period, as the Industrial Revolution progressed, cities often grew up around factories. How is the current change from an industrial to a service- and information-based economy affecting the places where people live and work?

Project

Research current and projected population trends in the United States. What factors account for the growth of some areas and the decline of others? Where will people work in the future?

Preparation

1. Working with a partner or a small group, use brainstorming or the *5W-How?* questions (*Who? What? When? Where? Why? How?*) to develop questions to guide your research.
2. Exchange ideas about the kinds of information that will help you answer your research questions and about possible sources, including the Internet and government publications.

Procedure

1. One way to gain an overview of your topic is to read several newspaper or magazine articles written for a general audience. (Check a library's indices to newspapers, essays, and articles.) Such articles may mention other sources as well as authors who are experts in the field.
2. Two good secondary sources for data on population distribution are *The World Almanac and Book of Facts* and the *Statistical Abstract of the United States*. The Census Bureau also issues numerous publications, such as *Current Population Reports* (available on microfiche in some libraries).
3. As you review the facts, opinions, and theories you find, draw your own conclusions about the relationship between the nation's transformation to a service- and information-based economy, the distribution of the population, and changes in the places where people work.

Presentation

Use one of the following formats (or another that your teacher approves):

1. **Communicating Graphically**

   Communicate your findings in a graphic display combining two or more types of illustrations, such as maps, charts, and graphs. Include only essential information, so that the finished product will be legible and uncluttered, and use color, patterns, or both to make the display accurate and attractive. Ask one of your high school's American history or economics teachers to field-test the display with his or her students at a suitable point in the course.
2. **Persuading**

   Write an editorial summarizing your findings and expressing your views on why students should use the information in planning their careers. Persuade your readers to take your ideas seriously by using a formal tone and by tailoring your appeals to their needs and interests. Submit your editorial to the school newspaper or to a local newspaper.
3. **Speaking Out**

   Prepare a speech explaining what your research suggests about your community's future. Since your investigation focused on national trends, you'll need to extrapolate from your findings—that is, to speculate on the basis of what you discovered. Present your speech to a meeting of a civic or professional group, such as the Rotary Club or the American Business Women's Association.

Processing

Did this activity make you rethink your career plans? Did it change your ideas about where you're likely to live and work in the future? Write a brief reflection for your portfolio.

LEARNING FOR LIFE 779

OBJECTIVES

1. Research current and projected population trends
2. Determine the factors influencing population growth or decline
3. Present research findings

Teaching the Lesson

Remind students that printed data goes out of date very rapidly. Whenever they take data from a source, students should always note the date of collection of the information, not just the date of publication. Encourage students to draw data from as many different sources as possible. Some federal, state, and local agencies maintain Websites that include statistical information on population and job statistics. Information updates will appear on these sites before being published in print.

Grading Timesaver

Rubrics for this Learning for Life assignment appear on p. 169 of the *Portfolio Management System*.

Developing Workplace Competencies

Preparation	Procedure	Presentation
• Generates related ideas • Makes inferences • Recognizes relationships • Predicts consequences	• Uses resources well • Works well on teams • Acquires data • Processes information • Evaluates data	• Interprets information • Communicates ideas • Teaches others • Demonstrates responsibility and self-esteem

OBJECTIVES

1. Read literature from the Victorian period on the themes of "Love and Loss" and "The Paradox of Progress"
2. Interpret literary elements
3. Apply a variety of reading strategies, with special emphasis on context and figurative language
4. Respond to the literature in a variety of modes
5. Learn how English became an international language in the Victorian period; compare and contrast British and American English
6. Learn and use new words
7. Plan, draft, revise, proofread, and publish a persuasive evaluation
8. Develop skill in analyzing and strengthening meaning through sentence style
9. Demonstrate ability to read and interpret a historical map
10. Evaluate a community through a variety of projects

The Victorian Period 1832–1901

Selection Readability

This Annotated Teacher's Edition provides a summary of each selection in the student book. Following each Summary heading, you will find one, two, or three small icons. These icons indicate, in an approximate sense, the reading level of the selection.

- ■ One icon indicates that the selection is easy.
- ■■ Two icons indicate that the selection is on an intermediate reading level.
- ■■■ Three icons indicate that the selection is challenging.

The Railway Station (detail) (19th century) by William Powell Frith.

781

Responding to the Art

William Powell Frith (1819–1909), whose lifetime spanned the Victorian age, was, for a time, the most popular artist in England. At the Royal Gallery, some of his paintings had to be roped off to protect them from the masses that swarmed around them. Ironically, the pictures themselves also teem with crowds. Frith strove for a photographic realism in his paintings, so they are a good guide to the daily lives and customs of his middle-class subjects.

Activity. Ask students to discuss these questions: What do you learn about Victorian society by looking at this painting? In what ways does the painting depict an active, vital group of people? In what ways does the painting offer a positive view of Victorian society? What anecdotes, or little stories, seem to be taking place within the larger context of the picture?

Resources

Viewing and Representing

Videocassette B, Segment 9

This segment explores the underside of Victorian progress by presenting the deplorable conditions spawned by the Industrial Revolution. For full lesson plans and worksheets, see *Visual Connections Teacher's Manual.*

The Victorian Period

by Donald Gray

So many worlds, so much to do,
So little done, such things to be . . .

—Alfred, Lord Tennyson

Transept of the Crystal Palace
by G. Hawkins (19th century). Published by Day and Son and Ackerman and Co.
Stapleton Collection, London.

(Inset) F
lid depic
ing Cry
Palace,
Dale Ha
Longpo
Stafford
shire
(1851),
T. J. and
J. Mayer
Fitzwilliam
Museum,
University
Cambridge

go.hrw.com
LEO 12-Victorian

OBJECTIVES

1. Understand the historical and social forces that shaped the Victorian era
2. Interpret the influence of historical context on the literary works of the era
3. Use a time line to locate information
4. Make connections between the issues and events of the Victorian era and those of today

Responding to the Quotation

? In this quotation, Tennyson captures the mood of the times. What is it? [He is expressing exuberant optimism and a vision of the world as a busy, bright place, teeming with possibilities.]

RESPONDING TO THE ART

Call students' attention to the fact that Tennyson's optimistic quotation is set against an illustration of the Crystal Palace. This building was the setting for the Great Exhibition of 1851, one of the earliest international exhibitions ever held.

Activity. Victorians were enraptured not only by the exhibit but by this building. Ask students why they think the Victorians responded so positively to the Crystal Palace. [Students may note the vaulted ceiling made of glass and steel, the interior fountain, the lavish statuary, the ingenious tiers, and the interior landscaping. All these features impressed the Victorians with their modernity, inventiveness, and style.] You might explain that some objected to the erection of the "palace" because it would involve cutting down three tall elms on the site. The undaunted architect Joseph Paxton saved the day, however, when he found a way to incorporate the trees into his design.

Professional Notes

Critical Comment:
The Inspired Amateur

Novelist and critic Margaret Drabble, writing on the Crystal Palace, notes that "Paxton's whole concept was, in fact, based on nature; he is thought to have devised the rib structure from his study of the huge South American water lily, *Victoria Amazonica,* which he had seen at Chatsworth; its giant leaves were strong enough to bear the weight of Paxton's small daughter. Like so many of the great Victorians, Paxton was strictly an amateur, as he had no professional qualifications as architect, engineer, or scientist; this was an age when the inspired amateur, his imagination unshackled by a narrow professional training or discipline, could achieve astonishing results."

Many Victorians thought of themselves as living in a time of great change. They were right. But the changes during Queen Victoria's long reign (1837–1901) occurred in a period of relative political and social stability, and many were the result of conditions that began before Victoria and most of her subjects were born.

Cotton handkerchief probably produced for Queen Victoria's Golden Jubilee in 1887 (PC86).
Museum of London.

Peace and Economic Growth: Britannia Rules

After Napoleon's defeat at Waterloo in 1815, Britain was not involved in a major European war until World War I began in 1914. The empire that had begun in the seventeenth and eighteenth centuries with British interests in India and North America grew steadily, until by 1900, Victoria was queen-empress of more than two hundred million people living outside Great Britain.

At the same time, the Industrial Revolution of the eighteenth century greatly expanded. It moved through booms and depressions, but over the course of the century it steadily created new towns, new goods, new wealth, and new jobs for tens of thousands of people climbing through the complicated levels of the middle class. These social and economic changes were expressed in gradual political reforms. Piece by piece, middle-class and ultimately working-class politicians and voters achieved political power while leaving the monarchy and aristocracy in place.

The Victorian era was a time of relative peace and economic growth. The British Empire grew steadily, the Industrial Revolution expanded, and political power was extended to the middle and working classes.

The Idea of Progress: "An Acre in Middlesex"

The English historian Thomas Babington Macaulay eloquently voiced the middle-class Victorian attitude toward government, history, and civilization. For Macaulay, history meant progress, and progress largely meant material improvement that could be seen and touched, counted and measured. "An acre in Middlesex is better than a principality in Utopia," he once

> The history of England is emphatically the history of progress.
> —Thomas Babington Macaulay

Ⓐ Cultural Connections

Personifying Nations

The word *Britannia* is a female personification of the British Empire or Great Britain. Ask students what similar personifications are applied to the United States. [Possible responses: Uncle Sam, Lady Liberty.]

Ⓑ Exploring the Historical Period

Progress Toward Democracy

The push for greater democracy was embodied in the Chartist movement, which got its name from the fact that its demands were first presented to Parliament in a petition called the People's Charter of 1838. Among other things, the Chartists called for salaries for members of Parliament, use of the secret ballot, and repeal of property requirements for serving in Parliament. Eventually, almost all the Chartists' demands were met. In addition, most adult men in Britain gained the right to vote by 1884.

Ⓒ Critical Thinking

Evaluating

? Do you agree or disagree with Macaulay's view? Why? [Possible responses: Some students will agree on the basis that it is better to live in the real world than in some impossible fantasy. Others will disagree, arguing that we all need to dream of better ways to live.]

Reaching All Students

Struggling Readers

Ask students to create a KWL chart. Before they read the unit essay, have students record what they already know about the Victorian era and what they want to learn. After they finish reading, ask students to record what they have learned. Follow up by asking students what more they would like to know about the Victorian period and brainstorm with them on ways of finding resources for answering their questions.

English Language Learners

Suggest students begin by previewing the unit essay, noting all the major headings as well as the illustrations which help tell the Victorian "story." Urge students to preview and review, as often as they need to, the statements in bold italic type that sum up the key ideas under each heading.

Advanced Learners

Invite students to choose a historical or cultural topic, such as theater in the Victorian age or the orphans of Victorian London, and to supplement the information provided in the text with additional research. Provide an opportunity for students to share what they learn in an oral report. Urge them to use graphic aids and other visual documentation if possible.

Time Line

This time line shows major events that occurred during the Victorian Period, 1832–1901.

- **1832–1846**

Dickens Portrays Victorian Poverty
Charles Dickens depicts the poverty and the criminal underground that existed in Victorian England in his novel *Oliver Twist.* Dickens may have drawn from his own memories when he wrote about Oliver's impoverished childhood. When Dickens's father was thrown into debtors' prison, young Charles was forced to leave school and work in a factory.

Texans Defeated at the Alamo
Americans living in the part of Mexico that later became the state of Texas had originally been invited by Mexico to help settle the part of Mexico that lies north of the Rio Grande. In 1835, however, the Texans, led by Stephen Austin, began a revolt for independence. Antonio Lopez de Santa Anna, who had helped Mexico gain its independence from Spain in 1821, was president of the Mexican province of Texas at the time. It was under Santa Anna's generalship that the Mexican army defeated the Texas rebels at the Alamo in 1836.

- **1847–1859**

Sojourner Truth Speaks Out
A feminist and abolitionist, Sojourner Truth delivered her famous "Ain't I a Woman?" speech at a women's rights convention in Akron, Ohio, in 1851. Although born into slavery and unable to read or write, Sojourner Truth was an inspiring speaker who eloquently championed freedom for African Americans and political rights for women. It was not until the twentieth century, however, that women in England and the United States won the right to vote.

Perry Opens Up Japan
In 1854, under enormous pressure from an American fleet under Commodore Perry, Japan reluctantly signed the Treaty of Kanagawa, which opened two Japanese ports to trade with American ships. Within a few years, other Western powers also gained trading rights with Japan. Many Japanese, however, were angry about this Western intrusion, and by 1867, the government had fallen. The new Meiji emperor, Mutsuhito, decided to resist Western influence by undertaking his own program to modernize Japan.

The Victorian Period, 1832–1901

LITERARY EVENTS

1832–1846

Elizabeth Barrett and **Robert Browning** elope; during their courtship, she writes poems included in *Sonnets from the Portuguese,* 1846

William Wordsworth becomes poet laureate, 1843

Nikolai Gogol draws attention to the plight of Russian serfs with his comic epic *Dead Souls,* 1842

Margaret Fuller helps found *The Dial,* a U.S. Transcendentalist journal that publishes Henry David Thoreau and Ralph Waldo Emerson, 1840

Edgar Allan Poe publishes "The Fall of the House of Usher," 1839

Charles Dickens publishes *Oliver Twist* in periodical form, 1837–1838

1847–1859

Charles Darwin publishes *On the Origin of Species by Means of Natural Selection,* 1859

Mary Ann Evans publishes stories in *Blackwood's Magazine,* using her pen name, George Eliot, 1857

Sojourner Truth delivers her "Ain't I a Woman?" speech in Akron, Ohio, 1852

Nathaniel Hawthorne publishes *The Scarlet Letter,* 1850

Alfred, Lord Tennyson becomes poet laureate, 1850

Karl Marx and Friedrich Engels publish *The Communist Manifesto,* 1848

Charlotte Brontë publishes *Jane Eyre;* Emily Brontë publishes *Wuthering Heights,* 1847

CULTURAL/HISTORICAL EVENTS

1832–1846

First Reform Bill extends vote to men who own property worth £10 or more annually, 1832

Mexican army defeats Texans at the Alamo, 1836

Victoria becomes queen of the United Kingdom of Great Britain and Ireland, 1837

Reforms included in Custody Act allow divorced women legal access to their children, 1839

First of what China terms "unequal treaties" makes Hong Kong a British colony, 1842

Potato famine begins in Ireland; close to one million people die from starvation or famine-related diseases; massive emigration begins, 1845

1847–1859

Ten Hours Act limits the number of hours that women and children can work in factories, 1847

Seneca Falls, New York, women's rights convention is led by Elizabeth Cady Stanton and Lucretia Mott, 1848

Social and political revolutions in France, Germany, and the Austrian Empire mostly fail, 1848

Japan opens trade to West, 1854

Change in laws allows Lionel de Rothschild to become first Jewish member of Parliament, 1858

Medical Act closes loophole that briefly allowed women to become physicians in Great Britain, 1858

- **Imperial State Crown (1837) made for Victoria's coronation.**

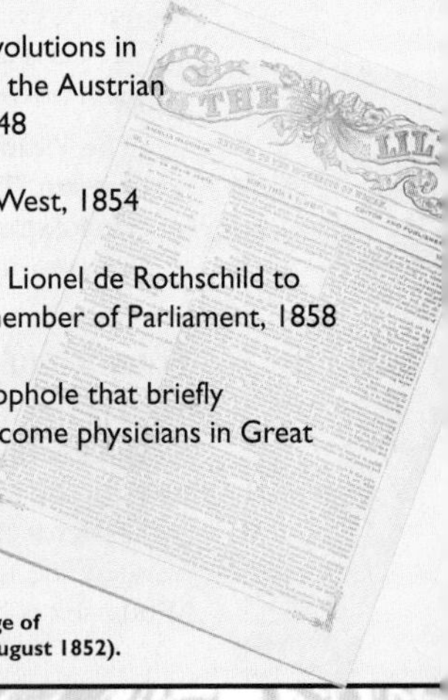

- **Front page of *The Lily* (August 1852).**

Using the Time Line

Have students use encyclopedias or other print or nonprint resources and databases to find the dates of the following events. When they have discovered the dates, have them add them to the time line.

- Schubert's "Unfinished Symphony" is first performed. [1865]
- Halley's comet appears; Mark Twain is born. [1835]
- Charles Goodyear develops a process to make rubber commercially available. [1839]
- Sigmund Freud publishes *The Interpretation of Dreams.* [1899]
- The first skeletal remains of *archaeopteryx,* the link between birds and reptiles, are discovered. [1861]
- Alexander II frees the serfs in Russia. [1861]
- Quantum theory is developed by Max Planck. [1900]
- Britain abolishes slavery in its empire. [1833]
- Henrik Ibsen publishes *A Doll's House.* [1879]

• Charles Darwin.

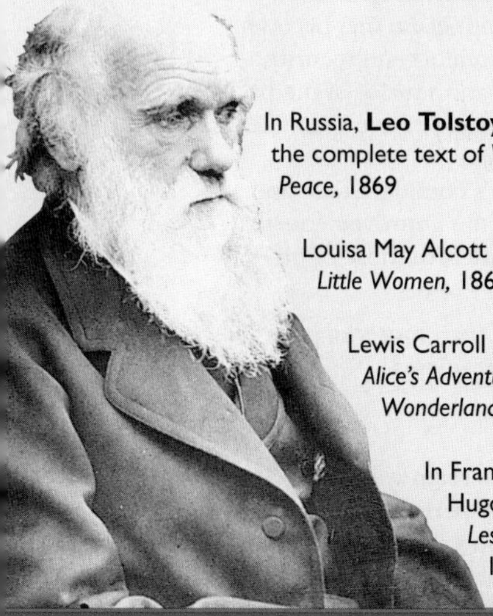

• English or French lady's fan with yellow pansies (1880–1900). Lace and painted silk leaf with mother-of-pearl sticks.

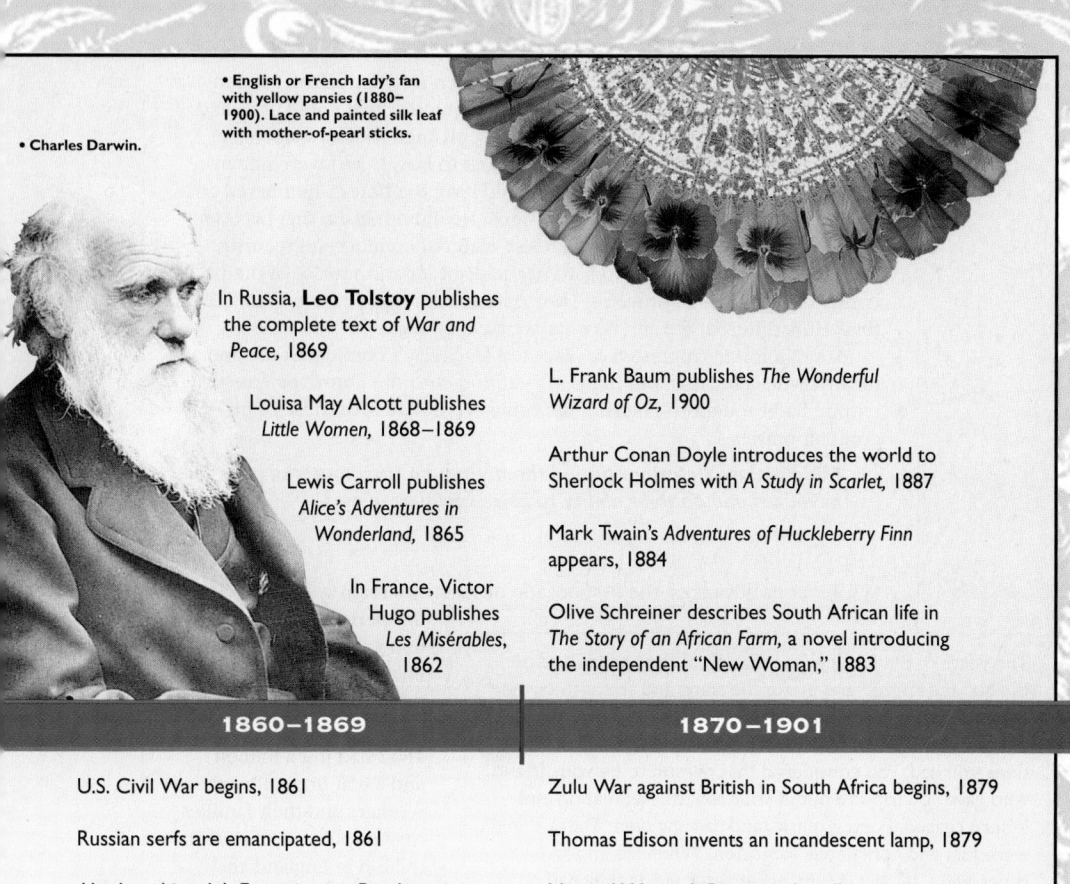

In Russia, **Leo Tolstoy** publishes the complete text of *War and Peace,* 1869

Louisa May Alcott publishes *Little Women,* 1868–1869

Lewis Carroll publishes *Alice's Adventures in Wonderland,* 1865

In France, Victor Hugo publishes *Les Misérables,* 1862

L. Frank Baum publishes *The Wonderful Wizard of Oz,* 1900

Arthur Conan Doyle introduces the world to Sherlock Holmes with *A Study in Scarlet,* 1887

Mark Twain's *Adventures of Huckleberry Finn* appears, 1884

Olive Schreiner describes South African life in *The Story of an African Farm,* a novel introducing the independent "New Woman," 1883

1860–1869

U.S. Civil War begins, 1861

Russian serfs are emancipated, 1861

Abraham Lincoln's Emancipation Proclamation declares slavery illegal in Confederate territories, 1863

Last Japanese shogun resigns; power returns to emperor, 1867

Second Reform Act gives vote to most male industrial workers, doubling the number of voters, 1867

Britain ends eighty-year practice of sending convicts to Australia, 1868

Debtors' prisons are abolished in England, 1869

Suez Canal opens, 1869

Mohandas K. Gandhi born in India, 1869

1870–1901

Zulu War against British in South Africa begins, 1879

Thomas Edison invents an incandescent lamp, 1879

Married Women's Property Act allows wives possession of property held before and after marriage, 1882

Indian National Congress is formed; begins agitating for Indian self-rule, 1885

Emmeline Pankhurst forms Women's Franchise League, arguing for British women's suffrage, 1889

More than 140 Sioux villagers are killed by U.S. soldiers at Wounded Knee Creek, South Dakota, 1890

Home Rule Bill (to create an Irish Parliament) defeated by British Parliament for second time, 1893

French scientists Pierre and Marie Curie discover radium, 1898

Queen Victoria dies, 1901

• 1860–1869

British Convicts Shipped to Australia

The tens of thousands of convicts sent to Australia from England made up a large proportion of the population of Australia for more than fifty years. Today, Australia maintains strong ties with Great Britain; the two countries share a common language, are close trading partners, and have similar legislative systems. During the Victorian period, the English people enjoyed books about Australia, such as Charles Rowcroft's *Tales of the Colonies* (1843) and Henry Kingsley's *The Recollections of Geoffrey Hamlyn* (1859). Convicts themselves, such as James Vaux, published memoirs that told their Australian story.

Britain Controls the Suez Canal

The French and the British both eyed Egypt hungrily for its valuable position at the mouth of the Red Sea. The Suez Canal was built with French financing, but Egypt also put enormous resources into it, which destabilized Egypt and made it possible for Britain to take control of the country in 1882. Britain maintained control of Egypt and the canal until the 1950s.

• 1870–1901

Europe Carves Up Africa

All the European nations decided how best to divide up Africa between them at the Berlin Conference of 1884–1885. (No African ruler attended this meeting.) Within twenty years, all of Africa was claimed by European countries with the exception of Ethiopia and Liberia. These artificial borders created by Europeans later contributed to the destabilizing conflicts which developed within and between African countries after they regained their independence from Europe in the twentieth century.

Crossing the Curriculum

Geography

Prompted by the time line entries, students might do research to find additional important events that occurred in different parts of the world during the Victorian period. Ask each student to prepare a brief presentation, using visuals to show how the selected event relates to events occurring in Victorian England.

Ⓐ Historical Connections

Thomas Babington Macaulay

Macaulay was primarily a historian—in fact, he began his first history of the world before he was ten. He was also a minor literary figure who wrote poetry and contributed to the notable literary magazines of his day. As a politician, Macaulay became a leading Whig in the House of Commons.

Ⓑ Exploring the Historical Period

The 1840s

A key reason for the hard economic times of the 1840s was the overcapitalization of the textile industry, which was subject to increasing competition from America. New inventions demanded new capital outlays, even as the return on capital was dwindling. In this atmosphere, real wages did not keep pace with the rising cost of urban living. Only a new and extraordinary industrial development could save England's economy: By the 1850s salvation came along in the shape of the railroads.

Ⓒ Reading Skills and Strategies

Modifying Reading Strategies

Tell students that the information presented in the box is set apart from the rest of the running text of the essay for specific reasons. Ask students how the information in this box differs from the text in the rest of the essay and how they might change their reading strategy as a result. [Possible responses: This is primary-source material, information about a historical event written by an eyewitness. Though written in the third person, the account has the immediacy, realistic details, and drama of a first-person account. To read it, students might shift from concentrating on facts and information to responding on a more emotional level.]

Maire ni Grianna, from Rannafast, County Donegal, recorded these memories of the 1847 famine on May 5, 1945, when she was eighty-one years old. She spoke in Irish; her oral history was translated by Emer Deane and is now part of the Department of Irish Folklore in University College, Dublin.

wrote. Macaulay admired cleanliness and order. He wanted the London streets free of garbage, drained and paved, lighted at night, and patrolled by a sober police force. He wanted the city planned so that residents of respectable neighborhoods did not live next to hovels and were not annoyed by beggars and peddlers. He would have the houses numbered and a population literate enough to read signs. He did not claim that his own time had entirely met these standards of material comfort and security, but his cool, almost amazed regard of the disorder and squalor of the past conveyed his sense of progress: How could those people have lived like that? How different we are; how far we have come.

Ⓐ Many Victorians regretted or disputed Macaulay's confident tone and materialistic standards. But in his satisfaction with the improvements that empire had brought to England, his views were typical of those of his contemporaries.

Middle-class Victorians prided themselves on their material advances and on their ability to solve social problems.

The "Hungry Forties"

Whatever its advances, the first decade of Victoria's reign was troubled— Ⓑ the period came to be known as the "Hungry Forties." Victoria came to the throne in the first year of a depression that by 1842 had put a million and a half unemployed workers and their families (in a population of sixteen million in England and Wales) on some form of poor relief. Government commissions investigating working conditions learned of children mangled when they fell asleep at machines at the end of a twelve-hour working day. They discovered young girls and boys hauling sledges of coal through narrow mine tunnels, working shifts so long that in winter they saw the sun only on Sundays.

Ⓒ The years of the Famine [in Ireland], of the bad life and of the hunger, arrived and broke the spirit and strength of the community. People simply wanted to survive. Their spirit of comradeship was lost. It didn't matter what ties or relations you had; you considered that person to be your friend who gave you food to put in your mouth. Recreation and leisure ceased. Poetry, music, and dancing died. These things were lost and completely forgotten. When life improved in other ways, these pursuits never returned as they had been. The famine killed everything.

The old people said that in the summer of 1846 the potato blight struck for the first time. People went to sleep at night with the potato fields looking green and healthy; when they got up the next day, every stem in the fields was ruined by the disease. . . .

They [the starving people] used to stay inside in their cabins, not able to walk, so weak were they with hunger. They would go out in the fields on all fours and eat their fill of grass and weeds and then they'd be able to walk home. Mothers lay in their beds with the children beside them and they were so weak they were not able to get up. They used to lie there until one after another they died of hunger.

—Maire ni Grianna, *from Memories of the Famine*

London Street Scene (1835) by J. O. Parry.

Alfred Dunhill Collection.

In Ireland, the potato blight (1845–1849) caused a famine that killed perhaps a million people and forced two million others—more than 25 percent of Ireland's population—to emigrate. Some went to English cities, where they lived ten or twelve to a room in slums that had two toilets for every 250 people.

The rapid growth of cities often made them filthy and disorderly. Nearly two million people lived in London during the 1840s, and commercial and industrial cities such as Manchester and Liverpool expanded rapidly. In Manchester in the 1840s, 40 percent of the streets were still unpaved. The Thames River in London was polluted by sewage, industrial waste, and the drainage from graveyards where bodies were buried in layers six or eight deep. In the 1850s, Parliament sometimes had to adjourn from its new riverside building because of the stench from the Thames.

> From the butchers' and greengrocers' shops the gaslights flared and flickered, wild and ghastly, over haggard groups of slipshod dirty women, bargaining for scraps of stale meat and frostbitten vegetables, wrangling about short weight and bad quality. Fish stalls and fruit stalls lined the edge of the greasy pavement, sending up odors as foul as the language of sellers and buyers. Blood and sewer water crawled from under doors and out of spouts, and reeked down the gutters among offal, animal and vegetable, in every stage of putrefaction.
>
> —Charles Kingsley

Serious problems surfaced during the early years of Victoria's reign: economic depression, widespread unemployment, famine in Ireland, and deplorable living and working conditions brought on by rapid urbanization and a lack of measures safeguarding young workers.

D Exploring the Historical Period

The Potato Famine and Emigration

The mass Irish emigration, which began in the hard times of the early 1840s and became essential for survival in the late 1840s, continued during the next decade and reached its peak in 1855. Besides going to England, the Irish also went to the United States and Canada, as well as to New Zealand and Australia (particularly to the gold fields of New South Wales). Historian J. B. Priestley suggests that while these immigrants undoubtedly sought a living wage, they also sought "a chance at last of sun and air, well away from overcrowded and disease-ridden hovels."

E Cultural Connections

Cities and Literature

Cities were important in Victorian society—a result of the rise of industry and the increasing wealth of the business class. Some Victorian novelists, notably Charles Dickens, dealt memorably with life in urban settings, looking unflinchingly at the cramped lives of the workers, not just at the smug prosperity of the middle and upper classes. Others, such as George Eliot and Thomas Hardy, continued to turn to village and country life for the settings of their fiction.

Using Students' Strengths

Intrapersonal Learners

Ask students to keep a journal of their responses to the information in this essay. In it, students might note their opinions of the Victorians; comparisons and contrasts with people, events, and ideas in their own age; and questions they have about the era in general or about individual events or personalities.

Verbal Learners

After students finish reading the essay, they may enjoy using the letters of the words *Victorian Period* as a mnemonic device for devising a list of characteristics of the period. For example, for *V,* they might write "Victoria, beloved queen, rules." If students are having difficulty recalling characteristics of the period, have them review the headings in the text, the boldfaced summary sentences, and the time line entries.

Visual Learners

It may help students to understand and remember the many contradictions of the Victorian era if they summarize them on a chart or graphic that highlights their relationship, such as a pair of balanced scales. For example, while the Victorians were enthusiastic church-goers, they also lived in an era when the very foundations of religious faith were being shaken by Darwin's theories and other scientific discoveries.

A Closer Look

This feature examines the social reforms made by women like Octavia Hill and Florence Nightingale in Victorian Britain.

Ⓐ Exploring the Historical Period

Women in Victorian England

High-profile, reforming women were the exception and not the rule. Writing about the role of women in Victorian England, Richard Altick in *Victorian People and Ideas* says, "Upper- and middle-class women were sedulously set apart from the worlds of commerce and, generally, of intellect. This represented a marked reversal of attitude and custom. In the seventeenth century, aristocratic ladies had actively managed their family's household and estates. In the eighteenth century, there had been plenty of middle-class businesswomen, engaged in a variety of occupations. . . . But the nation's increasing wealth and the growing complexity of the mercantile economy . . . [as well as] separation of business premises from the home, encouraged the detachment of women from the money-making world, and they began to aspire to a state of gentility devoid of responsibility."

Ⓑ Exploring the Historical Period

Florence Nightingale

Nightingale was a meticulous statistician who collected convincing data about the benefits of improved sanitation. In her *Notes on Matters Affecting the Health, Efficiency, and Hospital Administration of the British Army,* she explains that inadequate food, clothing, and unsanitary conditions—more than wounds from the fighting—contributed to the disastrous mortality rate among soldiers in the Crimean War.

A CLOSER LOOK

Ⓐ An Age in Need of Heroines: Reform in Victorian Britain

Be good, sweet maid, and let who will be clever;
Do noble things, not dream them, all day long.

—Charles Kingsley

Great Britain was the world's first industrialized nation, and its smoky cities illustrated the dangers of "progress": Unsanitary housing and rampant disease were unremarkably common. There were legal remedies for abuses, but Victorian social reform was not only a parliamentary process. It was also a passionate struggle to change public opinion through hard work and education.

"Do noble things." Following the Reverend Charles Kingsley's urging to "Do noble things, not dream them," many women approached social reform as a moral and religious duty. The social worker Octavia Hill (1838–1912) believed that adequate housing could "make individual life noble, homes happy, and family life good," and she became an authority on housing reform. She was also a conservationist, founding the National Trust to protect historic buildings and scenic spots from industrial development. Because of Hill's efforts, the public can visit sites such as the Runnymede meadow. Thanks to the National Trust, it looks much as it did when King John accepted the Magna Carta there in 1215.

Spoiling the "brutes." Perhaps the best-known Victorian reformer is Florence Nightingale (1820–1910), who transformed the public's perception of modern nursing during the Crimean War. Two unlikely inventions—the camera and the war correspondent—made her career possible. Newspaper reports revealed that bureaucratic bungling had cost thousands of lives in the army's hospitals in Scutari, Turkey. Public indignation gave Nightingale the unprecedented opportunity to become an army nurse. In Turkey, she saw scores of wounded soldiers dying from diseases caused by poor hygiene, lack of medical supplies, and sheer neglect. The ordinary British soldier was thought to be, in the words of the duke of Wellington, "the scum of the earth." When Nightingale asked medical authorities for clean bedding or warm clothing, she was told: "You will spoil the brutes."

Ⓑ Nightingale believed British soldiers were "murdered" by incompetence, and she vowed to avenge them. With gritty tenacity, she became an authority on public health, observing that sanitation could save lives. Queen Victoria read her meticulous reports and said, "I wish we had her at the War Office." Nightingale's efforts fundamentally changed hospital management and made nursing a respected career.

The Movement for Reform: Food, Factories, and Optimism

Violence broke out at massive political rallies called in the 1840s to protest government policies that kept the price of bread and other food high and deprived most working men (and all women) of the vote and representation in Parliament. In 1848, a year of revolution in Europe, nervous British politicians got the army ready and armed the staffs of museums and government offices when working-class political reformers organized what they called a "monster rally" in London to petition Parliament and the queen.

Still, most middle-class Victorians believed that things were better than in the past and that they were going to be better yet in the future. Their opinion was in part founded on a steady improvement throughout the Victorian era in the material condition of people in all social classes. The

Crossing the Curriculum

Social Studies

Ask students to find out what was going on in continental Europe in 1848 while the British establishment was readying itself to resist political reformers. Then have them compare and contrast the events in England with those on the continent. [That year, Marx and Engels drafted the *Communist Manifesto*; the French working classes rose up against Louis Philippe; there was unrest in Berlin, Vienna, and the (not yet unified) states of Italy. By contrast, the Chartists in 1848 planned nothing more dramatic than a march to London with a petition. Thousands of special constables were hired for the occasion but the Chartists left peacefully.]

Science

Have students work in groups of three or four to report on a signficant technological or scientific advancement made during the Victorian period. Students can provide a replica, schematic drawing, or other physical representation of the innovation. Background information can be given in the form of a bulletin board display or videotape presentation.

Florence Nightingale tending the wounded during the Crimean War (19th century).

"We make no compromise." Reformers such as Nightingale and Hill devoted themselves to aiding the victims of Victorian "progress," agitating for better conditions and for improved educational opportunities. In the name of charity, they often stepped outside the bounds of "ladylike" behavior. Josephine Butler (1828–1906) exposed the exploitation of women and girls, working to repeal acts that deprived poor women of their constitutional rights. In the name of reform, she declared that "we make no compromise; and we are ready to meet all the powers of earth and hell combined."

These reformers redefined the idea of "women's work"; in the process, they set public policies that curbed many abuses and saved countless lives. As we enter the twenty-first century, we continue to benefit from their efforts to improve the Victorian quality of life.

price of food dropped after midcentury, largely because of trade with other countries and the growing empire. Diet improved as meat, fruit, and margarine (a Victorian invention) began to appear regularly in working-class households. Factories and railroads made postage, newspapers, clothing, furniture, travel, and other goods and services cheap.

A series of political reforms gave the vote to almost all adult males by the last decades of the century. In 1832, the First Reform Bill extended the vote to all men who owned property worth ten pounds or more in yearly rent. Continued pressure led to the Second

> The principle which regulates the existing social relations between the two sexes—the legal subordination of one sex to the other—is wrong in itself, and now one of the chief hindrances to human improvement.
>
> —John Stuart Mill, *from The Subjection of Women*

Ⓒ Cultural Connections

"Ladylike" Behavior

This was the age—in the middle and upper classes—of the overdressed, underemployed wife. Almost as if she were part of the expensive decoration of the house, the typical Victorian lady would pass the day in a way totally unlike Florence Nightingale and Josephine Butler. The Victorian lady was relegated to trivial social and cultural pursuits and had little or no say in important family decisions. Direct students to the novels of John Galsworthy for a detailed portrait of middle-class life in the Victorian era.

Ⓓ Exploring the Historical Period

Women's Rights

When John Stuart Mill married in 1851, he signed a document giving up his legal rights to his wife's "person, property, and freedom of action." His legal right to his wife's property, however, was not repealed until about thirty years later. In 1882, the Married Women's Property Act finally allowed women to keep their money and property after they married.

Taking a Second Look

Review: Identifying the Main Idea
Remind students that identifying the main idea usually involves rereading a paragraph or passage to determine the stated or unstated main point. On the other hand, the details in a passage usually explain, support, or lead up to this main idea.

Activities

1. Work with students to identify the main idea of the first paragraph under "A Closer Look."
2. Have students work in pairs to determine the main idea of the three remaining sections.
3. Have students look at the main ideas of the four subsections to distill the main idea of the entire piece.
4. As a check, ask students how well the title of the essay expresses its main idea.
5. Discuss why finding the main idea is a valuable strategy for reading nonfiction.

Ⓐ Literary Connections

Refer students to William Blake's poems from *Songs of Innocence* and *Songs of Experience* on pp. 652 and 653 on the subject of child labor.

A Closer Look

This feature focuses on the controversial art of the Pre-Raphaelite Brotherhood and how it was received during Victorian times.

Ⓑ Humanities Connections

Change from Romantic to Realistic Art

Remind students that the artists of the Romantic era (which preceded Millais) were interested in presenting idealized beauty and transcendent moments of union between humans and the natural world. In the shift to Realism, the "dreams" of Romanticism were abandoned and life was portrayed more as it is. The movement toward Realism was aided also by the development of photography.

Ⓒ Humanities Connections

The Pre-Raphaelites

Into this growing emphasis on Realism and obsession with material progress waltzed the Pre-Raphaelites. In some ways, they revived Romanticism with their interest in beautiful form and their understanding of art as visual expression rather than as a means of reforming society or offering moral or spiritual inspiration.

Responding to the Art

English painter **John Everett Millais** (1829–1896) was the youngest student ever to attend the Royal Academy of Arts in London. He and his friends and fellow painters Dante Gabriel Rossetti and William Holman Hunt had passionate convictions on what art should be and together they formed the Pre-Raphaelite Brotherhood.

Activity. Have students describe paintings of Christ by some of the old Renaissance masters whom the Pre-Raphaelites rejected, showing reproductions if possible. Ask them to point out the differences between these paintings and Millais' work.

Reform Act in 1867, which gave the right to vote to most working-class men except for agricultural workers. Decades of agitation by Victorian women for suffrage succeeded only in the next century. Strengthened by their domestic contributions during the Great War, women age thirty and over won the vote in 1918. Universal adult suffrage in 1928 extended the vote to women at age twenty-one.

Ⓐ A series of Factory Acts limited child labor and reduced the usual working day to ten hours, with a half-holiday on Saturday. State-supported schools were established in 1870, made compulsory in 1880, and made

A CLOSER LOOK

The Pre-Raphaelite Brotherhood: Challenging Artistic Authority

Ⓑ *The Times* called it "plainly revolting." The *Literary Gazette* found it "a nameless atrocity." Charles Dickens thought its central character "a hideous, wry-necked, blubbering, red-haired boy in a nightgown." The painting that elicited such scathing abuse was *Christ in the House of His Parents* (1850) by John Everett Millais (1829–1896). Millais shocked the art world with his innovative techniques and the treatment of his subject—he portrayed the Holy Family as ordinary people in a shavings-strewn carpentry shop.

Ⓒ Millais belonged to the Pre-Raphaelite Brotherhood (PRB), a group that embraced the ordinary while rejecting "conventionalities and feeble reminiscences from the Old Masters." Dissatisfied with Victorian complacency, a group of seven young men modeled their work after medieval painters—those *before* the Renaissance painter Raphael—that they believed had a more natural vision. Founded in 1848, the PRB never shared a unifying style or principle. But they were united in their sense, as the artist Sir Edward Burne-Jones (1833–1898) said, that "the time is out of joint."

Christ in the House of His Parents (1850) by Sir John Everett Millais.

Tate Gallery, London.

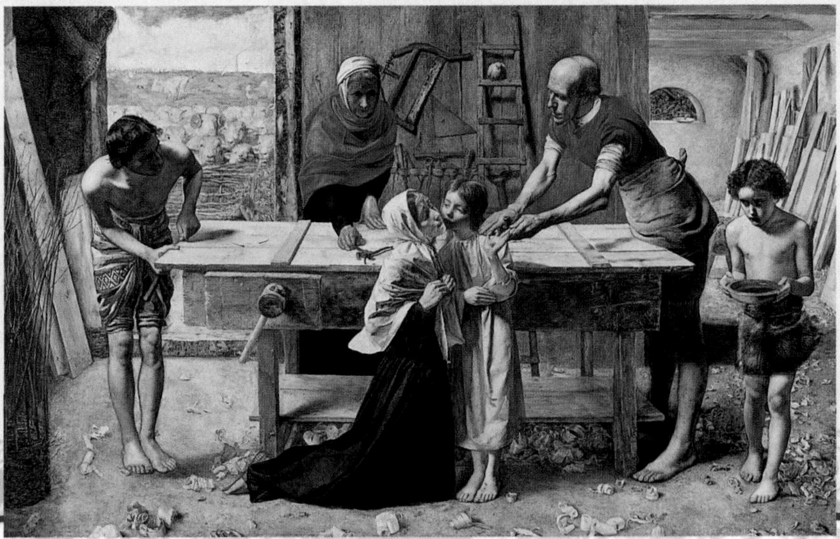

free in 1891. In the 1840s, 40 percent of the couples getting married could not write their names on their marriage certificates. By 1900, using that simple definition of literacy, more than 90 percent of the population was literate.

As the nineteenth century progressed, living conditions gradually improved. Food and other commodities became more readily available, most adult males won the right to vote, laws regulated the use of child labor, and compulsory education brought about widespread literacy.

Artistic "treason." The PRB is widely known for Dante Gabriel Rossetti's sensuous portraits. A favorite model was Jane Morris, and her long neck and abundant, wavy hair in works such as *Proserpine* (1874) are a PRB trademark. D

To members of the Royal Academy of Art, however, PRB members were artistic outlaws. Their shading techniques violated the academy's guidelines that one "principal light" should focus a painting's main elements. Their minute rendering of details seemed busy and bewildering, "a strange disorder of the mind or the eyes." PRB member William Holman Hunt (1827–1910) prided himself on botanical and geologic accuracy, laboring over his paintings' individual rocks and flowers. "Our talk is the deepest treason against our betters," Hunt said.

Proserpine (1874) by Dante Gabriel Rossetti.

Tate Gallery, London.

Art and cultural values. The PRB disbanded in 1853, but it attracted followers, drawn by the PRB's medieval models, who had turned away from industrial Britain's materialism. The art critic John Ruskin (1819–1900) asserted that art and artists suffered from mechanization: He argued that the way art was produced could shape a culture's values.

The artist William Morris (1834–1896) applied these theories in a decorating firm that revived traditional methods of producing furniture, tapestries, and stained glass. His Kelmscott Press crafted fine books with the painstaking detail of hand-printed engravings and hand-sewn bindings. Morris, Ruskin, and former PRB members taught artisans these skills and principles at the Working Men's College, an educational experiment begun in London in 1854.

Modern viewers delight in the PRB's exuberant excess of elaborate designs and glorious medieval trappings. Yet the Pre-Raphaelites' work also made a social statement. The tensions of the Industrial Revolution bonded the Brotherhood, and their rebellious movement raised difficult questions about the place of art and artists in a rapidly changing society. E

D Humanities Connection

Pre-Raphaelite Subjects

About the sensuousness of the Pre-Raphaelite portraits, Richard Altick writes: "The Pre-Raphaelites were famed, in some quarters notorious, for their mixture of mysticism and 'fleshliness', especially in connection with female subjects. The typical Pre-Raphaelite woman was . . . long-necked, reddish-haired, slender, and tending toward consumption—but to the Victorians, if not to us, there was something unsettlingly fascinating about her. They were better accustomed to the rosy-cheeked country maidens who figured in the genre paintings. . . ."

E Critical Thinking

Making Connections

? What do you think is the place of art and artists in today's rapidly changing technological society? [Possible response: The artist today must be a thoughtful and original voice in an anonymous world of instant information.]

Skill Link

Producing a Research Report

The last half of the nineteenth century saw a burst of cultural activity that would change ways of looking at art and literature forever. Interested students might pursue one of these topics for a written research report:

- the writings of Walter Pater and John Ruskin
- the rise of the salon in Paris
- the advent of Impressionism
- the phenomenon of photography
- the theater of Henrik Ibsen
- cultural events in your own state

Urge students to draw conclusions based on their research and to share these with the class, quoting passages and showing reproductions of artwork to illustrate their conclusions. Students may also wish to present their reports in other classes as a form of cross-curricular learning.

Ⓐ Humanities Connections

Thomas Bowdler

Perhaps the most famous literary censor of all times was Thomas Bowdler, who is best known for changing hundreds of words and even cutting entire scenes from Shakespeare's plays. Although Bowdler's *Family Shakespeare* was published in 1818 and therefore predates the Victorians, it was embraced by Victorian readers. The English language immortalizes Bowdler's well-meaning but clumsy efforts with the verb to *bowdlerize*. The word means "to cut or modify a work," and it carries connotations of prudery and violations of textual integrity.

Ⓑ Literary Connections

Victorian Censorship

Among the greatest victims of Victorian censorship was novelist Thomas Hardy. Magazine editors (who published novels in serial form) constantly rejected scenes from his novels or suggested ridiculous ways to alter them or to avoid any mention of sex altogether. Hardy stubbornly resisted these efforts to change his work.

Ⓒ Literary Connections

Stern Father Figures

Ask students to recall examples of autocratic father figures in the Victorian literature they have read. They may be familiar with the figure of Mr. Murdstone in Charles Dickens's *David Copperfield*, for example.

The Drawing Room (late 19th or early 20th century) by Paul Gustav Fischer.

Decorum and Authority

Many Victorians thought of themselves as progressing morally and intellectually, as well as materially. In fact, the powerful, mostly middle-class Ⓐ obsession with gentility or decorum has made *prudery* almost a synonym for *Victorianism*. Book publishers and magazine editors deleted or Ⓑ altered words and episodes that might, in the phrase of the day, bring a blush to the cheek of a young person. In art and popular fiction, sex, birth, and death were softened by sentimental conventions into tender courtships, joyous motherhoods, and deathbed scenes in which old people became saints and babies became angels. In the real world, people were arrested for distributing information about sexually transmitted diseases. Victorian society regarded seduced or adulterous women (but not their male partners) as "fallen" and pushed them to the margins of respectability.

Victorian decorum also supported powerful ideas about authority. Many Victorians were uneasy about giving strong authority to a central government (although it is revealing of the fundamental decorum of British society that its version of the 1848 European revolutions was a meeting to petition Parliament). In Victorian private lives, however, the autocratic father of middle-Ⓒ class households is a vivid figure in both fact (Elizabeth Barrett Browning's father, for example) and fiction.

> I still cling fondly to the hope that some system of female instruction will be discovered, by which the young women of England may be sent from school to the homes of their parents, habituated to be on the watch for every opportunity of doing good to others; making it the first and the last inquiry of every day, "What can I do to make my parents, my brothers, or my sisters, more happy? . . . I hope to pursue the plan to which I have been accustomed, of seeking my own happiness only in the happiness of others."
>
> —Sarah Stickney Ellis, essayist who argued that women's education should cultivate "the heart," not the mind

Skill Link

Generating Relevant, Interesting, and Researchable Questions

As students read the historical introduction and work on various projects related to the Victorian period, it may help to remind them of the following methods of generating questions for research:

- Interesting research questions should appeal to you and your readers.
- A good research question should help you discover new information on a familiar subject.
- To make your questions relevant, they should be limited to a manageable topic.
- To generate researchable questions, make sure there are a variety of sources related to your topic and that the sources of information are readily available.

Activity

Based on the listed criteria, ask students to pose at least three relevant, interesting, and researchable questions on the following topics:

1. the life of Charles Dickens
2. economic growth in Victorian Britain
3. the Pre-Raphaelite Brotherhood
4. the Great Famine in Ireland
5. child labor

Women in particular were subject to male authority. Middle-class women especially were expected to marry and make their homes a comfortable refuge for their husbands from the male domains of business, politics, and the professions. Women who did not marry had few occupations open to them. Working-class women could find jobs as servants in affluent households, while unmarried middle-class ladies could become governesses or teachers. Many middle-class women remained unmarried because men often postponed marriage until they achieved financial security. The problem of these unmarried, "redundant women," as they were called, was painful, although in literature, especially literature written by men, the figure of the middle-aged maiden was often played for comedy.

The excesses, cruelties, and hypocrisies of all these repressions were obvious to many Victorians. But the codes and barriers of decorum changed slowly because they were part of the ideology of progress. Prudery and social order were intended to control the licentiousness that Victorians associated with the political revolutions of the eighteenth century and the social corruption of the regency of George IV (1811–1820).

> When the views advanced by me in this volume . . . are generally admitted, we can dimly foresee that there will be a considerable revolution in natural history.
> —Charles Darwin, *from On the Origin of Species*

The Victorian emphasis on decorum grew from the conviction that life would be improved if it steadily became more refined, more rationally organized, better policed, and therefore safer.

VI

Intellectual Progress: The March of Mind

The intellectual advances of the Victorian period were dramatically evident to those living in it. Humans began to understand the earth, its creatures, and its natural laws. Geologists worked out the history written in rocks and fossils. Based on countless

Applicants for Admission to a Casual Ward (1874) by Luke Fildes. Oil on canvas.

Royal Holloway and Bedford New College, University of London.

D Cultural Connections

Male Authority

Historian Daniel Pool sheds light on the subject of patriarchy in Victorian culture in this way: "When the husband and wife exchanged vows, they became one person, and, in the words of jurist William Blackstone, 'the husband is that person.'"

E Historical Connections

Charles Darwin

No other work rocked the nineteenth century as profoundly as Darwin's *On the Origin of Species*. It shook religious faith by suggesting that human beings may not result from a special act of God's creation but, instead, may have evolved from nonhuman ancestors. Darwin himself was disturbed by the implications of his ideas and delayed publication of his work for many years. Yet he was moved to write of his theory: "There is grandeur in this view of life."

RESPONDING TO THE ART

Through a recommendation by fellow English artist John Millais, **Sir Luke Fildes** (1844–1927) was commissioned to illustrate Charles Dickens's unfinished last novel, *The Mystery of Edwin Drood*. Dickens's themes remained with Fildes when he painted this picture of impoverished people awaiting aid. The painting's realism and honesty won Fildes immediate fame.

Activity. Ask students how they think the Victorian upper classes may have responded to this painting. Invite them to describe any similar contemporary scenes they may have witnessed. What role do they think art can or should play in helping to correct social injustice?

Getting Students Involved

Cooperative Learning

Signs of the Times. Have students work in groups of three or four to create a time capsule for the Victorian era, a vessel whose contents give a well-rounded impression of the period. Encourage students to make or find objects, such as patent medicine bottles, and to collect copies and drawings of documents and pictures which sum up the times in a concise way. Paging through an illustrated history of the era may be a good starting point.

Suggest that one student in each group be responsible for directing and monitoring research, another for the physical work of creating and assembling the capsule, and a third for presenting the project to the class.

A Historical Connections

History of Science

Defining the Age of Progress as roughly the second half of the nineteenth century to the early years of the twentieth, S. C. Burchell writes that the era "saw the formation of four of the major concepts on which modern science is based: the idea of evolution; the idea of conservation of energy; the idea of space as a continuum that is pervaded by fields of physical activity (such as electromagnetic fields); and the idea that all action is dependent on the existence of certain basic units—the atom in chemistry, the cell in biology, the quantum in physics and so on."

B Critical Thinking

Interpreting

? Who are the players in Huxley's chess game? [Possible response: The players are the individual human being and the laws of the physical universe administered by an omnipotent but fair God.] How do you respond to his view of life? [Possible response: It is cold and terrifying, leaving no room for mercy on the part of God or vulnerability on the part of humans.]

RESPONDING TO THE ART

For information about the artist, see p. T781.

Activity. Tell students that Dickens had a strong dislike for the painting of Millais. Have them discuss how they think Dickens might have reacted to Frith's work, especially to this portrait of himself.

observations, Charles Darwin and other biologists theorized about the evolution of species. The industrialization of England depended on and supported science and technology, especially chemistry (in the iron and textile industries) and engineering.

Those who made and used scientific and technological knowledge had a confidence of their own. Thomas Huxley, a variously accomplished scientist who wrote and lectured frequently on the necessity of scientific education, imagined science as an exhilarating, high-stakes chess game with the physical universe.

> The chessboard is the world, the pieces are the phenomena of the universe, the rules of the game are what we call the laws of Nature. The player on the other side is hidden from us. We know that his play is always fair, just, and patient. But also we know, to our cost, that he never overlooks a mistake, or makes the smallest allowance for ignorance. To the man who plays well, the highest stakes are paid, with that sort of overflowing generosity with which the strong shows delight in strength. And one who plays ill is checkmated—without haste, but without remorse.
>
> —Thomas Huxley, *from A Liberal Education*

Huxley resembles those confident Victorians who built railways and sewers, organized markets and schools, and pushed through electoral reforms and laws regulating the conditions of work. These reformers believed that the world offered a challenging set of problems that could be understood by human intelligence and solved by science, government, and other human institutions. Huxley made the game exciting by warning that humans could lose. But so long as the game is played in the material world, Huxley and others like him saw no reason that they would not win.

Charles Dickens (1859) by William Powell Frith.

Victoria and Albert Museum, London.

Advances in science and technology convinced nineteenth-century intellectuals and reformers that human efforts could overcome all material problems.

Questions and Doubts

The Victorian period, and especially its literature, was filled with voices asking questions and raising doubts. Speaking for many of their contemporaries, and speaking to others they thought shallow and complacent, Victorian writers asked whether material comfort fully satisfied human needs and wishes. They questioned the cost of exploiting the

> There is no law of history any more than of a kaleidoscope.
> —John Ruskin

earth and human beings to achieve such comfort. They protested or mocked codes of decorum and authority.

In the first half of the period, some writers complained that materialist ideas of reality completely overlooked the spirit or soul that made life beautiful and just. Later in the century, writers like Thomas Hardy and A. E. Housman thought that Macaulay's and Huxley's ideas of history and nature presupposed a coherence and generosity that did not really exist. Literature in Victorian culture often reassured its readers that, rightly perceived, the universe made sense. But some writers unsettled their readers by telling them that they were not rightly perceiving the universe, or by asking them to consider whether human life and the natural world made as much sense as they had once hoped.

Charles Dickens, the most popular and most important figure in Victorian literature, is a case in point. The son of a debt-ridden clerk, Dickens lived out one of the favorite myths of the age: Through his own enormous talents and energy, he rose from poverty to become a wealthy and famous man. His was a peculiarly Victorian success, made possible by the increasing affluence and literacy, which gave him a large reading public, and by improved printing and distribution, which made book publishing a big business.

The conventional happy endings of Dickens's novels satisfied his readers', and probably his own, conviction that things usually work out well for decent people. But from the beginning of his career in the 1830s to the publication of his last complete novel in 1865, many of Dickens's most memorable scenes showed decent people

Who Were the Victorians?

Here are some of the social and material changes that marked the long reign of Queen Victoria.

- Industrialism made England the workshop of the world, with a mechanized factory system and extensive railways.
- Much of the British population moved from rural areas to rapidly growing cities.
- Expanded educational opportunities increased literacy; flourishing lending libraries and cheap periodicals created a mass reading public. (C)
- Continued advances in science and technology gave Victorians hope that all social problems—disease, poverty, even immorality—could be resolved by the march of "progress." (D)
- The human cost of industrialization was heavy: abuses of child labor, unsafe conditions in factories, and widespread disease from contaminated air and water.
- By the end of the century, the disruption and materialism of the era made people question changes brought on by rapid industrialization and reevaluate their definitions of progress.

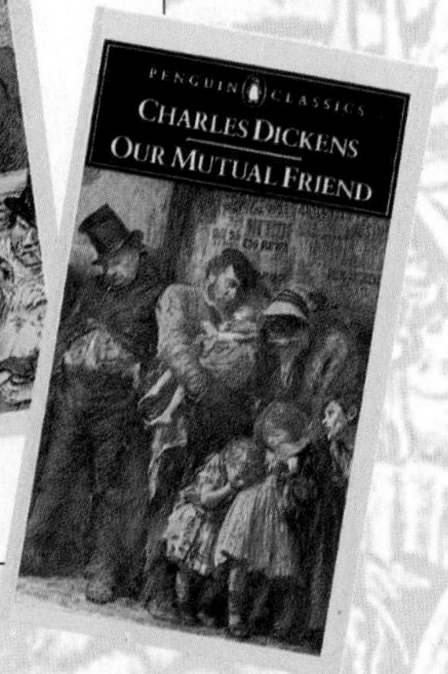

(C) Critical Thinking

Extending

Ask students to consider how many of these issues still have relevance today. Invite them to give modern examples of such Victorian concerns as rampant materialism and migrant populations. They may also want to discuss some modern responses to these issues.

(D) Reading Skills and Strategies

Using Graphic Aids

Remind students that boxed lists like this one summarize some of the most important ideas in the essay and provide a good review of what they have read. Urge students to use the heading and introductory sentence to focus their reading and to digest the content of each bulleted item fully before moving on to the next one. Encourage students to make summary lists like this one whenever they are reading informative material in textbooks and other nonfiction sources.

Professional Notes

Critical Comment: Dickens and Victorian Society

R. C. Churchill comments that the common feature of Dickens's novels of the late 1840s and 1850s is "a criticism of Victorian society, which, like that of the workhouse chapters of *Oliver Twist,* goes deep enough to be a universal criticism of human nature."

A Literary Connections

Oliver Twist as Social Commentary

The first few chapters of *Oliver Twist,* in which Oliver is in a workhouse, are arguably among the best chapters Dickens ever wrote. There Dickens attacks not just the material deprivation of the workhouse, but the additional (and heartwrenching) stipulation by the authorities that workhouse inmates be housed apart, resulting in the cruel separation of husbands and wives, parents and children.

B Appreciating Language

Denotation and Connotation

? What is the meaning of the word *veneer* on which Dickens based his characters' name? What are its connotations? [Possible response: A *veneer* is a surface overlay on wood; it does not go very deep. The Veneerings are "surface" people, interested only in appearances.] Students might be interested in other clever character names in Dickens. For example, Mr. Gradgrind, the schoolmaster, in *Hard Times* has all the roughness of spirit and grinding quality that his name suggests. Other notably named characters include Mrs. Sparsit, Mr. Skimpole, Mr. Bumble, Mr. Sowerberry, and, in this passage, Mrs. Podsnap. Invite students to speculate on the personalities and appearances of these characters.

C Elements of Literature

Repetition

Dickens often uses repetition for dramatic effects. Here the repetition of "Reflects" emphasizes that the Veneerings do not have any light of their own; rather, they "shine" with the false light of material wealth.

RESPONDING TO THE ART

For information on the artist, see p. T781.

Activity. Note how Frith's paintings present an almost *photographic* slice of Victorian life. Ask what students can infer from the painting about Victorian upper-class manners and customs. Students should be able to infer the occasion based on the painting's title, but can they figure out who is being honored?

A neglected, abused, and exploited. The hungry Oliver Twist asks for more gruel in the workhouse; the crippled Tiny Tim in *A Christmas Carol* cheerfully hobbles toward his possible early death; and David Copperfield is beaten and exiled by the cold, dark Mr. Murdstone.

In his later novels, Dickens also created characters and scenes to show that even the winners in the competition for material gain had reason to B be as desperate and unhappy as the losers. In *Our Mutual Friend,* his last novel, he describes a dinner party at the home of a family called the Veneerings, a name that emphasizes the family's superficial qualities. They are "bran-new people in a bran-new house in a bran-new quarter of London":

> C The great looking-glass above the sideboard reflects the table and the company. Reflects the new Veneering crest, in gold and eke in silver, frosted and also thawed, a camel of all work. The Herald's College found out a Crusading ancestor for Veneering who bore a camel on his shield (or might have done it if he had thought of it), and a caravan of camels take charge of the fruits and flowers and candles, and kneel down to be loaded with the salt. Reflects Veneering; forty, wavy-haired, dark, tending to corpulence, sly, mysterious, filmy. . . . Reflects Mrs. Veneering; fair, aquiline-nosed and fingered, not so much light hair as she might have, gorgeous in raiment and jewels. . . . Reflects Podsnap; prosperously feeding, two little light-colored wiry wings, one on either side of his else bald head, looking as like his hairbrushes as his hair. . . . Reflects Mrs. Podsnap; . . . quantity of bone, neck, and nostrils like a rocking horse, hard

Many Happy Returns of the Day (19th century) by William Powell Frith.

Harrogate Museums and Art Gallery, North Yorkshire, England.

features, majestic headdress in which Podsnap has hung golden offerings. . . . Reflects . . . mature young gentleman; with too much nose in his face, too much ginger in his whiskers, too much sparkle in his studs, his eyes, his buttons, his talk, and his teeth.

—Charles Dickens, *from Our Mutual Friend*

Attacks like Dickens's on the hollowness, glitter, superficiality, and excesses of Victorian affluence were common in Victorian literature, for example, in Robert Browning's portrayal of the murderously possessive duke in "My Last Duchess." Dickens also raised questions about the costs of progress in his descriptions of the huddle and waste of cities and the smoke and fire of industrial landscapes. In 1871, the art historian and social critic John Ruskin noted a new phenomenon that we call smog; he called it the plague wind, or "the storm-cloud of the nineteenth century," and concluded, chillingly, ". . . [M]ere smoke would not blow to and fro in that wild way. It looks more to me as if it were made of dead men's souls."

Lady Bracknell. . . . I do not approve of anything that tampers with natural ignorance. Ignorance is like a delicate exotic fruit; touch it and the bloom is gone. The whole theory of modern education is radically unsound. Fortunately in England, at any rate, education produces no effect whatsoever. If it did, it would prove a serious danger to the upper classes, and probably lead to acts of violence in Grosvenor Square.

—Oscar Wilde, *from The Importance of Being Earnest*

The materialism, secularism, vulgarity, and sheer waste that accompanied Victorian progress led some writers to wonder if their culture was really advancing by any measure.

From Trust to Skepticism and Denial

Trust in a transcendental power was characteristic of the early Victorian writers. They were the immediate heirs of the Romantic idea of a finite natural world surrounded by and interfused with an infinite, ideal transcendental reality. The highest purpose of a poet, of any writer, was to make readers aware of the connection between earth and heaven, body and soul, material and ideal. Fundamentally, as Thomas Carlyle wrote in his essay "The Hero as Poet," reality is spiritual, a divine idea. "All Appearances, from the starry sky to the grass of the field, but especially the Appearance of Man and his work, is but *vesture,* the embodiment that renders it [the divine idea] possible." The poet penetrates to the divine idea and makes it palpable in language and story to those of lesser power and vision. "That is always his message; he is to reveal that to us—that sacred mystery which he more than others lives ever present with."

If we had a keen vision of all that is ordinary in human life, it would be like hearing the grass grow or the squirrel's heart beat, and we should die of that roar which is the other side of silence.

—George Eliot, *from Middlemarch*

With some exceptions—Gerard Manley Hopkins is one and Christina Rossetti another—writers younger than Alfred Tennyson and Ruskin found it increasingly difficult to believe in an infinite power and order that

D Humanities Connections

Ruskin and Carlyle

Point out that John Ruskin (1819–1900) wrote on social, political, and artistic subjects. His proposals for social improvement were less grand and aggressive than those of another Victorian critic of society, Thomas Carlyle (1795–1881). Carlyle admired strong national leaders such as Oliver Cromwell and Frederick the Great, but Ruskin urged individual responsibility and collective action to combat injustice, such as boycotting the products of industrial and economic systems that demean human labor.

E Literary Connections

Oscar Wilde

Known for his sparkling wit and flamboyant personality, the Irish-born Oscar Wilde wrote plays, fiction, and literary criticism but is best known for four comedies: *Lady Windermere's Fan* (1892), *A Woman of No Importance* (1893), *An Ideal Husband* (1895), and *The Importance of Being Earnest.* This passage is typical of Wilde's hilarious and rather cutting wit, aimed squarely at the British upper classes.

Skill Link

Analyzing and Evaluating Literary Performances

The Importance of Being Earnest and adaptations of novels by George Eliot and Thomas Hardy are available on videotape. Assign students in small groups to view one of these and to critique the performance. Students might formulate their own criteria or respond to the following:

1. How faithful is the performance to the original work? Is its fidelity or lack of fidelity an asset or a problem? What has been lost or gained?
2. How convincing are the performances of the individual actors? How could they be improved?
3. Has the setting remained Victorian? How authentically has the time period been re-created?
4. What are the high points of this performance, and why? What would you change if you were the director?

Ⓐ Struggling Readers

Modifying Reading Strategies

Point out to students that poetry is a far more compressed form of expression than prose and generally requires the reader to slow down and pay more attention to the connotations of words. Be sure students notice that *alone* is italicized, and ask them to explore the connotations of *straits, shoreless*, and *watery*. Then have students share their responses to these words.

Ⓑ Literary Connections

George Eliot

The real name of George Eliot (1819–1880) was Mary Ann Evans. Her use of a pseudonym was one of a series of self-defining acts. After her father's death, she left her family's strongly religious household and went to London, where she edited an important magazine of liberal intellectual opinion. Eliot became one of the most accomplished of the Victorian novelists. Her fiction is based on her intimate knowledge of the world of provincial families in small towns. Her novels include *Adam Bede* (1859), *The Mill on the Floss* (1860), *Silas Marner* (1861), and *Middlemarch* (1871–1872). Cass in *Silas Marner* is a squire who seduces and abandons a young woman. The child born of this union is found and reared by a miser, Silas Marner, who is redeemed by his love for his young ward.

A Closer Look

This feature examines some of the comic relief and realistic drama that appeared in the Victorian literary scene.

Ⓒ Cultural Connections

Drury Lane Theater

First built in 1663 and rebuilt several times, the Drury Lane Theater remains standing today, making it the oldest theater in England still in use.

made sense of material and human existence. Some simply thought it unnecessary. Algernon Charles Swinburne and Rudyard Kipling, in their different ways, celebrated a relation between humans and the natural world that could be joyous and even redemptive.

Ⓐ
Yes! in the sea of life enisled,
With echoing straits between us thrown,
Dotting the shoreless watery wild,
We mortal millions live *alone*.

—Matthew Arnold, *from* "To Marguerite—Continued"

Other writers at midcentury, sometimes reacting to explanations of the world that excluded the spiritual, were saddened by what seemed to them to be the withdrawal of the divine from the world. The dominant note of much mid-Victorian writing was struck by Matthew Arnold in his poem "Dover Beach": "The Sea of Faith," Arnold wrote, had ebbed. There was no certainty; or if there was, what was certain was that existence was not governed by a benevolent intelligence that cared for its creatures.

By the end of the century, this skepticism and denial had become pervasive in the works of Hardy, Housman, and others. Early- and mid-Victorian novelists such as Dickens and George Eliot had dramatized a Ⓑ human ideal achieved through sympathy and unselfishness. They made sad or frightening examples of people like the Murdstones in *David Copperfield* and Godfrey Cass in *Silas Marner*—all hard surface and no

A CLOSER LOOK

Victorian Drama: From Relief to Realism

Ⓒ *Interior of Drury Lane Theater, 1808* (19th century) by Thomas Rowlandson and A. Pugin.

Guildhall Library, Corporation of London.

Though Queen Victoria, who came to the throne in 1837, loved the theater, it was she who once remarked, "We are not amused." And certainly the theater of the early part of her reign provided little to amuse anyone. Comedy must have license to explore, to expose, to look under the bed, and to ridicule, but Victoria's England was marked by prudery, good taste, repression of natural feelings, high-mindedness, and official censorship.

Irreverent ridicule. The operettas that William S. Gilbert wrote to Arthur Sullivan's music, beginning with *Trial by Jury* (1875), provided some delightful comic relief. Though today we think of these operettas (such as *The Pirates of Penzance* and *H.M.S. Pinafore*) merely as charming, tuneful, witty entertainments, in their period they irreverently ridiculed the law, the navy, the world of aesthetes, and the aristocracy.

soul. Their heroes and heroines learned to find happiness in nurturing marriages and in small communities of family and friends. But there were few such marriages and communities in the fiction and poetry of Hardy and Housman. These late-Victorian writers told stories of lovers and friends bereft and betrayed by unfaithfulness, war, and the other troubles that humans add to the natural troubles of mortal life.

Over the century, the trust in a transcendental power inherited from the Romantics eroded, giving way to uncertainty and spiritual doubt. Late-Victorian writers turned to a pessimistic exploration of the human struggle against indifferent natural forces.

Revealing Reality, Creating Coherence

Victorian writers had purposes as various as the ideas of reality they believed in. Some writers wanted to scare or shame readers into effective moral and political actions that they optimistically believed were possible. Some wanted to show readers what it is like to live in a pleasurable moment of intense feeling like that caught in a lyric or in the interesting perspectives of a character in a dramatic monologue or novel. Victorian literature entertained, informed, warned, and reassured.

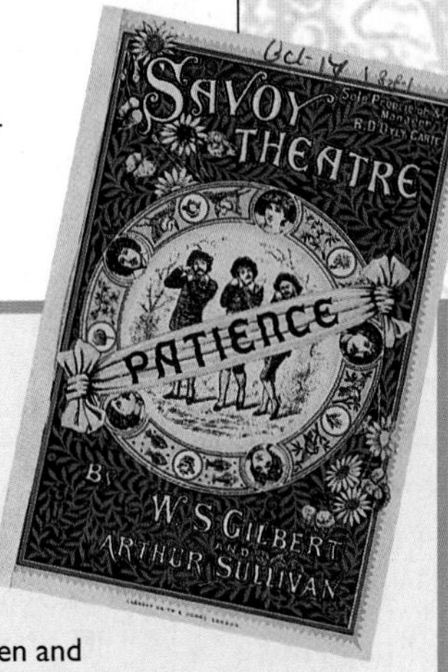

Program cover for October 17, 1881, Savoy Theatre production of *Patience* by Sir W. S. Gilbert and Sir Arthur Sullivan.

Victoria and Albert Museum, London.

Intrinsic to Gilbert and Sullivan operettas was a world-turned-on-its-head view of life that would influence both Oscar Wilde and Bernard Shaw. In Gilbert and Sullivan, "Things are seldom what they seem. / Skim milk masquerades as cream."

Moving toward realism. Coming into the era of Oscar Wilde and Bernard Shaw, drama was moving toward realism, which has been the dominant dramatic mode for the last hundred years. In England and in Europe, fiction writers were dealing with the social realities of the time—Charles Dickens among others in England, Émile Zola in France. From Scandinavia came the revolutionary voices of Henrik Ibsen in plays such as *An Enemy of the People* (1882) and of August Strindberg in *Miss Julie* (1888).

While some playwrights were assimilating new points of view and style, the theaters were also undergoing changes to accommodate the new plays. For years, London had been dominated by two huge theaters, Covent Garden and Drury Lane, each seating well over three thousand people—large theaters not congenial to intimate realistic drama.

In the early part of the nineteenth century, new, smaller theaters were built. The forestage, or apron, was removed, and gaslight (and soon electricity) took the place of candles once used to illuminate the stage. These changes cleared the way for the staging of smaller-scale realistic dramas, which an audience might view as though through an invisible "fourth wall," allowing the audience to eavesdrop on the action. In smaller theaters, on such a stage with new lighting, playwrights could now achieve an illusion of reality.

D Literary Connections

George Bernard Shaw

The Irish-born playwright George Bernard Shaw is considered by many to be the greatest British dramatist after Shakespeare. Like Wilde, he wrote late in the Victorian period and was critical of many of the so-called Victorian virtues. Like Wilde also, he shocked his Victorian audience. For example, an early play *Mrs. Warren's Profession* (1893) takes on the scandalous topic of prostitution. Shaw continued writing plays well beyond the Victorian period, publishing his well-known *Pygmalion* (upon which the play and movie *My Fair Lady* are based) in 1913 and *Saint Joan* in 1923.

E Critical Thinking

Making Connections

Encourage students to compare this information about Victorian stagecraft with what they read in the essay on "The Renaissance Theater" (pp. 282–288). Then ask them how today's directors have adapted, used, or discarded the theatrical conventions of the past.

Assessing Learning

Check Test: Multiple Choice

1. The Victorian era was a time of ____. [c]
  a. increased hardships for all classes
  b. civil wars at home
  c. peace and economic growth

2. Middle-class Victorian women were encouraged ____. [a]
  a. to marry and obey their husbands
  b. to become politically active
  c. to remain unmarried and educate the young

3. The paradox of progress means that ____. [b]
  a. success is the reward of hard work
  b. progress has drawbacks as well as benefits
  c. hardship is incompatible with progress

4. Religious faith was shaken by the theories of ____. [c]
  a. George Bernard Shaw
  b. George Eliot
  c. Charles Darwin

Quickwrite

Some students may argue that progress should not be measured only in improvements in material comforts and security but also in the growth of individual and social awareness and in concern for the community and the environment.

Even the playfulness of Lewis Carroll and Oscar Wilde shows the two most important and consistent purposes or effects of Victorian literature. The first was to make readers hope, or wonder if, reality was really like that—really as whole and satisfying as in Tennyson's *In Memoriam,* as briskly coherent as in a poem by Browning or an essay by Macaulay. The second principal purpose or effect was to demonstrate that, however bleak and chaotic reality seemed to be, the writer and reader could make a pleasing order in it. Even when a story or poem said that the world was ugly or made no sense, the story or the poem could seem beautiful and make sense to its audience. In every successful act of writing and reading literature, one more satisfyingly coherent thing in the world is created or discovered.

Finally, it is important to remember that these purposes and effects happened first to readers who were living Victorian lives. Victorian literature did not exist above or outside the comfortable and often confident lives of its readers. Many of the people who read Dickens settled down with his books after dining in rooms as garishly decorated as the Veneerings'. Most of the young men and women who thrilled to Dante Gabriel Rossetti's sensualism and to Housman's tender gloom probably moved on to make proper and modestly happy marriages and to find worthy occupations. People who were making a lot of money listened to Carlyle and Ruskin telling them that they were foolish and damned. People who were disturbed by how much money was being made listened to Macaulay reminding them that a century or so before they might not have been able to afford, or even to read, his book.

> **Lord Darlington.** . . . we are all in the gutter, but some of us are looking at the stars.
>
> —Oscar Wilde, *from Lady Windermere's Fan*

Victorian literature needs to be read not just as a comment on the complexity of its culture, but also as an important part of that culture. Its writers sent their words to work in the world to alter, to reinforce, to challenge, to enlarge, or to temper the ideas and feelings with which their contemporaries managed their lives.

Victorian writing reflects the dangers and benefits of rapid industrialization, while encouraging readers to examine closely their own understanding of the era's progress.

Quickwrite What do you think of the Victorian idea of progress? Do you agree that tangible improvements in material comfort and security constitute human progress? Or do you think there's more to it than that? Why? Jot down your thoughts about what progress means to you. If you'd like to, ask a classmate to respond to your written ideas.

(Opposite) *The Daydream* (19th century) by Dante Gabriel Rossetti.

Victoria and Albert Museum, London.

Getting Students Involved

Cooperative Learning

Then and Now. Have students work in groups to devise a list of contemporary American values. Then ask students to create a chart like the one that follows, comparing today's values to those of Victorian England. They may want to consider family, social, and political values. After students complete their small-group work, reconvene as a class to discuss the groups' findings and to discuss the question: Who defines the values of a society?

Modern Values in the United States	Values of Victorian England
[individual freedom]	[social order]

Collection 10

Love and Loss

Theme

The Human Condition *The Victorian era was characterized by a spirit of inquiry and a reverence for stability and decorum. Reflecting their era, the Victorian poets both embraced and questioned tradition, looking to the past and the future for new ways of understanding love, grief, nature, and God.*

Reading the Anthology

Reaching Struggling Readers

The *Reading Skills and Strategies: Reaching Struggling Readers* binder provides materials coordinated with the Pupil's Edition (see the Collection Planner, p. T800B) to help students who have difficulty reading and comprehending text or students who are reluctant readers. The binder for twelfth grade is organized around ten individual skill areas and offers the following options:

- **MiniRead** MiniReads are short, easy texts that give students a chance to practice a particular skill and strategy before reading selections in the Pupil's Edition. Each MiniRead Skill Lesson can be taught independently or used in conjunction with a Selection Skill Lesson.
- **Selection Skill Lessons** Selection Skill Lessons allow students to apply skills introduced in the MiniReads. Each Selection Skill Lesson provides reading instruction and practice specific to a particular piece of literature in the Pupil's Edition.

Reading Beyond the Anthology

Read On At the end of the Victorian Period collections, the grade twelve book includes a Read On, an annotated bibliography of books suitable for extended reading. To preview the Read On for the Victorian Period, please turn to p. T895.

HRW Library The *HRW Library* offers novels, plays, and short-story collections for extended reading. Each book in the Library includes one or more major works and thematically or topically related Connections. Each book in the *HRW Library* is also accompanied by a Study Guide that provides teaching suggestions and worksheets. The two titles shown here will work well to extend the theme of Collection 10.

A TALE OF TWO CITIES
Charles Dickens
Against the backdrop of the French Revolution, Dickens tells a tale of the redemptive powers of love. Sydney Carton is forced to choose between his own interests and those of the woman he loves.

JANE EYRE
Charlotte Brontë
A young governess, Jane Eyre, is the unconventional heroine of this romantic tale. Shy and plain, Jane manages to captivate her employer, Edward Rochester, a man with a terrible secret.

Collection 10 Love and Loss

Resources for this Collection

Note: All resources for this collection are available for preview on the *One-Stop Planner CD-ROM 2 with Test Generator.* All worksheets and blackline masters may be printed from the CD-ROM.

Internet Resources
go.hrw.com LE0 12-10

Selection or Feature	Reading and Literary Skills	Vocabulary, Language, and Grammar
• **Tears, Idle Tears** (p. 803) • **The Eagle: A Fragment** (p. 805) • **Flower in the Crannied Wall** (p. 806) • **The Lady of Shalott** (p. 807) **Critical Comment: Escaping a World of Shadows** (p. 813) • *from* **In Memoriam A.H.H.** (p. 814) • **Ulysses** (p. 821) • **Crossing the Bar** (p. 824) Alfred, Lord Tennyson **Spotlight On: The Enduring Arthurian Legend,** *from* **Morte Darthur** (p. 826)	• *Graphic Organizers for Active Reading,* Worksheet pp. 72, 73, 74, 75, 76, 77 • *Literary Elements:* Transparency 21 Worksheet p. 64	• *Words to Own,* Worksheet p. 22 • *Grammar and Language Links:* Noun Clauses, Worksheet p. 43 • *Language Workshop CD-ROM,* Types of Subordinate Clauses • *Daily Oral Grammar,* Transparencies 27, 28

• **My Last Duchess** (p. 829)
Connections: Scenes from a Modern Marriage (p. 832)
Julia Markus
• **Porphyria's Lover** (p. 833)
Robert Browning
	• *Reading Skills and Strategies: Reaching Struggling Readers*
	  • MiniRead Skill Lesson, p. 44
	  • Selection Skill Lesson, p. 51
	• *Graphic Organizers for Active Reading,* Worksheet pp. 78, 79
		• *Words to Own,* Worksheet p. 22
		• *Grammar and Language Links:* Revision Worksheet, p. 45

Sonnet 43 (p. 837) Elizabeth Barrett Browning	• *Graphic Organizers for Active Reading,* Worksheet p. 80	
• **Spring and Fall: To a Young Child** (p. 841) • **Pied Beauty** (p. 843) Gerald Manley Hopkins	• *Graphic Organizers for Active Reading,* Worksheet pp. 81, 82	• *Words to Own,* Worksheet p. 22

Other Resources for this Collection

- *Cross-Curricular Activities,* p. 10
- *Portfolio Management System,* Introduction to Portfolio Assessment, p. 1
- *Test Generator,* Collection Test

Writing	Listening and Speaking Viewing and Representing	Assessment
• *Portfolio Management System,* Rubrics for Choices, p. 170	• *Audio CD Library,* Disc 13, Tracks 2, 3, 4, 5, 6, 7, 8, 9, 10, 11 • *Viewing and Representing:* Fine Art Transparencies 12, 13 Worksheet pp. 48, 52 • *Portfolio Management System,* Rubrics for Choices, p. 170	• *Formal Assessment,* Selection Tests, pp. 156, 157, 159, 161, 163, 164 • *Test Generator (One-Stop Planner CD-ROM)* • *Preparation for College Admission Exams,* p. 39
• *Portfolio Management System,* Rubrics for Choices, p. 172	• *Audio CD Library,* Disc 13, Tracks 12, 13 • *Portfolio Management System,* Rubrics for Choices, p. 172	• *Formal Assessment,* Selection Tests, pp. 165, 166 • *Test Generator (One-Stop Planner CD-ROM)*
• *Portfolio Management System,* Rubrics for Choices, p. 173	• *Audio CD Library,* Disc 13, Track 14 • *Portfolio Management System,* Rubrics for Choices, p. 173	• *Formal Assessment,* Selection Test, p. 167 • *Test Generator (One-Stop Planner CD-ROM)*
• *Portfolio Management System,* Rubrics for Choices, p. 174	• *Audio CD Library,* Disc 13, Tracks 15, 16 • *Portfolio Management System,* Rubrics for Choices, p. 174	• *Formal Assessment,* Selection Tests, pp. 168, 169 • *Test Generator (One-Stop Planner CD-ROM)*

Transparency CD-ROM Video Audio CD

Collection 10 Love and Loss

Skills Focus

Selection or Feature	Reading Skills and Strategies	Elements of Literature and Language	Writing	Listening and Speaking	Viewing and Representing
Tears, Idle Tears (p. 803) **The Eagle: A Fragment** (p. 805) **Flower in the Crannied Wall** (p. 806) **The Lady of Shalott** (p. 807) *from* **In Memoriam A.H.H.** (p. 814) **Ulysses** (p. 821) **Crossing the Bar** (p. 824) Alfred, Lord Tennyson	Dialogue with the Text, pp. 805–806 Noting Text Structures: Oppositions, pp. 807, 813	Tone, p. 804 Tercet, pp. 805–806 Simile, p. 806 Symbol, p. 806 Meter, p. 807 Rhyme, pp. 807, 813 Alliteration, pp. 807, 813 Assonance, pp. 807, 813 Plot, p. 813 Climax, p. 813 Rhyme Scheme, pp. 813, 820 Image, p. 813 Contrasting Images, p. 813 Foreshadow, p. 813 Contrast, p. 813 Setting, p. 820 Contrast, p. 823 Character, p. 823 Extended Metaphor, p. 825	Make a Preliminary Evaluation of a Poem, p. 825 Compare Draft and Final Endings, p. 825 Compare and Contrast Heroes, p. 825 Write Telemachus's Reply to His Father's Speech in "Ulysses," p. 825		Create a Storyboard for a Film Version of "The Lady of Shalott," p. 825
My Last Duchess (p. 829) **Porphyria's Lover** (p. 833) Robert Browning	Draw Inferences from Textual Clues, pp. 829, 831	Dramatic Monologue, p. 829 Character, pp. 829, 831, 836 Situation, p. 829 Motive, pp. 829, 831 Relationship, p. 831 Rhyme, p. 831 Meter, p. 831 Setting, p. 836	Create Criteria for Evaluating a Dramatic Poem, p. 836 Write an Essay Comparing the Themes of "My Last Duchess" and "Porphyria's Lover," p. 836 Write a Dramatic Monologue from the Point of View of the Wife in "My Last Duchess," p. 836	Improvise a Scene Based on the Characters in "Porphyria's Lover," p. 836	
Sonnet 43 (p. 837) Elizabeth Barrett Browning		Petrarchan Sonnet, p. 838 Turn, p. 838 Rhythm, p. 839 Sonnet, p. 839 Metaphor, p. 839	Write a Dialectical Journal Entry Comparing Two Sonnets, p. 839 Write a Love Poem Based on "Sonnet 43," p. 839	Stage a Poetry Reading, p. 839	
Spring and Fall: To a Young Child (p. 841) **Pied Beauty** (p. 843) Gerald Manley Hopkins	Recognize Multiple Meanings of Words, pp. 841–842 Context, p. 841	Assonance, pp. 841–842 Alliteration, pp. 842–843 Imagery, p. 843 Antithesis, p. 843 Rhythm, p. 843	Identify and Evaluate Elements of Style, p. 844 Write a Prose Paraphrase of "Spring and Fall," p. 844 Create a Catalog, p. 844 Write Definitions for Unusual and Coined Words, p. 844		

Collection 10

LOVE AND LOSS

Tennyson
Browning
Barrett Browning
Hopkins

I cannot say what loves have come and gone;
I only know that summer sang in me
A little while, that in me sings no more.

—Edna St. Vincent Millay (American, 1892–1950),
from "What Lips My Lips Have Kissed"

OBJECTIVES

1. Read literature from the Victorian period on the theme of "Love and Loss"
2. Interpret literary elements
3. Apply a variety of reading strategies to literature of the Victorian period
4. Respond to the literature in a variety of modes

Responding to the Quotation

? How do you think Millay feels about loves that "have come and gone"? [Possible responses: She is sorry that they are over, but she is not sorry that she has loved. Or, love, like summer, is warm and beautiful but does not last.]

RESPONDING TO THE ART

Dante Gabriel Rossetti (1828–1882), both a poet and a painter, lived in London in an artistic household that was more Italian than English. His sister Christina was also a poet. Rossetti disliked the industrial development of Victorian England, preferring to look back and idealize the life and art of the Middle Ages and early Renaissance.
Activity. Ask students how this painting captures the mood or feeling of lost love. Have them point out specific details. [Students may point to the wilted flower, the unattended book, and the woman's sad, distracted expression.]

WORK IN PROGRESS

Writing Focus: An Evaluation

The following **Work in Progress** assignments build to a culminating **Writer's Workshop** at the end of Collection 11.

- Tennyson's poems — Take notes on a single poem (p. 825)
- Browning's poems — List criteria for a strong dramatic poem (p. 836)
- Sonnet 43 — Compare poem with another love sonnet (p. 839)
- Hopkins's poems — Take notes on effectiveness of experimental techniques (p. 844)

Writer's Workshop: Persuasive Writing / An Evaluation (p. 899)

OBJECTIVES

Tears, Idle Tears / The Eagle / Flower in . . . Wall / The Lady of Shallott / In Memoriam . . . / Ulysses / Crossing the Bar

1. Read and interpret the poems
2. Identify and analyze a tercet
3. Interpret sources of word music
4. Analyze text structures
5. Express understanding through critical and creative writing

SKILLS

Literary
- Identify and analyze a tercet
- Interpret sources of word music

Reading
- Analyze text structures

Writing
- Collect ideas for an evaluation
- Respond to a generalization
- Evaluate a revision
- Compare and contrast heroes
- Reply from a different point of view

Literature and Film
- Sketch a storyboard

Viewing/Representing
- Interpret details of paintings (ATE)

Planning

- **Block Schedule**
  Block Scheduling Lesson Plans Including Pacing Guide
- **Traditional Schedule**
  Lesson Plans Including Strategies for English-Language Learners
- **One-Stop Planner**
  CD-ROM with Test Generator

Alfred, Lord Tennyson

(1809–1892)

The Granger Collection, New York.

Caricature of Alfred, Lord Tennyson (1872) by Frederick Waddy.

When Alfred Tennyson learned that Lord Byron had died while helping Greek nationalist rebels, he went to the woods and carved on a piece of sandstone, "Byron is dead." Tennyson was fourteen years old. He felt sure that he would be a poet, and he was already practicing the dramatic gestures of the Romantic poets he admired.

Tennyson's father was a clergyman of good family but little money, who encouraged young Alfred's interest in poetry. At Cambridge University Alfred joined a group of young intellectuals, called the Apostles, who believed that their friend was destined to become the greatest poet of their generation.

In 1831, when his father died, lack of funds forced Tennyson to leave Cambridge, and he entered a troubled period. In 1832, he published his first significant book of poems, which some reviewers derided for its melancholy themes and weak imitations of Keats's language. The next year Tennyson was devastated by the death of his closest friend, Arthur Henry Hallam. He became engaged to marry in 1836, but the marriage was postponed for fourteen years because of his uncertain financial prospects. In 1843, his family invested in a woodcarving machine and lost what little remained of their money.

During this difficult period, when both his physical and mental health suffered, Tennyson apparently never considered any career but poetry. He polished his style to develop the melodious line and rich imagery of poems like "The Lady of Shalott." Tennyson published almost nothing in his "ten years' silence" from 1832 to 1842, but the friends to whom he read his poems remained convinced of his promise.

Gradually, Tennyson began to make his way. The two-volume *Poems* (1842) was favorably reviewed, and in 1845 the government granted him an annual pension of two hundred pounds. In 1850, he published *In Memoriam,* an elegy to Hallam that was immediately successful. It tells the story of his own recovery of faith in the immortality of the soul and of the harmony of creation—despite the new, unsettling discoveries of science and his deep sense of the unfairness of Hallam's death. That year, he was named poet laureate (after Wordsworth's death), and he finally married. Now Tennyson settled into the long, successful career that had been expected of him, and for the rest of his life he was considered the greatest living English poet.

In the forty years before his death in 1892, Tennyson published nearly a dozen volumes of poems. These include *The Idylls of the King,* which makes the rise, fall, and possible return of King Arthur into a kind of parable about the moral qualities of good political leaders and of their betrayal by the rest of us. His books sold like best-selling novels and made him rich. In 1884, he was made a peer of the realm and became Alfred, Lord Tennyson.

Tennyson never lost the melancholy and sense of chaos that friends and reviewers found in his early poems. He was immensely popular with his contemporaries because he spoke in a beautiful, measured language of their sense of the precariousness and sadness of life. And he also assured his readers that his own experience of sadness and disorder had taught him that everything was part of a benevolent plan in which eventually all losses would be made good.

go.hrw.com
LEO 12-10

Resources: Print and Media

Reading
- *Graphic Organizers for Active Reading,* pp. 72, 73, 74, 75, 76, 77
- *Audio CD Library*
  Disc 13, Tracks 2, 3, 4, 5, 6, 7, 8, 9, 10, 11

Elements of Literature
- *Literary Elements*
  Transparency 21
  Worksheet, p. 64

Writing and Language
- *Daily Oral Grammar*
  Transparencies 27, 28
- *Grammar and Language Links*
  Worksheet, p. 43
- *Language Workshop CD-ROM*

Viewing and Representing
- *Viewing and Representing*
  Fine Art Transparencies 12, 13
  Fine Art Worksheet, pp. 48, 52

Assessment
- *Formal Assessment,* pp. 156, 157, 159, 161, 163, 164
- *Portfolio Management System,* p. 170
- *Preparation for College Admission Exams,* p. 39
- *Test Generator (One-Stop Planner CD-ROM)*

Internet
- go.hrw.com (keyword: *LEO 12-10*)

Before You Read

TEARS, IDLE TEARS

Make the Connection

Shadows of the Past

Remembering the past: Do you find it sad or satisfying to look backward? You're probably thinking, "Obviously, that depends on what's being remembered—happy or sad times." But is that the only view? Is there a way in which memory itself—the very *fact* of the past—always shadows life in the present?

Quickwrite

How can tears be "idle"—can you cry without knowing why? Write a quick response.

Background

This poem is the most famous of eleven lyric songs that are interspersed in *The Princess,* a long narrative poem about women's education and emancipation. Tennyson wrote the lyric while visiting Tintern Abbey in the autumn, the same site Wordsworth contemplated in his famous meditation (page 658).

Disappointed Love (1821) by Francis Danby.

By Courtesy of The Board of Trustees of the Victoria and Albert Museum, London.

Summary ■■

The speaker says he cries when remembering the past. Though he does not fully understand the cause of his sorrow, he thinks it arises from some "divine despair." Through images such as autumn fields and birds singing to dying eyes, he expresses not only regret but a sense of death in life.

BROWSING IN THE FILES

About the Author. Tennyson was as celebrated in his own day as some of today's athletes and rock stars. Not only was Tennyson stalked at his own home by devoted admirers, but his every action was reported in the press. In *Tennyson: Aspects of his Life, Character and Poetry,* Harold Nicolson says that Tennyson's birthdays had all the gravity of a national celebration. People sent large and generous gifts ranging from rolls of woven cloth to garden chairs. Lakes, cliffs, and roses were named in his honor. News about Tennyson's actions, clothes, and even his tobacco were standard newspaper fare.

Reaching All Students

Struggling Readers

Explain that one meaning of the word *idle* is "useless." Ask students to work together to list three reasons or motives why a person might shed "idle tears." Students might also make predictions about the tone of voice of a speaker who is concerned about his idle tears. Invite students to record their predictions and to revise them after reading each stanza.

English Language Learners

To help students grasp the mood of the poem, call their attention to the repeated phrase at the end of each stanza: "the days that are no more." For further strategies for engaging English language learners with the literature, see

- *Lesson Plans Including Strategies for English-Language Learners*

Advanced Learners

Have students make a list of images that are frequently used by poets to suggest loss or death. They may begin with Tennyson's images in this poem and then read other poems with similar themes to enlarge their lists and see if some images are used repeatedly to express the same mood or emotion.

(A) Reading Skills and Strategies

Drawing Conclusions

? Why might you expect the speaker of this poem to be an older person? [Possible responses: The speaker is looking back on the past. The image of autumn fields might suggest a speaker in the autumn of life.] In fact, Tennyson said that in this poem he was attempting to capture "the yearning that young people occasionally experience for that which seems to have passed away from them for ever."

(B) Critical Thinking

Interpreting the Author's Purpose

? Why do you think Tennyson makes so many appeals to the readers' senses? [Possible responses: He is trying to make an abstract idea easy to understand; he wants to show that the experience of loss has affected every aspect of the speaker's life.]

Resources

Audio CD Library

A dramatic reading of this selection is available in the *Audio CD Library:*

- Disc 13, Track 2

Formal Assessment

- Selection Test, p. 156

MAKING MEANINGS

First Thoughts [Respond]

1. Students may say that after reading the poem they have a clearer idea of why the speaker is moved to tears.

Shaping Interpretations [Interpret]

2. Scenes include fields in autumn, sunrise on a sail, and remembered kisses after a loved one has died. The order is roughly chronological.

3. Most will agree that the poem begins with an autumn field and moves to darker images that are suggestive of death.

4. *Divine despair* may refer to the Biblical Fall; human beings are destined to struggle, to experience sorrow, and to die.

Tears, Idle Tears

Alfred, Lord Tennyson

Tears, idle tears, I know not what they mean,
Tears from the depth of some divine despair
Rise in the heart, and gather to the eyes,
In looking on the happy autumn fields,
And thinking of the days that are no more.

Fresh as the first beam glittering on a sail,
That brings our friends up from the underworld,
Sad as the last which reddens over one
That sinks with all we love below the verge;
So sad, so fresh, the days that are no more.

Ah, sad and strange as in dark summer dawns
The earliest pipe of half-awakened birds
To dying ears, when unto dying eyes
The casement slowly grows a glimmering square;
So sad, so strange, the days that are no more.

Dear as remembered kisses after death,
And sweet as those by hopeless fancy feigned
On lips that are for others; deep as love,
Deep as first love, and wild with all regret;
O Death in Life, the days that are no more!

The Offer (1866) by Thomas Faed.

MAKING MEANINGS

First Thoughts

1. After reading this poem, would you change what you wrote about "idle tears" in your Quickwrite notes? Why or why not?

Shaping Interpretations

2. What is the scene of each stanza of "Tears, Idle Tears"? Why do you think Tennyson orders the stanzas as he does?

3. Do you think the poem's sequence of images creates an increasingly dark **tone**? Explain.

4. What do you think the "divine despair" is in line 2? Could you relate it to Adam and Eve's fall in Genesis (page 416)—would that story explain the speaker's existential sadness? Explain.

5. Stanzas 2–4 present a series of comparisons that attempt to make concrete the abstract memory of "the days that are no more." What are these comparisons?

Connecting with the Text

6. Does the contradiction in the phrase "Death in Life" (line 20) make sense to you? Explain. What is your response to this line?

5. In stanza 2, the days past are as fresh as the first beam of the rising sun and as sad as the last sunbeam. In stanza 3, they are as sad as the morning sound of birds piping to dying ears, as sad as the morning light to dying eyes. In stanza 4, they are as dear as kisses remembered after death, as sweet as imagined kisses and as deep as first love.

Connecting with the Text [Respond]

6. Possible responses: Thinking of the past is like experiencing death in the midst of life. Or, times of great sorrow or times when people are bent on self-destructive paths are like death in life.

Before You Read

The Eagle: A Fragment
Flower in the Crannied Wall

Make the Connection

Lessons Large and Small

The poet, the scientist, and the religious believer don't necessarily have conflicting ideas about the phrase *mysteries of nature.* Yet to some nineteenth-century artists and believers, modern science's scrutiny of nature was a threat—a fearful one. Would a microscope reveal the secrets of matter, but at the expense of our traditional concepts of beauty and faith?

Part of Tennyson's immense popularity was that he addressed these philosophical issues and, for many, offered ways of resolving them.

Reading Skills and Strategies

Dialogue with the Text

Stop after reading each poem, and jot down the quality of nature that you think each poem evokes.

Elements of Literature

Tercet

Although Tennyson called "The Eagle" a fragment, its verse form and organization give it a feeling of completeness. Each stanza is a **tercet:** three lines with one rhyme. The eagle and the world are at rest in the first stanza and are moving in the second.

The Eagle: A Fragment

Alfred, Lord Tennyson

He clasps the crag with crooked hands; (A)
Close to the sun in lonely lands,
Ringed with the azure world, he stands.

The wrinkled sea beneath him crawls; (B) (C)
He watches from his mountain walls,
And like a thunderbolt he falls.

Summary

This poem spotlights a lone eagle perched high above the sea, stationary in the first stanza and in motion in the second. The word choices suggest strength, independence, loftiness, and a capacity for violence. As a symbol, the eagle might stand for Nature's power or for the individual's will to survive.

Resources

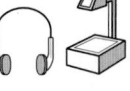

Audio CD Library

A dramatic reading of this selection is available in the *Audio CD Library:*

- Disc 13, Track 3

Viewing and Representing

Fine Art Transparency

To build background about eagles and to emphasize their majestic power, use the Fine Art transparency of Edward Julius Detmold's *The Eagle and the Beetle.* See the *Viewing and Representing Transparencies* and *Worksheets:*

- Transparency 12
- Worksheet, p. 48

(A) Reading Skills and Strategies

Dialogue with the Text

? How does this first line give you the sense that the eagle has both animal and human characteristics? [Possible responses: The eagle perches on a crag, or natural place, yet the author depicts it as having hands rather than talons.]

(B) Critical Thinking

Synthesizing

? What details combine to create the dominant impression of a solitary yet lordly creature? [Possible responses: Lordliness is suggested by the eagle's position above the everyday world, while the sea "crawls" beneath his gaze. The eagle is solitary in the poem; no other creature seems to exist in its "azure world"; all the surroundings are inanimate.]

(C) Elements of Literature

Tercet

? What are the rhymes in each stanza, and why is each a tercet? [In stanza 1, the rhymes are *hands, lands, stands;* in stanza 2, *crawls, walls, falls.* Each is a tercet because it has three rhyming lines.]

Using Students' Strengths

Naturalist Learners

Invite students to learn just how "close to the sun" the eagle flies and whether it, among all birds, has the loftiest nest sites and swoops fastest and longest. Students might also select other details about the eagle given in the poem, such as its habitat, and check them against what they know or can find out about eagles. Encourage students to compile a fact chart about eagles.

Verbal Learners

Students might compare Tennyson's word pictures describing an eagle with the images created by Ted Hughes in "Hawk Roosting" (p. 961) or by Gerard Manley Hopkins in "The Windhover." Urge students to pay particular attention to the bird as a symbol in each poem. Invite students to develop their comparisons and contrasts in a short paper.

Summary

The speaker plucks a tiny flower and its root out of a chink in a wall. Marveling at its ability to thrive in such unpromising conditions, the speaker realizes that if he could understand this small miracle of life, he might penetrate the larger mysteries of who we are and where we come from.

Resources

Audio CD Library

A dramatic reading of this selection is available in the *Audio CD Library:*

- Disc 13, Track 4

Ⓐ Vocabulary Note

? Explain that a *cranny* is a narrow opening or crack. What would you expect a crannied wall to look and feel like? [Possible responses: It would be rough to the touch. It would be uneven, with many small cracks or openings. It would probably appear weathered or broken.]

Ⓑ Reading Skills and Strategies

Dialogue with the Text

As students read, have them keep a double-entry chart. In the left column, they can note words and phrases that catch their attention. In the right column, they may offer comments or interpretations.

Ⓒ Critical Thinking

Interpreting

? What qualities make this flower so remarkable to the speaker? [Possible responses: Its delicate beauty; its ability to survive where there is so little to nourish it. The flower represents the tenacity of life, against all odds.]

Ⓓ Elements of Literature

Slant Rhyme

? What is the rhyme scheme of this poem? [*abccab*] Note that ll. 2 and 6 rhyme, but their rhyme is slanted, or inexact. How does this emphasize the final line? [Possible response: It makes the last line more startling; or, as unusual or unpredicatable as life springing from stone.]

Flower in the Crannied Wall

Alfred, Lord Tennyson

Flower in the crannied wall,
I pluck you out of the crannies,
I hold you here, root and all, in my hand,
Little flower—but *if* I could understand
What you are, root and all, and all in all,
I should know what God and man is.

Lord Tennyson (1903) by George Frederick Watts. The statue stands outside Lincoln Cathedral in Lincolnshire, England.

Making Meanings

The Eagle: A Fragment
Flower in the Cranned Wall

First Thoughts

1. What contrasting qualities of nature do you think Tennyson captures in these lyrics? (Check your reading notes.)

Shaping Interpretations

2. How does Tennyson use the **tercet** form to describe what is happening in "The Eagle"?
3. How could the sea, in "The Eagle," be "wrinkled"? What is suggested about the eagle's power in the last **simile**?
4. What do you think "all in all" (line 5) means in "Flower in the Crannied Wall"? What does the speaker seek to learn from the flower?
5. Suppose the eagle and the flower are used as **symbols.** What would you say they symbolize to Tennyson?

Challenging the Text

6. Do you agree with what Tennyson says a flower could tell us? How would a scientist regard the same flower?

Making Meanings

First Thoughts [Respond]

1. Answers may include power and delicacy; beauty and tenacity.

Shaping Interpretations [Interpret]

2. The first tercet vividly captures the eagle at rest; the second captures the eagle in motion.
3. From high above, the waves look like wrinkles on the flat surface of the sea. Like a thunderbolt, the eagle in flight is strong and powerful.
4. Possible responses: "All in all" may refer to life itself or nature or creation. If the speaker could understand the creation of a delicate but hardy flower, he might better understand the relationship between God and all living things.
5. The eagle may symbolize Nature's power or the isolation of the individual; the flower may stand for the mystery, beauty, or tenacity of life.

Challenging the Text [Evaluate/Apply]

6. Students may agree that the flower represents the beauty of life and its ability to triumph over adversity. A scientist might explain the same phenomenon in terms of its parts and functions or its adaptation to its environment.

Before You Read

THE LADY OF SHALOTT

Make the Connection

Shattering Glass

One of the main symbols in this dreamlike ballad is a mirror that the Lady uses with her weaving. Watch for how the mirror with its reflected images is in opposition to the "real" world. This is only one opposition, or tension, in the world of the Lady of Shalott, of whom Tennyson said: "The newborn love for something, for someone in the wide world from which she had been so long secluded, takes her out of the region of shadows into that of realities."

Reading Skills and Strategies

Noting Text Structures

As you read, be alert to **oppositions**—in setting, actions, or imagery—and record the first example you notice. Then, when Sir Lancelot appears in Part III, jot down at least one other contrast that he introduces.

Elements of Literature

Word Music

Be sure to read this poem aloud to hear the famous music of Tennyson's language. That music is created by the expert use of **meter** and by the dazzling use of **rhymes, alliteration,** and **assonance.** For many years schoolchildren in both England and the United States could recite the mysterious story of the Lady of Shalott from memory. You might try it.

Tate Gallery, London.

The Lady of Shalott (1888) by John William Waterhouse.

Summary ■■

In Part I, the speaker sets the scene and introduces the plot: The Lady, on her remote island, is under a curse: She must keep to her weaving and ignore Camelot. However, she is attracted by the reflections of the active world that she sees in her mirror. At the sight of two lovers, she declares that she is "half sick of shadows." In Part II, the shining figure of Sir Lancelot pierces the island gloom, and the lonely Lady chooses to leave her retreat and follow him. The mirror cracks. She then places her name upon the prow of a boat and floats toward Camelot, singing. By the time she reaches the first house, she is dead. Moved, the lords and ladies stare at her lifeless form, while Lancelot utters a prayer.

FROM THE EDITOR'S DESK

Hypnotic and lulling, "The Lady of Shalott" casts a spell as powerful as any the wizard Merlin ever cast. We hope students find in this rich ballad the same enchantment that we do.

Resources

Audio CD Library

A dramatic reading of this selection is available in the *Audio CD Library:*

- Disc 13, Track 5

Formal Assessment

- Selection Test, p. 159

Reaching All Students

English Language Learners

As students read, ask them to write a short summary of one or two sentences, capturing the main events of each part of the poem. Call their attention to the side glosses that define the more difficult and archaic language and encourage them to visualize the scenes in their imagination as they read.

Advanced Learners

Encourage students to gather information about medieval tapestries (for example, *The Hunt of the Unicorn* series in The Metropolitan Museum of Art in New York City). Then have students describe in words or sketch in pencil what they think the Lady of Shallot is creating on her loom. Have students share their work and discuss how their research affected their visualization of the Lady's creation.

A Reading Skills and Strategies

Noting Text Structures

? What oppositions do you find in the first stanza? [Possible responses: An island is set off from the land and the flow of human activity. There is also opposition suggested in "many-towered Camelot," which seems lofty and almost fantastic in contrast with the simple life of farmers "below."]

B Reading Skills and Strategies

Noting Text Structures

? How do the details in this stanza suggest opposition? [Possible response: The details in ll. 10–14 suggest a setting alive with color and movement; the details in ll. 15–18 suggest drabness and silence.]

C Elements of Literature

Word Music

? What sound devices contribute to the music of these lines? [Possible responses: alliteration in words such as "reapers, reaping" and "bearded barley"; assonance in "reaper weary" and "listening, whispers 'Tis." Short, rhythmic lines with consecutive rhyming words and the rhyme and repetition of *Camelot* and *Shalott* contribute to the poem's music.]

The Lady of Shalott

Alfred, Lord Tennyson

Part I

On either side the river lie
Long fields of barley and of rye,
That clothe the wold° and meet the sky;
And through the field the road runs by
    To many-towered Camelot;°
And up and down the people go,
Gazing where the lilies blow°
Round an island there below,
    The island of Shalott.

Willows whiten,° aspens quiver,
Little breezes dusk and shiver
Through the wave that runs forever
By the island in the river
    Flowing down to Camelot.
Four gray walls, and four gray towers,
Overlook a space of flowers,
And the silent isle imbowers°
    The Lady of Shalott.

By the margin, willow-veiled,
Slide the heavy barges trailed
By slow horses; and unhailed
The shallop° flitteth silken-sailed
    Skimming down to Camelot:
But who hath seen her wave her hand?
Or at the casement seen her stand?
Or is she known in all the land,
    The Lady of Shalott?

Only reapers, reaping early
In among the bearded barley,
Hear a song that echoes cheerly°
From the river winding clearly,
    Down to towered Camelot;
And by the moon the reaper weary,
Piling sheaves in uplands airy,
Listening, whispers "'Tis the fairy
    Lady of Shalott."

3. wold: rolling plain.

5. Camelot: legendary city, site of King Arthur's court and Round Table.

7. blow: blossom.

10. whiten: show the white undersides of their leaves when blown by the wind.

17. imbowers: shelters with trees, gardens, and flowers.

22. shallop: small, open boat.

30. cheerly: archaic for "cheerily."

Using Students' Strengths

Kinesthetic Learners

Have volunteers re-create the scene in the Lady's room, showing how she might have been using the mirror while weaving and at the same time have seen in it a reflection of the world outside. Then have students discuss what seeing merely "shadows" of the world suggests about the Lady's character and experience.

Visual Learners

Have students sketch a rough map of the setting of the poem, showing the river and its island, the barley and rye fields, the rolling hills, the highway, and the towers of Camelot itself. Students might then reread the poem aloud with a partner, pointing to the various locations on their map as they read.

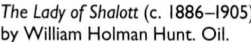

The Lady of Shalott (c. 1886–1905) by William Holman Hunt. Oil.

©Manchester City Art Galleries, England.

Part II

There she weaves by night and day
A magic web with colors gay.
She has heard a whisper say,
A curse is on her if she stay
        To look down to Camelot.
She knows not what the curse may be,
And so she weaveth steadily,
And little other care hath she,
        The Lady of Shalott.

And moving through a mirror clear°
That hangs before her all the year,
Shadows of the world appear.
There she sees the highway near
        Winding down to Camelot;
There the river eddy whirls,
And there the surly village churls,°
And the red cloaks of market girls,
        Pass onward from Shalott.

46. mirror clear: Weavers worked on the back of the tapestry so that they could easily knot their yarns. To see the front of their designs, weavers looked in a mirror that reflected the front of the tapestry.

52. churls: peasants; country folk.

RESPONDING TO THE ART

William Holman Hunt (1827–1910), an English painter, was a founder of the Pre-Raphaelites, along with Dante Gabriel Rossetti and John Everett Millais. Many of his works are of Biblical scenes. His goals in painting were moral uplift, historical authenticity, and direct study of nature. Hunt's paintings are often crowded with precise details and bright colors.

Activity. Invite students to use a magnifying glass to locate precise details and to discuss their effect on the painting as a whole.

D Struggling Readers

Identifying Cause and Effect

? Why does the Lady stay indoors and weave night and day? [A curse has been placed upon her if she looks at Camelot.]

E Reading Skills and Strategies

Using Glosses

Remind students to use the marginal notes as they read. Ask why the note about the "mirror clear" is of particular importance. [Possible response: It explains that the Lady sees only the front of her tapestry and sees life itself as a reflection in the mirror, emphasizing her detachment and isolation.]

F Critical Thinking

Interpreting

? What role does the mirror play in the Lady's life? [Possible responses: The Lady must rely on her mirror to catch any glimpses of the outside world. The mirror reflects life for her, though it does not enable her to participate in it.]

Getting Students Involved

Cooperative Learning

Who Was She? Assign students to groups of four. Each group can act as a team of newspaper reporters out to get the scoop on the Lady of Shalott. Each team should interview a different character or group of characters from the poem (played by other class members), such as the reapers, the lovers the Lady sees in the mirror, those who hear the Lady's song as she floats down to Camelot, and those who find her dead in the boat. The goal of each reporting team is to elicit as much newsworthy conjecture about this mystery maiden as possible. Students may report "live" or go on "location" with videotape. After each group makes its presentation, the group members can collaborate on an assessment of their group effort.

Ⓐ Reading Skills and Strategies

Noting Text Structures

? What oppositions do you find in ll. 55–70? [Possible responses: There is a contrast between the bustling, active world outside and the quiet, isolated life of the Lady looking in the "mirror blue." She can weave a web of magic sights, but they are fantasy; outside is reality. Also, a funeral is followed by a wedding.]

Ⓑ Reading Skills and Strategies

Making Predictions

? Tennyson himself said these two lines are a key to the poem (see Critical Comment, p. 813). If the Lady means what she says, what do you think she will do? [Possible responses: She might leave her island and go to Camelot, despite the curse; or, she might attempt to thwart the curse by luring people from Camelot to Shalott.]

Ⓒ Literary Connections

Arthurian Legend

In Arthurian legend, Lancelot is something of an enigma—he is the most noble of the knights of the Round Table, yet he seduces King Arthur's queen and plays a role in Camelot's demise. (In chasing after Lancelot and Guinevere, Arthur loses his unguarded throne to the villain Mordred and, in the resulting fight for kingship, is killed. See p. 171.) Point out that the arrival of Sir Lancelot in the poem is so momentous that Tennyson chooses to rhyme *Lancelot* (l. 77) with *Shalott* (l. 81)—the only place in the poem where *Camelot* is not the rhyming word.

Ⓓ Elements of Literature

Word Music

Encourage students to whisper these lines to hear their word music. Then ask them to identify the sound devices used. [Possible responses: There is alliteration in "golden galaxy" and "bridle bells"; there is repetition of *b* and *g* sounds throughout the stanza; there is both alliteration and consonance in "rode his armor rung." All together, the verse seems to ring as merrily as the bridle bells.]

Sometimes a troop of damsels glad,
An abbot on an ambling pad,°
Sometimes a curly shepherd lad,
Or long-haired page in crimson clad,
Goes by to towered Camelot;
And sometimes through the mirror blue
The knights come riding two and two:
She hath no loyal knight and true,
The Lady of Shalott.

But in her web she still delights
To weave the mirror's magic sights,
For often through the silent nights
A funeral, with plumes and lights
And music, went to Camelot;
Or when the moon was overhead,
Came two young lovers lately wed:
"I am half sick of shadows," said
The Lady of Shalott.

Part III

A bowshot from her bower eaves,
He rode between the barley sheaves,
The sun came dazzling through the leaves,
And flamed upon the brazen greaves°
Of bold Sir Lancelot.
A red-cross knight° forever kneeled
To a lady in his shield,
That sparkled on the yellow field,
Beside remote Shalott.

The gemmy° bridle glittered free,
Like to some branch of stars we see
Hung in the golden Galaxy.°
The bridle bells rang merrily
As he rode down to Camelot;
And from his blazoned baldric° slung
A mighty silver bugle hung,
And as he rode his armor rung,
Beside remote Shalott.

All in the blue unclouded weather
Thick-jeweled shone the saddle leather,
The helmet and the helmet feather
Burned like one burning flame together,
As he rode down to Camelot;
As often through the purple night,
Below the starry clusters bright,
Some bearded meteor, trailing light,
Moves over still Shalott.

56. pad: easy-gaited horse.

76. greaves: armor for the lower legs.

78. red-cross knight: The red cross is the emblem of St. George, England's patron saint.

82. gemmy: set with jewels.

84. Galaxy: Milky Way.

87. blazoned baldric: richly decorated sash worn across the chest diagonally.

Skill Link

Analyzing Text Structures: Chronological Order

Note that this ballad is written in chronological order. There are no flashbacks and events are presented as they occur. Ask students to consider the following questions:

1. **From the moment readers hear of the curse, they sense the Lady is doomed. How does chronological order contribute to this sense of inevitable doom?** [Possible response: The sequence of events leads inexorably ahead. There is never any turning back. The doom is as certain as the water flowing to Camelot.]
2. **What is the effect of the poem's rhythm? How does it affect the reader's sense of time?** [Possible response: The poem has a steady, predictable rhythm that has a hypnotic or lulling effect. Time seems to be moving slowly but inevitably forward.]

His broad clear brow in sunlight glowed;
On burnished° hooves his war horse trode;
From underneath his helmet flowed
His coal-black curls as on he rode,
As he rode down to Camelot.
From the bank and from the river
He flashed into the crystal mirror,
"Tirra lirra," by the river
Sang Sir Lancelot.

She left the web, she left the loom,
She made three paces through the room,
She saw the waterlily bloom,
She saw the helmet and the plume,
She looked down to Camelot.
Out flew the web and floated wide;
The mirror cracked from side to side;
"The curse is come upon me," cried
The Lady of Shalott.

Part IV

In the stormy east wind straining,
The pale yellow woods were waning,
The broad stream in his banks complaining,
Heavily the low sky raining
Over towered Camelot;
Down she came and found a boat
Beneath a willow left afloat,
And round about the prow° she wrote
The Lady of Shalott.

And down the river's dim expanse
Like some bold seër° in a trance,
Seeing all his own mischance—
With a glassy countenance
Did she look to Camelot.
And at the closing of the day
She loosed the chain, and down she lay;
The broad stream bore her far away,
The Lady of Shalott.

Lying, robed in snowy white
That loosely flew to left and right—
The leaves upon her falling light—
Through the noises of the night
She floated down to Camelot;
And as the boat head wound along
The willowy hills and fields among,
They heard her singing her last song,
The Lady of Shalott.

101. burnished: polished.

125. prow: front part of a boat.

128. seër: prophet.

E Critical Thinking

Evaluating

? How does Lancelot's arrival increase the narrative tension? [The Lady's desire for a better look at Lancelot causes her to defy the curse. Somewhere between that first glance and that final step to the window, she has to weigh the threat of the curse against the fulfillment of her own desire.] **Point out the irony that Lancelot continues on to Camelot, never realizing the effect that he has had upon the Lady.**

F Elements of Literature

Pathetic Fallacy

? A pathetic fallacy occurs when a writer assigns human emotions and moods to a force of nature. How does this stanza qualify as a pathetic fallacy? [Possible response: The Lady of Shalott knows that she is doomed. The disquiet of the wind and the river reflect her doom (or may be Nature's protest against it); the sky too may be mourning her fate.]

G Elements of Literature

Imagery

? What is the significance of the Lady's dressing in white? [Possible responses: Perhaps it represents the purity of the isolated, artistic life she is leaving behind; if she is traveling to Camelot out of devotion to Lancelot, she may imagine herself a bride.]

Making the Connections

Connecting to the Theme: "Love and Loss"

Point out that the Lady of Shalott's decision—or her impulse—to follow Lancelot puts her at risk. She lives in one world and functions well in it, but she is attracted to another, about which she knows nothing. She decides that love, or life, is worth risking everything for. She takes the risk and dies.

Crossing the Curriculum

Music

Have pairs of students attempt a musical interpretation of "The Lady of Shalott," either creating melodies or using established musical works. (They may want to find and play Irish singer Loreena McKennitt's interpretation, for example.) Have students share their music with the class.

Ⓐ Reading Skills and Strategies

Noting Text Structures

? How does this stanza suggest opposition? [Possible responses: The Lady is traveling to her death, yet singing; she is headed toward life, yet dying; she is leaving her tomblike cloister only to find death.]

Ⓑ Elements of Literature

Word Music

? How are the last two stanzas musical? [Possible responses: There is continued alliteration, as in *gallery* and *garden*, *houses* and *high*; consonance in repeated *l* sounds and blends; and assonance in *high* and *silent*, as well as *out*, *round*, and *prow*. The continued regular meter, with its repeated rhymes, carries the reader to the end of the poem in the same inexorable way as the Lady is carried to her death.]

RESPONDING TO THE ART

John William Waterhouse (1849–1917) painted not only this picture but the one on p. 807. Often classified as a Pre-Raphaelite, he was strongly influenced by literature, as is evident in these two paintings.

Activity. Have students compare the two paintings and tell how each one interprets the Lady of Shalott and her plight.

Ⓐ
Heard a carol, mournful, holy,
Chanted loudly, chanted lowly,
Till her blood was frozen slowly,
And her eyes were darkened wholly,
    Turned to towered Camelot.
For ere she reached upon the tide
The first house by the waterside,
Singing in her song she died,
    The Lady of Shalott.

Ⓑ
Under tower and balcony,
By garden wall and gallery,
A gleaming shape she floated by,
Dead-pale between the houses high,
    Silent into Camelot.
Out upon the wharfs they came,
Knight and burgher,° lord and dame,
And round the prow they read her name,
    The Lady of Shalott.

Who is this? and what is here?
And in the lighted palace near
Died the sound of royal cheer;
And they crossed themselves for fear,
    All the knights at Camelot:
But Lancelot mused a little space;
He said, "She has a lovely face;
God in his mercy lend her grace,
    The Lady of Shalott."

160. **burgher:** townsperson.

The Lady of Shalott (19th century) by John William Waterhouse.

Assessing Learning

Check Test: Short Answers

1. **Where does the Lady of Shalott live?** [on an island in a river that flows downstream past Camelot]
2. **How does she spend her time?** [She continually weaves a colorful "magic web," catching glimpses of the outside world only through a mirror.]
3. **Why does she go to her window—and what happens when she does?** [She goes to watch Sir Lancelot as he rides toward Camelot, realizing that she may have activated a curse placed upon her.]
4. **How does she travel to Camelot?** [She lies in a boat with her name written upon it and lets the river carry her.]
5. **How do the people in Camelot respond to her arrival?** [They are confused and somewhat frightened upon seeing her corpse; Lancelot reflects upon her beauty and prays for her soul.]

Critical Comment

Escaping a World of Shadows

Readers may differ in regard to the meaning or moral of the simple story this richly ornamented and carefully wrought poem tells. As you learned before you read the poem, no one should disregard the clue offered by Tennyson himself: "The newborn love for something," he said of the Lady of Shalott, "for someone in the wide world from which she had been so long secluded, takes her out of the region of shadows into that of realities." He is referring particularly to the last lines of Part II when, having watched a young bride and groom in the moonlight, the Lady declares that she is "half sick of shadows." (A)

Like the weaving that perpetually occupies the heroine—"A magic web with colors gay"—the narrative moves from scene to scene with a tapestried grace that quietly captures the romantic heart of the Age of Chivalry. The Lady is appropriately beautiful, wan, sequestered, and mysterious. Sir Lancelot, panoplied to the hilt with every object in the book of heraldry, is less a man than a vision of a man. And Camelot itself, "many-towered," exists like a little city afloat in time.

The "mirror clear" in line 46 is crucial both to the poem's narrative line and to its meaning. In the custom of weavers, the Lady has placed this mirror in a spot facing the loom from which she is able to see at a glance how her work is going. But, for the purposes of the story, the more important function of the mirror is to allow the Lady glimpses or "shadows" of the world in which she takes no part.

Making Meanings

First Thoughts

1. What do you think the Lady's "curse" is? Why do you think so?

Shaping Interpretations

2. Summarize the main events in the **plot** of this narrative poem. What moment marks its **climax**?

3. Scan the poem to find its metrical form. What is its **rhyme scheme**? What examples of **alliteration** and **assonance** help create the haunting music?

4. Point out **images** of dazzling light associated with Sir Lancelot in Part III. Find **contrasting images** associated with the Lady. What do you think is the meaning of this contrast? (Refer to your reading notes.)

5. Explain why lines 66–72 could **foreshadow** Lancelot's arrival and the Lady's actions in the second half of the poem. What yearning do you think the Lady expresses when she exclaims, "I am half sick of shadows" (line 71)?

6. How does Tennyson **contrast** the Lady's life with the lives of the villagers and court in Camelot? Do you think that Tennyson indicates a preference for any of these ways of life?

7. This poem was written during Tennyson's ten years of silence. Can you see any connection between the poem and his own life? Explain.

Challenging the Text

8. Think of the "magic web" the Lady weaves and the conditions under which she creates her art. What commentary do you think Tennyson is making on the role and life of an artist? How do you feel about his ideas? When would artistic seclusion be necessary, and when might it be undesirable?

Critical Comment

This feature explains that the shadows seen by the Lady of Shalott symbolize the world from which she is excluded.

(A) Critical Thinking

Expressing an Opinion

? Do you think there is any significance in Tennyson's choice of the expression "half sick" instead of "sick"? [Possible response: The Lady is only partly ready to give up her secure life as an observer and recorder of events rather than a full-fledged participant.]

Making Meanings

First Thoughts [Respond]

1. The Lady must die if she leaves her weaving. When she finally decides to look out the window and leave her room, she acts as if she knows she is doomed. Then the mirror cracks, shattering her art and her former view of the world.

Shaping Interpretations [Interpret]

2. The exposition reveals the Lady's lonely weaving and the curse that warns her not to look directly at the world outside. The climax occurs when a song entices the Lady to look out the window and she is compelled to leave her secluded world.

3. The poem is written mostly in iambic tetrameter. (The last line of each stanza is iambic trimeter.) For emphasis, many lines are trochaic and open with a stressed syllable (ll. 7–8, 10–17). The rhyme scheme is *aaaabcccb*. The poem's lilt comes from alliteration such as "Willows whiten" (l. 10) or "silken-sailed" (l. 22) and assonance such as "Listening, whispers" (l. 35).

4. The sun flames on his "brazen greaves"; his shield sparkles; his bridle glitters like a branch of stars. Lancelot contrasts with the Lady's world of shadows; even her castle is gray. The contrast is between life and a reflection of life or between life and death.

5. The Lady notices two young lovers and is envious of them. These feelings could foreshadow her falling in love with Lancelot and her decision to leave her isolation. When she says she is "half sick of shadows," she means she is tired of living life apart and wants to experience life firsthand.

6. The Lady lives alone in a world of shadows while the villagers and courtiers move and mingle in a bright world. The poet suggests participation in life is alluring, though perhaps falsely so.

7. Tennyson may have seen himself to be as isolated by his art, grief, or temperament as the Lady is isolated on her gloomy island.

Challenging the Text [Evaluate]

8. Tennyson may be commenting on the private versus the public roles of an artist, suggesting that isolation is unsatisfying but necessary, because public participation destroys both art and artist. Some turning away from the world may be required to produce art. Others may say that detachment from life, which should be the subject matter of art, is not possible or desirable for the artist.

Summary ■■■

Printed here are just four lyrics from the 131 that make up Tennyson's elegy for his close friend Arthur Henry Hallam. In Lyric 55, the speaker wonders if belief in God is contradicted by the study of nature, because Nature reveals an order concerned only with the survival of the species rather than of the individual. Though the speaker's faith falters, he does not give up his "larger hope."

In Lyric 56, Nature speaks, claiming power over life and death and expressing indifference to human ideals, hopes, and accomplishments. The speaker is horrified by this view, suggesting as it does that life and all human endeavor are meaningless. Lyric 95 is set at evening in a country-house garden where the speaker reads a letter written long ago by his friend. Later while sleeping, he experiences a mystical vision and awakes to a dawn in which previously irreconcilable forces move in harmony.

In Lyric 130, the speaker now sees his friend in all of Nature's manifestations and finds consolation and joy in his new-found sense of the unity of God and nature.

Before You Read

FROM IN MEMORIAM A.H.H.

Make the Connection

Surviving Grief

Why? That is often the first question an early or terrible death wrings from us. Tragic loss can make life seem arbitrary or ruthless; grief can even cause us to question our personal beliefs.

Quickwrite

Think of someone (perhaps a public figure) you admire who has died. What questions and feelings did that death raise for you?

Background

In Memoriam (Latin for "in memory of") is Tennyson's elegy for Arthur Henry Hallam, his closest friend at Cambridge and his sister's fiancé. Hallam, who died of a sudden brain seizure, was thought to be an extraordinarily promising young man, and his death shook the poet deeply. Tennyson struggled to survive not only his grief but also the religious doubt that Hallam's death bred. In the 131 separate lyrics of his elegy, which was written over seventeen years, Tennyson asks and gradually answers profound questions about life and death, religion and science, and the immortality of the soul.

Autumn Morning (19th century) by John Atkinson Grimshaw.

Christopher Wood Gallery, London.

Reaching All Students

Struggling Readers

Explain that while all the lyrics are about the death of Tennyson's dear friend, each expresses a different view or mood. Have students read each lyric separately, paraphrase it, and characterize its mood. Make sure students understand that the speaker, like all people who have endured a great loss, is going through a process of grieving and is trying to find meaning in his experience.

English Language Learners

Words such as *kine*, *empyreal*, and *freshlier* are archaic and likely to give English language learners difficulty. Encourage students to consult the side glosses and to keep a written log of unfamiliar words and their meanings.

from In Memoriam A.H.H.

Alfred, Lord Tennyson

55

The wish, that of the living whole
No life may fail beyond the grave,
Derives it not from what we have
The likest God within the soul?

Are God and Nature then at strife,
That Nature lends such evil dreams?
So careful of the type° she seems,
So careless of the single life,

That I, considering everywhere
Her secret meaning in her deeds,
And finding that of fifty seeds
She often brings but one to bear,

I falter where I firmly trod,
And falling with my weight of cares
Upon the great world's altar stairs
That slope through darkness up to God,

I stretch lame hands of faith, and grope,
And gather dust and chaff, and call
To what I feel is Lord of all,
And faintly trust the larger hope.°

56

"So careful of the type?" but no.
From scarpèd° cliff and quarried stone
She° cries, "A thousand types are gone;
I care for nothing, all shall go.

"Thou makest thine appeal to me:
I bring to life, I bring to death;
The spirit does but mean the breath:
I know no more." And he, shall he,

Man, her last work, who seemed so fair,
Such splendid purpose in his eyes,
Who rolled the psalm to wintry skies,
Who built him fanes° of fruitless prayer,

Who trusted God was love indeed
And love Creation's final law—
Though Nature, red in tooth and claw°
With ravine, shrieked against his creed—

7. type: species.

20. larger hope: Tennyson explains this phrase in his *Memoirs:* "that the whole human race would through, perhaps, ages of suffering, be at length purified and saved."

2. scarpèd: eroded to a steep slope.
3. She: Nature.

12. fanes: temples.

15. red . . . claw: The phrase refers to the view of all life as a ruthless struggle for survival.

Crossing the Curriculum

Science

In sections 55 and 56 of *In Memoriam A. H. H.,* Tennyson refers to his era's contrasting views of nature. Have interested students research and report on the various theories of natural science at the time (1835–1850), including Lyell's *Principles of Geology*. Then have them report on how today's scientists regard these Victorian theories.

Art

Invite students to create a collage or painting, using grief as a theme or commemorating the life of a deceased individual. Students may wish to work together to create a visual tribute to a public figure, such as Martin Luther King, Jr., or work individually to express a more personal loss. Encourage students to discuss how artistic expression might help a person cope with loss.

Resources

Audio CD Library

A dramatic reading of this selection is available in the *Audio CD Library:*

- Disc 13, Tracks 6, 7, 8, 9

Viewing and Representing

Fine Art Transparency

For a visual representation of questions of immortality, use the Fine Art transparency *The Doubt: Can These Dry Bones Live?* by Henry Alexander Bowler. See the *Viewing and Representing Transparencies and Worksheets:*

- Transparency 13
- Worksheet, p. 52

A Struggling Readers

Paraphrasing

Ask students to express the speaker's wish in their own words. [Possible responses: that life would not end at death; that the essence of a person would live on after death.]

B Cultural Connections

Science Versus Faith

In Victorian times, expanding knowledge of science began to challenge religious views of God and Nature. When the speaker finds God and Nature "at strife," he is embodying not just his own conflict but a prevailing conflict of his times.

C Reading Skills and Strategies

Drawing Conclusions

? Why does the speaker grasp only "dust" and "chaff" (that which is discarded when grain is winnowed)? [Possible responses: His faith is weak, and he doesn't find anything more sustaining.]

D Vocabulary Note

Word Origins

Tell students that the line "The spirit does but mean the breath" states an etymological fact. The Latin word *spiritus* means "breath"; it is the root of words that refer to breathing, such as *respiration* and *transpiration*.

E Struggling Readers

Breaking down Syntax

Tell students that in l. 8 Tennyson begins a question but then interrupts it. Where does he take up the question again? [in ll. 19–20] What is the question? [Shall he, man, be blown about the desert dust, or sealed within the iron hills?]

Literature and Society

It's not surprising that Queen Victoria, after the death of her beloved Prince Albert, found comfort in Tennyson's elegiac poem, for her world was shaken to the core by the loss of Albert, just as Tennyson was thrown into the most fundamental despair and faltering of faith by the loss of Hallam. In fact, Victoria sought and found innumerable ways to memoralize Albert. In addition to commissioning the Albert Memorial, she had Albert's speeches published, his biography written, and numerous pictures, statues, and busts commissioned. She even arranged for a plaque to be placed on the spot where he shot his last stag.

A Critical Thinking

Interpreting

? What is Tennyson suggesting by bringing up the violence of dragons? [Possible responses: The dragons fighting each other are mellow in comparison to a God who will let humans simply die and turn to dust. Or, humans without souls are out of step with the world, discordant, and more horrible than raging dragons.]

Literature and Society

The Victorian Reputation: The Queen and the Poet Laureate

Queen Victoria's reign (1837–1901) is often associated with prudery and acts of repression such as rejecting the works of bawdy Aphra Behn or, as in Thomas Bowdler's *Family Shakespeare,* censoring the exuberance of the Elizabethan bard. If, today, we imagine that Victorians were moralistic and restrained, the idea results in part from two nineteenth-century voices famous for their inconsolable yet dignified grief: Queen Victoria and Alfred, Lord Tennyson.

Grieving poet, grief-stricken queen. *In Memoriam A.H.H.* is Tennyson's tribute to Arthur Henry Hallam, the Cambridge soul mate who helped Tennyson find his poetic voice. Hallam died from a brain seizure at age twenty-two, and much of Tennyson's best poetry—"Ulysses," *Morte d'Arthur,* "Tears, Idle Tears"—indicates that Tennyson never recovered from the loss. One critic called *In Memoriam* "the solace and delight of every house where poetry is loved." England's queen put that solace to the test.

Queen Victoria's love of Prince Albert was legendary. Her private journal describes her 1840 wedding day as "bliss beyond belief" as she basked in her husband's "excessive love and affection." What is less well known is the frankness of Victoria's passion, which belies her reputation for stuffiness. "It is quite a pleasure to look at Albert when he gallops and valses [waltzes]," the queen wrote in 1839.

Who loved, who suffered countless ills,
  Who battled for the True, the Just,
  Be blown about the desert dust,
Or sealed within the iron hills?°

No more? A monster then, a dream,
  A discord. Dragons of the prime,
  That tare° each other in their slime,
Were mellow music matched with him.

O life as futile, then, as frail!
  O for thy° voice to soothe and bless!
  What hope of answer, or redress?
Behind the veil, behind the veil.°

20. **sealed . . . hills:** preserved like fossils in rock.

23. **tare:** archaic for "tore."

26. **thy:** Hallam's.

28. **veil:** the veil of death.

Skill Link

Evaluating the Credibility of Information Sources

As students work on various research projects suggested in this collection, it may be helpful to remind them of the following steps they can use to evaluate sources of information:

- Make sure the source is relevant and has information directly related to your research topic.
- Your source should be accurate and objective.
- The source should be up-to-date.
- Check Internet sources to make sure they are reliable.

Activity

Ask students to explore the library and community as well as the Internet to find five or six useful information sources for their research topics. Then have them evaluate their sources by checking them against the above criteria.

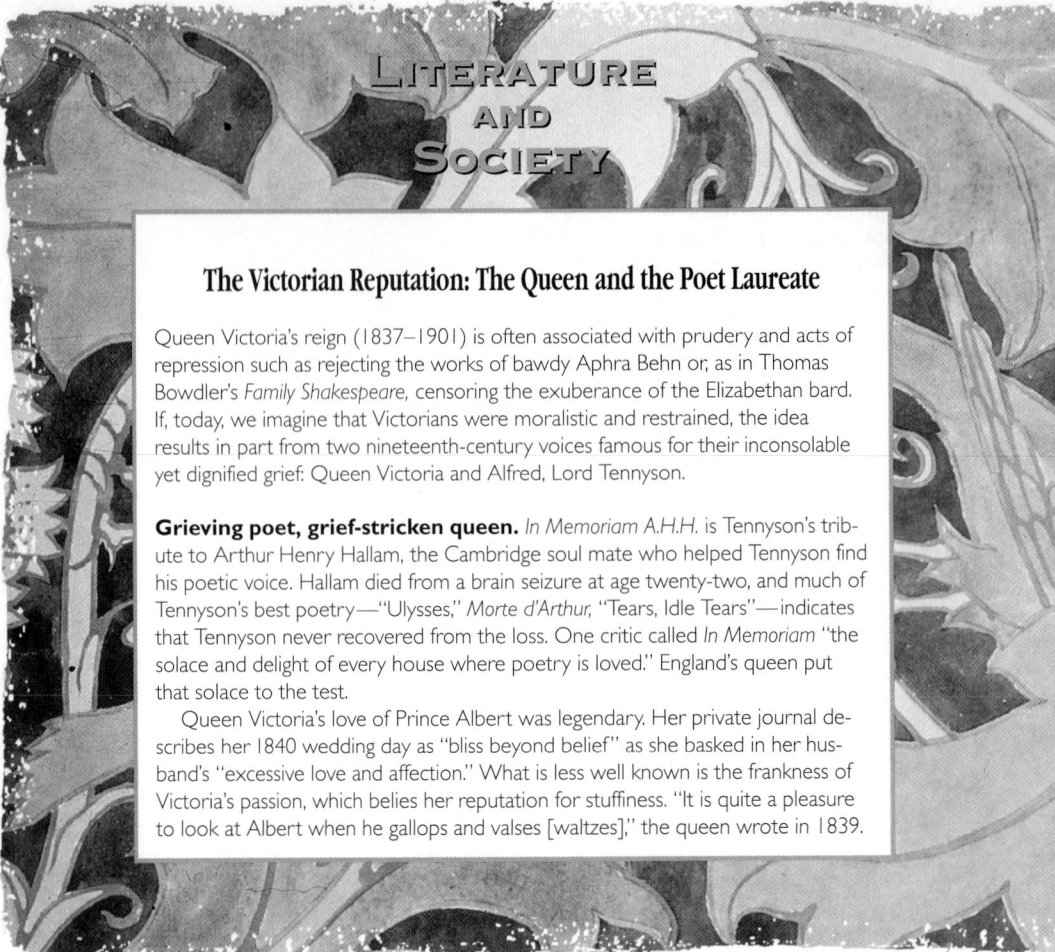

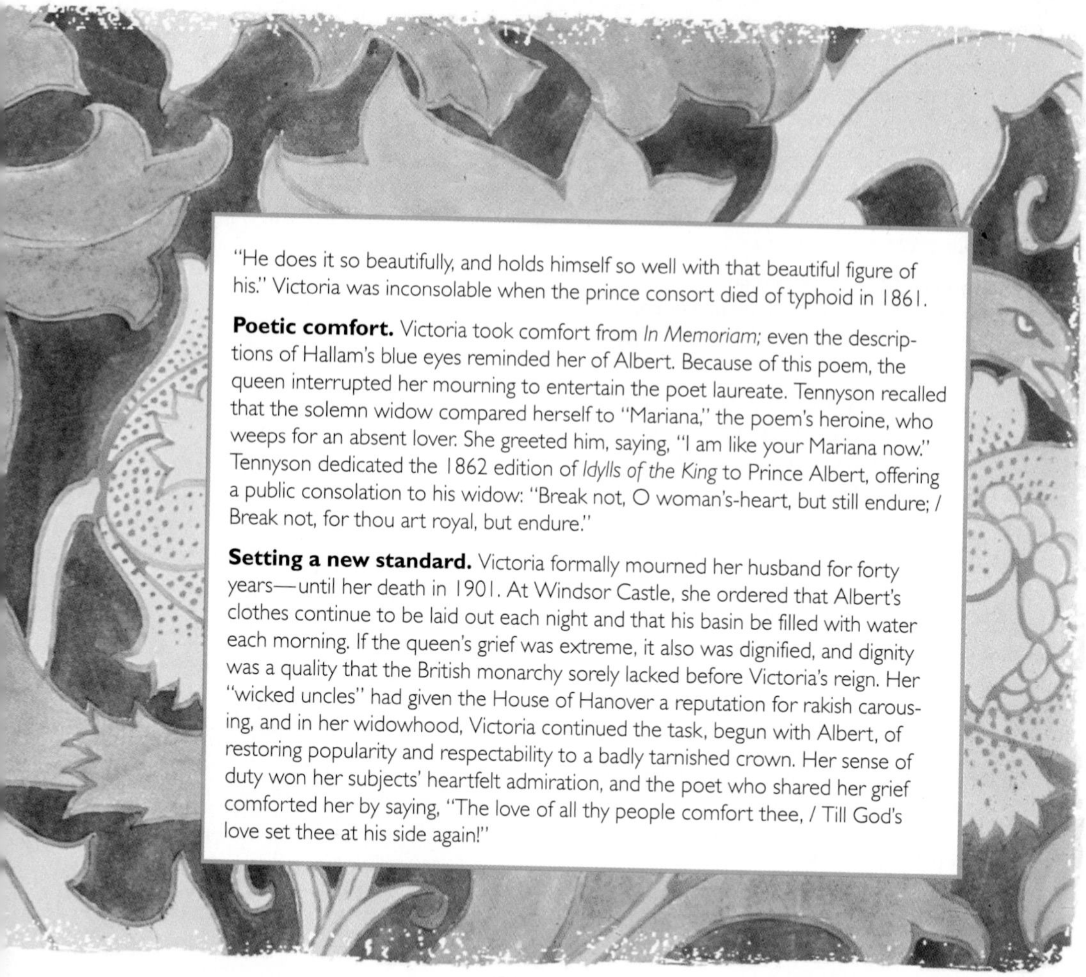

"He does it so beautifully, and holds himself so well with that beautiful figure of his." Victoria was inconsolable when the prince consort died of typhoid in 1861.

Poetic comfort. Victoria took comfort from *In Memoriam;* even the descriptions of Hallam's blue eyes reminded her of Albert. Because of this poem, the queen interrupted her mourning to entertain the poet laureate. Tennyson recalled that the solemn widow compared herself to "Mariana," the poem's heroine, who weeps for an absent lover. She greeted him, saying, "I am like your Mariana now." Tennyson dedicated the 1862 edition of *Idylls of the King* to Prince Albert, offering a public consolation to his widow: "Break not, O woman's-heart, but still endure; / Break not, for thou art royal, but endure."

Setting a new standard. Victoria formally mourned her husband for forty years—until her death in 1901. At Windsor Castle, she ordered that Albert's clothes continue to be laid out each night and that his basin be filled with water each morning. If the queen's grief was extreme, it also was dignified, and dignity was a quality that the British monarchy sorely lacked before Victoria's reign. Her "wicked uncles" had given the House of Hanover a reputation for rakish carousing, and in her widowhood, Victoria continued the task, begun with Albert, of restoring popularity and respectability to a badly tarnished crown. Her sense of duty won her subjects' heartfelt admiration, and the poet who shared her grief comforted her by saying, "The love of all thy people comfort thee, / Till God's love set thee at his side again!"

Design for printed linen (detail) (1893) by Charles Francis Annesley Voysey, printed by G. O. and J. Baker.
Victoria and Albert Museum, London.

95

By night we lingered on the lawn,
For underfoot the herb was dry;
And genial warmth; and o'er the sky
The silvery haze of summer drawn;

And calm that let the tapers° burn
Unwavering: Not a cricket chirred;
The brook alone far off was heard,
and on the board the fluttering urn.°

And bats went round in fragrant skies,
And wheeled or lit the filmy shapes°
That haunt the dusk, with ermine capes
And woolly breasts and beaded eyes;

5. **tapers:** candles.

8. **fluttering urn:** teapot or coffee urn heated by a candle.

10. **filmy shapes:** moths.

B Reading Skills and Strategies
Making Predictions

Lyric 95 is widely regarded by critics as the climax of the poem. Based on this information, ask students to predict what will happen in this lyric. [Students may predict a return to faith from the somber tone and mood of doubt in Lyrics 55 and 56.]

C Appreciating Language
Word Choice

? What is particularly effective about the word choices *chirred* and *fluttering?* [Possible responses: They help contrast the silence or distant, muffled sounds of the natural world with the intimate, comforting presence of domestic objects; they are both onomatopoetic in that their sounds imitate their meanings.]

D Critical Thinking
Analyzing Details

? What is happening in terms of time? [Time is passing. Evening is progressing into night.]

Skill Link

Analyzing and Responding to a Critical Review

According to literary critic Timothy Peltason, "*In Memoriam A.H.H.* is a poem about many things, but especially about the arranging impulse in human consciousness, about the conditions under which we find ourselves pressed into making new sense of experience. . . . For the poet, the impulse to arrange his life into some meaningful order is simultaneously the impulse to identify his own life with all other lives and with the course of human history. And so he finds his loss of Hallam analogous to the fall of man and looks forward to reunion with Hallam as he does to the 'far-off divine event' that is the goal of the race. Or he finds his history of trials and sufferings analogous to the geological history of the planet or the evolution of the species. Or he finds the model for his own expression of grief and renewal in the forms of pastoral and romantic elegy."

Work with students to analyze Peltason's comments, and ask students to decide whether or not they agree with his perspective.

Ⓐ Reading Skills and Strategies

Connecting with the Text

? Recall an instance when you saved a letter and reread it at a much later time. How did time change your perspective? [Possible responses: Time added a layer of memories; time made some events and responses seem less important yet brought the overall meaning of the experience into sharper focus.]

Ⓑ Appreciating Language

Oxymorons

"Silent-speaking words" is a compact verbal paradox, or oxymoron. Challenge students to find another oxymoron in this stanza ["love's dumb cry"] **and to comment on the effect of these expressions.** [Possible responses: By pairing contradictions, oxymorons suggest that things are not what they seem or that emotions defy logic.]

Ⓒ Advanced Learners

Making Connections

? In what ways is this passage what you would expect from a Romantic writer? [Possible responses: The speaker's vision, especially his sense of the "deep pulsations of the world" and of "Aeonian music," suggests the concerns of a Romantic writer. Here, the speaker, in line with the Romantics, sees Nature as a kindly force or as a source of solace; there is also some sense of finding God in Nature.]

Ⓓ Struggling Readers

Paraphrasing

? How would you paraphrase this stanza? [Possible response: Words, intellect, and memory all fail to convey what the speaker has just experienced.]

Ⓔ English Language Learners

Archaic Words and Spellings

Point out the word "knolls." Ask students to use context clues to figure out its meaning. [mounds] **Point out that the initial *k* is left over from a time in the development of English when every letter was pronounced.**

While now we sang old songs that pealed
  From knoll to knoll, where, couched at ease,
  The white kine° glimmered, and the trees
Laid their dark arms about the field.

But when those others, one by one,
  Withdrew themselves from me and night,
  And in the house light after light
Went out, and I was all alone,

A hunger seized my heart; I read
  Of that glad year which once had been,
  In those fallen leaves which kept their green,
The noble letters of the dead.

And strangely on the silence broke
  The silent-speaking words, and strange
  Was love's dumb cry defying change
To test his worth; and strangely spoke

The faith, the vigor, bold to dwell
  On doubts that drive the coward back,
  And keen through wordy snares to track
Suggestion to her inmost cell.

So word by word, and line by line,
  The dead man touched me from the past,
  And all at once it seemed at last
The living soul° was flashed on mine,

And mine in this was wound, and whirled
  About empyreal° heights of thought,
  And came on that which is, and caught
The deep pulsations of the world,

Aeonian° music measuring out
  The steps of Time—the shocks of Chance—
  The blows of Death. At length my trance
Was canceled, stricken through with doubt.

Vague words! but ah, how hard to frame
  In matter-molded forms of speech,
  Or even for intellect to reach
Through memory that which I became;

Till now the doubtful dusk revealed
  The knolls once more where, couched at ease,
  The white kine glimmered, and the trees
Laid their dark arms about the field;

And sucked from out the distant gloom
  A breeze began to tremble o'er
  The large leaves of the sycamore,
And fluctuate all the still perfume,

15. kine: archaic for "cattle."

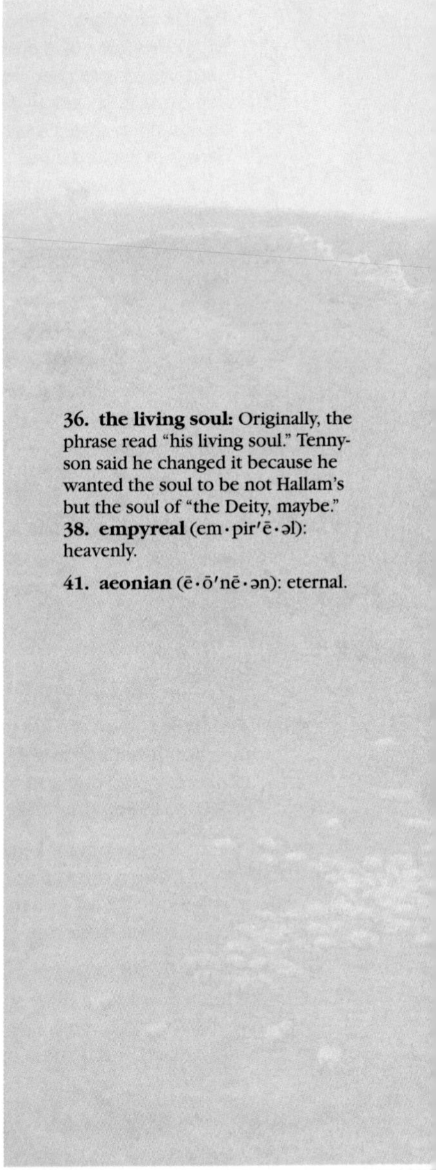

36. the living soul: Originally, the phrase read "his living soul." Tennyson said he changed it because he wanted the soul to be not Hallam's but the soul of "the Deity, maybe."
38. empyreal (em·pir′ē·əl): heavenly.

41. aeonian (ē·ō′nē·ən): eternal.

Making the Connections

Connecting to the Theme: "Love and Loss"

Students may discuss these questions:

- **How do the clashes between science and religion in Tennyson's time help to intensify his sense of loss?** [The comforting security of unquestioning faith has been lost; certainty has been replaced with unsettling doubt.]
- **Where do you find the sense of personal loss most keen? Where do you find it relatively manageable?** [Personal loss is most keen when the speaker can find no larger context in which to understand his friend's death. His grief is most managable when he senses the unity of all in God.]
- **How do feelings of love and connection both intensify loss and help to alleviate it?** [His love for Hallam intensifies the speaker's grief when his friend dies, but his sense of connection with all things in Lyric 130 gives him hope.]

And gathering freshlier overhead
    Rocked the full-foliaged elms, and swung
    The heavy-folded rose, and flung
The lilies to and fro, and said,

"The dawn, the dawn," and died away;
    And East and West, without a breath,
    Mixed their dim lights, like life and death,
To broaden into boundless day. **F**

View on the Coast of Cornwall (detail) (19th century) by Frank Goodwin.
Maidstone Museum and Art Gallery, Kent, England.

Assessing Learning

Check Test: Short Answers

1. **Why, at first, does the speaker find no comfort for his grief in Nature?** [Nature seems uncaring about individual survival.]
2. **Where does he later learn that answers and comfort lie?** ["behind the veil"]
3. **In Lyric 95, what activity prompts a vision that takes the speaker beyond his time and place?** [reading letters that Hallam once wrote to him]
4. **In Lyric 130, where does the speaker find his friend?** [Hallam is now "mixed" with God and Nature. All are one in the world the speaker inhabits.]
5. **How would you describe the development, or movement, of the speaker's feelings in these stanzas?** [He moves from a confused sense of loss and troubling doubts about God and Nature to a reaffirmation of life's essential unity and purposefulness.]

F Appreciating Language
Poetic Expression

? How does Tennyson combine image and symbol in this stanza to create a sense of renewal? [Possible response: He uses the image of the dawn breaking into day. He relies upon classical symbols of life and death: the East (place of the rising sun and therefore of life) and the West (place of the setting sun and therefore of death). He ends with the broadening into boundless day, or the sense of light flooding the horizon, bringing hope and fresh possibilities.]

(A) Critical Thinking
Synthesizing

? How does Tennyson's speaker resolve the conflict between God and Nature, which caused him such anguish earlier in the poem? [Possible response: He concludes that his departed friend not only is with God but remains a part of the physical world that the speaker inhabits.]

(B) Reading Skills and Strategies
Identifying Cause and Effect

? How have the speaker's experiences changed his attitude toward his departed friend? [Possible response: He finds that his love is greater than ever before and he feels his friend is still with him.]

Resources

Formal Assessment

- Selection Test, p. 161

Making Meanings

First Thoughts [Respond]

1. Possibilities include hopeful, blessed, renewed by nature. The speaker feels a renewed sense of faith and believes he is reunited with his lost friend.

Shaping Interpretations [Interpret]

2. The speaker wishes to believe in life after death but finds no evidence of it in Nature. Nature has no regard for individual life.
3. Nature claims she does not care. She brings life and death to all.
4. The setting is the lawn of a country house on a summer night, where people gather and sing. At the poem's end, the speaker is alone in the same or a similar setting but at dawn.
5. In the earlier lyrics, Nature is portrayed as a cold, unfeeling force that cares nothing about an individual soul. In Lyric 130, Nature is seen as a positive force no longer in conflict with God. The speaker senses his friend Hallam's soul diffused throughout Nature; images of air, water, sunrise, sunset, star, and flower are all positive.
6. Lyrics 55 and 56 express the speaker's doubt and despair and Lyric 130 expresses his joyful celebration of faith in life and death. In this change of heart, as well as that of Lyric 95, the speaker returns to the original scene—but with a new perspective.

130

Thy° voice is on the rolling air;
   I hear thee where the waters run;
   Thou standest in the rising sun,
And in the setting thou art fair.

What art thou then? I cannot guess;
   But though I seem in star and flower
   To feel thee some diffusive power,
I do not therefore love thee less.

My love involves the love before;
   My love is vaster passion now;
   Though mixed with God and Nature thou,
I seem to love thee more and more.

Far off thou art, but ever nigh;
   I have thee still, and I rejoice;
   I prosper, circled with thy voice;
I shall not lose thee though I die.

1. **Thy:** Hallam's.

Making Meanings

First Thoughts

1. What word or phrase would you use to describe the speaker's final emotional state? Why?

Shaping Interpretations

2. In Lyric 55, why does the speaker envision the possibility that God and Nature may be "at strife" (line 5)? What complaint does the speaker voice against Nature in this poem?
3. How does Nature answer this complaint in Lyric 56?
4. Describe the **setting** at the beginning of Lyric 95. How does this setting contrast with the setting at the end of the poem?
5. What is the difference between the aspects of Nature described in Lyrics 55 and 56 and those in Lyric 130?
6. Lyric 95 moves from a local scene to "empyreal heights of thought" to the original scene. How is this movement related to the speaker's mood in Lyrics 55 and 56 as well as in Lyric 130?
7. Describe the **rhyme scheme** of these lyrics. How do the poem's short lines and stanzas and the rhyme scheme affect you as the reader?
8. Did Tennyson address the issues you raised in your Quickwrite notes? Were any of his questions, worries, or doubts surprising to you? Why or why not?

Challenging the Text

9. This poem was popular because it satisfied readers who believed poetry should deal with serious subjects, such as grieving. Do you agree or disagree with such expectations for poetry? What do you think are the proper functions of poetry?

7. The rhyme scheme is *abba*. Students may say the short lines and stanzas and the regular rhyme sustain their interest and allow them to hear the poem's music.
8. Students may have addressed issues like these: a sense of wavering or renewed faith, of reassurance through a transformative experience, or of a cold, uncaring universe.

Challenging the Text [Apply/Evaluate]

9. Students may say the purpose of poetry is to delight the senses, amuse the mind, expand the imagination, stir emotions, or discuss serious subjects. You might refer students to various examples of "ars poetica" (the art of poetry): Archibald MacLeish's "Ars Poetica," Marianne Moore's "Poetry," and Wallace Stevens's "Of Modern Poetry" are all in *Elements of Literature, Fifth Course*.

Before You Read

ULYSSES

Make the Connection

Acting Your Age

An old adage says that youth is wasted on the young—that only older people have the experience and perspective to appreciate the joys of youthful health and exuberance. Stereotypes of "proper" activities for older adults may not take into account the skills and talents honed in a lifetime of living. Tennyson's adventure-seeking Ulysses may appear to be pursuing a young man's dream, but how can he abandon the passions of a lifetime merely because of his age?

Quickwrite

Some famous singers, dancers, and athletes continue their careers long after their skills have peaked. What (besides money) do you think motivates them, and would you do the same in their place?

Background

Ulysses (*Odysseus* in Greek) is one of the Greek leaders who fought in the ten-year-long Trojan War. Homer's epic poem *The Odyssey* tells of his equally long journey home from Troy to Ithaca. In Tennyson's poem, Ulysses, an old king, is at home with his wife and son, Telemachus (tə•lem′ə•kəs). After a tumultuous life of both marvels and horrors, the old king might finally rest—either thankfully or regretfully. But here Ulysses wants to leave home again for a final journey. He knows lost youth cannot be regained, but he seeks something else.

Tennyson said of this poem, "'Ulysses' was written soon after Arthur Hallam's death, and gave my feeling about the need of going forward, and braving the struggle of life perhaps more simply than anything in *In Memoriam*."

Ulysses Deriding Polyphemus (19th century) by J.M.W. Turner.

The National Gallery, London.

Summary ■■

The aging Ulysses recalls his past adventures, both happy and sad, and longs for the intensity of his younger days. He rejects the security of a settled life and desires instead to keep testing his limits and expanding the boundaries of his experience. In the second half of the poem, Ulysses speaks of passing his responsibilities as a ruler on to his mild, reliable son, Telemachus. Ulysses realizes, however, that his true soulmates are his fellow mariners with whom he shared his former toils and troubles. It is with them that he wishes to set sail again in search of "some work of noble note."

RESPONDING TO THE ART

J. M. W. Turner (1775–1851) continued the tradition of Romantic painting by expressing human emotions through depictions of nature, especially in landscapes and sea settings. The intensity of the background often dissolves the outline and structure of his subjects (like the ships in this painting) into near liquid impressions.

Activity. What attitude toward nature does this painting express? [awe, admiration] Where do human beings seem to fit in Turner's vision of nature? [subordinate to natural forces] See if students can find Polyphemus, the Cyclops. [He is up on the crag, hurling a rock at the Greeks.]

Reaching All Students

Struggling Readers

Ask students to stop after ll. 5, 17, 32, 43, and 57 and summarize what they have read. Be sure they understand how Ulysses feels at each point about his present and past experiences. When they finish reading, ask them to speculate about Ulysses' future.

English Language Learners

Pair English language learners with more proficient English speakers to help them with uncommon phrasing and rarely used vocabulary, such as "it little profits" (it does little good), and, in l. 10, "scudding drifts" (wind-driven spray). Also call their attention to the side glosses.

Advanced Learners

Have students relate "Ulysses" to "Do Not Go Gentle into That Good Night" (p. 1039), a poem written by Dylan Thomas a century after Tennyson's poem. Encourage students to consider whether Thomas's line "Old age should burn and rave at close of day" describes Tennyson's Ulysses. Have students discuss whether Ulysses fits Thomas's classification of people who "rage against the dying of the light."

A Struggling Readers

Summarizing

? How would you summarize Ulysses' complaint in the first five lines? [Possible response: Ulysses is tired of life at home, where all he does is spend time with his wife and attempt to govern people who are difficult to rule.]

B Exploring the Historical Period

Victorians as Explorers

Many of the values Ulysses expresses (such as his pride in having seen so much of the world and in having lived such an active, adventurous life) were values of the age in which the poem was written and perhaps of Tennyson himself. Victorians, in general, were eager explorers of little-known areas of the globe and of the new intellectual terrain opened up by scientific inquiry.

C Reading Skills and Strategies

Comparing/Contrasting

? How is Telemachus like or unlike his father? [Possible responses: Telemachus appears to respect convention; he willingly does what is expected of him. He is characterized by "slow prudence" and "soft degrees." Ulysses, on the other hand, was once, and still desires to be, spontaneous, adventurous, resourceful, and unconventional.] You might explain that Telemachus can be seen as representing another aspect of Victorian life, the ordered world of life at home.

Resources

Formal Assessment

- Selection Test, p. 163

Ulysses

Alfred, Lord Tennyson

It little profits that an idle king,
By this still hearth, among these barren crags,
Matched with an aged wife, I mete and dole°
Unequal laws unto a savage race,
That hoard, and sleep, and feed, and know not me.
I cannot rest from travel; I will drink
Life to the lees.° All times I have enjoyed
Greatly, have suffered greatly, both with those
That loved me, and alone; on shore, and when
Through scudding drifts the rainy Hyades°
Vexed the dim sea. I am become a name;
For always roaming with a hungry heart
Much have I seen and known,—cities of men
And manners, climates, councils, governments,
Myself not least, but honored of them all,—
And drunk delight of battle with my peers,
Far on the ringing plains of windy Troy.
I am a part of all that I have met;
Yet all experience is an arch wherethrough
Gleams that untraveled world whose margin fades
Forever and forever when I move.
How dull it is to pause, to make an end,
To rust unburnished, not to shine in use!
As though to breathe were life! Life piled on life
Were all too little, and of one to me
Little remains; but every hour is saved
From that eternal silence, something more,
A bringer of new things; and vile it were
For some three suns to store and hoard myself,
And this gray spirit yearning in desire
To follow knowledge like a sinking star,
Beyond the utmost bound of human thought.
This is my son, mine own Telemachus,
To whom I leave the scepter and the isle,°—
Well-loved of me, discerning to fulfill
This labor, by slow prudence to make mild
A rugged people, and through soft degrees
Subdue them to the useful and the good.
Most blameless is he, centered in the sphere
Of common duties, decent not to fail
In offices of tenderness, and pay
Meet° adoration to my household gods,
When I am gone. He works his work, I mine.

3. mete and dole: measure and give out.

7. lees: dregs or sediment.

10. Hyades (hī′ə·dēz′): stars that were thought to indicate rainy weather.

34. isle: Ithaca, Ulysses' island kingdom off the west coast of Greece.

42. meet: proper.

Using Students' Strengths

Intrapersonal Learners

Encourage groups of three students to engage in a silent dialogue about Ulysses' goals and desires. Each member of the group can assume the identity of either Ulysses, Telemachus, or Ulysses' wife. Have students, in character, converse by passing a sheet of paper back and forth with their responses to this question: "Why can't Ulysses be content with his past adventures?"

Interpersonal Learners

Invite students to role-play a conversation between a twenty-first-century Ulysses and his wife. Direct students to create a Ulysses who is faithful in character to the Ulysses in Tennyson's poem. The wife they create, however, should express values more typical of today's woman than of Homer's Penelope or Tennyson's Victorian version of the classically faithful wife.

There lies the port; the vessel puffs her sail;
There gloom the dark, broad seas. My mariners,
Souls that have toiled, and wrought, and thought with me,—
That ever with a frolic welcome took
The thunder and the sunshine, and opposed
Free hearts, free foreheads,—you and I are old;
Old age hath yet his honor and his toil.
Death closes all; but something ere the end,
Some work of noble note, may yet be done,
Not unbecoming men that strove with Gods.
The lights begin to twinkle from the rocks;
The long day wanes; the slow moon climbs; the deep
Moans round with many voices. Come, my friends,
'Tis not too late to seek a newer world.
Push off, and sitting well in order smite
The sounding furrows;° for my purpose holds
To sail beyond the sunset, and the baths
Of all the western stars, until I die.
It may be that the gulfs will wash us down;
It may be we shall touch the Happy Isles,°
And see the great Achilles,° whom we knew.
Though much is taken, much abides; and though
We are not now that strength which in old days
Moved earth and heaven, that which we are, we are,—
One equal temper of heroic hearts,
Made weak by time and fate, but strong in will
To strive, to seek, to find, and not to yield.

59. **smite . . . furrows:** row against the waves.

63. **Happy Isles:** in Greek mythology, Elysium (ē·liz′ē·əm), where dead heroes lived for eternity.
64. **Achilles** (ə·kil′ēz′): Greek warrior and leader in the Trojan War.

MAKING MEANINGS

First Thoughts

1. "Ulysses" is about a brave, or foolish, response to the securities and comforts of an orderly life very like that of middle-class mid-Victorian England. What do you think of Ulysses' decision? (Refer to your Quickwrite notes.)

Shaping Interpretations

2. How does Ulysses **contrast** his past and present lives? From this comparison, what conclusions can you draw about his values?
3. In lines 19–21, what does Ulysses claim about "all experience"?
4. Whom does Ulysses address in the second half of the poem? In the concluding lines of the poem, what qualities does he say that he shares with his mariners?
5. Where does Tennyson emphasize Ulysses' great endurance and insatiable curiosity? How would you **characterize** Ulysses?
6. Find Ulysses' references to his wife and son, and tell what you think his words reveal about his underlying feelings toward them. Then, explain whether you accept Ulysses' point of view.
7. What do you think Ulysses is determined not to "yield" to (line 70)?

Connecting with the Text

8. What lines in this poem do you think would encourage someone who needed to go forward despite the temptation to give up the struggle?

Challenging the Text

9. Ulysses knows that his journey is like pursuing the horizon. Do you think he is foolish for setting out on a journey he cannot complete? Explain.

D Reading Skills and Strategies

Comparing/Contrasting

? How does Ulysses' attitude toward his companions contrast with his attitude toward his son? [Possible response: Ulysses identifies with his companions and their exploits and feels close to them. Ulysses may love his son, may even admire him, but he does not want to live like him.]

E Humanities Connection

Achilles

Achilles was the greatest of the Greek warriors who fought against Troy; his death caused great mourning among his comrades. Achilles may represent Tennyson's friend Arthur Hallam, the subject of *In Memoriam A. H. H.* (pp. 815–820).

MAKING MEANINGS

First Thoughts [Respond]

1. Students may regard the decision as courageous and admirable because it shows strong will and determination; as selfish because it would cause Ulysses to leave his family and kingdom again; or, as foolish because he cannot repeat in old age his youthful triumphs.

Shaping Interpretations [Interpret]

2. His present life is boring and unsatisfying to him compared with his past. Students may say Ulysses values adventure over security.
3. Experience is an arch through which he sees a boundless, untraveled world.
4. Ulysses first addresses his son Telemachus and then his loyal sailors, comrades in past adventures. Ulysses says he shares a heroic heart and strong will with his sailors.
5. Lines 6–7, 12, 30–32, 45–48, 51–52, 56–65, and 70. Students may see Ulysses as immature or may view him as desiring to live life fully.
6. In l. 3, he calls his wife "aged," suggesting she no longer excites him. He says he loves his son, but he does not wish to remain with him. Students may agree with Ulysses since the poem is written from his perspective, or they may step back and see flaws in his inability to let go of the past.
7. Ulysses is determined not to yield to old age, to domestic comfort, or to complacency.

Getting Students Involved

Enrichment Activity

Planning the Journey. If Ulysses sails away again, where might he go? Will he return to the scenes of his previous adventures or will he set out for new territory? Have students research the route of Homer's Ulysses and consult historical atlases to plot an itinerary for Ulysses. Ask them to make a presentation to the class, using maps and other graphic devices.

Connecting with the Text [Apply]

8. Students may suggest ll. 56–57 or ll. 65–70.

Challenging the Text [Synthesize]

9. Students may judge Ulysses' goals as foolish and inappropriate to his age and station; or, they may admire his drive and determination to continue the life he loves.

Summary ■

In this poem of farewell, crossing the bar, or leaving the last shoal before the open sea, stands for dying. The speaker represents the passage from life to death as a gentle, inevitable pull of the tide. He requests no "moaning" or "sadness of farewell" from those left behind and expresses the hope of seeing his "Pilot" when he reaches his destination.

Resources

Audio CD Library

A dramatic reading of this selection is available in the *Audio CD Library:*

- Disc 13, Track 11

Formal Assessment

- Selection Test, p. 164

Ⓐ Elements of Literature

Imagery

? The first stanza establishes the two controlling metaphors of the poem: Crossing the bar represents dying and the sea represents the mystery of whatever comes after death. What might the auditory image "moaning of the bar" suggest? [Possible responses: It may refer to the cries of people who will mourn the speaker's departure; more literally, it may be the sound of waves or the hull of a boat dragging across the sandbar.]

Ⓑ Appreciating Language

Varying Line Lengths

? What do you think Tennyson was trying to accomplish by alternating long and short lines? [Possible responses: He was imitating the ebb and flow of the tides; he wished to surprise his readers and thereby hold their interest.]

Ⓒ Reading Skills and Strategies

Making Generalizations

? How would you characterize the speaker's attitude toward death? [Possible responses: The speaker is awed by the mysteries of death and the afterlife but determined to meet both with dignity; he is at peace with the natural cycle of life and death.]

Before You Read

CROSSING THE BAR

Make the Connection

Riding the Tide

In the last forty years of his life, Tennyson lived in the country like an affluent gentleman. Occasionally, he went to London to walk about in his black cloak and broad-brimmed hat and meet with distinguished writers, scientists, churchmen, politicians, and sometimes the queen. Tourists hung around his country house on the Isle of Wight and climbed trees to get a glimpse of him. People sent him mountains of poetry; he once estimated that he had received a verse for every three minutes of his life. How would you expect such a person to face death?

Quickwrite

What do you predict the images of harbor, bar (sandbar), and sea in this poem will stand for?

Background

Tennyson wrote this poem in 1889, at the age of eighty, while crossing the channel that separates England from the Isle of Wight. Before his death in 1892, he directed that the poem be printed at the end of all editions of his collected verse.

Crossing the Bar

Alfred, Lord Tennyson

Ⓐ
Sunset and evening star,
  And one clear call for me!
And may there be no moaning of the bar,
  When I put out to sea,

Ⓑ
But such a tide as moving seems asleep,
  Too full for sound and foam,
When that° which drew from out the boundless deep
  Turns again home.

Twilight and evening bell,
  And after that the dark!
And may there be no sadness of farewell,
  When I embark;

Ⓒ
For though from out our bourne° of Time and Place
  The flood may bear me far,
I hope to see my Pilot face to face
  When I have crossed the bar.

7. **that:** the soul.
13. **bourne** (bōrn): archaic for "boundary."

Sunset on Wet Sand (1845) by J.M.W. Turner. Watercolor over pencil.

The Whitworth Art Gallery, University of Manchester, England.

Making the Connections

Connecting to the Theme: "Love and Loss"

The speaker's acceptance of death implies a life well lived, presumably full of love but inevitably bringing loss and separation. The poem also suggests that death is a part of the natural ebb and flow of life and may not be so much a loss as a return "home" where a loving "Pilot" awaits.

Assessing Learning

Standardized Test Preparation

For practice with ACT and SAT formats, see

- *Preparation for College Admission Exams,* p. 39

MAKING MEANINGS

First Thoughts

1. Do you find this poem personally comforting, or do you feel some other emotion? Explain.

Shaping Interpretations

2. Explain how Tennyson **extends** his **metaphor** of life as a voyage. How close did you come in your Quickwrite notes to predicting what those three images would stand for?
3. Who might the "Pilot" be in line 15?
4. Paraphrase each of the speaker's wishes and hopes, and explain what you think they show about the feelings of an older person. Is the speaker accepting, afraid, or both?
5. What mental image does Tennyson's poem create for you? Describe it.

CHOICES: Building Your Portfolio

Writer's Notebook

1. Collecting Ideas for an Evaluation

Suppose you're a critic assigned to review one of Tennyson's poems. Your review can be high praise, harsh criticism, or some judgment in between. Which poem could you sink your teeth into? State whether you'll give the poem a positive or negative evaluation, and write the quality or element of the poem that influences your initial reaction. Save your work for the Writer's Workshop on page 899.

Responding to a Generalization

2. An Overview

Tennyson's poems are about how to respond to the losses and disorders of love, death, old age, the passing of leaders, and challenges to old standards of political and moral authority.

In an essay, respond to this generalization about Tennyson's poems. Take your evidence from the poems in this collection.

Evaluating a Revision

3. New Ending, New Meaning

When Tennyson published the first version of "The Lady of Shalott" in 1832, the last stanza ended thus:

"The web was woven curiously
The charm is broken utterly
Draw near and fear not—this is I,
The Lady of Shalott."

In an essay, compare this scenario to what occurs in the last stanza on page 812. What do you think of Tennyson's revision? Which ending do you think is more moving? Explain.

Comparing and Contrasting Heroes

4. Ulysses Across Time

Research the plot of Homer's *Odyssey,* and read portions of the epic, especially from Books 8, 13, and 19. In an essay, compare and contrast Homer's and Tennyson's hero figures. At the end of your essay, draw conclusions about what Tennyson's alterations to Homer's text reveal about Tennyson and his times.

Creative Writing

5. Man to Man

Write Telemachus's reply (poetry or prose) to his father's speech in "Ulysses." How does Telemachus feel about his father's leaving him and his mother for more adventures?

Literature and Film

6. Visualizing the Enchantment

"The Lady of Shalott" is vividly descriptive. Sketch a storyboard of shot-by-shot illustrations for a filmed version of the story. Show Tennyson's sparse dialogue (including the "whispers" of the curse) in captions.

MAKING MEANINGS

First Thoughts [Respond]

1. Students may sense the comfort the speaker feels; some may find the talk of death depressing.

Shaping Interpretations [Interpret]

2. The voyage is a metaphor for leaving the harbor of life for the sea (death and perhaps an afterlife). The sandbar may be the transition between life and death.
3. The "Pilot" is God or Divine Providence.
4. The speaker hopes there will be no sadness when it is time for him to go; he hopes to see his Pilot when he reaches the other side. Student responses to an older person's view of death will vary; many will agree that the speaker accepts death and that faith has given him hope of life after death.
5. Students' images will vary. Remind them to refer to the text to stimulate their imagination.

Grading Timesaver

Rubrics for each Choices assignment appear on p. 170 in the *Portfolio Management System.*

CHOICES: Building Your Portfolio

1. **Writer's Notebook** Suggest that students read some book reviews from their local newspaper before they get started.
2. **Responding to a Generalization** Students may benefit from making a chart that lists reasons to support and oppose this generalization.
3. **Evaluating a Revision** Students may wish to brainstorm in small groups or as a class to come up with reasons for why a particular ending is more moving.
4. **Comparing and Contrasting Heroes** Before they begin writing, suggest that students work in pairs to create a Venn diagram of the similarities and differences between the heroes.
5. **Creative Writing** If students decide to write their response in poetry form, they may wish to consider writing it in imitation of Tennyson's style.
6. **Literature and Film** Make sure students cover all the major events of the poem in their storyboard.

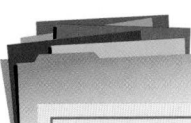

Spotlight On

This feature traces the recurrence of King Arthur in literature as an ideal of chivalrous behavior. It also charts the renewal of interest in Arthurian legend among the Victorians. Unlike some earlier interpretations, which stressed Arthur's physical prowess or mystical dimensions, Arthur, for the Victorians, was an enlightened and mature leader. In the excerpt from Tennyson's *Morte d'Arthur,* the dying Arthur humbly requests God's mercy and gracefully accepts the new order which will follow him. This contrasts with Thomas Malory's fifteenth-century version of Arthur's death (p. 171), in which Arthur seems not to die exactly but to fade from the scene until needed again. After discussing the text, challenge students to find a modern re-creation of the myth in art or popular culture and comment on its interpretation.

Ⓐ Literary Connections

Thomas Malory

Malory borrowed from French tales of the King Arthur legend to create *Le Morte Darthur* (The Death of Arthur), which is the first real masterpiece of English prose. Malory's story centers on Arthur, who as a child gained a kingdom by pulling a magic sword from a stone. Arthur is guided by the magician Merlin as he fights to create order in a lawless land.

Ⓑ Literary Connections

Tennyson Takes on the Legend

Tennyson called the Arthurian legend "the greatest of all poetical subjects." When he was just twenty-four, Tennyson set out to write an epic about Arthur. After five years, he had written only one poem, *Morte d'Arthur.* Later, Tennyson incorporated this poem into the long cycle of narrative poems he called *The Idylls of the King,* where it is renamed "The Passing of Arthur." Completed in 1888, *The Idylls of the King* was truly a life's work: Its composition spanned fifty years, and the scope of its twelve books is no less than the rise and fall of an entire civilization.

Be sure students discuss the famous lines in the episode from *Morte d'Arthur* excerpted here, especially "The old order changeth, yielding place to new, / And God fulfills Himself in many ways, / Lest one good custom should corrupt the world" and "More things are wrought by prayer / Than this world dreams of. . . ."

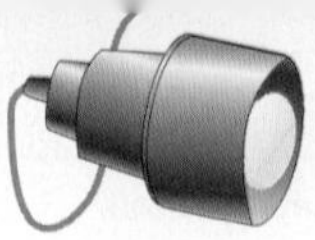

SPOTLIGHT ON

The Enduring Arthurian Legend

Chivalry rediscovered. Blame King George IV, who remodeled Windsor Castle with the feudal embellishments of arms and chivalric heraldry. Or perhaps blame the immensely popular Sir Walter Scott, whose novels were packed full of jousting tournaments and knights errant. With the help of these influential figures and many more, the ideals of King Arthur's royal city, Camelot, flourished in the nineteenth century. The model of chivalry had seemed barbarous in the elegant, classical eighteenth century; however, as scholars looked back on English history, they rediscovered fascinating rituals and antiquities. Historians republished medieval ballads, printed illustrations of medieval architecture, and, in the process, piqued public interest in the Middle Ages. Tennyson's "The Lady of Shalott" (page 808) is just one example of the nineteenth century's medieval mania, which reintroduced images of "many-towered Camelot" into popular culture.

Hope, honor, and nobility. Chivalry's message was, in part, one of hope. Kenelm Henry Digby's 1844 manual on chivalry asserts that "the noble fellowship of the Round Table cannot be broken forever; but fresh aspirants will again appear to . . . keep ahead of the degraded world." In describing the renewal of "noble fellowship," Digby provides a Victorian interpretation of an enduring English legend. The myth of King Arthur combines Christian morals with ancient pagan fertility rites to form a fascinating story of romance, magic, and betrayal. Ⓐ Key to an understanding of the Round Table and its code of chivalry is the work of Sir Thomas Malory (see page 169).

Ⓑ Tennyson made the story of Arthur into a kind of parable about the ideal political leader. Here is how Tennyson describes Arthur as he faces death. The king is mortally wounded. Sir Bedivere, who knows Arthur will die, remains with him.

> Then loudly cried the bold Sir Bedivere,
> "Ah! My Lord Arthur, whither shall I go?
> Where shall I hide my forehead and my eyes?
> For now I see the true old times are dead,
> When every morning brought a noble chance,
> And every chance brought out a noble knight.
> Such times have been not since the light
> that led
> The holy Elders with the gift of myrrh.
> But now the whole Round Table is dissolved
> Which was an image of the mighty world;
> And I, the last, go forth companionless,
> And the days darken round me, and the
> years,
> Among new men, strange faces, other minds."
> And slowly answered Arthur from the
> barge:
> "The old order changeth, yielding place
> to new,
> And God fulfills Himself in many ways,
> Lest one good custom should corrupt the
> world.
> Comfort thyself: what comfort is in me?
> I have lived my life, and that which I
> have done
> May He within Himself make pure! but thou,
> If thou shouldst never see my face again,
> Pray for my soul. More things are wrought
> by prayer
> Than this world dreams of. . . ."
>
> —Alfred, Lord Tennyson,
> *from Morte d'Arthur*

Professional Notes

Critical Comment:
Mania for Arthurian Mist

J. B. Priestley explains the lure of the Arthurian as an antidote to industrialization in Victorian England: "From the poets and painters . . . there came a kind of Arthurian colored mist, soon hovering over one grim industrial city after another. . . . There might be even more violence in these legends than in the dark, drunken streets behind the mills, but it was a dream violence, in which no real blood flowed, no guts spilled out. Here was sex but it was as delicate as that of flowers. . . . Everything happened in an entrancing landscape of fields rich with blossom or harvest, shining white towns, dusky forests between magicians' towers and huge castles, milky lakes darkening with enchantment, a land from which all railways, black factories, pitheads, and cholera-stricken hovels had vanished. . . ."

© Manchester City Art Galleries, England.

La Mort d'Arthur (1860) by Jones Archer. Oil on millboard (17″ × 20″).

According to Tennyson, the mission of the knights is to "live pure, speak true, right wrong, [and] follow the king." Sir Lancelot becomes the ideal of chivalrous behavior. Sir Ector describes Lancelot as "the courteoust knight that ever bore shield! And . . . the kindest man that ever struck with sword."

Beguiling contradictions. The story of Camelot is a bundle of contradictions. Lancelot, the perfect flower of knighthood, betrays his king by falling in love with Queen Guinevere. The revelation of their affair plunges the court into a war in which Arthur is killed. Arthur encourages his knights to undertake religious quests, yet he himself is not without sin: His illegitimate son seals his own downfall. The darker side of chivalry, it seems, is bound up inextricably with compelling ideals of bravery and honesty. The novelist John Steinbeck describes how these contradictions captured his attention the moment he read the tales of Camelot. "In that scene were all the vices that ever were—and courage and sadness and frustration, but particularly gallantry. . . . I was not frightened to find that there were evil knights, as well as noble ones. . . . Children are violent and cruel—and good—and I was all of these—and all of these were in the secret book."

In an age of industrial change, Victorians were drawn to images of simple feudal loyalties. They romanticized an age when disputes could be settled by the king's champion, a knight on horseback who threw down his gauntlet to anyone challenging royal authority. Similarly, modern readers are drawn to the magic of Camelot, nostalgically hoping for goodness and nobility to succeed in the face of overwhelming odds. Or, as the youthful King Arthur is taught in T. H. White's *The Once and Future King* (1958), "right" *can* prevail over "might." Malory tells us that "King Arthur is not dead" but "shall come again, and he shall win the Holy Cross." For five hundred years, readers have believed.

Responding to the Art

Jones Archer (1823–1904) was a Scottish painter who created a series of paintings on Arthurian subjects.

Activity. Ask students to speculate on the meaning of the figure that is barely visible in the painting's upper-right-hand corner.

C Humanities Connections

Twentieth-Century Camelot

The presidential administration of John F. Kennedy was sometimes referred to as Camelot. In many ways, Kennedy embodied an Arthurian ideal of youthful vigor and enthusiasm in an era of change and optimism in American history.

D Cultural Connections

Arthur Past and Present

Sir Thomas Malory's work has been the chief source of Arthurian material in modern times although mention of a legendary Celtic king was made as early as the seventh century in a Welsh poem called "Gododdin." In the ninth century, a Welsh historian described twelve battles in which a figure named Arthur led the Britons against the Saxons. In the twentieth century, T. H. White's novel (based on Malory) *The Once and Future King* (1958) served as the basis for the musical *Camelot* (1960) and the animated film *The Sword in the Stone* (1963). Director John Boorman's *Excalibur* is another contemporary cinematic interpretation of Arthurian material.

Assessing Learning

Check Test: True-False

1. The popularity of the Arthurian legend during the nineteenth century created a new interest in the history of the Middle Ages. [True]
2. Arthurian chivalry was a combination of Christian morality, courtly love rituals, and pagan fertility rites. [True]
3. Sir Lancelot was a chivalrous knight who would never betray King Arthur. [False]
4. John Steinbeck said that reading the tales of Camelot taught him that there is both good and bad in the world. [True]
5. In his re-creation of the Arthurian tales, Tennyson stresses Arthur's mystical powers and mysterious origins over his idealism and leadership qualities. [False]

OBJECTIVES

My Last Duchess / Porphyria's Lover

1. Read and interpret the poems
2. Interpret a dramatic monologue
3. Draw inferences from textual clues
4. Express understanding through critical and creative writing and improvisation

SKILLS

Literary
- Interpret a dramatic monologue

Reading
- Draw inferences from textual clues

Writing
- Collect ideas for an evaluation
- Compare themes
- Write a dramatic monologue

Speaking /Listening
- Improvise a scene

Viewing/Representing
- Analyze and interpret various works of fine art (ATE)

Planning

- **Block Schedule**
  Block Scheduling Lesson Plans with Pacing Guide
- **Traditional Schedule**
  Lesson Plans Including Strategies for English-Language Learners
- **One-Stop Planner**
  CD-ROM with Test Generator

Robert Browning

(1812–1889)

Robert Browning (1858) by Michele Gordigiani. Oil on canvas (29″ × 23″).
By Courtesy of the National Portrait Gallery, London.

Robert Browning wrote of his first published book, a long poem about the spiritual development of a poet, that it was part of a "foolish plan." He intended, he said, to write in many forms and under different names. Browning eventually gave up this idea, but he held on to his ambition of dazzling the world with his range and variety.

Browning's education allowed him to indulge his wide-ranging interests in music, art, the history of medicine, drama, literature, entomology, and other oddly assorted topics. Browning attended boarding school briefly but was mainly educated at home in a London suburb by tutors and by his omnivorous reading in his banker father's extensive library. As a teenager, Browning was brilliant, undisciplined, and determined to be a poet like his idol, Percy Bysshe Shelley. After a term at the University of London, he published (at his family's expense) several poems, plays, and pamphlets, but not until he began writing the short dramatic monologues of the 1840s—poems like "My Last Duchess" and "Porphyria's Lover"—did Browning find his proper form. While Browning struggled to gain recognition for his writing, he lived comfortably at home, supported by his parents, until he married at thirty-four.

In 1845, Browning wrote to Elizabeth Barrett, already an established poet: "I do . . . love these books with all my heart—and I love you too." Barrett was then a semi-invalid in her father's London house, where she submitted to his sternly protective care. Four months after the two poets began their correspondence, they met and fell in love. They secretly married in 1846, and a week later eloped to Italy. Mr. Barrett estranged himself from his famous daughter for the rest of his life.

Browning's happy marriage confirmed his belief that only by acting boldly can one wrest what is good from an imperfect world. "I was ever a fighter," he wrote in "Prospice." He liked to see himself in strenuous but joyous contests with difficulties. In his dramatic poems, he also liked to emphasize the error, weakness, and even the viciousness of his characters. His standing as a poet grew slowly in the 1840s and 1850s, for readers did not know how to react to speakers like the Duke in "My Last Duchess" and the lover in "Porphyria's Lover," who act boldly but for selfish and perverse motives. It was also hard for readers used to Tennyson's melodic lyrics to hear the music in Browning's quick, rough sounds.

Browning lived in Italy until Elizabeth's death in 1861, when he returned to England with their twelve-year-old son. During the 1860s, his fame began to grow. His first immediate success came with *The Ring and the Book* (1868–1869), a long poem spoken by characters involved in a seventeenth-century murder in Rome. Gradually, readers understood that by asking them to figure out and judge wicked men like the Duke in "My Last Duchess," Browning was really challenging them to discover what is virtuous and healthy, when love nourishes, and when and why it kills. Browning believed that human beings must act by a moral standard, just as he believed that those who love constantly and act bravely will be rewarded.

During the 1880s, admirers all over England and the United States founded Browning Societies and met to read and discuss his work and philosophy. By the time of his death in 1889, Browning had won a place next to Tennyson as the other great Victorian poet. Like Tennyson, he was read as a kind of sage who assured his contemporaries that "This world's no blot for us, / Nor blank; it means intensely, and means good" ("Fra Lippo Lippi").

Resources: Print and Media

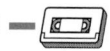

Reading
- *Reading Skills and Strategies*
  MiniRead Skill Lesson, p. 44
  Selection Skill Lesson, p. 51
- *Graphic Organizers for Active Reading*, pp. 78, 79
- *Audio CD Library*
  Disc 13, Tracks 12, 13

Writing and Language
- *Grammar and Language Links*
  Worksheet, p. 45

Assessment
- *Formal Assessment*, pp. 165, 166
- *Portfolio Management System*, p. 172
- *Test Generator (One-Stop Planner CD-ROM)*

Internet
- go.hrw.com (keyword: *LE0 12-10*)

Before You Read
My Last Duchess

Make the Connection
Portrait of a Marriage
The speaker in this poem is a powerful nobleman of Renaissance Italy. The poem opens with the speaker describing a painting of a woman whom he calls his "last Duchess." By the poem's end the speaker has suggested an entire relationship. Yet we get the feeling that he does not realize just how much he has revealed.

Reading Skills and Strategies
Drawing Inferences from Textual Clues
As you read, jot down the names of the three characters that Browning introduces, starting with the speaker. Next to each name, write down details from the poem that give clues to that person's **character, situation,** and **motives.** After several readings, try to reconstruct the relationships among the characters and the motives for their actions by drawing **inferences,** or logical conclusions, from the clues you have recorded. Of course, another basis for your inferences will be your own experience with people.

Elements of Literature
Dramatic Monologue
"My Last Duchess" is one of Browning's earliest and most popular **dramatic monologues,** poems in which a speaker who is not the poet addresses a listener who does not speak. Instead of telling us directly what the speaker and the other characters are like, Browning allows the speaker to indirectly reveal himself, the other characters, and the situation by dropping clues that we must piece together.

Background
Browning identified his speaker as the Duke of Ferrara, who married three times. In the poem the Duke is negotiating to marry the daughter of a Count. He is addressing the Count's representative.

© Manchester City Art Galleries, England.

A Lady with a Gold Chain and Earrings (1861) by Robert Braithwaite Martineau. Oil on panel (14″ × 10″).

go.hrw.com
LEO 12-10

Summary ■■
The speaker, a Duke, points out a painting of his "last" Duchess to an unnamed listener. In a dramatic monologue, the Duke provides clues about the Duchess and his relationship to her. The listener learns the Duke is wealthy, powerful, and jealous of the attention his late wife bestowed on others. The listener is identified toward the end of the poem as a man in the employ of a Count whose daughter the Duke is negotiating to marry.

Browsing in the Files
About the Author. Robert Browning once said about his wife Elizabeth Barrett, "The simple truth is that *she* was the poet, and I the clever person by comparison." Many would disagree. In his poetry, Browning excelled in character portrayal, compression of feeling, and sharp, descriptive imagery. He brought to perfection the dramatic monologue and was a pioneer in the art of psychological poetry.

Reaching All Students

Struggling Readers
Drawing inferences from textual clues was introduced on p. 829. For a lesson directly tied to this selection that teaches students to make inferences by using a strategy called "It Says I Say," see the *Reading Skills and Strategies* binder:
- MiniRead Skill Lesson, p. 44
- Selection Skill Lesson, p. 51

English Language Learners
Build background by focusing on the title with students before they begin to read. Point out that *last* means "previous" here. Make sure students understand that the speaker is showing off a portrait of his deceased wife to a visitor. The speaker is offering *his* views of the portrait and its subject.

Advanced Learners
Challenge interested students to write a prequel to "My Last Duchess," in either prose or poetry. They can expand on the circumstances surrounding the painting of the portrait and the events leading up to the day that "all smiles stopped together." Others might attempt a sequel, focusing on the Duke's next marriage.

A Historical Connections

The Duke of Ferrara

Browning identified his speaker as Alfonso II, the fifth Duke of Ferrara, a Renaissance nobleman. The Duke's first wife, of three in all, was a fourteen-year-old girl whom the Duke, shortly after marrying, left for two years. She died about a year after his return. It is believed that she was poisoned.

B Elements of Literature

Dramatic Monologue

? What clues in these lines tell you that while the speaker is addressing someone, the "conversation" is a monologue, that is, coming exclusively from one person? [Here the speaker asks a question but there is no answer given. He simply goes straight onto his next thought.]

C Reading Skills and Strategies

Drawing Inferences from Textual Clues

? Based on these clues, what inferences can you make about the Duchess? What inferences can you make about the Duke? [Possible reponses: The Duke thought his wife bestowed her attention and affection too freely. He suspected that she was unfaithful. As readers, we have no evidence of her infidelity other than the Duke's suspicions.]

Responding to the Art

Titian (c. 1485–1576) is generally considered the greatest of the Venetian painters of the Italian Renaissance due largely to his free and expressive brushwork and marvelous use of color. He painted portraits, religious subjects, and scenes from classical mythology. He had a long and successful career, including a stint as court painter to the King of Spain. An art critic of his own time wrote that the people in Titian's paintings "appear alive."

Activity. Ask what students can infer about this young man's character based on his facial expressions and general demeanor. What do they make of the single gloved hand?

My Last Duchess

Robert Browning

That's my last Duchess painted on the wall,
Looking as if she were alive. I call
That piece a wonder, now; Frà Pandolf's° hands
Worked busily a day, and there she stands.
Will 't please you sit and look at her? I said
"Frà Pandolf" by design, for never read
Strangers like you that pictured countenance,
The depth and passion of its earnest glance,
But to myself they turned (since none puts by
the curtain I have drawn for you, but I)
And seemed as they would ask me, if they durst,
How such a glance came there; so, not the first
Are you to turn and ask thus. Sir, 'twas not
Her husband's presence only, called that spot
Of joy into the Duchess' cheek; perhaps
Frà Pandolf chanced to say, "Her mantle° laps
Over my lady's wrist too much," or, "Paint
Must never hope to reproduce the faint
Half flush that dies along her throat." Such stuff
Was courtesy, she thought, and cause enough
For calling up that spot of joy. She had
A heart—how shall I say?—too soon made glad,
Too easily impressed; she liked whate'er
She looked on, and her looks went everywhere.
Sir, 'twas all one! My favor° at her breast,
The dropping of the daylight in the West,

3. **Frà Pandolf's:** Brother Pandolf, a fictitious painter and monk.

16. **mantle:** cloak.

25. **favor:** gift; token of love.

Man with Glove (16th century) by Titian (Tiziano Vecellio).
Louvre, Paris.

Using Students' Strengths

Logical/Mathematical Learners

Throughout his monologue, the Duke always feels that he is in the right; he entertains no views contradictory to his own. His guest is a kind of captive with no alternative but to accept the Duke's version of events. Challenge students to look for the "logic" in the Duke's thinking (possibly relating his views to those of the Italian political philospher Niccolò Machiavelli) and to explain how he has come to such views.

Auditory/Musical Learners

Invite students to prepare a dramatic reading of the poem that highlights the inferential nuances of the monologue. When they perform, students might stand before a portrait and enhance their reading with changes of facial expressions and bodily movements such as pacing or finger pointing. Remind them also to vary the pitch, volume, and rate of speed of their voices.

The bough of cherries some officious fool
Broke in the orchard for her, the white mule
She rode with round the terrace—all and each
Would draw from her alike the approving speech,
Or blush, at least. She thanked men—good! but thanked
Somehow—I know not how—as if she ranked
My gift of a nine-hundred-years-old name
With anybody's gift. Who'd stoop to blame
This sort of trifling? Even had you skill
In speech—(which I have not)—to make your will
Quite clear to such an one, and say, "Just this
Or that in you disgusts me; here you miss,
Or there exceed the mark"—and if she let
Herself be lessoned so, nor plainly set
Her wits to yours, forsooth,° and made excuse,
—E'en then would be some stooping; and I choose
Never to stoop. Oh sir, she smiled, no doubt,
Whene'er I passed her; but who passed without
Much the same smile? This grew; I gave commands;
Then all smiles stopped together. There she stands
As if alive. Will 't please you rise? We'll meet
The company below, then. I repeat,
The Count your master's known munificence
Is ample warrant° that no just pretense
Of mine for dowry will be disallowed;
Though his fair daughter's self, as I avowed
At starting, is my object. Nay, we'll go
Together down, sir. Notice Neptune,° though,
Taming a seahorse, thought a rarity,
Which Claus of Innsbruck° cast in bronze for me!

41. forsooth: archaic for "in truth."

50. warrant: guarantee.

54. Neptune: in Roman mythology, god of the sea.

56. Claus of Innsbruck: an imaginary sculptor.

MAKING MEANINGS

First Thoughts

1. What do you think happened to the Duchess?

Shaping Interpretations

2. According to the Duke, what happened to his last Duchess?
3. In a graphic form, identify the **characters** in this poem, their **relationships,** and their **motives.** (Refer to your reading notes.)
4. What impression of himself do you think the Duke intends to create by his remarks to the Count's emissary? Why would he choose to present himself in this way?
5. What do you think of the Duke's description of his last Duchess? Do you question his assessments? Why or why not?
6. Describe the poem's **rhyme** and **meter.** Read aloud two passages that strike you as examples of natural, colloquial speech.

Extending the Text

7. Can you imagine the events implied in this poem taking place today? Explain.
8. Many people like to read autobiographical details into literature. How does the marriage in this poem compare with the Brownings' own marriage? (See "Scenes from a Modern Marriage," the ***Connections*** on page 832.)

D Reading Skills and Strategies

Drawing Inferences from Textual Clues

? What inferences can you draw about the Duke from these lines? [Possible responses: It would have been beneath his dignity, beneath his high rank and status (his "nine-hundred-years-old name") to tell the Duchess what was bothering him. He was an arrogant, egotistical man who expected others to please him totally without his even having to tell them what he expected from them.]

E Literary Connections

Browning on Browning

When asked the meaning of these lines, Browning said that "the commands were that she should be put to death, . . . or he might have had her shut up in a convent."

F Elements of Literature

Dramatic Monologue

? What is the overall effect of hearing this narrative in the form of a dramatic monologue? [Possible responses: The Duke seems not only to have extraordinary power but to take great pride in his power. There is not only the suggestion of a hideous deed but also no hint of regret or remorse. The duke condemns himself unconsciously with his own words.]

MAKING MEANINGS

First Thoughts [Respond]

1. Many students will conclude, based on the hints in the poem, that the Duke had his wife killed.

Shaping Interpretations [Interpret]

2. He says he gave commands (l. 45) and all smiling stopped.
3. Students can create a three-column chart showing three characters, their relationships, and motives. The listener is an intermediary from the father of the woman the Duke wants to marry next. The Duke wishes to intimidate the visitor, perhaps flatter the prospective father-in law, but most certainly obtain the dowry he desires. The listener wishes to remain deferential, and the Duchess can no longer speak for herself.
4. He intends to present himself as cultured, confident, and wealthy—a man who gets what he wants.
5. The Duke presents the Duchess's actions as grossly improper and defiant. He may be misinterpreting her friendliness and youthful high spirits for infidelity. His assessments are highly questionable, for he is a cold, possessive, and self-centered man who cannot see anything beyond his own selfish desires.
6. The poem is written in couplets of iambic pentameter. Examples include ll. 21–23, 31–34, and 43–45.

Extending the Text [Apply]

7. Students may say that women have more legal rights today and would be more likely to assert themselves; others may point out that abuses of power still occur and go unpunished.
8. Possible response: While Robert, like the Duke, does seem to be the stronger personality in his marriage, he treats his wife with respect and affection, unlike the Duke, who sees his wife as his possession and expects her to bend to his will.

Connections

Before students read the article, tell them that they will be reading a contemporary journalist's account of the Brownings' marriage, including some of the challenges the couple faced and an overall assessment of their success as a couple. Ask students to consider the evidence the writer presents and make their own evaluation of the Brownings' marriage.

A Reading Skills and Strategies

Comparing/Contrasting

? What would make a marriage "modern," as opposed to Victorian? [Possible responses: A modern marriage might include more honesty and equality between husband and wife. In a modern marriage both husband and wife might have careers, and unlike Victorian marriages, the wives would probably not be relegated solely to domestic affairs and child-rearing.]

B Background

Elizabeth Barrett's Illness

Although critics debate the illnesses suffered by Elizabeth Barrett, some suggest she had a lung problem that began in childhood, as well as an injured spine from a fall she took as a teenager. Her brother's accidental drowning, while he and Elizabeth were nursing her condition by the sea at Torquay, no doubt intensified her mental—if not her physical—suffering.

C Critical Thinking

Synthesizing

? What picture of Robert and Elizabeth Browning as human beings does this article convey? [Possible responses: It shows a woman who asserted herself and practiced her art in Victorian times; it shows a man who was not shackled by the stereotypical ideas of his age about women's roles.]

Connections — A News Feature

Scenes from a Modern Marriage

BY JULIA MARKUS

The letter that began the most famous courtship of the 19th century opened, "I love your verses with all my heart, dear Miss Barrett." The writer, Robert Browning, a thirty-three-year-old poet respected in literary circles, was writing to a woman six years his senior, an invalid and a poet of national and international fame. Elizabeth Barrett had not long before recognized his own genius in a poem, "Lady Geraldine's Courtship," likening his poetic heart to a pomegranate "blood-tinctured" with "a veined humanity."

Cloistered in the airless bedsitting room she never left, Elizabeth Barrett was a famous yet mysterious poet. Little could Robert know that her household on Wimpole Street was one of enforced celibacy. Her father, scion of Jamaican wealth, forbade any of his nine adult children, male or female, to marry; all were still living at home. Elizabeth's allowing Robert to visit for the first time was in its own way a dangerous act, a rebellion.

The courtship that followed—daily letters for more than twenty months, secret weekly visits while Papa Barrett was at work—is one of the most romantic and obsessively documented love stories in our tradition.

They met 150 years ago, but their successful marriage has something to say to us today as we race toward the millennium wondering if we have learned anything at all about the art of love.

Not that any marriage is easy. Robert was disturbed by his wife's lifelong use of morphine, which she believed kept her alive, and he was skeptical of her attraction to spiritualism and furious at some of the mediums she befriended. Elizabeth also suffered four miscarriages, giving birth at the age of forty-three to one healthy son. But the birth of Pen Browning came on the day Robert's mother died in England, and his despondency drew him away from his son.

Desperate to help, Elizabeth told Robert she had once secretly written poems about him, during the courtship. She hesitantly handed him the *Sonnets from the Portuguese* as if to say, Look how love led me from despair; can I now lead you from it? "How I see the gesture, and hear the tones," he remembered years after her death, "and, for the matter of that, see the window at which I was standing, with the tall mimosa in front, and the little church court to the right."

The careers of these two poets were on different levels, which could have led to the kind of troubled celebrity marriage we read about today in the tabloids. Though they both wrote their best poetry during their marriage, Robert Browning's greatest collection, "Men and Women"—still in print—was hacked to death by the critics and sold fewer than two hundred copies. This failure added to his money worries—and, since the interest on her money supported them through most of their marriage, to his grave discomfort.

She in the meantime had written a daring novel in verse, "Aurora Leigh," which exposed the abuses against women in Victorian society and suggested, among other things, that what a female artist needed was not a husband but enough money for a garret of her own.

Elizabeth defied conventions only to find her book a best-seller that quickly went through five editions and was read and discussed everywhere. Yet while he was bitter about the critics who destroyed his hopes of critical and commercial success, "golden-hearted" Robert was thrilled by her success. He could talk of nothing else, and he always considered her the superior artist. To her sister Arabel she wrote, when people "write & talk of the 'jealousy' of authors & husbands, let them look at him!"

If this all seems too good to be true, let it be known the couple quarreled. They had very different ideas about child rearing, for one thing. Elizabeth, coming from a home in which her father's "thunder" dictated obedience and having been a child prodigy, wished for her son happy, carefree, unstructured days. Robert, who was doted on by his parents, wanted Pen to take his piano lessons seriously and learn to count. She kept Pen in long curls and velvet frocks; he wanted him to look like a real boy.

But both believed that arguments were important to the marriage. "You know I do think for myself (if the thought is right or wrong) and I do speak the truth (as I am capable of apprehending it) to my husband always," Elizabeth wrote to Arabel. "What you used to call 'our quarreling' is an element of our loving one another, & a very important element too."

—from The New York Times, February 14, 1995

Reaching All Students

Struggling Readers

Drawing Inferences from Textual Clues was introduced on p. 829. For a lesson directly tied to this selection that teaches students to draw inferences using a strategy called It Says . . . I Say, see the *Reading Skills and Strategies* binder:

- MiniRead Skill Lesson, p. 44
- Selection Skill Lesson, p. 51

Connecting Across Texts

Connecting with "My Last Duchess"

Offer these questions for discussion:

- Contrast the ways the Duke and Robert Browning treated their wives. [Possible response: The Duke is self-centered, insecure, arrogant. He insists his wife be submissive and appreciative. Browning in his day was eclipsed by his wife's fame and money, yet he respected and strongly supported her success.]
- Contrast Elizabeth Barrett and the Duchess. [Possible response: The Duchess is young and perhaps unwise or indiscreet; she appears to have had no role to play beyond that of duchess. Elizabeth Barrett Browning was a mature, independent woman who had a literary vocation.]

Victorian valentine (19th century) with decorative envelope showing a "Penny Black" stamp.

Private Collection.

Before You Read

PORPHYRIA'S LOVER

Make the Connection

Mad for Love

Readers might expect a poem titled "Porphyria's Lover" to be a romance. The speaker in the poem is a man whose character and identity we can deduce only by what he says. However, one thing is clear: He is a man of intense emotion. Impressed by his direct speech and unruffled manner, we then shudder at what we learn late in the poem. Yet we continue to hear the man out—fascinated, however uneasy—and are eventually led to ask, "Is he lovesick or genuinely disturbed?"

Quickwrite

Someone has said that the opposite of love is not hate but control. Think about some examples from history or fiction. What is your reaction to this idea?

Background

Like his American contemporary Edgar Allan Poe, Browning had a taste for morbid psychology; he once accused his wife, Elizabeth Barrett Browning, of lacking "a scientific interest in evil." In poems such as "Porphyria's Lover," he pursues that interest, exploring the complexity of human motivations. Browning is different from other nineteenth-century authors. This psychological poet seems more modern to us than his Victorian contemporaries.

Summary ■■

This dramatic monologue opens with a description of the setting: a violently windy and rainy night. Such an opening creates a sense of foreboding and foreshadows an evil deed. The speaker waits for Porphyria; then he describes her entrance and her loving embrace. Still, he complains that although she worships him, she is too weak to commit herself to him totally. He then strangles Porphyria with her own hair to make her his forever, imagining that Porphyria welcomes her death as a release from unwanted bonds. At the end of the poem, the speaker notices that God has not reacted to his deed.

Resources

Audio CD Library

A dramatic reading of this selection is available in the *Audio CD Library:*

- Disc 13, Track 13

Formal Assessment

- Selection Test, p. 166

Reaching All Students

Struggling Readers

Suggest students stop and think after every ten lines or so of the poem. At each stopping point, students can summarize what has happened, ask questions, seek help and verification from peers, or go back and reread. When they have gone through the entire poem in this fashion, they can begin to evaluate the speaker's perceptions and motives.

English Language Learners

Monitor comprehension by having students create a time line on which they list, chronologically, the events of the poem. Then as a class activity, have students name, one at a time, the events that lead up to the dramatic conclusion.

For more strategies for engaging English language learners with the literature, see

- *Lesson Plans Including Strategies for English-Language Learners*

Advanced Learners

Invite students to use this dramatic monologue to create a television or magazine interview in which the speaker of the poem is questioned about his relationship to Porphyria and his role in her death. Students should prepare some questions that can be answered by quoting directly from the poem and others that can be answered on the basis of their understanding of the events of the poem and the speaker's character.

(A) Elements of Literature
Setting and Mood

? What mood do you think this setting is meant to evoke? [Possible responses: The violence of the weather may be an outward reflection of the speaker's inwardly troubled state; the darkness suggests mystery or dark deeds and creates a sinister mood; the lake and trees suggest a remote setting or isolated locale, where whatever happens will be out of the sight of witnesses.]

(B) Reading Skills and Strategies
Drawing Inferences

? What appears to be the main external obstacle to this relationship? [Possible responses: Porphyria is already committed to some other relationship, possibly a marriage, and she is not able or willing to break the ties of that relationship: Perhaps the disapproval of her family prevents her from openly commiting herself to the speaker.]

(C) Elements of Literature
Dramatic Monologue

? What does the speaker reveal about himself and his perceptions in these lines? [Possible reponse: He is obsessed with Porphyria and believes that she too worships him.]

(D) Reading Skills and Strategies
Comparing/Contrasting

? What does the speaker in this poem have in common with the speaker of "My Last Duchess"? How do they differ? [Possible responses: While the speaker here is certain Porphyria worships him, at least at this moment, the Duke feels no such certainty about his wife's devotion; both men are obsessed by a woman whom they wish to possess totally. To ensure their mastery, both are willing to destroy what they desire, without a trace of self-doubt or remorse.]

Porphyria's Lover

Robert Browning

The rain set early in tonight,
The sullen wind was soon awake,
It tore the elm tops down for spite,
(A) And did its worst to vex the lake:
I listened with heart fit to break.
When glided in Porphyria; straight
She shut the cold out and the storm,
And kneeled and made the cheerless grate
Blaze up, and all the cottage warm;
Which done, she rose, and from her form
Withdrew the dripping cloak and shawl,
And laid her soiled gloves by, untied
Her hat and let the damp hair fall,
And, last, she sat down by my side
And called me. When no voice replied,
She put my arm about her waist,
And made her smooth white shoulder bare,
And all her yellow hair displaced,
And, stooping, made my cheek lie there,
And spread, o'er all, her yellow hair,
Murmuring how she loved me—she
Too weak, for all her heart's endeavor,
(B) To set its struggling passion free
From pride, and vainer ties dissever,°
And give herself to me forever.
But passion sometimes would prevail,
Nor could tonight's gay feast restrain
A sudden thought of one so pale
(C) For love of her, and all in vain:
So, she was come through wind and rain.
Be sure I looked up at her eyes
Happy and proud; at last I knew
Porphyria worshipped me: Surprise
Made my heart swell, and still it grew
While I debated what to do.
That moment she was mine, mine, fair,
Perfectly pure and good: I found
A thing to do, and all her hair
(D) In one long yellow string I wound
Three times her little throat around,
And strangled her. No pain felt she;
I am quite sure she felt no pain.
As a shut bud that holds a bee,
I warily oped° her lids; again
Laughed the blue eyes without a stain.

24. dissever: separate.

44. oped: archaic for "opened."

Using Students' Strengths

Intrapersonal Learners

The speaker in "Porphyria's Lover" offers the reader many clues to his introverted nature and isolated existence. Have students examine the monologue for evidence that the speaker is a troubled personality who has lost touch with a larger reality outside his own mind. Have them write their conclusions about his mental state in a letter to a social worker or therapist.

Auditory Learners

Invite students to prepare and perform part or all of "Porphyria's Lover" as a dramatic reading. Encourage students to try to capture not only Browning's poetic rhythm and imagery but also what they imagine to be the speaker's mental condition. Students should make creative use of the pitch, tone, and volume of their voices and of body language and dramatic timing.

And I untightened next the tress
  About her neck; her cheek once more
Blushed bright beneath my burning kiss:
  I propped her head up as before,
  Only, this time my shoulder bore
Her head, which droops upon it still;
  The smiling rosy little head,
So glad it has its utmost will,
  That all it scorned at once is fled,
  And I, its love, am gained instead!
Porphyria's love: She guessed not how
  Her darling one wish would be heard.
And thus we sit together now,
  And all night long we have not stirred,
  And yet God has not said a word!

April Love (1856) by Arthur Hughes.
Tate Gallery, London.

E Reading Skills and Strategies

Drawing Inferences

? What do the speaker's comments suggest about him? [Possible responses: These lines suggest that he is deranged. His obsession with Porphyria is so strong that he is happy to embrace her dead body and he thinks she is glad to be dead.]

F Critical Thinking

Evaluating

? Do you find the ending of the poem effective? Why or why not? Give your reasons. [Possible responses: Yes, it is effective because it leaves the reader with the dreadful realization that the speaker is so deranged that he would expect a congratulatory word from God on his murderous act. No, the speaker's behavior is so bizarre that the poem becomes a study in abnormal psychology, shocking rather than interesting or moving.]

RESPONDING TO THE ART

Arthur Hughes (1832–1915) was associated with the Pre-Raphaelites. Many of his paintings explore the theme of love, especially doomed courtships. Brilliant shades of green, purple, and blue characterize his art.

Activity. Engage students in a discussion about what the young woman in the painting might be doing and what the next frame might look like if the painting were a scene from a movie or one of a set of illustrations for a story or novel.

Making the Connections

Connecting to the Theme: "Love and Loss"

Ask students to comment on how Browning's "My Last Duchess" and "Porphyria's Lover" fit in with—or offer a macabre comment on—the theme of love and loss. [Possible responses: These poems reflect twisted love or love confused with control. In both, the men would rather lose the women to death than live with any doubt of their fidelity or commitment. When desire becomes an obsession, love and life are lost.]

Making Meanings

First Thoughts [Respond]

1. Most students will point to ll. 37–42, the murder; some may cite the last line.

Shaping Interpretations [Interpret]

2. In the beginning, he is sad and irritable, although Porphyria's devotion cheers him; in the end, he seems calm and satisfied.

3. He wants to preserve forever the moment when she is totally his. He complains (ll. 21–25) that she is too weak to commit herself to him forever. Students should relate his reasons to their Quickwrite notes.

4. The speaker thinks he sees Porphyria's blue eyes laugh (ll. 44–45) and her cheek blush (ll. 47–48) after he has killed her. Most students will agree that these perceptions are proof of his derangement. He confuses his feelings with hers.

5. The speaker's action is less surprising if readers already associate him with a madhouse. Students may think the poem is set in a cabin or country house.

6. The speaker seems to recognize the enormity of his deed and perhaps is surprised that God has not felt it necessary to pass judgment. Or, perhaps he is so deranged that he interprets God's silence as approval. The line implies that the speaker has some concern about the consequences of his action.

Connecting with the Text [Apply]

7. Students may say the speaker is clearly insane and cannot distinguish right from wrong and therefore should not be held accountable; others may say he performed a willful murder, knowing it was wrong, and is therefore guilty.

Extending the Text [Evaluate]

8. Responses will vary. Browning clearly links this crime with insanity, so perhaps he would agree with such a plea. On the other hand, the speaker appears to expect some sort of divine reaction, suggesting, perhaps, an awareness that he deserves condemnation.

Grading Timesaver

Rubrics for each Choices assignment appear on p. 172 in the *Portfolio Management System.*

Making Meanings

First Thoughts

1. What, to you, is the most disturbing passage in the poem? Why?

Shaping Interpretations

2. What are the speaker's different moods in the poem?

3. What reasons does the speaker give for strangling Porphyria? Do any of his reasons relate to the ideas in your Quickwrite notes?

4. What leads the speaker to assert that Porphyria "felt no pain"? What do you think of this claim?

5. Browning first published this poem, with another, under the general title *Madhouse Cells.* How does a knowledge of that **setting** affect your response to and interpretation of the poem? Where did you think the poem was set before you knew about Browning's original title?

6. "And yet God has not said a word!" Why do you think the speaker expects God to say something? What does the line tell you about the speaker's **character** and his awareness of what he has done?

Connecting with the Text

7. If you were serving on a jury for a trial of Porphyria's lover, would you find him not guilty by reason of insanity? Why or why not?

Extending the Text

8. From this poem, what do you think Browning's views might be on the legal plea not guilty by reason of insanity? What details in the poem make you think so?

Choices: Building Your Portfolio

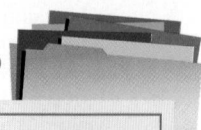

Writer's Notebook

1. Collecting Ideas for an Evaluation

An evaluation doesn't depend on personal taste. Your dislike of westerns, for instance, doesn't mean there are *no* good westerns. In evaluation, you use criteria, or standards of judgment, specific to the type of work, whether westerns or dramatic monologues. Use the Before You Read information (pages 829 and 833) and the Making Meanings questions (pages 831 and 836) to list criteria for a strong dramatic poem—for example, realistic dialogue. Save your work for the Writer's Workshop on page 899.

Comparing Themes

2. Love Stories?

In a brief essay, compare the themes of "My Last Duchess" and "Porphyria's Lover." Which poem do you consider the more effective monologue? Cite reasons to support your opinion.

Creative Writing

3. The Duchess Talks Back

Write a **dramatic monologue,** in prose, using the voice of the wife in "My Last Duchess." Base your monologue on an imaginary incident, and take into account the personality portraits of both the Duchess and the Duke in Browning's poem.

Improvisational Theater

4. Prelude to a Crime

Working with other students, imaginatively reconstruct the relationship between Porphyria and her lover before Porphyria's last visit. Look for clues in the poem that help you set up the speaker's state of mind and the time, place, and basic circumstances of a next-to-last meeting. Improvise the scene for the class.

Elizabeth Barrett Browning

(1806–1861)

Elizabeth Barrett Browning was one of the most famous poets of her day—more successful during her lifetime than her husband, Robert Browning. She is remembered today for her *Sonnets from the Portuguese,* of which "How Do I Love Thee?" is the best known.

During her lifetime, Barrett Browning was well known as an audacious, versatile poet who frequently wrote on intellectual, religious, and political matters. As a girl, she studied Greek, Latin, French, Italian, history, and philosophy—an uncommon education for a woman in nineteenth-century England. She published long narratives, a novel in verse, translations of Greek plays, and poems that dealt with the abolition of slavery, the exploitation of children in factories, religious belief, and Italian nationalism.

Elizabeth Barrett Browning (1858) by Michele Gordigiani. Oil on canvas (73.7 cm × 58.4 cm).
By Courtesy of the National Portrait Gallery, London.

Through the first half of her busy literary career, Elizabeth Barrett was a semi-invalid. Her illnesses have been variously diagnosed, but it is certain that their effect was enlarged by the sometimes bullying protectiveness of her father and perhaps by the drugs routinely prescribed in those days for a "nervous collapse." She wrote to Robert Browning during their courtship, "Papa says sometimes when he comes into this room unexpectedly and convicts me of having dry toast for dinner, . . . that obstinacy and dry toast have brought me to my present condition, and if I *pleased* to have porter and beefsteaks instead, I should be as well as ever I was, in a month!"

In 1845, she met Robert Browning, and the next year they married secretly and eloped to the Continent. Her father never forgave her for the marriage (he had forbidden all his children to marry), nor did he ever see her again. Barrett Browning flourished in Italy and bore a son when she was forty-three years old: her own "young Florentine" with "brave blue English eyes."

The Browning Readers (late 19th or early 20th century) by Sir William Rothenstein.
Bradford Galleries and Museums, London.

go.hrw.com
LEO 12-10

Objectives

1. Read and interpret the poem
2. Identify the Petrarchan sonnet form
3. Express understanding through writing or performance

Skills

Literary
- Identify the Petrarchan sonnet form

Writing
- Collect ideas for an evaluation
- Write a poem

Speaking/Listening
- Give oral readings of poems on the subject of love

Planning

- **Block Schedule**
  Block Scheduling Lesson Plans with Pacing Guide
- **Traditional Schedule**
  Lesson Plans Including Strategies for English-Language Learners
- **One-Stop Planner**
  CD-ROM with Test Generator

Browsing in the Files

About the Author. Elizabeth Barrett Browning wrote forty-four sonnets tracing the course of her love for Robert. On the issue of finally showing these sonnets to her husband, biographer Margaret Forster quotes Elizabeth Browning as saying, "I felt shy about them altogether" and Forster went on to explain that this was because Elizabeth Browning once heard Robert Browning "express himself strongly against 'personal' poetry." How did Robert Browning react to these sonnets when he finally read them? According to Elizabeth Browning—in what must surely be a great understatement—"he was much touched and pleased."

Resources: Print and Media

Reading
- *Graphic Organizers for Active Reading,* p. 80
- *Audio CD Library*
  Disc 13, Track 14

Assessment
- *Formal Assessment,* p. 167
- *Portfolio Management System,* p. 173
- *Test Generator (One-Stop Planner CD-ROM)*

Internet
- go.hrw.com (keyword: *LEO 12-10*)

Summary

This Petrarchan sonnet begins with the question "How do I love thee?" and follows with seven descriptions of how the speaker loves, concluding with the hope that her love will continue after death. Although the speaker compares her love to the simple faith she had as a child, she also reveals an adult realization that love includes "tears" and an inevitable encounter with death.

Ⓐ Elements of Literature

Petrarchan Sonnet

? Why do you think the poet chose the sonnet form to express her thoughts? [Possible responses: The sonnet form has often been used for love poems. The form contains the intense emotion of the poem by expressing it in regular rhyme and meter. The formal discipline orders and perfects the boundlessness of passion.]

Ⓑ Critical Thinking

Interpreting

? What do these lines mean? [Possible response: The speaker says that her love is as great as the urge she feels to reach for ideals ("the ends of Being and ideal Grace") that are beyond her grasp.]

Before You Read

SONNET 43

Make the Connection

Love Without Limits

This poem expresses an ardent, joyful love—a truly transforming love. And yet, it is not a blind, infatuated love. Amid the fervor, you may find hints that love must weather more than joy.

Quickwrite

Expressions of love are often exaggerated. Robert Burns wrote a love poem in which the speaker vows to love until the seas go dry. Think of some exaggerations you could use to say "I love you."

Elements of Literature

Petrarchan Sonnet

All forty-four poems in *Sonnets from the Portuguese* are written in traditional **Petrarchan,** or Italian, **sonnet** form: an octave (eight lines) and sestet (six lines) in iambic pentameter, rhyming *abbaabba cdcdcd.* Sonnet 43 does not have the usual **turn,** or break in thought, at the sestet. Rather, the poem is broken into short units of thought.

Background

Barrett Browning wrote her sonnets before her marriage, but did not show them to her husband until three years later. Reluctant to publish the poems because they were so autobiographical, she deliberately gave them a title that suggested that they were a translation into English from an original Portuguese source.

Ⓐ Sonnet 43

Elizabeth Barrett Browning

How do I love thee? Let me count the ways.
I love thee to the depth and breadth and height
My soul can reach, when feeling out of sight
For the ends of Being and ideal Grace.
I love thee to the level of everyday's
Most quiet need, by sun and candlelight.
I love thee freely, as men strive for Right;
I love thee purely, as they turn from Praise.
I love thee with the passion put to use
In my old griefs, and with my childhood's faith.
I love thee with a love I seemed to lose
With my lost saints°—I love thee with the breath,
Smiles, tears, of all my life!—and, if God choose,
I shall but love thee better after death.

12. lost saints: childhood faith.

Love Among the Ruins (1894) by Sir Edward Burne-Jones.
Wightwick Manor/National Trust Photographic Library, London.

Reaching All Students

Struggling Readers

Because the sonnet is so concise and so lacking in concrete detail, students may have difficulty following the speaker's thoughts. Take a cue from "Let me count the ways," and work with students (or have them work with partners) to complete a numbered list of "I love thee . . ." statements that will outline the poem. Ask students to put each statement in their own words and discuss why they think Barrett Browning expressed herself as she did.

English Language Learners

To check that English language learners have understood the poem, have them reconstruct it line by line. After students have read the poem several times, present the lines of the sonnet in random order on the chalkboard or on a transparency. Ask students to draw upon their comprehension of the poem as well as their knowledge of the sonnet's rhyme scheme to arrange the lines in their original order.

Advanced Learners

Invite students to compare and contrast this sonnet in form and meaning with another sonnet they have read on the subject of love, such as one of Spenser's sonnets on pp. 218–219 or one of Shakespeare's on pp. 225–229. Ask them to discuss their opinions on which sonnet speaks more wisely about love in an informal panel format.

Student to Student

Tu B'shvat
(A Jewish holiday that celebrates trees)

When I turn to look for you
the door swings back and forth
chilling the air
and smoke wavers in the empty doorway. **A**
I become a tree
capable of nothing
but to stand here
and watch you go
hoping one of my branches **B**
will snag
on your mulberry silk skirt
and bring you back.

—Michelle Dorrien
Clarkstown High School North
New City, New York

Making Meanings

First Thoughts

1. If someone sent Sonnet 43 to you, how would you feel?

Shaping Interpretations

2. How many distinct ways does the speaker say that she loves her beloved?
3. What do you think the poem expresses about the speaker's religious faith?
4. How are the pauses in the last three lines different in **rhythm** from those in the rest of the poem? What do you think is the effect of this change in rhythm?

Challenging the Text

5. In your opinion, has Barrett Browning described all of the important aspects and emotions of love? Explain your response. (Refer to your Quickwrite notes for ideas.)

Choices: Building Your Portfolio

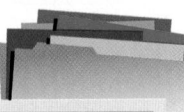

Writer's Notebook

1. Collecting Ideas for an Evaluation

In an evaluation of a literary work, you can find evidence for your position by comparing the work to another of the same type. What do you think is the best love sonnet you've read in this book? (There are many examples in the lyrics of the Renaissance poets, including William Shakespeare on pages 225–229.) Reread that other poem and Sonnet 43, and then create a dialectical journal entry comparing the two. On the left, write a positive statement about the earlier poem; on the right, freewrite a response about Sonnet 43. Save your work for the Writer's Workshop on page 899.

Creative Writing

2. Counting the Ways

Write a short love poem that answers the question: How do I love you? You might even try to write your poem in **sonnet** form. Before you begin, examine the ways that Barrett Browning and the student writer of "Tu B'shvat" (left column) use **metaphor** in their love poems.

Oral Performance

3. How Do You Say Love?

Select some other love poems from this book, and present an hour of "love talk." You might be able to arrange your poems as a series of statements and responses. Which poems should be spoken by men? Which by women? If you are interested in adding a modern woman's voice, read Edna St. Vincent Millay's "What Lips My Lips Have Kissed" (lines from the poem are quoted on page 801). Don't forget the love poem by E. E. Cummings on page 213.

Student to Student

In this student poem, a speaker describes watching a loved one leave a room. Using a tree metaphor, the speaker suggests her rootedness and also her desire to detain the leave-taker.

A Critical Thinking

Speculating

? What do you think has happened? [Possible response: Someone, perhaps a parent or lover, has left a room; perhaps this is a metaphor for a more significant or permanent leave-taking. The speaker watches the departure in a state of near immobility.]

B Reading Skills and Strategies

Drawing Inferences from Textual Clues

? Will the speaker wait for the one who has left to return? What textual clues support your inference? [Possible response: The speaker is compared to a tree that will stand fast. The metaphor of a branch snagging the leave-taker's skirt seems to indicate that the speaker feels some small hope that she can influence the leave-taker's decision.]

Making Meanings

First Thoughts [Respond]

1. Students may feel flattered, moved, humbled, or embarrassed by the depth of emotion.

Shaping Interpretations [Interpret]

2. In addition to the expectation of love continuing after death, there are seven ways.
3. The speaker expresses a religious faith that has matured from innocent childhood belief (ll. 10–12) to a deeper, more adult faith (ll. 13–14).
4. Possible responses: The choppy rhythm of the final lines, created primarily through the use of dashes, contrasts with the earlier, more measured declarations. The pauses in the final lines suggest an upwelling of emotion and possible challenges to love's smooth course.

Challenging the Text [Respond]

5. Responses will vary. Students may add the importance of similar values and interests or of physical attraction. They also may mention emotions such as fear of rejection and jealousy.

Connecting Across Texts

Connecting with Sonnet 43

Invite students to discuss the responses of the speaker of the student poem and of the speaker of Sonnet 43 to the threat of losing a loved one. [Possible responses: The speaker of the student poem expresses only a slight hope that she can "snag" the leave-taker and regain what has been lost. The speaker of Sonnet 43 expresses a strong faith that not even death can weaken her love. Both speakers express a steadfast devotion for the beloved.]

Grading Timesaver

Rubrics for each Choices assignment appear on p. 173 in the *Portfolio Management System*.

OBJECTIVES

Spring and Fall / Pied Beauty

1. Read and interpret the poems
2. Identify assonance
3. Interpret imagery
4. Recognize multiple-meaning words
5. Express understanding through writing or research

SKILLS

Literary

- Identify assonance
- Interpret imagery

Reading

- Recognize multiple-meaning words

Writing

- Collect ideas for an evaluation
- Paraphrase a poem in prose
- Create a list of "dappled" things
- Use a dictionary to find word meanings

Planning

- **Traditional Schedule**
  Lesson Plans Including Strategies for English-Language Learners
- **One-Stop Planner**
  CD-ROM with Test Generator

BROWSING IN THE FILES

Writers on Writing. In 1879, Hopkins wrote to Robert Bridges, "No doubt my poetry errs on the side of oddness." Thirty-nine years later when Bridges finally published the first of Hopkins's poems, times had changed so much that the oddest thing about the poems was the fact that they had been written so many years earlier. What appeared odd in 1879 was considered innovative in 1918, especially when placed in the context of the work of Yeats, Pound, and Eliot.

Gerard Manley Hopkins

(1844–1889)

Hopkins was the eldest son of highly educated parents who were devoted to the Church of England. His father, British consul-general of the Hawaiian Islands, sent the young Hopkins to Highgate, a London boarding school, where he won a poetry prize and later a scholarship to study classics at Oxford University. Hopkins intended to prepare himself for the Anglican ministry, but after much soul-searching, he converted to Roman Catholicism in 1866—a radical and shocking thing to do at the time.

In 1868, when he entered the Jesuit order, Hopkins burned almost all his poetry (a few poems remain) and "resolved to write no more, as not belonging to my profession, unless it were by the wish of my superiors." He wrote no poetry for seven years, but in 1875, he was asked to write an ode in memory of five Franciscan nuns who had drowned at sea. He sent "The Wreck of the *Deutschland*" to a Jesuit periodical, whose editors "dared not print it."

Hopkins, an unusually conscientious man, was ordained as a Jesuit priest in 1877 and devoted himself to the immediate demands of the priesthood. He served in parishes in poor sections of English and Scottish cities, writing sermons and ministering to the sick. As a teacher of classics at a Jesuit seminary and later as a professor of Greek at the Roman Catholic university in Dublin, Hopkins worked hard at lecturing, grading papers, and planning a series of scholarly papers. In 1889, at the age of forty-four, he died of typhoid fever in Dublin.

Hopkins published one of his poems in 1863, the year he entered college, but after that only a few insignificant poems appeared during his lifetime. He composed a small but very powerful body of poetry that he sent to his friends with careful instructions about how to understand them. In his letters, he elaborated on his ideas about using the stock of native English words for the diction of his verse. Hopkins's poems are also characterized by what he called **sprung rhythm,** and by **assonance, alliteration,** and **internal rhyme.** Robert Bridges, a friend and fellow poet, published the first edition of Hopkins's poems after his death.

Hopkins attempted in his sprung rhythm to imitate the sound of natural speech. He explained: "It consists in scanning by accents or stresses alone, . . . so that a foot may be but one strong syllable or it may be many light and one strong." In conventional metrics, a foot consists of a prescribed number of stressed and unstressed syllables (an *iamb,* for example, is an unstressed syllable followed by a stressed syllable). Sprung rhythm is not concerned with using only one kind of foot in a poem; in Hopkins's poems, a line may consist of many kinds of feet: iambs, trochees, dactyls, spondees, and so on.

For a while, literary critics regarded Hopkins as a twentieth-century poet—rather than a Victorian poet—because of his strongly individual language, compression of meaning, unconventional forms, and singular sound. But Hopkins is unmistakably rooted in the nineteenth century. In his almost ecstatic love of nature, his passionate conviction of a transcendental power, and his striving for individuality, Hopkins resembled the Romantic poets. In the "terrible sonnets" of his last four years, Hopkins expressed the doubts and spiritual anguish of many late-nineteenth-century writers.

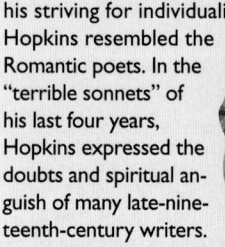

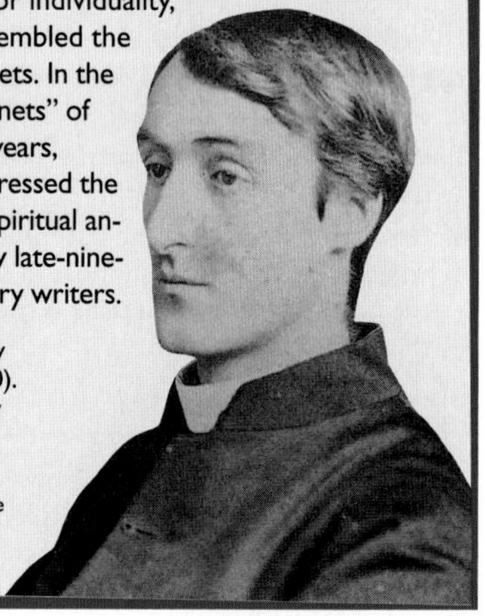

Gerard Manley Hopkins (1880). Photograph by Forshaw and Coles.

By Courtesy of the National Portrait Gallery, London.

go.hrw.com
LEO 12-10

Resources: Print and Media

Reading

- *Graphic Organizers for Active Reading,* pp. 81, 82
- *Audio CD Library*
  Disc 13, Tracks 15, 16

Assessment

- *Formal Assessment,* pp. 168, 169
- *Portfolio Management System,* p. 174
- *Test Generator (One-Stop Planner CD-ROM)*

Internet

- go.hrw.com (keyword: *LEO 12–10*)

Before You Read

SPRING AND FALL

Make the Connection

A Change of Seasons
Human life is often compared to the year's seasons, and in that metaphor, youth is springtime. In this deceptively simple lyric, Hopkins combines autumn, a child, and an adult speaker for a layered, poignant effect. From the girl's sorrow and sense of loss over falling leaves, the speaker moves to a much deeper grief.

Reading Skills and Strategies

Recognizing Multiple-Meaning Words
When you first read the poem aloud, be alert to words that could have more than one meaning. Then, read it again silently, jotting down multiple-meaning words and their line numbers in one column and their meanings in the other. Remember: A single word can function as more than one part of speech. For example, *spring* can be a noun naming a season or a water flow *and* a verb describing a movement upward or forward. It is a word's **context,** or placement in the text, that gives it its meaning.

Elements of Literature

Assonance
Assonance is the repetition of similar vowel sounds followed by different consonants in words that appear near one another. *Hate* and *pale* create assonance. *Hate* and *fate* are exact rhymes. Read "Spring and Fall" aloud to hear its unusual music.

Autumn Leaves (1856) by Sir John Everett Millais.
Oil on canvas (41$\frac{1}{16}$″ × 57$\frac{1}{16}$″).

© Manchester City Art Galleries, England.

Summary ■■

The speaker asks a child named Margaret what reasons she might have for grieving. In the first eight lines, the speaker suggests that Margaret as a child may grieve over the falling leaves in autumn, but as she grows older, she will no longer weep over such things. Instead, she will have other unmistakable reasons for grief. In the final line, the speaker states that Margaret is in mourning for herself or, in other words, that all her losses are subsumed in the greatest loss of all, her own inevitable death.

Background

Hopkins created new words in his poems. For example, both *wanwood* and *leafmeal* in "Spring and Fall" are original to Hopkins. Each invention brilliantly condenses and "compounds" sound and meaning in ways that are exactly right in their context.

Reaching All Students

Struggling Readers

This poem was written in a style that more closely resembles natural speech than many other poems from this era. To demonstrate this, read the poem aloud and then direct the class in a choral reading. Finally, do similar readings of a poem by Tennyson. Ask students to identify those passages that sound most like natural speech and to discuss the reasons for their choices.

English Language Learners

These learners will need help with Hopkins's unusual vocabulary and invented words. Have them work with more proficient students to make up lists of unfamiliar words and to use any context clues, the side glosses, and a dictionary to discover the meanings of the words they have listed. Make sure they understand that Hopkins uses some words like puns, exploiting their various meanings in the same line.

Advanced Learners

Invite students to scan "Spring and Fall" and to research Hopkins's use of "sprung rhythm," an unusual metrical line that he invented. Have students give an oral report to their classmates on Hopkins's rhythm, featuring oral readings of several poems by Hopkins as well as poems with more traditional meters. They might also display the scanned poems on the chalkboard while reading.

Ⓐ Elements of Literature
Assonance

? What examples of assonance do you find in these lines? What is its effect? [Assonance occurs in the repetition of the long *o* sound, which lends a sorrowful note to the lines. The long *o* sound is heard in *over, Goldengrove, grows, older, colder.*]

Ⓑ Reading Skills and Strategies
Recognizing Multiple-Meaning Words

? In how many ways can you interpret the word *springs* in l. 11? [Possible responses: The word might refer to the sources or origins of sorrow, or it might refer to the action of coming forth in the sense that all human sorrows spring from the same cause. Finally, it might be a reference to water, suggesting that Margaret's tears are like springs welling up from the sorrow deep in her soul.]

MAKING MEANINGS

First Thoughts [Respond]

1. Students may wonder if Margaret is in fact crying for the reasons the speaker suggests or if she is sad for some private reason of her own.

Shaping Interpretations [Interpret]

2. Margaret is grieving for the autumn leaves that have fallen from the trees, but the speaker says she is actually mourning for her own mortality.

3. Margaret will grow "colder" and not care about fallen leaves; she will have more personal reasons for grief.

4. One meaning of l. 11 is that all sorrow springs, or comes from, human mortality. Line 14 refers to the Biblical Fall: All human beings, due to original sin, are destined to experience sorrow and to die.

5. Lines 1–8 suggest Margaret will outgrow her sensitivity, but in ll. 10–12, the speaker says Margaret's sadness is for a larger grief. The speaker says Margaret grieves for her future losses.

Spring and Fall:
To a Young Child
Gerard Manley Hopkins

Márgarét, áre you gríeving
Over Goldengrove unleaving?°
Leáves, líke the things of man, you
Ⓐ With your fresh thoughts care for, can you?
Áh! ás the heart grows older
It will come to such sights colder
By and by, nor spare a sigh
Though worlds of wanwood° leafmeal° lie;
And yet you will weep and know why.
Now no matter, child, the name:
Ⓑ Sórrow's spríngs áre the same.
Nor° mouth had, no nor mind, expressed
What heart heard of, ghost° guessed:
It ís the blight man was born for,
It is Margaret you mourn for.

2. **Goldengrove unleaving:** grove of trees whose autumn leaves are falling.

8. **wanwood:** pale wood. **leafmeal:** reduced to decaying leaves (a pun on "piecemeal").

12. **nor:** neither.
13. **ghost:** spirit.

MAKING MEANINGS

First Thoughts

1. What questions do you have after reading this poem twice?

Shaping Interpretations

2. What is Margaret grieving for at the opening? Whom does the speaker say she is really grieving for?

3. What does the speaker predict about Margaret's feelings when her "heart grows older"?

4. What do you think the speaker means by saying "sorrow's springs are the same" (line 11)? Think back to the account of Adam and Eve in Genesis (page 416), and explain the "blight man was born for" (line 14).

5. How does the speaker's attitude toward Margaret and her grief shift in the course of the poem? How would you interpret the poem's last line?

6. Read the poem aloud. Identify at least four examples of **alliteration** and **assonance.**

7. Discuss the multiple meanings of *spring, fall,* and *leaves* in the poem. (Refer to your reading notes.)

Extending the Text

8. How does the source of grief in this poem compare with the "divine despair" in Tennyson's "Tears, Idle Tears" (page 804)?

6. Alliteration: ll. 1–2, *grieving/Goldengrove*; l. 6, *such/sights*; l. 8, *worlds/wanwood*; l. 11, *Sorrow's/springs/same.* Assonance: l. 5, *grows/older*; ll. 7–9, *by/by/sigh/lie/why*; ll. 8–9, *leafmeal/weep*; l. 13, *heart/heard.*

7. *Spring* and *fall* refer to the seasons, with their multiple connotations of life, birth, rebirth, death, and decay. *Springs* refers to a source of water; it may also be a verb suggesting movement from a source. The Fall of man is suggested in l. 14; *fall* is also a general decline. *Leaves* suggests the leaves of trees as well as the action of departing, and it may even refer to the Tree of Knowledge in the Garden of Eden, the source of original sin.

Extending the Text [Synthesize]

8. Possible responses: Both poems suggest that despair arises from a deep source in the human psyche that is aware of sin, suffering, and mortality; there is a spiritual sorrow that transcends personal losses.

Before You Read
PIED BEAUTY

Make the Connection
In Praise of Imperfection
This poem, perhaps not surprising from a poet as unconventional as Hopkins, is his song of praise to God for all things that are *pied:* covered with different-colored spots. As you read, think of the poem as being like a psalm—a praise song.

Quickwrite
What examples of spotted things do you think Hopkins will offer? Give two guesses, and tell why you do or don't find them beautiful.

Elements of Literature
Imagery
Imagery is language that appeals to the senses. In this poem, Hopkins's images follow one another with the instantaneous clarity of a movie's quick cuts. Most of his images are visual, but a few tap other senses, too.

Pied Beauty
Gerard Manley Hopkins

Glory be to God for dappled things—
For skies of couple-color as a brinded° cow;
For rose-moles all in stipple° upon trout that swim;
Fresh-firecoal chestnut-falls;° finches' wings;
Landscape plotted and pieced°—fold, fallow, and plow;
And áll trádes, their gear and tackle and trim.
All things counter, original, spare, strange;
Whatever is fickle, freckled (who knows how?)
With swift, slow; sweet, sour; adazzle, dim;
He fathers-forth° whose beauty is past change:
Praise him.

2. **brinded:** archaic for "brindled"; streaked with a darker color.
3. **stipple:** random dots or spots.
4. **fresh-firecoal chestnut-falls:** freshly roasted chestnuts.
5. **pieced:** parceled into fields.
10. **fathers-forth:** creates.

Evening Shadows (late 19th or early 20th century) by Viggo Christien Frederik Wilhelm Pedersen.

Summary ■■
In an awed, exuberant tone, the speaker praises God for His varied creation. In ll. 2–5, the speaker gives a number of specific, visual images of dappled, or spotted, things. In ll. 7–9, he singles out for praise all that is unconventional, surprising, or unpredictable in God's creation. In l. 10, he points out that the father of creation, unlike His creatures, possesses an unchanging beauty. The final line states the poem's theme: praise of God.

A Reading Skills and Strategies
Making Generalizations
? What overall impression does this list create? [Possible responses: The world is wonderfully varied; Nature delights in complexity.]

B Critical Thinking
Classifying
? What do the adjectives in ll. 7–9 have in common? [Possible response: All express the speaker's fascination with unconventional things, things that run counter to typical expectations. In ll. 7–8, that idea is expressed in single-word adjectives; in l. 9, it comes through pairings of opposites.]

C Elements of Literature
Imagery
? What types of images do each of the adjectives in l. 9 call to mind? [Possible responses: Hopkins evokes images of movement and, tangentially, touch with notions of "swift" and "slow"; of taste with "sweet" and "sour"; of sunlight and shadow with "adazzle" and "dim."]

D Elements of Literature
Theme
? What is Hopkins's main idea as summed up in the final line? [Hopkins's purpose and theme is praise of God through praise of His creations.]

Making the Connections

Connecting to the Theme: "Love and Loss"
Help students connect these poems with the collection theme by asking these questions:

- **What types of loss are referred to in "Spring and Fall"?** [Possible responses: There are several losses. Literally, there is the loss of leaves on the trees and the end of the season of growth. There is also the loss of childhood. Underlying all is an allusion to the loss of innocence and of immortality in the Garden of Eden.]
- **What types of love are evoked in "Pied Beauty"?** [Students may reasonably say that the poem expresses love of "dappled things" or even love of Nature, but more fundamentally, it expresses love and praise of God and God's creation.]

MAKING MEANINGS

First Thoughts [Respond]

1. The poet is filled with faith and awe. Some students may share his sense of wonder at Nature's intricate beauty.

Shaping Interpretations [Interpret]

2. He mentions a multicolored sky, a brindled cow, rose-colored spots on trout, roasted chestnuts, finches' wings, and a patchwork landscape.

3. This refers to anything unlike the norm.

4. The line contains three pairs of words with opposite meanings. Two pairs repeat *s* and *sw* sounds; one pair repeats the *d* sound.

5. He praises God as the creator of this beauty.

6. The beauty of the physical world is transitory; God's beauty is eternal.

7. Its abruptness and brevity give it emphasis.

Extending the Text [Analyze]

8. Both praise God's creations.

CHOICES: Building Your Portfolio

1. Writer's Notebook It may be helpful to students to come up with one example of each as a class before they find the others on their own.

2. Paraphrasing a Poem Students may want to consult a thesaurus to find replacements for some of Hopkins's colorful words.

3. Creative Writing Students may wish to share their ideas with a partner and get feedback as well as additional ideas before they begin writing.

4. Research/Special Vocabulary As an additional exercise, students may want to replace Hopkins's words with the dictionary definitions they find to see how the more ordinary words change the poem as a whole.

MAKING MEANINGS

First Thoughts

1. How would you describe the speaker's emotional state, and did this poem make you share it?

Shaping Interpretations

2. What specific examples of pied beauty does the poet mention in lines 2–6?
3. What do you think the poet means by saying "all things counter" (line 7)?
4. How does the poet combine **alliteration** with **antithesis** (opposites) in line 9?
5. According to the last two lines, why does the poet offer glory and praise to God?
6. In line 10, what contrast does the poet suggest between the beauty of the physical world and the beauty of God the creator?
7. How does the **rhythm** of the last line make it especially effective?

Extending the Text

8. How is this poem, like Psalm 23 (page 422), a "praise song"?

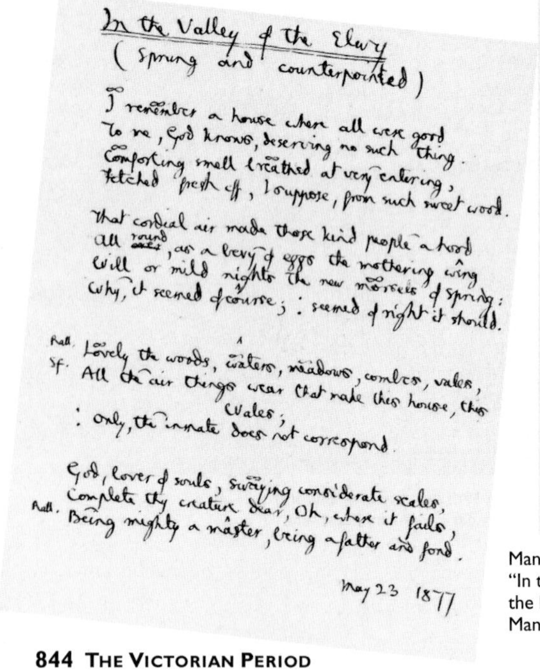
In the Valley of the Elwy
(Sprung and counterpointed)

I remember a house where all were good
To me, God knows, deserving no such thing.
Comforting smell breathed at very entering,
Fetched fresh off, I suppose, from such sweet wood.
That cordial air made those kind people a hood
All round, as a bevy of eggs the mothering wing
Will or mild nights the new morsels of Spring:
Why, it seemed of course; seemed of right it should.

Lovely the woods, waters, meadows, combes, vales,
All the air things wear that make this house, this Wales;
Only, the inmate does not correspond.

God, lover of souls, swaying considerate scales,
Complete thy creature dear, Oh, where it fails,
Being mighty a master, being a father and fond.

May 23 1877

Manuscript of "In the Valley of the Elwy" by Gerard Manley Hopkins.

CHOICES: Building Your Portfolio

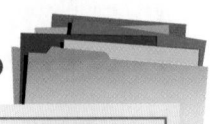

Writer's Notebook

1. Collecting Ideas for an Evaluation

A highly original and unconventional text is always a challenge to evaluate. Is the newness a breakthrough we should learn to admire, or is it merely odd (as it first seems)? In Hopkins's case, what is your judgment? Review both poems and find three examples of inverted word order, of unusual compounds, and of invented words. For each example, write what you feel is Hopkins's intended effect and your judgment of its success. Save your work for the Writer's Workshop on page 899.

Paraphrasing a Poem

2. Literal Meanings

Rewrite "Spring and Fall" in a prose paraphrase, using normal syntax and changing figurative language. Be sure to include all the poem's major ideas in your paraphrase.

Creative Writing

3. Another Look at Loveliness

Hopkins catalogs a number of "dappled" things whose beauty he celebrates. Starting from your Quickwrite notes, make your own list of things that are "original, spare, strange" in Hopkins's sense.

Research/Special Vocabulary

4. Pied Lexicon

Hopkins's poem contains a number of unusual words, such as "brinded" and "stipple." The poet also coins some compound words, such as "couple-color" and "fresh-firecoal." Use a dictionary to help you define at least six unusual terms from the poem. If illustrations will help, provide them.

(Opposite) *The Astrologer* (detail) (19th century) by Sir Edward Burne-Jones. Agnew and Sons, London.

Grading Timesaver

Rubrics for each Choices assignment appear on p. 174 in the *Portfolio Management System*.

The Paradox of Progress

Theme

Loss and Gain *In an age when great advances were made in science and the material lives of many were improved, people were confronted with the price of this progress. For each gain that was made, it seemed a loss had to be borne. The literature of the era reflects this ambivalence.*

Reading the Anthology

Reaching Struggling Readers

The *Reading Skills and Strategies: Reaching Struggling Readers* binder provides materials coordinated with the Pupil's Edition (see the Collection Planner, p. T844B) to help students who have difficulty reading and comprehending text or students who are reluctant readers. The binder for twelfth grade is organized around ten individual skill areas and offers the following options:

- **MiniRead** MiniReads are short, easy texts that give students a chance to practice a particular skill and strategy before reading selections in the Pupil's Edition. Each MiniRead Skill Lesson can be taught independently or used in conjunction with a Selection Skill Lesson.
- **Selection Skill Lessons** Selection Skill Lessons allow students to apply skills introduced in the MiniReads. Each Selection Skill Lesson provides reading instruction and practice specific to a particular piece of literature in the Pupil's Edition.

Reading Beyond the Anthology

Read On

At the end of the Victorian Period collections, the grade twelve book includes an annotated bibliography of books suitable for extended reading. To preview the Read On for the Victorian Period, please turn to p. T895

HRW Library

The *HRW Library* offers novels, plays, and short-story collections for extended reading. Each book in the Library includes one or more major works and thematically or topically related Connections. Each book in the *HRW Library* is also accompanied by a Study Guide that provides teaching suggestions and worksheets. The two titles shown here will work well to extend the theme of Collection 11.

THE RETURN OF THE NATIVE
Thomas Hardy
Clym Yeobright returns from Paris to rural Egdon Heath, hoping to build a life with purpose and meaning. His marriage to the selfish Eustacia Vye puts his dream in peril.

FRANKENSTEIN
Mary Shelley
The conflict between scientific progress and nature is highlighted in this monster tale. A young student, Victor Frankenstein, gives life to a creature, but Victor soon discovers that even a monster needs love.

Collection 11 The Paradox of Progress

Resources for this Collection

Note: All resources for this collection are available for preview on the *One-Stop Planner CD-ROM 2 with Test Generator.* All worksheets and blackline masters may be printed from the CD-ROM.

Internet Resources
go.hrw.com LE0 12-11

Selection or Feature	Reading and Literary Skills	Vocabulary, Language, and Grammar
Dover Beach (p. 847) Matthew Arnold **Critical Comment: Love Is Itself a Faith** (p. 849)	• *Graphic Organizers for Active Reading,* Worksheet p. 83	
• **The Darkling Thrush** (p. 853) • **Channel Firing** (p. 855) • **Ah, Are You Digging on My Grave?** (p. 857) Thomas Hardy **Spotlight On: Victorian Novelists** (p. 859)	• *Graphic Organizers for Active Reading,* Worksheet pp. 84, 85, 86	• *Grammar and Language Links:* Cliches, Worksheet p. 47 • *Language Workshop CD-ROM,* Improving Your Writing Style
• **When I Was One-and-Twenty** (p. 863) • **To an Athlete Dying Young** (p. 865) • **Is My Team Ploughing** (p. 867) A. E. Housman **Connections: Death and Other Grave Matters** (p. 868) Daniel Pool	• *Graphic Organizers for Active Reading,* Worksheet pp. 87, 88, 89	• *Daily Oral Grammar,* Transparency 29
The Mark of the Beast (p. 871) Rudyard Kipling	• *Reading Skills and Strategies: Reaching Struggling Readers* • MiniRead Skill Lesson, p. 66 • Selection Skill Lesson, p. 72 • *Graphic Organizers for Active Reading,* Worksheet p. 90	• *Words to Own,* Worksheet p. 24 • *Grammar and Language Links:* Repetition and Wordiness, Worksheet p. 49 • *Language Workshop CD-ROM,* Revising to Reduce Wordiness • *Daily Oral Grammar,* Transparency 30
World Literature: Russia How Much Land Does a Man Need? (p. 883) Leo Tolstoy *translated by* Louise and Aylmer Maude	The World Literature feature offers students the opportunity to explore thematically linked literature from different world cultures. Structured activities called Finding Common Ground are provided in the Pupil's Edition to guide students' explorations of these thematic connections between British and other world literature.	
The English Language: One Language—Many Nations (p. 896) John Algeo		
Writer's Workshop: Evaluation (p. 899)		
Language Workshop: Ways of Strengthening Meaning (p. 903)		• *Workshop Resources,* p. 57 • *Language Workshop CD-ROM,* Sentence Style
Learning for Life: Evaluating A Community (p. 905)		

Other Resources for this Collection

- *Cross-Curricular Activities,* p. 11
- *Portfolio Management System,* Introduction to Portfolio Assessment, p. 1
- *Formal Assessment,* Literary Period Test, p. 181
- *Test Generator,* Collection Test

Writing	Listening and Speaking Viewing and Representing	Assessment
• *Portfolio Management System,* Rubrics for Choices, p. 175	• *Audio CD Library,* Disc 14, Track 2 • *Portfolio Management System,* Rubrics for Choices, p. 175	• *Formal Assessment,* Selection Test, p. 170 • *Test Generator (One-Stop Planner CD-ROM)*
• *Portfolio Management System,* Rubrics for Choices, p. 176	• *Audio CD Library,* Disc 14, Tracks 3, 4, 5 • *Viewing and Representing:* Fine Art Transparency 14 Worksheet p. 56 • *Portfolio Management System,* Rubrics for Choices, p. 176	• *Formal Assessment,* Selection Tests, pp. 171, 172, 173 • *Test Generator (One-Stop Planner CD-ROM)* • *Preparation for College Admission Exams,* p. 41
• *Portfolio Management System,* Rubrics for Choices, p. 178	• *Audio CD Library,* Disc 14, Tracks 6, 7, 8 • *Portfolio Management System,* Rubrics for Choices, p. 178	• *Formal Assessment,* Selection Tests, pp. 174, 175, 176 • *Test Generator (One-Stop Planner CD-ROM)*
• *Portfolio Management System,* Rubrics for Choices, p. 180	• *Audio CD Library,* Disc 14, Track 9 • *Portfolio Management System,* Rubrics for Choices, p. 180	• *Formal Assessment,* Selection Test, p. 177 • *Test Generator (One-Stop Planner CD-ROM)* • *Preparation for College Admission Exams,* p. 43
	• *Audio CD Library,* Disc 15, Track 2	
		• *Formal Assessment,* The English Language Test, p. 179
• *Workshop Resources,* p. 33 • *Writer's Workshop 2 CD-ROM,* Evaluation	• *Viewing and Representing,* HRW Multimedia Presentation Maker	• *Portfolio Management System* • Prewriting, p. 181 • Peer Editing, p. 182 • Assessment Rubric, p. 183
		• *Portfolio Management System,* Rubrics, p. 184

Transparency CD-ROM Video Audio CD

Collection 11 The Paradox of Progress

Skills Focus

Selection or Feature	Reading Skills and Strategies	Elements of Literature and Language	Writing	Listening and Speaking	Viewing and Representing
Dover Beach (p. 847) Matthew Arnold		Mood, pp. 847, 850 Atmosphere, p. 847 Setting, p. 850 Image, p. 850 Figures of Speech, p. 850 Contrasting Imagery, p. 850	Determine a Poem's Meaning, p. 850 Write an Essay Focused on the Contrasting Imagery in "Dover Beach," p. 850 Write a Dialogue, p. 850		
Reading Skills and Strategies: Context Clues and Figurative Language (p. 851)	Context and Figurative Language, p. 851 Context Clues, p. 851	Simile, p. 851 Metaphor, p. 851			
The Darkling Thrush (p. 853) **Channel Firing** (p. 855) **Ah, Are You Digging on My Grave?** (p. 857) Thomas Hardy		Setting, p. 854 Foreshadow, p. 854 Speakers, p. 856 Irony, p. 856 Theme, pp. 856, 858 Diction, pp. 856, 858 Anticlimax, pp. 857–858 Narrator, p. 857 Tone, p. 858 Situational Irony, p. 858	Cite Evidence to Support an Evaluation, p. 858 Compare Two Poems Based on Their Use of Bird Images, p. 858 Write a Poem or Prose Passage Reflecting on the Past and Future, p. 858 Write a Persuasive Editorial, p. 858 Write a Biography of a Fictional Character, p. 858	Prepare and Present a Dramatic Reading of "Channel Firing," p. 858	
When I Was One-and-Twenty (p. 863) **To an Athlete Dying Young** (p. 865) **Is My Team Ploughing** (p. 867) A. E. Housman		Repetition, p. 864 Theme, p. 864 Literary Ballads, p. 867 Speaker, p. 869 Tone, p. 869 Message, p. 869	Compare Specific Elements in Two Poems, p. 869 Write an Essay Comparing Renaissance and Victorian Poetry, p. 869 Write a Tribute to an Athlete, p. 869 Write Diary Entries Responding to Events in Three Poems, p. 869	Select a Musical Background for an Oral Reading of a Housman Poem, p. 869	
The Mark of the Beast (p. 871) Rudyard Kipling	Identify Conflicts and Resolutions, pp. 871, 881	Allusion, pp. 871, 881 Conflict, p. 881 Characterization, p. 881 Theme, p. 881	Make and Support Generalizations, p. 881 Outline a Story Sequel, p. 881	Research and Present a Report on Life in the Raj, p. 881	Create a Story Map, p. 881 Prepare a Multimedia Report on Werewolf Myths in Different Cultures, p. 881
World Literature: Russia How Much Land Does a Man Need? (p. 883) Leo Tolstoy	The World Literature feature offers students the opportunity to explore thematically linked literature from different world cultures. Structured activities called Finding Common Ground are provided in the Pupil's Edition to guide students' explorations of these thematic connections between British and other world literature.				
The English Language: One Language—Many Nations (p. 896) John Algeo		Dialects of English, p. 896 British and American English, pp. 896–897 Pronunciation, Spelling, and Grammar, p. 897	Compare British and American Vocabulary Terms, p. 898 Rewrite British Sentences in American English, p. 898 Compare British and American Spellings, p. 898 Investigate Word Origins, p. 898		
Writer's Workshop: Evaluation (p. 899)			Write an Evaluation, pp. 899–902		
Language Workshop: Ways of Strengthening Meaning (p. 903)		Style, p. 903 Sentence Style, p. 903 Parallelism, p. 903	Revise Sentences to Improve Style, p. 903		
Reading for Life: Reading a Historical Map (p. 904)	Types of Maps, p. 904 Map Features, p. 904 Inferences Based on Maps, p. 904				Make Inferences Based on a Comparison of Two Maps, p. 904 Plan an Expedition Using a Map, p. 904
Learning for Life: Evaluating a Community (p. 905)	Gather Information from Sources, p. 905		Determine the Qualities Essential to a Livable Community, p. 905	Stage a Debate, p. 905	Design and Build a Scale Model of a Livable Community, p. 905

Collection 11

THE PARADOX OF PROGRESS

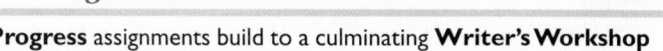

Arnold
Hardy
Housman
Kipling
Tolstoy

Wandering between two worlds, one dead,
The other powerless to be born . . .

—Matthew Arnold, *from Stanzas from the Grande Chartreuse*

OBJECTIVES

1. Read literature of the Victorian Period on the theme of "The Paradox of Progress"
2. Interpret literary elements
3. Apply a variety of reading strategies, particularly using context clues
4. Respond to the literature in a variety of modes
5. Learn and use new words
6. Learn how English became an international language
7. Plan, draft, and revise an evaluation
8. Write sentences that reflect an awareness of style
9. Demonstrate the ability to interpret a historical map
10. Explore through a variety of projects the qualities essential to a livable community

Responding to the Quotation

? Some Victorians realized that, despite technological progress, humanity had changed little inwardly. What "world" might be "dead," and what world might be "powerless"? [Possible response: The "dead" world might be the simpler, more confident past; the world "powerless to be born" could be the future or a present that makes sense or has meaning.]

RESPONDING TO THE ART

Sir Edward Burne-Jones (1833–1898) was an English painter, designer, and illustrator. Influenced by the art criticism of John Ruskin, he studied with the Pre-Raphaelite master Dante Gabriel Rossetti and took up the Pre-Raphaelite program to revive the artistic ideals of the Middle Ages. Burne-Jones held the medieval belief that art should promote morality and noble behavior. (For other art by Burne-Jones, see pp. 630 and 838.)

Activity. Have students jot down ideas on why an astrologer makes a fitting illustration for this collection.

Writing Focus: An Evaluation

WORK IN PROGRESS

The following **Work in Progress** assignments build to a culminating **Writer's Workshop** at the end of this collection.

• Dover Beach	Take notes on meaning and message (p. 850)
• Hardy's poems	Find passages to support evaluation (p. 858)
• Housman's poems	Use a chart to compare poems (p. 869)
• The Mark of the Beast	Find details to support generalizations (p. 881)

Writer's Workshop: Persuasive Writing / An Evaluation (p. 899)

OBJECTIVES

1. Read and interpret the poem
2. Analyze mood, or atmosphere
3. Use context clues and figurative language to determine word meanings
4. Express understanding through critical and creative writing

SKILLS

Literary
- Analyze mood, or atmosphere

Reading
- Use context clues and figurative language to determine word meanings

Writing
- Collect ideas for an evaluation
- Analyze imagery
- Create a dialogue

Viewing/Representing
- Connect art subject to collection theme (ATE)
- Respond to mood (ATE)
- Compare landscapes (ATE)

Planning

- **Block Schedule**
  Block Scheduling Lesson Plans with Pacing Guide
- **Traditional Schedule**
  Lesson Plans Including Strategies for English-Language Learners
- **One-Stop Planner**
  CD-ROM with Test Generator

Matthew Arnold

(1822–1888)

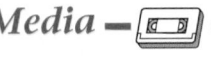

Portrait of Matthew Arnold (1880) by George Frederic Watts.

By Courtesy of the National Portrait Gallery, London.

Unlike the other major Victorian poets, Matthew Arnold achieved fame as both a poet and a critic. He is as famous today for his essays of literary and social criticism as he is for his poetry. His poems stand with the achievements of Tennyson and Browning, their quiet tones and carefully shaped figures of speech expressing his reflections on what Victorian society was like, what it would become, and what it had cost.

Arnold had difficulty in his youth living up to the expectations of his famous father, Dr. Thomas Arnold, one of the leading thinkers of the Victorian era and headmaster of Rugby School. An uneven student at Rugby, Arnold nevertheless won a scholarship to Oxford University in 1841. Although he was less than enthusiastic as a student, he seemed to thoroughly enjoy playing the role of a dandy. His performance at Oxford was a failure by Rugby standards, and he graduated without knowing clearly what he wanted to do. In 1847, he became private secretary to Lord Lansdowne, head of the Council of Education.

Arnold had won prizes for his poetry at both Rugby and Oxford. In 1849, he published his first book of poetry, *The Strayed Reveller,* to mixed reviews. Two more volumes of poetry followed in 1852 and 1853, and as a result Arnold was elected an Oxford professor of poetry in 1857.

After his marriage in 1851, Arnold became a government inspector of schools for poor children, a job he held for thirty-five years. His work was exhausting, requiring him to travel all over England and write daily reports. Though he continued to write poetry in his free time, he found it increasingly difficult. In 1853, he told a friend, "I am past thirty, and three parts iced over—and my pen, it seems to me, is even stiffer and more cramped than my feeling."

After 1860, Arnold almost completely stopped writing poetry and began a second career as a critic. His travels and his work had given him firsthand knowledge of pressing social problems, and he became an energetic essayist and lecturer on literary, political, social, and religious questions. *Essays in Criticism,* his first work on literary topics, was published in 1865; a second series appeared after his death in 1888. During the 1870s, Arnold's essays addressed religion and education. In *Culture and Anarchy* (1869) and in his essays on literature and religion, Arnold urged his readers to acquire a knowledge of history and to study "the best that has been thought and known in the world"—the Greeks, Dante, and Shakespeare—in order to judge ideas and personal conduct. Without the steadying influence of what he called culture, Arnold warned, the nineteenth century's technological and political changes would accelerate into a grossly materialistic democracy. He feared also an intellectual anarchy in which every opinion was seen to be as good as any other.

All through his life, Arnold was capable of knowing both the excitement of trying to change the temper of his age and the loneliness of not being comfortable in his own time. Lionel Trilling, the twentieth-century literary critic, writes that as both poet and critic, Arnold remains fresh and relevant for modern readers: "As a poet he reaches us not more powerfully but, we sometimes feel, more intimately than any other. As a critic he provided us with the essential terms for our debate in matters of taste and judgment."

go.hrw.com
LEO 12-11

Resources: Print and Media

Reading
- *Graphic Organizers for Active Reading*, p. 83
- *Audio CD Library*
  Disc 14, Track 2

Viewing and Representing
- *Visual Connections*
  Videocassette B Segment 9

Assessment
- *Formal Assessment*, p. 170
- *Portfolio Management System*, p. 175
- *Test Generator (One-Stop Planner CD-ROM)*

Internet
- go.hrw.com (keyword: LEO 12-11)

Before You Read
DOVER BEACH

Make the Connection
On a Darkling Plain
Where do people look for answers in times of crisis? Do they look to science? to religion? to government? Enormous problems may seem to call for sweeping solutions. Instead of thinking big, however, what if we thought *small*? Arnold reminds people that they also can look to personal relationships to find the hope, love, and integrity that can make sense of the world.

Quickwrite
What do you think people cling to in troubled times? Write down a short list of people, places, or things you value the most when times are tough.

Elements of Literature
Mood
Arnold creates a **mood** that shifts at certain points in the poem like the ebb and flow of the tide he describes. **Mood** is the feeling, or **atmosphere,** in a work created by the writer's choice of descriptive details, images, and sounds.

Background
Arnold's first draft of "Dover Beach" dates from 1851, when he and his wife spent a night at Dover during their honeymoon trip on the English coast.

At the Gallery (late 19th or early 20th century) by Paul Gustav Fischer.

Summary

The speaker is looking out at Dover Beach on the English coast. It is a moonlit night, and he calls his beloved to the window to breathe the sweet night air. He hears the endless roar of the waves flinging pebbles on the shore, and the sound suggests eternal sadness. The speaker remarks that the ancient Greek dramatist Sophocles long ago heard the same sound and it also reminded him of the ebb and flow of human misery. According to the speaker, the Sea of Faith, once full like the tide, is now retreating to the edges of the earth. The speaker cries out to his beloved, imploring that they be true to one another. Although the world seems beautiful and fresh, the speaker believes it is actually joyless, cruel, dark, and uncertain. Conflict and pain, he believes, are unavoidable and people fight without knowing why. Thus there is only consolation and meaning in honest and loving human relationships.

BROWSING IN THE FILES
Writers on Writing. It should come as no surprise that Arnold, a literary critic, wrote about the craft of writing. Share the following comment, and encourage students to apply it to "Dover Beach" and to their own writing.

> "Poetry is nothing less than the most perfect speech of man, that in which he comes nearest to being able to utter the truth."

Reaching All Students

Struggling Readers
Have struggling readers identify each complete thought in the poem by disregarding the breaks at the ends of lines and by interpreting the semicolons and the dash as if they were periods. Have students read aloud the sentences they identify and point out the subject and the verb(s) in each sentence. Also, to be sure students understand all the pronoun antecedents, ask them when they read to replace the word *it* each time it occurs with the noun to which it refers.

English Language Learners
Each of the four stanzas of this poem builds upon the previous one to convey Arnold's overall theme. To help students determine his message, have four small groups focus on one of each of the four stanzas in order to discover its main idea. Next, have each group write one sentence that captures their stanza's most important idea. Then, have groups share their generalizations about each stanza and collaborate on a main-idea statement for the whole poem.

Resources

Viewing and Representing

Videocassette B, Segment 9

Available in English and Spanish

This segment presents the working conditions of the Industrial Revolution. For full lesson plans and worksheets, see the *Visual Connections Teacher's Manual.*

A Elements of Literature

Mood

? If the first six lines establish a setting and mood in the poem, how do the words "Only" and "Listen!" in ll. 7 and 9 affect that setting and mood? [Possible responses: "Only" introduces a contrast or an exception to the peaceful setting that begins the poem. The strong interjection "Listen!" breaks the calm mood.]

B Elements of Literature

Metaphor

To help students appreciate the significance of the sea metaphor, ask them what powers the speaker attributes to the sea in these lines. [Possible response: The sea has the power to change the world by altering the shape of the shore. It is eternal with its endless rhythm and "note of sadness."]

C Cultural Connections

Despite their zest for progress, the Victorians were, in many ways, plagued by doubts. One of their greatest challenges was to reconcile their traditional religious beliefs with the new discoveries of science. The speaker voices the concerns of many in his day, who felt that if the new scientific theories were accepted, religious faith could not stand. Thus, Arnold (like Tennyson in "In Memoriam") can be said to speak not merely for himself but for his era.

D Reading Skills and Strategies

Connecting with the Text

? "Dover Beach" was first published in 1867. Does this closing image strike you as prophetic? Explain. [Possible response: Great wars were to come—particularly World Wars I and II. Throughout the twentieth century, new international alliances and new enemies would emerge, fueled by complex economic and political factors. "Ignorant armies" would continue to fight for causes they did not understand very well.]

Dover Beach

Matthew Arnold

The sea is calm tonight.
The tide is full, the moon lies fair
Upon the straits°—on the French coast the light
Gleams and is gone; the cliffs of England stand,
Glimmering and vast, out in the tranquil bay.
Come to the window, sweet is the night air!
Only, from the long line of spray
Where the sea meets the moon-blanched land,
Listen! you hear the grating roar
Of pebbles which the waves draw back, and fling,
At their return, up the high strand,°
Begin, and cease, and then again begin,
With tremulous cadence slow, and bring
The eternal note of sadness in.

Sophocles° long ago
Heard it on the Aegean,° and it brought
Into his mind the turbid ebb and flow
Of human misery; we
Find also in the sound a thought,
Hearing it by this distant northern sea.

The Sea of Faith
Was once, too, at the full, and round earth's shore
Lay like the folds of a bright girdle° furled.
But now I only hear
Its melancholy, long, withdrawing roar,
Retreating, to the breath
Of the night wind, down the vast edges drear
And naked shingles° of the world.

Ah, love, let us be true
To one another! for the world, which seems
To lie before us like a land of dreams,
So various, so beautiful, so new,
Hath really neither joy, nor love, nor light,
Nor certitude, nor peace, nor help for pain;
And we are here as on a darkling plain
Swept with confused alarms of struggle and flight,
Where ignorant armies clash by night.

3. straits: Strait of Dover, a body of water separating southeastern England and northwestern France.

11. strand: shore.

15. Sophocles (säf′ə•klēz′) (c. 496–406 B.C.): one of the principal writers of ancient Greek tragedies.
16. Aegean (ē•jē′ən): sea between Greece and Turkey.

23. girdle: belt.

28. shingles: beaches covered with pebbles.

Using Students' Strengths

Auditory Learners

To help set the scene for an oral reading, play a recording of the sound of surf pounding on the shore. Have students comment on the images and thoughts that come to mind as they listen. Briefly explain that the endlessly repeating sound of the waves is the essential image in Arnold's poem. Then play the recording again softly while a volunteer reads the poem aloud to the class.

Interpersonal Learners

Arnold's speaker concludes that in a world, offering at best only illusions of security, people need to "be true/To one another!" Invite students to work with partners. Ask them to focus on the last stanza, particularly on the speaker's world view as embodied in the closing image. Have each pair write a paraphrase of Arnold's image and then work together to present an alternative image, one that conveys their own view of human existence.

Pegwell Bay, Kent—A Recollection of October 5, 1858 (1859–1860) by William Dyce.
Tate Gallery, London.

Critical Comment

Love Is Itself a Faith

More than any other poem written in the nineteenth century, "Dover Beach" continues to echo through the consciousness of every generation of the twentieth century. To say why involves matters of both technique and meaning.

Compared with the characteristic product of the Romantic or Victorian poets, "Dover Beach" is low-keyed. The speaker's tone is largely that of quiet conversation in which iambs and anapests are congenially mixed. For all its conversational tone, however, the poem is remarkably ambitious in its claim to render a universal condition.

Unlike his predecessors and contemporaries, Arnold neither reaches for the sublime nor dwells on the sentimental in this poem. Instead, he writes a love poem that, incidentally, expresses the crisis of conscience brought about by the dwindling of religion—"the Sea of Faith"—and the rise of science. Science has transformed human life through industrialism and through the mass warfare that scientific inventions made possible. Against these bewildering developments, Arnold poses the notion that love is itself a faith to cling to and, by implication, that individual integrity and a humanistic vision broad enough to include the tragic conclusions of Sophocles are the only defenses against a world moving toward anarchy. **E**

RESPONDING TO THE ART

William Dyce (1806–1864) was a Scottish painter, designer, and writer who first gained prominence in the 1840s for his neoclassical renderings of Biblical subjects.

On the one hand, this painting seems almost as realistic as a photograph; on the other, Dyce has carefully built symbols of time into it. The setting is late afternoon. The cliffs display the march of geologic time, and the people gathering shells on the shore remind us how short human life is.

Activity. Ask students to describe their reactions to the mood of the painting. Does it seem optimistic to them? Nostalgic? Ambiguous? Students might compare this landscape to other landscapes in this book (such as *A Flemish Fair* on p. 282, *Covent Garden with St. Paul's Church* on p. 476, or *Worcester* on p. 622). In each case, have students focus on the relationship of the people to the landscape. Do the people dominate? Are they at home in the world around them? Why or why not?

Critical Comment

This comment focuses on Arnold's faith, expressed in "Dover Beach," that love can provide comfort as religion did before science and industrialism transformed society.

E Critical Thinking

Challenging the Text

Challenge students to defend or oppose the writer's claim that "Dover Beach" is primarily a love poem. [Possible responses: The poem is a love poem because the speaker's answer to the sadness and trouble he sees is to reaffirm love. Or, the poem is about the emptiness of the modern era, and the call for love is secondary to the main theme of the poem.]

Crossing the Curriculum

Music

In 1931, American composer Samuel Barber set "Dover Beach" to music for baritone and string quartet. Several recordings of Barber's deeply touching version are available, including one with Barber himself singing. Play a recording of the song for students and encourage them to discuss what qualities or effects they think the music adds to the poem.

Science

The meaning and value of scientific progress troubled the Victorians. In our time, science still creates controversies, often solving one problem only to reveal another. Have students focus on one scientific advance in medicine, space technology, communications, or another field and make an oral presentation of an issue that has arisen as a result of that scientific discovery. Issues might be moral, psychological, social, or artistic.

Making Meanings

First Thoughts [Respond]

1. Possible responses: Students will probably have the strongest emotional responses either to the first stanza, whose vivid images evoke a quiet melancholy, or to the final stanza, in which the speaker cries out for a loving commitment to help face a difficult world.

Shaping Interpretations [Interpret]

2. It is night in a room in Dover, England, overlooking the moonlit sea. The speaker is addressing a loved one.
3. The mood is calm, peaceful, perhaps even content. The mood is created by images of the calm sea, the moonlight, the vast cliffs, the tranquil bay, and the sweet air.
4. The "grating roar" and the sea flinging pebbles change the mood.
5. Referring to the "tremulous cadence" of the sea, which brings in the "eternal note of sadness," the speaker says that the same sound was heard centuries ago by Sophocles.
6. The "Sea of Faith" (a metaphor for religious belief) once surrounded the earth, encompassing it like the folds of a bright belt (a simile) which supported and decorated the earth. The speaker's faith has weakened; it has withdrawn, leaving the speaker as barren as the beaches he describes.
7. The speaker urges that the couple be true to one another because life is difficult and painful. Students may have similar comforts on their lists.

Extending the Text [Evaluate]

8. The speaker sees the world as chaotic, painful, and joyless. Students may suggest that the view is still relevant because the struggles of competing nations and groups still erupt into wars, armies still clash, and new conflicts continue to arise.
9. Possible response: Progress is always a double-edged sword. The paradox seems to be that attempts to create a "better" world often result in a world that many people find alien and inhospitable.

Grading Timesaver

Rubrics for each Choices assignment appear on p. 175 in the *Portfolio Management System.*

Making Meanings

First Thoughts

1. Which lines of the poem do you respond to most strongly? Why?

Shaping Interpretations

2. What is the **setting** of the first stanza? Who is the speaker, and whom is he addressing?
3. What **mood** do the first six lines evoke for you? What details in these lines create that mood?
4. What **images** in the second half of the first stanza begin to change this mood?
5. Where does the poem begin to move from a personal experience to a timeless and universal theme? What does the speaker imagine Sophocles also heard long ago?
6. Explain the **figures of speech** used to describe faith in lines 21–23. What do you think has happened to the speaker's faith, according to lines 24–28?
7. What does the speaker urge in the last stanza, and why? How does the speaker's resolution compare with the comforting things you cited in your Quickwrite entry?

Extending the Text

8. What is the speaker's view of his world as it is presented in the last stanza? Do you think this view is relevant to today's world? (Do "ignorant armies" still "clash by night"?) Explain why or why not.
9. Certainly the world had progressed when Arnold wrote his poem in the mid-1800s, but industrialization and scientific advances had also brought problems. (This is the "paradox of progress.") How is progress a paradox for us today—that is, how has progress both helped us and hurt or confused us?

Choices: Building Your Portfolio

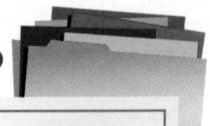

Writer's Notebook

1. Collecting Ideas for an Evaluation

In evaluating a poem, one of the things you will most likely focus on is **meaning.** The reader of any poem asks: What is the poet telling me, and how do I feel about that "message"? Ask yourself these questions about "Dover Beach." Save your notes about the poem's meaning and your response to it for the Writer's Workshop on page 899.

Analyzing Imagery

2. A Changing Picture of the World

Arnold starts his poem with a moonlit sea and ends with a dark plain. Write a brief essay focusing on the **contrasting imagery** in "Dover Beach." Discuss the importance of these contrasts in developing the universal **theme** of the poem.

Creative Writing

3. Newlywed Dialogue

Working with another student, write the **dialogue** between newlywed Arnold and his wife, Fanny Lucy (Arnold called her Flu), that might have inspired this poem. Be sure to express the feelings of both characters.

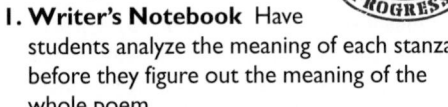

Matthew Arnold (1871), published in *Vanity Fair.*

Choices: Building Your Portfolio

1. **Writer's Notebook** Have students analyze the meaning of each stanza before they figure out the meaning of the whole poem.
2. **Analyzing Imagery** Encourage students to jot down a list of details to support the contrasting imagery before they begin writing.
3. **Creative Writing** Have the class brainstorm ideas about a situation that might have prompted the dialogue.

Reading Skills and Strategies

Vocabulary: Context and Figurative Language

You can sometimes figure out the meaning of a new word—or a familiar word used in a new way—by using **context clues.** These are hints that are found in the surrounding words, phrases, and sentences.

Similes and **metaphors** often provide excellent context clues. In a **simile,** words such as *like, as, than,* or *resemble* are used to compare one thing to another, as in "an inquisitive child is like a blossoming flower." In a **metaphor,** one thing is referred to as if it were something else, either directly, as in "an inquisitive child is a blossoming flower," or indirectly, as in "an inquisitive child grows and blossoms."

Because each of the two equivalent parts of the comparison describes the other, each part provides clues to the meanings of words in the other part. For example, if you read "an inquisitive child is like a blossoming flower" and do not know what *inquisitive* means, you can probably at least figure out that it is a desirable and pleasant quality because you know that in the equivalent part of the comparison the word *blossoming* signifies a desirable and pleasant quality.

Simile. In Robert Browning's poem "Porphyria's Lover" (page 834), the lover uses a simile to describe how he opens Porphyria's eyes after strangling her to death.

> As a shut bud that holds a bee,
> I warily oped her lids.

In this simile, the word *as* is used to compare the two similar actions. The lover warily opens the dead woman's eyes, as he would open a bud that holds a bee. The following diagram shows the almost equivalent relationship of the two parts.

open a bud that holds a bee	as ≈	warily open the dead woman's eyes

If *warily* is an unfamiliar word, knowing that it describes an action similar to opening a bud that holds a bee gives you a clue. You might guess that it means "cautiously."

Metaphor. In the following passage from "Ulysses" by Alfred, Lord Tennyson (page 822), Ulysses, who had been a warrior and world traveler, uses a metaphor that equates his "pause"—his current retirement—to an unused sword.

> How dull it is to pause, to make an end,
> To rust unburnished, not to shine in use!

This metaphor includes what might be an unfamiliar word—*unburnished.* However, like many metaphors, this one is rich with context clues. It contains three clues. First, the metaphoric comparison implies that an inactive warrior is an unburnished sword. The following diagram shows the equivalent relationship of the two parts.

inactive warrior	=	unburnished sword

The equivalent descriptive word for *unburnished,* then, is *inactive,* meaning "idle, retired, dull, sluggish." Second, the sword is rusting, and third, it does not "shine in use." From these clues, you may not yet know that *unburnished* means "unpolished," but you can probably guess that it does have something to do with a neglected condition in which the blade is not brilliantly shiny.

Try It Out

On your own paper, identify the first of the two figures of speech in the following passage from "Dover Beach" by Matthew Arnold as either a metaphor or a simile. Then, draw two boxes as in the preceding diagrams. For a metaphor, use = (equals) between the two boxes; for a simile, use ≈ (almost equals). Write one of the things being compared in each box. Repeat this procedure for the second figure of speech. Finally, write your guess at the meaning of the italicized word, *furled.* Check your guess in a dictionary.

> The Sea of Faith
> Was once, too, at the full, and round earth's shore
> Lay like the folds of a bright girdle *furled.*

Reading Skills and Strategies

This feature focuses on using context clues and figurative language to determine word meanings. These strategies are applied to Robert Browning's "Porphyria's Lover," Alfred, Lord Tennyson's "Ulysses," and Matthew Arnold's "Dover Beach."

Mini-Lesson: Context and Figurative Language

After the class has read the explanation in the text, give students additional practice in identifying the context clues in similes and metaphors by using clichés such as "packed like sardines," "a sea of faces," and "the road to victory." Ask students to contribute any clichéd similes and metaphors that they can recall. After writing the clichés on the chalkboard, have students tell exactly what each one means. Then add a challenging vocabulary word to each simile or metaphor, such as "packed like abject sardines" or "the formidable road to victory." Finally have students define the new words based on the meanings of the clichés.

Try It Out

Possible Answers

Diagrams for the two figures of speech should be similar to these:

Sea	=	Faith

sea surrounding the shore	≈	folds of a furled sash

Students will probably guess from context clues that *furled* has something to do with a folded or rolled-up piece of cloth; they also may know its antonym, *unfurled,* from associations with flags. Students should be able to verify in a dictionary that *furled* means "curled or rolled up." The sea clings to or holds the shore like an unfolded sash or belt.

Using Students' Strengths

Visual Learners

To help visual learners grasp the metaphors in the exercise on this page, have them draw the sea and the shore. Also ask students to draw an island with a sea all around it and to label the sea "Faith." Have volunteers display their drawings and use them as springboards to discuss how Arnold portrays the sea as a once protective force whose receding waves no longer embrace the shore.

OBJECTIVES

The Darkling Thrush / Channel Firing / Ah, Are You Digging on My Grave?

1. Read and interpret the poems
2. Identify and analyze anticlimax
3. Express understanding through persuasive writing, creative writing, or oral interpretation

SKILLS

Literary
- Identify and analyze anticlimax

Writing
- Collect ideas for an evaluation
- Compare poems
- Write an essay or poem on the past and the future
- Write a persuasive editorial about war
- Write a short fictional biography

Speaking/Listening
- Present a dramatic reading

Viewing/Representing
- Respond to details in a landscape painting

Planning

- **Block Schedule**
  Block Scheduling Lesson Plans with Pacing Guide
- **Traditional Schedule**
  Lesson Plans Including Strategies for English-Language Learners
- **One-Stop Planner**
  CD-ROM with Test Generator

Thomas Hardy

(1840–1928)

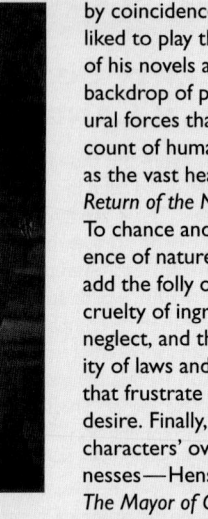

Thomas Hardy (1894).

Thomas Hardy was one of the principal novelists of late-Victorian Britain, but he began and ended his literary career as a poet. The oldest of four children, Hardy was born in a small village in Dorsetshire in southwestern England, the setting (under its ancient name of Wessex) of many of his novels and poems. His father was a stonemason and carpenter who loved music and taught Hardy to play the violin. Hardy went to the village school until he was sixteen, when he became an apprentice to an architect. He read widely on his own for the next six years, "reading the *Iliad,* the *Aeneid,* or the Greek Testament from six to eight in the morning, would work at Gothic architecture all day, and then in the evening rush off with his fiddle under his arm . . . to play country dances, reels, and hornpipes at an agriculturist's wedding." In 1862, Hardy began working as an architect in London, writing poems and stories in his free time. He tried unsuccessfully to publish his poems, but by the time he returned to Dorset in 1867 as an architect specializing in church restoration, he had started to publish fiction.

Hardy's fourth novel, *Far from the Madding Crowd* (1874), was enough of a popular success to enable him to stop working as an architect. During the next twenty years, he published ten novels and three collections of stories. The plots and themes of Hardy's fiction, like those of his poetry, express his belief in a world governed by chance and natural laws that are not hostile, but simply indifferent, to what humans want and deserve. Chance gives us pain when we try for gladness or glory; sometimes in his novels the entire course of lives is determined by coincidence. Hardy liked to play the big scenes of his novels against the backdrop of powerful natural forces that take no account of human life, such as the vast heath of *The Return of the Native* (1878). To chance and the indifference of nature, humans add the folly of war, the cruelty of ingratitude and neglect, and the irrationality of laws and customs that frustrate talent and desire. Finally, the central characters' own weaknesses—Henshard in *The Mayor of Casterbridge* (1886), Jude in *Jude the Obscure* (1895), even Tess in *Tess of the D'Urbervilles* (1891)—make them vulnerable to the destructive powers of nature and society.

The bleakness, pessimism, and irony of Hardy's novels disturbed many of his readers. In 1892, after reading an unfavorable review of *Tess of the D'Urbervilles,* he wrote, "Well, if this sort of thing continues no more novel-writing for me. A man must be a fool to deliberately stand up to be shot at." In 1895, when *Jude the Obscure* was severely denounced by readers and critics (some called it "Jude the Obscene"), Hardy decided to have his say thereafter in poetry: "Perhaps I can express more fully in verse ideas and emotions which run counter to the inert crystallized opinion—hard as a rock—which the vast body of men have vested interests in supporting."

He began collecting old, new, and revised poems in a series of volumes. He published the first in 1898 and was putting together an eighth collection thirty years later, the year of his death. "My poetry was revolutionary," he wrote, "in the sense that I meant to avoid the jeweled line." Twentieth-century critics have praised Hardy's poems for their simple, compressed forms and their sad, ironic tone.

go.hrw.com
LEO 12-11

Resources: Print and Media

Reading
- *Graphic Organizers for Active Reading,* pp. 84, 85, 86
- *Audio CD Library*
  Disc 14, Tracks 3, 4, 5

Writing and Language
- *Grammar and Language Links*
  Worksheet, p. 47
- *Language Workshop CD-ROM*

Viewing and Representing
- *Viewing and Representing*
  Fine Art Transparency 14
  Fine Art Worksheet, p. 56

Assessment
- *Formal Assessment,* pp. 171, 172, 173
- *Portfolio Management System,* p. 176
- *Preparation for College Admission Exams,* p. 41
- *Test Generator (One-Stop Planner CD-ROM)*

Internet
- go.hrw.com (keyword: LEO 12-11)

Before You Read
THE DARKLING THRUSH

Make the Connection
Difficult Transitions

A stark winter scene can suggest physical and emotional desolation. Yet the gloom of winter is followed by springtime renewal. Gloomy though it may appear at the time, the midwinter death of an old year marks the birth of a new one, and with it the hope for a new beginning.

Quickwrite

Why, in your opinion, do people have such strong feelings about the last day of the year or the last day of the century? Do you share those feelings? Write down your responses.

Background

Hardy wrote this poem on December 31, 1900, the last day of both the year and the century. As night falls, the speaker in the poem hears a thrush (a bird) singing joyfully. His thrush, like the century, is worn out and diminished—but still singing.

The Darkling Thrush (A)

Thomas Hardy

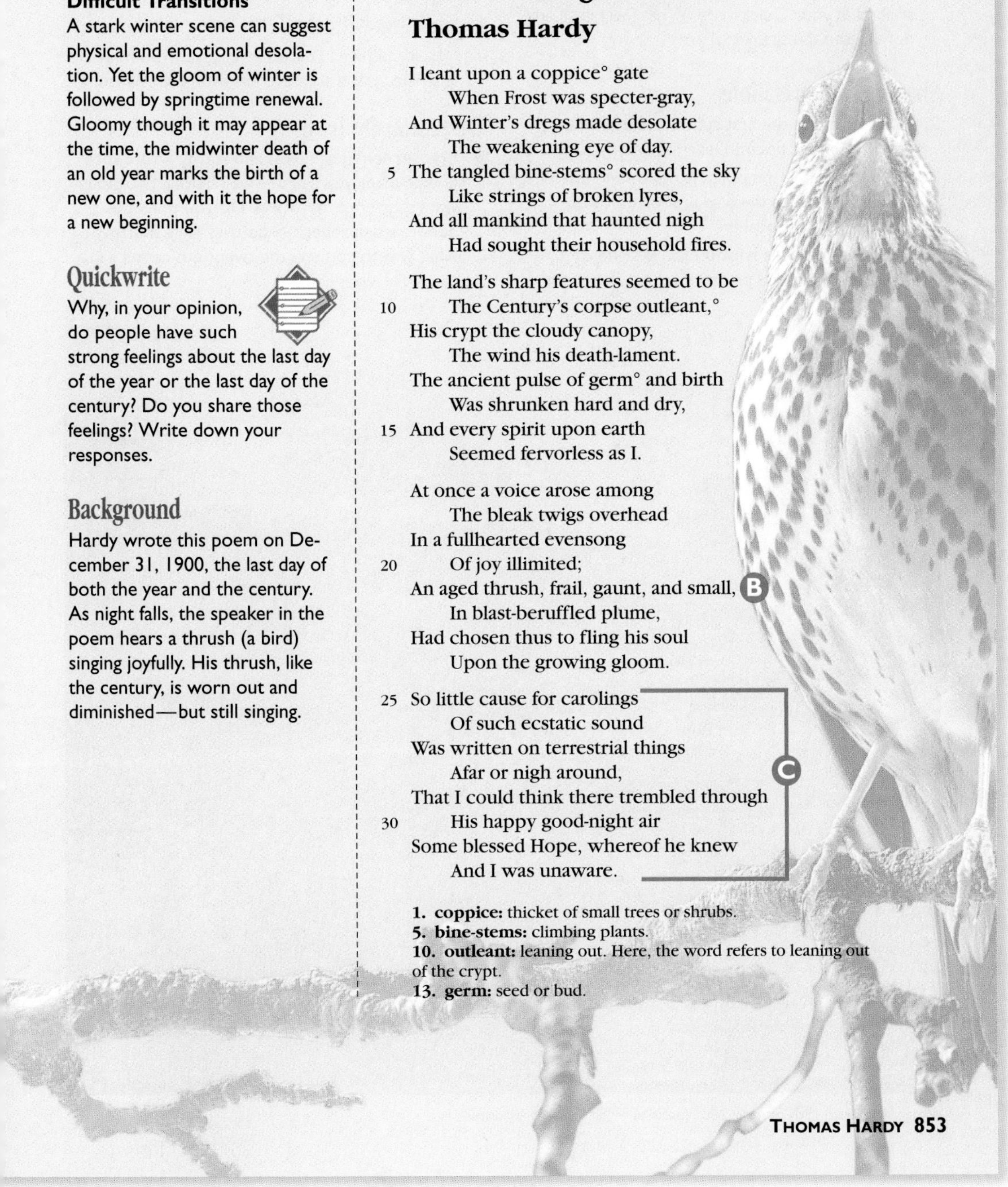

I leant upon a coppice° gate
When Frost was specter-gray,
And Winter's dregs made desolate
The weakening eye of day.
The tangled bine-stems° scored the sky
Like strings of broken lyres,
And all mankind that haunted nigh
Had sought their household fires.

The land's sharp features seemed to be
The Century's corpse outleant,°
His crypt the cloudy canopy,
The wind his death-lament.
The ancient pulse of germ° and birth
Was shrunken hard and dry,
And every spirit upon earth
Seemed fervorless as I.

At once a voice arose among
The bleak twigs overhead
In a fullhearted evensong
Of joy illimited;
An aged thrush, frail, gaunt, and small, (B)
In blast-beruffled plume,
Had chosen thus to fling his soul
Upon the growing gloom.

So little cause for carolings
Of such ecstatic sound
Was written on terrestrial things
Afar or nigh around,
That I could think there trembled through (C)
His happy good-night air
Some blessed Hope, whereof he knew
And I was unaware.

1. coppice: thicket of small trees or shrubs.
5. bine-stems: climbing plants.
10. outleant: leaning out. Here, the word refers to leaning out of the crypt.
13. germ: seed or bud.

Summary

In a desolate winter landscape, the speaker hears the joyful song of an old, frail thrush—a hearty sound in stark contrast to the dying and spiritless earth. The speaker is deeply moved by the bird's song, which seems to express a hope that the speaker himself does not possess.

(A) Vocabulary Note

Have students briefly discuss the word *darkling*. You might suggest they compare Hardy's use of it with the use of this word in Keats's "Ode to a Nightingale" (p. 757, l. 51) and in Arnold's "Dover Beach" (p. 848, l. 35).

(B) Reading Skills and Strategies
Making Inferences

? What do you infer from Hardy's choice of an old, frail, common thrush instead of a young, exotic songbird? [Possible responses: The thrush is common enough so that everyone can relate to it. Its age may reflect the age of the world, and its weakness may suggest that even a weak creature can generate hope.]

(C) Elements of Literature
Tone

Remind students that **tone** is the writer's attitude to the subject, and point out that the tone of the last stanza conveys a deep ambiguity toward the bird's joy. The first three stanzas are a grim portrait of a dead world, and although the old bird sings, in the last stanza, the speaker looks near and far and sees "little cause" for any positive outburst. He admits that he "could think" that the bird has some reason for hope, but the speaker leaves readers with the sober thought that, no matter what the bird knows, he himself is unaware of any reason to hope.

Reaching All Students

Struggling Readers

To stimulate students' interest in the theme of the poem, ask them for examples of how people project into nature the ideas and emotions they want to find there. For example, what associations do people often make with the sun, an eclipse, thunder and lightning, or a rainbow? Discuss with students how valid they think these associations are. Ask students what other associations Hardy's speaker might have made with the song of the thrush.

English Language Learners

Have English language learners work with English proficient partners to divide the poem into individual sentences. Then have them work together to identify the subject and the verb(s) of each sentence. You may also want to ask students to paraphrase each sentence, using standard English prose. Students may also substitute modern equivalents for some of Hardy's archaic word choices (e.g., *leant—leaned, nigh—near, whereof—of which*) when writing their paraphrases.

Advanced Learners

Encourage advanced learners to research the ideas, attitudes, and emotions that people express during millennium celebrations. What expectations, doubts, and even terrors rise to the surface when one millennium passes into another? Have students present oral reports on their findings.

MAKING MEANINGS

First Thoughts [Respond]

1. Responses will vary, but students may note gloomy details that would fit the mood of the first two stanzas or reasons for hope that would fit the mood of the final two stanzas.

Shaping Interpretations [Interpret]

2. "Coppice gate" (l. 1), "Frost" (l. 2), "Winter's dregs" (l. 3), "weakening eye of day" (l. 4). Students will probably see a gray, snowy, bleak scene.

3. The thrush's song signals its appearance in the third stanza.

4. Most students will sense some hope in the speaker; others may feel that his hopeless mood remains.

5. The speaker suggests the bird knows of a "blessed Hope" (l. 31).

6. *Darkling* means "in the dark"; it suggests emotional gloom as well as physical darkness. Interpretations of the song will vary; encourage students to see the song as part of an overall view of nature.

Connecting with the Text [Synthesize]

7. Students may mention a beautiful sunset, rainbow, or flower.

Extending the Texts [Evaluate]

8. Possible response: The poems are insightful and prophetic; they also show how the horror of war and uncertainty about the future exist in all centuries.

RESPONDING TO THE ART

Sir George Clausen (1852–1944) began his career as an interior decorator. He studied in London and Antwerp, sketched in Dutch fishing villages, and became an admirer of rustic landscapes rendered in a basically naturalistic style. After a stay at an artists' colony in Brittany in 1882, Clausen began to produce the paintings of rural scenes and fieldworkers for which he is best known. Clausen's landscapes depict the slow weathering of people in an unromanticized environment.

Activity. Ask students to list details in the painting that describe the way of life of the workers (clothing, tools, activities).

MAKING MEANINGS

First Thoughts

1. Compare the speaker's feelings about the end of the century with what you described in your Quickwrite. What feelings, if any, do you and the speaker share?

Shaping Interpretations

2. What details in the first stanza establish the **setting** for the poem? Describe what you see.

3. At what point in the poem is the thrush introduced? How does the bird first come to the attention of the speaker?

4. Does the speaker's **mood** change significantly in the course of the poem? If so, how?

5. What does the speaker say about the thrush's "air," or song, in the last stanza?

6. What do you think is the significance of the word *darkling* in the title? Do you think the thrush's song seems hopeful or hopeless? Explain.

Connecting with the Text

7. Has something in nature ever given you hope or cheered you? If so, describe your experience.

Extending the Texts

8. Both Arnold (page 846) and Hardy wrote their poems many years ago—well before two global wars shattered the world. Do you think the poems are prophetic—do they **foreshadow** what was to come in the twentieth century in a particular way? Explain.

Winter Work (late 19th or early 20th century) by Sir George Clausen.

Making the Connections

Connecting with the Theme: "The Paradox of Progress"

Paradox and ambiguity are at the core of "The Darkling Thrush," reflecting the doubts that plagued the Victorian imagination. Hardy wonders how the bird's joyful song should be interpreted, just as the Victorians questioned how nature itself should be understood. Have interested students research and report on Victorian attitudes toward nature and the effects of industrialization on nature.

Cultural Connections

Point out that different cultures attach various meanings and emotions to certain species of birds. For example, if Hardy's speaker were American and had seen an eagle soaring in the sky, he or she might have been filled with feelings of national pride and patriotism. Ask students to research and discuss the significance of specific birds to particular cultures or countries.

Before You Read
CHANNEL FIRING

Make the Connection
Wake-up Call
In an age of almost miraculous technological advances, humanity sometimes stops to ask itself: When will we be too advanced, or too civilized, or too sane to wage war? Hardy's poem brings a different perspective to that question. He imagines what the dead would say if they were awakened by violence in the land of the living.

Quickwrite
If they could speak, what do you think the dead would say to the living? Briefly write down your ideas.

Background
The subject of "Channel Firing" is the testing of guns at sea and on the shores of the English Channel. Hardy wrote this poem in April 1914, when a naval rivalry was growing between Great Britain and Germany. Four months later, World War I began.

The word *chancel* (line 3) refers to the part of a church nearest the altar; a *glebe* (line 9) is a plot of land attached to a church or its rectory. In the poem's last stanza, the sound of guns reaches three sites famous in British history: Alfred's Tower, near Stourton, which honors King Alfred's defeat of the Danes in 879; Camelot, the legendary site of King Arthur's court; and Stonehenge, the prehistoric arrangement of huge stones on the Salisbury Plain (see page 2).

Channel Firing

Thomas Hardy

That night your great guns, unawares,
Shook all our coffins as we lay,
And broke the chancel window-squares,
We thought it was the Judgment Day

And sat upright. While drearisome
Arose the howl of wakened hounds:
The mouse let fall the altar-crumb,
The worms drew back into the mounds,

The glebe cow drooled. Till God called, "No;
It's gunnery practice out at sea
Just as before you went below;
The world is as it used to be:

"All nations striving strong to make
Red war yet redder. Mad as hatters **(A)**
They do no more for Christés sake
Than you who are helpless in such matters.

"That this is not the judgment hour
For some of them's a blessed thing,
For if it were they'd have to scour
Hell's floor for so much threatening. . . .

"Ha, ha. It will be warmer when
I blow the trumpet (if indeed **(B)**
I ever do; for you are men,
And rest eternal sorely need)."

So down we lay again. "I wonder,
Will the world ever saner be,"
Said one, "than when He sent us under
In our indifferent century!"

And many a skeleton shook his head.
"Instead of preaching forty year,"
My neighbor Parson Thirdly said,
"I wish I had stuck to pipes and beer."

Again the guns disturbed the hour,
Roaring their readiness to avenge,
As far inland as Stourton Tower,
And Camelot, and starlit Stonehenge.

Summary ■■
The dead speakers report that gunnery practice woke them one night and they thought Judgment Day had arrived. God, however, explained to them that the noise was coming from human beings preparing for war. After God denounces war, the dead return to their rest, wondering if the living will ever learn.

Background
By 1914, Europe was divided into two powerful camps—the Triple Alliance (Germany, Austria-Hungary, and Italy) and the Triple Entente (France, Great Britain, and Russia). On June 28, 1914 Archduke Franz Ferdinand of Austria-Hungary and his wife were assassinated by a Serbian nationalist. Diplomacy failed to heal the breach, and Austria-Hungary declared war on Serbia on July 28. When Russia, which had promised to protect the Serbs, mobilized, Germany declared war on Russia. On August 3, Germany declared war on France and invaded neutral Belgium, causing Britain to enter what was to become World War I.

Resources
Viewing and Representing
Fine Art Transparency
A Fine Art Transparency of Sir John Lavery's *The Cemetery, Etaples, 1919* can be used to complement this lesson. See the *Viewing and Representing Transparencies and Worksheets:*
- Transparency 14
- Worksheet p. 56

(A) Critical Thinking
Making Connections
? Are nations still making "Red war yet redder"? Explain. [Possible responses: Yes, war is becoming bloodier and bloodier because weapons are increasingly more effective in killing and maiming.]

(B) Elements of Literature
Allusion
Divine laughter may refer to the fourth verse of the Second Psalm, in which God's reaction to warring nations is predicted as follows: "He that sitteth in the heavens shall laugh: the Lord shall have them in derision."

Reaching All Students

Struggling Readers
Extend the situation in the poem by having students reflect on what their ancestors might say about today's world situation if they were to speak from their graves. Have students work in pairs to create dialogues with their great-grandparents about the present state of the world. Students should address issues similar to those treated in Hardy's poem. Invite volunteers to present their dialogue to the class.

English Language Learners
Point out to English language learners that Hardy deliberately mixes everyday speech (the casual contraction "It's" in l. 10), idioms ("mad as hatters" in l. 14), and archaic expressions ("for Christés sake" in l. 15) in God's response. Tell students that Hardy may have combined these vocabularies to suggest God's timelessness and universality.

Making Meanings

First Thoughts [Respond]

1. Students may be surprised by God's laughter and by the good person who regrets his life of upright living because he did not improve the world.

Shaping Interpretations [Interpret]

2. The speakers are the dead, buried in a churchyard near the English Channel, who are addressing those still living. "Your" in l. 1 refers to the living people firing the guns.
3. God sees the firing as a pointless activity that accomplishes no more than do the actions of the dead.
4. The guns disturb the dead but not the living; Parson Thirdly wishes he had stuck to pipes and beer; the threatening sound of the guns reaches inland, shaking what it is meant to protect.
5. God declares that it is a good thing for some of the living that it is not Judgment Day because they would be condemned to scour the floors of Hell in punishment for their violence.
6. Students are likely to agree with the speakers' distaste for war and consider most wars foolish and unjustifiable. However, some students may acknowledge the necessity of war, at times, for a just cause.

Challenging the Text [Evaluate]

7. Students may suggest that the roughness of Hardy's language befits the harshness of his subject. If the speakers used perfect, upper-class English, the poem might have an elitist, unrealistic quality.

L'Enfer (Hell) (detail) (early 20th century) by Georges Paul Leroux.

Imperial War Museum, London. © 1997 Artists Rights Society (ARS), New York / ADAGP, Paris.

Making Meanings

First Thoughts

1. Does any detail in the poem surprise or even shock you? Explain why or why not. (Be sure to check your Quickwrite notes.)

Shaping Interpretations

2. What do you know about the **speakers** in the poem? To whom are the speakers talking? (To whom does "your" in line 1 refer?)
3. What do you make of God's irritation at those who fire the guns?
4. Point out at least three examples of **irony** in the poem.
5. What does God say about Judgment Day in the fifth stanza?
6. What do you think this poem says about war? Explain whether you agree or disagree with the **theme** of the poem.

Challenging the Text

7. In his own time, Hardy was criticized for his deliberate use of "unpoetic" **diction** (such as "drooled" in line 9 and "mad as hatters" in line 14). What is your response to Hardy's critics? Would the poem have a different effect if the speakers used perfect "king's English"?

Using Students' Strengths

Auditory Learners

Have students list sounds they would expect to hear (not only the guns, for example, but the scurrying of mice or the lowing of the cow) if they were present at the scene the poem describes. Then, encourage individuals to give an interpretive reading of the poem that reflects its meaning and mood.

Visual Learners

Have visual learners render the scene of the poem in a drawing or painting. Encourage them to include as many specific details from the poem as they can, such as the landscape, the hounds, and the graves of the individual speakers. Students may also want to consider drawing a bird's-eye view of the setting.

Before You Read
AH, ARE YOU DIGGING ON MY GRAVE?

Make the Connection
Do You Miss Me?
It's comforting to know that people miss us when we're gone. What if we could come back from the dead and find out how *much* they miss us? We all have expectations of how loved ones would respond to our absence, but we might be surprised at what they say about us when we're not around.

Quickwrite
Write a few sentences explaining what you think this poem is about, based on its title.

Elements of Literature
Anticlimax
The power of this poem in part depends on Hardy's use of **anticlimax,** the surprising occurrence of something trivial when something significant is expected. In this poem, Hardy challenges our conventional beliefs about death and grieving by creating a **narrator,** or speaker, who has only limited information about her situation—she therefore receives some very unexpected answers to her repeated question.

Ah, Are You Digging on My Grave?

Thomas Hardy

"Ah, are you digging on my grave,
My loved one?—planting rue?"°
—"No: Yesterday he went to wed
One of the brightest wealth has bred.
'It cannot hurt her now,' he said,
'That I should not be true.'" **A**

"Then who is digging on my grave?
My nearest dearest kin?"
—"Ah, no: They sit and think, 'What use!
What good will planting flowers produce?
No tendance of her mound can loose
Her spirit from Death's gin.'"° **B**

"But some one digs upon my grave?
My enemy?—prodding sly?"
—"Nay: When she heard you had passed the Gate
That shuts on all flesh soon or late,
She thought you no more worth her hate,
And cares not where you lie."

"Then, who is digging on my grave?
Say—since I have not guessed!"
—"O it is I, my mistress dear,
Your little dog, who still lives near,
And much I hope my movements here
Have not disturbed your rest?"

"Ah, yes! *You* dig upon my grave . . .
Why flashed it not on me
That one true heart was left behind!
What feeling do we ever find
To equal among human kind
A dog's fidelity!"

"Mistress, I dug upon your grave
To bury a bone, in case
I should be hungry near this spot
When passing on my daily trot.
I am sorry, but I quite forgot
It was your resting place." **C**

2. **rue:** yellow-flowered herb associated with grief.
12. **gin:** trap.

Summary

The speaker, a dead woman, asks if the digger on her grave is her beloved, but she is told that he has just married someone else. She asks if her kin are digging, but she is told that they see no point in tending her grave. She asks if it's her enemy who digs, but she is told that her enemy no longer cares about her. Finally, she learns that the digger is her dog, merely burying a bone.

A Reading Skills and Strategies
Drawing Conclusions

? Why might the "loved one" have been concerned about hurting the speaker? [Possible responses: If she were still alive, she would have been hurt to learn that the man could love another so quickly.]

B Critical Thinking
Extending the Text

? Many people would agree with the "nearest dearest kin" that tending the grave will do nothing to restore the person buried in it. Why, then, do you think that people often spend thousands of dollars on elaborate funerals, ornate headstones, and perpetual care of beautiful gravesites? [Possible responses: out of love or respect for the one who has died; out of the need (or pressure) to make a public show of their grief; because of tradition or a hope that their survivors will be as attentive as they have been.]

C Elements of Literature
Anticlimax

? In the poem Hardy has raised the speaker's hopes, only to let them down. How does this use of anticlimax affect you? [Possible responses: It creates sympathy for the dead woman; makes the reader wonder how well anyone is remembered after death.]

Reaching All Students

Struggling Readers
Struggling readers might benefit from a review of the use of quotation marks. The first two stanzas of the poem make use of single quotation marks within double quotation marks. Be sure students understand that such punctuation indicates that one speaker is repeating the exact words of another. It may help students to rewrite the poem in the form of a dialogue with the words of each speaker following his or her name.

English Language Learners
Have English language learners identify and list in sequence the people the speaker thinks are digging on her grave (lover, kin, enemy, dog).

Advanced Learners
Have students read some of the poems in Edgar Lee Masters's *Spoon River Anthology* and compare some of Masters's characters to Hardy's. What, for example, might Masters's Lucinda Matlock say to Hardy's speaker in this poem?

MAKING MEANINGS

First Thoughts [Respond]

1. Students probably will conclude that Hardy is mocking sentimentality about death. If the premise of this poem is accepted at face value, then a person who dies is quickly forgotten. Students may have predicted only human diggers.

Shaping Interpretations [Interpret]

2. One can assume she had a husband or fiancé and a family and that she had a conflict with another woman. The dog's answers reveal that the speaker's family is no longer grieving, that her enemy (like the dog) has forgotten her, and that her beloved has married someone else.
3. Animal traits include routine surveillance of territory and burying bones. More human traits include apologizing for having disturbed the woman's grave and preparing for the future.
4. Every time the woman speculates about the identity of the digger and the motives for his or her actions, she turns out to be wrong. In fact, no one is grieving for her.
5. Students will probably agree that the tone is wry, ironic, even bitter.

Challenging the Text [Evaluate]

6. Students will probably agree that Hardy's use of irony is quite effective. Even if the responses to the woman's questions seem comical at first, upon reflection students will empathize with the sadness of her situation.

Grading Timesaver

Rubrics for each Choices assignment appear on p. 176 in the *Portfolio Management System*.

MAKING MEANINGS

First Thoughts

1. After reading this poem, tell how you think Hardy feels about sentimental attitudes toward death. How close did you come in your Quickwrite notes to predicting what the poem would be about?

Shaping Interpretations

2. In the first three stanzas, what information about the dead woman's life do you get from her guesses and from the dog's answers?
3. In the last stanza, how does the dog's answer combine animal traits with qualities we consider human?
4. **Anticlimax** is the deflating effect we feel when our lofty expectations are let down. How does Hardy employ the device of anticlimax in each of the first three stanzas?
5. How would you describe the **tone** of this poem?

Challenging the Text

6. In **irony of situation,** there is a sharp discrepancy between what is expected and what actually happens. Do you think that Hardy's use of irony is effective in this poem? Why or why not?

CHOICES: Building Your Portfolio

Writer's Notebook

1. Collecting Ideas for an Evaluation

WORK IN PROGRESS

On page 856, questions 6 and 7 ask you to evaluate the elements of **theme** and **diction** in "Channel Firing." Whatever your evaluations were, you need concrete evidence from the poem to support them in an essay. Cite two quotations from the poem to support each of your responses to questions 6 and 7. Save your notes for the Writer's Workshop on page 899.

Comparing Poems

2. Bird Sightings

In a brief essay, compare "The Darkling Thrush" with any poem in this book in which the poet uses the conventional Romantic **images** of bird and song—for example, Keats's "Ode to a Nightingale" (page 755) or Shelley's "To a Skylark" (page 739).

Creative Writing

3. Passages and Reflections

Imagine that you are in a creative mood on the final evening of the year or the century. Write a short essay or poem summing up your view of the past and your hopes or fears for the future.

Persuasive Writing

4. What's Your Opinion?

Hardy's "Channel Firing" indirectly makes a point about war through the use of an imaginary dialogue. Write a persuasive editorial that directly expresses your ideas about war.

Creative Writing

5. The Rest of the Story

Write a short biography of the woman who speaks in "Ah, Are You Digging on My Grave?"

Oral Interpretation

6. Acting the Part

In a small group, present a dramatic reading of "Channel Firing" or "Ah, Are You Digging on My Grave?" Decide who will speak each line, and rehearse your interpretation. Include music, costumes, and sound effects to make your presentation more dramatic. Ask your listeners to evaluate your interpretations of the poems.

Assessing Learning

Standardized Test Preparation

For practice with ACT and SAT formats, see

- *Preparation for College Admission Exams,* p. 41

Informal Assessment

Self Assessment. To help students become more aware of how well they grasp Hardy's themes and tones, ask students to complete these two sentences:

What I understand best about Hardy's poems is ______________.

What I understand least about Hardy's poems is ______________.

SPOTLIGHT ON

Victorian Novelists

I am neither a man nor a woman but an author. **A**

—Charlotte Brontë, 1849

Victorian tastes seem remarkable today for the excesses of abundant hoop skirts and living rooms crowded with knickknacks. Literary fashions of the period were no different.

Magnificent Storytelling, Huge Books

The most remarkable product of Victorian literature was the novel—hefty volumes regularly published in three-volume editions called three-deckers. The lucrative phenomenon of magazine serialization encouraged authors to write long texts sometimes criticized as "loose, baggy monsters"; in this wealth of pages, however, novelists of the period perfected the art of storytelling. Victoria's reign produced notable poetry, but the period is best known for the passion, scope, and originality of its novels. **B**

A nineteenth-century audience recognized categories of novels including historical fiction, suspenseful detective stories, and "Newgate" or criminal novels with tales taken directly from prison records. Novels became a medium for instruction and were considered a legitimate way to learn history and etiquette. Writers also could address the social problems caused by the nineteenth century's rapid industrialization. For example, Charles Dickens lampoons the abuses of the court system in *Bleak House* (1852–1853) and exposes the horrors of workhouses in *Oliver Twist* (1837–1838). These books reached an increasingly large audience through lending libraries, periodicals, and affordable "cheap editions," ensuring a diverse Victorian readership that included a growing middle class and increasing numbers of female readers.

"Lady Novelists"

In the nineteenth century, the novel was a relatively new genre that was still developing its own traditions. The originality of this format, combined with the increase in literacy and the explosion of nineteenth-century publishing, presented large numbers of average, middle-class women with unprecedented opportunities to showcase their talents. Women no longer had to have exceptional wealth or education in order to write, and, though their work was often slighted by the literary men of the period, female novelists were no longer in danger of being branded "outrageous" or "unladylike" merely because they wrote. **C** The success of "lady novelists" is reflected in the American writer Nathaniel Hawthorne's complaint about "the d——d mob of scribbling women" whom he saw as competition. William Thackeray, a well-known novelist, could grumble at the success of Frances Trollope's *The Vicar of Wrexhill* (1837) by saying that the author "had much better remained at home, pudding making or stocking mending." The complaints of such established writers only confirm the success of female novelists. Prohibited from entering many lucrative professions, the "lady novelists" produced profitable books that often addressed the difficulties faced by talented, literary women.

George Eliot (1819–1880)

The author Mary Ann Evans adopted the pen name George Eliot to keep her identity secret at a time when serious literature by women could receive **D**

Reaching All Students

Struggling Readers

Help students make an outline of the content of each section in this feature. On the chalkboard or on a transparency, write the frame of a formal outline, providing students with the main points and asking them to fill in the supporting details. For example, you might write in "Types of Novels" as a main entry in the outline for the first section and then ask students to provide details such as "historical fiction" or "crime novels."

English Language Learners

Pair students and have each pair create a list of five to ten words or phrases that describe some aspect of the Victorian novel, as discussed in the Spotlight On. Items on their lists can include authors and titles; characters, subjects, and themes; and other details that help them characterize the Victorian novel. Have pairs share their lists; then help students work cooperatively to develop three important generalizations from the details on their lists.

Spotlight On

This feature gives an overview of the development of the novel in the Victorian period, charting the greater availability of affordable books and the larger, more diverse reading public, including growing numbers of women. During this period, women, for the first time, began to write and publish with such success that some of the established male authors, like Thackeray, resented the competition. Passages from the groundbreaking works of three female novelists—George Eliot, Charlotte Brontë, and Emily Brontë—illustrate their creation of strong female protagonists who grapple with the constraints all women faced in the Victorian era. After discussing the feature, urge interested students to research the publishing histories of Dickens, Thackeray, Eliot, or any of the Brontës.

A Reading Skills and Strategies

Drawing Conclusions

? What do you think Brontë means by this comment? [Possible response: She wants to be judged by the quality of her writing, not by her gender.]

B Humanities Connections

Serials

Perhaps the best contemporary parallel to magazine serialization is daytime television soap operas. Like magazine serials, the "soaps" have long, convoluted story lines and their plots move forward in very small steps; in addition, soap audiences, like the audiences for Victorian serials, eagerly anticipate each new installment.

C Exploring the Culture

? Why do you think writing was considered "unladylike"? [Possible responses: Women were entering a male-dominated area and were displaying a worldliness and competitive spirit that surprised and threatened many men.]

D Background

Other Victorian Novels

Adam Bede (1859), George Eliot's first novel, established her as a leading writer of serious fiction. Her masterpiece *Middlemarch* (1871–1872) is still considered one of the finest novels, by man or woman, of the Victorian age.

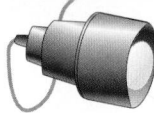

Ⓐ Reading Skills and Strategies
Predicting Outcomes

? Why is Maggie cutting her hair? [Possible response: It is an act of defiance, a declaration of independence by which Maggie hopes to get her family to see her as a person, not just a face.] **Do you think Maggie's action will get her what she wants? Why or why not?** [Possible response: Undoubtedly she will get attention, but her action may not get her the respect she desires.]

Ⓑ Cultural Connections
Pseudonyms

? When and why do people today use pseudonyms? [Possible responses: Today, a writer might choose a pseudonym to protect his or her privacy; an actor might change his or her name to increase "star appeal"; a well-known artist might produce a work under another name, hoping (as the Brontës did) that it will be judged on its own merit apart from the identity of the person who created it.]

Ⓒ Critical Thinking
Making Inferences

? How does Woolf imply that the Brontës were innovative writers? [She says that the Brontës actively struggled against the repressive forces of tradition and convention in their writing.]

Ⓓ Literary Connections
Other Victorian Viewpoints

Have students compare the view of love in *Wuthering Heights* (a power that can transcend death) to the attitudes toward love and death expressed in Matthew Arnold's "Dover Beach" and Thomas Hardy's "Ah, Are You Digging on My Grave?"

biased criticism—like Thackeray's. Known for her ability to capture rural village life in novels such as *Silas Marner* (1861), Eliot created talented heroines limited by circumstance and social propriety. For example, the young protagonist of *The Mill on the Floss* (1860) tires of her troublesome long hair and asks for her brother Tom's aid. In the process, Maggie Tulliver calls our attention to the Victorians' emphasis on "proper" feminine appearance.

> Tom followed Maggie upstairs into her mother's room, and saw her go at once to a drawer, from which she took out a large pair of scissors.
>
> "What are they for, Maggie?" said Tom, feeling his curiosity awakened.
>
> Maggie answered by seizing her front locks and cutting them straight across the middle of her forehead.
>
> "Oh, my buttons, Maggie, you'll catch it!" exclaimed Tom; "you'd better not cut any more off."
>
> Snip! went the great scissors again while Tom was speaking; and he couldn't help feeling it was rather good fun: Maggie would look so queer. . . .
>
> Ⓐ Maggie felt an unexpected pang. She had thought beforehand chiefly of her own deliverance from her teasing hair and teasing remarks about it, and something also of the triumph she should have over her mother and her aunts by this very decided course of action: she didn't want her hair to look pretty—that was out of the question—she only wanted people to think her a clever little girl, and not to find fault with her.
>
> —George Eliot, *from The Mill on the Floss*

Eliot's novels show that a clever little girl's problems only increase when she grows into a clever young woman. Unlike Dickens, who provides his audience with miraculous happy endings, George Eliot looks unflinchingly at heroines whose intelligence and talent have no place in their culture. Her perspective indicates the limitations of Victorian progress and prosperity.

George Eliot (1849), age 30.
Engraving by G. J. Stodart from a painting by M. D'Albert-Durand.

The Sisters Brontë: Charlotte (1816–1855) and Emily (1818–1848)

The Brontë sisters offer a striking example of the novel's success because they produced two of the most perpetually popular novels, *Jane Eyre* and *Wuthering Heights,* while living in the same Yorkshire household. The daughters of a minister, Charlotte and Emily determined that they could support themselves as novelists, and they wrote Ⓑ passionately of the isolated moor country they loved. Like George Eliot, they adopted men's names, Currer Bell and Ellis Bell, in the hopes of receiving fair, unbiased responses to their work. Ⓒ Describing the sisters, the writer Virginia Woolf said, "There is in them some untamed ferocity perpetually at war with the accepted order of things which makes them desire to create instantly rather than to observe patiently."

Ⓓ We can see this "ferocity" in Emily's *Wuthering Heights* (1847), a disturbing love story that draws on the Gothic themes of the Romantic poets she loved. Brontë attributes to her characters Catherine Earnshaw and Heathcliff a love that transcends even death, with Cathy haunting her soul mate from the grave. Heathcliff recalls these events from the day of her funeral:

Using Students' Strengths

Verbal Learners

Encourage students to respond to this feature by imagining themselves a Victorian reader writing a letter to the editor of a Victorian newspaper. In their letter, they may either praise or condemn a novel they are reading. Tell them to identify the novel and use examples from it to support their positive or negative evaluation.

Interpersonal Learners

Help students record the feature's main points by dividing the class into five groups, one group focusing on each heading/section. Have each group record the section's main points in a cluster diagram and then explain their diagram to the class. Finally ask each group to copy and distribute their clusters so that every group has a complete set.

"Being alone, and conscious two yards of loose earth was the sole barrier between us, I said to myself—

"'I'll have her in my arms again! If she be cold, I'll think it is this north wind that chills *me;* and if she be motionless, it is sleep.'

"I got a spade from the toolhouse, and began to delve with all my might—it scraped the coffin; I fell to work with my hands, the wood commenced crackling about the screws, I was on the point of attaining my object, when it seemed that I heard a sigh from some one above, close at the edge of the grave, and bending down.—'If I can only get this off,' I muttered, 'I wish they may shovel in the earth over us both!' and I wrenched at it more desperately still. There was another sigh, close at my ear. I appeared to feel the warm breath of it displacing the sleet-laden wind. I knew no living thing in flesh and blood was by—but as certainly as you perceive the approach to some substantial body in the dark, though it cannot be discerned, so certainly I felt that Cathy was there, not under me, but on the earth. . . ."

—Emily Brontë, *from Wuthering Heights*

Emily's novel shocked Victorian audiences by bringing Gothic evil, violence, and horror into a seemingly safe domestic setting. Charlotte's *Jane Eyre* (1847) was no less shocking in its rejection of docile, sentimental heroines. The popular novelist Margaret Oliphant wrote in 1855, "Ten years ago we professed an orthodox system of novel making. Our lovers were humble and devoted, when suddenly, without warning, *Jane Eyre* stole upon the scene." Charlotte constructs a love story containing a scandalous secret marriage and a madwoman hidden in the attic of a country mansion. Just as daring, though, is the independence of Jane Eyre, the self-possessed governess who refuses to accept the limitations of her social station or her sex:

The Brontë Sisters (1834) by Patrick Branwell Brontë.

By Courtesy of the National Portrait Gallery, London.

Nobody knows how many rebellions besides political rebellions ferment in the masses of life which people earth. Women are supposed to be very calm generally: but women feel just as men feel; they need exercise for their faculties, and a field for their efforts as much as their brothers do; they suffer from too rigid a restraint, too absolute a stagnation, precisely as men would suffer; and it is narrow-minded in their more privileged fellow creatures to say that they ought to confine themselves to making puddings and knitting stockings, to playing on the piano and embroidering bags. It is thoughtless to condemn them, or laugh at them, if they seek to do more or learn more than custom has pronounced necessary for their sex.

—Charlotte Brontë, *from Jane Eyre*

Three-Deckers and Victorian Values

Novels offered Victorian audiences opportunities to discuss, explore, and explain the rapid changes in the nineteenth-century social fabric. Female authors often described the friction between the period's social constraints and their own need for autonomy. Many modern authors reject the idea that stories can—or should—convey lessons in morality, just as they reject the notion that simple remedies exist for difficult social problems. Yet in Victoria's reign, with its proud, growing empire, Britons could still harbor bright hopes for social and scientific progress. The novels of the era could capture audiences with three-deckers that examined conflicts in fascinating detail; their hope, whether stated or not, was that solutions could be found.

E Reading Skills and Strategies

Connecting with the Text

? Margaret Oliphant wrote that *Jane Eyre* made novelists rethink the "orthodox," or traditional, aspects of their stories. Can you think of a story that made you look at something in a new way? [Possible responses: The movie version of Shakespeare's *Twelfth Night* made the play seem more modern. The novel *Beloved* by Toni Morrison put freedom in a new perspective.]

F Exploring the Culture

Contrary Opinions

Jane Eyre has been widely praised for its narrative power. The moral values it presents would not cause controversy today; however, the novel, when first published, was considered unacceptable, even immoral. Matthew Arnold, for example, wrote that Charlotte Brontë's mind contained "nothing but hunger, rebellion, and rage."

G Reading Skills and Strategies

Responding to the Text

Ask students to make some notes about the ways in which they believe "women feel just as men feel." Allow volunteers to share responses in small-group settings; also encourage students to refer to these notes when they are looking for ideas for original writing.

H Literary Connections

Audience Participation

Contemporary computer technology has created new ways for readers and writers to collaborate in the writing of fiction. Now, through hyperfiction, readers can invent their own ways of interacting with a novel, choosing to follow different characters and selecting from a variety of settings, plots, and even themes. In addition, some novelists post their work on the Internet and invite readers to contribute to their works-in-progress.

Assessing Learning

Check Test: True-False

1. Characteristics that make Victorian novels remarkable are their passion, scope, and originality. [True]
2. Many of Charles Dickens's novels criticize Victorian society. [True]
3. The endings of both George Eliot's and Dickens's novels are always happy. [False]
4. *Jane Eyre* was considered a "shocking" novel because of its strong-willed, unsentimental heroine. [True]
5. One way Victorian novels differ from many novels today is that they express a confidence that problems can be solved. [True]

Objectives

When I Was One-and-Twenty / To an Athlete Dying Young / Is My Team Ploughing

1. Read and interpret the poems
2. Identify literary ballad
3. Express understanding through critical writing, creative writing, music, or dramatic reading

Skills

Literary
- Identify literary ballad

Writing
- Collect ideas for an evaluation
- Write an essay comparing poems
- Write a tribute in prose or poetry
- Create fictional diary entries

Speaking/Listening
- Present a dramatic reading with music

Viewing/Representing
- Interpret body language in a painting (ATE)

Planning

- **Block Schedule**
  Block Scheduling Lesson Plans with Pacing Guide
- **Traditional Schedule**
  Lesson Plans Including Strategies for English-Language Learners
- **One-Stop Planner**
  CD-ROM with Test Generator

A. E. Housman

(1859–1936)

Housman said that he was careful not to think of poetry while he was shaving, for "if a line of poetry strays into my memory, my skin bristles so that the razor ceases to act." For Housman, poetry was all feeling. The feelings produced physical effects (shivers along the spine, tears, the sensation of being pierced by a spear) that came from what Housman said was the source of his own poems, "the pit of the stomach."

Housman's poetry is more restrained than his comments suggest. His poems evoke a narrow range of subdued feelings that are controlled by simple, tight verse forms and clear language and syntax. Although he uses simple words, his diction is precise and carefully polished: Each word is the right word in the right place.

Alfred Edward Housman (1926) by Francis Dodd. Pencil drawing (14¾″ × 10¾″).
By Courtesy of the National Portrait Gallery, London.

Alfred Edward Housman was born in Worcestershire in western England, the oldest of seven children. He was close to his mother, who died on his twelfth birthday. His father, a lawyer, allowed his practice, money, and talent to dwindle away in despondency and drink. At sixteen, Housman won a scholarship to Oxford, where he prepared for a career as a scholar and teacher of classical literature. But he attended classes irregularly, preferring to study on his own, and failed his final examinations.

In 1882, Housman entered the civil service as a clerk in the patent office, determined to prove himself as a classical scholar despite his failure at Oxford. For the next ten years, he set himself a rigorous program: writing and publishing papers on Greek and Latin literature while working as a patent clerk. In 1892, his series of scholarly papers won him an appointment as professor of Latin at London University. He stayed until 1911, when he moved to Cambridge University as professor of Latin and fellow at Trinity College. Housman spent the rest of his life as a formal and rather aloof teacher, a reserved participant in the small world of his college, and an authority in the yet smaller world of classical scholarship.

During his lifetime, Housman published only two books of poems containing a little more than one hundred poems. His first collection, *A Shropshire Lad* (1896), became popular because its graceful recollection of youthful pleasures and their transience fit a late-century mood of disillusionment in a world that has "much good, but much less good than ill." In "Terence, This Is Stupid Stuff," Housman acknowledged that his poems could be dismissed as self-indulgent bellyaching. The test of poetry, he believed, is not what is said but how it is said. In the refined elegance of his poems, he expressed his pessimistic vision of a cold, empty world. Unlike the major Romantic and Victorian poets who preceded him, Housman saw no hope of improvement or change, but only the possibility of enduring and making bearable the painful conditions of human existence.

go.hrw.com
LEO 12-11

Resources: Print and Media

Reading
- *Graphic Organizers for Active Reading,* pp. 87, 88, 89
- *Audio CD Library*
  Disc 14, Tracks 6, 7, 8

Writing and Language
- *Daily Oral Grammar*
  Transparency 29

Assessment
- *Formal Assessment,* pp. 174, 175, 176
- *Portfolio Management System,* p. 178
- *Test Generator (One-Stop Planner CD-ROM)*

Internet
- go.hrw.com (keyword: LE0 12-11)

Before You Read

WHEN I WAS ONE-AND-TWENTY

Make the Connection

Advice to the Lovelorn

Thousands of poems have been written about the experience of falling in love, and not all of the stories end happily. The tale told in "When I Was One-and-Twenty" is an ancient one, and the young speaker isn't the first to be disillusioned.

Quickwrite

What is "first love" like? How do people feel about love as they grow older? Jot down your thoughts about these questions.

Background

The tone of Housman's poetry is often nostalgic and bittersweet. This brief lyric from *A Shropshire Lad* is a good example. In fact, its lesson may have come from events in the poet's own life. At age twenty-two, Housman fell in love and was rejected. He became severely depressed and failed his Oxford examinations.

When I Was One-and-Twenty

A. E. Housman

When I was one-and-twenty
  I heard a wise man say,
"Give crowns and pounds and guineas°
  But not your heart away; (A)
Give pearls away and rubies
  But keep your fancy free."
But I was one-and-twenty,
  No use to talk to me. (B)

When I was one-and-twenty
  I heard him say again,
"The heart out of the bosom
  Was never given in vain;
'Tis paid with sighs a plenty
  And sold for endless rue."° (C)
And I am two-and-twenty,
  And oh, 'tis true, 'tis true. (D)

3. crowns and pounds and guineas: units of money in Great Britain.

14. rue: sorrow; regret.

Summary ■■

The twenty-two-year-old speaker recalls that when he was twenty-one, a wise man warned him not to give himself over to love. The speaker was headstrong and did not take the advice. Now he is suffering the pain of a failed love affair and believes that the wise man was right.

Background

The poetry collection *A Shropshire Lad*, published in 1896 and set in the English countryside, made Housman a famous poet. Other poems of his were published later, but most of them were written at about the same time as the poems in *A Shropshire Lad*.

(A) Struggling Readers

Summarizing

Have students rephrase the wise man's advice in these lines. [Possible response: "Spend a little money or spend a lot, but don't fall in love."]

(B) Reading Skills and Strategies

Connecting with the Text

? Do you think the young speaker's attitude, expressed in l. 8, is a common one? Why or why not? [Possible response: Most people, especially teenagers, go through a stage in which they think they "know it all"; eventually, they mature and realize their limitations.]

(C) Critical Thinking

Evaluating an Interpretation

? Housman is often described as one of the late Victorian writers who held a grim view of life. Do you see that view at work in this poem? Explain. [Possible response: His view is rather grim. In these lines, the wise man's words (with which the speaker comes to agree) express a belief that love is always painful and disappointing.]

(D) Elements of Literature

Irony

Point out to students that, on the surface, the speaker seems to have learned a hard lesson: At the ripe old age of 22, he seems to have acquired a valuable bit of "wisdom." However, the rather melodramatic last two lines suggest that the poet is smiling knowingly at the speaker and thinking (but not saying): What further, deeper "wisdom" will you acquire at the age of 42? 62? 82?

Reaching All Students

Struggling Readers

"When I Was One-and-Twenty" explores the tension between learning from elders and finding one's own answers. Have students chart the course of the poem with summary sentences in boxes: box #1, advice; box #2, attitude of the narrator; box #3, result of the narrator's attitude; box #4, conclusion. Point out that some details and motives for actions are not given in the poem. Ask students to identify these and make inferences about what is left out.

English Language Learners

Point out to students that the poet interrupts the predicate "Give away" in ll. 3 and 4 with the compound direct object "*crowns* and *pounds* and *guineas* / But not your *heart*." Help them to restate the sentence in normal word order: Give away crowns and pounds and guineas / But not your heart.

Making Meanings

First Thoughts [Respond]

1. Students who have experienced a failed relationship will probably sympathize with the speaker.

Shaping Interpretations [Interpret]

2. A year, or part of a year, has passed. Possible response: The speaker has learned the truth of what the wise man said.

3. The repetition of "'tis true" emphasizes the speaker's agreement and brings the poem to an emphatic close. Some students may sense the narrator's irony. Students may also note the repetition of whole lines (1 and 9), similar lines (2 and 10), and syntactical structures in the two stanzas.

4. Students may suggest themes such as "falling in love is foolishness" or "young love does not last." Most students will agree that Housman's attitude is one of ironic humor.

Connecting with the Text [Evaluate]

5. More cynical students might agree with the wise man, believing that the pain and disillusionment of a failed relationship should be avoided; others may be more optimistic, feeling that the experience of being in love is worth the risk of pain.

Responding to the Art

William Mulready (1786–1863) was an Irish-born painter who spent his life in England. Inspired by the Dutch masters, he became adept at "cottage subjects"—scenes of unpretentious domestic life, picturesque poverty, and everyday events in the lives of common people—scenes like those depicted in Housman's *A Shropshire Lad. The Sonnet* is typical of Mulready's bent for affecting narrative—the viewer seems to have arrived at the climax of a love story.

Activity. What do you think is written on the paper the woman is reading? How do you think the young man feels? Is the woman suppressing a laugh, a sigh, or a sob? How might the scene be one that results in "sighs a plenty" and "endless rue"?

The Sonnet (1839) by William Mulready.
Victoria and Albert Museum, London.

Making Meanings

First Thoughts

1. Did the speaker's story move you? Why or why not?

Shaping Interpretations

2. How much time has passed between the first and second stanzas? In your opinion, what has the speaker learned in this time?
3. What is the effect of Housman's use of **repetition** in the last line of the poem? What other kinds of repetition do you find in the poem?
4. What do you think is the poem's **theme,** or message? Do you think Housman is being serious or humorous in his attitude toward falling in love?

Connecting with the Text

5. If the wise man advised you that it is better to give away money than to give away your heart, what would you say in reply? Refer to your Quickwrite notes, and explain your response.

Using Students' Strengths

Visual Learners

Have students illustrate the poem, choosing a specific style that they can defend as appropriate to the poem. They might use modern costumes or research and use Victorian costumes for the characters, or illustrate the poem as if it were a song or nursery rhyme. Ask them to include the text, or part of the text, in their renderings.

Kinesthetic Learners

Have pairs of students respond to "When I Was One-and-Twenty" by assuming the "characters" of Housman's speakers—one the inexperienced twenty-one-year-old and the other the more experienced wise man. Have the students, in character, enact a meeting between the two in which they discuss the following: How much a person's world can change in just one year, and why.

Before You Read
To an Athlete Dying Young

Make the Connection
The Prime of Life
The strong, healthy athletes who earn fame and fortune seem to live charmed lives. But what happens when the cheering stops? When an athlete dies in the prime of life and at the peak of fame, faithful supporters discover a very sobering truth: Even these special young men and women are not invincible.

Quickwrite
At what age do you think you might be in the prime of your life—in top physical and mental condition? Jot down your thoughts about when you expect to achieve your peak and what you hope to be doing at that time.

Background
In 1896, Housman himself paid to have the first edition of *A Shropshire Lad* published. He scarcely made a profit from his book of sixty-three verses, which often tell stories in the voice of a young soldier or farm boy. However, Housman lived to see his poems become enormously popular during World War I. Soldiers saw themselves in the homesick lad from Shropshire and heard in his voice the echo of their own melancholy.

To an Athlete Dying Young

A. E. Housman

The time you won your town the race
We chaired you through the marketplace;
Man and boy stood cheering by,
And home we brought you shoulder-high.

Today, the road all runners come,
Shoulder-high we bring you home,
And set you at your threshold down,
Townsman of a stiller town.

Smart lad, to slip betimes° away
From fields where glory does not stay
And early though the laurel° grows
It withers quicker than the rose.

Eyes the shady night has shut
Cannot see the record cut,
And silence sounds no worse than cheers
After earth has stopped the ears:

Now you will not swell the rout
Of lads that wore their honors out,
Runners whom renown outran
And the name died before the man.

So set, before its echoes fade,
The fleet foot on the sill of shade,
And hold to the low lintel° up
The still-defended challenge cup.

And round that early-laureled head
Will flock to gaze the strengthless dead,
And find unwithered on its curls
The garland briefer than a girl's.

9. betimes: archaic for "early."
11. laurel: classical symbol of victory. Victorious Greek and Roman athletes were crowned with laurel wreaths.
23. lintel: top of a doorframe.

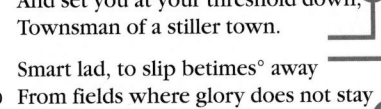

Young man, from *Penelope and Her Suitors* (detail) (1912) by John William Waterhouse.
City of Aberdeen Art Gallery and Museums Collection, Scotland.

Summary
The speaker addresses a young athlete who once received the townspeople's adulation and was carried aloft in victory who now is held high in a funeral procession. The speaker claims that the youth is lucky to have died young, while still in his glory.

A Reading Skills and Strategies
Drawing Conclusions
? Suppose you did not know the title of this poem. What clues in this stanza would help you to conclude that this is a funeral procession? [Possible responses: The road is one along which "all runners come," for all people die; "shoulder-high" suggests carrying a coffin; "a stiller town" suggests a graveyard or the realm of the dead.]

B Elements of Literature
Tone
? How would you describe the speaker's tone, or attitude, regarding the death of the young athlete? [Possible response: The tone seems ironic but sympathetic. The speaker is trying to justify the death of a young man in his prime.]

C Advanced Learners
Point out that the last stanza suggests an allusion to the classical Greek concept of the afterlife in Hades, where pale and bloodless shades gather to stare at a soul newly arrived from the land of the living.

Reaching All Students

Struggling Readers
This poem with its archaic diction and sentence structure will be difficult for struggling readers, but the subject matter (an athlete who has died young) will appeal to them. Listening to the poem on the audio will help their comprehension. You might also have students work in pairs to paraphrase what the speaker is saying to the dead athlete in each stanza.

English Language Learners
Point out that l. 2 offers an example of a noun being converted into a verb—*chaired.* Ask students to name other verbs that have developed from nouns, such as *faxed* and *filed.* Be sure they understand the two references to "shoulder-high." In l. 4, the triumphant athlete is being carried on the townspeople's shoulders in celebration. In l. 5, his dead body is being carried "home" in mourning.

Responding to the Art
This detail from *Penelope and Her Suitors* by the English painter **John William Waterhouse** (1849–1917) reflects the painter's frequent use of classical subjects (in this case, the young Greek suitors who try to induce the wife of Odysseus to give up waiting for him). This young man is not an athlete; however, his profile suggests the classical ideal of male beauty—young, intense, with well-defined, sculpted features. (For other art by Waterhouse, see pp. 807 and 812.)
Activity. Ask students to describe their own athletic ideal, focusing on physical appearance, mental abilities, and personality.

MAKING MEANINGS

First Thoughts [Respond]

1. Some students would hope for accounts of athletic successes and achievements in other facets of life. Some would object to the reminder that the athlete's career would have ended eventually. Others may appreciate the poem's realistic words about athletic careers.

Shaping Interpretations [Interpret]

2. Both stanzas mention being brought home "shoulder-high" by a crowd. The first is an act of adulation, the second an act of mourning. The repetition of "shoulder-high" emphasizes the ironic parallel between the two processions.

3. The speaker suggests that, although the athlete probably did not anticipate an early death, his departing at the prime of life is better—"smarter"—than lingering on after glory has passed. If students have sensed the disillusionment in "When I Was One-and-Twenty," they may conclude that the speaker's words are tinged with irony but are nonetheless sincere.

4. Possible response: The dead athlete is stepping over the threshold of the afterlife, where the spirits of the dead will gather to meet him and gaze upon him.

5. Some students might prefer a short, intense career of brilliant accomplishment; others might prefer a long, reliable career that mellows with age.

Challenging the Text [Evaluate]

6. Possible response: The death of a young person is poignant, with the unexpectedness of its tragedy and its implications of lost potential. However, an aging athlete can also be a moving subject, with its elements of inevitability and nostalgia.

MAKING MEANINGS

First Thoughts

1. How would you react to this poem if it were written about you or a close friend?

Shaping Interpretations

2. What parallel events are described in the first and second stanzas? What is the significance of repeating "shoulder-high"?

3. In line 9, why does the speaker call the athlete "smart"? Do you think the speaker means what he says in lines 9–20? Explain.

4. What scene do you see in the last two stanzas of the poem? (Where is the athlete now?)

5. The speaker suggests that it's best to die at one's peak, before glory begins to fade. After thinking about your Quickwrite entry, describe your response to this idea.

Challenging the Text

6. Housman's poem movingly describes a young athlete's death. If he had written a similar poem about an aging athlete, could the poem be as powerful? Explain your answer.

By Unfrequented Ways (late 19th or early 20th century) by William Henry Gore.

Assessing Learning

Standardized Test Preparation

For practice in proofreading and editing, see

- *Daily Oral Grammar,* Transparency 29

Crossing the Curriculum

Music

British composer George Butterworth, born in 1885 and killed at the Battle of the Somme in 1916, created two song cycles based on *A Shropshire Lad.* His deeply moving songs include settings of "When I Was One-and-Twenty" and "Is My Team Ploughing." Have students listen to a recording of these songs and tell what qualities of the poems they think the music captures. Also ask students if listening to the songs affected them in ways that reading the poems did not.

Fine Art

Ask students to research and create a display of fine art or photographs with athletic themes. They might, for example, look into the work of painter Leroy Neiman or of contemporary sports photographers. Encourage them to provide captions for the images, identifying those qualities of the athlete that are being emphasized.

Before You Read

IS MY TEAM PLOUGHING

Make the Connection

Remember Me?

When friends tell you they missed you while you were away, it confirms that you're an important part of their lives. But how long should loyalty—and love—last?

Quickwrite

Imagine you have moved away from your friends. What kinds of questions would you ask them after a long absence? Briefly record your response.

Elements of Literature

Literary Ballads

Housman once claimed that his inspiration came from "Shakespeare's songs, [and] the Scottish Border ballads." To describe the country life of a "Shropshire lad," Housman borrows from the simple style of traditional folk ballads, featuring a question-and-answer format in a conversation. In **literary ballads,** such as this one by Housman, poets adapt the structure and spirit of traditional ballads to modern uses. Hardy also used the structure of the old ballads, as in his poems told in the form of dialogues (pages 855 and 857).

Is My Team Ploughing

A. E. Housman

"Is my team ploughing,
  That I was used to drive
And hear the harness jingle
  When I was man alive?" **(A)**

Ay, the horses trample,
  The harness jingles now;
No change though you lie under
  The land you used to plough.

"Is football playing
  Along the river shore,
With lads to chase the leather,
  Now I stand up no more?"

Ay, the ball is flying,
  The lads play heart and soul;
The goal stands up, the keeper
  Stands up to keep the goal. **(B)**

"Is my girl happy,
  That I thought hard to leave,
And has she tired of weeping
  As she lies down at eve?"

Ay, she lies down lightly,
  She lies not down to weep:
Your girl is well contented.
  Be still, my lad, and sleep.

"Is my friend hearty,
  Now I am thin and pine,
And has he found to sleep in
  A better bed than mine?"

Yes, lad, I lie easy,
  I lie as lads would choose;
I cheer a dead man's sweetheart,
  Never ask me whose. **(C)**

Summary ■■

From his grave, the speaker quizzes an old friend about life on earth. The friend tells him the dead man's horses still work the fields, boys play ball as they did before the speaker's death, the dead man's sweetheart no longer weeps for him, and the friend himself has found contentment because he helps cheer a dead man's sweetheart. The friend urges the speaker not to ask whose sweetheart he comforts.

(A) Elements of Literature

Literary Ballad

? Review the ballads you read in Collection 2, pp. 90–96. What in this poem is reminiscent of the folk ballad form? [Possible responses: The questions and answers create a ballad pattern. The "yes" answers form a refrain of sorts.]

(B) Reading Skills and Strategies

Comparing and Contrasting

? Compare this reply to the reply in the second stanza. How does this new reply add tension to the poem? [Possible responses: The first reply is fairly matter of fact. Here, however, more emotion is involved.] **Point out that the response in stanza 6 is even more personal and heart-rending; thus, the poem is structured to be progressively more intimate and touching.**

(C) Elements of Literature

Tone

? What is the tone at the end of this poem? Explain. [Possible response: It is bittersweet, a mix of irony and sympathy much as in "To an Athlete Dying Young." There is irony in the fact that the living friend has taken his dead friend's place in the girl's heart; yet the living friend seems to be genuinely concerned that the dead man not be hurt by the truth.]

Resources

Selection Assessment

Formal Assessment

- Selection Test, p. 176

Test Generator (One-Stop Planner)

- CD-ROM

Reaching All Students

Struggling Readers

Have struggling readers create a drawing with a brief caption, describing the relationship that the primary speaker had, when alive, with each subject he asks about: his work animals, his teammates, his beloved, his best friend.

English Language Learners

Have two students read the poem aloud, each taking the part of one of the speakers. Be sure they understand that the dead man speaks first and his friend replies in the next stanza and that the same pattern continues throughout the poem. Ask them to look for other repeated patterns in the stanzas.

Advanced Learners

Ask students to compare (orally or in writing) "Is My Team Ploughing" with Hardy's "Ah, Are You Digging on My Grave?" (See p. 857.) Have them use the questions in each poem to determine the issues the speakers consider important. Do the responses to their questions suggest similar or different views of humanity?

Connections

This feature describes the elaborate customs and rituals with which Victorians observed the death of loved ones and neighbors. These included tolling bells in prescribed numbers at precise times and wearing mourning garments for prescribed periods, depending upon the closeness of the relationship with the deceased. Funerals were generally solemn—formal occasions for which undertakers often provided professional mourners, called "mutes," who were meant to lend an air of dignified melancholy.

A Critical Thinking

Analyzing Details

? Think about hearing the sound of the "passing bell" echoing across town. In what sense would this be a sound of respect? of rejoicing? of warning? [Possible responses: The bell and its tolling offer a tribute to the deceased's life. It could signal rejoicing in that a neighbor is entering heaven. It also could be a warning, as if to say, "This person has died. One day the bells will also toll for you."]

B Literary Connections

Remind students of the famous quotation from John Donne's "Meditation 17" (see p. 251): "And therefore never send to know for whom the bell tolls; it tolls for thee."

C Critical Thinking

Challenging the Text

? Do these "rules" about what people could and could not wear and how long people were supposed to mourn make sense to you? Why or why not? [Possible responses: They make sense because they provide some structure for mourners, who may feel emotionally lost; they make less sense in our pluralistic culture, since individuals express grief in a variety of personal ways.]

Connections — A History

Housman's poems somberly explore death. In the following excerpt, Daniel Pool explains the rituals the Victorians developed to respond to death.

Death and Other Grave Matters

Daniel Pool

Death—early death—was no stranger to the nineteenth-century English family, and perhaps that is why they loved to weep over the lingering demises of Dickens's small heroes and heroines. Certainly, they made a big production out of it in every other respect.

A In some rural communities the ritual began even before one died, with the ringing of a "passing bell" in the parish church to signal that a member of the community lay on his or her deathbed. B Characteristically, the bell tolled six times to indicate the passing of a woman, nine (the famous "nine tailors") to indicate the passing of a man, followed by a peal for each year of the dying person's life.

When a person died, a large funeral was held with everyone dressed in black (unless the deceased were a child or a young, unmarried girl, when the costume was white); mourners received black gloves and black scarfs. . . .

In most communities, funerals were an important social event, and propriety and due regard for the family's social standing necessitated that they be done right. . . . Characteristically, the undertaker would provide professional mourners, or "mutes," dressed in black to stand about and lend dignity to the affair. "There's an expression of melancholy in his face, my dear," says Mr. Sowerberry, the undertaker, to his wife when he takes on Oliver Twist as an apprentice, "which is very interesting. He would make a delightful mute, my love . . . I don't mean a regular mute to attend grown-up people, my dear, but only for children's practice. It would be very new to have a mute in proportion." When the body was actually brought to the gravesite for burial, there was often an additional tolling of the bells—the death knell—to let the parish know of the final laying to rest of the deceased. . . .

The departed were always to be mourned for specifically prescribed periods of time, which, in practice, affected mostly the clothes the survivors were permitted to wear and whether they could have fun or not. Men had it easy; they needed only to wear black armbands, a custom adopted from the military in the early years of the century. Women, however, were supposed to dress all in black. "My dear Celia," says Lady Catherine Chettam of Dorothea Casaubon [in George Eliot's novel *Middlemarch*] after her husband's death, "a widow must wear mourning at least a year." This meant an all-black wardrobe (the so-called widow's weeds), frequently of bombazine, a material especially favored because it did not gleam in light, and no jewelry or ornaments except for beads made of jet, a kind of coal. . . . C A widow was expected to mourn her husband for two years, but she could moderate her funereal clothing a bit after a while to "half mourning," which consisted of pinstripe black. Parents and children were to be mourned for a year, a brother, sister, or grandparent for six months, an uncle or aunt for three months, and a first cousin got six weeks. (In-laws were mourned too, but for lesser periods of time.) Some women remained in their mourning garb for the rest of their lives. . . .

Of course, the lead in this fashionable mourning was set in part by the queen. After the death of her beloved Albert in 1861 until her own death in 1901, portraits generally show Victoria in the somber black and white attire suitable for honoring the memory of a late departed.

—*from What Jane Austen Ate and Charles Dickens Knew*

Connecting Across Texts

Connecting with "Death and Other Grave Matters"

Ask students to discuss the psychological and social elements of Hardy's and Housman's poetry which are reflected in Pool's essay. First they should choose specific words from the essay—such as *death, ritual, dignity, melancholy, mourning*—and then relate each of these words to the poems. [Students should focus on Hardy's sad and ironic "Ah, Are You Digging on My Grave?" and on Housman's "To an Athlete Dying Young" and "Is My Team Ploughing." They might cite the graveside mourners, the ritual processions and religious ceremonies, the questions and prayers of both the living and dead, and the overall tones of loss and bitterness. They might also discuss whether they think the poems exhibit an element of irony that is suggested by Pool's quotation from Dickens's practical-minded Sowerberry.]

MAKING MEANINGS

First Thoughts

1. Why do you think the speaker has been forgotten so quickly? Is this cruel, or is it just realistic?

Shaping Interpretations

2. Housman's dialogue format doesn't explain the speakers' identities. Who are the two **speakers**?
3. What significance do you find in the order of the four questions asked in the poem? How do these questions compare with the ones you asked in your Quickwrite entry?
4. How would you describe the speaker's attitude in the last stanza? Was he a true friend to his dead companion? Why or why not?

Extending the Text

5. Why do you think people write poetry about death and practice rituals like the ones Daniel Pool describes in "Death and Other Grave Matters" (see ***Connections*** on page 868)? What are some of the ways we deal with death today?

CHOICES: Building Your Portfolio

Writer's Notebook

1. Collecting Ideas for an Evaluation

WORK IN PROGRESS

Housman's "Is My Team Ploughing" and Hardy's "Ah, Are You Digging on My Grave?" (page 857) have many similarities. Reread both poems now, and decide quickly which you think is more effective. Then make a chart comparing specific elements in the two poems (you *may* change your judgment). You could focus on such elements as theme, imagery, emotional content, and music. Save your notes for the Writer's Workshop on page 899.

Comparing Poems

2. Heartaches

In a brief essay, compare Housman's treatment of death and loss in these three poems. What is his attitude toward suffering and pain? Do you think he is a pessimist?

Comparing Poems Across the Centuries

3. Renaissance Versus Victorian Poetry

Collection 3, "Love, Death, and Time," opens on page 213. In an essay, compare and contrast the **tones** and **messages** of Housman's poems with the tones and messages of any three poems from that collection (if you wish, include the poem by the American poet E. E. Cummings that opens the collection).

Creative Writing

4. To an Athlete Today

Write a tribute to an athlete you admire. Write in either prose or poetry, and address your tribute directly to the athlete. You might open with Housman's words: "The time you . . ."

Creative Writing

5. In Your Own Voice

Imagine that you are the speaker, the Shropshire lad, in all three poems by Housman. (In "Is My Team Ploughing," assume that you are the speaker who answers.) Write three diary entries that tell about the events suggested in each poem.

Music and Literature

6. Housman's Soundtrack

Find a musical background for one of Housman's poems. Tape a dramatic reading of the poem with the music you selected for presentation, or present it live.

MAKING MEANINGS

First Thoughts [Respond]

1. Some students may note that "forgetting" is a natural part of putting aside grief—that survivors, out of necessity, must focus on their own lives. Others may feel that "forgetting" is callous and inappropriate.

Shaping Interpretations [Interpret]

2. The first speaker is a dead farmer, a man who enjoyed playing football and who had a girlfriend or wife ("my girl"). The other speaker is a living friend of the dead man.
3. The questions move from the objective to the more personal and emotional. Housman establishes an order of importance in which each succeeding question draws in the reader more, making the reader nearly as vulnerable to the answers as the dead man.
4. The attitude seems sympathetic but evasive. Students may disagree over whether he is a true friend (for taking care of someone that the dead man can no longer help) or a traitor (for loving the woman the dead man loved).

Extending the Text [Analyze]

5. Possible responses: When people are grieving, ritual can provide ways to release and channel their emotions and help them get through a difficult time. Poetry gives people the opportunity—whether as writers or as readers—to express grief and to share ideas and feelings about life and death. Today, people deal with death through a variety of ways, including small- and large-scale memorials.

Grading Timesaver

Rubrics for each Choices assignment appear on p. 178 in the *Portfolio Management System.*

CHOICES: Building Your Portfolio

WORK IN PROGRESS

1. and 2. With the class, brainstorm a list of elements and a list of "losses" for each poem.

3. Make sure students take detailed notes on each poem before they begin the essay.

4., 5., and 6. Have pairs of students read the poems aloud to get a feel for the emotional dialogue before they begin writing or presenting.

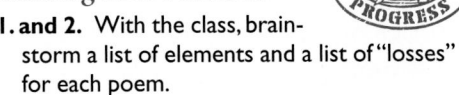

OBJECTIVES

1. Read and interpret the story
2. Identify conflicts and resolutions
3. Express understanding through creative writing, research, or speaking
4. Understand new words

SKILLS

Reading
- Identify conflicts and resolutions

Writing
- Collect ideas for an evaluation
- Create a story outline

Speaking/Listening
- Present a multimedia report about werewolves
- Present an informal report on Anglo-Indian ways of life

Vocabulary
- Use new words

Planning

- **Block Schedule**
  Block Scheduling Lesson Plans with Pacing Guide
- **Traditional Schedule**
  Lesson Plans Including Strategies for English-Language Learners
- **One-Stop Planner**
  CD-ROM with Test Generator

BROWSING IN THE FILES

Writers on Writing. Kipling rewrote his drafts again and again until he was satisfied with them. Here is his recipe for what he calls "Higher Editing": "Take of well-ground Indian ink as much as suffices and a camel-hair brush proportionate to the interspaces of your lines. In an auspicious hour, read your final draft and consider faithfully every paragraph, sentence and word, blacking out where requisite. Let it lie by to drain as long as possible. At the end of that time, re-read it aloud alone and at leisure. Maybe a shade more brushwork will then indicate or impose itself. If not, praise Allah and let it go . . . I have had tales by me for three or four years which shortened themselves almost yearly. The magic lies in the Brush and the Ink."

Rudyard Kipling

(1865–1936)

Rudyard Kipling was born in Bombay, India, where his father was a professor at the University of Bombay. Since it was customary for English citizens living in India (Anglo-Indians) to send their children home for their education, the six-year-old Kipling and his sister were left in the care of foster parents in England. Kipling recalled some of the unhappiness and rebelliousness of his school years in a novel called *Stalky & Co.* (1899).

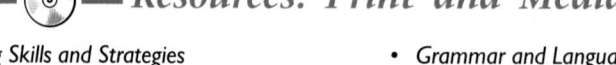

Rudyard Kipling (1899) by Philip Burne-Jones. Oil on canvas (29½" × 24½").
By Courtesy of the National Portrait Gallery, London.

At seventeen, Kipling returned to India to work as a journalist on a newspaper in Lahore. He quickly became popular for his stories, sketches, and poems that were published in newspapers and then collected in cheap editions sold at Indian railroad stations. His books were distributed in England as well, preparing the way for his return to England as a writer in 1889. *Barrack-Room Ballads* (1892), his first collection of poems published in England, went into three editions in its first year, and fifty more editions over the next thirty years. By the end of Queen Victoria's reign, Kipling had become the most popular British poet since Tennyson, and the most popular prose writer since Dickens. Kipling's popularity and public influence can be attributed in part to his strong endorsement of the British Empire.

But Kipling's ideas about "empire" were not simple. He was fascinated by the contrast and conflict of European civilization with the ancient cultures of the places into which it intruded. This conflict is the theme of many of his Indian stories, beginning with *Plain Tales from the Hills* (1888) and continuing in *Kim* (1901), his novel about a British boy submerged in the mystery of India.

Kipling did not always see European culture as superior (though he nearly always presented it as such), and he knew that empires do fall. He urged readers not to trust in guns to justify their dominion over large parts of the earth. The purpose of the British Empire, he argued, was not to make the imperial nation rich, but rather to extend British efficiency, decency, and comfort throughout the world. Today, however, many readers—even as they admire Kipling's craft—view his argument as a rationalization of the often brutal practices of British imperialism.

In 1907, Kipling became the first British writer to win the Nobel Prize in literature.

go.hrw.com
LEO 12-11

Resources: Print and Media

- *Reading Skills and Strategies*
  MiniRead Skill Lesson, p. 65
  Selection Skill Lesson, p. 71
- *Graphic Organizers for Active Reading,* p. 90
- *Words to Own,* p. 24
- *Audio CD Library*
  Disc 14, Track 9

Writing and Language
- *Daily Oral Grammar*
  Transparency 30
- *Grammar and Language Links*
  Worksheet, p. 49
- *Language Workshop CD-ROM*

Assessment
- *Formal Assessment,* p. 177
- *Portfolio Management System,* p. 180
- *Preparation for College Admission Exams,* p. 43
- *Test Generator (One-Stop Planner CD-ROM)*

Internet
- go.hrw.com (keyword: LEO 12-11)

Before You Read
THE MARK OF THE BEAST

Make the Connection
When Cultures Collide

As a member of the English ruling class in colonial India, Kipling was a witness to the conflicts that inevitably occur when two cultures are brought into contact by force. Although the battle lines between imperial Britain and colonial India seem clearly drawn in this story, the identity of the victor (if there is one) is less obvious. Indeed, what is most unsettling about Kipling's story may be the questions he poses, which go well beyond the specifics of this strange tale.

Reading Skills and Strategies
Identifying Conflicts and Resolutions

As you read, fill in the first column of a chart like the one below. Write down the names of individuals, groups, and ideas that come into conflict in the story. After you have completed the story, review the conflicts and decide if there is a clear-cut victor. If you think there is, write that name in the second column. If not, write *unclear*.

Conflict	Victor?

The first conflict on your chart should be the one suggested by the proverb that opens the story.

Elements of Literature
Allusion

An **allusion** is an indirect or passing reference to a person, event, place, quotation, or work of art the reader might be expected to know. Through allusion, a reader's knowledge can supply enriching details and relevance, without the writer's explicitly providing them.

Background

Kipling's writing reveals both a respect for the religions of India and a thorough knowledge of the Christian Bible. The title of this story is an allusion to the final book of the New Testament, the prophetic and mystical Book of Revelation. According to Chapter 13 of that book, great evil will take over the world at some unknown time. A beast somewhat like a leopard will rule that evil world, and all the beast's followers will be branded with his mark. Like the Book of Revelation, Kipling's story is more symbolic and suggestive than literal and realistic.

Elephants and pilgrims, Sonepur Fair in Binhar, India (1988).

Summary ■■

The British narrator tells a story about a strange adventure that he, a British police officer named Strickland, and another British man named Fleete had in colonial India. The three are returning from a party when Fleete, who is drunk, enters a temple and grinds his cigar into a statue of the Hindu god Hanuman. After this desecration, a leper, whom the narrator calls the Silver Man, touches Fleete's chest. A priest ominously suggests that the god will take his revenge.

The next day a black mark appears on Fleete's chest, and he begins to behave like a wolf—craving barely cooked meat, frightening horses, and howling and snarling. He degenerates quickly into a wild beast, forcing his friends to tie him up. A doctor can do nothing, and Strickland and the narrator agree that the Silver Man must be responsible. They capture the leper and force him to remove the curse. The next morning Fleete acts normally, with no memory of his transformation. The narrator wonders if anyone will believe the story.

Background

Read aloud Revelation 13:16–17: "And he causeth all, both small and great, rich and poor, free and bond, to receive a mark in their right hand, or in their foreheads: And that no man might buy or sell, save he that had the mark, or the name of the beast, or the number of his name." As students read Kipling's tale, have them look for references to the "mark of the beast." Have them consider who the "beast" of the story really is.

Preteaching Vocabulary

Words to Own

Have students read the Words to Own on the selection pages. Then have them use the words to complete the following sentences.

1. They thought the exchange student was pleasant and [*genial*].
2. Cold-hearted Lisa [*trifled*] with his affections.
3. Mark will realize someday that his self-importance is a [*delusion*].
4. Some people embarrass themselves by [*groveling*] before their bosses.
5. He was so [*distraught*] he forgot his car keys.
6. The neighborhood found ways to deal with [*ruffians*] who destroyed the playground.
7. He was only an athlete, but the media turned him into a kind of [*divinity*].
8. Proceed [*dispassionately*], and you'll make sound decisions.
9. The jewels were hidden in a [*recess*].
10. They believed they had been abused and they were looking for [*redress*].

Ⓐ Elements of Literature
Allusion
The story's title is an allusion to the book of Revelation in the Bible. Ask students what, even without knowledge of the allusion, the title suggests about the mood of the story. [The title suggests ferocity, dread, and evil.]

Ⓑ Critical Thinking
Hypothesizing
? What does this epigraph lead you to believe about the events of the story? [Possible responses: The epigraph sounds an ominous note of uncertainty and powerlessness with suggestions that some sort of battle is going to take place between religions or cultures.]

Ⓒ Reading Skills and Strategies
Identifying Conflicts and Resolutions
? What is the narrator suggesting about the story's conflict and its resolution by the statement that "direct control" resides with "the Gods and Devils of Asia"? [Possible response: He is suggesting that, whatever conflicts arise between people or between people and divinities, it is the divinities that determine the outcomes.]

Ⓓ Reading Skills and Strategies
Making Predictions
? What do the narrator's comments regarding Strickland and Dumoise hint about the story that he is preparing to tell? [Possible response: The story will seem mysterious and even unbelievable; yet it is not a fantasy, for witnesses were present. It somehow will involve the native culture of India.]

Ⓐ The Mark of the Beast

Rudyard Kipling

Ⓑ Your Gods and my Gods—do you or I know which are the stronger?

—*Indian Proverb*

Ⓒ East of Suez, some hold, the direct control of Providence ceases; Man being there handed over to the power of the Gods and Devils of Asia, and the Church of England Providence only exercising an occasional and modified supervision in the case of Englishmen.

This theory accounts for some of the more unnecessary horrors of life in India; it may be stretched to explain my story.

Ⓓ My friend Strickland of the Police, who knows as much of natives of India as is good for any man, can bear witness to the facts of the case. Dumoise, our doctor, also saw what Strickland and I saw. The inference which he drew from the evidence was entirely incorrect. He is dead now; he died in a rather curious manner, which has been elsewhere described.

When Fleete came to India he owned a little money and some land in the Himalayas, near a place called Dharmsala. Both properties had been left him by an uncle, and he came out to finance them. He was a big, heavy, genial, and inoffensive man. His knowledge of natives was, of course, limited, and he complained of the difficulties of the language.

He rode in from his place in the hills to spend New Year in the station, and he stayed with Strickland. On New Year's Eve there was a big dinner at the club, and the night was excusably wet.[1] When men foregather from the uttermost ends of the Empire they have a right to be riotous. The Frontier had sent down a contingent o' Catch-'em-Alive-O's[2] who had not seen twenty white faces for a year, and were used to ride fifteen miles to dinner at the next Fort at the risk of a Khyberee[3] bullet where their drinks should lie. They profited by their new security, for they tried to play pool with a curled-up hedgehog found in the garden, and one of them carried the marker round the room in his teeth. Half a dozen planters had come in from the south and were talking "horse" to the Biggest Liar in Asia, who was trying to cap all their stories at once. Everybody was there, and there was a general closing up of ranks and taking stock of our losses in dead or disabled that had fallen during the past year. It was a very wet night, and I remember that we sang "Auld Lang Syne" with our feet in the Polo Championship Cup, and our heads among the stars, and swore that we were all dear friends. Then some of us went away and annexed Burma, and some tried to open up the Sudan and were opened up by Fuzzies[4] in that cruel scrub outside Suakim,[5] and some found stars and medals, and some were married, which was bad, and some did other things which were worse, and the others of us stayed in our chains and strove to make money on insufficient experiences.

Fleete began the night with sherry and bitters, drank champagne steadily up to dessert, then raw, rasping Capri with all the strength of whiskey, took benedictine with his coffee, four or five whiskeys and sodas to improve his pool strokes, beer and bones[6] at half-past two, winding up with old brandy. Consequently, when he came out, at half-past three in the morning, into fourteen degrees of frost, he was very angry with his horse for coughing, and tried to leapfrog into the saddle. The horse broke away and went to his stables;

1. **the night was excusably wet:** In other words, they drank a lot.

2. **Catch-'em-Alive-O's:** men who were forced into service as soldiers.
3. **Khyberee:** reference to the people of Khyber (kī′bər), a region now part of Pakistan and Afghanistan.
4. **Fuzzies:** Sudanese natives. British soldiers gave them this name because of their long, frizzy hair. In the poem "Fuzzy-Wuzzy" (1890), Kipling calls the Sudanese soldier "a first-class fightin' man."
5. **Suakim:** Suakin (swä′kən), Sudan; city on the Red Sea.
6. **bones:** dice.

WORDS TO OWN
genial (jēn′yəl) *adj.:* mild-mannered; friendly.

Reaching All Students

Struggling Readers
Identifying Conflicts and Resolutions was introduced on p. 871. For a lesson directly tied to this selection that teaches students to identify conflicts and resolutions using a strategy called Somebody Wanted But So, see the *Reading Skills and Strategies* binder:
- MiniRead Skill Lesson, p. 65
- Selection Skill Lesson, p. 71

English Language Learners
Have English language learners create their own vocabulary lists as they read, noting any words that give them trouble (such as *palliative* or *paroxysm*). After they have read the whole story, students can share their word lists and form groups to discuss troublesome words and infer meanings from context when possible.

Advanced Learners
Have students read more of Kipling's wonderful stories of India. Suggest "The Phantom Rickshaw," "The Strange Ride of Morrowbie Jukes," "The Man Who Would Be King," "The Miracle of Purum Bhagat," and "The Return of Imray."

Shrine to the Monkey-god in Chamundi Hill Temple, Mysore, India.

so Strickland and I formed a Guard of Dishonor to take Fleete home.

Our road lay through the bazaar, close to a little temple of Hanuman, the Monkey-god, who is a leading divinity worthy of respect. All gods have good points, just as have all priests. Personally, I attach much importance to Hanuman, and am kind to his people—the great gray apes of the hills. One never knows when one may want a friend. **E**

There was a light in the temple, and as we passed we could hear voices of men chanting hymns. In a native temple the priests rise at all hours of the night to do honor to their god. Before we would stop him, Fleete dashed up the steps, patted two priests on the back, and was gravely grinding the ashes of his cigar butt in to the forehead of the red stone image of Hanuman. Strickland tried to drag him out, but he sat down and said solemnly:

"Shee that? Mark of the B—beasht! *I* made it. Ishn't it fine?" **F**

In half a minute the temple was alive and noisy, and Strickland, who knew what came of polluting gods, said that things might occur. **G** He, by virtue of his official position, long residence in the country, and weakness for going among the natives, was known to the priests and he felt unhappy. Fleete sat on the ground and refused to move. He said that "good old Hanuman" made a very soft pillow.

Then, without any warning, a Silver Man came out of a recess behind the image of the god. He was perfectly naked in that bitter, bitter cold, and his body shone like frosted silver, for he was what the Bible calls "a leper as white as snow." Also he had no face, because he was a leper of some years' standing, and his disease was heavy upon him. **H** We two stooped to haul Fleete up, and the temple was filling and filling with folk who seemed to spring from the earth, when the Silver Man ran in under our arms, making a noise exactly like the mewing of an otter, caught Fleete round the body and dropped his head on Fleete's breast before we could wrench him away. Then he retired to a corner and sat mewing while the crowd blocked all the doors.

The priests were very angry until the Silver Man touched Fleete. That nuzzling seemed to sober them.

At the end of a few minutes' silence one of the priests came to Strickland and said, in perfect English, "Take your friend away. He has done with Hanuman but Hanuman has not done with him." The crowd gave room and we carried Fleete into the road.

Strickland was very angry. He said that we might all three have been knifed, and that Fleete should thank his stars that he had escaped without injury. **I**

Fleete thanked no one. He said that he wanted to go to bed. He was gorgeously drunk.

We moved on, Strickland silent and wrathful, until Fleete was taken with violent shivering fits and sweating. He said that the smells of the bazaar were overpowering, and he wondered why

---

WORDS TO OWN

divinity (də·vin′ə·tē) *n.:* god; sacred being.
recess (rē′ses) *n.:* indentation.

E Cultural Connections

In the Hindu tradition, Hanuman, chief of the monkeys, is described as perfect in learning. He is a hero god in the *Ramayana*, one of India's sacred epic poems, for in it he helps to reunite Rama (one human incarnation of the god Vishnu) with Sita, his kidnapped wife. Hanuman sometimes is called Mahavira—"The Great Hero." He also is seen as a fertility god and as a sympathetic helper of humans.

F Elements of Literature

Allusion

Here Kipling directly employs the title's allusion to the Book of Revelation. Ask students how the allusion relates to the story at this point. [Possible response: It suggests, ironically, that Fleete is the "beast," who has set his mark upon the forehead of a pagan god.]

G Critical Thinking

Speculating

? What do you think Strickland "knew" about "what came of polluting gods"? [Possible answer: He knew that Fleete's action could cause a riot and that the trio could be hurt or even killed by Hanuman's followers.]

H Cultural Connections

In times past, lepers were forced to live in isolation from other people, because of fear of contagion. Today, leprosy can be treated (although a universal, permanent cure has not been found yet). In Kipling's day, however, the fear of leprosy was intense and almost universal.

I Reading Skills and Strategies

Identifying Conflicts and Resolutions

Here, Kipling eases the tension temporarily with a false resolution: He allows the characters to walk away, believing they have "escaped without injury."

Using Students' Strengths

Visual Learners

Have students draw representations of pivotal moments in the story. This will help them to remember, for example, what happened at the temple and during Strickland and the narrator's encounters with the deranged Fleete. Have the students post the illustrations in chronological order around the classroom and retell the events of the story while pointing to the drawings.

Auditory/Verbal Learners

Invite a pair of interested students to present part or all of this story as a radio drama, complete with sound effects and background music. Have them direct an audition in which other students can try out for each of the speaking parts, including that of the narrator. Suggest that a writing team be chosen to create a script for the story.

A Critical Thinking
Challenging the Text

? To make these comments, Kipling must stop the action of the story. Of what value are the comments? If you were telling this story, would you have stopped to make these comments? [Possible responses: Yes, the comments help characterize Strickland and inject a note of ironic humor into a tense scene. No, the comments are distracting and slow down the action.]

B Critical Thinking
Analyzing Character

? What connections, suspicions, or worries have made the narrator "cold, depressed, and unhappy"? [Possible responses: The narrator's gloom probably stems from worry that the Silver Man has somehow infected Fleete or from uncertainty about the meaning of the upset at the temple.]

C Elements of Literature
Symbol

? Is this "the mark of the beast"? What do you think it represents? [Many students will agree that it is the mark in the title, but interpretations will vary. Students may suggest that it represents the animal kingdom, which Fleete could have offended when he defiled Hanuman's temple.]

D English Language Learners

Point out to students that the idiom "the one from the other" (used more often in British English than in American) is another way of saying "from each other."

slaughterhouses were permitted so near English residences. "Can't you smell the blood?" said Fleete.

We put him to bed at last, just as the dawn was breaking, and Strickland invited me to have another whiskey and soda. While we were drinking he talked of the trouble in the temple, and admitted that it baffled him completely. Strickland hates being mystified by natives, because his business in life is to overmatch them with their own weapons. He has not yet succeeded in doing this, but in fifteen or twenty years he will have made some small progress.

"They should have mauled us," he said, "instead of mewing at us. I wonder what they meant. I don't like it one little bit."

I said that the Managing Committee of the temple would in all probability bring a criminal action against us for insulting their religion. There was a section of the Indian Penal Code which exactly met Fleete's offense. Strickland said he only hoped and prayed that they would do this. Before I left I looked into Fleete's room, and saw him lying on his right side, scratching his left breast. Then I went to bed cold, depressed, and unhappy, at seven o'clock in the morning.

At one o'clock I rode over to Strickland's house to inquire after Fleete's head. I imagined that it would be a sore one. Fleete was breakfasting and seemed unwell. His temper was gone, for he was abusing the cook for not supplying him with an underdone chop. A man who can eat raw meat after a wet night is a curiosity. I told Fleete this and he laughed.

"You breed queer mosquitoes in these parts," he said. "I've been bitten to pieces, but only in one place."

"Let's have a look at the bite," said Strickland. "It may have gone down since this morning."

While the chops were being cooked, Fleete opened his shirt and showed us, just over his left breast, a mark, the perfect double of the black rosettes—the five or six irregular blotches arranged in a circle—on a leopard's hide. Strickland looked and said, "It was only pink this morning. It's grown black now."

Fleete ran to a glass.

"By Jove!" he said, "this is nasty. What is it?"

We could not answer. Here the chops came in, all red and juicy, and Fleete bolted three in a most offensive manner. He ate on his right grinders only, and threw his head over his right shoulder as he snapped the meat. When he had finished, it struck him that he had been behaving strangely, for he said apologetically, "I don't think I ever felt so hungry in my life. I've bolted like an ostrich."

After breakfast Strickland said to me, "Don't go. Stay here, and stay for the night."

Seeing that my house was not three miles from Strickland's, this request was absurd. But Strickland insisted, and was going to say something, when Fleete interrupted him by declaring in a shamefaced way that he felt hungry again. Strickland sent a man to my house to fetch over my bedding and a horse, and we three went down to Strickland's stables to pass the hours until it was time to go out for a ride. The man who has a weakness for horses never wearies of inspecting them; and when two men are killing time in this way they gather knowledge and lies the one from the other.

There were five horses in the stables, and I shall never forget the scene as we tried to look them over. They seemed to have gone mad. They reared and screamed and nearly tore up their pickets;[7] they sweated and shivered and lathered and were distraught with fear. Strickland's horses used to know him as well as his dogs; which made the matter more curious. We left the stable for fear of the brutes throwing themselves in their panic. Then Strickland turned back and called me. The horses were still frightened, but they let us "gentle" and make much of them, and put their heads in our bosoms.

"They aren't afraid of *us,*" said Strickland. "D'you know, I'd give three months' pay if *Outrage* here could talk."

But *Outrage* was dumb, and could only cuddle up to his master and blow out his nostrils, as is the custom of horses when they wish to explain things but can't. Fleete came up when we were in the stalls, and as soon as the horses saw him, their

7. **pickets:** hitching posts.

Words to Own
distraught (di·strôt′) *adj.:* agitated.

Getting Students Involved

Film

Have students research how the British Empire has been portrayed in British and American films. They might prepare reports, for example, on such films as *Gunga Din, A Passage to India,* and *Gandhi.* Students might also research Indian films or films made in other parts of the former British Empire.

Skill Link

Analyzing Repetition and Word Choice

Have students read aloud the paragraph beginning "There were five horses." Ask them to pay special attention to the list of verbs used to describe the actions of the horses and to the cumulative effect of that list. Point out that Kipling piles one verb upon another after the word *and,* thus creating an impression of increasing fury among the animals. Finally, the horses and the paragraph wind down together with the words "gentle" and "heads in our bosoms."

fright broke out afresh. It was all that we could do to escape from the place unkicked. Strickland said, "They don't seem to love you, Fleete."

"Nonsense," said Fleete; "my mare will follow me like a dog." He went to her; she was in a loose box;[8] but as he slipped the bars she plunged, knocked him down, and broke away into the garden. I laughed, but Strickland was not amused. He took his moustache in both fists and pulled at it till it nearly came out. Fleete, instead of going off to chase his property, yawned, saying that he felt sleepy. He went to the house to lie down, which was a foolish way of spending New Year's Day.

Strickland sat with me in the stables and asked if I had noticed anything peculiar in Fleete's manner. I said that he ate his food like a beast; but that this might have been the result of living alone in the hills out of the reach of society as refined and elevating as ours for instance. Strickland was not amused. I do not think that he listened to me, for his next sentence referred to the mark on Fleete's breast, and I said that it might have been caused by blister flies, or that it was possibly a birthmark newly born and now visible for the first time. We both agreed that it was unpleasant to look at, and Strickland found occasion to say that I was a fool.

"I can't tell you what I think now," said he, "because you would call me a madman; but you must stay with me for the next few days, if you can. I want you to watch Fleete, but don't tell me what you think till I have made up my mind."

"But I am dining out tonight," I said.

"So am I," said Strickland, "and so is Fleete. At least if he doesn't change his mind."

We walked about the garden smoking, but saying nothing—because we were friends, and talking spoils good tobacco—till our pipes were out. Then we went to wake up Fleete. He was wide awake and fidgeting about his room.

"I say, I want some more chops," he said. "Can I get them?"

We laughed and said, "Go and change. The ponies will be round in a minute."

"All right," said Fleete. "I'll go when I get the chops—underdone ones, mind."

He seemed to be quite in earnest. It was four o'clock, and we had had breakfast at one; still, for a long time, he demanded those underdone chops. Then he changed into riding clothes and went out into the veranda. His pony—the mare had not been caught—would not let him come near. All three horses were unmanageable—mad with fear—and finally Fleete said that he would stay at home and get something to eat. Strickland and I rode out wondering. As we passed the Temple of Hanuman the Silver Man came out and mewed at us.

"He is not one of the regular priests of the temple," said Strickland. "I think I should peculiarly like to lay my hands on him."

There was no spring in our gallop on the racecourse that evening. The horses were stale, and moved as though they had been ridden out.

"The fright after breakfast has been too much for them," said Strickland.

That was the only remark he made through the remainder of the ride. Once or twice, I think, he swore to himself; but that did not count.

We came back in the dark at seven o'clock, and saw that there was no lights in the bungalow. "Careless ruffians my servants are!" said Strickland.

My horse reared at something on the carriage drive, and Fleete stood up under its nose.

"What are you doing, groveling about the garden?" said Strickland.

But both horses bolted and nearly threw us. We dismounted by the stables and returned to Fleete, who was on his hands and knees under the orange bushes.

"What the devil's wrong with you?" said Strickland.

"Nothing, nothing in the world," said Fleete, speaking very quickly and thickly. "I've been gardening—botanizing, you know. The smell of the earth is delightful. I think I'm going for a walk—a long walk—all night."

Then I saw that there was something excessively out of order somewhere, and I said to Strickland, "I am not dining out."

8. **loose box:** stall in which the horse is free to move about.

Words to Own

ruffians (ruf'ē·ənz) *n. pl.:* hoodlums; lawless persons.
groveling (gräv'əl·iŋ) *v.:* crawling with the face close to the ground.

E Humanities Connection

The "mark of the beast" imposed upon those who defy the gods or defile their sacred places is a theme with a long tradition. The ancient Greek myth of Actaeon is the classic example. Actaeon, a hunter, accidentally saw Artemis bathing; as punishment, he was transformed into a stag and torn apart by his own hounds. Similarly, Pentheus offended Dionysus by refusing to allow the god to be worshipped; as punishment, Pentheus was torn apart by maenads who perceived him to be an animal. (The story is dramatized brilliantly by Euripides in his play *The Bacchae.*) These tales remind humans that denying or defiling the divine is an "inhuman" act, the act of an animal.

F Reading Skills and Strategies

Identifying Conflicts and Resolutions

This moment offers the first suggestion that violence—specifically, violence against the Silver Man—will be part of the resolution of the story's conflicts. Ask students how Strickland's comment makes them feel. [Students may feel suddenly wary of the Englishmen or surprised at Strickland's lack of compassion.]

G Reading Skills and Strategies

Identifying Cause and Effect

? Up to now, the narrator has tried to rationalize Fleete's behavior. What do you think brings him to the realization that "there was something excessively out of order somewhere"? [Possible responses: Fleete's increasingly bizarre behavior; or Fleete's extraordinary statement that he plans to stay out all night in the Indian wilderness.]

Crossing the Curriculum

Architecture/Fine Arts

Have students research and report on some of the architectural and artistic treasures of India. Examples might include the Taj Mahal in Agra; the ancient Buddhist monasteries and shrines at Ajanta with their marvelous frescoes; and the miniature paintings of scenes from Hindu mythology. Students should report their findings, using visuals whenever possible.

Health

Students might research three medical conditions germane to this story: (1) leprosy (the Silver Man's affliction); (2) hydrophobia, or rabies (the "official" cause of Fleete's condition); and (3) lycanthropy, a mental disorder in which a person believes that he or she is a wolf. Students may share their research in a format of their own choosing but should relate their findings to the story.

Music

Have students find or create music that could be used as a soundtrack for "The Mark of the Beast." They might choose a particular theme song for each character or use music to set the moods of different scenes. As time permits, have volunteers play and explain their musical selections.

LITERATURE AND HISTORY

While Kipling's father was a civil servant in India, Schreiner's father was a missionary in South Africa. Both writers used fiction to bring the land of their childhood to life for British readers. Schreiner's work is also known for its strong feminist themes.

Ⓐ Struggling Readers

Connecting to the Text

Encourage struggling readers to compare the narrator's description and Strickland's comment with familiar scenes from classic horror movies. You might ask students how often they have heard variations of the line "There's going to be trouble tonight." Suspense, the expectation of violence, and exaggerated physical and mental deformity combine to make some of Kipling's scenes seem like parts of *Friday the 13th, Halloween, Scream,* as well as many werewolf movies.

Ⓑ Elements of Literature

Hyperbole

Hyperbole—a figure of speech that uses exaggeration to express strong emotion or create a comic effect—often plays a large role in tales of the fantastic. Kipling has his narrator go beyond literal truth when he speaks of "blood running cold," his heart stopping "as though a knife had been driven through it," and turning "as white as the tablecloth."

LITERATURE AND HISTORY

The Age of Empire

A breakfast table during the time of Queen Victoria's reign held many of the same items that we expect to find today: Indian tea, Kenyan coffee (more popular in the United States and Germany), perhaps Brazilian cocoa—all sweetened with Caribbean sugar.

Victorians were keenly aware that traders circled the globe to provide their morning beverages. Their knowledge came in part from writers such as Rudyard Kipling and Olive Schreiner (1855–1920), who so carefully documented the experience of Europeans abroad. (Schreiner wrote of South Africa.) Kipling's descriptions of the British presence in India capture the controversies of a period known as the Age of Empire. The nineteenth century provided European scholars with opportunities to study ancient civilizations, but the emphasis on indigenous peoples was eclipsed by the lucrative market for raw tropical materials: rubber, oil, cotton. The relationship between Europe and its colonies is summarized by the remark of an administrator, who observed in 1862 that "the traffic with half-civilized peoples has risks of its own, which are generally compensated by more than ordinary profits."

European powers were in such keen competition for colonies that, between 1876 and 1914, more than a quarter of the globe's land surface was distributed as colonies among a half-dozen countries. In Victoria's reign, the British prided themselves on the fact that the sun never set on their far-flung empire.

"Bless you!" said Strickland. "Here, Fleete, get up. You'll catch fever there. Come in to dinner and let's have the lamps lit. We'll dine at home."

Fleete stood up unwillingly, and said, "No lamps—no lamps. It's much nicer here. Let's dine outside and have some more chops—lots of 'em and underdone—bloody ones with gristle."

Now a December evening in Northern India is bitterly cold, and Fleete's suggestion was that of a maniac.

"Come in," said Strickland sternly. "Come in at once."

Fleete came, and when the lamps were brought, we saw that he was literally plastered with dirt Ⓐ from head to foot. He must have been rolling in the garden. He shrank from the light and went to his room. His eyes were horrible to look at. There was a green light behind them, not in them, if you understand, and the man's lower lip hung down.

Strickland said, "There is going to be trouble—big trouble—tonight. Don't you change your riding things."

We waited and waited for Fleete's reappearance, and ordered dinner in the meantime. We could hear him moving about his own room, but there was no light there. Presently from the room came the long-drawn howl of a wolf.

Ⓑ People write and talk lightly of blood running cold and hair standing up, and things of that kind. Both sensations are too horrible to be trifled with.

WORDS TO OWN

trifled (trī′fəld) *v.:* mocked; treated lightly.

Skill Link

Analyzing and Responding to a Written Review

Referring to Kipling's stories about India, critic James Harrison says, "In some ways Kipling's whole output of stories about India can be viewed as a search for equilibrium, whether between East and West, action and contemplation, or youth and age. So many of them turn out, ultimately, to be about a balance between the 'civilization' and discipline the British try to impose on India . . . and the variety, the richness, the vitality, even the intractable wisdom of the raw material these artists of law and order seek to imbue with their sense of form. And any such balance is a model, of course, of what Kipling the artist was striving to achieve in his writing." Have students analyze this comment and compare it with their own response. Ask them if they agree that "The Mark of the Beast" shows a search for balance between British "civilization" and the "raw material" of India; ask also if students detect a search for personal balance in the story.

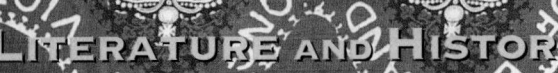

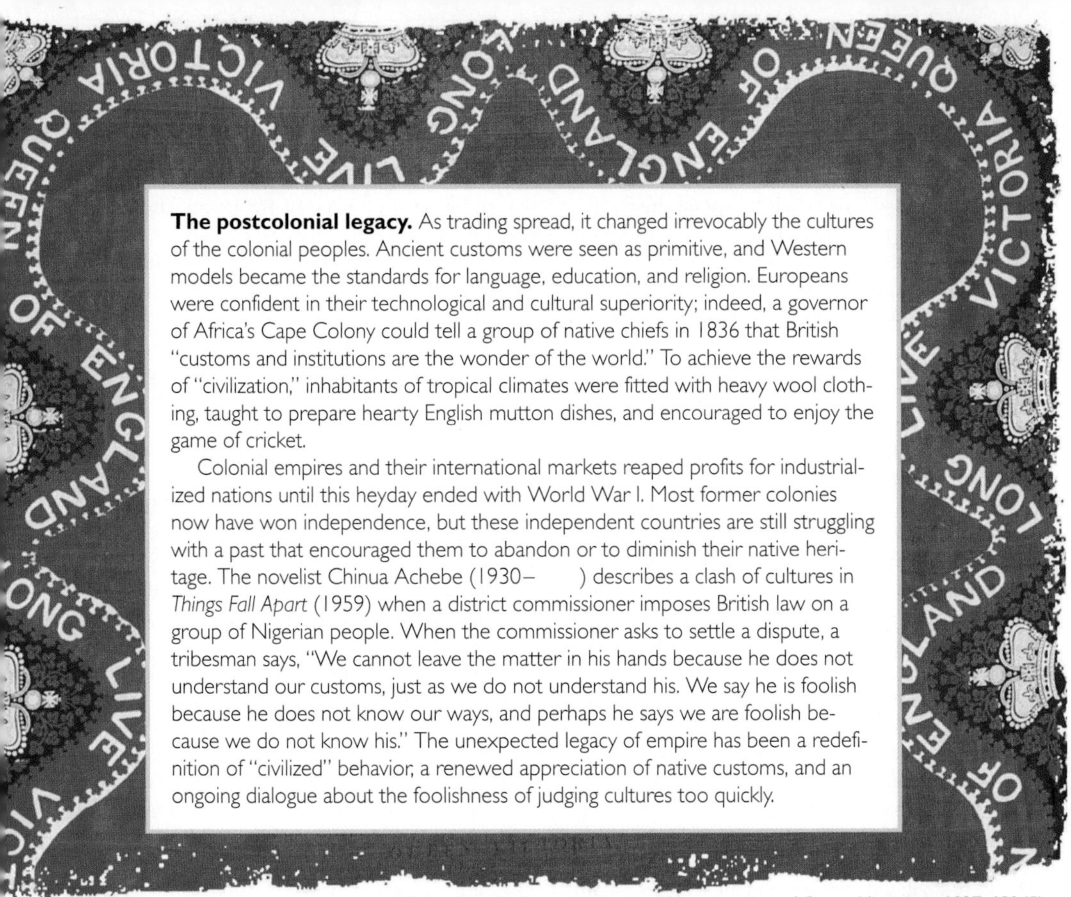

The postcolonial legacy. As trading spread, it changed irrevocably the cultures of the colonial peoples. Ancient customs were seen as primitive, and Western models became the standards for language, education, and religion. Europeans were confident in their technological and cultural superiority; indeed, a governor of Africa's Cape Colony could tell a group of native chiefs in 1836 that British "customs and institutions are the wonder of the world." To achieve the rewards of "civilization," inhabitants of tropical climates were fitted with heavy wool clothing, taught to prepare hearty English mutton dishes, and encouraged to enjoy the game of cricket.

Colonial empires and their international markets reaped profits for industrialized nations until this heyday ended with World War I. Most former colonies now have won independence, but these independent countries are still struggling with a past that encouraged them to abandon or to diminish their native heritage. The novelist Chinua Achebe (1930–) describes a clash of cultures in *Things Fall Apart* (1959) when a district commissioner imposes British law on a group of Nigerian people. When the commissioner asks to settle a dispute, a tribesman says, "We cannot leave the matter in his hands because he does not understand our customs, just as we do not understand his. We say he is foolish because he does not know our ways, and perhaps he says we are foolish because we do not know his." The unexpected legacy of empire has been a redefinition of "civilized" behavior, a renewed appreciation of native customs, and an ongoing dialogue about the foolishness of judging cultures too quickly.

Museum of London.

Silk handkerchief commemorating the coronation of Queen Victoria in 1837. (C245).

My heart stopped as though a knife had been driven through it, and Strickland turned as white as the tablecloth.

The howl was repeated, and was answered by another howl far across the fields.

That set the gilded roof on the horror. Strickland dashed into Fleete's room. I followed, and we saw Fleete getting out of the window. He made beast noises in the back of his throat. He could not answer us when we shouted at him. He spat.

I don't quite remember what followed, but I think that Strickland must have stunned him with the long bootjack,[9] or else I should never have been able to sit on his chest. Fleete could not speak, he could only snarl, and his snarls were those of a wolf, not of a man. The human spirit must have been giving way all day and have died out with the twilight. We were dealing with a beast that had once been Fleete. **C**

The affair was beyond any human and rational experience. I tried to say "hydrophobia,"[10] but the word wouldn't come, because I knew that I was lying. **D**

We bound this beast with leather thongs of the punkah[11] rope, and tied its thumbs and big toes together, and gagged it with a shoehorn, which makes a very efficient gag if you know how to **E**

9. **bootjack:** device for pulling off boots, often made of cast iron.

10. **hydrophobia:** rabies. One of the effects of rabies is an inability to swallow water.

11. **punkah** (puŋ′kə): swinging fan suspended from the ceiling. It is operated by pulling an attached cord or rope.

C Reading Skills and Strategies
Identifying Conflicts and Resolutions

Draw students' attention to this sentence and ask them what it implies about a conflict in the story. [Possible response: "Giving way all day" indicates that a long, internal conflict has been taking place within Fleete.]

D Critical Thinking
Analyzing Details

The only scientific explanation offered for Fleete's behavior is that he is suffering from rabies, which is sometimes called hydrophobia because one of its symptoms is difficulty swallowing water. Although the restlessness that Fleete has been displaying is one sign of rabies, even the narrator knows by this point that mere physical illness cannot sufficiently explain Fleete's condition.

E Appreciating Language
Pronoun Shift

? What justification is there for the narrator to switch from referring to Fleete as *he* to referring to him as *it*? [Possible response: Just a few lines earlier, the narrator says "We were dealing with a beast that had once been Fleete." The narrator can no longer consider Fleete human; he shows that view in his pronoun choice.]

Making the Connections

Connecting to the Theme: "The Paradox of Progress"

After students have read "The Mark of the Beast," ask them what "paradox of progress" they see in the circumstances in which the British characters find themselves. [Possible response: These characters, so sure of the superiority of everything British, are first mystified and then horrified by the power of the native Indian culture.]

Cultural Connections

Ask students to research their own cultural backgrounds or another culture that interests them to find legends or stories of beings who change their form from human to animal. Encourage students to draw conclusions about the themes or messages of these stories and to compare them to the theme of "The Mark of the Beast."

Ⓐ Reading Skills and Strategies

Making Inferences

? What would the doctor give as the cause of Fleete's death? [rabies, or hydrophobia] What is the "reality" that Strickland and the narrator can only whisper? [Fleete is suffering from a curse or spell placed upon him by the Silver Man.]

Ⓑ Struggling Readers

Using Context Clues

Encourage readers who struggle with the word *paroxysm* to examine the words around it. "Struggling" suggests violent physical effort, and the fear that the thongs "would give way" suggests straining against being held down. Students should be able to determine that a *paroxysm* is a sudden convulsion or outburst.

Ⓒ Critical Thinking

Analyzing Details

? Notice the items that Strickland brings into Fleete's room. How do you think these items relate to Strickland's character, to his muttered statement to the narrator, and to the overall plot of the story? [Possible response: The items can be used for violence, possibly torture, and Strickland already has suggested a desire to harm the Silver Man. He may use those items to keep the Silver Man from killing Fleete.]

Ⓓ Critical Thinking

Evaluating an Interpretation

In *Rudyard Kipling: Realist and Fabulist*, Bonamy Dobrée says of the "deliberate cruelty" that begins at this point in the story: "Kipling, we see, could understand cruelty; possibly he could be aware of tendencies towards it in himself, as he seems to confess: but the man or woman who can honestly say that he has not at some time or other felt this when sufficiently provoked by some horror must be rare indeed." As students read the rest of the story, ask them to comment on Dobrée's interpretation. [Students may point to "sufficiently provoked" as the key to Dobrée's comment, agreeing unknowingly with Dobrée's conclusion that the action is justified when its "purpose is the saving of a human soul."]

arrange it. Then we carried it into the dining room, and sent a man to Dumoise, the doctor, telling him to come over at once. After we had dispatched the messenger and were drawing breath, Strickland said, "It's no good. This isn't any doctor's work." I, also, knew that he spoke the truth.

The beast's head was free, and it threw it about from side to side. Anyone entering the room would have believed that we were curing a wolf's pelt. That was the most loathsome accessory of all.

Strickland sat with his chin in the heel of his fist, watching the beast as it wriggled on the ground, but saying nothing. The shirt had been torn open in the scuffle and showed the black rosette mark on the left breast. It stood out like a blister.

In the silence of the watching we heard something without mewing like a she-otter. We both rose to our feet, and, I answer for myself, not Strickland, felt sick—actually and physically sick. We told each other, as did the men in *Pinafore,*[12] that it was the cat.

Dumoise arrived, and I never saw a little man so unprofessionally shocked. He said that it was a heart-rending case of hydrophobia, and that nothing could be done. At least any palliative measures would only prolong the agony. The beast was foaming at the mouth. Fleete, as we told Dumoise, had been bitten by dogs once or twice. Any man who keeps half a dozen terriers must expect a nip now and again. Dumoise could offer no help. He could only certify that Fleete was dying of hydrophobia. The beast was then howling, for it had managed to spit out the shoehorn. Dumoise said that he would be ready to certify to the cause of death, and that the end was certain. He was a good little man, and he offered to remain with us; but Strickland refused the kindness. He did not wish to poison Dumoise's New Year. He would only ask him not to give the real cause of Fleete's death to the public.

So Dumoise left, deeply agitated; and as soon as the noise of the cart wheels had died away, Strickland told me, in a whisper, his suspicions. They were so wildly improbable that he dared not say them out aloud; and I, who entertained all Strickland's beliefs, was so ashamed of owning to them that I pretended to disbelieve.

"Even if the Silver Man had bewitched Fleete for polluting the image of Hanuman, the punishment could not have fallen so quickly."

As I was whispering this the cry outside the house rose again, and the beast fell into a fresh paroxysm of struggling till we were afraid that the thongs that held it would give way.

"Watch!" said Strickland. "If this happens six times I shall take the law into my own hands. I order you to help me."

He went into his room and came out in a few minutes with the barrels of an old shotgun, a piece of fishing line, some thick cord, and his heavy wooden bedstead. I reported that the convulsions had followed the cry by two seconds in each case, and the beast seemed perceptibly weaker.

Strickland muttered, "But he can't take away the life! He can't take away the life!"

I said, though I knew that I was arguing against myself, "It may be a cat. It must be a cat. If the Silver Man is responsible, why does he dare to come here?"

Strickland arranged the wood on the hearth, put the gun barrels into the glow of the fire, spread the twine on the table, and broke a walking stick in two. There was one yard of fishing line, gut lapped with wire, such as is used for *mahseer*[13] fishing, and he tied the two ends together in a loop.

Then he said, "How can we catch him? He must be taken alive and unhurt."

I said that we must trust in Providence, and go out softly with polo sticks into the shrubbery at the front of the house. The man or animal that made the cry was evidently moving round the house as regularly as a night watchman. We could wait in the bushes till he came by and knock him over.

Strickland accepted this suggestion, and we slipped out from a bathroom window into the front veranda and then across the carriage drive into the bushes.

12. ***Pinafore:*** *H.M.S. Pinafore* (1878), a comic operetta by W. S. Gilbert and Arthur Sullivan. Lovers in the play attempt to elope. When they are discovered, the cast sings, "Why, what was that? . . . It was—it was the cat!"

13. **mahseer** (mä′sir): large Indian freshwater fish of the carp family.

Skill Link

Analyzing and Responding to a Critical Review

When Victorian critic Lionel Johnson reviewed some of Kipling's stories in 1891, he cited what he considered to be an "unfortunate mannerism" in "The Mark of the Beast." He focused on such expressions as "the scene was beyond description"; "several other things happened also, but they cannot be put down here"; and "this part is not to be printed." Johnson wrote: "Now this suggestion of unmentionable horror is a piece of the very worst possible art: Mr. Kipling means to thrill us with absolute horror, to fill us with shuddering apprehensions of absolute fearfulness. He fails: we feel nothing but wonder and contempt, to find so able a writer fall into so pitiable a device." Ask students to summarize Johnson's main point. Then ask if they do or do not agree with Johnson and why.

In the moonlight we could see the leper coming round the corner of the house. He was perfectly naked, and from time to time he mewed and stopped to dance with his shadow. It was an unattractive sight, and thinking of poor Fleete, brought to such degradation by so foul a creature, I put away all my doubts and resolved to help Strickland from the heated gun barrels to the loop of twine—from the loins to the head and back again—with all tortures that might be needful.

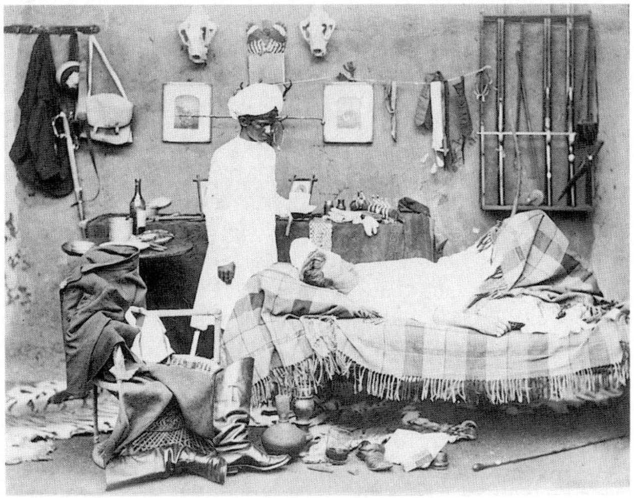

English officer attended by his Indian servant (1870s).
Albumen print by Willoughby Wallace Hooper and George Western.
By permission of the British Library, London.

The leper halted in the front porch for a moment and we jumped out on him with the sticks. He was wonderfully strong, and we were afraid that he might escape or be fatally injured before we caught him. We had an idea that lepers were frail creatures, but this proved to be incorrect. Strickland knocked his legs from under him and I put my foot on his neck. He mewed hideously, and even through my riding boots I could feel that his flesh was not the flesh of a clean man. Man vs man

He struck at us with his hand- and feet-stumps. We looped the lash of a dog-whip round him under the armpits, and dragged him backward into the hall and so into the dining room where the beast lay. There we tied him with trunk straps. He made no attempt to escape, but mewed. **E**

When we confronted him with the beast the scene was beyond description. The beast doubled backward into a bow as though he had been poisoned with strychnine, and moaned in the most pitiable fashion. Several other things happened also, but they cannot be put down here.

"I think I was right," said Strickland. "Now we will ask him to cure this case."

But the leper only mewed. Strickland wrapped a towel round his hand and took the gun barrels out of the fire. I put the half of the broken walking stick through the loop of fishing line and buckled the leper comfortably to Strickland's bedstead. I understood then how men and women and little children can endure to see a witch burnt alive; for the beast was moaning on the floor, and though the Silver Man had no face, you could see horrible feelings passing through **F** the slab that took its place, exactly as waves of heat play across red-hot iron—gun barrels, for instance.

Strickland shaded his eyes with his hands for a moment and we got to work. This part is not to be printed. torture leper

The dawn was beginning to break when the leper spoke. His mewings had not been satisfactory up to that point. The beast had fainted from exhaustion and the house was very still. We unstrapped the leper and told him to take away the evil spirit. He crawled to the beast and laid his hand upon the left breast. That was all. Then he fell face down and whined, drawing in his breath as he did so.

We watched the face of the beast, and saw the **G** soul of Fleete coming back into the eyes. Then a sweat broke out on the forehead and the eyes—they were human eyes—closed. We waited for an hour, but Fleete still slept. We carried him to his

Shantel wouldn't open her book so I opened it. She said, "I'm not going to read it."

E Vocabulary Note

Point out to students that Kipling repeatedly uses *mewed* to describe sounds made by the Silver Man. Have students define the word and discuss what it suggests about the character. [To *mew* is to whimper like a cat, suggesting that the Silver Man has become animal-like, robbed of the human gift of speech.]

F Literary Connections

The Victorians' desire to "see horrible feelings" and their fascination with macabre transformations are displayed in two novels of the time. In Robert Louis Stevenson's *Dr. Jekyll and Mr. Hyde* (1886), the "beast" takes over a man who crosses scientific boundaries. In Oscar Wilde's *The Picture of Dorian Gray* (1891), the "mark of the beast" becomes visible in the slowly transforming portrait of a morally degenerate man.

G Reading Skills and Strategies

Identifying Conflicts and Resolutions

The climax—the torture of the Silver Man—is left to the reader's imagination, but the resolution is quickly apparent. Ask students to find a phrase or sentence that seems to signal the resolution. [Possible response: "We . . . saw the soul of Fleete coming back into his eyes."]

Assessing Learning

Check Test: Questions and Answers

1. What crime does Fleete commit in his state of drunkenness? [He defiles a temple of Hanuman.]
2. Why do the temple priests let the British intruders go? [The Silver Man embraces Fleete—a sign, according to the priests, that Hanuman will avenge himself.]
3. What are the first signs that something strange is happening to Fleete? [Fleete demands bloody meat to eat, and he develops a dark spot on his chest where the Silver Man touched him.]
4. What does Dumoise believe has happened to Fleete? [He thinks Fleete is suffering from hydrophobia, or rabies.]
5. How do Strickland and the narrator restore Fleete to his former self? [They trap the Silver Man and torture him until he removes the curse.]

Standardized Test Preparation

For practice with ACT and SAT formats, see
- *Preparation for College Admission Exams,* p. 43

For practice in proofreading and editing, see
- *Daily Oral Grammar,* Transparency 30

A Reading Skills and Strategies

Identifying Conflicts and Resolutions

? Fleete awakens with no memory of what has happened; thus, he learns nothing from his experience. How do you think this realization affects the resolution of the story? [Possible responses: Even if Fleete has learned nothing, the narrator has, and he shares what he has learned with the reader. It is disappointing that Fleete is no wiser than when he started, but such a less-than-complete resolution is more true to life.]

MAKING MEANINGS

First Thoughts [Respond]

1. Possible responses: Kipling's story is less scary because it is hard to visualize; Kipling's use of suspense and the unknown makes the story at least as scary.

Shaping Interpretations [Interpret]

2. The first conflict is one that the narrator names: "Providence" and "the Church of England" vs. "the Gods and Devils of Asia." The first conflict to arise directly from the action of the story comes when Fleete grinds his cigar into the statue of Hanuman, offending the worshippers and perhaps the god himself. Both conflicts arise because of a clash of cultures. An external conflict arises between Fleete and his friends as the curse takes hold; an internal conflict takes place as animal instincts begin to dominate and Fleete's "human spirit" gives way. Strickland and the narrator also struggle internally to make sense of the situation.
3. The immediate victors in the conflict between the British and the Indians would seem to be the British, by virtue of their use of force on the Silver Man. However, it is strongly suggested that "the Gods and Devils of Asia" are stronger than any physical force or scientific knowledge that the British can bring to bear. The overall conflict of cultures has no clear-cut victor, neither in the story nor in history.

room and bade the leper go, giving him the bedstead, and the sheet on the bedstead to cover his nakedness, the gloves and the towels with which we had touched him, and the whip that had been hooked round his body. He put the sheet about him and went out into the early morning without speaking or mewing.

Strickland wiped his face and sat down. A night gong, far away in the city, made seven o'clock.

"Exactly four-and-twenty hours!" said Strickland. "And I've done enough to ensure my dismissal from the service, besides permanent quarters in a lunatic asylum. Do you believe that we are awake?"

The red-hot gun barrel had fallen on the floor and was singeing the carpet. The smell was entirely real.

That morning at eleven we two together went to wake up Fleete. We looked and saw that the black leopard rosette on his chest had disappeared. **A** He was very drowsy and tired, but as soon as he saw us, he said, "Oh! Confound you fellows. Happy New Year to you. Never mix your liquors. I'm nearly dead."

"Thanks for your kindness, but you're over time," said Strickland. "Today is the morning of the second. You've slept the clock round with a vengeance."

The door opened, and little Dumoise put his head in. He had come on foot, and fancied that we were laying out Fleete.

"I've brought a nurse," said Dumoise. "I suppose that she can come in for . . . what is necessary."

"By all means," said Fleete cheerily, sitting up in bed. "Bring on your nurses."

Dumoise was dumb. Strickland led him out and explained that there must have been a mistake in the diagnosis. Dumoise remained dumb and left the house hastily. He considered that his professional reputation had been injured, and was inclined to make a personal matter of the recovery. Strickland went out too. When he came back, he said that he had been to call on the Temple of Hanuman to offer redress for the pollution of the god, and had been solemnly assured that no white man had ever touched the idol, and that he was an incarnation of all the virtues laboring under a delusion. "What do you think?" said Strickland.

I said, "'There are more things . . .'"[14]

But Strickland hates that quotation. He says that I have worn it threadbare.

One other curious thing happened which frightened me as much as anything in all the night's work. When Fleete was dressed he came into the dining room and sniffed. He had a quaint trick of moving his nose when he sniffed. "Horrid doggy smell, here," said he. "You should really keep those terriers of yours in better order. Try sulfur, Strick."

But Strickland did not answer. He caught hold of the back of a chair, and, without warning, went into an amazing fit of hysterics. It is terrible to see a strong man overtaken with hysteria. Then it struck me that we had fought for Fleete's soul with the Silver Man in that room, and had disgraced ourselves as Englishmen forever, and I laughed and gasped and gurgled just as shamefully as Strickland, while Fleete thought that we had both gone mad. We never told him what we had done.

Some years later, when Strickland had married and was a churchgoing member of society for his wife's sake, we reviewed the incident dispassionately, and Strickland suggested that I should put it before the public.

I cannot myself see that this step is likely to clear up the mystery; because, in the first place, no one will believe a rather unpleasant story, and, in the second, it is well known to every right-minded man that the gods of the heathen are stone and brass, and any attempt to deal with them otherwise is justly condemned.

14. **"There are more things":** a reference to William Shakespeare's *Hamlet,* Act I, scene 5, lines 166–167: "There are more things in heaven and earth, Horatio, than are dreamt of in your philosophy."

WORDS TO OWN

redress (rē′dres′) *n.:* compensation for wrong.
delusion (di·lo͞o′zhən) *n.:* false belief.
dispassionately (dis·pash′ə·nət·lē) *adv.:* without emotion; impartially.

Reading Check

Possible responses appear below in an unmapped format.

Main conflict: West vs. East; ways of the English vs. Indian traditions.

Important events: Fleete pollutes a temple; where the Silver Man has touched him, Fleete develops a mark; Fleete begins to act inhuman; Strickland and the narrator tie him up; the Englishmen capture the Silver Man and torture him; the Silver Man finally releases Fleete from his strange state; Fleete has no memory of what has happened.

Points of keen suspense: the Silver Man's first embrace of Fleete; the discovery of Fleete groveling in the dirt; Fleete's wolflike howl; Strickland's suggestion that Fleete is under a curse from Hanuman; the torture of the Silver Man; the wait to see if the curse has been lifted.

Climax: Strickland and the narrator capture the Silver Man and torture him into restoring Fleete.

Outcome: Fleete returns to normal; Strickland and the narrator are left to wonder about what has happened.

MAKING MEANINGS

First Thoughts

1. Is Kipling's story as scary as other werewolf stories or movies you know? Why or why not?

Reading Check

Working with others, map the **main conflict, important events,** points of keen **suspense, climax,** and **outcome** of the story.

Shaping Interpretations

2. Complete the chart that you filled out as you read the story. How many **conflicts**—external and internal—did you find? Which conflicts resulted from cultural misunderstandings?
3. What about the victors in these conflicts? Were some conflicts left unresolved? Be sure to compare your answers in class.
4. Compare the **characterizations** of Fleete, Strickland, and the narrator. How does **point of view** affect what you know about each character?
5. Who or what is the Silver Man? What details in the story support your interpretation?
6. What does this story reveal about the British presence in India?
7. What **allusions** to the Book of Revelation in the Bible are made in this story? Consider these allusions, and tell what you think the story's **theme** is.
8. Do you think the events of this story illustrate the "paradox of progress"? Explain why or why not.

Challenging the Text

9. Do you think this story has something important to say to us today despite—or even because of—its racist elements? Cite details from the story to support your answer.
10. Critics have called this story "nasty," "poisonous," and even "sadistic." Explain why you agree or disagree with these assessments.

CHOICES: Building Your Portfolio

Writer's Notebook

1. Collecting Ideas for an Evaluation

WORK IN PROGRESS

How do you rate Kipling's story? Is it a well-told, suspenseful horror story? Is it a racist story? Are its characters stereotypes? Is it offensive or problematic in other respects? Make three general statements evaluating Kipling's story. Then list at least two details from the text to support each evaluation. Keep your notes for the Writer's Workshop on page 899.

Creative Writing

2. A Silver Man Sequel

The Silver Man survives, and the temple priests deny the whole incident. Use these facts to create a story outline for "The Mark of the Beast II."

Research / Speaking

3. The Evolution of a Myth

Werewolfism, or lycanthropy, is an ancient, enduring myth, but its significance can change. In Kipling's 1890 story and in the 1985 American film *Teen Wolf,* the werewolves have different characteristics. Prepare a multimedia report about werewolf stories in different periods and cultures, showing both the universal and specific social concerns they reflect.

Historical Research

4. The Jewel in the Crown

India was part of the British Empire until 1947; Victoria referred to it as the jewel in her crown. Explore the Anglo-Indian connection by researching the kind of life a British civil servant like Kipling might have lived in late-nineteenth-century India. As a contrast, describe the way of life of most Indians. Present your findings in an informal report.

4. Fleete is characterized as boorish, with little interest in India and its people. Strickland seems to have a greater understanding of India, but he is intense and nervous throughout. The narrator seems more balanced, although he follows Strickland's lead. Readers know no more about Fleete or Strickland than the facts and opinions the narrator provides.

5. The Silver Man is a leper, but there is also something mysterious about him. He may be under the special protection of Hanuman's temple; Strickland suggests that Fleete's transformation is the result of the Silver Man's having "bewitched Fleete for polluting the image of Hanuman."

6. The British tried to make their contact with the Indian population as British as possible; they sometimes did not even try to understand Indian ways; even an Englishman with some respect for Indians would sacrifice an Indian to save another Englishman.

7. Fleete's mark and the story's title refer to the book of Revelation. Students may suggest themes such as "culture clash" or "rational vs. the supernatural."

8. Possible response: The story illustrates the "paradox of progress" in the inability of science, the pride of the West, to explain Fleete's transformation.

Challenging the Text [Evaluate]

9. Most students will agree that Kipling's story has something important to say about the need to respect other cultures. They may argue that the expression of racism—as displayed in Fleete's disrespectful behavior—is an essential plot element and helps to make the story's point.

10. Some students might agree, pointing especially to the treatment of the Silver Man. Others, while noting that it is a sinister tale, may feel that adjectives such as *nasty, poisonous,* and *sadistic* reflect a prim view of storytelling and that stories today are "poisonous" and "sadistic" in ways Kipling never dared think of!

Grading Timesaver

Rubrics for each Choices assignment appear on p. 180 in the *Portfolio Management System.*

Objectives

1. Read and interpret the story
2. Generate relevant, interesting, and researchable questions
3. Recognize distinctive and shared characteristics of cultures
4. Compare text events with personal experiences
5. Recognize and discuss themes that cross cultures

Browsing in the Files

About the Author. Tolstoy's final flight from his home attracted a great deal of publicity. As he traveled, Tolstoy followed the newspaper accounts of his journey. "Everything is known already," he complained when he saw headlines like "LEO TOLSTOY LEAVES YASNAYA POLYANA." Journalists pursued him relentlessly, as they dog famous people today, continually telegramming their editors with every shred of information they could glean. As he was dying at Astopovo, frequent bulletins about his condition were released to the press.

Planning

- **Block Schedule**
  Block Scheduling Lesson Plans with Pacing Guide
- **Traditional Schedule**
  Lesson Plans Including Strategies for English-Language Learners
- **One-Stop Planner**
  CD-ROM with Test Generator

Resources

Listening

Audio CD Library

A recording of this story is included in the *Audio CD Library:*

- Disc 15, Track 2

World Literature

Russia

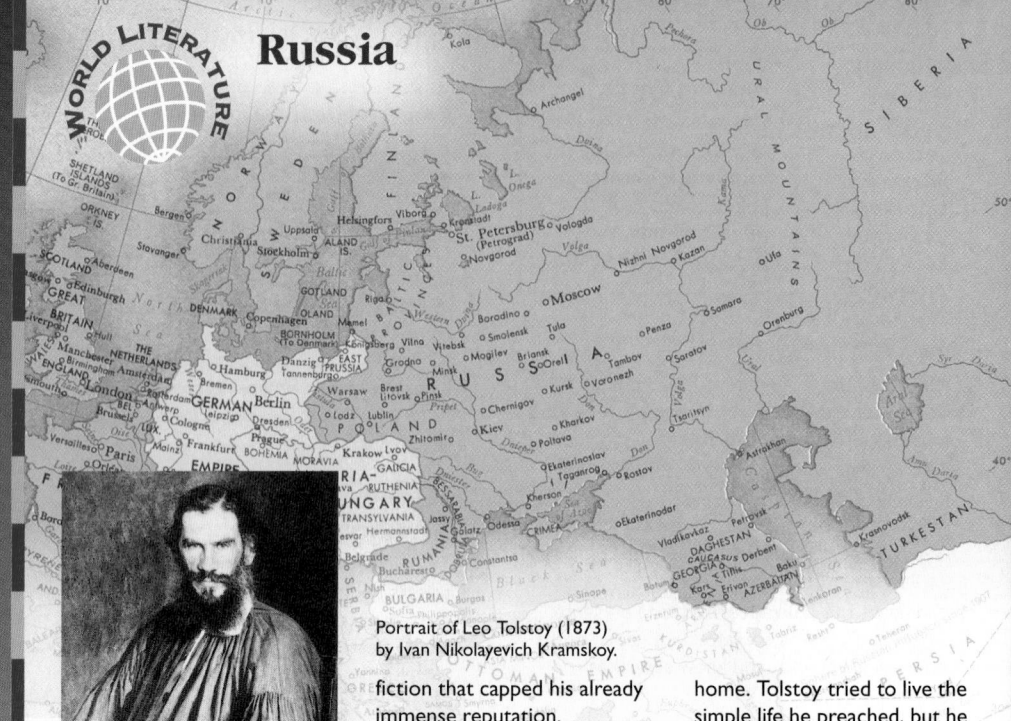

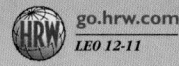

Portrait of Leo Tolstoy (1873) by Ivan Nikolayevich Kramskoy.

Leo Tolstoy

(1828–1910)

Ironically, Tolstoy, whose story provides a surprising answer to the title question, was born into wealthy, landed aristocracy. Count Leo Nikolayevich Tolstoy was orphaned at nine; at age nineteen, he took possession of a huge rural estate. There he wrote *War and Peace* and *Anna Karenina,* masterpieces of realistic fiction that capped his already immense reputation.

But by age fifty, Tolstoy had reached a moral and spiritual crisis. Aspiring to be holy and to do good, he found his best models in Russia's self-sufficient Christian peasants. His writings became fervent attacks on the government, church, and private ownership (because he felt all three operated by threat of force). Instead, Tolstoy celebrated communal, utopian ideals of pure love and honest labor.

Because he was already a famous writer, educational reformer, and war hero, the repressive Russian government left him alone as pilgrims worldwide journeyed to his home. Tolstoy tried to live the simple life he preached, but he was a man with many children and a wife who did not share his extreme views. With much bitter quarreling, she obtained Tolstoy's substantial royalties to support the family. Finally, as an old man of eighty-two, Tolstoy decided to lead a poor, reclusive life. He fled his home in secret, at night, with his doctor and youngest daughter. At a tiny, remote railroad station, the fugitives got off the train, and Tolstoy, ill with a high fever, was taken to the stationmaster's house. There, amid a mob scene of reporters and family who had eventually tracked him down, Tolstoy died of pneumonia.

(Map) Europe in 1914. Map © Rand McNally #98-S-116.

go.hrw.com
LEO 12-11

Reaching All Students

Struggling Readers

Each time Pahom is preparing to obtain more land, have students stop and reflect on what they think will happen next. Ask them to jot down one or two sentences stating their predictions. Then have them continue reading, stopping to revise their statements if any details in the story lead them to expect an outcome different from the ones they originally predicted.

English Language Learners

Easy-to-read reference books can provide English language learners with visual aids, especially drawings and photographs, which will help them understand Tolstoy's setting and characters. One such reference is *Tolstoy—The Making of a Novelist.* It includes many photographs of Tolstoy and of the people about whom he wrote, as well as paintings and drawings that were used to illustrate many of his stories.

Before You Read
HOW MUCH LAND DOES A MAN NEED?

Background

You will have no trouble seeing why this story is included under the theme "The Paradox of Progress." Very early, one character proclaims, "Loss and gain are brothers twain." Yet the historical setting makes the paradox much deeper. The nineteenth-century Russia that Leo Tolstoy is describing had just abandoned feudalism—a way of life dead in England since the Middle Ages.

Until Czar Alexander II ordered an emancipation in 1861, Russian peasants, called serfs, were virtual slaves of landowners and aristocrats: They could be bought or sold, and they owned no property. When Tolstoy wrote this story, serfs had had twenty-five years of freedom and rights. No one, certainly not the reformer Tolstoy, would wish to see them in bondage again. Yet in this parable he could wonder—with sharp humor—whether the peasants' progress had brought losses they would regret.

Quickwrite

Answer these questions as honestly as you can. First, if you could have everything you wanted, how much property (a home and land) would you wish for? Second, how much property do you think you really need?

How Much Land Does a Man Need?

Leo Tolstoy
translated by **Louise** *and* **Aylmer Maude**

An elder sister came to visit her younger sister in the country. The elder was married to a tradesman in town, the younger to a peasant in the village. As the sisters sat over their tea talking, the elder began to boast of the advantages of town life: saying how comfortably they lived there, how well they dressed, what fine clothes her children wore, what good things they ate and drank, and how she went to the theater, promenades, and entertainments.

The younger sister was piqued, and in turn disparaged the life of a tradesman, and stood up for that of a peasant.

"I would not change my way of life for yours," said she. "We may live roughly, but at least we are free from anxiety. You live in better style than we do, but though you often earn more than you need, you are very likely to lose all you have. You know the proverb, 'Loss and gain are brothers twain.' It often happens that people who are wealthy one day are begging their bread the next. Our way is safer. Though a peasant's life is not a fat one, it is a long one. We shall never grow rich, but we shall always have enough to eat."

The elder sister said sneeringly:

"Enough? Yes, if you like to share with the pigs and the calves! What do you know of elegance or manners! However much your goodman may slave, you will die as you are living—on a dung heap—and your children the same."

"Well, what of that?" replied the younger. "Of course our work is rough and coarse. But, on the other hand, it is sure, and we need not bow to anyone. But you, in your towns, are surrounded

Making the Connections

Connecting to the Theme: "The Paradox of Progress"

After students have finished reading the story, discuss with them the various ways in which it reflects the collection theme:

- As Pahom progresses financially, he puts himself in greater and greater danger of material ruin.
- As Pahom progresses up the economic ladder, he regresses socially, making more and more enemies.
- As Pahom progresses materially, he loses sight of the moral aspects of his actions.
- As Pahom seeks to enlarge his lands, his mental "vision" becomes more and more narrow, confined, and obsessive.
- As Pahom becomes a model of "modern" commercial success, he loses touch with traditional ways of living on the land which may be more spiritually satisfying.

Summary

In this parable, Pahom, a Russian farmer, overhears his wife and his sister-in-law arguing over the merits of city versus country life. Privately, he boasts that if he had enough land, he would not fear the Devil. The Devil overhears him and plots to exploit his greed. Pahom soon succeeds in buying land, yet he quickly becomes dissatisfied with what he has. He treats the local peasants as badly as he was once treated and continues to amass land. When a traveling dealer tells Pahom about the region of the Bashkirs, where fertile land is available at low prices, he decides to make the trip. The Bashkirs welcome Pahom and agree to let him have, for only one thousand rubles, as much land as he can circumscribe in one day. The catch is that he must return before sunset to the place from which he began. Pahom walks a great distance, trying to cover as much land as possible. In his mad rush back to the distant starting point, however, he exhausts himself and dies. He ends up with six feet of land—enough for his grave.

A Elements of Literature
Conflict and Theme

? Tolstoy's story begins with a conflict. What do the sisters argue about? [whose way of life is better] **How does their quarrel help establish the theme of the story?** [Possible response: Their quarrel raises the main issue—What do people need to have a satisfying life?]

B Reading Skills and Strategies
Responding to the Text

Give students a few minutes to freewrite about their initial reactions to the younger sister's argument. Then ask if her reasons seem valid, and why, or why not. [Possible responses: Her reasons seem valid since she and her husband are not risk-takers. Or, they are not valid since the younger sister is making excuses for her poverty.]

C Elements of Literature
Foreshadowing

? From the younger sister's warning, what do you think will happen to her or her family? Explain. [Possible response: Her warning may foreshadow some kind of temptation or even ruin that is in store for her or her family.]

A Cultural Connections

The Temptress in Literature

Remind students of the account in Genesis of the fall of Adam and Eve (pp. 416–418). As the Genesis story has Eve leading Adam into temptation, so folk tales, fairy tales, and other works of literature often present women as temptresses of men. In Tolstoy's story, however, the husband is clearly susceptible to temptation without his wife's prompting.

B Critical Thinking

Challenging the Text

? Do you think it is necessary to include the Devil as a character in this story? Defend your answer. [Possible responses: Having the Devil introduce the temptation makes the story less realistic, less believable; or, the inclusion of the Devil makes the story more like a folk tale or fable, thus making it more universal and calling attention to its moral purpose.]

C Reading Skills and Strategies

Making Generalizations

? What advantage might there be in group ownership of the land? [Possible responses: There might be fewer fines and taxes (or if there were fines, they might be agreed upon by the group); all of the farmers would have a personal stake in making the venture succeed.] Why, then, were the farmers unable to come to an agreement? [The narrator says that the Devil caused them to argue; perhaps they argued because each wanted more than his neighbor.]

by temptations; today all may be right, but tomorrow the Evil One may tempt your husband with cards, wine, or women, and all will go to ruin. Don't such things happen often enough?"

Pahom, the master of the house, was lying on the top of the stove[1] and he listened to the women's chatter.

"It is perfectly true," thought he. "Busy as we are from childhood tilling mother earth, we peasants have no time to let any nonsense settle in our heads. Our only trouble is that we haven't land enough. If I had plenty of land, I shouldn't fear the Devil himself!"

The women finished their tea, chatted a while about dress, and then cleared away the tea things and lay down to sleep.

But the Devil had been sitting behind the stove, and had heard all that was said. He was pleased that the peasant's wife had led her husband into boasting, and that he had said that if he had plenty of land he would not fear the Devil himself.

"All right," thought the Devil. "We will have a tussle. I'll give you land enough; and by means of that land I will get you into my power."

Close to the village there lived a lady, a small landowner who had an estate of about three hundred acres. She had always lived on good terms with the peasants until she engaged as her steward an old soldier, who took to burdening the people with fines. However careful Pahom tried to be, it happened again and again that now a horse of his got among the lady's oats, now a cow strayed into her garden, now his calves found their way into her meadows—and he always had to pay a fine.

Pahom paid up, but grumbled and, going home in a temper, was rough with his family. All through that summer, Pahom had much trouble because of this steward, and he was even glad when winter came and the cattle had to be stabled. Though he grudged the fodder when they could no longer graze on the pastureland, at least he was free from anxiety about them.

In the winter the news got about that the lady was going to sell her land and that the keeper of the inn on the high road was bargaining for it. When the peasants heard this they were very much alarmed.

"Well," thought they, "if the innkeeper gets the land, he will worry us with fines worse than the lady's steward. We all depend on that estate."

So the peasants went on behalf of their Commune,[2] and asked the lady not to sell the land to the innkeeper, offering her a better price for it themselves. The lady agreed to let them have it. Then the peasants tried to arrange for the Commune to buy the whole estate, so that it might be held by them all in common. They met twice to discuss it, but could not settle the matter; the Evil One sowed discord among them and they could not agree. So they decided to buy the land individually, each according to his means; and the lady agreed to this plan as she had to the other.

Presently Pahom heard that a neighbor of his was buying fifty acres, and that the lady had consented to accept one half in cash and to wait a year for the other half. Pahom felt envious.

"Look at that," thought he, "the land is all being sold, and I shall get none of it." So he spoke to his wife.

"Other people are buying," said he, "and we must also buy twenty acres or so. Life is becoming impossible. That steward is simply crushing us with his fines."

So they put their heads together and considered how they could manage to buy it. They had one hundred rubles laid by. They sold a colt and one half of their bees, hired out one of their sons as a laborer, and took his wages in advance; borrowed the rest from a brother-in-law, and so scraped together half the purchase money.

Having done this, Pahom chose out a farm of forty acres, some of it wooded, and went to the lady to bargain for it. They came to an agreement, and he shook hands with her upon it and paid her a deposit in advance. Then they went to town and signed the deeds, he paying half the price down, and undertaking to pay the remainder within two years.

So now Pahom had land of his own. He borrowed seed, and sowed it on the land he had bought. The harvest was a good one, and within a year he had managed to pay off his debts both

1. **lying . . . stove:** Pahom's house is lacking in luxury if the family's oven, made of brick or tile, is used as an item of furniture.

2. **Commune:** village council.

Crossing the Curriculum

Economics

In nineteenth-century Russia some land was owned communally by groups of peasants, but most of it was owned privately. In the United States, both then and now, most farm land is owned privately by individuals or corporations. Ask students to research the benefits and disadvantages of private ownership versus communal ownership of farm land and to summarize what they discover in an oral report.

Using Students' Strengths

Visual Learners

To Pahom, each chance to buy land is like a door opening to a better life. Students might map out the story by drawing a series of "open door" diagrams. On each diagram, they can note the circumstances that provide the "open door" and how each opening affects Pahom.

Cause	Effect
buys first plot of land	takes pride in owning land

Verbal Learners

Have pairs of volunteers create and present dialogues for one of the following pairs:

- Pahom and his wife
- Pahom and Simon
- the Bashkir chief and Pahom's servant

The subject of the dialogue can be the question asked in the story's title. Remind students to match each character's words to the behavior and values he or she displays in the story.

to the lady and to his brother-in-law. So he became a landowner, plowing and sowing his own land, making hay on his own land, cutting his own trees, and feeding his cattle on his own pasture. When he went out to plow his fields, or to look at his growing corn,[3] or at his grass meadows, his heart would fill with joy. The grass that grew and the flowers that bloomed there seemed to him unlike any that grew elsewhere. Formerly, when he had passed by that land, it had appeared the same as any other land, but now it seemed quite different. D

So Pahom was well contented, and everything would have been right if the neighboring peasants would only not have trespassed on his cornfields E

3. **corn:** any plants producing grain, such as wheat, rye, or oats.

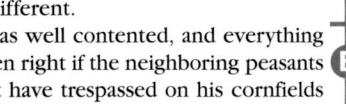

The Gleaners (1885–1886) by Isidore Verheyden. Oil on canvas (92 cm × 69 cm). Collection Crédit Communal, Brussels, Belgium.

D Critical Thinking

Interpreting

? Why does the land now appear more wonderful than and different from any other land? [Possible response: It now belongs to Pahom. When it wasn't his, he took no special notice of it.]

E Elements of Literature

Conflict

? What conflict arises from Pahom's new situation? [Possible response: He becomes protective of his property and sees his neighbors as trespassers.]

RESPONDING TO THE ART

Isidore Verheyden (1846–1905) was a Belgian painter best known for his landscapes. Although initially influenced by Impressionism, with its emphasis on the effect of light on surfaces, Verheyden later protested vigorously against what he thought were Impressionism's excesses. As his painting *The Gleaners* demonstrates, Verheyden's landscapes have a somber quality unlike the light and delicate tone of most Impressionist landscapes.

Activity. Invite students to work together on a mixed-media presentation of Impressionism. Suggest that students volunteer for activities that match their interests and abilities. One group, for example, might gather information on and reproductions of the work of Impressionist painters such as Pierre Auguste Renoir, Alfred Sisley, and Claude Monet. Others might contribute their own Impressionist-style paintings or drawings. Still others might read from the works of poets such as Stéphane Mallarmé, Edgar Allan Poe, Carl Sandburg, and E. E. Cummings. Music-minded students might select and play recordings of Impressionist works by composers like Claude Debussy or the American Charles Tomlinson Griffes.

Professional Notes

Critical Comment: Arnold on Tolstoy

The Victorians were impressed by artists who grappled with issues of culture and values. Matthew Arnold (see p. 846) wrote of Tolstoy, "Whatever else we have or have not in Count Tolstoi, we have at least a great soul and a great writer. . . . Whatever he may do in the future, the work which he has already done . . . is more than sufficient to signalise him as one of the most marking, interesting, and sympathy-inspiring men of our time. . . ." Have students discuss Arnold's evaluation. What qualities does Arnold praise in Tolstoy? Do students feel that any of these qualities detract from Tolstoy's effectiveness as a literary artist? Why, or why not?

A Elements of Literature

Character

? How do you see Pahom's character changing in these few sentences? [Possible response: Pahom goes from sympathy for his neighbors (an understanding that it was "no evil intent on their part that caused the trouble") to a desire to help them mend their ways (a wish to teach them a lesson) to a more aggressive retaliation (using the District Court to give them "one lesson, and then another," until the neighbors turn against him).] **What accounts for these changes in his personality?** [being a landowner]

B Reading Skills and Strategies

Identifying Cause and Effect

? What is the result of Pahom's feud with his neighbors? [There is so much resentment against him that he loses standing in the Commune, even though he owns land.]

C Elements of Literature

Theme

? Relate Pahom's "As it is, I am still too cramped to be comfortable" to the title of this story. How much land does Pahom think he needs at this point? [Possible response: enough to put a greater distance between himself and the other villagers, allowing him the "comfort" of not always worrying about trespassers.]

D Reading Skills and Strategies

Finding the Main Idea

? How does Pahom's comment here underscore a main idea of this story? [Possible response: Having improved his life materially by buying a small plot of land, he has become even more dissatisfied with what he has; whenever he sees the possibility of getting more land, he cannot rest until he has obtained it.]

and meadows. He appealed to them most civilly, but they still went on: Now the Communal herdsmen would let the village cows stray into his meadows, then horses from the night pasture would get among his corn. Pahom turned them out again and again, and forgave their owners, and for a long time he forbore to prosecute anyone. But at last he lost patience and complained to the District Court. He knew it was the peasants' want of land, and no evil intent on their part, that caused the trouble, but he thought:

"I cannot go on overlooking it or they will destroy all I have. They must be taught a lesson."

So he had them up, gave them one lesson, and then another, and two or three of the peasants were fined. After a time Pahom's neighbors began to bear him a grudge for this, and would now and then let their cattle on to his land on purpose. One peasant even got into Pahom's wood at night and cut down five young lime trees[4] for their bark. Pahom passing through the wood one day noticed something white. He came nearer and saw the stripped trunks lying on the ground, and close by stood the stumps where the trees had been. Pahom was furious.

"If he had only cut one here and there it would have been bad enough," thought Pahom, "but the rascal has actually cut down a whole clump. If I could only find out who did this, I would pay him out."

He racked his brain as to who it could be. Finally he decided: "It must be Simon—no one else could have done it." So he went to Simon's homestead to have a look round, but he found nothing, and only had an angry scene. However, he now felt more certain than ever that Simon had done it, and he lodged a complaint. Simon was summoned. The case was tried, and retried, and at the end of it all Simon was acquitted, there being no evidence against him. Pahom felt still more aggrieved, and let his anger loose upon the Elder and the Judges.

"You let thieves grease your palms," said he. "If you were honest folk yourselves you would not let a thief go free."

So Pahom quarreled with the Judges and with his neighbors. Threats to burn his building began to be uttered. So though Pahom had more land, his place in the Commune was much worse than before.

About this time a rumor got about that many people were moving to new parts.

"There's no need for me to leave my land," thought Pahom. "But some of the others might leave our village and then there would be more room for us. I would take over their land myself and make my estate a bit bigger. I could then live more at ease. As it is, I am still too cramped to be comfortable."

One day Pahom was sitting at home when a peasant, passing through the village, happened to call in. He was allowed to stay the night, and supper was given him. Pahom had a talk with this peasant and asked him where he came from. The stranger answered that he came from beyond the Volga,[5] where he had been working. One word led to another, and the man went on to say that many people were settling in those parts. He told how some people from his village had settled there. They had joined the Commune, and had had twenty-five acres per man granted them. The land was so good, he said, that the rye sown on it grew as high as a horse, and so thick that five cuts of a sickle made a sheaf. One peasant, he said, had brought nothing with him but his bare hands, and now he had six horses and two cows of his own.

Pahom's heart kindled with desire. He thought:

"Why should I suffer in this narrow hole, if one can live so well elsewhere? I will sell my land and my homestead here, and with the money I will start afresh over there and get everything new. In this crowded place one is always having trouble. But I must first go and find out all about it myself."

Toward summer he got ready and started. He went down the Volga on a steamer to Samara,[6] then walked another three hundred miles on foot, and at last reached the place. It was just as the stranger had said. The peasants had plenty of land: Every man had twenty-five acres of Communal land given him for his use, and anyone who had money could buy, besides, at a ruble an acre as much good freehold land as he wanted.

4. **lime trees:** linden trees.

5. **Volga:** river in western Russia flowing into the Caspian Sea.

6. **Samara** (su·mä′rə): city on the Volga River in southwestern Russia.

Getting Students Involved

Enrichment Activity

Words of Wisdom. In 1904 Tolstoy published a collection of aphorisms and quotations called *A Calendar of Wisdom.* In this book, he gathered nuggets of spiritual advice from the spiritual teachers and sacred texts he admired. To this treasury he added many of his own insights on how to live a moral life.

Have students read the book (Scribner, 1997, translated by Peter Sekirin) and select quotations which they think illuminate the moral lessons of "How Much Land Does a Man Need?" Or, you may put the following quotations from *A Calendar of Wisdom* on the chalkboard and ask students how Pahom might have applied the offered advice.

- It is better to know a few things which are good and necessary than many things which are useless and mediocre. (Tolstoy)
- You should study more to understand that you know little. (Montaigne)
- A wise man seeks wisdom; a madman thinks he has found it. (Persian proverb)
- The reason for rage is always inside of you. (Tolstoy)
- People live by love: love of yourself is the beginning of death, love of other people and of God is the beginning of life. (Tolstoy)

Having found out all he wished to know, Pahom returned home as autumn came on, and began selling off his belongings. He sold his land at a profit, sold his homestead and all his cattle, and withdrew from membership in the Commune. He only waited till the spring, and then started with his family for the new settlement.

As soon as Pahom and his family reached their new abode, he applied for admission into the Commune of a large village. He stood treat to the Elders[7] and obtained the necessary documents. Five shares of Communal land were given him for his own and his sons' use: that is to say—125 acres (not all together, but in different fields) besides the use of the Communal pasture. Pahom put up the buildings he needed, and bought cattle. Of the Communal land alone he had three times as much as at his former home, and the land was good corn land. He was ten times better off than he had been. He had plenty of arable land and pasturage, and could keep as many head of cattle as he liked. (E)

At first, in the bustle of building and settling down, Pahom was pleased with it all, but when he got used to it he began to think that even here he had not enough land. (F) The first year, he sowed wheat on his share of the Communal land and had a good crop. He wanted to go on sowing wheat, but had not enough Communal land for the purpose, and what he had already used was not available; for in those parts wheat is only sown on virgin soil or on fallow land. It is sown for one or two years, and then the land lies fallow till it is again overgrown with prairie grass. There were many who wanted such land and there was not enough for all; so that people quarreled about it. Those who were better off wanted it for growing wheat, and those who were poor wanted it to let to dealers, so that they might raise money to pay their taxes. Pahom wanted to sow more wheat, so he rented land from a dealer for a year. He sowed much wheat and had a fine crop, but the land was too far from the village—the wheat had to be carted more than ten miles. After a time Pahom noticed that some peasant dealers were living on separate farms and were growing wealthy; and he thought: (G)

"If I were to buy some freehold land and have a homestead on it, it would be a different thing altogether. Then it would all be nice and compact."

The question of buying freehold land recurred to him again and again.

He went on in the same way for three years, renting land and sowing wheat. The seasons turned out well and the crops were good, so that he began to lay money by. He might have gone on living contentedly, but he grew tired of having to rent other people's land every year, and having to scramble for it. Wherever there was good land to be had, the peasants would rush for it and it was taken up at once, so that unless you were sharp about it you got none. It happened in the third year that he and a dealer together rented a piece of pastureland from some peasants; and they had already plowed it up, when there was some dispute and the peasants went to law about it, and things fell out so that the labor was all lost. (H)

"If it were my own land," thought Pahom, "I should be independent, and there would not be all this unpleasantness."

So Pahom began looking out for land which he could buy; and he came across a peasant who had bought thirteen hundred acres, but having got into difficulties was willing to sell again cheap. Pahom bargained and haggled with him, and at last they settled the price at 1,500 rubles,[8] part in cash and part to be paid later. They had all but clinched the matter when a passing dealer happened to stop at Pahom's one day to get a feed for his horses. He drank tea with Pahom and they had a talk. (I) The dealer said that he was just returning from the land of the Bashkirs,[9] far away, where he had bought thirteen thousand acres of land, all for 1,000 rubles. Pahom questioned him further, and the tradesman said:

"All one need do is to make friends with the chiefs. I gave away about one hundred rubles' worth of silk robes and carpets, besides a case of tea, and I gave wine to those who would drink it; and I got the land for less than a penny an acre." And he showed Pahom the title deeds, saying:

"The land lies near a river, and the whole prairie is virgin soil."

7. **stood treat to the Elders:** provided the Elders with a meal.

8. **rubles:** units of money in Russia, Ukraine, and other countries.

9. **Bashkirs** (bash·kirz′): Turkish-speaking peoples who live on the Russian steppes, or plains.

(E) Reading Skills and Strategies

Making Predictions

? **Notice how well-off Pahom is now. Do you think he will be content? Why or why not?** [Most students will predict that he will grow dissatisfied as he has done before.] **Students will not have to read far to confirm their prediction.**

(F) Critical Thinking

Extending the Text

? What advice would you give Pahom or people like him? [Possible response: Look at how far you have progressed. Be grateful, enjoy what you have, and share your prosperity with others.]

(G) Background

Land Rights

Pahom has been leasing land to grow crops. If he could not pay the rent or were to die, the land would revert to its owner. Freehold land, on the other hand, would be his outright and would pass on to his descendants.

(H) Critical Thinking

Making Connections

? **Does this turn of events seem familiar? Explain.** [Possible response: Yes, we already have seen potential purchasers of land disagreeing over the terms of the purchase, thereby losing a good opportunity; we also have seen Pahom willing to go to court to get the better of his neighbors.]

(I) Cultural Connections

The Tradition of Tea

Several times in this story, discussions are held (and sometimes business is transacted) over tea. While not having the spiritual associations of the Japanese tea ceremony, the sharing of tea is a traditional social ritual in Russian culture.

Skill Link

Analyzing and Responding to a Critical Review

In this quotation from *Tolstoy: A Critical Introduction*, R. F. Christian discusses the characteristics of the folk tale and the religious parable in Tolstoy's popular stories, such as "How Much Land Does a Man Need?"

"The virtues of Christian love and forgiveness; the folly of harboring resentment; the evils of litigation, drink, violence and the craving for money are the most common themes of Tolstoy's popular stories. Their starting-point is nearly always a legend or parable. Their style is a model of lucidity and precision. The syntax is simple, the sentences short. . . . The untutored and unadorned speech of the peasantry; the wisdom of the proverb, moral precept, and example; the edifying coda and, occasionally, the element of the miraculous—these are the basic ingredients of the great majority of the stories for the people, which belong to the same category of literature and affect the same area of the human consciousness as the great parables of the religious teachers and prophets of the world."

Ask students to sum up the main points in this critique. Then ask them to find examples in Tolstoy's story of some of the characteristics that Christian cites.

Responding to the Art

Fiodor Vasilyev (1850–1873), a largely self-taught Russian painter, did not have any academic art training but studied informally with a landscape painter when he was seventeen. By the time he was twenty years old, he was well known for poetic landscapes, especially spacious and powerful pictures of the Volga River area. Tragically, he contracted tuberculosis. He moved to Yalta where he completed a good number of works with nature motifs before dying at the age of twenty-three.

Activity. Ask students to discuss how this painting might reflect themes in the Tolstoy story. How might the road in the painting suggest the road Pahom takes to get new land? In a metaphorical sense, could this be Pahom's "road to ruin"? To help students explore the iconography of the painting, ask them to look for trees in three life-stages (young, mature, dead) and speculate on the possible symbolism of those images.

Ⓐ Reading Skills and Strategies

Responding to the Text

? What is your reaction when you read this description of the Bashkirs and their land? [Possible responses: curious whether the people really are "as simple as sheep"; wary for Pahom, whose greed for land makes him vulnerable to manipulation.]

Road in the Woods (detail) (late 19th century) by Fiodor Vasilyev.

Pahom plied him with questions, and the tradesman said:

Ⓐ "There is more land there than you could cover if you walked a year, and it all belongs to the Bashkirs. They are as simple as sheep, and land can be got almost for nothing."

"There now," thought Pahom, "with my one thousand rubles, why should I get only thirteen hundred acres, and saddle myself with a debt besides? If I take it out there, I can get more than ten times as much for the money."

Pahom inquired how to get to the place, and as

Crossing the Curriculum

Geography

Although Tolstoy's story has universal application, it is realistically set in a specific Russian locale. Display a map of Russia and ask volunteers to point out the steppes, the Volga River, and Bashkiriya (Bashkortostan). Also, ask students to find photographs or drawings that show some of the physical and topographic features of the Russian landscape.

Social Sciences

Invite students to learn more about (1) the Russian system of serfdom which was abolished by Czar Alexander II, (2) the land-use system which replaced it, and (3) the ownership of land under Communist rule. How did each economic system affect those who dreamed of owning their own land? Under which system did the most Russians have the greatest chance of owning land? Have students organize their information in outlines and comparison charts and share it.

Mathematics

Have students compute how fast Pahom would have to walk to cover the perimeter of a 35-mile-square area in a day. Suggest that they agree on certain givens before they begin, such as the number of hours of daylight, the weather, the terrain, and the number and length of rest stops that Pahom will take. Students who have hiked may offer information on how long it takes to cover a certain distance, under various conditions.

Tretyakov Gallery, Moscow.

soon as the tradesman had left him, he prepared to go there himself. He left his wife to look after the homestead, and started on his journey taking his man with him. They stopped at a town on their way and bought a case of tea, some wine, and other presents, as the tradesman had advised.

On and on they went until they had gone more than three hundred miles, and on the seventh day they came to a place where the Bashkirs had pitched their tents. It was all just as the tradesman had said. The people lived on the steppes, by a river, in felt-covered tents. They neither tilled the ground, nor ate bread. Their cattle and horses grazed in herds on the steppe. The colts were tethered behind the tents, and the mares were driven to them twice a day. The mares were milked, and from the milk kumiss[10] was made. It was the women who prepared kumiss, and they also made cheese. As far as the men were concerned, drinking kumiss and tea, eating mutton, and playing on their pipes, was all they cared about. They were all stout and merry, and all the summer long they never thought of doing any work. They were quite ignorant, and knew no Russian, but were good natured enough. **B**

As soon as they saw Pahom, they came out of their tents and gathered round their visitor. An interpreter was found, and Pahom told them he had come about some land. The Bashkirs seemed very glad; they took Pahom and led him into one of the best tents, where they made him sit on some down cushions placed on a carpet, while they sat round him. They gave him some tea and kumiss, and had a sheep killed, and gave him mutton to eat. Pahom took presents out of his cart and distributed them among the Bashkirs, and divided the tea amongst them. The Bashkirs were delighted. They talked a great deal among themselves, and then told the interpreter to translate.

"They wish to tell you," said the interpreter, "that they like you, and that it is our custom to do all we can to please a guest and to repay him for his gifts. You have given us presents, now tell us which of the things we possess please you best, that we may present them to you."

"What pleases me best here," answered Pahom, "is your land. Our land is crowded and the soil is exhausted; but you have plenty of land and it is good land. I never saw the like of it." **C**

The interpreter translated. The Bashkirs talked among themselves for a while. Pahom could not understand what they were saying, but saw that they were much amused and that they shouted and **D**

10. **kumiss** (ko͞o′mis): fermented drink made from mare's milk.

B Cultural Connections

Descended primarily from the Turks, the Bashkirs were nomads, and Tolstoy's description of their traditional way of life is accurate. By the middle of the nineteenth century, most of the Bashkirs' land had been bought by people like Pahom. Finding it impossible to continue as pastoral nomads, most turned to agriculture and village life. Today, the Bashkirs are a Muslim minority in the lands they used to roam.

C Reading Skills and Strategies

Making Inferences

? Why do you think Pahom describes his situation in this way? Do you think that he is being honest? [Possible responses: He is trying to flatter his hosts, hoping to make them more willing to sell him land. He may be correct in his evaluation of the Bashkirs' land, but he was recently quite happy with the land that he now describes as overcrowded and "exhausted."]

D Reading Skills and Strategies

Making Predictions

? Based on the Bashkirs' response, what do you think will happen to Pahom? [Possible response: Their laughter, which Pahom seems to interpret as pleasure with the offer he has made, appears to be a form of ridicule. They seem to be sure they will get the better of this greedy stranger.]

Getting Students Involved

Enrichment Activity

Russian Writers. Have students form small groups to jointly research and report on other Russian writers. Possibilities include Alexander Pushkin, Ivan Turgenev, Anton Chekhov, Fyodor Dostoyevsky, Nikolai Gogol, and Alexander Solzhenitsyn. Encourage students to work together to create a visually interesting presentation which

- covers the main biographical facts
- identifies and comments on the writer's major works
- compares and contrasts the writer's themes with those of Tolstoy
- compares and contrasts the writer's style with that of Tolstoy
- includes a summary of adaptations of the writer's works for other media, especially films

A Critical Thinking
Analyzing Persuasive Techniques

What are the main points of Pahom's appeal? [Possible responses: He wants just a small part of their land; to guarantee that it remains his, he needs to have the proper papers drawn up; they are good people; God oversees all.] **How does the statement "Life and death are in God's hands" strengthen Pahom's case?** [Possible response: The statement makes him seem pious and thus less likely to deceive the Bashkirs.]

B Reading Skills and Strategies
Identifying Details

How much money does Pahom have to bargain with? [When he considered the stranger's words earlier, he thought about his own one thousand rubles.] **In essence, what does this price amount to?** [everything Pahom has]

C Critical Thinking
Evaluating Details

Do you think that this arrangement is fair? Why or why not? [Possible responses: The arrangement seems odd but fair; anyone could buy land under these terms; however, they also present everyone with a real temptation to be greedy.]

D Critical Thinking
Making Judgments

How wise do you think it is for Pahom to be making all these plans? [Possible responses: Pahom cannot help dreaming a bit; or, a circuit of thirty-five miles may be too optimistic, and Pahom should be more realistic about the distance he can cover.]

laughed. Then they were silent and looked at Pahom while the interpreter said:

"They wish me to tell you that in return for your presents they will gladly give you as much land as you want. You have only to point it out with your hand and it is yours."

The Bashkirs talked again for a while and began to dispute. Pahom asked what they were disputing about, and the interpreter told him that some of them thought they ought to ask their chief about the land and not act in his absence, while others thought there was no need to wait for his return.

While the Bashkirs were disputing, a man in a large fox-fur cap appeared on the scene. They all became silent and rose to their feet. The interpreter said, "This is our chief himself."

Pahom immediately fetched the best dressing gown and five pounds of tea, and offered these to the chief. The chief accepted them, and seated himself in the place of honor. The Bashkirs at once began telling him something. The chief listened for a while, then made a sign with his head for them to be silent, and addressing himself to Pahom, said in Russian:

"Well, let it be so. Choose whatever piece of land you like; we have plenty of it."

"How can I take as much as I like?" thought Pahom. "I must get a deed to make it secure, or else they may say, 'It is yours,' and afterward may take it away again."

"Thank you for your kind words," he said aloud. "You have much land, and I only want a little. But I should like to be sure which bit is mine. Could it not be measured and made over to me? Life and death are in God's hands. You good people give it to me, but your children might wish to take it away again."

"You are quite right," said the chief. "We will make it over to you."

"I heard that a dealer had been here," continued Pahom, "and that you gave him a little land, too, and signed title deeds to that effect. I should like to have it done in the same way."

The chief understood.

"Yes," replied he, "that can be done quite easily. We have a scribe, and we will go to town with you and have the deed properly sealed."

"And what will be the price?" asked Pahom.

"Our price is always the same: one thousand rubles a day."

Pahom did not understand.

"A day? What measure is that? How many acres would that be?"

"We do not know how to reckon it out," said the chief. "We sell it by the day. As much as you can go round on your feet in a day is yours, and the price is one thousand rubles a day."

Pahom was surprised.

"But in a day you can get round a large tract of land," he said.

The chief laughed.

"It will all be yours!" said he. "But there is one condition: If you don't return on the same day to the spot whence you started, your money is lost."

"But how am I to mark the way that I have gone?"

"Why, we shall go to any spot you like, and stay there. You must start from that spot and make your round, taking a spade with you. Wherever you think necessary, make a mark. At every turning, dig a hole and pile up the turf; then afterward we will go round with a plow from hole to hole. You may make as large a circuit as you please, but before the sun sets you must return to the place you started from. All the land you cover will be yours."

Pahom was delighted. It was decided to start early next morning. They talked a while, and after drinking some more kumiss and eating some more mutton, they had tea again, and then the night came on. They gave Pahom a featherbed to sleep on, and the Bashkirs dispersed for the night, promising to assemble the next morning at daybreak and ride out before sunrise to the appointed spot.

Pahom lay on the featherbed, but could not sleep. He kept thinking about the land.

"What a large tract I will mark off!" thought he. "I can easily do thirty-five miles in a day. The days are long now, and within a circuit of thirty-five miles what a lot of land there will be! I will sell the poorer land, or let it to peasants, but I'll pick out the best and farm it. I will buy two ox teams, and hire two more laborers. About a hundred and fifty acres shall be plow land, and I will pasture cattle on the rest."

Pahom lay awake all night, and dozed off only just before dawn. Hardly were his eyes closed

when he had a dream. He thought he was lying in that same tent and heard somebody chuckling outside. He wondered who it could be, and rose and went out, and he saw the Bashkir chief sitting in front of the tent holding his sides and rolling about with laughter. Going nearer to the chief, Pahom asked: "What are you laughing at?" But he saw that it was no longer the chief, but the dealer who had recently stopped at his house and had told him about the land. Just as Pahom was going to ask, "Have you been here long?" he saw that it was not the dealer, but the peasant who had come up from the Volga, long ago, to Pahom's old home. Then he saw that it was not the peasant either, but the Devil himself with hoofs and horns, sitting there and chuckling, and before him lay a man barefoot, prostrate on the ground, with only trousers and a shirt on. And Pahom dreamt that he looked more attentively to see what sort of a man it was that was lying there, and he saw that the man was dead, and that it was himself! He awoke horror-struck.

"What things one does dream," thought he.

Looking round he saw through the open door that the dawn was breaking.

"It's time to wake them up," thought he. "We ought to be starting."

He got up, roused his man (who was sleeping in his cart), bade him harness, and went to call the Bashkirs.

"It's time to go to the steppe to measure the land," he said.

The Bashkirs rose and assembled, and the chief came too. Then they began drinking kumiss again, and offered Pahom some tea, but he would not wait.

The Rainbow by Arkhip Kuindzhi (1842–1910).

Russian State Museum, St. Petersburg.

E Reading Skills and Strategies

Verifying Predictions

? Did you already guess that the people in Pahom's dream were either the Devil or one of his emissaries? [Some students may have suspected that each person who offered Pahom land was in some sense leading him into temptation.] Why do you think Pahom has such a vivid dream? [Possible response: The dream is one last warning to Pahom to curb his greed.]

RESPONDING TO THE ART

Arkhip Ivanovich Kuindzhi (1842?–1910) was a Ukrainian painter who made his career in Russia. He was self-taught and struggled against poverty in his early years. Light, especially light on landscapes, was Kuindzhi's greatest interest, and he created powerful effects by means of *chiaroscuro*—a technique in which light and shadow are dramatically contrasted. He painted rolling fields, groves of birch trees, snow-covered mountains, and moonlit nights. Many of his paintings, including *The Rainbow*, achieve a mystical dimension, like that of a lyric poet attempting to render an experience of the sublime.

Activity. Ask students what the image of a rainbow has traditionally represented. (Some students may know that in the Bible a rainbow suggests reconciliation between the human and the divine.) Students may also compare images of the roads in other paintings in this book. (See, for example, the Canterbury pilgrims on the road on p. 106, the falcon hunt on p. 156, the Worcester road on p. 622, and the Scarborough road on p. 756.) What does the road seem to signify in each painting? Focus students' attention on how the different artists portray the roads, their environs, and the people in the paintings.

Connecting Across Texts

Connecting with "How Much Land Does a Man Need?"

Remind students to consider similarities of setting, character, plot, theme, imagery, style, and tone. Here are some examples:

- The plot of Shakespeare's *Macbeth* (see p. 301) involves an overreaching main character, like Pahom, who schemes for more and more until he destroys himself.
- The Zen parables (see p. 431) have a simple, folk-like tone and also offer a wise, moral message.
- Milton's *Paradise Lost* (see p. 441) relates the downfall of Satan, the ultimate overreacher, whose goal like Pahom's, was far greater than what he could realistically achieve.
- Bunyan's *The Pilgrim's Progress* (see p. 451) involves an Everyman character on an allegorical journey for the purpose of learning a moral lesson.

Ⓐ Elements of Literature

Rising Action

The chief's words present Pahom with a temptation too great to pass up. These few sentences push the action into a higher gear; from here on, the element of suspense will intensify as Pahom tries to outpace the sun.

Ⓑ Reading Skills and Strategies

Drawing Conclusions

? What obstacle stands between Pahom and his goal? [Possible response: his own physical inability to complete the circuit that he has in mind.] Which details from this passage helped you reach this conclusion? [Possible responses: his pace, which he quickens very early in his trek; the rapidity with which Pahom goes from feeling "cool" to "quite warm"; his need to stop for breakfast.]

Ⓒ Elements of Literature

Theme

? How do Pahom's thoughts relate to the theme of the story? [Possible response: His comment "The further one goes, the better the land seems" is an apt metaphor for Pahom's increasing compulsion to possess more land.]

Ⓓ Elements of Literature

Character

? Is this action consistent with what you know of Pahom's character? Explain. [Most students will agree that his action is consistent, for it shows that even at this critical moment he can be tempted by the chance to obtain more.]

"If we are to go, let us go. It is high time," said he.

The Bashkirs got ready and they all started: some mounted on horses, and some in carts. Pahom drove in his own small cart with his servant and took a spade with him. When they reached the steppe, the morning red was beginning to kindle. They ascended a hillock (called by the Bashkirs a *shikhan*) and dismounting from their carts and their horses, gathered in one spot. The chief came up to Pahom and stretching out his arm toward the plain:

Ⓐ "See," said he, "all this, as far as your eye can reach, is ours. You may have any part of it you like."

Pahom's eyes glistened: It was all virgin soil, as flat as the palm of your hand, as black as the seed of a poppy, and in the hollows different kinds of grasses grew breast high.

The chief took off his fox-fur cap, placed it on the ground, and said:

"This will be the mark. Start from here, and return here again. All the land you go round shall be yours."

Pahom took out his money and put it on the cap. Then he took off his outer coat, remaining in his sleeveless undercoat. He unfastened his girdle and tied it tight below his stomach, put a little bag of bread into the breast of his coat, and tying a flask of water to his girdle, he drew up the tops of his boots, took the spade from his man, and stood ready to start. He considered for some moments which way he had better go—it was tempting everywhere.

"No matter," he concluded, "I will go toward the rising sun."

He turned his face to the east, stretched himself, and waited for the sun to appear above the rim.

Ⓑ "I must lose no time," he thought, "and it is easier walking while it is still cool."

The sun's rays had hardly flashed above the horizon, before Pahom, carrying the spade over his shoulder, went down into the steppe.

Pahom started walking neither slowly nor quickly. After having gone a thousand yards he stopped, dug a hole, and placed pieces of turf one on another to make it more visible. Then he went on; and now that he had walked off his stiffness he quickened his pace. After a while he dug another hole.

Pahom looked back. The hillock could be distinctly seen in the sunlight, with the people on it, and the glittering tires of the cart wheels. At a rough guess Pahom concluded that he had walked three miles. It was growing warmer; he took off his undercoat, flung it across his shoulder, and went on again. It had grown quite warm now; he looked at the sun, it was time to think of breakfast.

"The first shift is done, but there are four in a day, and it is too soon yet to turn. But I will just take off my boots," said he to himself.

He sat down, took off his boots, stuck them into his girdle, and went on. It was easy walking now.

Ⓒ "I will go on for another three miles," thought he, "and then turn to the left. This spot is so fine, that it would be a pity to lose it. The further one goes, the better the land seems."

He went straight on for a while, and when he looked round, the hillock was scarcely visible and the people on it looked like black ants, and he could just see something glistening there in the sun.

"Ah," thought Pahom, "I have gone far enough in this direction, it is time to turn. Besides I am in a regular sweat, and very thirsty."

He stopped, dug a large hole, and heaped up pieces of turf. Next he untied his flask, had a drink, and then turned sharply to the left. He went on and on; the grass was high, and it was very hot.

Pahom began to grow tired: He looked at the sun and saw that it was noon.

"Well," he thought, "I must have a rest."

He sat down, and ate some bread and drank some water; but he did not lie down, thinking that if he did he might fall asleep. After sitting a little while, he went on again. At first he walked easily: The food had strengthened him; but it had become terribly hot and he felt sleepy, still he went on, thinking: "An hour to suffer, a lifetime to live."

Ⓓ He went a long way in this direction also, and was about to turn to the left again, when he perceived a damp hollow: "It would be a pity to leave that out," he thought. "Flax would do well there." So he went on past the hollow, and dug a hole on the other side of it before he turned the corner. Pahom looked toward the hillock. The heat made the air hazy: It seemed to be quivering, and through the haze the people on the hillock could scarcely be seen.

"Ah!" thought Pahom, "I have made the sides too long; I must make this one shorter." And he went

Assessing Learning

Informal Assessment

Peer Assessment. Groups of five to seven students can gather to discuss "How Much Land Does a Man Need?" Each group should select a leader who will initiate discussion by asking, "Why do you think Tolstoy's story is in this collection?" Each group can also choose a secretary to record the main ideas discussed. After leaders share their groups' ideas, ask each group to assign a holistic score to another group based upon its ability to relate the story to the collection's theme and upon the depth of thought exhibited. Students might use a simple three-point rating scale: 1=excellent; 2=satisfactory; 3=unsatisfactory.

The Foundation E. G. Bührle Collection, Zurich, Switzerland.

The Sower (1888) by Vincent van Gogh.

along the third side, stepping faster. He looked at the sun: It was nearly halfway to the horizon, and he had not yet done two miles of the third side of the square. He was still ten miles from the goal.

"No," he thought, "though it will make my land lopsided, I must hurry back in a straight line now. I might go too far, and as it is I have a great deal of land."

So Pahom hurriedly dug a hole, and turned straight toward the hillock.

Pahom went straight toward the hillock, but he now walked with difficulty. He was done up with the heat, his bare feet were cut and bruised, and his legs began to fail. He longed to rest, but it was impossible if he meant to get back before sunset. The sun waits for no man, and it was sinking lower and lower.

"Oh dear," he thought, "if only I have not blundered trying for too much! What if I am too late?"

He looked toward the hillock and at the sun. He was still far from his goal, and the sun was already near the rim.

Pahom walked on and on; it was very hard walking but he went quicker and quicker. He pressed on, but was still far from the place. He began running, threw away his coat, his boots, his flask, and his cap, and kept only the spade which he used as a support.

"What shall I do," he thought again. "I have grasped too much and ruined the whole affair. I can't get there before the sun sets."

And this fear made him still more breathless. Pahom went on running, his soaking shirt and trousers stuck to him, and his mouth was parched. His breast was working like a blacksmith's bellows, his heart was beating like a hammer, and his legs

Responding to the Art

Vincent van Gogh (1853–1890), one of the major painters of the last two centuries, was born in Holland but did most of his best work in the south of France. Neither understood nor accepted during his lifetime, van Gogh struggled mightily with isolation, self-doubt, and recurring mental illness; however, he remained true to his unique artistic vision, and his mature work has a vitality and energy not seen in that of any of his contemporaries. His violent brushstrokes of bright, intense pigments create tension between colors.

Activity. Ask interested students to read the Parable of the Sower in the New Testament (Matthew 13, Mark 4, and Luke 8) and relate the parable to the painting. Some students may also research and report on van Gogh's extraordinary letters to his beloved brother Theo, his sole unswerving supporter.

E Critical Thinking

Challenging the Text

? Do you think that Tolstoy wants readers to feel sympathy for Pahom or not? Why? [Possible responses: Yes, even though Pahom has brought this situation upon himself and can free himself from it (at the cost of one thousand rubles), it is hard not to feel some sympathy for his suffering—especially for the sense of being trapped that he must feel. No, it is his own greed that brought him to this state.]

F Elements of Literature

Symbolism

? Notice what Pahom tosses aside and what he keeps. What do you think these items represent? [Possible responses: His discarded coat, boots, flask, and cap represent clothing and sustenance—the essential things of life; the spade, which he keeps, is not necessary for his survival; however, it represents his obsession to acquire more and more land.]

Making the Connections

Cultural Connections: Land Ownership

Use Tolstoy's story to discuss traditions of land ownership in various cultures. Ask students to draw from their own backgrounds and their knowledge of world cultures to explore customs and values concerning the owning of land. For example, in many traditional Native American cultures, land was considered part of the natural inheritance of all and was not "owned" by anyone. In fact, people "belonged to" the land; the land did not belong to the people. To extend the discussion, note that many people in the United States today rent land instead of owning it; ask what these renters lose or gain by not owning the land they live on.

A Reading Skills and Strategies

Identifying Cause and Effect

Tolstoy clearly shows that Pahom is afraid that he will not survive the run. Why, then, does he continue? [Possible response: According to Tolstoy, Pahom keeps running so that the Bashkirs will not consider him a fool.]

B Critical Thinking

Supporting an Interpretation

Is the Bashkir chief the Devil? Defend your interpretation. [Students who support this interpretation may point to the vividness of Pahom's "last chance" dream; students who disagree may suggest that Pahom's own greed makes the appearance of the Devil unnecessary and that the chief is just one of several characters who bring out Pahom's greed.]

C Elements of Literature

Climax

The rising action of the story reaches its highest point here, as Pahom's heart is strained to its limits; then the tension suddenly ceases, as Pahom's life ends.

D Elements of Literature

Irony

What irony or ironies do you find in this conclusion? [Possible responses: It turns out that the only land Pahom really needs is a burial plot. In addition, Pahom's own spade—the one thing he refused to give up during his run—is used to dig his grave. Furthermore, the Bashkirs seem to express pity over Pahom's death, but by now one suspects that they knew his greed would be the death of him.]

FINDING COMMON GROUND

As its name suggests, this feature requires students through lively discussion to discover areas of commonality between works of literature from different times and places and between the students' own experience and that of others in the literature.

After students have read "How Much Land Does a Man Need?" ask them to review their responses to the Quickwrite activity on p. 883. Invite them to comment on the ways in which their original responses may have been changed or confirmed as a result of reading about Pahom's experience. Have students work first in small groups and then share their responses in whole class discussions.

were giving way as if they did not belong to him. Pahom was seized with terror lest he should die of the strain.

Though afraid of death, he could not stop. "After having run all that way they will call me a fool if I stop now," thought he. And he ran on and on, and drew near and heard the Bashkirs yelling and shouting to him, and their cries inflamed his heart still more. He gathered his last strength and ran on.

The sun was close to the rim, and cloaked in mist looked large, and red as blood. Now, yes now, it was about to set! The sun was quite low, but he was also quite near his aim. Pahom could already see the people on the hillock waving their arms to hurry him up. He could see the fox-fur cap on the ground and the money on it, and the chief sitting on the ground holding his sides. And Pahom remembered his dream.

"There is plenty of land," thought he, "but will God let me live on it? I have lost my life, I have lost my life! I shall never reach that spot!"

Pahom looked at the sun, which had reached the earth: One side of it had already disappeared. With all his remaining strength he rushed on, bending his body forward so that his legs could hardly follow fast enough to keep him from falling. Just as he reached the hillock it suddenly grew dark. He looked up—the sun had already set! He gave a cry: "All my labor has been in vain," thought he, and was about to stop, but he heard the Bashkirs still shouting, and remembered that though to him, from below, the sun seemed to have set, they on the hillock could still see it. He took a long breath and ran up the hillock. It was still light there. He reached the top and saw the cap. Before it sat the chief laughing and holding his sides. Again Pahom remembered his dream, and he uttered a cry: His legs gave way beneath him, he fell forward and reached the cap with his hands.

"Ah, that's a fine fellow!" exclaimed the chief. "He has gained much land!"

Pahom's servant came running up and tried to raise him, but he saw that blood was flowing from his mouth. Pahom was dead!

The Bashkirs clicked their tongues to show their pity.

His servant picked up the spade and dug a grave long enough for Pahom to lie in, and buried him in it. Six feet from his head to his heels was all he needed.

FINDING COMMON GROUND

Tolstoy's story of a Russian farmer's land acquisition illustrates the perils of greed. In describing his disillusionment with private land ownership, Tolstoy provides today's readers with a parable about the "progress" of materialism. In small groups, talk about the contrast the story presents between the attitude of the Russians of Tolstoy's day and that of the traditional peoples, who are said to be "simple as sheep." Be sure to check your Quickwrite notes as you discuss the story.

- Find examples in the text that reveal the Bashkir culture's attitudes about property and values. How would you compare them with the beliefs of your own culture?
- The nomadic Bashkirs come into contact with outsiders who buy their land for a token sum. How is this clash of cultures similar to or different from the one depicted in Kipling's "The Mark of the Beast" (page 872)?
- You have seen British writers questioning the benefits of nineteenth-century industrialization and modernization. Does this questioning change in a Russian setting? In what ways does Tolstoy share or extend the debate about progress?
- Pahom's dreams of wealth are mocked in the story's ironic last line. Think of the stark contrast between what he wanted and "all he needed." What parallels do you find with our culture today? How and why do people's wants differ from their actual needs?

Assessing Learning

Check Test: Short Answers

1. **Why is the Devil willing to provide Pahom with land?** [He has heard Pahom boasting that with enough land he would not even fear the Devil; the Devil knows that a lust for land will bring Pahom under his control.]
2. **Whom does Pahom take to court, and why?** [He takes some of his neighbors to court because they have trespassed on his land and he is determined to protect what he has.]
3. **Why does Pahom go to see the Bashkirs?** [He hears that the Bashkirs are simple folk who will sell their land for almost nothing.]
4. **What do the Bashkirs offer Pahom in return for his presents?** [For a thousand rubles, Pahom can have as much land as he can circumscribe on foot in a day.]
5. **How much land does Pahom end up needing, and why?** [In the end, he needs only enough land for a grave. In his greed, he travels too far and dies while racing to get back.]

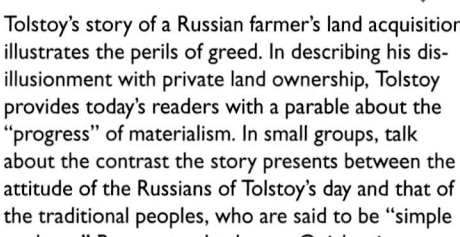

READ ON

Dark Shadows

Although there have been numerous movie (and stage) versions in the twentieth century, Bram Stoker's *Dracula* (Putnam) is rooted firmly in the Victorian psyche. Written in 1897, this Gothic masterpiece is not only a supreme story of horror and suspense, but also a reflection of the dark underside of an extremely moralistic age. The progressive values of high Victorian culture are pitted against—and ultimately triumph over—the deep-rooted desires and dreads of the subconscious.

Romantic Rebellion

"If there's one thing Papa will never, *never* permit, it's a marriage in the family." Rudolf Besier's play *The Barretts of Wimpole Street* (Little, Brown) is based on the relationship between Elizabeth Barrett and Robert Browning, which developed under less than auspicious circumstances: Elizabeth's father forbade any of his nine adult children to marry. But in spite of Mr. Barrett's extraordinary attitude, his whole house is literally seething with romance and rebellion.

A Peek at Victorian Private Lives

Welcome to nineteenth-century England! In *What Jane Austen Ate and Charles Dickens Knew* (Simon and Schuster), Daniel Pool gives new life to the daily life of the last century. Both the nitty-gritty details (How did they keep clean?) and the posh etiquette (How did one address a duke?) of the time are covered. Find out what the Victorians ate, what they wore, how they traveled, and whom they married.

Found in a Handbag

Much of the satire in Oscar Wilde's play *The Importance of Being Earnest* (Penguin) is targeted at the British class system. Wilde openly flouted Victorian ideas of respectability and presented his own philosophy as an alternative. The seemingly contradictory logic of the play is part of this philosophy: "The truth is rarely pure and never simple." The play is also available as a film, made in England in 1952, with Michael Redgrave. (This title is available in the HRW Library.)

Pastoral Problems

Thomas Hardy's *Far from the Madding Crowd* (Oxford University Press) is about one very beautiful woman and the profound effect she has on three very different men. Opening on a note of almost lighthearted comedy, the novel gradually evolves into a starker tale of thoughtlessness, abandonment, death, and derangement. The 1967 British film version of the novel, with Julie Christie, Peter Finch, and Alan Bates, is available on videotape.

READ ON

This feature provides suggestions for further readings by Victorian authors and about life in the Victorian age.

Portfolio Assessment Options
The following projects can help you evaluate and assess your students' reading accomplishments outside of class. Videotapes or audiotapes of completed projects may be included in students' portfolios.

- **Create a Silent Dialogue** Encourage pairs of students to respond to their reading by assuming the identities of two characters—from the same book or from different books. Have them, in character, create a silent dialogue by passing a paper back and forth and "conversing" about these questions: What obstacles did I have to face to achieve my goals? How did I deal with the obstacles? Was I successful?
- **Join a "Proper Patrol"** Ask a group of students to plan and present a panel discussion on the topic of "propriety" in the books they have read. As they discuss their books, encourage students to focus on what the authors set forth as "proper" behavior and what they suggest are the results of "impropriety."
- **Advertise a Miniseries** Ask students to imagine that the book they have read is being produced as a television miniseries. Have them decide how many episodes would be needed; then, have them write (1) a summary of each segment, which could be printed in a television program guide, and (2) some promotional copy for a TV or newspaper ad for each segment. Student writers and artists might get together to plan an advertising campaign and present it to the class.

OBJECTIVES

1. Learn how English became an international language.
2. Learn about different English dialects
3. Recognize differences between British and American English
4. Compare American and British vocabularies, syntax, spellings, and word origins

A Background

As the Victorian age saw English become a world language, it also saw the establishment and development of "the Queen's English"—the spoken standard to which all classes were expected to aspire.

B Cultural Connections

American Regional Dialects

There are three main regional dialects of American English: Northern, Midland, and Southern. Within these broad categories, however, there are differences; for example, a Bostonian and a New Yorker will not sound exactly the same, and someone from Charleston will speak differently from someone from New Orleans. Still, American English as a whole remains relatively uniform. One of the very few exceptions is Gullah, a dialect of English spoken on some islands off the southeastern coast of the United States. In Great Britain, on the other hand, a large number of striking speech variations can be found in a small geographical area.

C Exploring the Culture

In some countries (Japan and Saudi Arabia, for example), students choose the English dialect they will learn—British or American.

Resources

Formal Assessment

- English Language Test, p. 179

The English Language

One Language—Many Nations

by John Algeo

Although the spread of English outside the British Isles began in the early seventeenth century, it was during the Victorian Age that English became a world language. Primarily because of the influence of the British Empire, English became either the first or an important second language in the British Isles, the United States, and Canada, as well as in Jamaica, Trinidad and Tobago, Australia, New Zealand, Malaysia, Myanmar, India, Sri Lanka, Pakistan, Israel, Ghana, Sierra Leone, Nigeria, Sudan, Kenya, Tanzania, Malawi, Zambia, Zimbabwe, Swaziland, and South Africa. American expansion, although modest by comparison, extended English to the Philippines, Liberia, and a few other places.

English as an International Language

English first spread around the world as a result of political and commercial activities, empire building, and colonization. In addition, scientific and technological advances, movies and television programs, popular music, and fashions of clothing have all served to reinforce the prestige of English as an international language. Today, English is used more widely and for more purposes as a second language than any other human tongue.

To take only one example: English is the language of international aviation. If a Swedish pilot is landing an airplane in Greece, he or she uses English to converse with the controller on the ground. Having a single language for international aviation is obviously sensible. It would not do for a pilot who spoke only Swedish to ask for landing instructions from ground controllers who spoke only Greek. A common language is needed as a safety measure for international flights, and English was chosen because of the prominence of English-speaking people in making and flying airplanes. It is for such reasons that English has become the most widely used international language.

Dialects of English

Today, there are dialects of English all over the world. Each place where it is spoken has its own variety of the language, and old countries like England or large ones like the United States have many regional dialects. However, standard English—the English found in books, magazines, and large newspapers—is relatively uniform. That uniformity also helps to make English useful as an international language. Differences exist, to be sure, but they are minor fluctuations in what is obviously a single language.

Each country in which English is the main language of communication has its own national standard that differs in small, but recognizable, ways from the standards of other English-speaking lands. Among these national standards are those of Australia, Canada, the United Kingdom (England, Scotland, Wales, and Northern Ireland), Jamaica, New Zealand, the Republic of Ireland, and the United States.

Two Close Cousins: British and American English

The two most important national standards are those of the United Kingdom and of the United States: British and American English. The differences between them can be illustrated by a few expressions:

American	**British**
baby stroller	push-chair
baked potato	jacket potato
barrette	hair slide
coffee with cream	coffee white
daylight saving time	summer time

go.hrw.com
LEO 12-English Language

divided highway	dual carriage way
hood (of a car)	bonnet
Main Street	High Street
pharmacist	dispensing chemist
public restroom	convenience
savings and loan association	building society
subway	underground *or* tube
traffic circle	roundabout
trunk (of a car)	boot
wastepaper basket	bin
Watch your step.	Mind your step.
whole-wheat bread	brown bread
yield (highway sign)	give way

Entrance to the underground station at Piccadilly Circus, London.

The differences tend to occur especially in technical areas like automotive terms, in domestic matters like food names, and in specialized commercial terms like names for kinds of businesses. The specialized terminologies of American and British English differ considerably, but the words of the ordinary language—the everyday nouns and most verbs, adverbs, adjectives, and connecting words like prepositions and conjunctions—are very much alike in the two national standards.

Each national standard also has words for which there is no exact equivalent in the other. For example, in England a *bap* is a soft roll that may be used to make a sandwich; a *crumpet* is a kind of muffin; a *gateau* is a kind of cake; *chips* are French fries; a *free house* is a *pub* or bar where more than one brand of beer is sold; and a *purveyor* is a company that sells or deals in some product.

Each country has influenced the language of the other. In America, people who drive British cars may begin to use British automotive terms because they appear in the cars' operating manuals. The expression "Not to worry" is a Briticism that has become popular here. On the other hand, American expressions like "nitty-gritty" turn up in England, as do many technical terms.

Strange combinations of the two national standards sometimes emerge. American clothing, food, and television programs are very popular in England. A store in the Chelsea area of London announces itself as the "Texas Lone Star Saloon, Purveyors of the Best Chili, Tacos, Nachos." Everything about the store's sign is pure American—except the word *purveyors,* which is as British as crumpets and chips.

Pronunciation, Spelling, and Grammar

British and American English obviously differ in pronunciation. The British pronounce words like *bath, class,* and *can't* with the vowel sound of *father,* rather than with the vowel sound of *cat.* Like people from eastern New England, New York City, and the coastal South, but unlike most other Americans, the British drop *r* sounds unless they have a vowel after them, so that *poppa* and *popper* sound alike. American English tends to have more stresses on its words than does British English; so we pronounce *secretary* as sek′rə·ter′ē, whereas the British say it as sek′rə·trē. Perhaps the most striking difference between the two national standards, however, is in intonation, the "tune" of the sentence. To British ears, American speech sounds flat and dull—it has a more uniform, lower pitch and minimizes the difference between high and low notes. To

D Exploring the Culture

While British and American English are closely related, there are, in fact, enough differences between the two that the Associated Press, the American news agency, and Reuters, the British news agency, have to "translate" the English of one into the English of the other.

E Appreciating Language

The expression *nitty-gritty* (meaning "the basic facts or elements of a situation") became part of American slang in the 1960s. It is thought to have originally referred to nits, the gritlike eggs or larvae of head lice, which can be very hard to get rid of.

F Vocabulary Note

In its transition from British to American English, the word *missile* lost the long *i* and the stress which British speakers put on the final syllable. In America, *missile* rhymes with *whistle.*

G Background

In addition, Britons generally speak more quickly than Americans.

Reaching All Students

Struggling Readers

Before students read this feature, ask them to create a KWL chart. In the first column, have them record three things that they already know about the use of English outside the United States; in the second, they should write three questions about the topic that they would like to have answered. After they read the feature, they can fill in the third column with answers to the questions or clues about how to find the answers.

English Language Learners

Suggest that students find more examples of British English vocabulary by watching British television programs or movies and writing down unfamiliar words and expressions. Encourage them to try to figure out the meanings of the words from their contexts before consulting a dictionary of British English. Allow students to present their words and definitions to the class in formats of their own choosing.

Advanced Learners

Invite students to highlight some of the differences between British and American pronunciation and vocabulary by illustrating them in a humorous skit or an exchange of letters. The humor might arise from a misunderstanding stemming from dialect differences. After they share their writing, ask students to comment on what they learned about the differences in vocabulary and pronunciation in British and American English.

Ⓐ Literary Connections

Webster's Dictionary

We can trace these changes to Noah Webster (1758–1843), a schoolteacher from Connecticut. The 1828 edition of his dictionary included several Americanisms and the American meanings of some older British terms. It also set forth a distinctly American spelling and pronunciation for many words.

Ⓑ Background

Linguists theorize that the languages of approximately one third of the human race come from a common ancestral language, which they call Indo-European. Some of the languages that derive from this common source are the European descendants of Latin (including French, Spanish, Italian, and Portuguese); Russian; the Celtic languages (Irish and Scottish Gaelic); and various offshoots of German, with Dutch and English among them.

Folklorist Jakob Grimm established that the German word *vater* (the English word *father*) has the same root as the Sanskrit/Latin *pitar/pater*. This breakthrough, known as Grimm's Law, supports the thesis of a common Indo-European proto-language.

Try It Out

Answers

1. **Comparing Vocabulary.** accumulator=car battery; banger=sausage; flog=sell (especially illegally); lift=elevator; nous=savvy or intelligence; queue=line (of people, cars, and so on); rates=property taxes; scoff=gobble up; toffee-nosed=stuck-up; wellies=high rubber boots
2. **Rewriting British Syntax.**
   a. What do you want to do this afternoon?
   b. She says that she tried to call us, but she didn't.
   c. It looks as if the vote will be close.
   d. After long discussions, they agreed on the plan.
   e. I carry two pencils in case I lose one.
3. **Comparing Spellings.** ageing=aging; analyse=analyze; centre=center; labour=labor; marvelled=marveled
4. **Investigating Word Origins.** boomerang=a curved stick, used as a weapon, which returns to the point from where it is thrown (Australia); boondocks=any remote rural region (Philippines); thug=a hoodlum, robber, murderer, or other tough criminal (India); trek=a journey on foot (South Africa); walkabout=a walking tour (Australia)

American ears, British speech sounds fluting, high-pitched, quavering, and slightly hysterical—British speech has a more varied, higher pitch and exaggerates the difference between high and low notes.

Ⓐ Spelling also differs slightly in the two countries. British English uses *-our* in words like *colour* and *honour,* where American English uses *-or.* British uses *-re* in words like *centre* and *metre,* where American uses *-er.* British doubles the *l* at the end of unstressed syllables before adding a suffix beginning with a vowel in words like *travelling,* for which American usage typically keeps a single *l, traveling.* There are also a few miscellaneous differences: British *pyjamas* versus American *pajamas.* The differences are all trivial, although the British often insist that American books published in England be reset using British spelling. Americans seldom notice the difference.

Grammatical differences between the two forms of English are also few and unimportant. The British sometimes omit the definite article where we would use it: "in hospital" (British) versus "in the hospital" (American). They use a plural verb with some collective nouns (the word *government* and names of sports teams) for which we use a singular verb: "The government *have* decided . . ." "Nebraska *are* winning the bowl game." They treat *have* as a special verb that does not require an auxiliary in questions: "Have you the answer?" versus "Do you have the answer?" The British use only the past participle *got,* whereas we use both *got* and *gotten,* in different ways: "I've got it" versus American "I've got it" (meaning "I have it") and "I've gotten it" (meaning "I've obtained it"). Other British and American grammatical differences are equally minor.

> Oscar Wilde said that the English "have really everything in common with America nowadays, except, of course, language."

Actually, the differences between British and American English have often been exaggerated, as they were by Oscar Wilde, who said that the English "have really everything in common with America nowadays, except, of course, language." Ⓑ In fact, not only these two countries, but all the nations of the English-speaking world share a common linguistic heritage that goes back to the Anglo-Saxons and, before them, to Proto-Indo-European tribes that wandered from Asia across Europe. Today, despite the linguistic differences that divide us—the small distinctions of grammar, spelling, and pronunciation, and the greater but still not insuperable ones of terminology—English is a unified language. The core of English—our basic words and how we use them—is one.

Try It Out

1. **Comparing vocabularies.** What are the American counterparts of the British English terms listed below? (Look up the British words in a dictionary.)

accumulator	queue
banger	rates
flog	scoff
lift	toffee-nosed
nous	wellies

2. **Rewriting British English.** The following sentences in British English have grammatical constructions that differ from American usage. Rewrite each sentence as you would say it.
   a. What had you in mind to do this afternoon?
   b. She says she tried to ring us, but she can't have done.
   c. It looks like being a close vote.
   d. After long discussions, they agreed the plan.
   e. I carry two pencils in case one goes missing.
3. **Comparing spellings.** The following words are spelled in the British fashion. Write the American spellings.

ageing	labour
analyse	marvelled
centre	

4. **Investigating word origins.** The following words come from several different national varieties of English. Use a dictionary to see what they mean and where they originated.

boomerang	trek
boondocks	walkabout
thug	

Assessing Learning

Check Test: True-False

1. English became the first language, or a major second language, in many parts of the world as a result of British trade and imperialism. [True]
2. Two other factors that have helped to establish English as an international language are its general superiority as a language and the fact that it is easy to learn. [False]
3. Dialects of English are spoken only in countries other than England. [False]
4. Speakers of British English use a more varied intonation than do speakers of American English. [True]
5. Dialects of English are spoken widely in Canada, New Zealand, and the Republic of Ireland. [True]

Writer's Workshop

The history of the written word is rich a

Page 1

PERSUASIVE WRITING

AN EVALUATION

"I love it!" "I hate it!" "It's boring." "It's great!" Every day of our lives we make a range of judgments. Some are based on personal preference or whim, but others are careful, reasoned evaluations. Many Victorian writers considered it a *duty* to evaluate the changes taking place around them: Hardy, Arnold, and Dickens each made judgments, carefully measuring the benefits of industrial growth against the misery of the working-class English. Often our own judgments concern smaller things than what makes an ideal society, but they are still vital—our lives would be chaos if we failed to evaluate the opportunities and choices available to us, from jobs to political candidates. Evaluation, or judging something against a definite standard, is one of the most basic forms of writing—and thinking.

Prewriting

1. **Checking your Writer's Notebook.** By doing the Writer's Notebook activities in Collections 10 and 11, you may already have done some of the prewriting necessary for an evaluation. Look back through your entries for usable ideas, and then proceed with the prewriting activities that follow.

2. **Exploring the possibilities: art or life?** What will you evaluate? Because you've studied literature for several years, you're probably prepared to make some judgments about poetry, drama, or fiction—perhaps one of the selections you've recently read. Other possible subjects related to literature and the arts include movies, television shows, music, and dance or theater performances. You should also consider subjects from the real world: candidates for local or national office, sports equipment, or ideas about the formation of black holes in space. For a few minutes, freewrite a list of things that pique your interest or that you remember well—stories, shows, theories you've read or heard about, consumer goods. Then circle the one or two that you have strong feelings about. (It doesn't matter whether these feelings are positive or negative. The important thing is that you choose something to write about that prompts strong feelings in you.)

3. **How do I judge thee?** With a firm subject to evaluate, you can now determine the criteria for your evaluation. **Criteria** are the characteristics a particular thing must have to be judged an excellent example of its type or kind—that is, an excellent lyric poem, mystery story, sports car, action movie, economic theory, or some other thing. You need to look beyond your subject to the particular type, or genre, it belongs to. For example, if you're going to evaluate a poem, is the poem a narrative or a lyric? Ask

Technology HELP

See Writer's Workshop 2 CD-ROM. *Assignment: Evaluation.*

ASSIGNMENT
Write an evaluation, based on appropriate criteria and supported by reasons and evidence.

AIM
To persuade your readers to accept your informed judgment.

AUDIENCE
Your classmates or a specialized audience within your school—a literary society, a film club, or the student council, for example.

WRITER'S WORKSHOP 899

MAIN OBJECTIVE
Write an evaluation

PROCESS OBJECTIVES

1. Use appropriate prewriting techniques to identify and develop a topic
2. Create a first draft
3. Use Evaluation Criteria as a basis for determining revision strategies
4. Revise the first draft incorporating suggestions generated by self- or peer-evaluation
5. Proofread and correct errors
6. Create a final draft
7. Choose an appropriate method of publication
8. Reflect on writing progress

Planning

- **Block Schedule**
 Block Scheduling Lesson Plans with Pacing Guide
- **One-Stop Planner**
 CD-ROM with Test Generator

 Resources: Print and Media

Writing and Language
- *Portfolio Management System*
 Prewriting, p. 181
 Peer Editing, p. 182
 Assessment Rubric, p. 183

- *Workshop Resources*
 Revision Strategy Teaching Notes, p. 33
 Revision Strategy Transparencies 17, 18
- *Writer's Workshop 2 CD-ROM*
 Evaluation

Introducing the Writer's Workshop

Hand out copies of a variety of news magazines and ask students to tally the number of evaluation articles—generally reviews, columns or editorials—and make a list of the topics covered. Discuss the importance of evaluative essays and the wide range of possible topics. Explain to students that learning to write an evaluation is a way of becoming a better reader and a better-informed consumer.

Teaching the Writer's Workshop

Prewriting

If you limit choices for this assignment, allow students who wish to write about similar topics to get together in small groups to discuss evaluation criteria. If students decide to evaluate a film, they may find the criteria listed in the model useful. However, you may want students to have the experience of developing criteria of their own.

Using the Model

Discuss with the class other criteria they could add to the two provided in the model. Are there criteria for a film that would not be relevant when evaluating a book? [We expect different things from a CD-ROM, a movie, a television show, and a book. These expectations are often an unstated part of our criteria.]

Try It Out
Possible Answers

1. influence on others; economic worth; changes in the world because of him or her; moral character, etc.
2. quality and variety of food; quality of service; cost; cleanliness, etc.
3. impact of new procedure: financial, physical, moral; difference between old way and new; reaction of people affected, etc.
4. cost; value; taste; beauty, etc.
5. timeliness; honesty; reliability; thoroughness, appearance, coverage, etc.

Try It Out

What criteria would you apply to evaluate the following subjects?

1. An extraordinary person (a politician, an artist, an athlete, or some other noteworthy figure)
2. A local restaurant
3. A new way of doing things (such as a medical advancement or a governmental policy)
4. A product (such as a car or a brand of cereal)
5. A magazine or newspaper

yourself: *What makes this a lyric poem?* or *What makes this a narrative poem?* You can't evaluate a narrative and a lyric poem with the same criteria any more than you can evaluate a four-wheel-drive utility vehicle and a luxury car with the same criteria.

4. **Making a judgment, backing it up.** Establishing criteria is an important step in evaluating something, but it's just one step on the way. You also have to measure your subject against the criteria you've developed, *and* you have to convince your audience that the judgments you develop are sound. To be convincing, you need to supply reasons and evidence for your judgments. **Reasons** tell why a judgment should be accepted; **evidence** provides proof for each reason: quotations, examples, facts, details, or expert opinions. Generating reasons and evidence will build a convincing argument—the informed judgment that makes your evaluation worth reading (and accepting).

   One way to develop your case is to create a three-column chart. In the first column, list each of your criteria for judging your subject, starting with your most important criterion. In the second column, list each **reason** for judging your particular subject successful or unsuccessful, worthy or unworthy. In the third column, supply specific **evidence** for the judgments you've made in the second column. The following chart lists criteria, reasons, and evidence for evaluating *Sense and Sensibility*, a 1995 film adaptation of Jane Austen's 1811 novel.

Model

Criteria	Reasons	Evidence
Well-developed characters	Characters complex enough to seem real; flaws and strengths both shown.	Sisters reveal different facets with family, with suitors, and alone; Elinor's humor tempers her moral highhandedness.
Theme	Without preaching, story reveals a truth about the real world.	By end, Marianne realizes what Elinor already knows—that ordinary pleasures of *real* love outweigh any grand passion.

This writer draws evidence from the movie itself. Other kinds of evidence often used in evaluations include

- personal anecdotes (your own experiences with the subject, particularly those your readers might have shared)
- illustrations (quotations, descriptive details, paraphrases)
- statistics (for example, published data indicating that the car you're evaluating gets 35 miles per gallon while similar ones get 25)
- testimony (what others, especially those with personal experience or authoritative knowledge, have said about your topic)

Using Students' Strengths

Auditory Learners

Some students may benefit from using an audiotape recorder as a writing aid. Allow students to take oral notes on a tape recorder after they have done their prewriting. Then they may listen to the tape and transcribe it. When they evaluate and revise their drafts, they may listen to the tape again while following the written text to pinpoint any necessary revisions.

Visual Learners

Having students illustrate their evaluations is a good way to highlight key points and relevant supporting details. Students may draw pictures of characters, scenes, or essential points, or they may create a larger picture, such as a mural, that illustrates their basic criteria. These pictures may be posted in the classroom or attached to the students' essays for inclusion in their portfolios.

5. **Whittling away.** Winnow your list down to the most compelling criteria, reasons, and evidence you have. The less convincing material you've thought about can be eliminated or briefly described in your essay. If you think your audience will expect you to deal with aspects of your subject for which you don't have a strong case, think about how you will discuss them without weakening your overall argument.

   This involves analyzing your **audience.** Are they beginners or experts? The members of your school's film club will probably have more knowledge about filmmaking than a general audience, so you'll want to address some fine points of direction and cinematography in a movie review. If your subject is personal computers, and you're writing for your classmates, think about how you will explain your technical points.

6. **Shaping your argument.** The points you make in your evaluation should be arranged in some logical order. You may decide to proceed from most obvious to least obvious, from most general to most complicated, from least important to most important, or the reverse. Whatever pattern you choose, your readers should be able to easily follow your argument. At this point, try to outline your evaluation, at least in rough form.

Communications Handbook HELP

See Taking Notes and Documenting Sources; Proofreading.

Strategies for Elaboration: Avoiding Pitfalls

As you evaluate and refine your points and shape your argument, make sure you've avoided the following pitfalls:

- **Avoid using criteria based merely on personal tastes.** Make sure that your praise for a television show doesn't rely on the fact that the main character reminds you of your nice neighbor Hank.
- **Avoid using irrelevant criteria.** Are your criteria appropriately connected to the subject of your essay? Don't fault a certain model bicycle because you don't like the salesperson's shoes.
- **Avoid making hasty generalizations.** Don't praise something because you have overvalued a certain part of it. A play is not worthy of praise just because you've always liked the leading actor's work; a novel is not good just because the novelist's other novels are considered classics.
- **Avoid making one-sided comparisons.** No one will believe you if you claim your subject is absolute perfection (or thoroughly horrible) when compared with other things like it. To appear thoughtful and convincing, you must mention weaknesses in the things you praise and strengths in the things you criticize.
- **Avoid including straw-man arguments.** If there are closer comparisons to be made, don't compare the subject of your essay with something clearly inferior (or clearly superior). Your audience will suspect you have unfairly rigged your argument in favor of your judgment. (A straw man is something easily knocked down or dismissed.)
- **Don't avoid accepting the burden of proof.** Make sure that you can supply concrete evidence for all the judgments you make in your essay. It's up to you to show why your judgment is sound.

Professional Notes

Technology Tip

Encourage students to use a word-processing program to draft their essays. When they finish, have them print out their essays double-spaced for use in the evaluation and revision stages. Encourage students to save their work on floppy disks rather than on the computer's hard drive. The disks may be stored in the students' portfolios and used again.

Reaching All Students

Struggling Writers

Since students may want to quote from characters in literary works or films in their evaluations, you may want to review how quotations are punctuated. Also, refresh students' memories on the use of square brackets to indicate text changes by the writer of the essay.

Drafting

Before students begin to draft, have them assemble their prewriting notes. Work through the Strategies for Elaboration on p. 901, and ask students to evaluate each of their criteria against the list.

Evaluating and Revising

Have students use the Evaluation Criteria provided here to review their drafts and determine needed revisions.

Reflecting

As students reflect on this assignment, they should consider the following questions. (Have them date their responses and their evaluations for their portfolios.)

1. How original were the criteria I used for this assignment?
2. Should I care if other people have different criteria or do not agree with mine?
3. Will I be more or less inclined to read a book or movie review in the future? Why?

Resources

Peer Editing Forms and Rubrics

- *Portfolio Management System*, p. 182.

Revision Transparencies

- *Workshop Resources*, p. 33

Grading Timesaver

Rubrics for this Writer's Workshop assignment appear on p. 183 of the *Portfolio Management System.*

Evaluation Criteria

An effective evaluation

1. *orients the reader to the subject being evaluated*
2. *includes a clear statement of the writer's judgment*
3. *includes criteria that are appropriate, clear, and, if necessary, explained by the writer*
4. *includes relevant, convincing, and logically ordered reasons for the writer's judgment*
5. *includes sufficient evidence to support each reason*
6. *has a tone that is authoritative, consistent throughout, and appropriate for the intended audience*
7. *has an engaging beginning and an ending that restates the judgment in a satisfying way*

Revision STRATEGIES

Consider your readers one last time. Do you need to explain anything more clearly? Or have you overexplained anything they probably know already? Working with a writing partner, mark any explanations that need further clarification or some that need cutting. Revise, and then consult with your writing partner again to discuss your revisions.

Language Workshop HELP

Sentence style: page 903.

Drafting

1. **Reflecting on purpose and audience: the message and the messenger.** Before you begin drafting, think again about what you want your readers to believe after they read your evaluation. Who are your readers? Will they need extensive description or definitions of unfamiliar terms before you move into the meat of your evaluation?

   Your **tone** should be authoritative and convincing but engaging. It should also be consistent throughout your essay. Think about what kind of tone will suit your subject *and* your audience: formal or casual, serious or humorous?
2. **The introduction: finding a hook.** How will you capture your readers' attention right from the start? You might begin with an anecdote, a startling image, or a quote from an authority. Or you could just throw down the gauntlet and begin by announcing your judgment (of course, you'll still need to justify it later on). You've already thought quite a bit about your readers, so you know how much knowledge they have about your subject and whether you'll need to begin with a thorough description before moving into your evaluation.
3. **The body: building your case.** Your judgment of your subject is the controlling idea, or thesis, of your evaluation. Now you must construct the case to support your judgment, brick by brick. Before you begin writing, consult the outline you formulated in prewriting. Do you still think the order of reasons and evidence you established is the most effective? If not, reorder them. (And remember that even this order isn't engraved in stone—often a different or more logical pattern will emerge as you're writing.) Make sure that each reason for your judgment is adequately reinforced with evidence, and explain any criteria you think your readers will question or mistrust. Also, try to achieve balance, giving proper emphasis to description, reasons, and evidence without overexplaining or scrimping on any of them.
4. **The ending: driving it home.** Here's your chance to leave your readers thoroughly convinced that your evaluation is solid. You might end with a summary of the reasons you've presented or a restatement of your judgment, or you might refer to the beginning of the essay. In any event, leave your readers with something memorable—some ideas to turn over in their minds. (Any essay that just ends leaves readers feeling as though they were engaged in conversation with someone who abruptly walked away.)

Evaluating and Revising

1. **Peer review.** One of the most helpful ways to respond to someone else's writing is to ask questions. As you read, pause where you have a question, and write it either in the margin or on a separate sheet of paper. Then discuss your questions with the writer of the evaluation.
2. **Self-evaluation.** Using your peer reviewer's comments as a map, go through your essay again. Address any concerns about your criteria and evidence first. Put a check mark next to each criterion; then underscore the evidence that supports it. If your reviewer has raised any counterarguments to your case, think about how to defuse them. Finally, check to see if you should vary your sentence style.

Crossing the Curriculum

Democratic Values

If this is an election year, have your students compare two or more election advertisements or other campaign materials. What criteria for holding office is each candidate stressing? Is either candidate suggesting that the other cannot meet a criterion? What evidence is given to support either positive or negative claims?

CLAVDIVS
ONSOLDE
Language Workshop
The history
of the written
word is rich and
Page 1

OBJECTIVE
Use sentence style to strengthen meaning

Sentence Style: Ways of Strengthening Meaning

Most writers tend to have an identifiable general style that distinguishes their writing. For example, Matthew Arnold's poetic style differs from that of Gerard Manley Hopkins. **Style** is the way a writer uses language to express ideas and adapts language to suit the occasion. Style involves both the kinds of words a writer chooses (or **diction,** which you studied in the Language Workshop on page 777) and the way that writer joins those words to form sentences. In all good writing, the **sentence style** reflects the substance, or content, of the work. The beginning of Charles Dickens's *A Tale of Two Cities* contains one famous example of meaning reinforced by style. Notice how the use of **parallelism** contributes to the paradoxical nature of the passage—each statement is weighed against another, and both appear to be true:

> It was the best of times, it was the worst of times, it was the age of wisdom, it was the age of foolishness, it was the epoch of belief, it was the epoch of incredulity, it was the season of Light, it was the season of Darkness, it was the spring of hope, it was the winter of despair. . . .
>
> —Charles Dickens, *from A Tale of Two Cities*

Strategies for Analyzing Sentence Style

The following questions are useful in analyzing a writer's style. When answering each question, make notes about how each characteristic affects the meaning and overall impact of the writing.

- Are the sentences long, short, or varied?
- Are the sentences primarily declarative, interrogative, or imperative?
- Are the sentences simple, compound, complex, compound-complex, or varied in structure?
- Are the sentences primarily in the active or passive voice?
- Do the sentences follow the normal word order of English, or is the syntax inverted or varied in some way?
- Do the sentences use stylistic devices such as repetition or parallelism?

Writer's Workshop Follow-Up: Revision

Look back at the evaluation you wrote for the Writer's Workshop on page 899. Use the questions given above to analyze the sentence style of your evaluation. Working with a writing partner, identify at least three sentences you can revise to reinforce their meaning; then, share your revisions with your partner.

Technology HELP

See Language Workshop CD-ROM. *Key word entry: sentence style.*

Language Handbook HELP

See Sentence Style, page 1236.

Try It Out

How does Kipling's style affect the impact of the passage below? Rewrite the passage in other styles: Is the impact changed?

Everybody was there, and there was a general closing up of ranks and taking stock of our losses in dead or disabled that had fallen during the past year. It was a very wet night, and I remember that we sang "Auld Lang Syne" with our feet in the Polo Championship Cup, and our heads among the stars, and swore that we were all dear friends.

—*from* "The Mark of the Beast"

Resources

Workshop Resources
- Worksheet, p. 57

Try It Out
Possible Answers

1. "Everybody was there" is an ironic opening, followed as it is by the idea that it was necessary to "close ranks" because of the missing and take stock of the dead or disabled. "Everybody" is obviously not there.
2. The tone of disillusionment continues with the group defiling a "team" trophy, and their heads, like their feet, being somewhere they don't belong. These details build to the bitter realization that, despite the oath, they are not "dear friends."
3. Kipling achieves his effect by using simple language and linking ideas so closely that the contrast is immediate and apparent. If students separate the ideas in their rewrites, they will see that the passage loses its impact.

Assessing Learning

Quick Check: Sentence Style

Evaluate the following passage from Matthew Arnold's essay "Wordsworth" for elements of sentence style, using the questions in "Strategies for Analyzing Sentence Style" (p. 903).

"Wordsworth has been in his grave for some thirty years, and certainly his lovers and admirers cannot flatter themselves that this great and steady light of glory as yet shines over him. He is not fully recognized at home; he is not recognized at all abroad, yet I firmly believe that the poetical performance of Wordsworth is, after that of Shakespeare and Milton, of which all the world now recognizes the worth, undoubtedly the most considerable in our language from the Elizabethan age to the present time." [Possible answer: Arnold's lengthy, compound-complex sentences give an air of dignity and almost of majesty to his opening argument about the greatness of Wordsworth.]

OBJECTIVES

Read and interpret a historical map

Using the Strategies

Answers

1. India, Ceylon, Burma, Malaya, Sarawak, North Borneo
2. Persia, Afghanistan, Tibet, Nepal, Bhutan
3. approximately 2,225 miles
4. Singapore

Reading for Life

Reading a Historical Map

Situation

You've read about the British Empire during the Victorian era and you're curious about how far it extended into Asia. While browsing in a bookstore, you find a book on British history in which there's a map of the empire in the East. To interpret the map, you can apply these map-reading strategies.

Strategies

Identify the category of map you're reading. The two principal categories into which maps fall are political maps and special-purpose maps.

- Political maps show political units, such as states and nations. They often use different colors to show different countries. A historical map shows political boundaries at a certain time in history.
- Among the numerous kinds of special, or thematic, maps are road maps, aviation maps, navigational maps, geologic maps, and maps that show the amount of rainfall, the distribution of populations and crops, or agricultural and industrial areas.

Know how to use special map features. Most maps include one or more of the following:

- a compass rose, indicating directions on the earth's surface
- lines of longitude and latitude
- a distance scale

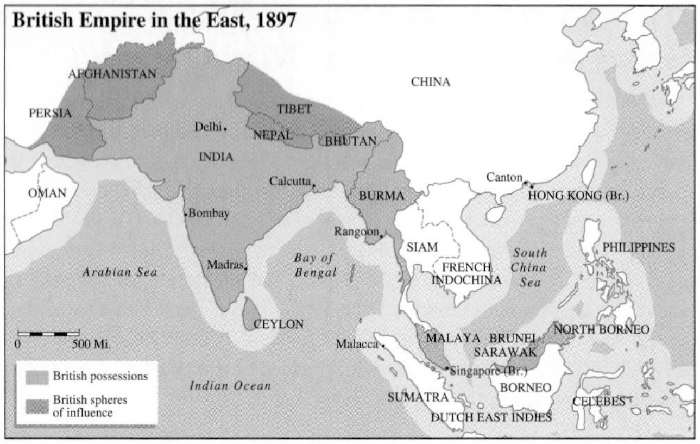

British Empire in the East, 1897

- a grid with labeled coordinates to help readers locate places on the map
- a map key, or legend, identifying special symbols

Using the Strategies

Answer these questions, using the map above.

1. Which countries were British possessions?
2. Which countries or parts of countries were within the sphere of British influence?
3. If Queen Victoria had traveled by land from Bombay to Delhi to Calcutta and then to Madras and back to Bombay, approximately how many miles would she have traveled?
4. Which British-controlled city between India and the Dutch East Indies is likely to have been an important trading center?

Extending the Strategies

- Compare a contemporary map of Central Asia with the historical map above. What inferences can you make about political changes that took place in the twentieth century?
- Plan an expedition to one of Great Britain's former colonies. Use an appropriate map to develop your itinerary.
- Use the Internet to obtain current information on one of the countries on the map.

Reaching All Students

English Language Learners

If you have Asian students, ask them to supplement their reading of the historical map and practice their English vocabulary at the same time by making some brief commentary on the political evolution of Asia since the period represented in the map. For example, a Thai student could point out that modern Thailand was called Siam in 1897; a Sri Lankan could tell the class that his or her country was once called Ceylon; a Cambodian, Laotian or Vietnamese student could briefly discuss the evolution of French Indochina into three separate national entities; an Indian or Pakistani student could explain the division of then-British India into the respective Hindu- and Muslim-majority nations of India and Pakistan.

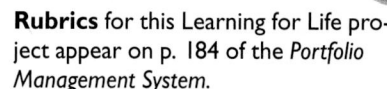

Learning for Life

Evaluating a Community

Problem
Progress in the form of rapid growth made some cities in Victorian England practically unlivable. How has progress affected communities today? What makes a good community?

Project
Identify the qualities you consider essential to a livable community. Are job opportunities an absolute necessity? What about size, location, climate, and quality of life? How has progress affected these qualities in communities in your area?

Preparation
1. Use brainstorming or freewriting to generate an initial list of qualities essential to a livable community.
2. With a group, examine the ways progress has changed your target community.

Procedure
1. From the group's master list, select the three or four qualities you consider most important, keeping in mind that this winnowing process will involve a series of trade-offs—for example, would you be willing to give up recreational facilities for more industry and thus more jobs? Then, rank the items in order of their importance to you.
2. Gather evidence—facts, statistics, examples, or anecdotes—to support each of your essential qualities.
3. Examine your list of the ways progress has affected your target community. Divide your list into positive effects and negative effects. Try to think of ways each negative effect could be corrected. Be sure to cite situations that might block the correction of the negative effects.

Presentation
Use one of the following formats (or another that your teacher approves):

1. **Agreeing to Disagree**
   With a classmate whose list of essential qualities differs significantly from yours, plan a debate. First, agree on two or three judges for the debate. Next, develop a proposition in the form of an evaluation—for example: *Resolved,* That job opportunities are more important in a community than recreational facilities. Finally, decide which one of you will take the affirmative position. After you've each prepared a debate brief, stage the debate in front of judges.
2. **Down to Scale**
   Design and build a scale model of a community that incorporates your choice of essential qualities. Before you begin construction, think about how you'll allocate space for residential, commercial, and industrial areas and how you'll lay out the streets. Display your model at the public library along with comment cards for viewers' responses.
3. **Appealing to Residents**
   If your investigation of the effects of progress on your target community has generated broad interest, prepare a report that includes your suggestions for changes. In your report, be sure to take into account the reasons why change may be difficult. Give convincing reasons why your recommendations should be considered. Your report should include a list of the qualities you think are essential to a livable community. You might ask the editor of your local newspaper to publish your report.

Processing
Did doing this activity change your feelings about your community? Why? Write a reflection for your portfolio.

OBJECTIVES
Identify the qualities essential to a livable community

Teaching the Lesson

Students from other countries may have different notions of what constitutes an ideal community. Reinforce the notion of citizen participation in American life, and ask students from other countries to define the similarities and differences between their American communities and their communities of origin.

Grading Timesaver

Rubrics for this Learning for Life project appear on p. 184 of the *Portfolio Management System.*

Developing Workplace Competencies

Preparation	Procedure	Presentation
• Works on teams • Evaluates data • Ranks alternatives • Makes decisions	• Processes information • Interprets information • Designs systems • Evaluates arguments	• Communicates information and ideas • Thinks creatively • Draws conclusions • Demonstrates integrity

OBJECTIVES

1. Read literature from the twentieth century on the themes "The Center Cannot Hold," "The Transforming Imagination," "Ourselves Among Others," and "Clashes of Culture"
2. Interpret literary elements used in the literature, with special emphasis on irony and the modern short story
3. Apply a variety of reading strategies to the literature, with special emphasis on recognizing how new words are formed and analyzing word analogies
4. Respond to literature in a variety of modes
5. Learn and use new words
6. Learn how English became an international language; compare and contrast British and American English
7. Plan, draft, and revise an informative report and a problem-solution essay
8. Write varied sentences that clearly reflect the relationships between ideas
9. Demonstrate the ability to read business memos and electronic mail
10. Predict the effect of a recent technological development on the future of society

Landscape from a Dream **(1936–1938) by Paul Nash. Oil on canvas (26¾″ x 40″).**
Tate Gallery, London, Great Britain.

Selection Readability

This Annotated Teacher's Edition provides a summary of each selection in the student book. Following each Summary heading, you will find one, two, or three small icons. These icons indicate, in an approximate sense, the reading level of the selection.

■ One icon indicates that the selection is easy.

■■ Two icons indicate that the selection is on an intermediate reading level.

■■■ Three icons indicate that the selection is challenging.

The Twentieth Century

Responding to the Art

Paul Nash (1889–1946) was a largely self-taught English painter, designer, printmaker, writer, and photographer. He served on the Western front in World War I and was an Official War Artist in 1917–1918. His painting *The Menin Road,* shown on p. 924, reflects this experience. The Surrealist painting shown here was painted during a transitional phase in Nash's career when, like other artists of his day, Nash created dreamlike landscapes with jarring, unexpected juxtapositions of objects and backgrounds.

Activity. Have students contrast this painting with the one that introduces the Victorian period (pp. 780–781). Then, have pairs of students discuss the following questions:

- How do the subjects vary?
- What, in your opinion, is the most radical difference between the two paintings?
- What mood or atmosphere does each painting create? What overall feeling does each leave you with?
- How does each painting help express or sum up the age it was selected to introduce?

The Twentieth Century

This essay presents highlights of British history since the turn of the century, with special emphasis on literary and artistic trends.

Responding to the Quotation

Among Britain's greatest modern writers is essayist and novelist George Orwell, whose biography appears on p. 1137. The Raj (British rule over India from 1757 until 1947) had a great impact on his life, since his father was in the Indian civil service and Orwell himself served as a member of the Indian Royal Police in Burma. At the peak of its power, which included rule over not only India but colonies on six continents, the British Empire was a place where "the sun never set": The empire did, in fact, appear to have the power to go on forever. Ask students whether they think Britain still has the same enormous influence that it had when Orwell wrote. Also ask them to comment on ways in which a colonial power's influence might persist long after its direct rule has ended.

Responding to the Art

Cyril E. Power was an artist and architect known for his linocuts—prints made from carved linoleum blocks. During the 1930s, he worked on poster designs for the London Passenger Transport Board. Power's style in this work owes a great deal to a short-lived early twentieth-century movement called Vorticism. Closely related to Futurism, Vorticism emphasized the use of simplified geometric forms presented in angular compositions that suggest dynamic movement and fragmentation. *Tube* is an informal word that the British use to refer to the subway system.

Activity. Have students comment on the following aspects of the painting:

- the arrangement of riders in a row, all exactly alike in posture and activity
- the exaggerated use of geometric shapes, such as swirling arcs and multiple angles
- the use of color, especially the nearly ubiquitous yellow

The Twentieth Century

by **John Leggett**

. . . England will still be England, an everlasting animal stretching into the future and the past, and, like all living things, having the power to change out of recognition and yet remain the same.

—George Orwell

The Tube Train (c. 1934) by Cyril E. Power.

© British Museum, London.

A View of Fleet Street (20th century) by Christian Snijders. Ⓐ

What a story of change, of the erosion of a proud, complacent, well-ordered society, is told by the early years of the twentieth century in Great Britain!

If we had lived in the era of Victoria, which ended with the great queen's death in 1901, or during the nine-year reign of her son Edward VII, we would have believed that Britain, with its moral and economic dominance of the world, would sail on majestically forever. But of course that is the misconception of every stable age and society—that life will go on just as it always has.

Even during this long, fairly stable period in Great Britain, though, profound changes were taking place, both externally and internally. Although the British imperial policy remained much the same throughout the Victorian era, several major colonies—Australia, South Africa, and New Zealand—gained their independence in the first decade of the twentieth century. Internally, Ⓑ Britain was experiencing social reforms that were to have far-reaching consequences. The rise in literacy, the growing power and influence of the Labour party, the widespread interest in socialist ideology—all were to dramatically change Great Britain and the world.

Political and social events during the early twentieth century would alter Great Britain's preeminent position as a world power and would dramatically change its society.

The Arrival (1923–1924) by Christopher R. W. Nevinson.
Tate Gallery, London.

Ⓐ Background

Fleet Street

Fleet Street is a central London thoroughfare that runs from Temple Bar to Christopher Wren's masterpiece, St. Paul's Cathedral. Famous for being the longtime home of many national newspapers, the street takes its name from the River Fleet. You might wish to have students return to this image of teeming streets in the early twentieth century when they read Eliot's "Preludes" on pp. 939–940.

Ⓑ Exploring the Historical Period

New Zealand and Australia

Australia gained its independence on January 1, 1901, when it proclaimed itself the Commonwealth of Australia. Since then, its ties to Britain have weakened, and it has aligned itself more closely with the United States. New Zealand loosened its ties to Britain much more reluctantly: The country was given dominion status in 1907 and autonomy in 1931, but it did not formally accept the latter until 1947.

RESPONDING TO THE ART

The Arrival, by **Christopher R.W. Nevinson,** is another example of the movement called Vorticism (see p. T908). Vorticism was England's answer to Futurism. Two of Vorticism's major proponents were American Imagist poet Ezra Pound (1885–1972) and English writer and painter Wyndham Lewis (1882–1957).

Activity. Ask students to compare *The Arrival* to *The Tube Train* on p. 908. Have them discuss the use of angles and geometric shapes in each. What is peculiarly "modern" about this style?

Reaching All Students

Struggling Readers

As they read, ask these students to take notes, which they can use later as the basis for making several generalizations about the twentieth century. Point out the section headings throughout this introduction and the summary statement that ends each section. Paying attention to these features will help students form their generalizations. They can also refer to the outline on p. 917, which summarizes the ideas and events of the twentieth century. Remind students that they can combine information they already know with the information they learn in this text in order to form their generalizations.

English Language Learners

Be sure these students understand that there are differences between British English and American English. Introduce the term *Briticism,* a word or phrase characteristic of British English. Share with students terms from British life that they may not know, such as *Labour Party, the House of Windsor, the royals,* and *dependencies.*

Advanced Learners

Encourage these students to read a recent work by Martin Amis, Margaret Drabble, A. S. Byatt, Anita Brookner, Graham Swift, Pat Barker, or another contemporary British novelist. Students might comment on what seems distinctively British in the work and what seems more to be a product of a global culture.

Time Line

• 1911–1916

Causes of World War I

World War I developed from many complex causes, including the steady rise of both nationalism and militarism and fears about the balance of power in Europe. The specific event that triggered armed conflict, however, was the assassination of Archduke Francis Ferdinand of Austria by a Serbian nationalist in Sarajevo on June 28, 1914.

Einstein and Modern Science

Albert Einstein (1879–1955) published four research papers in the same year he obtained his doctorate at the Polytechnic Academy in Zurich, and each paper contained an important discovery in physics. One of Einstein's theories, that of relativity, brought him international fame when it was verified in 1919. Two years later he was awarded the Nobel Prize in physics. Einstein became a U.S. citizen in 1940 and alerted the U.S. government to the fact that nuclear energy could be used to fuel weapons.

• 1917–1926

World War I Casualties

The devastating effects of World War I cannot be overstated. Horrific loss of life, staggering numbers of wounded (an estimated 21 million), and economic devastation of some nations (most notably Germany) were among its legacies.

• 1927–1939

European Market in Trouble

When the crash hit, Americans immediately pulled money out of European economies. Investments in Europe dropped or disappeared, and Europeans who had relied on exporting goods to America suddenly saw their markets disappear. With their war debts and dependence on American loans, Germany and Austria were among the first countries to suffer.

The Twentieth Century

• Sir Winston Churchill.

LITERARY EVENTS

1900–1910

- Swedish writer Selma Lagerlöf is first woman awarded the Nobel Prize in literature, 1909
- Dublin's Abbey Theatre founded by **W. B. Yeats** and Lady Gregory to produce plays by and about the Irish, 1904
- Joseph Conrad's *Heart of Darkness* published, 1902

1911–1916

- **James Joyce** publishes *A Portrait of the Artist as a Young Man,* 1916
- Czech writer Franz Kafka's *The Metamorphosis* published, 1915
- G. B. Shaw's *Pygmalion* first produced; **D. H. Lawrence**'s *Sons and Lovers* published, 1913

1917–1926

- African American writer Langston Hughes publishes first book of verse, *The Weary Blues,* 1926
- E. M. Forster's *A Passage to India* published, 1924
- **W. B. Yeats** receives the Nobel Prize in literature, 1923
- Publication of **Joyce**'s *Ulysses* and **T. S. Eliot**'s *The Waste Land,* 1922

1927–1939

- Spanish writer Federico García Lorca's play *Blood Wedding* produced, 1933
- **W. H. Auden**'s *Poems* published; Noel Coward's play *Private Lives* produced, 1930
- **Virginia Woolf** publishes *To the Lighthouse,* 1927

CULTURAL/HISTORICAL EVENTS

1900–1910

- Queen Victoria dies and is succeeded by her son Edward VII, 1901
- Sigmund Freud visits U.S. to lecture on psychoanalysis, 1909
- South Africa gains independence from Britain; Union of South Africa formed; racial segregation becomes governing rule, 1910

• Food coupon issued by the Ministry of Food during World War I.

1911–1916

- In New York City, the Armory Show introduces postimpressionism and cubism in art; in Paris, the first performance of Stravinsky's *Rite of Spring* causes a riot among bewildered spectators, 1913
- World War I begins after the assassination of Archduke Francis Ferdinand, 1914
- Albert Einstein announces his general theory of relativity, 1915
- Easter Rebellion in Dublin; uprising's leaders executed by British, 1916

1917–1926

- U.S. enters the war in Europe; Russian Revolution begins, 1917
- World War I ends with nearly 10 million dead; voting rights in England extended to women over 30, 1918
- Ireland is divided by treaty, with six northern counties remaining part of United Kingdom; civil war begins in Ireland, 1922

1927–1939

- U.S. stock market crashes, triggering worldwide depression, 1929
- Adolf Hitler appointed chancellor of Germany; Germans build first concentration camp, at Dachau, 1933
- In Russia, Stalinist purges force over 10 million people into labor camps, 1934–1938
- Spanish Civil War fought, 1936–1939
- Pablo Picasso paints *Guernica,* protesting German firebombing of the Spanish city, 1937
- Germany invades Poland; World War II begins, 1939

• Formerly unemployed men go to work selling apples.

Using the Time Line

Have students use an encyclopedia or other print or nonprint resources to find the dates of the following events and achievements in history, science, and the arts and add them to the time line.

- Stalin becomes dictator in the Soviet Union [1929]
- Landing vehicles from *Viking I* and *Viking II* set down on Mars and transmit photos of its surface [1976]
- Robert E. Peary reaches the North Pole [1909]
- Piet Mondrian paints *Broadway Boogie-Woogie* [1943]
- In China, the civil war between the Nationalists and Communists begins [1946]
- Fourth World Conference on Women is held in Beijing [1995]
- Biafra secedes from Nigeria and civil war erupts there [1967]
- Gandhi is assassinated in India [1948]
- The National Party of South Africa begins policy of apartheid [1948]
- Insecticides used for first time [1924]
- Chaplin's *Modern Times* comes to the screen [1936]
- Magritte paints *The Empire of Light;* O'Keeffe paints *Poppies* [1950]
- James D. Watson publishes *The Double Helix* [1968]
- Frank Lloyd Wright designs Unity Temple in Oak Park, Illinois [1906]

© 2000 The Estate of Pablo Picasso/Artists Rights Society (ARS), New York.

• ***Guernica* (1937) by Pablo Picasso.** Museo Nacional Centro de Arte Reina Sofia, Madrid. On permanent loan from the Museo del Prado, Madrid.

Winston Churchill receives Nobel Prize in literature; Samuel Beckett's play *Waiting for Godot* first produced in Paris, 1953

George Orwell's *Animal Farm* published; Chilean poet Gabriela Mistral awarded Nobel Prize in literature, 1945

Colombian writer Gabriel García Márquez publishes *One Hundred Years of Solitude,* 1967

Nigerian writer **Chinua Achebe**'s *Things Fall Apart* published, 1958

Irish writer **Seamus Heaney** receives Nobel Prize in literature, 1995

Japanese writer Kenzaburo Oe awarded Nobel Prize in literature, 1994

St. Lucian writer **Derek Walcott** publishes *Omeros,* a long poem inspired by Homer's *Odyssey,* 1990

Egyptian writer **Naguib Mahfouz** awarded Nobel Prize in literature, 1988

1940–1954

In the Battle of Britain, British Royal Air Force prevents German invasion of England, 1940

U.S. declares war on Italy, Germany, and Japan, 1941

Germany surrenders; U.S. drops atom bombs over Hiroshima and Nagasaki, ending World War II, 1945

Development of ENIAC at the University of Pennsylvania marks first generation of modern computers, 1946

India gains independence from Britain, 1947; Mohandas Gandhi assassinated, 1948

UN partitions Palestine, 1947; State of Israel created, 1948

Twenty-six of thirty-two counties in Ireland achieve full status as an independent republic, 1949

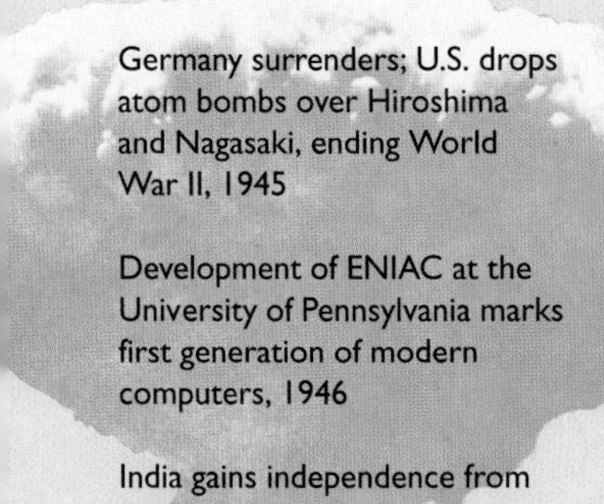

• **Mushroom cloud (August 9, 1945) from the atomic bomb dropped on Nagasaki, Japan, during World War II.**

1955–1974

Martin Luther King, Jr., leads boycott of buses in Montgomery, Alabama, 1955

Nigeria wins independence from Britain, 1960

British singing group the Beatles revolutionizes popular music, 1960s

Apollo 11 astronauts are first men to walk on the moon, as 600 million people watch live telecast, 1969

• **Astronaut Edwin E. Aldrin, Jr., lunar module pilot (1969).**

1975–2000

• **The Beatles (1964).**

Fall of Saigon marks end of Vietnam War, 1975

Nuclear disaster at Chernobyl plant in Ukraine, 1986

Berlin Wall is dismantled; Chinese army cracks down on pro-democracy students in Tiananmen Square, 1989

Soviet Union is dissolved, 1991

Nelson Mandela elected president of South Africa, 1994

Britain returns Hong Kong to China, 1997

Peace plan for Northern Ireland signed and ratified by referendum, 1998

• **1940–1954**

The Atomic Bomb

The atomic bomb dropped on Hiroshima on August 6, 1945, instantly killed about 66,000 of the city's inhabitants. The atomic bomb dropped on Nagasaki on August 9, 1945, had the force of 21,000 tons of TNT and killed approximately 39,000 people on impact.

• **1955–1974**

Martin Luther King, Jr.

Martin Luther King, Jr. (1929–1968), an important leader of the civil rights movement in the United States, was awarded the Nobel Peace Prize in 1964. He was assassinated in 1968. The U.S. Congress voted to establish a national holiday in his honor, and in 1986, the third Monday in January was declared Martin Luther King, Jr. Day.

• **1975–2000**

Vietnam: The Background

Even the official close of the Vietnam War did not end the controversy or speculation surrounding U.S. involvement in that conflict. From 1946 to 1954, France battled the Vietnam Independence League, or Viet Minh, in order to maintain French influence in Indochina. When the French forces were badly defeated in a key battle, peace was negotiated, and the country was separated into the Communist North and the French-controlled South. War broke out again shortly afterward. The United States feared a unified Communist Vietnam and became involved, taking over the French role in the conflict. By 1973, when the United States withdrew from the area, approximately 58,000 U.S. troops had been killed in the fighting. Vietnamese casualties on both sides totaled approximately 2 million.

China and Democracy

After the crackdown in Tiananmen Square, many students called for reforms and for the resignation of Deng Xiaoping, who then ordered a further crackdown. Meanwhile, China's economic boom continued to bring enormous change to the country. After Deng Xiaoping's death in 1997, Communist Party General Secretary Jiang Zemin became president. Despite the cloud of human rights abuses, China and the United States made diplomatic progress during President Clinton's 1998 visit.

Ⓐ Exploring the Culture

Social Darwinism

Although Social Darwinism enjoyed popularity in the second half of the nineteenth century (largely through the work of British sociologist Herbert Spencer, who coined the phrase "survival of the fittest") and into the beginning of the twentieth century, it fell out of favor after World War I. People began to view Social Darwinism as fueling such ills as racism, militarism, and nationalism. Also, the groundbreaking work in anthropology conducted by Margaret Mead, Franz Boas, and others (which showed that the creation of culture separates humans from animals) helped to dispel the myths of Social Darwinism.

Ⓑ Exploring the Historical Period

Marx and Engels

Karl Marx and his friend and close collaborator Friedrich Engels (1820–1895) co-authored the *Communist Manifesto* (1848), which sought to address many of the persistent problems in European industrialized society. Later in 1848, both participated in the German revolution that attempted to replace an authoritarian government with a representative one; when it failed, they both moved to England. There they finished the three volumes of *Das Kapital*, with Engels revising Marx's notes for the last two volumes, which were published after Marx's death in 1883.

Ⓒ Exploring the Culture

Freud and the Unconscious Mind

Sigmund Freud (1856–1939) founded the field of psychoanalysis, and a great many of his ideas have entered into common parlance and become part of the theory and practice of other fields and sciences. Freud himself applied his theories to the areas of anthropology, mythology, and religion with such works as *Totem and Taboo* (1913) and *Civilization and Its Discontents* (1930).

Ⓓ Responding to the Quotation

? What does Freud mean here? In what sense did poets and philosophers discover the unconscious? [Students may suggest that poets—and other artists—have always been able to express the contents of the unconscious through their creativity, and that philosophers indirectly described the human unconscious by tackling issues that have always perplexed humanity.]

Darwin, Marx, and Freud: Undermining Victorian Ideas

Many of the social and intellectual changes that were taking place in the early years of the twentieth century had their roots in the nineteenth-century work of three men: Charles Darwin (1809–1882), Karl Marx (1818–1883), and Sigmund Freud (1856–1939).

> The proletarians have nothing to lose but their chains. They have a world to win. Working men of all countries, unite!
>
> —Karl Marx and Friedrich Engels

Darwin's *Origin of Species* (1859) sets forth a theory of the evolution of animal species based on natural selection—those species that successfully adapt to their environments survive and reproduce; those that do not become extinct. This theory, which seems to contradict the Biblical account of the special creation of each species, fueled a debate that has continued from Victorian times to the present. Ⓐ So-called social Darwinism, the notion that in society, as in nature, only the fittest should survive and flourish, was a nasty extension of Darwin's scientific theories—although Darwin had nothing to do with its formulation. "Social Darwinism" was used to justify unrestricted competition, rigid class distinctions, indifference to social problems, and even doctrines of racial superiority.

In *Das Kapital* (1867), Karl Marx, a German philosopher and political economist who spent the last thirty years of his life in London, advocates Ⓑ the abolition of private property. Marx traces economic injustices to the capitalist system of ownership and argues that workers should own the means of production. His theories of social and economic justice revolutionized political thought and eventually led to sweeping changes in many governments and economic systems, including those of Britain.

> Ⓓ The poets and philosophers before me discovered the unconscious; what I discovered was the scientific method by which the unconscious can be studied.
>
> —Sigmund Freud

Ⓒ The psychological theories of Sigmund Freud, a doctor in Vienna, were equally revolutionary and far-reaching in their effects. In *The Interpretation of Dreams* (1900) and later works, Freud finds the motives for human behavior not in our rational, conscious minds but in the irrational and sexually driven realm of the unconscious, which is manifest mainly in our dreams. Conservative Victorians were outraged by Freud's claims that sexual drives influenced their behavior, but artists and writers found the notion of the unconscious and its mysterious, illogical workings fascinating.

Portrait of Charles Darwin (1840) by George Richmond.

Karl Marx.

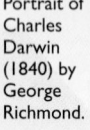

Sigmund Freud.

Using Students' Strengths

Musical/Auditory Learners

Students might enjoy creating a musical time line of the century by recording short pieces or bars of music that are representative of the music heard or composed during each decade of the twentieth century in Britain. Invite students to play their tapes for the class and to make available a play list, naming the composer of each selection, its date of composition, and its title.

The work of these thinkers helped to undermine the political, religious, and psychological assumptions that had served as the foundation of British society and the British Empire for generations. With the calamity of the Great War and the events that followed, that foundation was largely swept away.

The writings of Charles Darwin, Karl Marx, and Sigmund Freud caused people to question many of the social, religious, and economic beliefs of the Victorian period.

The Great War: "A War to End All Wars"

The truly great disaster of the first half of the century was the breakdown of the European balance of power. In 1914, Britain, France, and Russia, bound by treaties, were locked in opposition to Germany and Austria-Hungary. The confrontation plunged the whole of Europe into World War I, or what was known as the Great War. (E)

Return to the Front, 1917 by Richard Jack.
York City Art Gallery, York, England.

The Victorian writer Rudyard Kipling celebrated the British character as essentially patriotic, and he was right. When war broke out, a young Englishman felt that to be called on to defend his nation was likely to be the most exalted experience of his life. For centuries, in all sorts of wars and skirmishes, the ordinary youth of England had donned smart uniforms and marched off to faraway battlefields, just as they might go off to a sports event. On the battlefield, they would perform heroic acts, and for the most part they would return to be honored at home and to add their tales to the romantic lore of their regiments.

> You are ordered abroad as a soldier of the king to help our French comrades against the invasion of a common enemy. . . . Do your duty bravely. Fear God. Honor the king. (F)
>
> —Lord Kitchener to the British Expeditionary Force, 1914

When Britain declared war on Germany in 1914, young Britons crowded to the recruiting stations to enlist. Six months later, hordes of them lay slaughtered in the miserable, rain-soaked, vermin-infested trenches of France. (G) Sixty thousand young British men were killed or wounded on the first day of the Battle of the Somme alone. Three hundred thousand were killed, wounded, or frozen to death at the Battle of Ypres. (H) The generals would not stop the terrible—and in the end futile—carnage, and over the

(E) Exploring the Historical Period

Triple Trouble

By 1907, the major powers of Europe had committed themselves to one of two rival groups: the Triple Alliance, consisting of Germany, Austria-Hungary, and Italy, or the Triple Entente, consisting of Great Britain, France, and Russia. At the time, Bosnia was ruled by Austria-Hungary, but there was a strong desire on the part of Serbia to take it over. This led a Serbian nationalist in Sarajevo (Bosnia) to shoot Archduke Ferdinand. In response, Austria quickly made strong demands on Serbia, most of which Serbia was willing to meet. Nevertheless, Austria soon declared war on Serbia. Consequently, Serbia's strong ally Russia took action against Austria the same day.

(F) Exploring the Historical Period

Lord Kitchener

As soon as war broke out, Prime Minister Herbert Henry Asquith named Lord Kitchener Secretary of State for War. Considered a military hero for his conquests abroad, especially in the Sudan, Kitchener commanded the respect of the recruits and was widely regarded as the embodiment of the lofty ideals he expresses here.

(G) Exploring the Historical Period

Enlistment

When the war began, Britain had a small army and no policy of conscription (draft). Recruitment was restricted to volunteers. In fact, volunteerism brought in more recruits in the early years of the war than conscription did when it was finally adopted after May 1916.

(H) Background

The Battle of Ypres

Ypres is a city in northwestern Belgium, near the French border.

Using Students' Strengths

Interpersonal Learners

Some students might enjoy creating imaginary meetings between the luminaries of different time periods of the twentieth century. For example, what if Freud could meet and chat with actor/comedian John Cleese? What would Lord Kitchener have to say to Nigerian writer Wole Soyinka? Invite pairs or teams of students to create a dialogue that might occur at such a meeting and to share it with the class.

Visual Learners

Suggest that students re-create the time period—or a particular portion of the twentieth century—by means of a mixed-media collage. Encourage them to represent a wide variety of developments by showing key events and personalities in history, science, music, and the performing arts, as well as images that reflect changing lifestyles and trends. Urge students to draw, paint, or download images from a variety of sources.

A Exploring the Historical Period

Deep Trenches, High Casualties

The Great War was fought on two key fronts: the Western front and the Eastern front. On the Eastern front, Russians and Serbs fought against Germans, Austrians, and Turks. It was on the Western front, a small deadlocked area consisting mostly of northern France, that the British fought alongside their allies. There, both sides dug long, parallel trenches in order to protect themselves from the heavy bombardment of the enemy. While there were advances in weaponry at this time—better airplanes, machine guns, the tank (introduced by the British in 1916), and poison gas (introduced by the Germans in 1915 but used by both sides)—these innovations seemed to bring additional carnage rather than a quicker end to the hideous war.

B Exploring the Culture

Prevailing Pessimism

One reason for the prevailing pessimism is that so many people had gone off to war convinced that their cause was right and just. David Lloyd George, the British prime minister, had been instrumental in rallying the people in 1914, when he declared that it was a holy cause "on behalf of liberal principles, a crusade on behalf of the 'little five-foot nations,' like Belgium, flagrantly invaded by the Germans, or Serbia and Montenegro. . . ." Yet, afterward, the British would question what, indeed, they had fought so long and tragically for, and at such great cost to an entire generation.

C Background

Henry VIII and Royal Scandal

The marital problems of Henry VIII, who reigned from 1509 to 1547, and his desire for a divorce led to the creation of the Church of England as a separate entity from the Roman Catholic Church. Henry's wives were, in order, Catherine of Aragon (mother of the future queen Mary I), Anne Boleyn (mother of the future queen Elizabeth I), Jane Seymour (mother of Henry's successor, Edward VI), Anne of Cleves, Catherine Howard, and Catherine Parr.

A To be in the trenches was to experience an unreal, unforgettable enclosure and constraint, as well as a sense of being unoriented and lost. One saw two things only: the walls of an unlocalized, undifferentiated earth and the sky above. . . . It was the sight of the sky, almost alone, that had the power to persuade a man that he was not already lost in a common grave.

—Paul Fussell

course of four years an entire generation of young Englishmen was fed to the insatiable furnace of the war.

B With the armistice in 1918, a new cynicism arose. The old values of national honor and glory had endorsed a war whose results were gradually recognized as a weakened economy, a tottering colonial empire, and a loss of life equal to that caused by many plagues. Out of disillusionment came a pessimism about the state and the individual's relation to society. A new realism swept in, an antidote to the "romantic nonsense" of the past and in particular to the propaganda machine that had led a whole people into war.

After the Great War, in which nearly one million British soldiers died, many people in Great Britain developed a cynical attitude toward government and such values as national honor and glory.

A CLOSER LOOK

Royal Tradition and Scandal

C In its thousand-year history, England's monarchy has seen turbulent times. The fates of Henry VIII's wives (divorced, beheaded, died, divorced, beheaded, survived) provide a notorious example. Britons pride themselves on their love of ritual and tradition, but their liege lords often appear to be awkward anachronisms. When the extravagant and hugely unpopular George IV died in 1830, the London *Times* reflected, "There never was an individual less regretted by his fellow creatures."

The House of Windsor. As the British monarchy enters the twenty-first century, the House of Windsor rules a kingdom in transition from its colonial past. Today, the crown's functions are mostly ceremonial. Royals serve at official functions and charitable affairs, and the family's joking reference to itself as "the firm" indicates they take their business seriously.

Yet, with the business of ceremony comes the pressure of public scrutiny.

The royal family with Princess Diana in 1992.

Crossing the Curriculum

Geography

What made World War I a world war? What countries, besides Russia and those in Europe already mentioned, were involved? Ask students to present their findings by means of an annotated world map. [Among the countries involved were India, which provided more than 1 million soldiers to fight alongside the British; Australia and New Zealand, which also provided soldiers to the Allied cause; Japan, which declared war on Germany and took over its colonies in China and the Pacific; numerous African colonies, which became actual battlefields; Brazil, which supported the Allied cause; Arabs in Southwest Asia who were also involved in a battle with their Turkish rulers; and, of course, the United States.]

Experimentation in the Arts: Shocking in Form and Content

The decade before the war had seen the beginnings of a transformation in all the arts, especially on the Continent. In Paris, Henri Matisse and other new painters exhibiting in 1905 were called *les fauves* (the wild beasts) by critics for their bold, new use of line and color. Pablo Picasso's first cubist painting, *Les Demoiselles d'Avignon,* was finished in 1907, the same year that John Millington Synge's play *The Playboy of the Western World* caused a riot at its première at Dublin's Abbey Theatre. (The audience was outraged by the suggestion that the Irish would make a hero out of a boy who claimed to have murdered his father.) **D** In 1913, Igor Stravinsky's revolutionary music for the ballet *The Rite of Spring,* which was marked by strong, primitive (read "sexual") rhythms and dissonant harmonies, caused a riot at its première in Paris. The year after that, James Joyce's *Dubliners,* containing stories written up to a decade before, finally found an Irish publisher brave enough to publish it. All these works challenged traditional values of beauty and order and opened new avenues of expression. **E**

> Never trust the artist. Trust the tale.
>
> —D. H. Lawrence

Queen Elizabeth II called 1992 the *annus horribilis,* or "horrible year," because during that time two of her children separated from their spouses and several were caught in scandals highly publicized by the British tabloids. The year also saw another disaster: Ancient Windsor Castle caught fire, and the public balked at paying for the restoration of Elizabeth's family home. Responding to public opinion, Queen Elizabeth instituted a number of reforms. In 1992, she voluntarily agreed to pay income taxes on her fortune and to publish an annual accounting of spending on royal palaces.

In 1997, however, the royal family faced an even greater challenge when the much loved Princess Diana, the former wife of Prince Charles, was killed in a car accident. When the queen and the prince were slow to respond publicly to the tragedy, they were bitterly criticized by the public for their apparent coldness and formality. For many, Diana had represented the warmth and humanity that the royal family lacked. The queen once again responded to what her people wanted, however, and arranged a funeral for Diana of such great dignity that many British subjects reembraced the House of Windsor.

Institution or anachronism? Still, the larger question remains: What is the monarchy's role in postcolonial Britain? Prince Philip, the queen's husband, has said that if "people feel it has no further part to play, then for goodness' sake let's end the thing on amicable terms without having a row about it." Ending the monarchy might be economical, but such a pragmatic solution would end a thousand years of tradition. **F** The monarchy has endured not only because it provides historical continuity, but also because it captures the public imagination and, in an unromantic age, feeds the public appetite for pageantry and for a need to escape.

D Literary Connections

John Millington Synge

In Ireland, a spirit of nationalism was being revived at the same time that a new Irish literary theater was coming to the fore. One of the great playwrights of this period was John Millington Synge (1871–1909), who joined the movement to revive the ancient Irish language and legends.

E Exploring the Culture

Shock and Censorship

Both D. H. Lawrence and James Joyce had lifelong problems with censorship of their work, and both reacted in much the same way: leaving their home countries and seeking independent publication of their work. James Joyce left Ireland and, except for a brief return to Dublin, lived the rest of his life in Paris, Trieste, and Zurich. Lawrence left England shortly after the banning of his novel *The Rainbow* in 1915 and spent his remaining years writing and wandering in Italy, Australia, Mexico, southern France, and the American Southwest. Today, visitors can visit the D. H. Lawrence Shrine (containing the writer's ashes) in Taos, New Mexico, near the D. H. Lawrence Ranch.

F Background

History of the Monarchy

The British monarchy traces its roots back to Egbert of the House of Wessex, who was king from 802 to 825. The House of Windsor, which was known as the House of Saxe-Coburg-Gotha until 1917, has been in power since 1901. Royal powers are strictly limited now; the United Kingdom is a constitutional monarchy and a parliamentary democracy.

Taking a Second Look

Producing Research Projects

Have students learn more about the Great War by researching and reporting on one of the great battles on the Western front, such as Verdun, Somme, or Amiens. Have students learn what happened at one of these battles, being sure to note the numbers of casualties and the overall effect on the war. Students might also research the experience of battle on the front lines as it was lived by the average soldier on either side. Diaries and personal journals are good sources of this kind of information. Finally, students can research how returning soldiers reassimilated into society.

Students' reports can be written or oral. They may also wish to share their findings with their history classes.

Responding to the Art

Henri Matisse (1869–1954), one of the twentieth century's greatest artists, gained fame as a painter, sculptor, printmaker, and designer. The leader of the Fauves (literally, "wild animals"), a group of artists who broke traditional constraints by painting with bright colors and wild brushstrokes, Matisse invented an innovative style and was a master of the use of colors and form. *The Sadness of the King* uses a technique Matisse developed near the end of his life—"drawing with scissors." He painted large sheets of paper with striking colors and then cut and arranged shapes or "cutouts" to create a composition.

Activity. Ask students to explain what this work has to do with either sadness or a king. What makes this a particularly modern work of art?

A Literary Connections

Virginia Woolf

Woolf wrote a series of modern stream-of-consciousness novels. This method, which relies on the use of first-person narration, records the flow of thought in all its disjointed and unpredictable mystery, revealing with enormous fluidity the subtleties of human character.

B Exploring the Culture

Lifting the Ban on *Ulysses*

On December 6, 1933, in the same week that Prohibition was repealed, Judge Woolsey lifted the ban on *Ulysses* in the United States. The book had been censored as "obscene." In his decision, Woolsey wrote that the book did not, in fact, "tend to excite sexual impulses or lustful thoughts" and that "its net effect . . . was only that of a somewhat tragic and very powerful commentary on the inner lives of men and women." He added that he believed *Ulysses* to be a "sincere and serious attempt to devise a new literary method for the observation and description of mankind." In 1998, in a controversial list drawn up by the editorial board of the Modern Library, *Ulysses* was voted number one among the "Top 100 English-Language Novels of the Twentieth Century."

The Sadness of the King (1952) by Henri Matisse. Gouache cutout pasted on canvas (292 cm × 386 cm).

Musée Nationale d'Art Moderne, Paris. © 1997 Succession H. Matisse, Paris / Artists Rights Society (ARS), New York.

The twentieth century's vision of the future might well be summed up in the final line of Joseph Conrad's *Heart of Darkness* (1902): "The offing was barred by a black bank of clouds, and the tranquil waterway leading to the uttermost ends of the earth flowed somber under an overcast sky—seemed to lead into the heart of an immense darkness."

The novelists that followed Conrad were moving from a concern with society to a focus on introspection. Virginia Woolf even rejected traditional chronological order in storytelling. Experimenting with novelistic structure and with a shifting point of view, Woolf probed the human mind with the delicacy of a surgeon, examining all its shifts of moods and impressions. A

In his novels, D. H. Lawrence was expressing his own strong resentment against British society, with its class system, industrialism, militarism, and prudery. Lawrence shocked the British with his glorification of the senses and his heated descriptions of relations between the sexes. His novel *Lady Chatterley's Lover* (1928), about an affair between an upper-class woman and her gamekeeper, is explicitly sexual, and its full publication was banned in England until 1960.

Most influential of all was the Irish poet and novelist James Joyce, whose novel *Ulysses* appeared to a storm of controversy in 1922. *Ulysses,* based on Homer's *Odyssey,* narrates the events of a single day in the B

Les Demoiselles d'Avignon. Paris (June–July 1907), by Pablo Picasso. Oil on canvas 8′ × 7′8″ (243.9 x 233.7 cm).

The Museum of Modern Art, New York. Acquired through the Lillie P. Bliss Bequest. Photograph © 2000 The Museum of Modern Art, New York. © 2000 Estate of Pablo Picasso / Artists Rights Society (ARS), New York.

Crossing the Curriculum

Art

Direct students' attention to Pablo Picasso's *Les Demoiselles d'Avignon (Young Ladies of Avignon)* on this page or to *Guernica* on p. 911. Is their response to these paintings fiercely positive or negative? What is it about either painting that challenges previously accepted ideas about presenting the human form or using shape, line, and color? What has become of beauty and order? Invite students to find out more about Picasso, one of the key artists of the twentieth century. Students should report in a general way about the innovations Picasso made in art and his effect on the art world. Alternatively, they might present a time line showing the evolution of Picasso's various styles. The time line should include the two works mentioned above, as well as *The Old Guitarist* (a work from his earlier "Blue Period"), shown on p. 936.

> Signatures of all things I am here to read, seaspawn and seawrack, the nearing tide, that rusty boot. Snotgreen, bluesilver, rust: coloured signs.
>
> —James Joyce, *from Ulysses*

lives of a Jewish Dubliner named Leopold Bloom and a young man named Stephen Dedalus, as they unwittingly recapitulate the actions of Homer's Odysseus and his son Telemachus. Joyce drew, in a wholly revolutionary way, on myth and symbol, on Freudian explorations of sexuality, and on new conceptions of time and the workings of human consciousness.

Joseph Conrad, James Joyce, Virginia Woolf, and D. H. Lawrence experimented with form and content to challenge the conventions and limits of the novel.

The Rise of Dictatorships: Origins of World War II

The Great War, which had been called a war to end all wars, ironically led to another war. The League of Nations, the idealistic dream of U.S. president Woodrow Wilson, had no sooner been created than it was abandoned by a newly isolationist U.S. government. A worldwide economic depression that began in 1929 fostered the rise of dictators in Germany, Italy, and Russia.

In Italy and Germany, the form of totalitarianism that developed was fascism, a type of government that relies on the rule of a single dictator whose power is absolute and backed by force. Benito Mussolini, who came to power in Italy in 1922, held control through brutality and manipulation. Adolf Hitler and the Nazi party capitalized on Germany's economic woes to convince many Germans that their problems were caused by Jews, Communists, and immigrants.

> You cannot make a revolution with silk gloves.
>
> —attributed to Joseph Stalin

Russia's totalitarian government, based on the political theories of the economist Karl Marx, was Communist. Its founder, Nikolai Lenin, had sought in the 1920s to create a society without a class system, one in which the state would distribute the country's wealth equally among the people. But, in reality, the new government became as repressive as the rule of the czars had been. After Lenin's death in 1924, Joseph Stalin took power. In 1941, he became premier and continued to rule with an iron fist. Under Stalin's rule, as many as 15 million people were sent to the gulag, or system of forced-labor and detention camps.

The Twentieth Century

The following ideas and events distinguished the twentieth century:

- Radically new thinking in science, psychology, and economics challenged many treasured convictions of the Victorian period.
- With the huge British losses suffered in the Great War, conventional patriotism and romantic notions of bravery were swept away.
- Disillusioned by the war, British and European artists radically experimented with, even rejected, traditional notions of beauty and order.
- After a worldwide economic depression, Fascist dictatorships arose in Spain, Germany, and Italy, along with an equally brutal Communist regime in Russia.
- By the end of World War II, the Nazis had murdered 6 million Jews in what is now known as the Holocaust. Between 35 and 60 million people perished in World War II.
- Its postwar economy in shambles, Britain could not hold on to the territories that had constituted its empire; one after another, most of Britain's colonies won their independence.
- Since the 1960s, many extraordinary writers in English have come from Britain's former colonies.

C Literary Connections

Joyce's Innovations

When they read this excerpt, most students will be quick to note that reading *Ulysses* is not for the timid. Literary historian Harry Blamires explains Joyce's style in *Ulysses* in this way: "In Joyce's seven years of labour on *Ulysses,* from 1914 to 1921, he experimented with a vast range of stylistic devices including pastiche and parody from the worlds of literature, scholarship, journalism, and commerce. He broke through the fetters of syntax in presenting the flow of inner thought and feeling, and invented a system of annotational continuity that strings together unstructured impressions, mental jottings, evanescent half-thoughts, and the fleeting inarticulacies of cerebral and gut reaction that trail off into reverie or reminiscence."

D Exploring the Historical Period

Two Dictatorships Unite

Germany and Italy announced their "Axis" coalition on October 25, 1936, and then included Japan in an agreement made on November 25, 1936. The three countries solidified their forces and intentions with the Tripartite Pact, signed on September 27, 1940.

E Critical Thinking

Synthesizing

? What insights do these eight words provide, and how do they deepen your understanding of the historical period, with its rise of dictatorships? [Possible answers: This statement suggests there is nothing pretty, easy, or refined about revolution. The statement could be used to justify a ruthless efficiency or cruelty. It justifies or glorifies the kinds of radical thoughts and actions on which dictatorships often rest.]

Getting Students Involved

Enrichment Activity

Direct students' attention to the outline on this page. Assign each student—or a small group of students—one of the bulleted items, and ask them to regard it as the topic sentence in an essay about the twentieth century. Challenge students to develop the paragraph that would follow the topic sentence, reminding them to use explanatory sentences, as well as supporting facts and examples. When students have finished, have them share their paragraphs orally. Have the class vote on the best paragraph for each topic sentence. Then, call for a small group of volunteers to put these best paragraphs together in a well-crafted essay. The volunteer group should compose an introduction, a body, and a conclusion, using transitional elements in order to create a coherent class essay.

Responding to the Art

Henry Moore (1898–1986) was an important twentieth-century English sculptor. In his drawings, Moore created disturbing images that came out of his experiences in World War II. He drew Londoners hiding and waiting in underground shelters. These catacomb dwellers are haunting figures that seem neither dead nor alive. His renderings of the human form in the shelter drawings are more naturalistic than much of his other work, and he once said that he thought the war released his humanist impulses.

Activity. Ask students to make associations with Moore's shelterers. For example, does the drawing remind them of any other urban or contemporary scenes? What does the body language of the figures suggest about their emotions? What other words might students apply to the figures besides *apprehensive*?

Ⓐ Vocabulary Note
Word History

The word *Nazi* arose through the process of language change called *shortening*. (Students will read about this process on pp. 1176–1177.) A Nazi was a *nationalsozialist*—that is a member of the National Socialists, the fascist party controlling Germany from 1933 to 1945. (In German, the beginning of *national* sounds like *nazi*.)

Ⓑ Appreciating Language
Style

? This is one of the most famous speeches in history. What makes these lines so powerful, so compelling? [Possible answers: The most obvious device is repetition—in just eighty-one words, the clause *we shall fight* is repeated seven times. This places enormous weight on the collective pronoun *we* and on the shared identity and shared concerns of speaker and listeners. In its hypnotic repetition and in its recital of the list of places where the fight will go on, the speech gains a pounding momentum and becomes a rallying cry to a higher cause.]

Walter Hussey Bequest, Pallant House, Chichester, England. © The Henry Moore Foundation.

Two Apprehensive Shelterers (1942) by Henry Moore.

Ⓐ By 1939, the Nazis were sweeping through Europe with their motorized army and crack air force. Hitler's plan for the systematic destruction of the Jews and other minorities, scapegoats on whom he blamed Germany's economic woes, resulted in the deaths of millions of innocent men, women, and children—including the 6 million Jews who were killed in the Holocaust. Only twenty years after the "war to end all wars," Europe had again plunged into a bloody, brutal conflict. In 1940, Germany defeated France and then prepared to invade Britain by launching devastating air attacks against London and other cities. Prime Minister Winston Churchill declared: "We shall go on to the end." The British *did* persevere, but only after the Soviet Union and the United States entered the war did Germany's defeat become inevitable. In Japan, the war ended in the ultimate horror. On August 6, 1945, the entire city of Hiroshima was wiped out by a single atomic bomb dropped from an American plane. Small wonder, then, that much of the literature following the Second World War was dark and pessimistic.

Ⓑ We shall not flag or fail. We shall go on to the end, we shall fight in France, we shall fight on the seas and oceans, we shall fight with growing confidence and growing strength in the air, we shall defend our island, whatever the cost may be, we shall fight on the beaches, we shall fight on the landing grounds, we shall fight in the fields and in the streets, we shall fight in the hills; we shall never surrender.

—Sir Winston Churchill, June 4, 1940

The worldwide depression of the 1930s gave rise to dictatorships in Europe and led to the horrors of World War II.

Skill Link

Evaluating Sources of Information on the Net

Invite small groups of students to collaborate on an Internet search. Using their favorite search engine, have each group conduct a keyword search on one of the topics in this introduction. Ask them to print out a listing of the first twenty matches they find. Then, ask each group to divide up the work of evaluating those matches for credibility and usefulness by applying the following criteria:

1. Evaluate the site.
   - What kind of site is this? For example, is it government (gov), education (edu), or commercial (com)? What do these terms tell you about the site?
   - Who contributes information to this site?
2. Evaluate the authorship.
   - Is authorship stated? If so, who are the authors?

Britain After World War II: The Sun Sets on the Empire

After the war ended in Europe, Winston Churchill and his Conservative party were defeated by the Labour party, and Britain was transformed into a welfare state. The government assumed responsibility for providing medical care and other basic benefits for its citizens. While recovering from the war and rebuilding its own economy, Great Britain could not hold on to its many colonies. Most of them, including India, the "jewel in the crown," became independent nations, and the sun now sank nightly over the British Empire.

> Little do town dwellers know how the semistarved masses of India are slowly sinking to lifelessness. Little do they know that their miserable comfort represents the brokerage they get for the work they do for the foreign exploiter, that the profits and the brokerage are sucked from the masses. Little do they realize that the government established by law in British India is carried on for this exploitation of the masses. No sophistry, no jugglery in figures can explain away the evidence that the skeletons in many villages present to the naked eye. I have no doubt whatsoever that both England and the town dwellers of India will have to answer, if there is a God above, for this crime against humanity which is perhaps unequaled in history.
>
> —Mohandas K. Gandhi, 1922

In the spring of 1998, an end to thirty years of violent conflict over the status of the six British-controlled counties of Northern Ireland seemed near at hand. After years of fighting in the streets of Ulster and a bombing campaign by the Irish Republican Army (IRA) that at times extended into England, representatives of the Catholics and Protestants of Northern Ireland and the prime ministers of Great Britain and Ireland hammered out a promising formula for peace. An amazing 71 percent of the population of Northern Ireland and 94 percent of the population of the republic of Ireland voted yes in a referendum on the historic agreement on May 24, 1998.

After World War II, most of Great Britain's colonies became independent, and Britain's role in world affairs decreased.

British Writing Today: A Remarkable Diversity

Two of the most conspicuous literary figures in England before World War II were the poets W. H. Auden and Stephen Spender (see "Twentieth-Century British Poetry," pages 932–934). They shared a common intellectual background and a left-wing, antifascist political point of view. But after the war, a group of younger novelists and playwrights emerged who disliked the values of the Auden group. These writers, who became known as the Angry Young Men, criticized the pretensions of intellectuals and the bland lives of the newly prosperous middle class. One of the major works of the period was Kingsley Amis's novel *Lucky Jim* (1953), a scathing satire of British university life.

The period since the 1960s has been marked by great diversity, though it is still satire that the British excel at. Landmark novels published in Britain from the 1960s on include the sharp and witty novels of Muriel Spark (*The Prime of Miss Jean Brodie,* 1961), the moral and linguistic experiments of Anthony Burgess (*A Clockwork Orange,* 1963), the feminist novels of Margaret Drabble (*Gates of Ivory,* 1991), and the exuberant novels of Dubliner Roddy Doyle (*Paddy Clarke Ha Ha Ha,* 1993).

Skill Link (cont'd)

- What is their purpose in posting this information on the net?
- Are any credentials given? What are they?

3. Evaluate the information.
   - Is the information credited to a reliable source, such as a major newspaper, an established authority, or a well-known and established reference work?
   - Are any facts and statistics credited to reputable sources?
   - Are sources listed and fully documented?
4. Evaluate the writing.
   - Is the topic covered in a careful way, with biases either avoided or directly stated?
   - Does the work appear to have been edited—that is, is it grammatical, free from typos, and clearly written?
5. Decide for what purpose each source could be used or why it should be avoided. Explain.

C Background

Sir Winston Churchill

After the war, Sir Winston Churchill (1874–1965) served again as prime minister from 1951 to 1955, when he resigned. He was awarded the Nobel Prize in Literature in 1953 for his many writings, especially *The Second World War,* which comprises six volumes.

D Exploring the Historical Period

Independence for India

Call attention to the date of this quotation. Although full Indian independence was not achieved until 1947, the seeds of discontent were growing much earlier. In the Great War, well over a million Indians had fought on behalf of the British; in return, they were promised—and fully expected—a greater role in their own government. When this did not take place, acts of violence began. This led quickly to Gandhi's policy of civil disobedience and nonviolence, the strategy that eventually led to self-rule for India.

E Humanities Connections

Progress Toward Peace in Ireland

A few months after the referendum vote, John Hume, the Catholic head of the Social Democratic and Labor Party, and David Trimble, the Protestant leader of the Ulster Unionists, were awarded the 1998 Nobel Peace Prize.

F Literary Connections

Angry Young Men

The Angry Young Men criticized the institutional, the conventional, and the conforming. The upper classes were an invariable target of their criticism. Other Angry Young Men included Alan Sillitoe, who wrote about working-class life in the Midlands in *Saturday Night and Sunday Morning,* and John Braine, who wrote about social climbing in *Room at the Top.* Although a woman, Doris Lessing, author of *The Golden Notebook,* is sometimes included in this group.

G Literary Connections

A Clockwork Orange

This groundbreaking novel, popularized by Stanley Kubrick's 1971 film, is a dark satire directed against both liberal humanitarianism and totalitarianism. Its protagonist, a teenage thug, is emotionally neutered and behaviorally reconditioned into a benign but mechanical victim of social engineering.

Ⓐ Appreciating Language

Humor

? What makes this a particularly witty and quotable comment? [Possible answers: The statement is blatantly contradictory or oxymoronic: It pairs seriousness and humor. The statement itself relies on the dry wit (understated irony) associated with the English.]

Ⓑ Humanities Connections

Monty Python

Monty Python's Flying Circus is a nonsensical name taken by six performers: John Cleese, Graham Chapman, Eric Idle, Terry Gilliam, Terry Jones, and Michael Palin. In 1974, the troupe's BBC-TV shows (forty-five half-hour episodes) began airing in the United States on public television and today are considered cult classics.

Ⓒ Literary Connections

Multicultural Expression

These contemporary British writers from diverse backgrounds have often portrayed societies in transition, especially those former colonies in Asia, Africa, and other parts of the world that are struggling to maintain independence, encourage emerging democracy, and join the global economy. One writer who gained extreme and unwanted notoriety in 1989 was Salman Rushdie, whose novel *Satanic Verses* resulted in a threat on his life by militant Islamic groups. It was not until 1998 that the Iranian government finally withdrew this threat, enabling Rushdie to come out of hiding in London for the first time in more than nine years.

A CLOSER LOOK

DRY, DELICIOUS PARODY

Ⓐ *Humor is practically the only thing about which the English are utterly serious.*

—Malcolm Muggeridge

In "London Homesick Blues," the unamused American songwriter Gary P. Nunn offers to "substantiate the rumor that the English sense of humor is drier than the Texas sand." British humor is a source of national pride, although uncomprehending foreigners may not get the joke. Their comedy is notable for its ability to parody the national reputation for stiff-upper-lip reserve. For example, the novelist Sir P. G. Wodehouse mocks the notoriously poor traveling skills of British tourists, describing his character's "look of furtive shame, the shifty hangdog look which announces that an Englishman is about to talk French."

"Fabulous" silliness. British comedy revels in the ridiculous, and the television series *Absolutely Fabulous* brought that absurdity to its spoof of the fashion industry. American audiences clamored to see the ruthless fashion sitcom, even acquiring bootleg tapes of *AbFab* when no American network would buy the series.

Bubble: I've booked every model in the world. . . .
Edina: I know, darling, but what about the party?
Bubble: That is all completely under control. We've moved Stonehenge to a tent in Hyde Park.
Edina: Did you get permission for that, darling?
Bubble: They were very happy for us to use it, as long as it's back for the summer solstice. They realize how important the fashion industry is to this country.

When they recognized the program's devoted American followers, television officials aired *AbFab* in the United States. Yet, despite its success, one American public television official explained that his station does not buy British comedies because "most . . . are quite silly."

Ⓑ **Pythons and dead parrots.** The comedy troupe Monty Python's Flying Circus made silliness its specialty. In a scene well known to Python followers, a customer complains to a pet-shop proprietor that he has been sold a dead parrot. As the store owner ignores the obvious

An important development in the years since the war is the growing eminence of writers from Britain's former dependencies. One result of Great Britain's empire was the spread of English around the world. We are now seeing the effects of that linguistic dominance, with works written in English from the Caribbean (V. S. Naipaul, Derek Walcott), Africa (Doris Lessing, Wole Soyinka, Nadine Gordimer, Chinua Achebe, Ben Okri), and India (R. K. Narayan, Ruth Prawer Jhabvala, Salman Rushdie, Anita Desai). Ⓒ

Contemporary British literature is marked by great diversity, though satire is still a dominant mode.

World Literature: Writing from Afar Near at Hand

Though our world isn't really a global village, innovations in technology and transportation have linked us in ways our ancestors couldn't have imagined. Ideas travel as fast as myriad channels can carry them, and one writer may profoundly influence another living continents away. Today,

Getting Students Involved

Cooperative Learning

Have students work in groups of three to simulate an interview they could have conducted with "a person on the street" during one of the newsworthy events or periods mentioned in this essay: at the outbreak of World War I; during Hitler's rise to power; during the time Joyce's *Ulysses* was banned as obscene; or when Freud published *The Interpretation of Dreams*. Ask all three team members to write and revise interview questions and answers. Then two students can practice enacting the interview while a third directs and provides feedback. After students enact the interview for the class, each team member should write a self-assessment of his or her own contribution to the project, as well as an assessment of the success of the interview as a whole.

evidence, the exasperated customer finds increasingly imaginative ways to describe the dead bird.

> It's not pining. It's passed on. This parrot is no more. It has ceased to be. It's expired and gone to meet its maker. This is a late parrot. It's a stiff. Bereft of life, it rests in peace. If you hadn't nailed it to its perch, it would be pushing up the daisies. It's rung down the curtain and joined the choir invisible. This is an ex-parrot. (D)

The Pythons began their career by horrifying audiences with their bawdy, outrageous performances. Yet the parrot speech became so celebrated that the former prime minister Margaret Thatcher mentioned it in a political speech—which just goes to show that British humor is an acquired taste. (E)

A scene from *Monty Python's The Meaning of Life* (1983), with John Cleese, Terry Jones, and Eric Idle.
Globe Photos.

when important British, Asian, European, or Latin American authors write in their native languages, enterprising publishers have the work promptly translated for eager book buyers around the world. Thus, readers of English can go to bookstores or libraries and find translations of works by Naguib Mahfouz (Egyptian), Julio Cortázar (Argentine), Pablo Neruda (F) (Chilean), Aleksandr Solzhenitsyn (Russian), and hundreds of others.

> All paths lead to the same goal: to convey to others what we are. And we must pass through solitude and difficulty, isolation and silence, in order to reach forth to the enchanted place where we can dance our clumsy dance and sing our sorrowful song.
>
> —Pablo Neruda, on receiving the Nobel Prize in literature, 1971

Political concerns appear more often in current world literature than they have appeared in past British literature. The Nobel Prize–winner Aleksandr Solzhenitsyn, for example, has written much about human suffering and loss of freedom under the totalitarian government of the Soviet Union. Literally hundreds of writers from former British colonies explore the problems of personal identity and the effects of cultural domination and racism.

(D) Literary Connections

Allusions

The Pythons' humor is laden with allusions. Here, the phrase "choir invisible" refers to a poem by Victorian author George Eliot. The poem reads in part:

O may I join the choir invisible
Of those immortal dead who live
again
In minds made better by their
presence.

(E) English Language Learners

Idioms/Frozen Metaphors

Much of the language in this feature may be incomprehensible to English language learners. Be sure students understand the common, if informal, idiom *goes to show.* You might also explore some of the many euphemistic and idiomatic expressions for death, such as "pushing up daisies" and "meet [one's] maker," used in the excerpt from the Python sketch.

(F) Literary Connections

Pablo Neruda

Students may recall reading two of Neruda's sonnets (pp. 269–270) in Collection 3. Remind students that although they have read Neruda alongside Renaissance writers, his is very much a modern voice. You might also ask students to explain how this quotation, especially the second sentence, could be regarded as poetry written in prose.

Assessing Learning

Check Test: Short Answers

1. Which three nineteenth-century thinkers had an enormous impact on twentieth-century developments? [Charles Darwin, Karl Marx, and Sigmund Freud]
2. What similar political development occurred in Italy, Germany, and Russia before World War II? [Dictators rose to power.]
3. What quality characterizes the important works of art of the twentieth century before World War II? [experimentation]
4. What attitude is conveyed by most works of British literature just after World War II? [pessimism]
5. What are some of the reasons for contemporary British literature's amazing diversity? [the influence of different social and philosophical movements; the influx of literature from Britain's former colonies; innovations in technology and communication; and the effects of various political concerns]

Responding to the Art

Penelope Beaton (1886–1963) is one of Scotland's most celebrated artists. In this painting, Beaton uses the flat planes and decorative style reminiscent of Matisse (see p. 916) to present a quiet, domestic scene.

Activity. Ask students whether the image of a traditional English tea time fits with their conception of modern Britain. How does the painting point to the preservation of the old in the face of the new? Can students name other customs or national habits that still characterize the British people?

(A) Humanities Connections

The "Raw Struggle"

The United Nations Human Development Report of 1998 reflects the raw struggle of the have-nots. *The New York Times* summed up some of the UN facts in this way: "Of the 4.4 billion people in developing countries, nearly three-fifths lack access to safe sewers, a third have no access to clean water, a quarter do not have adequate housing, and a fifth have no access to modern health services of any kind." Meanwhile, "the world's 225 richest individuals . . . have a combined wealth of over one trillion dollars—equal to the annual income of the poorest 47 percent of the entire world's population."

Quickwrite

Suggest that students use a three-column chart to organize their thoughts. In the first column, students can list types of creative expression, such as poetry, films, comic books, best-selling fiction, painting, performance art, and dance. In the second column, they can list one or more specific examples of each type of creative work. In the third column, students can reflect on what these works reflect about our society and our times.

Tea Time (20th century) by Penelope Beaton.

Photograph by kind permission of Waterman Fine Art Ltd., St. James, London.

(A) And many writers in developing nations, to whom the niceties of Western living are foreign, document their raw struggle for existence. Such a variety of writing can only broaden and deepen our understanding of the human condition. As Solzhenitsyn said in his Nobel Prize acceptance speech, "The only substitute for what we ourselves have not experienced is art and literature. They have the marvelous capacity of transmitting from one nation to another—despite differences in language, customs, and social structure—practical experience, the harsh national experience of many decades never tasted by the other nation."

Twentieth-century technology has made an extraordinary amount of world literature available to readers around the world.

Quickwrite

Throughout the first half of this century, writers and artists responded to the general disillusionment of the times. Many works portrayed a civilization in ruins, traditional beliefs and morals challenged. What do you think the artistic expression of our day—from television to painting, music to comic books—reveals about our own society? List a few examples; then jot down some ideas about how our art and entertainment reflect where we are today.

The Center Cannot Hold

Theme

Things Fall Apart *In the first half of the twentieth century, two world wars devastated not only the landscape but human psyches as well. The psychological dislocation caused by the wars was compounded by the work of Freud, Marx, and Darwin, which seemed to prove that the old certainties no longer had meaning or power to comfort. The literature of this period mirrors a sense of loss, confusion, and despair. The dominant mode is irony.*

Reading the Anthology

Reaching Struggling Readers

The *Reading Skills and Strategies: Reaching Struggling Readers* binder includes a Reading Strategies Handbook that offers concrete suggestions to help students who have difficulty reading and comprehending text or students who are reluctant readers. When a specific strategy is most appropriate for a selection, a correlation to the Handbook is provided at the bottom of the teacher's page under the head Struggling Readers. This head may also be used to introduce additional ideas for helping students read challenging texts.

Reading Beyond the Anthology

Read On

At the end of the Twentieth Century collections, the grade twelve book includes an annotated bibliography of books suitable for extended reading. The suggested books are related to works in these collections by theme, by author, or by subject. To preview the Read On for this period, please turn to p. T1174.

HRW Library

The *HRW Library* offers novels, plays, and short-story collections for extended reading. Each book in the Library includes a major work and thematically or topically related Connections. The Connections are magazine articles, poems, or other pieces of literature. Each book in the *HRW Library* is also accompanied by a Study Guide that provides teaching suggestions and worksheets. The two titles shown here will work well to extend the theme of Collection 12.

THINGS FALL APART
Chinua Achebe

In the 1890s, Okonkwo, an Ibo leader, survives a seven-year exile but returns to discover that the British have assumed control of his village. Okonkwo's support for the traditional culture and values of the tribe brings him into conflict with other villagers and British colonial officials.

Collection 12 The Center Cannot Hold

Resources for this Collection

Note: All resources for this collection are available for preview on the *One-Stop Planner CD-ROM 2 with Test Generator.* All worksheets and blackline masters may be printed from the CD-ROM.

Internet Resources
go.hrw.com LE0 12-12

Selection or Feature	Reading and Literary Skills	Vocabulary, Language, and Grammar
The Rear-Guard (p. 924) Siegfried Sassoon **Dulce et Decorum Est** (p. 929) Wilfred Owen **Spotlight On: Twentieth-Century British Poetry** (p. 932) John Malcolm Brinnin	• *Graphic Organizers for Active Reading,* Worksheet p. 91	• *Grammar and Language Links:* Diction, Worksheet p. 51
World Literature: Spain **La Guitarra/The Guitar** (p. 936) Federico García Lorca *translated by* Robert Bly *and* Elizabeth du Gué Trapier	The World Literature feature offers students the opportunity to explore thematically linked literature from different world cultures. Structured activities called Finding Common Ground are provided in the Pupil's Edition to guide students' explorations of these thematic connections between British and other world literature.	
World Literature: Russia **Lot's Wife** (p. 945) Anna Akhmatova *translated by* Richard Wilbur	The World Literature feature offers students the opportunity to explore thematically linked literature from different world cultures. Structured activities called Finding Common Ground are provided in the Pupil's Edition to guide students' explorations of these thematic connections between British and other world literature.	
The Destructors (p. 948) Graham Greene	• *Graphic Organizers for Active Reading,* Worksheet p. 92 • *Literary Elements:* Transparency 22 Worksheet p. 67	• *Words to Own,* Worksheet p. 25 • *Grammar and Language Links:* End Punctuation, Worksheet p. 53 • *Language Workshop CD-ROM,* Using End Marks • *Daily Oral Grammar,* Transparency 31
• **Hawk Roosting** (p. 960) • **Chaucer** (p. 962) Ted Hughes	• *Graphic Organizers for Active Reading,* Worksheet p. 93	
World Literature: Russia • **Freedom to Breathe** (p. 965) • **The Bonfire and the Ants** (p. 966) Aleksandr Solzhenitsyn *translated by* Michael Glenny	The World Literature feature offers students the opportunity to explore thematically linked literature from different world cultures. Structured activities called Finding Common Ground are provided in the Pupil's Edition to guide students' explorations of these thematic connections between British and other world literature.	
World Literature: Vietnam **Thoughts of Hanoi** (p. 968) Nguyen Thi Vinh *translated by* Nguyen Ngoc Bich	The World Literature feature offers students the opportunity to explore thematically linked literature from different world cultures. Structured activities called Finding Common Ground are provided in the Pupil's Edition to guide students' explorations of these thematic connections between British and other world literature.	
In the Shadow of War (p. 970) Ben Okri **Connections: Zagreb: A Letter to My Daughter** (p. 974) Slavenka Drakulíc	• *Graphic Organizers for Active Reading,* Worksheet p. 94	• *Words to Own,* Worksheet p. 26 • *Grammar and Language Links:* Dangling and Misplaced Modifiers, Worksheet p. 55 • *Language Workshop CD-ROM,* Misplaced or Dangling Modifiers • *Daily Oral Grammar,* Transparency 32

Other Resources for this Collection

- *Cross-Curricular Activities*, p. 12
- *Portfolio Management System*, Introduction to Portfolio Assessment, p. 1
- *Test Generator*, Collection Test
- *Formal Assessment*, Literary Period Introduction Test, p. 185

Writing	Listening and Speaking Viewing and Representing	Assessment
• *Portfolio Management System*, Rubrics for Choices, p. 185	• *Audio CD Library*, Disc 16, Tracks 2, 3 • *Viewing and Representing:* Fine Art Transparency 15 Worksheet p. 60 • *Portfolio Management System*, Rubrics for Choices, p. 185	• *Formal Assessment*, Selection Test, p. 187 • *Test Generator (One-Stop Planner CD-ROM)*
	• *Audio CD Library*, Disc 16, Tracks 4, 5, 6	
	• *Audio CD Library*, Disc 16, Track 7	
• *Portfolio Management System*, Rubrics for Choices, p. 187	• *Audio CD Library*, Disc 16, Track 8 • *Portfolio Management System*, Rubrics for Choices, p. 187	• *Formal Assessment*, Selection Test, p. 189 • *Test Generator (One-Stop Planner CD-ROM)* • *Preparation for College Admission Exams*, p. 45
• *Portfolio Management System*, Rubrics for Choices, p. 188	• *Audio CD Library*, Disc 16, Tracks 9, 10 • *Portfolio Management System*, Rubrics for Choices, 188	• *Formal Assessment*, Selection Test, p. 191 • *Test Generator (One-Stop Planner CD-ROM)*
	• *Audio CD Library*, Disc 16, Tracks 11, 12	
	• *Audio CD Library*, Disc 16, Track 13	
• *Portfolio Management System*, Rubrics for Choices, p. 190	• *Audio CD Library*, Disc 16, Track 14 • *Portfolio Management System*, Rubrics for Choices, p. 190	• *Formal Assessment*, Selection Test, p. 193 • *Test Generator (One-Stop Planner CD-ROM)* • *Preparation for College Admission Exams*, p. 47

Transparency CD-ROM Video Audio CD

Collection 12 The Center Cannot Hold

Skills Focus

Selection or Feature	Reading Skills and Strategies	Elements of Literature and Language	Writing	Listening and Speaking	Viewing and Representing
The Rear-Guard (p. 924) Siegfried Sassoon **Dulce et Decorum Est** (p. 929) Wilfred Owen		Oxymoron, pp. 924, 927, 930 Onomatopoeia, p. 927 Irony, p. 927 Rhyme Scheme, p. 930 Half Rhyme, p. 930 Simile, p. 930 Theme, pp. 930–931 Tone, pp. 930–931 Imagery, p. 931 Structure, p. 931 Sound Devices, p. 931 Figurative Language, p. 931	Identify Possible Topics for Research, p. 931 Write an Essay Comparing and Contrasting Two Poems, p. 931 Write an Essay Evaluating a Poet's Stance, p. 931 Write an Essay Comparing and Contrasting Two Poems About War, p. 931 Write an Essay Analyzing the Way Elements in a Painting Create an Overall Effect, p. 931		Analyze the Elements of a Painting, p. 931
World Literature: Spain **La Guitarra** (p. 936) **The Guitar** (p. 937) Federico García Lorca *translated by* Robert Bly *and* Elizabeth du Gué Trapier	Compare Translations, p. 937	The World Literature feature offers students the opportunity to explore thematically linked literature from different world cultures. Structured activities called Finding Common Ground are provided in the Pupil's Edition to guide students' explorations of these thematic connections between British and other world literature.			
World Literature: Russia **Lot's Wife** (p. 945) Anna Akhmatova	Draw on Personal Experience, pp. 945–946	The World Literature feature offers students the opportunity to explore thematically linked literature from different world cultures. Structured activities called Finding Common Ground are provided in the Pupil's Edition to guide students' explorations of these thematic connections between British and other world literature.			
The Destructors (p. 948) Graham Greene	Inferring Motives, pp. 948, 959	Setting, pp. 948, 959 Motive, p. 959 Irony, p. 959 Image, p. 959 Atmosphere, p. 959 Theme, p. 959	Determine Basic Research Questions and Resources, p. 959 Write an Essay Interpreting a Central Image, p. 959	Prepare and Present Oral Arguments, p. 959 Evaluate Oral Arguments, p. 959	
Hawk Roosting (p. 960) **Chaucer** (p. 962) Ted Hughes	Paraphrase, p. 963	Personification, pp. 960, 963 Image, p. 963 Theme, p. 963 Tone, p. 963 Sound Structure, p. 963	Develop Research Questions, p. 963 Write an Analysis of a Poem's Theme, p. 963 Write an Essay Comparing Views of Nature, p. 963 Write an Essay Comparing "Chaucer" with a Renaissance Love Poem, p. 963		
World Literature: Russia **Freedom to Breathe** (p. 965) **The Bonfire and the Ants** (p. 966) Aleksandr Solzhenitsyn		Allegory, p. 966	The World Literature feature offers students the opportunity to explore thematically linked literature from different world cultures. Structured activities called Finding Common Ground are provided in the Pupil's Edition to guide students' explorations of these thematic connections between British and other world literature.		
World Literature: Vietnam **Thoughts of Hanoi** (p. 968) Nguyen Thi Vinh	The World Literature feature offers students the opportunity to explore thematically linked literature from different world cultures. Structured activities called Finding Common Ground are provided in the Pupil's Edition to guide students' explorations of these thematic connections between British and other world literature.				
In the Shadow of War (p. 970) Ben Okri	Analyzing the Time Frame, p. 970	Point of View, p. 970 Limited Third-Person Point of View, pp. 970, 976 Motive, p. 976 Symbol, p. 976	Identify Research Topics, p. 976 Write an Essay Analyzing a Central Symbol, p. 976 Write an Essay Comparing Thematic Development in Diverse Works, p. 976		

Collection 12 THE CENTER CANNOT HOLD

Sassoon	Greene
Owen	Hughes
Lorca	Solzhenitsyn
Eliot	Nguyen
Akhmatova	Okri

The title of this poem refers to a prophecy that Jesus will return to earth one day and usher in an era of peace. The First Coming was the birth of Jesus in Bethlehem two thousand years ago. The theme is introduced in the first two lines: A falconer is unable to control his hawk as it spirals out of control. This poem was written after the horrors of World War I. Yeats asks: Have we, like the falconer, lost control of the means to halt our descent into chaos?

The Second Coming

Turning and turning in the widening gyre
The falcon cannot hear the falconer;
Things fall apart; the center cannot hold;
Mere anarchy is loosed upon the world,
The blood-dimmed tide is loosed, and everywhere
The ceremony of innocence is drowned;
The best lack all conviction, while the worst
Are full of passionate intensity.

Surely some revelation is at hand;
Surely the Second Coming is at hand.
The Second Coming! Hardly are those words out
When a vast image out of Spiritus Mundi
Troubles my sight: somewhere in sands of the desert
A shape with lion body and the head of a man,
A gaze blank and pitiless as the sun,
Is moving its slow thighs, while all about it
Reel shadows of the indignant desert birds.
The darkness drops again; but now I know
That twenty centuries of stony sleep
Were vexed to nightmare by a rocking cradle,
And what rough beast, its hour come round at last,
Slouches towards Bethlehem to be born?

—William Butler Yeats

OBJECTIVES

1. Read literature from the twentieth century on the theme of "The Center Cannot Hold"
2. Interpret literary elements used in the literature
3. Apply a variety of reading strategies
4. Respond to the literature in a variety of modes
5. Learn and use new words
6. Plan, draft, and revise an informative report

Responding to the Poem

? What is the overall feeling you get from reading this poem? Which images help create that feeling for you? [Possible response: The poem evokes a feeling of fear and horror. This results from the vivid, apocalyptic imagery of a blood-dimmed tide, the Sphinx getting up and walking, and the shadows of dark, predatory birds reeling in the desert sky. It also comes from the images of darkness falling and the "rough beast," which has monstrous, threatening connotations. The poem is full of prophecy and portent, suggesting the end of the world.]

RESPONDING TO THE ART

Students will probably recognize the Sphinx; be sure they link it with Yeats's lines: "A shape with lion body and the head of a man, / A gaze blank and pitiless as the sun."

Activity. Invite students to discuss the use of this image suddenly moving "in sands of the desert" to evoke a wordless horror.

Writing Focus: An Informative Report

WORK IN PROGRESS

The following **Work in Progress** assignments build to a culminating **Writer's Workshop** at the end of Collection 13.

• Sassoon's and Owen's poems	Take notes on topics suggested by poems (p. 931)
• The Destructors	Explore topic using 5W-How? (p. 959)
• Hughes's poems	Note how poetry subject could be approached in informative paper (p. 963)
• In the Shadow of War	Note questions raised by story (p. 976)

Writer's Workshop: Expository Writing / An Informative Report (p. 1053)

OBJECTIVES

The Rear-Guard / Dulce et Decorum Est

1. Read and interpret the poems
2. Identify and interpret oxymorons
3. Express understanding through comparing and contrasting poems, evaluating a poet's stance, and analyzing and writing about art

Literary

- Identify and interpret oxymorons

Writing

- Collect ideas for an informative report
- Compare and contrast poems
- Evaluate a poet's stance

Art

- Analyze art

Viewing/Representing

- Relate artistic representations of historical events to themes conveyed in poetry (ATE)

Planning

- **Block Schedule**
  Block Scheduling Lesson Plans with Pacing Guide
- **Traditional Schedule**
  Lesson Plans Including Strategies for English-Language Learners
- **One-Stop Planner**
  CD-ROM with Test Generator

Before You Read
THE REAR-GUARD
DULCE ET DECORUM EST

Make the Connection

No Man's Land

In war, *no man's land* is the few hundred yards that separate one army's lines from another's. But for the group of writers who became known as the Trench Poets, war itself became a no man's land: a dehumanizing, horrific experience that made a mockery of civilization. Each of the Trench Poets either died in the muddy trenches of World War I (as Wilfred Owen did) or survived as a bitter but articulate ghost trapped by memories from which there was no escape (see page 932).

Quickwrite

During World War I, it was poetry that first brought home war's full brutality to many English people. Today people who have never been in battle see vivid images of war in movies and newspapers or on TV.

What is your most vivid mental image of war's horror? Recall impressions you've absorbed from film, photographs, the nightly news, what veterans have told you, literary works, or other sources. Close your eyes, think "war," and then record, in words, what you saw in your mind.

Elements of Literature

The Oxymoron

Have you ever had a bittersweet moment, a moment when you felt happy and sad at the same time? The word *bittersweet* is an example of an **oxymoron,** a figure of speech that combines apparently contradictory ideas to create a strong emphasis. Other oxymorons common in ordinary speech are *cold comfort, honest thief,* and *tough love.* In literature, "darkness visible" is a famous example from Milton. The Trench Poets found oxymorons useful in describing the unimaginable slaughter of trench warfare.

An **oxymoron** is a figure of speech that combines apparently contradictory ideas.

For more on Oxymorons, see the Handbook of Literary Terms.

The Menin Road, 1919 by Paul Nash.

Imperial War Museum, London.

Resources: Print and Media

Reading

- *Graphic Organizers for Active Reading*, p. 91
- *Audio CD Library*
  Disc 16, Tracks 2, 3

Writing and Language

- *Grammar and Language Links* Worksheet, p. 51

Viewing and Representing

- *Viewing and Representing*
  Fine Art Transparency 15
  Fine Art Worksheet, p. 60

Assessment

- *Formal Assessment*, p. 187
- *Portfolio Management System*, p. 185
- *Test Generator (One-Stop Planner CD-ROM)*

Internet

- go.hrw.com (keyword: LE0 12-12)

Siegfried Sassoon

(1886–1967)

Siegfried Sassoon was born into that high level of English society at which lifelong privilege is sustained by income from landed estates and assured inheritances. Educated at Cambridge University, and under no pressure to adopt a profession, he lived the life of a country gentleman until the outbreak of World War I. Along with the pursuit of leisure—which he would later write about in a famous book called *Memoirs of a Fox-Hunting Man* (1928)—Sassoon also wrote poetry. He had sufficient skill to win a place in the anthologies of the Georgian movement, in which the value of all things English was celebrated—from scones and honey at teatime to the bells of Winchester Cathedral.

Siegfried Sassoon (1915). Photograph by Beresford.

The war would change all that. For Sassoon, it would also lead to a career entirely at odds with his earlier expectations. Enlisting in the army as a patriot and an idealist determined to put an end to "Teutonic barbarism," he distinguished himself as an officer and was awarded a prestigious medal for bravery under fire. But, within two years of his enlistment, Sassoon's attitude toward the war underwent a change amounting to a total reversal of his earlier commitment. His new attitude was expressed in stark, almost savage poems detailing the brutality and debasement of trench warfare. The publication of these bitter testaments sent a shock wave of doubt through the minds of the English (among them, Winston Churchill, then minister of munitions, whose secretary, Edward Marsh, was the leader of the comforting Georgian poets and their most outspoken publicist).

Dissatisfied even with the depth of response his poems evoked, Sassoon wrote to the war department to protest a war he now believed was "being deliberately prolonged by those who have the power to end it." In a statement handed to his commanding officer, which Sassoon himself regarded as "an act of willful defiance," he spelled out his disillusionment: "I believe that this war, upon which I entered as a war of defense and liberation, has now become a war of aggression and conquest."

Expecting court-martial, and entirely prepared to sacrifice himself for his own cause, Sassoon was thwarted by the unsolicited and unwanted kindness of some of his friends, notably the poet Robert Graves, who shunted him toward a medical board of examiners. Diagnosed as shellshocked, Sassoon was committed to a military hospital in Scotland. There he met fellow patient Wilfred Owen, and the two began one of the most famous and mutually beneficial relationships in modern literature.

Disgust controlled by irony gives Sassoon's war poems their indelible imprint; the poems stand by themselves in an otherwise pedestrian career marked by one great parenthesis—the Great War itself.

Summary

During the grim trench warfare of World War I, a British officer, weary and irritable from lack of sleep, prowls a tunnel fifty feet below ground while a battle rages overhead. He is in search of his headquarters, guided only by a flashlight. He trips over a soldier and becomes abusive when the soldier does not respond to his demand for directions. Then the officer realizes that the soldier has been dead for days. Horrified, the officer continues moving until he finds a stairway lit by a shaft of dawn's light and makes his way above ground.

Browsing in the Files

Writers on Writing. Remarking on the lightheartedness and success of a fellow poet, Siegfried Sassoon once wrote in his diary: "For him literature is a glorious game. For me it is a struggle against disillusionment and disgust." Sassoon's greatest struggle, of course, was against the war, and he was aware that his pen was his best weapon. To Wilfred Owen (see p. 928) he gave his best advice on writing: "Sweat your guts out writing poetry! Sweat your guts out, I say!" Owen was understandably impressed, not only by the man (whose "general expression," he noted, was "one of boredom") but by the poet, about whose work Owen remarked: "There is nothing better this century can offer. . . ."

Reaching All Students

Struggling Readers

Build background by reading aloud the headnote on p. 926 and asking students to imagine what it would be like to be alone in such darkness, day after day and night after night, with the sounds of battle raging overhead. Then ask students to predict what the "grisly trench episode," referred to in the last sentence of the headnote, might be.

English Language Learners

For both poems, have students use a chart to record *who, what, where,* and *when.*

Advanced Learners

Challenge students to learn more about the Hindenburg Line and the progress or stalemate of the war in April 1917. Ask them to relate what they find out to the content of this poem and to report back to the class.

Resources

Viewing and Representing

Fine Art Transparency

Gassed, a painting by John Singer Sargent (1856–1925), shows the horror of one of the new weapons that made World War I so tragic. See *Viewing and Representing Transparencies and Worksheets:*

- Transparency 15
- Worksheet 60

(A) English Language Learners

Specialized Vocabulary

Students may not know what a military rear-guard is. Ask a volunteer to explain. [A rear-guard is a detachment of troops that protects the rear of a military force.] Ask students what this word suggests. [Possible answer: It suggests traditional battle formations, above the ground, in which one large group of soldiers is protected by another.] Note that the wartime setting of this poem is not the one of traditional, open battle and visible military formations but an underground one in which an isolated individual gropes his way along dark tunnels.

(B) Elements of Literature

The Oxymoron

? Why is "rosy gloom" an oxymoron, and what effect does it have on you as a reader? [Possible answer: The word *rosy* is usually cheerful, but it is contradicted by the word *gloom*. The use of this oxymoron is disturbing because it suggests a sky lit by explosives.]

(C) Critical Thinking

Drawing Conclusions

? Why does the soldier respond so violently to the "sleeper"? [Possible responses: He is disoriented and exhausted from days of no sleep and is both desperate and afraid; he is obviously used to giving orders and has no time for someone who is sleeping on the job.]

(D) Critical Thinking

Interpreting

? Where is the officer now headed, and how does he feel about it? How is this ironic? [Possible responses: He is heading above ground and feels relief at leaving "hell behind him." The experience underground almost makes the light of battle seem "rosy" by comparison. The relief he feels is ironic, however, since he is emerging into an aboveground world of battle and terror.]

In the battlefield trenches of World War I, enlisted men lived for weeks, sometimes years, in interconnected underground caverns infested by rats, with no drainage, poor ventilation, and only occasional dim shafts of natural light. In this poem, the "he" who recalls a grisly trench episode is the officer-poet, Siegfried Sassoon himself.

(A) The Rear-Guard

Siegfried Sassoon

(Hindenburg Line,° April 1917.)

Groping along the tunnel, step by step,
He winked his prying torch° with patching glare
From side to side, and sniffed the unwholesome air.

Tins, boxes, bottles, shapes too vague to know,
A mirror smashed, the mattress from a bed;
And he, exploring fifty feet below
(B) The rosy gloom of battle overhead.

Tripping, he grabbed the wall; saw someone lie
Humped at his feet, half-hidden by a rug,
And stooped to give the sleeper's arm a tug.
(C) "I'm looking for headquarters." No reply.
"God blast your neck!" (For days he'd had no sleep.)

"Get up and guide me through this stinking place."
Savage, he kicked a soft, unanswering heap,
And flashed his beam across the livid face
Terribly glaring up, whose eyes yet wore
Agony dying hard ten days before;
And fists of fingers clutched a blackening wound.

Alone he staggered on until he found
Dawn's ghost that filtered down a shafted stair
To the dazed, muttering creatures underground
Who hear the boom of shells in muffled sound.
(D) At last, with sweat of horror in his hair,
He climbed through darkness to the twilight air,
Unloading hell behind him step by step.

Hindenburg Line: German defensive barricade running across northern France. It was made of massive barbed-wire entanglements and deep trenches.
2. torch: flashlight.

Using Students' Strengths

Kinesthetic Learners

Encourage students to stage or recreate "The Rear-Guard" as a vignette. Players might include a narrator, the officer, and the dead man. Simple props, such as a flashlight and something giving the appearance of a tunnel, could be used. Remind students to evoke both the outward horror of the setting and the inward horror that the officer experiences.

Musical/Auditory Learners

Both "The Rear-Guard" and "Dulce et Decorum Est" use rhythm and rhyme. What do these musical elements add to, or take away from, one or both poems? Invite students to listen to the music of each poem as they read it aloud. Ask them to determine the ways in which the rhythms carry the reader forward and complement or contradict the message. Then ask them to prepare a dramatic reading of one or both poems that accents musical and metrical qualities.

Imperial War Museum, London.

Oppy Wood, 1917 by John Northcote Nash.

Making Meanings

First Thoughts

1. What did you feel when you finished this poem? What do you think the poet *wanted* you to feel?

Shaping Interpretations

2. Why is the man in the tunnel, and what happens there? How is the man's behavior simultaneously brutal and pathetic?
3. Where does **onomatopoeia** help you hear the sounds in the tunnel? What **oxymoron** does the poet use to describe the battle overhead?
4. The poet uses many strong present and past participles, such as *groping, prying, smashed,* and *humped*. What do these words help you *see*?
5. Explain the **irony** of what the speaker says in line 13.
6. How do you interpret the phrase "unloading hell" in line 25?

Connecting with the Text

7. How do the images in "The Rear-Guard" compare with your own mental pictures of war? (Recall what you recorded in your Quickwrite notes on page 924.) Are visual depictions of war more or less powerful than verbal descriptions—like the ones in Sassoon's poem?

Connecting with the Text [Evaluate]

7. Possible response: Students may say that the images in the poem mirror their ideas of war but that the poem is a detailed and personal account that they could not create. Students may say that a visual depiction of war more immediately expresses war's horrors, while words or phrases may endure longer in a reader's memory.

Responding to the Art

In this painting, **John Nash** (1893–1977) uses sharply defined forms and simplified coloring to create an image of war as something primitive and elemental. **Activity.** Have students compare and contrast this work with the work by the artist's brother on p. 924. How are their styles similar and different? Which portrayal is more realistic? Which is more haunting? Which has a greater effect on the viewer?

Making Meanings

First Thoughts [Respond]

1. Students may feel horror, shock, disgust, and sadness; these reactions square with the poet's intent.

Shaping Interpretations [Interpret]

2. The man is a soldier looking for headquarters, but he is lost in the dark tunnel and asks a huddled figure to direct him. When he gets no response, the man brutally curses and kicks the man, assuming that he is asleep. This action is revealed as pathetic because the man is not sleeping—he is dead.
3. In l. 22, the tunnel echoes with the "boom" of war overhead. The battle is described by the oxymoron "rosy gloom" in l. 7.
4. The reader may visualize the soldier "groping" in the darkness of the passageway making fumbling attempts to navigate it; the "prying," or disturbing, light of the flashlight; the "smashed" mirrors in bits and pieces; and the "humped" position of the fallen, swollen, and decomposing corpse. These verbs strongly depict specific actions and physical states.
5. The officer is asking a dead man to guide him.
6. "Hell" is the trench and death; "Unloading hell" means casting it off, if only temporarily, by ascending the stair and leaving the grisly scene.

Summary ■■

The speaker is marching with a group of battle-weary soldiers when a poison-gas shell explodes nearby. The soldiers scramble to don their gas masks, but one fails, and the others watch helplessly while the fumes choke him to death. The speaker says that, in all his dreams, he still sees the man dying. Then, he directly addresses the reader, asserting that if "you" could see that too, you would not teach children the vicious lie that it is sweet and honorable to die for one's country.

Browsing in the Files

About the Author. In France, Wilfred Owen gathered together his first poetic efforts under the title *Minor Poems—in Minor Keys—by a Minor.* Though the poems were never published, the title provides insight into Owen's humble sense of humor and his enthusiasm for poetry. When he became friends with Siegfried Sassoon (see p. T925) in June 1917, Owen's understanding of poetry and his writing style underwent an extremely rapid maturation. But Owen was to enjoy the height of his creative powers for only a short time; he was killed in action in the autumn of the following year. During that brief period, he composed some of the most poignant war poems in English literature. A volume of his poetry was published posthumously by Siegfried Sassoon.

Wilfred Owen

(1893–1918)

Wilfred Owen is one of the most poignant figures in modern literature. "The Poetry is in the pity," he said, and this famous remark could serve as his epitaph. Within the few adult years granted to him, Owen pursued a course of development that went from strength to strength. His interest in experimental techniques led him to master the use of half rhyme; this would become his most easily recognizable poetic signature. He also had a gift for lyricism that was bitterly tempered by "the truth untold, / The pity of war, the pity war distilled." The result was a series of elegies and metrical statements as terse and stark as those carved on tombstones.

Wilfred Owen.

Like an apprentice determined to master his art, Owen immersed himself in the long history of English poetry. He chose for his model and mentor the poet John Keats, whose astonishing life's work ended with his death at twenty-five (about the same age Shakespeare was when he began to write his plays). As a tutor in France for two years, Owen studied the French poets who were producing the tradition-shattering art that would become known as modernist. But all these literary influences were to become secondary to the devastating impact of a war Owen witnessed firsthand.

World War I broke out when Owen was twenty-one; he joined the British army, and the course of his life was determined. His progress in poetry was not made in the arcades of an ancient university or in the pastoral retreats where his literary forerunners were privileged to pursue their careers. His progress took place in the muddy purgatory of trench warfare and in the twilight existence of military hospitals.

In one of those hospitals, Craiglockhart, in Edinburgh, the young Owen met Siegfried Sassoon, a fellow officer and poet who had already distinguished himself for bravery in battle. Ironically, Sassoon was also the author of some of the most biting antiwar verses ever written. Temperamentally, the two men were far apart. Owen was an idealistic youth thwarted by circumstance; Sassoon was an aristocrat appalled by the wartime complacency of his own class. Even so, they became friends and artistic colleagues at once. After Owen's death, Sassoon became the first important British writer to herald the younger man's genius and to call attention to what he had accomplished under the most appalling conditions. By that time, events had told the sad story.

In 1918, Owen was listed among those killed in action—a mere seven days before the war ended with a joyous ringing of bells and dancing in the streets.

go.hrw.com
LEO 12-12

Professional Notes

Critical Comment: War Poet Rupert Brooke

In Choices on p. 931, students will read a poem by Rupert Brooke, who conveyed an entirely different attitude toward war. According to critic Harry Blamires, Brooke expressed the public mood of hope and lofty idealism that characterized England at the beginning of the war. He says that "[f]or Brooke personally the war supplied a central and moral purpose and a focus for self-transcendence that rescued him from complex neurotic conflicts. Thus his rhetoric distanced human sacrifice from the realities of the battlefield and was seized upon by a public hungrier for heady heroics than for nearer acquaintance with grief. The final sonnet, 'The Soldier,' . . . summed up a mood of dedication to England which the poet's early death rendered poignantly unanswerable."

This poem's title is taken from the Latin statement *Dulce et decorum est pro patria mori,* meaning "It is sweet and honorable to die for one's country." The statement originally appeared in an ode by the ancient Roman poet Horace and has been used for centuries as a morale builder—and an epitaph—for soldiers. Here the motto is given a bitter twist by a soldier-poet who cannot reconcile the thought it expresses with the reality he has experienced.

After the introduction of poison gas as a battlefield weapon during World War I, every man in the trenches was equipped with a gas mask: lifesaving armor, if donned in time. This poem describes the horrible consequences of not getting the mask on promptly.

Dulce et Decorum Est

Wilfred Owen

Bent double, like old beggars under sacks,
Knock-kneed, coughing like hags, we cursed through sludge,
Till on the haunting flares we turned our backs
And toward our distant rest began to trudge.
Men marched asleep. Many had lost their boots
But limped on, blood-shod. All went lame; all blind;
Drunk with fatigue; deaf even to the hoots
Of tired, outstripped Five-Nines° that dropped behind.

Gas! GAS! Quick, boys!—An ecstasy of fumbling,
Fitting the clumsy helmets just in time;
But someone still was yelling out and stumbling
And flound'ring like a man in fire or lime . . .
Dim, through the misty panes and thick green light,
As under a green sea, I saw him drowning.

In all my dreams, before my helpless sight,
He plunges at me, guttering, choking, drowning.

If in some smothering dreams you too could pace
Behind the wagon that we flung him in,
And watch the white eyes writhing in his face,
His hanging face, like a devil's sick of sin;
If you could hear, at every jolt, the blood
Come gargling from the froth-corrupted lungs,
Obscene as cancer, bitter as the cud
Of vile, incurable sores on innocent tongues,—
My friend, you would not tell with such high zest
To children ardent for some desperate glory,
The old Lie: *Dulce et decorum est*
Pro patria mori.

IT IS SWEET AND HONORABLE TO DIE FOR ONE'S COUNTRY

8. Five-Nines: gas shells measuring 5.9 inches each.

A Struggling Readers

Visualizing

? **What do you see in your mind's eye as you read these first two lines?** [Possible response: a group of soldiers with packs on their backs, bent over like old men, coughing and cursing, as they try to move through mud.] **Challenge students to compare this image with the (then) more traditional sight of upright soldiers marching in formation.**

B Elements of Literature

The Oxymoron/Hyperbole

? **In order to show the horror of war, Owen uses oxymorons and hyperbole, or gross exaggeration. What are some examples?** [Possible oxymorons: The idea of marching asleep (l. 5) is contradictory, yet it shows the numbed state of the men. "Drunk with fatigue" (l. 7) is another contradiction, yet it vividly conveys the soldier's weakened, stumbling movements; "desperate glory" (l. 26) is another oxymoron. Possible hyperboles: "All went lame; all blind" (l. 6); to say the men are deaf (l. 7) is also an exaggeration.]

C Exploring the Historical Period

Gas as a Weapon

Gas was first introduced as a battlefield weapon in World War I. Explain that gas masks, which Owen calls "helmets" here, were standard issue for soldiers in the trenches.

D Critical Thinking

Evaluating

? **Why is the comparison to drowning especially effective here?** [Possible answers: Drowning is an image that most people can identify with; it suggests a death that is not immediate but takes place as the available oxygen disappears; the green of the gas suggests the green of water; inside the mask, the presence of the gas might appear watery, adding to the look of a drowning man.]

E Advanced Learners

Theme

One motif in this poem is age and innocence: Soldiers go into battle as innocently as children, but battle ages or kills them. Challenge students to identify all the references in the poem to youth, innocence, aging (physical or emotional), and death.

Making the Connections

Connecting to the Theme: "The Center Cannot Hold"

In this poem, Owen hopes to dispel an "old Lie," but what is the new truth that replaces it? And in what ways does this truth help convey a new world in which the center is no longer holding, in which things are falling apart? Invite students to work in small groups to relate the horrific images of Yeats's "The Second Coming" (p. 923) to the moods and themes presented in the poems of Sassoon and Owen.

Listening to Music

War Requiem, Op. 66, by Benjamin Britten, performed by the New York Philharmonic Orchestra with the American Boychoir and Westminster Symphonic Choir, conducted by Kurt Masur

Activity

Have students listen to part or all of the *War Requiem* and then discuss how Britten wove Owen's poetry into his oratorio. How effective is the combination of the Latin mass and anti-war poetry?

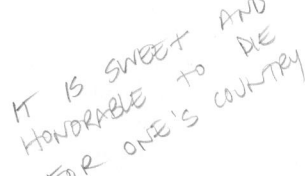

RESPONDING TO THE ART

The English painter **Christopher R.W. Nevinson** (1889–1946) returned from working with the Red Cross in France and painted bleak visions of the waste of war. Among his greatest works, his war paintings of 1915–1917, while stylistically conservative, run counter to the dominant patriotic sensibilities of the day.

Activity. Ask students to identify the ways in which Nevinson's title, *Paths of Glory* (an allusion to Thomas Gray's "Elegy Written in a Country Churchyard," p. 601), not only fits his own painting but also echoes Owen's poem and its title.

Imperial War Museum, London.

Paths of Glory, 1917 by Christopher R. W. Nevinson.

MAKING MEANINGS

First Thoughts

1. Do you think a poem like this has any relevance to wars as they are fought today? Why or why not?

Shaping Interpretations

2. What are the "misty panes" in line 13 through which the speaker glimpses the dying man?
3. What **oxymorons** can you find in the poem's second and last stanzas? Why is a figure of speech that expresses contradiction appropriate for the speaker's purposes?
4. What is the poem's **rhyme scheme**? Can you find any **half rhymes**?
5. Who is the "you" addressed in the final stanza?
6. Explain the **similes** in lines 23–24. How do they relate to the **theme** of the poem?
7. How would you describe the speaker's **tone**? How does it compare to the tone of today's war stories or war movies? (Cite some examples in your answer.)

Extending the Text

8. In recent years, the U.S. Army has recruited with the slogan "Be all that you can be," referring to educational and job opportunities in the military. Compare this slogan with the one mentioned in the poem. Which emotion or value does each slogan appeal to?

MAKING MEANINGS

First Thoughts [Respond]

1. Possible responses: Some students may say that people still engage in combat, as in the fighting in Bosnia and Kosovo in the late 1990s; others may point out that even when destruction is carried out by bombs, the suffering of the victim is just as hideous.

Shaping Interpretations [Interpret]

2. The "misty panes" are the panes of plastic that the wearer looks through; they are misty from the clouds of gas inside and out.
3. The oxymorons "An ecstasy of fumbling" and "desperate glory" describe the complex mix of fear and enthusiasm involved in donning one's gas mask in time and in enlisting in the military to die in patriotic sacrifice.
4. The rhyme scheme is *ababcdcd efefgh gh ijijklklmnmn.* One half-rhyme is *glory* / *mori* (ll. 26 and 28).
5. The "you" is collective. It can refer to anyone who preaches a simplistic patriotism.
6. The similes compare the soldier's dying responses to something "obscene" like "cancer" and to "cud" from an "incurable sore." They relate to the poem's anti-war theme by suggesting that war is a disease; that it is hideous and obscene; that it corrupts and destroys the innocent; that it reveals the lie that it is good, or decorous, or sweet to die for one's country.
7. The tone is tormented and desperately bitter. The tone of modern war movies and stories varies, but may be sarcastic or ironic as in the TV series *M*A*S*H,* elegiac and moving as in the film *Gallipoli,* bitter and serious as in the film *Welcome to Sarajevo,* or brutally realistic and terrifying as in *Saving Private Ryan.*

Extending the Text [Evaluate]

8. The slogan "Be all that you can be" promises personal development and advancement for the would-be soldier, appealing less to national patriotism than to individual self-realization. "Dulce et decorum est . . ." suggests patriotism and the glory of war above all—that is, the right and virtuous thing is to die for one's country without consideration of personal goals.

Choices: Building Your Portfolio

Writer's Notebook

1. Collecting Ideas for an Informative Report

Reading can give you ideas for informative reports. Think about the biographies of the two Trench Poets and what the poems themselves suggest about their experiences of World War I. Brainstorm for a few minutes, and jot down topics suggested by the poems that you might want to learn more about. It's possible that you might focus on details in the lives of the two young poets themselves. (Both are subjects of a 1997 film called *Regeneration,* based on an acclaimed trilogy about World War I by Pat Barker.) Save your notes for the Writer's Workshop on page 1053.

Comparing / Contrasting Poems

2. Side-by-Side Poems

In an essay, compare and contrast the **imagery, structure,** and **sound devices** of "The Rear-Guard" and "Dulce et Decorum Est."

Evaluating a Poet's Stance

3. It's Your Turn

In the last lines of his poem, Owen refers to an honorable death for one's country as "the old Lie." Do you agree that patriotism's high-minded idealism is a lie? Or is Owen perhaps stacking the deck by including so many gruesome battle details? Or do you think the poem presents a valid but insoluble conflict? In a brief essay, relate Owen's poem to your own concept of patriotism.

Comparing / Contrasting Poems

4. Another View

In an essay, point out the similarities and differences between Owen's "Dulce et Decorum Est" and the poem below by Rupert Brooke. (Brooke served in World War I but did not experience trench warfare; he died of blood poisoning en route to Europe.) Consider how each poet uses at least three of these elements: **imagery, theme** and sentiments about war, **tone, sound devices,** and **figurative language.**

Viewing and Representing

5. Through the Artists' Eyes

Review the art used to illustrate the introduction to "The Twentieth Century" (pages 906–922) and these poems by the Trench Poets. In an essay, analyze one of the pieces of art. First, describe what you see in the painting, and then analyze how the painting's elements work together to create an overall effect (consider such elements as **"story," color, light, form, tone**). You might also want to consider the work's **title.** Conclude your essay by describing your response to the work.

The Soldier

If I should die, think only this of me;
  That there's some corner of a foreign field
That is forever England. There shall be
  In that rich earth a richer dust concealed;
A dust whom England bore, shaped, made aware,
  Gave, once, her flowers to love, her ways to roam,
A body of England's breathing English air,
  Washed by the rivers, blest by suns of home.

And think, this heart, all evil shed away,
  A pulse in the eternal mind, no less
  Gives somewhere back the thoughts by England given;
Her sights and sounds; dreams happy as her day;
  And laughter, learnt of friends; and gentleness,
  In hearts at peace, under an English heaven.

—Rupert Brooke (1887–1915)

Grading Timesaver

Rubrics for each Choices assignment appear on p. 185 in the *Portfolio Management System.*

Choices: Building Your Portfolio

1. **Writer's Notebook.** Students may also be interested in the fact-based novel *Regeneration* (made into a film in 1997), the first novel in Pat Barker's World War I trilogy. In it, Siegfried Sassoon is committed to a mental hospital as an alternative to court-martial for his public denouncement of the war and is treated by psychiatrist Dr. William Rivers, who is moved by Sassoon's sentiments and ideals.
2. **Comparing/Contrasting Poems** Remind students to use a two-column chart to help them find and organize ideas before they begin to draft their essay.
3. **Evaluating a Poet's Stance** For another point of view, students may read Douglas MacArthur's famous essay, "Duty, Honor, Country," in which the World War II general asserts that "the soldier who is called upon to offer and to give his life for his country is the noblest development of mankind." This perspective may help balance Owen's point of view.
4. **Comparing/Contrasting Poems** Encourage students to begin by identifying the speaker in "The Soldier" and the speaker's attitude toward England, as well as the overall feeling conveyed by the poem.
5. **Viewing and Representing** Suggest that students devote separate paragraphs to different elements, such as the painting's subject or "story," its use of color, and its mood or feeling. Similarly, students might structure their prewriting so that they list and develop ideas in several categories before drafting.

Spotlight On

This feature provides an overview of British poetry during the twentieth century, with special emphasis on the Trench Poets, the English Group, Dylan Thomas and the poets of the "New Apocalypse," and the contemporary poets Philip Larkin and Ted Hughes.

After discussing the text, challenge students to create a time line of developments in twentieth-century poetry. They can add to and refine this time line as they read Collections 12–15.

A Literary Connections

John Malcolm Brinnin

Ask students if they can identify this person. [He is one of the program authors.] You might point out the biographical note about Brinnin, which appears on p. 3. You might also note that Brinnin has often been included in anthologies of twentieth-century poetry along with many of the same poets he introduces here.

B Critical Thinking

Synthesizing

? Do the war poems you just read by Sassoon, Owen, and Brooke appear to support this conclusion? What is conventional about them, and what is unconventional? Is Yeats's poem "The Second Coming" conventional—that is, is it like poems you have read by the Victorians and the Romantics? [Possible answer: The use of rhyme and rhythm in the war poems is highly conventional; Brooke even uses a sonnet form. However, Owen's and Sassoon's depiction of war as shocking, horrifying, and dehumanizing is very much a twentieth-century construct, and therefore unconventional. Yeats's poem is a departure from earlier poetry in both subject matter and form.]

C Literary Connections

Isaac Rosenberg

A Jew from a poor background, Isaac Rosenberg brought his painterly eye to the art and craft of writing poetry. Like Owen and Sassoon, he was unsparing in his descriptions of the horror of trench warfare and wrote about its unsavory details, such as rats and lice. Unlike Rupert Brooke, Rosenberg was an outsider. His poverty—and to some extent his Jewishness—cut him off from the splendors of England that Brooke loftily memorialized; no such subject matter ever mediated the grim realities Rosenberg recorded about life at the front.

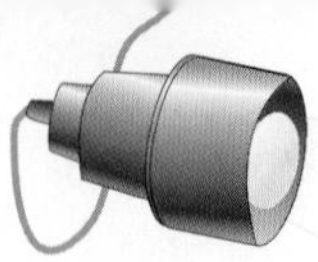

SPOTLIGHT ON

Twentieth-Century British Poetry

(A) *by* **John Malcolm Brinnin**

British poets in the early twentieth century were not experimenters. They did not make the daring adaptations that their American cousins **(B)** were quick to try out. Instead, the main concern of British poets in the twentieth century has been to express themselves in very conventional forms—even when they are responding to the most violent of experiences.

The Trench Poets: Poetry and Pity

You will see this use of traditional forms in a group of poets who wrote about the first great war of our war-torn century: the Trench Poets. What these poets wrote was categorized as "war poetry." Yet the poets themselves hoped their works would stand as testaments beyond the usual reach of poetic art—and as warnings.

As **Wilfred Owen** wrote, "The Poetry is in the pity," meaning that the shame of war overwhelms every attempt to make sense of it, in verse or by any other means. Intimately acquainted with miseries and horrors inconceivable to civilians, the Trench Poets stripped war of its glory. They positioned themselves against the Romantic rhetoric of their immediate predecessor, **Rupert Brooke** (himself a casualty of the Great War), who put into rhyme the expected patriotic response.

In contrast, the Trench Poets dwelt on the degradation of body and soul caused by trench warfare, and the humiliation that the trenches represented. In their view, the war that began as an assertion of righteousness and a test of national will became an exercise in slaughter. To them, the war demeaned the very idea of civilization and turned history itself into a "no man's land"—the few hundred yards of dead terrain that divided German trenches from British trenches, a terrain that bore all the features of hell. Killed in action, or crippled, blinded, gassed, and shellshocked, the Trench Poets, dead and alive, spoke to and for the youth of generations to come.

(C) The two poets among them who most clearly showed signs of genius were the young soldiers Wilfred Owen and **Isaac Rosenberg.** On April 1, 1918, Rosenberg was killed in action. Owen, whose poems later formed the libretto for Benjamin Britten's *War Requiem,* met the same fate six months later.

The English Group: A Political Agenda

One of the most exciting developments of the early 1930s was the emergence of four poets popularly known in America as "the English Group." The group consisted of the British writers **W. H. Auden** (page 1091) and **Stephen Spender** and the Irish-born writers **Cecil Day-Lewis** and **Louis MacNeice.** The audience for these poets was a generation that blamed the failure of capitalism for the devastation of World War I. This failure, they felt, was made even more apparent in the social unrest of the 1920s and in the economic collapse of 1929 that led to the Great Depression. The English Group's audience was also the generation that began to look toward socialism as an alternative to Great Britain's capitalist class system, and to the unequal distribution of wealth that perpetuated that system.

The most important concern in these poets' political thinking, however, was the rise of fascism. Fascism was the dictatorial, militaristic system that swept Germany, Italy, and Spain—it would eventually unite the democracies of the world in opposition to it and lead to World War II.

Without quite being aware of the fact, poetry, like everything else, was becoming politicized:

Using Students' Strengths

Logical/Mathematical Learners

Tell students that the development or evolution of a new "school" of writers, poets, or painters often comes as a reaction to pre-existing schools. Challenge students to create a flow chart in which they trace in chronological order the assertions and reactions of the various movements in British poetry. They might begin with the Renaissance (or even earlier) and trace developments up to and including the poets and schools covered in this essay.

Verbal Learners

Ask students to think of reasons that might explain the name given to each school of poetry. In what ways are the names accurate and descriptive? In what ways might they be misleading? What alternate names can students come up with for each of these schools of poetry?

> The qualities which distinguished us from the writers of the previous decade lay not in ourselves, but in the events to which we reacted. These were unemployment, economic crisis, . . . fascism, approaching war. . . . The older writers were reacting . . . to the exhaustion and hopelessness of a Europe in which the old regimes were falling to pieces. We were a "new generation," but it took me some time to appreciate the meaning of this phrase . . . that we had begun . . . in circumstances strikingly different from those of our immediate predecessors and that a consciousness of this was shown in our writing. . . . We were the 1930s.
>
> —Stephen Spender, *from World Within World*

Already entrenched in Italy and Germany, fascism threatened to spread to Spain when General Francisco Franco overthrew the elected Spanish Republican government in 1936. Franco's move was supported by Benito Mussolini, dictator of Italy, and Adolf Hitler. More than any other event of the decade, the Fascist threat to Spanish democracy unified the artists and intellectuals of a generation. The Spanish Civil War became *their* war. Some, unwilling to remain bystanders, enlisted as volunteers in the Republican Army and were counted among its casualties. As in World War I, some of the most brilliant poets of an era were silenced by the Spanish Civil War before they could fulfill their promise.

Dylan Thomas: A Return to Romanticism

When Auden, whose poetry surpassed that of others in the English Group, became an American citizen and established residence in New York City, it was the opinion of at least one critic that British poetry was "up the creek," but not "without a paddle." The paddle that he thought might rescue British poetry was **Dylan Thomas** (page 1032). This young man from Wales effectively ended one phase of poetic history and set the stage for another.

Never a part of any group, Thomas established his own poetic goals as a very young man. On the evidence of the remarkable notebooks he left behind, he pursued these goals throughout the brief course of his adult life. Yet, in the minds of critics who are more comfortable with poetry when it comes as the product of a "school" or a movement than from an individual of genius, Thomas was associated with certain writers more or less his own age. As time would tell, these other writers were more gifted as theorists than as poets.

Ambitious and bold, they called themselves "the New Apocalypse." In their opinion, it was time to halt the tendency of British poets to be concerned with politics and psychology—a concern that had turned poetry into a form of intellectual debate. They wanted a return to poetry as incandescent language—the language of the great English Romantics. They wanted to render individual experience in sacramental imagery—such as that found in the Psalms and in the high rhetoric of the King James Bible, in the visionary world of William Blake, and in the compacted wordplay and religious wit of Gerard Manley Hopkins. The young poets also admired the dream imagery of the subconscious, which had been dredged up and used by the spectacular new painters who called themselves surrealists.

These poets of the New Apocalypse believed that a new wave of Romanticism was about to break, bringing with it a heightening of verbal music and a delight in language for its own sake. They believed that this kind of poetry had been curbed by other kinds of poetry that emulated public speech and demanded clarity, logic, and a message. True to

Expansion of the Lyric (1913) by Leonardo Dudreville.
Richard Miller Collection, New York.

D Literary Connections
Spender and His "New Generation"

Not only did this group of English poets politicize poetry, but they also incorporated the symbols of the new technological age into their poetry. Spender, in particular, believed that images of machines were as important to the new poetry as the pre-twentieth-century images of, for example, roses and gardens.

E Humanities Connections
The Spanish Civil War

Refer students to Picasso's *Guernica,* shown on p. 911. This quintessentially Modernist painting, which shocked viewers when it first appeared, was painted in response to the Nazi firebombing of Guernica in Spain. It has since become emblematic of the chaos and fragmentation of the twentieth century.

F Literary Connections
Dylan Thomas

Writing about the newness, vigor, and charm of the early poetry of Dylan Thomas, poet and critic Louis Untermeyer says, "It startled readers with its strange word magic and its driving force," noting also its "image-crowded lines."

G Literary Connections
The New Apocalypse

The lesser poets to whom Brinnin alludes but does not name include George Barker and David Gascoyne.

Responding to the Art

Italian painter **Leonardo Dudreville** (1885–1975) was one of the early participants in the Futurist movement, which blended the Cubist vocabulary of fragmented geometric shapes with a new sense of movement and dynamism. *Expansion of the Lyric* demonstrates his use of simple geometric forms to suggest the movement of shapes and colors.

Activity. Ask students to speculate about the title. In what sense is the artist "expanding a lyric" in this painting? Or is he changing the definition of *lyricism,* making it less personal and more abstract?

Skill Link

Analyzing Characteristics of Clear Text

This is a short essay on a broad topic. Still, the author covers a great deal of ground by making good use of citations and examples to support the points he makes about twentieth-century British poetry. Ask students to do the following:

1. Review the article to find four examples of the author's use of supporting facts or quotations. [Possible example: In the first section, Owen's exact words typify the group of poets under discussion and the facts about Owen's and Rosenberg's deaths in action link the tragic aspects of their poetry to those of their brief lives.]
2. Compare findings in a class discussion.
3. Point out and discuss passages where other supporting facts and quotations could have been added to make the exposition more complete.

A Literary Connections

Philip Larkin

Characteristics of Larkin's poetry include the use of everyday language and rhythms, impressionistic sensory details, and a distinctive tone that is at once ironic, detached, and humane. Ask students to look for these qualities in "The Mower."

B Critical Thinking

Making Connections

? In what ways does "The Mower" remind you of Robert Burns's "To a Mouse" (p. 642)? In what ways is it different? [Possible responses: In both poems, the situation of a small animal imperiled by impersonal, deadly forces is a springboard for a meditation on a larger, more philosophical theme. In "To a Mouse," a mouse is unearthed, but not killed, by a farmer's plow, whereas here, a hedgehog is caught and killed in the blades of a mower; in "To a Mouse," the speaker addresses the mouse, whereas in this poem, the speaker merely reflects on the death of the hedgehog and its significance to human life.]

C Literary Connections

T. S. Eliot

Eliot became a British citizen in 1927, after some of his most famous work was behind him. "The Love Song of J. Alfred Prufrock" had appeared in 1915 and *The Waste Land* in 1922. Eliot's last major work, "Four Quartets," was concluded in 1943.

the name they chose, they saw themselves as apocalyptic: They regarded poems not as arguments or conclusions but as revelations, not as commentaries upon experience but, literally, as re-creations of experience still in the process of becoming intelligible.

The poets of the New Apocalypse got their message across, but they did not have the talent to give it substance. As they faded from the scene, Dylan Thomas alone was left to carry on their ideas. His famous career brought a new dimension to British poetry, reminding readers that poetry could be both as sensually exciting as music and as philosophically profound as Greek tragedy.

The Contemporary Scene

But Dylan Thomas died at the age of thirty-nine, and British poetry again entered a conservative and technically unadventurous phase. Then, out of this fallow period, two exceptional poetic personalities arose. Each in his own way showed that individual talent can make a mark and still have nothing to do with groups or movements. Each poet also rejected the nineteenth-century belief that—like sermons or editorials—poetry should be morally uplifting, or, at least, addressed to public issues.

These two poets were **Ted Hughes** (page 960), who was poet laureate of England, and **Philip Larkin** (1922–1985). Philip Larkin was the most widely admired poet in the generation succeeding that of Dylan Thomas. In their quiet, low-keyed way, his poems reflect all the great themes of contemporary experience. In his handling of these themes, Larkin keeps to an intimately human scale, in which the balance lies somewhere between disgust and disdain on the one hand, and heartbreak and despairing humor on the other.

The Mower

The mower stalled, twice; kneeling, I found
A hedgehog jammed up against the blades,
Killed. It had been in the long grass.

I had seen it before, and even fed it, once.
Now I had mauled its unobtrusive world
Unmendably. Burial was no help:

Next morning I got up and it did not.
The first day after a death, the new absence
Is always the same; we should be careful

Of each other, we should be kind
While there is still time.

—Philip Larkin

Today, British poetry is closer to its twentieth-century beginnings than it has been for many years. British poetry was never modern in the energetically experimental ways that produced the extraordinary succession of American poets that includes Ezra Pound, T. S. Eliot, Hart Crane, Wallace Stevens, William Carlos Williams, Elizabeth Bishop, Robert Lowell, and James Merrill. But now that the age of poetic schools, movements, and other kinds of labeled association seems to have run its course, certain older British poets who followed no program but their own have begun to shine more brightly than ever. Chief among these are Thomas Hardy and D. H. Lawrence. As it comes full circle, British poetry may have surrendered some of its vitality, but none of its character. The individual voice is still the one to listen for, and the measure of English poets today is still the degree to which they make our common language sound like their own.

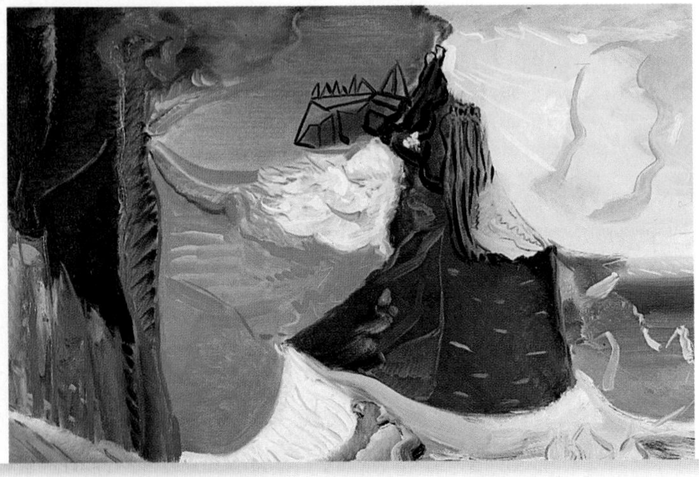

Diurnal Rhythm (20th century) by Maurice Cockrill.
Richard Miller Collection, New York.

934

Assessing Learning

Check Test: Questions and Answers

1. Wilfred Owen and Isaac Rosenberg are grouped in what school of poetry? [the Trench Poets]
2. Name two members of the English Group. [The group includes W. H. Auden, Stephen Spender, Cecil Day-Lewis, and Louis MacNeice.]
3. Dylan Thomas's poetry marked a return to what movement in poetry? [the Romantic movement]
4. Which two poets made a strong mark on contemporary British poetry without being part of a specific school or movement? [Ted Hughes and Philip Larkin]

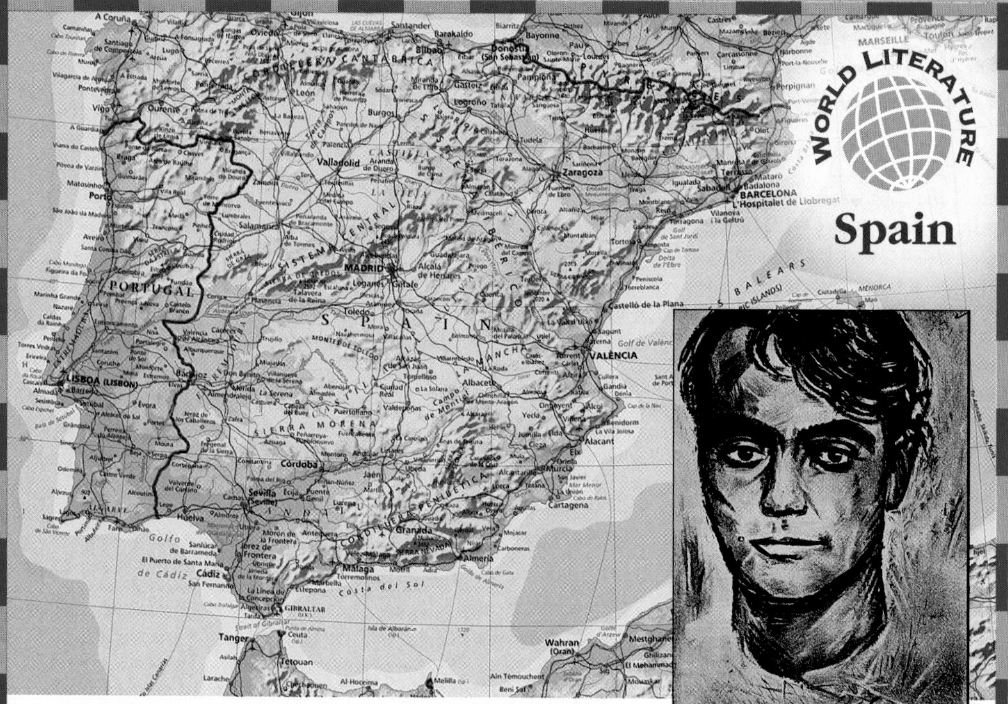

Drawing of Federico García Lorca, by Gregorio Prieto.

Federico García Lorca

(1898–1936)

In 1936, Spain was in the grip of a civil war. Republicans and Fascist-oriented Nationalists were locked in a bloody struggle for control of the government. On the night of July 19, 1936, in Granada, Nationalist fighters seized a popular young writer named Federico García Lorca, took him to a graveyard, forced him to dig his own grave, and then shot him. The world was outraged—Lorca was not political. It's possible that the Nationalists had felt threatened by the poet's work, which was at once deeply rooted in Spain and very modern.

Lorca was born on a prosperous farm just outside of Granada, in Andalusia, that sunny part of Spain where Moorish and Gypsy elements have mixed with a conservative Catholic culture. In 1919, he went to Madrid to study. Immensely handsome, charming, and intelligent, Lorca mingled easily with avant-garde artists there, including the surrealist painter Salvador Dali. But when Lorca began writing poetry and dramas of his own, he turned to the folklore and Gypsy music of Andalusia for inspiration.

Lorca wrote a series of dark tragedies, including *Bodas de sangre (Blood Wedding),* still produced on American stages today, about a bride who runs away on her wedding day with the man she secretly loves and who is murdered by her husband. *La casa de Bernarda Alba (The House of Bernarda Alba),* like a Greek tragedy, traces the workings of malignant fate in a family trapped by stifling tradition from which there is no escape but death. Lorca's most famous poem, lamenting the fatal goring of his friend, a bullfighter, is also one of the great elegies in all literature. *Llanto por Ignacio Sánchez Mejías (Lament for Ignacio Sánchez Mejías)* seemed also to prophesy the young writer's own violent death.

(Map) ©Rand McNally.

go.hrw.com
LEO 12-12

OBJECTIVES

1. Read and interpret the poem
2. Evaluate different translations of the poem, and present English and Spanish versions of the poem in oral performance
3. Recognize distinctive and shared characteristics of cultures
4. Compare the poem's content with students' own experiences
5. Recognize and discuss themes and connections that cross cultures

Planning

- **Block Schedule**
  Block Scheduling Lesson Plans with Pacing Guide
- **Traditional Schedule**
  Lesson Plans Including Strategies for English-Language Learners
- **One-Stop Planner**
  CD-ROM with Test Generator

BROWSING IN THE FILES

About the Author. The American poet and translator Robert Bly (see p. 937) writes this about the beloved poet of the Spanish people: "There is no other poet like him in the history of poetry. Everyone who reads a poem of Lorca's falls in love with him, and has a secret friend. All the rest of his life, whenever he thinks of Lorca, he notices a red ray of sunlight hit the ground a few inches from his feet."

Summary ■■

When the cry of the guitar begins at dawn, it cannot be stopped. It weeps as continuously and eternally as wind and water, mourning for life's pain and losses. The guitar is itself a wounded heart.

Reaching All Students

Struggling Readers

Build background by talking about the importance of the guitar in Spain, where it is almost a national icon, as an instrument of both folk and classical music. Have students identify the kinds of music in which guitar plays a major role. Ask them to brainstorm descriptive lists of all the emotional effects that can be achieved with the guitar (both acoustic and electric). Why is the image of a guitarist such a romantic one even today? (You might try playing a recording of the Beatles' song "While My Guitar Gently Weeps," which has some thematic similarities to García Lorca's poem.)

English Language Learners

Remind students that this is as much a poem of sound and emotion as it is of meaning. Assure them that some of the words and images are not meant to make perfect, rational sense and encourage them to listen attentively to the tone and rhythms of the poem. Students may want to draw some of their impressions.

Background

For many years up to approximately 1800, the guitar had five courses, or pairs of strings. Later, it was modernized to its familiar classical form: six single strings. At the end of this poem, when Lorca says that the guitar is a heart wounded by five swords, one way for students to grasp this image is by visualizing the five pairs of strings coursing across the middle, or heart, of the guitar.

RESPONDING TO THE ART

The work of **Pablo Picasso** (1881–1973) is often classified into periods, one of which is the Blue Period. At this time, when Picasso was deep in mourning for a beloved friend, he produced many canvasses in the same melancholy hues as those shown here.

Activity. Ask students to identify details that contribute to the mood of this painting. What major geometric shapes underlie the composition of this work?

Ⓐ Critical Thinking

Analyzing

? Even if you don't know one word of Spanish, what can you tell about this poem before you read the English version? [Students can at least make inferences based on the form of the poem. They can see that it is a short poem with short lines of approximately equal length. They can see the poem is all one stanza. If they look closely, they can see that certain words are repeated, such as *llanto* and *llora*, and they might note that these repeated words are also similar to one another.]

Before You Read
THE GUITAR

Background

Music and song were essential to Lorca. Even before his feet could reach the pedals, he was composing songs at the piano. He seemed to breathe the native music of Andalusia, what is called *cante jondo,* or "deep song." This dirgelike music is believed to have come with the Gypsies from India. In Spain it melded with Iberian and Moorish elements to form a wailing, almost obsessive rhythm that is hauntingly primitive and extraordinarily expressive. Best known abroad in its derivative form, flamenco, *cante jondo* is the wellspring of Lorca's intense, dramatic, and richly musical poetry. His themes, emotions, and images echo those ancient songs, which he compared to "the trilling of birds, the crowing of the rooster, and the natural music of forest and fountain."

Since no translation, no matter how accomplished, can ever completely capture Lorca's Andalusian sounds, it is important to hear his poetry in the original Spanish.

Quickwrite

Can you remember a time when the sound of music moved you deeply? What did you feel? What did the music remind you of?

Helen Birch Bartlett Memorial Collection, 1926.253. Photograph ©1998, The Art Institute of Chicago. All Rights Reserved.

The Old Guitarist (1903) by Pablo Picasso. Oil on panel (122.9 cm × 82.6 cm).

La guitarra

Federico García Lorca

Empieza el llanto
de la guitarra.
Se rompen las copas
de la madrugada.
Empieza el llanto
de la guitarra.
Es inútil callarla.
Es imposible
callarla.
Llora monótona
como llora el agua,
como llora el viento
sobre la nevada.
Es imposible
callarla.
Llora por cosas
lejanas.
Arena del Sur caliente
que pide camelias blancas.
Llora flecha sin blanco,
la tarde sin mañana,
y el primer pájaro muerto
sobre la rama.
¡Oh guitarra!
Corazón malherido
por cinco espadas.

Resources: Print and Media

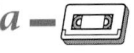

Reading
- *Audio CD Library*
  Disc 16, Tracks 4, 5, 6

Internet
- go.hrw.com (keyword: LE0 12-12)

The Guitar

Federico García Lorca

translated by **Robert Bly**

The crying of the guitar
starts.
The goblets
of the dawn break.
The crying of the guitar
starts.
No use to stop it.
It is impossible
to stop it.
It cries repeating itself
as the water cries,
as the wind cries
over the snow.
It is impossible
to stop it.
It is crying for things
far off.
The warm sand of the South
that asks for white camellias.
For the arrow with nothing to hit,
the evening with no dawn coming,
and the first bird of all dead
on the branch.
Guitar!
Heart wounded, gravely,
by five swords.

The Guitar

Federico García Lorca

translated by **Elizabeth du Gué Trapier**

Now begins the cry
Of the guitar,
Breaking the vaults
Of dawn.
Now begins the cry
Of the guitar.
Useless
To still it.
Impossible
To still it.
It weeps monotonously
As weeps the water,
As weeps the wind
Over snow.
Impossible
To still it.
It weeps
For distant things,
Warm southern sands
Desiring white camellias.
It mourns the arrow without a target,
The evening without morning.
And the first bird dead
Upon a branch.
O guitar!
A wounded heart,
Wounded by five swords.

FINDING COMMON GROUND

Extending themes across cultures. First, in a group, discuss the poem's meaning. Be sure to consider how the poem relates to the theme of this collection, "The Center Cannot Hold." Do any of the images remind you of images in the poem that opens the collection, "The Second Coming" (page 923)?

Evaluating oral presentations and performances. Next, assign different readers in your group to prepare the poems—the Spanish version and each English translation—for performance. Before you evaluate the performances, work together to draw up **criteria** that you think should characterize an effective performance. After the performances, analyze the readings in a group discussion, and evaluate their effectiveness.

Evaluating translations. With your group, discuss the translations of the poem. Before you open your discussion, agree on the **criteria** you look for in an effective translation of a poem into another language.

Translating the poem. If you or anyone else in your group is fluent in Spanish, try a new translation of "La guitarra."

Connecting Across Texts

Connecting with "Twentieth-Century British Poetry"

Students may now have read "The Second Coming" and some World War I poems, as well as Larkin's "The Mower." You might discuss the significant ways in which Lorca's poem differs from these other examples of twentieth-century poetry by asking students to contrast its subject matter, form, tone, and use of inventive images with those of the other poems. Students might even be asked to comment on which of the poems studied so far seems most modern in its sensibility, and why. As an aid to understanding or visualizing what is modern, students can return to the painting on pp. 906–907 and discuss the ways in which "The Guitar" is similar in spirit or execution to this image.

B Elements of Literature

Tone

? What tone do you hear as you read this poem? [Possible responses: The tone is one of sadness; it is softly musical and sorrowful; the tone is one of lament.]

C Critical Thinking

Interpreting

? García Lorca, like other poets of his day, was interested in the dreamlike and the allusive. Here, he is not so much naming precise, factual events as creating a mood and resonance. Why does he refer to sands that yearn for camellias and arrows without a target? [Possible responses: Through these images, he is suggesting the inevitability of sorrow and loss; he is mourning or "weeping" for the ephemeral quality of beauty and love.]

D Reading Skills and Strategies

Drawing Conclusions

? Why does the poet present the guitar as a wounded heart? [Possible answers: Like a wounded lover, the guitar sings sadly, unable to stop either longing or mourning; it mourns not only for its own losses but for the transient nature of time.]

E Critical Thinking

Expressing an Opinion

? Which of these two translations do you prefer, and why? [Responses will vary.]

FINDING COMMON GROUND

This feature will help students deepen their understanding of the poem by relating it to the collection theme, to cross-cultural themes, and to the multiplicity of ways in which poems can be translated and interpreted. Have students work in groups to complete all the activities; groups of four might rotate leadership roles as they conduct each of the activities.

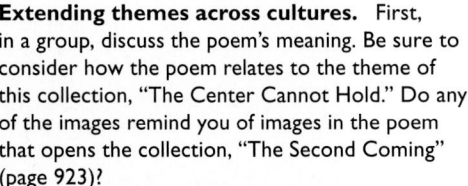

Spotlight On

This feature introduces perhaps the most frequently echoed poetic voice of the twentieth century. After discussing the introductory essay, ask students to summarize the key points made about Eliot. They might comment on what was so new about him, why he had such monumental influence, or what the poems included here reflect about his themes and concerns.

A Literary Connections

Fellow Expatriates

Other influential American expatriate writers include Ezra Pound, Ernest Hemingway, F. Scott Fitzgerald, and Gertrude Stein.

B Background

Eliot's Influence

Eliot was not only a poet; he was an editor, a critic, and a playwright. Between the two wars, he probably had more influence on modern poetry, at home and internationally, than any other living poet. How did he change poetry? There are no simple answers, but Eliot's own words, from an essay entitled "The Metaphysical Poets" (1921), may guide students: "The poet must become more and more comprehensive, more allusive, more indirect, in order to force, to dislocate if necessary, language into his meaning." As students read the poems included here, they might ask the following questions: Is this comprehensive—is it about something important? What are the allusions, and what do they mean? What is the meaning of this poem, and how has Eliot expressed it indirectly? Is the language "dislocated"—that is, is the language jarring, original, dissonant, full of new associations?

C Cultural Connections

The Voice of an Age

So famous and so influential was Eliot's great poem *The Waste Land* that the term itself, like "Lost Generation" and "Jazz Age," was an often-used expression of post–World War I disillusionment.

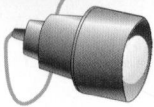

SPOTLIGHT ON

T. S. Eliot: The Voice of an Age

by **John Malcolm Brinnin**

Unlike poets whose long, outstanding careers eventually turn them into cultural monuments, T. S. Eliot was a monument who later became known as a man. Internationally famous at an early age, he was the product of an aristocratic New England family. The Eliots valued privacy and regarded self-exploitation and public exposure—even fame itself—as a form of vulgarity. Consequently, millions of readers knew T. S. Eliot less as a real personality than as a presence. Eliot was remote, austere, and self-possessed, a man whose sparse output was nevertheless the most celebrated and influential poetry written in English over a span of three decades.

T. S. Eliot was born in 1888 in St. Louis, Missouri, where his grandfather had established Washington University. In spite of this geographical displacement, the Eliots remained New Englanders. They could trace their ancestry back to the first Puritan settlements in North America. Young Tom Eliot was educated at Harvard College, after which he did graduate studies at the Sorbonne in Paris. Like many other young American writers of his generation, he found life abroad so stimulating that he decided not to return home. Settling in London before World War I, he worked in a bank, married an Englishwoman, and became an editor and a publisher. He made his expatriation complete by becoming a British citizen in 1927. In 1948, he was awarded the Nobel Prize. Not long before his death in 1965, on one of his several visits to the United States, so many people wanted to see and hear Eliot read his poetry that a football stadium had to be taken over to hold the audience.

Eliot had a vast influence as a poet. His techniques, along with those of his friend and fellow American, Ezra Pound, became the hallmarks of modern poetry. For over thirty years, in classrooms and in critical studies, his was *the* voice that expressed the dislocation and despair of the twentieth century. Eliot's world-weariness, his grave, restrained, and impersonal cadences, so much like the voices he heard in New England pulpits, were widely imitated and instantly recognized. Eliot dominated English literature in a way not seen since the days of Dr. Johnson.

Eliot's critical studies were also far-reaching. He argued against the commonly held view that

T. S. Eliot (1907) during his first year at Harvard, age 19.

By permission of the Houghton Library, Harvard University, Cambridge, Massachusetts.

go.hrw.com LEO 12-12

Professional Notes

Critical Comment: Eliot's Genius

In 1986, on what would have been T. S. Eliot's ninety-eighth birthday, Britain's poet laureate Ted Hughes (1930–1998) unveiled a plaque outside the London apartment where Eliot lived from 1957 until his death in 1965. Hughes praised Eliot as "*the* poet of our times" and "the prophet of a new world." He added, "It is the world which has already, in its soul, and throughout all its peoples, suffered the global holocaust, and must now, somehow, find in its own ashes the spiritual strength to resurrect itself. And it was Eliot's humility to know, with what seemed like knowledge inborn, that nothing matters now but to search for this strength, and to find it." Eliot's genius, Hughes pointed out, lies in his "attempts to deal with inner devastation" and the "general spiritual catastrophe" around him, so that his poetry speaks not only to "Western man, [but] perhaps, even, simply spiritual man."

poets were romantics who had superior powers of observation and expression. Eliot regarded poets as craftspeople who used traditional literary materials not for personal revelations but for the creation of better-made poems. The poet, according to these theories, was like those anonymous master artisans who made individual contributions to the great medieval cathedrals but who remained personally unknown. Like these humble artisans, the poet was just part of the background. What is important is the poem (or the cathedral), not the worker who made it. This point of view deplored the notion that a search through the poet's life would give clues to the meaning of the work. The work, all-important, stood apart from its creator. Submitting to Eliot's instruction, poets, students, and critics for generations studied a poem not for its messages or meaning, but for its method and structure—for its architecture.

In 1950, when I was director of New York's Poetry Center, Eliot made a visit to the United States. I recalled the event in a book called *Sextet:*

"This late in his life (he was sixty-one) Eliot had given less than a handful of readings in the United States and had read only once before in New York. The response to our announcement of the event suggested that many people thought his reading at the Poetry Center might well be his last. On the morning after we had named his date in *The New York Times,* fifteen or twenty requests were made for every seat available. Pursued and badgered to use my influence to produce tickets, I found that people who'd never read a sonnet since the seventh grade were suddenly lovers of poetry whose devotion I was implored not to dismiss."

A Vision of the Street

In music, *preludes* are brief works, usually free in form, that introduce larger and more formal compositions. When Eliot chose a musical title, he no doubt meant to suggest that these short poems introduced the mood and method of longer works written in the same period.

The images in "Preludes" are all drawn from city life. Horse-drawn carriages had not yet been replaced by automobiles, nor gas lamps by electricity, but nevertheless the dehumanizing aspects of a growing metropolis like Eliot's Boston were already sadly in evidence. Eliot saw multitudes of workers every day moving to and fro like debris washed in and out by the tides. He saw massive slums that blocked out forever the gentle rural landscapes of a preindustrial age.

"Preludes" are the observations of a wanderer through city streets. The speaker attempts to come to some conclusion about the meaning of the life around him, yet he finally gives up. Still, in the process, he gives us "a vision of the street," a scene for which he feels compassion but which, finally, he considers beyond redemption. Eliot wrote these poems when he was in his twenties. How many images suggest life as a wasteland? How do these descriptions of city life relate to urban landscapes today? (Note: In line 2, "steaks" refers to cheap cuts of meat.)

Preludes

T. S. Eliot

I

The winter evening settles down **D**
With smell of steaks in passageways.
Six o'clock.
The burnt-out ends of smoky days.
And now a gusty shower wraps
The grimy scraps
Of withered leaves about your feet **E**
And newspapers from vacant lots;
The showers beat
On broken blinds and chimney-pots,
And at the corner of the street
A lonely cab-horse steams and stamps.
And then the lighting of the lamps.

II

The morning comes to consciousness
Of faint stale smells of beer
From the sawdust-trampled street
With all its muddy feet that press **F**
To early coffee-stands.
With the other masquerades
That time resumes,
One thinks of all the hands
That are raising dingy shades
In a thousand furnished rooms.

D Elements of Literature
Word Choice

Note the three key words in the first line that set the poem's tone: *winter,* a time of death; *evening,* the prelude to night; and *down,* the direction of defeat, death, and hell.

E Struggling Readers
Finding Details

? What is one image in these lines that you can identify as positive or negative, and why? [Possible responses: All the images are negative. Examples include the burnt-out ends, like cigarette butts, of smoky (unclear, blurred) days; grimy scraps (unwanted, unusable remains) of withered (dying, dried-out) leaves; and vacant lots (places of disrepair and abandonment).]

F Critical Thinking
Evaluating

? In what ways are these lines "indirect"? What "big idea" do they suggest without directly saying it? [Possible response: Eliot is commenting on the lives of poor working-class people who wake up to the smell of stale beer and tramp off to work, stopping at coffee stands on streets strewn with sawdust (probably to cover the waste of horses). He is implying that lives lived in such a way, in such an environment, are shabby and spiritually void, marked by meaningless and unrelieved labor, with seemingly no hope for improvement.]

Reaching All Students

Struggling Readers

Suggest that students read the "Preludes" one at a time. Suggest also that they find just one image they can identify or explain in each poem. This image can serve as their own entrance into the poem.

English Language Learners

Have students listen to the audio recording, stopping it and replaying it as many times as needed in order to form some idea of a poem's meaning before reading it on their own or in a small group.

Advanced Learners

After they have read "The Hollow Men" (pp. 942–943), ask students to comment on the allusions they recognize or have learned about by reading the footnotes to the poem. Encourage students to work individually or in pairs to create a chart showing the "borrowed lines"—in other words, the lines that are direct quotations from other sources. Students should identify each source and explain the ways in which these lines add layers of meaning to the poem. What are the advantages and disadvantages of Eliot's reliance on allusions?

Ⓐ Critical Thinking

Interpreting

? This section of "Preludes" appears to become more personal. What shift has occurred? [Possible responses: There is a shift in person. The poem is now addressed to a "you"; the poem refers to "your soul."] **You might point out that despite the use of the second person, the identity of the "you" being addressed is unknown. Who might this "you" be?** [Possible response: the speaker.]

Ⓑ Critical Thinking

Evaluating

? Which of these images do you find most negative? [Students might cite the gutters, which collect stagnant water and are often blocked up with dead leaves and other debris. Another negative image is of dirty hands grasping yellow soles of feet.]

Ⓒ Reading Skills and Strategies

Making Inferences

? Another person is introduced. Who is it? [Possible response: Because the person referred to in Section III seems to be a woman, perhaps this is her companion. There is no clue to the person's identity, other than that he is male.]

Ⓓ Reading Skills and Strategies

Comparing/Contrasting

? How is the final stanza related to the four lines that precede it? [Possible answer: The final stanza dispels the hopefulness expressed by the preceding lines, in which a speaker is "moved" and senses something "infinitely gentle"—images that have positive connotations. In the final lines, that speaker disappears along with any sense of hope; the reader is told to laugh (as if in scorn) since the world keeps going around as it always has, with its eternal pattern of toil in "vacant lots."]

III

You tossed a blanket from the bed,
You lay upon your back, and waited;
You dozed, and watched the night revealing
The thousand sordid images
Of which your soul was constituted;
They flickered against the ceiling.
And when all the world came back
And the light crept up between the shutters
And you heard the sparrows in the gutters,
You had such a vision of the street
As the street hardly understands;
Sitting along the bed's edge, where
You curled the papers from your hair,
Or clasped the yellow soles of feet
In the palms of both soiled hands.

IV

His soul stretched tight across the skies
That fade behind a city block,
Or trampled by insistent feet
At four and five and six o'clock;
And short square fingers stuffing pipes,
And evening newspapers, and eyes
Assured of certain certainties,
The conscience of a blackened street
Impatient to assume the world.

I am moved by fancies that are curled
Around these images, and cling:
The notion of some infinitely gentle
Infinitely suffering thing.

Wipe your hand across your mouth, and laugh;
The worlds revolve like ancient women
Gathering fuel in vacant lots.

City Square (*La Place*) (1948) by Alberto Giacometti. Bronze (8½" × 25⅜" × 17¼") (21.6 × 64.5 × 43.8 cm).

The Museum of Modern Art, New York. Purchase. Photograph © 2000 The Museum of Modern Art, New York. © 1997 Artists Rights Society (ARS), New York, ADAGP, Paris.

Using Students' Strengths

Visual Learners

Have students create a mixed-media collage of images that represent the content and theme of "Preludes." Students may begin by identifying the most essential images, including a pervading sense of half-light or near-darkness, smoke, gutters, shutters, and city streets. They may use images cut from magazines or newspapers, as well as downloaded computer images, photocopies, clip art, found objects, and images they have drawn or painted themselves.

Naturalist Learners

Nature is turned upside down or subverted in this poem. Call attention to the line "sparrows in the gutters," and ask students to use their knowledge of sparrows and their behavior to discuss what this image suggests about the fate of the natural world. Students may search for other images of soiled nature that help create the grimy urban world of the poem where light creeps rather than shines and where skies fade behind a block of buildings.

A Lament for the Weary

There are many references to religion in Eliot's poem "The Hollow Men," which follows. You may, for instance, recognize on sight a line from the Lord's Prayer (see lines 77 and 91–94). But Eliot's main concern here is not to affirm his Christianity, but to give us a picture of a world of godless despair, a world without religion or the promise of salvation.

Taken from Joseph Conrad's famous story *Heart of Darkness,* the first line after the title is significant in two ways. First, it calls attention to the story of a man named Kurtz, who journeys to the center of Africa and falls into degradation. Kurtz is redeemed by self-awareness, only to find that this painful knowledge is not liberating but useless. Second, the line strikes the note of futility heard throughout the poem. **E**

The next line—"A penny for the Old Guy"—refers to one of the most notorious incidents in British history, the Gunpowder Plot. On November 5, 1605, a band of conspirators made plans to kill King James I by planting barrels of gunpowder in the underground vaults of Parliament. The man chosen to light the fuse that would result in a fatal explosion was a soldier named Guy Fawkes. But before the plot could be carried out, the conspirators were discovered. Guy Fawkes was arrested and, in the cruel custom of the day, first hanged, then drawn and quartered.

To commemorate this grisly event, every year on November 5, huge bonfires are set all over England. When these fires are lit, straw-filled effigies of Fawkes—the "stuffed men" of the poem—that look like scarecrows go up in flames, lighting up the skies. Children join in the fun by becoming beggars who ask passersby to give them "a penny for the guy."

The last four lines of this poem are among the most famous in modern poetry. What is the difference between ending with a "bang" and ending with only a "whimper"? **F**

E Literary Connections

Heart of Darkness

"Mistah Kurtz—he dead" is a line with many ramifications in Joseph Conrad's *Heart of Darkness.* This is because even before he dies in a physical sense, Kurtz is emotionally dead: In fact, he is described as "hollow at the core." (Incidentally, all the colonialists in the novel are described as "hollow men.") Kurtz comes to realize that evil is at the very heart of life, and his last chilling words are "The horror! The horror!"

F Critical Thinking

Interpreting

These powerful lines ("This is the way the world ends / Not with a bang but a whimper") are often quoted by people who have never read—or even heard of—Eliot's poem. Why do you think these lines have become emblematic of the twentieth century? [Possible response: With the almost constant threat of war throughout the twentieth century, there is an underlying sense of apocalypse—the "bang" that will end everything. There is also a play on words here, since "going out with a bang" means going out at a high point, with flash and style.]

Responding to the Art

Italian sculptor and painter **Alberto Giacometti** (1901–1966) is best known for his thin, attenuated human figures, which suggest a human consciousness pared down to its bare essence. In *City Square (La Place)*, anonymous figures are surrounded by empty space, each figure seemingly isolated from the others and reduced to its most fundamental form. Many people view Giacometti's works as visual metaphors of the post-war, anxiety-ridden world. His vision is of a world unable to recover from the horrors of war and the loss of faith.

Activity. Ask students how this sculpture reflects the world described by Eliot. Have them list lines or images in Eliot's poems that might serve as an alternate title for this work.

Taking a Second Look

Review: Using Context Clues

Some of the words in this Spotlight On feature may be unfamiliar to students. Suggest that when students read the expository text on this page, they use context clues to determine the meanings of unfamiliar words.

Activity

1. Have students find the following words on this page: *affirm, despair, degradation, conspirators, grisly, bonfires, effigies.*
2. Regardless of whether students already know the word or not, have them list context clues they could use to determine each word's meanings.
3. Have students identify the kinds of context clues they cite, including examples, definition, restatement, and contrast.
4. Have students use context to determine a meaning for each word, and then verify each word's meaning in a dictionary.

Ⓐ Appreciating Language
Repetition and Sound

? Which words and sounds are repeated most often in this stanza? [The word *dry* is repeated; *dried* is also used. Students may also notice the use of sibilants (the sounds of *s* and *sh*, as in *grass, headpiece*, and *whisper*).] Have students discuss how suggestions of dryness and the hissing sounds of the sibilants help create the dry and rustling tone of the poem.

Ⓑ Literary Connections

The hollow men are like the souls who live in the first circle of Dante's *Inferno* in *The Divine Comedy*. They are the people who lived life only for themselves and never committed themselves to anything; they failed to stand for any principles. Beatrice, who represents the heavenly or the beatific in *The Divine Comedy*, has "direct eyes." She is so holy—and so "whole"—that Dante cannot meet her pure, spiritually direct gaze.

Ⓒ Struggling Readers
Summarizing/Paraphrasing

? According to this stanza, what is "death's dream kingdom" like? [Possible response: In "death's dream kingdom" there is no one with "direct eyes" (l. 14), for a whole person with spiritual strength would have entered Paradise and would not be in the realm of the hollow men. Instead, in this dream kingdom, everything is shadowy, obscure, and ill-defined.]

Ⓓ Critical Thinking
Interpreting

? To what does the speaker wish to be "no nearer"? What is he trying to avoid by wearing disguises? [Possible responses: He does not want to approach the final judgment of death; he wants to avoid the eyes (ll. 19–22) that can look right through him and that are more penetrating and direct than his own; he wants to avoid the eyes of a soul that is whole and committed and engaged with life, because such eyes would be a reproach to him.]

Ⓔ Elements of Literature
Imagery

? How does Stanza III hearken back to the initial evocation of dryness? [Possible answer: It states that "This is the dead land . . . cactus land"—conjuring up the image of a dry, barren desert.]

The Hollow Men
T. S. Eliot

Mistah Kurtz—he dead.

A penny for the Old Guy

I

Ⓐ
We are the hollow men
We are the stuffed men
Leaning together
Headpiece filled with straw. Alas!
Our dried voices, when
We whisper together
Are quiet and meaningless
As wind in dry grass
Or rats' feet over broken glass
In our dry cellar.

Shape without form, shade without color,
Paralyzed force, gesture without motion;

Ⓑ
Those who have crossed
With direct eyes, to death's other Kingdom°
Remember us—if at all—not as lost
Violent souls, but only
As the hollow men
The stuffed men.

II

Ⓒ
Eyes I dare not meet in dreams
In death's dream kingdom
These do not appear:
There, the eyes are
Sunlight on a broken column
There, is a tree swinging
And voices are
In the wind's singing
More distant and more solemn
Than a fading star.

Ⓓ
Let me be no nearer
In death's dream kingdom
Let me also wear
Such deliberate disguises
Rat's coat, crowskin, crossed staves°
In a field
Behaving as the wind behaves
No nearer—

Not that final meeting
In the twilight kingdom

III

Ⓔ
This is the dead land
This is cactus land
Here the stone images
Are raised, here they receive
The supplication of a dead man's hand
Under the twinkle of a fading star.

Is it like this
In death's other kingdom
Waking alone
At the hour when we are
Trembling with tenderness
Lips that would kiss
Form prayers to broken stone.

IV

The eyes are not here
There are no eyes here
In this valley of dying stars
In this hollow valley
This broken jaw of our lost kingdoms

13–14. Those . . . Kingdom: Those with "direct eyes" have crossed from the hollow men's haunts into Paradise. The allusion is to Dante's *Paradiso.*

33. staves: rods or staffs; "crossed staves / in a field" form a scarecrow.

Getting Students Involved

Speaking and Listening

Divide the class into five groups, and assign each group a section of "The Hollow Men" to read aloud. Have students concentrate on the sounds of the language. For example, be sure they evoke the variety of rhythms in the free verse in Part II; also be sure they create the singsong quality of the nursery rhyme and the haunting sound of the prayer in Part V. Groups may decide whether to read their section chorally or to assign parts to individuals. Offer groups the option of adding echoic effects, a beat, or even musical accompaniment. After the groups perform their sections, ask students to discuss which parts of the poem they found most dramatically "musical."

In this last of meeting places
We grope together
And avoid speech
Gathered on this beach of the tumid river°

Sightless, unless
The eyes reappear
As the perpetual star
Multifoliate rose°
Of death's twilight kingdom
The hope only
Of empty men.

V

Here we go round the prickly pear°
Prickly pear prickly pear
Here we go round the prickly pear
At five o'clock in the morning.

Between the idea
And the reality
Between the motion
And the act°
Falls the Shadow
For Thine is the Kingdom°

Between the conception
And the creation
Between the emotion
And the response
Falls the Shadow
Life is very long

Between the desire
And the spasm
Between the potency
And the existence
Between the essence
And the descent
Falls the Shadow
For Thine is the Kingdom

For Thine is
Life is
For Thine is the

This is the way the world ends
This is the way the world ends
This is the way the world ends
Not with a bang but a whimper.

60. tumid river: Hell's swollen river, the Acheron (ak′ər·än′), in Dante's *Inferno.* The damned must cross this river to enter the land of the dead.
64. multifoliate rose: Dante describes Paradise as a rose of many leaves (*Paradiso,* Canto 32).
68. prickly pear: cactus.
74–75. Between . . . act: a reference to Shakespeare's *Julius Caesar:* "Between the acting of a dreadful thing / And the first motion, all the interim is / Like a phantasma or a hideous dream" (Act II, Scene1, lines 63–65).
77. For . . . Kingdom: closing lines of the Lord's Prayer: "For thine is the kingdom, and the power, and the glory, forever and ever."

F Reading Skills and Strategies
Determining the Author's Purpose

? What is Eliot trying to achieve by distorting a common children's rhyme in this manner? [Possible response: The use of the rhyme may suggest that the hollow men are like children who have no direction but simply go round and round. Unlike playing children, however, the hollow men do not go round the mulberry bush—a plant associated with the lush landscape of abundant water—but around the prickly pear, a desert plant with spines.]

G Reading Skills and Strategies
Determining the Author's Purpose

? What purpose is served by quoting this fragment of the Lord's Prayer? [Possible answers: It conveys the fragmented nature of the lives of the hollow men; it suggests the dream kingdom in which they live; it makes prayer seem like a desperate act, a supplication that cannot even yield results.]

H Vocabulary Note
Connotations

? Why does Eliot end the poem with the word *whimper*? [Possible response: A whimper is not only less bold than a cry—it is pathetic, supporting the idea that the hollow men's lives have no meaning or purpose.]

Listening to Music

"Memory" by Andrew Lloyd Webber, lyrics by Trevor Nunn and T. S. Eliot, from *Cats,* Original Broadway Cast (1982).

Probably the most famous composer of British stage musicals since Noel Coward, London native Andrew Lloyd Webber (1948–) has produced a string of transatlantic hits, including *Jesus Christ Superstar, Evita,* and *The Phantom of the Opera.* He began working on *Cats* in 1977, when he picked up a favorite book of poems from childhood, *Old Possum's Book of Practical Cats* by T. S. Eliot, and became interested in setting it to music.

Activity

Have students listen to "Memory" and identify lines from "Preludes" (p. 939) that appear in the song. Ask them if any of the lines not adapted from Eliot could have been written by the poet. Then, have them work in small groups, designing or describing a set that they think would be appropriate for staging "Memory."

Making the Connections

Connecting to the Theme: "The Center Cannot Hold"

Ask students to work in pairs or small discussion groups to list reasons why this Spotlight On feature is included as part of the "The Center Cannot Hold" collection. What do the themes and images in Eliot's poetry have in common with Yeats's "The Second Coming"? What other selections in this collection can Eliot's poems be compared with?

OBJECTIVES

1. Read and interpret the poem
2. Generate relevant, interesting, and researchable questions
3. Recognize distinctive and shared characteristics of the culture
4. Compare the poem's content with personal experiences
5. Recognize and discuss themes that cross cultures

Planning

- **Block Schedule**
  Block Scheduling Lesson Plans with Pacing Guide
- **Traditional Schedule**
  Lesson Plans Including Strategies for English-Language Learners
- **One-Stop Planner**
  CD-ROM with Test Generator

BROWSING IN THE FILES

About the Author. Akhmatova's biographer Amanda Haight explains, "In a time when a poem on a scrap of paper could mean a death sentence, to continue to write, to commit one's work to faithful friends who were prepared to learn poems by heart and thus preserve them, was only possible if one was convinced of the absolute importance and necessity of poetry." Though often ill—and near starvation from subsisting on a diet of mainly black bread and tea—Akhmatova continued to write and to share her poems.

WORLD LITERATURE

Russia

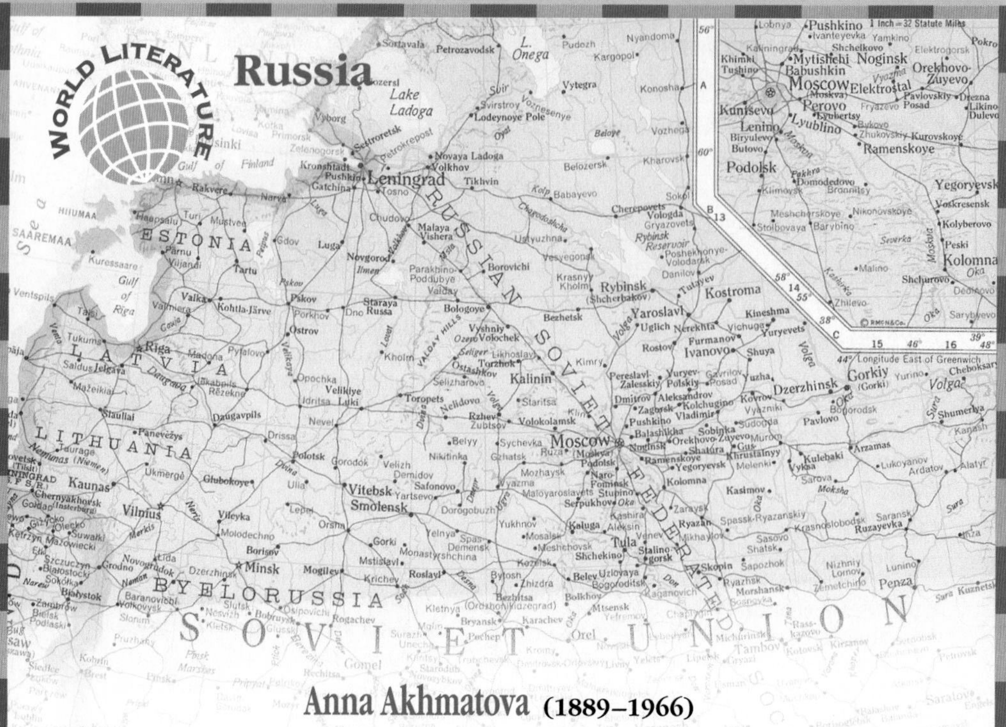

Anna Akhmatova (1889–1966)

Anna Akhmatova grew up near St. Petersburg, the capital of Russia before the 1917 revolution that led to a Communist takeover of the government. As a young writer just before the revolution, she was one of the founders of a literary movement called *acmeism* (ak′mē·iz′əm), which rejected ambivalent symbols in poetry and strove instead to present clearly etched ideas. (Just as Yeats is almost synonymous with Ireland, Akhmatova is regarded as a major Russian lyric poet.)

After the revolution, however, Akhmatova's poetry did not find a sympathetic ear with the new Communist regime. The official outlook was that art should exist in the service of the state and should treat themes that were politically and socially "useful." Akhmatova's first husband, the poet Nikolai Gumilev, was executed as a counterrevolutionary in 1921, and Akhmatova herself was forbidden to publish. As the terrifying years of Joseph Stalin's dictatorship wore on, she saw more and more of her friends arrested and her own son imprisoned. Throughout this period, however, she continued to write and to serve as mentor for a younger generation of Russian poets.

After Stalin's death in 1953, the works of many Russian writers were again publicly accepted. Akhmatova was finally able to enjoy a brief period of official recognition in the last years of her life. Boris Pasternak, a Russian novelist and poet who was himself threatened with banishment, paid tribute to Akhmatova in these words: "Your work throbs high with our remembered past."

Anna Akhmatova.

(Map) ©Rand McNally R. L. #98-S-116.

go.hrw.com
LEO 12-12

Reaching All Students

Struggling Readers

Be sure these students read the Background section before reading the poem. To ensure their understanding of the poem, you might ask them to make a storyboard of the Biblical story of Lot and his wife in Sodom. Check their storyboards to see whether they understand the sequence of events that lead up to the action in the poem.

English Language Learners

The flowing rhythm and clear rhyming pattern provide ideal material for English language learners to practice their pronunciation and intonation. First, go through the text as a choral reading so that all students can recite the poem together. Then, do an echo reading, in which you read each line and have students repeat it, modeling their pronunciation on yours.

Advanced Learners

The following four-line poem begins a longer work of Akhmatova's called *Requiem.* Challenge these students to compare and contrast it with "Lot's Wife":

No foreign sky protected me,
No stranger's wing shielded my face.
I stand as witness to the common lot,
Survivor of that time, that place.

Before You Read

LOT'S WIFE

Background

Besides its significance as a religious document, the Bible has served over the centuries as a source of literary inspiration for countless writers. In "Lot's Wife," the speaker focuses on a Biblical incident recounted in Genesis 19. Angered by the wickedness of the city of Sodom, God sends angels to punish the inhabitants. When the angels arrive in disguise as men, only Lot treats them hospitably. Lot's reward is a warning of the city's wholesale destruction. He is told to flee Sodom with his family and not to look back under any conditions. As Lot's family escapes, however, his wife disobeys the angels' command and turns her head to gaze upon the city. She is immediately turned into a pillar of salt.

For the twentieth-century Russian poet Anna Akhmatova, this ancient story assumed a poignant, almost painful relevance. She lived under a totalitarian regime that dictated the terms under which artists and writers could work. Yet, when Akhmatova had an opportunity to flee oppression in her homeland, she remained. In the following poem, Akhmatova views the story of Lot's wife, an ancient, unwilling exile, from the perspective of a modern woman who was sorely tempted by the lure of exile but who resisted.

Reading Skills and Strategies

Drawing on Personal Experience

As you read, jot down notes on how you might feel if you came under intense pressure to leave your homeland because life there had become intolerable. Would you regard such a departure as an act of desertion, or as a wise investment in the future? After you have thought about your own reactions, try to gauge the degree of sympathy with which the speaker regards Lot's wife.

Lot's Wife

Anna Akhmatova

translated by **Richard Wilbur**

The just man followed then his angel guide
Where he strode on the black highway, hulking and bright;
But a wild grief in his wife's bosom cried, [A]
Look back, it is not too late for a last sight

Of the red towers of your native Sodom, the square [B]
Where once you sang, the gardens you shall mourn,
And the tall house with empty windows where
You loved your husband and your babes were born.

She turned, and looking on the bitter view
Her eyes were welded shut by mortal pain; [C]
Into transparent salt her body grew,
And her quick feet were rooted in the plain.

Who would waste tears upon her? Is she not
The least of our losses, this unhappy wife?
Yet in my heart she will not be forgot [D]
Who, for a single glance, gave up her life.

Summary ■

As Lot and his wife retreat from Sodom, Lot's wife succumbs to an urge to look back at the place where she sang, planted gardens, loved her husband, and gave birth to her children. For disobeying the angel's command not to look back, she is immediately turned into a pillar of salt. In the final stanza, the speaker sympathizes with the urge to look back at one's homeland, even at such an awful cost.

[A] Reading Skills and Strategies

Drawing on Personal Experience

? If you were in the same position as Lot's wife, would you also have the urge to look back? Would you give in to the urge? Explain your answer. [Possible responses: Yes, it would take a great act of will not to do so; no, the consequences would be too dire.]

[B] Reading Skills and Strategies

Making Inferences

? To what city other than Sodom might the "red towers" and "the square" refer? [It might refer to Moscow, where Red Square is a famous landmark.]

[C] Vocabulary Note

Word Choice

? Why is *welded* a better word choice than, for example, *closed*? [Possible response: The word *welded* suggests a mechanical and involuntary act achieved through the application of intense heat; *welded* suggests the force and finality of an angry, punishing God who is swift to anger and unyielding in his retribution.]

[D] Appreciating Language

Shift in Point of View

? How does the point of view shift in the final stanza? What is the purpose of this shift? [Possible response: It shifts from third person to first person. The shift allows the voice of the speaker to express sympathy and identification with Lot's wife; it underscores the fact that the experience of Lot's wife is linked—on a metaphorical level—to the speaker's life and times.]

Using Students' Strengths

Intrapersonal Learners

Encourage students to find their own methods for expressing their understanding of both the meaning of the poem and the emotions conveyed by it. Students might wish to write a journal entry or even their own poem in order to express their responses to the direct questions posed by the poem: "Who would waste tears upon her? Is she not / the least of our losses, this unhappy wife?"

Verbal Learners

Pairs or small groups of students might argue or debate why Lot's wife has no name, or why Akhmatova does not give her one. They might also discuss whom this poem seems to show in a more positive light: Lot or Lot's wife. Do students find any feminist messages in the poem, or is the poem about issues that have nothing to do with gender? Encourage students to present, discuss, and debate their own opinions and interpretations.

Responding to the Art

Kasimir Malevich (1878–1935) was the founder of the art movement called Suprematism. He coined this term to express a new approach to art in which communicating "pure feeling" was the only objective for the artist. He used bold shapes and strong colors to simplify and purify his visual language.

Activity. Ask students how they might expect a woman with a rake to be pictured. Have them consider the clothes she might wear, her posture, the look on her face, the background against which she might be set, and even the position of the rake. Then, have students contrast the image in the painting with the one they have imagined. Students might also be asked why there seems to be nothing to rake in the picture. What does the pose of the woman suggest? Is there a "message" in this painting, or is it simply an aesthetic expression?

Finding Common Ground

This feature encourages lively discussion of students' responses to the poem. Suggest that students work in groups of four or five. In addition to discussing the imaginative use of the Biblical story, students might also consider why Akhmatova turned to the Bible at all when her message and purpose seem to be so entirely rooted in her own time and place.

Woman with a Rake (late 19th or early 20th century) by Kasimir Malevich.

Tretyakov Gallery, Moscow.

Finding Common Ground

Meet in small groups to discuss this poem. Your first task will be to formulate the questions you'd like to focus on. In your discussions, be sure to consider your reading notes and how your responses to exile compare with those of the speaker. Also, be sure to address how Akhmatova imaginatively used this Biblical story to stand for something else. Assign a recorder for your group. At the completion of your discussion, have the recorder report to the class at large on your responses to the poem.

As a class, try to agree on at least three responses to the poem—in other words, try to find some common ground.

Making the Connections

Connecting to the Theme: "The Center Cannot Hold"

You can link this poem to the collection theme by asking questions like these:

- **What kind of "center" is failing to "hold" in this poem?** [Possible answer: Both home and country can be thought of as centers of personal and political life, and this poem suggests banishment or exile from both.]
- **In what ways does this poem remind you of "The Second Coming," the Yeats poem that opens this collection and helps to state its theme?** [Possible answers: Both poems contain Biblical references; both poems suggest destruction on a huge scale; both poems contain images of immobility, of frozen action—Yeats's Sphinx and Akhmatova's pillar of salt; both poems evoke a sense of apocalyptic, cosmic horror—in "The Second Coming," the Sphinx begins to move, and in "Lot's Wife," a woman is turned to salt. Yet both poems suggest compassion and humanity. In "The Second Coming," Yeats recalls the "rocking cradle," a hopeful image referring to the birth of Christ; in Akhmatova's poem, the speaker shows empathy and asserts that she will not forget Lot's wife.]

Graham Greene

(1904–1991)

Graham Greene (1957).

For his serious idealistic novels dealing with contemporary moral dilemmas and for his light "entertainments" and thrillers, Graham Greene has won a rare combination of popular and critical admiration. His intention in his writing was always to tell the truth, which he saw as a primary duty of the artist, and, as you will see, Greene often wrote about life's losers—at least those whom we conventionally think of as losers.

Henry Graham Greene was born to a comfortable family in Berkhamsted, Hertfordshire. His father was the headmaster of Berkhamsted School, which Greene attended as a child. For reasons that are not clear, as Greene grew into adolescence, he became increasingly depressed and unhappy at school, which he described as his first impression of hell. After he tried to run away, he was sent to London to undergo psychoanalysis. He would later recall those six months in London as among the happiest of his life.

While he was still at Berkhamsted, Greene had a story published by a local newspaper, and he recalled feeling a sense of true literary triumph "for the first and last time." The experience convinced him to become a professional writer. He attended Oxford University, wrote a novel that failed to find a publisher, and published a book of poems in 1925, the year he graduated. As an apprenticeship, he went to work as a reporter for the Nottingham *Journal*.

In 1926, Greene became engaged to a Roman Catholic woman, Vivien Dayrell-Browning, and agreed to take instruction in her faith. Although he had been a confirmed atheist, he became convinced of "the probable existence of something we call God." His Catholic faith would turn out to be an important factor in his writing.

Greene took a job with the London *Times* and worked there until his first novel, *The Man Within,* was published in 1929. His next books were adventure stories, but they received little attention. Greene began to come into his own with the thriller *Stamboul Train* (1932; also published under the title *Orient Express*). This story of a train journey to Istanbul was the first of Greene's works that were made into movies.

Greene brought his religious concerns into his fiction with the novel *Brighton Rock* (1938), in which he explored the nature of good and evil and the inexplicable workings of divine grace. Pursuing the theme further in *The Power and the Glory* (1940), Greene revealed an unorthodox kind of Catholicism in which naturally sinful men and women, living in a fallen world, are often given a last-minute chance at redemption. As one critic notes, Greene's characters live "on the border between love and hate, good and evil, heaven and hell."

During World War II, Greene worked for the British Foreign Office, and afterward he became a director for a publishing house. During the 1950s, he was a celebrated foreign correspondent assigned to Malaysia, Indochina, Africa, and Cuba. His experiences as a journalist were reflected in novels such as *The Quiet American* (1955), which prophetically dealt with the implications of American involvement in Vietnam.

Greene's novels came out steadily, among them *The Heart of the Matter* (1948), *The End of the Affair* (1951), and *A Burnt-Out Case* (1961). Many of his books have been made into films, including *The Third Man* (1950) and *Our Man in Havana* (1958). He also published several plays, as well as a number of travel books describing his journeys.

In the first volume of his autobiography, *A Sort of Life* (1971), Greene revealed his motives for writing fiction as "a desire to reduce the chaos of experience to some sort of order, and a hungry curiosity. We cannot love others, so the theologians teach, unless in some degree we can love ourselves, and curiosity too begins at home."

go.hrw.com
LEO 12-12

OBJECTIVES

1. Read and interpret the story
2. Identify and analyze the story's setting
3. Make inferences about characters' motives
4. Express understanding through writing and role-playing
5. Learn and use new words

SKILLS

Literary
- Identify and analyze the story's setting

Reading
- Make inferences about characters' motives

Writing
- Collect ideas for an informative report
- Interpret imagery and make connections with other works

Speaking
- Evaluate oral persuasion by role-playing a part in a trial

Vocabulary
- Learn and use new words

Viewing/Representing
- Gain historical perspective on a story through visual representation (ATE)

Planning

- **Traditional Schedule**
  Lesson Plans Including Strategies for English-Language Learners
- **One-Stop Planner**
  CD-ROM with Test Generator

Resources: Print and Media

Reading
- *Graphic Organizers for Active Reading*, p. 92
- *Words to Own*, p. 25
- *Audio CD Library*, Disc 16, Track 8

Elements of Literature
- *Literary Elements*
  Transparency 22
  Worksheet, p. 67

Writing and Language
- *Daily Oral Grammar*
  Transparency 31
- *Grammar and Language Links*
  Worksheet, p. 53
- *Language Workshop CD-ROM*

Viewing and Representing
- *Visual Connections*
  Videocassette B, Segment 10

Assessment
- *Formal Assessment*, p. 189
- *Portfolio Management System*, p. 187
- *Preparation for College Admission Exams*, p. 45
- *Test Generator (One-Stop Planner CD-ROM)*

Internet
- go.hrw.com (keyword: LE0 12-12)

Summary ▪

"T." (Trevor) takes the leadership of the Wormsley Common gang away from Blackie when he suggests the organized destruction of a historic house that survived the German blitz. While the house's owner, Mr. Thomas (whom the gang calls "Old Misery"), is away, the gang thoroughly demolishes the inside of the house. When the owner returns unexpectedly early, they lock him in his outhouse. During the night Mr. Thomas spends there, the gang weakens the foundation of the house and rigs a truck parked nearby so that, on the next morning, the unwitting driver pulls down the gutted house as he drives away. When the driver releases Mr. Thomas from the outhouse, Mr. Thomas is devastated by the loss of his house, but the driver cannot stop himself from laughing uncontrollably at the situation.

Resources

Viewing and Representing
Videocassette B, Segment 10
This video shows the British response to World War II. For full lesson plans and worksheets, see *Visual Connections Teacher's Manual.*

Ⓐ Elements of Literature

Setting

? What is the time and place? [It is August, on the eve of a holiday. The place is Wormsley Common.] Note that the name *Wormsley* suggests an apple gone rotten; there is also a play on words in the use of the word *Common*, with its suggestion of commoners.

Ⓑ Reading Skills and Strategies

Inferring Motives

? What kind of emotional environment do you think T. has come from? [Because his family has "come down in the world," yet his mother still considers herself better than the neighbors, we might assume that T. has been raised in an atmosphere of bitterness and resentment.]

Before You Read

THE DESTRUCTORS

Make the Connection

The Rage to Destroy

This story is set in 1954, nine years after the end of World War II. During the war, the city of London had been regularly "blitzed" by German planes dropping firebombs, which destroyed many buildings in the city. Years after the war, the people of London still walked along bomb-blasted streets. More troubling than this physical destruction, though, was what many people saw as the moral destruction of society, the collapse of goodness and hope, especially among gangs of young people. Before you read, think about your own knowledge of or experience with vandalism. What motivates some people to want to destroy beautiful things?

Reading Skills and Strategies

Inferring Motives

Each section of this story gives you a bit more insight into the enigmatic main character, T. After each section, jot down how you see him, and note details of his words and actions that you find revealing. What needs or conflicts do you think motivate him to act as he does?

Elements of Literature

Setting

At one point in this story, the word *beautiful* appears several times. As readers, we are struck by the word's incongruity. We recognize, as do certain characters in the story, that the word somehow doesn't belong here. Until this scene and in all the scenes that follow, we are immersed in the seediness of Greene's **setting.** Greene's characteristic use of coarse imagery and language has created a drab world full of shabby violence.

The Destructors

Graham Greene

1

Ⓐ It was on the eve of August Bank Holiday that the latest recruit became the leader of the Wormsley Common gang. No one was surprised except Mike, but Mike at the age of nine was surprised by everything. "If you don't shut your mouth," somebody once said to him, "you'll get a frog down it." After that Mike had kept his teeth tightly clamped except when the surprise was too great.

The new recruit had been with the gang since the beginning of the summer holidays, and there were possibilities about his brooding silence that all recognized. He never wasted a word even to tell his name until that was required of him by the rules. When he said "Trevor" it was a statement of fact, not as it would have been with the others a statement of shame or defiance. Nor did anyone laugh except Mike, who finding himself without support and meeting the dark gaze of the newcomer opened his mouth and was quiet again. Ⓑ There was every reason why T., as he was afterward referred to, should have been an object of mockery—there was his name (and they substituted the initial because otherwise they had no excuse not to laugh at it), the fact that his father, a former architect and present clerk, had "come down in the world" and that his mother considered herself better than the neighbors. What but an odd quality of danger, of the unpredictable, established him in the gang without any ignoble ceremony of initiation?

WORDS TO OWN
ignoble (ig·nō′bəl) *adj.:* shameful; degrading.

Preteaching Vocabulary

Words to Own

Have pairs of students read the meanings of the Words to Own listed at the bottom of the selection pages. Then, have them collaborate to write original sentences using the words. After checking students' sentences, ask them to match each of these numbered words with its meaning.

1. altruistic	[j]	a. shameful
2. implacable	[c]	b. unplanned
3. abstain	[e]	c. inflexible
4. façades	[h]	d. huge mess
5. shambles	[d]	e. refrain from
6. ignoble	[a]	f. impatient
7. exhilaration	[i]	g. last name
8. surname	[g]	h. fronts of buildings
9. restive	[f]	i. high excitement
10. impromptu	[b]	j. unselfish

Private Collection.

Juvenile Counsel: Boys on a Doorstep (20th century) by Henry Lamb.

The gang met every morning in an impromptu car-park, the site of the last bomb of the first blitz. The leader, who was known as Blackie, claimed to have heard it fall, and no one was precise enough in his dates to point out that he would have been one year old and fast asleep on the down platform of Wormsley Common Underground Station. On one side of the car-park leaned the first occupied house, number 3, of the shattered Northwood Terrace—literally leaned, for it had suffered from the blast of the bomb and the side walls were supported on wooden struts. A smaller bomb and some incendiaries had fallen beyond, so that the house stuck up like a jagged tooth and carried on the further wall relics of its neighbor, a dado,[1] the remains of a fireplace. T., whose words were almost confined to voting "Yes" or "No" to the plan of operations proposed each day by Blackie, once startled the whole gang by saying broodingly, "Wren[2] built that house, father says."

"Who's Wren?"

"The man who built St. Paul's."[3]

"Who cares?" Blackie said. "It's only Old Misery's."

Old Misery—whose real name was Thomas—had once been a builder and decorator. He lived alone in the crippled house, doing for himself: Once a week you could see him coming back across the common with bread and vegetables, and once as the boys played in the car-park he put his head over the smashed wall of his garden and looked at them.

1. **dado** (dā′dō): wood paneling along the lower part of the walls of a room.

2. **Wren:** Sir Christopher Wren (1632–1723), a celebrated English architect.

3. **St. Paul's:** cathedral in London.

WORDS TO OWN

impromptu (im·prämp′tōō′) *adj.:* unplanned.

C Historical Connections

The Blitz

The blitz took place in 1940–1941. The word *blitz* is a shortened form of the German word *blitzkrieg*—literally, "lightning war," an offensive strike, often of bombs from the air, launched with great violence and speed. Though historically associated with the Germans in World War II, *blitz* also means any "sudden, overwhelming bombardment." Watch for this word at the story's end.

D Elements of Literature

Setting

? In what ways is this already a setting of destruction? [The neighborhood is rubble. Blasts have torn away some of the foundation and walls of the only house still remaining. The house is unsupported and isolated. As if anticipating that there will one day be a vacant lot in this space, people are already parking cars next to the house.]

E Reading Skills and Strategies

Inferring Motives

? Note that some details about T. are introduced here that will be useful for understanding what motivates him later in the story. What are these details? [Possible responses: His father understands the significance of a house by Wren and has communicated this to his son; T. deems the information about Wren to be worth both remembering and repeating.]

Reaching All Students

Struggling Readers

Encourage these students to visualize the setting, events, and characters as they read. As an aid to this process, you might make available pictures of London after the blitz. Be sure students also understand what is meant by the "impromptu car-park": This helps explain the presence of the truck at the end of the story and its ability to inflict the final damage.

English Language Learners

Explain that there are many Briticisms in this story, and be sure to define the most fundamental ones: *bank holiday* (a legal holiday) and *common* (a large open space intended to be shared). Point out the glosses that define and explain other Briticisms such as *loo* (bathroom) and *lorry* (truck).

Advanced Learners

T. and Mr. Thomas share some similarities, including their initial *T.* and the fact that T. is the child of an architect, who would value a Christopher Wren building just as keenly as Old Misery (Mr. Thomas) does. What else unites these two characters? Is one Old Misery and the other "young misery"? In each one's existence or worldview, are there "only things" (p. 953, para. 14)? Urge students to read with this focus in mind and to record their ideas on paper.

(A) Struggling Readers
Visualizing

? What details of the setting can you visualize? [Possible responses: The outhouse, or loo, is removed from the house by some distance and a "narrow garden." Though only a wooden "shed," the outhouse is completely intact, unlike the house itself.] **Note that the distance of the outhouse from the house will become an important detail later.**

(B) Reading Skills and Strategies
Inferring Motives

? Why do you think Mr. Thomas gives the boys the candy? [Possible responses: He is lonely. He can see the boys are a tough group, and he would rather be on good terms with them. He hopes kindness will do some good—and perhaps help protect his property. He is basically a compassionate person and believes that boys in their situation might respond to some small kindnesses.]

(C) Critical Thinking
Interpreting

? What motives do the boys attach to Mr. Thomas's offering of candy? What does this suggest about their general attitudes concerning adults? [Possible responses: They guess he has found the candy dropped somewhere, has stolen it, or is offering it as a bribe to stop them from bouncing balls on his wall. The boys are suspicious, distrusting, and used to bad treatment and dishonesty from adults.]

(D) Reading Skills and Strategies
Making Generalizations

? What kind of mischief does the Wormsley Common gang get into under Blackie's leadership, and what does this say about the character of both the gang and Blackie? [Possible responses: The gang catches free rides on the city buses, not a very serious infraction of the rules; this example suggests that neither Blackie nor his gang is engaged in any major destruction or rebellion.]

(E) English Language Learners
British Dialect and Usage

Be sure students understand that an expression like "He showed it me" is characteristic of the boys' dialect and means "He showed it to me"; be sure they also understand that *pinch*, in this story, means "to steal."

"Been to the loo,"[4] one of the boys said, for it was common knowledge that since the bombs fell something had gone wrong with the pipes of the house and Old Misery was too mean to spend money on the property. He could do the redecorating himself at cost price, but he had never learned plumbing. The loo was a wooden shed at the bottom of the narrow garden with a star-shaped hole in the door: It had escaped the blast which had smashed the house next door and sucked out the window frames of number 3.

The next time the gang became aware of Mr. Thomas was more surprising. Blackie, Mike, and a thin yellow boy, who for some reason was called by his surname Summers, met him on the common coming back from the market. Mr. Thomas stopped them. He said glumly, "You belong to the lot that play in the car-park?"

Mike was about to answer when Blackie stopped him. As the leader he had responsibilities. "Suppose we are?" he said ambiguously.

"I got some chocolates," Mr. Thomas said. "Don't like 'em myself. Here you are. Not enough to go round, I don't suppose. There never is," he added with somber conviction. He handed over three packets of Smarties.

The gang were puzzled and perturbed by this action and tried to explain it away. "Bet someone dropped them and he picked 'em up," somebody suggested.

"Pinched 'em and then got in a bleeding funk," another thought aloud.

"It's a bribe," Summers said. "He wants us to stop bouncing balls on his wall."

"We'll show him we don't take bribes," Blackie said, and they sacrificed the whole morning to the game of bouncing that only Mike was young enough to enjoy. There was no sign from Mr. Thomas.

Next day T. astonished them all. He was late at the rendezvous, and the voting for that day's exploit took place without him. At Blackie's suggestion the gang was to disperse in pairs, take buses at random, and see how many free rides could be snatched from unwary conductors (the operation was to be carried out in pairs to avoid cheating). They were drawing lots for their companions when T. arrived.

"Where you been, T.?" Blackie asked. "You can't vote now. You know the rules."

"I've been *there*," T. said. He looked at the ground, as though he had thoughts to hide.

"Where?"

"At Old Misery's." Mike's mouth opened and then hurriedly closed again with a click. He had remembered the frog.

"At Old Misery's?" Blackie said. There was nothing in the rules against it, but he had a sensation that T. was treading on dangerous ground. He asked hopefully, "Did you break in?"

"No. I rang the bell."

"And what did you say?"

"I said I wanted to see his house."

"What did he do?"

"He showed it me."

"Pinch anything?"

"No."

"What did you do it for then?"

The gang had gathered round: It was as though an impromptu court were about to form and to try some case of deviation. T. said, "It's a beautiful house," and still watching the ground, meeting no one's eyes, he licked his lips first one way, then the other.

"What do you mean, a beautiful house?" Blackie asked with scorn.

"It's got a staircase two hundred years old like a corkscrew. Nothing holds it up."

"What do you mean, nothing holds it up. Does it float?"

"It's to do with opposite forces, Old Misery said."

"What else?"

"There's paneling."

"Like in the Blue Boar?"

"Two hundred years old."

"Is Old Misery two hundred years old?"

Mike laughed suddenly and then was quiet again. The meeting was in a serious mood. For the first time since T. had strolled into the car-park on the first day of the holidays his position was in danger. It only needed a single use of his real name and the gang would be at his heels.

4. **loo:** British slang for "bathroom." *Loo* comes from the French word *lieux,* short for *les lieux d'aisances* (lā lyö de·zäns′), which means "places of convenience."

WORDS TO OWN
surname (sʉr′nām′) *n.:* last name.

Crossing the Curriculum

Architecture

Greene could have chosen any architect, but he chose Sir Christopher Wren. Why? Invite students to find out by researching Wren's career, influences, and philosophy. Students will learn that Wren was a Renaissance man (who actually lived just after the Renaissance), gifted in mathematics and science (he was once a professor of astronomy) as well as in architecture. For the purposes of this story, however, the key facts of interest are that Wren was most notably and consistently a church architect. Wren was obsessed with beauty and how it could arise from the strong clarity of geometry; he reaffirmed the classical style.

"What did you do it for?" Blackie asked. He was just, he had no jealousy, he was anxious to retain T. in the gang if he could. It was the word "beautiful" that worried him—that belonged to a class world that you could still see parodied at the Wormsley Common Empire by a man wearing a top hat and a monocle, with a haw-haw accent. He was tempted to say, "My dear Trevor, old chap," and unleash his hell hounds. "If you'd broken in," he said sadly—that indeed would have been an exploit worthy of the gang.

"This was better," T. said. "I found out things." He continued to stare at his feet, not meeting anybody's eye, as though he were absorbed in some dream he was unwilling—or ashamed—to share.

"What things?"

"Old Misery's going to be away all tomorrow and Bank Holiday."

Blackie said with relief, "You mean we could break in?"

"And pinch things?" somebody asked.

Blackie said, "Nobody's going to pinch things. Breaking in—that's good enough, isn't it? We don't want any court stuff."

"I don't want to pinch anything," T. said. "I've got a better idea."

"What is it?"

T. raised his eyes, as gray and disturbed as the drab August day. "We'll pull it down," he said. "We'll destroy it."

Blackie gave a single hoot of laughter and then, like Mike, fell quiet, daunted by the serious implacable gaze. "What'd the police be doing all the time?" he said.

"They'd never know. We'd do it from inside. I've found a way in." He said with a sort of intensity, "We'd be like worms, don't you see, in an apple. When we came out again there'd be nothing there, no staircase, no panels, nothing but just walls, and then we'd make the walls fall down—somehow."

"We'd go to jug," Blackie said.

"Who's to prove? And anyway we wouldn't have pinched anything." He added without the smallest flicker of glee, "There wouldn't be anything to pinch after we'd finished."

"I've never heard of going to prison for breaking things," Summers said.

"There wouldn't be time," Blackie said. "I've seen housebreakers at work."

"There are twelve of us," T. said. "We'd organize."

"None of us know how—"

"I know," T. said. He looked across at Blackie. "Have you got a better plan?"

"Today," Mike said tactlessly, "we're pinching free rides—"

"Free rides," T. said. "You can stand down, Blackie, if you'd rather. . . ."

"The gang's got to vote."

"Put it up then."

Blackie said uneasily, "It's proposed that tomorrow and Monday we destroy Old Misery's house."

"Here, here," said a fat boy called Joe.

"Who's in favor?"

T. said, "It's carried."

"How do we start?" Summers asked.

"He'll tell you," Blackie said. It was the end of his leadership. He went away to the back of the car-park and began to kick a stone, dribbling it this way and that. There was only one old Morris[5] in the park, for few cars were left there except lorries:[6] Without an attendant there was no safety. He took a flying kick at the car and scraped a little paint off the rear mudguard. Beyond, paying no more attention to him than to a stranger, the gang had gathered round T.; Blackie was dimly aware of the fickleness of favor. He thought of going home, of never returning, of letting them all discover the hollowness of T.'s leadership, but suppose after all what T. proposed was possible—nothing like it had ever been done before. The fame of the Wormsley Common car-park gang would surely reach around London. There would be headlines in the papers. Even the grown-up gangs who ran the betting at the all-in wrestling and the barrow-boys[7] would hear with respect of how Old Misery's house had been destroyed. Driven by the pure,

5. **Morris:** car made by the Morris firm, a British automaker.
6. **lorries:** British for "trucks."
7. **barrow-boys:** boys who sold fruit or vegetables from a barrow, or cart.

Words to Own
implacable (im·plā′kə·bəl) *adj.:* inflexible; relentless; obstinate.

F Cultural Connections

Class in British Culture

? What details in this paragraph convey the distrust of the "common" boys for a higher-class world? [Possible responses: The word *beautiful* worries Blackie; he mocks expressions associated with the upper classes ("my dear Trevor" and "old chap").]

G Reading Skills and Strategies

Inferring Motives

? What do you think has led T. to devise this cold-blooded, destructive plan? [Possible responses: Since T. has come close to being ousted from the gang for the upper-class taste he has revealed in his appreciation of Old Misery's house, he may be trying to prove that he is not only one of the gang, but its most determined member; his "disturbed" eyes suggest that he is a young man beyond hope and conscience; seeing the beauty of the house has brought out an urge to spoil and destroy what he—and, by extension, his family—cannot have; perhaps he has an unconscious urge to destroy something his father stands for—architecture.]

H Appreciating Language

Levels of Diction

After pointing out that *jug* is British slang for "jail," ask students what differences in speech patterns they can see between T. and the rest of the gang. [Possible answers: T. tends to use longer sentences and more sophisticated words, including the highly suspect *beautiful.* The other gang members use more dialect, more slang, and simpler sentences.]

I Reading Skills and Strategies

Inferring Motives

? Why does Blackie decide to support T.'s plan? [Possible response: The gang voted to support it, and he must go along; he rationalizes that, because what T. is planning has never been done before and is on such a "monumental" scale, it will bring fame and respect to the gang.]

Using Students' Strengths

Kinesthetic Learners

Several scenes in this story consist primarily of dialogue, such as the conversation between T. and the gang after T. has seen Old Misery's house. Have students work in small groups to choose a scene and prepare a dramatic reading. To guide their rehearsals and performance, ask groups to discuss beforehand the traits they will focus on to represent each character and the specific words, lines, or pauses they wish to emphasize.

Logical/Mathematical Learners

When a house is demolished by conventional methods, how is it done? Is the process of destruction described in this story realistic, or even feasible? Invite students to conduct research or to consult a local construction firm to find out. Students may present the actual conventional process of demolition by means of a flow chart, beginning with the legal step of getting authorization to demolish a building.

Ⓐ Elements of Literature

Setting

? Why do you think the story is set on a Sunday and includes references to going to church? [Possible responses: The Sunday setting heightens the irony of destruction, because Sunday is the Christian Sabbath, or day of rest; it is also the day when, according to the Bible, Christ rose after death; also, ironically, Sunday is the day when Christians are often reminded in church sermons to do right and good.]

Ⓑ Elements of Literature

Symbolism

Greene's Catholicism was an important part of his life. Advanced students may be challenged to agree or disagree with the idea that references to the garden and the apple in this story are symbolic, alluding to the events of Genesis in the Bible.

Ⓒ Reading Skills and Strategies

Inferring Motives

? Why do you think the gang is putting so much effort into the destruction of this house? [Possible response: They want to achieve the notoriety this act will bring them; they have nothing constructive to do, and unconsciously they feel empty and meaningless; destroying things gives them a thrill and, ironically, a sense of purpose and efficacy. Having grown up in an atmosphere of death and destruction, they want to smash and destroy what they see as the useless remains of war.]

Ⓓ Reading Skills and Strategies

Inferring Motives

? Mike "sat happily . . . clipping the wires," while T. "sat moodily . . . listening." What can you infer about each boy's motivations and reactions to this destructive enterprise? [Possible answers: Mike, perhaps because he is the youngest member of the gang, is busy, excited, and impressed with the importance and danger of what they are going to do. T., a more disturbed and complex boy, is less outwardly emotional, seeing only what is left to be done, methodically destroying for the sake of destroying.]

simple, and altruistic ambition of fame for the gang, Blackie came back to where T. stood in the shadow of Misery's wall.

T. was giving his orders with decision: It was as though this plan had been with him all his life, pondered through the seasons, now in his fifteenth year crystallized with the pain of puberty. "You," he said to Mike, "bring some big nails, the biggest you can find, and a hammer. Anyone else who can better bring a hammer and a screwdriver. We'll need plenty of them. Chisels too. We can't have too many chisels. Can anybody bring a saw?"

"I can," Mike said.

"Not a child's saw," T. said. "A real saw."

Blackie realized he had raised his hand like any ordinary member of the gang.

"Right, you bring one, Blackie. But now there's a difficulty. We want a hacksaw."

"What's a hacksaw?" someone asked.

"You can get 'em at Woolworth's," Summers said.

The fat boy called Joe said gloomily, "I knew it would end in a collection."

"I'll get one myself," T. said. "I don't want your money. But I can't buy a sledgehammer."

Blackie said, "They are working on number fifteen. I know where they'll leave their stuff for Bank Holiday."

"Then that's all," T. said. "We meet here at nine sharp."

"I've got to go to church," Mike said.

"Come over the wall and whistle. We'll let you in."

2

On Sunday morning all were punctual except Blackie, even Mike. Mike had had a stroke of luck. His mother felt ill, his father was tired after Saturday night, and he was told to go to church alone with many warnings of what would happen if he strayed. Blackie had had difficulty in smuggling out the saw, and then in finding the sledgehammer at the back of number 15. He approached the house from a lane at the rear of the garden, for fear of the policeman's beat along the main road. The tired evergreens kept off a stormy sun: Another wet Bank Holiday was being prepared over the Atlantic, beginning in swirls of dust under the trees. Blackie climbed the wall into Misery's garden.

There was no sign of anybody anywhere. The loo stood like a tomb in a neglected graveyard. The curtains were drawn. The house slept. Blackie lumbered nearer with the saw and the sledgehammer. Perhaps after all nobody had turned up: The plan had been a wild invention: They had woken wiser. But when he came close to the back door he could hear a confusion of sound, hardly louder than a hive in swarm: a clickety-clack, a bang bang bang, a scraping, a creaking, a sudden painful crack. He thought, It's true, and whistled.

They opened the back door to him and he came in. He had at once the impression of organization, very different from the old happy-go-lucky ways under his leadership. For a while he wandered up and down stairs looking for T. Nobody addressed him: He had a sense of great urgency, and already he could begin to see the plan. The interior of the house was being carefully demolished without touching the outer walls. Summers with hammer and chisel was ripping out the skirting-boards[8] in the ground floor dining room: He had already smashed the panels of the door. In the same room Joe was heaving up the parquet[9] blocks, exposing the soft wood floorboards over the cellar. Coils of wire came out of the damaged skirting and Mike sat happily on the floor, clipping the wires.

On the curved stairs two of the gang were working hard with an inadequate child's saw on the banisters—when they saw Blackie's big saw they signaled for it wordlessly. When he next saw them a quarter of the banisters had been dropped into the hall. He found T. at last in the bathroom—he sat moodily in the least cared-for room in the house, listening to the sounds coming up from below.

"You've really done it," Blackie said with awe. "What's going to happen?"

8. **skirting-boards:** baseboards; boards placed along the base of the walls of a room.

9. **parquet** (pär·kā′): fancy wood floor made of boards arranged in geometric patterns.

Words to Own

altruistic (al′tro͞o·is′tik) *adj.:* unselfish.

Getting Students Involved

Cooperative Learning

Read All About It! After they've read the story, have students work in groups of three to write the news story that might have followed this event. Remind groups to include a short, attention-getting headline; a powerful lead that tells *who, what, when, where, why,* and *how;* and a detailed report of what happened, in order from most interesting to least interesting events. Reports should include quotations from Mr. Thomas, the truck driver, and the parents of gang members who might have been interviewed after the event. The group should work together to plan or outline the article. Then, one person should be responsible for the draft, a second for the revision, and a third for putting the article in final form, proofreading it, and publishing it in the classroom. Groups can assess their work by establishing their own criteria beforehand (based on the assignment criteria) and deciding how well they met them when the article is finished.

"We've only just begun," T. said. He looked at the sledgehammer and gave his instructions. "You stay here and break the bath and the washbasin. Don't bother about the pipes. They come later."

Mike appeared at the door. "I've finished the wire, T.," he said.

"Good. You've just got to go wandering round now. The kitchen's in the basement. Smash all the china and glass and bottles you can lay hold of. Don't turn on the taps—we don't want a flood—yet. Then go into all the rooms and turn out drawers. If they are locked get one of the others to break them open. Tear up any papers you find and smash all the ornaments. Better take a carving knife with you from the kitchen. The bedroom's opposite here. Open the pillows and tear up the sheets. That's enough for the moment. And you, Blackie, when you've finished in here crack the plaster in the passage up with your sledgehammer."

"What are you going to do?" Blackie asked.

"I'm looking for something special," T. said.

It was nearly lunchtime before Blackie had finished and went in search of T. Chaos had advanced. The kitchen was a shambles of broken glass and china. The dining room was stripped of parquet, the skirting was up, the door had been taken off its hinges, and the destroyers had moved up a floor. Streaks of light came in through the closed shutters where they worked with the seriousness of creators—and destruction after all is a form of creation. A kind of imagination had seen this house as it had now become.

Mike said, "I've got to go home for dinner."

"Who else?" T. asked, but all the others on one excuse or another had brought provisions with them.

They squatted in the ruins of the room and swapped unwanted sandwiches. Half an hour for lunch and they were at work again. By the time Mike returned, they were on the top floor, and by six the superficial damage was completed. The doors were all off, all the skirtings raised, the furniture pillaged and ripped and smashed—no one could have slept in the house except on a bed of broken plaster. T. gave his orders—eight o'clock next morning—and to escape notice they climbed singly over the garden wall, into the car-park. Only Blackie and T. were left; the light had nearly gone, and when they touched a switch, nothing worked—Mike had done his job thoroughly.

"Did you find anything special?" Blackie asked.

T. nodded. "Come over here," he said, "and look." Out of both pockets he drew bundles of pound notes. "Old Misery's savings," he said. "Mike ripped out the mattress, but he missed them."

"What are you going to do? Share them?"

"We aren't thieves," T. said. "Nobody's going to steal anything from this house. I kept these for you and me—a celebration." He knelt down on the floor and counted them out—there were seventy in all. "We'll burn them," he said, "one by one," and taking it in turns they held a note upward and lit the top corner, so that the flame burnt slowly toward their fingers. The gray ash floated above them and fell on their heads like age. "I'd like to see Old Misery's face when we are through," T. said.

"You hate him a lot?" Blackie asked.

"Of course I don't hate him," T. said. "There'd be no fun if I hated him." The last burning note illuminated his brooding face. "All this hate and love," he said, "it's soft, it's hooey. There's only things, Blackie," and he looked round the room crowded with the unfamiliar shadows of half things, broken things, former things. "I'll race you home, Blackie," he said.

3

Next morning the serious destruction started. Two were missing—Mike and another boy, whose parents were off to Southend and Brighton in spite of the slow warm drops that had begun to fall and the rumble of thunder in the estuary like the first guns of the old blitz. "We've got to hurry," T. said.

Summers was restive. "Haven't we done enough?" he said. "I've been given a bob for slot machines. This is like work."

"We've hardly started," T. said. "Why, there's all the floors left, and the stairs. We haven't taken

Words to Own

shambles (sham′bəlz) *n.:* scene of great disorder. Derived from *schamel,* a Middle English name for a bench used to display raw meat for sale, the word came to mean a butcher shop or slaughterhouse and, by extension, any great mess.

restive (res′tiv) *adj.:* impatient; nervous.

E Vocabulary Note

Word History

The word *chaos*—at the heart of this collection's theme—comes from the Greek word for "empty space." *Chaos* is also the etymological basis of the word *gas,* the chemical state in which matter expands and contracts significantly, diffuses readily, and distributes itself spontaneously in any container.

F Struggling Readers

Visualizing

? What kinds of destruction do you see in your mind's eye? [Possible responses: broken glass and china; floors without their wood surfaces; ripped-out baseboards; doors pulled off their hinges; ripped and broken furniture; broken plaster everywhere.]

G Reading Skills and Strategies

Inferring Motives

? Why do you think T. chooses Old Misery's money as the "something special" he wants to destroy himself? [Possible responses: The boys regard Old Misery as a miser, and T. knows the hoard of money is important to him; since the money may represent what T. and his family have lost, burning it, rather than stealing it, may seem to T. the ultimate way to show that he finds no value in what the world finds meaningful—thus showing his contempt for life.]

H Reading Skills and Strategies

Responding to the Text

? How do you respond to T.'s speech about hate and love? [Possible responses: It is chilling because it makes T. seem like pure evil in human form—someone who destroys passionlessly and calculatedly, with no motive other than a desire to do harm; these tough words are a cover-up for some terrible anger, shame, or deep sorrow relating to his father, to his family, or to the loss of his family's status.]

Taking a Second Look

Review: Drawing Inferences from Textual Clues

As in any conversation, much is unstated in a story. Remind students that knowing what is implied, as well as recognizing what is stated, is a crucial reading skill.

Activities

1. Return to the Inferring Motives annotation on this page. Remind students that Trevor's motives are not stated; the reader must use clues from the text to draw inferences.
2. Have students work in groups to list all possible reasons for destroying the house, recalling that different members of the gang probably have different motives. Remind students that causation is complex, and motivations may be psychological, social, religious, economic, environmental, or even aesthetic (or, in this case, anti-aesthetic). For any motives students list, be sure that they can cite actual textual evidence that leads them to their conclusion.
3. Provide time for groups to share ideas.

A Vocabulary Note

Destroy or Destruct?

? Here Greene chooses and emphasizes the word *destroy*, yet, for this story's title, he decided against *destroyers* and instead created the word *destructors*. Why do you think he made this choice? [Possible responses: With its root *struct*, *destructor* seems more clearly the opposite of *constructor*; the suffix of *destructor* matches the suffix of another of its antonyms, *creator*.]

B Elements of Literature

Characterization

? The author says clearly that T. was never a child. What type of characterization is this? [direct] What does this statement suggest about Trevor? [Possible responses: He was never innocent. For whatever reasons—inner character, life circumstances, the influence of bitter parents—he never experienced a carefree childhood; perhaps he was always tainted with a destructive impulse and lack of conscience.]

C Reading Skills and Strategies

Inferring Motives

? Why does Blackie come to T.'s aid? [Possible responses: He wants not only to reclaim his leadership but also to do so through daring; he feels a moment of pity and understanding for T.; he wants the plan to be a success and the fame of the gang to spread.]

D Elements of Literature

Characterization

? What do T.'s responses in this stressful moment reveal about him? [Possible responses: He is calculating and able to think quickly; he shows qualities of leadership; he is single-mindedly focused on his goal; he is bright and is not distracted by emotions; he has the cold efficiency of a machine.]

out a single window. You voted like the others. We are going to *destroy* this house. There won't be anything left when we've finished."

They began again on the first floor picking up the top floorboards next the outer wall, leaving the joists exposed. Then they sawed through the joists and retreated into the hall, as what was left of the floor heeled and sank. They had learned with practice, and the second floor collapsed more easily. By the evening an odd exhilaration seized them as they looked down the great hollow of the house. They ran risks and made mistakes: When they thought of the windows it was too late to reach them. "Cor,"[10] Joe said, and dropped a penny down into the dry rubble-filled well. It cracked and span among the broken glass.

"Why did we start this?" Summers asked with astonishment; T. was already on the ground, digging at the rubble, clearing a space along the outer wall. "Turn on the taps," he said. "It's too dark for anyone to see now, and in the morning it won't matter." The water overtook them on the stairs and fell through the floorless rooms.

It was then they heard Mike's whistle at the back. "Something's wrong," Blackie said. They could hear his urgent breathing as they unlocked the door.

"The bogies?"[11] Summers asked.

"Old Misery," Mike said. "He's on his way." He put his head between his knees and retched. "Ran all the way," he said with pride.

"But why?" T. said. "He told me. . . ." He protested with the fury of the child he had never been, "It isn't fair."

"He was down at Southend," Mike said, "and he was on the train coming back. Said it was too cold and wet." He paused and gazed at the water. "My, you've had a storm here. Is the roof leaking?"

"How long will he be?"

"Five minutes. I gave Ma the slip and ran."

"We better clear," Summers said. "We've done enough, anyway."

"Oh, no, we haven't. Anybody could do this—" "This" was the shattered hollowed house with nothing left but the walls. Yet walls could be preserved. Façades were valuable. They could build inside again more beautifully than before. This could again be a home. He said angrily, "We've got to finish. Don't move. Let me think."

"There's no time," a boy said.

"There's got to be a way," T. said. "We couldn't have got thus far . . ."

"We've done a lot," Blackie said.

"No. No, we haven't. Somebody watch the front."

"We can't do any more."

"He may come in at the back."

"Watch the back too." T. began to plead. "Just give me a minute and I'll fix it. I swear I'll fix it." But his authority had gone with his ambiguity. He was only one of the gang. "Please," he said.

"Please," Summers mimicked him, and then suddenly struck home with the fatal name. "Run along home, Trevor."

T. stood with his back to the rubble like a boxer knocked groggy against the ropes. He had no words as his dreams shook and slid. Then Blackie acted before the gang had time to laugh, pushing Summers backward. "I'll watch the front, T.," he said, and cautiously he opened the shutters of the hall. The gray wet common stretched ahead, and the lamps gleamed in the puddles. "Someone's coming, T. No, it's not him. What's your plan, T.?"

"Tell Mike to go out to the loo and hide close beside it. When he hears me whistle he's got to count ten and start to shout."

"Shout what?"

"Oh, 'Help,' anything."

"You hear, Mike," Blackie said. He was the leader again. He took a quick look between the shutters. "He's coming, T."

"Quick, Mike. The loo. Stay here, Blackie, all of you till I yell."

"Where are you going, T.?"

"Don't worry. I'll see to this. I said I would, didn't I?"

10. **cor:** British exclamation of strong surprise or irritation. *Cor* is from *Gor,* or *Gord,* an earlier regional dialect pronunciation of "God."

11. **bogies** (bō′gēz): slang for "police."

Words to Own

exhilaration (eg·zil′ə·rā′shən) *n.:* excitement; high spirits.

façades (fə·sädz′) *n. pl.:* fronts of buildings.

Professional Notes

Critical Comment: Greene on Evil

In his autobiographical essay "The Lost Childhood," Graham Greene describes the amazement he experienced as a result of reading, calling it "a key turned in a lock." The books he read during his childhood were to have a lasting effect on him. The memory of a scene from one book grew into a scene in one of his own novels; the magic of another work kept him going when, later in life, he was working in "a little stuffy office in Freetown, Sierra Leone." The ideal characters of the fantastical tales he read as a child, however, failed to ring true after a while, and his expanded reading revealed a startling truth. As Greene describes it, "Goodness has only once found a perfect incarnation in a human body and never will again, but evil can always find a home there. Human nature is not black and white but black and gray." Greene's writing is a lifelong study of these finer shadings.

Old Misery came limping off the common. He had mud on his shoes and he stopped to scrape them on the pavement's edge. He didn't want to soil his house, which stood jagged and dark between the bomb sites, saved so narrowly, as he believed, from destruction. Even the fanlight had been left unbroken by the bomb's blast. Somewhere somebody whistled. Old Misery looked sharply round. He didn't trust whistles. A child was shouting: It seemed to come from his own garden. Then a boy ran into the road from the car-park. "Mr. Thomas," he called, "Mr. Thomas."

"What is it?"

"I'm terribly sorry, Mr. Thomas. One of us got taken short, and we thought you wouldn't mind, and now he can't get out."

"What do you mean, boy?"

"He's got stuck in your loo."

"He'd no business—Haven't I seen you before?"

"You showed me your house."

"So I did. So I did. That doesn't give you the right to—"

"Do hurry, Mr. Thomas. He'll suffocate."

"Nonsense. He can't suffocate. Wait till I put my bag in."

"I'll carry your bag."

"Oh, no, you don't. I carry my own."

"This way, Mr. Thomas."

"I can't get in the garden that way. I've got to go through the house."

"But you *can* get in the garden this way, Mr. Thomas. We often do."

"You often do?" He followed the boy with a scandalized fascination. "When? What right . . ."

"Do you see . . . ? The wall's low."

"I'm not going to climb walls into my own garden. It's absurd."

"This is how we do it. One foot here, one foot there, and over." The boy's face peered down, an arm shot out, and Mr. Thomas found his bag taken and deposited on the other side of the wall.

"Give me back my bag," Mr. Thomas said. From the loo a boy yelled and yelled. "I'll call the police."

"Your bag's all right, Mr. Thomas. Look. One foot there. On your right. Now just above. To your left." Mr. Thomas climbed over his own garden wall. "Here's your bag, Mr. Thomas."

"I'll have the wall built up," Mr. Thomas said. "I'll not have you boys coming over here, using my loo." He stumbled on the path, but the boy caught his elbow and supported him. "Thank you, thank you, my boy," he murmured automatically. Somebody shouted again through the dark. "I'm coming, I'm coming," Mr. Thomas called. He said to the boy beside him, "I'm not unreasonable. Been a boy myself. As long as things are done regular. I don't mind you playing round the place Saturday mornings. Sometimes I like company. Only it's got to be regular. One of you asks leave and I say Yes. Sometimes I'll say No. Won't feel like it. And you come in at the front door and out at the back. No garden walls."

"Do get him out, Mr. Thomas."

"He won't come to any harm in my loo," Mr. Thomas said, stumbling slowly down the garden. "Oh, my rheumatics," he said. "Always get 'em on Bank Holiday. I've got to go careful. There's loose stones here. Give me your hand. Do you know what my horoscope said yesterday? 'Abstain from any dealings in first half of week. Danger of serious crash.' That might be on this path," Mr. Thomas said. "They speak in parables and double meanings." He paused at the door of the loo. "What's the matter in there?" he called. There was no reply.

"Perhaps he's fainted," the boy said.

"Not in my loo. Here, you, come out," Mr. Thomas said, and giving a great jerk at the door he nearly fell on his back when it swung easily open. A hand first supported him and then pushed him hard. His head hit the opposite wall and he sat heavily down. His bag hit his feet. A hand whipped the key out of the lock and the door slammed. "Let me out," he called, and heard the key turn in the lock. "A serious crash," he thought, and felt dithery and confused and old.

A voice spoke to him softly through the star-shaped hole in the door. "Don't worry, Mr. Thomas," it said, "we won't hurt you, not if you stay quiet."

Mr. Thomas put his head between his hands and pondered. He had noticed that there was only one lorry in the car-park, and he felt certain that the driver would not come for it before the morn-

WORDS TO OWN

abstain (ab·stān′) *v.:* refrain from; hold oneself back from.

E Elements of Literature

Irony

? What is ironic about Old Misery's stopping to scrape mud off his shoes? [Possible response: He is worried about getting his house muddy, a trivial problem when a plan to destroy his house is well underway.]

F Struggling Readers

Identifying Pronoun Antecedents

? Who is *me* in these lines? [T.] **Usually a reader can trace a pronoun antecedent to the preceding text, but here the author is deliberately mysterious about T.'s identity, describing him only as "a boy" who "ran into the road." Therefore, to find this pronoun reference, students have to use prior information in the story—the fact that T. was the boy to whom Mr. Thomas showed the interior of his house.**

G Elements of Literature

Setting

? What details of the setting are emphasized here? [Possible answers: the garden that is about to be trespassed; the lowness of the garden wall.] **What significance do you find in these details?** [Possible responses: The presence of the wall may be ironic, since no wall can shut out evil. The lowness of the wall may suggest that Old Misery has inadequate defenses against incursions of evil.]

Skill Link

Generating Relevant, Interesting, Researchable Questions

What information about the blitz would add depth and meaning to a reading of this story? Ask students to generate researchable questions on the following topics:

- dates (beginning, ending, duration)
- numbers (attacks, planes, bombs, people killed and wounded, property damage)
- loss of priceless things (such as buildings by Wren, artworks)
- first-person accounts (A good source is *Children of the Blitz* by Robert Westall.)

Have students exchange their questions with a classmate to rank them in two ways: most interesting to least interesting; most researchable to least researchable. Encourage partners to discuss reasons for their rankings and ways of refining questions to make them more interesting or researchable.

Literature and the Movies

As mentioned in the biography on p. 947, many of Graham Greene's novels and short stories have been adapted as films. In fact, from the 1930s through the 1990s, about forty films, both for television and for the big screen, have been based on Greene's works. The majority of these films, including the classic *The Third Man* (1949), have been suspense thrillers, and some, like *This Gun for Hire* (1942) and *Ministry of Fear* (1944), are identified as pure film noir. To help students understand how this film genre relates to the collection theme, tell them that film noir presents a vision of the world as a place where "the center cannot hold." What distinguishes film noir from any other crime or suspense thriller? The answer would have to be in the dark, existential vision of the world film noir creates. Words and themes that set the film noir standard are *anxiety, death, obsession, betrayal, despair, violence.*

A Background

Early Film Noir Successes

One of the earliest and most successful films in this genre was *Farewell, My Lovely,* a 1944 film based on a novel by Raymond Chandler, with tough-guy private detective Philip Marlowe. Other early film noir classics include *The Killers* (1946), *The Postman Always Rings Twice* (1946), and *Out of the Past* (1947). Later, in 1958, Orson Welles crafted one of the darkest examples of film noir in American cinema, *Touch of Evil.*

B Background

Updated Film Noir

Two Martin Scorsese classics in the film noir genre are *Mean Streets* (1973) and, especially, *Taxi Driver* (1976). *Blood Simple* (1984), a film by the brothers Joel and Ethan Coen, meets the film noir definition and in some ways goes even deeper into blackness. The "vocabulary" of film noir has also made its way into other genres, such as Ridley Scott's science fiction classic *Blade Runner* (1982).

Literature and the Movies

Shadows on the Screen

You've probably seen movies in which the men are wisecracking tough guys, weak liars, or devious criminals and the women are treacherous temptresses. Everybody is looking for an angle but expecting the worst from life. And around them all, the city lies bleak, dark, menacing, and violent.

Springing from World War II's legacy of disillusionment and anxiety, the black-and-white American movies of the 1940s and 1950s known as film noir (French for "black film") were the first to use the formula described above. You probably also know recent films that fit this description, because many film noir techniques are still popular today.

Edgy heroes and dirty deeds. The gritty detective novels of Raymond Chandler, Dashiell Hammett, and James M. Cain were brought to the screen in seedy realism. Chandler's private eye Philip Marlowe and Hammett's Sam Spade (in director Edward Dmytryk's *Murder, My Sweet* and John Huston's *The Maltese Falcon*) were as alienated and violent as the "bad guys" they pursued.

But film noir isn't just a detective genre. The category includes tales of obsessive love (*Scarlet Street*), radioactive poisoning (*D.O.A.*), insurance scams (*Double Indemnity*), and even aliens (*Invasion of the Body Snatchers*). What links all these movies is a mood of nightmare and paranoia, a theme of corruption and fatalism, and a visual style of dramatic contrasts.

Setting the scene. World War II had a direct influence on the development of film noir. European directors who immigrated to the safety of the United States during the war favored stark dark-and-light contrasts, ominous shadows, strange camera angles, and low-key lighting (partly a result of equipment shortages). They found in America new supersensitive lenses, smaller rolling cameras, and portable generators: all the means to capture—on location—the rainy-night streets, fog, eerily echoing buildings, blinking neon signs, and panicked foot chases that built suspense in film noir.

Tension, conflict, pessimism, sorrow: perhaps these are twentieth-century conditions that will never wholly disappear—as film noir never has, though its sinister scenes are now washed in color. Many contemporary directors—from Martin Scorsese to the Coen brothers—regularly pay homage to film noir techniques in their work. If you've seen their movies, you've seen film noir in a modern guise.

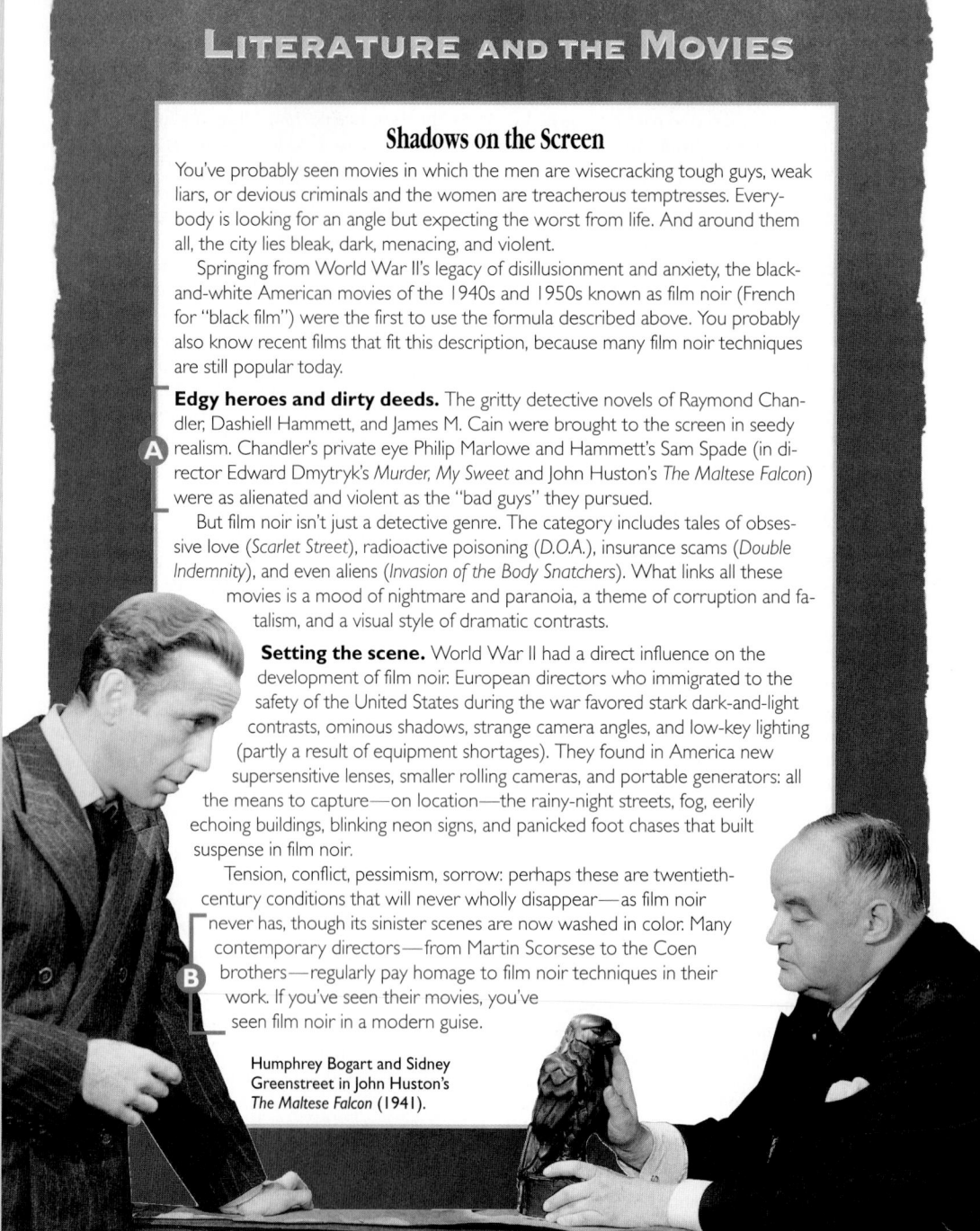

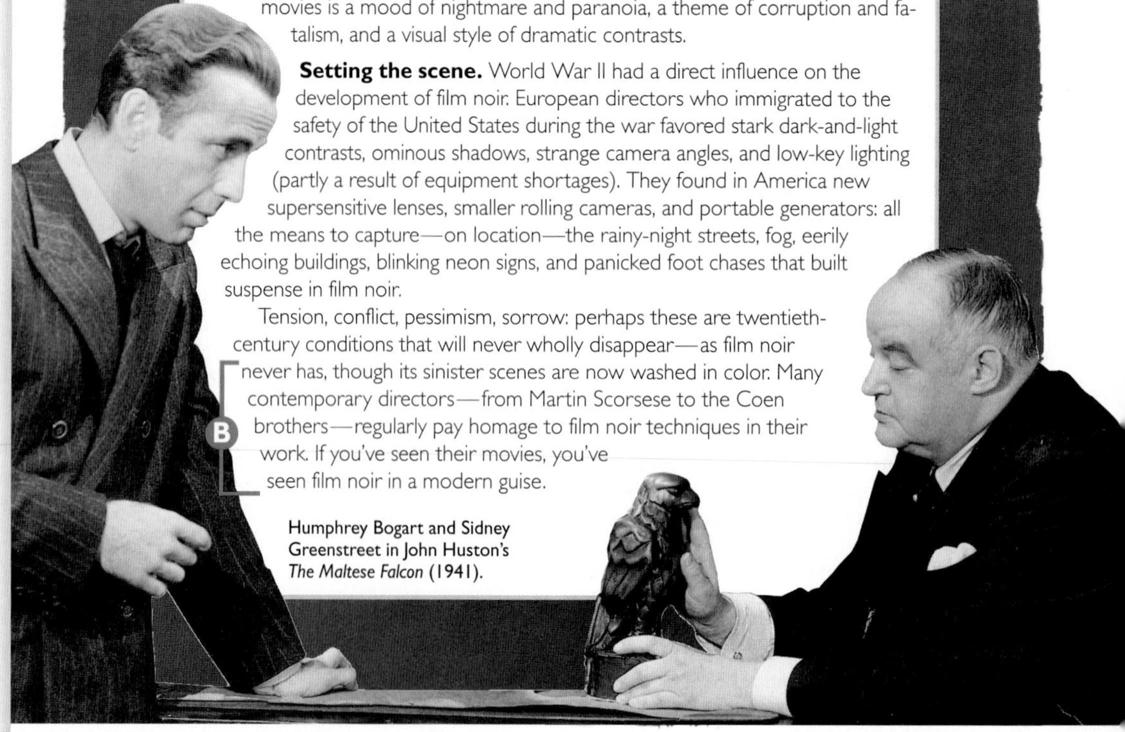

Humphrey Bogart and Sidney Greenstreet in John Huston's *The Maltese Falcon* (1941).

Assessing Learning

Check Test: Questions and Answers

1. What plan does T. propose? [He proposes that the gang destroy Mr. Thomas's house.]
2. What is the "something special" that T. finds to destroy? [Old Misery's money]
3. What does T. say when Blackie asks him if he hates Mr. Thomas? [He says if he hated Mr. Thomas, the destruction would not be fun.]
4. How do the boys prevent Mr. Thomas from finding them before they have finished their task? [They trap him in the outhouse.]
5. How does the truck driver react to what happens to the house? [He laughs uncontrollably.]

ing. Nobody could hear him from the road in front, and the lane at the back was seldom used. Anyone who passed there would be hurrying home and would not pause for what they would certainly take to be drunken cries. And if he did call "Help," who, on a lonely Bank Holiday evening, would have the courage to investigate? Mr. Thomas sat on the loo and pondered with the wisdom of age.

After a while it seemed to him that there were sounds in the silence—they were faint and came from the direction of his house. He stood up and peered through the ventilation-hole—between the cracks in one of the shutters he saw a light, not the light of a lamp, but the wavering light that a candle might give. Then he thought he heard the sound of hammering and scraping and chipping. He thought of burglars—perhaps they had employed the boy as a scout, but why should burglars engage in what sounded more and more like a stealthy form of carpentry? Mr. Thomas let out an experimental yell, but nobody answered. The noise could not even have reached his enemies.

4

Mike had gone home to bed, but the rest stayed. The question of leadership no longer concerned the gang. With nails, chisels, screwdrivers, anything that was sharp and penetrating they moved around the inner walls worrying at the mortar between the bricks. They started too high, and it was Blackie who hit on the damp course[12] and realized the work could be halved if they weakened the joints immediately above. It was a long, tiring, unamusing job, but at last it was finished. The gutted house stood there balanced on a few inches of mortar between the damp course and the bricks.

There remained the most dangerous task of all, out in the open at the edge of the bomb site. Summers was sent to watch the road for passers by, and Mr. Thomas, sitting on the loo, heard clearly now the sound of sawing. It no longer came from his house, and that a little reassured him. He felt less concerned. Perhaps the other noises too had no significance.

A voice spoke to him through the hole. "Mr. Thomas."

"Let me out," Mr. Thomas said sternly.

"Here's a blanket," the voice said, and a long gray sausage was worked through the hole and fell in swathes over Mr. Thomas's head.

"There's nothing personal," the voice said. "We want you to be comfortable tonight."

"Tonight," Mr. Thomas repeated incredulously.

"Catch," the voice said. "Penny buns—we've buttered them, and sausage-rolls. We don't want you to starve, Mr. Thomas."

Mr. Thomas pleaded desperately. "A joke's a joke, boy. Let me out and I won't say a thing. I've got rheumatics. I got to sleep comfortable."

"You wouldn't be comfortable, not in your house, you wouldn't. Not now."

"What do you mean, boy?" but the footsteps receded. There was only the silence of night: no sound of sawing. Mr. Thomas tried one more yell, but he was daunted and rebuked by the silence—a long way off an owl hooted and made away again on its muffled flight through the soundless world.

At seven next morning the driver came to fetch his lorry. He climbed into the seat and tried to start the engine. He was vaguely aware of a voice shouting, but it didn't concern him. At last the engine responded and he backed the lorry until it touched the great wooden shore[13] that supported Mr. Thomas's house. That way he could drive right out and down the street without reversing. The lorry moved forward, was momentarily checked as though something were pulling it from behind, and then went on to the sound of a long rumbling crash. The driver was astonished to see bricks bouncing ahead of him, while stones hit the roof of his cab. He put on his brakes. When he climbed out the whole landscape had suddenly altered. There was no house beside the car-park, only a hill of rubble. He went round and examined the back of his car for damage, and found a rope tied there that was still twisted at the other end round part of a wooden strut.

The driver again became aware of somebody shouting. It came from the wooden erection which was the nearest thing to a house in that desolation of broken brick. The driver climbed the smashed wall and unlocked the door. Mr. Thomas came out of the loo. He was wearing a

12. damp course: layer of waterproof material placed between two layers of brick in a house's foundation to keep moisture from rising up through the walls.

13. shore: beam

C Appreciating Language

Narrative Clincher

Students are probably familiar with clincher statements in expository paragraphs; point out that they can also be effectively used in narration or fiction. Ask what makes this a clincher statement. [Possible responses: The final statement is dramatic and lends closure not only to the paragraph but to section 3 of the story; it directly states, for the first time, that the boys are Old Misery's enemies and emphasizes Old Misery's state of utter aloneness and his victim status.]

D Critical Thinking

Speculating

? Why is the gang no longer concerned with the question of who is the leader? [Possible responses: Both Blackie and T. have taken control, in turn, and are now cooperatively running the show; the obsession with pulling the house down has taken on a life of its own, irrespective of who the "leader" is; the boys are now wholly engaged with their "work."]

E Reading Skills and Strategies

Inferring Motives

? Why do you think the boys give Mr. Thomas a blanket and some food? [Possible response: The boys' motives are irrational and confused—they want to stay true to their purpose of not harming the man physically, even though they are harming him psychologically; although they are set to wreck his house, the boys do not hate Mr. Thomas, but are motivated by less clear-cut reasons.]

F Critical Thinking

Challenging the Text

? Does the boys' action here make sense? [Possible responses: No, because these children have not shown any signs of consideration before this point; yes, because the boys have been able to separate destruction from robbery, and now they are separating destruction of the house from physical harm to the man.]

Making the Connections

Connecting to the Theme: "The Center Cannot Hold"

This story reflects an impulse not simply to destruction but to destruction on a grand scale, with no real motive. In some ways, the story seems to suggest that the bombing of London destroyed the world in which the boys live, taking away its logical or emotional center. Have students discuss these questions:

- Did the boys learn violence from experiencing violence? How are the London blitz and the blitz that takes place in this story alike, and how are they different?
- What kinds of "centers" (or values and emotional supports) appear to be missing or corrupted in these children's lives?
- In what sense are the members of the Wormsley Common gang like worms in an already rotten apple?

Ⓐ Critical Thinking

Evaluating

? Why is or isn't this a fitting ending for the story? [Possible responses: It's a fitting ending because it suggests that people in this ruined postwar environment suffer from a sense of meaninglessness and see the dark irony in life. It is not a fitting ending because it does not provide an alternative, more rational perspective on the distorted values of T. and his gang. It suggests that the whole world is perverse.]

RESPONDING TO THE ART

Lawrence Stephen Lowry (1887–1976) painted this scene in response to the bombing of major British cities by the German Luftwaffe in 1940. For 57 nights, an average of 160 bombers attacked London. During these raids, almost one Londoner in seven was hiding in a subway, a railroad tunnel, or some other form of municipal shelter. These raids set buildings on fire and killed civilians—and were meant to break the will of the British people.

Activity. Challenge students to find elements of hope in the painting. [A steeple is shown and is bathed in light; survivors are shown in purposeful, upright postures; there is a suggestion of teamwork for the common good.] Ask whether they think this painting shows that the bombings broke the British will. [Possible response: No, the destruction is physical—the people are alive, their wills intact.]

Courtesy of Mrs. Carol Ann Danes.

After the Blitz, 7th September 1940 by Lawrence Stephen Lowry.

gray blanket to which flakes of pastry adhered. He gave a sobbing cry. "My house," he said. "Where's my house?"

"Search me," the driver said. His eye lit on the remains of a bath and what had once been a dresser and he began to laugh. There wasn't anything left anywhere.

"How dare you laugh," Mr. Thomas said. "It was my house. My house."

Ⓐ "I'm sorry," the driver said, making heroic efforts, but when he remembered the sudden check to his lorry, the crash of bricks falling, he became convulsed again. One moment the house had stood there with such dignity between the bomb sites like a man in a top hat, and then, bang, crash, there wasn't anything left—not anything. He said, "I'm sorry. I can't help it, Mr. Thomas. There's nothing personal, but you got to admit it's funny."

Reading Check (on p. 959)

a. At the beginning of the story, Blackie is the leader, but T. takes over when he proposes to wreck Old Misery's house.

b. His father is a former architect, and his mother has an inflated sense of her worth.

c. It was built by renowned architect Christopher Wren; it has such dazzling features as a flying staircase.

d. First the gang destroys the inside. On the second day, they start destroying the structure itself. Finally on the third day, they tie a wooden support to a truck, which, when it drives away, pulls down the house.

MAKING MEANINGS

First Thoughts

1. What acts of vandalism and destruction in our culture does this story remind you of?

Reading Check

a. Who is the gang's leader at first? Who takes over? Why?
b. What is T.'s family background?
c. Why is Mr. Thomas's house valuable?
d. Describe how the house is destroyed.

Shaping Interpretations

2. T.'s **motives** for destroying Old Misery's house are important. What motives can you *eliminate* based on how the boys treat Old Misery and on what they do with the money?
3. What *are* T.'s motives? Support your answer with details from the story. (Your reading notes will help.)
4. How are these elements of the story **ironic:** (a) T.'s special talents, (b) T.'s father's former profession, (c) the history of the house, (d) Old Misery's horoscope?
5. A gang is a social group with a shared set of values. What are this gang's values, and where do you think they spring from?
6. What **images** are used to describe the setting of the Wormsley Common car-park and its surroundings? How does the **setting** contribute to the story's emotional **atmosphere**?
7. Consider the following excerpt from the story:

   ". . . they worked with the seriousness of creators—and destruction after all is a form of creation. A kind of imagination had seen this house as it had now become."

   Do you think it expresses the story's **theme**? Explain.
8. When Blackie asks T. whether he hates Mr. Thomas, T. answers, "Of course I don't. . . . There'd be no fun if I hated him." How would you explain T.'s answer? Do you think children are capable of this kind of cruelty? Explain.

CHOICES: Building Your Portfolio

Writer's Notebook

1. Collecting Ideas for an Informative Report

Even though "The Destructors" takes place half a century ago in London, the problem it examines is a timeless one. Explore what you know about the prevalence of random violence and vandalism in your own community, using the *5W-How?* questions (*Who? What? When? Where? Why? How?*). Then jot down your ideas about what library and community resources you might use to gather additional details for an informative paper. Save your work for the Writer's Workshop on page 1053.

Interpreting Imagery

2. Rotten to the Core?

Images of hollowness—of rotting from within—pervade the story. In the first part of an essay, cite these **images,** and discuss how they apply to the house, to Wormsley Common, and even to the story's characters. In the second part of the essay, discuss the ways "The Destructors" connects with images in W. B. Yeats's "The Second Coming" (page 923) and in T. S. Eliot's "The Hollow Men" (page 942).

Evaluating Oral Persuasion

3. The Destructor Trial

Is T. a vicious criminal who should be punished or a disturbed victim of society who deserves understanding? Prepare speeches to persuade people to accept your position on what should happen to T. (You might assume the roles of defense and prosecuting attorneys.) Your audience (the jury?) should analyze and evaluate your persuasive arguments and your performance. To review the techniques of persuasion, see pages 612–616. Before the speeches are presented, be sure the presenters and the evaluators agree on the criteria that should be used to analyze and evaluate oral persuasion.

Grading Timesaver

Rubrics for each Choices assignment appear on p. 187 in the *Portfolio Management System.*

Assessing Learning

Standardized Test Preparation

For practice in proofreading and editing, see

- *Daily Oral Grammar,* Transparency 31

MAKING MEANINGS

First Thoughts [Respond]

1. Students may name any destruction or defacement of public or private property—smashed windows, graffiti, and so on.

Shaping Interpretations [Interpret]

2. The boys are not motivated by material gain or a desire to physically harm Mr. Thomas; they're motivated by destruction for its own sake.
3. T. may be motivated by an association of the house and Old Misery with his father's former occupation. Clues are his knowledge of the renowned architect and his emphasis on the house's beauty.
4. T.'s special talents for destruction and leadership are ironic because such leadership is usually constructive; his father's former occupation as an architect—a creator of buildings who can appreciate the house's significance—is ironic; that the house, a landmark by Christopher Wren, survived the bombing but not the destruction by the boys is ironic; and Old Misery's horoscope ironically predicts a "serious crash."
5. The gang values daring and destruction, which may spring from a postwar malaise or from a conflict of old and new values in society.
6. Wormsley Common car-park is described as an "impromptu" parking lot on the site of the last bomb of the first blitz. On one side, Mr. Thomas's house sticks up like a jagged tooth. The encroachment of the parked cars where houses once stood further dehumanizes the setting, creating an atmosphere of destruction and chaos.
7. Students may say that creative imagination is now focused on destruction. They may also say that the evil portrayed in this story is neither a matter of creation nor destruction but a human impulse rooted somewhere deep in personal despair. Both responses express the story's theme.
8. Students may say that having a reason would diminish the pure, inexplicable fun of the evil act. They may also say that Mr. Thomas is a link to T.'s father, and the act is a way of expressing rage over the war's effect on his family or his sense that his father has failed him.

OBJECTIVES

Hawk Roosting / Chaucer

1. Read and interpret the poems
2. Identify and analyze personification
3. Express understanding through writing

SKILLS

Literary

- Identify and analyze personification

Writing

- Collect ideas for an informative report
- Analyze theme
- Compare views of nature
- Compare and contrast poems

Planning

- **Traditional Schedule**
  Lesson Plans Including Strategies for English-Language Learners
- **One-Stop Planner**
  CD-ROM with Test Generator

BROWSING IN THE FILES

About the Author. In "Visit," in *The Birthday Poems*, Hughes calls himself "the male lead in [Plath's] drama." He concludes by saying that what has happened to them is "only a story. Your story. My story."

Ted Hughes

(1930–1998)

Ted Hughes (1959).
© Rollie McKenna.

Ted Hughes, who often used violent nature imagery to symbolize the human condition, has been called "a twentieth-century Aesop whose fables lack an explicit moral." Hughes was born in West Yorkshire, where his father was a carpenter. After serving two years in the Royal Air Force, he studied archaeology and anthropology at Cambridge. In 1956, he married the brilliant young American poet Sylvia Plath. In 1963, after the couple had been separated for a short time, Plath, ill and depressed, took her own life in an unheated flat during one of the worst winters in London history.

An intensely private person, Hughes maintained an almost complete silence about his relationship with Sylvia Plath and the accusations that he somehow (because he had separated from her) was responsible for her death. That silence was broken in 1998 with the publication of a collection of poems called *Birthday Letters*. One of those poems is reprinted on page 962. (Also see Background on that page.)

The titles of Hughes's other books of poetry reveal his recurring subjects: *The Hawk in the Rain* (1957), *Animal Poems* (1967), *A Few Crows* (1970), *Cave Birds* (1975), and *Wolfwatching* (1991). Although Hughes writes of nature, he has nothing in common with the Romantics, who saw in nature a reflection of divine providence and primeval innocence. In Hughes's poems, nature represents the darkest impulses of the human heart; violence is not only an accepted fact of life, but also the impulse that links all creatures on earth. In 1984, Hughes was named poet laureate of England.

Before You Read

HAWK ROOSTING

Make the Connection

Deadly Instincts

Is violence really part of the natural order of things in the world? And what about the human capacity for murder and war? Is it *natural*, too, or a *distortion* of a natural force? This poem—or rather its unusual speaker, a hawk—makes us face these troubling questions.

The single-minded feathered killing machine of this poem presents us with a shocking truth: There are forces in nature that destroy without remorse or rationalization.

Quickwrite

Quickly write down whatever comes to mind when you hear the word *hawk:* characteristics, images, behavior, your emotional response.

Elements of Literature

Personification

We're so accustomed to discussing our pets' "personalities"—a haughty cat, a mischievous puppy—that we don't think of these descriptions as a form of **personification,** but in reality they are. When Ted Hughes tries to imagine what it's like to be a hawk, he gives the creature characteristics akin to human consciousness, desire, and will. His entire poem is a personification.

go.hrw.com
LEO 12-12

Resources: Print and Media

Reading

- *Graphic Organizers for Active Reading*, p. 93
- *Audio CD Library*
  Disc 16, Tracks 9, 10

Assessment

- *Formal Assessment*, p. 191
- *Portfolio Management System*, p. 188
- *Test Generator (One-Stop Planner CD-ROM)*

Internet

- go.hrw.com (keyword: LE0 12-12)

Hawk Roosting Ⓐ

Ted Hughes

I sit in the top of the wood, my eyes closed.
Inaction, no falsifying dream
Between my hooked head and hooked feet:
Or in sleep rehearse perfect kills and eat.

The convenience of the high trees!
The air's buoyancy and the sun's ray
Are of advantage to me; Ⓑ
And the earth's face upward for my inspection.

My feet are locked upon the rough bark.
It took the whole of Creation
To produce my foot, my each feather:
Now I hold Creation in my foot

Or fly up, and revolve it all slowly—
I kill where I please because it is all mine.
There is no sophistry° in my body:
My manners are tearing off heads—

The allotment of death.
For the one path of my flight is direct
Through the bones of the living.
No arguments assert my right:

The sun is behind me. Ⓒ
Nothing has changed since I began.
My eye has permitted no change.
I am going to keep things like this.

15. sophistry: clever but unsound reasoning.

Summary

The speaker is a hawk, roosting in a treetop. The hawk exults that it has no false dreams; when it sleeps, it rehearses kills and eats its prey. The hawk surveys its domain and declares itself ruler of this world. It presumes that all processes of nature work for its benefit. The hawk approves of life as it is and permits and anticipates no change.

Ⓐ Vocabulary Note

Word Choice

? What associations do you have with the word *roost?* In what expressions or idioms is this word found? [Possible responses: *Roost* suggests a place to perch, often on high; a roost may be to a bird as a throne is to a king; roosting suggests domesticity—to "rule the roost" is to control or dominate.] Ask students to come back to these associations and choose one or more appropriate ones after they finish reading the poem. They may use a dictionary to find related expressions.

Ⓑ Reading Skills and Strategies

Drawing Conclusions

? How would you describe the character of this hawk and its relationship to the world? [Possible responses: The hawk is self-assured and imperious, seeing itself at the center of all things. The hawk views the world as existing for the hawk's pleasure, and it is a world that suits the hawk perfectly; the hawk lives in harmony with the laws of nature; the hawk claims to hold creation in its foot, like a creator-god.]

Ⓒ Elements of Literature

Personification

? How does Hughes personify the hawk in these lines? [Possible response: The hawk speaks as if he were the lord of all creation. This is an ironic echo of human claims of dominion over the earth and its creatures.]

Reaching All Students

Struggling Readers

Before these students read, have them look at the hawk pictured and discuss their prior knowledge of hawks or other predatory birds. What associations do they make with such creatures? Have students brainstorm a list of characteristics associated with such birds.

English Language Learners

Be sure students read the Background (p. 962) before they read "Chaucer." Emphasize that the speaker in that poem is the poet himself, recounting a memory of an afternoon with the young woman who would become his wife. Remind students of the Chaucer selections (pp. 100–147) they have studied.

Summary

Hughes recalls a spring day when "you," probably Sylvia Plath, recited all or part of "The Prologue" and "The Wife of Bath's Tale" from *The Canterbury Tales,* enthralling an "audience" of cows who seemed fascinated by her recitation and, amazingly, drew around her in a ring. The speaker admits that he doesn't remember how the incident ended, for his attention had grown "too full."

Ⓐ Critical Thinking

Making Connections

? Where have you read these lines? [These are the first two lines—in Middle English—of "The Prologue" to *The Canterbury Tales* (p. 105).]

Ⓑ Reading Skills and Strategies

Making Inferences

? What is so extraordinary about this day, and about what Plath is doing? [Possible response: It is a beautiful spring day, and Plath is reciting, from memory, huge sections of *The Canterbury Tales* in Middle English. A herd of cows, enthralled by the sounds, comes close as if to listen.] To appreciate just how extraordinary this recitation is, students might be challenged to memorize the first two lines of Chaucer's Prologue, quoted here.

Ⓒ Elements of Literature

Personification

? How are the cows personified in this poem? [Possible responses: They are described as "enthralled"; the speaker says they "appreciated Chaucer." They gaze into Plath's face; they exclaim, renew their attention, try to "catch every inflection," and keep a reverent distance of six feet.]

Ⓓ Reading Skills and Strategies

Drawing Conclusions

? Why do you think this poem is entitled "Chaucer"? [Possible responses: Plath is reciting Chaucer and invoking the enchantment of poetry; she "becomes" Chaucer, the father of English poetry, for the span of time she recites, and thus she is identified with the great poet; the "spell" of Chaucer is so strong that cows stop to listen, suggesting that not only is poetry a kind of magic, but that Plath herself wields the power of the great poets—and so has achieved a kind of immortality.]

Before You Read

Chaucer

Background

In the many years since Sylvia Plath's suicide, controversy about her relationship with Ted Hughes and the extent of his responsibility for her death has swirled around Hughes. He maintained absolute silence on the subject, however, until the release in 1998 of *Birthday Letters.* In this collection of poems, all but two of which are addressed directly to Plath on the occasion of what would have been her sixty-fifth birthday, Hughes gives an intimate account of their relationship and the forces that, in his view, led to her poetry and to her death.

In this poem, Hughes speaks to a woman (we assume she is the young Sylvia) who is passionately reciting from Chaucer's *Canterbury Tales* in an English field in spring. The couple met in England when Plath arrived to study literature on a Fulbright grant.

Quickwrite

Imagine yourself in a field in the country on a sunny day in April with someone you love. How would you be feeling? Would you want to shout out to the world any snatch of poetry or song? Take some notes.

Chaucer

Ted Hughes

"Whan that Aprille with his shoures soote
The droghte of March hath perced to the roote . . ."
At the top of your voice, where you swayed on the top of a stile,°
Your arms raised—somewhat for balance, somewhat
To hold the reins of the straining attention
Of your imagined audience—you declaimed Chaucer
To a field of cows. And the Spring sky had done it
With its flying laundry, and the new emerald
Of the thorns, the hawthorn, the blackthorn,
And one of those bumpers of champagne
You snatched unpredictably from pure spirit.
Your voice went over the fields towards Grantchester.
It must have sounded lost. But the cows
Watched, then approached: they appreciated Chaucer.
You went on and on. Here were reasons
To recite Chaucer. Then came the Wyf of Bath,
Your favorite character in all literature.
You were rapt. And the cows were enthralled.
They shoved and jostled shoulders, making a ring,
To gaze into your face, with occasional snorts
Of exclamation, renewed their astounded attention,
Ears angling to catch every inflection,
Keeping their awed six feet of reverence
Away from you. You just could not believe it.
And you could not stop. What would happen
If you were to stop? Would they attack you,
Scared by the shock of silence, or wanting more—?
So you had to go on. You went on—
And twenty cows stayed with you hypnotized.
How did you stop? I can't remember
You stopping. I imagine they reeled away—
Rolling eyes, as if driven from their fodder.
I imagine I shooed them away. But
Your sostenuto° rendering of Chaucer
Was already perpetual. What followed
Found my attention too full
And had to go back into oblivion.

3. stile: steps over a wall or fence.
34. sostenuto (sôs′te nōō′tô): at a slower but sustained tempo. *Sostenuto* is a musical direction.

Getting Students Involved

Cooperative Learning

Speak for the Speaker. Who is this man who is speaking, and what is it he is saying? Invite students to prepare a short monologue in which the speaker tells—in prose, as if to a good friend—exactly what happened that day and how he felt about it. Students should work in groups of three to discuss the speaker's real feelings (which may be ambivalent and contradictory). One student can be responsible for prewriting, another for drafting, and a third for revising and proofreading the monologue. Provide time for a group member to read their monologue aloud and to compare and contrast the various interpretations. Also, provide time for students to assess their group's work as well as their individual contributions.

Making Meanings

Hawk Roosting

First Thoughts

1. How did you react to the hawk's philosophy?

Shaping Interpretations

2. What human qualities does the poet give the hawk in this **personification**? How do these qualities compare with your Quickwrite associations?
3. What does the hawk mean by saying it holds Creation in its foot? How is this different from the idea that God has "the whole world in His hands"?
4. How would you **paraphrase** lines 16–20?
5. What two meanings can you propose for the line "The sun is behind me"?
6. How is the hawk like some people?

Chaucer

First Thoughts

1. What do you *see* when you read this poem?

Shaping Interpretations

2. How did the cows respond to the recitation of Chaucer? Is the speaker's response like that of the cows? Explain.
3. Chaucer's great poem opens in the spring. What **images** of spring can you find in this poem?
4. In line 35, the speaker says that the woman's rendering of Chaucer was "already perpetual." What could he be suggesting about Sylvia Plath's poetry?
5. In the tragic story of Plath and Hughes, the "center could not hold." Does it surprise you that such joy could turn into pain? Explain.
6. How would you **paraphrase,** or restate in your own words, the poem's final sentence? (Is there agreement on what it means?)

Connecting with the Text

7. Do the feelings in this poem connect in any way to the ones you wrote about in your Quickwrite notes?

Choices: Building Your Portfolio

Writer's Notebook

1. Collecting Ideas for an Informative Report

WORK IN PROGRESS

Hughes's aim in "Hawk Roosting" is neither to inform nor to explain, yet he manages to distill a great deal of information about hawks into these few lines. To explore how you might approach the same subject in an informative paper, reread the poem slowly, jotting down questions it raises about the hawk's physiology and place in the food chain. Save your work for the Writer's Workshop on page 1053.

Analyzing Theme

2. What's It All About?

In a paragraph, state and discuss what you take to be the main **theme** of "Hawk Roosting" or "Chaucer." In a second paragraph, present your response to the theme.

Comparing Views of Nature

3. Birds of a Feather?

In a brief essay, compare the view of nature expressed in "Hawk Roosting"—and Hughes's bird itself—with those of Shelley's "To a Skylark" (page 739) and Keats's "Ode to a Nightingale" (page 755). Be sure to discuss how the poems differ and how they are alike.

Comparing and Contrasting Poems

4. Be My Love

Compare "Chaucer" with one of the robust love poems of the Renaissance (see pages 214–266) or with any other love poem in this book. In your essay, focus on one or two elements in the poems that are either very similar or very different—perhaps **themes, images, tones, sounds.** At the end of your essay, describe your response to each love poem.

Grading Timesaver

Rubrics for each Choices assignment appear on p. 188 in the *Portfolio Management System.*

Making Meanings

Hawk Roosting

First Thoughts [Respond]

1. Students may admire or disagree with the hawk's philosophy.

Shaping Interpretations [Interpret]

2. The hawk is capable of reflection; it is cold-eyed and egocentric.
3. Possible response: The hawk means that all the world serves as its prey, its domain. The idea of God holding the world in His hands seems merciful and beneficent, while the thought of the hawk holding the world in its claws seems horrific and predatory.
4. Possible paraphrase: The only manners I need are those required for getting my fair share by tearing off heads. My power is death, and no one need tell me that what's mine is mine.
5. The hawk attacks its prey's blind side, where the sun is; the sun supports the hawk's existence; the sun follows, or is subservient to, the hawk.
6. People can be as cruelly egocentric as the hawk.

Chaucer

First Thoughts [Respond]

1. Students should see a woman in a field, atop a wall, reciting Chaucer to an attentive audience of cows.

Shaping Interpretations [Interpret]

2. The speaker says the cows appreciated Chaucer and approached, "enthralled" and "hypnotized." He too was caught up in the spell.
3. Images include the "Spring sky" and the "new emerald" buds.
4. Possible response: Plath's poetry lives on forever.
5. Students may mention, among other things, that the pressures of modern life often work against stable relationships, and that deep love, once lost, often turns to great pain.
6. Possible response: The line could mean that the memory of how that special day ended was later lost among all the other things—including times of trouble and hardship in the marriage—that claimed his attention in the years to come.

Connecting with the Text [Apply]

7. Students may have imagined themselves speaking, singing, or joking while happily enjoying the company of someone they loved.

Objectives

Freedom to Breathe / The Bonfire and the Ants

1. Read and interpret the two prose poems
2. Generate relevant, interesting, and researchable questions, and share perceptions of the writer's perspective
3. Recognize distinctive and shared characteristics of the culture
4. Compare the text content with students' own experiences
5. Recognize and discuss themes and connections that cross cultures

Browsing in the Files

About the Author. The novella *One Day in the Life of Ivan Denisovich* was the first of Solzhenitsyn's works to be published in the Soviet Union, and it catapulted him to worldwide fame. He has not left the literary spotlight since. Nevertheless, despite the brief period of forgiveness for Solzhenitsyn marked by the publication of *Ivan Denisovich*, by 1965 his relationship with the Soviet government had turned so sour that the KGB confiscated his personal papers. By 1966, the Soviet Union refused to allow his work to be published. Nevertheless, Solzhenitsyn has been an amazingly prolific and internationally successful writer. His novels *The First Circle* and *The Cancer Ward* were first published abroad; and it was the publication abroad of the first volume of *The Gulag Archipelago,* which exposed the horrors of the Soviet prison camps, that led to his exile. Since his return to Russia in 1994, Solzhenitsyn has distanced himself from direct participation in politics.

World Literature

Russia

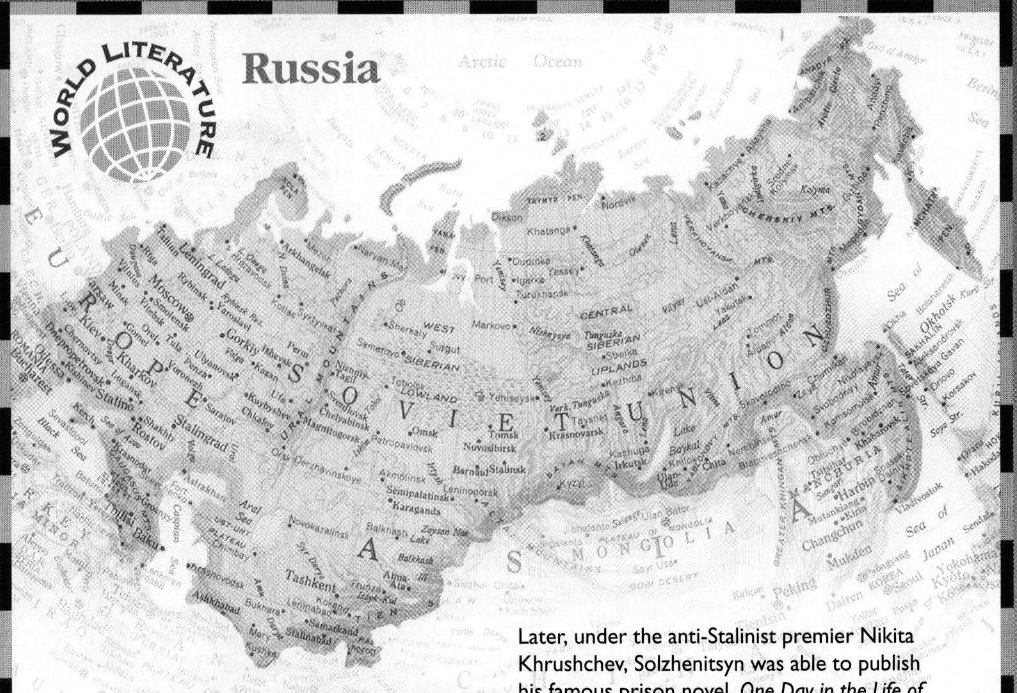

Aleksandr Solzhenitsyn

(1918–)

If to Aleksandr Solzhenitsyn (sōl′zhə·nēt′sin) his Soviet homeland was the burning log of "The Bonfire and the Ants," you could say he was swept from the fire in 1974. That's when he was arrested and exiled—for writing *The Gulag Archipelago,* a factual account of Soviet labor camps. Yet twenty years later, in May 1994, his apparently unquenchable love for his country drew him back to live again, as a free citizen, in Moscow.

Solzhenitsyn's troubled relationship with his homeland began much earlier. After becoming a decorated front-line officer in World War II, he was suddenly arrested in 1945 and served eight years in prison and labor camps for criticizing the premier, Joseph Stalin, in a letter to a friend. Later, under the anti-Stalinist premier Nikita Khrushchev, Solzhenitsyn was able to publish his famous prison novel, *One Day in the Life of Ivan Denisovich* (1962). But during the 1960s and 1970s, the Soviet government continually harassed him, attempting to silence his criticisms of political realities. On winning the Nobel Prize in 1970, Solzhenitsyn did not travel to Sweden for the ceremonies because he feared the Soviet regime would bar his return.

In 1974, the Soviet government revoked Solzhenitsyn's citizenship. Solzhenitsyn was deported and, for most of his twenty-year exile, lived quietly and wrote prolifically in Cavendish, Vermont. Now on Russian soil again, he is a world-famous symbol of both the former Soviet Union's repression and the ongoing search for a renewed Russia.

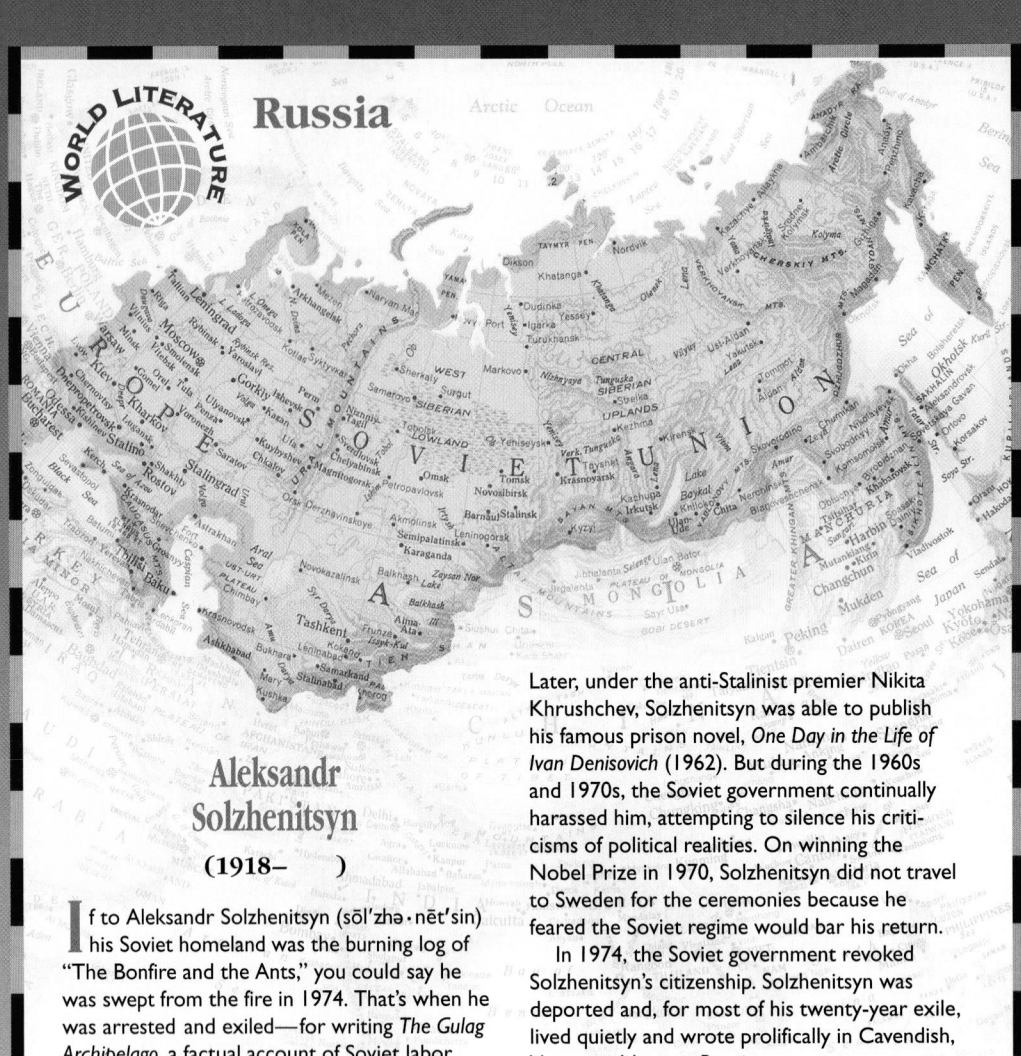

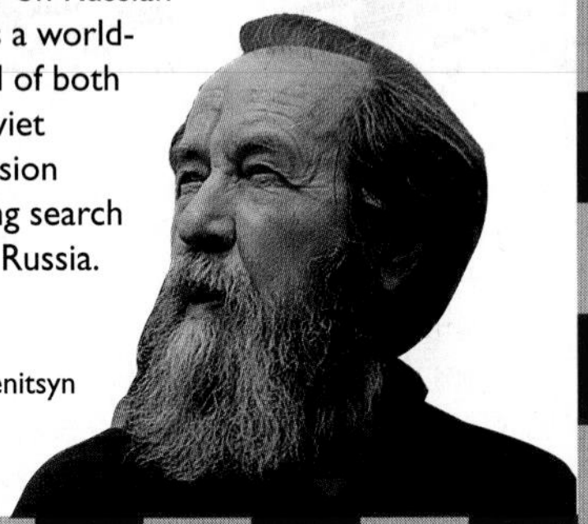

Aleksandr Solzhenitsyn (1994).

(Map) ©Rand McNally R. L. #98-S-116.

go.hrw.com LEO 12-12

Resources: Print and Media

Reading

- *Audio CD Library*
  Disc 16, Tracks 11, 12

Internet

- go.hrw.com (keyword: LE0 12-12)

Before You Read

FREEDOM TO BREATHE
THE BONFIRE AND THE ANTS

Quickwrite

Take a minute to brainstorm images of the place that you think of as home. Don't stop with your physical dwelling, though. Include the neighborhood, the section of the city or countryside, the whole city or county—whatever gives you a sense of the place and the people that are your own.

Once you've done your brainstorming, consider how you feel about home. Are you dying to get away, or do you hope you never have to leave?

Whatever your answer, your feelings would probably be different, or sharper, if you were forced out of your homeland and exiled to a faraway place. They would almost certainly be affected if danger suddenly loomed—perhaps gunfire or a raging flood—and common sense said, "Leave *now!*"

The two prose poems you are about to read were written by a Russian who had to contemplate his homeland from a prison cell and, later, from a twenty-year exile. Keeping in mind the powerful emotions and images that make up your idea of "home," jot down notes on how you might feel if you were suddenly forced to leave it.

Freedom to Breathe

Aleksandr Solzhenitsyn

translated by **Michael Glenny**

A shower fell in the night and now dark clouds drift across the sky, occasionally sprinkling a fine film of rain. **A**

I stand under an apple tree in blossom and I breathe. Not only the apple tree but the grass round it glistens with moisture; words cannot describe the sweet fragrance that pervades the air. I inhale as deeply as I can, and the aroma invades my whole being; I breathe with my eyes open, I breathe with my eyes closed—I cannot say which gives me the greater pleasure. **B**

This, I believe, is the single most precious freedom that prison takes away from us: the freedom to breathe freely, as I now can. No food on earth, no wine, not even a woman's kiss is sweeter to me than this air steeped in the fragrance of flowers, of moisture and freshness. **C**

No matter that this is only a tiny garden, hemmed in by five-story houses like cages in a zoo. I cease to hear the motorcycles backfiring, radios whining, the burble of loudspeakers. As long as there is fresh air to breathe under an apple tree after a shower, we may survive a little longer. **D**

Summary ■

After a rain, the speaker stands under an apple tree in bloom and consciously inhales and exhales, drinking in the sweet-smelling air. He reflects that this freedom to breathe freely is the most precious freedom of all.

A Struggling Readers
Prose Poem

Remind students that even though a prose poem takes the form of sentences and paragraphs, it must be read like other poems: as a compressed form of expression in which words are likely to have multiple and symbolic meanings, and in which every choice—whether of word or structure—is deliberate and significant.

B Reading Skills and Strategies
Determining the Author's Purpose

? Why does the speaker repeat "I breathe"? [Possible response: The repetition of the phrase "I breathe" has a lulling effect that parallels the speaker's relaxed mood. "I breathe" seems synonymous with "I am free."]

C Appreciating Language
Word Choice

? What makes the word *steeped* such an effective word choice? [Possible responses: The word emphasizes the saturation of the air with the scent of flowers; it suggests that the air, like tea that has been steeped, is saturated and infused with nature's scents.]

D Elements of Literature
Setting

? What effect does this sudden revelation of the larger setting have? [Possible response: It is surprising or even ironic that such a pure and cleansing experience of nature can happen in a chaotic urban setting.]

Assessing Learning

Check Test: Questions and Answers

"Freedom to Breathe"

1. Where does the speaker in "Freedom to Breathe" take his breaths? [under an apple tree after a rainfall, in a "tiny garden" in an urban setting]
2. According to the prose poem, what is the speaker's greatest pleasure? [breathing freely]

"The Bonfire and the Ants"

3. How do the ants come to be in the fire? [The speaker unwittingly throws the log in which they live onto a bonfire.]
4. What do the ants do after the speaker tries to free them? [They return to the burning log.]

Summary ■

Without realizing that a rotten log is filled with ants, the speaker throws it into the fire. First, the ants scramble out of the log, but then, drawn by some inexplicable force, they return to their burning home to die.

A Elements of Literature

Tone

? Based on the first sentence, how would you describe the prose poem's tone? [Possible answer: It is straightforward, matter-of-fact, and meditative, like a parable.]

B Reading Skills and Strategies

Determining the Author's Purpose

? What does the use of the word *homeland* suggest to you about the purpose of the poem? [Possible response: The prose poem symbolizes the speaker's relationship to his homeland.]

C Elements of Literature

Theme

? What is the theme of this prose poem? [Possible response: Ties to one's homeland can be so hard to break that sometimes a person is willing to make great sacrifices rather than leave.]

Finding Common Ground

This feature encourages students to discuss their experience of reading both selections and to discover questions and challenges they might pose in response to the prose poems. Urge students to imagine that they can present their challenges to Solzhenitsyn himself and to theorize about how he might answer their questions.

The Bonfire and the Ants

Aleksandr Solzhenitsyn

translated by **Michael Glenny**

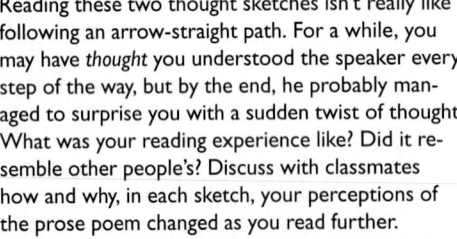

A I threw a rotten log onto the fire without noticing that it was alive with ants.

The log began to crackle, the ants came tumbling out and scurried around in desperation. They ran along the top and writhed as they were scorched by the flames. I gripped the log and rolled it to one side. Many of the ants then managed to escape onto the sand or the pine needles.

But, strangely enough, they did not run away from the fire.

B They had no sooner overcome their terror than they turned, circled, and some kind of force drew them back to their forsaken homeland. There C were many who climbed back onto the burning log, ran about on it, and perished there.

Finding Common Ground

Reading these two thought sketches isn't really like following an arrow-straight path. For a while, you may have *thought* you understood the speaker every step of the way, but by the end, he probably managed to surprise you with a sudden twist of thought. What was your reading experience like? Did it resemble other people's? Discuss with classmates how and why, in each sketch, your perceptions of the prose poem changed as you read further.

Once you've absorbed Solzhenitsyn's surprises, though, here's the question: What do these writings mean to *you*? In the Quickwrite on page 965, you were invited to think of your own home and how you might respond to being exiled from it—a fertile field for discussion. Another way of "finding common ground," of connecting with Solzhenitsyn or any other writer, is by digging into the differences between your perspective and the writer's—just as a discussion of differences can sometimes bring friends into a closer relationship with one another. You aren't necessarily expected to understand or agree with everything a writer says.

For each prose poem, challenge or query Solzhenitsyn on some point, whether an idea, an experience, an image, or something else. Here are examples of two challenges:

- Isn't it possible to have "fresh air to breathe" and not be free?
- Isn't an **allegory,** or symbolic story, that equates people with ants already manipulating readers? Would all humans drawn back to a homeland just "run about" and perish pointlessly?

Making the Connections

Connecting to the Theme: "The Center Cannot Hold"

"Freedom to Breathe" and "The Bonfire and the Ants" seem on first reading to have different messages. What do these pieces have in common, and how do they tie into the theme of the collection? [Possible responses: Both pieces show the power of certain intangible needs—whether that means personal freedoms or attachment to one's home. The center cannot always hold; things do not always make sense. "Freedom to Breathe" shows that, in a world in which the most basic freedoms cannot be taken for granted, simply being able to stand beneath a tree and breathe can be a precious gift, no matter how oppressive the larger surroundings. "The Bonfire of the Ants" shows another side of freedom—that, when faced with the freedom to leave one's home to escape danger, some people will instinctively maintain their attachment to a homeland rather than risk an unknown future. (Compare this message to that of Anna Akhmatova's poem "Lot's Wife" on p. 945.)]

WORLD LITERATURE

Vietnam

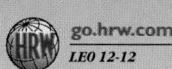

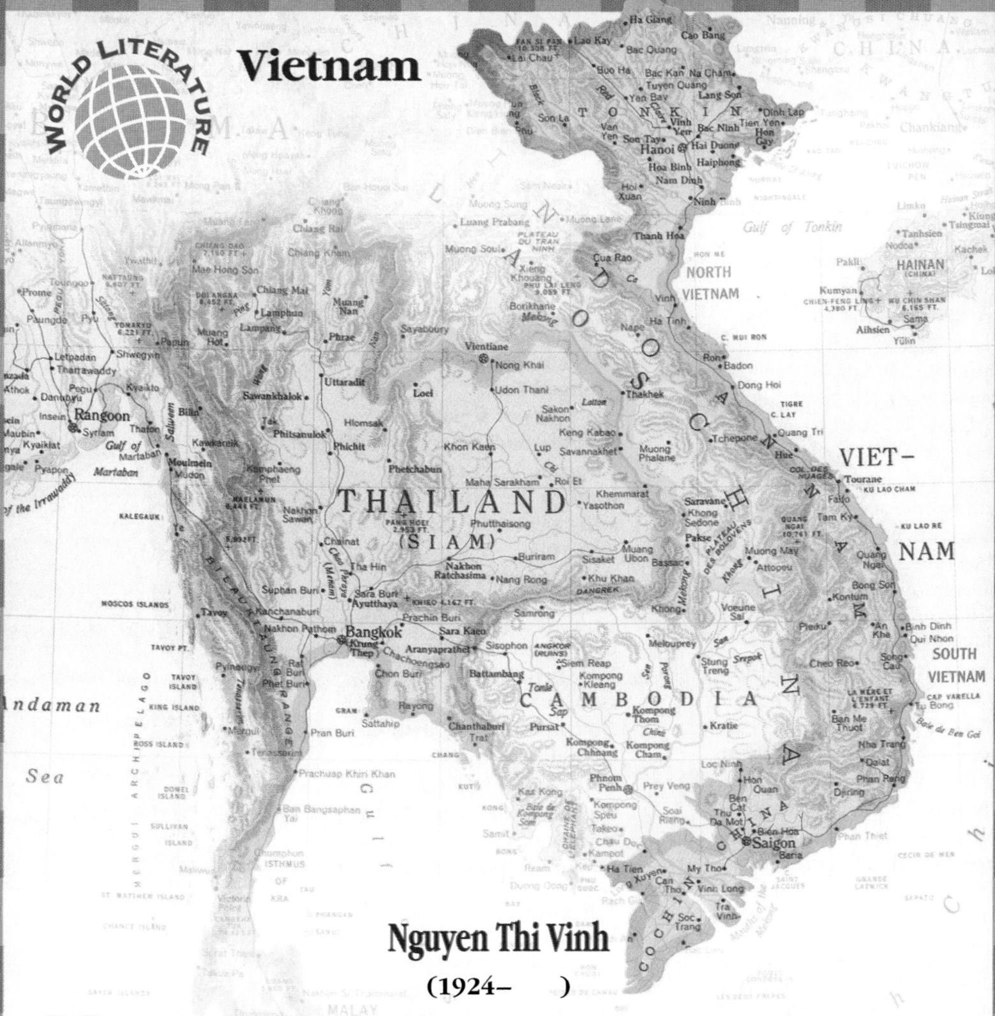

Nguyen Thi Vinh

(1924–   )

Nguyen Thi Vinh (nōō'yin tī vin'), while never a soldier, drew on her own experience for "Thoughts of Hanoi." Born in North Vietnam, she fled south to Saigon, the capital of newly created South Vietnam, in the 1950s to escape Communist rule. She quickly gained acclaim as a fiction writer with *Two Sisters* (1953), beginning a distinguished and successful literary career.

Her work constantly probed the pain, loss, and dislocation of a civil war that transformed friends into foes. When the Communists gained control of all of Vietnam in 1975, Nguyen stayed, despite the danger that made millions in the south flee.

Finally, however, in 1983, she followed others in her family to Norway. Her exile seems particularly wrenching since Nguyen's ancestors, for centuries, were members of one of Vietnam's two ruling families.

(Map) ©Rand McNally R. L. #98-S-116.

go.hrw.com
LEO 12-12

OBJECTIVES

1. Read and interpret the poem
2. Generate relevant, interesting, and researchable questions
3. Recognize distinctive and shared characteristics of cultures
4. Compare the poem's content with students' own experiences
5. Recognize and discuss themes and connections that cross cultures

BROWSING IN THE FILES

About the Author. Nguyen Thi Vinh was born in the Red River delta of what became North Vietnam. Her family name has a long history: From the sixteenth through the nineteenth centuries, the house of Nguyen was one of the two ruling families in Vietnam. In 1773, a member of the Nguyen family became the emperor of Vietnam, and his descendants ruled the country until its conquest by French forces in the late nineteenth century.

Although best known in Vietnam for her fiction—which, in addition to *Two Sisters*, includes *A Poor Hamlet* (1958) and *Birthmark* (1973)—it is Nguyen's poetry that has appeared most frequently in English translation.

Resources: Print and Media

Reading
- *Audio CD Library*
  Disc 16, Track 13

Internet
- go.hrw.com (keyword: LE0 12-12)

Summary ■■

One night, during civil war, the speaker—a South Vietnamese soldier—recalls the city of Hanoi, where he was raised. He addresses his "brother"—a former schoolmate and now a North Vietnamese soldier—and wonders if the city's life is still as he remembers it. He asks about the trains, the girls and boys engaging in daily activities, and the community he once knew. He fears that he and his old friend may meet and kill each other in battle but hopes that if they do, they will not do so with hatred. He also asks, plaintively, how this tragedy of war and division can be happening to them.

Ⓐ Appreciating Language

Style

? What is the effect of the repetition in ll. 10 and 11 of the words "still I . . ."? [Possible response: The repetition emphasizes the recurring nature of the two emotions and the length of time the speaker has endured being away from home.]

Ⓑ Elements of Literature

Apostrophe

In l. 14, the speaker addresses his "brother" directly. Explain that addressing an absent person as if that person were present is a figure of speech known as **apostrophe.** Ask students if they think the speaker is addressing an actual brother or someone else. Why is this term effective, regardless of the relationship? [Possible responses: The speaker could be addressing a real brother, or even a close childhood friend, but he might be using "brother" in the more figurative sense of "countryman," referring to any soldier from North Vietnam that he, as a South Vietnamese soldier, might have to confront in combat. The allusion to a family tie and to "roots" is effective because it emphasizes the extent of the damage done by the political division of the country, and it recalls the tragic and bitter intrafamilial divisions common during civil wars.]

Ⓒ Struggling Readers

Using Graphic Aids

? In poetry, the arrangement of text on a page often offers clues to meaning. What is different about the text in this stanza, and what meaning or mood change does it signal? [Possible answer: The lines are shorter with staggered indents, giving the impression of lively movement, and, perhaps, of a more lighthearted mood.]

Before You Read

THOUGHTS OF HANOI

Make the Connection

If you've ever been caught up in a feud, or observed one from the sidelines, you know how senseless the consequences can sometimes be. Often entire communities are divided—sometimes for generations—over a simple misunderstanding or a perceived slight.

Other feuds, of course, aren't trivial. They start over important and painful issues, and people are drawn into dangerous conflicts with those they love. That is what happens in the poem you are about to read. The "feud" is the devastating civil war between North and South Vietnam, which lasted from 1957 to 1975. The speaker, a southern soldier who grew up in the north, is addressing his "brother." His longing for his old way of life and the people from his past is heartfelt. The stakes are the ultimate: life itself.

Quickwrite

Make a list of some of the civil wars that have torn countries and peoples apart in the past fifty years or so. What caused each conflict? How could "friends" become "foes"? Have any of these wars been resolved?

Thoughts of Hanoi

Nguyen Thi Vinh

translated by **Nguyen Ngoc Bich**

The night is deep and chill
as in early autumn. Pitchblack,
it thickens after each lightning flash.
I dream of Hanoi:
Co-ngu° Road
ten years of separation
the way back sliced by a frontier of hatred.
I want to bury the past
to burn the future
still I yearn
still I fear
those endless nights
waiting for dawn.

Brother,
how is Hang Dao° now?
How is Ngoc Son° temple?
Do the trains still run
each day from Hanoi
to the neighboring towns?
To Bac-ninh,° Cam-giang,° Yen-bai,°
the small villages, islands
of brown thatch in a lush green sea?

The girls
  bright eyes
    ruddy cheeks
  four-piece dresses
    raven-bill scarves°
  sowing harvesting
    spinning weaving
  all year round,
the boys
  ploughing
    transplanting
  in the fields
    in their shops
  running across
    the meadow at evening
  to fly kites
    and sing alternating songs.°

5. Co-ngu (kō′no͞o′).

15. Hang Dao (häng′ dou′).

16. Ngoc Son (nōk′ sōn′).

20. Bac-ninh (bäk′nin′), **Cam-giang** (käm′gyäng′), **Yen-bai** (yen′bī′): towns near Hanoi.

27. raven-bill scarves: head scarves folded into straight-edged triangular forms, like the bill or beak of a raven.

39. alternating songs: songs sung in rounds, with singers beginning at staggered intervals.

Reaching All Students

Struggling Readers

Because students may have just read poems in which the poets themselves are the speakers (Hughes, Solzhenitsyn), remind students that the speaker of a poem is not necessarily the writer of the poem; the speaker may be an imaginary voice, or persona, through which the poet expresses ideas. Most of the time, the characteristics of the speaker are not stated directly and must be inferred. Emphasize that although the speaker in this poem is a male soldier, the poem was written by a woman.

English Language Learners

Present students with a map showing North Vietnam and South Vietnam, the location of Hanoi, and as many of the other locations named in the poem as possible. Use a pushpin or marker of one color to place the speaker in the poem in the South and a pin or marker of a different color to place his "brother" in the North.

Stainless blue sky,
jubilant voices of children
stumbling through the alphabet,
village graybeards strolling to the temple,
grandmothers basking in twilight sun,
chewing betel leaves°
while the children run—

Brother,
how is all that now?
Or is it obsolete?
Are you like me,
reliving the past,
imagining the future?
Do you count me as a friend
or am I the enemy in your eyes?
Brother, I am afraid
that one day I'll be with the March-North Army°
meeting you on your way to the South.
I might be the one to shoot you then
or you me
but please
not with hatred.

For don't you remember how it was,
you and I in school together,
plotting our lives together?
Those roots go deep!

Brother, we are men,
conscious of more
than material needs.
How can this happen to us
my friend
my foe?

45. **betel** (bĕt′'l) **leaves:** leaves of the betel pepper. These and the nuts of the betel palm are mild stimulants, often chewed like chewing gum in Southeast Asia.

56. **March-North Army:** that is, the South Vietnamese army marching into North Vietnam.

Finding Common Ground

With a small group of classmates, discuss the subject of civil war in the past fifty years or so. Use this poem and the human dimension it provides as a springboard for your discussion. Be sure to establish an agenda: Decide what questions you wish to discuss. (Refer to the Quickwrite notes you took before reading the poem.) At the conclusion of your group meeting, write a summation of your discussion, highlighting the topics you talked about and the group's responses to those topics.

After you have completed writing your discussion reports, meet together as a class and exchange views. Can you, as a class, find common ground in your responses?

D Vocabulary Note

Word History

The word *alphabet* comes from the first two letters of the Greek alphabet, *alpha* and *beta.* Its creation through combining and shortening makes its word history somewhat similar to that of our more informal term for the alphabet, the *ABCs.*

E Reading Skills and Strategies

Drawing Conclusions

? What conclusion can you draw about the relative roles of the speaker and the person he addresses in ll. 53–57? [Possible answer: They are soldiers in opposing armies.]

F Advanced Learners

Evaluating

Invite students to decide whether this poem meets T. S. Eliot's standards that modern poetry be comprehensive, allusive, and indirect. Alternatively, students might propose their own standards for what makes great poetry and determine whether this poem meets those standards.

Finding Common Ground

This feature encourages students to develop a deeper understanding of the poem through lively discussion of related historical contexts. Remind students of the ravages of the American Civil War, which also pitted family against family in a North-South conflict, and which resulted in more American deaths than all the other wars from the Revolutionary War through the Vietnam War combined. Then, remind students of these other countries where civil war has raged in the last fifty years: Nigeria, Angola, Yugoslavia, Korea, Nicaragua, Sri Lanka, and Algeria. Urge students to focus discussion by learning, in detail, about one or more of these conflicts.

Making the Connections

Connecting to the Theme: "The Center Cannot Hold"

Use the following questions to tie this poem to the collection theme.

- How do ll. 6–7 echo both the theme of Yeats's "The Second Coming" and the theme of this collection? [Possible responses: The phrase "ten years of separation" repeats the idea of things falling apart, of the center not holding; the "frontier of hatred" may remind readers of the "anarchy" and "blood-dimmed tide" in ll. 4–5 of Yeats's poem.]
- What other works in this collection have shown that political realities "loose" anarchy in individual lives? [Students have seen this in "The Destructors," with the blitz leaving behind boys who are "the worst" yet full of "passionate intensity." This idea is also apparent in the poems of Sassoon, Owen, Akhmatova, and Solzhenitsyn.]

OBJECTIVES

1. Read and interpret the story
2. Identify and analyze the point of view
3. Analyze the time frame
4. Express understanding through writing
5. Understand new words

SKILLS

Literary
- Identify and analyze the point of view

Reading
- Analyze the time frame

Writing
- Collect ideas for an informative report
- Analyze a symbol
- Write an essay comparing three works

Vocabulary
- Use new words

Planning

- **Traditional Schedule**
  Lesson Plans Including Strategies for English-Language Learners
- **One-Stop Planner**
  CD-ROM with Test Generator

Ben Okri

(1959–   )

Ben Okri.

Ben Okri grew up in the delta area of southern Nigeria. Although he later moved to London, his stories are set in Nigeria. Okri seems especially haunted by remembrances of the Nigerian Civil War (1967–1970), often called the Biafran War. This war began when the Ibo (ē′bō) people tried to secede from Nigeria and form their own state, called the Republic of Biafra. Thousands of people were killed in the civil war that ensued, and many more died of starvation. In fact, the very word *Biafra* today suggests images of swollen-bellied children holding up bowls and begging for food. The image of the starving child in Okri's story is a stark reminder of the horror of this war.

Okri first gained recognition in England with the publication of two novels, *Flowers and Shadows* (1980) and *The Landscapes Within* (1981), and a collection of short stories, *Incidents at the Shrine* (1986). The short story that follows, "In the Shadow of War," is from *Stars of the New Curfew* (1988), Okri's first book to be published in the United States.

Okri's awards include the Commonwealth Writers' Prize for Africa and the *Paris Review* Aga Khan Prize for fiction. His 1991 novel, *The Famished Road,* received England's Booker Prize. *Songs of Enchantment,* a sequel to *The Famished Road,* appeared in 1993 and *Astonishing the Gods,* in 1995.

Before You Read

IN THE SHADOW OF WAR

Make the Connection

Siege Mentality

The United States has not known war on its own soil since 1865. But in some parts of the world, a state of war is almost constant, especially in places where ethnic and religious strife runs high.

Reading Skills and Strategies

Analyzing the Time Frame

This story is set in a village in the heart of Nigeria during the Nigerian Civil War (1967–1970). We are not given this information in the story itself, however, because the story is told through the eyes of a child who would neither know nor understand these details. What we are given instead is a vivid picture of what the child, Omovo, sees and hears immediately around him. As you read, keep a two-column chart. In the first column, jot down details about his surroundings that Omovo gives. In the second column, note the conclusions that you draw from these details. Then, decide if it is necessary to know anything more than the story tells you about its historical context.

Elements of Literature

Point of View

Ben Okri was only eight years old when the Nigerian Civil War broke out, so it's not surprising that his main character, Omovo, is a child. Okri uses the **limited third-person point of view** to tell the story from Omovo's perspective.

War is a frightening, confusing time for children. Are the soldiers in this story good or evil? Is the veiled woman supernatural or mortal? Because Omovo's understanding is limited, the point of view deepens these enigmas.

go.hrw.com
LEO 12-12

Resources: Print and Media

Reading
- *Graphic Organizers for Active Reading*, p. 94
- *Words to Own*, p. 26
- *Audio CD Library*
  Disc 16, Track 14

Writing and Language
- *Daily Oral Grammar*
  Transparency 32
- *Grammar and Language Links*
  Worksheet, p. 55
- *Language Workshop CD-ROM*

Assessment
- *Formal Assessment*, p. 193
- *Portfolio Management System*, p. 190
- *Preparation for College Admission Exams*, p. 47
- *Test Generator (One-Stop Planner CD-ROM)*

Internet
- go.hrw.com (keyword: LE0 12-12)

In the Shadow of War

Ben Okri

That afternoon three soldiers came to the village. They scattered the goats and chickens. They went to the palm-frond bar and ordered a calabash[1] of palm wine. They drank amidst the flies.

Omovo watched them from the window as he waited for his father to go out. They both listened to the radio. His father had bought the old Grundig[2] cheaply from a family that had to escape the city when the war broke out. He had covered the radio with a white cloth and made it look like a household fetish.[3] They listened to the news of bombings and air raids in the interior of the country. His father combed his hair, parted it carefully, and slapped some after-shave on his unshaven face. Then he struggled into the shabby coat that he had long outgrown.

Omovo stared out of the window, irritated with his father. At that hour, for the past seven days, a strange woman with a black veil over her head had been going past the house. She went up the village paths, crossed the Express road, and disappeared into the forest. Omovo waited for her to appear.

The main news was over. The radio announcer said an eclipse of the moon was expected that night. Omovo's father wiped the sweat off his face with his palm and said, with some bitterness:

"As if an eclipse will stop this war."

"What is an eclipse?" Omovo asked.

"That's when the world goes dark and strange things happen."

"Like what?"

His father lit a cigarette.

"The dead start to walk about and sing. So don't stay out late, eh."

Omovo nodded.

"Heclipses hate children. They eat them."

Omovo didn't believe him. His father smiled, gave Omovo his ten kobo[4] allowance, and said:

"Turn off the radio. It's bad for a child to listen to news of war."

Omovo turned if off. His father poured a libation[5] at the doorway and then prayed to his ancestors. When he had finished he picked up his briefcase and strutted out briskly. Omovo watched him as he threaded his way up the path to the bus stop at the main road. When a danfo bus[6] came, and his father went with it, Omovo turned the radio back on. He sat on the windowsill and waited for the woman. The last time he saw her she had glided past with agitated flutters of her yellow smock. The children stopped what they were doing and stared at her. They had said that she had no shadow. They had said that her feet never touched the ground. As she went past, the children began to throw things at her. She didn't flinch, didn't quicken her pace, and didn't look back.

The heat was stupefying. Noises dimmed and lost their edges. The villagers stumbled about their various tasks as if they were sleepwalking. The three soldiers drank palm wine and played draughts[7] beneath the sun's oppressive glare. Omovo noticed that whenever children went past the bar the soldiers called them, talked to them, and gave them some money. Omovo ran down the stairs and slowly walked past the bar. The soldiers stared at him. On his way back one of them called him.

"What's your name?" he asked.

Omovo hesitated, smiled mischievously, and said:

"Heclipse."

The soldier laughed, spraying Omovo's face with spit. He had a face crowded with veins. His companions seemed uninterested. They swiped flies and concentrated on their game. Their guns

1. **calabash** (kal′ə·bash′): cup made from a calabash, a type of gourd.
2. **Grundig:** German brand of radio.
3. **fetish** (fet′ish): object believed to have magical powers.
4. **kobo** (käb′ō): Nigerian monetary unit.

5. **libation** (lī·bā′shən): liquid poured onto the ground as a sacrifice to the gods.
6. **danfo bus:** small bus. In the region surrounding Lagos, *danfo* means "in disrepair."
7. **draughts** (drafts): British game of checkers.

WORDS TO OWN

stupefying (sto͞o′pə·fī′iŋ) *v.* used as *adj.:* dulling the mind and senses; bringing on a state of lethargy.
oppressive (ə·pres′iv) *adj.:* hard to bear.

Summary

In a Nigerian village, in a time of civil war, soldiers offer a young boy, Omovo, a bribe to betray the whereabouts of a strange woman. He refuses. Later, Omovo follows the soldiers as they pursue the woman. Omovo sees her give supplies to starving people, probably refugees, who are living in a cave. The soldiers catch the woman as she returns; they interrogate, abuse, and kill her. Terrified, Omovo runs away, but he trips and falls, losing consciousness. When he wakes up, he finds himself back home, where he is shocked to find his father drinking with the soldiers. Omovo's father carries him to bed as Omovo tries in vain to tell what he has seen.

A Reading Skills and Strategies

Analyzing the Time Frame

? What do you learn about the time in which this story is set? [Possible responses: It is a time of civil conflict or all-out war, since soldiers come to the village; it is afternoon.]

B Elements of Literature

Foreshadowing

? When do you think the key action in this story will take place? Why? [Possible response: The eclipse of the moon seems to foreshadow something dark and strange, so the key action will probably occur that night.]

C Elements of Literature

Character

? What kind of man is Omovo's father? [Possible responses: He is both modern—he carries a briefcase—and traditional—he honors his ancestors. He is not forced to escape the city when the war breaks out. He stays informed about the war. He teases his son and wants to shield him from knowledge of the war.]

D Elements of Literature

Point of View

? What clues show Omovo's limited understanding? [Possible responses: The woman is just a blur of images; Omovo cannot make sense of who she is or what she represents; he also cannot understand the soldiers' intentions.]

Preteaching Vocabulary

Words to Own

Have pairs of students find each of the five Words to Own within the selection text. After they check the definitions at the bottom of the pages, have students see if they can use context to corroborate each word's meaning. Then, have them use each word in an original sentence that also supplies a context for the word. Finally, ask students to complete the analogies at right with the five words they have learned.

1. *Joke* is to *comical* as *burden* is to *[oppressive]*.
2. *Joyful* is to *grim* as *understated* is to *[ostentatious]*.
3. *Commandingly* is to *imperiously* as *crazily* is to *[dementedly]*.
4. *Traffic* is to *yielded* as *temptation* is to *[succumbed]*.
5. *Lively* is to *stimulating* as *dull* is to *[stupefying]*.

A Reading Skills and Strategies

Analyzing the Time Frame

? What time is it now, and what has happened since the beginning of the story? [Possible responses: It is late afternoon, almost evening. The torpor of the afternoon has ended, the woman has passed by, and the soldiers (and Omovo, in his own way) will now take action; there is a sense of foreboding, of the coming of darkness and evil.]

B Advanced Learners

Comparing/Contrasting

? How is the imagery used to describe the soldiers different from the imagery used to describe the strange woman? [Possible responses: The soldiers are solid, earthy, and coarse—one soldiers's buttocks are so large his pants have begun splitting; they sit and drink, stumble in the heat, and wield money and power. In contrast, the mysterious woman is an ethereal, veiled presence wafting through the setting like a ghost; the woman is dressed in the faded gray of poverty and seems to float through the town rather than walk.]

C Struggling Readers

Finding Details

? What details reveal that there is a war going on? [Possible responses: There are dilapidated signs and fences, a deserted factory, the ominous skeleton (p. 973), and the singing of war slogans (p. 973). Bombings, air raids, news of war on the radio, and soldiers in the bar are all details of war that have been mentioned earlier.]

D Elements of Literature

Point of View

? Using the third-person, limited point of view, the author permits the reader to see what Omovo sees without analyzing what it might mean. What is going on here that the boy is not mature or experienced enough to interpret? [Possible responses: The details of the unfinished estates, empty cement factory, and deserted workers' sheds all show the devastating effect of war on the landscape and suggest that people have fled the violence.]

At Obudu Cattle Ranch on Sonkwala Mountain, Nigeria (May 1989).

were on the table. Omovo noticed that they had numbers on them. The man said:

"Did your father give you that name because you have big lips?"

His companions looked at Omovo and laughed. Omovo nodded.

"You are a good boy," the man said. He paused. Then he asked, in a different voice:

"Have you seen that woman who covers her face with a black cloth?"

"No."

The man gave Omovo ten kobo and said:

"She is a spy. She helps our enemies. If you see her, come and tell us at once, you hear?"

A Omovo refused the money and went back upstairs. He repositioned himself on the windowsill. The soldiers occasionally looked at him. The heat got to him and soon he fell asleep in a sitting position. The cocks, crowing dispiritedly, woke him up. He could feel the afternoon softening into evening. The soldiers dozed in the bar. The hourly news came on. Omovo listened without comprehension to the day's casualties. The announcer <u>succumbed</u> to the stupor, yawned, apologized, and gave further details of the fighting.

B Omovo looked up and saw that the woman had already gone past. The men had left the bar. He saw them weaving between the eaves of the thatch houses, stumbling through the heat-mists. The woman was further up the path. Omovo ran downstairs and followed the men. One of them had taken off his uniform top. The soldier behind had buttocks so big they had begun to split his pants. Omovo followed them across the Express road. When they got into the forest the men stopped following the woman, and took a different route. They seemed to know what they were doing. Omovo hurried to keep the woman in view.

He followed her through the dense vegetation. She wore faded wrappers and a gray shawl, with the black veil covering her face. She had a red basket on her head. He completely forgot to determine if she had a shadow, or whether her feet touched the ground.

C He passed unfinished estates, with their flaking, <u>ostentatious</u> signboards and their collapsing fences. D He passed an empty cement factory: Blocks lay crumbled in heaps and the workers' sheds were deserted. He passed a baobab[8] tree,

8. **baobab** (bā′ō·bab′): thick-trunked African tree; often called "upside-down tree" because its branches look like roots.

WORDS TO OWN

succumbed (sə·kumd′) *v.:* yielded; gave way to.

ostentatious (äs′tən·tā′shəs) *adj.:* showy.

Reaching All Students

Struggling Readers

Remind these students that each detail is a clue to a world that Omovo can observe but not fully understand. Suggest that students work in pairs to make sense of these details. They may wish to draw some of the details in order to make the images tangible and understandable, and then to discuss the atmosphere these details create.

English Language Learners

These students may find it helpful to place key story events on a time line, thereby separating the events of the story from the description of the characters and setting.

Advanced Learners

Encourage students to research the Nigerian Civil War (1967–1970). Based on their findings, have them make conjectures about the respective ethnic groups to which the woman in this story and Omovo's father belong.

under which was the intact skeleton of a large animal. A snake dropped from a branch and slithered through the undergrowth. In the distance, over the cliff edge, he heard loud music and people singing war slogans above the noise.

He followed the woman till they came to a rough camp on the plain below. Shadowy figures moved about in the half-light of the cave. The woman went to them. The figures surrounded her and touched her and led her into the cave. He heard their weary voices thanking her. When the woman reappeared she was without the basket. Children with kwashiorkor[9] stomachs and women wearing rags led her halfway up the hill. Then, reluctantly, touching her as if they might not see her again, they went back.

He followed her till they came to a muddied river. She moved as if an invisible force were trying to blow her away. Omovo saw capsized canoes and trailing, waterlogged clothes on the dark water. He saw floating items of sacrifice: loaves of bread in polythene[10] wrappings, gourds of food, Coca-Cola cans. When he looked at the canoes again they had changed into the shapes of swollen dead animals. He saw outdated currencies on the riverbank. He noticed the terrible smell in the air. Then he heard the sound of heavy breathing from behind him, then someone coughing and spitting. He recognized the voice of one of the soldiers urging the others to move faster. Omovo crouched in the shadow of a tree. The soldiers strode past. Not long afterward he heard a scream. The men had caught up with the woman. They crowded round her.

"Where are the others?" shouted one of them.

The woman was silent.

"You dis witch! You want to die, eh? Where are they?"

She stayed silent. Her head was bowed. One of the soldiers coughed and spat toward the river.

"Talk! Talk!" he said, slapping her.

The fat soldier tore off her veil and threw it to the ground. She bent down to pick it up and stopped in the attitude of kneeling, her head still bowed. Her head was bald, and disfigured with a deep corrugation.[11] There was a livid gash along the side of her face. The bare-chested soldier pushed her. She fell on her face and lay still. The lights changed over the forest and for the first time Omovo saw that the dead animals on the river were in fact the corpses of grown men. Their bodies were tangled with riverweed and their eyes were bloated. Before he could react, he heard another scream. The woman was getting up, with the veil in her hand. She turned to the fat soldier, drew herself to her fullest height, and spat in his face. Waving the veil in the air, she began to howl dementedly. The two other soldiers backed away. The fat soldier wiped his face and lifted the gun to the level of her stomach. A moment before Omovo heard the shot a violent beating of wings just above him scared him from his hiding place. He ran through the forest screaming. The soldiers tramped after him. He ran through a mist which seemed to have risen from the rocks. As he ran he saw an owl staring at him from a canopy of leaves. He tripped over the roots of a tree and blacked out when his head hit the ground.

When he woke up it was very dark. He waved his fingers in front of his face and saw nothing. Mistaking the darkness for blindness he screamed, thrashed around, and ran into a door. When he recovered from his shock he heard voices outside and the radio crackling on about the war. He found his way to the balcony, full of wonder that his sight had returned. But when he got there he was surprised to find his father sitting on the sunken cane chair, drinking palm wine with the three soldiers. Omovo rushed to his father and pointed frantically at the three men.

"You must thank them," his father said. "They brought you back from the forest."

Omovo, overcome with delirium, began to tell his father what he had seen. But his father, smiling apologetically at the soldiers, picked up his son and carried him off to bed.

9. **kwashiorkor** (kwä′shē·ôr′kôr′): severe disease of young children, caused by deficiency of protein and calories and marked by stunted growth and a protruding belly.
10. **polythene** (päl′i·thēn′): term used in most English-speaking countries other than the United States for *polyethylene* (päl′ē·eth′ə·lēn′), a synthetic substance used to make tough, lightweight plastics, films, and the like.

11. **corrugation** (kôr′ə·gā′shən): groove or furrow.

WORDS TO OWN
dementedly (dē·ment′id·lē) *adv.:* madly; wildly.

E Reading Skills and Strategies
Making Inferences

? What can you infer about the woman, her mission, the people in the cave, and the contents of the basket? [Possible response: The people in the cave are probably war refugees to whom the woman is carrying food or other supplies in the basket.]

F Vocabulary Note
Varied Sources of English Vocabulary

This paragraph shows many sources of English vocabulary. In addition to words with Latin roots (some varied through the addition of affixes) and words from Old English, there are words from Spanish (*capsize*) and from Carib (*canoe*). There is a word that has entered the language as a trademark (*Coca-Cola*), a word from technology (*polythene*), and three words that have resulted from compounding (*waterlogged, outdated, riverbank*).

G English Language Learners
Dialect

Nigeria is a former British colony, where the use of English is widespread. The word *eh,* meaning, roughly, "right?," is a Briticism. "You dis witch" is dialect. Ask students what it may mean. [Possible responses: "You're this witch." "You're the witch."]

H Elements of Literature
Point of View

? Terror increases as the plot moves forward. What is Omovo feeling at this moment, and how is that the same or different from what the reader is feeling? [Possible responses: Omovo is terrified and feels the threat of impending violence, because he is seeing frightening things he has never seen before—dead bodies, a scarred woman. The reader feels all these things, in addition to fear for Omovo and a greater understanding of who this woman is and what she has been through.]

I Elements of Literature
Irony

? What is ironic about this final scene? [Possible response: The soldiers, whom Omovo so feared, and whom he has witnessed doing horrible violence, have brought him home to safety. Furthermore, his father, who has been trying so hard to keep him ignorant of the war, is friendly with them.]

Assessing Learning

Check Test: Questions and Answers

1. What item has Omovo's father disguised as a household fetish? [a radio]
2. How do the village children react to the "strange woman"? [They throw things at her.]
3. What are the soldiers giving the village children? [money]
4. What startles Omovo before he hears the shot? [a bird]
5. How does Omovo get back from the forest? [The soldiers bring him home.]

Connections

This letter from a mother to her daughter recounts the tragic start of war in the former Yugoslavia and how it impacted both of their lives.

A Struggling Readers
Identifying Pronouns

Who is "I," and who is "you" in this letter? ["I" is the writer of the letter, a mother. "You" is the writer's daughter, a woman in early adulthood.]

B Historical Connections
Croatia

In June 1991, the province of Croatia voted to form a republic independent of Yugoslavia. The separation was opposed by the area's Serbian minority, a group of about 600,000 people that had voted to form its own autonomous regions in Croatia. When President Franjo Tudjman refused to recognize Serbian autonomy, a civil war began.

C Critical Thinking
Challenging the Text

In what ways does this seem like a personal letter, and in what ways does it seem like a report intended for a general audience? [Possible answer: It seems like a personal letter in that the reader feels the writer's emotions. However, it does not seem as intimate as most personal letters; it also recounts information that the intended audience—the writer's daughter—would already know about.]

D English Language Learners
Briticisms

Explain that *tram* is a British term for "streetcar."

Connections — A Letter

The letter below was written on April 7, 1992, shortly after full-scale war erupted in the former Yugoslavia over land claimed by several ethnic groups. Sent from Zagreb, the historical capital of Croatia, Drakulíc's letter provides a poignant and personal history of the conflict in her homeland. She had thought, however hopefully, that her daughter might be able to live free of the past, outside the shadow of war.

Zagreb: A Letter to My Daughter

Slavenka Drakulíc

My dear R,

This morning I went to your empty room. Its tidiness was so strange: your usually unmade bed now covered with a blue quilt, a spotless desk, a chair without your T-shirts hanging from it, a carpet free of your scattered shoes. I miss you, I miss your voice, the notes that you left on the table when you came in late at night and that I read with my first morning coffee.

Today marks nine months since you left the country. I knew that you would go eventually, that you'd leave me, this house, your room where your childhood toys and books sit side by side with your evening dresses and makeup. That thought comforts me. *Living on her own will make her stronger, she will see the world, it is good for a young person to live abroad, and Vienna is only six hours away:* I keep repeating this to myself like some kind of mantra. Except that I know you didn't intend to leave so soon and so abruptly, didn't expect to leave me and your room, your university, and, more important, your friends here. You left so many things unfinished. You left because of the war.

It began on June 26, 1991, when the Yugoslav Federal Army attacked Slovenia. I was in London at that time, glued to a TV screen and a telephone. We both cried. "What do I do, Mama?" you asked on that first day of the war, but I didn't know how to advise you. What does one say to one's child when war begins? I didn't want you to panic after the army attacked Slovenia—even though it is only a hundred miles from Zagreb. One part of me could not believe that it was a real war because a real war could not happen—it would be too stupid, too absurd—here in Europe. But there was another part of me that knew it was real and knew there was no turning back.

One afternoon while I was still in London—I remember with great clarity that it was Tuesday, July 2—we were speaking on the telephone, and in the middle of our conversation you started screaming, "Mama, they're shooting next door!" I could hear the shots in the garden next to ours; I could visualize its high wall covered with roses and bunches of grapes hanging from the vine, the way the sun shone through its leaves at that particular moment of the late afternoon. And I could see you standing there, by the window overlooking it, lost and pale, trembling. You dropped the receiver, and then I heard your voice, half-cry and half-whimper, a voice I did not recognize. I don't think I have ever experienced such helplessness. I can hear it now, every sound that entered the receiver on that day, the distant hum of radio news in the background, the tram that passed by outside, and the sudden silence that followed it. Then the frightened yet soft voice of your boyfriend, Andrej, trying to calm you down. *Hush, it's nothing, it's nothing, just a drunken soldier,* he said, but it was too late,

Skill Link

Using Induction to Think Critically

This letter presents a few facts of one mother-daughter relationship against the backdrop of war. How can this particular, specific information be used to draw more general conclusions? Using the letter, ask students to do the following:

1. Find information about Yugoslavia that suggests conflicts and issues faced by Serbians and Croats not named in this article.
2. Identify information about the Serbo-Croatian conflict that suggests challenges faced by people other than this mother and daughter.
3. State generalizations that can be reasonably made about war, families, and ethnic groups in the former Yugoslavia.

because at that moment the war began for both of us.

Recent events here have led me to think about your father, sitting in Toronto. We married when I was eighteen and he was nineteen. He was from a Serbian family and I was from a Croatian one, but that didn't mean anything to us then. World War II had long been over by the time we were born, and people of my generation were trying to escape the war's shadow, to forget and just live our lives. Your father and I never discussed our family's different nationalities. Not because it was forbidden but because it felt unimportant. Perhaps our attitude was a consequence of the repression of the Communist regime, of the brainwashing of our education system, the plan to create an artificial "Yugoslav" nation. All I know is that we were interested not in the past, in who killed whom and why, but in our own lives.

The tragedy and the paradox of this situation now is that you will have to decide to take his side or mine, to become Serb or Croat. In this war there is no middle ground. You as a Croat or a Serb become responsible for what all other Croats or Serbs do. You are reduced to a single nationality—almost sentenced to it, since nationality in a war brings a danger of getting killed just because of it. You are now in a situation where you are forced to choose, to identify with something that has always been irrelevant to you, a total abstraction. "I am from Zagreb," you used to say, and perhaps it is the only right answer—to be a citizen. But not now. Not here.

—from Harper's Magazine

Horror and Scream by Dinko, age 12, from Pozega, from *I DREAM OF PEACE: Images of War by Children of Former Yugoslavia.* Preface by Maurice Sendak.

Copyright © 1994 UNICEF. Reprinted by Permission of HarperCollins Publishers, Inc.

E Historical Connections

The kingdom of Yugoslavia was invaded during World War II, and the country was divided among Germany, Italy, Hungary, and Bulgaria. The partition caused great political unrest, and Serbian nationalists waged guerrilla warfare against the pro-Fascist puppet government that was formed in Croatia. In retaliation, Croat nationalists initiated a campaign to exterminate the Serbs.

F Background

Communist Rule of Yugoslavia

Josip Tito, who ruled Yugoslavia from 1945 to 1980, unified the country under communism. In 1990, ten years after Tito's death and one year before the breakup of the Soviet Union and the beginning of the civil war in Yugoslavia, the Yugoslav party voted to end communism.

G Critical Thinking

Synthesizing

? Why is the fate of having to identify with one side or the other so horrible? [Possible responses: It robs the daughter of her own identity; it forces the daughter to become what she is not, to choose sides when she has no one side she wishes to choose.]

Connecting Across Texts

Connecting with "In the Shadow of War"

Invite students to explore the similarities and differences between Ben Okri's work of fiction and this letter by considering these points:

- the historical context of both works
- the amount and types of facts that emerge
- the roles of parents and children in each story
- the ways in which war determines not only ways of life but relationships between people
- point of view
- tone

MAKING MEANINGS

First Thoughts [Respond]

1. The point of greatest fear may be the moment at which the gun is raised to the woman's stomach or the moment at which the soldiers chase Omovo.

Shaping Interpretations [Interpret]

2. Omovo seems suspicious of the soldiers and sympathetic toward the woman.
3. Omovo's father tells him to come home early, so Omovo will be safe inside on that particular night. Omovo does not believe his father.
4. The soldiers want Omovo to reveal the veiled woman's location. Omovo may refuse out of some unspoken sympathy for the woman or because he instinctively distrusts the soldiers.
5. Possible responses: Omovo is curious; he is compelled by the mystery of the veiled figure.
6. The details show the physical and economic destruction of war.
7. Details about the malnourished children suggest she is bringing desperately needed food.
8. Possible responses: Omovo may feel a range of conflicting emotions, in which his relief at being safe is undercut by feelings of frustration, embarrassment, anger, or betrayal.
9. Possible responses: Omovo cannot immediately take in the brutality he sees around him; he has never seen such horrors and may be subconsciously masking the horror with gentler images.
10. Both show war's horror, but the child's perspective in Okri's story intensifies the sense of violence and scarring brutality.

Grading Timesaver

Rubrics for each Choices assignment appear on p. 190 in the *Portfolio Management System.*

MAKING MEANINGS

First Thoughts

1. At what point in Okri's story were you most worried about what might happen to Omovo?

Reading Check

a. What does Omovo's father say might happen during an eclipse of the moon?
b. What do the children believe about the veiled woman? What happens to her?

Shaping Interpretations

2. What are Omovo's feelings toward the soldiers? toward the woman?
3. Why do you think Omovo's father tells him about the eclipse? How does the boy react?
4. What is the soldier's **motive** for offering Omovo money? Why does Omovo refuse it?
5. Why do you think Omovo follows the soldiers who are following the veiled woman?
6. The story's **limited third-person point of view** means that we see the action and setting through a child's eyes. How do you interpret details that Omovo sees on the riverbank—such as the unfinished estates, the empty factory, the skeleton, the outdated currencies? (Be sure to check your reading notes.)
7. What do you think the woman brings to the people in the cave? What clues are provided?
8. At the end of the story, Omovo wakes up to find his father drinking with the soldiers. When Omovo tries to tell his father what happened, his father smiles "apologetically" at the soldiers. How do you think Omovo feels toward his father at this point? Explain.
9. How do you explain the transformations Omovo observes (canoes to dead animals to dead men)? Is he frightened? delirious? Or is there some other explanation?
10. Both Okri's story and "Zagreb: A Letter to My Daughter" (see ***Connections*** on page 974) concern war, but they are told from different points of view. How are the two narratives alike? How are they different?

CHOICES: Building Your Portfolio

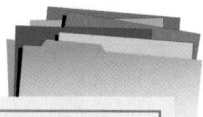

Writer's Notebook

1. Collecting Ideas for an Informative Report

Unless you're already familiar with the Ibo people's customs and culture, reading "In the Shadow of War" probably made you curious about them. What questions come to mind as you reflect on the story and think about the Nigerian Civil War or the current situation in Nigeria? (See Okri's biography on page 970.) Jot down your thoughts, and save your notes for the Writer's Workshop on page 1053.

Analyzing a Symbol

2. Tuned In

The radio plays a **symbolic** role in Okri's story. Find all the references to the radio, and then write a short essay explaining its significance. Here are some questions to get you started: Why is the brand name of the radio (a trivial detail) given? What is significant about the radio's resembling a fetish? What does Omovo listen to on the radio? What is the difference between hearing a disembodied voice on a radio and actually seeing an event?

Comparing Literary Works

3. Holding the Center

In an essay discuss the connections between the famous poem that opens this collection (W. B. Yeats's "The Second Coming") and the two prose selections here: Ben Okri's story and Slavenka Drakulíc's letter to her daughter (see ***Connections*** on page 974). Find specific details and images from the Yeats poem that relate to images and details in Okri's story and in the mother's letter. You might also discuss in your essay the child's painting on page 975.

Reading Check

a. He says that the world might go dark and the dead might walk around. He adds that "heclipses" eat children.
b. The children say she has no shadow and believe she is not human. She is later captured, brutalized, and shot.

Assessing Learning

Standardized Test Preparation

For practice with ACT and SAT formats, see
- *Preparation for College Admission Exams,* p. 47

For practice in proofreading and editing, see
- *Daily Oral Grammar,* Transparency 32

The Transforming Imagination

Theme

The Power of Memory *With the collapse of shared public values and meaning, people in the modern era looked inward for a sense of order and a source of hope. Many writers expressed romantic longings for a lost or perfect world. The chief mode still is irony.*

Reading the Anthology

Reaching Struggling Readers

The *Reading Skills and Strategies: Reaching Struggling Readers* binder provides materials coordinated with the Pupil's Edition (see the Collection Planner, p. T976B) to help students who have difficulty reading and comprehending text or students who are reluctant readers. The binder for twelfth grade is organized around ten individual skill areas and offers the following options:

- **MiniRead** MiniReads are short, easy texts that give students a chance to practice a particular skill and strategy before reading selections in the Pupil's Edition. Each MiniRead Skill Lesson can be taught independently or used in conjunction with a Selection Skill Lesson.
- **Selection Skill Lessons** Selection Skill Lessons allow students to apply skills introduced in the MiniReads. Each Selection Skill Lesson provides reading instruction and practice specific to a particular piece of literature in the Pupil's Edition.

Reading Beyond the Anthology

Read On

At the end of the Twentieth Century collections, the grade twelve book includes an annotated bibliography of books and films suitable for extended study. The suggested titles are related to works in these collections by theme, by author, or by subject. To preview the Read On for this period, please turn to p. T1174.

Collection 13 The Transforming Imagination

Resources for this Collection

Note: All resources for this collection are available for preview on the *One-Stop Planner CD-ROM 2 with Test Generator.* All worksheets and blackline masters may be printed from the CD-ROM.

Internet Resources
go.hrw.com LE0 12-13

Selection or Feature	Reading and Literary Skills	Vocabulary, Language, and Grammar
• **The Lake Isle of Innisfree** (p. 979) **Elements of Literature: Assonance and Alliteration** (p. 980) • **The Song of Wandering Aengus** (p. 981) • **The Wild Swans at Coole** (p. 982) William Butler Yeats	• *Graphic Organizers for Active Reading,* Worksheet pp. 95, 96, 97 • *Literary Elements:* Transparency 23 Worksheet p. 70	
Araby (p. 985) James Joyce **Elements of Literature: Irony: Things Are Not as They Seem** (p. 991) **Spotlight On: The Influence of James Joyce** (p. 993)	• *Graphic Organizers for Active Reading,* Worksheet p. 98 • *Literary Elements:* Transparency 24 Worksheet p. 73	• *Words to Own,* Worksheet p. 27 • *Grammar and Language Links:* Varying Sentence Length, Worksheet p. 57 • *Language Workshop CD-ROM,* Revising for Variety • *Daily Oral Grammar,* Transparency 33
• **The Rocking-Horse Winner** (p. 996) **Primary Sources: D. H. Lawrence on Money** (p. 1006) • **Snake** (p. 1007) D. H. Lawrence **Spotlight On: Film As Literature: More Than Meets the Eye** (p. 1012) William V. Costanzo	• *Reading Skills and Strategies: Reaching Struggling Readers* • MiniRead Skill Lesson, p. 76 • Selection Skill Lesson, p. 83 • *Graphic Organizers for Active Reading,* Worksheet p. 99 • *Literary Elements:* Transparency 25 Worksheet p. 76	• *Words to Own,* Worksheet p. 28 • *Grammar and Language Links:* Varying Sentence Length, Worksheet p. 59 • *Language Workshop CD-ROM,* Revising for Variety • *Daily Oral Grammar,* Transparency 34
The Demon Lover (p. 1018) Elizabeth Bowen	• *Reading Skills and Strategies: Reaching Struggling Readers* • MiniRead Skill Lesson, p. 55 • Selection Skill Lesson, p. 62 • *Graphic Organizers for Active Reading,* Worksheet p. 100	• *Words to Own,* Worksheet p. 29 • *Grammar and Language Links:* Varying Sentence Beginnings, Worksheet p. 61 • *Language Workshop CD-ROM,* Revising for Variety • *Daily Oral Grammar,* Transparency 35
World Literature: Argentina Axolotl (p. 1027) Julio Cortázar	The World Literature feature offers students the opportunity to explore thematically linked literature from different world cultures. Structured activities called Finding Common Ground guide students' explorations of thematic connections between British and other world literature.	
• **Fern Hill** (p. 1033) • **In my craft or sullen art** (p. 1036) **Elements of Literature: Wordplay** (p. 1037) • **Do Not Go Gentle into That Good Night** (p. 1038) Dylan Thomas **Elements of Literature: The Villanelle** (p. 1040)	• *Graphic Organizers for Active Reading,* Worksheet pp. 101, 102	
B. Wordsworth (p. 1042) V. S. Naipaul	• *Graphic Organizers for Active Reading,* Worksheet p. 103	• *Words to Own,* Worksheet p. 30 • *Grammar and Language Links:* Commas, Worksheet p. 63
Mushrooms (p. 1050) Margaret Atwood	• *Graphic Organizers for Active Reading,* Worksheet p. 104	
Writer's Workshop: Informative Report (p. 1053)		
Language Workshop: The Value of Variety (p. 1057)		• *Workshop Resources,* p. 59 • *Language Workshop CD-ROM,* Sentence Style

Other Resources for this Collection

- *Cross-Curricular Activities*, p. 13
- *Portfolio Management System*, Introduction to Portfolio Assessment, p. 1
- *Test Generator*, Collection Test

Writing	Listening and Speaking Viewing and Representing	Assessment
• *Portfolio Management System*, Rubrics for Choices, p. 191	• *Audio CD Library*, Disc 17, Tracks 2, 3, 4 • *Portfolio Management System*, Rubrics for Choices, p. 191	• *Formal Assessment*, Selection Tests, pp. 195, 196, 197 • *Test Generator (One-Stop Planner CD-ROM)*
• *Portfolio Management System*, Rubrics for Choices, p. 193	• *Audio CD Library*, Disc 17, Track 5 • *Portfolio Management System*, Rubrics for Choices, p. 193	• *Formal Assessment*, Selection Test, p. 198 • *Test Generator (One-Stop Planner CD-ROM)* • *Preparation for College Admission Exams*, p. 49
• *Portfolio Management System*, Rubrics for Choices, p. 195	• *Audio CD Library*, Disc 17, Tracks 6, 7 • *Portfolio Management System*, Rubrics for Choices, p. 195	• *Formal Assessment*, Selection Tests, pp. 200, 202 • *Test Generator (One-Stop Planner CD-ROM)* • *Preparation for College Admission Exams*, p. 51
• *Portfolio Management System*, Rubrics for Choices, p. 197	• *Audio CD Library*, Disc 18, Track 2 • *Viewing and Representing:* Fine Art Transparency 16 Worksheet p. 64 • *Portfolio Management System*, Rubrics for Choices, p. 197	• *Formal Assessment*, Selection Test, p. 203 • *Test Generator (One-Stop Planner CD-ROM)*
	• *Audio CD Library*, Disc 18, Track 3	
• *Portfolio Management System*, Rubrics for Choices, p. 199	• *Audio CD Library*, Disc 18, Tracks 4, 5, 6 • *Viewing and Representing:* Fine Art Transparency 17 Worksheet p. 68 • *Portfolio Management System*, Rubrics for Choices, p. 199	• *Formal Assessment*, Selection Tests, pp. 205, 207 • *Test Generator (One-Stop Planner CD-ROM)*
• *Portfolio Management System*, Rubrics for Choices, p. 201	• *Audio CD Library*, Disc 18, Track 7 • *Portfolio Management System*, Rubrics for Choices, p. 201	• *Formal Assessment*, Selection Test, p. 208 • *Test Generator (One-Stop Planner CD-ROM)*
• *Portfolio Management System*, Rubrics for Choices, p. 202	• *Audio CD Library*, Disc 18, Track 8 • *Portfolio Management System*, Rubrics for Choices, p. 202	• *Formal Assessment*, Selection Test, p. 210 • *Test Generator (One-Stop Planner CD-ROM)*
• *Workshop Resources*, p. 37	• *Viewing and Representing*, HRW Multimedia Presentation Maker	• *Portfolio Management System*, pp. 203, 204, 205

Transparency CD-ROM Video Audio CD

Collection 13 The Transforming Imagination

Skills Focus

Selection or Feature	Reading Skills and Strategies	Elements of Literature and Language	Writing	Listening and Speaking	Viewing and Representing
The Lake Isle of Innisfree (p. 979) **The Song of Wandering Aengus** (p. 981) **The Wild Swans at Coole** (p. 982) William Butler Yeats	Paraphrase, p. 983	Sound effects, pp. 979–980 Image, p. 981 Symbol, pp. 981–983 Mood/Elegy, p. 983 Theme, p. 983 Tone, p. 983	Develop Research Questions, p. 983 Analyze an Author's Stance, p. 983 Write an Essay comparing "The Wild Swans at Coole" with "Ode to a Nightingale," p. 983 Describe a Place of Peace, p. 983		
Araby (p. 985) James Joyce **Spotlight on the Influence of James Joyce** (p. 993)	Use a Graphic Organizer, p. 985 Connotations, p. 990	Epiphany, pp. 985, 990, 992 Point of View, p. 990 Setting, p. 990 Tone/Irony, p. 990 Stream of Consciousness, p. 993	Freewrite on Potential Topics, p. 992 Explain an Epiphany in "Araby," p. 992 Explore Multiple Meanings, p. 992 Use Another Point of View, p. 992 Write a Sketch Using Stream-of-Consciousness Techniques, p. 992	Prepare and Perform an Oral Reading of "Araby," p. 992	Create a Story Map for an American Setting, p. 992 Create Two Visions of Araby, p. 992
The Rocking-Horse Winner (p. 996) **Snake** (p. 1007) D. H. Lawrence	Identify Allusions, p. 1009	Symbol, pp. 996, 1006, 1009 Character, p. 1006 Theme, pp. 1006, 1010 Tone, p. 1006 Setting, pp. 1007, 1009 Conflict, p. 1009 Simile/Metaphor, p. 1009 Allusion, p. 1009 Sensory Images, p. 1010	Identify Research Questions on the Mind-Body Connection, p. 1010 Support a Thesis, p. 1010 Write a Stream-of-Consciousness Narrative from the Point of View of a Character, p. 1010 Write an Essay on the Theme of Transgression in Three Works, p. 1010 Write a Free-Verse Poem, p. 1010	Adapt a Scene from "The Rocking-Horse Winner" for Performance, p. 1010	
Reading Skills and Strategies: Formation of New Words (p. 1011)	Formation of New Words, p. 1011				
Spotlight On: Film as Literature: More Than Meets the Eye (p. 1012)		Elements of Film, p. 1013 Adaptation, p. 1014			Guidelines for Evaluating Film, p. 1016
The Demon Lover (p. 1018) Elizabeth Bowen	Modify Predictions, pp. 1018, 1024	Flashback, pp. 1018, 1023 Setting/Mood, pp. 1023, 1025 Omniscient Narrator, p. 1023 Dramatic Irony, p. 1023 Theme, pp. 1023, 1025	Identify Topics for a Report, p. 1024 Write an Essay Comparing a Short Story with a Ballad, p. 1024 Write a Descriptive Paragraph, p. 1025 Write an Essay Comparing Texts, p. 1025		Create a Story Map, p. 1023 Create a Story Illustration, p. 1025 Propose a Film Adaptation, p. 1025
World Literature: Argentina Axolotl (p. 1027) Julio Cortázar	Monitor Reading, p. 1027	Point of View, p. 1031 Conflict, p. 1031 Theme, p. 1031	The World Literature feature offers students the opportunity to explore thematically linked literature from different world cultures. Structured activities guide students' explorations of these thematic connections between British and other world literature.		
Fern Hill (p. 1033) **In my craft or sullen art** (p. 1036) **Do Not Go Gentle into That Good Night** (p. 1038) Dylan Thomas		Lyric, pp. 1033, 1037 Sound Effects, pp. 1033, 1037 Figures of Speech, p. 1033 Personification, p. 1037 Paradox, p. 1037 Pun, p. 1037 Villanelle, p. 1040	Prepare a Biographic Bibliography, p. 1040 Identify the Theme of a Poem, p. 1040 Write a Narrative of a Childhood Episode, p. 1040 Write a Response to "Do Not Go Gentle into That Good Night," p. 1040 Write a Response to an Author, p. 1040		
B. Wordsworth (p. 1042) V. S. Naipaul	Chronological Order, p. 1048 Analyzing the Vernacular, p. 1049	Setting, pp. 1042, 1048 Imagery, pp. 1042, 1048 Dialogue, p. 1042 Theme, p. 1048 Character, p. 1049	Develop a Thesis Statement, p. 1049 Write an Essay Exploring the Meaning of "the Poet's Eye," p. 1049 Analyze a Character, p. 1049 Write a Character Sketch, p. 1049	Research and Present an Oral Report on Calypso Music, p. 1049	Use a Graphic Organizer, p. 1049
Mushrooms (p. 1050) Margaret Atwood		Free Verse, pp. 1050, 1052 Image/Metaphor, p. 1052 Assonance, p. 1052 Alliteration, p. 1052	Develop a List of Possible Subjects for Research, p. 1052 Write a Free Verse Poem, p. 1052		
Writer's Workshop: Informative Report (p. 1053)			Write an Informative Report, pp. 1053–1056		
Language Workshop: The Value of Variety (p. 1057)		Varied Sentences, p. 1057	Revise Sentences by Varying the Placement of the Subject, p. 1057		
Reading for Life: Reading a Persuasive Speech (p. 1058)	Analyze a Speech, p. 1058			Prepare a Persuasive Speech, p. 1058	

Collection 13

THE TRANSFORMING IMAGINATION

Yeats
Joyce
Lawrence
Bowen
Cortázar
Thomas
Naipaul
Atwood

If one is lucky, a solitary fantasy can totally transform one million realities.

—Maya Angelou, *from The Heart of a Woman* (American, 1928–)

OBJECTIVES

1. Read literature of the twentieth century on the theme of "The Transforming Imagination"
2. Interpret literary elements with special emphasis on irony, word play, and the villanelle
3. Apply a variety of reading strategies, including understanding the formation of new words
4. Respond to the literature in a variety of modes
5. Learn and use new words
6. Plan, draft, and revise an informative report
7. Develop skill in forming effective sentences by varying length and word order
8. Demonstrate the ability to read a persuasive speech

Responding to the Quotation

? How can fantasy transform reality? [Possible responses: When a person fantasizes about something, reality can be totally blocked out and thus become irrelevant; a fantasy, or a dream, can help shape one's reality.] **Why would a person be lucky if such a transformation were to happen?** [Possible response: Fantasy is usually more desirable than reality because it is born out of our imagination or desires. It is not often that we can get exactly what we want.]

Writing Focus: Informative Report

WORK IN PROGRESS

The following **Work in Progress** assignments build to a culminating **Writer's Workshop** at the end of this collection.

• Yeats's poems	Use questions to find a topic (p. 983)
• Araby	Find topics in story or biography (p. 992)
• The Rocking-Horse Winner; Snake	Brainstorm questions for investigation (p. 1010)
• The Demon Lover	Find topic in literature (p. 1024)
• Thomas's poems	Research poet's life (p. 1040)
• B. Wordsworth	Trace character development (p. 1049)
• Mushrooms	Brainstorm subjects from nature (p. 1052)

Writer's Workshop: Expository Writing / An Informative Report (p. 1053)

OBJECTIVES

The Lake Isle of Innisfree / . . . Wandering Aengus / The Wild Swans at Coole

1. Read and interpret the poems
2. Identify and interpret verbal music
3. Identify assonance and alliteration
4. Interpret symbols
5. Express understanding through critical and creative writing

SKILLS

Literary

- Identify assonance and alliteration
- Interpret symbols

Writing

- Develop questions for an informative report
- Analyze the author's stance
- Compare two poems
- Write about an ideal place of peace

Viewing and Representing

- Relate fine art to the selections (ATE)

Planning

- **Block Schedule**
  Block Scheduling Lesson Plans with Pacing Guide
- **Traditional Schedule**
  Lesson plans Including Strategies for English-Language Learners
- **One-Stop Planner**
  CD-ROM with Test Generator

William Butler Yeats

(1865–1939)

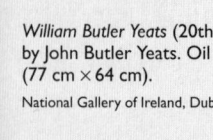

William Butler Yeats (20th century) by John Butler Yeats. Oil on canvas (77 cm × 64 cm).
National Gallery of Ireland, Dublin.

Generally regarded as the twentieth century's greatest poet writing in English, William Butler Yeats (rhymes with *crates*) was born in Dublin, Ireland, the son of a well-known portrait painter. He came on to the literary scene when the Pre-Raphaelite movement of the mid-nineteenth century was reviving as a result of new influences from the Continent.

The revival, called Art Nouveau in the world of painting, emphasized the mysterious and unfathomable—especially those recesses of the mind just then being scrutinized by the great pioneers in psychology, Sigmund Freud and Carl Jung. Particularly in poetry, the revival recommended evocation above statement, symbols above facts, and musical measures above common speech. It was within this atmosphere that the young Yeats established a reputation as a lyricist of great delicacy and as a versifier of old tales drawn from Irish folklore and mythology. In a collection of his early poems, *The Wanderings of Oisin and Other Poems* (1889), Yeats was a romantic dreamer, evoking the mythic and heroic past of Ireland. At this stage of his career, he was a pioneer of the Celtic Revival, determined to make the Irish conscious of their heroic past.

Yeats came abruptly into a new phase in 1914 when, heeding the advice of the American poet Ezra Pound, he set out to create a stark, chiseled, and eloquently resonant kind of poetry. That same year, he published a volume aptly titled *Responsibilities*. The man who had once seen himself as the prophet-priest of Ireland's national destiny was now grappling with his own personal realities. For years, Yeats had idolized and yearned for Maud Gonne, the beautiful Irish political activist who rejected his hand and instead chose another, more politically radical suitor. Finally, Yeats accepted that rejection and in 1917, at fifty-two, married Georgie Hyde-Lees, an Englishwoman who would remain his "delight and comfort" for the next twenty-two years.

With his private life settled, Yeats then cultivated a public role. From 1922 to 1928, he served as a senator of the newly formed Irish Free State. He also toured the United States, giving ritualized readings of the poems for which, in 1923, he was awarded the Nobel Prize in literature.

As a poet, Yeats may be said to have carved out of English a language distinctly his own. Monumentally spare and unadorned, "cold and passionate as the dawn" in Yeats's own words, it confirms the basic definition of poetry as "heightened speech."

Yeats was also a dramatist, and in this role he helped his friend Lady Gregory establish Dublin's Abbey Theatre as a monument to Irish culture and high literary standards. As a playwright, he dealt in poetic drama, allegories, and other nonrealistic approaches, often making adaptations of the ceremonial choreography of the Japanese Nō theater. Although Yeats's dramas are more theatrical than dramatic, they continue to be produced by small theater groups. Some audiences may agree with Yeats himself, who felt that some of his most memorable poems are embedded, like gems, in the scripts of his plays.

Yeats dramatized himself in the grand manner, which was entirely in keeping with his accomplishments and aristocratic pretensions. Nearly ten years after his death and burial in the south of France, his body was disinterred and returned to Ireland, like that of a primitive king, with full ceremony and military pomp, on the deck of a battleship.

Resources: Print and Media

Reading

- *Graphic Organizers for Active Reading,* pp. 95, 96, 97
- *Audio CD Library,* Disc 17, Tracks 2, 3, 4

Elements of Literature

- *Literary Elements*
  Transparency 23
  Worksheet, p. 70

Assessment

- *Formal Assessment,* pp. 195, 196, 197
- *Portfolio Management System,* p. 191
- *Test Generator (One-Stop Planner CD-ROM)*

Internet

- go.hrw.com (keyword: LE0: 12-13)

Before You Read

THE LAKE ISLE OF INNISFREE

Make the Connection

A Place of Peace

Our imagination can transport us from our busy lives to the calm of a peaceful retreat.

Quickwrite

What is your own vision of a peaceful retreat from everyday, routine life? Briefly describe your ideas, or draw a sketch of an ideal place of peace.

Elements of Literature

Verbal Music

As a young man, Yeats inherited much of the vocabulary and poetic posturing of his nineteenth-century predecessors. Phrases in the poem like "veils of the morning" and "midnight's all a glimmer" come from this old-fashioned vocabulary, and Innisfree itself represents all the impossibly idyllic, great good places that weary Victorians "on the roadway, or on the pavements gray" yearned for. Nevertheless, Yeats's lyrical skills, especially his haunting use of **assonance** (the repetition of similar vowel sounds), have created a poem whose verbal music has echoed in readers' memories for over a hundred years.

Background

Innisfree is a real island in Sligo, the beautiful county in the west of Ireland where Yeats spent many summers as a child, visiting his grandparents. Yeats once said that the poem came to him when he was in London on a dreary day. He passed a store display that used dripping water in a fountain, and he thought at once of the lake island of his childhood. Yeats's father had once read Thoreau's *Walden* to him. The bean rows and cabin in this poem are straight from Thoreau's account of his life in Walden Woods in Massachusetts.

The Lake Isle of Innisfree

William Butler Yeats

I will arise and go now, and go to Innisfree,
And a small cabin build there, of clay and wattles° made:
Nine bean-rows will I have there, a hive for the honey-bee,
And live alone in the bee-loud glade. **A**

And I shall have some peace there, for peace comes dropping slow,
Dropping from the veils of the morning to where the cricket sings;
There midnight's all a glimmer, and noon a purple glow,
And evening full of the linnet's° wings. **B**

I will arise and go now, for always night and day
I hear lake water lapping with low sounds by the shore;
While I stand on the roadway, or on the pavements gray,
I hear it in the deep heart's core. **C**

2. **wattles:** interwoven twigs or branches.
8. **linnet's:** A linnet is a European songbird.

go.hrw.com
LEO 12-13

Resources

Listening

A recording of Yeats's poems is provided in the *Audio CD Library*:

- Disc 17, Tracks 2, 3, 4

Elements of Literature

For additional instruction on symbol, see *Literary Elements*:

- Transparency 23
- Worksheet, p. 70

Summary ■■

In a lyric that is both decisive and dreamlike, the speaker determines that he will now leave his urban home and go to the lake island of Innisfree. There he will build a cabin and live alone in harmony with nature. He looks forward to the peace and transcendent natural beauty of the island. He states that one reason for his departure is that he constantly hears, deep in his heart, the sound of the lake water lapping along the shoreline.

A Critical Thinking

Classifying

? How would you classify the kind of life the speaker wishes to lead on the island? [Possible responses: simple, solitary, peaceful.]

B Elements of Literature

Verbal Music

? What sound elements create verbal music in ll. 5 and 6? [the alliterative *s* and *p* sounds; the repetition of *peace, dropping,* and the *-ing* sound]

C Reading Skills and Strategies

Drawing Conclusions

? What does the last stanza suggest about the speaker's relationship with nature? [Possible response: It suggests a mystical connection or basic identification with nature that endures despite the effects of city life.]

Reaching All Students

Struggling Readers

Each stanza consists of two two-line independent clauses. Ask students to read the poem a clause at a time and paraphrase each clause as they read it. [Stanza 1: I will get up and go to Innisfree and build a cabin; I'll have nine rows of beans and a beehive and live alone.]

English Language Learners

To bring the poem's imagery to life, ask students to draw a picture of the cabin and its surroundings. Suggest they begin by listing the visual images in the poem and then using these to visualize the cabin before they begin to draw.

Advanced Learners

Ask students to trace the influences of Romanticism in the poem. [Possible responses: use of the lyric form to express feeling; emphasis on nature; focus on imagination and naturalness.]

Using Students' Strengths

Auditory/Musical Learners

Ask students to list all the auditory images in the poem and then try to create the sounds, using both their voices and any objects or instruments that are available in the classroom.

Responding to the Art

Paul Henry (1876–1958), an Irish painter, designed posters for the London, Midland, and Scottish Railway. That experience contributed to the vigor and simplicity of his landscapes.

Activity. Ask students what elements in Yeats's poem appear in the painting. What mood is common to both poem and painting? [cabin, wattles, lake water, peaceful mood]

Making Meanings

First Thoughts [Respond]

1. Responses will vary. Though students may not have sketched a pastoral scene, they may have included soft sounds and images similar to Yeats's.

Shaping Interpretations [Interpret]

2. Go to Innisfree, build a small cabin, and live in it alone.
3. Bees, a cricket singing, and lake water lapping the shore.
4. Peace is like the fall of morning dew.
5. The island is beautiful, natural, and tranquil, while the speaker's actual location has noisy roadways and gray pavements.
6. Possible response: He evidently loves nature and the stillness one finds away from cities.

Connecting with the Text [Apply]

7. Possible responses: The memory would provide mental retreat from dreary surroundings and give hope of returning to the lake island.

Challenging the Text [Analyze]

8. Possible responses: The tone is lyrical, nostalgic, yearning, and muted. Because the speaker seems to value the tranquility and beauty of natural surroundings, the poem could be called a Romantic work.

Elements of Literature

Assonance and Alliteration
Possible Responses

1. Examples of assonance, *I/arise, go/go, cabin/build,* and *nine/bean/hive/bee,* dominate the stanza.

Lakeside Cottages (c. 1929) by Paul Henry. Oil on canvas (16″ × 24″).
Hugh Lane Municipal Gallery of Modern Art, Dublin.

Making Meanings

First Thoughts

1. How does the place of peace you sketched in your Quickwrite notes compare with Yeats's "lake isle"?

Shaping Interpretations

2. In the first stanza, what does the speaker say he will do?
3. What sounds does the speaker describe in the poem?
4. What does the speaker compare peace to?
5. How do the surroundings of the lake island contrast with the speaker's actual location?
6. Why do you think the speaker cannot find peace in the city setting?

Connecting with the Text

7. How might the memory of a place like Innisfree affect you if you found yourself in dreary surroundings?

Challenging the Text

8. How would you describe the **tone** of this poem? Do you think it could be called a Romantic poem? Explain why or why not.

Elements of Literature

Assonance and Alliteration

The music of this poem comes in part from Yeats's use of **assonance,** the repetition of similar vowel sounds in nearby words. The poem is also notable for a famous line (line 10) of **alliteration**—the repetition of consonant sounds in nearby words.

1. What vowel sounds dominate the first stanza?
2. What vowel sounds are emphasized by the rhyming words?
3. In line 10, what repeated consonant sounds echo the sound of lake water?
4. How would you describe the total effect of the vowel sounds in the poem? (How would the poem have been different if the poet had used more hard consonants, like *k, d,* or *p*?)

2. The rhyming words repeat the short *i* sound and the long *e, a,* and *o* sounds.
3. The repeated *l* and *w* sounds echo the sound of lake water. Some students also may suggest that the *k* and *p* sounds echo the little waves hitting the shore.
4. The repeated vowel sounds make the poem musical and haunting. Harder consonant sounds would have produced a more guttural and harsh effect.

Making the Connections

Connecting to the Theme: "The Transforming Imagination"
Ask students to discuss in what way the speaker's thoughts about Innisfree transform his reality. [Possible answers: By thinking about going to Innisfree, the speaker makes his reality—life in the dreary city—easier to bear. The speaker's thoughts about Innisfree actually will transform his reality if he leaves the city and goes to the isle of his dreams.]

Before You Read

THE SONG OF WANDERING AENGUS

Make the Connection

The speakers of Yeats's early poems are like the lovers in nineteenth-century romantic poetry: The beloved they search for is usually not of this world. As a young writer, Yeats was captivated by the old Celtic fantasies he heard in western Ireland. Here is what he writes in *The Celtic Twilight*: "It is far easier to be sensible in cities than in many country places I could tell you of. When one walks on those gray roads at evening by the scented elder bushes of the white cottages, watching the faint mountains gathering the clouds upon their heads, one all too readily discovers beyond the thin cobweb veil of the sense, those creatures, the goblins, hurrying from the white square stone door to the north, or from the Heart Lake in the south."

Yeats said that Aengus, the speaker of this poem, is the master of love in Celtic stories.

Quickwrite

What stories, including those told in film, present romantic love as a passionate encounter that ends quickly and is forever remembered and longed for? Jot down what you think of this scenario.

The Song of Wandering Aengus

William Butler Yeats

I went out to the hazel wood,
Because a fire was in my head, **A**
And cut and peeled a hazel wand,
And hooked a berry to a thread;
And when white moths were on the wing,
And moth-like stars were flickering out,
I dropped the berry in a stream
And caught a little silver trout.

When I had laid it on the floor
I went to blow the fire aflame,
But something rustled on the floor,
And some one called me by my name:
It had become a glimmering girl **B**
With apple blossom in her hair
Who called me by my name and ran
And faded through the brightening air.

Though I am old with wandering
Through hollow lands and hilly lands, **C**
I will find out where she has gone,
And kiss her lips and take her hands;
And walk among long dappled grass,
And pluck till time and times are done
The silver apples of the moon,
The golden apples of the sun.

MAKING MEANINGS

First Thoughts

1. What do you think of the romantic notion behind this poem?

Shaping Interpretations

2. Could the poem be read **symbolically** as a quest for beauty, especially the poet's search for beauty in his art? Use details in the poem to justify your response.

3. This poem makes an intensely visual impression. What **images** does the poet make you see? (Look especially at the use of color.)

4. How does the story of Aengus and his "glimmering girl" compare with Keats's romantic poem "La Belle Dame sans Merci" (page 751)?

Summary ■■

The speaker goes to the woods, hooks a berry to a thread, and drops it in a stream. He catches a silver trout and lays it on the ground. While he goes to tend the fire, the fish turns into a "glimmering girl" who calls the speaker by name and then runs away. Enchanted by the lovely creature, the speaker, now old with wandering, still hopes to find her again.

A Reading Skills and Strategies

Identifying Cause and Effect

? Why did the speaker go into the woods? [because a fire was in his head.] What does this suggest about his state of mind? [Possible answer: He was agitated or excited about something.]

B Struggling Readers

Identifying Pronoun Antecedents

? To what does "it" refer in ll. 9 and 13? [the silver trout] Describe in your own words what happens to "it" while the speaker goes to "blow the fire aflame." [Possible response: The trout rustles, transforms into a girl, calls the speaker's name, and runs away.]

C Critical Thinking

Expressing an Opinion

? Do you think Aengus is wise to go looking for the girl? Why or why not? [Possible responses: no, because the girl could just be a hallucination; no, she is an unknown entity that is better left alone; yes, there is every reason to search for that which captivates our imagination and stirs our desire for beauty.]

MAKING MEANINGS

First Thoughts [Respond]

1. Some students may find the romantic notion of a great love forever out of reach to be frustrating and immature. Others may find it charming and poignant.

Shaping Interpretations [Interpret]

2. Possible response: The poem could be read symbolically as a quest for beauty. The "fire" in the speaker's head could be his burning desire to create. When he tries to "blow the fire aflame," the "glimmering girl" mysteriously appears. This elusive figure could symbolize the ideal beauty the poet attempts to portray through his art. Although the ideal is unattainable for now (symbolized by the girl's vanishing), the speaker vows to continue searching for this ideal though he is "old with wandering."

3. Possible responses: The hazel wood; the threaded berry; white moths; little silver trout; a glimmering girl with apple blossoms in her hair; silver apples of the moon; golden apples of the sun.

4. Both speakers meet and are enchanted by a beautiful, otherwordly girl who vanishes as quickly as she comes. However, the speaker in Keats's poem is left lifeless and forlorn by the experience, whereas Aengus is invigorated and determined to regain the vision.

Summary ■■

On a lakeshore in Coole Park, in an October twilight, the speaker counts fifty-nine swans. He recalls counting them nineteen years before and remarks that "[t]heir hearts have not grown old" and they have remained faithful to their mates. The speaker, however, has a sore heart, and he acknowledges that much has changed in his life since he last saw the swans.

A Vocabulary Note

Multiple Meanings

? Yeats uses *still* in l. 4 as an adjective to mean "motionless" or "tranquil." *Still* can also be used as an adverb to mean "up to this or that time." How is *still* used in ll. 19, 24, and 25? [In ll. 19 and 24, *still* means "up to this or that time"; in l. 25, it means "motionless."]

B Reading Skills and Strategies

Making Inferences

? What is the speaker's mood in the third stanza? [Possible response: regretful; disappointed.] Why do you think that viewing the swans elicits such a mood? [Possible response: He grieves when he remembers a happier time nineteen years earlier when he first viewed the swans.]

C Critical Thinking

Interpreting

? In the fourth stanza, what does the speaker appear to imply about himself in contrast to the swans? [Possible answer: Everything has changed in his life since he first saw the swans, but they remain as they were nineteen years ago.]

D Elements of Literature

Symbol

? In order to be a symbol, the swans must possess general characteristics that allow them to stand not only for themselves but also for something beyond themselves. What descriptions used in ll. 25–29 help establish the swans' status as symbols? [mysterious, beautiful, delightful in men's eyes]

Before You Read

THE WILD SWANS AT COOLE

Make the Connection

Time Marches On

Yeats first saw the scene described in this poem when he was thirty-two. He wrote the poem at the age of fifty-one. How might the passing of time transform an experience?

Quickwrite

Think of a familiar scene you have returned to over the years. Describe how time has affected your responses to the scene.

Elements of Literature

Symbol

Yeats's swans can be regarded as **symbols,** but what do they represent? As you read the poem, keep in mind that symbols, by their very nature, are open-ended: Their meanings are various and open to interpretation.

Background

Yeats's good friend and fellow writer Lady Gregory lived on an estate known as Coole Park in Ireland's County Galway. When Yeats first visited there in 1897, he was in love with Maud Gonne, the beautiful activist for Irish independence, who was more interested in politics than in marriage. This poem, written in 1916, recalls Yeats's first view of the swans; now, nineteen years later, he realizes that "All's changed."

The swans are "wild," or migratory. Like the poet, they return annually to familiar places. Yeats knew that swans were monogamous, that "lover by lover" they continued to live in a state of mated bliss denied to him. But the larger meanings of the poem lie in the relation between memory, time, loss, and the inflexible patterns of natural life represented by the swans.

The Wild Swans at Coole

William Butler Yeats

The trees are in their autumn beauty,
The woodland paths are dry,
Under the October twilight the water
Mirrors a still sky;
Upon the brimming water among the stones
Are nine-and-fifty swans.

The nineteenth autumn has come upon me
Since I first made my count;
I saw, before I had well finished,
All suddenly mount
And scatter wheeling in great broken rings
Upon their clamorous wings.

I have looked upon those brilliant creatures,
And now my heart is sore.
All's changed since I, hearing at twilight,
The first time on this shore,
The bell-beat of their wings above my head,
Trod with a lighter tread.

Unwearied still, lover by lover,
They paddle in the cold
Companionable streams or climb the air;
Their hearts have not grown old;
Passion or conquest, wander where they will,
Attend upon them still.

But now they drift on the still water,
Mysterious, beautiful;
Among what rushes will they build,
By what lake's edge or pool
Delight men's eyes when I awake some day
To find they have flown away?

Reaching All Students

Struggling Readers

Place students in small groups to write a paraphrase of one of the five stanzas. Have a spokesperson from each group present the paraphrase to the class and then invite questions.

Advanced Learners

Encourage students to consider the poem in light of the following events: 1) World War I was raging; 2) the Easter uprising of 1916 had cast a pall on Irish political life; 3) Maud Gonne had given Yeats a final rebuff.

Using Students' Strengths

Auditory/Musical Learners

Ask students to locate or invent a melody that captures the essence of this poem. Point out that the tone and mood of the poem change as it progresses and suggest that the music they create reflect these changes. Students may wish to play their musical selections as they read the poem to the class.

Making Meanings

First Thoughts

1. What do you think is the most important word or passage in this poem? Be sure to compare your responses with those of other readers.

Shaping Interpretations

2. How is the speaker feeling as he gazes at the swans? How did he feel nineteen years earlier when he heard the beating of their wings?
3. The second, third, and fourth stanzas offer hints about the personal experience that underlies the poem. What are these hints? Why do you think the speaker's heart is "sore" (line 14)?
4. **Paraphrase,** or state in your own words, the question the speaker asks in the last stanza.
5. What qualities of the swans do you think the speaker envies? Why? What might the swans **symbolize** to the speaker?
6. How are the time of year and the time of day in this poem appropriate to its **mood**?
7. The word *awake* in the next-to-last line is mysterious at first reading. Do you think it signifies that the poem has all been a dream? Or could it mean something else? How might this word offer a clue to the **theme** of the poem?
8. How could this poem be said to be in the **elegiac** mode? How does the poem relate in **theme, tone,** and **imagery** to any of the other famous elegies in this book?

Connecting with the Text

9. Review your Quickwrite notes about how time and experience affected your response to a familiar place. How are your changed responses similar to the speaker's? How are they different?

Choices: Building Your Portfolio

Writer's Notebook

1. Collecting Ideas for an Informative Report

WORK IN PROGRESS

Many scholars believe that the 1916 Easter Rebellion in Ireland against the British might not have happened without the reawakening of Irish cultural identity that Yeats and his circle spearheaded. Develop a series of questions on the Celtic Revival and on Yeats's impact on Irish nationalism. Save your notes for the Writer's Workshop on page 1053.

Analyzing the Author's Stance

2. Time and Tide

Some critics consider Yeats the first modern poet. Others see him as continuing in the Romantic tradition of Shelley and Keats. On the basis of the poems you have read, including "The Second Coming," on page 923, analyze in a brief essay Yeats's attitude toward the past and toward modern life as he experienced it. Consider also his expectations for the future.

Comparing Poems

3. Birds of a Feather

In a brief essay, compare the **themes, imagery,** and **progression of thought** in "The Wild Swans at Coole" with those of Keats's "Ode to a Nightingale" (page 755).

Creative Writing

4. Your Own "Bee-Loud Glade"

The first line of "The Lake Isle of Innisfree" is often quoted. Write your own poem or paragraph beginning with the words "I will arise and go now." Then, go on to describe your own ideal place of peace. (You may want to refer to the Quickwrite notes you made for page 979.)

Making Meanings

First Thoughts [Respond]

1. Sample responses: "And now my heart is sore"; "All's changed"; " Their hearts have not grown old".

Shaping Interpretations [Interpret]

2. He feels melancholy. Line 18 suggests that nineteen years ago he felt more carefree.
3. Hints include the image of nineteen autumns, which means he is much older. Line 15 suggests that everything in his life is now changed. Lines 22–24 imply his heart has grown old; perhaps he has lost a lover or his ability to love. His "sore" heart indicates he has undergone a sad or sobering experience.
4. Possible response: Where will the swans go, and where will they build nests and delight others' eyes when they leave here?
5. Possible responses: He envies their brilliance, timelessness, passion, mystery, and ability to delight, perhaps because he has lost these qualities or never possessed them. The swans might symbolize beauty, youth, and permanence.
6. The melancholy mood is reinforced by the twilight setting in autumn, both symbols for old age or decline.
7. Possible response: The word might suggest that the speaker's life is as fleeting as a dream; thus, the word *awake,* paradoxically, could imply the speaker's death, and it could point to themes of mortality and lost innocence.
8. Elegies are characterized by imagery drawn from nature, formal language and structure, and a solemn or even melancholy tone, all of which appear in this poem. The poem is similar to "The Wanderer," "The Seafarer," and "In Memoriam."

Connecting with the Text [Apply]

9. Students' changed responses may be similar to the speaker's in that both may regret change, and they may be different in that students may like the changes in their lives or may feel that their lives have not changed that much.

Grading Timesaver

Rubrics for each Choices assignment appear on p. 191 in the *Portfolio Management System.*

OBJECTIVES

1. Read and interpret the story
2. Identify epiphany
3. Analyze irony
4. Use a graphic organizer
5. Create a comparison/contrast chart
6. Express understanding through writing, art, or performance
7. Learn and use new words

SKILLS

Literary

- Identify epiphany
- Analyze irony

Reading

- Create a comparison/contrast chart

Writing

- Freewrite ideas for an informative report
- Write an essay using textual evidence
- Write an essay applying different meanings of *vanity* to the narrator
- Create a story map
- Write a sketch of the story's events from another point of view
- Write a sketch using stream of consciousness

Speaking/Listening

- Prepare and perform an oral reading

Art

- Create original art

Vocabulary

- Learn and use new words

Viewing and Representing

- Relate an artwork to the selection (ATE)

Planning

- **Block Schedule**
  Block Scheduling Lesson Plans with Pacing Guide
- **Traditional Schedule**
  Lesson Plans Including Strategies for English-Language Learners
- **One-Stop Planner**
  CD-ROM Test Generator

James Joyce

(1882–1941)

James Joyce (1934) by Jacques-Émile Blanche.

Courtesy of the National Gallery of Ireland, Dublin.

James Joyce's masterpiece, *Ulysses* (1922), has probably had a greater effect on twentieth-century fiction than any other work of our times. Yet while he lived, Joyce was known largely as the author of what was thought a nearly unintelligible and scandalous book. Based on Homer's *Odyssey,* Joyce's *Ulysses* describes the events of a single day in Dublin, the city where Joyce grew up. And just as Homer's epic interpreted the world of the ancient Greeks, so does Joyce's epic mirror and interpret for us our own lives in the twentieth century.

Joyce was born in Rathgar, Ireland, a Dublin suburb. One of ten children of an improvident tax collector, he was educated at a series of Roman Catholic schools, but by the time he entered University College, Dublin, he had lost his faith. After graduating, he went to Paris and existed frugally by giving English lessons and writing book reviews.

In 1903, Joyce returned home to be at his dying mother's bedside. Afterward he lived briefly in a Martello Tower (a former military fortification) on the coast near Dublin, a site that has now become Ireland's James Joyce Museum. There he began an autobiographical novel, *Stephen Hero,* and also wrote some of the stories later published in *Dubliners* (1914).

In June 1904, Joyce met and fell in love with a Galway girl named Nora Barnacle. The date of their first walk, June 16, 1904, was later immortalized as Bloomsday, the date on which the action of *Ulysses* takes place. When Joyce's debts mounted, he persuaded Nora to leave Ireland with him; Joyce was never to live in Ireland again.

The penniless couple settled first in the Italian city of Trieste, where their two children, George and Lucia, were born. Joyce's book of poems, *Chamber Music,* was published in 1907 but brought him no royalties. His luck began to turn after 1914, when the influential American poet Ezra Pound reviewed *Dubliners* favorably and persuaded a British magazine to serialize *A Portrait of the Artist as a Young Man,* Joyce's rewritten version of *Stephen Hero.*

When Italy entered World War I in 1915, the Joyces left Trieste for Zurich, where Joyce worked on the early chapters of *Ulysses.* Because of sizable gifts from anonymous patrons, Joyce's financial troubles had begun to ease, but his physical problems increased. Between 1917 and 1930, he endured twenty-five operations for glaucoma and cataracts. Sometimes he was totally blind, yet he continued work on *Ulysses,* which appeared in magazine installments from 1918 through 1920, when it was suppressed.

The completed *Ulysses* did not easily find its way into print. Indeed, British printers found it so scandalous that they refused to set it in type. Finally, in 1922, Sylvia Beach, the American owner of a bookstore in Paris called Shakespeare & Co., agreed to put out an edition of one thousand copies. Many of the reviews were favorable, but the book was banned in both Britain and the United States. Not until 1934, after a famous court case, was *Ulysses* published in America. A British edition soon followed, and the book's fame spread rapidly worldwide.

Meanwhile, Joyce had completed a new novel, *Finnegans Wake,* about a Dublin barkeep named Earwicker. This complex experimental work finally was published in 1939 to inconclusive reviews. Some critics took it as a bad joke, others as madness, and Joyce, who considered it his masterpiece, grew morose over the dismal response. The Joyces, who had been living in Paris, returned to Zurich in 1940, when France fell to Nazi Germany. There Joyce became increasingly ill, his eye troubles complicated by a duodenal ulcer. He died on January 13, 1941, one month short of his fifty-ninth birthday.

Resources: Print and Media

Reading

- *Graphic Organizers for Active Reading,* p. 98
- *Words to Own,* p. 27
- *Audio CD Library,* Disc 17, Track 5

Elements of Literature

- *Literary Elements*
  Transparency 24
  Worksheet, p. 73

Writing and Language

- *Daily Oral Grammar*
  Transparency 33
- *Grammar and Language Links*
  Worksheet, p. 57
- *Language and Workshop CD-ROM*

Assessment

- *Formal Assessment,* p. 198
- *Portfolio Management System,* p. 193
- *Preparation for College Admission Exams,* p. 49
- *Test Generator (One-Stop Planner CD-ROM)*

Internet

go.hrw.com (keyword: LE0 12-13)

Before You Read

ARABY

Make the Connection

When Dreams Meet Reality

Have you ever taken on a task that seemed vital to your happiness—or hoped, fervently, that a childhood dream would come true? Perhaps you can remember just wishing to accomplish something grand, to win the admiration and praise of others.

Reading Skills and Strategies

Using a Graphic Organizer

In "Araby," the main character has a vivid imagination that sometimes causes him to misconstrue the realities of his life. As you read the story, look for differences between the way he imagines things to be and the way they really are. List these discrepancies in a two-column comparison-contrast chart like the one below.

Imagination	Reality

Elements of Literature

Epiphany

Joyce called the moments of revelation that occur in his stories "epiphanies." Here is an excerpt from *Stephen Hero,* an early draft of Joyce's semiautobiographical novel *A Portrait of the Artist as a Young Man,* in which his hero explains what he means by *epiphany:*

> A young lady was standing on the steps of one of those brown brick houses which seem the very incarnation of Irish paralysis. A young gentleman was leaning on the rusty railings of the area. Stephen as he passed on his quest heard the following fragment of colloquy out of which he received an impression keen enough to afflict his sensitiveness very severely.
>
> The Young Lady—(drawling discreetly) . . . O, yes . . . I was . . . at the . . . cha . . . pel . . .
>
> The Young Gentleman—(inaudibly) . . . I . . . (again inaudibly) . . . I . . .
>
> The Young Lady—(softly) . . . O . . . but you're . . . ve . . . ry . . . wick . . . ed . . .
>
> This triviality made him think of collecting many such moments together in a book of epiphanies. By an epiphany he meant a sudden spiritual manifestation, whether in the vulgarity of speech or of gesture or in a memorable phase of the mind itself. He believed that it was for the man of letters to record these epiphanies with extreme care, seeing that they themselves are the most delicate and evanescent of moments. —James Joyce

In fiction, an **epiphany** is a moment of sudden insight or revelation experienced by a character.

For more on Epiphany, see the Handbook of Literary Terms.

Background

On May 14, 1894, a five-day charity bazaar came to the city of Dublin. The bazaar was called Araby, a reference to Arabia, where bazaars—markets with long rows of stalls or shops—are common. For the children of Dublin, Arabia seemed a mysterious, exotic place, very different from the dark, all-too-real streets of the dreary city in which they lived.

The house in this story is based on one in which Joyce and his family actually lived. It stood on the same "blind," or dead-end, street as the Christian Brothers' School Joyce attended. When the Joyce children moved to this musky, dark house, they missed the open fields and woods of their former home.

go.hrw.com
LEO 12-13

Summary ■■

The young narrator has a crush on a neighborhood girl. She tells him she longs to go to Araby, a visiting bazaar, but cannot. He then plans to go and bring her something from what he imagines will be a thrillingly romantic place. After a series of frustrations, he arrives late as the bazaar is closing. Instead of fulfilling his dreams of exotic luxury, Araby is dreary. It features cheap trinkets and ordinary workers. The narrator has a desultory conversation with a young vendor. He leaves feeling disillusioned and ashamed of his vanity.

Resources

Listening

A recording of this story is provided in the *Audio CD Library*:

- Disc 17, Track 5

Elements of Literature

For additional instruction on epiphany, and on irony, see *Literary Elements*:

- Transparency 24
- Worksheet, p. 73

BROWSING IN THE FILES

Writers on Writing. Joyce was a proponent of writing about everyday life. He writes ". . . I think out of the dreary sameness of existence, a measure of dramatic life may be drawn. Even the most commonplace, the deadest among the living, may play a part in a great drama. It is a sinful foolishness to sigh back for the good old times, to feed the hunger of us with the cold stones they afford."

Preteaching Vocabulary

Words to Own

Have students read the Words to Own and their definitions listed at the bottom of the selection pages. Then have them choose partners. The first student gives his or her partner a word. The second student has to use the word correctly in a sentence. Have partners alternate roles.

In the following exercise, match each word with its definition.

1. imperturbable [g]
2. somber [c]
3. gauntlet [j]
4. diverged [e]
5. impinge [h]
6. incessant [a]
7. luxuriated [i]
8. garrulous [d]
9. improvised [b]
10. pervades [f]

a. continuous
b. made on the spot
c. dreary
d. talkative
e. separated
f. spreads throughout
g. composed
h. strike
i. took great delight
j. series of challenges

Ⓐ Appreciating Language
Word Choice

? In the first paragraph, Joyce describes the narrator's house with words that might also apply to the narrator himself. What words point out the house's isolation and confinement? [uninhabited, blind, detached]

Ⓑ Reading Skills and Strategies
Using a Graphic Organizer

Ask students to select one detail from this description that appeals to the senses of sight, smell, touch, and hearing. Have them record their responses on a chart, such as the one that follows.

Sensory Images	
Sight	[the ever-changing violet sky]
Smell	[odorous stables]
Touch	[cold air that stung]
Hearing	[shouts echoed in the street]

Ⓒ Reading Skills and Strategies
Comparing/Contrasting

? How does the image used to describe Mangan's sister differ from that used to describe the other characters? [She is in the light, while they are in darkness.] What does this suggest about her? [The halo of light portrays her as angelic; it suggests that she is special and superior.]

Ⓓ Elements of Literature
Irony

? What is ironic about the narrator's love for Mangan's sister? [Possible response: There is a discrepancy between the narrator's romantic view and the way things really are; he has a crush on someone he imagines but does not really know.]

Araby

James Joyce

North Richmond Street, being blind, was a quiet street except at the hour when the Christian Brothers' School set the boys free. An uninhabited house of two stories stood at the blind end, detached from its neighbors in a square ground. The other houses of the street, conscious of decent lives within them, gazed at one another with brown imperturbable faces.

The former tenant of our house, a priest, had died in the back drawing-room. Air, musty from having been long enclosed, hung in all the rooms, and the waste room behind the kitchen was littered with old useless papers. Among these I found a few paper-covered books, the pages of which were curled and damp: *The Abbot,* by Walter Scott, *The Devout Communicant,* and *The Memoirs of Vidocq.*[1] I liked the last best because its leaves were yellow. The wild garden behind the house contained a central apple-tree and a few straggling bushes under one of which I found the late tenant's rusty bicycle-pump. He had been a very charitable priest; in his will he had left all his money to institutions and the furniture of his house to his sister.

When the short days of winter came dusk fell before we had well eaten our dinners. When we met in the street the houses had grown somber. The space of sky above us was the color of ever-changing violet and toward it the lamps of the street lifted their feeble lanterns. The cold air stung us and we played till our bodies glowed. Our shouts echoed in the silent street. The career[2] of our play brought us through the dark muddy lanes behind the houses where we ran the gauntlet of the rough tribes from the cottages, to the back doors of the dark dripping gardens where odors arose from the ashpits, to the dark odorous stables where a coachman smoothed and combed the horse or shook music from the buckled harness. When we returned to the street light from the kitchen windows had filled the areas. If my uncle was seen turning the corner we hid in the shadow until we had seen him safely housed. Or if Mangan's sister came out on the doorstep to call her brother in to his tea we watched her from our shadow peer up and down the street. We waited to see whether she would remain or go in and, if she remained, we left our shadow and walked up to Mangan's steps resignedly. She was waiting for us, her figure defined by the light from the half-opened door. Her brother always teased her before he obeyed and I stood by the railings looking at her. Her dress swung as she moved her body and the soft rope of her hair tossed from side to side.

Every morning I lay on the floor in the front parlor watching her door. The blind was pulled down to within an inch of the sash so that I could not be seen. When she came out on the doorstep my heart leaped. I ran to the hall, seized my books, and followed her. I kept her brown figure always in my eye and, when we came near the point at which our ways diverged, I quickened my pace and passed her. This happened morning after morning. I had never spoken to her, except for a few casual words, and yet her name was like a summons to all my foolish blood.

Her image accompanied me even in places the most hostile to romance. On Saturday evenings when my aunt went marketing I had to go to carry

1. ***The Abbott . . . Vidocq*** (vē·duk′): in order, a historical romance about Mary, Queen of Scots, by Sir Walter Scott; an 1813 religious manual written by a Franciscan friar; and the memoirs (though not actually written by François Vidocq) of a French criminal who later became a detective.
2. **career:** course; path.

Words to Own

imperturbable (im′pər·tur′bə·bəl) *adj.:* calm; impassive.
somber (säm′bər) *adj.:* gloomy.
gauntlet (gônt′lit) *n.:* series of challenges. Derived from *gatlopp,* Swedish for "running down a lane," the term originally referred to a form of military punishment in which a wrongdoer had to run between two rows of soldiers who struck him as he passed.
diverged (dī·vurjd′) *v.:* branched off; separated.

Reaching All Students

Struggling Readers
After you read the first six paragraphs of the story aloud, ask students to summarize the events. Then, have them predict what will happen in the rest of the story. They should write down the answers to the following questions: Will the girl find out how the boy feels? If so, how will she react? What might the boy do to show his love? Will the girl fall in love with the boy? When they finish the story, have students compare their predictions with what actually happens.

English Language Learners
Students may be confused by the word *bazaar,* whose meaning varies from culture to culture. Explain how the word is used in this story to mean "fair," describing the various features of this kind of bazaar. Then, invite students to tell what comparable fairs take place in their own cultures.

© 1997 The Munch Museum/The Munch-Ellingsen Group/ARS, New York.

Summer Night's Dream (The Voice) (1893) by Edvard Munch.

some of the parcels. We walked through the flaring streets, jostled by drunken men and bargaining women, amid the curses of laborers, the shrill litanies[3] of shop-boys who stood on guard by the barrels of pigs' cheeks, the nasal chanting of street-singers, who sang a *come-all-you* about O'Donovan Rossa,[4] or a ballad about the troubles in our native land. These noises converged in a (E) single sensation of life for me: I imagined that I bore my chalice[5] safely through a throng of foes. Her name sprang to my lips at moments in strange prayers and praises which I myself did not understand. My eyes were often full of tears (I could not tell why) and at times a flood from my heart seemed to pour itself out into my bosom. I thought little of the future. I did not know whether I would ever speak to her or not or, if I spoke to her, how I could tell her of my confused adoration. But my body was like a harp and her words and gestures were like fingers running upon the wires. (F)

One evening I went into the back drawing-room in which the priest had died. It was a dark rainy evening and there was no sound in the house. Through one of the broken panes I heard

3. **litanies:** repeated sales cries. Literally, a litany is a prayer composed of a series of specific invocations and responses.

4. ***come-all-you . . .* Rossa:** A come-all-you (kum·al′yə) is a type of Irish ballad that usually begins "Come all you [young lovers, rebels, Irishmen, and so on]." O'Donovan Rossa was Jeremiah O'Donovan (1831–1915) from County Cork. He was active in Ireland's struggle against British rule in the mid-nineteenth century.

5. **chalice** (chal′is): cup; specifically, the cup used for Holy Communion wine. Joyce's use of the term evokes the image of a young man on a sacred mission.

RESPONDING TO THE ART

Edvard Munch (1863–1944), Norwegian painter and printmaker, produced works that convey intense human emotion, particularly states of acute suffering and anxiety. His preference for the reduction of his subject to its psychological content and to its most striking compositional elements set him apart from Naturalist painters, as well as from Impressionists and Neo-Impressionist painters. He was among the vanguard of the Expressionists, artists who reveal their highly personal reactions to the world, rather than strive for realistic representations.
Activity. Ask students if they think the spectral woman in *Summer Night's Dream (The Voice)* is the dreamer or part of the dream. Have them discuss what "the voice" might be saying.

(E) Appreciating Language

Religious Allusions

? What words link the boy's feelings for Mangan's sister with religious devotion? ["chalice," "strange prayers and praises," "confused adoration"] What does this reveal about the boy's feelings? [Possible response: In the boy's mind, his love has become something sacred.]

(F) Critical Thinking

Interpreting

? What does the narrator imply through the harp simile about the girl's effect on him? [Possible responses: He is completely under the girl's control. She is able to bring out the best in him, just as a musician can bring out the best in a musical instrument. The harp simile identifies her with the angelic, as does the halo of light. It enhances the boy's idealization of her.]

Using Students' Strengths

Visual Learners

The Araby bazaar is advertised in such a way that the boy imagines it as a place of Eastern enchantment and mystery. Ask students to design and execute posters advertising Araby. The posters should include images that give the bazaar a romantic aura and text that gives information about the time and place the bazaar will occur. Designate areas where the posters can be displayed.

Kinesthetic Learners

Have pairs of students role-play one or more of the following hypothetical scenes:

- The narrator's uncle and aunt discuss his strange behavior.
- The narrator tells Mangan's sister about his trip to the bazaar.
- Mangan's sister tells Mangan how she feels about the narrator.

After all pairs have performed, encourage the class to discuss the various interpretations.

A Reading Skills and Strategies

Responding to the Text

? What does the description of the lamplight falling on the young woman remind you of? [Possible responses: an angel, an entertainer in a spotlight, a ghostlike figure.] **What effect do you think this has on the boy?** [Possible response: He is in awe of her.]

B Vocabulary Note

Prefix *inter-*

Explain that the prefix *inter-* means "together," "between," or "among." The word *intervene* is a combination of the prefix *inter-*, meaning "between," and the Latin root *venire,* meaning "to come." Intervene means "to come, be, or lie between." Invite students to name other words using this prefix and indicate the meaning of each. [Possible responses: *interpose,* "put between"; *international,* "between or among nations"; *interact,* "act together."]

C Appreciating Language

Connotation

? The word *Araby* is an archaic form of *Arabia.* Why is this word associated with romance and enchantment? [The word suggests lands, places, and people often considered exotic and mysterious by Westerners.]

D Elements of Literature

Irony

? Why does something one would not expect to cheer a person—the cold gloom of the empty rooms—cheer the boy? [Possible responses: The solitude allows him to be alone with his thoughts. He feels liberated—free of obligation and of the commonplace surroundings of his everyday life.]

the rain impinge upon the earth, the fine incessant needles of water playing in the sodden beds. Some distant lamp or lighted window gleamed below me. I was thankful that I could see so little. All my senses seemed to desire to veil themselves and, feeling that I was about to slip from them, I pressed the palms of my hands together until they trembled, murmuring: *O love! O love!* many times.

At last she spoke to me. When she addressed the first words to me I was so confused that I did not know what to answer. She asked me was I going to *Araby.* I forget whether I answered yes or no. It would be a splendid bazaar, she said; she would love to go.

—And why can't you? I asked.

While she spoke she turned a silver bracelet round and round her wrist. She could not go, she said, because there would be a retreat that week in her convent.[6] Her brother and two other boys were fighting for their caps and I was alone at the railings. She held one of the spikes, bowing her head toward me. The light from the lamp opposite our door caught the white curve of her neck, lit up her hair that rested there and, falling, lit up the hand upon the railing. It fell over one side of her dress and caught the white border of a petticoat, just visible as she stood at ease.

—It's well for you,[7] she said.

—If I go, I said, I will bring you something.

What innumerable follies laid waste my waking and sleeping thoughts after that evening! I wished to annihilate the tedious intervening days. I chafed against the work of school. At night in my bedroom and by day in the classroom her image came between me and the page I strove to read. The syllables of the word *Araby* were called to me through the silence in which my soul luxuriated and cast an Eastern enchantment over me. I asked for leave to go to the bazaar on Saturday night. My aunt was surprised and hoped it was not some Freemason[8] affair. I answered few questions in class. I watched my master's face pass from amiability to sternness; he hoped I was not beginning to idle. I could not call my wandering thoughts together. I had hardly any patience with the serious work of life which, now that it stood between me and my desire, seemed to me child's play, ugly monotonous child's play.

On Saturday morning I reminded my uncle that I wished to go to the bazaar in the evening. He was fussing at the hallstand, looking for the hat-brush, and answered me curtly:

—Yes, boy, I know.

As he was in the hall I could not go into the front parlor and lie at the window. I left the house in bad humor and walked slowly toward the school. The air was pitilessly raw and already my heart misgave me.

When I came home to dinner my uncle had not yet been home. Still it was early. I sat staring at the clock for some time and, when its ticking began to irritate me, I left the room. I mounted the staircase and gained the upper part of the house. The high cold empty gloomy rooms liberated me and I went from room to room singing. From the front window I saw my companions playing below in the street. Their cries reached me weakened and indistinct and, leaning my forehead against the cool glass, I looked over at the dark house where she lived. I may have stood there for an hour, seeing nothing but the brown-clad figure cast by my imagination, touched discreetly by the lamplight at the curved neck, at the hand upon the railings and at the border below the dress.

When I came downstairs again I found Mrs. Mercer sitting at the fire. She was an old garrulous woman, a pawnbroker's widow, who collected used stamps for some pious purpose. I had to endure the gossip of the tea-table. The meal was prolonged beyond an hour and still my uncle did not

6. **retreat . . . convent:** temporary withdrawal from worldly life by the students and teachers at the convent school, to devote time to prayer, meditation, and studies.
7. **It's well for you:** "You're lucky" (usually said enviously).
8. **Freemason:** The Freemasons are a secret society whose practices were originally drawn from those of British medieval stonemasons' guilds; its members, almost exclusively Protestant, were often hostile to Catholics. The aunt apparently associates the exotic bazaar with the mysterious practices of Freemasonry.

WORDS TO OWN

impinge (im·pinj′) *v.:* strike; touch.
incessant (in·ses′ənt) *adj.:* never ceasing; constant.
luxuriated (lug·zhoor′ē·āt′id) *v.:* took enormous pleasure.
garrulous (gar′ə·ləs) *adj.:* talkative.

Skill Link

Discriminating Between Denotative and Connotative Meanings

Remind students that **denotation** is the literal, dictionary definition of the word, while **connotation** indicates the figurative meaning, association, or emotion that a word suggests. Joyce makes extensive use of the connotations of words in this story.

Ask students to work in pairs, and assign one paragraph (or part of a long paragraph) to each pair of students. Students should list the words from their paragraphs that seem to have been chosen as much for their connotations as for their denotations. The lists should include the literal definition of each word, as well as the associations each word suggests. Work with the pairs to create a master list of words on the chalkboard, and discuss their connotations with the whole class.

Fairground, Tottenham (1925) by Allan Gwynne-Jones. Watercolor.
Waterman Fine Art Ltd., London, UK.

come. Mrs. Mercer stood up to go: She was sorry she couldn't wait any longer, but it was after eight o'clock and she did not like to be out late, as the night air was bad for her. When she had gone I began to walk up and down the room, clenching my fists. My aunt said:

—I'm afraid you may put off your bazaar for this night of Our Lord.

At nine o'clock I heard my uncle's latchkey in the halldoor. I heard him talking to himself and heard the hallstand rocking when it had received the weight of his overcoat. I could interpret these signs. When he was midway through his dinner I asked him to give me the money to go to the bazaar. He had forgotten.

—The people are in bed and after their first sleep now, he said.

I did not smile. My aunt said to him energetically:

—Can't you give him the money and let him go? You've kept him late enough as it is.

My uncle said he was very sorry he had forgotten. He said he believed in the old saying: *All work and no play makes Jack a dull boy.* He asked me where I was going and, when I had told him a second time he asked me did I know *The Arab's Farewell to his Steed.*[9] When I left the kitchen he was about to recite the opening lines of the piece to my aunt.

I held a florin[10] tightly in my hand as I strode down Buckingham Street toward the station. The sight of the streets thronged with buyers and glaring with gas recalled to me the purpose of my journey. I took my seat in a third-class carriage of a deserted train. After an intolerable delay the train moved out of the station slowly. It crept onward among ruinous houses and over the twinkling river. At Westland Row Station a crowd of people pressed to the carriage doors; but the porters moved them back, saying that it was a special train for the bazaar. I remained alone in the bare carriage. In a few minutes the train drew up beside an improvised wooden platform. I passed out on to the road and saw by the lighted dial of a clock that it was ten minutes to ten. In front of me was a large building which displayed the magical name.

I could not find any sixpenny entrance and, fearing that the bazaar would be closed, I passed in quickly through a turnstile, handing a shilling to a weary-looking man. I found myself in a big hall girdled at half its height by a gallery. Nearly all the stalls were closed and the greater part of the hall was in darkness. I recognized a silence like that which pervades a church after a service. I walked into the center of the bazaar timidly. A

9. ***The Arab's . . . Steed:*** popular sentimental poem by the English writer Caroline Norton (1808–1877).
10. **florin:** British coin worth, at the time, the equivalent of about fifty cents.

Words to Own

improvised (im′prə·vīzd′) *v.* used as *adj.:* made for the occasion from whatever is handy.
pervades (pər·vādz′) *v.:* spreads throughout.

Responding to the Art

Dame Laura Knight (1877–1970) was best known as a painter of ballet and circus scenes in a bright, realistic style. During the London visits of Sergei Diaghilev's famed Ballet Russe, she painted backstage in order to be as close as possible to the authentic atmosphere of the dance. For the same reason, she also traveled with a circus. *Penzance Fair* reflects her love of the circus ambiance, with its blend of people of all classes and ages.
Activity. Ask students to describe the atmosphere of the painting. [Possible responses: merry, fantastic, exotic.] Then ask how they think the fair in the painting relates to the narrator's experience of Araby in fantasy and in reality. [Possible response: The tents, carousel, and merry crowds probably come close to what the boy imagines Araby to be like before he actually sees it.]

E Critical Thinking

Analyzing Character

? How would you characterize the aunt and uncle's relationship with the boy? [Possible responses: They seem to care for the boy but are somewhat distant from him. Their understanding of him is superficial.]

F Elements of Literature

Irony

? In what way is Araby very different from what the boy imagined? [Possible response: Araby is dark, silent, and ominous. The boy probably expected to encounter an exotic bazaar full of bright lights and people.]

Assessing Learning

Check Test: Sentence Completion

1. The former tenant of the narrator's house was a ________. [priest]
2. The narrator went to the bazaar to buy a gift for ___________. [Mangan's sister]
3. The word *Araby* suggests ______ to the narrator. [romance/enchantment]
4. At the end of the story, the boy's eyes burn with ___________. [anguish/anger]

Self-Assessment

Informal Assessment. Answer the following questions about how you read the story.

1. Did you attempt to predict what would happen next as you read?
2. Did you look up words or try to figure out unfamiliar words from context clues?
3. Did you jot down questions as they occurred to you while reading?
4. While you were reading, did you ask why the boy acts or speaks as he does?

Standardized Test Preparation

For practice with ACT and SAT formats, see
- *Preparation for College Admission Exams,* p. 49

For practice in proofreading and editing, see
- *Daily Oral Grammar,* Transparency 33

A Reading Skills and Strategies

Comparing/Contrasting

? What emotions overwhelm the boy at the end? [humiliation, futility, disillusionment] **How do they differ from what he expected, creating a central irony?** [He expected to buy a gift that would make the girl favor him, an act which would make him feel triumphant, valued, and even loved.]

B Elements of Literature

Epiphany

? What does the boy realize about himself? [Possible responses: He realizes that his hopes were unrealistic; he sees himself as vain for having had such hopes.]

MAKING MEANINGS

First Thoughts [Respond]

1. Some students may feel let down because they think the ending is anticlimactic. Others may feel deep sympathy for the boy.

Shaping Interpretations [Interpret]

2. The narrator has spoken only a few words to Mangan's sister. Their relationship is very casual in reality, but in his imagination the boy has given her great importance.
3. Possible responses: Their lives are restricted by limited routines. The boy goes only to school or to the market with his aunt on Saturdays. The young people are physically restricted by their elders. Both young and old are restricted by the elders' insensitivity and lack of imagination.
4. At the market, the boy imagines that he bears his chalice safely through a throng of foes, uniting reality with his fantasy. At school, he ignores reality, letting his thoughts wander; he considers the classwork "child's play."
5. At the end of the story, the boy realizes his romantic fantasies are illusions. His tears at the very end indicate his frustration and disappointment at this realization.
6. Possible responses: The death of the priest may represent the passing of religion as the source of mystery and passion in the boy's life. In the boy's quest, love replaces religion; hence, the religious references in the description of Mangan's sister.

(Answers continue on p. T991.)

few people were gathered about the stalls which were still open. Before a curtain, over which the words *Café Chantant*[11] were written in colored lamps, two men were counting money on a salver.[12] I listened to the fall of the coins.

Remembering with difficulty why I had come I went over to one of the stalls and examined porcelain vases and flowered tea-sets. At the door of the stall a young lady was talking and laughing with two young gentlemen. I remarked their English accents and listened vaguely to their conversation.

—O, I never said such a thing!

—O, but you did!

—O, but I didn't!

—Didn't she say that?

—Yes. I heard her.

—O, there's a . . . fib!

Observing me the young lady came over and asked me did I wish to buy anything. The tone of her voice was not encouraging; she seemed to have spoken to me out of a sense of duty. I looked humbly at the great jars that stood like eastern guards at either side of the dark entrance to the stall and murmured:

—No, thank you.

The young lady changed the position of one of the vases and went back to the two young men. They began to talk of the same subject. Once or twice the young lady glanced at me over her shoulder.

I lingered before her stall, though I knew my stay was useless, to make my interest in her wares seem the more real. Then I turned away slowly and walked down the middle of the bazaar. I allowed the two pennies to fall against the sixpence in my pocket. I heard a voice call from one end of the gallery that the light was out. The upper part of the hall was now completely dark.

A B Gazing up into the darkness I saw myself as a creature driven and derided by vanity; and my eyes burned with anguish and anger.

11. ***Café Chantant*** (kȧ·fā′ shän′tän′): The name refers to a coffeehouse with musical entertainment.

12. **salver** (sal′vər): serving tray.

MAKING MEANINGS

First Thoughts

1. Briefly describe how the ending of this story made you feel.

Reading Check

a. Who is the narrator of the story? Though the story uses **first-person point of view,** is the narrator the same age as the hero? Cite evidence to support your answer.

b. What is the **setting** at the opening of the story? Which adjectives paint a gloomy scene?

c. What is the purpose of the narrator's quest, or journey to the bazaar? What obstacles prevent him from achieving his goal?

d. What **connotations** does the word *Araby* have for the narrator? What is Araby really like?

Shaping Interpretations

2. How often have the narrator and Mangan's sister spoken to each other? How would you describe his relationship with her?
3. In what ways are the lives of these characters narrow or restricted?
4. How does the narrator deal with intrusions of reality into his fantasy—at the market, for example?
5. What **epiphany** has the boy experienced by the end of the story? What details support your answer?
6. Why do you think the dead priest appears in the story? In your opinion, what do the story's religious references contribute to the significance of the boy's quest?
7. Look back at the chart you made while reading, in which you compared what the narrator imagined with what was real. How could the story be seen as presenting a conflict between romance, or imagination, and reality?
8. How would you describe the writer's **tone**—his attitude toward the characters and what happens to them?
9. In medieval legends, a knight often rode off on

Reading Check

a. The narrator is an adult who remembers an episode from his childhood. The narrator is older than the boy of the story. This is indicated by use of the past tense.

b. The setting is the narrator's house on North Richmond Street. Among the adjectives that paint a gloomy scene are *blind, brown, somber, rusty, musty, old, damp, wild, rough, muddy, silent, dark,* and *feeble.*

c. The purpose of the quest is to buy a gift at the bazaar for Mangan's sister. Obstacles include his uncle's lateness, Mrs. Mercer's visit, the train's delay, and the narrator's failure to find a sixpenny entrance to the bazaar.

d. Araby connotes "Eastern enchantment" to the narrator, but he discovers that the bazaar is in reality only a dark, tacky, commercial enterprise run by ordinary English people.

a quest to prove himself worthy to his beloved, whom he worshiped from afar. How is the narrator of "Araby" like a questing knight? How is the story really a distortion of a quest tale?

Elements of Literature

Irony: Things Are Not As They Seem

Here is the plot of a story: A boy has a crush on a girl. He promises to get her something from a bazaar, but he gets there late and is unable to buy anything. The story ends with him standing in the darkened hall of the bazaar.

When you consider this bare-bones plot, "Araby" doesn't seem to be much of a story. A traditional story deals with some significant action, but "Araby" deals with a thwarted action. The protagonist fails to reach the goal he has been struggling to achieve, and in the end he is revealed to himself as the very opposite of the person he dreamed he was. "Araby" is ironic—both in its form and in many of its details.

In Greek comedy, an *eiron* was a character who was not what he appeared to be. From that Greek term comes **irony,** which in all its varieties also refers to things that are not what they appear to be.

Verbal irony. The most common form of irony is **verbal irony,** in which you say the opposite of what you really mean. We often use verbal irony in conversation. When asked how you feel after a really terrible day, you might say, for example, "I feel just great." We would know by the tone of your voice that you are being *ironic*—in reality, you feel anything but great. **Sarcasm** is a very broad and cutting form of verbal irony.

Situational irony. Another form of irony is **situational irony,** in which things turn out differently from what is expected. In its simplest form, this can involve a cartoon character laughing so hard at someone who has slipped on a banana peel that she herself walks right into an open manhole. In its most sophisticated form, as in Sophocles' *Oedipus Rex,* the hero Oedipus, in trying to escape a curse, brings it down upon himself. Surprise endings invariably feature situational irony.

Dramatic irony. A third form of irony, **dramatic irony,** occurs when readers or an audience knows something that a character does not know. In "Little Red Riding Hood," we know the wolf has dressed in the grandmother's clothes, but Red Riding Hood does not. This discrepancy between what we know and what the characters know creates a sense of irony and a degree of dramatic tension.

Romance versus reality. In "Araby," almost all of the irony stems from the discrepancy between the narrator's romantic view of things and the way things really are. His love for Mangan's sister is obviously overblown, an adolescent crush on someone he does not actually know. In pursuit of his love, he seeks some exotic gift from Araby, but this, too, becomes an ironic quest: In reality, he has simply taken a suburban train to a charity bazaar and returned empty-handed. In addition, through the aunt and uncle, the story shows that love in the real world—at least married love in Dublin—is not the ideal the boy imagines. It is, rather, marriage between an ineffectual woman and a man who comes home late and drunk.

But the ironies in "Araby" go still further. The hero's love and the quest he undertakes are directly associated with religion: "I imagined that I bore my chalice safely through a throng of foes. Her name sprang to my lips at moments in strange prayers and praises which I myself did not understand." Worshiping Mangan's sister is as much a religious act as an emotional one, and when his romantic dreams are shattered, his disillusion is not just with love, but with all of his spiritual values. Just as the aunt and uncle represent the reality of love, the reality of the religious part of the narrator's quest is represented by the dead priest and his rusty bicycle pump.

For Joyce, modern Ireland—its society, religion, and culture—was in a state of decay. The discrepancy between the ideals of Ireland's past and the reality of its present was the chief source of his irony.

Finding examples of irony. Illustrate the three types of irony with examples of your own. Your examples might be drawn from actual life, books, plays, films, personal experience, or your imagination. Do you think there is still today a discrepancy between social ideals and reality?

(Continued from p. T990)

7. Possible response: The conflict lies in the fact that the boy's ideas about Mangan's sister and Araby are sheer illusion. Neither the relationship as the boy imagines it nor Araby as a place of mystical enchantment exist in reality.

8. Sample responses: The tone is sympathetic and melancholy. The tone is amused and slightly embarrassed, revealing the amazement of a man looking back on his foolishness as a boy.

9. The boy is like a questing knight in that he idealizes his beloved and seeks to please her with a gift from an exotic place. The story is a distortion of the quest tale in that the boy's disillusionment gives an ironic turn to the traditional form.

Resources

Elements of Literature

For additional instruction on irony, see *Literary Elements*:

- Transparency 24
- Worksheet, p. 73

Elements of Literature

Mini-Lesson: Irony

After the students have read the various definitions of irony, explain that they are surrounded by irony every day—verbal irony in conversations, situational irony in many aspects of their own lives, and dramatic irony in countless movies and TV shows. Help students become more aware of irony by asking them to collect examples of all three types during the course of a single day.

Possible Responses

Verbal irony: Your friend is wearing ugly clothes, and you say "Nice outfit."

Situational irony: You wake up late for school, madly get your clothes on, tear out of the house, and arrive at school only to realize it is a holiday.

Dramatic irony: In *Oedipus Rex,* the audience knows that Oedipus has killed his father and married his mother, but he does not. This makes his promise to punish the murderer highly ironic. As a social ideal, criminals are jailed and innocent people are exonerated; in reality guilty people may go free while innocent people are convicted.

Using Students' Strengths

Visual Learners

Students might find it easier to handle the material presented in the feature if they take notes as they read, organizing them into a chart like the one that follows.

Type of Irony	Definition	Example
Verbal		
Situational		
Dramatic		

Auditory/Musical Learners

Some students may have difficulty recognizing verbal irony when they encounter it in print, because they do not have the tone of voice of the speaker to cue them that irony is intended. Have students take turns reading aloud the examples of verbal irony they listed on their index cards. Have them read the statements in two ways—first in a neutral and then in a sarcastic tone. The listeners should note how tone of voice can convey ironic intent.

Grading Timesaver

Rubrics for each Choices assignment appear on p. 193 in the *Portfolio Management System.*

CHOICES: Building Your Portfolio

WORK IN PROGRESS

1. **Writer's Notebook** Brainstorm with the class to come up with a list of possible topics.
2. **Using Textual Evidence** Students may find it helpful in the prewriting phase of this assignment to construct a pyramid. On the left side, students may list the events leading up to the boy's trip to Araby, moving upward in the order of events. At the zenith, students may write "arrival at Araby." On the right side of the pyramid, moving downward, students may list the events at the bazaar that lead directly to the epiphany.
3. **Expository Writing** Students will have to collect details from the story that support each of the three definitions of vanity.
4. **Creative Writing** For their story maps, students may use the following elements: setting, basic situation, conflict, characters, events, climax, resolution.
5. **Creative Writing** Encourage students to think about what they know of the girl by carefully reviewing what she says in her brief conversation with the narrator.
6. **Creative Writing** Encourage students to write some of their own thoughts in a stream-of-consciousness style before they write those of a character.
7. **Art** If students wish, they may do research to find out what art, if any, already exists in connection with "Araby."
8. **Performance** You may wish to have students evaluate each other's performances based on how well they convert the story into a script and set the scene and mood.

CHOICES: Building Your Portfolio

Writer's Notebook

1. Collecting Ideas for an Informative Report

WORK IN PROGRESS

Ideas for an informative report can come from what you read. Think back to your reading of "Araby." Review also what you read about Joyce's life. Is there any topic suggested by your reading that you might want to learn more about? "Araby," for example, might make you curious about Dublin life in the early 1900s—especially the general political situation in Ireland at that time. Freewrite for a few minutes, focusing on topics suggested by the story and by Joyce's life. Keep your notes for use in the Writer's Workshop on page 1053.

Using Textual Evidence

2. Significant Moments

Joyce used the term **epiphany** to describe a moment of sudden insight or revelation. The word *epiphany* comes from a Greek word meaning "a showing forth or revelation." In an essay, explain the epiphany that the narrator experiences at the end of the story. Show how the narrator's experiences have led to this revelation, and cite the passage of the story in which the epiphany is described.

Expository Writing

3. Vanity's Many Sides

At the end of the story, the narrator sees himself "driven and derided by vanity." One meaning of *vanity* is "the state of being empty, idle, valueless." Another meaning is "exaggerated self-love." Still another is "hunger for praise or admiration." In an essay, explain how all these definitions could apply to the narrator.

Creative Writing

4. The Universal Joyce

In a review of *Dubliners* in *The Egoist* (July 15, 1914), the poet Ezra Pound wrote that you could erase the local names, a few specifically local allusions, and a few historic events of the past, and substitute other names, allusions, and events, and these stories could be retold of any town. Is Pound right? Create a story map for "Araby," changing the setting to an American town in the early 2000s. Which details of plot and character will you have to change? Share your story map with classmates.

Creative Writing

5. Through Another's Eyes

Based on what you know of the young girl in the story, write a brief sketch of the story's events as seen through her eyes. What does she think of her neighborhood? of the bazaar? of the boy?

Creative Writing

6. The Thinking Mind

Read the material on pages 993–994 about stream of consciousness. Then try your hand at writing a sketch that reflects the associations and sensory impressions that occur in a character's mind. Start by placing your character in a specific setting. Then let his or her mind start to work.

Art

7. The Artist in You

Respond to the story by creating original art. You may want to contrast how Araby looked in the narrator's vivid imagination and in drab reality by painting two conceptions of the bazaar, by creating a collage, or by designing stage sets for a dramatization.

Performance

8. Araby Alive

With several classmates, prepare an oral reading of Joyce's story. You will have to make these decisions: (a) How many readers will you need? (b) Will you use any props? (c) Will you use lighting or music? (d) Will your readers be costumed in some way? You'll also have to appoint a director and create a script for your readers.

Making the Connections

Connecting to the Theme: "The Transforming Imagination"

Ask students to consider in what way the boy's reality is transformed by his fantasies. [Possible response: He makes the dreary reality of his life fade, at least temporarily, with his fantasies of love and enchantment.] **How does this transformation prove harmful?** [Possible response: By clinging to his fantasies, he totally deludes himself. Thus, he is hit hard when he actually experiences Araby.]

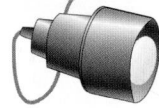

SPOTLIGHT ON

The Influence of James Joyce

Joyce's influence on twentieth-century writing is hard to overstate. His impact on world literature derives from his innovations in narrative techniques.

Portraying the flow of thought. Language for Joyce had an important psychological and social element. For Joyce (following St. Thomas Aquinas, who was following Aristotle), there is nothing in the mind which does not enter through the senses. We come to know the world through our senses, and our thought processes follow a pattern of association based on what we experience through our senses. Joyce's use of point of view in his writing and his presentation of thoughts directed by association led to the best-known characteristic of his mature style, called **stream of consciousness.** This is an attempt to portray the thinking mind directly, without "organizing" the thoughts and without the intervention of the author. **A**

Joyce's early novel *A Portrait of the Artist as a Young Man* (1916) contains the germ of his experiments with this technique. The method is most apparent, though, in his second novel, *Ulysses* (1922). Much of the action in this novel is presented through the thoughts of its protagonists. Here, for example, is one of the main characters, Leopold Bloom, standing in front of a Dublin tea shop, reading the labels on the cans of tea and thinking:

> His right hand once more more slowly went over his brow and hair. Then he put on his hat again, relieved: and read again: choice blend, made of the finest Ceylon brands. The far east. Lovely spot it must be: the garden of the world, big lazy leaves to float about on, cactuses, flowery meads, snaky lianas they call them. . . . Where was the chap I saw in that picture somewhere? Ah yes, in the dead sea floating on his back, reading a book with a parasol open. Couldn't sink if you tried: so thick with salt. Because of the weight of the water, no, the weight of the body in the water is equal to the weight of the what? Or is it the volume is equal to the weight? It's a law something like that. Vance in High School cracking his finger joints, teaching. The college curriculum. Cracking curriculum. What is weight really when you say the weight? Thirty-two feet per second per second. Law of falling bodies: per second per second. **B**
>
> —James Joyce, *from Ulysses*

James Joyce with Sylvia Beach, his publisher, in Paris during the Roaring Twenties. **C**

Spotlight On

This feature gives students a brief look at an individual writer or a literary genre that cannot be covered in full.

After discussing this feature, urge interested students to do research on any author mentioned in the last paragraph or on films using the montage technique.

A Background

Joyce's Technique

One technique that Joyce uses to approximate on the page the stream of a character's thought is the elimination of most punctuation. This practice has the effect of making his prose seem less like writing and more like speech.

B Critical Thinking

Analyzing

? Follow the train of thought in this passage. How does Joyce go from tea to tropical vines? [Bloom reads the label on a packet of tea and thinks about blends of tea made of the best brands from Ceylon, the country now known as Sri Lanka. The thoughts about a tropical land in turn make him think of flowery meadows *(meads)* and of tropical vines *(lianas)* that resemble snakes.]

C Background

Sylvia Beach

After meeting Sylvia Beach in 1920, Joyce became a frequent visitor to her bookshop-library, *Shakespeare & Co.*, and often sought her aid in literary matters. After Joyce was unable to find a publisher for the controversial *Ulysses*, Beach offered to publish the work. However, she did not find it easy to deal with the inconsiderate and demanding Joyce. Fed up with Joyce's demands, Beach wrote to him: "The truth is that as my affection and admiration for you are unlimited, so is the work you pile on my shoulders. When you are absent, every word I receive from you is an order. The reward for my unceasing labour on your behalf is to see you tie yourself into a bowknot and hear you complain."

Using Students' Strengths

Intrapersonal Learners

To illustrate how the stream-of-consciousness technique works, ask students to close their eyes, let their minds wander, and record the shifts in their thoughts. Students can do this by placing a sheet of notebook paper horizontally on their desks and drawing a straight line, from the far left of the sheet to the right, to represent their first thought; then, after that, they can indicate changes in thoughts by drawing lines in alternate directions. After three minutes, ask students to count the number of shifts in their thoughts and share this information with the class.

Visual Learners

Have students create a collage to illustrate the stream of consciousness in the *Ulysses* passage. They may draw their own illustrations or cut out images from newspapers and magazines.

Ⓐ Background

Finnegans Wake

This novel deals with the nightly dreams of a family of five, which, in addition to the events of the preceding day, recount the fears, hopes, desires, anxieties, and secret thoughts of the dreamers. The language of the novel is original and extremely demanding, consisting of foreign words, elaborate puns, and made-up vocabulary. In addition, the novel is completely circular in structure: It begins with the second half of a sentence and ends with the first half of the same sentence.

Ⓑ Literary Connections

Stream of Consciousness

The earliest attempt at stream of consciousness in English was made by Laurence Sterne in *Tristram Shandy* (1759–1767). In this novel, one of the first in English, Sterne allows the stream of thought to occur independently of logical progression, but he portrays this stream through the speech of his characters rather than through a direct presentation of their thoughts. The interior monologue (one person's train of thought) was used for the first time in 1888 by the French writer Edouard Dujardin.

Ⓒ Background

Joyce's Style

An even more hostile view of Joyce's work than Virginia Woolf's was voiced by critic Edmund Gosse in a letter to French academician Louis Gillet: "He [Joyce] is of course not entirely without talent, but he is a literary charlatan of the extremist order. His principal book, *Ulysses,* has no parallel that I know of in French. It is an anarchical production, infamous in taste, in style, in everything."

Bloom's mind moves by association from the tea label to the Far East to the picture he saw of a man who, he realizes, wasn't in the Far East but in the Near East, on the Dead Sea. This makes him think of the principles behind floating and falling, which reminds him of his school days and of a teacher who cracked his knuckles. Bloom's mind, as this passage demonstrates, contains a mix of personal memories, sensations, and half-remembered bits of information.

Ⓐ Joyce worked on his last novel, *Finnegans Wake,* for seventeen years, from 1922 to 1939. When it appeared, some critics claimed that it announced the death of the novel as a literary form. In the book, the author has completely disappeared, and the consciousness is that of a dreamer. Finnegan is a bricklayer's helper who falls from a ladder and dies on the first page of the novel.

Ⓑ Ⓒ **The experiments of others.** Joyce's experiments with stream of consciousness were soon adopted by Virginia Woolf (see page 1122). (Woolf detested *Ulysses,* however, which she called illiterate and underbred.) Woolf's novel *Mrs. Dalloway,* published three years after *Ulysses* in 1925, focuses on the memories, dreams, and feelings of a central character in the course of just one day in London. Like Joyce, Woolf aimed at compressing time so that she could present an entire way of life through the detailed examination of a tiny part of it.

As the book opens, Mrs. Dalloway is on her way to buy flowers for a party she will give that evening:

> Mrs. Dalloway said she would buy the flowers herself. For Lucy had her work cut out for her. The doors would be taken off their hinges; Rumpelmayer's men were coming. And then, thought Clarissa Dalloway, what a morning—fresh as if issued to children on a beach.
>
> —Virginia Woolf, *from Mrs. Dalloway*

Stream of consciousness, as this passage shows, can place unusual demands on the reader. For example, we have to infer from the context that Lucy is one of the household servants, that the doors will be removed for the party, and that Mrs. Dalloway is leaving her house to go shopping on a glorious summer's morning in London.

James Joyce (1902) in Paris, age 20.

The narrative method that Joyce and Woolf pioneered has grown so popular that we no longer regard it as unusual. Among its practitioners have been some of the greatest twentieth-century novelists in world literature, including William Faulkner (United States) and Samuel Beckett (Ireland). Its influence has extended even into film, into the technique of *montage,* in which images shown in rapid succession suggest a train of thought.

Assessing Learning

Check Test: True-False

1. Joyce's greatest contribution to world literature is the narrative techniques he pioneered. [True]
2. Joyce thought that the senses have little or nothing to do with how we come to know the world. [False]
3. Stream of consciousness is an attempt to portray the thinking mind directly. [True]
4. Stream of consciousness places little demand on the reader because everything is directly stated. [False]
5. No other writers experimented with stream of consciousness. [False]

D. H. Lawrence

(1885–1930)

David Herbert Lawrence was born in the English Midlands, the frailest child of a coal miner and a former schoolteacher. An able scholar, he too chose to become a teacher, for he resented the physical and spiritual ugliness that the mines had engendered in the Midlands.

While he was teaching, Lawrence began publishing poems and stories in magazines. In 1912, a year after publishing his first novel, Lawrence called on his former professor, Ernest Weekley, and became enchanted with Weekley's German-born wife, Frieda. Within weeks, Frieda Weekley had left her husband and three children and fled with Lawrence to Germany. For the next two years, the couple traveled through Austria and Italy. During this short time, Lawrence finished his novel *Sons and Lovers* (1913) and began work on two others, *The Rainbow* (1915) and *Women in Love* (1920).

Reviews of *Sons and Lovers* were cautiously favorable, but the moral controversy over Lawrence's work (a debate that continued for decades) was already heating up. While in Italy, Lawrence began to see industrialized England as corrosive and oppressive and the Victorian world he had known as overcivilized and prudish. He embraced a belief in "blood knowledge," in putting one's animal self in balance with one's intellect. Returning to England in 1914, he announced that "the source of all life and knowledge is in man and woman, and the source of all living is in the interchange and the meeting and mingling of these two." When a privately printed edition of Lawrence's novel *Women in Love* was published in 1920, one London critic judged it "a loathsome study of sex depravity leading youth to unspeakable disaster."

Around this time, a wealthy American writer, Mabel Dodge Luhan, who deeply admired Lawrence's work, invited him to come to Taos, New Mexico. Lawrence found New Mexico gorgeous, but he had his doubts about Americans, calling them "a host of people who must all have a sense of inferiority complex somewhere, striving to make good over everybody else." Meanwhile, in New York, those Lawrence called "the vice people" had been trying to suppress publication of *Women in Love*. Lawrence rejoiced to learn that a magistrate had declared that his novels were not obscene. On the contrary, he found they made a "distinct contribution to the literature of the present day."

By now, however, Lawrence was growing inured to the invective his work provoked on each publication day. But then he learned that he had incurable tuberculosis. Knowing he had only a few years remaining, Lawrence left the United States and returned to Italy. He now wrote continually, producing *Lady Chatterley's Lover* (1928), the work for which he is best remembered. The novel draws on his favorite theme—that of the sleeping beauty, the sexual awakening of a woman. The book drew new waves of anger from the censors. U.S. customs officers seized copies as they arrived on the docks, and the novel was banned in Britain. Ironically, as a result of this tremendous publicity, all of Lawrence's work, including his poetry, was in demand.

Giving in at last to doctors' advice, Lawrence retreated in early 1930 to a sanitarium in southern France, where he wrote every day until the end of his life. On March 2, 1930, with Frieda at his bedside, Lawrence died. He is buried at Taos.

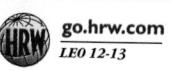

D. H. Lawrence.

go.hrw.com
LEO 12-13

OBJECTIVES

The Rocking-Horse Winner / Snake

1. Read and interpret the short story and poem
2. Interpret the story's symbolism
3. Use techniques for the formation of new words
4. Express understanding through critical and creative writing and performance
5. Learn and use new words

SKILLS

Literary
- Identify and interpret symbolism

Writing
- Collect ideas for an informative report
- Write an essay supporting a thesis statement
- Explore a theme
- Write a sketch using stream of consciousness
- Write a free-verse poem

Speaking/Listening
- Stage a theatrical performance

Vocabulary
- Use techniques for the formation of new words
- Learn and use new words

Viewing and Representing
- Relate fine art to the story (ATE)

Planning

- **Block Schedule**
  Block Scheduling Lesson Plans with Pacing Guide
- **Traditional Schedule**
  Lesson Plans Including Strategies for English-Language Learners
- **One-Stop Planner**
  CD-ROM with Test Generator

Resources: Print and Media

Reading
- *Reading Skills and Strategies*
  MiniRead Skill Lesson, p. 76
  Selection Skill Lesson, p. 83
- *Graphic Organizers for Active Reading*, p. 99
- *Words to Own*, p. 28
- *Audio CD Library*
  Disc 17, Tracks 6, 7

Elements of Literature
- *Literary Elements*
  Transparency 25
  Worksheet, p. 76

Writing and Language
- *Daily Oral Grammar*
  Transparency 34
- *Grammar and Language Links*
  Worksheet, p. 59
- *Language Workshop CD-ROM*

Assessment
- *Formal Assessment*, pp. 200, 202
- *Portfolio Management System*, p. 195
- *Preparation for College Admission Exams*, p. 51
- *Test Generator (One-Stop Planner CD-ROM)*

Internet
go.hrw.com (keyword: LEO 12-13)

Summary ■ ■

Paul, a young boy, desperately wants to gain the love of his mother, who is distant and depressed. When he asks her why their family always seems short of money, she tells him about the family's need for "luck." The confused but determined boy discovers that when he rides his rocking horse in a mad frenzy, he can foresee the winners of actual horse races. Paul uses these uncanny revelations to change the family's fortunes. Working with the gardener and Uncle Oscar, the boy makes a great deal of money and has it turned over to his mother through the family lawyer. He hopes the money will finally stop mysterious voices in the house from "whispering" for more money; however, the voices only "whisper" more madly. Finally, in order to predict the winner of the Derby, Paul makes a last, frenzied rocking-horse ride. He successfully predicts the winner, after which he collapses. Critically ill, Paul is informed by the gardener that he has won over seventy thousand pounds. After asserting to his mother that he is lucky, the boy dies in the night, leaving her to contemplate what she has gained and what she has lost.

Resources

A recording of this story is provided in the *Audio CD Library:*

- Disc 17, Track 6

Elements of Literature

For additional instruction on symbol, see *Literary Elements:*

- Transparency 25
- Worksheet, p. 76

Before You Read

THE ROCKING-HORSE WINNER

Make the Connection

The Root of All Evil

The old saying that "the love of money is the root of all evil" dates back to the Bible. Over the centuries, immeasurable evil—hatred, war, murder—has sprung from the lust for riches. Even on the most personal level—wife to husband, parent to child, friend to friend—the craving for wealth can have devastating effects.

Quickwrite

Jot down some associations about money that come to your mind—and what people will do to get it.

Elements of Literature

Symbol

Beginning with the title, the image of a child's rocking horse dominates this story. The horse is associated with every important development in the plot. As this story's tragedy unfolds, the horse seems to take on more than its literal meaning as a child's toy. It is slowly transformed into a **symbol,** richly suggestive of themes and meanings for the story as a whole.

Background

Lawrence saw men and women as torn between the promptings of their instincts (which he saw as natural and therefore good) and the demanding voices of their upbringing and education (which he saw as destructive). As you read "The Rocking-Horse Winner," which is told like a modern fable, notice which voices permeate the house and what effects these voices have on the characters.

Ride a Cock Horse (detail) (c. 1952) by Derek H. Clarke.

John Noott Galleries, Broadway, Worcester, England.

Preteaching Vocabulary

Words to Own

Have students in small groups read the Words to Own and their definitions. Then have a volunteer from each group present a sentence in which one of the vocabulary words is left out. Have the others try to figure out the missing word. The student who supplies it should devise another incomplete sentence for another vocabulary word. Have students continue until you are satisfied that they have a grasp of the definitions of all the words.

Complete each analogy with a vocabulary word.

1. favored : hated : : continued : [arrested]
2. replied : responded : : deflected : [parried]
3. weary : energetic : : famous : [obscure]
4. farce : amusing : : ghost : [uncanny]
5. strolled : ambled : : restated : [reiterated]

The Rocking-Horse Winner

D. H. Lawrence

There was a woman who was beautiful, who started with all the advantages, yet she had no luck. She married for love, and the love turned to dust. She had bonny children, yet she felt they had been thrust upon her, and she could not love them. They looked at her coldly, as if they were finding fault with her. And hurriedly she felt she must cover up some fault in herself. Yet what it was that she must cover up she never knew. Nevertheless, when her children were present, she always felt the center of her heart go hard. This troubled her, and in her manner she was all the more gentle and anxious for her children, as if she loved them very much. Only she herself knew that at the center of her heart was a hard little place that could not feel love, no, not for anybody. Everybody else said of her: "She is such a good mother. She adores her children." Only she herself, and her children themselves, knew it was not so. They read it in each other's eyes. **A**

There were a boy and two little girls. They lived in a pleasant house, with a garden, and they had discreet servants, and felt themselves superior to anyone in the neighborhood.

Although they lived in style, they felt always an anxiety in the house. There was never enough money. The mother had a small income,[1] and the father had a small income, but not nearly enough for the social position which they had to keep up. The father went into town to some office. But though he had good prospects, these prospects never materialized. There was always the grinding sense of the shortage of money, though the style was always kept up. **B**

At last the mother said: "I will see if *I* can't make something." But she did not know where to begin. She racked her brains, and tried this thing and the other, but could not find anything successful. The failure made deep lines come into her face. Her children were growing up, they would have to go to school. There must be more money, there must be more money. The father, who was always very handsome and expensive in his tastes, seemed as if he never *would* be able to do anything worth doing. And the mother, who had a great belief in herself, did not succeed any better, and her tastes were just as expensive.

And so the house came to be haunted by the unspoken phrase: *There must be more money! There must be more money!* The children could hear it all the time, though nobody said it aloud. They heard it at Christmas, when the expensive and splendid toys filled the nursery. Behind the shining modern rocking horse, behind the smart doll's house, a voice would start whispering: "There *must* be more money! There *must* be more money!" **C** And the children would stop playing, to listen for a moment. They would look into each other's eyes, to see if they had all heard. And each one saw in the eyes of the other two that they too had heard. "There *must* be more money! There *must* be more money!"

It came whispering from the springs of the still-swaying rocking horse, and even the horse, bending his wooden, champing head, heard it. The big doll, sitting so pink and smirking in her new pram,[2] could hear it quite plainly, and seemed to be smirking all the more self-consciously because of it. The foolish puppy, too, that took the place of the teddy bear, he was looking so extraordinarily foolish for no other reason but that he heard the secret whisper all over the house: "There *must* be more money!"

Yet nobody ever said it aloud. The whisper was everywhere, and therefore no one spoke it. Just as no one ever says: "We are breathing!" in spite of the fact that breath is coming and going all the time.

"Mother," said the boy Paul one day, "why don't we keep a car of our own? Why do we always use uncle's, or else a taxi?"

"Because we're the poor members of the family," said the mother.

"But why *are* we, mother?"

"Well—I suppose," she said slowly and bitterly, "it's because your father has no luck."

1. **income:** money from an inheritance or investments—not a salary.

2. **pram:** chiefly British for "baby carriage." The word is short for *perambulator*.

A Reading Skills and Strategies

Comparing/Contrasting

This opening paragraph reveals a conflict between appearance and reality. Have students contrast how things appear in the house with how they actually are. [Possible response: The woman appears to love her husband and children, but in actuality she cannot feel love for anybody.]

B Cultural Connections

Lawrence wrote this story for his friend Lady Cynthia Asquith. Like the woman in the story, Cynthia was born into the upper class of British society, the daughter of the eleventh Earl of Wemyss. She married a man with too little money and was always short of cash. At times, Lawrence scolded Cynthia for her materialism. Her sons found her a neglectful mother, with her love conditional on their successes. Lawrence translated his impressions of the Asquith family into "The Rocking-Horse Winner."

C Elements of Literature

Symbol

? Why is the pervasive "whispering" in the house an effective symbol for the family's financial problem? [Possible response: The problem is persistent, troubling, and never spoken of openly.]

Reaching All Students

Struggling Readers

Help struggling readers understand this selection by using the strategy, Most Important Word. Using this strategy, students will be able to summarize the story and understand the important points. See the *Reading Strategies Handbook* in front of the *Reading Skills and Strategies* binder.

- MiniRead Skill Lesson, p. 76
- Selection Skill Lesson, p. 83

English Language Learners

To keep students actively engaged in reading the text, have them read in small groups and make predictions about what is to come. Students should stop at least six times as they read and jot down a statement that expresses what they believe will be the next major development in the plot. (For example, they might stop on this page just before the conversation between Paul and his mother begins.) Once students complete the story, they can evaluate their predictions.

Advanced Learners

This story has been referred to as a fairy tale, a fable, and a satire. As they read, ask students to think about which category best fits the story. Encourage students to decide on a category and defend their decision with their classmates.

A Critical Thinking
Speculating

? What might Paul's mother be trying to hide from him? [Possible responses: her fear that she herself might be the source of bad luck; her insecurity or lack of faith in her own abilities; her feeling that getting married and having children was unlucky.]

B Reading Skills and Strategies
Making Inferences

? What is it the boy wants from his mother that he does not get? [Possible responses: attention, warmth, love, security.]

C Reading Skills and Strategies
Understanding Cause and Effect

? What effect does the conversation with his mother have on Paul? [Paul desperately seeks "luck" to please his mother.] **What evidence suggests that this effect is not a positive one?** [Possible responses: Paul becomes heedless of others, self-absorbed, and sly. Words and phrases such as "charging madly," "frenzy," "wildly," and "strange glare" suggest a somewhat sinister and supernatural aspect to Paul's ride.]

D Appreciating Language
Style

? What do the words *mad* and *furious* suggest about how Paul rides the rocking horse? [Possible responses: He rides it without pleasure, in a frenzy, with no thought for his own health or safety. He seems to be possessed by his quest for luck.]

The boy was silent for some time.

"Is luck money, mother?" he asked, rather timidly.

"No, Paul. Not quite. It's what causes you to have money."

"Oh!" said Paul vaguely. "I thought when Uncle Oscar said *filthy lucker,* it meant money."

"*Filthy lucre*[3] does mean money," said the mother. "But it's lucre, not luck."

"Oh!" said the boy. "Then what *is* luck, mother?"

"It's what causes you to have money. If you're lucky you have money. That's why it's better to be born lucky than rich. If you're rich, you may lose your money. But if you're lucky, you will always get more money."

"Oh! Will you? And is father not lucky?"

"Very unlucky, I should say," she said bitterly.

The boy watched her with unsure eyes.

"Why?" he asked.

"I don't know. Nobody ever knows why one person is lucky and another unlucky."

"Don't they? Nobody at all? Does *nobody* know?"

"Perhaps God. But He never tells."

"He ought to, then. And aren't you lucky either, mother?"

"I can't be, if I married an unlucky husband."

"But by yourself, aren't you?"

"I used to think I was, before I married. Now I think I am very unlucky indeed."

"Why?"

"Well—never mind! Perhaps I'm not really," she said.

A The child looked at her to see if she meant it. But he saw, by the lines of her mouth, that she was only trying to hide something from him.

"Well, anyhow," he said stoutly, "I'm a lucky person."

"Why?" said his mother, with a sudden laugh.

He stared at her. He didn't even know why he had said it.

"God told me," he asserted, brazening it out.[4]

"I hope He did, dear!" she said, again with a laugh, but rather bitter.

"He did, mother!"

"Excellent!" said the mother, using one of her husband's exclamations.

B The boy saw she did not believe him; or rather, that she paid no attention to his assertion. This angered him somewhere, and made him want to compel her attention.

C He went off by himself, vaguely, in a childish way, seeking for the clue to "luck." Absorbed, taking no heed of other people, he went about with a sort of stealth, seeking inwardly for luck. He wanted luck, he wanted it, he wanted it. When the two girls were playing dolls in the nursery, he would sit on his big rocking horse, charging madly into space, with a frenzy that made the little girls peer at him uneasily. Wildly the horse careered,[5] the waving dark hair of the boy tossed, his eyes had a strange glare in them. The little girls dared not speak to him.

D When he had ridden to the end of his mad little journey, he climbed down and stood in front of his rocking horse, staring fixedly into its lowered face. Its red mouth was slightly open, its big eye was wide and glassy-bright.

"Now!" he would silently command the snorting steed. "Now, take me to where there is luck! Now take me!"

And he would slash the horse on the neck with the little whip he had asked Uncle Oscar for. He *knew* the horse could take him to where there was luck, if only he forced it. So he would mount again and start on his furious ride, hoping at last to get there. He knew he could get there.

"You'll break your horse, Paul!" said the nurse.

"He's always riding like that! I wish he'd leave off!" said his elder sister Joan.

But he only glared down on them in silence. Nurse gave him up. She could make nothing of him. Anyhow, he was growing beyond her.

One day his mother and his Uncle Oscar came in when he was on one of his furious rides. He did not speak to them.

"Hallo, you young jockey! Riding a winner?" said his uncle.

"Aren't you growing too big for a rocking

3. **filthy lucre** (lo͞o′kər): riches (a derogatory usage).
4. **brazening it out:** acting boldly.

5. **careered:** rushed.

WORDS TO OWN
asserted (ə·sʉrt′id) *v.:* declared.

Skill Link

Analyzing Exclamations for Their Effect

Have students skim the beginning of the story to see where D. H. Lawrence intersperses his declarative sentences with exclamations. As they continue reading, students should note that the exclamations become more frequent as the child persists in his riding. The result is an increasingly desperate and despairing tone as the child eventually rides to his death.

Have students rewrite the following paragraph, adding exclamation points to achieve the variety and tone that D. H. Lawrence does. Then, have them compare their work.

She reached the top of the hill and looked down. The sidewalk stretched away, a concrete ribbon, unfurling to the street below. Seeing it filled the child with both delight and dread. She started down, skates making their familiar metallic grating. Down and down. Trees and houses became a blur. Cars zipped by, indistinguishable in the speed of her racing. Vainly, she wondered where the bottom was.

horse? You're not a very little boy any longer, you know," said his mother.

But Paul only gave a blue glare from his big, rather close-set eyes. He would speak to nobody when he was in full tilt. His mother watched him with an anxious expression on her face.

At last he suddenly stopped forcing his horse into the mechanical gallop and slid down.

"Well, I got there!" he announced fiercely, his blue eyes still flaring, and his sturdy long legs straddling apart.

"Where did you get to?" asked his mother.

"Where I wanted to go," he flared back at her.

"That's right, son!" said Uncle Oscar. "Don't you stop till you get there. What's the horse's name?"

"He doesn't have a name," said the boy.

"Gets on without all right?" asked the uncle.

"Well, he has different names. He was called Sansovino last week."

"Sansovino, eh? Won the Ascot.[6] How did you know this name?"

"He always talks about horse races with Bassett," said Joan.

The uncle was delighted to find that his small nephew was posted with all the racing news. Bassett, the young gardener, who had been wounded in the left foot in the war and had got his present job through Oscar Cresswell, whose batman[7] he had been, was a perfect blade of the "turf."[8] He lived in the racing events, and the small boy lived with him.

Oscar Cresswell got it all from Bassett.

"Master Paul comes and asks me, so I can't do more than tell him, sir," said Bassett, his face terribly serious, as if he were speaking of religious matters.

"And does he ever put anything on a horse he fancies?"

"Well—I don't want to give him away—he's a young sport, a fine sport, sir. Would you mind asking him himself? He sort of takes a pleasure in it, and perhaps he'd feel I was giving him away, sir, if you don't mind."

Bassett was serious as a church.

6. **Ascot:** famous horse race held annually at Ascot Heath in England. Several traditional British races are mentioned in the story.
7. **batman:** an officer's personal attendant.
8. **blade of the "turf":** stylish young racing fan.

The uncle went back to his nephew and took him off for a ride in the car.

"Say, Paul, old man, do you ever put anything on a horse?" the uncle asked.

The boy watched the handsome man closely.

"Why, do you think I oughtn't to?" he parried.

"Not a bit of it! I thought perhaps you might give me a tip for the Lincoln."

The car sped on into the country, going down to Uncle Oscar's place in Hampshire.

"Honor bright?" said the nephew.

"Honor bright, son!" said the uncle.

"Well, then, Daffodil."

"Daffodil! I doubt it, sonny. What about Mirza?"

"I only know the winner," said the boy. "That's Daffodil."

"Daffodil, eh?"

There was a pause. Daffodil was an obscure horse comparatively.

"Uncle!"

"Yes, son?"

"You won't let it go any further, will you? I promised Bassett."

"Bassett be damned, old man! What's he got to do with it?"

"We're partners. We've been partners from the first. Uncle, he lent me my first five shillings, which I lost. I promised him, honor bright, it was only between me and him; only you gave me that ten-shilling note I started winning with, so I thought you were lucky. You won't let it go any further, will you?"

The boy gazed at his uncle from those big, hot, blue eyes, set rather close together. The uncle stirred and laughed uneasily.

"Right you are, son! I'll keep your tip private. Daffodil, eh? How much are you putting on him?"

"All except twenty pounds," said the boy. "I keep that in reserve."

The uncle thought it a good joke.

"You keep twenty pounds in reserve, do you, you young romancer?[9] What are you betting, then?"

9. **romancer:** imaginative storyteller.

WORDS TO OWN

parried (par′ēd) *v.:* replied evasively.
obscure (əb·skyoor′) *adj.:* little-known.
comparatively (kəm·par′ə·tiv′lē) *adv.:* relatively; in comparison to others.

E Reading Skills and Strategies
Drawing Conclusions

? What state does Paul appear to be in when he is riding the rocking horse? [Possible response: He appears to be in a trance or to be hypnotized by the movement of the rocking horse.]

F Critical Thinking
Analyzing Details

? It is odd that the boy has not named one of his favorite toys. Then, we find out that he has changed its name, and the name it had last week was that of a winning racehorse. How would you explain these details? [Possible responses: The boy does not name the toy horse because he does not really love it, just as his mother cannot really love him. The boy names the horse after race winners because he wants the toy to bring him luck. There is some significance about the horse's names of which the reader is not yet aware.]

G Cultural Connections
Horse Racing

Horse racing was a popular pastime in England many years before the discovery of America. Today it is still looked upon as one of the country's chief pastimes, much as baseball is in the United States. British royalty usually has been keen on racing, which is referred to as the "sport of kings." It is no wonder, then, that Uncle Oscar delights in his nephew's interest in horse racing. It is an interest he would consider fitting for a gentleman.

H Elements of Literature
Symbol

? Why are religious images used in describing Bassett's attitude toward Paul's interest in horse racing? [Possible response: The religious references suggest a supernatural connection between Paul and racing. Bassett seems to know he is toying with something beyond his comprehension.]

Getting Students Involved

Cooperative Learning

Character Groups. Assign the roles of Paul, the mother, Uncle Oscar, and Bassett to members of the class so that each student is assigned one of the four roles. Ask students to form character groups of four. Have each group member make up a set of questions for each of the other three characters, asking why they behave the way they do, how they view the other characters, and how they feel about what happens in the story.

Responding to the Art

Mark Gertler (1891–1939) was an English painter who survived a background of poverty to win several art prizes and scholarships. He tried to reconcile his own predilection for realism with his European contemporaries' emphasis on defined form and heightened color. His 1916 antiwar masterpiece, *The Merry-Go-Round,* is a bitter and brutal vision of human beings reduced by war to endlessly spinning mechanical dolls. Students may be interested to know that Gertler was a frequent guest at the home of Lady Ottoline Morell, where he became acquainted with D. H. Lawrence.

Activity. Have students imagine the feelings of the people on the horses. How are they like Paul as he rides his rocking horse? How are they different? [Possible responses: The people seem to be in a daze, unaware of what is going on around them. Paul, too, enters a trancelike state when he rides his horse, but he is frantic, whereas these people seem anesthetized and robotic.]

The Merry-Go-Round (20th century) by Mark Gertler.

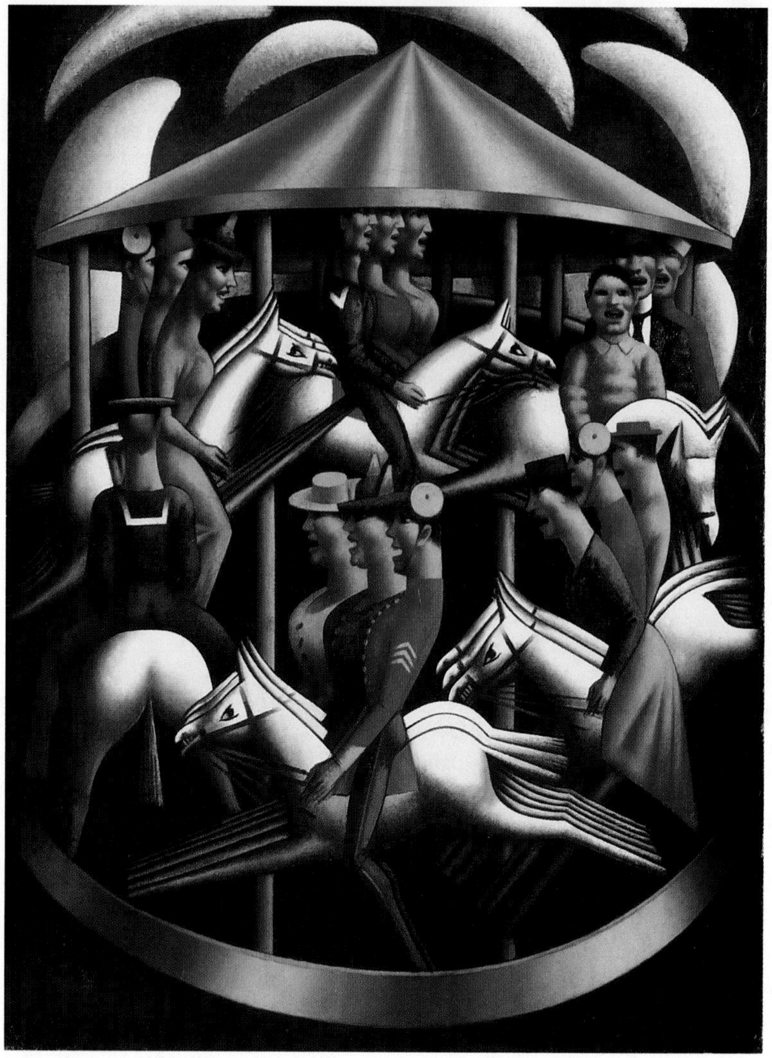

Tate Gallery, London.

A "I'm betting three hundred," said the boy gravely. "But it's between you and me, Uncle Oscar! Honor bright?"

The uncle burst into a roar of laughter.

"It's between you and me all right, you young Nat Gould,"[10] he said, laughing. "But where's your three hundred?"

"Bassett keeps it for me. We're partners."

"You are, are you! And what is Bassett putting on Daffodil?"

"He won't go quite as high as I do, I expect. Perhaps he'll go a hundred and fifty."

"What, pennies?" laughed the uncle.

"Pounds," said the child, with a surprised look at his uncle. "Bassett keeps a bigger reserve than I do."

B Between wonder and amusement Uncle Oscar was silent. He pursued the matter no further, but he determined to take his nephew with him to the Lincoln races.

"Now, son," he said, "I'm putting twenty on Mirza, and I'll put five on for you on any horse you fancy. What's your pick?"

10. **Nat Gould:** famous British authority on racing.

A Struggling Readers

Reading Aloud

This story contains a great deal of relatively simple dialogue. Students may benefit from taking roles and reading some of the dialogue aloud.

B Reading Skills and Strategies

Comparing/Contrasting

? How does Uncle Oscar's attitude toward Paul differ from Bassett's? [Uncle Oscar is amused and skeptical; Bassett is a serious believer in Paul's knowledge.]

Using Students' Strengths

Auditory/Musical Learners

Ask students who have musical talent to write a ballad that tells the story of Paul. It should include a refrain and should cover the major events of the story. Students may find or compose a melody that fits the ballad. Ask volunteers to perform their work for the class.

Verbal Learners

Have students work in pairs to improvise a telephone conversation between Paul's mother and a friend after Paul has died. This conversation should summarize the details of the story from the mother's point of view and include the mother's ideas about why Paul acted as he did. Allow students to make an audiotape of the conversation to play back later. Students also can do the same activity with Uncle Oscar or Bassett talking to a friend.

"Daffodil, uncle."

"No, not the fiver on Daffodil!"

"I should if it was my own fiver," said the child.

"Good! Good! Right you are! A fiver for me and a fiver for you on Daffodil."

The child had never been to a race meeting before, and his eyes were blue fire. He pursed his mouth tight and watched. A Frenchman just in front had put his money on Lancelot. Wild with excitement, he flayed his arms up and down, yelling *"Lancelot! Lancelot!"* in his French accent.

Daffodil came in first, Lancelot second, Mirza third. The child, flushed and with eyes blazing, was curiously serene. His uncle brought him four five-pound notes, four to one.

"What am I to do with these?" he cried, waving them before the boy's eyes.

"I suppose we'll talk to Bassett," said the boy. "I expect I have fifteen hundred now; and twenty in reserve; and this twenty."

His uncle studied him for some moments.

"Look here, son!" he said. "You're not serious about Bassett and that fifteen hundred, are you?"

"Yes, I am. But it's between you and me, uncle. Honor bright?"

"Honor bright all right, son! But I must talk to Bassett."

"If you'd like to be a partner, uncle, with Bassett and me, we could all be partners. Only, you'd have to promise, honor bright, uncle, not to let it go beyond us three. Bassett and I are lucky, and you must be lucky, because it was your ten shillings I started winning with. . . ." C

Uncle Oscar took both Bassett and Paul into Richmond Park for an afternoon, and there they talked.

"It's like this, you see, sir," Bassett said. "Master Paul would get me talking about racing events, spinning yarns, you know, sir. And he was always keen on knowing if I'd made or if I'd lost. It's about a year since, now, that I put five shillings on Blush of Dawn for him: And we lost. Then the luck turned, with that ten shillings he had from you: That we put on Singhalese. And since that time, it's been pretty steady, all things considering. What do you say, Master Paul?"

"We're all right when we're sure," said Paul. "It's when we're not quite sure that we go down."

"Oh, but we're careful then," said Bassett.

"But when are you *sure*?" smiled Uncle Oscar.

"It's Master Paul, sir," said Bassett in a secret, religious voice. "It's as if he had it from heaven. Like Daffodil, now, for the Lincoln. That was as sure as eggs." D E

"Did you put anything on Daffodil?" asked Oscar Cresswell.

"Yes, sir. I made my bit."

"And my nephew?"

Bassett was obstinately silent, looking at Paul.

"I made twelve hundred, didn't I, Bassett? I told uncle I was putting three hundred on Daffodil."

"That's right," said Bassett, nodding.

"But where's the money?" asked the uncle.

"I keep it safe locked up, sir. Master Paul he can have it any minute he likes to ask for it."

"What, fifteen hundred pounds?"

"And twenty! And *forty,* that is, with the twenty he made on the course."

"It's amazing!" said the uncle.

"If Master Paul offers you to be partners, sir, I would, if I were you: if you'll excuse me," said Bassett.

Oscar Cresswell thought about it.

"I'll see the money," he said.

They drove home again, and sure enough, Bassett came round to the garden house with fifteen hundred pounds in notes. The twenty pounds reserve was left with Joe Glee, in the Turf Commission[11] deposit.

"You see, it's all right, uncle, when I'm *sure*! Then we go strong, for all we're worth. Don't we, Bassett?"

"We do that, Master Paul."

"And when are you sure?" said the uncle, laughing.

"Oh, well, sometimes I'm *absolutely* sure, like about Daffodil," said the boy; "and sometimes I have an idea; and sometimes I haven't even an idea, have I, Bassett? Then we're careful, because we mostly go down."

"You do, do you! And when you're sure, like about Daffodil, what makes you sure, sonny?"

"Oh, well, I don't know," said the boy uneasily. "I'm sure, you know, uncle; that's all." F

11. **Turf Commission:** committee of the Jockey Club, the chief governing body for horse racing. This committee operates a bank in which bettors can deposit money for future bets.

C Reading Skills and Strategies
Making Inferences

? Why is Paul so anxious that his uncle not get anyone else involved in the betting partnership? [Possible response: He is afraid that another partner might be unlucky and ruin the winning streak.]

D Critical Thinking
Speculating

? Why do you think that Bassett is so quick to attribute Paul's knowledge to the supernatural? [Possible responses: As a simple man with little education, Bassett cannot imagine any other source of Paul's knowledge. A religious man, Bassett actually believes Paul to be divinely inspired.]

E English Language Learners
Interpreting Idioms

The British idiom (in full, *as sure as eggs is eggs*) is uncommon and might not be understood by all students. Explain that the origin of the phrase is obscure, but it means "something is certain" or "will definitely happen." Encourage students to jot down any other idioms they don't understand as they read. Work with them to discover the meanings through context clues.

F Reading Skills and Strategies
Drawing Conclusions

? Why is the boy uneasy about telling his uncle how he gets his racing tips? [Possible responses: He may be afraid that telling will bring bad luck. He may not completely trust his uncle. He may be embarrassed about the way he is getting the tips.]

Crossing the Curriculum

Health

Inform students that Lawrence's characterization of Paul may have been partly inspired by Cynthia Asquith's son John, who was thought to have been brain damaged by the use of forceps at birth. However, John was probably autistic, although never diagnosed. John Asquith often disobeyed and was subject to frenzied outbursts, like those Paul exhibits when riding his rocking horse. Interested students may research autism, its symptoms, and how it is treated today.

A Vocabulary Note

Unlocking Meaning

Tell students that they can often unlock a word's meaning by breaking it down into its parts. For example, the word *inconsiderable* consists of the prefix *in-* (meaning "not") plus the Latin root *considerare* (meaning "to look at closely") and the suffix *-able* (meaning "worthy of"). Putting these parts all together suggests a meaning such as "not worthy of being looked at closely." A look in the dictionary will confirm that *inconsiderable* means "not important" or "insignificant."

B Critical Thinking

Expressing an Opinion

? Paul fears his mother would stop him from betting, while his uncle does not think she would. Who do you think is right? Why? [Possible responses: Paul, because his mother would find his betting an embarrassment; Uncle Oscar, because Paul's mother would be so happy to get the money that she wouldn't care where it came from.]

C Critical Thinking

Analyzing Character

? Why does Paul's mother work secretly? [Possible responses: She thinks working is beneath her. She fears she will not succeed.] What does her dissatisfaction reveal about her? [Possible responses: She wants big rewards without working for them; she is very competitive and snobbish and cannot stand being anywhere but at the top.]

D Reading Skills and Strategies

Connecting with the Text

? If you were Paul, how would your mother's reaction to the gift make you feel? [Possible responses: disappointed, confused, hurt, angry.]

"It's as if he had it from heaven, sir." Bassett reiterated.

"I should say so!" said the uncle.

But he became a partner. And when the Leger was coming on Paul was "sure" about Lively Spark, which was a quite inconsiderable horse. The boy insisted on putting a thousand on the horse, Bassett went for five hundred, and Oscar Cresswell two hundred. Lively Spark came in first, and the betting had been ten to one against him. Paul had made ten thousand.

"You see," he said, "I was absolutely sure of him."

Even Oscar Cresswell had cleared two thousand.

"Look here, son," he said, "this sort of thing makes me nervous."

"It needn't, uncle! Perhaps I shan't be sure again for a long time."

"But what are you going to do with your money?" asked the uncle.

"Of course," said the boy, "I started it for mother. She said she had no luck, because father is unlucky, so I thought if *I* was lucky, it might stop whispering."

"What might stop whispering?"

"Our house. I *hate* our house for whispering."

"What does it whisper?"

"Why—why"—the boy fidgeted—"why, I don't know. But it's always short of money, you know, uncle."

"I know it, son, I know it."

"You know people send mother writs,[12] don't you, uncle?"

"I'm afraid I do," said the uncle.

"And then the house whispers, like people laughing at you behind your back. It's awful, that is! I thought if I was lucky——"

"You might stop it," added the uncle.

The boy watched him with big blue eyes, that had an uncanny cold fire in them, and he said never a word.

"Well, then!" said the uncle. "What are we doing?"

"I shouldn't like mother to know I was lucky," said the boy.

"Why not, son?"

"She'd stop me."

"I don't think she would."

"Oh!"—and the boy writhed in an odd way—"I *don't* want her to know, uncle."

"All right, son! We'll manage it without her knowing."

They managed it very easily. Paul, at the other's suggestion, handed over five thousand pounds to his uncle, who deposited it with the family lawyer, who was then to inform Paul's mother that a relative had put five thousand pounds into his hands, which sum was to be paid out a thousand pounds at a time, on the mother's birthday, for the next five years.

"So she'll have a birthday present of a thousand pounds for five successive years," said Uncle Oscar. "I hope it won't make it all the harder for her later."

Paul's mother had her birthday in November. The house had been "whispering" worse than ever lately, and, even in spite of his luck, Paul could not bear up against it. He was very anxious to see the effect of the birthday letter, telling his mother about the thousand pounds.

When there were no visitors, Paul now took his meals with his parents, as he was beyond the nursery control. His mother went into town nearly every day. She had discovered that she had an odd knack of sketching furs and dress materials, so she worked secretly in the studio of a friend who was the chief "artist" for the leading drapers.[13] She drew the figures of ladies in furs and ladies in silk and sequins for the newspaper advertisements. This young woman artist earned several thousand pounds a year, but Paul's mother only made several hundreds, and she was again dissatisfied. She so wanted to be first in something, and she did not succeed, even in making sketches for drapery advertisements.

She was down to breakfast on the morning of her birthday. Paul watched her face as she read her letters. He knew the lawyer's letter. As his mother read it, her face hardened and became more expressionless. Then a cold, determined

12. **writs:** legal papers; here, those demanding payment.

13. **drapers:** dealers in cloth and dry goods.

WORDS TO OWN

reiterated (rē·it′ə·rāt′id) *v.:* repeated.
uncanny (un·kan′ē) *adj.:* strange; eerie; weird.

Professional Notes

Critical Comment: Paul as Hero and Symbol

This discussion of some elements in "The Rocking-Horse Winner" is excerpted from "A Rocking Horse: The Symbol, the Pattern, the Way to Live," by W. D. Snodgrass: "[T]he story resembles many well-known fairy tales or magical stories in which the hero bargains with evil powers for personal advantages or forbidden knowledge. These bargains are always 'rigged' so that the hero, after his apparent triumphs, will lose in the end—this being, in itself, the standard 'moral.' . . . So, in some sense, Paul *is* demonic, yet a poor devil; though he has compacted with evil, his intentions were good and he has destroyed only himself. At first metaphorically, in the end literally, he has committed suicide. But that may be, finally, the essence of evil. . . . Paul is destroyed, we have said, by his desire to 'know.' It is not only that he has chosen wrong ways of knowing or wrong things to know. The evil is that he *has* chosen to know, to live by intellection." In a letter, Lawrence wrote: ". . . Paul is a symbol of civilized man, whipping himself on in a nervous endless 'mechanical gallop,' an 'arrested prance,' in chase of something which will destroy him if he ever catches it, and which he never really wanted anyway."

look came on her mouth. She hid the letter under the pile of others, and said not a word about it.

"Didn't you have anything nice in the post for your birthday, mother?" said Paul.

"Quite moderately nice," she said, her voice cold and absent.

She went away to town without saying more.

But in the afternoon Uncle Oscar appeared. He said Paul's mother had had a long interview with the lawyer, asking if the whole five thousand could not be advanced at once, as she was in debt.

"What do you think, uncle?" said the boy.

"I leave it to you, son."

"Oh, let her have it, then! We can get some more with the other," said the boy.

"A bird in the hand is worth two in the bush, laddie!" said Uncle Oscar.

"But I'm sure to *know* for the Grand National; or the Lincolnshire; or else the Derby. I'm sure to know for *one* of them," said Paul.

So Uncle Oscar signed the agreement, and Paul's mother touched the whole five thousand. Then something very curious happened. The voices in the house suddenly went mad, like a chorus of frogs on a spring evening. There were certain new furnishings, and Paul had a tutor. He was *really* going to Eton,[14] his father's school, in the following autumn. There were flowers in the winter, and a blossoming of the luxury Paul's mother had been used to. And yet the voices in (E) the house, behind the sprays of mimosa and almond blossom, and from under the piles of iridescent cushions, simply trilled and screamed in a sort of ecstasy: "There *must* be more money! Oh-h-h; there *must* be more money. Oh, now, now-w! Now-w-w—there *must* be more money!—more than ever! More than ever!"

It frightened Paul terribly. He studied away at his Latin and Greek with his tutor. But his intense hours were spent with Bassett. The Grand National had gone by: He had not "known," and had lost a hundred pounds. Summer was at hand. He was in agony for the Lincoln. But even for the Lincoln he didn't "know," and he lost fifty pounds. He became wild-eyed and strange, as if something (F) were going to explode in him.

"Let it alone, son! Don't you bother about it!" urged Uncle Oscar. But it was as if the boy couldn't really hear what his uncle was saying.

"I've got to know for the Derby! I've got to know for the Derby!" the child reiterated, his big blue eyes blazing with a sort of madness.

His mother noticed how overwrought he was.

"You'd better go to the seaside. Wouldn't you like to go now to the seaside, instead of waiting? I think you'd better," she said, looking down at him anxiously, her heart curiously heavy because of him.

But the child lifted his uncanny blue eyes.

"I couldn't possibly go before the Derby, mother!" he said. "I couldn't possibly!"

"Why not?" she said, her voice becoming heavy when she was opposed. "Why not? You can still go from the seaside to see the Derby with your Uncle Oscar, if that's what you wish. No need for you to wait here. Besides, I think you care too (G) much about these races. It's a bad sign. My family has been a gambling family, and you won't know till you grow up how much damage it has done. But it has done damage. I shall have to send Bassett away, and ask Uncle Oscar not to talk racing to you, unless you promise to be reasonable about it: Go away to the seaside and forget it. You're all nerves!"

"I'll do what you like, mother, so long as you don't send me away till after the Derby," the boy said.

"Send you away from where? Just from this house?"

"Yes," he said, gazing at her.

"Why, you curious child, what makes you care about this house so much, suddenly? I never knew you loved it."

He gazed at her without speaking. He had a secret within a secret, something he had not (H) divulged, even to Bassett or to his Uncle Oscar.

But his mother, after standing undecided and a little bit sullen for some moments, said:

"Very well, then! Don't go to the seaside till after the Derby, if you don't wish it. But promise

14. **Eton:** Eton College, a private prep school for boys, near London.

WORDS TO OWN

iridescent (ir′i·des′ənt) *adj.:* showing rainbowlike colors.

overwrought (ō′vər·rôt′) *adj.:* overly excited.

(E) Elements of Literature

Symbol

In note C on p. T997, the pervasive whispering in the house is read as a symbol for the family's problems. Ask students why the whispering increases at this point in the story. [Possible response: It is mirroring the mother's neurosis: The more she has the more she needs.] **What human foible might the whispering symbolize?** [Possible responses: greed, insecurity, materialism.]

(F) Critical Thinking

Hypothesizing

? Paul is "wild-eyed and strange." He doesn't hear what his uncle is saying. His eyes are "blazing with a sort of madness." What do you think accounts for these frightening changes in the boy? [Possible responses: He is possessed by evil spirits. He is desperately afraid that the whispering in the house will overcome him if he doesn't win more money. His fears of inadequacy, the lack of affection from his mother, and his strange powers have actually driven him mad.]

(G) Elements of Literature

Irony

? What is ironic about Paul's mother telling him he cares too much about the races? [Possible responses: He cares so much about them because he wants to win money for her. She has passed her materialism, her craving for money, on to him.]

(H) Reading Skills and Strategies

Drawing Conclusions

? What is the "secret within a secret"? [Some students may have guessed that Paul is getting the names of the winning horses on his frenzied rides. Others may not know this yet but may conclude from the fact that he does not want to leave home that there is something in the house that gives Paul the winners.]

Making the Connections

Connecting to the Theme: "The Transforming Imagination"

After students have finished reading the selection, explain that imagination and reality become blurred in this story. Have them consider what in the story is imagined and what is real. They may organize their thoughts on a chart such as this one.

Paul's Imagination	Reality

Next, ask in what way Paul's imagination transforms his reality? [Possible responses: In Paul's case, imagination actually becomes reality: He believes that the rocking horse can bring him luck in the form of racehorse winners, and this actually happens. Paul's imagination overpowers his reality and leads him to madness and death.]

A Elements of Literature
Irony

? How does this passage ironically underscore the identification between mother and son? [Possible responses: He is trying to help her, but since he doesn't understand the true nature of her problem, he is destroying himself in a reckless pursuit of money. She senses that he is in danger but is incapable of giving him love, the one thing that would save them both.]

B Reading Skills and Strategies
Understanding Cause and Effect

? Paul's mother has felt anxious about him before but has been able to ignore it. What is the cause of her anxiety now and why can she no longer ignore it? [Possible responses: Paul's mother is anxious because her son's frenzy is at a fever pitch; he looks and behaves very oddly. She senses some crisis is at hand; perhaps she is beginning to feel some responsibility for his altered state.]

C Reading Skills and Strategies
Determining the Author's Purpose

? The father is hardly mentioned in the story. Why do you think Lawrence does this? [Possible response: By hardly mentioning the father, Lawrence shows that he is physically absent from his family in the same way the mother is emotionally absent.]

me you won't let your nerves go to pieces. Promise you won't think so much about horse racing and *events,* as you call them!"

A "Oh no," said the boy casually, "I won't think much about them, mother. You needn't worry. I wouldn't worry, mother, if I were you."

"If you were me and I were you," said his mother, "I wonder what we *should* do!"

"But you know you needn't worry, mother, don't you?" the boy repeated.

"I should be awfully glad to know it," she said wearily.

"Oh, well, you *can,* you know. I mean, you *ought* to know you needn't worry," he insisted.

"Ought I? Then I'll see about it," she said.

Paul's secret of secrets was his wooden horse, that which had no name. Since he was emancipated from a nurse and a nursery-governess, he had had his rocking horse removed to his own bedroom at the top of the house.

"Surely you're too big for a rocking horse!" his mother had remonstrated.

"Well, you see, mother, till I can have a *real* horse, I like to have *some* sort of animal about," had been his quaint answer.

"Do you feel he keeps you company?" she laughed.

"Oh yes! He's very good, he always keeps me company, when I'm there," said Paul.

So the horse, rather shabby, stood in an arrested prance in the boy's bedroom.

The Derby was drawing near, and the boy grew more and more tense. He hardly heard what was spoken to him, he was very frail, and his eyes were really uncanny. His mother had sudden strange seizures of uneasiness about him. Sometimes, for half an hour, she would feel a sudden anxiety about him that was almost anguish. She wanted to rush to him at once, and know he was safe.

B Two nights before the Derby, she was at a big party in town, when one of her rushes of anxiety about her boy, her firstborn, gripped her heart till she could hardly speak. She fought with the feeling, might and main, for she believed in common sense. But it was too strong. She had to leave the dance and go downstairs to telephone to the country. The children's nursery-governess was terribly surprised and startled at being rung up in the night.

"Are the children all right, Miss Wilmot?"

"Oh yes, they are quite all right."

"Master Paul? Is he all right?"

"He went to bed as right as a trivet. Shall I run up and look at him?"

"No," said Paul's mother reluctantly. "No! Don't trouble. It's all right. Don't sit up. We shall be home fairly soon." She did not want her son's privacy intruded upon.

"Very good," said the governess.

C It was about one o'clock when Paul's mother and father drove up to their house. All was still. Paul's mother went to her room and slipped off

Words to Own

remonstrated (ri·män′strāt′id) *v.:* protested.

arrested (ə·rest′id) *v.* used as *adj.:* checked or halted in motion.

Assessing Learning

Check Test: Multiple Choice

1. Paul's mother lacks [a].
 a. peace of mind c. a comfortable home
 b. a family d. beauty

2. After speaking with his mother, Paul believes that what the family needs is [b].
 a. help c. work
 b. luck d. prayers

3. As he rides his rocking horse, Paul is [c].
 a. fearful c. frenzied
 b. content d. angry

4. Oscar's attitude toward Paul's death is [d].
 a. great sadness c. disgust
 b. outrage d. resignation

Standardized Test Preparation

For practice with ACT and SAT formats, see
- *Preparation for College Admission Exams,* p. 51

For practice in proofreading and editing, see
- *Daily Oral Grammar,* Transparency 34

Informal Assessment

Observation Assessment. As students work in groups, observe their behavior, and note the following on a scale of one to five (five being the best rating).

1. Do all students in a group seem engaged?
2. Are students performing assigned group roles?
3. Are students staying on the assigned task?
4. Are all students contributing to the task?
5. Is the atmosphere of the group conducive to participation by all members?

her white fur cloak. She had told her maid not to wait up for her. She heard her husband downstairs, mixing a whiskey and soda.

And then, because of the strange anxiety at her heart, she stole upstairs to her son's room. Noiselessly she went along the upper corridor. Was there a faint noise? What was it?

She stood, with arrested muscles, outside his door, listening. There was a strange, heavy, and yet not loud noise. Her heart stood still. It was a soundless noise, yet rushing and powerful. Something huge, in violent, hushed motion. What was it? What in God's name was it? She ought to know. She felt that she knew the noise. She knew what it was. **D**

Yet she could not place it. She couldn't say what it was. And on and on it went, like a madness.

Softly, frozen with anxiety and fear, she turned the door handle.

The room was dark. Yet in the space near the window, she heard and saw something plunging to and fro. She gazed in fear and amazement.

Then suddenly she switched on the light, and saw her son, in his green pajamas, madly surging on the rocking horse. The blaze of light suddenly lit him up, as he urged the wooden horse, and lit her up, as she stood, blonde, in her dress of pale green and crystal, in the doorway.

"Paul!" she cried. "Whatever are you doing?" **E**

"It's Malabar!" he screamed in a powerful, strange voice. "It's Malabar!"

His eyes blazed at her for one strange and senseless second, as he ceased urging his wooden horse. Then he fell with a crash to the ground, and she, all her tormented motherhood flooding upon her, rushed to gather him up.

But he was unconscious, and unconscious he remained, with some brain fever. He talked and tossed, and his mother sat stonily by his side.

"Malabar! It's Malabar! Bassett, Bassett, I *know*! It's Malabar!"

So the child cried, trying to get up and urge the rocking horse that gave him his inspiration.

"What does he mean by Malabar?" asked the heart-frozen mother.

"I don't know," said the father stonily.

"What does he mean by Malabar?" she asked her brother Oscar.

"It's one of the horses running for the Derby," was the answer.

And, in spite of himself, Oscar Cresswell spoke to Bassett, and himself put a thousand on Malabar: at fourteen to one.

The third day of the illness was critical: They were waiting for a change. The boy, with his rather long, curly hair, was tossing ceaselessly on the pillow. He neither slept nor regained consciousness, and his eyes were like blue stones. His mother sat, feeling her heart had gone, turned actually into a stone.

In the evening, Oscar Cresswell did not come, but Bassett sent a message, saying could he come up for one moment, just one moment? Paul's mother was very angry at the intrusion, but on second thoughts she agreed. The boy was the same. Perhaps Bassett might bring him to consciousness.

The gardener, a shortish fellow with a little brown moustache and sharp little brown eyes, tiptoed into the room, touched his imaginary cap to Paul's mother, and stole to the bedside, staring with glittering, smallish eyes at the tossing, dying child.

"Master Paul!" he whispered. "Master Paul! Malabar came in first all right, a clean win. I did as you told me. You've made over seventy thousand pounds, you have; you've got over eighty thousand. Malabar came in all right, Master Paul."

"Malabar! Malabar! Did I say Malabar, mother? Did I say Malabar? Do you think I'm lucky, mother? I knew Malabar, didn't I? Over eighty thousand pounds! I call that lucky, don't you, mother? Over eighty thousand pounds! I knew, didn't I know I knew? Malabar came in all right. If I ride my horse till I'm sure, then I tell you, Bassett, you can go as high as you like. Did you go for all you were worth, Bassett?" **F**

"I went a thousand on it, Master Paul."

"I never told you, mother, that if I can ride my horse, and *get there,* then I'm absolutely sure—oh, absolutely! Mother, did I ever tell you? I *am* lucky!"

"No, you never did," said his mother.

But the boy died in the night.

And even as he lay dead, his mother heard her brother's voice saying to her: "My God, Hester, you're eighty-odd thousand to the good, and a poor devil of a son to the bad. But, poor devil, poor devil, he's best gone out of a life where he rides his rocking horse to find a winner." **G**

D Elements of Literature
Symbol

? What could the "soundless noise" symbolize? [Possible responses: The "soundless noise" (Paul's rocking) could symbolize the boy's doom or a sense of impending sorrow; it could be the guilt the mother refuses to face; or it could be the greed that the house whispers about.] **Why should the mother be able to recognize the sound?** [Possible responses: because Paul has been rocking on the horse furiously for a long time; because it is the sound of her own greed; because she is responsible for Paul's reckless riding.]

E Critical Thinking
Analyzing Climax

Explain how this scene could be considered the climax, the point of greatest emotional intensity at which the conflict of the story is decided. [Possible response: The story has been building up to this point—Paul's most daring and dangerous ride. It is also the point at which his mother finally sees the consequences of her greed and materialism.]

F Critical Thinking
Making Connections

? What other characters does the boy's raving and desperation remind you of? [Possible responses: Faust, Macbeth. It is almost as if Paul has made some kind of a pact with a supernatural force to bring enough luck or money into the household to quiet the incessant voices.]

G Reading Skills and Strategies
Drawing Conclusions

? Why does Uncle Oscar think Paul is better off dead? [Possible responses: He realizes Paul was mad and feels that Paul has been saved from a life of agony. He believes Paul is lucky to have escaped a world driven by a materialism that can never be satisfied.]

Skill Link

Generating Questions for Further Study

Lawrence also wrote the following on the subject of materialism: "I don't want to own a house, nor land, nor a motor-car, nor shares in anything. I don't want a fortune—not even an assured income. . . . There is deep inside one a revolt against the fixed thing, fixed society, fixed money, fixed homes, even fixed love."

After students have read Lawrence's thoughts about natural human energy and money in Primary Sources on p. 1006, ask them to apply his ideas to "The Rocking-Horse Winner." They can begin their analysis by developing questions, such as the following: How could being "simple and direct, and a bit free from oneself above all" have helped Paul and his mother? How does Lawrence portray the evil of "money-fear" and "money-lust" in the story? How applicable are Lawrence's ideas to modern society?

Making Meanings

First Thoughts [Respond]

1. Possible responses: Because the mother is distant and unable to love, her treatment of her son is only superficially kind. Her outlook on life is selfish and negative; it is disturbing.

Shaping Interpretations [Interpret]

2. Possible responses: The voices represent the parents' materialism; as their greed increases, so does the volume of the voices. The parents are made oblivious to the voices by their own greed.
3. Possible responses: He becomes completely possessed by the demon of materialism as he attempts to control events; he wills himself into a psychic frenzy from which he cannot escape.
4. Possible responses: devotion to materialism, greed, Paul's desire for his mother's affection, temptation.
5. Possible response: Lack of money and pursuit of money lead to the destruction of love and even of life itself.
6. Possible responses: ominous, mystical, satirical.

Connecting with the Text [Apply]

7. Students may cite examples of crimes committed in the pursuit of money.

Challenging the Text [Evaluate]

8. Possible responses: The typical fairy tale ends happily, but here Paul dies and his mother is left to consider the consequences of her greed. Although happy endings are nice, this ending emphasizes Lawrence's point about the evils of materialism. The mother will have a lot of money, but it is unlikely to satisfy her since she has lost something priceless—her son.

Primary Sources | **A Letter**

D. H. Lawrence on Money

A theme that runs through nearly all Lawrence's works is the celebration of life—the human energy and force that express the joy of existence. Opposing this natural energy is materialism, which Lawrence believed misdirects our energies and warps the soul.

Rolf Gardiner, one of Lawrence's first admirers, managed a large farm in Dorset. In 1926, Lawrence wrote to Gardiner: "And don't be too ernest—earnest—how does one spell it?—nor overburdened by a mission: neither too self-willed. One must be simple and direct, and a bit free from oneself above all."

In another letter to Gardiner, Lawrence makes a rare, brief mention of the evils of materialism.

Villa Mirenda, Scandicci
Florence
18 Dec., 1927

Dear Rolf Gardiner,

. . . If I were talking to the young, I should say only one thing to them: Don't you live just to make money, either for yourself or for anybody else. Don't look on yourself as a wage slave. Try to find out what life itself is, and live. Repudiate the money idea.

And then I'd teach 'em, if I could, to dance and sing together. The togetherness is important.

But they must first overthrow in themselves the money-fear and money-lust. . . .

Making Meanings

First Thoughts

1. What did you think of the mother's treatment of her son? of her outlook on life generally?

Reading Check

a. The opening, written in the style of a fairy tale, tells of a woman who "had no luck." How had she been unlucky? What else does the writer tell directly about the mother's **character**?

b. How does Paul's mother define *luck* when Paul asks her what it means? What is Paul's confusion about the word *luck*?

c. What step does Paul take to ease his mother's anxiety over the family's debts? How does she react when she learns of her birthday surprise?

d. Who is Bassett? Why does he keep Paul's secret?

e. Does Paul solve his mother's problem? Why or why not?

Shaping Interpretations

2. How do you explain the ever louder voices in the house? In your opinion, why do only Paul and his sisters hear and react to the voices?
3. How would you describe what has happened to Paul by the end of the story?
4. What might the rocking horse **symbolize**?
5. State the **theme** of the story, using the words *love* and *money*.
6. How would you describe the **tone** of the story?

Connecting with the Text

7. Review your Quickwrite notes. Can you think of any current examples of tragedy resulting from an obsession with wealth?

Challenging the Text

8. In what ways is the story's ending a distortion of the usual fairy-tale ending? What do you think of Lawrence's decision to end it as he did?

Reading Check

a. The woman's love has turned to dust; she finds herself unable to love her children; she feels flawed. The woman is ambitious and eager for social position; she is not as rich as she hoped to be and is never satisfied.

b. She says that luck is what causes people to have money. Paul can't understand why God does not reveal the reason one person is lucky and another isn't. He confuses *luck* with *lucre*. He believes luck and money are the same—that one can't be lucky in other ways.

c. Paul bets on horses and wins a great deal of money. He asks his uncle to make an anonymous birthday present to his mother of a thousand pounds a year for five years. His mother is disappointed because she wants the whole amount right away; she appears cold and indifferent.

d. Bassett is the gardener and Paul's gambling partner. Bassett keeps the secret for several possible reasons: He respects the boy's talent, which he feels is somehow divine; they are making money; as an employee, Bassett must obey Paul, who wants the secret kept.

e. Paul fails to solve his mother's problem because her problem is not that she does not have enough money or enough luck. Her problem lies within herself, probably stemming from false values or feelings of inadequacy.

Before You Read

SNAKE

Make the Connection

Lords of Life

Are we the rulers of the natural world, or does nature in some way rule us? D. H. Lawrence, who was intensely interested in this question, came down on the side of nature. He believed that we are connected to nature through our instincts and that we are misguided by a social education that teaches us to rely on our intellect and distrust our senses. Thus, it is not surprising that when Lawrence writes about a snake, his vision is far from the conventional literary one that sees the snake as loathsome and evil.

Quickwrite

Write down what you see, hear, and feel when you imagine a snake.

Background

The water trough in the first line was part of the garden fountain at a house where Lawrence lived in the early 1920s. The house was in the outskirts of the Sicilian town of Taormina, not far from the snowcapped and ever-smoking Mount Etna, one of the world's active volcanoes. This **setting** is important in that "the burning bowels of the earth" (line 20) is not just a figurative description but also a literal one. It is from this "infernal region" that the snake emerges, recalling the Genesis account (page 416) of the garden of Eden.

Bacchus on Mt. Vesuvius. Fresco from the Casa del Centenario, Pompeii, 1st century A.D.).

Museo Archeologico Nazionale, Naples, Italy.

Snake

D. H. Lawrence

A snake came to my water trough
On a hot, hot day, and I in pajamas for the heat,
To drink there.

In the deep, strange-scented shade of the great dark carob tree **A**
I came down the steps with my pitcher
And must wait, must stand and wait, for there he was at the
trough before me.

He reached down from a fissure° in the earth-wall in the gloom
And trailed his yellow-brown slackness soft-bellied down, over
the edge of the stone trough
And rested his throat upon the stone bottom,
And where the water had dripped from the tap, in a small
clearness,
He sipped with his straight mouth,
Softly drank through his straight gums, into his slack long body,
Silently.

Someone was before me at my water trough,
And I, like a second-comer, waiting.

He lifted his head from his drinking, as cattle do,
And looked at me vaguely, as drinking cattle do,
And flickered his two-forked tongue from his lips, and mused a
moment,
And stooped and drank a little more,
Being earth-brown, earth-golden from the burning bowels of
the earth **B**
On the day of Sicilian July, with Etna smoking.

7. **fissure:** (fish′ər): long, narrow, deep cleft or crack.

Summary ■■

On his way to fill his pitcher with water, the speaker sees a snake at his water trough. Waiting for the snake to finish drinking, the speaker thinks about how his education dictates that he should kill the snake; however, he confesses that he likes the snake and is glad the animal has come to accept his hospitality. The speaker's inner "voices" call him a coward for not killing the snake, and he admits that he is afraid. As the snake is leaving, the speaker protests the animal's withdrawal by throwing a log at it. The snake hastens away and the speaker is left to consider his "pettiness."

A Reading Skills and Strategies

Making Inferences

? How does the speaker view the snake when he first encounters it in ll. 1–6? [Possible response: He views the snake as another being who deserves to use the trough first because he arrived first.]

B Appreciating Language

Repetition

? Point out that Lawrence makes much use of repetition in this poem. What word is repeated in l. 20? [earth] How is an idea carried from l. 20 into l. 21? [The smoke from Etna comes from deep in the earth.] What does this repetition suggest about the snake? [Possible response: The snake is a force of nature, belonging to the volcanic Sicilian land itself; it is closely associated not only with the earth's "burning bowels" but with "Etna smoking."]

Reaching All Students

English Language Learners

Much of this poem is simple and direct. However, some students may find it difficult to read the longer passages, such as the third stanza. Have students break these passages down a line at a time to ensure comprehension. Then read each stanza aloud so students can appreciate the rhythm of the poem.

Advanced Learners

Point out that Lawrence deliberately varies the rhythm of this poem. Short, matter-of-fact, somewhat staccato lines are followed by longer, more sinuous passages. After students have read the poem, ask them how these contrasting rhythms suggest the snake's mode of being and the speaker's inner voice. [Possible response: The fluidity of the longer lines reflects the snake's movement, natural and unhurried. The agitated quality of the shorter lines reflects the speaker's attempt to deny his instinctual feelings and obey the voice of his "accursed human education."]

Ⓐ Critical Thinking

Expressing an Opinion

? How would you answer the question that the speaker poses? Explain. [Possible responses: Yes, the speaker is a coward because he admits in l. 37 that he is afraid of the snake. No, he isn't a coward for feeling an instinctual connection with the snake and not wanting to kill it.]

Ⓑ Elements of Literature

Imagery

? In l. 40, the speaker refers to the hole from which the snake emerges as "the dark door of the secret earth." What imagery indicates a change in the speaker's attitude in ll. 50–52? ["dreadful hole"; "horrid black hole"] **What accounts for this change?** [Possible response: The voices of the speaker's education have temporarily convinced him that the snake is indeed a dangerous creature that should be killed.]

Ⓒ Reading Skills and Strategies

Responding to the Text

? In ll. 55–57, the speaker throws a log at the snake. How do you feel about this? [Possible responses: It is time he took some action against the dangerous creature. Throwing the log is a cowardly, half-hearted effort to pacify the voices of his education. Throwing the log is a betrayal of his innermost conviction that the snake deserves his respect and protection.]

The voice of my education said to me
He must be killed,
For in Sicily the black black snakes are innocent, the gold are
venomous.

And voices in me said, If you were a man
You would take a stick and break him now, and finish him off.

But I must confess how I liked him,
How glad I was he had come like a guest in quiet, to drink at
my water trough
And depart peaceful, pacified, and thankless
Into the burning bowels of this earth.

Ⓐ
Was it cowardice, that I dared not kill him?
Was it perversity, that I longed to talk to him?
Was it humility, to feel so honored?
I felt so honored.

And yet those voices:
If you were not afraid, you would kill him!

And truly I was afraid, I was most afraid,
But even so, honored still more
That he should seek my hospitality
From out the dark door of the secret earth.

He drank enough
And lifted his head, dreamily, as one who has drunken,
And flickered his tongue like a forked night on the air, so
black,
Seeming to lick his lips,
And looked around like a god, unseeing, into the air,
And slowly turned his head,
And slowly, very slowly, as if thrice adream
Proceeded to draw his slow length curving round
And climb again the broken bank of my wall-face.

Ⓑ
And as he put his head into that dreadful hole,
And as he slowly drew up, snake-easing his shoulders, and
entered further,
A sort of horror, a sort of protest against his withdrawing into
that horrid black hole,
Deliberately going into the blackness, and slowly drawing
himself after,
Overcame me now his back was turned.

Ⓒ
I looked around, I put down my pitcher,
I picked up a clumsy log
And threw it at the water trough with a clatter.

I think it did not hit him;
But suddenly that part of him that was left behind convulsed in
undignified haste,

Mt. Etna erupting, from *Campi—Phlegraei: Observations on the Volcanos* (1776–1779) by Sir William Hamilton. Plates etched and hand-colored by Petro Fabris.

Crossing the Curriculum

Social Studies

Interested students may like to know more about Mt. Etna. Have students form small groups to research various aspects of the subject, such as the following: the volcano's exact size and location, the dates of major eruptions and the damage caused by each, and the measures taken to control the lava flow. Invite the groups to present their findings to the class in an oral report.

Science

Encourage students to find out just what kind of snake Lawrence writes about in the poem. Have them use the descriptions Lawrence gives to narrow the field of possibilities. Suggest they search in books that provide pictures as well as descriptions of various poisonous snakes found in Sicily. When they think they have identified the kind of snake, have them share their conclusion with classmates and support their choice with details from the poem.

Writhed like lightning, and was gone
Into the black hole, the earth-lipped fissure in the wall-front
At which, in the intense still noon, I stared with fascination.

And immediately I regretted it.
I thought how paltry, how vulgar, what a mean act!
I despised myself and the voices of my accursed human education.

And I thought of the albatross,°
And I wished he would come back, my snake.

For he seemed to me again like a king,
Like a king in exile, uncrowned in the underworld,
Now due to be crowned again.

And so, I missed my chance with one of the lords
Of life.
And I have something to expiate:°
A pettiness. **D**

66. **albatross** (al′bə·trôs′): allusion to large seabird used as a symbol of guilt in the poem *The Rime of the Ancient Mariner* by Samuel Taylor Coleridge (see page 684).

73. **expiate** (eks′pē·āt′): atone, or make amends, for.

Making Meanings

First Thoughts

1. How did you respond to the speaker's feelings for the snake? How do your responses compare with the responses you recorded in your Quickwrite notes and with other readers' responses?

Shaping Interpretations

2. Describe the **setting** of the poem. What details help you see, hear, and feel what the speaker is experiencing?
3. Find the lines that describe the forces in **conflict** within the speaker's mind.
4. Why do you think the speaker refers to himself as "a second-comer" in line 15? How does he see himself in relationship to the snake?
5. List all the **similes** and **metaphors** used to describe the snake. What do these comparisons reveal about the speaker's attitude toward the snake?
6. Why does the speaker throw a log at the snake? Why does he immediately regret his action?
7. In line 66, the speaker connects the snake with the albatross, the central **symbol** in Coleridge's *The Rime of the Ancient Mariner* (page 684). How does Lawrence's experience connect with the ancient Mariner's story?
8. What do you think Lawrence's snake **symbolizes**?
9. What is the effect of the speaker's referring to "my snake" in line 67? How does this detail add to the speaker's sense of transgression, or wrongdoing, at the end of the poem?
10. Where in this poem can you find **allusions** to Pluto (or Hades), the king of the underworld in Greek mythology? Where can you spot allusions to the serpent in the Book of Genesis (see page 416)?

Extending the Text

11. Can you think of occasions when the voices of our "human education" might make us do something that would later cause shame or regret?
12. What solution does the poem suggest to the conflict between nature and culture, or "human education"? How do you feel about the poem's message?

Making Meanings

First Thoughts [Respond]

1. Students initially may have experienced the speaker's positive feelings for the snake as a bit odd, but they probably found them more understandable as the poem progressed. Many students probably recorded negative responses to snakes in their Quickwrite notes.

Shaping Interpretations [Interpret]

2. The setting is a hot summer day in the garden of a house on the outskirts of Taormina, Sicily, not far from Mt. Etna. Sensory details include the "strange-scented shade of the great dark carob tree," the colorful imagery used to describe the snake, "Etna smoking," and the "voices" in the speaker's head.
3. The voices of the speaker's education in ll. 22–26 are in conflict with the speaker's instinctual affinity for the snake, as expressed in ll. 27–30.
4. Possible responses: The speaker is "a second-comer" because the snake arrived at the water trough first or because, in the Bible, the snake was created before man. In some ways, he views the snake as superior.
5. "Come like a guest," "looked around like a god," "like a king," "one of the lords of life." These comparisons reveal the speaker's reverence for the snake.
6. The speaker throws a log at the snake because he feels a "sort of horror, a sort of protest against his withdrawing into that horrid black hole." He regrets his action because he realizes he committed a mean act just to pacify the "voices."
7. Possible response: The Mariner is punished for his sin against life in slaying the albatross. The speaker sees his throwing of the log as a comparable sin.
8. Possible responses: the forces of nature, divine creation, the spontaneous self.
9. Possible responses: By referring to "my snake," the speaker creates a stronger bond between himself and the animal. Thus, mistreatment of the snake becomes even more disgraceful, like mistreating a part of oneself.
10. Pluto: "like a god"; "king in exile, uncrowned in the underworld." Book of Genesis: "Being earth-brown, earth-golden from the burning bowels of the earth."

Extending the Text [Apply]

11. Possible responses: segregation in the United States; apartheid in South Africa.
12. When there is a conflict between nature and culture, nature should win. Some students may agree that natural instincts are more reliable than cultural dictates. Others may argue that without some cultural rules, civilization would crumble.

D Reading Skills and Strategies

Drawing Conclusions

? The speaker feels he must atone for his treatment of the snake. How do you suppose he believes he should have conducted himself? [Possible response: He should have allowed the snake to depart in its own time.]

Grading Timesaver

Rubrics for each Choices assignment appear on p. 195 in the *Portfolio Management System.*

CHOICES: Building Your Portfolio

1. **Writers Notebook** You may want to brainstorm with the class to come up with a list of topics.
2. **Supporting a Thesis** You can suggest that students first brainstorm a list of events and statements from the story that support this thesis. Then, suggest that students put their evidence in order by skimming the story. In doing this, they may find additional pieces of evidence to add to their lists.
3. **Exploring a Theme** Students should begin by identifying the violation and its results in each work. Suggest that they use a chart to organize this information.
4. **Creative Writing** Ask students to recall Paul's motivations and the frenzy with which he rides his horse. Then, as a prewriting activity, ask them to jot down words or phrases that might come into Paul's mind while he is riding his horse. Give them a time limit for this activity, such as two minutes.
5. **Creative Writing** Have students start by constructing a graphic organizer that lists the when, where, why, who, what, and how of their encounter. Then, tell students to expand on these facts by listing sensory details describing the setting.
6. **Playwriting/Performance** You may wish to encourage small groups of students to perform so that each performance will reflect a different interpretation of the mysterious aspects of the story.

CHOICES: Building Your Portfolio

Writer's Notebook

1. Collecting Ideas for an Informative Report

In linking Paul's illness to his emotional state, Lawrence draws on his knowledge of a subject that has lured writers and thinkers for centuries: the mind-body connection. Brainstorm to develop a set of questions you could use to investigate the current status of research on the role of the emotions in health and illness. Save your work for the Writer's Workshop on page 1053.

Supporting a Thesis

2. Keeping Up with the Joneses

The mother's extravagance results partly from social pressure—the need to keep up appearances. Find evidence in the story to support this statement, and write a brief essay presenting what you find.

Exploring a Theme

3. A Sense of Sin

In the Genesis account of the temptation of Adam and Eve (page 416), in Coleridge's *The Rime of the Ancient Mariner* (page 684), and in Lawrence's "Snake," there is a sense that a sacred prohibition has been violated. In a brief essay, explore the ways in which this **theme** of transgression is handled in the three works. Be sure to identify the violation and its results.

Creative Writing

4. Inside His Mind

Review the information on stream of consciousness as a narrative form (pages 993–994), and write a sketch in which you reveal the workings of Paul's mind as he rides his rocking horse to that tragic victory. What is he sensing? What associations come to his mind?

Creative Writing

5. Close Encounters

Write a free-verse poem in which you describe an encounter you had with an animal. Before you begin, think about whether the encounter taught you anything about nature. As Lawrence does, use **sensory images** and **figures of speech** to make the scene come alive.

Playwriting / Performance

6. Staging the Mysterious

Working with a partner or a small group, outline notes for how you would prepare a portion of Lawrence's story for the stage. How would you set the scene? What kinds of lighting and music would you use? How would you communicate the more intangible or mysterious aspects of the story, like what really happens to Paul as he rides? Then get together with other groups in your class to compare notes. If you feel you have some good ideas, try giving a live performance. (Be sure to read the discussion of the film version of the story, on page 1015.)

Using Students' Strengths

Intrapersonal Learners

For any of the writing activities above, assist students in the revision stage of the writing process by asking them to read their writing aloud and to record the reading on audiotape. Then, have the student replay the tape, stopping it after every paragraph for evaluation. Students should immediately revise any words or sentences that do not communicate the intended effect.

Reading Skills and Strategies

VOCABULARY: FORMATION OF NEW WORDS

Much as your vocabulary is constantly growing and changing as you learn, the English language is constantly growing and changing to accommodate what is new and different. There are at least four ways in which new words are commonly formed. Established words are joined to form new words, called **compounds** or **blends.** Words are shortened in a process called **shortening.** And when established words are used in new ways and assume new grammatical functions, they are said to undergo a **functional shift.**

Compounds. Speakers create **compounds** to describe or name something new with words that already exist. *Briefcase,* for example, is a compound formed to name the piece of luggage designed to encase legal documents, called briefs.

Blends. Like compounds, **blends** come from two or more established words. However, blends partially omit or slightly alter at least one of the established words in the process. Consequently, blends are sometimes more difficult to recognize and analyze than compounds. Would you have guessed that the common word *alone* is a blend of *all* and *one?*

Shortenings. Established words are sometimes abbreviated for the sake of convenience. The resulting new words are called **shortenings.** If the length of a frequently used word is cumbersome, you might give the word a "nickword" of sorts, just as you might give someone you know well a nickname. For instance, the more you talk about telephones, the more inclined you might be to call them *phones.*

Acronyms and back-formations are two specific kinds of shortenings. An **acronym,** the most extreme shortening, is a word formed from the first letter or letters of the words in a name or phrase. *Scuba* is an acronym for s(elf)-c(ontained) u(nderwater) b(reathing) a(pparatus).

A **back-formation** is a shortening that results when a syllable or syllables, usually affixes, are removed from a word. Affixes are usually added on, not taken away—thus the name back-formation. The word *photo,* for example, is a back-formation from *photograph.*

Functional shifts. Established words can assume new grammatical functions and meanings, resulting in **functional shifts.** For example, the noun *telephone* very quickly gave rise to a new verb, *to telephone,* meaning "to speak to by telephone."

New Word Forms

Form	Example	Analysis
compound	sweatshop	sweat + shop, to depict an unhealthy workplace
blend	smog	sm(oke) + (f)og, to describe fog polluted by smoke
shortening	flu	shortening of *influenza* by removing syllables
acronym	radar	abbreviation of *ra(dio), d(etection), a(nd) r(anging)*
back-formation	sulk	removal of *y* affix from adjective *sulky* to form noun meaning "a state of sullen aloofness"
functional shift	spoon (v.)	Noun for a utensil shifted to serve as a transitive verb, as in "to spoon soup into a bowl."

Try It Out

Speculate about how each of the following words was formed. Then, based on the way you think each one was formed, identify it as one of the following: compound, blend, shortening, back-formation, or result of a functional shift. Confirm or correct your guesses by finding each word in a dictionary.

bosun • overwrought • taxi • curio • parry

Resources

Elements of Literature

For additional instruction on how new words are formed, see Literary Elements:

- Transparency 25
- Worksheet, p. 76

Reading Skills and Strategies

Mini-Lesson:
Formation of New Words

In English new words can be formed by making functional shifts of nouns to verbs and by inventing compound adjectives. Point out to students that they probably form new words by these two processes without realizing it.

Ask students to compose sentences using the following nouns as verbs:

lamp [Possible responses: The interior decorator lamped our house for us. The evil magician lamped the genie.]

peanut [Possible responses: I peanutted the brittle before I should have. The farmer will peanut that field next week.]

wastebasket [Possible responses: The editor wastebasketed my first draft. The committee wastebaskets every idea from the board of directors.]

Ask students to invent compound adjectives for each of the following.

- A senator who is dodging an issue [an issue-dodging senator]
- A dog that is dialing a telephone [a telephone-dialing dog]

Try It Out

Possible Responses

1. bosun: a variant of *boatswain,* which is a compound word: *boat* + *swain* (boy), is a blend of *boat* and *swain*
2. overwrought: a compound of *over* and *wrought* (alternate past participle of *work*)
3. taxi: a shortening of *taxicab*
4. curio: a shortening of *curiosity*
5. parry: a functional shift or a shortening of *prepare* or *parade*

Getting Students Involved

Cooperative Learning

A Briefcase Is Not a Brief Case! Some words that make up compounds also function individually in phrases but with very different meanings. For example, a *briefcase* is a piece of luggage used to carry documents (or legal briefs), but a *brief case* is a case that does not last long. Work with the class to help them notice the differences in oral inflection or emphasis that sometimes tell whether a term is part of a compound or a phrase. You might use the following examples:

- She carried her *briefcase* to work every day. He had a common disease, a *brief case* of the measles.
- The students were *all ready* for their exam. The teacher *already* had it prepared.
- "Good *afternoon,*" said the teacher. They ate lunch *after noon* yesterday.

Now have students work in small groups of four or five to come up with as many examples of their own as possible. You can make this into a contest by setting a time limit of ten or fifteen minutes and declaring the group that comes up with the most correct examples in that time the winner. Have all groups share their examples with the class.

Spotlight On

After discussing the feature, urge interested students to do research on additional works of literature that have been made into films. Or, students may wish to view one of the literary adaptations mentioned and discuss their impressions of it.

A Historical Connections

Film in the United States

The history of film in the United States began on April 23, 1896, in a New York City music hall. The program for the evening featured a film of dancers, surf breaking on a beach, a comic boxing match, and other vaudeville comedy routines. This was not the first time people had seen moving pictures, though, because penny arcades had for some time exhibited "movies" by pasting still pictures on circular drums. When spun, these images appeared to be in motion. It is to a Frenchman named Georges Méliès that we owe the concept of motion pictures as an art form. Méliès "discovered" by accident the magical effects that can be produced with a movie camera when the film he was using got stuck. In trying to free the film, he inadvertently created a scene in which a bus appeared to turn into a hearse.

B Background

The fact that so many movies are available on television or can be rented or purchased on videotape largely accounts for the ever-growing amount of time Americans spend watching movies.

C Reading Skills and Strategies

Connecting with the Text

? What films have you seen that portray what it means to be human or to feel alienated from human society? [Responses will vary year by year.]

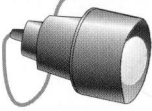

SPOTLIGHT ON

Film as Literature: More Than Meets the Eye

by **William V. Costanzo**

The Anglo-Saxons who assembled in great wooden halls to hear the *Beowulf* bard recite his epic poem of monsters and heroic feats lived in a land of menacing forests and incessant warfare. We can picture the bard singing his tale to the strumming of a harp while his listeners huddled round, delighted to be part of the evening's entertainment, protected from the mournful wind, enthralled by the exploits of their epic hero, their dragon slayer. Nearly thirteen hundred years later, we live in a different world. The dazzling variety of modern life reflected in the windows of our shopping malls and in the images of music videos would have baffled the Anglo-Saxons or even the Victorians. Yet the basic human need for stories has never been stronger than it is today. We still enjoy listening to stories. Our bookstores teem with works of fiction. But for the past one hundred years, we have been turning with increasing relish to a new form of storytelling: the movies.

Audience wearing 3-D electronic headsets.

Enlarging the House of Fiction

Statistics tell us that Americans now spend more time watching movies—in theaters, on television, and on VCRs—than they do reading books. Does this mean that movies are replacing literature? Or does it mean that movies are enlarging the house of fiction, building new rooms out of earlier literary forms, just as the sonnet grew from a tradition of love songs and the novel grew out of such forms as the novella and the pastoral romance. If films can be understood and appreciated as literature, then some attention to film literacy—our ability to view, interpret, analyze, evaluate, and communicate with movies—can enrich our understanding and appreciation of good films.

Seeing film as literature helps us to trace important continuities in the stream of stories that has flowed from the lips of bards, the pens of novelists, and the cameras of our film directors. For example, a comparative look at heroes and their adversaries—from Beowulf and Macbeth to Frankenstein and Forrest Gump—might reveal common themes about humanity: what it means to be human or to feel alienated from human society. A comparative look at the characters of Shakespeare, the Brontës, and Jerry Seinfeld might show a gradual decline in the stature of our heroes and heroines, from nobility to common citizens and antiheroes. By focusing this way on **content,** what literature is about, we can take a measure of our personal values and cultural beliefs.

We can also focus on **craft,** how different types of literature communicate their meanings. In Britain, storytelling began as a spoken art and evolved into a written literary tradition. New tools for shaping messages developed with each new literary form. The *Beowulf* poet was a master of

Taking a Second Look

Using a Graphic Organizer

Graphic organizers can assist a reader in extracting important ideas, facts, and details from a text. As students read the feature, ask them to construct a Venn diagram that compares books and film. In the left circle, ask them to write those aspects of printed literature that are unique. In the right circle, ask them to note those aspects of film that are unique to that medium. In the overlapping section of the circles, ask them to jot down aspects that the two media can share.

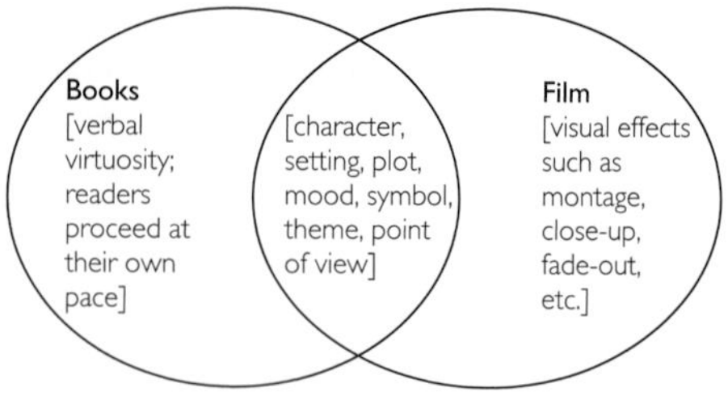

rhythm, alliteration, and the other tools of epic poetry. Dickens mastered dialogue, description, and other elements of written fiction to tell his stories in the form of novels. The craft of cinema borrows from these previous forms yet offers something new. Like other narrative artists, filmmakers give us stories with strong characters and settings depicted from particular points of view. But the filmmaker's toolbox includes cameras, actors, microphones, and lights. With such instruments of sight and sound, filmmakers coax their characters and settings to life.

Elements of Fiction, Elements of Film

Character, setting, plot, mood, symbol, theme, point of view: these elements are found in nearly every work of fiction, on the page or screen. Writers shape these elements with words. Filmmakers use actors and technology as well, moving through distinct stages of development.

Typically, a film begins with an idea. The idea for a story may be sketched out in a brief synopsis or in a longer treatment, which may contain some scenes, character development, and dialogue. Later, the complete story may be fleshed out in a screenplay or in a shooting script, a shot-by-shot blueprint for the film. This is the development stage of film production.

The next stage, preproduction, consists of preparations for the shooting. Here the elements of character, setting, and symbol begin to take on physical forms. The actors are cast; the locations are selected; the sets and props are built.

Production, the third stage, is led by the director, whose job is to turn the shooting script into a film. **D** Particular attention is given to mood and point of view. For every shot, the camera must be placed to show the action from a particular vantage point. For **E** example, a close-up might emphasize a revealing gesture or some symbolic detail. Every shot must also be lighted. Bright illumination (high-key lighting) might create a cheerful mood; dim light and contrasting shadows (low-key lighting) might communicate tension and suspense. Meanwhile, a sound crew works the microphones, recording dialogue and sound effects.

Other hands join in during the postproduction stage. The editor assembles each day's film into a continuous sequence, trimming here, inserting

Production shot from Terry Gilliam's film *The Adventures of Baron Munchausen* (1989).

D Background

The Director

The director of a movie is often compared to the conductor of an orchestra or the captain of a ship. Just as conductors or captains determine what happens in their realms, directors organize almost all the aspects of the production of a film. Different directors focus on different aspects of production: Some concentrate on the structure of the script, some on the performance of the actors, some on the camera work, and some on the editing process. Directors answer to producers, who are in charge of the financing and coordination of all the practical activities involved in the making of a film.

E Vocabulary Note

Technical Words

The following terms are often used in moviemaking. Each of the processes referred to by these terms produces specific effects on screen and, therefore, affects the film's level of artistry. *Continuity* refers to making sure people, costumes, and props are the same in a scene, even when parts are filmed at different times. A *dissolve* is a gradual merging of images. A *fade,* either "in" or "out," is a gradual movement from a black screen to a normally bright one, or vice versa. To *pan* is to move the camera angle horizontally, and to *tilt* is to move the angle vertically. To *track* is to move the camera backward, forward, or sideways to follow a moving object. To use *subjective tracking* is to view a scene through the eyes of a moving character.

Using Students' Strengths

Logical/Mathematical Learners

When students work on the section titled "Elements of Fiction, Elements of Film," ask them to make two sets of index cards. The first should contain the elements of fiction mentioned in the first sentence. (They may find it useful to consult the Handbook of Literary Terms for definitions for each of these elements and write the definitions on their cards.) The second set of index cards should contain the stages in the production of a film. Students can then practice matching the first set of cards with the second to see the relationship between the elements of fiction and film.

Intrapersonal Learners

Suggest to students that as they read this feature, they jot down the titles of books they have read that they think would make good movies. When they finish reading the feature, they can create a film production plan for one book on their list. The plan should indicate such decisions as who they would cast in the major roles, what scenes they would concentrate on in the film, and how the film would differ from the book.

Ⓐ Historical Connections

Computerization

Expanding technology, especially computerization, is creating new possibilities for filmmakers. Computers are being used to control camera movement, to create special effects, and to produce animation, which early filmmakers could not have imagined.

Ⓑ Cultural Connections

Academy Awards

Adaptations of books have always held a privileged place in the American film industry. They have been nominated for Academy Awards more often than any other kind of film. In 1939, almost all of the films competing for Oscars were adaptations of books: *Wuthering Heights; The Wizard of Oz; Of Mice and Men; Goodbye, Mr. Chips;* and *Gone With the Wind.* More recently, *Sense and Sensibility* and *Emma* have been made into films.

Ⓒ Cultural Connections

Boris Karloff

Boris Karloff (1887–1969) was born in South London into a family with diplomatic connections. He emigrated to Canada in 1909 and worked as a farmer for a while until he became a touring actor. His first movie role, in 1916, was as an extra. Karloff acted in a host of second-rate pictures during his long career but is best known for his role as the monster in the 1931 version of *Frankenstein.*

there, until a final cut is approved by the director. Ⓐ A sound lab may add music, sound effects, dialogue, and perhaps a voice-over narration. An optical lab may contribute special effects. By the time the film is ready for release, the original idea has gone through many transformations. Creative artists, technicians, and business interests have all shaped the final outcome. Unlike most written works, few movies have a single author.

The Art of Adaptation

Nearly all the heroes of great literature have appeared in movies. From Sir Gawain and Macbeth to Gulliver and Robinson Crusoe, from Jane Eyre and David Copperfield to Stephen Dedalus and Orlando, the leading figures of British fiction and their imagined worlds have been adapted for the screen. Ⓑ Why so many adaptations? Some reasons are economic. A published book offers a ready-made plot and a receptive audience; it takes less work to develop the story or publicity. But the appeal of adaptations lies in something deeper. The stories that have endured as classics speak to us across broad boundaries of time and space. We like to have them told again in a familiar medium. But what happens when a book is translated into the language of film?

Poster from James Whale's film version of *Frankenstein* (1931).

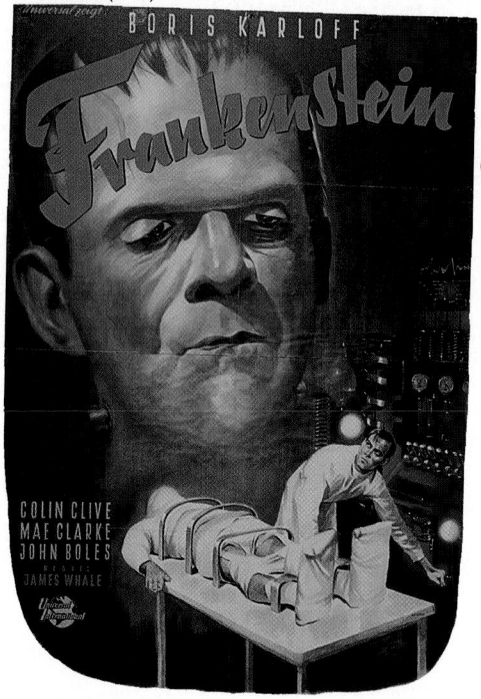

A scene from Michael Anderson's film version of *1984.*

A good way to explore the differences between film and written fiction is to compare a book to its film version. When you read a book like George Orwell's *1984* or Mary Shelley's *Frankenstein* before or after you see the film version, you notice differences in your experience. Some differences are a matter of content. For example, the 1931 film adaptation of *Frankenstein* eliminates the seagoing narrator and simplifies the plot as a struggle between the monster and its victims. Other differences lie in the medium itself, the particular methods by which films appeal to our emotions Ⓒ and imagination. Shelley's description provokes our visual imagination but leaves more room for us to picture the monster than do Boris Karloff's makeup and performance. Shelley's nineteenth-century prose is a steady, rational vehicle for ideas that seem to be eclipsed by the frightening faces, places, and special effects on the screen.

Every film adaptation is a performance, an interpretation of the text. Just as an orchestra can translate a sheet of music into the vibrant sounds of a recorded symphony, the creators of a film cooperate to transform the written work into a performance, an experience that will be seen and heard in countless movie theaters. Of course, every reading of a novel or short story is an interpretation, too. When we read, we cast the characters in our imagination. We construct sets and create the sound effects on a kind of mental movie screen. That's

Professional Notes

Critical Comment: A Case Against Adaptations

Not all people look favorably on film adaptations of works of literature. Critic Hannah Arendt holds the following view: "The entertainment industry is confronted with gargantuan appetites, and since its wares disappear in consumption, it must constantly offer new commodities. In this predicament, those who produce for the mass media ransack the entire range of past and present culture in the hope of finding suitable material. This material, however, cannot be offered as it is; it must be prepared and altered in order to become entertaining. . . . The danger is . . . precisely that it may become very entertaining indeed; there are many great authors of the past who have survived centuries of oblivion and neglect, but it is still an open question whether they will be able to survive an entertaining version of what they have to say."

why we're often disappointed when we see a film adapted from a book we like. It's also why a movie sometimes limits our experience of reading; if we see the movie first, its images keep getting in the way. Yet a faithful adaptation can be rewarding in its own right. D

"The Rocking-Horse Winner": A Case in Point

Consider "The Rocking-Horse Winner" (page 997). D. H. Lawrence's story opens like a fable. "There was a woman who was beautiful, who started with all the advantages, yet she had no luck." If you were filming the story, how would you capture its fairy-tale quality? How would you communicate the abstract concept that the woman had no luck? The story's narrator goes on to say that "she felt she must cover up some fault in herself. Yet what it was that she must cover up she never knew." Without a narrator, how would your film convey this insight into her character? You might invent a scene to reveal the woman's feelings. You might direct the actor to behave a certain way. Yet how can you know if your audience will interpret her performance as intended? How can you even know that the audience will think she's beautiful?

Already, your efforts to adapt the story have come up against some basic differences between written language and the visual language of film. First, abstract concepts like beauty and luck are easier to specify in words. How do you show luck on the screen without showing someone who is lucky? Second, writers can make precise statements through narration while filmmakers generally depend on the viewer's interpretation of images and sounds. How long would it take for a film to show that a character doesn't know what she feels she must cover up? Such a complex thought might require a whole scene, drawing on the resources of acting, camera work, lighting, and music to capture its complexities. On the other hand, a single shot of the woman's home at Christmas might convey in an instant what a writer couldn't describe in a thousand words.

Beyond these questions of setting, character, and theme is the question of genre. What kind of story is it? A moral fable? A supernatural tale? A psychological study of a dysfunctional family? How do other stories—or films—of this kind create the right mood for their genre? How, for example, would you shoot the frenzied rocking-horse scenes? How would you handle the voices in the house that whisper "There *must* be more money"? E

"The Rocking-Horse Winner" was adapted in 1949 by Anthony Pelissier, a British film director. Pelissier expands Lawrence's story to a ninety-minute film. He develops some characters, like the father and the nurse, and invents other characters, including a repugnant pawnbroker and an insolent bailiff. Uncle Oscar becomes a middle-aged gentleman, reproachful to his sister but kindly to her son. Pelissier also adds some scenes. Paul first meets Bassett in the gardener's shed. This provides an opportunity to reveal some background information through dialogue. Paul gets the rocking horse on Christmas Day, an occasion for displaying the F

A scene from Anthony Pelissier's film version of *The Rocking Horse Winner* (1949).

material values of the household. A scene in which Paul's mother puts her children to sleep is set against a scene between the children and the nurse, both scenes working together to reveal the mother's haughtiness and the limits of her maternal love. If you have an opportunity to view the film, compare it to the story as you saw it in your mind. Notice what is missing, what is added, what is different. Pay particular attention to the movie's ending, which continues beyond Uncle Oscar's final words. How might the changes be explained? How faithful is the movie to the letter and the spirit of Lawrence's story? Is the film a valid work of literature in its own terms?

D Reading Skills and Strategies

Connecting with the Text

Encourage students to discuss their reactions to film adaptations that they have seen. [Students may have seen one or more of the following: *Little Women, The Age of Innocence, Tess* (based on Thomas Hardy's *Tess of the D'Urbervilles*), *The Crucible, The Wings of the Dove, Emma,* or *Les Misérables.*]

E Background

Sound Devices

Filmmakers have certain sound devices at their disposal to help them portray the characters' thoughts or the sounds they imagine. The voice-over or the use of subjective sound allows movie audiences to hear what given characters are thinking or imagine what they hear.

F Historical Connections

Post-War British Cinema

Before World War II, the British film industry was much weaker than its American counterpart. During and after the war, however, the British became very successful in the production of literary adaptations. Some examples are as follows: actor-director Sir Laurence Olivier's film adaptations of Shakespeare's *Henry V* (1944), *Hamlet* (1948), and *Richard III* (1955); David Lean's adaptations of Charles Dickens's *Great Expectations* (1946) and *Oliver Twist* (1948); Anthony Asquith's adaptations of Terence Rattigan's plays *The Winslow Boy* (1948) and *The Browning Version* (1951), and of Oscar Wilde's *The Importance of Being Earnest* (1952).

Getting Students Involved

Cooperative Learning

Panel Discussion. Have students use the guidelines on p. 1016 to write a film review. (You may wish to provide a list of films that you feel are suitable for your students.) Assign groups of two to four to see the same film. When they have written their reviews, have the group members organize a panel discussion in which they compare their assessments of various aspects of the film. Encourage them to discuss specifics of style and to avoid plot summaries. Suggest they end the discussion with a recommendation to their classmates. They can give the movie a rating or simply recommend that students see the movie or skip it.

Ⓐ Literary Connections

Film as Literature

Although the term *literature* is usually applied to the written word, a broader interpretation applies here. Movies and written narratives share not only many of the same literary elements and storytelling strategies but also the same fundamental attraction. We go to movies for the same basic reason we read fiction: to enter an imagined world where we are able, for a time, to identify with other humans and to participate vicariously in their lives.

Ⓑ Critical Thinking

Challenging the Text

An opposing viewpoint is that the movie theater audience tends to disappear when the lights go out, allowing the moviegoer to lose all self-awareness while watching a film. This is why, when we have been absorbed by a film, we can be quite jarred when the lights suddenly come back on. Of his childhood experience at the cinema, Jean-Paul Sartre writes, "What an uneasy feeling when the lights went on. In the street I found myself superfluous." Have students discuss whether they agree with Sartre's view or the one expressed in the feature.

Ⓒ Background

Emma Thompson

Emma Thompson is a distinguished British actress who has appeared in Kenneth Branagh's film adaptations of *Henry V* and *Much Ado About Nothing* and in other notable films, such as *The Remains of the Day* and *Howards End,* winning an Academy Award for her acting in the latter. She also received an Academy Award for her screenplay for Jane Austen's *Sense and Sensibility.*

Ⓐ Evaluating Film as Literature

To answer the last question, consider your evaluative criteria. What do you look for in a film? Do you like action, drama, or romance? Your preference for a particular genre, like mysteries or science fiction, might be a good place to begin a self-study, but try to probe deeper. Why are some romantic movies more appealing than others? What makes an action film successful? In other words, focus on the craft of film as well as on the content. Most of us like a good story well told. We respond to characters that draw us into their lives. We enjoy the intensity of a strong scene or the working out of a provocative idea. This absorption in the elements of fiction makes us responsive viewers, sensitive to artistic merit. But we can also look beyond the immediate screen experience to the many hands that shaped the film, to the technical and artistic choices made by scriptwriters, actors, editors, and camera operators. In this way, we also become critical viewers, able to understand the reasons for our response.

This does not mean that moviegoing ought to be an exercise in cataloging camera angles. We need to ask what makes a scene significant for us. We need to explore our own sense of the film, our emotional and intellectual engagement, and we need to take into account other films and other viewers.

Ⓑ Finally, we should consider the experience of watching films as members of an audience. The sense of community that we feel in a theater is quite different from the experience of reading alone. In this respect, our multiplex cinema has much in common with the Anglo-Saxon hall. The next time that you watch those flickering images on the movie screen, think back to the origins of British literature. Remember the Anglo-Saxons gathering together, focusing their collective imagination on a flickering fire while the voices and visions of *Beowulf* emanated from their bard. Today, as then, the stories that come to us through literature connect us to others and to our humanity. Whether we hear them, read them, or watch them on a movie screen, these stories belong to a great tradition that reminds us where we're from, who we are, and what we might become.

GUIDELINES FOR EVALUATING FILMS

General Responses

1. How does the film make you feel? What does it make you think about?
2. Which scenes engage you most or least? Why?
3. What keeps you interested throughout the film?
4. What other films or literary works does the film remind you of?
5. How does the director use the elements of fiction: plot, character development, setting, theme, mood, symbol, point of view, and suspense?

Elements of Film

1. **Acting.** Are the performances believable? Are they overstated? understated?
2. **Camera work.** How does the camera frame events? When does it move, shift angles, or otherwise change our focus of attention?
3. **Lighting and set design.** Consider the location chosen for each scene. Is the set realistic and believable? How was the place made to look as if it belonged to a certain era? How does the lighting or use of color contribute to the atmosphere?
4. **Sound.** What kind of music sets the mood? Are any sound effects especially significant? Does the film use the voice of an unseen narrator to tell part of the story?
5. **Editing.** How are separate shots combined into a continuous sequence? How often does the camera cut, fade, or dissolve to a new view of events?

Ⓒ Hugh Grant and Emma Thompson in Ang Lee's film version of *Sense and Sensibility* (1995).

Assessing Learning

Check Test: True-False

1. Americans spend less time watching movies than they do reading books. [False]
2. The same basic elements are found in both literature and film. [True]
3. Sometimes film adaptations of literary works change the plots of the literary works. [True]
4. Critical viewers are able to understand and express the reasons for their responses to a film. [True]
5. The elements of films are in no way connected to the ancient literary traditions, stretching back to the Anglo-Saxons. [False]

Elizabeth Bowen

(1899–1973)

Elizabeth Bowen.
Photograph by Robin Adler.

Elizabeth Bowen was born in Dublin, Ireland, and spent her early years in Ireland's County Cork, on her family's splendid country estate, Bowen's Court. As Bowen later wrote, her family strove "to live as though living gave them no trouble." An only child, Bowen was looked after by a governess, taken to the Anglican church on Sundays, and taught to dance, wear gloves, and pay attention to manners. On her mother's orders, she was not taught to read until she was seven. When Bowen's father, a lawyer, was confined to a mental hospital, Elizabeth was not allowed to dwell on it. By her twelfth year, her father had recovered, but her mother had contracted fatal cancer. ("Good news," her mother is reported to have remarked, with her characteristic optimism. "Now I'm going to see what Heaven's like.") Elizabeth was not allowed to attend her mother's funeral or to mourn her.

Bowen's fiction clearly bears the stamp of her early years. Much of her writing is concerned with the processes of growing up, of losing innocence, of coming to terms with reality. Her main characters are often wealthy, sensitive, and well-mannered women; yet her novels also reveal a sense of insecurity, a feeling that life cannot be trusted, that existence is a struggle. Dislocation is a major theme, as is the brittleness of romance.

At seventeen, after attending a boarding school in England, Bowen moved to London to write stories. There she attended readings at the Poetry Bookshop, where she made the first of the literary friendships that were to become the fabric of her life. Among these literary friends were Rose Macaulay, Edith Sitwell, Ezra Pound, and Aldous Huxley.

In 1923, Bowen published her first collection of stories, *Encounters,* to little notice. She also married Alan Cameron, a teacher. For most of the next ten years, the couple lived in the university town of Oxford, where Cameron taught and his wife wrote industriously. Her first novel, *The Hotel,* was published in 1927. Thereafter, she produced story collections regularly and wrote nearly a novel a year.

In 1935, the couple moved back to London, where Bowen won acclaim for her novel *The Death of the Heart* (1938) and became a notable hostess of the literary world. During World War II, with its nightly air raids on London, Bowen was a dedicated air-raid warden, but she also went right on giving parties.

Once, while entertaining guests on her balcony, she took no notice of the magnesium flares, but when she had gathered everyone inside, she said, in a typical understatement, "I feel I should apologize for the noise." During the same period, she was writing the stories published in 1945 in *The Demon Lover,* a collection she called a "diary" of her reactions to the war. She described the stories as "flying particles of something enormous and inchoate." *The Heat of the Day* (1949), perhaps Bowen's finest novel, is a classic love story also set in wartime London.

After the war, Bowen and her husband returned to Bowen's Court but had barely begun this new, serene era when Cameron died of a heart attack. Predictably, Bowen became more active than ever. She traveled to Europe, visited her American publishers in New York, and lectured at Princeton, Vassar, Bryn Mawr, and the University of Wisconsin. All the while, she wrote steadily.

Although Bowen had been irrepressibly healthy all her life, a persistent cough proved to be a symptom of lung cancer. She died in 1973 and is buried in an Irish churchyard.

go.hrw.com
LEO 12-13

Objectives

1. Read and interpret the story
2. Identify and analyze flashback
3. Make and modify predictions
4. Express understanding through critical and creative writing
5. Learn and use new words

Skills

Literary
- Identify and analyze flashback

Reading
- Make and modify predictions

Writing
- Take notes on ideas for an informative report
- Compare a ballad with the story
- Describe a character
- Write a film proposal
- Compare texts

Vocabulary
- Learn and use new words

Viewing and Representing
- Relate fine art to the story (ATE)

Planning

- **Block Schedule**
  Block Scheduling Lesson Plans with Pacing Guide
- **Traditional Schedule**
  Lesson Plans Including Strategies for English-Language Learners
- **One-Stop Planner**
  CD-ROM with Test Generator

Browsing in the Files

About the Author. Although Bowen lived outside Ireland for much of her literary career, she maintained her connection with the country and kept her ancestral home in County Cork. She wrote about her early life in Ireland in her autobiography *Seven Winters* and about the history of her family in a work entitled *Bowen's Court,* both published in 1942. However, Ireland seldom figures in her novels; one exception is *The Last September,* which deals with the Irish Civil War of the 1920s.

Resources: Print and Media

Reading
- *Reading Skills and Strategies*
  Miniread Skill Lesson, p. 55
  Selection Skill Lesson, p. 62
- *Graphic Organizers for Active Reading,* p. 100
- *Words to Own,* p. 29
- *Audio CD Library*
  Disc 18, Track 2

Writing and Language
- *Daily Oral Grammar*
  Transparency 35
- *Grammar and Language Links*
  Worksheet, p. 61
- *Language Workshop CD-ROM*

Viewing and Representing
- *Viewing and Representing*
  Fine Art Transparency 16
  Fine Art Worksheet, p. 64

Assessment
- *Formal Assessment,* p. 203
- *Portfolio Management System,* p. 197
- *Test Generator (One-Stop Planner CD-ROM)*

Internet
go.hrw.com (keyword: LE0 12-13)

Summary ■ ■

During World War II, a married woman in her forties returns to her closed-up London house to collect a few belongings. Entering the house, she discovers a recent letter from a soldier she promised to marry twenty-five years earlier, but who was reported lost in action in France during World War I. In the letter, the man reminds the woman that she made a promise to him; he claims he is confident she will keep their appointment. In a flashback to 1916, the woman recalls their loveless affair and the man's intimidating ways. To escape the memory, she rushes from the empty house and enters the only cab at the taxi stand. The taxi pulls away. When the driver turns to face her, she screams, apparently recognizing him as the dreaded former fiancé. She beats on the closed windows as the driver speeds away into the empty streets.

Responding to the Art

Edward Bawden (1903–1989) was an English graphic designer, illustrator, and painter who produced covers, illustrations, posters, ads, and calendars. As an official war artist during World War II, he also painted a number of large-scale murals. *Cat on a Pile of Blankets* displays his typically simple lines and touches of wit.

Activity. Ask students to speculate on the identity of the figure in the mirror and why it appears only as a shadow or silhouette. What associations do the mirror, the shadow, and the cat arouse in students?

Before You Read

The Demon Lover

Make the Connection

Did I Scare You?

Ghost stories can be mesmerizing—even when they're scaring us to death. And part of why we're so drawn to them is that they make us think about which events are real and which are happening only in our imagination, or in the imagination of a character. See how well you can figure out what's real and what's not in this story. Is it a ghost story at all?

Reading Skills and Strategies

Modifying Your Predictions

Think about the title of this story. Then, freewrite for a few minutes, predicting what you think the story will be about. As you read, **modify,** or change, your predictions based on what happens in the story. Note the details that lead you to modify a prediction. You may find yourself changing your predictions several times as you learn more about the characters and the situation.

Elements of Literature

Flashback

A **flashback** is a scene in a narrative or dramatic work that interrupts the present action to tell what happened at an earlier time. "The Demon Lover" uses a **flashback** to provide important background information about the main character, Mrs. Drover. To recognize where the flashback begins, look for the sudden appearance of a verb in the past perfect tense (that is, preceded by the helping verb *had*).

Background

"The Demon Lover" has been compared to the movies of the director Alfred Hitchcock, a master of style, mood, and suspense. An amusing Hitchcock trademark is his appearance as a walk-on character somewhere in each of his films. Generations of moviegoers have delighted in trying to discover Hitchcock's fleeting but very recognizable presence. In a similarly unobtrusive way, Bowen is present in her work for those who recognize her. As you read "The Demon Lover," watch for a few descriptive words or emotional remarks that suddenly remind you of something you read in her biography.

"The Demon Lover" takes place in London in the early 1940s during World War II, when frequent German air raids over the city drove many Londoners to find temporary lodgings in the country. In the story, Mrs. Drover visits her "shut-up house," which is being looked after by a caretaker.

Cat on a Pile of Blankets (1985) by Edward Bawden.
The Fine Art Society, London.

Preteaching Vocabulary

Words to Own

Have students in small groups study the Words to Own. Then have a volunteer in each group start a game of Password and give a clue to the meaning of one of the vocabulary words. The other members try to guess the word, as another clue is added after each wrong guess. The person who correctly identifies the word begins providing clues for another word.

Choose the word that fits in each blank.

1. She smiled her [assent] to the plan.
2. The blackout left us in [utter] darkness.
3. The cat jumped [precipitately], startling me.
4. The aloof star [impassively] greeted her fans.
5. Light is [refracted] in water.
6. Good smells [emanated] from the kitchen.
7. The flashing of the [intermittent] light gave me a headache.
8. School lunches are often [prosaic].
9. I looked through the [aperture] in the wall.
10. The generous man gave without [stint].

The Demon Lover

Elizabeth Bowen

Toward the end of her day in London Mrs. Drover went round to her shut-up house to look for several things she wanted to take away. Some belonged to herself, some to her family, who were by now used to their country life. It was late August; it had been a steamy, showery day: At the moment the trees down the pavement glittered in an escape of humid yellow afternoon sun. Against the next batch of clouds, already piling up ink-dark, broken chimneys and parapets[1] stood out. In her once familiar street, as in any unused channel, an unfamiliar queerness had silted up; a cat wove itself in and out of railings, but no human eye watched Mrs. Drover's return. Shifting some parcels under her arm, she slowly forced round her latchkey in an unwilling lock, then gave the door, which had warped, a push with her knee. Dead air came out to meet her as she went in. **A**

The staircase window having been boarded up, no light came down into the hall. But one door, she could just see, stood ajar, so she went quickly through into the room and unshuttered the big window in there. Now the prosaic woman, looking about her, was more perplexed than she knew by everything that she saw, by traces of her long former habit of life—the yellow smoke stain up the white marble mantelpiece, the ring left by a vase on the top of the escritoire;[2] the bruise in the wallpaper where, on the door being thrown open widely, the china handle had always hit the wall. The piano, having gone away to be stored, had left what looked like claw marks on its part of the parquet.[3] Though not much dust had seeped in, each object wore a film of another kind; and, the only ventilation being the chimney, the whole drawing room smelled of the cold hearth. Mrs. Drover put down her parcels on the escritoire and left the room to proceed upstairs; the things she wanted were in a bedroom chest.

She had been anxious to see how the house was—the part-time caretaker she shared with some neighbors was away this week on his holiday, known to be not yet back. At the best of times he did not look in often, and she was never sure that she trusted him. There were some cracks in the structure, left by the last bombing, on which she was anxious to keep an eye. Not that one could do anything—

A shaft of refracted daylight now lay across the hall. She stopped dead and stared at the hall table—on this lay a letter addressed to her.

She thought first—then the caretaker *must* be back. All the same, who, seeing the house shuttered, would have dropped a letter in at the box? It was not a circular, it was not a bill. And the post office redirected, to the address in the country, everything for her that came through the post. The caretaker (even if he *were* back) did not know she was due in London today—her call here had been planned to be a surprise—so his negligence in the manner of this letter, leaving it to wait in the dusk and the dust, annoyed her. Annoyed, she picked up the letter, which bore no stamp. But it cannot be important, or they would know . . . **B** She took the letter rapidly upstairs with her, without a stop to look at the writing till she reached what had been her bedroom, where she let in light. The room looked over the garden and other gardens: The sun had gone in; as the clouds sharpened and lowered, the trees and rank lawns seemed already to smoke with dark. Her reluctance to look again at the letter came from the fact that she felt intruded upon—and by someone contemptuous of her ways. However, in the tenseness preceding the fall of rain she read it: It was a few lines.

> Dear Kathleen: You will not have forgotten that today is our anniversary, and the day we said. The years have gone by at once slowly and fast. In view of the fact that nothing has changed, I shall rely upon you to keep your promise. I was sorry to see you leave London, but was satisfied **C**

1. **parapets** (par′ə·pets′): low walls around rooftops.
2. **escritoire** (es′kri·twär′): writing table.
3. **parquet** (pär·kā′): wood floor made of boards arranged in geometric patterns.

Words to Own

prosaic (prō·zā′ik) *adj.:* ordinary; dull.

refracted (ri·frakt′id) *v.* used as *adj.:* bent by its passage from one medium to another.

Resources

Viewing and Representing

Videocassette B

Segment 10

Available in English and Spanish

The *Visual Connections* segment "Britain Battles On" explores how the British dealt with World War II.

Viewing and Representing

A fine art transparency of Leo Whelan's *The Kitchen Window* can be used with this lesson as a prereading motivator. See the *Viewing and Representing Transparencies and Worksheets:*

- Transparency 16
- Worksheet, p. 64

A Elements of Literature

Setting/Mood

? Here Bowen describes an eerie, menacing setting. What words and phrases help to define this setting? [Possible responses: "escape," "ink-dark," "unfamiliar queerness," "unwilling lock," "dead air."]

B Reading Skills and Strategies

Making Inferences

? What is mysterious about the arrival of the letter? [It is inside the house; the caretaker is away; it bears no stamp.] How do you think it was delivered? [Possible response: Somehow the "demon lover" got inside the house.]

C Reading Skills and Strategies

Modifying Your Predictions

Have students look at the predictions they made after reading the title of the story. Give them the opportunity to change their predictions at this point and ask them to make new predictions concerning the meaning of the letter.

Reaching All Students

Struggling Readers

To emphasize that the story includes a long flashback to past events, you may want to create an audiotape of the story using two readers with distinctly different voices. One would read the present action of the story and the other, the flashbacks. Alert students to the fact that they will hear two readers when they listen to the tape; afterward, ask them to discuss why the tape was created in this way.

English Language Learners

The descriptions of the setting are important in establishing the atmosphere of the story. To make sure that students appreciate the setting, read the first four paragraphs aloud to them. Then ask how they would feel if they walked into this house. Students who have difficulty expressing their feelings verbally may feel more comfortable drawing a picture of the house, perhaps showing shadowy elements that express their feelings of foreboding.

Advanced Learners

Have students discuss how war can change people. Ask them to draw on books they have read, movies they have seen, or any personal or family experiences with war. As they read the story, ask students to note whether or not any of the points brought up in the discussion apply to the main character, and if so, to what extent.

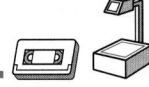

Ⓐ Reading Skills and Strategies
Making Inferences

? **What does the change in Mrs. Drover's coloring suggest about the letter or its writer?** [Possible response: She recognizes the handwriting and is shocked or frightened by it.]

Ⓑ English Language Learners
Understanding Ellipses

Point out that ellipses are used when words are omitted. Explain that sometimes a writer uses them to help indicate a character's state of mind. Read the elliptical sentences aloud for the students. Ask them what they think Mrs. Drover's state of mind is. [Possible responses: She cannot seem to complete a thought. She is nervous, upset, and fearful as she tries to remember something from her past.]

Ⓒ Elements of Literature
Flashback

? **What are the signals that a flashback begins here?** [The girl is young, and the reader can assume that the girl is Mrs. Drover. The space between paragraphs indicates that this is a break from the main action.]

Ⓓ Critical Thinking
Speculating

? **Why does Kathleen feel free when the soldier is gone? Why has she made the "unnatural promise" and why is it a "sinister" betrothal?** [Possible responses: She is free of the man's threatening presence and the intimidation with which he extracted the promise. She has made the promise out of fear, or perhaps because she can't refuse a man about to go off to the front. Perhaps she secretly hopes he will die in battle so that she won't have to fulfill her promise.]

that you would be back in time. You may expect me, therefore, at the hour arranged. Until then . . . K.

Mrs. Drover looked for the date: It was today's. She dropped the letter onto the bedsprings, then picked it up to see the writing again—her lips, beneath the remains of lipstick, beginning to go Ⓐ white. She felt so much the change in her own face that she went to the mirror, polished a clear patch in it, and looked at once urgently and stealthily in. She was confronted by a woman of forty-four, with eyes starting out under a hat brim that had been rather carelessly pulled down. She had not put on any more powder since she left the shop where she ate her solitary tea.[4] The pearls her husband had given her on their marriage hung loose round her now rather thinner throat, slipping in the V of the pink wool jumper her sister knitted last autumn as they sat round the fire. Mrs. Drover's most normal expression was one of controlled worry, but of assent. Since the birth of the third of her little boys, attended by a quite serious illness, she had had an intermittent muscular flicker to the left of her mouth, but in spite of this she could always sustain a manner that was at once energetic and calm.

Turning from her own face as precipitately as she had gone to meet it, she went to the chest where the things were, unlocked it, threw up the lid, and knelt to search. But as rain began to come crashing down she could not keep from looking over her shoulder at the stripped bed on which the letter lay. Behind the blanket of rain the clock of the church that still stood struck six—with rapidly heightening apprehension she counted each of the slow strokes. "The hour arranged . . . Ⓑ My God," she said, "*what* hour? How should I . . . ? After twenty-five years . . . "

Ⓒ The young girl talking to the soldier in the garden had not ever completely seen his face. It was dark; they were saying goodbye under a tree. Now and then—for it felt, from not seeing him at this intense moment, as though she had never seen him at all—she verified his presence for these few moments longer by putting out a hand, which he each time pressed, without very much kindness, and painfully, on to one of the breast buttons of his uniform. That cut of the button on the palm of her hand was, principally, what she was to carry away. This was so near the end of a leave from France that she could only wish him already gone. It was August 1916. Being not kissed, being drawn away from and looked at intimidated Kathleen till she imagined spectral glitters in the place of his eyes. Turning away and looking back up the lawn she saw, through branches of trees, the drawing-room window alight: She caught a breath for the moment when she could go running back there into the safe arms of her mother and sister, and cry: "What shall I do, what shall I do? He has gone."

Hearing her catch her breath, her fiancé said, without feeling: "Cold?"

"You're going away such a long way."

"Not so far as you think."

"I don't understand?"

"You don't have to," he said. "You will. You know what we said."

"But that was—suppose you—I mean, suppose."

"I shall be with you," he said, "sooner or later. You won't forget that. You need do nothing but wait."

Only a little more than a minute later she was free to run up the silent lawn. Looking in through the window at her mother and sister, who did not for the moment perceive her, she already felt that Ⓓ unnatural promise drive down between her and the rest of all humankind. No other way of having given herself could have made her feel so apart, lost and forsworn.[5] She could not have plighted a more sinister troth.[6]

Kathleen behaved well when, some months later, her fiancé was reported missing, presumed killed. Her family not only supported her but were able to praise her courage without stint because

4. **tea:** in Britain, a light, late-afternoon meal, served with tea.

5. **forsworn** (fôr·swôrn'): having lied under oath; perjured.

6. **plighted . . . troth:** made a more sinister promise of marriage.

WORDS TO OWN

assent (ə·sent') *n.:* acceptance.
intermittent (in'tər·mit''nt) *adj.:* starting and stopping at intervals; periodic.
precipitately (pri·sip'ə·tit'lē) *adv.:* suddenly.
stint *n.:* limitation.

Crossing the Curriculum

History

Inform students that World War I, known as the "Great War," generated casualties greater than in any previous war. Mrs. Drover's fiancé went to France in August 1916, to fight the Germans. Ask students to research information about the fighting in France in that year, including the number of casualties suffered, and have them give a brief oral report on their findings to the class.

Psychology

The Germans relentlessly bombed London from September 6 through October 12, 1940. During this time, 12,696 London civilians were killed by bombs. In September alone, the Germans dropped more than ten thousand bombs on the city. These attacks resulted in psychological trauma as well as physical damage. Have students research the psychological effects of the bombing on London citizens at the time.

they could not regret, as a husband for her, the man they knew almost nothing about. They hoped she would, in a year or two, console herself—and had it been only a question of consolation things might have gone much straighter ahead. But her trouble, behind just a little grief, was a complete dislocation from everything. She did not reject other lovers, for these failed to appear: For years she failed to attract men—and with the approach of her thirties she became natural enough to share her family's anxiousness on this score. She began to put herself out,[7] to wonder; and at thirty-two she was very greatly relieved to find herself being courted by William Drover. She married him, and the two of them settled down in this quiet, arboreal[8] part of Kensington: In this house the years piled up, her children were born, and they all lived till they were driven out by the bombs of the next war. Her movements as Mrs. Drover were circumscribed, and she dismissed any idea that they were still watched.

As things were—dead or living the letter writer sent her only a threat. Unable, for some minutes, to go on kneeling with her back exposed to the empty room, Mrs. Drover rose from the chest to sit on an upright chair whose back was firmly against the wall. The desuetude[9] of her former bedroom, her married London home's whole air of being a cracked cup from which memory, with its reassuring power, had either evaporated or leaked away, made a crisis—and at just this crisis the letter writer had, knowledgeably, struck. The hollowness of the house this evening canceled years on years of voices, habits, and steps. Through the shut windows she only heard rain fall on the roofs around. To rally herself, she said she was in a mood—and for two or three seconds shutting her eyes, told herself that she had imagined the letter. But she opened them—there it lay on the bed.

On the supernatural side of the letter's entrance she was not permitting her mind to dwell. Who, in London, knew she meant to call at the house today? Evidently, however, this had been known. The caretaker, *had* he come back, had had no cause to expect her: He would have taken the letter in his pocket, to forward it, at his own time, through the post. There was no other sign that the caretaker had been in—but, if not? Letters dropped in at doors of deserted houses do not fly or walk to tables in halls. They do not sit on the dust of empty tables with the air of certainty that they will be found. There is needed some human hand—but nobody but the caretaker had a key. Under circumstances she did not care to consider, a house can be entered without a key. It was possible that she was not alone now. She might be being waited for, downstairs. Waited for—until when? Until "the hour arranged." At least that was not six o'clock: Six has struck.

She rose from the chair and went over and locked the door.

The thing was, to get out. To fly? No, not that: She had to catch her train. As a woman whose utter dependability was the keystone of her family life she was not willing to return to the country, to her husband, her little boys, and her sister, without the objects she had come up to fetch. Resuming work at the chest she set about making up a number of parcels in a rapid, fumbling-decisive way. These, with her shopping parcels, would be too much to carry; these meant a taxi—at the thought of the taxi her heart went up and her normal breathing resumed. I will ring up the taxi now; the taxi cannot come too soon: I shall hear the taxi out there running its engine, till I walk calmly down to it through the hall. I'll ring up—But no: the telephone is cut off . . . She tugged at a knot she had tied wrong.

The idea of flight . . . He was never kind to me, not really. I don't remember him kind at all. Mother said he never considered me. He was set on me, that was what it was—not love. Not love, not meaning a person well. What did he do, to make me promise like that? I can't remember—But she found that she could.

She remembered with such dreadful acuteness that the twenty-five years since then dissolved like smoke and she instinctively looked for the weal[10] left by the button on the palm of her hand. She

7. **put herself out:** vex or distress herself.
8. **arboreal** (är·bôr′ē·əl): full of trees.
9. **desuetude** (des′wi·to͞od′): disuse.

10. **weal** (wēl): lump; welt.

WORDS TO OWN
utter *adj.:* total.

E Critical Thinking
Interpreting

? Why do you think Kathleen is not able to attract men? [Possible responses: She is "prosaic," that is, rather dull. She appears unapproachable because of her mixed feelings about the man she promised to marry. Because of her "unnatural promise," she feels a "complete dislocation from everything"; thus there is a wall "between her and the rest of all humankind."]

F Elements of Literature
Flashback

? Some flashbacks end abruptly, while others flow right back into the present. How does this flashback end? What signal returns the story to the present? [The events in Mrs. Drover's life are summarized up to the present, after which the story just continues in the present. The words "As things were" signal a return to the present.]

G Reading Skills and Strategies
Modifying Your Predictions

Once again, provide students with an opportunity to modify their predictions. Also, ask them to make a new prediction, indicating what they think will happen to Mrs. Drover. Will her former fiancé come to get her? Will the letter turn out to be a joke? Will the whole incident prove to be a figment of her imagination? Or, will the story be resolved in some other manner? [Predictions will vary but should be based on details given in the story.]

H Reading Skills and Strategies
Connecting with the Text

? What would you do if you were in Mrs. Drover's position at this point in the story? [Possible responses: Run. Get out of the house immediately. Find a telephone. Find someone to help.]

Taking a Second Look

Review: Drawing Inferences from Textual Evidence

Remind students that an **inference** is an educated guess based on information in the text and on the reader's prior knowledge and experience. Encourage them to back up their inferences with specific details from the text. Remind them to do the following when making inferences about a character: Pay attention to the character's speech, appearance, thoughts, actions, and what others say and think about the character.

Activities

1. As they read, have students list clues to Mrs. Drover's character suggested by her appearance, thoughts, and actions. Next to each clue, have them indicate what they infer about Mrs. Drover from the clue.
2. Have students form groups to discuss their inferences and consider how Mrs. Drover's character contributes to her dilemma.

RESPONDING TO THE ART

Vilhelm Hammershoi (1864–1916) was a Danish painter whose works allow the viewer to enter into quiet interiors and escape into timeless moments. Gray tones and a few strong accents provide the atmospheric ingredients of his mystical scenes. In *Rainy Weather,* a woman gazes out the window of a sparsely furnished, tidy dining room. She is seen from the back and no indication of her emotions is given; instead, the room itself, and the weather, establish the mood.
Activity. Ask students for their initial reactions to the atmosphere of the painting. To what extent are their reactions affected by Bowen's story? [Possible responses: The atmosphere appears dismal, menacing, and forlorn. The story has a decided effect because we apply Mrs. Drover's anxiety to the woman in the picture. To some the painting will suggest peace.]

A Reading Skills and Strategies
Drawing Conclusions

? Why can't Mrs. Drover remember her former fiancé's face? [Possible responses: The thought of him is so distressing that she has blocked it from her mind. Time has dulled her memory.]

B Critical Thinking
Speculating

? Who might be leaving the house? [Possible responses: The caretaker who has been there all along; the ghost of Mrs. Drover's presumed-dead fiancé or the man himself, who is still alive; nobody—it is just her imagination playing tricks on her.]

Rainy Weather (late 19th or early 20th century) by Vilhelm Hammershoi.

remembered not only all that he said and did but the complete suspension of *her* existence during that August week. I was not myself—they all told me so at the time. She remembered—but with one white burning blank as where acid has dropped on a photograph: *Under no conditions* could she remember his face.

So, wherever he may be waiting, I shall not know him. You have no time to run from a face you do not expect.

The thing was to get to the taxi before any clock struck what could be the hour. She would slip down the street and round the side of the square to where the square gave on the main road. She would return in the taxi, safe, to her own door, and bring the solid driver into the house with her to pick up the parcels from room to room. The idea of the taxi driver made her decisive, bold: She unlocked her door, went to the top of the staircase, and listened down.

She heard nothing—but while she was hearing nothing the *passé*[11] air of the staircase was disturbed by a draft that traveled up to her face. It emanated from the basement: Down there a door or window was being opened by someone who chose this moment to leave the house.

The rain had stopped; the pavements steamily shone as Mrs. Drover let herself out by inches

11. **passé** (pä·sā′): no longer fresh; rather old.

WORDS TO OWN
emanated (em′ə·nāt′id) *v.:* flowed; came forth.

Assessing Learning

Check Test: True-False
1. Mrs. Drover is returning to her London home to retrieve a few items. [True]
2. The empty, closed-up house unsettles Mrs. Drover. [True]
3. A letter from a former fiancé makes Mrs. Drover fearful. [True]
4. She had loved the letter writer passionately when they were young. [False]
5. A friendly, cheerful taxi driver eases Mrs. Drover's feelings of panic. [False]

Informal Assessment
Self-Assessment. Ask students to reflect on how they read the story and answer the following questions:
1. Did you try to anticipate how the story would end?
2. Did you ask "why" after each event to try to understand the characters' motivations?
3. Did you take note of specific descriptions to determine the atmosphere of the story?

from her own front door into the empty street. The unoccupied houses opposite continued to meet her look with their damaged stare. Making toward the thoroughfare and the taxi, she tried not to keep looking behind. Indeed, the silence was so intense—one of those creeks of London silence exaggerated this summer by the damage of war—that no tread could have gained on hers unheard. Where her street debouched[12] on the square where people went on living, she grew conscious of, and checked, her unnatural pace. Across the open end of the square two buses impassively passed each other: Women, a perambulator,[13] cyclists, a man wheeling a barrow signalized, once again, the ordinary flow of life. At the square's most populous corner should be—and was—the short taxi rank. This evening, only one taxi—but this, although it presented its blank rump, appeared already to be alertly waiting for her. Indeed, without looking round the driver started his engine as she panted up from behind and put her hand on the door. As she did so, the clock struck seven. The taxi faced the main road: To make the trip back to her house it would have to turn—she had settled back on the seat and the taxi *had* turned before she, surprised by its knowing movement, recollected that she had not "said where." She leaned forward to scratch at the glass panel that divided the driver's head from her own.

The driver braked to what was almost a stop, turned round, and slid the glass panel back: The jolt of this flung Mrs. Drover forward till her face was almost into the glass. Through the aperture driver and passenger, not six inches between them, remained for an eternity eye to eye. Mrs. Drover's mouth hung open for some seconds before she could issue her first scream. After that she continued to scream freely and to beat with her gloved hands on the glass all round as the taxi, accelerating without mercy, made off with her into the hinterland of deserted streets.

12. **debouched** (dē·bo͞oshd′): came out; emerged.
13. **perambulator** (pər·am′byo͞o·lāt′ər): chiefly British for "baby carriage." The word is often shortened to *pram.*

Words to Own
impassively (im·pas′iv·lē) *adv.:* calmly; indifferently.
aperture (ap′ər·chər) *n.:* opening.

Making Meanings

First Thoughts

1. Did you feel emotionally involved in Mrs. Drover's story? Why or why not?

Reading Check

Using the following schema, create a story map for "The Demon Lover."

Basic situation
Conflict
Characters
Event
Event
Event, etc.
Climax
Resolution

Shaping Interpretations

2. In some stories, descriptions of the **setting** provide much more than the physical background—they also create a particular **mood.** List the **images** in the story's first paragraph that help create a strong mood of foreboding.
3. Why has the Drover family left their London home? Cite two places in the text that make the reason clear. For what purpose has Mrs. Drover returned?
4. What details in the lovers' last meeting **foreshadow** a sinister, threatening reunion? What does Mrs. Drover tell us about her fiancé that explains why she is terrified of him?
5. The use of an **omniscient narrator** allows Bowen to give readers information about Mrs. Drover's psychological makeup that Mrs. Drover herself is not consciously aware of. Identify several such passages in the text.
6. **Dramatic irony** occurs when the audience is aware of something that a character does not know. What is the central dramatic irony of the story?
7. Contributing to the story's richness and depth is the interplay between present and past. Think about the **flashback** that tells what happened earlier in Mrs. Drover's life. Do you think the abrupt shift into the past is effective or merely confusing? Why?

Making Meanings

First Thoughts [Respond]

1. Most students will probably feel emotionally involved because of the story's suspense. Others may not feel involved because the story does not seem realistic to them or they cannot relate to Mrs. Drover.

Shaping Interpretations [Interpret]

2. Possible responses: The shut-up house, the "steamy, showery day," the "humid yellow . . . sun," the clouds that pile up "ink-dark," "broken chimneys," the "unwilling lock," the warped door, and the dead air inside the house.
3. Wartime bombings caused the Drovers to leave their home. Mrs. Drover finds "cracks . . . left by the last bombing" (p. 1019), and notes "the damage of war" later in the story (p. 1023). Mrs. Drover has returned to collect some things the family needs.
4. Possible responses: The lover hurts Kathleen's hand; she imagines "spectral glitters" in place of his eyes (p. 1020); he says ambivalently, "I shall be with you sooner or later" (p. 1020). Mrs. Drover reflects, "He was never kind to me . . . . He was set on me, that was what it was—not love. Not love, not meaning a person well" (p. 1021).
5. Possible responses: references to Mrs. Drover as a "prosaic woman" (p. 1019), the comment on her "intermittent muscular flicker" (p. 1020), and the descriptions of her reactions to her fiancé.
6. The reader suspects that the taxi driver is the demon lover; Mrs. Drover does not. Even though she is unnerved by the letter and is afraid her lover may return, she feels safe in the taxi until the driver turns around.
7. Possible responses: The abrupt shift to Mrs. Drover's past is effective, given her disorientation and anxious frame of mind. The abrupt shift is confusing because the reader doesn't see the connection between Mrs. Drover and the young girl until well into the flashback.

(Answers continue on p. T1024.)

Reading Check

Below are samples for a story map.

Basic situation: [Mrs. Drover has returned to her closed-up London house during World War II to retrieve some items.]

Conflict: [She fears harm from her former fiancé, or worse, from his ghost.]

Characters: [Mrs. Drover and her former fiancé]

Event: [Mrs. Drover finds a letter from her former fiancé, an intimidating man who supposedly died during World War I. The letter indicates that he is holding her to her promise of marriage and will arrive for their appointment.]

Event: [Mrs. Drover recalls their loveless affair and the man's cruelty and coldness.]

Climax: [Afraid, she hurries from the house and escapes into a waiting taxi cab.]

Resolution: [When the driver turns to face her, she recognizes him as her former fiancé. She screams and beats on the windows as the taxi takes off into the deserted streets.]

(Continued from p. T1023)

8. Possible response: During the disruption of wartime, people experience "complete dislocation from everything," even love.
9. Responses will vary, but students should be able to support their interpretation with evidence from the text. The hallucination theory, which must cover the letter as well as the taxi, is supported by the atmosphere of the house, with its "dead air" and memories, and by the fact that Mrs. Drover is completely alone. The ghost story, while it, too, draws on the atmosphere of the house, is supported by the mysterious appearance of the letter and Mrs. Drover's reactions in the final scene.

Grading Timesaver

Rubrics for each Choices assignment appear on p. 197 in the *Portfolio Management System.*

CHOICES: Building Your Portfolio

1. **Writer's Notebook** You may wish to brainstorm a list of topics with the class.
2. **Comparing Texts** Students may have some difficulty deciding how much similarity must exist between the story and the ballad in order for them to say that the story is based on the ballad. You may want to lead a discussion on this point before students begin the assignment.

(Notes continue on p. T1025.)

8. The two world wars bracket this story like bookends. During each war, Mrs. Drover experiences dislocation and confusion. During each war, the demon lover is part of her life. Yet he doesn't appear during the intervening twenty-five years. Use these strands of the story (war, Mrs. Drover's inner turmoil, and the lover's appearances) in a statement of the story's **theme.**

Challenging the Text

9. One possible interpretation of the story is that Mrs. Drover's experience is a hallucination: Her powers of imagination have combined with the pressures of wartime life to transform everyday reality into a waking nightmare. Another way of looking at the story is to consider it an out-and-out ghost story. Which interpretation do you favor, or do you have another? Support your interpretation with evidence from the text.

CHOICES: Building Your Portfolio

Writer's Notebook

1. Collecting Ideas for an Informative Report

The setting of Bowen's story is critical to the plot: It is wartime London, when German bombing raids were terrifying the populace, destroying neighborhoods and landmarks with an unnerving randomness. Reread the opening of the story, and review Bowen's biography. Jot down some topics about wartime London that you might be interested in researching. The air raids and their psychological effects might be one topic. Another might be the deportation of children from London (some came to the United States). Save your notes for the Writer's Workshop on page 1053.

Comparing Texts

2. The Same Old Song?

"The Demon Lover" is also one title of the following famous ballad. In an essay, compare the ballad to Bowen's story. Before you write, gather the material for your comparison by filling out a chart like the one below. (Consider also the prediction you made in your reading notes based on the story's title.)

Elements	Bowen Story	Ballad
Characters		
Plot		
Mood		
Theme		

Conclude your essay by indicating whether or not you believe the story is based in any way on the old song.

The Demon Lover

"O where have you been, my long, long love,
This long seven years and mair?"
"O I'm come to seek my former vows
Ye granted me before."

"O hold your tongue of your former vows,
For they will breed sad strife;
O hold your tongue of your former vows,
For I am become a wife."

He turned him right and round about,
And the tear blinded his ee:
"I wad never hae trodden on Irish ground,
If it had not been for thee.

I might have had a king's daughter,
Far, far beyond the sea;
I might have had a king's daughter,
Had it not been for love o thee."

"If ye might have had a king's daughter,
Yer sel ye had to blame;
Ye might have taken the king's daughter,
For ye kend that I was nane.

Using Students' Strengths

Auditory Learners

In Choice 2, some students may better understand the ballad "The Demon Lover" if they hear it read aloud as they follow the text. You can ask one or two students to prepare a reading of the poem ahead of time and have them present it in class. You may want to tape-record the reading so that students can play it back as often as they need.

Visual Learners

Instead of writing, drawing, or painting a likeness of the demon lover for Choice 3, some students may prefer to find a picture of a person that looks the way they imagine the character. Students may cut pictures from old magazines and newspapers and display them in class. Ask students to write a brief explanation for their choice, and have the class decide which picture they consider the best representation of the demon lover.

"If I was to leave my husband dear,
And my two babes also,
O what have you to take me to,
If with you I should go?"

"I hae seven ships upon the sea—
The eighth brought me to land—
With four-and-twenty bold mariners,
And music on every hand."

She has taken up her two little babes,
Kissed them baith cheek and chin:
"O fair ye weel, my ain two babes,
For I'll never see you again."

She set her foot upon the ship,
No mariners could she behold;
But the sails were o the taffetie,
And the masts o the beaten gold.

She had not sailed a league, a league,
A league but barely three,
When dismal grew his countenance,
And drumlie grew his ee.

They had not sailed a league, a league,
A league but barely three,
Until she espied his cloven foot,
And she wept right bitterlie.

"O hold your tongue of your weeping," says he,
"Of your weeping now let me be;
I will shew you how lilies grow
On the banks of Italy."

"O what hills are yon, yon pleasant hills,
That the sun shines sweetly on?"
"O yon are the hills of heaven," he said,
"Where you will never win."

"O whaten mountain is yon?" she said,
"All so dreary wi frost and snow?"
"O yon is the mountain of hell," he cried,
"Where you and I will go."

He strack the tap-mast wi his hand,
The foremast wi his knee,
And he brake that gallant ship in twain,
And sank her in the sea.

Creative Writing

3. No Prince Charming

At no time in the story are we given a description of the demon lover's face. At the end of the story, however, when Mrs. Drover is finally within six inches of his face, she begins to scream. Describe what you imagine Mrs. Drover sees. You might also do a drawing or painting of him.

Film

4. The Silver Screen

Suppose that you are the producer-director of a movie version of "The Demon Lover." You have to consider these tasks:

a. Casting both the younger and the older Mrs. Drover, her lover, and the minor characters of the family

b. Creating scenery, lighting, and background music to establish atmosphere

c. Creating suspense by such means as the chiming of the clock

d. Telling your screenwriters how you would expand parts of the story for a feature-length film

Write a proposal outlining your ideas on how you would convert the story into a film. Will you film the story as a horror tale or as a psychological study of love? (You may wish to consult the essay "Film as Literature," on page 1012.)

Comparing Texts

5. Lovers—Romantic and Demonic

In an essay, compare Bowen's story with these other accounts of encounters with a romantic or demonic lover: Keats's "La Belle Dame sans Merci" (page 751) and Yeats's "The Song of Wandering Aengus" (page 981). In your essay, consider **plot, characters, theme,** and **mood.**

(Continued from p. T1024)

3. Creative Writing You may want to remind students that the fiancé was listed as missing in action, so there is a good chance that he was wounded, possibly in the face. On the other hand, if he is a ghost, his appearance may be changed in other significant ways. Encourage students to let their imaginations loose as they describe the demon lover.

4. Film This assignment has several parts, and you may want to divide it and let small groups work on separate parts. Another way to handle the assignment is to let a group of four be responsible for a proposal, with each member of the group handling one of the key points. In either case, students should probably spend some time discussing the general direction the proposal will take before they begin working independently.

5. Comparing Texts Students may find it useful to create a chart in which to list the comparisons.

Element	Demon Lover	Belle Dame	Aengus
plot			
characters			
theme			
mood			

Objectives

1. Read and interpret the story
2. Monitor reading
3. Generate relevant and interesting questions
4. Compare text events with students' own experience and that of others
5. Recognize and discuss themes that cross cultures

Planning

- **Block Schedule**
  Block Scheduling Lesson Plans with Pacing Guide
- **Traditional Schedule**
  Lesson Plans Including Strategies for English-Language Learners
- **One-Stop Planner**
  CD-ROM with *Test Generator*

Browsing in the Files

About the Author. Cortázar has been compared to the great Argentine writer Jorge Luis Borges, especially because both writers tend to write about metaphysical themes such as life, death, the nature of reality, and the power of the imagination. Cortázar was employed as a translator for UNESCO after moving to Paris in 1951. He wrote a number of novels, several collections of short stories, and a book of poetry that was published posthumously.

Resources

Listening

Audio CD Library

A dramatic reading of this selection is available in the *Audio CD Library:*

- Disc 18, Track 3

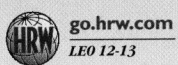

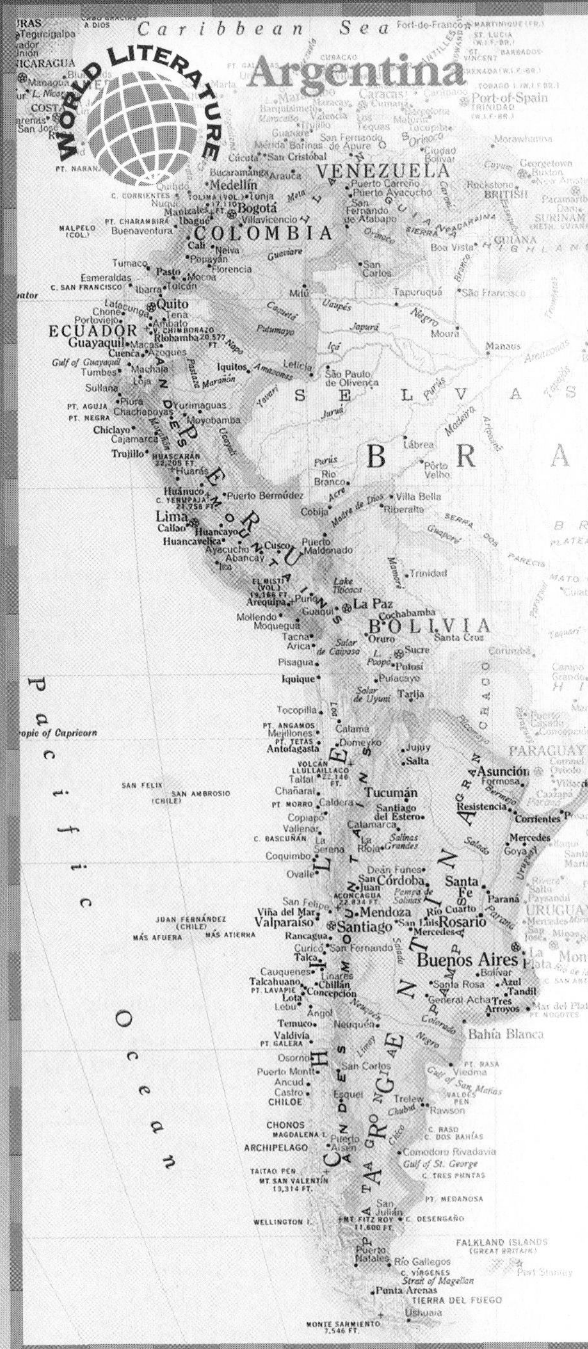

Julio Cortázar.

Julio Cortázar

(1914–1984)

Julio Cortázar (kho͞ol′yō kôr·tä′sär) believed that fantasy and reality, the rational and the irrational, exist on intersecting planes. In part, this philosophy surely stemmed from the fact that Cortázar himself had a foot in two very different worlds—Latin America and Europe. He was born in Brussels to Argentine parents, but his family returned to Argentina when he was five years old. After attending the University of Buenos Aires, he first taught high school and then taught French literature at a university. In 1946, he was briefly jailed for his opposition to Juan Perón's military dictatorship of Argentina and was forced to give up his academic career. At about this time, his first short story, "House Taken Over," was published, the first in a long and prolific career. Cortázar worked for a short time as a literary translator in Buenos Aires (fittingly, he translated the stories of Edgar Allan Poe into Spanish) before he moved to Paris to work as a translator for the United Nations. He continued in this post until his death in 1984.

Cortázar's works are always playful and experimental. In 1963, his masterpiece, *Rayuela* (translated into English as *Hopscotch*), was published to great acclaim. Named for a child's game, this dizzying and demanding novel includes instructions for the different ways it can be read. Although Cortázar traveled widely and was granted French citizenship in 1981, he always thought of himself as Argentine.

(Map) ©Rand McNally R. L. #98-S-116.

go.hrw.com
LEO 12-13

Before You Read

AXOLOTL

Background

Fantastical occurrences are often the stuff of sleep. Surreal images and irrational happenings flood our dreams, yet during the day, our lives seem ordered, routine, rational. What happens when these two worlds overlap or intersect—when we can't distinguish between them?

In "Axolotl," as in all literature of the fantastic, the impossible and the possible, fantasy and reality are set in opposition. The author often introduces some surrealistic element or extraordinary event into an otherwise entirely realistic environment, and the two become so intertwined that neither character nor reader can separate them.

In Julio Cortázar's fantastical short stories—among the best of the genre—daily life is often mysteriously subverted by unknown forces. This "invasion by the imaginary," as Cortázar called it, creates a tension that both exhilarates and disturbs.

The creatures shown on pages 1029 and 1030 are not from a sci-fi movie. They are real axolotls.

Reading Skills and Strategies

Monitoring Your Reading

As you read the story, keep track of when you yourself are unsure about what is *really* happening.

Axolotl

Julio Cortázar

translated by **Paul Blackburn**

There was a time when I thought a great deal about the axolotls. I went to see them in the aquarium at the Jardin des Plantes[1] and stayed for hours watching them, observing their immobility, their faint movements. Now I am an axolotl.

I got to them by chance one spring morning when Paris was spreading its peacock tail after a wintry Lent. I was heading down the boulevard Port-Royal, then I took Saint-Marcel and L'Hôpital and saw green among all that gray and remembered the lions. I was friend of the lions and panthers, but had never gone into the dark, humid building that was the aquarium. I left my bike against the gratings and went to look at the tulips. The lions were sad and ugly and my panther was asleep. I decided on the aquarium, looked obliquely at banal fish until, unexpectedly, I hit it off with the axolotls. I stayed watching them for an hour and left, unable to think of anything else.

In the library at Sainte-Geneviève, I consulted a dictionary and learned that axolotls are the larval stage (provided with gills) of a species of salamander of the genus *Ambystoma.* That they were Mexican I knew already by looking at them and their little pink Aztec faces and the placard at the top of the tank. I read that specimens of them had been found in Africa capable of living on dry land during the periods of drought, and continuing their life under water when the rainy season came. I found their Spanish name, *ajolote,* and the mention that they were edible, and that their oil was used (no longer used, it said) like cod-liver oil.

I didn't care to look up any of the specialized works, but the next day I went back to the Jardin des Plantes. I began to go every morning, morning and afternoon some days. The aquarium

1. **Jardin des Plantes** (zhär·dan′ dä plänt): Paris botanical garden, part of the French National Museum of Natural History. The name literally means "garden of plants" in French.

Summary ■■■

The narrator first recounts his obsession with visiting a public aquarium to watch a group of axolotls—larval salamanders—and then relates his eventual metamorphosis into one of these animals. The story ends as the axolotl wonders whether the man looking into the tank will write a story about axolotls.

Background

"Magic realism" is a term that is sometimes applied to the kind of writing that Cortázar produced. This term was coined in 1949 by the Cuban novelist Alejo Carpentier to denote writing that blurs the lines between the real and the fantastic. Carpentier was deeply influenced by French Surrealism, which tried to suppress the conscious mind and let the deeper reality of the subconscious emerge.

A Reading Skills and Strategies

Monitoring Your Reading

Students may be confused when they come to the final sentence of the first paragraph. Ask them what they think the narrator means when he says, "Now I am an axolotl." [Possible responses: Like the axolotls, he is quiet and doesn't move much. Or, he actually changed into a salamander.]

B English Language Learners

Interpreting Idioms

Explain to students that the idiom "hit it off" means "got along well together." Encourage them to keep a list of other idioms in the story that they find confusing. You can explain each idiom or have other students do so.

Reaching All Students

Struggling Readers

The long paragraphs and complex content may prove difficult for students. One helpful approach is to have students break the story down by paragraphs and write a brief summary of each paragraph on a chart, such as the following:

Paragraph	Summary	Paragraph	Summary
1		7	
2		8	
3		9	
4		10	
5		11	
6			

Advanced Learners

Invite interested students to read all or part of Ovid's *Metamorphoses* or Kafka's *The Metamorphosis* and discuss how what they have read relates to Cortázar's story.

A Elements of Literature

Point of View

? Point of view is the vantage point from which a writer tells a story. From what point of view is this story told? [first person] Knowing this, how reliable is the narrator's comment that there is nothing strange in his daily visits to the axolotls? [Possible response: The narrator may believe his assessments are perfectly reliable, but they may in fact be unreliable; there are other clues that his behavior is strange, such as the perplexed smile the guard gives him when he enters the aquarium.]

B Reading Skills and Strategies

Drawing Conclusions

? If you refer to the last sentence of the first paragraph and read the parenthetical statement here, what might you conclude has happened to the narrator? [Possible responses: The narrator identifies with the axolotl. The narrator has gone mad and thinks he is an axolotl. The narrator has become an axolotl.]

C Critical Thinking

Interpreting

? The narrator anthropomorphizes the axolotls when he credits them with a "secret will." Who might really have the secret will to abolish space and time? [Possible responses: the narrator himself; people in contemporary society.]

D Cultural Connections

Surrealism

Surrealism was a twentieth-century intellectual and artistic movement founded by André Breton. It grew out of the post-World War I movement known as Dada. Dada followers, including Breton, used absurdity to attack what they viewed as the false values of a so-called rational society. Here Cortázar attacks the tenets of evolution by making the absurd assumption that the less an animal resembles humans, the closer it is to humans on the evolutionary scale.

guard smiled perplexedly taking my ticket. I would lean up against the iron bar in front of the tanks and set to watching them. There's nothing strange in this, because after the first minute I knew that we were linked, that something infinitely lost and distant kept pulling us together. It had been enough to detain me that first morning in front of the sheet of glass where some bubbles rose through the water. The axolotls huddled on the wretched narrow (only I can know how narrow and wretched) floor of moss and stone in the tank. There were nine specimens, and the majority pressed their heads against the glass, looking with their eyes of gold at whoever came near them. Disconcerted, almost ashamed, I felt it a lewdness to be peering at these silent and immobile figures heaped at the bottom of the tank. Mentally I isolated one, situated on the right and somewhat apart from the others, to study it better. I saw a rosy little body, translucent (I thought of those Chinese figurines of milky glass), looking like a small lizard about six inches long, ending in a fish's tail of extraordinary delicacy, the most sensitive part of our body. Along the back ran a transparent fin which joined with the tail, but what obsessed me was the feet, of the slenderest nicety, ending in tiny fingers with minutely human nails. And then I discovered its eyes, its face. Inexpressive features, with no other trait save the eyes, two orifices, like brooches, wholly of transparent gold, lacking any life but looking, letting themselves be penetrated by my look, which seemed to travel past the golden level and lose itself in a diaphanous[2] interior mystery. A very slender black halo ringed the eye and etched it onto the pink flesh, onto the rosy stone of the head, vaguely triangular, but with curved and irregular sides which gave it a total likeness to a statuette corroded by time. The mouth was masked by the triangular plane of the face, its considerable size would be guessed only in profile; in front a delicate crevice barely slit the lifeless stone. On both sides of the head where the ears should have been, there grew three tiny sprigs red as coral, a vegetal outgrowth, the gills, I suppose. And they were the only thing quick about it; every ten or fifteen seconds the sprigs pricked up stiffly and again subsided. Once in a while a foot would barely move, I saw the diminutive toes poise mildly on the moss. It's that we don't enjoy moving a lot, and the tank is so cramped—we barely move in any direction and we're hitting one of the others with our tail or our head—difficulties arise, fights, tiredness. The time feels like it's less if we stay quietly.

It was their quietness that made me lean toward them fascinated the first time I saw the axolotls. Obscurely I seemed to understand their secret will, to abolish space and time with an indifferent immobility. I knew better later; the gill contraction, the tentative reckoning of the delicate feet on the stones, the abrupt swimming (some of them swim with a simple undulation[3] of the body) proved to me that they were capable of escaping that mineral lethargy in which they spent whole hours. Above all else, their eyes obsessed me. In the standing tanks on either side of them, different fishes showed me the simple stupidity of their handsome eyes so similar to our own. The eyes of the axolotls spoke to me of the presence of a different life, of another way of seeing. Glueing my face to the glass (the guard would cough fussily once in a while), I tried to see better those diminutive golden points, that entrance to the infinitely slow and remote world of these rosy creatures. It was useless to tap with one finger on the glass directly in front of their faces; they never gave the least reaction. The golden eyes continued burning with their soft, terrible light; they continued looking at me from an unfathomable depth which made me dizzy.

And nevertheless they were close. I knew it before this, before being an axolotl. I learned it the day I came near them for the first time. The anthropomorphic[4] features of a monkey reveal the reverse of what most people believe, the distance that is traveled from them to us. The absolute lack of similarity between axolotls and human beings proved to me that my recognition was valid, that I was not propping myself up with easy analogies. Only the little hands . . . But an eft,[5] the common newt, has such hands also, and

2. **diaphanous:** transparent.

3. **undulation:** wavelike movement.

4. **anthropomorphic:** having human shape or characteristics; humanlike.

5. **eft:** archaic for "newt," kind of amphibious salamander.

Using Students' Strengths

Spatial Learners

Have students draw illustrations or create a collage for this story. Encourage them to depict the transformation of the man into an axolotl. Does it happen gradually or suddenly? Perhaps it doesn't happen at all; he just imagines it. Ask them how they will resolve this issue before they draw.

Naturalist Learners

Ask students to imagine that they have turned into an axolotl. Have them write a journal entry in which they answer the following questions: Where do you live? What do you eat? Who are your natural enemies? Do you prefer to live in groups or are you a loner? What is your relationship with humans? Encourage students to use the story and do additional research to flesh out their entries.

we are not at all alike. I think it was the axolotls' heads, that triangular pink shape with the tiny eyes of gold. That looked and knew. That laid the claim. They were not *animals*.

It would seem easy, almost obvious, to fall into mythology. I began seeing in the axolotls a metamorphosis which did not succeed in revoking a mysterious humanity. I imagined them aware, slaves of their bodies, condemned infinitely to the silence of the abyss, to a hopeless meditation. Their blind gaze, the diminutive gold disc without expression and nonetheless terribly shining, went through me like a message: "Save us, save us." I caught myself mumbling words of advice, conveying childish hopes. They continued to look at me, immobile; from time to time the rosy branches of the gills stiffened. In that instant I felt a muted pain; perhaps they were seeing me, attracting my strength to penetrate into the impenetrable thing of their lives. They were not human beings, but I had found in no animal such a profound relation with myself. The axolotls were like witnesses of something, and at times like horrible judges. I felt ignoble in front of them; there was such a terrifying purity in those transparent eyes. They were larvas, but larva means disguise and also phantom. Behind those Aztec faces, without expression but of an implacable cruelty, what semblance was awaiting its hour?

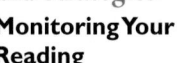

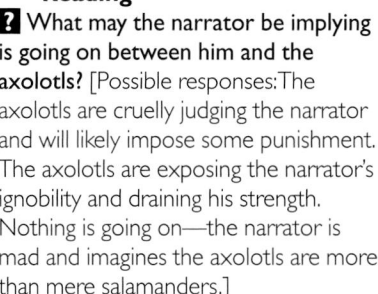

E Literary Connections

Here Cortázar evokes both Ovid's *Metamorphosis* and Kafka's *The Metamorphosis*. Ovid's is a work of mythology: The stories often include miraculous transformations, for example, a woman changing into a bird. Kafka wrote about alienated humans in an impersonal world. In *The Metamorphosis* a man finds himself transformed into a gigantic cockroach.

F Vocabulary Note

Latin Roots

? The word *larva* comes from a Latin root, meaning "mask" or "ghost"; thus Cortázar extracts the meanings "disguise" and "phantom." Why does he bring in these meanings? [Possible response: *Mask* and *ghost* suggest dual identity. *Disguise* and *phantom,* their synonyms, add further mystery and strangeness to the story.]

G Reading Skills and Strategies

Monitoring Your Reading

? What may the narrator be implying is going on between him and the axolotls? [Possible responses: The axolotls are cruelly judging the narrator and will likely impose some punishment. The axolotls are exposing the narrator's ignobility and draining his strength. Nothing is going on—the narrator is mad and imagines the axolotls are more than mere salamanders.]

Getting Students Involved

Cooperative Learning

Man or Axolotl? Ask students to imagine that the narrator is being interviewed by two specialists—a psychiatrist and an investigator of paranormal phenomena. Have students in groups of three role-play the parts of the narrator, the psychiatrist, and the investigator. After the interview, have the psychiatrist and investigator decide if the narrator is insane or has actually experienced some sort of metamorphosis. Then have them compare their conclusions with those of other groups. Before students begin, you might encourage them to first consider the following question: If the narrator has become an axolotl, what part of him still exists in the form of the man who visits the aquarium?

Enrichment Activity

Writing a News Article. Have pairs of students collaborate to write an article for a newspaper about the incident described in the story. Each article should have a suitable headline, answer who, what, when, where, why, and how questions, and include a photograph or drawing (with an appropriate caption) that presents some aspect of the story. You can let students publish their articles by displaying them in the classroom.

A Elements of Literature
Point of View

? In what way would the story differ if it were told from the guard's point of view? [Possible response: The guard would probably portray the man as crazy, being able to observe his strange behavior but not to discern his thoughts.]

B Appreciating Language
Repetition

? Cortázar uses repetition for various effects in the story. For example, his protestations that there is nothing strange going on make us feel just the opposite. What is the effect of his repeatedly stressing the axolotl's eyes? [Possible response: As the "mirrors of the soul," the eyes are thought to expose a creature's innermost being. By stressing the axolotl's eyes, Cortázar makes the reader feel that the narrator may be correct in assuming that there really is a mystery to penetrate.]

C Critical Thinking
Analyzing Motivation

? Why does the narrator want to prove that he is projecting a nonexistent consciousness upon the axolotls? [Possible responses: He has already admitted that he is frightened by the creatures and would thus like to prove to himself that they really are no more than salamanders. Part of him wants to cling to rational thought even as he is being taken over by irrational ideas about the axolotls.]

I was afraid of them. I think that had it not been for feeling the proximity of other visitors and the guard, I would not have been bold enough to remain alone with them. "You eat them alive with your eyes, hey," the guard said, laughing; he likely thought I was a little cracked. (A) What he didn't notice was that it was they devouring me slowly with their eyes, in a cannibalism of gold. At any distance from the aquarium, I had only to think of them, it was as though I were the tank each morning, the recognition was greater. They were suffering, every fiber of my body reached toward that stifled pain, that stiff torment at the bottom of the tank. They were lying in wait for something, a remote dominion destroyed, an age of liberty when the world had been that of the axolotls. Not possible that such a terrible expression which was attaining the overthrow of that forced blankness on their stone faces should carry any message other than

being affected from a distance. It got to the point that I was going every day, and at night I thought of them immobile in the darkness, slowly putting a hand out which immediately encountered another. (B) Perhaps their eyes could see in the dead of night, and for them the day continued indefinitely. The eyes of axolotls have no lids.

I know now that there was nothing strange, that that had to occur. Leaning over in front of one of pain, proof of that eternal sentence, of that liquid hell they were undergoing. (C) Hopelessly, I wanted to prove to myself that my own sensibility was projecting a nonexistent consciousness upon the axolotls. They and I knew. So there was nothing strange in what happened. My face was pressed against the glass of the aquarium, my eyes were attempting once more to penetrate the mystery of those eyes of gold

Making the Connections

Connecting to the Theme: "The Transforming Imagination"

After students have finished reading the selection, ask how the narrator's reality is transformed. [The narrator's imagination transforms him into an axolotl.] **Then have students discuss the following question: While the actual transformation is not believable, is there something that is believable in this story?** [Possible response: It is possible that the narrator suffers just as he imagines the axolotl does. It is believable that he identifies with the axolotl: an odd creature that is isolated and incapable of communication; a creature that seems to see and understand everything but do nothing.]

without iris, without pupil. I saw from very close up the face of an axolotl immobile next to the glass. No transition and no surprise, I saw my face against the glass, I saw it on the outside of the tank, I saw it on the other side of the glass. Then my face drew back and I understood.

Only one thing was strange: to go on thinking as usual, to know. To realize that was, for the first moment, like the horror of a man buried alive awaking to his fate. Outside, my face came close to the glass again, I saw my mouth, the lips compressed with the effort of understanding the axolotls. I was an axolotl and now I knew instantly that no understanding was possible. He was outside the aquarium, his thinking was a thinking outside the tank. Recognizing him, being him himself, I was an axolotl and in my world. The horror began—I learned in the same moment—of believing myself prisoner in the body of an axolotl, metamorphosed into him with my human mind intact, buried alive in an axolotl, condemned to move lucidly among unconscious creatures. But that stopped when a foot just grazed my face, when I moved just a little to one side and saw an axolotl next to me who was looking at me, and understood that he knew also, no communication possible, but very clearly. Or I was also in him, or all of us were thinking humanlike, incapable of expression, limited to the golden splendor of our eyes looking at the face of the man pressed against the aquarium.

He returned many times, but he comes less often now. Weeks pass without his showing up. I saw him yesterday, he looked at me for a long time and left briskly. It seemed to me that he was not so much interested in us any more, that he was coming out of habit. Since the only thing I do is think, I could think about him a lot. It occurs to me that at the beginning we continued to communicate, that he felt more than ever one with the mystery which was claiming him. But the bridges were broken between him and me, because what was his obsession is now an axolotl, alien to his human life. I think that at the beginning I was capable of returning to him in a certain way—ah, only in a certain way—and of keeping awake his desire to know us better. I am an axolotl for good now, and if I think like a man it's only because every axolotl thinks like a man inside his rosy stone semblance. I believe that all this succeeded in communicating something to him in those first days, when I was still he. And in this final solitude to which he no longer comes, I console myself by thinking that perhaps he is going to write a story about us, that, believing he's making up a story, he's going to write all this about axolotls.

Finding Common Ground

When we first hear the narrator of "Axolotl" speak, he has already undergone his fantastic transformation. "Now I am an axolotl," he confides to the reader in one of the very first sentences of the story. He seems to accept fully this extraordinary event and wishes to convince us that it really did occur, that it could occur, that its occurrence was *logical.* The narrator wishes to make the impossible—a psychological identification so complete that it becomes a physical transformation—appear as rational as a trip to the zoo.

In a group, discuss this strange short story. It might be helpful, given the suggestiveness of the story, to have it read aloud once before your discussions begin. The notes and questions you take as you read or listen to the story can form the basis for your discussion.

The first task of your discussion group is to set an agenda for your conversation. Be sure you cover these elements in your discussion: **point of view, conflict,** and **theme,** as well as connections to your own life and connections to other selections in this collection.

When your discussions are completed, report to the class. In your report, include questions you could not answer or could not agree on answers to.

Assessing Learning

Check Test: Fill-in-the-Blank

1. This story is written in the ______ person. [first]
2. The narrator is particularly fascinated by the _____ of the axolotl. [eyes]
3. The narrator believes that the "terrible expression" on the axolotls' faces carries a message of ___________. [pain, suffering]
4. According to the narrator, the only strange thing that happened after the metamorphosis was that he continued to ______. [think]
5. At the end of the story, the narrator consoles himself by thinking that the man might write a story about _______. [axolotls]

D Critical Thinking
Synthesizing

? Why does the narrator insist there is nothing strange throughout the story and then finally admit to one strange thing? [Possible response: Cortázar uses this refrain to set up the moment of the transformation. When the narrator becomes an axolotl, he continues to think as a man, and this, ironically, is the strange part to him.]

E Reading Skills and Strategies
Monitoring Your Reading

? The point of transformation may be very confusing. In what sense can the narrator be an axolotl in the tank and at the same time still be a man looking in from the outside? [Possible responses: The narrator now leads a dual existence of sorts—his consciousness is inside the axolotl, but his body remains outside the tank. The point of view has shifted from the man to the axolotl. The reader knows what the axolotl is thinking but has no idea what is going on inside the head of the man looking into the tank.]

F Critical Thinking
Extending the Text

? What is the parallel in this passage between human experience and that of the axolotl? [Possible answers: The axolotls can't communicate, but perhaps humans can't either. The narrator may once have felt as trapped in his humanity as he later feels trapped among the axolotls.]

Finding Common Ground

As its name suggests, this feature requires students, through lively discussion and questioning, to discover areas of agreement between their experience and the themes or issues raised in the literature.

To help students focus their discussions, ask them to come up with questions they think should be asked about the story. Provide examples similar to these: Do you ever begin to believe the narrator? Is there a moment when the extraordinary seems possible? Remind students to identify point of view [first-person], conflict [internal identity problem], and theme [the fantastic can occur; metamorphosis is possible; all creatures are mysteriously linked] when they report to the class.

OBJECTIVES

Fern Hill / In my craft . . . / Do Not Go Gentle into That Good Night

1. Read and interpret the poems
2. Identify and analyze lyric poetry
3. Identify the characteristics of an elegy
4. Understand and evaluate the villanelle
5. Express understanding through critical and creative writing

SKILLS

Literary

- Identify and analyze lyric poetry
- Identify the characteristics of an elegy
- Understand and evaluate the villanelle

Writing

- Prepare a bibliography for an informative report
- Write an essay about a theme
- Imitate lyrical style in a narrative
- Write a response to a poem
- Write to an author

Viewing and Representing

- Make inferences about an artwork (ATE)

Planning

- **Block Schedule**
  Block Scheduling Lesson Plans with Pacing Guide
- **Traditional Schedule**
  Lesson Plans Including Strategies for English-Language Learners
- **One-Stop Planner**
  CD-ROM with Test Generator

BROWSING IN THE FILES

About the Author. Dylan Thomas's father encouraged him to read widely and to speak English at home instead of his native Welsh. Even so, partly due to the influence of his uncle William, a poet who wrote in Welsh, Thomas maintained a traditional Welsh attitude toward poetry. He believed that it should exhibit artful wordplay and sound beautiful.

Dylan Thomas

(1914–1953)

Portrait of Dylan Thomas by Augustus John.

Born in Swansea, Wales, Dylan Thomas was a prodigy—a poet who wrote some of his most famous works before he was twenty. By that time, he had also sketched out themes, ideas, and angles of perspective for poems that he drew on for the rest of his life. Largely self-educated, he chose the rough-and-tumble life of a newspaper reporter over the comparative serenity of a university education. His recognition by the leading poets and literary critics of Britain and the United States came early, and with it came international fame. Neither was enough to prevent him from having to live on the edge of poverty until his death.

The only son of parents who lived by a code of "good appearances" among their neighbors, Thomas as a child was continually torn between a deep-seated wish to live up to the expectations of his schoolmaster father and an equally strong impulse to please his doting mother. At the same time, he rejected both parents' pretensions to gentility. This conflict was later intensified by a strangely childish self-indulgence that continually defeated his attempts to be a devoted husband to his wife, Caitlin, and a loving father to their three children. The temporary solace he found in alcohol led to that "insult to the brain" that caused his early and sudden death, in St. Vincent's Hospital in New York City. At the time, Thomas was making his fourth visit to the United States and preparing to collaborate on an opera with the composer Igor Stravinsky.

A man of magical presence, with an endless flow of wit and a transparent hunger for affection, Thomas charmed both his British and his American contemporaries. When he first came to America in 1950, he was regarded as the most charismatic British visitor since Oscar Wilde in 1885. His first reading tour of American colleges and universities was followed by ever more extensive trips, in which he crisscrossed the continent from Florida to British Columbia. Beyond their response to his personal magnetism, those who attended Thomas's oral readings heard something new in modern poetry—a kind of expression combining the oratorical *hywl,* or chanting eloquence, of the Welsh chapel service with the theatrical delivery of the Victorian actors who once thrilled American audiences with thunderous recitations from Shakespeare and Marlowe. Thomas's poems are a mixture of intricate complication and preacherlike eloquence, of sonorous solemnity combined with a playful use of language apparent even in his most serious works.

In his last years, Thomas found that the concentration needed to write poetry was more and more difficult to achieve. Consequently, he turned to less demanding forms of expression and produced two works that became familiar around the world: *Under Milk Wood* (1954), which he called a "play for voices," and his lyrical memoir *A Child's Christmas in Wales* (1955), now a holiday classic.

Celebrated by critics, sought after by American lecture agencies, and idolized almost like a rock star, Thomas died at the height of a fame he could neither accept nor enjoy. "Once I was lost and proud," he told a reporter from *The New York Times;* "now I'm found and humble. I prefer that other."

go.hrw.com
LEO 12-13

Resources: Print and Media

Reading

- *Graphic Organizers for Active Reading,* pp. 101, 102
- *Audio CD Library*
  Disc 18, Tracks 4, 5, 6

Viewing and Representing

- *Viewing and Representing*
  Fine Art Transparency 17
  Fine Art Worksheet, p. 68

Assessment

- *Portfolio Management System,* p. 199
- *Test Generator (One-Stop Planner CD-ROM)*

Internet

go.hrw.com (keyword: LEO 12-13)

Before You Read
FERN HILL

Make the Connection
Memories of Childhood
Childhood is often remembered as a time of carefree innocence. Therefore, most of us have some memory of an idyllic moment from childhood, when the world was a glorious place and everything seemed just right.

Quickwrite
Sketch one happy childhood memory of your own. Then, list three adjectives besides *happy* that describe your emotions as you recall this experience.

Elements of Literature
Lyric Poetry
Lyric poetry focuses on expressing emotions or thoughts rather than on telling a story. In the lyric poem "Fern Hill," Dylan Thomas uses a full range of **sound effects** and **figures of speech** to convey vivid memories of a young boy's enchanted life in the Welsh countryside. Although the speaker's memories are colored by reflection and experience, it is the exuberance of his feelings, above all, that claims our attention.

Background
As a child, Thomas spent his summers among relatives who worked on a farm that, in his poem, he calls Fern Hill. Set in an apple orchard, the farmhouse is of the whitewashed stucco typical of Wales and has a number of outlying barns for livestock and hay storage. Not far from the sea, Fern Hill looks down upon enormous tidal flats in an ever-changing seascape that provides a bountiful habitat for thousands of water birds.

"Fern Hill" is a memory of childhood joy, a vision of an earthly paradise as well as the playground of a boy for whom every day is an enchanted adventure. Yet, typical of Thomas, joy is never unadulterated or unshadowed. At the end of this extended song of praise, "time" holds him not, as we might expect, "green and growing," but "green and dying." Here we have a variation on one of Thomas's persistent themes—the lurking presence of death in life, of the worm in the seed.

Dylan Thomas and his family.

© Rollie McKenna.

Resources
A recording of Thomas's poems is provided in the *Audio CD Library*:
- Disc 18, Tracks 4, 5, 6

Viewing and Representing
Fine Art Transparency
A transparency of John Constable's *The Cornfield* complements "Fern Hill." See the *Viewing and Representing Transparencies and Worksheets:*
- Transparency 17
- Worksheet, p. 68

Summary ■■■
The speaker recalls his idyllic childhood at Fern Hill, a Welsh farm where he spent his days in carefree, imaginative play. To him, Fern Hill was like the Garden of Eden, a place where he was the lord of nature, ecstatic, independent, and unaware of the passage of time. He concludes by musing that he did not know then, as he does now, that time would take him from that magic land and reveal to him his mortality.

Reaching All Students
Struggling Readers
"Fern Hill" requires a close reading for its literal meanings to be understood. Read the poem aloud as students follow along in their texts. To monitor comprehension, pause frequently, perhaps using the commas as pacing guides. After reading a passage, ask students to paraphrase it. Once the entire poem has been read in this way, play the CD recording for the students.

A **Critical Thinking**

Analyzing Figurative Language

? What kinds of games does the speaker play? [Possible response: He plays imaginative games in which he pretends to be a prince and a lord.]

B **Vocabulary Note**

Multiple Meanings

? The word *green* has various meanings. What do you think the word *green* means in l. 10? [Possible responses: innocent, fresh, young, inexperienced.]

C **Elements of Literature**

Lyric Poetry

? What feelings do the images of earth, air, fire, and water evoke in ll. 19–22? [Possible responses: The images evoke feelings of joy, freedom, and serenity.]

D **English Language Learners**

Biblical Allusions

Some students may miss the allusions to Genesis. You can refer them to the excerpt from Genesis beginning on p. 416. Point out the following: "Adam and maiden" is Adam and Eve; "the birth of the simple light" occurred when God said, "Let there be light"; and "the first, spinning place" may refer to the creation of the universe.

Fern Hill

Dylan Thomas

Now as I was young and easy under the apple boughs
About the lilting house and happy as the grass was green,
The night above the dingle° starry,
Time let me hail and climb
Golden in the heydays of his eyes,
And honored among wagons I was prince of the apple towns
And once below a time I lordly had the trees and leaves
Trail with daisies and barley
Down the rivers of the windfall light.

And as I was green and carefree, famous among the barns
About the happy yard and singing as the farm was home,
In the sun that is young once only,
Time let me play and be
Golden in the mercy of his means,
And green and golden I was huntsman and herdsman, the calves
Sang to my horn, the foxes on the hills barked clear and cold,
And the sabbath rang slowly
In the pebbles of the holy streams.

All the sun long it was running, it was lovely, the hay
Fields high as the house, the tunes from the chimneys, it was air
And playing, lovely and watery
And fire green as grass.
And nightly under the simple stars
As I rode to sleep the owls were bearing the farm away,
All the moon long I heard, blessed among stables, the nightjars°
Flying with the ricks,° and the horses
Flashing into the dark.

And then to awake, and the farm, like a wanderer white
With the dew, come back, the cock on his shoulder: it was all
Shining, it was Adam and maiden,
The sky gathered again
And the sun grew round that very day.
So it must have been after the birth of the simple light
In the first, spinning place, the spellbound horses walking warm
Out of the whinnying green stable
On to the fields of praise.

3. dingle: little wooded valley, nestled between steep hills.

25. nightjars: common, gray-brown nocturnal birds, named for their jarring cries.

26. ricks: haystacks.

And honored among foxes and pheasants by the gay house
Under the new made clouds and happy as the heart was long,
In the sun born over and over,
I ran my heedless ways,
My wishes raced through the house high hay
And nothing I cared, at my sky blue trades, that time allows
In all his tuneful turning so few and such morning songs
Before the children green and golden
Follow him out of grace, **E**

Nothing I cared, in the lamb white days, that time would take me
Up to the swallow thronged loft by the shadow of my hand,
In the moon that is always rising,
Nor that riding to sleep
I should hear him fly with the high fields
And wake to the farm forever fled from the childless land.
Oh as I was young and easy in the mercy of his means,
Time held me green and dying
Though I sang in my chains like the sea. **F**

E Critical Thinking

Interpreting

? In ll. 42–45, the speaker says that as a child he ignored the fact that time allows few carefree days before leading children out of grace. What does he mean by this? [Possible response: The days of carefree childhood are numbered; children become adults, grow old, and eventually die.]

F Reading Skills and Strategies

Making Inferences

? What does the speaker imply about childhood innocence? [Possible responses: Innocence is destined to end. Innocence shields us from comprehending that time is our master; even in our youth, we are headed toward death.]

Dylan Thomas's youngest child, Colm, four years old (1953).
© Rollie McKenna.

Responding to the Art

The photographer **Rollie McKenna** visited Dylan and Caitlin Thomas in Wales in late summer 1953, only two months before the poet would die in a New York hospital. McKenna's photographic record of that visit, plus that of other visits with Thomas, is found in her book *Portrait of Dylan* (1982). The photographs on pp. 1033, 1035, 1036, and 1039 are from that book. John Malcolm Brinnin, one of the authors of *Elements of Literature,* wrote in a preface to McKenna's book that her photographic record of Thomas's last years is unmatched. John Brinnin accompanied Rollie McKenna on that 1953 visit to Wales. At the time, Brinnin was director of the Poetry Center at New York's YMHA. His mission, which proved to be unsuccessful, was to dissuade Thomas from undertaking another (destructive) American tour. Shortly after this visit the poet set off for the American journey from which he would not return.

We thought that this lovely photograph of Thomas's youngest child caught the innocence celebrated and mourned in "Fern Hill."

Crossing the Curriculum

Geography

Have students research various Welsh geographical features such as rivers, seacoast, and mountains. Encourage students to look in library books for photographs of farms like the one Thomas describes in the poem. In addition, you may ask students to watch the film *The Englishman Who Went up a Hill but Came down a Mountain* (1995) and then create a map of the Cambrian Mountains. Have students share their findings with the class in oral reports.

History

Ask students to work in small groups to research various aspects of Welsh history, culture, and language. After they have gathered information on these and other related topics, have the groups conduct panel discussions for the class in which they present the information they have obtained.

Summary ■■

The speaker explains when, for whom, and why he writes poetry. He writes at night while others are asleep. He writes for the "most secret heart" of people. He writes for lovers, "their arms/Round the griefs of ages," even though they pay no attention to his poetry.

A Elements of Literature

Wordplay

? "Singing" is an odd adjective to modify light. To what might the phrase "singing light" refer? [Possible responses: to the noise which the poet's lamp is making or to the fact that it's by the light of the lamp that the poet "sings." It may also indicate that the poet "sings" with a light heart.]

B Reading Skills and Strategies

Making Inferences

? What are the "common wages" the poet writes for in ll. 10–11? [Possible responses: The poet writes to touch the hearts of lovers. His common wages are the effects, unconscious though they may be, he creates on his audience.]

C Critical Thinking

Interpreting

? Who might the "towering dead" be and why doesn't the speaker write for them? [Possible responses: The "towering dead" might be literature's great deceased writers. Perhaps "nightingales" refers to Keats's "Ode to a Nightingale." The speaker doesn't write for them because his interest is in reaching ordinary people.]

Before You Read

IN MY CRAFT OR SULLEN ART

Make the Connection

For Whom the Poet Writes

Do you think poets have an image of their audience in mind when they write? Or do they write mostly for themselves and other poets? Perhaps each poet works differently, and we would have to speak to each one to get an answer to our question. Dylan Thomas describes his audience in this poem.

Quickwrite

What ideas and feelings come to mind when you hear the word *sullen*? Track your association on a cluster diagram like the one below.

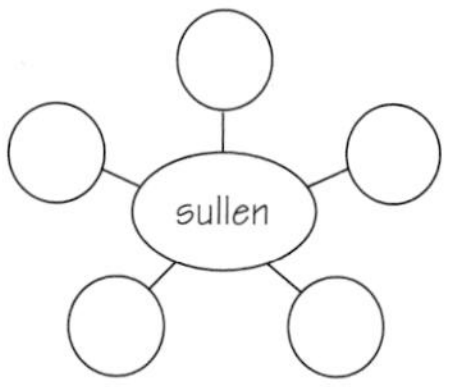

After you read the poem, look back at your diagram to see if any of your ideas and feelings match the meaning suggested in this poem.

In my craft or sullen art

Dylan Thomas

In my craft or sullen art
Exercised in the still night
When only the moon rages
And the lovers lie abed
With all their griefs in their arms,
I labor by singing light
Not for ambition or bread
Or the strut and trade of charms
On the ivory stages
But for the common wages
Of their most secret heart.

Not for the proud man apart
From the raging moon I write
On these spindrift° pages
Nor for the towering dead
With their nightingales and psalms
But for the lovers, their arms
Round the griefs of the ages,
Who pay no praise or wages
Nor heed my craft or art.

14. spindrift (spin′drift′): literally, spray blown from a rough sea or surf.

Thomas's writing shack, Laugharne, Wales.

©Rollie McKenna.

Reaching All Students

Struggling Readers

To focus their reading, ask students to read the poem to find the answers to these questions: When does the poet/speaker write? Why does he write? For whom does he write?

English Language Learners

Help students rephrase each stanza. [Possible responses: stanza 1: I write poetry at night when the moon glows and lovers lie in bed. I labor by lamplight for admission to their hearts, not for ambition or money or fame.]

MAKING MEANINGS

Fern Hill

First Thoughts [Respond]

1. Possible responses: It is not universal because not all children can play on a farm. It is universal insofar as all children can have summers full of fun and adventure.

Shaping Interpretations [Interpret]

2. Possible responses: "prince of the apple towns" (l. 6), "singing" (l. 11), "sang to my horn" (l. 16), "ran my heedless ways" (l. 40).
3. Lines 29–36 in the fourth stanza.
4. Possible responses: The speaker's childhood, like life in the garden of Eden, was innocent, carefree, and filled with joy in nature (represented by the references to rivers, stars, calves, foxes, owls, etc.). The boy's "awakening" into the reality of adulthood may be compared to Adam and Eve's loss of the garden of Eden.

(Answers continue on p. T1037.)

MAKING MEANINGS

Fern Hill

First Thoughts

1. Is the experience described in "Fern Hill" universal? Explain your response. (You may want to refer to your Quickwrite notes.)

Shaping Interpretations

2. What details tell how the speaker felt when he was "young and easy"?

3. What lines in the poem seem to refer to the Biblical account of paradise?

4. In what specific ways was the speaker's childhood like the life Adam and Eve led in the Biblical garden of Eden? In what ways is the boy's "waking" in the last stanza like the "waking" of Adam and Eve as they left the garden?

5. Where is time **personified** in the poem? Describe the different kinds of intentions that time seems to have regarding the boy.

6. How would you explain the **paradox,** or seeming contradiction, in the next-to-last line of the poem?

7. Read this entire **lyric poem** aloud, or listen to a recording of it, and try to hear the many elements that produce its music. Where does Thomas use **alliteration** and **onomatopoeia** to provide the sound effects?

Connecting with the Text

8. Which lines in "Fern Hill" could apply to all our lives?

Challenging the Text

9. Years after this poem was published, Thomas told a friend that one line continued to bother him because it was "bloody bad." The friend asked what line it was. "I ran my heedless ways," said Thomas, and he winced. Why do you think Thomas felt so strongly about a line that most people accept and even quote as part of his most celebrated poem? How do you feel about the line?

In my craft or sullen art

First Thoughts

1. Does the last line surprise you? Why, or why not?

Shaping Interpretations

2. *Sullen* means "sad" or "gloomy" today, but an older sense of the word is "solitary." (Its root is *solus,* which is Latin for "alone.") How might this explain why the speaker calls his art sullen? (What ideas and feelings did you associate with the word *sullen* in your Quickwrite?)

3. Describe the picture you see of the poet at work.

4. The speaker says that he writes "for the lovers, their arms / Round the griefs of the ages." What kind of people do you think he is describing? What might some of their griefs be?

5. For whom or for what is the poet *not* writing?

6. The speaker says that his readers "pay" him "no praise or wages / Nor heed my craft or sullen art." Why, then, does he write for them? (Lines 10–11 may give you a clue.)

7. Think about the word *spindrift* (line 14). Could this word suggest that the poet thinks his art might not last? Why, or why not?

Connecting with the Text

8. Do you feel that you are one of the people for whom the poet-speaker is writing? Give reasons for your answer.

ELEMENTS OF LITERATURE

Wordplay

Even at his most somber, Thomas continually indulges in wordplay—sometimes turning a **cliché** upside down, sometimes making chilling or amusing **puns,** sometimes using modifiers in surprising ways, often giving a twist of emphasis and new luster to an old saying.

How many instances of wordplay can you identify in "Fern Hill" and in "In my craft or sullen art"?

(Continued from p. T1036)

5. In ll. 4 and 13, time is obliquely personified as an indulgent parent who allows the boy the freedom to be happy. But in l. 53, time is a parent who holds a dying child in his arms. Thus, time seems to have intended the speaker to be happy but also to grow up, lose the paradise of childhood, and eventually die.

6. The phrase "green and dying" is paradoxical because it suggests innocent freshness and mortality at the same time.

7. Examples of alliteration occur in ll. 2, 15, 26–27, 34, and 41. Onomatopoeia occurs in ll. 2 ("lilting") and 35 ("whinnying").

Connecting with the Text [Apply]

8. Students may suggest that although not everyone experiences a childhood as idyllic as what Thomas describes, many remember youth as a time of innocence and beauty. They may cite the first line of each stanza.

Challenging the Text [Evaluate]

9. Some students may suggest that this line didn't satisfy Thomas because it doesn't contain an original image or figure of speech, and others may find the line to be a cliché.

MAKING MEANINGS

In my craft or sullen art

First Thoughts [Respond]

1. Possible responses: yes, because it sounds as if the speaker is happy to be ignored; no, because ll. 10–11 show the speaker's motives.

Shaping Interpretations [Interpret]

2. Possible response: The poet must pursue his vocation in unintrusive silence, away from people.

3. The poet is alone at night, toiling over his work, which could be illuminated by a nearby lamp.

4. Possible responses: everyday people who love life and each other; some of their griefs might be the inevitability of death, lost love, or unfulfilled dreams.

5. The poet does not write for "ambition or bread" or "the strut and trade of charms / On the ivory stages." He doesn't write for "the proud man" or "the towering dead."

6. Possible responses: He writes for them because he wants somehow to touch their hearts, even if they are unconscious of it.

7. Some may say *spindrift* suggests that poetry is ephemeral since poems are forgotten and the books in which they are written decay.

Connecting with the Text [Apply]

8. Some students may feel they are "lovers" of life and therefore belong to the poet's audience. Others may feel their "secret hearts" unreached by his poetry.

ELEMENTS OF LITERATURE

Possible Responses

Clichés turned upside down: "happy as the grass was green," "once below a time," "fire green as grass." Pun: "morning songs." Surprising use of modifiers: "lilting house," "sky blue traders," "lamb white days," "singing light," "towering dead." Old sayings with new twists: "the calves sang to my horn," "honored among foxes and pheasants."

Summary

The speaker urges his father not to submit quietly to death, contending that people near death should struggle against "the dying of the light." He asserts that those with true wisdom, even though they know death is inevitable, nevertheless rage against dying. He looks for a sign that his father, at the end of his life, will challenge death, whether through cursing, blessing, or crying.

Background

Dylan Thomas's poetic development was shaped in part by his schoolmaster father, D. J. Thomas, who passed on to his son a great enthusiasm for poetry. Although never going beyond Swansea Grammar School, young Dylan read widely and was knowledgeable about English poetry. During Dylan's late teens, his father suffered from a progressively worsening cancer of the throat and tongue. Seeing his father lose his battle with this devastating illness instilled in the son a dread of death and an obsession with human mortality.

Responding to the Art

Francis Bacon (1909–1992) was an English painter whose distorted depictions of the human body shocked many of his contemporaries. In the 1950s, Bacon painted a series of portraits based on the life mask of William Blake in the National Portrait Gallery. *Study for Portrait V* is one of these. It shows an indistinct head which seems to float like a hologram in a void.

Activity. What are your reactions to the painting? Do you find it eerie? Calm? Beautiful? Ugly? How appropriate do you think it is as an accompaniment to an elegy?

Before You Read

Do Not Go Gentle into That Good Night

Make the Connection

Challenging Death

Death may conquer every living thing in the end, but the instinct for survival remains remarkably strong. In contemporary literature, as in the *Gilgamesh* epic of four thousand years ago (page 53), heroes often battle against death's inevitability. Literature also records the frequent, fierce refusal of the living to accept a loved one's death. Suppose you knew someone who was facing death. How would you advise that person to behave? What attitude would you want that person to have?

Quickwrite

How would you personify death? Would you compare it to a grim reaper? an impartial judge? Would you picture it as a fearsome, skeletal figure? Jot down some images for death.

Elements of Literature

Elegy

The typical **elegy** is a poem that mourns a death that has already occurred. This poem is an elegy that speaks to a dying man, urging him not to surrender but to meet death in a spirit of challenge. As he often did in his poetry, here Thomas gives his own twist to a familiar subject. The poem may invite charges of irreverence, but its lyrical solemnity, not its argument, is what reverberates in the reader's mind.

Only two end-rhyme sounds occur in the poem, but both are blended into iambic pentameter with such skill that the many repetitions of similar sounds become a somber and delicate music. The use of *gentle* instead of the adverb *gently* may seem ungrammatical. But when we read the line as "Do not go, gentle, into that good night," as Thomas insisted, we gain the additional meaning of all that is gentle, including the gentle man who was Thomas's father.

Study for Portrait V (after life mask of William Blake) (1956) by Francis Bacon.

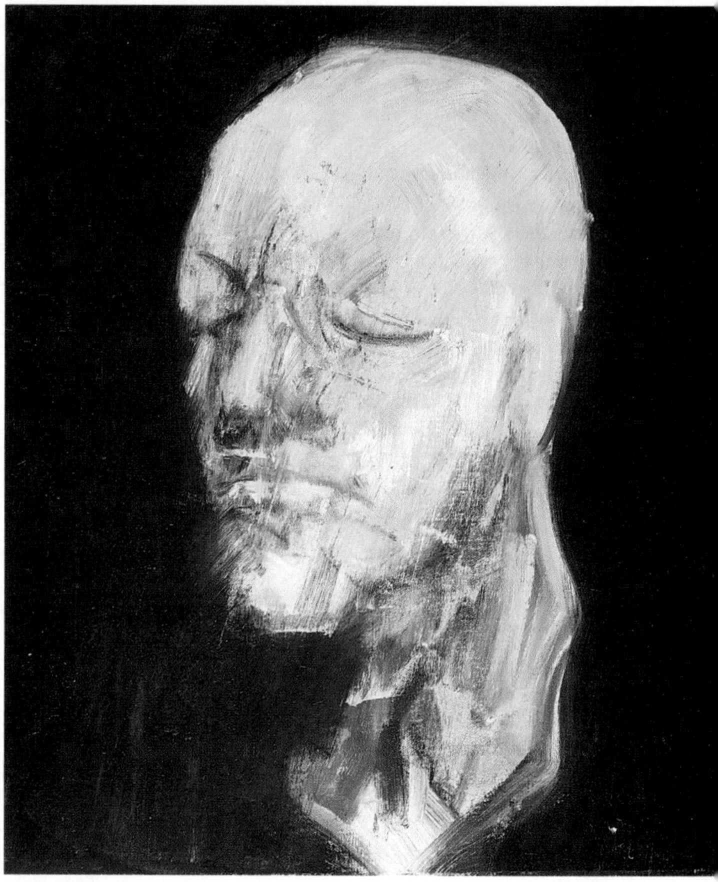

Reaching All Students

English Language Learners

Attitudes toward death vary from culture to culture. Explain that the speaker of this poem views death as something to be resisted. Encourage students to share their own or another culture's attitude toward dying.

Advanced Learners

Have students look for comparisons and contrasts between Thomas's attitude toward death and that of other poets they've read in this text.

Using Students' Strengths

Spatial Learners

Ask students to create a mural depicting the images that appear in the poem. They can draw pictures or cut them out of magazines. Suggest that they divide the mural into sections, one for each type of person who refuses to die without a fight. If they choose, students can also reserve a section for how they feel the speaker's father should "rage against the dying of the light."

Do Not Go Gentle into That Good Night

Dylan Thomas

A memorial to Dylan Thomas at the edge of a small pond, Cwmdonkin Park, Swansea, Wales.

© Rollie McKenna.

Do not go gentle into that good night,
Old age should burn and rave at close of day; (A)
Rage, rage against the dying of the light.

Though wise men at their end know dark is right,
Because their words had forked no lightning they
Do not go gentle into that good night.

Good men, the last wave by, crying how bright
Their frail deeds might have danced in a green bay,
Rage, rage against the dying of the light. (B)

Wild men who caught and sang the sun in flight,
And learn, too late, they grieved it on its way,
Do not go gentle into that good night.

Grave men, near death, who see with blinding sight
Blind eyes could blaze like meteors and be gay,
Rage, rage against the dying of the light. (C)

And you, my father, there on the sad height,
Curse, bless, me now with your fierce tears, I pray. (D)
Do not go gentle into that good night.
Rage, rage against the dying of the light.

MAKING MEANINGS

First Thoughts

1. What feelings does the poet reveal about his father's death? Are they at all contradictory?

Shaping Interpretations

2. What four types of people are described in stanzas 2–5? How do all these people respond to the dying of the light?
3. What does the speaker pray for at the end?
4. What is the "good night"? What **pun** on the phrase do you catch?
5. Given Thomas's feelings about the "good night," do you see anything contradictory in his use of the word *good*? Explain your answer.
6. Identify at least three **metaphors** in the poem. How do the ideas you recorded in

(A) Struggling Readers

Interpreting Metaphors

? To what does the speaker compare death and life? [death to night, life to light]

(B) Reading Skills and Strategies

Making Comparisons

? What four kinds of men does the speaker compare? [wise men, good men, wild men, grave men] What do they have in common? [They all find reason for sorrow or repentance at the coming of death; they all fight against it.]

(C) Critical Thinking

Expressing an Opinion

? Do you agree with the speaker that dying people should rage against death? [Possible responses: Yes, life is too precious to be let go of easily; no, people should die in peace, not angrily.]

(D) Elements of Literature

Elegy

? The elegy form goes back to the ancient Greeks and Romans, who used the term to refer to any serious meditation, including poems about love, war, and death. Today "elegy" is used exclusively to refer to poems of mourning. In what way does Thomas's poem fit both definitions? [Possible response: The poem mourns the imminent death of Thomas's father, but it also reflects on human mortality and how to face death. It speaks of a love for life and a battle against death.]

MAKING MEANINGS

First Thoughts [Respond]

1. In general, Thomas resents the fact that his father is dying but says that wise men know death must come, but they don't go without a struggle.

Shaping Interpretations [Interpret]

2. Wise men, good men, wild men, and grave men. The wise men are angry because their counsels failed to influence others; the good men deplore the ineffectuality of their deeds; the wild men learn too late that time is fleeting; the grave men regret their failure to enjoy life.
3. He asks his father to both curse and bless him.
4. Death. Ordinarily "good night" is used as a casual farewell, not as a synonym for death.
5. The word *good* is paradoxical since Thomas wants his father to resist death.
6. Metaphors include old age burning and raving (l. 2), wise men's words forking no lightning (l. 5), "frail deeds" dancing in a "green bay" (l. 8), and the singing of the sun in flight (l. 10). Students' images may be simpler and more graphic.
7. The speaker may feel that whether his father's tears constitute a curse or a blessing, they would be better than a gentle and terrible silence.

Challenging the Text [Synthesize]

8. Some students may think Thomas should have shown the poem to his father so the man could have prepared for death. Others may think Thomas did the right thing to protect his father.

ELEMENTS OF LITERATURE

Mini-Lesson: The Villanelle
Although the villanelle form does not require it, Thomas further restricts himself in this poem by limiting each line to ten syllables. This has the effect of adding further balance and symmetry to an already well-balanced and highly symmetrical verse form. This degree of discipline is ironic considering Thomas's message: Resist the natural order of events and rebel against the inevitable.

Possible Responses

1. Thomas has been completely faithful to the three rules for the villanelle.
2. Lines 1 and 3, which are repeated, carry the central theme: Resist the approach of death.

Grading Timesaver

Rubrics for each Choices assignment appear on p. 199 in the *Portfolio Management System.*

CHOICES: Building Your Portfolio

1. **Writer's Notebook** Review with students the correct format for a bibliography before they begin.
2. **Identifying a Theme** You may want students to discuss the theme of their chosen poem before they begin working on their essays. They can do this in small groups or with the whole class. Then, encourage them to reread the poem carefully, noting details that support the theme. Suggest that students think of how they would handle the theme and compare their ideas with Thomas's method.
3. **Creative Writing** Have students consider how their choice of details will convey feelings about their subject. Suggest they first think about the emotions the experience evokes and then jot these down as headings on a sheet of paper. Have them list appropriate images and figures of speech under each heading.
4. **Creative Writing** Have students brainstorm a list of possible topics before they begin writing.
5. **Creative Writing** If students choose to write a poem as a response they may want to imitate Thomas's poetic style.

your Quickwrite notes compare with the images that Thomas uses?

7. Why would any son beg his father to "Curse, bless, me now with your fierce tears"? What might this strange request indicate about the relationship between this father and son?

Challenging the Text

8. Soon after this poem was finished, Thomas sent it to Princess Caetani in Rome, hoping she might publish it in her literary magazine. In an accompanying letter, he wrote: "The only person I can't show the little enclosed poem to is, of course, my father, who doesn't know he's dying." Given the fact that the poem became one of the most famous elegies of the century, do you think Thomas's reluctance was justified? What would you have done in his situation?

ELEMENTS OF LITERATURE

The Villanelle

Thomas has written his poem in an old form called a **villanelle,** invented by French poets. At first this term, which means "rural" or "countrylike," was limited to light, lyric poems about the countryside. Today, villanelles are written on many topics and, as Thomas's illustrates, do not require a light **tone.**

The villanelle is a complex form. The trick is to make it sound spontaneous and fresh, yet still adhere to its strict limits:

- It should have nineteen lines divided into five three-line stanzas (tercets) and a concluding four-line stanza (quatrain).
- It can use only two end-rhyme sounds in this rhyme scheme: *aba aba aba aba aba abaa.*
- It should repeat line 1 in lines 6, 12, and 18, and it should repeat line 3 in lines 9, 15, and 19.

1. How faithfully has Thomas followed the rules for a villanelle?
2. The repeated lines in a villanelle must be significant. Has Thomas repeated ideas important to his poem? Explain your answer.

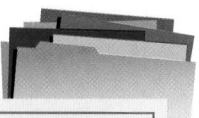

CHOICES: Building Your Portfolio

Writer's Notebook

1. Collecting Ideas for an Informative Report

You might be interested enough in Dylan Thomas's work to do research on the poet's tempestuous life. To start with, you might prepare a bibliography of books about Thomas that would give you the information you are interested in. Save your work for the Writer's Workshop on page 1053.

Identifying a Theme

2. What's It All About?

In a brief essay, state the **theme** of "Fern Hill" or "In my craft or sullen art," and cite the details from the poem that support that theme. At the conclusion of your report, tell how you respond to Thomas's handling of this theme.

Creative Writing

3. The Way Things Were

Narrate a joyful episode from your own childhood. In some of your sentences, try to imitate the lyrical style of "Fern Hill." Open with the words "Now as I was young and easy . . ."

Creative Writing

4. Feedback

Write a response to "Do Not Go Gentle into That Good Night," using the voice of a very old person who is facing death. Your response might be a poem, an essay, or a letter.

Creative Writing

5. The Audience Answers

As a reader of Dylan Thomas's poetry, write a response to his claim in "In my craft or sullen art" that his audience does not "praise" him or even "heed" his craft or art. Tell the poet in a letter or poem how you feel about his poetry.

Using Students' Strengths

Logical/Mathematical Learners
Some students may appreciate the mathematical aspects of prosody. As they work on the Elements of Literature feature, ask these students to develop mathematical formulas that express the rules for the villanelle. Also, ask these students to develop rules for other verse forms of their own devising. You also can specify subject matter and ask students to invent verse forms appropriate for each subject.

V. S. Naipaul

(1932–   )

When V. S. (Vidiadhar Surajprasad) Naipaul was born, his homeland, the Caribbean island of Trinidad, was still under the colonial rule of Britain. Like many Asian Indians, Naipaul's family had immigrated to Trinidad in the nineteenth century to work as indentured servants on the sugar plantations. With their Asian background and Hindu religion, the Naipauls felt themselves to be members of a transplanted society. As a result, from his earliest days, Naipaul felt a degree of rootlessness. He also felt—on the small island—a sense of the world as a kind of prison.

Fortunately, he was an outstanding student. Scholastic honors won him a place at Trinidad's Queen's Royal College and provided him a chance to leave the island. Granted a scholarship to England's prestigious Oxford University, Naipaul was one of only a few dark-skinned students at a university famous for educating England's privileged white upper classes.

Naipaul's father had pursued a faltering career as an island journalist, and this background inspired Naipaul to become a writer. Leaving Oxford in 1954, with no desire to return to Trinidad's narrow possibilities, he sought his identity in writing. He worked part time for the British Broadcasting Corporation (BBC) and tried his hand at writing fiction about the island life he had fled. His first short stories, which later became *Miguel Street,* went begging until he was able to publish his two earlier novels set in Trinidad, *The Mystic Masseur* (1957) and *The Suffrage of Elvira* (1958).

Naipaul's first masterpiece, *A House for Mr. Biswas,* came along in 1961. The novel, which some critics compared to Dickens's comic satires, tells about a poor, ineffectual Trinidadian (much like Naipaul's father) who finds stability by marrying into an influential family. Deprived of independence, Mr. Biswas's rebellion takes shape in the desperate quest for a house of his own. The novel reveals Naipaul's special gifts as a storyteller: his unique, ironic voice; his clear vision of so-called Third World people; and his understanding of life's essentials. The book established him as a major novelist throughout the world of letters.

Naipaul's search for roots has sent him traveling, first back to the West Indies and then to Africa, the Middle East, and India itself, as he pursues the meaning of his own mixed heritage. These voyages and inquiries have led Naipaul to produce more than twenty books, both fiction and nonfiction, including *A Bend in the River* (a 1979 novel set in Africa), *India: A Million Mutinies Now* (a 1991 travel book about his return to India), and *A Way in the World* (a 1994 autobiographical novel about a writer's journey toward self-understanding). All of Naipaul's works have been acclaimed for their clear and bitter yet compassionate insights into the human struggle for identity and survival.

Naipaul has won virtually all the major British literary prizes available to a prose writer and is a perennial nominee for the Nobel Prize in literature.

V. S. Naipaul (1981).

go.hrw.com
LEO 12-13

Resources: Print and Media

Reading
- *Graphic Organizers for Active Reading,* p. 103
- *Words to Own,* p. 30
- *Audio CD Library*
  Disc 18, Track 7

Writing and Language
- *Grammar and Language Links*
  Worksheet, p. 63
- *Language Workshop CD-ROM*

Assessment
- *Formal Assessment,* p. 208
- *Portfolio Management System,* p. 201
- *Test Generator (One-Stop Planner CD-ROM)*

Internet
go.hrw.com (keyword: LE0 12-13)

OBJECTIVES

1. Read and interpret the story
2. Identify and analyze setting
3. Analyze vernacular speech
4. Express understanding through writing, social studies, and music
5. Learn and use new words

SKILLS

Literary
- Identify and analyze setting

Reading
- Analyze vernacular speech

Writing
- List changes in a character for an informative report
- Write an essay on poetic vision
- Analyze a character
- Write a character sketch

Social Studies/Music
- Research and present an oral report on calypso music

Vocabulary
- Learn and use new words

Viewing/Representing
- Make inferences about an artwork (ATE)

Planning

- **Block Schedule**
  Block Scheduling Lesson Plans with Pacing Guide
- **Traditional Schedule**
  Lesson Plans Including Strategies for English-Language Learners
- **One-Stop Planner**
  CD-ROM with *Test Generator*

BROWSING IN THE FILES

Writers on Writing. Naipaul's attitude toward writing is far from romantic. He relates, "I began to write, I am afraid, for no other reason than because I thought it would be nice to be a writer. . . . One assumed it was all very interesting, writing these fabulous things, without pausing to consider what went before—and during—the writing of the fabulous things. . . . In fact writing is just a sort of disease, a sickness. It's a form of incompleteness, it's a form of anguish, it's despair."

Summary ■■

A small, neatly dressed stranger asks to come inside a boy's yard to watch bees. He tells the boy that he is "Black" (B.) Wordsworth, a poet who shares "White" Wordsworth's heart; however, he has never sold a poem. The man insists that the boy is also a poet, and the two become friends. B. Wordsworth encourages the boy to approach even mundane events with reverent delight. He tells him a story of two poets who married and lived happily until the girl poet and her unborn baby died in childbirth. He claims to be writing "the greatest poem in the world" at the rate of one line per month, but he reveals only one line: "The past is deep." One day, the boy finds his friend lying ill in his spare, one-room hut. B. Wordsworth tells the boy that he invented what he said about the two poets and asks him never to return. A year later, the boy finds the hut and its lush garden replaced by a modern building.

Resources

A recording of this story is provided in the *Audio CD Library*:

- Disc 18, Track 7

Before You Read

B. WORDSWORTH

Make the Connection

A Touch of the Poet

How would you describe a poet? Would you know one if you met him or her in the street? In the story you are about to read, a young boy's encounter with a poet transforms his world into "a most exciting place." Would you agree that part of a poet's function is to suggest new angles of vision for the rest of us? Do poets really help "transform" the world?

Quickwrite

Jot down four or five qualities that you associate with poets. Then, as you read, see how your image of a poet corresponds with that of the poet in the story.

Elements of Literature

Setting

The story's **setting** is the back streets of Port-of-Spain, the capital of Trinidad, the Caribbean island where Naipaul lived as a child. As you read, notice how Naipaul uses **imagery** and **dialogue,** as well as factual details, to bring this setting to life.

Background

A story about the magical world of childhood innocence, "B. Wordsworth" brims with all the surprise and joy that children feel when they glimpse a road to the future opening before their eyes. The humor of the story, of which there is plenty, springs from the contrast between the young narrator's view of things and his mother's more cynical view. Whereas Ma sees a funny old geezer at the back gate, the boy sees a poet, a man who lives for beauty, for mango trees, for the stars of heaven, and for ice cream. He sees a man with a wildly romantic and tragic history, someone who can feel for all the creatures of the world. What an opening of a boy's narrow horizon!

The poet in the story is a black Trinidadian who calls himself B. Wordsworth. Before you read, review what you know of another Wordsworth, the one with the first initial W. You might reread page 656 of this book.

Laventille (1984), Port-of-Spain, Trinidad.

Preteaching Vocabulary

Words to Own

Have students read the Words to Own and their definitions listed at the bottom of the selection pages. Then have them choose partners. The first student chooses a word and draws a simple picture suggesting the word's meaning. The second student tries to guess the word. For each incorrect guess, the first student draws another picture until the word is identified. Have partners alternate roles.

Ask students to choose the vocabulary word that fits each blank in the following paragraph:

During the day, I like to [patronize] that outdoor café and enjoy the beautiful [botanical] gardens nearby. As a nightly [rite], I sit sipping my coffee and gaze up at the sky to identify each and every [constellation]. What knowledge can I [distill] from these experiences at the café? You'll have to go there to find out for yourself.

B. Wordsworth

V. S. Naipaul

Three beggars called punctually every day at the hospitable houses in Miguel Street. At about ten an Indian came in his dhoti[1] and white jacket, and we poured a tin of rice into the sack he carried on his back. At twelve an old woman smoking a clay pipe came and she got a cent. At two a blind man led by a boy called for his penny. **A**

Sometimes we had a rogue.[2] One day a man called and said he was hungry. We gave him a meal. He asked for a cigarette and wouldn't go until we had lit it for him. That man never came again.

The strangest caller came one afternoon at about four o'clock. I had come back from school and was in my home clothes. The man said to me, "Sonny, may I come inside your yard?"

He was a small man and he was tidily dressed. He wore a hat, a white shirt, and black trousers.

I asked, "What you want?"

He said, "I want to watch your bees."

We had four small gru-gru palm trees[3] and they were full of uninvited bees.

I ran up the steps and shouted, "Ma, it have a man outside here. He say he want to watch the bees."

My mother came out, looked at the man, and asked in an unfriendly way, "What you want?" **B**

The man said, "I want to watch your bees."

His English was so good, it didn't sound natural, and I could see my mother was worried.

She said to me, "Stay here and watch him while he watch the bees."

The man said, "Thank you, Madam. You have done a good deed today."

He spoke very slowly and very correctly as though every word was costing him money.

We watched the bees, this man and I, for about an hour, squatting near the palm trees.

The man said, "I like watching bees. Sonny, do you like watching bees?"

I said, "I ain't have the time."

He shook his head sadly. He said, "That's what I do, I just watch. I can watch ants for days. Have you ever watched ants? And scorpions, and centipedes, and *congorees*[4]—have you watched those?" **C**

I shook my head.

I said, "What you does do, mister?"

He got up and said, "I am a poet."

I said, "A good poet?"

He said, "The greatest in the world."

"What your name, mister?"

"B. Wordsworth."

"B for Bill?"

"Black. Black Wordsworth. White Wordsworth was my brother. We share one heart. I can watch a small flower like the morning glory and cry." **D**

I said, "Why you does cry?"

"Why, boy? Why? You will know when you grow up. You're a poet, too, you know. And when you're a poet you can cry for everything."

I couldn't laugh.

He said, "You like your mother?"

"When she not beating me."

He pulled out a printed sheet from his hip pocket and said, "On this paper is the greatest poem about mothers and I'm going to sell it to you at a bargain price. For four cents."

I went inside and I said, "Ma, you want to buy a poetry for four cents?"

My mother said, "Tell that blasted man to haul his tail away from my yard, you hear."

I said to B. Wordsworth, "My mother say she ain't have four cents."

B. Wordsworth said, "It is the poet's tragedy."

And he put the paper back in his pocket. He didn't seem to mind.

I said, "Is a funny way to go round selling poetry like that. Only calypsonians[5] do that sort of thing. A lot of people does buy?"

He said, "No one has yet bought a single copy."

"But why you does keep on going round, then?"

1. **dhoti** (dō′tē): loincloth worn by many Hindu men.
2. **rogue** (rōg): archaic for "wandering beggar."
3. **gru-gru** (grōō′grōō′) **palm trees:** spiny-trunked West Indian palm trees.
4. ***congorees*** (käŋ′gə·rēz′): conger eels; long, scaleless eels found in the warm waters of the West Indies.
5. **calypsonians** (kə·lip′so′nē·ənz): West Indian folk musicians who traditionally perform satirical, syncopated songs that are improvised, or composed on the spot. *Calypso* possibly comes from *kaiso,* a Trinidadian dialect word meaning "town crier."

A Elements of Literature
Setting

? What details help you visualize the scene? [Possible responses: "hospitable houses," "an Indian came in his dhoti and white jacket," "an old woman smoking a clay pipe," "a blind man led by a boy."]

B Reading Skills and Strategies
Analyzing the Vernacular

Read the dialogue aloud to students. Ask them how it differs from standard English. ["It have" is used in place of "There is." The third-person singular pronoun "he" is paired with the first-person singular verbs "say" and "want." The verb "do" is missing from the question.] **How would the dialogue of the boy and his mother be phrased in standard English?** [Possible response: "Ma, there's a man outside. He says he wants to watch the bees." "What do you want?"]

C Critical Thinking
Analyzing Character

? What does the man's habit of watching insects for long periods of time suggest about him? [Possible responses: He has nothing else to do; he is very patient, and he loves nature.] **What does his use of standard English suggest?** [Possible response: that he is educated.]

D Literary Connections

? Who is "White Wordsworth," and what do the two "Wordsworths" share? ["White" Wordsworth is a reference to the English poet William Wordsworth. "Black" Wordsworth is the title character of Naipaul's story, a man of African ancestry. The two "Wordsworths" share "one heart"—a love for poetry and nature.]

Reaching All Students

Struggling Readers
This story is a series of episodes that are loosely tied together through the two characters. To help students follow the sequence of events, ask them to list the important events as they read. Students can use the sequence chart, found on Transparency 12 in the Transparency Package, to track the narration. Later, they can use their sequence charts to complete the Reading Check on p. 1048.

English Language Learners
The unfamiliar Trinidad Creole dialect of English will make the dialogue challenging for these students. They can read the story aloud in groups with the understanding that this reading is not a performance but a way to understand the story better. When a reader comes to dialogue in Creole, he or she can pause and discuss the meaning of the dialect with the group.

Advanced Learners
As students read the story, ask them to consider the validity of the title character's declaration that he and William Wordsworth "share one heart." In what ways is this true? In what ways are the two men very different? Have students refer to specific Wordsworth poems to support their conclusions in a postreading discussion.

A Elements of Literature

Setting

? The setting of William Wordsworth's poetry is the Lake District in the north of England. How does the tropical setting of Trinidad help form B. Wordsworth's ideas about life? [Possible response: Insects, flowers, and fruits abound in the tropical climate. B. Wordsworth has an appreciation for these things and takes the time to notice them.]

B Critical Thinking

Making Connections

? What Romantic attitudes are stressed in Naipaul's description of B. Wordsworth's home? [Possible responses: a love of nature, a dislike of urban life.]

C Struggling Readers

Rereading

? Reread this paragraph to try to get inside the boy's head and experience what he is feeling as he looks up. Why does looking at the sky help him? [Possible responses: It makes him forget about his problems; he realizes that he and his difficulties are insignificant; he feels connected to something larger than himself.]

D Reading Skills and Strategies

Analyzing the Vernacular

Ask students to make some generalizations about the Trinidad vernacular from these lines of dialogue. [Possible responses: Interrogative words are directly followed by a personal pronoun in a question. A second-person singular pronoun takes a third-person singular verb. The word "ain't" is used to introduce a question.]

He said, "In this way I watch many things, and I always hope to meet poets."

I said, "You really think I is a poet?"

"You're as good as me," he said.

And when B. Wordsworth left, I prayed I would see him again.

About a week later, coming back from school one afternoon, I met him at the corner of Miguel Street.

He said, "I have been waiting for you for a long time."

I said, "You sell any poetry yet?"

He shook his head.

(A) He said, "In my yard I have the best mango tree in Port-of-Spain.[6] And now the mangoes are ripe and red and very sweet and juicy. I have waited here for you to tell you this and to invite you to come and eat some of my mangoes."

(B) He lived in Alberto Street in a one-roomed hut placed right in the center of the lot. The yard seemed all green. There was the big mango tree. There was a coconut tree and there was a plum tree. The place looked wild, as though it wasn't in the city at all. You couldn't see all the big concrete houses in the street.

He was right. The mangoes were sweet and juicy. I ate about six, and the yellow mango juice ran down my arms to my elbows and down my mouth to my chin and my shirt was stained.

My mother said when I got home, "Where you was? You think you is a man now and could go all over the place? Go cut a whip for me."

She beat me rather badly, and I ran out of the house swearing that I would never come back. I went to B. Wordsworth's house. I was so angry, my nose was bleeding.

B. Wordsworth said, "Stop crying, and we will go for a walk."

I stopped crying, but I was breathing short. We went for a walk. We walked down St. Clair Avenue to the Savannah[7] and we walked to the racecourse.

(C) B. Wordsworth said, "Now, let us lie on the grass and look up at the sky, and I want you to think how far those stars are from us." I did as he told me, and I saw what he meant. I felt like nothing, and at the same time I had never felt so big and great in all my life. I forgot all my anger and all my tears and all the blows.

When I said I was better, he began telling me the names of the stars, and I particularly remembered the constellation of Orion the Hunter,[8] though I don't really know why. I can spot Orion even today, but I have forgotten the rest.

Then a light was flashed into our faces, and we saw a policeman. We got up from the grass.

The policeman said, "What you doing here?"

B. Wordsworth said, "I have been asking myself the same question for forty years."

We became friends, B. Wordsworth and I. He told me, "You must never tell anybody about me and about the mango tree and the coconut tree and the plum tree. You must keep that a secret. If you tell anybody, I will know, because I am a poet."

I gave him my word and I kept it.

I liked his little room. It had no more furniture than George's front room,[9] but it looked cleaner and healthier. But it also looked lonely.

(D) One day I asked him. "Mister Wordsworth, why you does keep all this bush in your yard? Ain't it does make the place damp?"

He said, "Listen, and I will tell you a story. Once upon a time a boy and girl met each other and they fell in love. They loved each other so much they got married. They were both poets. He loved words. She loved grass and flowers and trees. They lived happily in a single room, and then one day, the girl poet said to the boy poet, 'We are going to have another poet in the family.' But this poet was never born, because the girl died, and the young poet died with her, inside her. And the girl's husband was very sad, and he said he would

6. **Port-of-Spain:** seaport on the island of Trinidad; capital of Trinidad and Tobago.

7. **Savannah** (sə·van′ə): two-hundred-acre park in the center of Port-of-Spain. The racecourse is located there.

8. **Orion** (ō·rī′ən) **the Hunter:** constellation named for a hunter in Greek and Roman mythology whom Diana—the goddess of the moon and of hunting—loves but accidentally kills.

9. **George's front room:** George is a character in another story in Naipaul's book *Miguel Street.*

WORDS TO OWN

constellation (kän′stə·lā′shən) *n.:* group of stars, usually named after the object, animal, or mythological being its outline, or configuration, suggests.

Crossing the Curriculum

Geography

Ask students to locate Trinidad and Tobago on a map of the Caribbean region. Then, ask them to draw a larger map of the islands on a sheet of poster board. Have students indicate where Port-of-Spain and other cities are located, and have them note such geographical features as mountains, rivers, and lakes. Display these maps in the classroom.

Skill Link

Producing a Research Report

V. S. Naipaul writes, "The society I came from was colonial, and was originally a slave society, to which, later, people like myself, from Asia, went." Ask students to research the history of Trinidad and to report their findings in a written report. The report should include the effects of being a part of the British Empire on the people of Trinidad. For example, Naipaul reports, "When I was a child in Trinidad . . . there were eight or perhaps twelve free places in the secondary schools. Twelve free places in an island that had a population of over half a million. What an attitude to human beings!"

Remind students to credit the sources of all exact quotations and any original ideas or theories that they include.

The Trial (1986) by Julio Larraz. Oil on canvas.

© Julio Larraz, Private Collection, Courtesy Nohra Haime Gallery, New York City.

never touch a thing in the girl's garden. And so the garden remained, and grew high and wild."

I looked at B. Wordsworth, and as he told me this lovely story, he seemed to grow older. I understood his story. **E**

We went for long walks together. We went to the Botanical Gardens and the Rock Gardens. We climbed Chancellor Hill in the late afternoon and watched the darkness fall on Port-of-Spain, and watched the lights go on in the city and on the ships in the harbor.

He did everything as though he were doing it for the first time in his life. He did everything as though he were doing some church rite. **F**

He would say to me, "Now, how about having some ice cream?"

And when I said, yes, he would grow very serious and say, "Now, which café shall we patronize?" As though it were a very important thing. He would think for some time about it, and finally say, "I think I will go and negotiate the purchase with that shop."

The world became a most exciting place.

One day, when I was in his yard, he said to me, "I have a great secret which I am now going to tell you."

I said, "It really secret?"

"At the moment, yes."

I looked at him, and he looked at me. He said, "This is just between you and me, remember. I am writing a poem."

"Oh." I was disappointed.

He said, "But this is a different sort of poem. This is the greatest poem in the world."

I whistled.

He said, "I have been working on it for more than five years now. I will finish it in about twenty-two years from now, that is, if I keep on writing at the present rate." **G**

WORDS TO OWN

botanical (bə·tan′i·kəl) *adj.:* of plants or plant life; connected to the science of botany, which is the study of plants, their structure, growth, and so on.

rite *n.:* formal ceremony.

patronize (pā′trən·īz′) *v.:* be a customer of.

RESPONDING TO THE ART

Julio Larraz (1944–) is a Cuban painter who works in the United States. Since the late 1970s, Larraz has painted in a realistic yet vaguely symbolic style that makes the viewer think twice about ordinary objects. Paintings like *The Trial* suggest multiple interpretations, requiring the viewer to participate in creating meaning.
Activity. Ask students what event or narrative they think is represented in the painting. Is the man attending a trial? Is he on trial? Why can't his face be seen? Encourage students to interpret freely. Remind them that a "trial" may not be a legal proceeding: It can be any struggle.

E Reading Skills and Strategies

Making Inferences

? What does Naipaul manage to tell you about B. Wordsworth in these two sentences? [Possible responses: The man in the story who lost his wife and child is B. Wordsworth himself. Even retelling the story is painful, causing him to appear to age.]

F Critical Thinking

Extending the Text

? What do B. Wordsworth's attitudes suggest about how a poet should face everyday experience? [Possible response: A poet should bring to the day-to-day world a fresh eye and a sense of wonder or religious awe.]

G Reading Skills and Strategies

Drawing Conclusions

? Do you think B. Wordsworth will finish this poem? Explain. [Possible responses: Yes, he's a man of great patience who probably believes that great poetry takes a long time to write. No, he just wants to impress the boy or give himself something to strive for.]

Getting Students Involved

Cooperative Learning

A Résumé for Wordsworth. Divide the class into groups of four, and ask them to compose a résumé for B. Wordsworth. Students can get most of the basic identifying information (name, address, occupation, and so on) from the story. Then they can be creative and invent the information about his education, work experience, and accomplishments that would ordinarily appear on a résumé. After the groups have finished, have them share their résumés with the class.

Enrichment Activity

Discussing Current Events. Ask students to work in groups to list ten problems often discussed in the news. These can range from how to prevent pollution to how to encourage people to vote. When the list is completed, ask groups to exchange them. When a group gets a new list, students can discuss how B. Wordsworth, with his poet's sensibility, would respond to the problems. Have each group report to the class on three problems from their list.

LITERATURE AND SOCIETY

The Romantic poet William Wordsworth did his part to glorify childhood in his "Ode: Intimations of Immortality from Recollections of Early Childhood." In this poem, Wordsworth says that children come freshly from God, trailing clouds of glory. As they mature and become engrossed in the mundane tasks of daily life, the glory fades. Wordsworth views childhood as a state distinct from adulthood. This state fades gradually as people mature, but it leaves a significant mark on the rest of their lives. This view is a considerable departure from the idea of children as miniature adults.

A Reading Skills and Strategies

Drawing Conclusions

? Why does Naipaul include the anecdote about the pin? [Possible response: B. Wordsworth is experimental, and he compares the rules of the real world to the rules of the poet's idealized world.]

B Reading Skills and Strategies

Making Inferences

? What does this paragraph imply about B. Wordsworth's poem? Explain your reasoning. [Possible response: There really is no poem. He would have talked about the poem more if he were really working on it.]

LITERATURE AND SOCIETY

The Invention of Childhood

In our century, we often think of childhood as a time free of responsibilities and full of imaginative adventure. But this wasn't always so. Childhood wasn't seen as a special period until the early nineteenth century, when poets and philosophers began to idealize childhood in their writings.

Conflicting views, difficult lives. Before the Romantic period, children were seen as miniature adults. In many medieval and Renaissance paintings, children were drawn exactly as the adults were, only smaller. Until quite recently, children also lived mostly as part of an adult community: They conversed, ate, and worked with adults as soon as they were able to. If any distinction was made, it was merely that children were slightly more primitive—they required constant interaction with adults in order to be properly "civilized."

In the late eighteenth century, the French philosopher Jean Jacques Rousseau challenged this belief, dramatically proclaiming childhood to be the purest human state and society's process of "civilization" to be corrosive and corrupt. Yet upper-class European families continued to mold their children in traditional ways, and lower-class families, often reliant on every family member's contribution to the communal pot, packed their children off to work in factories as soon as they could hold a broom or thread a needle.

"You does write a lot, then?"

He said, "Not any more. I just write one line a month. But I make sure it is a good line."

I asked, "What was last month's good line?"

He looked up at the sky, and said, "*The past is deep*."

I said, "It is a beautiful line."

B. Wordsworth said, "I hope to distill the experiences of a whole month into that single line of poetry. So, in twenty-two years, I shall have written a poem that will sing to all humanity."

I was filled with wonder.

A Our walks continued. We walked along the sea wall at Docksite one day, and I said, "Mr. Wordsworth, if I drop this pin in the water, you think it will float?"

He said, "This is a strange world. Drop your pin, and let us see what will happen."

The pin sank.

I said, "How is the poem this month?"

B But he never told me any other line. He merely said, "Oh, it comes, you know. It comes."

Or we would sit on the sea wall and watch the liners come into the harbor.

But of the greatest poem in the world I heard no more.

I felt he was growing older.

"How you does live, Mr. Wordsworth?" I asked him one day.

He said, "You mean how I get money?"

When I nodded, he laughed in a crooked way.

WORDS TO OWN

distill (di·stil′) *v.:* to draw out the essence of.

Assessing Learning

Check Test: True-False

1. William Wordsworth is a famous Trinidadian poet. [False]
2. B. Wordsworth asks to watch bees in the boy's yard. [True]
3. The boy's mother welcomes the older man's friendship with her son. [False]
4. B. Wordsworth makes a meager living by singing calypsos. [True]
5. After B. Wordsworth's death, all signs of his house and yard disappear. [True]

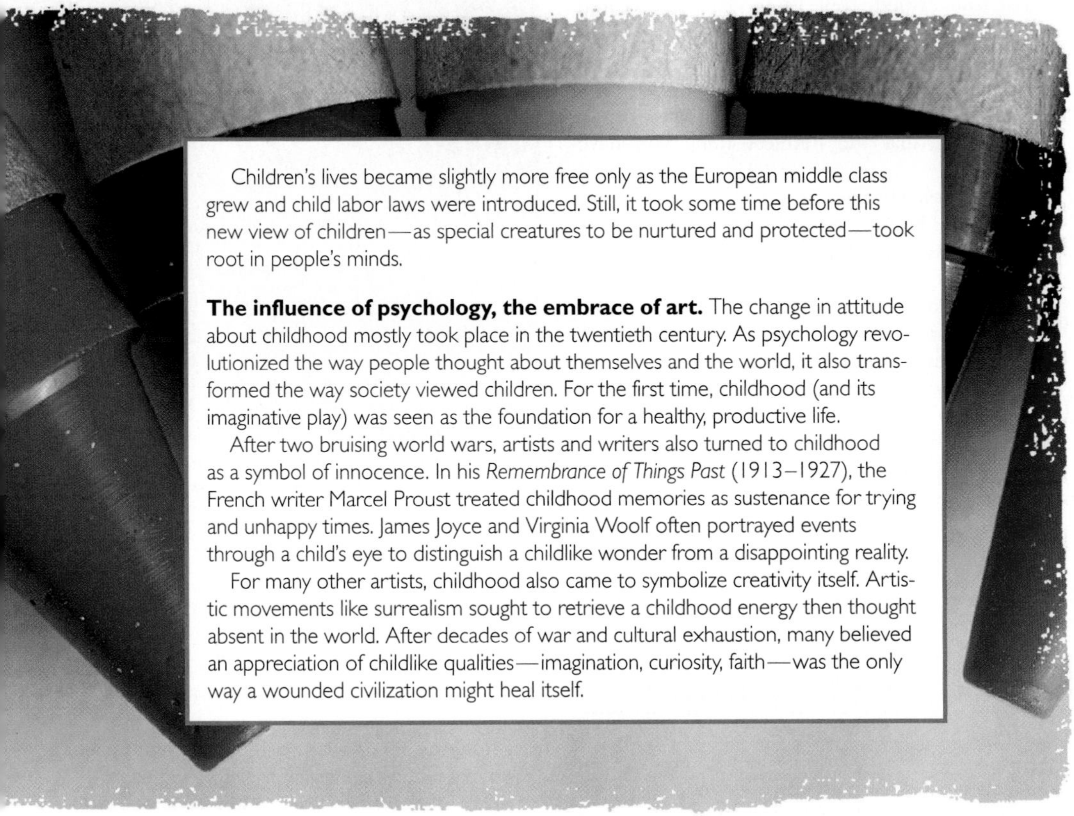

Children's lives became slightly more free only as the European middle class grew and child labor laws were introduced. Still, it took some time before this new view of children—as special creatures to be nurtured and protected—took root in people's minds.

The influence of psychology, the embrace of art. The change in attitude about childhood mostly took place in the twentieth century. As psychology revolutionized the way people thought about themselves and the world, it also transformed the way society viewed children. For the first time, childhood (and its imaginative play) was seen as the foundation for a healthy, productive life.

After two bruising world wars, artists and writers also turned to childhood as a symbol of innocence. In his *Remembrance of Things Past* (1913–1927), the French writer Marcel Proust treated childhood memories as sustenance for trying and unhappy times. James Joyce and Virginia Woolf often portrayed events through a child's eye to distinguish a childlike wonder from a disappointing reality.

For many other artists, childhood also came to symbolize creativity itself. Artistic movements like surrealism sought to retrieve a childhood energy then thought absent in the world. After decades of war and cultural exhaustion, many believed an appreciation of childlike qualities—imagination, curiosity, faith—was the only way a wounded civilization might heal itself.

He said, "I sing calypsos in the calypso season."

"And that last you the rest of the year?"

"It is enough."

"But you will be the richest man in the world when you write the greatest poem?"

He didn't reply.

One day when I went to see him in his little house, I found him lying on his little bed. He looked so old and so weak, that I found myself wanting to cry. **C**

He said, "The poem is not going well."

He wasn't looking at me. He was looking through the window at the coconut tree, and he was speaking as though I wasn't there. He said, "When I was twenty I felt the power within myself." Then, almost in front of my eyes, I could see his face growing older and more tired. He said, "But that—that was a long time ago."

And then—I felt it so keenly, it was as though I had been slapped by my mother. I could see it clearly on his face. It was there for everyone to see. Death on the shrinking face.

He looked at me, and saw my tears and sat up.

He said, "Come." I went and sat on his knees.

He looked into my eyes, and he said, "Oh, you can see it, too. I always knew you had the poet's eye." **D**

He didn't even look sad, and that made me burst out crying loudly.

He pulled me to his thin chest, and said, "Do you want me to tell you a funny story?" and he smiled encouragingly at me.

But I couldn't reply.

He said, "When I have finished this story, I want you to promise that you will go away and never come back to see me. Do you promise?"

I nodded.

C Reading Skills and Strategies

Making Inferences

? In light of his poor health, what does B. Wordsworth's statement suggest about his poem? [Possible responses: His "poem" is really the manner in which he lives his life. His poem is not going well because he is sick.]

D Reading Skills and Strategies

Responding to the Text

? What does B. Wordsworth mean by saying that the boy possesses "the poet's eye"? [Possible responses: He means that the boy sees things as a poet would or that the boy has the capacity of a poet for experiencing great emotion.]

Using Students' Strengths

Auditory Learners

As part of the Reading Skills and Strategies lesson on p. 1049, students may benefit from hearing passages written in the vernacular read aloud. If possible ask students in your school who come from the Caribbean area to help two or three student volunteers to prepare oral readings and perform them for the class. If possible, readers should use the pronunciation typical of Trinidad and Tobago.

Visual Learners

For Choices #4 on p. 1049, have students list the details they want to use in describing a person. Then have them find illustrative pictures in newspapers and magazines. Students can assemble the pictures in a collage, describe the person they have selected, and explain how the collage illustrates the written description.

RESPONDING TO THE ART

Julio Larraz, a Cuban artist, suggests in *Papiamento* a relationship among the sea, the tree, and the lone female figure. The combination of realism and poetic vision complements Naipaul's story.

A Critical Thinking

Extending the Text

? What do these changes signify? [Possible responses: the encroachment of modern urban life on nature, the tendency of modern life to stifle ideas; the idea that poetry has no lasting effect on modern life.]

MAKING MEANINGS

First Thoughts [Respond]

1. Possible responses: B. Wordsworth is presented very sympathetically, so it's easy to like him and regret his death. He is peculiar and lies to the boy, so it's difficult to have positive feelings toward him.

Shaping Interpretations [Interpret]

2. The boy learns sensitivity to the world.
3. Possible response: The story, which explains much of his behavior, is true. He denies it because he doesn't want the boy to be saddened by his story or his death.
4. In saying "I have been asking myself the same question . . .," he is questioning the purpose of his life and of human existence in general. Many poets do seek to answer "What are we doing here?"
5. Possible responses: Poetry involves observation (watching the natural world), enjoying (eating from the mango tree), sharing, questioning, and remembering experience. Poetry touches all aspects of life.
6. Possible responses: the palm trees humming with bees, the poet's yard, and the clear, starry skies.
7. Possible response: Naipaul was influenced by people who, like Wordsworth, looked for beauty in the world. He was encouraged to remember his experiences. The last scene in the story suggests that the poet's role includes acting as a witness, so that the things he or she sees won't be forgotten.

He said, "Good. Well, listen. That story I told you about the boy poet and the girl poet, do you remember that? That wasn't true. It was something I just made up. All this talk about poetry and the greatest poem in the world, that wasn't true, either. Isn't that the funniest thing you have heard?"

But his voice broke.

I left the house, and ran home crying, like a poet, for everything I saw.

A I walked along Alberto Street a year later, but I could find no sign of the poet's house. It hadn't vanished, just like that. It had been pulled down, and a big, two-storied building had taken its place. The mango tree and the plum tree and the coconut tree had all been cut down, and there was brick and concrete everywhere.

It was just as though B. Wordsworth had never existed.

Papiamento (1987) by Julio Larraz. Oil on canvas.

© Julio Larraz, Private Collection, Courtesy Nohra Haime Gallery, New York City.

MAKING MEANINGS

First Thoughts

1. How did this story make you feel about B. Wordsworth? How do you account for your reaction?

Reading Check

With two other students, devise a story map that shows all the important events in **chronological order.** Who is B. Wordsworth? How does he explain his connection with W. Wordsworth, the great nineteenth-century Romantic poet?

Shaping Interpretations

2. What does the boy learn from B. Wordsworth?
3. Do you think B. Wordsworth's tragic love story is true? If it is true, why would he deny it?
4. Consider what B. Wordsworth says to the policeman who asks, "What you doing here?" What deeper significance do you see in his reply? (Is this what poets also seek to know?)
5. Find some of B. Wordsworth's statements about poetry, and then consider the story's **theme.** What might Naipaul want to express about the nature of poetry?
6. What specific pictures of the **setting** are most vivid in your mind? If you were going to illustrate the story, what **images** would you concentrate on?
7. If we think of the narrator in the story as the author's recollection of himself at that age, what does the story suggest about the influences that made Naipaul a writer? What does it suggest about his view of the poet's position and role in society?

Connecting with the Text

8. Review your Quickwrite notes about poets. Then, find passages in the story that contrast the mother's no-nonsense ways with the poetic vision of B. Wordsworth. Do you find these two types of people in your own world? Explain.

Connecting with the Text [Apply]

8. Students should cite passages showing the mother as pragmatic and Wordsworth as a visionary. [Possible responses: The mother is wary of the stranger who wants to watch her bees and tells her son to watch him. Later, she refuses to buy Wordsworth's poem for four cents. On the other hand, Wordsworth can sit for hours and observe nature. He does everything with a sense of joy and discovery. Students will probably agree that both types of people exist in the world.]

Reading Check

Students should include the following events in their story maps: The boy meets B. Wordsworth, the boy learns about Wordsworth's life and his "poem," they spend time together, Wordsworth becomes ill and dies, the house and garden disappear. B. (Black) Wordsworth is the poetic "soulmate" or brother of W. (White) Wordsworth.

READING SKILLS AND STRATEGIES

Analyzing the Vernacular

The speech recorded in this story sounds unusual to people who live outside Trinidad. What Naipaul has captured is the **vernacular,** or everyday speech, of people who live on the island. The Trinidad vernacular is a creole form of English, which means it incorporates **idioms, pronunciations,** and **grammatical constructions** of the island's African, Spanish, Asian Indian, and other settlers.

1. Find three conversations in the Trinidad vernacular in this story, and read them aloud to hear their special rhythm.
2. Try to make a generalization describing how this Trinidad vernacular uses verb forms.

CHOICES: Building Your Portfolio

Writer's Notebook

1. Collecting Ideas for an Informative Report

WORK IN PROGRESS

One kind of informative report traces a character's development throughout a story. What changes does the boy undergo from the beginning to the end of "B. Wordsworth"? Make a list of the changes, and list evidence from the story to support your ideas. What thesis statement, or controlling idea, could you write to express what you've determined about the boy's development? Save your work for the Writer's Workshop on page 1053.

Expository Writing

2. Seeing Things Differently

Near the end of the story, the poet pays the boy the highest of compliments, saying "I always knew you had the poet's eye." In a brief essay, explain what you think the poet's eye sees. How is poetic vision different from an everyday perspective, both in the story and in your own world?

Analyzing a Character

3. Heart of a Poet

Write a brief essay in which you analyze the **character** of B. Wordsworth. What is he like? Why does he call himself B. Wordsworth? Before you write, gather your details by skimming the story and filling in a chart like the following:

Methods of Characterization	Details	What They Reveal
Actions		
Speech		
Responses of others		
Appearance		
Writer's direct evaluations		

Creative Writing

4. People Portraits

Naipaul has immortalized an unusual character by describing him in words. Think of someone you have known who is unusual in some way, and write a character sketch of that person. Describe his or her home, appearance, job, personality, and actions. Be sure you show how you feel about your subject.

Social Studies / Music

5. Day-o

Find out more about calypso—its origins, developments, and influence. Present your findings in an oral report accompanied by recorded (or live) music.

Using Students' Strengths

Verbal/Linguistic and Interpersonal Learners

For the Reading Skills and Strategies lesson, have students role-play a conversation between the boy and his mother, using the Trinidadian vernacular. The students can use a hypothetical scene, such as the boy telling his mother about Wordsworth's death or about his own intentions to be a poet when he grows up. Encourage students to keep the personalities of the characters in mind as well as their peculiarities of speech.

READING SKILLS AND STRATEGIES

Possible Responses

1. The first encounter between the boy and man, beginning with "The man said, 'I like watching bees. . . .' " (p. 1043); the conversation beginning with ". . . he said to me, 'I have a great secret which I am now going to tell you . . ." (p. 1045); and the one beginning with " 'How you does live, Mr. Wordsworth?' I asked him one day . . ." (p. 1046).
2. The verb forms are almost always in the present tense; third-person pronouns are used with first-person verbs; second-person pronouns take a third-person verb.

Grading Timesaver

Rubrics for each Choices assignment appear on p. 201 in the *Portfolio Management System.*

CHOICES: Building Your Portfolio

WORK IN PROGRESS

1. **Writer's Notebook** Review with students the best way to write a thesis statement and have them practice writing them.
2. **Expository Writing** Before they begin writing, ask students to brainstorm the different elements of a poetic vision. You might encourage them to use clustering to generate ideas, with "poetic vision" placed in the circle in the center of a word web.
3. **Analyzing a Character** One way to handle this assignment is to let students work together in groups of five. Each member of a group can be responsible for one aspect of characterization listed in the chart, and they can all share the details they uncover. Each student may then interpret individually what the details reveal about the character and how aspects of the character's personality relate to one another.
4. **Creative Writing** Students might organize their thoughts by listing the various aspects they wish to include about the person across a page as headings on a chart. Then they can fill in the chart with appropriate details.
5. **Social Studies/Music** You may suggest that students work in groups, with each member researching a different aspect of calypso music.

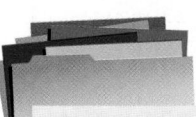

OBJECTIVES
1. Read and interpret the poem
2. Identify free verse
3. Express understanding through critical and creative writing

SKILLS
Literary
- Identify free verse

Writing
- List subjects from the natural world for an informative report
- Write a free verse poem using sensory images

Planning

- **Block Schedule**
  Block Scheduling Lesson Plans with Pacing Guide
- **Traditional Schedule**
  Lesson Plans Including Strategies for English-Language Learners
- **One-Stop Planner**
  CD-ROM with Test Generator

Summary ■■

In Part i, the speaker notes the quickness and ease with which an astonishing variety of mushrooms appear in the moist season. In Part ii, the speaker wonders about the mushrooms' origins because they seem to appear suddenly, with the speed and energy of thunderstorms. In Part iii, she notes a more disturbing aspect of mushrooms—how they spring from decay, sometimes glow in the dark, and have various tastes, some of which are unpleasant. In Part iv, the speaker admits that she gathers mushrooms partly because they remind her of death and of the life that springs from death. She concludes by linking mushrooms to decay, hope, and the creative process of her poetry.

Margaret Atwood
(1939–   )

One of Canada's foremost writers and critics, Margaret Atwood was born in Ottawa and now lives in Toronto. Her often bizarre short stories have frequently appeared in *The New Yorker* and have been collected in *Dancing Girls* (1977) and *Bluebeard's Egg* (1983). Her many novels often feature unusual heroines, like the daughter of the wilderness in *Surfacing* (1972) and the highwaywoman in *The Robber Bride* (1993). Atwood also frequently explores the problems of living in an increasingly technological—and often alien—environment. Her 1986 novel *The Handmaid's Tale* is a nightmarish vision of a future dictatorship in which women are used chiefly for breeding purposes. *Alias Grace* (1996) is a disturbing, mysterious novel based on a notorious nineteenth-century Canadian murder case, in which a young Irish maid, Grace Marks, was accused and convicted of murdering her employer and his mistress. The book grew out of Atwood's research into women and their roles in Canada's early history.

Margaret Atwood (1989).

Atwood's father was an expert on insects, and as a child, Atwood spent a good part of each year with her parents in the wilderness. Consequently, she developed a keen eye for nature, as her poem "Mushrooms" demonstrates. In speaking about her poems, Atwood once said, "I don't think of poetry as a 'rational' activity but as an aural one. My poems usually begin with words or phrases which appeal more because of their sound than their meaning, and the movement and phrasing of a poem are very important to me."

Before You Read
MUSHROOMS

Make the Connection
The Cycle of Life

A curious property of the imagination is its power to expand upon the most ordinary subjects. The growth and decay of a common plant, for example, can trigger reflections about the arc of human life or the vast, seemingly unending cycle of birth and death in nature.

Quickwrite
What do you associate with mushrooms? Before you read this poem, jot down a few notes.

Elements of Literature
Free Verse

You will notice striking imagery and hear sound effects in Atwood's poem, but you will not hear the regular repetition of stressed and unstressed syllables we call **meter.** That is because "Mushrooms" is written in **free verse,** poetry that does not use regular meter or a fixed rhyme scheme. To create music, free-verse poems use devices like internal rhyme, alliteration, assonance, and onomatopoeia. **Rhythm** is created by the use of irregular line lengths and repeated grammatical structures.

go.hrw.com
LEO 12-13

Resources: Print and Media

Reading
- *Graphic Organizers for Active Reading,* p. 104
- *Audio CD Library*
  Disc 18, Track 8

Assessment
- *Formal Assessment,* p. 210
- *Portfolio Management System,* p. 202
- *Test Generator (One-Stop Planner CD-ROM)*

Internet

go.hrw.com (keyword: LEO 12-13)

Mushrooms Ⓐ

Margaret Atwood

i

In this moist season,
mist on the lake and thunder
afternoons in the distance

they ooze up through the earth
during the night,
like bubbles, like tiny Ⓑ
bright red balloons
filling with water;
a sound below sound, the thumbs of rubber
gloves turned softly inside out.

In the mornings, there is the leaf mold
starred with nipples,
with cool white fishgills, Ⓒ
leathery purple brains,
fist-sized suns dulled to the color of embers,
poisonous moons, pale yellow.

ii

Where do they come from?

For each thunderstorm that travels
overhead there's another storm
that moves parallel in the ground.
Struck lightning is where they meet. Ⓓ

Underfoot there's a cloud of rootlets,
shed hairs or a bundle of loose threads
blown slowly through the midsoil.
These are their flowers, these fingers
reaching through darkness to the sky,
these eyeblinks
that burst and powder the air with spores.

iii

They feed in shade, on halfleaves
as they return to water,
on slowly melting logs,
deadwood. They glow
in the dark sometimes. They taste Ⓔ
of rotten meat or cloves
or cooking steak or bruised
lips or new snow.

Reaching All Students

English Language Learners
Difficulty with English pronunciations may prevent students from appreciating the sound of the poem. Read the poem aloud for them, stressing the onomatopoeic and alliterative qualities of words like *moist, mist, thunder, ooze, bubbles, balloons*.

Advanced Learners
Ask students to consider what Atwood's poetic vision is as they read the poem. Then have them compare and contrast her view of poetry with the views of Dylan Thomas and B. Wordsworth.

BROWSING IN THE FILES

About the Author. A central theme in Margaret Atwood's work is that of individual consciousness struggling to survive in a shifting, hostile world. In her poetry, this conflict is acted out against a background of "struck lightning"—where light and dark, life and death, and consciousness and unconsciousness join in a mysterious dance.

Ⓐ Literary Connections

Sylvia Plath
Sylvia Plath wrote a poem with the same title, in which the mushrooms are the speakers.

Ⓑ Elements of Literature

Free Verse
Identify some of the literary devices used to create music in this poem. [Possible responses: Assonance is woven throughout; for example, repeated *oo* sounds; alliteration (the *s* sounds) appears in ll. 1–3, 16, and 25.]

Ⓒ Reading Skills and Strategies

Making Inferences
? What is the speaker referring to with the words *nipples, fishgills, brains, suns,* and *moons?* [the shapes of different kinds of mushrooms]

Ⓓ Critical Thinking

Challenging the Text
? Does the metaphor comparing the roots of mushrooms to a storm blown through the soil make sense? Why or why not? [Possible responses: No, it's too fanciful because a storm cloud can't blow through solid soil; yes, the delicate white root tissue is reminiscent of clouds.]

Ⓔ Struggling Readers

Finding Details
? What three characteristics of mushrooms are revealed in part iii? [They feed in the shade; they glow in the dark; they have various tastes, such as that of rotten meat, bruised lips, or new snow.]

Making Meanings

First Thoughts [Respond]

1. Students may find the images in ll. 4–16 compelling. Most will prefer the more unusual and vivid images, such as "leathery purple brains."

Shaping Interpretations [Interpret]

2. Assonance: *flower* and *powder* in ll. 25 and 28; *feed* and *leaves* in l. 29. Alliteration appears in l. 7 and in l. 25, among others. Prepositional phrases using *in* begin two stanzas in the first section, and the repetition of *like* creates rhythm in l. 6.

3. The *b* sound.

4. Enriched soil.

5. Students will probably suggest that "bright red balloons" and "starred with nipples" describe the mushroom at the bottom of the photo on p. 1051. "Leathery purple brains" could refer to the mushroom at the top of the same photo. Original metaphors may include tables, cushions, or buttons.

6. The cycle of birth, death, and regeneration.

7. It appeals to sight, as in the reference to suns, embers, and pale yellow moons (ll. 15–16); it appeals to hearing and touch, as in the references to thunder (l. 2) and to balloons being filled (ll. 7–9), and through the choice of such words as *softly* (l. 10) and *leathery* (l. 14). Appeal to taste occurs in ll. 33–36 and to smell in ll. 40–42.

8. Possible responses: The mushrooms suggest decay because they feed on decaying matter and will decay themselves, but their sudden appearance suggests hope. They suggest dirt because they are nourished in soil and some varieties have an earthy taste. They suggest poetry because they embody both bright and dark aspects of existence.

Challenging the Text [Evaluate]

9. Possible responses: Mushrooms pop up overnight, much as poems are thought to "pop" into the minds of poets; their process of birth, death, and regeneration reflects distressing and uplifting elements of existence—the subject of much poetry. Some may find the metaphor too obscure to be effective; others will appreciate the subtlety.

iv

It isn't only
for food I hunt them
but for the hunt and because
they smell of death and the waxy
skins of the newborn,
flesh into earth into flesh.

Here is the handful
of shadow I have brought back to you:
this decay, this hope, this mouthful of dirt, this poetry.

Making Meanings

First Thoughts

1. What do you feel is the poem's strongest **image**? Why?

Shaping Interpretations

2. Read the poem aloud. What uses of **assonance** and **alliteration** help create its music? Where do repeated grammatical structures help create a **rhythm**?

3. In lines 6–10, what repeated consonant suggests the sound of the fingers of rubber gloves turning inside out?

4. "Leaf mold" can be defined as "soil enriched by decayed leaves" or "mold that grows on leaves." Which definition applies in line 11?

5. In lines 6–16, the poet describes various kinds of mushrooms, some against the background of leaf mold. Which mushrooms in the photographs on pages 1051 and 1052 would you match up with Atwood's descriptions? After you review your Quickwrite notes, think up a **metaphor** of your own for each of the photographs.

6. What biological process does line 42 refer to?

7. What senses does the poem appeal to? Quote examples from the poem.

8. Explain the poem's last four lines. How could mushrooms suggest decay, hope, mouthfuls of dirt, and poetry?

Challenging the Text

9. Explain the poem's **extended metaphor** in your own words. In your view, how effective is it?

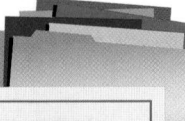

Choices: Building Your Portfolio

Writer's Notebook

1. Collecting Ideas for an Informative Report

Atwood's clinical and unsentimental poem certainly shows that she knows a great deal about mushrooms. Brainstorm to develop a list of subjects from the natural world—animal, vegetable, or mineral—that you want to know more about. Save your notes for use in the Writer's Workshop on page 1053.

Creative Writing

2. Poetry of the Everyday

Choose a simple subject from nature such as butterflies, lions, sand, or worms. What sounds do you associate with your subject? List words that have these sounds and also have some meaning associated with your subject. Then, use these words in a four- or five-line **free verse** poem about your subject. Try to include sensory images.

Grading Timesaver

Rubrics for each Choices assignment appear on p. 202 in the *Portfolio Management System.*

Choices: Building Your Portfolio

1. Writer's Notebook You may want to brainstorm a list of topics with the class.

2. Creative Writing Encourage students to list on a chart the sensory images they wish to include. Transparency 7: Sensory Details Chart in the Transparency Package may be useful.

BUILDING YOUR PORTFOLIO

Writer's Workshop

EXPOSITORY WRITING

AN INFORMATIVE REPORT

In "Araby," James Joyce uses his extraordinary imagination to transform his native city into a fictional setting. Yet Joyce's writing was also firmly grounded in his comprehensive knowledge of Dublin. In this Writer's Workshop you'll write an informative report about something *you* know well. In the process, you'll use skills fundamental to other types of writing as you collect, synthesize, and organize information.

Prewriting

1. **Checking your Writer's Notebook.** By doing the Writer's Notebook activities in Collections 12 and 13, you've already begun the prewriting for an informative report. Check through your entries for usable material and ideas; then proceed with the prewriting activities that follow.

WORK IN PROGRESS

2. **Searching for subjects.** Nearly any subject can lend itself to an informative report, as long as you can answer yes to the following four questions:
   - Does it interest you?
   - Do you know something about it already?
   - Will it interest your particular audience (in this case, your classmates)?
   - Can you put together enough information to write about the subject clearly and accurately?

   Begin your search by taking five to ten minutes to brainstorm for possible subjects that meet these four requirements. Here's the list one writer came up with:

Model

volunteering at the animal shelter
stream of consciousness—Joyce, Woolf, Faulkner, others?
Rolling Stones retrospective
plots of soap operas
talk shows today
stepfamilies
computer-animated cartoons
Walt Disney

Technology HELP

See Writer's Workshop 2 CD-ROM. *Assignment: Informative Report.*

ASSIGNMENT
Write a factual report sharing information on a subject.

AIM
To inform your readers.

AUDIENCE
Your classmates or other people interested in your subject.

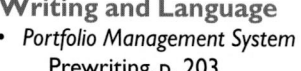

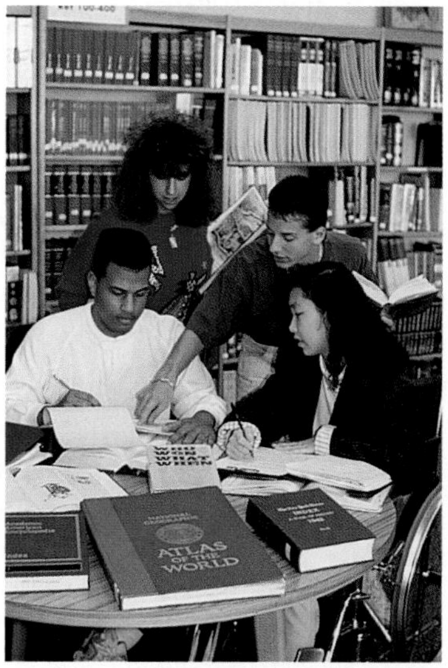

MAIN OBJECTIVE
Write an informative report

PROCESS OBJECTIVES

1. Use appropriate prewriting techniques to identify and develop a topic
2. Create a first draft
3. Use Evaluation Criteria as a basis for determining revision strategies
4. Revise the first draft incorporating suggestions generated by self- or peer evaluation
5. Proofread and correct errors
6. Create a final draft
7. Choose an appropriate method of publication
8. Reflect on progress as a writer

Planning

- **Block Schedule**
  Block Scheduling Lesson Plans with Pacing Guide
- **One-Stop Planner**
  CD-ROM with Test Generator

Introducing the Writer's Workshop

Have students write on a piece of scrap paper the name of one activity they enjoy. Have them be as specific as possible. For example, if a student names reading as a favorite activity, ask the student to specify what kind of reading—spy novels, sports biographies, computer books, and so on. Then, ask several volunteers to share their activities, and write these on the chalkboard. Point out that students probably already know a good deal about the activities they enjoy and that they could probably write about them without extensive research.

Survey the class to see which of the listed activities are of interest to other students. The activities with high scores have a built-in audience and are good potential topics for an informative report.

Resources: Print and Media

Writing and Language
- *Portfolio Management System*
  Prewriting, p. 203
  Peer Editing, p. 204
  Assessment Rubric, p. 205

- *Workshop Resources*
  Revision Strategy Teaching Notes, p. 37
  Revision Strategy Transparencies 19, 20
- *Writer's Workshop 2 CD-ROM*
  Informative Report

Teaching the Writer's Workshop

Prewriting

- Have students review the Prewriting steps developed on pp. 1053–1055. Remind students that memorable informative writing results from the combination of an interesting topic and an interesting method of presentation. A writer who is enthusiastic about a topic can sweep the reader along, even if the reader was not particularly interested in the subject at the start.
- Emphasize the necessity of identifying an audience before writing. Knowledge of the audience will help the writer determine the need to define basic terms and explain fundamental processes—neither of which may be neccessary with an informed audience.

Try It Out

Possible Answers

1. Any specific contemporary writer will serve as a suitable subject: Toni Morrison, Larry McMurtry, Amy Tan, etc.
2. Any specific part-time job will serve as a suitable subject. Some possibilities include working in a fast-food restuarant, working as a clerk in a clothing store, or working as a bagger in a grocery store.
3. Subjects related to computers should probably deal with the kinds of tasks computers can perform, rather than different makes or models of computers. Subjects can include word processing, games, exploring the Internet, or desktop publishing.

Try It Out

For each of the following broad subjects, suggest three or more subjects suitable for an informative report.

1. contemporary writers
2. part-time jobs
3. home computers

3. **Choosing a subject.** Look at the subjects you've listed, and circle the two or three that most appeal to you. Then write a few sentences telling how you might approach each subject. If some of your subjects are broad ones, such as "music," analyze them (break them down into parts or aspects) to determine how to make them more manageable for a short report. In analyzing music, for example, you might come up with "jazz," "alternative rock," or "reggae." Also, check to see whether any of your subjects suggest a comparison-contrast approach. If you jotted down "stream of consciousness—Joyce, Woolf, Faulkner, others?" for example, you might decide to compare and contrast Joyce's and Woolf's use of the technique.

   In choosing a subject, keep in mind that your purpose is to inform—not to describe, persuade, evaluate, or speculate about causes and effects. Check to make sure that the subject you select is one you can approach in an objective, impartial way.

4. **Exploring what you know.** To find out what you already know about your subject, you might simply list facts and examples in the order they occur to you. (Using the *5W-How?* questions—*Who? What? When? Where? Why?* and *How?*—can help you brainstorm.) Or you might create a cluster diagram like this one:

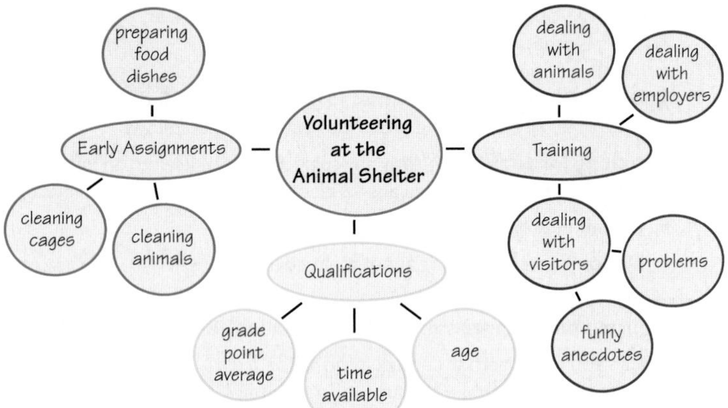

5. **Analyzing your audience.** Before you go on, stop to think about the audience you plan to share the information with. Jot down answers to these questions:
   - What do they already know about the subject?
   - What might they like to learn about the subject?
   - What background information will they need?
   - What terms will I need to define or explain?

   Analyzing your audience in this way will help you settle on an appropriate tone for your report, one that makes you sound knowledgeable and authoritative rather than pompous and pretentious. It will also help you decide whether you already have enough information or whether you need more.

Using Students' Strengths

Auditory Learners

Have students conduct informal oral surveys of classmates to determine whether the subjects for reports they are considering are interesting to others in the class. Ask students to prepare two or three questions ahead of time and to write these down for use during their interviews. Make a point of encouraging students to listen carefully to the responses of the students they interview and to write notes immediately after the other students have finished speaking.

Students should also use the interviews to determine whether or not key vocabulary or processes will have to be defined or explained in their reports.

6. **Gathering information.** Specific, interesting details are what make the difference between a so-so report and a spirited one. If you find that you need more information—facts and statistics, examples, sensory details, or perhaps an anecdote or two—to fulfill your purpose and to intrigue your audience, now is the time to track it down.

Strategies for Elaboration: Crediting Sources

Although you're not writing a formal research paper for this Writer's Workshop, you do need to acknowledge your sources when you use someone else's words or ideas. Otherwise, you'll be committing plagiarism. Use these guidelines to help you decide when to give credit to your sources.

Information you must credit:

- quotations, unless they're widely known, such as Patrick Henry's "Give me liberty or give me death."
- one-of-a-kind or little-known facts, such as data from scientific studies, surveys, and polls
- any original theory, opinion, or conclusion, even if you summarize or paraphrase it

Information you needn't credit:

- facts from standard reference works or multiple sources, such as the birth and death dates of James Joyce
- general information, such as the fact that a well-balanced diet is essential for sound nutrition

7. **Developing your thesis.** Look over the material you've gathered, and write one or two sentences stating the main idea you want your readers to take away from your report. The **thesis,** or **controlling idea,** should identify the subject and the focus of your report and suggest your purpose. Since it will point the way for your readers, make it as clear and specific as you can; but remember that you can always revise it later, if you need to.

8. **Organizing your support.** Clearly presenting the information you've gathered to support your thesis is essential for your readers. The wording of your thesis may suggest a natural order for your supporting material. For example, if your thesis focuses on three significant events in Dylan Thomas's childhood, you might group details about each of the events together and present them in **order of importance.** For a thesis that compares two part-time jobs, you could use the **block method,** presenting first the features of one job and then those of the other. Or you could use the **point-by-point method,** discussing one feature at a time, first for one job and then for the other. For a thesis focusing on change over time, such as one on computer advances in animation, you could use **chronological order.** Experiment until you find the arrangement that best suits your thesis and illustrates the relationships between your ideas.

Communications Handbook HELP

See Research Strategies.

Drafting

- Before beginning to write, have students make a conscious decision about the method of organization they will be using and create at least a brief outline.
- Remind students to use only every other line when they write their drafts. They should also leave extra space in the right margin. These blank spaces will be used for comments and editing marks.

Reaching All Students

English Language Learners

The informative report is a good opportunity for students learning English to present and explain some aspect of their native culture or country. Encourage students to select an aspect of daily life such as school, holidays, or sports. If they use a comparison-contrast method of developing their papers, students may need to interview their classmates to ensure that the information they have concerning the United States is accurate and complete.

Evaluating and Revising

Have students use the Evaluation Criteria to determine revisions that will improve the structure and style of their papers. Also, have students give their drafts a separate review for varied sentence structure, the focus of the Language Workshop in this collection (p. 1057).

Proofreading

Remind students that an error-free paper is an asset to the informative report. Mistakes in spelling, grammar, or usage undermine the authority of the writer and may cause the audience to question the writer's competence.

Publishing

If other classes are also writing informative reports, it may be possible to gather reports from all classes and publish them as topic-centered booklets. Circulate the booklets so that students in all classes have the opportunity to read reports by other students on topics of interest.

Reflecting

Have students respond to these reflection questions:

1. Did I select the right topic? Was there a better choice? If so, what was it?
2. Was I surprised by the reviewers' comments? Which ones? Did more than one reviewer have the same reaction?

Resources

Peer Editing Forms and Rubric

- *Portfolio Management System, p. 204*

Revision Transparencies

- *Workshop Resources,* p. 27

Language Workshop HELP

Effective sentences: page 1057.

Evaluation Criteria

An effective informative report

1. *clearly identifies the subject and the writer's thesis, or controlling idea, about the subject*
2. *supports the thesis and the writer's key points with relevant facts, examples, and other details*
3. *organizes the information so that the writer's ideas are easy to follow*
4. *includes enough direct references and transitional expressions to enable readers to follow the writer's ideas*
5. *establishes and maintains an objective, authoritative tone*
6. *concludes by refocusing on the writer's thesis*

Revision STRATEGIES

Are the ideas within and between your paragraphs clearly connected? If not, add direct references or transitional expressions.

Drafting

1. **The introduction: inviting them in.** Draw your readers in by grabbing their attention so that they'll want to read on to learn more. In setting the tone, try to sound objective, authoritative, and genuinely interested in sharing information about your subject. Be sure to include a thesis statement that identifies both your subject and your main idea about it.
2. **The body: escorting them through.** Devote a paragraph or two to each of your key points, including enough details to help readers understand and remember each point. Try to pace the details in such a way that readers aren't left feeling either overwhelmed or shortchanged. Where possible, use vivid images that will help them picture the information. Introduce sentence variety to keep your readers interested.

Strategies for Elaboration: Keeping Your Ideas Clear

You don't want your readers to misunderstand the gist of your report. To help keep your ideas clear, incorporate definitions and connections between ideas.

Definitions. If you use a term or concept that probably isn't familiar to your readers, include a brief definition. First identify the large group or class to which it belongs (A *plié* is "a ballet movement . . ."). Then identify features that distinguish the term or concept from all others in its class (". . . in which the back is held straight and the knees are bent outward").

Connections. In addition to arranging your ideas so that they're easy to follow, you can connect ideas within and between paragraphs with **direct references** and **transitional expressions.** Direct references refer to, repeat, or provide a synonym for a word or phrase used earlier. Transitional expressions show *how* ideas are connected. Since different transitional expressions indicate different relationships—time, space, or comparison/contrast, for example—choose such expressions carefully.

3. **The conclusion: showing them out.** In your conclusion, refocus on the main idea in your introduction, giving readers a sense that you've taken them where you said you would and that their time has been well spent.

Evaluating and Revising

As you evaluate and revise your report, make the changes *you* think will best help you share information on your subject. As you evaluate your paper, underline each point you've included to support your thesis. Then put a check mark next to the facts, examples, or other details you've included to explain each point. If supporting details are missing, add information to strengthen your points.

Grading Timesaver

Rubrics for this Writer's Workshop assignment appear on p. 205 of the *Portfolio Management System.*

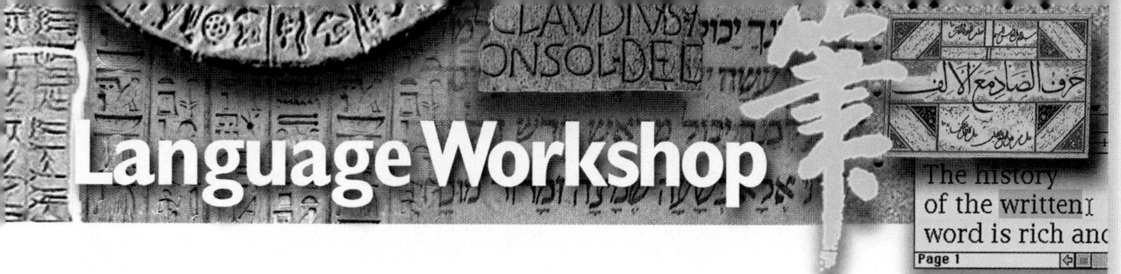
Language Workshop
The history
of the written
Page 1

OBJECTIVE
Write sentences varied in length and word order

EFFECTIVE SENTENCES: THE VALUE OF VARIETY

When you're reporting on a subject that truly interests you, the last thing you want to do is bore your readers with monotonous writing. Varying the length and word order of your sentences can help you create lively, energetic paragraphs that encourage readers to keep reading. Here are two techniques:

1. **Intersperse an occasional short sentence among longer ones.** Imaginative writers know the value of this technique, too, as Margaret Atwood's poem "Mushrooms" (page 1051) illustrates. Atwood devotes a total of seventy-six words to the two sentences that make up the first section of the poem. As the second section begins, the pace abruptly shifts: "Where do they come from?"
2. **Vary the subject-first order** that is normal in English sentences. By beginning some sentences with an introductory element—an appositive, a single-word modifier, or a phrase or clause modifier—you can not only add emphasis but also clarify the logical connections between sentences. Notice how D. H. Lawrence uses this technique:

> He went off by himself, vaguely, in a childish way, seeking for the clue to "luck." **Absorbed, taking no heed of other people,** he went about with a sort of stealth, seeking inwardly for luck. He wanted luck, he wanted it, he wanted it. **When the two girls were playing dolls in the nursery,** he would sit on his big rocking horse, charging madly into space, with a frenzy that made the little girls peer at him uneasily. **Wildly** the horse careered, the waving dark hair of the boy tossed, his eyes had a strange glare in them. The little girls dared not speak to him.
>
> —*from* "The Rocking-Horse Winner"

By using the different introductory elements indicated in boldface type, Lawrence sets up a fast pace in the paragraph, in which the rhythm of the sentence structures mirrors the action of the story. He makes us want to keep reading.

Writer's Workshop Follow-Up: Revision

Look back at the informative report you wrote for the Writer's Workshop on page 1053. Select one paragraph in the body to focus on. Underline the subject of each sentence in this paragraph. Do you ever depart from normal word order by not placing the subject first in each sentence? What sentences could you revise to introduce some sentence variety? Are there any places in the paragraph where a short sentence would create unexpected interest for the reader? Then look at the other paragraphs in your informative paper to see where else you might make revisions to improve sentence variety.

Technology HELP

See Language Workshop CD-ROM. *Key word entry: sentence style.*

Language Handbook HELP

See Revising for Variety, page 1238.

Try It Out

Revise the following paragraph, varying the length and word order of some of the sentences.

James Joyce's stream-of-consciousness technique is one of the most notable features of his later works. Joyce used the technique in his autobiographical novel *A Portrait of the Artist as a Young Man* (1916). It reveals the thought processes of Stephen Dedalus.

Resources

Workshop Resources
- Worksheet, p. 59

Language Workshop CD-ROM
- Sentence Style

Try It Out
Possible Answer

One of the most notable features of James Joyce's later works is his stream-of-consciousness technique. In his autobiographical novel *A Portrait of the Artist as a Young Man* (1916), Joyce used the technique to reveal the thought processes of Stephen Dedalus.

Assessing Learning

Quick Check: Effective Sentences

Ask students to rewrite the following sentences to vary them in length and/or word order.

Joyce uses a hodgepodge of ideas thrown together with no apparent order in the opening section of *A Portrait of the Artist as a Young Man* to create a picture of the mind of a young child. [Possible answers: (a) Using a hodgepodge of ideas thrown together with no apparent order, Joyce creates a picture of the mind of a young child in the opening section of *A Portrait of the Artist as a Young Man.* (b) In the opening section of *A Portrait of the Artist as a Young Man,* Joyce uses a hodgepodge of ideas thrown together with no apparent order to create a picture of the mind of a young child.]

In the final chapter of *A Portrait of the Artist as a Young Man,* Joyce includes a detailed philosophical discussion of aesthetics. [Possible answers: (a) A detailed philosophical discussion of aesthetics fills the final chapter of Joyce's *A Portrait of the Artist as a Young Man.* (b) The final chapter of Joyce's *A Portrait of the Artist as a Young Man* includes a detailed philosophical discussion of aesthetics.]

Reading for Life

Reading a Persuasive Speech

Using the Strategies
Possible Answers

1. His subject is to gain the support of the public by offering them potential work.
2. He tells them he will be honest. The word "truth" gives the sentence special appeal.
3. His point of view is that the country will survive. He has unflagging faith in the country and the public. Specific words and ideas that support this are: "The great nation will endure. . ."; ". . . the only thing we have to fear is fear itself . . ."; "restoration"; and "victory."
4. The tone is enthusiastic, optimistic, and firm. The repetition of topics such as honesty and restoration support this judgment.
5. The speech probably achieved FDR's purpose to lift people's spirits and encourage them to think positively and work to ensure the future success of the country. It may also have strengthened their support for FDR himself.

Situation
The text on the right is an excerpt from one of the most effective speeches of the twentieth century. It was delivered by President Franklin Delano Roosevelt at his first inauguration, in 1933, at a time when the nation and a good part of the world were in the midst of a crippling economic depression.

Here are strategies you can apply to reading this speech and any other political speech.

> ***from* Franklin D. Roosevelt's First Inaugural Address, 1933**
>
> This is preeminently the time to speak the truth, the whole truth, frankly and boldly. Nor need we shrink from honestly facing conditions in our country today. This great nation will endure as it has endured, will revive, and will prosper. So, first of all, let me assert my firm belief that the only thing we have to fear is fear itself—nameless, unreasoning, unjustified terror which paralyzes needed efforts to convert retreat into advance. In every dark hour of our national life, a leadership of frankness and vigor has met with that understanding and support of the people themselves, which is essential to victory. I am convinced that you will again give that support to leadership in these critical days. . . .
>
> Restoration [of confidence] calls, however, not for changes in ethics alone. This nation asks for action, and action now.
>
> Our greatest primary task is to put people to work. This is no unsolvable problem if we face it wisely and courageously.

Strategies

Recognize the speaker's subject, main idea, and point of view.

- Does the speaker present a clear position on the issue? Is he or she a knowledgeable and believable source on the subject?

Recognize and evaluate rhetorical techniques.

- These techniques include defining terms, giving examples, using analogies, showing cause-and-effect relationships, comparing and contrasting, and appealing to emotions. Does the speaker use techniques to influence you, to persuade you to accept a political position? Does the speaker present several points of view? Or is the speech slanted toward only one position?

Recognize the tone.

- Does the speaker address the audience with respect? with condescension? Is the tone serious? cynical? humorous?

Evaluate the speaker's choice of words.

- Is the vocabulary appropriate to the audience and the purpose? Are any loaded words used to support a position or make a point?

Using the Strategies
Answer these questions about Roosevelt's first inaugural address.

1. What is FDR's subject?
2. How does he engage the audience's attention in the first sentence? What word gives the sentence special appeal?
3. What is his **point of view** toward the subject and toward the audience? What specific words and ideas illustrate his position?
4. How would you characterize the **tone** of the speech? What examples support your judgment?
5. As a **call to action,** do you think the speech achieves FDR's purpose? What actions might the audience have taken?

Extending the Strategies

- Identify an issue in your community, and prepare a persuasive speech designed to rouse people to action.
- Listen, read, and analyze effective speeches by politicians, community leaders, or national and world leaders. Identify reasons why each speech succeeds or fails to persuade or motivate.

Collection 14

Ourselves Among Others

Theme

A Place in the World *With the loss of the old cohesive communal values, modern writers search for a viable relationship between the self and the social group. Some acknowledge the inevitable isolation of the individual, whose attempts to reach out fail or are rejected.*

Reading the Anthology

Reaching Struggling Readers

The *Reading Skills and Strategies: Reaching Struggling Readers* binder includes a Reading Strategies Handbook that offers concrete suggestions to help students who have difficulty reading and comprehending text or students who are reluctant readers. When a specific strategy is most appropriate for a selection, a correlation to the Handbook is provided at the bottom of the teacher's page under the head Struggling Readers. This head may also be used to introduce additional ideas for helping students read challenging texts.

Reading Beyond the Anthology

Read On

At the end of the Twentieth Century collections, the grade twelve book includes an annotated bibliography of books suitable for extended reading. The suggested books are related to works in these collections by theme, by author, or by subject. To preview the Read On for this period, please turn to p. T1174.

HRW Library

The *HRW Library* offers novels, plays, and short-story collections for extended reading. Each book in the Library includes one or more major works and thematically related Connections. The Connections are magazine articles, poems, or other pieces of literature. Each book in the *HRW Library* is also accompanied by a Study Guide that provides teaching suggestions and worksheets. The two titles shown here will work well to extend the theme of Collection 14.

NIGHT
Elie Wiesel

This memoir is Wiesel's account of his experiences during the Holocaust. *Night* serves as his personal testimony to humanity's duty to stand against the forces of darkness so that *Dawn* and *Day* (the second and third books in his trilogy) will come.

ANIMAL FARM
George Orwell

This political fable satirizes totalitarian governments. When the idealistic animals on a farm rise up and drive out the human despots, they soon learn a painful lesson: "All animals are equal, but some animals are more equal than others."

Collection 14 Ourselves Among Others

Resources for this Collection

Note: All resources for this collection are available for preview on the *One-Stop Planner CD-ROM 2 with Test Generator.* All worksheets and blackline masters may be printed from the CD-ROM.

Internet Resources
go.hrw.com LE0 12-14

Selection or Feature	Reading and Literary Skills	Vocabulary, Language, and Grammar
The Doll's House (p. 1061) Katherine Mansfield **Primary Sources: Katherine Mansfield: On Being a Writer** (p. 1066) **Connections: Sisters** (p. 1067) Rita Dove **Elements of Literature: The Modern Short Story** (p. 1068)	• *Graphic Organizers for Active Reading,* Worksheet p. 105 • *Literary Elements:* Transparency 26 Worksheet p. 79	• *Words to Own,* Worksheet p. 31 • *Grammar and Language Links:* Transitional Expressions, Worksheet p. 65 • *Daily Oral Grammar,* Transparency 36
World Literature: Denmark The Ring (p. 1071) Isak Dinesen	The World Literature feature offers students the opportunity to explore thematically linked literature from different world cultures. Structured activities called Finding Common Ground are provided in the Pupil's Edition to guide students' explorations of these thematic connections between British and other world literature.	
Not Waving but Drowning (p. 1077) Stevie Smith **Primary Sources: The Truths About Poetry** (p. 1079) Stevie Smith	• *Graphic Organizers for Active Reading,* Worksheet p. 106	
My Oedipus Complex (p. 1081) Frank O'Connor	• *Graphic Organizers for Active Reading,* Worksheet p. 107	• *Words to Own,* Worksheet p. 32 • *Grammar and Language Links:* Ornate and Plain Style, Worksheet p. 67; Punctuating Dialogue, Worksheet p. 69 • *Language Workshop CD-ROM:* Analyzing Your Writing Style; Punctuating Quotations • *Daily Oral Grammar,* Transparency 37
• **Musée des Beaux Arts** (p. 1092) • **The Unknown Citizen** (p. 1095) W. H. Auden **Spotlight On: Contemporary British Drama** (p. 1098) Robert Anderson *from* **Waiting for Godot** (p. 1099) Samuel Beckett **That's All** (p. 1102) Harold Pinter	• *Graphic Organizers for Active Reading,* Worksheet pp. 108, 109	• *Daily Oral Grammar,* Transparency 38
World Literature: Algeria/France The Myth of Sisyphus (p. 1105) Albert Camus *translated by* Justin O'Brien	The World Literature feature offers students the opportunity to explore thematically linked literature from different world cultures. Structured activities called Finding Common Ground are provided in the Pupil's Edition to guide students' explorations of these thematic connections between British and other world literature.	

Other Resources for this Collection

- *Cross-Curricular Activities,* p. 14
- *Portfolio Management System,* Introduction to Portfolio Assessment, p. 1
- *Test Generator,* Collection Test

Writing	Listening and Speaking Viewing and Representing	Assessment
• *Portfolio Management System,* Rubrics for Choices, p. 206	• *Audio CD Library,* Disc 19, Track 2 • *Portfolio Management System,* Rubrics for Choices, p. 206	• *Formal Assessment,* Selection Test, p. 211 • *Test Generator (One-Stop Planner CD-ROM)* • *Preparation for College Admission Exams,* p. 53
	• *Audio CD Library,* Disc 19, Track 3	
• *Portfolio Management System,* Rubrics for Choices, p. 207	• *Audio CD Library,* Disc 19, Track 4 • *Portfolio Management System,* Rubrics for Choices, p. 207	• *Formal Assessment,* Selection Test, p. 213 • *Test Generator (One-Stop Planner CD-ROM)*
• *Portfolio Management System,* Rubrics for Choices, p. 208	• *Audio CD Library,* Disc 19, Track 5 • *Portfolio Management System,* Rubrics for Choices, p. 208	• *Formal Assessment,* Selection Test, p. 214 • *Test Generator (One-Stop Planner CD-ROM)*
• *Portfolio Management System,* Rubrics for Choices, p. 209	• *Audio CD Library,* Disc 20, Tracks 2, 3 • *Viewing and Representing:* Fine Art Transparency 18 Worksheet p. 72 • *Portfolio Management System,* Rubrics for Choices, p. 209	• *Formal Assessment,* Selection Tests, pp. 216, 217 • *Test Generator (One-Stop Planner CD-ROM)*
	• *Audio CD Library,* Disc 20, Track 4	

Transparency CD-ROM Video Audio CD

Collection 14 Ourselves Among Others

Resources for this Collection

Note: All resources for this collection are available for preview on the *One-Stop Planner CD-ROM 2 with Test Generator.* All worksheets and blackline masters may be printed from the CD-ROM.

Internet Resources
go.hrw.com LE0 12-14

Selection or Feature	Reading and Literary Skills	Vocabulary, Language, and Grammar
Games at Twilight (p. 1109) Anita Desai	• *Graphic Organizers for Active Reading,* Worksheet p. 110	• *Words to Own,* Worksheet p. 33 • *Daily Oral Grammar,* Transparency 39
• **Digging** (p. 1117) • **The Grauballe Man** (p. 1119) Seamus Heaney	• *Graphic Organizers for Active Reading,* Worksheet p. 111	• *Daily Oral Grammar,* Transparency 40

Other Resources for this Collection

- *Cross-Curricular Activities*, p. 14
- *Portfolio Management System*, Introduction to Portfolio Assessment, p. 1
- *Test Generator*, Collection Test

Writing	Listening and Speaking Viewing and Representing	Assessment
• *Portfolio Management System*, Rubrics for Choices, p. 211	• *Audio CD Library*, Disc 20, Track 5 • *Portfolio Management System*, Rubrics for Choices, p. 211	• *Formal Assessment*, Selection Test, p. 218 • *Test Generator (One-Stop Planner CD-ROM)* • *Preparation for College Admission Exams*, p. 55
• *Portfolio Management System*, Rubrics for Choices, p. 212	• *Audio CD Library*, Disc 20, Tracks 6, 7 • *Portfolio Management System*, Rubrics for Choices, p. 212	• *Formal Assessment*, Selection Test, p. 220 • *Test Generator (One-Stop Planner CD-ROM)*

Transparency CD-ROM Video Audio CD

Collection 14 Ourselves Among Others

Skills Focus

Selection or Feature	Reading Skills and Strategies	Elements of Literature and Language	Writing	Listening and Speaking	Viewing and Representing
The Doll's House (p.1061) Katherine Mansfield		Symbol, pp. 1061, 1068 Theme, p. 1068 The Modern Short Story, p. 1068 • Closure • Trick Ending • Realism • Slice of Life • Psychological Realism • Dramatic Irony Omniscient Point of View, p. 1069	Analyze a Modern Short Story, p. 1069 Identify Problems Related to Peer Pressure, p. 1069 Write an Essay Evaluating the Author's Choice of Point of View, p. 1069 Write the Opening Paragraphs for a Contemporary Version of "The Doll's House," p. 1069	Prepare a Group Reading of "The Doll's House," p. 1069	
World Literature: Denmark **The Ring** (p.1071) Isak Dinesen	Dialogue with the Text, pp. 1071, 1076	The World Literature feature offers students the opportunity to explore thematically linked literature from different world cultures. Structured activities called Finding Common Ground are provided in the Pupil's Edition to guide students' explorations of these thematic connections between British and other world literature.			
Not Waving but Drowning (p. 1077) Stevie Smith		Title, p. 1079	Freewrite to Identify Problems and Possible Solutions, p. 1079 Write an Essay Exploring a Metaphor, p. 1079		
My Oedipus Complex (p. 1081) Frank O'Connor		Dramatic Irony, pp. 1081, 1090 Conflict, p. 1090 Comedy, p. 1090 Theme, p. 1090 Plot, p. 1090 Tone, p. 1090	Take Notes for a Problem-Solution Essay, p. 1090 Write a Humorous Narrative, p. 1090		
Musée des Beaux Arts (p. 1092) **The Unknown Citizen** (p. 1095) W. H. Auden		Diction, pp. 1092, 1094 Colloquial Language, p. 1092 Technical Terms, pp. 1092, 1097 Theme, pp. 1094, 1097 Speaker, p. 1096 Tone, p. 1096 Jargon, p. 1097	Take Notes on a Group Discussion, p. 1097 Write an Essay Comparing Texts Across Cultures, p. 1097 Write an Essay Analyzing a Satire, p. 1097 Write a Poem, Story, or Essay Based on a Work of Art, p. 1097 Write an Obituary for "The Unknown Citizen," p. 1097 Write a Contemporary Epitaph, p. 1097		Interpret a Painting, p. 1097
Spotlight On: Contemporary British Drama (p. 1098) *from* **Waiting for Godot** (p. 1099) Samuel Beckett **That's All** (p. 1102) Harold Pinter		Theater of the Absurd, p. 1099 Farce, p. 1101			
World Literature: Algeria/France **The Myth of Sisyphus** (p. 1105) Albert Camus	Dialogue with the Text, p. 1105	Existentialism, p. 1105 Myth, p. 1108 Epigram, p. 1108	The World Literature feature offers students the opportunity to explore thematically linked literature from different world cultures. Structured activities called Finding Common Ground are provided in the Pupil's Edition to guide students' explorations of these thematic connections between British and other world literature.		
Games at Twilight (p. 1109) Anita Desai	Analyzing Evocative Words, pp. 1109, 1116 Chronological Order, p. 1116	Imagery, pp. 1109, 1116 Theme, p. 1116 Title, p. 1116 Mood, p. 1116 Discovery, p. 1116 Tone, p. 1116	Take Notes on an Issue, p. 1116 Write an Essay Comparing and Contrasting the Treatment of a Theme in Two Stories, p. 1116 Write a Short Narrative, p. 1116		
Digging (p. 1117) **The Grauballe Man** (p. 1119) Seamus Heaney		Metaphor, pp. 1117, 1120 Extended Metaphor, pp. 1117, 1120 Simile, pp. 1117, 1120 Image, p. 1120 Symbol, p. 1120	Write an Original Poem Based on Lines from "Digging," p. 1120	Conduct a Group Discussion of the Mistrust Between Scientists and Lay People, p. 1120	

Collection 14 OURSELVES AMONG OTHERS

Mansfield
Dinesen
Smith
O'Connor
Auden
Camus
Desai
Heaney

We live, as we dream—alone.

—Joseph Conrad, *from Heart of Darkness*

Nocturne in Blue and Gold, Old Battersea Bridge (c. 1872–1875) by James Abbott McNeill Whistler.

Tate Gallery, London

OBJECTIVES

1. Read literature of the twentieth century on the theme of "Ourselves Among Others"
2. Interpret literary elements with special emphasis on the modern short story
3. Apply a variety of reading strategies
4. Respond to the literature in a variety of modes
5. Learn and use new words

Responding to the Quotation

? One important theme in much of twentieth-century literature is isolation, the loneliness that many people experience, even in crowds. How does the quotation from Conrad reflect this theme? [Some students may feel that Conrad uses the word *live* in a figurative sense to mean "to experience the fullness of life." In that sense, human beings are isolated because of the difficulty of making meaningful emotional contacts with other people. Others may disagree with Conrad, saying people routinely give and receive support.]

RESPONDING TO THE ART

James Abbott McNeill Whistler (1834–1903) was an American painter, printmaker, and master etcher who spent most of his life in Europe. Whistler became a leader of the Aesthetic Movement, which strove to emphasize purely aesthetic principles (such as atmosphere, mood, and interplay of color) over realistic representation. Whistler often titled his works "Harmony," "Nocturne," or "Arrangement" to emphasize their formal qualities over their content. In fact, his most famous painting is *Arrangement in Gray and Black No. 1: Portrait of the Artist's Mother* (often called *Whistler's Mother*).
Activity. Ask students to describe the atmosphere of the painting.

Writing Focus: A Problem-Solution Essay

WORK IN PROGRESS

The following **Work in Progress** assignments build to a culminating **Writer's Workshop** at the end of Collection 15.

- The Doll's House — Explore problems of peer pressure (p. 1069)
- Not Waving but Drowning — Freewrite ideas on issue (p. 1079)
- My Oedipus Complex — Extend conflict in story to real life (p. 1090)
- Auden's poems — Discuss issues treated in poems (p. 1097)
- Games at Twilight — Take notes on ideal course of study (p. 1116)
- Heaney's poems — Discuss attitudes toward science (p. 1120)

Writer's Workshop: Persuasive Writing / A Problem-Solution Essay (p. 1179)

OBJECTIVES

1. Read and interpret the story
2. Identify and interpret a symbol
3. Identify and analyze the elements of the short story
4. Compare characters' motives
5. Express understanding through critical writing, creative writing, or listening and speaking
6. Understand new words

SKILLS

Literary
- Identify and interpret a symbol
- Identify and analyze the elements of the short story

Writing
- Collect ideas for a problem-solution essay
- Evaluate point of view
- In a group, write the opening of an updated version of the story

Speaking/Listening
- Prepare and present a group reading of the story

Vocabulary
- Use new words

Viewing/Representing
- Compare the styles and subjects of paintings (ATE)
- Choose an alternative title for a painting (ATE)

Planning

- **Block Schedule**
  Block Scheduling Lesson Plans with Pacing Guide
- **Traditional Schedule**
  Lesson Plans Including Strategies for English-Language Learners
- **One-Stop Planner**
  CD-ROM with Test Generator

BROWSING IN THE FILES

About the Author. Although Katherine Mansfield is associated with New Zealand, she lived there for only eighteen years. Most of her stories, however, are set in that country. She was born in Wellington, New Zealand's capital, but she and her family later moved to Karori, a rural area. After immigrating to London in 1908, Mansfield led a bohemian lifestyle, touring with a musical company.

Katherine Mansfield

(1888–1923)

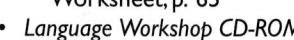

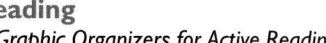

Katherine Mansfield.

Katherine Mansfield was born Kathleen Mansfield Beauchamp in Wellington, New Zealand, the third child of an ambitious merchant. As a child she was aware of the rugged beauty of her island home, but she shared her mother's distaste for being "out here," oceans away from England, the source of their culture.

At home she was "difficult" and prone to nightmares, a lonely, resentful child who saw her father as an adversary. At school she was moody and had few friends. She had her father's head for figures and could memorize verse at sight, yet she was a slovenly scholar.

When Mansfield was fifteen, the Beauchamp family sailed for England to enroll their daughters in Queen's College in London. Mansfield was delighted with every aspect of her new life, and when she was summoned home to New Zealand in 1906, she closeted herself in her room and grieved for lost London.

In 1908, when she was nineteen, Mansfield's family permitted her to return to London alone. But with only the meager allowance her father granted her, Mansfield was painfully poor and frequently sick. Her first literary encouragement came in 1910, when A. R. Orage, editor of the progressive journal *The New Age,* accepted several of her stories. These stories, which showed the strong influence of the Russian writer Anton Chekhov, were collected in a volume called *In a German Pension* (1911).

About the same time, an Oxford undergraduate named John Middleton Murry accepted a story and some of her poems for his new literary magazine, *Rhythm,* and the two began a long and stormy relationship. Eventually, they married and became publishing partners. The couple became close friends with D. H. Lawrence and his wife, Frieda; the friendship soured, however, and Lawrence later ridiculed Mansfield and Murry by using them as models for a couple in a destructive relationship in his novel *Women in Love* (1920).

When Mansfield's younger brother Leslie died in World War I, she was overcome with grief. When she at last emerged from this cloud, she vowed to write about New Zealand from then on as "a sacred debt . . . because my brother and I were born there." She called it a "debt of love. . . . I shall tell everything, even of how the laundry basket squeaked."

As her stories were published, Mansfield became recognized as a supremely gifted writer and an innovator of the short story. Up to this time, the short story had been seen as merely a finger exercise for the novel. People expected stories to have strong, chronological plots. Mansfield's stories downplayed attention to plot and action; instead, she tried to illuminate moments of significance.

Despite her growing success, Mansfield's personal life continued to be troubled. In 1917, she learned that she had tuberculosis. She and Murry were married the following spring, but three weeks later they separated. As Mansfield's health worsened, her characteristic verve gave way to loneliness, anger, and fear of death. But as she entered the final year of her life, she was reconciled to her illness. She renewed her relationship with Murry and showed a new compassion in her writing. In the brief time left to her, she also wrote some of her finest stories, many with New Zealand backgrounds, which are collected in *The Garden Party and Other Stories* (1922) and *The Dove's Nest and Other Stories* (1923).

A belief that some miracle might save her led Mansfield to an institute run by a healer named George Gurdjieff in France. The treatment did not work. There, with Murry at her side, she died in January 1923.

go.hrw.com
LEO 12-14

Resources: Print and Media

Reading
- *Graphic Organizers for Active Reading,* p. 105
- *Words to Own,* p. 31
- *Audio CD Library*
  Disc 19, Track 2

Elements of Literature
- *Literary Elements*
  Transparency 26
  Worksheet, p. 79

Writing and Language
- *Daily Oral Grammar*
  Transparency 36
- *Grammar and Language Links*
  Worksheet, p. 65
- *Language Workshop CD-ROM*

Assessment
- *Formal Assessment,* p. 211
- *Portfolio Management System,* p. 206
- *Preparation for College Admission Exams,* p. 53
- *Test Generator (One-Stop Planner CD-ROM)*

Internet
- go.hrw.com (keyword: *LEO 12-14*)

Before You Read
THE DOLL'S HOUSE

Make the Connection
Better Than You

Wherever people come together in groups, there is almost always competition for status, or high position. Some people will inevitably try to prove that they are superior to other people in the group, or that their group is superior to other groups.

Quickwrite
What gives one "superior" status in our society? Is status always dependent on material wealth?

In what environments do you think competition for status is especially fierce? Jot down your thoughts about competition.

Elements of Literature
Symbol

As you read, think about what this doll's house and its little lamp represent in a world where wealth and social position are important, in a society that mocks the ideal of compassion for the less fortunate.

A **symbol** is an object, an animal, a place, or a person used in fiction to stand for itself and for something broader than itself. The meanings of symbols are often elusive, and readers frequently disagree on their exact significance.

For more on Symbol, see the Handbook of Literary Terms.

Background
This story is set early in the twentieth century in a small village in New Zealand. At that time, New Zealand was still a British colony, and the British colonists had brought England's rigid class system with them to New Zealand. In this system, people's status in society was automatically determined by their family background. People with inherited wealth and privilege did not ordinarily associate with the poor or even with those who earn what we consider a middle-class income. In New Zealand, however, because of the shortage of schools, wealthy children attended school with children of different social classes.

Miss Miles's Dollhouse (c. 1890).

Bethnal Green Museum of Childhood. Courtesy of the Trustees of the Victoria and Albert Museum, London.

Summary ■■

The wealthy Burnell children—Isabel, Lottie, and Kezia—are given a large doll's house, a marvelous toy which fills them with delight and their schoolmates with admiration. The Burnells live in a rural area of New Zealand, where the school they attend admits all the local children, regardless of social standing. The Burnell children invite everyone at school, except the indigent Kelvey children, to see the doll's house; the Burnell sisters have been forbidden even to speak to the Kelveys, the daughters of a washerwoman. The Kelveys are mocked in school, shunned for their poverty, and taunted with the accusation that their absent father is in prison.

One day, however, Kezia Burnell (the youngest sister) sees Else and Lil Kelvey passing by the Burnells' house and invites the girls to look at the doll's house. Although fierce Aunt Beryl scolds Kezia and makes the Kelvey girls leave, the Kelvey sisters are deeply impressed by their brief glimpse of the doll's house and by Kezia's generosity.

Literary Connections
Women Writers Outside England

You might encourage students to compare and contrast the styles and subjects of one of the other twentieth-century women writers who, like Katherine Mansfield, wrote in English but did not grow up in England. These include Doris Lessing (p. 1146), Margaret Atwood (p. 1050), Nadine Gordimer (p. 1154), Isak Dinesen (p. 1070), and Anita Desai (p. 1109). Students might examine the various aspects of women's lives that these writers explored: personal and professional struggles, family relationships, and cultural conflicts.

Preteaching Vocabulary

Words to Own

Have students read the Words to Own and their definitions listed at the bottom of the selection pages. Then have them use the words to fill in the blanks of the following sentences:

1. We've been ___________ through the mall for six hours! [traipsing]
2. The children didn't expect the clown to stumble; they began to ___________. [titter]
3. Kim used thinner on all the spots where the paint had ___________. [congealed]
4. The center's energy ___________ in the last quarter of the closing game of the playoffs. [flagged]
5. You won't miss the huge landmark; it's too ___________. [conspicuous]

A Reading Skills and Strategies

Making Inferences

? What kind of person is Aunt Beryl? [Possible responses: condescending, unappreciative, easily offended.] **Explain to students that *beryl* is a very hard but lustrous mineral that occurs in hexagonal crystals; two varieties of beryl are emerald and aquamarine. How might that name reflect the qualities of Aunt Beryl's character?** [Possible responses: She is glittering but coldhearted; she places much importance on appearances or status.]

B Struggling Readers

Finding and Interpreting Details

Have students list the details that describe the house. [dark; oily; green; garish colors; lumps of paint] **What are the students' impressions of the doll's house based upon these details?** [Possible response: It has a showy, ornate, overdone quality.] **How do the children in the story see it?** [Possible response: They think it is perfect.]

C Appreciating Language

Point of View

? **Why does the author address "you" in this passage?** [Possible responses: The author takes the reader into her confidence by speaking directly to "you"; she creates an intimate tone.] **She also uses the conversational "isn't it," further drawing the reader into what seems to be a personal conversation.**

D Elements of Literature

Symbol

? **What might Kezia's liking of the lamp symbolize?** [Possible responses: She likes small, seemingly perfect things. Perhaps to her the lamp represents warmth or comfort.]

The Doll's House

Katherine Mansfield

When dear old Mrs. Hay went back to town after staying with the Burnells, she sent the children a doll's house. It was so big that the carter[1] and Pat carried it into the courtyard, and there it stayed, propped up on two wooden boxes beside the feed-room door. No harm could come of it; it was summer. And perhaps the smell of paint would have gone off by the time it had to be taken in. For, really, the smell of paint coming from that doll's house ("Sweet of old Mrs. Hay, of course; most sweet and generous!")—but the smell of paint was quite enough to make anyone seriously ill, in Aunt Beryl's opinion. Even before the sacking was taken off. And when it was . . .

There stood the doll's house, a dark, oily, spinach green, picked out with bright yellow. Its two solid little chimneys, glued onto the roof, were painted red and white, and the door, gleaming with yellow varnish, was like a little slab of toffee. Four windows, real windows, were divided into panes by a broad streak of green. There was actually a tiny porch, too, painted yellow, with big lumps of congealed paint hanging along the edge.

But perfect, perfect little house! Who could possibly mind the smell? It was part of the joy, part of the newness.

"Open it quickly, someone!"

The hook at the side was stuck fast. Pat pried it open with his penknife, and the whole housefront swung back, and—there you were, gazing at one and the same moment into the drawing room and dining room, the kitchen and two bedrooms. That is the way for a house to open! Why don't all houses open like that? How much more exciting than peering through the slit of a door into a mean little hall with a hatstand and two umbrellas! That is—isn't it?—what you long to know about a house when you put your hand on the knocker. Perhaps it is the way God opens houses at dead of night when He is taking a quiet turn with an angel . . .

"O-oh!" The Burnell children sounded as though they were in despair. It was too marvelous; it was too much for them. They had never seen anything like it in their lives. All the rooms were papered. There were pictures on the walls, painted on the paper, with gold frames complete. Red carpet covered all the floors except the kitchen; red plush chairs in the drawing room, green in the dining room; tables, beds with real bedclothes, a cradle, a stove, a dresser with tiny plates, and one big jug. But what Kezia liked more than anything, what she liked frightfully, was the lamp. It stood in the middle of the dining-room table, an exquisite little amber lamp with a white globe. It was even filled all ready for lighting, though, of course, you couldn't light it. But there was something inside that looked like oil, and that moved when you shook it.

The father and mother dolls, who sprawled very stiff as though they had fainted in the drawing room, and their two little children asleep upstairs, were really too big for the doll's house. They didn't look as though they belonged. But the lamp was perfect. It seemed to smile at Kezia, to say, "I live here." The lamp was real.

The Burnell children could hardly walk to school fast enough the next morning. They burned to tell everybody, to describe, to—well—to boast about their doll's house before the school bell rang.

"I'm to tell," said Isabel, "because I'm the eldest. And you two can join in after. But I'm to tell first."

There was nothing to answer. Isabel was bossy, but she was always right, and Lottie and Kezia knew too well the powers that went with being eldest. They brushed through the thick buttercups at the road edge and said nothing.

"And I'm to choose who's to come and see it first. Mother said I might."

For it had been arranged that while the doll's house stood in the courtyard they might ask the

Words to Own

congealed (kən·jēld′) *v.* used as *adj.:* thickened.

1. **carter:** delivery person.

Reaching All Students

Struggling Readers

Have struggling readers jot down all the references to rank, class, status, or hierarchy that occur in the story. For example, it is important to Isabel that she be the first "to tell" about the doll's house. Have students compare their notes; then, list the references chronologically (as they appear in the story) on the chalkboard to show the development of this central motif throughout the story.

English Language Learners

To help students understand the characters, pair English language learners with students who are more proficient in the language. Ask each pair to choose two characters and create a "silent dialogue." Have students assume the personae of their chosen characters, and pass a piece of paper back and forth as they "talk" to each other, writing down their conversation.

Advanced Learners

Have students read other stories set in New Zealand or Australia. They might look into *Some Other Country: New Zealand's Best Short Stories* or *The Oxford Book of Australian Short Stories*. The latter includes works by New Zealander Christina Stead and by Nobel Prize–winning Australian writer Patrick White. Have students use their reading to expand their awareness of the social and cultural conflicts presented in Mansfield's story.

girls at school, two at a time, to come and look. Not to stay to tea, of course, or to come traipsing (E) through the house. But just to stand quietly in the courtyard while Isabel pointed out the beauties, and Lottie and Kezia looked pleased . . .

But hurry as they might, by the time they had reached the tarred palings[2] of the boys' playground the bell had begun to jangle. They only just had time to whip off their hats and fall into line before the roll was called. Never mind. Isabel tried to make up for it by looking very important and mysterious and by whispering behind her hand to the girls near her, "Got something to tell you at playtime."

Playtime came and Isabel was surrounded. The girls of her class nearly fought to put their arms round her, to walk away with her, to beam flatteringly, to be her special friend. She held quite a court under the huge pine trees at the side of the playground. (F) Nudging, giggling together, the little girls pressed up close. And the only two who stayed outside the ring were the two who were always outside, the little Kelveys. They knew better than to come anywhere near the Burnells.

For the fact was, the school the Burnell children went to was not at all the kind of place their parents would have chosen if there had been any choice. But there was none. It was the only school for miles. And the consequence was all the children in the neighborhood, the Judge's little girls, the doctor's daughters, the storekeeper's children, the milkman's, were forced to mix together. Not to speak of there being an equal number of rude, rough little boys as well. But the line had to be drawn somewhere. It was drawn at the Kelveys. Many of the children, including the Burnells, were not allowed even to speak to them. They walked past the Kelveys with their heads in the air, and as they set the fashion in all matters of behavior, the Kelveys were shunned by everybody. Even the teacher had a special voice for them, and a special smile for the other children when Lil Kelvey came up to her desk with a bunch of dreadfully common-looking flowers.

They were the daughters of a spry, hardworking little washerwoman, who went about from house to house by the day. This was awful enough. But where was Mr. Kelvey? Nobody knew for certain. But everybody said he was in prison. So they were the daughters of a washerwoman and a jailbird. Very nice company for other people's children! And they looked it. Why Mrs. Kelvey made them so conspicuous was hard to understand. The truth was they were dressed in "bits" given to her by the people for whom she worked. Lil, for instance, who was a stout, plain child, with big freckles, came to school in a dress made from a green art-serge[3] tablecloth of the Burnells', with red plush sleeves from the Logans' curtains. Her hat, perched on top of her high forehead, was a grown-up woman's hat, once the property of Miss Lecky, the postmistress. It was turned up at the back and trimmed with a large scarlet quill. What a little guy[4] she looked! It was impossible not to laugh. (G) And her little sister, our Else, wore a long white dress, rather like a nightgown, and a pair of little boy's boots. (H) But whatever our Else wore she would have looked strange. She was a tiny wishbone of a child, with cropped hair and enormous solemn eyes—a little white owl. Nobody had ever seen her smile; she scarcely ever spoke. She went through life holding on to Lil, with a piece of Lil's skirt screwed up in her hand. Where Lil went our Else followed. In the playground, on the road going to and from school, there was Lil marching in front and our Else holding on behind. Only when she wanted anything, or when she was out of breath, our Else gave Lil a tug, a twitch, and Lil stopped and turned round. The Kelveys never failed to understand each other.

Now they hovered at the edge; you couldn't stop them listening. When the little girls turned round and sneered, Lil, as usual, gave her silly, shamefaced smile, but our Else only looked.

2. **palings** (pāl′iŋz): fence stakes.

3. **art-serge** (ärt·surj): type of woven wool fabric.

4. **guy:** British for "an odd-looking person." The word comes from the name of Guy Fawkes, an English conspirator executed for taking part in the 1605 Gunpowder Plot to bomb the king and the houses of Parliament. In England, handmade likenesses of Guy Fawkes are burned annually on November 5—Guy Fawkes Day.

WORDS TO OWN

traipsing (trāps′iŋ) *v.* used as *adj.:* colloquial for "wandering."

conspicuous (kən·spik′yo͞o·əs) *adj.:* attracting attention by being unusual.

(E) Cultural Connections

In many countries influenced by British tradition, afternoon tea became a fashionable ritual in the nineteenth century. It provided the newly prosperous middle and upper-middle classes with a pleasant way of socializing with friends and family while signaling their leisured status. Afternoon tea, served between 3:00 and 5:00 P.M., generally consisted of strong tea, crustless sandwiches, scones, pastries, and cakes.

(F) Elements of Literature

Symbol

The "ring" of a royal "court" symbolizes the unbridgeable gap between the classes. Just as a British commoner would not approach the Queen of England, so the Kelveys dare only come within earshot of the upper-class Burnells.

(G) Critical Thinking

Evaluating the Text

? Why does the author give such a complete description of the Kelveys, far more complete than that of the Burnells? [Possible response: She wants readers to identify with the Kelvey children and to focus on the common human feelings that readers share with the Kelveys.]

(H) Elements of Literature

Metaphor

? What do these comparisons indicate about "our Else"? [Possible responses: She is small, delicate, even fragile. She is wise and takes everything in.]

Using Students' Strengths

Visual/Kinesthetic Learners

Encourage students to draw or build their own versions of the doll's house in the story. You might suggest that groups work together to render the outside, the inside, or just one room of the house. Some students might take the role of researchers and find photographs of Victorian and early-twentieth-century architecture and domestic furnishings.

Intrapersonal Learners

Have students imagine Kezia's thoughts during various scenes of the story and write what they think she might record in her journal about these events. Remind students to consult the text and to gauge Kezia's feelings from her reactions, the dialogue, and their own feelings in similar circumstances.

Making the Connections

Connecting to the Theme: "Ourselves Among Others"

Encourage students to discuss how social status contributes to a person's overall sense of self-confidence and identity. They might ask themselves how they think most people react when their individual hopes and dreams are in conflict with the way others perceive them or when they move from one social group to another.

A Elements of Literature

Symbol

? Kezia's (and the author's) emphasis on the lamp suggests that, as a symbol, it has special importance in the story. Why do you think Kezia keeps thinking about the lamp? [Possible responses: She simply wants to talk about what she loves most. In a larger sense, the lamp symbolizes the importance of the light within, the sense of warmth in a home—or in a human being.]

B Reading Skills and Strategies

Drawing Conclusions

? How do the details of the girls' lunches further the distinction between the Kelveys and the other children? [Possible response: The Kelveys have only jam sandwiches, while the other children have thick meat sandwiches and buttered johnny cakes, indicating that their families have more money.]

C Critical Thinking

Interpreting

? Why does Kezia want to invite the Kelveys to look at the doll's house? [Possible responses: She wants to share her joy. She may not agree with their exclusion and sees them as human beings who feel as she does.]

D Reading Skills and Strategies

Making Inferences

? Why, on this particular day, do the girls decide to be spiteful to the Kelveys? [Possible response: The impact of the doll's house has worn thin, since everyone else has seen it, so the girls find another way to have fun with Lil and Else.]

E Critical Thinking

Interpreting

? Why do the girls have so much energy after they insult Lil and Else? [Possible responses: It makes them feel powerful and superior to put down the Kelveys. They are invigorated by Lena's daring.]

A

And Isabel's voice, so very proud, went on telling. The carpet made a great sensation, but so did the beds with real bedclothes, and the stove with an oven door.

When she finished Kezia broke in. "You've forgotten the lamp, Isabel."

"Oh, yes," said Isabel, "and there's a teeny little lamp, all made of yellow glass, with a white globe that stands on the dining-room table. You couldn't tell it from a real one."

"The lamp's best of all," cried Kezia. She thought Isabel wasn't making half enough of the little lamp. But nobody paid any attention. Isabel was choosing the two who were to come back with them that afternoon and see it. She chose Emmie Cole and Lena Logan. But when the others knew they were all to have a chance, they couldn't be nice enough to Isabel. One by one they put their arms round Isabel's waist and walked her off. They had something to whisper to her, a secret. "Isabel's *my* friend."

Only the little Kelveys moved away forgotten; there was nothing more for them to hear.

Days passed, and as more children saw the doll's house, the fame of it spread. It became the one subject, the rage. The one question was, "Have you seen Burnells' doll's house? Oh, ain't it lovely!" "Haven't you seen it? Oh, I say!"

B

Even the dinner hour was given up to talking about it. The little girls sat under the pines eating their thick mutton sandwiches and big slabs of johnny cake spread with butter. While always, as near as they could get, sat the Kelveys, our Else holding on to Lil, listening too, while they chewed their jam sandwiches out of a newspaper soaked with large red blobs . . .

C

"Mother," said Kezia, "can't I ask the Kelveys just once?"

"Certainly not, Kezia."

"But why not?"

"Run away, Kezia; you know quite well why not."

D

At last everybody had seen it except them. On that day the subject rather flagged. It was the dinner hour. The children stood together under the pine trees, and suddenly, as they looked at the Kelveys eating out of their paper, always by themselves, always listening, they wanted to be horrid to them. Emmie Cole started the whisper.

"Lil Kelvey's going to be a servant when she grows up."

"O-oh, how awful!" said Isabel Burnell, and she made eyes at Emmie.

Emmie swallowed in a very meaning way and nodded to Isabel as she'd seen her mother do on those occasions.

"It's true—it's true—it's true," she said.

Then Lena Logan's little eyes snapped. "Shall I ask her?" she whispered.

"Bet you don't," said Jessie May.

"Pooh, I'm not frightened," said Lena. Suddenly she gave a little squeal and danced in front of the other girls. "Watch! Watch me! Watch me now!" said Lena. And sliding, gliding, dragging one foot, giggling behind her hand, Lena went over to the Kelveys.

Lil looked up from her dinner. She wrapped the rest quickly away. Our Else stopped chewing. What was coming now?

"Is it true you're going to be a servant when you grow up, Lil Kelvey?" shrilled Lena.

Dead silence. But instead of answering, Lil only gave her silly, shamefaced smile. She didn't seem to mind the question at all. What a sell[5] for Lena! The girls began to titter.

Lena couldn't stand that. She put her hands on her hips; she shot forward. "Yah, yer father's in prison!" she hissed, spitefully.

E

This was such a marvelous thing to have said that the little girls rushed away in a body, deeply, deeply excited, wild with joy. Someone found a long rope, and they began skipping. And never did they skip so high, run in and out so fast, or do such daring things as on that morning.

In the afternoon Pat called for the Burnell children with the buggy and they drove home. There were visitors. Isabel and Lottie, who liked visitors, went upstairs to change their pinafores.[6] But Kezia thieved out at the back. Nobody was about; she began to swing on the big white gates of the courtyard. Presently, looking along the road, she

5. **sell:** slang for "trick."
6. **pinafores** (pin′ə·forz′): sleeveless, apronlike garments that young girls wear over dresses.

Words to Own
flagged (flagd) *v.:* declined; lost strength or interest.
titter (tit′ər) *v.:* to giggle.

Crossing the Curriculum

Social Sciences

Assign students to research and chart the way status is defined in various societies. Direct them to the work of anthropologists and social scientists, and prompt them with the following questions: Does the United States have a status system? Are there any universal markers that elevate an individual or family to higher status? Are status systems true designations of personal or social worth?

Geography

Encourage students to learn about the country of New Zealand by collecting information on its population and geography. Assign groups of three or four students to create short audio-visual documentaries that show how their research on New Zealand illuminates the setting of Mansfield's story.

Girl Sitting on the Steps (late 19th or early 20th century) by Peter Vilhelm Ilsted. Colored mezzotint.

Bonhams, London.

saw two little dots. They grew bigger, they were coming toward her. Now she could see that one was in front and one close behind. Now she could see that they were the Kelveys. Kezia stopped swinging. She slipped off the gate as if she was going to run away. Then she hesitated. The Kelveys came nearer, and beside them walked their shadows, very long, stretching right across the road with their heads in the buttercups. Kezia clambered back on the gate; she had made up her (F) mind; she swung out.

"Hullo," she said to the passing Kelveys.

They were so astounded that they stopped. Lil gave her silly smile. Our Else stared. (G)

"You can come and see our doll's house if you want to," said Kezia, and she dragged one toe on the ground. But at that Lil turned red and shook her head quickly.

"Why not?" asked Kezia.

Lil gasped, then she said, "Your ma told our ma you wasn't to speak to us."

"Oh, well," said Kezia. She didn't know what to reply. "It doesn't matter. You can come and see our doll's house all the same. Come on. Nobody's looking."

But Lil shook her head still harder.

"Don't you want to?" asked Kezia.

Suddenly there was a twitch, a tug at Lil's skirt. She turned round. Our Else was looking at her with big, imploring eyes; she was frowning; she wanted to go. For a moment Lil looked at our Else very doubtfully. But then our Else twitched her skirt again. She started forward. Kezia led the way. Like two little stray cats they followed across the courtyard to where the doll's house stood.

"There it is," said Kezia.

There was a pause. Lil breathed loudly, almost snorted; our Else was still as a stone.

"I'll open it for you," said Kezia kindly. She undid the hook and they looked inside.

"There's the drawing room and the dining (H) room, and that's the—"

"Kezia!"

Oh, what a start they gave!

"Kezia!"

It was Aunt Beryl's voice. They turned round.

(F) Vocabulary Note

Ask students why they think *clambered* is a more effective word than *climbed* to describe Kezia's action. [Possible response: *Clambered* suggests—with its rather awkward sound—the clumsiness and difficulty of the climb.]

(G) Elements of Literature

Character

? What do Kezia's actions indicate about her character? [Possible responses: She defies Aunt Beryl's orders; she thinks the Kelveys should be included; she is innately friendly and generous.]

(H) Critical Thinking

Analyzing Details

? What does Kezia *not* get to point out? [the lamp] **Why might this detail be especially important?** [Possible responses: The lamp is, to Kezia, the essential feature of the doll's house, the detail that makes it most human and welcoming. Aunt Beryl's coldness contrasts with the warmth of the lamp.]

RESPONDING TO THE ART

Peter Vilhelm Ilsted (1861–1933) was a Danish painter influenced by his brother-in-law, the painter Vilhelm Hammershoi (see p. 1022). Typical of his subdued and restrained style, Ilsted's *Girl Sitting on the Steps* reflects the quiet, lonely mood of "The Doll's House."

Activity. Ask students to compare Ilsted's painting with Whistler's *Nocturne in Blue and Gold,* which opens this collection (p. 1059). What elements of style and subject do the paintings have in common? [Possible responses: an isolated figure; a dark and desolate setting; emotional restraint.] Which character in Mansfield's story does *Girl Sitting on the Steps* bring to mind? [Possible responses: Lil or Else.]

Getting Students Involved

Cooperative Learning

Discuss with the class the three types of symbols—those universally recognized, those recognized by specific groups, and those that have personal significance. Then, ask students to bring to class an object or photograph that is symbolic in one of these ways. Divide the class into groups of five or six. Invite students to take turns displaying their symbols and allowing the group to determine which type(s) of symbol they are showing and what it might represent. After the group discusses the symbol, ask the student who brought it in to explain the meaning he or she has in mind. Point out that symbols often evoke multiple meanings, allowing readers and viewers some freedom of interpretation.

A **Critical Thinking**

Making Judgments

? What is the purpose of this paragraph? [Possible responses: It shows how, although feeling threatened by Willie Brent's proposal, Aunt Beryl feels powerful and in control after putting down the Kelvey girls. It compares Aunt Beryl's actions to those of the little girls who taunt Lil in the schoolyard. It shows that bullying can be used to cover up insecurity.]

B **Critical Thinking**

Analyzing Motives

? What moves Else to speak? [Possible response: She has been impressed with the lamp, even though she has only caught a glimpse of it.]

C **Elements of Literature**

Symbol

? The author ends the story with the symbol of the lamp, emphasizing once again its centrality to the story. What has the lamp come to mean for Else and for the reader? [Possible response: The lamp represents the inner light of human kindness that briefly shone out of Kezia.]

Primary Sources

In these two diary entries, Mansfield discusses her love of writing and her attachment to the "old masters."

D **Reading Skills and Strategies**

Making Inferences

Ask students to discuss the journal entry of May 30. Specifically, ask them what Mansfield means by "enough" in the first sentence. [Students will probably suggest that she means being alive and being a writer are all she needs to be happy.] **Then ask students to discuss why the sight of two people shaking hands and talking causes Mansfield's reaction.** [Possible responses: Being a writer gives her a chance to observe and study human behavior and to communicate what she sees. She can think of no greater satisfaction.]

At the back door stood Aunt Beryl, staring as if she couldn't believe what she saw.

"How dare you ask the little Kelveys into the courtyard?" said her cold, furious voice. "You know as well as I do, you're not allowed to talk to them. Run away, children, run away at once. And don't come back again," said Aunt Beryl. And she stepped into the yard and shooed them out as if they were chickens.

"Off you go immediately!" she called, cold and proud.

They did not need telling twice. Burning with shame, shrinking together, Lil huddling along like her mother, our Else dazed, somehow they crossed the big courtyard and squeezed through the white gate.

"Wicked, disobedient little girl!" said Aunt Beryl bitterly to Kezia, and she slammed the doll's house to.

A The afternoon had been awful. A letter had come from Willie Brent, a terrifying, threatening letter, saying if she did not meet him that evening in Pulman's Bush, he'd come to the front door and ask the reason why! But now that she had frightened those little rats of Kelveys and given Kezia a good scolding, her heart felt lighter. That ghastly pressure was gone. She went back to the house humming.

When the Kelveys were well out of sight of Burnells', they sat down to rest on a big red drainpipe by the side of the road. Lil's cheeks were still burning; she took off the hat with the quill and held it on her knee. Dreamily they looked over the hay paddocks,[7] past the creek, to the group of wattles[8] where Logan's cows stood waiting to be milked. What were their thoughts?

Presently our Else nudged up close to her sister. But now she had forgotten the cross lady. She put out a finger and stroked her sister's quill; she smiled her rare smile.

B "I seen the little lamp," she said, softly.

C Then both were silent once more.

7. **paddocks** (pad′əks): fenced pieces of land.
8. **wattles** (wät′'lz): acacia trees.

PRIMARY Sources | **LETTERS AND JOURNALS**

The following extracts are from *The Letters and Journals of Katherine Mansfield: A Selection.* The first is a journal entry dated May 30, 1917; the second is a letter to her painter friend Richard Murry.

Katherine Mansfield: On Being a Writer

D May 30 To be alive and to be a "writer" is enough. Sitting at my table just now I saw one person turning to another, smiling, putting out his hand—speaking. And suddenly I clenched my fist and brought it down on the table and called out—There is *nothing* like it!

20 June 1921

. . . About the old masters. What I feel about them (all of them—writers too, of course) is the more one *lives* with them the better it is for one's work. It's almost a case of living *into* one's ideal world—the world that one desires to express. Do you know what I mean? For this reason I find that if I stick to men like Chaucer and Shakespeare and Marlowe and even Tolstoy, I keep much nearer what I want to do than if I confuse things with reading a lot of lesser men. I'd like to make the old masters my *daily* bread—in the sense in which it's used in the Lord's Prayer, really—to make them a kind of essential nourishment. All the rest is—well—it comes *after*. . . .

Making the Connections

Cultural Connections

Invite students to study the economic and cultural influence of Great Britain on New Zealand. Ask them to develop posters or collages that show some of the changes British rule imposed on the country and the people of New Zealand—both the European settlers and the Maoris, the original inhabitants of New Zealand.

Assessing Learning

Check Test: True-False

1. The doll's house is a white Victorian wonder. [False]
2. The Burnells immediately want to tell their friends about the doll's house. [True]
3. Kezia's favorite part of the doll's house is the real glass windows. [False]
4. Kezia invites the Kelveys to see the doll's house. [True]
5. Aunt Beryl makes the Kelvey girls leave. [True]

Connections — A Poem

In this poem, written by the former U.S. poet laureate Rita Dove (1952–), the speaker gazes at a childhood photograph. Do her memories remind you of the events in "The Doll's House"?

Sisters

Rita Dove

for Robin Dove Waynesboro

This is the one we called
Bird of the Dead, Double Bird (A)
Who Feeds on Carrion. Dark
with a red organdy dress
for her third birthday,
she cried and cried,
snap-eyed imp whose brow sprouted horns
whenever she screwed up her face.

"Buzzard!" we shrieked
and when that was forbidden:
"Schmawk Schmawk Bird!"° after the local radio
personality. Several beatings later
the first literary effort appeared, a story
called "Blank the Buzzard,"
for which I claimed the First Amendment.
It was confiscated and shredded.

I can't believe she's taller
than me now, that my smile
lines sag where her Indian cheekbones soar. (B)
This is my home, my knothole
we're posing in front of. The palm tree
throws a boa° across our shoulders.
Light seals the cracks.

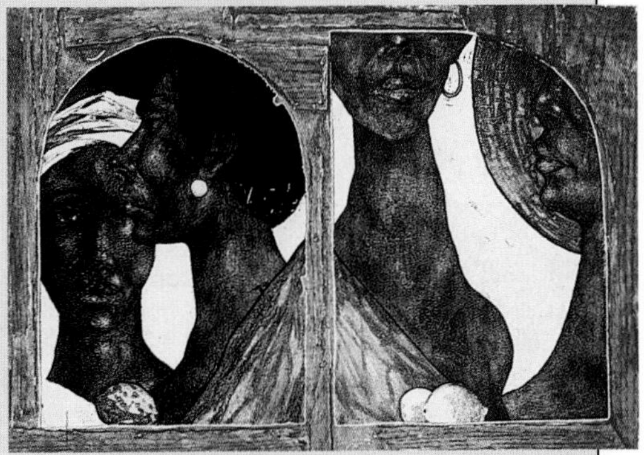

Environment No. V (1969) by Eldzier Cortor. Etching/intaglio (27″ × 35″).
Courtesy of the artist.

11. **Schmawk Schmawk Bird:** cartoonlike voice created by a radio disc jockey in Dove's childhood hometown of Akron, Ohio.

22. **boa** (bō′ə): long, fluffy scarf made of feathers or other soft material. Here, the shadow created by the palm tree looks like a boa.

Connections

The speaker is looking at a photograph of herself and another child (presumably her sister, as suggested by the title and the dedication). She recalls how, as a child, she harshly ridiculed the other girl, comparing her to a vulture and a little devil. In the last stanza, she returns to the present and, in a mood of reconciliation, admires the appearance of the sister, now grown up, whom she once demonized.

Background

Rita Dove writes frequently about family relationships, exploring what it means to know and love someone. In 1995 she published *Mother Love*, a collection of poems that use the Greek myth of Demeter and Persephone to examine the mother-daughter bond.

(A) Reading Skills and Strategies

Responding to the Text

? Why might the speaker have chosen this insult? [Possible responses: The speaker wants to make the girl feels ugly and inferior; since a buzzard eats the remains of other animals' kill, the label suggests low rank.]

(B) Reading Skills and Strategies

Making Inferences

? Why is this change particularly poignant? [Possible response: Although the speaker once ridiculed the other child's features, those same features now make her an attractive adult, while the speaker appears old.]

Responding to the Art

Eldzier Cortor (1916–) is an African American painter and lithographer who grew up in Chicago and studied at the Chicago Art Institute during the Depression. Cortor was strongly influenced by African art and Cubism, as well as by the realistic documentary style popular during the 1930s. Cortor is best known for his elegant and lyrical portraits of African American women, in which the figures seem both classical and romantic. **Activity.** Have students choose a few words from the Dove poem that would make a good alternative title for the Cortor etching.

Connecting Across Texts

Connecting with "The Doll's House"

The cruelty of children is one theme that surfaces in both Dove's "Sisters" and Mansfield's "The Doll's House." Another theme is the paradox of the seeming fragility of children and their extraordinary resilience in the face of pain and rejection. The theme of passing time also unites the two selections, since both Dove (explicitly) and Mansfield (implicitly) are looking at their characters from the perspective of years of experience. Both the poem and the story make readers have sympathy and even affection for the victimized characters.

Making Meanings

First Thoughts [Respond]

1. Answers will vary. Some students may say they identified most with Kezia because she is both imaginative and sensitive.

Shaping Interpretations [Interpret]

2. Isabel wants to show off. Kezia may invite the Kelveys because she wants to rebel against the exclusive social system of her family or because she wants to share the "light" of the lamp.
3. Else seems to depend on Lil and defer to her. Because Else rarely speaks, her words in the last line carry weight; her silence and her way of absorbing the events around her create the impression that she may be wise and intuitive.
4. The extravagant doll's house is a status symbol—a toy that symbolizes wealth and social standing. To Kezia, the lamp may symbolize the light of hospitality or the spiritual beauty of all human beings. To Else, it may represent hope, charity, love, or the possibility of a world illuminated by kindness instead of prejudice.
5. One theme is the desire for status, as gauged by material possessions and a sense of power and belonging. Although the Burnell girls and their friends are too young to have built their own status and reputation, they are already old enough to want to feel superior.
6. Most students will probably disapprove of the girls' meanness. Some students may see the meanness as a way the girls try to enhance their own status.

Connecting with the Text [Synthesize]

7. Lil and Else seem united against others; Dove's sisters seem to have fought as children but to have reconciled as adults. Students may think sibling rivalry is inevitable because of children's enormous need for parental attention and for asserting their own individuality.

Extending the Text [Compare/Contrast]

8. Students may recall situations in which a group of friends or family members has put down another group or an individual whom they considered inferior. Remind students to choose situations they would not mind sharing with others.

Making Meanings

First Thoughts

1. Which character in "The Doll's House" do you identify with most? Why?

> **Reading Check**
>
> a. With a partner, review the description of the doll's house. What do the furniture and the dolls themselves look like?
>
> b. Also, review the descriptions of the characters in the story. Who among them appears comfortable, or to truly "belong," in the world?

Shaping Interpretations

2. Why does Isabel invite friends to see the doll's house? Why does Kezia invite Lil and Else to see it?
3. Describe the relationship between Lil and Else. Is it significant that Else speaks the last line of dialogue in the story?
4. What do you think the doll's house **symbolizes** in the story? What does the little lamp symbolize to Kezia? What does it symbolize to Else as she says at the end, "I seen the little lamp"?
5. How would you state this story's **theme**—what does it reveal to you about cruelty, about status and families and outsiders? Be sure to compare your statements of theme in class.
6. How do you feel about the extraordinary meanness shown by Lil and Else's classmates? How do you account for it?

Connecting with the Text

7. How does the relationship between Lil and Else compare with that of the sisters in "Sisters" (see *Connections* on page 1067)? Do you think this kind of sibling rivalry is common? What causes it?

Extending the Text

8. Look back at your Quickwrite notes about status. What similarities, if any, exist between your world and the world of the story?

Elements of Literature

The Modern Short Story

People have been telling stories since the first campfire, but the short story as a separate form is really an invention of the nineteenth century. A number of factors probably contributed to the rise of the short story at roughly the same time in France, Germany, and the United States. Growing literacy, the consequent popularity of magazines, and the form's flexibility and appeal to a wide variety of writers were doubtless responsible for its success.

The American critic and writer Edgar Allan Poe created the most influential theoretical foundations for the short story in his 1842 review of Nathaniel Hawthorne's *Twice-Told Tales*. In this essay, Poe claimed that the story should be considered superior to the novel because, since a story could be read in one sitting, it could have a more unified aesthetic effect on the reader. To Poe, a unified effect was the most important literary goal. "A skillful artist," he wrote, "having conceived a certain *single effect* . . . then combines such events . . . as may best serve him in establishing this preconceived effect. . . . [T]here should be no word written of which the tendency, direct or indirect, is not to the one pre-established design." The effect that Poe aimed for in most of his stories was shock or horror.

The stories of other nineteenth-century writers frequently involved people in extreme states—physical, emotional, or both. It was not unusual for characters to go mad or die at the end. Such grand events satisfied both writers' and readers' need for **closure,** or the feeling that one has reached a satisfactory conclusion. Some writers, such as Guy de Maupassant in France and O. Henry in the United States, provided this closure through the use of a surprising twist, or **trick ending.**

Realism, a literary movement that developed in the latter part of the nineteenth century, served to decrease some of the excesses of earlier writers. The realists strove to portray life as it really is, not as we might wish or fear it to be. Some realists, such as the Russian Anton Chekhov, often wrote stories that had no strong beginning or end, but merely portrayed the events of daily life. These **slice-of-life** stories provided readers with snapshots

Reading Check

a. The furniture is realistic and consists of tables, chairs, beds with bedclothes, a cradle, a stove, a dresser, and a lamp. The dolls are too large for the house and look as though they do not belong in it.

b. One possibility is Kezia, who does not seem to have a sense of class distinction and is thus "comfortable" with all kinds of people. Students may also feel that Else is special, because she seems to look at the world squarely, as it is.

of life in a variety of places and social classes. The American Henry James wrote stories that faithfully depicted not only settings and ways of life, but also his characters' perceptions and motivations. This **psychological realism** also had a great effect on the modern short story.

Some writers today still agree with Poe that effect is the most important aspect of a story. However, the modern story more often aims not at a sensory effect *on* the reader but at *revelation to* the reader—the revelation of some essential truth implicit in the story. The main character of the story may remain ignorant of this truth even at the end, and **dramatic irony,** the result of the reader's knowing more than the character does, is a common element in modern fiction. Though readers may clearly see dramatic irony in "The Doll's House," the story doesn't at first appear to have the unity of form that Poe espoused. But closer examination reveals a coherence of language, theme, and imagery, in this case all related to the central symbol of the doll's house.

In a general sense, we can say three things about the modern short story:

1. It is more likely to be concerned with nuances of character than with the construction of a fast-paced plot.
2. It is more apt to imply important facts and psychological truths than to state them directly.
3. It is more apt to move toward a revelation of truth than toward an effect.

What would Poe think about the development of the modern short story? Some twentieth-century story elements might puzzle him, but he would certainly recognize the continuation of his own interest in coherence and care for detail.

Katherine Mansfield once wrote of another short story, "it seems to me there mustn't be one single word out of place, or one word that could be taken out." With that statement, Poe would heartily agree.

Analyzing a modern short story. With some classmates, choose a story from a recent periodical. Then, collaborate in writing a critique of the story for the entire class. As part of the critique, consider to what extent the story demonstrates the characteristics of the modern short story listed above.

CHOICES: Building Your Portfolio

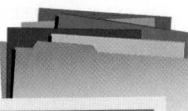

Writer's Notebook

1. Collecting Ideas for a Problem-Solution Essay

As in "The Doll's House," peer pressure often keeps people (of all ages) from befriending those outside their own cliques. Working with a partner or a small group, brainstorm to explore how widespread the problem is at your school and what could be done to ease its negative effects. Save your notes for use in the Writer's Workshop on page 1179.

Evaluating Point of View

2. Know-It-All Narrator

As you read "The Doll's House," you enter the minds of several characters. In an essay of at least three paragraphs, tell whether you think the author's **omniscient point of view** adds to the power of the story or makes the narrative confusing. Support your opinion with specific passages.

Creative Writing

3. "The Doll's House" Revisited

In a group, collaborate in writing the opening paragraphs of a new, updated story based on "The Doll's House." Decide together what might be different in the story if it were to take place in a contemporary setting.

Listening and Speaking

4. "The Doll's House" Dramatized

Prepare a group reading of "The Doll's House." First, determine how many readers are needed. Then, prepare a script and be sure each reader has his or her own copy. Practice various ways of interpreting the characters' feelings and various ways of delivering the lines. Before the final reading, rehearse before a small group, and ask for an evaluation of your performance.

Grading Timesaver

Rubrics for each Choices assignment appear on p. 206 in the *Portfolio Management System.*

CHOICES: Building Your Portfolio

1. **Writer's Notebook** Students might also choose to explore any positive effects of peer pressure. Remind students to choose a subject they would not mind sharing.
2. **Evaluating Point of View** Review the concept of the omniscient point of view before students begin work on this composition. Students might find it useful to organize their thinking with a chart like the one that follows.

Details That Add Power	Details That Make Story Confusing
[description of Beryl's feelings after she yells at the Kelveys]	[Who is Willie Brent, and why is Beryl afraid of him?]

3. **Creative Writing** Encourage students to think of a device, a toy, or an object—such as a pair of fancy sneakers or the latest video game—that might confer status on someone of middle-school age. You might also encourage some students to record their stories on tape before writing them down.
4. **Listening and Speaking** You might suggest that students cast the roles without regard to gender or even change the gender of a character in order to explore a different dimension of the rivalries in the story.

ELEMENTS OF LITERATURE

The Modern Short Story

To help students write their critiques, you might suggest that they also consider whether the story they are reviewing is part of a genre of fiction. These genres include mystery, romance, science fiction, fantasy, and thriller. Each genre has its own set of characteristics that students might explore as they write their critiques. For example, a mystery story usually requires the following:

- a clever and airtight plot
- detailed and intriguing clues
- a few red herrings or dead-end clues
- an engaging sleuth or problem solver
- a strong setting and atmosphere

Objectives

1. Read and respond to the story
2. Generate relevant, interesting, and researchable questions
3. Connect text events with students' own experience or with that of others

Planning

- **Block Schedule**
  Block Scheduling Lesson Plans with Pacing Guide
- **Traditional Schedule**
  Lesson Plans Including Strategies for English-Language Learners
- **One-Stop Planner**
  CD-ROM with Test Generator

Browsing in the Files

About the Author. As a young woman, Karen Christence Blixen studied English at Oxford and art in Paris and Rome. After her divorce from her cousin, Baron Bror von Blixen-Finecke, and a tragic love affair with Denys Finch-Hatton (who was killed in an airplane crash), she returned to Denmark from Africa in 1931 and began writing in both English and Danish. Her pseudonym, Isak, comes from a word that means "one who laughs" in Hebrew. Her stories often lean toward the Gothic, with supernatural elements, fantastic characters, and exotic settings.

Denmark

WORLD LITERATURE

Isak Dinesen.

Isak Dinesen

(1885–1962)

Isak Dinesen (the pen name of Baroness Karen Blixen-Finecke) led a series of lives, any one of which might be considered adventurous for a woman of her time. She first inherited a love of adventure and storytelling from her father, a dashing Danish aristocrat, and a sense of duty, obligation, and guilt from her mother, the daughter of a bourgeois merchant. As a young woman, she wrote stories and studied painting. Then, at the age of twenty-nine, she embarked on a new life. She defiantly married her cousin and moved to what is now Kenya, where the couple set up and operated a coffee plantation. Her husband, who was blatantly unfaithful to Dinesen, infected her with syphilis, a progressive disease from which she suffered for the rest of her life. In 1921 the couple divorced, and Dinesen ran the six-thousand-acre plantation by herself for another ten years. A collapse in coffee prices and her failing health forced Dinesen to return to Denmark in 1931.

Starting over with no money, Dinesen began revising stories she had drafted in her beloved Africa. Her first collection, *Seven Gothic Tales,* was published in 1934. Her best-known work, *Out of Africa,* an account of her life in Kenya, appeared in 1937 and established her as a major literary presence. Even in her seventies, although she was often so ill she had to dictate to a secretary, Dinesen continued to earn her living by writing.

(Map) ©Rand McNally R. L. #98-S-116.

go.hrw.com
LEO 12-14

Resources: Print and Media

Reading

- *Audio CD Library*
  Disc 19, Track 3

Internet

- go.hrw.com (keyword: *LEO 12-14*)

Before You Read

THE RING

Background

To her contemporaries, Isak Dinesen often seemed old-fashioned, for most of her stories are set between 1770 and 1870 and have the atmosphere of an era long past. During this time period, Dinesen's native Denmark was controlled by a few wealthy, aristocratic landowners. The wealthy often had little sympathy for the poor, who sometimes became outlaws, stealing fish or game on a landowner's property to feed themselves and their families. If they were caught, they risked being put to death.

"The Ring" was published in a collection of stories titled *Anecdotes of Destiny.* And to a large extent, all of Dinesen's stories are just what that title suggests. Each focuses on a turning point in human life, a moment when some important truth is revealed and a particular life is changed forever.

Reading Skills and Strategies

Dialogue with the Text

The rich young couple in "The Ring" seem at first to have a perfect relationship. As you read, jot down any indications that the young wife is heading toward a critical turning point, a moment when her life will be altered forever.

The Ring

Isak Dinesen

On a summer morning a hundred and fifty years ago a young Danish squire and his wife went out for a walk on their land. They had been married a week. It had not been easy for them to get married, for the wife's family was higher in rank and wealthier than the husband's. But the two young people, now twenty-four and nineteen years old, had been set on their purpose for ten years; in the end her haughty parents had had to give in to them.

They were wonderfully happy. The stolen meetings and secret, tearful love letters were now things of the past. To God and man they were one; they could walk arm in arm in broad daylight and drive in the same carriage, and they would walk and drive so till the end of their days. Their distant paradise had descended to earth and had proved, surprisingly, to be filled with the things of everyday life: with jesting and railleries,[1] with breakfasts and suppers, with dogs, haymaking, and sheep. Sigismund, the young husband, had promised himself that from now there should be no stone in his bride's path, nor should any shadow fall across it. Lovisa, the wife, felt that now, every day and for the first time in her young life, she moved and breathed in perfect freedom because she could never have any secret from her husband.

To Lovisa—whom her husband called Lise[2]—the rustic atmosphere of her new life was a matter of wonder and delight. Her husband's fear that the existence he could offer her might not be good enough for her filled her heart with laughter. It was not a long time since she had played with dolls; as now she dressed her own hair, looked over her linen press, and arranged her flowers, she again lived through an enchanting and cherished experience: One was doing everything gravely and solicitously, and all the time one knew one was playing.

It was a lovely July morning. Little woolly clouds drifted high up in the sky, the air was full

1. **railleries** (rāl′ər·ēz): good-natured ridicule; teasing acts or remarks.

2. **Lise** (lē′zə).

Reaching All Students

Struggling Readers

Before they read the story, have students discuss problems children from wealthy families may face growing up. Students might consider issues of personal freedom, decision making, and social responsibility. After students read the first paragraph, have them predict what the story will be about. As they continue to read, have them stop periodically and verify their predictions. Ask them to pinpoint specific details that lead them to make or revise a prediction.

English Language Learners

Help students understand the nonliteral levels of meaning that figurative language can convey. For example, in the second paragraph of the story, the narrator tells of the "bride's path," the lack of a "stone" in that "path," and the lack of a "shadow" across it. Have students discuss what a "stone" or a "shadow" in the "path" might represent on a nonliteral or symbolic level. Ask them to look for other examples of figurative language in the story.

Summary

A wealthy young woman named Lise has recently married a Danish squire, and their life together appears filled with love, trust, and happiness. One day, they go out walking around their estate. At the sheepfold, Lise learns that a thief has been stealing sheep and has murdered a man who tried to stop him. The killer has not been found. Hearing the details of the story gives Lise a strange thrill. While her husband takes care of some sick lambs, Lise wanders alone into a grove and discovers a bruised and ragged man holding a knife. Lise seems to see herself in the wild eyes of the desperate man. She silently offers him her wedding ring, but he brushes it aside. He and Lise study each other for a few moments, during which "something happened, things were changed." The man wraps his knife in Lise's handkerchief, sheathes the knife, and leaves. Lise tells her husband she has lost her wedding ring but does not mention her encounter in the grove.

A Reading Skills and Strategies

Dialogue with the Text

? The opening portrait of the marriage is one of perfect happiness, freedom, and honesty. Is this an indication that some dire change is going to take place? Why or why not? [Possible responses: Not necessarily; the couple may be able to cope well with any difficulties that arise. Yes, something must change because such perfection is an illusion.]

B Elements of Literature

Point of View

? What is the advantage of reading a story written in the third-person limited point of view? [Possible response: The reader has an intimate and intense knowledge of what is going on inside one character's mind.]

C Reading Skills and Strategies

Making Inferences

? What does this phrase indicate about Lise's daily life? [Possible response: It seems she has nothing worthwhile to occupy her; she thinks her duties are trivial and ceremonial.]

Responding to the Art

Icelandic painter **Jóhannes S. Kjarval** (1885–1972) was known for his primeval Icelandic landscapes. His mysterious scenes reveal a deep regard for nature but also an acknowledgement of a dark power hidden in the earth. *Forest Palace* can be viewed as a Symbolist landscape in which the trees invite the viewer to imagine another, less concrete reality.

Activity. You might ask students why they think the artist called the forest he painted a "palace"? What elements in the painting evoke either the setting or the mood of Dinesen's story? [Possible responses: the grove, the clearing, the somber mood.] Students might also contrast Kjarval's landscape with other landscapes in this book (such as John Northcote Nash's *Oppy Wood* on p. 927) and tell how they are alike or different in style and content.

A Critical Thinking

Hypothesizing

? How can a person hold two such contradictory ideas? [Students may suggest that intense feelings can induce complex thoughts that defy ordinary logic.] Do you trust Lise's perceptions of events? [Possible response: No, she seems mixed-up and immature, and she changes her opinions without good reason.]

Listasafn Islands, Reykjavík, Iceland.

Forest Palace (1918) by Jóhannes S. Kjarval (102 cm × 110 cm).

of sweet scents. Lise had on a white muslin frock and a large Italian straw hat. She and her husband took a path through the park; it wound on across the meadows, between small groves and groups of trees, to the sheep field. Sigismund was going to show his wife his sheep. For this reason she had not brought her small white dog, Bijou,[3] with her, for he would yap at the lambs and frighten them, or he would annoy the sheepdogs. Sigismund prided himself on his sheep; he had studied sheep breeding in Mecklenburg[4] and England, and had brought back with him Cotswold rams[5] by which to improve his Danish stock. While they walked he explained to Lise the great possibilities and difficulties of the plan.

A She thought: "How clever he is, what a lot of things he knows!" and at the same time: "What an absurd person he is, with his sheep! What a baby he is! I am a hundred years older than he."

But when they arrived at the sheepfold the old sheepmaster Mathias met them with the sad news that one of the English lambs was dead and two

3. **Bijou** (bē′zho͞o′): French for "jewel."
4. **Mecklenburg:** agricultural district in northeastern Germany.
5. **Cotswold rams:** the males of a kind of sheep with very long hair, originally from the Cotswold Hills of southwestern England.

Using Students' Strengths

Intrapersonal/Verbal Learners

Have students write Lise's journal entry for the day she faced the stranger. Tell them this entry is not limited to relating what happened. It may be a reflection on what the encounter means to her or a debate about what she will tell her husband. She may lament the change she has experienced or try to guess what the future holds for her.

Kinesthetic Learners

The narrator of "The Ring" says (p. 1074) that the scene with the stranger could only be rendered by pantomime. Have kinesthetic learners prepare and present a pantomime of the entire story or of the scene with the stranger. Students might want to perform in costume and use a few simple props, especially the ring itself.

Visual Learners

Have visual learners draw or paint one of the settings described in the story: the park, sheepfold, forest clearing, or meadow path. Students might also render their own ideas of the couple's house (inside or outside). Ask them to attach title cards to their work; each card should incorporate at least one specific detail taken directly from the story.

were sick. Lise saw that her husband was grieved by the tidings; while he questioned Mathias on the matter she kept silent and only gently pressed his arm. A couple of boys were sent off to fetch the sick lambs, while the master and servant went into the details of the case. It took some time.

Lise began to gaze about her and to think of other things. Twice her own thoughts made her blush deeply and happily, like a red rose, then slowly her blush died away, and the two men were still talking about sheep. A little while after, their conversation caught her attention. It had turned to a sheep thief.

This thief during the last months had broken into the sheepfolds of the neighborhood like a wolf, had killed and dragged away his prey like a wolf, and like a wolf had left no trace after him. **B** Three nights ago the shepherd and his son on an estate ten miles away had caught him in the act. The thief had killed the man and knocked the boy senseless, and had managed to escape. There were men sent out to all sides to catch him, but nobody had seen him.

Lise wanted to hear more about the horrible event, and for her benefit old Mathias went through it once more. There had been a long fight in the sheephouse, in many places the earthen floor was soaked with blood. In the fight the thief's left arm was broken; all the same, he had climbed a tall fence with a lamb on his back. Mathias added that he would like to string up the murderer with these two hands of his, and Lise nodded her head at him gravely in approval. She remembered Red Ridinghood's wolf, and felt a pleasant little thrill running down her spine. **C**

Sigismund had his own lambs in his mind, but he was too happy in himself to wish anything in the universe ill. After a minute he said: "Poor devil."

Lise said: "How can you pity such a terrible man? Indeed Grandmamma was right when she said that you were a revolutionary and a danger to society!" **D** The thought of Grandmamma, and of the tears of past days, again turned her mind away from the gruesome tale she had just heard.

The boys brought the sick lambs and the men began to examine them carefully, lifting them up and trying to set them on their legs; they squeezed them here and there and made the little creatures whimper. Lise shrank from the show and her husband noticed her distress.

"You go home, my darling," he said, "this will take some time. But just walk ahead slowly, and I shall catch up with you."

So she was turned away by an impatient husband to whom his sheep meant more than his wife. If any experience could be sweeter than to be dragged out by him to look at those same sheep, it would be this. She dropped her large summer hat with its blue ribbons on the grass and told him to carry it back for her, for she wanted to feel the summer air on her forehead and in her hair. She walked on very slowly, as he had told her to do, for she wished to obey him in everything. **E** As she walked she felt a great new happiness in being altogether alone, even without Bijou. She could not remember that she had ever before in all her life been altogether alone. The landscape around her was still, as if full of promise, and it was hers. Even the swallows cruising in the air were hers, for they belonged to him,[6] and he was hers.

She followed the curving edge of the grove and after a minute or two found that she was out of sight to the men by the sheephouse. What could now, she wondered, be sweeter than to walk along the path in the long flowering meadow grass, slowly, slowly, and to let her husband overtake her there? It would be sweeter still, she reflected, to steal into the grove and to be gone, to have vanished from the surface of the earth from him when, tired of the sheep and longing for her company, he should turn the bend of the path to catch up with her.

An idea struck her; she stood still to think it over. **F**

A few days ago her husband had gone for a ride and she had not wanted to go with him, but had strolled about with Bijou in order to explore her domain. Bijou then, gamboling, had led her straight into the grove. As she had followed him, gently forcing her way into the shrubbery, she had suddenly come upon a glade in the midst of it, a narrow space like a small alcove with hangings of thick green and golden brocade, big enough to hold two or three people in it. She had felt at that moment that she had come into the very heart of her new home. If today she could find the spot

6. him: that is, Sigismund. In Denmark at the time of the story, birds and other wild animals on an estate were the owner's property.

B Elements of Literature
Repetition

Point out to students that Dinesen repeats the word *wolf* three times in this sentence, an indication that this word is significant and may be symbolic. Remind students to look for clues as they continue to read that might explain the meaning of this symbol.

C Reading Skills and Strategies
Dialogue with the Text

? What does the reference to the tale of Little Red Ridinghood suggest about the action to come? [Possible response: The reference to the tale suggests that danger is imminent, and a crisis, possibly even a tragedy, is about to occur.] **Why do you think Lise reacts with "a pleasant little thrill"?** [Possible response: She is a romantic, and this exciting connection to the fairy tale delights her. She might also have a romantic love of danger.]

D Critical Thinking
Analyzing Character

? What does this exchange tell you about Sigismund? [Possible responses: Despite his wealth, he can put himself in the thief's shoes. He is so fortunate that other people's misfortunes do not disturb his equilibrium.]

E Critical Thinking
Interpreting

? What may Dinesen be showing about Lise as she walks away from her husband? [Possible response: She is spoiled, childlike, self-dramatizing, and overly romantic.]

F Reading Skills and Strategies
Making Inferences

? What is Lise's plan? [Possible response: She is going to disappear into the grove.] **Why does she hatch this plan?** [Possible responses: She wants to enjoy the sensation of knowing her husband is missing her. She wants to create a romantic scene.]

Skill Link

Critiquing a Literary Performance

Impress upon students that critiquing and evaluating a performance of a work of literature (a reading, a recitation, a play, or even a movie) requires the development and application of a set of appropriate criteria. Review with students the qualities they might expect to find in a good reading of a literary work.

Activity

Have students read two paragraphs of "The Ring" aloud while other students rank each performance on a scale of 1–5, 1 being the lowest for each criterion. Have students use each others' praise or suggestions to improve their communication. Criteria might include the following:

_____ Clear enunciation
_____ Sufficient volume
_____ Smooth and natural rhythm
_____ Correct pronunciation
_____ Variety of points of emphasis
_____ Appropriate tone

again she would stand perfectly still there, hidden from all the world. Sigismund would look for her in all directions; he would be unable to understand what had become of her and for a minute, for a short minute—or, perhaps, if she was firm and cruel enough, for five—he would realize what a void, what an unendurably sad and horrible place the universe would be when she was no longer in it. She gravely scrutinized the grove to find the right entrance to her hiding place, then went in.

She took great care to make no noise at all, therefore advanced exceedingly slowly. When a twig caught the flounces of her ample skirt she loosened it softly from the muslin, so as not to crack it. Once a branch took hold of one of her long golden curls; she stood still, with her arms lifted, to free it. A little way into the grove the soil became moist; her light steps no longer made any sound upon it. With one hand she held her small handkerchief to her lips, as if to emphasize the secretness of her course. She found the spot she sought and bent down to divide the foliage and make a door to her sylvan closet. At this the hem of her dress caught her foot and she stopped to loosen it. As she rose she looked into the face of a man who was already in the shelter.

He stood up erect, two steps off. He must have watched her as she made her way straight toward him.

She took him in in one single glance. His face was bruised and scratched, his hands and wrists stained with dark filth. He was dressed in rags, barefooted, with tatters wound round his naked ankles. His arms hung down to his sides, his right hand clasped the hilt of a knife. He was about her own age. The man and the woman looked at each other.

This meeting in the wood from beginning to end passed without a word; what happened could only be rendered by pantomime. To the two actors in the pantomime it was timeless; according to a clock it lasted four minutes.

She had never in her life been exposed to danger. It did not occur to her to sum up her position, or to work out the length of time it would take to call her husband or Mathias, whom at this moment she could hear shouting to his dogs. She beheld the man before her as she would have beheld a forest ghost: the apparition itself, not the sequels of it, changes the world to the human who faces it.

Although she did not take her eyes off the face before her, she sensed that the alcove had been turned into a covert.[7] On the ground a couple of sacks formed a couch; there were some gnawed bones by it. A fire must have been made here in the night, for there were cinders strewn on the forest floor.

After a while she realized that he was observing her just as she was observing him. He was no longer just run to earth and crouching for a spring, but he was wondering, trying to know. At that she seemed to see herself with the eyes of the wild animal at bay in his dark hiding place: her silently approaching white figure, which might mean death.

He moved his right arm till it hung down straight before him between his legs. Without lifting the hand he bent the wrist and slowly raised the point of the knife till it pointed at her throat. The gesture was mad, unbelievable. He did not smile as he made it, but his nostrils distended, the corners of his mouth quivered a little. Then slowly he put the knife back in the sheath by his belt.

She had no object of value about her, only the wedding ring which her husband had set on her finger in church, a week ago. She drew it off, and in this movement dropped her handkerchief. She reached out her hand with the ring toward him. She did not bargain for her life. She was fearless by nature, and the horror with which he inspired her was not fear of what he might do to her. She commanded him, she besought him to vanish as he had come, to take a dreadful figure out of her life, so that it should never have been there. In the dumb movement her young form had the grave authoritativeness of a priestess conjuring down some monstrous being by a sacred sign.

He slowly reached out his hand to hers, his finger touched hers, and her hand was steady at the touch. But he did not take the ring. As she let it go it dropped to the ground as her handkerchief had done.

For a second the eyes of both followed it. It rolled a few inches toward him and stopped be-

7. **covert** (kō′vərt): hiding place; shelter.

A Elements of Literature
Suspense
Point out how tension is increased in this scene by slowing down the action with a catalog of very specific details. Ask students to list some of these details. [Possible response: Lise's dress and hair getting caught.]

B Struggling Readers
Interpreting Details
? Who is this character? What do the details of his appearance tell about him? Might he also have a symbolic dimension? What will he do next? [Possible responses: He is the murderer and thief, or a harmless vagrant, or a figment of Lise's imagination. He represents the dark side of life or of Lise, and he may attack her.]

C Critical Thinking
Evaluating
? What kind of change do you think has taken place? [Possible responses: Because she has seen this strange, wild person near her home, she realizes she is vulnerable. Her idyllic existence is marred by this dangerous intrusion.]

D Critical Thinking
Analyzing Character
? How does Lise's observation reveal that she has already changed? [Possible response: She has become aware of the feelings of someone besides herself or her husband.] Point out that the stranger may also represent herself under different circumstances. Perhaps she recognizes that she and the stranger are vulnerable beings.

E English Language Learners
Interpreting Idioms
Suggest that students look up *mad* in a dictionary and examine its many meanings, including "mentally ill," "wildly excited," "foolish," "infatuated," "hilarious," and "angry." Point out that *mad* can also mean "having rabies," a particularly appropriate meaning for a man described as a *wolf*.

F Critical Thinking
Interpreting
? Have students discuss what happens in this passage. What might Lise's giving of the ring mean? [Possible responses: She thinks he intends to rob her. She offers the ring as a bribe, a gift, or a sign of friendship or kinship.]

Crossing the Curriculum

Social Sciences
Have students work in groups of four or five to find out as much as they can about life in Denmark at the time the story is set, around 1808. Invite students to explore what daily life (entertainment, work, education, travel) was like for the rich, landed gentry and for the landless poor. Have students use their research to write a short essay.

Science
Have students work in groups to study the breeding and raising of sheep. Have them consider how much sheep raising has changed since the early nineteenth century. After the groups report their findings in oral presentations, ask students to discuss how Sigismund's qualities as a sheep breeder shed light on his qualities as a husband.

fore his bare foot. In a hardly perceivable movement he kicked it away and again looked into her face. They remained like that, she knew not how long, but she felt that during that time something happened, things were changed.

He bent down and picked up her handkerchief. All the time gazing at her, he again drew his knife and wrapped the tiny bit of cambric round the blade. This was difficult for him to do because his left arm was broken. While he did it his face under the dirt and suntan slowly grew whiter till it was almost phosphorescent. Fumbling with both hands, he once more stuck the knife into the sheath. Either the sheath was too big and had never fitted the knife, or the blade was much worn—it went in. For two or three more seconds his gaze rested on her face; then he lifted his own face a little, the strange radiance still upon it, and closed his eyes.

The movement was definitive and unconditional. In this one motion he did what she had begged him to do: He vanished and was gone. She was free.

She took a step backward, the immovable, blind face before her, then bent as she had done to enter the hiding place, and glided away as noiselessly as she had come. Once outside the grove she stood still and looked round for the meadow path, found it, and began to walk home.

Her husband had not yet rounded the edge of the grove. Now he saw her and helloed to her gaily; he came up quickly and joined her.

The path here was so narrow that he kept half behind her and did not touch her. He began to

Svartbekken (1909) by Henrik Sørensen. (120 cm × 110.5 cm).

Bergen Kommunes Kunstsamlinger, Norway.

G Critical Thinking

Speculating

? Why does the stranger refuse the ring? [Possible responses: He wants to convey that he is more than just a desperate thief. He is impressed by Lise and wants her respect.]

H Elements of Literature

Symbol

? What might the handkerchief represent? [Possible responses: It could allude to ladies' silks that medieval knights carried into battle. It also could symbolize Lise's naiveté.]

I Critical Thinking

Evaluating Character

? Recall the repetition of *wolf* in the story Mathias tells. Do you think the stranger is a wolf? Why or why not? [Possible responses: No, the word is ironic, because, instead of being a wolf in sheep's clothing, the stranger is more like a sheep in wolf's clothing. Yes, he is wild and preys upon Lise's innocence.]

J Reading Skills and Strategies

Dialogue with the Text

? All of the previous indications of a crisis lead up to this point. What happens here and why? [Possible responses: Lise has been mesmerized by the man's gaze; by closing his eyes, he breaks their silent communion so that she can leave. He indicates that he has weighed all his options and made a decision; it is the story's turning point.]

RESPONDING TO THE ART

Henrik Sørensen (1882–1962) was a Norwegian painter, born in Sweden, who became one of the most influential voices in Norwegian cultural life. A student of Matisse, he painted landscapes, antiwar subjects, and religious works. *Svartbekken* was an early Norwegian Expressionist work, and it ignited much negative criticism. This picture shows a man alone in a landscape that suggests the shapes of claws, flames, and jaws of attacking animals.

Activity. Ask students what the relationship is between the man and the landscape around him.

Making the Connections

Connecting to the Theme: "Ourselves Among Others"

Ask students to discuss how this story fits the theme of the collection. [Possible response: For the first time in her protected life, Lise faces the fact that there are other people—people who feel and suffer—outside the confines of her fortunate circumstances.]

Reaching All Students

Advanced Learners

Many of Dinesen's stories have folk- or fairy-tale qualities, yet they also describe complex human emotions and relationships. Ask advanced learners to work in groups to compile a list of elements characteristic of fairy tales—such as an enchanted setting, magical interventions, and simple diction. Then have them apply the list to "The Ring" and summarize how Dinesen's story is like and unlike a fairy tale.

A Reading Skills and Strategies

Dialogue with the Text

? The story indicates decisively that "All is over." What do you think is now over? [Possible responses: The world as Lise has known it has changed. She reverses her resolution to share everything with Sigismund. She sees her husband as unable to share her understanding of what has occurred. In having denied him her thoughts, her "perfect" marriage is over.]

B Struggling Readers

Finding the Main Idea

? The author offers one final summarizing statement about the ring and uses it to reveal the heart of the story. What does this passage mean? [Possible responses: Lise grows from innocence to experience: she is now wedded to her awareness of evil, injustice, and hardship.]

C Critical Thinking

Challenging the Text

? Is it helpful that the author shifts to the husband's point of view here? [Possible responses: Yes, it emphasizes that Sigismund is following a completely different line of thought and is truly more separate from his wife than before. No, it is unnecessary, since the point is already clear.]

D Elements of Literature

Irony

? How is Lise's response here ironic in light of her promise at the end of the second paragraph? [She is doing the opposite of what she promised; she is now keeping secrets.]

Finding Common Ground

This feature requires students to discover through lively discussion areas of agreement with a theme or issue raised in the literature. When students work together in small groups, have one member keep notes on the discussion of each question. Once the groups have had time for a full discussion, have the recorder share a summary of the group's responses with the class.

explain to her what had been the matter with the lambs. She walked a step before him and thought: **(A)** All is over.

After a while he noticed her silence, came up beside her to look at her face, and asked, "What is the matter?"

She searched her mind for something to say, and at last said: "I have lost my ring."

"What ring?" he asked her.

She answered, "My wedding ring."

As she heard her own voice pronounce the words, she conceived their meaning.

Her wedding ring. "With this ring"—dropped by one and kicked away by another—"with this ring I thee wed." With this lost ring she had wedded herself to something. To what? To poverty, persecution, total loneliness. To the sorrows and the sinfulness of this earth. "And what therefore God has joined together let man not put asunder." **(B)**

"I will find you another ring," her husband said. "You and I are the same as we were on our wedding day; it will do as well. We are husband and wife today too, as much as yesterday, I suppose."

Her face was so still that he did not know if she had heard what he said. It touched him that she should take the loss of his ring so to heart. He took her hand and kissed it. It was cold, not quite the same hand as he had last kissed. He stopped to make her stop with him. **(C)**

"Do you remember where you had the ring on last?" he asked.

"No," she answered.

"Have you any idea," he asked, "where you may have lost it?" **(D)**

"No," she answered. "I have no idea at all."

Finding Common Ground

The couple in the story seem, at first, to live in a kind of fairy-tale paradise far from the concerns of unfortunates who might have to steal for food. All too soon, however, the troubles of the wider world intrude on their personal happiness.

Think about your own response to Lise's experience with the stranger. (Be sure to check your reading notes.) Get together with a small group to talk about the story. Here are some questions you might consider, though you also might want to set your own agendas:

- Why doesn't the stranger accept Lise's ring? Why doesn't he try to hurt her?
- Why doesn't Lise tell her husband about her experience with the stranger?
- How has Lise changed by the end of the story? How has her relationship with her husband changed?
- Be sure to comment on the relevance of the story to your life today. When your group has finished its discussion, assign one member to report to the class. Then see if, as a class, you can sum up your responses to the story—including your disagreements as well as any consensus you may reach.

Assessing Learning

Check Test: Short Answers

1. How long has the couple been married? [one week]
2. What work does Sigismund do? [He breeds sheep.]
3. What news shared by Mathias interests Lise? [the murder by the sheep thief]
4. What does Lise offer the thief? [her wedding ring]

Informal Assessment

Observation Assessment. As students discuss or write about their interactions with the story, use the following points to assess reading comprehension:

1=Rarely 2=Sometimes 3=Often

____1. Finds multiple levels of meaning
____2. Uses text to verify and clarify ideas
____3. Challenges the text
____4. Makes connections between the text and one's own experience

Stevie Smith

(1902–1971)

She was christened Florence Margaret Smith but got the nickname "Stevie" because she was short, like the British jockey Steve Donohue. She grew up in a suburb of London, abandoned by her father and raised by her mother and an aunt. Smith lived with her aunt for sixty-six years, until "Auntie Lion" died in 1968 at the age of ninety-six.

After finishing school, Smith worked as a secretary for a magazine publisher. She remained there for thirty years and began to publish poetry and fiction while in her early thirties. Her first publication, *Novel on Yellow Paper* (1936), is a playful monologue spoken by a character very much like Smith herself.

Smith's other early publications—mostly novels—also reflect her offbeat outlook and writing style. But it is in her poems that she fully displays her cleverness. The light side of her poetry often reflects a darker side as well, making her verse seriocomic (partly serious, partly humorous). Her poems often deal with death, loneliness, or despair, but Smith is never self-pitying. Her humor adds sparkle, allowing her to distance herself from her subject. Smith herself best summed up her paradoxical views when she claimed that she was "straightforward, but not simple." The poet Robert Lowell described her poetic "voice" as "cheerfully gruesome," and the poet-humorist Ogden Nash admired her "songs of deadly innocence."

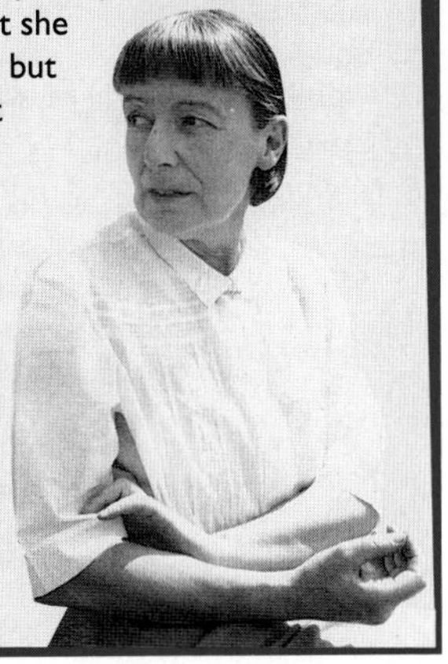

Stevie Smith (1954).

Before You Read

NOT WAVING BUT DROWNING

Make the Connection

Life's Misunderstandings

Everyone has misunderstandings. In fact, we misread each other's signals about nearly everything—from the most trivial to the most important things in life. We say one thing. People think we mean something else. We act a certain way for one reason. People think our action is motivated by something entirely different. The results of our misunderstandings can sometimes be tragic, as in this poem.

Quickwrite

Freewrite for a few minutes as you focus on Smith's **title:** What do you predict it means?

Background

Stevie Smith published ten volumes of verse, but, with the exception of this one poem, most of her poetry is unknown to American readers. Why this poem should have become more famous than all of her other poems is a question best answered by readers like you.

Here's what the poet reveals about her state of mind when she wrote the poem:

"I often try to pull myself together, having been well brought up in the stiff-upper-lip school of thought and not knowing whether other people find Death as merry as I do. But it's a tightrope business, this pulling oneself together, and can give rise to misunderstandings which may prove fatal, as in the poem I wrote about a poor fellow who got drowned. His friends thought he was waving to them but really he was asking for help."

go.hrw.com
LEO 12-14

OBJECTIVES

1. Read and interpret the poem
2. Express understanding through critical writing

SKILLS

Writing

- Collect ideas for a problem-solution essay
- Write an essay exploring the metaphor of the sea

Viewing/Representing

- Compare the scene in a painting with the scene in a poem (ATE)

Planning

- **Block Schedule**
  Block Scheduling Lesson Plans with Pacing Guide
- **Traditional Schedule**
  Lesson Plans Including Strategies for English-Language Learners
- **One-Stop Planner**
  CD-ROM with Test Generator

BROWSING IN THE FILES

About the Author. Stevie Smith wanted to be a poet all her life, but her first publication, *Novel on Yellow Paper*, was a prose work. This book is full of digressions and non sequiturs, and some critics compared it to the writing of Gertrude Stein. During the 1960s, interest in Smith's work increased, probably as the result of a series of public readings she gave. In 1969 she received the Queen's Gold Medal for Poetry.

Resources: Print and Media

Reading

- *Graphic Organizers for Active Reading,* p. 106
- *Audio CD Library*
  Disc 19, Track 4

Assessment

- *Formal Assessment,* p. 213
- *Portfolio Management System,* p. 207
- *Test Generator* (*One-Stop Planner CD-ROM*)

Internet

- go.hrw.com (keyword: *LE0 12-14*)

Summary

A man drowns when his cries and gestures for help are misinterpreted as playful waving. Some people speculate that he died of a heart attack caused by the icy water. The dead man himself responds that he always had been too "cold" and had lived "too far out" and separate from humanity.

(A) Reading Skills and Strategies
Making Inferences

? What two different meanings does this line suggest? [Possible responses: It suggests that he went farther into the water than people realized and that he lived at a great emotional distance from others.] Point out that in formal usage, *further* signifies quantity or degree, as opposed to *farther*, which indicates distance. This word choice adds an additional layer of meaning to the poem.

(B) Appreciating Language
Figurative Meanings

? Beyond the literal meaning, what might the "cold" associated with "his heart" represent? [Possible response: a lack of warm relationships or of love.]

(C) Elements of Literature
Rhythm

Ask students to listen to the poem's irregular rhythm, predominantly mixed trimeter and dimeter. Point out the ironic (and humorous) contrast in rhythm and length between ll. 7 and 8.

(D) Elements of Literature
Rhyme

The rhyme scheme is *abcb* in each stanza. The rhymes in stanzas 1 and 3 are approximate. The simplicity of the rhyme in ll. 2 and 4 (repeated in ll. 10 and 12) contrasts starkly with the content. Point out the repeated *o* sounds, especially in l. 9.

Not Waving but Drowning

Stevie Smith

Nobody heard him, the dead man,
But still he lay moaning:
(A) I was much further out than you thought
And not waving but drowning.

Poor chap, he always loved larking°
And now he's dead
(B) It must have been too cold for him his heart gave way,
(C) They said.

(D) Oh, no no no, it was too cold always
(Still the dead one lay moaning)
I was much too far out all my life
And not waving but drowning.

5. larking: playing; having a good time.

Blue and Silver—Chopping Channel (c. 1890) by James Abbott McNeill Whistler.
Courtesy of the Freer Gallery of Art, Smithsonian Institution, Washington, D.C.

Responding to the Art

The paintings of **James Abbott McNeill Whistler** (1834–1903) are generally elegant and restrained. *Blue and Silver—Chopping Channel* captures the open, rolling quality of the sea in a Japanese screen painting.
Activity. Ask students if the picture matches the scene in Smith's poem.

Reaching All Students

Struggling Readers
Ask three students to read the poem aloud: one taking the voice of the narrator, the second the voice of the dead man, and the third the voices of the man's friends.

English Language Learners
Help students see that the speaker acknowledges the tragedy of the man's failure to communicate with others but also maintains a detached stance and tone.

Crossing the Curriculum

Art
Stevie Smith accompanied many of her poems with line art that often adds another dimension to the poetry. For example, the illustration she attached to "Not Waving but Drowning" shows the head and torso of a young person with hair hanging like bars down his face. Ask students to create their own visual representation of the mood of this poem.

PRIMARY Sources | **AN AUTOBIOGRAPHY**

The Truths About Poetry

Here are some of the truths about poetry. She is an Angel, very strong. It is not poetry but the poet who has a feminine ending, not the Muse who is weak, but the poet. She makes a strong communication. Poetry is like a strong explosion in the sky. She makes a mushroom shape of terror and drops to the ground with a strong infection. Also she is a strong way out. The human creature is alone in his carapace. Poetry is a strong way out. . . .

Poetry does not like to be up-to-date, she refuses to be neat. ("Anglo-Saxon," wrote Gavin Bone, "is a good language to write poetry in because it is impossible to be neat.") All the poems Poetry writes may be called "Heaven, a Detail," or "Hell, a Detail." (She only writes about heaven and hell.) . . .

All Poetry has to do is to make a strong communication. All the poet has to do is to listen. The poet is not an important fellow. There will always be another poet.

—Stevie Smith, *from Me Again*

MAKING MEANINGS

First Thoughts

1. What does the **title** of the poem mean to you? (How do your ideas after reading the poem compare with your Quickwrite notes?)

Shaping Interpretations

2. How many different voices do you hear speaking in the poem?

3. What does the speaker mean by "it was too cold always" and "I was much too far out all my life"?

4. It seems bizarre that a dead man is talking. What might "dead" signify in the poem, besides its literal meaning? How is the dead man misunderstood or ignored?

Extending the Text

5. How could this poem be a summing up of one's whole life, or of the human condition in general?

Challenging the Text

6. Stevie Smith once said that good writing had to be "sad, true, economical, and funny." Does her poem meet these criteria? Do you agree with Smith's prescription for good writing?

CHOICES: Building Your Portfolio

Writer's Notebook

1. Collecting Ideas for a Problem-Solution Essay

WORK IN PROGRESS

Many people are "drowning" and in need of help. What obligation does society have to people in trouble, people who need a helping hand? Freewrite your ideas on this issue—focus on identifying the problems and listing possible solutions. You might want to jot down your response to the words of Joseph Conrad that open this collection (page 1059). Save your notes for the Writer's Workshop on page 1179.

Exploring a Metaphor

2. Sinking or Swimming

In an essay, explain how the sea is often used, in literature and in ordinary conversation, as a metaphor for life and death. What comparisons do we often make between living and swimming, floating, sinking, diving, or drowning?

MAKING MEANINGS

First Thoughts [Respond]

1. Students might say that the title sums up the literal meaning of the poem. Others might comment on ways in which a person can be "drowning" in the modern world.

Shaping Interpretations [Analyze]

2. Students may find three voices: the narrator (ll. 1–2, 8, 10); the drowned man (ll. 3–4, 9, 11–12); and bystanders (ll. 5–7).

3. The comment about the cold may mean his life has been lonely; "too far out" may mean he has lived outside the mainstream of society or at great emotional distance from others.

4. Students may suggest that failure to communicate well with others or to live fully could cause a person to feel dead emotionally. The drowning man's signal for help is misunderstood as "larking." Presumably earlier attempts to reach others emotionally were also not understood.

Extending the Text [Synthesize]

5. Students may suggest that although people try to communicate their needs, they may not always be heard.

Challenging the Text [Evaluate]

6. Students may agree that the poem meets her four criteria, but they may also point out the paradoxical requirement of being both sad and funny. Others may identify alternative criteria, such as beautiful, noble, and sincere writing.

Grading Timesaver

Rubrics for each Choices assignment appear on p. 207 in the *Portfolio Management System.*

Primary Sources

Smith's metaphorical remarks about poetry are taken from *Me Again,* a gathering of her uncollected writings. Students might be interested to know that, immediately after her death, her friend James MacGibbon assumed that some unpublished work would be found in her house. However, except for one poem on death that Smith had given MacGibbon in typescript, not one poem was found among her personal papers. Suggest that students approach Smith's comments about poetry as if the comments themselves were a poem. For example, they can discuss the figurative language she uses (the personification of poetry) and the comparisons of poetic expression to an atomic explosion or germ warfare. The concept that the poet is the instrument through which something larger expresses itself is not a new idea. Many poets speak of being the servant of poetry, not its master. Ask students which is more important—the artist or the work of art.

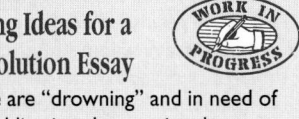

OBJECTIVES

1. Read and interpret the story
2. Identify and analyze dramatic irony
3. Identify supporting details (of an Oedipus complex)
4. Express understanding through critical and creative writing
5. Understand new words

SKILLS

Literary

- Identify and analyze dramatic irony

Reading

- Identify supporting details

Writing

- Collect ideas for a problem-solution essay
- Write an account of a humorous incident from childhood

Vocabulary

- Use new words

Planning

- **Block Schedule**
  Block Scheduling Lesson Plans with Pacing Guide
- **Traditional Schedule**
  Lesson Plans Including Strategies for English-Language Learners
- **One-Stop Planner**
  CD-ROM with Test Generator

BROWSING IN THE FILES

About the Author. Like the boy in "My Oedipus Complex," O'Connor spent his earliest years living alone with his mother, who supported the family by doing housework, while his father, a drummer in a British army band, was away on active duty. Minnie O'Donovan, O'Connor's mother, loved literature so much that she managed to borrow the complete works of Shakespeare from one of the families for whom she worked. She read every word. Her son developed a similar passion for reading. As a writer, O'Connor wanted to achieve absolute realism and touch the heart.

Frank O'Connor

(1903–1966)

Frank O'Connor.

Frank O'Connor was born Michael Francis O'Donovan in Cork City, Ireland. He was the only child of a bitterly poor couple whose battling shadowed his life.

O'Connor read endlessly, first boys' magazines and then, finding his way to the library, books of all kinds. Ironically, he particularly enjoyed stories of English schoolboys, and while he knew there would never be money for any such formal education in his own life, he imagined its privileges and yearned to be an educated man.

The reality of his own schooling was not half so appealing. O'Connor attended the Christian Brothers' school in Cork but in the end gave up on school, feeling it was a place where he would always be "useless, frightened, or hurt." But he had no intention of abandoning his dream of an education. At fourteen, he took a series of clerk's jobs that gave him money to buy the books he needed to educate himself.

In 1916, the long-standing hostility between England and Ireland flared into open rebellion, and O'Connor was caught up in the new patriotism. He read Irish history with new fervor and, along with other young Irishmen, thought of heroism. "I was improvising an education I could not afford," he said later, "and the country was improvising a revolution it could not afford." After England had brought up its artillery and "blown the center of Dublin flat . . . the country had to content itself with a make-believe revolution and I had to content myself with a make-believe education and the curious thing is that it was the make-believe that succeeded."

Truce with England came in 1921, when O'Connor was just short of eighteen, but its terms were unacceptable to a large number of Irish people. The treaty was immediately followed by a civil war in which O'Connor took the Republican side (the side that favored severing all ties to England and establishing an Irish republic). Throughout the next two years, he was active in the war, and while on a mission in the spring of 1923, he was arrested and imprisoned.

When at last he was released, he went on to educate himself further and to take part in the Irish literary revival, a movement that tried to restore the Irish language (it had been nearly wiped out by the English) and to create a purely Irish literature. For his pen name, he chose his beloved mother's maiden name.

O'Connor began writing stories, and in 1935, with his friend the poet W. B. Yeats, he became a director of the Abbey Theatre in Dublin. The theater was the heart of the Irish revival, which also involved Lady Gregory, Sean O'Casey, Seán O'Faoláin, and Liam O'Flaherty.

In his writing, O'Connor sought to capture the essence of Irish lyrical speech. His stories are all set in Ireland because "I know to a syllable how everything in Ireland can be said." O'Connor became a richly productive literary figure, bringing forth volumes of poetry, stories, a novel, an autobiography, plays, criticism, and translations. He was a regular contributor to such American magazines as *The New Yorker, The Atlantic Monthly,* and *Esquire.* Speaking of his mastery of the short-story form, Yeats said, "O'Connor is doing for Ireland what Chekhov did for Russia."

O'Connor came to the United States in 1952. In his later years, he taught at Harvard, Northwestern, and Stanford. For a poor boy with very little formal education, he had done quite well.

go.hrw.com *LEO 12-14*

Resources: Print and Media

Reading

- *Graphic Organizers for Active Reading,* p. 107
- *Words to Own,* p. 32
- *Audio CD Library*
  Disc 19, Track 5

Writing and Language

- *Daily Oral Grammar*
  Transparency 37
- *Grammar and Language Links*
  Worksheets, pp. 67, 69
- *Language Workshop CD-ROM*

Assessment

- *Formal Assessment,* p. 214
- *Portfolio Management System,* p. 208
- *Test Generator (One-Stop Planner CD-ROM)*

Internet

- go.hrw.com (keyword: *LEO 12-14*)

Before You Read
My Oedipus Complex

Make the Connection
Three's a Crowd
Have you ever heard the saying "Two's company; three's a crowd"? The saying reflects a basic human truth: Triangles often mean trouble in human relationships.

Many of us encounter our first troublesome triangle very early in life: If we're a first or an only child, we may compete with one parent for the attention of the other parent. In bigger families or families with a single parent, we may compete with a brother or sister to see who can capture a parent's attention. Among our childhood friends, alliances often shift daily.

Even later, with those we love deeply, a certain possessiveness may grip us when a third person enters the scene. Why do we have such a desire for the sole attentions of another? Are these feelings inevitable?

Quickwrite
Have you ever observed a young child competing with a father or mother for the attention of the other parent? Have you noticed any comical aspects of this earliest of all triangles in our lives? How about so-called sibling rivalry—what have you observed about brothers' and sisters' competing for the love and attention of the parents?

Elements of Literature
Dramatic Irony
The narrator of this story is a little boy competing with his father for his mother's love. In his innocence, the child assumes that he will marry his mother when he grows up. We, the readers, know, of course, that this will never happen. The child's lack of understanding of his parents' relationship fills the story with hilarious examples of **dramatic irony.**

Dramatic irony occurs when the reader knows something important that a character does not know.

For more on Irony, see the Handbook of Literary Terms.

Background
In Greek mythology, King Oedipus (ed′i·pəs) of Thebes, unaware of his true parentage, kills his father and marries his mother. The term *Oedipus complex* was first used in 1899 by the Austrian "father of psychoanalysis," Sigmund Freud, to describe the unconscious desire of a child for the exclusive love of the parent of the opposite sex. This desire results in rivalry with the parent of the same sex. In psychoanalytic theory, the Oedipus complex is a stage in normal human development, lasting from about age three to age five or six, and ending when the child identifies with the parent of the same sex.

Summary ■■

The narrator tells the story in the first person from the point of view of a five-year-old boy. He relates how his comfortable life with his mother changes when his father returns home from World War I. The boy, Larry, must now compete for his mother's attention, and he cannot grasp what she sees in such a crude and boring person as his father. His attempts to regain his mother's attention only anger his father and disturb his mother. He is told repeatedly not to interrupt, not to wake Daddy, but he persists until one morning his exasperated father strikes him. Outraged and confused, he announces that one day he will marry his mother.

When a new baby claims the mother's attention, the father-son relationship begins to change. They become allies when the father is "turned out" of the big bed, just as Larry was.

Background

According to O'Connor's biographer, James Matthews, two years before he wrote "My Oedipus Complex," O'Connor admitted (jokingly) that he believed he had always had an Oedipus complex. In a letter, he also said that he thought he had somehow bestowed this complex on his son Myles, whose desire at the age of eight was to kill his father and marry his mother. Matthews comments that O'Connor in the story uses a humorous tone, which enables him to deflect thoughts of the serious implications of such childhood emotions.

Preteaching Vocabulary

Words to Own
Have students read the Words to Own and their definitions listed at the bottom of the selection pages. Then have them match each word to the word or phrase in the following list that is most nearly its antonym:

1. winning [obnoxious]
2. insulted and irritated [cajoled]
3. obnoxious [winning]
4. mean-spirited [magnanimous]
5. comforting [ominous]
6. accusation [intercession]
7. gullibly [incredulously]
8. alert and attentive [preoccupied]
9. frown [guffaw]
10. befriend [alienate]

A Struggling Readers

Finding Details

? What do you learn about the narrator in the first paragraph? Distinguish between facts and assumptions. [Facts: His father is a soldier in World War I and is seldom home until the narrator is five. Assumptions: The narrator seems to be an imaginative child.]

B Elements of Literature

Language and Style

Discuss the sensory imagery, emphasizing the power of smell to create an intimate atmosphere. Point out the economy of O'Connor's language—how much he conveys in one sentence.

C Critical Thinking

Interpreting

? What does this passage convey? [Possible responses: The son believes that he and his mother are of one mind, even where his father is concerned. The mother is indulgent with the boy.]

D Elements of Literature

Dramatic Irony

There is a major discrepancy between the boy's perceptions and the adult reality. Point out that this passage is a superb example of **dramatic irony,** which occurs when the reader knows something (in this case, all about babies) that the character in a story does not know.

My Oedipus Complex

Frank O'Connor

Father was in the army all through the war—the first war,[1] I mean—so, up to the age of five, I never saw much of him, and what I saw did not worry me. Sometimes I woke and there was a (A) big figure in khaki peering down at me in the candlelight. Sometimes in the early morning I heard the slamming of the front door and the clatter of nailed boots[2] down the cobbles of the lane. These were Father's entrances and exits. Like Santa Claus he came and went mysteriously.

In fact, I rather liked his visits, though it was an uncomfortable squeeze between Mother and him when I got into the big bed in the early morning. He smoked, which gave him a pleasant musty (B) smell, and shaved, an operation of astounding interest. Each time he left a trail of souvenirs—model tanks and Gurkha[3] knives with handles made of bullet cases, and German helmets and cap badges and button sticks,[4] and all sorts of military equipment—carefully stowed away in a long box on top of the wardrobe, in case they ever came in handy. There was a bit of the magpie[5] about Father; he expected everything to come in handy. When his back was turned, Mother let (C) me get a chair and rummage through his treasures. She didn't seem to think so highly of them as he did.

The war was the most peaceful period of my life. The window of my attic faced southeast. My mother had curtained it, but that had small effect. I always woke with the first light and, with all the responsibilities of the previous day melted, feeling myself rather like the sun, ready to illumine and rejoice. Life never seemed so simple and clear and full of possibilities as then. I put my feet out from under the clothes[6]—I called them Mrs. Left and Mrs. Right—and invented dramatic situations for them in which they discussed the problems of the day. At least Mrs. Right did; she was very demonstrative, but I hadn't the same control of Mrs. Left, so she mostly contented herself with nodding agreement.

They discussed what Mother and I should do during the day, what Santa Claus should give a fellow for Christmas, and what steps should be taken to brighten the home. There was that little matter of the baby, for instance. Mother and I could never agree about that. Ours was the only house in the terrace[7] without a new baby, and Mother said we couldn't afford one till Father (D) came back from the war because they cost seventeen and six.[8] That showed how simple she was. The Geneys up the road had a baby, and everyone knew they couldn't afford seventeen and six. It was probably a cheap baby, and Mother wanted something really good, but I felt she was too exclusive. The Geneys' baby would have done us fine.

Having settled my plans for the day, I got up, put a chair under the attic window, and lifted the frame high enough to stick out my head. The window overlooked the front gardens of the terrace behind ours, and beyond these it looked over a deep valley to the tall, red-brick houses terraced up the opposite hillside, which were all still in shadow, while those at our side of the valley were all lit up, though with long strange shadows that made them seem unfamiliar; rigid and painted.

After that I went into Mother's room and climbed into the big bed. She woke and I began to tell her of my schemes. By this time, though I never seem to have noticed it, I was petrified[9] in my nightshirt, and I thawed as I talked until, the last frost melted, I fell asleep beside her and woke again only when I heard her below in the kitchen, making the breakfast.

After breakfast we went into town; heard Mass at St. Augustine's and said a prayer for Father, and did the shopping. If the afternoon was fine we either went for a walk in the country or a visit to

1. **first war:** World War I (1914–1918).
2. **nailed boots:** boots with short, broad-headed nails on the soles to prevent slipping and wear; also called hobnail boots.
3. **Gurkha** (goor′kä′): people of the mountains of Nepal, many of whom served in the British army.
4. **button sticks:** slotted strips of metal or wood that fit over a row of buttons on a military tunic, allowing the buttons to be polished without soiling the cloth.
5. **magpie:** type of bird that picks up all kinds of unlikely materials to build its nest.
6. **clothes:** bedclothes.
7. **terrace:** row of houses.
8. **seventeen and six:** seventeen shillings and sixpence.
9. **petrified** (pe′tri·fīd′): rigid from the cold.

Reaching All Students

Struggling Readers

Before students read the story, have them work in pairs to discuss the world of a five-year-old child. Perhaps they can remember their own childhood or that of a sibling or neighbor. Ask them to conclude by listing three things they think are very important to a child at this age.

English Language Learners

Students may have difficulty with some of the Irish expressions and idioms O'Connor uses as part of his narration and dialogue. Have students keep a running list of such words and expressions. Then by studying clues in the text and conferring with other students, have them jot down next to each item what they think it means. Finally, they can check their meanings with you or with a dictionary.

Advanced Learners

The tradition of Irish storytelling is a long and glorious one. Have advanced learners research other renowned Irish storytellers. Possibilities include James Stephens, Liam O'Flaherty, William Trevor, and James Joyce (see p. 984). Some students might read several stories and give a brief oral report on the storyteller's themes and style.

Mother's great friend in the convent, Mother St. Dominic. Mother had them all praying for Father, and every night, going to bed, I asked God to send him back safe from the war to us. Little, indeed, did I know what I was praying for!

One morning, I got into the big bed, and there, sure enough, was Father in his usual Santa Claus manner, but later, instead of uniform, he put on his best blue suit, and Mother was as pleased as anything. I saw nothing to be pleased about, because, out of uniform, Father was altogether less interesting, but she only beamed, and explained that our prayers had been answered, and off we went to Mass to thank God for having brought Father safely home.

The irony of it! That very day when he came in to dinner he took off his boots and put on his slippers, donned the dirty old cap he wore about the house to save him from colds, crossed his legs, and began to talk gravely to Mother, who looked anxious. Naturally, I disliked her looking anxious, because it destroyed her good looks, so I interrupted him.

"Just a moment, Larry!" she said gently.

This was only what she said when we had boring visitors, so I attached no importance to it and went on talking.

"Do be quiet, Larry!" she said impatiently. "Don't you hear me talking to Daddy?"

This was the first time I had heard those ominous words, "talking to Daddy," and I couldn't help feeling that if this was how God answered prayers, he couldn't listen to them very attentively.

"Why are you talking to Daddy?" I asked with as great a show of indifference as I could muster.

"Because Daddy and I have business to discuss. Now, don't interrupt again!"

In the afternoon, at Mother's request, Father took me for a walk. This time we went into town instead of out the country, and I thought at first, in my usual optimistic way, that it might be an improvement. It was nothing of the sort. Father and I had quite different notions of a walk in town. He had no proper interest in trams,[10] ships, and horses, and the only thing that seemed to divert him was talking to fellows as old as himself. When I wanted to stop he simply went on, dragging me behind him by the hand; when he wanted to stop I had no alternative but to do the same. I noticed that it seemed to be a sign that he wanted to stop for a long time whenever he leaned against a wall. The second time I saw him do it I got wild. He seemed to be settling himself forever. I pulled him by the coat and trousers, but, unlike Mother who, if you were too persistent, got into a wax[11] and said: "Larry, if you don't behave yourself, I'll give you a good slap," Father had an extraordinary capacity for amiable inattention. I sized him up and wondered would I cry, but he seemed to be too remote to be annoyed even by that. Really, it was like going for a walk with a mountain! He either ignored the wrenching and pummeling[12] entirely, or else glanced down with a grin of amusement from his peak. I had never met anyone so absorbed in himself as he seemed.

At teatime, "talking to Daddy" began again, complicated this time by the fact that he had an evening paper, and every few minutes he put it down and told Mother something new out of it. I felt this was foul play. Man for man, I was prepared to compete with him any time for Mother's attention, but when he had it all made up for him by other people it left me no chance. Several times I tried to change the subject without success.

"You must be quiet while Daddy is reading, Larry," Mother said impatiently.

It was clear that she either genuinely liked talking to Father better than talking to me, or else that he had some terrible hold on her which made her afraid to admit the truth.

"Mummy," I said that night when she was tucking me up, "do you think if I prayed hard God would send Daddy back to the war?"

She seemed to think about that for a moment.

"No, dear," she said with a smile. "I don't think he would."

"Why wouldn't he, Mummy?"

"Because there isn't a war any longer, dear."

"But, Mummy, couldn't God make another war, if He liked?"

10. **trams:** streetcars.

11. **got into a wax:** became upset.
12. **pummeling** (pum′əl·iŋ): hitting repeatedly with the fists.

WORDS TO OWN
ominous (äm′ə·nəs) *adj.:* threatening.

E Reading Skills and Strategies
Responding to the Text

? What effect does the narrator's extreme innocence have on the reader? [Possible responses: It is humorous; it evokes feelings of warmth, nostalgia, and empathy.]

F Critical Thinking
Challenging the Text

? Would a five-year-old boy think this way? How do you explain this paragraph? [Possible responses: No, the narrator has slipped into an adult perspective here, perhaps the grown-up Larry reflecting on his early thoughts. Yes, the fear of a mother's unsmiling face would naturally make a strong impression on a young child.]

G Elements of Literature
Conflict

In this passage O'Connor heightens the conflict with the word *ominous* and then hints that major changes are in store. Suggest that students watch how O'Connor repeatedly increases the tension, then gives some release (as in the beginning of the next paragraph).

H Elements of Literature
Dramatic Irony

? What does the reader know here that makes this a passage of dramatic irony? [Possible response: The reader is aware that the boy himself is totally self-absorbed.]

I Critical Thinking
Making Connections

? How is this conversation between Larry and his mother similar to the conversation between Paul and his mother regarding luck in "The Rocking-Horse Winner" (see pp. 997–998)? [Possible response: Both children ask a series of questions, and both look to God for help regarding their need for their mother's attention.]

Using Students' Strengths

Visual Learners

Ask students to draw three pictures of Larry's father: one as Larry perceives him before the war ends; another just after the father has returned; and a third at the end of the story, when the father seeks out Larry's company. Remind students to tie their artwork to the text, perhaps by captioning each picture with a quotation from the story.

Kinesthetic Learners

Allow volunteers to perform dramatic sketches based on scenes in the story. One person might read the scene while others act it out in pantomime; students could also combine narration with dialogue; or they could perform the scenes as mini-dramas. Remind them to match their body language, gestures, and facial expressions to the descriptions in the text.

Verbal Learners

Have verbal learners listen to a recording of the story. (O'Connor recorded his own version with Caedmon Records in 1954.) Then elicit student responses to the pace, rhythm, style, and tone of the reading. For example, do they think the reading is well-paced? Or would students prefer that it be read slower? faster? Is the tone appropriate to the text? Or should it be more humorous? more serious?

A Elements of Literature

Simile

? What makes this simile of a corked, carbonated beverage effective? [Possible response: It suggests that the boy feels fresh and is ready to "explode" with pent-up energy.]

B Critical Thinking

Challenging the Text

? Does the narrator's tone shift here in a way that is jarring or inconsistent? [Possible responses: Yes, the adult analysis interrupts the realistic feel of the childlike narration. No, the tone throughout the story suggests an adult looking back at his childhood self.]

C Reading Skills and Strategies

Identifying Cause and Effect

? What effect might it have on Larry to suspect that his mother is afraid? [Possible responses: The effects would be complex, including feelings of protectiveness and fear for himself and for his mother. He might also feel anger at the forced changes in his relationship with his mother.]

D Critical Thinking

Making Inferences

? Why do you think Larry's father does not bring him a cup of tea? [Possible responses: Since small children are not always given tea, this behavior may be perfectly natural. Or, it may indicate that, while the father was initially tolerant of his son, he is now purposefully ignoring, or is even resenting, Larry.]

E Elements of Literature

Dramatic Irony

? This touching, funny passage is an example of dramatic irony. What does the reader know that the child narrator does not? [Possible responses: The reader knows that the boy is not a true rival or equal of his father in the competition for his mother's affections. Also, the boy is not in an either/or situation in which he would have to "leave the house."]

"He wouldn't like to, dear. It's not God who makes wars, but bad people."

"Oh!" I said.

I was disappointed about that. I began to think that God wasn't quite what he was cracked up to be.

A Next morning I woke at my usual hour, feeling like a bottle of champagne. I put out my feet and invented a long conversation in which Mrs. Right talked of the trouble she had with her own father till she put him in the Home. I didn't quite know what the Home was but it sounded the right place for Father. Then I got my chair and stuck my head out of the attic window. Dawn was just breaking, with a guilty air that made me feel I had caught it in the act. My head bursting with stories and schemes, I stumbled in next door, and in the half-darkness scrambled into the big bed. There was no room at Mother's side so I had to get between her and Father. For the time being I had forgotten about him, and for several minutes I sat bolt upright, racking my brains to know what I could do with him. He was taking up more than his fair share of the bed, and I couldn't get comfortable, so I gave him several kicks that made him grunt and stretch. He made room all right, though. Mother waked and felt for me. I settled back comfortably in the warmth of the bed with my thumb in my mouth.

"Mummy!" I hummed, loudly and contentedly.

"Sssh! dear," she whispered. "Don't wake Daddy!"

This was a new development, which threatened to be even more serious than "talking to Daddy." Life without my early-morning conferences was unthinkable.

"Why?" I asked severely.

"Because poor Daddy is tired."

B This seemed to me a quite inadequate reason, and I was sickened by the sentimentality of her "poor Daddy." I never liked that sort of gush; it always struck me as insincere.

"Oh!" I said lightly. Then in my most winning tone: "Do you know where I want to go with you today, Mummy?"

"No, dear," she sighed.

"I want to go down the Glen and fish for thornybacks with my new net, and then I want to go out to the Fox and Hounds, and—"

"Don't-wake-Daddy!" she hissed angrily, clapping her hand across my mouth.

But it was too late. He was awake, or nearly so. He grunted and reached for the matches. Then he stared incredulously at his watch.

C "Like a cup of tea, dear?" asked Mother in a meek, hushed voice I had never heard her use before. It sounded almost as though she were afraid.

"Tea?" he exclaimed indignantly. "Do you know what the time is?"

"And after that I want to go up the Rathcooney Road," I said loudly, afraid I'd forget something in all those interruptions.

"Go to sleep at once, Larry!" she said sharply.

I began to snivel. I couldn't concentrate, the way that pair went on, and smothering my early-morning schemes was like burying a family from the cradle.

Father said nothing, but lit his pipe and sucked it, looking out into the shadows without minding Mother or me. I knew he was mad. Every time I made a remark Mother hushed me irritably. I was mortified. I felt it wasn't fair; there was even something sinister in it. Every time I had pointed out to her the waste of making two beds when we could both sleep in one, she had told me it was healthier like that, and now here was this man, this stranger, sleeping with her without the least regard for her health!

D He got up early and made tea, but though he brought Mother a cup he brought none for me.

"Mummy," I shouted, "I want a cup of tea, too."

"Yes, dear," she said patiently. "You can drink from Mummy's saucer."

E That settled it. Either Father or I would have to leave the house. I didn't want to drink from Mother's saucer; I wanted to be treated as an equal in my own home, so, just to spite her, I drank it all and left none for her. She took that quietly, too.

But that night when she was putting me to bed she said gently:

"Larry, I want you to promise me something."

"What is it?" I asked.

"Not to come in and disturb poor Daddy in the morning. Promise?"

WORDS TO OWN

winning (win′iŋ) *adj.:* charming.

incredulously (in·krej′o͞o·ləs·lē) *adv.:* disbelievingly.

Professional Notes

Critical Comment: O'Connor the Stylist

William Maxwell, an editor at *The New Yorker*, which published many of O'Connor's short stories, sees O'Connor as a master of language and style. Maxwell writes: "You cannot say that the man [O'Connor] who wrote 'The engine shrieked; the porter slammed the door with a curse; somewhere another door opened and shut, and the row of watchers, frozen into effigies of farewell, now dark now bright, began to glide gently past the window, and the stale, smoky air was charged with the breath of open fields' was indifferent to which word he used, or to the shape of his sentences. Or that he wasn't, indeed, a poet. . . ." Ask students to support Maxwell's evaluation of O'Connor by citing examples of poetic language from "My Oedipus Complex."

"Poor Daddy" again! I was becoming suspicious of everything involving that quite impossible man.

"Why?" I asked.

"Because poor Daddy is worried and tired and he doesn't sleep well."

"Why doesn't he, Mummy?"

"Well, you know, don't you, that while he was at the war Mummy got the pennies from the Post Office?"

"From Miss MacCarthy?"

"That's right. But now, you see, Miss MacCarthy hasn't any more pennies, so Daddy must go out (F) and find us some. You know what would happen if he couldn't?"

"No," I said, "tell us."

"Well, I think we might have to go out and beg for them like the poor old woman on Fridays. We wouldn't like that, would we?"

"No," I agreed. "We wouldn't."

"So you'll promise not to come in and wake him?"

"Promise."

Mind you, I meant that. I knew pennies were a serious matter, and I was all against having to go out and beg like the old woman on Fridays. Mother laid out all my toys in a complete ring round the bed so that, whatever way I got out, I was bound to fall over one of them.

When I woke I remembered my promise all right. I got up and sat on the floor and played—for hours, it seemed to me. Then I got my chair and looked out the attic window for more hours. I wished it was time for Father to wake; I wished someone would make me a cup of tea. I didn't feel in the least like the sun; instead, I was bored and so very, very cold! I simply longed for the warmth and depth of the big featherbed.

At last I could stand it no longer. I went into the next room. As there was still no room at Mother's side I climbed over her and she woke with a start.

"Larry," she whispered, gripping my arm very tightly, "what did you promise?"

"But I did, Mummy," I wailed, caught in the very act. "I was quiet for ever so long."

(G) "Oh, dear, and you're perished!"[13] she said sadly, feeling me all over. "Now, if I let you stay will you promise not to talk?"

"But I want to talk, Mummy," I wailed.

"That has nothing to do with it," she said with a firmness that was new to me. "Daddy wants to sleep. Now, do you understand that?"

I understood it only too well. I wanted to talk, he wanted to sleep—whose house was it, anyway?

"Mummy," I said with equal firmness, "I think it would be healthier for Daddy to sleep in his own bed."

That seemed to stagger her, because she said nothing for a while.

"Now, once for all," she went on, "you're to be perfectly quiet or go back to your own bed. Which is it to be?"

The injustice of it got me down. I had convicted her out of her own mouth of inconsistency and unreasonableness, and she hadn't even attempted to reply. Full of spite, I gave Father a kick, which she didn't notice but which made him grunt and open his eyes in alarm.

"What time is it?" he asked in a panic-stricken (H) voice, not looking at Mother but at the door, as if he saw someone there.

"It's early yet," she replied soothingly. "It's only the child. Go to sleep again. . . . Now, Larry," she added, getting out of bed, "you've wakened Daddy and you must go back."

This time, for all her quiet air, I knew she meant it, and knew that my principal rights and privileges were as good as lost unless I asserted them at once. As she lifted me, I gave a screech, enough to wake the dead, not to mind Father. He (I) groaned.

"That damn child! Doesn't he ever sleep?"

"It's only a habit, dear," she said quietly, though (J) I could see she was vexed.

"Well, it's time he got out of it," shouted Father, beginning to heave in the bed. He suddenly gathered all the bedclothes about him, turned to the wall, and then looked back over his shoulder with nothing showing only two small, spiteful, dark eyes. The man looked very wicked.

To open the bedroom door, Mother had to let me down, and I broke free and dashed for the farthest corner, screeching. Father sat bolt upright in bed.

"Shut up, you little puppy!" he said in a choking voice.

I was so astonished that I stopped screeching.

13. **perished:** frozen.

(F) Critical Thinking
Analyzing Details

? What do you learn about the mother during this conversation? [Possible responses: She is a devoted, patient, loving mother. She knows how to identify and appeal to her son's fear in order to persuade him to do what she wants.]

(G) Reading Skills and Strategies
Making Predictions

? Though she shows concern, the mother is firm during this conversation. Larry becomes spiteful. What might happen following this firm conversation? [Possible response: Larry might obey his mother, or he might wake his father in order to assert himself.]

(H) Reading Skills and Strategies
Identifying Causes and Effects

? What causes may underlie the father's actions here? [Possible responses: He is not used to having a child awaken him, and he is exhausted and worried from job hunting. As a result of his war experiences, he may be very sensitive to sudden or unexpected events while sleeping.]

(I) English Language Learners
Understanding Idioms

Point out that the expression "not to mind" indicates that the speaker is so sure of the first instance (that the screech is loud enough to wake the dead) that he has no doubt that the second instance would also occur (that the screech also would wake Father). In fact, he is so sure that he feels it is not even necessary to "mind" or think of saying it.

(J) Vocabulary Note
Using Context Clues

Help students to arrive at the meaning of the word *vexed* by looking at its context. The father has just "groaned" and complained vehemently about the boy. The mother responds "quietly." The word *though* indicates that her response contrasts with or covers up another feeling, a feeling that would not be in keeping with a calm and quiet response. In line with that reasoning, students should be able to guess that *vexed* means "troubled" or "irritated."

Skill Link

Speaking and Listening: Identifying and Analyzing Tone

Remind students that **tone** is the indication of the writer's attitude toward the reader, the subject, or a character. Although tone is generally suggested by the language of a piece of literature, tone can also be conveyed by the quality of the voice and body language of the reader.

Have students work in small groups to do multiple readings of the following line from O'Connor's story: "I had been through it all myself, and even at that age I was magnanimous" (taken from p. 1089, where Larry tries to comfort his father). Have them employ one of the following tones each time they read the sentence:

joyful	satiric	awed
resigned	self-pitying	bitter
somber	melancholy	ominous

Then have students suggest what each tone reveals about Larry's character and motives.

Literature and Psychology

Using his own psychoanalytic theories as the basis for literary criticism, Sigmund Freud published studies of a variety of literary characters, including Shakespeare's Hamlet, Macbeth, and Lady Macbeth. This type of criticism presumes that literary characters have the same needs and impulses as real human beings and thus can be analyzed by the same principles. Others, including Freud's biographer Ernest Jones, soon followed Freud's lead and applied psychoanalytic theories to literary questions. Jones interpreted Hamlet in terms of the Oedipus complex. Jones's theories are still cited today to explain why Hamlet cannot bring himself to promptly avenge his murdered father by killing his guilty uncle and stepfather, Claudius, and why he has such conflicted feelings toward his mother, Gertrude.

A Struggling Readers

Summarizing

? What emotional changes take place in the characters in this climactic scene? [Possible responses: Larry's father loses his temper. Larry first realizes that his father is jealous too. Larry feels spiteful anger toward his mother.]

Literature and Psychology

Mysterious Dreams and Secret Wishes

Frank O'Connor probably didn't read about the "Oedipus complex" in Sigmund Freud's twenty-four-volume collected works. This Freudian theory, and countless others, had already become a permanent part of twentieth-century culture by the time O'Connor wrote his story. Even today, Freud's work lives on in the very words we use to talk about the mind. You may have heard terms like "Freudian slip" or "wish fulfillment." But do you know where they come from?

Tell me what you're thinking. After early training as a physician, Sigmund Freud (1856–1939) became a leader in the new study of the mind. Cartoons of Freud often portray him as a bearded old man, scribbling away in a notebook while his patient lies on a comfortable couch and talks a blue streak. In fact, this was exactly the way Freud worked with his patients in Vienna: He thought that emotional problems were caused by memories his patients could not consciously remember, and he required his patients to "free associate," or speak their thoughts as randomly as they appeared in the mind. Freud believed such free association would lead back to an original traumatic experience, the discovery of which would cause the illness to dissolve.

Freud was also the first to propose that our deepest desires and fears lie buried in our unconscious, or "id." For Freud, the *id* (Latin for "it") represents our

Never, never had anyone spoken to me in that tone before. I looked at him incredulously and saw his face convulsed with rage. It was only then that I fully realized how God had codded[14] me, listening to my prayers for the safe return of this monster.

A "Shut up, you!" I bawled, beside myself.

"What's that you said?" shouted Father, making a wild leap out of the bed.

"Mick, Mick!" cried Mother. "Don't you see the child isn't used to you?"

"I see he's better fed than taught," snarled Father, waving his arms wildly. "He wants his bottom smacked."

All his previous shouting was as nothing to these obscene words referring to my person. They really made my blood boil.

"Smack your own!" I screamed hysterically. "Smack your own! Shut up! Shut up!"

At this he lost his patience and let fly at me. He did it with the lack of conviction you'd expect of a man under Mother's horrified eyes, and it ended up as a mere tap, but the sheer indignity of being struck at all by a stranger, a total stranger who had cajoled his way back from the war into our big

14. **codded:** British slang for "tricked."

Words to Own
cajoled (kə·jōld′) *v.:* coaxed with flattery.

Crossing the Curriculum

Performing Arts

Invite students to develop and present a monologue from the mother's or father's point of view about the period of time covered in the story. Encourage students to consider how the war and Larry's reactions may have affected the parents' feelings for each other. Ask students to consider the adjustments that all three family members are forced to make.

Social Sciences

Have students do further research on the Oedipus complex. Students could begin by studying the complete Oedipus myth as it originated in classical Greek mythology and was dramatized in the Greek theater (Sophocles' *Oedipus Rex* and *Oedipus at Colonus*). They can also read more about Freud's theory, as well as arguments against its validity. Students can summarize what they have learned and tell why they think the Oedipus complex is such a controversial theory.

Psychology

Have students work in small groups to research other theories of child development that might provide insight into the character of O'Connor's young narrator. Encourage students to find theories that are particularly applicable to Larry's age and situation.

infant selves, the part of us which seeks gratification of every desire—or "wish fulfillment." The *ego* corresponds to a more adult self, and the *superego* is an internalized parental voice, an inner censor that reminds us what is morally right. In Freud's view, the three parts of the mind work together, or in conflict, with every human action.

Buried truths and slips of the tongue. Some of Freud's most influential ideas appeared in *The Interpretation of Dreams,* published in 1900. Here, Freud holds that dreams, rich with strange objects and illogical events, can be decoded to reveal unconscious wishes, fears, and memories. He also thought that common mistakes in everyday speech are connected to unconscious thoughts that somehow slip past the watchful superego (hence the "Freudian slip"). At dinner, for example, when we wish to comment on anything but a friend's ridiculous purple hat, we might say "Please pass the purple," and immediately draw attention to what we most wanted to avoid.

Recent critics have suggested that Freud, who originally wanted to be a novelist, forced his patients' histories into tidy packages, with convenient beginnings and endings, thus making them more like fiction than actual life. Nevertheless, Freud's ideas have given us invaluable concepts—and a lasting vocabulary—with which to contemplate ourselves and others.

bed as a result of my innocent intercession, made me completely dotty.[15] I shrieked and shrieked, and danced in my bare feet, and Father, looking awkward and hairy in nothing but a short gray army shirt, glared down at me like a mountain out for murder. I think it must have been then that I realized he was jealous too. And there stood Mother in her nightdress, looking as if her heart was broken between us. I hoped she felt as she looked. It seemed to me that she deserved it all.

From that morning out my life was a hell. Father and I were enemies, open and avowed. We conducted a series of skirmishes against one another, he trying to steal my time with Mother and I his. When she was sitting on my bed, telling me a story, he took to looking for some pair of old boots which he alleged he had left behind him at the beginning of the war. While he talked to Mother I played loudly with my toys to show my total lack of concern. He created a terrible scene one evening when he came in from work and found me at his box, playing with his regimental badges, Gurkha knives, and button sticks. Mother got up and took the box from me.

15. **dotty:** crazy.

WORDS TO OWN
intercession (in'tər·sesh'ən) *n.:* pleading on behalf of another.

B Advanced Learners

The narration of this story in the first person is essential to its success. Have advanced learners review other works of literature written in the first person and compare the narrators. Possibilities include Swift's *Gulliver's Travels* (p. 488) and "A Modest Proposal" (p. 502), Keats's "When I Have Fears" (p. 748), Browning's "My Last Duchess" (p. 830), and Thomas's "Fern Hill" (p. 1034). Students might consider such topics as what each narrator reveals or does not reveal about himself and the tone each narrator takes.

C Elements of Literature

Dramatic Irony

Point out to students that Larry's use of hyperbole creates additional instances of dramatic irony. He believes that his life is "a hell" and that he and his father are "enemies." The reader knows that these are a child's exaggerations.

D Critical Thinking

Analyzing Character

? Do you think Larry is correct when he surmises that his father is jealous too? Explain. [Possible responses: Yes, the father competes with Larry for attention by losing his boots and making a fuss about his box of war treasures. No, the father is just going about his business, but Larry perceives a rivalry because he mixes up his own feelings with his father's.]

Getting Students Involved

Cooperative Learning

Resolving Conflicts. Much of the humor in this story hinges on misperceptions. In the following scenarios, ask students to determine how those involved might perceive the situation differently from each other and to summarize the two perspectives in the left-hand column. Then, have students suggest possible solutions for each situation in the right-hand column. The following graphic may be helpful.

Scenario 1: Rachel's father asks her not to borrow the new car to go to the mall on Saturday.

Scenario 2: Antonio tells his sister she should take a business class instead of an art class.

Description of Problem	Proposed Solutions
1a. [Rachel thinks he is being unreasonable.] 1b. [Father knows the parking lot will be busy and is worried about his car getting dented.]	1. [Rachel's father can take her to the mall and, over time, help her save for a car of her own.]
2a. [Antonio feels he is helping his sister to be practical.] 2b. [His sister feels he is bossy and insensitive to her interests.]	2. [Antonio and his sister should discuss the pros and cons of her taking each class.]

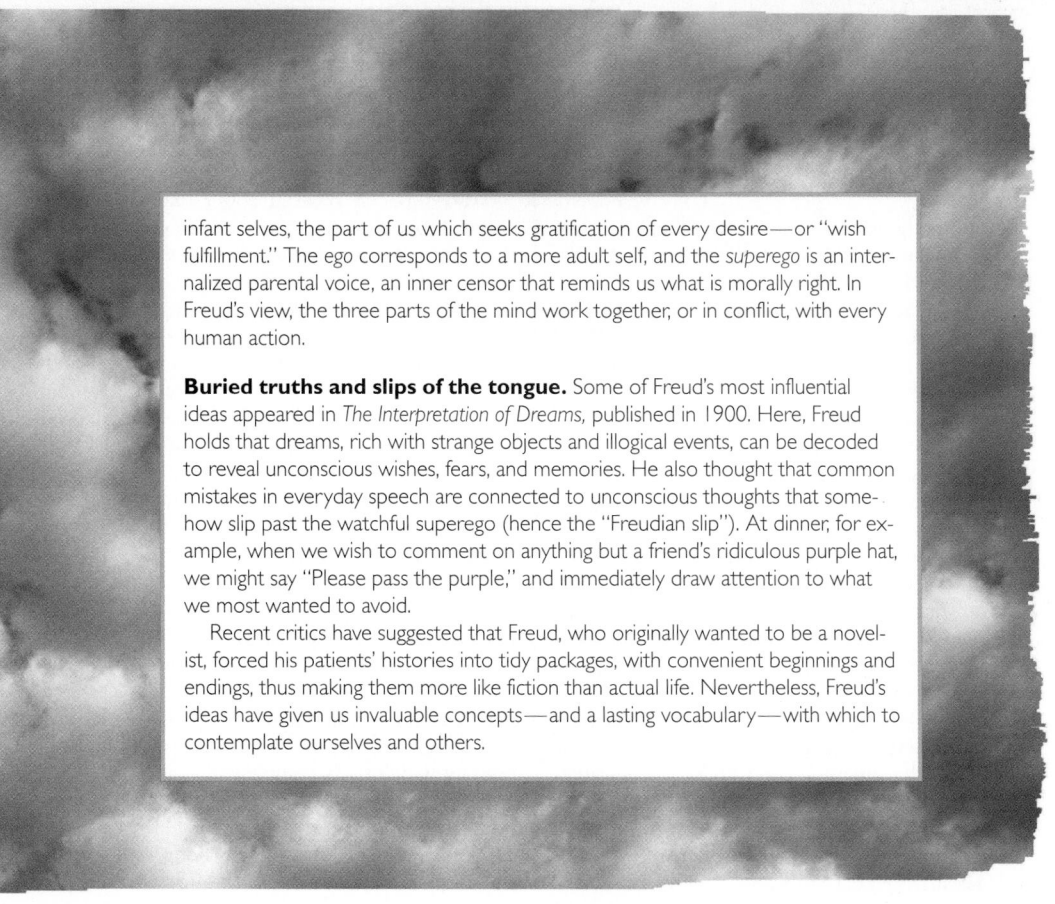

Ⓐ Vocabulary Note

Word Origins

Ask students what they think is the origin of the word *curio.* [shortened form of *curiosity*] Point out that shortening, clipping, or contracting words is a common way of creating new words. Other such words are *fan* (clipped form of *fanatic*), *phone* (shortened form of *telephone*), *auto* (clipped form of *automobile*), *punch* (contraction of *puncheon*), and *sub* (clipped form of *submarine*). Have students come up with some additional examples on their own.

Ⓑ Reading Skills and Strategies

Responding to the Text

? What is amusing and touching about Larry's predicament? [Possible responses: He mistakenly thinks he is the center and cause of everything in his world, even the arrival of the new baby. He does not understand the difference between his father and mother's relationship and his own love for his mother.]

Ⓒ Elements of Literature

Style

? What effect does the use of dashes in this passage have? [Possible response: The dashes interrupt the flow of the narrator's thoughts, showing some hesitation, disorientation, and a mix of emotions.]

"You mustn't play with Daddy's toys unless he lets you, Larry," she said severely. "Daddy doesn't play with yours."

For some reason Father looked at her as if she had struck him and then turned away with a scowl.

"Those are not toys," he growled, taking down the box again to see had I lifted[16] anything. "Some Ⓐ of those curios are very rare and valuable."

But as time went on I saw more and more how he managed to alienate Mother and me. What made it worse was that I couldn't grasp his method or see what attraction he had for Mother. In every possible way he was less winning than I. He had a common accent and made noises at his tea. I thought for a while that it might be the newspapers she was interested in, so I made up bits of news of my own to read to her. Then I thought it might be the smoking, which I personally thought attractive, and took his pipes and went round the house dribbling into them till he caught me. I even made noises at my tea, but Mother only told me I was disgusting. It all seemed to hinge round that unhealthy habit of sleeping together, so I made a point of dropping into their bedroom and nosing round, talking to myself, so that they wouldn't know I was watching them, but they were never up to anything that I could see. In the end it beat me. It seemed to depend on being grown-up and giving people rings, and I realized I'd have to wait.

But at the same time I wanted him to see that I was only waiting, not giving up the fight. One evening when he was being particularly obnoxious, chattering away well above my head, I let him have it.

"Mummy," I said, "do you know what I'm going to do when I grow up?"

"No, dear," she replied. "What?"

"I'm going to marry you," I said quietly.

Ⓑ Father gave a great guffaw out of him, but he didn't take me in. I knew it must only be pretense. And Mother, in spite of everything, was pleased. I felt she was probably relieved to know that one day Father's hold on her would be broken.

"Won't that be nice?" she said with a smile.

"It'll be very nice," I said confidently. "Because we're going to have lots and lots of babies."

"That's right, dear," she said placidly. "I think we'll have one soon, and then you'll have plenty of company."

I was no end pleased about that because it showed that in spite of the way she gave in to Father she still considered my wishes. Besides, it would put the Geneys in their place.

It didn't turn out like that, though. To begin with, she was very preoccupied—I supposed about where she would get the seventeen and six—and though Father took to staying out late in the evenings it did me no particular good. She stopped taking me for walks, became as touchy as blazes, and smacked me for nothing at all. Sometimes I wished I'd never mentioned the con- Ⓒ founded baby—I seemed to have a genius for bringing calamity on myself.

And calamity it was! Sonny arrived in the most appalling hullabaloo—even that much he couldn't do without a fuss—and from the first moment I disliked him. He was a difficult child—so far as I was concerned he was always difficult—and demanded far too much attention. Mother was simply silly about him, and couldn't see when he was only showing off. As company he was worse than useless. He slept all day, and I had to go round the house on tiptoe to avoid waking him. It wasn't any longer a question of not waking Father. The slogan now was "Don't-wake-Sonny!" I couldn't understand why the child wouldn't sleep at the proper time, so whenever Mother's back was turned I woke him. Sometimes to keep him awake I pinched him as well. Mother caught me at it one day and gave me a most unmerciful flaking.[17]

One evening, when Father was coming in from work, I was playing trains in the front garden. I let

16. **lifted:** British slang for "stolen."

17. **flaking:** spanking.

WORDS TO OWN

alienate (āl′ē·ən·āt′) *v.:* to drive apart.
obnoxious (əb·näk′shəs) *adj.:* offensive.
guffaw (gu·fô′) *n.:* loud laugh. "Guffaw" is an echoic word—one that imitates the sound it stands for.
preoccupied (prē·äk′yo͞o·pīd′) *adj.:* absorbed in one's own thoughts.

Making the Connections

Cultural Connections

Many cultures around the world provide games, religious ceremonies, and other rites of passage to signal the separation of boys from their mothers. Ask students to discuss how young boys, from their own cultural backgrounds or from a culture that interests them, are encouraged to leave their mothers or other female caretakers and join a more adult male world. At what age does this separation begin? What activities do the young boys and older males engage in?

Connecting to the Theme: "Ourselves Among Others"

What does this story suggest about Larry's relationship to others and how he may have to change? [Possible responses: The story examines the way a child feels about both parents and how these feelings change as the family structure shifts and the child matures. In this case, Larry must cope with the realization that he is no longer the center of his mother's attention or the only person in the world with needs.]

on not to notice him; instead, I pretended to be talking to myself, and said in a loud voice: "If another bloody baby comes into this house, I'm going out."

Father stopped dead and looked at me over his shoulder.

"What's that you said?" he asked sternly.

"I was only talking to myself," I replied, trying to conceal my panic. "It's private."

He turned and went in without a word. Mind you, I intended it as a solemn warning, but its effect was quite different. Father started being quite **D** nice to me. I could understand that, of course. Mother was quite sickening about Sonny. Even at mealtimes she'd get up and gawk at him in the cradle with an idiotic smile, and tell Father to do the same. He was always polite about it, but he looked so puzzled you could see he didn't know what she was talking about. He complained of the way Sonny cried at night, but she only got cross and said that Sonny never cried except when there was something up with him—which was a flaming lie, because Sonny never had anything up with him, and only cried for attention. It was really painful to see how simpleminded she was. Father wasn't attractive, but he had a fine intelli- **E** gence. He saw through Sonny, and now he knew that I saw through him as well.

One night I woke with a start. There was someone beside me in the bed. For one wild moment I felt sure it must be Mother, having come to her senses and left Father for good, but then I heard Sonny in convulsions in the next room, and Mother saying: "There! There! There!" and I knew it wasn't she. It was Father. He was lying beside me, wide awake, breathing hard and apparently as mad as hell.

After a while it came to me what he was mad about. It was his turn now. After turning me out of the big bed, he had been turned out himself. Mother had no consideration now for anyone but **F** that poisonous pup, Sonny. I couldn't help feeling sorry for Father. I had been through it all myself, and even at that age I was magnanimous. I began to stroke him down and say: "There! There!" He wasn't exactly responsive.

"Aren't you asleep either?" he snarled.

"Ah, come on and put your arm around us, can't you?" I said, and he did, in a sort of way. Gingerly, I suppose, is how you'd describe it. He was **G** very bony but better than nothing.

At Christmas he went out of his way to buy me a really nice model railway.

Words to Own

magnanimous (mag·nan′ə·məs) *adj.:* generous in rising above insults.

D Reading Skills and Strategies
Making Inferences

? What brings about the father's change in behavior? [Possible response: He realizes that Larry is hurt, as he is, by the mother's doting attention on the new baby.]

E Critical Thinking
Interpreting

? How do you interpret these comments about Larry's mother and father? [Possible responses: The comments signal a shift in Larry's perceptions, a tipping of the balance of his emotions. He is now capable of a serious criticism of his mother—she is "simpleminded." At the same time, he can now admit that his father has "a fine intelligence."]

F Elements of Literature
Dramatic Irony

? Point out to students that the dramatic irony continues even as the story draws to a close. What is the reader aware of here that Larry is not? [Possible responses: The reader realizes that Larry and his father are not in the same position regarding the new baby. Larry mistakenly sees himself as generous and comforting, while the reader realizes that the father is far more likely to understand and comfort his son than vice versa.]

G Elements of Literature
Resolution

The story ends with a new bond of affection developing between father and son.

Assessing Learning

Check Test: True-False

1. When the story begins, there is only one child in the family. [True]
2. The narrator refuses to pray for the safe return of his father from the war. [False]
3. After the father returns, the mother immediately forbids the boy to come into her bed in the morning. [False]
4. Larry believes that his father is also behaving jealously. [True]
5. The mother feels torn between the demands of father and son. [True]

Informal Assessment

Peer Assessment. As students present reports following group activities, have the audience evaluate each performance on a scale of 1 to 5, 5 being the highest. Develop the criteria you would like students to use when evaluating, or use a chart like the following:

Criteria	Score	Comments
Content		
Support		
Organization		
Presentation		

Making Meanings

First Thoughts [Respond]

1. Students may find the most humor in Larry's belief that he and his father are competing in the same way for his mother's love or that "it would be healthier for Daddy to sleep in his own bed."

Shaping Interpretations [Interpret]

2. Larry notices that whenever he is spending time with his mother, his father tries to distract her—once by looking for lost boots and another time by getting angry that Larry was playing with his curios.

3. The arrival of the new baby resolves the conflict because Larry and his father both lose the mother's attention and begin to sympathize with each other.

4. Larry assumes babies are purchased when the mother refers to the medical fees. He does not understand why his parents share a bed, since his mother told Larry that staying in his own room is healthier.

5. Larry identifies more with his father and "forgives" him. The new problem is Sonny, the baby and another rival.

6. O'Connor's story playfully turns some of the conventions of comedy on their head. Here the blocking figure is the father of the young comic hero, who really just wants to maintain his central position in the mother's affections. Reality dictates that his desire must be disappointed.

7. Students might see the theme as the humorous results of a child's misinterpretation of the adult world.

Extending the Text [Synthesize]

8. "Araby" centers more on the disappointing collapse of a young man's romantic fantasy; "My Oedipus Complex" is a comic presentation of a father-son conflict. The theme of "Araby" is coming-of-age disillusionment; the theme of "My Oedipus Complex" is also a kind of disillusionment but a less wounding one of a more resilient child. The tone of "Araby" is more serious than that of "My Oedipus Complex."

9. Students might respond that Larry's humorous misperceptions of adult reality undercut the possibility of taking the Oedipus complex too seriously.

Making Meanings

First Thoughts

1. Which of Larry's opinions or misunderstandings did you find most comical? Share your favorite passages with other readers.

> **Reading Check**
>
> Larry describes the war, ironically, as the most peaceful part of his life. Outline the details of Larry's peaceful morning ritual during the war. How does his life change when his father comes home?

Shaping Interpretations

2. At one point in the story, Larry realizes that he and his father are conducting "a series of skirmishes against one another, he trying to steal my time with Mother and I his." What details justify Larry's conclusion that his father is really jealous of him?

3. What event finally resolves the **conflict** between Larry and his father?

4. What is the **dramatic irony** in Larry's remarks about the cost of a baby? Find and explain one additional example of dramatic irony in Larry's comments about sharing his mother with his father.

5. At the end of the story, how can you tell that Larry's Oedipal stage is over? But what new problem has arisen in the household?

6. The plot of a **comedy** often involves a young person who is in love, who has to fight people who block his (or her) love, and who ultimately triumphs. How does O'Connor use this typical comic plot?

7. How would you state the **theme** of this story?

Extending the Text

8. How does O'Connor's story compare with Joyce's "Araby" (page 986) in **plot, theme,** and **tone**?

9. Do you think O'Connor is having some fun with psychoanalytic theory in this story, or is there a serious situation beneath the comic surface? Explain your opinion.

Choices: Building Your Portfolio

Writer's Notebook

1. Collecting Ideas for a Problem-Solution Essay

WORK IN PROGRESS

O'Connor takes a comical view of his young narrator's conflicts, but the problems of childhood can be serious. Read the comment by O'Connor below, taken from his autobiography *An Only Child* (1961), in which he talks about his father. Then, consider the conflicts young Larry has to struggle with, and take notes on how those struggles could have serious consequences in real life. How can children be helped to adapt to family problems that they are too young to understand? Save your notes for the Writer's Workshop on page 1179.

> . . . the house would be a horror. Only when he had money for drink would we have peace for an hour. . . . When I was old enough to go to school, I would come back at three o'clock and scout around to make sure that he was not at home. . . . When I talked of him to Mother, I always called him "he" or "him," carefully eschewing the name of "Father," which would have seemed like profanation to me.
>
> —Frank O'Connor, *from An Only Child*

Creative Writing

2. That Was Then

Refer to your Quickwrite notes. Have you ever observed a child struggling for the attention of a parent or coping with sibling rivalry? Using O'Connor's story as a model, write an account of a humorous incident from childhood—your own or someone else's. You will have to decide who will narrate your story, a child or an adult.

> **Reading Check**
>
> While his father is away at war, Larry awakens with the first light. He settles his daily plans, goes to his mother's room, and climbs into her bed to discuss them. After his father returns, his mornings are quite different: His mother now tries to prevent the child from disturbing the father.

Grading Timesaver

Rubrics for each Choices assignment appear on p. 208 in the *Portfolio Management System*.

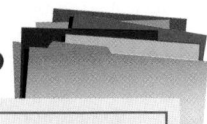

W. H. Auden

(1907–1973)

©Rollie McKenna.

W. H. Auden (1950s).

Wystan Hugh Auden gave a name to his times—"the Age of Anxiety"—and he lived to see the day when his influence was so broad and deep that, as far as poetry was concerned, that same era could have been called "the Age of Auden."

Auden was born in York, a city in northern England near the city of Leeds. He was the son of a physician and a nurse who encouraged his early interest in science and engineering. But in his adolescence, Auden discovered poetry, and he studied, with an analytical eye, all its forms, from Chaucer onward. By the time he entered Oxford, he was as much a teacher as he was a student, and he quickly gathered about himself other young poets, who accepted him as their leader.

Auden as a poet was difficult to classify, and he remains so to this day. By the time they have been recognized and acclaimed, most of the outstanding poets of any generation have produced individual works by which, rightly or wrongly, they will be identified. Sometimes these poems are masterpieces; sometimes they are rather run-of-the-mill poems which, for one reason or another, have caught the popular imagination. To this pattern, Auden is an exception. In spite of their virtuosity, uniform excellence, and formal variety, Auden's poems—lyrics, oratorios, ballads—tend to cohere as a body of work rather than to distinguish themselves as easily separable entities. For this reason, Auden is often regarded less as the author of certain individual poems than as the creator of a climate in which all things Audenesque thrive in an atmosphere uniquely his own.

Auden put his indelible stamp on the poetry of the 1930s, establishing his preeminence among the brilliant group of poets that included Stephen Spender, Louis MacNeice, and Cecil Day-Lewis. Auden caused his British compatriots shock and dismay when, in the critical year of 1939, as Hitler's divisions were about to march into Poland and initiate World War II, he decided to make his home in the United States. Auden had come to feel that, as the rise of fascism made war in Europe inevitable, his chances of enjoying creative freedom and of making a livelihood were available only in America. From 1939 to 1942, he taught at the University of Michigan and various other American universities. In 1946, he became a U.S. citizen.

For the next ten years, Auden lived mostly in New York City and California. He spent his summers in Kirchstetten, Austria, in a house he bought in 1957 with profits from his extensive reading tours—the first, and last, home of his own. This retreat, not far from Vienna, provided him with much-needed privacy and the opportunity to experience firsthand the culture of central Europe.

In England, Auden's emigration to the United States was, at the time, widely regarded as a defection, if not an outright betrayal. But the British eventually welcomed him back—first by electing him professor of poetry at Oxford, and later by making it possible for him to live on the campus of Christ Church College as a guest of the university whenever he returned to England.

go.hrw.com
LEO 12-14

OBJECTIVES

Musée des Beaux Arts/ The Unknown Citizen

1. Read and interpret the poems
2. Identify and analyze diction
3. Express understanding through critical and creative writing

SKILLS

Literary
- Identify and analyze diction

Writing
- Collect ideas for a problem-solution essay
- Compare texts across cultures
- Analyze a satire
- Write a poem, essay, or story inspired by a painting or piece of music
- Write an imaginary obituary
- Write an epitaph

Art
- Interpret and evaluate a painting

Viewing/Representing
- Analyze irony in a painting (ATE)
- Make associations among images in a painting (ATE)

Planning

- **Block Schedule**
  Block Scheduling Lesson Plans with Pacing Guide
- **Traditional Schedule**
  Lesson Plans Including Strategies for English-Language Learners
- **One-Stop Planner**
  CD-ROM with Test Generator

Resources: Print and Media

Reading
- *Graphic Organizers for Active Reading,* pp. 108, 109
- *Audio CD Library*
  Disc 20, Tracks 2, 3

Writing and Language
- *Daily Oral Grammar*
  Transparency 38

Viewing and Representing
- *Viewing and Representing*
  Fine Art Transparency 18
  Fine Art Worksheet, p. 72
- *Visual Connections*
  Videocassette B, Segment 10

Assessment
- *Formal Assessment,* pp. 216, 217
- *Portfolio Management System,* p. 209
- *Test Generator (One-Stop Planner CD-ROM)*

Internet
- go.hrw.com (keyword: *LEO 12-14*)

Summary

The speaker notes that the Old Masters always understood that acute individual suffering occurs while others simply go on with their daily lives. To illustrate this truth, he presents details from Pieter Bruegel the Elder's painting *The Fall of Icarus*. In the painting, a farmer continues plowing a field, barely aware that another man, Icarus, is falling to his death a short distance away. The onward flow of life seems to absorb even suffering and death.

BROWSING IN THE FILES

About the Author. In addition to teaching and writing, W. H. Auden served as a stretcher-bearer in the Spanish Civil War and later worked for a film company. By the time he was thirty-three, he had written four books of poetry, three plays, a collection of prose fiction, and two travel books and had edited two anthologies of poetry. He also wrote lyrics for blues songs, ballads, and operas. In 1951 he helped write the libretto for *The Rake's Progress*, an opera by Igor Stravinsky, and in 1964 he wrote the words for Stravinsky's *Elegy for J.F.K.*

RESPONDING TO THE ART

Flemish painter **Pieter Bruegel**, or Bruegel the Elder (1525–1569), depicted the vigor and coarseness of country life in rich detail, often with a humanist moral. Only about forty original paintings by Bruegel have survived, although copies of others exist. *The Fall of Icarus,* probably an early work, survives in two versions; scholars believe both versions are copies.

Activity. Ask students to tell how *The Fall of Icarus* is ironic, that is, how it deliberately frustrates viewers' expectations. Using Bruegel's painting as an example, have students discuss how an artist can convey a message by *refraining* from saying or showing something.

Before You Read

MUSÉE DES BEAUX ARTS
THE UNKNOWN CITIZEN

Make the Connection

The Value of the Individual

Every generation sees imperfections and injustices in the way things are. For Auden, during what he termed the Age of Anxiety, people had grown indifferent to human suffering, and society no longer treasured the individual. This indifference to the plight of others and disregard for the value of individuality were, to Auden, the symptoms of a society in need of reform.

Quickwrite

To what extent do you think individuality and compassion are valued or disregarded today? Jot down some thoughts and examples.

Elements of Literature

Diction

Auden's poems combine eloquent and elegant poetic language with down-to-earth **colloquial** words and **technical** terms, the jargon of trades and professions. Notice how he uses contrasting diction in these poems not only to surprise you but also to relate his language to his ideas.

> **Diction** is a writer's or speaker's choice of words.
>
> *For more on Diction, see the Handbook of Literary Terms.*

The Fall of Icarus (16th century) by Pieter Bruegel the Elder.
Musées Royaux des Beaux-Arts, Brussels, Belgium.

Reaching All Students

English Language Learners

Point out that the syntactical inversion in the first line—more naturally "They were never wrong about suffering"—has a purpose. It puts the key word "suffering" right at the very opening of the poem.

Advanced Learners

In his introduction to *The Oxford Book of Light Verse*, Auden wrote that in the nineteenth century, "The breakdown of the old village or small-town community left the family as the only real social unit, and the parent-child relationship as the only real social bond." Ask students to write a response to this comment, relating it to one of Auden's poems.

The source and inspiration for this poem are found in the famous painting by Pieter Bruegel showing Icarus drowning, permanently on display in the Musée des Beaux Arts (myoo·zā′ dā bō zär′), or Fine Arts Museum, in Brussels, Belgium. The painting depicts a dramatic moment in the Greek legend of Daedalus and his son, Icarus. According to the legend, the two were imprisoned on the island of Crete. In order to escape, Daedalus constructed wings of feathers and wax. Together they managed to take off from the island, but Icarus flew so high that the sun's heat melted the wax in his wings, causing him to fall into the sea and drown.

According to one critic, the painting represents "the greatest conception of indifference" in the history of art. The indifference, whether it is the artist's attitude or merely a strategy of technique, lies in its unexpected focus. The painting's center of interest is not Icarus, but a peasant plowing a field. He is handsomely dressed—in medieval rather than in Greek costume—and the furrows he tills are richly realistic. In the lower right-hand corner of the painting, almost as an afterthought, Icarus is seen splashing into the water not far from a passing ship.

Study the painting, and find the figure of the boy falling into the sea. Then, read the poem to see how Auden interprets the painting. Has he confirmed in words what the painter expressed with pigment?

Musée des Beaux Arts

W. H. Auden

About suffering they were never wrong,
The Old Masters: how well they understood
Its human position; how it takes place
While someone else is eating or opening a window or just walking dully along; **A**
How, when the aged are reverently, passionately waiting
For the miraculous birth, there always must be
Children who did not specially want it to happen, skating **B**
On a pond at the edge of the wood:
They never forgot
That even the dreadful martyrdom must run its course **C**
Anyhow in a corner, some untidy spot
Where the dogs go on with their doggy life and the torturer's horse **D**
Scratches its innocent behind on a tree.

In Bruegel's *Icarus,* for instance: how everything turns away
Quite leisurely from the disaster; the plowman may
Have heard the splash, the forsaken cry,
But for him it was not an important failure; the sun shone
As it had to on the white legs disappearing into the green **E**
Water; and the expensive delicate ship that must have seen
Something amazing, a boy falling out of the sky,
Had somewhere to get to and sailed calmly on.

Making the Connections

Cultural Connections: Mythology Today

Greek mythology played an enormous role in the development of Western culture. Time, however, has brought about new attitudes toward these old stories. Do people in contemporary America pay any more attention to Greek mythology than the plowman in the painting pays to the fallen Icarus? Why or why not? What has replaced mythology in today's culture? [Possible responses: pop culture, movies, and television.]

Connecting with the Theme: "Ourselves Among Others"

Students may readily see the connection between the collection theme and the issue raised in Auden's poem and Bruegel's painting—what is the proper relationship of the self to the sufferings of others? You might also ask them to discuss the poem in terms of the Biblical question "Am I my brother's keeper?" Or how can people create a balance between their personal needs and the needs of others?

A Reading Skills and Strategies

Finding the Main Idea

? What ironic contrast is Auden pointing out in the poem's first four lines? [Possible response: While intense suffering takes place, ordinary life goes on.]

B Cultural Connections

Point out that this poem was written during a time when the traditional values of Europe were shaken by the onslaught of fascism. Although the problems of suffering and of others' indifference certainly apply to this time of tumult, the issue itself is timeless. In fact, the painting that provides the poem's central image was finished in the mid-1500s.

C Elements of Literature

Allusion

? To what event might "the dreadful martyrdom" refer? [Possible responses: Christ's crucifixion; the martyrdom of a saint.]

D Elements of Literature

Diction

Auden's mix of elegant and colloquial diction is essential to creating the poem's detached yet sympathetic tone. Ask students to choose a line they find expressive, identify its tone, and explain how the word choice contributes to the overall effect of the poem. [Possible response: "[T]he dogs go on with their doggy life" is a down-to-earth comment in a casual tone; it brings the abstract concept of "real life" down to a visceral level that everyone can grasp.]

E Critical Thinking

Challenging the Text

? Is Auden's spare, almost understated style—such as the clause that begins "the sun shone/As it had to"—effective? [Possible responses: Yes, the matter-of-fact brevity accentuates the horror described. No, more dramatic language would have heightened the dichotomy at the heart of the poem.]

MAKING MEANINGS

First Thoughts [Respond]

1. Possible responses: wars, natural disasters, and famines in foreign countries that are not given wide coverage in the domestic media.

Shaping Interpretations [Interpret]

2. They are the great artists of the European Renaissance. The examples in ll. 3–13 show individuals' self-absorption while others suffer. Students might respond that some people are forced to ignore others' pain in order to survive or that some people make extraordinary efforts to assist others.
3. In the first painting, the subject is probably the birth of Christ; the indifferent children skate on a pond at the edge of a wood. The subject of the second may be Christ's crucifixion or the martyrdom of a saint; unperturbed dogs and horses are seen as an ironic counterpoint. These paintings resemble *The Fall of Icarus* in the indifference of the bystanders to extraordinary events.
4. The poet refers to Bruegel's painting *The Fall of Icarus*, in which neither the plowman nor the sailors take any interest because Icarus's fall does not affect them. Some students may point out that the bystanders simply do not see Icarus because they are engaged in their own pursuits; others may believe that the bystanders saw Icarus but chose to ignore his calamity.
5. The contrast is between formal and informal diction, between formal expressions like "miraculous birth," "the dreadful martyrdom," and "the expensive delicate ship" and informal ones like "doggy life" and "innocent behind."
6. Possible responses: People are indifferent to pain that is not their own. Human life, like nature, goes on in spite of individual suffering or death. Some students may choose ll. 1–4 because they state the theme most clearly.

Connecting with the Text [Challenge]

7. Students may cite public indifference to such problems as homelessness and disasters in far-off places. Some students may disagree, pointing to the willingness of many people to donate money and time to help others in need.

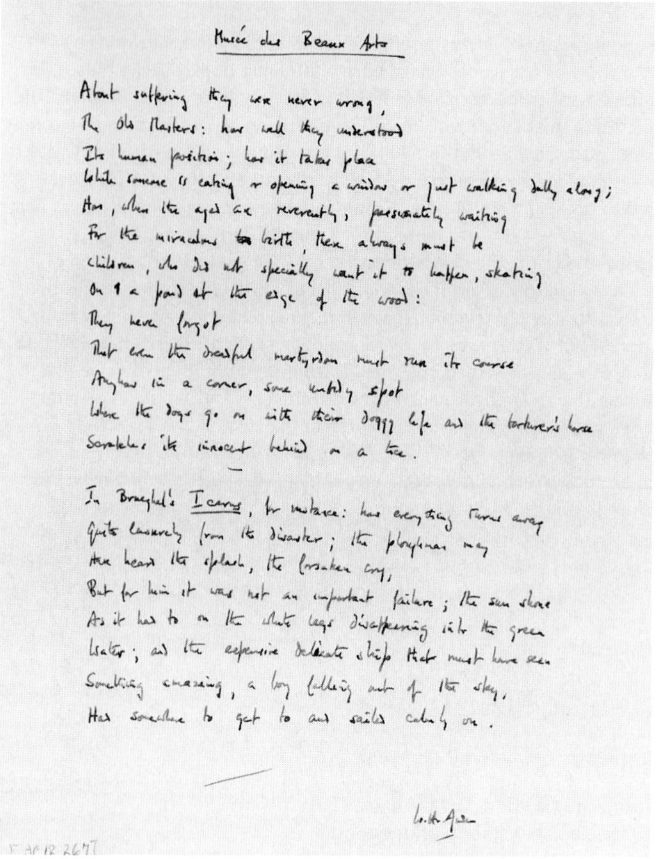

Musée des Beaux Arts

About suffering they were never wrong,
The Old Masters: how well they understood
Its human position; how it takes place
While someone is eating or opening a window or just walking dully along;
How, when the aged are reverently, passionately waiting
For the miraculous birth, there always must be
Children, who did not specially want it to happen, skating
On a pond at the edge of the wood:
They never forgot
That even the dreadful martyrdom must run its course
Anyhow in a corner, some untidy spot
Where the dogs go on with their doggy life and the torturer's horse
Scratches its innocent behind on a tree.

In Brueghel's Icarus, for instance: how everything turns away
Quite leisurely from the disaster; the ploughman may
Have heard the splash, the forsaken cry,
But for him it was not an important failure; the sun shone
As it had to on the white legs disappearing into the green
Water; and the expensive delicate ship that must have seen
Something amazing, a boy falling out of the sky,
Had somewhere to get to and sailed calmly on.

W. H. Auden's handwritten manuscript for "Musée des Beaux Arts."

Library of Congress, Washington, D.C.

MAKING MEANINGS

First Thoughts

1. Does this poem remind you of any times when the world seemed oblivious to individual suffering? Explain.

Shaping Interpretations

2. Who are the "Old Masters" (line 2)? What examples does the speaker provide to show how the Old Masters understood suffering? (Do you think Auden is right about this?)
3. Lines 5–13 describe two other paintings by Bruegel. What do you think are the events that Bruegel portrays? How do these paintings resemble *The Fall of Icarus*?
4. What example of his theory about suffering does the speaker offer in lines 14–21?
5. What contrast in **diction** can you see between expressions like "dreadful martyrdom" and "anyhow in a corner"? Find another example of contrasting diction.
6. What do you think is the overall **theme** of the poem? Which lines in the poem do you think are most important?

Connecting with the Text

7. Do you agree with the speaker that, in general, people are indifferent to the suffering they see around them? Why or why not? Look back at your Quickwrite notes as you answer.

Crossing the Curriculum

Social Sciences

Auden uses an ancient myth to make a timeless point. Have students work in pairs to discuss the purposes that any culture's mythology serves. Ask them to provide examples from their own culture or background or from one that interests them. How and why do some cultures absorb another culture's mythology (as the Romans did the Greek)? Invite students to create a display showing the role of mythology in any society.

Music

Have students find a libretto written by Auden, listen to the accompanying music, and study the lyrics. (*The Rake's Progress* would be an excellent choice.) They might consider these questions:

- What are the work's strengths and weaknesses?
- How does it compare with similar musical compositions?
- How might the music have affected Auden's poetry?

One of the persistent themes of twentieth-century literature is the anonymity of the individual in an ever more bureaucratic world. Here, Auden uses diction that mimics the jargon and technical language of officialdom in a report that covers everything except the fact that "the unknown citizen" had a heart and a soul.

The Unknown Citizen

W. H. Auden

(To JS/07/M/378
This Marble Monument Is Erected by the State)

He was found by the Bureau of Statistics to be
One against whom there was no official complaint,
And all the reports on his conduct agree
That, in the modern sense of an old-fashioned word, he was a saint,
For in everything he did he served the Greater Community.
Except for the War till the day he retired
He worked in a factory and never got fired,
But satisfied his employers, Fudge Motors Inc.
Yet he wasn't a scab° or odd in his views,
For his Union reports that he paid his dues,
(Our report on his Union shows it was sound)
And our Social Psychology workers found
That he was popular with his mates and liked a drink.
The Press are convinced that he bought a paper every day
And that his reactions to advertisements were normal in every way.
Policies taken out in his name prove that he was fully insured,
And his Health-card shows he was once in hospital but left it cured.
Both Producers Research and High-Grade Living declare
He was fully sensible to the advantages of the Installment Plan
And had everything necessary to the Modern Man,
A phonograph, a radio, a car, and a frigidaire.
Our researchers into Public Opinion are content
That he held the proper opinions for the time of year;
When there was peace, he was for peace; when there was war, he went.
He was married and added five children to the population,
Which our Eugenist° says was the right number for a parent of his generation,
And our teachers report that he never interfered with their education.
Was he free? Was he happy? The question is absurd:
Had anything been wrong, we should certainly have heard.

9. **scab:** slang term for a worker who refuses to join a union.
26. **eugenist** (yo͞o′jə·nist): specialist in controlling the population in order to effect an ideal gene pool.

Summary

Using the impersonal language of the bureaucratic state, the speaker dedicates a monument to an "unknown citizen." The eulogy reveals the deceased worker to have been obedient and to have led a thoroughly unremarkable life. The state dismisses as meaningless the question of whether the citizen was free or happy.

Resources

Viewing and Representing

Videocassette B, Segment 10
The World War II segment may provide a link to the theme of citizenship in "The Unknown Citizen."

Fine Art Transparency
A Fine Art transparency of Pol Bury's *16 Balls, 16 Cubes in 8 Rows* can be used as a prereading motivator for "The Unknown Citizen." See the *Viewing and Representing Transparencies and Worksheets:*

- Transparency 18
- Worksheet, p. 72

(A) Reading Skills and Strategies

Drawing Conclusions

? Point out that the dead man's "virtues" are presented in the negative ("no official complaint"). What other examples can you find? ["never got fired"; "wasn't a scab"; "never interfered"] What do you conclude about his personality from these statements? [Possible response: He was a bland and docile person who did what he was told.]

(B) Elements of Literature

Diction

? How would you describe the language and style Auden uses to convey his subject? [Possible responses: It is the language and style of a government report or of a detached journalist.]

(C) Critical Thinking

Interpreting

? What effect does the rhyme have in ll. 6 and 7? [Possible response: The rhyme draws attention to these lines and makes light of the man's death.]

(D) Critical Thinking

Evaluating

? Is this a good ending for the poem? Explain. [Possible response: It is effective because it states directly the problem Auden alludes to throughout the poem.]

Using Students' Strengths

Verbal Learners

Since diction is an important clue to the poem's meaning, have students research real-life examples of "officialese." *Quarterly Review of Doublespeak*, published by the National Council of Teachers of English, would be a good place to start. Ask pairs of students to compile a list of "official" words and phrases. Then have one student write a short eulogy in which he or she incorporates the officialese they have discovered. Finally, ask the other student to rewrite the eulogy in lively, direct prose that reveals a personal point of view.

Interpersonal Learners

After they read the poem, pair students and ask them to assume in turn the roles of a close friend of the "unknown citizen" and a bored government employee. Have the pair interview each other. Issues they might discuss include the relationship between the state and the individual, the pursuit of individual happiness, collective vs. individual values, and consumerism.

Responding to the Art

Oskar Schlemmer (1888–1943) was a German painter, sculptor, stage designer, and choreographer. Influenced by Cubism, he first developed a flat and abstract style but gradually adopted a more rounded sculptural approach, apparent in the masks and costumes he designed for plays, dances, and operas. He described his masks as "colored pieces of sculpture which, when worn by dancers, move in space." *Concentric Group* is from a 1925 series that combines Schlemmer's interest in abstract masks with an almost classical sense of harmony and proportion.

Activity. Ask students what associations the images in the painting bring to mind. Do the figures resemble masks? mannequins? robots? Does this image suggest an "unknown citizen"? Why or why not?

Making Meanings

First Thoughts [Respond]

1. Students may think the picture of the unknown citizen rings true, and that the citizen's anonymity, his reactions to advertisements, and his consumerism reflect a continuing trend in today's society.

Shaping Interpretations [Interpret]

2. He worked for Fudge Motors Inc. The Bureau of Statistics, the Union, the Social Psychology workers, the Press, Producers Research and High-Grade Living, the researchers into Public Opinion, and the Eugenist all report that he did what was expected of him by those in authority.
3. The speaker may be a government official. Although the speaker's tone is flat and impersonal, the poet's tone is satirical, almost bitter.
4. The person who asked may have been a person with his or her own ideas and values, perhaps a friend of the deceased.
5. Perhaps the numbers and letters indicate how the state reduces the individual to an impersonal function or a nameless representative of a group.

Concentric Group (1925) by Oskar Schlemmer. Oil on canvas.

© 2000 The Oskar Schlemmer Family Estate and Archive, courtesy Photo Archive C. Raman Schlemmer, 28824 Oggebbio, Italy.

Making Meanings

First Thoughts

1. Do you think this poem gives a true picture of our society today? Which details do or do not ring true? (Refer to your Quickwrite notes.)

Shaping Interpretations

2. What did the unknown citizen do for a living? What facts are reported on his conduct, and what agencies and groups contribute to this report?
3. Who do you think is the **speaker** of the poem? Although the poet does not directly state his opinions in this poem, they clearly emerge from the speaker's **tone.** How would you describe this tone?
4. Who do you think might have asked the questions in line 28?
5. What do you make of the inscription under the title? What other "monuments" are you reminded of?

Assessing Learning

Check Test: True-False

"Musée des Beaux Arts"

1. The speaker describes a painting by the Dutch Old Master Rembrandt. [False]
2. The painting shows farmers and sailors paying no attention to a drowning boy. [True]

"The Unknown Citizen"

3. The speaker praises the citizen for not being "odd in his views." [True]
4. The speaker believes that good parents should never interfere with the education that is provided for their children. [True]
5. The poem says that the unknown citizen was both free and happy. [False]

Standardized Test Preparation

For practice in proofreading and editing, see

- *Daily Oral Grammar,* Transparency 38

6. What would you say is the message, or **theme,** of the poem? How do you feel about Auden's message?
7. Find examples of impersonal, bureaucratic diction in the poem. Do you read or hear **technical vocabulary** and **jargon** like this today? If so, where?
8. The poem seems to depict the "unknown citizen" as a colorless stereotype. Did you, however, sympathize with the citizen? Explain your response to him.

Extending the Text

9. Auden's message about modern life is quite pessimistic. What sources of optimism do you find in modern life? Your Quickwrite notes may give you some ideas.

Challenging the Text

10. Could this poem have been written in any other time of history but the twentieth century? Why or why not?

CHOICES: Building Your Portfolio

Writer's Notebook

1. Collecting Ideas for a Problem-Solution Essay

WORK IN PROGRESS

As Auden's poems make clear, apathy and an impersonal bureaucracy can seriously affect not only the individual but also society as a whole. Is apathy or a mindless bureaucracy that ignores individual differences a serious problem in your school or community or in society as a whole? Get together with several other students to discuss this question and to explore the causes and effects of the problem. Take notes on your group's comments, and save them for possible use in the Writer's Workshop on page 1179.

Comparing Texts Across Cultures

2. Back to the Source

Read a translation or summary of Ovid's version of the myth of Daedalus and Icarus in Book 8 of the *Metamorphoses.* Then, in a brief essay, relate the myth to Auden's treatment of it in "Musée des Beaux Arts."

Interpreting a Painting

3. What Did Bruegel Mean?

Study the reproduction of Bruegel's *Icarus* on page 1092. In a paragraph, describe as precisely as you can what you see happening in the painting. Do you think Auden has correctly interpreted Bruegel's intent?

Analyzing Satire

4. Right on Target?

In a brief essay, analyze the targets and the methods of Auden's satire in "The Unknown Citizen." Does Auden manage to combine satire and sympathy? Explain your answer.

Creative Writing

5. Inspired by Art

Imitate Auden and write a poem, a brief essay, or a short story inspired by a painting or a piece of music. You might find a subject in a painting in this book.

Creative Writing

6. A Few Kind Words

Imagine that you are a good friend of the deceased citizen. Write your friend's obituary from this new point of view.

Creative Writing

7. Today's Unknown Citizen

Write your own epitaph for an unknown high school student, athlete, parent, or worker. Use the questions "Was he or she free? Was he or she happy?" as the focus of your account.

MAKING MEANINGS

(continued from p. T1096)

6. Possible response: The modern world emphasizes conformity at the expense of individuality, freedom, and happiness. Some students will agree that the modern world demands too much uniformity.
7. The poem never refers to the citizen by name or gives any individual traits. Impersonal, bureaucratic language is reflected in the use of passive voice ("He was found . . . to be") and the personfication of documents ("Policies . . . prove"). Jargon includes his being "fully sensible to the advantages of the Installment Plan" and such expressions as "fully insured" and "served the Greater Community."
8. Students may sympathize with the citizen, claiming that the society's drive for rigid conformity repressed his individuality.

Extending the Text [Synthesize]

9. Students may be optimistic about such developments as increased awareness of and respect for diversity and by people's heightened efforts to be actively involved in shaping their own values and communities.

Challenging the Text [Evaluate]

10. Some students will say that maintaining individuality became a more pressing problem in the twentieth century because of the spread of technology; others will say all societies exert pressures to conform.

Grading Timesaver

Rubrics for each Choices assignment appear on p. 209 in the *Portfolio Management System.*

CHOICES: Building Your Portfolio

WORK IN PROGRESS

1. Encourage students to consider the bureaucratic strategies their government might employ at times.
2. Read the myth aloud to the class, and keep a copy in the classroom for students to refer to as they write.
3. Students may benefit from doing some research on Bruegel's art before they begin writing.
4. Suggest that students cluster the targets of Auden's satire into two or more groups (such as government bureaucracy and commercial interests) and deal with these in separate paragraphs.
5. Prepare for this assignment by gathering posters, prints, and library books that contain pictures of works of art. Have these items available in the classroom.
6. Bring to class obituaries from newspapers that have a national focus as examples.
7. Remind students that an **epitaph** is a short inscription on a tomb or monument. It usually tries to capture the essence of the person it is commemorating.

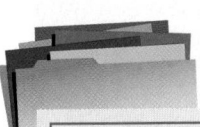

Spotlight On

This feature gives students an overview of British drama in the twentieth century. After introducing the feature, urge interested students to read plays by Samuel Beckett, Harold Pinter, Tom Stoppard, or other contemporary British playwrights and to see performances of their works either in person or on videotape.

A Exploring the Historical Period

Theater Censorship

Censorship of the theater began during the reign of Henry VII. It was intended to protect the king and members of the royal court from being offended by any play presented before them. The Master of the King's Revels was given the charge of making sure that the plays performed would not offend. When unorthodox religious ideas were added to the list of offensive topics, the job of censoring plays went to the Lord Chamberlain, who was responsible for running the king's household. Until the Theatres Act of 1968, producers of plays still had to submit a copy of the script, including any additions or changes, before they could receive a license to present the play to the public.

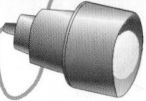

SPOTLIGHT ON

Contemporary British Drama

by **Robert Anderson**

It is difficult to know which of the playwrights of the twentieth century will stand the test of time—mostly because we are still too close to it. Plays are volatile creations, often written out of present concerns and emotions to reach an audience in the present. In a changing world with changing fashions, there is no way of knowing how people will respond to plays in the future. The highly regarded play of one generation is often viewed with contempt by the next generation: "How could they have thought that was a great play?"

Yet we can say with certainty that the twentieth century saw sweeping changes in both the content and the form of plays. Censorship of the stage in England ended in 1968, and since then there is virtually nothing that playwrights have not written about or cannot write about.

While the broadening of subject matter is a significant advance, some playwrights have been less interested in new subject matter than in new ways to get our attention—to shock us into recognizing old and new truths. These playwrights have followed various paths. Some have broken up the usual linear structure of a story—a beginning, a middle, and an end arranged in that order. In their plays they jump backward and forward in time,

Scene from a 1976 production of Samuel Beckett's *Waiting for Godot* at the Brooklyn Academy of Music, New York City.

Reaching All Students

Struggling Readers

Some students may be better able to follow the material in the Spotlight On feature if they see it presented in outline form, with main ideas separated from supporting details and examples. Help them begin by giving them the skeleton of a formal outline, and then ask them, as they read, to fill in the main and subordinate ideas. You might have students draft their outlines in pencil on large sheets of paper that they can share with other members of their reading group.

English Language Learners

English language learners may find the texts of Beckett and Pinter seemingly easier to read than the texts of Shakespeare or other earlier British playwrights. The diction of the later playwrights is simpler on the surface, and the style is less adorned. Encourage them, however, to see that the twentieth-century playwrights have incorporated multiple layers of meaning, stubborn ambiguities, and subtle depths of character into their deceptively bland and simple dialogue.

Advanced Learners

You might suggest that advanced learners research some of the essays and plays of Jean-Paul Sartre, the French philosopher and dramatist who dealt with many of the same themes of isolation and alienation that are found in the works of Samuel Beckett and Harold Pinter. Students might, for example, read Sartre's play *No Exit* and report to the class on its plot and themes.

hither and yon in space. Some, like the German playwright Bertolt Brecht, do not want to engage our sympathy for any character, but force us to keep our distance. Brecht called this "the alienation effect." Others, like the Irish playwright Samuel Beckett, ignore the usual ingredients of drama—character, conflict, development, and progression to a climax—and present us instead with a static situation. **B**

Playwrights who depart from the familiar conventions of playwriting take a great risk; they are like performers on a high wire without the safety net of a story. They had better be star performers every time out, or there will be a disaster. If they deny their audiences the pleasure of narrative ("Tell me a story!"), they have to keep them fascinated by other means.

Theater of the Absurd: Samuel Beckett

Though Samuel Beckett (1906–1989) was born in Ireland, he lived most of his life in France and wrote many of his plays in French, which he then translated into English. Whether or not he can be considered a British playwright, his *Waiting for Godot* (1953) is a modern classic, and his work is a prime example of what is known as the Theater of the Absurd. **C**

Deriving to some degree from James Joyce and surrealism, the Theater of the Absurd is an almost complete departure from the traditional theater of the preceding four hundred years. **D** The Theater of the Absurd, first of all, represents an attitude toward life expressed in part by the French writer Albert Camus:

> A world that can be explained even with bad reasons is a familiar world. But, on the other hand, in a universe suddenly divested of illusions and lights, man feels an alien, a stranger. . . . This divorce between man and his life . . . is properly the feeling of absurdity.
>
> —Albert Camus, *from* "An Absurd Reasoning"

The Absurdists do not want to tell us a story with characters arguing about the emptiness of life. They want instead to *present* us with this emptiness, this absurdity, moment by moment, so that we can experience it. There is usually no progression, no development in an Absurdist play. As we shall see in Beckett's *Waiting for Godot,* the "action" is waiting. The French title for Beckett's play is *En Attendant Godot,* literally, "While Waiting for Godot." The play is about the "while." Since the Absurdists' view is that the world is irrational, unmotivated, without cause and effect, they convey this idea not only as "the message" of the play but also in the fragmented, irrational method of the playwriting. *Waiting for Godot* was first produced in Paris in 1953 and in London in 1955. Two tramps, Vladimir and Estragon, are on a stage, bare except for a tree. **E**

Estragon. Charming spot. *(He turns, advances to the front, halts facing auditorium.)* Inspiring prospects. *(He turns to Vladimir.)* Let's go.
Vladimir. We can't.
Estragon. Why not?
Vladimir. We're waiting for Godot.
Estragon *(despairingly).* Ah! *(Pause.)* You're sure it was here?
Vladimir. What?
Estragon. That we were to wait.
Vladimir. He said by the tree. *(They look at the tree.)* Do you see any others?
Estragon. What is it?
Vladimir. I don't know. A willow.
Estragon. Where are the leaves?
Vladimir. It must be dead.
Estragon. No more weeping.
Vladimir. Or perhaps it's not the season.
Estragon. Looks to me more like a bush.
Vladimir. A shrub.
Estragon. A bush.
Vladimir. A ——. What are you insinuating? That we've come to the wrong place?
Estragon. He should be here.
Vladimir. He didn't say for sure he'd come.
Estragon. And if he doesn't come?
Vladimir. We'll come back tomorrow.
Estragon. And then the day after tomorrow.
Vladimir. Possibly.
Estragon. And so on.
Vladimir. The point is——
Estragon. Until he comes.
Vladimir. You're merciless.
Estragon. We came here yesterday.

B Literary Connections
Bertolt Brecht
Bertolt Brecht (1898–1956) was the leading Marxist playwright of his day. Born in Germany, Brecht served briefly as a medical orderly in World War I, and this experience made him a staunch pacifist. The work for which he is best known is *Mother Courage and Her Children,* set during the Thirty Years' War. The play criticizes a woman (who supplies both sides in the war with goods and services) for her dependence on war for her livelihood.

C Background
Theater of the Absurd
The phrase *Theater of the Absurd* describes drama that has its roots in the post–World War II philosophy of existentialism, which emphasized the necessity of individual choice in an essentially meaningless world. In the Theater of the Absurd, dramatists evoke that meaninglessness by means of black humor and morbid and grotesque situations that are simultaneously tragic and funny.

D Background
Surrealism
Surrealism was an artistic, literary, and philosophical movement that developed in Europe. The Surrealists attempted to represent a reality beyond the conscious mind. Using Sigmund Freud's theory of the unconscious, Surrealists looked to dream images and other products of unconscious association as keys to the true nature of reality. Some of the painters influenced by Surrealism were Salvador Dali, Max Ernst, Paul Klee, Joan Miró, and Pablo Picasso.

E Literary Connections
The Bald Soprano
Although *Waiting for Godot* is the play most closely associated with the Theater of the Absurd, it was not the first play of its type. That distinction belongs to *The Bald Soprano* by Eugène Ionesco, a Romanian who became a citizen of France. Subtitled "Anti-Play," *The Bald Soprano* pokes fun at the banal existence of two English couples. Much of the dialogue was lifted directly from an English phrase book that Ionesco had bought in order to learn the language. The play does not make apparent "sense," but the absurdity of the dialogue makes the point that language fails as a means of genuine communication between human beings.

Using Students' Strengths

Kinesthetic Learners
Allow interested students to act out one of the scenes excerpted in this feature. Have students work in groups of three, assigning one student to each character and one to serve as the director. Encourage students to experiment with facial and vocal expression, movement, and blocking. Invite groups to perform for the class and videotape their performances if possible.

Visual Learners
Invite visually oriented students to sketch the scenes or the characters in one of the dialogues. They may want to imagine themselves as illustrating the text for a printed edition of the play or as designing a set for a live performance or film. Emphasize that playwrights like Beckett usually provide little if any detailed physical descriptions of their sets or characters. Ask students to explain how they decided on the particulars of their drawings or designs.

Ⓐ Vocabulary Note

Point out to students that *riff* is a term derived from jazz. It is a constantly repeated musical phrase used as background for a soloist or as the basic theme of a final chorus. Here it suggests a short scene that offers a variation on one of the play's themes.

Ⓑ Elements of Literature

Theme

The themes of silence and nothingness can seem at first to be utterly bleak and without any glimmer of hope or optimism. You might mention to students, however, that the characters do manage to survive and continue their activities, and the play's humor may salvage an otherwise grim universe.

Ⓒ Literary Connections

Genêt and Albee

Jean Genêt (1910–1986) was a French novelist and playwright who wrote Absurdist plays about his characters' vain attempts to secure freedom from the personas imposed on them by others. A criminal all his life, Genêt was released from a life sentence in prison at the insistence of leading French writers and intellectuals in 1947.

Edward Albee (1928–) is an American playwright whose early plays, such as *The Zoo Story* and *The Sandbox*, are in the tradition of the Theater of the Absurd. In them, Albee dramatizes such Absurdist themes as illusion versus reality and the radical isolation of the individual. He has won the Pulitzer Prize for drama several times and continues to be one of the outstanding playwrights in the United States.

Scene from a June 1984 production of Samuel Beckett's *Endgame* at the Cherry Lane Theater, New York.

Vladimir. Ah no, there you're mistaken.
Estragon. What did we do yesterday?
Vladimir. What did we do yesterday?
Estragon. Yes.
Vladimir. Why . . . *(Angrily.)* Nothing is certain when you're about.
Estragon. In my opinion we were here.
Vladimir *(looking around).* You recognize the place?
Estragon. I didn't say that.
Vladimir. Well?
Estragon. That makes no difference.
Vladimir. All the same . . . that tree . . . *(turning toward auditorium)* that bog.
Estragon. You're sure it was this evening?
Vladimir. What?
Estragon. That we were to wait.
Vladimir. He said Saturday. *(Pause.)* I think.
Estragon. You think.
Vladimir. I must have made a note of it. *(He fumbles in his pockets, bursting with miscellaneous rubbish.)*
Estragon *(very insidious).* But what Saturday? And is it Saturday? Is it not rather Sunday? *(Pause.)* Or Monday? *(Pause.)* Or Friday?
Vladimir *(looking wildly about him as though the date was inscribed in the landscape).* It's not possible!
Estragon. Or Thursday?
Vladimir. What'll we do?
Estragon. If he came yesterday and we weren't here you may be sure he won't come again today.
Vladimir. But you say we were here yesterday.
Estragon. I may be mistaken. *(Pause.)* Let's stop talking for a minute. Do you mind?
Vladimir *(feebly).* All right.

—Samuel Beckett, *from Waiting for Godot*

Ⓐ Ⓑ Thus ends one of the series of "riffs" that make up the play. After a few moments' pause, the characters will start up again, terrified by the silence and the momentary view of nothingness.

Ⓒ Many people find the work of the Absurdists (Beckett, Eugène Ionesco, Jean Genêt, and Edward Albee) maddening. They say, "That's not a play!" just as some years ago, steeped in representational painting, some said of abstract expressionism,

Using Students' Strengths

Verbal Learners

Timing plays an important part in the delivery of the dialogue from *Waiting for Godot* and *That's All*, and some students may need to hear the passages presented orally in order to fully grasp their impact. Ask pairs of students to practice an oral reading of one of the two passages, giving due attention to the pace, pauses, and tone of the lines. Have the pairs present their readings, and have the class discuss the effect of each presentation.

Visual Learners

Ask interested students to research visual documentation of the many productions of Beckett's plays. In addition to photographs in books on Beckett and on the individual plays, students may find Internet links to specific productions and theaters and may be able to download the visuals. Suggest that they use their research to put together a posterboard display of Beckett's plays.

"That's not art!" Our expectations of what a play or a picture should be are deeply rooted in us, planted and nurtured by years of exposure to only certain kinds of dramatic experience or certain kinds of painting experience. The best we can do when faced with the strange is to try to remain open to the new, to let it try to educate us and broaden our appreciation, rather than to reject it because it is strange and new.

D Who is Godot? When someone asked Beckett this question, he answered that if he had known, he would have revealed it in the play. Possibly Godot is best explained by Tennessee Williams when he has Tom say in *The Glass Menagerie* that the Gentleman Caller is "the long delayed but always expected something that we live for."

Beckett's tramps, like Laurel and Hardy in the old movies, bicker in scene after scene, sometimes sounding like husband and wife in a standard domestic **farce,** or low comedy. E They seem to be derived in part from the end men who passed jokes and wisecracks back and forth in vaudeville and music halls. They also resemble the comedian and straight man in the comedy teams of movies, radio, and television. Though Beckett discarded all the ideas of progression and dramatic development, he employs a number of the appealing theatrical tricks of slapstick and vaudeville. There are pratfalls, difficulty getting shoes on and off, trousers falling down, futile efforts at suicide. The tramps are joined by a bizarre pair, Pozzo and Lucky, one a master, the other a slave on the end of a rope—a vivid theatrical picture.

Toward the end of Act I, a boy arrives from Godot to say he will not arrive today, but "surely tomorrow." Act II is almost a repetition of Act I, except that when Pozzo and Lucky enter, Pozzo is blind and Lucky is dumb. The boy again arrives at the end of the act to say that Godot will not arrive today, but tomorrow, "without fail."

Beckett regarded habit as "the lightning conductor" of our existence—in other words, the small habitual activities that keep us busy every day, all day, prevent us from being hit with the truth, which (as Beckett sees it) is loneliness, nothingness.

Regarding language, the Absurdist movement is antiliterary. The Absurdists believe that language has broken down and can no longer convey meaning. F When asked why, then, he used words, Beckett replied that words are all we have to work with. Actually, although Beckett turned his back on naturalism (the exact, detailed duplication of real life), he was a naturalist in his dialogue and sometimes even achieved a kind of poetry by his fidelity to real speech.

The nature of Beckett's work almost demands that it be performed in small, intimate theaters,

Scene from a 1979 production of Samuel Beckett's *Happy Days* at the Beckett Theater, New York.

Crossing the Curriculum

Art

Many graphic artists have displayed their talents on theatrical posters. Students interested in the visual arts might research and study such posters. Invite them also to create a poster for a contemporary play of their choice, using the posters they have researched as models. Remind them to strive for a distinctive image, composition, and style and to provide the viewer with the basic information about the production—title, dates, and place.

Technology

For a long time, plays have employed ingenious technologies to achieve special theatrical effects—from the appearance of Hamlet's father's ghost to the sinking of the *Titanic*. Have students research and report on how some of these special effects have been accomplished. They might use graphics and models to demonstrate such a device as the revolving stage or to show how thunder and lightning can be simulated on stage.

D Background

Who Is Godot?

Critic Ronald Hayman sums up Godot in this way: "Godot will never come but they will never be sure that he is not coming because there will always seem to be some reason for hoping that he will come tomorrow. And there will always be the possibility that he came today and that they failed to recognize him. . . . So in effect waiting for Godot is waiting for your life to be over, waiting for night to fall, waiting for the play to end." You might discuss with students the various experiences for which many people wait their whole lives—such as ideal love, scientific breakthroughs, a perfect society, even winning the lottery.

E Background

Vaudeville

The term *vaudeville* was first used in France to refer to satirical political ballads and later to light opera. Finally, in the United States, the term was used to describe live variety shows. Vaudeville was in its heyday in America from the 1890s to 1925, when it began to be overshadowed by motion pictures. The vaudeville era officially ended in 1932 with the closing of its most famous venue, the Palace Theater on Broadway.

Note that Beckett used many vaudeville devices, including engaging his characters in endless digressions, diversions, mistakes, and dead ends, so that in effect nothing ever "happens," but it takes a very long time. In fact, all of *Waiting for Godot* could be described as one long digression. Students who think this technique is rather old-fashioned might be reminded of the 1990s television sitcom *Seinfeld*, which was repeatedly described as being about "nothing."

F Background

Wordless Plays

In fact, Beckett does not use words at all in some of his plays. In 1957 he produced *Act Without Words*, a pantomime about a man unable to escape from a desert. Three of his pantomime plays were scheduled to be produced in Ireland in 1958; however, Beckett withdrew them from the International Theatre Festival in Dublin to protest festival officials' banning of a play by Beckett's fellow expatriate Sean O'Casey.

Ⓐ Background

Hearing Pinter

British actor Ben Kingsley, who starred in the film *Gandhi*, has been one of the best interpreters of Pinter's dialogue. To enable students to hear Pinter's peculiar halting and flat dialogue, obtain, if possible, a videotape of the movie version of *Turtle Diary* (starring Ben Kingsley), and select a portion to play for the class.

Ⓑ Background

Interpreting Pinter

The renowned director Sir Peter Hall offered this comment on playing Pinter's characters: "One of the worrying things for actors in Pinter is that you can never trust what is said to be literally true. It is much safer, in fact, to assume that it is a ploy, rather than the truth, unless you can actually discover that it is the truth. So when the actors have found how to wear their hearts on their sleeves and actually show their emotions, you then have to start a process where they hide their emotions, because to show emotion in Pinter's world is a weakness, which is mercilessly punished by the other characters." You might discuss with students this approach toward dramatic presentation. How do they feel about characters who do not show their emotions? What additional burdens does this place on the audience?

where every flutter of an eye can register. Beckett's plays are done in such theaters all over the world, and he is the "master," the point of reference for many of the experimenters now working in the theater. He was awarded the Nobel Prize in literature in 1969.

The Plays of Harold Pinter

Harold Pinter (1930–   ), an avowed disciple of Beckett and probably the most influential of the new English playwrights, is on the fringe of the Absurdist Theater. While Beckett deals with often grotesque characters in bizarre settings (the two tramps in *Waiting for Godot,* two old people in ashcans in *Endgame,* a woman buried in sand up to her neck in *Happy Days*), Pinter most often presents us with more or less real settings and identifiable characters speaking everyday language. The whole, however, is stylized in a manner that is now called Pinteresque.

With Pinter, we are not in a storytelling theater. To summarize what happens in these plays is as meaningless as trying to describe an abstract expressionist painting. Pinter's is a drama of ambiguities, implications, and contradictions. A critic reviewing a Pinter play might start by saying, "This is a play about a man who did or did not meet a woman a year ago in a restaurant." It is a world where the real is menacing, the pregnant pauses (all carefully indicated by Pinter) are full of terror, and the banal speech is full of mystery.

In a traditional play, we watch the gradual unfolding of a character, as though we were watching an onion being peeled, until the psychological center of the person is exposed. In Pinter's plays, we are not dealing with the complex psychology of character. Pinter's people are often without pasts—or they have self-contradicting pasts. Though Pinter avoids the conventional dramatic principles of progression and development, he starts from arresting situations, and he sustains mystery and suspense.

But it is Pinter's dialogue that is the hallmark of his art. He has taken the chitchat of everyday speech and stylized it to the point where it becomes a kind of poetry. The following revue sketch titled *That's All* was first presented on BBC Radio in 1964. This is the entire text.

That's All

Mrs. A. I always put the kettle on about that time.
Mrs. B. Yes. *(Pause.)*
Mrs. A. Then she comes round.
Mrs. B. Yes. *(Pause.)*
Mrs. A. Only on Thursdays.
Mrs. B. Yes. *(Pause.)*
Mrs. A. On Wednesdays I used to put it on. When she used to come round. Then she changed it to Thursdays.
Mrs. B. Oh yes.
Mrs. A. After she moved. When she used to live round the corner, then she always came in on Wednesdays, but then when she moved she used to come down to the butcher's on Thursdays. She couldn't find a butcher up there.
Mrs. B. No.
Mrs. A. Anyway, she decided she'd stick to her own butcher. Well, I thought, if she can't find a butcher, that's the best thing.
Mrs. B. Yes. *(Pause.)*
Mrs. A. So she started to come down on Thursdays. I didn't know she was coming down on Thursdays until one day I met her in the butcher.
Mrs. B. Oh yes.
Mrs. A. It wasn't my day for the butcher. I don't go to the butcher on Thursday.
Mrs. B. No, I know. *(Pause.)*
Mrs. A. I go on Friday.
Mrs. B. Yes. *(Pause.)*
Mrs. A. That's where I see you.
Mrs. B. Yes. *(Pause.)*
Mrs. A. You're always in there on Fridays.
Mrs. B. Oh yes. *(Pause.)*
Mrs. A. But I happened to go in for a bit of meat, it turned out to be a Thursday. I wasn't going in for my usual weekly on Friday. I just slipped in, the day before.
Mrs. B. Yes.
Mrs. A. That was the first time I found out she couldn't find a butcher up there, so she decided to come back here, once a week, to her own butcher.
Mrs. B. Yes.
Mrs. A. She came on Thursday so she'd be able

Making the Connections

Connecting with the Theme: "Ourselves Among Others"

After students have finished reading the feature, ask them how they think the works of Beckett, Pinter, and other twentieth-century British playwrights reflect the theme of the collection. What do they make of the paradox of the public, communal medium of drama presenting spectacles of individual isolation, alienation, and failure to communicate?

Skill Link

Evaluating Style

In *That's All* by Harold Pinter, the character Mrs. A speaks mostly in sentence fragments and elliptical expressions. Ask students to select three or four of Mrs. A's lines and rewrite them as complete sentences. Then, ask students to read the sentences aloud as part of the dialogue with Mrs. B. Ask students to evaluate which version of the lines, Pinter's or theirs, sounds more like real speech. What other effects do the fragments create that the complete sentences do not? [Most students will probably say that Pinter's fragments and elliptical expressions sound more like real speech and that they suggest or hint at emotional states.] Lead the class in a discussion of how the use of sentence fragments may be essential in accomplishing a dramatist's purpose.

to get meat for the weekend. Lasted her till Monday, then from Monday to Thursday they'd have fish. She can always buy cold meat, if they want a change.
Mrs. B. Oh yes. *(Pause.)*
Mrs. A. So I told her to come in when she came down after she'd been to the butcher's and I'd put a kettle on. So she did. *(Pause.)*
Mrs. B. Yes. *(Pause.)*
Mrs. A. It was funny because she always used to come in Wednesdays. *(Pause.)* Still, it made a break. *(Long pause.)*
Mrs. B. She doesn't come in no more, does she? *(Pause.)*
Mrs. A. She comes in. She doesn't come in so much, but she comes in. *(Pause.)*
Mrs. B. I thought she didn't come in. *(Pause.)*
Mrs. A. She comes in. *(Pause.)* She just doesn't come in so much. That's all.

—Harold Pinter

It is, of course, questionable how many situations, characters, or subjects can be dealt with in the Pinter manner. It would seem to be limiting. But over the last thirty years, he has written such notable full-length plays as *The Caretaker* (1960), *The Homecoming* (1965), *Old Times* (1971), and *Betrayal* (1978); and a series of highly effective short plays, including *The Dumb Waiter* (1960), *The Collection* (1961), *Landscape* (1968), *Silence* (1969), and *Moonlight* (1993). He has also adapted for motion pictures novels such as *The French Lieutenant's Woman* and *The Last Tycoon.*

British Theater Today

Beckett and Pinter are only two among the diverse lot of contemporary British playwrights. Many others—including John Osborne, Athol Fugard, Tom Stoppard, and Caryl Churchill—have written in a wide range of styles and forms, all more or less influenced by Beckett and Bertolt Brecht. Yesterday's avant-garde has become today's mainstream, and perhaps the avant-garde of tomorrow will be a return to some form of the conventional well-made play.

Americans have always considered London a great theater town, and it still is. Though seasons may vary in quality, in almost any year one may see productions from the rich dramatic literature of the country, past and present. The major British playwrights from Shakespeare to Shaw to Pinter form a galaxy to make Americans envious. Though the contemporary English theater may lack such tragic American masterworks as Eugene O'Neill's *Long Day's Journey into Night,* Arthur Miller's *Death of a Salesman,* and Tennessee Williams's *A Streetcar Named Desire,* we have nothing to match, as yet, the brilliance of Beckett or Pinter. But, as they say in baseball, "Wait until next year."

Poster for a 1995 production of Tom Stoppard's *Arcadia* in New York.
Art by James McMullan.

C Background
Stoppard and Fugard

Tom Stoppard was born Thomas Straussler in Czechoslovakia in 1937 and moved to England in 1946. Later, he became a journalist and then abandoned that career for playwriting. Stoppard has produced a series of witty and sophisticated plays for which he has won international renown. His major works include *Rosencrantz and Guildenstern Are Dead* (1967), *Jumpers* (1972), *Travesties* (1974), *Arcadia* (1993), and *The Invention of Love* (1997).

Athol Fugard was born in Middelburg, South Africa, in 1932 to parents who were English and Afrikaner (of Dutch ancestry). His abiding concerns are the sufferings imposed by prejudice and the forging of open and genuine relations between the races, not only in Africa but anywhere that racial conflict destroys human bonds. His most famous work is *Master Harold and the Boys* (1982). Other works include *Sizwe Bansi Is Dead* (1972) and *Valley Song* (1996).

D Background
The Well-Made Play

The term "well-made play" is used today to mean any play with a conventional multi-act structure, but the term originally referred to a play based on a very specific formula. The well-made play was extremely popular in the mid-nineteenth century and was raised to an art form by Norwegian playwright Henrik Ibsen.

Assessing Learning

Check Test: True-False

1. A play with a linear structure has a beginning, a middle, and an end. [True]
2. Theater of the Absurd is based on the idea that life is full, rich, and meaningful. [False]
3. The basic action in *Waiting for Godot* is waiting. [True]
4. *Waiting for Godot* employs comic techniques associated with vaudeville or movie slapstick. [True]
5. Harold Pinter is famous for his florid and sparkling dialogue, rich in metaphor and full of literary allusions. [False]

Objectives

1. Read and interpret the essay
2. Generate relevant, interesting, and researchable questions
3. Recognize and discuss myths that cross cultures
4. Compare text ideas with students' own experience

Browsing in the Files

About the Author. Perhaps because of his impoverished background, Camus maintained a strong affinity with workers. He joined the Communist party in 1934, but he soon rejected communism. He also rejected Christianity because he could not reconcile the intense physical suffering of innocent people with the concept of an all-merciful, all-powerful God. His rejection of communism led to a public disagreement with Jean-Paul Sartre, the leading French intellectual who had been Camus's close friend. Sartre believed that a commitment to communism, as embodied by the French Communist party, was essential for anyone who wanted genuine improvement in the lives of the working classes.

WORLD LITERATURE

Algeria/France

Albert Camus

(1913–1960)

For many people, Albert Camus (ka·mo͞o') was the very embodiment of the existential philosopher, a writer who asked questions about the foundations of our existence. Camus and his friends were associated with the Left Bank of Paris, where, in its smoky cafes, they argued about the meaning of human life. To Camus and other existentialists, we are uninvited guests in a meaningless universe.

Albert Camus was born in Algeria, at a time when Algeria was a colony of France. Raised in extreme poverty, he became one of the most influential writers of the twentieth century. When Camus was less than a year old, his father died of wounds suffered in World War I. His illiterate mother earned their living by cleaning houses. It is not surprising, therefore, that Camus viewed working-class people as individuals worthy of honor for their patient, silent labor, so like the toils of Sisyphus.

Albert Camus (1959).

One of Camus's teachers noticed his potential for learning and helped him pursue his education, first through high school and then through the University of Algiers, where Camus studied philosophy. When he was seventeen, an attack of tuberculosis ended Camus's dream of a sports career, and by 1935, he had turned to writing and the theater. In 1940, after writing a group of newspaper articles about injustices in Algeria, Camus was asked to leave, and he emigrated to Paris.

During World War II, Camus served as editor of *Combat,* an underground newspaper of the Resistance movement that courageously opposed the German occupation of France. In his plays, novels, and essays—of which the most famous is his 1946 novel *The Stranger*—he spoke out fearlessly against all forms of exploitation, cruelty, aggression, and hypocritical morality. Often ill and close to death, Camus kept writing and working in behalf of humanitarian causes throughout his life. In 1957, he was awarded the Nobel Prize in literature. Three years later, at the age of forty-six, he was killed in a car accident. A draft of Camus's unfinished autobiographical novel, *The First Man,* was found in the wreckage of his car. The book was not published until 1994.

(Map) ©Rand McNally R. L. #98-S-116.

go.hrw.com
LEO 12-14

Resources: Print and Media

Reading
- *Audio CD Library*
  Disc 20, Track 4

Internet
- go.hrw.com (keyword: *LEO 12-14*)

Before You Read
THE MYTH OF SISYPHUS

Background
Imagine that the year is 1942. Germany has invaded and is now occupying your country. Bombs are falling on cities all over Europe. Already millions of innocent people have been killed. You are desperately ill with tuberculosis. As everything that you thought was important in the world crashes around you, how would you react? Albert Camus chose to write "The Myth of Sisyphus," an essay that affirms life, no matter how meaningless or difficult it may be.

Camus based his essay on the Greek myth of Sisyphus, a clever but arrogant human who loved life and dared to defy the gods. After his death, Sisyphus even managed to escape from Pluto's dark underworld kingdom and return to life, a crime that deeply offended Zeus, king of the gods. To punish Sisyphus, Zeus condemned him to roll a huge rock eternally up a steep hill. As soon as Sisyphus reached the top of the hill, he had to stand by and watch while the rock rolled back downhill. Then he had to return to the bottom of the hill and roll the rock to the top again, and again, and again.

To Camus, the absurdity of Sisyphus's task symbolizes human existence. Camus's essay is often considered one of the important documents of **existentialism,** a philosophical and literary movement that holds that individuals must struggle to create their own meaning and morality in the absence of any absolute values. Many existentialists focus on a belief that the universe is indifferent to human suffering. However, Camus was an optimist. By becoming conscious of his terrible destiny, Camus's Sisyphus—and all of humanity—rises above it. For Camus, people achieve a kind of victory when they accept the meaninglessness of life with dignity, and even with joy.

Reading Skills and Strategies
Dialogue with the Text
As you read this challenging essay, make a note of any ideas in it that you find interesting, puzzling, or open to debate.

The Idleness of Sisyphus (1981) by Sandro Chia. Oil on canvas, in two parts, overall 10′ 2″ × 12′ 8¼″ (307 x 386.7 cm); top panel: 6′ 9″ × 12′ 8¼″ (205.5 x 386.7 cm); bottom panel: 41″ × 12′ 1¼″ (104.5 x 386.7 cm).

The Museum of Modern Art, New York. Acquired through the Carter Burden, Barbara Jakobson, and Saidie A. May Funds and purchase. Photograph © 2000 The Museum of Modern Art, New York. Sandro Chia/Licensed by VAGA, New York, N.Y.

Summary ■■■
In this essay Camus uses the Greek myth of Sisyphus to explain his existentialist philosophy. Sisyphus was condemned to spend eternity trying to roll a heavy rock to the top of a hill, only to have it roll back down each time, thus forcing him to begin again forever. Camus views Sisyphus as the absurd hero, a mortal who scorns the gods and embraces his fruitless labors with passion while fully conscious of their futility. To Camus, the labors of Sisyphus are ends in themselves. Sisyphus is stronger than his rock; his scornful dismissal of his imposed destiny enables him to surmount his fate and achieve personal freedom. Conscious of his situation, he embodies the "higher fidelity" to action that makes him both noble and happy.

RESPONDING TO THE ART
Sandro Chia (1946–   ) is an Italian painter and sculptor. Chia has referred to some of his works as "mythical conceptual art." A leader of the Italian art movement called Transavanguardia, he has produced large and colorful works replete with cultural allusions.
Activity. Students might compare Chia's Sisyphus with Bruegel's Icarus on p. 1092. Which character do students think is a more accurate reflection of people today, and why?

Using Students' Strengths

Visual Learners
Have visual learners draw two pictures of heroes. The first picture should represent what students consider to be a traditional hero, with the appearance and symbols that students usually associate with nobility or heroism. The second picture should represent the absurd hero as defined by Camus. (Students may want to borrow details from the description of Sisyphus and his labors in Camus's essay.) Ask students to choose a line or expression from literature as a caption for each picture.

Verbal/Interpersonal Learners
Divide verbal learners into teams of four, and have them stage a debate for the class on one of the following topics: "Sisyphus is (or is not) a hero for our time" or "Human fate is (or is not) in human hands." Encourage them to support their positions with evidence from both literature and real-world experience.

A Reading Skills and Strategies

Dialogue with the Text

? Do you agree with the gods' view that futile labor is the most dreadful punishment? Explain. [Possible responses: Yes, repetitive drudgery is unbearable. No, drudgery is difficult but still bearable; one is still free to choose to labor or not.]

B Critical Thinking

Analyzing Details

These sentences that describe the sea and earth are a poetic interlude in the midst of an often grim philosophical essay. Describe the sharp contrast these images create. [Possible response: The poetic lines make living on earth seem delightful and contrast starkly with the "infernal darkness" of the underworld or death.]

C Elements of Literature

Point of View

? Point out that Camus uses the third person throughout most of his essay but that in this one sentence he shifts to the second person. Why do you think he makes this switch here? [Possible responses: Talking directly to the reader makes the subject matter more immediate and more relevant. Camus discusses abstract ideas in a familiar way to make them seem accessible to the reader.]

D Reading Skills and Strategies

Making Inferences

? What does Camus mean by saying that Sisyphus is "superior to his fate"? [Possible responses: As Sisyphus follows his rock down the mountain, he has a respite from his labor, a time for reflection. Although he knows he will just have to return to his task, Sisyphus consciously embraces his fate, showing that he is a master, not a slave.]

The Myth of Sisyphus

Albert Camus

translated by **Justin O'Brien**

The gods had condemned Sisyphus to ceaselessly rolling a rock to the top of a mountain, whence the stone would fall back of its own weight. They had thought with some reason that there is no more dreadful punishment than futile and hopeless labor.

If one believes Homer, Sisyphus was the wisest and most prudent of mortals. According to another tradition, however, he was disposed to practice the profession of highwayman. I see no contradiction in this. Opinions differ as to the reasons why he became the futile laborer of the underworld. To begin with, he is accused of a certain levity[1] in regard to the gods. He stole their secrets. Aegina, the daughter of Aesopus, was carried off by Jupiter. The father was shocked by that disappearance and complained to Sisyphus. He, who knew of the abduction, offered to tell about it on condition that Aesopus would give water to the citadel of Corinth.[2] To the celestial thunderbolts he preferred the benediction of water. He was punished for this in the underworld. Homer tells us also that Sisyphus had put Death in chains. Pluto could not endure the sight of his deserted, silent empire. He dispatched the god of war, who liberated Death from the hands of her conqueror.

It is said also that Sisyphus, being near to death, rashly wanted to test his wife's love. He ordered her to cast his unburied body into the middle of the public square. Sisyphus woke up in the underworld. And there, annoyed by an obedience so contrary to human love, he obtained from Pluto permission to return to earth in order to chastise his wife. But when he had seen again the face of this world, enjoyed water and sun, warm stones and the sea, he no longer wanted to go back to the infernal darkness. Recalls, signs of anger, warnings were of no avail. Many years more he lived facing the curve of the gulf, the sparkling sea, and the smiles of earth. A decree of the gods was necessary. Mercury came and seized the impudent man by the collar and, snatching him from his joys, led him forcibly back to the underworld, where his rock was ready for him.

You have already grasped that Sisyphus is the absurd hero. He *is*, as much through his passions as through his torture. His scorn of the gods, his hatred of death, and his passion for life won him that unspeakable penalty in which the whole being is exerted toward accomplishing nothing. This is the price that must be paid for the passions of this earth. Nothing is told us about Sisyphus in the underworld. Myths are made for the imagination to breathe life into them. As for this myth, one sees merely the whole effort of a body straining to raise the huge stone, to roll it and push it up a slope a hundred times over; one sees the face screwed up, the cheek tight against the stone, the shoulder bracing the clay-covered mass, the foot wedging it, the fresh start with arms outstretched, the wholly human security of two earth-clotted hands. At the very end of his long effort measured by skyless space and time without depth, the purpose is achieved. Then Sisyphus watches the stone rush down in a few moments toward that lower world whence he will have to push it up again toward the summit. He goes back down to the plain.

It is during that return, that pause, that Sisyphus interests me. A face that toils so close to stones is already stone itself! I see that man going back down with a heavy yet measured step toward the torment of which he will never know the end. That hour like a breathing space which returns as surely as his suffering, that is the hour of consciousness. At each of those moments when he leaves the heights and gradually sinks toward the lairs of the gods, he is superior to his fate. He is stronger than his rock.

If this myth is tragic, that is because its hero is conscious. Where would his torture be, indeed, if

1. **levity** (lev′i·tē): disrespectful lightness or frivolity.
2. **Corinth** (kôr′inth): ancient city in Greece.

Reaching All Students

Struggling Readers

As they read, have students outline main ideas, details, and transitions between paragraphs by using a graphic organizer like the following. (This strategy may be more effective if students work in pairs, alternating between reading and writing.)

Main Idea/ Details	Transition	Main Idea/ Details	Transition	Main Idea/ Details

English Language Learners

Have students reread in context this sentence on p. 1107: "It echoes in the wild and limited universe of man." Point out the paradox in "wild and limited," and review the meaning of *paradox*. Have students keep an ongoing class list of the paradoxes presented by Camus, as well as any other paradoxes they can think of that express Camus's ideas. This activity will help students further their understanding of the concept of the absurd.

Advanced Learners

Suggest that advanced learners research and report to the class on the philosophy of existentialism. Students might, for example, report on the basic ideas and works of Jean-Paul Sartre, Simone de Beauvoir, Sören Kierkegaard, Martin Heidegger, and Karl Jaspers. Encourage students to relate existentialism's reliance on the individual to the theme of this collection and to other works of literature they have read.

at every step the hope of succeeding upheld him? The workman of today works every day in his life at the same tasks, and this fate is no less absurd. But it is tragic only at the rare moments when it becomes conscious. Sisyphus, proletarian[3] of the gods, powerless and rebellious, knows the whole extent of his wretched condition: It is what he thinks of during his descent. The lucidity that was to constitute his torture at the same time crowns his victory. There is no fate that cannot be surmounted by scorn.

If the descent is thus sometimes performed in sorrow, it can also take place in joy. This word is not too much. Again I fancy Sisyphus returning toward his rock, and the sorrow was in the beginning. When the images of earth cling too tightly to memory, when the call of happiness becomes too insistent, it happens that melancholy rises in man's heart: This is the rock's victory, this is the rock itself. The boundless grief is too heavy to bear. These are our nights of Gethsemane.[4] But crushing truths perish from being acknowledged. Thus, Oedipus[5] at the outset obeys fate without knowing it. But from the moment he knows, his tragedy begins. Yet at the same moment, blind and desperate, he realizes that the only bond linking him to the world is the cool hand of a girl. Then a tremendous remark rings out: "Despite so many ordeals, my advanced age and the nobility of my soul make me conclude that all is well." Sophocles' Oedipus, like Dostoevsky's Kirilov,[6] thus gives the recipe for the absurd victory. Ancient wisdom confirms modern heroism.

One does not discover the absurd without being tempted to write a manual of happiness. "What! by such narrow ways—?" There is but one world, however. Happiness and the absurd are two sons of the same earth. They are inseparable. It would be a mistake to say that happiness necessarily springs from the absurd discovery. It happens as well that the feeling of the absurd springs from happiness. "I conclude that all is well," says Oedipus, and that remark is sacred. It echoes in the wild and limited universe of man. It teaches that all is not, has not been, exhausted. It drives out of this world a god who had come into it with dissatisfaction and a preference for futile sufferings. It makes of fate a human matter, which must be settled among men.

All Sisyphus' silent joy is contained therein. His fate belongs to him. His rock is his thing. Likewise, the absurd man, when he contemplates his torment, silences all the idols. In the universe suddenly restored to its silence, the myriad wondering little voices of the earth rise up. Unconscious, secret calls, invitations from all the faces, they are the necessary reverse and price of victory. There is no sun without shadow, and it is essential to know the night. The absurd man says yes and his effort will henceforth be unceasing. If there is a personal fate, there is no higher destiny, or at least there is but one which he concludes is inevitable and despicable. For the rest, he knows himself to be the master of his days. At that subtle moment when man glances backward over his life, Sisyphus returning toward his rock, in that slight pivoting he contemplates that series of unrelated actions which becomes his fate, created by him, combined under his memory's eye, and soon sealed by his death. Thus, convinced of the wholly human origin of all that is human, a blind man eager to see who knows that the night has no end, he is still on the go. The rock is still rolling.

I leave Sisyphus at the foot of the mountain! One always finds one's burden again. But Sisyphus teaches the higher fidelity that negates the gods and raises rocks. He too concludes that all is well. This universe henceforth without a master seems to him neither sterile nor futile. Each atom of that stone, each mineral flake of that night-filled mountain, in itself forms a world. The struggle itself toward the heights is enough to fill a man's heart. One must imagine Sisyphus happy.

3. **proletarian** (prō′lə·ter′ē·ən): member of the working class.
4. **Gethsemane** (geth·sem′ə·nē): garden east of Jerusalem where Jesus Christ suffered intensely as he contemplated his possible death.
5. **Oedipus** (ed′i·pəs): character in Greek mythology who unknowingly kills his father and marries his mother. In *Oedipus at Colonus,* the last of three plays written by the Greek dramatist Sophocles (496–406 B.C.) about this tragic hero, Oedipus has blinded himself and is led by the hand by his daughter Antigone.
6. **Kirilov** (kē·rē′luf): character in Dostoevsky's 1872 novel *The Possessed.*

E Critical Thinking
Interpreting

? Why might Camus say that the fate of a worker is tragic only during moments of consciousness? [Possible response: Someone can be sad only if he or she recognizes that sadness.]

F Struggling Readers
Paraphrasing

Paraphrase Camus's statement about scorn. [Possible response: Once a person admits that something is true or real, its power over the individual is diminished.]

G Reading Skills and Strategies
Finding the Main Idea

? What is Camus's main point here? [Possible response: When we yearn for or remember happiness, we become melancholy and mired in grief.]

H Literary Connections
Camus and Voltaire

Reemphasize the horror of Oedipus's position: He unknowingly kills his father and marries his mother; he finds out what he has done, gouges out his eyes, and is banished from his homeland. Yet he still concludes that "all is well." Ask students to discuss why Oedipus might draw such a surprising conclusion. Remind students that in *Candide* (pp. 538–540), Pangloss teaches that "all is for the best." Have students consider how differently Voltaire and Camus evaluate the quality of human existence.

I Reading Skills and Strategies
Dialogue with the Text

? Do you agree that "[o]ne must imagine Sisyphus happy"? Why or why not? [Possible responses: Yes; he is at least able to see and acknowledge the reality of his existence. He will push the rock forever, but he also knows that he will forever walk down the mountain free of the rock. No, no matter what he thinks he knows, his actual existence is still miserable, futile, and immutable.]

Crossing the Curriculum

History

Have students work in groups to research and write an article on the French resistance against the Nazis in World War II. Encourage them to look for information about the underground newspaper *Combat* or the leadership of the Free French by General Charles de Gaulle. Students might also view the French film *The Battle of Algiers* (1965)—a compelling, documentarylike account of the Algerian guerilla revolt against the French, beginning in 1954.

Making the Connections

Connecting with the Theme: "Ourselves Among Others"

How does the lonely fate of Sisyphus relate to the collection theme? How does Camus's view of the individual compare and contrast with the views presented in some of the other selections in this collection? ["The Myth of Sisyphus" addresses the notion that each individual leads an isolated, unique existence, in which he or she tries to make the best of individual circumstances without reference to or support from others.]

Responding to the Art

René Magritte (1898–1967)—Belgian painter, printmaker, sculptor, photographer, and filmmaker—was a leader of the Surrealist movement. Influenced by the works of Giorgio de Chirico, Magritte developed a style in which objects were placed in unexpected or fantastical juxtapositions. Magritte's purpose was to suggest dimensions of experience or layers of consciousness that were out of the ordinary and to encourage the viewer to look at surface appearances in new ways. One of Magritte's most famous images is a realistic painting of a pipe with the caption *"Ceci n'est pas une pipe"* ("This is not a pipe"). He wanted to emphasize the distinction between a concrete object in the real world and an artistic representation of that object.

Activity. Ask students if they think every work of art needs to have a rational meaning that can be expressed in words. What do students think Magritte's *Castle of the Pyrenees* may "mean"? How may the expression *castles in the air* bear on the image? In what sense may Magritte's rock be like Sisyphus's mountain (or rock)?

Finding Common Ground

This feature requires students through lively discussion, research, and creative expression to discover areas of agreement between their experience and the ideas expressed in Camus's interpretation of the myth of Sisyphus as well as myths from other cultures. Have students read all of the alternative assignments and select the activity they find most interesting. Then allow students to form groups according to their interests. Students may observe that the human truths found in myths of all cultures—lessons about love, pride, sorrow, and so on—have validity today.

The Castle of the Pyrenees (1959) by René Magritte.

Israel Museum, Jerusalem
© 1997 C. Hersovici, Brussels / Artists Rights Society (ARS), New York.

Finding Common Ground

You can probably recognize in Camus's writing the voice of a man who wanted human labor and art to serve human needs. Perhaps you can also recognize the voice of someone with a lifelong commitment to the unfortunate of the world. Can you also hear that Camus was a man who faced hopelessness and despair in his own life, yet reacted to setbacks with renewed vigor and hope?

Explore your responses to Camus's essay (check your reading notes) and to his philosophy in one or more of these ways:

- According to Camus, "the workman of today works every day in his life at the same tasks, and this fate is no less absurd" than the tasks Sisyphus carries out. Imagine yourself as one of the workers Camus had in mind. Discuss the ways in which Camus's philosophy might help you face your life with hope and joy.
- A **myth** is an imaginative narrative, usually involving gods or other supernatural beings, that often explains something about the world or human beings. Myths reflect the beliefs and values of the society that produces them. Camus found meaning in the myth of Sisyphus. W. H. Auden (page 1091) was moved by the myth of Icarus, and Frank O'Connor (page 1080) was inspired by a modern interpretation of the ancient myth of Oedipus. In a group, make a list of myths from Greek and other cultures. Discuss connections between these myths and your own lives.
- Camus's writing has been called epigrammatic. That means he writes in **epigrams,** brief statements packed with meaning. Find one sentence in "The Myth of Sisyphus" that has particular meaning for you, and find a way to share it with the class. (For instance, use it on a poster.)

Assessing Learning

Check Test: Short Answers

1. Why did the gods choose to punish Sisyphus in the particular way that they did? [They thought futile labor was the worst possible punishment.]
2. What kind of hero does Camus claim Sisyphus is? [an absurd hero]
3. At what point does Camus claim that Sisyphus's fate becomes tragic? [when the hero becomes conscious of having no hope]
4. To what modern figures does Camus compare Sisyphus? [workers]
5. Whom does Camus see as the master of human fate? [the individual who consciously sees and accepts what cannot be altered]

Anita Desai

(1937–)

Anita Desai.

Born in Mussoorie, India, Anita Desai has been writing since the age of seven "as instinctively as I breathe." Desai's father was Bengali and her mother German, and Desai grew up hearing Hindi, English, and German spoken at home. However, it was in English that Desai learned to read and write. Educated at the University of Delhi, Desai began publishing in 1963.

Desai's fiction explores the struggles of contemporary Indian characters as they respond to cultural and social change. She sees her work as an attempt to discover "the truth that is nine-tenths of the iceberg that lies submerged beneath the one-tenth visible portion we call Reality." To evoke this "truth," Desai uses rich, sensual language and intense imagery. Because of her sensuous style and rich use of image and symbol, Desai has been referred to as an "imagist-novelist."

Desai's novels often focus on the emotional and spiritual lives of wives, older women, or sisters who take responsibility for others but are unable to create satisfactory lives for themselves. Her novels include *Cry, the Peacock* (1963), *In Custody* (1984), and *Baumgartner's Bombay* (1988).

Writing in *The New Republic,* Anthony Thwaite describes Desai "as such a consummate artist that she [is able to suggest], beyond the confines of the plot and the machinations of her characters, the immensities that lie beyond them—the immensities of India."

Before You Read

GAMES AT TWILIGHT

Make the Connection

Childhood Business

Work may be the business of adults, but play is often considered the "business" of little children. For it is through play that children do the hard work of learning many of life's important lessons. They learn about rules and strategies, strength and weakness. They learn that life is not always fair.

Elements of Literature

Imagery

Desai's vibrant **imagery** captures the smells, textures, shouts, and colors of a sizzling summer afternoon in India. From the beginning of the story, when the children burst out the door, to its end at twilight, Desai enables you to experience the world through the eyes and ears of her characters.

> **Imagery** is the use of language to evoke sensory impressions. Images are chiefly visual, but they can also appeal to the senses of smell, hearing, taste, and touch.
>
> *For more on Imagery, see the Handbook of Literary Terms.*

Reading Skills and Strategies

Analyzing Evocative Words

As you read, jot down words and phrases that help you imagine the scene and share the characters' experiences. When you have finished reading, discuss the impression created by these words.

Background

This story is set not long after India's independence from Britain, in 1947. During the long British rule in India, many upper-class Indian families adopted Western values and behaviors, including games like the one played in the story.

go.hrw.com
LEO 12-14

OBJECTIVES

1. Read and interpret the story
2. Identify and analyze imagery
3. Analyze use of evocative words
4. Express understanding through critical and creative writing
5. Understand new words

SKILLS

Literary
- Identify and analyze imagery

Reading
- Analyze use of evocative words

Writing
- Collect ideas for a problem-solution essay
- Compare and contrast stories
- Write a short narrative about the cost of cruelty

Vocabulary
- Use new words

Viewing/Representing
- Interpret images in a painting (ATE)

Planning

- **Traditional Schedule**
  Lesson Plans Including Strategies for English-Language Learners
- **One-Stop Planner**
  CD-ROM with Test Generator

BROWSING IN THE FILES

About the Author. In 1993 Desai joined the faculty of the Massachusetts Institute of Technology, and in 1995 she published the novel *Journey to Ithaca.*

Resources: Print and Media

Reading
- *Graphic Organizers for Active Reading,* p. 110
- *Words to Own,* p. 33
- *Audio CD Library*
  Disc 20, Track 5

Writing and Language
- *Daily Oral Grammar*
  Transparency 39

Assessment
- *Formal Assessment,* p. 218
- *Portfolio Management System,* p. 211
- *Preparation for College Admission Exams,* p. 55
- *Test Generator (One-Stop Planner CD-ROM)*

Internet
- go.hrw.com (keyword: *LEO 12-14*)

Summary ■■

On a hot afternoon in India, several children decide to play hide-and-seek. They scatter and hide, except for Raghu, who is It. A boy named Ravi finds a hiding place in a dark, spooky shed filled with discarded household goods.

Ravi spends hours in the shed, waiting and thinking of the thrill of winning the game. At twilight, when he finally emerges expecting victory and exultation, he discovers that the others have forgotten him and gone on to other pursuits. Ravi disappeared from their minds just as effectively as he disappeared during the game. He refuses to play anymore, finding the atmosphere of their new game funereal. He has experienced the "terrible sense of his insignificance."

Ⓐ Elements of Literature

Imagery

? Ask students to identify the sensory images in the passage. What is the effect of the imagery? [Images include red faces and stuffed lungs and noses. Possible response: Imagery helps readers feel the heat and empathize with the children.]

Ⓑ Reading Skills and Strategies

Analyzing Evocative Words

Point out that Desai deliberately puts the words *wailed, wild,* and *maniacal* into the same sentence. The long *a* and long *i* sounds evoke the outcries of the children.

Ⓒ Reading Skills and Strategies

Connecting with the Text

? Have you been in a setting like this one? What details help you imagine such a scene? [Possible responses: Yes, the glaring white walls may remind students of a blistering summer day in the southwestern United States. No, but Desai's description of the way nothing moves may help students imagine the scene.]

Ⓓ Cultural Connections

Ask students to consider the children's language: Is it similar to or different from language students used when playing games where they grew up? [Possible response: It sounds similar, and the interrupted sentences sound natural. But "eldest" sounds British.]

Games at Twilight

Anita Desai

It was still too hot to play outdoors. They had had their tea, they had been washed and had their hair brushed, and after the long day of confinement in the house that was not cool but at least a protection from the sun, the children strained to get out. Their faces were red and bloated with the effort, but their mother would not open the door, everything was still curtained and shuttered in a way that stifled the children, made them feel that their lungs were stuffed with cotton wool and their noses with dust and if they didn't burst out into the light and see the sun and feel the air, they would choke.

"Please, ma, please," they begged. "We'll play in the veranda and porch—we won't go a step out of the porch."

"You will, I know you will, and then——"

"No—we won't, we won't," they wailed so horrendously that she actually let down the bolt of the front door so that they burst out like seeds from a crackling, overripe pod into the veranda, with such wild, maniacal yells that she retreated to her bath and the shower of talcum powder and the fresh sari that were to help her face the summer evening.

They faced the afternoon. It was too hot. Too bright. The white walls of the veranda glared stridently in the sun. The bougainvillea[1] hung about it, purple and magenta, in livid balloons. The garden outside was like a tray made of beaten brass, flattened out on the red gravel and the stony soil in all shades of metal—aluminum, tin, copper, and brass. No life stirred at this arid time of day—the birds still drooped, like dead fruit, in the papery tents of the trees; some squirrels lay limp on the wet earth under the garden tap. The outdoor dog lay stretched as if dead on the veranda mat, his paws and ears and tail all reaching out like dying travelers in search of water. He rolled his eyes at the children—two white marbles rolling in the purple sockets, begging for sympathy—and attempted to lift his tail in a wag but could not. It only twitched and lay still.

Then, perhaps roused by the shrieks of the children, a band of parrots suddenly fell out of the eucalyptus tree, tumbled frantically in the still, sizzling air, then sorted themselves out into battle formation and streaked away across the white sky.

The children, too, felt released. They too began tumbling, shoving, pushing against each other, frantic to start. Start what? Start their business. The business of the children's day which is—play.

"Let's play hide-and-seek."

"Who'll be It?"

"You be It."

"Why should I? You be——"

"You're the eldest——"

"That doesn't mean——"

The shoves became harder. Some kicked out. The motherly Mira intervened. She pulled the boys roughly apart. There was a tearing sound of cloth, but it was lost in the heavy panting and angry grumbling, and no one paid attention to the small sleeve hanging loosely off a shoulder.

"Make a circle, make a circle!" she shouted, firmly pulling and pushing till a kind of vague circle was formed. "Now clap!" she roared, and, clapping, they all chanted in melancholy unison: "Dip, dip, dip—my blue ship——" and every now and then one or the other saw he was safe by the way his hands fell at the crucial moment—palm on palm, or back of hand on palm—and dropped out of the circle with a yell and a jump of relief and jubilation.

Raghu was It. He started to protest, to cry "You cheated—Mira cheated—Anu cheated——" but it was too late, the others had all already streaked away. There was no one to hear when he called out, "Only in the veranda—the porch—Ma said—Ma *said* to stay in the porch!" No one had

1. **bougainvillea** (bo͞o′gən·vil′ē·ə): woody, tropical vine with showy, purplish leaves.

WORDS TO OWN

maniacal (mə·nī′ə·kəl) *adj.:* crazed; wildly enthusiastic.
stridently (strīd′'nt·lē) *adv.:* harshly; sharply.

Preteaching Vocabulary

Have students read the Words to Own and their definitions at the bottom of the text pages. Then, have them fill in the blanks in the following sentences with the correct vocabulary words.

1. The song was supposed to be merely sad, but it was ________. [lugubrious]
2. Convinced of the justice of their cause, the protesters cried out _________. [stridently]
3. Do you have the ________ to challenge the boss's orders? [temerity]
4. What an _______ scent! [intoxicating]
5. He's ____ about practicing. [maniacal]
6. After the scandal broke, they endured only _________. [ignominy]
7. The monks were _________ their most sacred chant. [intoning]
8. It took a ________ effort to finish the marathon. [dogged]
9. She was _______ with anger at the insult. [seething]
10. Eyebrows raised, he glanced __________ at his opponent. [superciliously]

If All the World Were Paper and All the Waters Ink (1962) by Jess.
The Fine Arts Museums of San Francisco, California. Courtesy of the Odyssia Gallery, New York.

stopped to listen, all he saw were their brown legs flashing through the dusty shrubs, scrambling up brick walls, leaping over compost heaps and hedges, and then the porch stood empty in the purple shade of the bougainvillea, and the garden was as empty as before; even the limp squirrels had whisked away, leaving everything gleaming, brassy, and bare.

Only small Manu suddenly reappeared, as if he had dropped out of an invisible cloud or from a bird's claws, and stood for a moment in the center of the yellow lawn, chewing his finger and near to tears as he heard Raghu shouting, with his head pressed against the veranda wall, "Eighty-three, eighty-five, eighty-nine, ninety . . ." and then made off in a panic, half of him wanting to fly north, the other half counseling south. Raghu turned just in time to see the flash of his white shorts and the uncertain skittering of his red sandals, and charged after him with such a bloodcurdling yell that Manu stumbled over the hosepipe, fell into its rubber coils, and lay there weeping, "I won't be It—you have to find them all—all—All!" **E**

"I know I have to, idiot," Raghu said, superciliously kicking him with his toe. "You're dead,"

Words to Own
superciliously (so͞o′pər·sil′ē·əs·lē) *adv.:* disdainfully or scornfully; haughtily.

Responding to the Art

Jess (full name Jess Collins, 1923–) is a Pop and collage artist who has devised original ways of telling stories by using comic strips. *If All the World Were Paper and All the Waters Ink* takes its name from the following children's nursery rhyme:

If all the world were paper
And all the waters ink
And all the seas were bread and cheese,
What would we have to drink?

Activity. Open a discussion by asking students how they interpret the two large figures at the left and right of Jess's work. Ask students what nursery rhymes or games might be occupying the children in the picture. How might these pastimes have been learning experiences for the children, as in "Games at Twilight"?

E Critical Thinking

Speculating

? Point out the poignancy in this terse description of Manu caught in a dilemma. What effect do you think the author may have intended by including this scene? [Possible responses: The author may have wanted to help readers remember being in such a game and fearing they might get caught or to show how children everywhere share similar feelings and thoughts.]

Reaching All Students

Struggling Readers

Although it centers on a children's game, this story charts a complex psychological drama. Ask students to create a plot diagram showing all the major events in the story, especially external and internal conflicts. As a class or in groups, have students compare their diagrams and discuss how and if the various conflicts are resolved.

English Language Learners

Point out that Desai paints her scenes with well-chosen words and rarely uses vague or general diction. Encourage English language learners to keep a list of words whose meanings they are unsure of (such as *brassy, defunct,* and *sepulchral*). Then urge them to come up with a concrete object or experience to which they can relate the unfamiliar word. They can also confer with other students and check their associations in a dictionary.

Advanced Learners

Suggest that advanced learners research the work of another Indian writer, Ruth Prawer Jhabvala, and compare and contrast it with that of Anita Desai. Jhabvala's works include the novel *Heat and Dust* (1983); a superb collection of short stories, *Out of India* (1987); and numerous highly acclaimed screenplays, including *The Remains of the Day.*

Ⓐ Elements of Literature

Point of View

? How does the point of view shift during this part of the narrative? What is the effect of this shift on the reader? [The point of view shifts from third-person omniscient to third-person limited, allowing the reader to first get an overview of the children's game and then focus on Ravi's internal emotional experience.]

Ⓑ Struggling Readers

Reading Elliptical Constructions

Point out that "Also locked" is an elliptical construction, with the subject and the verb—"it was"— left out. Students will probably easily grasp that "Also locked" refers to the shed door. However, help them see that Desai uses these compressed constructions for a specific effect. The elliptical construction "Also locked" is abrupt, suggesting Ravi's quick, virtually automatic checking of the door. It verbally reflects Ravi's instantaneous action.

Ⓒ Elements of Literature

Simile

? What figure of speech does the writer use here? [Cleaning the shed is compared in a simile to looting a city.] Why is it appropriate in this context? [Possible response: The simile suggests the sense of chaos, fear, and disorientation that Ravi experiences.]

Ⓓ Critical Thinking

Synthesizing

? How would you summarize Ravi's mixed feelings in this passage? [Possible responses: He is pleased, scared, thrilled, wary, vulnerable, and uncertain.]

he said with satisfaction, licking the beads of perspiration off his upper lip, and then stalked off in search of worthier prey, whistling spiritedly so that the hiders should hear and tremble.

Ⓐ Ravi heard the whistling and picked his nose in a panic, trying to find comfort by burrowing the finger deep—deep into that soft tunnel. He felt himself too exposed, sitting on an upturned flowerpot behind the garage. Where could he burrow? He could run around the garage if he heard Raghu come—around and around and around—but he hadn't much faith in his short legs when matched against Raghu's long, hefty, hairy footballer legs. Ravi had a frightening glimpse of them as Raghu combed the hedge of crotons and hibiscus, trampling delicate ferns underfoot as he did so. Ravi looked about him desperately, swallowing a small ball of snot in his fear.

The garage was locked with a great heavy lock to which the driver had the key in his room, hanging from a nail on the wall under his workshirt. Ravi had peeped in and seen him still sprawling on his string cot in his vest and striped underpants, the hair on his chest and the hair in his nose shaking with the vibrations of his phlegm-obstructed snores. Ravi had wished he were tall enough, big enough to reach the key on the nail, but it was impossible, beyond his reach for years to come. He had sidled away and sat dejectedly on the flowerpot. That at least was cut to his own size.

Ⓑ But next to the garage was another shed with a big green door. Also locked. No one even knew who had the key to the lock. That shed wasn't opened more than once a year, when Ma turned out all the old broken bits of furniture and rolls of matting and leaking buckets, and the white anthills were broken and swept away and Flit sprayed into the spider webs and rat holes so that Ⓒ the whole operation was like the looting of a poor, ruined, and conquered city. The green leaves of the door sagged. They were nearly off their rusty hinges. The hinges were large and made a small gap between the door and the walls—only just large enough for rats, dogs, and, possibly, Ravi to slip through.

Ravi had never cared to enter such a dark and depressing mortuary of defunct household goods seething with such unspeakable and alarming animal life but, as Raghu's whistling grew angrier and sharper and his crashing and storming in the hedge wilder, Ravi suddenly slipped off the flowerpot and through the crack and was gone. He chuckled aloud with astonishment at his own temerity so that Raghu came out of the hedge, stood silent with his hands on his hips, listening, and finally shouted, "I heard you! I'm coming! *Got you*——" and came charging round the garage only to find the upturned flowerpot, the yellow dust, the crawling of white ants in a mud hill against the closed shed door—nothing. Snarling, he bent to pick up a stick and went off, whacking it against the garage and shed walls as if to beat out his prey.

Ravi shook, then shivered with delight, with self-Ⓓ congratulation. Also with fear. It was dark, spooky in the shed. It had a muffled smell, as of graves. Ravi had once got locked into the linen cupboard and sat there weeping for half an hour before he

Words to Own

seething (sēth′iŋ) *v.* used as *adj.:* surging; appearing constantly active or violently agitated.

temerity (tə·mer′ə·tē) *n.:* foolish or rash boldness; recklessness.

Two young girls, Rajasthan, India.

Crossing the Curriculum

Music

Have students work in groups of five or six to list childhood songs and chants, such as "The grass is green" (p. 1114) or "Ollie, Ollie, in free," and lyrics used to accompany rope jumping or other games. After students have recalled as many examples as possible, encourage them to find the origins of these songs and chants. Direct them to the music-history section of the library and also to special recorded collections of children's-game songs. Invite students to present their research findings to the class orally, using charts, recordings, and performance.

Science

Have students work in groups of four to investigate the vegetation in the setting of the story. They should list the plants that are mentioned, research what the plants look like, and create a drawing of the setting that incorporates the plants. Students might create a colored-chalk picture, a colored-pencil illustration with scientific labels, or a drawing in another medium.

Social Sciences

Have the class work in mixed-ability groups to conduct a study of modern India. Assign one of the following topics to each group: geography, population distribution, languages, agriculture, industry, education, government, recent history, and the arts. Have groups share their findings with the class in a format of their own choosing.

was rescued. But at least that had been a familiar place, and even smelled pleasantly of starch, laundry, and, reassuringly, of his mother. But the shed smelled of rats, anthills, dust, and spider webs. Also of less definable, less recognizable horrors. And it was dark. Except for the white-hot cracks along the door, there was no light. The roof was very low. Although Ravi was small, he felt as if he could reach up and touch it with his fingertips. But he didn't stretch. He hunched himself into a ball so as not to bump into anything, touch or feel anything. What might there not be to touch him and feel him as he stood there, trying to see in the dark? Something cold, or slimy—like a snake. Snakes! He leapt up as Raghu whacked the wall with his stick—then, quickly realizing what it was, felt almost relieved to hear Raghu, hear his stick. It made him feel protected.

But Raghu soon moved away. There wasn't a sound once his footsteps had gone around the garage and disappeared. Ravi stood frozen inside the shed. Then he shivered all over. Something had tickled the back of his neck. It took him a while to pick up the courage to lift his hand and explore. It was an insect—perhaps a spider—exploring *him.* He squashed it and wondered how many more creatures were watching him, waiting to reach out and touch him, the stranger. **E**

There was nothing now. After standing in that position—his hand still on his neck, feeling the wet splodge of the squashed spider gradually dry—for minutes, hours, his legs began to tremble with the effort, the inaction. By now he could see enough in the dark to make out the large solid shapes of old wardrobes, broken buckets, and bedsteads piled on top of each other around him. He recognized an old bathtub—patches of enamel glimmered at him, and at last he lowered himself onto its edge. **F**

He contemplated slipping out of the shed and into the fray. He wondered if it would not be better to be captured by Raghu and be returned to the milling crowd as long as he could be in the sun, the light, the free spaces of the garden, and the familiarity of his brothers, sisters, and cousins. It would be evening soon. Their games would become legitimate. The parents would sit out on the lawn on cane basket chairs and watch them as they tore around the garden or gathered in knots to share a loot of mulberries or black, teeth-splitting *jamun*[2] from the garden trees. The gardener would fix the hosepipe to the water tap, and water would fall lavishly through the air to the ground, soaking the dry yellow grass and the red gravel and arousing the sweet, the intoxicating scent of water on dry earth—that loveliest scent in the world. Ravi sniffed for a whiff of it. **G** He half-rose from the bathtub, then heard the despairing scream of one of the girls as Raghu bore down upon her. There was the sound of a crash, and of rolling about in the bushes, the shrubs, then screams and accusing sobs of "I touched the den——" "You did not——" "I did——" "You liar, you did *not*" and then a fading away and silence again.

Ravi sat back on the harsh edge of the tub, deciding to hold out a bit longer. What fun if they were all found and caught—he alone left unconquered! He had never known that sensation. **H** Nothing more wonderful had ever happened to him than being taken out by an uncle and bought a whole slab of chocolate all to himself, or being flung into the soda man's pony cart and driven up to the gate by the friendly driver with the red beard and pointed ears. To defeat Raghu—that **I** hirsute,[3] hoarse-voiced football champion—and to be the winner in a circle of older, bigger, luckier children—that would be thrilling beyond imagination. He hugged his knees together and smiled to himself almost shyly at the thought of so much victory, such laurels.

There he sat smiling, knocking his heels against the bathtub, now and then getting up and going to the door to put his ear to the broad crack and listening for sounds of the game, the pursuer and the pursued, and then returning to his seat with the dogged determination of the true winner, a breaker of records, a champion.

2. ***jamun*** (jä·mən): plumlike fruit.
3. **hirsute** (hur′so͞ot′): hairy; shaggy.

WORDS TO OWN

intoxicating (in·täks′i·kāt′iŋ) *v.* used as *adj.:* causing wild excitement or happiness, often to a point beyond self-control; heady.
dogged (dôg′id) *adj.:* persistent; stubborn.

E Reading Skills and Strategies
Making Inferences

? What is particularly frightening to Ravi about his situation? [Possible response: He is completely alone in an unfamiliar place in the dark.]

F Reading Skills and Strategies
Analyzing Evocative Words

Draw students' attention to the phrase "the wet splodge of the squashed spider." Point out that *splodge* is a British variant of the word *splotch* and that the words are carefully chosen to evoke a buggy, creepy sensation, especially through the use of the sibilant *s* sounds.

G Elements of Literature
Imagery

Point out the effectiveness of evoking the sense of smell, especially in the midst of a passage packed with powerful visual imagery.

H Reading Skills and Strategies
Making Predictions

? What do you think will happen to Ravi? [Possible response: He has hidden himself so well that he will hold out and win the game.] What details make you think so? [Possible responses: Raghu has already missed Ravi's hiding place; no one else has any reason to look in the shed.]

I Elements of Literature
Character

? What information in this passage adds to your understanding of Ravi? [Possible response: Ravi must be younger than most of the children. Part of his motivation may be to win despite his age.]

A Critical Thinking
Analyzing Details

? Does Ravi wait a long time, or does he just feel it has been a long time? How do you know? [He waits a long time; the afternoon light has turned to gray, and the sounds indicate the gardener is already watering.]

B Reading Skills and Strategies
Analyzing Evocative Words

Have students read this sentence aloud, noting the onomatopoetic quality of words like *quaked* and *twittered*. Then have them tell in their own words what the tree looks and sounds like. [Possible response: The tree has become a dark shaking mass, with vague moving shapes of noisy birds in it.]

C Critical Thinking
Interpreting

? What do you think the main conflict of this story is? [Possible response: Ravi feels a passionate need to win the game and defeat the older children.] Why does Ravi cry? [Possible response: He is embarrassed, disappointed, and hurt.]

D Elements of Literature
Imagery

? What visual imagery does Desai use here to help the reader picture the children? [In the light of dusk, the children's faces are pale, like death masks, and the vegetation is as dark as ink, casting long shadows.] How does the imagery add to an understanding of Ravi's emotions at this moment? [Possible response: The children look like ghosts, and the atmosphere is tomblike; the children are "dead" to Ravi, just as he has been forgotten by them.]

E Reading Skills and Strategies
Identifying Cause and Effect

? How can you explain the mother's response to Ravi's crying? [Possible response: She sees him as a small child who is probably fussing over some minor injury.]

F Reading Skills and Strategies
Making Inferences

? How does this chant relate to Ravi's experience? [Possible response: It emphasizes that the children have forgotten him; to him, to be forgotten is to be "dead."]

It grew darker in the shed as the light at the door grew softer, fuzzier, turned to a kind of crumbling yellow pollen that turned to yellow fur, blue fur, gray fur. Evening. Twilight. The sound of water gushing, falling. The scent of earth receiving water, slaking its thirst in great gulps and releasing that green scent of freshness, coolness. Through the crack Ravi saw the long purple shadows of the shed and the garage lying still across the yard. Beyond that, the white walls of the house. The bougainvillea had lost its lividity, hung in dark bundles that quaked and twittered and seethed with masses of homing sparrows. The lawn was shut off from his view. Could he hear the children's voices? It seemed to him that he could. It seemed to him that he could hear them chanting, singing, laughing. But what about the game? What had happened? Could it be over? How could it when he was still not found?

It then occurred to him that he could have slipped out long ago, dashed across the yard to the veranda, and touched the "den." It was necessary to do that to win. He had forgotten. He had only remembered the part of hiding and trying to elude the seeker. He had done that so successfully, his success had occupied him so wholly, that he had quite forgotten that success had to be clinched by that final dash to victory and the ringing cry of "Den!"

With a whimper he burst through the crack, fell on his knees, got up, and stumbled on stiff, benumbed legs across the shadowy yard, crying heartily by the time he reached the veranda so that when he flung himself at the white pillar and bawled, "Den! Den! Den!" his voice broke with rage and pity at the disgrace of it all, and he felt himself flooded with tears and misery.

Out on the lawn, the children stopped chanting. They all turned to stare at him in amazement. Their faces were pale and triangular in the dusk. The trees and bushes around them stood inky and sepulchral, spilling long shadows across them. They stared, wondering at his reappearance, his passion, his wild animal howling. Their mother rose from her basket chair and came toward him, worried, annoyed, saying, "Stop it, stop it, Ravi. Don't be a baby. Have you hurt yourself?" Seeing him attended to, the children went back to clasping their hands and chanting, "The grass is green, the rose is red. . . ."

But Ravi would not let them. He tore himself out of his mother's grasp and pounded across the lawn into their midst, charging at them with his head lowered so that they scattered in surprise. "I won, I won, I won," he bawled, shaking his head so that the big tears flew. "Raghu didn't find me. I won, I won——"

It took them a minute to grasp what he was saying, even who he was. They had quite forgotten him. Raghu had found all the others long ago. There had been a fight about who was to be It next. It had been so fierce that their mother had emerged from her bath and made them change to another game. Then they had played another and another. Broken mulberries from the tree and eaten them. Helped the driver wash the car when their father returned from work. Helped the gardener water the beds till he roared at them and swore he would complain to their parents. The parents had come out, taken up their positions on the cane chairs. They had begun to play again, sing and chant. All this time no one had remembered Ravi. Having disappeared from the scene, he had disappeared from their minds. Clean.

"Don't be a fool," Raghu said roughly, pushing him aside, and even Mira said, "Stop howling, Ravi. If you want to play, you can stand at the end of the line," and she put him there very firmly.

The game proceeded. Two pairs of arms reached up and met in an arc. The children trooped under it again and again in a lugubrious circle, ducking their heads and intoning

"The grass is green,
The rose is red;
Remember me
When I am dead, dead, dead, dead . . ."

And the arc of thin arms trembled in the twilight, and the heads were bowed so sadly, and their feet tramped to that melancholy refrain so mournfully, so helplessly, that Ravi could not bear it. He would not follow them, he would not be

Words to Own

lugubrious (lə·go͞o′brē·əs) *adj.:* very solemn or mournful, especially in a way that seems exaggerated or ridiculous.

intoning (in·tōn′iŋ) *v.* used as *adj.:* chanting.

Making the Connections

Connecting with the Theme: "Ourselves Among Others"

Discuss with students the ways in which they think childhood experiences form people's adult beliefs and personalities. What kind of adult do they think Ravi will become? What attitudes is he likely to have toward individuals or groups different from himself? In what ways do the other children treat him as an outsider? Is there any way in which Ravi's experience might reflect the history of the Indian people?

Assessing Learning

Check Test: Questions and Answers

1. What does Ravi want more than anything else? [to win the game of hide-and-seek]
2. Where does Ravi hide? [in a shed]
3. Who is Raghu? [an older boy, a soccer champion, who is It in the game]
4. Why does Ravi cry? [The older children have forgotten him, and his victory is hollow.]

included in this funereal game. He had wanted victory and triumph—not a funeral. But he had been forgotten, left out, and he would not join them now. The ignominy of being forgotten— **G** how could he face it? He felt his heart go heavy and ache inside him unbearably. He lay down full length on the damp grass, crushing his face into it, no longer crying, silenced by a terrible sense of his insignificance.

WORDS TO OWN
ignominy (ig′nə·min′ē) *n.:* shame and dishonor.

Student TO Student

Lesson of the Bamboo Crates

It's a soppy, rainy day. As I leave the subway station, I see a woman with one hand holding on to her daughter and the other hand grasping a big sack. This scene reminds me of another woman, miles away, in China.

She was my classmate Dai's mother. She only showed up in school on rainy days in the same worn, out-of-style clothes. Always, she brought a big bag of rice to pay for Dai's boarding expenses.

"Village people," we, the mean ones, **H** thought. When she and Dai stood together, with the same self-styled chopped haircut, we couldn't stop laughing.

One summer, I was assigned to a family in a nearby village to learn farming skills to get summer activity credits. Imagine my surprise to discover that Dai lived next door. My host told me that Dai had lost her father when she was a baby, and that her mother worked for a factory. All day she stood under the sun breaking bricks into little pieces. And when it rained, she worked from her home twining bamboo into crates.

I was such a city girl. Early in the summer, I twisted my ankle trying to work in the fields. I worried, "How will I earn my summer credits?" Just when I was about to give up, Dai's mom offered to teach me how to make bamboo crates. It was not easy. After many hours, I was still clumsy at it. I started feeling uncomfortable for keeping Dai's mother up way past her bedtime, but she was always patient.

"Don't rush," she said. "It takes time. There is plenty of laundry for me to wash while you are practicing."

The "sha-sha-sha" sounds of the wash started, and somehow, I couldn't concentrate. I raised my head and suddenly saw her as though **I** for the first time. Under the light of the moon, I saw a pair of deep eyes, full of light, and the wrinkles that years had marked on her face.

"Did Dai ever tell you about some of the mean kids in school?" I asked. "Did she tell you I was one of them?"

"Yes. She did."

"Then why do you help me—an almost stranger and a mean kid?"

"I told her that those mean children are just immature. They don't know anything about life. When Dai's father died, people in the village helped us out. And I know how much their **J** help meant to us. So now whenever I can help someone, I do. I help you because I don't like to see anyone give up. There aren't all that many next times."

She smiled. I nodded my head silently and smiled back.

I gained ten credits that summer, and I left the bamboo crate to her as a gift. When I returned to school, I never joined the mean kids again.

—Christy Ma
Seward Park High School
New York, New York

G Critical Thinking
Making Connections
Have students compare Ravi with Larry in "My Oedipus Complex" (p. 1082). [Possible responses: Both are self-centered and are hurt when events cause them to realize their insignificance. Larry is finally transformed by the realization that he is not his mother's only love. Ravi is inconsolable upon learning that he has been forgotten by his playmates.]

Student to Student

In this essay, the author, now living in New York City, flashes back to an incident that occurred in China that taught her the importance of kindness and respect for others who may seem different from oneself.

H Reading Skills and Strategies
Making Inferences
? What do you infer from the narrator's expression "we, the mean ones"? [Possible response: The narrator has already learned a moral lesson and disapproves of her past behavior and that of the group to which she belonged.]

I Critical Thinking
Drawing Conclusions
? What do you think the narrator sees "for the first time"? [Possible responses: She understands the hard life of the villagers, the goodness of Dai's mother, and her own small-mindedness in mocking Dai and her mother.]

J Reading Skills and Strategies
Finding the Main Idea
Tell in your own words the lessons Dai's mother teaches here. [Possible responses: Children should not be blamed for acts of meanness because they are too inexperienced to know better. Life is short; there will be fewer opportunities than we realize to be charitable.]

Connecting Across Texts

Connecting with "Games at Twilight"
Have students compare the behavior of the children in "Games at Twilight" with the behavior of "the mean ones" in "Lesson of the Bamboo Crates." [Possible response: The children in "Games at Twilight" are more self-centered than mean; they simply go on playing, forgetful of Ravi. The children in "Lesson of the Bamboo Crates" engage in mockery of a poor family because they have little experience of life and the hardships that others face.] Ask students to compare Ravi's realization with that of the narrator of "Lesson of the Bamboo Crates." [Possible response: Ravi comes face to face with a sense of his own unimportance to others; the narrator of "Lesson of the Bamboo Crates" comes face to face with an awareness of her own mean-spirited and narrow-minded behavior.]

Assessing Learning

Standardized Test Preparation
For practice with ACT and SAT for formats, see
- *Preparation for College Admission Exams,* p. 55

For practice in proofreading and editing, see
- *Daily Oral Grammar,* Transparency 39

Making Meanings

First Thoughts [Respond]

1. Many students will probably feel empathy for Ravi; they may recall similar childhood experiences.

Shaping Interpretations [Interpret]

2. Students may cite such words as *maniacal, bougainvillea, eucalyptus, phlegm-obstructed, hirsute*, and *lugubrious*. They may point to the tactile image of the insect crawling on Ravi or various images expressing the stifling heat. They may choose to illustrate Ravi in hiding or the children playing on without him.
3. Images include the dark, isolation in the shed, the waning light, and the funereal chant.
4. The other children have forgotten about Ravi and the earlier game.
5. They play a "funereal game." The chant, which talks about remembering the dead, mocks Ravi's futile hope for recognition.
6. Ravi is saddened by how quickly he has been forgotten; he gains a "terrible sense of his insignificance." Students may cite the final paragraph of the story.
7. Possible responses: The theme is a child's facing his insignificance and mortality. The associations of *twilight*, as well as the funereal game, support this theme. *Games* introduces associations of competition, struggle, rules of behavior, and "playing" at life.
8. In the shed, the psychological drama of the story takes place amidst a mood of somber struggle and isolation. Ravi braves the dark to win the game, which shows how much he wants to be recognized and thus heightens the tension.

Extending the Text [Evaluate]

9. Some students will say the children in the story are more realistic, citing the familiar disagreements and behavior. Others may point to realistic television shows that follow young people through difficult social and psychological struggles.

Making Meanings

First Thoughts

1. How much empathy for Ravi did you feel at the end of the story? Did his experience remind you of any of your childhood experiences?

Reading Check

Create a story map that outlines the important events in the story in **chronological order**—the order in which they happen.

Shaping Interpretations

2. What specific **words** and **images** in this story are most vivid to you? (Look over your reading notes.) If you had to draw one picture to illustrate the story, what would you draw?
3. Which **images** suggest loss and death to you? How do these images make you feel?
4. Why is everyone so surprised to see Ravi when he finally comes out of his hiding place?
5. What kind of game are the children playing at twilight?
6. What has Ravi discovered by the end of the story? Find a passage of the text that supports your answer.
7. How would you state the **theme** of this story—what revelation about human life does it make to you? As you think about the theme, think also about how the story's **title** reinforces its theme. (Think of the layers of meanings you can give to the word *games*.) Be sure to compare your statements of theme in class: Are there differences?
8. How do Ravi's experiences in the shed contribute to the **mood** of the story?

Extending the Text

9. Are the children in this story (and childhood itself) more realistically portrayed than the children in television situation comedies, or less so? Give examples to support your view.

Choices: Building Your Portfolio

Writer's Notebook

1. Collecting Ideas for a Problem-Solution Essay

Suppose you were designing a course of study in literature for seniors in high school. What problems do you see in the ways such courses are presently taught? What solutions would you propose for those problems? Take notes now on your thoughts on these issues. Base your ideas in part on your experience with the selections in this textbook. One thing you might consider is the kinds of literature you think seniors should be reading and the themes you think they should focus on. Save your notes for possible use in the Writer's Workshop on page 1179.

Comparing and Contrasting Stories

2. Comparing Childhoods

Here are three unusual stories about childhood: "The Doll's House" (page 1062), "My Oedipus Complex" (page 1082), and "Games at Twilight." In an essay, compare and contrast two of these stories. Focus on the **discoveries** made by the children in each story, the **theme** of each story, and the writer's **tone.** Remember that in a comparison-and-contrast essay, you are looking for similarities and differences.

Creative Writing

3. The Cost of Cruelty

The student essay on page 1115 deals with the theme "Ourselves Among Others." Write a short narrative of your own about a person (adult or child) who comes face-to-face with his or her own cruelty or unkindness.

Reading Check

Story maps should include the children going outside to play, the children choosing who is It, Ravi hiding behind the garage and in the storage shed, Ravi heading for the den, the children's responses to Ravi, and Ravi's reaction.

Grading Timesaver

Rubrics for each Choices assignment appear on p. 211 in the *Portfolio Management System.*

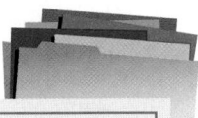

Seamus Heaney

(1939–)

Portrait of Seamus Heaney (1973) by Edward McGuire. Oil on canvas (56″ × 44″).

Reproduced with the kind permission of the Trustees of the Ulster Museum, Belfast.

Seamus Heaney was born to Roman Catholic parents in largely Protestant Northern Ireland. His boyhood on a farm in County Derry contributed profoundly to his identity as a poet. But Heaney never promoted himself as a rustic or regarded his work as an expression of regionalism. He earned his education as a scholarship student, first at a Catholic preparatory school and then at Queen's University in Belfast where, still in his midtwenties, he was appointed lecturer in English.

Instead of leading him away from his roots in Irish soil, Heaney's studies—particularly those having to do with the history and psychology of myth—opened for him a way of seeing anew not only the misty grandeur of his native landscape, but also the figures in it who, unknowingly, unite the past with the present. Heaney is an acute observer of rural life and of life lived on the industrial margins of cities, and he deals with both without romanticizing them.

Regarded by Robert Lowell as "the best Irish poet since William Butler Yeats," Heaney now occupies the chair at Harvard left vacant by Lowell's death in 1977. In 1995, commended for his works "of lyrical beauty and ethical depth, which exalt everyday miracles and the living past," Heaney was awarded the Nobel Prize in literature. He divides his time between Cambridge, Massachusetts, and a home in the republic of Ireland.

Before You Read

DIGGING
THE GRAUBALLE MAN

Make the Connection

Out of the Earth

Both of these poems, in their different ways, are about *digging.*

In 1969, Heaney read *The Bog People* by the archaeologist P. V. Glob, about the discovery in Denmark of the remarkably well-preserved bodies of several Iron Age men. One of those bog men was dug up near the village of Grauballe in Jutland in 1952. Heaney was particularly struck by the amazing photographs of those two-thousand-year-old humans who had been preserved in the boggy earth by a chemical process that resembles tanning. Here Heaney found a rich symbol of the earth's power to preserve the past. But Grauballe man, whose throat was slit in a ritual sacrifice, was also a reminder of the darker continuities in human experience—and of the earth's role as a tomb as well as a cradle.

Quickwrite

What do you associate with the word *digging?* Take a few minutes to make a list of your associations.

Elements of Literature

Metaphors and Similes

Up until the last line of "Digging," you may not realize that the poem contains an **extended metaphor,** a comparison between the father's work and the poet's that resonates throughout the poem.

In "The Grauballe Man," Heaney also uses a series of comparisons (**similes** and **metaphors**) to describe the extraordinary appearance of the bog man and the meaning the magnificent body has for the poet.

go.hrw.com
LEO 12-14

OBJECTIVES

Digging/The Grauballe Man

1. Read and interpret the poems
2. Identify and interpret simile, metaphor, and extended metaphor
3. Express understanding through critical and creative writing

SKILLS

Literary

- Identify and interpret simile, metaphor, and extended metaphor

Writing

- Collect ideas for a problem-solution essay
- Write a poem

Planning

- **Traditional Schedule**
  Lesson Plans Including Strategies for English-Language Learners
- **One-Stop Planner**
  CD-ROM with Test Generator

BROWSING IN THE FILES

About the Author. Much of Heaney's poetry reflects his rural Ulster upbringing and the extended sectarian conflict in Northern Ireland. Heaney analyzes the internecine violence in unique terms, protesting the unwillingness of both sides to speak out freely. As the speaker in "Digging" asserts, Heaney feels that through his writing, generations of his rural ancestors find a voice.

Resources: Print and Media

Reading

- *Graphic Organizers for Active Reading,* p. 111
- *Audio CD Library*
  Disc 20, Tracks 6, 7

Writing and Language

- *Daily Oral Grammar*
  Transparency 40

Assessment

- *Formal Assessment,* p. 220
- *Portfolio Management System,* p. 212
- *Test Generator (One-Stop Planner CD-ROM)*

Internet

- go.hrw.com (keyword: LE0 12-14)

Summary ■■

The speaker, clasping a pen, looks through a window at his father, who is digging in the garden with a spade. The speaker remembers his father's skill at digging potatoes and his grandfather's at cutting turf. He admits that he will never possess their talents for working the land but does acknowledge his own tool and talents. Metaphorically, he will dig in his imagination and memory and literally produce poetry with his pen.

Ⓐ Elements of Literature

Metaphor

The title establishes the metaphor that will extend to the end of the poem.

Ⓑ Elements of Literature

Simile

? Why do you think the speaker compares his pen to a gun? [Possible responses: His pen is his most powerful weapon. His pen gives him a sense of security.]

Ⓒ Elements of Literature

Setting

Help students detect the shifts from present to past. In l. 6 the speaker's father digs outside his window. In l. 7 the speaker's imagination moves back twenty years earlier, and he "sees" his father digging potatoes on the family farm. "Drills" here are furrows in which seeds are planted.

Ⓓ Reading Skills and Strategies

Finding the Main Idea

? What kind of experiences from his childhood does the speaker recall, especially in ll. 25–27? [Possible responses: vivid sensory experiences; acts of hard labor.]

Ⓔ Reading Skills and Strategies

Making Inferences

? Does the speaker feel alienated from his forebears? [Possible response: He is separated from them in time, but he feels united to them through blood, memory, and land.]

Ⓕ Elements of Literature

Extended Metaphor

? How can the speaker dig with a pen? [Possible responses: He can dig into his memory or the collective memory of his family or culture. He can dig into the minds and hearts of people, creating poems that illuminate human experience.]

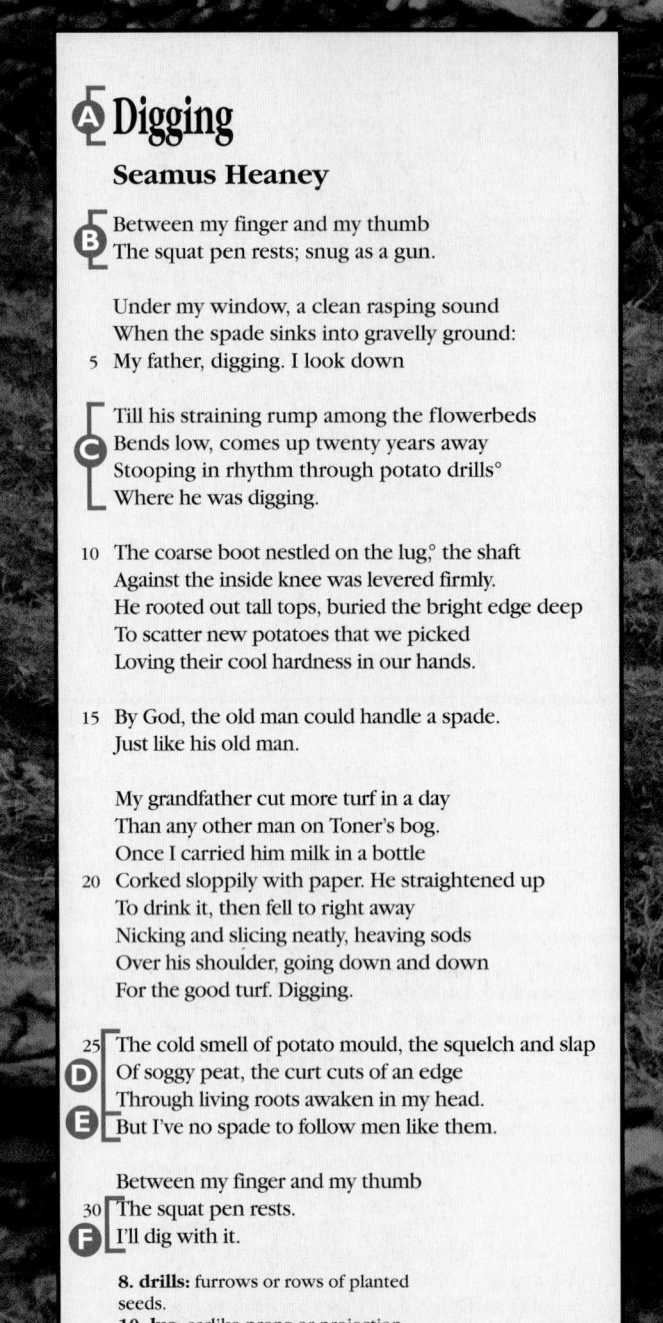

Ⓐ Digging

Seamus Heaney

Ⓑ Between my finger and my thumb
The squat pen rests; snug as a gun.

Under my window, a clean rasping sound
When the spade sinks into gravelly ground:
My father, digging. I look down

Ⓒ Till his straining rump among the flowerbeds
Bends low, comes up twenty years away
Stooping in rhythm through potato drills°
Where he was digging.

The coarse boot nestled on the lug,° the shaft
Against the inside knee was levered firmly.
He rooted out tall tops, buried the bright edge deep
To scatter new potatoes that we picked
Loving their cool hardness in our hands.

By God, the old man could handle a spade.
Just like his old man.

My grandfather cut more turf in a day
Than any other man on Toner's bog.
Once I carried him milk in a bottle
Corked sloppily with paper. He straightened up
To drink it, then fell to right away
Nicking and slicing neatly, heaving sods
Over his shoulder, going down and down
For the good turf. Digging.

Ⓓ The cold smell of potato mould, the squelch and slap
Of soggy peat, the curt cuts of an edge
Through living roots awaken in my head.
Ⓔ But I've no spade to follow men like them.

Between my finger and my thumb
Ⓕ The squat pen rests.
I'll dig with it.

8. drills: furrows or rows of planted seeds.
10. lug: earlike prong or projection by which a spade is supported.

Reaching All Students

Struggling Readers

Students may benefit from a brief discussion of how the tools or technology of people's work plays a major role in establishing their identities and self-esteem. Ask students to name some objects associated with a particular line of work or profession (such as a truck, basketball, telephone, camera, or computer) and tell how these objects (like Heaney's pen) can define a way of life, establish values, and confer meaning and satisfaction.

English Language Learners

Encourage students to read the poem aloud, paying special attention to the hard, rough sounds of words like *gravelly, lug, curt,* and *cuts.* Suggest to them that these sounds evoke the hard and violent physical labor that Heaney is describing.

The Grauballe Man

Seamus Heaney

As if he had been poured
in tar, he lies
on a pillow of turf
and seems to weep

the black river of himself.
The grain of his wrists
is like bog oak,
the ball of his heel

like a basalt° egg.
His instep has shrunk
cold as a swan's foot
or a wet swamp root.

His hips are the ridge
and purse of a mussel,
his spine an eel arrested
under a glisten of mud.

The head lifts,
the chin is a visor
raised above the vent
of his slashed throat

that has tanned and toughened.
The cured wound
opens inwards to a dark
elderberry place.

Who will say "corpse"
to his vivid cast?
Who will say "body"
to his opaque repose?

And his rusted hair,
a mat unlikely
as a fetus's.
I first saw his twisted face

in a photograph,
a head and shoulder
out of the peat,
bruised like a forceps baby,

but now he lies
perfected in my memory,
down to the red horn
of his nails,

hung in the scales
with beauty and atrocity:
with the Dying Gaul°
too strictly compassed

on his shield,
with the actual weight
of each hooded victim,
slashed and dumped.

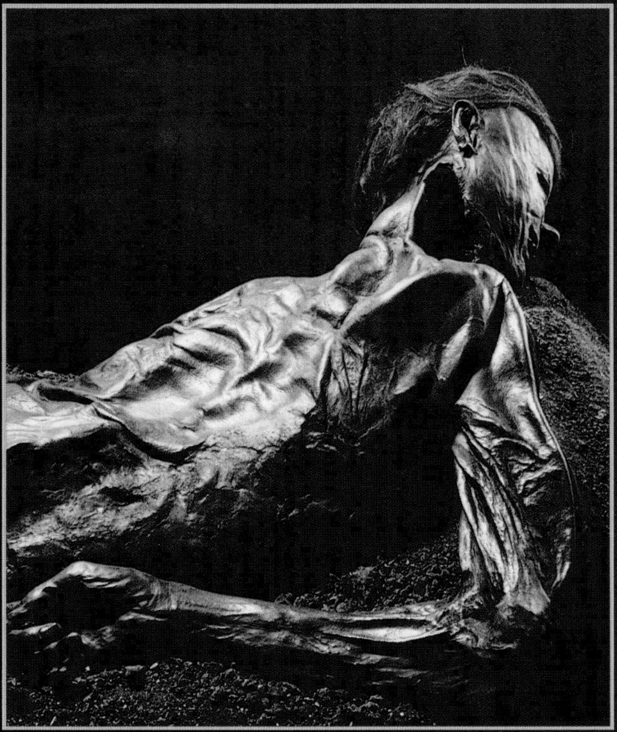

9. basalt: dark volcanic rock.
43. Dying Gaul: famous third-century B.C. statue of an Iron Age Celtic warrior dying on his shield.

Summary ■■

The speaker describes the preserved remains of a 2,000-year-old man found in a bog in Jutland, Denmark. He compares the dark body to a black river, a bog oak, volcanic rock, and a wet root, as well as to a swan, a mussel, and an eel. He notes that the throat was slashed. So vivid is the dead man's humanity, the speaker dares anyone to call him a "body" or a "corpse." To the speaker, the man, first seen in a photograph, is both an object of beauty and an atrocity. Although he is reminded of the beautiful, classical statue of the *Dying Gaul*, he is also horrified by the realization that the bog man was a victim of ritual sacrifice.

Ⓐ Elements of Literature

Metaphor

? Paraphrase "the black river of himself" for students as "his body is a black river." What does the metaphor suggest about the preserved body? [Possible responses: It suggests that the body is damp and dark, with grooves like waves, and that it seems a part of nature.]

Ⓑ Elements of Literature

Simile

? What is the body compared to in ll. 6–12? [an oak tree; basalt; a swan's foot; a swamp root] **What do all these comparisons have in common?** [They are all dark, wet, hard, or cold phenomena of nature.]

Ⓒ Reading Skills and Strategies

Responding to the Text

? The speaker dares the reader to call this a "corpse" or a "body." What would you call it? [Possible responses: a bog man; an artifact; a statue made by nature; a human being.]

Ⓓ Reading Skills and Strategies

Drawing Conclusions

? Against what does the speaker "weigh" the Grauballe Man? [Possible response: an image of beauty (the *Dying Gaul*) and an image of atrocity (bodies of people killed in sacrifices).] **What conclusion do you think he comes to?** [Possible response: The Grauballe Man has a horrible beauty, but he is still a slaughtered victim, bringing to mind a dark side of human behavior.]

Using Students' Strengths

Naturalist Learners

Encourage interested learners to research and report on the chemical process by which a human body could be preserved in a bog. Suggest that they pay particular attention to the properties of bog water. Have them create a display with diagrams and graphics to explain the process of preservation. Students may want to contrast the process responsible for preserving the bog man with the mummification process used in ancient Egypt.

Making the Connections

Connecting with the Theme: "Ourselves Among Others"

Ask students to discuss what archaeological finds like the Grauballe Man contribute to an overall picture of what it means to be a human being. Does Heaney's poem enlarge the everyday definition of "others"? What are the moral implications, for Heaney, of the discovery of the bog man? [Possible response: The poem reminds us that we have a relationship to "others" long dead—not only to victims but also to their slayers.]

Making Meanings

Digging/The Grauballe Man

First Thoughts [Respond]

1. For "Digging," students may mention the "rasping" of the spade, the smell of "potato mould," or the "straining rump" of a man digging. For "The Grauballe Man," they may cite the body "poured/in tar" or the "slashed throat."

Shaping Interpretations [Interpret]

2. The speaker sees his father stooping to dig with a spade.
3. The phrase signals the speaker's shift from the present moment to his memories. Students may have expected *feet, yards,* or *rows.*
4. He compares his pen to a gun and a spade. The gun comparison suggests the power of the written word. The pen-spade connects the speaker's heritage to his present occupation.
5. The speaker compares his work as a writer to that of his ancestors. As they dug the earth for food and warmth, he intends to dig into human experience for spiritual and emotional sustenance.
6. Similes: poured in tar; bog oak; a basalt egg; a swan's foot; a swamp root; a fetus; a baby. Metaphors: a black river; a mussel; an eel; a visor; a vent; an elderberry; rust; a mat; red horn. Students may respond that these comparisons suggest a close physical kinship between the human body and elemental nature.
7. Possible response: The man has ceased to appear human; he has been reincorporated into the earth and seems a part of a natural process.
8. The images reinforce the unity between the human and the animal, vegetable, and mineral worlds.
9. The Grauballe Man might symbolize the results of violent human impulses, a reminder that humans who are capable of making a beautiful statue are also capable of slitting a man's throat.

Connecting with the Text [Synthesize]

10. Students might mention delving into one's own past or that of one's culture, or uncovering lost or hidden artifacts. Both poems include "digging": writing as a way of searching for buried truths; archaeology as a means of uncovering truths about human history.

Making Meanings

Digging
The Grauballe Man

First Thoughts

1. What word or passage from each poem most vividly communicates to you what the speaker sees, hears, smells, or feels?

Shaping Interpretations

2. Describe what the speaker of "Digging" sees from his window.
3. Why do you think the father comes up "twenty *years*" away in line 7 of "Digging"? (What word did you expect to find there?)
4. What different things does the speaker compare his pen to in "Digging"? What significance can you find in these comparisons, particularly the one in the last stanza?
5. Explain the **extended metaphor** in "Digging." What kind of digging does the speaker intend to do?
6. List all the **similes** and **metaphors** the speaker uses to describe the Grauballe man. How do some of these comparisons make you feel about the man and his dark fate?
7. Why do you think Heaney dares anyone to call the man a "corpse" or "body" (lines 25–28)?
8. Why do you think the speaker uses **images** from the animal, vegetable, and mineral worlds in describing the Grauballe man?
9. Think about what the Grauballe man might **symbolize** for Heaney. What connections and contradictions in human experience might he represent? (Pay attention especially to lines 41–42.)

Connecting with the Text

10. What associations did you make with the word *digging*? How does the activity of digging link both these poems?

Choices: Building Your Portfolio

Writer's Notebook

1. Collecting Ideas for a Problem-Solution Essay

When the Grauballe man was discovered in Denmark, some of the local people were skeptical of the scientists' extraordinary claim that he was nearly two thousand years old. The locals did not know whether to trust the outside "experts" and feared they were the victims of a hoax. They preferred a more homely and less alarming explanation: The body was that of a local man named Red Christian, who, according to witnesses still living at the time, had gotten drunk and drowned in a bog seventy years earlier. With a small group, discuss other instances of mistrust or misunderstanding of scientists by ordinary people. What are some possible solutions to this problem? Take notes on your discussion, and save them for the Writer's Workshop on page 1179.

Creative Writing

2. Do Your Own Digging

Seamus Heaney once wrote that in "Digging" he truly found his own voice: "Finding a voice means that you can get your own feeling into your own words and that your words have the feel of you about them." Beginning with the last three lines of Heaney's poem "Digging," write your own poem, being careful to do your "digging" with words that suit your own voice. You might want to begin by recalling something about your parents, grandparents, or other older family members.

Assessing Learning

Standardized Test Preparation

For practice in proofreading and editing, see

- *Daily Oral Grammar,* Transparency 40

Grading Timesaver

Rubrics for each Choices assignment appear on p. 212 in the *Portfolio Management System.*

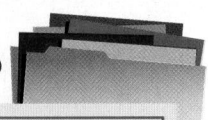

Collection 15

Clashes of Culture

Theme

Cultural Crossroads *In the late twentieth century, mobility and technology force people of different cultures, ages, genders, and religions to confront one another. The literature of the period reflects this diversity of voices and warns against the inevitable conflict that arises when one group tries to impose its will on another.*

Reading the Anthology

Reaching Struggling Readers

The *Reading Skills and Strategies: Reaching Struggling Readers* binder provides materials coordinated with the Pupil's Edition (see the Collection Planner, p. T1120B) to help students who have difficulty reading and comprehending text or students who are reluctant readers. The binder for twelfth grade is organized around ten individual skill areas and offers the following options:

- **MiniRead** MiniReads are short, easy texts that give students a chance to practice a particular skill and strategy before reading selections in the Pupil's Edition. Each MiniRead Skill Lesson can be taught independently or used in conjunction with a Selection Skill Lesson.
- **Selection Skill Lessons** Selection Skill Lessons allow students to apply skills introduced in the MiniReads. Each Selection Skill Lesson provides reading instruction and practice specific to a particular piece of literature in the Pupil's Edition.

Reading Beyond the Anthology

Read On

At the end of the Twentieth Century collections, the grade twelve book includes an annotated bibliography of books suitable for extended reading. The suggested books are related to works in these collections by theme, by author, or by subject. To preview the Read On for this period, please turn to p. T1174.

HRW Library

The *HRW Library* offers novels, plays, and short-story collections for extended reading. Each major work in the *Library* includes thematically related Connections. The Connections are magazine articles, poems, or other pieces of literature. Each book in the *HRW Library* is also accompanied by a Study Guide that provides teaching suggestions and worksheets. The title shown here will work well to extend the theme of Collection 15.

GREAT BRITISH STORIES

This anthology of classic works of British fiction includes stories by Kipling, Stevenson, Conrad, and other major writers. Many of these famous stories illustrate the conflicts between cultures that grew out of British imperialism.

Collection 15 Clashes of Culture

Resources for this Collection

Note: All resources for this collection are available for preview on the *One-Stop Planner CD-ROM 2 with Test Generator.* All worksheets and blackline masters may be printed from the CD-ROM.

Internet Resources
go.hrw.com LE0 12-15

Selection or Feature	Reading and Literary Skills	Vocabulary, Language, and Grammar
Shakespeare's Sister *from* **A Room of One's Own** (p. 1123) Virginia Woolf	• *Reading Skills and Strategies: Reaching Struggling Readers* • MiniRead Skill Lesson, p. 87 • Selection Skill Lesson, p. 94 • *Graphic Organizers for Active Reading,* Worksheet p. 112	• *Words to Own,* Worksheet p. 34 • *Daily Oral Grammar,* Transparency 41
World Literature: Egypt The Cairo Rooftop *from* **Palace Walk** (p. 1132) Naguib Mahfouz	The World Literature feature offers students the opportunity to explore thematically linked literature from different world cultures. Structured activities called Finding Common Ground guide students' explorations of thematic connections between British and other world literature.	
Shooting an Elephant (p. 1138) George Orwell	• *Reading Skills and Strategies: Reaching Struggling Readers* • MiniRead Skill Lesson, p. 98 • Selection Skill Lesson, p. 105 • *Graphic Organizers for Active Reading,* Worksheet p. 113	• *Words to Own,* Worksheet p. 35 • *Grammar and Language Links:* Revising Fused and Comma Splices, Worksheet p. 71 • *Daily Oral Grammar,* Transparency 42
No Witchcraft for Sale (p. 1147) Doris Lessing	• *Graphic Organizers for Active Reading,* Worksheet p. 114 • *Literary Elements:* Transparency 27 Worksheet p. 82	• *Words to Own,* Worksheet p. 36 • *Grammar and Language Links:* Semicolons and Colons, Worksheet p. 73 • *Daily Oral Grammar,* Transparency 43
Once Upon a Time (p. 1155) Nadine Gordimer	• *Graphic Organizers for Active Reading,* Worksheet p. 115	• *Words to Own,* Worksheet p. 37 • *Daily Oral Grammar,* Transparency 44
The Virgins (p. 1162) Derek Walcott	• *Graphic Organizers for Active Reading,* Worksheet p. 116	
Marriage Is a Private Affair (p. 1164) Chinua Achebe **Primary Sources: Diversity is Reality** (p. 1169) Chinua Achebe **Connections: Going Home** (p. 1169) Maurice Kenny	• *Graphic Organizers for Active Reading,* Worksheet p. 117	• *Words to Own,* Worksheet p. 38 • *Grammar and Language Links:* Revision Worksheet, p. 75 • *Daily Oral Grammar,* Transparency 45
Telephone Conversation (p. 1171) Wole Soyinka	• *Graphic Organizers for Active Reading,* Worksheet p. 118	
The English Language: English Today and Tomorrow (p. 1175) John Algeo		
Writer's Workshop: Problem-Solution Essay (p. 1179)		
Language Workshop: Relationships Between Ideas (p. 1185)		• *Workshop Resources,* p. 61 • *Language Workshop CD-ROM,* Subordinate Clauses
Learning for Life: Predicting Future Developments (p. 1187)		

Other Resources for this Collection

- *Cross-Curricular Activities,* p. 12
- *Portfolio Management System,* Introduction to Portfolio Assessment, p. 1
- *Formal Assessment:* Literary Period Test, p. 237; Literary Elements Test, p. 235
- *Test Generator,* Collection Test (CD-ROM)

Writing	Listening and Speaking Viewing and Representing	Assessment
• *Portfolio Management System,* Rubrics for Choices, p. 213	• *Audio CD Library,* Disc 21, Track 2 (Audio CD) • *Viewing and Representing:* Fine Art Transparency 19 (Transparency) Worksheet p. 76 • *Portfolio Management System,* Rubrics for Choices, p. 213	• *Formal Assessment,* Selection Test, p. 221 • *Test Generator (One-Stop Planner CD-ROM)* (CD-ROM) • *Preparation for College Admission Exams,* p. 57
	• *Audio CD Library,* Disc 21, Track 3 (Audio CD)	
• *Portfolio Management System,* Rubrics for Choices, p. 214	• *Audio CD Library,* Disc 21, Track 4 (Audio CD) • *Viewing and Representing:* Fine Art Transparency 20 (Transparency) Worksheet p. 80 • *Portfolio Management System,* Rubrics for Choices, p. 214	• *Formal Assessment,* Selection Test, p. 223 • *Test Generator (One-Stop Planner CD-ROM)* (CD-ROM) • *Preparation for College Admission Exams,* p. 59
• *Portfolio Management System,* Rubrics for Choices, p. 215	• *Portfolio Management System,* Rubrics for Choices, p. 215	• *Formal Assessment,* Selection Test, p. 225 • *Test Generator (One-Stop Planner CD-ROM)* (CD-ROM)
• *Portfolio Management System,* Rubrics for Choices, p. 217	• *Audio CD Library,* Disc 22, Track 2 (Audio CD) • *Portfolio Management System,* Rubrics for Choices, p. 217	• *Formal Assessment,* Selection Test, p. 227 • *Test Generator (One-Stop Planner CD-ROM)* (CD-ROM)
• *Portfolio Management System,* Rubrics for Choices, p. 218	• *Audio CD Library,* Disc 22, Track 3 (Audio CD) • *Portfolio Management System,* Rubrics for Choices, p. 218	• *Formal Assessment,* Selection Test, p. 229 • *Test Generator (One-Stop Planner CD-ROM)* (CD-ROM)
• *Portfolio Management System,* Rubrics for Choices, p. 219	• *Audio CD Library,* Disc 22, Track 4 (Audio CD) • *Portfolio Management System,* Rubrics for Choices, p. 219	• *Formal Assessment,* Selection Test, p. 230 • *Test Generator (One-Stop Planner CD-ROM)* (CD-ROM)
• *Portfolio Management System,* Rubrics for Choices, p. 221	• *Audio CD Library,* Disc 22, Track 5 (Audio CD) • *Portfolio Management System,* Rubrics for Choices, p. 221	• *Formal Assessment,* Selection Test, p. 232 • *Test Generator (One-Stop Planner CD-ROM)* (CD-ROM)
		• *Formal Assessment,* The English Language Test, p. 233

• *Workshop Resources,* p. 41
• *Writer's Workshop 2 CD-ROM,* Controversial Issues (CD-ROM)
	• *Viewing and Representing,* HRW Multimedia Presentation Maker	• *Portfolio Management System*
		  • Prewriting, p. 222
		  • Peer Editing, p. 223
		  • Assessment Rubric, p. 224

		• *Portfolio Management System,* Rubrics, p. 225

Transparency   CD-ROM   Video   Audio CD

Collection 15 Clashes of Culture

Skills Focus

Selection or Feature	Reading Skills and Strategies	Elements of Literature and Language	Writing	Listening and Speaking	Viewing and Representing
Shakespeare's Sister *from* **A Room of One's Own** (p. 1123) Virginia Woolf	Evaluate a Persuasive Message, pp. 1123, 1130 Main Idea, pp. 1123, 1130 Generalization, p. 1130	Biography, p. 1130 Irony, p. 1130 Tone, p. 1130	Identify Issues Suited to Problem-Solution Essays, p. 1130 Write an Essay Evaluating an Argument, p. 1130 Rewrite a Story to Achieve a Happy Ending, p. 1130 Write a Biographical Sketch, p. 1130		
World Literature: Egypt The Cairo Rooftop (p. 1132) Naguib Mahfouz	The World Literature feature offers students the opportunity to explore thematically linked literature from different world cultures. Structured activities called Finding Common Ground are provided in the Pupil's Edition to guide students' explorations of these thematic connections between British and other world literature.				
Shooting an Elephant George Orwell (p. 1138)		Irony, pp. 1138, 1143 Verbal Irony, p. 1138 Situational Irony, p. 1138	Identify Peer-Pressure Experiences, p. 1144 Write an Essay Explaining a Response, p. 1144 Write an Essay Interpreting a Symbol, p. 1144		Create a Storyboard for a Film Adaptation of "Shooting an Elephant," p. 1144
Reading Skills and Strategies: Analyzing Word Analogies (p. 1144)	Analogy, p. 1144 Types of Analogies, p. 1144				
No Witchcraft for Sale (p. 1147) Doris Lessing		Theme, p. 1147 Plot, p. 1152	Freewrite on Cultural Differences, p. 1153 Write an Essay Analyzing a Conflict, p. 1153 Write an Essay Analyzing Point of View, p. 1153 Write an Essay Comparing Texts, p. 1153	Research and Present an Oral Report on Folk Medicine, p. 1153	
Once Upon a Time (p. 1155) Nadine Gordimer	Outline, p. 1160	Parody, pp. 1155, 1160 Tone, p. 1160 Symbol, p. 1160 Moral, p. 1160	Write an Essay Comparing Texts, p. 1160 Write a Fairy Tale About a Clash of Cultures, p. 1160	Research, Write, and Present an Oral Report, p. 1160	Use a Graphic Organizer to Collect Ideas, p. 1160
The Virgins (p. 1162) Derek Walcott		Irony, p. 1163 Image, p. 1163	Investigate Causes and Effects, p. 1163 Write an Essay Supporting a Thesis, p. 1163 Write a Lyric with a Defined Speaker, p. 1163	Stage a Panel Discussion on "the American Dream," p. 1163	
Marriage Is a Private Affair (p.1164) Chinua Achebe		Irony, p. 1170 Conflict, p. 1170 Character, p. 1170 Symbol, p. 1170 Theme, p. 1170 Point of View, p. 1170	Develop a List of Intergenerational Problems and Their Causes, p. 1170 Write an Essay Interpreting an Ending, p. 1170 Write a Sequel, p. 1170	Organize a Debate, p. 1170	
Telephone Conversation (p. 1171) Wole Soyinka		Dialogue, pp. 1171, 1173 Theme, p. 1173 Character, p. 1173 Image, p. 1173 Irony, p. 1173	Write an Essay Analyzing a Character, p. 1173	Discuss Solutions to a Problem, p. 1173 Present an Oral Report on Housing Laws, p. 1173	
The English Language: English Today and Tomorrow (p. 1175) John Algeo	Word Origins, p. 1178 Etymologies, p. 1178 Use a Dictionary, p. 1178 Use Varied Sources of Information, p. 1178	Loanwords, p. 1175 Compounds, p. 1176 Affixed Forms, p. 1176 Shortenings and Back-Formations, p. 1176 Blends, p. 1177 Shifted Words, p. 1177			
Writer's Workshop: Problem-Solution Essay (p. 1179)			Write a Problem-Solution Essay, pp. 1179–84		
Language Workshop: Relationships Between Ideas (p. 1185)		Subordinating Conjunctions, p. 1185	Revise Sentences to Make Relationships Clearer, p. 1185		
Reading for Life: Reading a Business Memorandum or Electronic Mail (p. 1186)	Memorandum, p. 1186		Write a Memorandum, p. 1186		
Learning for Life: Future Developments (p. 1187)			Write a Futuristic Short Story, p. 1187	Plan a Talk Show, p. 1187	Design a Triptych, p. 1187

Collection 15

CLASHES OF CULTURE

Woolf
Mahfouz
Orwell
Lessing
Gordimer
Walcott
Achebe
Soyinka

As the traveler who has once been from home is wiser than he who has never left his own doorstep, so a knowledge of one other culture should sharpen our ability to scrutinize more steadily, to appreciate more lovingly, our own.

—Margaret Mead, *from Coming of Age in Samoa* (American, 1901–1978)

OBJECTIVES

1. Read literature of the twentieth century on the theme of "Clashes of Culture"
2. Interpret literary elements
3. Apply a variety of reading strategies, with special emphasis on analyzing word analogies
4. Respond to the literature in a variety of modes
5. Learn and use new words
6. Explore processes by which new words enter the English language
7. Plan, draft, and revise a problem-solution essay
8. Write sentences that correctly show relationships between ideas
9. Demonstrate the ability to read a business memorandum and electronic mail
10. Predict future developments through a variety of projects

Responding to the Quotation

Margaret Mead was a social anthropologist who became famous for her studies of tribal societies. She traveled far from home many times, conducting research in New Guinea, Samoa, and elsewhere. Hers was a lifetime of scrutiny of other cultures, a lifetime of appreciation of diversity and commonality. Students may explore the quotation by thinking of ways in which knowledge of another culture has helped them to deepen their understanding of their own traditions.

WORK IN PROGRESS

Writing Focus: A Problem-Solution Essay

The following **Work in Progress** assignments build to a culminating **Writer's Workshop** at the end of this collection.

- Shakespeare's Sister — Discuss problem treated in essay (p. 1130)
- Shooting an Elephant — Discuss pressure to conform (p. 1144)
- No Witchcraft for Sale — Freewrite about clashes in culture (p. 1153)
- Once Upon a Time — Brainstorm causes of crime (p. 1160)
- The Virgins — Investigate changes on way of life (p. 1163)
- Marriage Is a Private Affair — Brainstorm causes of generational clashes (p. 1170)
- Telephone Conversation — Discuss housing rights (p. 1173)

Writer's Workshop: Persuasive Writing / A Problem-Solution Essay (p. 1179)

Objectives

1. Read and interpret the essay
2. Evaluate the writer's persuasive message
3. Express understanding through critical and creative writing
4. Learn and use new words

Skills

Reading

- Evaluate the writer's persuasive message

Writing

- Collect ideas for a problem-solution essay
- Evaluate an argument
- Rewrite a story
- Create a life story for an imaginary person

Vocabulary

- Learn and use new words

Viewing/Representing

- Relate a painting's theme and mood to the essay's content (ATE)

Planning

- **Traditional Schedule**
  Lesson Plans Including Strategies for English-Language Learners
- **One-Stop Planner**
  CD-ROM with Test Generator

Browsing in the Files

About the Author. Although she was very well read, Virginia Woolf never had a formal education like her father and brothers who attended Cambridge University. Woolf delivered part of *A Room of One's Own* as a speech at the two women's colleges, Newnham and Girton, of Cambridge. Ironically, she spoke about the need for women's education at a school she was not able to attend.

Virginia Woolf

(1882–1941)

Virginia Woolf was born in Victorian London to the scholar and literary critic Sir Leslie Stephen and his artistic wife, Julia. In her youth, Woolf enjoyed all the advantages of a financially comfortable and intellectually challenging environment. Too frail to attend school regularly, she was privately tutored and given the luxury of her father's extensive library.

Virginia Woolf.

After her father's death in 1904, Virginia, her sister, Vanessa, and their two brothers moved to the area of London known as Bloomsbury. Soon they and their friends began to meet in what came to be called the Bloomsbury Group, an intellectual circle whose other prominent members included the writer E. M. Forster, the artist Duncan Grant, and the economist John Maynard Keynes. One member of the group was Leonard Woolf, a journalist and economist, whom Virginia married in 1912.

An informal gathering with the highest cultural standards, the Bloomsbury Group helped provide the right environment for Virginia Woolf's sensitive, experimental fiction. Only after her death, when her diaries were published, was it clear how powerful the emotional effect of her friends' praise or criticism had been on her.

Woolf had been writing since she was fourteen and reviewing books since her early twenties, but it was not until she was thirty-three, in 1915, that her first novel, *The Voyage Out,* was published. The publication of *Jacob's Room* (1922) and *Mrs. Dalloway* (1925) established her position as one of the foremost writers of her time. With these novels—and with subsequent novels such as *To the Lighthouse* (1927) and *The Waves* (1931)—Woolf pursued an experimental vision that emphasized personal impressions over external events and focused on the experience of life as it was being lived.

Like James Joyce, Woolf used the technique of stream of consciousness, although her version of it was somewhat different from his. For example, while *Mrs. Dalloway,* like Joyce's *Ulysses,* takes place on a single day, it covers, through the thoughts of its characters, an entire lifetime. Woolf was a great admirer of Joyce's *Portrait of the Artist as a Young Man,* but she considered *Ulysses* an "illiterate, underbred book." Still, she worried that "what I am doing is probably being better done by Mr. Joyce."

Woolf also wrote a great many reviews and essays, a number of them focusing on women authors who she felt had been neglected or exploring female writers in general. In 1917, she and her husband established the Hogarth Press, which published many of the most important writers—both male and female—of the day.

Troubled by sudden deaths and mental illness in her family, Woolf throughout her life suffered from bouts of depression and anxiety. These deepened with the German bombing raids over England in World War II, and in March 1941, she took her own life.

go.hrw.com
LEO 12-15

Resources: Print and Media

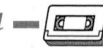

Reading

- *Reading Skills and Strategies*
  MiniRead Skill Lesson, p. 87
  Selection Skill Lesson, p. 94
- *Graphic Organizers for Active Reading,* p. 112
- *Words to Own,* p. 34
- *Audio CD Library,*
  Disc 21, Track 2

Writing and Language

- *Daily Oral Grammar*
  Transparency 41

Viewing and Representing

- *Viewing and Representing*
  Fine Art Transparency 19
  Fine Art Worksheet, p. 76

Assessment

- *Formal Assessment,* p. 221
- *Portfolio Management System,* p. 213
- *Preparation for College Admission Exams,* p. 57
- *Test Generator (One-Stop Planner CD-ROM)*

Internet

- go.hrw.com (keyword: LEO 12-15)

Before You Read

SHAKESPEARE'S SISTER

Make the Connection

Gender and Genius

Gender is perhaps the most basic difference between human beings in every culture. Beyond the biological differences are the social and cultural realities: the everyday concerns that men and women have and the work they are or are not able to accomplish. Virginia Woolf scrutinized those realities in her 1929 essay collection *A Room of One's Own,* from which the following selection is taken. Focusing on the creation of great literature, Woolf went back to Shakespeare's day and drew firm conclusions about the lack of equal opportunity for women through the ages.

Reading Skills and Strategies

Evaluating a Persuasive Message

After you read this essay, write Woolf's **main idea** across the top of a sheet of paper. Underneath it, list the arguments she makes to support her thesis. Next to each argument, indicate whether it appeals mainly to your intellect or to your emotions.

Background

A Room of One's Own is considered a pioneering work of feminist criticism, a field that did not even exist in 1929 but has since blossomed. Aims of feminist criticism include exposing sexist attitudes in or toward literature, reinterpreting earlier works from a feminist perspective, uncovering neglected women writers, and analyzing how gender affects a writer's subjects, themes, and even style. Some early feminists believed that "female language" is different from male language—richer in emotion, for example, and freer in patterns of meaning. Today, many feminists are exploring how cultural and economic forces help to shape the identities of women *and* men.

Virginia Woolf laid the foundation for much of this thinking. She was truly ahead of her time in insisting that social conditions can determine writing, that male literary language may not truly express women's experiences, and that the imagination can transcend gender.

Permission of Angelica Garnett.

Virginia Woolf in a Deck Chair (20th century) by Vanessa Bell.

Summary ■■

In this essay, Woolf imagines that William Shakespeare had a sister, Judith, who was as talented as her famous brother. Because Judith was a woman, Woolf theorizes, she would not have been allowed to develop her genius, and if she had, she probably would have been rejected by her family and society. Woolf guesses that Judith eventually would have committed suicide due to her frustrated ambition and unrecognized talent. Woolf also suggests that "Anonymous," the unknown author of so many works, was a woman. She describes the difficulties that a woman faced—and by implication still faces—in trying to succeed as a writer.

The artist who painted this portrait of Virginia Woolf was Woolf's sister, Vanessa Bell. Another painting by Bell is on p. 1178.

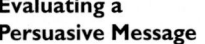

FROM THE EDITOR'S DESK

Famous as an innovative novelist who explored the stream-of-consciousness technique, Woolf is also regarded by scholars and critics as an influential and perceptive essayist, critic, and reviewer. She is known particularly for her writing on the role of women at a time when society was changing dramatically. We hope this provocative essay will make students think about other hidden geniuses whom the world has never known.

Preteaching Vocabulary

Words to Own

Ask pairs of students to read the definitions of each Word to Own at the bottom of the pages of the essay and then to create a sentence context for each word. Be sure that students understand that the words are defined in the footnotes as they are used in the context of the essay and that they have other meanings or connotations in different settings.

Then have students match each word with its opposite.

1. formidable	[e]	a. things that worsen
2. alleviations	[a]	b. domineering
3. notorious	[c]	c. famous in a positive way
4. servile	[b]	d. unfavorable
5. propitious	[d]	e. easy to handle or overcome

Resources

Viewing and Representing

Fine Art Transparency

A woman confined like a decorative object to a room is the subject of *Summer* by John Atkinson Grimshaw. See the *Viewing and Representing Transparencies and Worksheets:*

- Transparency 19
- Worksheet, p. 76

A Historical Connections

George Macaulay Trevelyan

Trevelyan's *The History of England* was the standard history book of Woolf's day.

B Reading Skills and Strategies

Evaluating a Persuasive Message

? Why do you think the author includes this seemingly irrelevant information about cats? [Possible response: Part of the job of the persuasive writer is to discredit contrary opinions. This foolish statement about cats discredits the gentleman's opinion about women and undermines him as an authority.]

C Humanities Connections

Ovid, Virgil, and Horace are among the most admired Latin poets. Latin was the language of learning in Europe for hundreds of years; studying it was an important part of a boy's education.

Shakespeare's Sister
from A Room of One's Own

Virginia Woolf

Here am I asking why women did not write poetry in the Elizabethan age, and I am not sure how they were educated; whether they were taught to write; whether they had sitting rooms to themselves; how many women had children before they were twenty-one; what, in short, they did from eight in the morning till eight at night. They had no money evidently; according to Professor Trevelyan[1] they were married whether they liked it or not before they were out of the nursery, at fifteen or sixteen very likely. It would have been extremely odd, even upon this showing, had one of them suddenly written the plays of Shakespeare, I concluded, and I thought of that old gentleman, who is dead now, but was a bishop, I think, who declared that it was impossible for any woman, past, present, or to come, to have the genius of Shakespeare. He wrote to the papers about it. He also told a lady who applied to him for information that cats do not as a matter of fact go to heaven, though they have, he added, souls of a sort. How much thinking those old gentlemen used to save one! How the borders of ignorance shrank back at their approach! Cats do not go to heaven. Women cannot write the plays of Shakespeare.

Be that as it may, I could not help thinking, as I looked at the works of Shakespeare on the shelf, that the bishop was right at least in this; it would have been impossible, completely and entirely, for any woman to have written the plays of Shakespeare in the age of Shakespeare. Let me imagine, since facts are so hard to come by, what would have happened had Shakespeare had a wonderfully gifted sister, called Judith, let us say. Shakespeare himself went, very probably—his mother was an heiress—to the grammar school, where he may have learnt Latin—Ovid, Virgil, and Horace—and the elements of grammar and logic. He was, it is well known, a wild boy who poached rabbits, perhaps shot a deer, and had, rather sooner than he should have done, to marry a woman in the neighborhood, who bore him a child rather quicker than was right. That escapade sent him to seek his fortune in London. He had, it seemed, a taste for the theater; he began by holding horses at the stage door. Very soon he got work in the theater, became a successful actor, and lived at the hub of the universe, meeting everybody, knowing everybody, practicing his art on the boards, exercising his wits in the streets, and even getting access to the palace of the queen. Meanwhile his extraordinarily gifted sister, let us suppose, remained at home. She was as adventurous, as imaginative, as agog to see the world as he was. But she was not sent to school. She had no chance of learning grammar and logic, let alone of reading Horace and Virgil. She picked up a book now and then, one of her brother's perhaps, and read a few pages. But then her parents came in and told her to mend the stockings or mind the stew and not moon about with books and papers. They would have spoken sharply but kindly, for they were substantial people who knew the conditions of life for a woman and loved their daughter—indeed, more likely than not she was the apple of her father's eye. Perhaps she scribbled some pages up in an apple loft on the sly, but was careful to hide them or set fire to them. Soon, however, before she was out of her teens, she was to be betrothed to the son of a neighboring wool stapler.[2] She cried out that marriage was hateful to her, and for that she was severely beaten by her father. Then he ceased to scold her. He begged her instead not to hurt him, not to shame him in this matter of her marriage. He would give her a chain of beads or a fine petticoat, he said; and there were tears in his eyes. How could she disobey him? How could she break his heart? The force of her own gift alone drove her to it. She made up a small parcel of her belongings, let herself down by a rope one summer's night, and took the road to London. She was not seventeen. The birds that sang in the hedge were not more musical than she was. She had the quickest fancy, a gift like her brother's, for the tune of words. Like him, she had

1. **Professor Trevelyan:** G. M. Trevelyan, author of *The History of England* (1926).

2. **wool stapler:** dealer in wool, a product sorted according to its fiber, or "staple."

Reaching All Students

Struggling Readers

Evaluating a Persuasive Message was introduced on p. 1123. For a lesson directly tied to this essay that teaches students to evaluate persuasive messages using a strategy called Save the Last Word for Me, see the *Reading Skills and Strategies* binder:

- MiniRead Skill Lessons, p. 87
- Selection Skill Lesson, p. 94

English Language Learners

Assist students to break up long paragraphs into shorter blocks of text. For example, read the first paragraph aloud to students and pause after the sentence that ends "at fifteen or sixteen very likely." Have students in pairs continue reading the rest of the essay, listening for natural breaks in the flow of the text.

Advanced Learners

Encourage students to investigate two famous feminist works that preceded *A Room of One's Own*—Mary Wollstonecraft's *A Vindication of the Rights of Woman* (1792) and John Stuart Mill's *The Subjection of Women* (1869). Ask students to compare and contrast the argument and tone of each work and present their findings in an oral report to the class.

a taste for the theater. She stood at the stage door; she wanted to act, she said. Men laughed in her face. The manager—a fat, loose-lipped man—guffawed. He bellowed something about poodles dancing and women acting—no woman, he said, could possibly be an actress. He hinted—you can imagine what. She could get no training in her craft. [D] Could she even seek her dinner in a tavern or roam the streets at midnight? Yet her genius was for fiction and lusted to feed abundantly upon the lives of men and women and the study of their ways. At last—for she was very young, oddly like Shakespeare the poet in her face, with the same gray eyes and rounded brows—at last Nick Greene the actor-manager took pity on her; she found herself with child by that gentleman and so—who shall measure the heat and violence of the poet's heart when caught and tangled in a woman's body?—killed herself one winter's night and lies buried at some crossroads where the omnibuses now stop outside the Elephant and Castle.[3]

That, more or less, is how the story would run, I think, if a woman in Shakespeare's day had had Shakespeare's genius. [E] But for my part, I agree with the deceased bishop, if such he was—it is unthinkable that any woman in Shakespeare's day should have had Shakespeare's genius. For genius like Shakespeare's is not born among laboring, uneducated, servile people. It was not born in England among the Saxons and the Britons. It is not born today among the working classes. How, then, could it have been born among women whose work began, according to Professor Trevelyan, almost before they were out of the nursery, who were forced to it by their parents and held to it by all the power of law and custom? Yet genius of a sort must have existed among women as it must have existed among the working classes. Now and again an Emily Brontë or a Robert Burns blazes out and proves its presence. [F] But certainly it never got itself onto paper. When, however, one reads of a witch being ducked, of a woman possessed by devils, of a wise woman selling herbs, or even of a very remarkable man who had a mother, then I think we are on the track of a lost novelist, a suppressed poet, of some mute and inglorious[4] Jane Austen, some Emily Brontë who dashed her brains out on the moor or mopped and mowed about the highways crazed with the torture that her gift had put her to. Indeed, I would venture to guess that Anon, who wrote so many poems without signing them, was often a woman. It was a woman Edward Fitzgerald,[5] I think, suggested who made the ballads and the folk songs, crooning them to her children, beguiling her spinning with them, or the length of the winter's night.

This may be true or it may be false—who can say?—but what is true in it, so it seemed to me, reviewing the story of Shakespeare's sister as I had made it, [G] is that any woman born with a great gift in the sixteenth century would certainly have gone crazed, shot herself, or ended her days in some lonely cottage outside the village, half witch, half wizard, feared and mocked at. For it needs little skill in psychology to be sure that a highly gifted girl who had tried to use her gift for poetry would have been so thwarted and hindered by other people, so tortured and pulled asunder by her own contrary instincts, that she must have lost her health and sanity to a certainty. No girl could have walked to London and stood at a stage door and forced her way into the presence of actor-managers without doing herself a violence and suffering an anguish which may have been irrational—for chastity may be a fetish invented by certain societies for unknown reasons—but were nonetheless inevitable. Chastity had then, it has even now, a religious importance in a woman's life, and has so wrapped itself round with nerves and instincts that to cut it free and bring it to the light of day demands courage of the rarest. To have lived a free life in London in the sixteenth century would have meant for a woman who was poet and playwright a nervous stress

3. **buried . . . Elephant and Castle:** Suicides were commonly buried at crossroads. The Elephant and Castle is a pub set at a busy crossroads in south London.

4. **mute and inglorious:** allusion to line 59 of "Elegy Written in a Country Churchyard" (page 601).

5. **Edward Fitzgerald** (1809–1883): English translator and poet.

Words to Own

servile (sur'vīl) *adj.:* like or characteristic of a slave; humbly submissive or yielding.

D Elements of Literature

Tone and Diction

? **What is the writer's attitude toward her subject in this passage?** [Possible response: ironic, perhaps contemptuous.] **What words and details support your interpretation of Woolf's tone?** [Possible responses: "Fat, loose-lipped," "guffawed," and "bellowed."]

E Reading Skills and Strategies

Evaluating a Persuasive Message

? **Do you agree that this is just how it would have been for Shakespeare's sister?** [Possible responses: Yes, the specific facts might have been somewhat different, but she surely would have met with similar obstacles. No, Woolf creates the story that best serves her own argument. She is presenting a lot of unprovable hypotheses as facts.]

F Literary Connections

Emily Brontë, a nineteenth-century English novelist and poet, wrote *Wuthering Heights.* Robert Burns, an eighteenth-century Scottish poet, was the son of a struggling tenant farmer. (See p. 640.)

G Reading Skills and Strategies

Evaluating a Persuasive Message

? **Here, Woolf admits that her story may be true or false. How does she use this statement to advance her own argument?** [Possible response: She implies that her argument is as good as any, since no one knows what Shakespeare's sister actually would have faced. By admitting the possible fallibility of her own argument, she preempts those who would challenge her to prove her thesis, and she preserves some of the emotional force of her hypothetical "life story."]

Getting Students Involved

Enrichment Activity

Speaking and Listening. *A Room of One's Own* was originally presented as a lecture to the women students of Cambridge. Ask small groups of students to practice reading the selection aloud in the manner in which they think Woolf may have presented it. Then have a member of each group choose a passage and present it to the class. Encourage students to dramatize their speeches with appropriate pauses, inflections, and gestures.

Skill Link

Analyzing Characteristics of Clear Text

Despite the fact that Woolf has few facts to go by concerning the life of a woman writer in Shakespeare's time, she backs up her argument by citing specific examples of how unfairly Elizabethan women were treated in general. Ask students to do the following:

1. Review the essay to find three examples of Woolf's use of historical instances in which women were treated unfairly. [For example, in the first paragraph she refers to a professor who wrote that in Shakespeare's time, women married very young and had little choice in the matter.]
2. Compare findings in a class discussion.
3. Point out and discuss passages in which other historical details could have been added to make the essay more complete.

Ⓐ Reading Skills and Strategies

Evaluating a Persuasive Message

? Is Woolf offering facts or opinions here? [She is offering facts since objective evidence supports the historical dearth of publications by women and the information about the women writers mentioned is verifiable.]

Ⓑ Literary Connections

In 1846, Charlotte Brontë and her two sisters published *Poems by Currer, Ellis, and Acton Bell.* George Eliot's Victorian novels, including *Middlemarch* and *The Mill on the Floss,* feature portrayals of strong, intelligent women. The novels of George Sand express strong feminist ideals. (See pp. 859–861.)

Ⓒ English Language Learners

Archaic Usage

Explain that this archaic usage refers to the days when people filled pens from ink wells and made corrections not by deleting or even erasing text but by covering mistakes with blots, or gobs, of ink. Once students understand this usage, they can appreciate how extraordinary is the claim that Shakespeare never changed a line.

Ⓓ Humanities Connections

Rousseau championed the educational importance of self-expression.

and dilemma which might well have killed her. Had she survived, whatever she had written would have been twisted and deformed, issuing from a strained and morbid imagination. And undoubtedly, I thought, looking at the shelf where there are no plays by women, her work would have gone unsigned. That refuge she would have sought certainly. It was the relic of the sense of chastity that dictated anonymity to women even so late as the nineteenth century. Currer Bell, George Eliot, George Sand,[6] all the victims of inner strife as their writings prove, sought ineffectively to veil themselves by using the name of a man. Thus they did homage to the convention, which if not implanted by the other sex was liberally encouraged by them (the chief glory of a woman is not to be talked of, said Pericles,[7] himself a much-talked-of man), that publicity in women is detestable. Anonymity runs in their blood. The desire to be veiled still possesses them. They are not even now as concerned about the health of their fame as men are, and, speaking generally, will pass a tombstone or a signpost without feeling an irresistible desire to cut their names on it, as Alf, Bert, or Chas. must do in obedience to their instinct, which murmurs if it sees a fine woman go by, or even a dog, *Ce chien est à moi.*[8] And, of course, it may not be a dog, I thought, remembering Parliament Square, the Sieges Allee,[9] and other avenues; it may be a piece of land or a man with curly black hair. It is one of the great advantages of being a woman that one can pass even a very fine negress without wishing to make an Englishwoman of her.

That woman, then, who was born with a gift of poetry in the sixteenth century, was an unhappy woman, a woman at strife against herself. All the conditions of her life, all her own instincts, were hostile to the state of mind which is needed to set free whatever is in the brain. But what is the state of mind that is most propitious to the act of creation, I asked. Can one come by any notion of the state that furthers and makes possible that strange activity? Here I opened the volume containing the Tragedies of Shakespeare. What was Shakespeare's state of mind, for instance, when he wrote *Lear* and *Antony and Cleopatra*? It was certainly the state of mind most favorable to poetry that there has ever existed. But Shakespeare himself said nothing about it. We only know casually and by chance that he "never blotted a line." Nothing indeed was ever said by the artist himself about his state of mind until the eighteenth century perhaps. Rousseau[10] perhaps began it. At any rate, by the nineteenth century self-consciousness had developed so far that it was the habit for men of letters to describe their minds in confessions and autobiographies. Their lives also were written, and their letters were printed after their deaths. Thus, though we do not know what Shakespeare went through when he wrote *Lear,* we do know what Carlyle went through when he wrote *The French Revolution;* what Flaubert went through when he wrote *Madame Bovary;* what Keats was going through when he tried to write poetry against the coming of death and the indifference of the world.

And one gathers from this enormous modern literature of confession and self-analysis that to write a work of genius is almost always a feat of prodigious difficulty. Everything is against the likelihood that it will come from the writer's mind whole and entire. Generally material circumstances are against it. Dogs will bark; people will interrupt; money must be made; health will break down. Further, accentuating all these difficulties and making them harder to bear is the world's notorious indifference. It does not ask people to

6. **Currer Bell, George Eliot, George Sand:** male pseudonyms for the female writers Charlotte Brontë, Mary Ann Evans, and Amantine-Aurore-Lucile Dupin.

7. **Pericles** (c. 495–429 B.C.): Athenian legislator and general.

8. ***Ce chien est à moi*** (sə shē·en′ ät ä mwä): French for "This dog is mine."

9. **Sieges Allee** (zē′gəs ä·lā′): busy thoroughfare in Berlin. The name—more commonly written as one word "Siegesallee"—is German for "Avenue of Victory."

10. **Rousseau:** Jean-Jacques Rousseau (1712–1778), French author whose candid, autobiographical *Confessions* began a vogue in literature for confessional accounts.

WORDS TO OWN

propitious (prō·pish′əs) *adj.:* favorable.

notorious (nō·tôr′ē·əs) *adj.:* widely but unfavorably known; famous.

Skill Link

Analyzing How the Writer's Motivation Affects Text Structure

Use the following questions to remind students that the order in which a writer presents information reflects the writer's purpose.

1. **What is Woolf's purpose for writing this essay?** [Possible responses: to counter the argument that women do not have the same creative genius as men; to broaden readers' perspectives on the female writer's plight, past and present.]
2. **In what order does Woolf present her arguments?** [Woolf begins by reporting a man's assertion that no woman could have written Shakespeare's plays. She follows up with a well-developed though hypothetical argument; she includes historical examples of literary women and ends with the assertion that writing is a "feat of prodigious difficulty" for both men and women but far more difficult for women.]
3. **How does Woolf's order of information serve her purpose?** [Possible response: Her opening example of either-or thinking draws readers into her point of view. Her hypothetical "life-story" adds a human dimension to her argument; her historical references substantiate her argument with facts. Her final point is her strongest and is likely to be received well because she has already gained readers' sympathy.]

write poems and novels and histories; it does not need them. It does not care whether Flaubert finds the right word or whether Carlyle scrupulously verifies this or that fact. Naturally, it will not pay for what it does not want. And so the writer, Keats, Flaubert, Carlyle, suffers, especially in the creative years of youth, every form of distraction and discouragement. A curse, a cry of agony, rises from those books of analysis and confession. "Mighty poets in their misery dead"[11]—that is the burden of their song. If anything comes through in spite of all this, it is a miracle, and probably no book is born entire and uncrippled as it was conceived.

Sheffield City Art Galleries, England.

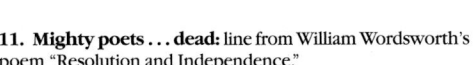

A Corner of the Artist's Room, Paris (late 19th or early 20th century) by Gwen John.

But for women, I thought, looking at the empty shelves, these difficulties were infinitely more formidable. In the first place, to have a room of her own, let alone a quiet room or a soundproof room, was out of the question, unless her parents were exceptionally rich or very noble, even up to the beginning of the nineteenth century. Since her pin money,[12] which depended on the goodwill of her father, was only enough to keep her clothed, she was debarred from such alleviations as came even to Keats or Tennyson or Carlyle, all poor men, from a walking tour, a little journey to France, from the separate lodging which, even if it were miserable enough, sheltered them from the claims and tyrannies of their families. Such material difficulties were formidable; but much worse were the immaterial. The indifference of the world which Keats and Flaubert and other men of genius have found so hard to bear was in her case not indifference but hostility. The world did not say to her as it said to them, Write if you choose; it makes no difference to me. The world said with a guffaw, Write? What's the good of your writing?

11. **Mighty poets . . . dead:** line from William Wordsworth's poem "Resolution and Independence."
12. **pin money:** small allowance given for personal expenses.

WORDS TO OWN
formidable (fôr′mə·də·bəl) *adj.:* difficult to handle or overcome.
alleviations (ə·lē′vē·ā′shənz) *n. pl.:* things that lighten, relieve, or make easier to bear.

RESPONDING TO THE ART

Gwen John (1876–1939) became well-known for her self-portraits and portraits of women. She settled in France in 1904, and *A Corner of the Artist's Room, Paris* is one of the muted interiors she produced there.
Activity. Ask students why they think this quiet interior, representing an artist's room, has been chosen to illustrate Woolf's essay. What objects would they put in an artist's room?

E Reading Skills and Strategies

Evaluating a Persuasive Message

? During Woolf's time, many scholars and politicians argued that biology made women inherently unfit to think about serious issues or to hold positions of responsibility. How does Woolf counter that argument? [She attributes inequalities to social causes rather than biological ones.]

F Critical Thinking

Evaluating

? What makes this a particularly effective last line? [Possible responses: It makes one final comparison with men; it underscores the difficulties women have faced; it ridicules the attitude that women are worthless. The word choice *guffaw* accentuates the condescension and impatience with which women have been met.]

Getting Students Involved

Cooperative Learning

Homer's Sister? Assign students to groups of three. Ask each group to create a fictional "vita" for a sibling of a famous male figure in the arts, sciences, entertainment, or other field. Students may imitate Woolf's approach in her essay, or they may compare and contrast the siblings by means of graphic organizers and oral presentations. Group members should collaborate on selecting the sibling they wish to profile and on their approach to the subject. Afterward, they may work together to divide the tasks necessary to complete the project. Each group member should present an oral or written summary of the group process or a self-assessment of his or her own contributions to the group effort.

Literature and Politics

This feature gives the details of one dramatic incident in the fight for women's right to vote in Britain. Encourage students to research the history of women's involvement in the local politics of their state or city.

Responding to the Art

This photograph shows the delivery of "human letters" to the Prime Minister of Great Britain, H. H. Asquith. He had tried to defend the Liberal party's refusal to enfranchise women by saying that there was no proof that women actually wanted the vote. So, women, like the ones in the photograph, responded not only by organizing enormous suffrage rallies and demonstrations but also by walking to the Prime Minister's home at 10 Downing Street carrying placards with the message "Votes for Women."

Activity. Ask students to describe other protest marches held in the twentieth century.

Ⓐ Historical Connections

A Broad Range of Tactics

One bold suffragist was so eager to make an impression on Prime Minister Asquith that she had herself hoisted up to a dining room window at a castle where he was vacationing. As he and his party were preparing to eat, she announced that women would continue to plague the Prime Minister until he gave them the vote.

Ⓑ Historical Connections

Joan of Arc

The liberty sought by Joan of Arc had nothing to do with women. Rather, she wished to rescue France from its English conquerors. Nevertheless, the association with Joan of Arc was a potent one for English suffragists because the English were much embarrassed by their defeat at the hands of a fifteen-year-old girl. Joan of Arc was unjustly condemned to death (burned at the stake) as much for supposed "witchcraft" as for political activity.

Suffragists with sandwich boards in London (c. 1910).

Votes for Women!

In December 1913, during an opera about Joan of Arc staged especially for the Ⓐ British royal family, three elegantly dressed women stood and addressed the king with a megaphone. The crowd was thrown into a panic as the women likened Ⓑ their struggle for the vote to Joan of Arc's fifteenth-century fight for liberty. When the police finally removed them, other women, hidden in the balcony, showered the audience with suffragist pamphlets. The king, of course, did not respond. But the dramatic protest joined the suffragists to Joan and other brave forerunners, just as Virginia Woolf's portrait of Shakespeare's fictional sister drew on the past to spur change in her own time.

Making the Connections

Connecting to the Theme: "Clashes of Culture"

Woolf's essay was published in 1929. Is it still relevant today? Would our own culture smother someone like Shakespeare's sister or nurture her? Encourage students to discuss these issues. Students might also discuss the extent to which they think genius is inherited or nurtured: Their opinions on this issue will affect their ideas about how culture encourages—or inhibits—individual achievement.

The vote—a right not granted to British women over the age of thirty until 1918, and not granted to women over twenty-one until 1928—was the key to meaningful change for women in Woolf's day. Woolf herself was among thousands of women who joined suffrage organizations during the first decade of the century. Although she could have written articles for publications such as *The Suffragette* or *Votes for Women*, she instead lent her support in more humble ways: She sat on the platform at public meetings and folded countless mailings (she later recalled spending "hours writing names like Cowgill on envelopes"). Yet Woolf was a pacifist, and her views against the use of physical force prevented her wholehearted involvement in the increasingly combative woman suffrage movement of the early 1900s.

A new phase in an old fight. Universal suffrage was not a new idea. Women and men had campaigned for it since the mid-1800s; in fact, the philosopher John Stuart Mill had brought a suffrage bill before the British Parliament in 1866. But the fight entered a new phase in 1904, when the ardent suffragist Christabel Pankhurst strode off to the Manchester Free Trade Hall to challenge Winston Churchill on the subject of voting rights for women. Churchill refused to acknowledge Pankhurst's demands, and she was howled down by the crowd, but she counted it as her first "militant" step.

Afterward, members of the Women's Social and Political Union, which Pankhurst and her mother, Emmeline, had founded in 1903, were emboldened to take other steps: They held rallies and marches, staged suffrage plays at public meetings, broke the windows of government buildings, and interrupted Parliament by shouting "Votes for women!" from their enclosed seats in the "Ladies' Gallery." (Later, several women chained themselves to the metal grille that separated this gallery from the main chamber.) From 1906 to 1914, more than a thousand suffragists were arrested and carted off to jail. Held in tiny cells, and prohibited from speaking to one another, these women still found other ways to protest, mostly through hunger strikes. In answer, the government force-fed the protesters until the procedure permanently damaged many women's health. Thereafter, in what came to be called "Cat and Mouse" licenses, hunger strikers were released from prison only until they regained their strength, then were rearrested.

Success at last. The sight of "respectable" women getting roughed up by hostile crowds and held for months in prison did alter public opinion: Many came to realize how badly women wanted the right to full citizenship. Yet protests continued without results until the beginning of World War I, when the Pankhursts and others abruptly turned their interests to the war effort. Ironically, many historians now think that women's work during the war, mostly as they filled the absent soldiers' jobs, was the turning point in the suffrage movement. When the war was over, most Britishers felt that women shouldn't—indeed couldn't—be deprived of the vote any longer.

C Background

Suffragist demonstrations in Great Britain were political events whose organizers placed a high premium on drama. Even actual plays by popular writers were staged to support women's rights. Suffragists (called suffragettes by their detractors) also marched in white dresses carrying elaborate banners in their movement's colors. For illustrations of these demonstrations and suffragists' art, see Lisa Tickner's book, *The Spectacle of Women: Imagery of the Suffrage Campaign* (1988).

D Struggling Readers

Creating a Time Line

Ask students to reread the feature and record important events in the struggle for female suffrage on a time line. Their last entry could be 1928, the year when all women in Britain over twenty-one were given the right to vote. Then ask students to use their time lines to help them orally summarize what they have read for the class.

Assessing Learning

Check Test: Questions and Answers

1. **For what purpose does Woolf invent Judith Shakespeare?** [to show why an Elizabethan woman could not have written plays of the caliber of Shakespeare's]
2. **Why does Judith run away to London?** [She wishes to escape family obligations and find a way to express her creative abilities.]
3. **According to Woolf, how does the repressed genius of women show itself in the Elizabethan age?** [Witches, women thought to be possessed by the devil, wise women selling herbs, and mothers of remarkable men may have been women struggling to find ways to express their creative genius.]
4. **How does the world treat male writers and female writers differently, according to Woolf?** [The world treats male writers with indifference and female ones with hostility.]

Standardized Test Preparation

For practice with ACT and SAT formats, see

- *Preparation for College Admission Exams,* p. 57

For practice in proofreading and editing, see

- *Daily Oral Grammar,* Transparency 41

Making Meanings

First Thoughts [Respond]

1. Students may say that Judith's story made the plight of female artists, especially in the past, easy to understand. Some may feel that most of the obstacles presented in the essay no longer exist for the contemporary female writer or artist.

Shaping Interpretations [Interpret]

2. Woolf's creation of a fictional biography enables her to present a sympathetic picture that gives emotional appeal to her thesis. Some students may find the biography psychologically convincing even if the facts cannot be verified. Others may find it emotionally manipulative and based purely on conjecture.

3. Woolf argues that women shun the limelight to avoid ridicule. Students may note that male and female public figures were held to different standards during Woolf's time and, to some extent, are so held in our own time.

4. The main idea is that women historically have been prevented from expressing creative genius by lack of opportunity and by crippling stereotypes and public rejection. Many will agree with Woolf, but some may argue that true genius will overcome adversity.

5. One place where Woolf's tone becomes ironic is at the end of the first paragraph when she mentions the bishop and his views. Students may read these passages with a tone of imperious contempt, of simple sarcasm, or of hissing anger.

Extending the Text [Evaluate]

6. Students may say that ample time, privacy, and freedom from worry about money are invaluable in the undertaking of almost any important endeavor, creative or otherwise. Students may also cite examples of artists who have overcome such obstacles.

Challenging the Text [Evaluate]

7. Unsupported generalizations occur throughout the essay since most of Woolf's "evidence" is anecdotal and hypothetical. Nevertheless, the absence of hard data makes the argument a difficult one to disprove by logic alone.

Making Meanings

First Thoughts

1. How did Judith's story make you feel about women's lives, past and present?

Reading Check

a. What happens to "Judith Shakespeare" when she goes to London?

b. According to Woolf, what general conditions make works of genius difficult to produce? What special conditions do women face?

Shaping Interpretations

2. Woolf uses an invented **biography** in this essay. Why do you think she uses such a device? Is her biography of Judith Shakespeare convincing to you? Cite reasons for your answer.
3. In her essay, Woolf says that for women "Anonymity runs in their blood." According to Woolf, why do women shy away from the limelight? What do you think of her reasons?
4. Woolf focuses on the unhappy psychological state of a gifted female writer in the age of Shakespeare. How would you state the **main idea** of her essay? Do you agree with Woolf's thesis? Why or why not? (Review the notes you took while reading.)
5. Where do you detect a tone of contemptuous **irony** in Woolf's essay? How would you read these passages aloud to convey Woolf's **tone**?

Extending the Text

6. In her essay, Woolf concludes that to write great literature, a woman *must* have money and a private place. Do you think this is still true today—for anyone, male *or* female? Explain your response.

Challenging the Text

7. Did Woolf make any **generalizations** in this essay that you think are unsupported by historical or contemporary evidence? Explain your response.

Choices: Building Your Portfolio

Writer's Notebook

1. Collecting Ideas for a Problem-Solution Essay

WORK IN PROGRESS

One way to identify a possible topic for a problem-solution essay is to focus on the local aspects of a far-reaching societal problem, such as the lack of equal opportunity for women that Woolf discusses in "Shakespeare's Sister." Spend a few minutes brainstorming or clustering to discover inequalities you perceive in the opportunities your school or community offers males and females of your age. Save your notes for the Writer's Workshop on page 1179.

Evaluating an Argument

2. The Gender Gap

Woolf's essay contains many ideas, both explicit and implicit, about gender roles. In an essay, (a) discuss how Woolf depicts men and women, (b) analyze how the characterizations work in her argument, and (c) evaluate her ideas. (Your reading notes may help you.)

Creative Writing

3. Reimagining Judith's Life

In Judith's story, where was her famous brother? What if Queen Elizabeth had heard of Judith's ambitions or her famous brother had recognized them? Rewrite Judith's life so that it *does not* end in tragedy.

Creative Writing

4. Another Mute Milton

Imagine a person of today or from the past who, if circumstances had been different, might have been a great writer, painter, or political leader. Write an imaginary life of that intensely creative but thwarted person.

Reading Check

a. Men laugh at her desire to act. She is seduced by an acting company's manager, becomes pregnant, and commits suicide.

b. Difficulties include lack of privacy and free time as well as financial insecurity. Most women also face additional family and domestic responsibilities that burden them but free their fathers and husbands.

Grading Timesaver

Rubrics for each Choices assignment appear on p. 213 in the *Portfolio Management System.*

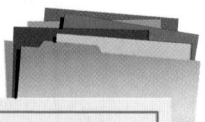

Naguib Mahfouz

(1911–   )

Naguib Mahfouz (nä'gēb' mä'fo͞oz), often heralded as Egypt's finest writer, grew up in a middle-class family similar to the family he traces in his acclaimed *Cairo Trilogy.* Mahfouz began sending stories to magazines when he was a philosophy student at Cairo University. When he first got paid for a story, he is reputed to have exclaimed, in disbelief, "One gets paid for them as well!"

Naguib Mahfouz.

For most of his life, Mahfouz worked as a civil servant for the Egyptian government, first in the Ministry of Religious Affairs, later in the Arts Administration, and still later as head of the State Cinema Organization. He has written more than forty novels and short-story collections, several plays, and many film scripts. Almost all his writing is set in Cairo. "Like their author," writes the translator Denys Johnson-Davies, "his stories never travel abroad, not even to the Egyptian countryside." Most of his novels are set in an area known as Khan al-Khalili, which is filled with mosques, restaurants, shops, and colorful people.

Despite their limited settings, Mahfouz's works are read widely throughout the Middle East and are considered highly influential. The subjects of his writings are the repression of women, social injustice, and the superficial values of modern life. Ironically, some of his books were banned in Arab countries, including Egypt, especially after he expressed support for the 1979 peace treaty between Egypt and Israel. Nevertheless, in Egypt and throughout the world, he is widely regarded as the outstanding writer of contemporary Arabic literature. In 1988, Mahfouz won the Nobel Prize in literature.

WORLD LITERATURE

Egypt

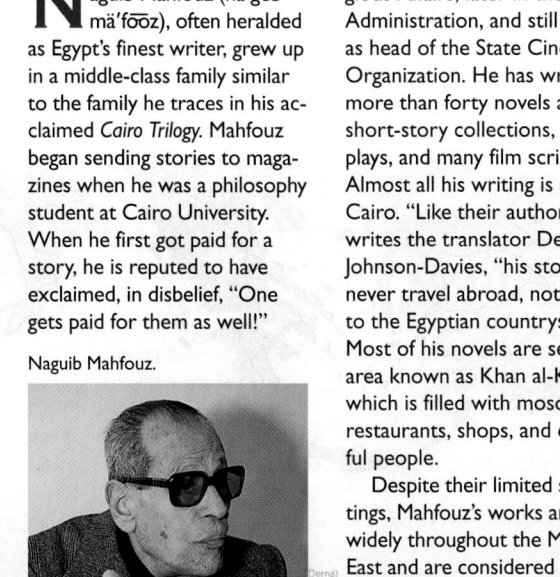

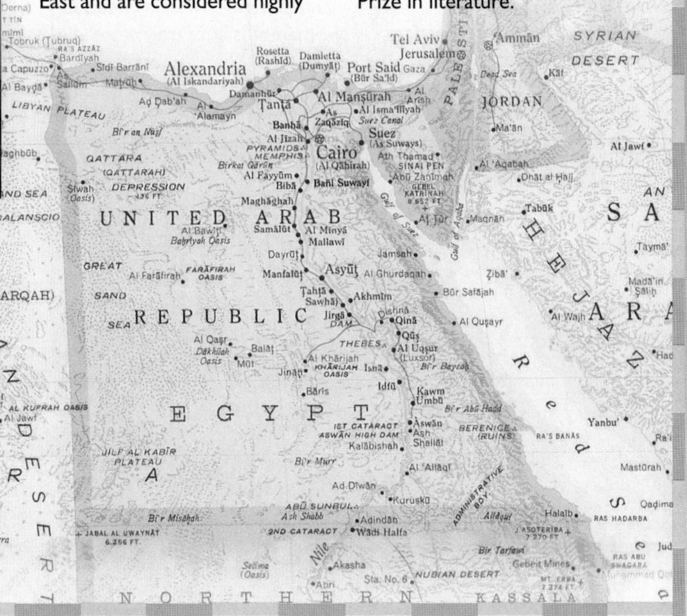

(Map) ©Rand McNally R. L. #98-S-116.

go.hrw.com
LEO 12-15

OBJECTIVES

1. Read and interpret the novel excerpt
2. Generate relevant, interesting, and researchable questions
3. Recognize distinctive and shared characteristics of cultures
4. Compare text events with students' own experience and that of others
5. Recognize and discuss themes and connections that cross cultures

BROWSING IN THE FILES

About the Author. Mahfouz is the first Arabic-language author to receive the Nobel Prize in literature. Although many critics consider him to be the leading literary figure of modern Egypt, his frank portrayal of characters, particularly women, has fostered controversy in the Arab world. Controversy has also surrounded his 1959 novel *Children of Gebelawi,* an allegory in which three characters thought to represent Moses, Jesus, and Mohammed wander the streets of modern Cairo. Soon after his Nobel Prize award in 1989, he began to receive death threats from religious zealots who objected to this novel. Despite the threats and one nearly successful assassination attempt in 1994, Mahfouz refuses to have bodyguards or vary his daily routine.

Writers on Writing. When asked about his ability to recreate the people of Cairo, Mahfouz replied, "I have always given thanks for the almost sacred privilege I have been granted of being able to 'identify' the human beings of this city which I know and love so well. Once those lives which go on around me enter my field of vision, they become characters. In other words, they become creatures of my own flesh and blood. My gratitude becomes a creative act."

Reaching All Students

Struggling Readers

One of Mahfouz's central preoccupations in *Palace Walk* is the many differences in the lives of men and women in the time and place he is describing. Invite students to make a Venn diagram and label the two large circles *Men* and *Women.* In each circle, students can record differences in the daily lives and opportunities of the genders and, in the overlapping area, any shared values and activities.

Advanced Learners

Students may wish to read the entire novel, or they may want to find and read the scene in which Amina ventures onto the street and has a mishap. Students may also explore the clash of cultures portrayed in the scenes in which Amina's husband learns what has happened to her and punishes her. Have the students prepare plot summaries and share them with the class.

Summary ■ ■

Amina, an energetic and meticulous Egyptian housewife, lives in a society in which women have extremely limited public lives. She has been mostly confined to her home throughout her twenty-five-year marriage. Amina finds moments of peace and reflection while tending the plants, pigeons, and chickens she has assembled on the roof of her family's Cairo house. Up on the roof, with its enchanting arbor garden, she senses a unity among all living things and feels that she participates in a unified and blessed life. Away from her bickering daughters—Aisha and Khadija—and her husband's watchful eye, Amina gazes at and wonders about the mysterious city. Neither resentful nor discontented, she prays for her family and her people, asking God to drive the English colonizers out of their land.

Planning

- **Block Schedule**
  Block Scheduling Lesson Plans with Pacing Guide
- **Traditional Schedule**
  Lesson Plans Including Strategies for English-Language Learners
- **One-Stop Planner**
  CD-ROM with Test Generator

Before You Read

THE CAIRO ROOFTOP

Background

Picture a world in which a girl marries at thirteen and from then on lives within the walls of her husband's home, unseen and unknown to those beyond the family circle. Her knowledge of the world outside is confined to what she can see from a rooftop.

Naguib Mahfouz introduces you to a woman who leads just such a confined life in "The Cairo Rooftop," a chapter from his novel *Palace Walk. Palace Walk* is one of three volumes in Mahfouz's *Cairo Trilogy,* which he wrote in Arabic and published in the mid-1950s. Because of translation delays, the trilogy was almost unknown outside the Middle East until 1988, when Mahfouz won the Nobel Prize in literature.

The English translation of the *Cairo Trilogy* opens the world of modern Egypt to Western readers. Spanning the years 1917 to 1952, the trilogy follows three generations of a middle-class Muslim family before, during, and after the 1919 uprising that led Britain to declare Egypt a sovereign state. The personal struggles within the family reflect not only Egypt's political history but also its increasing interest in education and science, the gradual emancipation of women, and the transformation of traditional attitudes toward Western life.

Palace Walk, the first book in the trilogy, chronicles the period from 1917 to 1919, two of the five years during which Egypt was a British protectorate. The main character in "The Cairo Rooftop" is Amina, who has been married to Ahmad, the family patriarch, since she was thirteen. Amina is totally, but willingly, dominated by her husband at a time when a virtuous woman of Islam rarely steps outside her husband's home, and never shows her face to a man who is not a close relative. There are five younger people in the family: Yasin, the twenty-one-year-old son of Ahmad's first wife; two other sons, Fahmy and Kamal; and two daughters, Khadija and Aisha.

Ahmad's family lives in a two-story house on Palace Walk, a street in Cairo that centuries ago connected two palaces. The street name that is the book's title can also be translated as "between two palaces" and refers not only to the street but also to the two political situations that frame the book and to the change from traditional to more modern ways that frames the family's experiences.

The map on page 1131 reflects the story's time frame: This is not the Middle East today.

Quickwrite

Start with what you know. Spend two or three minutes jotting down what you know about Egyptian history in the twentieth century.

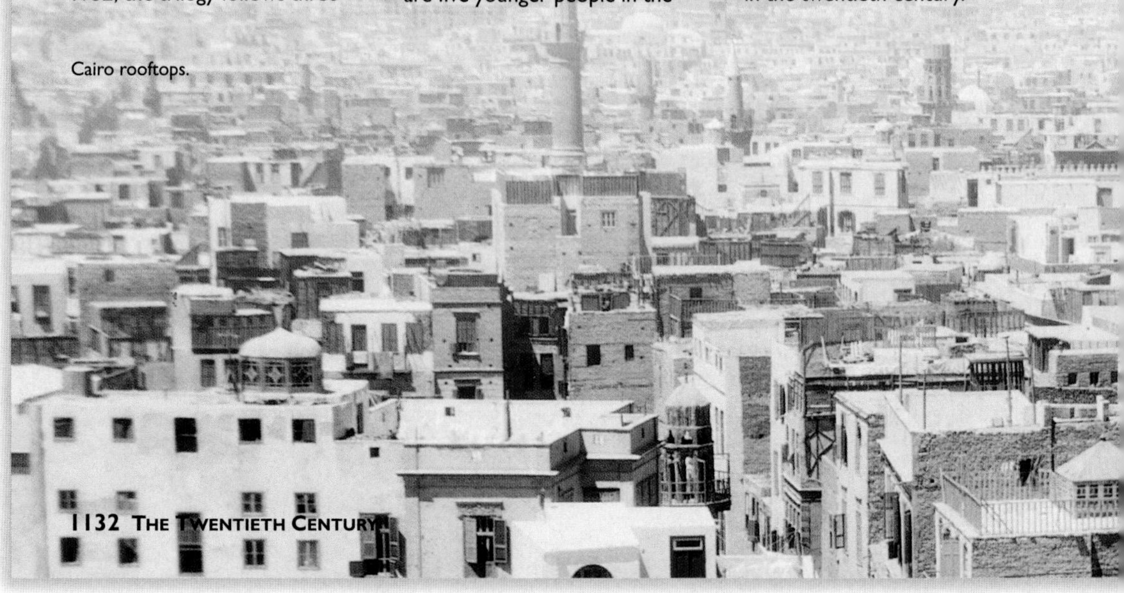

Cairo rooftops.

Resources: Print and Media

Reading
- *Audio CD Library*
  Disc 21, Track 3

Internet
- go.hrw.com (keyword: LE0 12-15)

The Cairo Rooftop *from* Palace Walk

Naguib Mahfouz

translated by **William Maynard Hutchins** *and* **Olive E. Kenny**

When they had finished breakfast, the mother said, "Aisha, you do the laundry today and Khadija will clean the house. Afterward meet me in the oven room."

Amina divided the work between them right after breakfast. They were content to be ruled by her, and Aisha would not question her assignment. Khadija would take the trouble to make a few comments, either to show her worth or to start a quarrel. Thus she said, "I'll let you clean the house if you think washing the clothes is too much. But if you make a fuss over the washing so you can stay in the bathroom till all the work in the kitchen is finished, that's an excuse that can be rejected in advance."

Aisha ignored her remark and went off to the bath humming. Khadija commented sarcastically, "Lucky for you that sound reverberates in the bathroom like a phonograph speaker. So sing and let the neighbors hear it."

Their mother left the room and went through the hall to the stairs. She climbed to the roof to make her morning rounds there before descending to the oven room. The bickering between her daughters was nothing new to her. Over the course of time it had turned into a customary way of life when the father was not at home and no one could think of anything pleasant to say. She had tried to stop it by using entreaty, humor, and tenderness. That was the only type of discipline she employed with her children. It fit her nature, which could not stand anything stronger. She lacked the firmness that rearing children occasionally requires. Perhaps she would have liked to be firm but was not able to. Perhaps she had attempted to be firm but had been overcome by her emotions and weakness. It seemed she could not bear for the ties between her and her children to be anything but love and affection. She let the father or his shadow, which dominated the children from afar, straighten them out and lay down the law. Thus their silly quarrel did not weaken her admiration for her two girls or her satisfaction with them. Even Aisha, who was insanely fond of singing and standing in front of the mirror, her laziness notwithstanding, was no less skillful and organized than Khadija.

Amina would have been justified in allowing herself long periods of relaxation, but she was prevented by a natural tendency that was almost a disease. She insisted on supervising everything in the house, no matter how small. When the girls

A Cultural Connections

The family's courtyard contains a well, a storeroom, and an oven room in which the meals are prepared. Inside this room are a large oven, piles of coal and wood for fuel, and shelves with pots, plates, and serving trays. Encourage students to comment on how this setting reflects a time, place, and culture different from their own.

B Struggling Readers

Finding Details

Point out to students that Khadija, at twenty, is the older daughter and represents the next generation of women. She resembles her mother with her indefatigable energy, proficiency in running the household, and fierce dedication to her family. Khadija is jealous of the voice and beauty of her spirited, sixteen-year-old sister, Aisha. As students read, remind them to look for details that reveal the character of each sister.

C Reading Skills and Strategies

Responding to the Text

? What is your impression of Amina as a mother? [Possible responses: She is a tender, loving mother; she is unassertive and does not know how to discipline her children.]

D Elements of Literature

Personification

? What does this personification indicate about the father's role as a disciplinarian? [Possible responses: That a shadow could dominate indicates that just the thought or mention of the father instills fear; the father is a dark and menacing power, even when not physically present.]

Using Students' Strengths

Intrapersonal Learners

Suggest that self-starters find their own way of expressing their response to the selection. They might do this in three stages: first, by creating a plan for how they will express themselves; second, by carrying out their plan and assessing the results; and, third, by recording and assessing their own work for their portfolio.

Naturalist Learners

What kind of natural life would be likely to thrive, year round, on a Cairo rooftop? Invite students to identify climate conditions (including both temperature and humidity) and to determine the types of plant and animal life that could live on a Cairo rooftop. Students might also draw pictures of plants and animals to illustrate their findings.

Ⓐ Background

Amina has three sons. Yasin, twenty-one, is Amina's stepson and a clerk in al-Nahhasin School. Fahmy attends law school, and Kamal is an elementary school pupil.

Ⓑ Cultural Connections

The Fez

A fez is a brimless felt cap, usually red, with a flat top from which a colored tassel hangs. Students can see a picture of a fez on p. 1148.

Ⓒ Struggling Readers

Rearranging Syntax

Call attention to the two sentences in this passage that begin with the word *How*. Explain that these sentences are tricky to comprehend for two reasons: First, the reader may expect a question, since *how* is often used to begin a question. Second, the object or complement precedes the subject and verb in each sentence. Ask students to recast each sentence in normal word order. ["She got so much joy from . . ." and "She felt good when she saw . . ."]

finished their work, she would go around energetically inspecting the rooms, living areas, and halls, with a broom in one hand and a feather duster in the other. She searched the corners, walls, curtains, and all the furnishings to eliminate an overlooked speck of dust, finding as much pleasure and satisfaction in that as in removing a speck from her eye. She was by nature such a perfectionist that she examined the clothes about to be laundered. If she discovered a piece of clothing that was unusually dirty, she would not spare the owner a gentle reminder of his duty, whether it was Kamal, who was going on ten, or Yasin, who had two clear and contradictory approaches to caring for himself. He was excessively fastidious about his external appearance—his suit, fez, shirt, necktie, and shoes—but shockingly neglectful of his underwear.

Naturally this comprehensive concern of hers did not exclude the roof and the pigeons and chickens that inhabited it. In fact, the time she spent on the roof was filled with love and delight from the opportunities it presented for work, not to mention the joys of play and merriment she found there. No wonder, for the roof was a new world she had discovered. The big house had known nothing of it until she joined the family. She had created it afresh through the force of her spirit, back when the house retained the appearance it had always had since being built ages before. It was her idea to have these cages with the cooing pigeons put on some of the high walls. She had arranged these wooden chicken coops where the hens clucked as they foraged for food. How much joy she got from scattering grain for them or putting the water container on the ground as the hens raced for it, preceded by their rooster. Their beaks fell on the grain quickly and regularly, like sewing-machine needles, leaving little indentations in the dust like the pockmarks from a drizzle. How good she felt when she saw them gazing at her with clear little eyes, inquisitive and questioning, while they cackled and clucked with a shared affection that filled her heart with tenderness.

She loved the chickens and pigeons as she loved all of God's creatures. She made little noises to them, thinking they understood and responded. Her imagination had bestowed conscious, intelligent life on all animals and occasionally even on inanimate objects. She was quite certain that these beings praised her Lord and were in contact, by various means, with the spirit world. Her world with its earth and sky, animals and plants, was a living, intelligent one. Its merits were not confined

Street scene in Cairo.

Crossing the Curriculum

Social Studies

The majority of Egyptians are Muslims, and Islam plays a central role in this selection. You may want to challenge students to find out the following:

- When and how Islam was introduced to Egypt [Arab Muslim invaders brought the religion to Egypt in A.D. 641.]
- Central beliefs of Islam [These include submission to the one God, Allah, and acknowledgment of his prophet, Mohammed.]
- The five Pillars of Islam [No god but Allah; prayer five times a day; the giving of alms; fasting; and pilgrimage.]

Students may also research attitudes toward women as expressed in the Koran, or Qur'an.

to the blessing of life. It found its completion in worship. It was not strange, then, that, relying on one excuse or another, she prolonged the lives of the roosters and hens. One hen was full of life, another a good layer. This rooster woke her in the morning with his crowing. Perhaps if it had been left entirely to her, she would never have consented to put her knife to their throats. If circumstances did force her to slaughter one, she selected a chicken or pigeon with a feeling close to anguish. She would give it a drink, seek God's mercy for it, invoke God's name, ask forgiveness, and then slaughter it. Her consolation was that she was exercising a right that God the Benefactor had granted to all those who serve Him. (D)

The most amazing aspect of the roof was the southern half overlooking al-Nahhasin Street.[1] There in years past she had planted a special garden. There was not another one like it in the whole neighborhood on any of the other roofs, which were usually covered with chicken droppings. She had first begun with a small number of pots of carnations and roses. They had increased year by year and were arranged in rows parallel to the sides of the walls. They grew splendidly, and she had the idea of putting a trellis over the top. She got a carpenter to install it. Then she planted both jasmine and hyacinth bean vines. She attached them to the trellis and around the posts. They grew tall and spread out until the area was transformed into an arbor garden with a green sky from which jasmine flowed down. An enchanting, sweet fragrance was diffused throughout.

This roof, with its inhabitants of chickens and pigeons and its arbor garden, was her beautiful, beloved world and her favorite place for relaxation out of the whole universe, about which she knew nothing. As usual at this hour, she set about caring for it. She swept it, watered the plants, fed the chickens and pigeons. Then for a long time, with smiling lips and dreamy eyes, she enjoyed the scene surrounding her. She went to the end of the garden and stood behind the interwoven, coiling vines, to gaze out through the openings at the limitless space around her.

She was awed by the minarets[2] which shot up, making a profound impression on her. Some were near enough for her to see their lamps and crescent distinctly, like those of Qala'un and Barquq. (E) Others appeared to her as complete wholes, lacking details, like the minarets of the mosques of al-Husayn, al-Ghuri, and al-Azhar. Still other minarets were at the far horizon and seemed phantoms, like those of the Citadel and Rifa'i mosques. She turned her face toward them with devotion, fascination, thanksgiving, and hope. Her spirit soared over their tops, as close as possible to the heavens. Then her eyes would fix on the minaret of the mosque of al-Husayn, the dearest one to her because of her love for its namesake.[3] She looked at it affectionately, and her yearnings mingled with the sorrow that pervaded her every time she (F) remembered she was not allowed to visit the son of the Prophet of God's daughter, even though she lived only minutes away from his shrine.

She sighed audibly and that broke the spell. She (G) began to amuse herself by looking at the roofs and streets. The yearnings would not leave her. She turned her back on the wall. Looking at the unknown had overwhelmed her: both what is unknown to most people, the invisible spirit world, and the unknown with respect to her in particular, Cairo, even the adjacent neighborhood, from which voices reached her. What could this world of which she saw nothing but the minarets and roofs be like? A quarter of a century had passed while she was confined to this house, leaving it only on infrequent occasions to visit her mother in al-Khurunfush. Her husband escorted her on (H) each visit in a carriage, because he could not bear for anyone to see his wife, either alone or accompanied by him.

She was neither resentful nor discontented, quite the opposite. All the same, when she peeked through the openings between the jasmine and the hyacinth bean vines, off into space, at the minarets and rooftops, her delicate lips would rise in a tender, dreamy smile. Where

1. **al-Nahhasin Street:** a main street in the Bayn al-Qasrayn, or Palace Walk, section of Cairo. This street is also called Coppersmiths Street for the artisans who line its sidewalks.

2. **minarets:** mosque towers. Minarets are often used by special criers to announce daily calls to worship.

3. **mosque . . . namesake:** mosque named for Husayn (626–680), a Shiite Muslim hero and grandson of the prophet Mohammed. A climactic moment in the novel comes when, against the wishes of her husband, Amina sneaks out to visit this mosque.

(D) Vocabulary Note

Latin Roots

The word *benefactor* comes from two Latin roots, *bene,* meaning "well" or "good" and *facere,* meaning "to do" or "to make." A benefactor is someone who does well by us: A benefactor gives aid. Encourage students to think of other words that contain the roots *bene* (for example, *benefits, benediction,* and *beneficial*) and *facere* (for example, *factory, manufacture*) and to relate the meanings of those words to the meanings of their Latin roots.

(E) Cultural Connections

A mosque is a place of worship for Muslims. The mosques' towers, from which the people are called to prayer, are called minarets. The section of Cairo referred to as the old quarter contains more than one thousand minarets.

(F) Advanced Learners

Connecting Character and Setting

Students may wish to learn more about this mosque or about Husayn, since Amina's later visit to this mosque is a pivotal episode in the novel.

(G) English Language Learners

Idioms

Students may need help with the phrase "break the spell." Explain that the "spell" was the state of reverie described in the previous paragraph. Ask what "break" means in this context. [Possible responses: end, stop.]

(H) Reading Skills and Strategies

Drawing Conclusions

? Key information is given here about the exact degree of Amina's isolation. What qualities of Amina's personality may have been formed by the conditions under which she lives? [Possible responses: Because she cannot leave the house, she focuses her energy on perfection in the home; because most of Amina's human contact is with her children, her lack of firmness may be attributed to her fear of losing or damaging that contact.]

Assessing Learning

Check Test: Questions and Answers

1. What is the "Cairo rooftop"? [the roof of Amina's house where she plants and raises animals]
2. Why is Amina in awe of the minarets? [She sees them only from the rooftop.]
3. What does Amina yearn for? [She wants to visit the mosque and see the city.]
4. How many years has Amina been confined to the house? [twenty-five years]
5. Is Amina resentful of her situation? [No, the opposite is true.]

Ⓐ Exploring the Historical Period

With the outbreak of World War I, Britain declared Egypt a protectorate and sent troops to defend the Suez Canal. In 1922, Britain granted Egypt independence but retained the right to station troops near the Suez Canal.

Finding Common Ground

The questions and activities in Finding Common Ground relate to the place of women in society. Have students work in groups to discuss the position of women in their own society in the past and present. Students might focus on the variety of goals and values that women themselves have expressed at different times and in different situations.

might the law school be where Fahmy was sitting at this moment? Where was the Khalil Agha School, which Kamal assured her was only a minute's trip from the mosque of al-Husayn? Before leaving the roof, she spread her hands out in prayer and called on her Lord: "God, I ask you to watch over my husband and children, my mother and Yasin, and all the people: Muslims and Ⓐ Christians, even the English, my Lord, but drive them from our land as a favor to Fahmy, who does not like them."[4]

4. **Fahmy . . . them:** Amina's son Fahmy, an Egyptian nationalist, fervently hopes for the end of English colonial rule.

Finding Common Ground

Review your Quickwrite notes, and think about what you would like to know about modern Egyptian history. Then, get together with others to discuss how you will respond to "The Cairo Rooftop." Discuss questions of your own, or try one of these questions or activities.

- How do you think this selection relates to the collection theme, "Clashes of Culture"?
- Is geography—and timing—everything? Suppose you had been born in Egypt or in China or anywhere else except the United States. Suppose you had been born in the early 1900s. What might your life have been like?
- Find out about dating and marriage customs or about educational and work opportunities for women in any country except yours. Take notes, and either give a talk to the class or hold a panel discussion with others who chose different countries.
- In many places in the world even today, the birth of a daughter causes less joy than the birth of a son. What do you think might be some reasons for this attitude?

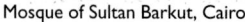

Mosque of Sultan Barkut, Cairo.

Connecting Across Texts

Connecting with "Shakespeare's Sister"

In "Shakespeare's Sister," Woolf rues the fact that women traditionally have had no "room" of their own—nowhere to be themselves, nowhere to express their own creativity. In this selection, Amina manages to create a private, creative space for herself in a crowded household in a teeming city. Ask students to discuss how they think Amina's experience relates to Woolf's argument. They might consider the following questions:

- What similarities and differences do you see between Amina's life and the life that the hypothetical Judith Shakespeare lived? To what extent were the destinies of each controlled by men or by society's attitude toward women?
- Judith is undermined by her circumstances, whereas Amina appears to have either made peace with or transcended hers. What accounts for this difference? Ask students if they attribute any significance to the fact that one selection was written by a female author and the other by a male. What other cultural or personal factors may account for the differences between the fates of these two characters?

George Orwell

(1903–1950)

George Orwell was born Eric Blair in Bengal, India, where his British father was a member of the Indian civil service. A few years afterward, his family returned to England. A lonely child, Orwell spent a good deal of time making up stories and poems. He later wrote that from an early age he knew he was going to be a writer.

After graduating from Eton, Orwell joined the Indian Imperial Police, serving in Burma from 1922 to 1927, when he resigned to devote more time to writing. Returning to Europe, he taught and took part-time, ill-paying jobs in France and England. His first book, *Down and Out in Paris and London* (1933), was based on these experiences. He based his next novel, *Burmese Days* (1934), on his life in Burma.

Although he published journalistic pieces under his real name, with his earliest books he began to publish as George Orwell, and he continued to do so until his death. After publishing three novels, Orwell was asked to write a study of conditions among industrial workers in northern England for the socialist Left Book Club. This became *The Road to Wigan Pier* (1937), a moving portrait of the difficult lives of working-class people.

Deeply disturbed by the rise of fascism in the 1930s, Orwell fought against the Fascists in the Spanish Civil War and published a book based on these experiences—*Homage to Catalonia* (1938). "The Spanish war," he wrote, "turned the scale and thereafter I knew where I stood. Every line of serious work that I have written since 1936 has been written, directly or indirectly, *against* totalitarianism and *for* democratic socialism."

His two most famous novels, *Animal Farm* (1945) and *1984* (1949), illustrate this point. *Animal Farm* is a political allegory that points out the dangers of totalitarianism, whether practiced by the left or the right. And *1984* has given us an entire vocabulary for the excesses of totalitarian regimes, including such terms as *newspeak* and *double-think.* In this book, Orwell stresses the connections between language, thought, and power, dramatizing in fiction the ideas he earlier explored in his famous essay *Politics and the English Language* (1946)—especially the idea that corrupt language can be used to promote political oppression.

George Orwell making a radio broadcast for the BBC.

go.hrw.com
LEO 12-15

OBJECTIVES

1. Read and interpret the narrative essay
2. Identify and explain the verbal and situational irony in the narrative
3. Understand and use analogies
4. Express understanding through critical and creative writing
5. Learn and use new words

SKILLS

Literary
- Identify and explain verbal and situational irony
- Understand word analogies

Writing
- Collect ideas for a problem-solution essay
- Explain a response
- Interpret a symbol
- Create a storyboard for a film

Vocabulary
- Learn and use new words

Planning

- **Block Schedule**
  Block Scheduling Lesson Plans with Pacing Guide
- **Traditional Schedule**
  Lesson Plans Including Strategies for English-Language Learners
- **One-Stop Planner**
  CD-ROM with Test Generator

Resources: Print and Media

Reading
- *Reading Skills and Strategies*
  MiniRead Skill Lesson, p. 98
  Selection Skill Lesson, p. 105
- *Graphic Organizers for Active Reading,* p. 113
- *Words to Own,* p. 35
- *Audio CD Library*
  Disc 21, Track 4

Writing and Language
- *Daily Oral Grammar*
  Transparency 42
- *Grammar and Language Links*
  Worksheet, p. 71
- *Language Workshop CD-ROM*

Viewing and Representing
- *Viewing and Representing*
  Fine Art Transparency 20
  Fine Art Worksheet, p. 80

Assessment
- *Formal Assessment,* p. 223
- *Portfolio Management System,* p. 214
- *Preparation for College Admission Exams,* p. 59
- *Test Generator (One-Stop Planner CD-ROM)*

Internet
- go.hrw.com (keyword: LE0 12-15)

Summary ■■

The narrator, Orwell himself, recounts an experience he had while serving as a police officer of the British Empire in colonial Burma. One day, an elephant terrorizes the district, killing one person. A large crowd of Burmese has gathered to watch the elephant by the time Orwell arrives on the scene. Although he hates his job (doing "the dirty work of the Empire") and does not want to kill the elephant, he feels pressured by the crowd to take action. He, therefore, repeatedly and awkwardly shoots the animal, causing its protracted and agonizing death.

BROWSING IN THE FILES

Writers on Writing. Orwell once offered this answer to the question why writers write. "All writers are vain, selfish, and lazy, and at the very bottom of their motives there lies a mystery. Writing a book is a horrible, exhausting struggle, like a long bout of some painful illness. One would never undertake such a thing if one were not driven on by some demon whom one can neither resist nor understand. For all one knows that demon is merely the same instinct that makes a baby squall for attention. And yet it is also true that one can write nothing readable unless one constantly struggles to efface one's own personality. Good prose is like a windowpane." You might ask students to discuss the final simile. What characteristics do good writing and a windowpane share? [Possible responses: Transparency, the capacity to reveal and to open up vistas of experience.]

Before You Read
SHOOTING AN ELEPHANT

Make the Connection
An Enemy Within

Wherever there were British colonies, there were British people who went to these colonies to live and to govern. No matter how long these people lived overseas, they generally remained outsiders, an alien minority holding power over a resentful people. As a police officer in British-controlled Burma in the 1920s, George Orwell did not just symbolize foreign rule—he was its agent. His awareness of being an enemy within another culture kindled enormous conflicts inside him. Just who was *his* enemy? Look for the answer that comes to him, elephant rifle in hand, in the upcoming essay.

Quickwrite

Have you ever witnessed a situation where group pressure forces someone to act in a way he or she might not really want to act? How can one's personality or individuality be taken away as a result of pressure from a crowd or any larger group? Jot down your thoughts on this issue of group pressure versus individuality.

Elements of Literature
Irony

The dominant literary mode in the twentieth century is irony (see page 991). Orwell's essay uses several strategies to evoke a sense of irony. He uses **verbal irony**—saying one thing and meaning something else, often something just the opposite. He also uses **situational irony**—in which something happens that is completely different from what we expect, or from what we think is appropriate. Irony cuts deeply into our feelings, perhaps because we sense that life itself is deeply and pervasively ironic.

> **Irony** is a discrepancy between expectations and reality or between appearances and reality. There are three types of irony: verbal irony, situational irony, and dramatic irony.
>
> *For more on Irony, see page 991 and the Handbook of Literary Terms.*

Background

This essay is set in Burma, a country in Southeast Asia. After a series of wars with Great Britain during the 1800s, Burma finally came under British control in the 1880s. Although allowed some self-rule in 1937, Burma became fully independent only in 1948, after a period of Japanese occupation during World War II. In 1989, the government changed the country's official name to the Union of Myanmar.

House used by British officers or planters. Chapra, India.

Preteaching Vocabulary

Words to Own

Ask pairs of students to read and discuss the definition of each vocabulary word. Then suggest that students work together to create mnemonic devices for remembering word meanings or spellings. Finally, read these sentences to the class and asks volunteers to choose the best vocabulary word to complete each sentence.

1. We could not leave grandfather alone any longer because of his ___. [senility]
2. Living conditions at the refugee camp are. ___. [squalid]
3. The streets of Cairo are like a ___. [labyrinth]
4. E-mail may ___ letter-writing. [supplant]
5. Josh came up with some silly ___ for his tardiness. [pretext]

Shooting an Elephant

George Orwell

In Moulmein, in Lower Burma, I was hated by large numbers of people—the only time in my life that I have been important enough for this to happen to me. I was subdivisional police officer of the town, and in an aimless, petty kind of way anti-European feeling was very bitter. No one had the guts to raise a riot, but if a European woman went through the bazaars alone somebody would probably spit betel juice over her dress. As a police officer I was an obvious target and was baited whenever it seemed safe to do so. When a nimble Burman tripped me up on the football field and the referee (another Burman) looked the other way, the crowd yelled with hideous laughter. This happened more than once. In the end the sneering yellow faces of young men that met me everywhere, the insults hooted after me when I was at a safe distance, got badly on my nerves. The young Buddhist priests were the worst of all. There were several thousands of them in the town and none of them seemed to have anything to do except stand on street corners and jeer at Europeans.

All this was perplexing and upsetting. For at that time I had already made up my mind that imperialism was an evil thing and the sooner I chucked up my job and got out of it the better. Theoretically—and secretly, of course—I was all for the Burmese and all against their oppressors, the British. As for the job I was doing, I hated it more bitterly than I can perhaps make clear. In a job like that you see the dirty work of Empire at close quarters. The wretched prisoners huddling in the stinking cages of the lockups, the gray, cowed faces of the long-term convicts, the scarred buttocks of the men who had been flogged with bamboos—all these oppressed me with an intolerable sense of guilt. But I could get nothing into perspective. I was young and ill-educated and I had had to think out my problems in the utter silence that is imposed on every Englishman in the East. I did not even know that the British Empire is dying, still less did I know that it is a great deal better than the younger empires that are going to supplant it. All I knew was that I was stuck between my hatred of the empire I served and my rage against the evil-spirited little beasts who tried to make my job impossible. With one part of my mind I thought of the British Raj[1] as an unbreakable tyranny, as something clamped down, *in saecula saeculorum,*[2] upon the will of prostrate peoples; with another part I thought that the greatest joy in the world would be to drive a bayonet into a Buddhist priest's guts. Feelings like these are the normal by-products of imperialism; ask any Anglo-Indian official, if you can catch him off duty.

One day something happened which in a roundabout way was enlightening. It was a tiny incident in itself, but it gave me a better glimpse than I had had before of the real nature of imperialism—the real motives for which despotic governments act. Early one morning the subinspector at a police station the other end of the town rang me up on the phone and said that an elephant was ravaging the bazaar. Would I please come and do something about it? I did not know what I could do, but I wanted to see what was happening and I got on to a pony and started out. I took my rifle, an old .44 Winchester and much too small to kill an elephant, but I thought the noise might be useful *in terrorem.*[3] Various Burmans stopped me on the way and told me about the elephant's doings. It was not, of course, a wild elephant, but a tame one which had gone "must."[4] It had been chained up, as tame elephants always are when their attack of "must" is due, but on the previous night it had

1. Raj (räj): rule over India. The word is derived from *rajya,* Hindi for "kingdom."
2. *in saecula saeculorum* (in sē′ko͞o·lə sē′ko͞o·lôr′əm): Latin for "forever and ever" (literally, "into ages of ages").
3. *in terrorem* (in ter·ôr′əm): Latin for "for terror." In other words, the gun might serve to frighten the elephant.
4. must: state of frenzy in animals. The word comes from *mast,* Hindi for "intoxicated."

WORDS TO OWN
supplant (sə·plant′) *v.:* to replace; displace.

Resources

Viewing and Representing

Fine Art Transparency

A legendary and ritual killing of an elephant is depicted in the Fine Art transparency *Krishna Kills the Elephant Kuvalayapida.* See the *Viewing and Representing Transparencies and Worksheets:*

- Transparency 20
- Worksheet, p. 80

(A) Historical Connections

After three Anglo-Burmese wars in the nineteenth century, Great Britain made Burma a province of India. Following an uprising in the early 1930s, four years after Orwell left, Britain gradually began to give Burma its independence.

(B) Reading Skills and Strategies

Making Connections

Explain to students that betel nut is chewed throughout much of Asia; it produces a reddish-brown juice that often stains the teeth of the chewer.

(C) Cultural Connections

Buddhist priests keenly felt the impact of colonialism. The British government refused to support Buddhism as the state religion, and monastic schools, which had given Burma's men a higher literacy rate than Britain's, declined. Ask students how these factors would have affected the young priests. [Possible response: They would have been idle, angry, and resentful.]

(D) Elements of Literature

Verbal Irony

? What is ironic about this statement? [Possible response: On the one hand, Orwell hates the notion of empire with its built-in assumptions of power and superiority; yet, in the same breath, he expresses a resentful and condescending attitude toward those he helps to oppress.]

Reaching All Students

Struggling Readers

Help struggling readers understand this selection by using the strategy, Anticipation Guides. Using this strategy, students will be able to evaluate their own responses to issues before and after they read the selection. See the *Reading Strategies Handbook* in front of the *Reading Skills and Strategies* binder.

- MiniRead Skill Lesson, p. 98
- Selection Skill Lesson, p. 105

English Language Learners

In his essay, Orwell often uses words that were borrowed from other languages and given English pronunciations and spellings. Before students begin reading, call attention to the terms *raj, mahout, must, coolie,* and *sahib* and point out the footnotes that give the pronunciation, derivation, and meaning of each of these words.

Advanced Learners

Urge students to explore another work by Orwell on a similar subject, such as the short essay "A Hanging" or the longer *Burmese Days.* Ask students to give a report to the class on what these works reveal about Orwell's attitude toward British colonialism. Suggest that they consider whether his attitude changes over time or remains the same.

A Reading Skills and Strategies

Connecting Literature to Historical Contexts

? What can you infer about the historical setting based on this passage? [Possible responses: At this time, Burma is comparatively poor and undeveloped. People live in bamboo huts. Fruit is sold in makeshift, open-air "stalls." Most significantly, the Burmese are unarmed and dependent on their British overlords for protection, perhaps even for survival.]

B English Language Learners

Understanding the Prefix *sub-*

Explain that *subinspector* is a British term denoting a role in the police hierarchy that is "below" or "under" the role of inspector. (An inspector is usually lower in rank than a police chief or superintendent.) The word *constable* is chiefly a British usage and means "police officer."

C Appreciating Language

Word Choice and Figurative Language

? What are some examples of powerful or effective language in this passage? [Possible responses: The verbs *ground, scored,* and *stripped* are precise and vivid; the descriptions of "arms crucified," "eyes wide open," and "head sharply twisted" are all precise and horrifying. Perhaps most chilling, and therefore most effective, is the simile comparing the removal of the man's flesh by the elephant's foot to the way in which a rabbit is skinned.]

D Reading Skills and Strategies

Predicting

? Based on what you have read so far, do you think the narrator will shoot the elephant? [Possible response: Yes, the presence of the gun, the title of the essay, and the expectations of the crowd suggest a shooting.]

E Elements of Literature

Situational Irony

? What is ironic about this situation? [Possible responses: The narrator, who is seen as having power, is "feeling a fool"; the person in charge is "unnerved" and seems to prefer following to leading.]

broken its chain and escaped. Its mahout,[5] the only person who could manage it when it was in that state, had set out in pursuit, but had taken the wrong direction and was now twelve hours' journey away, and in the morning the elephant had suddenly reappeared in the town. The Burmese population had no weapons and were quite helpless against it. (A) It had already destroyed somebody's bamboo hut, killed a cow, and raided some fruit stalls and devoured the stock; also it had met the municipal rubbish van and, when the driver jumped out and took to his heels, had turned the van over and inflicted violences upon it.

The Burmese subinspector and some Indian constables (B) were waiting for me in the quarter where the elephant had been seen. It was a very poor quarter, a labyrinth of squalid bamboo huts, thatched with palm leaf, winding all over a steep hillside. I remember that it was a cloudy, stuffy morning at the beginning of the rains. We began questioning the people as to where the elephant had gone and, as usual, failed to get any definite information. That is invariably the case in the East; a story always sounds clear enough at a distance, but the nearer you get to the scene of events the vaguer it becomes. Some of the people said that the elephant had gone in one direction, some said that he had gone in another, some professed not even to have heard of any elephant. I had almost made up my mind that the whole story was a pack of lies, when we heard yells a little distance away. There was a loud, scandalized cry of "Go away, child! Go away this instant!" and an old woman with a switch in her hand came round the corner of the hut, violently shooing away a crowd of naked children. Some more women followed, clicking their tongues and exclaiming; evidently there was something that the children ought not to have seen. I rounded the hut and saw a man's dead body sprawling in the mud. He was an Indian, a black Dravidian coolie,[6] almost naked, and he could not have been dead many minutes. The people said that the elephant had come suddenly upon him round the corner of the hut, caught him with its trunk, put its foot on his back, and ground him into the earth. This was the rainy season and the ground was soft, and his face had scored a trench a foot deep and a couple of yards long. He was lying on his belly with arms crucified and (C) head sharply twisted to one side. His face was coated with mud, the eyes wide open, the teeth bared and grinning with an expression of unendurable agony. (Never tell me, by the way, that the dead look peaceful. Most of the corpses I have seen looked devilish.) The friction of the great beast's foot had stripped the skin from his back as neatly as one skins a rabbit. As soon as I saw the dead man I sent an orderly to a friend's house nearby to borrow an elephant rifle. I had already sent back the pony, not wanting it to go mad with fright and throw me if it smelled the elephant.

The orderly came back in a few minutes with a rifle and five cartridges, and meanwhile some Burmans had arrived and told us that the elephant was in the paddy fields below, only a few hundred yards away. As I started forward practically the whole population of the quarter flocked out of the houses and followed me. They had seen the rifle and were all shouting excitedly that I was going to shoot the elephant. They had not shown much interest in the elephant when he was merely ravaging their homes, but it was different now that he was going to be shot. It was a bit of fun to them, as it would be to an English crowd; besides they wanted the meat. It made me vaguely uneasy. (D) I had no intention of shooting the elephant—I had merely sent for the rifle to defend myself if necessary—and it is always unnerving to have a crowd following you. I marched down the hill, looking and feeling a fool, with the (E) rifle over my shoulder and an ever-growing army of people jostling at my heels. At the bottom, when you got away from the huts, there was a metaled[7] road and beyond that a miry waste of

5. **mahout** (mə·hout′): elephant keeper. The word derives from *mahaut,* Hindi for "great in measure" and, thus, "important officer."

6. **Dravidian** (drə·vid′ē·ən) **coolie:** *Dravidian* denotes any of several intermixed races living chiefly in southern India and northern Sri Lanka. A coolie is an unskilled laborer. The word is derived from *quli,* Hindi for "hired servant," and has become offensive.

7. **metaled:** paved with cinders, stones, or the like.

WORDS TO OWN

labyrinth (lab′ə·rinth′) *n.:* maze; complex or confusing arrangement.

squalid (skwäl′id) *adj.:* foul or unclean; wretched.

Using Students' Strengths

Interpersonal Learners

Orwell was known as a socialist reformer, and his works can be read as protests against or exposés of economic or political injustice. In fact, a critic once wrote that Orwell "would not blow his nose without moralizing on conditions in the handkerchief industry." After students have finished reading, ask them to work in small groups to identify the social and political themes in this narrative, to infer Orwell's intended audience, and to speculate on the effect of this essay on that audience.

Verbal Learners

This essay is full of vivid word choices and figurative language. Invite pairs of students to identify and explain ten of Orwell's most effective uses of language.

paddy fields a thousand yards across, not yet plowed but soggy from the first rains and dotted with coarse grass. The elephant was standing eight yards from the road, his left side toward us. He took not the slightest notice of the crowd's approach. He was tearing up bunches of grass, beating them against his knees to clean them, and stuffing them into his mouth.

I had halted on the road. As soon as I saw the elephant I knew with perfect certainty that I ought not to shoot him. It is a serious matter to shoot a working elephant—it is comparable to destroying a huge and costly piece of machinery—and obviously one ought not to do it if it can possibly be avoided. And at that distance, peacefully eating, the elephant looked no more dangerous than a cow. I thought then and I think now that his attack of "must" was already passing off; in which case he would merely wander harmlessly about until the mahout came back and caught him. Moreover, I did not in the least want to shoot him. I decided that I would watch him for a little while to make sure that he did not turn savage again, and then go home.

But at that moment I glanced round at the crowd that had followed me. It was an immense crowd, two thousand at the least and growing every minute. It blocked the road for a long distance on either side. I looked at the sea of yellow faces above the garish clothes—faces all happy and excited over this bit of fun, all certain that the elephant was going to be shot. They were watching me as they would watch a conjurer about to perform a trick. They did not like me, but with the magical rifle in my hands I was momentarily worth watching. And suddenly I realized that I should have to shoot the elephant after all. The people expected it of me and I had got to do it; I could feel their two thousand wills pressing me forward, irresistibly. And it was at this moment, as I stood there with the rifle in my hands, that I first grasped the hollowness, the futility of the white man's dominion in the East. Here was I, the white man with his gun, standing in front of the unarmed native crowd—seemingly the leading actor of the piece; but in reality I was only an absurd puppet pushed to and fro by the will of those yellow faces behind. I perceived in this moment that when the white man turns tyrant it is his own freedom that he destroys. He becomes a sort of hollow, posing dummy, the conventionalized figure of a sahib.[8] For it is the condition of his rule that he shall spend his life in trying to impress the "natives," and so in every crisis he has got to do what the "natives" expect of him. He wears a mask, and his face grows to fit it. I had got to shoot the elephant. I had committed myself to doing it when I sent for the rifle. A sahib has got to act like a sahib; he has got to appear resolute, to know his own mind and do definite things. To come all that way, rifle in hand, with two thousand people marching at my heels, and then to trail feebly away, having done nothing—no, that was impossible. The crowd would laugh at me. And my whole life, every white man's life in the East, was one long struggle not to be laughed at.

But I did not want to shoot the elephant. I watched him beating his bunch of grass against his knees, with that preoccupied grandmotherly air that elephants have. It seemed to me that it would be murder to shoot him. At that age I was not squeamish about killing animals, but I had never shot an elephant and never wanted to. (Somehow it always seems worse to kill a *large* animal.) Besides, there was the beast's owner to be considered. Alive, the elephant was worth at least a hundred pounds; dead, he would only be worth the value of his tusks, five pounds, possibly. But I had got to act quickly. I turned to some experienced-looking Burmans who had been there when we arrived, and asked them how the elephant had been behaving. They all said the same thing: He took no notice of you if you left him alone, but he might charge if you went too close to him.

It was perfectly clear to me what I ought to do. I ought to walk up to within, say, twenty-five yards of the elephant and test his behavior. If he charged, I could shoot; if he took no notice of me, it would be safe to leave him until the mahout came back. But also I knew that I was going to do no such thing. I was a poor shot with a rifle and the ground was soft mud into which one would sink at every step. If the elephant charged and I missed him, I should have about as much chance as a toad under a steamroller. But even then I was not thinking particularly of my own skin, only of the watchful yellow faces behind. For at that

8. sahib (sä′ib′): master; sir. In colonial India, the title was used as a sign of respect for a European gentleman.

F Elements of Literature

Situational Irony

? What is ironic about this description? [Possible response: An "army" has set out in search of a supposedly crazy elephant, but the elephant is eating peacefully, concerned only about the cleanliness of the grass it is eating.]

G Critical Thinking

Interpreting an Analogy

? How does the analogy, or comparison, of the narrator to a conjurer, or magician, help to reveal the narrator's feelings? [Possible response: The narrator feels like the center of attraction from whom extraordinary and powerful action is expected. In a sense, he has come to embody the myth of the all-powerful Empire and cannot free himself from the role in which he has been cast.]

H Elements of Literature

Theme and Symbol

? Orwell began his narrative by remarking that a tiny incident revealed to him the nature of imperialism. What is the link between imperialism and the elephant? [Possible responses: Orwell is trapped because he must maintain the position of power taken by the imperial government. To maintain the image of British invincibility, he must ignore his humane instincts and shoot the "innocent" elephant.]

I Reading Skills and Strategies

Responding

? If you were Orwell, would you have shot the elephant? [Possible responses: Yes, it was necessary to maintain the crowd's respect. No, I would not allow myself to be an instrument of a government or policy with which I disagreed.]

Crossing the Curriculum

Geography/History

To learn more about Burma and its relationship to the British Empire as a whole, have students do the following:

- Locate a map showing Britain's Empire in the 1920s and find Burma on it.
- Note how many continents the empire spanned and which continent was primarily dominated by Britain.
- Explain the old saying, "The sun never sets on the British Empire."
- Offer historical explanations for why a tiny nation like Britain could have amassed such a large empire.
- Speculate on the feelings of the Burmese whose country was not considered as important to the British Empire as neighboring India, which was regarded as "the jewel in the crown," or the most important imperial holding.
- Research the role of Burma in the Second World War and in the fight for Indian independence from Britain.
- Find out about the human rights work in Burma of Daw Aung San Suu Kyi, the 1991 Nobel Peace Prize winner.

Ⓐ Reading Skills and Strategies

Making Connections

The narrator overcomes his fear for the sake of keeping up appearances. Ask students if they can identify with his desire to save face and live up to others' expectations. Invite them to write in their journals about a time when they may have suppressed fear in order to make a favorable impression.

Ⓑ Elements of Literature

Situational Irony

? What is ironic about this information? [Possible responses: The narrator is in charge of shooting the elephant and has been invested with a lot of power by the local people. However, he not only does not want to shoot the elephant, he does not know how and cannot do it competently.]

Ⓒ Critical Thinking

Expressing an Opinion

? Why do you think Orwell includes so much detail about the elephant's death? [Possible responses: In pivotal situations in life, or in situations when we are acting against our conscience, every detail becomes magnified and may replay in our memory at a later time. Also, the long, detailed description mirrors the agonizingly slow death of the elephant.]

Jumbo Elephant #2 (1988) by William Hawkins. Enamel and collage on masonite (48″ × 57″).
Ricco/Maresca Gallery, New York.

moment, with the crowd watching me, I was not afraid in the ordinary sense, as I would have been Ⓐ if I had been alone. A white man mustn't be frightened in front of "natives"; and so, in general, he isn't frightened. The sole thought in my mind was that if anything went wrong those two thousand Burmans would see me pursued, caught, trampled on, and reduced to a grinning corpse like that Indian up the hill. And if that happened it was quite probable that some of them would laugh. That would never do. There was only one alternative. I shoved the cartridges into the magazine and lay down on the road to get a better aim.

The crowd grew very still, and a deep, low, happy sigh, as of people who see the theater curtain go up at last, breathed from innumerable throats. They were going to have their bit of fun after all. The rifle was a beautiful German thing Ⓑ with cross-hair sights. I did not then know that in shooting an elephant one would shoot to cut an imaginary bar running from earhole to earhole. I ought, therefore, as the elephant was sideways on, to have aimed straight at his earhole; actually I aimed several inches in front of this, thinking the brain would be further forward.

When I pulled the trigger I did not hear the bang or feel the kick—one never does when a shot goes home—but I heard the devilish roar of Ⓒ glee that went up from the crowd. In that instant, in too short a time, one would have thought, even for the bullet to get there, a mysterious, terrible change had come over the elephant. He neither stirred nor fell, but every line of his body had altered. He looked suddenly stricken, shrunken, immensely old, as though the frightful impact of the bullet had paralyzed him without knocking him down. At last, after what seemed a long time—it might have been five seconds, I dare say—he sagged flabbily to his knees. His mouth slobbered. An enormous senility seemed to have settled upon him. One could have imagined him thousands of years old. I fired again into the same spot. At the second shot he did not collapse but climbed with desperate slowness to his feet and stood weakly upright, with legs sagging and head drooping. I fired a third time. That was the shot that did for him. You could see the agony of it jolt his whole body and knock the last remnant of strength from his legs. But in falling he seemed for a moment to rise, for as his hind legs collapsed beneath him he seemed to tower upward like a huge rock toppling, his trunk reaching skyward like a tree. He trumpeted, for the first and only time. And then down he came, his belly toward me, with a crash that seemed to shake the ground even where I lay.

I got up. The Burmans were already racing past me across the mud. It was obvious that the elephant would never rise again, but he was not

WORDS TO OWN

senility (si·nil′ə·tē) *n.:* state of deterioration that sometimes accompanies old age.

Assessing Learning

Check Test: Short Answers

1. **What internal conflict does the narrator face?** [He has to enforce colonial policy with which he disagrees.]
2. **Why does the narrator send for an elephant rifle?** [to protect himself against an animal he thinks may be dangerous]
3. **Why do the Burmese want the narrator to shoot the elephant?** [They want the diversion, and they want the meat.]
4. **Why does it take several shots to bring down the elephant?** [The narrator is inexperienced and does not know how to effectively shoot the animal.]
5. **What reason does the narrator give for killing the elephant?** [to avoid looking foolish]

Standardized Test Preparation

For practice with ACT and SAT formats, see
- *Preparation for College Admission Exams,* p. 59

For practice in proofreading and editing, see
- *Daily Oral Grammar,* Transparency p. 42

dead. He was breathing very rhythmically with long rattling gasps, his great mound of a side painfully rising and falling. His mouth was wide open—I could see far down into caverns of pale pink throat. I waited a long time for him to die, but his breathing did not weaken. Finally I fired my two remaining shots into the spot where I thought his heart must be. The thick blood welled out of him like red velvet, but still he did not die. His body did not even jerk when the shots hit him, the tortured breathing continued without a pause. He was dying, very slowly and in great agony, but in some world remote from me where not even a bullet could damage him further. I felt that I had got to put an end to that dreadful noise. It seemed dreadful to see the great beast lying there, powerless to move and yet powerless to die, and not even to be able to finish him. I sent back for my small rifle and poured shot after shot into his heart and down his throat. They seemed to make no impression. The tortured gasps continued as steadily as the ticking of a clock.

In the end I could not stand it any longer and went away. I heard later that it took him half an hour to die. Burmans were bringing dahs[9] and baskets even before I left, and I was told they had stripped his body almost to the bones by the afternoon.

Afterward, of course, there were endless discussions about the shooting of the elephant. The owner was furious, but he was only an Indian and could do nothing. Besides, legally I had done the right thing, for a mad elephant has to be killed, like a mad dog, if its owner fails to control it. Among the Europeans opinion was divided. The older men said I was right, the younger men said it was a damn shame to shoot an elephant for killing a coolie, because an elephant was worth more than any damn Coringhee[10] coolie. And afterward I was very glad that the coolie had been killed; it put me legally in the right and it gave me a sufficient pretext for shooting the elephant. I often wondered whether any of the others grasped that I had done it solely to avoid looking a fool.

9. **dahs** (däz): large carving knives.
10. **Coringhee** (kôr·ing′ē): port in southeastern India.

WORDS TO OWN
pretext (prē′tekst′) *n.:* excuse.

MAKING MEANINGS

First Thoughts

1. What do you think of Orwell's decision to shoot the elephant?

Reading Check

a. What problem is Orwell asked to solve?
b. About how big is the crowd following Orwell, and why does he say they have come along?
c. When Orwell finds the elephant, what are two reasons he gives for not shooting it?
d. How does the animal react when shot?

Shaping Interpretations

2. What seems to be Orwell's attitude toward the Burmese? Do you think he embodies an imperialist perspective? Use details from the story to support your answer.
3. Explain in your own words the meaning of Orwell's **ironic** insight: Tyrants destroy their own freedom. Then, identify three other ironies contained in this essay.
4. What do you think this essay reveals about the real nature of imperialism?
5. There are two Orwells in this essay: the one acting and the one looking back. Discuss the differences between the two observers, using examples from the text. How does the older Orwell feel about the younger one?

Connecting with the Text

6. The essay is filled with remarkable physical descriptions. Which description did you find most compelling? How did it make you feel?

Extending the Text

7. In what ways are Orwell's experiences like and unlike those of a contemporary police officer or of a soldier on a peacekeeping mission?

Reading Check

a. He is asked to rid the bazaar of a mad elephant.
b. At least two thousand people are following Orwell; they want the entertainment of seeing the elephant shot, and they want the meat from the animal.
c. To shoot a working elephant is like destroying expensive machinery; besides, the elephant's fit of madness has passed.
d. He dies slowly and in great agony.

MAKING MEANINGS

First Thoughts [Respond]

1. Some students may condemn Orwell's act as cowardly, and unnecessary; others may see that a complex of motives and competing loyalties causes him to act as he does.

Shaping Interpretations [Interpret]

2. Possible response: Orwell does not believe that the British should rule over the Burmese, but he is angry with individual Burmese who make it difficult for him to do his job. He also expresses himself in the language of the conqueror when he refers to the Burmese as "little beasts" or refers to their color or way of life disparagingly.
3. Tyrants no longer have the freedom to decide according to the needs of the situation but must instead decide according to the demands of power. Students may cite the following examples of irony: Orwell enforces a political philosophy of which he disapproves; the crowd is unaware that Orwell does not want to shoot the elephant.
4. Possible responses: Imperialism is harmful to both the oppressed and oppressor; imperialists are not as powerful or free as they seem.
5. The younger Orwell whose actions are presented in the narrative gets caught up in his situation; he is aware of the contradictions but unable to step outside the expectations of role and race. The narrator, on the other hand, can look back with greater perspective and maturity on his youthful actions and display a keener awareness of the ironies of his position.

Connecting with the Text [Evaluate]

6. Many students will comment on the description of the elephant's death; they may be drawn to it because the narrator emphasizes that the death is unnecessary.

Extending the Text [Analyze]

7. Possible responses: Like an ordinary police officer, Orwell is influenced by the pressure of the crowd. However, if the police officer is from the same community or culture as the people he or she is policing, the officer probably will not face the same contradictions that Orwell does.

Grading Timesaver

Rubrics for each Choices assignment appear on p. 214 in the *Portfolio Management System.*

CHOICES: Building Your Portfolio

1. **Writer's Notebook** Brainstorming as a class may be beneficial. Remind students to mention only those occasions that they do not mind sharing with the class.
2. **Explaining a Response** You may wish to build background by bringing in newspaper articles describing conflicts in colonies or former colonies. Continuing struggles in Africa, where colonialism often drew borders that ignored ethnic lines and where colonial governments often did little or nothing to prepare people for the transition to self-rule, may be good examples.
3. **Interpreting a Symbol** Remind students that there is no single correct interpretation of the elephant as symbol, but they must have evidence to support whatever interpretation they make. Suggest that while they reread the essay with this focus in mind, they use stick-on notes to mark significant details. They may want to outline or cluster the details they gather before writing.
4. **Creative Writing** To save time, assign small groups of students scenes from the essay, which they can use to create one panel for a class storyboard. In this way, students can focus on selecting the dialogue, and the various groups can present the entire essay to the class. To maintain the storyboard's continuity, groups should discuss their presentation with those who are working on scenes immediately before or after their own.

CHOICES: Building Your Portfolio

Writer's Notebook

1. Collecting Ideas for a Problem-Solution Essay

Pressure to conform is experienced by everyone who lives within a social group. Refer to your Quickwrite notes, and develop your ideas on group pressure. Think of specific occasions in your school or community when you or someone else experienced pressure to conform to group values or behavior. What happened, whom did it happen to, and why did it happen? Save your notes for possible use in the Writer's Workshop on page 1179.

Explaining a Response

2. A Significant Passage

Review the essay, and find one passage that you think is especially important, or controversial, or even upsetting. Write a brief essay in which you cite the passage and explain why you have chosen it. In your essay, be sure to describe your response to the passage and tell whether you think it connects to any situation in society as you know it today.

Interpreting a Symbol

3. Elephant Meanings

The elephant has tremendous importance in this essay. Could it **symbolize** the British Empire? Orwell himself? something else? Write an essay that presents your interpretation of the elephant's symbolic meaning. Cite details from the text to support your interpretation.

Creative Writing

4. Shooting "Shooting an Elephant"

Imagine that you are turning "Shooting an Elephant" into a short film. Create a storyboard, showing the scenes you'd include in your film. For which scenes would you add dialogue to move the film along? Which scene will mark the climax of your film?

Reading Skills

VOCABULARY: ANALYZING WORD ANALOGIES

An **analogy** is a similarity or likeness between two things that are unlike in other ways. When you state an analogy, you compare two things to show their likeness. A **word analogy** is a formally written statement that compares two pairs of words. The pairs of words are alike in that the relationship between the two words in the first pair is the same as the relationship between the two words in the second pair.

Standardized tests frequently include analogy questions, which measure your mastery of vocabulary and your ability to perceive relationships and patterns between words. Practice with analogies will help you develop the logical abilities to identify these relationships and patterns.

Reading word analogies. Although unlike in other ways, *cool* and *chilly* have a synonymous relationship to each other, just as *sad* and *unhappy* have. The following example shows how a word analogy using these words is written:

COOL : CHILLY :: sad : unhappy.

The colon (:) stands for the phrase "is related to." The double colon (::) between the two pairs of words stands for the phrase "in the same way that." Here are two ways to read the analogy:

- COOL [is related to] CHILLY
[in the same way that]
sad [is related to] *unhappy.*
- COOL is to CHILLY as *sad* is to *unhappy.*

Understanding word analogy problems. The word analogy items you will find in exercises and on tests will be one of the following two kinds:

- One pair of words is given, and you must select a second pair with the same relationship.
- One pair of words and one word from the second pair are given, and you must select the word that completes the second pair.

In both kinds of problems, the parts of speech and relative order of the words in each pair must match.

Making the Connections

Connecting to the Theme: "Clashes of Culture"

Students may discuss these questions:

- Orwell presents a clash of cultures that continues to resonate in our own times. What is it? [Possible responses: Nations or ethnic groups who try to dominate others culturally or economically set themselves up in untenable positions that inevitably lead to conflict with those they dominate or exploit.]
- This is a first-person account of a clash of cultures. In your opinion, would a more objective third-person account of the same issues be more or less effective? [Possible responses: No, it would be less effective because the reader would not feel the intensity of the narrator's self-doubt and self-recrimination. Yes, it would be more effective because it would provide a broader, more balanced picture of the issues.]

Identifying relationships. The chart on the right will help you identify some of the relationships that are frequently expressed in word analogies. Other possible relationships between words might include whole and part, function, action to object, action to performer, degree, and time sequence.

Solving word analogies. On standardized tests, analogy questions are usually presented in the two formats discussed on page 1144. You can use the following three steps to solve an analogy question:

- Analyze the first pair of words to identify the relationship between them.
- State the analogy in sentence or question form.
- Identify the best available choice to complete the analogy.

Try It Out

For each item, write, on your own paper, the type of relationship the words in the complete pair have to each other. Then, write the word from the following list that appropriately completes each word analogy. (An example is provided.)

conspicuous	obnoxious	senility
guffaw	pretext	squalid
labyrinth	propitious	temerity
magnanimous		

Relationship	Analogy
location	CLOUD : SKY :: student : school
1. ______	DUMP : ______ :: system : organized
2. ______	SOB : ______ :: grin : frown
3. ______	______ : FORGETFULNESS :: exercise : fitness
4. ______	THOUGHTFUL : CONSIDERATE :: ______ : offensive
5. ______	PATH : ______ :: piece : puzzle

Word Analogies		
Relationship	**Example**	**Explanation**
Antonym	SOILED : CLEAN :: careless : careful	*Soiled* is the opposite of *clean*, just as *careless* is the opposite of *careful*.
Synonym	COOL : CHILLY :: sad : unhappy	*Cool* and *chilly* are similar in meaning, as are *sad* and *unhappy*.
Cause and Effect	TRAGEDY : SADNESS :: comedy : happiness	*Tragedy* generally causes *sadness*, just as *comedy* generally causes *happiness*.
Characteristic Quality	OCEAN : LARGE :: pond : small	*Oceans* are characteristically *large*, just as *ponds* are characteristically *small*.
Part and Whole	CHAPTER : BOOK :: fender : car	A *chapter* is a part of a *book*, just as a *fender* is a part of a *car*.
Location	FISH : SEA :: moose : forest	A *fish* can be found in the *sea*, just as a *moose* can be found in a *forest*.
Classification	TANGO : DANCE :: neon : gas	The *tango* is classified as a kind of *dance*, just as *neon* is classified as a kind of *gas*.

OBJECTIVES

1. Use analogies to understand word meanings
2. Analyze relationships between words
3. Create original word analogies

Reading Skills and Strategies

This feature focuses on word analogies. This skill is applied, wherever possible, to reinforce comprehension of vocabulary included in the selections in this collection.

Mini-Lesson:
Analyzing Word Analogies

Have students make up their own analogies, using Words to Own from this collection and previous ones. Ask them to create an analogy illustrating each of the seven relationships listed in the first column of the chart on the left.

Try It Out
Answers

1. Relationship: characteristic, quality
   Word: SQUALID
2. Relationship: antonym
   Word: GUFFAW
3. Relationship: cause and effect
   Word: SENILITY
4. Relationship: synonym
   Word: OBNOXIOUS
5. Relationship: part and whole
   Word: LABYRINTH

OBJECTIVES

1. Read and interpret the story
2. Identify the story's theme
3. Express understanding through critical and creative writing, science, and research
4. Learn and use new words

SKILLS

Literary
- Identify the story's theme

Writing
- Collect ideas for a problem-solution essay
- Analyze conflict
- Evaluate point of view
- Compare and contrast texts

Science
- Research folk remedies and cures

Vocabulary
- Learn and use new words

Planning

- **Traditional Schedule**
  Lesson Plans Including Strategies for English-Language Learners
- **One-Stop Planner**
  CD-ROM with Test Generator

Doris Lessing

(1919–)

Doris Lessing was born in Persia (now Iran) to British parents who had fled England to escape its narrowness and provincialism. When she was five, her father gave up his job running a bank, and the family moved to a three-thousand-acre farm in Southern Rhodesia (now Zimbabwe). The farm employed some thirty to fifty black African laborers, each of whom earned the equivalent of about $1.50 a month and who lived in mud huts with no sanitation.

In Africa, Lessing's mother was homesick for England and often ill, while her father grew increasingly eccentric. Lessing describes her own childhood as "hellishly lonely"; the nearest neighbor was miles away. Only as an adult did she appreciate that her solitude had fostered a fine education, since the lack of company allowed her to spend her time slowly reading the classics of European and American fiction.

At fourteen, Lessing left school and went to work in Salisbury, the capital of Rhodesia, first as a nursemaid and then as a stenographer and telephone operator. The city had a white population of about ten thousand, and a larger black population that Lessing discovered "didn't count." When her first marriage collapsed, she entered radical politics. At twenty-six, she married a second time, but that marriage also ended in divorce.

"I can't remember a time when I didn't want to come to England," she later recalled. In 1949, she left Africa for England with her two-year-old son and the manuscript of her first novel, *The Grass Is Singing* (1950). Tracing a complex relationship between a white farmer's wife and her black servant, the book commanded attention as one of the earliest novels about Africa's racial problems.

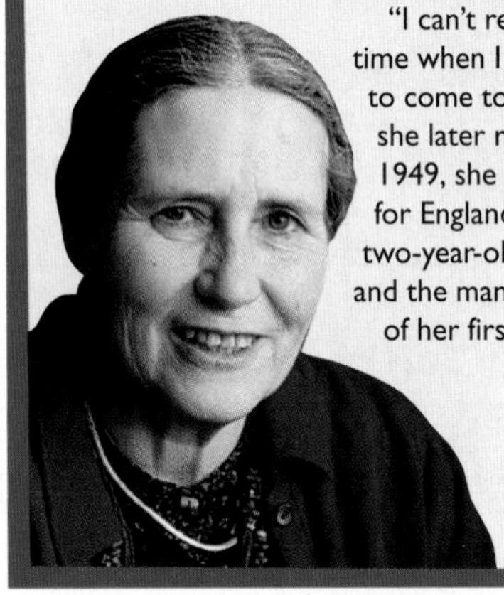

Doris Lessing (1984).

The short stories collected in Lessing's *African Stories* (1964) also take place in the Africa of her childhood. Also semiautobiographical is Lessing's quintet of novels, *Children of Violence* (1952–1969), which tells the story of the aptly named Martha Quest, who like her creator spent her childhood in Africa and her mature life in postwar Britain. The narrative continues to an apocalyptic ending in an unnamed city in the year 2000.

Lessing's most widely read and discussed book is probably *The Golden Notebook* (1962), an ambitious, complexly structured work that combines fiction, parody, and factual reporting to explore Lessing's concerns with politics, mental illness, and the problems of women in modern life. Another well-known book, *Briefing for a Descent into Hell* (1971), introduces readers to what Lessing calls "inner-space fiction," in which an individual mental breakdown is related to a wider social breakdown. In contrast, Lessing's five-volume series *Canopus in Argos: Archives* (1979–1983) is a sequence of fantasies set in outer space. However, one reviewer remarked that the series shows less of a relationship to typical space-travel science fiction than it does to the Book of Revelation in the Bible.

Among Lessing's more recent novels are *The Good Terrorist* (1985), about a group of young radicals in contemporary London, and *The Fifth Child* (1988), about the effects a "demon child" has on his family and society. She also continues to write nonfiction works on subjects ranging from political correctness to the 1980s war in Afghanistan. In 1994, she published *Under My Skin,* the first volume of her autobiography.

In all of Lessing's work, there is evidence of the responsibility she feels as a writer to be "an instrument of change." "It is not merely a question of preventing evil," she says, "but of strengthening a vision of a good which may defeat the evil."

go.hrw.com
LEO 12-15

Resources: Print and Media

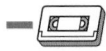

Reading
- *Graphic Organizers for Active Reading,* p. 114
- *Words to Own,* p. 36

Elements of Literature
- *Literary Elements*
  Transparency 27
  Worksheet, p. 82

Writing and Language
- *Daily Oral Grammar*
  Transparency 43
- *Grammar and Language Links*
  Worksheet, p. 73
- *Language Workshop CD-ROM*

Assessment
- *Formal Assessment,* p. 225
- *Portfolio Management System,* p. 215
- *Test Generator (One-Stop Planner CD-ROM)*

Internet
- go.hrw.com (keyword: LEO 12-15)

Before You Read

NO WITCHCRAFT FOR SALE

Make the Connection

The Power to Heal

The upcoming story asks troubling, complex questions about cultural conflict. Some of its cultural clashes are obvious, some are bridged by the unifying force of deep affection, and some remain mysterious—for the people involved, and perhaps for us. Do you think that some cultural differences cannot be bridged no matter how much goodwill the parties bring to their encounter? Or do you think that with effort, people truly *can* understand one another's beliefs and aspirations? See whether "No Witchcraft for Sale"—which really is not about witchcraft at all—clarifies, confuses, or changes your ideas.

Quickwrite

Think of someone you know or know about who comes from a culture or background very different from your own. What do you think that person would find difficult or impossible to understand about your culture? What is mysterious to you about that person's culture? Write down your ideas.

Elements of Literature

Theme

A story may have many threads. A wide assortment of ideas may be conveyed through characters' attitudes, through conflicts and their outcomes, through symbols, and even through a title. Yet despite the variety of ideas a reader may glean from a story, one dominant, central idea, or **theme,** will unify the work.

> **Theme** is a central idea or insight embodied in a work of literature.
>
> *For more on Theme, see the Handbook of Literary Terms.*

Background

This tale from Doris Lessing's *African Stories* takes place in Southern Rhodesia at a time when that southern African country was still under British rule. The Farquars in the story are part of the British ruling class; their servants are black Africans. In her preface to *African Stories,* Lessing writes: "If people had been prepared to listen, two decades earlier, to the small, but shrill-enough, voices crying out for the world's attention, perhaps the present suffering in South Africa and Southern Rhodesia could have been prevented. Britain, who is responsible, became conscious of her responsibility too late; and now the tragedy must play itself slowly out." In the 1960s, when Lessing wrote these words, Southern Rhodesia was an independent nation under minority rule by whites. Attempts by black African leaders to gain a voice in government were vigorously opposed by the white leadership. After much fighting between black nationalists and government troops, Southern Rhodesia emerged as the republic of Zimbabwe under the leadership of a black African, Robert Mugabe (moo·gäb′ē), in 1980.

Summary ■■

When the Farquars, a white couple living in South Africa, finally have a son, Teddy, their African cook, Gideon, lovingly nurtures the boy. From the beginning, Gideon knows there is an unbridgeable gap between Teddy and himself, but their friendship does not cool until the boy dismisses Gideon's own son as being "only a black boy." One day, a snake spits in Teddy's eyes, and he begins to go blind. Gideon, acting decisively, uses a root to cure him. The story of the cure spreads, and a white scientist arrives to ask Gideon to share his knowledge for the benefit of humanity. To the family's consternation, Gideon refuses. The whites do not understand that Gideon's knowledge of herbal medicine is part of the inherited culture of his people and that they are insulting him by expecting him to give it away.

BROWSING IN THE FILES

Writers on Writing. Doris Lessing has an abiding sense of the writer's responsibility. "Once a writer has a feeling of responsibility as a human being, for the other human beings he influences, . . . he must become a humanist, and . . . an instrument of change. . . ."

About the Author. Lessing is convinced of the human ability to change, even though she expresses some short-term pessimism about human limitations. She says, "[Humans] are supremely equipped to survive, to adapt, and even in the long run to start thinking."

Preteaching Vocabulary

Words to Own

Have pairs of students study the meanings of each vocabulary word and then sort the words into as many categories as possible. For example, they may sort them by structural attributes, such as prefixes and suffixes; by parts of speech; or by etymology, or origin. Encourage them to consult a dictionary for more information on each word.

Then have students complete each sentence.

1. Jamal's apology was halfhearted and [perfunctory].
2. Jenny's [reproachful] stare let me know I had said something wrong.
3. Native Americans expect their burial grounds to be treated [reverently].
4. The cook was [perversely] disappointed when the guests cut into the casserole.
5. Some injuries cannot be [annulled] by apologies.

A Historical Connections

When British colonists arrived in what they called Rhodesia, they took the country's most productive, fertile farmland for themselves. Africans were removed from their ancestral homes to communal lands, where the soil was poor and it was difficult to raise crops. As a result, many Africans who had made a living from the land were now displaced and became a source of cheap labor in cities and in mining operations. This resulted in the white community enjoying a very high standard of living while the black majority barely got by.

B Elements of Literature

Characterization

? What is your first impression of Gideon? [Possible response: He is patient and kind and very fond of Teddy.]

C Critical Thinking

? Why do you think Mrs. Farquar is pleased when Gideon says "we"? [Possible response: because he shares her joy in her son.]

D Elements of Literature

Irony

? What is ironic about Teddy's hair appearing "miraculous"? Explain. [Possible answer: The white child's hair is no more miraculous than the black child's. The only thing remarkable about his blond hair is that in this society it will confer power and prestige on him as he matures, which will be denied to the black boy.]

No Witchcraft for Sale

Doris Lessing

The Farquars had been childless for years when little Teddy was born; and they were touched by the pleasure of their servants, who brought presents of fowls and eggs and flowers to the homestead when they came to rejoice over the baby, exclaiming with delight over his downy golden head and his blue eyes. They congratulated Mrs. Farquar as if she had achieved a very great thing, and she felt that she had—her smile for the lingering, admiring natives was warm and grateful.

Later, when Teddy had his first haircut, Gideon the cook picked up the soft gold tufts from the ground, and held them reverently in his hand. Then he smiled at the little boy and said: "Little Yellow Head." That became the native name for the child. Gideon and Teddy were great friends from the first. When Gideon had finished his work, he would lift Teddy on his shoulders to the shade of a big tree, and play with him there, forming curious little toys from twigs and leaves and grass, or shaping animals from wetted soil. When Teddy learned to walk it was often Gideon who crouched before him, clucking encouragement, finally catching him when he fell, tossing him up in the air till they both became breathless with laughter. Mrs. Farquar was fond of the old cook because of his love for her child.

There was no second baby; and one day Gideon said: "Ah, missus, missus, the Lord above sent this one; Little Yellow Head is the most good thing we have in our house." Because of that "we" Mrs. Farquar felt a warm impulse toward her cook; and at the end of the month she raised his wages. He had been with her now for several years; he was one of the few natives who had his wife and children in the compound and never wanted to go home to his kraal,[1] which was some hundreds of miles away. Sometimes a small piccanin[2] who had been born the same time as Teddy, could be seen peering from the edge of the bush, staring in awe at the little white boy with his miraculous fair hair and Northern blue eyes. The two little children would gaze at each other with a wide, interested gaze, and once Teddy put out his hand curiously to touch the black child's cheeks and hair.

Gideon, who was watching, shook his head wonderingly, and said: "Ah, missus, these are both children, and one will grow up to be a baas,[3] and one will be a servant"; and Mrs. Farquar smiled and said sadly, "Yes, Gideon, I was thinking the same."

1. **kraal** (kräl): South African village.
2. **piccanin** (pik′ə·nin): black African child. Derived from *pequeno* (pä·kā′no͞o), Portuguese for "small," the term is often considered offensive.
3. **baas** (bäs): Afrikaans for "master." Afrikaans, a language developed from seventeenth-century Dutch, is spoken in South Africa.

WORDS TO OWN

reverently (rev′ər·ənt·lē) *adv.:* with deep respect, love, or awe, as for something sacred.

Reaching All Students

English Language Learners

Be sure students understand that Gideon's dialogue reflects the dialect of English spoken by blacks in Rhodesia at the time the story takes place. Help them to use the footnotes to learn the pronunciation and meaning of the dialect words. You may want to begin reading the story aloud and then have students themselves continue to read aloud in small groups of mixed proficiency.

Advanced Learners

Healers like Gideon did not disappear with the decolonization of Africa. Students may want to research their role in modern Zimbabwe. [Native practitioners, now often called "traditional healers" continue to dispense herbal medicines and to explore alternative treatments for such chronic illnesses as high blood pressure and asthma. Since independence, the Zimbabwean government has licensed thousands of traditional healers.]

She sighed. "It is God's will," said Gideon, who was a mission boy.[4] The Farquars were very religious people; and this shared feeling about God bound servant and masters even closer together. E

Teddy was about six years old when he was given a scooter, and discovered the intoxications of speed. All day he would fly around the homestead, in and out of flowerbeds, scattering squawking chickens and irritated dogs, finishing with a wide dizzying arc into the kitchen door. There he would cry: "Gideon, look at me!" And Gideon would laugh and say: "Very clever, Little Yellow Head." Gideon's youngest son, who was now a herdsboy, came especially up from the compound to see the scooter. He was afraid to come near it, but Teddy showed off in front of him. "Piccanin," shouted Teddy, "get out of my way!" And he raced in circles around the black child until he was frightened, and fled back to the bush.

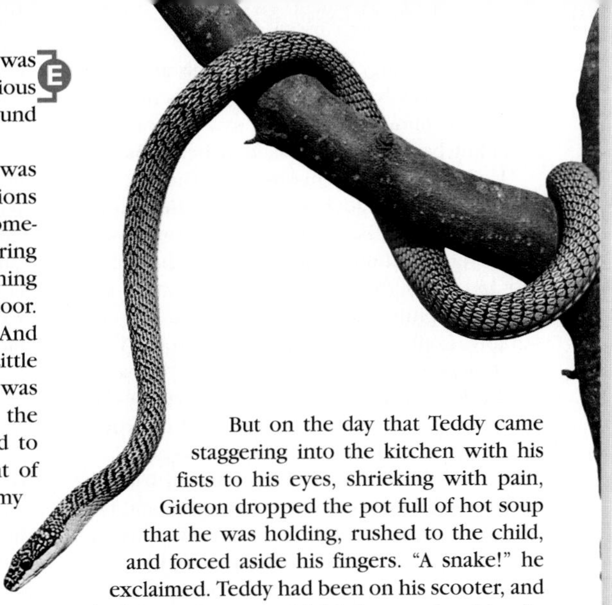

"Why did you frighten him?" asked Gideon, gravely reproachful.

Teddy said defiantly: "He's only a black boy," and laughed. Then, when Gideon turned away from him without speaking, his face fell. Very soon he slipped into the house and found an orange and brought it to Gideon, saying: "This is for you." He could not bring himself to say he was sorry; but he could not bear to lose Gideon's affection either. Gideon took the orange unwillingly F and sighed. "Soon you will be going away to school, Little Yellow Head," he said wonderingly, "and then you will be grown up." He shook his head gently and said, "And that is how our lives go." He seemed to be putting a distance between himself and Teddy, not because of resentment, but in the way a person accepts something inevitable. The baby had lain in his arms and smiled up into his face: The tiny boy had swung from his shoulders and played with him by the hour. Now Gideon would not let his flesh touch the flesh of the white child. He was kind, but there was a grave formality in his voice that made Teddy pout and sulk away. Also, it made him into a man: With Gideon he was polite, and carried himself formally, and if he came into the kitchen to ask for something, it was in the way a white man uses toward a servant, expecting to be obeyed.

4. **mission boy:** one educated by Christian missionaries.

But on the day that Teddy came staggering into the kitchen with his fists to his eyes, shrieking with pain, Gideon dropped the pot full of hot soup that he was holding, rushed to the child, and forced aside his fingers. "A snake!" he exclaimed. Teddy had been on his scooter, and had come to a rest with his foot on the side of a big tub of plants. A tree snake, hanging by its tail from the roof, had spat full into his eyes. Mrs. Farquar came running when she heard the commotion. "He'll go blind," she sobbed, holding Teddy close against her. "Gideon, he'll go blind!" Already G the eyes, with perhaps half an hour's sight left in them, were swollen up to the size of fists: Teddy's small white face was distorted by great purple oozing protuberances.[5] Gideon said: "Wait a minute, missus, I'll get some medicine." He ran off into the bush.

Mrs. Farquar lifted the child into the house and bathed his eyes with permanganate.[6] She had scarcely heard Gideon's words; but when she saw that her remedies had no effect at all, and remembered how she had seen natives with no sight in H their eyes, because of the spitting of a snake, she began to look for the return of her cook, remembering what she heard of the efficacy of native herbs. She stood by the window, holding the

5. **protuberances** (prō·to͞o′bər·əns·iz): swellings; bulges.
6. **permanganate** (pər·maŋ′gə·nāt′): dark purple chemical compound used as a disinfectant.

Words to Own
reproachful (ri·prōch′fəl) *adj.:* full of or expressing blame.

E Cultural Connections

Gideon is a "mission boy" because he attended a school run by Christian missionaries and learned the religion of his employers. Ask students what—for better or for worse—the missions may have provided for Africans. [Possible responses: Missions may have provided clinics and hospitals in addition to instruction, religious and otherwise, in their schools. They probably would aspire to instill European and Christian values, which would often conflict with traditional African beliefs and would tend to replace or obliterate African traditions and values.]

F Elements of Literature

Theme

This passage is central to the development of Lessing's theme. Ask students to tell why this moment in the story is so significant. [Possible responses: This is the most blatant example so far of racial conflict and injustice. Teddy's inability to apologize to Gideon shows white Rhodesians' lack of concern for the ramifications of their behavior on the black population whose lands they have appropriated. It also shows that Teddy regards Gideon as inferior.]

G Elements of Literature

Symbolism

? Why do you think Lessing decides on an injury to eyesight as the pivotal event in her plot? [Possible response: This story is about blindness of another sort, racial blindness. The whites appear to willfully disregard the humanity and dignity of the blacks whom they have reduced to a servant class in their own country.]

H Critical Thinking

Analyzing

? How does this incident affect the usual relationship between Mrs. Farquar and Gideon? [Possible response: Mrs. Farquar, who is usually in a position of power over her servant Gideon, is now totally reliant on Gideon, who is in control of Teddy's life.]

Using Students' Strengths

Visual Learners

Invite students to create a two-column chart to explore the motivations of the Farquars, Teddy, Gideon, and the scientist. Remind students to record both positive and negative motivations. Point out that no small measure of the story's power derives from the following irony: Although the characters are motivated, at least in part, by love or good intentions, a terrible divide still exists between them.

Naturalist Learners

Students might research and share information with the class about any of the following: the species of spitting snake that attacked Teddy and whether and how its venom could cause blindness; herbal and other natural cures for snakebite; attitudes toward traditional healing in American mainstream culture.

Ⓐ Reading Skills and Strategies

Responding to the Text

? If you were Mrs. Farquar, would you have trusted Gideon? [Possible response: Yes, he is her only hope, and although his actions seem strange, she knows he loves Teddy.]

Ⓑ Critical Thinking

Challenging the Text

? Were you curious to know how Teddy reacted to Gideon after his sight was saved? Would including this reaction have enriched the story? [Possible responses: No, Teddy's character has already been revealed and has served the purpose of demonstrating the white's feelings of superiority. Yes, Teddy's reaction is needed to show why he is deserving of Gideon's love and assistance.]

Ⓒ Elements of Literature

Theme

? Why do the Africans withhold the truth about their plants' medicinal properties? [Possible responses: White people do not respect the Africans or their medicine. Giving whites this knowledge would be like giving up part of their soul to those who would not appreciate the gift. The whites have already taken over enough of what rightfully belongs to the Africans.]

Ⓓ Critical Thinking

Comparing and Contrasting

? How does the scientist's motivation for finding out the cure compare with that of the Farquars? [While the Farquars appear to be motivated simply by a desire to share with others what they perceive to be a miracle, the scientist is motivated by the desire to make money.]

terrified, sobbing little boy in her arms, and peered helplessly into the bush. It was not more than a few minutes before she saw Gideon come bounding back, and in his hand he held a plant.

"Do not be afraid, missus," said Gideon, "this will cure Little Yellow Head's eyes." He stripped the leaves from the plant, leaving a small white fleshy root. Without even washing it, he put the root in his mouth, chewed it vigorously, and then held the spittle there while he took the child forcibly from Mrs. Farquar. He gripped Teddy (A) down between his knees, and pressed the balls of his thumbs into the swollen eyes, so that the child screamed and Mrs. Farquar cried out in protest: "Gideon, Gideon!" But Gideon took no notice. He knelt over the writhing child, pushing back the puffy lids till chinks of eyeball showed, and then he spat hard, again and again, into first one eye, and then the other. He finally lifted Teddy gently into his mother's arms, and said: "His eyes will get better." But Mrs. Farquar was weeping with terror, and she could hardly thank him: It was impossible to believe that Teddy could keep his sight. In a couple of hours the swellings were gone: The eyes were inflamed and tender but Teddy could see. Mr. and Mrs. Farquar went to Gideon in the kitchen and thanked him over and over again. They felt helpless because of their gratitude: It (B) seemed they could do nothing to express it. They gave Gideon presents for his wife and children, and a big increase in wages, but these things could not pay for Teddy's now completely cured eyes. Mrs. Farquar said: "Gideon, God chose you as an instrument for His goodness," and Gideon said: "Yes, missus, God is very good."

Now, when such a thing happens on a farm, it cannot be long before everyone hears of it. Mr. and Mrs. Farquar told their neighbors and the story was discussed from one end of the district to the other. The bush is full of secrets. No one can live in Africa, or at least on the veld,[7] without learning very soon that there is an ancient wisdom of leaf and soil and season—and, too, perhaps most important of all, of the darker tracts of the human mind—which is the black man's heritage. Up and down the district people were telling anecdotes, reminding each other of things that had happened to them.

"But I saw it myself, I tell you. It was a puff-adder bite. The kaffir's[8] arm was swollen to the elbow, like a great shiny black bladder. He was groggy after a half a minute. He was dying. Then suddenly a kaffir walked out of the bush with his hands full of green stuff. He smeared something on the place, and next day my boy was back at work, and all you could see was two small punctures in the skin."

This was the kind of tale they told. And, as always, with a certain amount of exasperation, because while all of them knew that in the bush (C) of Africa are waiting valuable drugs locked in bark, in simple-looking leaves, in roots, it was impossible to ever get the truth about them from the natives themselves.

The story eventually reached town; and perhaps it was at a sundowner party,[9] or some such function, that a doctor, who happened to be there, challenged it. "Nonsense," he said. "These things get exaggerated in the telling. We are always checking up on this kind of story, and we draw a blank every time."

Anyway, one morning there arrived a strange car at the homestead, and out stepped one of the workers from the laboratory in town, with cases full of test tubes and chemicals.

Mr. and Mrs. Farquar were flustered and pleased and flattered. They asked the scientist to lunch, and they told the story all over again, for the hundredth time. Little Teddy was there too, his blue eyes sparkling with health, to prove the truth of it. The scientist explained how humanity might benefit if this new drug could be offered for (D) sale; and the Farquars were even more pleased: They were kind, simple people, who liked to think of something good coming about because of them. But when the scientist began talking of the money that might result, their manner showed discomfort. Their feelings over the miracle (that was how they thought of it) were so strong and deep and religious, that it was distasteful to them

7. **veld:** in South Africa, open country with very few bushes or trees; grassland. *Veld,* also spelled *veldt,* is Afrikaans for "field."

8. **kaffir's** (kaf′ərz): *Kaffir* is a contemptuous term for a black African, derived from *kāfir,* Arabic for "infidel."

9. **sundowner party:** British colloquial term for "cocktail party." The term derives from the British custom of gathering for drinks at sunset.

Making the Connections

Connecting to the Theme: "Clashes of Culture"

After they finish reading, students may discuss these questions:

- What is the most important factor contributing to the racial tension that exists in this story? [the unjust society created by imperialism/colonialism that makes some people "haves" and others "have nots"]
- Can anyone in this story be condemned as bad or evil? Explain your answer. [Responses will vary, but students should note that Lessing takes pain to show instances of kindness and concern by both blacks and whites; she does not reduce her complex theme to a one-sided condemnation.]

to think of money. The scientist, seeing their faces, went back to his first point, which was the advancement of humanity. He was perhaps a trifle perfunctory: It was not the first time he had come salting the tail of a fabulous bush secret.[10]

Eventually, when the meal was over, the Farquars called Gideon into their living room and explained to him that this baas, here, was a Big Doctor from the Big City, and he had come all that way to see Gideon. At this Gideon seemed afraid; he did not understand; and Mrs. Farquar explained quickly that it was because of the wonderful thing he had done with Teddy's eyes that the Big Baas had come.

Gideon looked from Mrs. Farquar to Mr. Farquar, and then at the little boy, who was showing great importance because of the occasion. At last he said grudgingly: "The Big Baas want to know what medicine I used?" He spoke incredulously, as if he could not believe his old friends could so betray him. Mr. Farquar began explaining how a useful medicine could be made out of the root, and how it could be put on sale, and how thousands of people, black and white, up and down the continent of Africa, could be saved by the medicine when that spitting snake filled their eyes with poison. Gideon listened, his eyes bent on the ground, the skin of his forehead puckering in discomfort. When Mr. Farquar had finished he did not reply. The scientist, who all this time had been leaning back in a big chair, sipping his coffee and smiling with skeptical good humor, chipped in and explained all over again, in different words, about the making of drugs and the progress of science. Also, he offered Gideon a present.

There was silence after this further explanation, and then Gideon remarked indifferently that he could not remember the root. His face was sullen and hostile, even when he looked at the Farquars, whom he usually treated like old friends. They were beginning to feel annoyed; and this feeling annulled the guilt that had been sprung into life by Gideon's accusing manner. They were beginning to feel that he was unreasonable. But it was at that moment that they all realized he would never give in. The magical drug would remain where it was, unknown and useless except for the tiny scattering of Africans who had the knowledge, natives who might be digging a ditch for the municipality in a ragged shirt and a pair of patched shorts, but who were still born to healing, hereditary healers, being the nephews or sons of the old witch doctors whose ugly masks and bits of bone and all the uncouth properties of magic were the outward signs of real power and wisdom.

The Farquars might tread on that plant fifty times a day as they passed from house to garden, from cow kraal to mealie[11] field, but they would never know it.

But they went on persuading and arguing, with all the force of their exasperation; and Gideon continued to say that he could not remember, or that there was no such root, or that it was the wrong season of the year, or that it wasn't the root itself, but the spit from his mouth that had cured Teddy's eyes. He said all these things one after another, and seemed not to care they were contradictory. He was rude and stubborn. The Farquars could hardly recognize their gentle, lovable old servant in this ignorant, perversely obstinate African, standing there in front of them with lowered eyes, his hands twitching his cook's apron, repeating over and over whichever one of the stupid refusals that first entered his head.

And suddenly he appeared to give in. He lifted his head, gave a long, blank angry look at the circle of whites, who seemed to him like a circle of yelping dogs pressing around him, and said: "I will show you the root."

They walked single file away from the homestead down a kaffir path. It was a blazing December afternoon, with the sky full of hot rain clouds. Everything was hot: The sun was like a bronze tray whirling overhead, there was a heat shimmer over the fields, the soil was scorching underfoot, the dusty wind blew gritty and thick and warm in

10. **salting . . . bush secret:** An allusion to the ironic advice given to children about how to catch a bird: by putting salt on its tail. In other words, the scientist knows his search may be futile.

11. **mealie:** corn.

Words to Own

perfunctory (pər·fuŋk′tə·rē) *adj.:* halfhearted; indifferent.

annulled (ə·nuld′) *v.:* did away with; canceled.

perversely (pər·vurs′lē) *adv.:* disagreeably; contrarily.

E Appreciating Language

Stylistic Choices

? Why does Lessing choose to capitalize the common nouns *Big Doctor* and *Big City*? [Possible responses: The capital letters reveal the Farquars' belief that Gideon is unsophisticated and childlike. They may also reveal the Farquars' outsized respect for urban civilization (in contrast with the bush) and for science.]

F Reading Skills and Strategies

Monitoring Predictions

Ask students when they first suspected that Gideon would be asked to reveal his secret. [Possible response: when the scientist arrived.]

G Elements of Literature

Theme

? Theme is amplified here as a subtle shift in power occurs. What is the shift? [Possible response: Gideon assumes power by refusing to reveal his knowledge. He began to gain power when he saved Teddy's eyesight, but, for the first time here, he drops his usually compliant manner and becomes defiant.]

H Elements of Literature

Symbolism/Theme

? In what ways is this another instance of symbolic blindness and insensitivity? [Possible responses: The Farquars are shown as treading on, or "walking all over," something powerful and healing that their own culture does not recognize. The Farquars are blind to something valuable right in front of them just as they are blind to the humanity and dignity of the blacks they "see" everyday.]

Assessing Learning

Check Test: Short Answers

1. **Who is Teddy's best friend during his childhood?** [Gideon]
2. **At what point does their relationship change?** [when Teddy frightens Gideon's son and will not apologize]
3. **How does Gideon save Teddy's sight?** [He chews a root and spits the juice into Teddy's eyes.]
4. **Why does the scientist visit the Farquars?** [He hopes to learn about the medicine Gideon used to save Teddy's sight.]
5. **What does Gideon give the scientist?** [blue flowers instead of the actual cure]

Standardized Test Preparation

For practice in proofreading and editing, see

- *Daily Oral Grammar,* Transparency 43

Ⓐ Elements of Literature

Theme

? **In what ways does this exchange sum up the theme of the story?** [Possible response: First, it underscores the irony of the Farquars' request: Gideon did, in fact, show the Farquars the plant at the moment they most needed it; second, the Farquars seem to have forgotten what they "saw." The reply also underscores the unbridgeable racial divide between Gideon and the Farquars. The Farquars are asking a question that will never be answered, and Gideon is giving an opaque reply.]

Ⓑ Humanities Connection

In Hebrew history, Gideon led his people to victory. Afterward, he refused the crown of Israel, saying that only God was Israel's king. Ask students why Lessing might have named her character after this hero. [Possible response: Old Testament Gideon refuses a crown because he believes in a higher authority; Lessing's character refuses gifts because he does not want to violate the integrity of his knowledge and heritage.]

MAKING MEANINGS

First Thoughts [Respond]

1. Students may have been struck by the image of Gideon's own son watching the privileged white boy with the golden hair on his bicycle or by the white boy's cruelty to him. They may have been struck by words such as "Baas" or the name "Little Yellow Head."

Shaping Interpretations [Interpret]

2. The reality is that a racial divide will separate their children and control their destinies. The white boy will grow up to be a "baas" and the black boy, a servant.
3. Possible responses: They may be nice people, and yet their very existence rests on taking advantage of others. There is no cure for the Farquars' racial blindness. It is ironic that they have so little understanding of the man who saved their son.
4. These details suggest that race is destiny in this society and that the inequalities between the races are vast.

(Continued on p. T1153)

their faces. It was a terrible day, fit only for reclining on a veranda with iced drinks, which is where they would normally have been at that hour.

From time to time, remembering that on the day of the snake it had taken ten minutes to find the root, someone asked: "Is it much further, Gideon?" And Gideon would answer over his shoulder, with angry politeness: "I'm looking for the root, baas." And indeed, he would frequently bend sideways and trail his hand among the grasses with a gesture that was insulting in its perfunctoriness. He walked them through the bush along unknown paths for two hours, in that melting destroying heat, so that the sweat trickled coldly down them and their heads ached. They were all quite silent: the Farquars because they were angry, the scientist because he was being proved right again; there was no such plant. His was a tactful silence.

At last, six miles from the house, Gideon suddenly decided they had had enough; or perhaps his anger evaporated at that moment. He picked up, without an attempt at looking anything but casual, a handful of blue flowers from the grass, flowers that had been growing plentifully all down the paths they had come.

He handed them to the scientist without looking at him, and marched off by himself on the way home, leaving them to follow him if they chose.

When they got back to the house, the scientist went to the kitchen to thank Gideon: He was being very polite, even though there was an amused look in his eyes. Gideon was not there. Throwing the flowers casually into the back of his car, the eminent visitor departed on his way back to his laboratory.

Gideon was back in his kitchen in time to prepare dinner, but he was sulking. He spoke to Mr. Farquar like an unwilling servant. It was days before they liked each other again.

The Farquars made inquiries about the root from their laborers. Sometimes they were answered with distrustful stares. Sometimes the natives said: "We do not know. We have never heard of the root." One, the cattle boy, who had been with them a long time, and had grown to trust them a little, said: "Ask your boy in the kitchen. Now, there's a doctor for you. He's the son of a famous medicine man who used to be in these parts, and there's nothing he cannot cure." Then he added politely: "Of course, he's not as good as the white man's doctor, we know that, but he's good for us."

After some time, when the soreness had gone from between the Farquars and Gideon, they Ⓐ began to joke: "When are you going to show us the snake root, Gideon?" And he would laugh and shake his head, saying, a little uncomfortably: "But I did show you, missus, have you forgotten?"

Much later, Teddy, as a schoolboy, would come into the kitchen and say: "You old rascal, Gideon! Do you remember that time you tricked us all by making us walk miles all over the veld for nothing? It was so far my father had to carry me!"

Ⓑ And Gideon would double up with polite laughter. After much laughing, he would suddenly straighten himself up, wipe his old eyes, and look sadly at Teddy, who was grinning mischievously at him across the kitchen: "Ah, Little Yellow Head, how you have grown! Soon you will be grown up with a farm of your own. . . ."

MAKING MEANINGS

First Thoughts

1. What did you focus on most intently as you read the story—what word, phrase, image, or idea? Explain.

Shaping Interpretations

2. Mrs. Farquar and Gideon share a sense of sadness about the reality of their children's future lives. What is the reality that gives these two characters, and this whole story, a feeling of sadness?

Reading Check

a. Describe Gideon and Teddy's relationship at the story's start. What incident signals a change in their relationship?
b. What crisis sets the **plot** in motion?
c. What does Gideon do for Teddy?
d. Cite sentences showing that the Farquars do not really understand Gideon and his response to the doctor's request.
e. How does Teddy's relationship with Gideon change as he grows up?

Reading Check

a. Gideon and Teddy are great friends as the story begins. A change occurs when Teddy frightens Gideon's son and dismisses his cruelty by saying, "He's only a black boy."
b. A tree snake sprays poison in Teddy's eyes.
c. By means of quick action and an herbal cure, Gideon saves Teddy from blindness.
d. Sentences include "They were beginning to feel annoyed; and this feeling annulled the guilt that had been sprung into life by Gideon's accusing manner."
e. Gideon creates a distance between them. The relationship becomes more formal, polite, and guarded.

3. Does the narrator's presentation of the Farquars as people of goodwill seem **ironic** or straightforward? How did you respond to them?
4. What implicit criticism can you detect in the fact that while Teddy is riding a scooter, Gideon's son of the same age is a herdboy?
5. Why do you think Gideon refuses to share his wisdom with the Farquars? How do you feel about his refusal?
6. In what ways is this story about a clash of cultures? Reread Gideon's comment at the end of the story. What does it reveal about his understanding of the relationship between white European and black African cultures?
7. How would you state the **theme** of this story?

Connecting with the Text

8. Look back at your Quickwrite notes. How does the story affect your own notions about cultural differences?
9. Describe how you feel about the "Big Doctor." Did you find yourself identifying most with him, Gideon, or the Farquars? Explain your responses.

CHOICES: Building Your Portfolio

Writer's Notebook

1. Collecting Ideas for a Problem-Solution Essay

In this story, Lessing explores how different cultural values can lead to problems of misunderstanding and mistrust. What problems do you suppose you'd encounter if you were placed in a different culture? (You may want to expand on the Quickwrite notes you began on page 1147.) Freewrite for a few minutes about what you think you'd have to grapple with. Save your notes for the Writer's Workshop on page 1179.

Analyzing Conflict

2. Between Two Worlds

The conflict in the story between the scientist and the Farquars on the one hand and Gideon on the other comes about because Gideon does not wish to share his knowledge. The conflict is not between right and wrong, good and evil, or enlightened and unenlightened viewpoints. Rather, it is over cultural differences. In an essay, discuss the similarities in and differences between the Farquars' and the scientist's point of view and Gideon's. Use details from the story to back up your opinions.

Evaluating Point of View

3. Angle of Vision

In a brief essay, discuss the effects of the narrator's point of view. Also, consider how the story might be different if it were narrated by Gideon or by the adult Teddy Farquar. Cite passages to support your analysis.

Comparing Texts

4. Paradox or Progress?

In an essay, compare and contrast Lessing's story with Kipling's "The Mark of the Beast" (page 872). Consider **point of view, theme,** and **characters.** For help in writing a comparison-contrast essay, see the Writer's Workshop on page 185.

Science and Medicine / Research

5. Ancient Cures, Modern Proofs

Research and report orally on folk medicines and other traditional cures. (You may concentrate on a single culture if you wish or research remedies that are found in several cultures.) What sorts of studies have been done to determine their effects? Do these studies confirm or disprove a belief in the effectiveness of folk medicines and traditional cures?

5. Gideon believes that the plant is only for those "born to healing." Students may think the refusal shows selfishness, or they may believe it reflects cultural pride and personal integrity.
6. European culture has imposed itself on African culture; the Europeans are unwilling or unable to understand the traditions of Africa's indigenous peoples.
7. Possible response: Even if seemingly good people participate in a system of racial inequality, they will not be able to avoid clashing with those whose culture and rights they are suppressing.

Connecting with the Text [Respond]

8. Students may say that it makes them more aware of how people can be blind to their own prejudice and ignorance of others' cultures.
9. Students may choose any character as long as they explain their response with details, such as the frustration of the scientist, the disappointment of the Farquars, or the quiet determination and pride of Gideon.

Grading Timesaver

Rubrics for each Choices assignment appear on p. 215 in the *Portfolio Management System.*

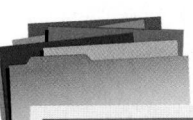

Objectives

1. Read and interpret the story
2. Identify and analyze parody
3. Express understanding through critical and creative writing, speaking, and research
4. Learn and use new words

Skills

Literary
- Identify and analyze parody

Writing
- Collect ideas for a problem-solution essay
- Compare texts
- Write a fairy tale

Speaking
- Present an oral report on a culture clash

Vocabulary
- Learn and use new words

Viewing/Representing
- Discuss the symbolic implications of an artwork and relate it to the story (ATE)

Planning

- **Block Schedule**
  Block Scheduling Lesson Plans with Pacing Guide
- **Traditional Schedule**
  Lesson Plans Including Strategies for English-Language Learners
- **One-Stop Planner**
  CD-ROM with Test Generator

Nadine Gordimer

(1923–   )

Nadine Gordimer was born in Springs, a small town located thirty miles from Johannesburg, on the gold-mining ridge that has brought South Africa much of its wealth. Her father was a Jewish jeweler who had emigrated from Lithuania as a teenager; her mother was a native of England. Gordimer grew up in a middle-class colonial society that imitated European conventions and values. She has said that she spent much of her childhood reading because she found that atmosphere extremely dull.

Nadine Gordimer.

Gordimer began writing at the age of nine when, as a sickly child, she was taken out of school for a time. At fifteen she published her first story in a Johannesburg weekly. When her first internationally published short-story collection, *The Soft Voice of the Serpent,* appeared in 1952, critics hailed Gordimer as a strong new voice who could draw fresh, authentic perceptions of African life. Her first novel, *The Lying Days,* appeared the following year to favorable reviews. Since then, she has continued to win praise and honors, and, in 1991, she won the Nobel Prize in literature.

Gordimer is known for her ability to show, as one critic said, "the infinite variety of human character, the rich and surprising drama inherent in human personality and in the clash of personality." She has been compared to Virginia Woolf for her talent in capturing the revealing moments in people's lives, what the critic Robert F. Haugh called "the illuminating moment, the quick perceptive glance of the author which sparkles like a gem."

Although she deals with universal themes and a variety of settings, much of Gordimer's writing concerns the troubles that her own nation has experienced. She has observed that "white culture imported from Europe never had a chance in the South African context. . . . All it did was to harm black culture. . . . In the process we suffered more than they." Commenting on Gordimer's writing about the effects of apartheid, the enforced separation of races, on South Africa, one critic called her "one of the very few links between white and black in South Africa. She is a bearer of culture in a barbaric society. And she is a luminous symbol of at least one white person's understanding of the black man's burden."

Perhaps Gordimer's greatest achievement is her ability to treat South Africa's problems from a literary rather than a political perspective. "Here I live in a society which is fundamentally out of joint. One can't but be politically concerned," she has said, but she disclaims a political allegiance. "I don't understand politics except in terms of what politics does to influence lives," she once observed. "What interests me is the infinite variety of effects apartheid has on men and women."

Among her best-known works are *A Guest of Honor* (1970) and *July's People* (1981), the latter set in an unnamed future when the whites in South Africa become the servants of the blacks.

Although Gordimer is respected around the world, she was a thorn in the side of her own country's government when apartheid was still in effect, and three of her novels were banned in South Africa. Nevertheless, she has always considered herself "an intensely loyal South African. I care deeply for my country. If I didn't, I wouldn't still be there."

go.hrw.com
LE0 12-15

Resources: Print and Media

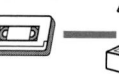

Reading
- *Graphic Organizers for Active Reading,* p. 115
- *Words to Own,* p. 37
- *Audio CD Library*
  Disc 22, Track 2

Writing and Language
- *Daily Oral Grammar*
  Transparency 44

Assessment
- *Formal Assessment,* p. 227
- *Portfolio Management System,* p. 217
- *Test Generator (One-Stop Planner CD-ROM)*

Internet
- go.hrw.com (keyword: LE0 12-15)

Before You Read
ONCE UPON A TIME

Make the Connection
Walls and Barriers
Isolation is one way to keep conflict at bay. Opposing parties cannot clash if they do not meet, or so the reasoning goes. The remedy has certainly been tried repeatedly throughout history and all over the world. Reservations, compounds, borders—these are all isolating walls, literal or figurative, that keep some people away from others. Even on the household level, we have today's "security systems," a phrase to keep in mind as you read Gordimer's "Once upon a Time." Does a security system do its job? Is it worth its price? Is it protecting life—or maintaining a fantasy of safety?

Quickwrite
When you think of a wall, what do you picture? What does your wall keep in and keep out? Record your ideas.

Elements of Literature
Parody
"Once upon a Time" is a **parody,** or imitation, of a fairy tale. Though parodies are often written for amusement, they also may make serious points. As you read Gordimer's story, consider why she chose to imitate a fairy tale.

Parody is the imitation of a work of literature, art, or music for amusement or instruction.

For more on Parody, see the Handbook of Literary Terms.

Blue at Noon (1955) by Adolph Gottlieb. Oil on canvas.
Collection Walker Art Center, Minneapolis. Gift of the T. B. Walker Foundation, 1963. Adolph and Esther Gottlieb Foundation/Licensed by VAGA, New York, N.Y.

Background
Until recently, South Africa, Nadine Gordimer's native land, practiced a policy called *apartheid,* the legal segregation of the races. Not only did black South Africans and other non-whites experience economic and political discrimination, but they were also forced to live in remote areas or in all-black "townships" bordering white cities. They could not leave these areas or enter white cities without "passbooks" that identified them by name, residency, and race.

Decades of rebellions, riots, and strikes left thousands of blacks dead and most of their leaders jailed. Finally, in 1991, the white government headed by F. W. de Klerk—under both internal and international pressure—repealed the apartheid laws. Three years later, the first all-race election swept the black South African Nelson Mandela, a former political prisoner and leader of the African National Congress, into office as president.

Preteaching Vocabulary

Words to Own
Ask pairs of students to read each definition and then to play a version of twenty questions, giving one clue at a time to each word's meaning, spelling, or structure. Then have students complete the following analogies.

1. collapse : explode :: shrink : [distend]
2. genius : brilliantly :: daredevil : [audaciously]
3. truth : ethics :: beauty : [aesthetics]
4. skirt : pleated :: knife : [serrated]
5. parochial : worldly :: stationary : [itinerant]

Summary

One night, the writer is awakened by ominous sounds in her house. Although it turns out there is no danger, she decides to make up a story to calm herself. The story is a kind of bitter parody of a fairy tale. In it, a wealthy white couple with one son seem to be happy and have everything, but they live in a society torn by racial strife. To protect themselves from the violence that is rocking their society, the couple installs a series of increasingly elaborate security devices. Finally, in desperate fear of intrusion, the wealthy couple installs a coil of serrated metal atop the walls surrounding their home and yard. One day their young son climbs into the tunnel of blades and is ensnared in its deadly grip. He is hacked out of the "razor teeth" and carried into the house—whether alive or dead, we are not told directly.

BROWSING IN THE FILES
About the Author. Gordimer resisted the former South African government's policy of apartheid, or racial segregation, by supporting the then outlawed African National Congress (ANC) and speaking out against censorship. **Writers on Writing.** Gordimer says, ". . . the best way to write [is] to do so as if one were already dead: afraid of no one's reactions, answerable to no one for one's views." Gordimer also explains that "writing is making sense of life."

Background

In Gordimer's story, the white family fears rioting "where people of another color were quartered." This allusion may refer to the 1976 riot in Soweto (an overcrowded suburb of the city of Johannesburg), where black Africans were forced to live apart from whites. Soweto residents protested a policy that would require some classes in community schools to be taught in Afrikaans, a language derived from Dutch and spoken by white South Africans. In the violence that followed, more than six hundred people were killed, most of them black South Africans.

A Reading Skills and Strategies
Analyzing Language Structures
? What is the effect of these three short paragraphs, consisting, respectively, of one sentence, a question, and a phrase? [Possible response: The technique creates suspense by singling out one detail at a time.]

B Reading Skills and Strategies
Identifying Cause and Effect
? Why is the narrator fearful? [Possible response: She hears a noise at night and has no protection. Murders occur in her neighborhood in daylight despite security devices.]

C Advanced Learners
Interpreting Symbolism
? What is symbolic about the narrator's house resting on an insecure foundation? [Possible responses: The house does not belong where it is and may come crashing down, mirroring the unsound foundations of a society built on racial injustice. The search for gold has undermined a basic human need: domestic security.]

Once upon a Time

Nadine Gordimer

Someone has written to ask me to contribute to an anthology of stories for children. I reply that I don't write children's stories; and he writes back that at a recent congress/book fair/seminar a certain novelist said every writer ought to write at least one story for children. I think of sending a postcard saying I don't accept that I "ought" to write anything.

A And then last night I woke up—or rather was wakened without knowing what had roused me.

A voice in the echo chamber of the subconscious?

A sound.

A creaking of the kind made by the weight carried by one foot after another along a wooden floor. I listened. I felt the apertures of my ears distend with concentration. Again: the creaking. I was waiting for it; waiting to hear if it indicated that feet were moving from room to room, coming up the passage—to my door. I have no burglar bars, no gun under the pillow, but I have the same fears as people who do take these precautions, and my windowpanes are thin as rime,[1] could shatter like a wineglass. B A woman was murdered (how do they put it) in broad daylight in a house two blocks away, last year, and the fierce dogs who guarded an old widower and his collection of antique clocks were strangled before he was knifed by a casual laborer he had dismissed without pay.

I was staring at the door, making it out in my mind rather than seeing it, in the dark. I lay quite still—a victim already—but the arrhythmia[2] of my heart was fleeing, knocking this way and that against its body-cage. How finely tuned the senses are, just out of rest, sleep! I could never listen intently as that in the distractions of the day; I was reading every faintest sound, identifying and classifying its possible threat.

But I learned that I was to be neither threatened nor spared. There was no human weight pressing on the boards, the creaking was a buckling, an epicenter[3] of stress. I was in it. The house that surrounds me while I sleep is built on undermined ground; far beneath my bed, the floor, the house's foundations, the stopes[4] and passages of gold mines have hollowed the rock, and when some face trembles, detaches, and falls, three thousand feet below, the whole house shifts slightly, bringing uneasy strain to the balance and counterbalance of brick, cement, wood, and glass C that hold it as a structure around me. The misbeats of my heart tailed off like the last muffled flourishes on one of the wooden xylophones made by the Chopi and Tsonga[5] migrant miners who might have been down there, under me in the earth at that moment. The stope where the fall was could have been disused, dripping water from its ruptured veins; or men might now be interred there in the most profound of tombs.

I couldn't find a position in which my mind would let go of my body—release me to sleep again. So I began to tell myself a story; a bedtime story.

In a house, in a suburb, in a city, there were a man and his wife who loved each other very much and were living happily ever after. They had a little boy, and they loved him very much. They had a cat and a dog that the little boy loved very much. They had a car and a caravan trailer for holidays, and a swimming pool which was fenced so that the little boy and his playmates would not fall in and drown. They had a housemaid who was absolutely trustworthy and an itinerant gardener who was highly recommended by the neighbors. For when they began to live happily ever after they were

1. **rime:** frost.
2. **arrhythmia** (ə·rith′mē·ə): irregular beating.
3. **epicenter:** central point.
4. **stopes:** excavations.
5. **Chopi** (chō′pē) **and Tsonga** (tsäŋ′gä): Bantu-speaking peoples of Mozambique in southeastern Africa. Tsonga is often spelled *Thonga.*

Words to Own
distend (di·stend′) *v.:* expand; stretch out; swell.
itinerant (ī·tin′ər·ənt) *adj.:* traveling.

Reaching All Students

Struggling Readers

You may want to use a strategy called Anticipation Guides to help connect this story to its historical context. For information on using this strategy, see p. 17 of the *Reading Strategies Handbook* in the front of the *Reading Skills and Strategies* binder.

English Language Learners

Gordimer's sentence structure is often complex. Suggest that students use the following strategies to work through the text:

- Skim a section quickly to get the general idea. Then, review it more slowly.
- Identify subjects and predicates of clauses.
- Pay attention to semicolons, commas, and dashes, which break sentences into smaller components.

warned, by that wise old witch, the husband's mother, not to take on anyone off the street. They were inscribed[6] in a medical benefit society, their pet dog was licensed, they were insured against fire, flood damage, and theft, and subscribed to the local Neighborhood Watch, which supplied (D) them with a plaque for their gates lettered YOU HAVE BEEN WARNED over the silhouette of a would-be intruder. He was masked; it could not be said if he was black or white, and therefore proved the property owner was no racist.

It was not possible to insure the house, the swimming pool, or the car against riot damage. There were riots, but these were outside the city, where people of another color were quartered. (E) These people were not allowed into the suburb except as reliable housemaids and gardeners, so there was nothing to fear, the husband told the wife. Yet she was afraid that some day such people might come up the street and tear off the plaque YOU HAVE BEEN WARNED and open the gates and stream in. . . . Nonsense, my dear, said (F) the husband, there are police and soldiers and tear gas and guns to keep them away. But to please her—for he loved her very much and buses were being burned, cars stoned, and schoolchildren shot by the police in those quarters out of sight and hearing of the suburb—he had electronically controlled gates fitted. Anyone who pulled off the sign YOU HAVE BEEN WARNED and tried to open the gates would have to announce his intentions by pressing a button and speaking into a receiver relayed to the house. The little boy was fascinated by the device and used it as a walkie-talkie in cops and robbers play with his small friends.

The riots were suppressed, but there were many burglaries in the suburb and somebody's trusted housemaid was tied up and shut in a cupboard by thieves while she was in charge of her employers' house. The trusted housemaid of the man and wife and little boy was so upset by this misfortune befalling a friend left, as she herself often was, with responsibility for the possessions of the man and his wife and the little boy that she implored her employers to have burglar bars attached to the doors and windows of the house, and an alarm system installed. The wife said, She is right, let us take heed of her advice. So from every window and door in the house where they were living happily ever after they now saw the trees and sky through bars, and when the little (G) boy's pet cat tried to climb in by the fanlight[7] to keep him company in his little bed at night, as it customarily had done, it set off the alarm keening[8] through the house.

The alarm was often answered—it seemed—by other burglar alarms, in other houses, that had been triggered by pet cats or nibbling mice. The alarms called to one another across the gardens in shrills and bleats and wails that everyone soon became accustomed to, so that the din roused the inhabitants of the suburb no more than the croak of frogs and musical grating of cicadas'[9] legs. Under cover of the electronic harpies'[10] discourse intruders sawed the iron bars and broke into homes, taking away hi-fi equipment, television sets, cassette players, cameras and radios, jewelry and clothing, and sometimes were hungry enough to devour everything in the refrigerator or paused <u>audaciously</u> to drink the whiskey in the cabinets or patio bars. Insurance companies paid no compensation for single malt, a loss made keener by the property owner's knowledge that the thieves wouldn't even have been able to appreciate what it was they were drinking.

Then the time came when many of the people who were not trusted housemaids and gardeners hung about the suburb because they were unemployed. Some importuned for a job: weeding or painting a roof; anything, *baas,*[11] madam. But the man and his wife remembered the warning about taking on anyone off the street. Some drank liquor and fouled the street with discarded bottles. Some

6. **inscribed:** enrolled.

7. **fanlight:** semicircular window over a door or a larger window.
8. **keening:** wailing.
9. **cicadas'** (si·kā′dəz): Cicadas are large, flylike insects.
10. **harpies':** Harpies are shrewish or grasping people. The word comes from the mythological Harpies, hideous winged monsters that have the head and trunk of a woman and the tail, legs, and talons of a bird.
11. ***baas*** (bäs): Afrikaans for "master." Afrikaans, a language developed from seventeenth-century Dutch, is spoken in South Africa.

WORDS TO OWN
audaciously (ô·dā′shəs·lē) *adv.:* boldly.

(D) Elements of Literature
Parody

? Elements of parody are interwoven with the description of the family's "fairy-tale" life. How is the fairy-tale dimension of their life subtly mocked here? [Possible response: Although they appear to have everything materially necessary "to live happily ever after," they are warned by a wise old witch (the mother-in-law) that they must take precautions to ensure their safety. They have everything but peace of mind.]

(E) Exploring the Historical Period

Under apartheid, many of South Africa's cities established separate residential and business sections for each race. In 1950, the Population Registration Act classified people as Bantu (black Africans of all nationalities), Colored (mixed race), and white. At one point, the South African government attempted to herd all blacks into outlying "homelands," leaving only those needed as laborers by white employers in the cities.

(F) Appreciating Language
Style

? Why might the author have decided not to use quotation marks and the standard conventions of paragraphing to set apart a character's exact words? [Possible response: The lack of punctuation makes the narrative seem more like a story the narrator is telling herself, a kind of stream of consciousness, rather than a report of events taking place in the world outside her imagination.]

(G) Elements of Literature
Parody

? In what way is this passage a parody of a fairy tale? [Possible responses: The "fairy-tale" phrase "living happily ever after" is used ironically; the family home is more like a jail or fortress than an enchanted castle; in it, simple, everyday acts, such as the cat coming in at night, have unwanted, alarming effects.]

Taking a Second Look

Review: Analyzing Language Choices

Remind students that authors carefully select the words in their stories to create specific effects and to emphasize their themes. Urge students to explore both the denotation and connotations of key words in Gordimer's story.

Activities

1. Each time the word "housemaid" appears, the word "trusted" modifies it. Why? What are the implications of these word choices? [Possible response: The family can never truly trust their black servants because of the fundamental racial injustice that underlies their relationship.]
2. The family's cat is consistently referred to as a "pet cat." What point may Gordimer be making by including the modifier "pet"? [Possible response: The family wants nothing out of control in their world. They want both their animals and servants to be tame.]

Responding to the Art

Jannis Kounellis (1936–) is a Greek painter, sculptor, and performance artist. *Untitled* combines limestone, plaster, and steel to create an ominous encasement of stone.

Activity. Ask students the following questions:

1. What does this wall make you think of, or feel? [Possible response: This barrier suggests entrapment, confinement, separation, isolation.]
2. What effect does the steel bracing give? [Possible response: Its purpose appears to be to keep the stones in place by force or containment. It creates a sense of tension and pressure.]
3. Why is a wall an appropriate image for this story? [The story is about the walls that separate people, or that people build around themselves. It might suggest the wall that eventually mangles (kills?) the beloved child.]

begged, waiting for the man or his wife to drive the car out of the electronically operated gates. They sat about with their feet in the gutters, under the jacaranda[12] trees that made a green tunnel of the street—for it was a beautiful suburb, spoiled only by their presence—and sometimes they fell asleep lying right before the gates in the midday sun. The wife could never see anyone go hungry. She sent the trusted housemaid out with bread and tea, but the trusted housemaid said these were loafers and *tsotsis,*[13] who would come and tie her up and shut her in a cupboard. The husband said, She's right. Take heed of her advice. You only encourage them with your bread and tea. They are looking for their chance. . . . And he brought the little boy's tricycle from the garden into the house every night, because if the house was surely secure, once locked and with the alarm set, someone might still be able to climb over the wall or the electronically closed gates into the garden.

You are right, said the wife, then the wall should be higher. And the wise old witch, the husband's mother, paid for the extra bricks as her Christmas present to her son and his wife—the little boy got a Space Man outfit and a book of fairy tales.

But every week there were more reports of intrusion: in broad daylight and the dead of night, in the early hours of the morning, and even in the lovely summer twilight—a certain family was at dinner while the bedrooms were being ransacked upstairs. The man and his wife, talking of the latest armed robbery in the suburb, were distracted by the sight of the little boy's pet cat effortlessly arriving over the seven-foot wall, descending first with a rapid bracing of extended forepaws down on the sheer vertical surface, and then a graceful launch, landing with swishing tail within the property. The whitewashed wall was marked with the cat's comings and goings; and on the street side of the wall there were larger red-earth smudges that could have been made by the kind of broken running shoes, seen on the feet of unemployed loiterers, that had no innocent destination.

When the man and wife and little boy took the pet dog for its walk round the neighborhood streets they no longer paused to admire this show of roses or that perfect lawn; these were hidden behind an array of different varieties of security fences, walls, and devices. The man, wife, little boy, and dog passed a remarkable choice: There was the low-cost option of pieces of broken glass embedded in cement along the top of walls, there were iron grilles ending in lance points, there

12. **jacaranda** (jak′ə·ran′də): tropical American trees with large clusters of blue or lavender flowers.

13. ***tsotsis*** (tsät′sis): colloquial expression for flashily dressed street thugs.

Untitled (1982) by Jannis Kounellis. Feather River travertine, cast plaster, and steel.

Collection Walker Art Center, Minneapolis. Walker Special Purchase Fund, 1987.

A Vocabulary Note

Prefix *sub-* and Latin Root *urb*

The word *suburb* contains the Latin prefix *sub-*, which means "near" or "next," and the root *urb* from the Latin *urbs,* meaning "city." Urge students to use the dictionary to find other meanings of the prefix *sub-* and examples of words in which it appears. Students may also go back to p. 1157, l. 5, to find the word *subscribed* and discuss its meaning and derivation.

B Elements of Literature

Parody

? What fairy-tale elements are parodied or given an ironic twist here? [Possible responses: The "wise old witch" appears again, apparently to do the family a good turn, but is she really making their life more secure? The child gets a book of fairy tales, suggesting that he is not being encouraged to explore the real world around him but rather to live in a world of fantasy.]

C English Language Learners

Briticisms

"Round the neighborhood" is an example of British English. American English speakers would be more likely to say "*around* the neighborhood."

Making the Connections

Connecting to the Theme: "Clashes of Culture"

Gordimer's story vividly distills the South African experience of apartheid. The family in the story represents the privileged white minority; the unwelcome loiterers represent the black majority, grown impatient with its poverty and oppression. Ask students to discuss how a clash of cultures is inevitable in situations like this one and what the results of such a clash might be.

Crossing the Curriculum

Social Studies

Ask students to work in groups to trace the development and dismantling of apartheid in South Africa. Have students research when the policy was begun, how it was enforced and challenged, and what the results of the policy and the efforts to end it were. Ask students to outline their findings and prepare an oral report with special emphasis on South Africa today.

were attempts at reconciling the aesthetics of prison architecture with the Spanish Villa style (spikes painted pink) and with the plastic urns of neoclassical façades (twelve-inch pikes finned like zigzags of lightning and painted pure white). **D** Some walls had a small board affixed, giving the name and telephone number of the firm responsible for the installation of the devices. While the little boy and the pet dog raced ahead, the husband and wife found themselves comparing the possible effectiveness of each style against its appearance; and after several weeks when they paused before this barricade or that without needing to speak, both came out with the conclusion that only one was worth considering. It was the ugliest but the most honest in its suggestion of the pure concentration-camp style, no frills, all evident efficacy. Placed the length of walls, it consisted of a continuous coil of stiff and shining metal serrated into jagged blades, so that there would be no way of climbing over it and no way through its tunnel without getting entangled in its fangs. There would be no way out, only a struggle getting bloodier and bloodier, a deeper and sharper hooking and tearing of flesh. The wife shuddered to look at it. You're right, said the husband, anyone would think twice. . . . And they took heed of the advice on a small board fixed to the wall: Consult DRAGON'S TEETH The People For Total Security.

Next day a gang of workmen came and stretched the razor-bladed coils all round the walls of the house where the husband and wife and little boy and pet dog and cat were living happily ever after. The sunlight flashed and slashed, off the serrations, the cornice of razor thorns encircled the home, shining. The husband said, Never mind. It will weather. The wife said, You're wrong. They guarantee it's rustproof. And she waited until the little boy had run off to play before she said, I hope the cat will take heed. . . . The husband said, Don't worry, my dear, cats always look before they leap. And it was true that from that day on the cat slept in the little boy's bed and kept to the garden, never risking a try at breaching security.

One evening, the mother read the little boy to sleep with a fairy story from the book the wise old witch had given him at Christmas. Next day he pretended to be the Prince who braves the terrible thicket of thorns to enter the palace and kiss the Sleeping Beauty back to life: He dragged a ladder to the wall, the shining coiled tunnel was just wide enough for his little body to creep in, and with the first fixing of its razor teeth in his knees and hands and head he screamed and struggled deeper into its tangle. **E** The trusted housemaid and the itinerant gardener, whose "day" it was, came running, the first to see and to scream with him, and the itinerant gardener tore his hands trying to get at the little boy. Then the man and his wife burst wildly into the garden and for some reason (the cat, probably) the alarm set up wailing against the screams while the bleeding mass of the little boy was hacked out of the security coil with saws, wire cutters, choppers, and they carried it—the man, the wife, the hysterical trusted housemaid, and the weeping gardener—into the house. **F**

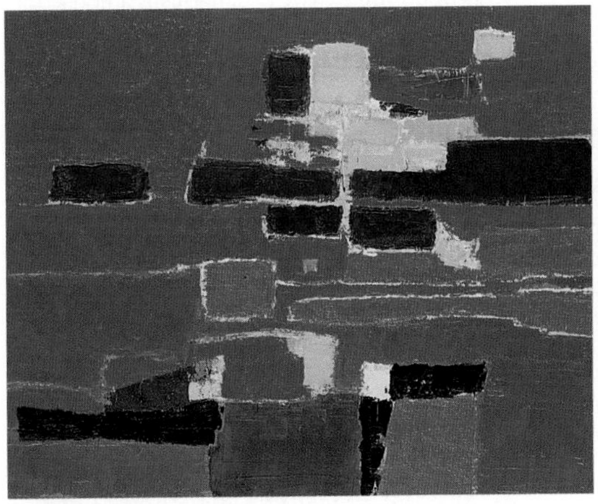

Le Ciel Rouge (*The Red Sky*) (1952) by Nicolas de Staël. Oil on canvas.

Collection Walker Art Center, Minneapolis.
Gift of the T. B. Walker Foundation, 1954.
©1997 Artists Rights Society (ARS), New York/ADAGP, Paris.

WORDS TO OWN

aesthetics (es·thet′iks) *n.:* principles of beauty.

serrated (sə·rāt′id) *v.* used as *adj.:* having jagged, sawlike notches along the edge.

D Elements of Literature

Parody

? What aspect of South African life is the author parodying here? [Possible response: She is parodying the ridiculous attempts of affluent whites to tastefully deter poor black burglars. Protective spikes, which are meant to cut or tear skin, are painted either pink to match the Mediterranean style of a Spanish villa or classic white to coordinate with simple Greco-Roman lines. Gordimer's parody shows how white suburbanites concentrate on the trivial details of their security systems while ignoring the very serious social realities of urban poverty, racism, and violence.]

E Elements of Literature

Foreshadowing

? What elements first suggested to you that Gordimer's story was not simply an entertaining fairy tale? [Possible responses: the references to riots, police, tear gas, guns, and racism.]

F Critical Thinking

Challenging the Text

? Do you think the violent ending and gruesome details are necessary to make the author's point? [Possible responses: No, the shocking ending is out of character with the rest of the story; or yes, the violence of the ending is foreshadowed sufficiently and is necessary to drive home the terrible irony—that the "protective devices" have harmed the very thing they were supposed to save.]

RESPONDING TO THE ART

Nicolas de Staël (1914–1955) was a French painter born in Russia. Here blocks of color collide and repel one another.

Activity. Why might this abstract painting have been chosen to illustrate the end of this story? Be sure to consider the title. [Possible response: The colors and figures create a violent, discordant mood. Order has given way and chaos threatens. A red sky could suggest fire, warfare, violence.]

Assessing Learning

Check Test: Short Answers

1. What initiates the author's bedtime story? [A noise in the house awakens and frightens her.]
2. Why does the family install electronically controlled gates? [The wife is afraid of the rioting she has heard about.]
3. Name at least two other security devices that the family installs. [burglar bars, an alarm system, a higher wall, and wire]
4. How does fear change the appearance of the neighborhood? [Fences, walls, and other security devices hide lawns and flowers.]
5. How does the child suffer as a result of his parents' fears? [He is brutally, if not mortally, injured in the wire coil.]

Standardized Test Preparation

For practice in proofreading and editing, see

- *Daily Oral Grammar,* Transparency 44

MAKING MEANINGS

First Thoughts [Respond]

1. Most students will be horrified that the parents helped cause this terrible event.

Shaping Interpretations [Interpret]

2. Humorous passages include descriptions of the "perfect" family and the son playing with the electronic gate. Gordimer's tone is ironic as she exposes the family's futile attempt to insulate themselves from the society in which they live.
3. Fairy-tale elements include living happily ever after; "Dragon's teeth" company; stock characters like the wise old witch. The parody emphasizes the gap between the real world the family lives in and the fantasy of security they are trying to create and believe in.
4. The opening grounds the story in reality. The reader is reminded that nothing in the story to come is really that long ago and far away.
5. Walls denote barriers just as race is a social and economic barrier in the story.
6. In most fairy tales, good triumphs and justice prevails. In this fairy tale, there is only the sense of continuing and perhaps escalating tragedy.

Connecting with the Text [Evaluate]

7. Some students may argue that the couple is racist because they accept the conditions of the racist society in which they live and do nothing to change or improve it. They merely try to protect themselves from its destructive effects. Others may see them as victims of a society they did not create.
8. If students envisioned a wall as protective, the story may have shattered this image.

Extending the Text [Analyze]

9. Ads for alarm systems promise security. They try to sell the illusion that total security can be achieved.

Challenging the Text [Evaluate]

10. Students may argue that the brutality is necessary to make the author's point, or they may say the description of the child's injury is gratuitously violent.

MAKING MEANINGS

First Thoughts

1. What were your feelings when you read the grisly end of this story?

Reading Check

Outline the course of this story through the four improvements to home security that the family makes. What is each improvement, what occasions it, and how well does it work?

Shaping Interpretations

2. Which passages in the story obviously have humorous intent? Did you find them funny? Overall, what is Gordimer's **tone**?
3. Point out elements of the fairy-tale genre that are used by Gordimer. (For example, the setting is not specified and the characters are not named.) How would you describe the effect of Gordimer's **parody**?
4. Why do you think Gordimer uses a nonfictional opening? How do you interpret the opening after reading the story?
5. How can the wall in the story be seen as a **symbol**?
6. Fairy tales often contain **moral** lessons. What are some of the morals of fairy tales you've read? What, in contrast, is the moral of "Once upon a Time"?

Connecting with the Text

7. In your opinion, are the husband and wife racists who cause their own tragedy? Explain your answer.
8. Look back at your Quickwrite notes. How does "Once upon a Time" support or change your picture of a wall?

Extending the Text

9. Think about ads for home protection systems. What messages do they give visually and verbally? What emotions do they play on?

Challenging the Text

10. Do you think this story is too brutal or violent? Compare and discuss your responses in class.

CHOICES: Building Your Portfolio

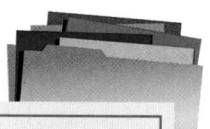

Writer's Notebook

1. Collecting Ideas for a Problem-Solution Essay

WORK IN PROGRESS

As Gordimer's story suggests, the fear of crime can have as powerful an impact as the experience of crime itself. In fact, polls in this country often reveal that people's perceptions of the crime rate usually exceed the actual rate. Yet crime is a very real problem. In a small group, brainstorm about what some of the causes of crime are and how they might be eliminated. Evaluate your proposed solutions by filling in a three-column chart headed "Possible Solutions," "Advantages," and "Disadvantages." Save your notes for the Writer's Workshop on page 1179.

Comparing Texts

2. The Great Divide

Both Gordimer's tale and George Orwell's "Shooting an Elephant" (page 1139) carry messages about cultural clashes. Compare the two works, focusing on **themes, genres, styles,** and **tone.**

Creative Writing

3. Not So Happily Ever After

Use "Once upon a Time" as a model to write your own fairy tale about a clash of cultures. Include in it some kind of wall or boundary.

Research / Speaking

4. Other Walls, Other Bridges

Investigate the current state of affairs in South Africa, or in another part of the world beset by long-standing divisions between groups of people. What separates people in this area, and what efforts are being taken to bring them together? Prepare a brief oral report, and present it to your classmates.

Reading Check

Electronically controlled gates are installed for fear of rioters, and the boy plays with the gates' intercom. Burglar bars and an alarm are added when nearby houses are robbed. Ironically, the noise of similar systems throughout the neighborhood masks the sound of burglaries. The wall is made higher, but the family still fears intruders. After razor wire is placed on the wall, the child is severely hurt by the wire.

Grading Timesaver

Rubrics for each Choices assignment appear on p. 217 in the *Portfolio Management System.*

Derek Walcott

(1930–   )

Derek Walcott was born and raised on St. Lucia, an island in the West Indies noted for its green valleys, vast banana plantations, and sleeping volcano. St. Lucia was a colony of Britain when Walcott was a boy, and its official language remains English.

The son of a schoolteacher father and a mother who was headmistress of the island's Methodist Infant School, Walcott was introduced to the classics of English literature at an early age and showed great promise in the use of language. As he grew older, he also enjoyed the peculiar brand of "Englishness" that belonged to even the most far-flung colonies of the British Empire. Yet, in spite of these skills and interests, no one ever dreamed that a boy from a tiny tropical island would one day be regarded as one of the leading English-language poets of his day or be awarded the 1992 Nobel Prize in literature.

A scholarship student at the University of the West Indies in Jamaica, Walcott stayed on after graduation to teach comparative literature. He then embarked on an independent career that took him to the island of Trinidad, where he lived for many years. Walcott has spent a good deal of time in the United States, where the scope of his activities has included not only writing poetry but also writing plays and teaching classes in creative writing at Harvard and Boston Universities. Among his best-known works are *Dream on Monkey Mountain and Other Plays* (1970), the long narrative poems *Another Life* (1973) and *Omeros* (1990), and the lyric collections *Sea Grapes* (1976) and *Midsummer* (1984).

Walcott's characteristic language is elegant, gracefully formal, and filled with the resourcefulness that comes only from a well-trained talent. Yet he has also tried, particularly in his plays, to capture the native rhythms, the diction, and the dialect variations of the speech of the islands he knows.

In his Nobel lecture, Walcott used a strong metaphor to describe how a poet must reject language imposed from outside the self:

> Tonally, the individual voice is a dialect; it shapes its own accent, its own vocabulary and melody in defiance of an imperial concept of language, the language of Ozymandias [see page 731], libraries and dictionaries, law courts and critics, and churches, universities, political dogma, the diction of institutions. Poetry is an island that breaks away from the main.

Derek Walcott.

go.hrw.com
LEO 12-15

OBJECTIVES

1. Read and interpret the poem
2. Express understanding through critical and creative writing and discussion

SKILLS

Writing

- Collect ideas for a problem-solution essay
- Support a thesis with examples
- Create a speaker and write a poem

Speaking

- Participate in a panel discussion

Planning

- **Block Schedule**
  Block Scheduling Lesson Plans with Pacing Guide
- **Traditional Schedule**
  Lesson Plans Including Strategies for English-Language Learners
- **One-Stop Planner**
  CD-ROM with Test Generator

BROWSING IN THE FILES

About the Author. Walcott grew up in a home filled with books and with a mother who recited Shakespeare to him. He says the Caribbean culture "is based on joy" and explains that seriousness is for those cultures "with four seasons."

Resources: Print and Media

Reading

- *Graphic Organizers for Active Reading,* p. 116
- *Audio CD Library*
  Disc 22, Track 3

Assessment

- *Formal Assessment,* p. 229
- *Portfolio Management System,* p. 218
- *Test Generator (One-Stop Planner CD-ROM)*

Internet

- go.hrw.com (keyword: LEO 12-15)

Summary ■ ■

As the speaker walks the streets of Frederiksted on the island of St. Croix, he sees a town that has in a sense died because its citizens have made tourism the foundation of the economy. Crime has risen; traditional values have degenerated; cheap commercialism dominates. The trade winds, once the signal of a fresh, new day, now stir little more than roulette wheels.

A Critical Reading

Making Inferences

? In what ways are the streets dead? [quiet, devoid of community life] What has killed the city? [Possible response: The city's own beauty has been its downfall because it attracted tourists.]

B Reading Skills and Strategies

Interpreting

? What does the speaker mean by "so cheaply underpriced"? [Possible response: He seems to suggest that no matter what price is put on goods, such as cameras and watches, the price will never be high enough to compensate for the losses commercialism causes, including the increasing crime rate.]

C Vocabulary Note

Multiple Meanings

? What multiple meanings are possible for "trade" and "banks of silver"? [Possible responses: "Trade" may refer to commerce, as well as to the cleansing and regenerative trade winds; "banks of silver" may suggest money or resplendent nature.]

Before You Read

THE VIRGINS

Make the Connection

Give and Take

Helping developing countries to strengthen their economies by sending international aid seems to be, and often is, a positive act. If poorer countries ask and richer countries give, isn't the result progress? Isn't this a co-operation of cultures, not a clash? That depends, Derek Walcott might say, on what is given—and on what is taken away.

Quickwrite

Throughout the developing world, many people yearn for the benefits of "the American dream." But just what is the American dream? And is achieving this "dream" always a sign of "progress"? Record your responses to these questions.

Background

"The Virgins," or Virgin Islands, form an island chain in the West Indies. The U.S. Virgin Islands, an American possession since 1917, has a republican government whose governor and other political leaders are elected by island residents. In this poem, Walcott describes Frederiksted, one of the old port cities on the U.S. Virgin Island of St. Croix (sānt kroi). Frederiksted is now a free port where tourists can purchase goods without paying custom duties. The economy of St. Croix, once based on sugar cane, is now dependent on tourism. As you read, keep in mind that *virgin* refers to the Virgin Islands, but that it can also mean "unspoiled or untouched," as in *virgin forest.*

Tourists at the Nassau Bazaar, the Bahamas.

The Virgins

Derek Walcott

Down the dead streets of sun-stoned Frederiksted,
the first free port to die for tourism,
strolling at funeral pace, I am reminded
of life not lost to the American dream;
but my small-islander's simplicities
can't better our new empire's civilized
exchange of cameras, watches, perfumes, brandies
for the good life, so cheaply underpriced
that only the crime rate is on the rise
in streets blighted with sun, stone arches
and plazas blown dry by the hysteria
of rumor. A condominium drowns
in vacancy; its bargains are dusted,
but only a jeweled housefly drones
over the bargains. The roulettes spin
rustily to the wind—the vigorous trade
that every morning would begin afresh
by revving up green water round the pierhead
heading for where the banks of silver thresh.

Reaching All Students

Struggling Readers

To help students relate to the poem's theme, ask them to recall a familiar place that they once enjoyed which has changed drastically due to some outside force. Tell them that Walcott is writing about the changes that have come over a Caribbean island he loves due to tourism. Then read the poem aloud, and ask students to form mental pictures of Frederiksted based on the details and images the poet includes.

Advanced Learners

Ask students to write a dialogue that might take place between a tourist and an island resident about the social, economic, and environmental changes that tourism has brought to St. Croix. Suggest that students do some research into the attitudes of Virgin Islanders to see if Walcott's opinion of tourism and development is widely shared.

Making Meanings

First Thoughts

1. Did you find yourself sympathizing with or questioning the speaker's viewpoint? Explain.

Shaping Interpretations

2. What is the tourist reminded of as he strolls the streets of Frederiksted?
3. How does Walcott **ironically** represent the "good life" of "the American dream"? How does his picture compare with your Quickwrite notes?
4. How do you explain line 2? What other **images** in the poem suggest decay and emptiness?
5. What positive images suggest the island "simplicities" that once existed in Frederiksted?
6. Sum up what you think Walcott is saying about the changes he sees. Who or what is responsible for the changes? Are the changes for the better or for the worse?

Extending the Text

7. Have places within the United States fallen victim to "the American dream" in ways similar to Walcott's description of Frederiksted? Explain your answer, and discuss your reactions.

Frederiksted, St. Croix, Virgin Islands.

Choices: Building Your Portfolio

Writer's Notebook

1. Collecting Ideas for a Problem-Solution Essay

In his poem, Walcott explores what happens when outside forces impose change on a way of life. Your response to question 7 under Extending the Text could be the starting point for an investigation into the causes and effects of a similar problem in your community. Use the *5W-How?* questions (*Who? What? When? Where? Why? How?*) to find out what you already know about the problem. Save your notes for the Writer's Workshop on page 1179.

Supporting a Thesis

2. Double Meanings

The scholar Laurence Perrine feels that Walcott's poems "are sharpened by his skillful use of irony and of words and phrases of double meanings." Support this statement in an essay, citing words and passages from the poem. Be sure to consider the title.

Creative Writing

3. My Own Islands

Imagine the other people who exist in this lyric's landscape, even if they are not mentioned: tourists, shopkeepers, fishers, and so on. Choose one, and write a lyric about Frederiksted in which he or she is the speaker.

Panel Discussion

4. What *Is* the American Dream?

Hold a panel discussion with some classmates about your own perceptions of "the American dream." What does each panel member see as ideal? What forces shape the dream you each hold? Do you feel pressure to conform to someone else's notion of what's ideal?

Making Meanings

First Thoughts [Respond]

1. Some students may agree with the speaker that tourism has blighted the natural beauty and traditional life of the island. Others may point out that living standards for the islanders have probably improved.

Shaping Interpretations [Interpret]

2. He is reminded of "life not lost" to commercialism and materialism.
3. He plays on the word *good* and represents the "good" life by goods: cameras and so forth. Students may well have equated the American dream with material wealth.
4. Paradoxically, the commercial development that is supposed to bring "the American dream," abundance for everyone, has brought spiritual death, as well as more crime, to the town. Images suggesting decay include "dead streets," "spin rustily," and "plazas blown dry."
5. Positive images include "vigorous trade" (if read in the sense of trade winds) and "banks of silver" (if read in the sense of unspoiled natural beauty).
6. American materialism has brought decay and death; from the speaker's perspective, the changes have been negative.

Extending the Text [Apply]

7. Students may mention the decay of the downtown centers of many older cities as an example of the failure of the American dream to sustain community life.

Grading Timesaver

Rubrics for each Choices assignment appear on p. 218 in the *Portfolio Management System.*

Objectives

1. Read and interpret the story
2. Express understanding through critical and creative writing
3. Learn and use new words

Skills

Writing

- Collect ideas for a problem-solution essay
- Interpret an ending
- Evaluate an opinion
- Add scenes to the story

Vocabulary

- Learn and use new words

Planning

- **Traditional Schedule**
  Lesson Plans Including Strategies for English-Language Learners
- **One-Stop Planner**
  CD-ROM with Test Generator

Chinua Achebe

(1930–)

Chinua Achebe.

Nigerian author Chinua Achebe (chin'wä' ä·chā'bā) planned to study medicine, but literature and his country's nationalist movement forever changed his plans. As a student, he came to realize the destructive effects of colonialism and dedicated himself to redefining Africa, to telling Africans' true story, including their achievements and failures. In his words, the European idea that "Africa was the Primordial Void, was sheer humbug; . . . Africa had a history, a religion, a civilization."

His novels, beginning with the celebrated *Things Fall Apart* (1958), focus on the changes in Nigerian life that occurred in the twentieth century. The novels trace life in Nigeria—sometimes presented as a fictionalized nation—from the arrival of early English missionaries, through years of colonial rule, to a post-independence era rife with corruption and political turmoil. Achebe believes that "Africa's meeting with Europe must be accounted a terrible disaster in this matter of human understanding and respect," yet his African characters are not idealized. They are held responsible for their private decisions and for solving the problems that threaten their nation's future.

Achebe is himself an Ibo, born in the eastern Nigerian town of Ogidi, where his father, a Christian convert, taught at the mission school. He has chosen to write in English, which he began to learn at age eight, in order to reach a wide audience.

During Nigeria's civil war of the late 1960s, Achebe worked for the cause of the secessionist Biafrans. Since then he has concentrated on teaching, and on encouraging and publishing promising young authors. Through his many works of fiction, nonfiction, and poetry, he has been a catalyst for an entire younger generation of African writers.

Before You Read

Marriage Is a Private Affair

Make the Connection

Coming Together

Like the United States, many nations are conglomerations of diverse peoples. And when people of diverse backgrounds come together, conflicts tend to arise. People may focus on differences in customs, religion, and ethnic heritage and fail to notice all the things they have in common. Yet, age-old distinctions often become less significant as people expand their horizons. They travel, they read, they watch, they listen. They go beyond "their kind."

Quickwrite

If your parents or guardians were to choose a perfect spouse for you, what kind of person would they choose? What qualities will *you* consider important in a partner? Jot down similarities and differences between your generation's attitudes toward love and marriage and those of the generation before you.

Background

The African nation of Nigeria has more than 250 ethnic groups. These groups have different languages and frequently differ in religion, customs, and traditions. The Ibo and Ibibio both live in southeastern Nigeria but traditionally did not intermarry. In Achebe's story, a young Ibo man and an Ibibio woman have moved from their native regions to Lagos, a large and modern city in southwestern Nigeria.

go.hrw.com
LEO 12-15

Resources: Print and Media

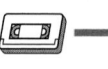

Reading

- *Graphic Organizers for Active Reading,* p. 117
- *Words to Own,* p. 38
- *Audio CD Library*
  Disc 22, Track 4

Writing and Language

- *Daily Oral Grammar*
  Transparency 45
- *Grammar and Language Links*
  Worksheet, p. 75

Assessment

- *Formal Assessment,* p. 230
- *Portfolio Management System,* p. 219
- *Test Generator (One-Stop Planner CD-ROM)*

Internet

- go.hrw.com (keyword: LEO 12-15)

Marriage Is a Private Affair

Chinua Achebe

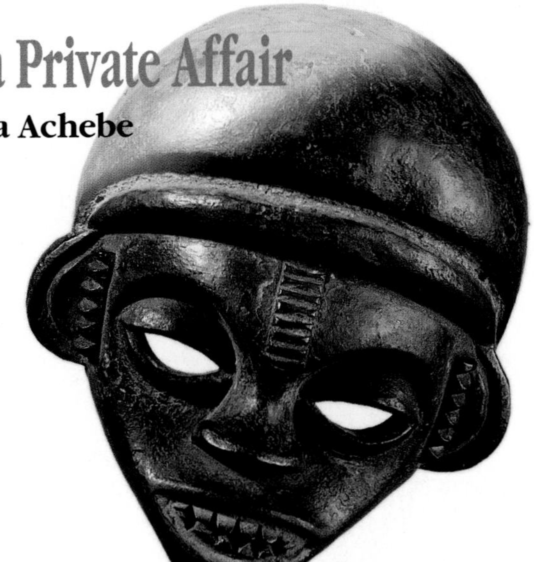

Old Ibibio mask.
© British Museum, London.

"Have you written to your dad yet?" asked Nene[1] one afternoon as she sat with Nnaemeka[2] in her room at 16 Kasanga Street, Lagos.[3]

"No. I've been thinking about it. I think it's better to tell him when I get home on leave!"

"But why? Your leave is such a long way off yet—six whole weeks. He should be let into our happiness now."

Nnaemeka was silent for a while, and then began very slowly as if he groped for his words: "I wish I were sure it would be happiness to him."

"Of course it must," replied Nene, a little surprised. "Why shouldn't it?"

"You have lived in Lagos all your life, and you know very little about people in remote parts of the country."

"That's what you always say. But I don't believe anybody will be so unlike other people that they will be unhappy when their sons are engaged to marry."

"Yes. They are most unhappy if the engagement is not arranged by them. In our case it's worse—you are not even an Ibo."[4] (A)

This was said so seriously and so bluntly that Nene could not find speech immediately. In the cosmopolitan atmosphere of the city it had always seemed to her something of a joke that a person's tribe could determine whom he married.

At last she said, "You don't really mean that he will object to your marrying me simply on that account? I had always thought you Ibos were kindly disposed to other people."

"So we are. But when it comes to marriage, well, it's not quite so simple. And this," he added, "is not peculiar to the Ibos. If your father were alive and lived in the heart of Ibibio-land[5] he would be exactly like my father." (B)

"I don't know. But anyway, as your father is so fond of you, I'm sure he will forgive you soon enough. Come on then, be a good boy and send him a nice lovely letter . . ."

"It would not be wise to break the news to him by writing. A letter will bring it upon him with a shock. I'm quite sure about that."

"All right, honey, suit yourself. You know your father."

As Nnaemeka walked home that evening he turned over in his mind different ways of overcoming his father's opposition, especially now that he had gone and found a girl for him. He had thought of showing his letter to Nene but decided on second thoughts not to, at least for the moment. He read it again when he got home and couldn't help smiling to himself. He remembered Ugoye[6] quite well, an Amazon[7] of a girl who used

1. **Nene** (nā′nā).
2. **Nnaemeka** (′n·nä·ā·mā′kə).
3. **Lagos** (lā′gōs′): former capital of Nigeria.
4. **Ibo** (ē′bō′): member of an African ethnic group living chiefly in southeastern Nigeria.
5. **Ibibio-land** (ib′ə·bē′o′land): area of southeastern Nigeria that is the traditional homeland of the Ibibio, another African ethnic group.
6. **Ugoye** (o͞o·gō′yā).
7. **Amazon:** tall, strong, aggressive woman. The term is taken from the name for the Amazons, a race of female warriors in Greek mythology.

WORDS TO OWN

cosmopolitan (käz′mə·päl′ə·tən) *adj.:* representative of many parts of the world; not constrained by provincial habits or prejudices.

Summary

A young Ibo man named Nnaemeka returns from the city of Lagos in Nigeria to the countryside where he was born to tell his father he plans to marry a girl, Nene, whom he met in the city. The father, Okeke, refuses to accept the marriage because Nene is not an Ibo. As tradition dictates, Nnaemeka's father has chosen an Ibo wife for him. Nnaemeka, however, is determined to marry the woman he loves and returns to the city. Equally adamant, Okeke returns the wedding picture his son sends with the image of the bride cut out. No reconciliation seems possible. However, years later, Nene writes to Okeke that her two sons want to see their grandfather, and the old man at last regrets the barriers he has placed between himself and his son's family.

Background

The dual setting (Lagos, Nigeria's largest city, and the traditional rural village) plays a key role in this story. The dichotomy between cosmopolitan city life and conservative rural life dramatizes the clash between old and new, modern and traditional, and Western and African that Acebe wishes to explore.

(A) Elements of Literature

Plot

? The author offers little exposition before introducing the story's conflict. What difficulty is introduced? [Nnaemeka is engaged to a woman who is not of his tribe.]

(B) Cultural Connections

Nigeria comprises many different ethnic groups, each with its own language, religion, and customs. Favored by the British colonial rulers because of their acceptance of Christianity, the Ibo became the nation's best-educated and most prosperous group. The Ibibio, the second-largest ethnic group, were traditionally farmers.

Preteaching Vocabulary

Words to Own

Have students work in pairs to study each vocabulary word and its definition. Ask them to discuss any structural clues to each word's meaning. For example, students can focus on suffixes that signal parts of speech or tense, the meaning of the prefixes *dis-*, *con-*, and *com-*, and any roots with which they are familiar, such as *cosmos*.

Then have students match each word with its meaning.

1. vehemently	[d]	a.	worldly
2. persevered	[b]	b.	kept on
3. commiserate	[c]	c.	sympathize with
4. disconcertingly	[e]	d.	forcefully
5. cosmopolitan	[a]	e.	in a way that bothers or distresses

Ⓐ Struggling Readers

Finding Sequence of Events

? The italicized text is a portion of a letter from Okeke to his son. When did this letter arrive, and what plot complications does it reveal? [The letter arrived sometime before the day on which the story opens; it shows that Nnaemeka's father has already identified the woman from his own tribe that he wants his son to marry.]

Ⓑ English Language Learners

Idioms

"Along the line of" is a common idiom but one whose meaning is far from transparent. Explain that it is most commonly used, as it is here, to mean "within the boundary of." Nnaemeka realizes that within the bounds of his father's values Nene will never be considered a suitable wife for him.

Ⓒ Critical Thinking

Speculating

? Why might Okeke mispronounce Nene Atang's name? [Possible responses: The name is from another tribe, and he would not be familiar with it. He may wish to show how alien the name is to him and what little respect he has for his son's choice.]

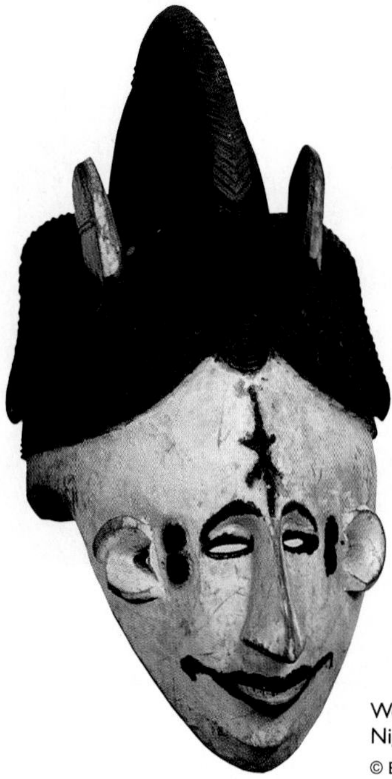

Wood mask. Ibo, Nigeria (37 cm).

© British Museum, London.

to beat up all the boys, himself included, on the way to the stream, a complete dunce at school.

Ⓐ *I have found a girl who will suit you admirably—Ugoye Nweke,[8] the eldest daughter of our neighbor, Jacob Nweke. She has a proper Christian upbringing. When she stopped schooling some years ago her father (a man of sound judgment) sent her to live in the house of a pastor where she has received all the training a wife could need. Her Sunday school teacher has told me that she reads her Bible very fluently. I hope we shall begin negotiations when you come home in December.*

On the second evening of his return from Lagos, Nnaemeka sat with his father under a cassia tree. This was the old man's retreat where he went to read his Bible when the parching December sun had set and a fresh, reviving wind blew on the leaves.

"Father," began Nnaemeka suddenly, "I have come to ask for forgiveness."

"Forgiveness? For what, my son?" he asked in amazement.

"It's about this marriage question."

"Which marriage question?"

"I can't—we must—I mean it is impossible for me to marry Nweke's daughter."

"Impossible? Why?" asked his father.

"I don't love her."

"Nobody said you did. Why should you?" he asked.

"Marriage today is different . . ."

"Look here, my son," interrupted his father, "nothing is different. What one looks for in a wife are a good character and a Christian background."

Ⓑ Nnaemeka saw there was no hope along the present line of argument.

"Moreover," he said, "I am engaged to marry another girl who has all of Ugoye's good qualities, and who . . ."

His father did not believe his ears. "What did you say?" he asked slowly and disconcertingly.

"She is a good Christian," his son went on, "and a teacher in a girls' school in Lagos."

"Teacher, did you say? If you consider that a qualification for a good wife I should like to point out to you, Emeka, that no Christian woman should teach. St. Paul in his letter to the Corinthians[9] says that women should keep silence." He rose slowly from his seat and paced forward and backward. This was his pet subject, and he condemned vehemently those church leaders who encouraged women to teach in their schools. After he had spent his emotion on a long homily he at last came back to his son's engagement, in a seemingly milder tone.

"Whose daughter is she, anyway?"

Ⓒ "She is Nene Atang."

"What!" All the mildness was gone again. "Did you say Neneataga, what does that mean?"

"Nene Atang from Calabar.[10] She is the only girl I can marry." This was a very rash reply and Nnaemeka expected the storm to burst. But it did

8. **Nweke** (′n·wā′kā).

9. **St. Paul . . . Corinthians:** reference to a passage in the Bible's New Testament (1 Corinthians 14:34).

10. **Calabar:** seaport city in southeastern Nigeria.

Words to Own

disconcertingly (dis′kən·surt′iŋ·lē) *adv.:* in a manner that embarrasses, confuses, or flusters.

vehemently (vē′ə·mənt·lē) *adv.:* passionately; strongly.

Reaching All Students

Struggling Readers

Students sometimes have difficulty determining who is speaking in a story that is primarily dialogue. Each time students come across a set of words enclosed in quotation marks as they read, have them fill in a double-column chart. Have them put the first and last word of the quoted dialogue in the first column and the speaker's name in the second column.

English Language Learners

To help students follow the plot of the story, have them fill out a cluster diagram with the label Major Conflicts in the circle at the center of the diagram. Encourage them to write the names of characters who are in conflict in the first round of radiating circles and then to specify the nature of the conflicts between characters in the next round of radiating circles.

Advanced Learners

Have students do research on contemporary Nigeria, especially on tensions between ethnic groups, regions, or city dwellers and rural people. Ask them to consider questions like these: Have the divisions eased or intensified since independence? What steps have been taken to unite the country and have they been effective? Students can present their findings in the form of an article for a magazine called *Today's Africa.*

not. His father merely walked away into his room. This was most unexpected and perplexed Nnaemeka. His father's silence was infinitely more menacing than a flood of threatening speech. That night the old man did not eat.

When he sent for Nnaemeka a day later he applied all possible ways of dissuasion. But the young man's heart was hardened, and his father eventually gave him up as lost.

D "I owe it to you, my son, as a duty to show you what is right and what is wrong. Whoever put this idea into your head might as well have cut your throat. It is Satan's work." He waved his son away.

"You will change your mind, Father, when you know Nene."

"I shall never see her," was the reply. From that night the father scarcely spoke to his son. He did not, however, cease hoping that he would realize how serious was the danger he was heading for. Day and night he put him in his prayers.

Nnaemeka, for his own part, was very deeply affected by his father's grief. But he kept hoping that it would pass away. If it had occurred to him that never in the history of his people had a man married a woman who spoke a different tongue, he might have been less optimistic. E "It has never been heard," was the verdict of an old man speaking a few weeks later. In that short sentence he spoke for all of his people. This man had come with others to commiserate with Okeke[11] when news went round about his son's behavior. By that time the son had gone back to Lagos.

"It has never been heard," said the old man again with a sad shake of his head.

"What did Our Lord say?" asked another gentleman. "Sons shall rise against their Fathers; it is there in the Holy Book."

"It is the beginning of the end," said another.

The discussion thus tending to become theological, Madubogwu, a highly practical man, brought it down once more to the ordinary level.

"Have you thought of consulting a native doctor about your son?" he asked Nnaemeka's father.

"He isn't sick," was the reply.

"What is he then? The boy's mind is diseased and only a good herbalist can bring him back to his right senses. The medicine he requires is *Amalile,* the same that women apply with success to recapture their husbands' straying affection."

"Madubogwu is right," said another gentleman. "This thing calls for medicine."

F "I shall not call in a native doctor." Nnaemeka's father was known to be obstinately ahead of his more superstitious neighbors in these matters. "I will not be another Mrs. Ochuba. If my son wants to kill himself let him do it with his own hands. It is not for me to help him."

"But it was her fault," said Madubogwu. "She ought to have gone to an honest herbalist. She was a clever woman, nevertheless."

"She was a wicked murderess," said Jonathan, who rarely argued with his neighbors because, he often said, they were incapable of reasoning. "The medicine was prepared for her husband, it was his name they called in its preparation, and I am sure it would have been perfectly beneficial to him. It was wicked to put it into the herbalist's food, and say you were only trying it out."

Six months later, Nnaemeka was showing his young wife a short letter from his father:

It amazes me that you could be so unfeeling as to send me your wedding picture. I would have sent it back. But on further thought I decided just to cut off your wife and send it back to you because I have nothing to do with her. How I wish that I had nothing to do with you either.

When Nene read through this letter and looked at the mutilated picture her eyes filled with tears, and she began to sob.

"Don't cry, my darling," said her husband. "He is essentially good-natured and will one day look more kindly on our marriage." But years passed and that one day did not come.

For eight years, Okeke would have nothing to do with his son, Nnaemeka. Only three times (when Nnaemeka asked to come home and spend his leave) did he write to him.

"I can't have you in my house," he replied on one occasion. "It can be of no interest to me

---

WORDS TO OWN

commiserate (kə·miz′ər·āt′) *v.:* to feel sorrow or pity for; sympathize.

---

11. Okeke (ō·kā′kā).

D Critical Thinking

Making Connections

Misunderstandings between generations often are caused by individuals' differing ideas about what is important and what is appropriate. Ask students to find examples from newspapers or books that illustrate conflicts between generations. Have students explain if and how the conflicts are resolved.

E Reading Skills and Strategies

Drawing Conclusions

? How do the reactions of the other men in the village shed light on Okeke's refusal to acknowledge his son's engagement? [Possible response: The comments of the other tribesmen show that Okeke's obstinacy is based on the deeply rooted and shared beliefs of his people.]

F Struggling Readers

Understanding Details

Explain that these details do not relate directly to the conflict between Nnaemeka and Okeke but do help to define the traditional values of the Ibo community and to reveal the character of Okeke: He is something of an independent thinker within the context of his people and their values and traditions.

Getting Students Involved

Enrichment

Speaking and Listening. Have students work in pairs to dramatize a conversation from the story. Encourage them to pay attention to nonverbal communication, such as gestures and movement, and to emphasize the importance of the inflection, speed, and volume of the voice in portraying emotion. Allow the pairs time for practice before they perform.

Professional Notes

Critical Comment: Achebe's Communication

Critic Margaret Laurence writes on the theme of communication in Achebe's writing: "In Ibo villages, the men working on their farm plots in the midst of the rain forest often shout to one another—a reassurance, to make certain the other is still there . . . on the other side of the thick undergrowth. The writing of Chinua Achebe is like this. It seeks to send human voices through the thickets of our separateness."

A Elements of Literature

Irony

? How does this passage indicate that the story's title is ironic? [Possible response: Nnaemeka's marriage is hardly private—it is the subject of village commentary and is even discussed by Ibo acquaintances in Lagos.]

B Struggling Readers

Finding Details

? Here, new information is revealed through correspondence. What is it? [Nnaemeka and Nene have had two sons.] **Where else have letters played a role in advancing the plot?** [A letter revealed the father's choice of a bride for his son; a letter also confirmed the couple's wedding and revealed the extent of Okeke's anger at the event.]

C Elements of Literature

Symbol

? What might the breaking storm marking the change of seasons symbolize? [Possible response: Okeke's attitude has changed.]

D Critical Thinking

Drawing Conclusions

? What do you think Okeke will do next? [Possible response: Okeke will allow his grandchildren to visit him.] **Do you think he is acting in or out of character? Explain.** [Possible responses: Love of family is a strong Ibo, as well as Christian, value, so Okeke has not strayed too far from his traditional beliefs. Getting older has tempered his formerly obstinate character.]

Ikenga headdress. Wood and feathers (76.1 cm).

UCLA Fowler Museum of Cultural History, Los Angeles. Gift of Wellcome Trust.

where or how you spend your leave—or your life, for that matter."

A The prejudice against Nnaemeka's marriage was not confined to his little village. In Lagos, especially among his people who worked there, it showed itself in a different way. Their women, when they met at their village meeting, were not hostile to Nene. Rather, they paid her such excessive deference as to make her feel she was not one of them. But as time went on, Nene gradually broke through some of this prejudice and even began to make friends among them. Slowly and grudgingly they began to admit that she kept her home much better than most of them.

The story eventually got to the little village in the heart of the Ibo country that Nnaemeka and his young wife were a most happy couple. But his father was one of the few people in the village who knew nothing about this. He always displayed so much temper whenever his son's name was mentioned that everyone avoided it in his presence. By a tremendous effort of will he had succeeded in pushing his son to the back of his mind. The strain had nearly killed him but he had persevered, and won.

Then one day he received a letter from Nene, and in spite of himself he began to glance through it perfunctorily until all of a sudden the expression on his face changed and he began to read more carefully.

B *. . . Our two sons, from the day they learnt that they have a grandfather, have insisted on being taken to him. I find it impossible to tell them that you will not see them. I implore you to allow Nnaemeka to bring them home for a short time during his leave next month. I shall remain here in Lagos . . .*

The old man at once felt the resolution he had built up over so many years falling in. He was telling himself that he must not give in. He tried to steel his heart against all emotional appeals. It was a reenactment of that other struggle. He leaned C against a window and looked out. The sky was overcast with heavy black clouds and a high wind began to blow, filling the air with dust and dry leaves. It was one of those rare occasions when even Nature takes a hand in a human fight. Very soon it began to rain, the first rain in the year. It came down in large sharp drops and was accompanied by the lightning and thunder which mark a change of season. Okeke was trying hard not to think of his two grandsons. But he knew he was now fighting a losing battle. He tried to hum a favorite hymn but the pattering of large raindrops on the roof broke up the tune. His mind immediately returned to the children. How could he shut his door against them? By a curious mental process he imagined them standing, sad and forsaken, under the harsh angry weather—shut out from his house.

D That night he hardly slept, from remorse—and a vague fear that he might die without making it up to them.

WORDS TO OWN

persevered (pʉr'sə·vird') *v.:* continued in a course of action despite difficulty or opposition; persisted.

Assessing Learning

Check Test: Short Answers

1. **Why doesn't Nnaemeka want to write to his father about his marriage plans?** [He knows his father will disapprove, so he wants to tell him in person.]
2. **What characteristics does Okeke require in a wife for his son?** [good character and Ibo background]
3. **How do the villagers react to the news of Nnaemeka's behavior?** [They agree with Okeke in condemning his son's actions.]
4. **What does Okeke do with his son's wedding picture?** [He returns it with Nene's image cut out.]
5. **What request does Nene make of Okeke?** [She asks that he allow his grandsons to visit.]

Standardized Test Preparation

For practice in proofreading and editing, see

- *Daily Oral Grammar,* Transparency 45

PRIMARY Sources — A SPEECH

This is an excerpt from Chinua Achebe's address to the graduating class of Bates College in Lewiston, Maine, on May 27, 1996.

Diversity Is Reality

The world is big. Some people are unable to comprehend that simple fact. They want the world on their own terms, its peoples just like them and their friends, its places like the manicured little patch on which they live. But this is a foolish and blind wish. Diversity is not an abnormality but the very reality of our planet. The human world manifests the same reality and will not seek our permission to celebrate itself in the magnificence of its endless varieties. Civility is a sensible attribute in this kind of world we have; narrowness of heart and mind is not.

Connections — A POEM

As you read the following poem by the poet Maurice Kenny (1929–   ), a member of the Mohawk people, who once lived in Brooklyn, New York, think back to the conflict between the father and son in "Marriage Is a Private Affair." How will Nnaemeka's own sons in that story relate to their grandfather's cultural legacy?

Going Home

Maurice Kenny

The book lay unread in my lap
snow gathered at the window
from Brooklyn it was a long ride
the Greyhound followed the plow
from Syracuse to Watertown
to country cheese and maples
tired rivers and closed paper mills
home to gossipy aunts . . .
their dandelions and pregnant cats . . .
home to cedars and fields of boulders
cold graves under willow and pine
home from Brooklyn to the reservation
that was not home
to songs I could not sing
to dances I could not dance
from Brooklyn bars and ghetto rats
to steaming horses stomping frozen
  earth
barns and privies lost in blizzards
home to a Nation, Mohawk
to faces I did not know
and hands which did not recognize me
to names and doors
my father shut

(E)

Primary Sources

In this excerpt from a 1996 commencement speech, Achebe advises listeners to beware of the current "anti-liberal atmosphere," which, he says, is like the atmosphere in Europe in the 1930s. Having lived through numerous coups, civil wars, and elections marked by violence in Nigeria, Achebe speaks with a deep awareness of the need for tolerance of diversity.

Encourage students to put Achebe's remarks in their own words and to think of situations in their own communities in which his advice might be relevant.

Connections

The Mohawk people were once part of the Iroquois League, an organization of six Native American nations. They inhabited what is now the eastern part of New York State. Mohawks supported the British during the American Revolution so after the British were defeated, many Mohawks moved to Canada. Other Mohawks live on the St. Regis Reserve, located on the U.S.-Canadian border and in the U.S. cities of New York, Buffalo, and Detroit. The speaker is traveling from Brooklyn in New York City to the reservation in rural New York State.

(E) Reading Skills and Strategies

Comparing and Contrasting

? What similarities and differences do you see between "Going Home" and "Marriage Is a Private Affair"? [Possible responses: Both pieces contrast modern urban life with a more traditional culture. In "Going Home," however, the speaker is a complete stranger to his ancestral culture, whereas Nnaemeka still has strong ties to his background.]

Connecting Across Texts

Connecting with "Marriage Is a Private Affair"

Students might discuss these questions:

- **What different attitudes toward traditional culture do the Achebe story and the Kenny poem express?** [The story establishes sympathy for the younger generation; it shows the desire of the urban young to move away from traditional values and adopt more modern behavior, such as marrying for love. The poem reflects the desire of the city-bred generation to return to, or at least learn about, the traditional ways that it has lost. The poem expresses more alienation and sense of loss than the story, which suggests the possibility of reconciling old and new.]
- **How might it come about that Nnaemeka's sons may one day feel the emotions expressed by the speaker in "Going Home"? Explain your answer.** [If their father abandons all connection with his traditional roots, he will have made a choice for his sons and, no matter how well-intentioned that choice might have been, they may later feel a sense of loss.]

MAKING MEANINGS

First Thoughts [Respond]

1. Most students will observe differences between generations. Some may say that the conflicts in the story are more or less extreme than those they have encountered.

Shaping Interpretations [Interpret]

2. For the Ibo, marriage is not at all a private affair: It is a tribal, or community, matter.
3. Conflicts occur between Nnaemeka and Okeke; Okeke and Nene; Okeke and his neighbors; and between traditional and modern values and customs. While the interpersonal conflicts are, for the most part, resolved or reduced, the conflict of cultural values continues, resolved in the course of history by forces often beyond individual control.
4. Okeke is proud and inflexible. He ignores his son and Nene for eight years, putting communal values before personal desires. Finally, he relents because he longs to see his grandchildren.
5. The herbalist was killed by Mrs. Ochuba, who gave him the medicine he prepared for her husband. The anecdote helps show the difference between Nnaemeka's world and his father's. It also shows that Okeke does not follow tradition blindly.
6. It could symbolize Okeke's renewal and hope for the next generation.
7. The theme is cultural conflict and change.
8. In the story, the narrator's third-person account makes it easy for the reader to sympathize with the younger generation's desire for change. In the poem, the use of the first person helps the reader to respond sympathetically to the speaker's feelings of loss.

Extending the Text [Evaluate]

9. Students may observe that, like Nigeria, the United States is a multicultural society where the values of various ethnic and religious groups are likely to clash. In the case of the United States, rapidly developing technology also contributes to divisions between generations. As in the story, individuals frequently are confronted with difficult value choices that cannot be easily resolved.

MAKING MEANINGS

First Thoughts

1. How would you compare the attitudes you described in your Quickwrite notes with the attitudes between generations in this story?

Shaping Interpretations

2. What is the **irony** of the story's title?
3. This story bursts with **conflicts** among people and ideas. What are at least two of these conflicts? Does the story resolve them? If so, how?
4. How would you describe Okeke's **character**? Use details from the story to support your answer.
5. What do you think happened to the herbalist, and why would Achebe include that anecdote?
6. What might the rain at the end of the story **symbolize**?
7. The story's subject is a marriage that occurs against a parent's wishes, but what is the story's **theme**?
8. Both Achebe's story and the poem "Going Home" (see *Connections* on page 1169) are about generational and cultural conflict, but they differ in narrative **point of view.** From whose point of view is each told? How does the point of view shape your response to each work?

Extending the Text

9. You hear much talk today about "traditional values" and about the "multicultural society." What are some contemporary examples of clashes in values, and how would you relate them to this story's plot and theme?

Reading Check

a. What are Okeke's objections to his son's marriage and choice of wife?
b. How much time passes from the marriage to the story's end? During that time, how does Okeke act toward his son?
c. How are Nnaemeka and his father different?
d. Why does Nene send a letter to Nnaemeka's father?

CHOICES: Building Your Portfolio

Writer's Notebook

1. Collecting Ideas for a Problem-Solution Essay

WORK IN PROGRESS

Personal problems such as Okeke's disapproval of his son's choice of a wife aren't suitable for a problem-solution essay, but their underlying causes—in this case, attitudes weighted by centuries of tradition—may be. Brainstorm to develop a list of intergenerational problems you're familiar with, and then work with a partner to analyze their underlying causes. Save your notes for the Writer's Workshop on page 1179.

Interpreting an Ending

2. Final Analysis

In an essay, present and support your interpretation of what happens at the story's end. Be sure to examine the nature **imagery.** Include your personal response to the way the story ends.

Evaluating an Opinion

3. A Failure of Imagination

In an interview, Chinua Achebe made this comment about poverty in Nigeria and elsewhere: "If we really could project into the skin of the beggar under the bridge in Lagos, we would immediately start doing something to bring about a just society. It is that lack of imagination which . . . is at the root of cruelty." Do you agree with Achebe, or would you explain the persistence of poverty differently? Organize a debate to discuss the issue.

Creative Writing

4. And Then What?

Working with a partner, continue the story. One of you, alone, will write a scene showing what Okeke does next; then the other will take up the action in a second scene. Be true to Achebe's characterizations.

Reading Check

a. Primarily, he objects to her being from a different tribe.
b. Eight years pass during which Okeke scarcely communicates with his son.
c. Nnaemeka does not feel the need to uphold tradition as his father does.
d. She asks him to see his grandsons.

Grading Timesaver

Rubrics for each Choices assignment appear on p. 219 in the *Portfolio Management System.*

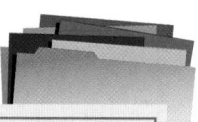

Wole Soyinka

(1934–)

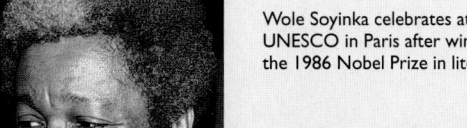

Wole Soyinka celebrates at UNESCO in Paris after winning the 1986 Nobel Prize in literature.

A voice of modern Africa, Wole Soyinka in 1986 became the first African to win the Nobel Prize in literature. Soyinka's favorite African deity is Ogun, god of both war and creative fire—a fitting muse for a multitalented writer and performer whose plays, songs, novels, and poetry combine political activism, universal themes, and African traditions.

Born Akinwande Oluwole Soyinka in a village in western Nigeria, Soyinka was the son of the principal of a Christian school and a teacher. His parents both supported European-style education, but his father also retained strong ties to his heritage as a member of the Yoruba tribe. Soyinka grew up respecting both traditions; his 1981 autobiography, *Aké: The Years of Childhood,* tells of his later struggle with this duality.

After attending University College at Ibadan, Nigeria, Soyinka studied English literature in England at the University of Leeds. In London in the late 1950s, he wrote plays and poetry for theater and radio. During this period of African nationalism and pressure for independence, Soyinka's themes were racism, injustice, tyranny, and corruption, all treated with satiric wit. Also concerned with the collision of ancient traditions and modern realities, he peppered his plays with vivid Yoruba masquerade ritual.

Soyinka felt brutal despotism firsthand during Nigeria's civil war of the late 1960s, when he was imprisoned for two years for the "crime" of meeting with secessionist leaders such as the writer Chinua Achebe. He describes these experiences in *The Man Died: Prison Notes,* published in 1972. Since then he has continued to record and dramatize, with both passion and humor, the struggle and spirit of modern-day Africa and Africans.

Before You Read

TELEPHONE CONVERSATION

Make the Connection

Subtle Discriminations

The following poem, written during Soyinka's college career in Britain in the late 1950s, records one of his own experiences with discrimination at a time when millions of people from former British colonies were arriving in England in search of economic and intellectual opportunity. As you read the poem, think about how Soyinka communicates this experience—is it presented as painful, or as humorously absurd? Is Soyinka's criticism straightforward or indirect?

Quickwrite

Think about the ways, both thoughtless and intentional, in which people practice discrimination. Then jot down some examples. How can those who are discriminated against make others mindful of what they've suffered?

Background

Soyinka's poem presents ideas primarily through a **dialogue.** The first speaker is talking from one of the red public telephone booths that were common in London years ago. To use such a phone, a person had to push one button to speak and another to listen. The first speaker is a well-educated black African and the second, a British woman who has property to rent. Soyinka's poem doesn't just describe their exchange; it re-creates it.

go.hrw.com
LEO 12-15

OBJECTIVES

1. Read and interpret the poem
2. Express understanding through critical writing or speaking

SKILLS

Writing
- Collect ideas for a problem-solution essay
- Analyze a character

Speaking
- Present an oral report

Planning

- **Traditional Schedule**
  Lesson Plans Including Strategies for English-Language Learners
- **One-Stop Planner**
  CD-ROM with Test Generator

BROWSING IN THE FILES

About the Author. During most of Soyinka's imprisonment, he was kept in solitary confinement. Denied writing materials, he wrote on toilet paper. After his release, Soyinka said his one theme, his one religion, was human liberty.

Resources: Print and Media

Reading
- *Graphic Organizers for Active Reading,* p. 118
- *Audio CD Library*
  Disc 22, Track 5

Assessment
- *Formal Assessment,* p. 232
- *Portfolio Management System,* p. 221
- *Test Generator (One-Stop Planner CD-ROM)*

Internet
- go.hrw.com (keyword: LEO 12-15)

Summary ■■

The black speaker is having a telephone conversation with a white landlady about renting an apartment. In an effort to spare himself a wasted trip, should the woman be racist, the speaker tells her over the phone that he is an African. She hesitates a moment, then impersonally asks whether he is dark- or light-skinned. Stunned, the speaker gives absurd details about his "color," in a flood of humiliation and fury which ends in a well placed insult to the fussy landlady.

(A) Appreciating Language
Word Choice

? What is ironic about the speaker's use of the word "self-confession"? [Possible response: The choice is ironic. The speaker has no reason to "confess"; yet, for someone like the landlady, the "wrong" skin color is apparently a crime.]

(B) Elements of Literature
Tone

? What is the speaker's tone? [Possible response: The speaker shows his anger by means of satirical and bitter humor.] **What word choices help you interpret the speaker's tone?** ["Stench," "rancid," the repetition of "red," "squelching," and "shamed" are among the words that show his anger and humiliation. His use of the word "considerate" in reference to his landlady is an example of verbal irony.]

(C) Critical Thinking
Classifying

? What kinds of words does the speaker use to describe his skin color? What is the effect? [After derisively joking about the colors of plain and milk chocolate, the speaker uses words that refer to hair color: "brunette" and "blonde." They reveal the absurdity of the landlady's color prejudice.]

(D) Elements of Literature
Irony

? What is ironic about the word "conversation" in the title? [Possible response: This has hardly been a conversation, or a dialogue. It has been, at best, an inquest instigated by prejudice and punctuated by ridicule and hostility.]

Telephone Conversation

Wole Soyinka

The price seemed reasonable, location
Indifferent. The landlady swore she lived
Off premises. Nothing remained
But self-confession. "Madam," I warned,
"I hate a wasted journey—I am African."
Silence. Silenced transmission of
Pressurized good-breeding. Voice, when it came,
Lipstick coated, long gold-rolled
Cigarette-holder pipped. Caught I was, foully.
"HOW DARK?" . . . I had not misheard . . . "ARE YOU LIGHT
OR VERY DARK?" Button B. Button A. Stench
Of rancid breath of public hide-and-speak.
Red booth. Red pillar-box.° Red double-tiered
Omnibus° squelching tar. It *was* real! Shamed
By ill-mannered silence, surrender
Pushed dumbfoundment to beg simplification.
Considerate she was, varying the emphasis—

"ARE YOU DARK? OR VERY LIGHT?" Revelation came.
"You mean—like plain or milk chocolate?"
Her assent was clinical, crushing in its light
Impersonality. Rapidly, wavelength adjusted,
I chose. "West African sepia"—and as an afterthought,
"Down in my passport." Silence for spectroscopic
Flight of fancy,° till truthfulness clanged her accent
Hard on the mouthpiece. "WHAT'S THAT?" conceding,
"DON'T KNOW WHAT THAT IS." "Like brunette."

"THAT'S DARK, ISN'T IT?" "Not altogether.
Facially, I am brunette, but madam, you should see
The rest of me. Palm of my hand, soles of my feet
Are a peroxide blonde. Friction, caused—
Foolishly, madam—by sitting down, has turned
My bottom raven black—One moment madam!"—sensing
Her receiver rearing on the thunderclap
About my ears—"Madam," I pleaded, "wouldn't you rather
See for yourself?"

13. pillar-box: chiefly British for "mailbox."
14. double-tiered / omnibus: bus with two decks, or tiers.

24. spectroscopic (spek'trō·skäp'ik) **. . . fancy:** wide range, or spectrum, of ideas.

Using Students' Strengths

Kinesthetic Learners
Students may enjoy giving a dramatic reading of the poem, with one student acting as the narrator and first speaker and another as the landlady. Others may want to create props that show the dialogue is taking place on the telephone. The conversation may be staged from two ends of the classroom and shouted across the "audience." Students should express the tone and feelings of each speaker. In the case of the landlady, her pauses are as important as her words.

Interpersonal Learners
Ask students to write a letter to the speaker of the poem expressing how they felt as they read the poem. Suggest that they share an experience in which they felt humiliated or angered by another person's prejudice or stereotypical responses. Have them compare their response to that of the speaker and discuss other ways that personal prejudice or discrimination can be confronted.

MAKING MEANINGS

First Thoughts

1. This poem dramatizes a battle. Who do you think finally wins, and why?

Shaping Interpretations

2. Paraphrase what happens in this poem, and then state what you feel is the poem's **theme.**
3. What does their **dialogue** reveal about these two **characters**?
4. This poem is full of colors—and not just of skin. What colors do you see in the poem? What does Soyinka want to communicate through these **images** of color?
5. What **irony** do you find in lines 23–26? What irony do you find in the description of the woman as well-bred?
6. What do you think of the speaker's final question?

Connecting with the Text

7. Since the speaker was prepared for prejudice, why do you think the woman's question disturbs him so much?
8. If you faced this kind of discrimination, how would you react to it?

Challenging the Text

9. Review your Quickwrite notes, and then think about whether Soyinka's poem is an effective way of making others aware of prejudice. Is it more, or less, effective than other ways? How so? Explain.

Nigerian bronze head, thought to be an Ife king (13th century).
British Museum, London.

CHOICES: Building Your Portfolio

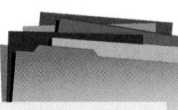

Writer's Notebook

1. Collecting Ideas for a Problem-Solution Essay

Newcomers to this country who encounter incidents of racial prejudice like the one Soyinka relates in "Telephone Conversation" may not realize that housing discrimination is illegal. What solutions could you pose for this problem? Working with a small group, discuss ways your class could work with existing community groups to educate newcomers about their housing rights. Save your notes for the Writer's Workshop on page 1179.

Analyzing Character

2. An Unpleasant Character

What kind of person is the landlady in Soyinka's poem? In an essay, analyze the character of Soyinka's landlady. What do you learn about her from the speaker's assumptions, judgments, and tone, and from the woman's own words? Cite specific details from the poem to support your analysis.

Law / Speaking

3. Home Sweet Home

Should laws restrict where a person can live? What about zoning laws that prohibit trailers in suburban neighborhoods? or laws that ban group homes in single-family developments? Research such laws in your community, and present an oral report, opening the issue for debate with your classmates.

Grading Timesaver

Rubrics for each Choices assignment appear on p. 221 in the *Portfolio Management System.*

MAKING MEANINGS

First Thoughts [Respond]

1. Students may say the speaker wins by virtue of his verbal acuity and wit. They may also say that the landlady wins because the speaker does not get the apartment. In either case, the cause of racial tolerance is not advanced.

Shaping Interpretations [Interpret]

2. A man phones a white woman about renting an apartment. When he announces that he is African, she asks how black he is. He answers her with derisive humor, revealing anger and humiliation. The theme is the absurdity of racial prejudice.
3. The speaker expects racism, yet, when he meets it, he is stunned by the woman's level of insensitive stupidity. His response is bitterly satiric. The woman is dense, hardly aware of her own offensiveness.
4. Soyinka uses red to communicate anger; gold ("gold-rolled cigarette holder") to communicate the landlady's gaudy pretentiousness; and sepia ("West African sepia") to display the speaker's sophistication and taste in contrast to the landlady's vulgarity.
5. The landlady's confession of ignorance contrasts ironically with the narrator's "confession" that he is African. The pretense of "good-breeding" is flatly contradicted by the woman's bad manners.
6. Students may find the final question well-deserved or jarring. The speaker who is deeply offended by the woman's ignorant and vulgar prejudice ends up flinging a polite translation of a vulgar retort at her. Has he joined her or beaten her?

Connecting with the Text [Analyze/Apply]

7. He was prepared for prejudice but not for the blunt and ignorant way the landlady expresses it.
8. Some students may say they would hang up; others might confront the woman's attitude or seek a legal remedy.

Challenging the Text [Evaluate]

9. Students may say this poem raises awareness and helps create sympathy for the victims of prejudice; others may say that political action is more effective than poetry.

READ ON

Portfolio Assessment Options
The following projects can help you evaluate and assess your students' reading outside of class. Videotapes or photographs of the completed projects, or the projects themselves, may be included in students' portfolios.

- **Capture an Image** Invite students to create an artistic representation that shows how the book they have read is related to some aspect of one or more of the selections in this unit. Students may work individually or cooperatively. Encourage the use of a variety of media, including watercolor, collage, photography, and clay sculpture. If students wish, have them work with you to set up a gallery area in the classroom.
- **Create Companion Copy** Invite pairs or groups of students who chose the same selection to write a companion piece for it—for example, a short story that serves as a prequel or sequel or a cycle of poems that captures the thoughts of one or more characters. Have students choose their own format for sharing their work with their peers.
- **Teach a Class** Ask students to prepare a lesson on a book they have read. They may give a brief talk; they may choose excerpts for their classmates to read and discuss; or they may prepare an experiential exercise that demonstrates the theme. Students who have read the same book may choose to work together.
- **Write to the Author** Students may express their opinions or ask questions about a work by writing a letter to the author. Students may actually send the letter in care of the publisher, or they may be able to track down an e-mail address. Students can also publish their letter on an author's chat board or web page.

READ ON

A Plea for Peace

Vera Brittain, born in England in 1893, grew up in an age of rich materialism and romantic idealism. But World War I suddenly and violently ended this time of comfortable isolation. After losing her fiancé and brother and serving as a volunteer nurse in France, she realized that "the world was mad and we were all victims." In her autobiography, *Testament of Youth* (Penguin), she explores how the war affected her and her generation and writes of her subsequent work for world peace.

In Black and White

Kaffir Boy (Macmillan) was one of the first accounts of growing up black in twentieth-century South Africa. When Mark Mathabane (mä·tä′bä·nā) published this autobiography in America in 1986, it became an international best-seller but was banned in his own country. Mathabane's exploration of South Africa's apartheid system, which has now been dismantled, shows the damage that ignorance of and contempt for other cultures can cause.

A Prophetic Voice

Brave New World (HarperCollins) was first published in 1932, but Aldous Huxley's satirical fantasy of the future has remained surprisingly contemporary. In the world-state portrayed in the novel, a supposedly scientific caste system determines social status, and individual freedom is forbidden. But Bernard Marx, a character whose social conditioning has gone wrong, disturbs all this.

An Angry Young Man

Alan Sillitoe was one of a group of young writers who emerged in the 1950s and 1960s and who were dubbed Angry Young Men. Their main themes were rebellion and isolation; they confronted society's mores and institutions head-on. Sillitoe's long short story *The Loneliness of the Long Distance Runner* (Penguin), about a young man in reform school, is among the best of the genre. (Director Tony Richardson's film of the story, available on videotape, was a key British film of the 1960s.)

Peaceful Protest

Mohandas K. Gandhi (1869–1948), also called Mahatma Gandhi, was a leader of the Indian nationalist movement against British rule. His doctrine of nonviolence advocated vigorous protest against social and political evils but did not sanction violence as a means to achieve change. The epic movie *Gandhi* (1982), a sweeping account of his life and times, is filmmaking at its best. Available on videotape, the film is directed by Richard Attenborough and features Ben Kingsley, Candice Bergen, John Gielgud, and Martin Sheen.

The English Language

English Today and Tomorrow

by John Algeo

In the twentieth century, English spread all over the world. It developed from a language spoken by a few wandering Germanic tribes to a world language used for more purposes than any other human tongue. Because its uses have continued to grow, it has continued to change. We can see change going on in English right now—especially in its vocabulary. **A**

Tracking New Words: Where They Come From

We are constantly in need of new words—to talk about new things or to talk about old things in new ways. We borrow new words from other languages, or we make them up by combining, shortening, blending, or shifting the use of old words.

Some words echo not other words but the sounds of things in the world around us. For example, the word *vroom* began as an imitation of how a car or motorcycle engine sounds when it is being raced. Then it was used as a verb referring to how a vehicle operates at very high speed: "The car vroomed around the corner and disappeared." **B**

Sacking Other Languages for Words: Loanwords

French is the modern language from which we have borrowed **C** most. French loanwords include *chief, choice, honor, machine, menu, picnic, police, prairie, restaurant, soup,* and a great many other familiar words, as well as more obvious loans such as *chauffeur, crepe, etiquette, rapport,* and *souvenir.* **D** From Spanish we have taken *canyon, lasso, patio, ranch, rodeo,* and, more recently, *macho;* from Portuguese, *flamingo, molasses, pagoda,* and others. From Italian we get musical terms, including *duet, soprano,* and *trombone,* and a variety of other words, such as *balloon, bandit, carnival, studio, umbrella,* and *volcano.*

Dutch has given us sailing terms such as *deck, dock,* and *yacht,* as well as *boss, dollar, knapsack, pickle, Santa Claus,* and *skate.* From German we have borrowed *frankfurter, hamburger, kindergarten, nickel,* and *pretzel.*

From more distantly related languages we have borrowed *banjo* (African, probably Bantu), *boomerang* (native Australian),

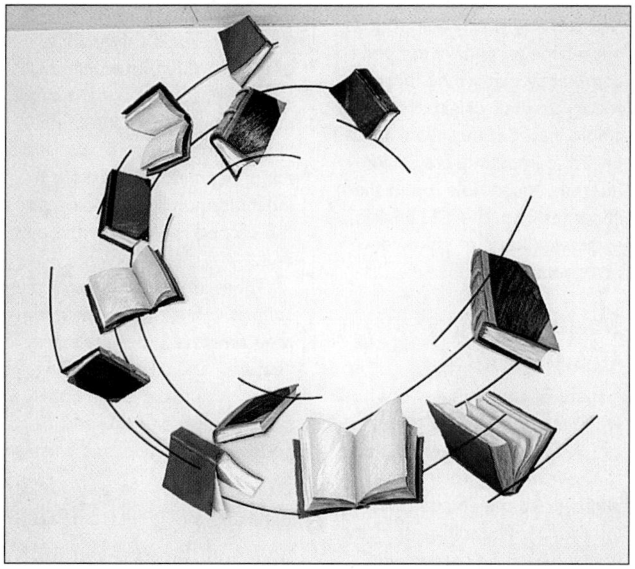

Incident in the Library (1983) by Julian Opie.
Oil paint on steel, wall installation (10 ft × 10 ft).
Photo courtesy Hal Bromm Gallery, New York.

go.hrw.com
LEO 12-English Language

OBJECTIVES

1. Understand and appreciate how languge grows and changes
2. Research word origins
3. Infer etymologies
4. Use a dictionary to find meanings of words
5. Locate sources of information on new words

In this final essay, John Algeo looks at our ever-changing vocabulary, tracing ways in which we have acquired words from other languages and in which we create new words every day.

A Background

English is spoken widely on six continents and is even the official language in several sub-Saharan African countries. Part of the reason for its success is its flexibility in function, composition, and syntax, but the same elements also make it a language that is easy to speak poorly.

B Appreciating Language

Another example is the word *plop.* Although *plop* imitates the sound of something dropping into water, it is also used informally as a verb to describe falling heavily, as in, "I plopped down into the soft chair."

C Historical Connections

Borrowing Words from French

Extensive borrowing from French (partly as a result of the Norman invasion of England in 1066) is one of the reasons why English has so many synonyms and near synonyms. For example, when English borrowed the verb *finish* from the French, it already had the perfectly good English word *end.* Both have remained in the language. Similar English/French pairings include (with English stated first) *wheel* and *cycle, act* and *deed, work* and *labor, building* and *edifice.*

D Cultural Connections

Modern Borrowing Across Cultures

Borrowing is not over, of course, and it works both ways. For example, today the French regularly use such words as *le weekend, le fastfood,* and *le jogging.*

Resources

Viewing and Representing

Videocassette A, Segment 2

The *Visual Connections* segment "English: A Living Language" includes information on recent change in language.

A Historical Connections

Borrowings from Native American Sources

English has been enriched by countless borrowings from Native American languages. Borrowed words include *caucus, chipmunk, moccasin, moose, opossum, papoose, powwow, raccoon, squaw, teepee,* and *woodchuck.* In addition, Native American languages have given us countless place names, including *Idaho, Dakota, Oklahoma, Mississippi, Texas, Tennessee, Iowa, Kansas, Michigan, Kentucky,* and *Illinois.*

B Appreciating Language

Prefixes

Some useful Greek prefixes are *anti-,* meaning "against"; *dys-,* meaning "bad"; *hyper-,* meaning "beyond" or "excess"; *hypo-,* meaning "under"; and *proto-,* meaning "first." Some useful Latin prefixes are *contra-,* meaning "against"; *extra-,* meaning "outside"; *inter-,* meaning "between"; *intra-,* meaning "within"; *juxta-,* meaning "near"; and *retro-,* meaning "backward."

C Appreciating Language

Back-Formations

Two of the relatively recent back-formations of our time are *net,* a shortened form of the word *internet,* and the slightly more complicated back-formation, *e-mail,* a shortened form of *electronic mail.*

D Critical Thinking

Speculating

? Where are acronyms most often used, and why? [Possible answers: They are frequently used in large institutions, especially governmental departments and military organizations, to make long names easier to say, spell, and recall.]

ketchup (Malay), *coffee* (Turkish, from Arabic), *mammoth* (Russian), *pal* (Romany), *pecan* (various Algonquian dialects), *shawl* (Persian), *shampoo* (Hindi), *soy* (Japanese), *tattoo* (Tahitian), *tea* (Chinese), *tom-tom* (Hindi), and *ukulele* (Hawaiian).

English is much richer for all these words we have borrowed from other languages.

Stacking Words Together: Compounds

We often make new words by joining existing words into a *compound.* A compound may mean something different from the literal sense of its parts. Thus, a *blackboard* is not necessarily black; it is often green instead.

Compounds have always been a favorite type of word formation in English. In Modern English, we have some words that were originally compounds but whose parts have merged so completely that we no longer recognize their origins. For example, *nostril* comes from an Old English compound, *nosu-thyrel* (literally, "nose-hole"), and *sheriff* comes from the Old English *scirgerefa* (literally, "shire-reeve" or "county official").

Tacking Parts On: Affixed Forms

Instead of combining two whole words to make a new one, we can add a word element (an *affix*) to the front of a word (as a *prefix*) or to the end of a word (as a *suffix*). The suffix *–ist* forms nouns meaning a person who believes in something or who has a particular profession. A *royalist* follows royalty, a *lobbyist* lobbies, and a *flat-earthist* believes that the earth is really flat as a pancake, despite what astronomers and geologists may say.

Q3 (1994) by Mark Wallinger. Acrylic on canvas (218.5 cm × 218.5 cm).

Private Collection. © The Artist, Courtesy Anthony Reynolds Gallery, London.

Some suffixes were originally independent words that dwindled into mere affixes. For instance, the suffix *–ful* is a dwindling of the word *full,* to which it is still close, though not the same, in meaning. A "handful of pennies" is not the same as a "hand full of pennies." The first is an indefinite number of coins, and the second is a hand with coins in it.

There are fewer prefixes than suffixes in English, but two common ones are *pre–* , meaning "before," and *post–* , meaning "after." We use them in combinations like *pregame* and *postgame* or *preteen* and *postteen.*

Hacking Parts Off: Shortenings and Back-Formations

We can also make new words by removing part of a word to shorten it. This process is quite common, probably because we don't like to use more energy than we have to in saying long words if short ones will do. *Gymnasium* is shortened to *gym; telephone* becomes *phone.*

Some shortenings are more complicated. The label *hazardous material* indicates that a container has dangerous chemicals or radioactive matter inside it. But the label is too long—a warning ought to be short and snappy. So both words in the expression are clipped, to produce *HAZMAT,* a short, easy to say, and (provided you know what it means) clear expression. When a phrase is shortened to the first parts of each of its words, the result is an *acronym* (from two Greek forms meaning "tip-name," that is, a name formed from the tips of other words).

The most extreme kind of acronym includes only the first letter of each original word. It may be said by pronouncing the names of the letters, like *CB*

Reaching All Students

Struggling Readers

As students read the article, have them take notes on the main ideas and details presented in each of the subsections. They may record these in classic outline form using Roman numerals and capital and lowercase letters to indicate main and subordinate ideas, or they may use any other convenient graphic organizer. Call their attention to the headings of the subsections since these will help them identify the topics covered in each. Encourage students to share their outlines and make revisions based on their discussions.

(citizens' band) or *RV* (recreational vehicle), or by pronouncing it as a word, like *ZIP* (zone improvement plan) *Code*.

A special kind of shortening occurs when an affix is taken off. Typewriters are more than a hundred years old now. When they first came into use, the word *typewriter* meant either the machine or the person who operated it. Then someone decided that a typewriter is for typewriting, and so the verb *to typewrite* was formed by taking off the suffix *–er.* Such words are called *back-formations* because the sequence of their formation is the reverse of the usual order of adding affixes.

A similar example is *to burgle,* which is what a burglar does. A difference between *burgle* and *typewrite,* however, is that while *typewrite* was shortened from *typewriter* very quickly (within twelve years after the longer word was introduced to English), *burgle* took a lot of time, more than three hundred years, to work its way out of *burglar.* And some people still don't like it.

Packing Words Together: Blends

A *blend* is a word that is made by combining two or more words while omitting part of at least one of them. Familiar examples are *brunch* (*breakfast* plus *lunch*) and *smog* (*smoke* plus *fog*). In Lewis Carroll's *Through the Looking-Glass,* Humpty Dumpty called such terms *portmanteau words.* A portmanteau is a suitcase with two sides that are folded together to make a single case. Humpty Dumpty said that in a portmanteau word, "There are two meanings packed up into one word."

An example of a technical blend is *shuttle craft,* from *space shuttle* plus *spacecraft.* A feminist example is *herstory* (meaning "history of women," or "history told from a woman's point of view"), from *her* plus *history.*

A special kind of blending is *folk etymology.* We sometimes take an unfamiliar word, especially a word borrowed from another language, and change its form by associating it with familiar English words. For example, we borrowed the Dutch word *koolsla* (which means "cabbage salad") as *coleslaw;* but then some people associated the first part of the word with the English word *cold* and came up with *cold slaw,* which makes sense because slaw is generally served cold.

Ramen Four Five Six (20th century) by Gregory B. Larson.
Private Collection.

Racking Up New Meanings: Shifted Words

Perhaps the most frequent way to make a new word is to use an old word in a new way. Today, *censure* means "to judge unfavorably" or "to condemn"; in Shakespeare's day, it meant simply "to judge or form an opinion." Shifts of meaning are going on all the time. *Bulletin board* can now be used for a computer service that provides information, instead of just for a board on which notices are posted.

A different kind of shift occurs when a word changes its part of speech. For example, we use the noun *hand* as a verb in "Hand me that book, please," the verb *sing* as a noun in "We are having a community sing," the adjective *tough* as a noun in "the young toughs," the noun *fun* as an adjective in "a really fun evening," the adverb *up* as a verb in "They upped the price," and so on. Such functional shifts are an easy and common way of making new words in Modern English.

Tomorrow's English

English is changing today even as we use it. Indeed, it is changing *because* we use it. Each change, however small, makes the language somewhat different from the English of yesterday. As the changes accumulate, little by little, day by day, they eventually make the language very different from what it was. But that is nothing to fear. Languages grow, as they must to live. By the way we speak English today and by the changes we introduce into

E Critical Thinking
Analyzing

? Can you "decipher" these blends: *twirl, bash, flare, smash, glimmer,* and *clash?* [*twist* and *whirl; bat* and *mash; flame* and *glare; smack* and *mash; gleam* and *shimmer; clap* and *crash*]

F Historical Connections
Shifted Words

The verb *compute* preceded the noun *computer* by a couple hundred years. The first recorded use of the word *computer* was in 1897, when it was used to mean "a calculating machine." The machine it referred to then was little more than a slide rule: It would be fifty years or more before there was anything resembling a hard drive in existence.

G Appreciating Language
Functional Shifts

When a word takes on a related but new meaning as a different part of speech, a functional shift has occurred. One example of this type of shift is the word *outfit.* It was originally used as a noun, as in "I wore a new *outfit* today," and shifted to include another use as a verb, as in "We have to *outfit* the entire team with uniforms."

Skill Link

Generating Relevant, Interesting, and Researchable Questions

As students work on various projects related to this feature on the English Languge, it may be helpful to remind them of the following methods of generating questions for research:

- An interesting research question should help you discover new information on a familiar subject.
- To make your questions relevant, they should be limited to a manageable topic.
- To generate researchable questions, make sure there are a variety of sources related to your topic and that the sources of information are readily available.

Activity

Based on the listed criteria, ask students to pose at least three relevant, interesting, and researchable questions on the following topics:

- the origins of modern English
- how new word meanings develop
- the ways in which English is continuing to change

Try It Out
Answers

1. blizzard—suggests a stormy blast or bluster; escalate—a shortened form of the word *escalator*; gas—from the Greek word for *chaos*; hiccup—an imitation of the sound; jeep—an abbreviation of *general purpose*; kitty-cornered—from *catercorner*; lengthwise—*length* plus *wise*; motel—blend of *motor* and *hotel*; pep—short for *pepper*; scarecrow—from its use, to scare birds, such as crows.
2. bonfire—in Middle English, this was a fire of bones; business—from *busy* plus *-ness* meaning the state of being busy; cupboard—from the Middle English words for *cup* and *board*; disease—not at ease; doff—from *to do off*.
3. Students are much more likely to encounter neologisms than archaic words in newspapers.
4. Remind students to identify the sources and meanings of the new words they find.

Resources

Assessment
Formal Assessment

- The English Language Test, p. 233

it, we are creating the English of tomorrow.

Over the years, English speakers have written some of the greatest literature known to humanity, literature that is read all over the world by people of diverse cultures. In the future, English will doubtless continue to be a medium for the expression of our common fears, hopes, aspirations, and exaltations.

> English belongs to all those all over the world who speak and write it, who read its literature, and who treasure it.

The English language, like English literature, is something we can take pride in. This language and this literature do not belong to one nation or to one people only, but are shared by many. English belongs to all those all over the world who speak and write it, who read its literature, and who treasure it.

Try It Out

1. **Finding word origins.** The following words illustrate various ways in which words are made. Look them up in a dictionary that gives etymologies, and describe their origins.

blizzard	kitty-cornered
escalate	lengthwise
gas	motel
hiccup	pep
jeep	scarecrow

2. **Inferring etymologies.** Words change their meanings over time, but some words keep evidence of their earlier meanings. Try to guess from their forms the earlier meanings of the following words. Then, look up their etymologies to see whether your guesses are correct.

bonfire	cupboard	doff
business	disease	

3. **Using a dictionary.** Look in a recent newspaper or magazine for words that are completely new to you. Find at least five such words, and on a sheet of paper, copy the sentences in which the words are used. Underline the unfamiliar words. Then, look up the words in a college or unabridged dictionary. If you find them, read their etymologies to find out where they come from. If you do not find them, do you think they may be new words or old but rare words?
4. **Locating sources of information.** Several dictionaries and periodicals list new words. Locate one of the following collections of new words in a library.
   - *The Oxford Dictionary of New Words,* eds. Elizabeth Knowles and Julia Elliot
   - *The Third Barnhart Dictionary of New English*
   - "Among the New Words" (a regular article in the magazine *American Speech*)
   - American Heritage Dictionary, WordStar, 1993 (an electronic dictionary that includes new words)

   Make a list of five new words from any of these sources. Tell what each word means.

A Conversation (1913–1916) by Vanessa Bell.

The Courtauld Gallery, London.

Assessing Learning

Check Test: Questions and Answers

1. How are new English words created? [Words may be borrowed from other languages, or existing English words may be combined, shortened, blended, or shifted.]
2. From which modern language has English borrowed the most? [French]
3. What is the difference between a suffix and a prefix? [A prefix is added to the beginning of a word; a suffix is added to the end.]
4. What is an acronym? [A new word produced by combining the first letter of each word of a phrase.]
5. Does the author view change in language as good or bad? [The author says change in language is good because it helps the language keep pace with change in society.]

BUILDING YOUR PORTFOLIO

Writer's Workshop

PERSUASIVE WRITING

A PROBLEM-SOLUTION ESSAY

Reading the selections in Collections 14 and 15 has shown you how twentieth-century writers used both fiction and nonfiction to explore social problems. By now, you've peered into the lives of an alienated bureaucrat, children shunned by their peers, and families and compatriots locked in conflict. Although many of these selections only hint at solutions, the clear-eyed portrayal of human problems, combined with the search for practical answers, is an important form of writing. Problem-solution essays, or proposals that call for definite action, are written every day—by scientists investigating solar energy, by citizens concerned about crime, by newspaper columnists proposing changes in the economy, and by politicians seeking office. In this Writer's Workshop, you'll write your own problem-solution essay, carefully analyzing a problem and proposing one or more specific solutions to it.

Prewriting

1. **Checking your Writer's Notebook.** By doing the Writer's Notebook activities throughout Collections 14 and 15, you may have already done some of the prewriting necessary for a problem-solution essay. Look back at your entries, and decide if you'd like to develop any of the ideas or problems you find there. Then proceed with the prewriting steps that follow.

WORK IN PROGRESS

2. **Identifying suitable problems.** Since you'll be presenting your findings to an audience, steer clear of strictly personal problems such as family squabbles or romantic entanglements. Instead, consider problems that significantly affect a number of people. For example, a family dispute over your plans to attend an unsupervised graduation party is too personal for a problem-solution essay. But the lack of an alternative to such private parties in your community would affect many seniors and their families. Another approach is to focus on the local aspects of a national or international problem. Instead of tackling "homelessness in the United States," for example, you might investigate the causes and effects of a local homeless shelter's policy of turning people back out onto the streets each morning.

   To identify suitable problems, try freewriting about problems you've noticed in your school, neighborhood, or city. You can also find ideas by reading newspaper and magazine articles, listening to radio and TV news and talk shows, and attending public meetings.

3. **Investigating a problem.** Once you start exploring the problem you've chosen, you may find that you need more information to understand it

Technology HELP

See Writer's Workshop 2 CD-ROM. *Assignment: Controversial Issue.*

ASSIGNMENT

Write an essay that explores a problem and proposes one or more solutions to it.

AIM

To persuade; to explore; to explain.

AUDIENCE

People who share (or can be led to share) your interest in solving the problem.

MAIN OBJECTIVE

Write a problem-solution essay

PROCESS OBJECTIVES

1. Use appropriate prewriting techniques to identify and develop a topic
2. Create a first draft
3. Use Evaluation Criteria as a basis for determining revision strategies
4. Revise the first draft, incorporating suggestions generated by self- or peer-evaluation
5. Proofread and correct errors
6. Create a final draft
7. Choose an appropriate method of publication
8. Reflect on progress as a writer

Planning

- **Block Schedule**
  Block Scheduling Lesson Plans with Pacing Guide
- **One-Stop Planner**
  CD-ROM with Test Generator

Resources: Print and Media

Writing and Language

- *Portfolio Management System*
  Prewriting, p. 222
  Peer Editing, p. 223
  Assessment Rubric, p. 224
- *Workshop Resources*
  Revision Strategy Teaching Notes, p. 41
  Revision Strategy Transparencies 21, 22
- *Writer's Workshop 2 CD-ROM*
  Controversial Issue

Introducing the Writer's Workshop

- Bring to class local newspapers that contain editorials and letters to the editor. Ask students to browse through the papers and to locate editorials and letters that describe problems and offer solutions. Have volunteers read aloud these editorials or letters.
- Be sure students understand the purpose of this assignment—to explain a problem, explore possible solutions, and persuade readers to take action.

Teaching the Writer's Workshop

Prewriting

- Brainstorming with the entire class is often an effective method of identifying problems and possible solutions. However, encourage students to avoid writing about the same problems as others unless they have some unique solutions.
- Remind students that school-related topics make gathering information easier, since the sources of information are usually on site, and sending students' essays to the school newspaper as letters to the editor is a convenient way to publish their writing. Also, students can develop a clear sense of their audience if they address their essays to school administrators.
- Have students work through the Prewriting techniques suggested on pp. 1179–84.

Try It Out

Possible Answers

1. social service agencies, real estate agents, mortgage bankers
2. people who fish in the lake, people who live near the lake, Environmental Protection Agency officials, scientific reports on conditions in the lake
3. school custodians, school administrators, teachers, students
4. local employment agencies, unemployed people, help-wanted ads
5. school administrators, teachers, students, newspaper articles on the low reading scores, analysis of reports from the testing agency

Try It Out

For each of the following problems, suggest at least three potential sources of information.

1. a lack of affordable housing in a community
2. pollution in a local lake
3. vandalism at a school
4. a town's lack of employment opportunities
5. low reading scores

fully. First, though, determine precisely what you *do* know about it by brainstorming or clustering or by asking yourself the *5W-How?* questions (*Who? What? When? Where? Why?* and *How?*). Then move outward, using a variety of sources to gather information: Read, listen, observe, and question others to discover their views. For example, if you're exploring the problem of flooding in your neighborhood, you might begin by jotting down an account of your own experiences and then reading newspaper articles on the causes and effects of the problem. You might also interview your neighbors and local officials, such as the county's director of stormwater engineering.

Strategies for Elaboration: Scrutinizing Your Subject

Looking at a problem from different points of view can help you understand it more fully. Try using these questions to analyze the problem you're investigating.

- What is the problem? How widespread is it?
- What is the history of the problem? What caused the problem? What effects has the problem had, and on whom?
- How is the problem like other problems? How is it different from them? What are the major parts of the problem?
- How serious is the problem? Why?

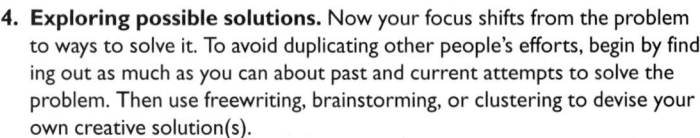

4. **Exploring possible solutions.** Now your focus shifts from the problem to ways to solve it. To avoid duplicating other people's efforts, begin by finding out as much as you can about past and current attempts to solve the problem. Then use freewriting, brainstorming, or clustering to devise your own creative solution(s).

Strategies for Elaboration: Reflecting on Solutions

Use these questions to explore other people's solutions and then your own ideas for solving the problem.

Other People's Ideas

- What solutions have already been tried?
- How well have those solutions worked?
- Why haven't they worked better?
- What solutions are now being considered?

Your Ideas

- Could some of the problem's causes be eliminated? If so, how?
- What could be done to ease or eliminate the effects of the problem?
- Does one part of the problem seem especially difficult to solve? Why?
- Which part of the problem seems easiest to solve? Why?
- What is the most promising solution (or part of the solution) you can think of?

Using Students' Strengths

Auditory Learners

As students use the Strategies for Elaboration on the pupil's page, have them work in pairs. One student in each pair can serve as an interviewer, asking the questions in the text and recording the ideas expressed by the other member of the pair. Students can take turns being the interviewer and then share their notes with one another as they write their drafts.

Visual Learners

Some students may find it useful to organize their ideas for the three major divisions of their essays in a chart like the one that follows. Students may jot down ideas or write whole paragraphs in the cells of the chart.

Introduction
Body
Conclusion

One student used two of the questions on page 1180 as prompts for a focused freewrite on the problem of traffic accidents on graduation night. Here are the ideas that resulted:

Model

Could some of the causes of traffic accidents on graduation night be eliminated? How? One cause of traffic accidents on graduation night is unsafe driving by students who have been drinking at unsupervised private parties. We could eliminate this cause by having a party at the Civic Center supervised by teachers and parents. But where would the money come from, and would students attend the party? Maybe local businesses would be willing to donate food, music, decorations, and door prizes in exchange for publicity. The donations would defray the cost of putting on the party and might also entice people to come to the party.

What is the most promising part of the solution you can think of? Maybe the Parent-Teacher Organization could hire buses to transport students to and from the party — maybe the school board would even allow school buses to be used. A student committee could decorate the buses with streamers and balloons.

5. **Evaluating alternative solutions.** A perfect solution to your problem may not exist. Usually, though, some solutions are clearly better than others, and in most cases, one solution can be shown to be the best choice. Use these questions to evaluate possible solutions and to identify the best solution to your problem.
   - What are the advantages and disadvantages of each solution?
   - Which solution is the most practical?
   - Does one solution have a comparative advantage? In other words, which solution will do the most good for the most people?

   Sometimes, two solutions may seem equally good—or none may seem feasible. In such cases, resist the urge to declare the problem unsolvable. Instead, search for a compromise. If your school doesn't have enough guidance counselors, for example, don't assume that students either have to do without career planning or have to pay an outside career-counseling service. A compromise solution might be for one of the guidance counselors to sponsor a student group offering peer counseling.

   In other cases, the problem may have more than one cause or may affect more than one group. Such situations may call for a variety of solutions. For example, if neighborhood residents object to the traffic and noise a new teen center will generate, one solution—having a new access road built—is not enough. You also need a solution for the noise.

   Making a chart like the one on page 1182 can help you analyze and evaluate alternative solutions. The writer is trying to discover solutions to the following problem: Not all students have home computers, which provide instant access to information needed for doing homework.

Getting Students Involved

Cooperative Learning

Identifying Problems. Have students work in groups to identify problems. Divide the class into groups of four, and assign each group an area of concern. For example, one group could identify problems at school; another, problems with traffic congestion; a third, a lack of recreational facilities; and so on. Each group should develop a list of at least four problems in their area. When the groups report to the class, make a master list that students can refer to when they begin selecting topics for their essays.

Model

Possible Solutions	Advantages	Disadvantages
Abolish homework	Eliminates inequity in grading; makes students' lives less stressful.	Removes valuable assessment tool; removes opportunity to apply research skills independently.
Keep school open two hours longer each weekday.	Gives students who need it access to computers in a familiar place; computers already budgeted for.	The school's budget can't cover additional costs for teachers' salaries, utilities, and school bus drivers' wages.
Establish next branch of county library at the school.	Opens services to all city residents, not just students; staff and equipment costs already budgeted for; saves cost of building a new facility.	County commissioners would have to be convinced of neighborhood support; residents of other parts of town might object.

Practicality
Keeping school open longer hours isn't practical—the school just doesn't have the money.

Comparative Advantage
Establishing the next branch of the county library at the school will do the most good for the most people and will make the best use of available money, staff, and facilities.

6. **Steps to success.** Once you've settled on a practical, workable solution—the end—turn your attention to the specific steps needed to make it a reality—the means. Focus on these questions:
   - What needs to be done?
   - How will it be done?
   - In what order will it be done?

   For example, establishing the next branch of the county library at your school might involve the following steps:
   - Develop support for the idea in your school zone by visiting or distributing literature to neighborhood residents.
   - Ask the newspaper to send a reporter to speak with students and residents about the need for and benefits of the proposal.
   - Contact your local county commissioner to arrange to have the proposal included on the commission's agenda.
   - Recruit students and other area residents to attend the commission meeting at which you will present the proposal and explain its benefits.

Crossing the Curriculum

Science

Much of science is concerned with identifying problems and developing solutions to them. Ask students to research and report to the class on famous problems that scientists have studied and on how these problems were solved.
A science teacher or librarian may be able to suggest specific resources that students can use to gather information.

7. **Analyzing your audience, setting your tone.** As in persuasive writing, audience considerations are central to a problem-solution essay. Here, your purpose is twofold: to *explain* the problem and possible solutions and to *prove* that the problem is serious and your solution is the best one. Use the questions in the following chart to plan your approach.

Questions	Analysis	Approach
What does the audience already know about the problem?	very little	Provide detailed background information.
	a little	Include some background details.
	a lot	Remind them of their stake in solving the problem.
What solutions might the audience favor?	the one you are proposing	Lead them from agreement to action.
	one you have rejected	Explain in detail the comparative advantage of your solution.
What kind of objections might the audience have to your solution?	major ones	Devote extra space to countering their objections and to explaining the benefits your solution offers.
	minor ones	Emphasize that your solution offers the greatest good for the greatest number of people.

In setting your tone, use objective language to demonstrate that your proposal isn't simply self-serving. Avoid emotionally charged words and, to keep from coming across as a know-it-all, qualify your recommendations: Use words such as *could, might,* and *perhaps* rather than *should, must,* and *unquestionably*. Using first-person pronouns can be especially effective in a problem-solution essay—*I, my, mine,* and *me* to recount your own experiences; *we* and *our* to describe the problem; and *ours* and *us* to underscore common concerns.

8. **Providing support.** Vague generalities and sweeping statements won't persuade readers to accept your analysis of the problem and its possible solutions or to accept your proposed solution as the best solution. Readers will expect you to provide sound reasons and specific evidence—facts, examples, and statistics. Compare the effectiveness of these two statements:

VAGUE Sixteen-year-old drivers are a lot more dangerous than older teen drivers.

Language Handbook HELP

See Personal Pronouns, page 1227.

Drafting

- Use editorials and letters to the editor of school and community newspapers as models. Select published items carefully to make sure they incorporate the methods and concepts that students are learning about in this Writer's Workshop.
- Before beginning their drafts, refer students to the three drafting steps on p. 1184.
- As students write, encourage them to imagine they are addressing a specific audience and to maintain a clear and consistent tone throughout.
- Remind students to use only every other line when they write their drafts. They should also leave extra space in the right margin. These blank spaces will be used for comments and editing marks.

Skill Link

Evaluating the Credibility of Information Sources

As students work on various research projects suggested in this collection, it may be helpful to remind them of the following steps they can use to evaluate sources of information:

- Make sure your source is relevant and has information directly related to your research topic.
- Make sure your source is accurate and objective.
- Make sure your source is up-to-date.
- Check Internet sources especially to make sure they are reliable and unbiased.

Activity

Ask students to explore the library resources as well as the Internet to find five or six useful information sources for their research topics. Then have them evaluate their sources by checking them against the above criteria.

Evaluating and Revising

Have students use the Evaluation Criteria provided here to review their drafts and determine needed revisions. Encourage students to look carefully at their sentences. A well-written sentence or paragraph is only effective if it convinces readers of its points, so students should cut any passages that are weak and unconvincing.

Proofreading

Have students proofread their own papers first and then exchange with another student. For this assignment, remind students to be particularly careful of the usage of personal pronouns in the nominative and objective cases.

If time permits, the edited copy should be put aside for at least a day before it is proofread for the final time by the author.

Publishing

Have students present their problems and solutions to an audience.

- Students may deliver their essays as oral proposals to classmates or to a local group that could solve the problem.
- Suggest ways students could distribute their essays to people who are affected by the problem.
- Have students rework their essays as letters to the editor, and send them to the editor of a school or local newspaper.

Reflecting

If students decide to add this essay to their portfolio, have them date it and write brief reflections on their writing experience by answering questions such as these:

1. What problems did I encounter in writing this problem-solution essay?
2. Which was harder, devising a solution or countering potential objections to my solution? identifying alternative solutions or analyzing their disadvantages?
3. What do I like best about my essay? What would I still like to improve?

Resources

Peer Editing Forms and Rubrics

- *Portfolio Management System*, p. 223

Revision Transparencies

- *Workshop Resources*, p. 41

Evaluation Criteria

An effective problem-solution essay

1. *opens with an attention-getting statement of the problem*
2. *provides sufficient information about the problem's causes and effects*
3. *clearly explains the seriousness of the problem*
4. *points out the disadvantages of alternative solutions*
5. *explains the proposed solution thoroughly, discussing its comparative advantage and countering objections*
6. *concludes with a strong restatement of the proposed solution*

Communications Handbook HELP

See Taking Notes and Documenting Sources.

Revision STRATEGIES

Are the steps needed to implement the solution clearly presented? Working with a writing partner, identify and discuss the steps you've included. If necessary, reorder the steps. Add any steps that are missing.

PRECISE Nationwide, according to the Insurance Institute for Highway Safety, sixteen-year-old drivers are involved in more than twice as many fatal crashes as seventeen-, eighteen-, and nineteen-year-old drivers.

Drafting

1. **The introduction: engage them.** Especially if your readers aren't aware of the problem or aren't convinced of its relevance to their lives, it's important to grab their attention immediately. Try beginning with an unusual fact, a stirring scenario, or a personal anecdote. Then define the problem explicitly, using descriptive terms that will help readers visualize the situation.
2. **The body: enlighten them.** As you explain the problem's seriousness, remember to support your reasons with facts, examples, and statistics. In discussing the alternative solutions you have rejected, clarify their specific disadvantages, again using solid evidence to back up your reasons. Then present your own solution, pointing out its comparative advantages and outlining the steps needed to implement it.

Strategies for Elaboration: Putting It All Together

- **Distributing emphasis.** The amount of space you devote to explaining the problem and its seriousness, describing your proposed solution, discussing rejected solutions, and countering possible objections to your solution will depend on your readers' concerns. If they're well aware of the problem, for example, you may spend more time discussing your solution. A very complex problem may call for a greater emphasis on its causes and effects than on your proposed solution.
- **Crediting your sources.** Your teacher may ask you to credit your sources formally, using parenthetical citations and a list of works cited. If not, you may credit your sources informally by weaving them into the sentences in which you refer to them, as in the "precise" example under "Providing Support," above.

3. **The conclusion: energize them.** To bring your essay to a compelling close, restate your proposed solution. Consider ending with a clear call to action—specific steps readers can take to help make your solution a reality.

Evaluating and Revising

Self-evaluation. Take a hard look at the solution you've proposed in your essay. Circle the solution, and number the necessary steps to achieve it that you've discussed. Next, underline each counterargument you've addressed. If you find few items to circle, number, or underline, you know what to focus on when you revise. Also, review your classmate's responses, looking especially for comments that will help you make your paper clearer and more persuasive. Then, revise your essay, making any necessary changes.

Grading Timesaver

Rubrics for this Writer's Workshop assignment appear on p. 224 of the *Portfolio Management System.*

Language Workshop
The history
of the written
word is rich and
Page 1

Effective Sentences: Relationships Between Ideas

A common problem in writing comes about when several clauses are strung together with only the word *and.* You can make your writing more precise by using subordinating conjunctions instead of *and,* when appropriate. A *subordinating conjunction* is a word that clarifies the relationships between ideas by indicating **time** (*after, as, before, until, when*), **cause** (*because, since, unless*), **purpose** (*so that*), or **condition** (*although, if, though*).

Here are some sentences that string together a series of ideas with the word *and.* Note that the relationships between the ideas are not too clear.

UNCLEAR Without even washing it, he put the root in his mouth, chewed it vigorously, and then held the spittle there, **and** he took the child forcibly from Mrs. Farquar.

He spoke incredulously, **and** he could not believe his old friends could so betray him.

Here is how Doris Lessing combined the same ideas using subordination. Notice that now the relationships between ideas are more precisely stated.

CLEAR Without even washing it, he put the root in his mouth, chewed it vigorously, and then held the spittle there **while** he took the child forcibly from Mrs. Farquar.

—*from* "No Witchcraft for Sale"

He spoke incredulously, **as if** he could not believe his old friends could so betray him.

—*from* "No Witchcraft for Sale"

Usually, there are several ways to indicate subordination. Here are two edited versions of the second sentence above:

He spoke incredulously **because** he could not believe his old friends could so betray him.

Because he could not believe his old friends could so betray him, he spoke incredulously.

Writer's Workshop Follow-Up: Revision

Review the essay you wrote for the Writer's Workshop on page 1179. Focus on one paragraph in the body of your essay to see where you can combine sentences to make relationships clearer; then study the other paragraphs. Share your changes with a writing partner.

Technology HELP

See Language Workshop CD-ROM. *Key word entry: subordinate clause.*

Language Handbook HELP

See Clauses, page 1232; Combining by Subordinating Ideas, page 1239; Commas, page 1245.

Try It Out

Combine the sentences below, using subordinating conjunctions to clarify relationships.

1. Gideon was a cook for the Farquar family. He would often play with their son, Teddy.
2. Gideon knew which plant had healing powers. He refused to identify it for the Farquars and he withheld his secret information.

Objectives

1. Use subordinating conjunctions to write effective sentences
2. Understand the uses of different types of subordinating conjunctions

Resources

Workshop Resources

- Worksheet, p. 61

Language Workshop CD-ROM

- Subordinate Clause

Try It Out

Possible Answers

1. While Gideon was a cook for the Farquar family, he would often play with their son Teddy.
2. Although Gideon knew which plant had healing powers, he refused to identify it for the Farquars, and he withheld his secret information.

Assessing Learning

Quick Check: Conjunctions

Choose a subordinating conjunction from the list to clarify the relationship between the main ideas in these sentences.

when although because even if

1. Learning to write clearly is important ___ writing is a primary means of transmitting ideas. [because]
2. ___ a person uses a computer, writing is a demanding skill. [Even if]
3. In fact, ___ people apply for jobs, they often have to demonstrate proficiency in the use of a computer word-processing program. [when]
4. ___ machines dominate the workplace, the human skill of writing clear, effective prose is still one of the most important assets a person can possess. [Although]

Objectives

1. Develop strategies for reading a memorandum or e-mail
2. Understand the purpose of writing and reading a memorandum or e-mail
3. Recognize the format of a memorandum or e-mail
4. Analyze the content of a memorandum or e-mail

Teaching the Lesson

Remind students that not all memos are alike. The order of information in the heading may be different, and RE (from Latin *in re,* meaning "in the matter of," "concerning," "as regards") may be used instead of SUBJECT. Point out that even though memos do have a format, they are still less formal than a business letter, so they should be used for internal correspondence only.

Using the Strategies

Possible Answers

1. The purpose is to provide information about respecting local customs. The subject.
2. U.S. Embassy Jakarta. Embassy employees also may benefit from the information in the memo.
3. Other employees who are not Indonesian also would want to know how to act respectfully.
4. Note differences in customs and change appropriately.
5. No. Action calls for a change in behavior not a written response.
6. Yes. Information is very precise and may need to be referred to later with specific incidents.

Reading for Life

Reading a Business Memorandum or Electronic Mail

Situation

Imagine you're working as a summer intern for an American company in Indonesia. During your first few days, you receive a memorandum (often shortened to *memo*) on the subject of respect for your co-workers' culture.

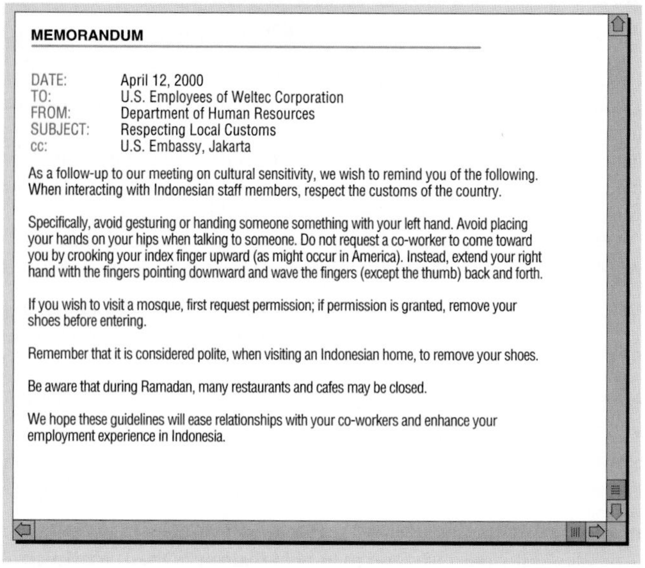

MEMORANDUM

DATE: April 12, 2000
TO: U.S. Employees of Weltec Corporation
FROM: Department of Human Resources
SUBJECT: Respecting Local Customs
cc: U.S. Embassy, Jakarta

As a follow-up to our meeting on cultural sensitivity, we wish to remind you of the following. When interacting with Indonesian staff members, respect the customs of the country.

Specifically, avoid gesturing or handing someone something with your left hand. Avoid placing your hands on your hips when talking to someone. Do not request a co-worker to come toward you by crooking your index finger upward (as might occur in America). Instead, extend your right hand with the fingers pointing downward and wave the fingers (except the thumb) back and forth.

If you wish to visit a mosque, first request permission; if permission is granted, remove your shoes before entering.

Remember that it is considered polite, when visiting an Indonesian home, to remove your shoes.

Be aware that during Ramadan, many restaurants and cafes may be closed.

We hope these guidelines will ease relationships with your co-workers and enhance your employment experience in Indonesia.

Strategies

Understand the purpose of a memorandum.

- A printed or electronic (e-mail) business memo is a method of sharing information among workers. Memos deal with issues such as workplace procedures and policies, records of meetings, and the status of projects.

Recognize the format of a memo.

- Print and electronic memos have these features: A heading indicates the date, the name of the person or department issuing the memo, the people to whom the memo is sent, and the subject of the memo. The heading is followed by the body of the memo. Either in the heading or below the body, there may be a list of names or initials following the abbreviation *cc.* This list refers to the people to whom copies of the memo are sent.

Read the memo.

- If there are abbreviations or special terms you don't recognize, ask someone to explain them to you.
- Take appropriate action. You may be expected to make changes in your behavior or your work routine.
- Determine whether the memo requires a written response.

Using the Strategies

Answer these questions about the memo above.

1. What is the purpose of this memo? What part of the memo tells you this succinctly?
2. Who receives a copy of the memo? Why might a copy be sent?
3. Can you think of any other individuals who might have been sent copies of this memo? Why?
4. What if any action is called for by this memo?
5. Does this memo require a written response?
6. Do you need to keep this memo?

Extending the Strategies

- Write a memorandum to your classmates on an issue of classroom procedure that is important to you.
- Ask someone you know to show you a business memo he or she has received.

Crossing the Curriculum

History

Have students choose an event in history in which the outcome could have been affected by information being sent to someone powerful enough to alter events. As they research the event, encourage students to consider how the outcome might have been influenced if a key person at the time had known more. Have students draft a memo in which they reveal the critical information. Students can write the memo from the point of view of an unknown, ordinary citizen or a famous historical figure.

Learning for Life

Predicting Future Developments

Problem
Many of the profound changes that occurred in the twentieth century grew out of Victorian-era developments. How might developments in the latter half of the twentieth century affect life in the twenty-first century?

Project
Predict how one twentieth-century development—social, cultural, or technological—may affect life in the next one hundred years. Will it change the pace and pattern of daily life? Will it alter the way people view themselves and the world around them?

Preparation
1. With a partner or a small group, brainstorm to generate a list of twentieth-century events, situations, and trends. To get started, you might focus on such categories as art, literature, computers, education, politics, medicine, and so on. Or you might begin with people: Who were the leading inventors, entrepreneurs, authors, artists, and scientists of the late twentieth century?
2. Choose the topic that interests you most, and freewrite to explore what you already know about it and what you think its long-range consequences may be.

Procedure
1. Using library and community resources, explore your topic through the eyes of others who share your interest. Look for facts, statistics, examples, anecdotes, and expert opinions that will answer as many of the *5W-How?* questions (*Who? What? When? Where? Why? How?*) as apply. Be sure to investigate what the experts called futurists suggest about future developments. You can cite the experts' views and give data to support your position.
2. Stimulate your imagination by asking, and answering, a series of *What if?* questions—for example, What if cities ban all cars in the future? Your answers needn't (in fact, can't) be provable, but they should be plausible.

Presentation
Use one of the following formats (or another that your teacher approves):

1. **Be a Television Star**
   Get together with two or three classmates who've chosen different topics to plan a talk show on your predictions for the future. Ask another student to serve as the show's host, and stage the show live (or ask a friend to videotape it for repeated showings) for your school's American history classes during their unit on the twentieth century.
2. **Display with Style**
   Design a triptych (a three-panel composition) illustrating your predictions for the future. Your triptych may be two- or three-dimensional, and you may choose the materials, medium (or media), and style. Give your finished work a title, and display it in the school cafeteria.
3. **Future Fiction**
   Write a short story, set in the late twenty-first century, in which you depict the consequences you foresee. Whether your story is fantastic or realistic, be sure to include in your story plan a basic conflict and a satisfying means of resolving it. With other students who have chosen this option, tape-record your story. Listen to one another's tapes, and share your responses to your stories. Then, add the tapes to your media center's books-on-tape collection.

Processing
Did this activity make you more (or less) optimistic about the future? Did it make you curious about what life will be like even further into the future? Write a brief reflection for your portfolio.

OBJECTIVES
1. Explain how a development in this century may affect society in the future
2. Conduct research
3. Choose and complete a project, summarizing and presenting research information

Grading Timesaver

Rubrics for this Learning for Life project appear on p. 225 of the *Portfolio Management System.*

Developing Workplace Competencies

Preparation	Procedure	Presentation
• Generates ideas • Identifies central issues • Recognizes relationships • Uses logic	• Uses resources • Processes information • Acquires and classifies data • Thinks creatively	• Works on teams • Communicates ideas and information • Interprets information • Solves problems

RESOURCE CENTER

HANDBOOK OF LITERARY TERMS

ALEXANDRINE **A line of poetry made up of six iambs**—that is, a line written in iambic hexameter. The following alexandrine is from Percy Bysshe Shelley's "To a Skylark" (Collection 9):

Our sweetest songs are those that tell of saddest
thought.

See page 221.

ALLEGORY **A story in which the characters, settings, and events stand for abstract or moral concepts.** Allegories thus have two meanings: a literal meaning and a symbolic meaning. Allegories were a popular literary form during the Middle Ages. Later, Edmund Spenser's *The Faerie Queene* (Collection 3) elaborately fused moral and political allegory: Spenser's Redcrosse Knight stands both for St. George, the patron saint of England, and for the more abstract idea of holiness. The best-known English allegory is John Bunyan's *The Pilgrim's Progress* (Collection 5), which recounts the adventures of a character named Christian. The hero's journey to the Celestial City brings him up against many trials that stand for the pitfalls facing the Christian traveling through this world toward the spiritual world.

See pages 221, 451, 495.

ALLITERATION **The repetition of consonant sounds in words that are close to one another.** Alliteration occurs most often at the beginning of words, as in "rough and ready." But consonants within words sometimes alliterate, as in "baby blue." The echoes that alliteration creates can increase a poem's rhythmic and musical effects and make its lines especially memorable. In this line from Alfred, Lord Tennyson's "The Eagle: A Fragment" (Collection 10), the alliteration of harsh *k* sounds reinforces the stark image of the bird:

He clasps the crag with crooked hands

Alliteration is an essential feature of Anglo-Saxon poetry; in most lines, two or three of the four stressed syllables alliterate.

See pages 49, 807, 980.

ALLUSION **A reference to a statement, person, place, event, or thing that is known from literature, history, religion, mythology, politics, sports, science, or popular culture.** For example, the concluding lines of Wilfred Owen's poem "Dulce et Decorum Est" (Collection 12) are *"Dulce et decorum est / Pro patria mori"* ("It is sweet and proper to die for one's country"). These lines allude to a line from an ode by the Latin poet Horace. The title of William Faulkner's *The Sound and the Fury* is an allusion to a line from Shakespeare's *Macbeth* (Collection 4). The cartoon above alludes to William Butler Yeats's poem "The Second Coming" (Collection 12).

See pages 414, 871, 941.

ANALOGY **A comparison of two things to show that they are alike in certain respects.** Writers often make analogies to show how something unfamiliar is like something well known or widely experienced. For example, people often draw an analogy between creating a work of art and giving birth to a child.

See page 1144.

"Basil, do you think the center is going to hold?"

Drawing by Booth; © 1984 The New Yorker Magazine, Inc.

ANTAGONIST **The character or force that opposes or blocks the protagonist, or main character, in a narrative.** Usually the antagonist is human, like Sir Mordred, the villainous rebel who destroys the Round Table in Sir Thomas Malory's *Le Morte Darthur* (Collection 2) or the schoolgirls who mercilessly taunt the Kelvey sisters in Katherine Mansfield's "The Doll's House" (Collection 14). Sometimes the antagonist is supernatural, like Satan, who opposes God in John Milton's *Paradise Lost* (Collection 5).

ANTICLIMAX See Climax.

ANTITHESIS **A contrast of ideas expressed in a grammatically balanced statement.** In the following line from Canto III of *The Rape of the Lock* (Collection 6), Alexander Pope balances noun against noun and verb against verb:

And wretches hang that jurymen may dine.

See pages 521, 844.

APHORISM **A concise, sometimes witty saying that expresses a principle, truth, or observation about life.** Alexander Pope's poetry contains some of the most famous aphorisms in the English language, as in this example from *An Essay on Criticism* (Collection 6):

To err is human, to forgive, divine.

APOSTROPHE **A figure of speech in which a speaker directly addresses an absent or dead person, an abstract quality, or something nonhuman as if it were present and capable of responding.** Apostrophe was a popular device with the Romantic poets: Wordsworth, for example, apostrophizes the river Wye in his "Tintern Abbey" (Collection 8). Among the second-generation Romantics, Shelley apostrophized the west wind and a skylark;

Reading Biographies

For further readings in biography, check the Read On pages in the pupil's edition. Biographies will supply students with excellent background information on the historical periods. The best biographies provide accurate historical information, at the same time using the elements of fiction to grip our interest: suspense, characterization, setting, climax, irony. Some excellent biographies that can supplement students' work in British literature are the following:

Shakespeare of London by Marchette Chute
Shakespeare Alive! edited by Joseph Papp and Elizabeth Kirkland
The Six Wives of Henry VIII by Antonia Fraser
Mary, Queen of Scots by Antonia Fraser
The Life of Thomas More by Peter Ackroyd
John Keats by W. Jackson Bate
Parallel Lives: Five Victorian Marriages by Phyllis Rose

For an unusual biography you might recommend Virginia Woolf's biography of Elizabeth Barrett Browning's spaniel, *Flush.* Several publishers are producing new lines of short paperback biographies of famous people, each one by a well-known writer. These biographies would be well worth students' investigation. Each biography is about 150 to 200 pages. One line is called Penguin Lives; the general editor is James Atlas. In that series, Edna O'Brien, for example, has a biography of James Joyce; Carol Shields, of Jane Austen.

Byron apostrophized the ocean; and Keats apostrophized a nightingale and a Greek urn (all in Collection 9).

See pages 672, 738.

ASIDE **Private words that a character in a play speaks to the audience or to another character and that are not supposed to be overheard by others onstage.** Stage directions usually tell when a speech is an aside. For example, in Act I, Scene 3, of Shakespeare's *Macbeth* (Collection 4), Macbeth makes numerous asides to the audience as he ruminates about the possibility of becoming king.

See page 383.

ASSONANCE **The repetition of similar vowel sounds followed by different consonant sounds in words that are close together.** Assonance differs from **exact rhyme** in that it does not repeat the consonant sound following the vowel. The words *face* and *base* rhyme, while the words *face* and *fade* are assonant. Like alliteration, assonance can create musical and rhythmic effects. In this line from Alfred, Lord Tennyson's "The Lotos-Eaters," the repetition of long *o* sounds is **onomatopoetic:**

All day the wind breathes low with mellower tone

See pages 683, 807, 841, 979, 980.

ATMOSPHERE **The mood or feeling in a literary work.** Atmosphere is usually created through descriptive details and evocative language. For example, Ben Okri sets the mood of his short story "In the Shadow of War" (Collection 12) with a dreamlike description of the war-torn forest around Lagos, Nigeria.

See page 847.

AUTOBIOGRAPHY **A written account of the author's own life.** Unlike **diaries, journals,** and letters, autobiographies are unified narratives usually prepared for a public audience. Also unlike memoirs, which often focus on famous events and people, autobiographies are usually quite introspective. George Orwell's "Shooting an Elephant" (Collection 15) is a well-known autobiographical essay.

See also Diary, Journal.

BALLAD **A song or songlike poem that tells a story.** Most ballads have a regular pattern of **rhythm** and **rhyme,** and they use simple language with a great deal of repetition. Ballads generally have a **refrain**—lines or words that are repeated at regular intervals. And they usually tell sensational stories of tragedy, adventure, betrayal, revenge, and jealousy. **Folk ballads** are composed by anonymous singers and are passed down orally from generation to generation before they are written down (often in several different versions). "Lord Randall" (Collection 2) is an example of a folk ballad. **Literary ballads,** on the other hand, are composed and written down by known poets, usually in the style of folk ballads. John Keats's "La Belle Dame sans Merci" (Collection 9) is a famous literary ballad.

The typical **ballad stanza** is a quatrain with the rhyme scheme *abcb.* The first and third lines have four stressed syllables, and the second and fourth lines have three. The number of unstressed syllables in each line may vary, but often the meter is primarily **iambic.**

See pages 90, 93, 96, 683, 750, 867.

BIOGRAPHY **An account of a person's life written by another person.** *The Life of Samuel Johnson* by James Boswell (Collection 7) is one of the most famous biographies ever written. Virginia Woolf's account of Shakespeare's sister in *A Room of One's Own* (Collection 15) is an invented biography.

See page 583.

BLANK VERSE **Poetry written in unrhymed iambic pentameter.** "Blank" means the poetry is unrhymed. "Iambic pentameter" means that each line contains five iambs, or metrical **feet,** each consisting of an unstressed syllable followed by a stressed syllable (˘ ′). Blank verse is the most important metrical form used in English dramatic and epic poetry. It is the verse line used in Shakespeare's plays and John Milton's *Paradise Lost* (Collection 5). One of the reasons blank verse has been so popular, even among modern poets, is that it combines the naturalness of unrhymed verse with the structure of metrical verse. Except for **free verse,** it is the poetic form that sounds the most like natural speech. It also lends itself easily to slight variations within the basic pattern. Like most of the English Romantic poets, William Wordsworth made extensive use of blank verse, as in these lines from *The Prelude:*

Oh! yet a few short years of useful life,
And all will be complete, thy race be run,
Thy monument of glory will be raised.

See pages 318, 385, 438, 450, 657, 662, 672.

CADENCE **The natural rise and fall of the voice.** Poets who write in **free verse** often try to imitate the cadences of spoken language.

See also Rhythm.

CAESURA **A pause or break within a line of poetry, usually indicated by the natural rhythm of the language.** A midline, or **medial,** caesura is a characteristic of Anglo-Saxon poetry; it divides the four-beat line in half. Later poets use the caesura less predictably, as in the following lines from Wilfred Owen's "Dulce et Decorum Est" (Collection 12). Here, the caesuras are indicated by the symbol ||.

Bent double, || like old beggars under sacks,
Knock-kneed, || coughing like hags, || we cursed
through sludge

See pages 49, 216.

CANTO **A subdivision in a long poem, corresponding to a chapter in a book.** Poems divided into cantos include Dante's *The Divine Comedy* (Collection 4), Pope's *The Rape of the Lock* (Collection 6), and Byron's *Don Juan* and

Childe Harold's Pilgrimage (both in Collection 9). Not all major subdivisions of long poems are called cantos: Milton's *Paradise Lost* (Collection 5) is divided into books, and Coleridge's *The Rime of the Ancient Mariner* (Collection 8), into parts.

The word *canto* comes from a Latin word for song and originally designated a section of a narrative poem that a minstrel could sing in one session.

See page 527.

CARPE DIEM **A Latin phrase that literally means "seize the day"—that is, "make the most of present opportunities."** The *carpe diem* theme is quite common in sixteenth- and seventeenth-century English poetry, as in this famous line from Robert Herrick's "To the Virgins, to Make Much of Time": "Gather ye rosebuds while ye may." The theme is also forcefully expressed in Andrew Marvell's "To His Coy Mistress" (both in Collection 3).

See pages 231, 239.

CHARACTER **An individual in a story or play.** A character always has human traits, even if the character is an animal, like the March Hare in Lewis Carroll's *Alice's Adventures in Wonderland;* or a god, as in the Greek and Roman myths; or a monster, as in *Beowulf* (Collection 1). A character may also be a godlike human, like Superman. But most characters are ordinary human beings, like Geoffrey Chaucer's colorful pilgrims in *The Canterbury Tales* (Collection 2), the eccentrics and paupers in Charles Dickens's novels, and the disillusioned boy in James Joyce's "Araby" (Collection 13).

The process by which the writer reveals the personality of a character is called **characterization.** A writer can reveal a character in the following ways:

1. By telling us directly what the character is like: humble, ambitious, impetuous, easily manipulated, and so on
2. By describing how the character looks and dresses
3. By letting us hear the character speak
4. By revealing the character's private thoughts and feelings
5. By revealing the character's effect on other people—showing how other characters feel or behave toward the character
6. By showing the character's actions

The first method of revealing a character is called **direct characterization.** When a writer uses this method, we do not have to figure out what a character's personality is like—the writer tells us directly. The other five methods of revealing a character are known as **indirect characterization.** When a writer uses these methods, we have to exercise our own judgment, putting clues together to figure out what a character is like—just as we do in real life when we are getting to know someone.

Characters can be classified as static or dynamic. A **static character** is one who does not change much in the course of a story. A **dynamic character,** on the other hand, changes in some important way as a result of the story's action. Characters can also be classified as flat or round. **Flat characters** have only one or two personality traits. They are one-dimensional—they can be summed up by a single phrase. In contrast, **round characters** have more dimensions to their personalities—they are complex, solid, and multifaceted, like real people.

See pages 103, 384, 1069.

CLASSICISM **A movement in art, literature, and music that advocates imitating the principles manifested in the art and literature of ancient ("classical") Greece and Rome.** Classicism emphasizes reason, clarity, balance, harmony, restraint, order, and universal themes. Classicism is often placed in direct opposition to **Romanticism,** with its emphasis on unrestrained emotions and personal themes. However, this opposition should be approached with caution, as it is sometimes exaggerated for effect.

See also Neoclassicism, Romanticism.

CLICHÉ **An expression that was fresh and apt when first coined but is now so overused that it has become hackneyed and stale.** "Busy as a bee" and "fresh as a daisy" are two examples. Clichés are often likened to **dead metaphors**—figures of speech ("leg of a chair," "mouth of a river") whose power to surprise has now been completely lost.

See page 1037.

CLIMAX **The point of greatest emotional intensity or suspense in a plot.** The climax usually marks the moment when the conflict is decided, one way or another. In Shakespeare's plays, the climax usually occurs in the last act, just before the final scene. Following the climax, the story is **resolved,** or closed.

Some critics talk of more than one climactic moment in a long work (though usually the greatest climax still occurs near the end of the plot). In drama, one such climactic moment is called the **turning point,** or **crisis.** In Shakespeare's plays, this moment usually occurs in the third act. The turning point is the pivotal moment when the hero's fortunes begin to decline or improve. All the action leading up to this turning point is **rising action,** and all the action following it is **falling action.** The turning point in *Macbeth* (Collection 4) occurs during the banquet scene in Act III, Scene 4, when Macbeth sees Banquo's ghost. From that point onward, it is downhill for Macbeth—everything goes wrong, culminating in the play's climax in Act V, Scene 8. It is at this point that we finally learn for certain that Macbeth will be defeated. The witches' prophecies are borne out: Birnam Wood does come to Dunsinane, and Macduff, "not born of woman," faces Macbeth. This confrontation is the climax of the play. After this point, the play moves rapidly toward its resolution, with Malcolm, Duncan's legitimate heir, assuming the throne.

In contrast, when something trivial or comical occurs at the point in a narrative when one expects something important or serious, the accompanying deflation is called an **anticlimax.** Thomas Hardy's poem "Ah, Are You Digging on My Grave?" (Collection 11) contains such an anticlimactic moment.

See pages 351, 388, 857.
See also Plot.

COMEDY **In general, a story that ends happily.** The hero of a comedy is usually an ordinary character who overcomes a series of obstacles that block what he or she wants. Often a comedy pits two young people who wish to marry against parental blocking figures who want to prevent the marriage. The wedding that concludes these comedies suggests the formation of a new society and a renewal of life. Comedy is distinct from **tragedy,** in which a great person comes to an unhappy or disastrous end, often through some lapse in judgment or character flaw. Comedies are often, but not always, intended to make us laugh. Two famous comedies are Oscar Wilde's play *The Importance of Being Earnest* and George Bernard Shaw's *Pygmalion.* Frank O'Connor's "My Oedipus Complex" (Collection 14) is a comedic short story.

See pages 283, 300, 393, 526, 798.
See also Farce, Tragedy.

CONCEIT **A fanciful and elaborate figure of speech that makes a surprising connection between two seemingly dissimilar things.** Although a conceit may be a brief metaphor, it usually forms the framework of an entire poem. One of the most important kinds of conceits is the **metaphysical conceit,** so called because it was widely used by the seventeenth-century metaphysical poets. This type of conceit is especially startling, complex, and ingenious. Two famous examples are John Donne's comparison of separated lovers to the legs of a compass in "A Valediction: Forbidding Mourning" (Collection 3) and George Herbert's comparison of belief in God to a pulley in "The Pulley."

See pages 220, 229, 247, 457.

CONFLICT **A struggle or clash between opposing characters, forces, or emotions.** In an **external conflict,** a character struggles against some outside force: another character, society as a whole, or some natural force. An **internal conflict,** on the other hand, is a struggle between opposing needs, desires, or emotions within a single character. Many works, especially longer ones, contain both internal and external conflicts. For example, in Shakespeare's *Macbeth* (Collection 4), Macbeth undergoes an internal conflict between his excessive ambition and his obsessive guilt. He also experiences various external conflicts with characters who attempt to block his ambition. In Doris Lessing's "No Witchcraft for Sale" (Collection 15), the conflict between Gideon and the scientist illustrates larger cultural conflicts.

See also Plot.

CONNOTATIONS **All the meanings, associations, or emotions that a word suggests.** For example, an expensive restaurant might prefer to advertise its "delicious cuisine" rather than its "delicious cooking." *Cuisine* and *cooking* have the same literal meaning—"prepared food." But *cuisine* has connotations of elegance and sophistication, while *cooking* does not. The same restaurant would certainly not describe its food as "great grub."

Notice the difference between the following pairs of words: *young/immature, ambitious/cutthroat, uninhibited/shameless, lenient/lax.* We might describe ourselves using the first word but someone else using the second. The English philosopher Bertrand Russell once gave a classic example of the different connotations of words: "I am firm. You are obstinate. He is a pigheaded fool."

See pages 513, 515, 650.
See also Denotation.

CONSONANCE **The repetition of final consonant sounds after different vowel sounds.** The words *east* and *west, dig* and *dog, turn* and *torn,* and Shakespeare's famous *"struts* and *frets"* (from *Macbeth,* in Collection 4) are examples of consonance. The term is also used sometimes to refer to repeated consonant sounds in the middle of words, as in *solemn stillness.* (Consonance, when loosely defined, can be a form of **alliteration.** Strictly speaking, however, alliteration is the repetition of initial consonant sounds.) Like **assonance,** consonance is one form of **approximate rhyme.**

See also Alliteration, Assonance.

COUPLET **Two consecutive lines of poetry that rhyme.** The couplet has been widely used since the Middle Ages, especially to provide a sense of closure. A couplet that presents a completed thought is called a **closed couplet.** Shakespeare used closed couplets to end his sonnets, as in this example from Sonnet 18 (Collection 3):

So long as men can breathe or eyes can see,
So long lives this, and this gives life to thee.

A couplet written in **iambic pentameter** is called a **heroic couplet.** Although the heroic couplet has been used in English literature since Chaucer, it was perfected during the eighteenth century. Here is an example from Pope's *Essay on Man:*

◡ / ◡ / ◡ / ◡ / ◡ /
Two principles in human nature reign;
◡ / ◡ / ◡ / ◡ / ◡ /
Self-love, to urge, and Reason, to restrain.

See pages 149, 522.

DENOTATION **The literal, dictionary definition of a word.** Ironically, the definitions Samuel Johnson provides in his famous *A Dictionary of the English Language* (Collection 7) are rarely denotative.

See page 515.
See also Connotations.

DENOUEMENT See Plot.

DEUS EX MACHINA **Any artificial or contrived device used at the end of a plot to resolve or untangle the complications.** The term is Latin, meaning "god from a machine." The phrase refers to a device used in ancient Greek and Roman drama: At the conclusion of the play, a god would be lowered onto the stage by a mechanical device so that he could save the hero and end the story happily. The term now refers to any device that resolves a plot in a forced or ridiculously implausible way: An orphan finds that he has inherited a fortune just as he is being packed off to the poorhouse; a hero is saved because the villain has forgotten to load his gun. Oscar Wilde's *The Importance of Being Earnest* and Charles Dickens's *Oliver Twist* both contain examples of *deus ex machina.*

See page 283.

DIALECT A way of speaking that is characteristic of a particular region or group of people. A dialect may have a distinct vocabulary, pronunciation system, and grammar. In the Middle Ages, when Latin was the "literary" language of Europe, writers such as Geoffrey Chaucer (Collection 2) began writing for middle-class audiences in their own regional languages, or what are now interchangeably called dialects or **vernaculars.** Today one dialect usually becomes accepted as the standard for a country or culture. In the United States, the dialect used in formal writing and spoken by most TV and radio announcers is known as standard English.

Writers often use other dialects, however, to establish character or to create local color. For example, Robert Burns (Collection 8) wrote his poetry in Scottish dialect, and V. S. Naipaul (Collection 13) has used the dialect spoken by Trinidad's Asian Indian population in many of his works. The East London cockney dialect, and the lower-class background it betrays, are at the very heart of George Bernard Shaw's famous play *Pygmalion* (1913). In this excerpt from the play, Henry Higgins, with his friend Colonel Pickering in attendance, begins to instruct the young flower girl Eliza Doolittle in how to speak "proper" English:

> **Higgins.** Say your alphabet.
>
> **Liza.** I know my alphabet. Do you think I know nothing? I dont need to be taught like a child.
>
> **Higgins** *(thundering)*. Say your alphabet.
>
> **Pickering.** Say it, Miss Doolittle. You will understand presently. Do what he tells you; and let him teach you in his own way.
>
> **Liza.** Oh well, if you put it like that—Ahyee, bəyee, cəyee, dəyee——
>
> **Higgins** *(with the roar of a wounded lion)*. Stop. Listen to this, Pickering. . . . (*To* Eliza) Say A, B, C, D.
>
> **Liza** *(almost in tears)*. But I'm saying it. Ahyee, Bəee, Cə-ee——

See pages 98, 641, 770, 896, 1049.

DIALOGUE Conversation between two or more people. Writers use dialogue to advance the action of a plot, to present an interplay of ideas and personalities, and to reveal the background, occupation, or social level of the characters through **tone** and **dialect.**

See pages 1102, 1171.

DIARY A day-by-day record of events and thoughts kept by an individual. A diary is usually an intimate **autobiographical** chronicle that is not intended for publication, although diarists sometimes have a reader in mind. The diary of Samuel Pepys (Collection 7) is a famous diary in English. Diaries of such modern writers as Virginia Woolf (Collection 15) have also been published.

See page 543.
See also Autobiography, Journal.

DICTION A writer's or speaker's choice of words. Speakers and writers use different types of words depending on the audience they're addressing, the subject they're discussing, and the effect they're trying to produce. For example, slang that would be suitable in a casual conversation with a friend ("He's a total nerd") would be unsuitable in a political debate. Similarly, the language that a nutritionist would use to describe a meal would be different from the language that a restaurant reviewer or a novelist would use.

Diction is an essential element of a writer's **style.** A writer's diction can be simple or flowery (*shop/boutique*), modern or old-fashioned (*pharmacy/apothecary*), general or specific (*sandwich/grilled cheese on rye*). Notice that the **connotations** of words (rather than their strict, literal meanings, or **denotations**) are an important aspect of diction.

See pages 513, 1092.

DISSONANCE A harsh, discordant combination of sounds. The opposite of **euphony,** a pleasant, harmonious combination of sounds, dissonance is usually created by the repetition of harsh consonant sounds. Dissonance is often used in poetry to communicate energy. The following lines from Gerard Manley Hopkins's "The Windhover" are dissonant:

> shéer plód makes plough down sillion
> Shine, and blue-bleak embers, ah my dear,
> Fall, gall themselves, and gash gold-vermilion.

Also called **cacophony,** dissonance is often used as a poetic device by John Donne (Collection 3) and Robert Browning (Collection 10).

DRAMATIC MONOLOGUE A poem in which a character addresses one or more listeners who remain silent or whose replies are not revealed. The occasion is usually a critical one in the speaker's life. Tennyson's "Ulysses" and Browning's "My Last Duchess" and "Porphyria's Lover" (all in Collection 10) are famous dramatic monologues.

See page 829.

ELEGY A poem that mourns the death of a person or laments something lost. Elegies may lament the passing of life and beauty, or they may be meditations on the nature of death. A type of **lyric,** an elegy is usually formal in language and structure and solemn or even melancholy in tone. Much of English poetry is elegiac, from the Anglo-Saxon lyric "The Seafarer" (Collection 1) to John Milton's "Lycidas," Thomas Gray's somber "Elegy Written in a Country Churchyard" (Collection 7), and the great elegy of the Victorian era, Alfred, Lord Tennyson's *In Memoriam A.H.H.* (Collection 10).

See pages 55, 435, 481, 606, 814, 1038.

END-STOPPED LINE A line of poetry in which the meter and the meaning conclude with the end of the line. Often the end-of-line pause is marked with punctuation, though it need not be. These lines from Alexander Pope's *An Essay on Man* (Collection 6) are end-stopped:

> Know then thyself, presume not God to scan;
> The proper study of mankind is man.

See also Run-on Line.

EPIC A long narrative poem that relates the great deeds of a larger-than-life hero who embodies the values of a particular society. Most epics include elements of

myth, legend, folklore, and history. Their tone is serious and their language grand. Most **epic heroes** undertake quests to achieve something of tremendous value to themselves or their society. Homer's *Odyssey* and *Iliad* and Virgil's *Aeneid* are the best-known epics in the Western tradition. The two most important English epics are the Anglo-Saxon poem *Beowulf* (Collection 1) and John Milton's *Paradise Lost* (Collection 5).

See pages 18, 20, 221, 393, 438, 526.

EPIGRAM **A brief, clever, and usually memorable statement.** Alexander Pope's writings are **epigrammatic** in style. Here is an example from his *Essay on Criticism:*

We think our fathers fools, so wise we grow,
Our wiser sons, no doubt, will think us so.

See pages 257, 525, 1108.

EPIPHANY **In a literary work, a moment of sudden insight or revelation that a character experiences.** The word comes from the Greek and can be translated as "manifestation" or "showing forth." The term has religious meanings that have been transferred to literature by many modern writers. James Joyce first gave the word its literary meaning in an early draft of *A Portrait of the Artist as a Young Man.* In Joyce's story "Araby" (Collection 13), the narrator experiences an epiphany at the end of the story when he recognizes the cheap vulgarity of the bazaar and the emptiness of his dream.

See pages 985, 992.

EPITAPH **An inscription on a tombstone or a commemorative poem written about a person who has died.** Epitaphs range from the solemn to the farcical. Ben Jonson's poem "On My First Son" (Collection 3) contains a famously poignant epitaph. The following epitaph, Robert Burns's "On William Graham of Mossknowe," is a more comic example:

"Stop Thief!" Dame Nature call'd to Death,
As Willie drew his latest breath:
"How shall I make a fool again?
My choicest model thou hast ta'en."

EPITHET **An adjective or other descriptive phrase that is regularly used to characterize a person, place, or thing.** Phrases such as "Peter the Great," "Richard the Lion-Hearted," and "America the Beautiful" are epithets. Homer created so many descriptive epithets in his *Iliad* and *Odyssey* that his name has been permanently associated with a type of epithet. The **Homeric epithet** consists of a compound adjective that is regularly used to modify a particular noun. Famous examples are "the wine-dark sea," "the gray-eyed goddess Athena," and the "rosy-fingered dawn."

See also Kenning.

ESSAY **A short piece of nonfiction prose that examines a single subject from a limited point of view.** There are two major types of essays. **Informal essays** (also called **personal essays**) generally reveal a great deal about the personalities and feelings of their authors. They tend to be conversational, sometimes even humorous, in tone, and they are usually highly subjective. **Formal essays** (also called **traditional essays**) are usually serious and impersonal in tone. Because they are written to inform or persuade, they are expected to be factual, logical, and tightly organized.

In English literature, the essay began with Sir Francis Bacon, who published his extremely formal *Essays* (Collection 5) in 1597. The English informal essay was pioneered by Joseph Addison and Sir Richard Steele (both in Collection 7) in the early eighteenth century. Notable twentieth-century English essayists include Virginia Woolf and George Orwell (both in Collection 15).

See pages 404, 567, 1123, 1138.

EXAGGERATION *See* Hyperbole.

FABLE **A very brief story in prose or verse that teaches a moral, or a practical lesson about life.** The characters in most fables are animals that behave and speak like humans. Some of the most popular fables are those attributed to Aesop, who was supposed to have been a slave in ancient Greece. Several of the pilgrims' tales in Geoffrey Chaucer's *The Canterbury Tales* (Collection 2) also contain fables.

See also Parable.

FALLING ACTION *See* Climax.

FARCE **A type of comedy in which ridiculous and often stereotyped characters are involved in far-fetched, silly situations.** The humor in farce is based on crude physical action, slapstick, and clowning. Characters may slip on banana peels, get pies thrown in their faces, and knock one another on the head with ladders. The movies featuring Abbott and Costello, Laurel and Hardy, and the Marx brothers are all examples of farces.

The word *farce* comes from a Latin word for "stuffing," and in fact farces were originally used to fill in the waiting time between the acts of a serious play. Even in tragedies, farcical elements are often included to provide **comic relief,** or a break from the pervading tension. Shakespeare frequently lets his "common" characters engage in farcical actions.

See pages 283, 332, 1101.

FIGURATIVE LANGUAGE **Language that intentionally departs from the normal construction or meaning of words in order to create a certain effect or to make an analogy between two seemingly dissimilar things.** Figurative language includes all **figures of speech.**

See page 389.

FIGURE OF SPEECH **A word or phrase that describes one thing in terms of another and is not meant to be understood on a literal level.** Figures of speech always involve some sort of imaginative comparison between seemingly unlike things.

Some 250 different types of figures of speech have been identified, but the most common are the **simile** ("My love is like a red, red rose"), the **metaphor** ("The Lord is my shepherd"), and **personification** ("Death, be not proud").

See also Hyperbole, Metaphor, Metonymy, Oxymoron, Personification, Simile, Symbol.

FLASHBACK **A scene in a movie, play, short story, novel, or narrative poem that interrupts the present action of the plot to "flash backward" and tell what happened at an earlier time.** "The Demon Lover" by

Elizabeth Bowen (Collection 13) includes a flashback that describes Mrs. Drover's farewell to her fiancé twenty-five years before the main action of the story takes place.

See page 1018.

FOIL **A character who sets off another character by strong contrast.** This contrast emphasizes the differences between two characters, bringing out the distinctive qualities in each. In *Macbeth* (Collection 4), Banquo is a foil to Macbeth. Though the witches prophesy similar fame for both Macbeth and Banquo, only Macbeth's appetite for power is excited by the prediction; Banquo remains loyal to the king.

FORESHADOWING **The use of clues to hint at what is going to happen later in the plot.** Foreshadowing arouses the reader's curiosity and builds up **suspense.** In *Macbeth* (Collection 4), the witches' prophecies foreshadow Macbeth's tragic end. Foreshadowing also occurs in Elizabeth Bowen's "The Demon Lover" (Collection 13) when Mrs. Drover imagines "spectral glitters in the place of" her fiancé's eyes, and when we learn that she made an "unnatural promise" to him—that she "could not have plighted a more sinister troth."

See pages 333, 813.
See also Suspense.

FRAME STORY **An introductory narrative within which one or more of the characters proceed to tell a story.** Perhaps the best-known example of stories contained in a frame story is the Persian collection called *The Thousand and One Nights.* In English literature, Geoffrey Chaucer's *The Canterbury Tales* (Collection 2) uses a frame story involving a group of people on a pilgrimage; within the narrative frame, each of the pilgrims then tells his or her own story. Giovanni Boccaccio's *Decameron* (Collection 2) contains another notable example of the frame-story device.

See pages 99, 103, 153.

FREE VERSE **Poetry that has no regular meter or rhyme scheme.** Free verse usually relies instead on the natural **rhythms** of ordinary speech. Poets writing in free verse may use **alliteration, internal rhyme, onomatopoeia,** and other musical devices to achieve their effects. They may also place great emphasis on **imagery.** Matthew Arnold's "Dover Beach" (Collection 11) is an early example of free verse, and T. S. Eliot's poems, including "The Hollow Men" (Collection 12), are especially fine and famous examples. Much of today's poetry is written in free verse: Margaret Atwood's "Mushrooms" (Collection 13) is one contemporary example.

See page 1050.

GOTHIC **A term used to describe literary works that contain primitive, medieval, wild, mysterious, or natural elements.** Such elements were frowned upon by eighteenth-century neoclassicists but hailed by the Romantic writers of the following era. The **Gothic novel,** a genre popular in the late eighteenth and early nineteenth centuries, is chiefly characterized by gloomy settings and an atmosphere of terror and mystery. Mary Wollstonecraft Shelley's *Frankenstein* is one of the most widely known Gothic novels.

See pages 516, 606, 636, 728.

HYPERBOLE **A figure of speech that uses exaggeration to express strong emotion or create a comic effect.** While hyperbole (also known as **overstatement**) does not express the *literal* truth, it is often used in the service of truth to capture a sense of intensity or to emphasize the essential nature of something. For instance, if you claim that it was 250 degrees in the shade, you are using hyperbole to express the truth that it was miserably hot.

See pages 245, 500.

IAMBIC PENTAMETER **A line of poetry made up of five iambs.** An **iamb** is a metrical foot, or unit of measure, consisting of an unstressed syllable followed by a stressed syllable (˘ ´). The word *suggest,* for example, is made up of one iamb. *Pentameter* derives from the Greek words *penta* (five) and *meter* (measure). Here are two lines from John Keats's "Ode to a Nightingale" (Collection 9) that are written in iambic pentameter:

Forlorn! the very word is like a bell
    To toll me back from thee to my sole self!

Iambic pentameter is by far the most common verse line in English poetry. Shakespeare's sonnets and plays, for example, are written primarily in this meter. Many modern poets, such as W. H. Auden (Collection 14), have continued to use iambic pentameter. Other than **free verse,** it is the poetic meter that sounds the most like natural speech.

See pages 99, 216, 318, 450.
See also Blank Verse.

IMAGERY **Language that appeals to the senses.** Most images are visual—that is, they appeal to the sense of sight. But imagery can also appeal to the senses of hearing, touch, taste, or smell. While imagery is an element in all types of writing, it is especially important in poetry, as in these lines from John Keats's "Sleep and Poetry":

What is more gentle than a wind in summer?
What is more soothing than the pretty hummer
That stays one moment in an open flower,
And buzzes cheerily from bower to bower?
What is more tranquil than a musk-rose blowing
In a green island, far from all men's knowing?

See pages 127, 384, 389, 415, 759, 843, 1109.

INCREMENTAL REPETITION **A device widely used in ballads whereby a line or lines are repeated with slight variations from stanza to stanza.** Each repetition advances the plot of the narrative. Incremental repetition is used in the folk ballad "Lord Randall" (Collection 2).

See page 96.

IN MEDIAS RES **The technique of starting a story in the middle and then using a flashback to tell what happened earlier.** *In medias res* is Latin for "in the middle of things." Traditional epics begin *in medias res.* For example, John Milton's *Paradise Lost* (Collection 5) opens with Satan and his cohorts in Hell, after the war in Heaven and their fall, events that are recounted later in a flashback.

INTERIOR MONOLOGUE See Stream of Consciousness.

IRONY **A contrast or discrepancy between expectation and reality—between what is said and what is really meant, between what is expected and what really happens, or between what appears to be true and what really is true.**

Verbal irony occurs when a writer or speaker says one thing but really means something quite different—often the opposite of what he or she has said. If you tell your friend that you "just love being kept waiting in the rain," you are using verbal irony. A classic example of verbal irony is Jonathan Swift's suggestion in *A Modest Proposal* (Collection 6) that the Irish solve their poverty and overpopulation problems by selling their babies as food to their English landlords.

Situational irony occurs when what actually happens is the opposite of what is expected or appropriate. In James Joyce's story "Araby" (Collection 13), the boy hears about a bazaar called Araby and imagines that it will be a splendid, exotic place. Yet when he arrives, he finds that in reality Araby is cheap and commonplace.

Dramatic irony occurs when the audience or the reader knows something important that a character in a play or story does not know. Forceful dramatic irony occurs at several points in Shakespeare's *Macbeth* (Collection 4). One example is in Act II, Scene 4: Macduff suspects that Duncan has been murdered by his own sons, but the audience knows that Macbeth is the murderer. Dramatic irony is also a powerful device in William Blake's "The Chimney Sweeper" from *Songs of Innocence* (Collection 8). The speaker is a child who believes what he has been told—that "if all do their duty they need not fear harm." But the reader, who is not so innocent, realizes that this is not so.

See pages 129, 487, 501, 991, 1069, 1081, 1138.

JOURNAL **A day-by-day record of events and personal impressions kept by an individual.** A journal is somewhat less intimate than a **diary** and more strictly chronological than an **autobiography,** which can jump back and forth in time in order to tell a coherent story or emphasize a particular theme. The term *journal* is also applied to periodicals that contain news or matters of current interest. In *A Journal of the Plague Year* (Collection 7), Daniel Defoe created a fictional journal.

See pages 557, 582, 583.
See also Autobiography, Diary.

KENNING **In Anglo-Saxon poetry, a metaphorical phrase or compound word used to name a person, place, thing, or event indirectly.** *Beowulf* (Collection 1) includes the kennings "whale-road" for the sea and "shepherd of evil" for Grendel.

See page 49.
See also Epithet.

LITERARY BALLAD See Ballad.

LYRIC POETRY **Poetry that focuses on expressing emotions or thoughts, rather than on telling a story.** Most lyrics are short, and they usually imply rather than directly state a single strong emotion. The term *lyric* comes from the Greek. In ancient Greece, lyric poems were recited to the accompaniment of a stringed instrument called the lyre. Today, poets still try to make their lyrics melodious, but they rely only on the musical effects they can create with words (such as **rhyme, rhythm, alliteration,** and **onomatopoeia**). Alexander Pushkin's "I Have Visited Again," William Wordsworth's "Tintern Abbey" (both in Collection 8), and Matthew Arnold's "Dover Beach" (Collection 11) are all lyric poems.

See pages 629, 631, 672, 1033.

METAPHOR **A figure of speech that makes a comparison between two seemingly unlike things without using a connective word *like, as, than,* or *resembles.*** You are using a metaphor if you say you're "at the end of your rope" or describe two political candidates as "running neck and neck."

Some metaphors are **directly** stated, like Percy Bysshe Shelley's comparison "My soul is an enchanted boat." (If he had written, "My soul is *like* an enchanted boat," he would have been using a **simile.**) Other metaphors are **implied,** like John Suckling's line "Time shall molt away his wings." The words *molt* and *wings* imply a comparison between time and a bird shedding its feathers.

An **extended metaphor** is a metaphor that is extended, or developed, over several lines of writing or even throughout an entire poem. In the following stanza, from "My Beloved Is Mine and I Am His" by Francis Quarles, the speaker develops a comparison between two lovers and two separate streams that flow into the same river. (The title and last line allude to the Biblical Song of Songs.)

Even like two little bank-dividing brooks,
    That wash the pebbles with their wanton streams,
And having ranged and searched a thousand nooks,
    Meet both at length in silver-breasted Thames
    Where in greater current they conjoin:
So I my best-beloved's am, so he is mine.

A **dead metaphor** is a metaphor that has become so common that we no longer even notice that it is a figure of speech. Our everyday language is filled with dead metaphors, such as *foot of the bed, bone of contention,* and *mouth of the river.*

A **mixed metaphor** is the incongruous mixture of two or more metaphors. Mixed metaphors are usually unintentional and often conjure up ludicrous images: "If you put your money on that horse, you'll be barking up the wrong tree."

See pages 214, 841, 851, 1117.

METAPHYSICAL CONCEIT See Conceit.

METAPHYSICAL POETRY **A term applied to the poetry of John Donne, Andrew Marvell, and other seventeenth-century poets who wrote in a similarly difficult and abstract style.** Metaphysical poetry, which is

intellectual and detached in contrast to the Elizabethan love poetry that preceded it, is distinguished by ingenious, obscure imagery, philosophical meditation, rough-sounding meter, and verbal wit.

See pages 246, 247.

METER **A generally regular pattern of stressed and unstressed syllables in poetry.** When we want to indicate the metrical pattern of a poem, we mark the stressed syllables with the symbol ' and the unstressed syllables with the symbol ˘. Indicating the metrical pattern of a poem in this way is called **scanning** the poem, or **scansion.** Here is how to scan these lines from William Blake's "The Tyger" (Collection 8):

/ ˘ / ˘ / ˘ /
Tyger! Tyger! burning bright
/ ˘ / ˘ / ˘ /
In the forests of the night

Meter is measured in units called feet. A **foot** consists of one stressed syllable and usually one or more unstressed syllables. The basic metrical feet used in English poetry are the **iamb** (as in *cŏnvínce*), the **trochee** (as in *bórrŏw*), the **anapest** (as in *cŏntrădíct*), the **dactyl** (as in *áccŭrăte*), and the **spondee** (as in *séawéed*). A poem is described as iambic, trochaic, anapestic, dactylic, or spondaic according to what kind of foot appears most often in its lines.

A complete description of a metrical line indicates both the type and number of feet the line contains. For example, a line of iambic pentameter consists of five iambs, while a line of trochaic tetrameter consists of four trochees.

See pages 216, 385, 525, 712, 807.

METONYMY **A figure of speech in which something closely related to a thing or suggested by it is substituted for the thing itself.** You are using metonymy if you call the judiciary "the bench," the king "the crown," the president (or presidential staff) "the White House," or the race track "the turf." Closely related to metonymy is **synecdoche** (si·nek′də·kē), a figure of speech in which a part stands for the whole, as in "our daily bread," meaning food.

MOCK EPIC **A comic narrative poem that parodies the epic by treating a trivial subject in a lofty, grand manner.** A mock epic uses dignified language, elaborate figures of speech, and supernatural intervention. The style of the mock epic is called **mock heroic** (and short mock epics are often called mock heroics). Alexander Pope's *The Rape of the Lock* (Collection 6) is considered the supreme mock epic in the English language.

See page 526.

MOOD See Atmosphere.

MOTIF **In literature, a word, character, object, image, metaphor, or idea that recurs in a work or in several works.** The rose is a motif that runs through many love poems. The motif of ill-fitting clothes appears throughout Shakespeare's *Macbeth* (Collection 4). It starts in Act I, Scene 3, when Macbeth asks Ross: "The Thane of Cawdor lives: why do you dress me / In borrowed robes?" This is soon followed by Banquo's observation: "New honors come upon him, / Like our strange garments, cleave not to their mold / But with the aid of use." The motif of ill-fitting clothes reaches its culmination in Act V, Scene 2, when Angus says of Macbeth: "Now does he feel his title / Hang loose about him, like a giant's robe / Upon a dwarfish thief." A motif almost always bears an important relationship to the **theme** of a work of literature.

MOTIVATION **The reasons for or forces behind the action of a character.** Motivation is revealed through a combination of the character's desires and moral nature with the circumstances in which he or she is placed. In Shakespeare's *Macbeth* (Collection 4), the witches' prophecy and Macbeth's overweening ambition combine to provide the motivation for his killing of the king.

See page 948.
See also Character.

MYTH **An anonymous traditional story that usually serves to explain a belief, custom, or mysterious natural phenomenon.** Most myths grew out of religious rituals, and almost all of them involve the exploits of gods and heroes. Such myths make it possible to understand and cope with things beyond human control. Every culture has its own **mythology,** but in the Western world, the most important myths have been those of ancient Greece and Rome. In twentieth-century literature, **allusions** to myths are often **ironic,** intended to reveal how diminished humanity has become in comparison with grand mythological figures.

See pages 368, 1081, 1105, 1108.

NARRATOR **One who tells, or narrates, a story.** In fiction, the narrator occupies any one of a variety of relations to the events described: from the center of the action to a distant, even objective, observer. A narrator may also be reliable or unreliable—if unreliable, the reader is made aware that the narrator's perceptions and interpretations of the action are different from those of the author. Such unreliable narrators can be deceitful or bumbling, but are often just naive characters—like Larry, the young narrator who humorously misunderstands much of the story's action in Frank O'Connor's "My Oedipus Complex" (Collection 14).

See pages 557, 714, 857, 1031.
See also Point of View.

NEOCLASSICISM **The revival of classical standards and forms during the late seventeenth and eighteenth centuries.** The neoclassicists valued the classical ideals of order, reason, balance, harmony, clarity, and restraint. In particular, they studied and tried to emulate the Latin poets Horace and Virgil. Alexander Pope (Collection 6) and John Dryden (Collection 7) were leaders of the neoclassical movement in England.

See pages 469, 580.

NOVEL **A long fictional prose narrative, usually of more than fifty thousand words.** In general, the novel uses the same basic literary elements as the short story: **plot, character, setting, theme,** and **point of view.** The

novel's length usually permits these elements to be more fully developed than they are in the short story. However, this is not always true of the modern novel. Some are basically character studies, with only the barest plot structures. Others reveal little about their characters and concentrate instead on setting or tone or even the language of the novel itself.

Some of the greatest novels in English literature are *Tom Jones* by Henry Fielding, *Pride and Prejudice* by Jane Austen, *Jane Eyre* by Charlotte Brontë, *David Copperfield* and *Great Expectations* by Charles Dickens, *Middlemarch* by George Eliot, *Jude the Obscure* by Thomas Hardy, *Lord Jim* by Joseph Conrad, *Sons and Lovers* by D. H. Lawrence, and *Ulysses* by James Joyce.

See pages 482, 516, 726, 727, 795, 859, 916.

OCTAVE An eight-line stanza or poem or the first eight lines of an Italian, or Petrarchan, sonnet. The usual rhyme scheme of the octave in this type of sonnet is *abbaabba*. The octave, which is sometimes called the **octet,** is followed by a six-line **sestet** with the rhyme scheme *cdecde* or *cdcdcd*.

See pages 220, 838.
See also Sonnet.

ODE A complex, generally long lyric poem on a serious subject. In English poetry, there are basically two types of odes. One is highly formal and dignified in style and is generally written for ceremonial or public occasions. This type of ode derives from the choral odes of the classical Greek poet Pindar. John Dryden's "Song for St. Cecilia's Day" is an English version of the Pindaric ode. The other type of ode derives from those written by the Latin poet Horace, and it is much more personal and reflective. In English poetry, it is exemplified by the intimate, meditative odes of such Romantic poets as Wordsworth, Keats, and Shelley (Collections 8 and 9).

See pages 482, 672, 737.

ONOMATOPOEIA The use of a word whose sound imitates or suggests its meaning. Many familiar words, such as *clap, squish, sizzle,* and *wheeze,* are onomatopoeic. In poetry, onomatopoeia can reinforce meaning while creating evocative and musical effects. The following lines, from Alfred, Lord Tennyson's "Mariana," contain several imitative sounds:

The sparrow's chirrup on the roof,
  The slow clock ticking, and the sound
Which to the wooing wind aloof
  The poplar made, did all confound
Her sense. . . .

See pages 738, 927, 1037, 1050.

OTTAVA RIMA An eight-line stanza in iambic pentameter with the rhyme scheme *abababcc*. The form developed in Italy and was popularized by the fourteenth-century Italian poet Giovanni Boccaccio. The most famous example of ottava rima in English poetry is Lord Byron's *Don Juan* (Collection 9). William Butler Yeats's "Sailing to Byzantium" is another notable example.

See page 714.

OXYMORON A figure of speech that combines apparently contradictory or incongruous ideas. "Bitter sweet," "cruel kindness," and "eloquent silence" are oxymorons. The classic oxymoron "wise fool" is almost a literal translation of the term from the Greek—*oxys* means "sharp" or "keen," and *moros* means "foolish." A famous oxymoron in literature is John Milton's description of Hell in *Paradise Lost* (Collection 5):

No light, but rather darkness visible . . .

See page 924.

PARABLE A short, allegorical story that teaches a moral or religious lesson about life. The most famous parables in Western literature are those told by Jesus in the Gospels of the Bible.

See page 425.

PARADOX An apparent contradiction that is actually true. A paradox may be a statement or a situation; as a statement, it is a figure of speech. The metaphysical and Cavalier poets of the seventeenth century (Collection 3) made brilliant use of paradoxes, as in this famous example from John Donne's "Death Be Not Proud" (Collection 3):

One short sleep past, we wake eternally,
And death shall be no more; Death, thou shalt die.

The speaker in the cartoon below doesn't understand the famous series of paradoxes that open *A Tale of Two Cities* by Charles Dickens.

See pages 218, 254, 266, 318, 738.

"I wish you would make up your mind, Mr. Dickens. Was it the best of times or was it the worst of times? It could scarcely have been both."

© The New Yorker Collection 1987. J. B. Handelsman from cartoonbank.com. All Rights Reserved.

PARALLELISM The repetition of words, phrases, or sentences that have the same grammatical structure or that restate a similar idea. Parallelism is often used in

literature meant to be spoken aloud, such as poetry, drama, and speeches, because it can help make lines emotional, rhythmic, and memorable. It is also one of the most important techniques used in Biblical poetry. The parallelism in the following lines, from William Blake's "A Divine Image," heightens their emotional effect and sharpens their meaning:

Cruelty has a human heart
And Jealousy a human face;
Terror the human form divine,
And Secrecy the human dress.

See pages 405, 421, 521, 655.

PARODY The imitation of a work of literature, art, or music for amusement or instruction. Parodies usually use exaggeration or inappropriate subject matter to make a serious style seem ridiculous. Alexander Pope's *The Rape of the Lock* (Collection 6) is a parody of such serious and sweeping epics as the *Iliad* and the *Aeneid.* Richard Armour's portrayal of *Macbeth*'s famous witches (Collection 4) is a contemporary example of parody.

See pages 742, 920, 1155.

PASTORAL A type of poem that depicts rustic life in idyllic, idealized terms. The term *pastoral* comes from the Latin word for shepherd, and originally pastorals were about shepherds, nymphs, and rustic life. Today, the term has a looser meaning and refers to any poem that portrays an idyllic rural setting or that expresses nostalgia for an age or place of lost innocence. The most famous traditional English pastoral is Christopher Marlowe's "The Passionate Shepherd to His Love," which is satirized in Sir Walter Raleigh's "The Nymph's Reply to the Shepherd" (both in Collection 3). Examples of untraditional pastorals include William Wordsworth's "Tintern Abbey" (Collection 8), William Butler Yeats's "The Lake Isle of Innisfree" (Collection 13), and Dylan Thomas's "Fern Hill" (Collection 13).

See pages 233, 520, 606.

PERSONIFICATION A kind of metaphor in which a nonhuman thing or quality is talked about as if it were human. In these lines, from Percy Bysshe Shelley's "A Dirge," the speaker describes the wind as if it were capable of feeling the human emotion of grief:

Rough wind, that moanest loud
Grief too sad for song

See pages 669, 960.
See also Apostrophe, Figure of Speech, Metaphor.

PLOT The series of related events that make up a story or drama. The plot is the underlying structure of a story. Most plots are built on these "bare bones": A **basic situation,** or **exposition,** introduces the characters, setting, and, usually, the story's major **conflict.** Out of this basic situation, **complications** develop that intensify the conflict. **Suspense** mounts until a **climax**—the tensest or most exciting part of the plot—is reached, where something happens to determine the outcome of the conflict. Finally, all the problems or mysteries of the plot are unraveled in the **resolution,** or **denouement.**

See pages 153, 388, 1069, 1098.
See also Climax.

POINT OF VIEW The vantage point from which a writer tells a story. There are three main points of view: **first-person, limited third-person,** and **omniscient third-person.**

In the **first-person point of view,** the narrator is a character in the story. Using the pronoun *I,* this narrator tells us his or her own experiences but cannot reveal any other character's private thoughts. When we read a story told in the first person, we hear and see only what the narrator hears and sees. We may have to interpret what this narrator says because a first-person narrator may or may not be objective, honest, or perceptive. For example, in Frank O'Connor's "My Oedipus Complex" (Collection 14), the narrator is a young boy whose understanding and insight are limited by his age: He believes that babies are purchased for seventeen shillings.

In the **limited third-person point of view,** the narrator is outside the story—like an omniscient narrator—but tells the story from the vantage point of only one character. The narrator can enter the mind of this chosen character but cannot tell what any other characters are thinking except by observation. This narrator also can go only where the chosen character goes. For example, "In the Shadow of War" by Ben Okri (Collection 12) is told entirely from the point of view of Omovo, the main character. We experience the stupifying summer heat, the mysteriousness of the veiled woman, and the horror of the gruesome river scene through Omovo's eyes alone.

In the **omniscient** (or **"all-knowing"**) **point of view,** the person telling the story knows everything that's going on in the story. This omniscient narrator is outside the story, a godlike observer who can tell us what all the characters are thinking and feeling, as well as what is happening anywhere in the story. For example, in "The Rocking-Horse Winner" by D. H. Lawrence (Collection 13), the narrator enters into the thoughts and secrets of every character, revealing both the "hard little place" in the mother's heart and Paul's determination to "compel her attention" by being lucky.

See pages 646, 970, 990, 993, 1023.
See also Narrator, Stream of Consciousness.

PROTAGONIST The main character in fiction, drama, or narrative poetry. The protagonist is the character we focus our attention on—the person whose conflict sets the plot in motion. (The character or force that blocks the protagonist is called the **antagonist.**) In *Beowulf* (Collection 1), the title character is the protagonist and the monster Grendel his antagonist. Most protagonists are **rounded, dynamic** characters who change in some important way by the end of the story. Whatever the protagonist's weaknesses, we still usually identify with his or her conflict and care about how it is resolved.

PUN A play on the multiple meanings of a word or on two words that sound alike but have different

meanings. Many jokes and riddles are based on puns. ("Why was Cleopatra so negative? Answer: Because she was the queen of denial.") Shakespeare was one of the greatest punsters of all time. Some of his puns are humorous, but others are more serious and subtle wordplays. A sinister pun occurs in Act II, Scene 2, of *Macbeth* (Collection 4), after Macbeth has murdered Duncan:

I'll gild the faces of the grooms withal,
For it must seem their guilt.

Here, Lady Macbeth plays on the words *gild* (to coat something with gold leaf) and *guilt.*

See page 1037.

QUATRAIN **A four-line stanza or poem or a group of four lines unified by a rhyme scheme.** The quatrain is the most common verse unit in English poetry. This quatrain from Alfred, Lord Tennyson's *In Memoriam A.H.H.* (Collection 10) has the rhyme scheme *abba* (sometimes called the envelope stanza):

Thy voice is on the rolling air;
I hear thee where the waters run;
Thou standest in the rising sun,
And in the setting thou art fair.

See pages 96, 220.

REALISM **In literature and art, the attempt to depict people and things as they really are, without idealization.** Realism as a movement developed during the mid–nineteenth century as a reaction against Romanticism. Realist writers believed that fiction should truthfully depict the harsh, gritty reality of everyday life without beautifying, sentimentalizing, or romanticizing it. The Norwegian playwright Henrik Ibsen was among the first to introduce realism to the stage. The English novelists Charles Dickens, George Eliot, Thomas Hardy, and Joseph Conrad are all considered realists.

See pages 799, 1068.
See also Romanticism.

REFRAIN **A repeated word, phrase, line, or group of lines.** While refrains are most common in poetry and songs, they are sometimes used in prose, particularly speeches. Refrains are used to create rhythm, build suspense, or emphasize important words or ideas.

See pages 90, 96.

RESOLUTION *See* Plot.

RHYME **The repetition of accented vowel sounds and all sounds following them in words that are close together in a poem.** *Park* and *bark* rhyme, as do *sorrow* and *borrow.* The most common type of rhyme, **end rhyme,** occurs at the ends of lines. **Internal rhyme** occurs within lines. Both types are used throughout *The Rime of the Ancient Mariner* by Samuel Taylor Coleridge (Collection 8), contributing to the poem's bouncy, songlike rhythm:

The fair breeze blew, the white foam flew,
The furrow followed free;
We were the first that ever burst
Into that silent sea.

When words sound similar but do not rhyme exactly, they are called **approximate rhymes** (or **half rhymes, slant rhymes,** or **imperfect rhymes**). In the following stanza, from W. H. Auden's "Five Songs," *began/gun* and *flush/flash* rhyme by means of **consonance,** while *began/flash* and *flush/gun* rhyme (very loosely) by means of **assonance:**

That night when joy began
Our narrowest veins to flush,
We waited for the flash
Of morning's leveled gun.

The pattern of rhymed lines in a poem is called its **rhyme scheme.** A rhyme scheme is indicated by giving each new rhyme a new letter of the alphabet. For example, the rhyme scheme of Coleridge's lines is *abcb.* There are two interlocking rhyme schemes in Auden's stanza. The one based on consonance is *abba;* the one based on assonance is *abab.*

See pages 96, 149, 221, 683, 807, 840, 930.

RHYTHM **The alternation of stressed and unstressed syllables in language.** Rhythm occurs naturally in all forms of spoken and written language. The most obvious kind of rhythm is produced by **meter,** the regular pattern of stressed and unstressed syllables found in some poetry. But writers can also create less structured rhythms by using rhyme, repetition, pauses, and variations in line length and by balancing long and short words or phrases. (Poetry that is written without any regular meter or rhyme scheme is called **free verse.**) The rhythm of the following lines, from Gerard Manley Hopkins's "Pied Beauty" (Collection 10), reinforces their meaning. The words themselves seem dappled, as if a painter's brush has stippled them onto the page:

All things counter, original, spare, strange;
Whatever is fickle, freckled (who knows how?)
With swift, slow; sweet, sour; adazzle, dim

See pages 90, 712, 1050.
See also Free Verse, Meter.

RISING ACTION See Climax.

ROMANCE **Historically, a medieval verse narrative chronicling the adventures of a brave knight or other hero who must undertake a quest and overcome great danger for love of a noble lady or high ideal.** Such a heroic character is bound by the code of **chivalry,** which emphasizes loyalty to his lord and ready service to the oppressed. He also must adhere to the philosophy of **courtly love,** an idealized view of the relationship between the sexes in which a knight performs brave deeds to win the approval of his lady.

Today, the term *romance* has come to mean any story that presents a world that is happier, more exciting, or more heroic than the real world. Characters in romances "live happily ever after" in a world where good always triumphs over evil. Many of today's most popular novels, movies, TV shows, and even cartoons are essentially romances. *Sir Gawain and the Green Knight,* Sir Thomas Malory's *Le Morte Darthur* (both

in Collection 2), and Edmund Spenser's *The Faerie Queene* (Collection 3) are famous English romances.

See pages 82, 158, 167, 826.

ROMANTICISM **A literary, artistic, and philosophical movement that developed during the late eighteenth and early nineteenth centuries as a reaction against neoclassicism.** While classicism and neoclassicism emphasize reason, order, harmony, and restraint, Romanticism emphasizes emotion, imagination, intuition, freedom, personal experience, the beauty of nature, the primitive, the exotic, and even the grotesque. However, many critics feel that the traditional opposition between Romanticism and classicism is all too often forced and exaggerated.

In English literature, William Blake, Samuel Taylor Coleridge, William Wordsworth, Percy Bysshe Shelley, John Keats, Lord Byron (all in Collection 8 or 9), Mary Wollstonecraft Shelley, and Sir Walter Scott are the leading Romantic writers.

See pages 630, 635, 672.

RUN-ON LINE **A line of poetry that does not contain a pause or conclusion at the end, but rather continues on to the next line.** Run-on lines force the reader on to the next line. Only with the next line do they form a grammatical unit and thus make complete sense. Such lines are said to exhibit **enjambment** (French for "striding over"). The following lines from Margaret Atwood's "Mushrooms" (Collection 13) are run-on lines:

Here is the handful
of shadow I have brought back to you:
this decay, this hope, this mouthful of dirt, this poetry.

See page 662.
See also End-stopped Line.

SARCASM **A kind of particularly cutting irony, in which praise is used tauntingly to indicate its opposite in meaning.** The speaker's tone of voice can also be an important clue in understanding this kind of irony. When a mud-soaked, windblown friend arrives for dinner, one might say sarcastically, "Why, don't you look lovely!"

See pages 501, 991.

SATIRE **A kind of writing that ridicules human weakness, vice, or folly in order to bring about social reform.** Satires often try to persuade the reader to do or believe something by showing the opposite view as absurd or—even more forcefully—vicious and inhumane. Among the most brilliant and scathing satirists in English literature are Geoffrey Chaucer, Alexander Pope, John Dryden, Jonathan Swift, Jane Austen, George Bernard Shaw, and Evelyn Waugh.

See pages 481, 495, 500, 537, 714.

SCANSION See Meter.

SESTET **A six-line stanza or poem or the last six lines of an Italian, or Petrarchan, sonnet.** The usual rhyme scheme of the sestet in an Italian sonnet is *cdecde* or *cdcdcd.* It follows an eight-line **octave** with the rhyme scheme *abbaabba.*

See pages 220, 838.

SETTING **The time and place of a story or play.** Usually the setting is established early in a story. It may be presented immediately through descriptive details, as in Anita Desai's "Games at Twilight" (Collection 14), or it may be revealed more gradually, as in Rudyard Kipling's "The Mark of the Beast" (Collection 11). Setting often contributes greatly to a story's emotional effect. The wild heath at the opening of Shakespeare's *Macbeth* (Collection 4) produces an atmosphere of horror, while the green valley in William Wordsworth's "Tintern Abbey" (Collection 8) creates a contemplative calm. Setting may also play a role in a story's conflict, as the fortresslike suburban houses do in Nadine Gordimer's "Once upon a Time" (Collection 15). Two of the most important functions of setting are to reveal character and to suggest a theme, as the setting of blitzed London does in Graham Greene's "The Destructors" (Collection 12).

See pages 606, 675, 948, 990, 1042.
See also Atmosphere.

SHORT STORY **A brief work of fiction.** The short story generally has a simpler plot than a **novel** and often reveals character through significant moments, or **epiphanies,** rather than through the accretion of many incidents or detailed descriptions.

See page 1068.

SIMILE **A figure of speech that makes a comparison between two seemingly unlike things by using a connective word such as *like, as, than,* or *resembles.*** Here is a simile from William Wordsworth's "It Is a Beauteous Evening, Calm and Free" that makes a connection between two sound images:

The holy time is quiet as a Nun
Breathless with adoration. . . .

An **epic simile,** also called a **Homeric simile,** is an extended simile in which many parallels are made between two dissimilar things.

See pages 247, 449, 851, 1117.
See also Figure of Speech, Metaphor.

SOLILOQUY **A long speech in which a character who is usually alone onstage expresses his or her private thoughts or feelings.** The soliloquy is an old dramatic convention that was particularly popular in Shakespeare's day. Perhaps the most famous soliloquy is the "To be or not to be" speech in Shakespeare's play *Hamlet.* Another major soliloquy occurs in Act V, Scene 5, of *Macbeth* (Collection 4), when Macbeth bewails his wife's death in the celebrated "Tomorrow, and tomorrow, and tomorrow" speech.

See page 383.

SONNET **A fourteen-line lyric poem, usually written in iambic pentameter, that has one of several rhyme schemes.** There are two major types of sonnets. The oldest sonnet form is the **Italian sonnet,** also called the **Petrarchan sonnet** (after the fourteenth-century Italian poet Petrarch, who popularized the form). The Petrarchan sonnet is divided into two parts: an eight-line **octave** with the rhyme scheme *abbaabba* and a six-line **sestet** with the rhyme scheme *cdecde* or *cdcdcd.* The octave usually presents

a problem, poses a question, or expresses an idea, which the sestet, or **turn,** then resolves, answers, or drives home. John Donne's sonnets (Collection 3) and John Keats's "On First Looking into Chapman's Homer" (Collection 9) are written in the Italian form.

The other major sonnet form, which was widely used by Shakespeare, is called the **Shakespearean sonnet,** or the **English sonnet** (Collection 3). It has three four-line units, or **quatrains,** followed by a concluding two-line unit, or **couplet.** The organization of thought in the Shakespearean sonnet usually corresponds to this structure. The three quatrains often express related ideas or examples, while the couplet sums up the poet's conclusion or message. The most common rhyme scheme for the Shakespearean sonnet is *abab cdcd efef gg.*

A third type of sonnet, the **Spenserian sonnet,** was developed by Edmund Spenser (Collection 3). Like the Shakespearean sonnet, the Spenserian sonnet is divided into three quatrains and a couplet, but it uses a rhyme scheme that links the quatrains: *abab bcbc cdcd ee.*

A group of sonnets on a related theme is called a **sonnet sequence** or a **sonnet cycle.**

See pages 219, 223, 268, 672, 746, 838.

SPEAKER **The imaginary voice, or persona, assumed by the author of a poem.** This voice is often not identified immediately or directly. Rather, the reader gradually comes to understand that a unique voice is speaking and that this speaker's characteristics must be interpreted as they are revealed. This process is an especially important part of reading a **lyric poem.**

See pages 264, 635, 759, 763, 1033.

SPENSERIAN STANZA **A nine-line stanza with the rhyme scheme *ababbcbcc.*** The first eight lines of the stanza are in iambic pentameter, and the ninth line is an **alexandrine**—that is, a line of iambic hexameter. The form was created by Edmund Spenser for his long poem *The Faerie Queene* (Collection 3). Several English Romantic poets have used the Spenserian stanza, including John Keats, Percy Bysshe Shelley, Lord Byron, and Robert Burns (Collections 8 and 9).

See pages 221, 725.

SPRUNG RHYTHM **A term coined by Gerard Manley Hopkins to designate his unconventional use of poetic meter.** Instead of the regular, musical **meter** of most poetry, Hopkins uses sounds that impede smooth reading and echo the sound of Anglo-Saxon poetry, which greatly influenced him. Sprung rhythm is based on the stressed syllables in a line without regard for the number of unstressed syllables; it also makes frequent use of **alliteration** and inverted syntax.

See page 840.

STANZA **A group of consecutive lines in a poem that form a single unit.** A stanza in a poem is something like a paragraph in prose: It often expresses a unit of thought. A stanza may consist of only one line or of any number of lines beyond that. The word *stanza* is Italian for "stopping place" or "place to rest."

See page 220.

STREAM OF CONSCIOUSNESS **A writing style that tries to depict the random flow of thoughts, emotions, memories, and associations rushing through a character's mind.** The term **interior monologue** is often used interchangeably with "stream of consciousness." James Joyce (Collection 13) and Virginia Woolf (Collection 15) were among the first to experiment with the stream-of-consciousness style in their novels.

See page 993.

STYLE **The manner in which writers or speakers say what they wish to say.** An author's style simultaneously expresses an individual's ideas and his or her unique way of expressing them. Style is closely connected to **diction,** or word choice, and, depending on what the author wants to communicate, can be formal or casual, plain or ornate, abstract or concrete, as well as comic, poetic, forceful, journalistic, and so on. Sir Francis Bacon (Collection 5) and Samuel Johnson (Collection 7) are both often cited as exemplars of style.

See pages 457, 578.
See also Diction.

SUSPENSE **The uncertainty or anxiety we feel about what is going to happen next in a story.** Writers often create suspense by dropping hints or clues that something—especially something bad—is going to happen. In "The Demon Lover" by Elizabeth Bowen (Collection 13), we begin to feel suspense when Mrs. Drover receives a mysterious letter that makes her lips "go white"; our anxiety increases sharply when the flashback reveals that the letter writer is her old fiancé; and our suspense reaches a climax when she escapes into a taxi and we discover who the driver is.

See pages 332, 333.

SYMBOL **A person, place, thing, or event that stands both for itself and for something beyond itself.** Many symbols have become widely recognized: A lion is a symbol of power; a dove is a symbol of peace. These established symbols are sometimes called **public symbols.** But writers often invent new, personal symbols, whose meaning is revealed in their work. For example, the old house in Graham Greene's "The Destructors" (Collection 12) is a symbol of civilization and beauty.

See pages 167, 393, 647, 739, 982, 996, 1061.

SYMBOLISM **A literary movement that began in France during the late nineteenth century and advocated the use of highly personal symbols to suggest ideas, emotions, and moods.** The French Symbolists believed that emotions are fleeting, individual, and essentially inexpressible—and that therefore the poet is forced to suggest meaning rather than directly express it. Many twentieth-century writers were influenced by the Symbolists, including T. S. Eliot, William Butler Yeats, James Joyce, Dylan Thomas, and Virginia Woolf (Collections 12, 13, and 15).

SYNAESTHESIA **In literature, a term used for descriptions of one kind of sensation in terms of another.** For example, color may be described as sound (a "loud" yellow), sound as taste (how "sweet" the sound), odor as tangible (a "sharp" smell), and so on. These lines from John Keats's "Ode to a Nightingale" (Collection 9) describe a sip of wine as tasting of color, motion, sound, and heat:

Tasting of Flora and the country green,
Dance, and Provençal song, and sunburnt mirth!

See page 759.

SYNECDOCHE See Metonymy.

TALL TALE **A type of folk literature characterized by humorous exaggeration and outlandish plot details.** Although part of the literature of many countries, it is mainly associated with Mark Twain and the American West.

See page 514.

TERCET **A triplet, or stanza of three lines, in which each line ends with the same rhyme.** It is also either of the two three-line groups forming the sestet of a **sonnet.**

See pages 525, 805.

TERZA RIMA **An interlocking, three-line stanza form with the rhyme scheme *aba bcb cdc ded* and so on.** Terza rima is an Italian verse form originally devised by Dante for *The Divine Comedy* (Collection 4). Among the many English poems that borrowed the form, Shelley's "Ode to the West Wind" (Collection 9) is one of the most famous.

See page 738.

THEME **The central idea or insight of a work of literature.** A theme is not the same as the subject of a work, which can usually be expressed in a word or two: old age, ambition, love. The theme is the idea the writer wishes to convey *about* that subject—the writer's view of the world or revelation about human nature. For example, one theme of James Joyce's "Araby" (Collection 13) might be stated this way: One of the painful aspects of growing up is that some of our dreams turn out to be illusions.

A theme may also be different from a **moral,** which is a lesson or rule about how to live. The theme of "Araby" stated above, for example, would not make sense as a moral.

While some stories, poems, and plays have themes that are directly stated, most themes are **implied.** It is up to the reader to piece together all the clues the writer has provided about the work's total meaning.

See pages 231, 959, 1116, 1147.

TONE **The attitude a writer takes toward the reader, a subject, or a character.** Tone is conveyed through the writer's choice of words and details. For example, Jonathan Swift's *A Modest Proposal* (Collection 6) is satiric in tone, while the tone of "Pied Beauty" by Gerard Manley Hopkins (Collection 10) might be described as awed.

See pages 263, 714, 849, 1096.

TRAGEDY **A play, novel, or other narrative depicting serious and important events, in which the main character comes to an unhappy end.** In a tragedy, the main character is usually dignified, courageous, and often high ranking. This character's downfall may be caused by a **tragic flaw**—an error in judgment or character weakness—or the downfall may result from forces beyond his or her control. The **tragic hero** usually wins some self-knowledge and wisdom, even though he or she suffers defeat, possibly even death. Tragedy is distinct from **comedy,** in which an ordinary character overcomes obstacles to get what he or she wants. *Beowulf* (Collection 1), Shakespeare's *Macbeth* (Collection 4), and John Milton's *Paradise Lost* (Collection 5) are all tragedies.

See pages 300, 591.
See also Comedy.

TURN See Sonnet.

TURNING POINT See Climax.

UNDERSTATEMENT **A figure of speech that consists of saying less than what is really meant or saying something with less force than is appropriate.** Understatement is the opposite of **hyperbole** and is a form of **irony.** You are using understatement if you come in from a torrential downpour and say, "It's a bit wet out there," or if you describe a Great Dane as "not exactly a small dog." Understatement can be used to create a kind of deadpan humor, but it can also function as a sustained ironic tone throughout a work, as in W. H. Auden's "The Unknown Citizen" (Collection 14).

See page 501.
See also Hyperbole, Irony.

VERNACULAR See Dialect.

VILLANELLE **A nineteen-line poem divided into five tercets (three-line stanzas), each with the rhyme scheme *aba,* and a final quatrain with the rhyme scheme *abaa.*** Line 1 is repeated entirely to form lines 6, 12, and 18, while line 3 is repeated as lines 9, 15, and 19. Thus, there are only two rhymes in the poem, and the two lines used as **refrains** (lines 1 and 3) are paired as the final couplet. The villanelle was originally used in French pastoral poetry. Dylan Thomas's "Do Not Go Gentle into That Good Night" (Collection 13) is an example of a modern villanelle.

See page 1040.

WIT **A quality of speech or writing that combines verbal cleverness with keen perception, especially of the incongruous.** The definition of *wit* has undergone dramatic changes over the centuries. In the Middle Ages, it meant "common sense"; in the Renaissance, it meant "intelligence"; and in the seventeenth century, it meant "originality of thought." The modern meaning of *wit* began to develop during the eighteenth century with the formulations of John Dryden (Collection 7) and Alexander Pope (Collection 6). In his *Essay on Criticism,* Pope said:

True wit is Nature to advantage dressed:
What oft was thought, but ne'er so well expressed

Perhaps the best examples of more modern wit can be found in the works of Oscar Wilde and George Bernard Shaw.

See pages 480, 533, 714.

Active Reading Strategies

Use the following reading strategies to help you discover meaning in what you read and relate that meaning to your life.

PREVIEWING AND SETTING A PURPOSE

Previewing the Text Preview a reading assignment or a book to get an overview of its organization. Read the title and any information included about the author. If you are assigned a book, flip through the pages and look at the table of contents, the index, and any illustrations, charts, or diagrams. Note the genre of the text—novel, history, biography, short story, play, or essay—and the difficulty of the vocabulary. Finally, consider what you already know about the subject and what you'd like to find out about it.

Setting a Purpose Before you begin to read, you should establish a clear purpose for reading. Purposes include (1) to be entertained, (2) to find out specific information, (3) to share an experience, (4) to learn about the craft of writing. You may have more than one purpose in mind as you read a particular text. Your purpose can dictate how closely you read and whether you take notes or use other study skills.

Activating Prior Knowledge As you read, you should use your prior knowledge and experiences to look for connections with the text. For example, as you read Orwell's essay "Shooting an Elephant" (page 1139), you might review what you know about colonialism in Burma and its effects on Burma (Myanmar) even up to the present day.

Constructing a KWL Chart To help you keep track of your prior knowledge, your purpose in reading, and your new learning, make a three-column chart and use it before, as, and after you read a work. In the first column, write what you already know (K) about the work. In the middle column, write what you want (W) to know. In the last column, record what you learned (L) as a result of your reading.

K	W	L
What I **know**	What I **want** to know	What I **learned**

READING ACTIVELY

Making and Confirming Predictions For some texts, such as short stories and novels, you should occasionally predict what will happen. To start the process of making predictions, ask yourself questions like *Where will the plot lead? How will the character act when he begins to lose his struggle?* Your answers will be predictions about what you are going to read. For example, in the first paragraph of D. H. Lawrence's "The Rocking Horse Winner" (page 997), the narrator tells you that a woman is incapable of feeling love. At once you should begin to ask questions and make predictions about what else you will learn about this character and what will become of her and, possibly, her children.

Making Inferences An **inference** is an educated guess. Inferences about a literary work are based on clues in the text and on your own knowledge. For instance, the title of Elizabeth Bowen's story "The Demon Lover" (page 1019) strongly suggests that something preternatural will happen to the main character. Ben Okri's title "In the Shadow of War" (page 971) suggests that the story will have to do with the violence of war.

Conclusions and generalizations are types of inferences. A **conclusion** is a judgment based on evidence in a text. You will probably conclude from the speaker's words in Wilfred Owen's "Dulce et Decorum Est" (page 929) that he is profoundly disillusioned by the patriotic slogans that mask the horror of war. A **generalization** is a broad statement based on specific examples. You might generalize from the selections in the collection of Anglo-Saxon literature that an elegiac strain is characteristic of the imaginative expressions of that period.

Noting Organization As you read, think about the way the writer presents ideas, people, and events. **Sequential,** or **chronological, order** arranges the events in a historical account or a story in the order in which they occur. You may find words such as *first, then, next, while,* and *finally.* Some great literary works, such as Virginia Woolf's novel *Mrs. Dalloway,* present events in **nonsequential order,** thereby "fragmenting" time. **Spatial order** tells you where one person or thing is in relation to another. Factual information is usually presented in **order of importance,** either from most to least important or from least to most important. **Logical order,** a

type of sequential order, organizes ideas in terms of meaning, so that one idea leads directly to the next. In an essay, an argument is best made in logical order, rather than scattering ideas so that a point in paragraph six is explained in paragraph two.

DEALING WITH DIFFICULT TEXTS

When you're having difficulty understanding a text, try one or more of these strategies:

1. **Rereading.** Stop reading and go back to the last point at which you had a grasp on the text. Reread from there.
2. **Reading on.** Keep reading to see whether context clues and/or new information clarify the text.
3. **Pausing to reflect.** Stop and think about what you've read so far. Perhaps construct a graphic organizer.
4. **Asking questions.** Ask *who, what, where, when, why,* and *how* questions about the text.
5. **Using resources.** Use a dictionary or other reference works to clarify the meaning of a passage.

MAKING SURE YOU UNDERSTAND A TEXT

Paraphrasing, outlining, and summarizing are useful strategies to make sure you understand a text. When you **paraphrase,** you restate an entire work or passage in your own words. Paraphrasing helps you to clarify anything that may have been fuzzy as you read. Here is a paraphrase of lines 1–4 of Shakespeare's Sonnet 116 (page 228):

> I won't be made to find impediments, or blocks, to the union of two minds that are true to each other. Love doesn't change even when other things are changing. Love doesn't adjust or alter itself even when other things are being altered or changed.

A work of nonfiction, such as Jonathan Swift's "A Modest Proposal" (page 502), can be **outlined** by showing its **main ideas** and **supporting details,** as below:

I. Main idea
  A. Supporting detail
    1. Supporting detail
    2. Supporting detail
  B. Supporting detail
[Etc.]

A **summary** is a concise restatement of the principal ideas and details of a text (usually prose). You can do a summary in different ways—for example, in paragraph form or in a story map like the following:

Story Map

Basic situation
Setting
Main character
His or her problem
Main events or complications
Climax
Resolution

STUDY SKILLS

USING A DICTIONARY

Use a dictionary to find the precise meaning (**denotation**) and usage of words. The elements of a typical entry are explained below.

1. **Entry word.** The entry word shows how the word is spelled (capitalizing the first letter if required) and divided into syllables.
2. **Pronunciation.** Phonetic symbols, sometimes with diacritical marks above them, show how to pronounce the entry word. Accent marks indicate which syllable is stressed. A key to symbols usually appears on every other page.
3. **Part-of-speech label.** This label classifies the entry word as noun, adjective, adverb, and so forth. When a word can be used as more than one part of speech, definitions are grouped by part of speech. The sample entry that follows shows four definitions for *derive* as a transitive verb (***vt.***) and one as an intransitive verb (***vi.***).
4. **Other forms.** Some dictionaries show the spellings of plural forms of nouns, principal parts of verbs (like ***-rived'*** and ***-riv'ing*** in the sample), and comparative and superlative forms of adjectives and adverbs.
5. **Word origin.** A word's **etymology** (et'ə·mäl'ə·jē) shows its linguistic history. According to the sample entry, the word *derive* comes from the Middle English word *deriven,* which in turn comes from the Old French word

deriver, which itself comes from the Latin word *derivare,* meaning "to divert." *Derivare* was created by adding the prefix *de-,* meaning "from," to the word *rivus,* meaning "stream." The sample entry shows that additional information on etymology appears in the entry for *rival.*

6. **Definitions.** If a word has more than one meaning, the meanings are numbered or lettered.
7. **Special-usage labels.** These labels identify special meanings or special uses of the word. Here, *Chem.* indicates that the fourth definition is a meaning of *derive* used in chemistry.
8. **Synonyms and antonyms. Synonyms** (words similar in meaning) and **antonyms** (words opposite in meaning) may appear at the end of an entry. Here, ***—SYN.*** RISE tells you that synonyms for *derive* are given in the entry for *rise.*
9. **Related word forms.** Different forms of the entry word are listed. Usually these are created by the addition of suffixes, such as in *derivable.*

Sample Dictionary Entry

(1) (2) (3) (4) (5)

de·rive (di rīv') **vt.** **-rived', -riv'ing** [ME *deriven* < OFr *deriver* < L *derivare,* to divert, orig., to turn a stream from its channel < *de-,* from + *rivus,* a stream: see RIVAL] (6) **1** to get or receive (something) *from* a source **2** to get by reasoning; deduce or infer **3** to trace from or to a source; show the derivation of **4** *Chem.* (7) to obtain or produce (a compound) from another compound by replacing one element with one or more other elements (8) ***—vi.*** to come *(from);* be derived; originate ***—SYN.*** RISE **—de·riv'a|ble** ***adj.*** **—de·riv'|er** ***n.*** (9)

Webster's New World Dictionary of American English, Third College Edition.

USING A THESAURUS

A **thesaurus** is a collection of synonyms. You use a thesaurus to find a word with a specific meaning. There are two basic formats for a thesaurus. The first, developed by Peter Mark Roget (1779–1869), groups words in categories. To use Roget's format, follow these steps:

- In the index, look up the word that expresses the general meaning of the word you are looking for. You may be looking for a synonym of the verb *thin,* for example. Under *thin,* you find the words *dilute, rarefy,* and *weed.*
- Choose the subentry closest to the meaning you have in mind. In this case, suppose you choose *dilute.*
- Note the number that follows the subentry, and find it in the body of the text. There, you will find synonyms of *dilute.*

The second kind of thesaurus presents words in alphabetical order, as in a dictionary:

Sample Thesaurus Entry

commencement, *n.* **1.** [A beginning] *—Syn.* genesis, start, initiation; see **origin** 1, 2. [Graduation ceremony] *—Syn.* convocation, graduation, commencement exercises, services; see **celebration** 1, 2, **ceremony** 2, **graduation.**

©1997 Webster's New World Thesaurus, Third Edition.

USING STUDY GUIDES

A **study guide** works as a reader's companion by providing help in understanding a text. It can clarify points and stimulate thinking. Study guides often include a biography of the author, critical reaction to the work, and analyses of characters, themes, and other literary elements. Many study guides also include suggestions for further reading and viewing.

A study guide usually examines a text in sections. A play by Oscar Wilde, for instance, might be examined scene by scene or act by act. Besides giving a summary of the section, a study guide might include commentary, helpful information, and questions to consider.

RECOGNIZING LOGICAL FALLACIES

When you are reading a piece of writing that aims to persuade you to share an opinion or adopt a course of action, you should be alert to the ways in which the writer argues his or her points. Writers should argue their points logically. Sometimes, however, they use incorrect or fallacious reasoning. Be on the lookout for **fallacies.** They appear at first glance to be based on sound reasoning but in fact contain mistakes of logic. Here are six common fallacies; there are many more.

1. **Circular reasoning or "begging the question."** The writer restates a point just made as if it were a new conclusion. In the sentence *Alison is lazy because she doesn't like to work,* the clause after *because* just restates the opening clause and doesn't tell you why Alison is lazy. The sentence *Alison is lazy because she enjoys sitting around and daydreaming* gives you a reason for Alison's laziness.
2. **Arguing ad hominem ("to the person").** The writer attacks the person or people presenting the issue rather than dealing logically with the issue itself. In the sentence *People who oppose a lower speed limit don't care about children,* "people" who oppose lower speed limits are attacked—but reasons for lowering the speed limit are not given.
3. **Hasty generalization.** The writer draws a conclusion from insufficient evidence or from exceptional or biased evidence. In the sentence *Today's films are loaded with foul language,* the writer incorrectly categorizes all films, failing

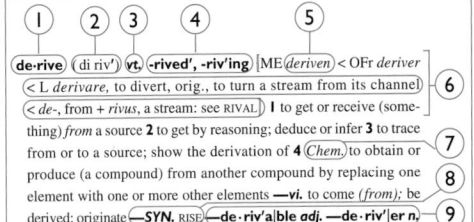

to account for the many films that have little or no foul language.

4. **Either-or fallacy** or **false dichotomy.** The writer presents only two alternatives when there are more than two. In the sentence *We have just two choices—either go to the ballgame or sit around the house,* the writer fails to mention additional choices, like seeing a movie.
5. **False analogy.** The writer assumes that because two things are alike in some ways, they must be alike in other ways. Notice the false analogy in the sentence *Since player A and player B are the same height and fast runners, they must have similar batting averages.* The writer ignores other important reasons for a particular batting average.
6. **False cause.** This fallacy is also known as *post hoc, ergo propter hoc,* meaning "after this, therefore because of this." In this fallacy, the writer argues that because *A* preceded *B, A* caused *B.* For example, *Right after Jim joined the Cardinals as a bench warmer, the team began a ten-game winning streak.* The writer makes a false connection between a winning streak and a player who rarely plays.

(For more on fallacies, see page 614).

Research Strategies

When you're looking for information, where should you begin? You might first create a research plan that outlines the topics you want to explore or the questions you want to answer. Then you can begin your search for print and nonprint resources that might be relevant to your plan. When doing research, do not rely solely on one source; instead, consult as many reliable sources as possible. The following research strategies can help you find resources in a library or media center or on a computer linked to the Internet.

USING A LIBRARY OR MEDIA CENTER

Library Catalogs

A library's main resources usually are printed volumes stored on shelves. More and more often, however, libraries (or, as they are sometimes called, media centers) feature holdings stored in electronic form and accessed from a computer terminal or other electronic device. To find information in a library, start by looking in the catalog. Most libraries record their holdings in an **on-line,** or **computer, catalog.**

On-line catalogs vary from library to library. With some, you begin by searching for resources by **title, author,** or **subject.** With others, you simply enter **key words** related to the subject you're researching. With either system, when you enter the relevant information in response to on-screen prompts, a new screen will display a list of materials or subject headings related to your request. When you find an item you want to examine, write down the title, author, and **call number,** the code of numbers and letters that shows you where in the library the item is located.

Some libraries still use **card catalogs.** A card catalog is a collection of index cards containing key information about each library holding. The cards are arranged in alphabetical order by surname of author, by the first word of title (omitting initial articles), and—for works of nonfiction—by subject.

Other Library Resources

Every library has a **reference section** containing materials you can use only in the library. Reference works include encyclopedias; yearbooks; dictionaries; directories; almanacs; atlases; and **indices,** extensive alphabetical lists (often of books or periodicals). *Books in Print* is a useful index, as is *The Reader's Catalog.* Reference works can appear in electronic or print format. Because many reference books are updated periodically, look for the most recent edition.

Electronic Databases These are large collections of information that you access at a computer terminal. Among the types of information stored on databases are statistics, biographical data, museum holdings, indices, and back issues of magazines.

There are two basic kinds of electronic databases. An **on-line database** is accessed at a computer terminal that is connected to a distant server computer that contains the database. Many computers can access the database at the same time. A **portable database** is available on magnetic tape, disk, CD-ROM, or other electronic medium not connected to a server computer. As a rule, only one person at a time can access the database.

A **CD-ROM** (compact disc–read-only memory) is a portable database stored on a disk that you access via a computer's CD-ROM drive. CD-ROMs can store not only text but also sound, images, and video clips. If you were to look up Thomas Hardy in a CD-ROM encyclopedia, you might find a clip from a film version of one of his novels.

Periodicals Most libraries hold a variety of periodicals as well as indices that help you locate information in them. To

find up-to-date magazine or newspaper articles on a topic, look in an electronic index such as *InfoTrac, ProQuest,* or *EBSCO*. Some electronic indices provide summaries, or **abstracts,** of articles. Other databases allow you to access the entire text of articles, which you can read on screen or print out. The *Readers' Guide to Periodical Literature* is an excellent index to hundreds of periodicals. Back issues of periodicals may be stored in print form or on **microfilm** (a reel of film), **microfiche** (a sheet of film), CD-ROM, or other information storage-and-retrieval device.

Audiovisual Resources Most libraries hold recordings of actors or authors reading books, videotapes of movies, and CDs and DVDs. These resources are useful when preparing a multimedia project.

USING THE INTERNET

The **Internet,** or **Net,** is a worldwide electronic network that connects millions of personal computers to other personal computers and to server computers containing vast amounts of data, words, and images. On the Net you can find information on almost any topic by accessing libraries, museums, electronic newspapers, government agencies, and many other sources. **E-zines** (often called **zines**) and **e-journals** are periodicals found only on-line. You gain access to the Net via Internet service providers (ISPs). The following are some ways in which the Internet can be used for research.

E-Mail

E-mail is an electronic message sent over a computer network. On the Internet you can use e-mail to contact institutions, businesses, and individuals. This is a quick and inexpensive method of consulting experts (located 1 mile or 10,000 miles away) on a topic you're researching. You can also use e-mail to exchange messages with students around the world.

Electronic Forums

Internet forums, or **newsgroups,** enable you to discuss and debate various subjects. You can post a question in a forum and receive responses from other knowledgeable people. Be careful, however: Responses may be incorrect.

The World Wide Web

The easiest way to conduct Internet research is on the World Wide Web (WWW). On the Web, information is provided on colorful, easy-to-access files called **Web pages.** A Web page may include text, images, sounds, and even video clips.

Using a Web Browser You can view Web pages with a **Web browser,** such as Netscape's *Navigator* or Microsoft's *Internet Explorer.* Every page on the Web has its own address, called a **URL,** or Uniform Resource Locator. If you know the URL of a Web page you want to access, enter it in the *location* field of your browser. See the accompanying illustration.

Web pages are connected by **hyperlinks,** which enable you to reach relevant data quickly by jumping from one page to another. These links are indicated by underlined or colored words or by images on your computer screen. When you click on hyperlink words or images, you are automatically transferred to another Web page.

Using a Web Directory and a Search Engine With many millions of linked Web pages, how do you find the information you want? If you're looking for general information on a topic, go to a **Web directory** (such as Yahoo), a list of topics and subtopics created to help you find an appropriate Web site. A directory is like a book's index. Begin with a broad category, such as <u>Literature.</u> Then, work your way down through the subtopics, from perhaps <u>English: Literature</u> to <u>Renaissance Literature: Authors</u> until you find a Web page that looks promising, such as one on Francis Bacon.

Sample Web-Browser Screen (1998)

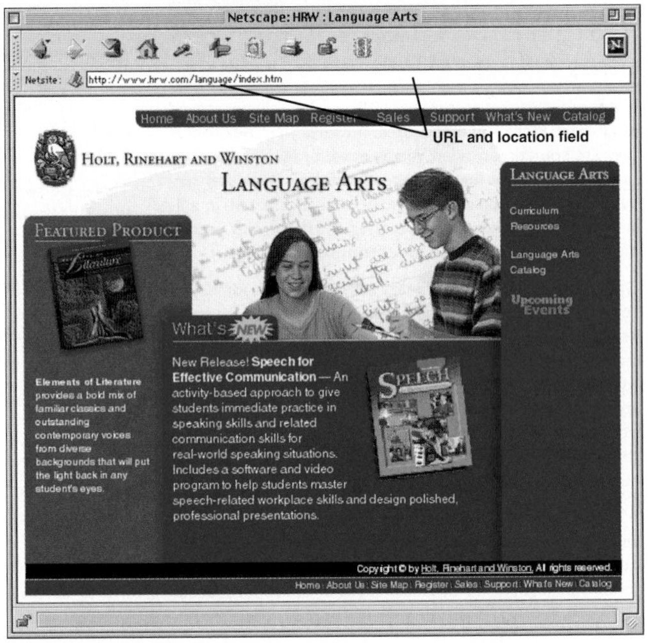

COMMON SEARCH OPERATORS AND WHAT THEY DO	
AND	Demands that both terms appear on the page; narrows search
+	Demands that both terms appear on the page; narrows search
OR	Yields pages that contain either term; widens search
NOT	Excludes a word from consideration; narrows search
–	Excludes a word from consideration; narrows search
NEAR	Demands that two words be in proximity; narrows search
ADJ	Demands that two words be in proximity; narrows search
" "	Demands the exact phrase; narrows search

If you are looking for more specific information, try using a **search engine,** an incredible software tool that indexes millions of Web sites. Some popular search engines are Lycos, Alta Vista, and Excite. To use a search engine, enter a **search term,** which is one or more keywords. The search engine will then list Web pages that contain your search term along with the first few lines of each page. A search term like the name *Bacon* can produce thousands of results, or **hits,** including Web pages dealing with the actor Kevin Bacon or smoked meats. If you're looking for information on the writer Francis Bacon, most hits will be irrelevant. It's important, therefore, to refine, or tailor, your search.

Refining a Keyword Search Searches using more than one keyword generally provide more focused results. Most search engines allow you to use **search operators** to create a string of keywords. Common search operators include the capitalized terms AND, OR, NOT, ADJ (adjacent), and NEAR. Use these operators to focus your search. Here's how the operators work. Let's assume, for example, that you're looking for material on Sir Francis Bacon and his treatise *The New Atlantis.* You might use this search term:

Bacon ADJ Francis AND Atlantis

This search term yields pages that contain the names *Francis, Bacon,* and *Atlantis* but most likely nothing about movies or smoked meats. Now suppose you want to learn more about Renaissance literature. If your first search turns up words about plays, you can expand your search by using OR:

plays OR poems

Doing a Phrase Search Exact phrases often produce better results than single words or strings of keywords. If you're looking for information on Renaissance poetry, for example, a search made with the unlinked keywords *Renaissance* and *poetry* will yield thousands of pages about the Renaissance and about poetry in general. On the other hand, a search using the exact phrase "Renaissance poetry"—signaled by quotation marks—will yield only pages containing that phrase.

Knowing Your Search Engine Not all search engines operate in the same way. Some have rules about using uppercase and lowercase letters. Some require a plus sign or minus sign between keywords, rather than the operator AND or NOT. Some require that you enter exact phrases within quotation marks. Some provide a list of options that enable you to search by exact phrases, individual words, and so on. Because the rules governing search engines differ, read the online Help information before you begin a search.

Evaluating the Credibility of Sources

Before you begin taking notes from any source—print or electronic or an interviewee—be sure your source provides information that is current, accurate, and free of strong bias. Evaluate both primary and secondary sources. **Primary sources,** or firsthand accounts, include letters, autobiographies, diaries, historical documents, and interviews. **Secondary sources,** which are derived from primary sources, include encyclopedias, documentary films, biographies, and

historical books. To evaluate the usefulness of a source, use this 4R test.

1. **Relevant.** The source must have information *directly* related to your topic. To find out if a book is relevant, you can check its table of contents and index. For some books and for articles, skimming can help. *Book Review Digest* offers, for selected titles, useful summaries and review excerpts; videotapes and audiotapes sometimes provide written summaries of their content; and periodical indices may include summaries of articles.
2. **Reliable.** The source must be accurate. A periodical whose reputation depends on accuracy, such as *Smithsonian* or *National Geographic,* or a well-regarded authority, such as a scholar, generally can be counted on to fact-check rigorously before publication. If in doubt about the reliability of a source, consult an expert, such as a teacher or librarian.
3. **Recent.** For most topics, use sources that are as current as possible. Ongoing research findings can change perceptions, generalizations, and opinions. For example, the discovery of a poet's childhood illness can lead to a new interpretation of her or his poems about childhood. Often, long-ago political events are reinterpreted in light of newly discovered information.
4. **Representative.** If there are opposing viewpoints on your topic, you should consult sources that provide a variety of interpretations. If one interpretation is strongly favored, you should also consult another source with a different slant.

TAKING NOTES AND DOCUMENTING SOURCES

If you use another person's words or ideas without giving credit, you are **plagiarizing,** which is a serious offense. Avoid plagiarizing by acknowledging in your work the source of each quotation, paraphrase, statistic, figure, and idea that you found through research. Careful documentation starts with accurate source cards and notes.

Preparing Source Cards

As you gather information, you can save time and ensure accurate documentation by preparing source cards in the format needed for your report's **sources cited** list (see page 1213). Put each source on a 3-inch × 5-inch card, or record it in a computer file. Follow these guidelines:

1. **Assign each source a different number.** When taking notes, it will save time to write the number rather than the author and title. Place the number at the top right of the card or computer entry.
2. **Record full publication data.** Data include subtitles, translators, and volume and edition numbers. Use a shortened form of the publisher's name, deleting initial articles and the type of business organization.
3. **Note the call number or location.** This information will help you reaccess the source quickly.

Sample Source Card

3

Goodrich, Norma Lovve. Merlin.
New York: Harper, 1988.

Westbank Community Library

Taking Notes

After evaluating your sources and preparing source cards, you are ready to read carefully and take notes. Use the following guidelines to prepare note cards that will be easy to use when writing your paper.

GUIDELINES FOR TAKING NOTES

1. Use a 4-inch × 6-inch note card, a half sheet of paper, or a separate computer file. Never put notes from more than one source on the same card or sheet of paper or in the same electronic file.
2. In the upper right, write the number you have assigned to the source.
3. In the upper left, use a word or phrase to identify the topic or main idea.
4. In the lower right, note the page numbers from which the information is taken.
5. Reread the note to be sure it is accurate.

Your notes may be direct quotations, summaries, or paraphrases. A **direct quotation** contains the author's exact words. When quoting directly, copy the statement word for word—including punctuation, capitalization, and spelling—and enclose the passage in quotation marks. A **summary** condenses the author's ideas and facts in your own words. A **paraphrase** restates information in your own words. To summarize or paraphrase, use lists and phrases instead of complete sentences.

Using Quotations

Relevant, interesting quotations add authority and punch to your research paper. The following chart describes several ways to use quotations effectively.

GUIDELINES FOR USING QUOTATIONS

- **Quote a whole sentence, introducing it in your own words.**

  EXAMPLE Woolf commented on Victorian conversation: "Nobody ever broke the convention. If you listened, as I did, it was like watching a game." (129).

- **Quote part of a sentence within a sentence of your own.**

  EXAMPLE Woolf wrote that the Victorian conversational style "allows one to say a great many things which would be inaudible if one marched straight up and spoke out" (129).

- **Quote just one or a few words within a sentence of your own.**

  EXAMPLE The essay draws attention to the lack of information on women writers and "call[s] for a history of women" (15).

- **Use an ellipsis (. . .) to indicate omissions from quotations.** Sometimes you need only a part of a quotation to make your point. Insert an ellipsis where words have been deleted.

  EXAMPLE Judith Shakespeare has a "poet's heart . . . caught and tangled in a woman's body" (50).

- **Set off longer quotations as extract blocks.** If a quotation will be more than four typed lines, start a new line and indent the entire quotation ten spaces from the left. Double-space, and do not use quotation marks.

Formatting Electronic-Source Citations

Writing electronic-source citations for a list of sources cited can be difficult. On-line sources often change, and many do not provide all the information required. For instance, many Web pages don't identify an author. In such cases, include in your citation whatever relevant information is available.

The format for citing electronic sources depends on (1) whether the source is on-line or portable and (2) whether the source has an identical print version or stands alone.

Listed below are the elements required for the citation of various kinds of electronic sources—in the order in which they should appear. Most elements likely to be included are listed, but many actual citations will not include all possible elements. (Note: If a URL runs onto a second line, divide the address immediately *after* a slash mark or *before* a dot. Never use a hyphen to divide a URL.)

Source from a Computer Network, such as the World Wide Web, with an Identical Print Version

- author's last name, then first name
- title of poem, short story, essay, document, or similar short work, set off by quotation marks
- title of book or periodical, underlined
- name of editor of book, preceded by the abbreviation *Ed.*
- publication data for print version
- title of scholarly project, database, or professional or personal site, underlined; or, for a professional or personal site with no title, a description such as *Home page*
- volume or issue number
- number range, or total number, of any numbered pages or paragraphs
- date of electronic publication or latest revision
- name of any sponsoring institution
- date you accessed the information
- full URL, in angle brackets

EXAMPLE Housman, A. E. A Shropshire Lad. London: K. Paul, Trench, Truebner, 1986. Project Bartleby. Jan. 1996. Columbia University. 22 Oct. 1999 <http://www.cc.columbia.edu/acis/bartleby/housman>.

Source from a Computer Network, such as the World Wide Web, with No Print Version

- author's last name, then first name
- title of poem, short story, essay, document, or similar short work, set off by quotation marks
- title of scholarly project, database, periodical, or professional or personal site, underlined; or, for a professional or personal site with no title, a description such as *Home page*
- name of editor of complete work or database, preceded by the abbreviation *Ed.*
- publication date or date of last revision
- number range or total number of any numbered sections
- name of any sponsoring organization
- volume, issue, or version number
- date you accessed the information
- the full URL, in angle brackets

EXAMPLE Patterson, Arthur Paul. "A Frankenstein Study." Watershed Online: Resources for a Literary Imagination. 1996. Watershed Online. October 1999. <http://www.watershed.winnipeg.mb.ca/index.html>.

CD-ROM with a Print Version

- author's last name, then first name
- title of document or article, set off by quotation marks
- title of print version, underlined
- publication data for print version
- database title, underlined
- edition, release, or version number
- publication medium (CD-ROM)
- city of publication
- name of publisher of electronic version
- date of electronic publication

EXAMPLE Miller, Arthur. The Crucible. New York: Bantam, 1959. The Crucible. CD-ROM. New York: Penguin, 1996.

CD-ROM with No Print Version

Omit the print information called for above.

EXAMPLE "American Renaissance." The History of American Literature. CD-ROM. Chicago: CLEARVUE/eav, 1995.

Citing Sources

Parenthetical Citations A short **parenthetical citation** gives source information in parentheses in the body of the text. It contains just enough information to lead a reader to the correct full entry in the sources cited list. Parenthetical citations include the author's last name and a page number, with these exceptions:

- a nonprint source such as an interview (Use name only.)
- a print source of only one page (Use name only.)
- a sentence that includes the author's name (Use page number only. See the first and fourth bulleted items in Guidelines for Using Quotations, page 1211.)
- an author with more than one entry on your list of sources cited (Add year of publication—for example: Roberts 1992, 65.)

For more information on specific kinds of parenthetical citations, see the chart below or the most recent edition of the Modern Language Association's *MLA Handbook for Writers of Research Papers*.

PARENTHETICAL CITATIONS
Works by One Author Author's last name and page(s): (Goodrich 100)
Works by More Than One Author All authors' last names (or first author and *et al.* if more than three) and page(s): (Radford and Swanton 78)
Multivolume Works Author's last name, volume number, and page(s): (Vinaver 1:81–82)
Works with No Author Listed on Title Page Full title (or a shortened version) and page(s): ("Arthurian Journey" 813)
Literary Works Published in Several Editions Full title and any information that would help readers find the quotation in any edition, such as chapter number or act, scene, and line numbers: (Macbeth II:2:34–39)
Indirect Sources *Qtd. in* ("quoted in") before the source and page(s): (qtd. in Goodrich 100)
More Than One Source in the Same Citation Relevant information for each source, separated by a semicolon: (Goodrich 195; Hopkins 47)

Use the following guidelines for correctly placing parenthetical citations.

Placement of Citations

- Place the citation as close as possible to the material it documents. If possible, place it at the end of a sentence.
- Place a citation after closing quotation marks and before the end punctuation mark.
- For an extensive quotation, set as an extract block (see Guidelines for Using Quotations, page 1211), place the citation *two spaces after* the final punctuation mark.

LIST OF SOURCES CITED

The **sources cited** list, which you should include at the end of your report, contains all the sources, print and nonprint, that you credit in your paper. Other names for this list are *bibliography* and *works* or *literature cited,* but they are only appropriate if your sources are limited to books and articles.

Formatting To prepare the sources cited list, center the words *Sources Cited* on a blank sheet of paper one inch from the top of the page. Double-space between "Sources Cited" and the first entry and between all subsequent entries. Double-space within entries as well. Begin each entry on a new line, even with the left margin. If an entry runs more than one line, indent the subsequent line or lines in the entry five spaces.

As a general rule, alphabetize your sources by the author's last name. If there is no author (or editor), alphabetize by title, ignoring *A, An,* and *The* as the first word of the title. For example, *The Cambridge History of Literary Criticism* would appear under *C* rather than *T*.

Publication Information When providing publication information, use shortened forms of publishers' names, unless this would lead to confusion. Abbreviate U.S. state names and months of the year (except May, June, and July).

Page Numbers You should include page numbers only for articles in periodicals or for other works that are part of a whole work, such as one essay in a book of essays. However, page and volume numbers aren't needed if entries are alphabetized, as in an encyclopedia.

SOURCES CITED: SAMPLE ENTRIES	
Standard Reference Works	
Encyclopedia	"Malory, Sir Thomas." The New Encyclopaedia Britannica: Micropaedia. 15th ed. 1988.
Biographical Reference	"Malory, Sir Thomas." Merriam-Webster's Biographical Dictionary. 1995 ed.
Books	
Book with One Author	Alcock, Leslie. Arthur's Britain: History and Archaeology A.D. 367–634. London: Penguin, 1971.
Book with Two or More Authors	Radford, C. A. Ralegh, and Michael J. Swanton. Arthurian Sites in the West. Devon: U of Exeter, 1975.
Book with No Author Listed	The Cambridge History of Literary Criticism. New York: Cambridge UP, 1989.
Book with One Editor	Brengle, Richard L., ed. Arthur, King of Britain. New York: Appleton, 1964.
Book with Two or More Editors	Pickford, Cedric E., Rex Last, and C. R. Barker, eds. The Arthurian Bibliography, II: Subject Index. Cambridge: Brewer, 1983.
Translation	Niane, D. T. Sundiata: An Epic of Old Mali. Trans. G. D. Pickett. London: Longman, 1965.

Selections from Books	
Selection from Book of Works by One Author	Tennyson, Alfred Lord. "To the Queen." The Works of Tennyson. Ed. Hallam, Lord Tennyson. London: Macmillan, 1913.
Selection from Book of Works by Several Authors	Oakeshott, W. F. "The Finding of the Manuscript." Essays on Malory. Ed. J.A.W. Bennett. Oxford: Clarendon Press, 1963. 1–6.
Selection from Collection of Longer Works	Steinbeck, John. The Acts of King Arthur and His Noble Knights: From the Winchester Manuscripts of Thomas Malory and Other Sources. Ed. Chase Horton. New York: Farrar, 1976. 51–98.
Articles from Magazines, Newspapers, and Journals	
Weekly Magazine Article	Porter, Andrew. "Purcell: King Arthur." The New Yorker 31 July 1989: 69.
Monthly or Quarterly Magazine Article	Converse, Florence. "Merlin Met Morgan-Le-Fay." Atlantic Monthly Sept. 1922: 376–377.
Article with No Author Listed	"An Arthurian Journey." Atlantic Monthly June 1980: 811–829.
Daily Newspaper Article, with Byline	Riding, Alan. "'King Arthur' Goes to Paris After 300 Years." New York Times 20 Feb. 1995, late ed.: C9+.
Daily Newspaper Article, No Byline	"Steinbeck Find Said to Be First 'Morte d'Arthur' Manuscript." New York Times 2 Jan. 1966, natl. ed.: 52.
Unsigned Daily Newspaper Editorial, No City in Title	"Supreme Injustice." Editorial. Star Ledger [Newark, NJ] 6 Oct. 1991: 17.
Scholarly Journal	Field, P.J.C. "Sir Thomas Malory, M.P." Bulletin of the Institute of Historical Research 47 (1974): 24–35.
Other Sources	
Personal Interview	Kibler, William W. Personal interview. 15 Oct. 1990.
Telephone Interview	Kibler, William W. Telephone interview. 12 Oct. 1990.
Published Interview	Campbell, Joseph. Interview with Bill Moyers. The Power of Myth. New York: Doubleday. 1988.
Radio or Television Interview	Harris, Richard. Interview with Scott Simon. Weekend Edition. Natl. Public Radio. WBUR Boston. 26 Mar. 1994.
Thesis or Dissertation	Couroux, Gerard Oliver. "Courtly Love in Malory's 'Le Morte Darthur.'" Diss. Loyola U of Chicago, 1968.
Cartoon	Stevens, Mick. Cartoon. The New Yorker Book of Lawyer Cartoons. New York: Knopf, 1994: 22.
Speech or Lecture	Bell, A.R.L. "The Road to Santiago de Compostela: The French Connection." Long Beach Ebell Club. 10 Oct. 1983.
Recording	Welcher, Dan. The Visions of Merlin. Cond. Akira Endo. LP. Louisville Orch. First Edition Records, 1989.
Film or Filmstrip	The Sword in the Stone. Dir. Wolfgang Reitherman. Walt Disney, 1963.
Videotape	Arthur the King. Dir. Clive Donner. CBS. KTBC, Austin. 26 Apr. 1985.

WRITING FOR LIFE

The writing you do now prepares you for the writing you will do in college and in your career. Your ability to write clear and effective memos, business letters, and résumés will be a major factor in your success as a professional. As a student, you will write letters of application for admission to colleges and universities, and you will write résumés to apply for jobs. As an employee, you may write interoffice memoranda and business letters.

When composing documents that others will read, follow the steps listed below. (Note: Computers and software programs make the writing process more efficient.)

1. **Prewriting.** Make notes about the key points you want to include in your document and how to present them.
2. **Writing a draft.** Compose a first draft, or version, of the document.
3. **Evaluating and revising.** Evaluate your draft closely, correcting any errors of spelling, grammar, and punctuation. Review the presentation of information and ideas for clarity and readability, and revise as necessary. Delete repetitive or irrelevant material.
4. **Preparing the final version.** Fine-tune the revised draft as necessary to prepare a final version. Make sure you proofread the document.

WRITING INTEROFFICE MEMOS

In the business world, writing is functional and is expected to be structured. One standard form of communication within a company or organization is the **memo** (or memorandum). Memos are concise messages that tell the reader *when, who, what, where, why,* and *how.* Memos contain guide words (*date, to, from, subject* or *re*) that immediately identify the date, destination, origin, and purpose of a message. Memos generally cover only one of the following categories.

- **Meeting notices.** Include the meeting date, time, place, purpose, and any other significant information, such as the agenda or the persons who will be attending.
- **Meeting summaries.** Provide a brief, factual report of discussions and decisions. Include the names and titles of individuals involved.
- **Requests for action or information.** Open by making the request, and then follow with details. If you have several requests, list them, phrasing each one similarly. Include a deadline stating when you need a response.

For more on memos, see page 1186.

WRITING EFFECTIVE BUSINESS LETTERS

Another essential form of business writing is the business letter. Whether you're writing to request information, make an offer, or register a complaint, your business letters can make a lasting impression on readers. If errors and inaccuracies or a sloppy appearance distract readers from the contents of a letter, you risk giving an impression of inefficiency or even incompetence. Keep these rules in mind:

1. Use formal, standard English.
2. Be clear.
3. Use the correct format.

Types of Business Letters

Request and Order Letters You write a **request letter** to ask for information about a job, college, product, service, policy, or procedure. You write an **order letter** to order merchandise. When writing a request or order letter, include all important details relating to time, location, size, style, cost, and so on.

Complaint or Adjustment Letters You write a **complaint** or **adjustment letter** when you are dissatisfied with a person, product, or service. Your letter should explain exactly what is wrong and should request a satisfactory resolution of the problem, such as a replacement of merchandise or a refund of your money. Keep the tone of your letter calm and courteous.

Letters of Application A **letter of application** introduces you to a selection committee or a potential employer. The letter should provide the reader with enough information to determine whether you are a good candidate for a job, scholarship, college, or university. Keep the following points in mind when writing a letter of application.

1. Identify the job or situation for which you are applying, and mention how you heard about it.
2. Depending on the situation, include
   - your age, grade in school, and grade point average
   - your experience, activities, awards, and honors
   - the personal qualities that make you a good choice
   - the dates or times you are available
3. Provide references—names of two or three responsible adults, other than relatives, who agree to recommend you. Include their addresses and telephone numbers.

Sample Letter of Application, Block Style

Heading
Your address, including city, state, and ZIP code.
Your e-mail address
Date you write the letter

1632 Garden View Drive
Anytown, PA 12345
mmanrique@ISP.com

September 23, 1999

Inside Address
Name, title, and address of person you are writing to. Use a title (*Mr., Ms., Mrs., Dr., Esq.,* etc.) with the person's name, and put his or her business title after the name.

Mr. John Lao
Director of Human Resources
XYZ Insurance Company
10 Central Avenue
Anytown, PA 12346

Salutation (greeting)
Use *Dear* followed by the person's title and last name and a colon. If the letter isn't addressed to a specific person, use a business title.

Dear Mr. Lao:

Body
Your message. If the body contains more than one paragraph, leave a blank line between paragraphs. Don't indent paragraph openings.

Are you looking for someone who carries out assignments efficiently and enjoys working with people? I have these qualities and other important business skills to bring to the position of administrative assistant you advertised in Sunday's Herald.

I am a 17-year-old senior at Jefferson High School and have completed courses in business English, word processing, and accounting. I can word-process at a rate of 50 words per minute while transcribing from recordings.

Last summer, as a receptionist at QRS Supply Company, I did filing and billing in addition to my regular duties. I feel at home in an office setting and enjoy taking on responsibility.

My résumé, which is enclosed, lists references who can tell you about my business skills and my personal strengths.

I believe that my background qualifies me for the position of administrative assistant. Please contact me by telephone at 555-1234 or by e-mail at mmanrique@ISP.com to set up an interview.

Closing
Use *Yours truly* or *Sincerely yours* followed by a comma.

Yours truly,

Signature
Type or print your name, leaving space for your signature. Sign your name in ink.

Marisol Manrique

Marisol Manrique

Use "Enclosure" if you're including something with your letter.

Enclosure

WRITING A PERSONAL RÉSUMÉ

Your **résumé** (or **curriculum vitae** [CV]) summarizes who you are, what you have learned, and what you have accomplished. The information in your résumé should include skills and achievements that give a potential employer a positive overview of your qualifications. When you apply for a job, you usually include your résumé with your letter of application to potential employers.

The structure, organization, and overall appearance of your résumé will give the reader an impression of you and your abilities. Print out or type your résumé on white or ivory paper. Proofread it carefully, making sure there are no factual or typographical errors, erasures, correction fluid, or stray marks. Your goal is to get an interview. Try your best to make a good first impression.

The following **model résumé** is written in reverse chronological order; it lists the most recent work experience first.

Sample Résumé

MARISOL MANRIQUE

1632 Garden View Drive
Anytown, PA 12345
Telephone: (215) 555-1234
E-mail: mmanrique@ISP.com

EDUCATION:	Senior, Jefferson High School Major studies: Business and foreign language courses Grade point average: 3.0 (B)		
WORK EXPERIENCE:	Summer 1999	Receptionist QRS Supply Company Anytown, PA	
	Summer 1996	Volunteer Office Worker YWCA Anytown, PA	
SKILLS:	Word processing:	50 wpm	
	Business machines:	Dictating, calculating, and copying machines; personal computers	
	Other languages:	Spanish (fluent)	
EXTRACURRICULAR ACTIVITIES:	Vice president, Future Business Leaders of America Member, Spanish Club		
REFERENCES:	Dr. Robert Robertson, Principal Jefferson High School Anytown, PA		(215) 555-6789
	Ms. Mary Jackson, English Teacher Jefferson High School Anytown, PA		(215) 555-4567
	Mr. Juan Ramos, Owner QRS Supply Company Anytown, PA		(215) 555-3456

COLLEGE ADMISSIONS

To apply to a college, you will have to complete an application. Most applications have two parts: the form and the essay.

Completing the College Application Form

Application forms usually ask for basic information about you: name, address, birth date, grade point average, extracurricular activities, and the educational background and occupations of your parents. Many colleges have adopted the Common Application form so that you need fill this form out only once and send it to all the schools you are applying to. The form can be downloaded from the Internet. It can also be sent by e-mail to many colleges. (Note: Some schools require their own forms instead of or in addition to the Common Application form.)

Be sure to ask your high school to send a copy of your **transcript** to the colleges you apply to. A transcript lists all the courses you have taken in high school and the grades you earned.

Writing the Admission Essay

Most colleges and universities ask for an admission essay because it tells them things about you that can't be gleaned from bare facts. An essay reveals how you approach a question, how you think, what is important to you, and how well your education and experience have prepared you to express yourself verbally.

Consider these points as you prepare to write your admissions essay:

1. Read the question carefully. Be sure you are answering what is asked.
2. Be yourself. Admissions staff ask for the essay because they want to get to know you. The essay is an opportunity to introduce yourself to the admissions staff. Write about something important to you. Your conviction will come across to the reader. Don't worry about what the reader might expect from you—say something you want to say.
3. Be neat. Write as many drafts as necessary. Fine-tune until your essay is the best you can make it. Then, check the revised draft carefully for any errors in spelling, grammar, and usage before you produce the final version.

PROOFREADING

Proofreading refines the mechanics of your writing. If you are using a computer to write, a spelling checker can help you with your spelling, but it cannot do everything. For example, spelling checkers will not help you determine if you should use *too, two,* or *to* or other homophones. A dictionary and a style book will serve as helpful reference tools when you proofread. As you review your writing, you might find this list of questions helpful: (1) Are all words spelled correctly? (2) Do subjects and verbs agree? (3) Do pronouns agree with their antecedents? (4) Are verb tenses consistent? (5) Are all proper nouns capitalized? (6) Are sentence fragments eliminated? (7) Are all punctuation marks appropriate?

As you proofread your work, use the standard proofreaders' marks listed in the chart below.

PROOFREADERS' MARKS

Symbol	Example	Meaning
≡	Twenty-second street	Capitalize lowercase letter.
/	Sarah's Uncle	Lowercase capital letter.
^	the capital Maine (of)	Insert.
℘	What's the the point?	Delete.
⁀ ‿	a heavy back pack	Close up space.
∿	tragedy	Change order (of letters or words). Transpose.
¶	¶"Help," he yelled.	Begin new paragraph.
⊙	Stay calm⊙	Add period.
^,	Of course you may be wrong.	Add comma.

Answering Essay Questions

Essay tests require you to think critically and to express your understanding of a topic clearly. Your answers to essay questions must be well organized and include details to support your generalizations. A well-written answer must contain a complete response to a question.

Scan the questions on the test before you start writing. If you have a choice of questions, identify the ones you can answer best. Budget your time so you can give adequate attention to each question.

1. Read each essay question carefully, and notice whether a question has several parts.
2. Identify the important terms in the questions. Find the key verbs, and identify the tasks you must accomplish. Identify how much evidence is required for an adequate treatment.
3. Take a few minutes to prewrite. Make notes or a simple outline on scratch paper, organize your material logically, and write a thesis statement. Write one paragraph for each point you wish to make, and end with a paragraph that summarizes or restates your main points.
4. Evaluate and revise as you write. Watch for spelling and grammatical errors. You will not have time to redraft the entire essay, but you can edit to strengthen specific parts. Keep your paper neat.

Essay questions usually ask you to perform specific tasks expressed by the verb in the question. The following chart lists the task required by some key verbs.

ESSAY TEST QUESTIONS

Key Verb	Task	Sample Question
analyze	Take something apart to see how it creates meaning.	Analyze the use of verbal music in "The Lake Isle of Innisfree."
argue	Take a stand on an issue, and give reasons supporting your opinion.	Argue whether high school students should be required to pass a skills test before they graduate.
compare/contrast	Discuss likenesses/differences. At times test makers use the verb *compare* to include "contrast."	Compare and contrast Roman Polanski's movie of *Macbeth* with Shakespeare's play.
define	Give specific details that make something unique.	Define the term *modernism* as it relates to literature.
demonstrate (also **illustrate, present, show**)	Provide examples to support a point.	Demonstrate an example of circular reasoning.
discuss	Examine in detail.	Discuss the character of Macbeth as portrayed in Polanski's movie.
explain	Clarify, expound on, or give reasons for, or a cause of, something.	Explain the function of the witches in *Macbeth.*
interpret	Discuss or explain the meaning or significance of something.	Interpret the symbolism of blood and water in *Macbeth.*
list (also **outline, trace**)	Give all steps (in order) or all details about a subject.	List the events that lead to the death of Lady Macbeth.
summarize	Give a brief overview of the main points in a piece of informative writing or of the main events in a narrative.	Summarize the plot of Coleridge's *The Rime of the Ancient Mariner.*

Speaking and Listening

Organizing Your Materials

Gather and organize information for your speech by following the basic process for writing a paper. If you are presenting an informative speech, use reliable sources of information, and take notes on what you find. Make an outline of the major points. Then, prepare note cards.

SPEECH NOTE CARDS
1. Put only one key idea, possibly accompanied by a brief example or detail, on each card.
2. Make a special note card for material that you plan to read word for word, such as a quotation, series of dates, or list of statistics.
3. Make a special note card to indicate when you should show a visual aid, such as a chart.
4. Number completed cards to keep them in order.

Unless you are presenting a memorized speech in a competition, you don't want to memorize your speech. You want your delivery to sound fresh and natural. If you use short phrases and signal words rather than full sentences to indicate key ideas on your note cards, you will not be tempted to read or memorize your speech.

Practicing Your Speech/Audience Evaluation

Practice your speech as often as you can to achieve a smooth, effective presentation. Practice at least once before an audience to get feedback. Be sure this audience evaluates your presentation based on criteria that you have agreed on.

Using Body Language Your body language can reinforce the impression you make on your audience. Body language includes facial expressions, eye contact, gestures, posture, and movement. Here are several tips for using body language effectively:

- Making eye contact when speaking can indicate honesty and sincerity. Make eye contact with individuals in your audience to make them feel you are talking *with* them.
- Posture conveys attitude. Stand confidently, and look alert and interested in what you are saying.

Using Your Voice Speak clearly and loudly enough for everyone in your audience to hear what you are saying. This sounds easy, but there are different aspects of speaking that affect how you sound to others:

- **Pitch** is how high or low a sound is or the natural rise and fall of your voice. Use pitch to emphasize various ideas and to avoid a monotone.
- **Volume** is the loudness or intensity of sound. You need to be loud enough to be heard when you are speaking. You also can raise or lower your voice for emphasis.
- **Stress,** or emphasize, important words or phrases to convey a point to your audience.
- **Rate** is the speed at which you talk. Speak at a comfortable, relaxed pace, and use changes in rate to communicate emotion and drama to your listeners.

Delivering Your Speech

Focus on your purpose for speaking. Think about what you want your listeners to do, know, believe, or feel.

Model Research Paper

Shakespeare's Sister: A Fable of Gender Inequality

"Let me imagine," muses Virginia Woolf, "since facts are so hard to come by, what would have happened had Shakespeare had a wonderfully gifted sister, called Judith, let us say" (Woolf, Room 48). Virginia Woolf, the great British novelist, essayist, and critic of the early twen-

Introductory Paragraph
Catches reader's interest.
Primary source citation.

tieth century, goes on to speculate about the destiny of Shakespeare's imaginary sister Judith. Like Shakespeare, Judith also has a genius waiting to be born. Unlike Shakespeare, however, Judith cannot attend school and is denied access to the London theater. Like other women of the sixteenth century, she is intended for an early marriage and a life confined to domestic duties. There is no opportunity for her gift to flourish. It dies, unborn, when Judith dies (Woolf, Room 49–50).

Thesis statement.

Virginia Woolf spoke of the fable of Judith in lectures she gave at two women's colleges at Cambridge University in 1928. Her talks became the well-known essay A Room of One's Own. The essay draws attention to the lack of information on women writers and "call[s] for a history of women" (Scott 15). It strongly criticizes gender discrimination. Woolf addressed her comments to an audience of young women who were experiencing inequality firsthand at Cambridge. Why, then, did Woolf not address the issue of Cambridge women directly? Why did she clothe her comments in the fable of Shakespeare's imaginary sister? The reason lies partly in the political climate of Cambridge at the time.

Body
Topic sentence.
Supporting details.

Secondary source citation.

Two women's colleges, Girton and Newnham, were established at Cambridge by 1873, allowing female students to attend men's lectures and take degree examinations exactly as male students did (Brittain 35–36). Women were not admitted to full status, however, and did not receive degrees from Cambridge until after World War II (Bradbrook 78–79). During those intervening years, men's attitudes toward female students ranged from reluctant toleration to outright hostility. Female undergraduates were accused, for example, of everything from "distracting" men in libraries to obscuring men's views with their picture hats (McWilliams-Tullberg 193). In 1920, when a proposal to admit women was defeated, male undergraduates appeared as a "howling mob" who chanted "we won't have women" and bribed children to do the same (McWilliams-Tullberg 193). . . . [The paper continues.]

Topic sentence.

Supporting details.

Secondary source citation.

In Judith Shakespeare, Virginia Woolf may have seen a reflection of herself. Certainly, she recognized the parallel when she wrote that her fictional heroine "lives in you and me, and in many other women who are not here tonight for they are washing up the dishes and putting the children to bed" (qtd. in Gilbert and Gubar 93). Then, too, there is another parallel in the two lives. Judith Shakespeare dies, her gift wasted. In 1941, Virginia Woolf died prematurely, her gifts also lost. "Who shall measure," Woolf wrote, "the heat and violence of the poet's heart when caught and tangled in a woman's body" (Woolf, Room 50)?

Conclusion

Sources Cited

Bradbrook, M. C. 'That Infidel Place': A Short History of Girton College, 1869-1969. London: Chatto, 1969.
Brittain, Vera. The Women at Oxford: A Fragment of History. New York: Macmillan, 1960.
Gilbert, Sandra M., and Susan Gubar. The War of the Words. New Haven: Yale UP, 1988, Vol. 1 of No Man's Land: The Place of the Woman Writer in the Twentieth Century. 3 vols. 1988-94.
Malcolm, Janet. "A House of One's Own." The New Yorker. 5 June 1995: 58-78.
McWilliams-Tullberg, Rita. Women at Cambridge: A Men's University--Though of a Mixed Type. London: Gollancz, 1975.
Scott, Joan Wallach. Gender and the Politics of History. New York: Columbia UP, 1988.
"Virginia Woolf." The Modern World: Ten Great Writers. Narr. Hermione Lee. London Weekend Television. London. 9 June 1988.
Woolf, Virginia. A Room of One's Own. New York: Harcourt, 1957.
[Note: This is a partial list of Sources Cited for this research paper.]

Resources

- *Language Handbook Resources,* pp. 1–4
- *Language Workshop CD-ROM,* Chapter 1: Parts of Speech

1 The Parts of Speech

PART OF SPEECH	DEFINITION	EXAMPLES
NOUN	Names person, place, thing, or idea	writer, Ben Okri, Anglo-Saxons, family, country, Wales, poem, "My Last Duchess," Romanticism
PRONOUN	Takes the place of one or more nouns or pronouns	
Personal	Refers to one(s) speaking (first person), spoken to (second person), spoken about (third person)	I, me, my, mine, we, us, our, ours you, your, yours he, him, his, she, her, hers, it, its, they, them, their, theirs
Reflexive	Refers to subject and directs action of verb back to subject	myself, ourselves, yourself, yourselves, himself, herself, itself, themselves
Intensive	Refers to and emphasizes noun or another pronoun	(See Reflexive.)
Demonstrative	Refers to specific one(s) of group	this, that, these, those
Interrogative	Introduces question	what, which, who, whom, whose
Relative	Introduces subordinate clause and refers to noun or pronoun outside that clause	that, which, who, whom, whose
Indefinite	Refers to one(s) not specifically named	all, any, anyone, both, each, either, everybody, many, none, nothing
ADJECTIVE	Modifies noun or pronoun by telling *what kind, which one, how many,* or *how much*	**a paperback** book, **an Anglo-Saxon** law, **this** one, **the seven brave** warriors, **less** space
VERB	Shows action or state of being	
Action	Expresses physical or mental activity	describe, travel, fight, believe, consider, remember
Linking	Connects subject with word identifying or describing it	appear, be, seem, become, feel, look, smell, sound, taste
Helping (Auxiliary)	Assists another verb in expressing time, voice, or mood	be, have, may, can, shall, must, would
ADVERB	Modifies verb, adjective, or adverb by telling *how, when, where,* or *to what extent*	walks **slowly, quite** different, **somewhat** boldly, coming **here soon**
PREPOSITION	Relates noun or pronoun to another word	about, at, by, for, from, in, on, according to, along with, because of
CONJUNCTION	Joins words or word groups	
Coordinating	Joins words or word groups used in the same way	and, but, for, nor, or, so, yet

(continued)

Correlative	A pair of conjunctions that join parallel words or word groups	both . . . and, either . . . or, neither . . . nor, not only . . . but (also)
Subordinating	Begins a subordinate clause and connects it to an independent clause	although, as if, because, since, so that, unless, when, where, while
INTERJECTION	Expresses emotion	ah, wow, ugh, whew

2 AGREEMENT

AGREEMENT OF SUBJECT AND VERB

2a. A verb should agree with its subject in number. Singular subjects take singular verbs. Plural subjects take plural verbs.

SINGULAR **He lives** in Camelot.
PLURAL **They live** in Camelot.

2b. The number of the subject is not changed by a phrase or a clause following the subject.

EXAMPLE
The **Lilliputians,** a nation of tiny people, **capture** Gulliver.

2c. Indefinite pronouns may be singular, plural, or either.

(1) The following indefinite pronouns are singular: *anybody, anyone, anything, each, either, everybody, everyone, everything, neither, nobody, no one, nothing, one, somebody, someone,* and *something.*

EXAMPLE
One of the most beautiful places in England **is** the Lake District.

(2) The following indefinite pronouns are plural: *both, few, many,* and *several.*

EXAMPLE
Both of the epics **were written** by John Milton.

(3) The indefinite pronouns *all, any, most, none,* and *some* are singular when they refer to singular words and are plural when they refer to plural words.

SINGULAR **None** of the equipment **was damaged.** [*None* refers to *equipment.*]
PLURAL **None** of the machines **were damaged.** [*None* refers to *machines.*]

2d. A *compound subject* may be singular, plural, or either.

(1) Subjects joined by *and* usually take a plural verb.

EXAMPLE
After rehearsal, **Juan, Anita,** and **Marcus are going** out to dinner.

A compound subject that names only one person or thing takes a singular verb.

EXAMPLE
His **wife** and **partner** in crime **is** Lady Macbeth.

(2) Singular subjects joined by *or* or *nor* take a singular verb.

EXAMPLE
Jill or **Jorge plans** to write a character analysis of Macduff.

(3) When a singular subject and a plural subject are joined by *or* or *nor,* the verb agrees with the subject nearer the verb.

EXAMPLE
Neither the **dancers** nor the **choreographer was** pleased with the routine.

2e. The verb agrees with its subject even when the verb precedes the subject, as in sentences beginning with *here, there,* or *where.*

SINGULAR Where **is** [*or* where's] **Malcolm**?
PLURAL Here **are** [*not* here's] **Malcolm** and his **brother.**

2f. A *collective noun* (such as *audience, flock,* or *team*) is singular in form but names a group of persons or things. A collective noun takes a singular verb when the noun refers to the group as a unit and takes a plural verb when the noun refers to the parts or members of the group.

Resources

- *Language Handbook Resources,* pp. 5–11
- *Language Workshop CD-ROM,* Chapter 2: Agreement

SINGULAR The tour **group is** on the bus. [The group as a unit is on the bus.]

PLURAL The tour **group are talking** about their plans. [The members of the group are talking to one another.]

2g. **An expression of an amount (a length of time, a statistic, or a fraction, for example) is singular when the amount is thought of as a unit or when it refers to a singular word and plural when the amount is thought of as many parts or when it refers to a plural word.**

SINGULAR **Fifty years is** how long Beowulf rules Geatland. [one unit]

PLURAL **One fourth** of the seniors **are working** on a production of *Macbeth*. [The fraction refers to *seniors*.]

Expressions of measurement (length, weight, capacity, area) are usually singular.

EXAMPLE

Four and seven-tenths inches is the diameter of a compact disc.

2h. **The title of a creative work (such as a book, song, film, or painting) or the name of an organization, a country, or a city (even if it is plural in form) takes a singular verb.**

EXAMPLES

"Tears, Idle Tears" was written by Alfred, Lord Tennyson.
The **United Nations was formed** in 1945.
Has the **Netherlands been flooded** recently?

2i. **A verb agrees with its subject, not with its predicate nominative.**

SINGULAR The **subject** of the lecture **was** epic heroes.

PLURAL **Epic heroes were** the subject of the lecture.

AGREEMENT OF PRONOUN AND ANTECEDENT

A pronoun usually refers to a noun or another pronoun. The word to which a pronoun refers is called its ***antecedent***.

2j. **A pronoun agrees with its antecedent in number and gender. Singular pronouns refer to singular antecedents. A few singular pronouns also indicate gender (feminine, masculine, or neuter). Plural pronouns refer to plural antecedents.**

EXAMPLES

Alfred, Lord Tennyson published *Idylls of the King* after **he** became poet laureate. [singular, masculine]
Lady Macbeth helps **her** husband. [singular, feminine]
The **Lilliputians** gave **their** captive food. [plural]

2k. **Indefinite pronouns may be singular, plural, or either.**

(1) Singular pronouns are used to refer to the indefinite pronouns *anybody, anyone, anything, each, either, everybody, everyone, everything, neither, nobody, no one, nothing, one, somebody, someone,* and *something.* The gender of any of these pronouns is determined by the word or words that the pronoun refers to.

EXAMPLES

Each of the **boys** has learned **his** part in *Macbeth*.
One of the **girls** has injured **herself.**

If the antecedent may be either masculine or feminine, use both the masculine and feminine pronouns to refer to it.

EXAMPLE

Anyone who is going on the field trip needs to bring **his** or **her** lunch.

(2) Plural pronouns are used to refer to the indefinite pronouns *both, few, many,* and *several.*

EXAMPLE

Many of the spectators leapt from **their** seats and cheered.

(3) Singular or plural pronouns may be used to refer to the indefinite pronouns *all, any, most, none,* and *some.* These indefinite pronouns are singular when they refer to singular words and are plural when they refer to plural words.

SINGULAR **None** of the renovated theater matches **its** original beauty. [*None* refers to the singular noun *theater.*]

PLURAL **None** of the geese have left on **their** annual migration. [*None* refers to the plural noun *geese.*]

2l. **A plural pronoun is used to refer to two or more singular antecedents joined by *and*.**

EXAMPLE

Malcolm and Donalbain left Scotland soon after **their** father was killed.

2m. **A singular pronoun is used to refer to two or more singular antecedents joined by *or* or *nor*.**

EXAMPLE

Neither **Malcolm nor Donalbain** felt **he** was safe.

2n. **A collective noun (such as *club* or *family*) takes a singular pronoun when the noun refers to the group as a unit and takes a plural pronoun when the noun refers to the parts or members of the group.**

SINGULAR The **jury** reached **its** decision less than one hour later. [The jury decided as a unit.]

PLURAL The **jury** disagree on how much importance **they** should give to one of the defendant's statements. [The members of the jury disagree.]

2o. **The title of a creative work (such as a book, song, film, or painting) or the name of an organization, a country, or a city (even if it is plural in form) takes a singular pronoun.**

EXAMPLES

I read ***Gulliver's Travels*** and wrote a report on **it.**
The **United Arab Emirates** generates most of **its** revenue from the sale of oil.

3 Using Verbs

THE PRINCIPAL PARTS OF VERBS

Every verb has four basic forms called the ***principal parts:*** the *base form,* the *present participle,* the *past,* and the *past participle.* A verb is classified as *regular* or *irregular* depending on the way it forms its past and past participle.

3a. **A *regular verb* forms the past and past participle by adding *–d* or *–ed* to the base form. An *irregular verb* forms the past and the past participle in some other way.**

COMMON REGULAR AND IRREGULAR VERBS

The following examples include *is* and *have* in italics to show that helping verbs (forms of *be* and *have*) are used with the present participle and past participle forms.

BASE FORM	PRESENT PARTICIPLE	PAST	PAST PARTICIPLE
REGULAR			
attack	*is* attacking	attacked	*have* attacked
drown	*is* drowning	drowned	*have* drowned
occur	*is* occurring	occurred	*have* occurred
risk	*is* risking	risked	*have* risked
try	*is* trying	tried	*have* tried
use	*is* using	used	*have* used
IRREGULAR			
be	*is* being	was, were	*have* been
bring	*is* bringing	brought	*have* brought
burst	*is* bursting	burst	*have* burst
come	*is* coming	came	*have* come
eat	*is* eating	ate	*have* eaten
go	*is* going	went	*have* gone
lead	*is* leading	led	*have* led
pay	*is* paying	paid	*have* paid
see	*is* seeing	saw	*have* seen
sing	*is* singing	sang	*have* sung
steal	*is* stealing	stole	*have* stolen
take	*is* taking	took	*have* taken
throw	*is* throwing	threw	*have* thrown

NOTE If you are not sure about the principal parts of a verb, look in a dictionary. Entries for irregular verbs give the principal parts. If no principal parts are listed, the verb is a regular verb.

TENSES AND THEIR USES

3b. **The *tense* of a verb indicates the time of the action or state of being that is expressed by the verb.**

(1) The ***present tense*** is used mainly to express an action or a state of being that is occurring now.

EXAMPLE

The article **compares** Beowulf with other epic heroes.

Resources

- *Language Handbook Resources,* pp. 12–23
- *Language Workshop CD-ROM,* Chapter 3: Using Verbs Correctly

The present tense is also used

- to show a customary or habitual action or state of being
- to convey a general truth—something that is always true
- to make a historical event seem current (such use is called the ***historical present***)
- to summarize the plot or subject matter of a literary work or to refer to an author's relationship to his or her work (such use is called the ***literary present***)
- to express future time

EXAMPLES

Every Friday, our teacher **gives** us a vocabulary quiz. [customary action]

Reptiles **are** coldblooded. [general truth]

The Greeks **establish** separate city-states, which **war** among themselves. [historical present]

In the land of the Lilliputians, Gulliver **appears** gigantic. [literary present]

The two-week seminar on Shakespeare **begins** on Monday. [future time]

(2) The ***past tense*** is used to express an action or state of being that occurred in the past but did not continue into the present.

EXAMPLE

An expert on T. S. Eliot's poetry **spoke** to our class.

(3) The ***future tense*** (*will* or *shall* + base form) is used to express an action or a state of being that will occur.

EXAMPLE

Laurie **will play** the part of Lady Macbeth.

NOTE *Shall* and *will* are both acceptable in forming the future tense.

(4) The ***present perfect tense*** (*have* or *has* + past participle) is used to express an action or a state of being that occurred at some indefinite time in the past.

EXAMPLE

Kenneth Branagh **has played** the roles of Henry V and of Iago.

The present perfect tense is also used to express an action or a state of being that began in the past and continues into the present.

EXAMPLE

Herot **has stood** empty for twelve years.

(5) The ***past perfect tense*** (*had* + past participle) is used to express an action or state of being completed in the past before some other past occurrence.

EXAMPLE

The kingdom **had suffered** before Beowulf arrived. [The suffering occurred before the arriving.]

Be sure to use the past perfect tense in "if" clauses that express the earlier of two past actions.

EXAMPLE

If you **had read** [*not* read *or* would have read] the article, you would have learned about Sutton Hoo.

(6) The ***future perfect tense*** (*will have* or *shall have* + past participle) is used to express an action or state of being that will be completed in the future before some other future occurrence.

EXAMPLE

By this time tomorrow, I **will** [*or* shall] **have memorized** "The Seafarer."

3c. Avoid unnecessary shifts in tense.

INCONSISTENT Wiglaf discovered the dragon's treasure and then brings it to Beowulf. [shift from past to present tense]

CONSISTENT Wiglaf **discovered** the dragon's treasure and then **brought** it to Beowulf. [past tense]

CONSISTENT Wiglaf **discovers** the dragon's treasure and then **brings** it to Beowulf. [present tense]

When describing events that occur at different times, use verbs in different tenses to show the order of events.

EXAMPLE

She **taught** school for several years, but now she **works** for a publishing company. [Because she taught at a specific time in the past, the past tense *taught* is correct. Because she works at the present time, the present tense *works* is correct.]

ACTIVE VOICE AND PASSIVE VOICE

3d. *Voice* is the form a transitive verb takes to indicate whether the subject of the verb performs or receives the action.

A verb is in the ***active voice*** when its subject performs the action (its object receives the action).

ACTIVE VOICE William Shakespeare **wrote** more than thirty-five plays.

A verb is in the ***passive voice*** whenever its subject receives the action (the verb has no object). A passive verb is always a verb phrase that includes a form of *be* and the past participle of an action verb.

PASSIVE VOICE More than thirty-five plays **were written** by William Shakespeare.

3e. Use the passive voice sparingly.

In general, the passive voice is less direct and less forceful than the active voice. In some cases, the passive voice also may sound awkward.

AWKWARD PASSIVE The sleeping grooms are smeared with King Duncan's blood by Lady Macbeth.

ACTIVE Lady Macbeth **smears** the sleeping grooms with King Duncan's blood.

Although you generally will want to use active voice rather than passive voice, the passive voice is not less correct than the active voice. In fact, the passive voice is useful in the following situations:

1. when you do not know the performer of the action

EXAMPLE
The Globe **was built** in 1599.

2. when you do not want to reveal the performer of the action

EXAMPLE
The actor **was criticized** for his portrayal of Macbeth.

3. when you want to emphasize the receiver of the action

EXAMPLE
King Duncan **was murdered** while he was asleep.

LANGUAGE HANDBOOK

4 Using Pronouns

CASE

Case is the form that a noun or a pronoun takes to indicate its use in a sentence. In English, there are three cases: *nominative, objective,* and *possessive.* Most personal pronouns have a different form for each case.

The Nominative Case

4a. A subject of a verb is in the nominative case.

EXAMPLES
They built the tower near the sea as **he** had requested. [*They* is the subject of the verb *built. He* is the subject of the verb *had requested.*]

4b. A predicate nominative is in the nominative case.

EXAMPLE
The only students who auditioned for the part of King Arthur were **he** and **Carlos.** [*He* and *Carlos* are predicate nominatives that follow the linking verb *were* and identify the subject *students.*]

PERSONAL PRONOUNS			
SINGULAR			
	NOMINATIVE	OBJECTIVE	POSSESSIVE
FIRST PERSON	I	me	my, mine
SECOND PERSON	you	you	your, yours
THIRD PERSON	he, she, it	him, her, it	his, her, hers, its
PLURAL			
	NOMINATIVE	OBJECTIVE	POSSESSIVE
FIRST PERSON	we	us	our, ours
SECOND PERSON	you	you	your, yours
THIRD PERSON	they	them	their, theirs

NOTE The form of a noun is the same for both the nominative case and the objective case. A noun changes its form for the possessive case, usually by adding an apostrophe and an *s* to most singular nouns and only an apostrophe to most plural nouns.

For more information about forming possessives of nouns, see page 1249.

Resources
- *Language Handbook Resources,* pp. 24–35
- *Language Workshop CD-ROM,* Chapter 4: Using Pronouns Correctly

The Objective Case

4c. **An object of a verb is in the objective case.**

EXAMPLES

The knight's answer pleases **her.** [*Her* is a direct object that tells *whom* the answer pleases.]

The Pardoner tells **them** a story about three greedy rioters. [*Them* is an indirect object that tells *to whom* the Pardoner tells a story.]

4d. **An object of a preposition is in the objective case.**

EXAMPLE

Are the Lilliputians afraid of **him**? [*Him* is the object of the preposition *of.*]

The Possessive Case

4e. **A noun or a pronoun preceding a gerund is in the possessive case.**

EXAMPLE

We were all thrilled by **Joetta's** [*or* **her**] scoring in the top 5 percent. [*Joetta's* or *her* modifies *scoring,* a gerund used as the object of the preposition *by.*]

Do not confuse a gerund with a present participle, which is a verb form that ends in *–ing* and may function as an adjective.

EXAMPLE

Macbeth found **them** [*not* their] standing around a caldron. [*Them* is modified by the participial phrase *standing around a caldron.*]

SPECIAL PRONOUN PROBLEMS

4f. **An appositive is in the same case as the noun or pronoun to which it refers.**

EXAMPLES

Duncan's sons, **Malcolm and he,** leave Scotland. [The compound appositive *Malcolm and he* refers to the subject, *sons.*]

Macduff suspects both of them, **Malcolm and him.** [The compound appositive *Malcolm and him* refers to *them,* the object of the preposition *of.*]

4g. **A pronoun following *than* or *as* in an elliptical construction is in the same case as it would be if the construction were completed.**

An ***elliptical construction*** is a clause from which words have been omitted.

NOMINATIVE I see him more often **than she.** [I see him more often *than she sees him. She* is the subject in the elliptical construction.]

OBJECTIVE I see him more often **than her.** [I see him more often *than I see her. Her* is the direct object in the elliptical construction.]

4h. **A pronoun ending in *–self* or *–selves* should not be used in place of a personal pronoun.**

EXAMPLE

Everyone except John and **me** [*not* myself] has read *Don Juan.*

4i. **The pronoun *who* (*whoever*) is in the nominative case. The pronoun *whom* (*whomever*) is in the objective case.**

EXAMPLES

Who wrote "Ozymandias"? [*Who* is the subject of the verb *wrote.*]

With **whom** did Wordsworth write *Lyrical Ballads*? [*Whom* is the object of the preposition *with.*]

CLEAR PRONOUN REFERENCE

The word that a pronoun stands for or refers to is called the ***antecedent*** of the pronoun.

4j. **A pronoun should always refer clearly to its antecedent.**

Avoid an ambiguous, a general, a weak, or an indefinite reference by

1. rephrasing the sentence, or
2. replacing the pronoun with an appropriate noun, or
3. giving the pronoun a clear antecedent.

AMBIGUOUS When the Green Knight was talking to Sir Gawain, he was holding his head in his hand. [The antecedent of *he* and *his* is unclear. Was the Green Knight holding Sir Gawain's head or his own?]

CLEAR The Green Knight was holding his head in his hand when he was talking to Sir Gawain.

GENERAL Macbeth will become king. This is one of the witches' prophecies. [*This* has no specific antecedent.]

CLEAR That Macbeth will become king is one of the witches' prophecies.

WEAK Our dog Hank is jealous of my new baby sister. To help him get over it, I try to give him extra attention. [The antecedent of *it* is not expressed.]

CLEAR To help our dog Hank get over his jealousy of my new baby sister, I try to give him extra attention.

INDEFINITE In this book it includes pictures of artifacts from the Sutton Hoo ship burial. [*It* is not necessary to the meaning of the sentence.]

CLEAR This book includes pictures of artifacts from the Sutton Hoo ship burial.

5 Using Modifiers

A ***modifier*** is a word or group of words that limits the meaning of another word or group of words. The two kinds of modifiers are *adjectives* and *adverbs.*

5a. **Use an *adjective* to limit the meaning of a noun or a pronoun. Use an *adverb* to limit the meaning of a verb, an adjective, or another adverb.**

COMPARISON OF MODIFIERS

5b. ***Comparison* refers to the change in the form of an adjective or an adverb to show increasing or decreasing degrees in the quality the modifier expresses.**

The three degrees of comparison are *positive, comparative,* and *superlative.*

1. Most one-syllable modifiers form the comparative and superlative degrees by adding *–er* and *–est.*

2. Some two-syllable modifiers form the comparative and superlative degrees by adding *–er* and *–est.* Other two-syllable modifiers form the comparative and superlative degrees by using *more* and *most.*

3. Modifiers of more than two syllables form the comparative and superlative degrees by using *more* and *most.*

4. To show a decrease in the qualities they express, all modifiers form the comparative by using *less* and the superlative by using *least.*

POSITIVE	COMPARATIVE	SUPERLATIVE
soft	softer	softest
thirsty	thirstier	thirstiest
slowly	more slowly	most slowly
skillfully	less skillfully	least skillfully

☞ For information about adding suffixes such as *–er* and *–est* to words, see page 1252.

5. Some modifiers form the comparative and superlative degrees in other ways.

POSITIVE	COMPARATIVE	SUPERLATIVE
bad (ill)	worse	worst
far	farther (further)	farthest (furthest)
good (well)	better	best
little	less	least
many (much)	more	most

5c. **Use the comparative degree when comparing two things. Use the superlative degree when comparing more than two.**

COMPARATIVE After reading *King Lear* and *The Winter's Tale,* I can understand why *King Lear* is the **more popular** play. [comparison of two plays]

SUPERLATIVE Of the three plays I saw, I think *Macbeth* was the **most powerful.** [comparison of three plays]

5d. **Avoid a double comparison or a double negative. A *double comparison* is the use of two comparative forms (usually *–er* and *more* or *less*) or two superlative forms (usually *–est* and *most* or *least*) to modify the same word. A *double negative* is the use of two negative words where one is enough.**

EXAMPLES

Who is the **noblest** [*not* most noblest] of King Arthur's knights?

I know **nothing** [*not* don't know nothing] about the Wars of the Roses.

Resources

- *Language Handbook Resources,* pp. 36–42
- *Language Workshop CD-ROM,* Chapter 5: Using Modifiers Correctly

5e. **Include the word *other* or *else* when comparing one member of a group with the rest of the group.**

ILLOGICAL Wiglaf is bolder than any of Beowulf's followers. [Wiglaf is one of Beowulf's followers. Logically, Wiglaf cannot be bolder than himself.]

LOGICAL Wiglaf is bolder than any of Beowulf's **other** followers.

5f. **Avoid comparing items that cannot logically be compared.**

ILLOGICAL I think Olivier's portrayal of Hamlet is more compelling than any other actor. [The sentence makes an illogical comparison between a portrayal and an actor.]

LOGICAL I think Olivier's portrayal of Hamlet is more compelling than any other actor's [portrayal]. [The sentence makes a logical comparison between portrayals.]

PLACEMENT OF MODIFIERS

5g. **Avoid using a *misplaced modifier*—a modifying word, phrase, or clause that sounds awkward because it modifies the wrong word or group of words.**

To correct a misplaced modifier, place the word, phrase, or clause as close as possible to the word or words you intend it to modify.

MISPLACED The old man told the three young rioters under a tree they would find Death. [What occurred under a tree: the telling or the finding?]

CLEAR The old man told the three young rioters they would find Death **under a tree.**

MISPLACED The anxious hunter watched the raging lion come charging at him as he readied his bow and arrow.

CLEAR **As he readied his bow and arrow,** the anxious hunter watched the raging lion come charging at him.

5h. **Avoid using a *dangling modifier*—a modifying word, phrase, or clause that does not sensibly modify any word or words in a sentence.**

You may correct a dangling modifier by

- adding a word or words that the dangling word, phrase, or clause can sensibly refer to
- adding a word or words to the dangling word, phrase, or clause
- rewording the sentence

DANGLING After becoming poet laureate, "The Charge of the Light Brigade" was written. [Who became poet laureate?]

CLEAR After becoming poet laureate, Alfred, Lord Tennyson wrote "The Charge of the Light Brigade."

CLEAR Alfred, Lord Tennyson wrote "The Charge of the Light Brigade" after he became poet laureate.

6 Phrases

WHAT IS A PHRASE?

6a. **A *phrase* is a group of related words that is used as a single part of speech and that does not contain a verb and its subject.**

EXAMPLE

***The Rime of the Ancient Mariner,* Coleridge's best-known poem, was published in 1798.** [*Coleridge's best-known poem* functions as a noun, *was published* is a verb, and *in 1798* functions as an adverb.]

THE PREPOSITIONAL PHRASE

6b. **A *prepositional phrase* begins with a preposition and ends with the *object of the preposition,* a word or word group that functions as a noun.**

EXAMPLE

From the rafters of Herot hung one **of Grendel's arms.** [The noun *rafters* is the object of the preposition *from.* The noun *Herot* is the object of the preposition *of.* The noun *arms* is the object of the preposition *of.*]

Resources

- *Language Handbook Resources,* pp. 43–50
- *Language Workshop CD-ROM,* Chapter 6—Lessons 23–25: The Phrase

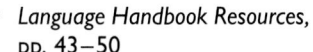

An object of a preposition may be compound.

EXAMPLE

The three men ignored the warnings **of the tavern-knave and the publican.** [Both *tavern-knave* and *publican* are objects of the preposition *of.*]

(1) An ***adjective phrase*** is a prepositional phrase that modifies a noun or a pronoun. An adjective phrase tells *what kind* or *which one.*

EXAMPLE

The three rioters found eight bushels **of gold coins.** [*Of gold coins* modifies the noun *bushels.*]

An adjective phrase usually follows the word it modifies. That word may be the object of another preposition.

EXAMPLE

They told stories on their journey **to Canterbury.** [*To Canterbury* modifies *journey,* the object of the preposition *on.*]

More than one adjective phrase may modify the same word.

EXAMPLE

Chaucer's trips **to Italy on important diplomatic missions** broadened his knowledge. [The phrases *to Italy* and *on important diplomatic missions* modify the noun *trips.*]

(2) An ***adverb phrase*** is a prepositional phrase that modifies a verb, an adjective, or an adverb. An adverb phrase tells *how, when, where, why,* or *to what extent* (*how long* or *how far*).

As you can see in the example below, more than one adverb phrase can modify the same word. The example also shows that an adverb phrase, unlike an adjective phrase, can precede the word it modifies.

EXAMPLE

In 1799, Wordsworth returned **with his sister to the Lake District.** [Each phrase modifies the verb *returned. In 1799* tells *when, with his sister* tells *how,* and *to the Lake District* tells *where.*]

VERBALS AND VERBAL PHRASES

A ***verbal*** is a form of a verb used as a noun, an adjective, or an adverb. A ***verbal phrase*** consists of a verbal and its modifiers and complements.

Participles and Participial Phrases

6c. A *participle* is a verb form that is used as an adjective. A *participial phrase* consists of a participle and all the words related to the participle.

The two kinds of participles are the *present participle* and the *past participle.*

(1) ***Present participles*** end in *–ing.*

EXAMPLE

Sir Gawain heard the Green Knight **sharpening his ax.** [The participial phrase modifies the noun *Green Knight.* The noun *ax* is the direct object of the present participle *sharpening.*]

(2) Most ***past participles*** end in *–d* or *–ed.* Others are irregularly formed.

EXAMPLE

Tormented by her guilt, Lady Macbeth lost her sanity. [The participial phrase modifies the noun *Lady Macbeth.* The adverb phrase *by her guilt* modifies the past participle *tormented.*]

Gerunds and Gerund Phrases

6d. A *gerund* is a verb form ending in *–ing* that is used as a noun. A *gerund phrase* consists of a gerund and all the words related to the gerund.

EXAMPLES

For Gulliver, **living in Brobdingnag** is quite different from **living in Lilliput.** [*Living in Brobdingnag* is the subject of the verb *is. Living in Lilliput* is the object of the preposition *from.* The adverb phrases *in Brobdingnag* and *in Lilliput* modify the gerund *living.*]

The Miller enjoys **playing the bagpipes.** [*Playing the bagpipes* is the direct object of the verb *enjoys. Bagpipes* is the direct object of the gerund *playing.*]

Infinitives and Infinitive Phrases

6e. An *infinitive* is a verb form that can be used as a noun, an adjective, or an adverb. An infinitive usually begins with *to.* An *infinitive phrase* consists of an infinitive and all the words related to the infinitive.

EXAMPLES

The three rioters vow **to kill Death.** [The infinitive phrase acts as a noun and is the direct object of the verb *vow. Death* is the direct object of the infinitive *to kill.*]

She had a great desire **to visit Stratford-on-Avon.** [The infinitive phrase acts as an adjective and modifies the noun *desire. Stratford-on-Avon* is the direct object of the infinitive *to visit.*]

Macbeth goes to the witches' haunt **to talk to them.** [The infinitive phrase acts as an adverb and modifies the verb *goes.* The adverb phrase *to them* modifies the infinitive *to talk.*]

Lady Macbeth helps her husband **become king.** [The sign of the infinitive, *to,* is omitted. The infinitive has a subject, *husband,* making the entire construction an ***infinitive clause.*** The infinitive clause acts as a noun and is the direct object of the verb *helps.*]

APPOSITIVES AND APPOSITIVE PHRASES

6f. An *appositive* is a noun or a pronoun placed beside another noun or pronoun to identify or explain it. An *appositive phrase* consists of an appositive and its modifiers.

An appositive or appositive phrase usually follows the word it identifies or explains.

EXAMPLES

Have you read Coleridge's poem **"Kubla Khan"**? [The appositive *"Kubla Khan"* identifies the noun *poem.*]

Shakespeare was born in Stratford-on-Avon, **a market town about eighty miles from London.** [The entire appositive phrase *a market town about eighty miles from London* identifies the noun *Stratford-on-Avon.*]

For emphasis, however, an appositive or an appositive phrase may precede the word that it explains or identifies.

EXAMPLE

A riot of colorful sights, intriguing aromas, and surprising noises, a Cairo bazaar is great fun to visit. [The appositive phrase explains why a Cairo bazaar is fun to visit.]

Resources

- *Language Handbook Resources,* pp. 51–65
- *Language Workshop CD-ROM,* Chapter 6—Lessons 26 and 27: The Clause

7 CLAUSES

7a. A *clause* is a group of words that contains a verb and its subject and that is used as part of a sentence. There are two kinds of clauses: the *independent clause* and the *subordinate clause.*

THE INDEPENDENT CLAUSE

7b. An *independent* (or *main*) *clause* expresses a complete thought and can stand by itself as a sentence.

EXAMPLE

SUBJECT VERB

William Shakespeare wrote more than 150 sonnets. [one independent clause]

THE SUBORDINATE CLAUSE

7c. A *subordinate* (or *dependent*) *clause* does not express a complete thought and cannot stand alone as a sentence.

EXAMPLE

SUBJECT VERB

that **Lord Byron swam** across the Hellespont

The thought expressed by a subordinate clause becomes complete when the clause is combined with an independent clause to create a complete sentence.

EXAMPLE

I read **that Lord Byron swam across the Hellespont.**

The Adjective Clause

7d. An *adjective clause* is a subordinate clause that modifies a noun or a pronoun.

An adjective clause always follows the word or words that it modifies. Usually, an adjective clause begins with a ***relative pronoun*** (such as *that, which, who, whom, whose*). A relative pronoun both relates an adjective clause to the word or words the clause modifies and performs a function within its own clause by serving as a subject, an object of a verb, an object of a preposition, or a modifier.

EXAMPLES

Mary Shelley, **who wrote *Frankenstein,*** liked reading ghost stories with her friends. [The relative pronoun *who* relates the adjective clause to the noun *Mary Shelley* and serves as the subject of the verb *wrote.*]

The knight **for whom Sir Gawain is searching** is the Knight of the Green Chapel. [The relative pronoun *whom* relates the adjective clause to the noun *knight* and serves as the object of the preposition *for.*]

An adjective clause may begin with a ***relative adverb,*** such as *when* or *where.*

EXAMPLES

My uncle Robert told us about the time **when he backpacked across the island of Luzon.** [The adjective clause modifies the noun *time.*]

Malcolm flees to England, **where he raises an army to attack Macbeth.** [The adjective clause modifies the noun *England.*]

The Noun Clause

7e. A *noun clause* is a subordinate clause that may be used as a subject, a predicate nominative, a direct object, an indirect object, or an object of a preposition.

Words that are commonly used to introduce noun clauses include *how, that, what, whether, who, whoever,* and *why.*

EXAMPLES

That Fleance escapes the murderers troubles Macbeth. [subject]

Power is **what Macbeth desires.** [predicate nominative]

Banquo suspected **that Macbeth had murdered Duncan.** [direct object]

The teacher will give **whoever can recite the soliloquy** ten points. [indirect object]

The teacher will give ten points to **whoever can recite the soliloquy.** [object of a preposition]

The word that introduces a noun clause may or may not have another function in the clause.

EXAMPLES

Do you know **who wrote *Don Juan***? [The word *who* introduces the noun clause and serves as the subject of the verb *wrote.*]

The witches predict **that Macbeth will become king.** [The word *that* introduces the noun clause but does not have any function within the noun clause.]

The Adverb Clause

7f. An *adverb clause* is a subordinate clause that modifies a verb, an adjective, or an adverb.

An adverb clause, which may come before or after the word or words it modifies, tells *how, when, where, why, to what extent,* or *under what condition.* An adverb clause is introduced by a ***subordinating conjunction***—a word or word group that relates the adverb clause to the word or words the clause modifies.

EXAMPLES

He acted **as though he had seen a ghost.** [The adverb clause modifies the verb *acted,* telling *how* he acted.]

Jane is taller **than her grandmother is.** [The adverb clause modifies the adjective *taller,* telling *to what extent* Jane is tall.]

They stayed longer **than I thought they would.** [The adverb clause modifies the adverb *longer,* telling *to what extent* their stay was longer.]

The Elliptical Clause

7g. Part of a clause may be left out when the meaning can be understood from the context of the sentence. Such a clause is called an *elliptical clause*.

EXAMPLES

While [he was] **painting,** Rembrandt concentrated completely on his work.

Ken may ride with us **if he wants to** [ride with us].

This job took longer **than the last one** [took].

For more about using pronouns in elliptical constructions, see page 1228.

8 Sentence Structure

SENTENCE OR FRAGMENT?

8a. A *sentence* is a group of words that has a subject and a verb and expresses a complete thought.

EXAMPLES

"My Last Duchess" is an example of a dramatic monologue.

For how many years was Winston Churchill the prime minister of Britain?

What an ambitious man Macbeth was!

Resources

- *Language Handbook Resources,* pp. 66–75
- *Language Workshop CD-ROM,* Chapter 7: Sentences

Only a sentence should begin with a capital letter and end with a period, a question mark, or an exclamation point. Do not be misled by a group of words that looks like a sentence but that either does not have a subject and a verb or does not express a complete thought. Such a word group is called a ***sentence fragment.***

FRAGMENT Awakens and finds himself surrounded by people six inches tall.

SENTENCE Gulliver awakens and finds himself surrounded by people six inches tall.

SUBJECT AND PREDICATE

8b. **A sentence consists of two parts: a subject and a predicate. A *subject* tells *whom* or *what* the sentence is about. A *predicate* tells something about the subject.**

In the following examples, all the words labeled *subject* make up the ***complete subject,*** and all the words labeled *predicate* make up the ***complete predicate.***

EXAMPLES

SUBJECT	PREDICATE
My sister and I	enjoyed *Gulliver's Travels.*

PREDICATE	SUBJECT	PREDICATE
For fifty years	Beowulf	ruled Geatland.

The Simple Subject

8c. **A *simple subject* is the main word or group of words that tells *whom* or *what* the sentence is about.**

EXAMPLE
The first **leader** of the gang was Blackie. [The complete subject is *the first leader of the gang.*]

The Simple Predicate

8d. **A *simple predicate* is a verb or verb phrase that tells something about the subject.**

EXAMPLE
Have you **read** "The Seafarer"? [The complete predicate is *have read "The Seafarer."*]

The Compound Subject and the Compound Verb

8e. **A *compound subject* consists of two or more subjects that are joined by a conjunction—usually *and* or *or*—and that have the same verb.**

EXAMPLE
A **nun** and three **priests** accompany the Prioress on the pilgrimage.

8f. **A *compound verb* consists of two or more verbs that are joined by a conjunction—usually *and, but,* or *or*—and that have the same subject.**

EXAMPLE
Truth **enlightens** the mind, **frees** the spirit, and **strengthens** the soul.

How to Find the Subject of a Sentence

8g. **To find the subject of a sentence, ask *Who?* or *What?* before the verb.**

(1) The subject of a sentence is never within a prepositional phrase.

EXAMPLES
A **group** of pilgrims gathered at the Tabard. [Who gathered? Group gathered. *Pilgrims* is the object of the preposition *of.*]

Out of the stillness came the loud **sound** of laughter. [What came? Sound came. *Stillness* is the object of the preposition *out of. Laughter* is the object of the preposition *of.*]

(2) The subject of a sentence expressing a command or a request is always understood to be *you,* although *you* may not appear in the sentence.

COMMAND Name the pilgrim accompanying the Plowman. [Who is being told to name? *You* is understood.]

The subject of a command or a request is *you* even when the sentence also contains a ***noun of direct address***—a word that names or identifies the one or ones spoken to.

REQUEST Marla, [you] please read the first stanza of "To a Skylark."

(3) The subject of a sentence expressing a question usually follows the verb or a part of the verb phrase. Turning the question into a statement will often help you find the subject.

QUESTION Have you read Lord Byron's poem "She Walks in Beauty"?

STATEMENT **You** have read Lord Byron's poem "She Walks in Beauty." [Who has read? You have read.]

QUESTION Were Shakespeare's plays popular during his own lifetime?

STATEMENT Shakespeare's **plays** were popular during his own lifetime. [What were popular? Plays were popular.]

(4) The word *there* or *here* is never the subject of a sentence.

EXAMPLES

There is **Canterbury Cathedral.** [What is there? Canterbury Cathedral is there.]

Here are my **drawings** of Chaucer's pilgrims. [What are here? Drawings are here.]

COMPLEMENTS

8h. **A *complement* is a word or a group of words that completes the meaning of a verb or a verbal. The four main kinds of complements are *direct objects, indirect objects, objective complements,* and *subject complements.***

The Direct Object and the Indirect Object

8i. **A *direct object* is a noun, a pronoun, or a word group that functions as a noun and tells *who* or *what* receives the action of a transitive verb.**

EXAMPLES

Banquo definitely suspected **him.** [Suspected whom? him]

Beethoven composed **sonatas** and **symphonies.** [Composed what? sonatas and symphonies—compound direct object]

8j. **An *indirect object* is a word or word group that comes between a transitive verb and a direct object. An indirect object, which may be a noun, a pronoun, or a word group that functions as a noun, tells *to whom, to what, for whom,* or *for what* the action of the verb is done.**

EXAMPLES

The Wife of Bath told the other **pilgrims** an interesting story. [Told to whom? pilgrims]

We should give **practicing for the concert** our full attention. [Should give our full attention to what? practicing for the concert]

The Objective Complement

8k. **An *objective complement* is a word or word group that helps complete the meaning of a transitive verb by identifying or modifying the direct object. An objective complement, which may be a noun, a pronoun, an adjective, or a word group that functions as a noun or an adjective, usually follows the direct object.**

EXAMPLES

Macduff called Malcolm **king.** [The noun *king* identifies the direct object *Malcolm.*]

He believed the money **his.** [The pronoun *his* modifies the direct object *money.*]

Everyone considered him **chivalrous.** [The adjective *chivalrous* modifies the direct object *him.*]

NOTE A ***transitive verb*** is an action verb that takes an object, which tells who or what receives the action.

The Subject Complement

8l. **A *subject complement* is a word or a word group that completes the meaning of a linking verb or a verbal and that identifies or modifies the subject. The two kinds of subject complements are *predicate nominatives* and *predicate adjectives.***

(1) A ***predicate nominative*** is a word or group of words that follows a linking verb and refers to the same person, place, thing, or idea as the subject of the verb. A predicate nominative may be a noun, a pronoun, or a word group that functions as a noun.

EXAMPLES

Of these three poets, Wordsworth was the most prolific **one.** [The pronoun *one* refers to the subject *Wordsworth.*]

The main characters are **Paul** and his **mother.** [The two nouns *Paul* and *mother* are a compound predicate nominative that refers to the subject *characters.*]

(2) A ***predicate adjective*** is an adjective that follows a linking verb and that modifies the subject of the verb.

EXAMPLES

Did King Hrothgar feel **powerless**? [The adjective *powerless* modifies the subject *King Hrothgar.*]

Iago is **sly** and **scheming.** [The two adjectives *sly* and *scheming* are a compound predicate adjective that modifies the subject *Iago.*]

☞ For a list of linking verbs, see page 1222.

SENTENCES CLASSIFIED ACCORDING TO STRUCTURE

8m. According to their structure, sentences are classified as *simple, compound, complex,* and *compound-complex.*

(1) A ***simple sentence*** has one independent clause and no subordinate clauses.

EXAMPLE
"Not Waving but Drowning" is one of my favorite poems.

(2) A ***compound sentence*** has two or more independent clauses but no subordinate clauses.

EXAMPLES
Othello is a great man, but his character is flawed.
Agatha Christie was a prolific writer; she wrote more than eighty books in less than sixty years.

(3) A ***complex sentence*** has one independent clause and at least one subordinate clause.

EXAMPLE
The poet who wrote "Ode on a Grecian Urn" is John Keats. [The independent clause is *the poet is John Keats.* The subordinate clause is *who wrote "Ode on a Grecian Urn."*]

(4) A ***compound-complex*** sentence has two or more independent clauses and at least one subordinate clause.

EXAMPLE
After Macbeth killed their father, Malcolm fled to England, and Donalbain escaped to Ireland. [The two independent clauses are *Malcolm fled to England* and *Donalbain escaped to Ireland.* The subordinate clause is *after Macbeth killed their father.*]

SENTENCES CLASSIFIED ACCORDING TO PURPOSE

8n. According to their purpose, sentences are classified as *declarative, interrogative, imperative,* and *exclamatory.*

(1) A ***declarative sentence*** makes a statement. It is followed by a period.

EXAMPLE
The lock on the front door is broken**.**

(2) An ***interrogative sentence*** asks a question. It is followed by a question mark.

EXAMPLE
Have you read Dylan Thomas's "Fern Hill"**?**

(3) An ***imperative sentence*** makes a request or gives a command. It is usually followed by a period. A very strong command, however, is followed by an exclamation point.

EXAMPLES
Please return this book to the library**.**
Give me the name of the warrior who succeeds Beowulf**.**
Stop making that noise**!**

(4) An ***exclamatory sentence*** expresses strong feeling or shows excitement. It is followed by an exclamation point.

EXAMPLES
What a talented writer she was**!**
We won**!**

For more information about using end marks, see pages 1243–1244.

9 SENTENCE STYLE

WAYS TO ACHIEVE CLARITY

Coordinating Ideas

9a. To *coordinate* two or more ideas, or to give them equal emphasis, link them with a connecting word, an appropriate mark of punctuation, or both.

EXAMPLE
I read the novel *Frankenstein***, and** then I saw the film.

Subordinating Ideas

9b. To *subordinate* an idea, or to show that one idea is related to but less important than another, use an adverb clause or an adjective clause.

EXAMPLES
Sir Gawain accepts the magic sash **because he wants it to protect him from the Green Knight.** [adverb clause]
Hrunting is the name of the sword **that Unferth gives Beowulf.** [adjective clause]

Resources

- *Language Handbook Resources,* pp. 76–90
- *Language Workshop CD-ROM,* Chapter 8—Lessons 31–33: Obstacles to Clarity; Lesson 34: Ways to Achieve Clarity; Lesson 40: Revising for Variety; Lesson 41: Revising to Reduce Wordiness

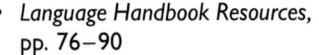

Using Parallel Structure

9c. **Use the same grammatical form (*parallel structure*) to express ideas of equal importance.**

(1) Use parallel structure when you link coordinate ideas.

EXAMPLE
In the winter I usually like **to ski** and **to skate.** [infinitive paired with infinitive]

(2) Use parallel structure when you compare or contrast ideas.

EXAMPLE
Einstein liked mathematical **research** more than laboratory **supervision.** [noun contrasted with noun]

(3) Use parallel structure when you link ideas with correlative conjunctions (*both . . . and, either . . . or, neither . . . nor,* or *not only . . . but also*).

EXAMPLE
Virginia Woolf was not only **a novelist** but also **an essayist.** [Note that the correlative conjunctions come directly before the parallel terms.]

When you revise for parallel structure, you may need to add an article, a preposition, or a pronoun before each of the parallel terms.

UNCLEAR I admire the poems of Byron more than Wordsworth.

CLEAR I admire the poems of Byron more than **those of** Wordsworth.

OBSTACLES TO CLARITY

Sentence Fragments

9d. **Avoid using a *sentence fragment*—a word or word group that either does not contain a subject and a verb or does not express a complete thought.**

For more information about sentence fragments, see pages 1233–1234.

Here are two common ways to correct a sentence fragment.

1. Add words to make the thought complete.

FRAGMENT Twelve Geats around Beowulf's tower. [The verb is missing.]

SENTENCE Twelve Geats **rode** around Beowulf's tower.

2. Attach the fragment to the sentence that comes before or after it.

FRAGMENT A doctor and a gentlewoman see Lady Macbeth. Walking in her sleep. [participial phrase]

SENTENCE A doctor and a gentlewoman see Lady Macbeth **walking in her sleep.**

NOTE Sentence fragments can be effective when used in expressive and creative writing and in informal writing.

Run-on Sentences

9e. **Avoid using a *run-on sentence*—two or more complete thoughts that are run together as if they were one complete thought.**

The two kinds of run-on sentences are *fused sentences* and *comma splices.* A ***fused sentence*** has no punctuation or connecting word at all between the complete thoughts. A ***comma splice*** has just a comma between the complete thoughts.

FUSED SENTENCE Wiglaf helps Beowulf the other warriors retreat in fear.

COMMA SPLICE Wiglaf helps Beowulf, the other warriors retreat in fear.

You can correct run-on sentences in several ways.

1. Make two sentences.

EXAMPLE
Wiglaf helps Beowulf**.** **T**he other warriors retreat in fear.

2. Use a comma and a coordinating conjunction.

EXAMPLE
Wiglaf helps Beowulf**, but** the other warriors retreat in fear.

3. Change one of the independent clauses to a subordinate clause.

EXAMPLE
Wiglaf helps Beowulf**, while the other warriors retreat in fear.**

4. Use a semicolon.

EXAMPLE
Wiglaf helps Beowulf**;** the other warriors retreat in fear.

5. Use a semicolon and a conjunctive adverb.

EXAMPLE
Wiglaf helps Beowulf**; however,** the other warriors retreat in fear.

Unnecessary Shifts in Sentences

9f. **Avoid making unnecessary shifts in subject, in tense, and in voice.**

AWKWARD Grandma goes to the farmers' market, where the freshest produce is. [shift in subject]
BETTER **Grandma** goes to the farmers' market, where **she** finds the freshest produce.

AWKWARD Macbeth sees Banquo's ghost, but no one else did. [shift in tense]
BETTER Macbeth **sees** Banquo's ghost, but no one else **does.**

AWKWARD Lyle spent four hours at the library, but no books on his research topic were found. [shift in voice]
BETTER Lyle **spent** four hours at the library, but he **found** no books on his research topic.

REVISING FOR VARIETY

9g. **Use a variety of sentence beginnings.**

Putting the subject first in a declarative sentence is not wrong, but starting every sentence with the subject can make your writing boring. To add variety to your sentences, rearrange sentence parts to vary the beginnings. The following examples show how a writer can revise sentences to avoid beginning with the subject every time.

SUBJECT FIRST Lady Macbeth is cunning and ruthless and goads her husband into committing murder.
SINGLE-WORD MODIFIERS FIRST **Cunning** and **ruthless,** Lady Macbeth goads her husband into committing murder.

SUBJECT FIRST ***In Memoriam,* which was published in 1850,** is Alfred, Lord Tennyson's elegy for his friend Arthur Hallam.
PARTICIPIAL PHRASE FIRST **Published in 1850,** *In Memoriam* is Alfred, Lord Tennyson's elegy for his friend Arthur Hallam.

APPOSITIVE PHRASE FIRST **An elegy for Alfred, Lord Tennyson's friend Arthur Hallam,** *In Memoriam* was published in 1850.

Varying Sentence Structure

9h. **Use a mix of simple, compound, complex, and compound-complex sentences in your writing.**

EXAMPLE
The three "weird sisters" greet Macbeth and Banquo with prophecies. [simple] According to the witches, Macbeth will become king, but Banquo will not, though his descendants will. [compound-complex] When Macbeth asks the witches to tell him more, they vanish. [complex] The subsequent conversation between Banquo and Macbeth lends insight into each man's character. [simple] That is, Banquo is skeptical of the witches' prophecies; however, Macbeth believes in them. [compound]

For information about the four kinds of sentence structure, see page 1236.

Revising to Reduce Wordiness

9i. **Avoid using unnecessary words in your writing.**

The following guidelines suggest some ways to revise wordy sentences.

1. Take out a whole group of unnecessary words.

WORDY Grendel's mother carried Beowulf to her home where she lived.
IMPROVED Grendel's mother carried Beowulf to her home.

2. Replace pretentious words and expressions with straightforward ones.

WORDY In *Lord of the Flies,* a group of males, all of whom are under thirteen years of age, is stranded on a land mass surrounded by water and totally free of inhabitants.
IMPROVED In *Lord of the Flies,* a group of **young boys** is stranded on an **uninhabited island.**

3. Reduce a clause to a phrase.

WORDY Sir Lancelot falls in love with Queen Guinevere, who is the wife of King Arthur.
IMPROVED Sir Lancelot falls in love with Queen Guinevere, **King Arthur's wife.**

4. Reduce a phrase or a clause to one word.

WORDY At that point in time, Mr. Thomas returns.
IMPROVED **Then,** Mr. Thomas returns.

10 Sentence Combining

COMBINING BY INSERTING WORDS AND PHRASES

10a. Combine related sentences by taking a key word (or using another form of the key word) from one sentence and inserting it into another sentence.

ORIGINAL The famous magician Harry Houdini performed impossible escapes. The escapes only seemed impossible.

COMBINED The famous magician Harry Houdini performed **seemingly** impossible escapes. [The verb *seemed* becomes the adverb *seemingly.*]

10b. Combine related sentences by taking (or creating) a phrase from one sentence and inserting it into another.

ORIGINAL Have you read the poem "The Hollow Men"? It was written by T. S. Eliot.

COMBINED Have you read the poem "The Hollow Men" **by T. S. Eliot**? [prepositional phrase]

COMBINING BY COORDINATING IDEAS

10c. Combine related sentences whose ideas are equally important by using coordinating conjunctions (*and, but, or, nor, for, so, yet*) or correlative conjunctions (*both . . . and, either . . . or, neither . . . nor, not only . . . but also*).

The relationship of the ideas determines which connective will work best. When joined, the coordinate ideas form compound elements.

ORIGINAL *Paradise Lost* was written by John Milton. *Paradise Regained* was also written by him.

COMBINED *Paradise Lost* **and** *Paradise Regained* were written by John Milton. [compound subject]

ORIGINAL *Adonais* is one of Shelley's best-known poems. Many critics think that *Prometheus Unbound* is his masterpiece.

COMBINED *Adonais* is one of Shelley's best-known poems**, but** many critics think that *Prometheus Unbound* is his masterpiece. [compound sentence]

Another way to form a compound sentence is to link independent clauses with a semicolon or with a semicolon and a conjunctive adverb (such as *however, likewise,* or *therefore*) followed by a comma.

EXAMPLES
She was willing to compromise**;** he was not.
They moved to Dorsetshire**; however,** they stayed there only a few months.

COMBINING BY SUBORDINATING IDEAS

10d. Combine related sentences whose ideas are not equally important by placing the less important idea in a subordinate clause (adjective clause, adverb clause, or noun clause).

ORIGINAL I read about the life of Queen Victoria. She ruled Great Britain from 1837 to 1901.

COMBINED I read about the life of Queen Victoria, **who ruled Great Britain from 1837 to 1901.** [adjective clause]

or

COMBINED Queen Victoria, **whose life I read about,** ruled Great Britain from 1837 to 1901. [adjective clause]

ORIGINAL Grendel's mother attacks Herot. King Hrothgar once again asks Beowulf for help.

COMBINED **When Grendel's mother attacks Herot,** King Hrothgar once again asks Beowulf for help. [adverb clause]

ORIGINAL They will find Death under an oak tree. An old man tells the three rioters that this will happen.

COMBINED An old man tells the three rioters **that they will find Death under an oak tree.** [noun clause]

For more information about subordinate clauses and subordinating ideas, see pages 1232–1233 and 1236.

LANGUAGE HANDBOOK

Resources

- *Language Handbook Resources,* pp. 91–104
- *Language Workshop CD-ROM,* Chapter 8—Lesson 38: Combining Sentences by Inserting Words and Phrases; Lesson 39: Combining Sentences by Inserting Clauses and by Coordinating Ideas

Resources

- *Language Handbook Resources,* pp. 105–112
- *Language Workshop CD-ROM,* Chapter 10—Lessons 54 and 55: Rules of Capitalization

11 CAPITALIZATION

11a. Capitalize the first word in every sentence.

EXAMPLE
The warrior who succeeds Beowulf as king is Wiglaf.

(1) Capitalize the first word of a sentence following a colon.

EXAMPLE
Mrs. Kelley asked me this question: **H**ow old is Beowulf when he fights Grendel?

(2) Capitalize the first word of a direct quotation.

EXAMPLE
After winning, Brian said, "**W**e couldn't have done it without the support of the good people of Raleigh."

When quoting from another writer's work, capitalize the first word of the quotation only if the writer has capitalized it in the original work.

EXAMPLE
After winning, Brian acknowledged "**t**he support of the good people of Raleigh."

(3) Traditionally, the first word of a line of poetry is capitalized.

EXAMPLES
If all the world and love were young,
And truth in every shepherd's tongue,
These pretty pleasures might me move
To live with thee and be thy love.
—Sir Walter Raleigh, "The Nymph's Reply to the Shepherd"

NOTE Some writers do not follow this rule. Whenever you quote from a writer's work, always use capital letters exactly as the writer uses them.

11b. Capitalize the first word in the salutation and the closing of a letter.

EXAMPLES
Dear John, **D**ear Sir or Madam: **S**incerely,

11c. Capitalize proper nouns and proper adjectives.

A ***common noun*** is a general name for a person, a place, a thing, or an idea. A ***proper noun*** names a particular person, place, thing, or idea. A ***proper adjective*** is formed from a proper noun. Common nouns are capitalized only if they begin a sentence (also, in most cases, a line of poetry), begin a direct quotation, or are part of a title.

COMMON NOUNS	PROPER NOUNS	PROPER ADJECTIVES
dramatist	**S**hakespeare	**S**hakespearean performer
country	**R**ussia	**R**ussian diplomat
mountains	the **A**lps	**A**lpine flora

In most proper nouns made up of two or more words, do not capitalize articles (*a, an, the*), short prepositions (those with fewer than five letters, such as *at, of, for, to, with*), the mark of the infinitive (*to*), and coordinating conjunctions (*and, but, for, nor, or, so, yet*).

EXAMPLES
Speaker of the **H**ouse of **R**epresentatives
American **S**ociety for the **P**revention of **C**ruelty to **A**nimals

NOTE When you're not sure whether to capitalize a word, check a dictionary.

(1) Capitalize the names of most persons and animals.

GIVEN NAMES	**V**irginia	**G**eoffrey
SURNAMES	**W**oolf	**C**haucer
ANIMALS	**L**assie	**R**ocinante

NOTE Some names contain more than one capital letter. Usage varies in the capitalization of *van, von, du, de la,* and other parts of many multiword names. Always verify the spelling of a name with the person, or check the name in a reference source.

EXAMPLES
La **F**ontaine **O'C**onnor al-**K**hansa **M**c**E**wen
Van **D**oren **I**bn **E**zra van **G**ogh de **V**ega

(2) Capitalize the names of nationalities, races, and peoples.

EXAMPLES
Japanese **C**aucasian **H**ispanic **C**elt

(3) Capitalize brand names. Notice that the noun that follows a brand name is not capitalized.

EXAMPLES
Sealtest milk **W**onder bread **C**rest toothpaste

(4) Capitalize geographical names.

TYPE OF NAME	EXAMPLES	
Towns, Cities	**S**tratford-on-**A**von **R**io de **J**aneiro	**D**ublin **S**outh **B**end
Counties, Townships	**M**arion **C**ounty **B**rooklyn **B**orough	**A**lexandria **T**ownship **L**afayette **P**arish
States, Territories	**O**klahoma **Y**ucatán	**N**orth **C**arolina **Y**ukon **T**erritory
Regions	the **M**iddle **E**ast **W**estern **H**emisphere	the **L**ake **D**istrict the **S**outhwest
Countries	**E**ngland	**C**osta **R**ica
Continents	**S**outh **A**merica	**E**urope
Islands	**L**ong **I**sland	**B**ritish **I**sles
Mountains	**H**imalayas **P**ikes **P**eak	**M**ount **R**ainier **S**ierra **N**evada
Other Landforms and Features	**C**ape of **G**ood **H**ope **D**eath **V**alley	**I**sthmus of **C**orinth **B**lack **F**orest
Bodies of Water	**I**ndian **O**cean **B**ering **S**trait	**R**ed **S**ea **S**an **F**rancisco **B**ay
Parks	**H**awaii **V**olcanoes **N**ational **P**ark **P**oint **R**eyes **N**ational **S**eashore	
Roads, Highways, Streets	**R**oute 42 **I**nterstate 75	**K**ing **A**venue **T**hirty-fourth **S**treet

NOTE Words such as *city, state,* and *county* are often capitalized in official documents such as proclamations. In general usage, however, these words are not capitalized.

OFFICIAL USAGE
the State of Iowa

GENERAL USAGE
the state of Iowa

NOTE Words such as *north, western,* and *southeast* are not capitalized when they indicate direction.

EXAMPLES
north of London
heading southwest

NOTE The second word in a hyphenated number begins with a small letter.

EXAMPLE
Forty-second Street

(5) Capitalize the names of organizations, teams, business firms, institutions, buildings and other structures, and government bodies.

TYPE OF NAME	EXAMPLES
Organizations	**D**isabled **A**merican **V**eterans **P**rofessional **P**hotographers of **A**merica
Teams	**R**iver **C**ity **E**astside **B**ombers **H**arlem **G**lobetrotters
Business Firms	**A**aron's **C**arpets **N**ational **B**roadcasting **C**orporation
Institutions	**O**xford **U**niversity **S**outhern **C**hristian **L**eadership **C**onference
Buildings and Other Structures	**L**incoln **C**enter for the **P**erforming **A**rts the **G**reat **W**all of **C**hina
Government Bodies	**U**nited **S**tates **C**ongress **H**ouse of **C**ommons

NOTE Do not capitalize words such as *democratic, republican,* and *socialist* when they refer to principles or forms of government. Capitalize such words only when they refer to specific political parties.

EXAMPLES
The citizens demanded **d**emocratic reforms.
Who will be the **R**epublican nominee for governor?

NOTE Do not capitalize words such as *building, hospital, theater, high school,* and *post office* unless they are part of a proper noun.

(6) Capitalize the names of historical events and periods, special events, holidays and other calendar items, and time zones.

TYPE OF NAME	EXAMPLES	
Historical Events and Periods	**M**iddle **A**ges	**R**eign of **T**error
Special Events	**S**uper **B**owl	**P**an-**A**merican **G**ames
Holidays and Other Calendar Items	**M**onday **N**ovember	**M**emorial **D**ay **N**ational **B**ook **W**eek
Time Zones	**E**astern **D**aylight **T**ime (**EDT**) **C**entral **M**ountain **T**ime (**CMT**)	

NOTE Do not capitalize the name of a season unless it is being personified or used as part of a proper noun.

EXAMPLES
We moved here last **f**all.
This month **F**all begins painting the leaves in brilliant hues.
The **F**all **F**estival is next week.

(7) Capitalize the names of ships, trains, aircraft, spacecraft, monuments, awards, planets and other heavenly bodies, and any other particular places and things.

TYPE OF NAME	EXAMPLES	
Ships	***M**errimac*	**U.S.S. N***autilus*
Trains	***Z**ephyr*	***H**ill **C**ountry **F**lyer*
Aircraft	***E**nola **G**ay*	***S**pruce **G**oose*
Spacecraft	***C**olumbia*	***M**agellan*
Monuments	**M**ount **R**ushmore **N**ational **M**emorial **E**ffigy **M**ounds **N**ational **M**onument	
Awards	**N**obel **P**rize	**M**edal of **F**reedom
Planets and Other Heavenly Bodies	**N**eptune **B**ig **D**ipper	**P**olaris **C**assiopeia
Other Particular Places and Things	**H**urricane **A**lma **M**arshall **P**lan	**S**ilk **R**oute **U**nion **J**ack

NOTE Do not capitalize the words *sun* and *moon*. Do not capitalize the word *earth* unless it is used along with the proper names of other particular places, things, or events.

EXAMPLES
The equator is an imaginary circle around the **e**arth.
Is Mercury closer to the **s**un than **E**arth is?

For more information about the names of particular places and things, see the discussion of proper nouns on page 1240.

11d. Do not capitalize the names of school subjects, except names of languages and course names followed by a number.

EXAMPLES
French **a**rt **A**lgebra **I**

11e. Capitalize titles.

(1) Capitalize a title belonging to a particular person when it comes before the person's name.

EXAMPLES
General Patton **D**r. Sanchez **P**resident Clinton

In general, do not capitalize a title used alone or following a name. Some titles, however, are by tradition capitalized. If you are unsure about capitalizing a title, check in a dictionary.

EXAMPLES
Who is the **p**rime **m**inister of Britain?
When was Ann Richards **g**overnor of Texas?
The **P**rince of **W**ales met earlier today with European leaders.

A title is usually capitalized when it is used alone in direct address.

EXAMPLE
Good afternoon, **S**ir [*or* **s**ir], may I help you?

(2) Capitalize a word showing a family relationship when the word is used before or in place of a person's name, unless a possessive comes before the word.

EXAMPLES
I asked **M**om if **U**ncle Bob is named after her **u**ncle Roberto.

(3) Capitalize the first and last words and all important words in titles of books, periodicals, poems, stories, essays, speeches, plays, historical documents, movies, radio and television programs, works of art, musical compositions, and cartoons.

TYPE OF NAME	EXAMPLES	
Books	*A Tale of Two Cities*	*Gulliver's Travels*
Periodicals	*National Geographic*	*Time*
Poems	"She Walks in Beauty"	"To His Coy Mistress"
Stories	"The Rocking-Horse Winner"	"Games at Twilight"
Essays and Speeches	"A Modest Proposal"	the Gettysburg Address
Plays	*The Tragedy of Macbeth*	*Pygmalion*
Historical Documents	Magna Carta	Treaty of Versailles
Movies	*Robin Hood: Prince of Thieves*	*Clueless*
Radio and TV Programs	*Adventures in World Music*	*Nova*
Works of Art	*The Kiss*	*March of Humanity*
Musical Compositions	*War Requiem*	"Tears in Heaven"
Cartoons	*For Better or Worse*	*Jump Start*

NOTE Unimportant words in a title include articles (*a, an, the*), short prepositions (those with fewer than five letters, such as *of, to, in, for, from, with*), and coordinating conjunctions (*and, but, for, nor, or, so, yet*).

For information about which titles should be italicized and which should be enclosed in quotation marks, see pages 1247 and 1248.

11f. Capitalize the names of religions and their followers, holy days and celebrations, holy writings, and specific deities and venerated beings.

TYPE OF NAME	EXAMPLES	
Religions and Followers	Christianity Muslim	Buddhist Judaism
Holy Days and Celebrations	Easter Passover	Ramadan Holy Week
Holy Writings	Bible Talmud	Koran I Ching
Specific Deities and Venerated Beings	Allah Dalai Lama	God Jehovah

NOTE The words *god* and *goddess* are not capitalized when they refer to mythological deities. The names of specific mythological deities are capitalized, however.

EXAMPLES
The Greek god of the sea was Poseidon.

12 PUNCTUATION

END MARKS

12a. A statement (or declarative sentence) is followed by a period.

EXAMPLE
The Ancient Mariner told an amazing tale.

12b. A question (or interrogative sentence) is followed by a question mark.

EXAMPLE
Do you know who played the leading role in the first movie version of *Hamlet*?

Resources

- *Language Handbook Resources,* pp. 113–124
- *Language Workshop CD-ROM,* Chapter 9—Lessons 42–46: Punctuating Sentences; Lesson 51: Conventional Uses of Punctuation

12c. **A request or command (or imperative sentence) is followed by either a period or an exclamation point.**

EXAMPLES
Turn the music down, please**.** [request]
Name the poet who wrote "The Lady of Shalott**.**" [mild command]
Watch out**!** [strong command]

12d. **An exclamation (or exclamatory sentence) is followed by an exclamation point.**

EXAMPLE
What an interesting story "My Oedipus Complex" is**!**

12e. **An abbreviation is usually followed by a period.**

If an abbreviation with a period ends a sentence, do not add another period. However, do add a question mark or an exclamation point if one is needed.

EXAMPLES
The store opens at 10 A.M**.**
Does the store open at 10 A.M.**?**

Some abbreviations, including those for most units of measurement, are written without periods.

EXAMPLES
AM/FM, CIA, CNN, PC, NASA, SOS,
cc, ft, lb, kw, ml, psi, rpm [*but* in. *for* inch]

TYPE OF ABBREVIATION	EXAMPLES
Personal Names	Howard G**.** Chua-Eoan W**.** H**.** Auden
Organizations, Companies	Co**.** Inc**.** Ltd**.**
Titles Used with Names	Ms**.** Sr**.** Dr**.**
Times of Day	A**.**M**.** (*or* a**.**m**.**) P**.**M**.** (*or* p**.**m**.**)
Years	B**.**C**.** (*written after the date*) A**.**D**.** (*written before the date*)
Addresses	St**.** Blvd**.** P**.** O**.** Box
States	S**.**C**.** Calif**.**

NOTE Use a two-letter state code when the ZIP Code is included. Two-letter state codes are not followed by periods, and no comma is placed between the state code and the ZIP Code.

EXAMPLE
Lexington, **KY** 40505

COMMAS

12f. **Use commas to separate items in a series.**

EXAMPLE
Virginia Woolf**,** James Joyce**,** and D. H. Lawrence are among the writers we are studying.

If all the items in a series are linked by *and, or,* or *nor,* do not use commas to separate them.

EXAMPLE
Byron **and** Shelley **and** Keats were contemporaries.

12g. **Use a comma to separate two or more adjectives preceding a noun.**

EXAMPLE
Gawain is the most gallant**,** honorable knight.

When the last adjective before a noun is thought of as part of the noun, the comma before the adjective is omitted.

EXAMPLE
I've finally found a decent, affordable used car. [*Used car* is thought of as one unit.]

12h. **Use a comma before *and, but, or, nor, for, so,* and *yet* when they join independent clauses.**

EXAMPLE
I read Seamus Heaney's "The Grauballe Man**,**" and now I want to read more of his poems.

You may omit the comma before *and, but, or,* or *nor* if the clauses are very short and there is no chance of misunderstanding.

12i. **Use commas to set off nonessential clauses and nonessential participial phrases.**

A ***nonessential*** clause or phrase is one that can be left out without changing the meaning of the sentence.

NONESSENTIAL CLAUSE W. H. Auden**, who was born in York, England,** became an American citizen in 1946.
NONESSENTIAL PHRASE The little blue sports car**, leaving all the others far behind,** forged into the lead.

☞ For more information about phrases, see Part 6: Phrases. For more on clauses, see Part 7: Clauses.

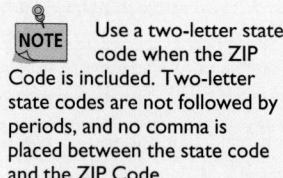

An ***essential*** clause or phrase is one that cannot be left out without changing the meaning of the sentence. Essential clauses and phrases are *not* set off by commas.

ESSENTIAL CLAUSE The writer **who received the Nobel Prize in literature in 1923** was William Butler Yeats.

ESSENTIAL PHRASE The pilgrims **riding along with the Knight** are the Squire and the Yeoman.

12j. Use commas after certain introductory elements.

(1) Use a comma after a one-word adverb such as *first, next, yes,* or *no* or after any mild exclamation such as *well* or *why* at the beginning of a sentence.

EXAMPLE
Yes, I have read *Don Juan.*

(2) Use a comma after an introductory participial phrase.

EXAMPLE
Looking calm, Jill walked to the podium.

(3) Use a comma after two or more introductory prepositional phrases or after a single long one.

EXAMPLE
With the help of Wiglaf, he killed the dragon.

(4) Use a comma after an introductory adverb clause.

EXAMPLE
After I had locked the car door, I remembered that the keys were still in the ignition.

12k. Use commas to set off elements that interrupt a sentence.

(1) Appositives and appositive phrases are usually set off by commas.

EXAMPLES
George Bernard Shaw's first play**, *Widowers' Houses*,** was published in 1893.
Is that she**, the one holding the sunflowers**?

Sometimes an appositive is so closely related to the word or words near it that it should not be set off by commas. Such an appositive is called a ***restrictive appositive.***

EXAMPLE
The poet **Edmund Spenser** died suddenly in 1599.

(2) Words used in direct address are set off by commas.

EXAMPLE
Your research paper**, Dylan,** is quite interesting.

(3) Parenthetical expressions are set off by commas.

Parenthetical expressions are remarks that add incidental information or that relate ideas to each other. Some common parenthetical expressions are *for example, I think, moreover,* and *on the other hand.*

EXAMPLE
Macbeth is superstitious and sensitive; Lady Macbeth**, on the other hand,** is logical and bold.

NOTE A contrasting expression introduced by *not, rather than,* or a similar term is parenthetical. Set it off by commas.

EXAMPLE
Percy Bysshe Shelley**, not John Keats,** wrote "Ode to the West Wind."

12l. Use a comma in certain conventional situations.

(1) Use a comma to separate items in dates and addresses.

EXAMPLES
On April 23**,** 1616**,** William Shakespeare died.
My grandparents' address is 505 King Street**,** Austin**,** TX 78701.

(2) Use a comma after the salutation of a personal letter and after the closing of any letter.

EXAMPLES
Dear Alicia**,** Yours truly**,**

(3) Use commas to set off abbreviations such as *Jr., Sr., RN, M.D., Ltd.,* or *Inc.*

EXAMPLES
Is Jorge Rivera**,** Jr.**,** in your class?
She is the owner of Flowers by Arthurine**,** Inc.

SEMICOLONS

12m. Use a semicolon between independent clauses that are closely related in thought and are not joined by *and, but, for, nor, or, so,* or *yet.*

EXAMPLE
The rain had finally stopped**;** a few rays of sunshine were pushing through breaks in the clouds.

12n. Use a semicolon between independent clauses joined by a conjunctive adverb or a transitional expression.

A ***conjunctive adverb***—such as *furthermore, however,* or *nevertheless*—or a ***transitional expression***—such

LANGUAGE HANDBOOK

as *for instance, in fact,* or *that is*—indicates the relationship of the independent clauses that it joins.

EXAMPLE

The snow made traveling difficult**;** **nevertheless,** we arrived home safely.

12o. **Use a semicolon (rather than a comma) before a coordinating conjunction to join independent clauses that contain commas.**

EXAMPLE

During the seventeenth century—the era of such distinguished prose writers as Sir Thomas Browne, John Donne, and Jeremy Taylor—the balanced compound sentence using commas and semicolons reached a high degree of perfection and popularity**;** but the tendency today is to use a fast-moving style with shorter sentences, fewer commas, and fewer semicolons. [commas within the clauses]

12p. **Use a semicolon between items in a series if the items contain commas.**

EXAMPLE

The summer reading list includes *Jude the Obscure,* by Thomas Hardy**;** *Lord Jim,* by Joseph Conrad**;** and *Lord of the Flies,* by William Golding.

COLONS

12q. **Use a colon to mean "note what follows."**

(1) Use a colon before a list of items, especially after expressions such as *as follows* and *the following.*

EXAMPLE

Collection 8 includes poems by the following authors**:** Robert Burns, William Blake, William Wordsworth, and Samuel Taylor Coleridge.

NOTE Do not use a colon before a list that directly follows a verb or a preposition.

EXAMPLES

Collection 8 includes poems by Robert Burns, William Blake, William Wordsworth, and Samuel Taylor Coleridge. [The list directly follows the preposition *by.*]

The main characters in Charles Dickens's *A Tale of Two Cities* are Dr. Manette, Lucie Manette, Charles Darnay, and Sydney Carton. [The list directly follows the verb *are.*]

(2) Use a colon before a quotation that lacks a speaker tag such as *he said* or *she remarked.*

EXAMPLE

His father's response surprised him**:** "I'm proud of you, son."

For information about punctuating quotations that do have speaker tags, see page 1247.

(3) Use a colon before a long, formal statement or quotation.

EXAMPLE

When he awoke, Gulliver found himself tied down**:** "I could only look upward; the sun began to grow hot, and the light offended my eyes. I heard a confused noise about me, but in the posture I lay, could see nothing except the sky."

12r. **Use a colon in certain conventional situations.**

EXAMPLES

12**:**01 A.M. [between the hour and the minute]

Mark 3**:**10 [between chapter and verse in referring to passages from the Bible]

To Whom It May Concern**:** [after the salutation of a business letter]

"A Valediction**:** Forbidding Mourning" [between a title and a subtitle]

13 PUNCTUATION

ITALICS

Italics are printed characters that *slant to the right like this.* To indicate italics in handwritten or typewritten work, use underlining.

13a. **Use italics (underlining) for words, letters, and symbols referred to as such and for foreign words that have not been adopted into English.**

EXAMPLES

The words *hiss* and *clang* are examples of onomatopoeia.

You typed *ie* instead of *ei.*

The motto *e pluribus unum* appears on all United States coins.

Resources

- *Language Handbook Resources,* pp. 125–132
- *Language Workshop CD-ROM,* Chapter 9—Lesson 44: Punctuating Interrupters; Lessons 47 and 48: Punctuating Possessives, Contractions, and Plurals; Lessons 49 and 50: Punctuating Titles and Quotations; Lesson 51: Conventional Uses of Punctuation; Lessons 52 and 53: Other Marks of Punctuation

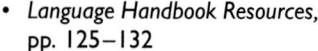

13b. Use italics (underlining) for titles of books, plays, long poems, periodicals, newspapers, works of art, films, television series, long musical compositions, recordings, comic strips, computer software, court cases, trains, ships, aircraft, and spacecraft.

TYPE OF NAME	EXAMPLE
Books	*The Canterbury Tales*
Plays	*The Taming of the Shrew*
Long Poems	*The Rime of the Ancient Mariner*
Periodicals	*Sports Illustrated*
Newspapers	*The Boston Globe*
Works of Art	*The Persistence of Memory*
Films	*It's a Wonderful Life*
TV Series	*American Playhouse*
Long Musical Compositions	*The Planets*
Recordings	*Unforgettable*
Comic Strips	*Doonesbury*
Computer Software	*Lotus 1-2-3*
Court Cases	*Marbury* v. *Madison*
Trains, Ships, Aircraft, and Spacecraft	*Orient Express* *Queen Elizabeth 2* *Enola Gay* *Apollo 13*

NOTE The article *the* before the title of a book, periodical, or newspaper is neither italicized nor capitalized unless it is part of the official title. The official title of a book appears on the book's title page. The official title of a periodical or newspaper is the name on its masthead, usually found on the editorial page.

EXAMPLES
What role does fate play in "The Seafarer"?
I found this information in ***The*** *New York Times.*
My mom looks through the *Sun-Times* every morning.

For a list of titles that are enclosed in quotation marks, see page 1248. For information about capitalizing titles, see page 1243.

QUOTATION MARKS

13c. Use quotation marks to enclose a *direct quotation*—a person's exact words.

(1) A direct quotation usually begins with a capital letter.

EXAMPLE
Sir Francis Bacon wrote, "**K**nowledge is power."

However, when the quotation is only a part of a sentence, do not begin it with a capital letter.

EXAMPLE
In Act 1, Scene 5, Lady Macbeth describes her husband's nature as "**t**oo full o' th' milk of human kindness."

Do not use quotation marks to enclose an ***indirect quotation*** (a rewording of a direct quotation).

DIRECT QUOTATION Al said, "I'm going fishing today."
INDIRECT QUOTATION Al said that he is going fishing today.

(2) When the expression identifying the speaker divides a quoted sentence, the second part begins with a lowercase letter.

EXAMPLE
"All good moral philosophy," according to Sir Francis Bacon, "**i**s but the handmaid to religion." [Notice that each part of a divided quotation is enclosed in quotation marks.]

When the second part of a divided quotation is a new sentence, the first word begins with a capital letter.

EXAMPLE
"On his first voyage, Gulliver finds himself in Lilliput," explained Ms. Chávez. "**T**he people there are only six inches tall."

(3) When used with quotation marks, other marks of punctuation are placed according to the following rules.

- Commas and periods are always placed inside the closing quotation marks.

EXAMPLES
"Read these lines**,"** he said, "and tell me what you think they mean**."**

- Semicolons and colons are always placed outside the closing quotation marks.

EXAMPLES
Gloria promised, "I'll go to the dance with you"; however, she said that several weeks ago.
Find examples of the following figures of speech in Wordsworth's poem "I Wandered Lonely as a Cloud": personification, metaphor, and simile.

- Question marks and exclamation points are placed inside the closing quotation marks if the quotation itself is a question or an exclamation. Otherwise, they are placed outside.

EXAMPLES
Did Keats write "Ode on a Grecian Urn"?
"What an imagination you have!" exclaimed Beth.

(4) When quoting a passage that consists of more than one paragraph, put quotation marks at the beginning of each paragraph and at the end of only the last paragraph in the passage.

EXAMPLE

"At Mr. Bowyers's, a great deal of company; some I knew, others I did not. Here we stayed upon the leads and below till it was late, expecting to see the fireworks; but they were not performed tonight. Only, the City had a light like a glory round about it, with bonfires.

"At last I went to King Street; and there sent Crockford to my father's and my house to tell them I could not come home tonight, because of the dirt and a coach could not be had."

—Samuel Pepys, *The Diary of Samuel Pepys*

(5) Use single quotation marks to enclose a quotation within a quotation.

EXAMPLE
Ms. Markham asked us, "What do you think John Donne meant when he said, 'No man is an island, entire of itself'?"

(6) When writing ***dialogue*** (a conversation), begin a new paragraph every time the speaker changes, and enclose each speaker's words in quotation marks.

EXAMPLE

This frighted the fellow that attended about the work; but after some pause John Hayward, recovering himself, said, "Lord, bless us! There's somebody in the cart not quite dead!"

So another called to him and said, "Who are you?"

The fellow answered, "I am the poor piper. Where am I?"

"Where are you?" says Hayward. "Why, you are in the dead-cart, and we are going to bury you."

—Daniel Defoe, *A Journal of the Plague Year*

13d. **Use quotation marks to enclose titles of short works, such as short stories, poems, essays, articles, songs, episodes of television series, and chapters and other parts of books.**

TYPE OF NAME	EXAMPLE
Short Stories	"The Doll's House" "Games at Twilight"
Poems	"Ode to a Nightingale" "Thoughts of Hanoi"
Essays	"Shakespeare's Sister" "The Myth of Sisyphus"
Articles	"How to Improve Your Grades"
Songs	"Wind Beneath My Wings" "Frankie and Johnny"
TV Episodes	"Tony's Surprise Party" "Inside the Earth"
Chapters of a Book	"The Age of Reform" "How Ecosystems Change"

NOTE Neither italics nor quotation marks are used for the titles of major religious texts or for the titles of historical or legal documents.

EXAMPLES
the Bible
Code of Hammurabi
Bill of Rights
Monroe Doctrine

For a list of titles that are italicized, see page 1247.

ELLIPSIS POINTS

13e. **Use three spaced periods called *ellipsis points* (. . .) to mark omissions from quoted material and pauses in a written passage.**

ORIGINAL At last she spoke to me. When she addressed the first words to me I was so confused that I did not know what to answer. She asked me was I going to *Araby*. I forget whether I answered yes or no. It would be a splendid bazaar, she said; she would love to go.

—James Joyce, "Araby"

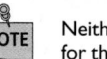

(1) If the quoted material that comes before the ellipsis points is not a complete sentence, use three ellipsis points with a space before the first point.

EXAMPLE
Of his conversation with Mangan's sister, the narrator says, "When she addressed the first words to me . . . I did not know what to answer."

(2) If the quoted material that comes before the ellipsis points is a complete sentence, use an end mark before the ellipsis points.

EXAMPLE
According to Mangan's sister, "It would be a splendid bazaar. . . ."

(3) If one sentence or more is omitted, ellipsis points follow any end mark that precedes the omitted material.

EXAMPLE
The narrator recalls his encounter with Mangan's sister: "At last she spoke to me. . . . She asked me was I going to *Araby*."

(4) To show that a full line or more of poetry has been omitted, use a line of spaced periods that is as long as the line of poetry above it.

ORIGINAL It fell about the Martinmas time,
And a gay time it was then,
When our goodwife got puddings to make,
And she's boild them in the pan.
—Traditional, "Get Up and Bar the Door"

ONE LINE OMITTED It fell about the Martinmas time,
. . . .
When our goodwife got puddings to make,
And she's boild them in the pan.

APOSTROPHES

Possessive Case

13f. The *possessive case* of a noun or a pronoun indicates ownership or relationship. Use an apostrophe in forming the possessive case of nouns and indefinite pronouns.

(1) To form the possessive of a singular noun, add an apostrophe and an *s*.

EXAMPLES
Beowulf**'s** shield the principal**'s** office

NOTE When forming the possessive of a singular noun that ends in an *s* sound, add only an apostrophe if the addition of *'s* will make the noun awkward to pronounce. Otherwise, add *'s*.

EXAMPLES
Ms. Rodgers**'** class the witness**'s** testimony

(2) To form the possessive of a plural noun ending in *s*, add only the apostrophe.

EXAMPLES
the players**'** uniforms the volunteers**'** efforts

(3) Form the possessive of only the last word in a compound word, in the name of an organization or business, or in a word group showing joint possession.

EXAMPLES
brother-in-law**'s** car
Ralph Merrill and Company**'s** products
Macbeth and Lady Macbeth**'s** plan

NOTE When a possessive pronoun is part of a word group showing joint possession, each noun in the word group is also possessive.

EXAMPLE
Chen**'s**, Ramona**'s**, and **my** project

(4) Form the possessive of each noun in a word group showing individual possession of similar items.

EXAMPLE
Byron**'s**, Shelley**'s**, and Keats**'s** poems

(5) Possessive forms of words indicating time, such as *minute, day, month,* and *year,* and words indicating amounts in cents or dollars require apostrophes.

EXAMPLES
four weeks**'** vacation a dollar**'s** worth

(6) To form the possessive of an indefinite pronoun, add an apostrophe and an *s*.

EXAMPLES
no one**'s** fault somebody else**'s** jacket

Contractions

13g. Use an apostrophe to show where letters, words, or numbers have been omitted in a contraction.

EXAMPLES
let us . . . . **let's** she would . . . . . **she'd**
you will . . . . . **you'll** 1998 . . . . **'98**

The word *not* can be shortened to *–n't* and added to a verb, usually without changing the spelling of the verb.

EXAMPLES
do not . . . . **don't** should not . . . **shouldn't**
EXCEPTION
will not . . . **won't**

Plurals

13h. Use an apostrophe and an *s* to form the plurals of all lowercase letters, some uppercase letters, numerals, and some words referred to as words.

EXAMPLES

There are two ***c*'s** and two ***m*'s** in *accommodate.*

Try not to use so many ***I*'s** in your cover letter. [Without the apostrophe, the plural of the pronoun *I* would spell *Is.*]

NOTE You may add only an *s* to form the plurals of words, numerals, and capital letters if the plural forms will not cause misreading. However, it is never wrong to use an apostrophe in such cases and is usually a good idea to do so.

EXAMPLE

James I ruled England during the early **1600s** [*or* **1600's**].

HYPHENS

13i. Use a hyphen to divide a word at the end of a line.

- Do not divide a one-syllable word.

EXAMPLE

Did the Green Knight know that Sir Gawain had **kissed** [*not* kis-sed] his wife?

- Divide a word only between syllables.

EXAMPLE

First, Macbeth was killed; then he was **decapi-tated** [*not* decapita-ted].

- Divide an already hyphenated word at the hyphen.

EXAMPLE

Queen Elizabeth I was ruler of England for **forty-five** [*not* for-ty-five] years.

- Do not divide a word so that one letter stands alone.

EXAMPLE

Paradise Lost by John Milton is a famous English **epic** [*not* e-pic].

13j. Use a hyphen with compound numbers from twenty-one to ninety-nine and with fractions used as modifiers.

EXAMPLES

thirty-seven

a **three-fourths** majority [*but* **three fourths** of the voters]

DASHES

13k. Use dashes to set off abrupt breaks in thought.

EXAMPLE

The playwright handles her material**—**I should say lack of material**—**quite well.

13l. Use dashes to set off appositives or parenthetical expressions that contain commas.

EXAMPLE

Several of the British Romantic poets**—**Shelley, Keats, and Byron, for example**—**led fascinating lives.

13m. Use a dash to set off an introductory list or group of examples.

EXAMPLE

Alliteration, caesuras, and kennings**—**these are features of Anglo-Saxon poetry.

PARENTHESES

13n. Use parentheses to enclose informative or explanatory material of minor importance.

EXAMPLES

A *roman à clef* **(**literally, "novel with a key"**)** is a novel about real people to whom the novelist has assigned fictitious names.

The Globe **(**see the drawing on page 284**)** was built in 1599. [The *s* in *see* is lowercase because the parenthetical sentence is within a complete sentence.]

The Globe was built in 1599. **(**See the drawing on page 284**.)** [The *S* in *See* is capitalized and a period follows *page 284* because the parenthetical sentence is not within another sentence but instead stands on its own.]

BRACKETS

13o. Use brackets to enclose an explanation within quoted or parenthetical material.

EXAMPLE

The newspaper article stated that "at the time of that Democratic National Convention **[**in Chicago in 1968**]** there were many protest groups operating in the United States."

14 SPELLING

UNDERSTANDING WORD STRUCTURE

Many English words are made up of roots and affixes (prefixes and suffixes).

Roots

The ***root*** of a word is the part that carries the word's core meaning.

ROOT	MEANING	EXAMPLES
–fin–	end, limit	final, infinite
–gram–	write, writing	grammar, epigram
–tract–	pull, draw	tractor, extract
–vit–	life	vitamin, vital

Prefixes

A ***prefix*** is one or more letters or syllables added to the beginning of a word or word part to create a new word.

PREFIX	MEANING	EXAMPLES
contra–	against	contradict, contrast
inter–	between, among	interstate, interact
mis–	not, wrongly	misfire, misspell
re–	back, again	reflect, refinance

Suffixes

A ***suffix*** is one or more letters or syllables added to the end of a word or word part to create a new word.

SUFFIX	MEANING	EXAMPLES
–fy	make, cause	verify, pacify
–ish	suggesting, like	smallish, childish
–ist	doer, believer	artist, humanist
–ty	quality, state	cruelty, certainty

SPELLING RULES

NOTE Always keep in mind that the best way to be sure you have spelled a word correctly is to look the word up in a dictionary.

ie and *ei*

14a. Write *ie* when the sound is long e, except after *c*.

EXAMPLES
rel**ie**ve ch**ie**f f**ie**ld conc**ei**t dec**ei**ve
EXCEPTIONS
either l**ei**sure n**ei**ther s**ei**ze prot**ei**n

14b. Write *ei* when the sound is not long e.

EXAMPLES
r**ei**gn for**ei**gn th**ei**r sover**ei**gn w**ei**ght
EXCEPTIONS
anc**ie**nt v**ie**w fr**ie**nd misch**ie**f consc**ie**nce

NOTE Rules 14a and 14b apply only when the *i* and the e are in the same syllable.

–cede, –ceed, and *–sede*

14c. The only English word ending in *–sede* is *supersede*. The only words ending in *–ceed* are *exceed, proceed,* and *succeed*. Most other words with this sound end in *–cede*.

EXAMPLES
con**cede** pre**cede** re**cede** se**cede**

Adding Prefixes

14d. When adding a prefix, do not change the spelling of the original word.

EXAMPLES
over + run = **over**run mis + spell = **mis**spell

Adding Suffixes

14e. When adding the suffix *–ness* or *–ly*, do not change the spelling of the original word.

EXAMPLES
gentle + ness = gentle**ness** final + ly = final**ly**

LANGUAGE HANDBOOK

Resources

- *Language Handbook Resources,* pp. 133–140
- *Language Workshop CD-ROM,* Chapter 10—Lessons 56 and 57: Basic Spelling Rules; Lesson 58: Homonyms

EXCEPTIONS
For most words ending in *y*, change the *y* to *i* before adding *–ness* or *–ly*.
heavy + ness = heav**iness**   ready + ly = read**ily**

NOTE One-syllable adjectives ending in *y* generally follow rule 14e.

EXAMPLES
shy + ness = shy**ness**   sly + ly = sly**ly**

14f. Drop the final silent e before a suffix beginning with a vowel.

EXAMPLES
awake + en = awak**en**   race + ing = rac**ing**
EXCEPTIONS
Keep the final silent *e*
- in a word ending in *ce* or *ge* before a suffix beginning with *a* or *o*
  peace**able**   courage**ous**
- in *dye* and in *singe* before *–ing*
  dye**ing**   singe**ing**
- in *mile* before *–age*
  mile**age**

NOTE When adding *–ing* to words that end in *ie*, drop the e and change the *i* to *y*.

EXAMPLES
die + ing = **dying**   lie + ing = **lying**

14g. Keep the final silent e before a suffix beginning with a consonant.

EXAMPLES
care + less = care**less**   sure + ty = sure**ty**
EXCEPTIONS
nine + th = nin**th**   judge + ment = judg**ment**
true + ly = tru**ly**   wise + dom = wis**dom**

14h. For words ending in y preceded by a consonant, change the y to *i* before any suffix that does not begin with *i*.

EXAMPLES
heavy + est = heav**iest**
accompany + ment = accompan**iment**
verify + ing = verif**ying**

14i. For words ending in y preceded by a vowel, keep the y when adding a suffix.

EXAMPLES
enjoy + ing = enjo**ying**   play + ed = pla**yed**
EXCEPTIONS
day + ly = da**ily**   lay + ed = la**id**
pay + ed = pa**id**   say + ed = sa**id**

14j. Double the final consonant before a suffix that begins with a vowel if the word *both* (1) has only one syllable or has the accent on the last syllable *and* (2) ends in a single consonant preceded by a single vowel.

EXAMPLES
rap + ing = ra**pping**   refer + ed = refe**rred**
EXCEPTIONS
- For words ending in *w* or *x*, do not double the final consonant.
  bow + ed = bow**ed**   tax + able = tax**able**
- For words ending in *c*, add *k* before the suffix instead of doubling the *c*.
  picnic + k + ing = picnic**king**

FORMING THE PLURALS OF NOUNS

14k. Remembering the following rules will help you spell the plural forms of nouns.

(1) For most nouns, add *–s*.

EXAMPLES
beagle**s**   senator**s**   taxi**s**   Saxon**s**

(2) For nouns ending in *s, x, z, ch,* or *sh,* add *–es*.

EXAMPLES
glass**es**   waltz**es**   brush**es**   Perez**es**

(3) For nouns ending in *y* preceded by a vowel, add *–s*.

EXAMPLES
journey**s**   decoy**s**   Saturday**s**   Kelley**s**

(4) For nouns ending in *y* preceded by a consonant, change the *y* to *i* and add *–es*.

EXAMPLES
comed**ies**   cavit**ies**   theor**ies**   sk**ies**
EXCEPTIONS
For proper nouns, add *–s*.
Gregory**s**   Kimberly**s**

(5) For some nouns ending in *f* or *fe*, add *–s*. For others, change the *f* or *fe* to *v* and add *–es*.

EXAMPLES
belief**s**   loa**ves**   giraffe**s**   wi**ves**
EXCEPTIONS
For proper nouns, add *–s*.
DeGroff**s**   Rolfe**s**

(6) For nouns ending in *o* preceded by a vowel, add *–s*.

EXAMPLES
radio**s**   cameo**s**   shampoo**s**   Matsuo**s**

(7) For nouns ending in *o* preceded by a consonant, add *–es.*

EXAMPLES
torpedo**es** echo**es** hero**es** potato**es**

For some common nouns ending in *o* preceded by a consonant, especially those referring to music, and for proper nouns, add only an *–s.*

EXAMPLES
photo**s** hairdo**s** solo**s** soprano**s** Spiro**s**

(8) The plurals of a few nouns are formed in irregular ways.

EXAMPLES
g**ee**se m**e**n child**ren** m**ice** t**ee**th

(9) For a few nouns, the singular and the plural forms are the same.

EXAMPLES
deer series Chinese Sioux

(10) For most compound nouns, form the plural of only the last word of the compound.

EXAMPLES
courthouse**s** seat belt**s** four-year-old**s**

(11) For compound nouns in which one of the words is modified by the other word or words, form the plural of the noun modified.

EXAMPLES
son**s**-in-law passer**s**by mountain goat**s**

(12) For some nouns borrowed from other languages, the plural is formed as in the original languages. In a few cases, two plural forms are acceptable.

EXAMPLES
analysis—analys**es** phenomenon—phenomen**a** *or* phenomenon**s**

(13) To form the plurals of figures, most uppercase letters, signs, and words referred to as words, add an *–s* or both an apostrophe and an *–s.*

EXAMPLES
1500**s** *or* 1500**'s** Bs *or* B**'s**
$**s** *or* $**'s** *and***s** *or and***'s**

NOTE To avoid confusion, add both an apostrophe and an *–s* to form the plural of all lowercase letters, certain uppercase letters, and some words used as words.

EXAMPLES
The word *fictitious* contains three ***i*'s.** [Without an apostrophe, the plural of *i* could be confused with the word *is.*]
Sebastian usually makes straight A**'s**. [Without an apostrophe, the plural of *A* could be confused with the word *As.*]
Because I mistakenly thought Evelyn Waugh was a woman, I used ***her*'s** instead of ***his*'s** in my paragraph. [Without an apostrophe, the plural of *her* would look like the pronoun *hers* and the plural of *his* would look like the word *hiss.*]

NOTE In names, ***diacritical marks*** (marks that show pronunciation) and capitalization are as essential to correct spelling as the letters themselves. If you're not sure about the spelling of a name, check with the person whose name it is, or consult a reference source.

EXAMPLES
Fran**ç**ois Lagerl**ö**f
Van **D**oren **v**an **G**ogh
M**á**rquez Mar**í**n
de **V**ega al-**K**hansa

15 Glossary of Usage

The Glossary of Usage is an alphabetical listing of expressions with definitions, explanations, and examples. Some of the examples are labeled *standard, nonstandard, formal,* or *informal.* The label ***standard*** or ***formal*** identifies usage that is appropriate in serious writing and speaking (such as in compositions and speeches). The label ***informal*** indicates standard English that is generally used in conversation and in everyday writing such as personal letters. The label ***nonstandard*** identifies usage that does not follow the guidelines of standard English usage.

accept, except *Accept* is a verb meaning "to receive." *Except* may be a verb meaning "to leave out" or a preposition meaning "excluding."

EXAMPLES
Does Sir Gawain **accept** the challenge from the Green Knight? [verb]
Certain states **except** teachers from jury duty. [verb]
I have read all of *Macbeth* **except** the last act. [preposition]

Resources
- *Language Handbook Resources,* pp. 141–145
- *Language Workshop CD-ROM,* Chapter 11: Usage

affect, effect *Affect* is a verb meaning "to influence." *Effect* may be either a verb meaning "to bring about or to accomplish" or a noun meaning "the result [of an action]."

EXAMPLES
How did the murder of King Duncan **affect** Lady Macbeth? [verb]
In this dispute, management and labor should be able to **effect** a compromise. [verb]
What far-reaching **effects** did the *Brown* v. *Board of Education of Topeka* decision have? [noun]

all ready, already *All ready* means "all prepared." *Already* means "previously."

EXAMPLES
Are you **all ready** for the audition?
We have **already** read "The Seafarer."

all right *All right* means "satisfactory," "unhurt; safe," "correct," or, in reply to a question or to preface a remark, "yes." *Alright* is a misspelling.

EXAMPLES
Does this look **all right** [*not* alright]?
Oh, **all right** [*not* alright], you can go.

all the farther, all the faster Avoid using these expressions in formal situations. Use *as far as* or *as fast as.*

EXAMPLE
Is that **as fast as** [*not* all the faster] Chris can run?

all together, altogether *All together* means "everyone in the same place." *Altogether* means "entirely."

EXAMPLES
The knights were **all together** for the celebration.
Sir Gawain was not **altogether** honest with the Green Knight.

allusion, illusion An *allusion* is an indirect reference to something. An *illusion* is a mistaken idea or a misleading appearance.

EXAMPLES
The speaker made an **allusion** to Emily Brontë's *Wuthering Heights.*
Before selecting a career, he had to abandon some of his **illusions** about his own abilities.
The director chose certain colors to create an **illusion** of depth on the small stage.

a lot Avoid this expression in formal situations by using *many* or *much.*

EXAMPLE
Many [*not* a lot] of my friends work part time after school and on weekends.

already See **all ready, already.**

altogether See **all together, altogether.**

among See **between, among.**

and etc. *Etc.* stands for the Latin words *et cetera,* meaning "and others" or "and so forth." Always avoid using *and* before *etc.* In general, avoid using *etc.* in formal situations. Use one of its meanings instead.

EXAMPLE
We are comparing the main female characters in Shakespeare's tragedies: Lady Macbeth, Cleopatra, Juliet, **and others** [*or* **etc.** *but not* and etc.].

any one, anyone The expression *any one* specifies one member of a group. *Anyone* means "one person, no matter which."

EXAMPLES
Any one of you could win the poetry contest.
Anyone who finishes the test early may leave.

as See **like, as.**

as if See **like, as if.**

at Avoid using *at* after a construction beginning with *where.*

NONSTANDARD	Where was Beowulf at when Grendel's mother attacked?
STANDARD	**Where** was Beowulf when Grendel's mother attacked?

a while, awhile *A while* means "a period of time." *Awhile* means "for a short time."

EXAMPLES
Herot remained empty for quite **a while.**
They stayed there **awhile.**

bad, badly *Bad* is an adjective. *Badly* is an adverb. In standard English, *bad* should follow a sense verb, such as *feel, look, sound, taste,* or *smell,* or other linking verb.

EXAMPLE
The prospects for fair weather look **bad** [*not* badly].

because In formal situations, do not use the construction *reason . . . because.* Instead, use *reason . . . that.*

EXAMPLE
The **reason** Sir Gawain accepts the green sash is **that** [*not* because] he thinks it will protect him from the Green Knight.

being as, being that Avoid using either of these expressions for *since* or *because.*

EXAMPLE
Because [*not* being as *or* being that] Sir Gawain is a knight, we expect him to behave chivalrously.

beside, besides *Beside* means "by the side of" or "next to." *Besides* means "in addition to" or "other than" or "moreover."

EXAMPLES

The Geats built Beowulf's tomb **beside** the sea.

No one **besides** Wiglaf helped Beowulf battle the dragon.

I have decided that I do not want to take journalism; **besides,** I cannot fit it into my schedule.

between, among Use *between* to refer to only two items or to more than two when comparing each item individually to each of the others.

EXAMPLES

The reward money will be divided **between** Chang and Marta.

Sasha explained the difference **between** assonance, consonance, and alliteration. [Each item is compared individually to each of the others.]

Use *among* to refer to more than two items when you are not considering each item in relation to each other item individually.

EXAMPLE

The reward money will be divided **among** the four girls.

bring, take *Bring* means "to come carrying something." *Take* means "to go carrying something."

EXAMPLES

I'll **bring** my copy of *Gulliver's Travels* when I come over.

Please **take** the model of the Globe Theater to the library.

bust, busted Avoid using these words as verbs. Instead, use a form of *break* or *burst,* depending on the meaning.

EXAMPLES

The window is **broken** [*not* busted].

The water main has **burst** [*not* busted] open.

can, may Use *can* to express ability. Use *may* to express possibility.

EXAMPLES

Can you play the guitar?

It **may** rain later.

cannot (can't) help but Avoid using *but* and the infinitive form of a verb after the expression *cannot (can't) help.* Instead, use a gerund alone.

NONSTANDARD	I can't help but laugh when I look at that photograph.
STANDARD	I can't help **laughing** when I look at that photograph.

compare, contrast Used with *to, compare* means "to look for similarities between." Used with *with, compare* means "to look for both similarities and differences between." *Contrast* is always used to point out differences.

EXAMPLES

The simile at the end of the poem **compares** the eagle's fall **to** a thunderbolt.

We **compared** Shakespeare's style **with** that of Christopher Marlowe.

The tour guide also **contrasted** the two castles' provisions for defense.

could of See **of.**

double subject Avoid using an unnecessary pronoun after the subject of a sentence.

EXAMPLE

George Bernard Shaw [*not* George Bernard Shaw he] wrote *Pygmalion.*

due to Avoid using *due to* for "because of" or "owing to."

EXAMPLE

All schools were closed **because of** [*not* due to] inclement weather.

effect See **affect, effect.**

either, neither *Either* usually means "one or the other of two." In referring to more than two, use *any one* or *any* instead. *Neither* usually means "not one or the other of two." In referring to more than two, use *none* instead.

EXAMPLES

Either of the two quotations would be appropriate to use at the beginning of your speech.

You should be able to find ample information about **any one** of those four poets.

Neither of the Perez twins is in school today.

None of the seniors have voted yet.

etc. See **and etc.**

every day, everyday *Every day* means "each day." *Everyday* means "daily," "ordinary," or "usual."

EXAMPLES

Every day presents its own challenges.

The party will be casual; wear **everyday** clothes.

every one, everyone *Every one* specifies every single person or thing of those named. *Everyone* means "everybody, all of the people named."

EXAMPLES

Elizabeth Bowen wrote **every one** of these stories.

Did **everyone** read "The Demon Lover"?

except See **accept, except.**

farther, further Use *farther* to express physical distance. Use *further* to express abstract relationships of degree or quantity.

EXAMPLES
Your house is **farther** from school than mine is.
The United Nations members decided that **further** debate was unnecessary.

fewer, less Use *fewer* to modify a plural noun and *less* to modify a singular noun.

EXAMPLES
Fewer students are going out for football this year.
Now I spend **less** time watching TV.

good, well Avoid using the adjective *good* to modify an action verb. Instead, use the adverb *well,* meaning "capably" or "satisfactorily."

EXAMPLE
We did **well** [*not* good] on the exam.

Used as an adjective, *well* means "in good health" or "satisfactory in appearance or condition."

EXAMPLES
I feel **well.**
It's eight o'clock, and all is **well.**

had of See **of.**

had ought, hadn't ought Do not use *had* or *hadn't* with *ought.*

EXAMPLES
Your application **ought** [*not* had ought] to have been sent in earlier.
She **ought not** [*not* hadn't ought] to swim so soon after eating lunch.

illusion See **allusion, illusion.**

imply, infer *Imply* means "to suggest indirectly." *Infer* means "to interpret" or "to draw a conclusion."

EXAMPLES
The speaker of "To a Skylark" **implies** that the skylark is a divine being.
I **inferred** from her speech that she would support a statewide testing program.

in, in to, into *In* generally shows location. In the construction *in to, in* is an adverb followed by the preposition *to. Into* generally shows direction.

EXAMPLES
Rudyard Kipling was born **in** Bombay.
He found the treasure and turned it **in to** his king.
Sir Gawain rode **into** the wilderness to find the Green Knight.

infer See **imply, infer.**

irregardless, regardless *Irregardless* is nonstandard. Use *regardless* instead.

EXAMPLE
Regardless [*not* irregardless] of the danger, he continued his journey.

its, it's *Its* is the possessive form of *it. It's* is the contraction of *it is* or *it has.*

EXAMPLES
The community is proud of **its** school system.
It's [it is] a symbol of peace.
It's [it has] been cooler today.

kind of, sort of In formal situations, avoid using these terms for the adverb *somewhat* or *rather.*

INFORMAL Macbeth appeared to be kind of worried.
FORMAL Macbeth appeared to be **rather** [*or* **somewhat**] worried.

kind of a(n), sort of a(n) In formal situations, omit the *a*(*n*).

INFORMAL What kind of a poem is "The Passionate Shepherd to His Love"?
FORMAL What **kind of** poem is "The Passionate Shepherd to His Love"?

kind(s), sort(s), type(s) With the singular form of each of these nouns, use *this* or *that.* With the plural form, use *these* or *those.*

EXAMPLES
This type of engine performs more economically than any of **those types.**

less See **fewer, less.**

lie, lay The verb *lie* means "to rest" or "to stay, to recline, or to remain in a certain state or position." Its principal parts are *lie, lying, lay,* and *lain. Lie* never takes an object. The verb *lay* means "to put [something] in a place." Its principal parts are *lay, laying, laid,* and *laid. Lay* usually takes an object.

EXAMPLES
Gulliver was **lying** on his back and could hardly move. [no object]
The Lilliputians **laid** baskets of food near Gulliver's mouth. [*Baskets* is the object of *laid.*]

like, as In formal situations, do not use *like* for *as* to introduce a subordinate clause.

INFORMAL John looks like his father looked twenty years ago.
FORMAL John looks **as** his father looked twenty years ago.

like, as if In formal situations, avoid using the preposition *like* for the compound conjunction *as if* or *as though* to introduce a subordinate clause.

INFORMAL The heavy footsteps sounded like they were coming nearer.

FORMAL The heavy footsteps sounded **as if** [*or* **as though**] they were coming nearer.

might of, must of See **of.**

neither See **either, neither.**

nor See **or, nor.**

of *Of* is a preposition. Do not use *of* in place of *have* after verbs such as *could, should, would, might, must,* and *ought* [*to*]. Also, do not use *had of* for *had.*

EXAMPLES
If I **had** [*not* had of] known about the shortcut, I **would have** [*not* would of] been here sooner.

Avoid using *of* after other prepositions such as *inside, off,* and *outside.*

EXAMPLE
Flimnap fell **off** [*not* off of] the tightrope.

off, off of Do not use *off* or *off of* for *from.*

EXAMPLE
You can get a program **from** [*not* off of] the usher.

on to, onto In the expression *on to, on* is an adverb and *to* is a preposition. *Onto* is a preposition.

EXAMPLES
The lecturer moved **on to** her next main idea.
She walked **onto** the stage.

or, nor Use *or* with *either;* use *nor* with *neither.*

EXAMPLES
The list of authors does not include **either** James Joyce **or** [*not* nor] D. H. Lawrence.
Neither James Joyce **nor** D. H. Lawrence is on the list of authors.

ought See **had ought, hadn't ought.**

ought to of See **of.**

raise See **rise, raise.**

reason . . . because See **because.**

refer back Since the prefix *re–* in *refer* means "back," adding *back* is generally unnecessary.

EXAMPLE
The writer is **referring** [*not* referring back] to the years when he lived in Ireland.

rise, raise The verb *rise* means "to go up" or "to get up." Its principal parts are *rise, rising, rose,* and *risen. Rise* never takes an object. The verb *raise* means "to cause [something] to rise" or "to lift up." Its principal parts are *raise, raising, raised,* and *raised. Raise* usually takes an object.

EXAMPLES
Her blood pressure **rose** as she waited. [no object]
The Green Knight **raised** the ax above his head. [*Ax* is the object of *raised.*]

should of See **of.**

sit, set The verb *sit* means "to rest in an upright, seated position." Its principal parts are *sit, sitting, sat,* and *sat. Sit* seldom takes an object. The verb *set* means "to put [something] in a place." Its principal parts are *set, setting, set,* and *set. Set* usually takes an object.

EXAMPLES
Banquo's ghost **sits** in Macbeth's place. [no object]
Please **set** the groceries on the table. [*Groceries* is the object of *set.*]

some, somewhat In formal situations, avoid using *some* to mean "to some extent." Use *somewhat.*

EXAMPLE
The Wedding Guest was somewhat shaken [*not* shaken some] by the Ancient Mariner's gaze and appearance.

sort(s) See **kind(s), sort(s), type(s)** and **kind of a(n), sort of a(n).**

sort of See **kind of, sort of.**

take See **bring, take.**

than, then *Than* is a conjunction used in comparisons. *Then* is an adverb meaning "at that time" or "next."

EXAMPLES
Is King Macbeth more superstitious **than** Lady Macbeth?
First, we will read "The Lamb"; **then,** we will read "The Tyger."

that See **who, which, that.**

their, there, they're *Their* is a possessive form of *they.* As an adverb, *there* means "at that place." *There* is also used to begin a sentence. *They're* is the contraction of *they are.*

EXAMPLES
They built a tomb for **their** fallen leader.
Macduff was not **there** at the time.
There is very little time left.
They're waiting for Banquo.

theirs, there's *Theirs* is a possessive form of the pronoun *they. There's* is the contraction of *there is.*

EXAMPLES
The treasure is **theirs** now.
There's an allusion to the Bible in the poem.

them Do not use *them* as an adjective. Use *those.*

EXAMPLE
Have you seen **those** [*not* them] murals by Judith Baca at the art museum?

then See **than, then.**

there See **their, there, they're.**

there's See **theirs, there's.**

they're See **their, there, they're.**

this here, that there Avoid using *here* or *there* after *this* or *that.*

EXAMPLE
This [*not* this here] poem was written by Robert Browning.

try and, try to Use *try to,* not *try and.*

EXAMPLE
I will **try to** [*not* try and] finish reading *The Diary of Samuel Pepys* tonight.

type, type of Avoid using the noun *type* as an adjective. Add *of* after *type.*

EXAMPLE
What **type of** [*not* type] character is the knight in "The Wife of Bath's Tale"?

type(s) See **kind(s), sort(s), type(s).**

ways Use *way,* not *ways,* when referring to distance.

EXAMPLE
Is Canterbury a long **way** [*not* ways] from the Tabard Inn?

well See **good, well.**

when, where Do not use *when* or *where* to begin a definition.

NONSTANDARD A caesura is where you break or pause in a line of poetry.
STANDARD A caesura is **a break or pause in a line of poetry.**

where Do not use *where* in place of *that.*

EXAMPLE
I read **that** [*not* where] you won a scholarship.

where . . . at See **at.**

who, which, that *Who* refers to persons only. *Which* refers to things only. *That* may refer to either persons or things.

EXAMPLES
Sir Gawain was the knight **who** [*or* that] accepted the Green Knight's challenge.
The Globe, **which** was built in 1599, burned down in 1613.
Is this the only poem **that** Sir Walter Raleigh ever wrote?

who's, whose *Who's* is the contraction of *who is* or *who has. Whose* is the possessive form of *who.*

EXAMPLES
Well, look **who's** [who is] here!
Who's [who has] read all of the play?
Whose treasure is it?

would of See **of.**

your, you're *Your* is a possessive form of *you. You're* is the contraction of *you are.*

EXAMPLES
Is that **your** car?
I can see that **you're** tired.

GLOSSARY

The glossary that follows is an alphabetical list of various words found in the selections in this book. Use this glossary just as you use a dictionary—to find out the meanings of unfamiliar words. (Technical, foreign, or more obscure words are not listed here but are defined instead in the footnotes that accompany each selection.)

Many words in the English language have more than one meaning. This glossary gives the meanings that apply to the words as they are used in the selections in this book. Words closely related in form and meaning are usually listed together in one entry (*agitated* and *agitation*), and the definition is given for the first form.

The following abbreviations are used:

adj.,	adjective	*n.,*	noun	*prep.,*	preposition
adv.,	adverb	*pl.,*	plural form	*v.,*	verb

Unless a word is very simple to pronounce, its pronunciation is given in parentheses. A guide to the pronunciation symbols appears at the bottom of each right-hand glossary page.

For more information about the words in this glossary or about words not listed here, consult a dictionary.

abasement (ə·bās′mənt) *n.:* humiliation.
abate (ə·bāt′) *v.:* to lessen.
abject (ab′jekt′) *adj.:* degrading; humiliating.
ablution (ab·lo͞o′shən) *n.:* washing of the body, especially as a religious rite.
abominable (ə·bäm′ə·nə·bəl) *adj.:* disgusting; hateful.
absolution (ab′sə·lo͞o′shən) *n.:* forgiveness.
abstain (ab·stān′) *v.:* to refrain from; hold oneself back from.
abyss (ə·bis′) *n.:* bottomless pit.
accentuate (ak·sen′cho͞o·āt′) *v.:* to emphasize.
accrue (ə·kro͞o′) *v.:* to increase over time.
acquit (ə·kwit′) *v.:* to clear of a charge; absolve.
admonish (ad·män′ish) *v.:* to scold mildly.
adversity (ad·vʉr′sə·tē) *n.:* trouble; misfortune.
aesthetics (es·thet′iks) *n. pl.:* principles of beauty.
affliction (ə·flik′shən) *n.:* deep suffering.
aggrieved (ə·grēvd′) *adj.:* offended; wronged.
agitated (aj′i·tāt′id) *adj.:* disturbed; upset. —**agitation** *n.*
agog (ə·gäg′) *adj.:* in a state of excitement and anticipation.
alienate (āl′ē·ən·āt′) *v.:* to drive apart.
allege (ə·lej′) *v.:* to declare or assert, often without proof.
alleviation (ə·lē′vē·ā′shən) *n.:* something that lightens, relieves, or makes easier to bear.
allotment (ə·lät′mənt) *n.:* distribution.
alms (ämz) *n. pl.:* goods donated to the poor as charity.
altruistic (al′tro͞o·is′tik) *adj.:* unselfish.
ambiguous (am·big′yo͞o·əs) *adj.:* having more than one meaning; unclear; vague.
amiability (ā′mē·ə·bil′ə·tē) *n.:* friendliness. —**amiable** *adj.*
amorous (am′ə·res) *adj.:* full of love.
anecdote (an′ik·dōt′) *n.:* brief, little-known fact or amusing story.
anguish (aŋ′gwish) *n.:* agony.
animosity (an′ə·mäs′ə·tē) *n.:* hostility; intense hatred or resentment.
annals (an′əlz) *n. pl.:* historical records.
annihilate (ə·nī′ə·lāt′) *v.:* to destroy completely.
annul (ə·nul′) *v.:* to do away with; cancel.
aperture (ap′ər·chər) *n.:* opening.
apparition (ap′ə·rish′ən) *n.:* strange figure, like a ghost, that appears suddenly.
apprehensible (ap′rē·hen′sə·bəl) *adj.:* able to be seen or understood. —**apprehend** *v.*
approbation (ap′rə·bā′shən) *n.:* approval.
arable (ar′ə·bəl) *adj.:* suitable for growing crops.
arboreal (är·bôr′ē·əl) *adj.:* full of trees.
ardor (är′dər) *n.:* passion; enthusiasm. —**ardent** *adj.*
arrears (ə·rirz′) *n. pl.:* overdue debts.
arrest (ə·rest′) *v.:* to check or halt in motion.
assail (ə·sāl′) *v.:* to attack. —**assailable** *adj.*
assent (ə·sent′) *n.:* acceptance.
assert (ə·sʉrt′) *v.:* to declare.
assignation (as′ig·nā′shən) *n.:* appointment; meeting.
asunder (ə·sun′dər) *adv.:* apart.
attenuate (ə·ten′yo͞o·āt′) *v.:* to make very slender or drawn out.
audacious (ô·dā′shəs) *adj.:* bold.
audit (ôd′it) *n.:* examination or accounting.
augment (ôg·ment′) *v.:* to increase.
avarice (av′ə·ris) *n.:* greed. —**avaricious** *adj.*
aversion (ə·vʉr′zhən) *n.:* dislike.
avow (ə·vou′) *v.:* to openly declare; acknowledge.

baleful (bāl′fəl) *adj.:* sinister; threatening.
baser (bās′ər) *adj.:* less valuable or worthy.
bastion (bas′chən) *n.:* fortified place; bulwark.
beguile (bē·gīl′) *v.:* 1. to pass the time in a pleasant way. 2. to charm.
benediction (ben′ə·dik′shən) *n.:* blessing.
benign (bi·nīn′) *adj.:* kind; gracious.
bequest (bē·kwest′) *n.:* gift left by means of a will.
blanch *v.:* to turn pale.
blasphemy (blas′fə·mē′) *n.:* mockery of God. —**blaspheme** *v.*
blight (blīt) *n.:* something that causes decay or withers one's hopes. —**blighted** *adj.*
botanical (bə·tan′i·kəl) *adj.:* of plants or plant life; connected to the science of botany, which is the study of plants, their structure, growth, and so on.
breach (brēch) *v.:* to break.
brevity (brev′ə·tē) *n.:* being brief.

fat, āpe, cär; ten, ēven; is, bīte; gō, hôrn, look, to͞ol; yoo, cure; yo͞o, use; oil, out; up, fʉr; get; joy; yet; chin; she; thin; *th*en; zh, leisure; ŋ, ring; ə for *a* in *ago*, e in *agent*, *i* in *sanity*, *o* in *comply*, *u* in *focus;* ′ as in *battle* (bat′'l).

brocade (brō·kād′) *n.:* richly woven cloth.
buffet (buf′it) *v.:* to hit or slap.
buoyancy (boi′ən·sē) *n.:* lightness.
burlesque (bər·lesk′) *n.:* derisive or comic spoof; satire.

cadence (kād′′ns) *n.:* rhythmic flow of sound.
cajole (kə·jōl′) *v.:* to coax with flattery.
calamitous (kə·lam′ə·təs) *adj.:* bringing great trouble.
candor (kan′dər) *n.:* honesty.
carouse (kə·rouz′) *v.:* to drink and celebrate noisily.
carrion (kar′ē·ən) *n.:* decaying flesh eaten by scavenging animals.
casement (kās′mənt) *n.:* window.
cavalcade (kav′əl·kād′) *n.:* parade of horses and carriages.
censure (sen′shər) *v.:* to condemn.
chaff (chaf) *n.:* 1. husks of grain. 2. anything worthless.
chalice (chal′is) *n.:* cup.
chasm (kaz′əm) *n.:* deep crack or fissure; abyss.
chasten (chās′ən) *v.:* to restrain from excess.
chastise (chas·tīz′) *v.:* to scold or punish.
circumambulate (sur′kəm·am′byoo·lāt′) *v.:* to walk around.
circumscribe (sur′kəm·skrīb′) *v.:* to limit; confine.
cistern (sis′tərn) *n.:* tank for collecting rainwater.
civility (sə·vil′ə·tē) *n.:* courtesy.
clamorous (klam′ər·əs) *adj.:* noisy.
clarion (klar′ē·ən) *n.:* clear, sharp, ringing sound.
clemency (klem′ən·sē) *n.:* compassion; mercy.
clinical (klin′i·kəl) *adj.:* detached; impersonal.
cloister (klois′tər) *v.:* to seclude; confine. —**cloistered** *adj.*
coalition (kō′ə·lish′ən) *n.:* temporary alliance or union for some specific purpose.
cohort (kō′hôrt′) *n.:* band of soldiers.
collateral (kə·lat′ər·əl) *adj.:* corresponding.
commiserate (kə·miz′ər·āt′) *v.:* to feel sorrow or pity for; sympathize.
commission (kə·mish′ən) *n.:* act of doing something.
companionable (kəm·pan′yən·ə·bəl) *adj.:* having the traits of a good companion; friendly.
comparatively (kəm·par′ə·tiv′lē) *adv.:* relatively; in comparison to others.
compel (kəm·pel′) *v.:* to force.
comprehensive (käm′prē·hen′siv) *adj.:* including all of the details; broad and sweeping.
concede (kən·sēd′) *v.:* to grant.
conceive (kən·sēv′) *v.:* 1. to form in the mind. 2. to cause life to begin. —**conception** *n.*
conciliate (kən·sil′ē·āt′) *v.:* to soothe the anger of; placate.
condescend (kän′di·send′) *v.:* to lower oneself; stoop.
confederate (kən·fed′ər·āt′) *v.:* to unite; form an alliance.
confiscate (kän′fis·kāt′) *v.:* to seize as a penalty.
conform (kən·fôrm′) *v.:* to become similar; adapt.
confound (kən·found′) *v.:* 1. to confuse. 2. to damn.
congeal (kən·jēl′) *v.:* to thicken.
conjecture (kən·jek′chər) *v.:* to reason; guess. —**conjectural** *adj.*
conjure (kän′jər) *v.:* to summon as by a magic spell. —**conjurer** *n.*
consecrate (kän′si·krāt′) *v.:* to dedicate to sacred use.
conspicuous (kən·spik′yoo·əs) *adj.:* attracting attention by being unusual.
constancy (kän′stən·sē) *n.:* loyalty.
constellation (kän′stə·lā′shən) *n.:* group of stars, usually named after the object, animal, or mythological being its outline, or configuration, suggests.
consternation (kän′stər·nā′shən) *n.:* alarm; bewilderment.
consummate (kän′sə·māt′) *v.:* to complete; fulfill.
contagion (kən·tā′jən) *n.:* spreading of disease.
contemptuous (kən·temp′choo·əs) *adj.:* scornful; disdainful. —**contemptuously** *adv.*
contend (kən·tend′) *v.:* to compete; struggle.
contingent (kən·tin′jənt) *n.:* group.
contortion (kən·tôr′shən) *n.:* unnatural form; distortion.
converge (kən·vurj′) *v.:* to come together at a point.
copious (kō′pē·əs) *adj.:* wordy; profuse.
cornice (kôr′nis) *n.:* decorative strip that runs along the top of a wall.
corporal (kôr′pə·rəl) *adj.:* bodily.
corrode (kə·rōd′) *v.:* to eat away, as by rust.
cosmopolitan (käz′mə·päl′ə·tən) *adj.:* representative of many parts of the world; not constrained by provincial habits or prejudices.
countenance (koun′tə·nəns) *n.:* face; appearance.
courtly (kôrt′lē) *adj.:* suitable for a royal court; with dignity or politeness. —**courtliness** *n.*
covet (kuv′it) *v.:* to long for with envy.
covetousness (kuv′ət·əs·nəs) *n.:* greed. —**covetous** *adj.*
cowed (koud) *adj.:* frightened by threats.
credulous (krej′oo·ləs) *adj.:* believing too readily.
crucial (kroo′shəl) *adj.:* of the greatest importance.
crystalline (kris′təl·in) *adj.:* transparent like crystal.
crystallize (kris′təl·īz′) *v.:* to assume definite form; harden.
culinary (kul′ə·ner′ē) *adj.:* of or about cooking.
cynical (sin′i·kəl) *adj.:* mistrustful.

dapple (dap′əl) *adj.:* spotted.
daunt (dônt) *v.:* to intimidate.
debar (dē·bär′) *v.:* to exclude; hinder.
decree (dē·krē′) *v.:* to officially order or decide.
decussate (dē·kus′āt′) *v.:* to cross so as to form an X; intersect.
defer (dē·fur′) *v.:* to postpone.
deference (def′ər·əns) *n.:* respect; courtesy.
definitive (di·fin′ə·tiv) *adj.:* conclusive; authoritative.
degrade (di·grād′) *v.:* to corrupt; dishonor. —**degradation** *n.*
deify (dē′ə·fī′) *v.:* to make divine; glorify.
delirium (di·lir′ē·əm) *n.:* uncontrollable excitement.
delusion (di·loo′zhən) *n.:* false belief. —**delude** *v.*
demented (dē·ment′id) *adj.:* mad; wild.
demise (dē·mīz′) *n.:* death.
denude (dē·nood′) *v.:* to strip; lay bare.
desolate (des′ə·lit) *adj.:* lonely; forlorn.
despondency (di·spän′dən·sē) *n.:* hopelessness.
despotic (des·pät′ik) *adj.:* tyrannical; oppressive.
deter (dē·tur′) *v.:* to prevent.
deviation (dē′vē·ā′shən) *n.:* a turning off from the usual or normal course.
diatribe (dī′ə·trīb′) *n.:* bitter criticism; rant.
diffusive (di·fyoo′siv) *adj.:* spread out; not concentrated. —**diffuse** *v.*

digress (di·gres′) *v.:* to wander off the subject.
diligent (dil′ə·jənt) *adj.:* patient; persistent.
diminutive (də·min′yo͞o·tiv) *adj.:* very small.
dire (dīr) *adj.:* dreadful.
dirge (durj) *n.:* funeral hymn; lament.
discern (di·surn′) *v.:* to perceive; understand.
discomfit (dis·kum′fit) *v.:* to embarrass; make uneasy.
disconcert (dis′kən·surt′) *v.:* to embarrass, confuse, or fluster.
discourse (dis′kôrs′) *n.:* conversation.
discreet (di·skrēt′) *adj.:* cautious about one's words and actions.
discriminate (di·skrim′i·nāt′) *v.:* to carefully distinguish between; differentiate.
disdainful (dis·dān′fəl) *adj.:* scornful.
disparage (di·spar′ij) *v.:* to speak disrespectfully of; belittle.
dispassionate (dis·pash′ə·nət) *adj.:* without emotion; impartial.
dispel (di·spel′) *v.:* to cause to vanish.
dispirit (di·spir′it) *v.:* to make sad or apathetic.
disposed (di·spōzd′) *adj.:* having a tendency toward.
dissuasion (di·swā′zhən) *n.:* advice or persuasion against.
distemper (dis·tem′pər) *n.:* disorder; disease.
distend (di·stend′) *v.:* to expand; stretch out; swell.
distill (di·stil′) *v.:* to draw out the essence of.
distraught (di·strôt′) *adj.:* agitated.
dither (di*th*′ər) *n:* excited or confused condition; nervousness.
diverge (dī·vurj′) *v.:* to branch off; separate.
divert (də·vurt′) *v.:* to amuse. —**diversion** *n.*
divinity (də·vin′ə·tē) *n.:* God; sacred being.
divulge (də·vulj′) *v.:* to make known.
docile (däs′əl) *adj.:* submissive; obedient.
dogged (dôg′id) *adj.:* persistent; stubborn.
dominion (də·min′yən) *n.:* governed territory.
dregs *n. pl.:* residue.
drone (drōn) *v.:* to hum or buzz continuously.
dubious (do͞o′bē·əs) *adj.:* doubtful; uncertain.
duly (do͞o′lē) *adv.:* as is right or required.
dumbfound (dum′found′) *v.:* to astonish; shock.
duress (do͞o·res′) *n.:* pressure; force.

eddy *n.:* little whirlpool.
edict (ē′dikt′) *n.:* official order.
efficacious (ef′i·kā′shəs) *adj.:* effective. —**efficacy** *n.*
effluvium (e·flo͞o′vē·əm) *n.:* flow of vapor and invisible particles.
ejaculation (ē·jak′yo͞o·lā′shən) *n.:* sudden impassioned utterance; exclamation.
emanate (em′ə·nāt′) *v.:* to flow; come forth.
emancipate (ē·man′sə·pāt′) *v.:* to set free.
eminent (em′ə·nənt) *adj.:* distinguished; noteworthy.
encumber (en·kum′bər) *v.:* to burden or hinder. —**encumbrance** *n.*
endeavor (en·dev′ər) *n.:* earnest attempt.
engender (en·jen′dər) *v.:* to create; produce.
entreaty (en·trēt′ē) *n.:* plea; sincere request. —**entreat** *v.*
enumerate (ē·no͞o′mər·āt′) *v.:* to count; list.
epicure (ep′i·kyoor′) *n.:* one who takes great pleasure in eating fine foods.
equivocate (ē·kwiv′ə·kāt′) *v.:* to be ambiguous; deliberately evade or lie. —**equivocation** *n.*
eradicate (ē·rad′i·kāt′) *v.:* to exterminate.
exhilaration (eg·zil′ə·rā′shən) *n.:* excitement; high spirits.
exorbitant (eg·zor′bi·tənt) *adj.:* excessive.
expedient (ek·spē′dē·ənt) *n.:* convenient means to an end.
expiate (eks′pē·āt′) *v.:* to make amends for wrongdoing; atone.
extort (eks·tôrt′) *v.:* to get by threats or violence.
exult (eg·zult′) *v.:* to rejoice. —**exultation** *n.*

façade (fə·säd′) *n.:* front of a building.
fallow (fal′ō) *adj.:* unplanted; uncultivated.
fanlight (fan′līt′) *n.:* fan-shaped window over a door.
feign (fān) *v.:* to make up; invent.
feint (fānt) *v.:* to pretend to strike.
fervent (fur′vənt) *adj.:* passionate. —**fervor** *n.*
fetter (fet′ər) *v.:* to chain.
flag *v.:* to decline; lose strength or interest.
foment (fō·ment′) *v.:* to stir up; incite.
forbear (fôr·ber′) *v.:* to avoid; cease.
formidable (fôr′mə·də·bəl) *adj.:* difficult to handle or overcome.
fortitude (fôrt′ə·to͞od′) *n.:* courage.
fraught (frôt) *adj.:* filled.
fray *n.:* noisy quarrel; commotion.
frugal (fro͞o′gəl) *adj.:* thrifty.
funereal (fyo͞o·nir′ē·əl) *adj.:* suitable for a funeral; solemn.
futile (fyo͞ot′'l) *adj.:* unable to succeed; useless.

gambol (gam′bəl) *v.:* to frolic; play animatedly.
garish (gar′ish) *adj.:* too showy or gaudy.
garret (gar′it) *n.:* attic.
garrulous (gar′ə·ləs) *adj.:* talkative.
gauntlet (gônt′lit) *n.:* series of challenges.
genial (jē′nē·əl) *adj.:* 1. mild-mannered; friendly. 2. pleasantly warm and healthful.
glut *v.:* to overfill.
gnome (nōm) *n.:* in folklore, a small being who dwells in the earth.
gorge (gôrj) *v.:* to stuff completely.
grovel (gräv′əl) *v.:* to crawl with the face close to the ground.
guffaw (gu·fô′) *n.:* loud laugh.
guile (gīl) *n.:* sly dealings.

haggard (hag′ərd) *adj.:* worn or tired looking.
harbinger (här′bin·jər) *n.:* indicator of what is to come.
hinterland (hin′tər·land′) *n.:* rural area; backwoods.
homage (äm′ij) *n.:* something done or given to show respect.

fat, āpe, cär; ten, ēven; is, bīte; gō, hôrn, look, to͞ol; yoo, cure; yo͞o, use; oil, out; up, fur; get; joy; yet; chin; she; thin; *th*en; zh, leisure; ŋ, ring; ə for *a* in *ago,* e in *agent, i* in *sanity, o* in *comply, u* in *focus;* ' as in *battle* (bat′'l).

homily (häm′ə·lē) *n.:* sermon.
hospitable (häs·pit′ə·bəl) *adj.:* friendly toward guests.
hue (hyo͞o) *n.:* shade of color.
hysteria (hi·ster′ē·ə) *n.:* outbreak of uncontrolled emotion. —**hysterical** *adj.*

ichor (ī′kər) *n.:* thin, watery substance from a sore. —**ichorous** *adj.*
idolatrous (ī·däl′ə·trəs) *adj.:* idol-worshiping; excessively devoted.
ignoble (ig·nō′bəl) *adj.:* shameful; degrading.
ignominy (ig′nə·min′ē) *n.:* shame and dishonor.
immaterial (im′mə·tir′ē·əl) *adj.:* 1. not consisting of physical matter. 2. unimportant.
impart (im·pärt′) *v.:* to share; tell.
impassive (im·pas′iv) *adj.:* calm; indifferent. —**impassively** *adv.*
impede (im·pēd′) *v.:* to hinder; obstruct. —**impediment** *n.*
impel (im·pel′) *v.:* to push forward.
imperceptible (im′pər·sep′tə·bəl) *adj.:* so gradual or subtle that it is not easily sensed.
imperialism (im·pir′ē·əl·iz′əm) *n.:* policy in which one country seeks power by conquering other countries and establishing colonies.
imperturbable (im′pər·tʉr′bə·bəl) *adj.:* calm; impassive.
impetuous (im·pech′o͞o·əs) *adj.:* sudden; uncontrolled.
impinge (im·pinj′) *v.:* to strike; touch.
impious (im′pē·əs) *adj.:* lacking reverence or respect.
implacable (im·plak′ə·bəl) *adj.:* inflexible; relentless; obstinate.
implore (im·plôr′) *v.:* to beg.
importune (im′pôr·to͞on′) *v.:* to make repeated demands of.
impromptu (im·prämp′to͞o′) *adj.:* unplanned.
improvise (im′prə·vīz′) *v.:* to make for the occasion from whatever is handy.
impudent (im′pyo͞o·dənt) *adj.:* shamelessly bold or disrespectful.
impute (im·pyo͞ot′) *v.:* to attribute to or accuse another.
inadvertent (in′ad·vʉrt′′nt) *adj.:* unintentional. —**inadvertently** *adv.*
inanimate (in·an′ə·mit) *adj.:* not alive.
incarnation (in′kär·nā′shən) *n.:* physical representation of an idea or quality; embodiment.
incendiary (in·sen′dē·er′ē) *n.:* firebomb.
incense (in·sens′) *v.:* to make angry.
incentive (in·sent′iv) *n.:* something that prompts one to take action or work harder.
incessant (in·ses′ənt) *adj.:* never ceasing; constant.
inclemency (in·klem′ən·sē) *n.:* harsh quality; severity.
inconsiderable (in′kən·sid′ər·ə·bəl) *adj.:* not worth consideration; unimportant.
inconstancy (in·kän′stən·sē) *n.:* unsteady loyalty; fickleness.
incorporeal (in′kôr·pôr′ē·əl) *adj.:* without substance.
incredulous (in·krej′oo·ləs) *adj.:* disbelieving.
indifferent (in·dif′ər·ənt) *adj.:* showing no concern or feeling.
indignant (in·dig′nənt) *adj.:* scornful.
indispensable (in′di·spen′sə·bəl) *adj.:* absolutely necessary.
indissoluble (in′di·säl′yo͞o·bəl) *adj.:* unable to be broken; permanent.
inevitable (in·ev′i·tə·bəl) *adj.:* certain to occur.
inference (in′fər·əns) *n.:* conclusion drawn by logical reasoning.
ingenious (in·jēn′yəs) *adj.:* clever.
inimitable (in·im′i·tə·bəl) *adj.:* difficult or impossible to imitate.
insatiable (in·sā′shə·bəl) *adj.:* unable to be satisfied; greedy.
intemperance (in·tem′pər·əns) *n.:* lack of restraint.
inter (in·tʉr′) *v.:* to bury.
intercession (in′tər·sesh′ən) *n.:* pleading on behalf of another.
interim (in′tər·im) *n.:* period of time between.
intermittent (in′tər·mit′′nt) *adj.:* starting and stopping at intervals; periodic.
interstice (in·tʉr′stis) *n.:* small or narrow place between things.
intone (in·tōn′) *v.:* to chant.
intoxicate (in·täks′i·kāt′) *v.:* to cause wild excitement or happiness, often to a point beyond self-control.
intrepid (in·trep′id) *adj.:* fearless.
invariable (in·ver′ē·ə·bəl) *adj.:* constant; without change.
invincible (in·vin′sə·bəl) *adj.:* unconquerable.
ire (īr) *n.:* anger.
iridescent (ir′i·des′ənt) *adj.:* showing rainbowlike colors.
irreconcilable (ir·rek′ən·sīl′ə·bəl) *adj.:* cannot be brought into agreement.
irrelevant (ir·rel′ə·vənt) *adj.:* not related to the subject; not important.
itinerant (ī·tin′ər·ənt) *adj.:* traveling.

jocund (jäk′ənd) *adj.:* in good humor; cheerful.
judicious (jo͞o·dish′əs) *adj.:* wise; prudent.

kindle (kin′dəl) *v.:* to set on fire; ignite.
knell (nel) *n.:* solemn sound of a bell.

labyrinth (lab′ə·rinth′) *n.:* maze; complex or confusing arrangement.
lament (lə·ment′) *n.:* cry of grief.
languish (laŋ′gwish) *v.:* to lose vitality; become weak.
laudable (lôd′ə·bəl) *adj.:* praiseworthy.
levy (lev′ē) *v.:* to impose.
lineage (lin′ē·ij) *n.:* ancestry.
livid (liv′id) *adj.:* 1. discolored by a bruise; gray blue. 2. red or white, as in "livid with rage." —**lividity** *n.*
loathsome (lōth′səm) *adj.:* disgusting.
lucid (lo͞o′sid) *adj.:* clearheaded; sane. —**lucidity** *n.*
lugubrious (lə·go͞o′brē·əs) *adj.:* very solemn or mournful, especially in a way that seems exaggerated or ridiculous.
lunacy (lo͞o′nə·sē) *n.:* madness.
luxuriate (lug·zho͞or′ē·āt′) *v.:* to take enormous pleasure.

magenta (mə·jen′tə) *adj.:* purplish red.
magnanimous (mag·nan′ə·məs) *adj.:* generous in rising above insults.
malady (mal′ə·dē) *n.:* illness.
malevolence (mə·lev′ə·ləns) *n.:* spite; ill will.

malicious (mə·lish′əs) *adj.:* intentionally mischievous or harmful; spiteful. —**malice** *n.*
malignity (mə·lig′nə·tē) *n.:* harmful or evil thing.
maniacal (mə·nī′ə·kəl) *adj.:* crazed; wildly enthusiastic.
marauder (mə·rôd′ər) *n.:* raider; plunderer.
martyrdom (märt′ər·dəm) *n.:* prolonged suffering or self-sacrifice.
maxim (maks′im) *n.:* general truth or rule of conduct.
meager (mē′gər) *adj.:* poor in quality or small in amount.
metamorphosis (met′ə·môr′fə·sis) *n.:* change of form.
mien (mēn) *n.:* manner; bearing.
mill *v.:* to move in a circular or random pattern, as a crowd or flock.
millennium (mi·len′ē·əm) *n.:* period of a thousand years.
mimic (mim′ik) *v.:* to imitate; mock.
mirth (murth) *n.:* joyfulness.
miry (mīr′ē) *adj.:* swampy; muddy.
monotonous (mə·nät′′n·əs) *adj.:* repeating without interruption.
mortal *adj.:* fatal.
mortify (môrt′ə·fī′) *v.:* to cause to feel shame or embarrassment.
multitudinous (mul′tə·to͞od′′n·əs) *adj.:* numerous.
munificent (myo͞o·nif′ə·sənt) *adj.:* very generous.
murky (murk′ē) *adj.:* shadowy.
mute (myo͞ot) *v.:* to muffle or soften.
myriad (mir′ē·əd) *n.:* great number of persons or things.

negligent (neg′lə·jənt) *adj.:* careless; lax.
nemesis (nem′ə·sis) *n.:* agent of retribution or punishment.
nicety (nī′sə·tē) *n.:* delicacy; elegance.
nimble (nim′bəl) *adj.:* moving quickly.
nonpareil (nän′pə·rel′) *adj.:* unrivaled; unequaled.
notorious (nō·tôr′ē·əs) *adj.:* widely but unfavorably known; famous.
noxious (näk′shəs) *adj.:* harmful.

oblique (ō·blēk′) *adj.:* slanting; indirect. —**obliquity** *n.*
obnoxious (əb·näk′shəs) *adj.:* offensive.
obscure (əb·skyoor′) *adj.:* little-known; vague. —**obscurely** *adv.*
obstinate (äb′stə·nət) *adj.:* unreasonably stubborn.
odious (ō′dē·əs) *adj.:* hateful; offensive.
officious (ə·fish′əs) *adj.:* eager to serve; obliging.
omen (ō′mən) *n.:* sign supposedly foretelling the future.
ominous (äm′ə·nəs) *adj.:* threatening.
oppressive (ə·pres′iv) *adj.:* hard to bear.
oracle (ôr′ə·kəl) *n.:* one capable of providing divine revelation or wisdom; seer.
ostentation (äs′tən·tā′shən) *n.:* showiness.
overture (ō′vər·chər) *n.:* proposal.
overwrought (ō′vər·rôt′) *adj.:* overly excited.

palliative (pal′ē·ə·tiv) *adj.:* easing; alleviating.
pallor (pal′ər) *n.:* paleness.
palpable (pal′pə·bəl) *adj.:* easily felt; tangible.
panegyric (pan′ə·jir′ik) *n.:* formal speech elaborately praising something.
parry (par′ē) *v.:* to reply evasively.
pathos (pā′thäs′) *n.:* a quality in something experienced or observed that evokes feelings of pity or sorrow.
patronize (pā′trən·īz′) *v.:* to be a customer of.
penance (pen′əns) *n.:* act of atonement for sin.
pensive (pen′siv) *adj.:* thinking deeply, often of something sad.
perceptible (pər·sep′tə·bəl) *adj.:* visible.
perfidious (pər·fid′ē·əs) *adj.:* treacherous. —**perfidy** *n.*
perfunctory (pər·fuŋk′tə·rē) *adj.:* halfhearted; indifferent. —**perfunctorily** *adv.*
pernicious (pər·nish′əs) *adj.:* wicked; extremely harmful.
perpetual (pər·pech′o͞o·əl) *adj.:* continuing forever; eternal.
perplexity (pər·pleks′ə·tē) *n.:* confusion; bewilderment. —**perplexedly** *adv.*
persevere (pur′sə·vir′) *v.:* to continue in a course of action despite difficulty or opposition; persist.
personable (pur′sən·ə·bəl) *adj.:* attractive in appearance and personality.
perturb (pər·turb′) *v.:* to upset; disturb. —**perturbation** *n.*
pervade (pər·vād′) *v.:* to spread throughout.
perverse (pər·vurs′) *adj.:* disagreeable; contrary.
pestilence (pes′tə·ləns) *n.:* plague; infection. —**pestilential** *adj.*
phosphorescent (fäs′fə·res′ənt) *adj.:* luminous; glowing.
pilgrimage (pil′grim·ij) *n.:* journey made to a place of religious or historical interest.
pious (pī′əs) *adj.:* devout or virtuous; sacred.
pique (pēk) *n.:* ruffled pride; displeasure.
placid (plas′id) *adj.:* calm; peaceful.
posterity (päs·ter′ə·tē) *n.:* all succeeding generations.
potent (pōt′′nt) *adj.:* powerful; mighty. —**potency** *n.*
prate (prāt) *v.:* to talk idly; chat.
precarious (prē·ker′ē·əs) *adj.:* uncertain; insecure.
precipitate (prē·sip′ə·tit) *adj.:* sudden. —**precipitately** *adv.*
predatory (pred′ə·tôr′ē) *adj.:* living by eating other animals.
predominant (prē·däm′ə·nənt) *adj.:* having the greatest influence or control.
preoccupied (prē·äk′yo͞o·pīd′) *adj.:* absorbed in one's own thoughts.
prerogative (prē·räg′ə·tiv) *n.:* right or privilege.
presumptuous (prē·zump′cho͞o·əs) *adj.:* boldly overconfident.
pretext (prē′tekst′) *n.:* excuse.
prevail (prē·vāl′) *v.:* to predominate; hold sway.
prevaricate (pri·var′i·kāt′) *v.:* to lie. —**prevarication** *n.*
pristine (pris′tēn′) *adj.:* pure; unspoiled.
procure (prō·kyoor′) *v.:* to obtain; get. —**procurement** *n.*
prodigious (prō·dij′əs) *adj.:* huge.
prodigy (präd′ə·jē) *n.:* genius.

fat, āpe, cär; ten, ēven; is, bīte; gō, hôrn, look, to͞ol; yoo, cure; yo͞o, use; oil, out; up, fur; get; joy; yet; chin; she; thin; *th*en; zh, leisure; ŋ, ring; ə for *a* in *ago, e* in *agent, i* in *sanity, o* in *comply, u* in *focus;* ′ as in *battle* (bat′′l).

profess (prō•fes′) *v.:* to openly declare.
proffer (präf′ər) *v.:* to offer; propose.
proficiency (prō•fish′ən•sē) *n.:* skill.
profound (prō•found′) *adj.:* deep.
promiscuous (prə•mis′kyo͞o•əs) *adj.:* casual; undiscriminating.
promontory (präm′ən•tôr′ē) *n.:* peak of land that juts into the sea.
prophetic (prō•fet′ik) *adj.:* foreshadowing; predicting.
propitious (prō•pish′əs) *adj.:* favorable.
propriety (prō•prī′ə•tē) *n.:* the quality of being proper or fitting.
prosaic (prō•zā′ik) *adj.:* ordinary; dull.
prostrate (präs′trāt′) *adj.:* lying face down in a show of submission or weakness. —**prostrating** *v.*
protract (prō•trakt′) *v.:* to draw out; extend.
prowess (prou′is) *n.:* outstanding ability or skill; bravery.
proximity (präks•im′ə•tē) *n.:* closeness.
prudent (pro͞od′'nt) *adj.:* careful and wise.
prurient (proor′ē•ənt) *adj.:* lewd; offensive.
pungent (pun′jənt) *adj.:* sharp-smelling.
purge (purj) *v.:* to get rid of; expel.
putrid (pyo͞o′trid) *adj.:* decayed; foul-smelling.

quaint (kwānt) *adj.:* pleasantly unusual.
quell (kwel) *v.:* to subdue.

rancid (ran′sid) *adj.:* stale or foul-smelling.
rancor (raŋ′kər) *n.:* ill will.
rank *adj.:* overgrown.
ravage (rav′ij) *v.:* to violently destroy.
ravenous (rav′ə•nəs) *adj.:* extremely hungry.
rebuke (ri•byo͞ok′) *v.:* to blame or scold.
recapitulate (rē′kə•pich′ə•lāt′) *v.:* to repeat; summarize.
recess (rē′ses) *n.:* indentation.
reckon (rek′ən) *v.:* to consider; judge.
recompense (rek′əm•pens′) *n.:* repayment; reward.
redress (rē′dres′) *n.:* compensation for wrong.
reflux (rē′fluks′) *n.:* a flowing back; ebb.
refract (ri•frakt′) *v.:* to cause a ray to bend as it passes from one medium to another.
reiterate (rē•it′ə•rāt′) *v.:* to repeat.
remonstrate (ri•män′strāt′) *v.:* to protest.
renown (ri•noun′) *n.:* great fame.
reparation (rep′ə•rā′shən) *n.:* payment to compensate for wrongdoing.
repose (ri•pōz′) *v.:* to lie calmly or quietly.
reprisal (ri•prī′zəl) *n.:* punishment in return for injury.
reproachful (ri•prōch′fəl) *adj.:* full of or expressing blame.
reprove (ri•pro͞ov′) *v.:* to express disapproval; rebuke.
repulse (ri•puls′) *v.:* to drive away.
requite (ri•kwīt′) *v.:* to repay.
resigned (ri•zīnd′) *adj.:* showing passive acceptance.
restive (res′tiv) *adj.:* impatient; nervous.
reticulate (ri•tik′yə•lit) *adj.:* having a network of veins like the threads of a net.
retinue (ret′'n•o͞o′) *n.:* string of attendants.
revelation (rev′ə•lā′shən) *n.:* awareness of something previously unknown; realization.
reverberate (ri•vur′bə•rāt′) *v.:* to echo a sound; resonate.
reverent (rev′ər•ənt) *adj.:* having deep respect, love, or awe, as for something sacred.
rhetoric (ret′ər•ik) *n.:* 1. art of speaking and writing. 2. showy but meaningless language.
rite *n.:* formal ceremony.
rudiments (ro͞o′də•mənts) *n. pl.:* basics.
rue (ro͞o) *v.:* to feel remorse; regret.
ruffian (ruf′ē•ən) *n.:* hoodlum; lawless person.

sacrilegious (sak′rə•lij′əs) *adj.:* violating something sacred.
sally *n.:* quick witticism or retort; quip.
sanctity (saŋk′tə•tē) *n.:* sacred quality; holiness.
sarcastic (sär•kas′tik) *adj.:* having biting irony; sneering.
saunter (sôn′tər) *v.:* to stroll.
score *v.:* to mark with a scratch or groove.
scrupulous (skro͞o′pyə•ləs) *adj.:* extremely careful and precise in deciding what is right or wrong.
scrutinize (skro͞ot′'n•īz) *v.:* to examine carefully.
secular (sek′yə•lər) *adj.:* not related to religion.
seethe (sēth) *v.:* to surge; appear constantly active or violently agitated.
semblance (sem′bləns) *n.:* appearance of something else; resemblance.
seminar (sem′ə•när′) *n.:* scholarly group discussion.
senile (sē′nīl′) *adj.:* showing the deterioration that sometimes accompanies old age. —**senility** *n.*
sensibility (sen′sə•bil′ə•tē) *n.:* capacity for being affected emotionally.
sepulcher (sep′əl•kər) *n.:* vault for burial.
sepulchral (sə•pul′krəl) *adj.:* gloomy.
sequel (sē′kwəl) *n.:* 1. something that comes after. 2. consequence or result.
sequester (si•kwes′tər) *v.:* to separate from others; isolate.
serene (sə•rēn) *adj.:* calm; peaceful.
serous (sir′əs) *adj.:* thin and watery. —**serosity** *n.*
serrate (ser′āt′) *adj.:* having jagged, sawlike notches along the edge.
servile (sur′vīl) *adj.:* like or characteristic of a slave; humbly submissive or yielding.
shambles (sham′bəlz) *n. pl.:* scene of great disorder.
sheaf (shēf) *n.:* stalks of grain bound up in a bundle. —**sheaves** *n. pl.*
shoal (shōl) *n.:* shallow place; sandbar.
signalize (sig′nəl•īz′) *v.:* to draw attention to.
silt *v.:* to fill up with sediment or residue.
sinew (sin′yo͞o) *n.:* tendon or connective tissue.
skeptical (skep′ti•kəl) *adj.:* doubting.
slake *v.:* to satisfy or quench.
slovenly (sluv′ən•lē) *adj.:* untidy.
sodden (säd′'n) *adj.:* soaked; soggy.
solace (säl′is) *n.:* peace; relief.
solicit (sə•lis′it) *v.:* to ask or plead earnestly.
solicitous (sə•lis′ə•təs) *adj.:* showing care or attention.
somber (säm′bər) *adj.:* gloomy.
sovereign (säv′rən) *adj.:* superior to all others.
spare *adj.:* meager; thin.
spawn (spôn) *v.:* to bring into being.
specter (spek′tər) *n.:* ghost. —**spectral** *adj.*
squalid (skwäl′id) *adj.:* foul or unclean; wretched.
squeamish (skwēm′ish) *adj.:* easily upset.
stagnate (stag′nāt′) *v.:* to become inactive or sluggish.

stature (stach'ər) *n.:* height.
statute (stach'o͞ot) *n.:* law.
stealth (stelth) *n.:* secret or sly behavior.
stifle (stī'fəl) *v.:* to suppress; hold back.
stint *n.:* limitation.
stratagem (strat'ə • jəm) *n.:* trick.
strident (strīd''nt) *adj.:* harsh; sharp.
stupefy (sto͞o'pə • fī') *v.:* to dull the mind and senses; make lethargic, as in a state of stupor.
subdue (səb • do͞o') *v.:* to conquer; overcome.
sublime (sə • blīm') *adj.:* awe-inspiring; majestic.
subsistence (səb • sis'təns) *n.:* existence; means of support or sustenance.
subtle (sut''l) *adj.:* delicately suggestive; not obvious.
succumb (sə • kum') *v.:* 1. to yield; give way. 2. to die.
suffice (sə • fīs') *v.:* to satisfy. —**sufficient** *adj.*
sundry (sun'drē) *adj.:* various.
supercilious (so͞o'pər • sil'ē • əs) *adj.:* disdainful or scornful; haughty.
superfluity (so͞o'pər • flo͞o'ə • tē) *n.:* excess.
supplant (sə • plant') *v.:* to replace; displace.
suppliant (sup'lē • ənt) *adj.:* requesting humbly. —**supplication** *n.*
surfeit (sʉr'fit) *v.:* to fill to excess.
surmise (sər • mīz') *n.:* guess; speculation.
surmount (sər • mount') *v.:* to rise above.
surname (sʉr'nām') *n.:* last name.
sustenance (sus'tə • nəns) *n.:* food or money to support life.
swathe (swäth) *n.:* long strip of cloth; bandage.
sylvan (sil'vən) *adj.:* of the woods.
symmetry (sim'ə • trē) *n.:* similarity of form on either side of a dividing line; balance.

taut (tôt) *adj.:* stretched tight.
tedious (tē'dē • əs) *adj.:* boring.
teem *v.:* to swarm.
temerity (tə • mer'ə • tē) *n.:* foolish or rash boldness; recklessness.
temperance (tem'pər • əns) *n.:* restraint; control.
temporal (tem'pə • rəl) *adj.:* limited to this world; not spiritual.
tenacity (tə • nas'ə • tē) *n.:* persistence; steadfastness.
tentative (ten'tə • tiv) *adj.:* hesitant; uncertain.
terrestrial (tə • res'trē • əl) *adj.:* of the earth.
theological (thē'ə • läj'i • kəl) *adj.:* having to do with the study of God.
theoretical (thē'ə • ret'i • kəl) *adj.:* in the realm of ideas, as opposed to practice or application.
timorous (tim'ər • es) *adj.:* full of fear; timid.
tincture (tiŋk'chər) *v.:* to color lightly; tint.
titillate (tit''l • āt') *v.:* to excite; stimulate.
titter *v.:* to giggle.
traipse (trāps) *v.:* colloquial for "to wander."
tranquil (tran'kwil) *adj.:* calm; peaceful.
transcend (tran • send') *v.:* to exceed; surpass.
transgress (trans • gres') *v.:* to overstep a limit or break a law.
transitory (tran'sə • tôr'ē) *adj.:* temporary or fleeting.
transom (tran'səm) *n.:* small hinged window directly above a door.
tremulous (trem'yo͞o • ləs) *adj.:* trembling; quivering.
tribulation (trib'yo͞o • lā'shən) *n.:* great misery; affliction.
tribute (trib'yo͞ot) *n.:* tax paid by a vassal to a lord or ruler.
trifle (trī'fəl) *v.:* to mock; treat lightly.
trivet (triv'it) *n.:* three-legged stand for holding pots.
tumult (to͞o'mult') *n.:* uproar; commotion.
turbid (tʉr'bid) *adj.:* thick; dense.
tyranny (tir'ə • nē) *n.:* cruel and unjust rule. —**tyrannical** *adj.*

uncanny (un • kan'ē) *adj.:* strange; eerie; weird.
uncouth (un • ko͞oth') *adj.:* crude; uncultured.
unfathomable (un • fath'əm • ə • bəl) *adj.:* unmeasurable; infinite.
unnerve (un • nʉrv') *v.:* to cause one to lose courage or confidence.
unprecedented (un • pres'ə • den'tid) *adj.:* not done or seen before; unique.
unscrupulous (un • skro͞o'pyə • ləs) *adj.:* dishonest; unprincipled.
unwary (un • wer'ē) *adj.:* not watchful or cautious.
usurper (yo͞o • zʉrp'ər) *n.:* one who seizes power unlawfully.
utter *adj.:* total.

vanquish (vaŋ'kwish) *v.:* to conquer.
vaulted (vôlt'id) *adj.:* arched.
vehement (vē'ə • mənt) *adj.:* passionate; forceful.
vellicate (vel'i • kāt') *v.:* to twitch; pluck.
velocity (və • läs'ə • tē) *n.:* speed.
verisimilitude (ver'ə • si • mil'ə • to͞od') *n.:* appearance of being real.
verity (ver'ə • tē) *n.:* truth.
vermin (vʉr'mən) *n.:* disease-carrying pest. —**vermin** *n. pl.*
vex *v.:* to annoy highly.
vigor (vig'ər) *n.:* strength; vitality.
viscous (vis'kəs) *adj.:* having the form of a sticky fluid.
vivacity (vī • vas'ə • tē) *n.:* liveliness; animation.
vociferate (vō • sif'ər • āt') *v.:* to speak loudly and vehemently. —**vociferous** *adj.*
void (void) *adj.:* empty.

waggish (wag'ish) *adj.:* prankish; playful.
wan (wän) *adj.:* pale; weak with sadness.
wanton (wän'tən) *adj.:* luxurious; unrestrained.
winning (win'iŋ) *adj.:* charming.
wither (with'ər) *v.:* to decay; wilt or shrivel.
wizened (wiz'ənd) *adj.:* dried up; withered.
wrath (rath) *n.:* great anger; rage.
wrought (rôt) *adj.:* shaped; fashioned.

zeal *n.:* enthusiasm; passion.

fat, āpe, cär; ten, ēven; is, bīte; gō, hôrn, look, to͞ol; yoo, cure; yo͞o, use; oil, out; up, fʉr; get; joy; yet; chin; she; thin; *th*en; zh, leisure; ŋ, ring; ə for *a* in *ago, e* in *agent, i* in *sanity, o* in *comply, u* in *focus;* ' as in *battle* (bat''l).

ACKNOWLEDGMENTS

For permission to reprint copyrighted material, grateful acknowledgment is given to the following sources:

Agencia Literaria Mercedes Casanovas: "La guitarra" from *Obras completas* by Federico García Lorca.

The Asia Society: "Thoughts of Hanoi" by Nguyen Thi Vinh from *A Thousand Years of Vietnamese Poetry,* translated by Nguyen Ngoc Bich. Copyright © 1974 by The Asia Society.

Stephanie Bailey: "Worn Out" by Stephanie Bailey from *Legends,* vol. X, May 1992. Copyright © 1992 by Stephanie Bailey. Published by Taylorsville High School.

Bantam Books, a division of Bantam Doubleday Dell Publishing Group, Inc.: From "Give Us This Day Our Daily Bread" from *Shakespeare Alive* by Joseph Papp and Elizabeth Kirkland. Copyright © 1988 by the New York Shakespeare Festival.

Robert Bly: "The Guitar" by Federico García Lorca from *Lorca and Jiménez: Selected Poems,* chosen and translated by Robert Bly. Copyright © 1973, 1997 by Robert Bly. Published by Beacon Press, Boston, 1973, 1997.

D. S. Brewer: From "The Day of Destiny" from *The Morte Darthur: Parts Seven and Eight* by Sir Thomas Malory, edited by D. S. Brewer. Copyright © 1968 by D. S. Brewer.

Curtis Brown Ltd., London, on behalf of the Estate of Sir Winston S. Churchill: From "Speech on Dunkirk, House of Commons," June 4, 1940. Copyright 1940 by Winston S. Churchill. From page 24 (retitled "A Scream of Rage") and from "The Black Death" from *The Birth of Britain* by Winston S. Churchill. Copyright © 1956 by Winston S. Churchill.

Cambridge University Press: From "The Medieval Situation" from *The Discarded Image* by C. S. Lewis. Copyright © 1964 by Cambridge University Press.

Delacorte Press/Seymour Lawrence, a division of Bantam Doubleday Dell Publishing Group, Inc.: From *Sextet: T. S. Eliot, Truman Capote and Others* by John Malcolm Brinnin. Copyright © 1981 by John Malcolm Brinnin.

Devin-Adair, Publishers, Inc., Old Greenwich, CT 06870: From *The Book of Margery Kempe* by Margery Kempe. Copyright © 1944 and renewed © 1972 by Devin-Adair, Publishers, Inc. All rights reserved.

Doubleday, a division of Bantam Doubleday Dell Publishing Group, Inc.: "Marriage Is a Private Affair" from *Girls at War and Other Stories* by Chinua Achebe. Copyright © 1972, 1973 by Chinua Achebe. From *How the Irish Saved Civilization* by Thomas Cahill. Copyright © 1995 by Thomas Cahill. "The Cairo Rooftop" from *Palace Walk* by Naguib Mahfouz. Copyright © 1990 by American University in Cairo Press.

Rita Dove and W. W. Norton & Company, Inc.: "Sisters" from *Grace Notes* by Rita Dove. Copyright © 1989 by Rita Dove.

Dutton Signet, a division of Penguin Putnam Inc.: From the annotations from *Macbeth* by William Shakespeare. Copyright © 1963 and renewed © 1991 by Sylvan Barnet for introduction and annotations. From *Beowulf,* translated by Burton Raffel. Translation copyright © 1963 by Burton Raffel; afterword copyright © 1963 by New American Library. From "The Unfed Dervish," "Information and Knowledge," "The Elephant-Keeper," "Safety and Riches," and "The Fox and the Camels" from *The Way of the Sufi* by Idries Shah. Copyright © 1968 by Idries Shah.

Faber and Faber Limited: "Hawk Roosting" and excerpt from *Lupercal* by Ted Hughes. Copyright © 1960 by Ted Hughes.

Famous Music Publishing Companies: Lyrics by Dean Pitchford from "Holding Out for a Hero." Copyright © 1984 by Ensign Music Corporation. International copyright secured. All rights reserved.

Farrar, Straus & Giroux, Inc.: From "On Keeping a Notebook" from *Slouching Towards Bethlehem* by Joan Didion. Copyright © 1966, 1968 and renewed © 1996 by Joan Didion. "Once upon a Time" from *Jump* by Nadine Gordimer. Copyright © 1991 by Felix Licensing, B.V. "Digging" from *Poems 1965–1975* by Seamus Heaney. Copyright © 1980 by Seamus Heaney. "The Grauballe Man" from *Selected Poems: 1966–1987* by Seamus Heaney. Copyright © 1990 by Seamus Heaney. "Chaucer" from *Birthday Letters* by Ted Hughes. Copyright © 1998 by Ted Hughes. "The Mower" from *Collected Poems* by Philip Larkin. Copyright © 1988, 1989 by the Estate of Philip Larkin. Canto XXXIV from *The Inferno of Dante: A New Verse Translation* by Robert Pinsky. Copyright © 1994 by Farrar, Straus & Giroux, Inc.; translation copyright © 1994 by Robert Pinsky. From "My Muse" and from "Too Tired for Words" from *Me Again* by Stevie Smith. Copyright © 1981 by James MacGibbon. "Freedom to Breathe" and "The Bonfire and the Ants" from *Stories and Prose Poems* by Alexander Solzhenitsyn, translated by Michael Glenny. Translation copyright © 1971 by Michael Glenny. "The Virgins" from *Sea Grapes* by Derek Walcott. Copyright © 1976 by Derek Walcott.

Grove/Atlantic, Inc.: From *Waiting for Godot* by Samuel Beckett. Copyright © 1954 by Grove Press, Inc.; copyright renewed © 1982 by Samuel Beckett. From "That's All" from *Complete Plays: Three* by Harold Pinter. Copyright © 1966 by H. Pinter Ltd.

Harcourt Brace & Company: "The Hollow Men" from *Collected Poems 1909–1962* by T. S. Eliot. Copyright 1936 by Harcourt Brace & Company, copyright © 1963, 1964 by T. S. Eliot. From "Warfare and Warlords" from *The Harbrace History of England, Part I: Ancient and Medieval England, Beginnings to 1509* by J. R. Lander. Copyright © 1973 by Harcourt Brace & Company. "Shooting an Elephant" from *Shooting an Elephant and Other Essays* by George Orwell. Copyright 1950 by Sonia Brownell Orwell and renewed © 1978 by Sonia Pitt-Rivers. From "A Sketch of the Past" from *Moments of Being* by Virginia Woolf, edited by Jeanne Schulkind. Text copyright © 1976 by Quentin Bell and Angelica Garnett; introduction and editorial material copyright © 1976 by Jeanne Schulkind. From *Mrs. Dalloway* by Virginia Woolf. Copyright © 1925 by Harcourt Brace & Company; copyright renewed © 1953 by Leonard Woolf. From "Shakespeare's Sister" and from page 64 from *A Room of One's Own* by Virginia Woolf. Copyright 1929 by Harcourt Brace & Company; copyright renewed © 1957 by Leonard Woolf.

John Hawkins & Associates, Inc.: "Macbeth and the Witches" from *Twisted Tales from Shakespeare* by Richard Armour. Copyright © 1957 by Richard Armour.

Hispanic Society of America: "The Guitar" by Federico García Lorca from *Translations from Hispanic Poets,* edited by Elizabeth du Gué Trapier.

Henry Holt and Company, Inc.: "Is My Team Ploughing," from "A Shropshire Lad," "To an Athlete Dying Young," and "When I Was One-and-Twenty" from *The Collected Poems of A. E. Housman.* Copyright 1939, 1940 by Henry Holt and Company, Inc.; copyright © 1967 by Robert E. Symons.

Houghton Mifflin Company: "Mushrooms" from *True Stories* from *Selected Poems II: Poems Selected and New 1976–1986* by Margaret Atwood. Copyright © 1987 by Margaret Atwood. All rights reserved. From *Gilgamesh,* translated by Herbert Mason. Copyright © 1970 by Herbert Mason. All rights reserved.

International African Institute, London: Four proverbs from *Jabo Proverbs from Liberia: Maxims in the Life of a Native Tribe* by George Herzog. Copyright © 1936 by the International African Institute. Published by Oxford University Press—London.

John Johnson Ltd.: "I Have Visited Again" from *The Bronze Horseman* by Alexander Pushkin, translated by D. M. Thomas. Translation copyright © 1982 by D. M. Thomas.

Estate of James Joyce: From *Stephen Hero* by James Joyce. Copyright © 1944, 1955, 1959, 1963 by James Joyce; copyright © by the Estate of James Joyce.

Alfred A. Knopf, Inc.: "The Demon Lover" from *The Collected Stories of Elizabeth Bowen* by Elizabeth Bowen. Copyright 1946 and renewed © 1974 by Elizabeth Bowen. "The Myth of Sisyphus" and from "An Absurd Reasoning" from *The Myth of Sisyphus and Other Essays* by Albert Camus, translated by Justin O'Brien. Copyright © 1955 by Alfred A. Knopf, Inc. From *Grendel* by John Gardner. Copyright © 1971 by John Gardner. "B. Wordsworth" from *Miguel Street* by V. S. Naipaul. Copyright © 1959 by V. S. Naipaul. "My Oedipus Complex" from *Collected Stories* by Frank O'Connor. Copyright 1950 by Frank O'Connor.

Liveright Publishing Corporation: "O sweet spontaneous" and "since feeling is first" from *Selected Poems* by E. E. Cummings. Introduction and commentary by Richard S. Kennedy. Copyright 1923, 1926, 1951, 1954, © 1991 by the Trustees for the E. E. Cummings Trust; copyright © 1976, 1985 by George James Firmage.

Arnulfo J. López: "A Poem Within a Poem" by Arnulfo J. López from *Heritage,* vol. 31, Spring 1991. Published by James Madison High School, Vienna, VA.

Macmillan General Reference USA, a division of Ahsuog, Inc.: From *Webster's New World Dictionary,* Third College Edition. Copyright © 1988, 1991, 1994, 1996, 1997 by Simon & Schuster, Inc.

Andrea D. Marzullo: "Mind" by A.D.M. from *Image,* Creative Arts Magazine, vol. 31, 1992. Copyright © 1992 by Andrea D. Marzullo. Published by Bellevue East Senior High School, Bellevue, NE.

Merlyn's Pen: The National Magazines of Student Writing: "Tu B'shvat" by Michelle Dorrien from *Merlyn's Pen,* Senior Edition, April/May 1994. Copyright © 1994 by Merlyn's Pen. First appeared in *Merlyn's Pen: The National Magazines of Student Writing.*

Melynn Minson: "Searching for a Future in the Dusk" by Melynn Minson from *Expressions,* vol. XXVII, 1992. Published by Hillcrest High School, Midvale, UT.

Edmund Morris: From "A Visit with Nadine Gordimer" by Edmund Morris from *The New York Times Book Review,* June 7, 1981. Copyright © 1981 by Edmund Morris.

New Directions Publishing Corporation: From "The Witness" from *Labyrinths* by Jorge Luis Borges, translated by James Irby. Copyright © 1962, 1964 by New Directions Publishing Corp. From *In Search of Duende* by Federico García Lorca, edited and translated by Christopher Maurer. Copyright © 1975, 1998 by the Estate of Federico García Lorca; copy-

right © 1975, 1998 by Christopher Maurer; copyright © 1955, 1998 by New Directions Publishing Corporation. "Dulce et Decorum Est" and from "Strange Meeting" from *The Collected Poems of Wilfred Owen.* Copyright © 1963 by Chatto & Windus, Ltd. "Not Waving but Drowning" from *Collected Poems of Stevie Smith.* Copyright © 1972 by Stevie Smith. "In my craft or sullen art" from *The Collected Poems of Dylan Thomas.* Copyright 1939, 1942, 1946 by New Directions; copyright 1952, 1953 by Dylan Thomas. "Fern Hill" and "Do Not Go Gentle into That Good Night" from *The Poems of Dylan Thomas.* Copyright © 1952 by Dylan Thomas. "Jade Flower Palace" by Tu Fu from *One Hundred Poems from the Chinese,* translated by Kenneth Rexroth. Copyright © 1971 by Kenneth Rexroth. All rights reserved.

The New York Times Company: Quote by David Ormsby Gore from *The New York Times,* October 28, 1962. Copyright © 1962 by The New York Times Company. "A Beam of Protons Illuminates Gutenberg's Genius" by Malcolm W. Browne from *The New York Times,* May 12, 1987. Copyright © 1987 by The New York Times Company. From "Scenes from a Modern Marriage" by Julia Markus from *The New York Times,* February 14, 1995. Copyright © 1995 by The New York Times Company. From "Lesson of the Bamboo Crates" by Christy Ma from *The New York Times,* April 5, 1997. Copyright © 1997 by The New York Times Company. From "A Collaboration Across 1,200 Years" by D.J.R. Bruckner from *The New York Times,* July 22, 1997. Copyright © 1997 by The New York Times Company.

North Point Press, a division of Farrar, Straus & Giroux, Inc.: From *Crow and Weasel* by Barry Lopez, illustrated by Tom Pohrt. Text copyright © 1990 by Barry Holstun Lopez; illustrations copyright © 1990 by Tom Pohrt.

W. W. Norton & Company, Inc.: "Fifth Day, Ninth Story" (retitled "Federigo's Falcon") from *The Decameron* by Giovanni Boccaccio, translated by Mark Musa and Peter Bondanella. Translation copyright © 1982 by Mark Musa and Peter Bondanella. "A Letter to My Daughter" from *The Balkan Express: Fragments from the Other Side of War* by Slavenka Drakulíc, translated by Maja Soljan. Copyright © 1993 by Slavenka Drakulíc; translation copyright © 1993 by Maja Soljan.

Gary P. Nunn: From lyrics to "London Homesick Blues" by Gary P. Nunn. Copyright © 1973 by Gary P. Nunn. Published by Nunn Publishing Company, BMI.

Harold Ober Associates Incorporated: From Commencement Address by Chinua Achebe, given on May 27, 1996, at Bates College. Copyright © 1996 by Chinua Achebe.

Oxford University Press, Inc.: From "The Troglodyte World" from *The Great War and Modern Memory* by Paul Fussell. Copyright © 1977 by Oxford University Press, Inc. From *Faust,* Parts I and 2, by Johann Wolfgang von Goethe, translated by Louis MacNeice; translation copyright 1951, 1954 by Frederick Louis MacNeice; renewed copyright © 1979 by Hedi MacNeice.

Pantheon Books, a division of Random House, Inc.: "A Clever Judge" by Chang Shih-nan and "Gold, Gold" by Lieh Tzu from *Chinese Fairy Tales and Fantasies,* translated and edited by Moss Roberts. Copyright © 1979 by Moss Roberts. "Axolotl" from *End of the Game and Other Stories* by Julio Cortázar, translated by Paul Blackburn. Copyright © 1967 by Random House, Inc.

Paulist Press: From *Julian of Norwich: Showings,* translated by Edmund Colledge, O.S.A., and James Walsh, S.J. Copyright © 1978 by The Missionary Society of St. Paul the Apostle in the State of New York.

Penguin Books Ltd.: From Introduction by Nevill Coghill, "The Prologue," "The Pardoner's Prologue and Tale," and "The Wife of Bath's Prologue and Tale" from *The Canterbury Tales* by Geoffrey Chaucer, translated by Nevill Coghill (Penguin Classics 1951, Fourth Revised Edition 1977). Copyright © 1951, 1958, 1960, 1975, 1977 by Nevill Coghill. "Night" from *The Koran,* translated by N. J. Dawood (Penguin Classics 1956, Fifth Revised Edition 1990). Copyright © 1956, 1959, 1966, 1968, 1974, 1990 by N. J. Dawood. "Question and answer among the mountains" by Li Po from *The Penguin Book of Chinese Verse,* translated by Robert Kotewall and Norman L. Smith, edited by A. R. Davis (Penguin Books, 1962). Translation copyright © 1962 by N. L. Smith and R. H. Kotewall.

Laurence Pollinger Limited and the Estate of Frieda Lawrence Ravagli: From "Letter to Rolf Gardiner, 18 December 1927," "Letter to Earl Brewster, 22 September 1922," and from "Letter to Rolf Gardiner, 17 July 1926" from *The Letters of D. H. Lawrence,* vol. IV–VI. Copyright 1932 by the Estate of D. H. Lawrence; copyright 1934 by Frieda Lawrence; copyright 1933, 1948, 1953, 1954, © 1956, 1957, 1958, 1959, 1960, 1961, 1962, 1967, 1969 by Stefano Ravagli and R. G. Seaman, executors of the Estate of Frieda Lawrence Ravagli; copyright © 1987 by the Estate of Frieda Lawrence Ravagli. Published by Cambridge University Press.

Random House, Inc.: From "Five Songs, II" [That night when joy began], "Musée des Beaux Arts," and "The Unknown Citizen" from *W. H. Auden: Collected Poems* by W. H. Auden, edited by Edward Mendelson. Copyright 1937, 1940 and renewed © 1965, 1968 by W. H. Auden. "The Ring" from *Anecdotes of Destiny* by Isak Dinesen. Copyright © 1958 by Isak Dinesen. From "Mecca" from *The Autobiography of Malcolm X* by Malcolm X with the assistance of Alex Haley. Copyright © 1964 by Alex Haley and Malcolm X; copyright © 1965 by Alex Haley and Betty Shabazz.

John Robinson for the Arthur Waley Estate: "To Tan-Ch'iu" by Li Po from *Chinese Poems,* translated by Arthur Waley. Copyright © 1946, 1961, 1983 by George Allen & Unwin (Publishers) Ltd.

Rogers, Coleridge & White Ltd., 20 Powis Mews, London W11 1JN, and Authors: From "The Seafarer" from *The Battle of Maldon and Other Old English Poems,* translated by Kevin Crossley-Holland. Copyright © 1965 by Kevin Crossley-Holland and Bruce Mitchell. From "Games at Twilight" from *Games at Twilight and Other Stories* by Anita Desai. Copyright © 1978 by Anita Desai.

St. James Press, a subsidiary of Gale Research Inc.: Quotes by Chinua Achebe and Anita Desai from *Contemporary Novelists,* Fifth Edition, edited by Lesley Henderson. Copyright © 1991 by St. James Press.

St. Martin's Press, Inc., New York, NY: From *World Within World* by Stephen Spender. Copyright © 1951 by Stephen Spender. Looking Back in 1994: A New Introduction to *World Within World.* Copyright © 1994 by Stephen Spender.

The Saturday Review: From "Black Man's Burden" by Maxwell Geismar from *The Saturday Review,* March 8, 1975. Copyright © 1974 by S. R. Publications Ltd.

Harriet O'Donovan Sheehy, c/o Joan Daves Agency as agent for the proprietor: From "After Aughrim's Great Disaster" from *An Only Child* by Frank O'Connor. Copyright © 1958, 1959, 1960, 1961 by Frank O'Connor.

Simon & Schuster: From *In Patagonia* by Bruce Chatwin. Copyright © 1977 by Bruce Chatwin. Number 17 from Book II, numbers 15 and 21 from Book VII, and number 23 from Book XV from *The Analects of Confucius,* translated by Arthur Waley. Copyright © 1938 by George Allen & Unwin, Ltd. "No Witchcraft for Sale" and from Preface from *African Stories* by Doris Lessing. Copyright © 1951, 1953, 1954, 1957, 1958, 1962, 1963, 1964, 1965, 1972, 1981 by Doris Lessing. "No Witchcraft for Sale" from *African Stories* by Doris Lessing. Copyright © 1951, 1953, 1954, 1957, 1958, 1962, 1963, 1964, 1965, 1972, 1981 by Doris Lessing. "Death and Other Grave Matters" from *What Jane Austen Ate and Charles Dickens Knew* by Daniel Pool. Copyright © 1993 by Daniel Pool.

The Society of Authors as the Literary Representative of the Estate of Katherine Mansfield: Excerpt from "Journal: May 30 [1917]" and "To Richard Murry [June 20, 1921]" from *The Letters and Journals of Katherine Mansfield,* edited by C. K. Stead.

Wole Soyinka: "Telephone Conversation" by Wole Soyinka from *Reflections: Nigerian Prose and Verse,* edited by Frances Ademola. Copyright © 1962 by Wole Soyinka.

Time Inc.: From "Life in 999: A Grim Struggle" by Howard G. Chua-Eoan from *Time,* vol. 140, no. 27, Fall 1992. Copyright © 1992 by Time Inc.

Charles E. Tuttle Co., Inc.: "The First Principle," "The Gates of Paradise," "The Moon Cannot Be Stolen," and "Temper" from *Zen Flesh, Zen Bones: A Collection of Zen and Pre-Zen Writings,* compiled by Paul Reps. Copyright © 1957 by Charles E. Tuttle Co., Inc.

University College of Dublin: Excerpt from *Memories of the Famine* by Maire ni Grianna from *Memories of the Famine* from Main Manuscript vol. 1071, pages 279–283, in the Department of Irish Folklore, University College, Dublin.

University of California Press: From *The Diary of Samuel Pepys,* vol. I, vol. II, vol. V, and vol. VII, edited by Robert Latham and William Matthews. Copyright © 1972–1986 by The Master, Fellows and Scholars of Magdalen College, Cambridge; Robert Latham; and the Executors of William Matthews.

The University of Chicago Press: From "Sir Gawain and the Green Knight" from *The Complete Works of the Gawain-Poet,* translated by John Gardner. Copyright © 1965 by The University of Chicago. From *The Panchatantra,* translated from the Sanskrit by Arthur W. Ryder. Copyright 1925 by The University of Chicago; copyright renewed 1953 by Mary E. Ryder and Winifred Ryder.

University of Texas Press: "Sonnet 17/Soneto 17" and "Sonnet 79/Soneto 79" from *100 Love Sonnets/Cien sonetos de amor* by Pablo Neruda, translated by Stephen Tapscott. Copyright © 1959 by Pablo Neruda and Fundacion Pablo Neruda; copyright © 1986 by University of Texas Press.

USA TODAY: From "Groundlings Get Close Look, Rowdy Adventures," by David Patrick Stearns from *USA TODAY,* June 12, 1997. Copyright © 1997 by USA TODAY.

Viking Penguin, a division of Penguin Putnam Inc.: "Top of the Food Chain" from *Without a Hero* by T. Coraghessan Boyle. Copyright © 1993 by T. Coraghessan Boyle. "The Destructors" from *Collected Stories of Graham Greene.* Copyright © 1955, 1983 by Graham Greene. "The Rocking-Horse Winner" from *Complete Short Stories of D. H.*

Lawrence. Copyright 1933 by the Estate of D. H. Lawrence; copyright renewed © 1961 by Angelo Ravagli and C. M. Weekley, Executors of the Estate of Frieda Lawrence Ravagli. "Snake" from *The Complete Poems of D. H. Lawrence* by D. H. Lawrence, edited by V. de Sola Pinto and F. W. Roberts. Copyright © 1964, 1971 by Angelo Ravagli and C. M. Weekley, Executors of the Estate of Frieda Lawrence Ravagli. "In the Shadow of War" from *Stars of the New Curfew* by Ben Okri. Copyright © 1988 by Ben Okri. "Unfortunate Coincidence" from *The Portable Dorothy Parker,* introduction by Brendan Gill. Copyright 1926 and renewed © 1954 by Dorothy Parker.

White Pine Press: "Going Home" from *Between Two Rivers: Selected Poems 1956–1984* by Maurice Kenny. Copyright © 1979, 1981, 1987 by Maurice Kenny.

Calen Wood: "Beowulf Shrinklet" by Calen Wood from *IKON, Literary-Arts Magazine,* 1994. Copyright © 1994 by Calen Wood. Published by Bakersfield High School, Bakersfield, CA.

Yale University Press: "Riddle #32: A Ship," "Riddle #33: Iceberg," "Riddle #47: Bookworm," and "The Seafarer" from *Poems from the Old English,* translated by Burton Raffel. Copyright © 1960, 1964, 1998 by Burton Raffel.

SOURCES CITED

From *How the Irish Saved Civilization* by Thomas Cahill. Published by Doubleday, New York, 1995.

From "What Lips My Lips Have Kissed" from *Collected Poems* by Edna St. Vincent Millay. Copyright 1923, 1951 by Edna St. Vincent Millay and Norma Millay Ellis. Published by HarperCollins.

From a letter to Princess Caetani from *The Collected Letters of Dylan Thomas,* edited by Paul Ferris. Letters copyright © 1957, 1966, 1985 by The Trustees for the Copyrights of Dylan Thomas.

From "A Brief Note About the River When Its Waters Rise Up Like the Sea" by Tu Fu from *An Introduction to Chinese Literature* by Liu Wu-chi. Published by Indiana University Press, Bloomington, 1966.

From "Literature and Conscientization: Interview with Chinua Achebe" by Biodun Jeyifo from *Nigeria Magazine,* Lagos, 1983.

From *A Sort of Life* by Graham Greene. Published by Simon & Schuster, New York, 1971.

From "Verse translation is a minor art . . ." from *The Translation of Verse* by Burton Raffel. Published by the University of Nebraska Press, Lincoln, 1960.

PICTURE CREDITS

The illustrations on the Contents pages are picked up from pages in the textbook. Credits for those illustrations can be found either on the textbook page on which they appear or in the listing below.

Page 1, Erich Lessing/Art Resource, NY; 2, David Parker/Science Photo Library/Photo Researchers, Inc.; 3, (bottom) Louis Jawitz/The Image Bank; 4, (middle) ©Sylvain Grandadam/Tony Stone Worldwide, (top) ©cliché Bibliothèque Nationale de France, Paris. Fr 95 fol. 173; 5, (top right) ©Meyer/Kunsthistorisches Museum, Vienna, (bottom, left to right) ©Justin Kerr; Art Resource, NY; ©Mario Corvetto/Comstock Inc.; 6, ©Farrell Grehan/Photo Researchers, Inc.; 7, Antony Edwards/The Image Bank; 8, (middle) Courtesy of Ted Spiegel; 9, Erich Lessing/Art Resource, NY; 10, (bottom) C. M. Dixon, (top) Ted Spiegel; 11, Michael Holford Photographs; 12, Ted Spiegel; 13, Werner Forman/Art Resource, NY; 14, Boltin Picture Library; 15, Art Resource, NY; 17, C. M. Dixon; 19, Werner Forman/Art Resource, NY; 20, ©Michael Holford; 22, Werner Forman/Art Resource, NY; 24, Art Resource, NY; 27, Boltin Picture Library; 28, Werner Forman/Art Resource, NY; 34, ©Michael Holford; 35, Courtesy of Ted Spiegel; 37, Erich Lessing/Art Resource, NY; 38, Werner Forman/Art Resource, NY; 39, ©Stephanie Berger; 43, Courtesy of Ted Spiegel; 44, 45, Werner Forman/Art Resource, NY; 50, The Kobal Collection; 51, Werner Forman/Art Resource, NY; 52, (top) Bridgeman Art Library, London/New York, (bottom) Giraudon/Art Resource, NY; 54, Scala/Art Resource, NY; 55, 56, 58, Cotton Coulson/Woodfin Camp & Associates; 60, Werner Forman/Art Resource, NY; 63, Boltin Picture Library; 64, Jules Zalon/The Image Bank; 65, (bottom) Art Resource, NY; 71, F. Cruz/Superstock; 72, Art Resource, NY; 74, Robert Harding Picture Library; 76, (top) Giraudon/Art Resource, NY, (bottom) Bridgeman Art Library, London/New York; 77, (top) Giraudon/Art Resource, NY, (bottom left) Bibiothèque Nationale/Archiv für Kunst und Geschichte, Berlin; 79, Photo: IndustrieFoto Hilbinger; 90, Robert Harding Picture Library; 93, Swedowsky/The Image Bank; 94, Photo AKG London; 96, Art Resource, NY; 100 (bottom), 101, Superstock, New York; 106, Bridgeman Art Library, London/New York; 113, Marvin E. Newman/The Image Bank; 125, Bridgeman Art Library, London/New York; 140, Archives G. Dagli Orti; 142, Corbis-Bettmann; 147, 151, 152 (top), Bridgeman Art Library, London/New York; 152, (bottom) Scala/Art Resource, NY; 156, Giraudon/Art Resource, NY; 160, Art Resource, NY; 166, Fine Art Photographic Library Ltd./Private Collection; 170, 173, Bridgeman Art Library, London/New York; 177, 181, Art Resource, NY; 189, F. Cruz/Superstock; 190, The Marquess of Salisbury, Hatfield House/Ted Spiegel; 192, 194 (top), Bridgeman Art Library, London/New York; 194, (bottom, left to right) Scala/Art Resource, NY; Erich Lessing/Art Resource, NY; Archiv für Kunst und Geschichte, Berlin; 195, (top and middle) Corbis-Bettmann, (bottom left) Bridgeman Art Library, London/New York, (bottom right) ©Lindsay Hebberd/Woodfin Camp & Associates; 196, 197, Bridgeman Art Library, London/New York; 198, (bottom) Archives G. Dagli Orti; 199, (top) Erich Lessing/Art Resource, NY; 202, Bridgeman Art Library, London/New York; 205, 206 (middle and right), 207, Bridgeman Art Library, London/New York; 213, Adam Woolfitt/Woodfin Camp & Associates; 218, Bridgeman Art Library, London/New York; 219, Art Resource, NY; 221, Ted Spiegel; 223, 225, 226, 228, 235, 236 (background), Bridgeman Art Library, London/New York; 239, Bridgeman/Art Resource, NY; 244, Bridgeman Art Library, London/New York; 246, 247, Art Resource, NY; 249, 250, Bridgeman Art Library, London/New York; 255, Taro Kumamoto/Photonica; 257, 258, 260, Bridgeman Art Library, London/New York; 261, Sotheby's Transparency Library, London; 263, Art Resource, NY; 264, Bridgeman Art Library, London/New York; 265, Art Resource, NY; 267, Dave Boyer/UPI/Corbis-Bettmann; 271, Bridgeman Art Library, London/New York; 281, Republic (Courtesy Kobal); 282, Bridgeman Art Library, London/New York; 283 (top right), 284, 288 (top), Walter Hodges, The Globe Restored, ©1973 by W. W. Norton & Co. By arrangement with Coward, McCann & Geohegan, Inc.; 288, (left and bottom) G. Swann/Sygma; 290, (top) Adam Woolfitt/Woodfin Camp & Associates, (bottom) Goldwyn (Courtesy Kobal); 291, (top) Ken Howard/Old Globe Theatre, (bottom) Photofest; 292, (top) Martha Swope © Time, Inc., (bottom) Paramount (Courtesy Kobal); 293, Photofest; 294, (top) ©Michal Daniel/NY Shakespeare Festival, (bottom) Two Cities (Courtesy Kobal); 295, (top) Photofest, (bottom) Sotheby's Transparency Library, London; 296, (top) Paramount (Courtesy Kobal), (middle) ©Paul Davis. Courtesy of the artist, (bottom) Photofest; 297, Republic (Courtesy Kobal); 298, (top to bottom) ©Paul Davis. Courtesy of the artist; Carol Rosegg; Art Resource, NY; 299, (top) Columbia (Courtesy Kobal), (bottom) Bridgeman Art Library, London/New York; 300, Columbia (Courtesy Kobal); 303, 306, Robert C. Ragsdale F.R.P.S./Stratford Festival, Canada; 311, Photofest; 312, Robert C. Ragsdale F.R.P.S./Stratford Festival, Canada; 315, Photofest; 320, Robert C. Ragsdale F.R.P.S./Stratford Festival, Canada; 322, Photofest; 324, 332, Robert C. Ragsdale F.R.P.S./Stratford Festival, Canada; 337, 338, Photofest; 340, Comstock; 342, Photofest; 344, 348, 352, 360, 366, 368, 370, Robert C. Ragsdale F.R.P.S./Stratford Festival, Canada; 376, Republic (Courtesy Kobal); 378, Robert C. Ragsdale F.R.P.S./Stratford Festival, Canada; 380, Photofest; 383, Robert C. Ragsdale F.R.P.S/Stratford Festival, Canada; 386, Carol Rosegg; 388, Robert C. Ragsdale F.R.P.S./Stratford Festival, Canada; 389, Photofest; 392, (top) Bridgeman Art Library, London/New York, (bottom) Scala/Art Resource, NY; 393, Fine Art Photographic Library Ltd.; 395, Art Resource, NY; 396, 399, Scala/Art Resource, NY; 401, Bridgeman/Art Resource, NY; 403, Scala/Art Resource, NY; 404, Bridgeman Art Library, London/New York; 405, 406, Archives G. Dagli Orti; 410, 413, 414 (top and bottom), Art Resource, NY; 415, 417, Scala/Art Resource, NY; 421, Art Resource, NY; 422, Foto Marburg/Art Resource, NY; 424, Corbis-Bettmann; 428, Bridgeman Art Library, London/New York; 433, (bottom) Corbis-Bettmann; 434, Boltin Picture Library; 439, Art Resource, NY; 440, Bridgeman Art Library, London/New York; 446, 448, Art Resource, NY; 462, The Cartoon Bank; 465, F. Cruz/Superstock; 466, 468, Bridgeman Art Library, London/New York; 470, (left to right) Mary Evans Picture Library; Boltin Picture Library; Bridgeman Art Library, London/New York; 471, (bottom, left to right) ©Michael Holford; Courtesy, Peabody Essex Museum, Salem, Mass.; ©Photothèque des Musées de la Ville de Paris; 472, 473, 475, 476, 477, Bridgeman Art Library, London/New York; 478, 479, Culver Pictures, Inc.; 480, Max A. Polster Archive; 481, Bridgeman Art Library, London/New York; 482, Mansell/Time, Inc.; 483, North Wind Picture Archives; 485, Bridgeman Art Library, London/New York; 487, Culver Pictures, Inc.; 489, Mary Evans Picture Library; 493, The Arthur Rackham pictures are reproduced with the kind permission of his family; 495, Mary Evans Picture Library; 498, 499, Bridgeman Art Library, London/New York; 501, Mary Evans Picture Library; 519, 520, Bridgeman Art Library, London/New York; 521, North

Wind Picture Archives; 522, Bridgeman Art Library, London/New York; 528, Robert Halsband Collection, New York; 530, Mansell/Time, Inc.; 532, (background) Adam Woolfitt/Woodfin Camp & Associates; 534, Bridgeman Art Library, London/New York; 536, North Wind Picture Archives; 537, Photo: Ullstein; 538, New York Public Library, General Research Division. Astor, Lenox and Tilden Foundations; 541, Bridgeman Art Library, London/New York; 545, Mary Evans Picture Library; 546, (background/border) Bridgeman Art Library, London/New York; 549, Mansell/Time, Inc.; 553, Janet Fries/Black Star; 555, e.t. Archive; 556, 562, Bridgeman Art Library, London/New York; 564, 568, Mansell/Time, Inc.; 569, 570, Bridgeman Art Library, London/New York; 571, Robert Harding Picture Library; 573, Bridgeman Art Library, London/New York; 574, Robert Harding Picture Library; 575, Art Resource, NY; 577, e.t. Archive; 581, Art Resource, NY; 584, North Wind Picture Archives; 586, Culver Pictures, Inc.; 587, Bridgeman Art Library, London/New York; 589, Mary Evans Picture Library; 590, Art Resource, NY; 591, Mary Evans Picture Library; 593, Bridgeman Art Library, London/New York; 594, Mary Evans Picture Library; 597, 598, Mansell/Time, Inc.; 619, F. Cruz/Superstock; 620, 622, Bridgeman Art Library, London/New York; 623, Art Resource, NY; 624, (middle left) Jacques-Louis David/Corbis-Bettmann, (bottom) Giraudon/Art Resource, NY; 625, (top left) Rare Book and Manuscripts Division, The New York Public Library. Astor, Lenox and Tilden Foundations, (bottom middle) Corbis-Bettmann; 626, Giraudon/Art Resource, NY; 627, Photo Bulloz; 628, Fine Art Photographic Library Ltd.; 629, (top) Bridgeman Art Library, London/New York, (bottom) Mary Evans Picture Library; 630, Sotheby's Transparency Library, London; 631, Fine Art Photographic Library Ltd.; 633, (middle) Archive Photos, (bottom right) Photofest; 638, 639, Bridgeman Art Library, London/New York; 641, 642, Fine Art Photographic Library Ltd.; 643, Sotheby's Transparency Library, London; 647, Bridgeman Art Library, London/New York; 648, 649, 651 (top left), Art Resource, NY; 651 (bottom left), 654, 658, 661, Bridgeman Art Library, London/New York; 662, Michael Jenner/The Robert Harding Picture Library; 663, Fair Street Pictures; 666, (border) Comstock; 667, Art Resource, NY; 669, Sotheby's Transparency Library, London; 670, Bridgeman Art Library, London/New York; (inset) Erich Lessing/Art Resource, NY; 674, Corbis-Bettmann; 675, Fine Art Photographic Library Ltd.; 676, Scala/Art Resource, NY; 709, 710, Sotheby's Transparency Library, London; 714, 718, 721, 723, Bridgeman Art Library, London/New York; 726, Art Resource, NY; 729, Robert Harding Picture Library; 732, (background/border) ©J. Polleross/The Stock Market; 733, Hulton Getty/Liaison Agency, Inc.; 741, Fine Art Photographic Library Ltd.; 743, Bridgeman Art Library, London/New York; 746, Giraudon/Art Resource, NY; 747, The Pierpont Morgan Library/Art Resource, NY; 748, Sotheby's Transparency Library, London; 750, 752, Bridgeman Art Library, London/New York; 754, North Wind Picture Archives; 756, 758, Bridgeman Art Library, London/New York; 762, Scala/Art Resource, NY; 766, 767, Bridgeman Art Library, London/New York; 780, Fine Art Photographic Library Ltd.; 782, Bridgeman Art Library, London/New York; 784, (bottom left) Crown copyright. Historic Royal Palaces, Hampton Court Palace, East Molesey, Surrey, (right) From the archives of the Seneca Falls Historical Society, Seneca Falls, NY; 785, (top left) Archive Photos, (top right) Art Resource, NY; 787, e.t. Archive; 789, Popperfoto/Archive Photos; 790, 791, Art Resource, NY; 792, Fine Art Photographic Library Ltd.; 793, Bridgeman Art Library, London/New York; 794, Art Resource, NY; 795, (bottom left) Fotomas; 795 (bottom right), 796, 798, Bridgeman Art Library, London/New York; 799, 801, Art Resource, NY; 804, Sotheby's Transparency Library, London; 805, Jack Barrie/Bruce Coleman, Inc.; 806, Betty Carpenter; 807, Art Resource, NY; 812, Mary Evans Picture Library; 814, 816 (border), 818, Bridgeman Art Library, London/New York; 830, Erich Lessing/Art Resource, NY; 833, e.t. Archive; 835, Art Resource, NY; 837, (bottom) Bridgeman Art Library, London/New York; 838, Photographer: Derrick E. Witty; 843, Fine Art Photographic Library Ltd./Waterhouse & Dodd; 844, Harry Ransom Humanities Research Center, The University of Texas at Austin; 845, Bridgeman Art Library, London/New York; 847, Sotheby's Transparency Library, London; 849, Art Resource, NY; 850, 852, Mary Evans Picture Library; 853, (background) Kim Taylor/Bruce Coleman, Inc.; 854, Fine Art Photographic Library Ltd.; 856, Bridgeman Art Library, London/New York; 857, (background) John P. Kelly/The Image Bank; 860, Archive Photos; 864, Art Resource, NY; 866, Fine Art Photographic Library Ltd./& By Courtesy of Cadogan Gallery; 871, ©Raghubir Singh; 873, ©1975 Bernard-Pierre Wolf/Magnum Photos, Inc.; 882, Archive Photos; 888, 891, Scala/Art Resource, NY; 897, William Carter/Bruce Coleman, Inc.; 905, F. Cruz/Superstock; 906, Art Resource, NY; 909, (top left) Sotheby's Transparency Library, London, (bottom) Art Resource, NY; 910, (top right) Max Nauta/Corbis-Bettmann, (bottom left) Bridgeman Art Library, London/New York, (bottom middle) UPI/Corbis-Bettmann; 911, (top) Giraudon/Art Resource, NY, (middle right) United Artists (Courtesy Kobal), (bottom left) Corbis-Bettmann, (bottom middle) NASA; 912, (left to right) Down House, Downe, Kent, UK/Bridgeman Art Library London/New York; Corbis-Bettmann; Culver Pictures; 913, Bridgeman Art Library, London/New York; 914, Lionel Cherruault/Sipa Press; 916, (top left) Giraudon/Art Resource, NY; 918, Bridgeman Art Library, London/New York; 921, Globe Photos; 922, (top) Bridgeman Art Library, London/New York, (bottom) Peter Grumann/The Image Bank; 923, Steve Vidler/Leo de Wys; 924, Bridgeman Art Library, London/New York; 925, Hulton Getty/Liaison Agency, Inc.; 927, Bridgeman Art Library, London/New York; 928, Hulton Getty/Liaison Agency, Inc.; 930, 933, 934, Bridgeman Art Library, London/New York; 936, ©2000 Estate of Pablo Picasso/Artists Rights Society (ARS), New York; 944, The Image Works; 946, Bridgeman Art Library, London/New York; 947, Corbis-Bettmann; 949, Bridgeman Art Library, London/New York; 956, Warner Brothers, 1941/The Kobal Collection; 958, Bridgeman Art Library, London/New York; 961, Joe Branny/Bruce Coleman, Inc.; 964, Sichov/SIPA Press; 965, ©Bonnie Sue/Photo Researchers, Inc.; 966, ©Patrick Donehue/Photo Researchers, Inc.; 968, (background) Geoffrey Clifford/Woodfin Camp & Associates; 969, (background) John Banagan/The Image Bank; 970, The Image Works, (insert) Mike Yamashita/Woodfin Camp & Associates; 972, ©Bruce Paton/Impact Visuals; 977, Jules Zalon/The Image Bank; 989, Bridgeman Art Library, London/New York; 993, Corbis-Bettmann; 994, e.t. Archive; 995, Corbis-Bettmann; 996, Bridgeman Art Library, London/New York; 1000, Art Resource, NY; 1004, ©Tom Croke/Gamma Liaison; 1007, ©Erich Lessing/Art Resource, NY; 1008, Christie's Images; 1010, Curtis Willocks/The Image Bank; 1012, Sony Theatres; 1013, Photofest; 1014, (top right) Globe Photos; 1014 (bottom left), 1015, Photofest; 1016, Columbia Pictures (Courtesy Kobal); 1017, The Image Works; 1018, Bridgeman Art Library, London/New York; 1022, Sotheby's Transparency Library, London; 1026, UPI/Corbis-Bettmann; 1029, Jane Burton/Bruce Coleman, Inc.; 1030, © Stephen Dalton/Photo Researchers, Inc.; 1032, 1038, Bridgeman Art Library, London/New York; 1041, UPI/Corbis-Bettmann; 1042, ©Bill Wassman/The Stock Market; 1046, (border) Thomas J. Peterson/Tony Stone Images; 1050, Wide World Photos; 1051, ©Jeff Lepore/Photo Researchers, Inc.; 1052, L. West/Bruce Coleman, Inc.; 1053, Jeff Greenberg/Photo Researchers, Inc.; 1058, F. Cruz/Superstock; 1059, Bridgeman Art Library, London/New York; 1060, Hulton Getty/Liaison Agency, Inc.; 1065, Bridgeman Art Library, London/New York; 1070, Archive Photos; 1076, ©Murray Alcosser/The Image Bank; 1077, Leslie Davis/Hulton Getty/Liaison Agency, Inc.; 1080, Brown Brothers; 1081, E. R. Degginger/Bruce Coleman, Inc.; 1086, (border) ©Terry Vine/Tony Stone Images; 1089, ©Horst Munzig/Woodfin Camp & Associates, Inc.; 1092, Scala/Art Resource, NY; 1098, 1100, 1101, Martha Swope © Time, Inc.; 1103, Courtesy of the artist; 1104, UPI/Corbis-Bettmann; 1108, Herscovici/Art Resource, NY; 1109, ©Nancy Crampton; 1111, Museum purchase, Roscoe and Margaret Oakes Income Fund, Museum Society Auxiliary, Mr. and Mrs. John N. Rosekrans, Jr., Walters H. and Phyllis J. Shorestein Foundation Fund, Mrs. Paul L. Wattis, Bobbie and Mike Wilsey, Mr. and Mrs. Steven MacGregor Read, Mr. and Mrs. Gorham B. Knowles, Mrs. Edward T. Harrison, Mrs. Nan Tucker McEvoy, Harry and Ellen Parker in honor of Steven Nash, Katherine Doyle Spann, Mr. and Mrs. William E. Steen, Mr. and Mrs. Leonard E. Kingsley, George Hopper Fitch, Princess Ranieri de San Faustino, Mr. and Mrs. Richard Madden (1994. 32); 1112, Jon Hicks/Leo De Wys, Inc.; 1118, (background) ©Nicholas Devore III/Bruce Coleman, Inc.; 1119, C. Gascoigne/Robert Harding Picture Library; 1121, Benn Mitchell/The Image Bank; 1122, Wide World Photos; 1123, Sotheby's Transparency Library, London; 1127, Bridgeman Art Library, London/New York; 1128, Hulton Getty/Liaison Agency, Inc.; 1131, Wide World Photos; 1132, 1134, Corbis-Bettmann; 1136, UPI/Corbis-Bettmann; 1137, Globe Photos, Inc., 1995; 1138, e.t. Archive; 1146, UPI/Corbis-Bettmann; 1148, ©E. Sparks/The Stock Market; 1149, ©Hans Reinhard/Bruce Coleman, Inc.; 1154, Wide World Photos; 1161, Wide World Photos; 1162, ©Geoff Gove/The Image Bank; 1163, ©Robert Frerck/Woodfin Camp & Associates; 1164, Wide World Photos; 1168, Photographer: Richard Todd (X65.7994); 1169, ©Bill Binzen/The Stock Market; 1171, Reuters/Corbis-Bettmann; 1172, ©Masa Uemura/Tony Stone Images; 1173, Werner Forman Archive/Art Resource, NY; 1177, Bridgeman Art Library, London/New York; 1180, ©Masa Uemura/Tony Stone Images; 1187, F. Cruz/Superstock.

Borders for The English Language features and for Language Workshops and Writer's Workshops, Paul Kazmercyk.

Macintosh window elements and icons © 1984 Apple Computer, Inc. All rights reserved. Used with the permission of Apple Computer, Inc.

Portions copyright Netscape Communications Corporation, 1998. All rights reserved. Netscape, Netscape Navigator, and the Netscape N Logo are registered trademarks of Netscape in the United States and other countries.

INDEX OF SKILLS

LITERARY TERMS

The boldface page numbers indicate an extensive treatment of the topic.

READING AND CRITICAL THINKING

LANGUAGE (GRAMMAR, USAGE, AND MECHANICS)

VOCABULARY AND SPELLING

WRITING

SPEAKING, LISTENING, AND VIEWING

RESEARCH AND STUDY

CROSSING THE CURRICULUM

CRITICAL COMMENTS

CREATIVE PROBLEM SOLVING

INDEX OF ART

FINE ART/ILLUSTRATIONS/CRAFTS

ORIGINAL MANUSCRIPTS

MAPS

CARTOONS

INDEX OF AUTHORS AND TITLES

Page numbers in italic type refer to the pages on which author biographies appear.